HANDBOOK OF RUSSIAN LITERATURE

Handbook of
RUSSIAN LITERATURE

Edited by

VICTOR TERRAS

Yale University Press
New Haven and London

Designed by Margaret E.B. Joyner
and set in Linotron Times New Roman type by
Asco Trade Typesetting Ltd., Hong Kong.
Printed in the United States of America by
Vail-Ballou Press, Inc.
Binghamton, New York

Library of Congress Cataloging in Publication Data
Main entry under title:

Handbook of Russian literature.

Bibliography: p.
Includes index.
1. Russian literature—Dictionaries.   I. Terras, Victor.
PG2940.H29   1985   891.3′03′21   84–11871
ISBN   0–300–03155–6

The paper in this book meets the guidelines for permanence
and durability of the Committee on Production Guidelines
for Book Longevity of the Council on Library Resources.

10 9 8 7 6 5 4 3 2 1

Contents

PREFACE

This handbook is a collective venture. It was planned and organized, at the suggestion of Yale University Press, by a committee consisting of Robert L. Jackson (Yale), Robert A. Maguire (Columbia), Frank R. Silbajoris (Ohio State), and myself. It contains articles by 106 scholars. It was made possible by a grant from the National Endowment for the Humanities.

The principle applied in soliciting contributions was that contributors would write one or two major articles and a group of minor articles from their general area of specialization. Each contributor was allotted a specific amount of space, and although a word count was suggested for each entry, the contributor could "borrow" space from one entry in favor of another. Some contributors proposed using a portion of their space allotment for entries not on the original list. Their suggestions were sometimes accepted, but many potential entries had to be excluded.

Because the writing spanned a year and a half, ending in the summer of 1983, documentation and bibliography are more up-to-date in some articles than in others.

This handbook is aimed at a broad spectrum of users: students of Russian literature, of course, but also those engaged in other branches of Russian studies who need to verify literary information relevant to their disciplines; teachers of literature in other languages who want to acquaint themselves with Russian literature; and, last but not least, the general reader. There exist, of course, works from which the information gathered in this handbook may also be obtained. Many of them are listed in the Bibliography. The raison d'être of this handbook is to make this information available in English under a single cover.

It is assumed that many of the users of this handbook do not read Russian. Therefore, Russian names are given in their familiar spelling (Dostoevsky, Gogol) in the English text. They are exactly transliterated (Dostoevskii, Gogol') when part of a Russian phrase, such as in the Russian entries of the bibliographic part of each article. Also, titles of Russian works are given in translation, usually followed by the Russian title in parentheses. The few instances in which a work is referred to by different titles are explained by the fact that the work is known in the English speaking world under different titles. For example, Dostoevsky's novel *Besy* is generally known under the title *The Possessed*, though the literal translation, *(The) Devils*, is actually preferred by some authors. Russian periodicals, though, are identified by their Russian title to avoid misunderstandings. For translation, if not given in the text, see the list of Russian periodicals.

The purpose of the bibliography added to most articles is to give the reader a head start, no more. With limited space available, only the more important primary texts and translations could be listed. Secondary literature given will be, in most instances, sufficient for general orientation only. In some cases, contributors have decided to use more of the space at their disposal for bibliographic information. In particular, more bibliographic information is desirable in the case of émigré authors, on whom references are difficult to obtain. In order to save space, publisher and, in many instances, place of publication have been omitted. In the case of Russian works, knowing that a work has appeared in St. Petersburg (Leningrad) and/or Moscow is of little help, but publication in a provincial city will at least suggest that the work will be less likely to be found on library shelves outside the Soviet Union. In the case of English translations from the Russian, no place of publication suggests that the book has appeared in Britain and/or the United States (ordinarily London and/or New York). But whenever an English translation has appeared in the Soviet Union (the much rarer case), place of publication (Moscow, as a rule) is given. Likewise in the case of works written in Russian and published in the West, place of publication is given. As a general principle, secondary literature in languages other than English and Russian has been included only when it contains information not available in English. By and large, the secondary literature given in the bibliographic part of each article ought to suffice as a lead to whatever further literature there may be available on the subject.

Entries which have received ample attention in the nine-volume Soviet encyclopedia of literature (*Kratkaya literaturnaya entsiklopediya*, 1962–78) have sometimes been treated cursorily or omitted entirely, while material disregarded by *KLE* is often given more attention. The word count of an entry should not be seen as an absolute or relative measure of its importance. The suggested word count given to contributors was based on my judgment, with which some of the contributors disagreed. In some instances contributors substantially exceeded the suggested word count of an entry and justified this by the long-time neglect of their charge. I had to respect their judgment.

Recent literature published in the USSR as well as in the West posed many problems. The very inclusion of authors still active and with much of their career probably still ahead of them is risky. Information on such authors is difficult to obtain and any analysis of their work would have to contain a dose of *critique du jour*, an approach in conflict with the nature of a handbook which is expected to remain in use for a number of years. After some attempts, I gave up the initial plan to obtain a major article on dissident literature. The scholars whom I contacted were probably right in suggesting that the topic was too elusive and ill-defined to be treated in an organized scholarly manner.

It is my pleasant duty to give credit to those who were instrumental in producing this handbook. My colleagues Robert L. Jackson, Robert A. Maguire, and Frank R. Silbajoris watched over its progress almost from its inception and gave much valuable advice, as did Edward Tripp of Yale University Press. Without a grant from the National Endowment for the Humanities this project would have never materialized. Brigitte Agna, Alan Cienki, Sheila McCarthy, and Christine Tomei, Brown University graduate students, helped me at various stages of the project. Judith Hickey, the copy editor, had a particularly difficult job on her hands, since many of the contributors, including myself, write English with less than native ease. I thank her in the name of all contributors for doing her job with skill and patience. Finally, I give thanks to those who wrote the articles which make up this handbook. As the only person who read every single line of the handbook from the beginning, I can sincerely say that it was a great educational experience.

VICTOR TERRAS

CONTRIBUTORS

Agna, Brigitte (Brown University) — B. A.
Altshuller, Mark (U.C.L.A.) — M. A.
Baehr, Stephen L. (Virginia Polytechnic Institute) — S. B.
Baer, Joachim T. (University of North Carolina, Greensboro) — J. B.
Bailey, James O. (University of Wisconsin, Madison) — J. O. B.
Baran, Henryk (S.U.N.Y., Albany) — H. B.
Barnes, Christopher J. (St. Andrews University, Scotland) — C. B.
Barooshian, Vahan D. (Wells College) — V. D. B.
Belknap, Robert L. (Columbia University) — R. L. B.
Berry, Thomas E. (University of Maryland) — T. E. B.
Beshenkovsky, Eugene (New York City) — E. B.
Birkenmayer, Sigmund S. (Pennsylvania State University) — S. S. B.
Blinov, Valery (Yale University) — V. B.
Bowlt, John E. (University of Texas) — J. E. B.
Bristol, Evelyn (University of Illinois) — E. Br.
Brostrom, Kenneth N. (Wayne State University) — K. N. B.
Brown, Edward J. (Stanford University) — E. J. B.
Clyman, Toby W. (S.U.N.Y., Albany) — T. W. C.
Condee, Nancy (Wheaton College) — N. C.
Danow, David K. (University of South Carolina) — D. K. D.
Dienes, Laszlo (University of Massachusetts, Amherst) — L. D.
Driver, Claire (University of Rhode Island) — C. D.
Dryzhakova-Altshuller, Elena (U.C.L.A.) — E. D. A.
Duran, James A. (Canisius College) — J. A. D.
Dyck, J. W. (University of Waterloo) — J. W. D.
Ehre, Milton (University of Chicago) — M. E.
Ermolaev, Herman (Princeton University) — H. E.
Fanger, Donald L. (Harvard University) — D. L. F.
Filippov, Boris (University Hills, Md.) — B. F.
Friedberg, Maurice (University of Illinois) — M. F.
Gasiorowska, Xenia (University of Wisconsin, Madison) — X. G.
Glad, John (University of Maryland) — J. G.
Glasse, Antonia (Ithaca, N.Y.) — A. Gl.
Gleason, Abbott (Brown University) — A. G.
Goldblatt, Harvey (Yale University) — H. G.
Grabowicz, George G. (Harvard University) — G. G.
Gregg, Richard (Vassar College) — R. G.
Harkins, William E. (Columbia University) — W. E. H.
Harris, Jane G. (University of Pittsburgh) — J. G. H.

Hart, Pierre R. (Louisiana State University)	P. R. H.
Holquist, James M. (Indiana University)	J. M. H.
Hoover, Marjorie (New York City)	M. H.
Hunt, Priscilla (Brown University)	P. H.
Ivask, George (University of Massachusetts, Amherst)	G. I.
Jahn, Gary (University of Minnesota)	G. J.
Johnson, D. Barton (University of California, Santa Barbara)	D. B. J.
Kagan-Kans, Eva (Indiana University)	E. K. K.
Ketchian, Sonia (Smith College)	S. K.
King, Janet M. (Cambridge, Mass.)	J. M. K.
Kjetsaa, Geir (University of Oslo, Norway)	G. K.
Kline, George L. (Bryn Mawr College)	G. L. K.
Lawton, Anna (Purdue University)	A. L.
Lee, C. Nicholas (University of Colorado)	C. N. L.
Lehrman, Alexander (Yale University)	A. Le.
Leighton, Lauren G. (University of Illinois, Chicago)	L. G. L.
Levitsky, Alexander (Brown University)	A. Lev.
Luckyj, George (University of Toronto)	G. L.
Maguire, Robert A. (Columbia University)	R. A. M.
Mathiesen, Robert (Brown University)	R. M.
McLean, Hugh (University of California, Berkeley)	H. McL.
Moser, Charles A. (George Washington University)	C. A. M.
Natov, Nadine (George Washington University)	N. N.
Nepomnyashchy, Catherine T. (Columbia University)	C. T. N.
Oinas, Felix J. (Indiana University)	F. J. O.
Oulanoff, Hongor (Ohio State University)	H. O.
Pachmuss, Temira (University of Illinois)	T. A. P.
Page, Tanya (University of Rochester)	T. P.
Perlina, Nina (Rutgers University)	N. P.
Picchio, Riccardo (Yale University)	R. P.
Polakiewicz, Leonard (University of Minnesota)	L. P.
Poltoratzky, Nikolai P. (University of Pittsburgh)	N. P. P.
Pomar, Mark G. (University of Vermont)	M. G. P.
Pomorska, Krystyna (M.I.T.)	K. P.
Randall, Francis B. (Sarah Lawrence College)	F. B. R.
Rannit, Aleksis (Yale University)	A. R.
Reeder, Roberta (Cambridge, Mass.)	R. R.
Rice, Martin P. (University of Tennessee)	M. P. R.
Richter, Manfred (University of Waterloo)	M. R.
Rosen, Nathan (University of Rochester)	N. R.
Rosenthal, Bernice G. (Fordham University)	B. G. R.
Rzhevsky, Nicholas (S.U.N.Y., Stony Brook)	N. Rz.
Scherr, Barry P. (Dartmouth College)	B. S.
Schillinger, John (Oklahoma State University)	J. S.
Segall, Helen (Dickinson College)	H. S.
Segel, Harold B. (Columbia University)	H. B. S.
Shane, Alex M. (S.U.N.Y., Albany)	A. M. S.
Shein, Louis J. (McMaster University)	L. J. S.
Silbajoris, Frank R. (Ohio State University)	F. R. S.
Stacy, Robert H. (Syracuse University)	R. H. S.
Stankiewicz, Edward (Yale University)	E. S.

CONTRIBUTORS

Stephan, Halina (University of Southern California)	H. St.
Tall, Emily (S.U.N.Y., Buffalo)	E. T.
Tamarchenko, Anna (Boston University)	A. T.
Tamarchenko, Grigory (Boston University)	G. T.
Terras, Victor (Brown University)	V. T.
Thompson, Ewa M. (Rice University)	E. Th.
Titunik, I. R. (University of Michigan)	I. R. T.
Todd, William M. (Stanford University)	W. M. T.
Tomei, Christine (Brown University)	C. T.
Twarog, Leon I. (Ohio State University)	L. T.
Urbanic, Allan (Harvard University)	A. U.
Venclova, Tomas (Yale University)	T. V.
Weeks, Albert L. (New York University)	A. L. W.
Welsh, David (University of Michigan)	D. W.
Woll, Josephine (Howard University)	J. W.
Worth, Dean S. (U.C.L.A.)	D. S. W.

ABBREVIATIONS

CASS	*Canadian-American Slavic Studies*
CSP	*Canadian Slavonic Papers*
CSS	*Canadian Slavic Studies*
Foster	Ludmila Foster, *Bibliografiya russkoi zarubezhnoi literatury, 1918–1968.* 2 vols. Boston: G. H. Hall, 1970.
IAN	*Izvestiya Akademii Nauk S.S.S.R., Seriya Literatury i Yazyka* (Moscow)
IJSLP	*International Journal of Slavic Linguistics and Poetics*
KLE	*Kratkaya literaturnaya entsiklopediya.* 9 vols. 1962–78.
Lewanski	*The Literatures of the World in English Translation: A Bibliography.* Vol. II: The Slavic Literatures. Comp. Richard C. Lewanski. New York: The New York Public Library, 1967.
MERSL	*The Modern Encyclopedia of Russian and Soviet Literature.* Ed. Harry Weber. Gulf Breeze, Fla.: Academic International Press, 1976– .
OSP	*Oxford Slavonic Papers*
PSS	*Polnoe sobranie sochinenii* (Collected Works)
RFolk	*Russkii fol'klor*
RLJ	*Russian Language Journal*
RLit	*Russkaya literatura*
RLT	*Russian Literature Triquarterly*
RusL	*Russian Literature* (The Hague and Paris)
RusR	*Russian Review*
SEEJ	*Slavic and East European Journal*
SEER	*Slavonic and East European Review*
SlavR	*Slavic Review*
TODRL	*Trudy Otdela Drevnerusskoi Literatury* (Moscow)
VLit	*Voprosy literatury*
ZS	*Zeitschrift für Slawistik* (Berlin)

RUSSIAN LANGUAGE JOURNALS AND ALMANACS
REFERRED TO IN THE TEXT

Adskaya pochta	Infernal Mail
*Aglaya	Aglaia
Aonidy	The Aonids
*Apollon	Apollo
Babochka	Butterfly
Beseduyushchii grazhdanin	The Citizen Conversing
Bibliograf	The Bibliographer
Bibliograficheskie listy Otechestvennykh zapisok	Bibliographic Sheets of the National Annals
*Biblioteka dlya chteniya	Library for Reading
Birzhevye vedomosti	Stock Exchange News
Blagonamerennyi	The Loyal Citizen
Budil'nik	Alarm Clock
Byloe	Bygone Days
Chisla	Numbers
Chizh	Siskin
Chtenie v besede lyubitelei russkogo slova	Reading in the Collegium of Lovers of the Russian Word
Chteniya obshchestva istorii i drevnosti	Readings of the Society of Russian History and Antiquities
Damskii zhurnal	Ladies Journal
Delo	The Cause *or* The Deed
Delo naroda	The People's Concern
Den'	Day
Detskaya literatura	Children's Literature
Detskoe chtenie dlya serdtsa i razuma	Children's Readings for Heart and Mind
Dnevnik pisatelya	A Writer's Diary
Dobroe namerenie	Good Intention
Dom iskusstv	House of Arts
Drakon	The Dragon
Drug chestnykh lyudei ili Starodum	Friend of Honest People or Oldthink
*Epokha	The Epoch
Eralash	Hotchpotch
Etnograficheskoe obozrenie	Ethnographic Review
Ezh	Hedgehog
Ezhemesyachnye sochineniya	Monthly Essays
Ezhemesyachnye sochineniya k pol'ze i uveseleniyu sluzhashchie	Monthly Compositions for Profit and Amusement
Golos	Voice
Gorn	The Forge
Gostinitsa dlya puteshestvuyushchikh v prekrasnom	The Inn for Travellers in the Beautiful
*Grani	Facets
Gryadushchee	Future
Gudki	Sirens
Gudok	The Factory Whistle
*Iskra	The Spark
Iskusstvo	Art
Iskusstvo kommuny	Art of the Commune
Istoricheskii vestnik	Historical Herald
Izvestiya Akademii nauk, otdelenie russkogo yazyka i slovesnosti	Communications of the Academy of Sciences, Department of Russian Language and Literature
Khudozhestvennoe slovo	Artistic Word
Khudozhestvennyi sbornik	Art Anthology
Knizhnaya letopis'	Book Chronicle
Knizhnyi vestnik	Book Announcer
*Kolokol	The Bell
*Kontinent	The Continent
Koshelek	The Purse
*Krasnaya nov'	Red Virgin Soil
Krasnaya zvezda	Red Star
Krug	Circle
*Kuznitsa	The Smithy
*Lef	Left Front of Art
Literatura i marksizm	Literature and Marxism
*Literaturnaya gazeta	Literary Gazette
Literaturnoe obozrenie	Literary Survey
Literaturnye pribavleniya k Russkomu invalidu	Supplement to the Russian Invalid
Literaturnyi kritik	Literary Critic
Mayak	Lighthouse
Mech	Sword
Mesyachnye istoricheskie, genealogicheskie i	Monthly Historical, Genealogical and

geograficheskie primechaniya v Vedomostyakh	Geographical Notes in the News
Mir Bozhii	God's World
Mir iskusstva	The World of Art
Mnemozina	Mnemosyne
Molodaya gvardiya	Young Guard
Molva	Rumor
Moskovskie gubernskie vedomosti	Moscow Province News
Moskovskie vedomosti	Moscow News
Moskovskii gorodskoi listok	The Moscow Municipal Bulletin
Moskovskii nablyudatel'	The Moscow Observer
Moskovskii sbornik	Moscow Miscellany
Moskovskii telegraf	Moscow Telegraph
Moskovskii vestnik	The Moscow Herald
Moskovskii zhurnal	The Moscow Journal
Moskovskii zritel'	The Moscow Observer
Moskovskoe ezhemesyachnoe izdanie	Moscow Monthly Edition
Moskva	Moscow
Moskvityanin	The Muscovite
Murzilka	Little Smeary
Nabat	Alarm
Nachalo	The Beginning
Nakanune	On the Eve
Na literaturnom postu	On Literary Guard
Na postu	On Guard
Narodnaya Volya	People's Will
Nashe vremya	Our Times
Nash sovremennik	Our Contemporary
Nauchnoe obozrenie	Scientific Review
Nevinnoe uprazhnenie	Innocent Exercise
Nevskii al'manakh	The Neva Almanac
Nevskii zritel'	The Neva Spectator
Niva	The Grainfield
Novaya Rossiya	New Russia
Novaya Zhizn'	New Life
Novoe russkoe slovo	The New Russian Word
Novoe slovo	The New Word
Novoe vremya	New Times
Novosti literatury	News from Literature
Novye Aonidy	The New Aonids
Novyi Giperborei	The New Hyperborean
Novyi korabl'	The New Ship
Novyi mir	New World
Novyi put'	The New Path
Novyi zhurnal	New Review
Odesskie novosti	Odessa News
Ogni	Fires *or* Lights
Ogonek	The Flame
Oktyabr'	October
Orlovskii vestnik	The Orel Herald
Oskolki	Fragments *or* Slivers
Osnova	The Foundation
Otechestvennye zapiski	National Annals
Parus	Sail
Pechat' i revolyutsiya	Press and Revolution
Pereval	The Crossing
Permskie gubernskie vedomosti	Perm Province News
Peterburgskaya gazeta	The Petersburg Gazette
Peterburgskii glashatai	The Petersburg Herald
Pioner	The Pioneer
Pionerskaya pravda	The Pioneer's Truth
Plamya	Flame
Pochta dukhov	The Spirits' Post (*or* Mail)
Pokoyashchiisya trudolyubets	The Toiler in Repose
Poleznoe uveselenie	Useful Diversion
Polyarnaya zvezda	Polar Star
Poryadok	Order
Posev	Sowing
Poslednie novosti	The Latest News
Pravda	Truth
Pravitel'stvennyi vestnik	Government Announcer
Prazdnoe vremya v pol'zu upotreblennoe	Idle Time for Good Use
Proletarskaya kul'tura	Proletarian Culture
Protalina	Thawed Patch
Pustomelya	The Windbag
Rassvet	Dawn
Rodina	The Motherland
Rossiiskaya bibliografiya	Russian Bibliography
Rossiya i slavyanstvo	Russia and Slavdom
Russkaya beseda	Russian Talk (*or* Conversation, *or* Colloquy)
Russkaya mysl'	Russian Thought
Russkaya rech'	Russian Speech
Russkaya starina	Russian Antiquities
Russkaya zhizn'	Russian Life
Russkie novosti	Russian News
Russkie vedomosti	Russian News
Russkie zapiski	Russian Annals
Russkii arkhiv	Russian Archive
Russkii golos	The Russian Voice
Russkii invalid	The Russian Invalid
Russkii mir	Russian World
Russkii sovremennik	The Russian Contemporary
Russkii vestnik	The Russian Herald
Russkoe bogatstvo	Russian Riches
Russkoe slovo	The Russian Word
Sadok sudei	A Trap for Judges
Samarskii vestnik	Herald of Samara
Sankt-Peterburgskie vedomosti	St. Petersburg News
Sankt-Peterburgskii Merkurii	St. Petersburg Mercury
Sanktpeterburgskii vestnik	St. Petersburg Herald
Satirikon	Satiricon
Sever	The North
Severnaya lira	The Northern Lyre
Severnaya pchela	The Northern Bee
Severnoe siyanie	Northern Lights
Severnye tsvety	Northern Flowers

Severnyi arkhiv	Northern Archive
Severnyi vestnik	The Northern Herald
Shtyk	Bayonet
Sibirskie ogni	Siberian Lights
Sintaksis	Syntax
Sirena	Siren
Slavyanin	The Slav
Sobesednik lyubitelei russkogo slova	Companion of Lovers of the Russian Word
Sovetskaya Sibir'	Soviet Siberia
Sovetskaya zhenshchina	Soviet Woman
Sovremennik	The Contemporary
Sovremennye zapiski	Contemporary Annals
Sovremennyi zapad	The Contemporary West
Soyuz molodezhi	Union of Youth
Spisok knig vyshedshikh v Rossii	List of Books Published in Russia
Strekoza	Dragonfly
Svistok	The Whistle
Svobodnoe slovo	The Free Word
Svobodnye chasy	Free Hours
Syn otechestva	Son of the Fatherland
Teatr i iskusstvo	Theater and Art
Teleskop	Telescope
Trudolyubivaya pchela	Busy Bee
Truten'	The Drone
Tsekh poetov	The Poets' Guild
Tsvetnik	Flower Garden
Tvorchestvo	Creation
Uchenye vedomosti	Learned News
Ukazatel' po delam pechati	Index for Publishing Affairs
Ukazatel' vnov' vyshedshikh knig	Index of Recently Published Books
Ukrainskii vestnik	Ukrainian Herald
Utrennii svet	Morning Light
Vechernyaya krasnaya gazeta	Red Evening Gazette
Vechernyaya zarya	Twilight
Vereteno	The Spindle
Versty	Milestones
Vesna	Springtime
Vestnik Evropy	The Herald of Europe

Vestnik narodnoi voli	Herald of the People's Will
Vestnik russkogo khristianskogo dvizheniya (RKhD)	Herald of the Russian Christian Movement
Vestnik zhizni	Messenger of Life
*Vesy	The Scales
Vokrug sveta	Around the World
Vol'naya russkaya pechat'	Russian Free Press
Volya Rossii	The Will of Russia
Voprosy literatury	Questions of Literature
Voprosy zhizni	Questions of Life
Voronezhskie izvestiya	Voronezh News
Vozdushnye puti	Aerial Ways
Vozrozhdenie	Renaissance
Vpered!	Forward!
Vremya	Time
Vremya i my	Time and We
Vsemirnaya illyustratsiya	World Illustration
Vsemirnyi sledopyt	Universal Pathfinder
Vstrechi	Encounters
Vsyakaya vsyachina	All Sorts of Things *or* Potpourri
Yasnaya Polyana	Yasnaya Polyana
Yunost'	Youth
Zarnitsy	Summer Lightning
Zarya	Dawn
Zavety	Behests
Zemlya Kolumba	Columbus' Land
Zerkalo sveta	Mirror of the World
Zhenskii vestnik	Herald of Women
Zhivopisets	The Painter
Zhivopisnoe obozrenie	Picturesque Review
Zhizn'	Life
Zhurnal ministerstva narodnogo prosveshcheniya	Journal of the Ministry of Public Education
Zhurnal zhurnalov	Survey of Journals
*Znamya	Banner
*Znanie	Knowledge
*Zolotoe runo	The Golden Fleece
Zritel'	Observer
*Zvezda	The Star
Zvezdochka	The Little Star

* Asterisk indicates an article in the text.

TRANSLITERATION TABLE

А	а	A a
Б	б	B b
В	в	V v
Г	г	G g
Д	д	D d
Е	е	E e
Ё	ё	Yo yo
Ж	ж	Zh zh
З	з	Z z
И	и	I i
Й	й	I i*
К	к	K k
Л	л	L l
М	м	M m
Н	н	N n
О	о	O o
П	п	P p
Р	р	R r
С	с	S s
Т	т	T t
У	у	U u
Ф	ф	F f
Х	х	Kh kh
Ц	ц	Ts Ts
Ч	ч	Ch Ch
Ш	ш	Sh sh
Щ	щ	Shch shch
	ъ	″ **
	ы	y
	ь	′ ***
Э	э	E e
Ю	ю	Yu yu
Я	я	Ya ya

*The adjectival endings -*yi* and -*ii* are rendered by -*y* in the English text: *maly* instead of *malyi*, *Dostoevsky* instead of *Dostoevskii*.
** The "hard sign" is rendered by a *y* in the English text.
*** The "soft sign" is omitted in proper names in the English text: *Gogol* rather than *Gogol'*.

HANDBOOK OF RUSSIAN LITERATURE

Ablésimov, Aleksándr Onísimovich (1742–83), composer of odes, eclogues, epistles, and fables. His *Tales and Fables* (Skazki i basni) was printed in 1769. He was also a contributor to satirical journals (1769–70). His three-act "original" (i.e., not translated) comic opera *The Miller, Sorcerer, Cheat and Matchmaker* (Mel'nik, koldun, obmanshchik i svat, 1779) greatly pleased audiences in Moscow and St. Petersburg (1781). It compared favorably to the more conventional pastoral comic operas of MAIKOV and NIKOLEV. It continued to be revived in both capitals throughout the 19th century as vaudeville, and was performed thirty-four times at the Maly Theater in Moscow between 1867 and 1877. His one-act comic opera *Fortune by Lot* (Schast'e po zhereb'yu, also 1779) was less successful. In 1780, Ablesimov wrote a dialog *The Wanderers* (Stranniki) for the reopening of the Petrovsky Theater in Moscow, which had burned down. In a wood near Moscow ("which is visible in the distance"), Satire seeks to join the Muses who, however, reject his advances. The three-act comic opera *March from Permanent Quarters* (Pokhod s nepremennykh kvartir, 1782) depicts the splendors and miseries of military life. (Only the first two acts survive.) Ablesimov translated nine cantos of the *Iliad*, which constitute the bulk of his published works.

Works: Sochineniya. St. Petersburg, 1849.
Translations: The Miller (Act 1, scenes 1–2). In *Anthology of Russian Literature*. Ed. Leo Wiener (1902–03), Vol. 1.
Secondary literature: A. A. Gozenpud, *Muzykal'nyi teatr v Rossii.* 1959.
D. W.

Acmeism, like any literary movement, is difficult to date exactly. The year of its formal establishment as a movement with a name, a defined membership, manifestoes, programmatic poems, a journal, and publishing ventures is 1913. The six self-declared Acmeists whose programmatic poems appeared in the March issue of APOLLON for 1913 as "illustrations" of the "theoretical ideas" expressed in the manifestoes published in the January issue, included Nikolai GUMILYOV and Sergei GORODETSKY, founders of the movement and its first self-appointed theoreticians, Anna AKHMATOVA and Osip MANDELSHTAM, its finest and most celebrated poets, and Vladimir NARBUT and Mikhail Zenkevich, its minor poets. They had already formed a nucleus within Gumilyov's first GUILD OF POETS founded in November, 1911.

The year 1913 is actually the peak of Acmeist consciousness as a movement, as a closed circle of poet-friends sharing a consciously prescribed poetics. Interrupted by World War I and the Revolution, the existence of the Acmeist group is usually given as a "mere two years." Nevertheless, efforts to keep Acmeism alive after 1918 included Gumilyov's establishment of a second Poets' Guild, Narbut's 1919 publication of Mandelshtam's manifesto, "Morning of Acmeism," and the redefinition of Acmeism in Mandelshtam's essay, "On the Nature of the Word," published in 1922. Following Gumilyov's tragic death in 1921, the surviving members (with the notable exception of Gorodetsky) not only persisted in referring to themselves as Acmeists, but attempted to redefine Acmeism in terms of their own work and as a worldview. Acmeism thus came to signify more than a short-lived movement; it was perceived as an autonomous "moral" and "aesthetic" force. As late as 1961, in her autobiographical statement, "Something about Myself," Akhmatova described herself as "an Acmeist." In her *Memoirs*, Nadezhda MANDELSHTAM recalls her husband's ultimate redefinition of Acmeism as the "yearning for world culture," and praises Zenkevich's continued reverence for his Acmeist past.

The history of Acmeism traces its roots back to late 1909–early 1910 with the coincidental appearance of the magazine *Apollon* (the *de facto* organ of the Acmeist movement), the closing of *The Scales* (VESY, the symbolist organ), the subsequent debates over the "crisis" of SYMBOLISM and the reassessment of the entire MODERNIST movement, as well as the less frequently mentioned posthumous cult of Innokenty ANNENSKY which developed following his sudden death on November 30, 1909. Hence, the beginnings of Acmeism go back to the conscious reassessment of symbolism and the self-conscious initiation of as yet unnamed and unfocused new directions, new tastes, and new aesthetic values, all of which appeared on the pages of *Apollon*, under the editorial leadership of Nikolai Gumilyov and Sergei MAKOVSKY.

Apollon must be credited as the best single forum for the airing of pre-Acmeist and Acmeist ideas and values. It is associated with the gradual definition of Acmeism as both a symbolist legacy and symbolist heresy. It published Annensky's critique of symbolism, a series of three articles entitled "On Contemporary Lyricism" (O sovremennom lirizme), in its first three issues. It carried the symbolist debates of 1910 as represented by Vyacheslav IVANOV, Aleksandr BLOK, Valery BRYUSOV and Andrei BELY. It printed tributes to Annensky, a reassessment of *Vesy*, the pre-Acmeist essays of KUZMIN and Gumilyov, all in 1910. Furthermore, it provided a continual commentary on contemporary Russian prose and poetry in the form of Kuzmin's "Notes on Russian Belles-Lettres" and Gumilyov's "Letters on Russian Poetry." Finally, in 1913, the Acmeist manifestoes, programmatic poems, and other essays and translations of the Acmeist circle appeared in the pages of *Apollon*.

Annensky's contribution, "On Contemporary Lyricism," provided the first critical survey of the "fifteen years of our lyrical modernism." In calling for discussions of poetry from an aesthetic rather than a philosophical or ideological perspective, he recognized the failure of the symbolist movement to continue to be "daring" or to view "complexity" as an aesthetic element. Annensky's profound interest in Classicism emerged in his explicit humanism, in his emphasis on the poet as "maker," and in his lyrical commitment to express the experience of the world in which he lived. The posthumous cult of Annensky developed by his followers among the third generation of modernist poets identified their dissatisfaction and disillusionment in symbolist values with Annensky's critique. Annensky represented a potential alternative to the poetry of *Vesy*, the mystical symbolism of Ivanov's theories, and the second generation of modernist poets. Unlike Ivanov's, Annensky's professed relationship to God and immortality was ambivalent: although he repudiated such concepts in the name of rationality, he was also acutely sensitive to an ultimate reality. He sought escape from the confrontation with death, however, neither in mysticism nor in abstract transcendence, but in his classical studies and in the world of artistic form. Gumilyov's definition of Annensky's aesthetic goal as "the precise embodiment of emotional experience" is thus a far cry from Ivanov's mystical view of poetry as the instrument for attaining "true reality."

In the January 1910 issue of *Apollon*, Mikhail Kuzmin published his essay, "On Beautiful Clarity," the first appeal to contemporary writers to value "clarity" above "obscurity" and the "beauty" of this world above "transcendence." In April, Gumilyov's essay, "Life of Verse" appeared, emphasizing the "organic" nature of poetry. While "art," he said, is "not an analogue of life," it has an autonomous existence: "Beautiful poems, like living beings, enter the circle of our life."

It was precisely at this time that the symbolist debates began in earnest at Vyacheslav Ivanov's Tower. Formal speeches presented at the bimonthly meetings included Ivanov's "Tenets of Symbolism" and Blok's "On the Current State of Russian Symbolism," published in the August 1910 issue of *Apollon*. Bryusov's rebuttal, "On Slavish Speech," followed in November.

Most significant, however, for the development of specificially Acmeist tenets, as opposed to the gradual rejection of mystical symbolist ideals, was Gumilyov's "Letter on Russian Poetry" reviewing Annensky's *Cypress Chest*, which appeared concurrently in August.

Gumilyov acknowledged the older poet as his mentor and model, juxtaposing Annensky's devotion to his craft to the "poets of *Vesy* fighting ideological battles." Second, in underscoring poetry's task as "the precise embodiment of emotional experience," Gumilyov opposed it to Ivanov's ideal of poetry as a vehicle for some higher experience, as a means to transcendent escape from this world's "baseness and torments." Third, he praised Annensky for capturing "the harmonic balance between image and form," ascribing to "balance" a primary position in his hierarchy of poetic values. Fourth, he evaluated Annensky's "range of ideas" in the context of their effect on the reader, rather than for their ideological values. "Sharpness," "unexpectedness," and "paradox" he perceived both as "ideas" and expressive devices. Gumilyov also identified particular humanistic values in Annensky's poetry and worldview: individualism, originality and strength of character, as well as poetic perspicacity, the ability to penetrate the depths of "the human soul." Summing up, he declared "... most seekers of new paths inscribe Annensky's name on their banner as our 'Tomorrow.'"

Hence, by the end of 1910, Gumilyov not only synthesized his aesthetic opposition to mystical symbolism, but began to formulate a new aesthetic. By 1911, the abstract philosophical issues of the debates were replaced by the more pragmatic tasks of the poet-craftsman. Gumilyov's key words in his "Letters on Russian Poetry" were "talent," "taste," and "poetic craft." *Apollon* had become the de facto organ of the third generation modernists. Other publications now printed the symbolists' philosophical debates.

Certain theoretical attempts were also made in 1910 to redefine the role of the poet and the function of poetry. Gumilyov's essay, "Life of Verse," already expounds certain basic ideas: "the organic nature" of poetry; the poet's calling as somewhere between the extremes of "mission" and escapism; the universality of language or "the word" as the aesthetic medium; the effects of poetry on "the reader;" the functional significance of poetic craft with respect to ideas and emotions.

Models cited by Gumilyov range from Homer to Oscar Wilde, from Dante to Pushkin. Examples of poetry include works of Bryusov, Ivanov, Annensky, and Kuzmin.

In asking, "What is necessary for a poem to live ... to make the world reckon with the fact of its existence ..." Gumilyov offers the idea of the "organic" nature of poetry discussed in detail in Mandelshtam's 1922 essay, "On the Nature of the Word." Mandelshtam specifically refers to the Acmeists as:

> The organic school of Russian poetry which developed as a result of the creative initiative of Gumilyov and Gorodetsky early in 1912, and which Akhmatova, Narbut, Zenkevich and the author of these lines officially joined, took upon itself the task of constructing just such a poetics.

> We can consider verbal representations not only as objective data of consciousness, but also as human organs, just like the liver or the heart.

To define the poet's calling as somewhere between the polar positions of the art-for-art's sake theorists and the art-for-life or utilitarian approach, Gumilyov cites Homer:

> Homer sharpened his hexameters, unconcerned with anything except vowel and consonant sounds, caesurae and spondees, and adapted his content to them. However, he would have considered himself a poor craftsman if, upon hearing his songs, youth had not striven for martial glory, if the clouded gaze of maidens had not increased the desire for beauty in the world.

Most significant, perhaps, for establishing the tenets of Acmeism, was Gumilyov's paraphrase of Oscar Wilde's evaluation of "the word" as the most universal aesthetic medium:

> The material used by musicians and artists is poor in comparison to the word. The word contains not only music, tender music like that of the alto or lute; not only color, vivid and luxurious like those which enchant us on Venetian and Spanish canvases; not only plastic forms, more lucid and distinct than those revealed to us in marble or bronze—those which contain thought and passion and spirituality. Words contain all these qualities.

Gumilyov further emphasized the clarity and distinctiveness of "the word," while Mandelshtam, in his essay, "Morning of Acmeism," advocated raising the "word" to the position of honor held by "music" in the symbolist canon: "For the Acmeists the conscious sense of the word, the Logos, is just as magnificent a form as music for the symbolists." Thus, both underscored the denotative value of "the word," as opposed to the Symbolist emphasis on obscurity, on making words as "vague" as "music" so as to transcend rational meaning and achieve metaphysical "harmony."

In addition, Gumilyov began to identify at this time those aspects of the incipient acmeist canon pertaining to the "reader's" vicarious physiological and psychological experience. He states that a poem must have

> thought and feeling ... the softness of outline of a young body where nothing is superfluous ... simplicity ... and refinement ... and, above all, style and gesture.... By gesture, I mean be so arranged ... that the reader strikes the pose of its hero, copies his facial expressions and movements and ... experiences exactly what the poet experienced, so that the spoken idea becomes ... the truth.

Mandelshtam's first extant essay, "François Villon," also written in 1910, but not published until 1913, is a paean to Villon as a "transitional" figure superficially bound by the restraints of the Middle Ages, but not yet a son of the Renaissance. Villon metaphorically captures the status of the third generation modernist poets between 1909–10 and 1912–13, when the acmeist credo was taking shape both theoretically and in practice.

> Obliged to the Middle Ages for his integrity, his temperament, for the source of his spiritual values ... Villon, last-born child of the Middle Ages, epigone of the feudal disposition, proved unreceptive to its ethical aspect, to its mutual guarantee! Gothic stability and morality were completely alien to him. On the other hand, greatly attracted by its dynamics, he elevated the Gothic to the heights of amoralism.

Similarly, while the third generation modernist poets were greatly attracted by the dynamics of symbolist technique and obliged to symbolism for the source of their aesthetic values, they were "unreceptive" to the "restraints" of symbolist ideology and semantics.

In 1910, Mandelshtam was concerned with the impulse behind Villon's human and poetic vitality: "I think that Villon was captivated not by the demonic, but by the dynamics of criminal life." He distinguished between Villon's not very profound "spiritual experiences" and the "brilliant complexity" of his "human relationships":

> If, for all their originality, Villon's spiritual experiences are not distinguished by particular profundity, his human relationships ... represent a composite of brilliant complexity.... How precise he was, how detailed!... The reader can imagine himself using the data, and can experience the life of the poet's contemporaries. The passing moment can thus endure the pressure of centuries ... remaining forever the same "here and now." One only needs to know how to extract that "here and now" from the soil of Time.... Villon knew how to extract it.

Thus, Mandelshtam perceived the function of poetry as the actualization of the human experience in all its precision, vitality, and complexity. The means to this end, he indicated, are in the precision of details as opposed to the "suggestive" language expounded by the symbolists. Poetic craft allowed the reader to relive the poet's human experiences vicariously, making the "passing moment ... endure the pressure of centuries." Mandelshtam thus added to Gumilyov's ideal of poetry as the "precise embodiment of emotional experience" a sense of historicity, the idea that the revelation or extraction of the historical moment or experience is a poetic challenge.

Indeed, the publication of Mandelshtam's essay, "François Villon," in the March 1913 issue of *Apollon*, accompanied as it was by Gumilyov's translation of fragments from the *Grand Testament* and by a carefully selected group of programmatic poems, may be regarded as Mandelshtam's first *printed* manifesto. "Morning of Acmeism," published in 1919, reiterates in more elegant and complex language most of the aesthetic ideals elaborated in 1910: balance, precision, dynamism, complexity, and physiological power as expressed through "the word."

Gumilyov's "Letters on Russian Poetry," published in *Apollon* between 1909 and 1917, record the transitional phase between the decline of symbolism and the rise of the post-symbolist "heresies," Acmeism and FUTURISM. They reveal the gradual formulation of the Acmeist credo based on his practical experience as poet-reviewer in contrast to the theoretical precepts of Ivanov, the poet-philosopher. While the "Letters" of 1909 to mid-1911 indicate how Gumilyov was still seeking ways to revive the symbolist legacy, the July 1911 "Letter" reviewing the older poet's *Cor ardens* contained Gumilyov's clear rejection of Ivanov's principles and practice. This review appeared only a few months after Ivanov had sharply criticized Gumilyov's new poem, "Prodigal Son," read at the April meeting of the Society for the Adepts of the Poetic Word. According to Akhmatova, the tone of Ivanov's attack so enraged Gumilyov and his younger disciples that it served as the necessary "pretext" to leave the Society and organize the Poets' Guild.

In his August "Letter," he generalized his attack against the poetry of *Vesy (The Scales)*, condemning it as passé: "What was good six or seven years ago in *The Scales*, supported by articles and critiques, seems somehow helplessly unconvincing now."

Furthermore, by August 1911, not only did Gumilyov repudiate the credo of *Vesy*, and the aesthetic theory and practice of the major symbolist spokesmen, but he also named particular poets as models of genuine poetry: PUSHKIN, LERMONTOV, Bryusov and Blok. Indeed, as early as mid-1910, he began to identify the "new directions" which certain older poets were taking, for instance, Blok and Bryusov. Of Bryusov's poem, "To Someone," Gumilyov noted: "[He] resolutely approaches the contemporaneity of which poets are so afraid, and comes out the victor."

Two years later, he called Bryusov

> a conqueror but not an adventurer, careful but decisive, as calculating as a brilliant strategist ... assimilating the characteristic traits of all literary schools before him.... But he added a certain something that made them blaze with a new fire.... Perhaps this something is the basis of a new school coming to replace Symbolism.

By August, 1912, in reviewing Blok's *Collected Works*, Gumilyov perceived a "purely Pushkinian ability to provide a feeling for the eternal in the momentary, to show the shadow of the genius watching over his fate behind every accidental image." Of Blok's second volume, he exclaimed: "Blok seems to have regarded the world of objects surrounding him for the first time, and having looked about, became indescribably joyful." At the same time, Gumilyov praised Kuzmin for being one of "the best contemporary Russian poets ... a poet of this earth, and finally, his fully developed technique never overshadows the image, but only inspires it."

By August 1912, therefore, Gumilyov's as yet unnamed aesthetic credo included a complete reinterpretation of the poet's mission in terms of his craft (as opposed to doctrine) and the redefinition of the poet-craftsman's ideal as "the precise embodiment of emotional experience." Gumilyov recognized poetry as a phenomenon of this world, of Man's experience on earth. He demanded that the poet seek poetry, "music," "beauty" in his immediate emotional experiences, seek a proper balance between details and the whole, and that he unite the details of the moment with "a feeling for the eternal." In singling out Pushkin, Annensky, Bryusov and Blok, among others, as his models, Gumilyov emphasized his doctrine of poetic humanism as opposed to occult, mystical or religious transcendence.

Gumilyov first used the term "Acmeism" in his September 1912 "Letter," reviewing his fellow Acmeist, Sergei Gorodetsky's fifth volume of verse, *Willow* (Iva). Although he uses "Acmeism" with specific reference to Gorodetsky's practice, it represents a synthesis of the comments made in his various "Letters" and essays. It includes Oscar Wilde's concept of the aesthetic universality of "the word," Kuzmin's "technique which never overshadows the image," the "feeling for the eternal in the momentary," "irony" as a fundamental element in poetry. In addition, Gumilyov clearly rejects the extremism of Parnassian aestheticism as well as the perception of Acmeism as mere "imaginism." He emphasizes that experience or thought cannot become poetic material until it is "clothed in the live and tangible flesh of the image, active and valuable in itself." And, perhaps even more significant, he underscores "mythopoesis" as essential to Acmeism:

Acmeism is in essence mythopoeism, because what, if not myth, will the poet create who repudiates both the exaggeration peculiar to youth and the uninspired moderation of old age, who uniformly strains all the powers of his spirit, who accepts the word in all its dimensions—musical, pictorial and ideological, and who demands that every creation be a microcosm. Criticism has frequently noted the domination of the subject over the predicate in Symbolist poems. Acmeism found this predicate in the logically musical and continuously developing movement of the image-idea throughout the entire poem.

Finally, in January 1913, *Apollon* published two Acmeist manifestoes, Gumilyov's "Acmeism and the Precepts of Symbolism" (reprinted in 1923 as "Acmeism and the Legacy of Symbolism"), and Gorodetsky's "Some Currents in Contemporary Russian Poetry." Mandelshtam's "Morning of Acmeism," although dating from 1913, was not published until 1919.

Gumilyov's manifesto endeavors to provide a theoretical justification for the new, post-symbolist movement based on a synthesis of the ideas published in *Apollon* since the end of 1909. It is not a particularly harsh attack against symbolism, but rather a historically oriented and pragmatically focused assessment of the symbolist legacy and a creative, relatively precise attempt to define Acmeism's "new directions" with clear examples:

> To replace Symbolism there is a new movement, which whatever it is called, Acmeism (from the Greek *akme*, meaning "the highest degree of something," "a blossom," "time of blossoming") or Adamism (a manly, clear, firm view of life), demands more balance, and a more precise knowledge of the relationships between subject and object than is found in Symbolism. However, for this trend to become fully established and be a worthy successor, it must accept the latter's legacy and answer all the questions it posed....
>
> French Symbolism as a school moved purely literary questions to the fore ... the new trend ... gives a decided preference to the Romanic over the Germanic spirit.... The notorious "theory of correspondences" betrays its Germanic origins. This Symbolist merging of all images and objects ... could have arisen only in the misty gloom of Germanic forests. [French] Symbolist metaphors trained [us] in bold turns of thought ; irony appearing ... in the Romanic writers has now replaced that hopeless German seriousness which our Russian Symbolists so cherished.... Finally, while we value the Symbolists for having shown us the significance of the symbol in art, we cannot agree to sacrifice other methods ... to it; we seek the complete coordination of all poetic methods.

Precise in his observations, Gumilyov criticized Russian symbolism primarily for directing "its main energies into the realm of the unknown." He emphatically differentiated between the poet and the mystic, theologian or philosopher, refusing to identify the function of poetry with means to transcendence or description of the mystical experience.

He acknowledged, however, that "certain quests" of the Russian symbolists "almost approached the creation of myth" and hence, the symbolists have the "right" to ask of any new movement, "how it regards the unknowable." Hence, in expounding the principles of Acmeism, Gumilyov emphasized the need to recognize "the unknowable" and accept it, for there is beauty in the "naive but wise and painfully sweet sensation of one's own lack of knowledge: this is what the unknown gives us." However, while recognizing and respecting the unknown, Acmeists distinguish between "the artist's material," which can include "angels, demons, or other spirits," indeed, any phenomena as "poetic images," and thought systems, dogmas and doctrines, which require justification outside the realm of poetry.

In criticizing German symbolism, he indicated that the poet's proper emphasis is on "existence," not on seeking "to serve some objective goal or dogma." The acmeist poet does not seek answers or resolutions in social, philosophical or religious doctrine, because what matters is "being," "the existence of the phenomenon":

> For us, hierarchy in the world of phenomena is only the specific gravity of each one, whereby the weight of the most insig-

nificant is yet immeasurably greater than the absence of weight, than nonexistence....

Sensing ourselves as phenomena among phenomena, we become part of the world rhythm, accepting all the forces which act upon us and, in turn, become forces ourselves....

After comparing the Acmeists to their symbolist predecessors and defending the new movement, Gumilyov cited his models and their particular contributions to Acmeism, providing both theoretical and practical justifications for his choices. Shakespeare, Rabelais, Villon and Théophile Gautier best expressed Man and his inner world, Man and his physical delights and powers, Man's capacity for experiencing life, and Man's need to express his experience of life in artistic form. "To unite these four elements is the dream of those who boldly call themselves Acmeists."

Gorodetsky's manifesto is more of an anti-symbolist polemic. Not only is it simpler, harsher and more pragmatic in its attack on the ultra-mystical precepts of Ivanov, but it is particularly hostile toward Blok, Bely, Bryusov, SOLOGUB and BALMONT.

What is basically in question in determining the differences between Acmeism and Symbolism is our resounding and colorful world: *This world* made of time, volume, and form, this planet—the earth. By filling the world with "correspondences," Symbolism essentially transformed it into a phantom whose importance is determined only by the degree to which other worlds are visible through its translucencies. Symbolism depreciated its great intrinsic worth. For the Acmeists, a rose has again become beautiful in itself, for its petals, fragrance, and color, and not for its purported likeness to mystical love or something else. Not only is a rose an object of beauty, but so is any earthly phenomenon, even something deformed. Henceforth, the ugly (*bezobrázno*) is only that which is formless (*bezóbrazno*), not fully realized, for it disappears somewhere between being and non-being.

Gorodetsky's manifesto also discussed his concept of "Adamism," defining it as perceiving the world anew: "to see things as Adam saw them at the dawn of creation." Hence, to Gumilyov's definition of "virility," he added the emphasis on optimism and primacy expressed in both his own and Mandelshtam's programmatic poems.

"Equilibrium" is also an essential element in Gorodetsky's aesthetic: "Art is first of all a state of equilibrium; it is solid, firm, durable." Hence, the artist's search for stability in word meanings and in the concreteness of everyday speech. Indeed, both manifestoes called for a return to "precision" and "clarity" of word meanings as opposed to the symbolist concept of "suggestiveness."

However, it is Mandelshtam who, both in his highly poetic manifesto, "Morning of Acmeism," and later, in "On the Nature of the Word," emphasizes semantic or philological consciousness as a distinctive difference between symbolism and Acmeism. For Mandelshtam the ultimate "reality" *is* "the word":

Too often we fail to see that the poet raises a phenomenon to its tenth power, and the modest exterior of a work of art often deceives us with regard to the monstrously condensed reality contained within. In poetry this reality is the word as such.

He even points out the nature of the confusion:

"The word as such" was born very slowly. Gradually, one after another, all the elements of the word were drawn into the concept of form. To this day the conscious sense, the Logos, is still taken erroneously and arbitrarily for the content.... The Logos demands nothing more than to be considered on an equal footing with the other elements of the word. The Futurists, unable to cope with the conscious sense as creative material, frivolously threw it overboard and essentially repeated the crude mistake of their predecessors.

For the Acmeists the conscious sense of the word, the Logos, is just as magnificent a form as music for the symbolists.

Most of the ideas, values and even imagery shared by the manifestoes are realized in the programmatic poems printed in the March 1913 issue of *Apollon*. These include the ideas of daring and challenge combined with the imagery of the architect-craftsman who al-

ways "takes the line of greatest resistance" for it is "harder to build a cathedral than a tower" (Gumilyov); creation as a proof of "existence," of "being," for a man is "not born to build if he does not hear metaphysical proof in the sound of a chisel splitting rock" (Mandelshtam), or "faced with non-being, all phenomena are brothers" (Gumilyov); equilibrium or balance as an aesthetic ideal, for "art itself is first of all a state of equilibrium" (Gorodetsky), and man's relationship to his world ought to be based on "a noble mix of rationality and mysticism as well as a feeling for the world as a living equilibrium" (Mandelshtam). Other shared concepts include the artist's need or impulse to celebrate the earth, all earthly phenomena, Man and man-made culture because "not only is a rose an object of beauty, but so is any earthly phenomenon" (Gorodetsky), and because "genuine piety before the three dimensions of space is the first condition of successful building: [he] regards the world neither as a burden nor an unfortunate accident, but as a God-given palace" (Mandelshtam); the idea of beauty as the full, vital and dynamic realization of form, or the revelation of the essence of existence or reality, because ugliness is "only that which is formless, not fully realized, for it disappears between being and non-being" (Gorodetsky), and because "the artist ... considers his world view a tool ... like the hammer in the hands of a stonemason ... his only reality is the work of art itself ..." though it may be a "monstrously condensed reality" (Mandelshtam).

The programmatic poems appeared in *Apollon* in the following order: Gumilyov's "Iambic Pentameters" (Pyatistopnye yamby), Gorodetsky's "Adam" and "The Stars" (Zvezdy), Narbut's "She is not beautiful" (Ona—nekrasiva) and "How swiftly the rooftops dry" (Kak bystro vysykhayut kryshi), Akhmatova's "I came to relieve you, sister" (Ya prishla tebya smenit', sestra) and "Cabaret artistique," Zenkevich's "Death of an Elk" (Smert' losya), and Mandelshtam's "Hagia Sophia" and "Notre Dame." An editorial footnote declared that they were intended as "illustrations" for the "theoretical views" expressed in the January manifestoes.

Gumilyov's "Iambic Pentameters" contain an autobiographical reckoning with his youth as well as an inspired and self-confident forecast for his future. The poet ironically derides his "dazzling dreams" as he details the nature of his failure and his subsequent break with his beloved. He affirms his new-found love in the joy of working with a community of poet-masterbuilders creating monuments "pleasing both the heavens and the earth." The sharp, relatively spare imagery of the love lyric is juxtaposed to the physical and metaphysical imagery conjoining the poet's emotional commitments to poetry, Acmeism and Freemasonry. For example, the first half of his poem contains the lines:

> I was young, ardent and over-confident,
> But the Earth's Spirit was silent, reserved,
> And my dazzling dreams died
> Just as birds and flowers die....
>
> I didn't dare to kiss your hair,
> Nor even press your fine, cold hands ...
> Every sound wounded and frightened me,
> And you walked out, in a simple dark dress.

The second half concludes with:

> Piously we raise cathedral walls
> Pleasing both the heavens and the earth.
> . . . .
> With hammers many have gathered here,
> We work more joyously together;
> One love unites us all....
>
> Triumphant and wondrous, a temple rises ...
> And we, harkening our master's voice,
> Are masons of all times and nations.

The image of the poet as a confident and joyous craftsman, the builder of monuments "pleasing both the heavens and the earth," as well as a representative of "all times and nations," is also developed by Mandelshtam in his manifesto, "Morning of Acmeism" and in his programmatic poems. However, Mandelshtam's focus derives not from autobiographical reckoning with his personal past as an impulse to poetic creation, but rather from his intellectual and mystical awe before the very fact of "existence," his astonishment that Man and Art "exist" in this world, and from his architectural metaphor of "the word" as the poet's "material," which he likens to the "keystone" of the Acmeist edifice. His intellectual awe and spiritual reckoning with mankind's cultural heritage, specifically with the power of the great architectural monuments, Notre Dame and Hagia Sophia, provide him with constant sources of moral and aesthetic inspiration.

In "Morning of Acmeism" he stated: "To exist is the artist's greatest pride. He desires no other paradise than existence.... Love the existence of the thing more than the thing itself and your own existence more than yourself: that is Acmeism's highest commandment." Hence, Mandelshtam's metaphorical association of the "existence of the thing," the artist's "reality," poetic language or "the word" and the poet-architect's material. To celebrate his physical and metaphysical love of "existence," the Acmeist poet-architect uses "the word" to build monuments whose "monstrously condensed reality" expresses the "noble mingling of rationalism and mysticism and the perception of the world as a living equilibrium."

In "Notre Dame," Mandelshtam combines the doctrines of "Adamism" and "Acmeism" expressed by Gorodetsky, Gumilyov and his own "Morning of Acmeism." As an "Adamist," he figuratively associates the physical attributes of Notre Dame with Adam's physiological characteristics, creating an image of the cathedral as a dynamic, living organism like Adam, the forefather of the human race. In addition, the cathedral is revealed as if joyously perceived anew by Adam, the first man as well as the first human creator or poet—the giver of names. As an "Acmeist," Mandelshtam underscores the significance of the historicity as well as the continuity of art's highest forms, the "peaks" of human creativity, both at the moment of their creation and as constant sources of inspiration for posterity. Beauty, for Mandelshtam, is awesome both in its external and internal construction and composition, in both its physiological and metaphysical manifestations. Meaning is simultaneously rational and mystical, historical and eternal, momentary and recurrent. Through the mediation of his art the poet merges what might appear to be antithetical values, perceptions, and images, thus converting complexity and mystery into forms comprehensible to man's common cultural experience.

It is within this context that Mandelshtam presents the poet's role as a kind of apprentice-craftsman to the monuments of the ages. The poet, through his aesthetic experience of such monuments as Notre Dame and Hagia Sophia, can resolve the tension between the rational and the mystical, the physical and metaphysical. In structuring his own poetic monuments, he joins the material of his craft and his cultural heritage, juxtaposing the concrete act of external observation of the material phenomena and their organization with his emotional and aesthetic experience; by studying and experiencing the inner organic logic of the aesthetic "organism" of Notre Dame, he perceives it anew and transforms it into yet a newer and more dynamic aesthetic monument appropriate to his own age. Thus the monuments of the past are revealed as the dynamic impulses of poetic inspiration and concrete reminders of cultural continuity.

The first stanza of "Notre Dame" contrasts its inner, organic structure with Man's organic nature or physiological essence—the cathedral, compared to Adam, is perceived as "tautening its nerves" and "flexing its muscles." Indeed, Mandelshtam realizes Gorodetsky's metaphor of "Adamism" quite literally. In the second stanza, he views the exterior form of the cathedral—"its secret plan"—with the observant eye of the Acmeist poet-craftsman: he regards the technical details making the complex structure a reality. Stanza three focuses on the complexity of art and reiterates the doctrine of "Morning of Acmeism" which links his worldview to the ideal of the Middle Ages: "... the noble mingling of rationality and mysticism and the perception of the world as a living equilibrium." Mandelshtam concludes his poem with the poet's self-confident assertion. The pronoun "I" is repeated three times, although it had been completely absent from the preceding three stanzas:

> The more attentively, O fortress Notre Dame,
> I studied your monstrous ribs,
> The more I thought: from dead weight
> Some day, I too shall create a thing of beauty.

The acmeist poet's function is thus to recognize "the existence" of the phenomena of this earth and to reveal their physical and metaphysical beauty to his fellow men so that they, in turn, may celebrate their "existence." In his later essay, "On the Nature of the Word,"

Mandelshtam emphasized the moral and social, as well as the aesthetic, essence of Acmeism, and centered his discussion on "the word" as "verbal representation." In "Morning of Acmeism" and his programmatic verse, however, he focused on the aesthetic autonomy and complexity of "the reality" and continuity of art, as opposed to the symbolists' emphasis on other-worldliness and the futurists' disdain for their cultural heritage.

While Gumilyov and Mandelshtam's emphasis on the unity of the physical and metaphysical worlds and on the continuity of artistic creativity does not resound as strongly in the programmatic poems of Gorodetsky, Akhmatova, Narbut, and Zenkevich, neither is it denied. Their focus is simply more concentrated on this world, and on the revelation, representation and celebration of its concrete and tangible phenomena, emotions and experiences.

Gorodetsky's "Adam" is a restatement of his doctrine of "Adamism" in verse. His poem concludes:

> To name, to recognize, to lift the cover
> Off solemn mystery and the gloom of old
> Is the first act. The second is
> To sing paeans to the living earth.

By interpreting the Acmeist poet's function in terms of his capacity to reveal the "living earth" and sing its praises, Gorodetsky formulates the optimistic tendency of the young Acmeists who chose to oppose symbolist "mystery" and "gloom," and hence, the desire to escape the confines of this world.

Akhmatova's poems, on the other hand, highlight the Acmeist capacity for irony, laconicism and precision in intimate mini-dramas of human relationships. Akhmatova realizes in poetic form Gumilyov's assessment of Annensky's goal as a poet: "the precise expression of emotional experience."

"I have come to take your place, sister" reveals Akhmatova's imaginative and highly concentrated depiction of the moment when youth and age recognize each other, and each in her own way poignantly perceives her own frailty, uncertainty, and sense of self in time. "Cabaret artistique" evokes the more common and more tangible pain of jealousy and desire dramatized against a background of concrete details of time and place as well as mood and tone. Dialogue is used in the former poem to heighten the drama of the encounter and to achieve a sense of distance:

> Your hair has turned gray. A tear
> has dimmed, misted your eyes.
>
> You no longer comprehend the song of the birds
> Nor notice either the stars or the glow of lightning.
>
> And the tambourine beat ceased long ago,
> Although I know you fear the silence.
>
> I have come to take your place, sister....

In "Cabaret artistique," the speaker gradually reveals her inner emotions. The setting ironically heightens the protagonist's emotional drama by providing the appropriate time and place for all the potential pleasures which she is denied. The concrete reality is the Stray Dog Café, New Year's 1913, disclosed in the title and in the imagery of the first stanza referring to the walls painted by the artist, Sergei Sudeikin, in birds and flowers. The famous Petersburg nightclub, frequented by the artists and poets of the period, provides the setting appropriate to the emotional expectations of the moment, emphasizing the total psychological incompatibility of the narrator and addressee.

> We are all here, carousers and harlots.
> How unhappy we are together!
> On the walls the flowers and birds
> Languish after the clouds.
>
> You sit smoking your black pipe ...
> I put on a narrow skirt
> To make me appear more slim.
> . . . .
> Oh, how my heart is yearning!
> . . . .
> And she who is dancing now,
> Will certainly end in hell.

Above all, the keenness of Akhmatova's ironic stance makes the reader conscious of the experiences portrayed. Both the more abstract, and indeed mysterious, context of the former, and the more tangible setting of the latter reveal what Mandelshtam termed the "monstrously condensed reality" of the moment. The emotional reality of this world is informed by the recognition of the self in time and space, and is gradually disclosed through the ironic juxtaposition of expectation and desire.

Narbut and Zenkevich's poems represent the work of the minor poets of the Acmeist circle. Their composition indicates a capacity for technical perfection associated with the original ideals of Acmeism. Their themes indicate the variety of interests and experiences of this world: humble, simple pleasures as well as denials of everyday life, the expression of ugliness and the grotesque, of physiological and elemental forces as well as the expression of sensitivity to physical texture and sensations, the experience of ordinary and everyday beauty as well as violence and death, filth and decay. Zenkevich's "Death of an Elk," for example, focuses neither on the specifics nor the metaphysics of death, but on the details of dying and decay. Narbut's "She is not beautiful" contradicts the symbolist ideal of the beautiful woman as the "eternal feminine," as ideal, alluring and distant. These poems also reflect the unlimited spectrum of tones and voices of which the Acmeists were capable, ranging from simple joy and astonishment to more complex attitudes of perversity, hostility, jealousy, disdain, humiliation.

Although World War I and the Revolution parted the members of the Acmeist group, the dominant values of Acmeism were continued and reaffirmed in the activities, poetry and critical writings of the three major Acmeist poets. Gumilyov established a second Poets' Guild after the war, taught poetry and drama, and continued his critical writing. Following his death in 1921, Mandelshtam and Akhmatova continued to broaden the definition of Acmeism. Mandelshtam's famous essay, "On the Nature of the Word," focuses on the word, developing several ideas suggested in his earlier writings but emphasizing both the moral and metaphysical nature of his Acmeist aesthetic in addition to the physiological characteristics stressed in "Morning of Acmeism." His Bergsonian metaphysics was shared by Gumilyov and remained a significant element in his work until his death in 1938. Akhmatova's ideals were expressed in her poetry, in particular in her longer poems, in her studies of Pushkin, and in her friendship with Nadezhda Mandelshtam.

In sum, Acmeism developed as a symbolist heresy, as an attempt to re-evaluate and reformulate modernist poetics as a verbal craft, as "art" rather than as a vehicle for mystical (otherworldly or escapist, religious or aesthetic) experience. That heresy became a full-fledged, if short-lived, movement, with manifestoes, a membership, and a canon of its own, persisting until about 1915. However, certain Acmeist values were to transcend time and continue to influence the poetry of its members throughout their lives. Indeed, Mandelshtam persisted in redefining Acmeism throughout his poetic career.

As opposed to the symbolists, the Acmeists sought their inspiration in the world of Man and in man-made culture, in the dynamism of the phenomenal world as opposed to the relative stasis of the noumenal world. Acmeism strictly opposed abstract otherworldly or mystical subject matter, and concentrated instead on the depiction of objects of divine and human creation: people, places, monuments, things of beauty, visible, tangible, and physiological. In this sense, Acmeism, as opposed to symbolism, may be considered both more objective than subjective, and more concrete than abstract.

Like the symbolists, the Acmeists placed a high value on technique and craft. However, the favorite techniques of the latter included irony, poetic distance, and a sensitive use of visual and psychological imagery, indeed, psychophysiological imagery, while the former showed a general preference for a more ideological (theoretical, philosophical, religious) vision, immersion in "the moment of transcendence," and an emphatic, often superimposed or artificial use of musical and religious imagery.

Nevertheless, like the symbolists, the Acmeists did not forgo thematic content in favor of technique as Mandelshtam accused the futurists of doing. The Acmeists never advocated "throwing Pushkin overboard," but on the contrary, created a cult of Pushkin and his neoclassical style. Furthermore, like the symbolists, Gumilyov, Mandelshtam and their fellow Acmeists retained the idea of the "word" as an autonomous entity, the sacred "Logos," which had to include both content and form. Mandelshtam in particular emphasized the semantic value of words, the basic "verbal fabric" of poetry, in contrast to the symbolist ideal of "suggestiveness," making words as "vague" as possible so as to achieve metaphysical "harmony," or the "music" of transcendence.

Bibliography: A. Akhmatova, "Mandel'shtam: Listki iz dnevnika." In *Vozdushnye puti: Al'manakh.* New York, 1965. N. L. Brodskii, et al., eds., *Literaturnye manifesty: Ot simvolizma k Oktyabryu.* 2d ed., 1929. Reprint. Munich, 1969. W. Chalsma, "Russian Acmeism: Its History, Doctrine, and Poetry." Ph.D. diss., University of Washington, 1967. S. Driver, "Acmeism." *SEEJ* 12 (1968), pp. 141–56. O. Mandel'shtam, *Sobranie sochinenii.* 4 vols. 1967–81. O. Mandelstam, "Morning of Acmeism" and "On the Nature of the Word." In *Mandelstam: The Complete Critical Prose and Letters.* Ed. J. G. Harris. Ardis, 1979. D. Mickiewicz, "The Problem of Defining Acmeism" and "The Acmeist Conception of the Poetic Word," *RLJ: Special Supplement,* Spring 1975, pp. 1–20, 59–76. E. Rusinko, "Russian Acmeism and Anglo-American Imagism," *Ulbandus Review* 1, no. 2 (1978), pp. 37–49. P. Steiner, "Poem as Manifesto: Mandelstam's 'Notre Dame,'" *RusL* 5 (1977), pp. 239–56. R. D. Timenchik, "Zametki ob akmeizme," *RusL* 7/8 (1974); 5, no. 3 (1977); 9, no. 2 (1981). V. Weidlé, "Peterburgskaya poetika." In N. Gumilev, *Sobranie sochinenii.* Ed. G. Struve and B. Filippov. 1968. Vol. 4, pp. v–xxxvi. V. Zhirmunskii, "Preodolevshie simvolizm." In *Voprosy teorii literatury.* 1928. Pp. 302–13.　　　　J. G. H.

Adamism, see ACMEISM.

Adamóvich, Geórgy Víktorovich (1884–1972), influential émigré critic and minor poet who left the Soviet Union in 1922. Chief literary critic for the literary review *Zveno* (1923–28) and the daily *Poslednie novosti* (1928–39). Occasional contributor to a large number of other émigré publications.

Adamovich is generally credited as being a major influence in the formation of the so-called Parisian Note (PARIZHSKAYA NOTA) among émigré poets in the period between the two world wars. He believed that literature should serve as a medium for the exchange of thoughts on the eternal themes of the human condition: life, death, love, etc. If the artist was to achieve anything of lasting value, he had to search out those themes which had concerned all men in all times. At the same time he advanced the moral message of art and believed strongly in the affective power of literature to deepen the sensitivity of the individual. Art, he believed, should not be a verbal, formalistic game but a sincere statement of author to reader. Literature is of value only if the author has something to say: "In art the theme is important."

Adamovich's pre–World War II essays were generally quite brief in nature, but after the war (and particularly after 1949) he wrote longer, more theoretical articles.

A recurrent topic in Adamovich's theoretical writings is the legacy and legitimacy of Russian émigré literature. He was convinced that émigré literature would form an essential part of the greater Russian tradition, but he was not particularly sanguine about the benefits of interaction between Western European literature and the Russian émigré tradition. Russian Soviet literature, he believed, presented greater opportunities for interaction, and he deplored the fact that such a dialogue had not occurred.

Although virtually all of Adamovich's critical articles appeared after emigration, he published two collections of verse in Russia: *Clouds* (1916) and *Purgatory* (1922).

A student of GUMILYOV, he was strongly influenced by ACMEISM. He avoided contemporary themes and settings and preferred a rather traditional poetic vocabulary. His poems are often written in a pensive mood, and the transitoriness of existence is a frequent theme.

Works: Chistilishche. 1922. *Na Zapade.* 1947. *L'autre patrie.* 1947. *Odinochestvo i svoboda.* 1955. *Kommentarii.* 1967.

Secondary literature: Roger Muir Hagglund, *A Study of the Literary Criticism of G. V. Adamovich.* Ph.D. diss., 1969, University of Washington. ———. "The Adamovič-Xodasevič Polemics," *SEEJ* 20 (1976), pp. 239–52. Yurii Ivask, "Razgovory s Adamovichem (1958–1971)," *Novyi zhurnal,* no. 134 (1979), pp. 92–101.　　J. G.

Aesopian language, a literary term (after the Greek fabulist Aesop), refers to the common efforts of writers, critics, and publicists, who, deprived of freedom of expression under the tsarist regime, tried from the late 18th through the early 20th century to circumvent the concentrated efforts of the censorship. Characterized by various forms of circumlocution, the devices of Aesopian language included the utilization of imagery borrowed from fables, allegorical fairy tale descriptions, the use of periphrasis and pseudonyms, hidden allusions at times coupled with fairly direct references (e.g., to official repression), irony, and various juxtapositions and contrasts. As a polemical device, Aesopian language concealed irony under the guise of general satisfaction and acceptance of the status quo. Denunciations of Russian realities were disguised as "foreign" thematics. "Innocent" everyday expression was transformed into veiled criticisms. Aesopian language might thus be characterized as a wholly convoluted, inverted manner of expression, yet one commonly accessible to the general readership. For as M. SALTYKOV-SHCHEDRIN asserts, all of these devices and tricks were for the Russian reader "a uniquely normal manner of expression. Literature had taught the people to read between the lines to such a degree that there was no hint so obscure as to remain uninterpreted, no allusion that would not be comprehended utterly.... Only the censorship understood nothing...."

Having developed as a special subtext of "literature between the lines," Aesopian language became not only a powerful means of political struggle and debate, but an important manifestation of realistic verbal art. To what extent the devices of Aesopian language have influenced general literary techniques has not yet been comprehensively studied; however, with time the stylistic demands of satire have incorporated the devices of Aesopian language independent of political realities and necessity, as in the works of M. BULGAKOV.

D. K. D.

Aesthetics in the sense of an explicitly stated theory of artistic creation did not appear in Russia before the 18th century. There existed, however, since the very beginnings of Russian literature, certain aesthetic principles which evolved along with other aspects of culture. Medieval architecture, icon and fresco painting, music, and literature were aesthetically integrated by virtue of being a part of religious services. The connection of an icon with the Holy Word is as natural as tales of miracle working icons, and the structure of a cathedral follows the same aesthetic principles as a holiday sermon. The aesthetics of Old Russian art and literature is utilitarian, as every work directly serves a specific purpose, yet it is also ideal. For example, a historical personage, such as a prince or martyr, will be made into an ideal scheme even in disregard of historical veracity. There is a tendency to adapt subject matter to the existing canon, rather than vice versa. Traditional devices are assiduously cultivated. Novelty was of little importance, since a work was read or seen many times and its content was known beforehand. Medieval literature and art are saturated with symbols. Descriptive details must be understood symbolically, e.g., Christ and the apostles are painted barefooted to signify their renunciation of earthly comforts. The author remains in the background, assuming a communal point-of-view, such as that of his monastery. Genre is functionally determined and hierarchically arranged, depending on the work's position in religious life.

The first change in the aesthetics of Russian literature was connected with the Second SOUTH SLAVIC INFLUENCE. The rhetorical style of *pletenie sloves* (weaving of words) featured an elaborate syntax, accumulation of synonyms, tautological compounds, neologisms, rhythmic organization of sentences, frequent exclamatory phrases, and direct apostrophe to the reader. Descriptions of the hero's emotions are now common. This new style has been interpreted as the ascendancy of an emotional attitude in art, superseding the more austere, theologically determined aesthetics of earlier literature. A similar development may be observed in icon painting.

After a period of consolidation in the reign of Ivan IV, the aesthetics of Russian literature experienced its first changes induced by Western influence. The baroque aesthetics of Polish literature of the Counter-Reformation entered 17th-century Russian literature via the Ukraine. The allegoric figures of classical poetics (Apollo, the Muses, and Sibyls) made their appearance in the writings of Nikolai Spafary (1636–1706) and SIMEON POLOTSKY.

Eighteenth-century literature is dominated by the aesthetic canon of classicism. Still during the reign of Peter I, the *Poetics* and *Rhetoric* of Aristotle, as well as the *Ars poetica* of Horace were trans-

lated. V. K. TREDIAKOVSKY translated Boileau's *Art poétique* in 1752. Subsequently, other theoretical works such as Voltaire's *Essai sur la poésie épique* and Batteux's *Les Beaux-Arts réduits a un même principe* were also translated. The writings of Marmontel, Laharpe, Gottsched, Burke, and Home were also known to Russian classicists. Some Russian authors stated their own theoretical positions, for example, A. P. SUMAROKOV in his *Two Epistles, the First dealing with the Russian Language, and the Second with Versification* (Dve epistoly, v pervoi predlagaetsya o russkom yazyke, a vo vtoroi o stikhotvorstve, 1747) and M. V. LOMONOSOV in *Preface on the Usefulness of Sacred Books in the Russian Tongue* (Predislovie o pol'ze knig tserkovnykh v rossiiskom yazyke, 1757), where he outlined his celebrated theory of "three styles." The aesthetic ideas which were current in Russia in the 18th century were eclectic and did not form a coherent aesthetic theory, but neither did their Western sources. No contradiction was seen between "imitation of nature" and a demand for *bienséance* and moral responsibility, between practical concerns such as the didactic and entertainment value of art and a notion that art's ultimate object is to attain the perfection of the True, the Good, and the Beautiful.

A key concept of 18th-century aesthetics is taste (*vkus*), defined by M. N. MURAVYOV (1757–1807) as "an accurate and delicate perception of beauty in nature and in art." It is often connected with an endorsement of Batteux's principle of art as "imitation of beautiful nature." The classicist canon of genres, based on a social hierarchy of values, has linguistic corollaries, set down in Lomonsov's doctrine of "three styles."

N. M. KARAMZIN was the first major writer to be actively aware of aesthetics as a scholarly discipline. He was familiar with the aesthetic theories of Lessing, Kant, and Schiller, but the greatest single influence on him was still Batteux's. Karamzin's sentimentalist aesthetics was still centered in imitation of nature, moralism, didacticism, and *bienséance*, but the mimetic conception of art was now wed to an emotionalist view of the creative process. Karamzin advocated the natural expression of human emotions in a "personal manner" (*lichnost'*) which, he said, "assures us of the truthfulness of what is described—often deceiving us, though." Karamzin was an aesthetic agnostic, believing that art could not reveal anything about the objective world, though it could reveal the artist's soul. While "taste" is still a focal concept in Karamzin's aesthetics, its laws are no longer the rational and immutable ones of earlier classicists, but subject to historical change.

While ROMANTICISM was gaining ground, largely through the efforts of V. A. ZHUKOVSKY, a classicist aesthetics was still taught at Russian schools and universities well into the 1820s and beyond, by scholars such as M. T. Kachenovsky (1775–1842) and A. F. MERZLYAKOV. The latter's *Kratkaya ritorika* (1817) still featured the Lomonosovian doctrine of "three styles." Also, there were some writers and poets of the younger generation whose aesthetics combined the traits of classicism, German storm and stress, and romanticism, the latter mostly in the version of Mme de Staël's *De l'Allemagne*. Poets and writers gathered around the FREE SOCIETY OF AMATEURS OF LITERATURE, THE SCIENCES, AND ARTS (Vol'noe obshchestvo lyubitelei slovesnosti, nauk i khudozhestv, 1801–25), in particular, belonged to this group, characterized by some as "neoclassicist." Among them were A. S. GRIBOEDOV, I. M. Muravyov-Apostol (1765–1851), N. I. GNEDICH, K. N. BATYUSHKOV, and V. K. KYUKHELBEKER. The "neoclassicist" aesthetics lacks the characteristic features of Jena romanticism (a dialectic model of the creative process and the work of art, art as "myth" and "symbol," romantic irony), but has other romantic traits, such as nationalism, idealization of the artist as a leader and prophet, and a belief in free, inspired creation. Some of the members of this group participated in what became known as the DECEMBRIST movement. They believed in lofty and noble poetic undertakings of civic importance. The Decembrist K. F. RYLEEV, who coined the famous line, "I'm not a poet, but a citizen," declared that the goal of poetry should be "to remind youth of the feats of their ancestors, to acquaint them with the brightest epochs of their nation's history, and to combine love of one's country with the first impressions of memory."

In his aesthetic views, A. S. PUSHKIN also stood on the threshold between Classicism and Romanticism. He welcomed Romanticism as the bringer of freedom from the constraints of the poetic canon of Classicism, particularly in the drama. His penchant for poetic stylization may be called romantic. Even more important, his image of the poet was that of the romantics. But then, Pushkin would have none of the Teutonic mysticism of his friends, the Moscow WISDOM LOVERS (lyubomudry), who had embraced Schelling's organic aesthetics, nor of the liberties taken at the expense of poetic discipline, good taste and *vraisemblance* by Hugo and the French phrenetic school.

A romantic aesthetics emerges between 1822 and 1825 in essays by A. A. BESTUZHEV, V. F. ODOEVSKY, N. A. POLEVOI, D. V. VENEVITINOV, P. A. VYAZEMSKY, and particularly in a monograph by A. GALICH (pseud. of Aleksandr Ivanovich Govorov, 1783–1848), *Essay on the Science of the Beautiful* (Opyt nauki izyashchnogo, 1825). An essay by O. M. SOMOV (1793–1833), "On Romantic Poetry" (1823), helped to propagate romanticism, although it was critical of it. German romanticism was the main source of Russian romantic ideas, though the ideas of Victor Hugo were also influential, Polevoi being their main exponent. Wilhelm Wackenroder's *Herzensergiessungen eines kunstliebenden Klosterbruders* (1797) were translated under the title *Ob iskusstve i khudozhnikakh* (On art and artists) by S. P. SHEVYRYOV in 1825. The generation of the 1820s and 1830s was heavily influenced by Schelling, whose aesthetics left a lasting imprint on Russian thought. Schelling's dialectic which made the work of art a forever elusive synthesis of opposites (the finite: the infinite, the ideal: the real, the subjective: the objective, reason: intuition, etc.) was embraced by the Russian romantics: "By romanticism I mean the striving of the infinite spirit of humanity to express itself in finite forms," wrote Bestuzhev. And so were the other basic traits of Schelling's aesthetics: the notion that the work of art is itself created nature, rather than "imitation of nature;" a conception of the work of art as symbol and hence a belief in the cognitive power of art; a pervasive aesthetic organicism, which makes the work of art an organic expression of cosmic, national, and human truths. Other traits of romantic aesthetics were an emphasis on art's organic connection with the spirit of an age (*dukh vremeni*), an organic theory of genre (where, for instance, the Tragic and the Comic are the positive and negative expression of the Ideal) and a metaphysical definition of the Beautiful ("the sensibly perfect phenomenon of something that is *per se* invisible," according to Galich).

In some of the more conservative romantics (SLAVOPHILES, in particular), an intimate connection between, or even an identity of art and religion were postulated, so by Odoevsky ("Sebastian Bach") and GOGOL ("The Portrait," "What Is Ultimately the Essence of Russian Poetry and What Is Its Peculiar Nature," in *Selected Passages*). More progressive Schellingians, such as N. I. NADEZHDIN, rejected romantic mysticism and stressed the social role of art.

V. G. BELINSKY started out as a pure Schellingian in his "Literary Reveries" (Literaturnye mechtaniya, 1834), but was soon converted to a Hegelian aesthetics ("The Idea of Art," 1841), which he never abandoned. His aesthetics was based on the three pillars of historical, national, and social organicism. Belinsky saw literature as an organ of a nation's social evolution, which he conceived as a progression of ideas. Art, defined by him as "thinking in images" (*myshlenie v obrazakh*), was an idea made aesthetically palpable. Belinsky's organic conception of the work of art implied that no poetic idea exists independently of its artistic form, and *vice versa*. It led him to a rejection of aesthetic intellectualism, schematism, and allegory, on the one hand, and to an equally resolute rejection of aesthetic naturalism and formalism, on the other. In practice, Belinsky and his followers were, however, more concerned with social content than with aesthetic form. Belinsky's conception of the creative individual was Hegelian. He believed that it was given to artists of genius to discover new truths and to create new values, while artists of talent could merely give aesthetically adequate expression to the ideas and values of their age. Toward the end of his life, Belinsky occasionally abandoned his organic aesthetics for a social utilitarianism, justified, he felt, by the fact that during critical epochs of history, such as his own age, spreading the plain truth and the right ideas was more important than any aesthetic values.

Throughout the 19th century, the position of an author in the political spectrum may be generally deduced from the extent to which his aesthetics stresses either the autonomy of art or the importance of art's social role, while maintaining both. Conservatives such as Apollon GRIGORIEV or DOSTOEVSKY asserted that only if the artist remained true to his calling could his work properly fulfill its social mission, while radicals like DOBROLYUBOV or SALTYKOV-SHCHEDRIN maintained that only an artist who pursued the right ideological course could

realize his potential as an artist. Likewise, the former would place more stress on the intuitive aspect of the creative process, and the latter on its rational and experiential component, though agreeing that both were essential. Dostoevsky departed from almost everybody else when he asserted that the highly idiosyncratic and even extreme was more revealing of human truth, and hence more "typical," than the ordinary. However, everybody agreed that art was to be a synthesis of the "individual" and the "typical."

The pattern of an organic aesthetics which allowed art to have its autonomy, yet also let it march in the forefront of whatever one believed to be progress, was broken by the social utilitarianism of N. G. CHERNYSHEVSKY and D. I. PISAREV. In his celebrated dissertation, *The Aesthetic Relations of Art to Reality* (Esteticheskie otnosheniya iskusstva k deistvitel'nosti, 1855), Chernyshevsky undertook to reduce art to imitation of nature and the aesthetic categories of the Beautiful, the Sublime, the Tragic, etc. to sense experience not different in kind from the Pleasing, the Unusual, and the Sad. He minimized the importance of art: "Let art be satisfied with its exalted and beautiful calling: to serve, in the absence of reality, as a surrogate of the same, and to be for humanity a textbook of life." Chernyshevsky and his followers had a tendency to label all artists as either Epicureans and hypocrites, indulging in their perverse pleasures under the guise of "disinterested art," or honest, socially concerned enlighteners, with nothing in between. In his essay "The Abolition of Aesthetics" (1865), Pisarev claimed that Chernyshevsky had in effect demonstrated that, inasmuch as there was no such thing as the Beautiful, there was no justification for the existence of aesthetics as an independent discipline. He accordingly practiced a strictly social and utilitarian approach in his own literary criticism.

The aesthetics of Lev TOLSTOI, as stated in *What is Art?* (1897–98), was in significant ways close to Chernyshevsky's. Tolstoi declared all art that was not a direct expression of emotion and capable of "infecting" humanity with the same emotion to be nonart, fit only for the idle amusement of an effete upper class. Since art may "infect" humans with good or evil emotions (such as Christian love or jingo patriotism), Tolstoi saw two kinds of art: "good" and "bad." And since much of recent art and literature failed to meet these criteria, if only by virtue of being unintelligible to the uneducated masses, Tolstoi summarily dismissed Shakespeare, Beethoven, Pushkin, and his own early works as either "nonart," "bad art," or a mixture of both.

Tolstoi's aesthetics was an isolated phenomenon and had no great influence. The same is true of the more original aesthetics of K. N. LEONTIEV, stated mostly in his essays gathered in *Byzantinism and Slavdom* (Vizantizm i slavyanstvo, 1871–72). Leontiev took art to be the deepest and most universal mode of cognition, and the highest vital expression, both absolutely and historically. His aesthetic evolutionism sees history advancing dialectically through three stages: primary simplicity to complex flowering to secondary simplification, with the second most vigorous, violent, complex, and beautiful. A believer in the life-creating power of strife, and even oppression, Leontiev felt that no vigorous activity, including art, could flourish under conditions of *laissez-faire* and argued that true creative freedom was more current in times and places where political freedom and religious tolerance were unknown. Leontiev, himself a brilliant writer turned ascetic, pointed out that salvation of the soul depended on a denial of the very values which are the object of man's most vigorous strivings at their creative best. He suggested that through a fierce and ever-renewed struggle between religious and aesthetic impulses, religion would be refined and art would become more spiritual.

While Leontiev's aesthetics remained without a response, the less original aesthetics of Vladimir SOLOVYOV became the basis of the aesthetics of Russian SYMBOLISM. Solovyov returned to Schelling's Neoplatonic system, taking art to be not the mere presentation of an idea, but its actual incarnation in a sense object. Hence form was not to be neglected. Solovyov followed Schelling not only in his mystic idealism, but also in a teleological conception of creation: the Idea creates cosmos from chaos even in nature, generating a hierarchy of forms in inorganic nature, and up through the plant and animal kingdom. Human creativity then continues the work begun by Nature. Eventually matter, fully penetrated by the Idea, will become immortal. Art is "theurgic" in that it creates a transition from beauty in nature to the beauty of future life. Initially, Solovyov tended to see a mystic con-

nection between Art and the mysteries of Christian religion. But in the essays "Beauty in Nature" (Krasota v prirode, 1889) and "The Universal Meaning of Art" (Obshchii smysl iskusstva, 1890) his theurgic view of art became more generally spiritualist.

The aesthetics of the "decadents" of the 1890s (BALMONT, BRYUSOV, ANNENSKY) was influenced by French symbolism, and by Schopenhauer. For once, some Russians dared to declare that "perhaps everything in life is but a means for the sake of brightly melodious verse" (Bryusov) and that art could be a serious business even if it was not socially useful. Bryusov declared that the history of literature was the record of a continuous search for new forms (instead of a record of literature's social *engagement*) and stressed the element of craftsmanship in art. The "decadents" developed a consciously "impressionist" and "momentalist" aesthetics, meaning an orientation toward the fleeting grace of subjective experience and a preference for casual, fragmentary images which would allude and stimulate, rather than signify directly. The aesthetics of Baudelairean *correspondances* was realized in multiple associations between sound patterns, imagery, and emotional content. The reception of a work of art was conceived as a mirror image of the creative process through sympathetic experience, so in Annensky's *Book of Reflections* (Knigi otrazhenii, 1905). The whole "decadent" aesthetics was oriented toward music and musical metaphors.

The aesthetics of the later symbolists (Vyacheslav IVANOV, BLOK, BELY) was close to Solovyov's, featuring Neoplatonic principles such as an acceptance of the metaphysical as well as psychological reality of "inner vision" (Ivanov uses the term *forma formans*) and a belief in a dual world of mundane and metaphysical reality, with art a bridge between these (Ivanov: *a realibus ad realiora*). The latter lead to an emphasis on the symbolic, mythopoeic, and theurgic function of art. Nietzschean aesthetic categories, such as the Dionysian and Apollonian, as well as its various elements (the female vs. the male principle in art, creation from plenitude or from hunger, and an analysis of the creative process in terms of "ascent" and "descent"), appear in the aesthetics of Vyacheslav Ivanov.

Chernyshevsky's crude naturalism and utilitarianism were refined by the populists P. L. LAVROV and N. K. MIKHAILOVSKY, and by the Marxist G. V. PLEKHANOV, who all sought to find a synthesis of the autonomy of art and an active social role for it. Plekhanov criticized Chernyshevsky for having failed to consider the specifics of the aesthetic fact and for having taken an absolute, rather than historical view of art. He suggested that the work of art is produced by the artist's creative intuition, on the one hand, and by the volition of his social class, on the other. Somehow, inexplicably, these attitudes are synchronized. Plekhanov, like Belinsky, believed that great art could not espouse reactionary or anti-humanitarian ideas. He also believed that a definite relationship existed between art and its socio-economic base. Specifically, he saw the pessimism, formlessness, and irrationalism of fin de siècle "modernism" as a reflection of the disintegration of the bourgeoisie as a social class. Plekhanov's ideas influenced other Marxists, such as A. V. LUNACHARSKY, V. V. VOROVSKY, V. M. FRICHE, and P. N. SAKULIN. The leading critics of the PEREVAL group of the 1920s, A. Z. LEZHNEV and A. K. VORONSKY, also held aesthetic views similar to Plekhanov's. They all believed that a healthy and victorious social class, such as the proletariat, should have a natural preference for realist art and reject, as a bourgeois diversion, any art which would distort, embellish, or ignore reality. This position was branded "VULGAR SOCIOLOGISM," when SOCIALIST REALISM was declared the official aesthetic and critical teaching in the 1930s.

Each of the various schools of Russian modernism developed its own aesthetic ideas, but hardly a consistent philosophy of art. An expressionist aesthetics has been recognized in some writers, poets, playwrights, and artists of the early 20th century (Leonid ANDREEV, David BURLYUK, the early MAYAKOVSKY, Nikolai ZABOLOTSKY). It features the cultivation of an alienated "I," facing a world in a state of catastrophe; an ahistorical yet highly sympathetic approach to human misery; a pointed disregard of artistic proprieties; and a penchant for the grotesque and nightmarish. The poetic practice, if not the aesthetic theory, of IMAGISM is largely expressionist.

ACMEISM produced some fine criticism, but hardly a new aesthetics. When Osip MANDELSHTAM said that "a poem is alive by virtue of its inner form, that sounding mould of form which precedes the written poem," or that poetry is an *anamnesis* of ancient images and truths ("Word and Culture," 1921), he was restating positions of the

organic aesthetics of Goethe and the romantics. The conception of a poem as a "living organism" was stated quite literally by Gumilyov, and both he and Mandelshtam cultivated the images of the "living word" and "word soul."

Russian FUTURISM combined two diametrically opposed tendencies: the modernity, urbanism, and expressionism of the early Mayakovsky and the anthropological, primitivist, and archaist mysticism of KHLEBNIKOV and KRUCHONYKH. The futurists developed some radically new notions about the nature of poetry. Instead of departing from an "inner vision" or "poetic idea," they departed, much as the cubist painters who inspired them, from their material, the speech sounds of Russian. Poetry became an exercise in skillful and imaginative deformation of the units of language. A wholly new notion, which appears in various formulations in futurism, Acmeism, and CONSTRUCTIVISM, is that of the "thingness" (*veshchnost'*) of the speech sound, the word, and the work of art. The symbolist aesthetics of a subtle and precarious balance of the "real" and "ideal" is sublated to mean that the "real," i.e., the speech sound, the word, the image, the poetic structure is itself "the thing."

Russian FORMALISM developed an aesthetics that was close to that of Futurism. Its pursuit of "literariness" (*literaturnost'*) in literature was based on the Neo-Kantian notion that a work of art exists on a different ontological plane than empirical reality or the emotional experience of its creator. SHKLOVSKY's slogan, "art as device" (*iskusstvo kak priem*), dramatized this notion. The history of literature, which had been previously synchronized with social and political developments, was now seen as a succession of aesthetic systems, each built from the ruins of the preceding. However, art and literature were still seen as inherently progressive activities, since their very essence was to challenge the world by creating new, "estranged" or "defamiliarized" models of it.

The formalist strain of Russian modernism led, on the one hand, to an aesthetics which made art utilitarian by principle: the artist was no more and no less than a skilled professional, like an agronomist or engineer, and hence the aesthetics of *Lef* and the constructivists of the 1920s was geared to fit those branches of art and literature that were directly linked to life at large: commercial art, propaganda, journalism, and mass entertainment. On the other hand, a conception of art as pure form also led to a mystic hypostasis of form, so in the theosophic speculations of the painters Vasily Kandinsky (1866–1944) and Kazimir Malevich (1878–1935).

Formalism was immediately attacked by various group who were maintaining the standpoint of nineteenth-century organic aesthetics. An art that was detached from the artist's social identity seemed untrustworthy to the communist activists of RAPP: it smacked of onetime bourgeois *bohémiens*, who were now offering their services to the victorious proletariat. But factual objections were also voiced. Boris ARVATOV and Pavel Medvedev (1891–1938) objected that the aesthetic fact must be seen in a dialectic relationship with other human activities, and that even if it was correct that the aesthetic fact stands apart from subjective experience, this did not mean that it had no ideological relevance.

The aesthetics of socialist realism, which has been the officially sanctioned theory of art in the Soviet Union since 1934, is eclectic. Most of its theorists follow the principles of a Belinskian social, national, and historic organicism. Art is expected to state an ideal (that of socialism) in a realistic form. The work of art is hypostasized as an "artistic symbol" (*khudozhestvennyi OBRAZ*), defined as a "concrete and yet universal image of human life, created with the aid of the creative imagination and possessing aesthetic meaning" (L. I. Timofeev). The "artistic symbol" is considered to have great cognitive power. These theoretical conceptions are in conflict with the utilitarian requirements of Soviet art and literature. Also, a Chernyshevskian naturalist aesthetics fits the creative practice of most Soviet artists and writers better than an organic aesthetics. Nevertheless, even Party organs will pay at least lip service to the principles of an organic aesthetics.

Contemporary Soviet aesthetic theory moves essentially within the confines of concepts and questions that were current in the first half of the 19th century. It has retained the conventional aesthetic categories, and specifically that of the Beautiful (*prekrasnoe*). A controversy regarding the nature of the Beautiful has been going on for a long time, between *prirodniki* (naturists), who believe that Beauty is inherent in the object, and *obshchestvenniki* (societalists), who claim

that Beauty is in the beholder's eye. Soviet aesthetic thought, on the whole, holds on to the notion, developed by Belinsky and refined by Plekhanov, that art is not only a mirror of life, but also an active agent in its development. It agrees, then, with Schelling's paradox which makes artistic creation free, yet its ultimate product determinate: a socialist artist is to arrive at his progressive message freely without coercion, much as a bourgeois artist will inevitably arrive at a negative assessment of capitalist society.

Besides the official aesthetics of Socialist Realism, there have existed and still exist in the USSR some independent lines of aesthetic thought, the most significant of which leads to the structuralist school of Yu. M. LOTMAN, V. V. Ivanov, V. N. TOPOROV, B. A. Uspensky, and others. In the 1920s, P. A. FLORENSKY (1882–1943), Sergei EIZEN-SHTEIN, and M. M. BAKHTIN searched for archaic structures (in biology, prehistory, ethnology, and folk culture) which might be prototypes of structures found in modern literature and art. Eizenshtein speculated that film, an art form still in its infancy, might be recapitulating an early stage in the development of established art forms. Bakhtin stated many of the ideas which were to form the core of Soviet semiotic theory in the 1960s and 1970s. He suggested that each field of ideological activity forms a specific sign system and studied the interaction of different systems, specifically the difficulties involved in "translating" signs into the language of another system. Bakhtin characterized art as a semiotic system where the meaning of signs is inseparable from the details of their material form. Therefore, the analysis of a work of art should be concerned with establishing the exact connection between its different levels, such as, in a poem, its conscious meaning, its pathos, and its sound structure. Bakhtin also demanded that the social and ideological context of a work of art be an integral element of its definition.

Yu. M. Lotman has been the main spokesman of Russian STRUC-TURALISM since the appearance of his Lectures on Structural Poetics (1964). His general aesthetic principles are in accord with traditional organic aesthetics: the work of art is seen as a model of reality in which several semiotic systems (aesthetic, social, political, etc.) are integrated by the artist, with the intention to exert a certain influence on that reality. Lotman's conception of "art as a language" stresses the notion that art is a semiotic system among others. His concern is with the peculiarities of the inner, hierarchic structure of this system and its interaction with other systems. The novelty of Lotman's approach lies in his efforts to state his observations, which are based on solid philological evidence, in scientific terms, specifically those of information theory. There is a general tendency in Russian structuralism to look for ways in which aesthetic insights may be quantified or otherwise stated in scientific terms.

Bibliography: Innokentii Annenskii, "Simvoly krasoty u russkikh pisatelei." In Knigi otrazhenii. 1979. Pp. 128–35. V. G. Belinskii, "Ideya iskusstva." In Polnoe sobranie sochinenii. 1953–59. Vol. 4, pp. 585–601. Yu. B. Borev, Osnovnye esteticheskie kategorii. 1960. N. A. Gulyaev, A. N. Bogdanov, and L. G. Yudkevich, Teoriya literatury v svyazi s problemami estetiki. 1970. J. Holthusen, Studien zur Ästhetik und Poetik des russischen Symbolismus. 1957. P. L. Ivanov, O sushchnosti krasoty. 1967. Vyacheslav Ivanov, "Simvolika esteticheskikh nachal." In Po zvezdam: Stat'i i aforizmy. 1909. Pp. 21–32. M. S. Kagan, ed., Lektsii po istorii estetiki. 3 vols. 1973–76. M. S. Kagan, Lektsii po marksistsko-leninskoi estetike. 2nd rev. ed. 1971. V. A. Keldysh, "Novoe v kriticheskom realizme i v ego estetike." In Literaturno-esteticheskie kontseptsii v Rossii kontsa XIX–nachala XX v. 1975. Pp. 68–115. Yury Lotman, Analysis of the Poetic Text. Ed. and trans. D. Barton Johnson. 1976. Yu. V. Mann, Poetika russkogo romantizma. 1976. Rudolf Neuhäuser, The Romantic Age in Russian Literature: Poetic and Esthetic Norms. An Anthology of Original Texts (1800–1850). 1975. Krystyna Pomorska, Russian Formalist Theory and its Poetic Ambiance. 1968. G. N. Pospelov, "'Khudozhestvennaya sistema' russkogo klassitsizma." In Problemy literaturnogo stilya. 1970. Pp. 126–62. L. K. Shvetsova, "Tvorcheskie printsipy i vzglyady blizkie k ekspressionizmu." In Literaturno-esteticheskie kontseptsii v Rossii kontsa XIX–nachala XX v. 1975. Pp. 252–83. K. V. Shokhin, "Problema prekrasnogo v esteticheskikh vozzreniyakh Drevnei Rusi." In Iz istorii esteticheskoi mysli drevnosti i srednevekov'ya. 1961. Pp. 282–302. A. A. Sidorov and Yu. S. Kalashnikov, "Problemy razvitiya russkoi khudozhestvennoi kul'tury kontsa XIX–nachala XX v." In Russkaya khudozhestvennaya kul't-ura kontsa XIX–nachala XX veka. Book 1, 1968. Rimvydas Silbajoris, "Human Contact and Tolstoi's Aesthetics." In Papers in Comparative Studies. 1981. Vol. 1, pp. 9–40. Edward M. Swiderski, The Philosophical Foundations of Soviet Aesthetics: Theories and Controversies in the Post-war Years. 1979. Teoriya literatury. 3 vols. 1962–65. Victor Terras, Belinskij and Russian Literary Criticism: The Heritage of Organic Aesthetics. 1974. V. V. Vanslov, Estetika romantizma. 1966. James West, Russian Symbolism: A Study of Vyacheslav Ivanov and Russian Symbolist Aesthetic. 1970.   V. T.

Afanásiev, Aleksándr Nikoláevich (1826–71), historian and folklorist, the leader of the Russian Mythological School of folklore investigation. He was born in the town of Boguchar in the province of Voronezh, in the family of a district official. He studied law at the University of Moscow, and from 1849 to 1862 served in the Archives of the Ministry of Foreign Affairs. Denounced in 1862, he lost his position, but continued to concentrate on his mythological and folklore studies.

In 1855 to 1864 Afanasiev published the work by which he is best remembered, his collection of Russian folktales, Narodnye russkie skazki. (A selected English edition was published by Pantheon in 1945.) It remains the classic collection of Russian folktales, though a number of others have succeeded it. Afanasiev was not a fieldworker, and took almost all of the 640 tales in the collection from published or manuscript sources. He did not refrain entirely from making changes in his material, or even from combining several parts of a single tale taken from different sources. But he was largely able to select the best variants of tales for inclusion in his collection. His commentary, reflecting his mythological biases, is largely outdated.

Afanasiev's leading theoretical treatise, The Poetic Attitudes of the Slavs Toward Nature (Poeticheskie vozzreniya slavyan na prirodu, 1866–69), likewise expressed his mythological view of the nature of folklore. A follower of Jakob Grimm, Afanasiev saw folklore narratives as myths, symbolic embodiments of natural forces, and especially of the conflict between light and darkness. He also borrowed liberally from his contemporary, Max Müller. Like Müller, Afanasiev regarded metaphor and myth as rooted in the nature of language itself. Through the comparative study of philology, Afanasiev believed, it will become possible to reconstruct original mythic thought.

In 1859 Afanasiev published a small collection of Russian Folk Legends (Russkie narodnye legendy), which because of their seemingly blasphemous character were proscribed by the censor until 1914. A collection of Indecent Tales (Zavetnye skazki) collected by Afanasiev, some of which portrayed the Russian landowning gentry and the clergy in a satirical light, was published anonymously in Geneva in the 1860s.

Bibliography: Narodnye russkie skazki A. N. Afanas'eva. Postface by A. Nechaev. 1978. Russian Fairy Tales Collected by Aleksandr Afanas'ev. Trans. Norbert Guterman. Folkloristic commentary by Roman Jakobson. 1975. Russian Folk Tales. Trans. Robert Chandler. 1980.

Secondary literature: M. K. Azadovskii, Istoriya russkoi fol'kloristiki. Moscow, 1963. Vol. 2, pp. 73–84. A. N. Pypin, Istoriya russkoi etnografii. St. Petersburg, 1891. Vol. 2, pp. 350–74. Yu. M. Sokolov, Russian Folklore. New York, 1950. Pp. 69–76, 386–87.   W. E. H.

Afinogénov, Aleksándr Nikoláevich (1904–41), dramatist. A graduate of the Moscow Institute of Journalism, Afinogenov joined the Communist Party in 1922 and wrote his first play two years later. In 1926 he became affiliated with the Moscow Workers' PROLETKULT Theater, which staged his On the Other Side of the Crack (Po tu storonu shcheli), based on stories by Jack London, At the Crossroads (Na perelome), on the revolutionary struggle of the German proletariat, Be on Guard (Glyadi v oba), about student life, and Raspberry Jam (Malinovoe varen'e), depicting the intrigues of "agents" in a provincial Soviet town. Afinogenov's association with the Proletkult Theater lasted from 1926 to 1929. Besides writing plays for it, he also served as its literary manager and then as its director. His two most important plays date from the late 1920s and early 1930s: The Eccentric (Chudak, 1929), set in a paper factory and dealing with the first Five Year Plan; its staging by the Second Moscow Art Theater signaled Afinogenov's break with the Proletkult; and Fear (Strakh, 19

a reasonably sympathetic consideration of the difficulties in integrating non-Party intelligentsia into the program of postrevolutionary reconstruction. Afinogenov took an active role in the UNION OF SOVIET WRITERS following its creation and in 1934 became editor of the Union journal *Theater and Drama* (Teatr i dramaturgiya). He died during the bombing of Moscow on October 29, 1941. His total output of twenty-six plays includes also *Station Far Distant* (Dalekoe, 1935), about heroic railroad workers in a remote Soviet community; *Hail, Spain* (Salyut, Ispaniya, 1936), on the Spanish Civil War; *Moscow, the Kremlin* (Moskva, Kreml', 1938), a historical-revolutionary "popular drama" about Lenin which was never finished; *Hotel De Luxe* (Otel' Lyuks, 1940), an unfinished anti-imperialist play; *The Mother of Her Children* (Mat' svoikh detei, 1939), about a heroic mother of five; *Mashenka* (1940), a once popular play on the upbringing of children; and *On the Eve* (Nakanune), one of the better early Soviet war plays which he completed shortly before his death in September 1941. Like KIRSHON, Afinogenov was an advocate of a Soviet psychological drama.

Works: P'esy, stat'i, vystupleniya. 1977. *Pis'ma, dnevniki.* 1977.
Translations: Distant Point. A Play. Trans. and adapted by H. Griffith. London, 1941. *Fear.* Trans. N. Strelsky, D. Colman, A. Greene. New York: Theatre of Vassar College, 1934. *Listen Professor! A Play in Three Acts.* American Version by P. Phillips. New York, 1944. H. B. S.

Aglaya, first Russian literary almanac, published in Moscow by N. M. KARAMZIN. Two books of the almanac appeared, the first in 1794 and the second in 1795. A second edition was issued in 1796. The contents consisted almost exclusively of works by Karamzin, notably two excerpts from "Letters of a Russian Traveler" (about London in book 1 and about Paris in book 2) and "The Isle of Bornholm" (book 1). Book 1 also included works by I. I. DMITRIEV and M. M. KHERASKOV. *Aglaya* had a strong sentimentalist bias, although the publication of "The Isle of Bornholm" pointed to the beginnings of Russian romanticism. C. T. N.

Aitmátov, Chingíz (1928–   ). Born in a small settlement (Sheker) in the mountainous region of Central Asia near the Chinese border in what is now the Kirghiz Republic of the USSR, Kirghiz by birth, recipient of several Soviet literary prizes, Aitmatov is probably the best known non-Russian Soviet prose writer. Author of short stories, novels, novellas, plays, and film scenarios, he is completely bilingual in Russian and Kirghiz.

Through his parents Aitmatov learned the Russian language and was exposed to Russian culture and literature. Through his paternal grandmother and aunt he experienced the nomadic way of life, absorbed the oral traditions of his people, and grew to love the rich ancient Kirghiz customs and culture, with its songs, legends and tales. Because his father, Torekul, was a victim of Stalin's purges, Aitmatov experienced firsthand the injustice and hardship of Stalin's reign.

A veterinarian by training, Aitmatov later studied at the Gorky Literary Institute in Moscow (1956–58) and then worked as a correspondent for *Pravda* in the Kirghiz Republic. He began his literary activity in the late 1940s as a translator and writer in the Kirghiz language.

Aitmatov's works are regularly published and reprinted in large editions. Among his more important works are *Farewell Gulsary* (1966), *The White Steamship* (1970), *The Ascent of Mount Fuji* (1975), and *And the Day is Longer Than a Century* (in Russian, 1981). Although he has been writing exclusively in the Russian language since 1966, all of Aitmatov's works are set in the mountains and steppes of his native rural Kirghizia. His main characters are all ethnically Kirghiz. They are rooted in their nomadic tradition and rich colorful culture; their speech is filled with proverbs, sayings, songs and Kirghiz expressions; their physical appearance, dress, and mannerisms reflect local color.

The clash between the traditional, timeless, nomad existence and the intruding foreign Soviet industrial, collectivized way of life, together with the conflict between good and evil are central to Aitmatov's works. He focuses on the themes of exile and the end of an era. Aitmatov explores human potential for evil and reveals the truth about the nature of man in general and Soviet society in particular. He is concerned with human ethics and values. His positive charac-

ters (often children) are frequently characterized by their craving for love and their nostalgia for the past. Their youthful idealism and lofty dreams are trampled upon by callous adults. They often escape from the brutality of present reality into the realm of lyrical dreams, fantasy, and death.

A number of Aitmatov's works have been adapted for the stage and cinema. His best and most controversial play, *The Ascent of Mount Fuji*, written jointly with Mukhamedzhanov, played to packed audiences (1973) for almost a year at the Sovremennik in Moscow and later in the United States at the Arena Stage in Washington. It was initially published in the United States in 1975 and was the first book covered by the new Soviet-American copyright agreement of 1973. Its central theme deals with Stalin's purges and their aftermath and raises the question of moral responsibility. Although the author does not dwell on the detail and horror as did SOLZHENITSYN, he nevertheless shows the senselessness and morally corrupting impact of the Stalin era with its terrible waste of human talent and potential.

A member of the Communist party, officially praised, Aitmatov nevertheless is not a hack writer and his works do not adhere strictly to the demands of SOCIALIST REALISM. They are permeated with a tragic note. His characters are rarely positive and have psychological problems often caused by the new Soviet System. The new way of life under the Soviet rule is thus presented in a negative light. Aitmatov refers to such taboos as Stalin's concentration camps (*The Ascent of Mount Fuji*), agricultural failures (*The First Cranes*), abuses of Soviet power (*Farewell Gulsary*), the senseless destruction of an indigenous ethnic culture (*The White Steamship*), exile and a number of other themes. He publicly criticizes the Soviet System, and without penalty.

Aitmatov's major contribution to world literature is his ability to portray a people caught at a turning point in their lives. He is the first to depict the customs and the disappearing way of life of the Kirghiz people who depended upon their oral traditions and did not have a written language prior to the Revolution.

Works in Russian: Dzhamilia. 1959. *Rasskazy.* 1958. *Materinskoe pole.* 1963–64. *Verblyuzhii glaz.* 1962. *Pervyi uchitel'.* 1967, 1971. *Povesti.* 1967. *Povesti gor i stepei.* 1963, 1971. *Povesti i rasskazy.* 1970. *Proshchai, Gul'sary.* 1967, 1976. *Povesti i rasskazy.* 1971. *Pegii pes, begushchii kraem morya.* 1977. *Rannie zhuravli.* 1976. *Belyi parokhod; povesti.* 1980. *I dol'she veka dlitsya den'.* 1981.
Works in English: Short Novels. n.d. *Tales of the Mountains and Steppes.* 1969, 1973, 1978. *The White Steamship.* 1972. *The Ascent of Mount Fuji.* 1975. *The Day Lasts More than a Hundred Years.* 1983.
Secondary Literature. K. A. Asanaliev, *Zametki o tvorchestve Ch. Aitmatova.* Frunze, 1968. M. Azizov, *Khudozhestvennye osobennosti yazyka povestei Ch. Aitmatova.* Makhachkala, 1971. A. B. Gevorkyan, "Prostranstvenno-simvolicheskie obrazy v povestyakh Ch. Aitmatova," *Trudy Samarkandskogo universiteta,* no. 238 (1973). Aleksandr Khvatov, "Nravstvennoe bespokoistvo gumanista." In Chingiz Aitmatov, *Povesti—roman* (1982), pp. 471–79. *Literaturnaya gazeta,* nos. 27–29, 31 (1970). N. N. Shneidman, "Soviet Literature at the Crossroads: The Controversial Prose of Chingiz Aitmatov," *RLT* 16 (1979), pp. 244–63. V. Voronov, *Chingiz Aitmatov: Ocherk tvorchestva.* 1976. H. S.

Akhmadúlina, Bélla Akhátovna (1937–   ) was born and brought up in Moscow. Her first published verses appeared in 1955. After finishing school, she entered the Gorky Literary Institute, graduating in 1960. Her first collection, *The String* (Struna, 1962), was followed by two long poems, "Tale of the Rain" (Skazka o dozhde) and "My Family Tree" (Moya rodoslovnaya) in 1963. In 1967 she published two more long poems, "Adventure in an Antique Shop" (Priklyuchenie v antikvarnom magazine) and "The Chills" (Oznob), the latter of which was taken as the title for a major collection of her work, *Oznob* (1968), published by the émigré publishing house, Posev. In 1969 *Music Lessons* (Uroki muzyki) appeared, followed by *Verses* (Stikhi, 1975), *Candle* (Svecha, 1977), *Blizzard* (Metel', 1977), *Dreams of Georgia* (Sny o Gruzii, 1977) and *Secret* (Taina, 1983). The almanac *Metropolis* (Metropol', 1979) contains her surrealist prose piece, "Many Dogs and a Dog" (Mnogo sobak i sobaka).

The creative act, a prominent theme in Akhmadulina's work, is for the poet an act of mediation between animate and inanimate, past and present, nature and human society. Privy to the "secret speech" of objects around her, she frees them from their lifeless state by the act of writing, or naming things, as she has described it. Writing itself is described as a difficult task: her battle to overcome her own muteness (*nemota*) is depicted as physical torture for the poet, who lacks confidence in her ability and is overwhelmed by an awareness of her artistic indebtedness to the surrounding world. A recurrent lyrical character in her writing is the "other artist" who, in contrast to her poetic *persona*, is able to write without difficulty.

Fantastic tendencies abound in her work: her long poems involve dreamlike, symbol-laden events which go beyond the historically, medically, or physically possible and are told in a sustained, narrative fantasy. Historical memory is explored not for artistic contrast, as in VOZNESENSKY's work, nor for social comparison, as in EVTUSHENKO's, but rather for the lyrical evocation of an atmosphere of which the poet retains a dim but vital recollection. This lends a lyric, mysterious quality to descriptions of contemporary life as well. Akhmadulina's relation to her reader is a complex one: her poetic "I" is alternately egalitarian ("This is I ..." [Eto ya ...]) and an outsider ("I envy time-honored habit ..." [Zavidna mne izvechnaya privychka ...]). In essence, most of her long poems—"The Chills," "Tale," etc.—are concerned with her alienation from socially defined normalcy: even health itself becomes suspect, and illness, whether physical, as in "The Chills," or mental, as in "Lunatics" (Lunatiki), serves as a metaphor for the poet's insistence on or entrapment in an alternate state of being. Criticism of her work, which has been described as apolitical "drawing-room poetry," contains little truth: although generally avoiding larger social issues, she has on occasion confronted them either directly, as in her poem "I Swear" (Klyanus') on TSVETAEVA's death, or indirectly, as in her muted criticism of philistine values in "Tale." More often, however, her challenge to contemporary literature lies not in the content of her work, as is the case with Evtushenko, but in her artistic treatment of that content: in this sense she is more akin to Voznesensky. Unlike Voznesensky, however, she avoids metrical and verbal experimentation: predominant metres are four- and five-foot iambs and three-foot anapests. She makes frequent use of feminine rhymes, as well as assonance and consonance in place of exact end-rhymes.

Works: Oznob. Frankfurt, 1968. *Sny o Gruzii.* Tbilisi, 1977.

Translations: Fever and Other Poems. Trans. Geoffrey Dutton and Igor Mezhakoff-Koriakin. 1969.

Secondary literature: Christine Rydel, "The Metapoetical World of Bella Akhmadulina," *RLT* 1 (1971), pp. 326–41.   N. C.

Akhmátova, Ánna Andréevna, born Anna Gorenko on 11 June 1889 near Odessa, died on 5 March 1966 at Domodedovo. Her father Andrei Gorenko was a maritime engineer. Her aristocratic mother Inna Stogova was a former member of the radical political group *Narodnaya Volya* (People's Will). The young Akhmatova knew French poets by heart as well as the Russians. She grew up in Tsarskoe Selo where she attended school, completing her final year at Fundukleevskaya gimnaziya in Kiev (1907). The same year she enrolled at the Faculty of Law at the Kiev College for Women, later withdrawing to study literature in St. Petersburg. In 1903 Akhmatova met the poet Nikolai GUMILYOV whose persistent wooing led to their marriage in 1910. They traveled abroad in 1910 and 1911. In Paris Akhmatova became friendly with the yet unknown artist Modigliani who drew her as Egyptian queens and dancers. Together they visited the Louvre and recited French poetry.

Akhmatova's first poem appeared in 1907 in Gumilyov's journal *Sirius*. She participated in the GUILD OF POETS organized by Gumilyov and GORODETSKY. Soon it disassociated itself from the SYMBOLISTS, giving birth to ACMEISM, whose avowed principles were an emphasis on clarity, freshness, a return to earth and close ties with the literature and culture of Europe and of all ages. The symbolist ANNENSKY was their acknowledged teacher. The popular Gumilyovs frequented the fashionable artistic café *The Stray Dog*.

The first collection of Akhmatova's verse, *Evening* (Vecher, 1912), appeared under the pseudonym Anna Akhmatova, taken from her Tatar great-grandmother. Hailed for its Acmeist clarity, conciseness, compressed style and precise details, the collection concurrently espoused the romantic concept of evening as a time of awakening for the sensitive young adult to life, love, and grief. Its miniature love lyrics manifested subtlety of style and message. The collection *Rosary*

(Chetki, 1914) showed marked changes in the poet's voice, from wary expectation of betrayal to disillusionment with love coupled with the worldliness of a *femme fatale*. The lyrics generated numerous female epigones whom the poet deplored in her "Epigram":

> I taught women to speak ...
> But, Lord, how to force them to be still!

The long poem *By the Very Sea* (U samogo morya, 1915) synopsizes the two collections, bidding farewell to adolescent reveries and a pagan outlook on life. The persona, who spurned a fisherman's love in favor of an imaginary prince, encounters death and sorrow partly of her own doing. *The White Flock* (Belaya staya, 1917) presents poems on memories of lost love transformed into song in the crucible of grief. The persona evolves into a sybil whose "lips no longer kiss, but prophesy." *Plantain* (Podorozhnik, 1921) contains poems addressed to Boris Anrep in London as keepsakes designated for the journey to a foreign land. It concludes with Akhmatova's refusal to emigrate. In *Anno Domini* (1922) Akhmatova's wandering personas grow stronger and independent of their lover. Religious themes increase; there are some Biblical poems: "Lot's Wife."

Meanwhile, Gumilyov had made several trips abroad and volunteered for the cavalry in 1914. The birth of their son Lev in 1912 failed to stabilize their marriage. In 1918 Akhmatova married Vladimir Shileiko, an Assyrologist, who tried to stop his wife's writing by burning her poems. Akhmatova grieved over Gumilyov's execution (1921) for alleged involvement in a counterrevolutionary plot. She sought solace from friends with common interests. Her friendship with the poet Osip MANDELSHTAM stands out. She divorced Shileiko in 1928.

After 1922 no new works of Akhmatova were published because her apolitical work was considered incompatible with the new order. Labeled an "internal émigrée," she was given a meager pension. Critics believed that her time had passed. Yet her verse continued to be cited by scholars of the FORMALIST school and admired by poetry lovers.

During her forced silence Akhmatova applied herself to the investigation of the life and works of Pushkin, producing some seminal articles published posthumously under the title *On Pushkin* (O Pushkine). She worked on *The Reed* (Trostnik, 1926–40) which contains poems on creation and features dedications to the poets Mandelshtam, PASTERNAK, and Dante. From 1926 to 1940 Akhmatova lived with the art critic, Nikolai Punin. The mass arrests of the 1930s which included her son and Punin generated a dirge to human suffering, *Requiem* (1935–40), never published in the Soviet Union.

An edition of early works plus a new cycle, *From Six Books* (Iz shesti knig, 1940), was recalled after publication. The same year Akhmatova commenced the unique, cryptic, hauntingly beautiful *Poem without a Hero* (Poema bez geroya) which she perfected until her death. During the war she was evacuated to Tashkent. The Asian ambience, its color and motifs, found reflection in the cycle "From a Tashkent Notebook." A volume of her poetry, *Izbrannoe*, appeared in Tashkent in 1943.

The wartime relaxation of controls on her publications ended with the decision of the Central Committee concerning the journals *Zvezda* and *Leningrad* which unleashed attacks on Akhmatova and ZOSHCHENKO, resulting in their expulsion from the UNION OF SOVIET WRITERS without the right to publish. As a means of support and appearing in print Akhmatova began to translate from numerous languages. Six volumes have appeared as separate imprints. Despite her success, Akhmatova complained that for a poet translating was comparable to devouring one's own brains.

The "Thaw" brought the release from prison of Lev and the gradual lifting of the ban on Akhmatova's publications. An edition of her poetry, with recent works, *The Course of Time* (Beg vremeni), appeared under her supervision in 1958. It introduced her largest collection *The Seventh Book* (Sed'maya kniga), emphasizing new themes—literary craft, war, death and symbolism—as well as part of her *Poem without a Hero*. The ailing poet became the acknowledged *grande dame* of Russian letters. Young poets gathered around her. She met the American poet Robert Frost. International recognition brought the Taormina Prize for Poetry in Italy (1964) and the awarding of an honorary degree from Oxford University (1965). With Akhmatova's demise Russian literature lost a great poet.

Akhmatova's legacy consists primarily of verse incorporated in seven collections and several *poemas*; there are also some memoirs, mostly unpublished, literary criticism, translations of verse and of some prose. Her creative career falls into three periods: the early period—1910–1922; the period of forced silence—1922–1940; the late period—1940–1966. Granted that during the early period Akhmatova was associated with the Acmeists and her work served as an example for their tenets, symbolist and romantic influences were not totally excluded from her classical verse. Mainly, the early lyrics develop the dominant love theme and ensuing chagrin in brief, superbly crafted pieces. In terms of artistic perfection there was no immature Akhmatova. The poems are presented in ego form by numerous female personas who seem like different parts of the poet. The story unfolds without a sequential pattern of verbs; the narration instead advances through switches in focus from dialog to objects and to nature which convey compositely the emotional state of the persona. In Acmeist poetics, concrete objects and interior details further the story when emotion prevents proper expression. Indeed, the poems present in miniature dramatic form the high moment following the end of love. Despite an illusory air of exactness, the speaker's rendition remains vague where the personal circumstances concerning the two principals is concerned—rather as in Greek tragedy where, due to the familiarity of the story, the dramatist could concentrate on details and nuances. Given a plot and psychology, elements of the Russian novel surface. Typical examples are "Song of the Last Meeting" and "The Gray-Eyed King." The early collections evince hints of a personal poetic diary of the poet's personas, some of whom are victims of love: "I saw my friend to the front door" (Provodila druga do perednei), "Confusion" (Smyatenie), while others,—wayward, capricious, naively destructive, or *femme fatale*— inflict pain on the lover: "The boy said to me: 'How painful it is!'" (Mal'chik skazal mne: Kak eto bol'no!). The speaker often addresses a male beloved, quoting his reply or that of nature to compensate for his silence.

In some poems Akhmatova draws upon folklore through the characters of her speakers, language, imagery, composition, and details, bringing her work close to the women's lament in the Russian folk tradition, with overlapping subject matter: a cruel husband, unfaithful lover, abandoned women. Still, the poems are never imitative—tradition is used to produce greater impact. Always restrained and discreet, Akhmatova was the first Russian poet to present a woman's perception of love, be it longing for a virile youth: "The Fisherman" (Rybak), or a woman's attitude to an unresponsive male, "Don't you love me, don't you want to look?/Oh, how handsome you are, damned one!"

Certain syntactic features, such as the preponderance of lines beginning with the conjunctions "and" or "but," imparts to Akhmatova's verses the simplicity of the monumental style of Old Russian, which the poet buttresses through the use of religious motifs and objects. In the Old Russian ambience lie the roots of the wandering persona who renounces the world following lost love: "To My Sister" (Moei sestre). She is, however, not a nun, the hackneyed sobriquet of "half-nun, half-harlot" notwithstanding, which certain critics attributed likewise to Akhmatova the person. Akhmatova's religious motifs are often laced with superstition and vestiges of paganism such as the willow, tree of water nymphs.

Akhmatova's love lyrics, then, earned acclaim through their accessible beauty of content and form as well as for the novelty of a feminine voice expressing women's emotions. Scholars found subtle devices and honed imagery in these simple poems. The later poetry adds themes of poetic creation, readership, war, and death, along with longer lyric forms, sometimes achieved through cyclization, all contributing to a wider thematic scope and deepened content. Akhmatova's late hermetic works led some to insinuate a decline in talent, as others had done for Pushkin. Long unnoticed was the device of extending the limits of her concise verse by incorporating literary allusions, correspondences, and subtexts. Akhmatova burrowed deep into the recesses of modern and ancient literatures and culture to create three-tiered edifices in verse, for which she provided a hint in *Poem without a Hero*: "But the box has a triple bottom." Indeed, the allusions often had more than one source; for example, in "Oh, How Heady Is the Fragrance of the Carnation" correspondences to Mandelshtam in turn echo Pushkin. Moreover, to substantiate intimate knowledge and firsthand familiarity with the culture and history of all times, some of Akhmatova's personas undergo metempsychosis. Metempsychosis of the persona parallels the use of allusions and subtexts by Akhmatova the poet: the persona expands her experience—the poet extends the limits of her verse. For if the *oeuvre* of each poet is construed as one lifetime in the ongoing process of literature, then reverberations of other writers in the works of Akhmatova represent, as it were, an incorporation of other lives into her poetry. Granted, the poet's literary knowledge and the persona's familiarity with many lives do not in themselves create verse: the poet as a person must participate in life, love, and grief before transmuting her experiences into art with the aid of her Muse.

At the crux of Akhmatova's creative philosophy lies omnipresent fire, both in life, love, grief, and in the composing of verse. In *The White Flock* she evolves fire thematics into a recurring pattern: living for her persona means to burn with feeling and to love, which results in grief. To alleviate her suffering the persona prays at the altar of her deity, the Muse, who instills fiery inspiration giving birth to melody which transforms prayer into song. Like life and love, creation is a form of suffering whose fruit consoles through the medium of fire. When committed to paper, song translates into verse. Poems collected into notebooks are fired for preservation as independent entities: "The Burned Notebook." Fire and grief are Akhmatova's inherent birthright since the root of her inherited surname, *Gorenko*, combines burning and grieving (*gore*, "grief," *goret'*, "burn"), a fact she exploits artistically.

Akhmatova has bequeathed two masterpieces in verse. *Requiem*, immortalizing a mother's anguish over her son's imprisonment, reaches all peoples and times. The ten core poems are preceded by an epigraph and three introductory pieces, as if a work on imprisonment were difficult to commence. Once begun, the surge subsides but slowly, as evidenced by the ponderous bipartite Epilog. Lacking sequential narration, these poems of diverse rhythm shift their focus on the leitmotif of prison and suffering. Each poem has a different approach, as if grief had sent the mother's head reeling with her mind fixated to her loss. Religious overtones intensify with the mother's suffering. Trees that once murmured to her maintain silence in pain. With the son's sentencing, insanity hovers to obliterate memory, but, like death, it evades her. A picture of the Mother of Christ at the Crucifixion broadens the inexpressible sorrow: "And there, where the Mother silently stood,/No one even dared to glance." Even if things change, the persona vows to accept no monument to herself except beside the prison lest in blissful death she forget the suffering of millions. The *poema*'s impactful content is offset by a melodious, folkish, subdued form.

Poem without a Hero: A Triptych is a complex, ciphered, densely structured narrative in verse whose many layers and possible interpretations contribute to its magnificent mystique. It is permeated with literary and biographical allusions. Like Pushkin in *Eugene Onegin*, Akhmatova invented her own strophe. Part 1, "1913: A Petersburg Tale," termed "a polemics with Blok" by Akhmatova herself, confines numerous authors within itself. It is based on a stylized recollection of the tragic suicide in 1913 of the young cornet and poet Vsevolod Knyazev, out of love for Akhmatova's friend Olga Sudeikina, an actress who preferred the poet Blok. On New Year's Eve 1940 costumed shades from 1913, including the ones in the romantic triangle, visit the persona at her home. They are described enigmatically. Nothing is related; a re-creation is achieved through the Hoffmannesque visit of shades, masks, and a portrait stepping out of its frame which conjures up the final year before the cataclysm of 1914 as well as that before World War II. The second part, "Tails" (Reshka, as in "heads and tails"), claiming to illuminate the preceding, returns to the present to treat the fate of a writer's artistic freedom in the face of editorial philistinism; it parallels Pushkin's "Conversation of a Bookseller with a Poet." Akhmatova provides a coded explanation for the obtuse editor unable to distinguish between the three persons in the triangle. Part 3, "Epilog," returns to postwar Leningrad with the poet's departure from Asia. A vessel for memory and culture, the poem memorializes a bygone era. Form, as important in the poem as content, is more accessible since the former is easily appreciated while the latter must be mined for comprehension. Through this work the poet conquers time and space.

Works: Sochineniya. Ed. G. Struve and B. Filippov. 2d ed. 3 vols. Munich, 1967–83. *Stikhotvoreniya i poemy.* Ed. V. Zhirmunskii. (Bol'shaya biblioteka poeta.) 1976. *O Pushkine.* 1977.

Translations: Poems of Akhmatova. Trans. Stanley Kunitz. 1973.

Poem without a Hero and *Requiem*. Trans. D. M. Thomas. 1976. *Way of All Earth*. Trans. D. M. Thomas. 1979.

Secondary literature: L. Chukovskaya, *Zapiski ob Anne Akhmatovoi*. 3 vols. Paris, 1976– . S. Driver, "Akhmatova: A Selected, Annotated Bibliography," *RLT* 1 (1971), pp. 432–34. ———, *Anna Akhmatova*. (Twayne's World Authors Series, 198.) 1972. A. Haight, *Anna Akhmatova: A Poetic Pilgrimage*. 1976. E. Dobin, *Poeziya Anny Akhmatovoi*. 1968. B. Eikhenbaum, *Anna Akhmatova: opyt analiza*. 1923. K. Verheul, *The Theme of Time in the Poetry of Anna Akhmatova*. The Hague, 1971.   S. K.

Aksákov, Iván Sergéevich (1823–86), SLAVOPHILE ideologue and journalist, was born in the village of Nadezhino in Ufa Province. His father was the well known theater critic and writer, Sergei Timofeevich AKSAKOV, and both Ivan and his older brother KONSTANTIN were prominent figures in Slavophile and nationalist circles, although Ivan had the eventful public career that his brother conspicuously refused. Ivan received his early education at home, in the religious, patriotic and highly cultivated atmosphere of the Aksakov household. In 1838 he entered the Imperial School of Jurisprudence in St. Petersburg, from which he graduated in 1842. A nine-year career in several governmental organizations followed before a quarrel with several of his narrow-minded superiors precipitated his resignation from government service; he had already spent some days under arrest in 1849, on suspicion of nationalist views subversive of the established order.

Aksakov was active for the next ten years as a student of Slavic popular life, journalist, and editor, while his Slavophile and nationalist convictions became firmer and more consequent. Troubles with the censorship, however, prevented his *Moskovskii sbornik* (1852, 1856) from getting off the ground. He served as de facto editor of the RUSSKAYA BESEDA, but because of his difficulties with the censors, Aleksandr Koshelev had his name on the masthead. His newspaper, *Parus*, was closed down after two issues, almost certainly because of Aksakov's growing Pan-Slavism.

With the deaths of the KIREEVSKY brothers (1856), KHOMYAKOV (1860) and Konstantin Aksakov (1860), Ivan Sergeevich became the leading figure among self-proclaimed Slavophiles. (It is probably incorrect to speak of a Slavophile "movement" during the 1860s.) In his newspapers *Den'* and *Moskva*, he commented extensively on the foreign and domestic politics of the day, most notably on the "Great Reforms" of Alexander II which he by and large supported. But his nationalism became ever more strident during the 1860s and 1870s, as the historical and cultural criticism of the early Slavophiles tended to give way to simpler and more strident forms of nationalism, often directed against Poles, Germans, and Jews. In 1880, Aksakov began publishing his final journalistic venture, *Rus'*, in which he alleged that he had discovered a world-wide Jewish conspiracy with headquarters in Paris; the racism and chauvinism so marked in the last two decades of his career have been an embarrassment to the many attracted to the more courageous and generous aspects of his life and work.

Recent scholarship, both in the Soviet Union and in the West, has argued that Aksakov's definition and use of the term *obshchestvo* (roughly "society") represented a genuine, if not earth-shaking, contribution to Slavophile theory. Aksakov had need of some such terminology because by the 1860s his brother Konstantin's stark opposition of the vital popular forces of "the land" and the necessary—if perennially threatening—power of "the state" was clearly inadequate to describe either Russian political life or culture. *Obshchestvo* to Aksakov was not just the gentry élite—it meant people like himself, who were not exactly *of* the land (as were the peasants and merchants), but who were organically related to it and spoke for it: the intelligentsia, but only if they had the right, Slavophile ideas.

At the death of POGODIN in 1875, Aksakov became president of the Moscow Slavic Benevolent Committee, and for two years he led the agitation in Russia for a more forward policy in the Balkans, and raised money all over the country to equip volunteers to fight with the Serbs. Instrumental in bringing about Russia's war with Turkey, Aksakov was delighted by its outcome, but his satisfaction turned to rage and frustration when Russia was forced by the great powers to accept the less advantageous terms of the Congress of Berlin. His final years did not bring the Slavic triumphs for which he had hoped, and he died a disappointed man, but the enormous crowds at his funeral suggest that his name was still a most potent one among an important segment of the Russian public.

Works: Sochineniya. 7 vols. 1886–87. Nina Perlina, ed., "Ivan Aksakov's and Nikolaj Straxov's Correspondence from 1863 through 1865: Fifty-three Unpublished Letters," *RLJ*, no. 114 (1979), pp. 117–88.

Secondary literature: Stephen Lukashevich, *Ivan Aksakov (1823–1886): a study in Russian Thought and Politics*. 1965. Michael B. Petrovich, *The Emergence of Russian Panslavism, 1856–1870*. 1956. Nicholas Riasanovsky, *Russia and the West in the Teaching of the Slavophiles*. 1952. Edward Thaden, *Conservative Nationalism in Nineteenth-Century Russia*. 1964. Nikolai Ivanovich Tsimbaev, *I. S. Aksakov v obshchestvennoi zhizni poreformennoi Rossii*. 1978. Andrzej Walicki, *W kręgu konserwatywnej utopii*. Warsaw, 1964. Trans. into English as *The Slavophile Controversy* (Oxford, 1975).   A. G.

Aksákov, Konstantín Sergéevich (1817–60), SLAVOPHILE ideologue and journalist, was born in the village of New Aksakovo in Orenburg Province. His father, S. T. AKSAKOV, was a theater critic of originality and discernment, who in *A Family Chronicle* and other works written in his maturity, made a substantial contribution to Russian literature. His younger brother, Ivan Sergeevich AKSAKOV, became an important spokesman for the Slavophile point of view in the 1860s and 1870s, after I. V. KIREEVSKY and A. S. KHOMYAKOV were dead, and an important figure in Russian Pan-Slavism.

Konstantin entered Moscow University at the age of fifteen in 1832, where he became for several years a member of the STANKEVICH Circle, along with BAKUNIN and BELINSKY, and a devotee of Hegel; the most important shaping force in his life, however (as was true of several of the Slavophiles), was his traditional, closely knit family, whose way of life suggested to him the communal values he was to discover in early Russian history.

In the latter 1830s Aksakov drew close to Yu. F. SAMARIN, and in the early 1840s, both Aksakov and Samarin fell increasingly under the sway of A. S. Khomyakov. That curious phase of Aksakov's career when he attempted to reconcile his continuing interest in Hegel with his growing attraction to Slavophilism is most fully expressed in his Master's dissertation, *Lomonosov in the History of Russian Language and Literature* (1846).

By the end of the 1840s, Aksakov had lost all interest in Hegel and had become the most passionate and single-minded of the Slavophiles, especially in the way he regarded Russian history as a battleground between the common people, whose social existence was religiously grounded, moral and free, and those forces—both in "the West"and associated with the Westernized elite in Russia and "their state"—which opposed popular aspiration. In the work of Konstantin Aksakov, the anarchist potentialities of Slavophilism are most evident and its opposition to the centralized Russian state most clear. Aksakov died in the Ionian Islands, in the midst of a European trip.

Works: Polnoe sobranie sochinenii. Ed. I. S. Aksakov. 2 vols. 1861, 1875.

Secondary literature: P. Christoff, *K. S. Aksakov: A Study in Ideas*. Vol. 3 of *An Introduction to Nineteenth-Century Russian Slavophilism*. 1982. A. Walicki, *The Slavophile Controversy*. 1975.
                A.G.

Aksákov, Sergéi Timoféevich (1791–1859). Like GONCHAROV, Sergei Aksakov, scion of a great Russian SLAVOPHILE family, was a genius of reminiscence. Born in Ufa, in the borderlands of the Russian Empire, Aksakov spent his childhood amid the beauty of unspoiled nature. Then, while still in his teens, he launched upon a bureaucratic career in St. Petersburg, at the same time developing a lively interest in literature and the theater, and also becoming a confidant of artistic people. His much later memoirs of Admiral SHISHKOV and of St. Petersburg theatrical life provide a fascinating glimpse of Russian society just before the Napoleonic invasion.

Aksakov began writing artistic literature very late: his first important and long work appeared only when he was in his mid-60s, although he did publish a short story as early as 1834. In 1832 he met GOGOL, and struck up a close acquaintance with him, one chronicled in his *Reminiscences of Gogol* (Vospominaniya o Gogole).

On the way to his more strictly literary works, Aksakov wrote two books which are almost unique in Russian literature: *Notes on Fishing* (Zapiski ob uzhen'e ryby, 1847), and *Notes of a Hunter in Orenburg Province* (Zapiski ruzheinogo okhotnika orenburgskoi gubernii), which came out in 1852. The first is a remarkably systematic discussion of every aspect of fishing (there are sections specifically devoted to the fishing pole, line, float, sinker, hook, an extensive discussion of bait, etc.); the second includes essays on the various types of wildfowl which a hunter in the Orenburg region might seek to bring down. Although their subject matter at first glance might not seem promising, the limpid style and concrete content of these books made them contributions to Russian literature, and they were recognized as such by contemporaries.

Aksakov always claimed he had no gift for fiction: he was, he said, purely a "narrator" describing things he knew at first hand. That generalization holds, with a certain twist, for the works which are now best remembered: his thinly fictionalized reminiscences of his childhood and youth, collections of substantial sketches known under the collective title of *Family Chronicle* (Semeinaya khronika, 1856) and *Childhood Years of Bagrov the Grandson* (Detskie gody Bagrova-vnuka, 1856).

Family Chronicle is what might be called a "pre-reminiscence," a narrative based on family legends which ends, indeed, with the very birth of the narrator, Sergei. In it Aksakov creates a marvelous portrait of his grandfather, called Stepan Bagrov, a patriarch in the old mold living on an estate on the Russian borderlands, whose greatest dedication was to his family even though he terrorized it with fits of temper, especially since the womenfolk in particular tended to be petty and scheming. There was much which was hideous about the life of the despotic landowner who dwelt far from the representatives of moral authority: Aksakov sketches with unblinking eye the criminality of Kurolesov, a landowner given to indulging his most sadistic whims when alone on his estate, one who does not hesitate to imprison and mistreat even his wife when she threatens to expose him.

Much of the *Family Chronicle* deals with the courtship and marriage of Bagrov-Aksakov's parents. His mother, a sensitive and cultured woman, incurs the spiteful envy of her sisters-in-law when she marries their good-hearted but highly provincial brother. Aksakov is much more the realist than, say, TURGENEV: Turgenev sometimes brings his heroes to the brink of marriage, while Aksakov goes beyond to describe with great candor all the petty difficulties a married couple must surmount if they are to create a family: he describes the human frailties and misunderstandings, the petty hatreds as well as the romantic love, in short, the varied problems which a city girl faces in adjusting to country life among her in-laws. In the end the work is a remarkably honest depiction of human psychology, which changes very little in the midst of a strong cultural tradition which leaves a powerful imprint upon those who live within it.

Childhood Years is a fictionalized reminiscence in the formal sense, for it consists of the childhood memories of Aksakov-Bagrov, in the tradition of childhood reminiscences which LEV TOLSTOI had begun a few years before and which MAKSIM GORKY would continue in the early 20th century. As he approached the end, Aksakov returned to his beginnings, dying about a year after this last work's publication. He left to posterity a tangible picture of what it meant to grow up in Russia at the close of the 18th century.

Works: Sobranie sochinenii. 4 vols. 1955–1956.
Translations: The Family Chronicle. Trans. M. C. Beverley. Introd. Ralph E. Matlaw. 1961.
Secondary literature: Andrew R. Durkin, *Sergei Aksakov and Russian Pastoral.* 1983.   C. A. M.

Aksyónov, Vasily Pávlovich (1932–), writer, was born into a communist family. After a short career as a medical doctor, Aksyonov became a writer by 1960. His best known early work is the short novel *Ticket to the Stars* (1961) (translation published as *A Starry Ticket*, 1962). It presents the characteristic marks of Aksyonov's prose: a fast-moving narrative dialogue sprinkled with colloquialisms, slang, and foreign borrowings, especially Americanisms. Aksyonov is the first to use for his material of fiction the Soviet generation that came to adulthood in the late fifties. In *Ticket to the Stars* this generation is shown to be uninhibited, attracted toward Western subcultures, shunning double-speak, and aspiring after independent judgment.

This mode also characterizes Aksyonov's subsequent works. He identifies with this technological and creative intelligentsia of the early sixties. Aksyonov can write in a straightforward prose: *Love for Electricity* (Lyubov' k elektrichestvu, 1971). However, left to himself, he moves toward the grotesque, the fantastic, and the satirical. His works of the seventies are written in this mode: from the innocuous *The Overstocked Tare of Barrels* (1968) to those published in the United States: *Our Golden Zhelezka* (1980), *Ozhog* (1980), and *The Island Crimea* (1981). These narratives assert an anarchistic freedom of expression. Still, they convey deliberate purposes: respectively, to make one feel the euphoria of the post-Stalinist intelligentsia; the agonizing encounter of the former jailors and the former prisoners; the deadlock of freedom in a world of fantastically reshaped history and geography. These works were written in response to the unfulfilled expectations of the "men of the sixties." The apparent immediate cause of Aksyonov's exile in July 1980 was the affair of *Metropol'*, a collection of works that Aksyonov and 22 other authors tried unsuccessfully to publish in 1979 in Moscow.

Works: "Zvezdnyi bilet," *Yunost'*. June–July 1961. "Na pol-puti k lune," *Novyi mir*, no. 7 (1962). "Zatovarennaya bochkotara," *Yunost'*, no. 3 (1968). "Kruglye sutki non-stop," *Novyi mir*. no. 8. 1976. *Zolotaya nasha Zhelezka.* Ann Arbor, 1980. *Ozhog.* Ann Arbor, 1980. *Zatovarennaya bochkotara. Randevu. Povesti.* Ann Arbor, 1980. *Ostrov Krym.* Ann Arbor, 1981.
Translations: A Starry Ticket. 1962. "Halfway to the Moon." In *The New Writing in Russia.* Ed. and trans. Thomas Whitney. 1964.
Secondary literature: Vasily Aksenov, "Poiski zhanra," *Novyi mir*, 1978, no. 1. Lev Anninskii, "Zhanr-to naidetsya!" *Literaturnoe obozrenie*, 1978, no. 7, pp. 44–46. A. Makarov, "Cherez pyat' let. Stat'ya tret'ya: Idei i obrazy Vasiliya Aksyonova," *Znamya*, 1966, nos. 7, 8. St. Rassadin, "Shestero v kuzove, ne schitaya bochkotary (fantasticheskaya simvolika v tvorchestve V. Aksenova)," *VLit*, 1968, no. 10.   H. O.

Aldánov, Mark Aleksándrovich Lándau (1886–1957), writer and critic, was born Landau in Kiev, son of a wealthy industrialist. He earned degrees in law and natural sciences at Kiev University, and in social sciences at the University of Paris, and went on to publish several articles and monographs in chemistry and political science. Aldanov moved from Kiev to St. Petersburg, frequented Duma literary circles, and travelled extensively throughout the world, returning to Russia in World War I for chemical research. In 1919 he emigrated to Paris, then to Berlin, married, settled in Paris in 1924, moved to New York in 1940, and lived from 1947 until his death in Nice, France.

Aldanov published some scientific research, literary criticism, and political commentary in Russia, but it was the emigration that made him a writer, the only one of his generation who lived wholly by his pen. He contributed literary criticism, book reviews, essays, necrologies, and extracts from his fiction to several émigré periodicals, primarily SOVREMENNYE ZAPISKI, *Poslednie novosti*, and NOVYI ZHURNAL, which he co-founded with M. Tsetlin in 1942. In Paris he published *Lénine* (1919) and *Deux révolutions: la révolution française et la révolution russe* (1920). These monographs led to his first literary work, *St. Helena, Little Island* (Svyataya Elena, malen'kii ostrov, 1922), a glimpse of Napoleon in his last days. This became part of the *Thinker* (Myslitel') cycle, linking Russian and Western European personalities and events in the era of the Napoleonic Wars. The cycle comprises: *The Ninth of Thermidor* (Devyatoe termidora, 1923), *Devil's Bridge* (Chertov most, 1925), and *Conspiracy* (Zagovor, 1927). Their principal fictional characters are an inexperienced young Russian adventurer and a wise old Jewish cynic, who observe and interpret a wide variety of situations and people in attempts to understand the full meaning of the French Revolution.

Three more novels dealing with the October Revolution and its repercussions in the European Russian émigré community are: *The Key* (Klyuch, 1930), *Escape* (Begstvo, 1932), *The Cave* (Peshchera, 1934–36). In the tetralogy historical figures dominate, but they virtually disappear from the trilogy, where numerous fictional characters from Aldanov's own intelligentsia milieu struggle to make sense of the events that have catastrophically altered their lives. The series features debates between two equally brilliant *raisonneurs*, a former chief of the tsarist secret police and a radical scientist who may hold a key to a mysterious death with wide political implications. Fictional characters again dominate in *Beginning of the End* (Nachalo kontsa, 1938), a contemporary novel focusing on members of a Soviet delegation to a small unnamed European country during the Spanish Civil War. It appeared in English as *The Fifth Seal* (1943).

Aldanov wrote "philosophical tales" in which events and situations prompt various fictional and historical characters to express contrasting philosophies of life. *The Tenth Symphony* (Desyataya simfoniya, 1931) examines the irony of fate and the continuity in time that genealogically links the characters in all Aldanov's novels except *Delirium* (Bred, 1954–55). In *Vodka Punch* (Punshevaya vodka, 1940) Catherine II's accession to the throne provides the impetus for "a tale about all five happinesses." Alexander I and Lord Byron stand at the center of "a tale about wisdom," *A Warrior's Grave* (Mogila voina, 1940). *A Tale of Death* (Povest' o smerti, 1969) expands the same plot structure into a novel that examines numerous ramifications of the 1848 French Revolution.

Two more novels of 20th-century life reveal Aldanov's 19th-century turn of mind. An adolescent from the October Revolution novels becomes the main character of *To Live as We Wish* (Zhivi kak khochesh', 1952), a writer of historical plays and filmscripts. *Delirium* features a psychedelic hallucination that includes visions of ancient Rome. Aldanov's most considerable achievements combine his gifts as psychological novelist, historical portraitist, and interpretive essayist. *Origins* (Istoki, 1950) takes the October Revolution back to its sources in the assassination of Alexander II. In *Suicide* (Samoubiistvo, 1958) civilized Europe's unwitting suicide in beginning World War I leads to the suicide of the two chief fictional characters.

Aldanov preserved the highest traditions of Russian Europeanism: cultivation, rationalism, skepticism, uprightness, and materialism. He rejected all religious solutions to the problem of pain and concentrated on the tragic aspects of aging, death, love, and chance. *A Night at Ulm: The Philosophy of Chance* (Ul'mskaya noch': filosofiya sluchaya, 1953) uses stylized dialogues to apply his systematic Cartesianism to all areas of life.

Aldanov's range of themes is varied and entertaining, his mastery of plot structure impeccable, his style lucid and aphoristic, but his pessimistic skepticism alienates many readers, and intellect dominates over intuition in his fictional characterizations, which have been unfavorably compared to the brilliant historical essays and portraits he wrote for the periodical press, some of them collected in *Ogon' i dym* (1922), *Sovremenniki* (1928), *Portrety* (1931), *Zemli, lyudi* (1932), *Yunost' Pavla Stroganova i drugie kharakteristiki* (1934), and *Novye portrety* (1936). Several excellent short stories are found in *A Night at the Airport* (1949). *Bel'vederskii tors* (1938) includes a novella and a play, *Liniya Brungil'dy*.

Works: see *Foster*, 1, pp. 115–24.
Translations: Lewanski, pp. 189–90.
Secondary literature: C. N. Lee, "Aldanov, Mark." In *MERSL* 1, pp. 103–10. C. Nicholas Lee, *The Novels of Mark Aleksandrovič Aldanov*. The Hague, 1969.   C. N. L.

Aleksandriya. A conventional title applied to Orthodox Slavic texts which contain variations of the medieval legend on the life and deeds of Alexander the Great (356–323 B.C.). In the Russian lands the *Aleksandriya* is represented by two main versions, the "Chronographic" and the "Serbian." The former version is contained in collections of heterogeneous, historical documents called *Khronografy* (the oldest of which date from the 15th century); the latter version is based on textual material common to both the East Slavic (from the 15th century, the earliest copy being that of the well-known scribe and literary compiler Efrosin) and the South Slavic (not earlier than the 15th century) literary traditions.

The Old Russian *Aleksandriya* is dependent on the Greek account attributed to pseudo-Callisthenes. Nevertheless, it betrays its own particular features. Alexander is presented as the son not of Philip II of Macedonia but of the Egyptian ruler-magician Nectanebes; the love between Alexander and Roxane assumes a much more important role than in the Greek account.

The texts of the *Aleksandriya* are written in prose but reveal some poetic sophistication. Although the *Aleksandriya* might be seen as the literary expression of "secular" interests, certain formal devices connect it with important Old Russian works of ecclesiastical inspiration. It is possible to detect striking parallels between the techniques used in the *Aleksandriya* and those employed in EPIPHANIUS THE WISE's *Life of St. Stefan of Perm* and the *Discourse on the Life and Death of the Grand Prince Dmitry Ivanovich* (Slovo o zhitii i o prestavlenii velikago knyazya Dmitriya Ivanovicha). In particular, Roxane's lament has much in common with the lament of Dmitry's widow Evdokiya.

Given the absence of any exhaustive investigation of the *Aleksandriya*'s versions and their textual components, one cannot determine whether and to what extent earlier translations or adaptations from Greek might have undergone reelaboration in the 15th century or in later periods.

Bibliography: M. N. Botvinnik, I. S. Lur'e, and O. V. Tvorogov, *Aleksandriya. Roman ob Aleksandre Makedonskom po russkoi rukopisi XV veka.* 1965. V. Istrin, *Aleksandriya russkikh khronografov. Issledovanie i tekst.* 1893. F. Magoun, "Stojan Novaković on the so-called 'Serbian Alexander.'" *Byzantion* 16, no. 1 (1944), pp. 315–38. R. Marinković, *Srpska Aleksandrida. Istorija osnovnog teksta.* (Filološki fakultet Beogradskog univerziteta, Monografije, no. 31.) Belgrade, 1969. C. A. van den Berk, *Der "serbische Alexanderroman."* (Slavische Propyläen, Vol. 13, 1.) Munich, 1970. A. N. Veselovskii, "Iz istorii romana i povesti," *Sbornik Otdeleniya russkogo yazyka i slovesnosti Akademii nauk* 40, no. 2 (1886), pp. 129–511.
                                                                H. G.

Aleksandr Nevsky, Life of. A concise hagiographic composition which celebrates the majesty of Prince Aleksandr Nevsky (1220–63), his inspired bravery and victories over the Swedes and Teutonic Knights, and the exemplariness of his faith and wisdom. The nature, origins, and textual history of the *Life* have been studied by scholars of different orientations. One of the main points of dispute remains the work's relationship to the fragment entitled *Slovo o pogibeli Ruskyya zemli* (Tale on the Ruin of the Russian land), which precedes the *Life* in two codices. Another issue on which opinions are divided is whether the extant testimonies of the work are dependent on an older "secular life." The fact that the *Life* has not come down to us in a compact textual tradition makes these and other controversial problems extremely difficult to resolve. To date, no exhaustive comparison and evaluation of all extant testimonies has been carried out. Instead, scholars have tended to focus their attention on a group of interrelated manuscripts which are usually referred to as the "first redaction." This redaction is in turn divided into two groups of codices on the basis of narrative variants.

Yu. Begunov has concluded that the first redaction of the *Life* was produced in the early 1280s at the Rozhdestvensky monastery in Vladimir and might be linked with the circle of Metropolitan Kirill II. Yet what remains unclear is to what extent the large body of textual material which has not yet been adequately considered would affect our attempts to establish an "original text." What is also open to further discussion is whether one can attribute the *Life* as it has come down to us to one author (Metropolitan Kirill, as suggested by D. Likhachëv) or whether one should rather speak of adaptation or reelaboration for liturgical or other purposes. When attempting to define the *Life*, it is important to remember that the work does not contain the type of biographical information one might expect to find in a *vita*, but rather presents only selected images of exemplary events and scenes.

Bibliography: Yu. K. Begunov, *Pamyatnik russkoi literatury XIII veka* Slovo o pogibeli Russkoi zemli. 1965. J. Fennell and A. Stokes, *Early Russian Literature.* 1974. Pp. 107–23. D. S. Likhachëv, "Galitskaya literaturnaya traditsiya v *Zhitii Aleksandra Nevskogo*," *TODRL* 5 (1947), pp. 36–56. V. Mansikka, *Zhitie Aleksandra Nevskogo. Razbor redaktsii i tekst.* 1913.   R. P.

Aleksandrova, Véra (pen-name of Vera Aleksandrovna Shvarts, née Mordvinova, 1895–1966), Russian émigré critic specializing in Soviet literary-political developments, publicist, and editor. Aleksandrova studied at the Higher Women's Courses in Odessa, the Gerye Courses in Moscow, and, in the 1920s, at the University of Geneva, never graduating, however, from any of these institutions. Coming from a conservative and patriotic milieu and associating first with religious-philosophical circles, and personally with V. V. Rozanov, she later moved toward Socialism. In 1919 she married a Menshevik, S. M. Shvarts, and since 1921 became herself a Social-Democrat and Menshevik. In 1921 she also left Russia, accompanying her husband into exile. For eleven years she lived in Germany, for seven in France, and for the last twenty-six years of her life in the United States.

Aleksandrova's initiation to journalism took place during the Great War, at the Moscow *Kommercheskii telegraf*. In the 1920s she contributed to some German and Austrian Marxist publications. But her true career was connected mostly with the Russian Menshevik magazine *Sotsialisticheskii vestnik* (Socialist Herald), where her first article appeared when she was nearly 32 years old and where she published more than 350 articles between 1927 and 1965. Since the 1940s Aleksandrova was also a regular contributor to *Novoe russkoe slovo* and, to a much lesser extent, to *Novyi zhurnal*. In addition, she contributed occasionally to some American periodicals. Concurrently, Aleksandrova worked for the magazine *Amerika* (1946–48), for Margaret Mead's research project on human behavior at Columbia University (1948–50), and, as its editor-in-chief, for the Chekhov Publishing House (1951–56).

As a student of Soviet literature, Aleksandrova was concerned mostly with its sociological aspects. Proceeding from both main and secondary authors and works and sometimes from minute facts and hints, she would try to arrive at a more complex general picture, revealing new trends, developments and conditions in Soviet life, and in the psychology of various groups of Soviet society.

Works: A History of Soviet Literature, 1917–1962. Garden City, N.Y. 1963. *A History of Soviet Literature, 1917–1964; From Gorky to Solzhenitsyn.* Anchor Books paperback, 1964. *Literatura i zhizn'; Ocherki sovetskogo obshchestvennogo razvitiya; Do kontsa Vtoroi mirovoi voiny: Izbrannoe.* Comp. by S. Shvarts. 1969. (Essays published in *Sotsialisticheskii vestnik*, 1927–1945, with a biographical sketch of Aleksandrova, pp. 3–13). Books edited by Aleksandrova and published by Chekhov Publishing House: *Pestrye rasskazy; Sbornik emigrantskoi prozy* (1953) and *Opal'nye povesti; Proza sovetskikh pisatelei* (1955). N. P. P.

Aleksandróvsky, Vasíly Dmítrievich (1897–1934), poet. One of the better known "proletarian poets" of the early years of the Soviet regime, Aleksandrovsky had little formal schooling, but began publishing his verse as early as 1913. A member of the Communist Party since 1917, he was one of the more active participants in the Moscow studio of the Proletkult in 1918–19 and later of the *Smithy* (Kuznitsa) group. Aleksandrovsky's verse is typical of this ambience: it celebrates the proletarian revolution as an event of elemental power, using a great deal of cosmic, martial, and industrial imagery, coupled with hyperbolic expressions of seething enthusiasm and boundless devotion to the world proletariat. Aleksandrovsky's versification is conventional and the declamatory effectiveness of his verse vanished with the decline of revolutionary fervor among his public.

Works: Stikhotvoreniya i poemy. Introd. S. Rodov. 1957.
Translations: Three poems in *Popular Poetry in Soviet Russia.* Ed. George Z. J. Patrick. 1929. "We" in *Modern Russian Poetry.* Ed. Vladimir Markov and Merrill Sparks. 1967. Pp. 696–97.
Secondary literature: Proletarskie poety pervykh let sovetskoi epokhi. Introd. essay by Z. S. Papernyi. 1959. V. T.

Alekséev, Mikhaíl Pávlovich (1896–1981), literary scholar, academician (1958), chairman of the Division of Russian and Foreign Literary Relations in the Institute of Russian Literature (Pushkinskii Dom). He was born in Kiev and graduated from Kiev University in 1918. Having started his career as a musicologist and poet, he later became a world authority on Russian-Western literary relations and cultural contacts. Alekseev was one of the first to pay attention to Russian influence on world literature, and also studied the influence on Russian literature of Spanish, French, English, and Slavic literatures. He was sponsor and editor of many important studies on literary contacts, including a catalogue of Voltaire's library and studies of Voltaire's literary heritage in Russia, and Pushkin's relations with world literature.

Works: Sibir' v izvestiyakh zapadnoevropeiskikh puteshestvennikov i pisatelei. Irkutsk, 1941. *Slavyanskie istochniki Utopii Tomasa Mora.* 1955. *Iz istorii angliiskoi literatury: Etyudy. Ocherki. Issledovaniya.* 1960. *Ocherki istorii ispano-russkikh literaturnykh otnoshenii XVI–XIX vv.* 1964. *Shekspir i russkaya kul'tura.* 1965. *Stikhotvorenie Pushkina "Ya pamyatnik sebe vozdvig ..."* 1967. *Slovari inostrannykh yazykov v russkom azbukovnike XVII v.* 1968. *Pushkin.* 1972. *Russko-angliiskie literaturnye svyazi, XVIII vek–pervaya polovina XIX veka.* (Literaturnoe nasledstvo. Vol. 91.) 1982.

Secondary literature: P. N. Berkov, "M. P. Alekseev—istorik i teoretik literatury." In *Russko-evropeiskie literaturnye svyazi.* 1966. G. N. Finashina, *Mikhail Pavlovich Alekseev.* 1972. *Sravnitel'noe izuchenie literatur: Sbornik statei k 80-letiyu akademika M. P. Alekseeva.* 1976. (Bibliography of his works for 1972–75, pp. 555–58.) E. B.

Alekséeva (née Devel, married Ivannikov), Lídya Alekséevna (1909–), émigré poet, was born in Dvinsk into the family of a Russian officer descended from a French émigré. She spent her childhood in the Crimea. Then, having left Russia in 1920, she spent the next 22 years in Yugoslavia. She graduated from the Philosophical Faculty of Belgrade University and came to the United States in 1949. Alekseeva started to write verse at age seven and has published her poetry since the 1930s. She is a great, exacting, and refined master of verse, who is in no need of pursuing originality at any cost. Using traditional forms, she manages to say a great deal—freshly, brightly, and with supreme concision. Her poetic handwriting is idiosyncratic—Alekseeva could not be confused with any poet now living. She is a rare painter of psychologically charged landscapes, seen with a sharp and tenacious eye. She has "boats at their moorings barely moving their sleepy bottoms"; "the blackness of a melted puddle is filled to the brim with springtime blue"; and in the gorges of the streets of New York, "over the courtyard, like a rectangular abyss, a dingy house arose joylessly, crossed out by iron stairs, like a botched draft." There live in Alekseeva's verse not only her memories of the Crimea and the Black Sea, of Dalmatia or of the Tyrol, which she grew to love forever, but also a cityscape, blackened by smoke, strewn with refuse, bespattered and befouled, which infects her reader with a kind of silent, secret, slightly morbid beauty. For even in an urban "grass-plot, trampled down by people, where the grass is burnt by cigarette butts, where flat rings of beer cans lie, barely twinkling," one may find an acorn, and the grass still grows, it grows even through the concrete armor of sidewalks. In Alekseeva's lyric landscapes there exists a certain correspondence with Lev Tolstoi, especially with the beginning of his novel *Resurrection*—no matter how hard people try to pollute living nature, it will still come back. Alekseeva's lyrics, including erotic-meditative and philosophic pieces, almost invariably have a landscape for their background. For all that surrounds us is "a goldfield of small joys":

> I haven't the strength anymore, to bear
> Too heavy a burden of happiness.
> For the likes of me, feeble and tired,
> God has something else in store:
> Do you see the goldfield of small joys?
> Do you see how many there are? They are for us ...

We find in Alekseeva's lyrics a certain pantheist absorption in nature, perceived as a plenitude of being, replete with meaning and with spirit. Man's pilgrim existence—here, moreover, that of an exile, émigré—does not make the poet dream of a steady, sedentary life: "I don't feel any yearning, when I see a cat, sleeping on someone else's steps, or a geranium in someone else's window," says Alekseeva. But our loneliness in the cold air of freedom, our separation from God is a heavy burden:

> I slept, like grey marble in a block—
> An unincarnate thought of Thine.
> . . . .
> I am created. I am alone.
> I am free. Why then am I afraid?"

Human freedom is somehow too much for us who are not fully incarnate: "Free? Oh yes, I don't deny it—but then what? Why, a sliver in the open sea is free also ..." In a whole series of Alekseeva's poems we face the autumnal twilight of being. She also has optimistic, even joyous verses, though a light elegiac haze always appears in them as an overtone. This may be, however, a property of Russian lyric poetry in general, perhaps of all lyric poetry. Alekseeva's poetry is at its most optimistic when she finds herself altogether alone with nature. Alekseeva's poetry was held in high regard by Anna AKHMATOVA, her relative on her mother's side. N. I. Ulyanov, usually a very reserved critic, called Alekseeva "the Fevroniya of Russian poetry." "She has a certain affinity with BUNIN," Yu. K. TERAPIANO writes about her, "a fusion of the poet's 'I' with images of nature, and bold, plastic, palpable descriptions of the visible world".... Alekseeva is also the author of prose miniatures, which are just as lyrical and "pastel colored" as her verses. They were published in various periodicals and two of her stories are included in the anthology *Humor and Satire of Post-Revolutionary Russia* (Yumor i satira poslerevolyutsionnoi Rossii, London, 1983).

Works: (Collections of verse:) *Lesnoe solntse.* Frankfurt, 1954. *V puti.* New York, 1959 (2d ed. 1962). *Prozrachnyi sled.* New York, 1964. *Vremya razluk.* New York, 1971. *Stikhi* [selection]. New York, 1980. (Translation of Ivan Gundulić's verse epic:) *Slezy bludnogo syna.* Washington, 1965.

Secondary literature: S. M. Rafalsky, B. A. Nartsissov, N. I. Ulyanov, I. V. Kachurovsky, and Dr. G. Zabezhinsky have written about Alekseeva's poetry.

Reviews: Lesnoe solntse: Novyi zhurnal, no. 39 (1954); A. Neimirok, In *Literaturnyi sovremennik: al'manakh.* Munich, 1954. *V puti:* Yu. Ofrosimov, *Novyi zhurnal,* no. 63 (1960); Yu. Terapiano, *Russkaya mysl',* 6 February 1960. ———, *Edinenie* (Melbourne), 4 March 1960. *Prozrachnyi sled:* O. Anstei, *Novyi zhurnal,* no. 81 (1965). *Vremya razluk:* S. Rafal'skii, *Russkaya mysl',* 1971; E. Vasil'eva, "Ptitsa na kreste," *Russkaya mysl',* 16 September 1971; T. Fesenko, "Dve svetlykh knigi," *Russkaya zhizn',* 21 November 1973; ———, "Tikhaya muza," *Novoe russkoe slovo,* 14 September 1980; B. Filippov, "Rossyp' malykh chudes." In *Mysli naraspashku.* Book 2. Washington, 1982.   B. F.

Aliger, Margarita Iósifovna (1915–), poet. Born in Odessa, Aliger attended the Gorky Institute of Literature from 1934 to 1937 and published her first collection of poetry, *Year of Birth* (God rozhdeniya) in 1938. Her early poetry is held in the conventional tone of enthusiastic support of Stalin's five year plans. Aliger's war poetry is likewise patriotic in a conventional way. Her verse epic *Zoya* (1942), whose heroine is the schoolgirl partisan Zoya Kosmodemyanskaya, won a Stalin prize in 1943. After the war, Aliger continued to write lyric poetry and *poemy* in which public spirited attention to issues of the day is combined with personal warmth, so in the *poema* "Leninskie gory" (1953), devoted to the construction of Moscow University. Since the onset of the THAW, which Aliger supported, she has travelled a great deal and international themes have appeared in her poetry, so in "The Art to Compose a Bouquet" (Iskusstvo sostavlyat' bukety, 1963), with Japanese motifs. Aliger has been for many years a member of the Presidium of the UNION OF SOVIET WRITERS.

Works: Stikhotvoreniya i poemy. 2 vols. 1970. *Stikhi.* 1971. "V poslednii raz" [memoirs], *Moskva,* 1974, no. 12.

Translations: Lewanski, p. 190.

Secondary literature: Elaine Feinstein, "Poetry and Conscience: Russian Woman Poets of the Twentieth Century." In *Women Writing and Writing about Women.* Ed. Mary Jacobus. 1980. Pp. 133–58.   V. T.

Alyósha Popóvich, see BYLINA.

Amalrík, Andreí Alekséevich (1938–80), dissident writer, playwright, poet, historian. Amalrik was exiled to Siberia in 1965 as a "parasite" (a charge akin to that of vagrancy under American law) and published his first book *Involuntary Journey to Siberia,* describing his life as a cowherd in a Siberian village. Allowed to return to Moscow in 1966, he tried to maintain low-profile dissident activity during the trial of GALANSKOV and GINZBURG. In 1969 he wrote a long essay entitled "Will the USSR Last Until 1984?" In it he pointed out the weaknesses of the Soviet empire and questioned whether it would endure. Amalrik also wrote a number of plays (some of which were broadcast in translation in Britain) and a collection of published poetry of a traditional bent. On 12 November 1980, while travelling to the Madrid Conference dedicated to the observance by the Soviet Union

of the Helsinki Accords on Human Rights, he was killed in an automobile accident.

Works: SSSR i zapad v odnoi lodke. London, 1978. *Zapiski dissidenta.* 1982.

Translations: Involuntary Journey to Siberia. Trans. Manya Harari and Max Hayward. 1970. *Nose! Nose? No-se!, and other plays.* Trans. Daniel Weissbort. 1973. *Will the Soviet Union Survive Until 1984?* 1970.

Secondary literature: John Keep, "Andrei Amalrik and *1984.*" *RusR* 30 (1971), pp. 335–45.   J. G.

American Literature in Russia, see ENGLISH-RUSSIAN AND AMERICAN-RUSSIAN LITERARY RELATIONS

Amfiteátrov, Aleksándr Valentínovich (1862–1938), talented Russian journalist, critic, playwright, novelist, and short story writer. Born into the family of a Moscow priest, Amfiteatrov graduated from the Jurisprudence Faculty of Moscow University in 1885, then travelled to Italy to pursue an operatic career. While abroad he contributed articles to the Moscow newspaper *Russian Record* (Russkie vedomosti), then developed his journalistic career in the Tiflis newspaper *New Review* (Novoe obozrenie). Amfiteatrov became well-known in the 1890s due to his "Moscow" and "Sunday" feuilletons written under the pseudonym Old Gentleman in SUVORIN's *New Time* (Novoe vremya). In 1899 together with V. Doroshevich he founded the very popular *Rossiya,* a Petersburg newspaper that was closed in 1902 because of his satirical feuilleton against the Romanov dynasty, *The Cheater Family* (Gospoda Obmanovy), for which he was exiled to Minusinsk. Emigrating to Paris in 1905, he continued criticizing the autocracy in his own journal *Red Banner* (Krasnoe znamya, 1906). In the 1910s he returned to Russia taking an active role in the new journal *Contemporary* (Sovremennik, 1911–1915). Emigrating again after the Revolution, Amfiteatrov continued his now largely anti-Bolshevik journalistic activities in émigré newspapers such as *Renaissance* (Vozrozhdenie) in Paris, *For Freedom* (Za svobodu) in Warsaw, and *Segodnya* in Riga. His lifelong interest in the theater found final expression in the essay collection *Familiar Muses* (Znakomye muzy, 1928).

As a writer Amfiteatrov was more concerned in dealing with topical matters in a light, captivating style than in achieving sustained artistic mastery, often resorting to extensive quotations from other books, placards, newspapers, and the like in order to capture the flavor of the epoch. The breadth of his interests was reflected in the variety of his fiction: the life and mores of late 19th-century Russian intelligentsia in a five-novel cycle beginning with *Men of the Eighties* (Vos'midesyatniki, 2 vols., 1907–08) and *Men of the Nineties* (Devyatidesyatniki, 1910); women's emancipation and prostitution in *Viktoriya Pavlovna* (1903), *Mar'ya Lus'eva* (1904), and *Lilyasha* (3 vols., 1928); the theatrical world in *Twilight of the Little Gods* (Sumerki bozhkov, 1908); and frontier life in *Siberian Etudes* (Sibirskie etyudy, 1904). In the early 1910s Amfiteatrov had achieved a popularity and acclaim among the general reading public that was rivaled only by that of A. VERBITSKAYA.

Works: Sobranie sochinenii. Vols. 1–30, 33–35, 37. 1911–16. *Gorestnye zamety: ocherki krasnogo Petrograda.* 1922. *Vcherashnie predki.* 1928. *Zarya russkoi zhenshchiny.* 1929. *Oderzhimaya Rus':* *demonicheskie povesti 17-go veka.* 1929. *Russkii pop 17-go veka.* 1930.

Translations: Folk-tales of Napoleon: Napoleonder from the Russian. 1902.

Secondary literature: G. Struve, *Russkaya literatura v izgnanii.* 1956. P. 130. S. Vengerov, *Kritiko-biograficheskii slovar' russkikh pisatelei i uchenykh.* Vol. 6 (1904). Pp. 331–34. *Literaturnaya entsiklopediya.* Vol. 1 (1929). Pp. 116–17.   A. M. S.

Amphibrach, see SYLLABOTONIC VERSIFICATION.

Anapest, see SYLLABOTONIC VERSIFICATION.

Andréev, Leoníd Nikoláevich (1871–1919), Russian prose writer, dramatist, and publicist. Son of a provincial land surveyor, Andreev lost his father at an early age and spent his childhood and youth in very difficult material conditions. He inherited his father's alcoholism, and is known to have made three attempts at suicide. Andreev's first short story, characteristically titled "He, She, and Vodka" (On, ona i vodka), was published in 1895, in the newspaper *Orlovskii vestnik*, but his writing career began in earnest only three years later. Though he registered as an assistant barrister after graduation from the Moscow University Faculty of Law in 1897, his law career was a failure: his few criminal cases were free of charge, and his only civil suit was lost in all instances. Instead, he concentrated on writing court reports, topical satire, and short stories for Moscow newspapers, chiefly *Kur'er*. His story "Once upon a Time" (Zhili-byli), published in the magazine *Zhizn'* in 1901, showed particularly great promise, and a collection of stories published the same year further increased the interest toward its author among readers and men of letters. Andreev became close with Gorky and the circle of writers connected with the publishing house ZNANIE. However, having paid his dues to the intelligentsia's standard sympathizing with revolution (in his case, rather with revolutionaries), Andreev drifted away from that milieu after 1905, parted with Gorky, and in 1907 to 1909 was editor of the literary-artistic almanacs *Shipovnik* (Sweetbriar), which were conceived in opposition to Gorky's *Znanie* and in which Symbolists became the dominant force.

During the first World War, Andreev was in the grips of a strong anti-German patriotism and took part in the large pro-war newspaper *Russkaya volya* (Russian Will). He actively opposed the Bolshevik seizure of power in October 1917, and, living in Finland, sent to the Western world a passionate SOS signal—to help save Russia from the tyranny and darkness of Bolshevism: *Russia's Call to Humanity, "Save Our Souls"* (Spasite! SOS, London, 1919). Andreev died a broken man when the Civil War in Russia was at its height.

In the creative legacy of Andreev one could distinguish at an early stage, alongside traits that were common to many representatives of the critical neo-realism of that period, also traits which were to be characteristic of the mature Andreev. Many of his stories and tales, and later, plays, made, on their appearance, a great impression on the Russian reader or viewer and raised a clamor in the press. Such were, for instance, "The Abyss" (Bezdna, 1902) and "In the Fog" (V tumane, 1902), in which Andreev dealt with sexual problems, including three literary taboos: venereal disease, rape, and necrophilia. The stories caused a scandal both on the Right and on the Left, and Lev Tolstoi's wife even sent an indignant letter to the newspaper *Novoe vremya* (February 7, 1903), protesting against such "dirt" in fine literature. In another story of that early period, "The Life of Vasily Fiveisky" (Zhizn' Vasiliya Fiveiskogo, 1904), full of sufferings and nightmares, and of alcoholics, cripples, lunatics, and perverts, the hero, an Orthodox priest, becomes deranged and is led to rebellion against God, and blasphemy. This interest in all kinds of ugliness and abnormality, in the weakness and dimness of reason, in the power of destructiveness and of death, runs through a great number of Andreev's works. In his anti-militarist "The Red Laugh" (Krasnyi smekh, 1905) Andreev depicted the horror of contemporary war, leading to madness and death. In "The Curse of the Beast" (Proklyatie zverya, 1908) he rejected the faceless civilization of big cities, while in "My Notes" (Moi zapiski, 1908), written in the name of a man condemned to solitary confinement for life, he exposed the vanity of freedom and called the entire world a prison.

Some of Andreev's stories were directly inspired by the revolutionary ferment of 1905 and its aftermath. While in "And So It Was" (Tak bylo, 1906) Andreev pointed out the vanity of political revolutions, in his very successful "The Story of Seven Who Were Hanged" (Rasskaz o semi poveshennykh, 1908) he portrayed with sympathy a group of revolutionaries awaiting execution in prison.

After 1908 Andreev continued to write stories and even produced a novel, *Sashka Zhegulev* (1911), but turned mostly to play writing. In the short period between the first and the second Russian Revolution, he wrote twenty-one plays and seven miniatures for the stage: His first play, *To the Stars* (K zvezdam, 1905 [for plays the date of their writing is indicated]), was followed by plays which belonged essentially to two different categories. Some were closer to the more realistic tradition of GORKY and CHEKHOV: *Days of Our Life* (Dni nashei zhizni, 1908); *Anfisa* (1909); *Gaudeamus* (1909); *Professor Storitsyn* (1912); *Ekaterina Ivanovna* (1912), for example. Others were more symbolic or allegorical and rhetorical: *The Life of Man*

(Zhizn' cheloveka, 1906 and 1908); *King Hunger* (Tsar' Golod, 1907); *Black Masks* (Chernye maski, 1908); *Anathema* (Anatema, 1909); *He Who Gets Slapped* (Tot, kto poluchaet poshchechiny, 1915), for example. Especially successful were *The Life of Man*, in which Andreev represented the meaninglessness of man's life in general, and *He Who Gets Slapped*, where in a circus symbolizing life, a man is beaten for the entertainment of others, and where one finds thwarted love, murder, suicide, and other such Andreevian traits. Among Andreev's miniatures for the stage, *The Beautiful Sabine Women* (Prekrasnye sabinianki, 1911) was quite popular, but on the whole, satire was apparently not his main vocation.

Personally, Andreev was as extravagant and contradictory as much of his writing. His nihilism and pessimism, particularly after the death of his beloved first wife in 1906, were genuine, yet there still was much theatricality and pose in him. A handsome man, he wore velvet jackets and page-caps, impersonating a painter (which he partially was) of the Renaissance (to which he in no way belonged). He loved the sea, and needed such means of stimulation as extremely strong tea and alcohol. Brought up in poverty, he longed for lavish decors and furnishings, and his was a fast way of life, consuming all of the great deal of money that his writings brought him. As for his writings, Andreev's preoccupation with death and morbidity, and his perception of the vulnerability of human reason and of the futility of human endeavor in the face of dark and irrational forces of life, were all sincere. Yet much of what he published was melodramatic or unsupported by any convincing personal experience. It was this affectation and lack of existentiality that led Lev Tolstoi to his famous remark: "Andreev continuously tries to scare me, but I don't get scared."

All that, however, did not prevent Andreev from becoming, in the first decade of this century, one of the most popular writers in Russia: his fame was almost on a par with that of Chekhov and Gorky. The fact remains that his talent and topical themes, his literary techniques combining tradition and modernism, the boldness of his imagination, and a captivating sketchiness of thought in dealing with complex moral-psychological and philosophical problems, endeared him to a significant segment of the intelligentsia and made him consonant with the times. And though that readership and that epoch are gone forever, some of Andreev's characteristics, particularly his obvious talent, ensure for him a permanent place in Russian literature, albeit a significantly smaller one than the one projected for him at the beginning of the century.

Works: Polnoe sobranie sochinenii. 8 vols. 1913. *Sobranie sochinenii.* 17 vols. (Vols 1–13, St. Petersburg, 1911–13; vol. 14, Moscow, 1913; vols. 15–17, Moscow, 1915–17.)

Translations: (All of Andreev's major works and a great many secondary ones have been translated into English.) See *Lewanski,* pp. 190–93. See also: *Letters of Gorky and Andreev 1899–1912.* Ed. with an introd. by Peter Yershov. New York, 1958.

Secondary literature: K. Chukovskii, *Leonid Andreev bol'shoi i malen'kii.* 1908. *Istoriya russkoi literatury kontsa XIX–nachala XX veka: Bibliograficheskii ukazatel'.* Ed. K. D. Muratova. 1963. Pp. 71–95. R. V. Ivanov-Razumnik, *O smysle zhizni; F. Sologub, L. Andreev, L. Shestov.* 2d ed. 1910. Reprint. Bradda Books, 1971. Alexander Kaun, *Leonid Andreyev; A Critical Study.* 1924. Reprint. 1969. Angela Martini, *Erzähltechniken Leonid Nikolaevič Andreevs.* Munich, 1978. *Rekviem; Sbornik pamyati Leonida Andreeva.* Ed. D. L. Andreev and V. E. Beklemisheva. 1930. James B. Woodward, *Leonid Andreyev; A Study.* 1969. Josephine M. Newcombe, *Leonid Andreyev.* 1973. N. P. P.

Ánikst, Aleksándr Abrámovich (1910–), literary scholar and theater critic. Anikst holds a doctoral degree in Art Studies and is a specialist in English literature and theater (Shakespeare in particular). He has written several books on the history and theory of drama in Russia and in the West. He has also published translations as well as popular histories of English and American literature.

Works: Istoriya angliiskoi literatury. 1956. *Shest' rasskazov ob amerikanskom teatre.* 1963. *Teatr epokhi Shekspira.* 1965. *Teoriya dramy ot Aristotelya do Lessinga: Istoriya uchenii o drame.* 1967. *Teoriya dramy v Rossii ot Pushkina do Chekhova.* 1972. *Shekspir; remeslo dramaturga.* 1974. *Pervye izdaniya Shekspira.* 1974. E. B.

Ánnenkov, Pável Vasílievich (1813? 1811?–1887), literary critic, memoirist. Attended the philological faculty of Petersburg University. At the end of the 1830s he met BELINSKY, HERZEN, BAKUNIN, TURGENEV. In the 1840s he went abroad and formed a close friendship with GOGOL. His letters from Europe began to appear in *Otechestvennye zapiski*. In 1847–48 his new letters, "Letters from Paris," appeared in SOVREMENNIK. In Europe he met Karl Marx and corresponded with him. In 1849 he published his "Letters from the Province" (Provintsial'nye pis'ma). However, he is most interesting as literary critic and writer of memoirs. In 1857 there appeared his biography of STANKEVICH; a series of critical articles in the 1850s and 1860s came out in various journals, collected in a volume entitled *On the Significance of Literature for Society* (O znachenii khudozhestvennykh proizvedenii dlya obshchestva). The significance of Annenkov is the counterweight he offered to the Belinsky-Chernyshevsky-Dobrolyubov ideology. Annenkov was a partisan of poetic freedom and an opponent of all tendentiousness in literature. In 1855 Annenkov prepared the first scholarly edition of Pushkin's works (7 volumes), and *Materials for a Biography of A. S. Pushkin* (Materialy dlya biografii Aleksandra Sergeevicha Pushkina, 1855), an important source for future Pushkin studies. Further works on Pushkin followed. His most important work is *The Extraordinary Decade* (Zamechatel'noe desyatiletie, 1880), a study of the intellectual and literary history of an era remembered as an important turning point in the spiritual evolution of Russia. There are vivid portraits of Gogol, Turgenev, Belinsky, Stankevich, GRANOVSKY, BAKUNIN, among others. During the 1880 Pushkin celebrations, Annenkov was awarded an honorary doctorate from Moscow University.

Works: Nikolai Vladimirovich Stankevich. 1857. *Vospominaniya i kriticheskie ocherki.* 3 vols. 1877–81. *Literaturnye vospominaniya.* Comm. and biogr. sketch by B. M. Eikhenbaum. 1928. *Literaturnye vospominaniya.* 1960.

Secondary literature: Istoriya russkoi kritiki. Vol. 1. 1958. B. L. Modzalevskii, "Raboty P. V. Annenkova o Pushkine." In *Pushkin.* 1929. *Ocherki po istorii russkoi kritiki.* Vol. 1. 1928. D. Ryazanov, *Karl Marks i russkie lyudi sorokovykh godov.* 1918. A. S. Suvorin, ed., *P. V. Annenkov i ego druz'ya. Literaturnye vospominaniya i perepiska 1835–37 godov.* 1892. S. A. Vengerov, *Kritiko-biograficheskii slovar'.* Vol. 1. 1889.   E. K. K.

Ánnenkov, Yúry, see TEMIRYAZEV.

Ánnensky, Innokénty Fyódorovich (1856–1909), poet, playwright, literary critic, and translator of Euripides. Born in Omsk, he was reared in St. Petersburg by an older brother, a journalist and social activist. He was educated at St. Petersburg University and became a secondary school teacher of Greek and Latin languages and literatures and of Russian literature. His first original works were tragedies on subjects taken from the Greek myths. His original verse, however, was in the tradition of French symbolism, although he was never a member of the Russian SYMBOLIST movement. He was neither prolific nor varied; his poetic oeuvre is contained in *Quiet Songs* (Tikhie pesni, 1904), *The Cypress Chest* (Kiparisovyi larets, 1910) and *Posthumous Verse* (Posmertnye stikhi, 1923). Although his poetry fell outside any Russian literary movement and has never been popular, his reputation as a poet's poet was lively and his place in Russian literature is permanent. His literary criticism began to appear in the 1880s. His complete translation of Euripides was published between 1907 and 1921.

Annensky's original tragedies on Greek subjects include *Melanippa the Philosopher* (Melanippa-filosof, 1901) about a mother who defends her children by Poseidon, although blinded and imprisoned; *King Ixion* (Tsar' Iksion, 1902) about the king who coveted Hera, sired the centaurs and was racked on a wheel in the underworld; *Laodamia* (1906) about the faithful wife of Protesilaus who chose not to survive him; and *Thamyras Cytharoede* (Famira-Kifared, 1913) about the harpist who challenged Apollo.

Annensky's reputation rests on his lyric verse. It is all of a piece; its characteristic subject is insurmountable ennui as introduced into European literature by Charles Baudelaire, cultivated by Paul Verlaine, and to some extent by Stéphane Mallarmé. The word "anguish" (*toska*) occurs frequently in his titles. His scope is narrow, but his poems are consistently on a high level, and his oeuvre is re-

warding. He was antipathetic to the Russian symbolist movement because of its mysticism and occasionally strident metaphysical urgency. He inherited from French symbolism its subtlety of psychology, refinement of taste, and impotent witnessing of transience. His poems are the inner monologues of a mind that is atheistic, yet pure; alienated yet lonely, remembering love and yearning for it. He loves nature yet sees in it, even at its showiest, the signs of decline and pointless death. He appreciates the arts, especially music. His poems have ingenious structures that accommodate the ellipses and fantasies of inner monologue, but demand a creative effort from the reader; he resembles Mallarmé in this respect. His books are carefully arranged. *Quiet Songs* opens with many depictions of gaudy colors and sunsets, progresses through a dark night to the anticipation of dawn, but also of death. Much of *The Cypress Chest* consists in twenty-five triptychs which feature psychological states or landscapes. Annensky tended to imbue nature with more signs of life and mind (often through figures of speech) than human life—a displacement which creates, together with his organizational fastidiousness, the impression of an attenuated emotional life.

Annensky's literary criticism appeared in *Books of Reflections* (Knigi otrazhenii vol. 1, 1906; vol. 2, 1909). It includes essays on GOGOL, DOSTOEVSKY, TURGENEV, CHEKHOV, and Konstantin BALMONT. His own aesthetic appears incidentally in "The Portrait" (Portret), about Gogol's short story of that name: art allows for a joy of contemplation and thus a triumph of the spirit that is unique in existence, and which places art above reality. For Annensky art was a psychological, not a mystical, experience. In addition to Euripides, he also translated Baudelaire, Verlaine, Leconte de Lisle, and other French and German poets, as well as Horace.

He was considered a mentor by the ACMEIST poets, who rebelled against the mystical tendencies of symbolism, and especially by Nikolai GUMILYOV and Anna AKHMATOVA.

Works: Stikhotvoreniya i tragedii. 2d ed. Introd. and notes by A. V. Fedorov. (Biblioteka poeta: Bol'shaya seriya.) 1959. *Knigi otrazhenii.* 2 vols. 1906 and 1909. Reprint. Slavische Propyläen, 50 (Munich, 1969). *Knigi otrazhenii.* Ed. N. T. Ashimbaeva, I. I. Podol'skaya, and A. V. Fedorov. Moscow, 1979. *Lirika.* Introd. and comm. by A. V. Fedorov. 1979.

Translations: Lewanski, pp. 193–94. *Modern Russian Poetry.* Ed. Vladimir Markov and Merrill Sparks. 1967. Pp. 112–29. *The Cypress Chest: Bilingual Edition.* Trans. R. H. Morrison. Ann Arbor, 1982.

Secondary literature: David Borker, "Annenskij and Mallarmé: A Case of Subtext," *SEEJ* 21 (1977), pp. 46–55. ———, "Intrinsic and Extrinsic Aspects of Structure in Annenskij's 'Verbnaja nedelja'," *SEEJ* 23 (1979), pp. 491–504. Renato Poggioli, "Innokentij Annenskij." In *The Poets of Russia, 1890–1930.* 1960. Pp. 170–73. Vsevolod Setchkarev, *Studies in the Life and Work of Innokentij Annenskij.* The Hague, 1963.   E. Br.

Ansteí, Ólga Nikoláevna (1912–   ), émigré poet of the "second wave," published her first book of verse, *Door in the Wall* (Dver' v stene, 1949) in Munich. Since her immigration to America in 1950, Anstei has published her verse in various periodicals and produced another book of verse, *In the Way* (Na yuru, 1976). She is also known as an expert translator of verse and prose from German and English. Anstei's poetry is characterized by a religious perception of the world, often from a markedly feminine point of view, and skillfully poeticized colloquial speech. Her versification is remarkably subtle.

Translations: America's Russian Poets. Ed. and tr. R. H. Morrison. 1975. P. 21.

Secondary literature: Fabii Zverev, "Poety 'novoi' emigratsii." In *Russkaya literatura v emigratsii: Sbornik statei,* ed. N. P. Poltoratskii. 1972. Pp. 74–75.   V. T.

Antinihilism in Russian literature of the 1860s was a response to the radical intellectual hegemony established during that decade. The leading critics—men like DOBROLYUBOV, CHERNYSHEVSKY, and PISAREV—viewed literature merely as a means of encouraging radical social reform, indirectly through literary criticism, or more directly through literature itself. When no one else would produce a "nihilist" novel, Chernyshevsky wrote *What Is To Be Done?* (Chto delat'? 1863), in which he depicted the "new people" and the society they hoped would come into being in the future. Generally speaking, the radicals believed that social pathology derived from social organization, and that it could be cured only by a radical reconstitution of society along socialist lines.

By contrast to the radical authors, the "antinihilist" writers cherished individual differences and historic custom, disliked abstract theorizing, and viewed the individual rather than the collective as the basic component of society. They believed that radical theories would inevitably fail when put into practice, and tried to demonstrate this belief in works of the artistic imagination.

Antinihilism was inconsequential in the drama of the 1860s, emerged more strongly in poetry (in the work of such men as A. K. TOLSTOI and Yakov POLONSKY), and was most powerful in the novel.

Although it had some obscure predecessors, TURGENEV's novel *Fathers and Sons* (Ottsy i deti, 1862) set the tone of the 1860s and gave the very word "nihilist" its currency. The tragic hero Bazarov—who dies at the end because he has appeared on the scene before his time—combines the quintessential characteristics of the radical hero of the 1860s as Turgenev saw him: he is a self-confident medical doctor, a philosophical materialist, a negator of established social values, even a revolutionary. *Fathers and Sons* split the radical camp, with Chernyshevsky condemning Bazarov as a caricature while Pisarev accepted him as a good portrayal of what was best in the younger generation. The echoes of the dispute which broke out over the book in 1862 resounded for many years. Indeed *What Is To Be Done?* was a rebuttal to *Fathers and Sons*, and Dostoevsky's *Notes from Underground* (Zapiski iz podpol'ya, 1864) was a species of response to *What Is To Be Done?*.

Aleksei PISEMSKY's *Troubled Seas* (Vzbalamuchennoe more, 1863) depicted the young radicals as just as corrupt as the older generation against which they rebelled; and Nikolai LESKOV's *No Way Out* (Nekuda, 1864) centered about a young woman radical who became disillusioned with her socialist colleagues but could not return to the established society she had so decidedly rejected for their sake. The radicals of the 1860s anathematized Pisemsky and especially Leskov for their attempts to create an objective image of them. Images have consequences, as well as ideas.

Ivan GONCHAROV's third novel, *The Precipice* (Obryv, 1869), which sold quite well among general readers, had as one of its major characters a young radical who cleaned his ears with rolled-up pages torn from books and entered rooms through windows. Like virtually all the other antinihilist writers, Goncharov endured violent criticism for his failure to "understand" the younger generation better.

But the culminating point of the antinihilist tradition was reached in 1871–72, with the publication of DOSTOEVSKY's *The Possessed* (Besy), inspired in large part by the revolutionary Sergei Nechaev's trial for political murder which took place then. Pyotr Verkhovensky—whom his creator saw as simultaneously dangerous and comic—by the use of scandal and intrigue works to subvert the established order in a small Russian city, hoping for a collapse which will permit the organized radicals to seize power. He forms a group of revolutionaries and cements them in loyalty both to himself and to the revolutionary "cause" by the collective murder of a former member of the group who, he claims, may inform on them. Verkhovensky's schemes indeed come perilously close to succeeding, but when they ultimately fail he escapes abroad, leaving his associates to their fate. *The Possessed* portrays the radicals as a collection of criminals or dupes, and the radical movement as an engine of social disorder. This was the result, in the real world, of the theories which Bazarov debated with his hosts on a quiet country estate in 1859 (*Fathers and Sons*). As one of Dostoevsky's crazed but penetrating characters says of the arson which brings *The Possessed* to its climax, "the fire is in the minds of men and not in the roofs of houses."

Bibliography: Charles A. Moser, *Antinihilism in the Russian Novel of the 1860's*. The Hague, 1964. ———, "Antinihilism in Russian Poetry of the 1860's," *SEEJ* 9 (1965); pp. 155–73. P. G. Pustovoit, *Roman I. S. Turgeneva 'Ottsy i deti' i ideinaya bor'ba 60-kh godov XIX veka*. 1960. Wolf-Heinrich Schmidt, *Nihilismus und Nihilisten*. Munich, 1974.   C. A. M.

Antokólsky, Pável Grigórievich (1896–   ), poet, critic, publicist, and stage director, was born in St. Petersburg, the son of a lawyer. He studied law at Moscow University, but never graduated. He joined the drama studio of E. B. Vakhtangov in 1915 and eventually became a director at Vakhtangov's theatre. During World War II, Antokolsky ran a theatre for frontline troops. Antokolsky began to publish his poetry in 1921. His poetry of the 1920s and 1930s often deals with French and German themes, so his verse epics "The Commune of 1871" (Kommuna 71 goda, 1933) and "François Villon" (1934). Subsequently, Antokolsky falls in line with the prevailing trend, concentrating on themes of "building socialism" and, after the outbreak of the war, valor and devotion to his country of the Soviet fighting man, so in his verse epic "A Son" (Syn, 1943), which earned him a Stalin prize. After the war, Antokolsky returned to historical themes of the distant as well as of the more recent past: "Eighteen-Hundred Forty Eight" (Tysyacha vosem'sot sorok vos'moi, 1948) and "In an Alley back of the Arbat" (V pereulke za Arbatom, 1954). In several of his books of the 1950s and 1960s, Antokolsky combined poetry with prose essays, criticism, and aphorisms, so in his "On Pushkin" (1960).

Works: Sobranie sochinenii. 4 vols. 1971–73. *Poety i vremya.* 1957. *Puti poetov.* 1965.

Translations: "A Son." In Joshua Kunitz. *Russian Literature since the Revolution.* 1948. "Shakespeare." In *Modern Russian Poetry.* Ed. Vladimir Markov and Merrill Sparks. 1967. Pp. 712–13.

Secondary literature: Lev I. Levin, *Chetyre zhizni: Khronika trudov i dnei Pavla Antokol'skogo.* 2d ed. 1978. V. Lugovskoi, "Poet i vremya." In his *Razdum'e o poezii.* 1960. D. L. Reznikov, "Poeticheskaya pushkiniana P. Antokol'skogo." *RLit* 19 (1976), no. 4, pp. 166–77.   V. T.

Antónov, Sergeí Petróvich (1915–   ), writer and critic, graduated from the Leningrad Highway Institute in 1938 and began publishing prose in 1947. He is the author of short stories, novellas and novels (two have been adapted for films). Set in the contemporary Russian village, his works deal primarily with psychological problems associated with life on a collective farm. His earlier works tended to depict the positive aspects of rural life.

Recipient of the USSR State Prize (1951) Antonov is an "officially" approved writer. Yet, some of his works incited heated controversy and criticism. *Rains* (1951); *The Penkovo Affair* (1956); *The Torn Ruble Note* (1966); and *Alenka* (1960) were attacked by conservatives and hailed by liberals for their deviation from SOCIALIST REALISM. They depicted genuine conflict between the real and the ideal life on the collective (see also CONFLICTLESS LITERATURE) and gave a frank picture of the social, economic, intellectual, and moral poverty plaguing Soviet village life. Generally, however, Antonov's criticism is cautious and seldom exceeds the limits of what is allowed at a given time.

Antonov is a talented writer. His prose is conventional, realistic, and lyrical in the tradition of PAUSTOVSKY and CHEKHOV. His characters are realistically drawn and psychologically developed.

In addition, Antonov is the author of works about literature. These include *Letters About the Short Story* (Pis'ma o rasskaze, 1964), *First Person Narrative* (Ot pervogo litsa, 1973), and *The Word* (Slovo, 1974), in which he discusses various aspects of the short story as a genre. These works are addressed primarily to the beginning writer and amateur rather than the scholar.

Works in Russian: Fiction: *Lena.* 1948. *Po dorogam idut mashiny.* 1950. *Poddubenskie chastushki.* 1950. *Mirnye lyudi.* 1950. *Dozhdi, Novyi mir*, 1951, no. 10. *Pervaya dolzhnost'.* 1952. *Izbrannoe 1947–1953.* 1954. *Razgovor: Povest' i rasskazy.* 1956. *Delo bylo v Pen'kove.* 1956. *Porozhnii reis.* 1960. *Alenka.* 1960. *Povesti i rasskazy 1954–60.* 1961. *Razorvannyi rubl', Yunost'*, 1966, no. 1. *Raznotrav'e.* 1968. *Tsarskii dvugrivennyi.* 1970. *Serebryannaya svad'ba.* 1972. *Tri bogatyrya.* 1973.

Essays and Criticism: V strane pol'derov i tyul'panov. Ocherki. 1957. *Pis'ma o rasskaze.* 1964. *Ya chitayu rasskaz.* 1973. *Ot pervogo litsa.* 1973. *Slovo.* 1974.

Translations: Poddubki Songs. Moscow, 1953. *Spring: Short Stories.* Moscow, 1954. *It Happened in Penkovo.* Moscow, 1956. *Alenka.* Moscow, 1960.

Secondary literature: A. Ninov, "Osmyslenie sovremennosti," *Neva*, 1967, no. 2. A. Ognev, *S. Antonov: Kritiko-biograficheskii ocherk.* Saratov, 1968. S. Plekhanov, (Review article), *VLit*, 1975, no. 2. M. Shcheglov, "Chto sluchilos' v Pen'kove?" *Druzhba naro-*

dov, 1956, no. 11. Reprint in his *Literaturnaya kritika* (1971). E. Starikova, "V poiskakh novogo," *Znamya*, 1956, no. 10. ———, "Dve povesti S. Antonova." In *Poeziya prozy*. 1962.   H. S.

Antonóvich, Maksím Alekséevich (1835–1918), literary critic, philosopher, and publicist, was born in Belopolie in Kharkov province, the son of a sexton. Having studied for the priesthood in Kharkov and St. Petersburg (1855–59), Antonovich divorced himself from religious studies through the influence of N. G. CHERNYSHEVSKY. For a time a contributor to SOVREMENNIK, he became editor in charge of the section on Russian literature, after the death of DOBROLYUBOV (1861) and the arrest of Chernyshevsky in 1862. Antonovich's materialistic, democratic, and atheistic views were formed through the writings of BELINSKY, Chernyshevsky, Dobrolyubov, and Feuerbach. A staunch defender of Darwinism, he argued against the idealism of Kant and Schopenhauer, opposed the Russian idealists and reactionaries of his time, and polemicized with the reactionary views expressed in the journals of DOSTOEVSKY, VREMYA and EPOKHA. Antonovich favored the aesthetic views espoused by Chernyshevsky and Dobrolyubov, and supported the democratic writings of the RAZNOCHINTSY. In his negative critique of TURGENEV's *Fathers and Sons* ("Asmodeus of Our Time"—Asmodei nashego vremeni, 1862), Antonovich blames the author for caricaturing the *raznochintsy* and their views. With the closing of *Sovremennik* in 1866, Antonovich virtually withdrew from active involvement in questions of literature and social movements. Later, however, he took a stand against decadent art. Sharply criticizing the supposedly reactionary tendencies of Dostoevsky's novel, *The Brothers Karamazov* ("A Mystic-Ascetic Novel"—Mistiko-asketicheskii roman, 1881), Antonovich ignored the complex dialectics of the work. Antonovich also wrote valuable reminiscences of Chernyshevsky, Dobrolyubov, and NEKRASOV, with fine assessments of the decade of the sixties.

Works: Shestidesyatye gody: Vospominaniya. 1933. *Izbrannye stat'i. Filosofiya. Kritika. Polemika.* 1938. *Izbrannye filosofskie sochineniya.* 1945.

Secondary literature: V. Kirpotin, "Publitsisticheskaya deyatel'nost' Antonovicha do aresta Chernyshevskogo," *Pod znamenem marksizma*, no. 7–8 (1928). M. N. Peunova, *Mirovozzrenie M. A. Antonovicha.* 1960. A. N. Shishkina, "Antonovich." In *Istoriya russkoi kritiki.* Vol. 2. 1958.   D. K. D.

Apocrypha. The conventional term *Apokrify* applies to a broad category of Old Russian writings which for some reason were identified with the "hidden" or "secret" works rejected by ecclesiastical authorities. Literary and cultural considerations have played an important role in broadening the criteria of classification far beyond the conceptual bounds established by the Church. This situation explains the current uncertainties and contradictions which confront scholars engaged in selecting and describing heterogeneous materials loosely defined as Apocrypha.

From an ecclesiastical standpoint, one may divide Old Russian Apocrypha into categories such as deuterocanonical, pseudoepigraphical, Old Testament, New Testament, and so forth. One may also equate apocryphal writings with "prohibited literature" (*otrechennaya literatura*). However, classifications of this kind are not fully adequate to describe the situation in the Russian lands, where no unified canonic tradition existed until the end of the 15th century. For this reason, modern scholars have had recourse to other classificatory schemes based mainly on thematic or typological considerations. They have identified as Apocrypha various "visions" or "revelations," lives of biblical personages, diverse apocalyptic and eschatological writings, and works on astrology or other forms of divination. On other occasions, different types of Old Russian writings have been grouped together and defined as Apocrypha because of their connection with some "secret" or "heretical" movement. This is the case, for example, with the many works linked to Bogomilism, a dualistic sect which spread from Bulgaria throughout Christendom in the 10th century and which reached Kievan Rus very early (see the *Primary Chronicle* s. a. 1071).

It is often difficult to determine not only the origins of Old Russian Apocrypha but also the area of their diffusion. The greater part of Old Russian Apocrypha were translations or adaptations from Greek writings and widely circulated throughout Orthodox Slavdom. Although most of the Apocrypha appear to have reached the Russian lands from the South Slavic region, there are examples of Slavic apocryphal accounts and legends which are documented only in the Russian lands (e.g., the well-known *Tale on Solomon and Kitovras*, an expansion of the theme found in 3 [1] Kings 6 : 7).

The majority of texts which have been studied as monuments of Old Russian Apocrypha belong to the category of "prohibited literature." Lists of such works were provided by ecclesiastical indices. The earliest known index of forbidden books is contained in the IZBORNIK OF 1073, which originally was compiled for the Bulgarian tsar Symeon at the beginning of the 10th century. Another list of prohibited writings which was produced in Bulgaria (11th–12th century) eventually made its way to the Russian lands and is preserved in the 14th-century Pogodin *Nomokanon*. The Russian indices of prohibited literature increasingly broadened the scope of Apocrypha (especially in the 16th and early 17th century); when codified, they entered the so-called *Kirillova kniga* (1644), a work which was especially popular among the OLD BELIEVERS.

It is important to emphasize, however, that many works known to us as Apocrypha were included in such orthodox collections as the *Tolkovaya Paleya, Istoricheskaya Paleya*, and *Prolog*. The great popularity of Apocrypha in Old Russian literature should not be attributed to lack of vigilance. The widespread diffusion of Apocrypha suggests, instead, that they might not have been viewed as contrary to Orthodox teachings. Indeed, some Apocrypha apparently were regarded and used as anti-heretical documents. Although the majority of apocryphal texts have come down to us in younger codices (15th–17th century), the Apocrypha seem to have played a decisive role in the formation of an Old Russian literary system.

The great interest shown in Apocrypha by both modern scholars (N. S. TIKHONRAVOV, A. N. PYPIN, I. Ya. Porfiriev, I. Franko, N. A. Meshchersky, A. Vaillant) and writers (F. M. DOSTOEVSKY, A. N. TOLSTOI, A. M. REMIZOV) has established for us a corpus of Old Russian apocryphal writings. Among the better known Apocrypha are: the *Discourse on Adam and Eve*, the *Legend on How God Created Adam*, the *Book of Enoch*, the *Vision of Abraham*, the *Death of Abraham*, the *Exodus of Moses*, the *Testaments of the Twelve Patriarchs*, the *Gospel of Thomas*, the *Gospel of Jacob*, the *Gospel of Nicodemus*, the *Conversation of Three Holy Men*, the *Discourse on the Tree of the Cross*, the *Revelation of St. Paul*, the *Questions of John the Theologian to the Lord on Mount Tabor*, the *Revelation of Baruch*, the *Revelations of Methodius of Patara*, the *Descent of the Virgin into Hell*, the *Address of Adam to Lazarus in Hell*, the *Ascent of Isaiah*, the *Ascent of Agapius to Paradise*, the *Tale of Afrodotion*, the *Judgments of Solomon*, and the *Tale on Solomon and Kitovras*.

Bibliography: I. Franko, *Apokrify i lehendy z ukrajins'kykh rukopysiv.* 4 vols. Lvov, 1896–1906. I. Ivanov, *Bogomilski knigi i legendi.* Sofia, 1925 (2d ed. Sofia, 1970). N. A. Meshcherskii, "Apokrify v drevnei slavyano-russkoi pis'mennosti (vetkhozavetnye apokrify)." In *Metodicheskie rekomendatsii po opisaniyu slavyano-russkikh rukopisei dlya svodnogo kataloga rukopisei, khranyashchikhsya v SSSR.* Vol. II, 1, pp. 181–223. 1976. I. Ya. Porfir'ev, *Apokrificheskie skazaniya o vetkhozavetnykh litsakh i sobytiyakh po rukopisyam Solovetskoi biblioteki.* 1877. ———, *Apokrificheskie skazaniya o novozavetnykh litsakh i sobytiyakh po rukopisyam Solovetskoi biblioteki.* 1890. A. N. Pypin, *Lozhnye i otrechennye knigi russkoi stariny.* (Pamyatniki starinnoi literatury, vol. 3.) 1862. M. N. Speranskii, *Slavyanskie apokroficheskie evangeliya.* 1895. ———, *Iz istorii otrechennykh knig.* 4 vols. (Pamyatniki drevnei pis'mennosti i iskusstva, nos. 129, 131, 137, 171.) 1899–1908. N. S. Tikhonravov, *Pamyatniki otrechennoi russkoi literatury.* 2 vols. 1863. Reprint. London, 1973. ———, "Otrechennye knigi v drevnei Rusi." In his *Sochineniya.* Vol. 1. Pp. 127–255. 1898. A. Vaillant, *Le livre des secrets d'Hénoch. Texte slave et traduction française.* Paris, 1952. P. V. Vladimirov, *Nauchnoe izuchenie apokrifov—otrechennykh knig v russkoi literature vo vtoroi polovine XIX stoletiya.* (Universitetskie zapiski.) Kiev, 1900. A. I. Yatsimirskii, *Bibliograficheskii obzor apokrifov v yuzhnoslavyanskoi i russkoi pis'mennosti (spiski pamyatnikov).* Fasc. 1: *Apokrify vetkhozavetnye.* 1921.   H. G.

Apollón, the leading literary and art magazine of St. Petersburg's cultured elite, published from the end of 1909 to 1917, was conceived in the "Salon of 1909," the combined inspiration of N. GUMILYOV, the young poet and future founder of the GUILD OF POETS and the ACMEIST movement, and S. MAKOVSKY, leading art historian and art editor of such magazines as *Bygone Years* (Starye gody, 1907–1917) and *Russian Icons* (1913–1914). The first issue reflected its dual orientation. Although *Apollon* was devoted primarily to the re-evaluation and, consequently, re-definition of the Russian modernist literary movement during the first two years of the magazine's existence, by 1912 its art section had increased so much in quality and quantity that it became, for all intents and purposes, an art review. Nevertheless, the ideals represented by the art review were perfectly in accord with the trends established by the new modernist aesthetics of Acmeism which, by then, had come to dominate the magazine's literary direction.

The first issue of *Apollon* appeared on October 15, 1909, blessed by the literary contributions of the greatly respected poet and classicist, I. ANNENSKY, the art reviews and scholarship of A. Benois, and the financial support of M. Ushakov. Installments of Annensky's assessment of Russian modernist poetry, "On Contemporary Lyrics," in the first three issues helped to define the new magazine's original orientation: the re-evaluation and re-definition of Russia's modernist legacy. Gumilyov's "Letters on Russian Poetry" provided a more immediate evaluation of contemporary publications and trends in poetry, KUZMIN's analyses of current Russian fiction, "Notes on Russian Belletristic Literature," provided a similar service for prose while VOLOSHIN's reviews, "Literary Life," provided Petersburgers with insights into the current Moscow literary scene.

In 1910, after the closing of the major symbolist magazines, VESY and ZOLOTOE RUNO, *Apollon* published not only the "great symbolist debates" (formal speeches by V. IVANOV and BLOK delivered at the Academy of Verse in an attempt to redefine the basic tenets and current state of symbolism; plus BRYUSOV's answer and BELY's response to Bryusov), but also the major essays of the third generation Russian modernist poets, Gumilyov's "Life of Verse" and Kuzmin's "On Beautiful Clarity."

By 1912, *Apollon* had recognized and given its support to uphold the post-symbolist values of the Poets' Guild and Gumilyov's disciples, following their break with Ivanov's Academy of Verse: the emphasis of craft over theme, poetry over mysticism, and the concomitant veneration and assessment of European literature and cultural traditions in the Russian cultural heritage.

In early 1913, *Apollon* became the de facto organ of the Acmeist movement: it published the Acmeist manifestoes, translations of the poetry of Acmeist mentors, and original programmatic poems of all six Acmeist poets. The Acmeists' interest in the fine arts, especially in painting, sculpture, and architecture, was reflected in the choice of the articles and reproductions which came to dominate the pages of the magazine during the last four years of its existence.

Bibliography: Denis Mickiewicz, "Apollo and Modernist Poetics." In *The Silver Age of Russian Culture*. Ann Arbor, 1975.

J. G. H.

Apúkhtin, Aleksei Nikoláevich (1840–93), poet, was descended from an old gentry family which was French in origin. He was a sickly child and was spoiled in spite of his parents' modest means. He began writing poetry as a boy and continued in the Petersburg Institute of Jurisprudence where he studied from 1852 to 1859. Here Apukhtin became a close friend of the future composer P. I. Tchaikovsky, a fellow student, whose letters reveal much about Apukhtin during this period. After finishing his education, Apukhtin worked in the Ministry of Justice until 1862 when he retired to his estate in Oryol province. In 1863, suffering from incurable obesity, Apukhtin moved to St. Petersburg where he remained until his death. He continued to write verses, but rarely published from fear of "selling his talent." In 1886, Apukhtin condescended and approved the publication of a collection of his poetry. Three thousand copies were published and quickly sold. Apukhtin's reputation as a poet was established.

Apukhtin was noted for his worship of a timeless and abstract ideal of beauty. His themes are ideal love, solace for the unhappy and unfortunate, and a humanist's laments on the disorder of human affairs and the imperfections of life. After the success of his book of poetry, Apukhtin began submitting his verses to journals (*The Herald of Europe, Russian Thought*). Many of Apukhtin's poems were set to music by Tchaikovsky and others: "Venice," "In a Pauper's Tatters" (V ubogom rubishche), "The Old Gypsy Woman" (Staraya tsyganka), etc. In his later years, Apukhtin wrote several stories: "The Diary of Pavlik Dolsky" (Dnevnik Pavlika Dol'skogo), "The Archive of Countess D." (Iz arkhiva grafini D.), "Between Life and Death" (Mezhdu zhizn'yu i smert'yu), and one dramatic scene: "Prince Tavrichesky." His prose works were published posthumously.

Works: Sochineniya. 2 vols. 4th ed. 1895. *Stikhotvoreniya.* Orel, 1959. *Stikhotvoreniya.* Leningrad, 1961.

Translations: "The Archive of Countess D." In *Great Russian Short Stories*. Ed. Stephen Graham. London, 1959. *From Death to Life* (Mezhdu zhizn'yu i smert'yu). Trans. R. Frank and E. Huybers. New York, 1917. [Poetry:] See *Lewanski*, p. 194.

Secondary literature: A. Borozdin, *A. N. Apukhtin.* 1895. M. Protopopov, "Pisatel'-diletant," *Russkoe bogatstvo*, 1896, no. 2, pp. 44–62.

T. E. B.

Arbúzov, Aleksei Nikoláevich (1908–), playwright, actor, and director. Arbuzov started his career as early as 1923, with a theater of the PROLETCULT in Leningrad, for which he also wrote his first agitational skits. He scored his first big hit as a playwright with *Tanya* (1939), which features one of Arbuzov's characteristic devices: long time intervals separating each successive act from the preceding. In this case it serves the purpose of showing the growth of the heroine from a callow student to a mature woman and professional (physician). Arbuzov, who has run his own studio during much of his career, has tended to produce plays of undoubting loyalty to the regime, yet unconventional and sometimes innovative in their structure. His greatest hit, *An Irkutsk Story* (Irkutskaya istoriya, 1959), plays out the personal drama of a woman between two men against the background of the construction of a huge Siberian power plant. The play's action is commented upon by a chorus, after the fashion of Brecht's epic theater. Arbuzov does not avoid melodramatic effects, psychological "twists," or the introduction of atypical situations. Thus, his play *Tales of Old Arbat* (Skazki starogo Arbata, 1970) features the love of a sixty-year-old artist for a twenty-year-old woman. Arbuzov's plays have rarely met with the full approval of the critical establishment, but they are very stageworthy and have enjoyed phenomenally long runs.

Works: Dramy. 1969. *Skazki starogo Arbata, Teatr, 1970, no. 9 Vybor, Novyi mir*, 1971, no. 9. *V etom milom starom dome, Teatr*, 1972, no. 2. *Moe zaglyaden'e, Moskva*, 1972, no. 5. *Staromodnaya komediya, Teatr*, 1975, no. 6.

Translations: Selected Plays. Trans. Ariadne Nicolaeff. Pergamon Press, 1982. *Tanya.* Trans. Alex Miller. In *Classic Soviet Plays*. Moscow, 1979. Pp. 441–518.

Secondary literature: S. V. Fenina, "Aleksei Nikolaevich Arbuzov," *Russkii yazyk za rubezhom*, 1979, no. 5: 16–25. Frederick I. Kaplan, "Love and Labor, Soviet Style: A Study of Alexei Arbuzov's *Irkutskaia istoriia*," *Proceedings of the Fifth National Convention of the Popular Cultural Association*. 1975. Pp. 935–50. I. Vishnevskaya, *Aleksei Arbuzov: Ocherk tvorchestva dramaturga.* 1971.

V. T.

Artsybáshev, Mikhaíl Petróvich (1878–1927), novelist and short story writer. Artsybashev published his first story, "Tumanov," whose theme is that of adolescent suicide, in 1901. His next story, "Horror" (Uzhas, 1903), described a brutal rape in harrowing detail. The themes of suicide, murder, execution (in several stories set in the Revolution of 1905), and other forms of violence remained dominant in the works of this prolific writer. Artsybashev's first novel, *The Death of Ivan Lande* (Smert' Ivana Lande, 1904), was an unsuccessful attempt to create "a perfectly beautiful human being" *à la* DOSTOEVSKY's Myshkin. He gained wide notoriety with his second novel, *Sanin* (1907), a vulgarization of Dostoevsky's *Notes from Underground*, featuring an amoral, cynical, and lecherous antihero who rationalizes his behavior in long-winded discussions. Artsybashev's next novel, *Millions* (Milliony, 1912), again dealt with a Dostoevskian theme (from *A Raw Youth*), the loneliness of a millionaire.

Artsybashev was a typical epigone: he used the themes, characters, and devices of his great predecessors (TURGENEV, Dostoevsky, TOLSTOI), vulgarizing them, at times skillfully. He also responded alertly to the moods of his age, the years between the two revolutions. Artsybashev emigrated after the October Revolution, but produced nothing of significance thereafter.

Works: Sobranie sochinenii. 10 vols. 1905–17.
Translations: Lewanski, p. 195.
Secondary literature: Temira Pachmuss, "Mikhail Artsybashev in the Criticism of Zinaida Gippius." *SEER* 44 (1966), pp. 76–87.

V. T.

Arvátov, Borís Ignátievich (1896–1940), literary and art critic and theorist. He joined the Communist Party in 1919, served as a political commissar on the Polish front in the Civil War, and was active in both the PROLETKULT and LEF.

Of the various attempts made in the 1920s at reconciling FORMALISM and MARXISM, Arvatov's—known as "formal-sociologism"—was the most imaginative, controversial, and influential. For Arvatov, the work of art is the product of skilled craftsmanship, not the expression of the artist's psyche. But he denies it any self-sufficient aesthetic value, seeing it instead as strictly utilitarian, as much a part of society's material culture as other forms of technology, although the most "efficacious" one. Art "functions as part of the social system as a whole," and the process by which it incorporates and reworks its materials is shaped by the laws of historical development, as reflected, for instance, in the demands of the consumer and the socio-economic position of the artist. Thus, the move toward tendentious art in the 1920s reveals the craftsman's new position as a member of a collective which insists on political awareness. Arvatov's ideas offended both Formalists and Marxists, and eventually proved incompatible with the officially-proclaimed tenets of SOCIALIST REALISM.

Works: Iskusstvo i klassy. 1923. *Iskusstvo i proizvodstvo.* 1926. "O formal'no-sotsiologicheskom metode," *Pechat' i revolyutsiya,* no. 3 (1927). *Sotsiologicheskaya poetika.* 1928. *Ob agitatsionnom i proizvodstvennom iskusstve.* 1930.
Secondary literature: Victor Erlich, *Russian Formalism.* 3d. ed. 1981. Pp. 111–14.

R. A. M.

Arzamás, literary group (1815–18). Of the more than four hundred familiar literary groups of its time, Arzamas is one of few to have made a lasting reputation in Russian letters, in part because of the brilliance of its membership, in part because of the infectious levity of its proceedings, in part because of its impact on the youthful works of Aleksandr PUSHKIN. Its formal meetings—which parodied those of learned academies, the FREEMASONS, and the BESEDA—spanned only a few years, but its membership had informally coalesced shortly before the Napoleonic invasion and would remain loosely together until at least 1825, and some Arzamasians collaborated on literary and journalistic projects (such as the LITERATURNAYA GAZETA) into the 1830s. Among the regular and honorary members were many of the finest poets and prose writers of Petersburg (where the meetings took place) and Moscow: K. N. BATYUSHKOV, D. V. DAVYDOV, A. S. PUSHKIN, V. L. PUSHKIN, A. I. Turgenev, P. A. VYAZEMSKY, V. A. ZHUKOVSKY (the Secretary of the group, who kept the minutes in mock-heroic hexameters), I. I. DMITRIEV, and N. M. KARAMZIN. F. F. Vigel and S. P. Zhikharev left invaluable memoirs and diaries about the period, as did Vyazemsky.

Held together by a complicated network of literary, school, family, and service relationships, the Arzamasians did not constitute a monolithic intellectual body. N. M. Muravyov, A. S. Orlov, and N. I. Turgenev played important roles in the Decembrist conspiracy, while other members came to hold ministerial rank under Nicholas I (D. N. Bludov, D. V. Dashkov, and S. S. Uvarov). Publicly the Arzamasians defended Karamzin (who owned an estate near the town of Arzamas) and Zhukovsky in the debates about the literary language and about literary ballads, but in the privacy of their meetings and conversations they constructively criticized and playfully parodied these two writers no less than their public adversaries. They shared in the principal literary interests of cultivated amateurs of the time: familiar correspondence and verse epistles, the cult of friendship, attention to stylistic controversy, and the appeal to westernized polite

society for aesthetic norms. Most shared in the Enlightenment ideals of cosmopolitanism, education, and justice and expressed this commitment through public service. Several projects for an Arzamas periodical came to naught, but their scintillating correspondence—semi-public in their own time and clearly destined by them for posterity—fulfilled journalistic, critical, and aesthetic functions.

Bibliography: M. I. Aronson and S. A. Reiser, eds., *Literaturnye kruzhki i salony.* 1929. M. S. Borovkova-Maikova, ed., *"Arzamas" i "arzamasskie" protokoly.* 1933. M. I. Gillel'son, *Molodoi Pushkin i arzamasskoe bratstvo.* 1974. William Mills Todd III, *The Familiar Letter as a Literary Genre In the Age of Pushkin.* 1976.

W. M. T.

Arzhák, Nikolai see DANIEL.

Aséev, Nikolai Nikoláevich (1889–1963), poet and writer, came from a middle-class family. He studied at Moscow and Kharkov Universities and launched his literary career in 1911, when some of his poems were published in the journal *Spring* (Vesna). Even though Aseev belonged to the CENTRIFUGE group of FUTURISTS, the poetics of his first collection, "Nocturnal Flute" (1914), shows SYMBOLIST influence. In the preface to "Letorei" (1915; the title is a neologism, literally "soaring of years") he embraced the poetics of cubo-futurism, asserting that "a stream of sounds may generate thoughts, but will never be governed by them." Aseev eventually retreated from the extreme positions of KRUCHONYKH and KHLEBNIKOV, but his style retained elements of their poetics even in the 1920s: a penchant for metaphysical metaphors, realized metaphor, etymologism, and even verbal "cubism." A fondness for folk poetry, idiomatic expressions, and colloquialisms, as well as a preference for ACCENTUAL VERSE, assonance/consonance rather than conventional rhyme, and for strident consonantal sound patterns remained characteristic of Aseev's poetry to the end of his life.

After some years in the Far East (1916–21), Aseev returned to Moscow in 1922, joined the LEF group, and became a loyal collaborator of MAYAKOVSKY's. He enthusiastically accepted the utilitarian aesthetics of *Lef* and became a proponent of "factography" and "thingness" (*veshchnost'*). Much of his work was now versified journalism and propaganda. Aseev wrote some poems which became popular songs, including "Budyonny's March," "My Little Rifle," "Five-Pointed Star" (Marsh Budyonnogo, Vintovochka, Pyatikontsovaya). The "revolutionary romanticism" of his verse epics, such as "Budyonny" (1923), "Twenty-Six" (1925), and "Semyon Proskakov" (1928), appealed to simple readers.

Aseev's later years were marked by his devotion to the memory of Mayakovsky. His lengthy verse epic "Incipit Mayakovsky" (Mayakovskii nachinaetsya, 1937–50) is written entirely in Mayakovsky's style, uses Mayakovsky's favorite rhythms, and contains many echoes of his poetry. It is, however, an interesting attempt at literary history in poetic form. Many of Aseev's shorter poems are also devoted, directly or indirectly, to Mayakovsky. Aseev's poetic style is a smoother, more "cultured," and more "pleasing" version of Mayakovsky's. Toward the end of his life, Aseev wrote a good deal of unpretentious occasional poetry in which he all but abandoned his Mayakovskian mannerisms.

Works: Sobranie sochinenii v 5 tomakh. 1963–64.
Translations: Lewanski, pp. 195–96.
Secondary literature: A. S. Karpov, *Nikolai Aseev: Ocherk tvorchestva.* 1969. Vladimir Markov, *Russian Futurism: A History.* 1968. Pp. 235–52. (Also has a bibliography.) V. Mil'kov, *Nikolai Aseev: Literaturnyi portret.* 1973.

V. T.

Askóldov, Sergei (pseudonym of Sergei Alekseevich Alekseev, 1871–1945), philosopher, was the illegitimate son of Aleksei Aleksandrovich Kozlov (1831–1901), a prominent philosopher, to whom he devoted a monograph: *A. A. Kozlov* (1912). Since Kozlov's first wife refused to give him a divorce, Askoldov's surname was taken from his father's first name. Kozlov's panpsychist philosophy in many ways determined the views of his son, particularly as stated in his first work, *Basic Problems of Gnoseology and Ontology* (Osnovnye problemy teorii poznaniya i ontologii, 1900). In his second—and last printed—book, *Thought and Reality* (Mysl' i deistvitel'nost', 1914), Askoldov departs somewhat from his father's positions, linking philosophic thought more closely to religious experience and mystic revelation. Even in the 1910s Askoldov sharply criticized recent systems of gnoseology which excluded from the concept of "gnoseological subject" (or from "consciousness in general") any kind of psychological content, thus reducing this concept to a pure abstraction and making the boundary between cognizing subject and cognized object elusive and unimaginable. Rather, Askoldov asserted, "the cognizing subject dealt with by a gnoseology that has not embarked upon a road of arbitrary contrivance, is an *individual* subject" (*Thought and Reality*, p. 29). Rejecting the antipsychologism then in vogue, Askoldov restored the *primacy* of our immediate consciousness to its rights as something *given*: "Cognition begins, not as a cognitive relationship, but much rather as that which precedes all cognition, namely reality, i.e., something to which a clear gnoseological division into subject and object is still alien" (*Thought and Reality*, p. 130). Askoldov develops all cognition "from two sources: (1) immediate consciousness, which represents for us the most primary reality, giving cognition a necessary basis and point of departure, and (2) thought" (*Thought and Reality*, p. 116). Those who confuse cognition and thought lose the ability to distinguish between "that which is real and that which is thought," and then "the transcendent is eliminated as an object of possible experience" (*Thought and Reality*, p. 44); yet in spite of everything, "the transcendent, as something that is beyond the limits of a *given* consciousness, irrepressibly breaks through into any gnoseology" (*Thought and Reality*, p. 72). The only reality which is given us immediately is the reality of our "I," not the "psychic phenomena" of positivism. Rather, "psychic phenomena" are a semi-abstraction of sorts, the result of a breakaway, performed by our analytic thought, from our integral "I," our integral *soul*. Askoldov postulates a universally animate cosmos, which cannot be apodictically proven, but without which the reality of the external world must remain incomprehensible (*Basic Problems*, pp. 181 ff.). In *Thought and Reality*, Askoldov speaks of a "polarity of form and matter" which cannot be reduced to one another, and of a certain "functional dualism" (pp. 281 ff.), but also of the possibility of a complete fusion of "pure" matter and spirit. In the 1930s and 1940s he speaks of an unamalgamated-inseparable unity of soul and matter, as well as of an integral cosmic unity in which, as he had said earlier, "the lower merges with the higher" (*Basic Problems*, p. 246). This is a system of spiritual-corporeal monads, whose hierarchic structure somehow reminds one of Dante's cosmology. These monads are by no means windowless, as those of Leibniz, but are mutually penetrable, the key to such mutual penetrability being Eros and Agape. Unfortunately, Askoldov's last major work, *Four Discourses*, written in the form of dialogues (following the example of Vladimir SOLOVYOV's *Three Discourses*), apparently was lost forever during World War II.

The difficult problem of Evil is stated interestingly by Askoldov, who distinguishes four basic forms of evil: (1) *empirical personal evil*, the most ordinary and infinitely diverse evil of individual human passions, (2) empirical supraindividual evil, i.e., evil rooted in the conditions and organization of social life, (3) *personal evil of transcendent* (otherworldly) *origin*, evil of mystic nature and origin, which manifests itself in the human soul, but whose roots and causes are deeper and farther than human consciousness, quite beyond its limits, and (4) the most fateful form of evil, defined as *suprapersonal and transcendent evil*, whose essence lies not so much in the external objectivity of things and actions as in the principle which animates them, i.e., individual and social morality without God and Christ. ("Religiozno-eticheskoe znachenie Dostoevskogo," in *Dostoevskii: 1881–100–1981* [London, 1981], pp. 48–51) Following DOSTOEVSKY's lead, who had been tormented precisely by that form of evil, which he saw at the bottom of "those Genevan ideas" of atheism-materialism-socialism, Askoldov was concerned mainly with the latter form of evil. This problem arose before him with particular poignancy after the October Revolution, when he saw and personally experienced this breakout from the underground of the *beast* in the human soul. Quite early in 1918, seeking to realize "the religious meaning of the Russian Revolution" (in an article of that title in a collection of essays, *Iz glubiny* [Moscow, 1918/1921, 2d ed. Paris, 1967]), Askoldov saw the Revolution as both atonement as well as the ascendancy, in the individual and national soul, of the *beast*: "The Russian soul is, like every other, tripartite, and every soul has a part of the *holy*, of the *human*, and of the *beast*. Perhaps the main peculiarity of the Rus-

sian soul is that in it the specifically human principle appears incomparably more weakly than in the national psychology of other nations. In Russian man, as a type, the *holy* and the *beast* appear strongest" (p. 44 of the 2d ed.). Russia, according to Askoldov, is a "holy beast," and having renounced God and Christ in her bolshevik years, flung herself into the abyss of the beast in her soul. It may develop, he continues, that in this there lies an expiatory sacrifice, because there are in the beast enough flashes of an awakening holiness. Here Askoldov is close to BLOK and VOLOSHIN, both of whom he amply quotes. It is for this reason, according to Askoldov, that Russia has not developed a *culture* as a set of social values, a humanist culture of the European type: the specifically human, which is the source of such culture, is largely lacking in the Russian soul.

Only the expiatory Divine sacrifice—the Golgotha of the Word become Flesh—resolves the irresoluble tragedy of theodicy. Askoldov felt that the freedom of will given us by our Creator was not a sufficient justification of the evil and innocent suffering in the world of Creation, nor that such freedom of ours could be broken by the Creator's intervention into our earthly affairs.

Besides his philosophic writings, Askoldov authored a number of essays on Dostoevsky, BELY, AKHMATOVA, and others. He also wrote poetry, a part of which was published in periodicals of the 1940s.

Askoldov was repeatedly arrested and was removed from his chair of philosophy at Petrograd University in 1922. He then taught technological commodity science at the Polytechnic Institute until his next arrest. After years in prison and labor camps, and subsequent exile in the Komi ASSR, Askoldov lived in Novgorod, still in exile, but closer to his family, which had remained in Leningrad, in the 1930s. After the capture of Novgorod by Hitler's forces on 16 August 1941, Askoldov suffered the usual fate of a "displaced person," eventually reaching Riga and then Berlin. A heart attack prevented him from fleeing Potsdam at the approach of Soviet forces. He was immediately thrown in prison by the NKVD, but released, apparently by mistake. When they returned, having realized their mistake, Askoldov was dead. He died on May 23, 1945.

Works: "Psikhologiya kharakterov u Dostoevskogo." In *F. M. Dostoevskii: Stat'i i materialy*. Peterburg, 1922. (Reprinted in *Dostoevskii: 1881–100–1981*. London, 1981.) "Forma i soderzhanie v iskusstve slova." In *Literaturnaya mysl'*, Book 3. Leningrad, 1925.

B. F.

Autobiography. An autobiography is a written account of one's life viewed from a given moment in time and filtered through memory, with all memory's conscious and unconscious lapses and distortions. The autobiographer's perspective at the time of writing shapes and determines the nature of the autobiography. As a literary genre the autobiography is closely related to other forms of autobiographical writing, such as the diary, the travel account, the memoir, and the autobiographical novel. In its broadest sense all of literature is autobiographical, but for practical purposes we limit the autobiography "proper" to a purportedly truthful, retrospective account of one's life, in prose, written by the subject and composed as a single whole.

It is, at times, difficult to differentiate the autobiography from the memoir; the distinction is one of degree rather than kind. In contrast to the autobiographical focus on the self, the memoir centers more on occurrences and people around and outside the author. Recent examples are Nadezhda MANDELSHTAM's *Hope Against Hope* (1970) and *Hope Abandoned* (1974); while these memoirs reveal much about the author's personality, her primary intent is to focus on Osip MANDELSHTAM, on the grim realities of the Stalin era and its effect on artistic creativity. The emphasis in the memoir is on what is remembered rather than on the one remembering.

Retrospection, central to the autobiography, is largely lacking in the diary. The writer of the diary presents events from day to day without regard for continuity. In contrast to the conscious design of the autobiography, life itself orders the sequence of the diary; the entries are chronological. Events recorded and their occurrence are close in time. Examples are the diaries of Aleksandr PUSHKIN, Lev TOLSTOI, and Andrei BELY.

A thin line separates the autobiography from the autobiographical novel. Whereas the autobiographer is constrained by the form to draw his or her primary material from memory, the novelist is free to invent persons and situations. This line of distinction is virtually obliterated in such 20th-century autobiographies as Valentin KATAEV's *Mosaic of Life or Oberon's Magic Horn* (1972), where imagination and dream are guiding principles in the narration, and fantasy and fact are closely intertwined. Ultimately, what distinguishes such autobiographies from fictional forms is the autobiographer's claim to authenticity.

The word "autobiography" was coined in England and came into currency in 1809; in Russia it first appeared in 1817 in a letter from A. Turgenev to P. VYAZEMSKY. Prior to that, "my life", "notes", "reminiscences", and "memoir" were used in the sense we now use the word "autobiography."

Writings containing autobiographical elements date back to the beginnings of Russian literature. Among the earliest examples are *The Testament of* VLADIMIR MONOMAKH (12th century), THE SUPPLICATION OF DANIIL THE EXILE (12th century), and IVAN the Terrible's correspondence with KURBSKY (16th century). Not until the 17th century, however, does the first real autobiography appear, *The Life of Archpriest* AVVAKUM *Written by Himself.* Here the author's life, dramatic and rich in exotic setting, is the subject of the work. His singular point of view gives the work its unity and structures its terrain. The language and style of this narrative are bold and original for its time, as is the personality it reveals.

The actual growth of autobiography begins in the second half of the 18th century. Literature moves away from religious motifs, forms, and accepted canons of classicism, and the narrator assumes an increasingly prominent role. There is a generally growing interest in the uniqueness of the individual and his or her inner life. Nataliya Dolgorukaya (1714–71) most poignantly exemplifies this trend. Her *Memoirs of Princess Nataliya Dolgorukaya*, the earliest written 18th-century autobiography, focuses on personal themes of love, and the hardship and suffering she endured during the years of exile with her husband. The movingly lyric style in which she expresses her love for him is unusual for its time. Another notable 18th-century autobiography is the uncommonly long *Life and Adventures* by Andrei Bolotov (1738–1833), cast in the form of letters and characterized by the sentiment and rhetoric of the epistolary genre typical of this period. These letters provide Bolotov with the vehicle for expressing his views on events and people he encountered. His personality emerges through his observation and commentaries, rather than through self-conscious introspection. Two 18th-century autobiographies often mentioned together are those by CATHERINE II (1729–96) and Princess Ekaterina Dashkova (1743–1810). *The Memoirs of Catherine II* make for most absorbing reading, giving a fascinating and often amusing perspective of this Russian monarch and the people at the court. *The Memoirs of Princess Dashkova* in some way complements the former, providing an added view of Catherine and the life of the upper classes. Dashkova herself emerges as a woman admirable for her energy and independence of spirit. *Notes* (Zapiski) by Gavriil DERZHAVIN (1743–1816) is a rare example of autobiography written mostly in the third person. While Derzhavin here speaks infrequently about his literary activities, he gives considerable detail about his life and times, making this work a valuable historical document as well as an important source of information on the life of this prominent poet.

Throughout the 18th century and the first half of the 19th century autobiographers gave little attention to childhood years, placing importance on the accomplishments of the mature adult. Ivan I. DMITRIEV (1760–1837), casting his autobiography *A Glance at My Life* (Vzglyad na moyu zhizn') into three equal parts, typically devoted only a small section of the first part to his early years. Denis FONVIZIN (1745–92), in *An Open Hearted Confession of My Deeds and Thoughts*, written at the end of his life, already indicates a shift in this pattern. Taking Rousseau's *Confessions* as a model, Fonvizin saw autobiography as a way of revealing his spiritual identity, and the history of his personality. Although never completed, the plan for the autobiography had four equal divisions: "childhood, youth, mature years, and old age." For the first time an autobiographer put equal stress on childhood years. It is not until the second half of the 19th century that we see the publication of autobiographies centering exclusively on childhood. This shift of interest is largely credited to Rousseau's pervasive influence. His belief in the natural goodness of children and the notion that childhood should be the happiest time of life encouraged nostalgia for vanished bliss. Child-rearing became a much-debated issue in many of the journals of the time. In this cultural climate Sergei AKSAKOV published *The Childhood of Bagrov-*

Grandson (1858), a nostalgic evocation in which he traces his psychological development from ages three to nine, giving a penetrating insight into the world of the child. This childhood autobiography was the third of three volumes, following *A Family Chronicle* (1856), portraying the generation of his parents and grandparents; and *Reminiscences* (1856), focusing on the author's life at the gymnasium and the University of Kazan. Less known is Afanasy FET's *The Early Years of My Life* (Rannie gody moei zhizni, 1893), which, he tells us in the introduction, Lev TOLSTOI had encouraged him to write. This work, together with his earlier two volumes *My Reminiscences* (Moi vospominaniya, 1890), reveals a fascinating portrait of this poet's many-faceted personality. A woman's perspective on childhood in 19th-century Russia is captured in *Reminiscences of Childhood* (1890) by Sofiya Kovalevskaya, a mathematician and minor writer. Nineteenth-century Russia also produced a number of autobiographical novels of childhood and adolescence. Among the more notable examples are Lev Tolstoi's *Childhood, Boyhood, and Youth* (1852–57), and GARIN-MIKHAILOVSKY's *Tema's Childhood* (1892), *Schoolboys* (Gimnazisty, 1893), and *Students* (1895). Aleksandr HERZEN's monumental *Past and Thoughts* (1852–68) goes beyond the formative years and encompasses a broader historical perspective. His personal life is shown organically intertwined with the annals of larger historical events, underscoring the intrinsic connection between man and his milieu. Of note also is Nikolai GRECH's autobiography, *Notes About My Life* (Zapiski o moei zhizni, 1886). Grech, a journalist for *Severnaya pchela*, gives a valuable and interesting view on the history of Russian literature in the second half of the 19th century.

The early decades of the 20th century saw the publication of Vladimir KOROLENKO's autobiography *The Story of My Contemporary* (1904–20); GORKY's trilogy *Childhood* (1913), *My Apprenticeship* (1914), and *My Universities* (1923), and Konstantin STANISLAVSKY's *My Life in Art* (1924). The early 20th century, a time of literary experimentation, also produced two lyrically poetic autobiographies, Osip Mandelshtam's *The Noise of Time* (1925) and Boris PASTERNAK's *Safe Conduct* (1931). The Stalin era of censorship, from the early thirties to the mid-fifties, limited all sorts of literary expression. Autobiographies published during that period, like Fyodor GLADKOV's *The Story of Childhood* (1949), *The Free Gang* (1950), and *The Wicked Year* (1954), and Konstantin PAUSTOVSKY's *Distant Years* (1946), do not go beyond 1917, and the recollections are confined to the narrow circle of life in the village and town. When Mikhail ZOSHCHENKO published *After Sunrise* (1943), an autobiography in which he delves into the hidden causes of his melancholia, the work was suspended after two installments and Zoshchenko was branded a "pernicious Freudian."

Following Stalin's death the veil of silence was lifted and writers began to assert their right to express their individual perceptions of the world. There was an outpouring of diaries, war reminiscences, and autobiographies. The dramatic increase in autobiographies in the post-Stalin era is to be attributed not only to the relaxation of censorship but also to the general self-consciousness of the age. Most major Russian literary figures writing in the second half of this century have turned to this genre. Among the autobiographies published are: Ilya ERENBURG's *Years, People, Life* (1954–62); Evgeny EVTUSHENKO's *A Precocious Autobiography* (1962); Samuil MARSHAK's *In the Beginning of Life* (V nachale zhizni, 1962); Vsevolod Rozhdestvensky's *Life's Pages* (Stranitsy zhizni, 1962); and Paustovsky's completion of his memoirs, *The Story of Life* (1962). Olga BERGGOLTS's *Day Stars* (Dnevnye zvezdy, 1959) moves away from a chronologically structured plot; separate episodes and themes are connected not by logic of the ego but the logic of the unconscious. Fragmented structure and the absence of historically ordered events become characteristic of many autobiographies of the 1960s and 1970s. Representative of this trend are: Yury OLESHA's *No Day Without a Line* (1965); Viktor SHKLOVSKY's *Once Upon a Time* (Zhili byli, 1963); Valentin KATAEV's *The Holy Well* (1966), *The Grass of Oblivion* (1967), and *A Mosaic of Life or Oberon's Magic Horn* (1972), and Daniil GRANIN's *A Return Ticket* (Obratnyi bilet, 1978). Other innovative post-Stalin autobiographies of note are: Mikhail Isakovsky's *On Elnya Land* (Na Elninskoi zemle, 1974); Vera Ketlinskaya's *Evening, Windows, People* (Vecher, okna, lyudi, 1974); Leonid MARTYNOV's *Transparent Frigates* (Vozdushnye fregaty, 1974); and Marietta SHAGINYAN's *Man and Time* (Chelovek i vremya, 1980).

Notable among émigré autobiographies published in the second half of the 20th century are Vladimir NABOKOV's *Speak Memory* (1951), Nikolai BERDYAEV's *Dream and Reality* (1950), Nina BERBEROVA's *Italics are Mine* (1969), and Lev KOPELEV's *The Education of a True Believer* (1978). Theoretical and critical literature on autobiography in Russia is relatively scant. By comparison, scholars in the West have given considerable attention to this genre, and criticism in the past two decades has shifted its emphasis from the psychological insights expressed in the autobiography to the working of the text itself.

Bibliography: Elizabeth A. Bruss, *Autobiographical Acts: The Changing Situation of a Literary Genre.* 1976. Christine Downing, "Re-Visioning Autobiography: The Bequest of Freud and Jung," *Soundings*, 60 (1977), pp. 210–28. Lidiya Ginzburg, *O psikhologicheskoi proze.* 1971. Janet Varner Gunn, *Autobiography: Towards a Poetics of Experience.* 1982. James Olney, ed. *Essays, Theoretical and Critical.* 1980. Roy Pascal, *Design and Truth in Autobiography.* 1960. Wayne Shumaker, *English Autobiography: Its Emergence, Materials and Form.* 1954. William C. Spengemann, *The Forms of Autobiography: Episodes in the History of a Literary Genre.* 1980. Zoya Vatnikova-Prizel, *O russkoi memuarnoi literature: kriticheskie analizy i bibliografiya.* East Lansing, 1978. T. W. C.

Averbákh, Leopóld Leonídovich (1903–39), literary critic, theorist, and organizer. Averbakh cut short his formal education at the age of sixteen to take a leading part in the organization of the Komsomol. In 1920 he became editor of the Komsomol organ *Yunosheskaya pravda*, and later he edited the youth journal *Molodaya gvardiya*. Averbakh was a leading figure in the proletarian literary movement from its earliest days, and he was one of the founders of VAPP, which later became RAPP (Russian Association of Proletarian Writers). He was a member of the editorial board of the journal NA POSTU, which was uncompromising in its opposition to non-communist and non-proletarian writers, many of whom found outlets for their work in the Soviet press of the twenties. After the Party resolution on literature of 1925 decreed a milder line more receptive to the so-called FELLOW TRAVELLERS, Averbakh became editor in 1926 of the renamed RAPP journal *Na literaturnom postu*. His theoretical and critical articles in that journal defined the policies of the RAPP leadership on the burning questions of the day: the cultural revolution, the nature of proletarian literature and its right to primacy, the limits of tolerance of non-proletarian writers, evidences of bourgeois ideology in literature. Prolific as a writer of essays and not lacking in fluency, Averbakh was narrowly educated, sectarian, and oppressively dogmatic in his treatment of literary questions and literary works. After the liquidation of RAPP in 1932 Averbakh was blamed for its "errors" and "distortions," and he was never prominent in the UNION OF WRITERS organized in 1934. He was arrested in 1937 and his name figured briefly in the public purge trial of 1938. He was apparently executed in 1939. His name reappeared in 1978 in the ninth (supplementary) volume of *Kratkaya literaturnaya entsiklopediya*, but without any statement that he had been rehabilitated.

Works: Kul'turnaya revolyutsiya i voprosy sovremennoi literatury. Moscow, 1928. (With Vladimir Kirshon.) *S kem i pochemu my boremsya.* Leningrad, 1930.

Secondary Literature: E. J. Brown, *The Proletarian Episode in Russian Literature.* New York, 1953; 1971. S. E. Sheshukov, *Neistovye revniteli.* Moscow, 1970. E. J. B.

Avérchenko, Arkády Timoféevich (1881–1925), journalist, humorist, and playwright. The son of an indigent merchant, Averchenko did not complete his technical high-school education and began working as a clerk at the age of fifteen. He began publishing in 1903, soon after coming to Kharkov, where he later contributed to and edited the humorous journals *Shtyk* (1906–07) and *Mech* (1907). Moving to Petersburg in 1908, Averchenko soon gained recognition as humorist and editor of SATIRIKON (1908–14), the leading satirical weekly which lampooned social ills. His first collection of humorous stories *Jolly Oysters* (Veselye ustritsy, 1910), which went through 24 editions in less than seven years, was quickly followed by a three-volume *Stories* (Rasskazy, 1910–11) and four volumes of one-act plays and miniatures adapted for the stage. In 1913 he left *Satirikon*, taking a host of contributors with him, to edit *Novyi Satirikon* (1913–18) until it was closed for satirizing the Bolsheviks. Leaving Petrograd, Averchenko

made his way to Sevastopol, where he wrote for the local press and published the anti-Bolshevik collection *Unclean Power* (Nechistaya sila, 1920). Forced to flee Russia in November 1920, he first settled in Constantinople, contributing to the weekly *Zarnitsy* and publishing several collections including one on the initial trials and tribulations of emigration, *Notes of an Unsophisticate* (Zapiski prostodushnogo, 1921). In 1922 Averchenko settled in Prague where, with the exception of extremely popular public appearances throughout East Europe and Germany, he remained until his death. Despite Lenin's hostile review of his admittedly talented *A Dozen Knives in the Back of the Revolution* (Dyuzhinu nozhei v spinu revolyutsii, 1921), Averchenko was published in the Soviet Union until 1930 and, after a long silence, reprinted in the 1960s.

Works: [*Sobranie sochinenii*]. 4 vols. 1911–14. *Krugi po vode.* 1912. *Podkhodtsev i dvoe drugikh.* 1917. *Chudaki na podmostkakh.* 1918. *Deti.* 1922. *Dvenadtsat' portretov.* 1923. *Otdykh na krapive.* 1924. *Shutka Metsenata.* 1925. *Rasskazy tsinika.* 1925. *Izbrannoe.* 1961. *Yumoristicheskie rasskazy.* 1964. *Tri knigi.* 1979.

Translations: Lewanski, p. 196.

Secondary literature: D. Levitskii, *Arkadii Averchenko: Zhiznennyi put'*. 1973. (With "Prefatory Note" in English by M. Giergielewicz, pp. 7–24.) O. Mikhailov, "Arkadii Averchenko," foreword in *Yumoristicheskie rasskazy* (1964), pp. 3–22. A. M. S.

Avvakúm Petróvich, Protopop (1620–82). The Archpriest Avvakum, a key figure in both the cultural and literary history of Russia, was the leader of the OLD BELIEVER Schism in the Russian Church of the mid-17th century. He considered himself a saint and wrote his own *Life* (Zhitie) to prove his sainthood and justify his leadership of the Schism. This unusual work was unprecedented for its evocation of the protagonist's humanness, for its historical concreteness, and for its introduction of the vernacular as a literary language on a par with CHURCH SLAVONIC. The Old Believer Schism occurred in reaction to Patriarch Nikon's reform of the Russian Church ritual on the model of the contemporary Greek Orthodox. This reform signalled the beginning of Muscovy's ideological turn to the West, its transformation into an absolute monarchy, and its acceptance of the elitist aesthetic and religious culture of scholastic humanism. The reform indicated a turning away from the traditional messianic penitential ideal which had defined the sacred nature of the Tsar and the redemptive mission of Muscovy since the time of Ivan IV. Avvakum's *Life* polemicized against this new idea of the State through personal example. He presented himself as a healer of the schism between the westernizing elite and the traditional people which took place after Nikon became Patriarch and as a culture hero and prophet of national redemption, ultimately taking the place of the Tsar himself. His Life showed how he embodied the paternalistic authoritarian spirituality of the 16th century House Orderer, for which ascetic self-discipline, humility, and good works were the path to personal and national salvation. His self-portrait thus revealed how Russia could be restored to her former purity and be transformed from the Third Rome to the New Jerusalem.

Avvakum used the conventions of the saint's life to portray his own sacrifice for the sake of his ideals and establish his credentials as a national spokesman. The uniquely human and concrete qualities of the *Life* derive from the fact that he was himself a parish priest (rather than a monk, as was traditional) and a father confessor. His profession of penitential spirituality required that he establish his brotherhood with all men in sin and conquer his pride before he could presume to be their leader. His *Life* did this by exemplifying his "foolishness" or "simplicity in Christ." St. Paul in his Epistles to the Corinthians advocated "foolishness" as a way of exposing the hypocrisy of self-acknowledged righteousness. Avvakum the narrator began by exposing his own hypocrisy as protagonist in order to earn the right to expose that of the Nikonians, and in so doing introduced a comic-ironic tone heretofore alien to Russian literature. He even showed himself daring to challenge the divine justice of his suffering (likening himself to the biblical Job) and then roundly castigated himself for exhibiting Adam's pride.

Avvakum's revelation of his own self-righteous pride went beyond the conventional self-denigration of the humility topos because he had to compensate for daring to present himself as Russia's self-appointed leader. His focus on his lowliness and degradation as protagonist of his *Life* included the exhibition of his impulse to sacrifice others to his uncontrolled appetites and vanity, revealing him to be the first fallible saint in Russian literature, and making his *Life* a "sincere," earnest confession of sin as well as of faith, as was traditional. He addressed this confession to his own father confessor, the Solovetsk hermit and neighbor in exile, Epifany, as well as to his own confessional "children," the believing Russian people, to whom he served as an example. Moreover, his polemical portrayal of his lowliness and degradation called forth an innovative focus on the actual conditions of his milieu. His use of the earthy and passionate vernacular language accessible to all to describe the unpretentious simplicity and typicality of his surroundings create the impression of realism. The Archpriest Avvakum was the first to describe the fauna and landscape of Siberian Russia and Lake Baikal which he witnessed as the priest assigned to a Russian colonizing mission. He expressed his touchingly human awe before this gift of God to mankind in the intonations of the spoken language of the people. Because he was a parish priest with a wife and children who advocated the House Orderer's vision of the family as a microcosm of the sacred state, he portrayed his relations with his actual family as exemplary of the penitential life he wished all Christians to imitate.

For Avvakum a man's recognition of Adam's sin in himself was the necessary first step to conversion and transcendence of sin through voluntary suffering. His *Life* became less a confession of sin than of faith, saturated with rhetorical pathos, when it described at length the "persecutions" he endured for the sake of the Church. His resulting miraculous survival of almost unimaginable hardships, together with visions affirming his providential destiny and miracles of healing and prophesy, were the signs of election won by his self-abnegation and debasement. These in turn entitled him to compare himself to the Prophet Elijah and to take the revolutionary step of assuming the latter's role as an earthly precursor to God in judgement at the Second Coming. This justified the narrator's venting his wrath against the Nikonians and his self-appointed leadership. The emphasis on his conversion through suffering resulted in a unique portrait of the polarized self alternating between sinner and saint, victim and judge.

Avvakum's personal reenactment of the all-human drama of sin and redemption was meant to exemplify a traditional understanding of penitential spirituality as the way to fulfillment of the national destiny. Although he exposed the inability of scholastic humanism and the absolutist state to embody the spirit of the people and their traditions, he failed to stop the Nikonians from laying the ground for the aristocratic court culture of 18th century westernizing Russia. On the other hand, Avvakum's autobiographical *Life* crystallized deep-rooted tendencies which would surface in the mainstream of the national Russian literature of the 19th and 20th centuries, epitomized in the work of DOSTOEVSKY. His innovative self-portrait transformed the canons of the saint's life and the literary language itself, evincing a new "modern" focus on the human personality in the process of change as the mainspring of the divine economy. It raised its author's personal experience and spoken language to the level of national archetype with messianic eschatological significance, and created an epic image of a uniquely Russian capacity for suffering, endurance, and faith which has influenced Russian literature to the present.

The sense of personal mission motivating Avvakum to write his own *Life* derived from his participation in a penitential movement for reform in the Church on the part of the lower clergy. This movement arose in the 1630s in the northeastern Nizhny Novgorod province in response to the national crisis of the TIME OF TROUBLES. Its goals became national policy in the early reign of Aleksei Mikhailovich before Nikon became Patriarch. A native of the Nizhny Novgorod province and the son of a village priest, Avvakum revealed a commitment to the penitential ideal from the time of his ordination in 1644. By 1647 he had come to the attention of the young Tsar and his father confessor, the Archpriest Stefan Vonifatiev, for his zealous exposure of corruption in his parish of Lopatishchii and for the local rancor this aroused. In 1652 he was promoted to the rank of Archpriest in the town of Yurievets on the Volga in accordance with the Tsar's policy of placing reforming priests in positions of power. The monk Nikon, also a member of the reforming brotherhood, became patriarch in June of that year. Fifteen months later Nikon had crushed his former friends among the lower clergy, reestablished the primacy of the episcopate which had fallen into abeyance during the

ascendancy of the Tsar's confessor, and set the Russian Church on a new path away from the democratic penitential spirituality of the Brotherhood towards the acceptance of the imported scholastic enlightenment.

Nikon exiled Avvakum and his family and household first to the Siberian center of Tobolsk. Avvakum remained there from December 1653 to June 1655, flourishing under the protection of the traditionalist Archbishop Simeon of Tobolsk and Siberia. A series of local denunciations against him gave Nikon the opportunity to exile him further to Eniseisk to join the colonizing exploratory expedition of Afanasy Pashkov into the "wilderness" of Dahuria (the area beyond Lake Baikal inhabited by the Buryat and Tungus Mongols). The Tsar recalled Avvakum from exile after Nikon fell from power in 1658. Avvakum returned to Moscow in 1664 to find that the Tsar intended to dethrone Nikon but not his innovations. Nikon's reforms symbolized Russia's new acquiescence to the westernized "absolutist" concept of both Church and State now being defined by churchmen from the Near East, White Russia, and the Ukraine. In response, Avvakum renewed his opposition to the Nikonian innovations and their adherents. This resulted in his second exile to Mezen with his family a few months later. He remained in Mezen a year and a half until recalled to Moscow in preparation for the Church Council of 1666–67 being organized by SIMEON POLOTSKY and Paisios Ligarides. This council officially deposed Nikon from the Patriarchal See and condemned as heretical the opponents of Nikon's reforms, thus destroying all obstacles to the subordination of the Church to the goals and ideology of the westernizing State. The Council placed Avvakum under anathema when he alone among the traditionalists refused to recant. His resistance made him a rallying point for the groundswell of opposition to the official Church which emerged immediately afterwards, opposition which achieved the dimensions of a mass movement by the end of the century. Avvakum and three other outspoken opponents of the new ritual were exiled to Pustozersk on the White Sea in 1667. All four Pustozersk fathers were burned at the stake in 1682 in the dragnet of government reprisals for the Old Believer demonstration in Moscow led by Nikita Pustosvyat.

Avvakum produced his large, polemical literary corpus in defense of the Old Belief after his exile to Pustozersk. He smuggled his works to his wife and children in Mezen, who copied them and distributed them in an underground network throughout Russia. His more than sixty separate works, addressed to his natural and his spiritual families, included letters, epistles, sermons in the form of biblical exegesis, homilies on specific issues in the dispute between the old and new world view, such as how to make the sign of the cross, how icons should be painted, and what fast and feast days should be observed. He also produced autobiographical notes of a documentary nature, his autobiographical saint's life, five petitions to Tsar Aleksei Mikhailovich and one to Tsar Feodor Alekseevich. Finally, his polemic with his co-exile at Pustozersk, the Deacon Feodor, over dogmatic issues resulted in writings on Christological and other questions concerned with the knowledge of God and the Word.

A preacher during most of his life, all of his works mimic his oratorical vernacular style and method of elucidating scriptural truth on the basis of concrete examples from his own life and that of his contemporaries. For Avvakum the written word was a form of moral accountability second only to a life devoted to confession, repentance of sin through expiatory suffering, and good works. To Avvakum's mind the artificial and abstract writings of his poetic and ideological enemies, the syllabic poets, justified the elite status of the ruling class, and divested it of moral responsibility. Reflecting the acknowledged influence of St. John Chrysostom, his homiletic writings revolve around a narrative core and use the portrayal of real experience and emotion to elucidate a spiritual lesson. A disciple of Dionysios the Areopagite as well, Avvakum brought to light the immanent unity of all phenomena in the spirit through the use of metaphor and symbol. The metaphorical texture of his writings interrelated all aspects of the diverse polarized dynamic world he portrays. This texture symbolized the transfigured flesh of Christ and testified to the organic wholeness of His creation. Indeed, symbol and metaphor created unity in a poetic world as polarized as the author's self. Language alternated between low and high, tone between comic and pathetic, reality, between material and spiritual. Among all his works, Avvakum's *Life* represented a holistic metaphorical system in which oppositions on all levels dynamically coexisted and interpenetrated. This system created an integral continuum symbolic of Avvakum's transfigured flesh and prophetic of his future resurrection.

Avvakum's *Life* stands at the center of his corpus because it expressed his moral accountability, showing how his personal experience testified to the beliefs expounded in all his works. He worked on it continuously between 1669 and 1676, producing four redactions which enable us to witness his creative process. The first, so-called Pryanishnikov redaction is shorter than the others and concerned with documenting the events of the Schism. However, Avvakum indicated his intent of writing about personal and cultural self-renewal by calling it a book of Genesis (*Kniga bytiya*). By the second edition (B) Avvakum focused on the stages of his own moral transformation as a promise of Russia's imminent transfiguration. This edition served as the source of the "mature" versions, the frequently anthologized and translated dramatic third redaction (A), and the longer and more tendentious fourth redaction (V). Only these last two redactions have come down to us in Avvakum's own hand.

The autograph of edition A appeared in a compilation composed around 1673 together with the autobiographical saint's life of Avvakum's coexile at Pustozersk. Epifany, Avvakum's confessor, wrote the dedication of Avvakum's *Life* to himself in his own hand, as well as a forgiveness and blessing of the protagonist and his family at the midpoint of Avvakum's narrative. Avvakum, in his turn, concluded his *Life* with a request that Epifany write his own *Life*, which indeed follows immediately upon his own: "You loved to hear from me what I am ashamed about—say at least a little yourself." This compilation also includes the autograph of Avvakum's Fifth Petition to the Tsar to which Avvakum referred the reader of his *Life* for the description of certain visions briefly referred to in his narrative. This rhetorical strategy served the purpose of protecting himself from the accusation of pride by shifting the onus from himself to the reader for making public the miracles communicated privately by him to the Tsar in the Fifth Petition. Only there can the reader learn about Avvakum's visions of his merging with God and the expansion of his body to union with heaven and earth.

The autograph of the last edition of the *Life* appeared in a compilation of 1675 and was also followed by Epifany's *Life*. To suggest that it was an act of prophesy and revelation, Avvakum called it a Book of Eternal Life and accompanied it in the compilation with his writing on Divinity and Creation. There his exegesis of the Book of Genesis reflects on the end of the world and on the visions of the Prophets. This compilation also contains an apology for his use of the vernacular: He claimed that his native Russian was a more sacred language of revelation than the Hebrew, Greek, and Latin used by the "philosophers" and "rhetoricians" dominating the Church, because his language in its lowliness expressed love rather than the intellectual pride of the elite. A citation from the Instruction of Abba Dorotheus added to the introduction of his *Life* indicated how a man may embody the power of love and become the word, travelling from the periphery to the center of the circle of Being and merging with God through "sincerity." Avvakum accompanied this with a drawing in his own hand portraying five Old Believer saints inside a circle at whose center is written "God," and the five main enemies of the Old Believers outside the circle, beginning with Nikon.

Avvakum's *Life* makes personal the aesthetic and religious principles defining the sacredness and integrity of the Muscovite State when this state was on the verge of extinction. Two centuries later Avvakum's *Life* entered elite Russian culture when N. S. TIKHONRAvov first published it in 1861. Russian writers, ranging from TURGENEV to SOLZHENITSYN, have discovered in the *Life* of the Archpriest Avvakum a key to the mythic and linguistic potential of Russian literature to unite national and personal identity, and in the Archpriest Avvakum the first Russian writer to address the problem of schism in the culture and the self.

Best Editions in Russian: The Pryanishnikov redaction, ed. by N. Sarafanova-Demkova, and other selected works are found in: N. K. Gudzii, *Zhitie protopopa Avvakuma im samim napisannoe i drugie ego sochineniya*. Pp. 305–45. Redaction B, see: P. S. Smirnov, ed., *Pamyatniki istorii staroobryadchestva XVII v.* Book 1, fasc. 1 (Russkaya istoricheskaya biblioteka 29.) 1927. Pp. 84–149. Redaction A, see: A. N. Robinson, *Zhizneopisanie Avvakuma i Epifaniya*. 1963. Pp. 139–78. Redaction V, see: V. I. Malyshev, N. S. Demkova, and

L. A. Dmitriev. *Pustozerskii sbornik*. 1975. Pp. 40–83. For almost the entire published corpus of Avvakum's works, see: P. S. Smirnov, *Pamyatniki istorii staroobryadchestva XVII v.* (as above).

Translations: Redaction A with bibliography and historical commentary, see: K. Brostrom, *The Archpriest Avvakum: The Life Written by Himself*. (Michigan Slavic Publications) 1979. Pp. 35–115. Pierre Pascal, *La Vie de L'Archprêtre Avvakum écrite par lui-même et sa dernière* [Fifth] *Epître au Tsar Alexis*. Paris, 1960.

Secondary literature: Historical and Cultural Background: M. Cherniavsky, "The Old Believers and the New Religion," *SlavR* 25 (1966), pp. 1–39. P. Pascal, *Avvakum et les débuts du raskol*. Paris, 1934. S. A. Zenkovsky, "The Russian Church Schism." In Thomas Riha, *Readings in Russian Civilization*. 1964. Pp. 145–57. ———, *Russkoe staroobryadchestvo*. Munich, 1970. Avvakum: K. N. Brostrom, "Further Remarks on the Life of the Archpriest Avvakum." In K. Brostrom, *The Archpriest Avvakum: The Life Written by Himself*. (Michigan Slavic Publications) 1979., pp. 147–207. John M. Gogol, "The Archpriest Avvakum and Quirinus Kuhlmann: A Comparative Study in the Literary Baroque," *Germano-Slavica* 2 (1973), pp. 35–48. P. Hunt, "The Structure and Function of the Autobiography of the Archpriest Avvakum," *Ricerche Slavistiche* 23 (1975–76), pp. 57–70. ———, "The Mythic Structure of the Autobiography of the Archpriest Avvakum." In *Formal Techniques and Cultural Models in Orthodox Slavic Literature*. Ed. Riccardo Picchio (Michigan Slavic Publications.) In press. V. Vinogradov, "On the Tasks of Stylistics: Observations Regarding the Style of the *Life of the Archpriest Avvakum*." In K. Brostrom, *The Archpriest Avvakum* (as above), pp. 117–47.   P. H.

Azóv. **Story of the Defense of.** The heroic capture of Azov from the Turks in 1637 by the autonomous Don Cossack horde and the victory of a small Cossack force over the large Turkish army besieging Azov in 1641 gave birth to three literary works: A Historical Tale of the Taking of Azov from the Turks of 1637, a poetical Story of the Defense of Azov of 1642, and a Fabulous History of the Taking of Azov and of its Defense against Tsar Ibrahim by the Don Cossacks of the 1680s. The first two works arose in the Military Chancery of the Horde. The most important of these was the poetic story because of its dialogic narrative structure. The individualized voice of a first person narrator, speaking both for the Cossack collective and for the Turks, tells the tale of the siege and its ideological significance for the Cossacks. The story was a poetic parallel to the Cossacks' official war memorandum to Muscovy about the siege, meant to influence the convening Muscovite Assembly of the Land to accept Azov as part of the Tsar's patrimony. Its own dialogic form expanded on the memorandum's device of reporting diplomatic parleys in the first person. The oratorical and narrative devices of folkore and of the military tale, together with vernacular expressions, enriched the language of the chancery and endowed the narrative with a national Cossack flavor. The story's innovative use of a stylized first-person narration to speak for the collective foreshadowed the development of "skaz" in late 19th-century literature.

Bibliography: For the text of all three tales, see: V. P. Adrianova-Peretts, *Voinskie povesti drevnei Rusi*. Moscow and Leningrad, 1949. Pp. 41–115. For criticism see: A. N. Robinson's articles in *Voinskie povesti*, pp. 166–255 and in *TODRL* 7 (1949), pp. 98–130. The basic textological study has been done by A. Orlov, *Istoricheskie i poeticheskie povesti ob Azove. Teksty*. Moscow, 1906; and *Skazochnye povesti ob Azove, "Istoriya 7135 goda"*. Warsaw, 1900.

P. H.

Bábel, Isaák Emmanuílovich (1894–1941), writer. An exceptionally meticulous and demanding craftsman, he would repeatedly revise and polish his short stories to a high gloss. Konstantin PAUSTOVSKY, novelist and author of reminiscences of Babel, informs that the text of "Lyubka the Cossack" evolved through twenty-two variants prior to publication. Babel's predilection for painstaking textual revision, coupled with a reluctance to publish original work during the increasingly menacing atmosphere of Stalinist terror of the 1930s, made him singularly unprolific. His complete works (so far never collected)

31

would probably not exceed two volumes. Yet, Babel's "silence" of the 1930s, like that of Yury OLESHA, a fellow writer of short prose from Odessa, is true as a designation only with regard to his published imaginative writing. For both, the 1930s were a period of unsuccessful attempts to find politically praiseworthy, or at least safe subjects, coupled with near-feverish work of journalistic and editorial nature in order to earn a livelihood. In Babel's instance, money-making activities included also adaptation of literary works, his own and other authors', for the screen, while efforts to produce ideologically acceptable writing are attested by "Gapa Guzhva," a 1930 fragment of what was apparently intended as a novel about collectivization of Soviet agriculture. Another excerpt from that work in progress which was to be named "The Great Well" (Velikaya krinitsa) appeared posthumously. Responding to frequently voiced criticism, Babel also attempted to reinforce in his work motifs of "positive" Soviet nature (as in *The Jewess*, written probably in 1934, but published only in the West in 1969) and generally broaden his assortment of settings and genres (the set of characters of the 1935 play *Maria* includes several personages reminiscent of *The Cherry Orchard*. Babel's only other play, *Sunset*, published in 1928 but rarely performed, is a pastiche of characters and motifs from *The Odessa Tales*). According to some sources, Babel even intended to write a book that would extol the courage and selflessness of the Soviet secret police. These efforts notwithstanding, Babel was to share in the fate of countless compatriots who fell victims to the Great Purge. On 15 May, 1939, Babel was arrested and his manuscripts confiscated. His exact fate remains unknown. Official Soviet accounts report the date of his death as 17 March 1941. It may well be that Babel's friendship with Nikolai Yezhov, the then just arrested chief of the Soviet secret police, and with Yezhov's wife, sealed Babel's fate, but that is pure conjecture. In 1956 Babel was posthumously cleared of charges against him, but the confiscated manuscripts were declared lost. Though no longer officially proscribed, Babel's writings are only rarely published in the USSR. Their moral and political ambiguities and equivocation as well as their demonstratively Jewish subject matter do not endear them to most Soviet critics, and his strong eroticism is as objectionable today as it was in tsarist Russia where the writer had once been indicted on charges of pornography.

Reliable biographical information is scarce. In his "autobiographical" tales, some of which are among the best of his work as a whole, Babel refracted factual data through his creative imagination. Moreover, there are also reasons to believe that he consciously tried to refashion his life story to suit the ideological predilections of the Communist authorities. Thus Babel appears to minimize the importance in his life of a thorough, Jewish religious education and more generally of his traditional middle-class Jewish family background, reasonably prosperous and religiously observant. (A brief attempt to portray these may be found in Alexander SOLZHENITSYN's *August 1914*). Isaak Emmanuilovich Babel was born in Odessa on July 13, 1894, the son of a salesman of agricultural machinery who then became owner of a small warehouse. After some ten years in Nikolayev, a nearby small port city, the family returned to Odessa, then a busy, cosmopolitan commercial center with a polyglot population made even more conspicuously exotic by visiting sailors from distant lands. Odessa was then also not only heavily Jewish (Jews constituted about a third of the population), but also a major center of Jewish culture. The city's Jews were predominantly Yiddish-speaking, but at the turn of the century their literature was written in three languages. Jewish Odessa's writers included at that time Mendele Mocher Sforim, dubbed "the grandfather of Yiddish literature"; Chaim Nachman Bialik, to this day the most important poet writing in modern Hebrew; and the Zionist leader Vladimir Zhabotinsky who, like Babel himself, wrote in Russian. All these traditions were to influence Babel's later work, which also bears a strong imprint of French writing, in particular of Flaubert and of Maupassant. But then, French influences were in many ways much in evidence in Odessa, a city called sometimes the Marseilles of Russia, though in plebeian Odessa their manifestations were understandably different from those in aristocratic Russian culture. Nevertheless, in company with earlier Russian writers descended from the gentry, Babel, only a generation away from unemancipated Yiddish-speaking Jews, produced his first literary efforts in French. Unlike the Russian authors of aristocratic origin, Babel learned French not from private tutors on the family estate, but in a classroom of Odessa's Nicholas I Commer-

cial School, an institution attended by a motley crew of students from varying social and ethnic backgrounds. By contrast, Babel's private tutors taught him music and also imparted to him a solid knowledge of Hebrew, of the Bible and of rabbinic commentaries. Echoes of all permeate Babel's work, imparting to it a flavor rare in Russian writing, though not uncommon in literatures where Biblical motifs abound, such as the English.

In 1915 Babel moved to St. Petersburg and published several articles in *Zhurnal zhurnalov* which he signed "Bab-El'," Hebrew for "Gates of God." In one of them he predicted a rebirth in Russian literature of a Ukrainian Gogolian tradition and the advent of an "Odessa Maupassant." The first came true with the formation in the 1920s and 1930s of an Odessa group of writers that included Eduard BAGRITSKY, Ilya ILF and Evgeny PETROV, Valentin KATAEV, Vera INBER, Paustovsky and Olesha. And it was Babel himself who became Odessa's Maupassant. Babel's first literary efforts, the short stories "Mama, Rimma and Alla" and "Ilya Isaakovich and Margarita Prokofyevna," appeared the following year in Maksim GORKY's journal *Letopis'*. Both were sentimental and strongly erotic; the latter, in fact, featured a prostitute with a heart of gold.

In October 1917 Babel volunteered for army service but was soon sent home because of illness. Returning to St. Petersburg once more, Babel resumed his journalistic activity. He participated in 1918 in food requisitioning expeditions and also worked briefly for the Commissariat of Education. It was also then that Babel worked for a time for the Cheka, the newly organized Soviet secret police, although it is not clear in what capacity. In 1919 he rejoined the Soviet army, but returned to Odessa after a few months, married, and joined the staff of the State Publishing House. Four short stories about the brutality of World War I, all adaptations from the French writer Gaston Vidal ("On the Field of Honor," "The Deserter," "The Family of Papa Marescot" and "The Quaker") were printed in the Odessa journal *Lava* in June 1920. It was also in the summer of 1920 that Babel was assigned as war correspondent and propagandist for a military newspaper to the Mounted Cavalry which, commanded by Semyon Budënny, then fought in the Ukraine against Poland and a variety of anti-Soviet forces. The diary and notebooks from that campaign form the foundation of *Red Cavalry*, Babel's most important collection of short prose. It is primarily to this cycle (and also, to a lesser extent, to *The Odessa Tales*) that Babel owes his reputation as one of this century's masters of the short story. The four *Odessa Tales* ("The King," "How Things Were Done in Odessa," "The Father," and "Lyubka the Cossack") were published individually between 1921 and 1923, although they did not appear as a cycle in book form until 1927. Several of the thirty-four stories of *Red Cavalry* were completed as late as 1924 and 1925. The collection appeared in book form in 1926. A thirty-fifth, "Argamak," was added in 1931. It now concludes the collection, imparting to it a more "optimistic" flavor than did the somber "Rabbi's Son" which had hitherto served as the cycle's final story.

The Odessa Tales and *Red Cavalry* fascinated and shocked with their unusual subject matter, stylistic manner and, if only by implication, moral position. The first presented in luxuriant, lush colors a vast canvas of Jewish Odessa. It was not, however, a customary panorama of smug bourgeoisie or the oppressed poor, of a conflict of generations, of anti-Semitism or class consciousness. Babel's Odessa of a highly stylized and romanticized Jewish underworld appeared to contemporaries as exotic as tales of mysterious far-away lands. Its central characters, such as the larger-than-life Jewish gangster, Benya Krik (a translation of his full first name, Ben Zion, and of the last, is "The Yell of a Son of Zion"), the amazon innkeeper, madam and fence Lyubka the Cossack, or the majestic, patriarchal sexton Arieh-Leib (literally, "lion-lion," in Hebrew and in Yiddish) appear as protagonists of mock-heroic sagas. Their exploits are related in what is (as Victor Terras aptly defines it) a travesty of traditional epic and Biblical narratives, an effect Babel achieves by incongruously combining in the speech of both narrators and protagonists majestic grandiloquent locutions with Odessa slang, ungrammatical Russian and Yiddishisms. (This latter comic device of the inapposite calque may have been suggested to Babel by the Yiddish writings of Sholom Aleichem, which use for this purpose mistranslations of Biblical Hebrew.)

If Yiddish-flavored *skaz* is employed to paint the Breughel-like canvases of *The Odessa Tales*, analogous illiterate Cossack speech is often resorted to in the miniatures that form *Red Cavalry*. Whether related in this manner, or by a narrator who bears a strong resemblance to the author (the narrator is named Kirill Lyutov, which was also Babel's own *nom de guerre*), these are for the most part tightly woven, understated accounts of individual scenes of the war. Horrors of the war, with emphasis on grotesque, premeditated cruelty toward civilians as well as toward the foe, brutality unjustified by military necessity, are recorded with matter-of-fact brevity. Murder, rape, robbery, desecration, vandalism are all shown as routine occurrences. The effectiveness of these accounts is greatly enhanced by their exotic settings (e.g., a Polish aristocrat's residence, a Roman Catholic church, a Hasidic rabbi's court, an antiquarian store). The dispassionately impartial attribution of blame for the atrocities to both warring sides is summarized in the puzzled question of Gedali (the Hebrew name means "God is great"), an old pious man in the story bearing his name, how one can tell the Revolution from the Counterrevolution. Indeed, even an enthusiastic convert to the revolutionary cause who dies for his new faith ("The Rabbi's Son") appears to have carried among his belongings not only a portrait of Lenin, but also one of Maimonides, the medieval Jewish physician and theologian, author, significantly, of *The Guide for the Perplexed*.

Babel's avoidance of simplistic political tendentiousness, his partiality for contradiction and paradox, and above all the equivocation and ambiguity of the didactic message contained in his work—in short, precisely those attributes that endear Babel to sophisticated non-Soviet readers—have always been held against him in the USSR. Perhaps the most notorious early attack was the article by Semyon Budënny, commander of the army Babel depicted, expressing outrage over the writer's "slanderous" portrayal of his men. While Babel's influential friends (Gorky among them) helped deflect Budënny's ire at the time, the misgivings he voiced still echo occasionally in Soviet appraisals of Babel's work.

The Odessa Tales reflect an aspect of Russian, including early Soviet writing that is rarely discussed by scholars in the USSR. That problem is the important influence on turn-of-the-century Russian literature of Friedrich Nietzsche, and particularly of his *Birth of Tragedy*, with its indictment of Christianity for its alleged "condemnation of the passions, fear of beauty and sensuality, a beyond invented the better to slander this life." To Nietzsche, "the unconditional will of Christianity to recognize *only* moral values ... [is] at the very least, a sign of abysmal sickness, weariness, discouragement, exhaustion, and the impoverishment of life" (Walter Kaufman, ed. and trans., *The Basic Writings of Nietzsche*. 1968. P. 23). One manifestation of Nietzsche's impact was the fascination of a number of Russian authors, including Babel's friend and protector Gorky, with physical prowess and stamina, with undisguised sensuality and fearlessness. Because of historical circumstances, Nietzsche's strictures against Christianity were also all too easily applicable to Judaism in the Diaspora. (This, incidentally, runs counter to conventional wisdom according to which Babel's protagonists dream of escaping ascetic Judaism for the joyously sensual Christian world. More importantly, such traditional interpretations of Babel—by Lionel Trilling, for instance—ignore such weighty evidence as the writings of Vasily Rozanov, a Russian writer and far more profound scholar of religion and sexuality than his contemporary Babel, who maintained that it is Christianity, not Judaism, that extols ascetic values and should become "phallic"). Moreover, glorification of a new breed of physical Jews capable of striking fear into the hearts of their traditional Gentile oppressors could also have been suggested to Babel by Zionist teachings. There is some evidence of Babel's participation, as a student, in Zionist youth organizations. It is thus Nietzsche and, possibly, Zionism that inspired such giants as Mendel Krik and his two sons and daughter, Lyubka the Cossack, and Froim Grach and his daughter, physical men and women filled with zest for life and altogether unconcerned with ethics and morals, to say nothing of religion.

Wartime violence stripped natural physical man of his glory, revealing his unseemly side. Strength, it was demonstrated, rarely begets joy; more often it causes suffering and death. Similarly, sexuality near the battle field normally inspires painful, violent and humiliating rape rather than torrid lovemaking. In peacetime, physical man is an athlete; in war time he wreaks brutal destruction. It is for that reason that moral and ethical concerns, largely absent from *The Tales of Odessa*, reappear prominently in *Red Cavalry*. Justice and mercy,

dignity and compassion, are discussed here even by religious believers employing religious categories and questioning moral agnosticism of the Revolution. Their arguments are reported, with respect and even a degree of sympathy, by the non-believing Communist narrator Lyutov, though one proposed solution, "an International of good men," a Revolution that would also accept the Sabbath, is dismissed as an impractical dream ("Gedali").

A leftist, Russian, Jewish intellectual, particularly one strongly influenced by the adamant anti-clericalism of the French Left, could hardly be expected to return to the fold of organized religion. (Babel's ties to France had grown closer after the emigration in 1925 of his mother and sister to Belgium, and of his wife to Paris, where his daughter Nathalie was born in 1929. Babel spent two years abroad, from late 1927 to late 1928, and from late 1932 to late 1933. He made his final brief visit to Paris in June 1935). Moreover, institutionalized religion appeared to him as an abstraction divorced from human affairs. In *Red Cavalry*, however, there are some inklings of a possible bridge, by means of painting and literature, between the ethical and moral dimensions of religious teachings and humanity's concerns and aspirations. This may be seen in "Pan Apolek," in which paintings of saints in a Roman Catholic church boldly portray local peasants and Jews; similar art in St. Valentine's Church in a story of the same name; and from a rabbi's verdict that the narrator's effort to render in verse the adventures of Hershele Ostropoler, a picaresque hero of Yiddish folklore, is lofty ambition ("The Rabbi"). That in his later years Babel was more optimistic about the possibility of some sort of coexistence of Communism and religious ethics, is suggested by "Karl-Yankel," a 1931 story in which an infant, circumcized unbeknownst to his atheist parents, emerges with the hybrid name of Patriarch Jacob (in the Jewish tradition, synonymous with Israel) and of Karl Marx, and with the narrator's confidential prediction of a happy future. At the same time, Babel's late work exudes a wistful quality particularly noticeable in loving evocations of childhood (for instance, in "Awakening" and "In the Basement," both published in 1931). Another theme of Babel's last writings is that of the relation between art and reality, as in "Guy de Maupassant" and "Di Grasso" (1937), both testimonies that Babel was silenced at the height of his creative powers.

Works: Selected Stories and Plays. English introd. by A. B. Murphy, Russian introd. by Ilya Ehrenburg. Chicago, 1965. *Zabytye proizvedeniya*. Ann Arbor, 1979.

Translations: The Collected Stories. Ed. and trans. Walter Morison, introd. Lionel Trilling. New York, 1955. *The Lonely Years 1925–1939. Unpublished Stories and Private Correspondence*. Ed. and introd. Nathalie Babel, and trans. Andrew R. MacAndrew. New York, 1964. *You Must Know Everything, Stories 1915–1937*. Trans. Max Hayward and ed. Nathalie Babel. New York, 1969.

Secondary literature: Patricia Carden, *The Art of Isaac Babel*. Ithaca, 1972. James E. Falen, *Isaac Babel, Russian Master of the Short Story*. Knoxville, 1974. Maurice Friedberg, "Yiddish Folklore Motifs in Isaac Babel's *Konarmija*." In *American Contributions to the Eighth International Congress of Slavists*, Victor Terras, ed. Columbus: Slavica, 1978. Pp. 192–203. Carol Luplow, *Isaac Babel's* Red Cavalry. Ann Arbor, 1982. Arkadii L'vov, *Utolen'e pechal'yu. Opyt issledovaniya evreiskoi mental'nosti*. New York, 1983. Danuta Mendelson, *Metaphor in Babel's Short Stories*. Ann Arbor, 1982. Victor Terras, "Line and Color: The Structure of I. Babel's Short Stories in *Red Cavalry*," *Studies in Short Fiction* 3, no. 2 (Winter, 1966), pp. 141–56.   M. F.

Bagritsky (pseud. of Eduárd Geórgievich Dzyúbin, 1897–1934), poet. Born and educated in Odessa, Bagritsky wrote some modernist verse before the Revolution, publishing it locally. He enthusiastically embraced the Revolution, fought with a Bolshevik guerilla group in the civil war, and wrote agitational pieces of poetry and prose. In the years following the Revolution Bagritsky's poetry followed a line of revolutionary romanticism. In 1925 he moved to Moscow, where he became associated with the Pereval and later with the constructivist group. In 1926 he wrote his most famous work, "The Lay about Opanas" (Duma pro Opanasa), loosely patterned after the Ukrainian folk ballad, the duma. It tells the story of the peasant Opanas who joins the wrong side in the civil war and pays for it with his life. But the real hero of the "Lay" is a Bolshevik commander. The "Lay" is written in a lively and free-changing rhythm which gives it a popular flair. Among the many heroic revolutionary poems of the 1920s, "The Lay about Opanas" is probably the best. The poems of Bagritsky's first volume of verse, *South-West* (Yugo-zapad, 1928) still deal mostly with the Revolution and civil war, and still in an exuberantly romantic manner. Poems dealing with other subjects are equally romantic. The volume was well received. In 1930 Bagritsky joined RAPP and his poetry now addressed itself to the first Five-Year Plan. The poems and verse epics collected in *Victors* (Pobediteli, 1932) and *The Last Night* (Poslednyaya noch', 1932) still have the same ring of genuine romantic enthusiasm. Bagritsky died of a respiratory ailment. He was a talented poet of some originality. His vigorous fantasy and untrammelled emotionality are cast into a mold of imagery which is always fresh and concrete, familiar yet sufficiently defamiliarized. Poeticized colloquialisms and a verse rhythm which approaches that of lively speech contribute to the sense of immediacy conveyed by Bagritsky's better poems. Bagritsky also translated from Ukrainian, English, French, and Turkish.

Works: Sobranie sochinenii. 2 vols. 1938. *Stikhotvoreniya i poemy.* 1964. *Dnevniki. Pis'ma. Stikhi.* 1964.

Translations: "The Bird-Catcher" and "The Smugglers." In *Modern Russian Poetry.* Ed. Vladimir Markov and Merrill Sparks. 1967. Pp. 672–81. "Verses about a Nightingale and a Poet" and "Insomnia." Trans. Luba Halat Kowalski, *RLT* 8 (1974), pp. 65–68. *See also* Lewanski, p. 197.

Bibliography: Luba Halat Kowalski, "Eduard Bagritsky: A Selected Bibliography," *RLT* 8 (1974), pp. 540–42.

Secondary literature: Walenty Cukierman, "The Odessa Myth and Idiom in Some Early Works of Odessa Writers," *CASS* 14 (1980), pp. 36–51. I. I. Grinberg, *Eduard Bagritskii.* 1940. Luba H. Kowalski, "Eduard Bagritsky: A Biographical Sketch with Three Unpublished Letters," *RLT* 8 (1974), pp. 472–86. V. Narbut, ed., *Eduard Bagritskii. Al'manakh.* 1936. Wendy Rosslyn, "Bagritskii's *Duma pro Opanasa*: The Poem and its Context," *CASS* 11 (1977), pp. 388–405. ———, "The Path to Paradise: Recurrent Images in the Poetry of Eduard Bagritsky," *Modern Language Review* 71 (1976), pp. 97–105. A. D. Sinyavskii, "Eduard Bagritskii." In *Istoriya russkoi sovetskoi literatury.* Vol. 1. 1917–1929. 1958. G. Struve, *Russian Literature under Lenin and Stalin, 1917–1953.* 1971. Pp. 191–92.   V. T.

Bakhtín, Mikhaíl Mikhaílovich (1895–1975), literary theorist, scholar, and philosopher of language. Bakhtin was born 16 November 1895 in Orel. His family was of the old nobility, but no longer owned property at the time of his birth. His father was manager at different times of various state banks, so the family moved around a good deal in Bakhtin's childhood, from Orel to Vilnius to Odessa, where Bakhtin finished gymnasium and entered the philological faculty of the local university in 1913. The following year he transferred to St. Petersburg University where his older brother, Nikolai, was a student. The two were very close, although they never saw each other again after 1918 when Nikolai joined the Whites and—after many adventures—emigrated to England, where he became a professor of classics and linguistics at Birmingham University. Bakhtin did well at the university, studying with the distinguished Hispanist and student of Baudouin de Courtenay, D. K. Petrovsky, the philosopher A. I. Vvedensky and other leading lights of the time. But his most intense work was done under the great classicist F. F. Zelinsky, some of whose ideas clearly had an influence on the young Bakhtin, particularly those in Zelinsky's treatise on Homeric narrative tragedy. It was during these years Bakhtin laid the foundation for his prodigious knowledge of literature and philosophy, especially those of Germany and ancient Greece.

In 1918 Bakhtin left the university and moved to the small West Russian city of Nevel, where he taught high school for the next two years. It was here the first of several "Bakhtin circles" was formed, composed mainly of V. N. Voloshinov (1894–1936); M. V. Yudina (1899–1970) the concert pianist; L. V. Pumpyansky (1894–1940), later a professor of literature at Leningrad University, and M. I. Kagan (1889–1937), who had just returned from Germany where he had been a favorite student of Hermann Cohen, leader of the Marburg Neo-Kantians. The group organized concerts and lectures at the Nevel House of Culture; the activity that attracted most attention was a series of debates in which Bakhtin and Pumpyansky opposed a number of local Bolsheviks on the religious question. It was during

this period that Bakhtin was first published (a two-page piece on "Art and Responsibility") and where he began a large philosophical treatise on values in art, religion, and politics, *The Architectonics of Responsibility*, containing most of the positions he would spend the rest of his long life working out in more detail.

In 1920 Bakhtin moved to Vitebsk, which was at that time an island of light amidst the dark events of revolution and civil war, a refuge for such artists as El Lisitsky, Malevich, and Marc Chagall. Several prominent scientists had also sought haven from the cold and hunger of Petrograd, as well as leading musicians from the former Mariinsky theater, who formed a conservatory. A lively newspaper was founded, *Iskusstvo*, whose main force was a local Party activist, P. N. Medvedev (1891–1938), who now joined the new Bakhtin circle, which was augmented as well by I. I. Sollertinsky (1902–43), later musical director of the Leningrad Philharmonic. Kagan had left the group, ending up as editor of the great Soviet *Encyclopedia of Energy Resources* in Moscow. But even after his departure the group continued to discuss philosophical topics, especially recent developments in Neo-Kantianism, Phenomenology, and the Bergsonian version of Vitalism.

Two events of great personal importance occurred in Vitebsk. In 1921 Bakhtin married Elena Aleksandrovna Okolovich, who for fifty years took care of Bakhtin and shared all his hardships until her death in 1971. During this period the osteomyelitis, which had plagued Bakhtin since his teen years, was complicated by typhoid, making him a semi-invalid for the rest of his life, even after amputation of a leg in 1938. In 1924 Bakhtin moved back to Leningrad, where he led the most precarious existence, giving private lectures and reading manuscripts for a number of publishing houses. In 1924 he tried to enter the debate between FORMALISTS and sociologically oriented critics, but the journal that was to publish the article (*Russkii sovremennik*) was closed before it could appear. These were nevertheless fruitful years for Bakhtin, during which he continued his constant discussions with yet another Bakhtin circle, this time made up of such stalwarts as Yudina, Voloshinov, Medvedev, Sollertinsky, and Pumpyansky, plus such new faces as the poets N. A. KLYUEV and B. M. Zubakin, the biologist I. I. Kanaev, the experimental writers Konstantin VAGINOV and Daniil KHARMS, and the Indologist M. I. Tubyansky. He was also close at this time to a number of Leningrad Church groups, such as The Brotherhood of St. Sophia, *Voskresenie* and the Brotherhood of St. Seraphim of Sarov.

He wrote a number of works during these years that were published under the names of his friends Voloshinov (who died of tuberculosis) and Medvedev (who was shot). There is some dispute about who actually wrote such texts as *The Formal Method in Literary Scholarship* (1928), published under Medvedev's name, or *Freudianism: a Critical Sketch* (1927) and *Marxism and the Philosophy of Language* (1929) published as the work of Voloshinov. The original manuscripts are no longer extant and all the principals are dead, but there is no doubt among those still alive who were close to the group in the 1920s and later, that Bakhtin was the author of these books. There is at least one other author still alive who has testified that Bakhtin wrote an article using his (the other author's) name. The reasons why Bakhtin resorted to so extreme a tactic to get his books published are several and complex. Essentially he did so as a matter of expediency: it was one thing for a figure who was well known to be a believer to write a book about DOSTOEVSKY, quite another for him to write a book on topics more directly touching on Marxist ideology.

In 1929 Bakhtin did publish *Problems of Dostoevsky's Poetics*, in which the Dialogism that he had been meditating since his days in Nevel was announced to the world as "polyphony." The book was well received, even by Party intellectuals such as LUNACHARSKY. But the impact of the book was muffled when, just as it appeared, Bakhtin was arrested and exiled to Kustenai (in Kazakhstan) for the next six years. Even here Bakhtin continued to write, and some of his most important work (such as "Discourse in the Novel") was written while he was in Kustenai. In 1936 he was able to teach a course at the Mordovian Pedagogical Institute in Saransk; in 1937, fearful of rearrest, he moved to Kimry, where he finished a book devoted to Goethe and the *Bildungsroman*. The manuscript was accepted by the *Sovetskii pisatel'* publishing house, but during the German invasion the galleys were lost forever. Bakhtin had one other copy of the manuscript, but rifled it for paper with which to roll his constant flow of cigarettes during the Second World War.

Bakhtin spent the war years in Moscow. In 1940 he had submitted a long dissertation on Rabelais. In 1946 his defense of the dissertation split the examining committee into two camps. After several stormy sessions the State Accrediting Bureau stepped in, and Bakhtin received the degree of *Kandidat*, but not the more honorific Doctor, which members of the original committee had wanted to award. Nineteen more years were to elapse before the Rabelais book emerged in 1965. In the meantime Bakhtin had been invited back to Saransk, where he taught until 1961. In 1963 the Dostoevsky book was reissued to great acclaim and in 1969 he returned to Moscow, where he died on 7 March 1975.

These last years finally brought him the fame and influence he had been so long denied. A group of young scholars at the Gorky Institute, most notably V. Kozhinov and S. Bocharov, took up his cause, as did other leaders of Moscow intellectual life, such as V. V. Ivanov. In 1975 a collection of essays outlining a historical poetics for the novel appeared, and in 1979 appeared another collection of essays from various periods of his life, including a long fragment of the philosophical treatise he had begun while still in Nevel.

Since the 1963 republication of the Dostoevsky book, Bakhtin's reputation has continued to grow as his influence has been felt in such otherwise disparate schools of criticism as those associated with *Tel Quel* (Julia Kristeva) on the one hand and Tartu Semiotics (LOTMAN, Ivanov) on the other. It may very well be the case that in future Bakhtin will be remembered primarily as a philosopher of language, but at present the two areas of his activity which have excited the widest interest are his attempts to work out a historically based poetics, and his essays relating to theory of the novel. While each area calls for attention in its own right, both share a common base in Bakhtin's conception of literature as a system, one which reveals itself *as* a system only when viewed as a continuously ongoing enterprise, not as a discrete series of passive, isolated texts, but as a living web of intricately connected utterances.

Bakhtin began his career during the heyday of Formalism, clearly a healthy antidote to the unchecked impressionism or dry-as-dust philology which preceded it. The Formalists' polemical formulation that a text was no more than the sum of its devices was an extreme Bakhtin found useful in formulating his own position. From the outset he opposed the two major assumptions of the early Formalists: reification of the text, conceiving of the work as a crafted *thing*; and secondly, a conscious disregard for specific historical circumstances. If, then, the Formalists concentrated on the mechanics of versification and narrative, what PROPP would call the morphological aspects of analysis, Bakhtin called attention to a work's semantics. In this he anticipated a direction that became apparent in later Formalism, particularly in the work of TYNYANOV. But in Bakhtin there is an emphasis on *social* factors as the ground of meaning: understanding comes about as a function of factors deriving from the whole culture.

Bakhtin had in common with the Formalists (and later STRUCTURALISTS) an emphasis on language, but the way Bakhtin understands language is quite different from the essentially Saussurean model on which so many other movements have been based. Bakhtin's conception of language is based on an a priori sense of opposition and struggle at the heart of existence, a ceaseless battle between centrifugal forces that seek to keep things apart, and centripetal forces that strive to make things cohere. This manichean clash is present in culture as well as nature, in the specificity of the individual human consciousness and in the even greater particularity of actual utterances. There is no such thing as a "general language," of a sort that professional linguists sometimes posit: language when it *means* is always somebody talking to somebody else, even when that someone else is one's own inner addressee.

Bakhtin's basic model for this conception of language is two people talking to each other in a specific dialog at a given time and in a particular place. These persons would not confront each other as sovereign egos capable of sending messages to each other through uncluttered semiotic space. Rather, each would be a consciousness at a specific point in the history of defining itself through the choice each has made—out of all the possible existing languages, the heteroglossia available to it at that moment—of a discourse to transcribe its intention *in this specific exchange*. The two will, like everyone else, have been born into an environment in which the air is already aswarm with words. Their development as individuals will have been prosecuted as a gradual appropriation of a specific mix of discourses

that are capable of best mediating their *own* intentions, rather than those which sleep in the words they use before they use them. Thus, each will seek, by means of intonation, pronunciation, lexical choice, and gesture, to send out a message to the other with a minimum of interference from the otherness constituted by pre-existing meanings of the kind present in dictionaries and ideologies and the otherness of the intentions present in the other person in the dialog.

A key concept in Bakhtin's thought, then, is "discourse" (*slovo*), the dynamic conception of language that is sensitive to the fact that no word can be understood *in itself*, but must be put into a situation—not only linguistic, but historical and cultural—if its meaning is to be grasped. And, of course, the meaning will not be singular, but as plural as its possible contexts. This emphasis on a relational whole over isolated parts became, to be sure, a fundamental aspect of later structuralism, but without Bakhtin's openness to the historical dimension. It was only when semiotics was "rediscovered" in Tartu and Paris as an antidote to the ultra-Formalism of the more militant structuralists that the deeper significance of Bakhtin's work became widely apparent (see STRUCTURALISM AND SEMIOTICS).

His work falls into four periods. The first, from 1918 to 1924, may be called his metaphysical period, for it is during these years that his thought finds expression in the genre of axiology, the philosophical study of values. This work includes Bakhtin's first publication, "Art and Answerability," in a local Nevel anthology of 1919, the *Architectonics of Responsibility* (partially published as "Author and Hero" in 1979), a number of lost notebooks on Dostoevsky (some of the ideas from which went into the 1929 book), and the 1924 "Problem of Context," scheduled to appear in *Russkii sovremennik* but when that journal was closed, not published until 1975. It was during this period, especially in the *Architectonics*, that Bakhtin laid down the groundwork for all the work he was to do for the rest of his life.

The second, or Leningrad period, from 1924 to 1929, is the period during which Bakhtin published a number of books and articles, most of them under the names of his friends. These would include under Voloshinov's name, *Freudianism: A Critical Sketch* (1927) and *Marxism and the Philosophy of Language* (1929), and under Medvedev's, *The Formal Method in Literary Study* (1928). During these years Bakhtin—quite according to his own formula for self appropriation—found his own voice as an author by ventriloquating others. This period is crowned by the appearance of *Problems of Dostoevsky's Poetics*, published under Bakhtin's own name in 1929.

The next period, the long years of exile (officially in Kustenai and unofficially in Saransk) stretches from 1930 to 1960. During these years Bakhtin concentrated on the novel as an even more concrete means for expressing his ideas than attempts in the previous decade to do the same thing in psychology, philosophy of language, and Vitalism. The essays on novel theory published for the first time in 1975 were written during these years, as were the lost Goethe book and the dissertation on Rabelais. While in Saransk after World War II he gradually returned to the more directly philosophical concerns of his youth.

In his last period, dating from the time he began revisions for the second edition of his Dostoevsky book in 1961, Bakhtin saw many of his earlier, unpublished texts emerge into the light of day, including the Rabelais book, published in 1965, and his essays on novel theory, published in 1975. After his move to Moscow, he wrote a number of essays that sought to extend some of his earlier ideas on the nature of language and the distinctive place of the humanities among the sciences. These were published posthumously in 1979.

While there is an apparent constancy in Bakhtin's career, there is development as well. The 1929 version of the Dostoevsky book makes rather extravagant claims for Dostoevsky's uniqueness: Dostoevsky's achievement appears as something of an aberration in literary history. The second edition of 1963 has attached to it new material that seeks rather to place the Dostoevskian novel into a tradition. The new material and the point of view which it entails are drawn from work on the history of the novel Bakhtin pursued during the thirty-four years that intervened between the two editions. In those years Bakhtin came to regard the Dostoevskian novel to be not so much an absolutely unprecedented event in the history of the genre but rather the purest expression of what always had been implicit in it. Viewing the history of the novel through the optic of the Dostoevskian example had revolutionary consequences. The novel ceases to be "simply one genre among other genres" (Bakhtin, 1975, p. 449). It becomes not only "the main hero of the drama of modern literary development" (p. 451), but the most significant force at work even in those early periods when most other scholars would argue that there were no novels being written at all.

Such scholars would, within their own terms, be correct in asserting that there were no novels in Plato's Athens or during the Middle Ages, or at least no novel as we have come to know it. But Bakhtin is clearly not referring to that concept of a novel which begins with Cervantes or Richardson. These books, and especially the nineteenth-century psychological novel which evolved from them, have become the canon of the genre-novel. The majority of literary scholars are most at home when dealing with canons, which is why Bakhtin said that "literary theory reveals its complete helplessness when dealing with the novel" (Bakhtin, 1975, p. 448). Rather, "novel" is the name Bakhtin gives to whatever force is at work within a given literary system to reveal the limits, the artificial constraints of that system. Literary systems are comprised of canons, and "novelization" is fundamentally anti-canonical. It will not permit generic monologue. Always it will insist on the dialogue between what a given system will admit as literature on one hand, and those texts which are otherwise excluded from such a definition of literature on the other. What is more conventionally thought of as the novel is simply the most complex and distilled expression of this impulse.

The history of the novel so conceived is very long, but it exists outside the bounds of what traditional scholars would think of as strictly *literary* history. Bakhtin's history would be charted, among other ways, in devaluation of a given culture's higher literary forms: the parodies of knightly romances (Cervantes), pastorals (Sorel), sentimental fictions (Sterne, Fielding), etc. But these texts are merely late examples of a tendency that had been abroad since at least the ancient Greeks. Bakhtin comes very close to naming Socrates as the first novelist, since the gadfly role he played, and which he played out in the drama of the dialogue precisely, is more or less what the role of the novel has always been. That role has been assumed by such unexpected forms as the confession, the utopia, the epistle, or the Menippean satire, in which Bakhtin is particularly interested. Even the drama (Ibsen and other Naturalists), the long poem (*Childe Harold* or *Don Juan*), or the lyric (as in Heine) become masks for the novel during the 19th century. As formerly distinct literary genres are subjected to the novel's intensifying anti-generic power, their systematic purity is infected and they become "novelized."

Bakhtin's *Rabelais* is perhaps the best demonstration of his general thesis that any poetics worthy of the name must ground itself in a new definition of its subject: the literary text must be conceived of as a problem in understanding and therefore as a social process deeply embedded in history. At the same time *Rabelais* advances Bakhtin's particular view of the novel, since it argues that the key to grasping that much misunderstood book *Gargantua* is the manner in which it deploys the resources of medieval carnival.

Carnival is conceived by Bakhtin as an armory of attitudes and forms, ritual weapons opposed to the reigning status quo: "As opposed to the official feast (which sanctioned existing political, religious, and social habits) ... carnival celebrated temporary liberation from the prevailing truth and the established order.... Carnival was the true feast of time, the feast of becoming, change and renewal. It was hostile to all that was ageless, completed, at an end...." (Bakhtin, 1965, p. 13). Its effect was a "gay relativity" of all fixed values.

Bakhtin provides an intricate analysis of the various aspects of folk laughter which find their most structured articulation in the world of the carnival: special patterns of dress, interpersonal behavior, emphasis on gross body imagery, etc. Each of these aspects is treated as if it were a language with its own rules for meaning. Thus *Rabelais* can be read as a textbook example of semiotic analysis, a highly detailed justification for the earlier but necessarily abstract call of the Vitebsk circle (in Bakhtin's 1924 article and Voloshinov's *Marxism and the Philosophy of Language*) for a new "science of ideologies, that is, the study of a given culture in terms of its various sign systems or discourses." *Rabelais* is also an opportunity to show in detail what Bakhtin means by novel, since *Gargantua* is shown to use all the subversive, but life-enhancing, structures and energies of carnival in pursuit of the novel's traditional, system-debunking task.

The essays which are included in the posthumous 1975 anthology once again address the problem of how to conceive a historical poetics for the novel. They open up several new avenues of investigation.

The essays were written over a period stretching from 1924 to the 1970s; most were composed during the dark decades of the 1930s and 1940s, yet Bakhtin's originality and energy remained unimpaired. "Epic and Novel" is perhaps the most concise of Bakhtin's various formulations of the novel as an anti-generic, constantly innovating force. The longest essay in the volume introduces what might be called Bakhtin's answer to the phoneme in linguistics, a basic unit of study he calls a "chronotope," which is the way in which a given text defines itself by means of the time/space relations its structure presupposes. All the essays are studded with surprising but apt illustrations drawn from diverse ages and languages. They bespeak a life of intense scholarship, rarely found in combination with the kind of bold theoretical speculation Bakhtin permits himself. There are further unpublished manuscripts yet to come, and we can only hope they will not suffer the vicissitudes which plagued the publishing career of the texts already available.

Works: Problems of Dostoevsky's Poetics. (Trans. of 2d ed. of 1963.) 1973. [*A new translation is soon to appear.*] *Rabelais and His World.* 1968. *The Dialogic Imagination.* 1981. *Books published under other names*: V. N. Voloshinov, *Freudianism: A Marxist Critique.* 1976. ———, *Marxism and the Philosophy of Language.* 1973. P. N. Medvedev, *The Formal Method in Literary Scholarship.* 1978.

Secondary literature: Caryl Emerson, "The Outer Word and Inner Speech," *Cherez* (Spring, 1978). Michael Holquist, "The Politics of Representation." In *Allegory and Representation.* Ed. Stephen J. Greenblatt. 1981. Julia Kristeva, "A Ruined Poetic." In *Russian Formalism.* Ed. John Bowlt and Stephen Bann. 1973. Gary Saul Morson, "The Heresiarch of Meta," *PTL* 3, no. 3 (October 1978). Anna Tamarchenko, "Mikhail Mikhailovich Bakhtin." In M. M. Bakhtin—V. N. Voloshinov, *Freidizm: Kriticheskii ocherk.* New York, 1983. Pp. 225–80.   J. M. H.

Baklánov, Grigóry Yákovlevich (pseud. of Fridman, 1923–), short-story writer and novelist, was born in Voronezh. He fought in World War II and graduated from the Gorky Literary Institute in 1951. He began his literary career in the early 1950s with short stories about the postwar village. During de-Stalinization he was one of the first Soviet authors to depict World War II without embellishment. His short novels, *South of the Main Offensive* (Yuzhnee glavnogo udara, 1958), *An Inch of Ground* (Pyad' zemli, 1959), and *The Dead Should Not Be Shamed* (Mertvye sramu ne imut, 1961) portray not only the heroism and self-sacrifice but also the selfishness and cowardice of Soviet combatants. In the novel *July 1941* (Iyul' 41 goda, 1965), which reflects some influences of Lev Tolstoi, descriptions of war alternate with flashbacks into the purges of the 1930s to reveal their crippling impact on the Red Army.

The novel *Friends* (Druz'ya, 1975) draws a moral contrast between two provincial architects. Decency is at last rewarded, but the impression remains that Soviet society is fertile soil for the growth of careerism and obsequiousness. In the short novel *The Youngest among the Brothers* (Men'shii sredi brat'ev, 1981) Baklanov depicts, with a light sense of humor, the life of a middle-aged Moscow professor dominated by his shallow wife. In both of the last works the plot moves slowly and lacks the dramatic quality of Baklanov's war novels. His recent, largely autobiographical stories are set during and immediately after the war.

Works: V Snegiryakh. 1954. *Iyul' 41 goda, Znamya,* 1965, nos. 1–2. *Izbrannoe.* 1974. *Druz'ya.* 1976. *Izbrannye proizvedeniya.* 1979–80. *Men'shii sredi brat'ev, Druzhba narodov,* 1981, no. 6. *Rasskazy, Druzhba narodov,* 1982, no. 1.

Translations: The Foothold [An Inch of Ground]. 1962. *South of the Main Offensive.* 1963.

Secondary literature: B. Anashenkov, "Istselisya sam ...", *VLit,* 1976, no. 1, pp. 54–57, 60–75. D. Brown, *Soviet Russian Literature since Stalin.* 1978. Pp. 277–78. N. Ivanova, "Pered zerkalom," *Oktyabr',* 1981, no. 10, pp. 215–17.   H. E.

Bakúnin, Mikhail Aleksándrovich (1814–76), anarchist theoretician and revolutionary leader, was born on the ancestral estate of Premukhino, in Tver province (now Kalinin), of an hereditary noble family. His father was a liberal who obtained his doctorate in philosophy at Padua University, Italy. Young Mikhail was intended for the diplomatic service but he chose to study the natural sciences. He was enrolled in the Artillery School in St. Petersburg, was commissioned, and served in Lithuania. In 1835 Bakunin left the military because he was bored with it. His interest in literature and philosophy led him to join the STANKEVICH Circle in Moscow. He was first influenced by Fichte's philosophy while translating some of his works for the periodical TELESKOP. Later he became interested in Hegel's philosophy, which he used to challenge the views of HERZEN and other liberal thinkers.

In 1840 Bakunin went to Berlin to continue his studies in philosophy. There he frequented different literary and radical circles. In 1842 he moved to Dresden where he met Arnold Ruge, leader of the Young Hegelians. Bakunin published an essay in Ruge's *Deutsche Jahrbücher für Wissenschaft und Kunst*, entitled "Reaction in Germany—a Fragment by a Frenchman." In this article Bakunin glorified the idea of perpetual revolt.

Bakunin later moved to Paris where he became associated with Karl Marx, which intensified his revolutionary zeal. Meanwhile he was concerned with the liberation of the Poles and other Slav peoples from oppression. His anti-Russian government speeches led to his expulsion from Paris.

Bakunin is a unique phenomenon in the history of 19th-century revolutionary history. He was both a socio-philosophical thinker and a man of action. Herzen characterized him as "everything about this man is colossal, his energy, his appetite, yes, even the man himself." Bakunin played an important role in the February revolution of 1848 in France and the March revolution in Berlin. During 1848–49 Bakunin became involved in uprisings in France, Prague, and Dresden, where he was arrested. Jailed in Saxon and Austrian prisons, he was eventually turned over to the Russian authorities, who imprisoned him in the Peter and Paul Fortress, where he spent six years. In 1857 he was exiled to Siberia after submitting his *Confession* to the Tsar. He managed to escape to the United States via Japan and from there made his way to Western Europe.

In 1863 Bakunin left for Italy and in1865 he founded the International Brotherhood in Naples. This organization served as a conspiratorial avenue for promoting revolution whenever the opportunity presented itself. He also became involved in the League for Peace and Freedom. His essay "Federalism, Socialism and anti-Theologism" contains the essence of anarchist philosophy. In 1868 Bakunin left the League to found the International Alliance of Social Democracy, which was later dissolved when his followers joined the International Workingmen's Association. In his *Revolutionary Catechism* Bakunin advocates the abolition of the state and organized religion and the fostering of communal autonomy within a federal structure. Violence became for him a positive element as a means of bringing about a social revolution. Bakunin and his followers challenged the power wielded by Marx. The disagreement centered on Marx's insistence that after the workers have seized power there must be a transitional period under the dictatorship of the proletariat. Bakunin argued that power by the proletariat is just as evil as that of any state. He argued that a communist state would only magnify the evil of other states. In 1872 Bakunin was expelled from the *International* when the Congress met at the Hague. Bakunin maintained that there can be no revolution without passionate destruction, since this would be instrumental in bringing about a new world. Destructive action, according to Bakunin, is determined by the positive ideal. Bakunin's central ideas are stated in his *God and the State*. These are: (1) propagation of atheism; (2) destruction of the State, to be replaced by a system of anarchist-communism; and (3) political action cannot achieve the destruction of the State, rebellion being the only method. Bakunin envisioned a federalist organization which would be based on mutual co-operation without any political organization. Despite his deteriorating health, Bakunin participated in the Lyons Rebellion in 1870 and in the abortive Bologna uprising in 1874. He died in Bern, Switzerland, in 1876.

Works in Russian: Izbrannye sochineniya. 5 vols. 1919–21. *Sobranie sochinenii i pisem.* 4 vols. 1934–35.

Works in English: God and the State. Trans. Benjamin Tucker. Boston, 1893. *Marxism, Freedom and the State.* Trans. K. J. Kenafick. London, 1950. *The Political Philosophy of Bakunin.* Ed. G. P. Maximoff. 1953. *Stratism and Anarchy.* Trans. C. H. Hummer, ed. J. F. Harrison.

Works in French: Oeuvres. Ed. J. Guillaume. 6 vols. Paris, 1896–

1914. Editions of Bakunin's selected works have also appeared in German and Spanish.

Secondary literature: Paul Avrich, "The Legacy of Bakunin," *RusR* 29 (1970), pp. 129–42. E. H. Carr, *Bakunin.* London, 1937. H. E. Kaminski, *Bakounine, la vie d'un revolutionnaire.* Paris, 1938. Yu. M. Steklov, *Mikhail Aleksandrovich Bakunin, ego zhizn' i deyatel'-nost', 1814–1876.* 4 vols. 1926–27. George Woodcock, "Bakunin," *The Encyclopedia of Philosophy,* Vol. 1, pp. 244–46. There is a useful discussion of Bakunin and anarchism in Bertrand Russell's *Proposed Roads to Freedom,* Chap. 2. L. J. S.

Balakshin, Pyotr P. (1898–), Russian journalist, historian, and short story writer. Born and raised in the Far East in the family of a government official, Balakshin graduated from the Aleksandrovsk Military School in Moscow. Voluntarily enlisting in the Russian army, he fought in Romania during World War I and in the Far East under General Kolchak during the Civil War. After several years in Japan and China, Balakshin emigrated to America in the late 1920s, eventually settling in San Francisco and attending the University of California for three years. Continuing the literary and journalistic activities which he had begun in 1917, Balakshin founded the newspaper *Russkie novosti*, became a regular contributor to San Francisco's *Russkaya zhizn'*, and edited a literary miscellany *Zemlya Kolumba* (2 nos., 1936–1937) under the pseudonym B. Miklashevich. After World War II he spent ten years in Korea and Japan serving as a military historian for the U. S. Army.

Balakshin is best known for his short stories describing the life of Russian émigrés in the 1930s and 1940s on Fillmore Street in San Francisco, which he characterized as "one of the most interesting and grotesque streets in the whole world, attractive and repugnant, enticing in its distorted beauty and human sores laid bare." Of equal importance, however, is his 800-page pioneering history *Finale in China* (Final v Kitae, 2 vols., 1958–59), in which he chronicled the rise, development, and decline of the Russian emigration in the Far East.

Works: Sobranie sochinenii, Vol. 1 (*Povest' o San Frantsisko: rasskazy,* 1951), Vol. 2 (*Vesna nad Filmorom: rasskazy,* 1951), Vol. 3 (*Vozvrashchenie k pervoi lyubvi: rasskazy,* 1952), Vol. 4 (*Planirovshchiki: roman,* 1955). A. M. S.

Ballad. The Russian ballad emerged as a direct imitation of the European pre-romantic and romantic ballad, largely through ZHUKOVSKY's excellent translations and adaptations of ballads by Bürger, Goethe, Schiller, Southey, Walter Scott, Thomas Campbell, and others. Zhukovsky also wrote some original ballads. The genre was popular in the romantic period and was cultivated by PUSHKIN ("The Hussar," "The Bridegroom"), LERMONTOV ("The Airborne Ship," "Tamara"), Aleksei TOLSTOI ("Vasily Shibanov"), and many others. The genre became firmly established in Russian poetry and is cultivated even in 20th-century poetry, by Eduard BAGRITSKY, Nikolai TIKHONOV, and others.

Texts: Russkaya ballada. Introd., ed. and comm. by V. I. Chernyshev. Introd. essay by N. P. Andreev. 1936.

Secondary literature: Kenneth H. and Warren U. Ober, "Zhukovsky's Early Translations of the Ballads of Robert Southey," *SEEJ*, 9 (1965), pp. 181–90. ———, "Zhukovsky and Southey's Ballads: The Translator as Rival," *Wordsworth Circle* 5 (1974), pp. 76–88. ———, "Zhukovsky's Translation of Campbell's 'Lord Ullin's Daughter'," *Germano-Slavica* 2 (1977), pp. 295–305. V. T.

Balmont, Konstantin Dmitrievich (1867–1942), poet, translator, novelist, essayist, and author of travel books. Balmont concluded his studies at a gymnasium in Shuya and entered Moscow University Law School in 1886, but left after a nervous breakdown in 1887. He then worked as a free-lance poet, translator, and writer, and after 1896 travelled restlessly in Western Europe and on all continents until his final exile in France from 1920 on. Balmont's journeys account for the exotic vein in his poetry and prose, and especially illuminate his discussions of Mexican and Mayan symbolism. Balmont's early books of verse, *Buildings on Fire* (Goryashchie zdaniya, 1900) and *Let Us Be as the Sun* (Budem kak solntse, 1903), indicate the stages of his development from sentimentalism and aestheticism-made-music to an intellectually aggressive, in part Nietzschean, decadent emotionalism which brought him great popularity and made him an inspirer of two generations of SYMBOLISTS and others. His influence can be detected in BRYUSOV, Vyacheslav IVANOV, BLOK, BELY, SEVERYANIN, TSVETAEVA, and POPLAVSKY. Balmont's strongest verse was produced in the years 1900 to 1917, and then in exile for the collection *In the Parted Distance* (V razdvinutoi dali, 1930).

It is difficult to characterize for the English-speaking reader Balmont's artistic singularity, but certain similarities can be drawn between his poetics and those of Keats, Shelley, Poe, and especially Swinburne. Balmont issued twenty-nine volumes of poetry, but his published collections contain only a part of his production; he could compose ten poems a day, and even improvise "wreaths" of SONNETS. Balmont's long lines, especially his slowly streaming anapestic, trochaic, and amphibrachian verses, are structurally anti-Pushkinian; with their experimental, vibrant rhythms he made an intoxicating psychic impact on the reader, and his sensual themes shocked and delighted Russian late-Victorian, early 20th-century readers. Balmont's singular vogue was due, in addition, to his stormy exhibitionist personality, to his erotogenic tunefulness and spontaneous prosodic ingenuity. A born virtuoso, the Paganini of Russian verse, Balmont believed in the first, "divinely inspired" version of a poem and opposed revisions.

A polyglot, having studied some forty languages, Balmont admired English above all and translated the complete works of Shelley and nearly all of Whitman and Poe. His verse renderings, especially of Shelley and Poe, done in precise metrical and rhyme schemes, are true, living poetry. In addition, he translated works by Shakespeare, Marlowe, Blake, Coleridge, Byron, Tennyson, Swinburne, and Wilde as well as German, Spanish, French, East European, Georgian, and Oriental poets. But so complete was Balmont's immersion in the watercolor fluidity of the English language, that he may paradoxically be considered an English poet writing in Russian.

While not lacking in originality of thought, Balmont was interested in becoming a pure poet-musician and agitated sorcerer, not a poet-thinker like Vyacheslav Ivanov or an intellectual poet-tragedian like MANDELSHTAM. His famous lines "Five senses are the way of the lie,/but there is an upswing of ecstasy/when the truth becomes visible by itself" show that he believed above all in revelation. He tried to maintain this ecstasy, but, writing too much, he often failed, especially in his political verse. Of the body of some 7,000 poems (including translations) about a hundred are masterpieces important to the development of Russian poetic culture in general. During the first decade of the century Balmont was highly praised by the poet-critics ANNENSKY, Blok, and V. Ivanov, but after 1920 younger significant critics and poets, both in the Soviet Union and in exile, became unjust to him, with two great exceptions: Tsvetaeva, who remained enthusiastic about his poetry and poetics to the very end of her life, and ZHIRMUNSKY, who called him "The master of intrinsic form." Since the late 1960s, however, starting with the pioneering critical essay of Vladimir Markov, Balmont has been partly rehabilitated both abroad and in the Soviet Union. His place as one of the finest Russian lyrists of purely euphonic style is today secure.

Works: Polnoe sobranie stikhov. 10 vols., incomplete. 1908–13. *Zmeinye tsvety.* 1910. *Krai Ozirisa.* 1914. *Poeziya kak volshebstvo.* 1915. *Slovo o muzyke.* 1917. *Sobranie liriki.* 6 vols. 1917. *Sonety mëda, solntsa i luny.* 1917. *Svetozvuk v prirode i svetovaya simfoniya Skryabina.* 1917. *Tropinkoi ognya.* 1919. *My.* 1920. *Persten'.* 1920. *Sem' poem.* 1920. *Marevo.* 1922. *Pod novym serpom.* 1923. *Moë-ei.* 1924. *Stikhi o Rossii.* 1924. *Severnoe siyanie.* 1931. *Stikhotvoreniya.* 1969. *Izbrannye stikhotvoreniya i poemy.* 1975. *Izbrannoe: Stikhotvoreniya, perevody, stat'i.* 1980.

Translations: Modern Russian Poetry. Vladimir Markov and Merrill Sparks, eds. 1967. Pp. 2–29. *See also: Lewanski,* pp. 198–99.

Secondary literature: A. Belyi, "Konstantin Dmitrievich Bal'mont," *Vesy,* 3 (1904): 9–12. I. Annenskii, "Bal'mont—lirik." In his *Kniga otrazhenii* 1906. Pp. 169–213. V. Ivanov, "O lirizme Bal'monta," *Apollon,* 3–4 (1912), pp. 36–42. P. Lebesgue, "Un grand poète slave: Constantin Balmont," *Revue politique et littéraire,* 69 (1931), pp. 460–75. R. Poggioli, *The Poets of Russia.* 1960. Pp. 82–96. K. Muratova, *Istoriya russkoi literatury kontsa XIX–nachala XX veka: bibliograficheskii ukazatel'.* 1963. Pp. 106–11. V. Markov, *Modern Russian Poetry.* 1967. Pp. liii-liv. ———. "Bal'mont: A Reappraisal," *SlavR,* 28 (1969), pp. 221–64. V. Orlov, "Bal'mont: Zhizn' i poeziya." Introd. to K. D. Bal'mont, *Stikhotvoreniya.* 1969. Pp. 45–

74. Silvia Althaus-Schönbucher, *Konstantin D. Bal'mont—Parallelen zu Afanasij A. Fet: Symbolismus und Impressionismus.* Bern, 1975. R. Patterson, "Bal'mont." In *Izbrannye stikhotvoreniya i poemy.* 1975. Pp. 15–80. A. Rannit, "Konstantin Balmont and His Letters to Dagmar Shakhovskaia," *Yale University Gazette* 51, no. 2 (1976), pp. 86–97. L. Ozerov, "K. Bal'mont i ego poeziya." In *Izbrannoe: Stikhotvoreniya, perevody, stat'i.* 1980. Pp. 3–26.　　A. R.

Baltrushaitis, Yúrgis Kazimírovich (Jurgis Baltrušaitis, 1873–1944), a Russian and Lithuanian SYMBOLIST poet and translator of poetry from many languages into Russian. Born on a Lithuanian farm, he was educated in mathematics and natural sciences at Moscow University. Turning to literature, he helped found the SKORPION publishing house in 1899, and became head of the Writers' Union in 1919. Baltrushaitis served as the Lithuanian diplomatic representative to the Soviet Union from 1920 and, from 1939, as Councillor to the Lithuanian Legation in Paris.

Baltrushaitis's Russian verse is sparse in its vocabulary, parsimonious of image, ponderous in style and unyielding in the pursuit of the basic symbolist concern with, as he put it, "the proximity to another world, with which the measure of our contact is the only measure of our value, and the search for which, it must be, constitutes our only purpose and meaning." It is distinguished by dignified humility and a reticent severity of faith in the infinite wonders of Creation, of which humanity is one, in an unbroken continuum that starts with the plainest wayside flower and ends at the feet of the Lord.

Most of Baltrushaitis's Lithuanian poems were written between 1939 and 1943. They are marked by three different language textures: a symbolist vocabulary carried over directly from the Russian poems, a rich and earthy peasant idiom raised to the level of abstract conceptions, and reintroduced, or reconstituted, old linguistic forms carrying symbolic meanings equivalent to the highest concepts Baltrushaitis had developed in his Russian verse. The humble, enduring faith in an ultimate realm of the spirit is adorned in the Lithuanian poems with an idyllic country ambiance.

Works: Gornaya tropa. 1911. *Zemnye stupeni.* 1912. *Liliya i serp.* 1948. *Poezija.* 1948. *Poezija.* 1967. *Derevo v ogne.* 1969.

Secondary literature: J. Aistis, "Jurgis Baltrušaitis." In *Baltrušaitis, poezija.* 1967. Valerii Ya. Bryusov, *Dalekie i blizkie.* Moscow, 1912. S. S. Rozanov, *Yu. Baltrushaitis.* Moscow, 1913. *Russkaya literatura XX veka, 1890–1910.* Book 5. Ed. S. A. Vengerov. Moscow, n. d. Rimvydas Šilbajoris, "Some Special Features of Baltrušaitis' Lithuanian Poetry," *Journal of Baltic Studies* 9, no. 2 (1978), pp. 147–54. Delija Valiukėnaitė, "Jurgis Baltrušaitis and William Blake: A Brief Comparison," *Lituanus* 10, no. 3–4 (1964), pp. 58–77. Bronius Vaškelis, "Jurgis Baltrušaitis: a Lithuanian and Russian Symbolist," *Lituanus* 10, no. 3–4 (1964), pp. 5–8.　　F. R. S.

Baratýnsky, Evgény Abrámovich (1800–44), poet. The son of a disgraced favorite of Emperor Paul, Baratynsky entered the Corps of Pages in St. Petersburg, an aristocratic military school, in 1813. Three years later, by personal resolution of the Emperor, he was expelled for taking active part in a theft. This catastrophe, preventing him from entering service except as a private in the army, was forever to leave the brand of Cain on Baratynsky, sustaining the profound melancholy in his character. He had received the gift of sorrow, a gift that was soon to make him a poet.

In 1819, introduced to "the family of the good Muses" by DELVIG, and becoming a friend of PUSHKIN, he joined a St. Petersburg regiment as a private, but was soon transferred to Southeastern Finland. Just like Pushkin, who had to leave St. Petersburg at about the same time, he proudly developed the romantic pose of an exile. However, the capital was not far off, and he had ample opportunity to maintain his literary contacts, especially in the FREE SOCIETY OF AMATEURS OF RUSSIAN LITERATURE, where he was admitted as "a poet of feasts and languid melancholy" (Pushkin). In the galaxy of young poets gathering around Pushkin, Baratynsky was early recognized to have the most brilliant talent.

Prizing Finland as the cradle of his poetry, and strongly influenced by the *Songs of Ossian*, Baratynsky describes the country as the wild fatherland of "Odin's children," with "mountains rising up to heaven." Far from being a realistic observer of a stern but not very impressive landscape, the poet obviously subscribes to the romantic view of Wordsworth that the task of poetry is "to treat of things not as they are, but as they seem to exist to the senses, and to the passions." His love for Finland is especially evident in the narrative poem *Eda* (1824), about a local girl who is seduced by a Russian hussar. Narrated by a noncommissioned officer in the Russian forces of occupation, the plot is abundant with political overtones shared by the DECEMBRIST poets, among whom Baratynsky had several friends.

At last, in the summer of 1825, Baratynsky was made an officer, thanks to the untiring efforts of ZHUKOVSKY, pledging for his friend at the Imperial court. A few months later the poet moved to Moscow to see his sick mother, a woman of strong personality, who made him leave service and marry Anastasia Engelhardt, the daughter of a General. Soon afterwards, the publication of his *Poems* (Stikhotvoreniya, 1827) and his narrative poem *The Ball* (Bal, 1825–28), a satire of society life in Moscow with the favorite romantic contrast of a dark and a fair beauty, established his reputation as a first-class poet.

From now on his life was outwardly uneventful, divided between his increasing family, his modest estates, and his literary work. To live in Moscow, more or less isolated from his friends in St. Petersburg, proved very hard for him. However, the change of intellectual milieu also opened up new horizons to a poet deeply rooted in French traditions. Thus in the early 1830s his friendship with the young philosopher Ivan KIREEVSKY and his close relations with the members of the former SOCIETY OF LOVERS OF WISDOM (*lyubomudry*) gave him a thorough insight into German romanticism and the idealist teachings of Schelling. His poem "On the Death of Goethe" (Na smert' Gete, 1832) is probably the finest eulogy ever written to the great German.

When toward the end of the 1830s Moscow intellectual life turned to SLAVOPHILISM, Baratynsky felt increasingly uncomfortable. Himself a great admirer of Western thought and literature, he could not stand the aggressive and chauvinistic talk of "rotten Europe." Neither did he find a new anchorage among the young WESTERNIZERS, people like STANKEVICH, BELINSKY, HERZEN, and OGARYOV, who estranged him with their radicalism and blind admiration for Hegel. Fallen between two stools, he retired to Muranovo, some thirty miles from the city. Today the estate of Muranovo, erected according to drawings made by the poet, is a highly recommendable museum dedicated to the memory of Baratynsky and TYUTCHEV.

A model gentleman-farmer, Baratynsky at this time found little leisure to write poetry. He was not very much encouraged to write by the critics either. As early as 1831 his narrative poem *The Concubine* (Nalozhnitsa), about a dark beauty who kills her unfaithful lover, trying to reconquer his love by what she believes to be a love potion, met with harsh criticism on account of its "base" plot and "rude" language; reluctantly the poet later changed the title to *The Gypsy Girl* (Tsyganka). No better was the reception of a two-volume edition of his collected works (*Stikhotvoreniya I-II*, 1835). He continued to write, however, and after a visit to his beloved St. Petersburg in 1840, when he was hailed by old friends like Zhukovsky, VYAZEMSKY and ODOEVSKY and became acquainted with the genius of LERMONTOV, he was inspired to publish his last volume of verse, bearing the pessimistic and symbolic title of *Twilight* (Sumerki, 1842). Although vehemently criticized by Belinsky for its romanticism and lack of actuality, *Twilight* is today considered to be one of the finest volumes of verse in the Russian language.

In the autumn of 1843, deeply disappointed in Moscow salons, some of which reminded him of "hospitals," others of "nurseries," Baratynsky realized a long-cherished plan, going abroad on what he called "a pilgrimage." Spending the winter in Paris, flattered by the attention paid to him by Russian émigrés and reading French translations of his poems in various salons, he established personal contacts with a number of French writers, such as Lamartine, Vigny, Nodier, and, possibly, George Sand.

Finally, in the spring of 1844, the Baratynsky family left Marseilles for Naples, the chief goal of the journey. *The Steamer* (Piroskaf), written during the voyage, is filled with new hope and zest for life. However, the end was near. Enraptured by the beauty of Naples and thriving among the carefree "children of the sun," the poet suddenly fell ill and died from a mysterious disease, at 44 years of age.

In his famous treatise *On Naive and Sentimental Poetry*, Schiller defines the contrast between the unified, "naive" poet and the divided, "sentimental" poet. While the naive poet restricts himself to spontaneous imitation of nature, the sentimental poet reflects on the impression made by nature, striving for an infinite ideal contrary to reality. In Russian literature the two foremost representatives of the Golden Age of Poetry may be taken to illustrate this typology: Pushkin is the naive poet who transforms the personal and subjective into universal and objective harmony, whereas Baratynsky expresses the yearning for this harmony, a yearning for a reconciliation with life that can never be reached. Throughout Baratynsky's life this philosophical conflict grows deeper and deeper, making him, together with Tyutchev, the most eminent poet of thought in Russian literature.

In accordance with Schiller's definition of the sentimental poet, Baratynsky set out as a writer of elegies, in which the conflict of ideal and real is predominant. Unlike less talented contemporaries whose elegies are often marred by fixed phrases and worn-out expressions, he makes the elegy an instrument for analyzing genuine feelings of sorrow and yearning. A favorite theme of his is love that is no more to be revived: "Dissuasion" (Razuverenie, 1821), "Confession" (Priznanie, 1823). The latter was judged by Pushkin to be the best elegy ever written in Russian. Treating the theme of unhappy love in its movement and development, Baratynsky's elegies have been aptly characterized by Kireevsky as "psychological miniatures."

In Baratynsky's opinion, "to express a feeling means to untie it, to command it." No wonder, then, that his poetry often attains a stern and chilly character, with a clear and dry atmosphere. Feeling is not absent from his poems: His thought is a poetically feeling thought, with the feeling as an undercurrent between theme and form, not direct, but living as an echo in the reader, behind the words. All this lends his poems a flavor of their own. A just estimate of his conscious efforts to write differently is given by Baratynsky himself: "My Muse is no raving beauty, she will never draw a throng of eager lovers after her, yet now and then the men will be struck by the uncommon expression of her face and by the calm simplicity of her speech" ("The Muse," 1828). Among these men was Pushkin: "Baratynsky belongs to the number of our excellent poets. With us he is original, for he thinks. He would be original everywhere, for he thinks in his own way, truly and independently, while he feels intensely and deeply. The harmony of his verse, the freshness of his style, the verve and precision of expression must impress everyone, even someone poorly endowed with taste and feeling."

A constant endeavor to "conquer the feeling of the heart by means of reason" makes the conflict between intellect and spontaneity the main theme in Baratynsky's poetry. His mature poems are to be regarded as philosophical poetry first and foremost. Of course, this does not imply that the poet is rhyming philosophical propositions; it is hardly possible to derive a philosophical system from his poetry. However, if the point of departure of his earlier poetry is his personal experience, the aim of his later works becomes essentially philosophical: to investigate the fate of man.

A modern reader is involuntarily struck by the immediate importance of this poetry. Thus, "The Last Death" (Poslednyaya smert', 1827) is one of the first examples of anti-utopian literature in Russia. Describing, not without pride, the achievements of industrialized and mechanized man in a distant future (people move around in aircraft and have solved the problems of hunger and overpopulation), the poet forebodes that universal happiness will be bought at the cost of all higher values and will subsequently lead to complete degeneration: indulging themselves in the pursuits of intellectual knowledge, unable to strike a balance between thought and feeling, people neglect the emotional side of their nature and die from impotence.

Related to this apocalyptic vision of inner destruction is "The Last Poet" (Poslednii poet, 1835), a disturbing description of a modern "iron age" when people, completely involved in the accumulation of goods, become utterly indifferent to "the childish dreams of poetry." However, when the poet has been driven to suicide by ridicule and contempt, people are left behind with "a yearning soul": something is obviously missing in their paradise of materialism.

On the whole, in Baratynsky's mature poetry the movement of mankind away from nature becomes a major concern. While primitive man felt an inner bond with nature, which responded to him with "mutual love," modern man puts his trust in reason and does not receive new prophecies from nature: "Omens" (Primety, 1839).

Himself an intellectual poet, Baratynsky has now become a rebel against intellect.

In a world of materialism the poet is more and more alienated. His only joy is his rhymes, and even they are voices from beyond: "Rhyme" (Rifma, 1840). Describing his alienation, the poet calls himself "a prematurely born child," "a sigh with wings" unable to find a place in either heaven or earth: "The Stillborn" (Nedonosok, 1835). There is a note of tragic irony in the description of this symbolic creature, aspiring to heaven and yet cursing the splendor of "senseless eternity"; the reader is reminded of Shakespeare's words in *Hamlet*: "What should such fellows as I do crawling between earth and heaven?"

A unique masterpiece in the grand style is "Autumn" (Osen', 1836–37), a majestic ode to dejection in which the poet compares human life to the activities of the farmer: Both have sown with hope, but whereas the farmer is rewarded by a rich harvest, the human being only faces death. The fate of man is to be alone. Even if you have gained an insight in life that might be useful to other people and the communication of which might bring you considerable relief, you have to bear the whole burden of this insight yourself: "You can never translate your Innermost into earthly sounds." Torn by inner conflicts and filled with doubts as to the meaning of life, Baratynsky found a difficult way to faith. One of his latest poems is "Prayer" (Molitva, 1842 or 1843), in which he implores "the king of heaven" to quiet his ailing spirit, and to give him strength for his "stern paradise."

Baratynsky was a Hamlet striving for harmony in a world of discord. "Oh, lyre! If I could only bestow thy harmony on life!" Outside poetry, life prevented him from reaching this harmony. He therefore felt himself entitled to meditate on life, inquiring why it was as it was, "and not otherwise." He hardly found any answer, but he posed questions that will never cease to occupy thinking and feeling people.

"It is high time that Baratynsky finally get the place on the Russian Parnassus that has long belonged to him." Today this wish of Pushkin has come true. Almost completely forgotten in the latter half of the 19th century, Baratynsky met with a triumphal revival with the SYMBOLISTS (BRYUSOV, BALMONT, BLOK), who rightfully felt him to be a forerunner of their poetic pursuits. In later years he has been highly prized by eminent poets such as MANDELSHTAM, ASEEV, and VINOKUROV. Nevertheless, Baratynsky is still little known outside Russia; in book form he is only known to have been translated into French, German and Norwegian.

Works: Polnoe sobranie stikhotvorenii. Ed. E. N. Kupreyanova. (Biblioteka poeta, Bol'shaya seriya, 2d ed.) 1957.

Translations: Lewanski, p. 199. (French:) *Recueil de poésies d'Eugène Baratinsky*. Cette, 1858. (German:) J. A. Boratynskij, *Ausgewählte Gedichte*. Introd. and trans. Heinrich Stammler. Munich, 1948. (Norwegian:) Jevgenij Baratynskij, *Stjernen*. Gjendiktning og forord ved Geir Kjetsaa. Oslo, 1977.

Secondary literature: G. R. Barratt, *Selected Letters of Evgenij Baratynskij*. The Hague, 1973. ———. "A Note on the Development of Baratynsky's Elegiac Verse," *SEER* 55 (1977), pp. 172–84. Benjamin Dees, *E. A. Baratynsky*. (Twayne's World Authors Series, 202.) 1972. Geir Kjetsaa, *Evgenii Baratynskii: Zhizn' i tvorchestvo*. Oslo, Bergen, and Tromsø, 1973. (With a comprehensive bibliography of Baratynsky's works and the literature about the poet.) Nils Åke Nilsson, "Baratynskij's Elegiac Code." In *Russian Romanticism: Studies in the Poetic Codes*. Stockholm, 1979. Pp. 144–66. Joseph Thomas Shaw, *Baratynskii: A Dictionary of the Rhymes and a Concordance to the Poetry*. (Wisconsin Slavic Publications, 3.) 1975.

G. K.

Barkóv, Iván Semyónovich (1732–68), parodic-burlesque poet. As many other Russian 18th-century literary men of plebeian origin, Barkov succeeded in securing education and high culture by dint of powerful ambitions, native abilities, and defiance of endless hardships. Employed at the Academy of Sciences in St. Petersburg, he, in connection—or parallel—with his duties, became editor-commentator of the first Russian edition of KANTEMIR and published a number of his own translations (also with commentaries) of the satires of Horace and the fables of Phaedrus. Meanwhile, he also produced, in great quantity and variety, unprintable travesties on virtually all the canonical genres of Russian classicism, their unprintabil-

ity stemming from Barkov's deliberate, unstinting use of indecent language and sexual frankness. These works circulated in manuscript collections, copies of which proliferated throughout the 18th and early 19th centuries, and were well known and much appreciated by the Russian literary community, as praises from such notables as NOVIKOV, KARAMZIN, and PUSHKIN testify. MAIKOV's masterpiece "Elisei" owed a vital debt to Barkov, as indeed did the entire, very ample parodic-burlesque tradition in Russia. The often-made claim that it was Barkov's intention to ridicule and discredit classicism overlooks the fact that classicism itself made provision for just such a tradition. Needless to say, the casual status of Barkov's main oeuvre encouraged numerous spurious accretions over time ("Barkovshchina"). Serious scholarly investigation of Barkov has only recently begun and to this time his unprinted works have been made available only in heavily censored excerpts.

Works: Poety XVIII veka. Ed. G. P. Makogonenko and I. Z. Serman. (Biblioteka poeta, bol'shaya seriya.) Leningrad, 1972.

Secondary literature: A. G. Cross, "'The Notorious Barkov': An Annotated Bibliography," *Study Group of Eighteenth Century Russia Newsletter*, 1974, no. 2, pp. 41–52. G. P. Makogonenko, "Vrag parnasskikh uz," *RLit* 7, no. 4 (1964), pp. 136–48. I. Z. Serman, "Biograficheskaya spravka." In *Poety XVIII veka*. Ed. G. P. Makogonenko and I. Z. Serman. Biblioteka poèta, bol'shaya seriya. Leningrad, 1972. Pp. 189–93.

I. R. T.

Baroque, the Russian. The baroque period in the history of Russian literature is a relatively recent (from the 1950s) and highly controversial topic whose scholarly discussion remains beset with unresolved conflicts and contradictions, with factional assumptions and prejudices, with far from adequate research, study and publication of primary materials. No summary of the Russian baroque undertaken at the present time can possibly avoid an argumentative, tentative and partisan complexion. (*Caveat emptor*.)

The fact can hardly be disputed that Russia did not participate directly in the historical developments which preceded and conditioned the emergence of the European baroque: Russia's *contemporary* experience of the Renaissance, the Reformation, the Counter-Reformation, was in every way "marginal." Nor does the known and the presumable evidence justify claiming for Russia a body of literary works equal in stature, scope, or quality to any of the baroque literatures of the West or of other Slavic peoples. To acknowledge these evident disparities in cultural development and literary inventory is not, however, tantamount to disproving the validity of recognizing an authentic baroque culture and its literary products in Russia.

At the very crux of the problem stand the characteristics of the 17th and early 18th century in Russian history—the period claimed, and denied, as that of the Russian baroque. Flanked emblematically, on the one side, by the TIME OF TROUBLES and, on the other, by the Reforms of Peter the Great, and with the Great Church Schism marking its midpoint, this era, as no other in Russian history, witnessed the fundamental dislocation, convulsion, and restructuring of the entire configuration of Russian life. It was a time of severe contradiction and struggle between the old Russian ways, whose very imperilment aroused powerful consciousness and fervor (often, and signally, of an eschatological kind), and the new Western ways which galvanized Muscovy into an empire and society within the European orbit. Of exceptional significance for developments throughout the period was Russia's confrontation with the West at the very intersection of Eastern and Western worlds—Poland and the Ukrainian and Byelorussian territories. Scene of constant wars and international diplomatic maneuverings, and of massive, virulent conflict between Orthodoxy and Catholicism, these frontiers were also, far more than anywhere else, the very corridors through which the new influences of the Western world flooded into Russia.

These turbulent, contradictory and fermentative times were reflected no less in the cultural than in the political, social and religious spheres of Russian life (indeed, such spheres were inseparable from one another). Precisely in the 17th century, upon the age-old, now decidedly parochial medieval culture of Russia converged en masse the effects of virtually all the stages of European cultural history from ancient to contemporary times which Russia had previously experienced remotely at best or not at all. The result was a radical expansion and transformation of all the arts. To speak of literature exclusively, along with the continued existence of medieval types of literature, which themselves tended to hybridization and contamination as the medieval system failed, all of the following appeared in Russia essentially for the first time: poetry as a major vehicle of literary expression with regular systems of versification and a variety of genres; dramaturgy (and all other aspects of theater, as well—professional acting, stagecraft, etc.); fiction in the then modern forms—anecdotes, tales, romances; parody, satire, facetiae—indeed, the comic in general; a host of new themes, especially that of erotic love but also a broad spectrum from secular and plebeian life; the study of letters—grammar, rhetoric, poetics, prosody. Translation, which had, of course, figured vitally in Russian medieval culture, now assumed vastly more varied dimensions.

The problem of the 17th and early 18th century, thus, principally resides in what certainly seems the period's motley, chaotic and, from the angle of European cultural history, exceedingly telescoped character. Various expedients have been proposed to contend with that problem in its literary aspect. Some scholars regard all the expansion and ferment in the literature of the period as, so to speak, eleventh-hour stirrings of the medieval system itself which, in their view, ceases only with the reforms of Peter the Great. Others mark out the 17th and early 18th century as a "period of transition" between the medieval and the modern eras in whose "pot-pourri" make-up they generously allow for an "*imported* baroque." Still others, somewhat similarly, posit three autonomous literary-cultural strains for the period—the medieval, the "democratic," and the "pre-classicist"—subsuming under the third category what the others had called "imported Baroque." Another tack altogether is taken by proponents of the idea of a Russian baroque. While acknowledging the motleyness of the constituent features of the period, they reject the notion of their autonomous, inert co-existence, seeing them rather as constituents brought into relationship by a unified system in which motleyness has functional value. The baroque, with its catholicity, its polymorphism and its capacious "accommodation of disparates," proved, they aver, such a system just as it had under different, but analogous, circumstances elsewhere. The positing of the baroque as the cultural dominant in 17th and early 18th century Russia, they argue, enables us to view, and study, the seeming miscellaneousness of the period as composing a certain order—an epochal style.

The phenomenon called the "imported baroque" provides special access to a consideration of this epochal style. The term refers to a literary repertoire derived chiefly from Polish practices as selected and codified in the pedagogy of Polish Jesuit academies and instituted, along with the whole of that pedagogy, at Ukrainian and Byelorussian schools, above all the KIEV ACADEMY (later the Moscow Academy, as well), where it evoked a flourishing baroque literary culture. Most of its practitioners in Russia were resident Ukrainian and Byelorussian clerics from the Kiev Academy, outstandingly SIMEON POLOTSKY, who, in the second half of the 17th century, together with his Russian disciples Silvestr MEDVEDEV and Karion ISTOMIN, firmly established and proliferated this writing practice in Moscow, and, in the early 18th century, Stefan YAVORSKY, Dmitry ROSTOVSKY and, partly, Feofan PROKOPOVICH. The works produced by these men represent the repertoire's range: religious tracts (mainly polemics), sermons, school dramas and, especially, syllabic verses of paraliturgical, moralistic-didactic, and panegyric kinds. This was a highly bookish literature written by erudites and polyglots (all wrote in Latin and Polish, as well), its most blatantly baroque features being a rhetorically elaborated, mannered style and frequent recourse to the ingenuities of *poesis curiosa*: acrostics, anagrams, carmina figurata, palindromes, paradoxes, paronomasias, "conceits" and the like—all features easily aligned with Western baroque practices. But far more fundamentally this literature vividly and copiously illustrates the general baroque tendency of comprehending and incorporating together the most disparate and even incongruous things, e.g., Christian dogma and the Bible/pagan mythology and philosophy, the "new science"/the old lore, humanism/mysticism, church and state ceremonials/folkways, not to speak of the spiritual/the natural, the serious/the comic, word/picture, verse/prose, etc. This constructive confrontation and combination of different types and spheres (among whose sources was the literal-moral-allegorical-anagogic hermeneutic model of the biblical exegetes) provides a poetic *differentia specifica* for the Russian 17th and early 18th century as a distinct period set off

from the staid etiquette system of the preceding medieval era and from the rationalistic decorum of the later Russian classicism which condemned baroque dynamic pluralism as "disorder" and "barbarity." Thus viewed, the "imported Baroque" becomes one key sector of a Russian literary baroque of wide and indigenous diapason.

A good deal of the poetry produced during this period is closely related to, or overlaps with, the "imported Baroque." Two poems are particularly extraordinary and exemplary as Russian baroque works. The first, of the late 17th century, the "Pentateugum," an apocalyptic vision of the "four last things" and the "vanity of human life," is a pastiche of passages from several then-renowned Western poems translated and adapted into a composite vernacular Russian/Church Slavic language by a Pole, A. Kh. Belobotsky (in its Russian spelling). The other, dated 1734, is the "Spiritual contemplation" (Umozritel'stvo dushevnoe) of the Muscovite Pyotr BUSLAEV, which, with a numerically symmetrical organization of parts and with intense drama and emotion, depicts physical death and spiritual ascension. Still another set of works of exemplary baroque character, but for different reasons, is found in the hymnography of the Monk German (1670s and 1680s) whose poetic texts mediate between elaborate acrostic designs (which can only be seen) and music (which can only be heard).

The dramaturgy of the period displays an ample, indeed sometimes lavish, multifarious and multiform complexion, both in its texts and their performance. Moreover, the seriocomic biblical and historical dramas, the mystery plays and dramatized saints' lives that made up the bulk of the repertoire were typically combined with "interludes" whose buffoonery and plebeian language and themes created complex counterpoint with the more elevated, even sacred, dramas. In the late 17th and especially in the early 18th century came translations or adaptations or original equivalents of the so-called "English comedy" with its Elizabethan style of violence, eroticism, and character psychology. During the time of Peter the Great, religious allegorical drama was transformed into political allegory and staged as outdoor public spectacles with pageantry, music, and even allegorical fireworks displays.

Prose of the 17th and early 18th century, especially parodies, satires, facetiae (many of which had verse doubles), but also the romances and adventure tales, hardly allows of isolation from the baroque under the spurious rubric "democratic literature." The very effect of these works depended on an appreciation for the sacrosanct which they travestied or the taboo which they featured, and therefore they are inextricably interrelated with the whole literary culture of the times. Some of these prose works were regular omnibuses of baroque features (including the feature of "omnibus" itself), perhaps the most outstanding in this regard being *The Tale of the Russian Cavalier Alexander* (probably 1730s).

Also hailed as "democratic literature" is the masterpiece of the era, *The Life of the Archpriest* AVVAKUM *Written by Himself* (1672–75). Generally regarded as wholly alien to the baroque of any shape or color, this work, from the point of view outlined above, proves eminently interpretable as an outstanding example precisely of the indigenous Russian baroque. Among the myriad of its other pertinent features: it is an autobiography modelled on a "life of a saint"; its language is a fabulous hybrid of Church Slavic and Russian with Biblisms and dialecticisms, even obscenities, cheek by jowl; its tone constantly swings between the author's self-abasement and his self-exaltation, between invective and endearment, between "mirth and misery" ("i smekh i gore!"); its ideological motif consists in the antinomy of glad-hearted acceptance of suffering and martyrdom and vociferous revilement of those who bring them about. The *Life* is certainly not written in the artificial, ornate, learned style of the Polotsky school but its style is unquestionably a powerful and purposeful, complexly structured rhetoric in its own terms. As A. Morozov has declared, Avvakum and Polotsky are not alien phenomena but only the different poles of the same phenomenon of the Russian baroque of the 17th century. It is hardly a mere irony of history that successors to the OLD BELIEVER leadership in the early 18th century, the Denisov brothers, the elder of whom was educated incognito at the Kiev Academy, established a school on the model of that institution at the important Old Believer settlement on the River Vyg and began the practice of writing syllabic verses!

With the rise of Classicism in the 1740s, the era of the Russian baroque may be said to come to an end but its spirit and many of its specifics continued to play a vital role in 18th-century Russian literary culture. The seminaries, particularly the Moscow Academy, remained a veritable bastion of the baroque well into the 19th century. *Poesis curiosa* found adepts even outside that domain, most remarkably in the classicist Aleksei Rzhevsky. The baroque entered as a strong component into that extraordinary and idiosyncratic poetic system concocted and practiced by V. TREDIAKOVSKY. But most importantly and powerfully the baroque predominated throughout the entire tradition of Russian panegyric and spiritual odes from LOMONOSOV to PETROV, DERZHAVIN, BOBROV, and even RADISHCHEV.

Bibliography. An exceptionally full bibliography on the baroque, including the Russian baroque, is given in: I. A. Chernov, *Iz lektsii po teoreticheskomu literaturovedeniyu. I. Barokko.* Tartu, 1976. Pp. 172–85. *Works of special importance:* D. S. Likhachev, *Razvitie russkoi literatury X-XVII vekov.* Leningrad, 1973. (Esp. Chapter 5.) A. A. Morozov, "Problema Barokko v russkoi literature XVII-nachala XVIII veka," *RLit* 5, no. 3 (1962) pp. 3–38. A. M. Panchenko, *Russkaya stikhotvornaya kul'tura XVII veka.* Leningrad, 1973. A. N. Robinson, *Bor'ba idei v russkoi literature XVII veka.* Moscow, 1974.

I. R. T.

Bátyushkov, Konstantin Nikoláevich (1787–1855), lyric poet, essayist, epistolarian. Born to an old gentry family and a nephew of the poet M. N. MURAVYOV, Batyushkov was educated at private French and Italian schools in St. Petersburg, where he acquired an excellent command of these languages. He also learned German and Latin. Batyushkov first served in the Ministry of Education, then entered the military and participated in campaigns against the French, the Swedes, and again the French. During these years he formed friendships with the poets GNEDICH, KRYLOV, ZHUKOVSKY, and VYAZEMSKY, and took part in the circle of A. N. Olenin, who arranged for him to serve in the Public Library. After reaching Paris with the victorious Russian army, he returned to Moscow and joined ARZAMAS. With his fellow Arzamasian Uvarov he translated a dozen poems from the Greek anthology (pub. 1820), and these, together with a collection of his works (1817) received virtually unanimous critical approval. Batyushkov was hailed as the cofounder, with Zhukovsky, of a new poetic school. Nevertheless, this recognition and a diplomatic post in Naples (1819–20) failed to relieve the depression and pessimism that had been building up in him since the invasion of Moscow, and he succumbed to incurable mental illness in 1822.

Batyushkov's earliest verse followed the precedent of the DMITRIEV-KARAMZIN school in its predilections for "small" genres and fugitive themes. But Batyushkov's intense commitment to perfecting a precise, harmonious language for the expression of the life, sentiments, and values of a modern poet-gentleman led him to pursue his own course of literary development through a series of creative "translations" of Tibullus, Parny, Millevoye, Petrarch, Tasso, and other Romance-language poets. This process culminated in two important poems: a deft literary satire ("A Vision on the Banks of Lethe," 1809) in which Batyushkov separated himself both from the epigones of Karamzin and from Admiral SHISHKOV and his followers; and an epistle to Zhukovsky and Vyazemsky ("My Penates," 1811) in which Batyushkov crafted, in swiftly moving iambic trimeters, a persona for himself as carefree devotee of simple pleasures, refined idleness, poetry, and friendship. Although Batyushkov's growing pessimism would subsequently find expression in elegiac themes of separation and early death, this persona formed for many contemporaries the image of Batyushkov, especially when it came to be reinforced by the sensuous concreteness of his anthology verses. It was in this poetry that Batyushkov developed the style that would have such an impact on his imitators: highly kinetic in its quick transitions, precise in linking nouns and epithets of similar semantic orders, and dedicated to rendering emotions by finely detailing physical gestures. In its harmonious sound orchestration and use of such devices as hiatus, Batyushkov's poetry struck contemporaries by its "Italian" quality.

Batyushkov's finest work of the last years, aside from his anthology translations and imitations, often took elegiac form: "On the Ruins of a Castle in Sweden" (1814) and "The Dying Tasso" (1817) are notable examples.

Batyushkov's verse had many imitators during the 1810s and 1820s, among them PUSHKIN, whose marginal notes to Batyushkov's works (1830) reveal a respectful, but critical, perspective on his tutor

in what Pushkin called the school of "harmonious precision." FET and Apollon MAIKOV learned from Batyushkov's anthology verses, and Batyushkov enjoyed renewed attention during the post-symbolist period. MANDELSHTAM's "Batyushkov" (1932) brilliantly invokes the spirit and manner of the elegist's work.

Batyushkov's "Speech on the Influence of Light Poetry on Language" (1816) served as a cultural and poetic manifesto. In it he defended the interaction through which salon society had taught poets "to fathom the secret play of passions, to observe manners, to maintain all social conventions and relationships, and to speak clearly, lightly and pleasantly." In other essays, Batyushkov moved toward what he called "the science of the poet's life," which anticipated the expression-oriented aesthetics of ROMANTICISM. In "Something About the Poet and Poetry" (1815) he manipulated the lives of a number of poets to show how they had followed his rule "live as you write and write as you live." Here—as in his essays on LOMONOSOV, KANTEMIR, and Voltaire—Batyushkov's ideal poet is a person of lively sensibility and commitment to ameliorating social conditions through the spread of enlightenment.

Batyushkov's splendid familiar letters feature keenness of observation, self-irony, and the interpenetration of literary topics and details from everyday life.

Works: Sochineniya. Ed. L. N. Maikov and V. I. Saitov. 3 vols. 1885–87. *Polnoe sobranie stikhotvorenii.* Ed. N. V. Fridman. 1964.

Translations: Lewanski, p. 200.

Secondary literature: I. Z. Serman, *Konstantin Batyushkov.* New York, 1974. N. V. Fridman, *Poeziya Batyushkova.* 1971. ———, *Proza Batyushkova.* 1965.

W. M. T.

Bédny ("Poor"), Demyán (pseud. of Efim Alekséevich Pridvórov, 1883–1945), poet and satirist. Of peasant origin, Bedny attended a school for army medics (1900–04) and served as a medic in World War I. He took courses in the humanities at Petersburg University (1904–08) and began to publish early. In 1911 his poem "On Demyan the Poor, an Ornery Fellow" (O Dem'yane Bednom, muzhike vrednom) appeared in the Bolshevik newspaper *Zvezda* and henceforth he published under the pen name Demyan Bedny. He joined the Communist Party in 1912 and was one of its most active and effective propagandists for many years, particularly during the Civil War. Bedny produced snappy propaganda jingles, catchy Red Army songs, racy satires directed at the Regime's enemies of the moment, caustic antireligious tracts, such as "New Testament, without a Flaw, of Demyan the Evangelist" (Novyi zavet bes iz"yana evangelista Dem'yana, 1925) and, first and foremost, versified journalism, following the Party line. Bedny's folksy style features a sharp ear for current usage, frequent use of the rhythms and devices of folk poetry (CHASTUSHKA, rayoshnik, song). His pieces often close in a popular saying or proverb. Bedny, who was very much in the good graces of LENIN and TROTSKY, survived a period of disgrace (including expulsion from the Party) for having vilified the Russian historical past in his libretto of a comic opera, *The Heroes* (Bogatyri) and, unlike other old Bolsheviks, lived to do his thing even during World War II.

Works: Polnoe sobranie sochinenii. 19 vols. 1925–33. *Sobranie sochinenii.* 5 vols. 1953–54. *Izbrannye proizvedeniya.* 1959.

Translations: Lewanski, p. 200.

Secondary literature: I. S. Eventov, *Dem'yan Bednyi.* 1953.

V. T.

Bégichev, Dmitry Nikitich (1786–1855), novelist. Of ancient nobility, Begichev had a successful career, first in the military and then in the civil service. He was governor of Voronezh (1830–36) and was appointed a senator in 1840. Begichev's literary fame rests with his first novel, *The Kholmsky Family: Some Traits of the Manners and Way of Life, Family and Single, of the Russian Gentry* (Semeistvo Kholmskikh: Nekotorye cherty nravov i obraza zhizni, semeinoi i odinokoi, russkikh dvoryan. 1832. 3rd ed., 1841). The novel was published anonymously and Begichev's subsequent works were signed by "Author of the Kholmsky Family." Begichev's works contain a wealth of information about the life of the Russian provincial gentry, seen with a critical eye. *The Kholmsky Family* follows the tradition of the English family novel and is a forerunner of "All's well that ends well," an early version of TOLSTOI's *War and Peace.* Tolstoi knew Begichev's work and was very much interested in it.

Bibliography: A. D. Kitina, "D. N. Begichev." In *Ocherki lite-raturnoi zhizni Voronezhskogo kraya XIX–nach. XX v.* 1970.

V. T.

Bek, Aleksándr Alfrédovich (1902–72), writer, was born in Saratov, the son of a military doctor. He participated in both the Civil War and the Second World War. Bek appeared in print for the first time in 1919, having contributed a series of sketches to his divisional newspaper. Later he published essays and reviews in various journals. From 1931, Bek served on a number of editorial staffs. The novel, *Volokalamsk Highway* (Volokalamskoe shosse, 1943–44), portrays the heroism of the defenders of Moscow in 1941. Sequels to the work are the tales, "A Few Days" (Neskol'ko dnei, 1960) and "General Panfilov's Reserves" (Rezerv generala Panfilova, 1960).

Bek's interest in the efforts of the Soviet worker and in problems of technological creativity is reflected in such works as "Kurako" (about a Soviet hero of labor, 1934), in the collection, *Blast Furnace Workers* (Domenshchiki, 1946), and in the novel, *Young Folk* (Molodye lyudi, 1954, in collaboration with N. Loiko). Bek's concern with problems of innovation in technology is central to his documentary novel, *The Life of Berezhkov* (Zhizn' Berezhkova, 1956), in which, as in many other of his works, fictional portraits are interwoven with depictions of historical figures. Soviet criticism credits Bek with the ability to write about the worker and the challenges facing him in an engaging manner, thus demonstrating his view that labor is the central feature of human existence. Bek's novel, *The New Appointment* (Novoe naznachenie), a *roman à clef* about I. Tevosyan, Minister of Steel Production under Stalin, appeared in the West in 1972, its publication in the Soviet Union having been blocked (in 1965) by Tevosyan's widow.

Works: Moi geroi: Povesti. 1967. *Pochtovaya proza.* 1968. *Sobranie sochinenii.* 1971. *Novoe naznachenie.* Frankfurt, 1972.

Translations: Lewanski, p. 200.

Secondary literature: T. A. Khmel'nitskaya, "A. Bek, Volokalamskoe shosse," *Zvezda,* 1945, no. 3. I. Sakharova, "Neispol'zovannye vozmozhnosti," *Oktyabr',* 1955, no. 1. Anatolii Mednikov, "Voennye fotografii," *VLit* 22 (1978), no. 5, pp. 225–38.

D. K. D.

Belínsky, Vissarión Grigórievich (1811–48), important and influential critic of the first half of the 19th century, the first professional Russian critic, and the founder of (in Marxist-Leninist terms) "revolutionary-democratic" criticism. Born in Sveaborg (Finland) the son of a doctor, Belinsky attended Moscow University for three years but was expelled before taking a degree. (He had written a play critical of serfdom.) His incomplete formal education was well supplemented, however, by extensive reading throughout the remaining years of his life. In 1833 he began to write for NADEZHDIN's TELESKOP, but this journal was suppressed in 1836 for publishing CHAADAEV's *Philosophical Letter.* In 1838 he became editor of the *Moskovskii nablyudatel',* but this publication lasted only a year. In 1839 Belinsky moved to St. Petersburg, becoming chief critic for OTECHESTVENNYE ZAPISKI. In 1846 NEKRASOV invited him to join the staff of the SOVREMENNIK. Suffering from tuberculosis, Belinsky went abroad briefly in 1847 and died the following year at St. Petersburg shortly after his return to Russia.

Belinsky's life and career were short but exemplarily arduous and *engagé.* This intense engagement in the study of literature and its place in Russian life earned him the epithet of *neistovyi* ("frenzied"), while contemporaries as different in outlook as HERZEN and TURGENEV have the highest praise for him, both as man and as critic. To the present day, even among scholars opposed to Marxist-Leninist literary and critical canons and who decry Belinsky's execrable style, his critical acumen is frequently lauded: "His judgments on writers who began their work between 1830 and 1848 may be accepted almost without qualification. This is high praise for a critic, and one that few deserve." (Mirsky) Nevertheless, Belinsky's judgment was on occasion fallible and, in one or two instances, absurd (especially from the 20th-century Western point of view). But Belinsky, we should remember, was engaged in the most challenging and risky form of criticism, namely, the judgment and evaluation of the works (often on their first appearance in print) of contemporary writers, a form of criticism many critics cautiously avoid. It is much safer to write learned articles on writers of the past whose reputations, one way or the other, were established years or even centuries ago.

Belinsky's name is closely associated with and representative of four important aspects of Russian intellectual history in the early decades of the 19th century. He was, first, an *intelligent* (or member of the *intelligentsia*), that is, an educated member of society but one with radical political views. Second, he was a RAZNOCHINETS—in his case, a man of other than gentry or noble origin who entered upon a career not traditional for his class. Third, he was a *zapadnik* or "WESTERNIZER," holding (as opposed to the SLAVOPHILES) that Russia must continue to borrow from and maintain affiliations with the intellectual currents of Western Europe. And, fourth, Belinsky as thinker and critic was greatly influenced by and indebted to German romantic/idealist thought, which was, without exaggeration, inundating Russian intellectual life in the 1830s. Indeed, his career as a critic is frequently divided into phases, varying according to the particular German ideology of interest to him at any given time, whether that of Schiller, Schelling, Fichte, or Hegel. In general, this German philosophy or metaphysic offered an organic (or holistic) interpretation of the whole of reality, something which lent it the qualities and the appeal of a substitute religion. This organic outlook, especially that of Schelling's *Naturphilosophie,* is clearly evident at the very beginning of (e.g., in "Literary Reveries," 1834) and throughout Belinsky's career as a critic, while his attitude towards Schiller almost exactly parallels that of DOSTOEVSKY.

All of Belinsky's important theoretical canons of analysis and judgment—his views, for instance, on such polar concepts as form/content, universals/particulars, objective/subjective art, prose/poetry, etc.—are also of German inspiration and are often treated as sequiturs of organicism. But whereas "orthodox" organicism sees a work of art as an organic whole and would require a merging and equating of form and content, of universals and particulars (the "concrete universal"), Belinsky in fact almost always gives priority to content over form and stresses universal concepts. Thus he sees an ideal marriage of the universal and the particular in Walter Scott's novels (immensely popular in Russia) but distinguishes between the genius of PUSHKIN and that of LERMONTOV by asserting that the latter was inferior to Pushkin in form but superior in content. When Lermontov's *A Hero of Our Time* appeared in 1840, it was criticized by many as a distortion of reality and for lacking unity; but Belinsky reviewed it enthusiastically and defended its unity in no uncertain terms. It should be pointed out here that the pre-eminence of such writers as Pushkin, Lermontov, GOGOL, Dostoevsky, Turgenev, GONCHAROV, and Nekrasov in subsequent Russian letters is in considerable part due to Belinsky's favorable reviews and judgments (along with outspoken criticism when this was pertinent).

Another concept of German origin taken up by Belinsky (in, for example, "The Idea of Art," 1841) is the definition of art as "thinking in images" (*myshlenie v obrazakh*). This formula, handy but not very helpful, has had a long history in subsequent Russian aesthetics and criticism and is still especially favored in present-day Soviet Russian critical and aesthetic theory. For Belinsky, the ability to think in images constituted what we call the creative imagination. For this latter concept he sometimes uses the word *voobrazhenie* and sometimes *fantaziya,* but he does not elaborate on essential differences as Coleridge does (whose debt to German thought in this area is also considerable). Colored, too, by earlier German thought is Belinsky's concern for types: the true literary artist must be able to create types or symbolic characters which are both specifically individual and of general or universal significance—such as Shakespeare's Hamlet or even Gogol's Lt. Pirogov in "Nevsky Prospect."

Belinsky had little sympathy for Old Russian literature or for 18th-century pseudoclassical literature or for works reflecting this earlier world. In his 1840 essay on GRIBOEDOV's classical comedy in verse, *Woe from Wit,* Belinsky contrasts this work with Gogol's *Inspector General* and finds the latter superior: Gogol's play represents a "closed world" with a central idea and a central figure, a totality that "resembles reality more than reality itself," whereas Griboedov's comedy is merely clever satire of an earlier society and lacks universal significance. But most modern Western critics would, we think, reverse this particular judgment. It is in his essay on *Woe from Wit* that Belinsky makes a most revealing statement: "A man drinks, eats, and dresses—this is a world of phantoms ... but a man feels, thinks, and recognizes himself as an organ, a vessel of the spirit, a finite particle of the general and infinite—this is the world of reality (*deistvitel'nost'*)." This both reminds us of earlier German "romantic realism" (e.g., Novalis) and suggests something akin to what is really meant by "SOCIALIST REALISM." It is also clear from this statement that Belinsky would automatically reject—as in fact he did—what we call NATURALISM (in, say, the manner of Zola).

Belinsky wrote almost a dozen articles on Pushkin whom he acknowledged as Russia's national poet. Although he criticized Pushkin's works as inferior to those of Lermontov in significant, relevant content, and in fact (this is one of Belinsky's *gaffes*, fit for inclusion in something like Henri Peyre's *The Failures of Criticism*) ranked him lower than Walter Scott and George Sand, he nevertheless recognized a universal quality in the poet. For Belinsky, Pushkin's poetry (to borrow a phrase from one of Pushkin's own poems, *Rus'yu pakhnet*) "smells of Russia," and yet has an appeal for all men. Pushkin, furthermore, is a poet of objective reality, little given to metaphysical or other reflections, even though there is everywhere evidence of his gentry connections and even though the particularly French 18th-century background, so inimical to Belinsky, is apparent in Pushkin's very language. But still, since the form of Pushkin's verse is superb, he is essentially an artist; here Belinsky comes close to praising Pushkin in terms of pure aestheticism, something he elsewhere resolutely condemns.

Belinsky's comments on Gogol are perhaps his most controversial. In the 1840s another critic, Faddei BULGARIN, referred disparagingly to a group of writers, including Gogol, as the "natural school." Belinsky seized upon the term "natural" and employed it in a positive, laudatory sense as a synonym for "realistic." As noted above, Belinsky considered Gogol's *Inspector General* superior to *Woe from Wit*; he also thought highly of *Dead Souls*. While other critics (such as SHEVYRYOV) recognized—as we do today—that Gogol was a romantic writer par excellence, a master of the grotesque and the absurd, Belinsky insisted almost perversely that it was "Russian reality," with all its hateful aspects, that was reflected in Gogol's works and that the author himself was a great social critic. Belinsky does not even recognize the satire in *Dead Souls* but refers (in Hegelian terms) to its *pafos* (pathos). In distinguishing—not always too clearly—between "real" and "ideal" literature (which distinction comes from Friedrich Schlegel and recalls Schiller's earlier one between "naive" and "sentimental" art), Belinsky believed that "real" literature reflects or deals with life, while "ideal" literature is concerned primarily with ideas. Thus *Don Quijote, Evgeny Onegin,* and *Dead Souls*, for example, are "real," while Goethe's *Faust* is "ideal." For Belinsky, Gogol was moreover the founder of Russian realism and a greater writer than Pushkin in the sense that he was (in the 1840s) more socially relevant. True, Gogol does not have the universality of Pushkin and is, in Belinsky's view, primarily a Russian national genius. But there is no consideration of foreign literary influences (such as the writings of E. T. A. Hoffmann) on Gogol and no appreciation of Gogol's Ukrainian background (Belinsky's harsh criticism of the great Ukrainian poet SHEVCHENKO is a serious blot on his reputation).

Belinsky did not live long enough to know Dostoevsky's major novels, but he wrote favorably of Dostoevsky's *Poor Folk* (1846), since it showed an awareness of social ills as well as humanitarian sympathies; but when Dostoevsky's fantasy, *The Double*, appeared later in 1846, Belinsky reacted negatively (and, indeed, this work by Dostoevsky even today strikes a mature reader as inchoate, derivative, and amateurish). Belinsky, however, objected mainly to the elements of irrational fantasy and, especially, to the theme of insanity which, he felt, had no place in literature. Yet in reviewing Nekrasov's almanac *Peterburgskii sbornik* (in which *Poor Folk* had appeared) Belinsky prophesied about the *future* fame of Dostoevsky and this is often cited in support of the critic's perspicuity. Nor did Belinsky know the major novels of Turgenev. He reviewed enthusiastically such early poetic works by Turgenev as *Parasha* (1843) and *A Conversation* (1845) but very soon his enthusiasm cooled and he felt that Turgenev lacked true poetic talent. But the two remained friends and Turgenev's admiration for Belinsky, for his enthusiasm and devotion to literature, was immense. (One of the most sympathetic memoirs we have of Belinsky is that included in Turgenev's *Literary Reminiscences*). Belinsky personally disliked GONCHAROV and knew only his first novel, *The Same Old Story* (1847). This he recognized as an example of "mere" or objective art, but a work by a man of talent and it

is this talent or artistry which makes up for, in part at least, the absence of ideas.

As we have seen, Belinsky was an outspoken critic of naturalism, of romantic escapism, of "pure" or autotelic art, and of mere, irrational fantasy in literature; he could, however, accept certain romantic elements, provided these were balanced by or, rather, organically and artistically combined with a serious concern for real life. Although Belinsky had a keen sense of style and differentiated between language and style (*slog*), he neither devoted attention to anything approaching an analysis of the language and the linguistic style of those Russian authors he considers; nor did he pay any attention to polishing or refining his own style as a critic. The reason for Belinsky's negligence in these matters is again his dominating concern for content and for language used to communicate and not as an end in itself. As for Belinsky's own style, it is frequently criticized (especially in the West) as labored, diffuse, repetitive, journalistic, and as having had a pernicious influence on the language of subsequent Russian literary criticism. But it should be pointed out that the late Soviet scholar, Viktor VINOGRADOV, in his *History of the Russian Literary Language*, writes that Belinsky "refashioned the Russian literary language" and ascribes great importance to the critic for having introduced into Russian usage a large body of abstract philosophical and literary terminology. We must note, too, the excellent example of Belinsky's passionate, condemnatory rhetoric in his famous "Letter to N. V. Gogol" (1847), written in answer to Gogol's *Selected Passages from Correspondence with Friends*: here Belinsky castigates Gogol for his betrayal of both literature and the Russian people. (It was for a reading of this prohibited letter at a meeting of the Petrashevsky Circle that Dostoevsky was arrested in 1849.)

So far as Belinsky's legacy is concerned, his approach and methods set the tone for the bulk of later 19th-century Russian literary criticism and, following the Revolution, these became a central part of official Marxist-Leninist "socialist realist" aesthetic and critical theory. His principal epigones in the 19th century were the Civic Critics who narrowed the Belinskian focus, emphasized the utilitarian aspects of literature, and, in one case (PISAREV), produced something close to a *reductio ad absurdum*. The so-called Aesthetic Critics (e.g., BOTKIN, ANNENKOV, DRUZHININ) and the Symbolists turned their attention, to some extent, away from the social significance of literature and gave greater emphasis to literary form and to personal aesthetic sensibilities. But the major reaction (in some ways, an overreaction) against the Belinskian heritage was that of the FORMALISTS of the early 20th century and their few successors among the émigrés and within Soviet Russia itself. Formalism, however, has been officially condemned and the Soviet STRUCTURALISTS take great pains to disavow any connection with it.

Works: Polnoe sobranie sochinenii. 13 vols. 1953–59. *Works in English: Selected Philosophical Works.* Moscow, 1956. *Belinsky, Chernyshevsky, and Dobrolyubov: Selected Criticism.* Ed. R. Matlaw. 1962.

Secondary Literature: P. V. Annenkov, *The Extraordinary Decade.* Ed. A. P. Mendel. 1968. Herbert Bowman, *Vissarion Belinski, 1811–1848: A Study in the Origins of Social Criticism in Russia.* 1954. Thelwall Proctor, *Dostoevskij and the Belinskij School of Literary Criticism.* The Hague, 1969. R. Stacy, *Russian Literary Criticism: A Short History.* 1974. Chap. 3. Victor Terras, *Belinskij and Russian Literary Criticism: The Heritage of Organic Aesthetics.* 1974. *Turgenev's Literary Reminiscences.* Trans. David Magarshack. 1968. Chap. 2. René Wellek, *A History of Modern Criticism, 1750–1950.* 1955–65. Vol. 3, chap. 7.   R. H. S.

Bell, The see *Kolokol*.

Belóv, Vasíly Ivánovich (1932–   ), writer. Of peasant background, Belov began to publish early (1956) and graduated from the Gorky Institute of Literature in 1964. But he has spent much of his life in his native Vologda, in the North of Russia, whose nature and people are the subject of most of his works. Belov's long short-story "That's How Things Are" (Privychnoe delo, 1966) is considered the beginning of the new "COUNTRY PROSE," one of whose leading exponents Belov has remained to date. In a series of subsequent works, such as *A Carpenter's Tales* (Plotnitskie rasskazy, 1968), *Vologda Whimsies* (Bukhtiny vologodskie, 1969), and *The Eve* (Kanuny, 2 vols. 1972–

77), a "historical novel" set in the days of Collectivization of Agriculture (1928–29), Belov probes deeply into the effects of collectivization, urbanization, and destruction of old ways (including religion) on the Russian countryside and its inhabitants. His works are clearly in violation of the "socialist" component of the canon of SOCIALIST REALISM, in that human problems and relationships are viewed without regard to the progress of Soviet society towards communism. Although no explicit political statement is made in these works, their message is that the Russian peasant may still possess values which are incompatible with the official ideology, and that ignoring these values has been a mistake on the part of the Soviet regime. Belov is anything but an unsophisticated or provincial writer. Ostensibly regional and socially limited, his fiction is replete with allusions and ambiguities which conjure much broader issues. Belov's reflective and lyric passages are done with skillful precision, and while he introduces a great deal of local color and uses many of the devices of prose folklore, the implied author created by him is modern and sophisticated.

Works: Sel'skie povesti. 1971. *Kholmy: Povesti i rasskazy.* 1973. *Tseluyutsya zori ... Povesti i rasskazy.* 1975.

Secondary literature: Deming Brown, *Soviet Literature since Stalin.* 1978. Pp. 245–49. Geoffrey A. Hosking, "Vasilii Belov, Chronicler of the Soviet Village," *RusR* 34 (1975), pp. 165–85. ———, *Beyond Socialist Realism: Soviet Fiction since Ivan Denisovich.* 1980. Pp. 57–70. (With bibliography, pp. 226–29.) T. V. Krivoshchapova, "Rol' prozaicheskikh fol'klornykh zhanrov v tvorchestve Vasiliya Belova," *Vestnik Moskovskogo Universiteta* (filologiya), 1976, no. 4, pp. 33–44. Larisa Kuznetsova, "Semeinaya zhizn' Konstantina Zorina," *Literaturnoe obozrenie,* no. 5 (1977), pp. 56–60. V. T.

Bély, Andreí (pseud. of Bugáev, Boris Nikoláevich, 1880–1934), a leading representative of Russian SYMBOLISM, poet, novelist, literary critic, polemicist, and theorist. Born on 26 October 1880, Bely was the only child of Nikolai Vasilievich Bugaev, a well-known mathematician at Moscow University, and of his wife Aleksandra Dmitrievna, a beautiful society woman with considerable musical talent. They were an ill-matched pair: the eccentric, autocratic, but brilliant father was deeply committed to the natural sciences and to his own mathematics, while the emotionally unstable mother apparently feared these rational disciplines and proclaimed—often with the vigor of hysteria—her own highly subjective allegiance to the arts. A precocious, impressionable child, Bely was often both victim and prize in family frays, as his loving but possessive parents sought to shape him in their own images. As an adult Bely was both quirky and capable of sustained, concentrated labor, both emotionally volatile and intellectually gifted, in many ways a predictable and yet altogether unusual amalgam of these parental impresses.

Quite out of the ordinary was Bely's ability to discern in his childhood the collision of principles ultimately of historical and metaphysical significance (e.g., *At the Turn of the Century,* 1930). Rationalism versus emotionalism, harmonious order versus chaotic disorder, creation versus destruction, love versus hatred, morality versus amorality, unity and community versus distintegration and estrangement—these dualities and their corollaries were at the center of Bely's vision; they are also familiar rubrics attached to fundamental tensions and currents of thought in modern psychology, philosophy, and theology. These antinomies have their primary historical source in the scientific revolution, the complex, mutually reinforcing aftershocks of which contributed substantially to the shape of the intellectual history in Russia to which Bely was an heir. A scientifically based vision of cosmic chaos, of aimless and meaningless causation, contended with a variety of philosophical and theological efforts to discover behind the mask of causality a mysterious Meaning beyond reason, or to affirm man's capacity to create meaning for himself. As a young man Bely was influenced by both Russian and Western thinkers who reflected these general tendencies (Schopenhauer, Nietzsche, SOLOVYOV, and Kant); their often disharmonious cosmologies continued to manifest themselves indirectly in certain problems which arise in his literary and especially philosophical efforts to discover and describe a principle of synthesis powerful enough to reconcile all contradictions. Bely's childhood also seemed particularly auspicious to him because of the Symbolist *fin de siècle* mentality itself, in which apocalyptic premonitions mixed foreboding with exhilaration in contemplating history's imminent demise: All contradictions, all that militates against reconciliation, against community, communion, and oneness will—perhaps—disappear in the catastrophic dawn of the Millennium.

Although Bely graduated from Moscow University in 1903 with a degree in the natural sciences, an interest he retained, he had already begun his literary career, most importantly in his work on his four prose *Symphonies* (the *First* and the *Second* appeared in 1903 and 1902 respectively). Owing to their experimental, "decadent" character, he published them under a pseudonym, perhaps to avoid embarrassing his father, who had not been hindered in his rise to Dean of the University by his quite pedestrian literary tastes. An older friend of the family, Mikhail Solovyov, the younger brother of the famous philosopher Vladimir Solovyov, had proposed the name Andrei Bely (Andrew White); more importantly, he gave Bely encouragement as well as direct contact with a thinker who was to influence his thought significantly, especially with regard to the principle of duality as it manifests itself in the nature of the universe and in history. In particular Bely was moved, like other Symbolists, by Solovyov's understanding of cosmological and historical process as a movement toward reunification with God. This apotheosis will reconcile the transcendent "all-in-oneness" (*vseedinstvo*) of the Divine Logos the multiplicity of the phenomenal world and, with regard to human history, the endless contradictions, symbolized by Christ and Antichrist, which spring from man's spiritual aspirations, his freedom, and his egotism. Solovyov also spoke of a world-soul, the common subject uniting all creatures, which once voluntarily separated itself from God (who in his love grants creation freedom) but which is linked again to the Divine Logos through Christ; this, as it were, "resurrected" world-soul is manifest in SOPHIA—Holy Wisdom, the Eternal Feminine—whose appearance heralds the advent of the Millennium and final reunification, who mysteriously embodies the goal of history. This vision of a "Lady Most Beautiful," a "Woman Clothed in the Sun," became an evocative symbol for several symbolists (Bely included); their passionate engagement with such eschatological thinking also explains in part the popularity of imagery drawn from the Book of Revelation in symbolist poetry.

The period 1903 to 1910 was an astonishingly productive one for Bely; he published over two hundred articles, book reviews, and essays, as well as three collections of poetry and two more *Symphonies.* But the apocalyptic promise which he and his associates had discerned in the revolution of 1905 had not been fulfilled, and sectarian squabbles were fragmenting the symbolist movement. Bely's frenetic activities both reflected and stoked the fires of these controversies, while his frequently irregular personal life exacerbated tensions which kept him near the brink of physical and mental exhaustion. Especially painful was his relationship with the great poet Aleksandr BLOK and his wife Lyubov, which began propitiously in 1903 but degenerated by 1905 into something bizarre and almost farcical. The hothouse atmosphere in which disputes were conducted and the intensity with which these intellectuals not only thought but lived their ideas can be seen in Bely's identification of Lyubov Blok with the Divine Sophia, and in the worshipful service of love he dedicated to her. (Bely finally fled to Germany to escape the impossible situation.)

However peculiar his behavior at times, Bely was engaged in a fervent spiritual quest that depended on ideas always open to question. The resultant strain, extended over years, may explain his rather sudden, lengthy immersion in Rudolph Steiner's anthroposophical "Spiritual Science," beginning in 1912. Accompanied by Asya Turgeneva, whom he now considered his wife, Bely met Steiner in Europe and quickly fell under his influence. Bely spent four years abroad, studying Steiner's occult teachings, taking lessons in German, and even assisting in the construction of the Anthroposophical Temple in Dornach, Switzerland.

In 1916 Bely was called to military service. Leaving Asya in Switzerland, he returned to Russia but somehow avoided the army. During the period of revolution and civil war, he earned a paltry living as an archivist and librarian while lecturing under the auspices of the Free Philosophical Society (Vol'fila), of which he was a founder, and at the House of Arts and the Academy of Spiritual Culture. Bely's lectures generally dealt with literary topics or with the anthroposophical ideas he was committed to propagating in Russia. Like many other established writers he also worked for PROLETKUL'T, primarily as a critical reader of manuscripts. With regard to the Revolution itself, Steiner's conception of a process of cosmic evolution punctuated by violent periods of transition contributed to the reawakening of Bely's old apocalyptic visions; at first he understood the upheaval as a spiritual apotheosis, a synthesis emerging from the ancient antinomy of matter and spirit ("Christ is Risen," 1918). But events belied his hopes, and his euphoria waned as his mental condition worsened. By 1921, when he returned to Europe, Bely was often behaving in an erratic, anti-social manner, and his mood was not improved by Steiner's cool reception and Asya's refusal to renew their relationship. But another woman, Klavdiya Vasilieva, accompanied him on his return to Russia in 1923, where they were married. There he lived quietly, trying to avoid political difficulties and continuing to write. During his final decade Bely completed the trilogy of Moscow novels, three volumes of memoirs, a new study of poetry and another on Gogol.

Ironically, Bely's pronounced literary influence on others was primarily stylistic, not ideological; and yet his own works cannot be understood adequately without reference to philosophy. Both the dualism prominent in his thinking and his sense of being caught in the "scissors" of historical crisis, at the explosion point between moribund past and nascent future, were noted above (e.g., *At the Turn of the Century* [literally, *On the Boundary of Two Centuries*] and *Between Two Revolutions*, 1934); so too was his compulsive desire to locate a principle of synthesis which would transfigure existence forever. However, Bely's approach to these problems was fundamentally epistemological, and he found the necessary principle in mind, not matter. He was thus inclined to recognize the symptoms of historical crisis primarily in man's disrupted inner life, especially in the paralysis induced by dualistic thinking. Such thinking represents an inadequate understanding of the world; it can be rectified only by the spiritual transformation of man himself by himself, so that he might then transform the world: "The transformation of the reality outside us depends on the transformation of the reality within us" (*Symbolism*, 1914).

This idealist perspective places special value upon the artist; it also kept Bely forever on the brink of subjectivism and relativism. His orientation was toward the experiencing consciousness: It is in the experience of reality that consciousness brings meaningful order to its own, otherwise chaotic, contents—a process which is fundamentally creative. Cognition is a second step, generating "symbols" of human creativity which produce a meaningful, value-bearing, objective reality. All creative activity, and especially art, produces symbols, which are a synthesis of mind-generated form and of content taken from reality. Inasmuch as thought is primary in this fusion, it follows that true reality is made and transformed by human creativity, especially the artist's; Bely therefore found himself between the philosophical tendencies noted above: Man creates meaning for himself in the context of chaos; and belief in a transcendent Meaning inaccessible to scientific reason. Although Bely's critics pointed out that his philosophical position could not lead to God, he preferred to argue that man is the agent of the Divine Logos in his acts of creation. Human creation thus becomes the process of reunification with God. This statement of faith apparently has its source in St. John's identification of the "Word" (Logos) with Christ and with God, the principle of ultimate meaning (John 1 : 1). While admitting the importance of religious affirmation for Bely, his epistemologically centered thought often pressed him toward solipsism in his own art.

With a few exceptions, Bely's most memorable verse was written early in his career, when the Symbolist poets dominated the Russian literary scene. The title of his first collection, *Gold in Azure* (Zoloto v lazuri, 1904), alludes directly to Solovyov's ideas and to his famous poem "Three Encounters," in which the poet meets the "Woman Clothed in the Sun." Sun imagery and an array of symbolic colors are major vehicles here for Bely's apocalyptic anticipation of the New Age. The sun remained the center of a constellation of imagery involving light and color in his work, and in his life as well (e.g., his fanatical dedication to sunbathing); his next two collections, *Ashes* and *The Urn* (Pepel and Urna, both 1909), were pessimistic extensions of this central symbol. The exuberance and affirmation inherent in a golden sunset in an azure sky are replaced here by images of deep twilight, cold, violence, and destruction; the forces of chaos and death turn the poet's anguished attention to the suffering of his people in the first volume, and provoke melancholy philosophical

meditations in the second. These collections are, on one level, a record of Bely's emotional and philosophical experience between the advent of the 1905 revolution and his immersion in anthroposophy.

Other, later collections (*The Princess and Her Knights*—Korolevna i rytsari, 1919, *The Star*—Zvezda, 1922, *After Parting*—Posle razluki, 1922) are interesting primarily as experimental extensions of Bely's earlier poetic innovations and as they reflect his more recent theoretical ideas on versification. Few readers find these later poems emotionally affective, however, with the single great exception of "The First Encounter" (Pervoe svidanie, 1921), a verse memoir in four parts which is widely viewed as Bely's finest poetic achievement.

Bely's experiments with rhythm, sound, and typography in poetry carried into his prose, for indeed he made no essential distinction between the two. The four *Symphonies*, written between 1899 and 1908, represented in part a response to Solovyov's principle of "all-in-oneness," as they attempted to create a new unitary form which fused poetry, prose, and music. All except the *Third* were structured in imitation of the four movements of the classical symphony, reflecting the special importance Bely (and some other Symbolists) attached to music as the supreme art form. The thematic complexity of the *Symphonies* taken together is suggested, for example, by the recurrent image in them of Sophia, in both serious and satirical incarnations. Dreams that touch the absolutely real and dreams that plunge into illusion and madness reflect the estrangement of this world from *that* one, and they point to the rich development of this theme in later works, especially in *Petersburg*. Although Bely abandoned overt imitation of musical form after completing the *Fourth Symphony* in 1908, he continued to utilize techniques developed in these works. Beyond the categories noted above, critics have discussed his intricate and involute use of the leitmotif, sometimes extended into entire passages which are repeated with, or without, thematically significant alteration.

The Silver Dove (Serebryanyi golub', 1910) draws its material from the Russian intelligentsia's movement "to the people," which began during the 19th century largely in response to ideas associated with SLAVOPHILISM, one major source of the revolutionary tradition. Bely's use of revolutionary intrigues and activities in his plots follows logically from his ideas. But the inherent interest of such materials is sometimes reduced by the astonishing verbal virtuosity, and occasionally the overwrought embellishments, of his ornamental prose. In *The Silver Dove*, the variety of narrative styles partially obscures a story about a young poet, disenchanted with urban life, who joins a group of peasant religious sectarians and is murdered by them after he fails to sire a new Savior by one of their women. The second volume grew into *Petersburg*, considered by many to be one of the 20th century's great novels. Of its five editions (one posthumous, in 1935), those of 1916 and 1922 are usually preferred, the latter being the shorter by one-third. Probably no single work had a greater impact on postrevolutionary writers familiar with symbolism's allusive, ornamental treatment of historical themes (e.g., PILNYAK). In scope the novel encompasses by implication all of Western European culture set against the dark, anarchic forces of Mongolianism, and compresses it into a year of historical crisis, 1905. During that revolutionary year the city's inhabitants are being torn to pieces by dualistic forces that are manifested politically, socially, and above all psychologically. At the center of this spiritual-historical powder keg is a bomb in fact and in symbol, to be delivered to a high official by his own half-demented, neo-Kantian son. The geometrically precise city, long before Bely a symbol of Russia's cultural schizophrenia, is now sinking into the amorphous swamp upon which it was once raised by Peter I, whose great statue moves menacingly at times through the spectral landscape.

Themes with epistemological relevance such as dementia and illusion or intuition and prophecy are the principal links between *Petersburg* and *Kotik Letaev* (1922), which depicts the emergence of self-consciousness in a small boy. The novel's material is fundamentally autobiographical, reflecting Bely's own "family apocalypse." It has been praised for its insights into child psychology, its harmonious blending of prose and poetry, and its accretionary integration of a complex symbolic system through an expanding spiral structure which encloses ever larger areas of experience. Its sequel, *The Baptized Chinaman* (Kreshchenyi kitaets, 1922), deals with a subsequent stage in Kotik's development; its title once again refers to the fundamental, many-faceted dualism comprised by the symbols East and West in Bely's work. This work and the trilogy of Moscow novels written during his last period (*The Moscow Eccentric* [*Moskovskii chudak*, 1926], *Moscow Under Siege* [*Moskva pod udarom*, 1926], *Masks* [*Maski*, 1931]) are considered less successful than *Petersburg* and *Kotik Letaev*; they have also received less scholarly attention. The interiorization of experience, evident in the earlier works, becomes more pronounced in the later works, despite plots that incorporate sensational events and dark intrigues. Their further study from the perspective of epistemology will undoubtedly uncover features of considerable interest.

Bely wrote four famous, but factually unreliable, volumes of memoirs: *Recollections of A. A. Blok* (*Vospominaniya ob A. A. Bloke*, 1922), *At the Turn of the Century* (*Na rubezhe dvukh stoletii*, 1930), *The Beginning of the Century* (*Nachalo veka*, 1933), and *Between Two Revolutions* (*Mezhdu dvukh revolyutsii*, 1934). He also produced a significant study of Gogol (*Masterstvo Gogolya*, 1934) and investigations of verse rhythm which were important initiatives in the study of this problem of poetics.

Works: (The following bibliographical listing includes most of the works mentioned above; listings including lesser works can be found in the critical literature.) *Chetyre simfonii*. Munich, 1971. *Khristos voskres*. Ann Arbor, 1971. *Kotik Letaev*. Munich, 1964. *Korolevna i rytsari*. Tumba, Sweden, 1968. Microfiche. *Kreshchenyi kitaets*. Munich, 1969. *Maski*. Munich, 1969. *Masterstvo Gogolya*. Munich, 1969. *Mezhdu dvukh revolyutsii*. Chicago, 1966. *Moskva*. Ann Arbor, 1969. *Na perevale*. Ann Arbor, 1970. *Na rubezhe dvukh stoletii*. Chicago, 1966. *Nachalo veka*. Chicago, 1966. *Pamyati Aleksandra Bloka*. Paris, 1971. *Pepel*. Tumba, Sweden, 1968. Microfiche. *Pervoe svidanie*. Tel-Aviv, 1970. *Peterburg*. Letchworth, 1967. *Serebryanyi golub'*. Munich, 1967. *Simvolizm*. Munich, 1969. *Stikhotvoreniya i poemy*. Leningrad, 1966. *Urna*. Ann Arbor, 1970. *Zapiski chudaka*. Letchworth, 1973. *Zoloto v Lazuri*. Ann Arbor, 1970.

Translations: *St. Petersburg*. Trans. John Cournos. New York, 1957. *Kotik Letaev*. Ann Arbor, 1971. *The Silver Dove*. New York, 1974. *Petersburg*. Trans. John Malmstad and Robert Maguire. Bloomington, Ind., 1977. *The First Encounter*. Princeton, 1979. *See also Lewanski*, p. 201.

Secondary literature: B. Christa, *The Poetic World of Andrey Bely*. Amsterdam, 1977. S. Cioran, *The Apocalyptic Symbolism of Andrej Belyj*. The Hague, 1973. J. Elsworth, *Andrey Bely*. Letchworth, 1972. ———, "Andrei Bely's Theory of Symbolism," *Forum for Modern Language Studies* 11 (1975). J. Holthusen, *Studien zur Ästhetik und Poetik des russischen Symbolismus*. Göttingen, 1957. G. Janecek, ed., *Andrey Bely: A Critical Review*. Lexington, Ky., 1978. ———, "An Acoustico-Semantic Complex in Belyj's *Kotik Letaev*," *SEEJ* 18 (1974), pp. 153–59. S. Karlinsky, "Symphonic Structure in Andrej Belyj's 'Pervoe svidanie,'" *California Slavic Studies* 6 (1971). A. Kovac, *Andrej Belyj: The "Symphonies" (1899–1908): A Re-Evaluation of the Aesthetic-Philosophical Heritage*. Bern, 1976. O. Maslenikov, *The Frenzied Poets: Andrej Biely and the Russian Symbolists*. Berkeley, 1952. K. Mochul'skii. *Andrei Belyi*. Paris, 1955. H. Stammler, "Belyj's Conflict with Vjačeslav Ivanov over War and Revolution," *SEEJ* 18 (1974), pp. 259–70. F. Stepun, *Mystische Weltschau*. Munich, 1964. G. Struve, "Andrej Belyj's Experiments with Novel Technique." In *Stil und Formprobleme in der Literatur*. Heidelberg, 1959. James West, *Russian Symbolism*. London, 1970.

K. N. B.

Bem, Álfred Lyúdvigovich (1886–1945), scholar, editor, critic. Born in Kiev and trained at St. Petersburg University under S. A. VENGEROV, Bem edited and contributed to several of the first serious collections of articles studying the ways Russian classics reflected earlier works, Russian and foreign. He emigrated to Prague in 1919, where he taught at Charles University and the Russian Pedagogical Institute, and remained there until his death. He published studies of old Russian literature, Pushkin, Lermontov, Turgenev, Tolstoi, and Blok, and reviewed much of the current Russian literature for Prague periodicals, but his greatest contributions involved Dostoevsky, especially the four invaluable collections: *O Dostoevskom*, I (1929), II (1932), III (1936), all in Prague, and *Dostoevskii, Psikhoanaliticheskie etyudy*, Berlin, 1938.

Bibliography: See *Foster*, pp. 214–22. S. V. Belov, "Bibliografiya rabot A. L. Bema o Dostoevskom." In *O Dostojevském, Sborník statí a materialů*. Prague, 1972.

R. L. B.

Benedíktov, Vladímir Grigórievich (1807–73), poet. An officer by education, Benediktov took part in the suppression of the Polish uprising in 1831. From 1832 to his retirement in 1860 he was an official in the Ministry of Finance, devoting his spare time to mathematics, astronomy, and poetry. The enormous success of *Poems by Vladimir Benediktov* (2d ed., 1836) has been explained by the decline of poetry from the high standards set up during the Golden Age. However, this can hardly be the only explanation, since his verse was hailed by a number of the greatest poets of the time, including ZHUKOVSKY, VYAZEMSKY and TYUTCHEV. Obviously, readers accustomed to harmony, distinction, and restraint, were looking for a more showily attractive form of poetry, and Benediktov offered them exactly what they wanted. Rhetorical and declamatory, his poems are characterized by an extravagant use of poetic ornamentation. "To express mysterious torments," Benediktov wrote, "in order that the fire of the heart rise up in your words, invent sounds that have never before been heard, devise an unknown language!" Indeed, rich in euphony, his poems abound in striking metaphors and surprising epithets. The heart of a beautiful woman is "an abyss at the bottom of which a crocodile lies in repose," her eyes are "two Ouch diamonds," and her waist is "infinitely capricious." Subsequently the reputation of Benediktov was ruined by BELINSKY, who charged him with "sins against language and common sense," and with reducing his poems to "verse toys." After a short-lived comeback as a poet of progressive ideas in the latter 1850s he was rediscovered by the SYMBOLISTS, who experienced the influence of his rich rhymes and sound imagery. Today the star of Benediktov is timidly rising, but there is still no comprehensive study of his controversial poetry.

Works: *Sochineniya*. Ed. Ya. P. Polonskii, 2 vols. St. Petersburg, 1902; *Stikhotvoreniya*. Ed. L. Ginzburg, Leningrad 1939.

Secondary literature: Dmitrij Čiževskij, *History of Nineteenth-Century Russian Literature*. Vol. 1: The Romantic Period. Nashville 1974. St. Rassadin, "Neudachnik Benediktov," *VLit*, 1976, no. 10, pp. 152–83.

G. K.

Berbérova, Nína Nikoláevna (1901–), poet, prose writer, and critic. Born and educated in St. Petersburg, Berberova left Russia in 1922 with the poet Vladislav KHODASEVICH and lived in Berlin, Prague, Italy, and Paris. She later taught Russian literature at Princeton University. Berberova has contributed to *Sovremennye zapiski*, *Novyi zhurnal*, *Vozrozhdenie*, *Opyty*, *Grani*, and *Zveno*, among many other Russian and American journals and anthologies. Her autobiography, *The Italics Are Mine* (1969) was published in Russian as *Kursiv moi: avtobiografiya* (1972). Her play *Madame* was staged in Paris in 1938.

Works: (Novels:) *Poslednie i pervye*. 1930. *Pobeditel'nitsa*. 1932. *Bez zakata*. 1938. *Zheleznaya zhenshchina*. 1980. (Biographical Works:) *Chaikovskii: istoriya odinokoi zhizni*. 1936. *Borodin*. 1938. *Alexandre Blok et son temps*. 1948. (A Collection of short stories:) *Oblegchenie uchasti*. 1949. (Major Articles:) "25 let posle smerti A. A. Bloka." *Orion*, 1947. "Iz peterburgskikh vospominanii." *Opyty*, 1953, no. 1. "Vladislav Khodasevich, russkii poet 1886–1939," *Grani*, no. 12 (1951).

T. A. P.

Berdyáev, Nikolaí Aleksándrovich (1874–1948), religious philosopher, was born in Lipky, a suburb of Kiev. On his father's side he was descended from a long line of military men. His mother, a Princess Kudasheva, descended from a French noble family, the Choiseuls, who were given asylum in Russia by Catherine the Great.

Young Nikolai was enrolled in the Corps of Cadets in Kiev but was later transferred to the Corps of Pages. Berdyaev was never really interested in a military career as intended by his father. Instead, he steeped himself in Kant, Schopenhauer, Nietzsche, Ibsen, Boehme, Franz Baader, Marx, TOLSTOI and DOSTOEVSKY.

During his student period Berdyaev became interested in Marxism, and in 1894 joined the Social Democratic Party which led to his being exiled to Vologda for three years. In 1901 he went to Germany to study at the University of Heidelberg. He returned to Russia in 1904 and settled in St. Petersburg where he embarked upon his literary activities. He and Sergei BULGAKOV edited the periodical *Novyi Put'*.

Berdyaev's intellectual and spiritual development may be divided into four main periods. In the first period Berdyaev, while still under the influence of Kantian philosophy, concentrated on ethical problems. The second and most creative period is marked by his interest in religious and mystic philosophy. The third period is centered in the problem of the philosophy of history, with particular emphasis on the eschatological element in the historical process. The fourth period marks the culmination of his personalistic philosophy which permeated his whole life and thought.

After the 1917 October Revolution Berdyaev was appointed professor of philosophy at the University of Moscow. In 1922 Berdyaev was exiled along with a number of Russian intellectuals because of his strong religious views. He settled in France where he continued his literary activities.

Berdyaev's personalism and existentialism are rooted in his metaphysics which has its basis in Boehme's *Ungrund*. For Boehme the *Ungrund* is pure, indeterminate and contentless will, and freedom is found in the Godhead. The two basic concepts in Berdyaev's *Weltanschauung* are freedom and the supreme value of the human personality. These two concepts merge into one since freedom exists in the human personality. Freedom for Berdyaev is "primal, irrational, dark, and indeterminate ... is pre-existent to all being which is already determined." Berdyaev distinguishes between God the Creator and the Godhead which is the "ground of God." He maintains that freedom has its source in the *Ungrund* and not in God. He calls it "meonic freedom," which is the creative energy underlying the forms and directions of all processes. Freedom is bound up with the "cosmic aim," and God as Creator brings value into being out of pure potentiality, which is termed the "theogonic process."

God and His creatures, according to Berdyaev, are mutually related in the pursuit of realizing maximum value. All positive value experience is regarded as the immanence of God. For Berdyaev only the subject is ultimately real since it is the subject that begets the object. Berdyaev's solution to the depersonalization of man is to be found in transforming man from the human into the divine-human—a view fully developed by Vladimir SOLOVYOV in his *Lectures on Godmanhood*. Such a transformation can only take place at the end of human history and the reign of the true existential communion of man with God and with each other. Only an eschatological and teleological view of history, according to Berdyaev, gives meaning to history. Eschatology entails man's active, dynamic, and conscious striving towards the goal of bringing about the "end of time." A society that furthers the goal of the development of selves into persons is a true community, or *sobornost'*.

Berdyaev's ethical views are rooted in his concept of man's freedom and creativity. Berdyaev rejects a utilitarian ethics which treats man as a means to an end. According to Berdyaev, man is free not only to act morally or immorally but also to decide what is moral or immoral. The ethics of freedom is also the ethics of love. The moral ideal for Berdyaev is a complete harmonious being, who by his creative energy seeks to unify the entire world in the realization of value. It should be noted that Berdyaev was painfully aware that this ideal is impossible of realization because of the very structure of our existence. History is tragic for it proposes a goal that is never fully attainable. Nevertheless, tragedy is meaningful and history has meaning in that those spirits whose lives constitute history achieve their divine purpose even if it entails suffering and failure, which are ultimately justified in that historical beings actualize a community of personal values, which for Berdyaev is the Kingdom of God.

Works: For a complete bibliography of Berdyaev's works, see: *Bibliographie des oeuvres de Nicolas Berdiaev*. Comp. Tamara Klépinine. Introd. Pierre Pascal. Paris, 1978.
Works in English: The Meaning of History. 1936. *The Destiny of Man.* 1937. Reprint, 1979. *The Origin of Russian Communism.* 1937. *The Russian Idea.* 1937. Reprint, 1979. *The Beginning of the End.* 1952.
Secondary literature: Igumen Gennadi [Eikalovich], "Filosofiya

neravenstva," *Grani*, no. 102 (1976), pp. 202–26. Alexis Klimov, *Berdiaeff*. Paris, 1967. Donald A. Lowrie, *Rebellious Prophet*. 1960. Jean-Claude Marcadé, ed., *Colloque Berdiaev*. Paris, 1978. Matthew Spinka, *Nicolas Berdyaev*. 1940. James C. S. Wernham, an essay in *Berdyaev and Shestov*. 1968.   L. J. S.

Berggólts, Olga Fyódorovna (1910–75), poet, was born in St. Petersburg, the daughter of a doctor. In 1925 she joined the literary group *Smena* (Change). Her early publications were primarily children's stories and journalistic writings. After graduation from the Philology Department of Leningrad University in 1930, she published her first collection of verse, *Poems* (Stikhotvoreniya, 1934), followed by *Book of Songs* (Kniga pesen, 1935) and *Fall* (Listopad, 1938). Berggolts's most significant contribution to Soviet poetry is her writings about her war experience. Her *Leningrad Notebook* (Leningradskaya tetrad', 1942), which contains "A February Diary" (Fevral'skii dnevnik) and "A Poem of Leningrad" (Leningradskaya poema), as well as *Leningrad* (1944) and *Your Road* (Tvoi put', 1945) are lyric documentation of the nine-hundred-day siege of Leningrad, through which she herself lived and worked at Leningrad Radio: her radio commentary from this period was collected as a separate volume, *Leningrad Speaking* (Govorit Leningrad, 1946).

In 1951 she received a State Prize for her verse epos "Pervorossiisk" (1950). The siege of Sevastopol is the subject of her verse tragedy "Loyalty" (Vernost', 1954). Her prose work *Diurnal Stars* (Dnevnye zvezdy, 1959), is a lyrical autobiography of her youth interwoven with war experiences. Many of her later publications—*Verses* (Stikhi, 1962), *The Knot* (Uzel, 1965), *Diaries of Bygone Years* (Dnevniki dalekikh let, 1967), *The Trial* (Ispytanie, 1967), and *Memory* (Pamyat', 1972)—recapitulate themes of earlier works. Most characteristically, Berggolts writes of her generation's common experiences. Predominant themes in her work—loss, memory, the reconciliation of individual and collective responsibility—reflect the moral decisions of that era. Although modest in its attempts at technical variety, her work frequently mixes chronological sequences to heighten emotional impact. The Leningrad works are monuments to the human potential under siege.

Works: Sobrannye sochineniya. 3 vols. 1972–73.
Translations: Two poems in *Modern Russian Poetry*. Ed. and trans. V. Markov and M. Sparks. 1967. Pp. 756–59.
Secondary literature: Andrei Sinyavsky, "The Poetry and Prose of Olga Berggolts." In *For Freedom of Imagination*. Trans. Laszlo Tikos and Murray Peppard. 1971. Pp. 37–62.   N. C.

Berkov, Pável Naúmovich (1896–1969), literary scholar, bibliographer, archeographer. A professor of Leningrad University, Berkov was a Senior Researcher and chairman of the 18th-century group at the INSTITUT RUSSKOI LITERATURY (Pushkinskii Dom). He was also a correspondent member of the Academy of Sciences (1960). Berkov had a broad knowledge of Russian literary history and studied PUSHKIN, Kozma PRUTKOV, literatures of other Soviet nationalities, history of the theater, techniques of literary study, theoretical problems, and techniques of bibliography and bibliophily. His main contributions were in 18th-century literary history where he left several standard monographs. Berkov played an important role as editor and sponsor of many 18th-century publications including the serial *XVIII vek: Sbornik statei i materialov*, the main source for the study of 18th-century literary history.

Works: "Izuchenie russkoi literatury inostrantsami v XVIII veke," *Yazyk i literatura* 5 (1930), pp. 87–136. *Lomonosov i literaturnaya polemika ego vremeni*. 1936. *Istoriya russkoi zhurnalistiki XVIII veka*. 1952. *Vvedenie v tekhniku literaturovedcheskogo issledovaniya*. 1955. *Bibliograficheskaya evristika; k teorii i metodike bibliograficheskikh razyskanii*. 1960. "Ocherk literaturnoi istoriografii XVIII veka." Part 1 of *Vvedenie v izuchenie russkoi literatury 18 veka*. 1964. *Istoriya russkoi komedii XVIII veka*. 1977.
Secondary literature: Pavel Naumovich Berkov (k 60-letiyu so dnya rozhdeniya: Spisok pechatnykh trudov). 1956. H. Grasshoff, "Pavel Naumovich Berkov in memoriam," *ZS* 15 (1970), pp. 319–20. P. N. Berkov, *Izbrannoe: Trudy po knigovedeniyu i bibliografii*. 1978. (Bibliography: pp. 247–57)   E. B.

Besé da lyubítelei rú sskogo sló va (Collegium of Amateurs of the Russian Word, 1811–16), a society of Petersburg men of letters which met at the house of G. R. DERZHAVIN, who headed the Society together with Admiral A. S. SHISHKOV. Most of the members, among whom the better known were S. A. SHIRINSKY-SHIKHMATOV, D. I. KHVOSTOV, A. A. SHAKHOVSKOI, I. A. KRYLOV, and N. I. GNEDICH, held conservative views in most matters. They supported Shishkov in his controversy with the KARAMZINIAN school of Russian literature. The patriotic and nationalist orientation of *Beseda* caused some of the future DECEMBRISTS and their sympathizers, such as P. I. KATENIN, V. K. KYUKHELBEKER, A. S. GRIBOEDOV, V. F. Raevsky, and others, to side with the ideas of *Beseda*.

Bibliography: N. I. Mordovchenko, *Russkaya kritika pervoi chetverti XIX v.* 1959.   V. T.

Bestúzhev (pseud. Marlinsky), Aleksándr Aleksándrovich (1797–1837), writer, poet, critic, translator, DECEMBRIST revolutionary. TURGENEV called him Russia's first most beloved writer, and he has been likened to Victor Hugo as an ultra-romantic writer of exotic tales in an unrestrained style. He began his career in 1819 as a translator of English and French criticism, and for the next six years wielded great influence as a polemicist on behalf of romantic aesthetics. He published his first prose tale in 1821 and soon became known as a writer of Gothic horror tales from Livonian and Russian history ("Wenden Castle," "Eisen Castle," "The Traitor"), historical adventure tales ("Tournament at Reval," "Roman and Olga"), and society tales of unrequited love ("An Evening at a Bivouac," "A Second Evening at a Bivouac"). From 1823 through 1825 he co-edited the literary almanac POLYARNAYA ZVEZDA with Kondraty RYLEEV. He was not a very good poet in his early years, but the "Agitational Songs" he wrote with Ryleev as part of their revolutionary activities are of high quality. He was a leader of the Northern Society of the Decembrist conspiracy from 1823, and he led the key rebel unit during the revolt of 14 December 1825. After his arrest he confessed freely and implicated Ryleev and others in plots to assassinate Alexander I. He spent almost five years in Siberia and was then transferred to the Caucasus and allowed to return to an active literary life under the pseudonym Marlinsky. His prose of the 1830s—society tales ("The Test"), stories of the supernatural ("The Terrible Divination," "The Cuirassier"), naval adventures ("The Frigate *Hope*," "Lieutenant Belozor"), and exotic tales of the Caucasus ("Ammalat-Bek," "Mulla Nur")—brought him unprecedented popularity in Russia and abroad. His deeply romantic poetry of this time on lonely exile, religious meditation, and Death and the Grave is quite good. His long review essay on a historical novel by N. A. POLEVOI, subtitled "On Romanticism and the Historical Novel," is a remarkable manifesto of Romanticism and a theory of history. He was an excellent ethnographer and linguist who mastered languages with ease and commemorated Caucasian cultures in newspaper reports and travel essays. His notoriety grew when a young girl was killed in his bed, and his relationships with rebels and bandits suggest that he might have been a secret agent. Bestuzhev was killed in a skirmish with Circassian mountaineers under mysterious circumstances that gave rise to even wilder legends.

As a critic Bestuzhev is known for his defense of the Russian language against the "barbaric" influence of French, his attacks on Neoclassicism, and his advocacy of Romanticism. He is most often noted for the civic or socio-political content of his criticism, especially in the "Glances" (*Vzglyad*) at Russian literature that prefaced the *Polyarnaya zvezda*, but his criticism is more valuable for his consistent interest in questions of language, style, and modern literary theory. In his early years he decimated the reputations of Neoclassical or more traditional writers such as A. A. SHAKHOVSKOI and P. A. KATENIN with detailed analyses of lexicon and style. His essay "On Romanticism" is a credible, if too fanciful, synthesis of romantic idealist notions into a theory of history and Romanticism. BELINSKY considered him a far better critic than writer.

Belinsky called Bestuzhev the "instigator" of the Russian prose tale, and by this he meant that while the genre was well established in Russia by the early 1820s (KARAMZIN), Bestuzhev helped turn Russian literature from poetry to prose and developed the genre on the models of Goethe, Schiller, Richter, Florian, Madame de Genlis,

Chateaubriand, Hugo, Ann Radcliffe, and Sir Walter Scott. Bestuzhev worshipped Byron, and his prose tale has been called a "transposition" of the Byronic verse tale into Russian prose. In both form and characters his tales are the epitome of BYRONISM. His career falls into two periods: 1821 to 1825 and 1830 to 1837. He developed the prose tale in five generic categories: the Byronic society tales known as the tales of men and passions, the historical tales, the horror tales, the sea adventures, and the tales of the Caucasus. The early tales are derivative, beset by false heroics, and awkwardly experimental; the tales of the 1830s are notable for their graceful form and their originality. The style known as Marlinism is filled with colliding metaphors, aphorisms and witticisms, exclamations and hyperbole, and complex yet smooth syntax. Among his best early tales are "Wenden Castle," a tone poem of medieval revenge, the two evenings at a bivouac, which adroitly mix witty hussar anecdotes with sad stories of love, and "The Traitor," a sophisticated psychological treatment of fratricide and lust for power. The best mature tales include "The Test," in which two hussars outwit themselves in a test of a lady's fidelity, "The Frigate *Hope*," about a ship's captain who abandons his duty for a woman, and "Ammalat-Bek," on the theme of the tormented primitive man in confrontation with civilization.

Bestuzhev's ultra-romantic manner was his downfall. He ruled his age and his popularity far exceeded PUSHKIN's but he was quickly forgotten in serious literature. His survival after 1840 was as a marvelous moment in the adolescence of generations of spellbound Russians.

Works: *Sochineniya*. 2 vols. 1958.
Translations: "Ammalat Bek." In *Anthology of Russian Literature*. Ed. Leo Wiener. Vol. 2. 1902–03. "An Evening on Bivouac." In *Russian Romantic Prose: An Anthology*. Ed. Carl R. Proffer. 1979.
Secondary literature: Lauren G. Leighton, *Aleksandr Bestuzhev-Marlinsky*. 1975.   L. G. L.

Betáki, Vasíly (1930–   ), poet, translator, and critic.
Betaki studied at the Pedagogical Institute and the Soviet Writers Union's Literary Institute in Moscow, and taught literature and language at several schools. From 1956 to 1962 he was the assistant director of scholarly research at the Pavlovsk palace-museum, and since 1962 a free-lance writer. Elected a member of the UNION OF SOVIET WRITERS in 1966, he was expelled for political dissidence and forbidden to publish in 1972. In 1973, Betaki received the status of a political exile in France and since then has lived in Paris, working for Radio Liberty and the quarterly KONTINENT. He is a prolific translator, primarily of English and American poetry, and the author of three collections of his own work: *Earthly flame* (Zemnoe plamya, 1960), *Closing the Current of Time* (Zamykanie vremeni, 1974), and *Europe-Island* (Evropa-ostrov, 1981).

Betaki creates visions either of intimacy and tenderness in his love and meditative verse or of violence and ferocity in his political poems, of which the masterpiece is "In memory of Czechoslovakia" (Pamyati Chekhoslovakii). His poems convey both indirect and dramatic color, light, movement, and most of all, sound, and are never simply descriptive. Somehow he succeeds in reconciling the opposite characteristics of the poetics of symbolism and expressionism. Haunting the borderlands of the unconscious, he remains a formalist, and his rhythmic density, proliferation, and order run counter to the spirit of free verse, making exceptional demands on the interpretative discipline of the critic and the sensibility of the reader.

In all three collections of verse, Betaki appears as a poet-critic of contemporary and historical Russia, holding that a man should symbolize and extract experiences from the transitory, and transpose them to the artist-thinker key. Against the varieties of intellectual suffering arising from a desperate sense of the flux and impermanence of Russia as well as of the contemporary Western world, he counterposes his convictions of philosophical and moral value. Betaki's importance lies not so much in his technical and stylistic innovations as in his aptitude for creative synthesis and, finally, in the ideal which he posits and realizes, namely, that a split, alienated, and public man may yet produce a deeply personal art by turning to pure sources of musical poetry, however sharp and atonal his verse might occasionally become.

Bibliography: A. Rannit, "Zametka o dvukh knigakh Vasiliya Betaki," *Kontinent* 33 (1982), pp. 393–96. W. Weidlé, Preface to *Zamykanie vremeni* (1974), pp. vii-x.   A. R.

Bezyménsky, Aleksándr Ilyích (1898–1973). A poet and an early activist in the organization of proletarian literature, Bezymensky was prominent in VAPP and later in RAPP. In the latter organization he was a member of the minority opposition known as *Litfront,* which opposed the program and the slogans of the leadership, favoring instead the direct participation of poetry and prose in the political and economic struggles of the Five-Year Plan. His early poetry shows some influence of the PROLETKUL'T and Smithy (KUZNITSA) poets in its symbolic striving for "the sun" and the proletarian "dawn," but he soon came under the influence of MAYAKOVSKY's post-revolutionary publicistic poetry, and, like Mayakovsky, engaged his verse in the campaigns and struggles of the day, always articulating the Party line of the moment. His verse drama *The Shot* (Vystrel, 1930) demonstratively rejected the psychological realism favored by the leadership of RAPP and dealt directly with shock workers and bureaucrats, exposing hindrances to production and offering heroic remedies to remove them. In 1930 Stalin favored Bezymensky with a personal letter in which he said that *The Shot* "should be considered as a model of revolutionary proletarian art for the present day." Bezymensky continued to write poetry supporting the Party program: collectivization and the Five-Year Plan in the thirties, and in 1949 his *Angry Lines* (Gnevnye stroki) attacked Western capitalist warmongers. His verse lines are not without a certain epigrammatic verve.

Works: Vystrel. 1952. *Izbrannye proizvedeniya, 1918–1958.* 2 vols. 1958.

Translations: See *Lewanski,* p. 203.

Secondary literature: E. J. Brown, "The Year of Acquiescence." In *Literature and Revolution in Soviet Russia.* Ed. M. Hayward and L. Labedz. 1963. A. Selivanovskii, *V literaturnykh boyakh.* 1959.

                                              E. J. B.

Bibliography of Russian Literature. The student of Russian literature has at his disposal an impressive array of bibliographic materials to guide him through the varied topics of the field. Both Soviet scholars and their pre-revolutionary counterparts have demonstrated remarkable skill in the art of bibliography. Early efforts, however, did not focus specifically on the compilation of bibliographies of literature but rather upon the formation of a general publishing record. Nevertheless, many literary sources can be found within these general bibliographies of the 18th and early 19th centuries.

Russian bibliography prior to the 18th century is fragmentary and represented chiefly by descriptions of private collections. These were located either in monastic repositories or in the private libraries of Russian noblemen. [For a survey of these works consult: N. V. Zdobnov, *Istoriya russkoi bibliografii do nachala XX veka* (Moscow, 1942, and subsequent editions.)] In the mid-17th century an interesting work of unknown authorship appeared, entitled "Oglavlenie knig, kto ikh slozhil" [The contents of books, who composed them] and was later published by V. M. Undolsky in *Chteniya obshchestva istorii i drevnostei rossiiskikh,* 1846, no. 3 [Readings of the Society of Russian History and Antiquities]. The "Oglavlenie" was the first general list of manuscripts and printed books existing in the Russian lands.

In the 18th and 19th centuries, more systematic Russian bibliography began to evolve. Works from this period fall into three basic categories: (1) bibliographic departments in journals or in supplements to them, the nearest example of what is called "tekushchaya" bibliography, the "current" chronicle of book and journal publications, (2) catalogues of book dealers, valuable for their grouping of materials into general subject classes, and (3) various retrospective bibliographies and bibliographic encyclopedias designed to cumulate and classify the listings of the first two categories.

The first grouping, the bibliographic departments of journals, covers portions of the latter part of the 18th century and most years in the 19th century. Since the editorial positions of these journals varied, as did the skills of the bibliographers involved, the quality of these listings often appears uneven and the coverage is frequently incomplete. Also, because many of these works fall under the class of "obshchaya" or "general" bibliography, their employment in literary

study can be a painstaking process. Despite these deficiences, this type of bibliography still provides a useful literary history of the period.

The first of this type is *Russische Bibliothek zur Kenntnis des gegenwärtigen Zustandes der Litteratur in Russland* (Leipzig, Riga, and St. Peterburg, 1772–89, Russian Library for Knowledge of the Contemporary State of Literature in Russia), edited by H. L. Ch. Bachmeister. The *Russische Bibliothek* covered publications from 1770 to 1787. It was not until 1814, with "Sovremennaya russkaya bibliografiya," a department of N. I. GRECH's journal *Syn otechestva* that another attempt at a current record of publications was made. Grech's journal provided this service until 1826 and in turn was followed in this task by several other periodical publications throughout the 1830s and 1840s. Many members of Russia's intelligentsia were involved in the editorship of these journals and participated in their bibliographic compilations. N. A. POLEVOI's MOSKOVSKII TELEGRAF, A. S. PUSHKIN's SOVREMENNIK, employing at different times not only Russia's premier poet, but also the writer N. V. GOGOL and the radical critics N. G. CHERNYSHEVSKY and N. A. DOBROLYUBOV, F. BULGARIN's SEVERNAYA PCHELA, O. SENKOVSKY's BIBLIOTEKA DLYA CHTENIYA, and A. A. Kraevsky's OTECHESTVENNYE ZAPISKI, at various times listed and reviewed the "belles lettres" of the second quarter of the 19th century.

These privately organized bibliographies were paralleled between 1837 and 1855 by the government-sponsored periodical *Zhurnal Ministerstva narodnogo prosveshcheniya* (Journal of the Ministry of Public Education). Under the editorship of S. S. Uvarov, this journal acted both as an organ of censorship and as an official registry of publications. In its first two years a bibliographic section appeared under the title "Ukazatel' vnov' vyshedshikh knig" (Index of recently published books). From 1837 until it ceased publication, the "Ukazatel'" was published as a supplement to the journal at irregular intervals.

Shifts in political atmosphere made "current" bibliography in the latter half of the 19th century a complex affair. The government ended the official list of publications and did not resume this task until 1869. In the meantime various bibliographic journals endeavored to maintain a current listing. For 1855, P. P. Lambin provided a systematic listing of published works in a supplement to the *Izvestiya Akademii nauk, Otdelenie russkogo yazyka i slovesnosti* (News of the Academy of Sciences, Department of Russian language and literature). V. I. Mezhov, the most prolific bibliographer of the mid-19th century and a staff member of the Public Library in Petersburg, covered works from 1856–59 in supplements to *Bibliograficheskie listy Otechestvennykh zapisok* (Bibliographic Sheets of Otechestvennye zapiski, 1856–57), RUSSKAYA BESEDA (1859), and in the *Zhurnal Ministerstva vnutrennykh del* (Journal of the Ministry of Internal Affairs, 1860).

Other journals which engaged in "current" bibliography (with the years of participation in parentheses) are: *Knizhnyi vestnik* (Book Announcer, 1860–67), *Bibliograf* (1869, The Bibliographer), *Zhurnal Ministerstva narodnogo prosveshcheniya* (1869–70), *Rossiiskaya bibliografiya* (Russian Bibliography, 1879–81), *Bibliograf* (1885–94) and *Knizhnyi vestnik* (1884–1908).

When the official government register of publications resumed in 1869, it was under the auspices of the journal *Pravitel'stvennyi vestnik* (Government Announcer). From 1869 to 1876 the listing appeared within the journal in chronological arrangement. The same list appeared in subject arrangement between 1872 and 1879 in *Ukazatel' po delam pechati* (Index for Publishing Affairs), but again resumed its chronological listing between 1879 and 1902 in the former periodical. After 1902 and until 1907 this listing of publications was issued independently under the title *Spisok knig, vyshedshikh v Rossii* (List of books, published in Russia).

In 1907 under the editorship of A. D. Toporov and under the control of the *Glavnoe upravlenie po delam pechati* (Main Administration for Publishing Affairs) began a monthly chronicle of publications, the journal *Knizhnaya letopis'* (Book Chronicle), inaugurating the modern period of Russian national bibliography.

Russian current bibliography was fortuitously augmented by private book dealers, who provided systematic catalogues of their inventories. With the dual purpose of offering bibliographic services and promoting their business enterprise, these merchants have left a valuable record of literary publishing in the 18th and 19th centuries.

One of the earliest of such catalogues was *Rospis' rossiiskim knigam dlya chteniya iz biblioteki V. Plavil'shchikova ... v 3-kh ch.* (List of Russian books for reading from the library of V. Plavilshchikov ... in three parts. St. Petersburg, 1820, with yearly supplements in 1821–26). Part three was devoted entirely to literature and related topics. The *Rospis'* was compiled by V. G. Anastasevich, a member of the staff of the Petersburg Public Library and the leading bibliographer of his day. When Plavilshchikov died in 1823, his business was inherited by his assistant, A. F. SMIRDIN, who continued the task of producing catalogues, retaining Anastasevich to compile *Rospis' rossiiskim knigam dlya chteniya iz biblioteki Aleksandra Smirdina ...* (St. Petersburg, 1828, with supplements in 1829, 1832, and 1847).

Publications between 1831 and 1845 appear in the catalogue of the firm of M. D. Olkhin, *Sistematicheskii reestr russkim knigam s 1831 po 1846* (St. Petersburg, 1846, compiled by I. P. Bystrov).

The latter half of the 19th century saw the collaboration of V. I. Mezhov (see above) and P. A. Efremov, a talented bibliographer and editor, with several book dealerships. The *Sistematicheskii katalog russkim knigam, prodayushchimsya v knizhnom magazine A. F. Bazunova ...* (St. Petersburg, 1869, with supplements in 1870–71, 1873, and 1875, compiled by Mezhov) attempted to cover most publications from 1825 to 1874. Mezhov also organized the *Sistematicheskii katalog russkikh knig v knizhnom magazine Ya. A. Isakova ...* (St. Petersburg, 1877, supplement 1880), the firm's inventory between 1875 and 1878. Both Efremov and Mezhov at different times compiled the *Sistematicheskaya rospis' knigam ... v knizhnom magazine I. I. Glazunova ...* (St. Petersburg, 1876, with supplements at various intervals between 1869 and 1889). Glazunov's catalogues list publications between 1855 and 1887, though materials prior to this period were included, depending on the firm's stock in any given year.

Publications from the latter portion of the 19th century can be found in *Katalog knizhnogo magazina "Novoe vremya" A. S. Suvorina s alfavitnom ukazatelem 1878–1901 gg.* (St. Petersburg, 1902).

"Retrospective" bibliography developed and became popular during the 19th century. Compilations appeared which attempted to reconstruct the publishing history of Russia, and as the art of bibliography became specialized, bibliographies devoted specifically to literary study made their way into print.

The earliest of the first type was V. S. Sopikov's *Opyt rossiiskoi bibliografii ili polnyi slovar' sochinenii i perevodov ... do 1813* (An Attempt at Russian Bibliography or A Complete Dictionary of Works and Translations ... to 1813, 5 vols., St. Petersburg, 1813–21), not only a valuable record of Russian literary output, but also of European materials that had an important influence upon Russian culture. In 1904, V. N. Rogozhin republished this work with corrections and further annotations.

Other contributions to the bibliographic record of this period are P. P. Pekarsky's *Opisanie slavyano-russkikh knig i tipografii 1679–1725 gg.* (Description of Slavonic-Russian books and typographies, St. Petersburg, 1862), V. M. Undolsky's *Ocherk slavyano-russkoi bibliografii* (Essay of a Slavonic-Russian bibliography, St. Petersburg, 1871), and N. V. Guberti's *Materialy dlya russkoi bibliografii: Khronologicheskoe obozrenie redkikh i zamechatel'nykh knig XVIII Stoletiya, 1725–1800* (Materials for Russian bibliography: A chronological survey of rare and remarkable books of the 18th century, 3 vols., St. Petersburg, 1878–91).

"Otraslevaya" (subject) bibliography made its appearance in the 19th century as Russian literature gained an international reputation. G. N. Gennadi's incomplete *Spravochnyi slovar' o russkikh pisatelyakh i uchenykh XVII i XIX stoletii* (Reference dictionary of Russian writers and scholars of the 18th and 19th centuries, 3 vols., Berlin and Moscow, 1876–1908, up to the letter R) provides a short biographical sketch plus a list of works and criticism. A similar study by A. V. Meyzer entitled *Russkaya slovesnost' s XI po XIX stoletiya vklyuchitel'no: bibliograficheskii ukazatel'* (Russian literature from the 11th to the 19th century inclusive, St. Petersburg, 1899–1902) is somewhat broader in scope, grouping materials by period with an index to individual authors. Both works not only included monographs but also attempted to include articles from periodical publications. V. V. Sipovsky provided an annotated bibliography of prose works of the 18th century in his *Iz istorii russkogo romana i povesti ...* (From the history of the Russian novel and tale, Pt. 1, 2d ed., St. Petersburg, 1903).

V. I. Mezhov, who figured prominently in the compilation of "current" bibliography and catalogues for bookdealers, provided a detailed account of Russian literary history and criticism of the mid-19th century in two works: *Russkaya istoricheskaya bibliografiya za 1865–76 vklyuchitel'no* (Russian historical bibliography for 1865–76 inclusive, 8 vols., St. Petersburg, 1882–90), where Vol. 4 is entitled *Istoriya russkoi slovesnosti i yazyka* (History of Russian literature and language) and contains nearly 8,000 references, and *Istoriya russkoi i vseobshchei slovesnosti: bibliograficheskie materialy 1855–1870* (History of Russian and world literature, St. Petersburg, 1872), covering works in Russian on both native and foreign literature.

D. D. Yazykov attempted a bibliographic dictionary of Russian writers organized by their date of death. His *Obzor zhizni i trudov pokoinykh russkikh pisatelei, umershikh v 1881–93 gg.* (Survey of the life and works of deceased Russian writers, who died between 1881 and 1893, 3 vols., St. Petersburg, 1885–1916; 2d ed., 1903–1915, 10 vols., only covers until 1890) provides useful lists of an author's works and criticism about them for many of the leading writers of the 19th century.

The end of the century marked the early bibliographic endeavors of S. A. VENGEROV, who became the first director of the *Vzesoyuznaya knizhnaya palata*. His "kartoteka," a card file of Russian publications, articles, biographical references, etc. now housed at Pushkinskii dom (Pushkin House), the literary center of the Academy of Sciences, remains the source of much of Soviet retrospective bibliography and literary study. Several works under his direction showed the great potential of Russian bibliography at the turn of the century. The most complete is *Istochniki slovarya russkikh pisatelei* (Sources for a dictionary of Russian writers, St. Petersburg, 1900–17, vols. 1–4), but it covers only Russian writers from A to Nekrasov. His *Russkie knigi ...* (Russian books, 3 vols., St. Petersburg, 1897–99) attempted to list all Russian publications from 1708 to 1893, but its publication ceased after listing only those writers whose surnames began with the first three letters of the Russian alphabet.

Three works of this period are devoted to a record of serialized publications. A. N. Neustroev's *Istoricheskoe rozyskanie o russkikh povremennykh izdaniyakh ... 1702–1802* (Historical investigation of Russian serialized publications, St. Petersburg, 1874) with its accompanying *Ukazatel'* (1898) not only provides a publishing history of journals and almanacs, but also attempts to index their contents. The publishing records of periodicals for the 18th and 19th centuries are: *Spisok russkikh povremennykh izdanii s 1703 po 1899* (St. Petersburg, 1901, compiled for the Academy of Sciences by V. I. Sreznevsky) and N. M. Lisovsky's *Russkaya periodicheskaya pechat'; 1703–1900* (2 vols., St. Petersburg, 1915). The first volume contains a bibliographic description of publications, and the second provides a chronological table of their publishing history.

Bibliography in the Soviet Period. The organ for current bibliography in the Soviet period was a holdover from earlier times, keeping its name and changing only in the government body which controlled its production. *Knizhnaya letopis'* began in 1907 under the auspices of the *Glavnoe upravlenie po delam pechati* and in 1917 was continued by the newly formed *Vsesoyuznaya knizhnaya palata* under the directorship of S. A. Vengerov. The value of *Knizhnaya letopis'* as a current record of Russian book production increased when it became mandated by law that all Soviet publications be deposited at the Palata. In 1925, *Ezhegodnik knigi SSSR* began as a yearly cumulation of the weekly *Knizhnaya letopis'*, however, the annual does not contain certain ephemera and pamphlets.

The *Letopis' periodicheskikh izdanii* (Chronicle of periodical publications, Moscow, 1933–) is the union list for journals, almanacs, and other serialized publications. Indexing of periodicals is accomplished by the *Letopis' zhurnal'nykh statei* (Moscow, 1926–). Literary topics are found under the category "Khudozhestvennaya literatura" in a single alphabetical listing by author. The lack of a more detailed subject division makes the use of this index a cumbersome task.

Two other lists of publications are of interest to literary scholarship: the *Katalog knig* of the Moscow publishing house "Nauka," and the yearbook *Bibliografiya izdanii Akademii nauk SSSR*. The former lists books in cumulations dating back to 1945, including the series *Literary Monuments* (Literaturnye pamyatniki). The latter began in 1956 and under the section "Literatura" one can find the publications of the Academy's center of literary study, *Pushkinskii dom*.

The Academy's *Institut nauchnoi informatsii po obshchestvennym naukam* (Institute of scientific information in the social sciences) organizes and publishes three indexes of scholarship devoted specifically to general literary matters. *Novaya sovetskaya literatura po literaturovedeniyu: Bibliograficheskii byulleten'* (New Soviet literature on literary scholarship, Moscow, 1953; in 1976 the name was changed to *Novaya sovetskaya literatura po obshchestvennym naukam: literaturovedenie*) is a monthly index of all Soviet literary scholarship with convenient subject divisions. *Referatnyi zhurnal. Seriya 7. Literaturovedenie* (Moscow, 1973–) reviews fifty to sixty works on literary topics in each issue. The index *Slavyanskoe yazykoznanie ...* (Slavic philology, Moscow, 1963–) offers useful information on research concerning the development of the Russian literary language, both current and retrospective to 1918.

Since 1956, Soviet dissertations have been indexed by the Lenin Library in Moscow. Its *Katalog kandidatskikh i doktorskikh dissertatsii, postupivshikh v biblioteku im. V. I. Lenina* is for most purposes a union list of doctoral research. For works prior to 1956, Leningrad University published *Dissertatsii zashchishchennye v Leningradskom gosudarstvennom universitete ... 1934–* (Dissertations defended at Leningrad State University, Leningrad, 1955–; ceased with 1961–68 index). Similarly, Moscow University published *Doktorskie i kandidatskie dissertatsii, zashchishchennye ... s 1934 po 1954 gg.* (3 vols., Moscow, 1956–60).

Soviet Retrospective Bibliography. Soviet scholars have continued the work begun in the 19th century to trace the production of manuscripts and printed books of earlier periods. They have also sought to accumulate and index early Soviet scholarship on literary topics, a task which alleviates the arduous work caused by the minimal subject divisions of the national bibliographies. The following is a selective list of such works divided by period.

For literature prior to and including the 17th century one can consult A. S. Zernova's *Knigi kirillovskoi pechati, izdannye v Moskve v XVI–XVII vv. Svodnyi katalog* (Books in Cyrillic published in Moscow ..., Moscow, 1958) and V. I. Pozdeeva's recently published *Katalog knig kirillicheskoi pechati XV–XVII v. v nauchnoi biblioteke Moskovskogo universiteta* (Catalogue of books in Cyrillic of the 15th–17th centuries in the research library of Moscow University, Moscow, 1980).

R. P. Dmitrieva's *Bibliografiya russkogo letopisaniya* (Bibliography of Russian Chronicles, Moscow and Leningrad, 1962) provides information both on the publication of Russian chronicles and on scholarship about them dating back to 1674. Additional information on the description of Russian manuscripts can be found in N. F. Belchikov's *Spravochnik-ukazatel' pechatnykh opisanii slavyano-russkikh rukopisei* (Reference-index of published descriptions of Slavonic-Russian manuscripts, Moscow and Leningrad, 1963).

Two works which provide an index to Soviet scholarship on this early period of Russian literature are D. S. LIKHACHEV's compilation for the Academy of Sciences entitled *Bibliografiya sovetskikh rabot po drevnerusskoi literature za 1945–55 gg.* (Moscow, 1956) and the more current N. F. Droblenkova's *Bibliografiya sovetskikh russkikh rabot po literature XI–XVIII vv....* (for 1917–57, Moscow and Leningrad, 1961; for 1958–67, 2 vols., Leningrad, 1978).

O. V. Danilova's *"Slovo o polku Igoreve": bibliograficheskii ukazatel'* (Moscow, 1940) and V. P. Adrianova-Peretts's *"Slovo o polku Igoreve"; bibliografiya ...* (Moscow and Leningrad, 1940) list publications, translations, and research on Russia's important early epic. These indexes also include pre-Soviet and Western sources.

The *povest'* (tale) in early Russian literature has been the subject of several bibliographies: V. P. Adrianova-Peretts, *Drevnerusskaya povest', bibliografiya* (Moscow and Leningrad, 1940, vol. 1, additional volumes were not published); N. K. Piksanov, *Starorusskaya povest', bibliografiya* (Moscow, 1923), and the Academy of Sciences's Institute of Russian Literature, *Bibliografiya drevnerusskoi povesti.* Ed. A. A. Nazarevskii (Moscow and Leningrad, 1955).

The literature of the 18th and 19th centuries has been more accessible to the bibliographer. Peter the Great organized libraries and academies and mandated the production of many works. Thus began a period of more systematic and controlled scholarly work. Soviet bibliographers have been able to record retrospectively the publishing record of this period. A joint effort by the Lenin Library in Moscow and the Saltykov-Shchedrin Library in Leningrad has resulted in the five-volume *Svodnyi katalog russkoi knigi grazhdanskoi pechati XVIII veka* (Union catalog of Russian books in civil type of the 18th century, Moscow, 1962–67), with *Dopolneniya* (Addenda, Moscow, 1975) based on their own vast collections and on the seminal work of Sopikov, Rogozhin, and other 19th-century bibliographers. Other works of this type include T. A. Bykova and M. M. Gurevich's *Opisanie izdanii napechatannykh pri Petre I* (Description of Publications printed under Peter I), which appears as two separate volumes: *Opisanie izdanii grazhdanskoi pechati, 1708–yan. 1725* (Moscow, 1955) and *Opisanie izdanii, napechatannykh kirillitsei 1689–yan. 1725* (Moscow, 1958), with *Dopolnenie* (Leningrad, 1972), based on the collection of the rare book department of the Saltykov-Shchedrin Library.

For serialized publications of the pre-revolutionary period, Soviet scholars have added to the pioneering work of Lisovsky and Sreznevsky (see above) with *Bibliografiya periodicheskikh izdanii Rossii, 1901–1916* (4 vols., Leningrad, 1958–64) under the editorship of L. N. Belyaeva. More selective in scope are A. G. Dementyev's *Russkaya periodicheskaya pechat', 1702–1894* (Moscow, 1959) and its companion volume by M. S. Cherepakhov and E. M. Fingirit, *Russkaya periodicheskaya pechat,' 1895–okt. 1917* (Moscow, 1957). For indexes which list the contents of this era's periodical literature, one can consult N. A. Vukotich, *Materialy dlya spiska ukazatelei russkoi periodicheskoi pechati* (Materials for a list of indexes to Russian periodicals, Leningrad, 1928). N. P. Smirnov-Sokolsky has compiled a descriptive listing of other types of serialized publications in *Russkie literaturnye al'manakhi i sborniki XVIII–XIX v.* (Russian literary almanacs and collections, Moscow, 1965).

Both the Academy of Sciences and the Lenin Library have published bibliographic guides to the original literature and criticism of Russian *belles lettres* in the 18th and 19th centuries. The former institution has produced: *Istoriya literatury XVIII v.* Comp. by V. P. Stepanov and Yu. V. Stennik (Leningrad, 1968). K. D. Muratova has edited the Academy's guides to the 19th century: *Istoriya russkoi literatury XIX v.* (Leningrad, 1962) and *Istoriya russkoi literatury kontsa XIX–nachala XX v.* (Leningrad, 1963). Each of the above provides a listing of an author's works, materials of biographical interest, and critical appraisals.

The Lenin Library has sponsored "recommended" bibliographies to the literature of this period. N. P. Zhdanovsky compiled *Russkie pisateli XVIII veka; rekomendatel'nyi ukazatel' literatury* (Moscow, 1954). R. M. Krendel presided over a committee of compilers to produce *Russkie pisateli pervoi poloviny XIX veka* (Moscow, 1951) and *Russkie pisateli vtoroi poloviny XIX–nachala XX vv.* (3 vols., Moscow, 1958–63). The above three works are somewhat more selective than the Academy bibliographies but in addition to listings by author, selected subject areas are also examined.

A valuable literary chronicle covering almost three decades of Russian literature is *Russkaya literatura kontsa XIX–nachala XX veka* (3 vols., Moscow, 1968–75), edited by V. A. Byalik. Each volume contains a monthly publication record of original works and criticism beginning with 1890 and continuing to 1917. Separate bibliographies of the works and/or of the critical literature about many of the major Russian authors, such as Pushkin, Dostoevsky, Tolstoi, Lermontov, Nekrasov, Saltykov-Shchedrin, Gorky, Esenin, and Leonov, have been published by IRLI (INSTITUT RUSSKOI LITERATURY or Pushkinskii Dom), IMLI (INSTITUT MIROVOI LITERATURY), publishing houses (Kniga, Vysshaya shkola, etc.), and by major libraries, such as the Leningrad Public Library.

Bibliography devoted to literature of the Soviet period is voluminous and only a representative sampling of retrospective compilations can be listed here. The Academy of Sciences has begun a series of cumulations designed to gather and classify criticism specifically of Soviet literature from the October Revolution to the present. *Sovetskoe literaturovedenie i kritika: Russkaya sovetskaya literatura* (Moscow, 1966–79) is now in four volumes and includes research published up to and including 1973.

The *Vsesoyuznaya knizhnaya palata* has completed a detailed record of serials, newspapers, etc. entitled *Periodicheskaya pechat' SSSR, 1917–49* (10 vols., Moscow, 1955–63). Volume eight is devoted to literary periodicals. The listing in each volume is chronological, but ample indexing is provided by title, place of publication, and issuing organization. The *Palata* has also published a four-volume cumulation *Literaturno-khudozhestvennye al'manakhi i sborniki; bibliograficheskii ukazatel'* (Moscow, 1957–60). This work covers publications between 1900 and 1937.

The Saltykov-Shchedrin Library in Leningrad is responsible for a retrospective look at the prosaists of the Soviet period. *Russkie sovetskie pisateli-prozaiki: biobibliograficheskii ukazatel'* (7 vols.,

Leningrad, 1959–72) gives a detailed record by writer of published works, biographical sources, and critical articles.

Sovetskaya literatura: Rekomendatel'nyi ukazatel' literatury (Moscow, 1976–79) is a four-volume work organized by literary genre. Each volume contains short bibliographic essays about selected authors and subjects. N. I. Matsuev has compiled a multi-volumed set of bibliographies covering works from 1938 to 1965 entitled *Sovetskaya khudozhestvennaya literatura i kritika* (Moscow, 1952–72, currently in its 9th volume). Matsuev's work is especially helpful for obtaining a listing of the original works of Soviet authors. A record of personal bibliographies of Soviet writers can be found in Yu. M. Laufer's *Bibliografiya russkoi sovetskoi literatury* (Moscow, 1963).

Other bibliographies, more specific in nature are: *Sovetskii roman, ego teoriya i istoriya; bibliograficheskii ukazatel', 1917–1964* (The Soviet novel, its theory and history, Leningrad, 1966); *Vosem' let russkoi khudozhestvennoi literatury (1917–25); bibliograficheskii spravochnik* (Moscow, 1926, A. M. Vitman et al. compilers); I. V. Vladislavlev (Gul'binskii), *Literatura velikogo desyatiletiya, 1917–27* (Literature of a great decade, Moscow, 1928); S. Stykalin, *Sovetskaya satiricheskaya pechat', 1917–63* (Moscow, 1963); and A. K. Tarasenkov, *Russkie poety XX veka, 1900–55: bibliografiya* (Moscow, 1966).

Russian literary bibliography in the West. There is a considerable amount of research devoted to Russian literature which does not originate in the Soviet Union, and the inability to read Russian need not be a hindrance to interested persons. Library catalogues, indexes to periodicals, encyclopedias and general reference works offer a wide array of materials on many topics of Russian literature and cultural life.

The *American Bibliography of Slavic and East European Studies* (Bloomington, Ind., 1956–) lists monographs and articles in English on literary history, theory, and individual authors. The *Bibliographic Guide to Soviet and East European studies* (Boston: G. K. Hall, 1978–) is an annual bibliography which uses the cataloguing records of the Library of Congress and the Slavonic Collection of the New York Public Library to provide a comprehensive listing of monographs, regardless of language or place of publication, on all aspects of life in that part of the world.

There are two annual bibliographies which are international in scope and provide listings not only of Russian publications, but of works in a variety of Western languages. The Modern Language Association's *MLA International Bibliography of Books and Articles on the Modern Languages and Literatures* (New York, 1957–) now indexes over 3000 scholarly journals, plus *Festschriften*, monographs, and collections. It contains a large section on Russian literature and in recent years has increased the number of cross-references to related subjects in order to facilitate comparative study. *Year's Work in Modern Language Study* (Oxford, 1952–), in essay form, offers a selective list of research in its section "Russian Literature."

A recent work by Garth M. Terry, *East European Language and Literature: a subject and name index to articles in English language journals. 1900–1970* (Oxford, 1978), is a time-saving cumulation which indexes and classifies articles in nearly 800 journals and includes approximately 10,000 citations.

Bibliographies of bibliography. The above listing contains only a sampling of the vast number of bibliographies devoted to the study of Russian literature. Personal bibliographies, bibliographic essays, and bibliographies attached to scholarly monographs have, for the most part, been omitted. Especially in the area of Western scholarship, non-scholarly material has been avoided as well as the many general works of national bibliography and periodical indexes. These often contain sections devoted to Russian literature and the works of individual authors, and the reader should be aware of their availability.

The following bibliographies of bibliography can provide additional avenues of inquiry:

Soviet and Russian Sources: B. S. Bodnarskii, *Bibliografiya russkoi bibliografii, bibliograficheskaya literatura s 1913 po 1925 gg. vklyuchitel'no.* 3 vols. Moscow, 1918–26. (Originally published as part of the journal *Bibliograficheskie izvestiya*). B. L. Kandel', et al. *Russkaya khudozhestvennaya literatura i literaturovedenie: Ukazatel' bibliograficheskikh posobii.* Moscow, 1976. M. V. Mashkova and M. V. Sokurova, *Obshchie bibliografii russkikh periodicheskikh izdanii, 1703–1954.* Leningrad, 1956. Vsesoyuznaya knizhnaya palata, *Bibliografiya sovetskoi bibliografii za 1939–.* Moscow, 1941–. (The official listing of all bibliographic work appearing in the Soviet Union).

———. *Obshchie bibliografii russkikh knig grazhdanskoi pechati, 1708–1955.* Leningrad, 1955, 2d ed. 1956. (Contains a table of the most significant works of Russian bibliography). N. V. Zdobnov, *Istoriya russkoi bibliografii do nachala XX v.* Moscow, 1942, 3d ed. 1955. (A bibliographic essay, well-indexed by compiler and title).

Western Sources: Yrjö Aav, *Bibliographies and books on librarianship in Russian characters in the Helsinki University Library.* Helsinki, 1965. (Contains a section on the History of Literature). Theodore Besterman, *A World Bibliography of Bibliographies.* 4th ed. Lausanne, 1966. (Lists only monographs and serials devoted to bibliography). *Bibliographic Index.* New York, 1937– . (Lists monographs, articles, and bibliographies appearing within monographs). *Bibliographische Berichte.* Frankfurt, 1959– . (Subject headings given in German and English). Louise Noëlle Maclès, *Les sources du travail bibliographique.* Genève, 1950–55. (Volume 2, part 2 contains a section on Russian bibliography). J. S. G. Simmons, *Russian Bibliography, Libraries and Archives. A Selective list . . .* Oxford, 1973. Alice F. Toomey, *A World Bibliography of Bibliography, 1964–74.* Totowa, N. J., 1977. (Continues Besterman). Serge A. Zenkovsky, and David Armbruster. *A Guide to the Bibliographies of Russian Literature.* Memphis, 1970.   A. U.

Biblioteka dlya chteniya, Zhurnal slovesnosti, nauk, khudozhestv, promyshlennosti, novostei i mod: (Library for Reading; Journal for Belles Lettres, Science, Art, Commerce, News and Fashions), 1834–65. A monthly journal and the first in Russia of encyclopedic scope. The history of this journal is inextricably linked to the fate of its first and most significant editor, O. I. SENKOVSKY. From 1834 to 1836, N. I. GRECH was officially listed as co editor. The Polish born Senkovsky, who wrote under the pseudonym of Baron Brambeus, created and breathed life into the journal. Financed by A. F. SMIRDIN and founded as a commercial venture, the journal was extremely successful in the 1830s. The title reflects its concerns; namely, an entertaining and easy way to acquire knowledge of existing literary and scholarly works. The significance of *Biblioteka* in the history of literature and journalism, in particular, is indisputable. By appealing to a wide range of readers (country gentry and urban bourgeoisie of all ages), Senkovsky succeeded in popularizing both literature and varied information in different realms of science. He also introduced readers to foreign literature with translations of George Sand, Balzac, Scott, Thackeray. As his contemporaries testify, his enormous talent and ceaseless activity were able to attract some of the foremost writers of the day: PUSHKIN, BESTUZHEV-Marlinsky, LERMONTOV, DAL, POLEVOI, later OSTROVSKY, MAIKOV, FET, L. TOLSTOI. However, his extremely pragmatic, at times cavalier, attitude towards his contributors helped to create a somewhat unsavory reputation. He asserted editorial prerogatives and dictatorial powers in rewriting and sometimes changing the work radically in order to make it more readable according to his lights. Under his guidance, the journal kept to a somewhat conservative political stance. The first blow to its authority was the appearance of OTECHESTVENNYE ZAPISKI in 1839. Gradually, the authority of *Biblioteka* began to diminish. In 1848, illness forced Senkovsky to retire. From 1847 to 1856 A. V. Starchevsky stood at the helm as co-editor and editor. A. V. DRUZHININ headed *Biblioteka* from 1856. At the end of 1860, A. F. PISEMSKY took over and tried his hand until 1863; P. B. BOBORYKIN then presided until the demise of the journal in 1865.

Bibliography: V. G. Belinskii, "Nichto o nichem" (1836). In *Polnoe sobranie sochinenii* (1953–59). Vol. 2, pp. 7–50. D. I. Bernshtein, "Biblioteka dlya chteniya," *Uchenye zapiski Moskovskogo gos. ped. instituta.* 1939. Vol. 2. L. Ya. Ginzburg, "Biblioteka dlya chteniya v 30-kh godakh. O. I. Senkovskii." In *Ocherki po istorii russkoi zhurnalistiki i kritiki.* Vol. 1. 1950. N. V. Gogol, "O dvizhenii zhurnal'noi literatury v 34 g." In *Polnoe sobranie sochinenii* (1937–52). Vol. 8. N. Panchenko, "Biblioteka dlya chteniya." In *Ocherki po istorii russkoi zhurnalistiki i kritiki.* Vol. 2. 1965.

E. K. K.

Bítov, Andreí Geórgievich (1937–), prose writer, was born in Leningrad. He served in the army for a period, and enrolled thereafter in the Leningrad Mining Institute (from which he had been expelled earlier). Summer geological expeditions provided material for his first works. When he completed his studies at the Institute in

1962, he signed agreements for his first book and a film scenario. His short stories have appeared in numerous journals and as a series of collections.

Bitov's stories contain psychological accounts of an urban hero and are largely comprised of "travel notes." The latter aspect seeks an understanding of man's place in both the world of nature and the world of man, a search whose intensity is heightened by the strain and isolation imposed by an alien environment. The cycles of stories in large measure chronicle the spiritual and psychological development of a hero, who consistently passes through moments of self-confrontation and resultant self-realization, while at the same time remaining essentially isolated from others. The frequent choice of the surname, "Monakhov," for the hero, emphasizes the sense of a certain spiritual isolation (*monakh* meaning "monk" in Russian).

Bitov is almost exclusively interested in his characters' inner world constructed from their own perceptions. At times, he suggests that fiction is itself a means of restoring one's perception analogous to that of a child. In this sense, Bitov's ultimate hero is literature, whose special function is to offer the possibility of attaining self-awareness and a revitalized vision of the world. In fact, Bitov's novel, *Pushkin House* (Pushkinskii dom), is dedicated to the Russian literary tradition, embodied in particular in Pushkin, Gogol, and Dostoevsky.

Works: Bol'shoi shar, Povesti. 1963. *Takoe dolgoe detstvo.* 1965. *Dachnaya mestnost', Povesti.* 1967. *Aptekarskii ostrov, Rasskazy i povesti.* 1968. *Obraz zhizni, Povesti.* 1972. *Sem' puteshestvii.* 1976. *Dni cheloveka.* 1976. *Pushkinskii dom.* Ann Arbor, 1978.

Secondary literature: L. Anninskii, "Tochka opory; eticheskie problemy sovremennoi prozy," *Don,* 1968, no. 6, pp. 168–81. Yu. Karabchievskii, "Tochka boli: O romane Andreya Bitova *Pushkinskii dom*," *Grani,* no. 106 (1977), pp. 141–203. Wolf Schmid, "Verfremdung bei Andrei Bitov." *Wiener Slavistischer Almanach,* 5 (1980): 25–53. V. Solov'ev, "Problema talanta." In *Puti k khudozhestvennoi pravde.* 1968. Pp. 262–95.   D. K. D.

Bitsílli, Pyotr Mikhaílovich (1879–1953), émigré historian, literary scholar, and linguist, a specialist in the history of the Renaissance and Russian 19th-century history. He was a professor of world history in his native Odessa (1917), Skopje (1920), and Sofia (1924–53). A scholar of broad erudition, Bitsilli left a variety of elegant essays on Russian literary history, in which he was able to combine methods of formal analysis and attention to particulars with an understanding of social ideas and historical intuition. His literary studies attract more and more attention both in the West and in the Soviet Union.

Works: (Only works relevant to Russian literature, or of general interest, are listed here.) *Elementy srednevekovoi kul'tury.* 1919. *Ocherki po teorii istoricheskoi nauki.* 1925. *Etyudy o russkoi poezii.* 1926. *Problema russko-ukrainskikh otnoshenii v svete istorii.* 1930. *Kratkaya istoriya russkoi literatury.* 1934. *K voprosu o kharaktere russkogo yazykovogo i literaturnogo razvitiya v novoe vremya.* 1936. "Puteshestvie v Arzrum." In *Belgradskii Pushkinskii sbornik.* 1937. *Pushkin i Vyazemskii: K voprosu ob istochnikakh pushkinskogo tvorchestva.* 1939. *Pushkin i problema chistoi poezii.* 1945. *K voprosu o vnutrennei forme romana Dostoevskogo.* 1946. (Reprint, 1966) *Problema cheloveka u Gogolya.* 1948. *Zametki o nekotorykh osobennostyakh razvitiya russkogo literaturnogo yazyka.* In *Godišnik na Sofijskija Universitet.* Filolog. fak. 47. 1954. Pp. 201–86. *Anton P. Čechov: Das Werk und sein Stil.* Trans. and supplemented from other works of the author by Vincent Sieveking. 1966. (Bibliography, pp. 239–43).

Translations: Chekhov's Art: A Stylistic Analysis. Trans. Toby W. Clyman and Edwina Cruise. Ann Arbor, 1982.

Secondary literature: Foster, 1, pp. 241–48. Belgrad. Russkii nauchnyi institut, *Materialy dlya bibliografii russkikh nauchnykh trudov za rubezhom.* Vols. 1–2 (1931–41). "Prof. Petr Mikhailovich Bitsilli." In *Istoričeski pregled,* 5 (1953): 560–61.   E. B.

Blank verse. Some prefer to limit the term blank verse to a specific form, the unrhymed pentameter line, which has been very widely used, especially for verse drama, in several literary traditions—most notably, English, German, and Russian. For Russian, at least, where poems may employ other meters and still be unrhymed, a more inclusive definition seems in order. It is still necessary to distinguish blank verse from FREE VERSE, which is usually unrhymed, but the term blank verse may be applied to all unrhymed *metrical* poetry.

The Russian phrase *belyi stikh* for blank verse apparently arose from the translation of a translation. The first literary blank verse was Italian, and the eleven-syllable unrhymed lines were called *versi sciolti* (literally, verse loosened or set free). From there unrhymed poetry entered the English tradition in the 16th century, where the word "blank" was applied because such poetry lacked the adornment of rhyme. French, where the tradition never really took hold, borrowed the term *vers blanc*; while *blanc* may mean empty or unmarked as well as white in French, Russians simply interpreted the word in its meaning of white; hence, *belyi stikh.*

Blank verse in Russian dates back to the 18th century. Kantemir employed it for his syllabic poem "To Elizabeth I" (Elisavete Pervoi, 1743), while some of the parodies that Sumarokov wrote in the 1750s are among the early examples of unrhymed verse in syllabotonic meters. Since then blank verse has remained a continuous if minor tradition in Russian poetry, the overwhelming majority of which is rhymed. The blank verse that has been written in Russian can be divided roughly into four groups:

(1) By far the most important use of blank verse has been in poems employing the unrhymed iambic pentameter. Here the direct influence of Shakespeare and other English poets, as well as of certain German poets (who had used it for original poetry since the second half of the 18th century) had a crucial impact. Thus it appears in Zhukovsky's translation of Schiller's *Die Jungfrau von Orleans* (1817–21), though Katenin's play "The Feast of John Lackland" (Pir Ioanna Bezzemel'nogo, 1820) appears to have been the first original dramatic work in Russian where the meter appears. Pushkin's *Boris Godunov* (1825) is written in iambic pentameter without caesura; after the late 1820s most works in this meter, including Pushkin's own "Little Tragedies" (Malen'kie tragedii, 1830), lack the caesura. From Pushkin's time on, the unrhymed iambic pentameter becomes the predominant form for verse drama: it occurs in A. K. Tolstoi's historical trilogy on Ivan the Terrible and his successors, in the historical chronicles of Ostrovsky, and in many other works. Somewhat later, in Annensky's plays, which employ more than one meter, the iambic pentameter is by far the most important. The meter has also appeared in many non-dramatic poems, including Blok's cycle "Free Thoughts" (Vol'nye mysli, 1907) and various short lyrics by poets who otherwise nearly always employ rhyme.

(2) Certain imitations of classical meters are unrhymed, such as the hexameter and its companion, the elegiac distich. Both were quite common from the establishment of the syllabotonic tradition until the middle of the 19th century; since then they have generally turned up, when at all, only in translations.

(3) Both imitations and stylizations of folklore frequently employ unrhymed verse. The longer folk genres were essentially unrhymed, although as a result of parallelisms grammatical rhymes did occasionally arise. Still, rhyme is not characteristic of the BYLINA or most folk songs. Thus Pushkin's "Tale of the Fisherman and the Fish" (Skazka o rybake i rybke, 1833), Lermontov's "Song of the Merchant Kalashnikov" (Pesnya pro ... kuptsa Kalashnikova, 1837), Nekrasov's "Who Can Be Happy and Free in Russia" (Komu na Rusi zhit' khorosho, 1863–77), and many of Koltsov's songs are all unrhymed. Similarly, numerous stylizations and translations of foreign folk verse also lack rhyme; for instance, the majority of Pushkin's "Songs of the Western Slavs" (Pesni zapadnykh slavyan, 1834) and Akhmatova's precise translations of the Serbian *deseterac* (a ten-syllable line with a caesura after the fourth syllable). Many attempts to imitate folk meters employ lines that are either trochaic or in a form of tonic versification known as strict accentual verse (sometimes called the *taktovik*); very often the unrhymed clausula is dactylic throughout the poem.

(4) Finally, lyric poetry written in meters other than iambic pentameter may also be unrhymed. Even though blank verse is not particularly common in any of the other meters, it can be found in nearly all the syllabotonic and tonic meters that have been commonly employed in literary Russian.

Bibliography: B. V. Tomashevskii, *Russkoe stikhoslozhenie.* Petrograd, 1923. Pp. 87–89. ———, *Stilistika i stikhoslozhenie.* Leningrad, 1959. Pp. 364–65. B. O. Unbegaun, *Russian Versification.* Oxford, 1956. Pp. 152–55.   B. S.

Blok, Aleksándr Aleksándrovich (1880–1921), poet and playwright, was born into a family of the gentry. His father, A. L. Blok, was a jurist, professor of Warsaw University, and a talented musician. His mother, A. A. Beketova, was a writer. His parents separated soon after his birth. Blok spent his childhood in the family of his grandfather A. N. Beketov, a botanist and Rector of Petersburg University, in Petersburg and the Beketov's estate Shakhmatovo, near Moscow. In 1889 Blok's mother obtained a formal divorce and married F. F. Kublitsky-Piottukh, an officer, whereupon she and her son moved to his apartment in an industrial section of Petersburg. Having graduated from a Gymnasium in 1898, Blok entered law school at Petersburg University, but transferred to its Historical-Philological Division in 1901, from which he graduated in 1906. In his early youth he had developed an interest in the theater (he played Hamlet, Romeo, and Chatsky in Griboedov's *Woe from Wit*) and intended to become an actor, but at 18 he began to write poetry seriously. In 1903 Blok married L. D. Mendeleeva, daughter of the famous chemist D. I. Mendeleev. This marriage, hardly successful in a conventional sense, proved important for Blok's inner development: L. D. Mendeleeva inspired almost all of his early and much of his later verse. Blok's rapprochement to A. BELY, S. SOLOVYOV, and other SYMBOLISTS occurred at the same time. In 1903 Blok's verses were first published in *Novyi put'*, a journal edited by D. MEREZHKOVSKY and Z. HIPPIUS.

In 1904 Blok's first book of verse appeared: *Verses on a Beautiful Lady* (Stikhi o Prekrasnoi Dame) was received with enthusiasm by the young symbolists. Blok's second book of verse, *Inadvertent Joy* (Nechayannaya radost', 1907), and his lyric drama *The Fair Show Booth* (Balaganchik), staged in 1906, made him famous. It was then that Blok became a professional man of letters, moving in the circles of the literary-philosophic intelligentsia and the theatrical Bohemia. His personal life and creativity were affected by his relations with the actress N. N. Volokhova (his cycles of verse, "Snow mask" [Snezhnaya maska], "Faina," and the play *Song of Fate* [Pesnya sud'by]) and the singer L. A. Del'mas (his cycle of verse, "Carmen"). Blok made several trips abroad, of which his journey to Italy in 1909 was particularly significant (his cycle "Italian Verses" and his series of essays, *Lightning Flashes of Art* [Molnii iskusstva]). His trip to Warsaw, occasioned by the death of his father in 1909, gave Blok the impulse for his verse epic *Retribution* (Vozmezdie, 1910–21). After the appearance of his books *Land in Snow* (Zemlya v snegu, 1907), *Lyric Dramas* (1908), *Nocturnal Hours* (Nochnye chasy, 1911), a three-volume collection of his poems (1911–12), the play *Rose and Cross* (Roza i krest, 1913), and the verse epic *Garden of Nightingales* (Solov'inyi sad, 1915) Blok's fame had spread all over Russia. He published many articles and gave many public lectures ("The People and the Intelligentsia"—Narod i intelligentsiya, 1908). In 1916 Blok edited and wrote an introduction to a collection of the poetry of A. GRIGORIEV, who influenced his late poetry in many ways.

Drafted in 1916, Blok was appointed, through the influence of friends, to serve as a record keeper with an engineering unit. He was stationed at the front near Pskov until March of 1917. He greeted the February Revolution with enthusiasm. Starting in May of 1917 he edited testimony given by former ministers of the Tsar before the Extraordinary Investigative Commission of the Provisional Government, which provided him with material for his book, *The Last Days of the Old Regime* (Poslednie dni starogo rezhima, 1919). The October Revolution initially also gave Blok much hope (his article, "Intelligentsia and Revolution," 1918). He worked for Soviet institutions, participated in the publishing house *Vsemirnaya literatura* (World literature), the Bolshoi dramatic theatre, and the *Vol'naya filosofskaya assotsiatsiya* (Vol'fila, Free Philosophic Association), which he helped to organize. In 1920 he was elected chairman of the Petrograd division of the All-Russian Union of Poets. Blok was close to the Left Social Revolutionaries' Party at the time. In February of 1919 he was briefly arrested in connection with the so-called "conspiracy of the Left SR's." The last two years of Blok's life were marked by his profound disappointment in the Revolution. Apathy, despair, hard living conditions, and a mysterious (possibly venereal) disease led to his mental illness and early death.

Blok is "the last romantic poet" (V. ZHIRMUNSKY). His creations are in all of their manifestations imbued with a profound lyric quality. It is important to be aware of the mythopoeic character of Blok's poetry: he gave his own life a supra-personal meaning, perceived it as a religious tragedy (in his mystic strivings he was close to the Gnostics and undogmatic branches of Christianity). The three volumes of his verse form, in his own words, "a trilogy of humanization" (*trilogiya*

vochelovecheniya), describing the spiritual becoming of the world and of the hero, the road to knowing the Truth through love. Blok was an innovator mainly in that he gave a new meaning to old, often archaic symbolic entities.

Blok's early poetry is linked to the traditions of ZHUKOVSKY, POLONSKY, FET, as well as to the epigonic lyrics of the 19th century. The spirit of German romanticism enters it through Zhukovsky. Impressions of the theater, poetic quotations and reminiscences play a significant role in his early verses. Later, Blok was fascinated by the poetry of Vladimir SOLOVYOV, and particularly by his cult of the World Soul, SOPHIA. This led him to theophanic and eschatological motifs, linked also to Novalis and Dante. In his *Verses on a Beautiful Lady*, Blok appears as a consistent symbolist and clairvoyant. These poems may be perceived as an intimate lyric diary; yet in terms of a symbolist "poetics of correspondences," the transcendent reveals itself to the poet in the mundane, and amatory, psychological, or landscape verse becomes timeless myth incarnate. The Beautiful Lady, an unearthly beloved, mediatrix between God and man, assumes certain traits of the Mother of God, yet on an earthly level becomes identical with the poet's fiancée, L. D. Mendeleeva, with the poet her servant and her knight. The peripeties of earthly love are interpreted on a philosophic plane, as participation in the spiritual foundation of being, as well as on a plane of mystic utopia, as anticipation of universal catastrophe, and the end and regeneration of the world. Motifs characteristic of the early Blok, such as those of distance, dawn, sundown, azure, mysterious premonitions and encounters, are connected to all this. These poems derive their structure from a complex intertwining of mythological motifs, they are saturated with Church symbolism, and in their tonality remind one of a prayer; every detail of landscape, every word, and every movement acquire hidden meaning. However, as early as in 1901 overtones of doubt and fear begin to invade Blok's poetry. They are followed by motifs of scepticism and cruel harlequinade, as in the cycle "Crossroads" (Rasput'ya, 1902–04).

The collections *Inadvertent Joy* and *Land in Snow* mark a transitional period in Blok's creative career. The revolution of 1905, in particular, is reflected in his changed worldview. Mystic presentiments and inner calm are replaced by moods of spiritual crisis and ruinous passions. The poet now proposes a plurality of avenues in the search of truth and leans himself toward moral relativism and anarchy. He downgrades and parodies the Solovyovian myth. The poet's friends A. Bely and S. Solovyov (and to some extent Blok himself) perceived this period as a betrayal of former ideals and even as religious apostasy. In Blok's poetry of this period the World Soul is replaced by another universal symbol, the unpredictable, irrational Power of nature. On the level of poetic imagery, the most significant transition is from the Beautiful Lady to the Unknown Woman (*Neznakomka*), an ordinary urban female who appears to the half-crazed imagination of the poet as an incarnation of mystery and beauty. While the symbolist duality of the real and unreal is retained, it turns to chaos and confusion. In place of dawn and sundown, the threatening and ominous motifs of blizzard, conflagration, and falling stars make their appearance. So do cityscapes, certainly in part under the influence of the urbanist poetry of BRYUSOV and the French symbolists to which Blok was attracted at the time. But in contrast to Bryusov, Blok sees the city as something deeply antispiritual, lifeless, infernal. Demonic nightmares of doubles and masks take shape in Petersburg's phantom world. Motifs of loneliness, doom, as well as social motifs originating with DOSTOEVSKY prevail. Blok fills the city with fantastic and grotesque creatures. An interest in popular demonology and folk magic also appears in the cycle *Bubbles of the Earth* (Puzyri zemli). Symbol is largely replaced by metaphor, often with traits of romantic satire. These phenomena, in spite of all their inner ambivalence, enrich Blok's lyrics and make them more complex. His poetry of this period is marked by boldness and irrationality of composition and imagery. The elevated lexicon of a religious cult is replaced by a concrete urban vocabulary. Also, Blok's metrics and strophics now tend to depart from classical norms, as DOL'NIKI, free verse, colloquial speech, and features of the gypsy romance make their appearance. The canon of exact rhyme is broken. In these respects, Blok is to some extent a precursor of FUTURISM. However, while he changes the structure of his verse, he still retains the romantic tone of his poetry: exaltedness, musicality, and a tendency toward synaesthesia and catachresis continue to be its dominant features.

The cycle *Free Thoughts* (Vol'nye mysli, 1907) is markedly different from Blok's other works of this period. Here his blank verse, striking in its energy and freedom of intonation, approaches the traditions of Russian realism.

Blok's mature poetry (the poems of his "third volume," 1907–16), enriched by new accomplishments, returns to classical models. Blok now moves close to Pushkin, whose level of artistry he almost reaches. As before, motifs of heartache, despair, cosmic dissonance, and chaos (the cycle *Terrible World*—Strashnyi mir), the absurdity of human existence (a group of poems entitled *Danse macabre*—Plyaski smerti) stand out. The cycle *Retribution* contains some magnificent penitential verse ("Of valor, feats, and glory"—"O doblestyakh, o podvigakh, o slave", "The Commander's Steps"—Shagi Komandora). Blok now looks back to his second period as to a fall, a substitution of modern decadence for living and creative symbolism; ecstatic transcendence beyond the limits of the mundane turned to sin. An ever present memory of his earlier symbolic systems imparts a metapoetic character to Blok's poetry of this kind. A striving emerges to leave lyric isolation for more objective genres. The cycle *Iambs* (Yamby) is imbued with political and social themes. In Blok's *Italian Verses* a vivid sense of history, a picturesque plasticity, and lively narrative appear; here Blok achieves an unsurpassed harmony of composition, rhythm, and sound symbolism ("Ravenna"). His short *poema* "Garden of Nightingales" in many ways resembles his *Italian Verses*.

The cycle *My Country* (Rodina), devoted to Russia's fate through history, occupies a central position in Blok's "third volume." It is full of anxiety and tragic premonitions. Here Blok turns to the traditions of Russian religious-philosophic thought and simultaneously to the heritage of NEKRASOV and "populist" lyrics. The image of Russia created in these poems is profoundly ambivalent. It flashes traits of a heavenly beloved, the Mother of God, but the savage, chaotic element is also present. Russia is humble and patient, yet possessed by an outlaw spirit of revolt. Rooted in her religious past (the cycle *On the Field of Kulikovo*—Na pole Kulikovom), poor and sinful in her present, Russia promises to become the New America of the future. The opposite poles of Blok's poetic ideal, whose outlines appeared in the first two volumes of his lyrics, are now fused in the image of Russia. Blok's myth becomes thus historically concrete: the Beautiful Lady and the Power of nature are reinterpreted as "my fateful native country" (*rokovaya, rodnaya strana*). The hero again becomes a knight who has broken the spell cast over his beloved and who foresees and helps to bring about the future New Life. By the same token, Blok now leans toward a radical revolutionary worldview. But even here he remains a symbolist and a romantic: entirely real objects and events become allegories, images of spiritual states.

The unfinished verse epic "Retribution" is, according to Blok, full of "revolutionary premonitions." In this work, Blok went back to his own roots, his personal genealogy: the poem was to delineate the history of the Beketov family from the 1870s to 1905. Most interesting is the historiosophic aspect of the poem, where the 19th century is characterized as "iron," and the 20th as "homeless." Blok sought to show the maturation of a spirit of music in the womb of an amusical civilization. "The spirit of music," related to Bergson's *élan vital*, which breaks down all boundaries and synthesizes culture, becomes a new Blokian myth (cf. his essay, *The Downfall of Humanism*—Krushenie gumanizma, 1919).

Blok's most famous and most controversial work is the verse epic *The Twelve* (Dvenadtsat', 1918), the first serious artistic response to the October Revolution. One hears in it familiar Blokian motifs such as a hatred for the lifeless and absurd world of the city, a rejection of the established way of life, destructive passion, murderous revolt which acquires a religious significance. Many of Blok's friends sharply protested against the poem. Soviet critics have interpreted it as a justification and acceptance of Bolshevism on Blok's part. In fact, *The Twelve* allows different, including mutually contradictory, interpretations. It seems most reasonable to understand the poem as a religious-moral tragedy, in which the basic problems of Blok's creative world are stated with the utmost acuity, yet are not given a definite solution. The poem is structured polyphonically, with abrupt rhythmic transitions. It uses the language of the city, the idiom of the popular romance, of the CHASTUSHKA, and of the revolutionary slogan. Blok destroys the harmonious and symmetric edifice of verse, introducing varied strophic patterns; yet at the same time, the poem

possesses a strict cyclic structure, and its twelve parts correspond to the number of twelve apostles, the red guards of the poem. The romanticism of *The Twelve* turns into a satire, praise becomes mockery, affirmation changes to negation. The whole poem leaves an impression of "a grandiose unresolved dissonance" (V. Zhirmunsky)

Almost simultaneously with *The Twelve*, Blok wrote the poem "The Scythians" (Skify), in which he develops some traditions of SLAVOPHILE thought, juxtaposing the sphinx that is Russia to civilized Europe. This poem, substantially rhetorical, enjoyed and still continues to enjoy great popularity.

The Twelve and "The Scythians" are usually considered to have been a last flash of Blok's creative genius. It is more correct, though, to consider as such Blok's last poem, "To Pushkin House" (Pushkinskomu domu), and his so-called discourse on Pushkin, "On the Poet's Calling" (O naznachenii poeta) (both 1921), where the poet expresses, nobly and with rare vigor, his protest against tyranny and his praise of the "secret freedom" which stands up to the power of vulgar officialdom.

Blok is important not only as a poet and essayist, but also as a dramatic poet. In 1906, having become close to the theatre of V. Komissarzhevskaya and the director V. MEYERHOLD, he wrote four plays. The best known of them, *The Fair Show Booth*, belongs to the same category of autopolemic and autoparodic works as many of Blok's poems of that period. Here Blok uncovers theatrical contrivance in mystery, mere posing in tragic experience, and emptiness in symbols. *The Fair Show Booth* can be interpreted on many levels, including the political. As far as structure and style are concerned, it is highly original: a mixture of tragedy and farce, a grotesque, with emphasis on the conventional and illusory. The play as well as its staging were a major event in the history of Russian and world avant-garde theater. The other three plays of that year were less successful. *The King in the Square* (Korol' na ploshchadi) and a dialogue connected with it, *On Love, Poetry, and Civil Service* (O lyubvi, poezii i gosudarstvennoi sluzhbe), state political problems in an ironic form which dates from German romanticism. *The Unknown Woman* (Neznakomka) develops the theme of the poem of that title. *Song of Fate* (1908) is not one of Blok's successes either: connected with the cycles "Snow Mask" and "Faina," and with the poet's "populist" moods, it presents these in an obtrusively allegoric manner. Blok's best play, *Rose and Cross*, is in verse. Here Blok brilliantly utilized the example of Calderon and Wagner. In contemporary literature, the plays of Paul Claudel may be considered analogous to it. The action of the play is set in a world of medieval legend and is connected with Gnostic myths. In 1916 K. STANISLAVSKY accepted the play for staging, but it was never performed. Blok's last play, *Ramses* (1919), was written for educational purposes and is of no serious importance. Blok also translated F. Grillparzer's drama *Die Ahnfrau* (Pramater', 1908).

Blok had a huge influence on Russian poetry, including schools that were hostile to him, ACMEISM and Futurism. AKHMATOVA and MAYAKOVSKY learned from him directly. He has entered history as a poetic witness of great changes and cataclysms, as a poet who transformed the Russian poetic idiom, and as one of the most controversial and remarkable Russian writers, "a monument to the beginning of a century" (Anna Akhmatova).

Works: Sobranie sochinenii. 12 vols. 1932–36. *Sobranie sochinenii.* 8 vols. 1960–63. *Zapisnye knizhki.* 1965.

Translations: Modern Russian Poetry. Ed. V. Markov and M. Sparks. 1967. Pp. 152–83. A. Pyman, ed., *Selected Poems.* 1972. Lucy E. Vogel, *Aleksandr Blok, The Journey to Italy.* 1973. *Selected Poems.* Moscow, 1981. See also: Lewanski, pp. 203–06.

Secondary literature: A. Blok i sovremennost'. 1981. *Aleksandr Blok v vospominaniyakh sovremennikov.* 2 vols. 1980. S. Alyanskii, *Vstrechi s Aleksandrom Blokom.* 2d ed. 1972. N. Ashukin, *Aleksandr Blok: Sinkhronicheskie tablitsy zhizni i tvorchestva, 1880–1921, Bibliografiya 1903–1923.* 1923. M. Beketova, *Aleksandr Blok.* 1922. 2d ed. 1930. ———, *Al. Blok i ego mat', vospominaniya i zametki.* 1925. A. Belyi, *Nachalo veka.* 1933. ———, *Mezhdu dvukh revolyutsii.* 1934. ———, *Vospominaniya o A. A. Bloke.* Munich, 1969. L. D. Blok, *Byli i nebylitsy.* Bremen, 1977. *Blok i muzyka: Khronika, Notografiya, Bibliografiya.* 1980. *Blokovskii sbornik*, 4 vols. Tartu, 1964–81. John E. Bowlt, "Aleksandr Blok: The Poem 'The Unknown Lady'," *Texas Studies in Literature and Language* 17 (1975), pp. 349–56. K. Chukovskii, *Kniga ob Aleksandre Bloke.* 1922.

———, *Aleksandr Blok kak chelovek i poet.* 1924. ———, *Sobranie sochinenii.* Vol. 2 (1965), pp. 264–316; vol. 6 (1969), pp. 505–79. ———, "Iz dnevnika (1919–1921)," *VLit* 24 (1980), no. 10, pp. 284–313. G. Chulkov, *Gody stranstvii.* 1930. Pp. 121–44. L. Dolgopolov, *Poemy Bloka i russkaya poema kontsa XIX–nachala XX vekov.* 1964. G. Donchin, *The Influence of French Symbolism on Russian Poetry.* The Hague, 1958. Victor Erlich, *The Double Image.* 1964. Pp. 99–119. E. Etkind, *Materiya stikha.* Paris, 1978. Pp. 16–43, 419–78. A. Fedorov, *Teatr A. Bloka i dramaturgiya ego vremeni.* 1972. ———, *Al. Blok—dramaturg.* 1980. L. Fleishman, "K interpretatsii blokovskogo tsikla 'Zaklyatie ognem i mrakom'," *Slavica Hierosolymitana* 1 (1977), pp. 102–08. B. Gasparov, "Poema A. Bloka 'Dvenadtsat' i nekotorye problemy karnavalizatsii v iskusstve nachala XX veka," *Slavica Hierosolymitana* 1 (1977), pp. 109–31. L. Ginzburg, *O lirike.* 2d ed. 1974. Pp. 243–310. Z. Gippius, *Zhivye litsa.* Prague, 1925. Pp. 5–70. P. Gromov, *A. Blok, ego predshestvenniki i sovremenniki.* 1966. Sergei Hackel, *The Poet and the Revolution: Aleksandr Blok's "The Twelve."* 1975. Robin Kemball, *Alexander Blok, a Study in Rhythm and Metre.* The Hague, 1965. R. Khlodovskii, "Blok i Dante." In *Dante i vsemirnaya literatura.* 1967. Pp. 176–248. E. Kolpakova, et al., *Materialy k bibliografii Aleksandra Bloka za 1928–1957 gg.* (Uchenye zapiski Vil'nyusskogo pedagogicheskogo instituta, 6.) 1959. Pp. 289–355. L. Krasnova, *Poetika Aleksandra Bloka.* Lvov, 1973. V. Lednitskii, "'Pol'skaya poema' Bloka," *Novyi zhurnal,* no. 2 (1942), pp. 309–24; no. 3 (1942), pp. 260–87. *Literaturnoe nasledstvo* 27–28 (1937); 92 (1980), books 1–4. S. Makovskii, *Na Parnase "Serebryanogo veka".* Munich, 1962. Pp. 143–75. D. Maksimov, *Poeziya i proza Al. Bloka.* 2d ed. 1981. Irene Masing, *A. Blok's "The Snow Mask"; An Interpretation.* Stockholm, 1970. P. Medvedev, *Dramy i poemy Al. Bloka.* 1928. Z. Mints, *Lirika Aleksandra Bloka.* 4 vols. Tartu, 1965–75. ———, *Chastotnyi slovar' "Stikhov o prekrasnoi dame" A. Bloka i nekotorye zamechaniya o strukture tsikla.* (Uchenye zapiski Tartuskogo universiteta, 198.) 1967. Pp. 180–316. ———, "Funktsiya reministsentsii v poetike A. Bloka," *Uchenye zapiski Tartuskogo universiteta* 308 (1973), pp. 387–417. K. Mochul'skii, *Aleksandr Blok.* Paris, 1948. Mon[akhinya] Mariya [E. Kuz'mina-Karavaeva], "Vstrechi s Blokom," *Sovremennye zapiski* 62 (1936), pp. 211–28. *O Bloke.* 1929. *Ob Aleksandre Bloke.* 1921. V. Orlov, *Poema Aleksandra Bloka "Dvenadtsat'."* 2d ed. 1967. ———, *Puti i sud'by.* 2d ed. 1971. Pp. 507–743. ———, *Pereput'ya.* 1976. Pp. 313–66. ———, *Gamayun.* 1978. (2d ed. 1980, English trans. 1980.) *Pamyati Aleksandra Bloka.* London, 1980. V. Pyast, *Vospominaniya o Bloke.* 1923. Avril Pyman, *The Life of Aleksandr Blok.* 1979– . F. D. Reeve, *Aleksandr Blok, Between Image and Idea.* 1962. T. Rodina, *Aleksandr Blok i russkii teatr nachala XX veka.* 1972. S. Solov'ev, "Vospominaniya ob Aleksandre Bloke." In *Pis'ma Aleksandra Bloka.* 1925. Pp. 9–45. G. Struve, *O chetyrekh poetakh.* London, 1981. Pp. 5–24. Kiril Taranovsky, "Certain Aspects of Blok's Symbolism." In *Studies in Slavic Linguistics and Poetics in Honor of Boris O. Unbegaun.* 1968. Pp. 249–60. ———, "Zelenaya zvezda i poyushchie vody v lirike Bloka," *RusL* 8, no. 4 (1980), pp. 363–76. *Tezisy I vsesoyuznoi (III) konferentsii "Tvorchestvo A. A. Bloka i russkaya kul'tura XX veka."* Tartu, 1975. V. Toporov, "K retseptsii poezii Zhukovskogo v nachale XX veka," *RusL* 5, no. 4 (1977), pp. 339–72. ———, *Akhmatova i Blok.* Berkeley, 1981. L. Trotsky, *Literature and Revolution.* 1968. Pp. 116–25. *V mire Bloka.* 1981. Jan van der Eng, "Aspects of Poetic Communication: Time and Space in Four Poems by A. Blok," *RusL* 8, no. 4 (1980), pp. 377–402. V. Veidle, *Posle "Dvenadtsati."* Paris, 1973. N. Vengrov, *Put' Aleksandra Bloka.* 1963. *Vospominaniya ob A. A. Bloke.* (Uchenye zapiski Tartuskogo universiteta, 104.) 1961. Pp. 296–378. A. Yakobson, *Konets tragedii.* New York, 1973. Pp. 7–195. *Zapiski mechtatelei,* no. 6, 1922. V. Zhirmunskii, *Poeziya A. Bloka.* 1922. ———, *Drama A. Bloka "Roza i krest."* 1964. "Anna Akhmatova i Aleksandr Blok," *RLit* 13 (1970), no. 3, pp. 57–82.

T. V.

Boborýkin, Pyotr Dmitrievich (1836–1921), novelist, and playwright, was born in Nizhny Novgorod, the son of a wealthy landowner, studied law at Kazan University, then physics and mathematics at the University of Dorpat, where he became interested in Russian and West European literature. He edited and published BIBLIOTEKA DLYA CHTENIYA from 1863 to 1865. Early in the 1890s he left Russia permanently and died in Lugano, Switzerland.

Boborykin was a very cultivated man, multi-lingual, a lecturer, teacher, literary and theatrical historian and commentator, feuilletonist, journalist, memoirist, author of more than 100 volumes. His immoderate productivity inspired the verb *boborykat'*: "to write badly on topical issues." For over six decades, in more than 30 plays and dozens of novels and short stories, he chronicled trends in Russian social and intellectual life. He is remembered chiefly as a novelist. *Bon Voyage* (V put'-dorogu, 1862–64) contains autobiographical material. *Vespertine Sacrifice* (Zhertva vechernyaya, 1868), like several plays, has passages censors labelled pornographic. *Solid Virtues* (Solidnye dobrodeteli, 1870) observes representatives from the liberal intelligentsia, including capitalists of various moral persuasions, who also figure in *Operators* (Del'tsy, 1872–73), *Kitai-gorod* (1882)—generally considered his best novel—and *Vasily Tyorkin* (1892), featuring an idealized peasant turned entrepreneur. The liberal intelligentsia also figures prominently in *Newcomers* (Iz novykh, 1882), *On the Wane* (Na ushcherbe, 1890), *Watershed* (Pereval, 1894), and *The Foot-Messenger* (Khodok, 1895). Boborykin treats controversies between Populists and Marxists ambivalently in *Another Way* (Po drugomu, 1897) and *Draft* (Tyaga, 1898), but the attitude to the 1905 revolution in *The Great Wreck* (Velikaya razrukha, 1908) is unequivocally anti-Marxist.

Boborykin's commitment to capitalism and naturalism isolated him from literary and political contemporaries. He is prolix and unimaginative, his characterizations static and schematic, his plots monotonous and cluttered by long descriptions that impede the flow of action.

Works: Sochineniya. 12 vols. 1884–86. *Sobranie romanov, povestei i rasskazov.* 12 vols. 1897 (complementary editions). *Evropeiskii roman v XIX stoletii.* 1900. *Za polveka: Moi vospominaniya.* 1929.

Secondary literature: "Boborykin." In *Istoriya russkoi literatury.* Vol. 2, pt. 2. 1956.

C. N. L.

Bobróv, Semyón Sergéevich (1763–1810), Russian poet, received his education at a seminary (starting 1772), the Gymnasium of Moscow University (starting 1780), and Moscow University (1782–85). After graduation he lived in Petersburg and later served as a translator for the Black Sea command of the Admiralty under Admiral N. S. Mordvinov. He returned to Petersburg around 1800, where he died of tuberculosis.

Bobrov was a contributor to the journals *Pokoyashchiisya trudolyubets, Zerkalo sveta, Beseduyushchii grazhdanin, Severnyi vestnik, Thalia, Lyceum,* and *Tsvetnik,* and a member of the "Amicable Learned Society" (Druzheskoe uchenoe obshchestvo) and the "Society of University Alumni" (Obshchestvo universitetskikh pitomtsev) at Moscow University, as well as of the "Society of Friends of Letters" (Obshchestvo druzei slovesnykh nauk) in Petersburg. Here he apparently met, and possibly befriended, N. A. RADISHCHEV. After his return to Petersburg, Bobrov actively participated in the activities of the FREE SOCIETY OF LOVERS OF LETTERS, SCIENCES, AND ARTS (Vol'noe obshchestvo lyubitelei slovesnosti, nauk i khudozhestv). Since his student years, Bobrov was under the strong influence of FREEMASONRY (he probably belonged to a Masonic lodge). His lyric poetry shows the influence of Edward Young's *Night Thoughts* and features their essential motives: meditation on life and death, the flow of time, apocalyptic moods, and such.

Bobrov wrote the first descriptive *poema* of Russian literature, *Tauris, or My Summer Day in the Tauric Chersonesus* (Nikolaev, 1798). He had the chapter "Summer" from Thomson's *The Seasons* for his model. In a poem, "Night" (1801), he condemned the assassination of Tsar Paul I. Bobrov's last work, a huge two-volume *poema, The Ancient Night of the Universe, or the Peregrine Blind Man* (Drevnyaya noch' vselennoi, ili Stranstvuyushchii slepets, 1801–09), is a mystic-philosophic allegory in the masonic manner, on the progress of the soul from base passions toward the light of true religious spirituality.

Works: Rassvet polnochi, ili Sozertsanie slavy, torzhestva i mudrosti porfironosnykh, branonosnykh i mirnykh geniev Rossii s posledovaniem didakticheskikh, eroticheskikh i drugikh raznogo roda v stikhakh i proze opytov Semena Bobrova. Pts. 1–4. St. Petersburg, 1804. [Poems and an excerpt from "Khersonida":] *Poety 1790–1810-kh godov.* (Biblioteka poeta. Bol'shaya seriya.) Comm. and biogr. by M. G. Al'tshuller. Leningrad, 1971. Pp. 67–160. *Proisshestvie v tsarstve tenei, ili Sud'bina rossiiskogo yazyka.* In *Trudy po russkoi i slavyanskoi filologii.* Vol. 24. *Uchenye zapiski Tartuskogo universiteta,* fasc. 358. Tartu, 1975. Pp. 255–322.

Secondary literature: M. G. Al'tshuller, "S. S. Bobrov i russkaya poeziya kontsa 18–nachala 19 v." In *Russkaya literatura 18 veka. Epokha klassitsizma.* (18 vek, 6.) 1964. Pp. 224–46. ———, "Poeticheskaya traditsiya Radishcheva v literaturnoi zhizni nachala 19 veka: Radishchev i Bobrov." In *A. N. Radishchev i literatura ego vremeni.* (18 vek, 12.) 1977. Pp. 114–24. ———, "S. Bobrov and E. Young" (forthcoming). S. Brailovskii, *Semen Sergeevich Bobrov.* (Izvestiya Istoriko-filologicheskogo instituta knyazya Bezborodko v Nezhine, 15.) Nezhin, 1895. Yu. Lotman and B. Uspenskii, "Spory o yazyke v nachale 19 veka kak fakt russkoi kul'tury," *Trudy po russkoi i slavyanskoi filologii* 24, pp. 168–254. Z. M. Petrova, "Zametki ob obrazno-poeticheskoi sisteme i yazyke poemy S. S. Bobrova 'Khersonida'." In *Poetika i stilistika russkoi literatury. Pamyati akademika V. V. Vinogradova.* 1971. Pp. 74–81.   M. A.

Bobróv, Sergeí Pávlovich (1889–1971). See FUTURISM.

Bóbyshev, Dimitry Vasílievich, born in 1936 in Mariupol, one of the most remarkable poets of his generation, essayist, and literary critic. His father, Vyacheslav Meshcheryakov, was an architect, his mother a research chemist. He was eventually adopted by his stepfather, Vasily Bobyshev, a naval engineer. Bobyshev graduated from the Leningrad Technological Institute. A number of his poems were published in Soviet periodicals. He moved to the United States in November, 1979. It was Anna AKHMATOVA who introduced Bobyshev to literature and Russian culture. Along with the poets Naiman, Rein, and BRODSKY, he is called an "orphan of Akhmatova," a label of his own coinage. Bobyshev's poetry is metaphysical. Even some of his early poems resemble psalms, devoted to a gracious and terrible God. Bobyshev was baptized by the well-known confessor, Fr. Dimitry Dudko. Fr. Aleksandr Men (Men'), another clergyman and theologian, was also his teacher. In his life and in his work, Bobyshev feels himself to be an Orthodox Christian. According to his own testimony, a mystic vision which he experienced in March of 1972 in Leningrad has been the most important event of his life. It somewhat resembled the visions of Vladimir SOLOVYOV and of Swedenborg. This spiritual epiphany is reflected in several cycles of his verse: "Material Comedy" (Veshchestvennaya komediya), "Meditations" (Meditatsii), and "Sigmates" (Sigmaty). Man is to Bobyshev "an intelligent, living particle." From men, "the Creator creates creators," and here Bobyshev's conception agrees with BERDYAEV's ideas, as stated in *The Meaning of Creation* (Smysl tvorchestva). But most of all, Bobyshev leans on his mystic experience. His Christianity is a cosmic one. The crucifixion appears to him in terms of coordinate axes of cosmic space. This is not pantheism, but panentheism, the revelation of a transcendent God in the cosmos. And yet Bobyshev's God is also personal: Father and Son, Savior and Redeemer. Excessive spiritualism is alien to Bobyshev. He captures the heavenly in the earthly. The human being is to him "matter plus deity." There is a certain dogmatic precision and credibility of actual religious experience in his Christian poetry. Bobyshev's lyric persona is not a flattened, ambivalent 20th-century Hamlet, but an integral religious individuality, much as is also the case in the poetry of the great Russian Christian poet Osip MANDELSHTAM. Bobyshev cultivates no Baudelairean infernal flowers of Evil, but rather the flowers of Good in a Dantesque *paradiso.* His verses have nothing of the decadence, nihilism, or grotesque buffoonery found in some other Soviet dissident poets. Bobyshev is of course far removed from any official Soviet versifiers. He is moved by the divine order of the world and by feats of human culture. His message is: "Flower, sacred Life, / in dirty, delicate work, / in pure sweat, on the road, / in the dark experience of the flesh, / even in your lethal flight, / die, but flower." A bright, positive faith speaks through his poetry. Bobyshev's message is one of this-worldly, rather than otherworldly Christianity, such as was established in Russia by DOSTOEVSKY, Vladimir Solovyov, and the thinkers of the so-called "new religious consciousness," Berdyaev, Fr. Sergei BULGAKOV, Semyon FRANK, and Nikolai LOSSKY. It is not always easy to solve Bobyshev's metaphysical puzzles, his very much "avant-garde," yet also carefully thought-out game of images and associations, often distant from one another. One may sometimes get lost in the thickets of Bobyshev's metaphysical lyrics, much as in

the verses of a John Donne or Luis Gongora. Bobyshev's neobaroque poetics originates from that of his favorite poet, DERZHAVIN. Perhaps inadvertently, he follows the canon of the Russian baroque, codified by the critic A. S. SHISHKOV, who recommended that Russian poets should mix Slavonic expressions with the vernacular, i.e., "high" and "low" style. Bobyshev's poetry features archaisms from the 18th century along with prosaisms, and even Soviet slang. Perhaps this is why even his most "bookish" verses are not abstract, but are invested with lyric energy and a dynamic faith. There are among Bobyshev's poems some which form a figure, such as a crucifix, a triangle, a six-pointed star, etc., like in the poetry of the 17th and 18th century, but also in some modern poets, Dylan Thomas, for example. There is also a certain similarity between Bobyshev's poetry and that of Iosif BRODSKY. What Brodsky looks for in the Old Testament, Bobyshev finds in the Gospel. In his most recent poems, written in the United States, Bobyshev writes about America. Americans remind him of the carefree lotus-eaters of the Odyssey. In his *Russian Tercines,* heeding SOLZHENITSYN's call for national penance, Bobyshev unveils many of the dark aspects of Russia, contemporary and historical, and senses the doom of "the last of the empires" (the USSR), yet continues to love his native Russia passionately. He also shows what is best about her: her culture and her saintliness. Bobyshev is particularly successful at painting landscapes of the Russian North. In his *Petersburg Cycle,* Bobyshev celebrates St. Xenia of Petersburg, who lived in the 18th century and was recently canonized by the Russian Synodal Church in the United States, after having been venerated locally for a long time. She is for Bobyshev the heavenly patroness of her native St. Petersburg, which Bobyshev envisages behind today's Leningrad. In the United States, Bobyshev has read his poetry, lectured, and given papers on many university campuses. His verses have been broadcast to the USSR by Radio Canada, Voice of America, BBC, and Vatican Radio.

Works: Ziyaniya: Sbornik stikhotvorenii i poem. Paris, 1979. Bobyshev's poetry has been published in *Kontinent, Vremya i my, Vestnik RKhD, Russkaya mysl',* and other periodicals. Interview with Bobyshev: *Russkaya mysl',* 10 September 1981.

Secondary literature: (Anon.) *The Post* (Wooster, Ohio), 8 October 1980, *The Milwaukee Journal,* 26 March 1981. A. Bakhrakh, *Novoe russkoe slovo,* 30 December 1979. K. Filips-Juswigg, "*Russkie tertsiny* Bobysheva," *Russkaya mysl',* 20 May 1982. N. Gorbanevskaya, *Kontinent* 22 (1980). Yu. Ivask, "Tsvety dobra" [Flowers of Good], *Russkaya mysl',* 25 September 1980, and *Vestnik RKhD,* 134 (1981). Yu. Mal'tsev, *Posev.* 1976.   G. I.

Bogatyrév, Pyotr Grigórievich (1893–1971), folklorist and literary scholar, hailed from Saratov. After graduating from Moscow University in 1918, he worked as Professor in Bratislava, Czechoslovakia, from 1921 to 1940. Having returned to the Soviet Union and received his doctorate in 1941, he taught at Moscow University and was director of the Folklore Sector of the Institute of Ethnography, Academy of Sciences, from 1943 to 1948. He was removed from both positions in 1948. Apparently rehabilitated in 1952, he was Professor at Voronezh University until 1963 and again at Moscow University, 1964 to 1971.

Bogatyrev was, with R. JAKOBSON, a cofounder of the Moscow Linguistic Circle in 1915 and later one of the most active members of the Prague Linguistic Circle, which laid the foundation for the "FORMAL SCHOOL" and the structural-semiotic trend in linguistics, folkloristics, and ethnography.

Bogatyrev published numerous books and articles on folklore, folk belief, ethnography, and literature of the Slavs (especially the West Slavs and Ukrainians). In folklore he utilized the functional-structural approach. In his first important study, *Actes magiques, rites et croyances en Russie Subcarpatique* (1929), Bogatyrev used the synchronic method advanced by F. de Saussure for the investigation of ethnographic and folklore material. He studied the forms and functions of popular customs, rites, and magical acts and demonstrated that the changes in them were affected by the changes in the functional hierarchy. His study *The Functions of Folk Costume in Moravian Slovakia* (Funkcie kroja na Moravskom Slovensku, 1937) investigated the everyday, holiday, ceremonial, and ritual costumes of Slovakia from the structural-functional standpoint, claiming that the costume functions simultaneously as a thing and a sign. His doctoral dissertation, *Czech and Slovak Folk Theater* (Lidové divadlo české a slovenské, 1940), dealt with the form and function of the folk theater as a structured art, unraveling its connection with popular rites and customs.

Bogatyrev also studied the Slavic folk epic, folk tales, folk songs, folk dance, and Russian-Czech literary relations. He fully recognized the strong mutual influences between oral and written verbal art and of folk arts and "high art" in general (R. Jakobson). He edited a textbook of Russian folklore and a chrestomathy of the epic of the Slavic peoples. His major monographs and articles were published in a volume, *Questions of the Theory of Popular Art* (Voprosy teorii narodnogo iskusstva, 1971).

Works: Actes magiques, rites et croyances en Russie Subcarpatique. Paris, 1929. *Funkcie kroja na Moravskom Slovensku.* Turčiansky Sv. Martin, 1937. *Lidové divadlo české a slovenské.* Prague, 1940. *The Functions of Folk Costume in Moravian Slovakia.* The Hague, 1971. *Voprosy teorii narodnogo iskusstva.* Moscow, 1971. "Ritual Games in the Funerals of Sub-Carpathian Russia," *Folklore Forum* 10, no. 2 (1977), pp. 41–59.

Secondary literature: N. N. Gratsianskaya and E. V. Pomerantseva, "Pyotr Grigor'evich Bogatyrev," *Sovetskaya etnografiya,* 1971, no. 6, pp. 192–94. Roman Jakobson, "Petr Bogatyrev: Expert in Transfiguration," *Sound, Sign, Meaning,* Michigan Slavic Contributions, 6 (1976), pp. 29–39.   F. J. O.

Bogdánov (real name: Malinóvsky), Aleksándr Aleksándrovich (1873–1928). A philosopher of MARXISM, a literary activist and writer, Bogdanov was an early member of the bolshevik faction of the RSDP, and an early associate of LENIN. Under the influence of the Viennese philosopher Ernst Mach he developed the system of philosophical views known as "empiriomonism" (1906) which Lenin attacked vigorously in his *Materialism and Empiriocriticism* (1909). Bogdanov was one of the organizers, along with LUNACHARSKY and Bazarov, of a Party school on Capri (1909) where he helped develop the ideas of working humanity as a "god-building" force, and of the Party as an expression of that force rather than a conspiratorial organization. Those ideas too met with Lenin's violent opposition. Bogdanov was the principal theoretician of the PROLETKUL'T, and he propounded the view that the cultural development of the proletariat should proceed independently of the Party apparatus. The heritage of past literature must, he maintained, be assimilated and "mastered" by the proletariat. Bogdanov had been educated as a doctor and he was a convinced exponent of an organization of the future society based on the exact sciences. He wrote two science fiction novels, *Red Star* (Krasnaya zvezda, 1908) and *Engineer Manni* (1912). The first of these was interesting for its anticipation of rocket travel, automation of production, and atomic fission. Bogdanov was the founder of an Institute for Blood Transfusion in Moscow, and his death occurred as the result of an experiment performed upon himself.

Works: Iskusstvo i rabochii klass. 1918. *O proletarskoi kul'ture.* 1924.

Secondary literature: E. J. Brown, *The Proletarian Episode in Russian Literature.* 1953, 1971. Jutta Scherrer, "Les écoles du parti de Capri et de Bologne: la formation de l'intelligentsia du parti," *Cahiers du Monde russe et sovietique* 19, no. 3 (1978). Jutta Scherrer and Georges Haupt, "Gor'kii, Bogdanov, Lenin: Neue Quellen zur ideologischen Krise in der bolschevistischen Fraktion (1908–1911)," *Cahiers du Monde russe et sovietique* 19, no. 3 (1978). ———, "Bogdanov e Lenin." In *Storia del Marxismo.* Vol. 2. Turin, 1979.
E. J. B.

Bogdanóvich, Ippolít Fyódorovich (1744–1803). Born in a family of Ukrainian gentry, Bogdanovich at the age of 15 introduced himself to M. M. KHERASKOV, the playwright and writer of Neoclassical verse, as a "youth interested in poetry and music." Kheraskov encouraged him to enter Moscow University (1761). In 1765, Bogdanovich published a versified treatise *Double Bliss* (Sugubnoe blazhenstvo) which proved a failure, and he published little until *The Lyre* (Lira, 1773), a collection of fables, epistles, epigrams, and odes. He translated various works of Voltaire, Jean-Jacques Rousseau and other enlightened French writers. In 1775, he was appointed editor of the official journal of the Academy of Sciences, which he enlivened by translations from foreign newspapers until 1782, when he was obliged to

resign. His major work was *Dushenka: An Ancient Tale in Free Verse* (Dushen'ka. Drevnyaya povest' v vol'nykh stikhakh, 1783). Book I had been published separately in 1778, but Bogdanovich revised it for the 1783 edition. A Russian version of the myth of Amor and Psyche, with acknowledgments to Apuleius and La Fontaine, *Dushenka* differs from other 18th-century mock-heroic poems in treating the subject poetically, rather than mockingly. In this respect it resembles Pope's *The Rape of the Lock.* The domestic arrangements, food, clothing are Russian, and Amor's court and gardens are a description of Tsarskoe selo (rebuilt in 1779). Bogdanovich's own voice is audible addressing the reader, thereby giving a tone of unforced intimacy new to Russian narrative poetry. Bogdanovich's *Collected Works* in six volumes (1809–10) were reprinted in 1818–19, when PUSHKIN was writing *Ruslan and Lyudmila,* which shows some evidence of Pushkin's admiration for *Dushenka.*

Works: Stikhotvoreniya i poemy. 1957.

Translations: "Dushen'ka: An Ancient Tale in Free Verse." In Harold B. Segel, *The Literature of Eighteenth-Century Russia: A History and Anthology.* 1967. Vol. 2. Pp. 180–238.

Secondary literature: I. Z. Serman, Introductory essay to *Stikhotvoreniya i poemy.* 1957.   D. W.

Bóndarev, Yúry Vasílievich (1924–   ), Soviet novelist, was born in Orsk. A veteran of World War II, Bondarev graduated from the Gorky Literary Institute in 1951. He began writing short stories in the late 1940s but eventually turned to novels with *The Commanders' Youth* (Yunost' komandirov, 1956). Bondarev's major concern has been the morality of his generation. His short novels, *The Battalions Are Asking for Fire* (Batal'ony prosyat ognya, 1957) and *The Last Volleys* (Poslednie zalpy, 1959), and the novel *The Hot Snow* (Goryachii sneg, 1969) all deal with war, focusing on the emotions and actions of combatants in critical situations. Themes of morality and Stalin's postwar repression dominate the novel *Silence* (Tishina, 1962) and its sequel *The Two* (Dvoe, 1964), while in the short novel *Relatives* (Rodstvenniki, 1969) children judge their parents' behavior during the purges.

The relation between man's youth and his middle age has been a prominent theme of Bondarev's recent novels. In *The Shore* (Bereg, 1975) a Soviet writer learns that a German woman, with whom he had a passionate romance as a young officer, still loves him. He dies, without reaching the promised shore of the dream of his youth. In *The Choice* (Vybor, 1980) a terminally ill expatriate kills himself on a visit to Moscow so that he may be buried in the city of his youth. His fate causes his former Soviet friend to engage in a painful exploration of existential questions. Bondarev is strong in his presentation of war and human relationships, while his ideology remains within official boundaries.

Works: Sobranie sochinenii. 4 vols. 1973–74. *Bereg.* 1975. *Vybor.* 1981.

Translations: The Last Shots (1961). *Silence* (1965). *The Hot Snow* (1971). *The Choice* (1980), *Soviet Literature,* 7–9 (1981). "The Vigil," trans. Robert Daglish. In *Anthology of Soviet Short Stories.* Vol. 2. Moscow, 1976.

Secondary literature: D. Brown, *Soviet Russian Literature since Stalin.* 1978. Pp. 273–75, 279–280. E. Gorbunova, *Yurii Bondarev: Ocherk tvorchestva.* 1981. B. Mai, "Auf der Suche nach einer neuen Synthese: Jurij Bondarevs Roman *Bereg,*" ZS 25 (1980), pp. 479–93. I. Rostovtseva, "The Responsibility of Memory," *Soviet Literature,* 1981, no. 9, pp. 118–25.   H. E.

Book of Degrees, see STEPENNAYA KNIGA.

Book of Generations, see STEPENNAYA KNIGA.

Boris and Gleb, SS. (died ca. 1015). Portrayed in Kievan hagiography as the first examples of obedience to the Christian political code of ethics in newly-converted *Rus'.* Upon the death of their father Grand Prince Vladimir in 1015, Boris and Gleb refused to enter into violent competition with their elder brother Svyatopolk over succession to the Kievan throne. The two brothers preferred a martyr's death to fratricide. The hagiographic accounts emphasize that the martyrdom of Boris and Gleb was not in vain—the "cursed" Svyatopolk eventually is vanquished by their righteous brother Yaroslav who establishes the reign of a blessed dynasty. Attempts at canonization undertaken by Yaroslav (reigned 1019–54) were ultimately successful: the sanctity of the two brothers was recognized by the Byzantine Church, and later by the Universal Church. After the relics of Boris and Gleb were transferred to Vyshgorod in 1072, they quickly became objects of legendary veneration.

The martyrdom of Boris and Gleb is celebrated in many works: (1) the account found in the *Primary Chronicle* (for the year 1015) entitled "On the Murder of Boris"; (2) the LEGEND (Skazanie) *and the Passion and the Encomium of the Holy Martyrs Boris and Gleb*; (3) the *Reading* (Chtenie) *on the Life and Slaying of the Blessed Passion-Sufferers Boris and Gleb*; (4) other accounts, including the *Offices of Boris and Gleb*, the *Encomia of Boris and Gleb*, the legends found in the PROLOG, and the readings contained in the *Paremiinik*. Given the presence of common textual material and themes, the relationship between these works (in particular, between the *Chronicle* account, the *Legend*, and the *Reading*) has been the object of considerable controversy. The following hypotheses have been advanced: (1) the *Reading*, attributed to the monk Nestor in our codices, was written on the basis of the *Legend*, whose compiler had made use of the *Chronicle* account (Bugoslavsky); (2) the *Reading* and the *Chronicle* account were already available to the anonymous compiler of the *Legend* (Shakhmatov, Serebryansky, Abramovich, Voronin); (3) the extant works all derive from a hagiographic saga, an "Ur-legend," and other (now lost) sources (Müller). Scholars generally agree that the *Legend* exhibits compilatory features, but disagree as to whether the so-called "Legend on Miracles" (Skazanie o chudesakh) belongs to an original compilatory scheme or represents a later addition.

The popularity of Boris and Gleb in the Old Russian literary tradition is well documented by the large number of manuscripts known to us which contain works on their life and martyrdom or relating to their cult. Exceptional in this regard is the widespread diffusion of the *Legend*—the thirteen testimonies of this work recently made known by G. Revelli bring the total to 180 codices.

Bibliography: D. I. Abramovich, ed., *Zhitiya svyatykh muchenikov Borisa i Gleba i sluzhby im.* (Pamyatniki drevnerusskoi literatury, no. 2.) Petrograd, 1916. L. A. Dmitriev and D. S. Likhachëv, eds., *Pamyatniki literatury drevnei Rusi: XI–nachalo XII veka.* 1978. J. Fennell and A. Stokes. *Early Russian Literature.* Berkeley and Los Angeles, 1974. Pp. 11–32. L. Müller, "Studien zur altrussischen Legende der Heiligen Boris und Gleb," *Zeitschrift für Slavische Philologie* 23 (1954), pp. 60–77; 25 (1956), pp. 329–63; 27 (1959), pp. 272–322; 30 (1962), pp. 14–44. G. Revelli, "Arkheograficheskie svedeniya o neizvestnykh rukopisyakh *Skazaniya o Borise i Glebe*," *Ricerche slavistiche* 24–26 (1977–79), pp. 11–21. N. N. Voronin, "'Anonimnoe' skazanie o Borise i Glebe, ego vremya, stil' i avtor," *TODRL* 13 (1957), pp. 11–56.   R. P.

Bótkin, Vasíly Petróvich (1811–69), literary, art, and music critic and publicist. The son of a wealthy merchant and brother of the well-known physician, Sergei Botkin, he was a moderate liberal in the thirties and forties, associating with both members of the STANKEVICH Circle and the WESTERNIZERS (BAKUNIN, BELINSKY, HERZEN). A man of elegant and expensive tastes, a connoisseur of art and music, and a polyglot, he traveled widely in Europe, meeting with such varied personalities as Karl Marx, Louis Blanc, and Victor Hugo. Although he was the first Russian publicist to acquaint Russian readers with the writings of the young Engels, his *Letters on Spain* (published 1847 to 1849 in *Sovremennik*) has remained his most popular work. Botkin was a prodigious letter writer and much of his aesthetic and critical theory, quite eclectically romantic and strongly colored by German idealist thought, is in fact scattered throughout his extensive correspondence, especially with Ivan TURGENEV. More of his general comments on aesthetics and critical theory may be found in his essay on the poetry of Afanasy FET (who married Botkin's sister), "The Poetry of A. A. Fet" (published in SOVREMENNIK in 1857). The "Year of Revolution" in Europe, 1848, seems to have frightened Botkin and thereafter he became more and more politically conservative. As a critic, he also moved further to the right after 1855, becoming eventually a spokesman for autotelic ("art for art's sake") theory and an "aesthetic" critic. In this connection, his name is frequently linked with those of Aleksandr DRUZHININ and Pavel ANNENKOV.

Works: Sochineniya. 3 vols. 1890-93. *Pis'ma ob Ispanii.* 1976. *V. P. Botkin i I. S. Turgenev.* Ed. N. Brodskii. 1930.
Secondary literature: Edmund Kostka, "A Trailblazer of Russian Westernism," *Comparative Literature* 18 (1966), pp. 211–24.
R. II. 3.

Bová Korolévich (Prince Bova), *Tale of*, a popular Russian chivalric romance of the 17th century. It circulated in manuscript as well as printed form in the so-called LUBOCHNAYA LITERATURA. The tale of Bova, along with several other chivalric tales of Western origin, was extremely popular with Russian readers of the 17th, 18th and even 19th centuries, and illustrates a new, Western, and secular orientation of Russian literature of that period. These tales introduced concepts such as chivalric honor, fidelity, and a mild eroticism new to Russian literature of the 17th century, and this was no doubt their appeal.

The source of the tale is a French romance of the 13th century about the Norman-French hero Beuve d'Antone (the English Bevis of Hampton). This tale spread to Italy, and in the 16th century a Serbian Slavic version was made along the Dalmatian coast; this in turn served as the basis for a Belorussian (West Russian) version from which the Russian 17th century tale derived.

The narrative is an extremely complex one, with many characters and episodes. The hero, Prince Bova, must fight for his inheritance against his evil stepmother, who has killed his father. Bova prevails after many contests over all his enemies, and at the end marries the beautiful Princess Druzhevna. Of great interest is the attempt to Russianize the story by adding many details of content and style from the Russian epic songs (see BYLINA) and the Russian FOLKTALES, and the figure of Bova himself actually appears in other Russian folk songs and folktales.

The romance about Bova was first popular among the upper classes, and the work appears in the list of "leisure reading" of the tsarevich, Aleksei Petrovich. Gradually, as happened to much of the older Russian literature, it moved down the social ladder and became favorite reading of the lower middle classes and literate peasants, for whom the *lubochnaya literatura* or "chap" literature was published.

The romance about Bova had considerable influence on later Russian literature. RADISHCHEV and PUSHKIN both wrote narrative poems about Bova. In *The Brothers Karamazov*, DOSTOEVSKY's Smerdyakov compares himself to the "faithful servant Licharda," a character in "Bova Korolevich."

Bibliography: W. E. Brown, *A History of Russian Seventeenth-Century Literature.* Ann Arbor, 1980. Pp. 45–47. Dmitrij Čiževskij, *History of Russian Literature from the 11th Century to the End of the Baroque.* The Hague, 1960. Pp. 236–37. N. K. Gudziy, *History of Early Russian Literature.* New York, 1949. Pp. 412–16. V. D. Kuzmina, "Povest' o Bove-koroleviche v russkoi rukopisnoi traditsii XVII–XIX vv." In *Starinnaya russkaya povest'.* Ed. N. K. Gudzii. 1941. Pp. 83–134.   W. E. H.

Brik, Osip Maksímovich (1888–1945), literary theorist and playwright. A graduate of the Law School at Moscow University, Brik was married to one of the Kagan sisters, Lili, who later became MAYAKOVSKY's mistress and inspired many of his poems. After the October revolution, Brik worked at the Commissariat for Education in the Department of Fine Arts. There he edited the journal *Iskusstvo kommuny* (1918–19) which propagated both Marxist ideals and FUTURIST poetry. He cofounded the journals LEF (1923–25) and NOVYI LEF (1927–28), which similarly supported literary experimentation combined with a devotion to the cause of the new Soviet state.

According to the testimony of his longtime friend V. B. SHKLOVSKY, Brik was a talented but modest person who did not attempt to make a name for himself by publishing literary scholarship. He seldom put down his thoughts on paper and preferred to inspire others rather than to write himself.

Brik's scholarly reputation rests on two essays investigating the ways in which auditory and semantic effects are achieved in poetry: "Sound Repetitions" (Zvukovye povtory, 1917) and "Rhythm and Syntax" (Ritm i sintaksis, 1927). In the first essay, Brik investigated sound repetitions which do not produce a rhyme and which occur in unaccented syllables. He discovered several patterns of such repetitions in the poetry of PUSHKIN, LERMONTOV and of other Russian poets. In the second essay, the same principle of investigation was applied to rhythm and syntax. Brik argued that in Russian poetry of various periods there exist "rhythmical and syntactical figures," or word combinations following the same grammatical pattern. This last study was a follow-up to the work of Andrei BELY who made a similar study in *Simvolizm* (1910).

Works: Radio-Oktyabr' (a play co-authored with V. V. Mayakovsky, 1926). *Ivan Groznyi: Istoricheskaya tragediya.* 1942.

Secondary literature: Vahan D. Barooshian, *Brik and Mayakovsky.* The Hague, 1978. B. Jangfeldt, "Osip Brik: A Bibliography, with an Introduction and a Post Scriptum," *RusL* 8 (1980), pp. 579–604. Rosemarie Ziegler, "Zu einer Bibliographie der Werke von O. M. Brik," *Wiener Slawistischer Almanach* 5 (1980), pp. 335–50.

E. Th.

Bródsky, Iósif Aleksándrovich (1940–   ), contemporary poet, born in Leningrad and currently teaching at universities in the United States. All of his collections of poetry were published in the West rather than in the Soviet Union; only separate poems appeared there. He was arrested in January of 1964, charged with "parasitism," sentenced in March to five years administrative exile, and sent to work on a state farm in the Arkhangelsk region. While he was there his first collection of verse was published in the West, and public opinion was roused in his support. In November of 1965 he was released and allowed to return to Leningrad, where he continued to write and translate from English. In 1972 he was all but required by the authorities to emigrate; no cause was given. His poetry is apolitical and universal in its themes; it achieves what may be called a modern Classicism. It shuns the conventions of SOCIALIST REALISM and shows links with the poetry of the Russian avant-garde generation, especially that of Anna AKHMATOVA and Osip MANDELSHTAM, and with English poetic traditions. At present Brodsky is a regular contributor to Russian émigré and English language magazines.

Brodsky's oeuvre consists in works in two traditional genres, the short lyric and the longer poem, called POEMA, which may be narrative, lyric, or dramatic. The presence of the longer poems signals the high seriousness which Brodsky attributes to the poetic calling. In both genres his poetry is pervaded by a sadness that arises from the contemplation of a rather broad range of common human experiences in such spheres as love, friendship, fame, art, cultural history and current events, as well as anxieties, misfortunes, and death. Thus his work appears to have an underlying philosophical premise which is pessimistic, but which is seldom stated; he is not didactic. Moreover, his tone is nostalgic rather than bitter. His pessimism is alleviated by humor, by many ironies, and by puns and other word plays. Many of his poems are autobiographical; some are linked with identifiable geographical locations, however varied, and his poems typically have a plausibility or verisimilitude that ties them closely to reality. He tends to work from the specific to the general. He has experimented seriously with meters, free verse, rhymes, and rhyme schemes.

His first collection, *Stikhotvoreniya i poemy* (Poems and Narrative Verse), which appeared in 1965, consists of fifty lyrics written before 1963, five long poems, and nine lyrics of 1964, several written in internment. Many traits of his mature verse are already present, including his melancholy view. The most significant piece is the tribute called "Great Elegy: to John Donne." (Bol'shaya elegiya. Dzhonu Donnu) in which the soul of the thinker weeps because of its ethereal elevation above the man and material objects, which slumber, unawakened. A retelling of the story of Isaac and Abraham leads to reflections that cast doubt on the efficacy of sacrifice or the existence of salvation. "The Procession" (Shestvie) consists of a series of monologues by diverse literary figures (Harlequin, Prince Myshkin, Hamlet, and others) which tend to show that each person is limited by his own crippling world-view. Throughout the long poems and the lyrics there runs a sense of helplessness in the face of evil, which inexplicably prevails in a world where humans desire its opposite. Violence, bloodshed, murder, and war are commonplace, as are loneliness, alienation, and vanities; meanwhile people strive for accomplishments and warmth, and death is both ubiquitous and pointless. Some titles and opening lines will illustrate: "And eternal

battle" (I vechnyi boi), "Monument to Pushkin" (Pamyatnik Pushkinu), "Jewish cemetery near Leningrad" (Evreiskoe kladbishche okolo Leningrada). Colloquial phrases, free verse, and inexact rhymes are prevalent.

The second volume, *A Halt in the Wilderness* (Ostanovka v pustyne) is Brodsky's most substantial collection to date. It contains fifty-eight lyrics, eight long poems, and a lengthy dramatic dialogue "Gorbunov i Gorchakov" (the surnames of two mental patients), all written between 1962 and 1969 (some poems are reprinted from the earlier collection). The tenor of his work is unchanged, but new devices and techniques make their appearance; they are the signs of a continuing concern for craftsmanship that imparts its own solemnity to the whole. The theme of love is given a new prominence in that a separate section is devoted to it. Within this group an ever greater role is played by the pain of separation and loss; one poem depicts Dido as she watches the retreating Aeneas. Moreover, the section of long poems is concluded by "Farewell, Mlle. Veronica" (Proshchaite, madmuazel' Veronika) in which the loss of love is symbolic of wider deprivations. The poems written in the north record a genuine interest in its bleak forests and marshes, as well as unexpected small joys. An impression of the suffering incurred by internment is to be had from the long poems, particularly from "Letter in a Bottle" (Pis'mo v butylke), which purports to be the tale of a shipwreck, which is plainly a metaphor for "sinking" feelings; in form it is a farewell to a love. The lyrics from the period after Brodsky's release are often autobiographical, but uneventful. Several of the long poems are broad statements about the nature of culture. The title poem "A Halt in the Wilderness" is a comment on the razing of a Greek church in Leningrad; he concludes that each culture must bring its own sacrifice to civilization. "Verses on the Death of T. S. Eliot" (Stikhi na smert' T. S. Eliota) is a tribute to Eliot's love for the world. The dramatic poem "Gorbunov i Gorchakov" shows through its two portraits that suffering comes not only from within; it can also be inflicted by other people. The volume is marked by a relative return to Classical prosody and a penchant for iambic pentameter.

Since his emigration in 1972 Brodsky has brought out two substantial volumes of poetry, *The End of a Beautiful Epoch* (Konets prekrasnoi epokhi, 1977) containing poems dated 1964 through 1971; and *A Part of Speech* (Chast' rechi, 1977) containing poems written between 1972 and 1976. The books are different. *The End of a Beautiful Epoch* gives the impression of a sterility and barrenness that results from withdrawal. Skepticism is now deeper and irony has not vanished, but almost no poems show the painful nostalgia for human warmth that the earlier books had. In the title poem, words, which are the poet's world, tell of a world of atrocities without vision. Hope too is gone, as becomes apparent in the poems with private subjects. *A Part of Speech*, most of whose poems were written in emigration, reflects the move, but not with joy. Western civilizations are portrayed as variously comfortable, or teeming with artifacts, but always missing the point and lonely. In "Thames in Chelsea" (Temza v Chelsi) a stolid, productive culture appears to have replaced God. In *Roman Elegies* (Rimskie elegii, 1982) the aesthetic inclinations and historical heritage of the city are densely present, but a suspicion of mere hedonism prevails.

Works: Stikhotvoreniya i poemy. Washington, D.C. and New York, 1965. *Ostanovka v pustyne. Stikhotvoreniya i poemy.* New York, 1970. *Konets prekrasnoi epokhi. Stikhotvoreniya 1964–1971.* Ann Arbor, 1977. *Chast' rechi. Stikhotvoreniya 1972–1976.* Ann Arbor, 1977. *Rimskie elegii.* New York, 1982.

Translations: The Funeral of Bobo. Trans. Richard Wilbur. Ann Arbor, 1974. *A Part of Speech.* New York, 1980. *Selected Poems.* Trans. George L. Kline. Foreword by W. H. Auden. New York, 1973.

Secondary literature: George L. Kline and Richard D. Sylvester, "Brodskii," *MERSL.* Ed. Harry B. Weber. Gulf Breeze, Fla., 1979. Vol. 3. Pp. 129–37. Jane E. Knox, "Iosif Brodskij's Affinity with Osip Mandel'štam: Cultural Links with the Past." Ph.D. diss., University of Texas at Austin, 1978.

E. Br.

Bryúsov, Valéry Yákovlevich, (1873–1924) poet, novelist, and critic, was born in Moscow, the son of Yakov Kuzmich Bryusov and Matryona Aleksandrovna Bakulina. His paternal grandfather, Kuzma

Andreevich Bryusov, was a former peasant who had purchased his freedom and had built a successful cork business in the capital, while Aleksandr Yakovlevich Bakulin, his maternal grandfather, was a small landowner and minor writer.

Bryusov was a precocious child and learned to read at a very early age. His father was a liberal, self-educated "man of the sixties" and as such in accordance with the philosophy of the times, placed little restriction on his oldest son, while, at the same time, paying little attention to his pastimes in general. As a result, Bryusov had the run of his father's extensive library and acquired a strong background in literature before attending school. Left to his own devices, the young Bryusov began inventing fictions in the form of histories of peoples and lands that he would then chronicle in stories and poems, the first of which he wrote at the age of eight in 1881.

Bryusov's childhood, however, was essentially a lonely one, and when, in the fall of 1884, he entered the second class in Frants Ivanovich Kreiman's Gymnasium he was an outsider who did not know how to play with children of his own age. This naturally led to great social difficulties, many fights, and considerable unhappiness, the end result being that he learned quickly that the only respect he could command from his peers was that accorded to him for his continually increasing erudition and eccentricities. Consequently, he spent his years at Kreiman's cultivating both. He continued to do the same at Polivanov's Gymnasium where he transferred from Kreiman's in 1890.

By 1893 Bryusov had already decided that his future would be bound to literature, and, more specifically, to the new school of SYMBOLISM. In a diary entry made on March 4 of that year he wrote that symbolism (it was still called DECADENCE at the time) was the wave of the future and that he would be its leader. To this end he embarked on a program of translations of leading French Symbolist poets such as Mallarmé, Rimbaud and others and continued to write poems based on the work of contemporary French poetry.

The true birth of the Russian Symbolist movement under Bryusov's leadership can most conveniently be dated from the first week in March, 1894, when, in collaboration with an old schoolmate, A. A. Lang (writing under the pseudonym A. Miropolsky), he published the anthology *The Russian Symbolists* (Russkie simvolisty). This collection of outrageous and sensational models of the "new poetry" brought Bryusov and his non-existent movement almost instant notoriety. Shortly after this, Bryusov published his translation of Verlaine's *Romances sans paroles* and began to attract the attention of more and more of Russia's young poets and of some Europeans who contacted him to find out more about this new development in Russian poetry.

In August, 1895, Bryusov published his first independent collection of poems, *Chefs d'Oeuvre*. For this effort he was awarded with even greater critical vituperation than he had previously received for *The Russian Symbolists*. The result of this new notoriety was Bryusov's virtual banishment from Russian literature for almost three years. However, in 1898 Bryusov's fortunes began to change, first when he acquired a job as an editor with P. Bartenev's *Russian Archive* (Russkii arkhiv), and then with his involvement in the founding of the SKORPION publishing house, the first publishing house devoted exclusively to the works of the Symbolists. It was beginning in 1898 that Bryusov, encouraged by his new successes, began publishing again, first some of his poems in a collection with works by BALMONT, Konevskoi, and Durnov entitled *Book of Meditations* (Kniga razdumii), and then, in 1900 his third collection of poems, *Tertia Vigilia*, the collection that brought Bryusov his first truly positive recognition as a poet.

It was, however, in 1904 that Bryusov reached the beginning of his undisputed reign as the leader of the Russian symbolists when he assumed the editorship of the critical journal VESY, published by "Skorpion" and serving as the symbolists' chief organ for the dissemination of their work, the work of their colleagues abroad, the theory of symbolism, and their polemical statements directed against those who would challenge Symbolism's hegemony in Russian literature.

In 1906 "Skorpion" published Bryusov's fifth collection of poetry, *Wreath* (Venok) or *Stephanos*, the title which appeared in Greek on the binding. Although *Tertia Vigilia* had given Bryusov the recognition as a poet that he was seeking, *Wreath* was his first major poetic success and the book in which he reached his mature poetic style. At the same time, it also showed how far Bryusov in fact was from the

other, generally younger, symbolist poets for whom he served as teacher and inspiration. In reading the poems contained in this collection, one easily sees that Bryusov was a poet more akin to the 19th century than to the 20th; that is, his aesthetic sensibilities, his subject matter, his poetics in general were much more firmly based in the long Russo-European poetic tradition than were those of his fellow Symbolists. Taking this into consideration, it becomes less difficult to see why, beginning in 1908, Bryusov began to make his break with Symbolism as a school and a movement in order to follow his own individual road of poetic development.

Having broken decisively with the symbolists, Bryusov began, after 1910, to be more involved with teaching than with writing, though he never really stopped writing until his death. Much of his writing after 1910, however, was more academic than belletristic, including many significant translations such as Virgil's *Aeneid*, the works of Edgar Allan Poe, and the monuments of Armenian literature. Between 1918 and 1924 he also published a series of instructional texts on versification.

After the Revolution, Bryusov became what might be called a literary bureaucrat as well as an academic. From 1918 through 1919 he was the manager of *Narkompros* (Department of Public Education), Division of Scientific Libraries; in 1919 he served in the State Publishing House; in 1920 he joined the Communist Party and organized LITO (the Literary Division of *Narkompros*), which was characterized as the "regulatory organ of the nation's literary taste." Bryusov died on October 9, 1924, in Moscow, of membranous pneumonia and pleurisy.

Bryusov's contributions to Russian literature were many and profound in his roles as poet, novelist, short story writer, essayist, literary historian, translator, polemicist, organizer, and teacher of poets greater than himself, such as A. BELY and A. BLOK. Through Bryusov's efforts many fine Russian poets attained a much wider public forum and much greater respect more quickly then they could have expected without his endeavors on their behalves. Bryusov had an abiding concern for the image of the poet and it was because of this concern that he successfully expended so much energy in raising the stature of modern poetry in Russia to the position he felt it deserved.

Although Bryusov should be remembered as a writer of poetry, fiction, essays, and literary history and theory, his greatest contribution to the history of Russian literature was his ceaseless effort to raise the poet, poetry, and culture in general to a point where they could most effectively exert their civilizing influence on our chaotic world.

Works: Moi Pushkin. (Repr. of 1929 ed.) Munich, 1970. *Opyty.* (Repr. of 1918 ed. With an introd. by Dmitrij Tschiževskij.) Munich, 1969. *Rasskazy i povesti.* (Reprint. With an introd. by Dmitrij Tschiževskij.) Munich, 1970. *Sobranie sochinenii.* 7 vols. 1973–75.

Translations: See *Lewanski*, pp. 207–8.

Secondary literature: N. Ashukin, *Valerii Bryusov v avtobiograficheskikh zapisyakh, pis'makh, vospominaniyakh sovremennikov i otzyvakh kritiki.* 1929. T. J. Binyon, "Bibliography of the Works of Valery Bryusov." *OSP* 12 (1965), pp. 117–40. I. Bryusova, "Materialy k biografii Valeriya Bryusova." In V. Ya. Bryusov, *Izbrannye stikhi.* 1933. Pp. 119–49. D. Maksimov, *Poeziya Valeriya Bryusova.* 1940. K. B. Mochul'skii, *Valerii Bryusov.* Paris, 1962. Martin P. Rice, *Valery Briusov and the Rise of Russian Symbolism.* 1975. V. P. Shcherbina et al., *Valerii Bryusov.* (Literaturnoe nasledstvo, Vol. 85.) 1976. Alexander Schmid, *Valerij Brjusovs Beitrag zur Literaturtheorie: Aus der Geschichte des russischen Symbolismus.* Munich, 1963. V. Zhirmunskii, *Valerii Bryusov i nasledie Pushkina.* 1922.

M. P. R.

Bulgákov, Mikhaíl Afanásievich (1891–1940), writer and playwright, was born in Kiev. His father was a professor at the Kiev Theological Academy. Mikhail, the eldest son, had two brothers and four sisters. Friendship, respect, and mutual love reigned in the house, and the image of a happy home appears in several of Bulgakov's works. Their home is now a historic landmark. From 1901 to 1909 Bulgakov attended Aleksandrovsky High School; theater became his favorite entertainment. In 1909 he enrolled at the Medical School of Kiev University, and graduated in the spring of 1916. In 1913, he married Tatiana Lappá who moved with him to the village of Nikolskoe and later to Vyazma where Bulgakov was assigned for his obligatory medical service. He returned to Kiev in February 1918 and began to practice medicine. Kiev was at that time the focal point of an intense struggle between several political forces—German troops, the Ukrainian Nationalist army, Red troops, and the Russian Volunteer Army. After his brothers had left Kiev for the south of Russia with the Volunteer Army, Bulgakov enlisted as a field doctor in a Volunteer Army regiment and went to the Caucasus. Toward the end of 1919, he resigned from military service and spent over a year in Vladikavkaz working as a journalist. His early plays, with which he was himself dissatisfied, were staged by the local theater, but still his income was minimal. In May 1921 he moved to Tiflis (Tbilisi) and later to Batum in search of a job. In September of that year he returned to Kiev and eventually left for Moscow, where he stayed until the end of his life and where literature and the theater were his only concerns.

The first few years in post-revolutionary Moscow were a continuous struggle for survival. Bulgakov wrote humorous sketches for various newspapers, especially for *Gudok*; in 1922 he became affiliated with the Berlin-based Russian paper *Nakanune*. His feuilletons and short stories published in this paper established his literary reputation. Many of Bulgakov's works of that time are semi-autobiographical, e.g., "The Extraordinary Adventures of a Doctor" (1922), "Notes on the Cuffs" (1922–23) and "Bohème" (1924), as well as the novel *The White Guard* (1924) and "Notes of a Young Country Doctor" (1926–27). In many of these works Bulgakov protested against the cruelty, violence, and murders he had witnessed during the Civil War. In 1924 Bulgakov's first marriage was dissolved, and he married Lyubov Belozersky, who has left valuable memoirs of her eight years with Bulgakov. In 1932 they separated and Bulgakov married Elena Shilovsky. From 1924 to 1926 two parts of *The White Guard* and two collections of short satirical stories, *Diaboliad* and *A Treatise on Housing*, were published. Two novelettes, "The Fatal Eggs" (1924) and "Heart of a Dog" (written in 1925 but never published in the Soviet Union), which contain bitter satire and elements of science fiction, are concerned with the fate of a scientist and the misuse of his discovery, a theme taken up again in the play *Adam and Eve* (1931). The most significant features of Bulgakov's satire, such as a skillful blending of fantastic and realistic elements, grotesque situations, and a concern with important ethical issues, had already taken shape; these features were developed further in Bulgakov's last novel *The Master and Margarita*.

In 1925 Bulgakov began his eleven-year association with the Moscow Art Theater. After many changes required by the Repertory Committee, his play *The Days of the Turbins* premiered on 5 October, 1926—an important date in the history of the Art Theater. The play continued the theme of *The White Guard*—the fate of Russian intellectuals and officers of the Tsarist Army caught up in revolution and civil war. The play *Flight* (1927), which was rehearsed but never staged in Bulgakov's lifetime, completed the topic of people involved in momentous, historical upheavals. The years 1926 to 1929 marked the peak of Bulgakov's career as a playwright. Besides *The Days of the Turbins*, two satirical comedies, *Zoika's Apartment* (at the Vakhtangov Theater, 1926–29) and *The Crimson Island* (at the Kamerny Theater, 1928–29), were staged with great success but, like *The Turbins*, provoked hostile attacks in the Soviet press. In the spring of 1929, all of Bulgakov's plays were banned, leaving him without any source of income. He sent a letter to the Soviet government in March of 1930 requesting permission to resume his publications. The result was a telephone call from Stalin and Bulgakov's assignment to the Art Theater, where he adapted GOGOL's novel *Dead Souls* for the stage (premiered 28 November 1932).

The fate of a writer fighting for his spiritual and artistic independence and his right to create became the subject of Bulgakov's drama *A Cabal of Hypocrites* (or *Molière*, 1930), the biographical novel *Life of Monsieur de Molière* (1933), and the drama *Alexander Pushkin*, later renamed *The Last Days* (1935). The novel was rejected by the publishing house to which it was submitted; *A Cabal of Hypocrites*, which had been rehearsed for 4 years, premiered on February 15, 1936 but a negative review in *Pravda* caused it to be banned after seven performances. This prompted the rejection of the fantastic comedy *Ivan Vasilievich*—a revision of the earlier comedy *Bliss*—and *Alexander Pushkin*.

For the second time Bulgakov saw his career as playwright ruined. In his *Theatrical Novel*, subtitled *Notes of a Dead Man* (1937), he described his experience with the Art Theater in tragicomic form. In the fall of 1936 Bulgakov left the Art Theater and accepted a position at the Bolshoi Opera Theater as a librettist. His last attempt to return to the Art Theater by writing the play *Batum* (previously titled *A Pastor*, 1939) failed; the play was banned before rehearsals began. Bulgakov would repeatedly ask for permission to go to Paris to see his brothers, but the Soviet authorities never granted him an exit visa. Despite the development of his illness and his failing eyesight, Bulgakov continued writing: he devoted his last years to his "sunset" novel *The Master and Margarita*. He died on 10 March, 1940, and was buried at the Novodevichye Cemetery in Moscow.

During his lifetime Bulgakov was known mostly as a playwright. With several of his plays banned, his reputation rested on *The Days of the Turbins*, re-premiered in February 1932, and on his adaptation of *Dead Souls*. Bulgakov emerged as an outstanding novelist only a quarter of a century after his death. In the 1960s his four novels were published in the Soviet Union and translated into several languages, assuring his posthumous fame. Bulgakov used a variety of genres and narrative styles. He possessed an astonishing faculty for transforming harsh reality into an almost jovial anecdote. His works abound in genuine humor and wit along with satire and bitter irony. However, sometimes the last scenes of Bulgakov's comic stories and plays create a tragic impression, as they suddenly end in destruction or death. From humorous sketches Bulgakov progressed through Gogolian grotesque and surrealist stories to end with a philosophical novel. He transformed ugly reality by elevating the problem of evil to the realm of metaphysics. Along with the castigation of everyday triviality, lies, dishonesty, and hypocrisy, the main themes of Bulgakov's works are crucial confrontations of an individual with the hostile forces of his environment, the arbitrariness of the authorities, and the cruelty of man to man. By introducing into his last novel the figures of Yeshua and Pilate, Bulgakov showed his concern for the significance of ethics in modern life, with a continuous struggle between light and darkness going on today as it did two thousand years ago. Bulgakov's bibliography is expanding rapidly. The best editions and secondary sources are: *An International Bibliography of Works by and about Mikhail Bulgakov*. Comp. by Ellendea Proffer. Ann Arbor, 1976.

Works: Diavoliada. 1925. *Dramy i komedii*. Introd. V. Kaverin. 1965. *Izbrannaya proza*. Introd. V. Lakshin. 1966. *P'esy*. Paris, 1971. *Romany*. Introd. K. Simonov. 1973 and 1978. *Izbrannoe*. Introd. E. Sidorov. Afterword by M. Chudakova. 1980. *Sobranie Sochinenii*. Vol. 1 of the 10-volume *Collected Works*, ed. and introd. E. Proffer. Ann Arbor, 1982.

Translations: The Master and Margarita. Trans. Mirra Ginsburg. 1967 (abridged version). Trans. M. Glenny. London, 1967 (complete version). *Black Snow: A Theatrical Novel*. Trans. M. Glenny. 1967. *Life of Monsieur de Molière*. Trans. Mirra Ginsburg. 1970. *The White Guard*. Trans. M. Glenny with "The House of the Turbins" by Victor Nekrasov. 1971. *Diaboliad and Other Stories*. Trans. C. R. Proffer, Introd. C. R. and E. Proffer. 1972. *The Early Plays*. Trans. and Introd. C. R. and E. Proffer. 1972.

Secondary literature: Two special issues devoted to Bulgakov: *RLT*, no. 15 (1978). Ed. C. R. and E. Proffer. *CASS*, 15, no. 2–3. (1981). Ed. Nadine Natov. M. O. Chudakova, "Arkhiv M. A. Bulgakova," *Zapiski otdela rukopisei* 37 (1976). Lesley Milne, *The Master and Margarita: A Comedy of Victory*. Birmingham, 1977. R. W. Pope, "Ambiguity and Meaning in *The Master and Margarita*: The Role of Afranius," *SlavR* 36, no. 1 (1977). E. Proffer, "On *The Master and Margarita*". In *Major Soviet Writers: Essays in Criticism*. Ed. E. J. Brown. 1973. A. Colin Wright, *Mikhail Bulgakov: Life and Interpretation*. Toronto, 1978.   N. N.

Bulgarian influence see SOUTH SLAVIC INFLUENCE.

Bulgárin, Faddeí Venediktovich (1789–1859), writer and journalist. Son of a Polish rebel, drifter, soldier of fortune with Alexander I's armies and then Napoleon's, prisoner of war, solicitor, associate of the DECEMBRISTS, police informer, plagiarist, cutthroat journalist (SEVERNAYA PCHELA, 1825–1859, and several others), pioneering feuilletonist, novelist, and landowner—Bulgarin's life was no less colorful than those of the heroes of his picaresque novels, which, beginning with the tremendous commercial success of *Ivan Vyzhigin* in 1829, seemed to usher in an age of prose and professional authorship in Russian letters. Indeed, the early 1830s hailed Bulgarin as no less a prose writer than PUSHKIN was a poet, although posterity has found these moralizing novels, as well as his historical ones (*Dimitry The Pretender*, 1830; *Mazepa*, 1833–34), verbose and tendentious.

Bulgarin's hypersensitivity to criticism and fear of commercial rivals led him to engage Pushkin and the LITERATURNAYA GAZETA in a vicious squabble (1829–31). Pushkin's devastating satires, "On the Memoirs of Vidocq" (O zapiskakh Vidoka, 1830), "A Triumph of Friendship" (Torzhestvo druzhby, 1831), and "A Few Words about Mr. Bulgarin's Little Finger" (Neskol'ko slov o mizintse g. Bulgarina, 1831) justly and effectively destroyed Bulgarin's reputation as man and author. Bulgarin's *Severnaya pchela* continued to be influential into the 1840s, although it attacked nearly every writer of talent who appeared during those years, among them Pushkin, GOGOL, BELINSKY, and the "NATURAL SCHOOL" (a title Bulgarin coined). "Morality" and "nationality" were his critical touchstones, although they generally served as a cover for commercial motives. Nevertheless, Bulgarin's feuilletons, denunciations to the secret police, and memoirs are occasionally quite perceptive, especially on such literary-sociological questions as authorial status and remuneration.

Works: Polnoe sobranie sochinenii. 7 vols. 1839–44. *Vospominaniya.* 1846–49.

Translations: Ivan Vejeeghen, or Life in Russia. Trans. G. Ross. 2 vols. London, 1831.

Secondary literature: M. K. Lemke, "Faddei Bulgarin i 'Severnaya pchela.'" In his *Nikolaevskie zhandarmy i literatura: 1826–1855 gg.* 2d ed. 1909. (Bulgarin's denunciations.) Jurij Striedter, *Der Schelmenroman in Russland.* Berlin, 1961. W. M. T.

Búlich, Véra Sergéevna (1898–1954), émigré poet, translator and prose writer. Bulich was born into the family of a professor of literature at St. Petersburg University and spent most of her life in Finland, where for many years she was a librarian in the Helsinki University Library. As a poet, she should be placed in the literary context of First Emigration feminine poetry cultivating the spectrum of intimate emotions and characteristic of the Russian Parnassus. Of her four volumes of poetry the first two, *The Pendulum* (Mayatnik, 1934) and *The Captive Wind* (Plennyi Veter, 1938), and especially the last one, *The Boughs* (Vetvi, 1954), represent her best. Bulich's themes are often conventional, but their execution is elegant in its ACMEIST simplicity and her emotional subtlety and psychological perceptiveness cannot be denied. G. ADAMOVICH wrote: "The impression of Vera Bulich's verse is that of something fragile, as if of porcelain perfection." At her best (and her last collection, with its foreboding of destruction, gives her additional credit) she is an earnest master, though she hardly achieves the captivating ease of L. CHERVINSKAYA or the transcendent lucidity of L. ALEKSEEVA, who later brought this kind of classical feminine poetry to the point of perfection. Bulich also published a collection of fairy tales, which was translated into Finnish. As a translator of modernist Finnish poetry of the circle of the so-called Torch Bearers, she has no competitors. The manuscript of her anthology of Finnish poetry, which was published only in part, is kept in the archives of the Finnish Literary Society in Helsinki.

Works: Satu pikkiriikkisestä prinsessasta. 1927. *Skazki,* 1 and 2. 1931. *Burelom.* 1947.

Secondary literature: T. Pakhmuss, "Vera Bulich, russkii poet Finlyandii," *Sovremennik,* 41 (1979), pp. 162–69. V. B.

Búnin, Iván Alekséevich (1870–1953) is a writer of the first rank. He was born in the heartland of Russia, the fertile countryside south of Moscow that nurtured among the gentry many writers, among them TURGENEV and TOLSTOI. The Bunins were an old aristocratic family who, like many of their class, came upon hard times during the rapid industrialization of the 1880s. The somber beauty of the landscape of central Russia affected Bunin deeply. Though his work shows repulsion at the oppressive aspects of traditional Russian society, he is a nostalgic writer, his mind turned back to a time when men lived close to nature. He is preoccupied by the passing of the way of life that nurtured him. Aristocratic nostalgia combines in him with aristocratic pride. Detached, self-enclosed, he maintains a persistent attitude of stoicism before the sorrows of existence.

Bunin first broke into print in 1888 and by the turn of the century his reputation was firmly established. As a young man he was briefly infatuated with Tolstoianism. In the early 1900s he gravitated to the realistic writers centered around GORKY's publishing house, ZNANIE. However, Bunin was a loner, impossible to pigeon-hole into any group. One of the few writers he felt personally close to was CHEKHOV. A first marriage failed; his second common-law wife, Vera Muromtseva, remained his closest companion to the end of his days. Few Russian writers travelled as much as the restless Bunin—besides the usual *grand tour* of Europe, he made trips to the Middle East, North Africa, India, and Ceylon, using their locales for numerous stories. He greeted the Bolshevik Revolution with scorn and emigrated to Paris. His corpus is not enormous but it is continuous, the product of over sixty years of creative activity. In 1933 he was awarded the Nobel prize, becoming the first Russian writer to achieve that distinction.

Bunin originally contemplated a career as a painter and an impulse to the purely pictorial is strong in his work. His poetry, of much less significance than his prose, is conservative in manner and Parnassian in temper. Its themes are the same as those of his fiction—the richness of nature, its melancholy beauty (night is Bunin's favorite time), loneliness, and death. Faced with the passing of things, he is elegiacally wistful or stoically accepting. Though his verse can be evocative, it is static and monotonous. Its strength lies in careful observation of externals. A prosiness in his poetry anticipates the reaction against the vague mellifluousness of SYMBOLISM of the post 1910 generation.

Bunin's prose is more poetical than his poetry. Here he proved himself one of the great masters of the Russian language. Many of his stories are actually lyrical monologues, and lengthy descriptions, usually of nature, fill almost all of them. His prose has an almost magical power to create and sustain a mood. Yet it is seldom flabby. His language resists vagueness by its extreme density. A typical Bunin passage, however lyrical its rhythms, is crowded with the minutiae of perception. He also has a marvelous ear for the nuances of common speech. His mimicries of Russian dialects rival LESKOV, though he is humorless. Too often in Bunin's work mastery is degraded into mere virtuosity, the exhibition of verbal powers for their own sake. Bunin was hostile to MODERNISM but he shares the modernist urge to subjugate experience to form. Although he is commonly regarded as a realist, his realism is closer to the impersonal aestheticism of Flaubert than the moral realism of the Russian tradition. He is also a serious writer and at times can be genuinely moving.

Much of Bunin's pre-Revolutionary work is a lyrical elegy over the dying countryside. Dying old peasants, and portraits of destitution and hunger are common. But underlying Bunin's regret over the decline of rural Russia is a theme that obsessed him all his life—the impenetrable isolation of men in their suffering. In the face of death—both of the individual and of the social order—nature provides solace. Its beauty consoles; its eternal renewals offer an image of constancy to oppose the decay of human things. Though his pantheistic recourse to nature sets him apart from DECADENCE and symbolism, he participates fully in the fin de siècle sense of historical crisis. Like his contemporaries, he is filled with foreboding over the seeming death of traditional culture. Of his early stories, "Antonov Apples" (Antonovskie yabloki, 1900) stands out for its exceptional lyric warmth and celebrative exuberance. But its celebration is purely commemorative, a song of praise for a way of life that is no more. *The Village* (Derevnya, 1909–10), a novella, is more typically grim. It is a harrowing tale of provincial rot. Stripped of Bunin's usual lyricism, thoroughly naturalistic, virtually plotless (as is most of Bunin's fiction), its power derives from its accumulation of convincing detail and an uncompromising concentration upon the failed lives of its protagonists. *Dry Valley* (Sukhodol, 1911) is one of the supreme masterpieces of modern fiction. In this haunting novella, Bunin's lyrical reverie achieves a mythic and tragic resonance unequalled in his fiction. Experience is filtered through layers of memory and multiple perspectives to evoke a consummate image of the patriarchal estate of Old Russia. The estate called Dry Valley, bereft of the natural vitality and warm generosity celebrated in "Antonov Apples," offers only scenes of violence and ruin. Memory is unable to uncover any value save the value of memory itself, and physical nature alone offers an anchor of permanence in the wasteland of history.

Russia, though the object of both his love and his hate, sustained Bunin's art. When he gets away from the Russian countryside he knew so intimately—as in his exotic Eastern tales and much of his work in emigration—he tends to become sentimental or abstract. Bunin's international style, though impressively elegant, lacks the vigor of his Russian manner. The lushly written "Brothers" (Brat'ya, 1914) is a schematic allegory, influenced by Bunin's reading in Buddhism, of the hopelessness of desire. The famous "Gentleman from San Francisco" (Gospodin iz San-Frantsisko, 1915), a work of cold jewel-like beauty, may be read as both a satire of bourgeois civilization and yet another allegory of the vanity of human ambition in the face of death. "Loppy Ears" (Petlistye ushi, 1916), an atypical urban story, is a chilling study of sadism.

Bunin's years in emigration saw an increased tendency to a purely meditative story, and also the cultivation of a decadent strain in his art. Sex, along with death, possesses his imagination. "Sunstroke" (Solnechnyi udar, 1925) is one of the best of his love stories and also paradigmatic. Sexual encounters in Bunin never develop into lasting ties. They are casual though intense—brief accidents of "sunstroke" that leave the male partner with an ache of yearning. His wistfulness is not so much over lost opportunity as, once again, the transitoriness of human relationships. "Mitya's Love" (Mitina lyubov', 1924) is a poetical treatment of youthful love, though somewhat marred by sentimentality. *Dark Avenues* (Temnye allei, 2d ed., 1946), his last collection of stories, describes shortlived erotic liaisons, all doomed, often by the sudden death of one of the partners. One of his more important later works is the fictionalized autobiography, *The Life of Arseniev* (Zhizn' Arsen'eva, first complete ed., 1952). Like the bulk of his fiction, Bunin's "autobiography" is neither a psychological exploration nor a history of moral growth but a way of converting experience into an object of aesthetic contemplation and reverie.

Works: Sobranie sochinenii. 9 vols. Moscow, 1965–67.
Translations: The Village. Trans. Isabel F. Hapgood. 1923. *The Gentleman from San Francisco and Other Stories.* Trans. Bernard Guilbert Guerney. 1933. *The Well of Days.* Trans. Gleb Struve and Hamish Miles. 1933. *The Dreams of Chang and Other Stories.* Trans. Gleb Struve and Hamish Miles. 1935. *The Elaghin Affair and Other Stories.* Trans. Bernard Guilbert Guerney. 1935. *Dark Avenues and Other Stories.* Trans. Richard Hare. 1949. *See also:* Lewanski, pp. 208–10.
Secondary literature: Serge Kryzytski, *The Works of Ivan Bunin.* The Hague, 1971. Renato Poggioli, "The Art of Ivan Bunin." In *The Phoenix and the Spider.* 1957. Gleb Struve, "The Art of Ivan Bunin," *SEER* 11 (1932–33). James D. Woodward, *Ivan Bunin: A Study of His Fiction.* 1980.
M. E.

Burlyúk, David Davídovich (1882–1967), poet and painter, was born in Kharkov, the son of an estate manager. The family had its own art studio. In 1897, Burlyuk began to write poetry. In 1899, he studied art in Kazan, and a year later in Odessa. He also studied art in Munich and Paris. In 1911, Vasily Kandinsky invited Burlyuk to exhibit his paintings at the Blue Rider exhibition in Munich. Burlyuk painted in many styles, but never developed his own. He was the father of CUBO-FUTURISM and discovered and cultivated MAYAKOVSKY's poetic talent. Burlyuk published many of the early cubo-futurist collections of poetry. In 1920, Burlyuk left Russia, and in 1922 settled in New York. Although he organized a major poetic movement, Burlyuk himself never attained any significant recognition.

Burlyuk was not a major poet or a theoretician of cubo-futurism. His poetry, like his art, was imitative, an awkward, disorganized mixture of disparate styles. He often imitated some of the features of Mayakovsky's, KHLEBNIKOV's and KRUCHONYKH's poetry to give his own poetry the appearance of innovation. He drew his themes from the poetry of Russian and French symbolists: an obsession and fascination with death, the ugly and the macabre; occultism, mysticism, eroticism, and escapism. The anti-aesthetic orientation of his poetry, with its crude language and typographical devices, was intended to shock readers and critics.

Secondary literature: Vahan D. Barooshian, *Russian Cubo-Futurism 1910–1930.* The Hague, 1974. Pp. 67–78. *David Burlyuk: K 25-letiyu khudozhestvenno-literaturnoi deyatel'nosti.* New York, 1924. E. Gollerbakh, *Poeziya Davida Burlyuka.* New York, 1931. Vladimir Markov, *Russian Futurism: A History.* Berkeley, 1968. Pp. 172–79, 318–26. I. Postupalskii, *Literaturnyi trud D. Burlyuka.* New York, 1930.
V. D. B.

Busláev, Fyódor Ivánovich (1818–97), philologist, folklorist, and art historian, graduated from Moscow University in 1838. He became a Professor at the same University in 1847 and a member of the Academy of Sciences in 1881.

Buslaev's studies belong to two areas, linguistics and folklore. In linguistics, he compared the Russian language with Indo-European and Old Church Slavonic; he also investigated and published a few ancient manuscripts.

Most of Buslaev's articles on folklore were published in three collections, the principal one of which is *Historical Sketches of Russian Folk Literature and Art* (2 vols., 1861). One of the founders of the MYTHOLOGICAL SCHOOL in Russia, Buslaev viewed folklore as the impersonal creative work of the people and as "fragments of ancient myths." He developed the theory of an ancient epic period, in which mythology, language, laws, rites, and customs were created. Language for Buslaev was "the essential component part of the unseparable moral activity of the whole people"; the same creative power that gave rise to language formed also the myths of the people and its poetry.

Buslaev's special area of interest was the mutual relationship of oral traditions with Old Russian apocryphal and hagiographic literature, as well as that of folklore and literature with the visual arts, particularly iconography. Typical of Buslaev was his romantic aestheticism; he gave special attention to the artistic quality of Russian folklore and its moral elevation.

Under the influence of new theories in folkloristics, Buslaev later abandoned the mythological school and gave preference to the theory of borrowing. Following Benfey, he recognized the East as the homeland of European folklore.

Works: Sochineniya. 3 vols. St. Petersburg and Leningrad, 1908–30. *Istoricheskaya grammatika russkogo yazyka.* Moscow, 1959. (1st ed. 1863.)
Secondary literature: M. K. Azadovskii, *Istoriya russkoi fol'kloristiki* 2 (1963): 53–70. A. N. Pypin, *Istoriya russkoi etnografii* 2 (1891): 75–109. Yu. M. Sokolov, *Russian Folklore.* Detroit, 1971. Pp. 64–69.
F. J. O.

Busláev, Pyotr (d. before 1755), poet, attended the Moscow Academy of Slavonic, Greek, and Latin. He was a deacon at the Moscow Cathedral of the Assumption, but eventually left ecclesiastic service. Much of Buslaev's reputation as a minor poet is attributed to the success of his poem, "Soulful Speculation Described in Verse about the Passing on of Her Excellency Baroness Mariya Yakovlevna Stroganova" (Dushevnoe umozritel'stvo opisannoe stikhami o pereselenii prevoskhoditel'noi baronessy Stroganovoi Marii Yakovlevny v vechnuyu zhizn', 1734). While the poem, written in syllabic verse, relies heavily on Slavisms, its language is both lucid and expressive. N. M. KARAMZIN, N. I. NOVIKOV, and V. K. TREDIAKOVSKY all praised Buslaev for his efforts.

Works: Sillabicheskaya poeziya 17–18 vekov. 1935. *Sobranie proizvedenii russkikh poetov.* Ed. S. A. Vengerov. Vol. 1, pt. 3, 1897.
B. A.

Butkóv, Yákov Petróvich (18?–1856), writer. Born a free townsman in the remote province of Saratov, Butkov was self-educated, experienced great privation throughout his life, and died in poverty. Praised by CHERNYSHEVSKY as perhaps the most talented of GOGOL's early followers, and by REMIZOV as the most gifted of all the Russian naturalists, Butkov first broke into print in St. Petersburg with a verse segment entitled "Gaidamak" (a name given to rebellious Ukrainian cossacks), which appeared inconspicuously in Nikolai GRECH's conservative journal, *Syn otechestva.*

Five years later, two of Butkov's stories were printed in Faddei BULGARIN's reactionary SEVERNAYA PCHELA. Butkov's work received little attention until his small collection *Petersburg Heights* [i.e., garrets] (Peterburgskie vershiny, 1845), followed shortly by *Petersburg Heights II* (1846), were published by Grech. In the depiction of the lowest social classes, Butkov's work offered a blend of humorous Gogolian narrative with the spirit of the French *physiologie* and *roman-feuilleton.*

The tone had been set earlier by *A Physiology of St. Petersburg* (Fiziologiya Peterburga, 1845), a collection of sketches by Russian authors which had been assembled by NEKRASOV and applauded by

BELINSKY. Though Belinsky denied that Butkov could rival Gogol, Bulgarin polemically asserted that Butkov had surpassed Gogol with a naturalism untainted by caricature. Most critics recognized in Butkov's work the combination of the author's originality and the influence of Gogol's comic detail. By combining these elements with extraliterary forms such as the vaudeville and the journal feuilleton, Butkov's work may be seen as a transition between Gogol's grotesque realism and DOSTOEVSKY's early works.

Butkov worked for Kraevsky's *Otechestvennye zapiski* from 1847 to 1849, publishing only a few short works. He subsequently disappeared from the literary scene when authors such as HERZEN and GRIGOROVICH provided a more unstylized naturalism. Butkov died in a charity hospital at about the age of 33.

Works: Russkie povesti XIX veka, 40–50 godov. 1952.

Secondary literature: V. G. Belinskii, "*Peterburgskie vershiny*, opisannye Ya. Butkovym. Kniga pervaia" (1845), *PSS* (1953–59), Vol. 9, pp. 354–62. I. S. Chistova, "Butkov i Dostoevskii: Iz istorii literaturnogo dvizheniia 40-kh godov XIX veka," *RLit* 14 (1971). ———, "Chernyshevskii i Butkov: Kommentarii k povestyam i povesti," *RLit* 21 (1978). Peter Hodgson, *From Gogol to Dostoevsky: Jakov Butkov a reluctant naturalist in the 1840's*. Munich, 1976. V. N. Maikov, "*Peterburgskie vershiny*, opisannye Ya. Butkovym, kn. vtoraia" (1846), *Sochineniia* (1901), vol. 1.   J. S.

Buturlin, P. D. (1859–96), see SONNET.

Bykov, Vasily Vladimirovich (Bykaŭ, Vasil', 1924–), Belorussian and Russian writer, was born in the village of Chernovshchina, Vitebsk region. Bykov's main theme is the Second World War and the effects of wartime Stalinism on the Soviet soldier and partisan. His writing is based largely on his own experience of war and events personally witnessed or told to him. His first stories date from 1951 but were published only in 1956. The tale, "The Cry of the Cranes" (Zhuravlinyi krik, 1960), attracted considerable critical attention for its forthright treatment of wartime themes. Other early works include "Frontline Pages" (Frontovye stranitsy, 1960), "The Third Rocket" (Tret'ya raketa, 1962), and "Alpine Ballad" (Al'piiskaya ballada, 1963). Bykov's main concern is with individual psychology and the motivations which lead one to take a certain course of action, be it heroic or cowardly, as a result of facing hardship and danger. For one critic, Bykov "represents war through the dialectics of the human soul."

Bykov's later more ambitious works, including "The Dead Feel No Pain" (Mertvym ne bol'no, 1966), "Cursed Height" (Proklyataya vysota, 1968), and "Kruglyansky Bridge" (Kruglyanskii most, 1969), while still dealing with moral problems of heroism and betrayal, also consider unflinchingly both the immediate results of Stalinist practices and their more current aftermath. Thus Bykov is concerned with the fact that those who had benefited earlier at the cost of the well-being of others are still managing to flourish unimpeded in present times. In the seventies, Bykov continued to expose the wartime manifestations of Stalinism: the incompetence of high-ranking military officers; the prevailing atmosphere of suspicion and denunciations; the terrible indifference to truth and the subsequent hardship which such disregard entails. Ultimately, while focusing upon the past, Bykov's works are rich in contemporary implication.

Works: Sotnikov. 1972. *Obelisk, Povesti*. 1973. *Kogda khochetsya zhit'* (play). 1974. *Volch'ya staya*. 1975.

Secondary literature: L. Lazarev, *Vasil' Bykov: Ocherk tvorchestva*. 1979. Arnold B. McMillin, "Vasil Bykaŭ and the Soviet Byelorussian Novel." In *The Languages and Literatures of the Non-Russian Peoples of the Soviet Union*. Hamilton, Ontario, 1977. Pp. 268–94. Igor' Shtokman, "The Growth of Crystal: Vasil' Bykov, Characters and Circumstances," *Soviet Studies in Literature* 15 no. 2 (1979), pp. 28–56.   D. K. D.

Bylina (pl. *byliny*) is a type of epic folk song of varying length, usually 300–400 lines. The term *bylina* ("what happened in the past") is a scholarly term which came into use in the 1830s. The popular term for both the *bylina* and the historical song is *starina*, "old story."

Collection

An important collection of *byliny* derives from the middle of the 18th century. It has been attributed to a Cossack named Kirsha Danilov, about whom nothing is known. The songs were recorded in Western Siberia, in the province of Perm, probably for the mill owner P. A. Demidov. Stylistic retouchings of the texts show Danilov's familiarity with official terminology and lead us to assume that he may have been a clerk in a military office (STENDER-PETERSEN). *Byliny* collected at various places in Russia in the first half of the 19th century were sent to P. V. KIREEVSKY, who included them in his large collection of folk songs.

Byliny, believed to be on the verge of extinction, were rediscovered in Olonets province as a genre still flourishing in the 1860s by P. N. Rybnikov, an exiled civil servant. This discovery was so surprising that it was first met with disbelief. Rybnikov's collection of 224 texts was published in the years 1861 to 1867. About ten years later, A. F. HILFERDING set out for the same region to supplement Rybnikov's work. His collection, published posthumously in 1873, contained 318 texts.

The work of Rybnikov and Hilferding initiated a systematic search for *byliny* everywhere in northern Russia, a search that has continued to the present. *Byliny* were found not only in Olonets, but on the shores of the White Sea, along the rivers flowing to the north, and in Siberia as well. This collecting resulted in extensive and valuable *bylina* collections by N. S. TIKHONRAVOV, A. V. Markov, A. D. Grigoriev, N. E. Onchukov, and others, at the end of the 19th and the beginning of the 20th century.

Origin and dissemination

Though *byliny* are unknown in southern Russia and the Ukraine, the evidence shows that they must have originated there. They frequently mention East Slavic cities (Kiev, Chernigov, Smolensk) and personages (the Kievan Duke Vladimir). There are a number of details that refer specifically to Old Kiev, such as the Pochaina River ("Puchai River" or "Puchainya" of the *byliny*) and the "Relics of Boris" as a designation for an ancient fort in Vyshgorod, a suburb of Kiev.

A majority of folklorists concur that the *bylina* as a genre arose in the Kievan period (10th–11th centuries). Some scholars (e.g., PROPP) are inclined to shift the origin to a considerably earlier time. It is plausible that mythological songs of the East Slavs were the predecessors of *byliny*, but the sweeping historical events of the Kievan period must have caused a mutation in these songs. These events began with the Christianization of *Rus* in the 10th century and skirmishes with waves of Asiatic intruders, the Pechenegs and Polovetsians. They culminated in the arrival of the Tatars in Russia in the 13th century and the devastation of the land.

In *byliny*, historical events are alluded to only vaguely and often allegorically. The conversion to Christianity is echoed as a battle with the dragon. The Polovetsian Tugorkan has become the dragon Tugarin, and Sharugan (or Sharakan) appears as Shark the Giant. A number of *byliny* have for their subject the Tatar invasion and the Russians' struggle against them. Contrary to historical truth, most of the *byliny* about the battles against the Tatars give the victory to the Russians. Similarly, in *byliny* whose theme is the payment of tribute to the Khans of the Golden Horde, the Russian heroes are shown as managing instead to collect it from them.

According to V. F. MILLER, *byliny* originated in the upper classes among the singers of the princes' retinue. Later they were taken over by the SKOMOROKHI, wandering minstrels, singers and buffoons of the lower classes. In their hands, *byliny* received their final form, with special stylistic peculiarities, formulas, and other embellishments. It may be assumed that the *skomorokhi* added to *byliny* a considerable portion of novelistic themes and farcical motifs. They were crucial to the dissemination of *byliny* and other folklore, since their profession involved constant travel. During the reign of Alexis Mikhailovich in the 17th century, the *skomorokhi* were subjected to cruel persecution. Their musical instruments were confiscated and burned and the entertainers themselves were whipped and—when caught repeatedly—exiled to the border regions. The *skomorokhi* took the *byliny* to the north, and through their mediation the tradition was handed over to the peasants and fishermen of that region.

When the Bolsheviks came to power, the *byliny* were at first looked down upon. Considered to be the creation of bards of the higher, princely class, *byliny* did not fit into the reality of a communist state. The emergence of patriotism in the Soviet Union in the mid-1930s necessitated a reinterpretation of *byliny* so that they might be used for the government cause. Such an opportunity offered itself in connection with the presentation of Demyan BEDNY's comic opera *Epic Heroes* (Bogatyri) at the Kamerny Theater in Moscow. In November, 1936, the opera was removed from the stage for misinterpreting Russian history and for portraying Russia's epic heroes as representatives of the nobility and in a derogatory way. At the same time a blustering discussion about the character and origin of the epic was started by *non*folklorists. Folklore scholars finally had to give in and to deny the "aristocratic origin" of *byliny*, insisting on their "folk origin." According to Yu. M. SOKOLOV, "the majority of *byliny* came from the masses of the working people."

This view, a cornerstone of Soviet folkloristics, has no foundation. The structure of *byliny* and its two basic themes—hunting and fighting—support V. F. Miller's conclusion that the *byliny* were created within princely circles of Old *Rus* (Oinas). Since the military retinue consisted not only of princes and boyars, but also of boyars' servants and peasants, the creators of *byliny* may have come from various social strata. Only in the 16th and 17th centuries did *byliny* become the exclusive property of the lower strata of society.

Bylina cycles

It is customary to classify *byliny* according to the principalities in which the action takes place: Kievan and Novgorodian. *Byliny* exhibiting mythological features are separated into another group. The *bogatyri*, valiant heroes of the mythical *byliny*, are usually referred to as "Older heroes" and those of the Kievan cycle as "Younger heroes." The heroes of the Novgorod cycle are not designated *bogatyri*.

Mythological Byliny

The mythological *byliny*, probably the most ancient category, have Volkh Vseslavevich, Svyatogor (holy mountain), and Mikula Selyaninovich (the villager's son) as their heroes. The *bylina* of Volkh (*volkhv* meaning magician) has some shamanistic overtones. By changing himself into a grey wolf, an aurochs, or a falcon, Volkh hunts all kinds of animals. In the shape of a bird, he penetrates the Indian realm where he overhears the plans of the emperor and empress. After he destroys the emperor's weapons, Volkh and his retinue attack and smash him, thus saving the country from peril. The *bylina* of Volkh obviously reflects the life of Prince Vseslav of Polotsk (d. 1101) (Jakobson-Szeftel).

Svyatogor is a giant, so powerful that Mother Earth cannot carry him, and he has to live in rocky mountains. He is destined to perish, and his eventual death is reported in different ways. In one *bylina*, he boasts that he could lift the whole world if only he could find a point of support. He finds a shoulder bag containing "the weight of the whole world," sent by God, and tries to lift it, but cannot do so and dies. In another *bylina*, Svyatogor and Ilya Muromets come across a coffin. When Svyatogor lies down in the coffin, he cannot get out and is doomed to die there. Before his death he manages to breathe a part of his strength into Ilya. There are some other rare *byliny*—partly told in prose—connected with Svyatogor: about his cuckoldry (Svyatogor's wife forces Ilya to be intimate with her while Svyatogor sleeps), and about his marriage (Svyatogor marries a girl whom he had found once on a dung pile and supposedly killed). These are clearly of later origin.

Mikula Selyaninovich is a prodigious plowman who works so fast that Duke Volga (probably from Oleg, one of the historical rulers) can overtake him on horseback only after three days. Volga persuades Mikula to accompany him as his companion on a mission to collect taxes from three towns presented to him by Duke Vladimir. Volga is put to shame when he and his retinue cannot remove a plow from the ground, whereas Mikula lifts it with one hand and throws it into a bush. There are a number of parallels (presented by A. MAZON and others) to the theme of the encounter of a ruler with a prodigious peasant, but the question of the actual source of the *bylina* has not been solved.

The Kievan cycle

The *byliny* of this largest cycle, the Kievan, center around Vladimir, Grand Duke of Kiev (usually referred to as "Vladimir the Fair Sun"), in the same way that the legends of the knights of the Round Table center around King Arthur. The figure of Duke Vladimir may incorporate various rulers of Old Russia, primarily Vladimir I (d. 1015) and Vladimir II Monomakh (d. 1125), who fought against the nomads of the steppe—Pechenegs and Polovetsians, respectively. In the *byliny*, all the hostile nomad armies are collectively called Tartars.

Duke Vladimir of the *byliny* arranges big feasts in his palace, gives various tasks to his heroes (*bogatyri*) and rewards and punishes them. However, he himself never functions as a principal figure. The *byliny* sing of the exploits of the heroes, whose primary duty while stationed either in Kiev or at Russian *bogatyr* outposts is to protect the Russian land against foreign invaders: heathen tsars, hostile heroes, and formidable monsters. They also fight internal enemies— robbers and brigands. Occasionally they collect or deliver tribute, seek a bride, and settle accounts between themselves or even quarrel with Duke Vladimir. Their leisure is spent in hunting game and having amorous adventures.

The most prominent heroes of the Kievan *byliny* are Ilya Muromets, Dobrynya Nikitich, and Alyosha Popovich (the priest's son). Of these, Ilya has the leading position. He is adorned with the ideal features of the epic hero. A brave, unselfish servant of his country, he protects it against numerous enemies and defends its orphans, widows, and poor.

Ilya appears as a peasant's son in several *byliny*. He is paralyzed for 33 years before being healed by Jesus and two apostles or by some holy men, who bestow exceptional strength upon him and tell him that he is not destined to die in battle. Ilya applies his strength first to clear the land on his parents' farm, then goes to Kiev to Duke Vladimir. On his way he conquers monstrous Solovei Razboinik (Nightingale the Robber), who controls the highway between Chernigov and Kiev. He takes Solovei to Duke Vladimir and kills him there.

Ilya's further feats include his victory over another monster, Idolishche (Big Idol), whom he approaches in pilgrim's garb. When Idolishche attacks him, Ilya grabs him by the legs and, using him as a weapon, destroys Idolishche's Tatar army.

Ilya occasionally displays his fiery temper, so that even Duke Vladimir is hard put to hold him in check. Once when he has not been invited to the Duke's feast, he goes berserk and begins raging and smashing up churches in Kiev, until Dobrynya succeeds in pacifying him. Sometimes Ilya is locked up by the Duke, to be released when danger threatens Russia. On one such occasion, Ilya is sent, together with a group of heroes, against Kalin Tsar, who demands the surrender of Kiev. However, he falls into a pit dug by the Tatars and is captured. When he is being taken to the place of execution, he prays fervently to God. His prayer is heard, and through divine intervention he finds himself freed from his fetters. He then destroys Kalin Tsar and his army. After several more exploits, including the destruction of a camp of brigands who want to rob him, Ilya finds a hidden treasure, gives it away, and descends to the Kievan crypts, where he is turned to stone.

The *byliny* about Ilya illustrate the evolution of the *bylina* genre—its creation and transformation over a long period of time (Astakhova). Ilya's development into a powerful hero is manifestly connected with Kiev's rise to prominence. When the power of the Kievan rulers increased, Ilya became a symbol of the self-image of the people. Some mythological songs and legends already in existence, such as those about the liberation of areas from highwaymen and monsters, were reinterpreted and attached to Ilya ("Ilya and Solovei Razboinik" and "Ilya and Idolishche") in the same manner as Theseus was developed into the national hero of Athens. The succeeding period of Tatar rule left its imprint on the *byliny* about Ilya: the enemies against whom he fought were called Tartars (Ilya's fight with Kalin Tsar and others); Idolishche became the leader of a Tatar army; and Solovei Razboinik received a Tatar patronymic, "Odikhmantiev" or "Rakhmatovich." In the 17th century Ilya acquired different attributes from the circles in which *byliny* about his exploits were sung. In the north, the peasants considered him one of them and attached the attribute "peasant's son" to him. In the south, the Cossacks in their turn proudly associated him with themselves and called him the "Old Cossack." During the peasant revolts of the 17th century (such as the uprising of Stenka Razin), the *byliny* about Ilya the Rebel were created (e.g., Ilya's quarrel with Duke Vladimir and Ilya's association with the poor people of the tavern). One of the most recent *byliny* (created in the 1930s) is about Ilya's marriage: since Ilya was known to have had a son, then consequently he must have had a wedding.

As to Ilya's origin, R. JAKOBSON and others consider his appellative "Muromets" a corruption of "Norman" (Old Norse *Nordmadr*) and suggest that Ilya was originally a Scandinavian (Varangian) leader active in Russia. Though rejected by Soviet scholars, the explanation gains support by the Russians' practice of attributing the highest valor to foreign heroes. Thus, the Estonian hero Kalev (Kolyvan) or Kalevipoeg (Kolyvanovich), transplanted into Russia, is considered stronger than any Russian hero. Ilya is warned not to fight him and the mothers of several other heroes deplore the fact that their sons are not as strong as Kalevipoeg.

Dobrynya Nikitich, sometimes represented as Duke Vladimir's nephew, is an ideal knightly diplomat. He has good manners and clever speech, and he enjoys great respect from the Duke and the heroes. Many-sided and talented, he plays well at dice, cards, and checkers, is an excellent shot, swims expertly, and plays and sings like a real minstrel.

The *bylina* "Dobrynya's Fight with the Dragon" graphically displays Dobrynya's heroic qualities as a dragon slayer. When Dobrynya, against the advice of his mother, goes swimming in Puchai River, he is attacked by a dragon. Their fight ends temporarily with a nonaggression pact, but when the dragon later violates this agreement, Dobrynya attacks and kills him. "Dobrynya and Marinka" shows him in the hands of an amorous witch, whom he finally succeeds in outwitting and killing.

Dobrynya is given the most complicated and delicate assignments. He is sent to verify the correctness of Dyuk Stepanovich's claim to great riches. Dispatched as a matchmaker to Lithuania, he forces the king's daughter to come to Duke Vladimir to be his bride. His mission to the Polovetsian tsar, undertaken together with a companion, is highly successful. Defeating the Polovetsian tsar at dice, cards, and in archery, then attacking his troops, Dobrynya makes the Polovetsian tsar Duke Vladimir's debtor and brings back tribute from the tsar to the Duke.

Dobrynya's prototype is conjectured to be Duke Vladimir I's maternal uncle, who was also called Dobrynya. Chronicles characterize Dobrynya as a significant historical figure, first as the protector and supporter of the Duke, and later as his collaborator.

Alyosha Popovich appears in several *byliny* as Ilya's and Dobrynya's companion and comrade-in-arms. He is distinguished by agility, prowess, and bravery, as well as by cheerfulness, craftiness, and cheekiness. After he kills Tugarin Zmeevich (dragon's son), he becomes a much-admired hero in Kiev. Alyosha's negative features may have been attributed to him because of his supposed priestly descent. In the *bylina* "Dobrynya and Alyosha," Alyosha deceives even his sworn brother Dobrynya. Dobrynya rides off into the open plain and advises his wife that if he does not return in six years, she may marry whomever she wants—except Alyosha. Alyosha, however, brings home false tidings that Dobrynya is dead and begins to besiege the young "widow" with marriage proposals. Dobrynya's wife, under pressure from Duke Vladimir and the Duchess, finally agrees to marry Alyosha. Dobrynya arrives home during the wedding celebration, attends the wedding party disguised as a minstrel, and claims his wife. This *bylina*, the most popular in Russia, is modelled on the international theme "The husband at the wedding of his wife." Alyosha Popovich originally may have been a retainer of the Duke of Rostov. Local legends as well as 14th- and 15th-century *byliny* about him became a part of the overall Russian tradition, and he became, anachronistically, one of Duke Vladimir's heroes. Through *byliny*, Alyosha was then introduced into chronicle accounts of the battle on the Kalka River in 1224 (Likhachov).

It is somewhat surprising that the heroes of *byliny* sometimes rely on various tricks or a *deus ex machina* to secure their victories. Thus Ilya and Alyosha use disguises: they don the clothes of wandering pilgrims to put their unsuspecting enemies off guard. Or Alyosha pretends to be deaf, so as to get close to the monster. In one *bylina*, Tugarin in the shape of a dragon flies high in the air and is out of

reach for the hero. Then Alyosha asks God to send rain. Rain comes, soaking the dragon's paper wings, and the dragon falls to the ground. In another *bylina*, Ilya's prayer saves him from certain death (see above).

These episodes show that *bylina* singers did not make any distinction between exploits based on the personal excellence of the hero and those due to cunning, miraculous intervention, or outside help. The same is true of other epics. In the *Iliad*, although Achilles conquers Hector with the crafty assistance of the goddess Athena, her help does not tarnish the victor's crown. Victory is victory, by whatever means it is won.

In the Kievan cycle there appear numerous other heroes, both romantic lovers and chivalrous, brave fighters, for example, Churilo Plenkovich, Dyuk Stepanovich, Solovei (Nightingale) Budimirovich, Mikhailo Potyk, and Sukhman. The handsome Churilo Plenkovich, who comes to Kiev from the southern frontier areas of Duke Vladimir's possessions, becomes a seneschal at the court. When even the Duke's wife cannot turn her eyes from him and wants him to be her chamberlain, the Duke has no other choice but to send him back home. Churilo is finally killed by an outraged husband, who surprises him in bed with his wife.

Dyuk Stepanovich arrives in Kiev as a visiting foreigner from the South and attracts attention by his sneering mockery of the poverty of the city and the court. He wins a wager with Churilo Plenkovich by parading in innumerable new suits and by jumping on horseback across the Dnieper River. Dyuk's possessions and wealth are so fantastic that the inventory takers sent by Duke Vladimir must ask the Duke to sell his cities in order to purchase sufficient writing paper, pens, and ink.

Solovei Budimirovich, a merchant and singer, comes to Kiev from the North with many ships, builds a palace there during a single night and—contrary to established custom—receives a marriage proposal from Duke Vladimir's niece, Zabava Putyatichna. The girl's proposal to the man is not at all surprising, if we interpret the building of the palace as a marriage trial. Scholars have sought to connect the *bylina* of Solovei Budimirovich with an historical wedding between a Norwegian Viking and the daughter of a Kievan Prince.

Mikhailo Potyk's love for the lady White Swan is so strong that, when she dies, he has himself buried with her. But when she is resuscitated, she turns out to be an unfaithful witch, and Mikhailo kills her.

The fate of the brave hero Sukhman is tragic. Having gone out to bring back a live bird to Duke Vladimir, he chances upon a Tartar army. He kills all the Tartars, but is himself wounded. When the Duke, distrusting his honesty and patriotism, humiliates him by incarceration, Sukhman commits suicide.

The Novgorod cycle

The Novgorod *byliny* are devoid of any heroism and as such are close in spirit to the medieval ballad. Their theme is the daily life of this rich commercial city connected by Hanseatic ties to Western Europe, and the marked antagonism between different Novgorodian social classes, which occasionally flares into real clashes and fights.

The main protagonists of the Novgorod cycle are Sadko and Vasily Buslaev. Sadko is a poor *gusli* (a type of harp) player who has commerce with the underwater kingdom. With the help of the Tsar of Lake Ilmen he becomes a rich merchant. When he sails out with his fleet of thirty ships, the sea is becalmed because taxes have not been paid to the Sea King, and Sadko's ships cannot proceed. Despite all his ruses, Sadko has to sacrifice himself to the Sea King to get the ships moving. However, he fares quite well in the kingdom of the sea ruler and eventually returns to his native Novgorod. The bylina reiterates the Jonah motif (Jon. 1:4 ff.), which is based on the age-old sailor's belief that if there is an evildoer on board a ship, the whole crew must suffer.

While the *byliny* about Sadko abound in fairy tale elements, those about Vasily Buslaev are rather realistic. They display the negative side of city life in this rich trading republic. In the *byliny* about Vasily Buslaev, the son of a boyar, we hear first of his childhood pranks and then of his and his retinue's fight against the men of Novgorod, whom Vasily has provoked. Vasily's group would have slain all the men of Novgorod had not his mother wrapped him in her sable cloak and carried him off to her manor. His brawling career ends with a pilgrimage to the Holy Land, evidently undertaken for the atonement of his earlier sins; he perishes on the return journey. Attempts have been made to identify both Sadko and Vasily Buslaev with certain historical figures mentioned in the old Novgorod chronicles.

Structure and form

Byliny consist of three basic parts—the introduction, the narrative portion, and the epilogue. In addition, some *byliny* have an introductory verse for disposing the audience favorably to listening to the epic narrative. The prevailing type of introduction to Kievan *byliny* describes a feast at Duke Vladimir's palace, at which the boasting heroes are given a task to fulfill. Some *byliny* begin with the description of how one or more heroes set out on a mission.

The narrative portion of a *bylina* relates an extraordinary adventure involving a hero and his foe. As A. P. Skaftymov has shown, the structure of the *bylina* is based on an effort to elicit surprise from the audience. The striving for strong effects leads to the abundant use of contrasts in the depiction of the hero and his opponent. At first the hero is minimized and the enemy is hyperbolized. The hero may appear as sick and helpless, or he may be too young or too plain, and his burst of bravado does not inspire any trust. The enemy, on the contrary, is shown as having invincible strength and power. He is terribly big and gluttonous (as e.g., Tugarin), or his whistling causes great destruction in nature (as Solovei Razboinik). People are afraid of him and overwhelmed by his violence. However, when they clash, the hero conquers his enemy with amazing ease.

The epilogue is either a hint to the host for a reward or treat, or a reference to the sea, e.g.: "And they tell the *bylina* about Dobrynya, / to calm down the blue sea, / and for you all to hear, good people." This latter type obviously reflects the magical function of the singing of *byliny* to calm a stormy sea or lake.

Byliny rely heavily on the use of commonplaces (*loci communes*)—formulaic, stereotypic descriptions of recurring situations; they often begin the *bylina* or appear in transitional passages that connect two episodes of the action (Arant). A few commonplaces, obviously the oldest, such as the description of the banquet at Duke Vladimir's, of the hero's entrance into the hall, of his galloping horse, and of the slaughter of the enemy, are found wherever *byliny* are sung. Some are known in a single region, some are restricted to narrators of a single district or a single school, and some are used only by individual bards. The study of commonplaces can be used for a variety of purposes, such as determining the singer and his teacher, pinpointing the areas of origin for certain variants, and discovering falsifications of texts (Ukhov).

There is a tendency in *byliny* to use fixed epithets, that is, to qualify a certain noun with a certain epithet. The horse, for example, in about ninety-five percent of all cases is "good," the field is "open," the birch tree, the day, the swan, and the tent are "white," the table and gate are "high," the wolf and goose are "grey," and the steppe, road, and yard are "broad." According to P. D. Ukhov, fixed epithets function as means of generalization and typification, pointing to the more characteristic, permanent, typical features of certain objects and phenomena.

Byliny have several types of meters, but the most common of them has three stresses per line and a varying number (one to three) of unstressed syllables between stresses. Usually the ending is dactylic and may receive a secondary stress on the last syllable. *Byliny* are stichic, presented line by line without stanzaic arrangement. Rhyme is not used, although syntactical parallels occasionally provide grammatical rhymes.

The singers do not learn long epic songs by heart, but compose them while singing. Studies by Arant and Harkins have proven that singers use the formulaic technique in their presentation. The *byliny* are sung to a rather monotonous melody. Most singers make use of only one melody in their *bylina* repertoire, though infrequently individuals may use two or three.

In former times musical instruments were generally used to accompany *bylina* singing. The oldest instrument was the *gusli*—a low, irregular, four-sided box with the strings stretched over the cover. I. Tõnurist has shown that the instrument itself is not Slavic, but was taken over from the Balto-Finns in the Old Novgorod area, where a Slavic name was given to it (cf. Serbocroatian *gusle*). When a

few centuries later, the *gusli*—its shape somewhat changed—came to be used primarily for the accompaniment of dancing, its place in the presentation of *byliny* was taken by the balalaika. In some areas, the balalaika was used until recent times; in others (like Olonets), it went out of use some time ago.

The singers of *byliny* come primarily from the peasantry, and among them a considerable number are women. The learning of songs is frequently a family tradition. Three or four generations of singers occasionally occur; the most outstanding is the Ryabinin clan of Olonets, initiated by Trofim Ryabinin in the second half of the 19th century. The best known female singers are Marya Krivopolenova from the Pinega River and Agrafena Kryukova from the White Sea coast, both active at the beginning of this century, and Agrafena's daughter Marfa Kryukova (died 1953), the most famous bard of the Stalin era.

In the north, *byliny* were cherished and preserved longer than anywhere else, partly because of the isolation of these areas from cultural centers. The northern way of life and northern climate provided an atmosphere and an eager and grateful audience which led to the continuation of the tradition.

Beginning with the turn of the century, the *bylina* genre has rapidly declined as a living oral tradition. The number of *bylina* singers has diminished drastically. The range of *bylina* themes has become smaller and the texts corrupt and fragmentary. Even the principal episodes have become distorted and schematic and epic ceremonialism (commonplaces, repetitions, fixed epithets, and so on) is being discarded. We are witnessing the rapid extinction of the *bylina* genre, if it has not become extinct already.

Collections: A. M. Astakhova, *Byliny Severa.* 2 vols. Moscow and Leningrad, 1938–51. ——— *Il'ya Muromets.* Moscow and Leningrad, 1958. A. M. Astakhova, V. V. Mitrofanova, and M. O. Skripil', *Byliny v zapisyakh i pereskazakh XVII–XVIII vekov.* Moscow and Leningrad, 1960. Kirsha Danilov, *Drevnie rossiiskie stikhotvoreniya, sobrannye Kirsheyu Danilovym.* Moscow and Leningrad, 1958. (1st ed., 1804.) A. F. Gil'ferding, *Onezhskie byliny, zapisannye A. F. Gil'ferdingom letom 1871 goda.* 4th ed. 3 vols. Moscow and Leningrad, 1949–51. (1st ed. in 1 vol., 1873.) A. D. Grigor'ev, *Arkhangel'skie byliny i istoricheskie pesni.* 3 vols. Moscow, 1904 (Vol. 1), Prague, 1939 (Vol. 2), St. Petersburg, 1910 (Vol. 3). M. S. Kryukova, *Byliny M. S. Kryukovoi.* 2 vols. Moscow, 1939–41. A. V. Markov, *Belomorskie byliny.* Moscow, 1901. N. E. Onchukov, *Pechorskie byliny.* St Petersburg, 1904. V. Ya. Propp and B. N. Putilov, *Byliny.* 2 vols. Moscow, 1958. P. N. Rybnikov, *Pesni, sobrannye P. N. Rybnikovym.* 2d ed. 3 vols. Moscow, 1909–10. (1st ed. in 3 vols., 1861–67.) Yu. I. Smirnov and V. G. Smolitskii, *Dobrynya Nikitich i Alesha Popovich.* Moscow, 1974. Yu. M. Sokolov, *Onezhskie byliny.* Moscow, 1948.

Translations: Nora K. Chadwick, *Russian Heroic Poetry.* 1964. Isabel Florence Hapgood, *The Epic Songs of Russia.* 1916. (1st ed., 1886.) L. A. Magnus, *The Heroic Ballads of Russia.* London, 1921.

Secondary literature: Alex E. Alexander, *Bylina and Fairy Tale: The Origins of Russian Heroic Poetry.* The Hague, 1973. Patricia Arant, "Formulaic Style and the Russian Bylina," *Indiana Slavic Studies,* 4 (1967), pp. 7–51. A. M. Astakhova, *Byliny: Itogi i problemy izucheniya.* 1966. ———, *Russkii bylinnyi epos na Severe.* Petrozavodsk, 1948. Alvin B. Carus, "The Affective 'Grammar' and Structure of Great Russian Charms," *Forum at Iowa on Russian Literature* 2 (1977), pp. 3–19. Wilfrid Chettéoui, *Un rapsode russe. Rjabinin le père. La byline au XIXᵉ siè* Paris, 1942. William Harkins, "O metricheskoi roli slovesnykh formul v serbokhorvatskom i russkom narodnom epose." In *American Contributions to the Fifth International Congress of Slavists, Sofia, September, 1963.* Vol. 2. The Hague, 1963. Pp. 147–65. Karl Hartmann, *Volksepik am Weissen Meer: A. M. Krjukova—Eine Sängermonographie.* 1974. Roman Jakobson and Marc Szeftel, "The Vseslav Epos," *Memoirs of the American Folklore Society* 42 (1949), pp. 13–36. A. Mazon, "Mikula, le prodigieux laboureur," *Revue des Études Slaves,* 11 (1931), pp. 149–70. ———. "Svjatogor ou Saint-Mont le Géant," *Revue des Études Slaves,* 12 (1932), pp. 160–201. V. F. Miller, *Ocherki russkoi narodnoi slovesnosti.* Moscow, 1897, 1910, 1924. Felix J. Oinas, "The Problem of the Aristocratic Origin of Russian Byliny," *SlavR* 30 (1971), pp. 513–22. Felix J. Oinas and Stephen Soudakoff, eds, *The Study of Russian Folklore.* The Hague, 1975. M. M. Plisetskii, *Istor-*

izm russkikh bylin. Moscow, 1962. V. Ya. Propp, *Russkii geroiche-skii epos.* 2d ed. Moscow, 1958. (1st ed., 1955.) A. P. Skaftymov, "Poetika i genezis bylin" (abbreviated). In *Stat'i o russkoi literature* Saratov, 1958. Pp. 3–76. (1st ed. [complete], 1924.) B. Sokolov, "Byliny." In *Literaturnaya entsiklopediya,* vol. 2. 1929. Pp. 1–38. Yu. M. Sokolov, "Byliny," In *Russian Folklore.* Detroit, 1971. Pp. 291–370. A. N. Stender-Petersen, "Problema sbornika Kirshi Dani-lova," *Scando-Slavica,* 4 (1958), pp. 70–93. I. Tõnurist, "Kannel Vepsamaast Setumaani." In *Soome-ugri rahvaste muusikapärandist.* Ed. I. Rüütel. Tallinn, 1977. Pp. 149–82. P. D. Ukhov, *Atributsii russkikh bylin.* Moscow, 1970. P. D. Ukhov, "Postoyannye epitety v bylinakh kak sredstvo tipizatsii i sozdaniya obraza." In *Osnovnye problemy eposa vostochnykh slavyan.* Ed. V. V. Vinogradov et al. Moscow, 1958. Pp. 158–71. V. M. Zhirmunskii, *Narodnyi geroiche-skii epos: Sravnitel'no-istoricheskie ocherki.* Moscow and Leningrad, 1962.   F. J. O.

Byronism. Byron's verse, mentioned in the Russian periodical press as early as 1815, became a major force in Russian culture only in the early 1820s, when French and Russian translations made Byron available to the Russian reading public, which knew little English, and when the optimism fostered by Russia's victory against Napoleon yielded to disillusionment with the harshness of the last years of Alexander I's reign. Under these circumstances Byron's Eastern tales (especially "The Giaour" and "The Corsair"), lyrics, dramas (*Cain, Heaven and Earth*), "The Prisoner of Chillon" (trans. by Zhukovsky, 1822), and "Childe Harold's Pilgrimage" provided a language and poetics for the expression of disillusionment and bitter rebelliousness. A few Russians of the 1820s to 1840s, such as A. S. PUSHKIN, were able to grasp the implications of Byron's *Don Juan* for the development of longer narrative works, including the novel. Fewer still, such as A. A. DELVIG, ignored Byron altogether.

Byronism, as a fashionable behavior model and as an ideology, featured elements of proud rebelliousness (vs. God, the social order, civilization, tyranny), aristocratic arrogance, melancholy, love of nature, misanthropy, passionate excess, and "demonism." In different manifestations it could foreground political aspiration or individual isolation. The model derived not only from the figures of titanic heroism in Byron's works but also from understandings of Byron's life culled from many articles in the press and from Thomas Moore's edition of Byron's letters and journals (1830)—lameness, aristocratic position, domestic disaster, incestuous love, exile, struggle for liberty, death in Greece; from the flood of Russian lyrical tributes after Byron's death; and from the many narrative poems that felt the impact of Byron—Pushkin's "Prisoner of the Caucasus," "Fountain at Bakhchisarai," and "Gypsies," KOZLOV's "The Monk," and LER-MONTOV's "Mtsyri" and "Demon." Two novels which subjected their Byronic heroes to critical scrutiny, Pushkin's *Eugene Onegin* and Lermontov's *Hero of Our Time,* have likewise contributed to the complex Russian understanding of Byronism.

Bibliography: N. Ya. D'yakova, "Bairon." In *Lermontovskaya entsiklopediya.* 1981. E. J. Simmons, *English Literature and Culture in Russia (1553–1840).* 1935. Chap. 10. A. N. Veselovskii, "Etyudy o baironizme." In his *Etyudy i Kharakteristiki.* 4th ed. Vol. 1. 1912. W. N. Vickery, "Parallelizm v literaturnom razvitii Bairona i Pushkina." In *American Contributions to the Fifth International Congress of Slavists.* 1963. V. M. Zhirmunskii, *Bairon i Pushkin.* 1978.   W. M. T.

Byt, a Russian word difficult to translate with all its connotations intact, is often left untranslated. The *Slovar' russkogo literaturnogo yazyka* defines its primary meaning as "general way of life; the aggregate of customs and mores characteristic of a particular people, class, social milieu, stratum, etc." In this sense it is attested in classic Russian authors from PUSHKIN (*krest'yanskii byt,* peasant life) to GON-CHAROV (*morskoi byt,* life aboard ship), and it is still in use (*novyi sovetskii byt,* the new Soviet way of life).

In the 19th century *byt* had no derogatory overtones, and its derivative, *bytopisanie,* was an elevated, SHISHKOV-style equivalent for "history." In 20th-century literary usage, however, *byt* came to denote especially the more mundane aspects of everyday life, the *intérieur* of kitchens, bathrooms, and bedrooms, as opposed to the great world outside, the arena of public life. Writers who concentrated on such quotidian realities were known as *bytoviki,* and in the

1920s contrasted with the neo-romantics who sang the heroics of revolution and civil war. Among them were Panteleimon ROMANOV, N. Ognev, and of course Mikhail ZOSHCHENKO.

However, it was in the work—and the mind—of MAYAKOVSKY that *byt* attained new status as a metaphysical category. For Mayakovsky *byt* was the enemy incarnate, the embodiment of everything routine and unchanging, the enslavement of man to physical, biological, and social necessity, even time itself. The "future" of Mayakovsky's futurism was, therefore, far more than the rhetoric of an aggressive, past-abhorring literary school; it was the heaven where man would at last be liberated from *byt.* Ultimately, as JAKOBSON explained, *byt* was the non-poet, everything outside the poet's self. Mayakovsky's war with *byt* is alluded to in many poems, most explicitly in *About That* (Pro eto, 1923); his tragic loss of the war is conveyed by the famous line from his suicide note, "Love's boat smashed against *byt*" (Lyubovnaya lodka razbilas' o byt). The hatred of *byt,* and the poet's fight against it, is also a crucial theme in the work of Marina TSVETAEVA and Nikolai ZABOLOTSKY.

Bibliography: Edward J., Brown, *Mayakovsky: A Poet in the Revolution.* 1973. Roman Jakobson, "On a Generation That Squandered Its Poets." In *Major Soviet Writers: Essays in Criticism.* Ed. Edward J. Brown. N.Y., 1973. Simon Karlinsky, *Marina Cvetaeva; Her Life and Art.* 1966. Lawrence Leo Stahlberger, *The Symbolic System of Majakovskij.* The Hague, 1964.   H. McL.

Byzantine influence created the higher culture and the written literature of the Russians and the other Orthodox Slavs. It predominated over all influences from other sources—Scandinavian, Mongol-Tatar, Latin, German, Italian, English, etc.—up to the end of the 17th century and beyond, and provided the background against which these other influences manifested themselves. Unlike other influences, it was all-pervasive: it affected not only individual written texts and other artifacts of higher culture, but gave that culture its structure and purposes, and the bulk of its material: the very techniques of writing and of making books, the kinds of texts to be committed to writing and the models on which they could be composed, the literary system into which these texts entered, and the very context—Christianity—in which they were read, all came to the Orthodox Slavs primarily from Byzantium. So basic was the Byzantine influence in this period that one perhaps ought not to speak of it as an influence, but rather as a transplant: a certain limited part of Byzantine higher culture and written literature was transplanted as a whole into Slavic lands, where it subsequently underwent a variety of influences, including Slavic ones.

During this period, the written literature of the Orthodox Slavs, including the Russians, was largely supra-national in character. It may be termed CHURCH SLAVONIC literature, after the supra-national language, Church Slavonic, in which most of it was written. Church Slavonic literature began with the work of two Greek missionaries, Constantine and Methodius, in Great Moravia and Pannonia during the second half of the 9th century. Their disciples and successors continued their literary work for a number of centuries in Macedonia, Bulgaria, Serbia and Kievan Russia, as well as on Mt. Athos and in other international centers of Orthodox monastic life. Later Church Slavonic literature flourished also in the Rumanian lands and in the Grand Principalities of Lithuania and of Moscow. Since it originated two hundred years before the schism between Rome and the four Eastern Patriarchates in the middle of the 11th century, Church Slavonic literature was cultivated by some of the Slavs who were under Roman ecclesiastical jurisdiction as well—chiefly by the Croats, and also by the Slovenes and the Czechs. Until the 13th century texts seem to have crossed the boundary between Orthodoxy and Catholicism with ease, but after that time each of these two branches of Church Slavonic literature developed in isolation from the other.

Church Slavonic literature is in great part a literature of translations; original Slavic works form an extremely small part of it, and consequently the line between translation and original composition is much less sharply drawn than is customary in modern European literatures. Not only are translations much more numerous than original compositions, but they are on the average much lengthier, and to judge by the surviving manuscripts they were copied much oftener. Moreover, most original compositions—sermons, lives of saints and services for their feasts, prayers, chronographs, etc.—follow closely the models provided by translated works. It is not until the 18th century that any Orthodox Slavs develop extensive vernacular literatures of their own in which original compositions greatly outweigh the heritage of translations, and need not be regularly modeled upon them.

To judge by what has come down to us, almost all of the early translations were made from Greek originals. There are a small number of translations from other languages (Latin, German, Hebrew, etc.), but not enough to challenge the predominance of Greek. The Greek texts chosen for translation were almost entirely ones which would commonly be found in Byzantine monastic libraries, and thus do not represent the full range of texts which a Byzantine scholar would have been able to read at Constantinople in the original Greek. Virtually everything that was translated into Church Slavonic is of a popular or a useful character; what might be described as Byzantine "highbrow" literature—works in the classical tradition, and works of a speculative or theoretical character—is conspicuously absent.

First place among the translations is easily held by the liturgical texts according to the Byzantine Rite. Perhaps as many as three fourths of all extant Church Slavonic manuscripts written before the end of the 16th century contain only texts of this character. These include the Lectionaries drawn from the Gospels, from the Acts and Epistles of the Apostles and from the Old Testament (*Evangelie*, *Apostol* and *Paremeinik*, respectively) and the Psalter (*Psaltyr'*), as well as the books containing texts for the various cycles of services which combine to make up the ecclesiastical year. The Horologion (*Chasoslov*) gives the services of the daily and weekly cycles, with the exception of the three Divine Liturgies, which are found in the Liturgiarion (*Sluzhebnik*). The services for the days of the fixed yearly cycle are contained in twelve large volumes, one for each month of the year; each volume is called a Menaion (*Sluzhebnaya mineya*). The moveable yearly cycle is linked to the date of Easter, which varies from year to year; its services are found in the Triodion (*Triod' postnaya*), the Pentekostarion (*Triod' tsvetnaya*) and the Oktoëchos (*Oktoikh*). Rituals which are not tied to any particular day in any of the cycles, but can be celebrated at need, are found in the Euchologion (*Trebnik*). Both the fixed and the moveable yearly cycle are combined in the Synaxarion (*Prolog*), which contains abridged sermons and saints' lives for liturgical use. Musical texts are sometimes extracted from the above volumes and copied by themselves, giving rise to several kinds of musical books, each of which contains a particular kind of musical composition: the Kontakarion (*Kondakar'*), the Sticherarion (*Stikhirar'*), the Heirmologion (*Irmologii*), the Kanonarion (*Kanonnik*), and others.

Second place is occupied by translations of various Greek collections of saints' lives and sermons in unabridged form, which were not normally used in the course of any service of worship, but rather were read aloud in monasteries or read privately. The majority of these volumes are arranged not by author, but according to the ecclesiastical year; each such volume normally covers one month, and is called a Menologion (MINEI CHET'YI). However, sermons ascribed to a single Father of the Church are sometimes found collected by themselves: John Chrysostom, Gregory of Nazianzus and Ephrem the Syrian are the ones most commonly treated in this way.

No sharp line can be drawn between such volumes and other Patristic writings. Generally speaking, three classes of Patristic writings were translated at an early date: theological manuals and compendia of an elementary sort, commentaries on certain books of the Bible, and works of a strongly monastic cast. To these were later added the translations of a number of mystical writings, which might constitute a fourth class. Among the theological manuals and compendia are an abridged translation of the *Fount of Knowledge* by John of Damascus, and complete translations of the catechetical lectures by Cyril of Jerusalem and by Theodore of Studios, of Athanasius of Alexandria's work *Against the Arians*, of Leo of Rome's *Tome*, and of the *Pandects* by Antioch and by Nikon of the Black Mountain. Among the Biblical commentaries are those by Theophylact of Ochrid on the Gospels, by pseudo-Oecumenikos on the Epistles, and by Andrew of Caesarea on the Apocalypse; the Old Testament is covered by Hesychios of Jerusalem's *Commentary on the Psalms*, Hippolytos of Rome's *Commentary on Daniel* (to which was added his work On the Antichrist), and Catenae, i.e. composite commentaries excerpting several Fathers, on Job, Ecclesiastes, the Song of Songs, and the Prophets. None of these are works of any great exegetical sophistication. Much more important were the Old Testament commentaries by the extremely sophisticated exegete Theodoret of Cyrrhus, some of which were translated at an early date; but it is indicative that they were much less frequently copied than the other translated commentaries, and that some of them have not survived in any copy, although quotations show that they were once available in translation. Among the monastic works, John of Sinai's *Ladder of Paradise* was widely copied, as were no less than five Paterica (i.e. collections of monastic anecdotes), and some of the ascetic writings attributed to Basil of Caesarea. The mystical works translated were mostly those important for the hesychast movement: pseudo-Dionysios the Areopagite's works and the scholia thereto by Maximos the Confessor, the sermons of Isaac the Syrian, and especially the works of Symeon of Thessalonica.

In comparison with the above translations, all others are relatively rare, and probably were much less widely circulated. Here belong a variety of florilegia, as well as what one might term the "scientific and pseudo-scientific" texts, volumes of canon and civil law, and, oddly enough, the Old Testament. Until the end of the 15th century, the only books of the Old Testament which were available in Church Slavonic translation without a commentary were the Octateuch (i.e. Genesis–Ruth), the Tetrabasileion (i.e. I–II Samuel, I–II Kings), Esther, Job, the Psalter, Proverbs, the Song of Songs, and the Wisdom of ben Sirach (i.e. Ecclesiasticus); most of these were translated from the Greek, as expected, but Esther was translated from the Hebrew. As noted above, some of these were also in circulation with translated commentaries, as were Ecclesiastes and the Prophets. The remaining dozen books were translated from the Latin Vulgate about 1493 in Novgorod, when Archbishop Gennadios of that city undertook to compile a complete Church Slavonic Bible for the first time.

Of greater interest to the modern reader, perhaps, are the Slavonic translations of popular Greek historical writings, for example the *Chronicles* by George Hamartolos, John Malalas, George Synkellos, John Zonaras and Constantine Manasses, and also Josephus' famous *Jewish War*, with its tantalizing passages (not found in the Greek) concerning John the Baptist, Jesus and the first Christians.

A literature is more than just the totality of its literary works: those works generally stand in close and well-defined relations to one another, thereby imposing a system or structure upon that literature as a whole. Moreover, as new works are added to a literature, and as old works cease to be read, the structure of that literature can change. The Greek works available to cultivated Byzantine readers had come to form two systems—one classical, the other ecclesiastical—which overlapped only to a limited extent. Only the ecclesiastical system was transplanted to the Orthodox Slavs, so that the very few works translated which belonged, however marginally, to the classical system had perforce to be worked into the ecclesiastical system, or to survive as isolated phenomena.

In Byzantine literature, the classical system was a hierarchy of genres, which was correlated to some extent with a hierarchy of literary dialects of the Greek language. To this system belonged not only the heritage of Greek Classical Antiquity, but also the works of a considerable number of Christian writers working in its traditions, such as Gregory of Nazianzus.

The ecclesiastical system, though it contains genres, is not organized principally in terms of them, but rather in terms of the uses to which the individual texts are put: it is not a system of textual forms, but of textual functions. Two kinds of use or function are considered: the given text's place in one or another of the four cycles of the ecclesiastical year, which determines when it will be used in worship or read aloud, and its level of canonical authority, which determines its value in theological argumentation. In the manuscripts at least, if not always in our modern scholarly editions, almost every text belonging to one or the other of the two yearly cycles has a "calendrical tag," which defines its place in the ecclesiastical year, for example "St. Cyril the Monk's Sermon about the Deposition of the Body of Christ from the Cross ... *for the Third Sunday after Easter*," or "*On April 6th*: the Feast and Life of our Blessed Father and Teacher Methodius, Archbishop of Moravia" (tags in italics). (The ways in which texts are tagged for the daily and weekly cycles are more complicated, and need not be treated here.) A text's level of canonical authority will often not be explicitly given, but must be inferred from other information; however, in the first of the two examples, the ascription to

"*Saint* Cyril the Monk" (i.e. Cyril of Turov) assures the reader that the sermon has at least a moderately high level of canonical authority, and is trustworthily Orthodox.

Levels of canonical authority are determined ultimately by the inspiration and the orthodoxy of the texts themselves, which have been made known by the Oecumenical Councils and by the Fathers of the Orthodox Church. They may be thought of as a pyramid with four levels, each more authoritative than the one below it. The highest level is occupied by the books of the Old and New Testaments (the exact list of these books differs slightly from the lists used by Catholic and Protestant Churches). The next level down is that of the liturgical books (which are to a great extent composed of Biblical texts) and the Canons of the Oecumenical Councils (including canons of other origin which have been sanctioned by an Oecumenical Council). On the third level down are the writings of the Fathers of the Church, i.e. of Orthodox bishops ("Father" is a title of a bishop), and of a few other saints. The fourth and lowest level is the most extensive of all: here are found the broad mass of Orthodox writings, including APOCRYPHA and pseudepigrapha which are free from heresy. There are also heretical and condemned writings which pretend to a position in the pyramid without truly having one. They might be arranged in an inverted pyramid of their own, separate from and far below the canonical pyramid. Canonical authority, therefore, is in large part a question of the orthodoxy of the text's content, which is most easily approached through the related question of the text's author. (In the case of HAGIOGRAPHY and its liturgical appendages, the text's subject also comes into question.)

A text's place in one or another of the four cycles of the ecclesiastical year is fixed, but as a consequence its contiguous texts will vary from one year to the next, since the four cycles do not align themselves with one another in the same way from one year to the next. The services of worship appointed for any given day in a particular ecclesiastical year are formed by "interweaving" texts drawn from the weekly and the two yearly cycles. Since any given day of, say, the fixed yearly cycle will be a different weekday and a different number of days before or after Easter from one year to the next, the exact combination of liturgical texts for that day will also differ. Because of the length of the cycles involved, the entire pattern repeats itself only after a period of 532 years. Thus, no text belonging to the ecclesiastical system will be read or heard in quite the same broad context as it was during the previous year, or as it will be during the following year, and the exact pattern of contexts will not repeat itself within the lifetime of any reader or hearer.

As texts are "interwoven" with one another, their parts can come to be separated by extraneous material. Not only are the books of the Bible treated in this way (being broken up into "lessons"), but also many of the longer hymnological compositions. There is, for example, a kind of hymn called a kanon, which in theory contains nine odes (in practice, one or more of the odes is generally omitted). The odes of a kanon are sung one after another, and there are breaks after the third and the sixth ode, where other texts are sung or read before proceeding to sing the fourth or seventh ode of the kanon. In one case, because of its extreme length, a kanon is spread out over several days' services of worship: this is the Great Kanon of St. Andrew of Crete, which is sung from Monday through Thursday during the first week of Lent. Moreover, if more than one kanon is prescribed for a particular day, they may be "interwoven" with one another: the first ode of each kanon is sung in turn, then the third ode of each, then the fourth, etc. (the second ode is generally omitted, except for Lenten kanons).

Moreover, a kanon is usually composed in a way which results in its containing recognizable fragments of earlier compositions by other hymnographers. Each of a kanon's odes may be compared roughly to a Western hymn in irregular meter, in that it will contain several "verses." The first "verse" is called the heirmos; it sets the meter and determines the music. The remaining "verses" are called troparia; they must conform to the meter of the heirmos and thus can be sung to its music. Almost without exception, the composer of a kanon will compose only the troparia himself, and will take his heirmoi from some earlier kanon still in use. As a result, one and the same set of heirmoi (both words and music) will eventually come to be found in a large number of kanons; although these kanons are not usually performed contiguously, they are indissolubly united with one another by their common heirmoi.

All these facts have far-reaching aesthetic consequences, which must be understood by whoever would appreciate or study the medieval literature, art, or music of the Orthodox Greeks and Slavs in its own terms. For the Greeks, the effect is somewhat attenuated by the persistent survival, alongside the ecclesiastical system, of writings in the classical system of verbal art; but the Orthodox Slavs, to whose soil only the ecclesiastical system was transplanted, show its implied aesthetics in pure form. The result is a literature which may not appear to merit the name "literature" upon first acquaintance, for it emphasizes function over form and conformity over originality. In line with its relative disregard for form, it does not insist on any sharp divisions within art according to the medium used: the verbal, musical, and visual (iconographic and architectural) works created by the Orthodox Slavs are not works of separate arts, but simply parts of one overreaching art; a work in one medium may have its strongest associative links with works in all media indifferently. In line with its relative disregard for originality, it does not insist on the sharply delimited integrity of any work of art: most of what has been created was meant to be taken in context, and not in just one context, but in a series of contexts varying from one year to the next; and these contexts press so tightly upon the work that they breach its boundaries, with the result that compositions interpenetrate one another textually. The best effects of this literature, its greatest artistic power, are achieved not explicitly, but implicitly, and remain totally invisible to anyone who approaches a single work in isolation. It is a literature which can be appreciated best as a totality of works, in which any particular work by itself is of little significance or effect, and the context of its appreciation is in principle more than just literature.

Bibliography: A. S. Arkhangel'skii. "Tvoreniya ottsov tserkvi v drevnerusskoi pis'mennosti (Obozrenie rukopisnogo materiala)." *Zhurnal Ministerstva narodnogo prosveshcheniya*, 257 (July 1888); pp. 1–49, 258 (August 1888); pp. 203–95. H. Birnbaum, "Toward a Comparative Study of Church Slavic Literature." In *On Medieval and Renaissance Slavic Writing: Selected Essays*. The Hague, 1974. Pp. 13–40. I. U. Budovnits, *Slovar' russkoi, ukrainskoi, belorusskoi pis'mennosti i literatury*. Moscow, 1969. Filaret (Gumilevskii), *Obzor russkoi dukhovnoi literatury 862–1863*. St. Petersburg, 1888. D. S. Likhachev, "Staroslavyanskite literaturi kato sistema." *Literaturna misul* 13, no. 1 (January-February 1969); pp. 3–38. N. A. Meshcherskii, *Istochniki i sostav drevnei slavyano-russkoi perevodnoi pis'mennosti IX–XV vekov*. Leningrad, 1978. I. Ševčenko, "Remarks on the Diffusion of Byzantine Scientific and Pseudo-Scientific Literature among the Orthodox Slavs," *SEER* 59 (1980–81), pp. 321–45. F. J. Thomson, "The Nature of the Reception of Christian Byzantine Culture in Russia in the Tenth to Thirteenth Centuries and its Implications for Russian Culture." *Slavica Gandensia* 5 (1978); pp. 107–39. L. P. Zhukovskaya, "Pamyatniki russkoi i slavyanskoi pis'mennosti XI–XIV vv. v knigokhranilishchakh SSSR," *Sovetskoe slavyanovedenie*, 1969, no. 1; pp. 57–71.   R. M.

Calendar poetry. The agricultural ritual year was divided into several major holidays during which rituals were performed. They can be divided into two cycles, the longer of which started at the beginning of the year and lasted up to the harvest. The various rituals in this cycle were to ensure a good harvest, fertile cattle, and family prosperity. The second cycle was performed during and after the harvest to guarantee next year's harvest would be plentiful and the peasants would have health and strength for the coming year. Based on the dual-belief system (*dvoeverie*) among the peasants, pagan celebrations coincided with important events in the Christian calendar, and thus some holidays were fixed while others depended on the date of Easter.

The peasants followed the solar calendar and began their new year on December 25th. The period from December 25 to January 6 was known as *svyatki* (from *svyat*, "holy"), during which special songs called *zimnie prazdnichno-pozdravitel'nye pesni* (winter holiday-greeting songs) were performed on Christmas Eve, New Year's and Epiphany (January 6th). One of the most common terms for this type of song was *kolyada*, which often appeared in the refrain. In central Russia and the Volga area the terms *ovsen'* or *tausen'* and in Northern Russia *vinograd'e* might appear instead. The performers were young people who would go from hut to hut singing these songs. The basic composition of the song consisted of an introduction, a panegyric to the host and his family, a request for a reward, then depending on the reward, wishes for prosperity or misfortune. Often the host and his surroundings are described in an idealized manner, which has been interpreted as a form of homeopathic magic, where through the power of the word, what has been depicted will come true. In some songs *kolyada* is personified as a female figure who brings Christmas. Many of the songs are limited to a request for a reward, then a wish for prosperity or misfortune based on whether the host rewards the singers or sends them away.

The next set of calendrical songs are platter (*podblyudnye*) songs which are sung on New Year's Eve. Girls would tell their fortune by dropping rings into a dish which would then be covered. The girls would sit on a bench and begin to sing as one of the girls would take a ring from the dish. The fortune foretold in the song would apply to the owner of the ring. The songs portray symbols which might have the same meaning in all regions or might differ according to area. While the solution to many of the songs still remains a mystery, others have been interpreted, for example: a pearl rolling up to a ruby signifies marriage; a sleigh means travel; a covered trough foretells death. The songs are relatively short. Sometimes every line is followed by the word *slava* (glory); most frequently the symbolic episode is followed by the refrain: *komu vynetsya/tomu sbudetsya* (for whom it is drawn, for her it will come true) and this may also be followed by the word *slava*.

Shrovetide (*Maslenitsa*) was celebrated the week before Lent. The songs accompanying the various rituals are often ribald. The welcoming of *Maslenitsa* in the form of a female straw effigy or a peasant dressed as a woman was accompanied by song. The greeting consisted of a merry procession of people in sleighs or on foot singing songs describing the welcoming of *Maslenitsa* with ritual food—bliny (round pancakes symbolizing the sun), butter, and cakes. During the week, games and various forms of entertainment such as sledding were accompanied by songs in which *Maslenitsa* would be associated with the particular activity to which the song was devoted. At the end of the week there was a mock funeral for *Maslenitsa*, which has been interpreted as the burying of winter, or the ritual burial of a natural force whose strength would enter into the earth and would be resurrected in the form of vegetation. The effigy, or in the case when *Maslenitsa* has been represented by a peasant, a sheaf of wheat or straw, is taken in a funeral procession with laughter and joking beyond the village and either trampled into the ground or burned, and the remnants are thrown into the field. The songs accompanying this ritual describe the burial or accuse *Maslenitsa* of deception: she has stayed only seven days and now Lent is coming for seven weeks. As PROPP suggests, the laughter has a particular significance: it reflects the idea that this is a death that ultimately will lead to resurrection and life in the form of vegetation.

The invocation to spring takes place on either March 1 (St. Eudocia's Day), March 9 (day of the forty martyrs), or March 25 (Annunciation). The peasants invoked birds, especially larks, and bees, who according to peasant belief brought the spring. These songs were called *vesnyanki* (from *vesna*, "spring") and were usually performed on high places such as roof tops of granaries or hills. Sometimes spring was personified and invoked to lock up winter and unlock summer.

The day cattle were first driven to pasture, St. George's (Egorii) Day (April 23), was accompanied by songs to protect the cattle from harm. On the eve of this holiday men went around the village and sang special songs at each hut. The songs are reminiscent of *kolyadki*. After invoking Egorii to protect the cattle, the singers ask the host for a reward and in relation to the response, the singers wish him either well or ill.

Zelenye svyatki (green *svyatki*), also known as *Rusalka* (mermaid week), was celebrated the seventh week after Easter, culminating on Trinity Sunday. On Thursday of that week, called *Semik*, girls went into the forest with fried eggs and decorated a birch with ribbons, twined the ends of its branches into wreaths, and danced a *khorovod* (round dance) around it. The girls also wove garlands from birch twigs and celebrated *kumlenie*, when they kissed through the wreaths and became friends for life. On Trinity Sunday they untwined the garlands on the birch, then wove separate wreaths and threw them into the water to tell their fortune. If the wreaths floated, it signified good fortune; if they sank, it meant death. Each aspect of the ritual is associated with particular songs describing the event. On Trinity Sunday in certain areas they would throw into the water a birch "mermaid" (*Kostroma*). The *Kostroma* would be in the form of a doll, which was put into a coffin. The girls would walk to the river in a funeral procession and throw the coffin into the water, all accompanied by appropriate songs. This has been interpreted as another form of the death of a natural spirit whose strength was returned to nature, and would thus help the growth of the crops.

The forces of nature were considered to be strongest on the eve of John the Baptist (Ivan Kupala), June 23. Some songs called the villagers to the celebration in the forest where they jumped through ritual bonfires or bathed in rivers or lakes. Other songs are invectives against witches to prevent them from spoiling the herds and the grain.

The last songs sung during the calendrical year were devoted to the harvest, which had no fixed date and depended on the climate. The beginning of the harvest was called *zazhinki*. The ritual aspect of the harvest was at the end, the *dozhinki*, when a few ears left in the field uncut, the "beard," were twisted, bent to the ground and buried, returning strength to the soil and thus ensuring a good harvest for the next year. The last sheaf was decorated and brought to the hut to provide strength and prosperity for the family. Both these rituals were accompanied by appropriate songs.

Bibliography: V. I. Chicherov, *Zimnii period russkogo zemledel'cheskogo kalendarya XVI–XIX vekov.* 1957. V. Ya. Propp, *Russkie agrarnye prazdniki.* 1963 Roberta Reeder, *Down Along the Mother Volga.* 1975. Yu. M. Sokolov, *Russian Folklore.* 1971. V. K. Sokolova, *Vesenne letnie obryady.* 1979. I. Zemtsovskii, *Poeziya krest'yanskikh prazdnikov.* (Biblioteka poeta, Bol'shaya seriya.) 1970. *See also:* "Obryadovaya poeziya." In *Russkoe ustnoe narodnoe tvorchestvo.* Ed. N. I. Kravtsov and S. G. Lazutin. 1977. Pp. 41–50.
R. R.

Catherine the Great (1729–96). An active if modestly talented contributor to the literary life of her nation, Catherine gave singular expression to the concept of enlightened absolutism. Her lively correspondence with the French philosophers, among whom she regarded Voltaire as her teacher, suggests a humanist and free thinker quite unlike the conservative preceptress who, despite her imperfect Russian, authored numerous comedies, satires, fairy tales and feuilletons for the edification of her subjects. Intent on the promotion of existing authority, her initial impulse was to depict innocuous human foibles rather than serious social deficiencies, appealing to a reason largely synonymous with government policy. In later works, a more direct and strident attack on liberal ideology became evident; several plays written in the late 1780s are comedies in name only, their purpose being to discredit FREEMASONRY.

In her choice of genres, Catherine followed prevailing European and domestic literary trends. The decision to found a satirical journal in 1769 was doubtlessly prompted by the English example of Addison's *Spectator*. If the tone and substance of her own *Vsyakaya vsyachina* (All Kinds of Things) failed to capture that of the model, it still held considerable importance as a catalyst for the creation of original Russian satire, first appearing in the short-lived journals of N. I. NOVIKOV and F. EMIN. Of Catherine's other writings, her comedies deserve mention, if only because of their number and popularity. The first, *O vremya!* (Oh Times!), dating from 1772 and loosely adapted from a German original, depicts the petty schemings of the Moscovite nobility. Subsequently inspired by translations of Shakespeare, she abandoned the Neoclassical dramatic conventions and used *The Merry Wives of Windsor* as a model for one comedy, *Vot kakovo imet' korzinu i bel'e* (A Basketful of Washing), and his chronicle plays as a source for her "historical representations." A mixed dramatic genre, the latter served monarchic purposes by celebrating the rule of Russia's ancient autocracy in the persons of Ryurik and Oleg.

Works: Sochineniya Imperatritsy Ekateriny II. Ed. A. N. Pypin., St. Petersburg, 1901–7.
Translations: The Literature of Eighteenth Century Russia. Ed. and trans. Harold B. Segel. Vol. 1. New York, 1967. *Voltaire and Catherine the Great: Selected Correspondence.* Ed. A. Lentin, Cambridge, 1974.

Censorship

Secondary Literature: Catherine the Great: A Profile. Ed. Marc
Raeff, New York, 1972. Michael von Herzen, "Catherine II—Editor
of *Vsiakaia Vsiachina*? A Reappraisal," *RusR* 38 (1979), pp. 283–97.
P. R. H.

Censorship, government control over all social activities involved in
the production of arts and letters. Censorship became institutionalized in the post-Gutenberg era. As an institution, censorship serves
as indirect evidence of the intellectual interests of a given society.

Early evidence of ecclesiastic censorship in Russia can be traced
back to 1589, when Moscow received its own Patriarchate. Lists of
anathematized religious books appeared in the mid-17th century, due
to the Schism. The first attempt to ban a secular work dates from 1591
when the Russian Company sought to suppress the first edition of
Giles Fletcher's *Of the Russe Common Wealth.* The history of secular
censorship in Russia might be divided into the following periods: (1)
1702–83, when the Western innovations of book-printing, book-
marketing, and the public press were promoted by the Tsars and protected by the government; (2) *1783–1804*, when censorship commissions for examination of foreign and Russian books were established;
(3) *1804–March 1917*, the period of official censorship functioning
under the auspices of several consecutive legal statutes: 1804, 1828,
1865, and 1914; (4) *March 1917–November 10, 1917*, a period of free,
uncensored press in Russia after the downfall of the Monarchy; (5)
November 1917–1919, a period when control was exercised by a set of
Revolutionary Decrees issued by the Council of Peoples Commissars
aimed at the counter-revolutionary press; (6) *1919–present*, complete
supervision of press, mass culture, and propaganda under the control
of the State Publishing House (Gosizdat, later Glavlit).

In the first half of the 18th century there was no censorship in
Russia. Moreover, European cultural tendencies were promoted and
the development of literacy and science was encouraged. In 1727, the
newly-formed Russian Academy of Sciences elaborated its supreme
organizational law, the Academy Statute, granting to all members the
privilege of free, uncensored creativity, and exempting Academy editions from censorship. (This privilege was revoked by the Soviet Government in 1928.) The first Russian newspaper, *The Gazette* (later the
St. Petersburg Gazette, 1702–27; 1728–1917) was not censored until
1763. In the same year CATHERINE II issued a rescript forbidding
distribution in Russia of those foreign books "which had already
been forbidden everywhere else in Europe." Yet by and large,
writers of the mid-1700s sought government protection and due to a
small readership were subsidized by the Senate, the Synod, and the
Tsars.

The period of ENLIGHTENMENT strongly influenced the development of satirical journalism. The progenitor of Russian satirical
periodicals, VSYAKAYA VSYACHINA (initiated by Catherine II in 1769)
spawned twenty-five "offspring," all free from censorship until 1783.
In January 1783, Catherine II and the Senate legalized the free establishment of book-printing houses in Russia (*vol'nye russkie tipografii*). However, the owners of these houses were responsible for
the character of books published and were supervised by the Police
(Uprava Blagochiniya) and ultimately, the Empress. Although moderate, the rescript of 1783 was the first attempt to impose bureaucratic control over the press. The French Revolution of 1789 turned
the government's fear of radicalism into hysteria. The banning of
RADISHCHEV's *Journey from St. Petersburg to Moscow*, the author's
subsequent trial and exile, the four-year imprisonment of Nikolai
NOVIKOV (1792–96), the ban on FONVIZIN's writings after his publication of "Questions addressed to Catherine II," as well as the persecution of the Masonic (see FREEMASONRY) movement put an end to the
era of imperial liberalism in Russia. To prevent further contacts between Russian intellectuals and revolutionary France, censorship
committees were established in the main port cities and in Moscow.
In September 1796 the free printing houses were closed. In 1797,
during the reign of Paul I, the position of Censor was placed within
the Table of Ranks of the civil service. In 1800, in addition to the
censoring of published material, preliminary censorship of manuscripts went into effect and a special rescript issued by Paul I forbade
the usage of several words (mainly social and philosophical terms).
With the accession of Alexander I, Russian censorship was eased and
the clock set back to 1783.

The First Censorship Statute, published on June 9, 1804, established committees for preliminary censorship of manuscripts. These
committees were governed by Universities or Educational Councils.
The censors were charged with preventing antigovernment, irrelig-
ious, immoral, and slanderous passages from reaching publication;
they were obliged to explain to the authors the reasons for rejecting
their works and to inform the Government of the most unacceptable
texts. The censors were instructed to ban only explicitly harmful
ideas: "If the statement allows for an ambivalent interpretation, it is
desirable to interpret it in favor of the author and not to persecute his
views" (sec. 21). Despite modifications made in the 1804 Statute between 1804 and 1826 (in 1811 ultimate supervision of censorship was
transferred to the Ministry of Police and later to the ministry of Internal Affairs), this bureaucratic control did not constrain culture, and
during this period the art of letters grew into the art of literature, the
most significant component of Russian social, intellectual, and
aesthetic awareness.

The suppression of the DECEMBRIST revolt by Nicholas I ushered
in a set of retrograde measures. In 1826 the Minister of Education,
SHISHKOV, introduced a statute (nicknamed "the iron statute") which
established a Supreme Censorship Council headed by three Ministers
(Education, Foreign Affairs, and Internal Affairs). The lower rungs
in the hierarchy were formed by the Main Censorship Committee in
Petersburg and by committees in Moscow, Derpt (now Tartu), and
Vilno (now Vilnius). Several items in the statute (Nos. 181, 190, 193)
prescribed special caution in the examination of manuscripts on social
history, the natural sciences, and medicine. Section 151 authorized
special censorship of translations from European sources. A modified
version of this statute was approved by the State Council in 1828 and
remained valid until the death of Nicholas I in 1855. Ultimate supervision remained with the Ministry of Education, but from 1830 on the
Third Department of the Secret Police came to play a leading role in
the Committee. In 1848, after the outbreak of revolution in Europe,
Nicholas I established a secret committee on censorship, the so-called
"censorship over censors" committee. As Aleksandr NIKITENKO,
himself a Petersburg censor, wrote in 1850, Russia had twelve
censorships altogether: "If one adds up all the officials in charge of
censorship, their number would exceed the number of books published in a year." The controls over literature, complemented by per-
lustration of private correspondence, and surveillance of Russians
travelling abroad were aimed at policing individual awareness and
eradication of liberal notions in Russia. Despite these controls, free-
minded sentiment was not strangled. As Isaiah Berlin puts it in his
essay "Russia and 1848," "the liberal journals... *Notes of the Fatherland* [National Annals] and *The Contemporary* took courage and began to print articles ... containing for those who could read between
the lines, vague hints and concealed allusions critical of the existing
regime." In the years of repression, frontiers between SLAVOPHILES
and WESTERNIZERS became dividing lines and the foundations of Russian political parties were laid. Journalism, the most persecuted component of Russian literature, played the leading role in this process.

After the death of Nicholas I the rescript of 1848 was annulled,
thus beginning the "thaw period" of 1856 to 1862. During the seven
years from 1848 to 1855, only 25 new periodicals appeared, whereas
in the six years from 1855 to 1862, 180 new journals were founded,
Russian contacts with Europe grew stronger, and liberalism dominated the epoch. In 1855 HERZEN established his Russian Free Press
in London. His uncensored publications, along with unofficially circulated handwritten literature, strongly influenced the social attitudes
of Russian readers and throughout the decade of 1855 to 1865 many
intellectuals, while officially working for periodicals within the
Empire, contributed to émigré editions abroad (N. Eidelman, *The
Hidden Correspondents of "The Polar Star"*, 1966). In 1862 a preliminary censorship statute, whose legislative idea was borrowed
from German and Turkish laws on the press, was promulgated in
Russia. It became law in 1865 and remained in effect until 1905. From
1865 on, the General Management of Press exercised control over
literature, journalism, and theater repertoires. Several local committees on foreign censorship, printing houses, and book-trade surveillance were also set into operation. Authors and editors were freed
from censorship by paying an officially established fee and by guaran-
teeing the loyalty of their publications. Censors were authorized to
impose monetary fines, prohibit harmful materials from distribution,
inflict penalties and ban magazines after several reprimands. This
combination of preventive and punitive measures was the practice
typical of Russian censorship until 1905. From 1905 on censorship

concentrated exclusively on punitive measures. Military and postal censorship was restored at the beginning of World War I. With the downfall of the Romanov Empire, censorship was abolished (March 1917). While censorship in Tsarist Russia ultimately served to precipitate the development of revolutionary ideas in Russia, it impeded the development of social awareness among its audience. The Russian reader, unprepared for active participation in political life and poorly trained in the use of a free press, did not have time to acquire these skills in the eight-month span when complete freedom of the word reigned.

On November 9, 1917, only two days after the Bolsheviks had seized power, the Council of Peoples Commissars issued a decree aimed "against the counter-revolutionary press of all shades" and banned newspapers of several political parties that had been legalized by the Provisional Government in March 1917. This broad definition produced a ban of the dailies published by the Constitutional Democrats and several newspapers published by the Mensheviks. Whereas the liberal and democratic Russian press possessed no structural model for its development, the basic model for the Bolshevik press was set up by Lenin as early as 1905, in his article "Party Organization and Party Literature." Although formally addressed to a like-minded group of Bolsheviks, the article allowed for a wider interpretation, and preshaped the idea of Communist Party control over the arts. Lenin wrote: "The socialist proletarian literary endeavour cannot be an instrument of individual or group advantage independent of common proletarian aims.... Literary work must be established as part of organized, systematic, social-democratic party work" (*Sochineniya*, 10, pp. 26, 31). After Nov. 7, 1917 Lenin's dicta achieved their widest possible interpretation, eventually leading to the concept of PARTIINOST' (party-mindedness), a categorical imperative imposed by the Party on all expressions of Soviet culture. Although the word "censorship" disappeared from everyday speech, government control over the press grew quite severe. On January 28, 1918, a Revolutionary Press Tribunal was set up, and in May of 1919 the State Publishing House (Gosizdat, later Glavlit) was established. With the emergence of Gosizdat, the publishing activities of all presses (Party, academic, and literary) became subject to its control, which included even such details as allocation of paper.

During the period of 1919 to 1929 Gosizdat nationalized the means of production, publication and distribution of literature, thus seizing material control. The years 1919 to 1929 still constitute a transitional period in the history of political control of literature in the USSR, since different political persuasions, aesthetic theories, and social attitudes were still to be found. During this transitional period slogans proclaimed by the Party changed, but the various slogans were all created by Party bureaucrats. Different "social laws" were to govern the creativity of the intelligentsia, but the privilege of "discovering the laws" belonged to the Party alone. According to TROTSKY (1923), "the law of social attraction toward the ruling class (proletariat) determines the creative work of the intelligentsia" and therefore it would not be advisable to "eliminate PILNYAK, the SERAPION BROTHERHOOD with Vsevolod IVANOV, TIKHONOV and POLONSKAYA." "If we will eliminate MAYAKOVSKY and ESENIN, is there anything that will remain for us?" asked Trotsky. A. LUNACHARSKY, the People's Commissar of Education, protected MAYAKOVSKY and the revolutionary FUTURISTS, yet attacked the FORMALISTS and EIKHENBAUM. Even during this transitional decade, all attempts made by writers to liberate themselves from Party control were thwarted. The Proletcult, which attempted to maintain independence from political control by setting up workshops for creative proletarians, was attacked by Lenin in 1922 and closed down in 1927. The group of Bolshevik sympathizers or "fellow travellers" was eliminated by 1930; the Russian Association of Proletarian Writers (RAPP) was dissolved in 1932. On April 23, 1932, a resolution from the Central Committee of the Communist Party announced the disbandment of all professional factions and approved the organization of the UNION OF SOVIET WRITERS, a single organization uniting writers "who wished to participate in the class struggle of the Proletariat and Socialist construction through their creative work." The First Union Congress (1934) mapped out the general trends of SOCIALIST REALISM, whose aesthetics were aimed at "the creation of artistic works worthy of the great epoch of Socialism."

With the formation of the Writers Union and with the adoption of the Union's statute, absolute bureaucratic control over press and writing had been achieved and continues to exist to this day. The Party bureaucracy controls intellectual life ideologically, economically, and politically, while Socialist Realism dictates a rigid system of creative practice. Gosizdat, or Glavlit (Main Management of Literature and State Publishing Houses) guarantees protection of "military and political secrets of the press." Glavlit officials, these unnamed censors, exercise complete control over the press. They impose a multi-leveled system of control upon all forms of print, be it literature, scientific works, periodicals, theater posters, or even greeting cards. While censorship in the Russian Empire was carried out in accordance with legal statutes, Soviet Glavlit has no rules whatsoever. It either grants permission for a work to be published or bans its publication. Censorship regulations in Tsarist Russia sought to create some sort of balance between permitted and desired freedom of thought. Glavlit does not seek any such balance. The existence of the Russian Free Press abroad and the illegal press within the Russian Empire introduced a corrective into the actual practice of Russian censorship. Today, Russian literature published in emigration, as well as the existence of SAMIZDAT and tamizdat (unapproved material printed abroad and distributed unofficially in the Soviet Union) cannot bring any correctives into the practices of Gosizdat. In fact, the existence of samizdat and tamizdat only demonstrates the stubborn inflexibility of Gosizdat. As D. Pospelovsky writes, "samizdat and tamizdat ... are phenomena born of totalitarian ideocratic *diktat* by the regime, its rejection by those who write, and a thirst for alternative values by the public. They are a product of a system which rejects and bans independent thought as a matter of principle, while the censorship of traditional absolutist states banned only that thought which it considered to be a direct threat to the public order."

Bibliography: Istoriya russkoi literatury XVIII veka: Bibliograficheskii ukazatel'. Leningrad, 1968. Pp. 101–04. *Istoriya russkoi literatury XIX veka: Bibliograficheskii ukazatel'*. Moscow and Leningrad. 1962. Pp. 86–87. *Istoriya russkoi literatury kontsa XIX–nachala XX veka: Bibliograficheskii ukazatel'*. Moscow and Leningrad, 1963. Pp. 47–49.

Works on Censorship. In Russian: N. Eidel'mann, *Tainye korrespondenty "Polyarnoi zvezdy."* Moscow, 1966. M. Lemke, *Ocherki po istorii russkoi tsenzury i zhurnalistiki.* St. Petersburg, 1904. ———, *Epokha tsenzurnykh reform, 1859–1865.* St. Petersburg, 1904. ———, *Nikolaevskie zhandarmy i literatura, 1826–1855.* St. Petersburg, 1909. V. Rozenberg and V. Yakushkin, *Russkaya pechat' i tsenzura v proshlom i nastoyashchem.* Moscow, 1905. D. Shamrai, "K istorii tsenzurnogo rezhima Ekateriny II," *XVIII vek*, 1958, no. 3, pp. 187–206. A. Skabichevskii, *Ocherki istorii russkoi tsenzury.* St. Petersburg, 1892.

In English: Zhores Medvedev, *Ten Years after Ivan Denisovich.* London, 1973. S. Monas, *The Third Section: Police and Society in Russia under Nicholas I.* 1961. A. Nikitenko, *The Diary of a Russian Censor.* Amherst, 1975. H. Papmehl, *Freedom of Expression in 18th-century Russia.* The Hague, 1971. D. Pospelovsky, "From Gosizdat to Samizdat and Tamizdat," *CSP* 20 (1978), pp. 44–62. E. J. Simmons, "The Origins of Literary Control," *Survey*, 36–37 (1961), pp. 60–67, 78–84. A. Solzhenitsyn, *The Calf and the Oak.* New York, 1980. H. Swayze, *Political Control of Literature in the U.S.S.R., 1946–1959.* Cambridge, 1962. L. Trotsky, *Literature and Revolution.* New York, 1957.

N. P.

Centrifuge (Tsentrifuga), Futurist literary group based in Moscow (1913–17). Centrifuge stemmed from the group, Lirika, founded by Yulian P. Anisimov in 1913. Early in 1914, Lirika split into Centrifuge and Archer. The central Centrifuge figures were: Sergei BOBROV (who headed the group), Nikolai ASEEV, and Boris PASTERNAK. They were joined one year later by Ivan Aksyonov. Centrifuge does not have a clear aesthetic identity. In its initial stage it leaned heavily towards SYMBOLISM. As a FUTURIST group, Centrifuge sided with the ego-futurists and waged a feud with rival groups such as cubo-futurism and Mezzanine of Poetry. Centrifuge was less radical than the cubo-futurists in the rejection of the past, in fact some Centrifugists were admirers of PUSHKIN. Centrifuge was connected with avant-garde art groups, and its publications were illustrated by painters, such as A. Ekster and El Lisitsky. In the year 1915, because of financial difficulties, Centrifuge was associated with the publishing enterprise, Peta, owned by Fyodor Platov.

The main Centrifuge theoretician, Bobrov, wrote essays and books on aesthetics. However, he was never able to define a clear program and goal for the group. In *The Lyric Theme* (Liricheskaya tema, 1914), he outlines the foundations of Centrifuge, and in *Notes of a Poet* (Zapiski poeta, 1916) he offers interesting ideas on verse rhythm. Other theoretical essays, provocative although vague in their formulation, are Pasternak's "Wasserman Test" (Vassermanova reaktsiya, 1914) and "Black Goblet" (Chernyi bokal, 1916). Aksyonov wrote an original and insightful book of criticism, *Picasso and Environs* (Pikasso i okrestnosti, 1917). Several books of poetry by individual members and associates were issued under the imprint of Centrifuge. *Invalid Foundations* (Neuvazhitel'nye osnovaniya, 1915) by Aksyonov is the most avant-garde Centrifuge work. Bolshakov's *Sun at the End of its Flight* (Solntse na izlete, 1916) is written in a Mayakovskian vein. Ivnev's *Gold of Death* (Zoloto smerti, 1916) is a decadent, rather than a futurist book. *Above the Barriers* (Poverkh bar'erov, 1917) by Pasternak clearly displays the typical aesthetic features of his later poetry. Bobrov is represented by *Diamond Forests* (Almaznye lesa, 1917) and *Lyre of Lyres* (Lira lir, 1917). Furthermore, Centrifuge published a book of translation by Aksyonov, *The Elizabethans* (Elizavetintsy, 1916). Aksyonov was a pioneer in that field of studies. Later, he wrote an imitation of a Greek tragedy, *The Corinthians* (Korinfiane, 1918), also published by Centrifuge.

Centrifuge issued two joint publications, *Brachiopod* (Rukonog, 1914) and *Second Centrifuge Miscellany* (Vtoroi sbornik Tsentrifugi, 1916). Both include poetry, theory, and criticism. In *Brachiopod*, the ego-futurists occupy a prominent place. In the second miscellany, KHLEBNIKOV figures among the main contributors. Although Centrifuge seems to have disbanded towards the end of 1917, books bearing its imprint kept appearing until the early 1920s. The last book published by Centrifuge is Bobrov's novel, *Uprising of the Misanthropes* (Vosstanie mizantropov, 1922).

Bibliography: V. Markov, *Russian Futurism: A History*. Berkeley and Los Angeles, 1968.   A. L.

Chaadáev, Pyotr Yákovlevich (1794–1856), philosopher. Born into a wealthy landowning family, educated at Moscow University, Chaadaev left his studies to serve as an officer in the Russian army during the campaign against Napoleon. He was in Alexander I's honor guard with the occupying armies in Paris in 1814. Having resigned his commission in 1821, he lived in Western Europe from 1823 to 1826, but thereafter in Moscow. He had met PUSHKIN in 1816 and the two remained close friends until Pushkin's death (1837). Their correspondence is a literary and intellectual document of both brilliance and depth. Pushkin considered Chaadaev his mentor in matters political; but Chaadaev in turn was persuaded by Pushkin to study KARAMZIN's *History* and to recognize (as he had failed to do earlier) the positive contributions to Russian history of Peter the Great.

Pushkin wrote several poems to and about Chaadaev, declaring in one of the latter: "In Rome he would have been a Brutus, in Athens a Pericles", but that in Russia he was condemned to the minor role of a "Hussar officer". In fact, following his resignation from military service, Chaadaev attempted to join the Russian diplomatic corps, but was rebuffed. He refused the civil-service position which was offered him in the Ministry of Finance, and remained an intensely private person, living out his lonely years in Moscow as what HERZEN later called "an embodied veto."

The publication in the journal TELESKOP (1836) of a Russian translation of the first and most harshly critical of the *Philosophical Letters* (written in 1829 in a forceful and elegant if slightly old-fashioned French, and circulated privately in manuscript) had aroused a storm: the journal was suspended, the editor, NADEZHDIN, penalized, and Chaadaev declared officially insane, placed under house arrest with daily medical supervision for more than a year. Not only was he denied the right to publish, but mention of his work, either favorable or unfavorable, was forbidden. The title of Chaadaev's *Apology of a Madman* (1837) is an ironic reference to his officially proclaimed "instant insanity."

The other seven Letters had all been written by 1831; but none of them, nor the *Apology*, was to be published during Chaadaev's lifetime. The first (partial) publication (in French in Paris, by I. S. Gagarin, S.J.) dates from 1862.

In the vivid image of Osip MANDELSHTAM, the mark which Chaadaev left on the consciousness of Russian society was as sharp and indelible as that which a diamond cuts into glass. It is now clear—and Chaadaev said as much himself in 1854 (cf. *Sochineniya*, vol. 1, pp. 308–09)—that his harsh critique of the Russia of his time was motivated by love rather than hatred, by the will to reform rather than the rage to repudiate. But the cultivated Russian public no less than the political and ecclesiastical authorities treated him as a renegade, almost a traitor.

Surveying the "world-historical" scene, Chaadaev found unity, universality, and "conciliarity" in Western Europe, with its tradition of Roman Catholic Christianity, but exclusiveness, divisiveness, and self-centeredness in Russia, with its tradition of Russian Orthodox Christianity. He had encountered certain of Hegel's writings; he had met and corresponded with Schelling; and he had studied such French "traditionalists" as Guizot, de Maistre, Bonald, and Lamennais. Under these combined influences, he meditated deeply on the role of religion in general, and Christianity in particular, in human history. He ascribed a special ontological status to the realm of the historical, and was uniquely sensitive to the "sacred flow" of history. He shared the "theurgical restlessness" of those who feel destined to do "God's work in history."

Separateness, fragmentation, and egoism are, for Chaadaev, so many forms of "falling away" from the ideal dynamic unity in which God holds the human and social, as well as the natural, world. He sees Christ as representing not just the spirit of sacrifice, but also "a horror of division, a passionate love of unity" (Ltr. VIII, p. 160; trans. Zeldin). Taking a cosmic view, Chaadaev discerns in the "totality of beings" a unity which is absolute, objective, and transempirical (Ltr. V, pp. 91, 92).

But Russia has broken away from the unity of the West, withdrawing into a self-isolation initiated by Photius (820–891), Patriarch of Constantinople, when he excommunicated Pope Nicholas I. Russians are locked into their spiritual separatism, ignorant of what is happening in Europe. "We [Russians] live only in the narrowest of presents, without past and without future, in the midst of a flat calm" (Ltr. I, p. 36). A chief symptom of Russia's willful self-centeredness, for Chaadaev, is the fact that, whereas in Europe Christianity brought about the abolition of slavery and serfdom, in Russia serfdom was introduced several centuries *after* the coming of Christianity.

Exemplifying unity and conciliarity, the nations of Western Europe, Chaadaev asserts, have walked "hand in hand" down the centuries. On any given day—at Christmas, say, or Easter—Christians throughout Europe take part in the same liturgy, using the same language (Latin), the same texts, gestures, and music. For Chaadaev, who called himself "quite simply ... a Christian philosopher" (letter to Princess Meshcherskaya, 27 May 1839; in *Sochineniya*, vol. 1, p. 236), the history and culture of Europe has been unified and made fruitful by Western (i.e., Roman Catholic) Christianity. "It is Christianity," he declared, "which has accomplished everything in Europe" (Ltr. I, p. 46).

Chaadaev is an even more outspokenly Europocentric thinker than Hegel. He is scornful toward the "culture" and "religion" of India and China and dismisses the alleged "civilization" of Japan and the alleged "Christianity" of Abyssinia (i.e., the Coptic Christianity of what is now Ethiopia) as "absurd aberrations" from "divine and human truths" (Ltr. I, p. 44; cf. Ltr. VI, pp. 120–21). One suspects that by "divine and human truths" he in fact means "the norms of 19th-century Western Europe."

The harsh view that Divine Providence guides the historical development of Western Europe but not that of backward, self-isolated Russia is somewhat softened in certain of the later Letters, and especially in the *Apology*, in which Chaadaev admitted that there had been "some exaggeration" in his earlier (1829) "quasi-indictment of a great nation" (*espèce de réquisitoire contre un grand peuple*) and that he had failed to give its due to "that [Russian Orthodox] church, so humble, at times so heroic, which alone attenuates the emptiness of our chronicles" (*Apology*, p. 176). Anticipating certain SLAVOPHILE themes, Chaadaev went so far as to suggest that Russia is in fact destined to solve a majority of the social problems and to "perfect the greater part of the ideas" which have had their origin in older societies (*ibid.*, p. 174). But he was wary of the extreme religious nationalism of the emerging Slavophiles and rejected their "retrospective utopia" as involving an "arrogant apotheosis of the Russian people." This, Chaadaev felt, threatened to turn Russia away from "that religious humility, ... that modesty of spirit, which has always been the distinctive trait of our national character" (letter to Schelling, 20 May 1842; *Sochineniya*, vol. 1, pp. 245, 46).

Works: François Rouleau, ed., *Pierre Tchaadaev: Lettres philosophiques adressées à une dame.* Paris, 1970. M. O. Gershenzon, ed., *Sochineniya i pis'ma.* 2 vols. Moscow, 1913, 1914; xerographic reprod., Ann Arbor, 1975.

Translation: Peter Yakovlevich Chaadayev, *Philosophical Letters and Apology of a Madman.* Trans. and introd. Mary-Barbara Zeldin. Knoxville, Tenn., 1969.

Secondary literature: Charles Quénet, *Tchaadaev et les Lettres philosophiques: contribution à l'étude du mouvement des idées en Russie.* Paris, 1931.

G. L. K.

Change of Landmarks, see *SMENA VEKH.*

Chastúshka, a short rhymed nonritual folk lyric which is usually sung to the accompaniment of a balalaika or accordion. The term *chastushka* first came into general usage through Gleb USPENSKY's work on Russian folk lyrics (1889), although it had been used before by other collectors. While the genre may have existed earlier, chastushkas began to appear in printed collections only in the 1860s and 1870s, which reflected the prejudice many collectors like DAL and KIREEVSKY had against them, preferring the older, more traditional folk genres. The first special edition devoted to chastushkas was D. K. Zelenin's *Pesni derevenskoi molodezhi* (1903). Folklorists such as KOSTOMAROV emphasized the need to study and collect this genre, since it was playing an increasingly important role among the people.

There has been an extensive polemic on the origins of the chastushka. Some see it as a derivation of the traditional folk lyric, and are able to show parallels between themes and devices in the two genres. Others point specifically to game and dance songs, since they are often rhymed, or the gathering and dispersal songs for *khorovody.* V. S. Bakhtin mentions a possible antecedent in the *pripevka*, which would be heard when a dance reached the height of emotion, for example: "Dance, lady, bolder, it'll make the musician merrier!" Wedding *prigovorki* are also mentioned as a possible source. It is important to keep in mind that whatever its origin, the chastushka did not replace previous genres, which continued to develop and change alongside the chastushka, and like it, continued to assimilate new themes and topics. In turn, while the chastushka shares certain features with other folk genres, it is a unique system adapting similar themes to its own particular form of expression.

The themes of the chastushka are extremely varied. Many relate to the theme of love, and as in the folk lyrics, they reflect its full range of emotions. Different chastushkas often convey very different attitudes toward the same event depending on the persona they represent. In one an obedient girl submissively says she will marry whomever her father chooses, while in another a willful girl defies her parents, in another is proud of having more than one lover, and generally plays hard to get. One group of chastushkas relate to recruiting, and cover the entire period from the actual selection as a recruit through the week of revelry before the recruit leaves, and his final farewell. These express the point of view both of the recruit himself and of the women affected by his leaving. Another set of chastushkas concerns the workers before the revolution and their grievances. Numerous chastushkas relate to political events and go back to the Russo-Turkish war of 1877. They are about major historical events that affected the peasants' and workers' lives, such as Stolypin's reform, World War I, the 1917 Revolution, the civil war, the NEP period, the first Five-Year Plan, and World War II. Sometimes they may express different views toward the same event. In one a peasant believes the Duma will provide him with more land, while in another he believes the Duma cares little about the peasants' needs and will only help the rich get richer. An example of a topical chastushka is one devoted to the Five-Year Plan:

> The Five-Year Plan is no twig,
> You can't break it;
> For this little Five-Year Plan
> We're ready to fight.

An interesting group of prerevolutionary chastushkas are devoted to the life of hooligans in St. Petersburg. The heroes brag about carrying knives, drinking vodka, and smoking tobacco, while their female counterparts drink and run after young men. There are also special songs devoted to thieves and vandals.

Some chastushkas are comic or satirical. They satirize the clergy, mock braggarts and bullies, or poke fun at those from other villages or even their own friends, for example:

> My dear is pretty,
> Looks like a hedgehog;
> Sable browed, like a cow,
> Round faced, like a pig.

Some songs, called *neskladukhi*, derive their comic effect from transferring features from one object to another where they are inappropriate: there are books with pockets, tea is drunk from galoshes. Sometimes the comic songs are just based on nonsense:

> Look there, down our street
> Rides the priest astride a hen;
> The priest's wife comes on foot,
> combing her braids with a comb.

While chastushkas often have universal themes without any specific temporal or local features, others reflect specific changes in modern life: A girl sends a telegram rather than letter to her boyfriend telling him about her impending marriage; locomotives and planes take one's beloved away; one's sweetheart is no longer the peasant or worker, but the young pioneer or tractor driver. Film, radio, phonographs, and bicycles begin to appear.

Some chastushkas are performed to specific dances. However, the dances are not traditional, but are related to the quadrille, the lancier, and other village versions of city dances. One set of such chastushkas is called the *tsyganochka* (gypsy girl), where the cycle begins with the line "in a gypsy's garden"; another group is the *eletskie* chastushkas, which begin with the lines "I'll dance the Eletsky" or "Listen, they're playing the Eletsky". These lines usually begin the first stanzas, then regular lyric content appears in the subsequent chastushkas of the cycle. Often, as in the *tsyganochka* songs, there is a competition between pairs of participants. Each tries to make up new figures in the dance or new chastushkas, and the song is often a retort to the preceding one.

One of the most popular cycles of chastushkas during the Civil War period was the *yablochko* songs, whose name comes from the first line, "Eh, my apple". They have four lines with the second and fourth rhymed. Such songs already existed before the revolution in northern Russia as well as in the Ukraine and in Belorussia. During the Civil War they were adopted by both the Reds and the Whites mainly for political purposes, for example:

> Eh, apple, green on one side,
> We don't want the Tsar, we want Lenin.

However, they also reflected more general themes. They were often accompanied by a sailor's dance, but could also be sung alone.

While the vast majority of chastushkas are composed of four lines, there are also six-line and two-line forms. In the six-line version the first two lines often set up a basic situation, and the following four develop it:

> Brother mine, brother mine,
> Shall we settle, you and I.
> You'll get the plough and harrow,
> I'll get to go to foreign parts.
> You'll get store-room and house,
> I'll get to go to foreign parts.

An important group of two-line chastushkas are the *Semenovna.* They were not transcribed in the prerevolutionary period, although older informants remember them having been sung. Two lines correspond to a musical phrase. They relate to the "cruel" romances of the middle class at the turn of the century. The heroine is depicted as headstrong and independent, she often stays out all night:

> Eh, Semenovna, where are you gadding about,
> Not coming home at night.

> There's Semenovna sitting on the steps,
> Doing nothing, singing songs.

However, many do not relate specifically to any Semenovna, and the content is often violent. One sister stabs another from jealousy, a girl commits suicide because she has been betrayed by her beloved. "Eh, Semenovna," "Oh, hill, hill" and "An airplane comes flying" are popular openings for the song cycles with different subjects.

Another group are the *stradanie*, which are also in the form of rhymed couplets. They were widespread before the revolution in the Volga region and central Russia. Most of them deal with love, but there are others concerning recruiting, workers, etc. Often the word *stradanie* (suffering) is included in the text:

> Oh, daddy, what punishment.
> My heart aches from suffering.

The chastushka has many formal features in common with other folklore genres, particularly the folk lyric. They can be in the form of a dialogue, which may be question and answer, third person narrative, monologue, or a combination of these. Parallelism is typical of many chastushkas, although others develop one single action. There is traditional parallelism, with a comparison of nature and man:

> All the flowers in bouquets,
> Only the lilac's missing;
> All the girls are at the party,
> Only my sweetheart isn't there.

Other images are more unique to the chastushka:

> Don't fret, my cap, —
> I'll sew a vizor on you;
> Don't fret, my sweetheart, —
> I'll come to see you in the evening.

Based on parallelism, the same or similar beginning or *zachin* can be applied to different songs with similar themes:

> It's good to mow grass
> Which is green,
> It's good to love a girl
> Who is merry.

> It's good to mow grass
> Which is burdock,
> One must love those kids
> Who have girlfriends.

However, this *zachin* often becomes neutral and has little or no relation to what follows; for example at first the following opening related directly to a human situation:

> A star fell from the sky,
> Like a silver coin.
> God and all good people know
> That I'm an orphan.

Here the falling star symbolizes the sad plight of the orphan. However, in the following chastushka the *zachin* is neutral.

> A star fell down the sky,
> From the blue sky.
> When you're with me I love you,
> When you're not, I love another.

This is not a chronological development; it is quite possible for later chastushkas to use the *zachin* in the traditional symbolic manner. Less frequently songs have the same endings and differ in the first two lines.

Another way songs are generated is by the substitution of similar actions:

> To the front porch,
> A letter came flying,
> Couldn't drink, couldn't eat,
> Wanted to read that letter.

> We went to work in the morning,
> Found a proclamation.
> Read it in the evening,
> Went all on strike next morning.

Once a particular formula has been created for treating a particular type of event or person, it can be used again later. For example, in World War II chastushkas attacking Hitler were based on earlier ones against Kaiser Wilhelm:

> Pray to God, my friend,
> That Wilhelm may die.
> He's at war for the third year,
> All countries are sick of him.

> Pray to God, my friend,
> That Hitler may die:
> He's at war for the third year,
> All are deathly sick of him.

Antithesis is another device sometimes used in the chastushka:

> Married women blame me for a tramp,
> Girls praise me for a hard worker,
> Married women blame me for a scoundrel,
> Girls praise me for a fine fellow.

As in traditional lyrics, certain images become fixed symbols in this genre, such as intertwining plants standing for a boy and girl together, green for health and black for death and grief.

Metonymy is also used symbolically. A girl will put her dancing slippers under the bench, indicating her married state; a recruit will remove his peasant jacket and replace it with a soldier's coat; a girl is getting thinner, reflecting her state of mind, her longing for her boyfriend who is far away.

Repetition in various forms is typical of the chastushka. There is tautology, for example "a hill, what a hill" or "rarely, quite rarely, rarely"; repetition of words or phrases; and repeated syntactical constructions such as:

> Otchego zhe les gustoi?—
> Znat', nikto ne rubit.
> Otchego ty slishkom zloi?—
> Znat', nikto ne lyubit.

> Why is the forest dense? —
> Must be, no one cuts it.
> Why are you too mean? —
> Must be, no one loves you.

Repeated prepositions can also be found, especially in older chastushkas, such as: "dlya lyuboi dlya devushki" (for any girl), "on na sivom na kone" (on a grey horse), "U nashikh u vorot" (at our gate).

Fixed epithets occur in numerous chastushkas. Sometimes they are traditional: "foreign parts," "blue sea," "auburn locks," as found in other folk genres. However, new ones have been added such as "educated" to describe one's beloved. One's sweetheart is often referred to as a "berry," "joy," "drolya," or "beau." Some are local terms, such as "drolya," which is typical of Vologda and the Archangel areas.

Various types of rhyme patterns appear in the chastushka. Crossed rhyme is popular, as well as rhymed couplets and rhyming of all lines. There is sometimes the pattern *a b c a*, where the first and last lines rhyme. Whereas in literature rhymes based on suffixes, verbs or tautology are generally avoided, they are typical of the chastushkas. Hemistichs may also rhyme, and sometimes internal rhyme appears. Assonance is frequent as well.

As both Sobolev and Kolpakova emphasize, the metrical pattern of the chastushka must be discussed in connection with the melodies with which they appear. Various texts when analysed by the verbal text alone may appear to be in different literary meters, but when sung the line falls into twelve beats. Almost all chastushkas are sung to the following model, and if necessary a syllable will be extended over several beats:

(Sobolev, p. 140)

For example, the following chastushka:

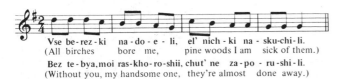

Vse be-rez-ki na-do-e-li, el' nich-ki na-sku-chi-li.
(All birches bore me, pine woods I am sick of them.)
Bez te-bya, moi ras-kho-ro-shii, chut' ne za-po-ru-shi-li.
(Without you, my handsome one, they're almost done away.)

(Sobolev, p. 139)

Thus the chastushka is provided with numerous devices and images to convey an emotion or thought as concisely as possible and the performer can improvise numerous of these little "poems in miniature," as they are referred to by many scholars.

Bibliography: Chastushka. Introd. V. S. Bakhtin. (Biblioteka poeta, Bol'shaya seriya.) 2d ed. 1966. N. P. Kolpakova, "Tipy narodnoi chastushki," *RFolk* 10 (1966), pp. 264–88. S. G. Lazutin, *Russkaya chastushka.* 1960. *Sbornik velikorusskikh chastushek.* Ed. E. N. Eleonskaya, 1914. V. I. Simakov, *Sbornik derevenskikh chastushek.* 1913. P. M. Sobolev, "K voprosu o ritmiko-metricheskoi strukture chastushek," *Khudozhestvennyi fol'klor*, 1927, nos. 2–3, pp. 130–44. Yu. M. Sokolov, *Russian Folklore.* Trans. Catherine Ruth Smith. 1971. Pp. 530–49. V. V. Straten, "Tvorchestvo gorodskoi ulitsy," *Khudozhestvennyi fol'klor*, 1927, nos. 2–3, pp. 144–65. I. V. Zyryanov, *Poetika russkoi chastushki.* 1974.   R. R.

Chékhov, Antón Pávlovich (1860–1904), great short story writer and dramatist. He was born on January 17, 1860, in Taganrog, the third of six children. His domineering father, a small shopkeeper, was himself the son of a former serf who had bought his family into freedom. Chekhov's mother was of merchant-class origin. He recalled his childhood as oppressive ("in my childhood there was no childhood"): long hours of duty in his father's shop and frequent beatings. The family did, however, encourage education. While Chekhov was in the *gymnasium* (1868–79), his father went bankrupt, and the family moved to Moscow, leaving Anton to finish school in Taganrog. He supported himself by tutoring.

In 1879 Chekhov enrolled in the medical faculty at Moscow University. Following the example of his older brother, Aleksandr, he helped support himself and his family by writing for humor magazines. (In view of the deterioration and frequent absence of his father and the irresponsibility of his older brothers, Chekhov now became the chief breadwinner and de facto paternal authority in the family.) He regarded his literary career as having begun in March, 1880, with the simultaneous publication in *Strekoza* (Dragonfly) of two little parodies. Written solely for money, Chekhov's earliest writings were ephemera without serious literary intent; nevertheless, the glimmers of talent began to show. His output grew in both quantity and quality during his years in medical school, though he still did not take himself seriously as a writer. All his early works were signed with pseudonyms, most frequently "Antosha Chekhonte." Two early "stories" were in fact full-length novels: *Useless Victory* (Nenuzhnaya pobeda, 1882), written in imitation of Mor Jókai's society tales; and *The Shooting Party* (Drama na okhote, 1884–85), a murder mystery.

Chekhov completed medical school in 1884. He practised medicine intermittently for several years, rather drifting away from the profession than breaking with it. His intellectual interest in medicine, and in biological science generally, remained strong all his life; and medical education and medical experience left a deep mark on his writings. Medical practice afforded opportunities for close, "unbuttoned" observation of people, often at critical junctures in their lives; and at a deeper level the point of view expressed in Chekhov's stories and plays is that of a good doctor—always compassionate, but clear-eyed and unsentimental. As an artist, Chekhov professed a scientist's credo: "For chemists there is nothing unclean on the earth. The writer must be as objective as the chemist."

Chekhov's stories continued to grow in depth and range. Until 1886 his chief outlets remained humor magazines, especially Nikolai Leikin's *Oskolki* (Fragments), published in Petersburg, for which he also wrote a regular column of Moscow gossip. However, many of Chekhov's stories of the mid-1880s were, in length and subject, no longer suitable for such publications. Though he still avoided the highbrow reviews, Chekhov found new media for his more serious work, the Petersburg daily newspapers—first *Peterburgskaya gazeta* and finally the biggest of all, *Novoe vremya*. With the latter's publisher, Aleksei SUVORIN, Chekhov formed a close personal friendship. Support from Suvorin, an encouraging letter from the writer GRIGOROVICH, and a serious critical article comparing him to KOROLENKO all helped induce Chekhov to raise his literary sights. His stories become longer, more varied, more complex; and one, "The Requiem" (Panikhida, 1886), at Suvorin's urging was at last signed "Anton Chekhov." Collections of stories appeared in book form beginning in 1884. The 1887 volume, *At Twilight* (V sumerkakh), was awarded the Pushkin prize for that year.

Most of Chekhov's earliest writings consist of formula jokes and anecdotes, pure verbal buffoonery. Some, however, have a satirical dimension, pointing to the theme of human weakness, absurdity, and pain, Chekhov was to develop more deeply later—for instance "Death of an Official" (Smert' chinovnika, 1883). A more realistic variant, without stress on comic absurdity, presents sketches of socio-psychological archetypes, such as the famous busybody and bully, Sergeant Prishibeev (Unter Prishibeev, 1885). A note of sadness is increasingly struck, even in these early stories, anticipating another favorite Chekhov theme, people's isolation and mutual incomprehension, as in "Heartache" (Toska, 1886).

The year 1886 marks the beginning of a transition, from the "early" to the "middle" Chekhov. It is not a sharp break, rather an expansion, an opening out. Though he had outgrown them, the experience of writing for humor magazines had not been injurious to Chekhov's artistic development. It had taught him conciseness, sharpness of line, clarity of exposition. Nevertheless, the severe space restrictions and thematic prescriptions of such organs as *Oskolki* were too inflexible; they left no room for growth. A notable feature of the newly expanded stories is the psychological close-up. Characters are no longer perceived satirically, as social archetypes, but seen from within. And the inner life revealed is often an unhappy one, the characters' "real life" being in sharp contrast with their "world of desire," reached only through memory or fantasy. Poignant stories of unhappy children are frequent, such as "Vanka" (1886), children's unhardened, "underdog" point of view revealing the wide gulf between their natural humanity and ugly social realities. An especially horrifying rendition of this theme is "Sleepy" (Spat' khochetsya, 1888). Not all Chekhov's stories of children are tragic, however; he was equally good at evoking children's vitality and exuberance (e.g., "Small Fry" [Detvora] and "Boys" [Mal'chiki], both 1887). As victims of a male-dominated society, women are also often used to articulate the "underdog" point of view, as in "Anyuta" or "The Chorus Girl" (Khoristka, both 1886). Always wary of ideological clichés, however, Chekhov in the latter story shows that cruelty is no male monopoly; women can be exploiters as well as victims. Class barriers are a frequent cause of mutual incomprehension, as in "A Nightmare" (Koshmar) or "The Privy Councilor" (Tainyi sovetnik, both 1886); but sometimes, especially when love is involved, it is simply that one person's feeling is not matched by the other's (e.g., "Verochka," 1887). Amazingly free of conventional moralism, Chekhov remains neutral on the issue of "licit" vs. "illicit" sexual relations; and his perception of female lust was equally un-Victorian—it is as strong and as prevalent as its male counterpart ("A Calamity" [Neschast'e] and "Agaf'ya" [both 1886]).

By 1888 Chekhov was a thoroughly committed professional writer. He had also undergone baptism of fire as a dramatist. Two short stories had been transformed into one-act plays (there were six more later), and there were now two full-length dramas: *Ivanov* (1887) and *The Wood Demon* (Leshii, 1888–89). *Ivanov* offers a multi-angled view—characteristically Chekhovian—of that hoary figure of Russian literary tradition, the "superfluous man," full of good intentions but ineffectual; Chekhov treats him with understanding, neither condemning nor exonerating. In *Ivanov*, Chekhov was still far from the diffuse, low-key dramatic technique he made famous in his four late plays; on the contrary, as he put it, he gives the audience "a punch on the nose" at the end of each act. *Ivanov* was successfully produced in 1887 and in a revised version again in 1889. Chekhov, however, remained dissatisfied with it: the public had not understood it properly, and he thought the fault must be his. Experience with *The Wood Demon* was even more discouraging. Though it contained several fine characterizations and embodied some of Chekhov's most cherished ideas—for instance, about ecology—it was rejected as unstageable by the Petersburg state theater committee, and its private production in Moscow in 1889 was not well received. Chekhov refused to allow any more productions of the play, but later (just when is unclear) miraculously transformed it into a masterpiece, *Uncle Vanya*.

The second major development in Chekhov's art of the latter 1880s was his experimentation with longer narrative forms. A long novel tentatively called "Stories from the Lives of My Friends" remained unfinished, but *The Steppe* (Step', 1888) proved a notable advance. Lacking a conventional plot, it is an account of a nine-year-old boy's experiences during a trip across the steppe, with detailed observations of the flora and fauna he encounters, the latter including human beings. Appearing in the literary review *Severnyi vestnik* (Northern Herald), *The Steppe* marked Chekhov's emergence from low- to high-brow media. Many superlative stories date from this period, remarkable especially for the unusual, "clinical" points of view Chekhov employs: in "The Name-Day Party" (Imeniny, 1888) that of a woman having a miscarriage; in "A Nervous Breakdown" (Pripadok, 1889), that of a student undergoing an acute depressive attack triggered by a visit to a brothel; in "A Dreary Story" (Skuchnaya istoriya, 1889), that of an old professor—unlike so many of Chekhov's characters, a man of real achievement and distinction— "alienated" from life by poor health, senescence, and approaching death.

Despite the successes of his literary career, Chekhov felt guilty about his abandonment of medicine. Moreover, he still owed a dissertation to obtain a full M. D. Partly to discharge this debt, partly to relieve the depression brought on by the death from tuberculosis of his brother Nikolai, partly for the sake of adventure, Chekhov in 1890 undertook a (pre-railroad) journey across Siberia to Sakhalin Island, paying for the trip by writing travel sketches for *Novoe vremya*. On Sakhalin he made a thorough study of social, economic, and medical conditions, both of the Russian settlers—mostly convicts—and the native Ainu and Gilyak populations, whose cultures were being systematically obliterated, to his sorrow. Chekhov's observations were eventually incorporated in a remarkable book, *Sakhalin Island* (Ostrov Sakhalin, 1893–95). He returned to Russia by sea, via Hong Kong, Singapore, Ceylon, and the Suez Canal. The journey inspired a beautiful short story, "Gusev" (1890). Soon after his return Chekhov went off with the Suvorins on his first trip to Western Europe.

The years 1891 to 1895 were a period of intense activity for Chekhov. Circumstances pushed him back into medical and public health activities—first the terrible famine of 1891 and then the cholera epidemic that followed. In 1892 he bought a country estate, Melikhovo, near Serpukhov, where he involved himself energetically in local affairs and served as doctor to local peasants. His literary output continued unabated, however, and includes some of his most famous works. Many of these are "problem" stories, encapsulating social or philosophical issues. In "The Duel" (Duel, 1891) characters embodying several divergent philosophies confront one another, a feckless "superfluous man" being attacked by a ruthless "social Darwinist," with a more tolerant, "Christian" position represented by other characters. In "The Wife" (Zhena, 1892), where the famine of 1891 is invoked, Chekhov raises the recurrent "drop in the ocean" question—the immensity of the country's problems, the depths of its poverty, and the puniness and apparent futility of efforts to grapple with them. The result is the discouragement and resignation endemic in the upper classes. This same problem is posed in even more poignant form in "Ward No. 6" (Palata No. 6, 1892): is it right (or even possible) to opt out of life and contemplate the world from a safe distance? "An Anonymous Story" (Rasskaz neizvestnogo cheloveka, 1893) cautiously raises the issue of revolutionary terrorism. "A Woman's Kingdom" (Bab'e tsarstvo, 1894) invokes the tensions of early industrialism and the stark, guilt-ridden confrontation of wealth and poverty. "Three Years" (Tri goda, 1895), providing a contrast of old vs. new life-styles in the wealthy merchant milieu, once again illustrates Chekhov's pessimistic view of the chances for reciprocated and enduring love between men and women. In all these and other "problem" stories, however, the problem is only an ingredient; the

abstract issue is fully embedded in fictional reality, in the lives of vital, believable characters.

The later 1890s witnessed Chekhov's return to the theater. During the seven years from 1896 to 1903 he produced the four masterpieces that have established his reputation as one of the great dramatists of modern times: *The Sea Gull* (Chaika, 1896), *Uncle Vanya* (Dyadya Vanya, 1899), *Three Sisters* (Tri sestry, 1901), and *The Cherry Orchard* (Vishnevyi sad, 1903). The initial Petersburg performance of *The Sea Gull*, for somewhat extraneous reasons, was a failure, but its revival at the Moscow Art Theater in 1898 was a triumph; and from then on, despite much disagreement with its director, STANISLAVSKY, Chekhov's work as a playwright was closely linked to that theater.

The four plays are strikingly innovative in method. First of all, Chekhov works from the premise that the real drama is found in the give-and-take of ordinary human relations, not in heightened, conventionally "dramatic," actions. Even when they occur in his plays, for instance Treplev's suicide in *The Sea Gull* or Uncle Vanya's shot at his brother-in-law, such actions never produce fundamental changes in relationships. Second, dramatic interest is always diffused among a substantial number of characters, not focussed on one or two stars. Third, just as he does in his stories, Chekhov stresses people's lack of emotional reciprocity and poor communication. They talk, but seldom listen to one another; they love and hate, but these emotions are seldom returned in kind or in proportion. Although he assiduously keeps a low profile and avoids all preachiness, Chekhov's plays nevertheless do express some of his cherished values: the importance of beauty, both natural and man-made, in enriching human life; the importance of the "little things" in life, and especially of mutual respect and consideration in human intercourse; the slow advance of civilization through the dedication and hard work of individuals.

Work for the theater did not deflect Chekhov from writing fiction; many of his greatest stories were written in his last years. Chekhov had earlier been influenced by TOLSTOI's social ideas, though he never shared their religious basis or condoned Tolstoi's wholesale rejection of science and culture. (After a visit to Yasnaya Polyana in 1895 Chekhov developed a cordial, though not close, personal relationship with Tolstoi.) In "My Life" (Moya zhizn', 1896) Chekhov gives a wonderfully fair and sympathetic, though never idealized, presentation of both the motives and the difficulties encountered by a person trying, in a Russian provincial town, to live by a Tolstoian moral code, one at odds with that of the people around him. "Peasants" (Muzhiki, 1897) created a sensation with its unsparing picture of poverty and brutishness in the village, particularly offensive to doctrinaire, peasant-worshipping populists. In 1898 appeared the trilogy of stories, "The Man in a Case" (Chelovek v futlyare), "Gooseberries" (Kryzhovnik) and "About Love" (O lyubvi), which are among Chekhov's finest achievements in fiction. Related orally by three characters in turn, à propos of a discussion, all deal with variations on the theme of waste, frustration, and lack of fulfillment in life. Chekhov's versatility is extraordinary, his subjects inexhaustible. "The Darling" (Dushechka, 1899) is a case study of the passive woman who acquires identity only from the males she associates with. "The Lady with the Pet Dog" (Dama s sobachkoi, 1899) is an acutely perceptive, totally unmoralistic study of an adulterous love affair. "In the Ravine" (V ovrage, 1900) is a complex, wonderfully poetic, deeply ambiguous treatment of the theme of exploitation, the strong vs. the weak. "Ionych" (1898) and Chekhov's last story, "The Bride" (Nevesta, 1903) both take up the recurrent theme of cultural and spiritual provincialism, both literal and figurative; in the latter story the heroine, Nadya, achieves liberation both from the vulgarity of her home town and the clichés of doctrinaire radicalism.

Clear symptoms of tuberculosis had appeared in Chekhov as early as 1884. Strangely, for a man otherwise so courageous about facing truths, and a doctor at that, for as long as he could Chekhov dealt with his illness ostrich-style, by denying its existence. Only in 1897 did massive hemorrhaging from the lungs force him to publicly acknowledge his condition and accept treatment by other doctors. For the remainder of his life he was a semi-invalid, living mostly in his "warm Siberia," Yalta, where he built a villa. He also spent two winters in Nice. It was too late, however, for a warm climate and somewhat, though not sufficiently, reduced activity to affect the disease, which continued its slow but relentless course. It allowed Chekhov just time for a love affair with Olga Knipper, an actress in the Moscow Art Theater, whom he married in 1901. Despite the frequent separations necessitated by her career and his illness, the marriage was notably happy. But Chekhov's life had only three years to run. His last public appearance, marred by a terrible coughing fit, took place at the Moscow premiere of *The Cherry Orchard* (17 January 1904). Later that spring he went to take the waters at Badenweiler in Germany and died there on 2 July.

Works: Polnoe sobranie sochinenii i pisem. 20 vols. 1944–55. *Polnoe sobranie sochinenii i pisem.* 26 vols. 1974–80.

Translations: The Oxford Chekhov. Trans. and ed. Ronald Hingley. 9 vols. 1964–80. *Anton Chekhov's Life and Thought: Selected Letters and Commentary.* Trans. Michael Henry Heim in collaboration with Simon Karlinsky. Selection, introd. and commentary by Simon Karlinsky. 1973. *Chekhov: Five Major Plays.* Trans. and introd. Ronald Hingley. 1977. *Six Plays of Chekhov.* Trans. and introd. Robert W. Corrigan. 1979. *Anton Chekhov's Short Stories: Texts of the Stories, Backgrounds, Criticism.* Selected and ed. Ralph E. Matlaw. 1979. *See also:* Lewanski, pp. 210–26.

Secondary literature: (The bibliography of books on Chekhov is immense, especially in Russian; the following is a highly selective list in English only:) Jean-Pierre Barricelli, ed., *Chekhov's Great Plays: A Critical Anthology.* 1981. Paul Debreczeny and Thomas Eekman, eds., *Chekhov's Art of Writing: A Collection of Critical Essays.* 1977. Thomas Eekman, ed., *Anton Čexov: Some Essays.* Leiden, 1960. Ronald Hingley, *A New Life of Anton Chekhov.* 1976. Robert L. Jackson, ed., *Chekhov: A Collection of Critical Essays.* 1967. Karl D. Kramer, *The Chameleon and the Dream; The Image of Reality in Čexov's Stories.* 1970. Maurice Valency, *The Breaking String: The Plays of Anton Chekhov.* 1966. Jan van der Eng, Jan Meijer, and Herta Schmid, *On the Theory of Descriptive Poetics: Anton P. Chekhov as Story-Teller and Playwright.* 1978. Thomas Winner, *Chekhov and His Prose.* 1966.

Recent Russian Works: G. Berdnikov, *Chekhov—dramaturg: Traditsii i novatorstvo v dramaturgii A. P. Chekhova.* 2d rev. ed. 1972. ———, *Chekhov.* 1978. V. B. Kataev, *Proza Chekhova: Problemy interpretatsii.* 1979. M. L. Semanova, *Chekhov—khudozhnik.* 1976.

H. McL.

Chernyshévsky, Nikolái Gavrílovich (1828–89), radical journalist, political thinker, literary critic, novelist, revolutionary, and martyr. Chernyshevsky was born in Saratov, the son of an obscure priest. His linguistic talents enabled him to go to the University of St. Petersburg (1846–50) where he became a member of the intelligentsia. A teacher at Saratov from 1851 to 1853, he married a shallow wife, Olga Vasilieva in 1853 and returned to St. Petersburg to write for the noted "thick" journal, SOVREMENNIK.

Here he found his career, advancing to co-editor in 1859, before the police closed the journal and arrested Chernyshevsky in 1862. In journalism he found his true vocation, for after Tsar Nicholas I's death in 1855 the much relaxed censorship allowed the radical intelligentsia more freedom to print their views. Chernyshevsky proved the most notable and influential of the new radical writers in the "thick" journals and became, like BELINSKY before him, a kind of literary-political "dictator" in opposition to the Tsarist régime. More than anyone, he formulated the ideals and aims of the young radicals, summoned "the generation of the 1860s" into existence, and simultaneously expressed their drives and led them further until his lasting exile to Siberia in 1864.

The basis of his ideas was the French Enlightenment; he exchanged faith in God for its alternate religion of humanity and confidence in science, culture, argumentation, and political action. He shared the great complex of "organicist" German romantic ideas which was common to much of the European Left: that nations progress in evolutionary stages, that the common people are the moral and practical heart of a nation, that history moves forward through resolute conflict between groups, classes, and nations, that literature and art arise from nations and people and evolve with them in successive stages, that it is writers and artists who first perceive and express social reality and change and thereby crystallize emerging phases of consciousness and move classes and nations, above all in their own

time. He was much influenced by Hegel, and by the Left Hegelian Feuerbach's materialism and radicalism. He preached a thoroughgoing materialism and, independently of Marx whom he never absorbed, combined it in some ways with Hegelian dialectics. He derived all this from reading his predecessor, Belinsky, and then directly from the Germans. Beyond Germany, Chernyshevsky called himself a Jacobin and also respected Bentham and the Mills, and, far more than most of the Russian intelligentsia, welcomed the British industrial revolution and the consequent machine, urban, and proletarian age of the future. French socialists and his sometime friend HERZEN made Chernyshevsky a socialist who favored decentralized agrarian and urban communes, *not* the centralized state socialism of Marx.

Believing that society and literature were always vitally interlinked, and forced by the censors to express his views chiefly by reviewing other books, Chernyshevsky subsumed most of his political career under his function as a literary critic. He took up Belinsky's role as literary "dictator" to the new age, but his own style was less self-deprecating, disjointed, and witty than Belinsky's, equally splendid in invective, and more sovereign, magisterial, and implacable in tone.

Chernyshevky became famous in 1855 with his master's essay, *The Aesthetic Relations of Art to Reality* (Esteticheskie otnosheniya iskusstva k deistvitel'nosti). In it he maintained that science is higher than art, that men take joy in beauty as they take joy in life, because "beauty is life," that the common people are the true arbiters of beauty and art, that "the tragic is a man's suffering and death," that beautiful art portrays far more beautiful nature, that science and art are a handbook for the study of life itself, a higher study than either. These vitalist and pro-realist positions strongly influenced all future Russian left literature.

Chernyshevsky's *Essays in the Gogol Period of Russian Literature* (Ocherki gogolevskogo perioda russkoi literatury, 1855–56) was his most ambitious critical work, a laudatory study of Russian realist writing, especially GOGOL's, and even more of Belinsky's radical-realist, political-literary criticism. In it he pushed for forthright sincerity in writing, blasted philosophical idealism as necessarily reactionary and expounded a moderate view of the goodness of human nature. This, too, became part of the Russian radical credo.

In the 1850s Chernyshevsky generally admired the tales of TURGENEV as they appeared. His notable review of *Asya*, 1858, is often quoted, "Forget about these erotic questions! They are not for the reader of our times ... preoccupied with the emancipation of the serfs!" as if this were a call to drop human literature for political propaganda, but in context these are contrary-to-fact sentences, part of high praise for Turgenev's portrayals of the human, private side of people as the highest insight into the conditions that determine politics. He greeted the first works of TOLSTOI, whom he called a "repentant nobleman," with joy and insight, emphasizing the use of "interior monologue" and defending Tolstoi's analyses of private, psychological life, too, against simple-minded radicals.

Chernyshevsky's most important philosophical-literary writing was *The Anthropological Principle in Philosophy* (Antropologicheskii printsip v filosofii, 1860). In it he held that philosophy and literature depend on the social situation, that thinkers and writers serve one party or another. He promoted materialism as the theoretical basis for revolution and praised chemistry above all sciences. He argued that men's good and evil actions are determined by their social situation: a poor man has to steal. He detailed man's motivation by egoism in a morally neutral sense, which allows educated, radical men to see that socially beneficial acts and public reforms coincide with their own legitimate self-interest. He ended with optimistic prose poems to a kind of "cosmos," a world guided forward progressively by impersonal natural law. This work provided much philosophical and moral structure and content for future Russian radical literature.

As Tsar Alexander II emancipated the serfs in 1861, Chernyshevsky, the dean of the radicals, led the attack on the terms of emancipation, especially what he saw as a heartlessly insufficient land grant. He helped inspire and became somewhat involved in a wave of student and peasant disturbances in 1861–62. The police closed *Sovremennik* for eight months in 1862 and on 19 July arrested Chernyshevsky and imprisoned him in the Fortress of Sts. Peter and Paul. In prison he managed to write his celebrated novel, *What is to Be Done?* (Chto delat'?), which, astonishingly, was legally published in the reopened *Sovremennik* in 1863 because each of two censors thought the other was supposed to suppress it. Subtitled *From Stories about the New People*, the novel aimed to replace Turgenev's recent *Fathers and Sons* (1862) as the preeminent picture of young revolutionaries in fiction. Barred from discussing political emancipation openly, Chernyshevsky wrote the tale of the emancipation of a woman, Vera Pavlovna, who stage by stage escapes a wretched background and parents to become an educated, autonomous and radical *intelligentka*, a socialist and the founder-leader of a dressmaking *artel* (communal shop) for poor, freedom-seeking women of St. Petersburg. To gain independence from her parents, Vera had contracted a purely "legal" marriage to a thoroughly decent radical medical student, Lopukhov. They live in separate rooms, in personal and economic autonomy and respect. This feminist theme of the novel enormously influenced the future liberation movement of Russian women.

Chernyshevsky avoids the cheap ending of having the couple fall in complete love. Instead, Vera falls in love with another radical medical student, Kirsanov. The two men discuss their dilemma with much rationality but also with anger and agony. Lopukhov nobly offers to give way to a free union of Vera and Kirsanov. Kirsanov nobly refuses because such an attempt to live future ethics in 1860s society could only lead to persecution of the woman as an adulteress. The rationalist Chernyshevsky constructed a novel in which three rational and decent new people worked themselves into a tragic dilemma from which there was no escape.

The plot, already punctuated by Vera's dreams of guilt and socialist hope, now deliberately abandons realism. Lopukhov fakes suicide, permitting Vera and Kirsanov to marry. Years later he returns from America with his own wife, and the two couples live rationally and happily forever after. Lopukhov's disappearance is announced by still another radical, the formidable Rakhmetev, whose brief appearance is a kind of last dream, a vision of a wholly revolutionary new man of the distant future, totally self-disciplined save for cigars. Witty as well as hortatory, the novel had an enormous inspirational effect on three generations of Russian radicals. LENIN said he was converted to the revolution by reading it. It has been scoffed at as stupid and wooden by Russian rightists and most Westerners, an equal and opposite political prejudice.

In 1864 Chernyshevsky, like DOSTOEVSKY before him, underwent a mock execution, and was sent to seven years of forced labor in the silver mines of the Irkutsk region and twelve years of exile in the Arctic village of Vilyuisk. Hardships and malaria destroyed his ability to write and ensured his lasting reputation as a martyr. He was allowed to return to Astrakhan in 1883 and to Saratov in 1889, where he died on 29 October. He has been a radical and Communist idol in Russia ever since, and a genuine inspiration to vigorous, value-laden, radical literature aiming to combine progressive effect with truthful, realist, human, complex art.

Works: Polnoe sobranie sochinenii. 16 vols. 1939–53. (Accurate texts, Stalinist commentary.)
Translations: Selected Philosophical Essays. Moscow, 1953. *What is to Be Done?* Trans. Benjamin R. Tucker. Rev. and abridged [by about one fifth] by Ludmilla B. Turkevich. Introd. by E. H. Carr. 1961.
Secondary literature: G. M. Fridlender, "Estetika Chernyshevskogo i russkaya literatura," *RLit* 21, no. 2 (1978), pp. 11–35. U. Gural'nik, *Nasledie N. G. Chernyshevskogo—pisatelya i sovetskoe literaturovedenie: Itogi, zadachi, perspektivy izucheniya.* 1980. Norman G. O. Pereira, *The Thought and Teachings of N. G. Černyševskij.* The Hague, 1975. Francis B. Randall, *N. G. Chernyshevskii.* (Twayne World Authors Series, 22.) 1967. G. A. Solov'ev, *Esteticheskie vozzreniya Chernyshevskogo.* 2d rev. ed. 1978. G. E. Tamarchenko, *Chernyshevskii—romanist.* 1976. William F. Woehrlin, *Chernyshevskii: the Man and the Journalist.* 1971.

F. B. R.

Chertkóv, Vladímir Grigórievich (1854–1936), editor, publisher, and publicist. Chertkov was born in St. Petersburg to a wealthy and aristocratic military family. His excellent education was followed by service in the cavalry. He left the army in 1881 following a period of ideological crisis in his personal life. Having heard of L. N. TOLSTOI's post-conversion teachings and attracted by their similarity to his own

views and aspirations, Chertkov made his acquaintance in 1883. Thereafter he became Tolstoi's disciple and closest collaborator. Late in 1884 they founded a non-profit publishing house called The Intermediary (POSREDNIK). The purpose of this enterprise was to make inexpensive editions of Tolstoi's works and other suitable writings readily available to the "popular" audience (i.e., the uneducated masses of the Russian people). In 1897 Chertkov was exiled from Russia because of his activities in behalf of the spread of Tolstoism. He went to England and there published a newspaper, *Svobodnoe slovo*, works by Tolstoi which had been banned in Russia, and a variety of materials on the student movement and religious sectarianism in his homeland. He was allowed to return to Russia in 1905. Because of the antipathy between him and Countess Tolstoi, however, Chertkov refrained from visiting Tolstoi at home. Their dealings were conducted primarily through correspondence or in the course of Tolstoi's occasional visits to Chertkov's estate. Chertkov played an important role in the preservation of Tolstoi's papers and served, until his death, as editor-in-chief of the definitive 90-volume edition of Tolstoi's *Complete Collected Works* (Polnoe sobranie sochinenii, 1928–58).

Works: Zlaya zabava: Mysli ob okhote. 1890. *O poslednikh dnyakh L. N. Tolstogo.* 1911. *Tserkov' i politika.* 1919. *Ukhod Tolstogo.* 1922.
Translations: The Last Days of Tolstoy. Trans. N. Duddington. London, 1922.
Secondary literature: P. A. Bulanzhe, *Tolstoi i Chertkov.* 1911. A. Maude, *The Life of Tolstoy.* Vol. 2. London, 1930. Passim. M. V. Muratov, *L. N. Tolstoi i V. G. Chertkov po ikh perepiske.* Moscow, 1934. V. D. Bonch-Bruevich, "V. G. Chertkov" (necrology), *Literaturnaya gazeta*, 11 November 1936. E. J. Simmons, *Leo Tolstoy.* 1946. M. A. Shcheglov, "Lev Tolstoi i V. G. Chertkov." In his *Literaturno-kriticheskie stat'i.* 1958. Pp. 164–95.

G. J.

Chervínskaya, Lídiya Davýdovna (1907–), émigré poet in Paris, also worked at Radio Station Liberty in Munich. Like Anatoly SHTEIGER, she wrote poems in the spirit of the "Parisian note" (PARIZHSKAYA NOTA). Her verse is diary-like, very personal, with muffled intonations, phrases expressing the persona's perplexity and queries about the world of finite experience. There are aphoristic statements, parentheses, dashes, and disconnected syntactical units. Her poetry is allegorical and dominated by the persona's analytical, inquisitive mind. The leitmotif of Chervinskaya's verse is approaching death, a call for silence. Her manner of expression seems direct, but the meaning is often complicated by ambiguous or obscure references and things are frequently left unsaid. Seldom do any bright colors enliven her poems; her favorite medium is India ink with black and white halftones. Chervinskaya also avoids paying much attention to the musical tonality of her verse and leans instead toward conversational intonations. She frequently breaks up the quatrain ending her poem, sometimes sonnet-fashion, or by introducing a new line, or by stopping in midsentence. Her verse portrays an "urban heart"— there are no descriptive portrayals of nature. It is populated by half-shadows, with vague outlines, diffused moods, and a duality of feelings, as in the lines: "I know—not knowing. I love—not loving." Many of her epithets are prefixed with the negative particle "not": "not hypocrisy, not indifference." Her style is marked by Parisian scenery, flower imagery, time perceived as time of day and season, often through a dreamy haze. Occasionally there are variations on themes from Russian classics (PUSHKIN, BLOK, AKHMATOVA). Her poems, interesting also because of their graceful refusal to be structured or pointed, are irreproachable in artistic taste.

Works: Priblizheniya. Paris, 1934, *Rassvety.* Paris, 1937, and *Dvenadtsat' mesyatsev.* Paris, 1956. Her verse and critical essays have appeared in various émigré literary journals, newspapers, and anthologies such as *Numbers, Contemporary Annals, The New Review, Russian Annals, Muse of the Diaspora, Experiments, The New House*, and *The Anchor: An Anthology of Emigré Poetry.*
Secondary literature: Temira Pachmuss, *A Russian Cultural Revival: A Critical Anthology of Emigré Literature before 1939.* Knoxville, TN, 1981. Pp. 364–68.

T. A. P.

Chét'i minéi, see MINÉI CHÉT'I.

Children, literature for (*detskaya literatura*). In Russia, as elsewhere, many works originally written for and read by adults have in due course become readings for children and adolescents, sometimes in an abbreviated or bowdlerized form. Foreign works (*Don Quixote, Robinson Crusoe*, the novels of Walter Scott, J. F. Cooper, Dickens, etc.) have suffered this fate no less than some Russian classics, such as PUSHKIN's *The Captain's Daughter*, GOGOL's Ukrainian tales, the historical novels of LAZHECHNIKOV and Aleksei Konstantinovich TOL-STOI, etc. Some classics of foreign and Russian literature have become a part of school curricula. A Russian high school graduate of the 1980s will have read most of the same books as his parents or even his grand-parents: *Eugene Onegin, Dead Souls, War and Peace*, GORKY's *Mother*, OSTROVSKY's *How the Steel Was Tempered*.

Literature designed specifically for young readers began to develop in the 18th century. Much of it was translated, for example, the extremely popular collection of biblical stories by the German Protestant theologian Johannes Hübner ("One Hundred and Four Holy Stories from the Old and New Testament for the Edification of the Young," 1714), which is fondly remembered by Father Zosima in DOSTOEVSKY's *The Brothers Karamazov*. A multi-volume *Library for Children* (Detskaya biblioteka, 1783–85) was translated and adapted by A. S. SHISHKOV from the German of J. H. Campe. The moral tale (*conte moral*) for children was likewise an early import. N. I. NOVI-KOV, among his other firsts, also published the first Russian magazine for children, *Juvenile Readings for the Heart and Mind* (Detskoe chtenie dlya serdtsa i razuma, 1785–89), as a weekly supplement to the *Moscow News*.

During the first half of the 18th century, a large part of Russian books for children continued to be translations, mostly from the French and German. Some writers, such as Vladimir Burnashev (1809–88) and Aleksandra Ishimova (1806–81), specialized in producing books for children of various ages. The quality of these works was generally low. Critics, such as BELINSKY and DOBROLYUBOV, who frequently reviewed books for children, found most of them pedantic, much too schematic, dry, and boring. Once the romantic period had established an attitude of interest, respect, and caring for the child's psyche, first-rate writers and poets not infrequently wrote works expressly addressed to children. Among them, we find Nikolai NEKRASOV, Apollon MAIKOV, Yakov POLONSKY, Vladimir DAL, Dmitry GRIGOROVICH, Konstantin Stanyukovich, etc. Aleksandr OSTROVSKY's dramatized fairy tale (in verse), *The Snow Maiden* (Snegurochka, 1873) stands out as one of his most successful pieces. Lev TOLSTOI, in particular, devoted years of his life to education and the composition of primers and readers for Russian children. His *New Primer* (Novaya azbuka, 1875) and *Russian Readers* (Russkie knigi dlya chteniya, 1–4, 1875–85) contained some fiction and non-fiction written by Tolstoi himself. In general, the rapid development of public education in the second half of the 19th century was accompanied by corresponding advances in the quantity and quality of literature for children.

The Soviet government, from the very outset, devoted a great deal of attention to literature for children. As early as 1919 Maksim GORKY organized the publication of the first Soviet magazine for children, *Northern Lights* (Severnoe siyanie). In the 1920s and 1930s, literature for children became a not insignificant outlet for some first rate poets and writers of a "modernist" bent, such as the OBERIUTY A. VVEDENSKY and D. KHARMS. Lev KASSIL, a talented prose writer, described the Revolution of 1917 in stories told from a child's point of view and presumably for children ("Conduit," 1930, "Shvambraniya," 1933), in what for an adult reader amounts to a brilliant technique of "making it strange." S. Ya. MARSHAK and K. I. CHUKOVSKY, whose talents were by no means limited to writing poetry for three- to ten-year-olds, devoted a great deal of their time to producing some of the best poetry for children in any literature. Marshak's *poema*, *The Mails* (Pochta, 1927) is a classic which has been translated into many languages, including English. Some of MAYAKOVSKY's most attractive post-revolutionary poems were for children, for example, "What Is Good, and What Is Bad" (1925).

Literature for children followed all the tendencies dictated by the Party line, including the unattractive and even the vicious ones. In Mayakovsky's lengthy "Fairy Tale about Petya, a Fat Child, and Sima, a Skinny One" (1925), Petya, a bourgeois child, is fat, gluttonous, greedy, lazy, stupid, and he mistreats animals, while Sima, a proletarian child, is bright, unselfish, frugal, and good to animals. In

the end, Petya stuffs himself with an enormous quantity of goodies, and bursts, showering Sima and his proletarian friends with the goodies, which they happily consume.

As constraints imposed on literature grew tighter with the advent of SOCIALIST REALISM, literature (as well as art and theater) for children became attractive as an outlet for the whimsical, the fantastic, and the eccentric, which were no longer tolerated in mainstream literature and art. As a result, a very large number of leading writers and poets wrote for children, while imaginative artists gladly illustrated their books. Among Soviet authors who have written for children, besides those already mentioned, we find S. ANTONOV, N. ASEEV, A. GAIDAR, V. KATAEV, V. KAVERIN, M. PRISHVIN, Yu. OLESHA, N. TIKHONOV, M. ZOSHCHENKO, and many others.

In some instances, literature for children has served as a vehicle for hidden political satire, so in the case of some "fairy tales" by Kassil and particularly in the plays "for children" by Evgeny SHVARTS (*The Dragon, The Shadow*). Even pieces of straightforward political indoctrination written for children may have, for the adult reader, the effect of political satire, for example, "Felix the Iron Man" by Yury German, whose hero is the infamous chief of the GPU, Feliks Dzerzhinsky. It is a peculiar phenomenon of the Soviet literary scene that literature addressed to children is widely read by adults, because it may create a more "estranged" and hence more interesting view of reality than literature addressed to adults.

The Soviet regime has paid a great deal of attention to the development of literature for children. Much of the literature for children of school and pre-school age is published by the publishing house *Children's Literature* (Detskaya literatura), founded in 1933. It produces a variety of series, such as The School Library (Shkol'naya biblioteka), The Golden Library (Zolotaya biblioteka), Library of Adventure and Science Fiction (Biblioteka priklyuchenii i nauchnoi fantastiki), Historico-Revolutionary Library (Istoriko-revolyutsionnaya biblioteka), etc. Included in these series are the works of many classics of Russian and world literature. A number of magazines for children appear in the Soviet Union, so *The Pioneer* (Pioner, since 1924) and *Little Smeary* (Murzilka, since 1924). A great deal of secondary literature on the subject of literature for children also exists.

Bibliography: "Detskaya literatura" in *KLE* 2 (1964), pp. 608–20. Miriam Morton, ed., *A Harvest of Russian Children's Literature*. Foreword by Ruth Hill Viguers. 1967. ———, *Through the Magic Curtain: Theater for Children, Adolescents and Youth in the U.S.S.R.: 27 Authoritative Essays*. 1979.   V. T.

Chinnov, Ígor Vladímirovich (1909–   ), poet and essayist. Born in Riga, Chinnov spent his childhood in Russia, returning to Latvia, where he took a law degree from the University of Riga in 1939. Having fled Latvia during the war, Chinnov settled in Paris, where he took his *licence ès-lettres* (1947) and supported himself as a free lance *littérateur* and language teacher. His first collection of verse, *Monologue*, came out in Paris in 1950. Subsequently Chinnov worked as a senior news editor and literary critic for Radio Liberty in Munich (1953–62). He immigrated to the United States in 1962 and held successive professorships of Russian literature at the University of Kansas, the University of Pittsburgh, and Vanderbilt University, where he taught until his retirement. He now lives in Florida. A regular contributor to *Novyi zhurnal*, Chinnov has published some critical essays, scholarly articles, and reviews, besides his poetry.

Chinnov's early poetry has much in common with the "Parisian note" (PARIZHSKAYA NOTA) of G. V. ADAMOVICH. It deals with life's crucial problems in a restrained and resigned way, and is marked by economy of means, traditional versification and vocabulary, and avoidance of picturesque and ornamental imagery. It is also autumnally pessimistic. In "Lines" (1960) and much more so in "Metaphors" (1969), a tendency toward freer rhythms, more elaborate sound patterns, and more colorful imagery signal a more serene outlook on life and a grateful appreciation of the beauty and plenitude of God's world. Chinnov's poetry of the 1970s gravitates toward composition controlled by the flow of a poem's sounds, which makes for a surrealistic dance of verbal phantoms, not without some method in its madness. A humanist despite his deep-rooted pessimism, Chinnov is a skeptic with a deep affection for religion, a sober observer of life who is, however, eager to catch glimpses of another, mystic reality.

Further collections: Partitura. 1970. *Kompozitsiya.* 1972. *Pastorali.* 1976. *Antiteza.* 1979.

Translations: Three poems, trans. Theodore Weiss and L. P. Izhorsky, in *TriQuarterly,* no. 28 (1973), pp. 433–34. R. H. Morrison, ed. and trans., *America's Russian Poets.* 1975. Five poems, in *Russian Poetry: The Modern Period.* Ed. John Glad and Daniel Weissbort. 1978. Pp. 289–92. William Tjalsma, trans. *Transfigurations: Igor Chinnov in English.* (Micromegas Chapbooks.) 1979.

Secondary literature: Lee B. Croft, "The Method to Madness in a Poem by Chinnov," *SEEJ* 17 (1973), pp. 408–13. Yurii Ivask, "Poeziya 'staroi' emigratsii." In *Russkaya literatura v emigratsii.* Ed. N. P. Poltoratskii. 1972. Pp. 63–65. Emmanuil Rais, "Poeziya Igorya Chinnova," *Vozrozhdenie,* no. 235 (1977), pp. 131–45. Vladimir Veidle, "O poetakh i poezii. 3. O stikhakh Igorya Chinnova," *Mosty* 7 (1961), pp. 143–47. *See also* "Foreword" by John Glad and Victor Terras, in *Antiteza.* Washington, D.C., 1979. Pp. 3–8. Reviews of Chinnov's collections have appeared in *Novoe russkoe slovo, Novyi zhurnal, Russkaya mysl', Vozrozhdenie,* and other periodicals.

V. T.

Chirikov, Evgény Nikoláevich (1864–1932), novelist, playwright, and publicist. Born in Kazan, into a family of the gentry, Chirikov studied mathematics at Kazan University, but was expelled in 1887 for participating in student demonstrations. He was for many years involved in the revolutionary movement and belonged to the ZNANIE group, of which GORKY was the leader. Chirikov's novels, stories, and plays dealt with topical questions, usually in a provincial setting. His plays, such as *Jews* (Evrei, 1904, translated into several languages, including Yiddish), *Peasants* (Muzhiki, 1906), and *The Sorceress* (Koldun'ya, 1909) were quite successful, though they lack psychological depth. Chirikov's best-known novel is *The Life of Tarkhanov* (Zhizn' Tarkhanova), whose first three parts appeared in 1911, 1913, and 1914, and the fourth and last in 1925, after Chirikov's emigration. In Prague, where Chirikov had settled after leaving Russia, Chirikov continued his literary activities. His long short-story, "A Devastated Soul" (Opustoshennaya dusha, 1921), was an effort to capture the inner life of a bolshevik revolutionary. His novel, *The Beast from the Abyss* (Zver' iz bezdny, 1926), is set in the south of Russia during the civil war. Chirikov drew an almost equally negative image of Whites and Reds and was roundly attacked by critics of both sides. Chirikov died in Prague.

Works: Sobranie sochinenii. 17 vols. 1910–16. *Yunost'.* New York, 1955. *Povesti i rasskazy.* Ed. E. M. Sakharova. Moscow, 1961. See also *Foster,* pp. 1164–66.

Translations: The Chosen People (trans. of *Evrei*). A Drama in Four Acts. New York, 1907. *Marka of the Pits.* Trans. L. Zarine. New York, 1930. *See also: Lewanski,* p. 226.

Secondary literature: S. V. Kastorskii, "Realisticheskaya proza." In *Istoriya russkoi literatury.* Vol. 10. 1954. ———. *Revolyutsiya 1905 goda i russkaya literatura.* 1956. Gleb Struve, *Russkaya literatura v izgnanii.* 1956. Pp. 124–25. V. T.

Chizhévsky (Čyževs'kyj, Tschižewskij), Dmítry (Dmytro) Ivánovich (1894–1977), historian, philosopher, literary scholar, a specialist in the history of Slavic literatures. Born in Aleksandriya (Ukraine), Chizhevsky studied mathematics, astronomy, and philosophy at St. Petersburg University and Slavic philology and linguistics at Kiev University. After his emigration from the Soviet Union in 1921, he studied philosophy in Heidelberg and Freiburg, and was a member of the Prague Linguistics Circle. Chizhevsky taught philosophy at the Ukrainian Free University (1924–32), and Slavic and Russian literature and civilization at Halle (1932), Marburg (1945–49), Harvard (1949–56), and Heidelberg (1956–63). He published many textbooks, including histories of Russian, Ukrainian, and Comparative Slavic literature, monographs on the history of Ukrainian and Russian literature, the history of philosophy in the Ukraine (including an important monograph on Skovoroda), the influence of German philosophy among the Slavs (Hegel, Boehme, J. Arndt, Oettinger), and the history of baroque literature in the Slavic countries. His broad knowledge of Slavic history, literature, linguistics, and philosophy enabled Chizhevsky to make important comparative studies of Slavic literatures. He also published some important source material (His

discovery and publication of an unknown manuscript by Comenius stands out.) and edited series of publications for Mouton (The Hague) and Fink (Munich).

Selected Works: Gegel' v Rossii. Paris, 1939. *On Romanticism in Slavic Literatures.* The Hague, 1957. *History of Russian Literature from the Eleventh Century to the End of the Baroque.* The Hague, 1960. *Comparative History of Slavic Literatures.* Nashville, 1971. *Skovoroda: Dichter, Denker, Mystiker.* Munich, 1974. *History of Nineteenth-Century Russian Literature.* 2 vols. Nashville, 1974–76. *Russian Intellectual History.* Ann Arbor, 1978.

Secondary literature: D. Gerhardt, "Schriftenverzeichnis von D. I. Čyževs'kyj (1912–54)." In *Festschrift für Dmytro Čyževs'kyj zum 60. Geburtstag.* (Veröffentlichungen der Abteilung für Slavische Sprachen und Literaturen des Osteuropa-Instituts [Slavisches Seminar] an der freien Universität Berlin, 6.) Berlin, 1954. Pp. 1–34. George G. Grabowicz, "Toward a History of Ukrainian Literature." In *Harvard Ukrainian Studies* 1, no. 4, pp. 407–523. Hugh McLean, "Chyzhevs'kyj, Dmytro Ivanovich." In *MERSL.* Ed. Harry Weber. Pp. 148–54. Omeljan Pritsak and Ihor Ševčenko, "Dmytro Čyževs'kyj: In Memoriam." In *Harvard Ukrainian Studies* 1, no. 3, pp. 379–406. Hans-Jürgen zum Winkel, "Schriftenverzeichnis von D. I. Tschižewskij (1954–1965)." In *Orbis Scriptus: Dmitrij Tschižewskij zum 70. Geburtstag.* Ed. Dietrich Gerhardt et al. Munich, 1966. Pp. 35–48.

E. B.

Chórny, Sásha (pseud. of Aleksandr Mikhailovich Glikberg, 1880–1932), satirist, poet, and prose writer. Since 1905, Chorny was one of the most active political satirists in St. Petersburg. His first collection of lyrics and satire, *Sundry motifs* (Raznye motivy, 1906), was stopped by the Censor. Subsequently, Chorny was one of the most active contributors to the SATIRIKON. He also translated German poetry and wrote some masterful verses for children. After the Revolution, Chorny emigrated, first to Poland, then in 1920 to Berlin, where he published a book of verse, *Thirst* (Zhazhda, 1923). He then moved on to Paris, where he wrote some excellent prose: *Unserious tales* (Neser'eznye rasskazy, 1928) and *Soldiers' Tales* (Soldatskie skazki, publ. posthumously in 1933). Chorny's satire is hardhitting and sarcastic. It is said to have had some influence on MAYAKOVSKY. Chorny's lyric poetry is sophisticated and deeply pessimistic.

Works: Stikhotvoreniya. Introd. essay by K. Chukovskii. Introd., ed. and comm. by L. A. Evstigneeva. 1960. *Satiry.* Paris, 1978.

Secondary literature: L. Evstigneeva, *Zhurnal 'Satirikon' i poety-satirikontsy.* 1968. Z. Papernyi, "Smekh Sashi Chernogo," *Novyi mir,* 1960, no. 9. E. Shneiderman, "Novoe o Sashe Chernom," *RLit* (1966), no. 3. V. Trenin and N. Khardzhiev. "Mayakovskii i 'satirikonskaya' poeziya." In *Poeticheskaya kul'tura Mayakovskogo.* 1970.

V. T.

Chukóvskaya, Lídiya Kornéevna (1910–), novelist, memoirist, dissident, daughter of writer Kornei CHUKOVSKY. Chukovskaya, whose second husband died in Stalin's purges, is the author of two novels on the topic: *The Deserted House* (Sof'ya Petrovna) and *Going Under* (Spusk pod vodu). Both deal with the psychological repercussions of living in constant terror. A close friend of Anna AKHMATOVA, Chukovskaya saved some of Akhmatova's poems by committing them to memory and also published a two-volume account of her conversations with Akhmatova. With time, Chukovskaya became more and more active in the dissident movement. In a famous open letter she violently criticized novelist Mikhail SHOLOKHOV for his condemnation of SINYAVSKY and DANIEL and his support of the regime. She also published abroad spirited defenses of PASTERNAK and SOLZHENITSYN. In 1974 she was expelled from the Writers' Union and described her experience in *The Process of Expulsion.* A professional editor (largely in the area of juvenile fiction), Chukovskaya has written a good deal on the art of editing and gathered her essays into a book entitled *In the Editor's Workshop.* Chukovskaya has also written some poetry, published in a collection entitled *On This Side of Death.*

Works: V laboratorii redaktora. 1963. *Zapiski ob Anne Akhmatovoi.* Paris, 1976.

Translations: The Deserted House. Trans. Aline B. Werth, 1967. *Going Under.* Trans. Peter Weston. 1972.

Secondary literature: E. Breitbart, "Khranitel'nitsa traditsii: Lidiya Korneevna Chukovskaya," *Grani,* no. 104 (1977), pp. 171–82.
J. G.

Chukóvsky, Korneí Ivánovich (pen-name of Nikolaí Vasílievich Korneichukóv, 1882–1969), writer, children's poet, critic and literary scholar, translator, and editor. Chukovsky's father, a student, abandoned his family, and the child was brought up by his mother, a woman of peasant origin. Due to his background and political conditions of the time, Chukovsky was unable to finish high school and remained a self-taught person for the rest of his long life. However, his contributions to literature and scholarship were such that in 1957 he was awarded the degree of doctor of philological sciences and in 1962 an Honorary D. Litt. by Oxford University.

Chukovsky began his literary career in 1901, in the newspaper *Odesskie novosti,* which later sent him to London as a correspondent. While in England (1903–04), he studied English literature and wrote on it for Russian publications. Returning to Russia, he moved to St. Petersburg, where V. Ya. BRYUSOV invited him to write for the symbolist magazine VESY and where, during the first Russian revolution of 1905, he edited a short-lived satirical magazine, *Signal.* After the revolution, he contributed to the liberal press and later collected his critical essays on contemporary writers in a number of books. In 1912 he moved to the Finnish village Kuokkala (now Repino, USSR), where he befriended the painter I. E. Repin, V. G. KOROLENKO, L. N. ANDREEV, A. N. TOLSTOI, A. I. KUPRIN, A. F. KONI, and others, all of whom were later depicted in his artistic memoirs.

Poetry—both Russian and English—was Chukovsky's other infatuation. Here his main attention was devoted to N. A. NEKRASOV, about whom he published several studies, culminating in his *Masterstvo Nekrasova* (Nekrasov's Craftsmanship, 1952).

Chukovsky's interest in verbal creativity of children and in literature for children started in the 1900s. When later, in 1916, M. Gorky invited him to direct the children's section of the publishing house *Parus* (Sail), he began to write for children himself. Though going against prevailing canons, Chukovsky's fairy tales in verse eventually brought him enormous popularity. He is famous also for his observations on children's speech and psychology: his book *From Two to Five* (Ot dvukh do pyati), published first as *Little Children* (Malen'kie deti, 1928) ran through more than twenty editions and was translated into many languages, incl. English.

Chukovsky's other fame is related to his art as a translator and theoretician of translation. The first edition of his translations from Walt Whitman appeared as early as 1907. Since 1918, when he became head of the Anglo-American department of the publishing house *Vsemirnaya literatura* (World Literature), Chukovsky translated, besides Whitman, some of the works of Mark Twain, G. K. Chesterton, Oscar Wilde, Fielding, Sir A. Conan-Doyle, O. Henry, Kipling, and others, and "retold" for children the writings of Daniel Defoe, R. Raspe, and J. Greenwood. He generalized his experience, and the experience of other translators, in a booklet, *Principles of Artistic Translation* (Printsipy khudozhestvennogo perevoda, 1919), later significantly expanded: *The Art of Translation* (Iskusstvo perevoda,* 1930, 1936) and *The Lofty Art* (Vysokoe iskusstvo, 1941, 1964, 1968).

Chukovsky's love for the word and the Russian language manifested itself during the public discussion on language which took place in the Soviet Union in the late 1950s. He published a number of articles and a book, *Alive as Life* (Zhivoi kak zhizn', 1962), in which he condemned the contemporary littering of the Russian literary language with Sovietisms and bureaucratese (*kantselyarit*).

As an editor, Chukovsky was in charge of several editions of N. A. Nekrasov's works (including the complete works in 12 vols., 1948–53), of the collections *The Craftsmanship of Translation* (Masterstvo perevoda, 1965–70), of the works of V. A. Sleptsov, A. F. Koni, A. I. Kuprin, Oscar Wilde, A. Conan-Doyle, of the memoirs of A. Ya. PANAEVA and I. E. Repin, and others.

Works: Sobranie sochinenii. 6 vols. 1965–69.

Translations: The Silver Crest: My Russian Boyhood. Trans Beatrice Stillman. 1976. *The Poet and the Hangman* (Nekrasov and Muravyov). Trans. R. W. Rotsel. 1977. *See also* Lewanski, p. 226.

Secondary literature: M. Petrovskii, *Kniga o Kornee Chukovskom.* 1966. *Vospominaniya o Kornee Chukovskom.* Comp. K. I. Lozovskaya, Z. S. Papernyi, and E. Ts. Chukovskaya. 1977. *Zhizn' i tvorchestvo Korneya Chukovskogo.* Comp. Valentin Berestov. 1978.
N. P. P.

Chulkóv, Geórgy Ivánovich (1879–1939). A minor symbolist writer, essayist, and critic, originator of a controversial doctrine called mystical anarchism. He was born in Moscow, studied medicine at Moscow University, was arrested for political activity in 1902, exiled to the Yakutsk region, settled in Nizhni-Novgorod, returned to St. Petersburg and published his first book of verse in 1904. He briefly edited the SYMBOLIST journal *Novyi put'* and was instrumental in the founding of another, *Voprosy zhizni.* He edited three volumes of a miscellany called *Torches* (Fakely, 1906, 1907, 1908) which included both symbolists (Vyacheslav IVANOV and others) and realists such as Maksim GORKY. In 1906 he published a pamphlet, *On Mystical Anarchism* (O misticheskom anarkhizme). The doctrine, which attempts to reconcile the aim of freedom with participation in a mystical communal life, attracted adherents during the period of political disappointment stemming from the abortive revolution of 1905 and was energetically supported by Ivanov. Adverse reactions by other symbolists, who rejected the idealization of collectivity (sobornost'), contributed to an atmosphere of conflict over goals which was to end the symbolist movement as a cooperative enterprise. Chulkov's poetry belongs to the DECADENT current and is otherwise undistinguished. He wrote several novels, beginning with *Satan* (Satana, 1911), which have almost been forgotten, as well as short stories and several plays. After the revolution he published memoirs, the most informative of which is *Years of Wandering* (Gody stranstvii, 1930), and essays on 19th century Russian authors, including DOSTOEVSKY and TYUTCHEV.

Works: Sochineniya. 6 vols. St. Petersburg. 1911–12. *Satana.* Moscow 1915. *Vchera i segodnya.* 1916. *Lyudi v tumane: Kniga rasskazov.* 1916. *Serezha Nestroev: Roman.* 1916. *Sud'ba Rossii.* 1916. *Metel': Roman.* 1917. *Mikhail Bakunin i buntari 1917 goda.* Moscow, 1917. *Posramlennye besy: Rasskazy.* 1921. *Nashi sputniki: Sbornik statei 1912–1922.* 1922. *Stikhotvoreniya.* 1922. *Tyutcheviana: Epigrammy, aforizmy i ostroty F. I. Tyutcheva.* 1922. *Vechernie zori: Rasskazy.* 1924. *Myatezhniki 1825 goda.* 1925. *Poslednyaya lyubov' Tyutcheva.* 1928. *Imperatory: Psikhologicheskie portrety.* 1928. *Brat'ya Borisovy.* 1929. *Gody stranstvii.* 1930. *Letopis' zhizni i tvorchestva F. I. Tyutcheva.* 1933. *Zhizn' Pushkina.* 1938. *Kak rabotal Dostoevskii.* 1939.

Secondary literature: William H. Richardson. "Chulkov." In *MERSL.* Ed. Harry B. Weber (1981) Vol. 4. Pp. 137–41.
E. Br.

Chulkóv, Mikhaíl (Mikhailo) Dmitrievich (1743?–1792), writer. After early years in Moscow, Chulkov worked as an actor at the court theater in St. Petersburg after which he served several years on the household staff at court. Finally, during the last twenty or so years of his life, he enjoyed a successful civil service career in the Department of Commerce. From the mid-fifties through the eighties Chulkov was also a writer.

First a comic-playwright, Chulkov made his greatest and most influential contribution to Russian letters as a prosaist. His talents were especially suited to humor, parody, and satire as evidenced by his biggest and most popular work, the omnibus of anecdotes, legends, short stories, and novels published under the apt title of *The Mocker* (Peresmeshnik). This work variously parodies the ambitions and pretensions of the serious cultivation of prose fiction, then only getting underway in Russia, and takes as its special target of satire the newly minted Russian urbanity.

Literary pretensions and social manners were featured in Chulkov's two, short-lived satirical journals on whose pages also appeared all of Chulkov's published poetry—three lengthy poems proving him a master of burlesque verse.

The novel *The Comely Cook* (Prigozhaya povarikha) is usually regarded as Chulkov's masterpiece. A first-person account of the adventures of a "debauched woman" replete with details frequently hailed as "realistic," this work also substantially shares Chulkov's typical comic-parodic-satiric orientation.

Significant contributions to Russian literary culture are also Chulkov's encyclopedic works on Slavic mythology and folklore (M. POPOV, collaborator) and his sizable collection of Russian songs—the first printed Russian songbook.

Works: "Stikhi na kacheli," "Stikhi na semik," and "Plachevnoe padenie stikhotvortsev." In *Iroi-komicheskaya poema*. Leningrad, 1933. Also in *Poety XVIII veka*. Vol. 1. Leningrad, 1958. *I To i Syo* (excerpts). In *Russkie satiricheskie zhurnaly XVIII veka*. 1940. "Gor'kaya uchast'" and *Prigozhaya povarikha*. In *Russkaya literatura XVIII veka*. 1970. *Peresmeshnik* (excerpts) and *Prigozhaya povarikha*. In *Russkaya proza XVIII veka*. 1971.

Translations: "A Bitter Fate" and *The Comely Cook*. In: Harold B. Segel, *The Literature of Eighteenth-Century Russia*. Vol. 2. New York, 1967.

Secondary literature: J. Garrard, *Mixail Čulkov*. The Hague and Paris, 1970. ———. "'Russkii Skarron' (M. D. Chulkov)," *XVIII Vek*, 1976, no. 11. J. Goodliffe, "Some Comments on Narrative Prose Fiction in Eighteenth-Century Russian Literature, with Special Reference to Chulkov," *Melbourne Slavic Studies*, 1970, nos. 5–6. V. Shklovskii, *Chulkov i Levshin*. Leningrad, 1933. I. R. Titunik, "Mikhail Chulkov's 'Double-Talk' Narrative," *CASS* 9 (1975).   I. R. T.

Church Slavonic. The term Church Slavonic is used here for two chronologically and functionally distinct languages, Old Church Slavonic (OCS) and Church Slavonic (CS) which are bound by historical continuity, by their supra-national literary character, and, to a lesser extent, by their ecclesiastical function. By Old Church Slavonic is meant the oldest language of the Slavs which was codified in the 9th century by the Slavic Apostles, Cyril and Methodius, and their followers, and which is preserved in the canonical Slavic texts of the 10th and 11th centuries A.D. Since Old Church Slavonic was used not only for strictly liturgical purposes (as witnessed by the semi-secular *Lives* of Cyril and Methodius written soon after their death), it is customary to refer to it also as *Old Slavonic* (Fr. *vieux slave*, Russ. *staroslavyanskii*) in contradistinction to Old Slavic, which designates the old phases of any Slavic language. Equally ambiguous is the term Church Slavonic which refers to the Slavic recensions that evolved from Old Church Slavonic and which experienced the influence of the local Slavic languages and dialects. Until the formation of the latter into national literary languages, Church Slavonic was the main literary vehicle of the Orthodox and Croatian Catholic Slavs, and it transcended by far its original ecclesiastical functions.

Older philological scholarship invested considerable effort in determining the cradle of Old Church Slavonic which it located first in Pannonia (the "Old Slovenian" theory of Kopitar and Miklosich) and later in the Balkans (the "Macedo-Bulgarian" theory developed most fully by Jagić). And indeed the canonical corpus of OCS includes only those texts which reveal the phonological and morphological peculiarities of early South-East Slavic, such as the reflexes *št*; *žd* (from *tj, kti; dj*), *rat, trat, tlat* (from *ort, tort, tolt; trět, tlět* (from *ort, tort, tolt; tert, telt*); *l* (from *tl, dl*), the presence of nasals ę, ǫ and of the jers ъ, ь ; the genitive singular and/or nominative-accusative pl. ending -ę in "soft" -*a* and -*jo* stems. The recognition that Old Church Slavonic was a supra-national literary language brought also the awareness that it cannot be identified with a single geographic region, since it absorbed from the very beginning dialectal (above all, lexical) features common to other Slavic areas. The importance of phonological features, however, overrides all other criteria and accounts for the fact that texts which betray local Slavic characteristics are relegated to CS, or to the history of the individual Slavic languages. Thus even such early East Slavic texts as the *Ostromir Gospel* (1056–57) and the Izborniki Svyatoslava (1073 and 1076) are treated as Russian-CS recensions, whereas such texts as the *Freising Leaflets* (of the 10th century) are assigned to the treasure-house of Slovenian literature.

The canonical OCS texts and inscriptions have come down to us in the two original alphabets of the Slavs, Glagolitic and Cyrillic. The older (10th century) and major portion of these texts was written in Glagolitic, the alphabet invented by St. Cyril himself. The two alphabets must have coexisted for some time, however, as evidenced by the fact that the oldest Slavic inscriptions on stone were written in the simpler Cyrillic which eventually replaced Glagolitic among all the Orthodox Slavs.

The spread of OCS among the Christianized Slavs brought about an ever deeper penetration of local peculiarities into this relatively unified literary language and hastened its breakdown into diverse CS recensions. The CS recensions never relinquished the bond of their common tradition and function, but they entered into a state of continuous tension with each other and with the emerging Slavic national languages which progressively expanded their range and literary functions.

The distinctive character of the CS recensions is defined by the phonetic and morphological features which they share with their local languages; e.g., the confusion of the nasal vowels in Bulgarian CS; the replacement of nasal by oral vowels in Russian, Serbo-Croatian (S.-Cr.) and Slovene CS; the confusion of the jers in Bohemian and S.-Cr. CS; the change of *y* to *i* and *v*- to *u*- in S.-Cr. CS; the use of *polnoglasie* and of *č, ž* in place of *št, žd* in Russian CS. The extent to which the local features penetrated into CS varied according to historical period, the nature of the text, and strength of local traditions (i.e., the prestige of schools or centers of learning). No less profound was the impact of CS upon the evolving literary languages which came to include texts of a legal, administrative, historiographic, or folkloristic nature. The use of formal characteristics is not, however, sufficient to assign a text to CS or a native literary tradition, for its linguistic character must be determined not only by external, but also by semantic, especially lexical and phraseological criteria. The interpenetration of the "learned" CS and the local, "popular" languages makes many an attempt at such an assignment rather futile.

The history of CS among the Orthodox Slavs is one of recurrent oscillation between a unified and archaizing CS, and the discrete and innovative vernaculars, a phenomenon which was far less pronounced among the Catholic Slavs who preserved the CS tradition only in Croatia (until the 18th century) from where it spread for a brief period of time to Bohemia and Poland (under Charles IV and under Jagiełło). The first major effort to overcome the pull of local traditions among the Orthodox Slavs emanated from Trnovo in 14th-century Bulgaria, and led to the formation of an archaic language and a complex literary style which took hold for some time in *Rus'* and in Serbia. The political and ecclesiastical decline of the South Slavic lands (especially after the battle at Kosovo in 1389) contributed, on the other hand, to the spread and growing importance of Russian-CS, which imparted some of its linguistic elements to the CS recensions and to the budding literary languages of the Southern Slavs. This influence became even more pronounced in the 17th century when outstanding Ruthenian scholars (Melety Smotritsky, Lavrenty Zizany) established a new norm of CS that was imitated by all Orthodox Slavs. The final emancipation of the South Slavic languages from the dominance of CS occurred only in the 19th century, when Bulgarian and Serbo-Croatian formed their own literary languages, though traces of Russian-CS have survived in these languages until today. Far more complete was the emancipation from CS of Ukrainian, Byelorussian, and Macedonian, which gained literary status respectively in the second half of the 19th and in the 20th century. As a result of these developments, contemporary ("Synodal") CS has come to earn its name, for it is now a language confined solely to the needs of the Church. (On the role of Church Slavonic in the history of literary Russian see The Russian language).

Bibliography: V. Jagić, *Entstehungsgeschichte der kirchenslavischen Sprache*. Berlin, 1913. J. Kur, "Cirkevněslovenský jazyk jako mezinárodní kulturní (literární) jazyk Slovanstva." In *Československé přednášky pro IV Mezinárodní Sjezd Slavistů*. Prague, 1958. Pp. 13–35. R. Picchio, "Church Slavonic." In *The Slavic Literary Languages: Formation and Development*. Ed. A. Schenker and E. Stankiewicz. New Haven, 1980. Pp. 1–33.   E. S.

Civic poets, see Shestidesyatniki.

Classicism, see Neoclassicism.

Collegium of Amateurs of the Russian Word, see Beseda lyubitelei russkogo slova.

Comedy, Russian. Comedy in the Russian folk theater of the 17th century, which preceded literary comedy by several generations, was provided by a gallery of comic types: bribe-taking officials, usurers, gentry wearing powdered wigs, and even clergy, though the Church suppressed these. But such characters had nothing to do with the plays proper. However, they were such a part of Russian life that they survived into the 1750s and appear in the comedies of the literary stage. A. P. SUMAROKOV (1718–77) who was appointed Director of the Imperial Theater in St. Petersburg in 1756 and provided numerous plays for the repertoire, including comedies, introduced these character types and added others—fops, pedants, misers, and gamblers. Sumarokov also used the stage to satirize his enemies in literature.

Despite its late beginnings, Russian dramaturgy developed rapidly. Between 1750 and 1786, over 300 plays in Russian had been performed in the Imperial Theater, mostly comedies and often translations or adaptations. These comedies were not intended primarily to divert audiences. The Russian theater was permeated by the moralizing and didacticism which prevailed in the literature of 18th-century Europe. The function of literature, including dramaturgy, was to improve society by furnishing moral precepts and examples. LOMONOSOV wrote in his *Rhetoric* (1748) that "the theater should serve a moral purpose," while Sumarokov formulated and practised the rule that "the attribute of comedy is to correct manners.... To amuse and cure is her direct role." In 1774, the journalist N. I. NOVIKOV appealed for Russian comedies "containing more moral lessons and examples," and ten years later. I. A. KRYLOV called the stage "a tribune for castigating moral and social vices."

Playwrights agreed that the most effective means of using the stage to correct "faults and vices" in contemporary society was satire, and three trends emerged in the 1760s: personal satire as practised by Sumarokov; more general satire, deriding vices common to all men (hypocrisy, bigotry, envy), and satire against specifically Russian social, economic and political abuses, such as faulty education of the gentry, Gallomania, even serfage. The trends were not mutually exclusive: individuals whom an audience could identify might be derided as an example of more general vices, or faults common to all might be satirized in a Russian setting.

Censorship began in the Imperial Theater as soon as original plays were produced. CATHERINE was relatively liberal toward the printed word (most Russians were illiterate), but less so toward the spoken word, especially when members of the public were admitted to performances. Her fear of the spoken, rather than written word, was characteristic of the Censorship in Russia until 1917, and later. At first she read plays herself, but in 1766, she appointed I. P. ELAGIN, a Minister at Court, to carry out the task. He was assisted by two secretaries, V. I. LUKIN and D. I. FONVIZIN. These both began by adapting French plays for the Russian stage by introducing Russian names, proverbs, even dialect. Fonvizin went further than Lukin in this respect: his original comedies *The Brigadier* (written in 1768 but not performed until 1780, in Moscow) and *The Minor* (Nedorosl', 1782) though both were ruthlessly cut for performances, nevertheless startled audiences by depicting recognizable Russian country landowners, officials, domestic tutors and serfs, placed in a Russian setting with detailed stage-directions (they play cards and drink tea). Fonvizin's understanding of "comedy" as a genre differed from that of his contemporaries who saw comedy in terms of *situations* (beatings, practical jokes), whereas to him, comedy was essentially a matter of relations between his *characters*, reflected in their speech. This view of comedy was inherited in the 19th century by GOGOL and OSTROVSKY. Both of Fonvizin's comedies remain in the standard repertoire, although his complete "authorized" version of *The Minor* was not permitted by the Censorship until 1882, when it had reached 100 performances at the Maly Theater in Moscow. Recently, it has been produced as a musical (Pushkin Theater, Moscow, 1975), and as a vaudeville "for young audiences" (in Kiev, 1978). Such "arrangements" of the classics of the Russian theater are common enough in the Soviet Union.

Russian comedy of the 18th century developed into several kinds, often imitating French comedy, especially Molière. Of these, the most highly regarded was the comedy of character, but the comedy of manners and of situation, as well as tearful comedy and comic opera, all found their way into the repertoire. *Woe from Wit* (1823) by A. S. GRIBOEDOV looks back to the comedy of manners, with satire directed against the "depraved and parasitical" society of fashionable Moscow in the 1820s. The young protagonist Chatsky is related to the fashionable *umniki* (wits) of the time, who had already appeared on the Russian stage in comedies such as A. A. SHAKHOVSKOI's *A Lesson to Flirts* (Urok koketkam, 1815). Here, the *umnik* Olgin visits Lipetsk spa to be cured of his "disordered nerves, migraines, and vertigo" which he has brought back from Paris. Olgin's conversation consists

of "improper couplets by French authors," and "free-thinking nonsense," for which he is considered "agreeable in society."

The fate of *Woe from Wit* at the hands of the Censorship was characteristic of the period, when comedy was regarded as more dangerous than tragedy, because the latter "did not depict real life." Although Griboedov wrote *Woe from Wit* in 1823, and it was widely known in manuscript copies, the first production was not given until 1831, in the censored version which was the only version allowed until 1871. By the 1880s, it was traditionally given for the opening night of the season in the Imperial Theaters. It has been called "the actor's university" in the Soviet Union (like *Hamlet*). Critics continue to discuss the comedy and how it should be produced for contemporary audiences, who might fail to recognize its "social significance."

A minor kind of comedy which was imported from Paris and flourished in the Imperial Theaters was the VAUDEVILLE: over 850 adaptations or originals were produced at St. Petersburg between 1826 and 1861 (as compared with 387 full-length "comedies"). They were comedies of situation—disguises, practical jokes, misunderstandings, and horse-play—featuring conventional character types— flirtatious young wives, rich elderly husbands, gallant young officers, elderly spinsters, benevolent grandfathers and the like. Dancing and the singing of "couplets" were common. By the 1840s, Russian characters appear—government officials, merchants, provincial actors, journalists and plebeians—set in Moscow or St. Petersburg. For decades, vaudeville was the only theatrical genre at all representative of contemporary Russian life, and writers took to describing them as "sketches from everyday life," or "physiological sketches," thus relating them to the "NATURAL SCHOOL" of prose fiction in the 1840s. P. A. Karatygin, a prolific writer of vaudevilles, composed *The Natural School* (Natural'naya shkola) in 1847. It became a scandalous success with 16 performances during the first season and frequent revivals until 1865.

Many players and writers made debuts in vaudeville, including M. S. Shchepkin (1788–1863), later the leading actor of the Maly Theater, and I. I. Sosnitsky (1794–1871) celebrated for his performances in comedies by Gogol and Ostrovsky. D. T. Lensky (1805–60) wrote over 150 vaudevilles and also made his name as an actor in Gogol's *Inspector-General*. NEKRASOV, TURGENEV and CHEKHOV wrote vaudevilles. They are still written and produced in the Soviet Union. V. KATAEV, V. Shkvarkin, and M. ZOSHCHENKO, among others, are authors of vaudevilles.

However, vaudeville exercised a baleful influence on the first production of Gogol's *The Inspector General* in St. Petersburg in 1836, as the players had been trained in the clowning style of vaudeville and naturally adopted it, much to the disgust of the playwright. M. O. Dyur (1807–38) was the original Khlestakov and made it a purely vaudeville performance. Similarly, Lensky as Khlestakov in the first Moscow production failed to understand Gogol's intentions. Only Shchepkin as the Mayor met with the approval of the author, and played the role 144 times until 1858.

By 1843, *The Inspector-General* had been greeted with acclamation not only in the capitals, but also in the provinces, from Odessa and Kiev to Kazan and Voronezh. But audiences not infrequently understood the comedy to refer to their own local authorities, who then withdrew it. *The Inspector-General* has remained in the repertoire although Gogol's final version (1842) was prohibited until 1870. By 1891, it had reached 334 performances in the Imperial Theaters. MEYERHOLD produced a celebrated version in 1926, and in 1972 it was staged with a musical accompaniment at the Leningrad Theater of Satire, Khlestakov's entrances being marked by a "St. Petersburg theme." In 1980, a "choreographic transcription" was given at the Kirov theatre.

Gogol spent the next several years writing comedies, including *Marriage* (Zhenit'ba, 1842). This piece only ran six nights that season, because the audience thought it was unfinished, and hissed (a fairly regular occurrence in the Imperial theaters, these being "the only place where the public could express its opinions.") However, it remained in the repertoire, and by 1861 had been performed over 120 times in both capitals. The relative failure of *Marriage* has shown producers that "it cannot be played as an ordinary comedy of manners, because behind the [front of a] Potemkin village are falsity and poverty of spirit," as a Soviet producer in Daghestan remarked (1975).

M. S. Shchepkin was instrumental in bringing about the debut of

I. S. Turgenev in the theater. In 1849, Shchepkin persuaded the directors and the Censor in St. Petersburg to accept both the three-act comedy *The Bachelor* (Kholostyak) and the one-act comedy *Luncheon at His Excellency's* (Zavtrak u predvoditelya). Turgenev's earlier, two-act comedy *A Charity Case* (Nakhlebnik, 1848) had been prohibited by the Censor because "the plot casts a shadow upon our gentry class" (heartless gentry taunt the impoverished "charity case"), and because "all the characters are heartless and despicable." Turgenev bore these remarks in mind when writing *The Bachelor*, but even so, the Censor cut references to the ownership of serfs and the use of the word "God" in oaths. Shchepkin himself took the part of the bachelor Moshkin, a poor clerk whose ward is jilted by an official because she is not "properly educated." However, it was withdrawn when Shchepkin returned to Moscow, as no one in St. Petersburg was competent to play the role. It has been revived from time to time.

During Turgenev's life, his one-act comedy *A Provincial Lady* (Provintsialka, 1851) was his most successful piece, because it "dealt with love and coquetry ... which are the essential elements of comedy." However, critics complained it was more of a comic episode, than a comedy. In the play, Darya Ivanovna, the provincial lady, aged twenty-eight, flirts with a Count who promises to arrange her husband's transfer to St. Petersburg; he then realizes she and her husband have been making fun of him. The part attracted such leading ladies as Marya Savina (1854–1915), who ruled the Imperial Theaters for thirty years, and chose *A Provincial Lady* for a benefit night in 1880, and again in 1900, for her 25th anniversary benefit. Savina also insisted upon the first production of *A Month in the Country* (Mesyats v derevne, 1855) in St. Petersburg in 1879, although the Imperial Theaters were not ready for it. (It had already been produced without success in Moscow, in 1872). Though published, the Censor objected to stage production partly because the young domestic tutor Belyaev, "a plebeian student," has attended "the political faculty" at Moscow University, where there was unrest at the time. It was revived infrequently (Savina appeared as Natalya Petrovna, aged twenty-nine, in St. Petersburg in 1903), and not until the Moscow Art Theater production in 1909, did critics begin to refer to Turgenev's "tender lyricism, gentlemanly delicacy, and aristocratic spirit." After the October Revolution, it was not produced in the Soviet Union until 1943: as a "psychological drama," rather than "a social comedy of manners."

When A. N. OSTROVSKY's three-act comedy *Don't Sit in a Sledge That Is Not Your Own* (Ne v svoi sani ne sadis') was given simultaneously in both capitals in 1853, it was an immediate success with 24 nights in St. Petersburg, and 31 in Moscow. Ostrovsky had already written several comedies, but this was the first to be permitted by the Censor, because Tsar Nicholas I had declared: "It is not a play, but a lesson in manners." Ostrovsky's next comedy *Poverty Is No Vice* (Bednost' ne porok, 1854) was even more successful, with its scenes of Russian manners and customs, songs, proverbs, and sayings, not to mention a heroine in muslin, with straight hair, instead of the conventional velvet and French coiffure. Ostrovsky "had revealed a country whose details are unknown, and have never been described." His use of language was striking, designed to persuade rather than impress. But the atmosphere prevailing in the early 1850s convinced Ostrovsky that satirical comedy was no longer possible in Russia. He turned to the SLAVOPHILE movement, with its idealization of patriarchal family life, old traditions, and some sentimentality, although critics now accused him of simplifying the "psychology" of his characters. But Ostrovsky preferred to depict Russians so that his audiences were pleased to see themselves on the stage, rather than upset. The Directors of the Imperial Theaters, and the Censorship, were hostile to Ostrovsky's plays from the start. His four-act comedy *We Aren't Strangers, We'll Square Our Accounts!* (Svoi lyudi—sochtemsya!), although published in 1850, was prohibited until 1861 (during a brief period of liberalization) on the grounds that "all the characters are villains," and "the entire play is an insult to Russian merchants." Likewise, the five-act comedy *A Profitable Position* (Dokhodnoe mesto) went into rehearsal at the Maly in 1857, but was suddenly withdrawn until 1863, when it ran for twenty-three nights in St. Petersburg.

By 1865, Ostrovsky's comedies were established as classics of the Russian stage in both capitals and especially in the provinces, although critics complained he was "written out," and repeating characters and plots ("We keep meeting the same old acquain-

tances"), and that he was out of touch with contemporary matters. Ostrovsky then turned to the writing of historical dramas.

In the 1870s, the older generation of actors who had established Ostrovsky's dramaturgy in the Imperial Theaters was dying out: Shchepkin died in 1863, Sadovsky in 1872, and Sosnitsky in 1873. Actresses began to dominate the Russian stage: in addition to the all-powerful Savina, there were M. I. Ermolova (1853–1928), G. N. Fedotova (1846–1925), and others. By 1900, the Aleksandrinsky company in St. Petersburg consisted of 54 actresses and 44 actors. Playwrights, including Ostrovsky, began writing parts with leading ladies in mind. But the leading ladies could be capricious: Savina never liked Ostrovsky's comedies, and refused to play in his four-act comedy *Slave Women* (Nevol'nitsy, 1880), because the part was "too old for her." Ostrovsky's last group of comedies began with the five-act *Wolves and Sheep* (Volki i ovtsy, 1875), his finest and last achievement in the satirical comedy of manners. Other comedies of the decade depict provincial actresses and provide parts for leading ladies.

Ostrovsky's comedies demanded a style of acting and production totally different from that of his contemporaries. They had no room for the hyperbole of Gogol nor even for the traditional round of applause which players in the Imperial Theaters expected after delivering a striking line or piece of "business." The conventional "pavilion" stage-sets fitted with two sofas, a table, some chairs and doors, and a chandelier, were totally inadequate. Ostrovsky demanded "truthful" settings, and "modest bourgeois interiors."

Audiences also changed. GONCHAROV said "The upper classes hardly know Ostrovsky," and remarked that audiences at his plays were often "unusual ... they wear galoshes and fur jackets." In fact they represented the second or third generation of the "merchant aristocracy of Moscow." These audiences remained faithful to Ostrovsky's plays and, despite official hostility and back-stage intrigues, the plays remained in the repertoire: by 1881, a total of 1,803 performances of Ostrovsky's plays had been seen at the Aleksandrinsky, and 1,003 in Moscow.

After Ostrovsky's death in 1886, critical comments became increasingly unfavorable: the 50th performance of *Don't Sit in a Sledge That Is Not Your Own* at the Maly in 1903 was said to be "too simplified, too didactic" for the time, and in 1909, A. I. Sumbatov-Yuzhin, director of the Maly, decided that "most productions of Ostrovsky no longer draw audiences." Other productions were described as "obsolete ... might safely be left in Ostrovsky's *Collected Works*." After the Revolution, however, Ostrovsky's works became "the artistic base for a new, revolutionary dramaturgy," and LUNACHARSKY's slogan "Back to Ostrovsky!" (1923) led to many revivals. In the thirties, his plays began appearing in Central Asia (Uzbekistan, 1938). In 1973, the 150th anniversary of his birth was celebrated by 15 productions across the Soviet Union, seen by 350,000 persons. Yet a revival of *We Aren't Strangers* at the Mayakovsky Theater (Moscow, 1974) caused "boredom to prevail in the auditorium," with "this tale of things long past, about a bankrupt merchant who offers his creditors ten kopecks on a ruble."

Although Ostrovsky's dramaturgy provided much of the Russian repertoire during the latter part of the century, a number of his contemporaries were also writing for the theater: A. V. SUKHOVO-KOBYLIN had his three-act comedy *Krechinsky's Wedding* (Svad'ba Krechinskogo) produced at the Maly in 1855. The Censor had banned it as "coarse" the previous year, but it was an immediate success, with thirty-six performances at the Maly and twenty-four at the Aleksandrinsky that season, and productions in the provinces. Critics declared there had been nothing like it since *The Inspector-General*. The players contributed greatly as always to the play's success: Shchepkin played Muromsky, P. M. Sadovsky was Rasplyuev, the "individual who has no right to exist," and S. V. Shumsky (1820–78) played Krechinsky. In St. Petersburg, Krechinsky was played by V. V. Samoilov (1818–72), who adopted a Polish accent entirely against the author's instructions, since Krechinsky is "a déclassé Russian gentleman." In the 1880s, the role of Rasplyuev was taken over by V. N. Davydov (1849–1925), who included it in his repertoire for the next forty years.

Krechinsky's Wedding is technically old-fashioned, like Ostrovsky's early comedies, with monologues, asides, and the traditional "mot à la fin." But, like Ostrovsky, Sukhovo-Kobylin recognized the importance of language in comedy, and his characters reveal themselves by what they say, as well as by their actions and appearance.

His comedy "introduced to the Russian theater a great number of new types, whose existence Gogol had not foreseen." By 1883, *Krechinsky's Wedding* had been played 168 times at the Maly. But the 1899 revival there failed, because the satire had become "alien to contemporary society," and the comedy was "basically an implausible anecdote." It has been revived in the Soviet Union. The "vaudeville situations" were emphasized at a Maly production in 1971. Musical versions were staged in Kiev in 1975, and at the Kuzbass Operetta in 1979.

Two years after the première of *Krechinsky's Wedding* a four-act comedy *Death of Pazukhin* (Smert' Pazukhina) was banned by the Censor "because all the characters without exceptions are liars, cheats, swindlers, and hypocrites" and the comedy "depicts the complete moral ruin of our society." The playwright, M. E. SALTYKOV-SHCHEDRIN, never wrote for the theater again, and the comedy was not produced for some thirty years, when it appeared in the provinces (Kharkov, Samara, Perm, Odessa). It reached the Aleksandrinsky in 1893, and was included in the repertoire of the Moscow Art Theater in 1914. It was last performed in the Soviet Union in 1927.

The Russian repertoire of the seventies and eighties was furnished by a number of competent hacks, skilled in devising effective situations and in providing players with roles which displayed their particular strength. Their well-made comedies stressed ingenuity and dexterity in construction; situations dominated characters and dialogue; and all their plays had big "scenes" and curtain lines meant to draw applause. But responsible critics, and even some players, despised such pieces. Unfortunately, their popular success deterred serious writers from writing for the stage.

The playwrights included V. A. Dyachenko (1818–76) whose comedy *The Domestic Tutor* (Guverner, 1864) was written for Samoilov. By 1878, it had been performed over 100 times in both capitals. His later comedies of family life dealt with unfaithful husbands and misalliances, but critics said he had "no principles," and could end a comedy with a liberal, or conservative, or patriotic phrase "to suit the climate of the day." A. A. POTEKHIN had a success with his four-act comedy *Tinsel* (Mishura) written in 1858 and produced in both capitals in 1862, where it remained in the repertoire until 1911. *Tinsel* exposes corrupt officials but, as DOBROLYUBOV wrote, "it might have been a major comedy, but Potekhin was not equal to the task." It was revived in the 1901 season, with Savina and Vera Komissarzhevskaya (1863–1910) in the cast.

The most prolific supplier of comedies, original or in translation, was V. A. Krylov. He was at the height of his fame in the Imperial Theaters in the 1880s, when 15 of his works were performed 1,500 times at the Aleksandrinsky. Over a period of some forty years, Krylov provided 120 "products," which critics unanimously condemned: Ostrovsky referred scornfully to his "kitchen," Sumbatov-Yuzhin called him "a clever fabricator," and Meyerhold described him as "a prolific dramatist, who overwhelmed the Russian stage with his wares." However, the all-powerful Savina found his plays to her liking (despite a notorious squabble she had with him) and appeared in at least thirty of them, in roles which required her to display "slyness and hypocrisy, coquetry and cajolery, pretended and real tears, laughter and grief."

Themes which interested Krylov, other playwrights, and audiences in the 1870s and 1880s included embezzlement, financial speculation, bankruptcy, theft of funds, malversions of financiers, and fashionable ladies of ill-repute, reflecting at least in the theater the rise of capitalism and its effect on Russian high society. An example was the four-act comedy *A Financial Genius* (Finansovyi genii, 1876) by A. F. PISEMSKY, first produced at the Maly but withdrawn after five nights because critics complained "all the characters were drawn from newspapers, not from life." Krylov was, in fact, skilled at turning sensational newspaper reports into plays. Nearly 30 years later, a five-act comedy *The Petrol Fountain* (Neftyanoi fontan, 1901) was produced at enormous expense at the Maly. The setting was the Caucasus, and the authors V. L. Veliko and M. G. Maro depicted wicked financiers attempting to embroil honest Russian officials in shady deals. It ran sixteen nights, largely on account of the settings.

In 1891, the critic Ivanov wrote: "Writers of comedy merely patch together some comic aspects of life, but have no idea how to create comic characters or situations. They insert comical little scenes to make the audience laugh ... and actors are forced to play in them, although they complain." By this time, however, new playwrights

were appearing: V. I. Nemirovich-Danchenko (1858–1943) wrote his first comedy *The Wild Rose* (Shipovnik, 1882) because he thought he could write something better than Krylov. It ran for eleven nights. In 1890, his comedy *New Business* (Novoe delo) had an unexpected success: Danchenko wrote it with character players in mind rather than leading ladies, and it "lacked powerful effects, such as hysteria, revolver shots, and swoons." Contemporaries regarded him as the heir of Ostrovsky at the Maly, but he turned to directing and teaching until 1894, when his four-act comedy *Gold* (Zoloto) was produced at the Aleksandrinsky, with Savina as the virtuous, wealthy Valentina Kochevnikova, who feels her wealth a moral burden, though neither she nor Nemirovich-Danchenko could decide how to dispose of it. Savina and the critics disliked the contrived happy ending (marriage), but agreed that refuge in a convent was not a solution either. His later comedies suffer from similar falsities and ambiguities.

A contemporary of Nemirovich-Danchenko was A. I. Sumbatov-Yuzhin (1857–1927), a leading player at the Maly (he played Chatsky in Griboedov's *Woe from Wit* for two decades from 1882). He became director of the Maly in 1909. His first success was *Husband of a Celebrity* (Muzh znamenitosti, 1884), dealing with the "problem" of whether an actress should retire from the stage when she marries. (The Imperial Theaters had this rule.) Sumptuously produced, it ran 47 nights at the Maly, and his next comedy *A Gentleman* (Dzhentel'men, 1897) was still more successful: a wealthy industrialist seeks to demonstrate his gentlemanly intellect and feelings, but is exposed as an oaf, as detestable as the *samodury* of Ostrovsky. Sumbatov's portrayal of frivolous society and his skill in devising dramatic or comic situations, reappear in his later comedies, which were produced splendidly at the Imperial Theaters—with countless tables and chairs, sofas, lamps, potted palms, staircases, French windows and the inevitable chandelier.

Both Sumbatov and Nemirovich-Danchenko were appointed to the "Theatrical Literary Committee" (T. K. L., established in 1858) in the nineties, as were Krylov and other popular writers. The Committee was an advisory body. In 1891, the members read 155 plays and rejected 116 as unsuitable for production. In 1895, they prevented the first production of Chekhov's *Seagull*. In 1905, they rejected thirty-five plays (out of sixty-eight). (A similar body currently functioning in the Soviet Union passed 706 plays submitted out of 2,175 in 1970.)

L. N. TOLSTOI's plays include four comedies of manners (1856, unfinished), and *An Infected Family* (Zarazhennoe semeistvo, 1864), in which he parodied the progressive ideas of CHERNYSHEVSKY's novel *What is to be Done?* Tolstoi submitted it to the Maly, but Ostrovsky had it rejected. Tolstoi later admitted Ostrovsky had been right. By 1890, Tolstoi's views had changed. In the four-act comedy *Fruits of Enlightenment* he depicted the empty, self-indulgent lives of Russian gentry—horse-racing, bicycling, spiritualist seances—as seen through the eyes of three peasants. At first, the Censor permitted amateur performances only because the comedy was a "caricature" of Russian gentry. Later it was produced at the Maly, as a conventional stage comedy, or "something by Krylov." Tolstoi protested but it was favorably received by audiences (fifty nights at the Aleksandrinsky by 1902). Critics, more discerning than audiences, praised the comedy as the first attempt in the Russian theater "to depict peasants genuinely attached to the soil." It was not staged as an "angry satire" until the Moscow Art Theater produced it in 1951. This production was later condemned as giving "a simplified and vulgar sociological interpretation."

V. N. Davydov (see above) played the third peasant in *Fruits of Enlightenment* and also appeared as Sorin in the first production of Chekhov's "comedy" *The Seagull* (Chaika) at the Aleksandrinsky in 1896. But Chekhov's comedy failed in St. Petersburg, partly on account of the stage direction by E. P. Karpov (1857–1926), who staged it like a comedy by Krylov, with the conventional "pavilion," sofas, tables, and chairs, and chandelier. The players learned their parts conscientiously, wore their best clothes and glued on mustaches when required.

After *Three Sisters* (1901) had been produced, Chekhov declared he had meant to write "a vaudeville in four acts," though the play was defined variously as a drama, or scenes from country life, and told Olga Knipper and STANISLAVSKY he had been written "comic parts" for each. *The Cherry Orchard* (1904) was not only a comedy "but, in places, a farce." Chekhov thought it more comical than *Three Sisters* and inquired why it was announced as "a drama"? The presence of vaudeville elements in Chekhov's plays is self-evident, although producers make them "tearful." However, by the 1920s, the Moscow Art Theater productions of his plays were "no longer tearful and sentimental, and audiences laughed more."

After 1917, playwrights in the Soviet Union frequently resorted to satirical comedy to attack many of the same aspects of contemporary society as their 19th-century predecessors had done, and were often as schematic in their portrayal of vices and faults as playwrights of the 18th century, even to the use of speaking names. Targets included careerism and bribe-taking in the State apparatus (A. Sofonov's *A Career*), bureaucracy (A. Bezymensky's *The Shot*, 1929, a comedy in verse commended by Stalin in 1930 as a "model of revolutionary art"), or the cowardice and ignorance of rural clergy (A. Neverov's *Laughter and Woe*, 1923, depicting Soviet life in 1919 sympathetically). Settings ranged from turbine or shoe factories to collective farms, or workers' Homes of Rest.

Vaudeville retained its popularity, though such pieces were often criticized as "unreal, conventional." V. Kataev's *Squaring the Circle* (1928) observes Chekhov's criteria for a successful vaudeville. V. Shkvarkin's *Someone Else's Child* (1933), which revolves around overhearing and misunderstanding, remained in the repertoire of the Moscow Theater of Satire for a decade, and was revived in the 1970s (with 260 performances in eight theaters in 1973).

"Comedy" was officially defined as an optimistic play, and the early comedies of N. F. Pogodin were well received: his *Tempo* (1929) had 100 performances in the 1930 season. "Lyrical comedy" included V. Gusev's *Spring in Moscow* (1940) which remains in the Soviet repertoire.

Official attacks on the repertoire of Soviet theaters occurred in 1946, when playwrights (e.g., Zoshchenko) and directors were accused of yielding to Western influences (Brandon Thomas' farce *Charley's Aunt* and J. K. Jerome's *Miss Hobbs* were perennial successes on the Soviet stage and productions of Somerset Maugham were in rehearsal). In 1952, the aftershock of Zhdanov's attack on the state of Soviet literature caused writers to avoid comedy: that year only one new comedy was produced: Kakhkhar's *On New Ground* (Na novoi zemle). Critics and audiences have complained for decades of the lack of "good" Soviet comedies, which has been especially apparent in the repertoire of the Moscow Theater of Satire, which has been described as "shallow ... the dramaturgy of anecdotes." Preoccupation with questions of genre has resulted in the production of such things as the "comedy-grotesque," "prologue and epilogue to a historical comedy," or "comedy in six parts." In answer to a questionnaire in 1977, a number of playwrights agreed that "dramaturgy is something flexible," so that the Soviet repertoire contains "comic tragedies" and "tragic farces." Those participating agreed that Korneichuk's *Front* (1942) is the outstanding example of a comedy in the best tradition, with its "grotesque, hyperbolic satire".

Bibliography: P. N. Berkov, *Istoriya russkoi komedii XVIII v.* Leningrad, 1977. Yu. Dmitriev *et al. Istoriya russkogo dramaticheskogo teatra v semi tomakh.* 1977, in progress. V. Frolov, *O sovetskoi komedii.* Moscow, 1954. Harold B. Segel, *Twentieth Century Russian Drama.* New York, 1979. Elizabeth Warne, *The Russian Folk Theatre.* The Hague, 1977. David Welsh, *Russian Comedy 1765–1823.* The Hague, 1966. Peter Yershov, *Comedy in the Russian Theatre.* Trans. T. Zuber. New York, 1956. D. W.

Comparative-historical method, see Folklore, Study of; Scholarship, Literary.

Conflictless literature (*beskonfliktnaya literatura*)—a term illustrative of the difficulties involved in reconciling quasi-Marxist theory with Soviet realities. About 1940 Soviet philosophers discovered that since "socialism" had been officially achieved, Soviet citizens for the first time in history lived in a society free of class conflict. This raised important theoretical problems. After the war some enterprising literary critics seized upon this promising idea and developed the "theory of conflictlessness." It runs as follows. Literary conflict, the source of plot interest, reflects social conflict. Social conflict is class conflict. In the USSR, however, class conflict has been eliminated. Ergo: literature—at least literature on contemporary themes—

cannot reflect conflict in the full sense. Only remnants are left, for instance, the clash between the "good" and the "excellent." Essentially the job of Soviet literature is to exult. "We need a holiday literature," one critic wrote, a literature that "lifts a person above trifles and contingencies."

Even before Stalin's death, however, the Party bosses had begun to worry about the lack of public response to official literary edification. Much praised novels lay unread in bookstores; theaters showing contemporary Soviet plays were half empty. The hapless critics who had thought up the theory of conflictlessness were chosen as scapegoats. No, no, the Party now insisted: Soviet life is not conflictless at all; it is full of heroism and struggle. Reflecting this struggle, Soviet literature must not "prettify" (*priukrashivat'*) reality nor cover up "contradictions." But of course non-typical, negative aspects of Soviet life must not be overstressed either.

The "theory of conflictlessness" was denounced as early as 1954 at the second Congress of Soviet Writers, and it is now defunct, a verbal symbol of the excesses and absurdities of the Stalinist past. The problem of literary freedom, however, and of public indifference to a didactic, "managed" literature, is very much alive.

Some relevant bibliography is cited in the (unsigned!) article "Beskonfliktnosti 'teoriya'" in the *Kratkaya literaturnaya entsiklopediya* (Vol. 1. pp. 577–80), which provides a good illustration of the verbal adroitness required to discuss this taboo-ridden topic in the Soviet press. H. McL.

Constructivism. The term was initially applied to a movement in the visual arts which developed under the influence of Picasso's "constructions" (relief forms from various materials). Russian sculptors and painters, such as Naum Gabo (1890–1978), Ivan Pougny (1894–1956), and Vladimir Tatlin (1885–1953) developed this technique, sometimes in suspended three-dimensional arrangements of nonrepresentational nature, while El Lissitzky (1890–1941) and others translated it into similarly non-objective three-dimensional geometric graphics. After the October Revolution the Russian constructivists volunteered their skills to the new regime, offering to apply them to utilitarian ends in industrial and commercial design. An offshoot of constructivism in the visual arts were the stage sets of Meyerhold's theater, such as Lyubov Popova's famous constructivist design (1922) for *The Magnificent Cuckold* by Fernand Crommelynck. Meyerhold's own principle of biomechanics, by which he proposed to convert his ensemble into a maximally effective mechanism geared to infuse the audience with proper social attitudes ("sociomechanics") was another constructivist idea.

In literature, constructivist ideas were advocated and applied mainly by the Futurists who eventually gathered around the journal Lef. Their theorists, such as Boris Arvatov and Osip Brik, advocated and their leading poet Vladimir Mayakovsky created utilitarian art, pointedly simplified and geared to be maximally functional. Significantly, *Lef* cultivated modern mass media (newspaper, film, radio, billboard advertising) as outlets of their work. Mayakovsky's essay "How to Make Verse" (1926) is "constructivist" in a general sense.

Constructivism in literature acquired a more specific meaning with the emergence of the *Literary Center of Constructivists* (Literaturnyi tsentr konstruktivistov or LTsK) in 1924. Among its members were E. G. Bagritsky, V. M. Inber, V. A. Lugovskoi, I. L. Selvinsky, and K. L. Zelinsky, among others. Zelinsky, the theorist of the group, developed a principle of constructive distribution of material with a maximal functional load per unit (he called it *gruzifikatsiya slova*, lit. "loadification of thw word"). The underlying idea was that the ever-growing complexity of the modern world made it progressively more difficult to grasp its meaning. The artist's job was to reduce this complexity to simple formulas and present these to the masses in an intelligible and provocative way. While none of the constructivists were very successful in this respect (in A. N. Chicherin's verse such literary reductionism led to non-objective poetry, not what the movement at large had in mind), another principle developed by Zelinsky, called the "local method" (*lokal'nyi priem*), found some practical application. It amounted to an integration of every level of a work (sound, rhythm, imagery, lexicon, syntax) with its intended meaning, i.e., a pointedly functional approach to composition. The poets Bagritsky and Selvinsky successfully applied this principle in their verse, using slang, regionalisms, local color, the rhythms of folk song, etc., when the theme of a poem would demand it. However, only Selvinsky applied this principle with any consistency.

Constructivist ideas reached their final stage in the aesthetics of *New Lef* (1927–30). Assuming that the old, imaginative literature was now only a vestige of the bourgeois past, the writers, artists, and film makers of *New Lef* claimed that the socialist present and future belonged to reportage, "factography," to the documentary and the newsreel—to art dealing with real life directly. Writers such as TRETYAKOV and SHKLOVSKY, film makers such as Sergei EISENSTEIN and Dziga Vertov, artists such as Aleksandr Rodchenko seriously tried to translate these ideas into practice. The staging of Mayakovsky's plays *The Bedbug* (1929) and *The Bathhouse* (1930) at Meyerhold's theater was a last gasp of the aesthetics of *Lef*. The *Literary Center of Constructivists* and *Lef* both ceased to exist in 1930.

Bibliography: Boris Arvatov, *Iskusstvo i proizvodstvo*. 1926. *Biznes. Sbornik Literaturnogo tsentra konstruktivistov*. 1929. John E. Bowlt, "Russkii konstruktivizm i khudozhestvennoe oformlenie stseny," *Novyi zhurnal*, no. 126 (1977), pp. 109–27. Herman Ermolaev, *Soviet Literary Theories, 1917–1934*. Berkeley, 1963. *Gosplan literatury. Sbornik Literaturnogo tsentra konstruktivistov*. 1925. *Literaturnye manifesty: Ot simvolizma k Oktyabryu*. Vol. 1. 2d ed. 1929. Reprint Munich, 1969. Pp. 258–64. K. Zelinskii, *Poeziya kak smysl. Kniga o konstruktivizme*. 1929.   V. T.

Contemporary, The, see SOVREMENNIK.

Contemporary Annals, see SOVREMENNYE ZAPISKI.

Content and form. The dichotomy of "content" vs. "form" has stood in the focus of Russian aesthetic and critical thought ever since BELINSKY put it there, having acquired it from German idealist aesthetics (Hegel's *Gehalt* and *Form*). For Belinsky and his followers it is one of several ways in which the dialectic quality of the work of art manifests itself. It often merges or overlaps with the "ideal" and the "real," the "universal" and the "particular," the "typical" and the "individual," "creation" and "craft," and other dialectic pairs. A work of art consists of form, whose excellence depends on the artist's talent, and content, whose value lies in its objective sociohistorical importance. Form and content are understood to be inseparable (the "body" vs. "soul" analogy is often used to underscore this). Hence it would be wrong to identify content with subject matter, intention, *sujet*, or plot, much as form is not identical with poetic devices, structure, or canon. Content, in Belinskian criticism, is subject to the historical process, while form belongs to the individual artist's genius. PUSHKIN, the poet of an as yet unformed national consciousness "is the equal of any poet in the world as far as form is concerned, while in his content he cannot stand comparison with any of the poets of world stature" (V. G. Belinsky, "Russian Literature in 1841," *PSS* 5, pp. 558). Belinsky also started a long-lasting trend in Russian criticism, to approach the work of art from the side of content rather than form, even while insisting on their unity. Russian literary criticism has been guided mostly by a Hegelian *Gehaltsästhetik* rather than by a Kantian *Formästhetik*.

In the utilitarian, naturalistic, and materialistic aesthetics of CHERNYSHEVSKY and his followers, form was separated from content, and content now meant that aspect of the work of art which reflected nature, and form the more or less superfluous niceties and embellishments added by the artist. The importance of form was downgraded accordingly, and critics such as DOBROLYUBOV were apologetic about giving any attention at all to details of dramatic or novelistic structure, versification, imagery, and style, all relegated to the domain of form.

This trend was reversed in SYMBOLIST aesthetics, which returned to the notion of an organic unity of content and form. Vyacheslav IVANOV's conception of a *forma formans* (an equivalent of the Plotinian *endon eidos*, Shaftesbury's and Goethe's "inner form") sees the creation of a work of art as the unveiling of an ideal vision through the artist's craft. While this conception (cultivated also by some of the leaders of the avant-garde, such as Kandinsky and Malevich) implied the presence of an ideal content in the work of art, the formalist aesthetics of Russian FUTURISM, CONSTRUCTIVISM, and other groups of the avant-garde limited the artist's and critic's concern to that aspect of the work of art which heretofore had been called form. Content and form were united once more, but now with a heavy emphasis on form.

The various schools of MARXIST-LENINIST AESTHETICS returned to the Belinskian (= Hegelian) dialectic conception of the creative process as a realization of an ideal content (*ideinoe soderzhanie*) in an artistic form (*khudozhestvennaya forma* or *khudozhestvennyi obraz*). The historicist component of this conception is, however, changed to say that in all true art a new historical content must generate new artistic forms. Like Belinsky's, Russian Marxist-Leninist aesthetics is content-oriented. Form is seen as a means to express content and only as such is given a right to exist. "Formalist" art is considered nonart. While Marxist-Leninist theorists insist on the unity of content and form, critical practice commonly follows a procedure once called "FORMALISM in reverse" by Konstantin FEDIN: ideological content is discussed at length, while *sujet*, structure, composition, and style are given a few perfunctory observations at the end of a review. There is, however, no agreement among Soviet aesthetic theorists regarding the question whether or not all elements of form (proportion, symmetry, rhythm) were at one time appropriated by man in the process of social labor, and hence, to what extent these elements may be an organic part of content.

Bibliography: Edward M. Swiderski, *The Philosophical Foundations of Soviet Aesthetics: Theories and Controversies in the Post-War Years*. 1979. Pp. 92–96. Victor Terras, "Content and Form," In *Belinsky and Russian Literary Criticism*. 1974. Pp. 142–45.   V. T.

Cosmic poetry, "Cosmism" (*kosmicheskaya poeziya, kosmizm*). While cosmic imagery plays a significant role in Russian classicist (LOMONOSOV, DERZHAVIN) and romantic (TYUTCHEV, FET) poetry, it is hardly pervasive or massive enough there to allow one to speak of a "cosmic" genre. In romantic poetry, elementary (air, water, earth, fire) as well as cosmic (the sun, the firmament, the stellar universe) imagery appear routinely as mystic symbols of man's affinity to the cosmos ("the inner sky," "the inner ocean," "the inner sun"), much as they do in romantic literature in the West. The same is true of Russian SYMBOLISM. Only in Vyacheslav IVANOV does the role of cosmic themes occasionally assume striking proportions. In Russian FUTURISM, cosmic themes and cosmic imagery assumed a central role, as signalled by Aleksei KRUCHONYKH's spectacle *Victory over the Sun* (1913) and poems by KHLEBNIKOV such as "The Lightning Sisters" (Sestry-molnii, 1919–21) or "Break-in of [or: "into"] the Universe" (Vlom veselennoi, posthumous). Khlebnikov wrote a number of poems whose message is one of a symbolic identity of language and cosmos, e.g., "Scratching the Sky: A Breakthrough into Languages. A Fusion of Stellar and Ordinary Language" (Tsarapina po nebu: Proryv v yazyki. Soedinenie zvezdnogo yazyka i obydennogo, 1922). In MAYAKOVSKY, cosmic imagery, as prevalent as in Khlebnikov, is mostly straightforwardly allegoric or of the order of Wellsian science fiction. But grandiose visions in which the poet's persona experiences cosmic events are found in "The Backbone Flute" (1915), "Man" (1918), and "About That" (1923). "Cosmism" came into its own in the revolutionary poetry of the first few years of the Soviet regime. In the revolutionary hymns of poets belonging to the PROLETCULT movement, such as Vasily ALEKSANDROVSKY, Ivan Filipchenko (1887–1939), Mikhail GERASIMOV, Vladimir KIRILLOV, and others, the October Revolution was treated as a cosmic event, with the appropriate imagery. Mayakovsky did likewise in his *poema* "150,000,000" (1919) and in his allegoric spectacle *Mystery-Bouffe* (1918).   V. T.

Country prose (*derevenskaya proza*), a term applied to a genre of post-THAW literature which deals in a sympathetic way with rural life and with people who are not in the mainstream of organized, Party-controlled, production-oriented life. The two mainsprings of this genre are, on the one hand, compassion with the social misfit or underdog and his alienated view of modern society, and on the other, a feeling that the very backwardness of a peasant unaffected by Party ideology and modern ways may have allowed him to retain certain values (Christian, or even pre-Christian, universally human) to which modern man is insensitive. An example of the former would be Vasily BELOV's short novel *That's How Things Are* (Privychnoe delo,

1966), and of the latter, SOLZHENITSYN's short story "Matryona's House" (Matrenin dvor, 1963). Both have of course many precursors in pre-revolutionary Russian literature, from DAL and GRIGOROVICH to TOLSTOI and CHEKHOV.

The *derevenshchiki* of the post-Thaw period, such as Aleksandr YASHIN, Vladimir SOLOUKHIN, Vasily BELOV, Fyodor Abramov, Sergei ZALYGIN, Vasily SHUKSHIN, Valentin RASPUTIN and others, differ from the "peasant writers" of the 1920s in that they take a detached view of their subjects, never pretending that the implied author himself shares their worldview or their alienation. But a wistful undertone in many of these works suggests that the author's compassion is mixed with a sense of loss. Soviet country prose has succeeded in circumventing the canon of SOCIALIST REALISM, creating a world that is both hauntingly real and intensely challenging to the principles of official socialism. As far as the art of fiction is concerned, country prose generally follows the tradition of Chekhov's understated impressionism, slice-of-life type plots, and low-key dialogue.

Bibliography: Deming Brown, *Soviet Russian Literature since Stalin.* 1978. Geoffrey Hosking, *Beyond Socialist Realism: Soviet Fiction since Ivan Denisovich.* 1980. E. Starikova, "Sotsiologicheskii aspekt sovremennoi 'derevenskoi prozy'," *VLit* 16 (1972), no. 7. Georg Witte, *Die sowjetische Kolchos- und Dorfprosa der fünfziger und sechziger Jahre.* Munich, 1983. (With bibliography.) Gleb Zekulin, "Aspects of Peasant Life as portrayed in contemporary Soviet Literature," *CASS* 1 (1967), no. 4.   V. T.

Criticism, see LITERARY CRITICISM.

Cubo-Futurism, see FUTURISM.

Cyrillic is one of the two oldest alphabets of the Slavs which has come down to us in Old CHURCH SLAVONIC texts of the 11th century (the *Codex Suprasliensis, Savvina kniga*), in the earliest (9th and 10th century) Slavic inscriptions (on stone, birch bark, and objects of usage) and in the oldest Russian-Church Slavonic manuscripts (the *Ostromir Gospel* of 1056–57). The name of the alphabet honors the first Slavic Apostle, St. Cyril, who was actually the inventor of the earlier and more complex GLAGOLITIC which Cyrillic replaced in time among all Orthodox Slavs. Until 1860 it was also used by the Orthodox Rumanians, and after the October Revolution it was adopted (with various modifications) by various non-Slavic minorities of the Soviet Union.

The Cyrillic alphabet consisted originally of 43 letters, 24 of which were based on the Greek uncial (capital) letters that were used in the 9th and 10th centuries; the other letters represent adaptations of Glagolitic and of some Greek letters (e.g., the letter Б). The breakdown of Old Church Slavonic into Church Slavonic recensions and the expansion of their literary functions gave rise to new typographic conventions, while the formation of national Slavic languages brought about changes in the number, shape, and phonetic value of individual Cyrillic letters. The oldest Cyrillic ductus (called *ustav*), which was used primarily in writings of a liturgical character, was soon complemented by the *poluustav* which rounded up the shape of the letters and introduced a greater number of abbreviatures and accent marks. This ductus, which was employed in a wider variety of religious texts, was, in turn, complemented by the *skoropis'* (cursive) which found its way into all kinds of ecclesiastical and secular writings. The East Slavic (or "Russian") *skoropis'* developed two variants of its own: a northeastern (or "Moscow") variant and a more ornamental western ("Lithuanian") variant. The earliest Slavic books were printed in all three types of ductus, though their use varied according to country; thus the *ustav* was used by the presses of Warsaw, Vilnius, and Prague, while the *poluustav* was favored in Russia until the introduction of the *graždanskij šrift* (in 1708). In addition to simplifying the shape of the letters, the Russian alphabet acquired in the 18th century three additional letters (й, э and ё). Further simplifications were introduced by the 1917 orthographic reform which dropped the use of several letters (v, ı, θ , ѣ) and eliminated the writing of the final ъ. The Slavic languages with recent literary status (Serbo-Croatian, Bulgarian, Ukrainian and Macedonian) have each modified the original alphabet by reducing its number, by assigning new values to some traditional letters and by adding letters suitable to their phonological systems. Even more drastic changes have been introduced into the Cyrillic alphabet of those non-Slavic languages of the Soviet Union which borrowed it from Russian.

Bibliography: L. V. Cherepnin, *Russkaya paleografiya.* 1956. H. Jensen, *Die Schrift in Vergangenheit und Gegenwart. Die slavischen Schriften.* Berlin, 1958. Pp. 460–74. E. F. Karskii, *Slavyanskaya kirillovskaya paleografiya.* 1928.   E. S.

Dactyl, see SYLLABOTONIC VERSIFICATION.

Dal (Russ. Dal', Danish Dahl), Vladímir Ivánovich (1801–1872), writer (mostly under the pseudonym "Kazak Lugansky") and scholar. The son of a physician of Danish and of a mother of German background, Dal received his early training from his mother and from private tutors. Later he was sent to the Naval Cadet School of St. Petersburg from which he graduated in 1819. He served for a period in the Russian fleet of the Baltic and the Black Sea. In 1826, Dal began to study medicine on a government grant at the University of Derpt (now Tartu). As a military physician he participated in the campaigns against Turkey (1828–29) and Poland (1831–32). His career at the Military Hospital in St. Petersburg was cut short by professional disagreements with his superiors. He resigned from medical practice and took an administrative position with the Ministry of the Interior in Orenburg Province. He served in similar positions in St. Petersburg and Nizhny-Novgorod until he retired in 1859. At that time he moved to Moscow and devoted his remaining years to the process of sorting and publishing his rich collections of proverbs and lexicological materials.

Dal attracted the attention of other writers by his first literary work, *Russian Fairy Tales—First Group of Five* (Russkie skazki—Pyatok pervyi, 1832). During a time when prose writing in Russia was still largely imitative of foreign models (French and English), this collection of Russian fairy tales, highly stylized by the invention of a folk narrator, was hailed as an imaginative and original contribution to Russian belles lettres by such writers as PUSHKIN. His work was seen as a product of native Russian genius, artistically transformed. Thus, Dal early in his artistic career distinguished himself as a man who drew his inspiration from Russian folklore rather than from literary sources. The same tendency of seeking inspiration in the life of simple Russian people revealed itself in his "physiological sketches" which he wrote in the forties and which critics regarded as exemplary samples of that widely practiced form of writing in Russia.

While Dal was a skilled observer, he lacked talent in developing a story and creating psychological depth for his characters. He was basically not an artist but a collector and recorder of native Russian culture. He was interested in the wealth of the Russian language, and he began collecting words while still a student in the Naval Cadet School. Later he collected and recorded proverbs, fairy tales, folk songs, birch bark woodcuts, and accounts of superstitions, beliefs, and prejudices of the Russian people. His industry in the sphere of collecting was prodigious. Much of what he gathered he turned over to other specialist collectors and under his own name published only *On the Beliefs, Superstitions and Prejudices of the Russian People* (1845–46), *Proverbs of the Russian People* (1862) and the *Reasoned Dictionary of the Living Russian Language* (Tolkovyi slovar' zhivogo veliko-russkogo yazyka, 1863–66), in four volumes. While an excellent collector, Dal had some difficulty ordering his material, and his so-called alphabet-nest system was not completely satisfactory until Baudouin de Courtenay revised it thoroughly in the third (1903–10) and fourth (1912–14) editions of the *Dictionary*.

Dal has his place in the history of Russian literature of the first half of the 19th century; but his unique contribution to Russian culture rests in the single-handed compilations of the *Proverbs* and his four-volume *Dictionary*, unsurpassed to this day for regionalisms and dialectal expressions.

Works: Polnoe sobranie sochinenii. 10 vols. 1897–98. *Tolkovyi slovar' zhivogo velikorusskogo yazyka.* 4 vols. 1955–56. (Reprint of 1880–82 2d ed.) *Poslovitsy russkogo naroda.* 1957.

Secondary literature: J. T. Baer, *Vladimir Ivanovich Dal' as a Belletrist.* The Hague, 1972. ———. "Vladimir Ivanovič Dal'—Collector and Recorder of Native Russian Culture," *Welt der Slaven*

22 (1977), pp. 225–41. M. Kankava, *V. I. Dal' kak leksikograf.* Tbilisi, 1958. V. Porudominskii, *Dal'.* 1971.　　　　J. B.

Daniél, Yúly Márkovich (pseudonym: Nikolai Arzhak, 1925–), prose writer, poet, and translator. Daniel first attracted attention to himself in the early 1960s when he used the pseudonym of Nikolai Arzhak to publish four satirical stories abroad without the permission of the authorities: "Hands," "This Is Moscow Speaking," "The Man from MINAP," and "The Atonement."

"Hands" tells of an executioner working for the secret police. The man's hands shake after his bullets are replaced with blanks when he is supposed to execute a priest. He believes a miracle has occurred and is discharged from the *Cheka*. "This Is Moscow Speaking" is a fantasy in which the government declares a "Day of Public Murders" and permits random murder. "The Man from MINAP" is a light-hearted farce in which a man is described as a hero for being able to control the sex of his offspring by imagining during intercourse either Karl Marx or Klara Zetkin. "The Atonement" deals with the guilt of those who knew of the political terror and did nothing about it.

Daniel's identity was discovered by the authorities, and in a 1966 trial, widely discussed in the Western press, he was sentenced to five years at hard labor. His co-defendant in the trial was Andrei SINYAV-SKY. Daniel was released in 1970 and ultimately permitted to return to Moscow, where he works as a translator. In 1971 he published abroad a collection of verse containing twenty-one rather conventional poems describing his experience in the forced-labor camps. Daniel's literary output has, for reasons beyond his control, been very small.

Translations: The Man from M.I.S.P. Trans. M. V. Nesterov. London, 1967. *This is Moscow Speaking, and other stories.* Trans. Stuart Hood, Harold Shukhman, and John Richardson. Foreword by Max Hayward. London, 1968. *Prison Poems.* Trans. David Burg and Arthur Rogers. Chicago, 1972.

Secondary literature: Margaret Dalton, *Andrei Siniavsky and Julii Daniel': Two Soviet "Heretical" Writers.* Würzburg, 1973.　　J. G.

Daniíl, Abbot, author of the oldest (early 12th century) example of pilgrimage literature (*palomnicheskaya literatura*, that is, literature of the "palmists," because the pilgrims often returned home with a palm branch from the Holy Land). Very little is known about Daniil. He was the abbot of a monastery in southern *Rus'*, probably in the principality of Chernigov. He undertook a journey to the Holy Land in the years 1104 to 1106 (or 1106 to 1108), a period when Palestine was occupied by the Crusaders and ruled by King Baldwin. During his sixteen-month stay in the Holy Land, Daniil was permitted to visit many places to which access was usually forbidden. His impressive retinue and the respect shown to him by King Baldwin have led some scholars to conclude that Daniil was not an ordinary pilgrim but had gone to Palestine in some official (diplomatic or ecclesiastic) capacity. Upon his return to *Rus'*, Daniil wrote the *Zhit'e i khozhen'e Danila Rus'skyya zemli igumena* (The Life and Pilgrimage of Daniil, Abbot of the Russian land).

Daniil's *Pilgrimage* was extremely popular in the Russian lands— approximately 150 manuscripts which contain the work (dating from the 15th-19th century) have come down to us. The popularity of the *Pilgrimage* derives from Daniil's ability to combine detailed descriptions of the Holy Places with legendary and apocryphal motifs. (For a time the *Pilgrimage* was listed in the index of forbidden books.) Daniil's adherence to the general scheme of pilgrimage literature does not cause him to lose sight of his Russian audience. He looks at Jerusalem and other Holy Places with "Russian eyes." It is also noteworthy that Daniil makes reference to a unified, undivided "Russian land," a rare occurrence in 12th-century *Rus'*.

Daniil's faithful exactitude and geometric precision confer upon his language a marked poetic effect. The language of the *Pilgrimage* has attracted the attention of many scholars, especially because of its documentation of local linguistic variants on both the lexical and morphological levels (e.g., embryonic articular use of the demonstrative pronoun).

Bibliography: V. V. Danilov, "K kharakteristike 'Khozhdeniya' igumena Daniila," *Trudy Otdela drevnerusskoi literatury,* 10 (1954), pp. 92–105. L. A. Dmitriev, and D. S. Likhachëv, *Pamyatniki literatury drevnei Rusi: XII vek.* 1980. K. Seeman, *Die altrussische Wallfahrtsliteratur. Theorie und Geschichte eines literarischen Genres.*

Munich, 1976. M. A. Venevitinov, *Zhit'e i khozhen'e Danila Rus'-kyya zemli igumena 1106–1108 gg.* (Pravoslavnyi palestinskii sbornik III [I, 3] and IX [III, 3].) St. Petersburg, 1883–85. Reprint *Slavische Propyläen.* Vol. 36. Munich, 1970. P. Zabolotskii, "Legendarnyi i apokrificheskii element v Khozhdenii ig. Daniila," *Russkii filologicheskii vestnik,* 41 (1899), nos. 1–2, pp. 220–37 and 3–4, pp. 237–73.　　H. G.

Daniíl, Metropolitan (?–1547). A central figure in the religious and political life of Muscovite Russia. A disciple of IOSIF VOLOTSKY, Daniil became abbot of the Volokolamsk monastery in 1515. As a protégé of the Muscovite prince Vasily III, he was appointed (without church sanction) metropolitan of "All *Rus'*" in 1522. After the death of Vasily III in 1533, the boyars who ruled the country deposed Daniil in 1539 and banished him to the Volokolamsk monastery, where he spent the remaining years of his life.

Daniil's struggles with both intransigent Orthodox believers such as the "Non-Possessors" (*nestyazhateli*) and various heretical movements such as the "Judaizers" (*zhidovstvuyushchie*) are clearly reflected in his theoretical and polemical writings. Among his principal adversaries (and victims) were MAKSIM GREK and Vassian Patrikeev. His works include: a *Council Book* (sobornik) containing sixteen "Orations" (slova); a collection of fourteen *Epistles* (poslaniya); and many other epistles and "instructions."

Daniil's writings represent an invaluable source of information for both religious and cultural historians. Given the wide variety of styles he uses, and his lexical and thematic innovations, they are equally important for literary historians. In particular, Daniil's vehement condemnation of vice and corruption in the customs of 16th-century Muscovy provides us with a unique picture of certain elements of society (such as SKOMOROKHI, drunkards, astrologists, and magicians) which hitherto had remained beyond the bounds of literary etiquette.

Secondary literature: I. D. Belyaev, "Daniil mitropolit Moskovskii," *Izvestiya Otdeleniya russkogo yazyka i slovesnosti Akademii nauk* 5 (1856), pp. 195–209. I. U. Budovnits, *Russkaya publitsistika XVI v.* 1947. V. Zhmakin, *Mitropolit Daniil i ego sochineniya.* 1881. A. A. Zimin, *Rossiya na poroge novogo vremeni.* 1972.　　H. G.

Daniíl, zatochnik, see MOLENIE DANIILA ZATOCHNIKA.

Danílov, Kírsha, see BYLINY

Davýdov, Denís Vasílievich (1784–1839), poet, ARZAMASIAN, memoirist, military theorist. Davydov was hailed as one of the finest prose writers and most original poets of his time. The son of a high-ranking army officer who fell afoul of the autocracy, Davydov himself was never fully trusted in official circles. Nevertheless, after taking part in battles against the French, Swedes, Turks, Persians, and Poles and after proposing and conducting successful partisan warfare against Napoleon's armies, he reached the rank of lieutenant-general. As in his poetic career, genuine ability combined with an extraordinary gift for self-promotion.

Davydov practiced all of the "small" genres of the KARAMZINIAN school, but he is remembered mainly as the "hussar-poet"—maker of a series of epistles, songs, and satires whose lyric hero is a fiery hussar who celebrates vodka, women, and song on the eve of battle. In their intimate thematics and intonations, these lyrics break with the tradition of the 18th-century battle ode; but their abrupt transitions and use of military jargon represent a departure from the harmonious salon style of his friends' (BATYUSHKOV'S, ZHUKOVSKY'S) verse. Nevertheless, he retained the admiration of these poets. His exuberant, conversational manner and endearing self-irony served as an important precedent for the youthful work of A. S. PUSHKIN and N. M. YAZYKOV.

The anonymous third-person biographical sketch that Davydov crafted (1828, 1832) and used as a preface to his collected works establishes a persona to match this style—the gentleman-poet and gentleman-soldier of simple pleasures, high enthusiasms, and inevitably quick successes. The liberties that Davydov took in his verses and in his military activities made him an attractive figure during the repressive 1820s and 1830s, and his works were published both in the BIBLIOTEKA DLYA CHTENIYA and in Pushkin's SOVREMENNIK. His military behavior made him a useful model for the partisan Denisov in TOLSTOI's *War and Peace*.

Works: Polnoe sobranie stikhotvorenii. Introd. V. M. Sayanov and B. M. Eikhenbaum. 1933. *Sochineniya.* Introd. and ed. V. Orlov. 1962.

Translations: "The Song of an Old Hussar." In Charles Fillingham Coxwell, *Russian Poems.* Introd. D. Mirsky. 1929. "Wisdom." In John Bowring, *Specimens of the Russian Poets with Preliminary Remarks and Biographical Notices.* 2d ed. 1821.

Secondary literature: G. A. Gukovskii, *Pushkin i russkie romantiki.* 1965. Pp. 147–61. I. M. Semenko, "Denis Davydov." In her *Poety pushkinskoi pory.* 1970. Pp. 95–120. W. M. T.

Decadence. A literary current which originated in France and had its florescence in Russia after the turn of the 20th century. It drew on some morbid and antisocial elements found in the works of Charles Baudelaire, Paul Verlaine, Joris Karl Huysmans, and, to some extent, Oscar Wilde. In Russia decadence both predated and succeeded SYMBOLISM, with which it was inextricably intertwined at its height. Decadence was the name most often given to Russian symbolism in its early years, and, indeed, most Russian symbolists, including the nominal maître d'école, Valery BRYUSOV, made use of decadent elements in their work. Russian decadence was characterized by aestheticism, sensationalism, and religious perverseness. Compared with Western decadence it had less of dandyism, insouciance, and the deliberate cultivation of the trivial; it was relatively more solemn and metaphysical, as was also true of Russian symbolism. Decadence met with more opprobrium in Russia than in France, not only on the part of utilitarian critics, but on the part of some symbolists, who wished at times to disassociate themselves from any imputation of moral degeneracy.

Decadence had an ample preparation in 19th century Russian poetry, if not in prose. Its principal subject since mid-century had been a melancholia which ascended to romantic irony, and which had been fed by political frustrations that could scarcely be examined (given the censorship). Allusions to decline were commonplace. Parnassianism had been effectively excluded, and a reaction against social commitment had already appeared, for example, in the transitional poetry of N. MINSKY and Dmitry MEREZHKOVSKY. Fantasies of an animated nature (as in Oscar Wilde) had already appeared in the poetry of Konstantin FOFANOV, and a real break with tradition had occurred in the feminine sensuality of Mirra LOKHVITSKAYA's verse.

The mid-nineties brought a flood of symbolist works, both in prose and poetry, which contained decadent elements. Investigations of pathological states appeared, as well as statements of a metaphysical pessimism; in time Nietzsche's influence brought a defiant amoralism and somewhat doctrinaire defenses of aestheticism. Konstantin BALMONT was the first successful decadent; his *Under Northern Skies* (Pod severnym nebom, 1894) introduced a causeless, splenetic melancholia, and his subjects in his next several books included Satanism and wider expressions of religious unease and frustration. After the turn of the century he abandoned sorrows for a pantheistic élan, pictured himself as a god-like superman who derives his strength from the cosmos and is guided only by inclinations "beyond good and evil"; *Let Us Be Like the Sun* (Budem kak solntse, 1902) contains examples. Fyodor SOLOGUB was the second popular decadent. His short stories in *Shadows* (Teni, 1896) depict schoolchildren who suffer from delusions and escapist reveries. The protagonist of his novel *Bad Dreams* (Tyazhelye sny, 1896) owes his morbid visions to Huysmans's hero Des Esseintes in *A Rebours*. Sologub's verse revealed, in addition to these themes, a desire for death. In the new century his verse reflected a pessimism which recalled both Gnosticism and Schopenhauer, and in some poems he posed as a solipsist who has created both good and evil. His imaginative imagery included depictions of Satan, witches, and other mythic representations of evil. A poet who was considered the quintessential decadent by other members of the symbolist movement, although little known to the public, was Aleksandr DOBROLYUBOV, who published *Natura naturans. Natura naturata* in 1895.

Other symbolists of the 1890s in whose works decadence played a large role were Valery Bryusov, Dmitry Merezhkovsky, and Zinaida HIPPIUS. Bryusov brought out a series of three miscellanies called *Russkie simvolisty* (Russian symbolists, 1894–95) which were imitative of Baudelaire and Verlaine, to some extent of Arthur Rimbaud. Bryusov's own, immature poetry adumbrates the notion that evil prevails in the world through human passions and lust for cruelties. His "scandalous" subjects included sexual desire and sadism. In his later verse Bryusov discovered in himself an amoral dedication to art. In *Tertia vigilia* (1900) he admires artists for their capacity to create beauty from earthly material, both good and evil. His short stories in *The Earth's Axis* (Zemnaya os', 1907) picture pathological states and cultural cataclysms. Merezhkovsky and Hippius were the center of a group aspiring to a Christian renovation of Russian culture, yet their work was also colored by decadence. A novel by Merezhkovsky called *The Outcast (Julian the Apostate)*—Otverzhennyi (Yulian-Otstupnik)—depicts not only a rejection of Christianity but "pagan" sensuality and barbarous customs as a philosophical revelation about human nature. Hippius' verse displayed religious struggles and a watery, or dusty, scenery that was typical of decadence.

With the new century an optimism, usually transient, entered the symbolist movement and resulted in a puristic tendency. But the political disillusionment which followed the failure of the Revolution of 1905 fostered a renewal of decadence. Vitalities, such as they were, now poured into a cultural brilliance. Sologub achieved fame with a grotesque satire of the Russian provinces called *The Petty Demon* (Melkii bes, 1907). Two young symbolists who had been sanguine in their metaphysical, or mystical, hopes now turned to decadence. Aleksandr BLOK, who had epitomized the idealist current in *Verses About the Beautiful Lady* (Stikhi o Prekrasnoi Dame, 1905), now symbolized the new spirit of irony, especially in his lyric dramas, *The Fair Show Booth* (Balaganchik, 1906) and *The Unknown Woman* (Neznakomka, 1906), which ridicule mystics; the same tendency appeared in his lyric poems. Andrei BELY turned to self-laceration and cultural despair in the verse of *Ashes* (Pepel, 1909) and *The Urn* (Urna, 1909); in his novel *Petersburg* (1916) he satirized both symbolism and the revolutionary expectations of 1905.

In the first decade of the new century there existed also an aesthetic decadence among writers who were akin to symbolism, but who lacked its mysticism. Foremost among them was the poet Innokenty ANNENSKY. He was a more genuine heir of Baudelaire, Verlaine, and Mallarmé than were the Russian symbolists in that he was attentive to the elusive, entranced by the beauty of artificial objects, loved art, especially evocative music, for its own sake, and preferred a showy, languorous nature. He was modern in his resignation to alienation. A writer who was devoted to delicate, attenuated, fragile, and cultural forms of beauty was Mikhail KUZMIN; he sometimes wrote of homosexual loves, as in the novel *Wings* (Kryl'ya, 1907). In his life he cultivated the dandyism, and in his poetry the airiness, which Russian symbolism shunned.

Decadence survived symbolism in some currents of the avant-garde, particularly of FUTURISM. The ego-futurist manifestos showed that faith in the efficacy of intuition that was an underpinning of all decadence. The cubo-futurists, particularly Vladimir MAYAKOVSKY, developed a brash new style of dandyism. Decadence has never claimed an entire era, it is always the dark side of epochs with more positive aspirations.

Bibliography: Evelyn Bristol, "Idealism and Decadence in Russian Symbolist Poetry," *SlavR* 39 (1980), no. 2, pp. 269–80. Georgette Donchin, *The Influence of French Symbolism on Russian Poetry.* The Hague, 1958. Vladimir Markov, "K voprosu o granitsakh dekadansa v russkoi poezii (i o liricheskoi poeme)." In *American Contributions to the Eighth International Congress of Slavists, vol. 2: Literature* (1978), pp. 485–98. Renato Poggioli, *The Poets of Russia. 1890–1930.* 1960. E. Br.

Decembrism, the sociopolitical literary trend of the romantic movement associated with the revolutionary conspiracy that culminated in the revolt of 14 December 1825. The terms Decembrist and Decembrism were devised later from the month of this, the first modern revolution, which became a symbol to later Russian revolutionaries. The conspiracy originated in the national trauma of the Napoleonic invasion of 1812 and the subsequent European campaigns that brought the Russian masses into contact with Europe. The conspiracy was first projected in discussion groups formed by young officers in Paris in 1814, and developed through several secret societies modeled on the German *Tugendbund* and FREEMASONRY. In the early 1820s the conspiracy became better organized in two groups, the Southern Society in the army near Kiev and the Northern Society in Moscow and Petersburg. The former was generally committed to a plan for a republican form of government, the latter to a constitutional monarchy. A radical wing which cut across both societies pursued the example of the French Revolution, a moderate wing was drawn to the ideal of the American Revolution. Never a mass movement, Decembrism was composed of idealistic army officers, noblemen, and intellectuals embittered by the failed promise of the liberal reforms of Alexander I, the backwardness of the feudal serfage system, the tyranny of the autocracy, and the corruption of the government. The Decembrists wrote treatises for the reform and modernization of Russia, plans for reorganization, and a constitution, and critiques of the tsarist system. The Decembrists agitated among the soldiery, but devoted most of their efforts to recruiting from their own class. They considered expulsion and even extermination of the imperial family, and several attempts were made to assassinate Alexander I. Too often, their revolutionism was expressed at champagne and oyster banquets where they sang revolutionary songs by PUSHKIN, A. A. BESTUZHEV (Marlinsky), and K. F. RYLEEV. During the interregnum following the unexpected death of Alexander I two hastily contrived revolts occurred, one in the south, the other on Senate Square in Petersburg. Caught by surprise, the Decembrists of the Northern Society set their revolt for 14 December, and were quickly suppressed by Nicholas I. Five of the leaders were hanged, the others were exiled to Siberia or transferred to the Caucasus. Russian culture was shattered by the removal of many of the brightest, most idealistic talents from active participation in national life and by the compromise of many others.

Literary Decembrism is variously defined and termed. Among the most common terms are Decembrist romanticism, civicism, Decembrist civicism, and Decembrist romantic civicism. The terms indicate the difficulty of defining a contradictory socio-political literary phenomenon. Most narrowly defined, it comprises only those actual members of the conspiracy who were literarily active and whose works expressed the ideals they were attempting to realize through political action. This definition implicates K. F. Ryleev as the conspiracy's most ardent proponent in both literature and action, A. A. Bestuzhev as a leader of the conspiracy and a literary propagandizer, V. K. KYUKHELBEKER and Prince A. I. ODOEVSKY as members of the conspiracy and cultivators of Decembrist themes, and N. A. and M. A. Bestuzhev as minor writers and active conspirators. This definition is usually broadened to include those sympathizers and fellow travelers who were generally aware of and even privy to the conspiracy and cultivated similar socio-political or civic themes in their works. Drawn in here are Pushkin, Prince P. A. VYAZEMSKY, A. S. GRIBOEDOV, N. M. YAZYKOV, P. A. KATENIN, and others who were cleared of complicity but nevertheless compromised by their sympathies. Also drawn in by this definition are such men as N. I. GRECH and F. V. BULGARIN who were close to the conspiracy but later became active supporters of the government. This creates a problem of distinguishing between Pushkin and the other literary aristocrats who wrote revolutionary songs and verses before 1825 and the literary plebeians Grech and Bulgarin who, however conservative, even reactionary, they became after 1825, were undeniably liberal in their literary and political activities of the early 1820s. The problem is complicated even further by drawing in virtually every romantic writer who cultivated socio-political themes and was associated in any way with the Decembrists. Literary Decembrism thereby becomes so broadly defined as to include the metaphysical romantics V. F. ODOEVSKY and D. V. VENEVITINOV, the loyal poet-hussar Denis DAVYDOV, and the poet A. I. POLEZHAEV who suffered for his post-1825 literary expressions of Decembrist sympathies.

Soviet scholars take Literary Decembrism very seriously as the most important trend of the romantic movement. The trend has been thoroughly studied, particularly by V. G. Bazanov in two books titled *Essays on Decembrist Literature*. Study ranges from the broadest consideration of any literary work that can be in any way interpreted as "progressive" or "revolutionary" to carefully defined distinctions of socio-political phenomena. The general view is that Literary Decembrism is a demand for original, passionate, lofty, and free creativity, including fullest expression of the ideals of patriotism and love for freedom. The slogan used for this literature is "national in form and civic in content." Literary Decembrism calls for "national-historical distinctiveness in poetry" and equates this with the concept of

NARODNOST'—native pride, national originality. It is devoted to the national past and thus to the cultivation of folklore, legends, chronicles, and all other available sources of historical themes. Literary Decembrism makes the assumption that literature has political value, even that literature and politics are identical. It is a literature of protest and revolution, and of sympathy for the people. It is democratic in both political and social terms.

The frequently used synonym civicism (*grazhdanstvennost'*) originates in the Decembrist ideal of civic Rome, dreams of a republic, and perception of the poet as a patriotic citizen. Civicism implies a literature of opposition to established authority, a yearning for individual freedom and dignity, a desire for equality and justice, a call for national originality and a glorification of the national past, a hatred of serfage and an attempt to enlighten the masses, an emphasis on democracy and the democratic past as represented by Novgorod. The civic ideal was most obviously expressed by Ryleev in the line, "I am a citizen, not a poet." Decembrist civicism is a romantic trend, and thus largely excludes the civic poetry of the 18th-century Neoclassicists and the later civicists of the realist period.

Literary Decembrism grew out of the national trauma of 1812, was shattered by the failure of the revolt of 14 December 1825, and existed thereafter only in anonymously published works of the surviving conspirators and covert, disguised reaffirmation of Decembrist ideals in the works of sympathizers. The trend reached its peak in the years 1823 to 1825 with the publication of the three annual issues of the literary almanac POLYARNAYA ZVEZDA edited by Ryleev and Bestuzhev. The literary-political platform of the almanac was enunciated in the "Glance" (vzglyad) at ancient and current Russian literature written by Bestuzhev as a preface to each issue. The editors emphasized socio-political works and managed to get several strong civic statements past the censors, but their first concern was to publish the best available works of the best poets and writers. In this they were successful until obliged to compete with SEVERNYE TSVETY, the almanac of the Pushkin pleiad. Among the chief concerns of the editors were the modernization of the Russian literary language and its liberation from the pernicious influences of the French language and its Neoclassical dictates; the championing of the "spirit of the time" in literature, which is to say an emphasis on content over form in romantic poetry; a preference for the style, as opposed to the political views, of the great national historian N. M. KARAMZIN's pro-autocracy *History of the Russian State*; cautious opposition to the prestigious older poets of the Karamzinian sentimental-elegiac school, more open opposition to the metaphysical romantics' Schellingian faith in poetry as philosophy, and outright rejection of outmoded Neoclassicism. The national past was glorified as a prelude to the post-1812 yearning for freedom and democracy. Byron was adored.

The genres of Literary Decembrism were conventionally Romantic, as were language and devices of prose and verse, but at least one form is so strongly identified with civic poetry as to be its unique specialty. This is the short historical poem known as the DUMA or "meditation," cultivated most successfully by Ryleev. Modeled on a late 17th-century Ukrainian song form, and introduced to the Russians from the Polish romantics by F. V. Bulgarin, the *duma* is a verse of varying lengths which celebrates and is titled after a hero of the national past interpreted as a leader of the people who expresses the "spirit of the time" at a crucial historical moment. In Ryleev's hands the *duma* was a lofty genre imbued with patriotic fervor and love of freedom. Ryleev preferred martyred heroes who bravely and selflessly sacrificed themselves in a noble cause. He chose for his subjects the ancient hero Svyatoslav who died rather than set off another fratricidal struggle for power in Kievan Rus, Boyan who sang of Igor's campaign, Dmitry Donskoi who defeated the Tatars, Prince KURBSKY who defied Ivan the Dread, and Nataliya Dolgorukaya who died a victim of Catherine's envy.

Literary Decembrism is remarkable for its high idealism and the poet's sense of his own lofty mission. The civic poet is at once an admirer of the past and a would-be liberator of the present. This comes out with particular force in Ryleev's historical verse tales *Nalivaiko* and *Voinarovsky*. In the latter work Voinarovsky, nephew of the hetman of the Ukraine, Mazepa, overcomes his misgivings about treason and gives himself to the cause of Ukrainian independence. In the former work Ryleev celebrated the hetman of the Cossacks who died for his people's freedom in the 16th century:

I know: destruction waits
For him who rises first
Against the people's oppressors;
I know that fate has chosen me,
But where, pray tell, and when
Has freedom been gained without cost?
Yes, I will perish for my homeland—
I feel this, I know it. . . .

In an ode titled "Civic Courage" Ryleev likens patriotic rebels to Aristides, "illuminated by glory," in whose heart "a love for the common good, a love for his fellow citizens" never perished, "neither in exile, nor in distant lands."

Not all the Decembrists were as committed as Ryleev. His close associate Aleksandr Bestuzhev shared his convictions, but hardly with such force. As the most popular writer of the time, especially in the 1830s when he was allowed to publish under the pseudonym Marlinsky, Bestuzhev was the "instigator" of the romantic prose tale in Russia. He created magnificent heroes out of the past, as in the patriotic tale "The Raiders," the historical tale à la Scott "Tournament at Reval," and the Novgorod legend "Roman and Olga." In the latter tale young Roman, aided by robbers, saves democratic Novgorod from autocratic Moscow and wins the hand of the beautiful Olga. Bestuzhev's historical heroes are also villains, however, as is the case with the main character of "The Traitor," Vladimir Sittsky, who betrays Russia out of envy of his popular brother, his lust for power, and his pitiful longing for admiration. Bestuzhev's tales of Livonian history, "Wenden Castle," "Neuhausen Castle," and "Eisen Castle," are Gothic tales of terrible vengeance, and even the tale from Russian history "Gedeon" is Gothic in its theme of bloody revenge. In his post-Decembrist tales Bestuzhev created civic heroes who are often beset by doubt, whatever their commitment to lofty ideals and love for their homeland. "The Frigate Hope," an 1832 tale of a naval captain who deserts his ship for an illicit love affair, and dies knowing he has failed both his love and his duty, is a psychologically painful confession of the author's own guilt. Even the hero of "Ammalat-Bek," Bestuzhev's most exotic and positive hero of the tales of the 1830s, is a man beset by terrible conflicts of loyalty which lead to death and dishonor.

A very popular genre of the civic trend is the revolutionary song, one of the strongest and most poignant forms of protest. Ryleev and Bestuzhev coauthored a series of "Agitational Songs" which were very well known to their fellow conspirators and others. One of these songs, "Tell me, say, how tsars are murdered in Russia," mocks the assassination of Paul I and other royal victims of palace revolts in the 18th century. "Our Tsar is a Russian German" satirizes the Romanov family and ridicules Alexander I in a strong jeering rhyme, "Ay-da Tsar, ay-da Tsar, Orthodoxy's Star!" It is hard to decide whether the "Agitational Songs" are more valuable for their political sensationalism or their rollicking cadence and lusty slang. "Akh, it makes me sick" is an attack on the banality and brutality of the autocracy in the language of serfs. The song complains of "Russian lords" who "rob us shamelessly" and "strip our skins." Russian landowners are "thieves, fleecers, they suck our blood like leeches."

The revolutionary song was cultivated far beyond the confines of Decembrism strictly defined. This and other political-satirical verse genres were favored by poets right up until the post-1825 suppression. Very early in the century the hussar-poet Denis Davydov wrote several ringing satires and songs against Petersburg society and the army command, and in the late 1830s he wrote a bitter invective under the title "Hungry Cur." Among authors of revolutionary songs and verses were P. A. Katenin, N. M. Yazykov, and P. A. Vyazemsky. Some of the most extreme political views were expressed by Pushkin in the early 1820s, most notably in "Liberty. An Ode," "Noel. Hurrah," and "The Dagger." The ode "Liberty" is addressed to "the menace of tsars, the singer of proud freedom." When Pushkin casts his eye over Russia he sees "everywhere scourges, everywhere irons, the destructive shame of laws, the impotent tears of slavery, everywhere unjust power." In "The Dagger" Pushkin celebrates Brutus, Marat, Charlotte Corday, and Karl Sand. He praises "the secret guard of freedom, the avenging dagger, the final arbiter of shame and insult."

After 1825 Literary Decembrism sounded notes of great despair.

Understandably, it was the Decembrists themselves who expressed the deepest regret and disillusionment. Indicative here are the verses written by A. I. Odoevsky while incarcerated in the Peter-and-Paul Fortress in Petersburg, and the sad poetry of exile written by V. K. Kyukhelbeker in Siberia. Undoubtedly the finest poetry of lonely exile belongs to Bestuzhev who expressed both regret and hope in many verses of the late 1820s while in Yakutsk. Among the best of these are "To a Cloud," "Shebutui," and "The Bark." In the latter poem Bestuzhev likens his life to a bark floating down a dark river between looming banks. Better known is Pushkin's post-Decembrist expression of his fate as a fellow-traveler of the Decembrists, "Arion." Despair and loss of hope frequently resulted in bitter contemplations of an inhuman Russia, and even outright denunciations of Russian backwardness. Typical here is D. V. Venevitinov's post-Decembrist poem "Homeland," in which he renounces all hope of change:

Dirt, villainry, stench, and cockroaches,
And over all the master's knout—
And this is what many fools
Call "our sacred homeland."

Hope was not fully lost, however, and faith in the ideals of Decembrism did not vanish. In 1827, in his "Message to Siberia," Pushkin reaffirmed his allegiance to his fallen friends and sent them words of hope:

Deep in your Siberian mine,
Keep your patience proud,
Your bitter toil is not in vain,
The rebel thought unbowed.

One year later the exiled Decembrist poet A. I. Odoevsky replied by expressing continued defiance and his comrades' faith that their example would live on:

Our bitter toil is not in vain,
Our spark shall light the fire again,
And an enlightened Russian nation
Shall heed proud freedom's inspiration.

Bibliography: V. G. Bazanov, *Ocherki dekabristskoi literatury: pubitsistika, proza, kritika.* 1953. ———. *Ocherki dekabristskoi literatury: poeziya.* Moscow, 1961. L. G. Leighton, *Russian Romanticism: Two Essays.* 1975.

L. G. L.

Délvig, Antón Antónovich (1798–1831), poet. Baron Delvig—the scion of a thoroughly Russified Baltic German family and no aristocrat, despite the title—is remembered not only as A. S. PUSHKIN's schoolmate and closest friend, but also as editor of the splendid almanac SEVERNYE TSVETY and of the newspaper LITERATURNAYA GAZETA, and as the maker of Neoclassical idylls and "folk" romances.

Delvig developed his genuine gift for the poetry of friendship, love, and sensuous delight in a variety of St. Petersburg's amateur literary assemblies—the Lycée at Tsarskoe Selo, the A. N. Olenin circle, the salons of S. D. Ponamareva and Z. A. Volkonskaya, the "GREEN LAMP," and the "FREE SOCIETY OF LOVERS OF RUSSIAN LITERATURE." Delvig and his wife themselves conducted a salon that attracted such prominent writers as Pushkin, GNEDICH, ZHUKOVSKY, KRYLOV, and GOGOL. Good-natured and indolent—his "laziness" was not merely a literary convention—Delvig was most unsuited to the demands of professional literary life of the 1830s (vicious polemics, publication deadlines, harsh censorship), and the *Literaturnaya gazeta* proved a commercial failure. Legend blames Delvig's early death on either domestic unhappiness or harsh treatment by the Chief of Gendarmes, Benkendorf. Pushkin called this death the end of an era.

However careless his editing and social behavior, Delvig was a meticulous craftsman of difficult meters and of such verse forms as the sonnet, the epigram, and the elegy. Inspired throughout his brief career by the classicism of the late DERZHAVIN and of BATYUSHKOV, Delvig created his own masterpieces in a series of idylls, especially "The Bathing Women" (Kupal'nitsy, 1825), "Friends" (Druz'ya, 1827), and "The End of the Golden Age" (Konets zolotogo veka, 1829), that are remarkable for their precise diction, fluent hexameters, and concreteness of imagery. Several of his "Russian Songs," such as "Nightingale, my Nightingale" (Solovei moi, solovei, 1826) have been set to music and have survived in this medium.

Works: Polnoe sobranie stikhotvorenii. Ed. B. Tomashevskii. Introd. I. Vinogradov and B. Tomashevskii. 1934. *Polnoe sobranie stikhotvorenii.* Ed. and introd. B. V. Tomashevskii. 1959.

Translations: See Lewanski, p. 227.

Secondary literature: L. Koehler, *Anton Antonovič Del'vig: A Classicist in the Time of Romanticism.* The Hague, 1970.

W. M. T.

Den' poézii (Day of Poetry), an annual almanac, published since 1956 by the publishing house *Sovetskii pisatel'* (Soviet Writer) in Moscow. It includes primarily poetry by contemporary poets who live in the capital, up to 200 authors in each issue. Publication of the almanac was initiated by V. Lugovskoi. In the course of the following twenty-five years, M. Lukonin, V. Fyodorov, V. Bokov, S. Kunyaev, A. SURKOV, E. VINOKUROV, Yu. Drunina, A. Zhegulin, L. Vasilieva (1979, 1980), A. Peredreev (1981), and others have acted as chief editor. *Den' poezii* ordinarily prints its authors in alphabetic order. Occasionally, special sections are assigned to prose appendices, materials from the archives of Russian poetry, propaganda texts occasioned by the celebration of certain anniversaries, etc. From time to time, *Den' poezii* will publish the works of "forgotten" or "repressed" poets, such as A. AKHMATOVA, M. TSVETAEVA, B. PASTERNAK, M. KUZMIN, N. KLYUEV, O. MANDELSHTAM, M. VOLOSHIN, and others. The twenty-five issues of *Den' poezii* which have appeared so far offer some interesting material toward a survey of tendencies in and the evolution of contemporary Soviet poetry.

In the mid-1950s, after the death and exposure of Stalin, Soviet poetry began to revive after twenty-five years of stagnation and total absence of any genuine poetic activity (those who printed poems in praise of Stalin and the "happy" life of Soviet people from the 1930s to the 1950s cannot be considered as poets, and the true poets who survived these years, such as Akhmatova, Pasternak, and ZABOLOTSKY, were almost entirely silent). Immediately after the 20th Congress of the CPSU, which had sanctioned a modicum of intellectual freedom (as compared to the days of Stalin), the poetic column of Soviet literature quickly reacted to the mood of the day. The central organs of the USSR, such as *Pravda, Izvestiya,* etc., began to publish quite routinely verses of sharply topical interest and the Soviet readership developed an interest in poetry, which they had ignored in the years of Stalin's rule. Also, it became customary to hold annual "days of poetry," when poets would appear at book stores and communicate with their readers. Very quickly, these meetings, which were attended by more and more people, turned into public appearances of poets in clubs, on city squares, in stadiums, drawing crowds of up to 75,000. It was in connection with this development that *Den' poezii* was established as an annual almanac. Similar almanacs, though not regularly (as in Moscow), appeared from time to time in Leningrad, Kursk, Petrozavodsk, Dyushanbe, and other places.

The first few issues of *Den' poezii* featured the names of poets of the older, pre-War generation: N. ASEEV, P. ANTOKOLSKY, D. Kedrin, V. Lugovskoi, M. SVETLOV, I. SELVINSKY, N. TIKHONOV, A. Prokofiev, etc. However, the "war" poets dominated, of course: M. ALIGER, E. Dolmatovsky, M. Isakovsky, S. SHCHIPACHOV, M. Lukonin, V. INBER, L. Oshanin, etc. Among them there were some who rather boldly catered to the moods of the "THAW" and in their quest for popularity found genuinely exciting themes and images (E. Vinokurov, B. SLUTSKY, K. Vanshenkin, O. BERGGOLTS, M. Lvov, A. TVARDOVSKY); others, apparently distrustful of the permanence of these new trends, continued their sterile "poetic" propaganda and, unsuccessful with readers and listeners alike, ceased being perceived as poets and proceeded to engage in other "genres," mostly administrative (A. Surkov, N. Gribachov, A. Sofronov, etc.)

The mid-1950s signal the birth of the so-called "poetic avant-garde," i.e., young poets who entered the literary scene largely after the death of Stalin: E. EVTUSHENKO, A. VOZNESENSKY, B. AKHMADULINA, R. KAZAKOVA, Yu. Morits, B. OKUDZHAVA, N. MATVEEVA, etc. Precisely this group of poets, unencumbered by the ghosts of Stalin's oppression, was able to seize upon the ideas of the "Thaw" quickly, temperamentally, and with talent. Their various forms of poetic interpretation of these ideas gained them immense popularity among their audiences, young audiences in particular. A. Voznesensky at one time defined this process profoundly and with fine poetic touch: "We are drawn to verse, as one suffering from scurvy is to grass, /

And joyfully, and timidly our souls begin to flower." It must be stated that between 1956 and 1962 the "poetic avant-garde" played a huge role in liberating Soviet youth from the deadening, thoroughly mendacious, and depressing propaganda "poetry" of SOCIALIST REALISM. For the first time since many years of Soviet rule poets were again *believed.* However, the editors of *Den' poezii* were in no hurry to open their pages to authors of the "poetic avant-garde." Thus, in the issue of 1958, E. Evtushenko, who had already published several volumes of his poetry and was particularly popular at mass recitals, was not represented; and neither was B. Okudzhava, whose songs were sweeping the country in tape recordings; Yu. Morits, whose "Discourse on Happiness" (Razgovor o schastii) had disappeared from bookstore shelves in a few minutes, was not there, either. A. Voznesensky, who had not as yet published a volume of his verse, but had become famous through his *poema* "Masters" (Mastera), printed in the *Literary Gazette,* was represented in the 1958 issue of *Den' poezii,* but by four entirely unsuccessful poems.

In the mid-1950s, an "anti-avant-garde" (I. Kobzev, E. Asadov, E. Isaev, A. Markov) also made its appearance. Its poetic specialty was to fight against so-called "nihilism," in defense of old revolutionary and Party dogma.

The issues of *Den' poezii* dating from the early 1960s, at the height of Khrushchevian liberalism, are the most poignant. In those years the proportion of young poets, leaning more and more toward the "avant-garde," and of poets of the older and the war generation changed significantly. The "poetic avant-garde" now occupied the place which rightfully belonged to it by virtue of its popularity, and more and more new names joined it: M. Borisova, M. Pavlova, R. ROZHDESTVENSKY, T. Zhirmunskaya, etc. This wave was followed by a second, more "nihilist" wave, whose renunciation of the socialist-realist past was bolder, and whose search for new poetic forms was more active. These were the so-called poets of the journal *Sintaksis,* some of whom occasionally made the pages of *Den' poezii:* V. Burich, I. Kharabarov, I. Belosinskaya, E. Kotlyar, etc. However, in the collections of those years political themes were still dominant, themes which then moved the whole country. Evtushenko's famous poems "Baby Yar" and "Stalin's Heirs" quite naturally never appeared in *Den' poezii,* but then the lines of a little known poet of the war generation, M. Lvov, gave unexpected encouragement to the whole country: "They carry out the sarcophagus. / They carry out the sarcophagus. // This is how history / puts leaders in their place. // No flag waves over him. / No flag weeps over him. // Nobody sheds tears. / Nobody gives him praise." (*Den' poezii,* 1962)

By the mid-1960s, after Khrushchev's fall, the collections of *Den' poezii* reflect the complex processes of the development of contemporary Russian poetry. To begin with, older dogmatists and the war generation for a while seized full control over the publication of poetic production. This is particularly obvious in the issue of 1964 which, neglecting alphabetic order, begins with the names of A. Prokofiev, N. Gribachov, and N. Tikhonov. Further on, "dogmatists" are obviously given precedence and only the most "quiet" among the young are given a place, while the most popular part of the avant-garde (Voznesensky, Evtushenko, Akhmadulina, Okudzhava, etc.) is absent. The second half of the 1960s shows little change: the "avant-garde" is hardly admitted to *Den' poezii,* but from time to time, new names of young poets make their appearance: V. SOSNORA, G. Gorbovsky, O. Chukhontsev, N. Korzhavin, and N. RUBTSOV. The so-called "Russophiles," such as S. Kunyaev and F. Chuev are clearly gaining in numbers. For a while, A. TARKOVSKY, a poet very popular among the young generation, author of profound meditations and a talented as well as intelligent craftsman, disappears from the pages of *Den' poezii.* However, two other poets gain a foothold there: N. Tryapkin, a poet of Russian nature of some originality, and V. SHALAMOV, known for his tragic fate as a 20-year prisoner of *GULag.*

By the end of the 1960s and the early 1970s, the "poetic avant-garde" gradually returns to *Den' poezii.* However, its members have clearly lost some of their poetic élan. Evtushenko went off into the major didactic genre ("Bratsk Hydro-Electric Plant"), while Voznesensky apparently sensed the end of the avant-garde charge, which had spent itself effectively killing Stalinite dogmatic poetry. Aside from this struggle for overcoming the past, the "avant-garde" had no spiritual banner that might have inspired poetic thought and feeling.

Far from gratuitously and with great pathos, Voznesensky asserted in 1973 that "Man lives by the Heavens alone." But his readers did not see those "Heavens" in Voznesensky's poetry and his popularity rapidly declined.

The early 1970s were in general a kind of "poetic desert" in contemporary Russian poetry (at least as far as its open, published part, represented by *Den' poezii*, was concerned), even though from time to time new and interesting names did appear: Yu. Kublanovsky (1975, 1981), E. Rein (1972, 1975), V. Vysotsky (1975, 1981), etc. A large number of poets, including even some who were actively publishing in the USSR (not mentioning those who dared to publish abroad), were not admitted to *Den' poezii* during those years. Such were A. KUSHNER, V. SOSNORA, G. Gorbovsky, etc. It was precisely during those years that *outside* Soviet poetry, *outside* its officially recognized status (participation in *Den' poezii* was exactly a sign of such status), another powerful and varied tendency developed in contemporary Russian poetry: I. BRODSKY, D. BOBYSHEV, A. GALICH, N. Korzhavin, Z. Afanasieva, E. Ignatova, Yu. Karabichevsky, V. Krivulin, O. Okhapkin, S. Stratanovsky, I. Burikhin, etc. All of these are poets of different degrees of talent, different age, and different personal histories, but they are united by one thing: official nonrecognition by the Union of Soviet Writers. By the end of the 1970s, the influence of this, officially unrecognized poetry is visibly on the rise, while *Den' poezii* continues to be the organ of three generations of Soviet poets: the older (of the 1920s and 1930s), the War generation (the 1940s and 1950s), and the avant-garde of the 1960s. To be sure, in addition to these, the last collections (1980, 1981) have begun to introduce more often and more substantially texts of so-called "old masters": O. Mandelshtam, N. Klyuev, M. Kuzmin, etc. In 1982, a jubilee edition of *Den' poezii* appeared: "A Selection, 1956–1981" (Izbrannoe, 1956–81). It reflects, more or less objectively, the evolution of Soviet poetry during those past twenty-five post-Stalin years. However, it has left out a whole poetic generation, that of the 1970s. Poets of that generation, published largely either abroad or in *Samizdat*, express quite different feelings and thoughts, and search for their own poetic forms.   E. D. A.

Derevenskaya proza, derevenshchiki, see COUNTRY PROSE.

Derzhávin, Gavrĭla Románovich (1743–1816), poet, statesman, and soldier. Born near Kazan, in a household of poor landowners, tutored in childhood by incompetents, Derzhavin entered the substandard Kazan high school in 1759 (at the time the second, after Moscow, in all the Russias) and, without finishing it, was called to serve in 1762 as a private with the Preobrazhensky Guards regiment in St. Petersburg. From these inauspicious beginnings, Derzhavin rose to become one of the most powerful and controversial government officials during the reign of Catherine II while at the same time justly earning his laurels as the greatest Russian poet of his day.

Derzhavin served in the ranks until 1772, when he finally received an officer's commission. While cleaning stables and saddling horses, he also dreamed of Pegasus, tried his hand at poetry and was noticed by the literati of St. Petersburg, among them MAIKOV, NOVIKOV and even TREDIAKOVSKY. When the Pugachev rebellion exploded in the Southeastern steppes, Derzhavin, a native of these parts, became an intelligence officer in the Imperial army, served with distinction, though not without controversy (he was accused of insubordination) until 1775, and received his discharge in 1777, with the rank of lieutenant colonel, on a fair-sized estate granted to him by the Empress.

While at war, Derzhavin continued to court the Muses and in 1774 wrote his first significant poetry, the so-called "Chitalagai odes" (published in 1776) among which the "Ode on the Death of General Bibikov," the Supreme Commander of Imperial Forces against Pugachev, stands out for its pathos and meditative lyricism in the presence of death. Back in civilian life, he gained the patronage of the powerful Prince Vyazemsky, obtained a good post in the Senate and was married in 1778. His wife, one of the three Dyakov sisters, helped bring him into the literary and personal companionship of the playwrights and poets KAPNIST and Lvov, husbands of the other two. Some of Derzhavin's basic views as an artist began to take shape in the intellectual exchange among the three writers, all of whom were inclined to turn away from the high solemnity of LOMONOSOV's odes, toward literary currents associated with pre-romanticism and with the

ideas of the French critic Charles Batteux who emphasized individual perception and choice in the imitation of nature, as against the prescriptive norms of classicism (see NEOCLASSICISM). Derzhavin's literary friends, among them also the poet DMITRIEV, were gentlemen cultivated in the arts, and they soon realized that they were dealing with a more rough-hewn, more assertive and possibly greater talent than their own; hence, their efforts to "tame" and polish Derzhavin's verse met with only limited success.

In 1778–79, the newly established literary *Sanktpeterburgskii vestnik* published a number of Derzhavin's poems, among them the powerful "Ode on the Death of Prince Meshchersky" and the "Verses on the Birth in the North of a Porphyrogennete Child," dedicated to the future Tsar Alexander I. This was one of the first odes by Derzhavin in which he disregarded the prescriptive classical requirements of the genre to the extent of mixing "high" and "low" styles, standard mythological references and Russian country scenes, to suit his own imagination. His paraphrase of Psalm 81 aroused a great deal of controversy in 1780, because its accusatory voice addressed to "rulers and judges" appeared downright "Jacobin" to Catherine II. The poem could not be published until 1787. Derzhavin soon improved his position with the Empress, however, when, in 1782, he dedicated to her his "Ode to Felitsa." Ostensibly an official panegyric, it broke all the rules by addressing the Russian autocrat in a personal, wittily conversational tone where satire directed against her courtiers was interwoven with cheerfully flattering portrayals of Catherine as a humble, thoroughly human and enlightened ruler. The "conceit" of the poem was Derzhavin's reference to Catherine's own "Tale of the Prince of Khlor" describing the mission of the future Tsar Alexander to find a "rose without thorns," i.e., a just and rational principle of worldly power. Catherine herself figures in it under the name of "Felitsa," ostensibly a Kirghiz-Kaizak Princess, representing the rule of reason. In his poem, Derzhavin wears the mask of one of her courtiers, a "Murza," who contrasts his own lazy, hedonistic and arrogant ways with the simplicity and wisdom of the Empress herself. The particular shortcomings of this "Murza," needless to say, very closely resembled those of some of Catherine's courtiers, to her amusement and the courtiers' consternation. The genre of "Oriental tale" was already popular in England and in France, where social commentators used it to satirize the evils of their time with impunity under this "exotic" mask. Derzhavin, however, had the imagination to use this device in a panegyrical ode, and the unexpected human warmth and wit of his style profoundly touched and flattered the Empress. Derzhavin's reputation as a poet was now established, and his career as a statesman well begun. In 1786 he was appointed Governor of the Olonetsk Province, in the far north, where he undertook his duties with far greater zeal and cantankerous honesty than the Russian bureaucracy could tolerate, and therefore, energetic and brilliant administrator though he was, soon became embroiled in conflicts with his superiors. Transferred in 1785 as Governor to the Province of Tambov, Derzhavin continued in his maverick ways, to the point where he was again, as once before in the military, accused of insubordination. Exonerated in court, Derzhavin nevertheless felt it was time to write another ode in the "Felitsa" style to regain the good graces of the Empress. His "Portrait of Felitsa" (1789) helped him to enter the intimate circle of the court through his appointment as Catherine's personal secretary for the receipt of petitions. Ambitious, argumentative, honest, though capable of intrigue, Derzhavin underwent some more ups and downs in his service as high government official in various posts, and was even made Minister of Justice by the next Tsar, Alexander I, in 1802, whereupon he promptly embroiled himself in a conflict with the powerful statesman Speransky and was pensioned off in 1803.

During the last years of his life, Derzhavin devoted himself more and more to literary pursuits, quite possibly because he came to realize that this, rather than the career of a statesman, was now to be his true vocation. Interestingly enough, at this late date, he turned his main attention to the theater. He was already famous for his "Felitsa" poems (in addition to the two mentioned above, he also wrote "The Vision of Murza," 1783, which began with a magnificent description of St. Petersburg at night, the first such urban landscape in Russian poetry, "Thanks to Felitsa," 1783, and "The Depiction of Felitsa," 1789) as well as for his major contemplative ode "God" (1784), and "The Waterfall" (1791–94), dedicated to the memory of Potemkin, a long and beautiful work touched by the spirit of so-called

"Ossianic" romanticism. The only truly major poem Derzhavin wrote in his retirement was "To Evgeny, Life at Zvanka" (1807), consisting of idyllic-philosophical stanzas dedicated to his friend, bishop Evgeny Bolkhovitinov, a cultivated literary historian, who would come and keep him company at Zvanka, Derzhavin's estate. In the theater, Derzhavin made a considerable effort in several genres: a musical, *Dobrynya* (1804), a historical tragedy, *Herod and Mariamna* (1807), another tragedy, *The Dark One* (Temnyi, 1808), on the Russian Tsar Vasily II, "The Blind"; the operas [Ivan] *The Terrible, or the Subjugation of Kazan* (Groznyi, ili pokorenie Kazani, 1814) and *Pozharsky, or the Liberation of Moscow* (Pozharskii, ili osvobozhdenie Moskvy, 1806), and even children's plays and comic operas. These theatrical works, although apparently very important to Derzhavin, had little success on the stage; indeed, with one exception, they were not produced at all. The reasons for their failure probably had to do with the formal obscurities of Derzhavin's language in the tragedies, with the sometimes wearisome complexity of plots, and, in the case of his only play to see the stage, *Herod and Mariamna*, dealing with incidents in ancient Jewish history as reported in Josephus Flavius, with the lack of sufficient historical knowledge, and therefore interest, on the part of the Russian spectators.

In 1811 Derzhavin joined the famous conservative Collegium of Lovers of Russian Literature (BESEDA LYUBITELEI ROSSIISKOI SLOVESNOSTI), headed by the retired Admiral SHISHKOV. As one of its most important members, Derzhavin also turned his attention to literary theory in his "Dissertation on Lyric Poetry, or the Ode," begun in 1811, for the most part still unpublished. At the very end of his life, Derzhavin had the opportunity to witness the graduation exercises of Aleksandr PUSHKIN in 1815 and, in Pushkin's words, "to note and bless" him "while stepping down into the grave."

Historians of literature, following their urge to classify things, have placed Derzhavin into several different categories, sometimes contradicting each other. Some consider him, after all, a classicist, because he did accept the view that poetry must have a public function in the affairs of state, must be dedicated to the promotion of the ideal of Virtue, and must, in this, be an imitation of Nature manifest as the work of God. Others have noted that Derzhavin took an anti-classicist position in the matter of "artistic taste," preferring the truth of personal experience to any prescriptive norms based upon the examples of antiquity. Similarly, Derzhavin would not accommodate his poems to the established rules of literary genres pertaining to language, style or to verse form. All this, combined with the notion that the imitation of nature most meaningful for a poet is actually an inspiration *by* nature and that therefore the colors, sounds and sights of life must be recreated and transformed in the poetic text, rather than merely represented by traditional stylistic and lexical means, has inclined some scholars to consider Derzhavin in the context of West European pre-romanticism, as a kind of transitional figure in Russian letters, summarizing one literary epoch and foreshadowing another. Derzhavin's tumultuous gift of words—his rich, colorful, dynamic images, exuberant and ornamental style, have led some others to characterize him as a BAROQUE writer, in spite of the difficulties with periodisation and meaning of the term that this entails. "Realism" is another anachronistic term that may come to mind, considering the vividness and accuracy with which Derzhavin reproduces in words the visual or tactile aspects of the physical world.

All these diverse notions may each claim some rational validity or intuitive truth, but we do need to have some sort of central conception of Derzhavin's talent and his place in Russian literature, lest we simply call him "eclectic" and thus abdicate our efforts at comprehension, or else become no wiser than our classificatory zeal. To begin with, it is worth noting, as W. E. Brown has done in his 1980 *History of 18th Century Russian Literature*, that, unlike the classicists, Derzhavin did not wear a succession of artistic masks, poetic *personae*, in accordance with the requirements of each particular genre, but "rode rough-shod" over it all, sustaining, imposing the unifying force of his own artistic temperament and personality upon his art, even if that personality itself was quite multifaceted and sometimes contradictory. This central thrust of highly personal artistic integrity acquires, for Derzhavin, an aspect of happy creative intoxication when it reaches the point of inspiration: "The poet, in the full intoxication of his feelings, inflamed by that fire that comes from above, or to speak more simply, by imagination, goes into a

rapture, seizes his lyre and sings what his heart commands him" (quoted in Brown, p. 409). This, of course, can only help us to classify Derzhavin in the category of truly inspired poets, from Ovid, who said "Est Deus in nobis, agitante calescimus illo," (there is a god in us through whose agency we get our warmth), to PASTERNAK, who felt that at the moment of inspiration reality lost its previous coherence in the mind, and everything needed a new name, that name being art. The notion of "new name," however, may lead us a step further in the comprehension of Derzhavin, because it resembles the Russian FORMALISTS' concept of *ostranenie*, defamiliarization, in which things whose meanings have become automatic and no longer perceptible to us, are made to seem strange, and therefore both real and mysterious in a personal way, as if seen for the first time; art, as Viktor SHKLOVSKY said, "makes a stone *stony* again." It may be precisely Derzhavin's most pivotal contribution to the history of Russian literature that he made stones "stony," communicated his astonishment and delectation at the discovery that the concreteness of things is poetic, not "again," but for the first time in Russian letters, with the possible exception\of the early Middle Ages. The "thingness" of the poetic word, so well understood by the 20th-century Russian ACMEISTS, becomes transmuted in Derzhavin's poetry into the moral force of his integrity, and this is what makes it possible, for instance, in his "Felitsa" poems to speak of the gorgeous colors and shapes of Imperial presence as well as of pickled cucumbers and the indolence of fools and yet forge it all into a perfectly coherent new artistic structure, a genre unto itself, however much it may or may not resemble the classical panegyric ode.

Pushkin once observed that Derzhavin's genius "thought in Tartar," and never knew the Russian grammar. We might, in turn, say that Pushkin's genius "thought in French"; what will matter is that the two writers worked with the Russian language at different stages with different results. Derzhavin's time was one of great turbulence in political affairs and in the structures of Russian society, thus also in the uses of the Russian language. Consequently, by wrenching the unsettled literary Russian into a shape that fit his talent, Derzhavin also became an innovator, even a revolutionary, in both language and style. Lomonosov's "high" and "middle" styles, even the "low," became thoroughly mixed up in Derzhavin's verse whenever his inner sense of style required this. Similarly, the mythological references of, say, the classical odes, were woven into a fabric that also contained realistic scenes from Russian life. Finally, even grammatical structures, discrete lexical categories, were conjoined in an original way, disquieting to the cultivated ear. Derzhavin would, for instance speak of a "darling-blue" bird (milosizaya ptichka), who was a swallow, who was also his deceased wife, his "Plenira," in a poem dedicated to her memory. On a grand scale, as in his poem "The Waterfall," a "mountain of diamonds," does not feel coldly abstract in its sparkle, because it makes us feel its reality as a particular waterfall in nature, and thus, instead of withdrawing from the "prosaic" natural order of things, the glittering cascade permeates everything with its own magnificence. In the "Ode on the Death of Prince Meshchersky," the "tongue of time, the clang of metal" seems both darkly elevated and materially concrete as it speaks to us in the terrifying voice of death.

The seizing and transforming of things to make them cohere into a new substance and image at the moment of inspiration has some sort of resemblance to what Derzhavin does in the sphere of ideas as well. The democratic directness and simplicity of address, "speaking the truth to the Tsars with a smile," as Derzhavin put it, does not distract from, but only enhances the magnificence of the royal idea, so powerfully felt by Derzhavin all his life in both his capacities—as a statesman and as a poet. His admiration for the great military hero Suvorov becomes deeply convincing for us across the centuries precisely when Derzhavin speaks of him as "sleeping on straw and eating dry bread" together with his soldiers. With equally simple sincerity, Derzhavin could say of himself in his poem "God": "A king—a slave; a worm—a god!" One might say, perhaps, that part of Derzhavin's talent was his ability to experience and to make us feel a certain higher, poetic sense of equivalence among disparate ideas and things.

Such a talent, of course, establishes itself as a pivotal point of reality and historical continuum in times of turbulent transition. In this sense, Derzhavin can be compared not only to Pushkin, but also to the Russian SYMBOLISTS, and perhaps particularly MAYAKOVSKY, since they all stood on thresholds of new epochs and transformed their fluid, uncertain time into enduring monuments of art.

Works: Sochineniya Derzhavina s ob"yasnitel'nymi primecha-niyami Ya. Grota. 9 vols. 1864–83. G. A. Gukovskii, ed, *G. R. Der-zhavin. Stikhotvoreniya.* 1933. V. P. Druzin, ed, *G. R. Derzhavin. Stikhotvoreniya.* (Biblioteka poeta, malaya seriya.) 1963. D. D. Bla-goi, ed, *G. R. Derzhavin. Stikhotvoreniya.* (Biblioteka poeta.) 1957.

Translations: Harold B. Segel, ed. and trans. *The Literature of Eighteenth-Century Russia.* 2 vols. 1967. Vol. 2, pp. 254–317. See also *Lewanski.* 227–28.

Secondary literature: M. G. Al'tshuller, "Literaturno-teoretiche-skie vzglyady Derzhavina i 'Beseda lyubitelei russkogo slova'," *XVIII vek,* no. 8 (1969), pp. 103–13. Claude Backvis, "Dans quelle mesure Derzhavin est-il un Baroque?" In *Studies in Russian and Polish Liter-ature.* Ed. Zbigniew Folejewski et al. The Hague, 1962. P. N. Ber-kov, "Derzhavin i Karamzin v istorii russkoi literatury kontsa XVIII—nachala XIX veka," *XVIII vek,* no. 8, (1969), pp. 5–18. D. D. Blagoi, "Gavrila Romanovich Derzhavin." In *G. R. Derzhavin. Stikhotvoreniya.* 1957. Pp. 5–74. W. E. Brown, "Gavriil Romanovich Derzhavin and the Beginnings of Sentimentalism." Chap. 13 in *A History of 18th Century Russian Literature.* 1980. Pp. 381–416. J. V. Clardy, *G. R. Derzhavin: A Political Biography.* The Hague, 1967. G. A. Gukovskii, *Russkaya poeziya XVIII veka.* 1927. ———, "Iz istorii russkoi ody 18-go veka," *Poetika,* 3 (1927), pp. 129–47. J. A. Harris, "In Defense of Derzhavin's Plays," *New Zealand Slavonic Journal,* no. 2, pp. 1–15. Pierre R. Hart, *G. R. Derzhavin: a Poet's Progress.* 1978. Helmut Kölle, *Farbe, Licht und Klang in der malen-den Poesie Derzhavins.* Munich, 1966. A. N. Kulakova, "O spornykh voprosakh v estetike Derzhavina," *XVIII vek,* no. 8 (1969), pp. 25–41. ———. *Ocherki istorii esteticheskoi mysli XVIII veka.* 1968. G. P. Makogonenko, "Pushkin i Derzhavin," *XVIII vek,* no. 8 (1969), pp. 113–27. E. A. Maimin, "Derzhavinskie traditsii i filosofskaya poeziya 20–30-kh godov XIX stoletiya," *XVIII vek,* no. 8 (1969), pp. 127–44. I. Z. Serman, *Derzhavin.* 1967. V. A. Zapadov, *Masterstvo Derzhavina.* 1958. ———. *Gavrila Romanovich Derzhavin.* 1965.

F. R. S.

Detective story. Novels and short stories with a plot organized around a baffling crime are not unknown in 19th-century Russian literature. *Crime and Punishment* and *The Brothers Karamazov,* for example, both feature an intelligent detective, who uses psychological deduc-tion in identifying a murderer, correctly in the former, incorrectly in the latter work. However, the genre of the detective story failed to attract a Russian writer of the caliber of Conan-Doyle, Gaboriau, or Anna Katharine Green. The huge demand for crime fiction was sat-isfied largely by translations of the Nick Carter (by John R. Coryell), Sherlock Holmes (by Conan-Doyle), and Nat Pinkerton (by Allan Pinkerton) series. As early as 1883, CHEKHOV parodied this genre in a story, "The Swedish Match, a Crime Story" (Shvedskaya spichka [Ugolovnyi rasskaz], 1883). With the arrival of film, in Russia as elsewhere, the detective story entered into a mutually enhancing relationship with this new medium.

The demand for detective stories (and films) continued unabated after the Revolution. The 1920s produced a new, albeit short-lived genre, "Red Pinkertonism" (a term coined by Nikolai Bukharin), in which the bourgeois detective was replaced by brave and ingenious workers fighting the evil machinations of capitalist tycoons and their henchmen. The best example of this genre is Marietta SHAGINYAN's serialized trilogy *Mess-Mend* (1924), published under the pseudonym "Jim Dollar." Other writers who engaged in Red Pinkertonism were Valentin KATAEV, Ilya ERENBURG, Aleksei TOLSTOI, and Viktor SHKLOVSKY, to mention only the best known. The end of the New Economic Policy (NEP) also spelled the end of Red Pinkertonism.

The detective genre lay dormant in the years of Stalin's reign. However, many of its traits resurfaced in SOCIALIST REALIST "produc-tion" literature, where the nefarious activities (spying, sabotage, wrecking, and murder) and eventual exposure by watchful Party cadres, of assorted enemies of the people (White Guards masquerad-ing as communists, foreign agents, corrupt intellectuals) are routine ingredients. Such socialist realist classics as Leonid LEONOV's *The Road to the Ocean* and *The Russian Forest,* Aleksandr AFINOGENOV's play *Fear,* or Yury OLESHA's film *Engineer Kochin's Mistake* have many of the features of a crime thriller. The THAW after Stalin's death made it possible to resuscitate the detective genre, to argue over its pros and cons, and even to discuss its theory. However, crime in the Soviet detective genre is socially or politically motivated, rather than pathological or gratuitous. There is also a heavy emphasis on the moral aspect, though some authors have been charged by critics with treating serious issues frivolously. More than in the West, the genre addresses itself to the young reader. Some Soviet writers of detective stories: Roman Kim (1899–   ), Lev Ovalov (real name: Shapovalov, 1905–   ), Matvei Roizman (1896–   ), Nikolai Toman (1911–   ), Lev Sheinin (1906–67), and Nikolai Shpanov (1896–1961).

Bibliography: A. Adamow, "Der sowjetische Kriminalroman," *Kunst und Literatur* 25 (1977), pp. 305–16. Natalia Ilyina and Arkadi Adamov, "Detective Novels: A Game and Life." *Soviet Literature,* 1975, no. 3, pp. 142–50. Robert Russell, "Red Pinkertonism: An Aspect of Soviet Literature of the 1920s," *SEER* 60 (1982), pp. 390–412. N. Toman, "Chto takoe detektivnaya literatura." In *O fanta-stike i priklyucheniyakh. O literature dlya detei.* Fasc. 5 (1960), pp. 277–84.

V. T.

Diaghilev, Sergei Pavlovich (1872–1929), impresario and journalist. With a formal background only in music (he was a student of Rimsky-Korsakov), Diaghilev was a powerful factor in the Russian MODERNIST movement and did more than anyone to bring Russian art, music, and theater, and thus Russian culture in general, to the attention of the Western public. He was one of the founders of the journal MIR ISKUSSTVA (1898–1904), was appointed a special assistant to the Director of the Imperial Theaters in 1899. Between 1906 and 1909 he organized a series of exhibitions of Russian and West European art, which acquainted Russians with French cubism, the fauves and the futurists, and German expressionism almost at the time of the inception of these movements, and caused the West to take note of Russian modernism (Larionov, Goncharova, Malevich, etc.). These connections had a significant influence on the development of Russian literature, FUTURISM in particular. Diaghilev went on to organize performances of Russian orchestral music, opera, and bal-let in Paris. He discovered Igor Stravinsky, whose ballets *The Firebird* (1910), *Petrushka* (1911), and *The Rite of Spring* (1913) created a sensation in Paris. Diaghilev was able to coordinate modernist music with the imaginative sets of artists such as Aleksandr Benois (1870–1960) and Lev Bakst (1868–1924), the brilliant choreography of Mikhail Fokine (1880–1942), and the dancing of Vatslav Nijinsky and Tamara Karsavina. Diaghilev continued to be an important factor in the fortunes of the Russian ballet in the West until his death.

Secondary literature: A. I. Haskell, *Diaghileff.* 1955. S. Lifar, *A History of Russian Ballet.* Trans. A. I. Haskell. 1954.

V. T.

Dissident literature, see *SAMIZDAT.*

Dmitriev, Ivan Ivanovich (1760–1837), poet, was born in the Sim-birsk region. He embarked early upon a military career. While serv-ing as a Guards officer in the capital, he was exonerated from a charge of plotting to assassinate Paul I and compensated for the in-dignity by an almost fairy-tale elevation to high rank and social posi-tion. He held various posts, lastly that of Minister of Justice.

A poet of repute from his youth on, Dmitriev shared the sensibil-ity, world-outlook, and antipathy for grandiloquence of KARAMZIN, with whom he was closely associated from the nineties. Dmitriev, therefore, must also be regarded as one of the founders of Russian SENTIMENTALISM. To that trend he contributed much-acclaimed verses in typical sentimentalist forms—songs, intimate epistles, and histori-cal tales. He also wrote satires, fables, and stories in verse in which he revealed more pronounced expertise in humor than did his fellow sentimentalists. As satirist he achieved special fame with "At second hand" (Chuzhoi tolk), wherein the fustian ode-writers of his day are mocked. His witty, light-touch fables were thought to rival KRYLOV's.

Out of fashion in the romantic era, Dmitriev retained the admira-tion of BATYUSHKOV, ZHUKOVSKY, and especially VYAZEMSKY. PUSH-KIN, however, tended to depreciate Dmitriev who, meanwhile, in his stories in verse, particularly "Wife à la mode" (Modnaya zhena), had displayed a flair for creating conversational speech in iambics closely approximating Pushkin's own brilliant achievements. Dmitriev was also much valued as a translator and adapter of French poetry.

Works: Sochineniya Ivana Ivanovicha Dmitrieva. Ed. A. A. Floridov. 2 vols. 1893. (With an autobiography, "Vzglyad na moyu zhizn'," vol. 2, pp. 1–151.) *Polnoe sobranie stikhotvorenii*. Ed. G. P. Makogonenko. (Biblioteka poeta, bol'shaya seriya.) 1967.

Translations: See Lewanski, p. 229.

Secondary literature: E. N. Kupreyanova, "Dmitriev i poety karamzinskoi shkoly." In *Istoriya russkoi literatury*. Vol. 5, pt. 1. 1941. Pp. 121–43. G. P. Makogonenko, "'Ryadovoi na Pinde voin' (Poeziya Ivana Dmitrieva)." In *Polnoe sobranie stikhotvorenii*. (Biblioteka poeta, bol'shaya seriya.) 1967. Pp. 5–68.   I. R. T.

Dobrolyúbov, Aleksándr Mikhaílovich (1876–1944?). A minor SYM-BOLIST poet, considered by some to be an extreme example of DECADENCE both because of his unusual poetry and because of his studied eccentricities in life. Born in Warsaw, he lived in St. Petersburg, made contact with BRYUSOV and the Moscow symbolists in 1894, and published a collection of poems, *Natura naturans. Natura naturata* in 1895. Subsequently he lived as a religious wanderer among peasants and laborers in Olonetsk province in the north, as a novice at Solovetsky Monastery, again as a wanderer in Orenburg province in the south, and in the Samara region, where he founded his own sect. He returned to literary circles sporadically and published two further books, *A Collection of Verse* (Sobranie stikhov, 1900) and *From the Invisible Book* (Iz knigi nevidimoi, 1905). He was lost from sight for many years after the Revolution and is presumed to have died in 1944 near Baku.

His verse, sometimes in the form of rhythmic prose, is ornate, highly allusive, and characterized by a dreamlike logic. In *Natura naturans. Natura naturata* his poems are concerned with death, religion, love, and nature. In *Sobranie stikhov* he speaks about the natural universe, perception, and the will. He recalls Schopenhauer in his philosophical concerns and Nietzsche's *Thus Spake Zarathustra* in his dramatic anecdotes. His nature poems, colored by fantasy and philosophy, resemble those of FOFANOV, BALMONT, SOLOGUB, and KHLEBNIKOV, but he lacked the steadfast literary purpose of these better-known poets.

Works: Sochineniya. Introd. Joan Delaney Grossman. Berkeley, 1981.

Secondary literature: Valery Y. Bryusov, *The Diary of Valery Bryusov (1893–1905)*. Ed. and trans., Joan Delaney Grossman. 1980. Georgii Chulkov, "A. Dobrolyubov." In *Pokryvalo Izidy*, 1909. Pp. 91–98. Samuel D. Cioran, "Aleksandr Dobroliubov: A Prophet of Silence," *CSS* 5 (1971), pp. 178–95. Vladimir Gippius, "A. Dobrolyubov." In *Russkaya literatura XX veka*. Ed. S. A. Vengerov, 3 vols. 1914. Vol. 1. Pp. 272–87. N. A. Poyarkov, "Al. Dobrolyubov." In *Poety nashikh dnei*. 1907. Pp. 8–14. S. A. Vengerov, "A. Dobrolyubov." In *Russkaya literatura XX veka*, ed. S. A. Vengerov, 3 vols. 1914. Vol. 1. Pp. 265–71.   E. Br.

Dobrolyúbov, Nikolaí Aleksándrovich (1836–61), influential critic. Born in Nizhny Novgorod the son of a priest who, ashamed of his lowly but typical social position, tried vainly to ingratiate himself with the local aristocracy, Nikolai also was enrolled in a theological seminary but withdrew at the age of seventeen. Tortured by feelings of inadequacy and torn between his early and deep religious devotion and then by growing doubts, he recorded his torments and his "sins" in a diary which has been called "the most outspoken diary in Russian 19th-century literature" (Lampert). His ungainly physical appearance and numerous brief and sad love affairs further complicated his life. Dobrolyubov moved to St. Petersburg and, following the death of his parents (and obliged now to support himself and seven siblings), began his brief career in journalistic criticism when he became associated with the journal SOVREMENNIK in 1857. This brief career ended some four years later with his premature death due to tuberculosis.

Making up, along with CHERNYSHEVSKY and PISAREV, the trio of Russian "Civic" critics, Dobrolyubov continued the radical tradition both in politics and criticism of Vissarion BELINSKY; indeed, like Chernyshevsky, he thought of himself as a successor to Belinsky, although particular differences and inconsistencies are apparent. Like Belinsky and Chernyshevsky, Dobrolyubov too was influenced by his reading of Feuerbach and such French utopian socialists as Saint-Simon, Louis Blanc, and Fourier. Although Dobrolyubov wrote many review articles, his reputation is based largely on four of these. In what is perhaps his best known critical essay, "What is

Oblomovism?" (Chto takoe oblomovshchina?, 1859), Dobrolyubov analyzes the character Oblomov in GONCHAROV's novel of the same name (1859) as a social type (the "superfluous man"), attributing the affliction or malady of "OBLOMOVISM" (sometimes rendered "Oblomovitis") to social conditions in Russia, particularly serfage. Dobrolyubov treats Goncharov's novel not at all as literature or art but rather as a social document, and he discusses the novelistic character as if this figure were a real person reacting to an actual environment. It is eminently clear from this and succeeding studies by Dobrolyubov that, for him, literature was merely a reflection of the real world; it is also clear that such an approach is not so very different from the later Marxist-Leninist concept of art and literature as aspects of a "superstructure," dependent on and functionally related to a given underlying socio-economic base.

Also published in 1859 was Dobrolyubov's article on the plays of Aleksandr OSTROVSKY, "The Kingdom of Darkness" (Temnoe tsarstvo); here, too, he reduces the wide variety of characters to a small number of representative types (such as the type of the over-bearing domestic tyrant among the merchantry, the *samodur*) and attempts to demonstrate socio-literary relationships. Again, Ostrovsky's plays are hardly treated as dramatic literature but rather as documents detailing the cruelty of the oppressors and the resignation of their victims. In another article on Ostrovsky's play *The Storm* (Groza, 1859) entitled "A Ray of Light in the Kingdom of Darkness" (Luch sveta v temnom tsarstve, 1860) Dobrolyubov departs even further from the text of the play (as most would read it), seeing in the pitiful figure of the ignorant and superstitious Katerina, the suicide, something like a symbol of revolution. And in the same year, having read Turgenev's novel *On the Eve* (Na kanune, 1860), Dobrolyubov wrote "When Will the Real Day Come?" (Kogda zhe pridet nastoyashchii den'?). Here he deprecates the subtle lyricism and psychological insights of the great novelist (who has been called "a novelist's novelist") as if these were so much *impedimenta*; and again Turgenev's novel serves merely as a corpus of socio-political data.

In 1861 shortly before he died Dobrolyubov wrote "Downtrodden People" (Zabitye lyudi), devoted to some short stories and the novel *The Insulted and the Injured* by DOSTOEVSKY. Claiming that the literary qualities in the works of Dostoevsky are unworthy of aesthetic analysis, Dobrolyubov argues that these works, therefore, merit only his own kind of sociological approach. But it is in this final critical essay by Dobrolyubov that we see the glimmerings of a deeper and more mature sensibility which, however, never had the chance to develop. Dostoevsky, incidentally, although he disagreed with Dobrolyubov in many respects, considered him the leading critic of the time.

Works: Sobranie sochinenii. 9 vols. 1961–64.

Works in English: Selected Philosophical Essays. Moscow, 1956. *Belinsky, Chernyshevsky, and Dobrolyubov: Selected Criticism*. Ed. R. Matlaw. 1962.

Secondary Literature: George Harjan, "Dobrolyubov's 'What Is Oblomovism?'; An Interpretation," *CSP* 18 (1976), pp. 284–92. V. S. Kruzhkov, *N. A. Dobrolyubov: Zhizn', deyatel'nost', mirovozzrenie*. 1976. E. Lampert, *Sons against Fathers: Studies in Russian Radicalism and Revolution*. 1965. Chap. 4. G. Lukács, *Studies in European Realism*. 1964. Chap. 5. R. Stacy, *Russian Literary Criticism: A Short History*. 1974. Chap. 4. René Wellek, *A History of Modern Criticism: 1750–1950*. Vol. 4. 1965. Pp. 245–53.   R. H. S.

Dobrýnya Nikítich, see BYLINA.

Dolínin (Iskoz), Arkády Semyónovich (1883 or 1880–1968), literary scholar, born into a Jewish family outside the Pale. Educated in Vienna, where he published his first work, "On Symbolism" (1906), and in Petersburg, where he studied under S. A. VENGEROV. Dolínin's entries in the commentary to the *Complete Works* of Pushkin and his article "The Gypsies" (*Pushkinist*, 1914, no. 1, pp. 17–44) deal with the treatment of Rousseau and the dichotomy of individual freedom and nature in PUSHKIN. In his early years Dolínin was interested in Russian symbolism, Acmeism, and the symbolic realism of CHEKHOV and Boris ZAITSEV. Of his eighty works, more than forty deal with DOSTOEVSKY, concentrating on the way Dostoevsky perceived cultural, socio-philosophical, and spiritual ideas produced in Russia and Europe and their artistic realization in his novels (*The Late Works of Dostoevsky*, 1963). Dolínin is able to convey the philosophic and poetic intensity of Dostoevsky's political interests and of his interpretation of other writers' ideological concepts ("Dostoevsky in the Petrashevsky Circle," *Zven'ya*, 1936, no. 6, pp. 512–45; "Turgenev in *The Possessed*," in *Dostoevskii: Materialy i issledovaniya* 2 (1925), pp. 119–38). Dolinin demonstrated that many of the burning issues of Dostoevsky's day, discussed in Russian periodicals of the 1860s and 1870s, became structural components of the latter's novels. His superb knowledge of the cultural ambience of Dostoevsky's epoch allowed Dolinin to advance new principles of textological interpretation for Dostoevsky's manuscripts and to demonstrate the poetic cohesion of his plots ("Dostoevsky in his Work on *A Raw Youth*," *Literaturnoe Nasledstvo*, vol. 77).

In his four-volume collection of Dostoevsky's letters, Dolinin developed a new type of textological commentary. Each gloss, formally a small historical reference, is in essence a condensed monograph. Each note in the commentary lays ground for a further discussion of Dostoevsky's personal, social, cultural, artistic, and ideological contacts with his correspondents. Dolinin served as an editor and main contributor to *Dostoevsky: Materials and Studies* (1922, 1925, 1935) and *Dostoevsky in the Memoirs of his Contemporaries* (1964, 2 vols.). Among his other works are articles on BELINSKY, HERZEN, Chekhov, and Pushkin.

Bibliography: "A. S. Dolinin." In *Pisateli Smolenshchiny*. Smolensk, 1965. N. P.

Dól'nik, see TONIC VERSIFICATION.

Dombróvsky, Yúry Ósipovich (1909–78), novelist and short-story writer. Born and educated in Moscow, Dombrovsky spent much of his life in Central Asia. He was arrested at one time and seems to have spent some time in a labor camp. His works, artistically on a high level, gained little official or popular recognition. Dombrovsky's historical novels, whether they deal with the distant past, as in *The Fall of the Empire* (Krushenie imperii, 1938) or *Derzhavin* (1939), or with more recent events, as in *The Ape Returns for his Skull* (Obez'yana prikhodit za svoim cherepom, 1959), set in Hitler's Germany, are well researched, but essentially oriented toward problems of the writer's own time and country. They tend to treat moral issues, specifically the plight of the isolated intellectual facing an oppressive power structure.

Works: Khranitel' drevnostei. 1964. *Smuglaya ledi: Tri novelly o Shekspire.* 1969. *Khudozhnik Kalmykov.* 1970.

Secondary literature: Olga Hassanoff, "Dombrovskij's 'The Keeper of Antiquities'," *Melbourne Slavonic Studies* 5–6 (1971), pp. 194–202. I. Shenfel'd, "Krugi zhizni i tvorchestva Yuriya Dombrovskogo," *Grani*, no. 111–12 (1979), pp. 351–77. V. T.

Domostroi (16th century). An Old Russian work which concerns itself with the "management of the household." Its models may include, in addition to works of the Kievan era such as the *Pouchenie* (Instruction) of VLADIMIR MONOMAKH, Greek writings of classical antiquity (above all, Xenophon's *Oeconomicus*) and Western humanistic works of didactic literature. An "original" version of the Domostroi probably was produced in Novgorod at the beginning of the 16th century in a milieu of merchants and boyars. The most complete version of the work which has been preserved (known as the "second redaction") apparently was compiled in mid-16th century Moscow by the protopope Silvestr, who for a time enjoyed the protection of Ivan IV.

The *Domostroi* consists of sixty-four chapters, the last of which is a didactic epistle addressed by Silvestr to his son Anfim. The work can be divided into three parts: (1) the first part focusing on civil obligations, that is, on the necessary behavior towards ecclesiastical and political tradition and authority; (2) the second part dealing with family responsibilities and functions; (3) the third part concentrating on the practical obligations connected with managing the household. Both the prevalence of a "plain" didactic style and the possibility that linguistic differences may correspond to compositional layers in the work have attracted the attention of scholars.

Together with works such as the STOGLAV (Book of One Hundred Chapters) and the *Azbukovnik* (Alphabet Book), the *Domostroi* is often regarded as an "official" document of 16th-century Muscovite ideology which aimed to establish new rules governing all aspects of social behavior. However, the emphasis on the family as the kernel of social life might also echo humanistic interpretations of classical intellectual clichés.

Bibliography: I. S. Nekrasov, *Opyt istoriko-literaturnogo issledovaniya o proiskhozhdenii drevne-russkogo Domostroya.* 1873. A. Orlov, ed., *Domostroi po Konshinskomu spisku i podobnym.* 2 vols. in 1. Moscow, 1908–10. Rprint. *Russian Reprint Series*, no. 37. The Hague, 1967. A. Orlov, *Domostroi: Issledovanie, chast' I.* 1917. Rprint. *Russian Reprint Series*, no. 53. The Hague, 1967. A. I. Sobolevskii, "Pop Sil'vestr i Domostroi." *Izvestiya po russkomu yazyku i slovesnosti Akademii nauk SSSR* 2, no. 1 (1929), pp. 187–202. M. A. Sokolova, *Ocherki po yazyku delovykh pamyatnikov XVI veka.* 1957. H. G.

Dórosh (real name: Gol'berg), Efim Yákovlevich (1908–72), writer and journalist, a minor figure before the THAW, emerged as a major representative of "COUNTRY PROSE" with his *Country Diary* (Derevenskii dnevnik), begun in 1956 and continued until the writer's death. The stories and sketches of *Country Diary*, told in the first person singular, often candidly describe the negative side of life on a collective farm and also speak up for the preservation of traditional values. Dorosh has been credited with a lively and precise manner of presentation and a good ear for the spoken language of rural Russia.

Works: Rasskazy. 1954. *Derevenskii dnevnik. Chetyre vremeni goda.* 1963. *Zhivoe derevo iskusstva.* 1970. *Ivan Fedoseevich ukhodit na pensiyu.* 1971.

Secondary literature: Deming Brown, *Soviet Literature since Stalin.* 1978. Pp. 226–31. Gleb Žekulin, "Efim Dorosh." In *Russian and Slavic Literature*. Eds. Richard R. Freeborn, R. R. Milner-Gulland, and Charles A. Ward. 1976. Pp. 425–48. V. T.

Dostoévsky, Fyódor Mikhaílovich (1821–81), novelist, short-story writer, journalist. Dostoevsky was born 30 October 1821 at St. Mary's Hospital for the Moscow poor, where his father, Mikhail Andreevich (1789–1839), had been on the staff for eight months after an eight-year career in the Army medical service. Mikhail's father was a Uniate priest in Podolia, but the family claimed descent from 17th-century nobility in Dostoevo, northeast of Pinsk, and was legally entitled to own land and serfs. Dostoevsky's mother, Maria Fedorovna Nechaeva (1800–37), was the daughter and granddaughter of Moscow merchants. She seems to have been loving and religious; her husband was strict and able, but sometimes alcoholic and violent. Dostoevsky's younger sisters, Lyubov (born and died in 1829), Vera (1829–96), and Aleksandra (1835–89), were seldom close to him, but Varvara (1822–92) was, and her marriage in 1840 to P. A. Karepin (1796–1850) helped to shape Dostoevsky's many responses to the fashionable literary theme of the helpless girl at the mercy of a rich older man. His younger brothers Andrei (1825–97), an engineer, and Nikolai (1831–83), an architect, played minor roles in his life, but Andrei wrote a useful memoir. His older brother, Mikhail (1820–64), shared Dostoevsky's literary and journalistic involvements, his early social ideals, and his education. They attended Moscow schools together for four years, and then the Military Engineering School in St. Petersburg from 1837 to 1843, followed by the minimum terms of military service. In 1839, they learned that their father had been murdered, perhaps justifiably, by the peasants on a small estate he had bought south of Moscow.

Beginning in the 1830s, Dostoevsky broadened his education by reading widely and with the enthusiasm of youth and a determination to master the literary craft. In his letters, he glories over the approved European classics, Homer, and Shakespeare, the French dramatists, Diderot, Voltaire, Goethe, and most often Schiller, whose depictions of nobility, sublimity, and beauty were often to delight the heroes and sometimes to amuse the sophisticates in his later novels. He naturally read the Russian classics, and owed a tremendous literary debt to KARAMZIN, PUSHKIN, LERMONTOV, and most of all GOGOL. In his own generation, he knew HERZEN, and debated with him in London; he wrote about TOLSTOI, but never met him; he maintained intense and often tortured personal, literary, and political relations with TURGENEV and NEKRASOV. In Europe, he admired and imitated Dickens, Hugo, and later Zola among the greatest figures, but his taste was broad, and he learned much about dark staircases and hypnotic eyes from the gothic and sensational writers of the time, "Monk" Lewis, Ann Radcliffe, Charles Maturin, E. T. A. Hoffmann, Thomas DeQuincey, Eugène Sue, and Edgar Allan Poe, whom Dostoevsky's journals introduced to Russian readers in the early 1860s. In the mid-1840s, he worked on translations of Honoré de Balzac and George Sand, and borrowed episodes, characters, and techniques from both authors all his life. In 1881, Melchior de Vogüé called Dostoevsky a "true Scythian," a writer alien to Western traditions and ways of thinking; but in fact, he drew heavily on Western writers and thinkers in those very passages that Western critics have sometimes found strange and foreign.

Early writings

In 1844, Dostoevsky resigned his engineering lieutenant's commission after a year's obligatory service, and entered the Petersburg literary world with his translation of Balzac's *Eugénie Grandet* (1833). Since Balzac had recently visited St. Petersburg, and the novel had already been adapted for the Russian stage, Dostoevsky was displaying a practical shrewdness about the literary scene which was to alternate with his frequent surrenders to financial desperation for much of his career. He also found in the novel, themes of obsessive greed and affection, criminality and self-sacrifice, which he would later explore on his own, and he made the translation a richly readable piece of Russian prose, conveying the fullness of the original partly by russifying the French settings, customs, weather, etc.

In 1846, he published his first novel, *Poor Folk* (Bednye lyudi). In the obsolete epistolary form, it presents a thoroughly modish hero, a poor Petersburg copy clerk who loves a woman he cannot possess. Makar Devushkin, the devoted forty-seven-year-old copyist, has lived a life of innocence for many years in a sort of urban pastoral. Varvara Dobroselova, the pathetic, but more sophisticated girl of seventeen, describes her own innocent days, when she devoted herself with heroic generosity to her dying mother and to the student Pokrovsky, who is older, educated, patronizing, irascible, and also dying. An ensuing year of shame and suffering at the hands of a procuress and her client, the bluffly lecherous squire Bykov, who is Pokrovsky's natural father, leaves her too worldly for further self-sacrifice; she rejects Bykov's continuing propositions until the subjugated old libertine offers marriage, which she accepts, regretfully abandoning Makar. As a text on morals, *Poor Folk* shows Varvara as one of the many Dostoevsky characters who are morally and spiritually worse after suffering than before; critical tradition has focused more on the Dostoevsky characters (mostly murderers) whom suffering redeems. As a text on aesthetics, *Poor Folk* exposes Makar's innocence to a band of compulsive literary imitators, invites comparison between Makar's articulate woe and the misery in Gogol's "Overcoat" or Pushkin's "Station Master," and in its epigraph calls upon the reader to speculate with Makar on whether literature should offer solace, or accurate representation, or simply be an activity that holds together the fragments of a human spirit. Taking *Poor Folk* as a social text, the grand cham of Russian literature at the time, Vissarion BELINSKY, read the novel as a moving protest and joined Dostoevsky's friends GRIGOROVICH and NEKRASOV in welcoming him as a new Gogol, to the detriment of Dostoevsky's modesty, which had never been great.

During the next four years, Dostoevsky published a dozen works of very different sorts. His next novel, *The Double* (Dvoinik, 1846), and one short story, "The Landlady" (Khozyaika, 1847), showed Dostoevsky mastering that technique in E. T. A. Hoffmann's tales which makes the reader search among conflicting data with increasing frustration in an effort to decide whether the events are the fantasies of an unbalanced character or the presentation of the supernatural as real. In *The Double*, the morbidly sensitive and pretentious clerk Golyadkin, already clinically deranged by the social pressures of his office, is driven finally to a madhouse by a series of encounters with a being who is sometimes clearly his own reflection in a glass, sometimes the embodiment of his own aggressive fantasies, sometimes an unpleasant ordinary mortal who happens to have the same name and appearance, and sometimes, in some supernatural way, himself. The massing of irreconcilable data leads the reader into a state of mind not unlike Golyadkin's. "The Landlady" plays with similar ambiguities when Ordynov, a susceptible student in the Hoffmannesque tradition, encounters a beautiful woman totally in the power of a dark and threatening master, Murin. Ordynov cannot tell whether this power is magic, hypnosis, blackmail, love, paternity, or some terrifying combination of these, but Murin's strange, barely comprehensible speech becomes more and more menacing as the story builds toward an ending whose frustrating inadequacy as a solution to the puzzle may constitute a major step in Dostoevsky's life-long search for new literary ways to exploit his reader's response.

Most of Dostoevsky's remaining works in the 1840s explore either an established literary formula or a pathological character type. "A Novel in Nine Letters" (Roman v devyati pis'makh, 1847), "Another Man's Wife and a Husband under the Bed" (Chuzhaya zhena i muzh pod krovat'yu, 1848), and "A Christmas Party and a Wedding" (Elka i svad'ba, 1848), all derive their impact primarily from the reader's familiarity with firmly fixed literary patterns. "A Christmas Party and a Wedding" is a Dickensian Christmas story, philanthropic, indignant, contrasting the self-satisfied calculation of an old sensualist with the despair of a helpless child. The other two stories approach sensuality in an equally mannered tradition, the mockery of the cuckold, a tradition less congenial to Dostoevsky's recurring themes and concerns. The humor here takes the form of literary travesty; Dostoevsky was apparently not ready to handle cuckolding psychologically, as he did in *The Eternal Husband* (Vechnyi muzh, 1870), or to improvise the runaway humanity of such self-dramatizing monologuists as Foma Opiskin, Razumikhin, Fyodor Karamazov, or Lebedev, and the other buffoons. Four stories and some fragments treat pathological or fatal exaggerations of common human flaws as seen by a decent, bewildered Petersburg narrator: "Mr. Prokharchin" (1846), presents a miser; "Polzunkov" (1848), a morbid self-consciousness; "A Faint Heart" (Slaboe serdtse, 1848), an incapacitating fear of human intercourse; and "An Honest Thief" (Chestnyi vor, 1848), a strange indecisiveness.

Personal life

"White Nights" (Belye nochi, 1848) and *Netochka Nezvanova* (1849) mark the beginnings of a period in Dostoevsky's creative career which was interrupted by his arrest and exile. In the spring of 1847, Dostoevsky had begun to attend the Friday meetings at the house of M. V. Butashevich-Petrashevsky (1821–66) to discuss social problems, most often from the utopian socialist viewpoint of Charles Fourier. In the books he read from the Petrashevsky library, Dostoevsky found a vision of a sunlit golden world so perfectly arranged that human potentialities were realized there. This vision of a golden age recurs in his later works, as does a mocking vision of the romantic posturing among the idealists of the 1840s. Dostoevsky probably maintained some ironic detachment from the PETRASHEVSKY CIRCLE because of its atheism, but probably also joined a particularly radical splinter group that even acquired a printing press. In any case, at one Petrashevsky meeting, he had read Belinsky's forbidden letter attacking Gogol for abandoning radicalism, and was jailed for this offense when the entire group was arrested on 22 April 1849. He took his interrogation with intelligence and courage, was condemned to death and taken out to a parade ground to be shot. Reprieved at the very last moment in accord with Nicholas I's cruel flair for melodrama (22 December 1849), he endured the hellish conditions of a prison labor camp in Tobolsk from January 1850 to January 1854, and had to remain in exile as an army private in Semipalatinsk until April 1857, and as a lieutenant until August 1859, when the more enlightened government of Alexander II let him return first to Tver and then to St. Petersburg.

The 1850s and early 1860s were the most difficult quarter of Dostoevsky's personal life. The fetters on his legs, the miserable food, the stench, noise, and lack of privacy in the prison barracks, coupled with the brutality of certain officers, and the class hostility of most of his fellow convicts left physical and psychological scars upon him that lasted a decade. He describes sharp and fearsome childhood hallucinations, and in these years his epilepsy worsened, sometimes incapacitating him for two or three days, and recurring several times a month. His affair and marriage with Maria Dmitrievna Konstant Isaeva, the wife and then the widow of a good friend, complicated his life further. She suffered from hysteria, tuberculosis, and dependents whose demands were to trouble Dostoevsky all his life. Her death on 15 April and Mikhail Dostoevsky's on 10 July 1864 deprived Dostoevsky of the two people closest to him. With no children of his own, he assumed the debts, expenses, and harassments of these two families. In the spring of 1865, he proposed marriage to a wealthy and radical young author Anna Korvin-Krukovskaya (later Zhaklar, 1843–1887). She had the good sense to refuse him. His several other efforts to find a congenial companion culminated in a miserable affair with the alternately admiring and hostile Apollinaria Suslova, who tormented him in Russia, Italy, Switzerland, France, and Germany, where he exacerbated his emotional and financial problems by gambling away whatever money he could earn or borrow. On 4 October 1866, to meet a 1 November deadline with a merciless publisher, Stellovsky, he hired a stenographer, Anna Grigorievna Snitkina (1846–1918), and dictated *The Gambler* to her. Together, they met the deadline, and on 15 February 1867 they were married. Anna Grigorievna was not an intellectual, but she set Dostoevsky's life on an even keel, became his publisher, copied out his writings from dictation, and organized and gradually reduced his debts; within a year or two, without nagging, she cured him of his gambling mania and of Suslova; she teased and coddled and adored him, and made him a solid family man for the last quarter of his life. She bore him four children, Sofia, who only lived a week or two in 1868; Lyubov (1869–1926), who wrote a prickly memoir; Fyodor (1871–1921), who became an engineer; and Aleksei (1875–78), whose death left Dostoevsky heartbroken. Partly to escape their importunate families and creditors, the Dostoevskys lived in western Europe from April 1867 to July 1871, returning after that to St. Petersburg. In summer, she would often take the children to a house he had bought in Staraya Russa, near Novgorod while he went to a German watering place, usually Ems, for his emphysema, which his smoking aggravated. In 1881, he suffered a hemorrhage in his throat and died three days later, on 29 January. He is buried in the Alexander Nevsky Monastery in Leningrad.

Journalism and polemic

Having learned from his work among the journals and ephemera of the 1840s that literature offered greater editorial and financial rewards to its purveyors than to its producers, Dostoevsky and his brother Mikhail started a journal of literature and opinion called VREMYA (1861–63). The articles of the social commentator Nikolai STRAKHOV and the organic critic Apollon GRIGORIEV, coupled with fiction by major Russian authors and translations from foreign works helped build *Vremya* into one of the most successful of the "fat" journals that dominated Russian 19th century intellectual life. Its circulation had passed 4,000 by April 1863 when it was closed by the censors, who had read unintended hostility into an article by Strakhov on the Polish uprising of 1862. In 1864 the brothers received permission to open another journal, *Epokha*, which collapsed in March 1865, after Mikhail's death and the attendant financial and editorial problems. In these journals, Dostoevsky and his brother worked as editor and publisher, but Dostoevsky also published the major works he wrote, and several minor works with political overtones, such as "A Vile Anecdote" (Skvernyi anekdot, 1861) and "The Crocodile, or Mauled in the Mall" (Neobyknovennoe sobytie, ili passazh v passazhe, 1865). The latter presents the pronouncements of a man in the belly of a crocodile in the Passage, a St. Petersburg shopping center, cruelly paralleling those of CHERNYSHEVSKY as a political prisoner. Dostoevsky also included a series of articles on Russian literature (1861) and a perceptively hostile picture of European poverty and godless money-grubbing in "Winter Notes on Summer Impressions" (1863). In this period of increasing tension between those who were willing or even eager to face a revolution for the triumph of scientism, atheism, feminism, socialism, or other Western values and those who, whether or not they had welcomed the great reforms of the 1860s, turned desperately to Russianness, Orthodoxy, and autocracy to restabilize society after them, Dostoevsky and his journals entered into increasingly vitriolic polemics with Chernyshevsky, DOBROLYUBOV, PISAREV, SALTYKOV-SHCHEDRIN, and other NIHILISTS whom Dostoevsky characterized as warring members of an isolated clique. Dostoevsky opposed to their views not a SLAVOPHILE repudiation of the West as such, nor a denial of the need to better the lot of Russia's poor, and certainly not any sympathy with the ideals of Russian aristocrats, bureaucrats, or plutocrats, but a doctrine that he and his associates called *pochvennichestvo*, or "grassroots." They argued that Peter the Great's Westernization had enriched Russia, but that now Russia must turn to the wisdom of its rural past if it is to say its own word in the history of man-

kind. The practical socialism of a Russian village meant far more, they thought, than the theories and experiments of Western faddists.

After his return from Europe in 1871, Dostoevsky became editor of *Grazhdanin* (The Citizen), a journal belonging to the difficult and not overly enlightened Prince Vladimir Petrovich MESHCHERSKY (1839–1914). Here he published his own strange short story about tawdry life beyond the grave, "Bobok" (1873), but most of his own writing took the form of a series of articles on literature, national and international politics, causes célèbres, and human nature, published under the heading of "A Writer's Diary." At the end of 1874, he left this work and devoted 1875 to writing *The Raw Youth*, which he published in Nekrasov's rather radical journal, *Otechestvennye zapiski*, before returning to journalism and opening *Dnevnik pisatelya* as a full scale monthly which he wrote and published by himself for 1876–77, and had resumed after *The Brothers Karamazov* with a single issue in 1881, when he died. This journal contained two of his greatest short stories, "A Gentle Creature" (Krotkaya, 1876) and "The Dream of a Ridiculous Man (Son smeshnogo cheloveka, 1877), but most of it weaves his own political, social, religious, and psychological views into a texture that has been called a special kind of art. On aesthetics, he argued against the controversial art-for-art's-sake doctrine, saying that literature (unless by a madman) is always contemporary and activist, but that censors or radical critics who try to harness that activity will stifle its capacity to influence people. On religion, he argued that Catholicism, like socialism, aspired to bring the kingdom of God into existence on earth, that this secular goal was doomed, and with it the Protestantism that opposed it, leaving Orthodoxy as the only bulwark against the atheists, Moslems, Jews, etc. He argued that the Russian autocracy's freeing of the serfs without a civil war was superior to the American oppression of ex-slaves or the godless and often mindless "isms" of the revolutionaries. Despite these anti-Semitic, anti-Turkish, anti-American, anti-French, and anti-German pronouncements, his eloquent last speech at the dedication of Pushkin's statue in Moscow (published in the 1881 *Dnevnik pisatelya*) called true Russianness the capacity to absorb and indeed to be all that is precious in all of Europe. Even if he had written no fiction at all, Dostoevsky's four journals would have made him one of the great Russian publicists, editors, and men of letters of his time. As a world figure, however, his reputation must rest on four great short stories, four novellas, four full-scale works in memoir form and the four greatest murder novels ever written.

A tetralogy of short stories

"White Nights" (Belye nochi, 1848), "Notes from Underground" (Zapiski iz podpol'ya, 1864), "A Gentle Creature" (Krotkaya, 1876), and "The Dream of a Ridiculous Man" (Son smeshnogo cheloveka, 1877) form a series of stories of which only the second has received the worldwide attention it deserves. Each of these stories presents the decisive moment in the lonely life of a nameless narrator who defines himself with bookish self-consciousness as a particular kind of Petersburg character. In each of these stories, the narrator encounters a girl who desperately needs his help, and he reacts in a way that seems to lead to a paradise, which he then loses. In the last three of these stories, the hero's unpardonable behavior destroys the real bliss which he might otherwise have enjoyed; in "White Nights" the paradise is more like that in Gogol's plots, a fairy-gift that was never really there: the implausible union of the nice and nubile Nastenka with a hopeless daydreamer who talks like a book and lives like a snail fixed to his dismal dwelling, but whose thirst for just such a companion turns the city and its buildings into girls when he describes them. Drawing on Dostoevsky's early journalistic sketches of St. Petersburg, this story recaptures the emotionalism, the valorization of individuality, and the self-deprecating mockery that characterized sentimental literature at its best, but it carries the reader from the playful hyperbole of its beginning to the high lyricism of the dreamer's final blessing upon Nastenka for having brightened four daylit evenings of a lonely life. "White Nights" is the loveliest thing that Dostoevsky wrote.

"Notes from the Underground" may well be the nastiest. Part I opens with an assault on the reader's intellectual and moral values by a narrator who is older than the dreamer in "White Nights," but so deeply embedded in his quarters too that he compares himself to a mouse lurking spitefully under the floor. He elaborates two sets of associations: with such things as ant hills, chemical retorts, piano keys, logarithm tables, the Crystal Palace Exposition in London, and the formula $2 \times 2 = 4$, he associates utilitarian social order, scientism, determinism, deadness, bull-like purposefulness, self-interest, and the mechanistic, mathematical laws of nature and reason; with the underground mouse hole, the chicken coop, tongues stuck out, pins stuck into people, beating one's head against a stone wall, and the formula $2 \times 2 = 5$, he associates consciousness, caprice, viciousness, paradox, freedom of will, life, and desire. With savage perversity and paradox he argues that caprice usually prevails over self-interest, and that it actually is one's real interest.

Part I of this story confesses the underground man's beliefs, and Part II confesses the actions and the daydreams which reflect and reinforce those beliefs. He recounts a series of incidents in which he has oscillated like his paradoxes between an impulse to reach out and enter into human contact and a drive to dominate, hurt, and be hurt. The latter eventually, inertially prevails. In the culminating episode, in hysterical spite, he deliberately misconstrues the spiritual rebirth of a prostitute whom he has redeemed according to the lessons of Chernyshevsky, Nekrasov, and other romantic seekers after moral beauty. Like the Underground Man, Dostoevsky distrusted scientistic and deterministic theories and despised utopian and utilitarian aspirations to bring the kingdom of heaven into existence on earth, but he uses the Underground Man less as his spokesman than as a victim struggling against such theories and aspirations. Dostoevsky's letters complain that the church censors had passed everything in the story that was blasphemous and had destroyed the resolution at the end because it was religious.

"The Gentle Creature" (also translated as "The Meek One") may contain our only clue to the nature of this lost ending. In this story, the narrator lacks even the savage appeal of the Underground Man. He is a despicable Petersburg pawnbroker driven from a military career for cowardice. He insinuates himself into the life of a girl so poor and helpless that she has nowhere to go except to marry him. And then to gratify a sick thirst for domination and a sicker fantasy of eventually revealing his true nobility in longed-for splendor, he tortures her with discipline and silence until she rebels, is crushed, and kills herself. She dies holding an icon, although suicide precludes repentance and is the one sin which Orthodoxy cannot pardon. For thirty pages, the pawnbroker recounts this story, justifying himself before her bier, but on the last page, he looks at her thin face and realizes what he has done: "I tortured her to death. That's what." With new-found eloquence, he gives a name to his incapacity to express, or understand, or even feel the dimensions of his love for her while she lived: "Inertia, oh nature, people are alone on earth, and that's our woe." In thirty pages, Dostoevsky has created as unredeemed a villain as exists in literature, and on this last page leads him to remember the command "Love one another," through the act of telling what he only realized was a love story after having told it.

"The Gentle Creature" ends with the question of a half-crazed, totally dependent lover, "But what will become of me when they take her away?" Though the question expects no real answer, it tempts readers to think of a strange Petersburger like the narrator of "The Dream of a Ridiculous Man," who is also a loner and who also says of the world, "it doesn't matter at all." On his way home to commit suicide, this ridiculous man encounters a desperate little girl but ignores her pleas for help. He dreams that he has taken his life, been wafted to paradise, and corrupted it, and out of this dream emerges a love of life more important than the meaning of life. The story differs from all of Dostoevsky's other work in its extreme abstractness. The man is abstractly ridiculous. We never laugh at him. He simply corrupts the paradise; there are no other characters in the story with any minds at all. It represents Dostoevsky's approach to a complex of ideas and images and literary techniques which had haunted his entire career, but from a new direction, an abstract style which he never lived to elaborate.

Four novellas and four memoir-like works

In addition to his journalism, his tetralogy of short stories, and his four world-famous novels, Dostoevsky devoted his mature talent to four full-length works that derive their form and much of their material from autobiography, and to four novellas (povesti) which he wrote in the decade after his exile. Like satirical dramas or society novels modeled on Scott's *St. Ronan's Well*, the novellas *Uncle's Dream* (Dyadyushkin son, 1859), *The Friend of the Family* (Selo Stepanchikovo, 1859), *The Gambler* (Igrok, 1867), and *The Eternal Husband* (Vechnyi muzh, 1870), all show the collision of normal and decent humanity with characters who carry such commonplace traits as provincial propriety, religiosity, weakness for roulette, or uxoriousness to the point of self-destructive hysteria. In these four works Dostoevsky experiments with his beloved scandal scenes, with explorations of emotion interworking with idea, and with his chief departure from the evolving European craft of novel-writing—his unimaginative chronicler of barely imaginable events. Like Pushkin's "Little Tragedies" these novellas humanize manias in a way that later readers have found psychologically shrewd and socially subtle, but Dostoevsky here stops short of morality and serious religious experience, the two areas in which his novelistic power is greatest. In these novellas, also, Dostoevsky may not have processed his sources as thoroughly as elsewhere. For *Uncle's Dream*, the town of Semipalatinsk and Turgenev's and SALTYKOV's ironic vision of the provinces, derived in turn from Dostoevsky's earliest favorites, Pushkin, Gogol, and Balzac, lie very near the surface of Dostoevsky's work. *The Friend of the Family* emerges from the same complex of literary and real life experience, with the addition of Molière's *Tartuffe* and a rebellion against Gogol's portentous political pronouncements in his later works. In the *Gambler*, Dostoevsky drew with understandable haste and passion on his visits to the German watering places, on Rousseau's vision of the trustworthy Englishman, and on the figure of Polina Suslova, who exploited his own weakness with such exquisite ingenuity; and in *The Eternal Husband*, he drew on the rich literature of cuckoldry for his picture of compulsive behavior.

Over a longer period of time, Dostoevsky undertook four full-length quasi-memoirs in which an innocent looks back upon a period of acculturation into some rather dark world of exaggerated character traits held in check by a rigid social structure: *Netochka Nezvanova* (1849), *The House of the Dead* (Zapiski iz mertvogo doma, 1860–62), *The Insulted and Injured* (Unizhennye i oskorblennye, 1861), and *The Raw Youth* (or *The Adolescent*, Podrostok, 1875). Netochka Nezvanova narrates her upbringing among poor musicians and wealthy aristocrats in St. Petersburg, and then her discovery of the secrets of her elders and of her own emotional life. Dostoevsky's arrest interrupted this novel, and he never finished it. It remains of interest for its early explorations of spiteful and gratuitous acts, for the intensity of passion, and for the light it throws on Dostoevsky's interest in the female psyche.

The House of the Dead claims to be the memoir of a very different person, the murderer Goryanchikov, entering a very different world, that of the prison camps where Dostoevsky had spent four terrible years. Unlike Dostoevsky, Goryanchikov emerges from prison empty of any spirit or capacity to deal with his fellow human beings, but other memoirists have identified most of the officers and convicts Dostoevsky describes, making *The House of the Dead* either a real memoir with a fictional narrator or else a novel with the first-person form and the experienced content of a memoir. Goryanchikov's account begins in an almost anthropological manner, with a distanced narrator describing a remote and remarkable society. Almost immediately, the cruelty and the uselessness of the prison system emerge in discussions of punishments and of the unrepentance of the prisoners. The hostility between peasantry and gentry, and their shared sympathy with escapees and released captives lead naturally back to the beginning, with its graphic depiction of the harm this prison system does, in the person of Goryanchikov, whom it has reduced from a man to a zombie. But the great power of the book lies not in such teachings but in the harrowing lives the inmates live as they eat, sleep, bathe, pray, go to the hospital, drink themselves into insensibility, work for themselves, or on labor details, or recount their deeds outside the camp. The raw, largely unplotted ugliness of peasant life and prison life overpowers the death-dealing order of the authorities, making this work one of the masterpieces in a tradition reaching from AVVAKUM to SOLZHENITSYN and SHALAMOV.

In *The Insulted and Injured*, Dostoevsky's memoirist again encounters an underworld, but the setting returns to St. Petersburg, and the emotional level and the subject matter are often Dickensian. The figures of Nellie and Natasha carry Dostoevsky's exploration of female psychology further than Netochka Nezvanova, and the memoirist, Ivan Petrovich seems to share a number of traits and experiences with the more successful and aggressive writer Fyodor Dostoevsky. The inherent limitations on what a quasi-memoirist can know also led Dostoevsky to use the self-abasing confession to convey plot elements beyond his narrator's ken. In general, *The Insulted and Injured* lacks the enormous power of *The House of the Dead*, but marks an important step in Dostoevsky's development of techniques and ways of understanding.

In *The Raw Youth*, Arkady Dolgoruky reminisces about his own assault on the sophisticated world. He begins with an outsider's vision in which power matters above all, and he daydreams about attaining such power as the Rothschilds have. But his pursuit and discovery of his natural father Versilov introduces him into a world of noble passion around Akhmakova, into a tawdry underworld around Lambert, and into a mysteriously holy world around his legal father, Makar Dolgoruky. Thematically, *The Raw Youth* forms an integral part of Dostoevsky's emotional, intellectual, and literary development, but the lost documents, secret passions, great misunderstandings, and other melodramatic apparatus that emerge automatically when an author presents a long, complicated plot through a first-person narrator, have made this, like the two other highly plotted quasi-memoirs, a private favorite of Dostoevsky lovers but not a world classic.

The four great murder novels

Like Shakespeare's, Dostoevsky's four most generally accepted masterworks deal with murder: one with murderous ambition and remorse (*Crime and Punishment*, Prestuplenie i nakazanie, 1866); another with unwise attachments and murderous jealousy (*The Idiot*, Idiot, 1868); a third with young arrivals from abroad laying waste their fathers' city and then annihilating themselves (*The Possessed*, Besy, 1872); and the fourth with an exploration of the ways a group of passionate siblings lives out the metamorphoses of parricide (*The Brothers Karamazov*, Brat'ya Karamazovy, 1880). Within these successive contexts Dostoevsky elaborates and develops a cluster of recurring themes, events, organizing patterns, and character types. The dramatization of one's own degradation, for example, emerges rather conventionally in the self-destructive drunkard Marmeladov, who inspires most readers of *Crime and Punishment* with harrowing pity and provokes laughter only in the sort of barflies who could laugh in a nightmare of Raskolnikov's at a horse being beaten to death. In *The Idiot*, these themes mingle in the infectious buffoonery of Lebedev and General Ivolgin, but also mature into the existential confession of the dying Ippolit, whose nihilism and exhibitionism recur in the central figures of *The Possessed*, Stavrogin and Pyotr Verkhovensky. As Dostoevsky's sense of humor grows richer and less traditionally literary, however, his presentation of buffoonery transcends the drunken self-congratulation of Lebyadkin in *The Possessed* and erupts in *The Brothers Karamazov* into an entire pathology of the self, embodied in Maksimov, Madame Khokhlakova, Snegiryov, and Kolya Krasotkin, and culminating in the inspired illogic of the arrantly disreputable Fyodor Karamazov. In much the same way, the curiously passive and childlike power of goodness evolves from novel to novel from the saintliness of Sonya and the puppy-like practicality of Razumikhin through the magnetic mysticism of Myshkin and then the religious nationalism of Shatov to the active love Alyosha Karamazov and Zosima practice.

Dostoevsky embodies evil in two character types. The petty villain Luzhin and his radical associate Lebezyatnikov evolve into the politically and existentially exacerbated Ippolit and the infuriating radicals around him, who reappear as the terrifying band of radicals around the manipulative villain Pyotr Verkhovensky, and finally decline into the ridiculous and repulsive radical Rakitin in *The Brothers Karamazov*. The first three of these novels balance their sets of petty political villains against single satanic sensualists of huge hypnotic authority, Svidrigailov, Rogozhin, or Stavrogin, while the single Rakitin has three such counterparts: Ivan Karamazov, whose agnostic passion summons up the Devil, Smerdyakov, who exploits the hypnotic suggestiveness of evil, and Mitya, who enunciates the destructive power of sensuality. In each of these novels, desire centers on a well-bred woman and a fallen woman: the gallant Dunya and the prostitute Sonya, the inaccessible Aglaya and the hysterical Nastasya Filippovna; the passionate Dasha and the deranged Marya; and finally, as Dostoevsky's own emotions matured, the self-lacerating Katerina Ivanovna, and the catlike Grushenka, with her overflow of angry pride, native Russianness, and sex.

Like the Cathedral of the Blessed Basil, *Crime and Punishment* derives much of its power from the symmetrical simplicity of the plan underlying its fierce intricacies. Raskolnikov believes he has reasoned himself into a sordid, pitilessly rehearsed and calculated murder, but his dreams, his mistakes, and his sudden impulses display a compassionate, liberating, generous humanity. This opposition between cruel, conscious, utilitarian, greedy, sick, superstitious suffocation and the breath of holy life with its instinctive decency and self-abnegation, organizes the characters, the actions, and the motives in the novel, right down to the name Raskolnikov, which suggests not only the fanaticism of a Russian schismatic, but also his transsected nature. To overrule the testimony of his own subconscious, Raskolnikov's rational self ascribes his murder of a vicious pawnbroker to his poverty in the oppressive city of St. Petersburg, to the need to demonstrate that his own status resembled that of Julius Caesar, whom Napoleon III called a great man whom the greatest good of the greatest number exempts from ordinary morality, and to the need to provide for his widowed mother and his gallant sister Dunya, who is threatened by the lecherous murderer Svidrigailov and about to be married off to the despicable businessman Luzhin. The prostitute Sonya and the detective Porfiry encourage Raskolnikov's aesthetic and moral revulsion against the murder. Sonya works religiously, weeping uncomprehendingly for Raskolnikov's second victim, the unresisting sister of the pawnbroker, and for the third precious life he has destroyed, his own. Porfiry works psychologically, giggling knowingly until Raskolnikov realizes what he already feels instinctively, that criminals suffer from a disease with two symptoms, first the drive to crime, and second, a drive to confess or get caught which leads to suicide unless satisfied. The nightmarish suicide of the other murderer, Svidrigailov, confirms one branch of this disjunction, and Raskolnikov's repeated blunders, suspicious acts, and near confessions confirm the other branch even before he brings himself to confess religiously to massed humanity, and socially, to a police lieutenant who is the only figure in the novel with both a public and a family life. Confession here does not result from repentance but enables it to happen. Only in a Siberian prison camp does Raskolnikov's subconscious humanity produce an ideological dream which unfolds the implicit argument that self-serving rationality is actually a symptom of an oppressive unrecognized disease of the spirit. Dostoevsky planned *Crime and Punishment* as a first person narration, and the published version retains much of the obsessive concentration on Raskolnikov which that plan would have offered. The narrative stays so close to Raskolnikov that readers hold their breath along with him when capture seems imminent, thus physically experiencing the sensation of a murderer trying to escape. By implicating his readers in Raskolnikov's escape and also in the contagious glory and contagious sordidness of the St. Petersburg Raskolnikov experiences, Dostoevsky ultimately involves them with equal power in Raskolnikov's vacillating progress from the rational necessity for murder and suicide to the religious necessity for life and resurrection.

In *The Idiot*, these impulses toward destruction and salvation emerge in a pair of characters who arrive in St. Petersburg together. Rogozhin, the debauched orphan of a rich merchant feels strangely attracted to Myshkin, the epileptic, visionary orphan of an impoverished prince. Unlike Raskolnikov, these two enter the St. Petersburg of successful merchants, entrepreneurs, and bureaucrats, with their shady hangers-on. Dostoevsky hoped to embody in Myshkin that magic goodness which he found in Don Quixote and Mr. Pickwick, but several characters in this worldly community find Myshkin too naive for belief. He does inspire immediate hospitality in some and candor in others, and his floundering efforts to find good in this demi-monde enrich the lives of those in whom he finds it, though his efforts to do good merely demonstrate his impotence, unless he is dealing with children or the childlike. He enchants the childlike wife and beautiful daughters of General Epanchin, but falls in love with the hysterical beauty of Nastasya Filippovna, the kept woman whom the exquisite Totsky is trying to marry off to Epanchin's mediocre aide Ganya Ivolgin.

This beauty drives the central action of the novel, motivating Totsky, Ganya, Rogozhin, Myshkin at crucial moments, operating on Myshkin even when abstracted from her person, since he falls in love with her picture before meeting her. He reacts to the aesthetic with overwhelming intensity: a calligraphic flourish, a Swiss valley with a waterfall, the horror of a Holbein Pietà, or the ghastly face of a man about to be beheaded all hold a richness of implication for him which relates to the totality of consciousness in the instant before an epileptic fit. But beauty can also belong to the doll-like vapidity of a dinner guest, and Ippolit's mind, even more diseased than Myshkin's, experiences a monster whose ugliness also approaches the absolute. These complexities make the aesthetic lesson of the book as problematical as the ineffectuality of goodness makes the moral lesson. As a whole, the novel has more of the gratuitous than *Crime and Punishment*, more psychologies driven by forces not perspicuous to the narrator or the characters themselves. The narrator's discovery of his own bewilderment halfway through the novel may mark Dostoevsky's discovery of a novelistic technique for bewildering his reader which he exploited fully in *The Possessed*.

Like *Crime and Punishment*, *The Possessed* has its center near the point where politics, morals, and religion intersect, but it begins where *Crime and Punishment* ends, with the vision of a society infested by evil creatures that produce devastating delusions of rationality. Here, Dostoevsky compares infectious radicalism with the devils that drove the Gadarene swine over a precipice. He draws his central inspiration from the anti-nihilist novels current at the time and from the trials (1871–73) of those around Sergei Gennadievich Nechaev (1847–82) whose violent writings had aroused a public reaction almost as angry as his use of a group murder to implicate his associates irrevocably in his plot. Dostoevsky depicts the disruption when a band of modish radicals move into a stultified provincial town where little has happened since the arrival of Stepan Trofimovich Verkhovensky, a pretentious hanger-on, first in the liberal 1840s circles in the capitals, and later in the provincial Stavrogin household. The novel contrasts his posturings with the murderousness of his son Pyotr and with the enigmatic power of his pupil Nikolai Stavrogin, whose apathy and gratuitous actions arouse immense expectations. Dostoevsky obscures Stavrogin's nature and motives, but gives him a central role in the past history of many characters, at least as they report it. Kirillov, the totally asocial being, ascribes to Stavrogin his theory that suicide can shake the world, and leaves the world unshaken by his suicide. Shatov ascribes his idealistic nationalism to Stavrogin, and Stavrogin fails to interfere with Pyotr's plan for the group murder of Shatov. *The Possessed* has more spectacular scandal scenes than any of Dostoevsky's novels, more deaths of major characters, and one confession by Stavrogin of a child rape so horrible it was censored. Dostoevsky made no effort to restore it in later editions, probably because he had adjusted the later chapters to compensate for its loss. As a political tract, a portrayal of sick minds, and a study of the manipulations of groups, *The Possessed* remains Dostoevsky's masterpiece.

In *The Brothers Karamazov*, Dostoevsky confronts the problem of faith and the problem of evil, drawing together many elements from his earlier fiction and journalism and also from a number of works he planned but never wrote, including, "The Russian Candide," "Atheism," a novel about children, a trilogy called *The Life of a Great Sinner*, and a play about the convict Ilyinsky, who served many years in Siberia for parricide before the real murderers confessed. The existing novel presents the murder of the vicious, drunken, avaricious, and perversely funny old lecher Fyodor Karamazov, who has three sons, Mitya, Ivan and Alyosha, and probably the bastard servant Smerdyakov as well. Old Fyodor mocks the faith of Alyosha and the monks Alyosha reveres; he debates the existence of God with Smerdyakov and with his intellectual son Ivan. Ivan in turn tempts Alyosha's faith with his legend of the Grand Inquisitor, who sees Christ perform miracles but rejects him for not using his divinity to forestall all human doubts and sins. Ivan shifts the argument from belief in God to the rejection of a God who permits innocent children to suffer in His universe, an argument Dostoevsky had told his editor was unanswerable. Abandoned, suffering, or tortured children appear in this novel in a dozen contexts, from the neglected Karamazov brothers at the start to the agonized Snegiryov's dying son Ilyusha at the end, persecuted by his classmates and their natural leader Kolya Krasotkin. In the town's monastery, Alyosha's holy mentor, the elder Zosima argues that in a world where universal causality links all actions, we should not blame God for all such evil, but bear the guilt ourselves because every human being at some time has started trains of evil actions leading ultimately to the horrors we

blame on God. Zosima also argues that when God's grace dies, through the death of a good person or the death of goodness in a person who survives, it never dies completely but will be revived and instill new grace in others. The careers of Mitya, Alyosha, and Zosima, all confirm this pattern. All receive the insemination of grace, in a blessing, an obeisance, or an embrace, and all fall into a state of mind where lust and anger leave grace dead. And all fall asleep and wake up saved by childhood memories which are the repository of apparently dead grace.

Reputation and influence

Dostoevsky has a reputation as a teacher of politics, religion, psychology, and ethics, and as a novelist. During his lifetime, political considerations dominated most literary discussion and his polemics with the radical critics established the outline of his subsequent reputation. Reactionaries praised and radicals blamed him for his anti-nihilism and support for autocracy, some claiming that his prison camp experience had crushed his early radicalism. In the 1920s, DOLININ and others argued against his suppression, citing his early radical ties, his compassion for the oppressed, his critique of the bourgeoisie, and his association with Nekrasov and other radicals in the mid-seventies. They lost, and as late as the 1950s a 500-page history of Russian literature did not mention Dostoevsky's name. In 1956 the Soviets reached a compromise which restored Dostoevsky to scholarly and popular attention as a critical realist who presented and embodied the contradictions of his time. In Western scholarship, his nationalism has attracted more attention than his conservatism and has offered a rather neat explanation for his rejection of the Westernized radicalism of the 1860s and his rapprochement with some of the more populist radicals of the 1870s.

Dostoevsky's religious beliefs attracted the wrath of the radical press from the 1860s on, and the support of the official church press from the 1870s on. His interest in N. K. FYODOROV, friendship with Konstantin Pobedonostsev, and close ties with Vladimir SOLOVYOV left legacies in different parts of the Orthodox community which lead eventually to writings like V. V. ROZANOV's, Vyacheslav IVANOV's, and Nikolai BERDYAEV's, and those of others who discover new religious liberations and new kinds of God–man interplay in "The Notes from the Underground," *The Possessed*, and *The Brothers Karamazov*.

Dostoevsky's reputation as a psychological novelist emerged chiefly in the West following de Vogüé's description of him as a spirit alien to Western ways of thought. French scholars turned to him for insights into murder, hallucination, and madness, and Freud's "Dostoevsky and Parricide" (1928) has helped to make Dostoevsky a seminal figure for the entire psychological community. Russian men of letters like N. K. MIKHAILOVSKY and Maksim GORKY often see Dostoevsky's interest in suffering and other extreme psychological states as a reflection of a sensual pleasure in suffering for which there is little non-literary evidence.

In France after World War II, the existentialists turned to Dostoevsky along with Kierkegaard as the Christian forerunners for their new ethic, just as they saw Nietzsche as their pagan ancestor. Lev SHESTOV, V. V. Rozanov, and others had paved the way for this awareness, but Camus, Malraux, and Sartre made it explicit in their drama, fiction and philosophical writings.

Although these four aspects of Dostoevsky's reputation had their beginnings at different times and in different places, all four persist actively and fruitfully down to the present day. Joseph Frank's ambitious presentation of Dostoevsky's thought in the context of intellectual history is the basis for a synthesis of these four approaches. As a practitioner of novel writing, Dostoevsky attracted little scholarly attention until just before World War I, when Leonid GROSSMAN wrote about the self-conscious way in which Dostoevsky used Russian and European models for his work. In 1921, the opening of the box of notebooks, letters, and other materials left by Dostoevsky's widow permitted Russian and German editions of the materials indispensable for the study of Dostoevsky's "creative laboratory." In France, André Gide's book removed the aura of exoticism, and in England the Constance Garnett translations made the texts widely available. Dolinin, V. S. Nechaeva, V. G. Komarovich, and others set the novels into literary history and theory. In the Stalinist period, the center of Dostoevsky studies shifted to the West, where most of the works were available in the major languages, and scholarship on Dostoevsky's sources and his techniques became as important as the more traditional studies of his life, his work, and his thought. Novelists from Ralph Ellison to Leonid LEONOV boast of studying his techniques, and his writing is part of the standard high school curriculum in the Soviet Union and elsewhere. The scholarship of FRIDLENDER, Toporov, Belov, Tunimanov, Vetlovskaya, and many others in the Soviet Union is indispensable to serious scholars in the West, and the thirty-volume edition of Dostoevsky's works now in progress will confirm the maturity and the breadth of Dostoevsky scholarship in the Soviet Union.

Works: Polnoe sobranie khudozhestvennykh proizvedenii; Dnevnik pisatelya; stat'i. Ed. B. Tomashevskii and K. Khalabaev. 13 vols. 1926–30. *Pis'ma.* Ed. A. S. Dolinin. Vols. 1–3, 1928–34, vol. 4, 1959. *Polnoe sobranie sochinenii v tridtsati tomakh.* Ed. G. M. Fridlender et al. 1972–
Recommended English translations: (The Penguin editions of the Magarshack translations of the major novels are somewhat more accurate than the graceful, competent, and enormously influential Constance Garnett translations of virtually all of Dostoevsky's fiction.) *Novels.* Trans. Constance Garnett. New York, 1912. *The Short novels of Dostoevsky.* Trans. Constance Garnett. New York, 1945, 1951. *The Short Stories of Dostoevsky.* Trans. Constance Garnett. New York, 1946, 1957. *Crime and Punishment.* Trans. Jessie Coulson; ed. George Gibian. Norton Critical Editions. New York, 1964. *The Brothers Karamazov.* Trans. Constance Garnett; ed. Ralph Matlaw. Norton Critical Editions. New York, 1976.
Translations of Dostoevsky's Non-Fiction: The Diary of a Writer. Trans. Boris Brasol. New York, 1949. *Dostoevsky's Occasional Writings.* Trans. and ed. David Magarshack. New York, 1963. *The Notebooks for* Crime and Punishment. Trans. Edward Wasiolek. Chicago, 1967. *The Notebooks for* The Idiot. Trans. Katharine Strelsky. Chicago, 1968. *The Notebooks for* The Possessed. Trans. Victor Terras. Chicago, 1968. *The Notebooks for* A Raw Youth. Trans. Victor Terras. Chicago, 1969. *The Notebooks for* The Brothers Karamazov. Trans. Edward Wasiolek. Chicago, 1971. *The Unpublished Dostoevsky, Diaries and Notebooks, 1860–1881.* 3 vols. Ann Arbor, 1973–76.
Secondary literature: [S. V. Belov,] *Dostoevskii, bibliografiya 1917–1965.* Moscow, 1968. M. M. Bakhtin, *Problemy tvorchestva Dostoevskogo.* Moscow, 1929. ———, *Problems of Dostoevsky's Poetics.* Trans. R. W. Rotsel. Ann Arbor, 1973. N. F. Bel'chikov, *Dostoevskii v protsesse petrashevtsev.* Moscow, 1971. A. L. Bem, ed, *O Dostoevskom, sbornik statei.* Prague, Vol. 1, 1929; Vol. 2, 1932; Vol. 3, 1936; Vol. 4, 1938. N. M. Chirkov, *O stile Dostoevskogo.* Moscow, 1963, 1967. Jacques Catteau, *Dostoïevski.* Paris, 1973. ———, *La création littéraire chez Dostoïevski.* Paris, 1978. A. G. Dostoevskaya, *Muzei pamyati F. M. Dostoevskogo.* St. Petersburg, 1906. ———, *Vospominaniya.* Moscow, 1925. ———, *Reminiscences.* Trans. Beatrice Stillman. New York, 1975. ———, *Dnevnik.* Moscow, 1923. ———, *Perepiska.* Leningrad, 1976. A. S. Dolinin, ed, *Dostoevskii, stat'i i materialy.* Petrograd, Vol. 1, 1922; Vol. 2, 1926. ———, ed, *Materialy i issledovaniya.* Moscow, 1935. ———, *V tvorcheskoi laboratorii Dostoevskogo.* Moscow, 1947. ———, *Poslednie romany Dostoevskogo.* Moscow, 1963. ———, ed. *F. M. Dostoevskii v vospominaniyakh sovremennikov.* 2 vols. Moscow, 1964. Donald Fanger, *Dostoevsky and Romantic Realism, a Study of Dostoevsky in Relation to Balzac, Dickens and Gogol.* Cambridge, Mass., 1965. ———, ed, *O Dostoevskom* [Articles by P. M. Bitsilli and others]. Providence, 1966. Joseph Frank, *Dostoevsky, The Seeds of Revolt.* Princeton, 1976. G. M. Fridlender, *Realizm Dostoevskogo.* Leningrad, 1964. ———, ed, *Dostoevskii, materialy i issledovaniya.* 6 vols. Leningrad, 1974–83. ———, ed, *Dostoevskii i ego vremya.* Leningrad, 1971. L. P. Grossman, *Biblioteka Dostoevskogo.* Odessa, 1919. ———, *Tvorchestvo Dostoevskogo.* Odessa, 1921–28. ———, *Seminarii po Dostoevskomu.* Moscow, 1922. ———, *Put' Dostoevskogo.* Leningrad, 1924, 1928. ———, *Poetika Dostoevskogo.* Moscow, 1925, 1928. ———, *Zhizn' i trudy Dostoevskogo, biografiya v datakh i dokumentakh.* Moscow, 1935. ———, *Dostoevskii.* Moscow, 1962, 1965. ———, *Dostoevsky.* Trans. M. Mackler. New York, 1973. ———, ed, *Tvorchestvo Dostoevskogo, Sbornik statei i materialov.* Moscow, 1970. Michael Holquist, *Dostoevsky and the Novel.* Princeton, 1977. International Dostoevsky Society, *Bulletin,* 1970–79. ———, *Dostoevsky Studies,* 1980– . Robert L. Jackson, *Dostoev-*

sky's Quest for Form. New Haven, 1965. ———, *The Art of Dostoevsky.* Princeton, 1981. ———, ed, *Twentieth Century Interpretations of* Crime and Punishment. Englewood Cliffs, N. J., 1974. Robin Miller, *Dostoevsky and* The Idiot. Cambridge, Mass., 1981. K. D. Mochul'skii, *Dostoevskii, zhizn' i tvorchestvo.* Paris, 1927. ———, *Dostoevsky, His Life and Work.* Trans. Michael Minihan. Princeton, 1967. Gary Morson, *The Boundaries of Genre.* Austin, 1981. V. S. Nechaeva, *Opisanie rukopisei F. M. Dostoevskogo.* Moscow, 1957. ———, *Rannii Dostoevskii, 1821–1849.* Moscow, 1979. ———, *Zhurnal M. M. i F. M. Dostoevskikh* Vremya, *1861–1863.* Moscow, 1972. Vladimir Seduro, *Dostoevsky in Russian Literary Criticism, 1846–1956.* New York, 1957. ———, *Dostoevsky's Image in Russia Today.* Belmont, Mass., 1975. Victor Terras, *The Young Dostoevsky (1846–1849).* The Hague, 1969. ———, *A Karamazov Companion: Commentary on the Genesis, Language and Style of Dostoevsky's Novel.* Madison, 1981. Yurii Tynyanov, *Arkhaisty i novatory, Dostoevskii i Gogol'.* Petrograd, 1921. V. V. Vinogradov, *Evolyutsiya russkogo naturalizma, Gogol' i Dostoevskii.* Leningrad, 1929. ———, *O yazyke khudozhestvennoi literatury.* Moscow, 1959. ———, *Problema avtorstva i teoriya stilei.* Moscow, 1961. M. V. Volotskoi, *Khronika roda Dostoevskogo, 1506–1933.* Moscow, 1933. Edward Wasiolek, *Dostoevsky, The Major Fiction.* Cambridge, Mass., 1964. ———, ed, Crime and Punishment *and the Critics.* San Francisco, 1961. René Wellek, ed, *Dostoevsky, A Collection of Critical Essays.* Englewood Cliffs, N. J., 1962. V. A. Zelinskii, ed., *Kriticheskie kommentarii k sochineniyam F. M. Dostoevskogo, sbornik statei.* 4 vols. Moscow, 1901–06. R. L. B.

Dostoévsky, Mikhail Mikhailovich, (1820–64), editor, publisher, critic, translator and storywriter. Born in Moscow and educated with his younger brother Fyodor in Moscow schools and the St. Petersburg Military Engineering Academy, Mikhail Dostoevsky returned to St. Petersburg in 1847 after five years' military service in Revel. Always very close to his brother, he also translated Goethe and Schiller, and wrote stories in the Gogolian and the "physiological" fashion, including "The Daughter" (Dochka, 1848), "Mr. Svetelkin" (1848), "The Sparrow" (Vorobei, 1848), "Two Oldsters" (Dva starika, 1849), "Fifty Years" (Pyat'desyat let, 1850), as well as the comedy *The Older and the Younger* (Starshaya i men'shaya, 1851). Among several unfinished works, the Dickensian novel *Money* (Den'gi) survives in a manuscript of the same period, with one chapter published in 1852 as "Brother and Sister" (Brat i sestra). Though arrested briefly along with Fyodor, he was exculpated of any serious involvement with the Fourierist PETRASHEVSKY circle. In 1852, he opened a small tobacco factory which he sold in 1860 to reenter the literary world with an article on OSTROVSKY and a number of translations, including Victor Hugo's *Last Day of a Condemned Man.* With Fyodor's return from exile, Mikhail found his real calling as editor and co-publisher of the monthlies *Vremya* (1861–63), and *Epokha* (1863–64), which collapsed soon after his death, leaving Fyodor desperate and destitute but devoted to Mikhail's memory and family.

Works: Mikhail M. Dostoevskii. *Sobranie sochinenii.* Petrograd, 1915.
Secondary literature: Fedor M. Dostoevskii, "Neskol'ko slov o M. M. Dostoevskom," *Epokha,* 1864, no. 6, pp. I–VI. V. S. Nechaeva, *Rannii Dostoevskii, 1821–1849.* 1979. ———, *Zhurnal M. M. i F. M. Dostoevskikh,* Vremya, *1861–63.* 1972. ———, *Zhurnal M. M. i F. M. Dostoevskikh* Epokha, *1864–1865.* 1975. R. L. B.

Drama, Russian. The opposition of the Orthodox Church to musical and theatrical entertainments delayed the appearance of drama in Russia until the late 17th century. The first recorded performance of a literary play took place on 17 October 1672 when a prose comedy based on the biblical book of Esther entitled *Artakserksovo deistvo* was staged for the benefit of the Tsar Aleksei Mikhailovich and his family at the newly built court theater in the palace at Preobrazhenskoe. Translated into a curious mixture of Church Slavonic and the contemporary idiom of the bureaucracy (the so-called "chancery language") from the original German of Johann Gottfried Gregory, the pastor of the Lutheran Church in Moscow's *nemetskaya sloboda,* or foreign quarter, the play took ten hours to perform and employed a cast of some sixty-four amateur actors recruited for the occasion by

Pastor Gregory. The Tsar's death in 1676 adversely affected the fortunes of the new Russian theater, for his son Fyodor, his immediate heir, forbade further dramatic presentations.

The situation was brighter in the Ukraine where the KIEV ACADEMY, founded in 1632 by Pyotr Mohyla, staged plays on the model of the Latin school drama of the Jesuit academies in Poland. At first, these plays were presented in Latin and served the pedagogical function of providing instruction in that language. Later, Latin was replaced by the local vernacular and CHURCH SLAVONIC. When scholars of the Kievan Academy were invited to Moscow in the time of Tsar Aleksei Mikhailovich to assist in the modernization of Muscovite education, it was from their ranks that the first native Slavic playwrights in the history of Russian drama were recruited. The first was the Belorussian SIMEON POLOTSKY (1629–80), the tutor to the Tsar's children, the first postmedieval poet in the Russian literary tradition, the codifier of the Polish-derived syllabic prosodic system then in use in Russia, and the first Russian playwright. Polotsky wrote two plays in syllabic verse, presumably for performance at court: *The Tragedy of King Nebuchadnezzar, the Golden Calf, and the Three Youths not Burned in the Furnace*, a short piece to be performed by just six actors and adapted from the Orthodox church ceremony of the "three youths in the fiery furnace"; and *The Comedy Parable of the Prodigal Son*, a five-act drama based on the New Testament parable. *The Prodigal Son* was published posthumously in 1685 and proved a great success.

More impressive a dramatist than Simeon Polotsky was Daniil Tuptalo, Metropolitan of Rostov, also known as St. Dimitry ROSTOV-SKY (1651–1709) after his canonization in 1751. Tuptalo was the author of several mostly short plays composed for (and performed by) the students in the monastery school founded by him in Rostov. The best known of these are *The Nativity of Christ* (Rozhdestvo Khristovo), *The Resurrection of Christ* (Voskresenie Khristovo), and *The Ascension Play* (Uspenskaya drama), which was discovered only in 1907. While on the whole faithful to the school drama tradition of didacticism and allegory, Tuptalo modified it by introducing comic and realistic characters and action into the play's serious scenes rather than relegating them, as was customary, to inter-act diversions known as "interludia" or "intermedia."

Tuptalo's plays date from 1702 to 1706. During this period, in 1705, the most original preclassicist Russian drama was written, the five-act syllabic *Tragicomedy of St. Vladimir* (generally referred to simply as *Vladimir*) by the outstanding ideologue of Peter the Great's reform program, Feofan PROKOPOVICH (1681–1733), Archbishop of Novgorod and former rector of the Kiev Academy. *Vladimir* was written while Prokopovich was a professor of rhetoric at the Academy on the occasion of the school's annual celebration.

Commemorating the conversion to Christianity of the Grand Duke Vladimir of Kiev in 988, the "tragicomedy" is greatly enlivened by the antics of the pagan priests Zherivol ("Bull-glutton"), Kuroyad ("Chicken-eater"), and Piar ("Drunkard") and the various temptations put before Vladimir in a vain attempt to dissuade him from his course. The play ends with a glorification of Hetman Mazeppa to whom the work was originally dedicated and who was present at the first performance in Kiev.

Aleksandr SUMAROKOV (1718–77), who eventually became the general manager of the first permanent Russian theater after its organization by the Empress Elizabeth in 1756, was Russia's first modern dramatist. He began his career writing tragedies for performance either at the Corps of Cadets, of which he was a graduate, or for the Empress's court theater. Between 1747 and 1751 he wrote five tragedies, all along strictly classicist lines and patterned after the tragedies of Voltaire: *Khorev*, *Semira*, and *Sinav and Truvor*, set in pre-Christian Russia, a classicist version of *Hamlet*, and *Aristona*, set in ancient Persia in the time of Darius. His most interesting tragic drama is undoubtedly *Dmitry the Pretender* (Dmitrii samozvanets), written in 1771. In part influenced by Shakespeare's *Richard the Third*, the play traces the Pretender's descent into evil and self-destruction. Impressed by Sumarokov's early tragedies, the Empress ordered the other major writers of the first half of the century, Vasily TREDIAKOVSKY (1703–69) and Mikhail LOMONOSOV (1711–65), to also write tragedies. Trediakovsky responded with *Deidamia*, which was indebted to the Italian Pietro Metastasio's opera libretto *Achille in Sciro* and was published only posthumously and never staged. Lomonosov wrote two tragedies, *Temira and Selim*, an "Oriental" tragedy

along the lines of Racine's *Bajazet* and Voltaire's *Zaire*, and the weaker *Demophon*, on an ancient Greek theme.

The writing of tragedy increased in the second half of the 18th century. Vasily MAIKOV (1728–78), best known for his mock epic poem *Elisei*, wrote *Agriope* and *Themistes and Hieronyma* (1773). The poet Aleksei Rzhevsky (1737–1804) was the author of *The False Smerdis* (1769), while the important poet and one-time rector of Moscow University, Mikhail KHERASKOV (1733–1807), used his tragedy *The Venetian Nun* (Venetsianskaya monakhinya, 1758), marked by elements of the new sensibility of sentimentalism, to attack religious intolerance. Kheraskov's political liberalism, manifest in his plays, changed drastically, however, under the impress of CATHERINE's sharpened reaction and the French Revolution. His tragedy *Liberated Moscow* (Osvobozhdennaya Moskva, 1798), was an unabashed celebration of the Romanov dynasty and autocracy. Nikolai NIKOLEV (1758–1815) wrote *Sorena and Zemir* (Sorena i Zamir, 1784), modelled after Voltaire's *Alzire, ou les américains* (1736). Like Trediakovsky before him, Yakov KNYAZHNIN (1742–91), Sumarokov's son-in-law, found inspiration for a tragedy in a work by Metastasio: his *Dido* (1769) is a free adaptation of the Italian writer's opera libretto *Didone abbandonata*. Other tragedies, with Russian settings, followed: *Vladimir and Yaropolk*, *Rosslav*, *Vladisan*, and *Olga*. On commission by the Empress Catherine he converted Metastasio's *La clemenza di Tito* into a musical tragedy with sung choruses and ballets. The Metastasio work as well as Corneille's *Cinna* were the sources of his best known and, in its time, controversial tragic drama, *Vadim of Novgorod* (1789). The play went into rehearsal the following year, but fearing adverse reaction to it in the wake of the French Revolution, Knyazhnin himself had the production stopped. The play was still denounced as subversive, and on Catherine's personal order all copies were confiscated and the work was burned publicly by an executioner. The full text, without deletions, was published for the first time only in 1914.

Catherine's opposition to whatever she regarded as threatening to her authority expressed itself also in literary form. While lacking in originality and any real feeling for the theater, her collected works for the stage, opera libretti included, fill three volumes in Russian and one in French, which she wrote more comfortably. There was hardly a genre of 18th-century classicist drama she did not essay, but few of her plays had any resonance. They do, however, shed much light on such pet peeves of the Empress as FREEMASONRY, reform-minded writers, and all forms of mysticism. In the field of tragedy her most interesting work was a historical drama about the first Varangian prince of Russia, Ryurik, titled *Historical Presentation, from the Life of Ryurik* (Istoricheskoe predstavlenie, iz zhizni Ryurika, 1786), which she subtitled "An Imitation of Shakespeare, without preservation of the customary theatrical rules." This was one year before KARAMZIN's translation of the complete text of *Julius Caesar*. Catherine's play focuses mainly on Vadim's unsuccessful attempt to topple Ryurik from the throne, and was clearly intended as an object lesson on political conspiracy. It was followed in 1790 by an even more unconvincing effort in the same spirit, *The Original Leadership of Oleg* (Nachal'noe upravlenie Olega).

The cultivation of dramatic COMEDY in 18th-century Russia produced a richer harvest than that of tragedy. Comic drama, like tragic, began with Sumarokov, but his comedies, at best pale imitations of Molière, compare unfavorably even with his own tragedies. All told, Sumarokov wrote 12 comedies from 1750 to 1772, including *Tresotinius* (a lampoon of the poet Trediakovsky), *The Monsters* (Chudovishcha), *An Empty Quarrel* (Pustaya ssora), *Dowry by Deceit* (Pridanoe obmanom), *The Guardian* (Opekun), *The Usurer* (Likhoimets), *Three Brothers, Partners* (Tri brata sovmestniki), *Venomous* (Yadovityi), *Narcissus* (Nartsiss), *The Imaginary Cuckold* (Rogonosets po voobrazheniyu), *The Mother, Her Daughter's Accomplice* (Mat' sovmestnitsa docheri), and *The Squabbler* (Vzdorshchitsa).

The development of Russian prose comedy along more original lines owed much to the contribution of Vladimir LUKIN (1737–94), a dramatist and translator from the French (Regnard and Marivaux, among others), who advocated an enrichment of the Russian repertoire by a skillful adaptation of foreign plays. According to Lukin's theory, which he exemplified in his successful adaptation (through an intermediate French version) of the the Englishman Robert Dodsley's *The Toy Shop* (1735), under the title *The Trinket Vendor*

(Shchepetil'nik, 1765), the foreign model could provide plot and, in general terms, characters, but the setting had to be russianized, and identifiable Russian types had to be found for the original dramatis personae wherever possible. Undoubtedly, Lukin's most important dramatic work was an original play *The Wastrel Reformed by Love* (Mot ispravlennyi lyubov'yu, first performance 19 January 1765), which deserves consideration as the first full-length modern comedy in Russian. The best Russian comedies of the 18th century came, however, from Denis FONVIZIN (1745–92), and Vasily KAPNIST (1757–1823). Fonvizin's *The Brigadier* (Brigadir, 1769), a satire on the Russian Gallomania of the period, and *The Minor* (Nedorosl', 1781), about the education of the young gentry in Catherine's time and the ignorance and greed of the provincial landowning class, come alive with excellent characterizations and good, natural Russian dialogue. Kapnist's best comedy was *Chicanery* (Yabeda, 1798), a verse satire aimed at corruption in the courts. Although most highly regarded for his many fables, Ivan KRYLOV (1769–1844) also wrote an amusing comedy, *Trump* (Trumf) or *Podshchipa* (1800), a parody of the genre of classicist tragedy.

The sentimentalism already manifest in Lukin's comedy *The Wastrel Reformed by Love* became pervasive in Russian comedy and, to a lesser extent, tragedy from the late 1760s to the end of the century. Inspired by the French *comédie larmoyante* (Destouches, Diderot, Nivelle de Chaussée) and the works of the English writers George Lillo and Edward Moore, Russian dramatists wrote a number of plays in the sentimental idiom. Following his *Venetian Nun* (1748), which already exhibits sentimental elements, Kheraskov wrote three other plays drenched in the then-fashionable lachrymosity: *The Atheist* (Bezbozhnik, 1761), *Friend of the Unfortunate* (Drug neschastnykh, 1774), and *The Persecuted* (Gonimye, 1775), an adaptation of Shakespeare's *The Tempest*. Other sentimental plays were written by Mikhail Veryovkin (1732–95)—*And So It Should Be* (Tak i dolzhno, 1773) and *Just Right* (Toch'-v-toch', 1774), both attacks on corruption, the latter set in the time of the Pugachyov rebellion; by Count Pavel Potyomkin (1743–96), a translator of Rousseau—*The Triumph of Friendship* (Torzhestvo druzhby, first performed 1773), on the familiar classicist theme of the conflict of duty and feeling; and by Pyotr PLAVILSHCHIKOV (1760–1812), one of the more interesting, less conventional Russian dramatists of the 18th century and the author of two sentimental comedies in prose—*The Landless Peasant* (Bobyl', 1790) and *The Sales Clerk* (Sidelets, 1803).

An immensely popular genre of 18th-century Russian drama was the comic opera, which was introduced in the early 1770s. Inspired by the French comic opera of the period, the Russians showed a special affinity for the rural settings, peasant characters, and social class conflicts of the genre. The comic opera was usually one or two acts in length and included songs and sometimes choruses; the musical score was not necessarily original, with the vocal numbers frequently sung to popular tunes. The first Russian comic opera was *Anyuta* (1772), by Mikhail POPOV (1742–90), which was performed for the Empress Catherine by members of her church choir at Tsarskoe Selo on 26 August 1772. This was followed by such well-known works in the same style as *Misfortune from a Carriage* (Neschast'e ot karety, performed 1779), by Yakov Knyazhnin; *Rozana and Lyubim* (Rozana i Lyubim, premiered 1778) by Nikolai Nikolev; *The Miller—a Wizard, Cheat, and Matchmaker* (Mel'nik—koldun, obmanshchik i svat, first performed 1779), by Aleksandr ABLESIMOV (1742–83); and *The St. Petersburg Bazaar* (Sankt-peterburgskii gostinyi dvor), the most original of all, dealing with the traditional Russian merchant class, by Mikhail MATINSKY (1750–ca. 1820).

Early 19th Century

Although early 19th-century Russian drama is not well known and produced no plays of international distinction, its influence on the playwrighting of such major figures as PUSHKIN, GRIBOEDOV, LERMONTOV, and GOGOL was hardly insignificant. In tragedy, a classicist style continued to be cultivated into the early years of the new century. Its principal practitioner was Vladislav OZEROV (1769–1816), the author of five tragedies, the best of which have classical antique settings, as in the case of *Oedipus in Athens* (performed 1804) and *Polyxena* (premiered 1809). *Fingal* (1805), a less impressive work, reflected the great popularity of the Ossianic poems in late 18th- and early 19th-century Russia, while the stirringly patriotic *Dimitry of the*

Don (Dimitrii Donskoi, 1807)—which Griboedov later parodied in *Dimitry of the Ludicrous* (Dimitrii Dryanskoi)—made Ozerov a national hero. Other generally weak classicist tragedies were written by Pavel KATENIN (1792–1853) and Vilgelm KYUKHELBEKER (1797–1846), whose most important work, the "mystery play" *Izhorsky*, a trilogy of dramatic poems the first two parts of which were published in 1835, is about a Byronic romantic who goes off to redeem himself by fighting against the Turks in the Greek liberation struggle.

More favorable results were achieved in the genre of verse comedy. Clearly the most talented comic dramatist before Griboedov was the prolific Prince Aleksandr SHAKHOVSKOI (1777–1846), whose comedies in verse and vaudevilles dominated the Russian stage in the decade from 1815 to 1825. Among Shakhovskoi's best comedies, which impress by virtue of their lightness, naturalness of diction, and relative sophistication, are the five-act comedy in verse, *A Lesson for Coquettes, or the Lipetsk Spa* (Urok koketkam, ili Lipetskie vody, 1815), *Semilordly Fancies, or the Home Theater* (Polubarskie zatei, ili Domashnii teatr, 1808), a five-act comedy in prose about serf theaters, which enjoyed the peak of their popularity during this period, and *All in the Family, or the Married Fiancee* (Svoya semya, ili Zamuzhnyaya nevesta, 1817), written together with Griboedov and Khmelnitsky.

Other writers of verse comedy in the first two decades of the 19th century before Griboedov were: Mikhail ZAGOSKIN (1789–1852), the author of *Comedy against Comedy* (Komediya protiv komedii, premiered 1815), a defense of Shakhovskoi's *The Lipetsk Spa* and a possible source for Gogol's *The Play Lets Out* (Teatral'nyi raz"ezd, 1836–1842), *The Noble Theater* (Blagorodnyi teatr, 1827), his major success about a performance by a group of amateur actors, and *The Malcontents* (Nedovol'nye, 1835), an attack on Griboedov's famous *Woe from Wit*; and Nikolai Khmelnitsky (1789–1845), known primarily for his vaudevilles and the author also of two verse comedies, *The Chatterbox* (Govorun, 1817) and *The Indecisive* (Nereshitel'nyi, 1819), similar in theme to Gogol's *Marriage*.

Shakhovskoi's one-act play with music, *Cossack Poet* (Kazakstikhotvorets, 1812), inaugurated the genre of Russian VAUDEVILLE. If Shakhovskoi's work retained strong links with Russian 18th-century comic opera, the vaudevilles of Khmelnitsky, among the best of the age, favored instead an upper-class milieu. Between 1817 and 1829, Khmelnitsky wrote 12 one-act comedies in verse and vaudeville. Also prolific as a writer of vaudevilles was Aleksandr Pisarev (1803–28), whose *Mr. Hustle-Bustle* (Khlopotun, first performed 1824) was a success, and who collaborated on occasion with Khmelnitsky. The principal structural feature of the vaudeville were the couplets (kuplety), which often contained topical allusions, especially in the plays of Khmelnitsky. Of other writers of vaudevilles in Russia in the first half of the 19th century—Pyotr Karatygin (1805–79), Dimitry Lensky (1805–60), and Fyodor Koni (1809–79)—Lensky was perhaps the most talented. His *Lev Gurych Sinichkin* (premiered fall 1839), regarded as a masterpiece of the vaudeville genre, recounts the efforts of a provincial actor to arrange a stage debut for his talented young daughter.

The first great comic dramatist of 19th-century Russia was Aleksandr Griboedov (1794–1829), the author of one of the greatest classics of the Russian stage, *Woe from Wit* (or *The Misfortune of Being Clever*, Gore ot uma, 1824). A verse play of sparkling dialogue, some of whose lines have become proverbial, *Woe from Wit* is close to 18th-century satiric comedy in its exposure of the obscurantism of contemporary Muscovite conservative society, yet features a hero, Chatsky, and a theatrical use of light and space influenced by romanticism. Griboedov's skill as a comic dramatist, particularly in the area of verse and diction, owed much to his earlier collaboration with Shakhovskoi and Khmelnitsky.

Although Pushkin's fame in the drama rests on his neo-Shakespearean history play *Boris Godunov* (1825, published 1830), which has survived in the theater only in the form of Mussorgsky's opera, it was in his "little tragedies" (which were also made into operas) that Pushkin displayed a genuine dramatic gift. Inspired by the *Dramatic Scenes* (1819) of Barry Cornwall (pseud. of Bryan Waller Procter, 1787–1874) in which brief dialogues in verse combine elements of drama and narrative poetry, these consisted of *The Covetous Knight* (Skupoi rytsar'), *Mozart and Salieri*, and *The Stone Guest* (Kamennyi gost'). Each work is devoted to a specific human passion: avarice, jealousy, and eros. *The Stone Guest*, the longest and dramatically most effective of the three, was inspired by the Don Juan legend. Sometimes reckoned among the "little tragedies" is *A Feast During the Plague* (Pir vo vremya chumy, 1830), an adaptation of scenes from *The City of the Plague* by John Wilson but more in the nature of a dramatic poem than a play. Pushkin also began writing a folk drama entitled *Rusalka* (1826, 1829, 1832), but it remained unfinished.

Far more in the mainstream of the romantic movement was the poet Mikhail Lermontov's (1814–41) major effort in the drama, the verse play *Masquerade* (Maskarad, 1835), a grim melodrama about a gambler named Arbenin who murders his wife in the belief that she has been unfaithul, only to learn after her death that she was innocent. The stunning production of the play in 1917 by the great Russian director Vsevolod MEYERHOLD accounts for much of its fame.

Twelve years after Griboedov's *Woe from Wit*, Russian drama had another comic masterpiece: *The Inspector General* (Revizor, 1836, revised for a second edition in 1841), by one of the greatest of Russian writers, Nikolai Gogol (1809–52). Gogol's first attempt at comedy, subsequently abandoned, was *The Order of Vladimir, Third Class*, which he began in 1832. The next year he began the farcical *Marriage* (Zhenitba), a satire on matchmaking and marriage for which a final draft was ready in 1835 and a complete one only in 1841. *The Gamblers* (Igroki), about a card-sharp made the butt of a swindle more clever than anything he could think of, came in 1842; while still entertaining, it is less of an achievement than *The Inspector General* and *Marriage*. Presumably based on a story he heard from Pushkin, *The Inspector General* is about the hoodwinking of a corrupt provincial town by a young adventurer from St. Petersburg mistakenly thought to be a government inspector. Shaped by such disparate traditions as Ukrainian comedy, puppet theater, pantomime, the Italian *commedia dell'arte*, the Spanish picaresque novel, and the ancient tradition of the braggart soldier, *The Inspector General* abounds in comic situations and hyperbolic characterization. Troubled, however, about the preponderance of "negative" types in the play and the successful flight at the end by the adventurer Khlestakov and his servant Osip, Gogol wrote two apologias for it in which he attempted to reconcile it with principles of Christian morality: "The Play Lets Out" (1836–1842) and "The Dénouement of 'The Inspector General'" (written 1846, but published posthumously). Gogol's interest in drama was not limited to playwriting. His "Petersburg Notes of 1836" (published in 1837) and "The Petersburg Stage of 1835–36" (written 1836, published posthumously) offer a number of interesting observations on the contemporary Russian stage.

The great tradition of Russian comedy established by Griboedov and Gogol continued in the works of Aleksandr OSTROVSKY (1823–86) and Aleksandr SUKHOVO-KOBYLIN (1817–1903) in the second half of the 19th century. In the interim between the plays of Gogol and those of his spiritual heirs, a school of historical drama came to the fore. Plays of a largely patriotic and melodramatic character celebrating autocracy and the subservience of the Russian people to their sovereigns were written by Nestor KUKOLNIK (1809–68), Nikolai POLEVOI (1796–1846), and others. The most talented of these writers was undoubtedly Kukolnik, the author of over a dozen plays, whose best-known work, *The Hand of the Almighty Has Saved the Fatherland* (Ruka Vsevyshnego otechestvo spasla, 1832), eulogizes the foundation of the Romanov dynasty in iambic pentameter blank verse and was immensely popular in its time. While most of Kukolnik's plays deal with Russian historical subjects, a few are based on the lives of Italian artists with whom Kukolnik felt certain affinities: *Torquato Tasso* (1830–31), *Giulio Mosti* (1832–33), *Giacobo Sannazaro* (1833), and *Domenichino*, about Giovanni Domenico Zampieri.

Russian HISTORICAL DRAMA finally came of age in the plays of Aleksei Tolstoi (1817–75). His major work consisted of a dramatic trilogy based on 16th-century Russian history: *The Death of Ivan the Terrible* (Smert' Ioanna Groznogo, premiered in 1867), the only part of the trilogy Tolstoi was able to see on stage; *Tsar Fyodor Ivanovich* (1868), which was kept from production by the censors until 1898; and *Tsar Boris* (1870), which was staged for the first time in 1881. The stage production of *The Death of Ivan the Terrible* at the Aleksandrinsky Theater in Petersburg in 1867 was a major event in the Russian theater. Far superior to other contemporary Russian historical drama by virtue of their stylistic polish and psychologically more complex portraiture, Tolstoi's three plays provided Konstantin STANISLAVSKY and the Moscow Art Theater with some of their greatest

successes in the late 19th and early 20th centuries, and were generally included as part of the repertoire on foreign tours.

One of the most prolific, influential, and highly regarded dramatists in the history of the Russian theater, Aleksandr Ostrovsky (1823–86) is remembered now chiefly for his early social comedies about the lives of the Moscow merchant class, whom Ostrovsky knew at first hand, and his modern tragedy *The Storm* (Groza, 1860), about an illicit love affair in a superstition-ridden provincial Volga town. All told, Ostrovsky wrote some fifty plays with about half of them in regular production in Russian theaters from the 1850s to the 1890s. Of the plays depicting the mores of the Moscow merchants, the best and most frequently performed are *It's a Family Affair, We'll Settle It Ourselves* (Svoi lyudi—sochtemsya, 1846), *The Poor Bride* (Bednaya nevesta, 1851), *Keep to Your Own Sleigh* (Ne v svoi sani ne sadis', 1852), and *Poverty Is No Crime* (Bednost' ne porok, 1853), all distinguished by lifelike characterizations and dialogue and great fidelity to the customs of the Moscow merchant milieu. In the 1860s, 1870s, and 1880s, Ostrovsky directed his attention to the social and economic changes brought about by the reforms of 1861 and the rise of a new Russian capitalist class. Characteristic plays of this period are *Mad Money* (Beshenye den'gi, 1870) and *Wolves and Sheep* (Volki i ovtsy, 1875). Of his later plays in this vein, in which elements of moralizing and melodrama emerge, the best by far is *Without a Dowry* (Bespridannitsa, 1879). Constituting a distinct segment of Ostrovsky's canon is a group of plays dealing with Russian theatrical life or featuring actors. These include *Talents and Admirers* (Talanty i poklonniki, 1882), *The Comic of the 17th Century* (Komik 17-ogo veka, 1873), *The Forest* (Les, 1871), and *The Guilty Are Guiltless* (Bez viny vinovatye, 1883). *The Forest*, about a pair of actors who rescue a poor young girl from the clutches of a tyrannical guardian somewhat related to the strong character of Mrs. Kabanov in *The Storm*, has been one of Ostrovsky's most popular and often-performed plays. The enthusiasm for historical drama in the second half of the 19th century, which brought to the fore the works of Aleksei Tolstoi as well as other lesser dramatists (Nikolai Chaev, 1824–1914; Dimitry Averkiev, 1836–1905), also touched Ostrovsky. But apart from *The Comic of the 17th Century*, such "historical chronicles" as *Koz'ma Zakharych Minin Sukhorukii* (1862) and *Dimitry the Pretender and Vasily Shuisky*, 1867, are among his weakest works.

Nineteenth-century Russian literature had few major writers who concentrated exclusively or predominantly on the drama. The greatest was Ostrovsky. The second most important, by virtue of only three plays, his sole major literary effort, was Aleksandr Sukhovo-Kobylin (1817–1903). A wealthy aristocrat, Sukhovo-Kobylin became embroiled in a sensational murder case involving his French mistress and spent a little time in jail. The case was eventually dismissed for lack of evidence, but the experience prompted Sukhovo-Kobylin to write a remarkable dramatic trilogy largely based on his own exposure to the contemporary police and judicial system. The first play, *Krechinsky's Wedding* (Svad'ba Krechinskogo, 1854), is in the tradition of the popular French well-made play and recounts the attempted fleecing of a well-to-do provincial family by a young aristocrat who has squandered his money on gambling. The second play, *The Case* (Delo, 1861), traces the later attempts of the Muromsky family to clear their daughter's good name after she is charged with being Krechinsky's accomplice. Much indebted to Gogol's Petersburg stories, the play is a bitter satire of the Russian bureaucracy and judicial system. The last play, *The Death of Tarelkin* (Smert' Tarelkina, 1869), is a grotesque satire of officialdom with surreal elements which was kept from the stage in its original form by the censors until 1917. The striking modernity of *The Death of Tarelkin* in particular attracted MEYERHOLD's attention, and his successful production of it on 23 October 1917, began the rediscovery of the *Trilogy* as a whole.

Of prominent writers who also essayed the drama between Gogol and CHEKHOV, the most important contributions to a Russian theatrical literature came from Ivan TURGENEV (1818–83), Mikhail SALTYKOV-SHCHEDRIN (1826–89), Aleksei PISEMSKY (1820–81), and Lev TOLSTOI (1828–1910). Although remembered primarily as a dramatist for his only full-length dramatic work, *A Month in the Country* (Mesyats v derevne, 1850), a well-crafted drama about romantic and other frustrations among the gentry, notable for its psychological realism and subtlety, Turgenev was a master of the one-act genre. His best short plays, which reflect the influence of the domestic Russian vaudeville tradition and the proverb plays especially of the French dramatist Alfred de Musset, are *Where It's Thin, It Tears* (Gde tonko, tam i rvetsya, 1847), *The Sponger* (Nakhlebnik, 1848), *The Bachelor* (Kholostyak, 1849), *The Provincial Lady* (Provintsialka, 1850), *An Evening in Sorrento* (Vecher v Sorrento, 1852), *Breakfast at the Marshal's* (Zavtrak u predvoditelya, 1849), and *Conversation on the Highway* (Razgovor na bol'shoi doroge, 1851). Features common to Gogol and the so-called NATURAL SCHOOL are discernible additionally in the short plays.

While not frequently associated with drama, the novelist Saltykov-Shchedrin was the author of several "dramatic scenes," monologues, one-act plays, and one major full-length play, the four-act comedy *The Death of Pazukhin* (Smert' Pazukhina, 1857), a negative picture of the Russian merchant class reflective of the author's antipathy toward the Slavophile movement.

Celebrated in his time as the author of the novel *A Thousand Souls* (1858), Pisemsky also wrote plays, the most important of which by far was *Bitter Fate* (Gor'kaya sud'bina, 1859), a tragic drama about the doomed romance between a married serf woman and the nobleman who owns her husband. Introduced into 19th-century Russian drama by a popular but second-rate playwright, Aleksei POTEKHIN (1829–1908), the peasant theme reached its apogee in the play for which Count Lev Tolstoi is most remembered as a dramatist, *The Power of Darkness* (Vlast' t'my, 1888), a grim naturalistic play about peasant life, featuring, among other examples of peasant brutality, the on-stage murder of a child. The more important of Tolstoi's other stage works are *The Fruits of Enlightenment* (Plody prosveshcheniya, 1891), a four-act satirical comedy on the then-fashionable spiritualism, the flawed but highly popular six-act *The Living Corpse* (Zhivoi trup, first published 1911), based on an actual court case, and which Tolstoi regarded as unfinished, and the five-act *A Light Shines in the Darkness*, a profoundly pessimistic play with autobiographical undertones on which Tolstoi worked sporadically for some twenty years from the early 1880s to 1902 and never succeeded in completing.

Of the many Russian playwrights active in the last decade and a half of the 19th century and the first years of the 20th, none achieved the international acclaim of Anton Chekhov (1860–1904), although his major plays are few in number. Chekhov first attempted dramatic writing while still a medical student, but his unfinished *Platonov* (the name assigned by later editors) is overburdened with character and incident. *Ivanov* (1888), though still weak in some respects, gives clearer hints of Chekhov's future greatness. After *Ivanov*, Chekhov turned to one-act farces such as *The Bear* (Medved', 1888), *The Proposal* (Predlozhenie, 1888–89), *The Wedding* (Svad'ba, 1889–90), and *The Anniversary* (Yubilei, 1891; revised 1902), with which his superb comic gifts found a natural outlet. The short plays are splendid examples of the genre and have retained their popularity to this very day. With *The Wood Demon* (Leshii, 1889), Chekhov returned to full-length drama. Although staged independently and occasionally re-vived, the play has long been overshadowed by its more concentrated reworking, *Uncle Vanya* (Dyadya Vanya, 1899). Chekhov's first great success as a playwright came with the famous Moscow Art Theater production of *The Seagull* (Chaika, 1896), his only dramatic work dealing with art and specifically the art of the theater. Its initial production in Petersburg in 1896 was a dismal failure, but the more sympathetic Moscow Art Theater staging in 1898 brought fame to both the new theater and Chekhov. It was from *The Seagull* that the Art Theater derived its curtain logo, in recognition of the great success of the production. Chekhov's last two major plays are his masterpieces: *Three Sisters* (Tri sestry, 1901), and *The Cherry Orchard* (Vishnevyi sad, 1904), both dealing with the theme of dispossession and portraying the inability of people of refinement and sensitivity to cope with change. While Chekhov never entirely dispensed with elements of melodrama, his style as a dramatist differed radically from that of his Russian predecessors and such giants of European drama as Ibsen and Strindberg. Deemphasizing plot, or external action, Chekhov created the dramatic experience out of the interplay of his character's emotions and the small incidents that make up everyday life. His remarkable nuanced yet natural dialogue, in which the unspoken is often more important than the spoken, illuminates the problem of communication among people, by revealing the gap between words and emotions.

Chekhov's immense reputation today obscures the fact that in the early 20th century he was less highly regarded as a dramatist than Maksim GORKY (1868–1936) whose entry into the drama Chekhov en-

couraged. As a playwright Gorky is best known for his naturalistic drama about the tenants of a flop house, *The Lower Depths* (Na dne, 1901–2). Actually, Gorky's first play (and among his best) was *The Philistines* (or *The Petty Bourgeois*, Meshchane, 1901), an attack on the contemporary Russian bourgeoisie whom Gorky loathed with a passion equal to his contempt for the intelligentsia. This latter group is the subject of such plays as the outwardly Chekhovian *Summer Folk* (Dachniki, 1904), *Barbarians* (Varvary, 1905), *The Last Ones* (Poslednie, 1908), and *Queer People* (Chudaki, 1910). In *Enemies* (Vragi, 1906), Gorky focuses on relations between workers and factory owners in the period of the Revolution of 1905. *Vassa Zhelezno-va*, written the same year (but revised in 1935 along more orthodox Soviet lines), features the portrait of a woman ready to do anything for her family, and merits attention chiefly as an extreme form of naturalism. Of Gorky's other pre-revolutionary plays—*The Zykovs* (Zykovy, 1913), *The Counterfeit Coin* (Fal'shivaya moneta, 1913), and *The Old Man* (Starik, 1915; revised 1922 and 1924)—the best is probably *The Zykovs* in which Gorky demonstrates an attraction for the earthiness and strength of will of the Russian merchant class while cognizant of its capacity for egomania and brutality.

After a long hiatus from the drama, caused most likely by his inability to adapt to the post-revolutionary demands for plays with a Soviet content, Gorky returned to the stage only in the early 1930s. His new work was a loosely related trilogy of plays dealing mostly with representatives of the old order unable to adjust to change as Russia stood on the threshold of the Revolution. The cycle comprises *Somov and Others* (Somov i drugie, 1930), *Egor Bulychov and Others* (Egor Bulychov i drugie, 1930–33), and *Dostigaev and Others* (Dosti-gaev i drugie, 1933). The best of the three is *Egor Bulychov* with its strong portrait of a Russian merchant going to death not fully comprehending the upheaval taking place around him. Although Gorky is frequently dismissed as a second-ranking dramatist for his heavy-handed social and political didacticism, his unsuccessful efforts to assimilate Chekhovian technique, and the occasional clumsiness of his dramatic style, he was very popular in his time in Europe as well as Russia and has enjoyed a revival in the English-speaking world in recent years.

Closely related to Gorky in outlook are writers whose careers he furthered under the auspices of his ZNANIE publishing house. The *Znanie* "circle" included such dramatists as Evgeny CHIRIKOV (1864–1932), Semyon Yushkevich (1868–1926) and Sergei Naidenov (1868–1922) whose plays deal for the most part with contemporary socio-economic issues and the status of minorities (especially Jews). Although largely forgotten now, Chirikov's *The Jews* (Evrei, 1905), Yushkevich's *Hunger* (Golod, 1905) and *Miserere* (1911), and above all Naidenov's *Vanyushin's Children* (Deti Vanyushina, 1901), set in the old merchant milieu, attracted attention in their day.

More markedly political in inspiration were the plays of Anatoly LUNACHARSKY (1875–1933), who shared Gorky's revolutionary views, though unaffiliated with *Znanie*, and who became the first People's Commissar of Education after the Revolution. Strongly interested in and supportive of theater, Lunacharsky was a prolific if ungifted dramatist whose playwriting spans the period 1906 to 1922. Although celebrated in the USSR as the author of the ponderous post-revolutionary historical dramas *Oliver Cromwell* (1920) and the *Thomas Campanella* trilogy (1920–22), Lunacharsky's better plays antedate the Revolution. Still burdened, as is most of his dramatic writing, by tendentiousness and verbosity, the philosophical *The King's Barber* (Korolevskii bradobrei, 1906) and *Faust and the City* (Faust i gorod, 1916) are clearly Lunacharsky's best stage works, intellectually and artistically.

During the time that Gorky's pre-revolutionary plays were becoming dominant on the Russian stage, the SYMBOLIST movement, with which Gorky had little sympathy, was also having an impact on the drama. Although the symbolists scored significant achievements in poetry and prose fiction, they were by and large unsuccessful as dramatists. Often marred by excessive lyricism and a lack of dramatic dynamism, their plays make better reading than theater. Beginning with possibly the earliest, the short verse "neo-mystery" *The Sun* (Solntse) by Nikolai MINSKY 1855–1937), most Russian symbolist plays, indebted to Mallarmé, Maeterlinck, and Villiers de l'Isle Adam, sought to transform the theater into a temple capable of achieving true spiritual communion between player and spectator. Representative of the new symbolist mystery play were such works as

Andrei BELY's (1880–1934) *He Who Has Come* (Prishedshii, published 1903) and *Jaws of Night* (Past' nochi, 1907), Konstantin BALMONT's (1867–1943) *Three Blossomings* (Tri rastsveta, staged January 1906), and Valery BRYUSOV's futuristic and apocalyptic *Earth* (Zemlya, 1904). Of the three plays with which she is credited—*Sacred Blood* (Svyataya krov', 1901), *The Red Poppy* (Makov tsvet, 1912, allegedly written with her husband Dmitry MEREZHKOVSKY and their friend D. V. Filosofov), and *The Green Ring* (Zelenoe kol'tso, 1914)—only the first can be regarded as a serious effort by Zinaida HIPPIUS (1869–1945) to write a play in a symbolist vein. While *The Red Poppy* and *The Green Ring* are realistic plays dealing with contemporary social problems (the impact of the Revolution of 1905 on an affluent Russian family, generational conflict), *Sacred Blood* combines elements of Hippius's symbolist mystical Christianity and the fin de siècle interest in folklore.

Folk and popular motifs, frequently linked to traditions of the medieval mystery play, pervade a number of symbolist dramatic works. Among the most convincing and theatrically viable in this vein are the plays *The Devil Play* (Besovskoe deistvo, 1907) and *The Tragedy of Judas, Prince of Iscariot* (Tragediya ob Yude, printse Iskariotskom, 1909), the latter based on an apocryphal legend of Judas, by Aleksei REMIZOV who at one time collaborated on symbolist productions with Meierkhold. After *The Triumph of Death* (Pobeda smerti, 1907), essentially a melodramatic revenge play garbed in fashionable turn-of-the-century medieval attire, the well-known symbolist prose writer Fyodor SOLOGUB (1863–1927) wrote two entertaining plays with folk elements, *Vanka the Butler and the Page Jehan* (Van'ka klyuchnik i pazh Zhean, 1908) and *Night Dances* (Nochnye plyaski, 1908). The last play served as a vehicle in part of Sologub's belief in the importance of dance for the theater, an idea he voiced as well in an article on the new drama, "The Theater of a Single Will" (Teatr odnoi voli), which appeared in an important collection of symbolist essays on theater published in 1908 under the title *Theater: A Book about the New Theater* (Teatr: kniga o novom teatre).

Two other contributors to the same volume were among the most important writers of a drama of symbolist persuasion: Aleksandr BLOK (1880–1921) and Mikhail KUZMIN (1875–1936). Keenly interested in drama and theater and a prominent figure in Russian theatrical life after the Revolution, Blok was responsible for two of the best plays to come out of the symbolist period: the short spoof of Maeterlinckian drama and the mystical proclivities of symbolism, *The Fair Booth Show* (Balaganchik, 1906), its title and format inspired by the puppet tradition of popular Russian fairs and a triumph in Meierkhold's production at the theater of Vera Komissarzhevsky in 1907, and *The Rose and the Cross* (Roza i krest, 1912), originally planned as a scenario for a ballet about Provençal troubadors with music by Glazunov. In its final form the play tells the story of the exemplary knight Bertran and his hopeless love for Izora, the wife of the master of his castle, and her search for the mysterious author of a haunting song whose meaning he does not fully comprehend. The play incorporates gnostic elements and dramatizes the theme of the nobility of pure sacrifice. Blok's other plays—*The King in the Square* (Korol' na ploshchadi, 1908), *The Unknown Woman* (Neznakomka, 1908), and *Song of Fate* (Pesnya sud'by, 1908; rewritten 1919), all three published under the collective title *Lyrical Dramas* (Liricheskie dramy), and *Rameses* (Ramzes, 1913), which has an ancient Egyptian setting—were much less successful although the *Lyrical Dramas* bring together romantic elements and social concerns in sometimes effective ways. As an active participant in the vibrant cabaret and intimate theater life of early 20th-century Russia, Mikhail Kuzmin wrote a number of theatrical works, including ballets and pantomime. But his most appealing (and stageworthy) plays consist of three short stylish "neo-mysteries" of which Blok had high praise in his article "On Drama" (1907): *Eudoxia of Heliopolis, or The Reformed Courtesan* (O Evdokii iz Geliopolya, ili Obrashchennaya kurtizanka), *Alexis, Man of God, or The Lost and Found Son* (O Aleksee cheloveke bozh'em, ili poteryannyi i obrashchennyi syn), and *Martinianus* (O Martiniane), all three published for the first time as a separate book in 1908. Kuzmin's later *The Venetian Madcaps* (Venetsianskie bezumtsy, 1912) sets a conflict of sexual love, hate, and, finally, murder in an opulent setting of late 18th-century Venice.

The new interest in tragedy among the symbolists rekindled enthusiasm for classical antiquity, especially the ancient Greeks, and resulted in a number of plays with classical settings. Probably the most interesting, from the comparative point of view, were those based on the legend of Laodamia and Protesilaus: *Laodamia* (Laodamiya, 1902, published 1906), by Innokenty ANNENSKY (1856–1909), and Fyodor Sologub's *The Gift of the Wise Bees* (Dar mudrykh pchel, 1907). Besides *Laodamia*, Annensky wrote *Melanippe the Philosopher* (Melanippa-filosof, 1901), *King Ixion* (Tsar' Iksion, 1902), and the best of his classical plays and the only one ever to be staged *Thamyras the Cythara Player* (Famira-kifared, 1906; published 1913; staged 1916), about a mortal artist who tried to challenge a Muse. Vyacheslav IVANOV (1866–1949), who had written extensively on a symbolist concept of liturgical and theurgical drama under the influence of Wagner and Nietzsche (especially in his book *Along the Stars* (Po zvezdam, 1909), was the author of two plays on classical themes: *Tantalus* (Tantal, 1905), and *Prometheus* (Prometei, 1919). The poetess Marina TSVETAEVA (1892–1941), who was also interested in the drama, wrote, in a classical vein, *Theseus* (Tezei) or *Ariadne* (Ariadna, 1924), and *Phaedra* (Fedra, 1927).

The most prolific major playwright of pre-Revolutionary 20th-century Russia, Leonid ANDREEV (1871–1919), a former associate of Gorky's Znanie, was only superficially related to the symbolist movement. Of his many plays on a variety of subjects, Andreev's best known and most important are *The Life of Man* (Zhizn' cheloveka, 1906), *Black Masks* (Chernye maski, 1908), *Professor Storitsyn* (1912), *Ekaterina Ivanovna* (1912), and *He Who Gets Slapped* (Tot, kto poluchaet poshchechiny, 1915). Symbolical and allegorical rather than symbolist, *The Life of Man* dramatizes a gloomy vision of the life cycle of bourgeois man. Andreev dealt with human wretchedness and the mysteries of existence in plays of similar style such as *King Hunger* (Tsar' Golod, 1907), *Anathema* (Anafema, 1910), and *Ocean* (Okean, 1910). *Black Masks* is an allegory on the darker side of the human psyche set in medieval Italy. While *Professor Storitsyn* and *Ekaterina Ivanovna* rank among Andreev's better plays on social themes they now seem dated and are rarely staged. *He Who Gets Slapped*, a bitter commentary on the dispossession of the righteous in a world of false values, set in a circus milieu, has been widely staged throughout the world and remains Andreev's best-known play.

Two other types of dramatic writing prominent in the second decade of the 20th century prior to the Revolution were plays of a romantic-escapist character and those embodying a "theatricalist" concept of both theater and life. The most outstanding practitioners of the first type were the poets Nikolai GUMILYOV (1886–1921) and Marina Tsvetaeva. Gumilyov's dramatic work includes *Don Juan in Egypt* (Don Zhuan v Egipte, published 1912), a one-act play in verse; *Actaeon* (Akteon, published 1913), similar in theme to Annensky's *Thamyras the Cythara Player*; *The Game* (Igra, 1916), a "dramatic scene" set in a Paris gambling casino in 1813; *Gondla* (1917), a four-act dramatic poem with a 9th-century Icelandic setting; *A Child of Allah* (Ditya Allakha, 1918), Gumilyov's best play, about the divine love of the medieval Persian poet Hafiz and written originally for the puppet theater; and *The Poisoned Tunic* (Otravlennaya tunika, 1918; published 1952), about the Byzantine Empress Theodora's revenge against the Bedouin poet Imr-ul Qais with whom her daughter Zoe is in love. Tsvetaeva's "romantic-escapist" plays were inspired by her fondness for late 18th-century France and her sense of affinities between that age and the Russia of her own time. Their heroes are the great lovers Giacomo Casanova de Seingalt (1725–98) and Armand Louis de Gontaut Biron, duc de Lauzun (1747–93). The "Casanova cycle" comprises *Casanova's End* (Konets Kazanovy, published 1922; a one-act play in verse); *Phoenix* (Feniks, published in Prague in 1924, and an expanded version of the first play); and *An Adventure* (Priklyuchenie, a five-act play in verse published in Prague in 1923). The play about Lauzun, *Fortune* (Fortuna), was published in Paris in 1923.

"Theatricalism," or "theatricality," in the early 20th century represented an attempt to counter the prevalent naturalistic and symbolistic trends in drama and staging by restoring what was felt to be the lost element of play in the performance and bringing to the fore the artifice of theatrical art. Parallel to the efforts in the theater in this respect by such Russian directors as Vsevolod Meierkhold and Nikolai EVREINOV (1879–1953), a type of theatricalist drama arose which was neither naturalistic or symbolistic and which sought to achieve the same revitalization of drama as was then taking place in theater.

This theatricalist drama often incorporated parodic and satirical elements and made frequent use of such traditional theatricalist techniques as the play-within-a-play, masks, puppetry, pantomime, and the Italian commedia dell'arte. Blok's *The Fair Booth Show* (1906) and Kuzmin's *The Venetian Madcaps* (1912) both exhibit features common to the genre. The leading exponent of a theatricalized drama, as indeed of a theatricalized theater, was the director and playwright Evreinov. A major contributor to contemporary dramatic and theatrical theory, Evreinov was a prolific playwright as well as an active director. Among his best and most frequently performed plays are the philosophical one-act Harlequinade *A Merry Death* (Veselaya smert', 1908) and the full-length *The Main Thing* (Samoe glavnoe, 1919) in which a company of actors, the play-within-a-play motif, and the masks of the commedia dell'arte are brought together to expound a concept of theatricality encompassing not only the theater, but life itself. The later parts of the trilogy initiated with *The Main Thing* were informed with a bleaker vision of man related to Evreinov's disenchantment with the course of the Revolution in Russia and his emigration to Paris in 1925. *The Ship of the Righteous* (Korabl' pravednykh, 1924), depicts the failure of a utopian society aboard ship, while *The Theater of Eternal War* (Teatr vechnoi voiny, 1927) makes use of the theatrical metaphor to argue the case that the eternal war is none other than life itself in which success rests on the skilled use of the guile of the theater.

The Soviet Period

The problem faced by Russian theaters after the Revolution was their inability to stage "Soviet" plays in response to political pressure at a time when there were hardly any plays on specific Soviet themes of any merit. Although a curious variety of theatrical forms came to the fore in the wake of the Revolution—particularly the *agitka*, or short agitational play on some topical issue, the "living newspaper," where news headlines were dramatized before live audiences, and mass spectacles celebrating triumphs of the Revolution including above all those staged in Petrograd by Evreinov—none had any lasting impact on the further development of Russian drama.

The play regarded as the first of significance in the Soviet period is *Mystery-Bouffe* (Misteriya-buff, 1918; revised 1921) by the great "poet of the Revolution" Vladimir MAYAKOVSKY (1893–1930). Interested in both film and theater already before the Revolution, Mayakovsky made his debut as a dramatist with the surreal *Vladimir Mayakovsky. A Tragedy* (Vladimir Mayakovskii. Tragediya, 1913), a celebration of the creative power of the poet who alone holds the possibility of a reordering of existence. *Mystery-Bouffe*, which was begun in fact before the Revolution, is a political play hailing the ultimate triumph of the workers of the world while at the same time mocking the Christian concept of paradise by means of a burlesque of the medieval mystery play form. The revised Prologue of 1921 reflects the impact on Mayakovsky of the ideas of the theatricalists, especially Evreinov. After *Mystery-Bouffe*, Mayakovsky wrote two satirical comedies—*The Bedbug* (Klop, 1928) and *The Bathhouse* (Banya, 1929)—in which elements of the absurd and grotesque are used to ridicule the new Soviet bourgeois in the period of the so-called New Economic Policy (NEP) (1921–28) and the self-centeredness and myopia of the new Soviet bureaucracy. Noticeable in both plays, apart from their grotesque satire, is the author's introduction of science-fiction motifs such as, for example, the time machine in *The Bathhouse*.

Before dramatists succeeded in devising credible plays on Soviet themes, they attempted to fill the gap in the Soviet repertoire by works depicting revolution elsewhere in Europe, principally Germany and China. There was also a reflection here of a genuine enthusiasm for the imminent world revolution predicated on the success of the Russian experience. The unsophisticated but not uninteresting dramatist Vladimir Bill-Belotserkovsky (1884–1970), who had been a factory worker for a while in the United States, wrote two plays about the political ramifications in America of the Russian Revolution: *Echo* (Ekho, 1922) and *Port the Helm* (Levo rulya, 1923). The former futurist poet and friend and collaborator of Mayakovsky, Sergei TRETYAKOV (1892–1939), was the author of the most impressive plays on the theme of the international revolution. *Are You Listening, Moscow?* (Slyshish', Moskva?!, first staged in 1923) depicts events in contemporary revolutionary Germany and formally combines elements of the early Soviet *agitka* and German expressionism which was becoming well known in Russia at the time. *Gas Masks* (Protivogazy, first performed in a Moscow gas plant in 1924), about the cynical and callous director of a gas works, vaguely recalls the *Gas* play cycle of the German Expressionist Georg Kaiser. *Roar, China!* (Rychi Kitai!), Tretyakov's most famous play, is an exercise in anti-Western sentiment against the background of revolutionary upheaval in China. Tretyakov knew China first-hand, having taught Russian literature there as a visiting professor in 1924–25. Instructive as examples of the extremes to which this type of Soviet drama could go are A. Faiko's *Lake Lyul* (Ozero Lyul, 1920), a melodrama about a revolutionary conspiracy set "somewhere in the far West or, perhaps, the extreme East," and *Bubus the Teacher* (Uchitel' Bubus, 1924), a political farce inspired by the revolutionary upheaval in Germany in the late 1910s and early 1920s.

Understandably, the first Soviet plays of any real merit after Mayakovsky's *Mystery-Bouffe* found their subjects in the Revolution and civil war. "Classics" of the Soviet stage in this idiom are *Storm* (Shtorm, 1924) by Bill-Belotserkovsky, *Armored Train No. 14–69* (Bronepoezd 14–69, 1927) by Vsevolod IVANOV (1895–1963), *Breakup* (Razlom, original version 1927), about a conspiracy to block the attempt by Red mutineers to sail up the Neva and force the capitulation of Petrograd, by Boris Lavrenyov (1891–1959), *Lyubov Yarovaya* (1925), about a husband and wife on opposite sides of the political fence during the civil war, by Konstantin Trenyov (1876–1945), and such plays by Vsevolod VISHNEVSKY (1900–51) as *The First Cavalry Army* (Pervaya konnaya, 1929), about the exploits of Budyonny, and *An Optimistic Tragedy* (Optimisticheskaya tragediya, 1933), about a woman commissar who whips into shape an unruly unit of sailors dominated by an anti-Bolshevik anarchist faction.

Generally speaking, as a Soviet drama on the Revolution and civil war began to develop, the matter of an appropriate form for such drama became a matter of debate. Beginning with Bill-Belotserkovsky's *Storm* and especially in the works of Vishnevsky, realistic elements were given a certain epic and romantic aura by techniques to which in the aggregate the term "monumental" came to be applied. What this meant was a loose episodic structure, typological characterization, striking sound effects, the use of choruses, narrators, prologues and epilogues, and occasionally screens in the manner of the German epic theater of Brecht and Piscator. Probably the archetype of this type of drama was Vishnevsky's *The First Cavalry Army* (1929). Plays of more traditional formal properties set in the time of the Revolution and the Civil War continued to be written, of course, the most famous of them being *The Days of the Turbins* (Dni Turbinykh, 1926) by the outstanding novelist and short-story writer Mikhail BULGAKOV (1891–1940). A dramatization of Bulgakov's controversial novel *The White Guard* (Belaya gvardiya, 1925)—which may account for the play's conservative style—*The Days of the Turbins* deals with political intrigue and military conflict in the Ukraine during the winter of 1918 and early 1919 and is noteworthy above all for its sympathetic depiction of a White family caught up in the turmoil of war. In the sequel, *Flight* (Beg, 1926–28), which was an original stage play, Bulgakov abandoned the conventional realism of *Days of the Turbins* in favor of a style owing much to film technique and the art of the grotesque. The play's theme—the unreality of the existence of Russians who sought haven from the Civil War in emigration—is underscored by a deft use of light and the division of the play not into acts but into "dreams." Among Bulgakov's other works for the stage, perhaps the most interesting are *The Crimson Island* (Bagrovyi ostrov, written 1927, staged 1928, son banned), an indictment of censorship, *A Cabal of Hypocrites* (Kabala svyatosh) or *Molière* (completed 1930, staged February 15, 1936, but cut after seven performances), a play ostensibly based on the life of Molière but alluding to Bulgakov's own problems with the authorities over *Days of the Turbins* and *Flight*, and *Zoya's Apartment* (Zoikina kvartira, 1926), a satirical comedy about an enterprising bordello-keeper set against the background of the severe housing shortage in the first decade after the Revolution.

Comedies such as Bulgakov's *Zoya's Apartment* and Mayakovsky's *The Bedbug* represent a species of satiric drama often of absurdist or grotesque character that came into prominence during the era of NEP and reflected the specific social conditions of the period. The targets of NEP satire were generally the would-be entrepreneurs who rushed to take advantage of the new economic policy with an astonishing variety of schemes to make money as fast as conditions permitted and the anomalies characteristic of the early Soviet state as it struggled to get on its feet after the severe dislocations of World War I, the Revolution, and the civil war. Apart from the comedies of Bulgakov and Mayakovsky, the best specimens of the genre were such comedies as *The Sweet Souffle* (Vozdushnyi pirog, 1924–25) by Boris Romashov (1898–1958), *A Harmful Element* (Vrednyi element, 1927) and *The Cardsharp* (Shuler, 1929) by Vasily Shkvarkin (1894–1967), *Comrade Tsatskin and Company* (Tovarishch Tsatskin i Ko, 1926), by Aleksandr Popovsky, and particularly the two "black comedies" for which Nikolai ERDMAN (1902–70) is best known, *The Mandate* (Mandat, 1925) and *The Suicide* (Samoubiitsa, 1928 or 1929), both of which have been staged in the West.

Closely related to NEP satirical comedy was a type of melodrama, frequently of a satirical nature, that dealt mainly with the misdeeds of malcontents and other "retrogressive" elements in the new Soviet society. Among the best-known melodramas of the 1920s were Aleksei Faiko's *Evgraf, Seeker of Adventures* (Evgraf, iskatel' priklyuchenii, 1926) and *The Man with the Briefcase* (Chelovek s portfelem, 1929), and Boris Romashov's *The End of Krivorylsk* (Konets Krivoryl'ska, 1925–26).

Among the more interesting developments in Russian drama during the 1920s and early 1930s were the plays written by two groups of writers whose social and aesthetic views brought them into confrontation with the official Soviet positions: the SERAPIONS and the OBERIUTY. Among the Serapions, the most talented dramatist was the critic and prose writer Lev LUNTS (1901–24). What stands out most in Lunts' plays, aside from anti-conformist, anti-utopian views of society in part shaped by ZAMYATIN, is the fine sense of theater they reflect. *Outside the Law* (Vne zakona, 1920), *Bertran de Born* (1922), and *The Apes are Coming!* (Obez'yany idut!, published 1923), and *The City of Truth* (Gorod pravdy, first published 1924) are rich in action and innovative stage techniques, especially *Outside the Law*, which calls for three simultaneous stages, and *The Apes are Coming*, in which the realistic and fantastic mingle in a play-within-a-play. Although known primarily for his prose fiction, especially the anti-utopian novel *We*, Zamyatin also wrote several plays, among them the historical plays *The Fires of St. Dominic* (Ogni sv. Dominika, 1923), set in Inquisition Spain, *Attila* (1928), and his best, the immensely successful *The Flea* (Blokha, 1925), a dramatization of the famous story by LESKOV. The principal dramatists of the Oberiu group, *The Society for Real Art* (Ob''edinenie Real'nogo Isskustva) were Aleksandr VVEDENSKY (born 1904, died during World War II) and Daniil KHARMS (1905–41). Vvedensky was the author of a spoof on Christmas entitled *Christmas at the Ivanovs* (Yolka u Ivanovykh), while Kharms is known for his Kafkaesque-absurdist *Elizaveta Bam*. As non-representational drama, the Oberiuty plays owe much to surrealism and at the same time anticipate the "theater of the absurd."

The beginning of the first Five-Year Plan in 1928 and the growing self-confidence of the Soviet state placed demands on Soviet dramatists for a drama responsive to the needs of "socialist construction" and, once it was promulgated, imbued with the ideology of SOCIALIST REALISM. During the 1930s a number of plays were written on the vast new program of national reconstruction, among them such "classics" of the Soviet stage as *Tempo* (Temp, 1929) and *Aristocrats* (Aristokraty, 1935), about the building of the White Sea Canal with prison camp inmates, by Nikolai POGODIN (1900–62); *The Rails Are Humming* (Rel'sy gudyat, 1927) and *Bread* (Khleb, 1930), the latter a strong play about the suppression of the *kulaks*, by Vladimir KIRSHON (1902–38), an able dramatist who was executed by a firing squad on July 28, 1938; *The Miraculous Alloy* (Chudesnyi splav, 1934), about the fledgling Soviet aircraft industry, was his most popular play. Dramatists also directed their attention during this period to the problems faced by individuals, above all intellectuals and artists, unable to adjust to the changes in society since the advent of the Soviet state. Addressed to this subject were some of the better plays of the 1930s: the melodramatic *A List of Assets* (Spisok blagodeyanii, 1931), by Yury OLESHA (1899–1960), about a Russian actress in Paris; *Fear* (Strakh, 1931), about a scientific institute attempting to adjust to the Soviet era, by Aleksandr AFINOGENOV (1904–41); *Tanya* (1938), about a young woman who develops a redeeming sense of the collec-

tive, by one of the most prolific and important Soviet dramatists, Aleksei ARBUZOV (1908–); and *The Chimes of the Kremlin* (Kremlevskie kuranty, 1940, 1956), about a recalcitrant engineer who is eventually won over to the Soviet regime, by Pogodin.

It was also during the 1930s and early 1940s that the dramatic gifts of Evgeny SHVARTS (1897–1958) brought some badly needed lightness and whimsy to the Russian stage. Long active in children's literature and the author of a few plays for children, Shvarts wrote three dramatic works of a satiric character inspired by fairy tales by Hans Christian Andersen and Charles Perrault: *The Naked King* (Golyi korol', 1934), *The Shadow* (Ten', 1940), and *The Dragon* (Drakon, 1943). Although universal in their satire, Shvarts' plays can also be read as commentaries on Soviet reality.

The approach of war, and World War II itself provided subject matter for a large number of Soviet plays of generally exhortatory and patriotic character. Of those set on the eve of the war, the most highly regarded are *The Orchards of Polovchansk* (Polovchanskie sady, 1938), by the major Soviet novelist and dramatist Leonid LEONOV (1899–), *Field Marshal Kutuzov* (Fel'dmarshal Kutuzov, 1939), by the historical dramatist Vladimir Solovyov (1907–), and *On the Eve* (Nakanune, 1941), by Aleksandr Afinogenov. Often more interesting and original for his form than the familiar Soviet issues with which he deals in his plays, Leonov was the author of several works for the stage: *Skutarevsky* (1934); a dramatization of his novel *The Badgers* (Barsuki, 1927); *Untilovsk* (1928), about a Siberian town; *The Taming of Badadoshkin* (Usmirenie Badadoshkina, 1930), about a NEP profiteer; *The Wolf* (Volk, 1939), on "enemies" within the Soviet state; *The Snowstorm* (Metel', 1939; revised 1962), about conflict between two brothers, one a corrupt Soviet official, the other an émigré; *An Ordinary Person* (Obyknovennyi chelovek, 1940–41), dealing with contemporary social values; *Invasion* (Nashestvie, 1942) and *Lyonushka* (1943), depicting Russian heroism during the war; and *The Golden Carriage* (Zolotaya kareta, 1946–55), on the subject of postwar reconstruction in a small town. Probably Leonov's best known play, *The Orchards of Polovchansk* portrays a provincial Russian family on the eve of the war in an outwardly Chekhovian ambience. Forced to revise the play on several occasions for ideological reasons, Leonov eventually compromised the integrity of his original conception. Known primarily as a historical dramatist on the basis of such works as *The Great Sovereign* (Velikii gosudar', 1943–55), *Denis Davydov* (1953–55), and *The Victors Are Judged* (Pobediteley sudyat, 1953), Vladimir Solovyov found inspiration for *Field Marshal Kutuzov* in the obvious historical parallels between the approach of World War II and the Napoleonic invasion of Russia in 1812. A rousing patriotic play dramatizing the rationale behind the wartime scorched-earth policy employed by the Soviets, *On the Eve* was written by Afinogenov after the war had broken out in 1941 and just a few months before his own death in it.

Following Afinogenov's *On the Eve*, the best of the Russian war plays were *Smoke of the Fatherland* (Dym otechestva, 1942), by the Brothers Tur (pseudonym of Leonid Tubelsky and Pyotr Ryzhei) and Lev Sheinin (1905–); *The Russian People* (Russkie lyudi, 1942), by the best-known Soviet writer to come out of World War II, Konstantin SIMONOV (1915–79); and *Invasion* (Nashestvie, 1942), by Leonid Leonov. Although the plays as a group are expectedly patriotic and melodramatic, they are not devoid of interest and have been performed outside the USSR.

Zhdanov's crack-down and the tensions of the postwar Cold War from 1946 to 1952 made a shambles of Russian drama. The very principle of "conflictless" literature now in force made all genuine drama impossible. The general barrenness of this period was relieved only by the ludicrous hysteria of anti-Western and anti-American plays of the time typified by such works as Simonov's *The Russian Question* (Russkii vopros, 1946) and Lev Sheinin's *At Mid-Century* (V seredine veka, 1950). With the waning of these tensions and an improvement in the domestic political climate in 1954 and again after the 20th Party Congress of 1956, new directions became possible in Soviet drama. These took several distinct forms: plays "exposing" corruption in high places and other dark aspects of the Stalin era while at the same time appealing for greater honesty in Soviet society; plays of an anti-heroic character aimed at undermining the foundations of Soviet "monumentalism" in the name of a more down-to-earth depiction of everyday Soviet reality; and finally plays advocating the rights of citizenship of the emotions, plays, in other words, about romance and love, often lyrical, often about young people, and often frank in dealing with such previously taboo subjects as marital conflict, separation and divorce, and extramarital relations. Among the most representative dramas of the THAW of 1953 and 1954 were *The Guests* (Gosti, 1954) by Leonid Zorin (born 1924), the author in 1967 of the popular romantic play *A Warsaw Melody* (Varshavskaya melodiya); *A Personal Matter* (Personal'noe delo, 1954), by Aleksandr Shtein (1906–); *Good Luck!* (V dobryi chas!, 1954), by Viktor Rozov (1913–), an exceptionally prolific and popular playwright who has frequently written about young people and the author of the well-known *Alive Forever* (Vechno zhivye, 1956), about young lovers during World War II; and *Years of Wandering* (Gody stranstvii, 1954), by the equally prolific and popular Aleksei Arbuzov. Reflecting the changed climate following the 20th Party Congress were such plays as *A Petrarchan Sonnet* (Sonet Petrarki) by Nikolai Pogodin, and *A Woman Alone* (Odna), by Samuil Alyoshin, both on the theme of love. In *Factory Girl* (Fabrichnaya devchonka, 1956), Aleksandr Volodin (born Lifshits, 1919) reiterated the need for greater honesty in the portrayal of Soviet life, while in his later *Five Evenings* (Pyat' vecherov, 1959) he combined an adult love story with a rejection of "monumentalism" and hero worship, emphasizing instead that ordinary people often accomplish the heroic in unglamorous work.

To a considerable extent, the thematics of the post-Stalinist 1950s have remained dominant in Russian drama to the present, a fact attested by the plays of such major figures as Rozov and Arbuzov. Rozov's plays from the late 1960s and early 1970s such as *The Day of the Wedding* (V den' svad'by, 1969), *The Social Director* (Zateinik, 1969), and *From Evening till Noon* (S vechera do poludnya, 1970) all deal generally with the joys and sorrows of love and strike only one new chord which resounds in a number of other comtemporary Soviet plays as well—the need to preserve personal moral integrity in the face of the growing materialism of a Soviet society become greatly bourgeois.

If Arbuzov hewed to much the same line in such plays as *It Happened in Irkutsk* (Irkutskaya istoriya, 1959), *My Poor Marat* (Moi bednyi Marat, 1964), *The Happy Days of an Unhappy Man* (Schastlivye dni neschastlivogo cheloveka, 1967), *Evening Light* (Vechernii svet, 1976), and *An Old Fashioned Comedy* (Staromodnaya komediya, 1967), he has demonstrated a greater capacity for experimentation with play structure than Rozov and indeed a number of younger Russian dramatists. Known primarily for plays of lengthy time spans somewhat on the order of dramatized chronicles, Arbuzov has also pioneered a type of neo-theatricalist play incorporating choruses, music, dance, visionary scenes, and unusual sound effects. To this group belong *It Happened in Irkutsk* (1959), with which he first moved in the direction of a new theatricalism, *In This Pleasant Old House* (V etom milom starom dome, 1976), a "vaudeville-melodrama," and *My Eye-Catcher* (Moe zaglyaden'e, 1976), an "optimistic comedy." With *An Old Fashioned Comedy* (1976), which has only two speaking parts and has been produced in the West, Arbuzov showed that he could satisfy a taste for sentiment with equal facility.

Arbuzov's reversion to vaudeville and farce points up the new interest in these old genres among Soviet dramatists in the 1970s as ways were sought to devise different play structures to accommodate dramatic works of little or no ideological substance. In 1974, Rozov wrote *Four Drops* (Chetyre kapli), consisting of four "tragicomic sketches," while a real talent for vaudeville was shown by a very promising younger dramatist named Aleksandr Vampilov (1937–72). Besides his incomplete two-act vaudeville *The Incomparable Nakonechnikov* (Nesravnennyi Nakonechnikov, 1972), Vampilov wrote two one-act comedies of a farcical nature, "Twenty Minutes with an Angel" and "An Incident with a Typesetter," which subsequently were grouped together and staged under the title *Provincial Anecdotes* (Provintsial'nye anekdoty). Vampilov's major plays—*Farewell in June* (Proshchan'e v iyune, 1965), *The Elder Son* (Starshii syn, 1967), *Duck Hunting* (Utinaya okhota, 1967), and *Last Summer in Chulimsk* (Poslednim letom v Chulimske, 1972)—are marked by lyricism, a deep feeling for nature, a keen sensitivity to the ironies of life, and fondness for dramatizing transitions from light-hearted self-centeredness to sobering self-awareness. If not altogether convincing, *Duck Hunting* (which has been staged in the United States) more than any other play by Vampilov exemplifies his preoccupation with irony and egocentricity. More lyrical and muted in tone, *Last Summer in Chulimsk*, Vampilov's most successful stage work, creates an unmistakable Chekhovian aura as dramatic tension arises out of an intertwining of seemingly unrelated private dramas in a provincial Siberian setting.

Besides Vampilov, whose untimely death by drowning in 1972 represented a severe loss to the Soviet stage, several other noteworthy dramatic talents came to the fore in the 1970s and early 1980s: the Kirghiz writer Chingiz AITMATOV (1928–), who together with Kaltai Mukhamedzhanov wrote *The Ascent of Mt. Fuji* (Voskhozhdenie na Fudziyamu, premiered 1973), which attracted considerable attention in and outside the USSR for its parable-like treatment of the theme of collective guilt; Mikhail Roshchin (1933–), the author of popular plays about contemporary Soviet youth, above all *Valentin and Valentina* (1971); Aleksandr Gelman, whose interest lies strongly in industrial themes and whose successful *Minutes of a Meeting* (Protokol odnogo zasedaniya, 1976) deals frankly with high-level bureaucratic mismanagement; Edvard Radzinsky (born 1936), a productive dramatist who has written on romantic subjects in such plays as *104 Pages about Love* (104 stranitsy lyubov', published 1973), *A Bit about Women* (Chut'-chut' o zhenshchine, published 1974), and *She in the Absence of Love and Death* (Ona v otsutstvii lyubvi i smerti, 1982), but who has also demonstrated a capacity for plays of philosophical interest: *Talks with Socrates* (Besedy s Sokratom, staged 1975); *Lunin, or the Death of Jacques Transcribed in the Presence of the Master* (Lunin, ili Smert' Zhaka zapisannaya v prisutstvii Khozyaina, about the last days of the Decembrist Mikhail Lunin); and a willingness to explore constraints on artistic creativity in the USSR, as in his play *Making a Film* (Snimaetsya kino, published 1973); Aleksandr Borshchagovsky, whose *A Lady's Tailor* (Damskii portnoi, 1980) is a moving drama of Jews in wartime Kiev; and two promising younger women dramatists who write mostly about the dilemmas of personal relationships, Lyudmila Petrashevskaya and Zoya Boguslavskaya whose play *Contact!* (Kontakt!, 1979) is a "psychological chronicle" with a New York setting.

Bibliography: A. Anikst, *Istoriya ucheniya o drame: Teoriya dramy v Rossii ot Pushkina do Chekhova.* 1972. John E. Bowlt, "Russkii konstruktivizm i khudozhestvennoe oformlenie stseny," *Novyi zhurnal* 126 (1977), pp. 108–127. Sharon M. Carnicke, "Naturalism to Theatricalism: The Role of Symbolism," *Ulbandus Review* 1, no. 1 (1977), pp. 41–58. A. V. Danovskii, "Slovo o dramaturgii epokhi klassitsizma," *Russkaya rech'*, 1979, no. 2, pp. 21–26. V. Frolov, *Sud'by zhanrov dramaturgii: Analizy dramaturgicheskikh zhanrov v Rossii XX v.* 1979. Michael Glenny, "The Soviet Theatre." In *An Introduction to Russian Language and Literature*, ed. Robert Auty and Dimitri Obolensky. 1977. Pp. 271–85. S. Hill and J. Dunkelberger, "Russian Drama after Chekhov: A Guide to English Translation, 1900–1969," *Theatre Documentation* 2, no. 1–2 (1969–70), pp. 85–108. George Kalbouss, "The Birth of Modern Russian Drama." In *Russian and Slavic Literature*, ed. Richard Freeborn et al. 1976. Pp. 175–89. V. P. Meshcheryakov, "Dva stoletiya russkoi teatral'noi kritiki," *RLit*, 1980, no. 4, pp. 225–32. *Ocherki istorii russkoi sovetskoi dramaturgii.* 3 vols. 1963–68. *Russkie dramaturgi.* 3 vols. 1959–62. Harold B. Segel, *Twentieth-Century Russian Drama: From Gorky to the Present.* 1979. S. E. Shatalov, "Polveka russkoi dramy: Turgenev, Ostrovskii, Chekhov." In *Colloquio italo-sovietico.* 1976. Pp. 121–34. Yu. Smelkov, "Obnovlenie konflikta: Zametki o sovremennoi dramaturgii," *Novyi mir* 52 (1976), no. 4, pp. 234–51. N. Vemer, "Osnovnye tendentsii razvitiya sovremennoi sovetskoi dramaturgii pervoi poloviny 70-kh godov," *ZS* 22 (1977), pp. 348–56. Leo Wiener, *The Contemporary Drama of Russia.* 1924.   H. B. S.

Drone, The, see TRUTEN'.

Druzhinin, Aleksándr Vasílievich (1824–64), novelist and critic. Of gentry origin, his moderate liberalism of the 1840s and 1850s is reflected in his "problem" novel, *Polinka Saks* (1847), much admired by BELINSKY. In this short novel, showing the marked influence of George Sand, a young married woman is "liberated" by her indulgent spouse to pursue an extra-marital affair but ultimately discovers that she really loves her husband. An admirer of English literature, Druzhinin wrote numerous articles on such writers as Dr. Johnson, Boswell, Crabbe, and Scott and tried his hand at translating

Shakespeare, In the 1850s he began taking a stronger and stronger anti-utilitarian stand and moved, as a critic, into the conservative camp, his views now representing a definite reaction against those of Belinsky and the "civic critics" (CHERNYSHEVSKY, DOBROLYUBOV, etc.). Indeed, Druzhinin was one of the first Russian critics to deny that literature should be subordinated to social or political ends; and, by the mid-fifties, as editor of BIBLIOTEKA DLYA CHTENIYA, he was making this publication a journal of aesthetic criticism. In "A Critique of the Gogolian Period of Russian Literature and Our Relations to It" (Kritika gogolevskogo perioda russkoi literatury i nashi k nei otnosheniya, 1856) Druzhinin speaks out in favor of the Pushkinian and against the Gogolian tradition (or, more accurately, the Belinskian interpretation of this tradition) in Russian literature. According to Druzhinin, the works of Ostrovsky and Lev TOLSTOI represent "pure art," while TURGENEV is criticized for damaging his art by sacrificing it to contemporaneity. Druzhinin together with Pavel ANNENKOV and Vasily BOTKIN make up an important trio of "aesthetic" critics.

Works: Sobranie sochinenii. 8 vols. 1865–67. *Polin'ka Saks.* 1955.

Secondary literature: Brief notice in R. Stacy, *Russian Literary Criticism: A Short History.* 1974. Anmartin-Michal Brojde. "Druzhinin's View of American Life and Literature," *CASS* 10 (1976), pp. 382–99.
R. H. S.

Dudintsev, Vladimir Dmitrievich (1918–   ) Graduated from law school in Moscow. His earlier works were written in a conventional socialist-realist manner: straightforward narratives about episodes of socialist construction. His novel *Not by Bread Alone* (Ne khlebom edinym, 1956) brought him fame. The novel details the fate of an inventor dedicated to the well-being of Soviet society who tries—unsuccessfully in the original version—to batter down the stone wall of vested interests. The novel conveys the author's indignation at the failure of the promised socialist millennium. The new socialist system has developed its own inherent flaws: the new managers (whom the author calls "monopoly") misuse socialist power to their own advantage and to perpetuate themselves. The monopoly tries to eliminate—and does eliminate in the original version—the idealistic inventor. The effectiveness of the novel derives from the forcefulness with which it raises doubts about the legitimacy of socialist construction. This explains why SIMONOV, editor of *Novyi mir*, had Dudintsev add a redeeming Part Four. A literary paradox underlies the novel: the author uses the apparatus of a literate SOCIALIST REALISM to discredit that which it would be expected to glorify. Therein lies the novel's particular literary interest. The publication of *Not by Bread Alone* unleashed against Dudintsev a violent campaign which subsided by 1959, when Khrushchev held out the olive branch. At about that time Dudintsev wrote *A Newyear's Tale* (Novogodnyaya skazka), retelling the *Not by Bread Alone* story in a short fairy-tale medium. In it Dudintsev signified a sly thanksgiving to the fairy-tale "head" of a "brotherhood" of "bandits."

Works: Ne khlebom edinym, Novyi mir, 1956, no. 8, pp. 31–118; no. 9, pp. 37–118; no. 10, pp. 21–98. "Novogodnyaya skazka," *Novyi mir,* 1960, no. 1. *Rasskazy.* 1963.

Translations: Not by Bread Alone. New York, 1957. (With a preface by Dudintsev.) *A New Year's Tale.* Trans. Max Hayward. London, 1960.

Secondary literature: Grigori Svirski, *A History of Post-War Soviet Writing: The Literature of Moral Opposition.* Trans. Robert Dessaix & Michael Ulman. 1981.
H. O.

Dudýshkin, Stepán Semyónovich (1820–66), journalist and minor literary critic. Born into a merchant family and educated in the law, he was influenced by the liberalism of the 1840s and lavished fulsome praise on BELINSKY. He himself tried to point up connections between literature and social problems in his early journalistic reviews and began to contribute to *Otechestvennye zapiski* in 1847. But Dudyshkin had associated with the circle of writers around the Maikov family (especially the critic, Valerian MAIKOV) and he moved in the direction of aesthetic criticism and "pure art" theory, no longer relating political and literary phenomena. By 1860 he was one of the co-editors of *Otechestvennye zapiski* and was in charge of its criticism section until his death. As an apolitical critic opposed to the "revolutionary-democratic" views of CHERNYSHEVSKY, and PISAREV, he was attacked in turn by the latter for his reactionary position.

But Dudyshkin never fully embraced autotelic aesthetic theory; rather, many of his reviews (such as his survey of Russian literature for 1852) are mere lists of names and titles accompanied by impressionistic comments. Somewhat eclectic in his tastes (he thought highly of the works of Lev TOLSTOI and admired French novels), Dudyshkin's romantic proclivities are clearly evident in his essays on GOGOL, LERMONTOV, TURGENEV, and PISEMSKY. He edited an edition (1860–62) of the works of Lermontov, whom he called "the poet of despair," and his essay on Turgenev (*Povesti i rasskazy I. S. Turgeneva,* 1857) is perhaps his most exemplary study.

Bibliography: V. I. Kuleshov, *Istoriya russkoi kritiki.* 1972. A. V. Starchevskii, "Odin iz zabytykh zhurnalistov," *Istoricheskii vestnik,* 1886, no. 2.
R. H. S.

Dukhóvnaya Akadémiya, see KIEV ACADEMY.

Dukhóvnye stikhí (spiritual verses) are based on church legends and the APOCRYPHA, on the Holy Scriptures, saints' lives (see HAGIOGRAPHY), and church teachings. They were usually performed by a special class of singers, the *kaliki,* blind wanderers who specialized in this verse. They would wander in small groups from village to village and to church festivals and fairs. One of the most famous poems is about the *Golubinaya kniga,* the book of profound wisdom. During the reign of King David the book allegedly fell from the clouds into the city of Jerusalem. It contained questions of King Volotoman Volotomanovich and the answers of King David concerning the origin of the world and cosmology in general. Animals from medieval bestiaries appear, such as the phoenix and the unicorn. Other *stikhi* are about saints such as ALEKSANDR NEVSKY, BORIS and GLEB, and Alexis the man of God. One *stikh* is about the struggle of Anika the Warrior with death, a subject which came from the West and later appeared in the folk LUDKI (broadsides) Many of the *stikhi* are different versions of various episodes in the life of Christ. There are verses devoted to the Virgin, including the Dormition of the Virgin, a favorite festival among the Russian people. In some cases the *dukhovnye stikhi* adapt the story of a non-Russian saint to Russian reality. St. Demetrius of Thessalonica, for example, is depicted defeating the Tatar Mamai instead of Koloyan, who is his opponent in the original saint's life. One of the most popular subjects of the *stikhi* is the Alleluya, the "Wife of Mercy," who according to the story saved Christ by taking him by the hand instead of her little boy, who was thrown into the oven, where he remained unharmed. Various sects adopted this legend because it was an example of immolation by which one could be saved from sin. Whereas many of the *stikhi* are narrative epics, there are also beautiful lyrics such as "The Complaint of Cain" and "The Complaint of Adam" before the gates of heaven. One of the favorite themes in the verses is the Last Judgement, with a description by Christ of the glories of heaven and the horrors of hell.

The verses include many devices typical of Russian folk poetry, such as tautology, gradual narrowing of images, fixed epithets, and repeated passages, as in the BYLINY, in which a character is given a series of orders, and carries them out in almost exactly the same words. The length of the *stikhi* vary; some are very short and others may consist of several hundred lines. Sometimes they are in the form of a monologue or dialogue, but most often they are a combination of descriptive narrative and dialogue.

Bibliography: Alex E. Alexander, *Russian Folklore: An Anthology in English Translation.* 1975. P. Bessonov, *Kaliki-perekhozhie,* 1861–64. nos. 1–6. *The Heritage of Russian Verse.* Ed. Dmitry Obolensky. 1965.
R. R.

Dúma, The, and Russian literature. A *duma* (pl. *dumy*) is a Ukrainian lyric-epic song, dating from the 16th to the 17th century, which is chanted to the accompaniment of either a *bandura* (sometimes called *kobza*) or a *lira.* Originally, a duma was performed by a blind wandering minstrel *banduryst* (or *kobzar*). These highly poetic songs came into being during and after the Cossack era in Ukrainian history. In content they deal with the fate of the Cossacks in Turkish captivity, the exploits of various Cossack heroes, or the pain of parting from relatives. In form they are the finest tragic songs in the Ukrainian oral tradition. They have no stanzas, vary in length, and were transmitted orally. As a genre they are related to funeral laments and music plays an important part in their performance. The lines of a *duma* are arranged in groups which may be called tirades or periods, similar to the *laisse* structure of French epic. There are very definite stylistic features (standard epithets, repetitions, and endings) in these songs, which, according to some scholars, have links with the earlier, Kievan epos.

The word *duma* (meditation), first recorded in 1587 in a Polish chronicle by S. Sarnicki (under the year 1506) may be of Polish origin. Many Polish classicists and pre-romantics used this term as a sub-title to their poems. One of them, J. U. Niemcewicz wrote several *dumy* and it was under his acknowledged influence that K. RYLEEV published in 1825 a collection of *Dumy*. As far as content and form are concerned, Ryleev's poems have nothing in common with the Ukrainian *dumy*. Only one of the twenty-one poems, "Khmelnitsky," is on a Ukrainian topic and is based not on folklore but on a history text by Bantysh-Kamensky. Others tell of Russian historical heroes. Like Niemcewicz, Ryleev aimed at evoking in his readers patriotic and heroic emotions, as well as a striving for justice. These objectives were only occasionally present in the Ukrainian *dumy*. However, the Decembrist Ryleev showed deep affection for the Ukraine and for Ukrainian strivings for independence in his later poems "Nalivaiko" (1825) and "Voinarovsky" (1825) which bear some resemblance to the Ukrainian *dumy*.

Some Ukrainian writers who wrote in Russian used the *dumy* as a base for their plots and characterization (Yevhen Hrebinka's *Chaikovsky*). Attempts have been made to discover elements of *dumy* in GOGOL's *Taras Bulba*. In modern times, E. BAGRITSKY wrote his *Duma pro Opanasa* (1926) with some motifs from Ukrainian folklore. As a genre, the Ukrainian *dumy* remained inimitable. They merely provided a convenient romantic label for historical heroic poems and occasionally inspired Ukrainian (Lysenko), Russian (Tschaikovsky), Polish (Moniuszko) and Czech (Dvořák) composers. In music the term *duma* was used, in the 19th century, interchangeably with its diminutive *dumka*.

Bibliography: K. Hrushevska, ed., *Ukrainski narodni dumy.* Kiev, 1927. *Ukrainian Dumy* (parallel Ukrainian and English text). Toronto-Cambridge, 1979.

Secondary literature: A. G. Tseitlin, *Tvorchestvo Ryleeva.* 1955.

G. L.

Ego-Futurism, see FUTURISM.

Eikhenbaum, Boris Mikhailovich (1886–1959), literary historian and theorist. Of middle-class background, Eikhenbaum graduated in philology from Petersburg University in 1912. Six years later he joined the faculty of the university and left that post only upon his retirement in 1949. His association with OPOYAZ and lifetime sympathy for some of the tenets of this group earned him a place in the FORMALIST movement. He was, however, primarily an academic critic, and most of his work is historical and traditional. His best known and innovative works are *The Melodics of Russian Lyric Verse* (Melodika russkogo liricheskogo stikha, 1923), *About Literature* (Skvoz' literaturu, 1924), and *Literature: Theory, criticism, polemic* (1927). His several books on TOLSTOI are also very important. In *The Melodics*, Eikhenbaum examined the Russian poetic tradition from DERZHAVIN to AKHMATOVA, coming to the conclusion that regardless of literary periods, there existed in Russian poetry three styles: the singsong (napevnyi), the oratorical (oratorskii), and the conversational (govornyi). In *About Literature*, he examined some classics of Russian literature, and offered a new interpretation of GOGOL's story *The Overcoat*, emphasizing a necessity of acting out the story, or at least reading it aloud, to recover its ironic meaning. He also pointed out a tendency to imitate oral narration in the stories of LESKOV and REMIZOV, and he dubbed this tendency the SKAZ technique. In *The Young Tolstoi* (Molodoi Tolstoi, 1922) and in *Lev Tolstoi* (3 vols., 1928–60), Eikhenbaum advanced the thesis that Tolstoi's philosophical quest and the crises of the later part of his life came about as a way of finding new novelistic techniques, rather than for personal reasons. In his academic capacity, Eikhenbaum acquired recognition as one of the editors of Tolstoi's *Polnoe sobranie sochinenii* (1928–58).

Works: Pushkin—poet i bunt 1825 goda. 1907. *Anna Akhmatova.* 1923. *Lermontov.* 1924. *Moi vremennik.* 1929. *Marshrut v bessmertie: Zhizn' i podvig chuklomskogo dvoryanina i mezhdunarodnogo leksikografa Nikolaya Petrovicha Makarova.* 1933. *Stat'i o Lermontove.* 1961. *O poezii: Sbornik statei.* 1969. *O proze: Sbornik statei.* 1969.

Translations: "The Theory of the 'Formal Method'." In *Russian Formalist Criticism: Four Essays.* Trans. L. T. Lemon and M. J. Reis. 1965. "O. Henry and the Theory of the Short Story." Trans. I. R. Titunik. Michigan Slavic Contributions, no. 1, 1968. *The Young Tolstoi.* 1972. *Lermontov: A Study in Literary-Historical Evaluation.* 1981. *Tolstoi in the sixties.* 1982. *Tolstoi in the seventies.* 1982.

Secondary literature: Harold K. Schefski, "The Changing Focus of Eikhenbaum's Tolstoi Criticism," *RusR* 37 (1978), pp. 298–307.

E. Th.

Eisenstein (Eizenshtein), Sergei Mikhailovich (1898–1948), film director, teacher, and theorist, began in the theater during military service (1918–20) as stage designer for troop entertainments and went on to design and teach in the PROLETKULT Theater in Moscow in 1920. With Sergei TRETYAKOV, he devised and directed a wildly satirical revue version of Ostrovsky's *The Diary of a Scoundrel* (Na vsyakogo mudretsa dovol'no prostoty, 1923). Instead of having the scoundrel Glumov's diary read aloud, Eisenstein showed its content in a brief film, his first. Thereafter he turned to film-making.

Both his first feature films, *Strike* (1925) and *Potyomkin* (1926), exemplified the principle he advocated in an article in the magazine LEF, "The Montage of Attractions." By this he meant the rapid succession of antipodal images sometimes called "collision montage." Thus in *Potyomkin* frames showing soldiers marching forward with guns levelled to fire were alternated with close-ups of frightened civilians retreating before them. The striking contrast of images achieved by such innovative editing or "montage" was meant to arouse justified resentment in the viewer against the tyranny of force. Another innovation was Eisenstein's choice, not of a trained actor, but of a "natural" for a part, his so-called *tipazh* or search for a real person who embodied the character he saw in the role. Finally, Eisenstein preferred real outdoor scenes to the constructed studio set.

Eisenstein's next films were *Ten Days that Shook the World* after a story by John Reed (1928), *The Old and the New* (1929), and the next projected, *Viva Mexico!*, was filmed during Eisenstein's trip to the United States and Mexico (1929–32). Unfortunately Eisenstein was recalled to the Soviet Union before he had finished the last film, and it was pieced together from Eisenstein's material with sound added by other hands. Eisenstein suffered other disciplinary setbacks, the removal of TROTSKY from the film *Ten Days*, and the shelving of his next project, *Bezhin Meadow* (1935), after a story by TURGENEV. But all difficulties were erased with the thrillingly patriotic sound film, *Alexander Nevsky* (1938), which Eisenstein made when World War II was threatening.

In a changed monumental style with professional actors, Eisenstein's last film, *Ivan the Terrible*, Parts I and II (1943–46), originally planned as a trilogy, was made during World War II in a studio in Alma Ata. Upon its release in 1945, Part I, in which the heroic young Ivan makes himself Tsar, earned a Stalin Prize for Eisenstein. Part II, however, shows the Tsar, protected by feudal underlings, but still fearing for his life and countering plots and treachery by ever worse cruelty. It was condemned in 1946 as alluding to Stalin's terror. Though Eisenstein pleaded that he would revise Part II and depict in Part III again a heroic Ivan conquering an outlet to the Baltic Sea, the director died before he could complete the trilogy. Part II was released only after Stalin's death in 1958.

In 1932 Eisenstein had begun teaching at the Government Film Institute in Moscow, and in 1933 he started a many-volume treatise on film directing—never completed. He taught composing each film frame with as much care as if it were one of the Japanese prints he so much admired. Eisenstein's teachings and highly personal art of the film are wholly out of fashion today.

Works: Izbrannye proizvedeniya. 6 vols. 1964–1971.
Translations: The Film Sense. Trans. and ed. Jay Leyda. 1942. *Film Form.* Trans. and ed. Jay Leyda. 1949. *Film Essays with a lecture.* Trans. Jay Leyda. 1968.
Secondary literature: Jay Leyda and Zina Voynow, *Eisenstein at Work.* Introd. Ted Perry. 1982. Herbert Marshall, ed, *The Battleship*

Potemkin. 1978. Jerry L. Salvaggio, "Between Formalism and Semiotics: Eisenstein's Film Language," *Dispositio* 4 (1979), pp. 289–97. Kristin Thompson, *Eisenstein's* Ivan the Terrible: *A Neoformalist Analysis.* 1981. Trevor Whittock, "Eisenstein on Montage Metaphor." In Brian Green, ed. *Generous Converse: English Essays in Memory of Edward Davis.* Cape Town, 1980. Pp. 136–44.　　M. H.

Eizenshtein, see EISENSTEIN.

Elágin, Iván (pseud. of Iván Venedíktovich Matvéev, 1918–　), born in Vladivostok, poet and translator, studied medicine in Kiev, but failed to get his degree as the War interrupted his studies. The end of the War found him in Munich, where he published his first collections of poetry, "On the Way from There" (Po doroge ottuda, 1947) and "You, my Century" (Ty, moe stoletie, 1948), and a comedy, *The Portrait of Mlle. Tarzhi* (1949). After his immigration to the United States Elagin embarked upon an academic career and continued his literary work. He received his Ph.D. from New York Univeristy in 1970, with a dissertation, *"John Brown's Body,* by Stephen Vincent Benét: Translated into Russian, with an Introduction and Notes" (published in 1979 by Ardis, Ann Arbor, Mich.), and has taught Russian literature at N.Y.U. and the University of Pittsburgh (since 1971). He regularly publishes his translations of American poets in the journal *Dialog-SShA* (Dialogue-USA). Elagin's poetry reflects successive stages in the life of a "displaced person": nostalgia, bewilderment, wonder, conflict, fascination with the New World, and continued estrangement. Elagin's view of New York City, in particular, is intriguing. Elagin's language is vigorous, modern, and often colloquial. He is at his best in satirical and grotesque verse, in which his traditional syllabotonic stanzas and echoes of the classics of Russian poetry contrast effectively with vivid modern imagery.

Works: Po doroge ottuda. 1953. (contains poems from Elagin's earlier collections and new poems). *Politicheskie fel'etony v stikhakh.* 1959. *Otsvety nochnye.* 1963. *Kosoi polet.* 1967. *Drakon na kryshe.* 1973. *Pod sozvezdiem topora.* 1976. A further collection, *V zale vselennoi,* was planned at the time of the writing of this article.
Translations: R. H. Morrison, ed. and trans. *America's Russian Poets.* 1975. Pp. 33–40.
Secondary literature: L. Rzhevskii, "O poezii Ivana Elagina," *Novyi zhurnal,* no. 126 (1977). V. Betaki, "Tri spora: O poezii Ivana Elagina," *Grani,* no. 103 (1977). Reviews of Elagin's collections have appeared in *Novoe russkoe slovo, Novyi zhurnal, Russkaya mysl', Vozrozhdenie,* and other periodicals.　　V. T.

Elágin, Iván Perfílievich (1725–94?), poet, translator, and dramatist. A member of the Russian Academy from 1783, Elagin began his career in literature and the theater soon after he completed military service in the Gentry Cadets Corps in 1743. He wrote elegies, songs and satires, and in the 1750s and 1760s contributed to the journals *Ezhemesyachnye sochineniya* (the *Monthly Essays* of the Academy) and *Vsyakaya vsyachina,* edited by A. P. SUMAROKOV and CATHERINE II, respectively. As an advocate of Sumarokov's poetic theory, Elagin gained notoriety with his satire, "On a Dandy and Coquettes" (Na petimetra i koketok), which provoked a heated polemic involving M. V. LOMONOSOV and other littérateurs of the time. Elagin also achieved recognition for his translations of Molière, Prévost, Bravo, Holberg, and others. According to N. M. KARAMZIN, Elagin's translations advanced the development of the Russian literary language. Further, from 1766 to 1779 Elagin was involved with theater administration.

Secondary literature: P. N. Berkov, *Istoriya russkoi zhurnalistiki 18 veka.* 1952. *Istoriya russkoi literatury.* Vol. 3. 1941. Pp. 356–58. A. O. Kruglyi, "I. P. Elagin, Biograficheskii ocherk." In *Prilozheniya k Ezhegodniku imp. teatrov za 1893–1894 gg.* Vol. 2. 1895. N. I. Novikov, "Opyt istoricheskogo slovarya o rossiiskikh pisatelyakh." In *Izbrannye sochineniya.* 1951. Pp. 300–01. V. N. Vsevolodskii-Gerngross, *Russkii teatr vtoroi poloviny 18 veka.* 1960.　　B. A.

Elegy (*elegiya*), a genre of lyric poetry, whose criterion in Greek and Latin poetry was its meter, the elegiac distich, rather than any particular theme or mood. The love elegies of Propertius and Tibullus, and Ovid's melancholy *Tristia* became models of Renaissance and baroque poetry. In the 18th century the elegy developed into a genre of lyric poetry, characterized formally by a certain length and a deliberate pace (six or five feet to a line), and thematically by melancholy philosophic meditation. The history of the Russian elegy begins with SUMAROKOV and continues uninterrupted to the present. It reaches its first peak in ZHUKOVSKY and BATYUSHKOV. Zhukovsky's two versions of Gray's "Elegy written in a Country Churchyard," the first (1802) in quatrains of Alexandrines, and the second (1839) in hexameters, are still the most famous examples of the genre in Russian poetry. The elegies of PUSHKIN, BARATYNSKY, and LERMONTOV tend to follow the romantic elegy, being somewhat shorter and more poignant expressions of moments of personal soul-searching, as Pushkin's "Elegy" (1830). The tradition was continued by FET, who effectively used the elegiac distich in "A Strange Feeling" (Strannoe chuvstvo, 1847), and attained great intensity of elegiac feeling in "In the Stillness of Midnight" (V polunochnoi tishi, 1888). The elegiac mode was popular with the symbolists, BRYUSOV and BLOK in particular, while Vyacheslav IVANOV cultivated the elegiac distich in explicit response to Propertius and Ovid ("Laeta," 1892). The ACMEISTS, AKHMATOVA and MANDELSHTAM in particular, continued the tradition. Mandelshtam's most famous poem, "Tristia" (1918) echoes both Ovid and Tibullus. The elegy is quite alive in modern poetry. Aleksandr TVARDOVSKY, Leonid MARTYNOV, Vadim Shefner, and Iosif BRODSKY, among others, have written poems explicitly or implicitly marked as elegies.

Bibliography: L. S. Fleishman, "Iz istorii elegii v pushkinskuyu epokhu," *Uchenye zapiski Latviiskogo gos. univ.* 106 (1968). L. G. Frizman, *Zhizn' liricheskogo zhanra: Russkaya elegiya ot Sumarokova do Nekrasova.* 1973. G. A. Gukovskii, "Elegiya v 18 v." In *Russkaya poeziya 18 v.* 1927. George Gutsche, "Pushkin's 'Andrei Shen'e' and Poetic Genres in the 1820s," *CASS* 10 (1976); pp. 189–204. Kenneth H. and Warren U. Ober, "Zhukovsky's First Translation of Gray's Elegy." *SEEJ* 10 (1966); pp. 167–72.　　V. T.

Emigré literature. More than sixty years have passed since the tragic exodus of many of Russia's eminent writers, critics, philosophers, scholars, and statesmen in the wake of the October Revolution of 1917 and the ensuing Civil War. Paris soon became the émigré capital of Russian culture, art, and literature. Other important émigré centers emerged throughout Europe in the early 1920s in Berlin, Prague, Warsaw, Belgrade, Sofia, Riga, Helsinki, and Tallinn. The Russian intellectual community of Paris, however, determined the tone of Russian belles-lettres abroad. Russian authors in the West practised the genres of the short story, the tale, the novel, travel notes, memoirs, and lyric poetry, often of a philosophic bent and concerned with the basic tenets of freedom and Christian optimism.

Many illustrious writers left the Soviet Union when they realized that the new government was determined to control and direct the themes, plots, and artistic techniques of their present and future works. This was the reaction of authors as diverse as Mark ALDANOV, Konstantin BALMONT, Ivan BUNIN, Don Aminado (literary pseudonym of Aminad Petrovich Shpolyansky), Zinaida HIPPIUS, Aleksandr KUPRIN, S. K. MAKOVSKY, D. S. MEREZHKOVSKY, Sasha CHORNY, Lev SHESTOV, and Nadezhda TEFFI. Their example was followed in 1920 to 1923 by Georgy ADAMOVICH, Boris ZAITSEV, Georgy IVANOV, Nikolai OTSUP, Aleksei REMIZOV, Vladislav KHODASEVICH, Marina TSVETAEVA, Ivan SHMELYOV, Irina ODOEVTSEVA, and Mikhail OSORGIN, as well as by such noteworthy philosophers, scholars, and statesmen as Nikolai BERDYAEV, N. O. LOSSKY, Fyodor Stepun, B. P. Vysheslavtsev, Semyon FRANK, Sergei Bulgakov, Anton Kartashev, Mark Vishnyak, Pavel Milyukov, V. D. Nabokov, Pyotr STRUVE, and Ilya Bunakov-Fondaminsky. The Soviet writer Evgeny ZAMYATIN moved to Paris in 1931. Russian émigrés dispersed all over Europe with Vyacheslav IVANOV settling in Italy (1924), Igor SEVERYANIN and Pyotr Pilsky in Estonia, Mikhail ARTSYBASHEV and Dmitry Filosofov, an intimate friend of the Merezhkovskys', in Warsaw; Vladimir NABOKOV went to Berlin after graduating from Cambridge (England); Marina Tsvetaeva moved first to Prague and then to Paris in 1925; Nikolai MINSKY lived in England; Sergei MINTSLOV in Yugoslavia; Pyotr BITSILLI in Bulgaria.

Before, during, and especially after the Second World War, the migration of Russian writers continued: Karl Hoerschelmann, Pavel Irtel, Meta Roos, and Elizaveta Bazilevskaya-Roos fled from Estonia to Poland and later to Germany; Yury IVASK left Estonia for Germany and then for the United States; Igor CHINNOV moved from Riga to Germany, France, and finally to the United States; Nikolai Belotsvetov left Latvia for Germany; Leonid Zurov and Ivan Lukash went to Paris; Valery PERELESHIN moved from Kharbin to Peking and then to Rio de Janeiro; Tamara Velichkovskaya arrived in France via Yugoslavia; Dmitry KLENOVSKY managed to escape from the Soviet Union to Germany during the war, as did Ivan ELAGIN, who later went to the United States. Boris Nartsissov travelled from Estonia to Germany, Australia, and the United States. Mark Aldanov, Mark Vishnyak, Mikhail Tsetlin and his wife Maria left Paris for New York; Nabokov moved from Berlin to Paris and then to America. Antonin LADINSKY returned to the USSR.

The literary reputation of the so-called "older" generation of poets and fiction writers had already been established in Russia. But the "younger" generation of émigré writers—among them Aleksandr GINGER, Dovid KNUT, Boris POPLAVSKY, Lidiya CHERVINSKAYA, Anatoly STEIGER, Alla Golovina, Viktor Mamchenko, Anna PRISMANOVA, Ladinsky, Vladimir Smolensky, Yury TERAPIANO, Yury FELZEN, Chinnov, Ivask, Belotsvetov, Nartsissov, Viktor Tretyakov, Irtel, Roos, Vera BULICH, and Bazilevskaya—developed their talents and emerged as significant artists while outside their country and virtually beyond the reach of Russian mentors. Several "older" writers, however (for example, Bunin, Hippius, Georgy Ivanov, Adamovich, and Khodasevich), took some of the emerging poets and fiction writers under their wings, urging them to master the Russian language and its rules of prosody. Zinaida Hippius was instrumental in the creation of two literary journals, Novyi dom (The New House) and Novyi korabl', where still unknown young writers like Nina BERBEROVA, Terapiano, Steiger, Felzen, and Vladimir Zlobine could publish their works. Another outlet for young writers in Paris was an almanac, Krug (The Circle), initiated by Bunakov-Fondaminsky and published by his literary group. Thus the new "aspirants" could learn their craft from Hippius, Adamovich, Khodasevich, and other established authors. Bunin held symposiums at his home on poetry and fiction, which were well attended by young émigré writers. Galina KUZNETSOVA and Zurov are often referred to as Bunin's disciples. By 1948, Velichkovskaya had opened her own literary salon in Paris, and Adamovich, Georgy Raevsky, Sofia Pregel, Terapiano, Prismanova, Zurov, and Professor V. N. Ilyin often attended her soirées.

Among the many literary groups in exile perhaps the most important and sophisticated was "The Green Lamp" (Zelenaya lampa), an émigré literary and philosophical society founded in Paris by Hippius and her famous writer husband, Merezhkovsky. Not only literary matters, but also religious and political questions were raised and debated at the meetings of the group. At the first meeting of "The Green Lamp" (5 February 1927), the society was inaugurated with discourses by Khodasevich and Merezhkovsky on its objectives and goals. Tsetlin spoke on "Literary Criticism," Hippius on "Russian Literature in Exile," Bunakov-Fondaminsky on "The Russian Intelligentsia as a Spiritual Order," and Adamovich discussed the question "Does Poetry Have a Goal?" "The Green Lamp" was in fact an offshoot of the famous Sunday salons at the Merezhkovskys', frequented by the Russian intellectual élite of Paris: Professor V. N. Speransky, Berdyaev, Vysheslavtsev, K. V. Mochulsky, Makovsky, Lev Shestov, Mark Aldanov, A. F. Kerensky, Kartashev, Bunin, Teffi, Remizov, Shmelyov, Zaitsev, Adamovich, Georgy Ivanov, Odoevtseva, Terapiano, Knut, Felzen, Poplavsky, V. S. Varshavsky, V. V. WEIDLÉ, and others. Discussions centering on poetry, philosophy, religion, and metaphysical concepts stimulated a lively exchange of ideas. The Holy Trinity, love, life, and death, the "Third Testament," Vladimir SOLOVYOV, Kierkegaard, Hegel, Nietzsche, and Marx were among the varied topics of discussion. The guests also analyzed and evaluated the latest developments in literature, periodicals, and the activities at other literary soirées.

In an enthusiastic response to the freedom enjoyed by Russians in the West but suppressed in their native land after the Bolshevik coup d'état in 1917, new literary unions, groupings, trends, publishing houses, and periodicals were established in many other countries as well. Russian literature flourished everywhere, witnessing experimentation in style and a search for new ways of expression. Particularly active was the "Literary Circle" in Tallinn, actually founded in 1896, which met every Monday in the salon of its secretary Mariya Ilyinishna Padva. The meetings were attended by Nikolai Andreev, Ivask, Boris Pravdin, Irtel, Vasily Nikiforov-Volgin, and other repre-

sentatives of Russian belles lettres in Estonia. The Circle was one of the first Russian literary and social organizations in exile. The members presented papers and gave reports on Russian poetry and prose. Vladimir Sergeevich Sokolov, a teacher of Russian literature and principal of the Russian High School in Narva (Estonia), organized a "Small Literary Circle" for his students. At the meetings of this Circle the students read their own papers on symbolism, Acmeism, futurism, and other literary trends in Russia. Sokolov is warmly remembered by his former students, among them Nikolai Andreev.

Another literary circle, the "POETS' GUILD," was organized in 1928 by the modernist poet and lecturer at the University of Tartu, Boris Vasilievich Pravdin. The group patterned itself after GUMILYOV's "Guild of Poets" in St. Petersburg. Pravdin introduced his young poets, Nartsissov, Ivask, Meta and Elizaveta Roos, Dmitry Maslov, Boris Dikoi (Vilde), and Boris Taggo (Novosadov), to "literary novelties" arriving from Russia and the West and urged them to be sensitive to new and striking elements in poetic form, image, strophe, and rhythm.

In 1934 a second "Guild of Poets" was formed by Pavel Irtel in Tallinn. Among its members were Hoerschelmann, Andreev, Nartsissov, Ivask, Meta and Elizaveta Roos, and Irina Borman. Ivask, Nartsissov, and Andreev recall with gratitude the efforts of both Guilds in Estonia to further the poetic talents and critical acumen of their participants. The name of the literary almanac Nov' (Virgin Soil) published by Irtel's "Guild of Poets" should be noted: these Russians intended to plant their literary roots in a new, fertile, virgin soil. "In the Boat of Words" was a literary circle of Russian poets in Riga which counted among its members Chinnov, Mikhail Klochkov, Georgy Matveev, Belotsvetov, and Tamara Mezhak-Schmelling. The circle issued a monthly journal, Mansarda (The Attic), edited by Klochkov and Matveev. In Viipuri (Finland), A. E. Prazhkova organized a Russian literary circle named "The Union of Poets" (Sodruzhestvo poetov). Vera Bulich often appeared at Prazhkova's literary soirées to read her poetry and to lecture on Russian literature.

Berlin had its own Russian House of Arts modelled after the famous House of Arts in St. Petersburg, created by Maksim GORKY to shelter Russian poets and writers during the hungry and cold years following the October Revolution and the Civil War. The two Houses of Arts were closely affiliated. Remizov, Khodasevich, SHKLOVSKY, MAYAKOVSKY, and Minsky often read their works at the Berlin House of Arts. Émigré and Soviet writers mixed freely there, and the meetings were well attended by Russians residing in Berlin. In 1922 Russian poets in Berlin also founded a "Club of Writers," where Berdyaev, Aldanov, Stepun, Pavel MURATOV, Remizov, Khodasevich, Shklovsky, Ilya Erenburg, Andrei BELY, and Yuly Aikhenvald presented their papers and held literary debates.

In Prague, A. L. BEM headed "The Heritage of Poets," including among its members the poets Vyacheslav Lebedev, Golovina, Tatyana Rathaus, Vladimir Mansvetov, Aleksei Eisner, Evgeny Gessen, Vadim Morkovin, and Emilia Chegrintseva. Whereas the émigré centers in Belgrade, Tallinn, Riga, and Warsaw were oriented largely toward the literary fashions of Paris and Prague, Bem's literary circle cultivated the style of PASTERNAK. Other literary groups in Prague were "The Russian Hearth" of Countess S. V. Panina; the literary society of B. A. Evreinov, and V. F. Bulgakov's circle. Warsaw had "The Tavern of Poets," and Helsinki the literary and philosophical society Svetlitsa (Parlor). Once a week the members of Svetlitsa gathered at the Club of "The Russian Colony" in Helsinki to discuss poetry and fiction. Vera Bulich, President of Svetlitsa, V. V. Drozdovich, Yu. Grigorkov, and a Navy officer, P. F. Svetlik, who was particularly interested in philosophy, regularly attended these meetings. Svetlitsa, moreover, organized book exhibits, poetry readings, lectures on Russian belles lettres, and supported the activities of Vereteno (The Spindle), a Russian literary and artistic society in Helsinki. Among the many celebrities of Russian art, theater, and belles lettres who visited Finland during the 1920s and 1930s were A. AMFITEATROV, A. Kuprin, Boris Zaitsev, Igor Severyanin, N. Plevitskaya, Shalyapin, Tamara Karsavina, Mikhail Fokin, tenor Dmitry Smirnov, and soprano Tatiana Menotti. Helsinki housed the publishing house Biblion, directed by the Russian playwright Fyodor Falkovsky, which issued, among other Russian books, Leonid ANDREEV's novella "Satan's Diary" (1921), its sequel "A Nocturnal

Conversation" (1921), and a collection of stories by Kuprin, *The Star of Solomon* (1920). *Biblion*, specializing in translations from Finnish into Russian and German, was another Russian center in Finland.

Several of these literary groups were engaged in heated polemics with one another and used almanacs and journals to voice their thoughts. Hippius, for example, attacked Berdyaev's journal *Put'* because of its "conciliatory position" toward the Soviet Union, and criticized E. E. Lazarev's journal *Volya Rossii*, an organ of the left-wing Socialist Revolutionary Party under the editorship of V. I. Lebedev, Marc Slonim, and V. V. Sukhomlin. The critical section of the magazine systematically reviewed all literary publications in the Soviet Union. In the eyes of some émigrés, this was a flirtation with the USSR. In Mark Slonim's words, "A considerable stir in traditional and conservative émigré circles was provoked by *Volya Rossii*'s challenging, unorthodox view of literature and art.... The monthly claimed that the study of [new Soviet literary] works was indispensable for the understanding of the changes brought about in Russian society by the Revolution.... In the 1920s the literary policy of *Volya Rossii* encountered strong resistance and disapproval, and it succeeded in gaining a favorable response only after a bitter struggle.... The role *Volya Rossii* played in the artistic and intellectual discussions of the 1920s and the heated polemics it provided abroad form a little known but fascinating chapter of émigré literary history" (quoted from *Russkaya literatura v emigratsii: Sbornik statei*, ed. N. P. Poltoratskii [Pittsburgh, 1972], pp. 382–83).

Another Russian journal, *Versty* (Milestones), edited by D. P. SVYATOPOLK-MIRSKY, P. P. Suvchinsky, and S. Ya. Efron, likewise irritated some Russian exiles, among them Hippius and Merezhkovsky, because its EURASIANISM emphasized the Asiatic factors in the history of Russia and Russian culture and advocated an "Exodus to the East." Hippius particularly denounced the journal's "politics of appeasement" with the Soviet government. In most émigré circles the idea, advanced by E. D. Kuskova, S. N. Prokopovich, and A. V. Reshetnikov, to end the "civil war" between the émigrés and the Soviet government was unacceptable. P. N. Milyukov's theory on the "evolution of Bolshevism"—that no opposition toward Bolshevism was necessary because it would, in due time, change of its own accord—similarly angered many Russian writers in exile. Another group of Russian exiles formed the circle *Smenovekhovtsy* and published a weekly journal, SMENA VEKH, edited by Yu. V. Klyuchnikov. The journal advised Russians abroad to consider themselves "conquered by the Soviet government." This attitude caused strong disapproval with many émigrés, who thought that these developments resulted from an alarming conspiracy originating in the Soviet Union. Mikhail Osorgin was criticized in Russian journals and newspapers for his belief in a necessary "spiritual return" to Soviet Russia. On 1 March 1924, Osorgin gave a lecture in which he encouraged young Russians living in Paris to return to Russia and participate in the destiny of their homeland. His appeal was condemned by all circles.

In the 1939 draft of her unfinished essay "A History of the Intelligentsia in Exile: A Sketch of Four Five-Year Plans," Zinaida Hippius provides an invaluable record of these manifold activities. She divides the history of the Russian émigré intelligentsia into four phases: the first Five-Year period, 1920 to 1925; the second, 1925 to 1930; the third, 1930 to 1935; and the fourth, 1935 to 1939. For each she presents a detailed picture of literary events (meetings, soirées, discussions, and conflicts), as well as a detailed account of various publishing efforts. Hippius adds her own witty observations and draws conclusions about each period. She describes the activities of the older and younger generations, M. M. Vinaver's journal *Zveno* (The Link), Kerensky's newspaper *Dni* (Days), V. L. Burtsev's *Obshchee delo* (Common Cause), Milyukov's *Poslednie novosti* (The Latest News), SOVREMENNYE ZAPISKI, *Illyustrirovannaya Rossiya* (Russia Illustrated), Tsetlin's almanac *Okno* (The Window), the literary group KOCHEVYE (Camp of the Wanderers), headed by Slonim, and its fortnightly journal *Novaya gazeta* (The New Gazette), the emergence of Bunakov-Fondaminsky's *Krug* (The Circle), in collaboration with Berdyaev, G. P. FEDOTOV, and E. Yu. SKOBTSOVA (Mother Mariya), and *Vechera poezii* (Evenings of Poetry) in Paris. Her discussion of *Sovremennye zapiski*, a review of literature, politics, and the arts (1919–40), is of particular interest as it was one of the more successful journals of the post-revolutionary emigration. Although Hippius is critical of Vishnyak's allegedly capricious and even suspi-

cious handling of material submitted for publication, she acknowledges the journal's value especially in the field of belles lettres, literary criticism, and history of literature. She also praises the weekly paper *Rossiya i Slavyanstvo* (Russia and Slavdom), which appeared in 1928 to replace Pyotr Struve's weekly paper *Rossiya* (Russia). Both the new title, which referred to the journal's intention to promote friendship and cultural ties between various Slavic countries, and the new editorial board consisting of Struve's associates, were in her opinion well chosen. Though Hippius' interpretation of the events and atmosphere of Russian Paris is not always serious and rarely objective, her "History" has considerable historical and literary significance and forms a welcome addition to the few works devoted to Russian literature in the West.

The Russian intellectual community abroad created a "conspiracy" of sorts to sustain and further the development of Russian—as distinct from Soviet—culture. Echoes of Russian SYMBOLISM, ACMEISM, and FUTURISM can be found in the works of both the older and the younger generation, but there is also ample evidence of a common striving toward innovation. Like the modernists at the turn of the century, both generations advocated freedom from prevailing norms and rebelled against the dogmatic conception of art made fashionable by BELINSKY, CHERNYSHEVSKY, DOBROLYUBOV, and their disciples in the Soviet Union. In protest against the 19th-century radicals and their 20th-century heirs who had imposed upon the arts a socially oriented materialistic ideology, émigré writers openly pleaded in favor of idealism, Christian optimism or Christian resignation, and a mystic-ethical weltanschauung.

The period 1923 to 1939 may be considered the apogee of the literary activities of the first-wave emigration. The era witnessed many literary masterpieces and was distinguished by Bunin's receipt of the Nobel Prize for literature in 1933. Noted works like Bunin's novella "Mitya's Love," his short story "Sunstroke," and his novel *The Life of Arsenyev*, Remizov's *The Image of Nikolai the Miracle Worker*, Zaitsev's novel *The House in Passy*, Shmelyov's novel *The Nanny from Moscow*, Merezhkovsky's historico-religious writings, and Aldanov's historico-philosophical works were published during these years. Poetry flourished equally in the years between 1923 and 1939 with the publication of numerous collections by eminent poets, such as Hippius, Tsvetaeva, Khodasevich, Adamovich, Georgy Ivanov, Otsup, and Bunin. Moreover, many young writers made their debut in the Russian press abroad.

A multitude of newspapers, literary journals, and almanacs were available in which Russian writers could publish their works. Russian newspapers and periodicals like *Poslednie novosti*, *Obshchee delo*, *Rossiya*, and VOZROZHDENIE in Paris; *Rul'* (The Rudder, Berlin), *Dni* (Berlin; from 1925, Paris), *Segodnya* (Today, Riga), *Vesti dnya* (The Latest News, Tallinn), *Russkaya zhizn'* (Russian Life) and *Russkie novosti* (Russian News, both Helsinki), *Za svobodu* (For Freedom, Warsaw), *Novoe vremya* (New Times, Belgrade), and *Novoe russkoe slovo* (The New Russian Word, New York) provided a forum for the creative endeavors of the émigré community. For the most part, these periodicals maintained high cultural standards, as did most Russian journals and almanacs published in émigré settlements throughout the world—for example, *Russkaya mysl'* (Russian Thought, Sofia, 1921; Prague, 1922; Berlin, 1922–23; Paris, 1927); in Paris: SOVREMENNYE ZAPISKI (Contemporary Annals), *Versty* (Milestones), *Zveno* (The Link), *Illyustrirovannaya Rossiya*, *Gryadushchaya Rossiya* (Future Russia), *Russkie zapiski* (Russian Annals, Paris-Shanghai), *Vstrechi* (Encounters), *Novyi grad* (The New City), *Novyi korabl'* (The New Ship), *Golos minuvshego* (Voice of the Past), *Obshchee delo*, *Orion*, *Put'* (The Road), *Russkaya nedelya* (The Russian Week, Paris, 1925; Prague, 1926), *Chisla* (Numbers), the almanacs *Krug* (The Circle) and *Okno* (The Window); in Berlin: *Russkaya kniga* (The Russian Book), later renamed *Novaya russkaya kniga* (The New Russian Book), *Utverzhdeniya* (Discussions), *Na chuzhoi storone* (In a Foreign Country, Berlin-Prague), and GRANI (Facets, Berlin, 1922–23; Frankfurt on Main, 1946–), *Spolokhi* (Northern Lights), and *Zhar-ptitsa* (Firebird, Berlin-Paris); in Brussels: *Blagonamerennyi* (The Loyalist); in Warsaw: *Mech* (The Sword); in Prague: *Volya Rossii* (The Will of Russia), *Svoimi putyami* (Along Our Path), and *Studencheskie gody* (Student Years); in Helsinki: *Zhurnal sodruzhestva* (Journal of Concord) and *Dni nashei zhizni* (Days of Our Life); in Riga: *Perezvony* (Chimes), *Liter-*

atura i zhizn' (Literature and life), *Mansarda* (Mansard), *Novaya nedelya* (The New Week), *Novaya niva* (The New Field), *Nord-ost* (North-East), *Otkliki* (Responses), and *Yunyi chitatel'* (The Young Reader); in Tallinn: *Via sacra*, *Na chuzhbine* (In a Foreign Country), *Oblaka* (Clouds), *Nov'* (Virgin Soil), and *Russkii magazin*; in Narva: *Knut* (The Whip); in New York: *Zarnitsa* (Summer Lightning), *Na chuzhbine* (In a Foreign Country), NOVYI ZHURNAL (The New Review), and *Opyty* (Experiments); in Kaunas: *Zarya* (Dawn) and *Zerkalo* (The Mirror); in Bucharest: *Zolotoi petushok* (The Golden Cockerel) and *Nedelya* (The Week); in Belgrade: *Meduza* and *Nashe budushchee* (Our Future); in Shanghai: *Na chuzhbine* (In a Foreign Country) and *Nash put'* (Our Path); in Constantinople: *Put'* (The Road); in Buenos Aires: *Nasha strana* (Our Country); in Kharbin: *Rubezh* (The Boundary); in Peking and Kharbin: *Russkoe obozrenie* (The Russian Review, 1920–21; Chicago, 1927–29); in Hamburg: *Put'* (The Road); after the Second World War, in Munich: *Mosty* (Bridges); in Frankfurt on Main: *Posev* (Crops); in Toronto: *Sovremennik* (The Contemporary); in New York: *Vozdushnye puti* (Aerial Ways). In addition to these older journals, many of which no longer exist, there are more recent periodicals initiated by Soviet émigrés of the "third wave", such as *Kontinent* (West Germany and Paris), *Gnosis* and *Novyi amerikanets* (The New American) in New York; *Ekho* (The Echo), *Vestnik* (The Messenger), *Tret'ya volna* (The Third Wave), *S 'A' do 'Ya'* (From A to Z) in Paris; and *My i nashe vremya* (We and Our Times) in Israel.

One salient feature of all literature written in exile, especially political exile, is its orientation toward the past. Emigré literature usually embraces the established traditions of the original national culture, since they provide a certain stability in an alien and largely hostile world. We can detect deep ties with the past in the works of the German writers who fled the Nazi regime as well as in the works of numerous Russian writers, poets, and philosophers who abandoned their homeland after the Bolshevik Revolution. Many a poignant passage describes the glory of a vanished past. The exiled writer experiences in his adopted country a series of evolutionary stages which are reflected in his work. During the first years of exile, the writer continues to write as he did at home; however, eventually the new experiences and conditions of the host country begin to affect his artistic sensibility. His homeland becomes a mere cherished memory, while the culture and civilization of the émigré's newly acquired home may now influence his artistic perception. The effect of his new culture is clear when traces of the language of the adopted country begin to appear in the writer's works. The strong attachment to one's home intensifies, but it blends with a renewed faith in mankind, confidence in life, and the search for new, individual values, as well as for a new literary technique. These fresh beginnings, projected against a backdrop of lost dreams and nostalgic aspirations, constitute one of the most remarkable and at the same time most dramatic chapters in the history of modern literature.

In Paris, Adamovich shaped and determined a literary movement sometimes known as the "Parisian note" (PARIZHSKAYA NOTA), which appealed especially to the younger poets. The main tenets of the movement were ascetic simplicity, the rejection of all forms of experimentation in versification, and the prominence of eschatological subject matter: truth, loneliness, suffering, and death. The technical features of its poetry include the use of parentheses, dashes, truncated syntactical units, and frequent subordinate clauses. Unexpected aphorisms, thoughts only partially phrased, the serenity of restrained epithets, an absence of motion verbs, a tendency to conceal the careful formal polish of their verse, and an occasional hint of irony are all characteristic of the "Parisian Note." Most poems deal with the "eternal" themes of love, solitude, nature, and pensive sadness without, however, being excessively didactic or moral; the focus is not on religious or philosophic questions. Of course, not all émigré poets were seduced by the quiet and restrained "Parisian Note"; accomplished poets like Hippius, Tsvetaeva, Poplavsky, Ginger, Prismanova, and Knut resisted the movement and continued to write in their own, inimitable fashion.

Between 1920 and 1939 and in the following years Russian intellectual communities integrated themselves to a considerable degree in adjacent cultures. In fact, while there had been no significant "cross-pollination" between the older Russian writers and the literatures of their host countries, the situation was different with the younger Russian writers who had been intellectually and artistically nurtured in the West. Poplavsky, Felzen, Gaito GAZDANOV, and Vilmar Adams-Aleksandrovsky, for example, eagerly embraced the rich Western literary tradition, as well as its many radical innovations. Western experimentation also transpires in the declamatory intonation of Knut's early poems; a new kind of irony and grotesque appear in the later poetry of Georgy Ivanov and Khodasevich; bizarre and surrealist visions, even features of dadaism, materialize in the creations of Poplavsky; enraptured sound, color chains, and emphasis on verbal mastery are characteristic of Ladinsky's verse. The stream-of-consciousness technique and the *monologue intérieur* developed in the works of Marcel Proust, James Joyce, Virginia Woolf, Valéry Larbaud, and other European avant-garde writers of the period, may also be found in the writings of Felzen. Ivask's highly personal chains of associations are fused with sound experiments, neologisms, and elliptical imagery resembling the English metaphysical and religious poets John Donne, Richard Crashaw, and George Herbert, as well as the Spanish poet Luis de Góngora who delighted in the poetic elaboration of philosophical conflict. Archaic words, different levels of diction, puns, neologisms, "nonsense" language, and whimsical wordplay highlight Remizov's ornamental patterns with their almost hypnotic combinations and recombinations of phrases. Boris Semyonov skillfully exploited the richness of the Russian language using colorful archaisms, dialectal forms, and neologisms; he developed a fanciful mixture of fairy tale, Russian *bylina*, and dreams to create a powerful, unforgettable impression of the passion and terror unleashed in a time of radical political upheaval. Pravdin's modernism resides to a large extent in the careful utilization of literary allusions ranging from the myths of ancient Greece to the style and manner of 17th-century neoclassical France in accordance with the strict aesthetic rules of Boileau. Ivan Belyaev's poetry is remarkable for its verbal experimentation, Dostoevskian intensity, and lyrical compactness; images, themes, concepts, and avant-garde systems of versification are interwoven to produce a volatile mosaic of ambivalent, highly subjective perspectives. Yury Shumakov, who was associated with Russo-Estonian circles fascinated by futurism, displays a definite tendency toward eccentric "trans-sense" language and the use of futurist devices in association with symbolist imagery. With its matter-of-fact portrayal of the basic duality of the world, enhanced by a masterful arrangement of rhyme, imagery, poetic vocabulary, and unexpected paradoxes, Rathaus' poetry is also experimental and European. The restrained, fragile, and pensive verse of Bulich resembles delicate Chinese porcelain with its exquisite design and color; she frequently uses aphoristic formulations to capture thoughts and emotions merely hinted at or only partially expressed. Freely mixing poetic and prosaic language, word games, free verse, and sound symbolism along with an increasing tendency toward the grotesque and fantastic, Chinnov's poetry has its own unmistakable ligature. Nartsissov's poems embody a scientific weltanschauung mythologized and expressed in poetic form. He often fuses the old with a new mythology, contrasting a modern view of the Apocalypse with Biblical imagery. The influence of E. T. A. Hoffmann and Edgar Allan Poe is evident in much of his work: in his preoccupation with the supernatural, metaphysics, *Naturphilosophie*, and in the romantic theme of the double. Tretyakov's filigree portrayal of medieval Kiev is reminiscent of the evocation of a distant golden past and the use of the supernatural to be found in the English romantic poets. His poem "Noontide" is similar in flavor to the imaginary Xanadu of Coleridge's "Kubla Khan." The avant-garde poetry of Taggo is more "left wing" than even the most "leftist" futurists including Mayakovsky. Taggo was fond of witty, even caustic aphorisms like *vozhdei vozhzhami!* "[Hit] the reigning—with the reins!" The early prose of V. Sirin (Pseud. of V. Nabokov) with its penchant for fantastic impressionism was certainly an organic part of this creative explosion. The primarily experimental nature of these works is symptomatic of a break, at least partially, with the 19th-century literary conservatism that characterized the works of some of the older representatives of Russian poetry and fiction. These influences and attitudes fostered creative ferment in all areas of art and learning and contributed to the development of a unique Russian culture, one distinct from (though not oblivious of) its 19th-century progenitor and its neighboring 20th-century Western European cultures. Russian émigré literature was unquestionably neither static nor irretrievably chained to its "mother" culture in Russia as some scholars have suggested.

Since World War II, the United States has become a major center for émigré poetry and the new home of numerous Russian poets. Lidiya ALEKSEEVA, Olga ANSTEI, Nonna Belavina, Dmitry BOBYSHEV, Iosif BRODSKY, Ivan Elagin, Tatyana Fessenko, Boris FILIPPOV, Gleb Glinka, Georgy GOLOKHVASTOV, Oleg ILYINSKY, Naum Korzhavin, Nikolai MORSHEN (Marchenko), Dmitry Shakhovskoi, (Archbishop John of San Francisco, who writes under the pen name Strannik), and Zinaida Trotskaya, among others, came to live in America. Despite the great influx of Russian poets, however, there does not appear to be much significant interaction between Russian émigré and American poetry. In the verse of more recent Russian poets there are clear indications of a strong mood of nostalgia, anguish, and a longing to return. Even when the poet responds positively to his new country, he does so largely in contrast with the old. In an effort to retain ties with his former culture, the émigré poet may often ignore the rich but alien tradition which surrounds him. While most Russian poets of the "second-wave" emigration in America reject experimental forms in verse, there are a few who, in an attempt to oppose this conservative stance, do espouse new trends. Eloquent alienation from conservatism can be heard in the oratorical voice of Elagin, in the quiet reflections of Brodsky, and in the fragile, meticulous, and refined contemplation of Alekseeva. Morshen combines nostalgia with a strong sense of the grotesque to create a very personal, ironic style. The freshness and innovations of these poets form a striking contrast with the static condition of Soviet Russian literature. While innovative, Elagin's work nevertheless reflects the heritage of Mayakovsky and even reaches back to the 18th-century ode. The poet Ilyinsky, influenced by Pasternak, reveals himself as a traditional poet in landscape descriptions, nature details, and delicate sound effects.

Among newer Russian poets in exile Dmitry KLENOVSKY (pseudonym of Dmitry Iosifovich Krachkovsky), who died in 1976 in Traunstein (West Germany), deserves special mention. Before the October Revolution he spent much time in France, where he discovered the works of Henri de Régnier, de Hérédia, Albert Samain, Coppée, and Sully-Prudhomme. Klenovsky was a poet of Russian and Western European culture who continued the great tradition of the St. Petersburg school of poetic craftsmanship distinguished by its exquisite artistic taste and impeccable technique and usually expressing philosophical or contemplative moods focussed on the poet's conflicting inclinations: the Platonic ideal versus sensual joy in earthly existence, faith and agnosticism, life and death. At times his poetic perception of the universe reaches Eucharistic depths, but generally Klenovsky creates restrained, even sparse imagery, which lends a sense of spaciousness to his verse. In harmony with the Acmeist poetics, turbulent emotions and intentional disorder are absent. Because of his direct exposure, at an early stage, to Western European art and culture, Klenovsky has come to stand apart from his contemporaries in Russian verse.

If one compares the first-wave emigration with the second wave, it appears that the first group had a much higher share of intellectuals who were well versed in Western European literary traditions and more inclined toward experimentation in prose and poetry, which led to intricate patterns in meter, rhyme, image, sound orchestration, color, and rhythm. The writers of the first wave saw the preservation and enrichment of Russian culture in exile as their special task and attempted to spread their spiritual ideals, convictions, aspirations, as well as to make their poetic credo known through their works. The task appears to have been beyond the capacities of the Russians who emigrated after World War II. Moreover, the poetry and fiction of the earlier Russian exiles graphically illustrate the divergent attitudes and philosophies prevalent among Russian intellectuals in the 1920s and 1930s. Their works manifest both a striving to preserve the native culture and language through literature in exile and, simultaneously, an impatient search for new artistic forms of expression. Although the first-wave émigrés often did not share each other's aesthetic and philosophical allegiances, they all strongly opposed the idea of coercion in artistic creation, whether in content or in form. A mood of nostalgia and anguish pervades many of their works, as well as an awareness of participating in the crystallization process of a culture, also reflecting their unique experiences in exile.

The émigrés of the second wave, with some exceptions, seemed unable to equal the degree of culture, education, and "Westernization" of the first-wave. At the turn of the century sophisticated Russian writers had eagerly identified with the cultural trends developing in Western Europe; indeed one of their early objectives was the propagation of Western culture and literature in Russia. They looked to Europe for stimulation, inspiration, and new models. This rich background produced remarkable poets and fiction writers, such as Hippius, Tsvetaeva, Georgy Ivanov, Adamovich, Khodasevich, Vyacheslav Ivanov, Balmont, Merezhkovsky, Bunin, Teffi, Otsup, Remizov, and Aldanov. So, too, to the younger generation the paths leading to Western culture and literature had been open, and all of its aesthetic and intellectual experiences accessible. But except for a few like Klenovsky, Russian authors of the second-wave emigration and even more so those of the third-wave had been largely severed from the culture tradition of Western Europe and its influences. With the possible exception of Elagin, no major poets or writers have emerged from among the émigrés of the second wave. As Leonid Rzhevsky has formulated it: "In comparison with the first or 'old' Russian emigration, which included such outstanding writers as Bunin and Remizov, the newer wave of emigrants did not produce any outstanding names. However, it yielded a number of books of widely acknowledged value which were translated into other languages. Many of these books ... are characterized by a documentary and autobiographical quality—a direct reflection of all that the individual authors witnessed and experienced during the years of Stalin's terror; in this, too, lies their additional informative value" (quoted from *Russkaya literatura v emigratsii: Sbornik statei*, ed. N. P. Poltoratskii [Pittsburgh, 1972], p. 370).

Russian literature in exile, while unique in some respects, may also be considered part of a larger phenomenon, almost a tradition, that of expatriate writing: Americans in Paris; Germans and Frenchmen in England and the United States during the Nazi period. The essentially modern character of Russian émigré literature, its stylistic experimentation, and its philosophical and psychological content are clearly of far-reaching significance within the international outline of the 20th-century avant-garde experience. The émigré phenomenon is not merely an isolated though interesting addendum to contemporary literature; it is organically linked to its development.

On the surface, the fate of Russian writers in exile may seem to resemble that of Henry James (1843–1916), who became a British citizen in 1915 in protest against American neutrality in World War I, of the great American-born poet T. S. Eliot (1888–1965), whose most celebrated works appeared in England, or of French writers like André Maurois (pseudonym of Emile Herzog, 1885–1967), who were opposed to the Nazi occupation of France and left for England. Thomas Mann (1875–1955) understood early on the evil nature of National Socialism and recognized it as a threat to his own personal safety: he left Germany, going into self-imposed exile first in Switzerland and later in the United States. He became an American citizen in 1944. The Germans Bertolt Brecht (1898–1956) and Carl Zuckmayer (1896–1977), poets and playwrights, fled the Nazi terror by emigrating to the United States, where both created some of their most significant works. But because their exile was largely voluntary (as was also the case with several Russian writers in the 19th century, among them DOSTOEVSKY), these authors could later return to their homeland. Moreover, they frequently moved to a country where they could use their mother tongue in everyday life (like Thomas Mann and Hermann Hesse in Switzerland).

Not so with the Russian writers in exile after the 1917 Revolution. Their "Diaspora" was as real as the dispersion of the Jews after the Babylonian exile. Completely severed from their homeland, often stateless and deprived of the hope of ever returning home, unable to speak their own language in the new country, these Russians met with a destiny quite unique in history. Their fate has been aptly described by Aleksandr Perfilyev in his poem "A Fig for the Nations": "Silently, we are spread out around the world ... and gloomily carry our passports, marked 'blacklisted'.... We're not accepted anywhere.... At every step: 'Declared an alien,'/Live where you like, go and live in the water.... The émigré is as ragged as ever, / And in his refugee's life, thrice-accursed / He has nowhere found peace." The social plight of the Russian exile as presented in the works of Russian émigré writers is complemented by an existential sense of estrangement and alienation—not only from Russia, but from all those things that are dear to his heart: from his language, his cultural tradition, and even from himself.

Russian émigré literature written between 1920 and 1940 clearly shows the authors' objection to outdated themes and lack of craftsmanship, a dissatisfaction with prevailing 19th-century criticism of art based on sociological and ideological considerations, and an increased if not exclusive interest in the aesthetic and metaphysical content of belles lettres. These early writers endeavored to re-establish the importance of the individual and stressed the validity of intuitive and spiritual revelations. Since their works also represent the prevailing social, religious, and political attitudes of the period, they are important for the study of both the pre-Revolutionary and the post-Revolutionary intelligentsia. The value of the poetry and fiction of the later Russian émigré writers is entirely different. They illustrate the effect of the laws of "dialectical materialism" imposed on prose, poetry, and criticism since the late 1920s. The influence of this methodology as the only guideline in the practice and study of literature is obvious in many of their works. The writings of later émigrés also reveal that it was only in the freedom of exile that they could continue and enhance the poetic experimentation and innovation of the 1920s and thus approximate the avant-garde literature of the West.

Bibliography: Ludmila A. Foster, *Bibliography of Russian Emigré Literature*. 2 vols. 1970. John Glad, "The American Chapter in Russian Poetry," *RLJ* 30, no. 106 (1976), pp. 173–84. Zinaida Hippius, "A History of the Intelligentsia in Exile: A Sketch of Four Five-Year Plans." Intro. Temira Pachmuss, *RLJ* 26, no. 93 (1972), pp. 3–13; nos. 94–95, pp. 3–19. Simon Karlinsky and Alfred Appel, Jr., eds., *The Bitter Air of Exile: Russian Writers in the West, 1922–1972*. Berkeley, 1977. ———, guest eds., *Russian Literature and Culture in the West: 1922–1972*. 2 vols. *TriQuarterly*, nos. 27 and 28 (1973). Temira Pachmuss, *Intellect and Ideas in Action: Selected Correspondence of Zinaida Hippius*. Munich, 1972. ———, *A Russian Cultural Revival: A Critical Anthology of Emigré Literature before 1939*. Knoxville, 1981. Nikolai P. Poltoratzky, "Russian Literature, Literary Scholarship and Publishing in the United States." In *Ethnic Literatures since 1776: The Many Voices of America*. Ed. Wolodymyr T. Zyla and Wendell M. Aycock. Lubbock, Texas, 1978. Pp. 455–501. ———, ed. *Russkaya literatura v emigratsii: Sbornik statei*. Pittsburgh, 1972. Gleb Struve, *Russkaya literatura v izgnanii*. New York, 1956. T. A. P.

Emín, Fyódor Aleksándrovich (1735?–1770), a satirist, an original thinker and the author of the first Russian novel. His origins, background and education are unknown. In fact, Emin may not even have been a native of Russia. Novikov reports that Emin was a young orphan when he travelled in Europe and Asia with a Jesuit tutor, and that in Turkey Emin served in the Turkish army and converted to Islam to save his life. In 1758, in London, Mohamed Emin applied to A. M. Golitsyn for Russian citizenship, which was granted him after his conversion to Russian Orthodoxy, and in 1761, Emin arrived in St. Petersburg, where he taught briefly at the Cadet Corps, then translated for the Foreign Department, and later served in Catherine's Cabinet. In 1763, Emin, who spoke many languages and was exceedingly well read, became a professional writer by necessity and by inclination. In 1769, he also wrote his popular satirical journal *Adskaya pochta* for which he was indebted to Lesage's *Diable Boiteux* (itself inspired by de Guevara) and three major articles for Novikov's Truten'. The twenty-five books which Emin wrote over seven years include his own novels, his translations, his "translations" of non-existent books (e.g., *The Garden of Love* [Lyubovnyi vertograd], 1763, 5 editions) and a *Russian History* with references to non-existent sources.

Miramond (1763), *Themistocles* (1763) and *Letters of Ernest and Doravra* (1766) are among Emin's major original novels. *Miramond* belongs to the tradition of the Russian novel of adventure (typified later, in 1782, by M. Komarov's *Georg*), and shares affinities with Prévost's popular *Mémoires d'un Homme de Qualité* (1728–31). Miramond is an educated, morally upright "Chevalier" native of Turkey. He travels abroad to enlighten his heart and mind, and in Egypt wins the heart of Zyumbulya, the Sultan's daughter, to whom he is happily wedded after countless adventures, misfortunes, and near-misfortunes on the cosmopolitan background of England, Portugal, Spain, Italy, Poland, etc. *Themistocles*, which Emin dedicated to Catherine, is cast in the loose form of a journey during which the Athenian general Themistocles and his son Neocles converse on a wide variety of philosophical topics. *Themistocles* illustrates well Emin's erudition in 18th-century thought, and is his own, updated version of Fénelon's very popular *Télémaque* (1699). Like Fénelon in writing *Télémaque*, Emin conceived this work as a pedagogical manual for the young heir (Paul I was nine years old). Emin's *Letters of Ernest and Doravra* consist of 126 letters divided into four volumes, and represent the first Russian epistolary novel. Emin was inspired by Richardson (first translated into Russian nearly three decades later), and he knew Rousseau's *New Héloïse* (1761). But Emin's epistolary novel is structured largely independently and contains his own discussions on topical issues.

Emin fell into oblivion after the advent of Karamzin. The eclipse is understandable inasmuch as Emin's dated, often unwieldy prose style, his erudition and predilection for the "huge" form of the novel were alien to the subsequent pre-romantic generations of Russian writers, as was also Emin's artful web of mystification around his person. It is nevertheless paradoxical that to this day there is still no extensive study of Emin, Russia's first novelist, and the first writer in Russia to introduce into prose fiction the exotic orient and the autobiographical mode. An unreliable "Life" of Emin is inserted in the last six editions of his *Put' ko spaseniyu*, first published posthumously in 1780, and in the 3d edition of *Miramond*.

Secondary literature: A. Blagosvetlov, "Istoricheskii ocherk russkogo prozaicheskogo romana," *Syn otechestva*, no. 28 (1856), pp. 27–33. N. M. Karamzin, "Emin." In *Panteon russkikh avtorov*. 1802. A. Lyashchenko, *K istorii russkogo romana. Publitsisticheskii element v romanakh F. A. Emina*. St. Petersburg, 1898. 18 pages. N. I. Novikov, "Emin." In *Opyt Istoricheskogo slovarya*. 1772. T. P.

English-Russian and American-Russian literary relations.

English and American Literature in Russia

Although regular Russian-English trade and diplomatic contacts began in the 16th century, large-scale Russian exposure to English literature had to wait until the 18th century, when Russia turned West for enlightenment. The first important English cultural influence came from journals such as Addison and Steele's *The Spectator*. These served as prototypes for similar Russian journals, which were numerous and widely read and popularized English enlightenment thought—mainly through the intermediary of French and German translations. The 18th century also saw the beginning of systematic publication of English literature: Empress Catherine II commissioned translations of Swift's *Gulliver's Travels* and Fielding's *Adventures of Joseph Andrews*, and the journalist Nikolai Novikov published Milton's *Paradise Lost*, Fielding, Smollett, Sterne, Pope, Sheridan, Bunyan, and Young.

In the second half of the 18th century there began the broad dissemination of the poetry and novels of English sentimentalism. The most influential poetic works were Edward Young's *Night Thoughts*, James Thomson's *The Seasons*, and the Ossianic poems of James Macpherson. Young and Thomson introduced the themes of melancholy, worship of night, meditations on death and the transience of human life, while Macpherson's Ossian stimulated interest in folk poetry and the national past. Two Russian writers important for the dissemination of sentimentalism in Russia were Nikolai Karamzin and Vasily Zhukovsky. Karamzin knew English literature and had been to England, while Zhukovsky did much to make English literature accessible to Russians, translating Dryden, Thomson, Southey, Scott, Moore, Campbell, and Byron.

The second half of the 18th century also saw the penetration of the English novel, which was an important factor in the development of Russian fiction. Among the most popular were Defoe's *Robinson Crusoe* (trans. 1762–64), Fielding's *Tom Jones* (trans. 1770–71) and *Joseph Andrews* (trans. 1772–73), Goldsmith's *Vicar of Wakefield* (trans. 1786), Richardson's *Pamela* (trans. 1787), *Clarissa Harlowe* (trans. 1791–92), and *Sir Charles Grandison* (trans. 1793–94), and the Gothic novels of Ann Radcliffe. The most influential novelist was Laurence Sterne, whose *A Sentimental Journey Through France and Italy* (pub. 1768, trans. 1793) influenced Aleksandr Radishchev's *Journey from Petersburg to Moscow* (1790) and Karamzin's *Letters of a Russian Traveller* (1791–92). Sterne's influence extended into the 19th century and included Gogol, Pushkin (who preferred *Tristram*

Shandy), and Lev TOLSTOI (who read *Sentimental Journey* in 1850 when he was twenty-two and translated parts of it).

The next wave of English influence came with the introduction of Byron, Shakespeare, and Scott, who represented for Russians the essence of ROMANTICISM. Byron's Oriental poems strongly influenced Pushkin's southern poems, *Prisoner of the Caucasus* (1822) and *The Fountain of Bakhchisarai* (1824), while his *Don Juan* influenced Pushkin's novel in verse, *Evgeny Onegin* (1823–31). Byron also inspired LERMONTOV, who read him in English in the early 1830s and translated many of his poems. The first living British novelist to be popular in Russia was Sir Walter Scott, whose works were first translated into Russian in the early 1820s and who reached the height of his popularity in the late 1820s and early 1830s. Russians made pilgrimages to his home in Scotland and wrote to him. In the 1830s his novels made their way to peddlers who sold them all over the Russian empire, and his heroes, plots, and scenes became part of the consciousness of Pushkin's generation. Pushkin was rereading Scott while writing his historical novel, *The Captain's Daughter* (1836), and both he and the critic Vissarion BELINSKY spoke of Scott's beneficial influence. Although Shakespeare's name was known in Russia in the 18th century, Russians learned to appreciate him only with the coming of romanticism. Pushkin used Shakespeare as a model for his historical drama *Boris Godunov* (1825, pub. 1831), with its blank verse and freedom from the restrictions of classicism. Shakespeare's popularity outlasted the romantic period and continues to this day. TURGENEV and DOSTOEVSKY were inspired by him; there are echoes of Shakespeare in the poetry of Aleksandr BLOK and Boris PASTERNAK; and Pasternak's translations of his plays are classics of the Russian stage.

The first American writer to be widely read in Russia was James Fenimore Cooper, whose historical novel, *The Spy*, was translated in 1825. Translations of his other works followed during the next two decades and by 1850 he was considered a classic. The year 1825 also saw the translation of Washington Irving's *Rip Van Winkle*. Like Cooper, Irving reached the height of his fame in the mid-1830s and remained popular throughout the 19th century.

The wave of English literature entering Russian crested in the 1840s with the works of Charles Dickens. Dickens's reputation was made in 1847 with the translation of *Dombey and Son*. *David Copperfield*, which came out in Russian in 1849–50, also enjoyed an enormous success. Dickens had a wide and diverse following both before and after the Revolution. Tolstoi, who read him in English, exalted his love for his characters and drew on *David Copperfield* in his presentation of a child's vision of life in *Childhood*. He also used Dickensian themes in *War and Peace* and *Anna Karenina*. Dostoevsky was absorbed with Dickens, valued him for the moral influence he could exert, and was influenced by many of his types—buffoons, angelic child figures, and neurotics. He especially admired his humble characters and called him a "great Christian." Among 20th-century writers, official publishing practices in the Soviet Union today tend to favor the more conventional writers, such as John Galsworthy, H. G. Wells, A. J. Cronin, Graham Greene, and Doris Lessing.

American authors favored in the second half of the 19th century include Thomas Mayne Reid, Bret Harte, Harriet Beecher Stowe, Thoreau (who influenced Tolstoi's views on civil disobedience), Emerson, Longfellow, Poe, and Mark Twain. In the early 20th century the works of Jack London and Walt Whitman became part of the Russian literary scene. Although Whitman's name had been known as early as 1861, the first collection of his poems came out only in 1907, rendered into Russian by the noted translator, Kornei CHUKOVSKY. Whitman's influence can be seen on the Russian futurists, especially KHLEBNIKOV, and the early MAYAKOVSKY. The 1920s brought new authors—O. Henry, Upton Sinclair, Zane Grey, Frank Norris, Sherwood Anderson, Dos Passos, Sinclair Lewis, Dreiser, and Eugene O'Neill. In the 1930s Steinbeck, Erskine Caldwell, Richard Wright, Langston Hughes, and Ernest Hemingway became popular. During the years of the Cold War, the list of acceptable American writers was restricted to old favorites like Twain and Dreiser, and leftists such as Howard Fast (quickly stricken from the list of approved writers when he left the Communist Party in 1957). The post-Stalin period has seen the publication of many new American writers, including Carson McCullers, John Cheever, J. D. Salinger, John Updike, Faulkner, James Baldwin, and (belatedly) Melville,

and the re-introduction and enormous popularity of Hemingway. Lately there has been a vogue for the works of Kurt Vonnegut, Jr.

Russian literature in England and America

Before the 19th century, Russian literature was little known in Britain, although some information was available from the press, travel descriptions, and encyclopedias, and there had been some translations of CATHERINE II, Lomonosov, DERZHAVIN, and SUMAROKOV. A landmark was Sir John Bowring's *Specimens of the Russian Poets* (1821–23), which included translations from some of the best poets of the 18th and early 19th centuries—Lomonosov, Derzhavin, Karamzin, Zhukovsky, KRYLOV, and VYAZEMSKY—and created a genuine burst of interest in Russian literature in both England and America. As for prose, some of Karamzin's tales had appeared beginning in 1800 and some of Scott's Russian disciples had been published as well. The first spell of sustained interest in Russian literature in England belongs to the period of the Crimean War (1853–1856), when England and Russia were enemies, and coincides with the presence in England of Ivan Turgenev, who came to that country in 1847 for the first of many visits. Turgenev's *A Sportsman's Sketches* came out in England in 1855, followed by *Fathers and Sons* and *A Nest of Gentlefolk* in 1868 and *Virgin Soil* in 1877. Turgenev knew many English writers, including George Eliot, Thackeray, Carlyle, Rossetti, Tennyson, Robert Browning, Trollope, and Swinburne, and in 1879 he received an honorary degree from Oxford. He was the most important emissary of Russian culture in Victorian England and he helped create a favorable climate of opinion for his own works and the Russian novel in general. In the United States, too, Turgenev was the first Russian writer to be widely read and appreciated—even more warmly than in England—and most of his principal works saw early American editions: *Fathers and Sons* in 1867, *Smoke* in 1872, *Rudin* in 1873, *Virgin Soil* in 1877, and *A Sportsman's Sketches* in 1885. William Dean Howells and others pointed to him as a model of the realism they wanted for American literature. This current of opinion reached England through Henry James, who went to Europe to meet Turgenev in 1875, became his close friend, and found in him a potent influence and inspiration.

In the 1880s Tolstoi and Dostoevsky began to make their mark. The first English translation of Dostoevsky was *The House of the Dead*, published in New York in 1881. Translations of other works followed: *Crime and Punishment*, *The Insulted and Injured*, *Uncle's Dream*, *The Eternal Husband* in 1886, and *The Friend of the Family* (*Selo Stepanchikovo i ego obitateli*), *The Gambler*, and *The Idiot* in 1887. Tolstoi, whose *Childhood and Youth* had been translated in 1862 and *The Cossacks* in 1878, neither attracting much attention, was introduced to the English-speaking world by some of his later confessional works in a volume called *Christ's Christianity* (1885). The novels *Anna Karenina* and *War and Peace*, the latter carelessly translated from the French, came out in 1886. Writers and critics, as well as translators, played an important role in introducing the two giants to the English-speaking public. Worthy of mention here are the critical appreciations of William Dean Howells and Matthew Arnold, but the most influential work of all was by Eugène Melchior Vicomte de Vogüé, a French diplomat who had spent time in Russia. De Vogüé's book, *The Russian Novel* (*Le Roman Russe*), which was first published as a series of articles in 1883 and as a book in 1886 (it was not translated into English until 1913 but was well known before then), had a profound influence in Europe and America. It brought Russian realism, especially Tolstoi and Dostoevsky, to the attention of the reading public and pointed to its significance as an acceptable alternative to French naturalism. Russian realism's emphasis on moral values and compassion appealed to the English and seemed to many the path which English fiction should now take. By 1900 the initial vogue for Dostoevsky was over, but it was renewed in 1910 by Maurice Baring's *Landmarks of Russian Literature*. Baring's praise of Dostoevsky's *The Brothers Karamazov* helped prepare the way for Constance Garnett's translation of that novel, which first appeared in English in 1912 and marked the beginning of a Dostoevsky craze in England that lasted until the 1920s. Garnett (1862–1946), who learned Russian on her own, translated about seventy volumes of Russian literature, including twelve volumes of Dostoevsky between 1912 and 1920 and the first serious translations of Tolstoi. The American Isabel Hapgood also deserves mention as an early and successful translator of Russian literature. Another great English translator of Tolstoi was Aylmer Maude (1858–1938), who was a close friend of Tolstoi and lived in Russia for twenty years, and whose translation of *War and Peace* came out in 1922–23. The fourth Russian writer to have a profound influence on English and American literature was Anton CHEKHOV, whose stories began to come out in English in the 1890s and whose reputation was established with Garnett's thirteen-volume translation of his work in 1916 to 1922.

The 20th century saw Russian writers visiting America and English and American writers in Russia. Perhaps the best-known visit was that of Maksim GORKY to America in 1906 to raise money for the Bolsheviks. Coming here with high hopes, he was disillusioned at the scandal created by the press in reaction to his common-law wife. He nevertheless stayed in the United States for the better part of a year and wrote his novel *Mother* in upper New York State. In 1922–23 ESENIN visited the United States; in 1925, MAYAKOVSKY; and in 1936, the humorists, ILF and PETROV. Visits of English and American writers to Russia and the Soviet Union include those by H. G. Wells, a good friend of Gorky, in 1914, 1920, and 1934, George Bernard Shaw in 1931, Lincoln Steffens in 1917, 1918, and 1923, John Dos Passos in 1921 and 1928, Theodore Dreiser in 1927, and the critic Edmund Wilson in 1935. Of Russian writers writing after the Revolution, Mikhail SHOLOKHOV and Isaak BABEL are the most widely known in the United States from the 1920s. Since 1956, Pasternak and Aleksandr SOLZHENITSYN are the two best-known names in fiction. The poets Anna AKHMATOVA and Osip MANDELSHTAM are highly regarded, as are the memoirs of Mandelshtam's widow, Nadezhda MANDELSHTAM, called in English *Hope Against Hope* (*Vospominaniya*) and *Hope Abandoned* (*Vtoraya kniga*). Since the Revolution, many Russian writers have settled in the United States, including Vladimir NABOKOV, Solzhenitsyn, and the poet Joseph BRODSKY.

Bibliography: Lars Ahnebrink, "The Influence of Turgenev." In *The Beginnings of Naturalism in American Fiction.* New York, 1961. Pp. 315–420. K. N. Atarova, "Lev Tolstoi i Lorens Stern," *IAN* 33, no. 6 (1974), pp. 508–15. Dieter Boden, *Das Amerikabild im russischen Schrifttum bis zum Ende des 19 Jahrhunderts.* Hamburg, 1968. N. N. Bolkhovitinov, *Russko-amerikanskie otnosheniya 1815–1832.* 1975. Dorothy Brewster, *East-West Passage: A Study in Literary Relationships.* 1954. Deming Brown, *Soviet Attitudes Toward American Writing.* Princeton, 1962. Donald Davie, ed., *Russian Literature and Modern English Fiction: A Collection of Critical Essays.* 1965. Boris Eikhenbaum, *The Young Tolstoi.* Trans. and ed. Gary Kern. 1972. A. Fedorov, *Tvorchestvo Lermontova i zapadnye literatury.* In *Literaturnoe nasledstvo.* Vols. 43–44, 1941. Pp. 129–226. Maurice Friedberg, *A Decade of Euphoria: Western Literature in Post-Stalin Russia 1954–64.* 1977. ———, "The U.S. in the U.S.S.R.: American Literature through the Filter of Recent Soviet Publishing and Criticism," *Critical Inquiry* 2, no. 3 (1976), pp. 519–83. Royal A. Gettman, *Turgenev in England and America.* 1941. Clare R. Goldfarb, "William Dean Howells: An American Reaction to Tolstoy," *Comparative Literature Studies* 8 (Dec. 1971), pp. 317–37. Joan Delaney Grossman, *Edgar Allan Poe in Russia: A Study in Legend and Literary Influence.* Würzburg, 1973. Henry James, "Ivan Turgenev." In *Henry James: Representative Selections,* 1966. Pp. 9–41. I. Katarskii, *Dikkens v Rossii.* 1966. V. I. Kuleshov, *Literaturnye svyazi Rossii i Zapadnoi Evropy v XIX veke (pervaya polovina).* 2d rev. ed. 1977. N. M. Lary, *Dostoevsky and Dickens: A Study of Literary Influence.* 1973. Yu. D. Levin, "Angliiskaya poeziya i literatura russkogo sentimentalizma." In *Ot klassitsizma k romantizmu.* 1970. Pp. 195–297. ———, "Angliiskaya prosvetitel'skaya zhurnalistika v russkoi literature XVIII veka." In *Epokha prosveshcheniya* 1967. Pp. 3–109. ———, "Russian Responses to the Poetry of Ossian." In *Great Britain and Russia in the Eighteenth Century: Contacts and Comparisons.* Ed. A. G. Cross. 1979. Pp. 49–64. V. A. Libman, *Amerikanskaya literatura v russkikh perevodakh i kritike: Bibliografiya 1776–1975.* 1977. Helen Muchnic, *Dostoevsky's English Reputation 1881–1936.* (Smith College Studies in Modern Languages, 20.) 1939. ———, "Edmund Wilson's Russian Involvement." In *Edmund Wilson: The Man and His Work.* Ed. John Wain, 1978. Pp. 86–108. Harold Orel, "English Critics and the Russian Novel 1850–1917," *SEER* 33, no. 81 (1955), pp. 457–69. Raisa Orlova, *Ernest Khemingvei v Rossii.* Ann Arbor, 1983. Gilbert Phelps, *The Russian Novel in English Fiction.* 1956. ———, "The Early Phases of British Interest in Russian Literature," *SEER* 35, no. 81 (1958), pp. 418–33. *Soviet Criticism of American Literature in the Sixties.* Ed. and trans. Carl R. Proffer. 1972. Roberta Rubenstein, "Virginia Woolf and the Russian Point of View," *Comparative Literature Studies* 9, no. 2 (1972), pp. 196–206. Peter Rudy, "Lev Tolstoy's Apprenticeship to Lawrence Sterne," *SEEJ* 15, no. 1 (1971), pp. 1–21. *Russian Studies of American Literature: A Bibliography.* Comp. Valentina A. Libman. Ed. Clarence Gohdes. 1969. *Russko-angliiskie literaturnye svyazi (XVIII vek-pervaya polovina XIX veka)* . (*Literaturnoe nasledstvo,* vol. 91, 1982.) *Russko-evropeiskie literaturnye svyazi.* 1966. Ernest J. Simmons. *English Literature and Culture in Russia (1553–1840).* 1935 (reprint. 1964). J. A. Sokolow, "Arriving at Moral Perfection: Benjamin Franklin and Leo Tolstoy," *American Literature* 47, no. 3 (1975), pp. 427–32. *Sravnitel'noe izuchenie literatur.* 1976. Patrick Waddington, *Turgenev and England.* 1981. Virginia Woolf, "The Russian Point of View." In *The Common Reader: first series.* 1962. Pp. 219–31. V. Zhirmunskii, *Bairon i Pushkin: Iz istorii romanticheskoi poemy.* 1924.

E. T.

Enlightenment, the. Eighteenth-century Russia was the stage of an impressive flourishing of the arts and sciences and ideas under the influence of West European culture. Such an impact from the West had not been felt since the time of the Christianization of *Rus'* when Western culture came from Byzantium. Beginning in the reign of Peter I (1689–1725) and until the end of the reign of Catherine II (1762–96), great Italian architects (Rastrelli and Quarenghi) were commissioned in Russia, and the modern period of Russian culture began: modern Russian painting, poetry, literary theory, drama and prose fiction, history, the main branches of the natural sciences, positivist and empirical philosophy, and modern natural-law jurisprudence date from the 18th century. The view that a much belated Russian "Renaissance" occurred in this period was irresistible for some literary historians: GUKOVSKY borrowed the term to describe the universal genius of LOMONOSOV. The notion of an 18th-century renaissance in Russia may have a certain historical validity from the Russian perspective; however, the fact remains that the West was no longer experiencing a Renaissance but the Enlightenment (époque des lumières, Aufklärung, Illuminismo, *prosveshchenie*) characterized by a flourishing of the sciences and of ideas, rather than of the arts. Scholars built a bridge between the concepts of an anachronistic renaissance and the Enlightenment with the amorphous term *prosvetitel'stvo*, which was coined in the 1930s, and denotes a Russian progressive spirit covering a period of two hundred years, from SIMEON POLOTSKY and other poets of the same period, who praised learning and the sciences in their *virshi*, up to CHERNYSHEVSKY in the 1860s. The concept of *prosvetitel'stvo* thus includes a rather diluted *prosveshchenie*. Nevertheless, the focus should properly be on the Enlightenment, or diffusion primarily of the empirical sciences and ideas. This movement was of considerable magnitude in Russia, suggesting that the unique Russian degree of responsiveness to Western ideas was already apparent in the 18th century, and confirming BERDYAEV's useful observation that the Russian intelligentsia, "schismatic" (*raskol'nichii*) and "fanatic" in its commitment to moral, social, and political ideas, in fact, was born in the 18th century.

One of the most important general attributes of Western and Russian thinkers of the Enlightenment was their dedication to the dissemination of learning, the natural sciences, and new ideas. The need for the dissemination of learning was acutely felt in Russia, where over 90 percent of the population was illiterate, and where, until the 1780s, institutions of learning, the number of printing presses and a book trade were virtually non-existent. The process of dissemination in the West, as in Russia, was compounded by qualitative differences of assimilation, not only between Russia and Western Europe, but within the different countries of Europe and varying also in different periods. For example, Locke was perceived differently in England and in France, by the early and by the radical French thinkers of the Enlightenment, and similarly, by the early Russian thinkers and by the thinkers of the 1760s and 70s (who absorbed Lockean gnoseology mainly through radical French works.) The Russian dissemination and assimilation of Western ideas in the 18th century may best be divided into an early Enlightenment (until the 1760s) and a radical phase (1760s to late 1770s), which approximate in character and time the corresponding periods of the Enlightenment in Western Europe.

In the early phase of Russian Enlightenment anticlericalism was nurtured by the Protestant Reformation (which in Russia combined with native popular anticlericalism). Feofan PROKOPOVICH, author of the *Dukhovnyi Reglament* (1720, Engl. trans. 1723), wittily satirized as pagan priests the Russian clerical obscurantists (*tserkovniki*) who opposed Peter's reforms (*Vladimir*, 1705); and at the KIEV ACADEMY, where Feofan taught poetics, rhetoric and philosophy, he expounded the Copernican system and Galileo. The circle of Feofan included Chr. Wolff (1679–1754), mathematician, physicist, and Leibnizian philosopher, with whom Feofan corresponded. V. N. Tatishchev (1686–1750), another prominent member of the circle, displayed a strong empirical bent in his scholarly and scientific interests, espoused the scepticism of Descartes and the positivism of Bacon, and was one of the first Russian thinkers to read P. Bayle (1646–1716). Tatishchev forcefully defended the virtues of education for the masses in *Discourse on the Usefulness of Learning and Schools* (Razgovor o pol'ze nauk i uchilishch, 1733; first published, 1887). Another important member of the group was Prince A. KANTEMIR, first Russian satirist, and a philosopher, to whom belongs one of the earliest (1744) uses by a Russian thinker of the metaphor of "Liberty" as a "heavenly goddess" (reported by F. Algarotti, "Viaggi in Russia," 1764). Already before 1731, in his first satire, Kantemir defended the diffusion of learning and the sciences in Russia and attacked Russian *tserkovniki*. During his tenure as Russian ambassador in London, Kantemir also lived in Paris, where he was close to Montesquieu who was composing *De l'Esprit des Lois* (1748), to Maupertuis, the French Newtonian mathematician and astronomer, and to Count F. Algarotti (1712–64), popularizer of Newton in Italy. V. K. TREDIAKOVSKY and M. V. Lomonosov, shared the views of Feofan and his circle. In 1730, Trediakovsky made naively explicit his attack against the Russian clergy (*popy*) in the "Introduction" to his *Voyage to the Isle of Love* (Ezda v ostrov lyubvi), a translation from the French, and the first printed book on love in Russian. Lomonosov, Russia's first modern scientist, satirized clerical opponents of the Copernican system; he founded in Russia the studies of physics, chemistry, mineralogy and geology, and conducted experiments to measure the force of electricity discharged by lightning (Franklin's contemporaneous but different experiments led him to the discovery of the lightning rod). Lomonosov was also the first Russian historian to attempt to disprove the theory of the Norman origin of the Russian state, and he dared to bring to the attention of Voltaire some of the factual inaccuracies in the first volume of *L'Empire de Russie sous Pierre le Grand* (2 vols., 1760–63).

The most striking method of dissemination adopted in France and in Russia in the early phase of the Enlightenment was that of popularizations and adaptations of the classics of the empirical sciences. Kantemir translated in 1730 (first published 1740) Fontenelle's adaptation of the Copernican system in his *Entretiens sur la pluralité des mondes* ("for women," 1686), and later in Paris (MS unpublished) Algarotti's *Neutonianismo per le donne* (1733, cf. Voltaire on Newton in *Lettres Philosophiques*, 1734, and his *Eléments de la physique de Newton*, 1736). In 1760, Trediakovsky, under the direct influence of Kantemir, translated A. Deleyre's popular adaptation of D. Mallet's "Life" of Francis Bacon with an "Analyse" of Bacon's philosophy. And Lomonosov in 1746 translated for use as a textbook in his classes Wolff's *Experimental Physics* from Tümmig's abridged version (1725). Lomonosov, however, polemicized with Wolffian physics and philosophy, and paved the way for a rebuttal of Wolffian-Leibnizian philosophies on the pre-ordained harmony in the universe. At the same time, Lomonosov rejected much of Newton (hypothesis on gravitation; optics), which discouraged Russian studies of Newton, and contributed little to the dissemination in Europe of Lomonosov's own work in physics and chemistry. (In 1774, Diderot left Russia with Lomonosov's *Grammar, History* and studies in geology.) A major Russian contribution to the Western movement of the Enlightenment in the early phase was the *History of the Growth and Decay of the Ottoman Empire* (2 vols., London, 1734) by Kantemir's father; Voltaire praised the work for its objectivity, used it for his tragedy *Mahomet* (1739–42) and cited it in his *Essai sur les moeurs* (1756).

Enlightenment in the West in its next, radical phase (1750s to late 1770s) was centered in France. Some of the most influential radical works published at this time included the *Encyclopédie* (1751–72) edited by Diderot, the mechanistic utilitarian moral and jurisprudential principles of Helvétius's *De l'Esprit* (1758, polemicized with Montesquieu's *De l'Esprit des Lois*) and the materialist and atheist works co-authored by d'Holbach and Diderot, such as *Le Système de la Nature* (1770). These works were widely read in Russia over the brief period from the 1760s to the late 1770s, when French radical ideas eclipsed German philosophy, contrary to the claims made by some scholars. The radical phase of the Russian Enlightenment was ushered in by a vogue of "vol'terizm," "vol'terianizm," later "vol'terianstvo" (the term implies mockery of the Russian church, even atheism, and is largely but not altogether unrelated to Voltaire's ironic wit and deism). This vogue, the first one in Russia of French or even European origin, reached the provinces, and even the illiterate classes, according to memoirs and private correspondence (A. T. Bolotov, I. V. Lopukhin, D. I. FONVIZIN, F. F. Vigel, F. V. Vinsky). It was launched in no small measure by Catherine II, Voltaire's pupil, who aspired to rival the model "enlightened monarch" Frederick II (1740–86). Catherine never implemented her *Instruction* (1767, where Montesquieu stood uncomfortably with Beccaria, pupil of Helvétius, and the ideas of both were distorted); she had no interest in or understanding of French free thought, and no Sansouci; and French thinkers (de la Rivière, Diderot, Grimm, and others) who accepted her invitation to stay at her court, stayed only briefly, and never returned. But Catherine for a while turned to French thinkers for recognition and at a time when some of the most innovative and far-reaching systems in Western philosophy were being conceived. For a while, her courtiers too turned to contemporary French thinkers for inspiration; and so did Russian thinkers, most of whom were trained in the finest European public institutions of learning (Glasgow University, Leipzig University; but not in French universities, where education was mainly in religious hands).

Beginning with the sessions of the Legislative Commission (1767–68), and with the "Question" (1767) on serfdom presented for international competition by the Free Economic Society, Russian thinkers (along with Marmontel) began to demand the total or gradual abolition of the bondage system: the brothers Kozelsky, A. Ya. Polenov (1736–1816, 2nd prize for the "Question," first published in 1865), I. A. Tretyakov (1735–76), S. E. Desnitsky (?–1789), Prince D. A. Golitsyn (1734–1803), and others. At this time, Desnitsky (graduate with Tretyakov of the Faculty of Law at Glasgow University), who taught Jurisprudence at Moscow University and later translated Blackstone, advocated the separation of powers in his *Representation on the Institution of Legislative, Judicial, and Executive Power in the Russian Empire* (Predstavlenie o uchrezhdenii zakonodatel'noi, suditel'noi i nakazatel'noi vlasti v Rossiiskoi imperii, 1767). And Ya. P. Kozelsky's (1728–1794) *Philosophic Propositions* (Filosoficheskie predlozheniya, 1768) in which the different branches of philosophical inquiry were categorized and described, classified jurisprudence and politics under the heading of "applied moral science" (*nauka iskaniya blagopoluchiya*). In Russian pedagogy, during this period an empirical science of education, I. I. Betskoi (1704–95), under the influence of the French Encyclopédistes conceived a project for the creation of a "new breed of men" which would fill the ranks of the nonexistent Russian *tiers état*. Upon his innovative principles, which were highly praised by Diderot, he founded at the Smolny monastery the Institute for Young Women. Similarly, gnoseology in this period was viewed as an empirical science, most strikingly in Kozelsky's *Filosoficheskie Predlozheniya* and D. S. Anichkov's (1733–88) *Discourse on the Properties of Human Cognition* (Slovo o svoistvakh poznaniya chelovecheskogo, 1770), who both traced the source of human understanding to "the senses" (*chuvstva*), or "physical organs." Finally, in the 1760s and 70s the anthropological origins of religion were explored, e.g., by Kozelsky, Anichkov in *Discourse, from Natural Theology, on the Beginning and Development of Natural Worship of God* (Rassuzhdenie iz natural'nogo bogosloviya o nachale i proizshestvii natural'nogo bogopochitaniya, 1769) and Desnitsky in *Juridical Discourses on Things Sacred* (Yuridicheskie rassuzhdeniya o veshchakh svyashchennykh, 1772).

The mainspring of Russian thought in the 1760s and 1770s was Locke's sensualist philosophy, especially in the form of its many first and distant French cousins (Condillac, Rousseau, but also Helvétius and his disciples, Beccaria and early J. Bentham, as well as Diderot and d'Holbach, who all relied heavily upon Locke for the principles of their systems). The 18th-century discovery of the senses "empiricized" natural-law jurisprudence in Russia and the various other branches of philosophy. But the radical systems of 18th-century

French sensualist philosophy raised difficult "truths" to embrace: (1) the absence of innate ideas of good and evil leading to the rejection of Cartesian dualism, the soul and, ultimately, the Divine being; and (2) the determining role of education and legislation, in place of traditional religious principles, in forming productive and virtuous citizens, and in ensuring the welfare of the people. An existential dilemma for the Russian thinker arose from these "truths" and expressed itself in the last quarter of the century in fierce attempts to cling to the radical principles of the 1760s and 1770s, as in the case of RADISHCHEV's *Journey from Petersburg to Moscow* (1790). Other Russian thinkers in the late 1770s experienced a traumatic spiritual reversal, and embraced the Christian mythic ethic and the "enlightenment" of the Russian FREEMASONS (late 1770s to 1792) under the persuasive leadership of Schwarz (d. 1789) and the organizational genius of NOVIKOV. Senator I. V. Lopukhin (1756–1816) exemplified the latter, when he recorded in his *Zapiski* (first published 1860) how in the late 1770s his moral ideology changed course overnight from his plans to disseminate underground his translation of the closing chapter of *Le Système de la Nature* to his decision to embrace the moral values of Masonry. In 1789 to 1792 Fonvizin similarly recorded in his *Candid Confession* (Chistoserdechnoe priznanie) an unconditional moral rejection of his former, freethinking ways. Also in the last quarter of the century the earlier xenophobic nationalism of Novikov (one of the few Russian Masons exempted from a spiritual reversal) and a nationalism tinged with "Slavophilism" came to the fore. By the 1780s the tide of radical thought was stemmed, and the spiritual reversal became the new, dominant trend, which works such as P. S. Baturin's (1740?–1803) *Inquiry into the Book of Error and Truth* (Issledovanie knigi o zabluzhdeniyakh i istine, 1790) and Radishchev's *Journey* were powerless to reverse. Another century elapsed in Russia until in the 1860s comparably radical ideas were revived. But from the 18th century existential quandary the Russian intelligentsia was born, and the government began to repress its two mutually antagonistic camps (Radishchev's arrest, 1790; Novikov's arrest, 1792). Indeed, the radical members were termed already by Catherine "schismatics" (*raskol'niki*); that is, were associated by her in their social, political, and moral purposefulness with a fanatic, religious phenomenon in Russian society.

Texts: I. Ya. Shchipanov, *Izbrannye proizvedeniya russkikh myslitelei vtoroi poloviny XVIII veka.* 2 vols. 1952.

Secondary literature: (There is no monograph in English devoted to the Russian Enlightenment.) M. P. Alekseev, ed., *Epokha prosveshcheniya.* 1967. P. N. Berkov, ed., *Problemy russkogo prosveshcheniya v literature XVIII veka.* 1961. A. G. Cross, *Russians in Eighteenth-Century Britain.* 1980. (The only thorough study on Russian contacts with Western Europe.) Yu. D. Lotman, "Die Frühaufklärung und die Entwicklung des gesellschaftlichen Denkens in Russland." In *Studien zur Geschichte der russischen Literatur des 18. Jahrhunderts,* 3 (1968). Pp. 93–119. G. P. Makogonenko, *Radishchev i ego vremya.* 1956. A. N. Pypin, *Istoriya russkoi literatury.* Vols. 3 (1902) and 4 (1903). Marc Raeff, "The Enlightenment in Russia and Russian Thought in the Enlightenment." In *The Eighteenth Century in Russia.* Ed. J. G. Garrard. Oxford, 1973. Pp. 25–47. I. Ya. Shchipanov, *Filosofiya russkogo prosveshcheniya: vtoraya polovina XVIII veka.* 1971. Studies of individual Russian thinkers are abundant. See especially the series *XVIII vek* (1935–   ). T. P.

Epic songs, see BYLINA.

Epifánii Premúdryi, see EPIPHANIUS THE WISE.

Epigram, literary genre. The word derives from Greek *epigramma,* 'inscription,' and has come to signify any wise or witty writing which achieves point and completion in a very brief space. The Greek epigram is usually written in a strict verse pattern of 2–8 lines, though it is also found in prose. The genre of epigram, now often taking the form of satire, was also popular in Latin literature. After some centuries of decline the genre regained its significance in the Age of Classicism. The first writers of epigrams in Russia (SUMAROKOV, DMITRIEV, V. L. PUSHKIN, VYAZEMSKY) are clearly influenced by classicist models, striving for biting wit, sustained brilliance, and perfection of form. Besides traditional epigrams against personal enemies, "cruel" women, and talentless writers, the poets of the Golden Age, especially PUSHKIN, BARATYNSKY, and the DECEMBRISTS, also wrote political

epigrams on burning topics of the day. Transmitted orally or in copies, such epigrams, often aiming at social evils or detested supporters of autocracy, could only be printed years later. Widespread were also the epigrams of TYUTCHEV, Sobolevsky, and MINAEV, distinguished by a sharp twist of phrase and meaning at the end, a kind of punch line. Well-known writers of epigrams in Soviet times are S. MARSHAK and A. BEZYMENSKY; the genre still enjoys popularity in literary journals.

Bibliography: V. Manuilov, ed., *Russkaya epigramma (XVIII–XIX v.v.).* 1958. V. E. Vasil'ev et al., eds. *Russkaya epigramma vtoroi poloviny XVII-nachalo XX v.* 1975. G. K.

Epiphanius the Wise (Epifanii Premudryi, ?–ca. 1420). One of the most learned and talented representatives of the new literary trends which developed in the Russian and Balkan Slavic lands in the late 14th and early 15th centuries. His literary works are usually examined against the background of the "Second SOUTH SLAVIC INFLUENCE." The scant details about his life known to us primarily are drawn from his hagiographic writings. Epiphanius spent most of his adult life in the Trinity Monastery founded by SERGIUS OF RADONEZH (ca. 1440). He must have arrived there before Sergius's death in 1391. Prior to that time, it appears that Epiphanius was a resident of the monastery of Gregory the Theologian in Rostov, where he met Stefan (?–1396), the future missionary to the Permian lands. Epiphanius seems to have known Greek and been acquainted with the Greek hagiographic tradition. It is likely that he travelled to Mount Athos, Constantinople, and Jerusalem. Since the middle of the 19th century, scholars have attempted to attribute to Epiphanius a considerable number of literary works, including the *Tale of Monk Epiphanius on his Journey to Jerusalem* (Skazanie Epifaniya mnikha o puti k Ierusalimu), the *Discourse on the Life and Death of the Grand Prince Dmitry Ivanovich* (Slovo o zhitii i o prestavlenii velikago knyazya Dmitriya Ivanovicha), and a letter to Abbot Kirill of Tver.

Epiphanius occupies a prominent place in Old Russian hagiography as the author of the *Life of St. Stefan of Perm* and the *Life of St. Sergius of Radonezh.* The *Life of St. Stefan* is known to scholarship through Druzhinin's edition of an early 16th-century manuscript contained in a Reading Menaea for the month of April (with variants from later 16th- and 17th-century codices). In the work Stefan's mission to the Permians is offered as proof that the Russian lands had acquired sufficient dignity to become a center for propagating the Christian faith. Epiphanius's style in the *Life of St. Stefan* has been the object of intense scrutiny. It has been regarded as the Russian facet of a pan-Orthodox Slavic mode of literary expression usually referred to as "word weaving" (*pletenie sloves*). In the work Epiphanius says: "I was not in Athens in my youth and I did not learn from the philosophers either rhetorical weaving or eloquent words." This statement can be interpreted as a rejection of uninspired "Hellenic" rhetoric. Word weaving is used as the expression of verbal inadequacy and is intimately bound up with the prayerful search for inspired words (conceived in accordance with the Platonizing theories of the Hesychast movement).

The *Life of St. Sergius* has come to us through a complex textual tradition, which is divisible into several redactions. Later re-elaborated by Pachomius Logothetes (Pakhomii Logofet) the Serb, the *Life of St. Sergius* is of great importance for the comparative study of Russian, Balkan Slavic, and Byzantine hagiographic schemes.

Bibliography: L. A. Dmitriev and D. S. Likhachëv, eds., *Pamyatniki literatury drevnei Rusi: XIV–seredina XV veka.* 1981. V. G. Druzhinin, ed., *Zhitie svyatogo Stefana, episkopa Permskogo napisannoe Epifaniem Premudrym.* St. Petersburg, 1897. Reprint *Apophoreta Slavica,* no. 2. Ed. D. Čiževskij. The Hague, 1959. F. Kitch, *The Literary Style of Epifanij Premudryj: Pletenije Sloves.* (Slavistische Beiträge, 96.) Munich, 1976. R. Picchio, "L' 'intreccio delle parole' e gli stili letterari presso gli Slavi ortodossi nel tardo Medio Evo." In *Studi Slavistici in ricordo di Carlo Verdiani.* Ed. A. M. Raffo. Pisa, 1979. Pp. 245–62. B. P. Zubov, "Epifanii Premudryi i Pakhomii Serb: K voprosu o redaktsiyakh Zhitiya Sergiya Radonezhskogo," *TODRL* 9 (1953), pp. 145–58. R. P.

Epistolary prose. The term includes two basic categories which are not always easily separated: intimate, private correspondence (not intended for a broad readership), and any work in prose written in the epistolary form. Letter-writing became a personal, expressive means of communication comparatively late in Russia. In the extant epistolography the spoken language of the 11th to 15th century birch-bark letters (found mostly in Novgorod) later gave way to an "administrative" (*prikaznyi*) language, possibly by contamination from bureaucratic epistolary forms, such as the *chelobitnaya, gramota, gramotka, gramotitsa*, etc. In the 17th century a Latinate syntax with polonisms was introduced, with a macaronic admixture of germanisms and gallicisms under Peter's reign, when the model letter-writer was *Priklady kako pishutsya komplimenty raznye* (Germ. trans. 1708; 4th ed. 1725). The date moved to the head of the letter, and after the 1720s, in intimate correspondence the *chelobitnaya* formula of self-abasement was discarded, and western forms of address (including *vy*) were adopted. In the 1760s to 1770s the aristocracy developed a remarkably simple, concise, and personal diction in French (the prevailing language in letter-writing of the aristocracy in Europe as well); however, in the 1780s to 1790s, under the influence of German pietism, the style became ponderously sentimental. The earlier qualities were subsequently reinstated, and in the 1830s to 1840s, at last Russian letter-writing became an artful form of communication and self-expression; in the course of the 20th century it lost this value, much as in Europe.

The Russian epistle in prose (*poslanie, slovo*) was by far the most widespread literary form of expression over the period from the Christianization of Kievan *Rus* until the end of the 16th century. It owed its origin to the Eastern Church, and ultimately, the apostles; it was written in a high literary, i.e., Church-Slavonicized language. Churchmen wrote epistles in controversies over dogma, to spread the Christian ideology in the monastic community, as in the case of the *Kievo-Pecherskii* PATERIK, but also to counsel the Grand Prince, and later the Tsar. In the 11th century THEODOSIUS wrote to Izyaslav on fasting, and to Svyatoslav, severely reprimanding the prince for usurping his brother's throne. The form flourished in the 16th century, as in the epistles of MAKSIM GREK (1480–1556), attacking Catholicism, monastic ownership and preaching the "God-chosen marriage" in Russia of the temporal power and the Church, in the epistles of Filofei which advanced the theory of "Moscow the Third Rome" and in Ivan PERESVETOV's (a layman) two *chelobitnye* epistles, in the correspondence of KURBSKY and IVAN IV, and in the epistle of Silvestr at the end of his redaction of the DOMOSTROI. The Old Russian epistle was a tool for religious, moral, social, and political indoctrination.

This Eastern orientation of Russian epistolary prose was tenacious and slowed down the assimilation of West-European epistolary forms in Russian belles lettres. In the Petrine tales the process of assimilation motivated the insertion of love letters; later, N. I. NOVIKOV borrowed for his satirical journals Steele and Addison's device of the "letter to the editor." But Russian epistolary prose continued to be invested with moral and social ideology by Novikov, by FONVIZIN in his satirical "Letters to Falalei" and famous letters from abroad (several were published in 1798), by RADISHCHEV in "Letter to a Friend Living in Tobolsk" and later by GOGOL in *Selected Passages* (Vybrannye mesta iz perepiski s druz'yami, 1847). The heyday of the epistolary novel in England and France in the second half of the 18th century produced in Russia one, solitary work in this genre, EMIN's *Pis'ma Ernesta i Doravry* (1766), which was flawed in style and tone. And at the turn of the century the Karamzinian cult of the small form presented an additional obstacle to the development of epistolary forms (although KARAMZIN significantly "Europeanized" Russian epistolary prose with his *Letters of a Russian Traveler*). The Russian Pamelas and Julies, St Preux, Werthers and "demonic" heroes wrote little. In the 1830s PUSHKIN and Marlinsky (BESTUZHEV) took the epistolary novel in hand, but only in 1846, with Dostoevsky's *Poor Folk* was epistolary prose used for the first time in Russia to reveal the intimate world, emotions, and psyche of the character with an intensity and pathos comparable to Rousseau's manner in the *New Heloise*. But by then epistolary forms in West-European belles lettres were moribund, and they did not thrive in Russia.

Bibliography: A. A. Elistratova, "Epistolyarnaya proza romantikov." In *Evropeiskii romantizm.* 1973. P. A. Orlov, ed. and introd., *Russkaya sentimental'naya povest'.* 1979. V. V. Vinogradov, *Ocherki po istorii russkogo literaturnogo yazyka XVIII–XIX vv.* 1934.

T. P.

Epókha, journal (1864–65). At the end of January, 1864, Mikhail Mikhailovich DOSTOEVSKY received permission to open a monthly, *Epokha*, continuing the work of *Vremya*, which the censor had closed after its April 1863 issue. The combined January–February issue appeared late in March, and it came out with comparable delays through the February, 1865 issue, when it closed, in financial and administrative disarray, following the death of Mikhail on 10 January, 1864. Fyodor DOSTOEVSKY was the driving force behind the journal from the start, and its chief editor after Mikhail's death. He published "Notes from Underground" in the first and fourth issues, and "The Crocodile" in the last, as well as a number of polemics with the nihilists in the name of his "grassroots" (*pochvennichestvo*) doctrine favoring a return to Russian rural values and ideas. Apollon GRIGORIEV's organic aesthetics and Nikolai STRAKHOV's political comments in *Epokha* were in tune with these beliefs, as were the fiction of Vsevolod KRESTOVSKY and Dmitry Averkiev. Ivan TURGENEV and Nikolai LESKOV also published major stories in the journal.

Bibliography: V. S. Nechaeva, *Zhurnal M. M. i F. M. Dostoevskikh* Epokha, *1864–1865.* 1975.

R. L. B.

Erdman, Nikolaí Robértovich (1902–70), dramatist. Erdman is known primarily for two riotous satires of early Soviet life: *The Mandate* (Mandat, 1924), a farcical comedy of situation in which a forged patent of residence assumes the significance of a certificate of membership in the Communist Party; and *The Suicide* (Samoubiitsa, 1928), a "black comedy" about an ordinary Soviet citizen who is driven by despair to attempt suicide which he is finally too cowardly to carry out. *The Mandate* was staged by MEYERHOLD on 20 April 1925 and proved a tremendous success. *The Suicide* was accepted for production by both Meyerhold's theater and the Moscow Art Theater and went into rehearsal. In 1932, however, both plays were placed under an official ban. It was only after Stalin's death that in 1956 a production of *The Mandate* was mounted by the Studio Theater of Film Actors in Moscow; *The Suicide*, on the other hand, has never been staged in the USSR, although productions have been undertaken in the West, including the United States. From 1927 on, Erdman alone or in collaboration with others, was engaged principally as a film script writer. It was probably during this period that he also wrote a third comedy under the title *A Session on Laughter* (Zasedanie o smekhe), but the text has apparently been lost. Most probably on the basis of the satire especially of *The Suicide*, Erdman was prohibited from further literary work and was restricted to residence only in the city of Kalinin. Early efforts to have the ban on him rescinded, most notably by BULGAKOV in a personal letter to Stalin, were in vain. Although Erdman was able to return at least to film work around 1942, it is impossible to determine exactly when he was permitted to resume residence in Moscow. Presumably this came some time after Stalin's death and may have coincided with the 1956 production of *The Mandate*, which inaugurated his rehabilitation.

Works: Mandat. P'esa v trekh deistviyakh. Ed. and introd. W. Kasack. Munich, 1976.
Translations: The Suicide. Trans. by Peter Tegel. London, 1979. *Two Plays: "The Suicide" and "The Mandate,"* trans. Genereux, Volkov, and Hoover. Ann Arbor, 1975.
Secondary literature: Marjorie Hoover. "Nikolai Erdman: A Soviet Dramatist Rediscovered," *RLT* 2 (1972), pp. 413–34.

H. B. S.

Erenbúrg (Ehrenburg), Ilyá Grigórievich (1891–1967), journalist, prose writer, memoirist, poet, and translator. He was a public figure, often representing the Soviet Union abroad. Prolific and versatile, he was probably the most Western Soviet writer of his generation. Unscathed by the Stalinist purges, his works served as a weather vane of the political atmosphere of his time. His novel, *The Thaw* (1954), coined the name of the cultural and political era in the more liberal post-Stalin Russia. (See the THAW.) His reminiscences, *People, Years, Life* (1961–65) dealt with such sensitive subjects as the destruction of a whole generation of writers and artists during the Stalin period and gave the "go ahead" signal to writers like PAUSTOVSKY, Nadezhda MANDELSHTAM, and SOLZHENITSYN to publish their memoirs.

Born in Kiev 14 January 1891 into an educated, well-to-do, middle-class Jewish family, in 1896 he moved to Moscow. As a student he became involved in revolutionary activities, was arrested, and after his release in 1908 left for Paris where he lived until 1917 when he returned to Russia. In 1921, he again left Russia and with minor intervals lived in Western Europe, mostly Paris, during the 1920s and 1930s as a foreign correspondent for *Izvestiya* and other Soviet dailies. In 1936–37 he was in Spain writing about the Spanish Civil War. Between 1940 and 1941 he witnessed and lived under the German occupation of Paris. He returned to Moscow in 1941 where he died 31 August 1967.

Erenburg began his literary career as a poet and published eleven collections of poems between 1911 and 1923. Even though he continued writing poetry all his life, he is known primarily as a prose writer and journalist. He became a reporter in 1913 and published his first prose work, *The Extraordinary Adventures of Julio Jurenito*, in 1922. A satire of the West, this work has been acknowledged to be his best. Its hero, the teacher Julio Jurenito, is the spirit of negation who says that "art is the hearth of anarchism, artists are heretics, sectarians, and dangerous rebels." He, therefore, proposes the "abolition of all art."

Julio Jurenito, Trust D.E. (1923), *Thirteen Pipes* (1923), *Summer of 1925* (1926) are set in and critical of Western Europe. On the other hand, *The Self-Seeker* (1925) and *A Street in Moscow* (1927) are set in Russia and deal with Soviet life during the NEP (New Economic Policy) period. They contrast the immoral, antisocial behaviour of "nepmen" and thieves to the nobility, moral righteousness, and selflessness of party activists. *Out of Chaos* (1933) is Erenburg's contribution to "Five-Year Plan" literature. It is a powerful novel and one of his best. It deals with the problems of building an industrial society.

The Fall of Paris (1941) returns Erenburg to Europe. Winning him a Stalin Prize, it deals with the corruption and fall of Western Europe. *The Storm* (1947) is Erenburg's contribution to World War II literature. His descriptions of the German invasion contain some of the first depictions of Nazi atrocities. *The Thaw* (1954), despite its artistic weakness, is Erenburg's best-known novel. It presents the themes and sets the tone for Russian literature during the Khrushchev era.

Erenburg's reminiscences, *People, Years, Life* (1961–65), were serialized in NOVYI MIR. Severely criticized by the establishment, but praised by the young and in the West, it is a cautiously written work by a self-conscious, self-censoring writer who was well traveled, and knew a large number of the people involved in the artistic and cultural life of Europe and Russia during the first half of this century. Erenburg presents a gallery of people: artists, writers, film-makers, impresarios, educators, statesmen and rulers. The most fascinating and brilliant sections describe people whom he loved and/or admired. Thus BABEL, Falk, Picasso, TSVETAEVA, and many others whose names had been taboo since the 1930s because they were nonconformist or purged come to life on his pages. He was the first to resurrect them and foreshadow their official "rehabilitation."

In assessing Erenburg's works, it is apparent that his novels and short stories are uneven in quality and output. Their central ideas are usually interesting and clever and his satire is biting. Yet often his characters are poorly developed, do not speak with their own voices, and remain flat. Thus, one can say that Erenburg was an outstanding journalist and memoirist, a mediocre poet, and a good and occasionally excellent novelist and short story writer.

Works: Polnoe sobranie sochinenii. 8 vols. 1928–29. *Sobranie sochinenii.* 9 vols. 1962–67. *Letopis' muzhestva.* 1974. *Stikhotvoreniya.* (Biblioteka poeta.) 1977.

Translations: See Lewanski, pp. 236–37. See also: Selections from People, Years, Life. 1972. *The Life of the Automobile.* 1976.

Secondary literature: G. Belaya, "Il'ya Erenburg," *Oktyabr',* 1961, no. 1. Edward J. Brown, *Russian Literature since the Revolution.* 1982. Pp. 198–204. V. Bryusov, "Stikhi o kanunakh," *Russkie vedomosti* 7, 6, (1916). V. Erlich, *Problems of Communism,* no. 12 (1963) and no. 14 (1965). Julian Laychuk, "The Evolution of I. G. Ehrenburg's Weltanschauung During the Period 1928–1934," *CSP* 12 (1970), pp. 395–416. H. Oulanoff, "Motives of Pessimism in Erenburg's Early Works," *SEEJ* 11 (1967), pp. 266–77. A. Rubashkin, *Publitsistika Il'i Erenburga protiv voiny i fashizma.* 1965. *Russkie sovetskie pisateli-prozaiki: Ukazatel'.* Vol. 6, pt. 2. 1969. K. Simonov, "Novaya povest' Il'i Erenburga (Ottepel')," *Literaturnaya gazeta* 17, 20 July 1954. Marc Slonim, *Soviet Russian Literature.* 1977. Pp.

213–22. T. K. Trifonova, *Il'ya Erenburg.* 1952. ———, "Erenburg." In *Istoriya russkoi sovetskoi literatury.* Vol. 4. 1971.   H. S.

Erofeev, Venedikt (1938 or1939–), writer, attended the Philological Division of Moscow University and Vladimir Pedagogic Institute. He has worked as a glassware inspector, stoker, watchman, highway construction hand, fitter, etc. There is some evidence for the existence of the following works by Erofeev: "Memoirs of a Psychopath" (Zametki psikhopata, 1956–57), "Good Tidings" (Blagaya vest'), a novel, *Shostakovich*, and some literary studies. Allegedly these works have been circulated by SAMIZDAT. In 1982, the publishing house *Serebryanyi vek* (Silver Age, New York) published an essay by Erofeev on Vasily ROZANOV, entitled "Through an Eccentric's Eyes" (Glazami ekstsentrika).

Erofeev's most significant work is his *poema* (in prose) "Moscow-Petushki" (Moskva-Petushki, 1969), a drunken confession in which the hero, who bears the author's name, tells of a train ride from Moscow to one of its suburbs. Erofeev's *poema* is as saturated with literary and cultural reminiscences as any work of Russian literature. These reminiscences, borrowed from what seems to be the surface layer of world culture (a case might be made for the hero's belonging to "mass culture"), form the basis of the poetics of "Moscow-Petushki." The author's irony and laughter are accompanied by allusions to the Bible, Aeschylus, Christ, Luther, Rabelais, and many others. (The mockery is on the wane toward the end of the *poema*, as the hero's perception of the world grows more tragic.) The main thrust of the hero's mockery and travesty is directed at Soviet pseudo-culture: GORKY, LENIN, Nikolai OSTROVSKY, the press, etc. All of this links Erofeev's work with the classical epos and the modern epopoeia (Homer, Dante, GOGOL's *poema* "Dead Souls"), on the one hand, and with the mock-heroic epic tradition, on the other. At the same time, the work may be interpreted as the story of the hero's death and resurrection (a variant, then, of the Christ myth). It may be also read as the ravings of a dying man in the last minutes of his life, in which case the *poema*'s time and space are condensed to a single moment and a single point, which would draw Erofeev's book into the orbit of the experimental prose of Proust and Joyce.

Works: Moskva-Petushki. Paris, 1977. 2d ed. 1981. *Glazami ekstsentrika.* Rego Park, N. Y., 1982.

Translations: Moscow to the End of the Line. Trans. H. W. Tjalsma. Introd. Vera Dunham. New York, 1980. *Moscow Circles.* Trans. J. R. Dorrell. New York, 1983.

Secondary literature: Mark Al'tshuller, "*Moskva-Petushki* Venedikta Erofeeva i traditsii klassicheskoi poemy," *Novyi zhurnal,* no. 146 (1982), pp. 75–85. (Anon. Review,) *RLT,* no. 17 (1982), pp. 266–67. Geoffrey Hosking, "Drinking Mystically, Travelling Sentimentally," *TLS,* 15 January 1982, p. 63. Sidney Monas, (Review), *SlavR* 40 (1981), p. 509. I. A. Paperno and B. M. Gasparov, "Vstan' i idi," *Slavica Hierosolymitana* 5–6 (1981), pp. 387–400. P. Vail' and A. Genis, "Strasti po Erofeevu," *Ekho,* 1978, no. 4.   M. A.

Ershov, Pyotr Pávlovich (1815–69), poet, playwright, and short story writer, who spent most of his life (1836 to his death) as a secondary school teacher at Tobolsk in Siberia. His fame rests with a single work, written in his student days in Petersburg, the fairy tale in verse "The Humpback Horse" (Konek-Gorbunok, 1834), deservedly a Russian classic. Quite in the manner of—and by no means inferior to—Pushkin's fairy tales in verse, it has a lively plot, sly satire, folksy language, and an irresistible, driving rhythm. Ershov's later works do not measure up to "The Humpback Horse."

Works: Konek Gorbunok. Stikhotvoreniya. Ed. M. K. Azadovskii. 1961.

Translations: Humpy. Trans. W. White. 1931. *The Little Humpbacked Horse.* Trans. L. Zellikof. Moscow, 1956. *Little Hunchback Horse.* Adapt. I. Wicker. 1942. *Little Magic Horse, a Russian Tale.* Trans. T. Drowne. 1942.

Secondary literature: V. G. Utkov, *Dorogi Kon'ka Gorbunka: Sud'by knig.* 1970. ———, *Grazhdanin Tobol'ska.* 1980.   V. T.

Ertel, Aleksándr Ivánovich (1855–1908), novelist and short-story writer. The self-educated son of a Russified German estate agent, Ertel was temporarily attracted to POPULISM, but rejected its illusory theories, convinced that progress depended not on revolutionary doctrines based on coercion and violence which fail to respect the individual's dignity and freedom, but on action by individuals imbued with high moral qualities. Like Tolstoi, Ertel regarded love toward one's fellow-men as all-important, but unlike him, felt that love must be linked with reason. Ertel's first literary effort, the lyric poem "A Night of Mowing" (Noch' na pokose, 1875), was inspired by the poetry of N. A. Nekrasov. His first story, "Migrants" (Pereselentsy, 1878), concerns the sad lot of peasants, a major theme in his work, while his first collection of stories, *Notes from the Steppes* (Zapiski stepnyaka, 1883) deals with the post-emancipation era, particularly the people (*narod*)-intelligentsia relationship. In 1884 Ertel was imprisoned in the Sts. Peter and Paul Fortress for his ties with the revolutionaries and afterwards exiled for four years to Tver. During the 1880s he published a series of novellas, including "The Miss of Volkhonsk" (Volkhonskaya baryshnya, 1883) and "The Greedy Peasant" (Zhadnyi muzhik, 1886), written in the spirit of Tolstoi's "Tales for the People," and a play, *Women's Riot* (Babii bunt, 1884). Ertel is best known for his two epic novels, *The Gardenins* (Gardeniny, 1889) and *Change* (Smena, 1891). The first, his best work, depicts the growth of capitalism in the countryside in the 1870s as a positive force; the second deals with the attendant political and cultural changes of the 1880s. Both are remarkable for their language, particularly "folk speech." After writing his last novella, "Strukov's Career" (Kar'era Strukova, 1895–96), which depicts lawyers of "small deeds," Ertel abandoned literature.

Works: Sobranie sochinenii. 7 vols. 1909. *Sobranie sochinenii.* 2 vols. 1918.

Translations: Lewanski, p. 237.

Secondary literature: I. I. Ignatov, "Ertel' i Bunin," *Don*, 1974, no. 1. G. A. Kostin, *A. I. Ertel': Zhizn' i tvorchestvo.* Voronezh, 1955. N. S. Parsons, "Aleksandr Ertel' as a Christian Humanist," *SEER* 46 (no. 106, 1969), pp. 176–91. A. P. Spasibenko, *A. I. Ertel': pisatel'-vos'midesyatnik.* Alma-Ata, 1966.

L. P.

Eruslán Lazarévich, *Tale of*, a popular Russian narrative of the 17th century, of Persian origin. The source is several episodes taken from Firdawsi's 10th-century epic poem *Shah-nama*. The hero, named Rustem, turns in the poem into an *araslan* (lion), hence the name Eruslan or Uruslan in the Russian work. The adaptation was made in the Southeast Russian Cossack milieu, and many Turkish words and details of Cossack life on the steppes have been added. The Russian version also contains many details and phrases from the Russian epic BYLINA and the Russian FOLKTALE.

The tale, which is extremely complex, is rich in colorful details of fantasy and magic, and served as an important source of the strand of Eastern exoticism in modern Russian culture and literature. There are many episodes, in all of which the hero triumphs; Eruslan is characterized by an urge to challenge all rival heroes, especially those reputed to be braver and stronger than he. Most celebrated are his encounter with a hero's live head and his victory over a three-headed monster. In the end he wins the Empire of India and there joins his "lawful" wife and puts aside an earlier "unlawful" wife who had proved insufficiently beautiful.

From manuscript the tale passed into the so-called LUBOCHNAYA LITERATURA to become favorite reading for the lower middle classes and literate peasants in the 18th and 19th centuries. It was the source of a Russian folktale, and served as a basis in part for Pushkin's long poem *Ruslan and Lyudmila* (1820).

Bibliography: W. E. Brown, *A History of Russian Seventeenth-Century Literature.* Ann Arbor, 1980. Pp. 47–49. N. K. Gudziy, *History of Early Russian Literature,* New York, 1949. Pp. 432–37. D. Rovinskii, *Russkie narodnye kartinki.* St. Petersburg, 1881. Vol. 4, pp. 27–34, 135–42; vol. 5, pp. 114–19.

W. E. H.

Esénin, Sergei Aleksándrovich (1895–1925), the most popular of the so-called PEASANT WRITERS. Having received an elementary-school education in his village school, Esenin moved in 1912 to Moscow and in 1915 to Petersburg, where he became acquainted with Nikolai GORODETSKY, Aleksandr BLOK, and Nikolai KLYUEV.

Esenin was lionized as a true "people's poet," and he soon became fast friends with Klyuev, whom he regarded as his mentor and with whom he may have had a homosexual relationship. While Klyuev was a poet of extreme complexity, however, Esenin's verse was simplicity itself—a circumstance which explains much of his popularity with the broad masses of Russian readers. Esenin presented himself as the simple Russian peasant calling for a return to the ideals of village life and warning against the evils of industrialization. His metaphors and comparisons are based on rural imagery and evidently were influenced by KOLTSOV.

In 1916 Esenin published his first verse collection—*Radunitsa*. The title is untranslatable and indicates a religious rite among the Eastern Slavs which probably dates back to pagan times—the funeral feast held on the grave during the first week after Easter.

There is a pervasive note of melancholy in Esenin's verse; while glorifying the simple pleasures of village life, he is oppressed by the futility of attempting to preserve it. This melancholy also extends to his attitude toward himself, and early on in his poetry there are ominous hints as to his own future fate. Related to this sense of melancholy is a strong sentimentality, and he could in many ways be compared with A. E. Housman.

In 1919 Esenin joined the IMAGINISTS—a group strongly influenced by Italian futurism, and closer to the latter than to the Anglo-American Imagists. Some prominent members of the group were Aleksandr Kusikov, Anatoly MARIENGOF, and Vadim SHERSHENEVICH, who was the primary theoretician of the Imaginists. The Imaginists proclaimed the primary nature of "the image per se" and spoke of the image actually "devouring" meaning. Even metaphors were referred to as "minor images." Esenin is nothing if not a poet of images, but he gradually drifted away from the group after a relatively short period.

In 1923 he met and married the American dancer Isadora Duncan and took a long trip with her abroad, visiting Germany, France, Belgium, Italy, and the United States, where he spent four months. Duncan spoke no Russian, and he knew no English; the relationship was obviously a difficult one. When they returned to Europe in 1924 he divorced her and went back to the Soviet Union, where he remarried.

Esenin's 1921 to 1924 cycle *Moscow of the Taverns* (Moskva kabatskaya) marked the beginning of his bohemian period. Esenin was an alcoholic, and his broken life was reflected in his verse. The term "Eseninism" (*eseninshchina*) became a popular negative epithet of the period. Esenin's poetry of the twenties is radically different from his early manner. Instead of glorifying traditional peasant values, he boasts of having chopped up icons to brew tea. Gone is the romantic lyricism of his youth. In 1924 and 1925 Esenin published his *Persian Motifs*, a romantic cycle based on Eastern themes.

Esenin was extremely unstable, was doubtful of the value of his own poetry, and was drinking constantly. Ultimately he committed suicide by hanging himself, first writing a poem in his own blood:

Goodbye, my friend, goodbye.
My dear, you are in my heart.
Predestined separation
Promises a future meeting.

Goodbye my friend, without handshake and words,
Do not grieve and sadden your brow;
In this life there's nothing new in dying,
But living, of course, is no newer.

Esenin began publishing in 1915, and thus his poetic career lasted only ten years. He was very prolific, although he paid for this with a certain facility and monotony of image. His long poems "Anna Snegina" and "Pugachov" as well as his prose are not particularly successful, but his brief lyric poetry truly captured the imagination of the average Russian.

Works: Sobranie sochinenii. 6 vols. 1967.

Translations: Confessions of a Hooligan: fifty poems. Trans. Geoffrey Thurley. 1973. See also Lewanski, pp. 395–97.

Secondary literature: V. G. Belousov, *Sergei Esenin: Literaturnaya khronika.* Pt. 1, 1969. Pt. 2, 1970. J. Davies, ed., *Esenin: A Biography in Memoirs, Letters, and Documents.* 1982. Gordon McVay, *Esenin: A Life.* 1976. ———, *Isadora and Esenin.* 1980. Yu. Prokushev, *Sergei Esenin: Obraz, stikhi, epokha.* 1975. Lynn Visson, *Sergei Esenin: Poet of the Crossroads.* (Colloquium Slavicum, 11.) Würzburg, 1980. A. Volkov, *Khudozhestvennye iskaniya Esenina.* 1976.

J. G.

Essay, see SKETCH.

Etymologism. A figure of speech in which a familiar root of the language is abstracted, deautomatized, or foregrounded, with attention drawn to its original meaning. It differs from "folk etymology" in that its originator has a claim to philological sophistication. It often serves as a basis for the formation of neologisms. An etymological approach to language was cultivated by the purists of the BESEDA group around A. S. SHISHKOV in the 1800s. It also played a role in the punning satirical poetry of the "civic poets" of the 1860s. Etymologism is important in the language theory and poetics of the FUTURISTS, KRUCHONYKH and KHLEBNIKOV in particular. The latter has a number of poems which are essentially morphological variations on one or two roots, e. g., "We are charmed and we shun" (My charuemsya i churaemsya, 1914), with the epigraph: (the roots *chur ...* and *char*). Some other poems of Khlebnikov's are wholly devoted to etymological conceits, e. g., "Oration on *L*" (Slovo o El', 1920), where the word *lyud*, arbitrarily given an "original" meaning "man," is associated with *lodka*, "boat," *ladon'*, "hand," and other words beginning with "l." The futurists' etymologisms often turned into outright folk etymologies and malapropisms. For instance, in Khlebnikov's "Iranian Song" (1921) the magic tablecloth (skatert' *samo*branka) becomes the airplane's (*samo*let) wife, and "life" is associated with a "tin can," because *zhestyanka*, "tin can," is taken to be a derivative of *zhist'* (dialect form of *zhizn'*, "life").   V. T.

Eurasianism (*evraziistvo, evraziitsy*), an ideological movement among Russian émigré intellectuals in the 1920s and 1930s, which emphasized the Asian elements in Russian civilization and was inclined to see the Soviet regime as a manifestation of these elements. Eurasianist ideas were voiced by D. P. SVYATOPOLK-MIRSKY, N. S. TRUBETSKOI, the historian G. Vernadsky, and others. Cf. SCYTHIANISM. See also SMENA VEKH.   V. T.

Evréinov, Nikolái Nikoláevich (1879–1953), playwright and director, historian and theorist of theater, reacted against the realism prevailing in turn-of-the-century theater, and with N. V. Drizen produced two seasons of naive or archaic theater in his so-called Ancient Theater (Starinnyi Teatr), the first (1907–08) of French medieval plays, the second (1911–12) of Spanish Renaissance dramas. After Vera Komissarzhevskaya's dismissal of MEYERHOLD, Evreinov replaced him as her director in D'Annunzio's *Francesca da Rimini* (1908). Evreinov wrote successful satiric sketches which he staged for the St. Petersburg cabaret theater, "The Crooked Mirror" (1908–13); thus he parodied the style in which various directors would stage GOGOL's *The Inspector General*. Theoretically he viewed the theater not as imitating life, but, on the contrary, life as theater in which we all constantly act a role. After emigrating to Paris in 1920, he wrote plays and a highly personal, rather than scholarly history of the Russian theater.

Works: Dramaticheskie sochineniya. 3 vols. 1915–17. *Istoriya russkogo teatra.* New York, 1955.
Works in English: Nikolai Yevreinov, *The Chief Thing.* 1926. Nicolas Evreinoff, *The Theatre in Life.* 1927.
Works in French: Histoire du théâtre russe. 1947.
Secondary literature: Christopher Collins, "Nikolai Evreinov as a Playwright," *RLT* 2 (1972), pp. 373–98. George Kalbouss, "The Plays of Nikolai Evreinov," *RLJ*, no. 92 (1971), pp. 23–33. C. Moody, "Nikolai Nikolaevich Evreinov 1879–1953," *RLT* 13 (1975), pp. 659–95. Ellendea Proffer, ed., *Evreinov: Fotobiografiya/Evreinov: A Pictorial Biography.* Ann Arbor, 1981.   M. H.

Evtushénko, Evgény Aleksándrovich (1933–), poet, was born in Zima Junction in the Irkutsk region. His father, a geologist, and his mother, a singer, moved with him to Moscow in 1935. His parents were divorced during the war years and in 1948 he ran away to join his father on a geological expedition in Kazakhstan. After his return to Moscow in 1949, his early attempts at writing met with success: his first published poem appeared that year. In 1951 Evtushenko entered the Gorky Literary Institute, where he studied until 1954. His first book, *Scouts of the Future* (Razvedchiki gryadushchego), strongly influenced by MAYAKOVSKY and KIRSANOV, appeared in 1952, followed by *Third Snow* (Tretii sneg, 1955). In 1956, the journal *Oktyabr'* published his long poem "Zima Junction" (Stantsiya Zima); in the same

year *Highway of Enthusiasts* (Shosse entuziastov) appeared, followed by *A Promise* (Obeshchanie, 1957) and *Bow and Lyre* (Luk i lira, 1959).

The appearance of his *Verses of Different Years* (Stikhi raznykh let, 1959) was the culmination of Evtushenko's early period of writing: although many poems in later collections—*Apple* (Yabloko, 1960), *A Wave of the Hand* (Vzmakh ruki, 1962), *Tenderness* (Nezhnost', 1962)—retain the declamatory expansive tone, others are mixed with a meditative quality bordering on melancholy. His verse of the sixties focuses more frequently on the apparently insignificant occurrences of daily life as a source of poetic content.

In 1961 his long poem "Baby yar" appeared, raising the spectre of enduring anti-Semitism in Soviet society, and caused considerable controversy, which had only just abated when "Stalin's Heirs" (Nasledniki Stalina, 1962), questioning the degree of official commitment to de-Stalinization, once again created a furor. However, evidence of his gradual acceptance by the literary establishment was his election to the editorial board of the journal *Yunost'*, on which he served from 1962 to 1969. During an official tour to France in 1963, Evtushenko's decision to publish his *Autobiographie précoce* serially in *L'Express* once again aroused controversy. After a period of relative eclipse during the bleak year of 1963, during which time he worked on the long poem "Bratsk Hydro-Electric Plant" (Bratskaya GES), Evtushenko returned to the center of literary discussion. The poem itself was published in 1965. His volume *Signal Launch* (Kater svyazi) appeared in the following year.

Evtushenko became a member of the Praesidium of the USSR Writers' Union in 1967. His retrospective collection of lyrics, *White Snow Is Falling* (Idut belye snegi, 1969), was followed by a series of new volumes: *I'm of Siberian Stock* (Ya sibirskoi porody, 1971), *Singing Dam* (Poyushchaya damba, 1972), *Road Number One* (Doroga nomer odin, 1972). His most recent works include *Paternal Rumor* (Ottsovskii slukh, 1975), *Full Size* (V polnyi rost, 1977), *Morning People* (Utrennii narod, 1978), *Fulcrum* (Tochka opory, 1981), the prosework, *Berry Country* (Yagodnye mesta, 1982), and a collection of articles, *Talent is a Planned Miracle* (Talant est' chudo nesluchainoe, 1980).

Unquestionably the most visible of the "young poets" of the post-Stalin generation, Evtushenko has led the fight, both in his work and in his career, against entrenched literary and political values. His verse often seeks out an opponent, imaginary or real, with whom the poet engages in a battle against hypocrisy, careerism, bureaucracy. His tone is often pugnacious, exuberant, conscious of the tradition of Mayakovsky. Evtushenko is, however, a conservative poet, both in technique and language: he eschews the metrical and linguistic experimentation of VOZNESENSKY, for example, and has no interest in the word as artifact, as does AKHMADULINA. In his more meditative lyrics, he is most akin to Esenin in his consciousness of his origins.

For Evtushenko, the poem is essentially episodic, editorial, or narrative: all other poetic elements are muted in relation to these characteristics. His works give the impression of belonging to an extended "lyrical biography" (SINYAVSKY), in which the poet, alternately self-affirming and self-critical, evaluates all experience in relation to his own creative development. The poet's vocation, a common theme in his work, is the communication of truth, as sincerely and accessibly as possible. Typically, therefore, his language is straightforward, seldom obscure or stylistically colored. The poet is often depicted as a means of transportation or communication, as in his poems "Signal Launch" (1963) or "Streetcar of Poetry" (Tramvai poezii, 1968). Evtushenko's verse is closely bound to everyday details or topical events, elevated to significance through oratorical style. He delights in triadic argumentation, contrasting two extreme positions and resolving them by a third which redefines an old concept: the people, the Party, patriotism. Equally characteristic is the use of apparent contradiction: "I make my career by not making it." Evtushenko frequently uses alliteration and assonance, and plays on verbal stems in place of direct rhymes. His verse, largely written in iambic meter, employs deliberately jarring metaphors and startling contrasts.

Works: Izbrannye proizvedeniya. 2 vols. 1975.
Translations: The Face Behind the Face. Trans. Arthur Boyars and Simon Franklin. 1979.

Secondary literature: Simon Karlinsky, "Yevtushenko and the Underground Poets," *The Nation*, 21 November 1966, pp. 549–53. Andrei Sinyavsky, "In Defense of the Pyramid." In *For Freedom of Imagination*. Trans. Laszlo Tikos and Murray Peppard. 1971. Pp. 167–95.

N. C.

Fables. The history of the fable in Russian literature begins with the Russian translations of Aesop's fables in the 17th century. Already the earliest manuscripts (1607) contained insertions by the translators or scribes of their own imitations. Russian 17th-century culture found Aesop's fables quite congenial; they were made use of in such disparate items as sermons and popular graphic art (LUBOK). Typically, Aesop's fables were seen as parables on a par with those of the Gospels (indeed, the word for parable, *pritcha*, also meant, and long continued to mean, fable, as well); they are so treated in the didactic-homiletic poems of SIMEON POLOTSKY. Polotsky's versifying of Aesop's fables itself is a particularly significant fact inasmuch as the fable was to achieve its greatest popularity and fullest development in Russian literature precisely as a genre of poetry in the middle decades of the 18th century.

Following the ancient precedent of Phaedrus and powerfully inspired by La Fontaine's more recent example, KANTEMIR, TREDIAKOVSKY, Lomonosov, and SUMAROKOV all cultivated the fable, but it was to Sumarokov, the grandmaster of Russian neoclassicism, that the Russian verse fable came to owe its specifics and its success. Operating basically within the parameters of the La Fontaine model (often adapting La Fontaine's fables themselves), Sumarokov took special advantage of the fable's being a classicist "low" genre to open his version to the wide use of colloquial language, the attributes of plebeian life and the techniques of comic art. Typically delivered in a style of chatty familiarity and replete with dialogue, the Sumarokov fable took on a decidedly racy, folksy, even burlesque tone. Undoubtedly, Sumarokov left his most permanent mark on the Russian fable in his choice of verse form: he used, almost exclusively, the free iambic line (from monometer to hexameter) which both aptly paced the fable's intonation and threw its rhymes into unusual prominence. Sumarokov's fables served as vehicle not only for the moral didacticism associated with the fable from ancient times but also for social satire, for literary lampoon and polemic, for anecdotes, jokes, and puns.

Thanks to Sumarokov's ingenuity and industry the fable became so popular a poetic genre as to be de rigueur for all Russian poets of the 18th century. MAIKOV, RZHEVSKY and most other disciples of Sumarokov adhered closely to the master's version in their own fables, but already KHERASKOV and BOGDANOVICH displayed a tendency to restrain and refine the Sumarokov model. The development of this more decorous version of the Russian verse fable found its highest expression in the work of the two most famous fabulists of the late 18th century, KHEMNITSER, who mainly adapted and followed the German fabulist Gellert, and DMITRIEV, whose witty and elegant fables were particularly inspired by late French classicists such as Florian. The more ribald Sumarokov style of fable also continued to find able practitioners in ABLESIMOV, P. A. Sumarokov, A. IZMAILOV and others.

The Russian verse fable reached the peak of its development with Ivan KRYLOV whose fables from their first appearance in the early decades of the 19th century to the present day have enjoyed repute as the supreme achievements of the genre in Russian literature. Krylov may be said to represent the final synthesis of the whole intensive cultivation of the fable preceding him, but it was predominantly the Sumarokov fable with its La Fontaine associations that he revived, re-invigorated and brought to perfection. Notwithstanding attribution to him of "realism" and quintessentially Russian folk wit, it can hardly be doubted that Krylov owes his preeminence as fabulist not so much to any uniqueness in his work but to the magnitude of his talent.

After Krylov the fable waned as a literary genre, retaining a permanent foothold in children's literature and also serving peripheral literary functions as vehicle of social satire. A bright spot in its later history came in the 1850s with the appearance of that figment of genius, Kozma PRUTKOV, among whose masterpieces of nonsense

literature fables are amply represented. In the early years of the 20th century the verse fable was revived on a broad scale by Demyan BEDNY and adapted to the needs of revolutionary agitation and, later, Soviet propaganda. A highly convoluted but, nevertheless, definite link with the tradition of the Russian fable can be seen in works by the OBERIU group, especially D. KHARMS.

Bibliography: G. A. Gukovskii, *Russkaya poeziya XVIII veka*. 1927. Pp. 151–82. N. L. Stepanov, ed., *Russkaya basnya XVIII–XIX vekov*. (Biblioteka poeta.) 1977. (With editor's introduction, "Russkaya basnya," pp. 5–62). R. B. Tarkovskii, "K istorii povestvovatel'nykh form russkoi basni XVII veka," *Trudy Otdela drevnerusskoi literatury* 27 (1972), pp. 247–56.

I. R. T.

Fábula (from Latin *fabula*, a story; a narration). In *O teorii prozy* (1925), SHKLOVSKY first enunciated the FORMALIST distinction between "material" of the story, or the raw outline of it, and treatment of this story in an actual work of art. In his terms, *fabula* is "the material which is ... molded by the writer into the *syuzhet*." Thus the fabula of PUSHKIN's Eugene Onegin is the romance between Eugene and Tatiana. It has never been made clear by Shklovsky, however, whether *fabula* is the events of life or their most schematic presentation in language. We assume that it is the latter. The *fabula* then is a chronological summary of the major events of the plot of a novel or a short story.

Of all the conceptualizing the formalists have done, the distinction between *fabula* and *syuzhet* is closest to the representational theory of art to which formalism was inimical. The distinction is based on the idea that things, events and concepts have ontological status before they are incorporated into a work of literature, and that language reflects life rather than creating its own reality. It presupposes a direct link between reality and literature which was explicitly denied by such radical formalists as JAKOBSON. TYNYANOV, who did not deny the existence of such link, qualified it in such a way as to make it irrelevant. Shklovsky's formulations disregard de Saussure's thesis with which the linguistically-oriented formalists agreed, namely, that "in language there are only differences," and they weaken the formalist thesis that literary investigation should concentrate on the discontinuity between life and literature rather than on the correspondences between them.

E. Th.

Fadéev, Aleksándr Aleksándrovich (1901–56), novelist, literary theorist, and administrator, was born in Kimry, Tver province, into the family of a school teacher. From 1908 to 1921 Fadeev lived in the Far East, where he attended commercial school in Vladivostok, joined the Communist Party, and fought on the Red side during the Civil War. As a delegate to the 10th Party Congress, he took part in the suppression of the Kronstadt rebellion and was severely wounded in battle. From 1922 to 1924 he attended the Moscow Mining Academy and then worked for two years in the Press Section of the North Caucasus Party Committee in Rostov-on-Don. In 1926 he returned to Moscow for permanent residence.

Fadeev's earliest published works were the stories "Against the Current" (Protiv techeniya, 1923) and "The Flood" (Razliv, 1924), both set in the Far East. The first describes the ruthless struggle of Red commissars against a mutinous unit of their army; the second deals with sociopolitical conflicts in a remote village shortly before the October Revolution. The stories are undistinguished, particularly "The Flood," which suffers from sketchy delineation of characters, fragmented narrative, and excessive use of metaphor. Fame came to Fadeev with *The Rout* (Razgrom, 1927), a novel about a Red guerrilla detachment fighting in the Far East during the Civil War. Despite Fadeev's avowed intention to show how Communists and workers lead and re-educate the masses, the novel is written in a restrained style. The guerrillas are depicted impartially, and their commander is not without weaknesses. The only biased portrait is that of Mechik, a young guerrilla of petty bourgeois origin. He is endowed with what Fadeev deemed the worst characteristics of his class: selfishness, individualism, and romantic daydreaming. Mechik is contrasted with Morozka, an uneducated miner, created to demonstrate the superiority of proletarian morality. At a crucial moment Morozka sacrifices himself to warn the guerrillas of an ambush, while Mechik deserts to save his own life. Although only nineteen guerrillas survive the destruction of their detachment by White Cossacks, the ending strikes an optimistic note. *The Rout* is short, well composed, clearly written, and almost devoid of ornamental excesses. Fadeev presents social psychology through individuals, and his methods of probing into their minds betray a strong influence of Lev TOLSTOI.

With the publication of *The Rout* Fadeev became a major figure in the Soviet literary establishment. As a leader of the Russian Association of Proletarian Writers (1928–32) he championed the so-called dialectical-materialist creative method and rejected romanticism, equating it with idealism, embellishment of life, and defense of the exploiting classes. He occupied high positions in the UNION OF SOVIET WRITERS and headed it from 1946 to 1954, dutifully carrying out the Party's repressive policy in literature.

Fadeev's second novel, *The Last of the Udege* (Poslednii iz udege, 1929–40), remained unfinished. It was conceived as a vast epic portraying various social strata before and during the Revolution. The description of a Far Eastern tribe, the Udege, was to illustrate the point that salvation from the ills of capitalist civilization lay not in the return to primitive ways of life but in the advancement toward socialism. The novel's four published parts are marked by a slow-moving plot and loose construction.

Among Fadeev's writings inspired by World War II are a collection of sketches, *Leningrad in the Days of the Blockade* (Leningrad v dni blokady, 1944), and the novel *The Young Guard* (Molodaya gvardiya, 1945). Mingling fact with fiction, the novel tells the dramatic story of an underground youth organization in the Ukrainian town of Krasnodon during the German occupation. The young Komsomol members are idealized and romanticized, reflecting Fadeev's new belief that romanticism is vital for the representation of ideals and dreams of the Soviet people. In 1946 Fadeev received the Stalin Prize for *The Young Guard*, but in 1947 articles prompted by Stalin attacked him for underrating the Party leadership in the Komsomol underground. In 1951 Fadeev produced an inflated version of the novel which, after some minor revisions, has become the definitive text in post-Stalin Russia.

In the early 1950s Fadeev worked on a novel, *Ferrous Metallurgy* (Crnaya metallurgiya). After Stalin's death it turned out that some of the novel's major themes were no longer politically acceptable. Despondent over the loss of time, removed from the top position in the Union of Soviet Writers, and haunted by the memories of his role in the political persecution of writers, Fadeev shot himself.

Works: Protiv techeniya. 1924. *Razliv.* 1924. *Razgrom.* 1927. *Molodaya gvardiya.* 1946. *Sobranie sochinenii.* 7 vols. 1969–1971. *Pis'ma, 1917–1956.* 2d. enl. ed. 1973.

Translations: The Nineteen [= The Rout]. 1929. *Leningrad in the Days of the Blockade.* Trans. R. Charques. 1946. *The Rout. A Novel.* Trans. O. Gorchakov. Moscow, 1956. *The Young Guard.* Moscow, 1958.

Secondary literature: Edward J. Brown, *Russian Literature Since the Revolution.* 1982. Pp. 134–40. A. S. Bushmin, *Aleksandr Fadeev: Cherty tvorcheskoi individual'nosti.* 1971. V. Ozerov, *Aleksandr Fadeev.* 4th ed. 1976. Helen von Ssachno, "Two Russian Writers: Fadeyev and Tvardovsky," *Encounter*, February 1975, pp. 56–60. S. Zaika, *O romane A. Fadeeva* Poslednii iz udege: *Istoriya sozdaniya, avtorskaya kontseptsiya, stil'.* 1972.   H. E.

Family novel (semeinyi roman), an epic genre that basically focuses on the range of problems inherent in families, and in which the life of the family, the "nest," creates a special system of plots, meetings, conflicts, and motivations. In a broader sense, the family novel may also comprise problems of several generations. In literature, as a rule, the individual is the primary unit of any collective, whether nation, state, or commune. In the family novel, however, it is the family, rather than the individual, which is the primary unit, and interrelationships within the family are similar to the relationship between different organs and the organism as a whole. The question arises of what constitutes the primary loyalty: biological or social, familial or state. As the whole gamut of human associations can occur within a family, from a purely biological-genetic grouping to social and class determinism, the family novel often serves as a microcosm of society. This, no doubt, accounts for the popularity of the genre in world literature. The family system is forcefully represented in such diverse works as Thomas Mann's *Buddenbrooks*, J. Galsworthy's *The*

Forsyte Saga, or the very contemporary Latin American novel by G. Garcia Marquez, *One Hundred Years of Solitude*.

The Russian family novel sees its beginning in the 19th century with S. T. AKSAKOV's *Family Chronicle* (Semeinaya khronika, 1856), and *Childhood of Bagrov Grandson* (Detskie gody Bagrova vnuka, 1858). These novels describe the solid, if authoritarian, virtues of the 18th-century grandfather, the weakening of character among the children, and the dissolution of family ties. *Fathers and Sons* (Ottsy i deti, 1861) by I. TURGENEV encompasses the conflict of generations, as well as family bonds. The sons (men of the 1860s) repudiate the values of the fathers (men of the 1840s) that they consider obsolete in the "new" world.

L. TOLSTOI expands the horizons of the traditional family novel. In *War and Peace* (Voina i mir, 1869), a classic blend of national epic and family novel, he unfolds a backdrop of grandiose dimensions that not only engages the fate of Russia, but that of Europe as well. Undoubtedly, war (or revolution) creates situations of tension and urgency that penetrate to the deepest levels of human essence, whether social or inborn. Tolstoi's parallel plots of family relations and the destiny of Russia during the 1812 Napoleonic invasion bring out his belief in family and national "likenesses," in the "call of the blood," in which the individual is subsumed. *Anna Karenina* (1877) also employs the microcosms of "clans" to reveal conflicting moral values.

The Golovlyovs (Gospoda Golovlevy, 1875–80) by E. SALTYKOV-SHCHEDRIN reflects the contemporary positivist belief in biological and cultural determinism. No doubt, Saltykov-Shchedrin was strongly influenced by E. Zola'a cycle *Les Rougon-Maquart* that depicts the gradual deterioration and disintegration of several generations.

On the other hand, F. DOSTOEVSKY's *The Brothers Karamazov* (Brat'ya Karamazovy, 1880) is a violent reaction to the prevailing views of determinism. While all four half-brothers participate, in various degrees, in a "blood" plot to murder their father, each is free to choose his individual path to either salvation or damnation.

M. SHOLOKHOV's *Quiet Flows the Don* (Tikhii Don, 1928–1940) continued the Tolstoian tradition of double plot that involves family fortunes and the sweeping national destruction of war and revolution.

Contemporary Soviet village prose, with its stress on patriarchal values, implicitly plays on "the call of the nest" to counter the corrupting forces of urban living. However, the favorite genre for the modern depiction of family fortunes is the smaller "novella" (*povest'*) rather than the extensive form of family novel.

Bibliography: Boris Eikhenbaum, *Lev Tolstoi.* Vol. 2. 1931. Pp. 228–48 and *passim.* Ralph E. Matlaw, "Sergey Aksakov: The Genius of Ingenuousness." In *The Family Chronicle* by S. T. Aksakov. 1961. Pp. vii–xxiv.   E. K. K.

Fedin, Konstantín Aleksándrovich (1892–1977), novelist, short story writer, author of war sketches, critical essays, and literary reminiscences, also an important official figure. He started his literary career with the SERAPION BROTHERS. His first novel *Cities and years* (Goroda i gody, 1924), one of the first major novels in Soviet literature, embodied Fedin's quest for a new literary statement. Its displaced chronological sequences bring "time out of joint," accentuating a sense of turmoil. Different kinds of speech and genres, telescoped together, also contribute to its dramatic effect. *Cities and Years* foreshadows a recurrent theme in Fedin's works: the Russian intelligentsia, typified by writers and artists, in their relation to history and society. In *Cities and Years* a representative of the intelligentsia fails to find his place in the Revolution. *The Brothers* (Brat'ya, 1928) is the drama of a musician who remains at odds with the Revolution and is doomed to solitude. Still, he is not a failure. The doctrine of SOCIALIST REALISM has become mandatory for Soviet writers since the early thirties. Fedin complied with it. However, both *The Rape of Europe* (Pokhishchenie Evropy, 1934–35) and *Sanatorium "Arcturus"* (Sanatorii "Arktur," 1936) remained short of the mark. Fedin's difficulty lay in the destructive effect of a transition from one novelistic system to another. His first two novels project the alienated intellectual who for moral or aesthetic reasons, cannot come to terms with the Revolution. Socialist realism has decreed a different system: one based on the "positive hero" motivated by an unequivocally communist ideology; he embodies the power center of revolutionary action; he has the right answers for all issues. If taken seriously, it postulated a new aesthetic approach. Fedin took this new approach in his trilogy. For his story material he selected three high points of history which coincide with momentous stages in the life of Fedin's positive hero: (1) The eve of World War I, the time of the making of the positive hero: *Early Joys* (Pervye radosti, 1946). (2) The turning point of history, when the positive hero helps achieve the victory of the Revolution. Here Fedin employs an astounding socialist-realist device: he mythologizes history by ascribing Trotsky's strategic victory to Stalin: *No Ordinary Summer* (Neobyknovennoe leto, 1948). (3) When the German-Soviet war starts, the positive hero rushes to the defense of the fatherland: *The Bonfire* (Koster, 1961). Fedin managed to attribute to this half-century sweep a sense of inevitable movement of history toward the triumph of a communist Russia. The positive hero wins all the important battles, wavering intellectuals are won over to the cause of socialism, enemies are destroyed. Fedin was enough of a good prose writer to imprint on his narrative material a degree of validity. Whether the trilogy, especially its third component, is a superior work depends on how one reads it. In his capacity as First Secretary of the UNION OF SOVIET WRITERS Fedin prevented the publication of SOLZHENITSYN's *Cancer Ward*. In his letter of January 1968 to Fedin about Fedin's infamous act, KAVERIN speaks of "a writer who puts the noose around the neck of another writer" (English translation in *Survey*, no. 68, 1968).

Works: Sobranie sochinenii. 10 vols. 1972.
Translations: Cities and Years. 1962. *Early Joys.* Trans. H. Kazanina. Moscow, 1948; *Early Joys.* New York, 1962. *No Ordinary Summer.* 2 vols. Moscow, 1950. *See also Lewanski*, pp. 237–38.
Secondary literature: Elizabeth K. Beaujour, "Some Problems of Construction in Fedin's *Cities and Years*," *SEEJ* 16 (1972), pp. 1–18. Julius M. Blum, *Konstantin Fedin: A Descriptive and Analytical Study.* 1967. N. I. Kuznetsov, "O tvorcheskoi istorii romana K. A. Fedina *Goroda i gody*," *RLit* 22 (1979), no. 2, pp. 158–68. *Tvorchestvo Konstantina Fedina.* I. S. Zil'bershtein, ed. 1966. B. Brainina, *Fedin i zapad.* 1979. H. O.

Fedótov, Geórgy Petróvich (1886–1951), historian, essayist, and religious thinker. Fedotov taught European medieval history at the Universities of St. Petersburg (1914–18) and Saratov (1920–22), emigrated to France in 1925, and was professor of Church history at the Russian Theological School in Paris from 1926 to 1940. He came to the United States in 1941 and taught at St. Vladimir's Theological Seminary until his death. Much of Fedotov's work was devoted to the role of religion (Christian as well as pre-Christian) in the history of Russia and its people. His monograph, *Russian Religious Folk Poetry* (Russkaya narodnaya religioznaya poeziya, Paris, 1935), is still an important text on this genre. Fedotov's monumental work, *The Russian Religious Mind* (2 vols., 1946–66), is an indispensable tool of any student of Russian culture and literature. Among Fedotov's many articles there are some that deal with Russian literature. His posthumous collection, *The New City* (Novyi grad, 1952), contains two essays on PUSHKIN and one on BLOK.

Works: The Collected Works of George P. Fedotov. Belmont, Mass., 1975– . (Vol. 2: *A Treasury of Russian Spirituality* contains *Lives* of Russian saints and works by Russian churchmen, most of which are highly relevant to Russian literature; vols. 3 and 4: *The Russian Religious Mind*.) V. T.

Fellow Travelers (*poputchiki*), a term coined, apparently by TROTSKY in 1923, to designate Soviet writers of non-proletarian and/or non-revolutionary background who were nevertheless willing to accept the ideals of the Revolution and to work constructively within and for the socialist order. The label "fellow traveler" was applied, with varying degrees of approbation, to writers belonging to the SERAPION BROTHERHOOD, CONSTRUCTIVISTS, IMAGISTS, and writers not affiliated with any particular group, such as Leonid LEONOV, Marietta SHAGINYAN, and Aleksei TOLSTOI. The critics of the "On Post" group and of RAPP insisted on applying it even to LEF and PEREVAL, many of whose members were card-carrying communists with impressive revolutionary records. MAYAKOVSKY, for one, angrily rejected any suggestion that he was a "fellow traveler," pointing out that he and his associates had served the Soviet regime from its very first days. The attitude of the Party was almost from the beginning favorable to fellow travelers, as its leaders—Trotsky, for one—had little faith in the future of pro-

letarian literature. A resolution of the Central Committee of the Communist Party, "On Party Policy in the Area of Belles Lettres" (O politike partii v oblasti khudozhestvennoi literatury, published 1 July 1925), stated that, while there were different fellow travelers, some more securely committed to the Soviet regime than others, the Party's "attitude" toward them should be in general "tactful and solicitous." The Party's solicitude for fellow travelers was quite justified in view of the fact that most works of Soviet literature that had any literary merit were produced by fellow travelers. The term "fellow traveler" lost its meaning when all literary groupings were disbanded in 1932 and the newly formed UNION OF SOVIET WRITERS embraced proletarian writers and fellow travelers alike.

Bibliography: Leon Trotsky, *Literature and Revolution.* Trans. Rose Strunsky. 1968. V. T.

Félzen, Yúry (pseudonym of Nikolaí Bernardovich Freidenstéin, 1895–1943), son of a St. Petersburg physician, wrote plotless psychological novels: *Deception* (Obman, 1930), *Happiness* (Schast'e, 1932), and *Letters About Lermontov* (Pis'ma o Lermontove, 1935–36). He also contributed to Russian-language journals and almanacs in Paris such as *Chisla, Novyi korabl'* (The New Ship), SOVREMENNYE ZAPISKI, and HIPPIUS' *Literaturnyi smotr: Svobodnyi sbornik* (Literary Review: A Free Collection). He died in a German concentration camp after the Nazis had arrested him, his father's German descent notwithstanding. Felzen's characters are weak, refined, fatigued, and meditative. They engage in endless conversations on love and death, the insanity of life and human endeavor. Frequently in love, their feelings are not reciprocated; or, like Lermontov, they do not wish "to love for a moment, and to love eternally is impossible." These attitudes, as well as Felzen's melancholia, clarity of vision, stream of consciousness, and *monologue intérieur* remind one of Marcel Proust, James Joyce, Virginia Woolf, and Valéry Larbaud. His style is uneven, careless, often even grammatically incorrect. Written in the form of a diary or letters and addressed by the "I" to his beloved, the novels develop along an inner plane, in long and complex sentences. The emotional intensity of Felzen's narrative, however, could hardly be rendered in a smooth and polished style. The theme of love and jealousy is developed against the background of philosophical considerations, commentaries on art and literature, and generalizations concerning human nature and man's plight. Felzen was an original and sophisticated writer whose work assimilated and sometimes surpassed Western European experiments in literary technique.

Further reading: Temira Pachmuss, *A Russian Cultural Revival: A Critical Anthology of Emigré Literature before 1939.* (Knoxville, Tenn. 1981). Pp. 254–60. T. A. P.

Feodósii Pechérskii, see THEODOSIUS, ST.

Fet, Afanásy Afanásievich (1820–92), poet. The name under which he is known in the history of Russian poetry comes from his mother, Charlotta Foeth. She left her husband Johann Wilhelm Foeth and followed the Russian nobleman Afanasy Neofitovich Shenshin, who had been taking watering treatments in Darmstadt, to Russia. Shortly after the arrival of the couple on the estate of Shenshin, a child was born and baptized Afanasy Shenshin. However, the marriage between Fet's mother and father was not made official until 1822, two years after Shenshin's return to Russia. As a result of this irregularity Afanasy Fet was denied the right to use the name Shenshin by the Holy Consistory in Orel and consequently was no longer a nobleman but a RAZNOCHINETS. As a boy and as a man he suffered greatly from this humiliation, which was not corrected until 1873, when Tsar Alexander II through a special edict restored Fet into the privileges and rights of the hereditary nobility and allowed him the use of the name Shenshin. As a poet, however, Fet retained his mother's name by which he was already known to the Russian public.

Fet studied in a German boarding school in Võru (Estonia), later in the philological division of Moscow University (1838–44). In order to retrieve his title as nobleman, he entered military service and served for eight years in various provincial towns. In 1853, he was transferred to the guards which gave him ample opportunity to visit St. Petersburg and to cultivate his contacts with Russian writers, particularly TURGENEV. Fet married the sister of the critic V. P. BOTKIN, bought an estate and in 1860 started the life of a country squire. In

1877, he purchased an even larger estate with a fine country house and in addition a house in Moscow where he spent his winters. In 1889, he was awarded the court title of Kammerherr (chamberlain), an honor which in some way expunged the injustice done to him as a fourteen-year-old boy. He died in Moscow in the early winter of 1892.

Fet started writing poetry while still a student at Moscow University in 1838. He belonged to a circle of young men in whose midst the future poet and critic Apollon GRIGORIEV played a prominent role. Both Grigoriev and Fet were devoted to poetry and in 1840, at the age of nineteen, Fet published his first collection of verse, *The Lyrical Pantheon* (Liricheskii panteon). While still a student, Fet published regularly both in the MOSKVITYANIN and the OTECHESTVENNYE ZAPISKI and many of the lyrics which later became widely known derive from those years. A second collection appeared in 1850, edited by Apollon Grigoriev and a third in 1856, edited and with a preface by Ivan Turgenev. Leading critics (Botkin) greeted his verse with applause. But in the late fifties and early sixties writers were challenged to commit themselves ideologically. Fet was inclined to political conservatism and to the notion that art had only one purpose—to serve the cause of beauty. He clarified his ideological position in two essays, one on the poetry of TYUTCHEV (in *Russkoe slovo*, 1859, Vol. 2, Pt. 2) and another one on the artist Ivanov (in *Khudozhestvennyi sbornik*, 1866). This affirmation of the artist's only duty to his muse and his denial of any didactic justification brought him the hostility of the vociferous leftist critics. CHERNYSHEVSKY, DOBROLYUBOV, SALTYKOV-SHCHEDRIN, PISAREV, and ZAITSEV heaped abuse on Fet, most of all Pisarev. As a result of these attacks Fet's lyre fell silent for a period of two decades. He reappeared on the literary scene in the early eighties on the eve of a revival of a taste for the kind of poetry he was able to write: *Evening Fires* (Vechernie ogni, 1883). This collection saw four editions before the poet's death.

Fet's poetry deals above all with two topics: nature and love. To these one might add a third: reflective, or philosophical poetry. His nature poetry is characterized by fine and precise observation. He sees everything and this sharpness of vision and the intensity of beauty he evokes is sometimes almost uncanny. Nature is alive in Fet, it communicates with man and man responds: "Willows and Birches" (Ivy i berezy); "On a Southern Night on a Hayrick" (Na stoge sena noch'yu yuzhnoi, one of L. Tolstoi's favorites); "I Stood Motionless for a Long Time" (Ya dolgo stoyal nepodvizhno). In this communion with nature Fet continues the romantic tradition.

His love lyrics are sometimes full of charm and delightfully airy: "I Came to You with a Greeting" (Ya prishel k tebe s privetom). At other times they contain a suggestion of a dark and ominous force: "Secret" (Taina). Many of his poems show a characteristic mellifluousness and many were put to music. Dreams, elusive feelings, vague sensations are the essence of Fet's poetry and coupled with his mellifluous singing voice create translucent, light, and airy patterns. In their irrational quality they became a prominent source of inspiration for the succeeding school of symbolism.

Fet has also written poems which reflect the pessimism of Schopenhauer whom he admired greatly and whose principal work, *Die Welt als Wille und Vorstellung* (Vol. I), he translated into Russian in 1881. He also translated several other works by Schopenhauer. Furthermore, he corresponded about him with his close friend, Lev Tolstoi, who was also a great admirer of the German philosopher, and with the literary historian Vladimir Ivanovich Shtein. Fet's poem "Tortured by Life, the Betrayal of Hope" (Izmuchen zhizn'yu, kovarstvom nadezhdy) is preceded by an epigraph from Schopenhauer's *Parerga und Paralipomena*, II. Aside from Schopenhauer, Fet translated many of the Latin classical poets (Catullus, Ovid, Propertius, Virgil, and others), Goethe's *Faust* and other works during the last seven years of his life. He left three volumes of memoirs.

Works: Polnoe sobranie stikhotvorenii. Ed. B. Ya. Bukhshtab. 1937. 2d ed. 1959. *Pis'ma* (Otryvki). In *Russkie pisateli o literature.* Vol. 1. 1939.

Translations: I Have Come to Greet You: Selected Poems. Trans. James Greene. 1982. *See also: Lewanski*, pp. 238–40.

Secondary literature: J. T. Baer, "Schopenhauer und Afanasij Fet." In *61. Schopenhauer-Jahrbuch für das Jahr 1980*. Ed. A Hübscher. Pp. 90–103. D. Blagoi, *Mir kak krasota: O* Vechernikh

ognyakh *A. Feta.* 1975. B. Ya. Bukhshtab, *A. A. Fet: Ocherki tvorchestva.* 1974. Richard F. Gustafson, *The Imagination of Spring: The Poetry of Afanasy Fet.* 1966. Lydia M. Lotman, *Afanasy Fet.* Boston, 1976.

J. B.

Feuilleton. The feuilleton (Fr. *feuille*, leaf, sheet) is a short work in a minor genre that ranges uncertainly between journalism and literature. Topical in subject matter, it tends to be humorous and satirical, sometimes parodying other genres. Its outstanding characteristic is that it has no specific subject matter or form; unity is imposed only by the author's presence as a first-person narrator. His style is easy, light, and colloquial, often maintaining the intimate tone of a personal confession to the reader. The feuilleton differs from an essay in important respects. The feuilleton is written for a newspaper, not a journal, and is designed for a mass audience. It is more responsive to contemporary issues; its style is lighter; it makes no attempt to exhaust a subject; and it has fewer literary pretensions than the essay.

In the West the feuilleton goes back to 18th-century France: to Voltaire, Diderot, and Fréron. The actual term "feuilleton," however, was used for the first time on 28 January 1800 by the Paris newspaper *Journal des Débats* to designate not a genre but the lower part of the newspaper where non-political and unofficial items were printed—announcements, theater and music reviews, articles on fashion, and light verse. Later the feuilleton became a separate sheet. From 1837 to 1848 it was enlarged from a chronicle of Parisian life to include literary contributions from important writers like Jules Janin, Balzac, Gautier, and Soulié. The feuilleton also featured serialized novels by Dumas and Eugène Sue—"romans-feuilletons."

French feuilletons were widely discussed and translated into Russian from the 1820s on. BULGARIN published a chronicle of Petersburg public events in his journal *Severnaya pchela*. In the 1830s SENKOVSKY, imitating Jules Janin, wrote many satirical feuilletons on contemporary mores for the magazine *Biblioteka dlya chteniya*. PANAEV was to remark that Russians were not successful in copying the light, clever, sparkling French chatter about trivia. The many Russian feuilletonists who wrote in this vein were regarded as working in a low genre and were treated with contempt, as seen in the portrait of Tryapichkin in GOGOL's *The Inspector General*. Social satire, going back to the 18th-century journals of NOVIKOV and KRYLOV, proved more successful. PUSHKIN, under the pen-name of Feofilakt Kosichkin, wrote feuilletons wittily attacking Bulgarin. BESTUZHEV-Marlinsky satirized literary foes. In the 1840s the feuilleton took on certain aspects of the popular physiological sketch. Satirists who valued the freedom afforded by the feuilleton were BELINSKY, GRIGOROVICH, PLESHCHEEV, SOLOGUB, TURGENEV, GONCHAROV, and SALTYKOV-SHCHEDRIN. HERZEN excelled in parody; NEKRASOV wrote feuilletons in verse as well as prose; Turgenev wrote chronicles of life in Berlin and Paris.

DOSTOEVSKY in particular was to demonstrate the high possibilities of the feuilleton as a literary genre in his writings of 1847 and 1861. Openly scorning the usual chronicling of Petersburg events, he chose to write about his subjective impressions of Petersburg, the character of the dreamer, and the creative process. These feuilletons, as Komarovich has shown, inspired the subject matter and style of many of Dostoevsky's early works as well as of *Notes from Underground* and *The Diary of a Writer*.

The feuilleton remained popular throughout the century. CHEKHOV wrote fifty feuilletons between 1883 and 1885, mostly under the heading "Fragments of Moscow Life," in which he chronicled the theater and literary life as well as topical themes. "Sergeant Prishibeev" and other stories grew out of these feuilletons. GORKY began writing feuilletons in 1895, lashing out at social injustice at home and abroad. Two talented feuilletonists at the turn of the century were A. V. AMFITEATROV (1862–1923) and V. M. Doroshevich (1864–1922). The latter invented the "short-line" paragraph, a single aphoristic line which became popular with Gorky and other writers. The magazines SATIRIKON (1908–14) and *Novyi Satirikon* (1913–18) featured the feuilletons of N. A. TEFFI and MAYAKOVSKY (the latter in verse).

In the early Soviet period the humorous and satirical feuilleton was brilliantly continued by OLESHA, BULGAKOV, ZOSHCHENKO, KATAEV, and ILF AND PETROV. The Soviet feuilleton in recent years has been extremely popular, but it has tended to be more journalistic than literary.

Bibliography: Dostoevsky's Occasional Writings. Trans. and ed. D. Magarshack. New York, 1963. "Feuilleton" in the *Great Soviet Encyclopedia* (English translation of 3d ed.), New York, 1977 (1981), vol. 27, p. 182. J. Frank, *Dostoevsky: The Seeds of Revolt.* 1976. Pp. 217–38. A. V. Zapadov, ed. *Russkii fel'eton.* 1958. "Fel'eton" in *Literaturnaya entsiklopediya*, 1939, vol. 11, pp. 689–95. E. I. Zhurbina, *Teoriya i praktika khudozhestvenno-publitsisticheskikh zhanrov.* 1969.
N. R.

Filíppov (Filistínsky), Borís Andréevich (1905–), Russian émigré prose writer, poet, literary critic and scholar, journalist, editor, and educator. Born in Stavropol in the Caucasus, Filippov studied at the Leningrad Oriental Institute (1924–28) and graduated from the Evening Institute of Industrial Construction in Leningrad (1929–33). He had been arrested by the Communist authorities in 1920, 1927, and 1929. In 1936 he was sentenced to a five-year term in the NKVD camps in accordance with the notorious article 58–10 of the Criminal Code: anti-Soviet propaganda. He was in Novgorod, when the German Army occupied that city in August 1941. Through Pskov and Riga he came to Germany and later to the United States, where he lived in New York (1950–1954) and then moved to Washington, D. C. In this country, Filippov worked for the Voice of America and for several research institutions, and taught at the American University from 1968 until his retirement in 1978.

Filippov was preoccupied with literary and philosophical problems from an early age. In 1920 he organized and led a literary-philosophical circle in Stavropol until it was broken up by the GPU in 1924. However, his literary activities began in earnest only in the 1940s. After the War, in Kassel and Munich, he wrote mostly for GRANI and *Posev.* For a great many years, he has been contributing to *Novoe russkoe slovo* (New York) and *Russkaya mysl'* (Paris).

In the last eighteen years, Filippov has published twenty-seven books of poetry, fiction, feature-stories, recollections, and essays. He has been highly productive also as an editor and coeditor. He has edited works by DOSTOEVSKY, FORSH, N. MANDELSHTAM, Yu. ANNENKOV, A. Volsky, A. Stavar, L. Bogdanov, Andrei SINYAVSKY, Yuly DANIEL, A. Esenin-Volpin, a.o. Together with G. P. STRUVE, he has edited the works of KLYUEV, GUMILYOV, AKHMATOVA, O. MANDELSHTAM, PASTERNAK, and ZABOLOTSKY; together with E. V. Zhiglevich, works by ZOSHCHENKO, LEONTIEV, REMIZOV, SHKAPSKAYA, K. Burzhuademov, and ZAMYATIN, as well as two collections of essays, on Dostoevsky and on BLOK. With G. P. Struve and N. A. Struve, Filippov undertook the edition of the works of O. Mandelshtam (vol. 4, supplementary), Akhmatova (vol. 3, suppl.), and VOLOSHIN (2 vols.).

With regard to Filippov's own creative writing, critics appear to be unanimous in pointing out the great variety of his themes, styles, and language. A. Sedykh calls him a master of the short story, B. NARTSISSOV—a master of *skaz* narration. His prose and poetry have a definite philosophical dimension, often sad, but often also enlightened and humorous.

Works: For a complete list of books authored or edited by Filippov to the mid-1970s see his *Skvoz' tuchi* (Washington, D. C., 1975), pp. 301–03.

Secondary literature: Tat'yana Fesenko, "Nezabytyi yubilei," *Novoe russkoe slovo*, 3 August 1975. Boris Nartsissov, "Master skaza," *Russkaya mysl'*, 14 August 1975. Andrei Sedykh, "Master korotkogo rasskaza," *Novoe russkoe slovo*, 3 November 1974. ———, "B. A. Filippovu—75 let," *Novoe russkoe slovo*, 3 August 1980.
N. P. P.

Film and Literature are by no means inevitably connected. The first silent black-and-white films shown to sizeable audiences by the middle of the first decade of this century were of such brief footage as hardly to allow story development. Two early literary subjects on film derived from ballads, and thus were quickly told: the popular *Stenka Razin*, produced by Aleksandr Drankov (1908), and LERMONTOV's *Song of the Merchant Kalashnikov*, by Aleksandr Khanzhenkov (1909). The initial exploitation of film as a technological wonder in penny arcades put it beyond the pale of art at first, but soon Moscow Art Theater actors deigned to appear in films. The wordlessness of silent film determined that the role of literature was only in providing "story," and literary subjects were pirated in the beginning without copyright. Thus, the Tolstoi estate protested the making of a film after Lev TOLSTOI's *The Living Corpse* (1911). Khanzhenkov won first critical approval of a literary subject with his *Queen of Spades* (1916) after PUSHKIN. Another film after Pushkin, *The Little House in Kolomna* (1913), launched Russian film comedy. Perhaps the finest film after a literary classic, Yakov Protazanov's *Father Sergius* after Tolstoi, was made in 1917, but released only after the October Revolution, possibly because of pre-revolutionary censorship.

The rich and *sui generis* aesthetic possibilities of the new medium were recognized by the Russian avant-garde. As early as 1913, the futurist MAYAKOVSKY asserted on the pages of *Cine-Journal*, a magazine devoted to the new art form, that the cinema was destined to rejuvenate a stagnant theater, enslaved by its various utilitarian commitments, and return it to its proper domain of free creativity. Mayakovsky was also the first of many major figures in Russian literature to be actively involved in film making as a script writer and actor (both since 1918).

World war and Revolution profoundly changed the Russian film. They promoted records of reality, such as the newsreel; forced the home film industry, isolated from foreign imports, to expand; and exploited film as a powerful means of persuasion. Lev Kuleshov, director and leader of a cinema workshop, reviewed two documentary features for *Novyi Lef*, although the editor, Sergei TRETYAKOV, published a disclaimer of agreement (1927, no. 4, pp. 31–34). Kuleshov views the history of the Russian war and post-war cinema dialectically as first factual films, then story films, culminating in a synthesis—real footage edited as feature film. He calls the two films under review, Esfir Shub's *Fall of the Romanov Dynasty* and Mikhail Kaufman's *Moscow*, examples of "subjective-artistic montage"; he emphasizes the individual, creative expressionism of film-cutting aimed at "calling forth a heightened impression, effects of a purely rhythmic nature with minimal idea meaning." Kuleshov further notes the formal purpose of montage in these purportedly factual films: "a combination of explosive shrieks or succession of symbolic frames, but not a calm view of events, persuasive in the montage of its material" (p. 32). The newsreel, of course, should show events truthfully, and the montage or cutting of the film should be dictated by the material, not by the film-maker. The notion that the material itself, rather than any extrinsic idea of the artist's, should determine the creative process was, of course, also a key position of the FUTURIST avant-garde.

How montage can substitute illusion for fact was a subject of experimentation in Kuleshov's film-editing workshop in 1923. A boy and girl are filmed in Moscow, but, by interposing footage of the White House in Washington, the viewer is led to believe the two are climbing the steps of the White House. A needed shot of the handshake between them had not been made, so the hands of two other persons wearing the overcoats of the two were filmed, and when this shot followed one of the featured couple, it seemed they were shaking hands.

Not illusion, but a dramatic emphasis of reality was the aim of the most famous practitioner of montage, Sergei EISENSTEIN. A student in Kuleshov's workshop, Eisenstein had also assisted Shub in the cutting room. In his first film, *Strike* (Stachka, 1925), beside the montage of antithetical images, Eisenstein showed masses instead of an individual hero. He achieved interesting rhythms, and composed shots from above and below to create impressive patterns within single frames.

Cross-fertilization between literature and film is difficult to distinguish from parallel development. In any case, two characteristics common to both were the simultaneous, seemingly superimposed presentation of various levels of large social units, such as a city or a political movement, and the technique of perceiving things from strange angles. Cities (against whose background individual heroes emerge only indistinctly), masses, or an entire culture become the focus internationally of novels in the 1920s: Andrei BELY's *Petersburg* (1913–22), John Dos Passos' *Manhattan Transfer* (1925), and Alfred Döblin's *Berlin Alexanderplatz* (1929). Vladimir Mayakovsky unindividualized his "masses" poem of the same period, *150,000,000*, which he first published without even an author's name. In "ornamentalist" prose of the 1920s (OLESHA, PILNYAK, VESYOLY), plot in a conventional sense is abandoned in favor of a cinematic or kaleidoscopic stream of mostly visual impressions.

The unfamiliar viewing angle is a technique which appears sooner in literature than on film. A horse which has fallen is seen from the unusual angle of the horse's point of view in Mayakovsky's "A Good Relationship With Horses" (1918): "I went up to him / and see / the horse's eyes. / The street has turned upside down...." In Olesha's prose, especially in his novel *Envy* (1927), every cinematic device then known is applied: stills and accelerated motion, fade-in and fade-out, shots from above and below, montage, visual symbolism, trick shots creating visual illusions, color schemes, etc.

Increasingly writers and film-makers collaborated. Mayakovsky, Olesha, and Nikolai ERDMAN, among others, wrote film scenarios. Olesha's script, *The Severe Youth* (Strogii yunosha), was made by Avram Room into a film of considerable interest (1936). Olesha's scenario, though it dates from the 1930s, the era of sound film, contains mostly descriptions of scene and action, and practically no dialogue. Nikolai ASEEV was employed to write dialogue for the film.

Though silent films could resort to titles, the best screen versions of the classics were without words. In his masterpiece *The Mother*, after Maksim GORKY (Mat', 1926), Vsevolod Pudovkin, another Kuleshov student, composed each scene like a painting, placing but a few objects with utmost simplicity, carefully determining angle and lighting. From the foot of the husband's white-draped bier we see a symmetrical cruciform composition, the mother standing at the head of the bier with two women in black profiled at each side. In the bare room, the icon, illuminated by a single candle, is centered above the bier.

Eisenstein's only projected filming of literature, *Bezhin Meadow* (1925–37), after a story by Ivan TURGENEV, unfortunately could not be completed. A series of stills assembled from the film's footage by Eisenstein's contemporary, the director Sergei Yutkevich, shows that Turgenev's slight, almost lyric subject had been moved forward in Eisenstein's plan to Soviet times and given political meaning, the opposition of peasants and priests to collectivization. The boy hero set to guard the collective grain fields is killed by his own father. Eisenstein selected a boy he felt to be naturally right for the role, without experience in acting, a practice (*tipazh*) usual with him. Also according to his usual practice, Eisenstein photographed the film on location in the south—on a government grain farm, and in a village.

In the 1930s, Soviet film had to join literature in a strict adherence to the canon of SOCIALIST REALISM. As a result, it lost its innovative quality and penchant for experimentation. With the arrival of sound, film and literature also moved much closer than they had been in the years of silent film. Whether studio sets and Art Theater actors, or location photography and characteristic "types" from the population are used, the important achievement of translating literary classics is the projection of the original in background and characters. And this has been achieved for over a half-century now, from the film after Tolstoi's *Polikushka* (1920) with the Moscow Art Theater actors Ivan Moskvin and Olga Gzovskaya to Nikolai Mikhalkov's 1970s rendering of Ivan GONCHAROV's *Oblomov* with Oleg Tabakov of the Moscow *Sovremennik* (Contemporary) Theater.

Eisenstein's conception of a pointed dialectic tension between picture and sound was abandoned. Films based on Soviet classics such as A. N. TOLSTOI's *Peter I*, FURMANOV's *Chapaev*, or Gorky's autobiographic trilogy add little to the literary original except for some decorative color. The parade of patriotic historical films in the 1930s and 1940s has its perfect equivalent, and often its source, in literature. Film versions of Russian classics, such as the monumental *War and Peace*, likewise show few creative departures from the literary original.

The "THAW" after Stalin's death in 1953 affected literature and film in a similar manner. The escape from—or better, the avoidance of—socialist realism led both in the direction of lyricism, loving presentation of detail, and a pursuit of the picturesque, rather than to any kind of radical innovation or experimentation.

Bibliography: Ephraim Katz, *The Film Encyclopedia*. New York, 1982. *Kinoslovar'*. 2 vols. Moscow: Sovetskaya entsiklopediya, 1966. Dieter Krusche, *Reclams Filmführer*. Stuttgart, 1973. Jay Leyda, *Kino*. London, 1960.   M. H.

Florénsky, Pável Aleksándrovich (1882–1943), scholar, religious philosopher, folklorist, and poet. In striking contrast to many figures of Russian thought, Florensky studied the natural sciences first, graduating from the Physico-Mathematical Faculty of Moscow Univer-

sity in 1904, and only then theology, graduating from the Moscow Theological Academy (Dukhovnaya Akademiya) in 1908. He was active primarily as a theologian before the Revolution, but was allowed to lecture on philosophy in VKhUTEMAS (Advanced Art and Technology Workshops) in the early 1920s and was an editor of *Tekhnicheskaya entsiklopediya* from 1927 to 1933. He was repeatedly arrested and eventually deported in Stalin's purges. He died in exile. Florensky's ideas were revived and some of his works published or republished by the Tartu STRUCTURALISTS in the 1960s and 1970s, when it was discovered that Florensky had anticipated certain structuralist conceptions. Florensky's *magnum opus*, *The Pillar and Foundation of Truth* (Stolp i utverzhdenie istiny, 1914), is a grandiose attempt at a universal theodicy, in which Florensky marshals all his great scientific, historical, literary, and linguistic erudition to defend Orthodox dogma from a position of Solovyovian all-unity (*vseedinstvo*). It contains a wealth of interesting detail and many judicious observations, but in an age of advanced specialization, Florensky's undertaking was doomed to frequent errors and dilettantism in many points of detail, and he hardly approached the great goal which he had set himself. Subsequently, Florensky departed more and more from dogmatic Orthodoxy and turned toward the Platonism of SOLOVYOV and the hellenizing aesthetic theories of the symbolist poet Vyacheslav IVANOV, who was pursuing a revival of the communal and religious function of art. Florensky himself, like Lev Tolstoi before him, saw the humanistic, anthropocentric tendency which had prevailed in European art since the Renaissance as a misdirected development which had led man away from his organic ties to the cosmos and made him pursue an illusory quest for the mechanical mastery of nature. A similar archaizing tendency appears in Florensky's studies of language, in which he follows KHLEBNIKOV's belief in the organic nature of "inner form" and, on its pristine and deepest level, even of the phonemic and morphemic building stones of language—an effort, then, to grasp the nature of language by way of glottogonic speculation.

Works: (Poetry) *V vechnoi lazuri*. 1904. (Philosophic works:) *Stolp i utverzhdenie istiny*. 1914. *Smysl idealizma*. 1914. "Obratnaya perspektiva." In *Uchenye zapiski Tartuskogo universiteta*. No. 198. 1967. "Symbolarium." In *Trudy po znakovym sistemam*. Vol. 5. Tartu, 1971. "Stroenie slova." In *Kontekst*. 1972.

Secondary literature: N. Lossky, *History of Russian Philosophy*. 1952. V. V. Zenkovsky, *A History of Russian Philosophy*. Vol. 2. 1953. *See also KLE* 9, pp. 760–61.   V. T.

Fófanov, Konstantín Mikháilovich (1862–1911), poet. A minor poet, Fofanov nevertheless possessed "a genuine gift of song" (Mirsky). Many of his lyrics were set to music. After early beginnings (1881), rather in the manner of FET, Fofanov developed a style which placed him with the decadents of the 1890s, evident in his collections *Shadows and Secrets* (Teni i tainy, 1892) and *Illusions* (Illyuzii, 1900). He might have earned a more important place in the poetry of the Silver Age, had he not been followed by BALMONT, BRYUSOV, and BLOK, who developed rather the same themes and techniques in a more profound and refined manner.

Works: Stikhotvoreniya. Introd. essay by M. Kleman. 1939. *Stikhotvoreniya i poemy.* Introd. essay by G. Tsurikova. 1962.

Translations: Lewanski, p. 240.

Secondary literature: V. Bryusov, *Dalekie i blizkie*. 1912.

V. T.

Folk drama. The Russian folk drama consists of a variety of miscellaneous forms; besides actual plays for human actors it includes a PUPPET THEATER featuring the comic farce about Petrushka. It has also been traditional to classify other phenomena, such as the *rayok*, an optical show of pictures accompanied by verses, parts of the folk wedding ritual, and other folk rituals, including holiday mummery, as belonging to the Russian folk theater.

The roots of Russian folk drama are difficult to trace. A number of theatrical elements accompany the performance of folk tales and folk songs, and at times "parts" are assigned to specific performers. There were also theatrical elements in folk rituals, such as those of weddings and funerals or the ritual celebration of festivals of the agricultural year. Holiday mummery, featuring masks including animal masks, has been recorded in Russia as early as the 11th century. Yet a "missing link" that would tie those folk genres to drama itself seems to be lacking. For one thing, the performance of folk drama generally depended on the availability of a written text and an experienced, literate person who could serve as director. The Russian Orthodox Church had a very small repertoire of pantomimes, the most important of which was the so-called "Fiery Furnace Play," portraying the miracle of the saving of the three holy youths from the wrath of Nebuchadnezzar. But it is likewise difficult to construct a bridge between church plays and later folk plays. Most likely the various forms of Russian folk drama and theater were brought from other countries, notably the West, by professional actors and performers: German *Spielmänner* are known to have visited Russia in the Middle Ages. The Russian SKOMOROKHI were professional actors who may have created the prototype of what is now the Russian folk theater.

The oldest known folk play and the most widespread, *The Comedy of Tsar Maximian and His Son Adolphe*, seems to have appeared very early in the 18th century. The subject apparently derives from a hagiographic narrative, possibly one concerning St. Dorothea, who underwent martyrdom under the Roman emperor Diocletian, whose successor was Maximianus (d. 310). In the play Tsar Maximian calls on his son Adolphe to renounce Christianity and recognize the father's pagan gods. Adolphe staunchly refuses and is executed. The original martyrological concept is heavily overlaid with comic scenes, as in the scene in which Tsar Maximian orders the deaf gravedigger to clear away the body and the latter delays with a kind of stubborn resistance expressed as farcical miscomprehension. The play may have been intended as a satirical reflection on political events of the reign of Peter the Great (1682–1725), such as Peter's marriage to a Lutheran woman in 1712 (Tsar Maximian is portrayed as just married, for the second time, to a pagan), or Peter's putting his son Alexis to death in 1718. If these events did not actually inspire the play, they most certainly gave it an additional resonance. But in later times it survived largely by virtue of its many farcical scenes.

The second most popular play is *The Boat*, variously known among the folk as "The Brigand Band," "The Black Raven," etc. It is frequently connected with Cossack heroes such as Stenka Razin or Ermak. It originated in the second half of the 18th century. The play depicts a boat on the Volga or Kama River, carrying a band of brigands: much of the theatrical interest depends on the stage imitation of rowing a boat. The brigands are portrayed sympathetically as righteous foes of the established order, a trait familiar in Russian and European folklore concerned with bandits. In a central episode a young man who joins the band of brigands recounts his own sad lot and that of his dead brother, a passage developed by PUSHKIN in his narrative poem, "The Brigand Brothers" (1821–22). *The Boat* also influenced OSTROVSKY's play *The Commander* (1864).

Plays were performed in holiday seasons, as in Shrovetide. Preparations and rehearsals were rather elaborate. A director was appointed who taught the actors their roles, including movements and intonations which were learned by heart. The few female roles were taken by young men. Properties were few but significant; stage decoration almost nonexistent. Costumes, make-up, and properties aimed, for the most part humorously, to characterize the part; thus, Tsar Maximian might wear an ordinary jacket, a wooden sword and a paper crown. Delivery was stiff and exaggerated, presumably for the sake of greater effect. The text included lines of verse and songs, and relied greatly for its effect on verbal devices such as pun and oxymoron.

A special form of folk theater is constituted by the *rayok*, a peepshow performance in which the spectator looks through a lens at enlarged pictures in a box. The first picture of the series was traditionally one that depicted the fall of man's first parents, and hence the name *rayok* (paradise). Other pictures showed cities of the world and remarkable sights such as the Lisbon earthquake. The performers recited special verses known as *virshi*, rhymed but apparently non-metrical, a form popular in Russia in the 17th century (distinct from the literary SYLLABIC VERSES, also often called *virshi*). These identified the scenes and commented, sometimes humorously or ironically, on the subjects.

Bibliography: P. N. Berkov, ed., *Russkaya narodnaya drama XVII–XX vekov.* 1953. P. G. Bogatyrev, ed., *Russkoe narodnoe poeticheskoe tvorchestvo.* 1956. Pp. 463–95. Yu. M. Sokolov, *Russian Folklore.* New York, 1950. Pp. 499–507. V. N. Vsevolodskii- Gerngross, *Russkaya ustnaya narodnaya drama.* 1959. Russell Zguta, *Russian Minstrels.* Philadelphia, 1978. Pp. 109–20.   W. E. H.

Folk epic, see BYLINA.

Folklore, Study of.

Collection and Study of Folklore in Tsarist Russia

Folklore has always been popular among all strata of Russian society, except for the clergy, who viewed it with hostility as unclean and containing rudiments of heathen ideology. Therefore it is not surprising that the first records of Russian folklore were made by foreigners—the Englishmen Richard James (1619–20) and Samuel Collins (the 1660s). Of older collections, that of Kirsha Danilov, which includes BYLINY and historical songs of the Ural region (mid-18th century), is the most significant.

Real interest in the collection and publication of folklore arose only in the first decades of the 19th century, in connection with the romantic movement and inspired by German philosophers and folklorists. The writers ZHUKOVSKY, PUSHKIN, GOGOL, and others used folklore for artistic purposes. P. V. KIREEVSKY, having become infatuated during his travels in Germany with the ideas of a "national spirit" and "national soul," compiled a grandiose collection of folk songs in the 1830s (published posthumously). In his struggle against the Westernizers, he made use of folklore to demonstrate the spiritual greatness of Russia. V. I. DAL collected FOLKTALES and especially proverbs (proverb collection, 1861). A. N. AFANASIEV published a collection of tales, primarily from materials of the Russian Geographic Society, Dal, and others (1855–64), the largest and most important folktale collection, comparable to that of the Brothers Grimm.

The discovery of a flourishing *bylina* tradition in northern Russia by P. N. Rybnikov and A. F. HILFERDING in the 1860s and 1870s resulted in an increase of interest in folklore which lasted unabated until World War I. In addition to several *bylina* collections, collections of other types of folklore were published: folktales (by N. E. Onchukov, D. K. Zelenin, and B. M. and Yu. M. SOKOLOV), lyric songs (by A. I. Sobolevsky and P. V. Shein, see FOLK SONG), LAMENTS (by E. V. Barsov), and riddles (by D. N. Sadovnikov). In collecting and publishing folklore, the personality of the individual singers and narrators was at the center of attention. To underline their role, the materials in significant collections of folklore have been arranged, since Hilferding's "Onega *Byliny*" (1873), according to performers.

Research into folklore began in the 1860s. Following the West European "mythologists" (the Brothers Grimm, A. Kuhn, M. Müller, W. Mannhardt, etc.), F. I. BUSLAEV and A. N. Afanasiev became the most significant representatives of the MYTHOLOGICAL SCHOOL. Afanasiev in his work *The Poetic Views of the Slavs toward Nature* (Poeticheskie vozzreniya slavyan na prirodu, 1865–69) interpreted Slavic and Indo-European myths as reflections of various forms of storms and clouds, or light and darkness.

The theory of borrowing (or migration), which had been elaborated by the German orientalist Theodor Benfey, was made known in Russia by the art critic V. V. Stasov (1868). Although Stasov's thesis that the *byliny* had been borrowed from the East was untenable, the theory of borrowing became largely accepted in Russian folkloristics. Even some of the supporters of the mythological school, like Buslaev and VESELOVSKY, admitted the superiority of the new school. Veselovsky investigated the routes followed by Eastern legendary tales from India into and within Europe. In his studies of some Eastern legends and *byliny* V. F. MILLER, a fervent advocate of the theory of borrowing, concentrated on the mediating role played between the East and Russia by Caucasian Iranians and Turks.

The historical school emerged from an endeavor to link folklore with history. This method was first applied by L. N. Maikov in his work on the *byliny* of the Vladimir cycle (1863). However, it was V. F. Miller, who had become aware of the inadequacies of Benfey's school, who became the chief exponent of the historical school. From the mid-1890s and for about two decades thereafter, Miller reexamined a great number of *byliny*, trying to establish their historical basis—the agreement of their subject matter with historical personages and events. His studies were published in three volumes of

Outlines of Russian Folk Literature (Ocherki russkoi narodnoi slovesnosti, 1897–1924). The historical school was accorded general recognition until the October Revolution.

Developments during the Soviet period

During the first decade of Soviet rule, the social sciences, including folklore, could thrive without interference on the part of the Party and government. In the study of folklore, different trends, such as the historical school, FORMALISM, and the so-called Finnish school, coexisted side by side. Tendencies of the historical school are found in the commentaries to the *bylina* collections of 1918–19 by M. N. Speransky and B. M. Sokolov, both followers of V. F. Miller.

The formalists V. Ya. PROPP, A. I. Nikiforov, A. P. Skaftymov, V. M. ZHIRMUNSKY, and others concentrated on certain formal aspects of folklore—structure, style, verse, and language—with complete disregard for ideology and historical conditions. Propp and Nikiforov studied the functions of its dramatis personae. Nikiforov also focused his attention on the complete folktale repertoires of certain regions. Skaftymov's "Poetics and Genesis of *Byliny*" (Poetika i genezis bylin, 1924) emphasized the significance of the study of structure over that of ideology; it succeeded in explaining certain disputed problems (such as the negative traits of Prince Vladimir) by pointing to the requirements of structure. Zhirmunsky contributed to the study of the poetics, particularly rhythm and metrics, of folk songs.

The historic-geographic method of the Finnish school was applied by N. P. Andreev. This method, devised in Finland by Julius and Kaarle Krohn and Antti Aarne, strove to present the complete life history of a work of folklore. By meticulous analysis of all available variants and by considering all historical and geographic factors, these scholars attempted to reconstruct its original form and to determine the place and time of its creation. Andreev was the student of one of the leaders of the historic-geographic method, the Estonian folklorist Walter Anderson. With his assistance, he translated Aarne's tale-type index into Russian and supplemented it with Russian material (1929). Andreev's two studies of Russian legends, which utilized this method, were published in an international series (Folklore Fellows Communications) in Finland.

Soviet folklorists continued the traditions of their predecessors in organizing extensive collection in the field. The first expedition, called "In the footsteps of Rybnikov and Hilferding," was arranged by the State Academy of Fine Arts in Moscow in 1926 to 1928 to investigate the Olonets region under the direction of the Sokolov brothers. It was followed by numerous other expeditions to Karelia, the White Sea region, the areas of the great Northern rivers, and Siberia. These expeditions brought to light quite a number of hitherto unknown variants of folktales, *byliny*, and other genres. A part of this material was published in large collections by M. K. Azadovsky, A. M. Astakhova, Yu. M. Sokolov, A. N. Nechaev, R. S. Lipets, and others.

The collectors in the field observed carefully the personality of the individual singer and narrator. This resulted in a few studies on narrators by B. M. Sokolov and especially by M. K. Azadovsky. The keen interest in the individual narrator led to a new type of folklore collection confined to the repertoire of a single person, the "collected works," so to speak, of a certain master narrator. Such special collections have been devoted to the folklore of the Siberian storyteller Natalya Vinokurova, the Voronezh storyteller Kupriyanikha (Anna Kupriyanovna Baryshnikova), and the White Sea storytellers Matvei Korguev and Marfa Kryukova.

The brief period of considerable freedom in folkloristics came to an end in the last years of the 1920s. With the creation of the UNION OF SOVIET WRITERS in 1932, literature and folklore were subjected to complete control by the government. In his keynote speech at the congress of Soviet writers in 1934, Maksim GORKY stressed the close connection of folklore to the life and working conditions of the people, the life optimism of folklore, and its high artistic value. His speech opened the eyes of the rulers of Russia to the significance of folklore as a powerful force to advance communism and served as a stimulus to initiate large-scale collecting activity. The collection of folklore was now strongly supported by Party leaders and organizations. Local centers of folklore were founded, and the collection of folklore was made obligatory for ethnographic organizations. The local intelligentsia, university students, and students of trade schools were mobilized for active collecting. Influential party papers such as *Pravda* and local papers and magazines published both appeals for collecting folklore and samples of collected materials.

With this new situation, the study of folklore passed "beyond the limits of narrow and impractical academism" and began following the principles and methods of Marxism-Leninism. Folklorists had to recognize that "Soviet folklore constituted an effective means of agitation and propaganda for communist ideas," and the singers and narrators had to view "their activity as agitatorial and propagandistic."

Former trends of study, especially formalism and the Finnish school, were declared harmful. Folklorists had to admit their errors and were made to recant. Thus Propp publicly admitted "the failure of the attempts of the formalists to get out of the blind alley into which the formal method of fairy-tale study had led them." Andreev unmasked the real goals of the Finnish school: "to deprive the fairy-tale material of its sociopolitical significance and to lead the scholar from the study of the actual reality of the tale into pointless formal-logical abstractness." Zhirmunsky subjected to self-criticism his formalistic works and his former "shortsighted" attitude toward the sociology of Hans Naumann. (On the supposed harmfulness of the historical school, see BYLINY.)

As studies of the social function of folkore had to take precedence over questions of origin and migration, folklorists devoted great attention to those genres of folklore which had been neglected or ignored before the Revolution, such as satires on priests and noblemen, folk traditions about revolutionary movements, and the folklore of workers. Satirical stories about priests and folk healers were extensively collected and published by Yu. M. Sokolov, E. D. Vishnevskaya, and others. These stories, widely disseminated in cheap popular editions, served as a means of intensifying anti-religious propaganda. Sokolov also published a collection of satires about the nobility. Folk traditions about revolutionary uprisings, especially those led by Stenka Razin and Pugachev, were collected and published by A. N. Lozanova and B. M. Blinova. Of the SOLDIERS' SONGS only the so-called recruits' songs had attracted any interest in tsarist Russia; now other genres, such as revolutionary soldiers' songs, also became the object of study (especially by I. S. Eventov). The old workers' songs, relating the hard life of workers in factories and mines, were collected not only by folklorists but also by the factory workers themselves in the industrial centers of Russia.

The genres which were the main subject of study before the October Revolution, such as fairy tales, *byliny* and historical songs, also received due attention. Soviet folklorists concentrated especially on the changes which these genres had undergone during the Soviet period. With reference to fairy tales they emphasized the trend from the fantastic and miraculous towards the realistic, and stressed the pervading antagonism towards the Tsar.

The genre of the CHASTUSHKA (folk rhyme), which had arisen in Russia only in the 1860s, became the most productive genre under the Soviet system. This is a short, usually 4-line rhymed ditty, easily improvised, comparable to the German *Schnaderhüpfel* and Japanese *haiku*. Typical is its epigrammatic and frequently nonsensical character, extreme brevity, and marked rhythm. *Chastushki* were eagerly collected and studied, and their creation was strongly encouraged because of their practical value. They were used for whipping up enthusiasm for various governmental actions such as collectivization, the Five-Year Plans, and the Stakhanovite movement, and for propagandizing the new, "Stalin" constitution.

Much attention was focused on the collection and study of entirely new folklore, i. e., creations that had emerged in the changed conditions of Soviet life—*skazy* (biographic narratives and memoirs), *noviny* (neo-epics), Soviet folktales, and letter-poems. *Skazy* were very popular in the 1920s and early 1930s. They were collected from folk singers and others, and dealt with their own lives, the events they had witnessed and the remarkable people they had met. Their purpose was to expose the negative side of the tsarist regime and, by contrast, to demonstrate the advantages of the Soviet order. These narratives were concerned with wives' sufferings under their despotic and drunken husbands in the past, events of the Revolution and the Civil War, life in the Red Army, and the like.

Soviet patriotism, propagated extensively since the mid-1930s, found its strongest expression in a new type of folk song, the *novina* (neo-epic), as opposed to the *starina* (old epic). *Noviny* imitated traditional *byliny*, making use of their motifs and poetic devices, but employing contemporary life as their subject. Their protagonists were no longer the ancient epic heroes, but the "new Soviet hero-innovators and defenders of the socialist fatherland," "kolkhoz heroes and factory heroes." Most often the Soviet government and military leaders, such as Lenin, Stalin, Chapaev, Voroshilov, and Budyonny, functioned as their heroes. Typical is the *novina* "The Lay of Lenin" by Marfa Kryukova. It begins with the execution of Lenin's older brother for his attempt on the life of the Tsar, and ends with the death of Lenin and Stalin's oath of loyalty to him. The song is a hodgepodge of folklore motifs and *bylina* clichés, communist propaganda, and distorted historical facts.

Noviny were paralleled by Soviet folktales on contemporary themes. Their heroes were Soviet leaders and military men, collective farmers, and workers. These tales, invented by the tellers, included only a few folktale motifs, mostly allegorical. The truth sought by the hero turned out to be the October Revolution. The magic ring became the symbol of the scientific tasks which the polar explorers (*chelyuskintsy*) had to solve, "the symbol of their scientific service to the people." Living and dead water was interpreted as "the immortality and invincibility of the Soviet people."

In the mid-1930s, a new lyro-epic genre appeared: letter-poems addressed to Stalin. Occasioned by important events in the life of workers or professional groups and drafted jointly by folk performers and professional poets, they were amended at successive mass meetings. After the final version had been adopted, it was sent to Stalin accompanied by tens of thousands (in some cases even several millions) of signatures. Though one may question their validity as folk tradition, what with their highest imaginable tributes to Stalin they no doubt belong to the curious phenomenon of "Soviet folklore" that developed during the "personality cult" of the Stalin era.

Folk singers and tellers of the older generation who were totally or partially illiterate were given special crash courses to prepare them for their high calling. They were invited to regional and Republic centers, where they attended lectures, concerts and theatrical performances, visited museums, and familiarized themselves with the achievements of science and technology, literature and art. Radios were installed in their homes, and subscriptions to newspapers and magazines were provided for them. Like writers, they were sent on so-called creative missions (*tvorcheskie komandirovki*). The greatest masters among them were assigned writers and professional folklorists as tutors to assist them with facts and ideology. The tutors suggested suitable topics from newspapers, novels, or history, recorded the works which the singers created, emended them, and arranged for their publication. Several of the bards were elected full members of the Union of Soviet Writers and were given the title of Honored Artist or awarded the Order of Lenin. Some were elected members of the Supreme Soviet. On the shore of the White Sea the government built for the singer Marfa Kryukova a medieval bower (*terem*) which looked as if it had been carried over from the *byliny*: it had glazed stoves in the prince's chambers and small gates on carved porches, decorated with "folk art" figures of horses and roosters. However, the singer preferred to continue living in her old hut.

It is obvious that under these circumstances the creations of folk singers were far removed from the genuine folklore spirit. Nevertheless, they were received by folklorists with high praise. Yury Sokolov wrote about Marfa Kryukova's *noviny*: "As a result, we have something new, original, independent, which in certain specific aspects . . . even recalls the 'ancient songs,' but as a whole is sharply distinguished from them, particularly by its great sustained lyric quality and by the free plan of its composition."

In the second half of the 1940s, after the war, a change in literary policy occurred which also affected the study of folklore. Now began a most intensive campaign, led by A. A. ZHDANOV, against all Western elements in Soviet literature and literary studies. The folklorists Propp and Azadovsky were accused of stressing the international character of folklore and following the comparativist line. After 1948, folklorists refrained from making any references to Western scholarship; instead they endeavored to demonstrate that Russian folklore had developed from indigenous national roots.

After Stalin's death (1953), and especially after the period of de-Stalinization beginning in 1956, a certain liberalization became noticeable in Russian folklore studies. Folklorists now felt free to criticize the gross mistakes of folklore research in bygone years, such as

the thesis of "the flourishing of Soviet folklore," the propagandizing of pseudo-folklore as genuine folklore, and the artificial grafting of the *novina* genre onto folklore. Soviet fairy tales were said to be "simply unsuccessful literary works" (Nechaev). Folklorists were sincere in their self-criticism concerning the idealization of Stalin: "'The tragic guilt' of many Soviet folklorists was the fact that they, yielding to the influence of the propaganda of the personality cult, tried to present matters in such a way as if the whole nation glorified Stalin from all its heart and created these idyllic, conflictless, gala works about the 'happy life'. . . ." (Gusev). Folklorists unanimously agreed that the "personality cult" had brought to the fore many creations that had scarcely any connection with folklore.

The following years witnessed a general relaxation among folklore scholars and folk singers alike. Folklorists turned their attention to serious scholarly problems. The excited debate on the nature of Soviet folklore in 1953 to 1955 and again in 1959 to 1961 that activated almost all Soviet folklorists, and the discussion of the specifics of folklore that followed, could have happened only in this atmosphere of temporary promise and hope. It became possible to devote more attention to problems of form than before. This was demonstrated by the re-publication of the formalistic studies by Skaftymov and Propp.

Complete freedom has, however, eluded Soviet folklorists, since their choice of genres and topics for collection and study is still restricted. Either due to actual encouragement by the government or to a desire to please it, some folklorists (e.g., Putilov) have slipped back into Stalin era practices. Some of the pseudo-folkloric works of that era have appeared in the 1960s, showing that not all folklorists have ceased to regard them as folklore. As in the past, folklorists continue to assist folk performers and, in general, supervise the development of folk art.

Scores of highly qualified folklorists have been actively engaged in collection, publication, and research. A number of these collections of folklore materials have been published, primarily in the series *Monuments of Russian Folklore* (Pamyatniki russkogo fol'klora) since 1960. Some significant studies on almost all genres, but especially on *byliny*, historical songs, ballads, and ritual songs have appeared. A. M. Astakhova, V. Ya. Propp, M. K. Azadovsky, V. I. Chicherov and P. G. Bogatyrev are worthy of special mention. Astakhova's study *The Russian Bylina Epic in the North* (Russkii bylinnyi epos na Severe, 1948) is a significant achievement. Unlike Miller and other leading prerevolutionary folklorists, Astakhova studies the *byliny* not as stagnant archaic phenomena, but as living processes. Propp, after abandoning formalism, turned to the social aspects of folklore. Azadovsky had started as an investigator of folktales and laments, with special emphasis on the role of the narrator, but became more and more attracted to the history of Russian folklore and problems of the interrelationship between literature and folklore. Chicherov contributed to the study of the same problems, to the theory of folklore, and to ritual poetry. Bogatyrev produced numerous studies on folk beliefs, folk theater, costumes, and various folklore genres.

In addition to those mentioned, there are many other important contemporary (or recently deceased) folklore scholars. M. O. Skripil (died 1957) and V. P. Adrianova-Peretts have studied folklore in Old Russian literary works; the latter's special sphere of interest has been the relationship between the styles of folk and art literature. D. S. LIKHACHEV has examined the origin and early development of *byliny* and historical songs. Various aspects of *byliny* have been studied also by R.S. Lipets, A. P. Evgenieva, M. M. Plisetsky, P. D. Ukhov (died 1962) and M. P. Shtokmar, and historical songs have been treated by V. K. Sokolova and B. N. Putilov. The folktale has been the concern of I. V. Karnaukhova, A. N. Nechaev, Isidor Levin, E. V. Pomerantseva (died 1981), and E. M. Meletinsky. Lyric songs have been studied by T. M. Akimova, N. P. Kolpakova, and V. M. Sidelnikov; workers' songs by P. G. Shiryaeva; revolutionary songs by A. M. Novikov. Research on the popular theater has been carried out especially by V. N. Vsevolodsky-Gerngross and also by V. Yu. Krupyanskaya and T. M. Akimova. The so-called small genres (riddles and proverbs) have been the object of study by M. A. Rybnikova, M. I. Shakhnovich, V. P. Anikin, and G. L. Permyakov.

Trends in the interpretation of folklore in the Soviet Union from 1917 to the 1970s can be summarized as follows:

(a) The position advocating an identity between folklore and literature, a legacy from the prerevolutionary period (A. F. Hilferding and others), has turned out to be the strongest current in Soviet folkloristics. Adhered to by the leading folklorists of the time (Yu. M. Sokolov, M. K. Azadovsky, and N. P. Andreev), if affected folklore research in the 1920s and 1930s; and it led to the encouragement of individual master singers to create new, individual works (*noviny*, Soviet tales, etc.) in the 1930s and 1940s. Since the 1940s this trend has asserted itself in the favorable attitude taken toward the use of literary models for mass verbal creations.

(b) The concept of folklore as part of ethnography, with emphasis on the archaic, relic character of folklore as a phenomenon of "living antiquity" was advocated in the beginning of the 1930s, primarily by V. M. Zhirmunsky. It was, however, met by a concentrated opposition on the part of the majority of folklorists.

(c) The principle of collectivity endorsed by Maksim Gorky in the 1930s has, since the 1950s, been considered the primary characteristic of contemporary Soviet folklore. It has been adhered to by almost all the leading folklorists (A. M. Astakhova, V. I. Chicherov, V. E. Gusev, E. V. Pomerantseva, V. P. Anikin, etc.). Attempts at denying it by some advocates of a broader notion of folklore (Chistov, etc.) have remained a cry in the wilderness.

(d) In connection with the spread of literary culture in the Soviet Union, the feature of orality has been relegated more and more to the background. Only exceptionally (e.g., by O. I. Shvedova) has it been ranked as equal to the criterion of collectivity. Among the various aspects of orality, the live oral performance has been singled out as exceptionally relevant to folklore (by A. N. Nechaev, M. A. Rybnikova, N. I. Gagen-Torn).

(e) Persistent attempts by several reputable folklorists (K. V. Chistov, M. F. Rylsky, for example) to broaden the notion of Soviet folklore through the inclusion of works of amateur artistic groups have been strongly disputed by others (V. E. Gusev, etc.), who have pointed out that such inclusion would leave as the only criterion of folklore a too general and indistinct notion of "social affiliation," i.e., the idea of its creation by working people. It has also been argued that amateur artistic activity should interest not only folklorists, but also scholars of theater, musicologists, and choreographers. Only the collective form of works by amateurs, the segment that has found acceptance by a group, could fall into the sphere of folklore.

(f) Soviet folklorists agree that works which meet all the criteria of folklore can pass as folklore *only* if they are *narodnye*, "popular" as well as "national," i.e., follow the Marxist-Leninist doctrine.

Bibliography. Collections: (For collections and studies of *byliny*, see BYLINY.) A. N. Afanas'ev, *Narodnye russkie legendy.* 1914. (1st ed., 1859.) ———. *Narodnye russkie skazki.* 3 vols. Ed. by V. Ya. Propp. 1957. (1st ed. in 8 vols., 1855–1863.) D. M. Balashov, *Narodnye ballady.* 1963. E. V. Barsov, *Prichitaniya Severnogo kraya.* 3 vols. 1872, 1882, 1886. V. G. Bazanov and I. P. Razumova, *Russkaya narodno-bytovaya lirika. Prichitaniya Severa.* 1962. P. A. Bessonov, *Kaliki perekhozhie.* 6 vols. 1861–64. V. Bokov, *Russkaya chastushka.* 1950. V. I. Chernyshev, *Russkaya ballada.* 1936. V. Dal', *Poslovitsy russkogo naroda.* 1957. (1st ed., 1861–62.) I. P. Karnaukhova, *Skazki i predaniya Severnogo kraya.* 1934. P. V. Kireevskii, *Pesni sobrannye P. V. Kireevskim.* 10 vols. 1860–74. Novaya seriya, 2 vols. (2nd vol. in 2 parts). 1911, 1918, 1929. A. N. Lozanova, *Pesni i skazaniya o Razine i Pugachove.* 1935. L. N. Maikov, *Velikorusskie zaklinaniya.* 1869. N. E. Onchukov, *Severnye narodnye dramy.* 1911. V. Ya. Propp, *Narodnye liricheskie pesni.* 1961. N. I. Rozhdestvenskaya and S. S. Zhislina, *Russkie chastushki.* 1956. M. A. Rybnikova, *Zagadki.* 1932. D. N. Sadovnikov, *Zagadki russkogo naroda.* 1959. (1st ed., 1876.) Aleksei I. Sobolevskii, *Velikorusskie narodnye pesni.* 7 vols. 1895–1902. G. S. Vinogradov, *Russkie plachi (prichitaniya).* 1937. Nikolai Vinogradov, *Zagovory, oberegi, spasitel'nye molitvy i proch.* 2 vols. 1907–09. Z. I. Vlasova and A. A. Gorelov, *Chastushki v zapisyakh sovetskogo vremeni.* Moscow, 1965.

Collections in English: Aleksandr Afanas'ev, *Russian Fairy Tales.* Trans. Norbert Guterman. Folkloristic commentary by Roman Jakobson. 1973. (1st ed., 1945.) Alex E. Alexander, *Russian Folklore: An Anthology in English Translation.* 1975. D. P. Costello and I. P. Foote, *Russian Folk Literature.* 1967. Adolf Gerber, *Great Russian Animal Tales: A Collection of Fifty Tales.* New York, 1970. W. R. S. Ralston, *Russian Folk-Tales.* 1873. ———. *The Songs of the Russian People, as Illustrative of Slavonic Mythology and Russian*

Social Life. 2d ed. 1970. (1st ed., 1872.) Roberta Reeder, *Down along the Mother Volga.* An Anthology of Russian Folk Lyrics with an Introductory Essay by V. Ya. Propp. 1975.

Secondary literature: N. P. Andreev, *Die Legende vom Räuber Madej.* (Folklore Fellows Communications [= FFC] 69.) Helsinki, 1927. N. P. Andreev, *Die Legende von den zwei Erzsündern.* (FFC, 54.) Helsinki, 1924. N. P. Andreev, *Ukazatel' skazochnykh syuzhetov po sisteme Aarne.* 1929. A. M. Astakhova et al., *Ocherki russkogo narodnopoeticheskogo tvorchestva sovetskoi epokhi.* 1952. Mark K. Azadovskii, *A Siberian Tale Teller.* Trans. James R. Dow. Austin, Texas, 1974. ———, *Istoriya russkoi fol'kloristiki.* 2 vols. 1958–63. ———, *Stat'i o literature i fol'klore.* 1960. P. G. Bogatyrev, ed., *Russkoe narodnoe poeticheskoe tvorchestvo.* 2d ed. 1956. (1st ed., 1954.) P. G. Bogatyrev, *Voprosy teorii narodnogo iskusstva.* 1971. H. Munro Chadwick, N. Kershaw Chadwick, "Russian Oral Literature." In *The Growth of Literature.* Vol. 2, 1936, pp. 1–296. V. I. Chicherov. *Russkoe narodnoe tvorchestvo.* 1959. ———, *Voprosy teorii i istorii narodnogo tvorchestva.* 1959. ———, *Zimnii period russkogo zemledel'cheskogo kalendarya XVI–XIX vekov.* 1957. K. V. Chistov, *Narodnaya poetessa I. A. Fedosova: Ocherk zhizni i tvorchestva.* 1955. ———, *Russkie narodnye sotsial'no-utopicheskie legendy XVII–XIX vv.* 1967. Stephen P. Dunn and Ethel Dunn, eds., *Introduction to Soviet Ethnography.* 2 vols. Berkeley, Cal., 1974. Andrew Guershoon, *Certain Aspects of Russian Proverbs.* 1941. V. E. Gusev, *Estetika fol'klora.* 1967. Felix Haase, *Volksglaube und Brauchtum der Ostslaven.* 1939. Harold L. Klagstad, "Great Russian Charm Structure," *Indiana Slavic Studies* 2 (1958), pp. 135–44. Maurice I. Levin, "The Structure of the Russian Proverb," In *Studies Presented to Professor Roman Jakobson by His Students,* ed. by Charles E. Gribble. 1968. Pp. 180–87. Ivan A. Lopatin, "What the People Are Now Singing in a Russian Village," *Journal of American Folklore,* 64 (1951), pp. 179–90. Elsa Mahler, *Die russische Totenklage.* 1935. ———, *Die russichen dörflichen Hochzeitsbräuche.* 1960. S. V. Maksimov, *Nechistaya, nevedomaya i krestnaya sila.* 1903. V. J. Mansikka, *Die Religion der Ostslaven,* Vol. 1. *Quellen.* (FFC, 43.) Helsinki, 1922. ———, *Über russische Zauberformeln mit Berücksichtigung der Blut- und Verrenkungssegen.* Helsinki, 1909. E. M. Meletinskii, *Geroi volshebnoi skazki.* 1958. M. Ya. Mel'ts, comp., *Russkii fol'klor: Bibliograficheskii ukazatel'.* 3 vols. 1961 (Vol. 2), 1966 (Vol. 1), 1967 (Vol. 3). V. F. Miller, *Ocherki russkoi narodnoi slovesnosti.* 3 vols. 1897, 1910, 1924. A. N. Nechaev, "O tozhdestve literatury i fol'klora." In *Voprosy narodno-poeticheskogo tvorchestva,* ed. by V. I. Chicherov and V. M. Sidel'nikov. 1960. Pp. 127–45. Felix J. Oinas, "The Political Uses and Themes of Folklore in the Soviet Union." In *Folklore, Nationalism, and Politics,* ed. Felix J. Oinas 1978. Pp. 77–95. ———, "The Problem of the Notion of Soviet Folklore." In *Folklore Today. A Festschrift for Richard M. Dorson,* ed. by Linda Dégh et al. 1976. Pp. 379–97. Felix J. Oinas and Stephen Soudakoff, eds., *The Study of Russian Folklore.* 1975. M. M. Plisetskii, *Istorizm russkikh bylin.* 1962. E. V. Pomerantseva, *Mifologicheskie personazhi v russkom fol'klore.* 1975. ———, *Sud'by russkoi skazki.* 1965. V. Ya. Propp, *Istoricheskie korni volshebnoi skazki.* 1946. ———, *Morfologiya skazki.* 2d ed. 1969. (1st ed., 1928.) ———, *Morphology of the Folktale.* 2d ed., rev. and ed. Louis A. Wagner, new intr. by Alan Dundes. 1968. (1st ed., trans. Laurence Scott, introd. Svatava Pirkova-Jakobson, 1958.) ———, *Russkie agrarnye prazdniki.* 1963. V. N. Putilov, *Russkii istoriko-pesennyi fol'klor XIII–XVI vekov.* 1960. *Russkii fol'klor: Materialy i issledovaniya 1– . 1956– .* V. A. Rybakov, *Drevnyaya Rus': Skazaniya, byliny, letopisi.* 1963. B. M. Sokolov, "Ekskursy v oblast' poetiki russkogo fol'klora," *Khudozhestvennyi fol'klor* 1 (1926), pp. 30–53. ———, *Skaziteli.* 1924. Yu. M. Sokolov, *Russian Folklore.* Trans. Catherine Ruth Smith. Introd. Felix J. Oinas. 1971. (1st ed., 1950.) ———, *Russkii fol'klor.* 1941. (1st ed., 1938.) V. K. Sokolova, *Russkie istoricheskie pesni XVI–XVIII vv.* 1960. ———, *Russkie istoricheskie predaniya.* 1970. Heinrich Stammler, *Die geistliche Volksdichtung als Äusserung der geistigen Kultur des russischen Volkes.* 1939. Brigitte Stephan, *Studien zur russischen Častuška und ihrer Entwicklung.* 1969. Carl Stief, *Studies in Russian Historical Song.* Copenhagen, 1953. S. A. Tokarev, *Religioznye verovaniya vostochnoslavyanskikh narodov XIX-nachala XX veka.* 1957. V. N. Vsevolodskii-Gerngross, *Russkaya ustnaya narodnaya drama.* 1959. D. K. Zelenin, *Ocherki russkoi mifologii,* I: *Umershie neestestvennoi smert'yu i rusalki.* 1916. Russell Zguta, *Russian Minstrels: A History of the Skomorokhi.* 1978.   F. J. O.

Folkloristics, see FOLKLORE, THE STUDY OF.

Folk Song. The Russian folk song represents a vast and varied tradition. Depending on the focus, this material can be classified according to function, mode of performance, or social group. One of the major attempts at classification is N. P. Kolpakova's system which divides Russian folk songs into : (1) invocations which appear in rituals such as those addressed to Cosmas and Damian in the wedding celebration or the invocations to spring in the calendrical rituals; (2) game songs which dramatize collective games, imitate aspects of peasant life such as planting, and songs connected with dance; (3) panegyrics such as those addressed to the head of a household during Yuletide or to participants of a wedding; (4) lyrics subdivided by mode of performance into *chastye* (rapid tempo) which may be love, satirical, or dance songs; *protyazhnye* (drawn-out) songs which may be about love, family, recruiting, soldier life, prison, and songs sung under specific circumstances such as *ulichnye* (sung on the street) and *zastol'nye* (sung at table) songs.

A more satisfactory classification of folk songs is Vladimir PROPP's which divides them into: (1) songs of peasants involved in agricultural labor; (2) songs of peasants engaged in non-agricultural work (soldiers, barge haulers, etc.), (3) songs of the proletariat. The peasant songs are then divided into ritual and non-ritual. Ritual songs include calendrical songs associated with the pagan holidays timed to those in the Christian calendar (see CALENDAR POETRY), such as Christmas, when special songs are sung to ensure a good harvest, or St. John's Eve which coincides with pagan Midsummer night festivities. Some of the harvest songs also belong to the category of work songs, since their rhythm is determined by the rhythm of the work of harvesting which they accompany.

The other basic ritual cycle is devoted to family rituals such as wedding and funeral celebrations where appropriate songs are associated with each episode in the course of the ritual. Within these two ritual cycles are different categories such as the LAMENT, ritual lyrics (e.g., wedding ritual songs), invocations, panegyrics, and songs reflecting a belief in homeopathic magic.

One category of non-ritual folk songs are "songs of peasant slavery." Some are about peasants who were forced to work in the manor. In one popular song a lackey tells the peasants working in the fields not to envy him, since his work is far more humiliating and difficult than theirs. This pattern is later adapted to a proletarian song telling the peasants in the field not to envy those working in the mines, for the miner's lot is harder than theirs. Other songs tell about forced recruitment or members of a family taken to be lackeys or stewards.

In another category are love songs, which are divided into vocal songs and those connected with movement, such as songs accompanying a round dance or *khorovod*. Most of these songs are of life seen through the eyes of a young girl. The song may describe a girl's shyness on meeting her beloved, her grief because her sweetheart has left her, or her praise of her sweetheart's handsome features. Sometimes the songs take the male point of view, as when a young man tells of the girl whom he loves, as he is riding off to Moscow to see her.

In a related category are love songs connected with movement. In the *khorovod*-game songs the participants may move in a circle in the direction of the sun, from right to left, with members of the group inside the circle acting out the subject of the song. However, the *khorovod* can also be performed with dancers in rows facing each other, in a figure eight, etc. They may walk like a snake, in single file, or in rows of four. All members sing while performing the *khorovod*. In a dance, however, only the onlookers sing. The dances are performed by individuals and are mainly for men. In some areas the *khorovod* is preceded by "gathering" songs, when a group goes around the village inviting young men and women to join the khorovod; there are also "dispersal" songs which mark the end of the performance. While a short plot is usually acted out in the *khorovod*, in the dance songs there may be only a series of images that are not closely connected, and the song ends when the dancers no longer wish to continue. In both types of songs the contents are generally cheerful, or even mischievous, as in the song where a girl's father tries to keep her locked up at home, but she does not heed him and sees her sweetheart in spite of him. Whereas the characters in the vocal love songs are referred to as "pretty girl" and "nice young

man," in *khorovod* and dance songs they are frequently more idealized and depicted as a *tsarevich* and a *tsarevna*.

Songs about family life are also divided into two groups, vocal and *khorovod*-game or dance songs. Vocal songs are invariably about the difficulties of family life. Whereas sometimes a man may complain about his wife's indifference to him, most of them are about the grievous lot of a wife who misses the carefree life she led in her parents' home when she had freedom and could play, in contrast to her present life in a strange household with a husband and inlaws who treat her cruelly. There are cheerful family songs, such as the one in which there is rejoicing when a son his just been born, but these are rare. There are also songs about widows grieving over the difficulty in getting food and raising their children without a husband.

The *khorovod*-game and dance songs about family life have a totally different tone. While they treat essentially the same subject matter as the vocal songs, the attitude is funny and satirical. The wife deceives her husband or talks back to him; a lazy wife is harnessed to a sleigh to drag wood; a mother-in-law treats her sons-in-law well with gifts of food.

Humorous and satirical songs may also be vocal or *khorovod*-game and dance songs. Many are ironic, such as the song about Dunya-fine-weaver, who produces fiber thicker than rope when she spins. One of the most famous songs is about the fools Foma and Eryoma, who try to plough with a cat and rooster instead of a horse, or are thrown out of church for bellowing their prayers. Foma buys a boat without a bottom to go fishing, and this adventure ends in disaster. Often the songs satirize the clergy, who are depicted as more interested in drink and amusement than prayers and fasting.

Lullabies often begin with the lulling sounds "bayú, bayushki-bayú." Animals, especially cats, are depicted engaging in human activities, such as weaving bast shoes or having a cradle almost as nice as a child's. The songs generally have short lines with frequent alliteration which helps fulfill the function of lulling a child to sleep.

Another set of songs are of peasants engaged in non-agricultural labor (soldiers, barge haulers, etc.) Many of the songs of the *burlaki* (barge haulers or loggers) are work songs which accompany labor and whose rhythm is determined by the work. The bargehaulers worked in teams and dragged heavy ships up the river under straps. The loggers cleared the forests, then bound the logs into rafts which they would navigate to the mills. In many cases the work of the haulers and loggers was similar, such as moving a boat or raft off a shoal, and both would accompany this labor with the same song. Propp and E. V. Hippius suggest an interpretation for the popular refrain in such songs, *dubinushka, ukhnem*. *Dubina* means oak or tree in general, and *ukhnem* means "let's throw it down." In clearing a forest, the tree roots were chopped, and a rope attached to the top of the tree was pulled when the roots were almost all chopped. The refrain was "Let's pull [the rope]. Let's throw it down." Later the song was applied to other forms of labor which required groups to work in unison. While these belong to the category of work songs, other *burlak* songs are lyrics about the life of *burlaki*. In one song there is a depiction of *burlaki* about to leave their village for work, as their families say farewell. In another, a girl grieves because she misses her *burlak* who has a lot of money in his knapsack. Another is about a girl upset because all the *burlaki* except her sweetheart have returned from the Volga, who then rejoices when he also returns.

Robber songs can be divided into those which represent the positive aspects of a brigand's life and others about the fate of the hero who is caught. In the first type the men are called *udaloi* (daring) or *usy* (moustaches) and are idealized, with sable hats, elegant kaftans, silken shirts, and boots of Moroccan leather. In these songs the bold robbers avenge themselves for the wrongs inflicted upon them and their families, or they find shelter with a stingy peasant who tries to trick them, and they end up punishing him and taking his money instead. In the songs of a captured robber the hero usually compares his plight with that of a preying bird who got caught and is now in captivity, or contrasts his fate with that of a free bird. Elements of the epic are evident in one song, "Oh, my dearest, my young wife" (Akh ty dushechka, zhena moya molodaya), in which the wife describes how she warned her husband not to carry on his robber's life, not to saddle his horse and leave at midnight. Her husband does not heed the warning and, whereas in an epic or fairy tale the hero usually ends up happily in spite of his errors, here the hero is punished and the song ends with him in prison.

SOLDIER SONGS cover the entire cycle of a soldier's life, from the time he is recruited to the time of his death. Recruiting is accompanied by special laments which are thematically related to the funeral laments, with the recruit's female relatives wailing over the fact they will be left alone to do hard labor and raise the children. These laments were motivated by the fact that from the time of Peter I until the end of the 18th century, when their term was reduced to twenty-five years, soldiers served for life. There are lyric songs of the recruit who receives the *nevzgoda*, the bad news that he has been selected, and his days of freedom are over. Many songs tell about the difficult life of the soldier, the sleepless nights and endless marches and campaigns. Some songs portray the thoughts of a soldier of the family he has left back home; others depict his "new family," as his rifle is his new wife and his new home is the steep mountains. Often the death of a soldier comes as he dies alone under a tree and tells his horse to convey the news to his family. There are also love songs such as the one about a girl whose sweetheart has just been recruited.

Prison and exile songs are related to robber songs about heroes who end up in prison, but whereas in the robber songs the heroes are punished specifically for their brigandage, in this category the songs are usually vague about any actual crimes committed. As in the robber-prison songs, the protagonists contrast their life of freedom to their life in captivity and compare themselves to caged birds. Some songs tell of the trek to exile on the Siberian highway—the prisoners are overcome by grief, but pride still shines in their eyes. There are also love songs told through the view of a young girl, such as the one about a girl who fell in love with a revolutionary worker, and now she follows him to prison. Some songs contain "nursing" imagery, typical of the robber and soldier songs, to convey the prisoner's reminiscences of his free life in wild nature which "nursed" him and "lulled" him to sleep. This category also includes the songs of the *brodyagi* (tramps) who end their lives in prison.

The last major category established by Propp are the workers' songs from the factories and mines. The early songs are similar in structure and style to peasant folk songs and often give an optimistic picture of a worker's life. There are also love songs about a village girl grieving because her sweetheart has left her to go to work in a factory. By the middle of the century the songs portrayed the extremely difficult life of the workers. Sometimes songs relating to one profession such as mining were adapted to describe the hardships in another profession such as textile mills. Later songs were created about work in the Don Basin coal mines. Sometimes the songs related to specific factories or mines; however, often a local song became generalized to mining or factory work in general. By the end of the century songs no longer merely protested the conditions under which workers lived, but called for revolutionary action or described strikes and uprisings. Workers' songs increasingly came under the influence of written poetry and were often written by proletarian poets or members of the intelligentsia, then were reworked as they were disseminated in leaflets or orally among the masses. New genres such as revolutionary marches and hymns were very popular during the 1905 Revolution, and in the demonstrations and strikes that occurred up until 1917.

Structure of the folk song

There is no single prosodic system for Russian folk songs; it varies with the genre. Whereas the pattern of a trochaic meter with a dactylic clausula was adopted by literary poets in their imitations of the Russian folk song, many genres do not follow this schema. Russian folk dance songs, for example, usually have a four-foot trochaic line with a stress on the third and seventh beat, with a truncated ending:

$$\grave{x}\, x\, \acute{x}\, x\, /\, \grave{x}\, x\, \acute{x}\, (x).$$

There are also dance songs in three-foot trochaic meter. The lament, however, is trochaic with a dactylic ending and includes four to seven syllables per line. Lyrics and ritual songs such as *kolyadas* are tonic but are characterized by different metrical patterns.

Rhyme is not typical of Russian folk songs. In literature, if a poem contains rhyme it occurs throughout the entire stanza, whereas in folk poetry if rhyme occurs at all it is generally sporadic and is based on syntactic parallelism. Rhymes are "grammatical," a characteristic considered inferior in written Russian literature by the beginning of the 19th century. Rhymes may occur at the beginning, middle or end of the line or in various combinations of this pattern. For example:

Ty podi, moya korovushka, domoi,
Propadi, moya golovushka, doloi!

(Go home, my little cow
Fall down, my little head!)

The rhyming may be in couplets, but it also may continue through several lines:

V ponedel'nik mlada zhala,
Vo vtornik vyazala,
V sredu vozila,
V chetverg molotila,
V pyatnitsu veyala,
V subbotu meryala,
V voskresen'e prodala
I denezhki propila.

(On Monday the young girl cut the corn,
On Tuesday she bound it,
On Wednesday she carted it,
On Thursday she threshed it,
On Friday she winnowed it,
On Saturday she measured it,
On Sunday she sold it,
And squandered the money on drink.)

Many lyrics are polyphonic *protyazhnye* (drawn-out) songs. The songs consist of eight-, nine-, or thirteen-syllable lines with five to seven unstressed syllables which is called the *raspetyi stikh* (extended verse line). This line often contains interrupted words (apocope), repetitions of words or phrases, inserted particles, exclamations, and interjections (the insertions may appear in the middle of a word as well). Melisma (*raspev*) is common, where an entire musical phrase may be sung to a single syllable of the text. The first few measures of a song are usually sung by the leader of the chorus (*zapevala*), and then the chorus joins in. This occurs at the beginning of each stanza. The number of parts can change from performance to performance or even within one performance, and at certain points in the song all voices sing in unison or in octaves.

The added components are typical of *chastaya* (rapid tempo) songs as well, which is the mode of performance for *khorovod*-game and dance songs. The examples below show interruption of words and insertion of interjections as delimiters in both types of songs:

Chastaya pesnya:

Vo piru-to byla,
Da ya ne chai pila,
Oi, da ya ne chai-to pila—
Da kofei kushala,
   Ya ne chai-to pila—
Da kofei kushala,
Oi, da kofei kushala
Da iz poluvedra,
   Ya ne ryumkami,
Da ya ne stakanami,
Oi, da ya pila-to, mlada,
Da iz poluvedra,
   Oi, da iz polu-to vedra . . .

Rapid Song

At a feast I was,
Yes I didn't drink tea,
Oi, yes, I didn't drink tea—
Yes, coffee I tasted,
   I didn't drink tea—
Yes, coffee I tasted,
Oi, yes, coffee I tasted
Yes out of half a pail,
   Not out of wineglasses,
Yes, not out of glasses,
Oi, yes did I drink, a young lass,
Yes, out of half a pail,
   Oi, yes, out of half a pail . . .

Protyazhnaya pesnya

1. Ne velyat-to Dune za re... /vot, za rechen'ku
   khodit'
2. Vot, za rechen'ku khodit', da,
   Ne velyat-to-Dune molo... /vot, molodchika lyubit'
3. Vot, molodchika lyubit', da,
   Ne velyat-to Dune molo... /vot, moloden'(i)kogo,
4. Vot, moloden'(i)kogo, da,
   Dushu-Vanyushku chernobro... /
   chernobroven'(i)kogo.

Drawn-out Song

1. Dunya was not allowed beyond the ri... /well,
   beyond the river to go
2. Well, beyond the river to go, yes,
   Dunya was not allowed a you... /well, a young man
   to love
3. Well, a young man to love, yes,
   Dunya was not allowed a you... /well, a young man
4. Well, a young man, yes,
   Sweetheart-Vanyushka the blackbro... /the
   blackbrowed

Often in the drawn-out songs the beginning and end of a musical phrase do not coincide with the verbal syntactic unit, and may begin in the middle of a verbal phrase or the middle of a word:

Protyazhnaya pesnya

Ne ve-lyat-to Du-ne___ za-re... vot, za re-chen'-ku-(u)kho-
dit'___ Vot, za-re-chen'ku___ kho-dit',___ da ne ve-
lyat-to___ Du-ne mo-lo... vot, mo-lod-chi-ka(a)lyu-bit'.___

The stanzas of lyric songs are varied and different from the composition of literary stanzas. They do not have cross rhyme (a b a b), but frequently there is a repetition of one or two lines or words. The repetitions may function differently from the initial statement of the words or phrase, since they may first appear at the end of a stanza and then at the beginning of the next, where they take on new meaning within the context, and mark the beginning rather than the end of a musical phrase. This structure is known as "chain composition" and thus the syntactic construction is distributed over several stanzas which is another distinction from the enclosed structure, marked by thematic completeness, in the literary stanza. Chain structure, however, is not the only form in which the syntactic construction extends to several stanzas, for example:

> We weeded the cabbages
> We repeated,
>   Ai lyuli, ai lyuli,
> We repeated:
>
> "Whoever needs a cabbage,
> Come buy,
> Ai lyuli, ai lyuli,
> Come buy."

There also may be anaphora, or repetition at the beginning of a line:

> A pretty girl was milking cows,
> Through a rag she strained the milk,
> With milk she fed the young man,
> Fed him, saying:
> "Don't marry, don't marry, young man,
> Don't marry, don't marry, brave one!

> Among us you must live,
> Among us, girls,
> Among us, doves!"

There also may be epiphora or repetition at the end of a line:

> Wasn't it a falcon,
> A falcon through the mountains flew,
> Through the mountains a falcon flew,
> Well, he flew, flew,
> Flew, swans he sought,
> Little swans he sought.

A. M. Novikova notes three basic types of lyric stanzas: (1) Songs with four line stanzas: AABB, but unlike the literary stanza, the content carries over to the next couplet:

> Between two white birches
> Between two white birches,
> Water flowed by,
> Water flowed by.

Variants of this are four-line stanzas where two or three lines of a refrain have been added. Another popular variant is the chain construction where the last two lines of one stanza are repeated in the next. (2) Songs with a three-line stanza with the second line repeated:

> Dear good man was walking down the road,
> Dear good down the high road,
> Dear good down the high road...
>
> And I after him, a girl,
> Ran following behind him,
> Ran following behind him...

A modification of this is a stanza of three lines with a repetition of one line, or three lines where there is a short refrain with the repetition of the second line:

> Mother gave me away
> To a large family,
> U-ukh, kha, kha, to a large family.

(3) Songs with two-line stanzas are very typical, particularly when the last line of the distich is repeated in the next stanza, another example of the chain composition.

> Willow, willow, my green one,
> Why, willow, are you standing so sadly?
> Why, willow, are you standing so sadly?
> Has the sun, willow, baked you?

Variations of this are when only the second half of the last line is repeated:

> Dear winter-winter, frosty one,
> Don't freeze me, a nice young man!
>
> A nice young man...
> A wife did not live with her husband in harmony.
>
> Did not live in harmony...
> She did not live in harmony and did in her husband....

The second line of the stanza may begin with a refrain and end with the last words of the first line:

> From out of the forest, the dark forest,
> Oi li, oi lyuli, dark forest,
>
> From out of the garden, the green garden,
> Oi li, oi lyuli, green garden...

In general, there are two types of refrains: (1) traditional, such as the *zvukopis'* ("oi, lyuli, lyuli" or "ukh kha-kha") used in different songs; (2) a refrain connected with the text and having a semantic or expressive function. Either lines of the basic text may be repeated or other lines may appear.

The major difference between the folk lyric and folk epic and drama cannot be based on Aristotle, who said lyric is basically monologue, epic narrative, and drama dialogue. There are numerous lyrics whose entire structure is based on dialogue or narrative, or narrative with a minimum of dialogue or monologue. The focus of the lyric is on the revelation of thought or emotion. Whereas an event or action of a hero may be emphasized in the epic, the lyric stresses the hero's attitude toward the event. Thus, for example, details are rarely given about reasons for the separation of lovers or concrete events connected with a betrayal; instead what is provided is a description of the effect this event has on the persona in the song. Similarly, events are connected in a song not through any logical tie in the real world, but through the emotional associations of the hero. Kolpakova has divided the lyrics into narrative and meditative. In the narrative type there is a situation which leads to action and creates a new situation, whereas in the meditative lyric there is mainly a complaint or an expression of an emotion. However, even in the narrative type the episode has no real plot in the Aristotelian sense of a complication-climax-dénouement. The subject is mainly a focus for expressing thoughts and feelings.

Symbolism is typical of many folk songs. Symbols may signify different things in different genres, and different aspects of the symbolic image may be emphasized. In wedding poetry, for example, the *kalina* (snowball bush) stands for maidenhood, or the image of the white snowball bush and its red berries may be compared to the bride's white face and red cheeks; in love lyrics, however, the bitter taste of the berry is emphasized and its bitterness may be compared to a life without joy. Within a genre, however, there is usually a set of symbols with relatively fixed meanings, for example in love lyrics a vineyard means joy, while wormwood, a rowan tree, and fog symbolize grief. Moreover, attributes that are fixed, such as the blossoming and withering of plants, where blossoming stands for life and joy and withering for sorrow and death, have the same associations in all folk songs. Sometimes, as in some of the ritual platter songs, the symbols were not noted by the collectors and are now difficult to decipher.

Many songs are characterized by PARALLELISM. Images from nature or the household are presented and then applied to the human situation. Usually a few lines at the beginning of a song present the symbolic image, which is then related to the human event; sometimes, however, an entire stanza is devoted to the symbolic image and the next stanza presents the human situation; more rarely lines within one stanza describing the symbolic situation alternate with the human event. In many cases certain images are typical of different types of songs. For example, often in bridal laments the bride tells of her dream, in which she walked through steep mountains and collected berries. The steep mountains are her grief and the berries her tears. In wedding lyrics the bride and her girlfriends are frequently depicted as swans, and the groom as a falcon who removes one of the swans from the flock. Sometimes the same type of images are used in different types of songs with similar situations. Both the robber and soldier, for example, live most of their life out-of-doors, away from their family, and in both robber and soldier songs we find nature images as a substitute family: their bed is the damp mother earth, the head of the bed the root of a tree, their blanket the gusty wind, and their weapon is their wife. There are also variations of these formulas, for example, their bed may be the feather grass, the head of the bed a white stone, their blanket the dark night. Both captured robbers and prisoners in general sing songs comparing their plight to that of a preying bird now sitting captured in a cage. The image of a caged bird also occurs in wedding lyrics, where the prospective bride visited by her girlfriends who try to comfort her is compared to a bird in a cage visited and comforted by its friends.

Negative parallelism with an implicit comparison through negation is another popular device in the folk songs. In a recruiting lament, for example, the song begins: "It is not a cuckoo cuckooing in a damp forest, not a nightingale loudly whistling in the green garden— a fine young man is sitting in slavery crying, pouring hot tears." A love song begins: "It is not a falcon flying in the sky,/not a falcon dropping a grey feather—/A young man is galloping down the road/ Hot tears pour from his bright eyes." The young man has had to leave his beloved. While most frequently parallelism compares objects or actions, sometimes it compares sounds, as when a trumpet's sound is compared to the crying of a young girl.

Often the parallelism at the beginning of the song takes the form of an address: "Why garden, garden of mine,/green garden,/why little garden have you withered, dried up?"—and then a girl asks her beloved why he is leaving her. In a variation of this, a cuckoo is asked why it is cuckooing, and it answers that it is alone in the garden which has dried up. Then a pretty girl is asked why she is grieving, and she answers she has been abandoned by her beloved. However, an

address does not necessarily take the form of parallelism. In many cases the address is descriptive and provides a setting or mood, for example a love song begins: "Oy, my birch/My curly, young one!" Then beneath the birch a young man parts with his sweetheart. In another address, the image symbolizes an obstacle that must be overcome before a girl can be reconciled with her beloved: "Oh, winter/you were nasty/, Kept snowing a snowstorm—/It's impossible to go to my beloved!" The song then continues that she will fly like a bird and reach her beloved, that is, the obstacles will be overcome.

A song may also begin with a narrative description of the setting, which is almost always generalized. An episode may take place in a meadow or on the road and rarely does a song get any more specific. Certain locations are typical of each genre, for example love songs usually are set in a garden, in the woods, or in a meadow, while soldier songs take place on the battlefield or if the soldier is wounded or dying, under a tree. Different parts of the day or seasons of the year may begin a song, depending on the emotional associations desired; for example, autumn or evening create a melancholy mood. Whereas the setting in certain genres such as love lyrics are usually realistic, those in others such as wedding panegyrics are idealized. Instead of a peasant hut the setting is in a palace, for example.

Another compositional device for beginning a song is termed "the gradual narrowing of imagery." There is movement from the general to the particular. The last image is considered the most important. Yu. M. SOKOLOV points to five types of narrowing of images: (1) the representation of nature (garden, meadow, tree, birds on the tree); (2) representations of dwellings (chamber, bedstead, table and feast); (3) description of apparel (costume or headdress); (4) family relationships (father, mother, young brothers and sisters); (5) social relationships (boyar, tradesman, peasant). While this occurs most frequently at the beginning of a song, it may also occur throughout the song.

Characterizations in folk songs are not portraits of particular individuals. Usually the characters are nameless or have typical names such as Dunya, Ivan, or Masha. There are formulaic descriptions for the various characters. In love lyrics there is the *dobryi molodets* (the nice young man) who has light brown curls, and the *krasnaya devitsa* (the pretty girl) with white face, crimson cheeks, and brows of sable. In other songs such as wedding lyrics, or wedding and agricultural panegyrics, the characters are idealized.

Fixed epithets which usually occur with particular nouns are typical of the folk songs. They fall into two basic categories: (1) descriptive, such as the green garden, bare field, and dark forest, and (2) emotional, such as dear friend, nasty mother-in-law. Epithets may appear before the noun, but frequently occur in postpositive position such as *polya chistye* (fields bare) or *tsvetki moi lazorevye* (flowers of mine azure). In wedding panegyrics the epithet is one of the main devices for praising the addressee, and each participant addressed is characterized by particular epithets. For example, the matchmaker is described as: *umna Aleksandrushka* (wise Alexandrushka) with a white face, crimson cheeks, and a peacock's gait. In a mocking song, however, similarly suitable epithets are applied to her characterization: she is unwashed and has a black face. The settings and costumes in these songs are similarly idealized or denigrated through epithets. In a wedding panegyric, for example, the participant may have velvet pants and a silken shirt, while in a mocking song his shirt may be full of holes and his pants ragged. Sometimes a series of epithets may appear to be illogical, such as "light-blue, crimson flower," but usually such epithets have taken on a more general meaning, as in this case where both "light-blue" and "crimson" are not descriptive of color but mean "bright."

Metaphor is another form of characterization. For example in a wedding lyric a bride may address her friends as *podruzhki-golubushki* (girlfriends-doves). Metaphors are also used to describe objects, such as when a soldier song describes a Cossack walking "with his comrade Sashenka, his sharp sword." In some songs an interrelated set of metaphors appears, such as in the soldier song where the hero says he has married another wife, a quick bullet gave him in marriage and a sharp sword betrothed him, where the underlying reference is death. Similes are not as typical of folk songs, although they do occur. Metonymy is sometimes used, as in a family lyric where the husband is not at home, but his whip is. Here, as in literature, the metonymy is symbolic, where the whip not only represents the husband, but his threatening relationship toward his wife. Synecdoche also appears in these songs, where, for example, an old man may be called "broad beard" or "grey beard."

TAUTOLOGY is frequently encountered in folk songs, where words which are different parts of speech but share a common root appear in sequence, such as *grom gromit* (thunder thunders). Another form of tautology which appears in the folk songs is that of paired synonyms, which can occur using different parts of speech, such as paired nouns—path-road, fate-lot, or paired verbs—got up-arose, walked-strolled.

Other devices include irony, where a word whose common meaning is the opposite in the given context, such as when a jealous husband comes home and is described as bringing a "dear guest"—a silken whip. There are also forms of personification, particularly of "grief" and "freedom." In a wedding song the bride addresses *volya* (personal will or freedom) and says *volya* came only before marriage, but after marriage there will only be hard labor. There are similar songs where a new recruit compares the freedom of his life now and the difficult life facing him as a soldier. In some lyrics grief is personified as a form of fate:

> I sow grief-sorrow
> Along the green meadow
> My sorrow grows
> Like tiny grass
> Does not fade or wither
> But blooms with the flowers.

Diminutives are used to provide emotional coloring toward what is depicted. Hyperbole is not typical of folk songs but does occur, as in the song where a girl "shed tears and drowned meadows."

The lexicon of folk songs is characterized by numerous words from local dialects. The syntax is often different from that of literary texts. Prepositions are frequently repeated, such as "*in the green, in the garden.*" Sometimes a noun will occur in one line and the adjective modifying it in the next in the same syntactic position, or more than one noun may be treated in this way as in: "It is not a sable rushing down the street, / It is not a black Siberian [sable] along the wide [street]." Similarly the first name and patronymic may occur in different lines: "You are my friend, Stepanida-dear! / You are my friend, Okhromeevna!" Lazutin has pointed out another typical syntactic feature of the songs. A word may appear first without a suffix, then with a diminutive suffix lending it emotional coloring, and finally with an epithet: "Vy lesa l', moi lesochki, lesa moi temnye" (You forest, my little forest, my dark forest).

Some genres are more fixed than others. While laments are always improvised, other songs within a given region may remain fixed over a period of time. However, a process called "contamination" often occurs, and a singer can create new songs based on formulae from other songs already known. This also applies to folk melodies. Sometimes this occurs not only within genres but across genres, as in the example described above, where a lackey, a manor house serf, tells the field serfs his life is harder. This is then adapted to a proletarian song where miners tell the field workers life in the mines is much harder. Parts of songs may be replaced by passages from other songs, related images may replace each other, as in the soldier song where the soldier's "bed" may be either the grass or damp mother earth; certain types of songs may disappear while others, like the CHASTUSH-KI, may appear, and songs may become more generalized, as when a proletarian song describing difficult conditions in one particular textile mill is then generalized to textile mills as a whole. In other genres such as the robber songs, some songs may describe a general setting, such as "on a river" while others may mention a specific river such as the Volga.

Thus the Russian folk singer is not only a performer but a creator who has available a rich store of traditional compositional structures, devices, and formulaic phrases, and the art of the singer is judged in terms of how well these possibilities have been employed.

Bibliography in English: Vladimir Propp, "Generic Structures in Russian Folklore," *Genre* 4 (1971), pp. 213–49. R. Reeder, *Down Along the Mother Volga.* 1975. Yu. M. Sokolov, *Russian Folklore.* Trans. C. Ruth Smith. 1971. I. I. Zemtsovsky, "Russian Folk Music." In *The New Grove Dictionary of Music and Musicians*, Vol. 19. 1980. Pp. 388–97. *Bibliography in Russian:* (1) Collections: E. B. Artemenko, *Russkie narodnye pesni.* 1974. P. V. Kireevskii, *Pesni. Novaya seriya*, vyp. 1 (1911), vyp. 2, chap. 1, (1917), chap. 2 (1929). S. G. Lazutin, *Russkie narodnye pesni.* 1965. P. V. Shein, *Velikorus v svoikh pesnyakh, obryadakh, obychayakh, verovaniyakh, skazkakh, legendakh i.t.p..* Vol. 1, vyp. 1–2. 1898. A. I. Sobolevskii, *Veliko-russkie narodnye pesni.* 7 vols. 1895–1902. V. Ya. Propp, *Narodnye liricheskie pesni.* 2d. ed. (Biblioteka poeta, bol'shaya seriya.) 1961. (2) *Specialized collections and secondary literature:* O. B. Alekseeva, *Ustnaya poeziya russkikh rabochikh.* 1971. L. A. Astaf'eva, "Simvolicheskaya obraznost' kak sredstvo psikhologicheskogo izobrazheniya," *RFolk* 14 (1974), pp. 109–18. D. M. Balashov, "O rodovoi i vidovoi sistematizatsii fol'klora," *RFolk* 17 (1977), pp. 34–35. V. Chistov, *Prichitaniya.* 2d ed. (Biblioteka poeta, bol'shaya seriya.) 1960. V. Dobrovol'skii, "Tsepnaya strofika russkikh narodnykh pesen," *RFolk* 10 (1966), pp. 237–47. V. I. Eremina, "Klassifikatsiya narodnoi liricheskoi pesni v sovetskoi fol'kloristike," *RFolk* 17 (1974), pp. 109–30. V. I. Eremina, *Poeticheskii stroi russkoi narodnoi liriki.* 1978. N. P. Kolpakova, *Lirika russkoi svad'by.* 1973. ———, *Russkaya narodnaya bytovaya pesnya.* 1962. N. N. Kravtsov, *Poetika russkikh narodnykh liricheskikh pesen.* 1974. A. M. Novikova, "O stroficheskoi kompozitsii traditsionnykh liricheskikh pesen," *RFolk* 12 (1971), pp. 47–54. M. P. Semenova, "Syuzhet i khudozhestvennoe vremya v pesennykh zhanrakh russkogo fol'klora." In *Voprosy poetiki literatury i fol'klora.* Voronezh, 1974. Pp. 32–44. I. I. Zemtsovskii, *Poeziya krest'yanskikh prazdnikov.* 2d ed. (Biblioteka poeta, bol'shaya seriya.) 1970.   R. R.

Folktales (*skazki* or *narodnye skazki*), the leading prose form of Russian folklore. Russian folktales are justly famous the world over, in particular the so-called magic tales (*volshebnye skazki*), corresponding to Western European fairy tales. Animal tales and moral tales are less well known outside Russia, though they are more specifically national and "Russian" in certain of their characteristics. The corpus of Russian folktales is extremely rich and diversified, so that it is difficult to make satisfactory generalizations concerning them.

Magic or fairy tales are usually regarded as a most ancient form of folklore, without question prehistorical and pre-Christian in their world view. Statistically they constitute approximately one-fifth of the entire repertoire of Russian tales. Well-preserved mythic elements are relatively rare in them, though there are some mythic references intended to explain the succession of the seasons, e.g., the figure of Ded-Moroz (Grandfather Frost) or the witch who keeps prisoner in a cage a bird representing spring, so that the bird must be liberated if spring is to come. The Russian folklorist Vladimir PROPP argued, nevertheless, that most magic tales are vestigial myths derived from passing rites, in particular the rite of male maturation; this principle is no longer understood by the folk, and hence mythic elements as such have greatly deteriorated.

Russian magic tales contain a rich trove of exotic characters and elements. Eastern influences seem to be more pronounced than Western, influencing the figure of the exotic Firebird (*Zhar-ptitsa*), which inspired the famous ballet by Igor Stravinsky (1910). The Russian witch, known as Baba Yaga, has quite specific characteristics: she lives at the edge of the forest in a hut on chicken feet; she rides into battle on a pig brandishing a pestle. Though evil, she may take pity on the hero and help him. A third figure is that of the evil enchanter Kashchei the Immortal, who cannot be killed because his soul is located at the bottom of the ocean on the head of a pin inside an egg, which in turn is inside a fish; he can, of course, be killed once the hero finds his soul. Ogres and dragons also figure in Russian tales as villains, though they are frequently replaced by the native bear in what is often a more comic and unquestionably more modern treatment.

The hero is usually nameless: he may be a king's son (Ivan tsarevich), but he may also be of common origin. Often he is one of three brothers (as in Western tales): his brothers fail to perform the exploit at hand, while he succeeds. As in the West, his success is often to be explained by the protection accorded him by some friendly power, sometimes won by an act of charity, such as giving a slice of bread to a poor old woman. His helper may be a Baba Yaga, but often it is a "wise woman" who befriends him and helps him achieve his goal. As in Western tales, animals play a considerable role as helpers of the hero: the most notable Russian example is the gray or gray-brown horse (*sivyi burets*). As Propp has shown, the hero rarely achieves his goal without assistance from his protector and without a talisman such as a magic sword or self-swinging club.

The hero's goals include winning a beautiful princess and an immense fortune; often magical labor-saving devices such as self-setting tables or flying carpets are won in the bargain. The quest accomplished, the tale ends, for there is no longer any suspense. It is obvious that these tales represent vicarious wish fulfillment on the part of tellers and listeners, especially since no very high level of virtue or courage is needed to win the prize.

Russian moral tales are likely of more recent origin. Though they lack much specific detail which would characterize them chronologically, they seem to be connected, for the most part, with the 17th and 18th centuries in Russia, and with a native Russian tradition and background (though Western, rather than Eastern influence seems detectable). No doubt the genre as such is far older than the 17th century, since similar tales are found in the Hindu *Rig-Vedas*; it seems to have been largely reformed in Russia during the 17th century, and even later. In Russian these tales are known as *bytovye skazki* (tales of everyday life); they are often satirical and invariably moral in their point of view. Similar tales are found in Western Europe, but it is interesting that the Russian repertoire of such tales is somewhat richer, and they constitute, taken together with the related anecdotes, almost sixty percent of the Russian stock of tales. Moral tales, unlike magic tales, usually avoid the supernatural.

Moral tales are often based on contrasts: the wise wife saves her foolish husband from trouble; the poor man triumphs over his rich brother; a wife is suspected of infidelity but exonerates herself by proving her chastity. Soviet scholars have tended to stress the "realism" in the portrayal of social life in such tales, but it is clear that they are highly stylized and schematic in their structure, and very like similar tales among other peoples.

As elsewhere, a group of "simpleton" tales is known, associated with the comic figure of *Ivan durak* (Ivan the Fool): the tales illustrate grotesque and hyperbolic examples of his folly, generally leading to his injury or death. It is curious that *Ivan durak* also plays a heroic role in certain Russian magic tales, where his folly is mere simplicity or the fraudulent characterization of his envious brothers.

Related to moral tales are anecdotes, shorter, often abruptly truncated narratives with a striking ending. Both genres, moral tales and anecdotes, contain many obscene examples.

A special subgenre of moral tales are tales of a deceived devil. These were more popular in the South, particularly in the Ukraine. In such tales a peasant often traps a devil who is trying to play some mischief on him, and forces the devil to do his will. This group of comic tales had a strong influence on Russian 19th-century literature, notably on PUSHKIN's poem narrative "The Tale of the Priest and His Workman Balda" (1830), and on GOGOL's story "The Night Before Christmas" (1832).

Animal tales are an extremely characteristic Russian group, accounting for some ten percent of Russian tales. Though they may well derive ultimately from primitive totemic conceptions, their modern function is ironic and satiric, and in this they are related to the Western European beast epos. Animals play human roles in these tales: they speak and dress like humans, and even get married and set up housekeeping together. Favorite figures are foxes, wolves, bears, cats, roosters, and hares, but birds and insects are also found. Dialogue is especially frequent in these tales, for which stylized, exaggerated intonations are used and striking contrasts prevail in the rendition of the speeches of the different animals.

Another group, considerably smaller, are soldiers' tales, usually of an adventurous character. Their details suggest that they are younger than most other tales, and they can most definitely be associated with the 18th and early 19th centuries. They have a pronounced picaresque character. In these tales a wandering soldier, often discharged from service and on his way home, undergoes adventures: he comes to a house of robbers, a house haunted by ghosts, or meets up with a witch.

There is a small body of Russian religious legends (*legendy*), often recounting miracles: in a popular example Christ and St. Peter wander over the world seeking to find a kind person and to reward him.

Traditions (*predaniya*) are hardly folktales at all and usually lack a developed literary form. They are short and recount unusual events, particularly associated with a given place or region. These may include natural phenomena (e.g., lakes and mountains are left by the

steps of a giant), as well as instances of witchcraft, sorcery, or demonology, such as the birth of monstrous children. Sometimes they etymologize local place names, e.g., the Russian city of Archangel (Arkhangel'sk), according to the tradition, was named for the appearance there of an archangel from Heaven.

In past centuries a certain professionalism is apparent among Russian tale-tellers, and Ivan the Terrible and Catherine the Great are known to have had their court tale-tellers. Tale-telling was very likely one of the occupations of the professional SKOMOROKHI or "minstrels" of past centuries. Even in the late 19th century, professional tellers were hired in North Russia and Siberia to tell tales to groups of men employed in guilds (*arteli*) doing common work together such as lumbering or fishing.

Still, in modern times tale-telling is primarily to be associated with amateur folk performers, usually peasant women. Some of these are also singers of epic songs (see BYLINA) or mourners, and these are still probably to be regarded as semi-professionals. But in most recent times folktales survive, if at all, among village mothers with infant children, and tale-telling generally ceases when the child starts to school. Recent times have also seen a tendency for tales to be formed out of popular literary narratives, such as Pushkin's *Dubrovsky*, A. K. TOLSTOI's historical novel *Prince Serebryany*, or Alexandre Dumas' *Count of Monte Cristo*.

Tale narration is associated with much use of exaggerated and often high-pitched intonation, particularly in the dialogue parts. There is a good deal of gesture. Dialogue tales exist, and these have sometimes been regarded as transitional forms between folktales and FOLK DRAMA.

Systematic collection of folktales began rather later than that of folk songs, and the first great collection was made by AFANASIEV, published 1855–1864; it has remained the classic Russian collection in spite of the appearance of many subsequent collections.

The literary influence of folktales has been enormous: notable examples include Pushkin's *Skazki* in verse, particularly the tale of the Workman Balda (1830–1834), certain of Gogol's stories, especially "A May Night" (1831) and "The Night Before Christmas" (1832), ERSHOV's verse tale *The Little Hunchbacked Horse* (1834), DOSTOEVSKY's novella *The Landlady* (1847), OSTROVSKY's play *Snegurochka* (The Snow Maiden, 1873), and many others. Besides these more or less specific reworkings of folktale motifs, one can find broad examples of folktale influence on narrative attitude and construction in many other works such as Pushkin's *Tales of Belkin* (1831) and AKSAKOV's *Family Chronicle* (1856). Folktales have also served as subjects for opera and ballet, sometimes operating through a literary intermediary, sometimes directly, e.g., Tchaikovsky's opera *The Red Slippers* (1876), or Stravinsky's ballet *The Firebird* (1910).

Texts in English: Russian Fairy Tales. Collected by Aleksandr Afanas'ev. Trans. Norbert Guterman. Folkloristic commentary by Roman Jakobson. New York, 1973.

Secondary literature: N. P. Andreev, *Ukazatel' skazochnykh syuzhetov po sisteme Aarne*. 1929. V. P. Anikin, *Russkaya narodnaya skazka*. 1959. E. M. Meletinskii, *Geroi volshebnoi skazki*. 1958. E. V. Pomerantseva, *Russkaya narodnaya skazka*. 1963. ———, *Sud'ba russkoi skazki*. 1965. Vladimir Propp, *Morphology of the Folktale*. Bloomington, Ind., 1958. S. V. Savchenko, *Russkaya narodnaya skazka*. Kiev, 1914. Yu. M. Sokolov, *Russian Folklore*. New York, 1950. Pp. 381–498.   W. E. H.

Folk versification. Broad distinctions based on mode of performance must first of all be made among sung or lyric verse (*pésennyi stikh*), recited or narrative verse (*retsitatívnyi stikh*), and spoken verse (SKÁZOVYI STIKH). Each mode has its own prosodic organization or metrical forms, and is associated with certain genres (PROPP).

The versification of Russian folk poetry has not been investigated nearly as thoroughly as that of literary poetry. This situation exists in part because of continuing disagreement over the prosodic principles operating in folk verse. In his historical survey on the study of folk versification, Shtokmar delineates four main approaches: the foot theory (HILFERDING), the tonic or accentual concept (VOSTOKOV), the syntactic foot (Golokhvastov), and the denial of any rhythmical organization (Shafranov). Many scholars reject the notion that literary and folk meters share any features; others express divergent opinions as to whether the musical or poetic rhythm predominates, or whether an interaction takes place between the two kinds of rhythm (Famintsyn).

The difficulties encountered in analyzing Russian folk meters are far more complex than those met in studying literary meters. Such factors as textual variation, reliability of recordings, genre differences, regional features, the gradual decline of the folk tradition, the distinctive language of folk poetry, accentuation, the process of rhythmic change, and the strong tendency to lose a fixed number of syllables per line (unlike the folk verse of other Slavic languages where isosyllabism is largely maintained) must all be constantly borne in mind. Nevertheless, detailed linguistic analysis based on the most accurate recordings of the most artistic performers can reveal many persistent rhythmical patterns and meters underlying individual realizations of a folk song (JAKOBSON, Taranovsky).

Many folklorists have noted that the poetic rhythm of songs disintegrates during a spoken retelling (a recording technique applied by many early collectors) and that accurate texts can be obtained only from a sung rendition. Consequently, one may conclude that folk songs normally exist in a musical performance and that some kind of dependent relationship arises between the musical and poetic rhythms. The rhythmical function of apparently meaningless filler particles, filler vowels, repeated prepositions, morphological variants, hypocoristics, elision, arbitrary rhythmical stresses, and various types of repetition emerges with full clarity only while a song is being sung.

Over the last two decades, investigation of the language of Russian folklore has developed into an independent field of inquiry (Artemenko, Khrolenko). While scholars on the whole concur that the linguistic medium of folklore constitutes a distinct subcode of the Russian language, they differ as to whether a folk work is expressed entirely within the regional dialect of the performers (Evgenieva) or is supradialectal (Desnitskaya). Ossovetsky considers that general Russian features outweigh dialectal elements and that folklore texts exhibit more linguistic uniformity than diversity. Jakobson and BOGATYREV suggest that folklore functions as the literary language of a local dialect.

One needs to maintain a healthy scepticism toward the reliability of printed transcriptions of folk songs. For instance, E. Gippius distinguishes several stages in the recording and publication of folk songs: the text actually performed on one occasion, the collector's field notes, the collector's subsequent final copy, and the published version. Textual changes, omissions, and errors may occur at each stage, but the chief modifications take place because recorders and editors intentionally or unintentionally tend to slant the language toward literary norms. While standardization of the phonetics makes a text more accessible to the general reader, changes in morphology and syllabification have serious consequences for linguistic and metrical study. Precisely for such reasons, Putilov and Chistov have stated that an awareness of textological questions should permeate all aspects in the study of folklore.

Accentuation must be taken into careful consideration during rhythmical analysis of folk songs because the stressing of numerous words may depart from literary norms (Korsh, Jakobson, Taranovsky). A few examples are: *bogátyr'*, *podnébes'e*, *ródnyi*, *sakhárnyi*, *séstritsa*, *sokól*, *svétlitsa*, and *tsvétnyi*. Some words, such as *mólódéts* or *zélénói*, may exhibit as many as three variant stresses. Accentuation in folk poetry has been little studied; unfortunately few collectors observe the practice of noting all non-literary stresses. Stressing can be generally classified as standard, substandard, dialectal, archaic, or arbitrary (stresses which have no linguistic correlates and are utilized solely for the sake of the rhythm). For instance, singers frequently stress the negative particle *ne*, verbal prefixes, prepositions in preposition-noun phrases, and the ending of adverbs with the suffix *o* (*bystró*); such accentuation was much more prevalent in Old Russian than it is in contemporary standard Russian.

While literary verse is founded on word prosody, folk poetry to a large degree is based on phrase or syntagmatic stress, although word stress still plays an important role. Such prosodic characteristics are most evident in traditional short-adjective and noun combinations, where the adjective acquires a phrase stress on the ending and the noun receives a word stress on the ending. These combinations usually contain four to six syllables; examples are *belá zaryà*, *na dobrá konyà*, and *za zelenó vinò*. It is often assumed that disyllabic nouns stressed on the first syllable lose their stress in phrases such as *na siné*

more or *vo chistó pole*, as would be the case in ordinary speech or in prose. However, in recordings where non-literary stresses have been consistently marked, the stressing will usually be *na siné morè* and *vo chistó polè*. Singers may employ this kind of arbitrary accentuation by analogy with pervasive rhythmical patterns, and also perhaps through an effort to coordinate the musical and poetic rhythms. Arbitrary stress shifts involve all parts of speech, and are so widespread that they should be regarded as being a traditional attribute of the language of folk songs and an inherent aspect of a musical performance.

Epics (BYLINY) and funeral LAMENTS (*prichitániya*) are performed in recited verse; historical songs, ballads, and spiritual verses (*dukhóvnye stikhi*) are ambivalent because they may appear in either epic or lyric verse. Narrative songs are usually "stichic," that is, they are executed line by line to a single repeated melody. While in north Russia epics are performed mainly by one singer, among the Cossacks in the south and east epic themes have been considerably shortened and have been transformed into lyrics sung in chorus. Epic reciters employ a number of different meters in their narrative repertory; most often they use an unrhymed dactylic clausula, but at times they resort to feminine or hyperdactylic endings as well. Although several subgenres may be discerned among the *byliny* (Astakhova, Propp), in the "high epics" the full epic line is composed chiefly in "free trochees" (*vol'nye khorei*) or in three-stress accentual verse (*aktsentnyi stikh, tonicheskii stikh, taktovík*); both meters ordinarily have a dactylic clausula, but accentual verse may also acquire hyperdactylic endings. "Free trochees" display a random mixture of line lengths containing mainly from four to eight feet (nine to eighteen syllables), but five- and six-foot trochees form the majority. Iambic lines constituting a variation of the anacrusis or line opening may occasionally develop. In three-stress accentual verse the intervals between main stresses usually range from one to three syllables. The original form of the short epic line, which is identified with the medieval minstrels (SKOMOROKHI) and is limited to songs about *Kostryuk, Gost' Terentii*, and *Shchelkan*, probably represents an eight-syllable line with stresses bound on the third and sixth syllables, and with a dactylic ending (anapest dimeter, x x x́ x x x́ x x), although singers may vary the number of syllables in the interval between main stresses and extend the clausula. North-Russian laments are also sung in shorter and longer lines, the trochaic tetrameter and trochaic hexameter, both of which have a dactylic ending (Jakobson, Taranovsky).

Other narrative meters appear in "lower epic genres" and are connected with specific themes. The ballad "Mat' knyazya Mikhaila ubivaet zhenu ego" is composed chiefly in trochaic tetrameter with feminine ending; the song "Vavilo i skomorokhi," which has been recorded only from Krivopolenova, consists mainly of trochaic pentameter lines with feminine ending; and some historical songs display basically a six-foot trochaic line with feminine clausula. The ballad "Brat'ya razboiniki i ikh sestra" appears essentially in two-stress accentual verse, which has a dactylic ending and an interval varying from two to five syllables between the main stresses. Three-stress accentual verse with feminine clausula is used in the satirical song "Ptitsy na more"; four-stress accentual verse appears in a few historical songs and spiritual verses (Gasparov).

On the basis of their studies of comparative Slavic metrics, Jakobson and Taranovsky have deduced that the Common Slavic epic line consisted of ten syllables with a caesura fixed after the fourth (4 + 6) and with a close marked by a long ninth syllable. The Serbo-Croatian *deseterac* and the Russian epic line developed from this single source; however, in Russian the caesura was eliminated and the quantitative close was replaced by a dactylic clausula so that the line received an additional syllable. After the loss of the weak jers and the emergence of stress as the distinctive prosodic feature, Russian epic verse acquired the form of the trochaic pentameter (x́ x x́ x x́ x x́ x x́ x); subsequently the line was gradually expanded between the second and third ictuses or metrical stresses (TRUBETZKOI). Such a historical perspective provides a means of explaining how the six-foot line became so common in trochaic epics recorded much later in the 19th and 20th centuries, and how the comparatively newer three-stress accentual verse came into existence. One pertinent instance of rhythmic change and of how the loss of isosyllabism could lead to the formation of accentual verse may be perceived in the two-stress line of the ballad "Brat'ya razboiniki" (x x x́ ... x́ x x); this meter probably developed from a syllabic loosening of the interval between the two bound phrase stresses in the lyric 5 + 5 form, which consists of two symmetrical five-syllable hemistichs divided by a caesura (x̀ x x́ x x̀ / x̀ x x́ x x̀).

Lyric verse appears in a wide variety of genres (Kolpakova, Propp), is performed chiefly by a chorus, and is usually stanzaic; however, some solo wedding laments sung by the bride may be stichic. Lyrics are differentiated by tempo; many dance songs (*plyasovýe pesni*) and round dance songs (*khorovódnye pesni*) may possess quick rhythms and regular poetic meters, while other lyrics may be performed slowly and have highly irregular verse. Stanzaic patterns, which are not always obvious in the poetic texts, are determined by the structure of the melody, which most often consists of a couplet corresponding to two poetic lines, although three- and four-line stanzas are also encountered (Dobrovolsky, Kulakovsky, Novikova). Many kinds of repetition and the use of a refrain may reflect adjustment of the text to the phrasing of the melody. The traditional Russian lyric song (*starínnaya pesnya*) is ordinarily unrhymed; when rhyme appears, it usually results from syntactic parallelism and occurs sporadically.

The "largo song" (*protyázhnaya pesnya*) represents a uniquely Russian manner of performing a lyric; the text is fragmented several ways according to the requirements of the highly embellished and continuously evolving melody (Zemtsovsky). Because isosyllabism is usually abolished in lyrics sung in the fashion of the largo song, the texts for the most part are unsuitable for metrical study. It is conceivable that the frequent loss of isosyllabism in Russian folk poetry may be ascribed to the development of the largo song. Nevertheless, in essence many lyrics still retain a set number of syllables per line and manifest a reasonably well-defined meter; one must turn to these songs for information about Russian lyric meters. One need not attribute all metrical verse in folk songs to the influence of literary versification after the syllabotonic reform in the middle of the 18th century. Singers create new works on the basis of long-existing rhythmical models in the same way that they compose new songs out of traditional linguistic materials (fixed phrases, motifs, and poetic devices) and adapt new melodies to older musical formulas (Goshovsky).

Metrists studying Russian folk versification have focused most of their attention on epic meters and have largely neglected lyric verse. For this reason, the typology of lyric meters proposed here is only tentative; more extensive investigation will probably reveal additional metrical forms, particularly those having a caesura. The first lines have been cited as examples from songs composed in each meter; the full notation for each meter is provided below the citations.

Meter	Clausula	Syllables	Example
Trochaic 3	fem.	6	Kák na réchke, réchke x́ x x́ x x́ x
Trochaic 3	dac.	7	V'étsya, v'étsya khmélyushko x́ x x́ x x́ x x
Trochaic 4	masc.	7	Na semnádtsatom godú x́ x x́ x x́ x x́
Anapest 2	dac.	8	Raznesló, razleléyalo x x x́ x x x́ x x
Trochaic 4	fem.	8	Kák u nás byló na Vólge x́ x x́ x x́ x x́ x
Trochaic 4	dac.	9	Otletála lébed' bélaya x́ x x́ x x́ x x́ x x
5 + 5	dac.	10	iz pod kámushka, kámnya bélogo x̀ x x́ x x̀ / x̀ x x́ x x̀
Trochaic 6	masc.	11	Kák po ránnei, ránnei útrennei zaré x́ x x́ x x́ x x́ x x́ x x́
Trochaic 6	fem.	12	Úzh vy kúmushki, golúbushki skazhíte x́ x x́ x x́ x x́ x x́ x x́ x
Trochaic 6	dac.	13	Chtó pod slávnym býlo górodom pod Shlyúshenom x́ x x́ x x́ x x́ x x́ x x́ x x

Dactylic or feminine endings are utilized most often in traditional lyrics, but a masculine clausula may be employed in satirical songs or in dance songs. Among the ten meters listed, the trochaic tetrameter with dactylic or feminine ending is the most frequent and appears in the widest range of genres; however, the 5 + 5 form and the anapest dimeter are also often used. The archaic 5 + 5 form may be the sole common lyric meter in Russian to have preserved a caesura. At least three kinds of accentual verse are utilized in lyric songs: a two-stress line with an interval between main stresses varying from two to five syllables and with a dactylic ending, and three-stress lines having either a feminine or dactylic clausula (Gasparov). Future study may elucidate specific genre associations for some meters.

The *chastúshka* is generally considered to have developed in the second half of the 19th century and to have been strongly influenced by literary verse. However, the chastushka, which is probably the most productive genre in present-day Russian folklore, did not achieve its definitive form until the beginning of the twentieth century. The chastushka, which is often sung to the briskly regular rhythm of an instrumental accompaniment, consists basically of a quatrain, which may be rhymed in several possible combinations and with various kinds of ending; the trochaic tetrameter is the most prevalent meter (Trubetzkoy, Lazutin).

Literary poets have often imitated folk meters, in particular trochaic verse. From the last part of the 18th century through the first half of the 19th century poets such as N. A. Lvov, Karamzin, Delvig, Tsyganov, and Koltsov employed trochaic meters in their folk song stylizations, which were in many cases termed "Russian song." The anapest dimeter and especially the so-called "Koltsov meter" (*koltsovskii razmer*), which was derived from the folk 5 + 5 form, were also often utilized (Gasparov). While writers such as Pushkin ("Pesni zapadnykh slavyan"), Lermontov ("Pesnya pro tsarya Ivana Vasil'evicha . . ."), and A. K. Tolstoi employed various types of folk accentual verse in the 19th century, literary poets developed accentual verse in poems not connected with the folk style only in the beginning of the 20th century. "Free trochees" with a widely varying number of feet per line have largely remained alien to literary poetry; nevertheless, Mayakovsky created his own form of this meter in a number of works (Gasparov). One could speculate that the history of Russian literary versification might have taken a quite different course if it had evolved out of indigenous folk meters instead of being modeled on Polish syllabic verse in the second half of the 17th and beginning of the 18th century, and then being patterned on German meters as a result of Lomonosov's reform.

In the final account, Russian folk meters should be studied within the context of comparative Slavic metrics in the way comparative Slavic linguistics, folklore, folk musicology, and belief systems are investigated. The results obtained from such a broader viewpoint lend support to the contention of Jakobson and Taranovsky that trochaic folk verse is much older than the syllabotonic reform of Trediakovsky and Lomonosov in the 1730s and 1740s.

Bibliography: E. B. Artemenko, *Sintaksicheskii stroi russkoi narodnoi liricheskoi pesni v aspekte ee khudozhestvennoi organizatsii.* 1977. A. M. Astakhova, *Byliny: Itogi i problemy izucheniya.* (Moscow and Leningrad, 1966). James Bailey, "Literary Usage of a Russian Folk Song Meter," *SEEJ* 14, no. 4 (1970), pp. 436–52. ———, "The Metrical Typology of Russian Narrative Folk Meters." In *American Contributions to the Eighth International Congress of Slavists* 1 1978. Pp. 82–102. ———, "The Trochaic Song Meters of Kol'-cov and Kašin," *RusL* 12 (1975), pp. 5–27. P. G. Bogatyrev, "O yazyke slavyanskikh narodnykh pesen v ego otnoshenii k dialektnoi rechi," *Voprosy yazykoznaniya*, 1962, no. 3, pp. 75–86. K. V. Chistov, *Sovremennye problemy tekstologii russkogo fol'klora.* 1963. A. V. Desnitskaya, *Naddialektnye formy ustnoi rechi i ikh rol' v istorii yazyka.* 1970. B. M. Dobrovol'skii, "Tsepnaya strofika russkikh narodnykh pesen," *RFolk*, 1966, no. 10, pp. 237–47. A. P. Evgen'eva, *Ocherki po yazyku russkoi ustnoi poezii.* 1963. M. L. Gasparov, "Taktovik v narodnom stikhe i ego literaturnykh imitatsiyakh." In *Sovremennyi russkii stikh*, 1974. Pp. 352–71. E. V. Gippius, "Tekstologicheskoe issledovanie." In M. Balakirev, *Russkie narodnye pesni.* 1957. Pp. 229–81. V. Goshovskii, *U istokov narodnoi muzyki slavyan.* 1971. R. Jakobson, "O sootnoshenii mezhdu pesennoi i razgovornoi narodnoi rech'yu," *Voprosy yazykoznaniya*, 1962, no. 3, pp. 87–90, and "Studies in Comparative Slavic Metrics,"

OSP 3 (1952), pp. 21–66. N. P. Kolpakova, *Russkaya narodnaya bytovaya pesnya* 1962. F. Korsh, "O russkom narodnom stikhoslozhenii," *Sbornik Otdeleniya russkogo yazyka i slovesnosti* 67, no. 8 (1901). L. Kulakovskii, *Stroenie kupletnoi pesni*. 1939. A. Maslov, "Byliny, ikh proiskhozhdenie, ritmicheskii i melodicheskii sklad," *Trudy Muzykal'no-etnograficheskoi komissii* 2 (1911), pp. 301–27. S. G. Lazutin, *Poetika russkogo fol'klora*. 1981. A. M. Novikova, "O stroficheskoi kompozitsii narodnykh traditsionnykh liricheskikh pesen," *RFolk*, 1971, no. 12, pp. 47–54. I. A. Ossovetskii, "O yazyke russkogo traditsionnogo fol'klora," *Voprosy yazykoznaniya* 1975, no. 5, pp. 66–77. V. Propp, "Zhanrovyi sostav russkogo fol'klora," *RLit*, 1964, no. 4, pp. 58–76. B. N. Putilov, "Voprosy tekstologii proizvedenii russkogo fol'klora." In *Izdanie klassicheskoi literatury*, ed. K. K. Bukhmeier. 1963. Pp. 17–58. M. P. Shtokmar, *Issledovaniya v oblasti russkogo narodnogo stikhoslozheniya*. 1952. K. Taranovsky, "The Identity of the Prosodic Bases of Russian Folk and Literary Verse." In *For Roman Jakobson*, ed. M. Halle et al. 1956. Pp. 553–58. ———, "M. P. Shtokmar, 'Issledovaniya v oblasti Russkogo narodnogo stikhoslozheniya,'" *Južnoslovenski filolog* 21 (1955–56), pp. 335–63. ———, "Roman Jakobson, 'Studies in Comparative Slavic Metrics,'" *Prilozi za književnost, jezik, istoriju i folklor* 20, no. 3–4 (1954), pp. 350–60. N. S. Trubetzkoy, "W sprawie wiersza byliny rosyjskiej," *Z zagadnień poetyki* 6 (1937), pp. 100–10. ———, "O metrike chastushki," In *Three Philological Studies*. Ann Arbor, 1963. Pp. 1–22. A. Vostokov, *Opyt o russkom stikhoslozhenii*. 2d ed. 1817. A. T. Khrolenko, *Leksika russkoi narodnoi poezii*. Kursk, 1976. I. I. Zemtsovskii, *Russkaya protyazhnaya pesnya*. 1967.

J. O. B.

Fonvízin, Denís Ivánovich (1745–92), playwright. A native of Moscow, Fonvizin obtained his secondary and university education at the newly founded Moscow University; in 1763, following his graduation, he moved to St. Petersburg and a bureaucratic career. In his spare time he undertook the translation of literary works from French and German, which served as preparation for the composition of his first original play, *The Brigadier*, written in 1768–69.

The Brigadier encountered an enthusiastic welcome, and proved a milestone in the history of the Russian theater. The plot revolves about a young couple, Sofya and Ivanushka, whose families are visiting as a means of becoming acquainted. There ensues a comedy of extra-marital intrigue, in which the fathers of the prospective couple pay court to the wives not their own, even as the fickle Ivanushka directs his attentions toward his prospective mother-in-law, thus competing with his own father. In the end those who sought to violate their marriage vows are put to shame, and Sofya finds her true mate in Dobrolyubov, a man who despises petty intrigue. And so Fonvizin upholds the ideal of the family founded upon mutual love and respect—between husband and wife, and also between parents and children. That ideal is embodied in the prospective union of Sofya and Dobrolyubov.

The Brigadier is better remembered in the history of Russian culture, however, as a satirical critique of contemporary Russian Gallomania, a critique voiced through Ivanushka and his prospective mother-in-law. Both pepper their speech with French phrases, and when Ivanushka learns of his father's interest in his prospective mother-in-law, he threatens to challenge him to a duel, for he has read of just such a thing in France and cannot bear to imagine he is "such a swine as not to imitate what has happened even once in Paris." More than any other single work, *The Brigadier* recalled Russian society to a sense of proportion in its infatuation with everything French.

Partly as a consequence of his initial literary success, Fonvizin advanced in the bureaucracy under the patronage of Count Nikita Panin, who at the time had a major hand in formulating Russian foreign policy. His personal situation improved in the 1770s: he was granted an estate in 1773 and married happily the following year, in addition to undertaking the first of several European trips in 1777–78. His bureaucratic star faded with Panin's resignation from government service in 1781, followed by his death in 1783 (Fonvizin eulogized him in a short biography published in 1784). But almost as if in compensation for this decline, his literary career achieved its zenith with the premiere in 1782 of his dramatic masterpiece, the comedy *The Minor* (Nedorosl'), now virtually the only 18th-century Russian play still sometimes staged in the Soviet Union.

Though humorous and witty, *The Minor* raises some very serious questions. The Prostakovs—brutal landowners given to abusing their servants—seek to marry their blockheaded son Mitrofan off to their ward, Sofya, when they discover she is heiress to Starodum, the voice of upright older traditions who suddenly appears upon the scene after a long absence. An attempted abduction leading to a forced marriage fails thanks to Sofya's beloved Milon; when Mrs. Prostakova attempts to punish her servants for their bungling she is relieved of her authority over them by order of the Empress, who will not tolerate further abuses. At the end Mrs. Prostakova, the play's negative hero, loses both her servants and her son's affections.

The central themes of *The Minor* are the problems of virtue and of social justice. Through the play's deus ex machina, Pravdin, the State acts to enforce virtue, to give force to its dictum that "no one is free to tyrannize over others"; in fact there is an absolute disjunction between the power of the State to enforce the good and the ability of Prostakova to bully her servants and even her family. Virtue is preached—often at great length—by Starodum ('Old Thought'), the play's *raisonneur* and positive hero. Starodum believes that a proper education should not so much train the intellect as inculcate moral values, and that, moreover, the State should so arrange things that those who behave virtuously receive material rewards. Indeed, Mrs. Prostakova's fate at play's end is an allegory of what ought to happen to those who violate the rule of virtue.

In 1785, while returning from a trip abroad, Fonvizin suffered a severe paralytic stroke, the results of which would affect him until his death. Toward the end of his brief life he was overcome with contrition for the sins which, he believed, were responsible for his physical ailment. He expressed that contrition in his unfinished *Open-Hearted Confession* (Chistoserdechnoe priznanie), a short but remarkable document of autobiographical revelation. During the 1780s Fonvizin also composed several fictional and journalistic works with political implications. In them he wrestled, among other things, with the precepts of virtue both in personal and public life.

Among Fonvizin's most interesting works are his travel letters, primarily those written during his trip to Germany and France in 1777–78, and to Germany and Italy in 1784–85. Fonvizin's reactions are always fresh as he records his responses to manmade marvels, his visits with leading writers and scholars, and particularly his observations on human nature and national characteristics. Fonvizin is very much the Russian patriot, although no chauvinist; his skeptical mind detected the weaknesses of nearly everyone, including individuals of great international reputation. He believed that intelligent and honest men were quite rare in any country, and that they formed a supranational class of people who recognized one another instantly; but that beyond this, Russian cultural achievements could hold their own with those of any other country, including France. Fonvizin believed the future belonged to Russia, and that the West was living on largely depleted cultural capital.

Works: Sobranie sochinenii. Ed. G. Makogonenko. 2 vols. 1959.
Translations: Dramatic Works of D. I. Fonvizin. Trans. and ed. Marvin Kantor. Bern and Frankfurt, 1974. See also: *Lewanski*, pp. 240–41.
Secondary literature: Charles Moser, *Denis Fonvizin*. (Twayne's World Authors Series, 560.) 1979. Kiril Pigarev, *Tvorchestvo Fonvizina*. 1954. S. Rassadin, *Fonvizin*. 1980. Alexis Strycek, *Denis Fonvizine*. Paris, 1976.

C. A. M.

Formalism, a trend in literary interpretation in Russia in the second and third decades of the 20th century. Its adherents emphasized the importance of studying the literary text rather than the author who had produced it. In particular, they addressed themselves to the study of literary language and its strategies. Thus formalism is flanked by two traditional disciplines: rhetoric and linguistics.

Formalism partially overlapped with FUTURISM, a trend in Russian poetry which likewise declared language rather than reality to be the focus of its attention. The formalist scholars SHKLOVSKY and JAKOBSON were also members of the futurist movement. Unlike futurism, however, formalism turned out to be remarkably influential abroad. Its methodology and assumptions about literature have contributed to a variety of developments in anthropology, linguistics, history, semiotics and of course literary theory. Some of its alleged influence might have been in fact mere convergence, a product of the zeitgeist rather than direct derivation. Even in such cases, however, the presence in formalism of the seeds of many important contemporary theories in the human sciences is worth noting.

The scholars associated with the movement were originally students at the Moscow and Petersburg universities and, later, teachers at the Institute of Art History at Petrograd: V. B. Shklovsky, Yu. N. TYNYANOV, R. O. Jakobson, and B. M. EIKHENBAUM. Among the lesser or otherwise peripheral figures, one should mention B. V. TOMASHEVSKY, V. Ya. PROPP, V. M. ZHIRMUNSKY, O. M. BRIK, L. P. Yakubinsky, B. M. Engelgardt, V. V. VINOGRADOV, and A. P. Skaftymov.

Several factors contributed to the emergence of formalism. The most important was the young scholars' impatience with the state of literary scholarship in Russia at the turn of the century and their desire to provide for literary study a solid methodology which would put it on a par with the natural sciences. The young students of philology and linguistics felt that their teachers of literary history taught history rather than literary analysis. Non-academic literary criticism, on the other hand, was dominated by SYMBOLIST poets and artists who were strangers to academic discipline and often identified idealist philosophy with criticism. In addition, cultural periodicals published works of "social" critics who saw in literature an expression of political and social ideas. None of these trends seemed satisfactory to the future formalists.

The second factor was the influence of Western and East European (including Russian) theories of language, literature, and culture. The Russian scholars A. A. POTEBNYA and A. N. VESELOVSKY, the Polish linguist Jan Baudouin de Courtenay, and several German philologists and historians influenced the formalists directly or indirectly at the time of their university studies. They sensitized them to problems of language and folklore, and they fostered in them an awareness of the necessity of minute documentation of one's theses and arguments.

The third factor was the rise of radical thought in Russia at the beginning of the 20th century. At that time, the Russian intelligentsia was becoming increasingly receptive to any inversion of old certitudes and fixed creeds in any areas of endeavor. The revolutionary atmosphere which it cherished provided a favorable breeding ground for any challenge to doctrines of the past. The formalists were ostensibly and defiantly radical in their irreverence toward both academic scholarship and symbolist philosophizing. Some of them adopted a dialectical and historicist method from the very beginning of their activity. Their revolutionary stance gained them the initial sympathy of those leaders of the October Revolution who were put in charge of art and scholarship. It allowed them to find employment and gave them an opportunity to teach their theories at the Petrograd Institute of Art History in the 1920s. Ironically, formalism was ultimately destroyed by the same forces whose support it initially enjoyed.

The fourth factor which helped to shape early formalism in particular ran counter to those mentioned above. It was a significant albeit convoluted influence of Kantian—or, more broadly, romantic—theories of language and literature which had been absorbed by the prolific symbolist writer Andrei BELY and which reached formalism through his writings. Bely's literary criticism anticipated Shklovsky's and Tomashevsky's classifications of literary devices culminating in statistical averages for the use of a certain device in an author's works. Bely engaged in the study of literary forms because he believed in their correspondences with the Absolute, whereas the formalists were interested in them for their own sake. Nevertheless, the overt results of their endeavors often were similar.

Furthermore, at the beginning of their activity some formalists adhered to the idea, essentially idealist and symbolist in nature, that literature, or art in general, makes one "see the world anew," deepening and refreshing one's perception of reality. The emphasis was on *how* this happens rather than on the nature of reality, but the positing of literature's ultimate goal was consistent with the thinking of the preceding generation of literary theorists. Shklovsky and Eikhenbaum were particularly prone to this symbolist influence. The other formalists did not argue against this idea but they did not pursue it any further.

The formalist movement dates back to the formation of two learned circles whose members maintained contact with one another: OPOYAZ in Petersburg and the Moscow Linguistic Circle in Moscow. The three collections of essays published by *Opoyaz* in the years 1916 to 1919 contain the first programmatic statements of the formalists. In 1923, *Opoyaz* was dissolved but its former members continued their activity in the Left Front of Art (LEF), as well as in the more academic setting of the State Institute of Art History in Petrograd.

While the formalists pushed forward with their articles, books, and occasional novels, criticism against them began to mount. It came from two directions. One was that of the official bureaucracy which saw in the formalists' insistence on the autonomy of the literary work a refusal to treat literature as a handmaiden of the Soviet state. Such was the criticism of the first Soviet Commissar of Education A. V. LUNACHARSKY. The other attack came directly from one of the leaders of the October Revolution, LEV TROTSKY. He, too, was dissatisfied with the route formalist criticism seemed to take. Instead of accusing the formalists of irrelevance or triviality of their pursuits, he accused them of maintaining links with the idealist philosophy of symbolism. What he objected to in particular was Shklovsky's idea of "seeing the world anew." In one of his essays he called the formalists "followers of St. John," i.e., believers in the metaphysical roots of language. He could have rested easy: formalism never developed in an idealist direction. Trotsky's and Lunacharsky's displeasure, however, ostracized the formalists and eventually forced them to modify or reorient their scholarly interests. In 1930, Shklovsky's public avowal of the "mistakes" of formalism officially ended the work of this movement in the Soviet Union.

What was new, or at least influential, in formalist research? Broadly speaking, its impact has taken two directions. The first is reducible to an addition of yet another layer to the fund of literary criticism, a new link in the positivistic progression from less knowledge to more. This aspect of formalism has captured the attention of many students of literature in the West who have used the critical tools developed by the formalists without inquiring into their philosophical implications. The development of this aspect of formalism proceeded as follows.

The Formalists placed great emphasis on the investigation of the literary work per se, and they insisted on the autonomy of literature and, by implication, of literary study. In "O literaturnoi evolyutsii" (1927) Tynyanov asserted that in order to become an independent branch of science, theory of literature has to review and revise its most fundamental concepts. In "Literaturnyi fakt" (1924) he said that such commonly used terms as *literature* and *genre* had not as yet been satisfactorily defined. Jakobson's insistence on "literariness" as the proper subject matter of the theory of literature, and Shklovsky's proclamation that "art is device" expressed similar views. At the same time, the formalists took issue with some current theories of literature. According to Shklovsky, literature is not "thinking in images," which is a shortcut to perception, but much rather consists in making the process of perception more difficult, in making the familiar unfamiliar and forcing the reader to reconsider reality rather than merely recognize it.

These programmatic declarations were followed by more specific studies dealing mainly with poetry. Yakubinsky and Brik investigated the arrangement of sounds in poetry and discovered in it various patterns which surpassed the generally known phenomena of alliteration and assonance. Zhirmunsky and Eikhenbaum analyzed individual poems from the point of view of both semantics and verse forms and arrived at readings somewhat similar to those of Cleanth Brooks in *The Well Wrought Urn* (1947). These and other poetic studies solved a number of disputed questions concerning the prosody of PUSHKIN and the relation between various schools in Russian poetry. They belong to the most indisputable achievements of the formalists.

Related to these are various attempts, more or less successful, to generalize these specific findings about poetry into a more abstract system. Tomashevsky singled out certain general features of poetic forms and literary genres, as he tried to systematize all literary genres in *Teoriya literatury. Poetika* (1925). On the periphery of formalism, Tomashevsky and Zhirmunsky wrote historical studies which rank among the most perceptive of their generation. Tynyanov tried to explicate his concept of literature by arguing in terms of "verse factors," "constructional principles," and "dominant features." He arrived at the concept of the literary work as a "system" which is a part of an even broader "system" of genre and, ultimately, of all literature. This and other formalist terminology (Shklovsky's "making it strange," "making it difficult," "slowing it down," "laying bare the device"; Eikhenbaum's "motivation") reappeared in the vocabulary of students of Russian literature in the United States in the 1960s and 1970s. Shklovsky's and Eikhenbaum's concepts have their roots in Aristotle's *Rhetoric* whereas Tynyanov's stem from a dialectical vision of literary development. This distinction, however, has passed unnoticed by those who saw in formalism merely a reservoir of technical concepts dealing with literature.

Formalist studies of prose fiction were grounded in a repudiation of the psychological approach. This led to a disregard for that dimension of prose fiction which has been of greatest interest to most readers. Shklovsky proclaimed Laurence Sterne's *The Life and Opinions of Tristram Shandy* to be the most typical novel of all times, because it fulfills best the precept (formulated by Shklovsky) that literature should turn upon itself, "lay bare its devices" and remind the reader of its artificiality. Clearly this judgement falls short of providing a profound insight into prose fiction. In the same vein, Shklovsky maintained that Cervantes' *Don Quixote de la Mancha* came about as a result of "stringing together" (*nanizyvanie*) anecdotes, proverbs, stories, and monologues for which the author wanted to find room in a single work of literature. The character of Don Quixote emerged as an accidental result of this process of stringing together motifs. Similarly, Eikhenbaum argued that TOLSTOI's works should be viewed as links in a chain of literary evolution rather than as expressions of personal convictions. Tolstoi's moral crises might have been unconscious attempts of a frustrated writer to find new means of expression and to invent new "motivation" for his characters and for the ideas they represented.

This method obviously runs counter to the common experience of literature. Its anti-empirical bias however proved valuable in analysing highly formulaic genres such as folktales. Accordingly, Skaftymov argued that the structure of the Russian folk epic (BYLINA) influenced the role in it of one of its standard heroes, Prince Vladimir. The role Vladimir plays in the *bylinas* is modest in comparison to those played by the less illustrious characters. This had to happen if suspense were to be maintained: the choice of roles for Vladimir has been limited by history and legend whereas the choice of roles for less well known heroes has practically unlimited. In his famous *Morfologiya skazki* (1928), Propp offered a classification of Russian folktales from the standpoint of the function which a hero, a situation, or a section of the plot fulfil in the tale. He listed the functions which in his opinion are essential to the folktale, and then proceeded to show how these functions could be fulfilled by very different characters or situations. Skaftymov's and Propp's analyses anticipate the semiotic studies of the 1960s and 1970s.

Among the studies which precede the rise of semiotics there is also the work of Roman Jakobson. Insofar as it concerns literature, it is centered in the idea that the function of literature consists in turning language upon itself, as it were, or turning the reader's attention from the referential aspect of an utterance to the utterance itself. Jakobson's concept of "literariness," first expressed in *Noveishaya russkaya poeziya* (1922), and his idea of "foregrounding the utterance" formulated in "Linguistics and Poetics" (1960) emphasize the structural aspect of literary expression and can easily be accommodated within the semiotic concept of encoded communication. Jakobson's contribution to semiotics (see STRUCTURALISM AND SEMIOTICS) however was channelled mainly through his post-formalist linguistic studies and therefore need not be considered here.

In these ways, then, formalism may be treated as "another contribution." But in other ways, it cannot easily be accommodated within the framework of the evolution of literary theory. In some ways, formalism was no less revolutionary than the October Revolution itself. And it is owing to this second set of features (related to the first but distinct nevertheless) that it gained so much popularity among strongly anti-traditionalist scholars in France and elsewhere.

This revolutionary aspect of formalism is perhaps most articulately expressed in the writings of Yu. N. Tynyanov, in such essays as "Literaturnyi fakt" and "O literaturnoi evolyutsii." Tynyanov's concept of literary dynamism which he formulated in the 1920s is a reworking for literary purposes of the Hegelian notion of dialectics as a theory of the unity and conflict of opposites. It is profoundly historicist in that it views literature not as the sum total of all literary works but rather as one colossal process of change. The struggle between literary forms is for Tynyanov the essence of the history of literature. The relationship between "material" and "form" in literature is forever changing. What is considered "material" in one literary period—

e.g., the genre of the personal letter in classicism—may become literary form in the following period. Elements considered marginal in one period may become primary in another, and some may disappear altogether and reappear sometime in the future. Such processes may appear obvious enough to a critic who believes in a representational function of literature; while such a critic would merely acknowledge them as such, however, Tynyanov wanted them to become cornerstones of a new literary theory.

Tynyanov regards dialectic as the logic of literature. In his view, all literary elements are perpetually at war with one another. It is this "war" rather than what literature overtly says, that constitutes the proper subject matter of literary study. The history of literature should be written from the standpoint of literary change because change is the essence of literature. In "Literaturnyi fakt" Tynyanov observes that to maintain that the psychology of the writer accounts for such and such literary phenomenon is like saying that the October Revolution derived from the personal characteristics of its leaders. Neither statement seemed acceptable to him.

The revolutionary nature of such postulates becomes apparent when they are juxtaposed with the approach represented by the otherwise similar studies of Andrei Bely or T. S. Eliot. Bely's literary scholarship implied a static view of literary forms and devices. The concept of literary dialectics was alien to him. Traditional Western theory of literature has likewise maintained that literary works derive from one another in a continuous sort of fashion, and that there exists a continuity of development of literary forms and genres. In contrast, Tynyanov maintained that the fundamental feature of every literary period is its discontinuity with the past. Shklovsky's remark that in literature, inheritance is not passed directly but goes "from uncle to nephew," somewhat like the moves of a knight in a chess game, is another instance of this way of thinking. Thus the idea of order implied, for instance, in T. S. Eliot's essay "Tradition and the Individual Talent" (1919) is foreign to Tynyanov's and Shklovsky's conceptions. Eliot's "alteration of the past by the present" is at odds with the formalist argument about the continuous struggle in each literary epoch between "recognized" and "underground" schools. Tynyanov's "evolution" is a misnomer: what he envisages is a revolution which takes place as one literary generation gives way to another. The "underground" schools are always ready to "pounce," should the established literary school falter. Only through such pouncing does literature develop. This perception of literary development finds its inspiration in the Hegelian principle of an incessant struggle between opposed elements of reality. Its profoundly dialectical basis is opposed to the similarly fundamental idea of Eliot's, namely, that there exists, in the mind or in reality, an absolute order which gives rise to meaning.

Disregard for the static concepts of traditional literary history led to a disregard for the evaluative procedures used by traditional scholarship. Tynyanov maintained that literary history should not be concerned with the "generals," i.e., it should not consist of description and praise of the great works of literature; rather, it should deal with second- and third-rate works in which the seeds of change can be seen more clearly. These works are frequently more indicative of the direction which a national literature will take in the future, and they are therefore more interesting than "canonical" works. Such assumptions generated Tynyanov's interest in political journalism and Shklovsky's fondness for the marginal works of Russian folklore.

An evaluation of formalism can be accomplished from several viewpoints corresponding to some extent with what has been indicated as the area of its impact. One of them has to do with the autonomy of literary studies. Since the times of romanticism and for a variety of reasons, the status of literary studies at European and American schools and universities has steadily grown at the expense of philosophy, logic, and other generalist disciplines. The formalists made their own unique contribution to this broad trend. By concentrating on the technical side of literature, they helped to strengthen the position of literary studies in the context of other humanistic scholarship. They helped to build up the current intellectual consensus that neither literary works nor literary research can be reduced to illustrations of historical or psychological developments. In this regard, they share credit with certain trends in literary scholarship of other countries, and Anglo-American New Criticism in particular. However, in many ways the formalists were more radical than the New Critics and therefore constituted the vanguard of the movement which claimed autonomy for literary research. While they have not succeeded in attuning the general public to technical problems of literature, they have strengthened the general adherence of literary scholars to the idea that literature cannot be treated primarily as a reflection of other areas of human activity. This idea has been fundamental to the teaching of literature at American universities since the 1950s.

Related to this idea of literary autonomy is the achievement of what may be called the methodological primacy of literary studies. Before the formalists came forth with their theories, literary scholarship derived its methodology from such disciplines as history or philosophy. Afterwards, this relationship has tended to reverse itself. In recent times, literary theory has posited certain general rules about language which were then applied by students of history, philosophy, anthropology, or indeed any other area of humanistic scholarship.

The best known instance of this methodological primacy is the development of the new generalist discipline called semiotics. Semiotics views all phenomena of signification as containing a common structure and therefore subject to certain common laws. The works of Propp and Jakobson were particularly important in this respect. Propp's study of the functions of characters in the folktale and Jakobson's work on the phonetic and semantic deformations of language in poetry, model the structure of literature in a way surpassing the ill-defined concern with "form" of the early formalists. Jakobson's emigration from the Soviet Union shortly after the October Revolution helped to disseminate this aspect of formalist research in the West.

The most significant aspect of formalist influence is to be found in the works of French and American structuralists. While the autonomy of literary study and the formulation of basic semiotic principles probably would have been achieved without the help of the formalists, the dialectical thrust of many structuralist studies seems to be directly derived from formalist theorizing.

The formalists, Tynyanov in particular, viewed literature as Marx viewed society (or, for that matter, as Hegel viewed all phenomena of nature and of the human world): as a process which consists of incessant struggle and entails unavoidable contradictions, or as a dynamic sequence of events whose ultimate importance depends not on some system or order external to them but on their relevance to the process itself. Inherent in this view is an absence of the concept of value which played a prominent role in literary theorizing until the 20th century. This concept of value was central to the works of the German neo-Kantian Rickert and of the Russian symbolist Bely. It obviously played a large role in those theories of literature which emphasized literature's didactic dimension. It was implied in the slogan of art of art's sake adopted by the French Parnassians. In all these cases, literature was valued because of things external to it: because it conveyed man's spiritual dimension, or because it represented man's idea of beauty, or because it prompted him to a good life, or simply because it was a characteristically human form of activity. On the basis of value, a selection and hierarchy of literary works could be established: some works could be considered better, or more valuable, others worse, or less valuable.

Such considerations are irrelevant to the dialectical framework adopted by the formalists. The implication of Tynyanov's programmatic essays is that all values inherent in literature are relative, subject to historicist reinterpretation and themselves products of it. A literary study which results from treating literature dialectically was postulated and practised by the French structuralists as well. Sometimes it merged with purely semiotic study, although the latter has tended toward a representational concept of knowledge rather than postulating a continuous and everchanging flow of signifiers whose signifieds are subject to incessant reinterpretation.

The dialectical concept of literary evolution returns to the social context of literature which the early formalists so vehemently denounced. In viewing literature as a part of the dialectical process of social change, Tynyanov anticipated the French structuralists who likewise reintegrated literature and society. This reintegration however has little in common with the traditional vision of literature as a product of human personality. The difference lies in the postulate of the dialectical relationship between society, the author, and his work. Thus, while on a certain level formalism can be said to advocate the autonomy of the literary work, on another level it claims rigid interdependence of social and cultural phenomena. On this more complex level, formalism and structuralism are again concerned with what literature "says," not in the sense, however, of conveying a message or "seeing the world anew," but in the sense of spelling out the relationship (usually unperceived by the writer) between the writer, the work and the social milieu. Accordingly, Shklovsky perceived Tolstoi's *War and Peace* as a result of a clash between class and genre, or between the form of the novel and the social realities of Russia at the time of Napoleon's invasion. Such readings are not intended to *uncover* a static meaning inherent in the work and grounded in some extraliterary order; rather, they *produce* a meaning. This produced meaning is in itself a result of a dialectical interchange between the social background of the reader, the work, and the author. Such concerns are perhaps best summarized in the French structuralist Claude Lévi-Strauss's remark in *La Pensée sauvage* that his work is meant "to contribute to that theory of superstructures which Marx barely sketched out."

It is ironic that the formalists were condemned in Soviet Russia for their allegedly bourgeois theories whereas in the West their links to a decisively anti-bourgeois ideology have been generally recognized. Soviet Marxists of the 1920s did not understand that in the long run, formalism could be made into an ally rather than an enemy of socialist literature because it proclaimed the demise of the traditional representational and value-oriented interpretation of literature. After World War II, however, revisionist Marxist scholars in the West correctly perceived that a significant part of formalist theorizing was grounded in a Marxist perception of the world.

It is also ironic that Western Slavicists have generally perceived formalist theory as a reservoir of technical concepts which could be used in discussing literature, rather than as an expression of a profoundly dialectical and historicist (as opposed to empirical or rationalist) world view. While Slavicists made use of the more traditional resources of formalism, the French structuralists seized primarily upon its ideological underpinnings. And when formalist concepts once more entered Slavic scholarship through the detour of French structuralism, many Slavicists failed to recognize in the strongly historicist writings of an Althusser or a Lévi-Strauss, the old and comfortable concern for craftsmanship which formalism once seemed to represent.

Selected texts: Formalism: history, comparison, genre. Ed. L. M. O'Toole and A. Shukman. Oxford, England, 1977. *Michigan Slavic Materials: Readings in Russian Poetics.* Ed. L. Matejka. Nos. 2(1962) and 5(1964). *Russian Formalism: a collection of articles and texts in translation.* Ed. S. Bann and J. E. Bowlt. 1973. *Russian Formalist Criticism: Four Essays.* Trans. and ed. L. T. Lemon and M. J. Reis. Lincoln, Nebraska, 1965. *Texte der russischen Formalisten.* 2 vols. Ed. W. Kośny. Munich, 1969–72. *Théorie de la littérature: textes des formalistes russes réunis.* Ed. and trans. T. Todorov. Paris, 1966. *Twentieth-century Russian Literary Criticism.* Ed. V. Erlich. 1975.

Secondary literature: Tony Bennett, *Formalism and Marxism.* London, 1979. Victor Erlich, *Russian Formalism: History-Doctrine.* 3d ed. 1981. Fredric Jameson, *The Prison-House of Language.* 1972. P. N. Medvedev and M. M. Bakhtin, *The Formal Method in Literary Scholarship: A Critical Introduction to Sociologist Poetics.* Trans. A. J. Wehrle. 1978. Originally published under the title *Formal'nyi metod v literaturovedenii,* 1928. Krystyna Pomorska, *Russian Formalist Theory and its Poetic Ambiance.* The Hague, 1968. R. H. Stacy. *Russian Literary Criticism: A Short History.* 1974. E. M. Thompson. *Russian Formalism and Anglo-American New Criticism: A Comparative Study.* The Hague, 1971.   E. Th.

Formalism, aesthetic concept. (Latin *forma*, figure, shape, model; *formalis*, pertaining to shape or form.) A trend in art criticism which posits that the value and originality of a work of art reside in its form. In this sense, formalism found its vigorous spokesmen in Central Europe toward the end of the 19th century and beginning of the 20th. The Austrian literary historian Oskar Walzel (1864–1944) postulated the existence in a literary work of a gestalt, or inner form, which "conforms to the purpose of an individual work of art" rather than being a reflection of some general pattern common to a certain literary genre. The Swiss art historian Heinrich Wölfflin (1864–1945) postulated that the change of form in art lies at the core of artistic change in general. To prove this, Wölfflin analysed the formal changes in neoclassical and romantic painting.

Walzel's and Wölfflin's ideas go back to the writings of European romantics. The German philosopher August Wilhelm Schlegel argued that Shakespeare's plays are possessed of "organic form" and therefore satisfy the "formal" requirement even though they do not conform to the rules for tragedy laid down by the French neo-classicists. In England, S. T. Coleridge spoke of "mechanical" and "innate" form in the works of literature. The Austrian music critic Eduard Hanslick (1825–1904) likewise postulated the existence of "inner form" in music. Ultimately, such ideas go back to Plotinus who saw artistic form as inseparable from the work of art and impossible to verbalize.

All these thinkers view the literary form as an organic part of a work of art. It is inseparable from content and is, in fact, a part of the content. In contrast, a "mechanical" approach to form can be found in the rules concerning style and genre in French neo-classicism, in Boileau's L'Art poétique (1674) in particular. A revival of interest in the perfection of artistic form occurred among the French Parnassians in the 1830s. The representative poet and critic Théophile Gautier maintained that the achievement of formal beauty (reflected in rhythm, versification and phraseology) was the most important poetic task.

In Russia, a content-oriented aesthetic has dominated at least since BELINSKY, who resolutely rejected all formalist thinking. Among Belinsky's successors, the radicals, such as CHERNYSHEVSKY and DOBROLYUBOV, considered any concern with form trivial or frivolous, while right wing critics, such as GRIGORIEV or STRAKHOV, who held form in higher esteem, believed nevertheless that form was secondary to ideal content, so that even "so-called technical blunders of an artist derive from some moral source, from an attitude toward the problem in question which is not perfectly straight and clear" (Grigoriev). Even members of the "aesthetic school" (DRUZHININ, ANNENKOV, etc.) insisted that form should be inseparably and organically linked with content. Only in symbolist aesthetic did form come into its own, with "decadents" like BRYUSOV assuming a position close to that of the French Parnassians, and mystics like Vyacheslav IVANOV perceiving the creative process as "inner form" (forma formans) growing into a manifest work of art (forma formata). In Russian FORMALISM, the concepts of "content" and "form" received an entirely novel treatment. The official position of Soviet criticism has been unalterably opposed to any kind of formalism.

Bibliography: Etienne Gilson, *Forms and substances in the arts.* Trans. S. Attanasio. 1960. Adolf von Hildebrand, *The Problem of Form in Painting and Sculpture.* Trans. M. Meyer et al. 1978. René Wellek, "Concepts of Form and Structure in Twentieth-Century Criticism." In *Concepts of Criticism.* 1963. Pp. 54–68.   E. Th.

Forsh, Ólga Dmítrievna (1873–1961), was born in Daghestan, the daughter of General D. V. Komarov, and studied painting in Kiev, Odessa, and St. Petersburg. She made her debut as a writer of articles and short stories about romantic seekers dissatisfied with empirical reality and tormented by ideas from various philosophies, including theosophy. After brief administrative and editorial assignments for the new Soviet government in Moscow and Kiev, she settled permanently in Leningrad, making the city and its history her major literary themes.

Dressed in Stone (Odety kamnem, 1924–25) juxtaposes true and false 19th-century revolutionaries against the backdrop of the Peter and Paul Fortress. *Contemporaries* (Sovremenniki, 1926) explores the opposition between mediocrity and talent in art and features GOGOL and the painter A. A. Ivanov. Other important historical novels include the *Radishchev* trilogy: *Jacobin Ferment* (Yakobinskii zakvas, 1932), *A Landed Lady of Kazan* (Kazanskaya pomeshchitsa, 1934), *Fateful Book* (Pagubnaya kniga, 1939). *Mikhailovsky Castle* (Mikhailovskii zamok, 1946) vividly depicts the Pauline era and its two foremost architects, V. Bazhenov and A. Voronikhin. Her last historical novel, *Firstborn of Freedom* (Perventsy svobody, 1950–53), gives an annalistic treatment of the Decembrist uprising. *Hot Shop* (Goryachii tsekh, 1926), *Crazy Ship* (Sumasshedshii korabl', 1931), and *The Raven* (Voron, 1933, as *Simvolisty*) are all fictionalized memoirs. The first portrays the revolutionary workers and soldiers of 1905 to 1907; the second recreates the Petrograd *Dom iskusstv* (House of the Arts) in the early 1920s, the third resurrects the Petersburg intelligentsia of the preceding decade. Of lesser importance are

the frequently satirical short stories and novellas, plays and filmscripts on contemporary and historical themes, and children's stories.

In her fondness for the grotesque and her overwrought, ornamental, expressionistic prose style, Forsh recalls Gogol, Dos-TOEVSKY, BELY, and REMIZOV. Her sketches of contemporaries reveal a flair for keen, laconic psychological portraiture.

Works: Sobranie sochinenii. 7 vols. 1928–1930. *Sobranie sochinenii.* 8 vols. 1962–1964. "Avtobiografiya." In *Sovetskie pisateli.* Vol. 2. 1959.

Translations: Palace and Prison. Trans. F. Solasko. Moscow, 1958. *Pioneers of Freedom.* Moscow, 1954.

Secondary literature: N. Lugovtsov, *Tvorchestvo Ol'gi Forsh.* 1965. R. Messer, *Ol'ga Forsh.* 1965. A. Tamarchenko, *Ol'ga Forsh: Zhizn', lichnost', tvorchestvo.* 1974. R. A. Skaldina, *O. D. Forsh: Ocherk tvorchestva 20–30 gg.* 1974.   C. N. L.

Fortunátov, Filipp Fyódorovich (1848–1914); Professor at Moscow University, academician, leading Russian Indo-Europeanist and student of contemporary Russian.

Fortunatov's career at Moscow University (1876–1902) coincided with the triumph of the Neogrammarian approach to language of which he was the foremost Russian representative, but which he partially overcame by rejecting the notion of a single Indo-European proto-language, by shifting attention from reconstruction to the history of individual languages and by his interest in the synchronic aspects of language. His many-sided scholarly and teaching activities established him as head of the Moscow School of Linguistics which produced a whole generation of distinguished Russian and foreign linguists (SHAKHMATOV, Porzhezhinsky, Peshkovsky, Peterson, Ushakov, Pokrovsky, Budde; Broch, Belić, H. Pedersen, Boyer, Berneker, Mikkola); his influence on Western linguistics was small, however, because of his limited written output. The significance of his contribution can be gleaned only from the lectures and articles gathered in his posthumous *Izbrannye trudy* (2 vols, 1956).

Like the Neogrammarians in the West, Fortunatov was interested primarily in the reconstruction of the early Indo-European (IE) sound system but, unlike them, he posited the existence of dialectal differences in the oldest phases of IE and assumed the existence of a large inventory of original sounds. He devoted special attention to the study of IE vowels and sonants and to their concomitant prosodic features. He is credited, together with F. de Saussure, with the discovery of the rules of Balto-Slavic accentuation, though his extension of the so-called Saussure law to Slavic (a law which Saussure formulated only for Lithuanian) has proven to be an over-hasty generalization.

In his analyses of modern Russian, Fortunatov pursued a strictly formal approach which ascribed primary importance to the inflectional peculiarities of Russian but which neglected their semantic properties. In the field of syntax he emphasized the binary and hierarchical organization of syntactic constituents, but his approach, which was largely psychological, failed to point out the distinction between the phrase (*slovosochetanie*) and the sentence.

Bibliography: F. M. Berëzin, *Ocherki po istorii yazykoznaniya v Rossii: Konets XIX – nachalo XX v.* Pp. 28–99. M. G. Bulakhov, *Vostochno-slavyanskie yazykovedy.* Vol. 1. 1976. Pp. 264–72. M. N. Peterson, Introduction to F. F. Fortunatov, *Izbrannye trudy* (1956), pp. 5–16.   E. S.

Frank, Semyón Lyúdvigovich (1877–1950), Russian religious philosopher, political economist, sociologist, and author of a number of original essays on Russian and West European writers; publicist and educator. In his youth Frank was a Marxist and an atheist. At the beginning of the century he came to philosophical idealism and later to religious philosophy and the Russian Orthodox Church (1912). Politically, he was a follower and, for many years, a close collaborator of P. B. STRUVE in several of his periodicals. He also took part in three famous Moscow collections of essays: *Problems of Idealism* (Problemy idealizma, 1902), *Landmarks* (VEKHI, 1909), and *From the Depths* (Iz glubiny, 1918; Paris, 1967). In 1922 he was expelled from Russia by the Soviet authorities. He then lived in Germany until 1937, in France until 1945, and for the rest of his life in England.

Frank studied political economy at Moscow University and economics and philosophy at the universities of Berlin and Munich. Since 1906 he taught at several private institutions of higher learning in St. Petersburg, at St. Petersburg University (1912–17), the University of Saratov (1917–21), Moscow University (1921–22), and, in exile, at the Russian Scientific Institute in Berlin (1923–32) and the University of Berlin (1931–33).

Like Vladimir SOLOVYOV and N. O. LOSSKY, Frank was a systematic philosopher. His writings cover epistemology, logic, metaphysics, anthropology, and ethics, and are unified by his concept of *Vseedinstvo* (all-unity).

Among Frank's numerous books, the posthumous *Studies on Pushkin* (Etyudy o Pushkine, Munich, 1957), is devoted entirely to one major literary figure. However, Frank also authored many important essays in Russian, German, and Dutch on Dostoevsky, L. Tolstoi, Gogol, Leontiev, Tyutchev, M. Gorky, Goethe, Nietzsche, Rainer Maria Rilke, and other writers. A distinguishing trait of Frank's writings is clarity of structure and thought and simplicity and elegance of style.

Bibliography: Bibliographie des Oeuvres de Simon Frank. Etablie par Vasily Frank. Paris, 1980. *Sbornik pamyati Semena Lyudvigovicha Franka*. Ed. Very Rev. Vasilii Zen'kovskii. [Munich], 1954. (Includes a bibliography by L. A. Zander, pp. 177–192).

Secondary literature: N. O. Lossky, *History of Russian Philosophy*. New York, 1951. Pp. 266–92. V. V. Zenkovsky, *A History of Russian Philosophy*. Two vols. Trans. George L. Kline. 1953. Pp. 852–72. S. A. Levitskii, "S. L. Frank," In *Russkaya religiozno-filosofskaya mysl' XX veka*. Ed. N. P. Poltoratskii. Pittsburgh, 1975. Pp. 372–82.   N. P. P.

Freemasonry in Russian literature. During the 18th and first quarter of the 19th centuries, many Russian writers were attracted to the Society of Freemasons. Begun in England in 1717 but tracing its rituals back to the building of the Temple of Solomon and the guilds of working stonemasons of the Middle Ages, Freemasonry reached Russia by the 1730s (when the first Russian lodges were founded by foreigners) but became a truly important factor in Russian literature only from the late 1770s through the first third of the 19th century. Although Freemasonry was frequently suppressed or temporarily banned from the early 1790s through 1802 and was officially prohibited with Alexander I's abolition of all secret organizations in Russia in 1822, Freemasonry figured prominently in Russian literature through the end of the 19th century.

Among the 18th-century writers who joined the Freemasons were A. P. SUMAROKOV, M. M. KHERASKOV, N. I. NOVIKOV, V. I. MAIKOV, A. N. RADISHCHEV, N. M. KARAMZIN, A. A Rzhevsky, and V. I. LUKIN; 19th-century Masons included A. S. PUSHKIN, A. S. GRIBOEDOV, V. A. ZHUKOVSKY, P. A. VYAZEMSKY, N. I. GRECH and such Decembrist writers as K. F. RYLEEV, A. A. BESTUZHEV (pseudonym Marlinsky), A. I. ODOEVSKY, and V. K. KYUCHELBEKER. Although some of these writers "played with Freemasonry like a toy" (in the phrase of N. I. Novikov) and others (especially the Decembrist writers) used Freemasonry as a base for their political activities, many writers (e.g. Kheraskov, Maikov, Novikov, and, to a lesser extent, Sumarokov) took their Masonry quite seriously and used it as a source for literary symbols and allegories. As a result, Masonic symbols and rituals occasionally provide important clues necessary for "decoding" 18th century novels (such as Kheraskov's *Cadmus and Harmonia* [Kadm i Garmoniya, 1st ed. 1789], which has recently been interpreted along Masonic lines).

In Russia, as elsewhere, Masonic literature often was "constructed" upon metaphors and symbols of building and architecture. Using the basic image of "construction" of an inner temple that would restore man to the lost spiritual state of Eden, Masonic literature frequently depicted the process of shaping "rough stone" (symbol of the post-Fall, pre-Masonic state of man) into a finished building (the Mason who has passed through all the stages or "degrees" of Freemasonry and been initiated into Masonic truths). Often, the hero of Masonic literature is sent on a journey, where he becomes entrapped in a labyrinth (representing the ruts of man's everyday life) but is ultimately freed with the help of a wiser man (representing

the Masonic master, who offers the lost man the "thread of the sciences of Solomon"). While entrapped, the Masonic hero often undergoes a ritual death, and upon his release he is reborn into an Edenic state of the kind lost by Adam in the Fall. This typical hero's adventures were well summarized by M. M. Kheraskov in the preface to the 1809 edition of his Masonic epic *Vladimir Reborn* (Vladimir vozrozhdennyi): "The wanderings of an attentive man along the path of truth, on which he meets with worldly enticements, is subjected to many temptations, falls into the darkness of doubt, and fights with his inner passions; he finally gains control over himself, finds the path of truth, and, after attaining enlightenment, is reborn." Such descriptions apply equally well to many works of European Masonic fiction (such as Schikaneder's libretto for Mozart's Masonic opera *The Magic Flute*) and reflect the fact that Masonic fiction throughout the world partook of similar plots, symbols, allegories, and sometimes even characters. The Masonic idea of life as a pilgrimage or a journey with distinct paths that lead to both "right" and "wrong" connects Masonic fiction to such other didactic genres as the chivalric romance, the BILDUNGSROMAN, and the baroque novel of testing (the *Prüfungsroman*), which all had influenced Masonic literature.

During the first decades of the 19th century Freemasonry provided a model for the organization and rituals of a number of secret societies and was perhaps more important as a social force than as a literary scheme. Since many of the Decembrists were at one time Masons it is not surprising that they borrowed ideas, images, initiation rites, "degrees," and in some cases even the names (e.g., the name *Les Slaves Réunis* used by the Southern Society) of Masonic lodges. More surprising is that some 19th-century literary Masons actually parodied Freemasonry at some point in their careers. For example, the "brotherhood" of ARZAMAS, which consisted largely of former Masons, included a mock-initiation ceremony devised by Zhukovsky which parodied the ceremony of the Masons, leading the poet Vyazemsky to jest that Arzamas was a kind of "literary Masonry." Recent research has also suggested that Pushkin's 1834 tale *The Queen of Spades* (Pikovaya dama) was probably intended as a parody of Masonic ritual and its Gothic reminder to "remember death" (*memento mori*).

As an important social force in 19th-century Russia, Freemasonry also figures in a number of historical novels written by non-Masons about the Napoleonic and Decembrist eras, including L. N. TOLSTOI's *War and Peace* (1869), where in Book II, Part 2 (= "Book Five" in some English translations) Pierre Bezukhov becomes a Freemason as part of his quest for the "meaning of life." Based on intensive manuscript research on Freemasonry and Masonic ritual conducted by Tolstoi at Moscow's Rumyantsev Museum in 1866, the Masonic sections reflect Tolstoi's distrust of artificial solutions to the problems of life and his sentiment expressed in a November 15, 1866, letter to his wife that "the sad thing about these Masons was that they were all fools." In *War and Peace*, Tolstoi is more negative to the Masons than he had been in his earlier work *Two Hussars* (Dva gusara, 1856), where he had simply referred to the "naive times of the Masonic lodges, the Martinists, and the Tugendbund." After meeting the Mason Bazdeev on (significantly) a journey, Pierre is inducted into the Masons and instructed in a most un-Tolstoian philosophy that "no one can reach the truth by himself": "Only by placing stone upon stone with the cooperation of everyone ... can the temple be built which is a worthy dwelling of the Great God [who dwells within man]." Throughout the Masonic sections, Tolstoi ridicules the naiveté, hypocrisy, and complacency of the Masons who pretend to be reforming the world but are often pursuing their own pleasure and self-interest.

Unlike Tolstoi, A. F. PISEMSKY in his historical novel *The Masons* (Masony, 1880), which deals with individual Masons in the 1830s after the prohibition of the Masonic movement, admires the idealism of sincere Masons like his hero Egor Marfin, who attempts to put his Masonic precepts into practice but is ultimately unable to defeat the evil realities of provincial Russia. Although Pisemsky (who had also devoted a chapter of an earlier work—*The Troubled Sea* [Vzbalamuchennoe more], 1863—to the Masons) occasionally derides the artificiality of Masonic rituals, he is far more balanced and positive towards individual Masons than was his famous contemporary.

Parallel to the literature of Freemasonry since the end of the 18th century, there has been a strong anti-Masonic current in Russian literature, reflected as early as the three anti-Masonic comedies written during the 1780s by CATHERINE the Great herself (*The Deceiver, The Deluded,* and *The Siberian Shaman*), who identified the Masons with charlatans like Cagliostro or those gullible enough to be deceived by them. Eighteenth-century sources ranging from N. G. Kurganov's *Russian Universal Grammar* (which in some editions contained a "Psalm on the Unmasking of the Freemason" claiming that the Masonic secret "is found in the sum 666") to DERZHAVIN's "Felitsa" (which praised Catherine the Great for "not going from the throne to the East," i.e. to the Masonic lodge to which many of her courtiers belonged) identified the Masons with evils ranging from the Antichrist through Stenka Razin and the robber Vanka Kain. In a similar vain, V. T. NAREZHNY in his *The Russian Gil Blas* (Rossiskii Zhil'blaz, 1814) depicted the Masons as organizing orgies. But one of the strongest condemnations of the Masons in 19th-century Russian literature appeared long after the prohibition of the Masons in F. M. DOSTOEVSKY's *The Brothers Karamazov* (1880) in the section entitled "The Grand Inquisitor" where Ivan Karamazov claims that the spirit of the Grand Inquisitor and of the Catholic Church as a whole lives on among the Masons. Both the Catholic Church and the Masons, according to Ivan, use the ideas of "miracle, mystery, and authority" (or, in an earlier draft, "slavery, servitude, and mystery") to keep weak men from having to use their "freedom of choice in the knowledge of good and evil" and to deceive them into thinking themselves happy. Like the Church, Ivan implies, the Masons are working not with Christ but with "him" (the devil), and thus the Church so strongly opposes the Masons because they provide competition and break the unity of the fold. At the conclusion of Ivan's story of the Grand Inquisitor, Alyosha Karamazov asks his brother whether he himself is a Mason since he does not believe in God, naively implying an equation between atheists and Masons.

Dostoevsky's condemnation of the Masons reflected his fear of all rationalist, utopian schemes which inevitably invite weak men to exchange their freedom for "happiness." In condemning the Masons, Dostoevsky recognized the utopian essence of their movement, which had striven to restore man's lost paradise through the improvement of morals. Given the central role of the search for heaven-on-earth in Russian culture since the 10th century, it is not surprising that the European currents of Freemasonry found many adherents in 18th and early 19th-century Russia. The specific impact of Freemasonry on individual works of Russian literature has still not been adequately explored and presents fertile ground for future research.

Bibliography: Stephen Baehr, "The Masonic Component in Eighteenth-Century Russian Literature." In A. G. Cross, ed. *Russian Literature in the Age of Catherine the Great.* Oxford, 1976. Pp. 121–40. ———, "Freemasonry in Russian Literature: Eighteenth Century," *MERSL,* forthcoming. Lauren Leighton, "Gematria in 'The Queen of Spades'," *SEEJ* 21 (1977), pp. 455–69. ———, "Freemasonry in Russian Literature: Nineteenth Century," *MERSL,* forthcoming. ———, "Pushkin and Freemasonry: 'The Queen of Spades'." In George Gutsche and Lauren Leighton, eds., *Studies in Nineteenth-Century Russian Literature.* 1982. Pp. 15–23. ———, "Freemasonry in Russia: The Grand Lodge of Astraea (1815–1822)," *SEER* 60 (1982), pp. 244–61. Harry Weber, "*Pikovaja dama*: A Case for Freemasonry in Russian Literature," *SEEJ* 12 (1968), pp. 435–47.
S. B.

Free Society of Amateurs of Letters, Sciences, and Arts (Vól'noe óbshchestvo lyubítelei slovésnosti, naúk i khudózhestv, 1801–25). Founded by a group of recent graduates of the *gimnaziya* (secondary school) of the Academy of Sciences in Petersburg, the Society was originally a focus of libertarian thought. Among its members were many RAZNOCHINTSY. Works by Voltaire, Diderot, Montesquieu, and other authors of the French Enlightenment were translated and discussed by the membership. Republican ideas were voiced, as in A. Kh. VOSTOKOV's ode "To the Worthy" (Oda dostoinym, 1801), published in the Society's almanac *Scroll of the Muses* (Svitok muz). Among the Society's more prominent members were I. M. Born, A. Kh. Vostokov, Nikolai and Vasily Radishchev, sons of Aleksandr RADISHCHEV, K. N. BATYUSHKOV, and S. S. BOBROV. After 1807, as the general mood in the Capital was turning more conservative, the Society was dominated by its more conservative members, ceased to

function from 1812 to 1816 and met only irregularly until its demise in 1825.

Bibliography: V. N. Orlov, *Russkie prosvetiteli 1790–1800-kh godov.* 2d ed. 1953.
V. T.

Free Society of Amateurs of Russian Letters (Vól'noe óbshchestvo lyubítelei rossiískoi slovésnosti, 1816–25). The Society was founded in St. Petersburg by a group of young men, civil servants for the most part, who met regularly to listen to readings of the members' works and to discuss various intellectual topics, especially the meaning of history. Initially conservative, the Society veered more and more toward republican ideas after F. N. GLINKA was elected president in 1819 and the future DECEMBRISTS, K. F. RYLEEV, A. A. BESTUZHEV, and V. K. KYUKHELBEKER, began to play a leading role in the Society. Other prominent members were N. I. GNEDICH, O. M. SOMOV, A. A. DELVIG, and A. S. GRIBOEDOV. The Society published a monthly, "Sorevnovatel' prosveshcheniya i blagotvoreniya" (The Champion of Enlightenment and Beneficence, 1818–25), which advanced many of the ideas of pre-romanticism, such as "national spirit," identification with the national historical past, an active interest in folk poetry, a strong concern with the creative individuality ("genius"), and with freedom of artistic expression. The general tone of the journal was one of patriotic fervor and civic idealism. The activities of the Society came to a sudden end with the collapse of the Decembrist revolt.

Bibliography: A. S. Kurilov, ed., *Istoriya romantizma v russkoi literature: Vozniknovenie i utverzhdenie romantizma v russkoi literature (1790–1825).* 1979. N. I. Mordovchenko, *Russkaya kritika pervoi chetverti XIX v.* 1959.
V. T.

Free verse. The term *free verse* could imply a poetry liberated from all restraints, but in that case it would be indistinguishable from prose. A more accurate term would be *freed verse* to indicate poetry that has abandoned the main organizing element or elements that are operative within a given tradition. For Russian the key factor has been the set of constraints imposed by meter. In Russian SYLLABOTONIC POETRY the ictuses can appear only at certain positions in the line and the number of stresses between ictuses is a constant. TONIC VERSIFICATION, which became established around the turn of the century, loosens these constraints: the number of syllables between ictuses can vary, usually within certain limits; the number of syllables before the first ictus (i.e., in the anacrusis) is no longer necessarily constant throughout the poem; and as a result of these changes the ictuses can appear in different positions from line to line. Free verse is another type of reaction to the metrical requirements of syllabotonic poetry, but instead of loosening the constraints it abandons them. Hence Russian free verse is *non-metrical* poetry, in which neither the number of syllables per line nor the number of unstressed syllables between stresses are regulated throughout. Most scholars feel that Russian free verse *may* be rhymed; some have tried to establish a distinction between rhymed free verse (*svobodnyi rifmennyi stikh*) and unrhymed (for which the French term *vers libre* is used), though the majority still use *vers libre* and *svobodnyi stikh* interchangeably.

Efforts to find a single feature common to all free verse, beyond the division into lines of verse that occurs on the printed page, have not met with much success. It is basically a type of writing that is denser and more tightly organized than most prose and in which metrical organization has been replaced by one or several other features (such as repetition, parallelism, arrangement of intonational patterns) that create a sense of order. The predominant feature may change from one part of the work to the next. Thus the graphic division into lines is still usually required to distinguish free verse from highly stylized prose writing.

Free verse is much less important for Russian poetry than it has been for, say, English, though it has existed in Russian almost since the beginning of the syllabotonic era. The earliest examples are generally considered to be several of SUMAROKOV's translations from the psalms; in the 19th century a number of translations were written in what today would be termed unrhymed variable *dol'niki,* but in the context of the period were seen as relatively free and therefore provided an intermediate step in the development of free verse. BLOK's experiments in free verse, like his work with the various tonic meters, were quite influential on modern developments; also important was the poetry of Mikhail KUZMIN, whose early "Alexandrian Songs" (Aleksandriiskie pesni, 1905–08) represents one of the more extensive free verse cycles in the history of Russian poetry. From the 1930s until the 1960s free verse was rare; perhaps the only poet to use it much was the little-known Kseniya Nekrasova. During the past couple of decades both VINOKUROV and SOLOUKHIN have written a significant amount of free verse, while many other poets have employed the form at least occasionally.

Bibliography: V. S. Baevskii *et al.*, "K istorii russkogo svobodnogo stikha," *RLit* 18 (1975), no. 3, pp. 89–102. O. A. Ovcharenko, "K voprosu o tipologii svobodnogo stikha," *Vlit* 23 (1979), no. 2, pp. 223–38. Jaak Põldmäe. "Tipologiya svobodnogo stikha." In *Uchenye zapiski Tartuskogo gosudarstvennogo universiteta*, vypusk 422: *Trudy po znakovym sistemam*, 9. 1977. Pp. 85–98. A. L. Zhovtis, *Stikhi nuzhny... : Stat'i*. Alma-Ata, 1968.   B. S.

French-Russian literary relations. Sustained contact between France and Russia did not begin until the middle of the 17th century, in the reign of Tsar Alexis, father of Peter the Great. With Peter's forced Westernization of the medieval, nearly Oriental Russian State, European contacts of all kinds grew immensely in number. In PUSHKIN's words, Russia burst upon Europe "like a ship being launched, to the sound of axes and the thunder of cannons." Because of Peter's maritime and engineering interests, English and Dutch influences were at first the stronger, but it was not long before France's brilliant ENLIGHTENMENT came to dominate the intellectual and literary spheres in Russia as indeed in all of Europe. The beginnings, however, were slow, and complicated by the lack of a suitable Russian literary language: the precision and wit of the grand siècle could scarcely be rendered into what were essentially church and chancery languages.

In 1732, Empress Anna founded the Nobles' Cadet Corps, a school expressly designed to impart a European education to Russian noblemen, but it was not until the reign of Elizabeth that an appreciable intelligentsia developed among the nobility. It undertook enthusiastically the acquisition of French culture. The process continued apace until reaching a peak in the first half of Alexander I's reign, in the early 19th century, when admission to polite society depended heavily on the quality of the French spoken.

The beginnings of 18th-century Russian literature coincide with and are inseparable from the importation of French literature. Returning from his studies at the Sorbonne in 1730, TREDIAKOVSKY translated Paul Tallement des Réaux's "Voyage à l'île d'amour;" in that same year, KANTEMIR translated Fontenelle's "Entretien sur la pluralité des mondes" and shortly thereafter, Montesquieu's "Lettres Persanes." (Kantemir served in diplomatic posts in Paris and London.) Of his "Satires," Kantemir said, "In composing them I followed mostly Horace and the Frenchman Boileau, from whom I took a great deal, after adapting it to our customs." In that neoclassical age, being derivative of antique or contemporary models was not at all considered a bad thing. SUMAROKOV, the "Russian Racine," observed, "Boileau didn't take everything from Horace, and I didn't take everything from Boileau."

The giant of the age, LOMONOSOV, who fixed the literary language, thus allowing some measure of order in translation, was not so directly connected with France—yet it is he whom we think of first as the 18th-century Russian *honnête homme*. At base, his theoretical positions—his hierarchy of styles, for example—are neoclassical, French, even though their corollaries are solidly founded on his sense of the Russian language. It is true that Lomonosov could scarcely countenance the more French-oriented Sumarokov, but it cannot be said that the French literary studies he undertook at Freiburg did not deeply influence his own literary theories.

It was the "Sumarokov School" including MAIKOV, KHERASKOV, NOVIKOV and FONVIZIN which dominated roughly the third quarter of the century; this period (the 1760s and 1770s) was one of great enthusiasm for Voltaire. A memoirist recalling the age recounts: "When I talk of French books, I have in mind the works of Voltaire, which are for Muscovites all of French literature." Voltairianism (*Vol'ter'yanstvo*) and freethinking (*vol'nodumstvo*) were synonymous; the phenomenon was for a time (superficially at least) fostered by CATHERINE II. She and a goodly number of her grandees corresponded directly with Voltaire, as they did with the Encyclopedists. Although D'Alembert refused to succumb to Catherine's blandishments, Diderot came

to Petersburg with an idea to publish there a second edition of the Encyclopedia. Catherine also tried to win over Rousseau, whom she hated, and whose works she forbade in Russia. (Rousseau, however, did correspond with admirers like Count Razumovsky, and translations of his works were circulated in good number, as were those of the more acceptable Diderot and Montesquieu.)

The peasant risings in 1773 to 1774 put an end to Catherine's liberal posturings, and there was a general swing to the right among the nobility, a movement away from French philosophy and toward German pietism. The wave of gallophobia was reflected by Fonvizin (as in his play *The Brigadier*), though largely on the level of satire on French dress, manners, and "Helvetianism." Most characteristic of the era was the great poet DERZHAVIN, who knew no French and was unfamiliar with French culture. (PUSHKIN was later to observe that "ignorance was the reason for his *narodnost*," i.e., specifically Russian national character.) Finally, the French Revolution resulted in a low ebb in French-Russian literary relations.

Curiously, the influence of French society's manners and mores continued and even increased, and a new incursion of French ideas penetrated into Russia, revolutionary ones (not the old ones of the Enlightenment), with RADISHCHEV as the chief bearer of the new values. Like Lomonosov, Radishchev had studied in Germany, but at a time when French democratism permeated the atmosphere there; his later philosophical writings have much in common with Holbach, Helvétius and Diderot, while in his belles lettres, the influence of Rousseau, Montesquieu and Voltaire are clear. In the violent reaction to the French Revolution, his exile would seem to have been inevitable.

Also a student of the French left, KARAMZIN, who dominated the last decade of the century and the first of the 19th, managed a politically less dangerous path by espousing Rousseauistic sentimentalism while ignoring or at least soft-pedaling its essentially democratic content. It was one of those eras of "double-think" that persistently occur in the history of Russian ideas: the reading public (the nobility) delighted in *La Nouvelle Héloïse* and *Emile* without troubling themselves much about the political implications of the works. Karamzin's anti-French period of interest in English and German literature passed into a "sanitized" French one of pleasant sentimentalism and elegiac contemplation in the manner of Jacques Delille. DMITRIEV, a senior member of the "Karamzin school" and reformer of the language of Russian poetry, was nicknamed "the pure-blooded Frenchman."

The great literary battle that was joined after the turn of the century, the battle of the "archaists and the innovators," was essentially between francophobe and francophile—in literary matters. The former are the nationalist/Orthodox/native Russian contingent; the latter, the Westernizing/liberal/French-leaning group. The first is represented by Admiral SHISHKOV, and the second by Karamzin, or his "school." It might be fairly said that both sides had good points, and that the battle was salutary for the development of the Russian literary language. The reason we tend to side against the Shishkov group is because Pushkin did—but for reasons as much extraliterary as not, and one has the feeling from his writings that he agreed full well with some of the opposition's points. It is touching to remember that when Pushkin's much-loved Uncle Vasily Lvovich lay on his deathbed and regained consciousness for a moment, recognizing his nephew, he spoke his last words: "O, qu'il est ennuyeux, ce Katénine." Then he died, peacefully, having shot a last barb at the anti-French party.

The wave of emigration that followed the French Revolution affected a whole generation of the nobility: a succession of abbés and gouvernantes passed through their houses and salons. Joseph de Maistre held forth for fourteen years in Petersburg. The young Pushkin spoke French from childhood, and had the run of the family's French libraries (his father and uncle were in practice essentially transposed French petits-maîtres). Pushkin's best subjects at the Lycée were French—and fencing. His schoolboy nickname was *frantsuz*, "the Frenchman." One of his masters was de Budri, incognito brother of Marat.

It was the mutual interest in each other's works of Pushkin and Prosper Mérimée that marked the first real literary exchange between France and Russia. Mérimée also acquainted the French public with GOGOL and TURGENEV.

The years before the Napoleonic Wars were ones in which the hegemony of French culture (pre-Revolutionary, to be sure) reached its peak. With the wars, anti-French sentiment naturally grew strong, but such was the hold of French culture that its international prestige continued even after Napoleon's depredations, even if diminishing gradually. Contributing to the process was the anglophilism which swept Russian society on the return of the officers from the wars, and especially after the Imperial Progress to London. In literature, ZHU-KOVSKY had turned away from France to Germany as early as 1808, as BATYUSHKOV turned to Italy. Interest in German universities and their philosophers grew throughout these years. By the 1820s, Push-kin's attraction to Byron, and later to Shakespeare, supplanted the French authors. Moreover, the evolution around this time of a con-siderable body of independent Russian literature, solving problems of the literary language, rendered French models less important. In-terest in writers like Mme de Stael and Benjamin Constant remained high, but the old standard of 18th-century French culture was too remote to survive in a Russia suffering the aftermath of the Decem-brist Rebellion. To be sure, French continued to be the language of the nobility, but more as a kind of class marker, oddly removed from French culture overall. With the "men of the forties" and the increas-ing leadership of the non-noble, "RAZNOCHINETS" intelligentsia, French as a means of communicating current ideas recedes even further.

On the other hand, this same development spurred a renewed interest in French literature itself, which either echoed or influenced the new Russian ideas: the works of Hugo, Sue, Dumas, Janin and later Balzac appeared in POLEVOI's MOSKOVSKII TELEGRAF. HERZEN wrote that "Saint-Simonisme lay at the base of our convictions."

In the literature of the 1840s, George Sand's social ideas played an immense role in the writings of BELINSKY, Herzen, DRUZHININ, CHERNYSHEVSKY and the early Turgenev. Proudhon and Fourier were endlessly discussed; French ideas were again on a par with Hegel-dominated German ones. For the young SALTYKOV-SHCHE-DRIN's generation, "France seemed a land of miracles." The liberals were horrified at the outcome of the Rebellion of 1848 in France; in Russia, the predictable repression occurred: Saltykov was exiled, the PETRASHEVSKY CIRCLE scattered.

In the following period, 1850s to 1870s, the period of the great Russian realists, contact—both direct and indirect—with French novelists was intense. Turgenev, of course, was a personal friend of both Flaubert and Mérimée, and was acquainted with George Sand, Hugo, Zola, Maupassant (as well as Taine and Renan). Balzac had an enormous influence on the young DOSTOEVSKY, who translated *Eugénie Grandet*. *Le Père Goriot* contributed to the genesis of *Crime and Punishment*. If in his later life Dostoevsky's growing disapprov-al of the French reflected on his appreciation of contemporary French literature, its influence on his career overall cannot be gainsaid.

TOLSTOI studied French literature all his life, but its influence on his writing is less marked than on Dostoevsky's. Still, one must recog-nize Rousseau's influence in his thought, "a great and salutary" one, in Tolstoi's words. Of Stendhal, he said: "I am more indebted to him than anyone. He taught me to understand war." The society he de-picts in *War and Peace* was at the apogee of French cultural influence. If later he had little patience for the NATURALISTS and none at all for the DECADENTS, he did come to admire Maupassant in his last years.

Coextensive with this period—from the 1890s into the teens of the 20th century—was a new and vital chapter in French-Russian literary relations, one which was totally alien to Tolstoi: the SYMBOLIST move-ment.

One must be careful not to overstress French symbolist in-fluences, for there was an organic tradition in Russian literature which was equally if not more important: in the Russian romantic movement, and in the ideas of Schopenhauer and other German phi-losophers as filtered through the Russian romantics. Especially im-portant in this regard is the poetry of FET and TYUTCHEV. It is difficult to find a salient characteristic of Russian symbolism (apart from the quirkier kind of religiomysticism indulged in by some of the symbol-ists) which is in some way or another not paralleled in Tyutchev and Fet.

Nevertheless, the beginnings of a symbolist consciousness date from articles in the early nineties on French symbolist poets by MEREZHKOVSKY and Zinaida Vengerova. The exciting thing is that for the first time, French-Russian literary relations were on a two-way street: France had "discovered" Russian literature, and the va-et-vient between the cultures was more than considerable. Shortly after

Vengerova's article appeared, a French critic observed that Venge-rova "est très amplement instruite de notre mouvement littéraire ... l'article est remarquable par l'abondance de l'information, et le liber-alisme du jugement."

The older of the two symbolist "generations" was probably the closer to the French poets: BRYUSOV translated them "to make the models more accessible;" Prince Urusov's translations of Baudelaire won over the recalcitrant BALMONT; SOLOGUB spoke of himself as "half-Parisian."

The symbolist and post-symbolist periods were an exciting time of syncretism and cosmopolitanism in the arts. Poets and artists of all kinds travelled regularly to Paris. According to BLOK, gossip at the "Stray Dog" consisted of "who had slapped whom in Paris"; there, GUMILYOV became acquainted with Sartre; AKHMATOVA conversed with Modigliani; both Russian poets attended the Paris openings of DIAGHILEV's *Ballets Russes*.

Close contact ceased with the onset of the war, revolution and civil war, if one does not count the emigration in the 1920s. (One notable exception is the relationship between Maksim GORKY and Romain Rolland.) Following the institution of the first Five-Year Plan, there soon developed a Soviet idea that literary relations of the pre-war kind constituted "kowtowing to the West"; such contacts were at first suspect and later dangerous. By the time relations could be more or less safely pursued in the post-Stalin era, French literature no longer occupied a special position, and it is now more or less on a par with the other major literatures of the West.

The story of French-Russian literary relations is a much shorter one, although for a time around the fin de siècle, they were intense. Apart from Mérimée, French interest in and knowledge of Russian literature was very limited. Leroy Beaulieu's monumental study touched on the topic, but it was mostly devoted to other fields of endeavor. Travel notes by littérateurs produced some degree of awareness (Custine, Dumas, Gautier), but by and large, as late as 1880, even the major writers were unknown. The Franco-Prussian War had predisposed France to interest in Russia. Melchior de Vogüé observed, "Until a few years ago, we left it to a handful of orientalists to busy themselves with checking the writings of these Sarmatians. We had a notion that a literature might exist in their midst, as in Persia or Arabia; we did not place much trust in it ..." It was de Vogüé, in the mid-eighties, who launched the "Russian inva-sion," with Tolstoi and Dostoevsky in the vanguard. His book, *Le Roman russe*, appeared just when a mass of translations from those authors was being published. By the end of the decade, their names were household words; they were a mine for critics, a model for aspir-ing writers and a check for established ones. Tired of positivist claims, fed up with naturalist excesses, the French public and intel-ligentsia were ready for what they perceived to be the mysticism of the Russians—including their moral, religious, and ethical concerns. "Tolstoism" as an influence was recognized in the early nineties (by such an unlikely figure as Théodore de Wyzéwa). Enthusiasm for Russian literature and all the arts peaked in the years before the Great War, and, it seemed, "Tout Pétersbourg" was in Paris. Now it was Dostoevsky's turn. In 1908, Gide published an article on Dos-toevsky's correspondence, initiating a whole series of critical studies. Dostoevsky was to remain crucial for Gide's own work until after World War II, when Gide, in connection with the existentialist move-ment, truly comes into his own as a Dostoevsky critic.

The French spokesman for Soviet literature is first and foremost Louis Aragon; though his standard *Littératures soviétiques* (1955) is now somewhat dated, he has continued a major link between Soviet and French letters.

Bibliography: Louis Aragon, *Littératures soviétiques*. 1955. Georgette Donchin, *The Influence of French Symbolism on Russian Poetry*. The Hague, 1958. *Èpokha prosveshcheniya: iz istorii mezh-dunarodnykh svyazei russkoi literatury*. Ed. by M. P. Alekseev. 1967. E. Haumant, *La Culture française en Russie* (1700–1900). Paris, 1910. V. I. Kuleshov, *Literaturnye svyazi Rossii i Zapadnoi Evropy*. 1965. *Ot klassitsizma k romantizmu: iz istorii mezhdunarodnyx svyazei russkoi literatury*. Ed. M. P. Alekseev. 1970. *Ot romantizma k realizmu: iz istorii mezhdunarodnykh svyazei russkoi literatury*. Ed. M. P. Alekseev. 1978. *La Poésie russe* (Edition bilingue). Ed. Elsa Triolet. Introd. Roman Jakobson. Paris, 1965. Aleksandr Rogalski, *Rosja-Europa: wzajemne związki, wpływy i zależności kulturalno-*

literackie. Warsaw, 1960. *Rossiya i Zapad: iz istorii literaturnykh otnoshenii.* Ed. by M. P. Alekseev. 1973. *Russkie pisateli o yazyke* (XVIII–XX vv.). Ed. by B. Tomashevskii. 1954. *Russkaya kul'tura i Frantsiya, Literaturnoe nasledstvo,* 29–30, 31–32. (1937). (See esp. S. Makashin, "Literaturnye vzaimootnosheniya Rossii i Frantsii," 29–30, V–LXXXII.) *Russko-Evropeiskie literaturnye svyazi.* Ed. by P. N. Berkov. 1966. I. Sozonovich, *K voprosu o zapadnom vliyanii na slavyanskuyu i russkuyu poeziyu.* Warsaw, 1898. (Reproduced by University Microfilms, Inc. Ann Arbor, 1962.)   C. D.

Freudianism in Russian literature. In the 1920s, Freudian theories awakened a lively interest among Russian thinkers. A. K. VORONSKY, a leading Marxist, redefined psychoanalysis. "Societal instinct," he thought, also belongs to the content of the subconscious. Voronsky tried to use the subconscious to investigate the hidden ideological motivation of behavior. He defended the concept of intuition in his polemic with the "Left Front" of Soviet literature about the nature of the poetic work. V. N. Voloshinov, a disciple of BAKHTIN, subjected Freudianism to scholarly critique in a book entitled *Freidizm* (1927). Soviet theoreticians would not accept a theory that appeared to reject the societal significance of literature. By 1927 Freudianism became a prohibited topic. In the official Soviet judgement, Freudianism is still a manifestation of bourgeois decadence. In our time, knowledgeable Freudian references are found in journalism and literature, authored by LAKSHIN, the STRUGATSKYS, and others.

As a critical interpretation of literature, psychoanalysis is an inquiry into the psychic life of the writer. A literary work conveys the history of how the repressed complexes of the author's subconscious were sublimated into a symbolization acceptable to "censorship." The pioneering Russian literary psychoanalytical study is *Essays on the Psychology of Gogol's Works* (Ocherki po psikhologii gogolevskogo tvorchestva) by I. D. Ermakov (1923). *The Nose* has the qualities of a dream that cries out to be interpreted in Freudian terms, and Ermakov does so with a relentless psychoanalytical consistency. Freud's own article "Dream and Parricide" (1928) discusses how Dostoevsky transforms "his intention of murdering his father" into a sublimated cultural form of aggression. Imposition of severe ethical injunctions by the superego also serves as a source of creative activity. This is the case of Tolstoi (Voloshinov).

Psychoanalysis may give us a deeper insight into man's mental world, but has its limitations. The aesthetic structure of a literary work need not convey an objective psychoanalytic fact; it transforms the empirical personality of the author. Therefore, psychoanalysis may misrepresent both author and work. An example of balanced psychoanalytical studies are those on Dostoevsky and Gogol published under the editorship of Professor Bem (e.g., A. L. Bem, *Dostoevskii: Psikhoanaliticheskie etyudy.* Prague, 1938).

Since the late twenties Freud's name appears mostly as petty critical abuse, as when the plot of Gladkov's novel *Cement* (1925) was labeled as "an unnatural blend of Marxism and Freudianism." Libedinsky's novel *Birth of Man* (Rozhdenie cheloveka, 1930) earned the epithet "Freudian."

Freudianism has left its imprint on major literary works, such as *Ulysses* (1922). At the time when *Ulysses* appeared, Soviet literature practiced "ornamental prose." Did Pilnyak, Nikitin, and Vsevolod Ivanov borrow this style of narrative from the Joycean stream-of-consciousness technique? This is unlikely. Joyce drew on the Freudian system. The Russian "ornamental prose" followed Russian traditions. Under socialist realism, Freud-inspired works of major dimensions cannot be written. At most, Freudian motives would have a marginal, grotesque function. Kaverin's *Revizor* (1926) is a take-off on Gogol's *Nose*: a mental patient relives Major Kovalev's experience. However, Kaverin does not disguise the sexual nature of the subject's latent thought. In his *Sparrow Night* (Vorobyinaya noch', 1927) a provincial cashier tries to identify with a small-time conquistador, and fails miserably in carrying out his "goal-oriented identification." OLESHA's play *The Black Man* (Chernyi chelovek) produces a villain intended to be a parody of Freud, Spengler, and Bergson. Apparently Olesha never completed this play.

In this area of marginal Freudianism, ZOSHCHENKO holds a particular place. His works deal often with neurosis, and a few of them relate to Freudianism. His grotesque characters come to grips with some facets of Freudian theory. In "A Medical Case" (Meditsinskii sluchai, 1928) an amateur psychiatrist tries to cure a girl who in con-

sequence of a "traumatic experience" has lost speech. Other stories deal in the same facetious key with the theory of libido: "Matrenishcha" (1926), "Personal Life" (Lichnaya zhizn', 1933). The title of his story "Doctoring and Psychics" (Vrachevanie i psikhika, 1933) is virtually a literal translation of Stefan Zweig's book, part of which is dedicated to Freud. Zoshchenko's later narrative *Youth Returned* (Vozvrashchennaya molodost', 1933) demonstrates great interest in psychoanalytic therapy. The Freudian substance of Zoshchenko's interest is made to appear to be focused on the theories of Pavlov. The most interesting work is *Before Sunrise* (Pered voskhodom solntsa, 1943). It could be interpreted as a psychoanalytic investigation in the form of an autobiographical tale. The author embarks on a quest for the source of his life-long neurosis. He identifies his neurosis. In the last lines, just "before sunrise," the cause of his neurosis starts dawning on the author. However, "sunrise" never comes.

Russian literature would offer a rich field for psychoanalytic study, such as study of mental states as synchronized with reality.

Bibliography: M. N. Afasizhev, *Freidizm i burzhuaznoe iskusstvo.* 1971. I. D. Ermakov, *Ocherki po psikhologii gogolevskogo tvorchestva.* 1923. Sigmund Freud, "Dostoyevsky and Parricide." In *Standard Edition of the Collected Psychoanalytical Works.* Ed. James Strachey. 1961. Vol. 21. Pp. 172–83. Iolan Neifel'd (Jolan Neufeld), *Dostoevskii: Psikhoanaliticheskii ocherk pod redaktsiei prof. Z. Freida.* Trans. from the German by Ya. Druskina. Leningrad and Moscow, 1925. A. V. Petrovskii, *Istoriya sovetskoi psikhologii.* 1967. Pp. 81–94. V. Voloshinov, *Freidizm.* 1927. (In English: V. N. Voloshinov, *Freudianism: A Marxist Critique.* Trans. I. R. Titunik, ed coll. Neal H. Bruss. 1976.) A. Voronskii, *Literaturnye zapiski.* 1926. (Articles: "Freidizm i iskusstvo" and "Ob iskusstve," pp. 7–56.) Mikhail Zoshchenko, *Pered voskhodom solntsa: Povest'.* New York, 1967. (Introd. articles by Vera von Viren-Garchinskaya and Boris Filippov.)   H. O.

Friche, Vladimir Maksimovich (1870–1929), literary scholar and theoretician of the sociological method. Friche got his degree in the philological faculty of Moscow University in 1894, and taught there for several years before the Revolution. From 1895 on he published a large number of articles and books on topics in West European literature. Friche was involved with Marxist groups already in the 1890s, becoming especially close to the Bolsheviks after 1905 and joined the Party in 1917. Friche was heavily influenced by PLEKHANOV and even his very early work attempts to develop a uniquely Marxist methodology in the study of world literature. After the Revolution Friche became head of the literary section of several important Party organizations, including the Communist Academy, as well as editor of several journals and the first two volumes of the *Literary Encyclopedia.*

In the 1920s he published a number of books (*Plekhanov and Scientific Aesthetics*, 1922; *Sketch for a Sociology of Literary Styles*, 1923; *Freudianism and Art*, 1925; *The Sociology of Art*, 1926) in which he argued that literary style was an aspect of social style. The history of literature was the story of conflict among styles representing the struggle between classes. Friche sought in literature the "social equivalent" in literature that shaped political history outside literature. He argued against individual heroes, whom he wished to replace with heroic group protagonists, a position that was to influence such groups as *LitFront* and *On Literary Guard.* In 1929 he was made an Academician.

Secondary literature: M. B. Khrapchenko, "Voprosy istorii russkoi literatury," *Literatura i iskusstvo,* 1931, no. 4. P. N. Sakulin, *Academik V. M. Friche* (nekrolog). 1930.   J. M. H.

Fridlénder, Geórgy Mikháilovich (1915–), literary scholar. Educated at Leningrad State University, and bilingual by upbringing, he contributes to comparative studies, history of German aesthetics and literature, and Russian REALISM. In 1957 Fridlender produced an annotated edition of Lessing's *Laokoon.* In his preface he introduced Lessing as a progenitor of the discipline which studies different systems of artistic signs. His *Marx and Engels and Problems of Literature* (1964), brought him the title of full professor. Here Fridlender discusses aesthetic aspects of the Marxist theory of reflection, according to which human cognitive awareness reflects, analyzes, and synthesizes the regularities of the material universe, as well as social and economic class relations. In the years 1965 to 1969 he complemented the central statements of this work by a number of articles on Marxist aesthetics in the version given it by Lenin.

Since 1955 Fridlender has worked for the INSTITUT RUSSKOI LITERATURY (Pushkin House), preparing Academy editions of Belinsky, Gogol, Turgenev, and Dostoevsky. Among his works published by the Institute are articles on the history of the Russian novel and criticism, several comparative studies of German and Russian authors, works on Pushkin's poems and elegies, and a number of articles on Tolstoi and Chernyshevsky. Fridlender is a contributor to and editor-in-chief of several Academy collections: *History of the Russian Novel* (1962), *Dostoevsky and his Time* (1971), *Dostoevsky: Materials and Inquiries* (Materialy i issledovaniya, 1974–1983, vols. 1–5), and *Dostoevsky in Foreign Literatures* (1978). His books *Dostoevsky's Realism* (1964) and *The Poetics of Russian Realism* (1971) discuss several key questions of the general structure of the reflection of reality by means of the verbal arts. Emphasis is given to the specificity of genre and plot development, as well as to the poetic image of time, space, and human personality within the framework of Russian and European realism of the 19th and 20th centuries.

Bibliography of Fridlender's works: Bibliografiya proizvedenii Dostoevskogo i literatury o nem. Moscow, 1968. P. 401. *Dostoevskii: Materialy i issledovaniia.* Leningrad, 1974. Vol. 1. P. 330. *Pushkinskii Dom. Bibliografiya trudov.* Leningrad, 1981. P. 371.

Secondary literature: J. W. Dyck, "G. M. Fridlender, *Realizm Dostoevskogo,*" *Books Abroad,* 1965, no. 4.   N. P.

Frol Skobeev, see PICARESQUE NOVEL.

Fúrmanov, Dmítry Andréevich (1891–1926), officially lauded Soviet Russian political prose writer and journalist. Furmanov studied literature at Moscow University (1909–12, 1924). He joined the Communist Party in 1918. During the Civil War (1919–21) he was a political Commissar with the 25th Division of the Red Army under General Chapaev, a legendary leader of Bolshevik guerrilla forces. With them, Furmanov roamed throughout the Southeastern steppes and the Urals. After the Revolution Furmanov devoted himself to literature and party work. His first novel, *The Red Landing Force* (Krasnyi desant), was published in 1921. He is best known for his novel *Chapaev* (1923), a chronicle of events surrounding General Chapaev's exploits during the Civil War. Based on Furmanov's own diaries and notes, it is a glorification of the Soviet folk hero Chapaev. Furmanov contrasts Chapaev, who accepts the Revolution on an emotional level, to the rational, dedicated party leader, Klychkov, modeled on Furmanov himself.

Chapaev has been hailed by the Soviet establishment as "the first great work depicting the Revolution," "a classic of Soviet literature" and the prototype of "the epic form in Soviet prose." During the 1930s it was adopted as an official model of SOCIALIST REALISM. Since 1923, *Chapaev* has been reprinted almost annually in huge editions and has been made into a popular film and opera. The central theme of Furmanov's works is the Revolution and the revolutionary struggle, presented from the point of view of the Communist Party. His style is laconic and "factographic."

Works: Sobranie sochinenii. 4 vols. 1960–1961. "Za kommunizm," *Literaturnoe nasledstvo* 74 (1965). *Na podstupakh oktyabrya (ocherk), Nezabyvaemye dni.* 1967.

Translations: Chapayev. London, 1935. (Repr. 1973). *Chapayev.* Moscow, 1974.

Secondary literature: Edward J. Brown, *Russian Literature since the Revolution.* 1963. Pp. 150–61.   H. S.

Futurism. Russian futurism is probably the major poetic movement in Russia of this century. But to characterize it as a unified movement would be highly inaccurate. If there is a single principle that united all the futurist groups, it is that poetry is an autonomous and experimental art of the "word." The futurist groups, especially the cubo-futurists, sought a radical departure from the literature of the "stifling past;" they assaulted the revered literary idols—PUSHKIN, DOSTOEVSKY, TOLSTOI, among others—and expressed their contempt for the poetic language of the past. They believed that each literary age sets its own artistic criteria and tasks. Unlike the Russian SYMBOLISTS, who valued the poetic word for its suggestive powers, ideas and the creation of myths, the Russian futurists saw the poetic word as an end in itself, without any reference to either meaning or reality. Experimentation with the poetic word was in theory the form and content of poetry, often with a view to directing poetic language to modern city life. Put differently, if a painting was the sum of its distortions, as Picasso once remarked, so too was poetry the sum of its linguistic distortions. Poetry was seen as technique, not a metaphysical quest for unattainable realities, which was the basic poetic pursuit of Russian SYMBOLISM. When one considers that futurist principles extended to painting, graphics, poster art, circus, music, theater, and typography, and led to the rise of other major movements, such as Russian FORMALISM and CONSTRUCTIVISM, Russian futurism takes on even greater historical significance. Scandal, outrage, sensation, and controversy mark most of its history, and it produced at least two of the greatest poets of this century: Viktor KHLEBNIKOV and Vladimir MAYAKOVSKY.

One gains a better perspective of the diversity and flexibility of Russian futurist principles by examining the four poetic groups that comprise Russian futurism: the ego-futurists, the Mezzanine of Poetry (which was the former's counterpart), Centrifuge, and the cubo-futurists.

Ego-futurism was formed by Igor SEVERYANIN and Konstantin Olimpov in St. Petersburg in 1911, and the poets associated with them (and the Mezzanine of Poetry) were Konstantin Bolshakov, Graal-Arelsky, Pyotr Fofanov, Vasilisk Gnedov, Ivan IGNATIEV, Georgy IVANOV, Ryurik IVNEV, Viktor Khovin, Pavel Kokorin, Dmitry Kryuchkov, Ivan Lukash, Pavel Shirokov, Sergei TRETYAKOV, Lev Zak, and Vadim SHERSHENEVICH, the last mentioned being the leader of the Moscow group of ego-futurists, the Mezzanine of Poetry. According to Vladimir Markov, the ego-futurists "never produced anything artistically successful...." (See bibliography below.)

Historically, however, ego-futurism, and its two most important representatives, Igor Severyanin and Vadim Shershenevich, deserve attention. In their poetic "program," the ego-futurists considered the poetry of the past a wasteland, and sought to create an "irrational poetry," to understand "the unclarity of the earth," and to experiment with new rhymes and words. Poetry was seen as an apotheosis of the ego, a quest for self-revelation. The ego-futurists were largely influenced by Italian futurism, especially in their view that poetic language had to keep pace with modern life and with the creation of a new language that would reflect it.

As for Igor Severyanin, his poetic themes were often banal and vulgar, but he enthralled his readers with descriptions of the "refined" tastes and pleasures of bourgeois high life. Although his style was crude and awkward, his experiments in rhyme and meter, along with his neologisms from French as well as Russian, were noteworthy, and gave his poetry the appearance of modernity. His recitals were analogous to a poetic concert and had a truly hypnotic effect on his audience. He would "croon" rather than read his poetry. Severyanin's popularity was striking; and as a measure of it, his *Thunder-Seething Goblet* (1913) underwent more than ten editions. Once Severyanin had seen his popularity as the fulfillment of his ego, he abandoned the ego-futurists in 1912, and later became temporarily associated with the cubo-futurists. His influence on Mayakovsky was not insignificant, as Nikolai Khardzhiev has recently pointed out.

In 1913, Vadim Shershenevich (and Lev Zak) organized the Mezzanine of Poetry. Shershenevich viewed poetic evolution as a "constant search for new forms, new means of expression, which would allow to express more deeply and adequately feelings and thoughts...." He also emphasized the creation of new words and experimentation with their semantic and sensory possibilities. He rejected the cubo-futurist notion of the autonomous word as a "phonetic entity." Italian futurism strongly influenced Shershenevich's poetry which is oriented to urban themes, and glorifies the modern technological age and its "beauty of speed." He translated the Italian futurist manifestos and other works into Russian, although his understanding of Italian futurism was limited and elementary. His *Futurism Without a Mask* (1913) was "the first attempt to provide a systematic account of futurism in Russia" (Anna Lawton). In 1914, Shershenevich, like Severyanin, was associated with the cubo-futurists, and was the chief editor of *The First Journal of Russian Futurists* (1914), to which he contributed eleven poems. In that same year, he also published his poems in the cubo-futurist *Croaked Moon* (Dokhlaya luna, 1914). Thereafter he published independently, and in 1918 he founded Russian IMAGISM.

In 1913, a much smaller, more talented lyrical futurist group, Centrifuge, was formed. Although it did not consider itself futurist, the group accepted the name when applied to it. The three basic poets of Centrifuge, Sergei Bobrov, Boris PASTERNAK, and Nikolai ASEEV, combined in their poetry Russian classical traditions with features of Russian and French symbolism and futurism. It is difficult to discern any poetic program in Centrifuge; in fact, the group explicitly rejected any "guidelines." Its major tie to futurism is the attention to urban themes, its efforts to renew poetic technique, and to seek new poetic directions. Even as an offshoot of futurism, Centrifuge expanded the range of futurist aesthetics (Markov).

Sergei Bobrov was the main inspiration of Centrifuge. He was also its teacher and theoretician, as well as an erudite poet who imitated Russian classical and symbolist poets. For Bobrov, all poetry was intrinsically "symbolic." Metrics were one of his major interests. He attempted to define fundamental poetic qualities, but his own sophistication ironically proved to be an impediment to any clear elaboration (Markov).

A far more important poet, who subsequently achieved international fame, was Boris Pasternak. His is the poetry of the landscape, replete with metaphors which are occasionally complex and opaque; but what lent his poetry an aura of freshness and novelty was the role of nature as the source and subject of action, the prime mover of events. In his poetry, nature interacts and becomes equated with the world of common, concrete things, and the blend of the "high" and the "low," in both theme and language, is a major feature of his poetry.

The early poetry of Nikolai Aseev, who later became an important Soviet poet, reflected classical themes, Hoffmannesque elements, and Russian and French symbolism. The phantasmagoric urban setting of his early poetry strongly links him with futurism. His maturation as a poet later was the result of the influence of Khlebnikov and Mayakovsky. In the 1920s, Aseev was a member of the cubo-futurist group.

Cubo-futurism is beyond dispute the central movement in Russian futurism, a truly revolutionary phenomenon, both creatively and politically. Many of the prominent art and literary figures of the immediate pre- and postrevolutionary period were in some way connected with cubo-futurism, partly because of its cult of novelty and innovation. Throughout their long, complicated, and turbulent history, which spans some twenty years, the cubo-futurists evinced much greater group solidarity and aesthetic consistency than any of the other futurist groups, which no longer existed after 1917.

In 1910, a group of poets who called themselves "those who will be" (*budetlyane*) attempted to mark its entry into the literary world by publishing a collection of poetry, *A Trap for Judges* (Sadok sudei). Among the poets who contributed to the collection and who came to be identified with cubo-futurism were Vasily KAMENSKY, Viktor KHLEBNIKOV, David, Nikolai, and Vladimir BURLYUK, Elena GURO, and Ekaterina Nizen. Because of the strong symbolist orientation of their poetry, the publication went largely unnoticed. What reviews there were, were negative. Valery BRYUSOV, one of the leading symbolist poets, wrote that the publication was "almost beyond the limits of literature. The collection is replete with puerile escapades in bad taste, and its authors aim above all to shock the reader and to harass the critics (what is called *épater les bourgeois*)." A year later, Vladimir MAYAKOVSKY and Aleksei KRUCHONYKH joined the group (originally called Hylaea, then cubo-futurists in 1913), and in 1912 it published another collection of poetry and its famous manifesto in the pamphlet *A Slap in the Face of Public Taste*. Through its manifesto, the group immediately gained the attention and recognition that had eluded it in 1910. The manifesto outraged its readers by calling for throwing Pushkin, Dostoevsky, and Tolstoi "from the Ship of Contemporary Life," and by attacking leading Russian literary figures. The attack on Russian classical writers became a permanent tactic of the cubo-futurists and posed enormous difficulties for them in the 1920s. Bolshevik leaders of conservative literary tastes considered the attack tantamount to blasphemy. The basic tenet of the group's poetic program was "the enlargement of the poet's vocabulary in its scope with arbitrary and derivative words (word-novelty)." The emphasis on experimentation with, and renewal of, poetic language echoes repeatedly in cubo-futurist history.

Khlebnikov, Mayakovsky, David Burlyuk, Kruchonykh and Kamensky are the principal poets of cubo-futurism, for they largely shaped the poetic and linguistic contours of the movement. Their aesthetic and poetic orientation invites attention.

Khlebnikov "is easily the most original poet Russia ever produced...." (Markov). He saw "futurism" as "the study of the influence of the future on the past." Khlebnikov is generally known for his neologisms, and his "trans-rational language" (*zaumnyi yazyk*, see ZAUM), which broadened the semantic range of his poetry. But his linguistic experiments were also directed to the creation of a "universal language" which would unite men, since Khlebnikov found so much human conflict and violence in history. His poetry has a "primitive," fragmentary and plotless character; it presents puzzles to the reader, who must "creatively" unravel its illogical, suggestive, mysterious, and allusive features. The linguistic, historical, and mythological dimensions of his poetry are truly extraordinary and almost inexhaustible. Khlebnikov devoted most of his life to a search for the laws of history and time. Hence the numerous mathematical equations and numbers in his poetry. These efforts seem to represent a fantastic struggle against death. After his death in 1922, the publication of Khlebnikov's works by the cubo-futurists brought Khlebnikov the recognition that he so justly deserved.

Mayakovsky is the dominant poet of cubo-futurism, the avatar of avant-garde poetry, however controversial and ambiguous his poetic legacy. He is mainly responsible for giving futurism its mass appeal and for establishing its "tradition." Although he supported the basic principles of cubo-futurism, he was not in any strict sense a theoretician, because he simply lacked the erudition. He was, however, by no means indifferent to the problems of poetic craft, and his "How to Make Poetry" (1926) is an impressive statement on the craft of poetry. Mayakovsky was such a "supreme *poetic* intellect" that he could give "his unique poetic shape to any topic essayed ..." (Markov), hence the difficulty in describing the themes of his poetry as a whole. In the pre-revolutionary period, however, one finds the themes of the poet in "nihilistic" rebellion against his time; of the suffering, terrified poet; of martyrdom; of unrequited love; of hatred toward war; of the city as a source of pain, vice, and violence; of the misunderstood poet. According to Markov, in Mayakovsky's poetry, "the surface reasons, which may be downright adolescent, do not count; what is important are the intensity and the dynamism of his emotion and his art." The formal aspects of his poetry were often directed against poetic traditions and conventions: in his neologisms, declamatory delivery "based on conversational intonation" (Markov), his striking innovations in rhyme and tonic verse.

The post-revolutionary years saw further development in Mayakovsky's poetry, which he put at the service of the Bolshevik regime. His lyric poetry, an integral part of his poetic legacy, unquestionably suffered; but Mayakovsky surely savored the role of a public and topical poet, regardless of his later regret that he had stifled his lyrical impulse. Political content or commitment did not necessarily detract from the craft and quality of his poetry, for Mayakovsky never shed "his belief that the poet must be a craftsman rather than an ideologist" (Halina Stephan). Roman JAKOBSON points out, in vindication of Mayakovsky's abiding adherence to cubo-futurism, that his "poetry of the last years was a massive laboratory of work on word and theme. It became clear how masterfully he could use this work in his first efforts in the area of theatrical prose, and what unlimited possibilities of development were contained in it." Mayakovsky's tragic death in 1930 marks the end of the avant-garde era.

David Burlyuk was the father of cubo-futurism, as well as its resourceful and energetic organizer of tours and lectures. He was responsible for publishing most of the cubo-futurist poetic collections, to which he contributed poetry and theoretical essays on art, his primary vocation. He discovered Mayakovsky's poetic talent and cultivated it ("my real teacher," as Mayakovsky noted in his autobiography). Like other cubo-futurists, Burlyuk viewed art as a distortion of reality, based on the three principles of "disharmony, dissymmetry and disconstruction." Burlyuk's poetry, like his art, was an imitation of various styles, particularly those of the Russian and French symbolists, whom he never transcended. His poetry has a strong strain of anti-aestheticism—a cubo-futurist characteristic—designed to outrage and shock his reader. Burlyuk never developed his own style, either in painting or in poetry.

When, in 1915, Mayakovsky formed a new friendship with Osip (and Lily) BRIK, Burlyuk's close association with him ended, although they remained friends and even worked together during the revolutionary years in promoting cubo-futurism. In 1920, Burlyuk left Russia, and two years later he settled in New York, where he continued to support the cubo-futurists in his numerous publications, although he never succeeded in describing or explaining the major avant-garde movement which he himself had so brilliantly organized.

Kruchonykh was the most prolific and effective "theoretician" of cubo-futurism, its most loyal and consistent proponent of the destruction of meaning in poetry. More than any other cubo-futurist, he enraged the critics of cubo-futurism by his irreverent attacks on Russian classical and symbolist poets for grappling with metaphysical problems that had no solution. He became the most militant advocate and practitioner of "trans-rational language" in poetry, which he derived from Khlebnikov's rational notion of it. For Kruchonykh, "trans-rational language" consisted of arbitrary and meaningless sound sequences, but expressive of certain emotions. Kruchonykh felt compelled by the confused and chaotic nature of the time to eliminate meaning from poetry so as to gain a new perception of the world. He justified "chaos" in poetry as follows: "Thought and language do not keep pace with the experience of the inspired person; therefore the artist is free to express himself not only in common language (of concepts), but also in a personal language (the artist is an individual) and in a language that has no definite meaning, in (an uncongealed) trans-rational [language]. A common language is binding; a free one allows one to express oneself more fully."

During the revolutionary years 1917–20, Kruchonykh propagated trans-rational poetry in Tiflis, Georgia, and organized (with Ilya Zdanevich) a poetic group, "41°". Its aim was "to make use of all great discoveries by its contributors and to put the world on a new axis." During the 1920s, Kruchonykh saw in the development of Soviet literature a triumphant affirmation of his notion of trans-rationalism. He staunchly supported the cubo-futurist journals, LEF and New Lef, which occasionally published his works; but the increasing emphasis on utility and ideology in literature brought an end to Kruchonykh's trans-rationalism.

Kamensky is the versatile, "enthusiastic" poet of cubo-futurism. He played a key role in its formation by introducing Khlebnikov to David Burlyuk and by suggesting that the former's neologistic experiments become the basis of a new poetic movement. Kamensky shared with Burlyuk a passion for democratizing art, for bringing art and poetry to the streets and squares so as "to beautify life, to make it joyful, to create inspiration for it ..." His poetry rings with a genuine zest for life and a love of nature. One also finds cosmic, historical, and folkloric themes in his poetry, and it also reflects some of the features of Mayakovsky's poetry—lyricism, declamatory delivery—and of Khlebnikov's and Kruchonykh's use of trans-rational language.

After the Bolshevik Revolution, Kamensky took a critical part in organizing, with Mayakovsky and Burlyuk, the Café of Poets, but his association with the cubo-futurists in the 1920s was rather marginal. His memoirs are a useful, if not always reliable, source for an account of cubo-futurism.

In 1915, Osip Brik established a close working relationship with Mayakovsky and guided the cubo-futurist movement to its end in 1930. Brik's personal publication of two of Mayakovsky's greatest works, *A Cloud in Trousers* (1915) and *The Backbone Flute* (1916), brought Mayakovsky poetic recognition. The relationship not only led to Brik's interest in, and research on, "sound repetition" in poetry, but also to the formation of a highly significant group, the Society for the Study of Poetic Language (OPOYAZ), which eventually came to represent Russian formalism. In 1917, Brik also published the first collection of linguistic studies by the formalists. Subsequently, Russian formalism became closely linked with cubo-futurism in the 1920s.

The Bolshevik Revolution regenerated the cubo-futurists and the avant-garde. For them, the Revolution was not only a political break with the past, but also a break with all "stifling" literary and cultural traditions, and the opportunity to undertake a revolution in art—all of which, in retrospect, has no historical precedent. Because of their support of the Bolshevik regime (with which many artists refused to cooperate) and its efforts to create a cultural organization to direct the art life of the country, the cubo-futurists and avant-garde artists became cultural commissars who "reigned almost unchallenged" (TROTSKY) in the Department of Fine Arts. As commissars of art, the cubo-futurists were obsessed with one fundamental idea: the perma-

nent integration of art into every facet of daily life. This idea was "new and profoundly revolutionary. It is not for nothing that it so gripped the minds of ... avant-garde artists that they ... were ready in the name of art 'to put to the wall' even art itself" (Yakov Tugendkhold). Moreover, "futurism," or experimentation and novelty in art, tended to become the official cultural policy of the regime, although it did seek to foster the free development of all art movements. The regime actually promoted the cubo-futurists by providing them with subsidies for a publishing concern (*IMO*—The Art of the Young) and a newspaper *Iskusstvo kommuny*, so as to propagate their views, avant-grade art, Mayakovsky's poetry, and the linguistic studies of the formalists.

In the course of their revolution in art, the cubo-futurists and the avant-garde created conflict and opposition. Despite warnings from Anatoly LUNACHARSKY, the Commissar of Education, the cubo-futurists relentlessly attacked the art and literature of the past, identified their art with "proletarian" art, often spoke of a "dictatorship" in art, and tended to discriminate against "academic" artists. In 1919, their publishing concern and newspaper were terminated. By the end of 1920, once the Revolution had been consolidated, LENIN, who frequently called Lunacharsky to task for his sympathetic support of the cubo-futurists during the revolutionary years, was able to devote attention to cultural matters. He dismissed the cubo-futurists from the Department of Fine Arts. Lenin had always been suspicious of them and never cared for avant-garde art or poetry.

Lenin's hostility, however, failed to blunt the revolutionary fervor of the cubo-futurists. In fact, during the immediate postrevolutionary years, their movement gained momentum and expanded to include many of the major figures of the art, theatrical, film, and photographic world. They were utterly determined to gain recognition for their art and to participate in shaping Soviet cultural development in the 1920s. In January 1921, they attempted unsuccessfully to form a "definite cultural-ideological movement within the Party as an art group with respect to the theoretical elaboration, manifestation and implementation of the fundamentals of a communist, and of the transition to a communist, culture."

In 1921, the cubo-futurist and avant-garde struggle continued in the Institute for Artistic Culture (*Inkhuk*), in which there were over fifty members, including some of the eminent figures of the time: Natan Altman, Boris ARVATOV, Aleksei Babichev, Osip Brik (who was Chairman of the Institute), Nikolai Chuzhak, Sergei EISENSTEIN, Aleksandra Exter, Pavel Filonov, Naum Gabo, Aleksei Gan, Ivan Klyun, Boris Kushner, Anton Lavinsky, El Lissitzky, Kazimir Malevich, Pavel Mansurov, Vladimir Mayakovsky, Vsevolod MEYERHOLD, Anton Pevzner, Lyubov Popova, Nikolai Punin, David Shterenberg, Varvara Stepanova, Aleksandr Rodchenko, Vladimir Tatlin, and Sergei Tretyakov. The ideological banner of the Institute was constructivism, which radically assaulted "pure forms of art" (such as easel painting) and attempted to shape the artistic consciousness of the masses by inserting artistic expression into production. As the constructivists were gradually removed from the art workshops, the activities of the Institute came to an end in the beginning of 1924.

The early 1920s saw the gradual revival of literature and literary groups. The Bolshevik regime consciously encouraged the growth and development of diverse literary tendencies to the extent that they did not criticize the Revolution or the regime. It believed that a "proletarian" literature, based on the best literary achievements of the past, would develop in the future.

In this context, the cubo-futurists realized that they could not effectively advance their literary and cultural program and preserve their group identity without a press. Early in 1923, they applied for and obtained permission to publish a journal that came to be known as *The Left Front of Arts* (*Lef*), which loosely grouped cubo-futurist poets, such as Mayakovsky (who was chief editor of *Lef*), Kruchonykh, Kamensky, Aseev, and Tretyakov; art and literary critics, such as Boris Arvatov, Brik, Nikolai Chuzhak, Boris Kushner, and Grigory VINOKUR; formalist (*Opoyaz*) critics, such as Viktor SHKLOVSKY, Boris EIKHENBAUM, Yury TYNYANOV, Boris TOMASHEVSKY; Constructivist artists, such as Anton Lavinsky, Lyubov Popova, Varvara Stepanova, Aleksandr Rodchenko; and also Sergei Eisenstein, Dziga Vertov, Boris Pasternak, Isaak BABEL, among others.

The *Lef* group did not project a unified program, nor did it seek one. Its aim was to yoke literary theory and practice, to discuss and investigate the art of literary and linguistic technique for the solution of literary problems, and thus contribute to the development of literature. The cubo-futurists firmly believed that literary creation was not a function of "ideology," but a function of formal innovation, devices, and craftsmanship. Brik explained that the purpose of *Opoyaz* was to "help proletarian art not by vague discussions about the new 'proletarian spirit' and 'communist consciousness,'" but by precise technical knowledge of the devices of contemporary poetic craft."

The cubo-futurists, however, never succeeded in transcending their Bohemian tactics and past. Their loud and strident manifestos in *Lef* were a direct continuation of early futurism. Their manifestos spoke of the Russian classics as "textbooks" for the elimination of illiteracy, and of "*the struggle against transferring the methods of the work of the dead to today's art.*" The primary purpose of literature was not to reflect or imitate the "passive" life and culture of the past, but to shape and build life for a new, revolutionary culture.

Many of the works that *Lef* published were impressive contributions to an understanding of poetic and linguistic technique and formalist literary theory. Ironically, though, Isaak Babel's prose works were seen to hold high promise both for their "formal design and for an interesting psychological dimension that the Lef group, true to futurist anti-psychologism, refused to acknowledge" (Halina Stephan). Likewise, the appearance in *Lef* of some of the best lyric poetry by Aseev, Mayakovsky, and Pasternak and of the trans-rational poetry by Kamensky and Kruchonykh contradicted the journal's aim to discover "a communist path for all varieties of art." The very diversity of the *Lef* group militated against a unified aesthetic program that became essential to its survival. Other problems arose: the journal's circulation had declined from 5,000 in 1923 to 1,500 in 1924, and thus it incurred heavy financial losses. The decline was partly a result of a rapidly growing interest in prose and its reflection of Soviet reality, and a corresponding lack of interest in lyric poetry. *Lef* was torn by internal dispute over its organization and its lack of unity and clear ideological direction. *Lef* also found itself in conflict with other literary groups and Party leaders for its acrid and polemical statements and manifestos. In January 1925, after publishing seven issues, *Lef* was discontinued, but it "made a lasting imprint on Soviet literary life and cultural politics. The existence of such a journal provided a mouthpiece for the avant-garde groups that were active in Soviet cultural life but could not hope for any impact without a published declaration of their position. Yet the futurists realized that permission to put out a journal represented only a very limited success, an unspectacular culmination of their plans for an avant-garde culture, plans that had found little support among political revolutionaries" (Halina Stephan).

In 1927, the cubo-futurists waged their last battle for their place in Soviet literature, even though their survival had been already doomed by the Party's policy shift in 1925 from neutrality in literary affairs to a future commitment to a proletarian group, the Octobrists, arch rivals of the cubo-futurists. The Party had also implied that the expression of "communist ideology" would eventually become the fundamental criterion of literature.

In 1927, the cubo-futurists once again obtained permission to publish their own journal, *New Lef*, in which they effectively combined literary theory and practice. With some historical cogency, the cubo-futurists mounted an assault on the thematic and formal irrelevance of the Russian classics to the new literary needs of the post-Revolutionary period. According to Brik, pre-Revolutionary literature was created largely by and for the Russian intelligentsia and satisfied its psychological needs because of its alienation from "practical work." The advent of the Bolshevik Revolution signified a radical break with that literature and with the Russian intelligentsia; it posed a new set of thematic, cultural and literary problems which past literary methods and forms could not contain or reflect. The Revolution had created a new "cultural consumer" and readership, and had given the new Soviet intelligentsia the opportunity for active participation in economic and cultural reconstruction. Thus, the difference between the intrinsically "distorted" facts of literature and "real" facts of Soviet life could now be discerned. "All attempts to find in the old literature models for today's literary art are hopeless. All attempts to apply political pressure on writers to write from the perspective of worker-peasant life are absurd" (Brik).

The cubo-futurist antidote to the literary "crisis" was the "literature of fact," the fixation and montage of the facts of Soviet reality, as expressed in diaries, memoirs, collections, biographies, travelogues, sketches, reports about factories and collective farms, and in newspaper and journalistic work. One of the basic objectives of the "literature of fact," implicit in its focus on economic and cultural problems and needs, was to arouse consciousness of these problems and thus enlist the participation of the reader in their solution. From a literary and political perspective, the "literature of fact" was a way of "liberating the writer from the much more confining demand that he *interpret* reality in the light of dialectical materialism. To fix the writer firmly on the ground of *fact* meant to free him from the obligation to produce ideologically tendentious 'imaginative literature'" (Edward J. Brown).

The cubo-futurist theory of "social commission" (*sotsial'nyi zakaz*) was another antidote to literary problems. Brik first expounded this theory during the revolutionary years, and it was extensively practiced by the Institute of Artistic Culture in the early 1920s. By 1927, the theory gained significant currency to the point of stirring a heated debate. Essentially, the theory entailed a client-producer relationship, by which an "artist" consciously and independently fulfills the cultural, social, and class needs or demands of his time. As far as the artist was concerned, being given a commission also involved the opportunity for formal experimentation: he was to create the forms adequate to the fulfillment of the commission. The theory had key implications: "artistic" production was similar to other forms of production or work, since it was fundamentally a function of craft or skill, not basically the expression of political ideology. Nor did it mean the imposition of any "tendency" in fulfilling the commission. Put differently, the "artist" was not a creative, spiritual entity above society, but a worker integrally related to the normal processes of production.

Russian cubo-futurism ended in 1930. It is not difficult to see that political and ideological urgencies failed to undermine its basic principles: revolt against literary traditions and the primacy of formal and linguistic innovation. The cubo-futurists saw the Bolshevik Revolution as an extension of their own aesthetic revolt and sought to give a content to the vague cultural aims of the Bolsheviks. The cubo-futurists "may have been radical in their attempt to blend art and politics, but they were extreme not in their commitment to the political system, but in their determination to use that system to create a new type of art" (Halina Stephan). In the 1920s, however, the cubo-futurists perhaps had already fulfilled their historical role of making their principles and literary achievements traditions in themselves. The history of avant-garde movements seems to demonstrate that revolt and innovation are at once the condition of their existence and destruction.

Bibliography: The Ardis Anthology of Russian Futurism. 1980. Vahan D. Barooshian, *Russian Cubo-Futurism 1910–1930*. The Hague, 1974. ———, *Brik and Mayakovsky*. The Hague, 1978. Edward J. Brown, *Mayakovsky: A Poet in the Revolution*. 1973. K. Chukovskii, *Futuristy*. 1922. Victor Erlich, *Russian Formalism: History—Doctrine*. 3d ed. 1981. Bengt Jangfeldt, *Majakovskii and Futurism 1917–1921*. Stockholm, 1976. Kjeld B. Jensen, *Russian Futurism, Urbanism and Elena Guro*. Aarhus, Denmark, 1977. Nikolai Khardzhiev, "Mayakovskii i Igor' Severyanin," *RusL*, 1978, no. 4, pp. 307–46. Anna Lawton, *Vadim Shershenevich: From Futurism to Imaginism*. 1981. Vladimir Markov, *Russian Futurism: A History*. 1968. (The best study of early Russian futurism; contains the most complete bibliography of futurist works.) Krystyna Pomorska, *Russian Formalist Theory and Its Poetic Ambiance*. The Hague, 1968. Halina Stephan, *"Lef" and the Left Front of Arts*. Munich, 1981.

V. D. B

Fyódorov, Nikolai Fyódorovich (1828–1903), librarian, religious thinker. The illegitimate son of Prince Pavel Gagarin, Fyodorov was born in Southern Russia, schooled in Tambov and Odessa until 1854, when he became a provincial schoolteacher and after 1868 a librarian in Moscow, serving for twenty-five years in the Rumyantsev library. An omnivorous reader and a charismatic polymath, Fyodorov turned V. A. Kozhevnikov and Nikolai Peterson into life-long disciples and played a significant part in the intellectual development of TOLSTOI, DOSTOEVSKY, Vladimir SOLOVYOV and others. He believed that humanity, properly controlled and regulated, could master nature so completely that the dead could be resurrected, perhaps in extraterrestrial space, and that this task of recreating our ancestors is the holiest undertaking for a Russian people whose sense of community and self-sacrifice equip them for it. In his own fanatically austere life, he published little, but Peterson and Kozhevnikov organized and printed his notes as *The Philosophy of the Common Task* (Filosofiya obshchego dela, 1906, 1913).

Works: Filosofiya obshchego dela: stat'i, mysli i pis'ma Nikolaya Fedorovicha Fedorova. Vol. 1 (Vernyi, 1906); vol. 2 (Moscow, 1913). Repr. with introd. by N. Zernov. Munich, 1973. Also by Gregg International Publishers, Farnsworth, Hants, England, 1970.
Works in English: Excerpts in *Russian Philosophy* ed. James M. Edie et al. 1965. Vol. 3. Pp. 11–54.
Secondary literature: Ludmila Koehler, *N. F. Fedorov: The Philosophy of Action.* 1979. Stephen Lukashevich, *N. F. Fedorov (1828–1903).* 1977. George M. Young, Jr., *Nikolai F. Fedorov: An Introduction.* 1979. (Detailed bibliography.) R. L. B.

Gaidár (pseud. of Arkády Petróvich Golikóv, 1904–41), war hero, journalist, and writer of children's books. Gaidar joined the Red Army in 1918 and commanded a regiment at 16. Forced into retirement by injuries received in battle, Gaidar became a journalist and soon discovered his vocation as a writer for children. His stories, including "School" (Shkola, 1930), "A Military Secret" (Voennaya taina, 1935), "Chuk and Gek" (1939), and "Timur and His Team" (Timur i ego komanda, 1940) immediately became Soviet classics. Several of them were made into films. Gaidar was killed in action in October 1941.

Works: Sobranie sochinenii. 4 vols. 1959–60.
Translations: Timur and His Comrades. Trans. R. Renbourn. London, 1942. *Timur and His Gang.* New York, 1943. *Timur and His Squad; Stories.* Trans. I. Flaxman. Moscow, 1948.
Secondary literature: B. Kamov, *A. P. Gaidar.* 1979. I. I. Rozanov, *Tvorchestvo A. P. Gaidara.* 1979. V. T.

Galanskóv, Yúry Timoféevich (1939–72), dissident poet. Born in Moscow, Galanskov studied law at Moscow University, but was expelled for his dissident activities after only two semesters. In 1961, Galanskov helped edit the SAMIZDAT publication, *Feniks No. 1* (Phoenix), where he also printed some of his own poems written in defense of human rights and social justice. Galanskov also edited *Feniks No. 2* (1966), which included Andrei SINYAVSKY's celebrated essay "What Is Socialist Realism?" and Galanskov's own essays and poetry of a democratic and pacifist tenor. Galanskov was arrested in January 1967, and was sentenced a year later to seven years imprisonment to be served in a "severe regime" labor camp. He died in a prison hospital after an operation for a duodenal ulcer. Galanskov is widely recognized as a martyr for the dissident cause.

Works: "Otkrytoe pis'mo delegatu XXIII s"ezda KPSS M. Sholokhovu," *Grani* 67 (1968), pp. 115–33. *Yu. T. Galanskov: Poet i chelovek.* Frankfurt, 1973. "Pis'ma rodnym i druz'yam," *Grani* 94 (1974).
Translations: (6 poems.) In *Russian Poetry: The Modern Period.* Ed. John Glad and Daniel Weissbort. 1978. Pp. 297–301.
Secondary literature: Deming Brown, *Soviet Literature since Stalin.* 1978. Pp. 355–56. Robert Figner, trans. and ed., "Chronique des événements," *Esprit* 386 (1969), pp. 658–75. *Protsess chetyrekh i sbornik Materialov po delu Galanskova, Ginzburga, Dobrovol'skogo i Lashkovoi.* Comp. and comm. Pavel Litvinov. Amsterdam, 1971. B. A.

Gálich, Aleksándr (pseudonym of Aleksándr Ginzburg, 1918–77), Russian poet who sang his work, accompanying himself on a guitar. Although he had written a number of plays and movie scripts, Galich became famous in the 1960s as one of Russia's unofficial "bards." His songs, sometimes satirical, sometimes tragic, dealt with everyday life and politics from a common-sense, usually satirical point of view. He wrote one song, for example, about a man who struggles to win the award "Shop of Communist Labor" for his shop—it manufactures barbed wire. In the song "Comrade Paramonova" Galich pokes fun at the intrusion of the Party into problems of family life. Other songs are in a more tragic key—of Khrushchev arranging a hunt over the

bodies of men who died in the battle of Narva, or of how Galich himself would one day return to Russia. In late 1971/early 1972 Galich was expelled from the Writers' Union at the insistence of Dmitry Polyansky, a member of the Politburo. He emigrated in June 1974 and died in Paris from electrocution while repairing a tape recorder. In an obituary Efim Etkind referred to him as the "most popular man in Russia."

Works: General'naya repetitsiya. Frankfurt, 1974.
Translations: Songs and Poems. Trans. G. S. Smith. Ann Arbor, 1984.
Secondary literature: D. Andreeva, "Rossii serdtse ne zabudet ... (O tvorchestve Aleksandra Galicha)," *Grani,* no. 109 (1978), pp. 215–28. Rosette C. Lamont, "Horace's Heirs: Beyond Censorship in the Soviet Songs of the *Magnitizdat,*" *World Literature Today* 53 (1979), pp. 220–27. Gene Sosin, "Magnitizdat: Uncensored Songs of Dissent." In *Dissent in the USSR,* ed. Rudolf L. Tokes. Baltimore, 1975. Pp. 276–309. J. G.

Gallicisms. With the Petrine Reforms, there was an immense influx of foreign words into Russian. By the time of Peter's death in 1725, there were some 3000 foreign words adopted into the language (about 25 percent administrative terms from German, another quarter seafaring terms from Dutch, English, French, Italian as well as German; the remainder mostly military and scientific terms, mostly from German and French). Because of the great appeal of the French culture of the 17th and 18th centuries, German soon yielded to French as a source of loanwords, and by the reign of CATHERINE II, there was a rampant gallomania which not only added lexical items but affected the very syntax of the language. During the process, many successful calques and borrowings evolved, but there was also a host of barbarisms and macaronisms which cluttered both the literary and everyday languages. Peter the Great complained that even military commands had become incomprehensible to subalterns and common soldiers ("Zanimat' mesto avantazhnoe" was taken to mean "Occupy a town named Avantazhnoe"). By the 1750s, LOMONOSOV was impelled to defend the expressiveness of the Russian language, and warned against too many borrowings (he had French in mind): "Foreign words are at first helpful, but later harmful." Even Francophile SUMAROKOV was appalled at what had become a kind of Russo-French pidgin, and recorded this extreme example: "Ya v distraktsii i dezespere, amanta moya sdelala mne infidelite, a ya ku syur protiv rivalya svoego budu revanshirovatsya." (I am distraught and in despair. My lover has been unfaithful to me, and I will certainly be avenged on my rival.)

FONVIZIN, during an anti-French phase, satirized contemporary gallicisms in *The Brigadier,* but himself made use of them (delat' dolzhnost'/faire son devoir; vzyat' otstavku/prendre congé; raduyus' sdelat' vashe znakomstvo/je suis heureux de faire votre connaissance).

In the latter part of the century, some measure of balance was struck between a colloquial Russian and the more erudite one (including loanwords), particularly in the periodical press of the time. KARAMZIN used loan translations with care, creating many of his own, ones which seemed to fit quite naturally into Russian (vliyanie, chelovechnyi, promyshlennost', sovershenstvovat'). Further, by replacing the heavy German-Latin syntax favored by Lomonosov with one closer to educated colloquial Russian, Karamzin was able to approximate the lightness of French speech in what sounded like pure Russian.

Ironically, Karamzin helped to introduce a new French literary taste which was contrary to these healthy developments: sentimentalism, with its "langue sentimentale" and predilection for "pleasantness." Pleasantness in speech was conceived as periphrasis. It is claimed that locutions like this could be heard in the salons of the Karamzinian school: "Voiturez-nous les commodités de la conversation" (Convey to us the commodities of conversation) meaning, "Bring us some chairs so we can sit down and talk."

It was against excesses of this sort in the early part of the 19th century that the "archaizers" (SHISHKOvians, supporters of native Russian against French influence) rose up to do battle against the "innovators" (Karamzinians). The battle raged during PUSHKIN's formative years, and while he and his partisans ridiculed the Shishkovians, one has the feeling that he actually agreed with their more sensible points. French culture in Russia reached its height around this time, before and during the Napoleonic Wars. TOLSTOI, in retrospect, plays on the gallicisms of the period in *War and Peace* (e.g., the color of Hippolyte's trousers was "cuisse de nymphe effrayée"). In any case, it was Pushkin who had settled the matter by developing a graceful literary style suitable for the great literature of the rest of the century. In the decade after Pushkin's death, French was losing its preeminence, and gallicisms in Russian no longer represented a question of special importance.

Bibliography: A. M. Babkin, *Slovar' inoyazychnykh vyrazhenii i slov.* 2 vols. 1966. V. A. Bogoroditskii, *Obshchii kurs russkoi grammatiki.* Kazan, 1913. Maurice Friedberg, "The Comic Element in War and Peace," *Indiana Slavic Studies* 4, pp. 100–19. Greta Hüttl-Worth, *Foreign Words in Russian: A Historical Sketch, 1550–1800.* 1963. L. P. Krysin, *Inoyazychnye slova v sovremennom russkom yazyke.* 1968.   C. D.

Gan (Hahn), née Fadéeva,, Eléna Andréevna (1814–42, published under the pseudonym Zeneida R-va), writer. She was the mother of the theosophist and writer Elena P. Blavatsky. In her highly successful novels and stories, such as *The Ideal* (Ideal, 1837), *The Medallion* (Medal'on, 1839), *The Judgment of Society* (Sud sveta, 1840), and *Theofania Abbiaggio* (Teofaniya Abbiadzhio, 1841), Gan undertook the mission of a Russian George Sand, advocating progressive ideas, and in particular the emancipation of women, demanding their right to an education and creativity, and to love and be loved as equal partners. Her statement of the plight of an educated woman caught up in the dull routine of an officer's wife, repeated in several of her works, has a ring of truth. Gan, a talented writer whose promising career was cut short by an untimely death, shared the virtues as well as the faults of the early George Sand: an emotionality which sometimes turns to sentimentality, a fluid style which too often becomes rhetorical, and sharply drawn characters which tend to become stereotypes.

Works: Sochineniya. 4 Pts. 1843. *Polnoe sobranie sochinenii.* 6 vols. 1905.

Secondary literature: V. G. Belinskii, "Sochineniya Zeneidy R-voi" (1843). In PSS (1953–59). Vol. 7. Pp. 648–78. E. S. Nekrasova, "Elena Andreevna Gan (Zeneida R-va), 1814–1842," *Russkaya starina*, 1886, nos. 8 and 9. Marit B. Nielsen, "The Concept of Love and the Conflict of the Individual versus Society in Elena A. Gan's *Sud sveta*," *Scando-Slavica* 24 (1978), pp. 125–38.   V. T.

Gárin, N. (pseudonym of Nikolaí Geórgievich Mikhailóvsky, 1852–1906), writer. Graduated from the Engineering Institute in 1878; worked in the Ministry of Communications on and off for many years. A talented engineer, he participated in the building of the Siberian and Batum railroads and other projects. Influenced by POPULISM, Garin also tried his hand at agrarian reforms; he bought various estates and tried to run them rationally. In 1890 he published *A Few Years in the Village* (Neskol'ko let v derevne), a cycle of sketches in which he described his farming experiences. From 1892 he devoted himself to literature, mortgaging his estate to join a group headed by the critic N. K. MIKHAILOVSKY which purchased the journal "Russkoe bogatstvo". In 1892 he also began to publish his most important work—the *Bildungsroman* trilogy: *Tema's Childhood* (Detstvo Temy, 1892), *In High School* (Gimnazisty, 1895), and *Students* (Studenty, 1895). A fourth book, *Engineers* (Inzhenery) appeared posthumously in 1907. In the central character, Tema Kartashev, Garin traced the spiritual and psychological evolution of a typical Russian intellectual of the time. In his peasant stories of the 1890s "Christmas Eve in a Russian Village" (Sochel'nik v russkoi derevne), "Village Scenes" (Derevenskie panoramy), and "Barge-Haulers" (Burlaki), Garin turned to describing the misery, ignorance, and poverty of village life. By the mid-1890s, Garin broke off with the Populists and began to collaborate with the Marxists. He was one of the founders of the first Marxist newspapers *Samarskii vestnik*, (1896–97). A story, "Klotil'da," appeared in the Marxist journal *Nachalo* in 1899. In his stories Garin often discussed controversial subjects: discrimination against Jews, debasement of women, abuse of children, and yet his work was imbued with optimism and faith in a better future. In 1898 Garin took a journey around the world, about which he wrote sketches entitled *Through Korea, Manchuria and the*

Liaotung Peninusula (Po Koree, Man'chzhurii i Lyaodunskomu poluostrovu). Garin wrote with great sympathy about the "yellow" races and he also compiled a book of Korean folklore. After 1905 Garin belonged to the "ZNANIE" group of writers, headed by M. GORKY, and contributed large sums to the Bolshevik Party.

Works: Polnoe sobranie sochinenii. 9 vols. 1903–10. Vols. 10–17. 1913–14. *Polnoe sobranie sochinenii.* 8 vols. 1916. *Iz dnevnikov krugosvetnogo puteshestviya.* 5 vols. 1952. *Sobranie sochinenii.* 5 vols. 1957–58.

Secondary literature: M. Gor'kii, *Portrety zamechatel'nykh lyudei.* 1936. G. N. Mironov, *Poet neterpelivogo sozidaniya.* 1965. V. M. Kolos, *N. G. Garin-Mikhailovskii: Problemy khudozhestvennogo tvorchestva.* 1967. N. D. Kurtysheva, *Tvorcheskii put' N. G. Garina-Mikhailovskogo.* 1955. I. M. Yudyan, *N. G. Garin-Mikhailovskii.* 1969.   E. K. K.

Gárshin, Vsévolod Mikhaílovich (1855–88), a gifted writer who managed to complete some 20 short stories before his suicide. He came from the middle gentry. His father, a weak-willed man, had pursued a military career, and Garshin briefly followed in his footsteps, serving in the Balkans in 1877 against the Turks. He enlisted in order to participate in the suffering of his fellow man. His mother, a self-centered and domineering woman, had abandoned him when he was five to run away with a revolutionary activist. Though she later took him back, the experience left deep scars. A victim of savage depressions and intermittent mental breakdowns, Garshin finally flung himself down a staircase when he could bear his life no longer.

Garshin entered Russian literature during an interval in which the great realist tradition was grinding to a halt and no dominant literary manner had stepped in to replace it. In the 1880s ambitions became smaller, the lyric and short story upstaged the novel, style was often tentative and eclectic. Also, a reaction against the utilitarian imperatives of the previous decades led to an interest in universal themes isolated from specific social circumstances. Garshin's own work combines a sharp eye for detail and psychological exactitude with a penchant for allegory that anticipates SYMBOLISM. His stories tend to be more dramatically concentrated than the short story of the earlier realist period, which was focused on the sketch. Their mood reflects the widespread spiritual depression of the European fin de siècle, intensified in Russia by harsh political reaction. Garshin is a writer compulsively drawn to suffering, whence his identification with the victim revealed in a streak of POPULIST pathos. He is not above indulging in sentimentality and melodrama—common blemishes of writing in the 1880s—but his best work is well disciplined.

Among his best are military tales. In "Four Days" (Chetyre dnya, 1877) a wounded soldier relates what it feels like to lie, unable to move, next to a putrefying corpse. Often compared to the war stories of TOLSTOI (along with TURGENEV and DOSTOEVSKY, a major influence), it displays a sensationalist NATURALISM and heightened emotionalism that are quite un-Tolstoian. The obsessive fascination with death of "Four Days" runs through Garshin's oeuvre, as does its basic format—the encounter of an idealistic, sensitive young man with the evil of the world. The collision may fill the young man with guilt, as in "Four Days," or it may cause him to reassess his evaluation of reality. Thus in "From the Reminiscences of Private Ivanov" (Iz vospominanii ryadovogo Ivanova, 1883), the innocent discovers hidden complexities in the apparently corrupt officer Ventsel. Though the thesis overruns the characters—a not infrequent fault of Garshin's—the story is distinguished by a dispassionate and compelling rendering of the daily lives of men at war. Perhaps because it treats characters quite unlike the author and hence unsusceptible to his excessive emotionalism, "Officer and Orderly" (1880) turned out to be the finest of his military tales. Understated in the way CHEKHOV is, it tells of two opposites—the vain, superficial officer Stebelkov and his brutishly simple-minded orderly Nikita—joined only by the accident of circumstance and by their parallel lives of meaningless routine and spiritual desolation.

Of Garshin's fables the most outstanding are "Attalea Princeps" (1880) and "The Red Flower" (Krasnyi tsvetok, 1883). Attalea Princeps is a palm tree who, in a supreme effort of will, grows through the glass roof of its imprisoning hothouse only to discover, instead of freedom, a bleak Russian sky. The fabulous inventions of the tale, as well as its theme of lonely failed rebellion, point to a resurgence of romanticism in Garshin's age. In "The Red Flower" a madhouse furnishes yet another metaphor of the world as a prison. More than any other work it crystallizes Garshin's central concern—the issue of evil. The madman of the story imagines that the world's evil is contained in three poppies growing in the courtyard of his asylum. He plucks them one by one, hoping to purify existence by draining off its corruption into his own body. Despite its allegorical abstraction, the story is an extremely convincing study of madness. In the Dostoevskian "Night" (1880) suicide is entertained (and rejected) as another path to perfection.

Garshin's most ambitious story, "Nadezhda Nikolaevna" (1885), is mere overblown melodrama, a case of Dostoevsky undigested. Once again it implicates a young idealist, now an artist, in the violence of the world. Another tale about artists, "The Artists" (Khudozhniki, 1879), though inconclusive, is revealing of Garshin's views of his calling. An intense artist of populist sympathies is so overwhelmed by the anguish of his subject, a terribly exploited worker, that he quits painting. Art ultimately proves impotent before human suffering.

Works: Sochineniya. 1963.

Translations: The Scarlet Flower: Stories. Trans. B. Isaacs. Moscow, n. d. *The Signal and Other Stories.* Trans. R. Smith. New York, 1915. *Last Translations: Three Stories by Vsevolod Garshin.* Trans. Eugene M. Kayden. 1979. *See also:* Lewanski, p. 242.

Secondary literature: Grigorii Byalyi, *Vsevolod Garshin.* 1969. Leland Fetzer, "Art and Assassination: Garshin's 'Nadezhda Nikolaevna'," *RusR* 34 (1975), pp. 55–65. Karl D. Kramer, "Impressionist Tendencies in the Work of Vsevolod Garshin." In *American Contributions to the Seventh International Congress of Slavists.* Vol. 2. Ed. Victor Terras. The Hague, 1973. Pp. 339–56.   M. E.

Gástev, Aleksei Kapitónovich (1882–1941), one of the most original and popular poets of the proletarian literary movement. He was a member of the Bolshevik faction from the early years of the century, was arrested and exiled, and twice emigrated to Paris. He began publishing in 1904, in Party journals, but his first book, published after the Revolution, *Poetry of the Working-Class Attack* (Poeziya rabochego udara, 1918), was for the most part a collection of his poetry and prose written earlier. Gastev was a poet of the factory worker, whom he saw "growing out of iron" into a new kind of human being, one psychologically in harmony with the hard objective calculus of machines and organized production. In his sometimes very moving rhythmic lines Gastev speaks of the coming might of the world proletariat and the triumph of a new working class culture stripped of any remnant of individualism. Hyperbolic passages on the total rationalization of the working class psychology are not infrequent, as when he speaks of "the mechanization, not only of gestures, not only of production methods, but of everyday thinking, coupled with extreme rationality …" Gastev was arrested in 1938 and and apparently died in prison in 1941. He was posthumously rehabilitated in 1957.

Works: Poeziya rabochego udara. Moscow, 1964.

Secondary literature: Z. Papernyi, "V pervye gody." In his *Samoe trudnoe.* 1963.   E. J. B.

Gazdánov, Gaitó (Geórgy Ivánovich, 1903–1971), émigré novelist and short story writer. Joined the White Army at the age of 16. After graduating from high school in Bulgaria, Gazdanov settled in Paris in 1923. His first short stories began to appear in 1926 and 1927, primarily in the Prague journal *Volya Rossii.* In 1930 Gazdanov became very well known in the emigration, as his first novel, *An Evening with Claire* (Vecher u Kler, Paris, 1930, reprinted by Ardis, Ann Arbor in 1979) was hailed as a major literary event and he was seen as the most promising young novelist besides NABOKOV. This impression was reinforced by the short story "Water Prison" (Vodyanaya tyur'ma) published in the first issue of the new, and controversial, journal *Chisla* in which Gazdanov's story was seen by most critics as the most accomplished piece of writing. As a result of his new-found fame, the gates of SOVREMENNYE ZAPISKI, the emigration's most prestigious journal, opened for Gazdanov and it was there that he published most of his work, including two novels, *The History of a Journey* (Istoriya odnogo puteshestviya), and *Night Roads* (Nochnye dorogi), and eight short stories, until the journal ceased publication in 1940. To make ends meet, however, Gazdanov had to work and after some very hard

times in the mid-1920s, he found the occupation that gave him both a living and enough time for writing—night-time taxi driving. It was only in 1953 that Gazdanov could finally give it up after accepting a post at Radio Liberty where he worked as an editor until his death. NOVYI ZHURNAL (New York) published all five novels that Gazdanov wrote after World War II. Only one book-form edition of a Gazdanov novel was published and that was a reprint of the pre-war *Night Roads* (New York, 1952). Even though two of these novels, *The Specter of Alexander Wolf* (Prizrak Aleksandra Vol'fa), and *Buddha's Return* (Vozvrashchenie Buddy) were translated into English and published in New York in 1950 and 1951, international recognition failed to come. Gazdanov was disappointed about the post-war decline in émigré cultural life, yet after a hiatus in the mid-fifties, he resumed work and published the novels *The Awakening* (Probuzhdenie, 1965–66) and *Evelyne and Her Friends* (Evelina i ee druz'ya, 1968–71) and several new short stories in *Novyi zhurnal.* His last, unfinished novel, *The Coup d'État* (Perevorot, 1972) appeared in the same journal posthumously. In 1983 La Presse Libre (Paris) announced the publication of a two-volume collection of Gazdanov's novels and short stories. Gazdanov's art is characterized by the unusual but attractive combination of high emotional intensity expressed in lucid, restrained, classically balanced prose of impeccably sustained rhythm. Most of his works have an episodic narrative structure; most paint emotional landscapes, the inner life of the psyche, the subtle "movements of the soul," as Gazdanov called them. Most of his characters undergo metamorphoses, are on an "emotional journey," in search of love, identity, or answers to the "cursed questions" of human existence. In several of his novels there is also a "metaphysical thriller," a suspenseful murder story deepened by philosophical meditations on the meaning of life, death, and chance. Gazdanov's fiction is remarkable both for being a distillation of literary Russian of great clarity and harmony, and for its modern, existential themes, a combination that makes him somewhat akin to Camus and rather unique among his Russian contemporaries.

Secondary literature: L. Dienes, *Russian Literature in Exile: The Life and Work of Gajto Gazdanov.* Munich, 1982. ———, *Bibliographie des oeuvres de Gaito Gazdanov.* Paris, 1982. T. Pachmuss, ed., *A Russian Cultural Revival.* Knoxville, Tenn., 1981. G. P. Struve, *Russkaya literatura v izgnanii.* New York, 1956.   L. D.

Gerásimov, Mikhail Prokófievich (1889–1939). A proletarian poet active in the political and literary affairs of the Russian Social Democratic Party before the Revolution. The son of a railway worker, he joined the Party in 1905, was arrested for his activities and spent many years in exile. In 1913 he began publishing his poems in Bolshevik journals. He was active in the PROLETKUL'T, in VAPP (see RAPP), and in KUZNITSA. Gerasimov's lyrics celebrate proletarian labor and the worldwide proletarian struggle. The factory and the iron world of machines are for him both the product and the natural element of the working class. His poetic figures are often derived from the tools and the processes of industrial production. The transition to NEP was a cruel disillusionment for Gerasimov as for other writers of *Kuznitsa,* and he resigned from the Party in 1921. He was arrested in 1937 and died in prison in 1939. He was rehabilitated posthumously and two collections of his verse have since appeared in the Soviet Union.

Works: Stikhotvoreniya. 1959.

Secondary literature: R. Shatseva. In *Proletarskie poety pervykh let sovetskoi epokhi.* 1959.   E. J. B.

Germanisms. Words and expressions which have come from German, both in the form of direct borrowings and derivational, semantic, or syntactic calques.

German words were adopted during all periods in the development of the Russian language, but particularly intensively during the first half of the 18th century. The process of Westernization of the economic, social, and cultural life, which set in during the reign of Peter the Great, brought with it many loanwords from West European languages, especially from German and French. Approximately one quarter of the foreign words which are part of the modern literary language were absorbed during this time. They belong mainly to the areas of administration, trade, and the military; e.g., *shtempel'* "stamp" (G. Stempel), *bukhgalter* "accountant" (Buchhalter), *slesar'* "locksmith" (Schlosser), *parikmakher* "barber" (Perücken-macher), *tseikhgauz* "armory" (Zeughaus), *shturm* "assault" (Sturm). Quite often—especially in the 17th and 18th centuries—German words were first borrowed by Polish or Byelorussian and then entered the Russian language in a Polish or Byelorussian form; e.g., *shturmovat'* "to take by storm" (stürmen), *gvalt* "uproar" (Gewalt), *fortel'* "trick" (Vorteil).

On the other hand, German frequently was the intermediary for words of Latin and French origin; e.g., *lampa* "lamp" (Fr. lampe, G. Lampe), *paket* "parcel" (Fr. paquet, G. Paket), *prezident* "president" (Fr. président, G. Präsident), *banket* (Fr. banquet, G. Bankett).

It is not always possible to determine with certainty whether a loanword was borrowed from German, Dutch, or other Germanic languages; e.g., *machta* "mast" (G. Mast, Dutch mast). This is one reason why some authors include among "Germanisms" all borrowings from Germanic languages.

Very often loanwords underwent certain changes in Russian. The older a borrowing is, the more likely is its adaptation to the phonological and morphological rules of the Russian language. In *gorn* "bugle" (Horn), for instance, the initial *h* was replaced by *g*; and *lozung* "slogan" (Losung) as well as *shtraf* "fine" (Strafe) changed their gender from feminine to masculine, since in Russian both end in a consonant.

Until approximately 1740 the influx of German loanwords was greater than that of French ones, but from then on, GALLICISMS outnumbered Germanisms. During the 18th century it was LOMONOSOV, RADISHCHEV, and KARAMZIN in particular who furthered the Europeanization of the literary language, making it more suitable for expressing abstract concepts, and adapting it to the international scholarly terminology. The leading writers of the 18th and the 19th centuries enriched the Russian language both by introducing loanwords and by creating calques, i.e., lexeme-by-lexeme translations of foreign words. Lomonosov, for instance, adopted the German loanwords *kolba* "retort" (Kolben) and *shtol'nya* "[mining] gallery" (Stollen) among others, but he also created such calques as *vozdushnyi nasos* "air pump" (Luftpumpe) and *zazhigatel'naya tochka* "focus" (Brennpunkt). Among the calques that Karamzin coined or popularized are *obrazovanie* "culture, education" (Bildung), *samonadezhnost'* "self-confidence" (Selbstvertrauen) and *blagotvoritel'-nost'* "charity" (Wohltätigkeit). Karamzin also introduced phraseological and syntactic calques; e.g., *slomat' led* "to break the ice" (das Eis brechen), *sidet' kak na igolkakh* "to be on tenterhooks" (wie auf Nadeln sitzen), *prinimat' uchastie* "to take part" (Anteil nehmen, teilnehmen).

During the 19th century further abstract terms became established in literary usage. Among them are the calques *mirovozzrenie* "world-view, philosophy of life" (Weltanschauung), *tselostnost'* "integrity" (Ganzheit), *predpolagat'* "to presuppose" (voraussetzen) and *isklyuchitel'nyi* "exceptional" (ausschließlich). BELINSKY in particular played a leading role in making such terms known to the educated Russian. The semi-calque *gumannost'* "humanity", modelled on the German word "Humanität", is another neologism frequently found in Belinsky's writings.

An example of a calque coined in the 20th century is *skorosshivatel'* "loose-leaf binder" (Schnellhefter).

At times Germanisms—and Gallicisms—became the target of PURISTS. Attempts were made, for instance, to replace *buterbrod* "sandwich" (Butterbrot) with *khleb s maslom* "bread with butter", and *fel'dsher* "medical attendant" (Feldscher) with *lekarskii pomoshchnik* and its abbreviated form *lekpom*, but these attempts failed. Other Germanisms, however, did not have to be replaced; they were short-lived or have become obsolete, e.g., words designating czarist institutions.

Bibliography: A. Bond, *German Loanwords in the Russian Language of the Petrine Period*. Bern, 1974. S. C. Gardiner, *German Loanwords in Russian 1550–1690*. 1965. G. Hüttl-Worth, *Foreign Words in Russian: A Historical Sketch, 1550–1800*. 1963.   M. R.

German-Russian Literary Relations. Even before Peter the Great broke through the wall of Greek Orthodoxy, which had surrounded the Muscovite Empire for centuries, many works of Western literature had entered Russia, mostly via Poland and the Ukraine. How-ever, the West learned of the existence of Russian literature rather late. Of great importance for the study of Russo-German literary relations is Paul Fleming's Russian experience during the Thirty Years War. His sonnet "An die große Stadt Moskau" (1636) calls for a good understanding between Volga and Rhine. Western mystic literature, too, came to Russia via the Ukraine and Poland. *Imitatio Christi*, by Thomas à Kempis, was translated and widely read. However, in Muscovite Russia the spirit of mysticism had yielded to a more formal piety. Yet, with the reforms introduced by Peter, the door to the West was opened. Even before, Quirinus Kuhlmann (1650–89), a religious fanatic and dreamer of the so-called "fifth Jesulite monarchy," travelled to the German settlement near Moscow from where he hoped to spread the teachings of Jakob Boehme (1575–1624) and other German mystics. His experiment failed. Nevertheless, with the help of several translations, the writings of "holy Jakob" soon were known beyond the boundaries of the German *sloboda*.

Around 1700, S. Poddorsky, a student in Halle and later bishop of Pskov, translated numerous German pietist writings. Poddorsky was influenced by A. H. Francke (1663–1727), whose *Anfang der christlichen Lehre* he translated into Russian. *Das wahre Christentum* and *Informatorium Publicum* by J. Chr. Arndt (1555–1621) were also widely read, until prohibited in 1743. German pietism had a definite influence on Russian religious life in the 18th century. Its spirit can be sensed in the writings of St. Tikhon Zadonsky. Generations of Russian children made their first contact with the Bible through a translation of Johannes Hübner's *Hundert und vier heilige Geschichten aus dem alten und Neuen Testament* (1714), as we are told in DOSTOEVSKY's *Brothers Karamazov*. Toward the end of the 18th century, the initiative for many translations of German mystics came from a circle of Russians led by the publisher N. I. NOVIKOV. Scholars, landowners, writers, and even monks showed great interest in non-Russian ecclesiastical writings. Among the translated works of Novikov's circle, we find excerpts from *Der Cherubinische Wandersmann* by Angelus Silesius (1624–77) as well as works by the Swabian mystic F. Chr. Oetinger (1702–82); the Genesis commentary by Valentin Weigel (1533–88); writings by A. von Franckenberg (1593–1652); the father of Swabian pietism, J. A. Bengel (1687–1752); and also new translations from works by Thomas à Kempis and J. Chr. Arndt. In 1794, Novikov was arrested and many translations were destroyed. Nevertheless, the Novikov tradition persisted.

In the beginning of the 19th century, Alexander I showed great interest in J. H. Jung-Stilling (1740–1817) whose works appeared in various abbreviated Russian translations. V. F. ODOEVSKY and his circle, the lyubomudry (see WISDOM LOVERS), as well as many theologians (Glukharyov, Borisov), scholars (Avseniev, Golubinsky), and writers and critics such as CHAADAEV, the AKSAKOVS, BAKUNIN, HERZEN, and BELINSKY read the philosophers Kant, Schelling, Franz von Baader, and G. H. Schubert, then popular in Russia, and were greatly influenced by their thinking. They were also active in spreading the works of Boehme, John Pordage, Saint-Martin, von Franckenberg and Jung-Stilling. The Russian romantic writer KYUKHELBEKER, while in prison after the Decembrist revolt, occupied himself extensively with German mysticism. Similarly, Aleksandr Herzen began his study of philosophy not only with Hegel, but read at the same time, and with great interest, Boehme, Swedenborg and other mystics. A detailed study of German mysticism was undertaken by the philosophical mentor of both Dostoevsky and Tolstoi, N. N. STRAKHOV (1828–96), who was first in Russia to include the name of Meister Eckhart in his list of German mystics. The Ukrainian philosopher P. D. Yurkevich, who named Leibniz, Swedenborg, and Boehme among the last great philosophers of the West, was the teacher of V. SOLOVYOV (1853–1900). Solovyov's theological and philosophical sources can be traced, in particular, to the mystical writings of Boehme and of Jung-Stilling. The philosophers S. N. Trubetskoi (1862–1905) and N. BERDYAEV (articles about Boehme) were followers of Solovyov.

In the area of literature, the symbolists, because of their kinship with the romanticists of the 19th century, found their way back to the philosophy of German idealism and German mysticism. Two of their themes were especially attractive to the Russian poets at the turn of the century. The psychological, as expressed by J. A. Bengel (translated by F. Levitsky) and Jung-Stilling, and developed by Solovyov, was taken over by BLOK, BELY, MEREZHKOVSKY, HIPPIUS, and also by Vyacheslav IVANOV and his circle. The speculative-philosophical approach to religion by Boehme was the ultimate source of a new avenue to Russian creative thinking. Other German mystics who influenced Russian thought during the last two centuries were: J. G. Arnold (translated by Levshin), J. Chr. Arndt, A. H. Francke, A. von Franckenberg, F. Chr. Oetinger, J. Scheffler (Angelus Silesius), and V. Weigel.

In 1693, Peter I met the great German philologist Heinrich Ludolf in the German suburb of Moscow. Ludolf had published, in Oxford, the first grammar of modern Russian and had contacts with the pietist circle of Francke to which Peter had been introduced. Much more important, however, were Peter's contacts with the philosophers Leibniz and Wolff of the German Enlightenment. After Peter's death and the creation of the Academy of Sciences, the exchange of information between Germany and Russia became more mutual. M. V. LOMONOSOV had studied in Germany with Wolff and became professor and one of the founders of Moscow University. In addition to his interest in the sciences, Lomonosov had become Russia's foremost linguistic scholar and poet. He studied Martin Opitz' *Buch von der teutschen Poeterey* and imitated J. C. Günther in his "Ode on the Capture of Khotin" (1739). Lomonosov's poetics was greatly influenced by J. G. Gottsched (1700–66) who dictated Germany's literary taste at the time. Many of Gottsched's followers (Kanitz, Reichel, König, etc.) were included in V. K. TREDIAKOVSKY's *New and Brief Method for the Composition of Russian Verse* (1735). J. G. Reichel (died 1788) became professor at the University of Moscow and the teacher of D. I. FONVIZIN.

The Russian THEATER, too, received its impetus from Western models. There was pastor J. G. Gregori's theater (1672–76); Johann Kunst's group came from Danzig by invitation of Peter I, and Caroline Neuber's group played in Russia during the reign of Empress Anna. A. P. SUMAROKOV became the first director of a theater established in 1756. As a dramatist, he imitated the French, but as a lyricist he turned to the German poets Ludwig Gleim, E. von Kleist, and Fr. G. Klopstock. Works by Sumarokov were soon translated into German. An ode and the tragedy *Semira* were translated by T. I. von Osterwald (1729–90), a German officer with the Corps of Cadets in Petersburg. Sumarokov's fables were rendered into German by A. L. Schlözer (1735–1809), historian of the Academy in St. Petersburg, and were published in a bilingual edition. Sumarokov's literary themes taken from history became models for some German writers.

Several other writers of Russian classicism became known in German translations. Among them were KANTEMIR, DERZHAVIN, and CATHERINE II. J. M. R. Lenz (1751–92) and A. von Kotzebue (1761–1819), trans. Derzhavin's poems, 1793) were among the most active translators, and F. Nicolai was the publisher of some of Catherine's works.

In the mid-sixties of the 18th century, the University of Leipzig attracted many Russian students. RADISHCHEV and Goethe were in Leipzig at the same time. Here, the greatest influence upon the Russians may have been exerted by Chr. F. Gellert's sensitivity to human suffering. Gellert's lectures and the Russian peasant revolt (Pugachov, between 1773 and 1775) may well have been the major cause for Radishchev's revolutionary *Journey from Petersburg to Moscow* (1790), which soon became known in Germany. Gellert's *Betschwestern*, together with other German works, were commissioned for translation by Catherine. Catherine's satirical comedy *O Time* imitates Gellert. The last quarter of the 18th century provided the German reader with a wealth of information about literature in Russia through the publications of the *Neue Bibliothek der Schönen Wissenschaften und Freien Künste* (see edition of 1768) and especially the *Russische Bibliothek zur Kenntnis des Gegenwärtigen Zustandes der Literatur in Russland*, published in Petersburg, Riga, and Leipzig. At the same time, the Russian poet G. R. Derzhavin, who was fluent in German, and his friend I. I. KHEMNITSER, the son of a German doctor, were active in introducing German literature in Russia. Derzhavin was well acquainted with A. von Haller, F. von Hagedorn, and E. von Kleist. He also translated parts of Klopstock's *Messias* and was among the first to recognize the greatness of Schiller. His own poetry was translated by Kotzebue and caused a sensation in Germany. Khemnitser wrote fables with profound Russian content, but their form imitated that of Lessing, Gellert, and Lafontaine. He also translated most of Gellert's fables into Russian.

In 1784, N. I. Novikov became the driving force behind the Moscow Freemasons. He also continued the work started by J. G.

Schwarz, a German from Siebenbürgen, and since 1779 professor at Moscow University. Schwarz introduced Kant to his students and published, with his seminar, some 500 German works in Russian translation. Among these publications were works by Lessing, Klopstock, Gellert, and Schiller. Lenz became an active member of Novikov's circle. He translated parts of KHERASKOV's heroic epic *Rossiada*, wrote some treatises about early Russian literature, and had great influence upon KARAMZIN who, too, had been active in Novikov's circle.

N. M. Karamzin received more attention in Germany than any other contemporary Russian. His sentimental stories, published in newspapers, periodicals, and in separate editions, were widely read in Germany. In his *Letters of a Russian Traveller* (1791), published in German from 1799 to 1802, Karamzin informed the German reader about Russia's emerging literature. At the recommendation of Lenz, Karamzin had visited Kant, Herder, Ramler, Wieland, Lavater, among others. *Poor Liza* became Karamzin's best known literary work in Germany. Perhaps the profoundest impression upon Karamzin was left by Herder. Herder's "Slawenkapitel" in *Ideen zur Philosophie der Geschichte der Menschheit* predicted a great future to the Slavs. Yet, Herder described the Russian national character, especially Russia's willingness and desire to learn from others, best in his famous *Journal meiner Reise*. Karamzin suggested to his Russian fellow writers many German sources for imitation. Traceable are, through his translations, Klopstock, Haller, Gessner, and some detailed studies of Schiller's poetry and drama.

F. M. Klinger (1752–1831), a German dramatist who became a Russian general, was instrumental in introducing Schiller in Russia, while Schiller's brother-in-law, Wolzogen, on the occasion of a visit to Petersburg, supplied Schiller with background material for his drama *Demetrius*. Kotzebue, who was equally at home in Germany and in Russia, had been strongly impressed by Sumarokov's great *Demetrius* tragedy. He was the first in Germany to introduce the Demetrius theme there.

Although several German studies of Russian literature, including one by J. G. Seume (1763–1810), had been previously produced, it was Ludwig Wachler (1767–1838) who made the attempt to sum up the achievements of Russian literature in his *Handbuch der allgemeinen Geschichte der literärischen Cultur* (1805). Two years earlier, the first anthology of Russian literature in German translation had been prepared by G. von Doppelmair, as well as a publication of several Russian folksongs, translated and edited by J. G. Richter. A discussion about Russian literature, however, was introduced some fifteen years later when Hofrat von Busse produced a collection of Russian literature, today known as the *Vladimir Anthology*, or officially *Fürst Vladimir und dessen Tafelrunde*. This anthology contradicted the popular notion that medieval Russia had remained barbaric, without literature and culture, and revealed an abundance of material of tales and sagas, showing convincingly that Kievan *Rus'* had occupied an important place within the structure of medieval Europe.

Blazing the trail for the introduction of Russian literature in Europe was Sir John Bowring's (1792–1872) anthology of representative works of Russian literature, published in English (1821–1823). The introduction to the book gives a thorough discussion of Russian literature from Lomonosov to ZHUKOVSKY. Goethe acquired his knowledge of Russian literature from this anthology. Almost every learned Russian traveller in Germany considered it his obligation (and an honor) to visit Goethe in Weimar, although not everyone agreed with Goethe's political views. It is questionable whether or not Goethe really understood the concerns of the Russian intelligentsia. Some literary minds, such as Herzen, Belinsky, PISAREV, and STANKEVICH, looked upon Goethe with some scepticism.

A second anthology, by K. F. von der Borg, appeared in 1823, two years after Bowring's work. It included samples of representative writings and biographical sketches of more than twenty Russian authors. Because of political circumstances, von der Borg's *Poetische Erzeugnisse der Russen* omitted leading Decembrist writers, but he introduced to the German reader many important authors of the 18th and early 19th centuries who were still unknown in Germany. Considerable attention was given to Lomonosov, Sumarokov, Derzhavin, Zhukovsky, and KRYLOV, among others. Kotzebue, in an earlier edition, had compared Derzhavin to the German Klopstock. Derzhavin's "Ode to God" became a favorite. In 1828, there appeared in

Stuttgart yet another anthology, with translations of eighty Russian folk songs by P. O. Götze.

Zhukovsky had many personal contacts (Goethe, Tieck, A. von Humboldt, Jean Paul, Fouqué) in Germany, while a celebrity and perhaps the most beloved poet in Russia. His kinship with Schiller is especially apparent in his elegies and heroic epics with highly ethical emphasis. Varnhagen von Ense at one time planned a study of Zhukovsky, which never materialized. Nevertheless, he praised his poetic skill, while rejecting his rigid conservatism. Zhukovsky's translations of Schiller's ballads, several poems by Goethe, and especially G. A. Bürger's "Lenore" soon made their way into Russian school texts.

Krylov entered Germany as the Russian Aesop. He, too, was first introduced through Borg's anthology. Journals such as *Blätter für literarische Unterhaltung* and *Magazin für die Literatur des Auslandes* praised Krylov's topical and poetic caricatures of national habits and follies very highly and F. Torney translated 307 Krylovian fables. Borg's anthology, the first substantial survey of Russian literature in Germany, dealt primarily with poetry.

One of the first Russian plays performed in Berlin was V. A. OZEROV's patriotic tragedy *Dmitry Donskoi*, translated by J. T. Wiedeburg. The Russian drama in Germany found a significant patron in F. A. Gebbard (1781–1861). Gebbard who had spent thirty years as an actor at the German theater in St. Petersburg made a modest beginning with the translation of the play *Modnaya lavka* (Das Mode-Magazin) by Krylov. Krylov's play had had good success in St. Petersburg, but Gebbard's free translation invited sharp criticism in reviews and discussions.

Up to the end of the first quarter of the 19th century, Russian prose literature in Germany was synonymous with Karamzin whose voluminous history of Russia had raised the eyebrows of scholars and writers all over Europe. Reviews had been favorable and expressed hope for good translators such as J. G. Richter who earlier in the century had rendered into German several of Karamzin's prose works. In any case, Karamzin's work was received well in Germany and was often used as source material for German literary works (Braunschweig, Hebbel, Schiller, and others). Karamzin the historian gave support to Karamzin's image as a creative writer.

In 1831 K. von Knorring published in Reval (Tallinn) three issues of his *Russische Bibliothek für Deutsche*. In the third booklet, he included GRIBOEDOV's *Woe from Wit* in a verse translation. Griboedov never acquired great fame in Germany, but the German reader recognized that a new beginning had been made in Russia with real people and real situations in literature.

Encouraged by Alexander von Humboldt, an anthology of Russian literature in German was compiled and published by Karolina von Jaenisch (PAVLOVA). Born in Yaroslavl, she was personally acquainted with PUSHKIN and Mickiewicz, and with other writers such as TURGENEV, the Aksakov brothers, and GRANOVSKY. She read from their works in her own literary circle. The anthology was favorably reviewed in several German journals. A great future was forecast for Russian literature, and Mickiewicz and Pushkin proclaimed the greatest poets of Europe.

After the Napoleonic wars and with Alexander I as "savior" of Europe, Germany's interest in Russia and the Russians grew. Many Russian poets and writers visited Germany, Zhukovsky made Germany his permanent home after 1841, and many Germans went to Russia. Between 1830 and 1840, a dozen of Russian novels and a collection of short stories appeared in German translation. Highly praised and soon considered as the best representatives of Russian literature were F. V. BULGARIN, N. I. GRECH, and O. I. SENKOVSKY. For a while they overshadowed Russia's greatest poet A. S. Pushkin.

The earliest translations of Pushkin appeared in von der Borg's anthology of 1823. Shortly thereafter, Pushkin's works or parts of them were regularly printed in such media as *Die Breslauer Zeitung* and *Die Zeitung für die elegante Welt*. Among the better known translators were A. Wulffert and F. Otto. The works most frequently published in German were *The Prisoner of the Caucasus, The Fountain of Bakhchisarai, Ruslan and Lyudmila*, and *The Gypsies*. *Boris Godunov* was received with some scepticism because of its down-to-earth realism. However, with the publication of *Eugene Onegin*, Pushkin had become the "Russian Byron."

With Pushkin, Russian literature had reached maturity. The flow of influence was no longer only from Germany to Russia. H. König's (1790–1869) book, *Die literarischen Bilder aus Russland* (1837), kin-

dled a lively debate with the result that Russian literature became a subject of everyday interest in Germany. Pushkin's *History of the Pugachov Rebellion* (1834) provided the source for Robert Prutz's ballad "Die Mutter des Kosacken" and Karl Gutzkow's drama *Pugatscheff* (1844). K. A. Varnhagen von Ense, acquainted with N. A. Melgunov, learned Russian and became one of Germany's most knowledgeable scholars and promoters of Russian literature. His essays on Russian literature were translated into Russian and thus opened the door to a rich literary exchange and friendship with Turgenev, TYUTCHEV, Bakunin, Zhukovsky, and many others. He was the first to translate from LERMONTOV's *Hero of our Time* and took great interest in the translations made by F. Bodenstedt, W. Wolfsohn, Metlerkamp, A. von Viedert, and others.

Friedrich Bodenstedt (1819–92), a private teacher in Moscow, made Lermontov (*Lermontows Poetischer Nachlass*, 2 vols., 1852) famous in Germany. Turgenev engaged him as his personal translator and Bodenstedt's publication of Pushkin's *Poetische Werke*, in three volumes, secured for him a niche in the history of both Russian and German literature.

N. V. Gogol had several translators. He was first introduced in Germany by a König-Melgunov translation of *The Memoirs of a Madman* (1839). Soon some of the short stories and *Dead Souls* were translated by H. Bode, Ph. Löbenstein, R. Lippert, and A. Lewald. An excellent translation of *The Inspector General* was made by A. von Viedert (1854), who in 1853 wrote an article about Gogol for the *Leipziger Illustrierte Zeitung* and several contributions on Russian literature for the Brockhaus encyclopedia. He was much impressed by H. Heine's work, knew Gutzkow, Storm, Heyse, Auerbach, and highly respected Belinsky's critical views. After 1857, von Viedert was primarily concerned with spreading German literature in Russian.

Another translator of great impact was W. Wolfsohn, born 1820 in Odessa. Theodor Fontane reports in *Von zwanzig bis dreissig* that he had learned Russian from him in order to read Pushkin, Karamzin, and other Russian writers in Russian. Wolfsohn had considerable influence on Berthold Auerbach, Otto Ludwig, and other German writers. His book, *Die schöne wissenschaftliche Literatur der Russen* (1843), included *The Igor Tale*; his journal, *Russische Revue* (started in 1862), printed first translations of works by TOLSTOI and Dostoevsky.

Turgenev's relationship with Western literature is well documented. In Germany, he lived mostly in Baden-Baden. His friendship with many German writers (especially Storm, Varnhagen, Bodenstedt, Heyse, Ebner-Eschenbach, Freytag, Spielhagen) helped to form his poetic style. It appears, however, that only a later generation of German writers (Th. Mann, Eduard von Keyserling) received some literary inspiration from Turgenev. D. von Liliencron claimed that his novellas were written in the spirit of Storm and Turgenev.

Tolstoi and Dostoevsky had the greatest impact on German literature. As early as 1847, Wolfsohn drew attention to *Poor Folk* and in 1863 he translated excerpts from *Memoirs from the House of the Dead*. In spite of this early introduction, Dostoevsky's influence in Germany became noticeable only with the writers of German Naturalism. Johannes Schlaf was struck by Dostoevsky's psychological and religious power, although most others at that time had little use for religious themes. Nevertheless, H. Bahr, A. Holz, and W. Heine were infected by Dostoevsky during their student years in Berlin. H. Conradi's novel, *Adam Mensch* (1889), is akin to *Crime and Punishment*, especially in depicting the moods of its characters. Conradi makes direct reference to Dostoevsky in his planned continuation to *Adam Mensch*. Dostoevsky's Raskolnikov can also be seen as the model for W. Walloth's novel *Neid*, and E. Zabel and E. Koppel went as far as writing a play called *Raskolnikov* ("Schauspiel in vier Akten nach F. M. Dostoevskij"). The psychological analysis so common in Dostoevky's works has attracted the interest of authors from Nietzsche, who discovered Dostoevsky rather late, to many authors of the present. The most prominent among them were Stefan Zweig and Hermann Hesse.

Lev Tolstoi, too, was an idol of German naturalism. During his visit in Germany, he made the acquaintance of Auerbach and some other writers. Tolstoi thought very highly of German music and of Schopenhauer's philosophy. However, only with the appearance of Gerhart Hauptmann's *Die Weber*, he felt that the Germans finally were in possession of their own national drama. The early Tolstoi translations came to Germany via the Baltic Germans and St. Petersburg. P. Heyse and H. Kurtz republished *War and Peace*, an earlier translation of which had first appeared in Prague. Soon *Anna Karenina* was published in book form. The *Kreutzer Sonata* appeared in German translation (R. Löwenfeld) before it was printed in the original. Tolstoi's collected works in thirty-three volumes were available to the German reader before 1914. Social criticism, environment, and the didactic tone in Tolstoi's works were of importance to the German naturalists. *The Power of Darkness* and Hauptmann's *Vor Sonnenaufgang* are akin with respect to characters, milieu, and motif. Tolstoi's influence can also be recognized in *Einsame Menschen*, *Fuhrmann Henschel*, and other plays. Hauptmann once wrote: "Meine literarischen Wurzeln gehen zurück auf Tolstoi." Other German writers under Tolstoi's influence were Max Halbe (*Mutter Erde*), J. J. David (*Hagars Sohn*), Stefan Zweig (*Untergang eines Herzens*), and Theodor Fontane (*Effi Briest*).

During the First World War, R. M. Rilke wrote with regard to Russia that the home of his instincts, all his inner origins lay there ("Alle Heimat meines Instinkts, all mein innerer Ursprung ist dort!"). At the turn of the century, he visited Russia twice; he spent some time with Tolstoi and S. D. Drozhzhin (1848–1930),and earlier, while acquainted with Lou Salomé, was introduced to and read the works of Turgenev, Dostoevsky, and Gogol. He read Chekhov somewhat later. Piety, patience, and humility, he felt, are needed to overcome suffering, and he found all of this in the Russian soul. His "Stundenbuch" is impregnated with the image of "becoming through suffering." Rilke wrote poetry in Russian and translated parts of Dostoevsky's *Poor Folk*, and the *Igor Tale*. His *Geschichten vom lieben Gott* and the cycle of poetry, *Die Zaren*, are full of Russian piety and folklore from the BYLINY. In Worpswede, and later in Paris, Rilke continued his intimacy with Russian literature. His dramatic sketch *Das tägliche Leben* reminds one of Chekhov's *Uncle Vanya*. Elements of Dostoevsky's Raskolnikov and Tolstoi's *The Death of Ivan Ilyich* found their way into *Malte Laurids Brigge*. The third part of the "Stundenbuch," although written in France, breathes the air of Tolstoi and Russia. The Rilke-Pasternak and Rilke-Tsvetaeva contacts are a chapter in themselves.

Another German writer much influenced by "Holy Russian Literature" was Thomas Mann. Mann himself has recorded how Tolstoi had become part of his *Bildung*. Turgenev, Tolstoi, and GONCHAROV were models for his *Buddenbrooks*. His famous comparison of Tolstoi and Goethe (article), and his novels *Der Zauberberg* and *Doctor Faustus*, to some degree variations of the *Grand Inquisitor*, demonstrate Mann's indebtedness to Russia's great novels. Although Mann showed at times a preference for Tolstoi, Dostoevsky became of great importance to him after he had read Merezhkovsky. *Doctor Faustus* reflects Dostoevsky's apocalyptic and grotesque world of suffering, and in his essay "Dostoewski—mit Massen," Mann draws a balance sheet, perhaps in anticipation of the Dostoevsky wave that flooded Germany after World War II.

There were many other 20th-century German authors who strongly leaned on the great Russian writers of the 19th and 20th centuries. In Franz Werfel's *Barbara oder die Frömmigkeit* and *Die vierzig Tage des Musa Dagh* a linkage to Dostoevsky's anthropocentric concept of man and of fallen man as a brother has been recognized. H. von Heiseler's admiration for Pushkin found expression in *Peter und Alexej*, *Die Kinder Godunofs*, *Grischa*, and perhaps, *Die magische Laterne*, as well as in his poetry. Social, psychological, and even mystical features, so prevalent in Tolstoi and Dostoevsky, are found in some of Heiseler's short stories. The spirit of 19th-century Russian literature can also be felt in H. Mann, Arnold Zweig (*Der Streit um den Sergeanten Grischa*), Frank Thiess (*Tsushima*), and also in some works of Ernst Barlach.

Soviet and East German literary contacts are extensive. Well documented are the parallels between *Die Mutter* by Brecht and GORKY's novel. The *Caucasian Chalk Circle*, too, has a Russian milieu. Mayakovsky influenced Brecht, as well as Johannes R. Becher, Willy Bredel, and Erich Weinert, all of whom spent some time in the Soviet Union. It is, perhaps, natural that two distinct peoples, linked by similar or identical socio-economic and ideological facts, in time develop similar problems in their respective literatures. Thus, one can find themes such as that of the creative individual, his struggle against reactionary elements in a socialist society, and how he copes with life, just as easily in the books of Strittmatter, Neutsch, Kant, Jakobs,

Wohlgemut, Reimann, Kirsch, etc., as in the books of their Russian counterparts, such as Kuznetsov, Aksyonov, Smirnov, Nikolaeva, Granin, Matveeva, and many more. A comparative topological study could be rewarding, especially in so-called Soviet and GDR *Ankunftsliteratur*.

Bibliography: E. Boehme and A. Luther, "Frühe dt. Übersetzungen aus dem Russischen," *Philobiblon*, 1933, nos. 8, 9. P. Yu. Danilevskii, '*Molodaya Germaniya*' i russkaya literatura. 1969. S. Durylin, "Russkie pisateli i Gete v Veimare," *Literaturnoe nasledstvo* 4–6 (1932), pp. 263–85. J. W. Dyck and S. Hoefert, eds., *Germano-Slavica*. Waterloo, Canada. 1973– . R. Fischer, *Schillers Widerhall in der russischen Literatur*. Berlin, 1958. M. Gorlin, *N. V. Gogol und E. Th. A. Hoffmann*. Leipzig, 1933. E. Hexelschneider, *Die russische Volksdichtung in Deutschland bis zur Mitte des 19. Jh.* Berlin, 1967. B. Kaiser, *Über Beziehungen der dt. und russ. Literatur im 19. Jh.* Berlin, 1948. H. Koenig, *Lit. Bilder aus Russland*. Stuttgart und Tübingen, 1837. E. Kostka, *Glimpses of Germanic-Slavic Relations from Pushkin to Heinrich Mann*. 1975. V. I. Kuleshov, *Literaturnye svyazi Rossii i Zapadnoi Evropy v XIX veke*. 1965. H. Raab, "Deutsch-Russische Literaturbeziehungen von der Aufklärung bis zur Romantik," *Zeitschrift der Ernst Moritz Universität*, *Gesellschafts- und Sprachwissenschaftliche Reihe*, No. 2/3. Greifswald, 1955–1956. A. Rammelmeyer, "Russische Literatur in Deutschland," *Deutsche Philologie im Aufriss* 3, pp. 439–80. E. Reissner, *Deutschland und die russische Literatur*. Berlin, 1970. ———, "Die Rezeption der russischen Literatur in Deutschland zwischen 1813 und 1848 im Spannungsfeld von Fortschritt und Reaktion," *ZS* 8 (1963), no. 5. W. Setschkareff, *Schellings Einfluss in der russischen Literatur der 20er und 30er Jahre des XIX Jh.* Leipzig, 1939. J. von Sievers, *Deutsche Dichter in Russland: Studien zur Literaturgeschichte*. Berlin, 1855. F. Stepun, "Nemetskii romantizm i russkoe slavyanofil'stvo", *Russkaya mysl'*, 1910, no. 3. Dmitrij Tschižewskij, "Hegel in Russland." In *Hegel bei den Slaven*. 2d ed. Darmstadt, 1961. Pp. 145–387. V. M. Zhirmunskii, *Gete v russkoi literature*. 1937. G. Ziegengeist, *I. S. Turgenev und Deutschland*. Berlin, 1965.

J. W. D.

Gershenzón, Mikhail Ósipovich (1869–1925), philologist and philosopher, a specialist in the history of 19th-century Russian literature and philosophy, Pushkin, Chaadaev, Pecherin, and the Decembrists, and a participant in the famous symposium, VEKHI (1909). Gershenzon was born in Kishinev, in a Jewish family. A graduate of Moscow University, he wrote several books on the 19th-century Moscow intelligentsia: *Ogaryov's Love* (Lyubov' Ogareva), *History of a Friendship* (Istoriya odnoi druzhby), *Ogaryov's Lyric Poetry* (Lirika Ogareva), 1900–04, *P. Ya. Chaadaev: His Life and Thought* (P. Ya. Chaadaev. Zhizn' i myshlenie, 1907), *A History of Young Russia* (Istoriya Molodoi Rossii, 1908), *A Life of Pecherin* (Zhizn' Pecherina, 1910), *The Decembrist Krivtsov and his Brothers* (Dekabrist Krivtsov i ego brat'ya, 1914). All of his studies feature a fortunate combination of an excellent style, deep knowledge of historical and literary sources, and an ability to create psychological portraits. The same combination is found in his books and brilliant essays on Pushkin, such as *The Wisdom of Pushkin* (Mudrost' Pushkina, 1919, reprint Ann Arbor, 1983). Gershenzon also published some important literary and historical source material, including *Russkie Propilei, Novye Propilei* (1923), *Sochineniya i pis'ma Chaadaeva* (1913). After the Revolution, Gershenzon wrote several books devoted to philosophy and religion: "Correspondence from Two Corners" (Perepiska iz dvukh uglov, 1922, with Vyacheslav Ivanov), *Gulfstream* (Gol'fstrem, 1922), and *The Destiny of the Jewish People* (Sud'by evreiskogo naroda, 1922).

Bibliography: Ya. Z. Berman, *M. O. Gershenzon: Bibliografiya*. Odessa, 1928. L. Grossman, "Gershenzon-pisatel'." In M. O. Gershenzon, *Stat'i o Pushkine*. 1926. M. Tsyavlovskii, "Predislovie." In M. O. Gershenzon. *Pis'ma k bratu*. 1927. Pp. iii–vii. *Istoriya istoricheskoi nauki v SSSR. Dooktyabr'skii period: Bibliografiya*. 1965. P. 254.

E. B.

Gértsen, see HERZEN.

Giléya, see HYLAEA.

Gilferding, see HILFERDING.

Ginger, Aleksándr Samsónovich (1897–1965), émigré poet, husband of the poet Anna PRISMANOVA. Ginger converted to Buddhism toward the end of his life. His poetry first appeared in the 1920s, in Parisian émigré journals. His early poetry imitates GUMILYOV, but in his mature years he leaned toward surrealism and Guillaume Apollinaire. A fusion of pathetic and comic motifs in solemn verses is characteristic of his poetry. His poem "The Torch" (Fakel), in which poets are likened to runners in a relay race, passing a torch to each other, has acquired a certain fame. He is the prototype of the main hero in Boris POPLAVSKY's novel *Apollon Bezobrazov*.

Works: (Collections of verse:) *Svora vernykh.* 1922. *Predannost'.* 1925. *Zhaloba i torzhestvo.* 1939. *Vest'.* 1957. *Serdtse.* 1965.

Secondary literature: A. Bakhrakh, *Po zapisyam, po pamyati.* 1980. Yu. Ivask, "Poeziya staroi emigratsii." In *Russkaya literatura v emigratsii*, ed. N. P. Poltoratsky, 1972. P. 65. Yu. Terapiano, Necrology in *Russkaya mysl'*, 11 September 1965. G. I.

Ginzburg, Aleksándr, see GALICH.

Ginzburg, Evgéniya Semyónovna (1896–1980). A Party activist from her earliest years, Ginzburg worked as a teacher, school principal, and propagandist among the Tartar population in Kazan. She was arrested in 1937, and after nearly two years of solitary confinement and repeated interrogation, she was sent to a hard-labor camp in the gold fields of Kolyma. Released in 1947 but still in exile, she elected to remain in Magadan in order to be near the camp where the man she loved was still a prisoner. There she lived for a time with her son Vasily (the writer AKSYONOV). She was rehabilitated in 1956 and became one of the most distinguished contributors to the literary revelations of the Soviet camp system.

The reminiscences of her early days as a teacher and propagandist, published in the journal *Yunost'*, revealed a gift for the artistic treatment of documentary materials. Her autobiographical work *Krutoi marshrut* (2 vols. 1967; 1978; translated into English as *Journey into the Whirlwind* and *Within the Whirlwind*), is a beautiful and moving account of arrests, interrogations, trials, various jails, and the harshest of the labor camps, Kolyma. One of very few accounts of camp life from the viewpoint of a female prisoner, Ginzburg's book is literary art of a high order. Her first volume tells of her arrest in 1937 and sentence to ten years imprisonment on a charge of "participation in a Trotskyist terrorist group." Thanks to her own tough vitality and, paradoxically, to sheer amazement and curiosity about the hideous world in which she found herself, she survived those years and set down her observations. The second volume tells of the final years of her sentence, her tender love for the prisoner Anton Walter, who became her second husband, her own release while he had still more years to serve, and her efforts to build a home near Anton's prison camp, an island of family intimacy always threatened by arbitrary rearrest and the renewal of misery. The two books are a record of the disillusionment, remorse, and re-education of a once-loyal communist. They place Ginzburg securely in the company of superb Russian autobiographers, writers able to transform the rude facts of history into artistic structures. Neither volume was ever published in the USSR, but they circulated widely in SAMIZDAT and have been translated into many languages.

Works: "Studenty dvadtsatykh godov," *Yunost'*, 1966, no. 8. *Krutoi marshrut.* Vol. 1. Frankfurt, 1967. *Krutoi marshrut.* Vol. 2. Milan, 1979.

Translations: Journey into the Whirlwind. 1967. *Within the Whirlwind.* 1981.

Secondary literature: E. J. Brown, "The Education of a Communist," *The New Republic*, 21 March 1981. E. J. B.

Giperborei (The Hyperborean), a monthly literary magazine, ten issues of which appeared in St. Petersburg in 1912 and 1913, was designated the official organ of the *Tsekh poetov* (POETS GUILD) established in 1911 by Nikolai GUMILYOV, as the focal point of the ACMEIST literary movement. *Giperborei* was edited by its publisher M. L. LOZINSKY, a patron of the arts and a minor poet. Each issue numbered only about thirty pages and consisted almost entirely of poetry, usually by the Acmeists, including Gumilyov, Anna AKHMA-

TOVA, Osip MANDELSHTAM, Sergei GORODETSKY, Vladimir NARBUT, M. A. Zenkevich, Lozinsky, and Georgy IVANOV. Other poets such as the symbolist Aleksandr BLOK, Mikhail KUZMIN, the peasant poet Nikolai KLYUEV, and Ilya ERENBURG, also appeared. The journal also had a small section of literary criticism. The more substantial journal associated with Acmeism, which arose in opposition to the mystical tendency of SYMBOLISM, was APOLLON (1909–1917).

Giperborei was also the name of the press which published several volumes of verse by the Acmeists, including Mandelshtam's *Kamen'* (The Stone) in 1916. After the revolution Gumilyov with several associates (Mandelshtam, V. A. Rozhdestvensky, I. V. ODOEVTSEVA, and N. A. OTSUP) issued in hectograph one issue each of a *Novyi Giperborei* (New Hyperborean, 1921), a *Drakon* (Dragon, 1921) and a *Tsekh poetov* (1922).

Bibliography: L. N. Chertkov "Giperborei." In *KLE*. Vol. 2. P. 186. E. Br.

Gippius, see HIPPIUS.

Gladilin, Anatóly Tíkhonovich (1935–), prose writer, born in Moscow, and emigrated to Paris April 1976. He studied at the Gorky Institute of Literature in Moscow. His first work, *The Chronicle of the Times of Viktor Podgurski* (1956) was published in *Yunost'* and was followed by numerous short stories and novels. Gladilin was a representative of the "new voices" of the 1960s. His protagonists during the 1950s and 1960s were mostly young men grappling with personal problems, and with moral and ethical issues.

In stories like "The First Day of the New Year" (1963) Gladilin portrays the conflict and generational gap between the son and his dying father focusing on what D. Brown calls their ideological and psychological differences. In "Forecast for Tomorrow" (1972), which was published abroad, although the main character is older, Gladilin continues to raise questions about the individual and his obligation to society. His collection, *Friday's Rehearsal* (Paris, 1978), contains four stories written between 1965 and 1976 which parody various aspects of Soviet life. Gladilin's major non-fiction work, *The Making and Unmaking of a Soviet Writer* (1979), is an autobiographical account of censorship and the pressures it exerts on Soviet artists.

Gladilin's prose is characterized by formal experimentation. One aspect is the experimentation with narrative point of view and another is the inclusion of what he calls "material from life": dreams, diaries, letters, newspaper announcements, excerpts from films, radio and television programs, and scientific facts.

Works in Russian: Khronika vremen Viktora Podgurskogo. 1958. *Brigantina podnimaet parusa; Istoriya odnogo neudachnika.* 1959. *Dym v glaza. Povest' o chestolyubii.* 1959. *Pesni zolotogo priiska.* 1960. *Vechnaya komandirovka.* 1962. *Idushchii vperedi.* 1962. *Pervyi den' Novogo goda.* 1963, 1965. "Istoriya odnoi kompanii," *Yunost'* 1965, nos. 9–10. *Evangelie ot Robesp'era.* 1970. *Prognoz na zavtra.* Frankfurt, 1972. *Sny Shlissel'burgskoi kreposti: povest' o Ippolite Myshkine.* 1974. *Dva goda do vesny: roman, rasskazy.* 1975. "Tigr perekhodit ulitsu," *Kontinent* 7 (1976). *Repetitsiya v pyatnitsu.* Paris, 1978. *Parizhskaya yarmarka: fel'etony, putevye zametki, literaturnye portrety.* Paris/Tel Aviv, 1980.

Works in English: The Making and Unmaking of a Soviet Writer: My Story of the "Young Prose" of the Sixties and After. 1979.

Secondary literature: Deming Brown, *Soviet Russian Literature since Stalin.* 1978. Pp. 204–06. E. J. Brown, *Russian Literature since the Revolution.* 1982. Pp. 369–70. E. Gromov, "V krivom zerkale paradoksov. Zametki o povestyakh Gladilina," *Smena* 22 (1960). V. Shitova, "Urok zhizni i prosto urok," *Yunost'*, 1960, no. 5. I. Solov'eva, "Material i priem," *Novyi mir*, 1963, no. 4. H. S.

Gladkóv, Fyódor Vasílievich (1883–1958), novelist and short story writer. Of Old Believer peasant background, Gladkov worked as an elementary and junior secondary school teacher from 1902 to 1917. He was also politically active in the Russian Social-Democrat Workers Party (since 1906) and suffered arrest and exile. He published his first story in 1900 but only after having served in the Red Army during the Civil War did Gladkov make his career as a journalist and writer. He belonged to the KUZNITSA group in the 1920s and established his reputation as a major writer with his novel *Cement* (Tsement, 1925), a milestone in the history of Soviet literature. *Cement* relates how a communist activist, returning after the civil war, puts a cement plant back into production, overcoming a formidable array of obstacles. It became the prototype of the "production novel." The novel's hero and heroine, Gleb and Darya Chumalov, who sacrifice their personal happiness to the cause of "building socialism," became the subject of a spirited controversy. The critics of LEF observed an unresolved contradiction between the Chumalovs as ideal figures of heroic proportions and Gladkov's attempt—ill-advised, in those critics' opinion—to endow them with individual human traits and a "psychology." Other critics, among them Maksim GORKY, with whom Gladkov had corresponded since 1902, claimed that there was nothing wrong with placing the ideal into a real setting. In this particular sense, *Cement* was, in fact, an adaptation to a contemporary Soviet ambience of the method used by Gorky in his novel *Mother* (1906), and quite in accord with the principles of SOCIALIST REALISM, as developed in the 1930s.

Gladkov's subsequent works, and specifically the novel *Energy* (Energiya, 1932–38), which dealt with the construction of the Dneproges hydroelectric plant, did not meet with the success of *Cement*. Toward the end of his life, Gladkov, emulating his master Gorky, wrote a trilogy of autobiographical novels about his own childhood and youth.

Works: Sobranie sochinenii. 8 vols. 1958–59. *Myatezhnaya yunost'. Ocherki. Stat'i. Vospominaniya.* 1961. *M. Gor'kii – F. V. Gladkov.* [Correspondence.] *Literaturnoe nasledstvo.* Vol. 70. 1963.
Translations: Cement. Trans. A. Arthur and C. Ashleigh. 1929.
Secondary literature: B. Ya. Brainina, *Fedor Gladkov: Ocherk zhizni i tvorchestva.* 1957. Robert L. Busch, "Gladkov's *Cement*: The Making of a Soviet Classic," *SEEJ* 22 (1978), pp. 348–61. L. N. Ul'rikh, *Gor'kii i Gladkov: K voprosu o gor'kovskikh traditsiyakh v sovetskoi literature.* 1961.
V. T.

Glagolitic is the oldest alphabet of the Slavs, probably invented by St. Cyril before the Moravian Mission (in 863) in connection with his translation of the Scriptures into Old CHURCH SLAVONIC. The alphabet which consists of forty letters and whose name is derived from the verb *glagolati* "to speak" appears in the oldest (10th century) Church Slavonic texts (such as the *Kiev Missal*, the *Codex Marianus*, the *Codex Zographensis*, the *Glagolita Clozianus*, several *abecedaria*) and was extant among all the Slavs who shared the Old Church Slavonic tradition.

The origin of Glagolitic, its relation to CYRILLIC and the historical changes it underwent in the various Slavic countries have been the subject of considerable research and controversy. It is now generally agreed that the Glagolitic letters were in part based on the Greek minuscules current in the 9th and 10th centuries, and on letters of Semitic origin and were in part invented by Cyril himself. Whatever the origin of the individual letters, the alphabet as a whole was admirably suited to the phonemic system of Old Church Slavonic. From the very beginning Glagolitic developed two typographic variants: a "round" (or "Bulgarian") ductus which has come down to us in the above-mentioned canonical texts of Old Church Slavonic and in a number of later texts of diverse geographical origin, and an "angular" ("Illyric" or "Croatian") ductus which became prevalent in the Slavic West and which survived in Croatia as late as the 18th century. The chronological primacy of Glagolitic over Cyrillic has been established on the basis of the correspondence of its letters to numerical values (a correspondence which is upset in Cyrillic), by the presence of Glagolitic glosses and letters in Cyrillic manuscripts, by references of copyists to Glagolitic originals (e.g., the colophon of Upyr Likhoi of 1047 which states that the work was copied *iz kurilovicě*) and by the older linguistic features of the Glagolitic canonical texts. Both systems of writing coexisted for some time among the Slavs, but were apparently used for different purposes, as witnessed by the fact that the oldest inscriptions on stone were carved in the simpler Cyrillic.

The replacement of Glagolitic by Cyrillic, which began in Bulgaria in the 10th century, was motivated by the greater simplicity of Cyrillic and by the rapprochement of the Orthodox Slavs to the Byzantine centers of power, while the suppression of Glagolitic among the Western Slavs came about with the prohibition of the Slavic liturgy in Moravia in 885 and with the Great Schism of 1054. The Orthodox Slavs of Serbia and Macedonia (in the Ohrid region) preserved Glagolitic until the 13th century while the Catholic Slavs of Croatia restored it after papal recognition of the Slavic liturgy in the 13th century. Glagolitic was henceforth employed in all forms of liturgical and secular literature and persisted in Croatia until the end of the 18th century. From here it was transplanted for some time by the *glagoljaši* to Bohemia and Poland (during the reign of Charles IV and Władysław Jagiełło).

Bibliography: N. Durnovo, "Mysli i predlozheniya o proiskhozhdenii staroslavyanskogo yazyka i slavyanskikh alfavitov," *Byzantinoslavica* 1 (1929), pp. 48–85. A. Vaillant, "L'alphabet vieux slave," *Révue des études slaves* 32 (1955), pp. 7–31. V. Yagich (Jagić), "Glagolicheskoe pis'mo." In *Entsiklopediya slavyanskoi filologii* 3 (1911), pp. 51–262.
E. S.

Glavlit, see CENSORSHIP.

Glinka, Fyódor Nikoláevich (1786–1880), poet, cousin of the famous composer. An officer by profession, Glinka took an active part in the wars against Napoleon. Archaic and rhetorical in form, his early patriotic poems reveal the influence of LOMONOSOV and DERZHAVIN. The classicist tragedy *Velzen or Holland Liberated* (1808; 1810) shares the liberalism of the time, announcing that "a country devoid of laws and freedom is not a kingdom but a prison." His works, especially his recollections of the Napoleonic Wars (*Letters from a Russian Officer*, 1808; 1815–16) made him a well-known figure in literary circles and a respected president of the FREE SOCIETY OF LOVERS OF RUSSIAN LETTERS (1819–1825). As a result of the DECEMBRIST uprising, although he was not active in it, Glinka was removed from service and exiled to Petrozavodsk. Here he became an ardent student of Karelian ethnography and folklore. Rich in colors, with magnificent descriptions of the severe northern landscape, his "Karelian poems" were highly praised, notably by his friend PUSHKIN. By now Glinka was a typical romanticist, attracted by the secret language of nature and devoted to the task of telling "the inexpressible." From the end of the 1830s he showed growing sympathies with the SLAVOPHILES. His interest in religious themes, evident even in his youth, gave birth to a series of religious poems, often with a mystical flavor: *Spiritual Poems* (1839), *Job* (1859), *The Mysterious Drop* (1861). Although known first and foremost as the author of songs in the folk style ("Troika," 1824; "The Prisoner," 1831), he should also be remembered for his religious poetry, which has never been sufficiently appreciated. On the whole, the absence of a comprehensive monograph on Glinka is a regrettable gap in the study of Russian poetry.

Works: Sochineniya, 3 vols. 1869–72. *Izbrannye proizvedeniya.* 1957.
G. K.

Gnédich, Nikolái Ivánovich (1784–1833), poet and translator, is remembered mainly for his meticulous, stately translation of the *Iliad* (1829)—an important cultural event in its own time and still the standard verse translation.

Familiar with soldierly and rural life through family background (Cossack leaders, Ukrainian gentry), Gnedich acquired his love of the Classics in the Seminary at Poltava and the Collegium at Kharkov and his considerable scholarly knowledge at the Nobles' Pension at Moscow University. He could also read and translate French (Voltaire's *Tancrède*), German (Schiller), and English (Milton, Byron). His version of *King Lear* (1808), however, was derived from a French neoclassical adaptation.

Gnedich took part in a number of familiar literary groups: the BESEDA, the "GREEN LAMP," the "FREE SOCIETY OF LOVERS OF RUSSIAN LETTERS," and the Olenin and Ponomareva salons. His taste and critical judgement were respected by his friends BATYUSHKOV, KRYLOV, DELVIG, and PUSHKIN. His work appeared in a variety of genres and meters: civic lyrics, informed by the ideals of the Enlightenment, "Peruvian to a Spaniard" (Peruanets k Ispantsu, 1805); Ossianic and Homeric hymns; a highly acclaimed original idyll in amphibrachs ("The Fishermen," 1822); a translation of Theocritus, "Women of Syracuse" (Sirakuzyanki, 1820–21) in appropriately lively, colloquial hexameters; and a collection of twelve folk songs, translated from modern Greek (1824).

Gnedich devoted over two decades to the *Iliad*. He began (1807) by continuing KOSTROV's unfinished version in Alexandrines (Books I–VI, 1787), but started his own version in hexameters (1811), publishing the first fragments of this translation in 1813 and the complete edition with a preface in 1829. Gnedich's preface defines the *Iliad* as an "encyclopaedia of antiquity," not an imaginary world, poetically adorned, and he sought to render the material realia and mores of that world precisely, even when this required him to violate the norms of the "salon style" by drawing upon CHURCH SLAVONIC, archaic Russian, folkloric terms, dialects, and even Ukrainian. The decision to use hexameters was also daring, because the meter had been compromised for early 19th-century readers by TREDIAKOVSKY's *Tilemakhida*. Gnedich realized these choices so well that both his contemporaries and posterity have acknowledged their rightness.

Works: Stikhotvoreniya. Ed. and introd. I. N. Medvedeva. 1956. (Includes his translations of the *Iliad* and of Voltaire's *Tancrède*.) *Iliada.* Ed. and commentary I. M. Tronskii and I. I. Tolstoi. 1935.

Secondary literature: P. Tikhonov, *N. I. Gnedich: Neskol'ko dannykh dlya ego biografii.* 1884.   W. M. T.

Gógol, Nikolaí Vasílievich (1809–52), is 19th-century Russia's greatest comic writer; he is also widely regarded as one of the supreme masters of Russian prose. His fame at home was established early in his career and his reputation has shown remarkably few fluctuations, though changing cultural viewpoints have produced radically differing interpretations of his enigmatic art. Foreign recognition was slower in coming, due to tardy and inadequate translations; modernism, however, at length created a climate in which the force and originality of Gogol's imagination could be appreciated in spite of verbal infelicities. Kafka drew on Gogol's story, "The Nose," to produce his own "Metamorphosis," and in so doing provided new terms for the understanding of his Russian predecessor. It is, however, within Russian literature that Gogol's importance and influence may be seen at their fullest.

Born in Sorochintsy in the Mirgorod district of the Ukraine, or Little Russia as it was then called, on 20 March 1809, Gogol was the first surviving child of Vasily Afanasievich Gogol-Yanovsky, a small landowner, and Mariya Ivanovna, who had married in her early teens. His father is remembered as an unpublished writer of verse epistles and comedies in Ukrainian. Mariya Ivanovna, only 18 at the time of Gogol's birth, was a credulous woman who later, in the days of his fame, attributed to him the invention of the steamship and the railroad. Vasily Afanasievich died around the time of Gogol's sixteenth birthday; his mother lived until 1868.

Gogol's formal education began in 1818 at the district school in Poltava and concluded with his graduation from the *gymnasium* in Nezhin, which he attended from 1821 to 1828. There, while superficially gregarious, Gogol nourished a sense of apartness from his fellows (his nickname among them was "the mysterious dwarf"); he seems to have taken pleasure in appearing to be a different person to each of them. His chief passions were for poetry and theater; his announced ambition was to achieve some grand personal exploit which would distinguish him from the colorless crowd, confer significance on his name, and bring benefit to his fellow-citizens (by which he seems to have meant Russians rather than Ukrainians; though he spoke Ukrainian, all his writings—save for one epigram and one letter—were in Russian).

In December 1828 he moved to Petersburg, capital of the Russian Empire and the most cosmopolitan of its cities, where he immediately sought—unsuccessfully at first—the acquaintance of Russia's premier poet and preeminent aristocratic dandy, Aleksandr PUSHKIN, ten years his senior and then at the height of his fame. His long poem, "Hanz Kuechelgarten," was published under a pseudonym in June of 1829. This, too, proved a fiasco; negative reviews led him to buy up and burn all the unsold copies, after which he fled for some six weeks to Germany, offering a series of vague and contradictory explanations in letters to his alarmed mother. The incident is worth noting because it inaugurates a pattern in which the elements of dissatisfaction with his writing, mystification, and physical evasion all combine.

Within a year of his arrival in Petersburg, Gogol had received the first of a series of appointments as a minor civil servant and written the first of the stories that were shortly to bring him fame. Office work gave way to private tutoring, then to a post as teacher of history at the Patriotic Institute, then to a year as adjunct professor of universal history at Petersburg University. But the largest part of Gogol's energy in this initial and most productive period of his career (which ended in July 1836 with his departure for Rome and thirteen years of expatriation) was devoted to sustained experimentation in almost all the forms of authorship then current, and to cultivating acquaintance with leading literary figures, the poets Pushkin and ZHUKOVSKY chief among them. Both lent encouragement, publicly and privately, to the young author, in whom they quickly recognized a unique and exceptional phenomenon. Gogol was later to credit Pushkin with "ceding" him the ideas for two of his supreme masterpieces, *The Inspector General* and *Dead Souls*.

Five published volumes represent no more than a part, albeit a significant one, of Gogol's remarkable productivity in these Petersburg years: the stories collected as *Evenings on a Farm Near Dikanka* (Part One, 1831; Part Two, 1832); *Arabesques*, a miscellany containing stories, essays and lectures (1835); *Mirgorod*, a cycle of four stories (1835); and *The Inspector General* (1836). There was, in addition, a considerable body of uncollected literary journalism, fiction and dramatic fragments. The year 1836, however, marked an abrupt turning point. Gogol's professional efforts had come to nothing; his hopes of supplying a program for Pushkin's journal, *Sovremennik*, were rebuffed; and perhaps most importantly, his comedy, *The Inspector General*, which premiered in April 1836, proved a theatrical success for what seemed to him all the wrong reasons. "The contemporary writer," he concluded, "the comic writer, the writer of manners should be as far as possible from his country."

The next six years, punctuated by two returns to Russia, were spent in European travel and residence in Italy; they are dominated by work on the novel he conceived as a paradoxical epic, *Dead Souls*, the first part of which appeared in 1842, almost simultaneously with his greatest short story, "The Overcoat." Where in Petersburg Gogol had been an enterprising participant in cultural life, in his European expatriation he practiced a monklike devotion to his great epic project, which he came to regard as a sacred legacy after Pushkin's death in 1837. Loans and subventions from friends and from the imperial family helped him meet his everyday needs, which were minimal.

By the time the first volume of *Dead Souls*—long awaited and much talked about in Russia—appeared, the project had grown to embrace two and possibly three parts, something on the model, apparently, of Dante's *Commedia*. The last ten years of Gogol's life (1842–52) center on his vain struggles to complete the next part; he deemed none of what he wrote worthy of publication. This period, often labelled as one of religious mania or mysticism, is marked by soaring ambitions and plummeting self-confidence. Their confluence lends a strange arrogance to his frequent protestations of humility, and his professed need to purify his soul through religious exercises lends a solemnly prophetic note to everything he writes. Abandoning (or abandoned by) the comic sense that had produced his best works, he comes increasingly to resemble one of his own caricatures. "O, believe my words," he writes in a characteristic letter, "I myself do not dare disbelieve them"! The fruit of this tendency is *Selected Passages from Correspondence with Friends* (1846), a deeply, often embarrassingly personal book prompted by Gogol's creative impasse and by a belief that he was dying; it was intended as his offering to a public long clamorous for the continuation of *Dead Souls* and it sought to deal directly with the central theme of that continuation: the spiritual and social transformation of Russia. *Selected Passages* marks the end of Gogol's career. Principled derision had been his stock in trade; now he himself received it in full measure. He was to publish no more books. The remaining half dozen years of his life were spent, as before on *Dead Souls*. He was frequently despondent; bouts of physical illness recurred. In February 1852, fasting and weak, he woke his servant and instructed him to burn the unpublished manuscripts of his novel. Ten days later, he—who had said that writing was tantamount to living and breathing for him—died, in the words of a contemporary, an "artist-monk, Christian-satirist, ascetic and humorist, martyr of the exalted ideal and the unsolved riddle."

Gogol fostered the enigmatic impression summed up here. He referred to his life as one of "non-events," identified it entirely with his writing, and claimed repeatedly that only the successful completion of his life's work would offer a key to the "riddle" of his existence. The life apart from the writing does indeed baffle biographers: it shows none of those involuntary relationships—whether with people or places—that provide that kind of experience which turns temperament into biography. Devious and secretive, Gogol resisted decisive involvement with anything other than his art. There is no record of amorous attachments, or of formative pressure from economic or political or social necessities. Nor are there any diaries or other direct records of his inner life which might illuminate what he published or be illuminated by it. Gogol's writing, which he once identified as the history of his own soul, stands alone, strangely luminescent, its power as easy to feel as it is hard to account for.

Gogol's career is framed by two failures— *Hanz Kuechelgarten*, a callow narrative poem published pseudonymously in 1829 in imitation of outworn models, and *Selected Passages from Correspondence with Friends*, a collection of oracular statements about how Russia and Russians might wake into spiritual and social unity. Between them his genius unfolds rapidly. The stories collected as *Evenings on a Farm Near Dikanka* show the young author capitalizing on the current vogue for operetta-like Ukrainian subjects and, at the time, exploring the possibilities of different narrative voices and manners. These stories, hailed by Pushkin as an event in Russian literature (not least for their comic flair and stylistic virtuosity), were published as the work of one Rudy (i.e., redheaded) Panko, an engagingly garrulous provincial beekeeper who has transcribed some of the stories told by visitors to his quarters. The stories themselves borrow freely from the works of earlier Ukrainian writers (including Gogol's own father) and from the puppet theater for their local color and sometimes for their plots, which involve deceptions and transformations, often supernatural in origin, presented by turns in a comic and a horrific key, and interlarded with landscape descriptions of great lyric power. It is Gogol's artful orchestration of all these elements that gives the stories their collective originality and such interest as they still retain; in them, stylistic virtuosity of a high order signals the presence of a highly individual artistic temperament. Already the Gogolian phrases and rhythms suggest that there is more here than meets the eye or can be easily accounted for. That suggestion was to become his hallmark, and it can be seen most clearly in the two stories which, by their differing intensities, stand out from the others in these two volumes: "A Terrible Vengeance," and "Ivan Fyodorovich Shponka and his Auntie." The first is a sombre folk opera, a kind of prose poem recounting the fruition of an ancient curse in terms that seem to beg for Freudian interpretation. Uncharacteristically, it is the only one of these stories completely devoid of humor; permeated with dread, it is written in a sustainedly rhythmic prose whose effect in the original is hypnotic, enforcing the truth announced by one of the characters that the conscious mind does not know "even a tenth part" of what the unconscious knows. "Shponka" represents the opposite extreme of Gogolian fiction, that manner which was to inform most of the Petersburg Tales, together with *Dead Souls*. As such it is anomalous in this collection. The expectation of some meaningful plot or action is constantly baffled; vast amounts of attention are lavished to great comic effect on characters and details that have no apparent significance whatsoever; and the narrative breaks off just at the point where it seems about to turn into a story. Gogol's reader is thus involved in a way and to a degree that were radically new, his own experience of the text eclipsing such absurd fragments of experience as can be found *within* the text.

The stories of Gogol's next cycle, *Mirgorod* (1835), are identified on the title page as "a continuation" of *Evenings on a Farm near Dikanka*, but that suggestion of continuity is deceptive. The manner of these stories is quite different, as is the governing, external vantage point. The book is signed with Gogol's name; Rudy Panko has disappeared along with the other storytellers of the *Evenings* to be replaced by a writer whose particular temperament more obviously shapes all the narrations, though each belongs to a different genre. The first, "Old-World Landowners," might be called a sentimental idyll since it describes in nostalgic tones a devotedly loving couple, simple to the point of cretinism, and the insulated (already vanished) way of life they represent. Complexity enters by way of the narrative perspective: the story opens, "I very much love the modest life of those isolated owners of remote villages," and the framing emphasis is on the value which that life can hold for those who are fated to live more actively and consciously in recognizably "modern" conditions. The subtle balancing of sympathy and derision marks "Old-World Landowners" as one of Gogol's enduring masterpieces—and it is precisely such ambivalence, conveyed through an elusively personal style, that was to distinguish the best of his later writing.

"Taras Bulba," the second of the stories in *Mirgorod*, is a cross between epic and historical novel, taking (especially in the revised version of 1842) the tone, drama and hyperbole of the first and the then-current clichés of the second. There is undeniable power, though often of an adolescent sort, in this hymn to a vanished Cossack brotherhood of heroic fighters and carousers; there is also, in the description of the young Andriy's erotically inspired treason and subsequent execution by his father, Taras, powerful temptation to Freudian analysis. Equally tempting in this respect, but more artistically mature, is the next story in the collection, "Viy." The Viy, Gogol assures his readers in a footnote, is a creature of Ukrainian folklore, "the chief of the gnomes." Competent investigators of the matter have branded that footnote a mystification; but they have also recognized the masterful way in which Gogol's imagination reproduces the effects of authentic folklore. This tale of terror deals with the intrusion of nocturnal, supernatural forces into the daylight world of a Ukrainian schoolboy, via symbolically rendered erotic experience; an obscure sense of guilt increases as the story moves to the hero's climactic vigil in a deserted church, which ends with the besieging demons' summoning the title character, a monster with iron eyelids whose glance kills. The concluding "Tale of How Ivan Ivanovich Quarreled with Ivan Nikiforovich" is, up to its last line, entirely comic—a brilliant exercise in generating and sustaining comic narration. The "story" of how two cretins quarreled over nothing is no more than a pretext; like so much of Gogol's future writing, it is a triumph of manner over matter. Even the famous concluding line— "It's dreary in this world, ladies and gentlemen!"—can perhaps best be understood as a comment on the perception that underlies Gogolian comic writing, a perception that cannot be masked indefinitely.

Mirgorod constitutes Gogol's farewell to the Ukrainian setting and themes which had established him as a writer of fiction. Indeed, within a year of its appearance he had published all but one of the stories known as his Petersburg Tales, stories set in the present and dealing with phantasmagoric life of the capital of the Russian empire. The Petersburg Tales (printed together only in 1842, in the third volume of the author's Collected Works) are a more strictly unified cycle than anything that had preceded them; each story makes its contribution to the emergent image of a city absurd, fantastic and dehumanized—a fateful and fated place which represents the intrusion into Russia of modern life and Europeanization. Three of the five—"Nevsky Prospect," "The Portrait," and "Diary of a Madman"—appeared in Gogol's *omnium gatherum, Arabesques*, in the spring of 1835. "Nevsky Prospect," which takes its name from the city's central avenue, contains virtually all the ingredients that appear, differently accented, in the other stories of the cycle. It presents the paired adventures, one "tragic," the other comic, of two young men, each of whom follows a beauty he has seen on the avenue, with fateful results. Piskarev, an innocent young artist, pursues "a perfect Bianca of Perugino," only to discover that she is a prostitute; sordid urban reality mocks his dreams of the ideal; he can sustain these dreams only with the aid of opium, and only for a while; at length he kills himself, "the victim of a mad passion" which is in fact a passion for art and purity, and as such foredoomed by the soulless nature of the city. That soullessness is satirically incarnated in Lieutenant Pirogov, the protagonist of the second adventure. Shallow and monumentally self-assured, he mistakes the wife of a German artisan for a woman of easy virtue, and receives a thrashing for his pains. Framing the two adventures are an ironic opening eulogy to the avenue which is the quintessence of Petersburg and a closing, impassioned warning not to trust impressions in this demonically deceptive place.

The demon, invoked ambiguously in "Nevsky Prospect," becomes an active and literal presence in "The Portrait," which is a romantically allegorical fable about the dangerous powers of art and its openness to corruption through money. "The Portrait" is the most derivative of these tales and, because it excludes any trace of the comic, the least characteristic. "Diary of a Madman," by contrast, presents Petersburg life as seen through the eyes of one of the innumerable petty civil servants who staffed the vast, mechanical bureaucracy of the capital. Brilliantly comic and deeply moving at the same time, this sole specimen of first-person narration adds to the cycle a new indictment of the city's crushing effect on human aspiration, and underlines at the same time the congruence between a madman's vision of Petersburg and the vision conveyed by all the other stories, though perhaps most notably by "The Nose," which appeared in a journal late in 1836, and which constitutes Gogol's most inspired foray into the poetics of the absurd. This tale about Major Kovalev, a puffed-up nullity, and his anguished pursuit of his runaway proboscis, has overtones of satire and undertones of parody, but its main comic value is the consistent and disquieting absurdity which now comes to characterize "the northern capital of our far-flung state."

The last of the Petersburg Tales, "The Overcoat," was written substantially later than the other four—and in Rome, rather than in Russia. Gogol's perspective here is broader, and the story—perhaps the best-known and most influential in all Russian literature—may be seen both to crown the Petersburg cycle and introduce the Gogol of *Dead Souls*. The comic fabric of "The Overcoat" is not very different from that of "The Nose" or "Diary of a Madman," and earlier Petersburg themes inform this story, too. Indeed, urban impersonality, rigid bureaucracy, thwarted desire, and the whole image of the unnatural and malevolent capital have a power here that exceeds anything else Gogol wrote on the subject. But this tale of a poor clerk, hyperbolically meek and puppet-like, who is set on the road to a minimal kind of manhood only to be robbed of the possession that triggered the change in him, shows new themes as well. It is, to be sure, a riddle, like "The Nose"; the questions forced on the amused but uneasy reader, however, involve ethical and spiritual values: love, humility, fellow-feeling, Christian brotherhood, the very question of what is significant in life (and in art). For well over a century critics have found it impossible to agree on the meaning or sense of "The Overcoat," despite a general recognition of the rich irony and subtle poetry of the author's performance, and that fact, perhaps, offers a key to how the story may ultimately be understood as the unresolved statement of a moral dilemma in one's attitude toward intellectually, psychologically and culturally "insignificant" people, when neither fellow-feeling nor indifference proves to be quite tenable.

From an indictment of Petersburg as symbol of corrupting Europeanization, Gogol's fiction moves to the timeless provinces, heartland of Russia. The transition may already be seen in his masterpiece of stage comedy, *The Inspector General* (1836), in which a vacuous minor clerk from the capital is mistaken by a corrupt set of provincial officials for the plenipotentiary investigator who, they have been warned, is on his way from Petersburg. The callow clerk, Khlestakov, is not a confidence man; he is drawn into the delusions of the mayor and his associates out of a kind of complaisant idiocy, and the extraordinary lies he tells about his position as the Tsar's right-hand man come not from calculation but from a kind of misplaced poetic inspiration. Satire here is overwhelmed by poetry and celebration as the characters take license from each other to embrace, in a kind of ecstasy, their own projected fictions. It is their idea of Petersburg—dream symbol of a banal glory—to which they all pay homage. In Act Four Khlestakov, laden with gifts and betrothed to the mayor's daughter, gallops off; in the last act, the thunderstruck provincials learn that he is not what they took him to be. The news coincides with the announcement that the real inspector has arrived; the characters freeze in terror and hold their poses while the audience contemplates them "for about a minute and a half." This sudden draining of comic animation is a Gogolian hallmark; here it serves to emphasize the way the play seeks to implicate the spectator by triggering, rather than representing, significant experience.

One story—the masterful miniature called "The Carriage" (1836)—anticipates Gogol's confrontation of the eventless, backwoods life of quintessential Russia in *Dead Souls*, the novel that was to absorb most of his energy from its inception in late 1835 to the year of his death. The initial impetus came, Gogol reports, from Russia's greatest living poet, Pushkin, who cited to the young author the example of Cervantes, asking what his place in history would have been if he had confined himself to writing shorter pieces and never undertaken a large, potentially major work. For the young Gogol, Pushkin's word verged on the sacred, and he immediately set about developing the picaresque situation Pushkin suggested, that of a rogue who travels through the Russian countryside buying up lists of deceased serfs (or "souls," as they were then called) whose death has not yet been officially registered. Gogol later recalled that he had thought at first only of the comic episodes this situation might provide, and how they might be interlarded with affecting ones. Indeed, the first chapters he drafted were crudely satiric, moving Pushkin to exclaim, "God, how sad our Russia is!" The project, however, rapid-

ly evolved in a different direction, one signalled by the paradoxical subtitle, "poema." *Dead Souls*, Gogol thereby warns his reader, must be read as poetic in nature and purpose, symbolic rather than realistic, and epic in intention. The novel, in other words, is an artistic document that sought to include, alongside comic and lyric delight, "all of Russia"—Russian types, manners, speech—presented as a statement about Russia's current spiritual state, and about its ultimate destiny. By the time the first volume was published in 1842, Gogol anticipated two more, very different in manner, as being necessary for its completion; after covert diagnosis was to come an exemplary story of moral rebirth. The author's consistent dissatisfaction with the drafts he produced, however, kept him from publishing any of the continuation; indeed, he burned it twice, and the five chapters of Volume Two which appeared after his death were accidental survivors of the last burning.

What is usually read and discussed under the title of *Dead Souls*, therefore, is in fact the first volume—a characteristic product of Gogol's genius in its very "incompleteness"; i.e., in its lack of plot or resolution. Many of Gogol's most original works had given a similar sense of fragmentariness or circularity, thereby stimulating readers to search for the meaning in the experience those works had so artfully put them through. In this case there were powerful thematic clues in the dual emphasis on Russianness and, in the frequent authorial digressions, on the seriousness and difficulty of writing such an extravagantly and idiosyncratically comic book. These clues reinforced the puzzle of the title (whose apparent denial of the soul's immortality made the censor uneasy, moving him to add a title of his own: "The Adventures of Chichikov"). The dead souls, it becomes clear as one reads, are not only the strange merchandise being sought by Chichikov, Gogol's picaresque protagonist; the term applies as well to virtually all the characters of the book, most of whom are solipsists and all of whom are caricatures, strikingly presented but radically incomplete.

The vitality in *Dead Souls* is largely linguistic. Gogol's Russian, full of oddity and surprise, is consistently eventful—in no other prose of his time was the sound, shape, rhythm, and suggestiveness of individual words given such prominence, or deployed so broadly. His style is one to be savored, perhaps ideally through reading aloud; the rationale for such a style—as for the mysterious mission of the protagonist—is suggested only at the end of the book (where it was meant to provide a transition to the succeeding volume).

Dead Souls opens with Chichikov's arrival in the sleepy town of N, and the first six chapters establish his mirror-like amiability as he visits a series of local landowners—the vapid and obliging Manilov, the thrifty and suspicious Korobochka, the bearlike and misanthropic Sobakevich, the headlong Nozdryov, who cannot separate fact from fiction in his own uncontrollable speech, and the pathetic miser, Plyushkin. Seeking to wheedle from each the legal title to his recently-deceased serfs, Chichikov falls in with the dominant obsession of each, so that the wonderfully varied series of reactions to the same shady proposition makes of these chapters a single symmetrical portrait gallery.

In chapters seven through eleven the locus shifts back to the town of N, where speculation and rumors about Chichikov's true identity fuel a comedy of errors reminiscent of *The Inspector General*, with the result that Chichikov is compelled to flee. The book ends as it began with Chichikov's carriage in motion. Nothing has been resolved, though Chichikov has, in the final chapter, been given an explanatory biography that points forward as well as back. Resolution is thus deferred, much as the character of Gogol's Russia is left to take shape in the future; the famous closing paragraph likening Russia to a speeding troika at once establishes the connection and constitutes the final mystification. But if the energy and power of Gogol's book seem to be propelling it, like the troika, toward an unclear destination, the ending may be seen, in retrospect, as symbolic of something more specific than national destiny or progress: the powerful energies of 19th-century Russian fiction itself, which Gogol's novel did so much to galvanize.

Gogol was to publish no significant new artistic works after 1842. The Collected Works that appeared in that year and the next contained "The Overcoat"; a fragment of a novel entitled "Rome," invidiously comparing Paris and Rome in much the terms he had earlier used in juxtaposing Petersburg with Moscow (humane tradition versus shallow "modernity"); a stage comedy first drafted nearly a decade before, *Marriage* (subtitled "A Completely Improbable Event in Two Acts"); *The Gamblers*, a one-act sketch of professional confidence men at work; *After the Play*, a defense of his lofty view of comedy, based on the mixed reception of *The Inspector General* in 1836; and revisions of a number of his earlier works, notably "Taras Bulba" and "The Portrait," which appeared in substantially new versions.

The last decade of his life was given to the continuation of *Dead Souls*; it is a chronicle of unrelieved frustration which often verged on desperation, giving rise to rumors of religious mania and other psychic disorders. In 1846 these rumors were stimulated by the preface Gogol wrote for the second edition of *Dead Souls*, in which he besought his readers to send him letters correcting his errors in the depiction of Russian life and suggesting material that might be used in the succeeding volumes. Then, in 1847, he produced his strangest book to date, *Selected Passages from Correspondence with Friends*. This is a collection of homilies, exhortations and selective personal confessions, offered to a public impatient for the next installment of his novel at a time when the author believed his death to be imminent. Alongside the very important "Four Letters Concerning *Dead Souls*," the book is a passionately (and humorlessly) rhetorical statement about the present confused state of Russia, and about the means, as Gogol conceived them, to a spiritual rebirth into active, Christian brotherhood. *Selected Passages* was disconcerting because it lacked completely that ironic, critical stance which had marked the best of Gogol's earlier writing. Those earlier writings, whatever their author's intentions, could be seen as politically and socially "progressive"; this book, in its language and concepts alike, appeared archaic and reactionary. Some later readers have assigned it an honorable place in the tradition of Russian spirituality; in purely literary terms it is perhaps most important as constituting the first proclamation by a major artist of the Russian writer's social obligation—an obligation on which Gogol proved unable to act, but one that was adopted by the brilliant generation of novelists who followed: DOSTOEVSKY, TOLSTOI, TURGENEV, GONCHAROV, SALTYKOV-SHCHEDRIN and others.

The question Gogol poses at the end of "The Nose"—"Why do authors write such things?"—can be applied to all his most important productions, which is to say that their intentionality is unusually difficult to account for; no other Russian writer combines a verbal magic so undeniable with so intractable an ambiguity of meaning. That fact has left his work open to the most various kinds of interpretation. In his lifetime and just after, he was championed by Vissarion BELINSKY, the founder of "civic" criticism in Russia, and by his successor, Nikolai CHERNYSHEVSKY. Though the former had early recognized the essence of Gogol's writing as "a comic animation, always in process of being overcome by a profound feeling of melancholy and dejection," his praise soon changed its emphasis, and Gogol became "the poet of reality," to such an extent that *Dead Souls* could be hailed as being exclusively "serious, calm, true, and profound"! Belinsky in his most influential years was championing a view of Russian literature as mirror of society and catalyst of enlightened public opinion. Gogol was his prime exhibit and was used accordingly as an instrument in the critic's social-political polemic.

Shortly after Belinsky's death in 1848, his self-appointed heir, Chernyshevsky, extended the heritage by purging his own criticism of the aesthetic sensitivity that had still marked that of his predecessor, concentrating even more narrowly on the revolutionary social function—actual and potential—of contemporary literature. It was Chernyshevsky who, in the middle fifties, strung together long excerpts from Belinsky's articles to make up his *Sketches of the Gogol Period in Russian Literature*. Here Gogol's significance was further generalized; with virtually no attention to his texts or to the actual manner of his writing, he was portrayed as the father of that Russian realism which, however different in fact, had already begun to make itself felt in the writings of Turgenev, Tolstoi, Dostoevsky, and company, one of whom is reported to have declared, "We all came out of Gogol's 'Overcoat.'" This view rapidly became an article of faith for the Russian intelligentsia, and as such it has persisted in the more orthodox writing of Soviet critics up to the present day.

Countervailing views (as expressed in the author's lifetime by SHEVYRYOV, PLETNYOV, and Apollon GRIGORIEV) enjoyed little currency before the end of the 19th century, when the SYMBOLIST school, interested in phenomena "more real" than the details of everyday reality, took a fresh look at Gogol's works and found there a world of unprecedented strangeness. Dmitry MEREZHKOVSKY, Andrei BELY, and Valery BRYUSOV all made major contributions to this radical reassessment, and their work led in turn to close textual studies by the Russian FORMALISTS (EIKHENBAUM, VINOGRADOV, Slonimsky) which confirmed once and for all the anti-realistic manner of Gogol's narratives, thus opening the way to further explorations of his artistry.

A full tracing of Gogol's fortunes in Russian criticism has yet to be written; the same is true of the much more problematic question of his influence on the writers who came after him. Broadly speaking, it may be said that "The Overcoat" dominates the major 19th-century reactions to Gogol's writing as these found expression in literary form: Dostoevsky's first novel, *Poor People*, is a transparently polemical reworking of that story; Turgenev's early sketches develop, in less ambiguous terms, the note of compassion for the "little man"; Saltykov-Shchedrin extends Gogol's use of irony and caricature into the area of pure satire. In the 20th century it is rather "The Nose," that lively and mysterious verbal artifact, which can serve as emblem for the widespread license to innovate that Russian prose writers took from Gogol. Here one can only list some of the more prominent names: ROZANOV, SOLOGUB, BELY, Remizov, ZAMYATIN, NABOKOV, OLESHA, MANDELSHTAM, ZOSHCHENKO, PLATONOV, SINYAVSKY ("Abram Tertz").

Gogol's influence on Russian dramaturgy and stagecraft, in his century and after, is a subject whose importance demands mention, though it lies beyond the purview of this article.

Works: Sochineniya N. V. Gogolya. N. S. Tikhonravov ed. 10th ed. Vols 1–5, 1889; vols 6–7, 1896. *Polnoe sobranie sochinenii*. 14 vols. 1937–52.

Translations: The Collected Tales and Plays of Nikolai Gogol. Ed. Leonard Kent 1969. *Dead Souls*. Trans. B. G. Guerney. 1963. (And see Carl R. Proffer, "*Dead Souls* in Translation," *SEEJ* 4 (1964), pp. 420–33.) *Arabesques*. Trans. Alexander Tulloch. 1979. *Selected Passages from Correspondence with Friends*. Trans. Jesse Zeldin. 1969. *Letters of Nikolai Gogol*. Ed. Carl R. Proffer. 1967.

Criticism: Donald Fanger, *The Creation of Nikolai Gogol*. 1979. V. V. Gippius, *Gogol*. Ed. and trans. Robert A. Maguire. 1981. *Gogol from the Twentieth Century*. Ed. Robert A. Maguire. 1974. Vladimir Nabokov, *Nikolai Gogol*. 1944. Vsevolod Setchkarev, *Gogol: His Life and Works*. 1965. Philip Frantz, comp., *Gogol: A Bibliography*. 1983.

D. L. F.

Gogolian Trend in Russian Literature, The. As early as in his "Literary Reveries" (1834), BELINSKY spoke of the "Pushkinian period of Russian literature." While he did not explicitly credit GOGOL with being the leader of the subsequent period, his writings certainly bear out such a notion. It was made explicit in CHERNYSHEVSKY's "Essays on the Gogolian Period of Russian Literature" (1855). Chernyshevsky saw Gogol as the founder of a civic trend in Russian literature, of a literature which was concerned with Russian social reality. At the same time, PUSHKIN was seen as Gogol's antipode, the model of a tradition of "pure poetry," remote from the concerns of "real life." Only V. V. ROZANOV, in his essays on Gogol in the 1890s, and SYMBOLIST critics of the 1900s reversed this approach, seeing Pushkin as the founder of Russian realism, and so a precursor of TURGENEV and TOLSTOI, and Gogol as the creator of a phantasmagoric world of grotesque and sublime visions, conjured up by virtuosic verbal artistry. Gogol's prose now became the model of an "ORNAMENTAL" school in Russian prose fiction (BELY, REMIZOV, PILNYAK, etc.).

V. T.

Golden Fleece, The, see *ZOLOTOE RUNO*.

Golokhvástov, Geórgy Vladimirovich (1898–1963), poet and translator. Little is known about Golokhvastov's life except that he spent most of his emigration in the United States. His work was almost never publicized and is now virtually in oblivion, though there is evidence that it enjoyed a high reputation within a narrow circle of admirers. Its undoubted artistic qualities and today's increased interest in émigré literature in general may suggest a possibility of his future revival. His opus magnum is a long and formidable epic, *The Destruction of Atlantis* (Gibel' Atlantidy, 1938), published in a limited edition and now a bibliographical rarity. An infrequent case of the genre in Russian poetry, this epic narrative, written in fine verse, metrically and rhythmically impeccable, treats an esoteric version of the Atlantis myth, presumably within the theosophic tradition, which attributes the collapse of the legendary continent to the attempts of its inhabitants to create an androgyny through artificial means. Golokhvastov's poem is in many ways fully original, though one may perceive in it distant echoes of MEREZHKOVSKY's imaginative essay "Atlantis-Europe" (1930), both being pessimistic meditations on the destructiveness of scientific progress, if deprived of its moral and religious correlations. Golokhvastov emphasizes, however, the psychological ambiguity of the endeavor and the poem can be read as an allegory on human hubris which cannot but result in cosmic catastrophe. Replete with rich texture and colorful imagery, the epic is an experienced and insightful elaboration on a given mythopoeic *thèse*. Besides a modest volume of lyric poetry, *Life and Dreams* (Zhizn' i sny, 1944), and his translation of SLOVO O POLKU IGOREVE (1951), Golokhvastov produced a volume of verse in another eccentric genre, that of semi-sonnets (*Polusonety*, 1931), that is poems composed of one quatrain and one tercet. In Russian poetry it seems to be a unique case of this form consistently utilized. Golokhvastov's semi-sonnets, dealing with a variety of philosophical and cultural topics, are written by a competent hand and with great technical skill in his usual rigid and detached, classically traditional style.

Works: *Chetyre stikhotvoreniya*. 1944. *Debri*. 1953.

Secondary literature: B. Brazol, "Vdokhnovennaya poema" (1936). V. Orelin, "Gibel' Atlantidy—poema G. V. Golokhvastova" (1939).   V.B.

Goncharóv, Iván Aleksándrovich (1812–91), writer, was born to a prosperous family of grain merchants in the middle Volga town of Simbirsk (now Ulyanovsk). Though legally members of the gentry, the Goncharovs were still rooted in the traditionalist culture of the old merchant class. The narrow religiosity of his family left few evident traces on the adult Goncharov, but its business background resulted in his lifelong commitment to the bourgeois virtues of hard work and practical achievement. After the death of his father when Ivan was seven, the godfather of the Goncharov children assumed responsibility for their upbringing. Nikolai Tregubov was an aristocrat not only by birth but by manner and culture. His enthusiasm for the liberal ideas of the French Enlightenment made him a typical figure of the Westernized gentry of his generation. Attracted by Tregubov and cultured aristocrats like him, the son of Simbirsk merchants also came to regard them as impractical dreamers incapable of action—victims of "OBLOMOVISM," the term he coins to describe the lethargy of his hero, Oblomov.

Goncharov's education proceeded through a local boarding school for children of the gentry, Moscow Commercial School, and, from 1831 to 1834, Moscow University. Goncharov attended Moscow University during the heyday of Russian romantic enthusiasm, especially for German romantic idealism. Always cautious of extremes of thought and feeling, he stayed aloof of the famous student circles, such as those of HERZEN and STANKEVICH. Nevertheless, the spirit of Russia's romantic age was evident in his abiding faith in the autonomy and supreme dignity of art, and the unconscious provenance of its products, as well as in his lifelong sense, often at odds with his own ironic scepticism, that men require some lofty, even if unattainable, ideal. His literary corpus may be seen as an ongoing dialectic with the romantic temper, parodying its excesses while simultaneously affirming some of its values, most particularly, the primacy of art and creative imagination.

In 1835 Goncharov entered the government service from which he finally retired in 1867, two years before the publication of his last novel. From 1855 until his retirement he was an official of the Russian censorship. He never married. Anxiously neurotic, he suffered bouts of paranoia. His accusation of plagiarism against TURGENEV caused a scandal. After the hostile critical reception of *The Precipice* he wrote little and lived out his last years in lonely seclusion.

A Common Story (Obyknovennaya istoriya, 1847) was hailed by BELINSKY as an important blow in the battle of the NATURAL SCHOOL against ROMANTICISM. It has been called Russia's first truly realistic novel. Its REALISM lies in its plain unadorned style and ironic attitude towards experience, as well as its systematic debunking of romanticism. A *Bildungsroman*, it describes a movement from country to city which is simultaneously a process of disillusionment in the life of its

hero. Aleksandr Aduev, a naive provincial, arrives in Petersburg with high hopes for love and glory as a writer, only to have his dreams dashed by the actualities of life in the cold impersonal city and by the biting mockery of his urbane uncle, an industrial entrepreneur and dry bureaucrat named Pyotr. A running dialogue between the two lends the work much of its humor, as Pyotr relentlessly parodies Aleksandr's inflated language and romantic enthusiasms. Though fullness of character is sacrificed to ironic design, *A Common Story* still manages to preserve a youthful freshness that makes it an entertaining if thin novel.

Aleksandr eventually surrenders his country ways and bookish idealism to become a sober bourgeois like his uncle. Goncharov uses Pyotr as a foil to make comedy of Aleksandr's inflated idea of himself, but he also makes it clear that Pyotr's calculating life is emotionally sterile. The novel turns in an ironic circle in which the uncle is shown to have gone through a romantic phase much like his nephew's, while the nephew, in becoming a carbon copy of his uncle, faces a maturity as empty as his mentor's. The novel, instead of siding with either Aleksandr or Pyotr, resolves in an ironic deadlock in which neither youthful enthusiasm nor worldly scepticism are regarded as sufficient solutions to the problem of living. *A Common Story* is a novel about coming of age, the loss of illusions, and the compromises of maturity, presented not as a didactic lesson, but as "a common story," a comedy that is the way of the world.

The Frigate Pallas (Fregat Pallada, 1855–57) grew out of Goncharov's experience as secretary to the admiral on a government-sponsored expedition to Japan—an exceptional adventure in his otherwise sedentary life. It is his second-best book. His distinctively smooth, lightly ironic prose was made to order for a travel book. The blend of warm sympathy and sly humor that fill the pages on the Japanese are surpassed in his writings only by *Oblomov*. The Orient for Goncharov was more comically curious than exotic. His adamant refusal to recognize romantic exotica resulted in a travel book shaped, like the novels, by parodic principles. *The Frigate Pallas* consistently moves from romantic expectations of idyllic landscapes, mysterious and sensual peoples, wild and stormy seas to an actuality of squalid ports, shabby hotels, sullen natives, and a sea that is mostly monotonous. As in *A Common Story* and *Oblomov* Goncharov creates a comedy out of the discrepancy between exceptional imaginings and "common" realities.

In *Oblomov* (1859) Goncharov once again confronts a dreamy character with the harsh demands of reality. It is, however, much richer and more profound than anything else Goncharov wrote. The characters, especially Oblomov, convey a sense of independent, felt life missing from his schematic first novel. Goncharov also places his hero's personal dilemma into the stream of history. It is Oblomov's tale but it is also the story of the demise of his class. An outsized comic figure, Oblomov has taken on mythic proportions, becoming for Russian criticism the archetypal "superfluous man" and the embodiment of the inertia Russians now call "Oblomovism." Humorous and keenly ironic, psychologically probing, the work is yet permeated by currents of lyricism and symbolic intimation that make it an exceptional, even eccentric, novel in the realist tradition.

The shifting tones of the novel are perhaps the result of its slow maturation—it was begun in 1847 and only completed in 1858. Part One, written in the forties, is most closely tied to the manner of the natural school. Static and plotless, it depicts with delicious humor a typical day in the life of its colossally indolent hero and his equally indolent servant Zakhar. Both master and man have become totally alienated from the "normal" world of activity and ambition. Goncharov, in turning despair into burlesque, shows himself a follower of GOGOL and predecessor of modern writers like Beckett. The famous chapter nine, "Oblomov's Dream," is in turn a picture of typical days on Oblomov's ancestral estate, Oblomovka. It is a piece of great imaginative appeal and poetic beauty. It moves in several directions at once, offering a humorous portrait of Russian provincial stagnation, a biography of Oblomov's childhood, the genesis of his crippling passivity, and evolving ultimately into a fairy-tale-like image of a pastoral idyll. This mythic projection of a homely, idiosyncratically Russian land of Cockaigne stands at the center of the novel, exerting a seductive fascination despite the ironic uses to which Goncharov puts it. Oblomov is doomed by his dream of paradise. Unwilling to relinquish it, he is unable to act in the real world.

Parts Two and Three recount his failed effort to enter the usual world through his love for Olga Ilyinskaya. Holding to an extremely idealized image of love, Oblomov sees Olga as a way to recapture his dreams of paradise. When she demands that he assume common human responsibilities, he folds and the romance collapses. Though the love story suffers from an excessive sweetness of tone, it is of central importance. By allowing Oblomov a last desperate attempt to escape his isolation, Goncharov draws us closer to his character, enriches our understanding of him, and lends his life a pathos largely absent from the earlier comic treatment.

The other weak point in the novel is the portrait of Stolz. He is everything Oblomov is not—active, energetic, sensible, and practical. Presented as a didactic counter to lazy Oblomov, he turns out to lack precisely those virtues that Oblomov embodies—tenderness and imagination. As in the instance of Pyotr and Aleksandr Aduev, each is a foil to the other. Stolz is wooden and unconvincing, but his relation with Oblomov is complex and contributes much to the novel's range of implication.

Part Four is the most powerful piece of writing in Goncharov's oeuvre. It traces Oblomov's final decline into a vegetative existence and death. Largely eventless, like Part One, its portrayal of Oblomov's massive inertness is no longer funny. As in "Oblomov's Dream," the hero sinks into a dreamlike hallucinatory state leading this time to oblivion. His demise is sad but it is not tragic. Having failed to enter the larger world of activity and purpose, Oblomov gradually learns to accept himself and his limitations. At the nurturing hands of his devoted housekeeper, Agafya Matveevna, he regains for a fleeting moment the idyllic childhood world of his dreams. This sense of acceptance and reconciliation places the novel, for all its very real pain, in the mode of comedy. The novel concludes on a note of continuity, as Oblomov passes on to his mourners—Olga, Stolz, Agafya, and his son by Agafya—an image of tenderness to sustain them in their lives. It is Goncharov's hope that, as the Russian gentry dies out, its finer virtues—love of art, aristocratic courtesy, cherishing of personal relationships— will survive in the cold impersonality of the modern world.

The Precipice (Obryv, 1869) was one of a flood of ANTI-NIHILIST novels of the 1860s and 1870s. The revolutionary intransigence of the radicals (dubbed "nihilists"), their philosophical positivism and ethical utilitarianism alienated and frightened writers of Goncharov's generation—"the men of the forties"—who had been reared in the climate of romantic idealism. Long and cumbersome, often digressive, *The Precipice* manages to plod through the story of the competition of three men for the love of the darkly mysterious Vera: the vacillating artist Boris Raisky, the solidly reliable and practical Ivan Tushin (the Pyotr Aduev or Stolz of this novel), and the villainous nihilist Mark Volokhov. Volokhov, who espouses "free love," seduces Vera at the bottom of the precipice of the novel's title; the community of Malinovka, the estate where Vera lives, roundly condemns him; Tatyana Markovna, the matriarch of Malinovka, forgives Vera; Vera will marry the dependable and "truly Russian" Tushin; and all, except the aimless Raisky (in many ways a self-portrait of Goncharov), seem destined to live happily ever after.

The politics of *The Precipice* seek a middle ground between reactionary traditionalism and revolutionary radicalism. Tushin, its positive hero, is a firm believer in progress, education, and social and economic amelioration. However, the concerns of the novel are not so much political as social. Through the figure of the nefarious Mark Volokhov, Goncharov condemns sexual licentiousness, while affirming the traditional Russian family as a bulwark against moral laxity. Art and the family are the two values the novel opposes to "nihilism."

Simpleminded in its politics, the novel as a work of art is bombastic and melodramatic. The only relief from its incessant moralizing and strident urgencies is in occasional sketches of daily life on the estate of Malinovka—the kind of genre painting at which Goncharov remained a master to the end. The reasons for the failure of *The Precipice* are many, but surely one was his inability to handle dramatic form. His usual literary manner is leisurely, introspective, ironic, and comical, and sometimes, as in *Oblomov*, softly lyrical. In the 1860s and 1870s the Russian novel moved to politically engaged and dramatically intense forms (compare the novels of DOSTOEVSKY), and in *The Precipice* Goncharov strained to accommodate his personal vision and idiosyncratic talents to the imperatives of his age. The result was disastrous.

Works: Sobranie sochinenii. 8 vols. 1952–55.

Translations: A Common Story. Trans. Constance Garnett. 1894. *Oblomov.* Trans. Ann Dunnigan. 1963. *The Precipice.* Trans. M. Bryant. 1916. (Abridged.) *The Voyage of the Frigate Pallada.* Ed. and trans. N. W. Wilson. 1965. *See also:* Lewanski., p. 247.

Secondary literature: A. D. Alekseev, *Bibliografiya I. A. Goncharova: 1832–1964.* 1968. ———, *Letopis' zhizni i tvorchestva I. A. Goncharova.* 1960. Milton Ehre, *Oblomov and His Creator: The Life and Art of Ivan Goncharov.* 1973. Robie Macauley, "The Superfluous Man," *Partisan Review,* no. 2 (1952). André Mazon, *Ivan Gontcharov: un maître du roman russe.* Paris, 1914. V. S. Pritchett, "The Great Absentee." In *The Living Novel.* 1946. Renato Poggioli, "On Goncharov and His *Oblomov*." In *The Phoenix and the Spider.* 1957. M. Ya Polyakov, ed., *I. A. Goncharov v russkoi kritike.* 1958. N. I. Prutskov, *Masterstvo Goncharova-romanista.* 1962. Vsevolod Setchkarev, *Ivan Goncharov: His Life and Works.* Würzburg, 1974.

M. E.

Gorbanévskaya, Natálya (1936–   ), poet, journalist, dissident. Gorbanevskaya published only a handful of her poems in officially authorized Soviet journals, although her verse was circulated privately in the Soviet Union and was published abroad. On 5 August 1968 she took part in a demonstration on Red Square protesting the invasion of Czechoslovakia. She also edited a letter to world public opinion which was reprinted in a large number of foreign newspapers in August and September of 1968. She was confined for a week in the Kashchenko Psychiatric Hospital with a diagnosis of "deep psychopathy and possible latent schizophrenia." Gorbanevskaya described her experience in an autobiographical sketch entitled "Free Medical Care." In 1975 she was permitted to emigrate.

Gorbanevskaya's verse is very intense and often contains allusions to her political experiences. The themes of pain, separation, and despair are prominent in her love lyrics as well.

Works: Stikhi. Frankfurt, 1969. *Polden': Delo o demonstratsii 25 avgusta 1968 goda na Krasnoi ploshchadi.* Frankfurt, 1970. *Poberezh'e: Stikhi.* Ann Arbor, 1973. *Tri tetradi stikhotvorenii.* Bremen, 1975. *Pereletaya snezhnuyu granitsu: Stikhi 1974–1978.* Paris, 1979. *Angel derevyannyi.* Ann Arbor, 1983.

Translations: Red Square at Noon. Introd. Harrison E. Salisbury. Trans. Alexander Lieven. New York, 1972. *Selected Poems.* Trans. Daniel Weissbort. London, 1972.

J. G.

Gorbátov, Borís Leóntievich (1908–54), writer, ardent adherent of SOCIALIST REALISM, was born in the Don Basin (Pervomaisk), the setting for a number of his works. His first story, "The Well Fed and the Hungry" (Sytye i golodnye), appeared in 1922. The short novel *The Cell* (Yacheika, 1928) is devoted to Komsomol life in the twenties. Gorbatov's first full-length novel, *Our Town* (Nash gorod, 1930), relates the hardships and struggles of party workers in naturalistic detail. This was followed by a series of sketches, *Expedition in the Mountains* (Gornyi pokhod, 1932), based on his military experience in the Red Army (1930–31). Subsequently, Gorbatov's frequent travels as a correspondent for *Pravda* resulted in several collections of sketches devoted to the Soviet worker, including *Komintern* (1932), *Masters* (Mastera, 1933), and *My Generation* (Moe pokolenie, 1933, a short novel), all of which romanticize the first Five-Year Plan. A sequel to the latter work, the play, *Our Fathers' Youth* (Yunost' ottsov, 1943), dealt with the writer's own generation's participation in World War II. Gorbatov's collection of stories, *Everyday Arctic* (Obyknovennaya Arktika, 1937–40), tells of the heroic exploits related to the opening up of the Far North. During the War, Gorbatov served as a war correspondent. His experiences and the events he witnessed provided the material for the impassioned accounts related in *Letters to a Comrade* (Pis'ma tovarishchu, 1941–42), "Aleksei Kulikov, Soldier" (Aleksei Kulikov, bots, 1942), *Tales of a Soldier's Soul* (Rasskazy o soldatskoi dushe, 1943), and *The Unvanquished* (Nepokorennye, 1943), winner of a Stalin Prize in 1946. Also to Gorbatov's credit are travel notes, "In Japan and in the Philippines" (1946–47), and a screen play, *Miners of the Donets* (1950, in collaboration with V. M. Alekseev), which received a Stalin

Prize in 1951. *Don Basin* (Donbass, 1951), a novel set in Gorbatov's birthplace, is concerned with Soviet youth of the thirties.

Works: Sobranie sochinenii. 5 vols. 1955–56.
Translations: See Lewanski, p. 247.

Secondary literature: A. Ionov, *B. L. Gorbatov: Ocherk zhizni i tvorchestva. Vospominaniya.* Stalino, 1956. V. Karpova, *Chuvstvo vremeni: Ocherk tvorchestva B. Gorbatova.* 2d ed. 1970. G. Kolesnikova, *Boris Gorbatov.* 1957.   D. K. D.

Góre-Zlochástie (Woe-Misfortune). This work was found by A. N. PYPIN in 1856 in a manuscript collection from the first half of the 18th century. It has been established that it is a 17th-century work which manifests a departure from traditional medieval Russian literature in its incorporation of many aspects of folk poetry. The story begins with the fall of Adam and Eve, and relates how even after the expulsion man continued to disobey God's commands and was severely punished. The story of the nameless youth exemplifies the relationship between man and God described in the introduction. His parents give the boy rules and precepts to follow, and he disobeys. After being tempted by a friend to drink, he loses all his wealth. At a feast the guests warn him not to follow the evil path. He agrees, but disobeys the admonition not to boast, for which Gore-zlochastie (Woe-Misfortune) punishes him by pursuing and tempting him throughout the story. In the end the youth is saved by seeking refuge in a monastery.

Certain aspects of the work relate it to the written tradition. The teachings of the parents and admonition of the guests are similar to medieval Russian instructions of parents such as the "Instruction to his Children" by VLADIMIR MONOMAKH and the later teachings of the DOMOSTROI. N. K. Gudzy has pointed out the relation of the work to other 17th-century works in prose and verse on the evils of drink. The story also fits into the context of other 17th-century works in which man is tempted by the devil and signs his fate over to him, such as the *Tale of* SAVVA GRUDTSYN. In many aspects, however, "Gore-Zlochastie" is typical of Russian folk literature. As in folk songs, the hero and other characters are nameless and no specific time or place is designated. The hero wanders from his parents' home to a "strange land." The prosodic scheme of unrhymed lines of four stresses per line is typical of the BYLINA, as are such passages as the arrival and boasting at a feast. Typical of folk poetry in general are fixed epithets such as "strange land," "swift river," "white body," and "oaken table;" tautologies such as "steal-rob," "feed-eat," "family-clan;" and repeated passages such as the description of the youth neither eating nor drinking nor making merry nor boasting at the feast, followed by lines in which the guests ask him in almost the same words why he is abstaining from the above. Gore is frequently personified in folk lyrics, where the character is saved from Gore's pursuit by the grave. However, there is an important difference between its representation in the folk lyric and this story, since in the lyric the protagonist is a passive victim, whose behavior does not influence the arrival of Gore, whereas in the story Gore comes to punish the youth for his boasting. Gore also does not undergo transformations in folklore as it does in the story, appearing as an archangel, a barefooted naked young man, and in other forms as well. Thus the tale is a unique combination of various aspects of literary and folk tradition.

Translation: "Misery-Luckless-Plight." In *Medieval Russia's Epics, Chronicles, and Tales.* Ed. Serge A. Zenkovsky. 1974. Pp. 489–501.   R. R.

Górky, Maksím (pseud. of Alekséi Maksímovich Peshkóv, 1868–1936), writer, playwright, poet, and critic. Though his talent hardly measured up to that of his major contemporaries, Gorky has been officially designated "the founder of socialist realism and originator of Soviet literature" (*KLE*) and is accorded the attention received only by authors of classics. He has had a powerful impact not only on many minor Soviet writers, but also on many writers of the Eastern bloc and of the Third World.

Gorky was born on 28 March 1868 in Nizhny Novgorod (later named Gorky in his honor) on the Volga, into a lower-middle-class family. He lost his parents early and at eleven years of age started life on his own as an errand boy, dishwasher on a Volga steamer, apprentice to an icon painter, stevedore, baker, etc., as described later in his autobiographic trilogy, *Childhood* (Detstvo, 1913), *In the World* (V lyudyakh, 1916), and *My University Years* (Moi universitety, 1922). All along, he read voraciously and gradually developed a political and literary consciousness. In 1889, in Nizhny Novgorod, he met the writer V. G. KOROLENKO, who helped him to make his debut in literature. In 1891 Gorky went to the Caucasus, where he worked on the railroad, learned about the workers' movement, and published his first story, "Makar Chudra," in the Tbilisi newspaper *Kavkaz* (1892). Having returned to Nizhny Novgorod later in 1892, Gorky began his career as a professional writer in earnest, publishing stories, sketches, essays, and poetry in various periodicals of the Volga region. In 1895 he broke into the "big time" of Moscow and Petersburg journals, and soon his two-volume collection, *Sketches and Stories* (Ocherki i rasskazy, 1898) made him famous. Along with the Norwegian Knut Hamsun and the American Jack London, he introduced a new kind of romanticism to world literature, that of the hobo and drifter.

Gorky's stories have the peculiar extra dimension of a decided sympathy with the *Lumpenproletariat*, coupled with an antipathy against the peasant. In the story "Chelkash," the hero, a professional thief who plies his trade in the port of Odessa, is presented as much the better man than the simpleminded peasant lad who is his helper. Gorky's romanticism is quite unabashed in some stylized pieces such as "Old Woman Izergil" (Starukha Izergil') and in his poems, such as the celebrated "Song of the Falcon" (Pesnya o sokole, 1895) and "Song of the Stormy Petrel" (Pesnya o burevestnike, 1901), both blatant encomiums to a romantic revolutionary hero. Gorky's best poetic work, "The Maiden and Death" (Devushka i smert'), with an equally life-affirming message, was also written in the 1890s, though it was published in 1917. "The Maiden and Death" is untranslatable into English, since its resolution, the maiden's escape from death, depends on death's grammatical gender, feminine in Russian, which makes her amenable to pity.

The novel *Foma Gordeev* (1899) is Gorky's first major effort at a panoramic presentation of what he thought to be the essence of recent Russian social history: the ascendancy of the bourgeois entrepreneur and the growth within the ranks of the bourgeoisie of a young generation of dissidents who become enemies of their own class. Later versions of the same conception are *The Life of Matvei Kozhemyakin* (1910–11) and *The Artamonov Business* (1925).

Gorky's success quickly made him a public figure, unequivocally a spokesman for the revolutionary left wing of the Russian intelligentsia. He published in journals, such as *Novoe slovo* and *Zhizn'*, among whose contributors were also PLEKHANOV and LENIN; signed revolutionary proclamations; got involved in a secret printing press, for which he was temporarily exiled to Arzamas in central Russia (1901). In 1902 Gorky was elected to the Russian Academy, but the government declared the election invalid, whereupon some members of the Academy, including CHEKHOV, resigned their membership. In 1900, Gorky joined the ZNANIE publishing house in Petersburg as an editor and in the following years was largely responsible for its orientation toward realistic works with a social tendency, contributing some himself.

In the 1900s Gorky wrote several plays, whose structure is clearly influenced by Chekhov, but whose whole emphasis is quite different. Gorky's plays have a definite political tendency. Reactionary types are set against progressive types. Their psychology is straightforward, lacking Chekhov's subtlety. But several of Gorky's plays were successful on stage, in particular *The Lower Depths* (Na dne, 1902), set in a flophouse and carrying the message of indicting the society that would allow its members to become human derelicts, thieves, and whores. The play was a hit at STANISLAVSKY's Moscow Art Theater. Other plays which are still staged outside the Soviet Union are *Summer Folk* (Dachniki, 1904) and *Enemies* (Vragi, 1906), the latter important in that it deliberately bases its dramatic conflict on class struggle (the plot hinges on a bitter strike of factory workers against unscrupulous owners) and in effect creates a new pair of types: "the enemy" and "the comrade," both defined in terms of social class. Gorky openly and actively supported the Revolution of 1905. He joined the Bolshevik Party in the summer of 1905 and soon thereafter his association with Lenin began, cordial at times, but also marred by serious disagreements.

To stay out of trouble's way and to collect funds for the Party, Gorky travelled to the United States in 1906. His impressions of

America, predictably negative, were recorded in "My Interviews" (Moi interv'yu, 1906) and "In America" (V Amerike, 1906). During his stay in America, Gorky also wrote his most famous work, the novel *Mother* (Mat', 1906). What is true of its author in general, is particularly true of *Mother*. It is not a very good novel artistically, yet it is difficult to name a work of Russian literature which has had more influence, political as well as literary. *Mother* tells the story of a middle-aged working class woman who, once a cowed, humble, and ignorant victim of all the injustices and cruelties to which a woman of her class is exposed, becomes a fearless, conscious, and eloquent worker for the cause of the Revolution. She is the mother of Pavel Vlasov, Gorky's version of the heroic revolutionary. Various other revolutionary types are also introduced, including Rybin, a peasant rather than a worker, whose spontaneous, undisciplined, albeit vigorous and heroic stand is presented as hopeless, even harmful to the cause. *Mother*, a propaganda novel, pointedly refuses to be objective: the moral makeup of each character is determined solely by his or her social identity: "comrades" are honest, upright, kind, courageous, wise, and strong, while "enemies" are tricky, unscrupulous, cruel, cowardly, and sickly. Even the best among those revolutionaries who are not of working class background but have joined the movement out of idealism, cannot approach the moral stature of the genuine proletarians. However, *Mother* is a work of genuine vision. It gloomily predicts the terrible bloodshed of the Revolution and the difficulties which the revolutionary regime will have with the peasantry. It underscores the religious nature of the movement, making an effort to present the revolutionary ideology as a legitimate successor of the Christian faith. The virtue and saintliness of the revolutionary heroes are underscored: they are chaste (Pavel Vlasov will not marry because a family will reduce his effectiveness as a revolutionary), utterly selfless, full of love and compassion for their working class brothers, disciplined and dedicated—altogether strikingly close to the ideal of the medieval saint's life. While the prophecy in *Mother* was a self-fulfilling one, Gorky created here an ideal image of revolutionary man which was soon to be accepted as the self-image of the revolutionary regime in Russia and elsewhere, an officially sanctioned myth. *Mother* is also the archetype of the SOCIALIST REALIST novel. When it was severely criticized for its blatant departure from the real facts of social and political life, and this even by sympathetic Marxist critics such as Plekhanov and VOROVSKY, Gorky produced a rejoinder which in a nutshell contains the essence of socialist realist aesthetics. In his play *Queer People* (Chudaki), Gorky let his hero, the writer Mastakov, exclaim: "Well, all right, my old woman is a lie, they'll say, I know it, they'll say it! 'There are no such women!' they'll scream. Well, Lena, today there are no such women, but tomorrow there will be some—do you believe me, Lena, that there will be such women?" Whereupon the heroine, Lena, answers: "Yes, you help them to be, and they'll be."

The years following *Mother* coincided with a period of political reaction in Russia, and a change of heart experienced by many intellectuals who were formerly inclined to support the Revolution. The celebrated symposium, *Landmarks* (VEKHI, 1909) highlighted this tendency. Gorky was also affected by the general change of mood. He established his residence on the island of Capri late in 1906 and went through a period of mystical searchings. Partly under the influence of A. A. BOGDANOV, he developed a philosophy of *bogostroitel'stvo* (lit. "godbuilding"), reflected in his short novel *A Confession* (Ispoved', 1908). Gorky's *bogostroitel'stvo* is an attempt to infuse the concepts of the dignity of man and the noble destiny of humanity with religious ardor. Gorky's cult of man (the familiar man-god of DOSTOEVSKY and Vladimir SOLOVYOV), with the people (*narod*) an object of worship as well as the "builder" of a new god, is not all that far removed from the ideas and moods of his contemporaries, the Russian symbolists Dmitry MEREZHKOVSKY, Vyacheslav IVANOV, and Andrei BELY.

In 1913 a general amnesty allowed Gorky to return to Russia, where he continued to be politically active, edited a *First Miscellany of Proletarian Writers* (1914), and founded a journal, *Letopis'* (Annals, 1915–17), around which he sought to gather writers of his own progressive and anti-war views. During this period, Gorky reached the pinnacle of his artistry in his autobiographic stories "All Over Russia" (Po Rusi, 1912–18) and memoirs, *Childhood, In the World*, and *My University Years*. Gorky is at his best when he can describe what he has himself seen and experienced. His landscape descriptions are among the most meticulous in Russian literature. He is also very good at describing the physical appearance of people, at rest as well as in action, and he has a fine ear for their speech. But most of all, he had really seen and heard a great deal about areas of life which had rarely or never been presented to the Russian reader with such immediacy and vigor. Gorky is at his best reporting his own experience in the first person singular. In many of his best short stories, plot is not the main thing—a character, a fact of life, or an ambience is. Therefore, many of his best pieces are essentially impressionistic sketches. Gorky's reminiscences, in particular those of TOLSTOI (1919), but also of Chekhov, Korolenko, Leonid ANDREEV, and others, tend to capture a side of his subject which no one else could see. In Gorky's *Reminiscences of Tolstoi*, said D. S. MIRSKY, "we have a picture of Tolstoy in his old age in which the irrational, the complete man stands before us in all the relief of life."

Gorky's reaction to the October Revolution was ambivalent. His series of articles, "Untimely Thoughts" (Nesvoevremennye mysli, 1917–18), published in the Menshevik newspaper *Novaya zhizn'*, took a critical view of it. However, Gorky was willing to collaborate with the Bolshevik regime and actively participated in several of its cultural projects, such as the launching of a series of popular editions of the classics of world literature by the publishing house *Vsemirnaya literatura* (World Literature). Gorky also used his credit with the new regime to save cultural values from destruction and also saved many lives, by direct intervention as well as by convincing his Bolshevik friends that it did not serve the best interest of the Revolution to let writers, artists, and scholars starve to death because they were not proletarians. Nevertheless, in summer 1921 Gorky left Russia, forced to do so by his failing health, according to the official version, and after having spent some years at various German and Czech spas, settled in Sorrento, where he lived until 1931 (with visits to the Soviet Union in 1928 and 1929). Gorky never broke with the Communist regime, continued to publish his new works in the Soviet Union, and stayed aloof from the émigré community, though on friendly terms with individual émigré writers, such as V. F. KHODASEVICH.

After a triumphant return to Russia, Gorky continued to be quite productive. He wrote two new plays, *Egor Bulychov and Others* (1932) and *Dostigaev and Others* (1933), as well as a new version of his prerevolutionary play *Vassa Zheleznova* (1935). He travelled widely in the Soviet Union and wrote a series of sketches of his impressions, all supportive of Stalin's Five-Year Plan. He also resumed his organizational activities and was involved in several publishing projects, such as the *Biblioteka poeta* (Poet's Library). Finally, he played a key role at the first All-Union Congress of Soviet Writers in 1934. He who had created the template of all socialist realist literature in his pre-revolutionary novel *Mother*, was now allowed to preside over the institutionalization of the practices which he had introduced under so very different conditions. It remains a question to what extent Gorky enjoyed freedom of action during these last years, or even if all the writings which appeared under his name were actually written by him. Gorky died on 18 June 1936 under faintly suspicious circumstances. He was given a magnificent state funeral. His fame and authority have not been allowed to diminish since and he continues to be officially considered Russia's greatest writer of the 20th century. It must be noted that Gorky himself had a modest opinion of his talent: he considered himself no more than an honest journeyman of his trade.

Gorky's main work, the lengthy novel *The Life of Klim Samgin* (Zhizn' Klima Samgina, begun in 1925), remained incomplete. While it suffers from the faults of his other longer works (an unsteady plot line, many *longueurs*, failure to maintain structural and stylistic patterns, absence of a unifying conception), it is a most intriguing and in some ways an impressive work. Gorky has chosen for his hero, whose life he follows through forty years of Russian history, including the revolutions of 1905 and 1917, a rather colorless bourgeois intellectual who is never earnestly committed to any particular political ideology. Official Soviet criticism has explained this by suggesting that Gorky thus "unmasked such 'thinkers' who deem themselves to be above partisan concerns and exposed the dependence of their ideology on the practice and the class interests of the bourgeoisie" (*KLE*). But a reader who, like Klim Samgin, is "above partisan concerns" may very well read the novel as a thoughtful and critical inquiry into the causes, the nature, and the meaning of the processes which led to the cataclysm of the Revolution.

Gorky's posthumous influence has been great. On the one hand, it has been instrumental in maintaining the positions of socialist realism. On the other, Gorky's humanism and his consistently fair judgment of "fellow travelers" (Babel, Bulgakov, Zoshchenko, etc.) even in the face of vicious attacks by "proletarian" critics have indirectly helped the partial rehabilitation of some writers who, together with their works, disappeared from the literary scene in the 1930s.

Works: Sobranie sochinenii. 25 vols. 2d ed. 1933–34. *Sobranie sochinenii.* 30 vols. 1949–56. *Sobranie sochinenii.* 1968– . *Nesvoevremennye mysli.* Paris, 1971. See also: *Arkhiv M. Gor'kogo.* 1939– .

Translations: See Lewanski, pp. 248–59.

Bibliography: S. D. Balukhatyi, *Literaturnaya rabota M. Gor'kogo. Spisok pervopechatnykh tekstov i avtorizovannykh izdanii, 1892–1934.* 1936. ———, *Kritika o M. Gor'kom. Bibliografiya statei i knig, 1893–1932.* 1934. S. D. Balukhatyi and K. D. Muratova, *Literaturnaya rabota M. Gor'kogo. Dopolnitel'nyi spisok. 1889–1937.* 1941.

Secondary literature: F. M. Borras, *Maxim Gorky, the Writer: An Interpretation.* Toronto, 1967. ———, *Maxim Gorky and Lev Tolstoy.* Leeds, 1968. B. Bursov, *Roman M. Gor'kogo* Mat' *i voprosy sotsialisticheskogo realizma.* 3d ed. 1962. B. A. Byalik, *M. Gor'kii—dramaturg.* 2d ed. 1977. ———, *M. Gor'kii—literaturnyi kritik.* 1960. ———, *Sud'ba Maksima Gor'kogo.* 2d ed. 1973. A. I. Goncharenko, *Publitsistika Gor'kogo.* 1961. Richard Hare, *Maxim Gorky: Romantic Realist and Conservative Revolutionary.* 1962. A. V. Lunacharskii, *Stat'i o Gor'kom.* 1938. A. Metchenko, *Zaveshchano Gor'kim: Rol' A. M. Gor'kogo v razvitii sotsialisticheskogo realizma.* 1969. A. S. Myasnikov, *M. Gor'kii, ocherk tvorchestva.* 1953. L. Jay Oliva, "Maxim Gorky Discovers America," *New York Historical Society Quarterly* 51 (1967), pp. 45–60. A. Ovcharenko, *M. Gor'kii i literaturnye iskaniya XX stoletiya.* 1978. Wolfgang Pailer, *Die frühen Dramen M. Gor'kijs in ihrem Verhältnis zum dramatischen Schaffen A. P. Čechovs.* (Slavistische Beiträge, 122.) Munich, 1978. Harold Segel, "Gorky's Major Plays," *Yale/Theater* 7, no. 2 (1976), pp. 56–77. P. Strokov, *Epopeya M. Gor'kogo* Zhizn' Klima Samgina. 1962. I. Vainberg, *Zhizn' Klima Samgina M. Gor'kogo: Istoriko-literaturnyi kommentarii.* 1971. V. V. Vorovskii, "O M. Gor'kom" (1902) and "Maksim Gor'kii" (1910). In his *Literaturno-kriticheskie stat'i.* 1956. Pp. 49–66, 253–72. Irwin Weil, *Gorky: His Literary Development and Influence on Soviet Intellectual Life.* (Studies in Language and Literature, 5.) 1966. Bertram D. Wolfe, *The Bridge and the Abyss: The Troubled Friendship of Maxim Gorky and V. I. Lenin.* (Hoover Institution Publications, 58.) 1967.
V. T.

Gorodétsky, Sergeí Mitrofánovich (1884–1967), poet, and co-founder of the POETS' GUILD and the ACMEIST movement. He was a student in the Department of History and Philology at St. Petersburg University. In 1912, GUMILYOV wrote, "Sergei Gorodetsky is a great joy to us all ... he has managed to do so much that one is dazzled.... His lack of restraint in creative power, his resolution in executing what has been conceived, and his uniformity of style in the most varied endeavors reveals an impetuous and strong nature, completely fitting for the heroic twentieth century."

Although Gorodetsky published more than ten volumes of verse, prose fiction, literary translations, and even a new libretto for M. I. Glinka's opera, *Ivan Susanin* (1937–1944), his reputation as a poet and a literary figure derives from the promise of his first book of poetry, *Spring Corn* (Yar', 1907), which brought him instant fame as it was welcomed by both V. BRYUSOV and A. BLOK, and from his role as co-founder (with N. Gumilyov) of the Poets' Guild (1911) and the Acmeist movement.

His best poetry was inspired by Slavic mythology and Russian folklore, an interest which he is credited with encouraging in the young futurist poet, Velimir KHLEBNIKOV. Gorodetsky's second collection of poems entitled *Perun* (the Slavic name of the Thunder god, 1907), and his fifth book, *Willow* (Iva, 1912), reviewed by

Gumilyov, were also well received. His prose tales left a far less favorable impression.

In November 1911, Gorodetsky joined Gumilyov in establishing the Poets' Guild and in 1913, along with his mentor and friend, he published an Acmeist manifesto entitled "Some Currents in Contemporary Russian Poetry," in the January issue of APOLLON. He also contributed two poems, "Adam" and "The Stars," to the March issue of *Apollon* as part of a set of programmatic poems.

Gorodetsky's manifesto is somewhat clearer, simpler and more direct than Gumilyov's in its attack against the ultra-mystical SYMBOLISM of Vyacheslav IVANOV and the extreme aestheticism of the first generation symbolist poets. In an endeavor to define his fundamental quarrel with the symbolist attitude toward the supernatural as the source of art and beauty, while asserting man's sense of his own moral and physical destiny as the basis of Acmeist ideals, he maintained: "What is basically in question in determining the differences between Acmeism and symbolism is our resounding and colorful world: *this world* made of time, volume, and form, this planet—the earth." He called on his fellow poets "to return poetry to the real world."

In his early post-revolutionary poetry, he expressed themes of revolutionary progress and the romanticism of man's heroic struggle. Outside the Soviet Union he has been morally condemned for his public repudiation of Gumilyov.

Works: Stikhotvoreniya i poemy. 1960. *Stikhi.* 1964.
Translations: Modern Russian Poetry. Ed. Vladimir Markov and Merrill Sparks. 1967. Pp. 636–41. See also: *Lewanski*, p. 259.
Secondary literature: N. A. Taktasheva, ed., "Avtobiografiya S. M. Gorodetskogo," *RLit* 12 (1970), no. 3, pp. 186–90.
J. G. H.

Gráni (Facets), Russian émigré review of literature, arts, science, and sociopolitical thought; initially published irregularly, later quarterly. The first issue of *Grani* was published in a camp for Displaced Persons, Moenchehof near Kassel, in West Germany, in July 1946; in 1982, No. 123 (for January–March) was published in Frankfurt on Main.

The first few issues of *Grani* were edited by E. Romanov, B. Serafimov, and S. Maksimov. Later, the composition of the editorial board changed several times, but two names stand out, those of E. R. Romanov (editor-in-chief, formally, from No. 5, 1949) and N. B. Tarasova (from No. 51, 1962). The review is published by the Posev publishing house and is thus closely linked with the NTS (Narodnotrudovoi soyuz), the political organization of Russian Solidarists.

The editorial article in *Grani* No. 1 stated that the purpose of the review was to serve "the Word of Truth," by showing the "paths, on which the bright facets of human souls are revealed" (hence the name of the review, *Facets*). On the occasion of the 15th anniversary of *Grani* (No. 50, 1961) the review's platform was expressed in three main propositions: to reestablish the forcibly broken tradition of the Russian past as represented by the prophetic literature of PUSHKIN, GOGOL, and DOSTOEVSKY; to contribute to the birth and development of a new Russian literature oriented toward spiritual values; and to work for the rapprochement and eventual merger of the two Russian literatures, presently estranged: émigré literature and literature under the Soviets.

Throughout the years, *Grani* succeeded in establishing significant contacts with authors and *Samizdat* publications in the Soviet Union. Poems and prose works received from the USSR were published as early as 1956 (No. 32). No. 52 (1962) was entirely devoted to materials from the Soviet Union. *Grani* was also first to publish certain works of PASTERNAK, AKHMATOVA, TARSIS, and SOLZHENITSYN.

Lately, *Grani* started the additional publication of collections of selected materials from its earlier issues. Specially designed for dissemination in the USSR, these collections are pocket-size (9.5 by 14.5 cm), on thin paper, containing each about 500 pages. No. 1 consists of selections from nos. 87/88–94, No. 2 from nos. 78–86, No. 3 from nos. 71–77, No. 4 from nos. 69–70, and No. 5 from nos. 53–68.

Bibliography: For "Contents" of *Grani* see Nos. 59 (1–58), 74 (52–74), 78 (75–78), 87/88 (79–86), 89/90 (75–89/90), 95 (91–95), 102 (96–102), 106 (101–06), 110 (107–10), 114 (111–14), 118 (115–18), 123 (119–22). On *Grani* see: Vyacheslav Zavalishin, "Chetvert'

veka zhurnala 'Grani.'" In: *Russkaya literatura v emigratsii*, Ed. Nikolai P. Poltoratzky. Pittsburgh, 1972. Pp. 301–07 (in Russian) and 383 (in English).   N. P. P.

Gránin, Daniíl Aleksándrovich (pseud. Gérman, 1918–   ), short-story writer and novelist. Granin graduated from the Leningrad Polytechnical Institute in 1940 and worked as an engineer until 1950. He published his first short story, "The Second Variant" (Variant vtoroi) in 1949 and gained recognition in the post-Stalin period. His first major success was the novel, *Those Who Seek* (Iskateli, 1955), followed by two further novels, *After the Wedding* (Posle svad'by, 1958) and *I Challenge the Storm* (Idu na grozu, 1962) both of which were adapted for the stage. Granin has also published a number of short stories including, "Yaroslav Dombrovsky" (1951) and "The House on the Fontanka" (Dom na Fontanke, 1968), and entertaining essays about his trips abroad in the late 1960s.

For the most part, Granin's work presents fictional accounts of Soviet technological society, drawn upon his own experience. However his treatment is romantic in that the hero is invariably a mediocre and yet dedicated scientist whose sole interest in his work is the quest for truth. Accordingly, contrasted with this virtuous example are brilliant scientists who are preoccupied with petty interests such as fame, power, financial security. Thus, in a broader sense, Granin's exploration of scientific quest is a critique of social values, a critique which moreover serves as both an indictment of Stalinist practices and an advocation of Soviet ideology in that he stresses the importance of science. In *Those Who Seek*, for example, Granin describes how an average scientist, Andrei, manages to unite his group of assistants into an efficient research team and perfect a new fault locator. Thus, unlike his former classmate, Viktor (a brilliant candidate turned factory boss), Andrei wins the respect and admiration of his fellow workers and scores a personal victory through creative initiative and selfless dedication. Nevertheless, Granin does not always adhere to this formulaic approach as evidenced by "The House on the Fontanka," a nostalgic recollection of pre-war Russia delivered with great skill and subtlety.

Works: Sobranie sochinenii.1978.
Translations: Those Who Seek. Trans by Robert Daglish. Moscow, 1958. "The House on the Fontanka." In *Modern Russian Short Stories.* Ed. M. Orga. London, 1980.
Secondary literature: Keith Armes, "Daniel Granin and the World of Soviet Science," *Survey* 90 (1974), pp. 47–59. L. Plotkin, "Novye povesti Daniila Granina," *Neva*, 1977, no. 5, pp. 183–87. A. G. Waring, "Science, Love and the Establishment in the Novels of D. A. Granin and C. P. Snow," *Forum for Modern Language Studies* (St. Andrews, Scotland), 14 (1978), pp. 1–15.   B. A.

Granóvsky, Timofeí Nikoláevich (1813–55), historian and professor, was born into the family of a small landholder in Orel province. He studied law at Petersburg University from 1832 to 1835, and in that final year his first article appeared: "The Fate of the Jewish People" (Sud'by evreiskogo naroda). In 1836, he continued his studies in Berlin, taking a particular interest in Hegel through the influence of N. V. STANKEVICH. Having returned to Russia in 1839, Granovsky was appointed professor of history at Moscow University. At the same time, he became acquainted with HERZEN and BELINSKY, and began to espouse the views of a WESTERNIZER deploring serfdom, despotism, and autocracy, while championing the ideals of enlightenment and individual freedom. His disputes with Herzen in 1845 and 1846, in which Granovsky's point of view came to be regarded as bourgeois liberalism, while Herzen tended towards revolutionary democratism, foreshadowed the later split among Westernizers. In his lectures, Granovsky projected thinly veiled criticism of the tsarist regime and its iniquities, criticism which Herzen, among others, thoroughly appreciated.

In 1845, Granovsky defended his Master's thesis, and in 1849 his doctoral dissertation, "Abbé Suger: On Communes in France" (Abbat Sugerii: Ob obshchinakh vo Frantsii). At this time, he contributed to such journals as the OTECHESTVENNYE ZAPISKI, MOSKVITYANIN, and (from 1847) SOVREMENNIK. The period of reaction between 1848 and 1855, which had its particular manifestations at Moscow University, were hard years for Granovsky, who suffered various "reprimands" but nevertheless remained true to his liberal convictions.

Granovsky proclaimed the need for a more scientific basis upon which to ground the study of history (his discourse, "On the Present Condition and Meaning of Universal History," 1852), while recognizing its close affinity with anthropology and other related fields. In this respect, his views paralleled those of CHERNYSHEVSKY. In both his scholarly and teaching roles, Granovsky opposed SLAVOPHILE views regarding the history and development of Russia as contrasted to Western Europe, their idealization of peasant traditions, and—from Granovsky's perspective—their vague, unscientific approach to the study of history in general. Granovsky stood at the center of the literary life of his times and exercised considerable influence upon his more famous literary contemporaries, especially Herzen and TURGENEV. Within his own field, he was consistent in his efforts to demonstrate the connections between works of literature and their historical basis. In DOSTOEVSKY's novel, *The Devils*, Granovsky served as the prototype for Stepan Trofimovich Verkhovensky.

Works: Polnoe sobranie sochinenii. 2 vols. 1905.
Secondary literature: N. G. Chernyshevskii, "Sochineniya T. N. Granovskogo." In *Polnoe sobranie sochinenii.* Vol. 3. 1947. A. I. Gertsen, "Publichnye chteniya g. Granovskogo ..." In *Sobranie sochinenii v 30 tt.* Vol. 2. 1954. ———. *Byloe i dumy.* In *Sobranie sochinenii.* Vol. 9. 1956. A. E. Kosminskii, "Zhizn' i deyatel'nost' T. N. Granovskogo," *Vestnik MGU*, 1956, no. 4. I. S. Turgenev, "Dva slova o Granovskom." In *Sobranie sochinenii v 12 tt.* Vol. 11. 1956. *T. N. Granovskii i ego perepiska.* 2 vols. 1897.   D. K. D.

Grebénka, Evgény (Ukr. Hrebinka, Jevhen; 1812–48), a writer more prominent for his Ukrainian than for his Russian works, whose varied and energetic literary activities constituted in the 1830s and 1840s the most important bridge between the two literatures. Born near Piryatyn (Ukr. Pyrjatyn) in the Poltava region, he completed in 1831 the Nezhin (Ukr. Nižyn) gymnasium (where GOGOL was an older classmate) and in 1834, after brief military service, settled in St. Petersburg, teaching literature in various military schools. Grebenka's first and ultimately most influential literary works were in Ukrainian (he began writing Ukrainian poetry in 1831); in 1834 he published his collection of fables, *Fables of Little Russia* (Malorossiiskie prikazki, 2d ed. 1836). The handful of lyrical poems included here have a basically pre-romantic, folkloric cast. His efforts in the late 1830s to publish a collective edition of various Ukrainian writers culminated in the 'almanac' *Lastivka* (1841), which included, among others, some early poems of SHEVCHENKO. The latter's release from serfdom and his introduction into Ukrainian intellectual circles in St. Petersburg was also organized by Grebenka. Less successful is his free translation of PUSHKIN's "Poltava" (first fragments published in 1831, the whole in 1836), which is marked by the broad burlesque tradition of Kotljarevs'kyj and at times approaches unintentional parody.

Grebenka's Russian writings are much greater in quantity and range. His lyrical poetry is often focused on Ukrainian themes and modelled on folk songs; some of them, such as "Dark Eyes" (Chernye ochi—Ochi chernye, ochi strastnye) attained great popularity as songs. His long dramatic poem *Bogdan* (1843) (on the seventeeth century Cossack Hetman Khmel'nyc'kyj) employs romantic conventions and continues the tradition of Ryleev and Maksymovyč in heroizing the Hetman and celebrating the union of the Ukraine and Russia.

Grebenka's greatest efforts were in prose. He wrote two novels and some two score *povesti* and short stories. Here his poetics evolved from the early sentimental-romantic *Tales from Piryatyn* (Rasskazy piryatyntsa, 1837), which drew on Ukrainian folk motifs and devices, to romantic treatments of the Ukrainian Cossack past, to, finally, his focus on social problems and the margins of society in the style of the natural school, as exemplified by his participation in Nekrasov's *Fiziologiya Peterburga* (1845). Throughout his prose there is evidence of Gogol's influence: in the narrative devices of the early Piryatyn stories (which also draw on Marlinsky), in his depictions of Ukrainian history and *byt* (though his major work here, the novel *Chaikovsky*, 1843, also relies on oral sources and family history), and his baring of the gamut of social iniquity, where, for example, the structure of *Adventures of a Blue Bank Note* (Priklyucheniya sinei assignatsii, 1847) is modelled on *Dead Souls.*

Secondary literature: S. D. Zubkov, *Russkaya proza G. F. Kvitki i E. P. Grebenki v kontekste russko-ukrainskikh literaturnykh svyazei.* Kiev, 1979.
G. G.

Grech, Nikolai Ivánovich (1787–1867), journalist, writer, and philologist. Son of a clerk, Grech occupied a leading position in Russian journalism. In the years 1812 to 1839 he was the publisher and editor of *Syn otechestva,* one of the first "thick journals" in Russia. Initially the journal had a liberal orientation, which it lost after the DECEMBRIST uprising, when BULGARIN, a secret agent of the police, became coeditor. On the other hand, Grech was coeditor from 1831 to 1859 of Bulgarin's newspaper SEVERNAYA PCHELA, a semi-official organ held in contempt by liberal writers. In Petersburg journalism Grech, together with Bulgarin and SENKOVSKY, formed a notorious triumvirate strongly opposed to new tendencies in Russian literature. Grech's novels (*The Black Woman,* 1834; *A Trip to Germany,* 1836) are rather unimportant, while his numerous works on the Russian language, especially his *Elementary Rules of Russian Grammar* (1828, 11 editions), enjoyed great popularity. Some of them were promptly translated and had a lasting influence on the study of Russian abroad. His important *History of Russian Literature* (1822, several editions) was the first book of its kind to appear in Russia. Narrow in scope, it concentrates on the writers' biographies. Most interesting are his *Notes from my Life,* offering a broad and critical picture of contemporary social and literary life. Because of his conservative or rather reactionary views, Grech has been little studied, in spite of his unquestionable influence on Russian literature.

Works: Grund-Regeln der Russischen Grammatik. St. Petersburg, 1828. *Grammaire raisonnée de la langue russe I–II.* St. Petersburg, 1828–29. *Sochineniya,* 3 vols. 1855. *Zapiski o moei zhizni.* St. Petersburg, 1886; Moscow and Leningrad, 1930.
G. K.

Green Lamp, The (Zelénaya lámpa), literary group (1819–20). A group of poets, theater enthusiasts, and political conspirators who met approximately twenty-two times between April 1819 and fall of 1820 in the Petersburg home of N. V. and A. V. Vsevolozhsky. The "Green Lamp" was affiliated with the proto-Decembrist "Union of Welfare." It is difficult, however, to draw absolute conclusions about the group's membership, interests, and activities because its records are fragmentary and because the Vsevolozhsky brothers also entertained a set of young libertines on Saturday nights (see A. S. PUSHKIN's letter to N. Vsevolozhsky of late October 1824), and their revels are often confused with the meetings of the "Green Lamp."

The group included the poets A. S. Pushkin, A. A. DELVIG, and N. I. GNEDICH; the essayist A. D. Ulybyshev; and several members of the "Union of Welfare" (S. P. Trubetskoi, Ya. N. Tolstoi, and F. N. GLINKA). Archival materials suggest that the "Green Lamp," which met after theatrical performances, devoted its meetings to the reading and criticism of verse, to reviewing theatrical events, studying ancient Russian history, and discussing politics. Ulybyshev's essays, especially his utopian fantasy "Un Rêve," display Enlightenment tendencies: anticlerical deism and constitutional monarchism. Pushkin's letter of 26 September 1822 (in prose and verse) to Ya. Tolstoi imaginatively recreates the spirit and style of their symposia.

Bibliography: B. L. Modzalevskii, "K istorii 'Zelenoi lampy.'" In *Dekabristy i ikh vremya.* Vol. 1. 1928. V. B. Tomashevskii, *Pushkin. Kniga I.* 1956. Pp. 193–224.
W. M. T.

Grékova, Irina Nikoláevna (pseud. of Eléna Sergéevna Vénttsel, 1907–   ). A Soviet Russian prose writer, born in Reval (now Tallinn), Grekova is by profession a mathematician and cyberneticist. Holder of a doctoral degree, she was Professor of Cybernetics at the Moscow Air Force Academy from 1955 to 1967. Literature is her avocation. Her pseudonym, "Igrek," stands for an unknown in Russian mathematical terminology. She published her first story in 1957 and was immediately acclaimed as one of the "new voices" in Russian literature. Not prolific, she is the author of short stories and novellas, most of which have been published in NOVYI MIR.

The setting for her first story, "Beyond the Entryway" (1962), is a science laboratory and the story deals with the value of science and lyric poetry. Indirectly, Grekova questions the application of scientific discoveries for destructive purposes.

In "The Lady's Hairdresser" (1963) Grekova moved the debate about art and creativity to the beauty parlor. She depicts how the young hairdresser Vitaly, a creative artist and dedicated worker, is resented for his success by his mediocre fellow workers, and by the unethical, bribe-taking administrators. They hound him for paying attention to the artistry and not fulfilling his quotas of "heads." He quits this job and goes to work in a factory. Grekova exposes the lack of integrity and pride in one's work and shows how the oppressive forces of conformity stifle initiative and creativity.

"During the Tests" (1967) is set in an isolated Siberian settlement in 1952 where a group of ballistics experts conduct a military experiment. The dullness, pettiness, and poverty of their spiritual lives are underscored by denunciation, suspicion, and fear. After its publication Grekova was dismissed from the Air Force Academy, and subjected to harsh criticism. Simultaneously, *Novyi mir* and its editor were attacked. As a result, according to Svirsky, *Novyi mir* was banned from distribution to the military.

Grekova's stories, told from a woman's point of view, and with humor, portray the daily life of a professional woman in the Soviet Union. She provides insight into the atmosphere of institutes, beauty shops, and homes. She raises moral and ethical questions but does not supply answers. Her prose is realistic, straightforward, and introspective. Her primary means of characterization are dialogues, and internal monologues which are artfully spliced into conversations.

Works: "Za prokhodnoi," *Novyi mir,* 1962, no. 7. "Damskii master," *Novyi mir,* 1963, no. 11. "Letom v gorode," *Novyi mir,* 1965, no. 4. *Pod fonarem.* 1966. "Na ispytaniyakh," *Novyi mir,* 1967, no. 7. "Malen'kii Garusov," *Zvezda,* 1970, no. 9. "Khozyaika gostinitsy," *Zvezda,* 1976, no. 9. *Kafedra: povesti.* 1981.
Translations: "The Lady's Hairdresser," *RLT* 5 (1973).
Secondary literature: Deming Brown, *Soviet Russian Literature since Stalin.* 1978. Pp. 163–67. E. J. Brown, *Russian Literature since the Revolution.* 1982. Pp. 321–22. E. Dobin, "Khozyaika gostinitsy," *Literaturnoe obozrenie,* 1977, no. 10. V. Kamyanov, "Sluzhba pamyati," *Novyi mir,* 1971, no. 5. V. Lakshin, "Pisatel', chitatel', kritik," *Novyi mir,* 1965, no. 4. B. Leonov, "Za i protiv . . ." *Moskva,* 1969, no. 5.
H. S.

Griboédov, Aleksándr Sergéevich (1795–1829), diplomat and dramatist. Born in Moscow of a comfortable if not wealthy family, Griboedov entered Moscow University in 1806 at the age of eleven. He studied law, literature, and science and intended to pursue an advanced degree when the French invasion changed his plans. On 26 July 1812 he joined the Moscow hussars but saw no action. In 1815 Griboedov moved to Petersburg and in March 1816 received his discharge from the army. Shortly thereafter, he entered the College of Foreign Affairs where his career as a diplomat began. Griboedov's first play, the one-act verse comedy *Young Wives* (Molodye suprugi), an adaptation of Creuzé de Lesser's *Le Secret du ménage,* was produced in September 1815. Together with Pavel KATENIN in 1817 he wrote the three-act prose comedy *Student,* a satire of the ARZAMAS literary circle. Another collaborative effort, with Prince SHAKHOVSKOI and Nikolai Khmelnitsky, resulted in a third comedy, *All in the Family* (Svoya sem'ya). An improvement over his previous works, it was produced in January 1818. With A. Gendre, Griboedov next wrote *Sham Infidelity* (Pritvornaya nevernost'), produced in February 1818 and, like *Young Wives,* also an adaptation of a French original.

In August 1818, Griboedov left Moscow to assume the post of secretary to the Russian legation in Persia. After a stay of nearly a year in Tiflis he finally reached Teheran where he was engaged in diplomatic work from February 1819 until late 1821. From then until early 1823 he was back in Tiflis as diplomatic secretary to General A. P. Ermolov, the commander of the Russian Army of the Caucasus. When he went on an extended leave in February 1823, he brought with him the first two acts of his most famous dramatic work, *Woe from Wit* (or The Misfortune of Being Clever, Gore ot uma). Griboedov finished the play between March 1823 and May 1824. Because of its satirical content, however, permission for publication was denied. In May 1825, Griboedov returned to the Caucasus. It was here that he was arrested after the outbreak of the Decembrist uprising because of his previous acquaintance with Ryleev and Bestuzhev. He was escorted back to Petersburg and imprisoned for four months. Following his release, he was promoted to the next grade in the civil service and posted again to the Caucasus. War with Persia had erupted in June 1826 and Griboedov was placed in charge of the peace negotiations on the Russian side. When the Peace of Turkmenchai was concluded on 10 February 1828, it was Griboedov who personally delivered the treaty to the Tsar. In recognition of his diplomatic achievement he was named Russian minister to Persia. He reached Teheran in January 1829 after a sojourn of several months in Tiflis where he married the daughter of the Georgian poet Prince Aleksandr Chavchavadze. The treaty that ended the hostilities with Persia produced deep resentment in that country so that by the time Griboedov reached the capital it was a tinderbox needing only a spark to ignite it. When an Armenian eunuch of the Shah's harem took refuge in the Russian legation, crowds of fanatic Persians stormed it on 30 January 1829 killing everyone in sight. Griboedov's mutilated body was eventually recovered and buried in Tiflis.

Woe from Wit remains Griboedov's greatest literary achievement. The play was published in 1833, but with cuts; the full text became available only in 1861. One of the most brilliant classics of the Russian stage, the comedy's greatest appeal lies in the naturalness and pithiness of its dialogue and the sparkling liveliness of its verse— rhymed iambics of one to thirteen syllables per line, a metric pattern first introduced by Sumarokov in his fables in the 18th century and used for comedy before Griboedov by Shakhovskoi. Within the confines of a single setting—the Famusov home—and a twenty-four hour time frame, *Woe from Wit* presents an unflattering picture of contemporary Moscow society dominated by political and cultural conservatives afraid of change and stubbornly resistant to it. Returning to this society is an angry young man named Chatsky who quickly recognizes his estrangement from it and the hopelessness of any reconciliation. He becomes outspokenly critical of everything around him and is ultimately compelled to run away. The conventional romantic intrigue is overturned as the young woman Chatsky loves and who he believes loves him, Sofya, is romancing with her father Famusov's sleazy secretary Molchalin who in turn is hotly pursuing Lizanka (Liza), Sofya's maid. Angered at Chatsky's boorishness and criticism, Sofya takes revenge by planting the rumor at a ball that he is crazy. Unable to bear the claustrophobia he feels closing in around him on all sides, Chatsky flees Sofya, the Famusov home, Moscow, and perhaps Russia itself. The play abounds in superbly drawn satirical characters who, while types, are also individuated. Apart from its satire, humor, and lively dialogue (a number of lines of which have become virtually proverbial in Russia), the play reflects romanticism as much as it looks back to 18th-century classicism. This is evident in its preference for verse over prose, its use of light and space, and its main protagonist, Chatsky, who embodies some traits of the romantic hero.

Works: Gore ot uma. Introd. and notes D. P. Costello. Oxford, 1951. *Sochineniya v stikhakh.* Ed. I. N. Medvedeva. 1967.

Translations: The Mischief of Being Clever. Trans. B. Pares. Introd. D. Mirsky. London, 1925.

Secondary literature: A. S. Griboedov: Tvorchestvo, biografiya, traditsii. Sbornik statei. 1977. Jean Bonamour, *A. S. Griboedov et la vie littéraire de son temps.* Paris, 1965. Yu. N. Borisov, Gore ot uma *i russkaya stikhotvornaya komediya: U istokov zhanra.* 1978. I. Medvedeva, Gore ot uma *A. S. Griboedova.* 2d ed. 1974. N. K. Piksanov, *Tvorcheskaya istoriya* Gorya ot uma. 1971. H. B. S.

Grigóriev (Grigór'ev), Apollón Aleksándrovich (1822–64), poet and critic, was born in Moscow, the son of a minor government official. He took a law degree at Moscow University in 1842, but never practiced law. He worked intermittently as a government official, teacher, and private tutor, but mostly as a literary and theater critic for the Otechestvennye zapiski (1849–50), Moskvityanin (1850–56), Vremya and Epokha (1861–64), and other journals. Brilliantly gifted, sociable, and of a pleasant disposition, Grigoriev was also a man of irregular habits, plagued by unhappy love affairs and a drinking problem. He died of a stroke on 7 October 1864, in St. Petersburg debtors' prison.

Grigoriev's poetry is post-romantic. Themes of Lermontovian *Weltschmerz* and Masonic mysticism (Grigoriev translated a cycle of Masonic hymns from the German) are given a personal, occasionally even a social touch. A fine guitar player, Grigoriev was a master of the Gypsy romance, which he helped to introduce into Russian poetry. As a poet and literary theorist, he anticipated some traits of Russian Symbolism and was held in high regard by the symbolists, Blok in particular. Grigoriev's autobiography, *My Literary and Moral Wanderings* (Moi literaturnye i nravstvennye skital'chestva, 1862–64), became a classic. Written, to some extent, in response to Herzen's *My Past and Thoughts*, it gives a warm and sympathetic close-up view of middle class life in the Moscow of Grigoriev's childhood and youth, and of the intellectual ferment among the developing intelligentsia.

Grigoriev was the foremost conservative literary critic of his age and is thought by some to have been the greatest Russian critic of the 19th century. He was a Slavophile with democratic and middle-class leanings, and without some of the archaist-reactionary and messianic-mystic quirks of other Slavophiles. Grigoriev, the Dostoevsky brothers, and Strakhov formed the nucleus of the *pochvenniki* ("men of the soil") group (see Pochva), which stood between the Slavophiles and the Liberals in the political spectrum of the 1860s. Grigoriev professed a well-defined philosophy of art, which he articulated, somewhat repetitiously, in several of his annual surveys of Russian literature and in theoretical essays, such as "On Truth and Sincerity in Art" (1856), "A Critical View of the Foundations, Importance, and Devices of Contemporary Art Criticism" (1858), "The Paradoxes of Organic Criticism" (1864), etc. His criticism was "philosophical," geared to understanding works of literature as expressions of ideas, the national spirit, and the drift of history. Grigoriev's theory of art is derived mainly from Goethe, Schelling, and Carlyle. Other influences, acknowledged by Grigoriev himself, were Coleridge, Emerson, Hugo, Renan, Buckle, and Lewes. Grigoriev also considered himself a disciple of Belinsky, whose later, Hegelian and socialist, phases he condemned, however.

To Grigoriev criticism is in relation to art, what art is in relation to life: an intuitive grasp of its light and warmth. The critic's main task is then to recognize and to appreciate all true and living art, while exposing the sham and falsehood of all that is artificial and stillborn. Grigoriev called his criticism "organic," implying that it took art to be an organic function of social and national life in its historical development. He rejected purely aesthetic or formalist criticism, as well as any "art for art's sake." But he also rejected the utilitarian and naturalist conception of art developed by Chernyshevsky, on the grounds that it ignored the autonomy of art and its ideal component. To Grigoriev a genuine work of art was quintessential reality. He therefore stressed the cognitive, visionary, and prophetic power of art. Great art, he said, not only mirrors a nation's growth, but also anticipates it and acts as its catalyst. Thus, Grigoriev declared that Pushkin had, in his life and works, created quintessential and prophetic symbols of the character and destiny of the Russian nation. Like Belinsky before him, Grigoriev saw literary types as the main achievement of creative intuition, in whom the individual, the national, and the universally human are fused. Grigoriev's criterion of great literature was that it should reveal the truth of life. He saw this truth in moral and religious terms, while his "progressive" opponents saw it in socio-political terms.

Grigoriev, whose prose style was ponderous and often prolix, was not effective as a practicing literary critic, but in retrospect it appears that he was often right and on occasion profoundly so. He was the first to point out the greatness of Pushkin's prose and the seminal importance of Ivan Petrovich Belkin as a symbol of the new Russian man, ready to face Russian reality without the crutch of an artificially acquired European civilization. Grigoriev was one of very few critics to recognize the importance of Gogol as a conservative political and religious thinker and to give his *Selected Passages from a Correspondence with Friends* (1847) a positive review. He rejected Lermontov's *A Hero of Our Time* as an ephemeral phenomenon, and not truly Russian. Grigoriev's analysis of Turgenev was subtle and perceptive. While agreeing with the common view that Turgenev was a herald and chronicler of every new movement in Russian life, Grigoriev suggested that Turgenev, in his many and varied subjects, was seeing ultimately himself only and projecting his personal sensibility upon everything he touched.

Grigoriev's interpretation of Goncharov's *Oblomov* was diametrically opposed to DOBROLYUBOV's in the latter's "What is Oblomov-ism?" Grigoriev stressed Oblomov's positive Christian qualities and saw the landowner Oblomov's marriage to Agafya, a simple Russian woman, as a symbolic detail of deep and positive significance. Grigoriev's understanding of the young TOLSTOI was profound and sympathetic. He recognized the writer's genius, but also the inner conflicts with which he was afflicted, specifically the danger posed by the interference of Tolstoi the moralist's analytic mind with the gifted artist's organic intuitions.

Grigoriev gave more attention and enthusiastic support to the playwright OSTROVSKY than to any other contemporary Russian au-thor, not only because he and Ostrovsky were friends and had come from the same social milieu of middle-class Moscow, or because Gri-goriev was fond of the theater, especially when it featured Russian songs and dances (which Ostrovsky's plays often do). Grigoriev found that Ostrovsky's sober realism and healthy sense of humor created a true mirror of Russian reality, yet were not devoid of a staunch belief in Russian ideals and a warm optimism. An excellent theater critic, Grigoriev did not hesitate to point out the technical weaknesses of Ostrovsky's plots and composition.

Grigoriev is in many ways an attractive figure. His conservatism lacks bitterness or malice. He has a great deal of warmth even for his opponents. His idealism is sincere, his love of literature genuine. He is widely read and handles philosophical concepts with the confidence of an academically trained scholar. His reviews and essays contain many just observations, and a brilliant insight here and there. But he has many weaknesses also. The link between theoretical thought and literary fact is often tenuous. His reviews ramble along and it will often take him pages to make a simple point. He repeats himself interminably. He is also diffuse: one gets the impres-sion that he has great good will and sympathy for all the right ideas and causes, yet these ideas and causes are never pinpointed.

Works: [N. N. Strakhov, ed.,] *Sochineniya.* Vol. 1. 1876. V. F. Savodnik, ed., *Sobranie sochinenii Apollona Grigor'eva.* Fasc. 1–14. 1915–16. Vasilii Spiridonov, ed., *Polnoe sobranie sochinenii i pisem Apollona Grigor'eva v dvenadtsati tomakh.* Vol. 1. 1918. *Izbrannye proizvedeniya* [Poetry]. 1959. *Literaturnaya kritika.* Ed. B. F. Egor-ov. 1967. *Sochineniya.* I. Kritika. Ed. V. S. Krupich. Villanova U. Press, 1970. All of these editions have a single volume. The first two are highly unreliable due to arbitrary editorial changes. Biography and Bibliography: *A. A. Grigor'ev: Materialy dlya biografii.* Ed. V. Knyazhnin. 1917. B. F. Egorov. "Bibliografiya kritiki i khudozhest-vennoi prozy Ap. Grigor'eva." *Uchenye zapiski Tartuskogo gos. uni-versiteta* 98 (1960); pp. 216–46.

Translations: My Literary and Moral Wanderings and Other Auto-biographical Material. Trans. and introd. Ralph E. Matlaw. 1962.

Secondary literature: Jürgen Lehmann, *Der Einfluss der Philo-sophie des deutschen Idealismus in der russischen Literaturkritik des 19. Jahrhunderts: Die "organische Kritik" Apollon A. Grigor'evs.* 1975. A. P. Marchik, "'Organicheskaya kritika' Apollona Gri-gor'eva." *IAN* 25 (1966), pp. 514–21. Boris Sorokin, *Tolstoi in Pre-Revolutionary Russian Criticism.* 1979. Chap. 3: The Slavophile and "Organic" Critics, pp. 78–94. Victor Terras, "Apollon Grigoriev's Organic Criticism and Its Western Sources." In *Western Philosophi-cal Systems in Russian Literature.* Ed. by Anthony M. Mlikotin. 1979. Pp. 71–88. René Wellek, *A History of Modern Criticism.* 1955–65. Vol. 4; pp. 266–70.
V. T.

Grigoróvich, Dmítry Vasílievich (1822–99), writer. Born a member of the landed gentry, Grigorovich spent his childhood on his father's estate in Simbirsk, studied in private German and French *pensions* in Moscow from 1832 to 1835, and continued coursework at the St. Petersburg School of Military Engineering and the Academy of Art until 1840. Grigorovich worked in the Directorate of the Imperial Theaters, and in a period of literary inactivity from the 1860s to the 1880s he was the secretary of the Society for the Encouragement of the Arts.

Attracted by French "physiologies" of Paris life which were sell-ing well in St. Petersburg, N. A. NEKRASOV invited Grigorovich to contribute to what became the almanac, *Fiziologiya Peterburga* (1845). The result, after extensive investigation, was Grigorovich's influential sketch, *Petersburg Organ Grinders* (Peterburgskie shar-manshchiki), a work in which he attempted to depict "reality as it

genuinely is," particularly as he saw the St. Petersburg setting in GOGOL's *The Overcoat* (1842).

Grigorovich's most important works are the tales *The Village* (De-revnya, 1846) and *Anton Goremyka,* 1847. Both aroused consider-able attention when they appeared in the progressive journal, SO-VREMENNIK. Important more for approach than for execution, the works were opposed to serfdom and were regarded as being written in the spirit of the NATURAL SCHOOL, though the compassionate de-scription of the misery of peasant life is more a form of sentimental naturalism. In them, Grigorovich went beyond the outward behavior and speech of the peasantry and attempted to paint peasant life from the point of view of the characters on a background of a lyrical depic-tion of Russian nature. His work had considerable impact upon prac-titioners of the new literature. *Anton Goremyka* was highly esteemed by BELINSKY, who saw in it the initiation of an era of exposés of rural life, while SALTYKOV-SHCHEDRIN praised Grigorovich for achieving the humanization of the Russian peasant.

Grigorovich's literary fame was soon eclipsed by TURGENEV's *A Sportsman's Sketches* which began appearing the same year in *So-vremennik;* but his initial contribution as a catalyst remains undimin-ished in importance. Grigorovich continued the tradition in the fifties, producing a number of works in which he sought to accurately but sympathetically describe peasant life, as in *The Fishermen* (Ryba-ki, 1853). One work from this period, *The School of Hospitality* (Shkola gostepriimstva, 1855) is also notable for its attacks on CHERNYSHEVSKY.

In 1858 and 1859, Grigorovich travelled through the Mediterra-nean, and subsequently described the experience in a series of sketch-es entitled *The Ship Retvizan* (Korabl' Retvizan, 1859, 1863). At the onset of political tensions in the 1860s, Grigorovich turned away from literature and *Sovremennik,* and returned to writing only in the eight-ies with the tale, *The Guttapercha Boy* (Guttaperchevyi Mal'chik, 1883), which became a well-known children's story about the tragic fate of a young circus acrobat. His *Literary Reminiscences* (Litera-turnye vospominaniya, 1892–93) are a rich source of literary and historical material. A friend of most of the prominent figures in 19th-century Russian literature, he is also remembered as the person who introduced DOSTOEVSKY to Nekrasov in 1845, and for his role in discovering and encouraging CHEKHOV.

Works: Polnoe sobranie sochinenii. 12 vols. 1896. *Izbrannye proizvedeniya.* 1959. *Literaturnye vospominaniya.* 1961.

Translations: The Fishermen. Preface by A. Rappoport. 1916. "New Year's Eve." In *Tales from the Russian.* Trans. by H. Suther-land Edwards. 1892. "The Peasant." In *The Russian Horizon: An Anthology.* Ed. Nagandranath Gangulee. 1943.

Secondary literature: Joachim T. Baer, "The 'Physiological Sketch' in Russian Literature." In *Mnemozina: Studia Litteraria in Honorem Vsevolod Setchkarev.* Ed. Joachim T. Baer and Norman W. Ingham. Munich, 1974. Pp. 1–12. V. G. Belinskii, "Vzglyad na russkuyu literaturu 1846 goda" and "Vzglyad na russkuyu literaturu 1847 goda." In *PSS* 10 (1956), pp. 42–43, 250–51. Rose L. Glickman, "Industrialization and the Factory Worker in Russian Literature," *CSS* 4 (1970), pp. 629–52. L. M. Lotman, "Grigorovich." In *Istoriya russkoi literatury.* Vol. 7. 1955. M. V. Otradin, "Peterburgskie povesti D. V. Grigorovicha: problema geroya," *Filologicheskie nauki* 19 (1977), no. 2. pp. 21–31.
J. S.

Grin, Aleksándr Stepánovich (1880–1932), writer. Son of a Polish exile, Stefan Grinevsky, Grin was born in the region of Vyatka (Kirov). The young Grinevsky relieved the drabness of his adoles-cence by reading adventure novels by Mayne Reid and G. Aimard or fantastic tales by E. T. A. Hoffmann and E. A. Poe. His aspirations to become a sailor failed. In the early 1900s Grin joined the Socialist Revolutionary Party. He wrote political proclamations and in this way discovered his literary talent.

Grin's literary lifework developed outside the mainstream of Rus-sian literature. He achieved a particular combination of the empirical and the fantastic: a prose in the nature of a fairy tale in the sense that he did not abide by the laws of probabilities of the "here and now." This enabled him to recombine the relations of reality in accordance with his poetic purpose: to set side by side a quaint exotic world and a recognizable modern one, both preserving equal poetic validity, e.g., 20th-century cruisers along with romantic sailships of another age.

Grin's fiction defied topicality. He created a whole romantic world: an exotic southern coast, radiant seas and ports. Exotic locale generates exotic characters: high-spirited adventurers, robbers and assassins, beautiful women, and sailors and captains. These exotic sites and characters do not pertain to any concrete historical setting, but are intended to be purely imaginary. By removing his characters from reality, Grin endowed them with a generalized human significance, which he conveyed by giving them non-Russian names. For the same reason, Grin's protagonists never have a concrete historical nationality. Imaginary as it is, Grin's world bears a striking resemblance to the empirical world. It is astoundingly tangible and of great visual effectiveness. This is what gives aesthetic validity to the invented setting of Grin's world.

Grin's important works are his stories and novels. The stories are marked by a sense of escape into romantic exoticism stimulated by ingenious plots, often with moral resolutions and philosophical lessons, e.g., the ennobling function of art ("Water Color," 1928). However, the splendor of representation does not muffle a voice of loneliness and despair. These stories form a fairly homogeneous system, related in theme, tense emotional atmosphere, landscape, names of cities and characters, and events. Grin's five novels could be described as adventure novels. *Red Sails* (Alye parusa, 1923) is a particular rendition of the Cinderella motif. *Luminous World* (Blistayushchii mir, 1923) describes a fight against self-satisfied mediocrity which ends in failure. *The Golden Chain* (Zolotaya tsep', 1925) is a story of wealth as a source of misery. *Gliding on the Waves* (Begushchaya po volnam, 1928) tells of a quest for happiness that both turns out well and fails. *The Road to Nowhere* (Doroga nikuda, 1930) is Grin's ultimate symbol, a novel about failure to do well in life. Grin was never well received by Russian critics. He died, forgotten and destitute, in the town of Stary Krym, but his romantic prose may have resisted the corrosion of time better than most of the romantic and fantastic literature of the twenties.

Works: Sobranie sochinenii. 6 vols. 1965.
Translations: A. Green, *Scarlet Sails.* A. Grin, *The Seeker of Adventure: Selected Stories.* Moscow, 1979. Alexander Grin, *Selected Short Stories.* Ed. and trans. Nicholas Luker. Ann Arbor, 1983.
Secondary literature: Avtobiograficheskaya povest'. In *Sobranie sochinenii.* Vol. 6. Pp. 228–361. V. Kovskii, *Romanticheskii mir Aleksandra Grina.* 1969. V. Sandler, ed., *Vospominaniya ob Aleksandre Grine.* 1972. Nicholas J. L. Luker, *Aleksandr Grin: The Forgotten Visionary.* Newtonville, Mass., 1980. ———, "A Selected Bibliography of Works by and about Alexander Grin (1880–1932)," *RLT* 8 (1974), pp. 543–65.
H. O.

Gronsky, Nikolai Pavlovich (1909–34), émigré poet. Having emigrated at the age of eleven, Gronsky belonged to the Parisian group of young émigré poets of the late twenties and early thirties. However, his work is in some respects markedly different from the nostalgic and melancholy PARIZHSKAYA NOTA on the Russian Montparnasse, advocated by G. ADAMOVICH. Gronsky's talent never developed fully, perhaps because of his untimely death by accident. M. TSVETAEVA, his personal friend, entertained high expectations in regard to his future achievements and devoted a panegyric review to his posthumous book. Gronsky's work, though rather heterogeneous and frequently unpolished, bears the unmistakable stamp of poetic energy and originality, both in vision and in expression. This is especially true in relation to his long poem "Belladonna," a fervent glorification of heroic alpinist exploits resulting in both ecstasy and catastrophe. This theme—of heroic exultation—is generally characteristic of Gronsky's work and puts him in sharp contrast with the pessimism and submissiveness of the main trend in the émigré literature of the period that was preoccupied with intimacy and subtleties of human feelings. Gronsky's verse is far from traditional: it is abrupt, and energetic, with a tendency for becoming grandiose. A certain influence of Tsvetaeva's poetic principles may be suggested and also, possibly, an echoing of DERZHAVIN, who was the subject of his thesis at the University of Brussels. One is tempted to call Gronsky's work "expressionistic," and it may well be so, but the question remains as to what extent those features are the product of conscious poetic choice and to what extent they may be the result of artistic immaturity. In contrast to the refined assonances of A. SHTEIGER or to the deliberate and effective con-

versationalism of G. IVANOV, Gronsky shares with his gifted and immature contemporary, B. POPLAVSKY, a carelessness in his versification which cannot be attributed to mastery, since it disregards any metrical or rhyme patterns as a matter of principle, thus giving immediate way to the release of emotional tension. His poetry is replete with suggestive imagery and penetrating insights, but there is hardly a piece which can be thought artistically accomplished.

Works: Stikhi i poemy. 1936.
Secondary literature: M. Tsvetaeva, "Posmertnyi podarok" (1934), *Vozdushnye puti* 5 (1967) (also in *Izbrannaya proza v dvukh tomakh*, Vol. 2. 1979. Pp. 122–30). ———, "O knige N. P. Gronskogo 'Stikhi i poemy'," *Sovremennye zapiski* 36 (1936) (also in *Izbrannaya proza v dvukh tomakh*, Vol. 2. 1979. Pp. 319–21).
V. B.

Grossman, Leonid Petrovich (1888–1965), literary critic and author, educated in Odessa and Paris. His first work was published in 1903. Grossman wrote historical and biographical novels which are stylizations of different cultural strata of 19th-century Russian life: *Death of a Poet: A Novel of the Last Years of Pushkin* (trans. E. Bone, 1947); *Roulettenburg* (1932), strongly influenced by Dostoevsky's *The Gambler; A Velvet Dictator* (1933), a portrait of the period of revolutionary terrorism, centered in the life of the writer Vsevolod GARSHIN. *The Love Story of Nina Zarechnaya*, posthumously published in *Prometei* 2 (1967) pp. 218–89, discusses the biographical subtext of Chekhov's play *The Sea Gull.* In his scholarly works, Grossman combines a biographical approach with a discussion of poetic, cultural, and philosophical influences on the personality and style of the writer (*Sketches on Pushkin*, 1923; *From Pushkin to Blok: Sketches and Portraits*, 1926; *Pushkin: A Biography*, 1939). Grossman is the author of more than ten works on Turgenev which discuss generic features of Turgenev's plays and the writer's contacts with the actors of his time. In his other works Grossman examines the reciprocity of aesthetic interests in the visual, verbal, and performing arts (*The Theater of Sukhovo-Kobylin*, 1940; *The Theater of Turgenev*, 1924; *Pushkin in the Theater Dress-Circle*, 1926). A thorough study of Dostoevsky constitutes the main corpus of Grossman's writings. He concentrated on generic and compositional features of Dostoevsky's works, whose poetics he characterized as a joining of varied and incompatible elements into the unity of novelistic construction (*Dostoevsky's Poetics*, 1926; "Dostoevsky the Artist", in *Tvorchestvo Dostoevskogo*, 1959, pp. 330–416). Grossman also examined Dostoevsky's reading interests and demonstrated a variety of aesthetic impressions which the writer drew from his readings in Russian and European authors: *Dostoevsky's Library* (1919), *Balzac and Dostoevsky* (trans. by L. Karpov, Ann Arbor, 1973); "Dostoevsky and the Chartist Novel," *VLit*, 1959, no. 4, pp. 147–58. His documentary treatise *The Life and Works of Dostoevsky* (Zhizn' i trudy Dostoevskogo, 1935) includes extracts from many hundreds of archival documents and serves as a fundamental basis for all sorts of historical and cultural studies of Dostoevsky.

Works: Sobranie sochinenii. 4 vols. 1928. For a bibliography of Grossman's works, see: *F. Dostoevskii. Bibliografiya proizvedenii i literatury o nem.* 1968. p. 382 (index). *Bibliografiya literatury o Turgeneve.* 1970. P. 170 (index).
Translations: Dostoevsky: A Biography. Trans. M. Mackler. 1975. *Confession of a Jew.* Trans. Ranne Moab. 1975.
Secondary literature: I. Andronikov, "L. P. Grossman," *Prometei* 2 (1967), pp. 218–19.
N. P.

Grossman, Vasily Semyonovich (1905–64), novelist and short story writer, was born in Berdichev in the Ukraine. Having taken a degree in the physics and mathematics division of Moscow University, he worked as a chemical engineer. His first story, "Glyukauf," about Soviet miners, was published in 1934. Another story of the same year, "In the Town of Berdichev" (V gorode Berdicheve), in which he describes an episode during the Civil War, received the attention of Maksim GORKY, who offered his support to the young writer. In his later stories, "Four Days" (Chetyre dnya), "Comrade Fyodor" (Tovarishch Fedor), "The Cook" (Kukharka), Grossman focuses upon such themes as the struggle against the tsarist regime, the sufferings endured during the Civil War, and the building of the new Soviet state. His four-part novel, *Stepan Kolchugin* (1937–40), traces the life of a young worker, while following essentially the same themes. During the Second World War, Grossman served as a war correspondent for the journal KRASNAYA ZVEZDA and published a series of sketches and stories about the war-time struggles of the Soviet people. Representative of this time are the stories, "Direction of the Main Strike" (Napravlenie glavnogo udara) and "The People is Immortal" (Narod bessmerten), both published in 1942. In 1946, Grossman published the play, *If to Believe the Pythagoreans* (Esli verit' pifagoreitsam), which received critical reviews; and in 1952, he began to publish an uncompleted novel, *In a Good Cause* (Za pravoe delo), projected as an historical epic of the Second World War. The second part of this work was deemed ideologically unacceptable by Soviet editors, but was published posthumously in the West. Grossman's last novel, *Everything is in Flux* (Vse techet …) is a bitter indictment of Soviet society. It was published by SAMIZDAT and eventually appeared in the West.

Works: Rasskazy. 1937. *Povesti i rasskazy.* 1950. *Za pravoe delo.* 1954. Pt. 2 in *Kontinent*, nos. 4–7 (1975–76). *Povesti. Rasskazy. Ocherki.* Introd. F. Levin. 1958. *Staryi uchitel'. Povesti i rasskazy.* 1962. *Vse techet …* Frankfurt, 1970.

Translations: Lewanski, p. 260.

Secondary literature: A. Myasnikov, "Literatura i voina," *Oktyabr'*, 1942, no. 11. V. Pertsov, "Podvig i geroi," *Znamya*, 1945, no. 9. A. Bocharov, *Vasilii Grossman: Kritiko-bibliograficheskii ocherk.* 1970.

D. K. D.

Guild of Poets, see POETS' GUILD.

Gukóvsky, Grigóry Aleksándrovich (1902–50), philologist, a specialist in the history of 18th- and 19th-century Russian literature. A graduate of Petrograd University, Gukovsky was a professor of Leningrad and Saratov Universities, as well as founder and chairman of the 18th-century group in the INSTITUT RUSSKOI LITERATURY (Pushkinskii Dom) in Leningrad. Gukovsky was among the first to engage in 18th-century studies among Soviet philologists and remains one of the main authorities on that period of Russian literature. In the 1920s he was close to the formalists and published several articles in the renowned collection *Poetica*. The most significant of them was an article on the nature of Russian classicism (O russkom klassitsizme; in *Poetica*, 1929, pp. 21–65), dealing specifically with problems of anonymity and literary borrowing in 18th-century literature. Another work of his which broke the ice in 18th-century studies was *Russkaya poeziya XVIII veka* (1927; earlier variant: "Von Lomonosov bis Deržavin," *Zeitschrift für Slavische Philologie* 2 (1925), pp. 323–65). In the 1930s, Gukovsky was interested in sociological interpretation of 18th-century literary movements and wrote *Essays in the History of 18th-century Russian Literature: the Aristocratic Fronde in the Literature of the 1750s and 1760s* (Ocherki po istorii russkoi literatury XVIII veka: Dvoryanskaya fronda v literature 1750–1760-kh godov, 1936). His last contributions to 18th-century studies were published in the Academy *History of Russian Literature*, vols. 3–5 (1943–47). In the 1940s, Gukovsky wrote several important monographs on 19th-century realism: *Pushkin i russkie romantiki* (1946, 2d ed. 1965), *Pushkin i problemy realisticheskogo stilya* (1957), and *Realizm Gogolya* (1959). Gukovsky was arrested in 1949 and died in prison.

Bibliography: V. P. Stepanov and Yu. V. Stennik, comps., *Istoriya russkoi literatury 18 veka: Bibliograficheskii ukazatel'.* 1968. (Index) K. D. Muratova, comp., *Istoriya russkoi literatury XIX veka: Bibliograficheskii ukazatel'.* 1962. (Index)

Secondary literature: P. N. Berkov, *Vvedenie v izuchenie russkoi literatury 18 veka.* Pt. 1. Ocherk literaturnoi istoriografii 18 veka. 1964. M. V. Ivanov, "Pamyati Grigoriya Aleksandrovicha Gukovskogo (1902–1950)," *RLit*, 1972, no. 4, pp. 232–34.

E. B.

Gul (or Goul, Russ. Gul'), Román Borísovich (1896–   ), émigré prose writer, memoirist, publicist, literary critic and journalist, belongs to the younger generation of the first emigration literati, having published his first book, *The Ice Expedition* (Ledyanoi pokhod) in 1921 almost immediately after he left Soviet Russia. This was the beginning of his distinguished career as a man of letters. Gul's activity is surprising in its variety: he is not only a literary, but also a public figure, and from 1959 on he has been the editor-in-chief of NOVYI ZHURNAL, an influential literary periodical founded by M. ALDANOV, which is in fact a kind of direct successor to the SOVREMENNYE ZAPISKI. Gul's own work is manifold: it includes historical novels, biographies of revolutionaries, red generals, and chiefs of the Soviet secret police, documentary as well as fictionalized, several collections of essays and memoirs. His literary output exceeds a dozen volumes, some of them translated into many languages, including Japanese. As a historical novelist and biographer Gul is most interested in controversial characters engaged in subversive activities and is fascinated by exploring their motives psychologically and mercilessly exposing the working of their minds. His most successful book is probably the novel *Azef* (1959; an earlier version was called *General Bo*, 1929) which is a fictionalized account of the life of the famous social revolutionary who was at the same time an agent-provocateur of the Tsar's secret police. This novel is popular not only within the Russian emigration, but was received warmly in Western European countries, especially in France, where it was praised by A. Malraux, who was impressed by its existential dimension. The two main characters, Azef and Savinkov, exemplify two facets of subversion: double-mindedness—which results in utter cynicism and almost causes a personality split in the search for accommodation—and pointless destructiveness—as the outcome of a conflict with absurd reality. Gul's style is crisp and economical, pregnant with hidden passion; his characters always memorable. His recent memoirs, *I Took Russia with Me* (Ya unes Rossiyu, 1981) were acclaimed in the émigré press for their comprehensiveness.

Works: V rasseyan'i sushchie. 1923. *Pol v tvorchestve.* 1923. *Zhizn' na fuksa.* 1927. *Belye po chernomu.* 1928. *Skif.* 1931. *Tukhachevskii.* 1932. *Krasnye marshaly.* 1933. *Dzerzhinskii.* 1936. *Oranienburg.* 1937. *Kon' ryzhii.* 1952. *Odvukon'.* 1973. *Solzhenitsyn.* 1976. (With Victor Trivas) *Tovarishch Ivan.* 1968. See complete list of the works of Roman Gul in *Ya unes Rossiyu*, pp. 363–65.

Secondary literature: C. Megret, "Un Malraux-Camus avant la lettre," *Carrefour*, 24 August 1955. Also in Roman Goul, *Azef.* 1974. Pp. 5–8.

V. B.

Gumilyóv, Nikolai Sergéevich (1886–1921), Acmeist poet and literary critic. Born in Kronstadt, the son of a naval surgeon, and raised in St. Petersburg, he attended the Tsarskoe Selo Lyceum whose director (1896–1906) was the famous poet and classicist, Innokenty ANNENSKY. Throughout his life he recognized his debt to Annensky as poet, critic, teacher and mentor. Eight months before his mentor's unexpected death, Gumilyov persuaded him to act as unofficial editor and advisor to the new literary and art magazine, APOLLON, founded by himself and S. MAKOVSKY in 1909.

Gumilyov was indebted to Annensky not only for fostering and supporting his literary talents, but for stimulating his interest in assessing SYMBOLISM as a literary movement and evaluating its legacy in the development of Russian literary MODERNISM. Annensky's own reassessment of the current state of lyric poetry, published in the first three issues of *Apollon*, helped to establish Gumilyov's rationale for organizing the POETS' GUILD in 1911 in opposition to Vyacheslav Ivanov's Academy of Verse and for clarifying and defining his concept of the poet's function and the role of poetry in the new literary movement known as ACMEISM, in 1912 and 1913. He spent 1907–08 in Paris, studying at the Sorbonne. He also founded the short-lived Paris review *Sirius* in which he published his own work—his first critical essay, and early verse of Anna AKHMATOVA. He returned to St. Petersburg in 1908.

In 1910, Gumilyov married Anna Akhmatova, also an admirer of Annensky and resident of Tsarskoe Selo, but was divorced from her by 1918. Soon after their marriage, he set out on two lengthy journeys to Africa, and in 1914, one month after the Russian declaration of war, he enlisted in the Imperial Army even though he had been granted a medical exemption. Toward the end of the war, he spent time in London and Paris where he had occasion to meet the leading literary figures of the day. Gumilyov's major literary activities after the Revolution, and until his execution for alleged counter-revolutionary activities in 1921, were serving as an instructor in creative writing—poetry and drama—in the literary studio of the House of the Arts (DISK) in Petrograd, where ZAMYATIN and SHKLOVSKY were instructors in prose, and preparing a manuscript on "The Theory of Poetry."

Gumilyov is best known as an Acmeist theoretician and teacher, and as a poet of romantic adventure and masculine heroism even though such themes are virtually absent from his most mature, later collections. His earliest collections of poetry, including *The Path of the Conquistadors* (Put' konkvistadorov, 1905), *Romantic Flowers* (Romanticheskie tsvety, 1908), and *Pearls* (Zhemchuga, 1910), are symbolist in inspiration and orientation. It is the middle period of his work that is most influenced by the life and scenery of Africa and characterized by the themes of physical bravery, adventure, and war. Nevertheless, some of the best poems from this period are neither romantic nor exotic, including: "Ballad," "The Pilgrim" (Palomnik), "I believed, I thought" from his fourth book, *Foreign Skies* (Chuzhoe nebo, 1912) and "In Memory of Annensky," "Rain," "Evening," and "The Invalid" (Bol'noi) from *The Quiver* (Kolchan, 1916). These volumes are also his most Acmeist in their concreteness and precision of style, in their man-centered thematic material, and in their non-mystical ideology. While Gumilyov's war poetry is indicative of his rhetorical power (indeed, even his intention to enlist is enunciated in the same rhetoric, "The voice of war calls me"), his series of prose sketches entitled *Notes of a Cavalryman*, reflect the keen visual emphasis of the Acmeist poet, the lucid power of direct observation and perception belonging to an astute and thoughtful eye-witness. Another interesting prose collection is entitled *In the Shade of a Palm* (published posthumously, 1922).

Gumilyov attained full poetic stature in his last three years, in the poems of *The Pyre* (Koster, 1918) and *The Pillar of Fire* (Ognennyi stolp, 1921; published posthumously). His later verse exhibits greater psychological and stylistic complexity, a more intense personal element, and more philosophical depth. The blending of rational and supra-rational stylistic and compositional elements in such works as "The Lost Streetcar" (Zabludivshiisya tramvai), "The Word" (Slovo), or "Memory," may be partly explained by the Acmeist interest in Henri Bergson's metaphysics, in particular, in his theories of memory, time, and space, and by Gumilyov's general attempt to synthesize the earlier basic tenets of Acmeism with a broader, more metaphysically oriented aesthetic.

Among Gumilyov's most impressive contributions to the literary life of the early 20th century are his essays, including "Life of Verse" (1910), and his series of nearly forty "Letters on Russian Poetry," originally published in *Apollon* (1909–1916) and reissued separately in 1923. In this series of reviews Gumilyov developed the canons of taste and craftsmanship which became Acmeism. His concept of the poet as craftsman is enhanced by his fellow poet KUZMIN's image of the poet as architect and by the ideal of the FREEMASONS building monuments to "both the heavens and the earth." His restrained language and laconic judgments reflect the style and images he singles out in the works under review. He was also responsible for several major translations, including François Villon's *Testaments*, Coleridge's *Rime of the Ancient Mariner*, and the Babylonian epic of Gilgamesh.

Works: Sobranie sochinenii. 4 vols. Ed. G. P. Struve and B. A. Filippov. Washington, 1962–68. Vol. 1 (Poetry 1903–15). 1962. Vol. 2 (Poetry 1916–21 and poems of various years). 1964. Vol. 3 (Drama and poems of early years not included in Vol. 1). Vol. 4 (Prose, incl. literary criticism and introductions to translations). Introd. V. V. Weidlé. 1968. *Naidennye stikhi i pis'ma*. Paris, 1980.

Translations: Selected Works of Nikolay Gumilev. Trans. B. Raffel and A. Burago. Ed. S. Monas. 1972. *On Russian Poetry: Selected Essays and Reviews*. Trans. D. Lapeza. Ann Arbor, 1977. (8 poems.) In *Russian Poetry: The Modern Period*. Ed. John Glad and Daniel Weissbort. 1978. Pp. 69–76. *See also* Lewanski, p. 261.

Secondary literature: Marie Maline, *Nicolas Gumilev: Poète et critique* acméiste. Brussels, 1964. Earl Sampson, *Nikolay Gumilev*. 1978. R. D. Timenchik, "Zametki ob akmeizme," *RusL* 7/8 (1974), 5 (1977), no. 3, 9 (1981), no. 2. Yu. N. Verkhovskii, "Put' poeta: O poezii N. S. Gumileva." In *Sovremennaya literatura*. 1925. Pp. 93–143.

J. G. H.

Guró, Eléna Génrikhovna (pseudonym of Eleonora von Notenberg, 1877–1913), poet, writer, and artist, was born in St. Petersburg and died of tuberculosis in her summer house in the Finnish village of Uusikirkko. She started writing and painting at a very early age. Throughout her life she pursued these two artistic activities and often combined them by illustrating her own books. Guro attended the school of "The Society for the Encouragement of the Arts"

(Obshchestvo pooshchreniya khudozhestv) which she completed in 1903, and then studied under the artists Tsionglinsky, Bakst, and Dobuzhinsky.

Guro published a short story in 1905. Her first book, *The Hurdy-Gurdy* (Sharmanka) appeared in 1909, and in the same year she participated in her first painting exhibition, "The Impressionists." In 1910, Guro formed the group *Venok* (Wreath), together with V. KAMENSKY and the brothers David and Vladimir BURLYUK, all of whom eventually became active participants in the group of the cubo-FUTURISTS. Guro was connected with the avant-garde not only professionally, but on a personal level as well, being the wife of the artist, composer, and musician Mikhail Matyushin. She contributed prose and poetry to the almanacs, *A Trap for Judges* (Sadok sudei) no. 1. (1910) and no. 2 (1913), whose publication she subsidized. These almanacs are closely connected with the history of Russian cubo-futurism. Her second collection (poetry, prose, a play), *Autumnal Dream* (Osennii son, 1912), was favorably reviewed by the SYMBOLIST poet Vyacheslav IVANOV. Some of Guro's works were published posthumously. *Baby Camels of the Sky* (Nebesnye verblyuzhata) appeared in 1914, although part of this collection was included in the second almanac, *A Trap for Judges*. Two small prose pieces appeared in the journal, *The Union of Youth* (Soyuz molodezhi, 1913). Several poems were published in the collection, *The Three* (Troe, 1913).

Guro's literary works present impressionist, symbolist, and futurist traits. Her poetic world includes the harmonious order of nature and the tragic reality of city life. Guro's urbanism is expressed in an impressionist manner. However, it shows many features typical of MAYAKOVSKY's poetry and Natalya Goncharova's paintings. Her sensitivity to the "word," as a poetic fact, and her skillful play with neologisms show her kinship with the futurist practitioners of "transrational poetry" (ZAUM). Guro's neologisms are often derived from children's language, and the child as a poetic persona often appears in her works. Guro's all pervading theme is love for all creatures and things, and a maternal concern for the rejected, the weak, and the defenseless.

Translations: "Little Camels in the Sky" and "An Impulse," *RLT* 12 (1975).

Secondary literature: M. Banjanin, "The Prose and Poetry of Elena Guro," *RLT* 9 (1974), pp. 303–16. B. Gusman, *100 poetov. Literaturnye portrety*. 1923. K. B. Jensen, *Russian Futurism, Urbanism, and Elena Guro*. Aarhus, 1977. V. Kamenskii, *Put' entuziasta*. 1931. N. Khardzhiev, "Mayakovskii i Elena Guro." In *Poeticheskaya kul'tura Mayakovskogo*. 1970. Pp. 193–95. B. Livshits, *The One And A Half-Eyed Archer*. Trans. John Bowlt. 1977. V. Markov, *Russian Futurism: A History*. 1968. M. Matyushin, "Russkie kubofuturisty." In *K istorii russkogo avangarda*. Stockholm, 1976.

A. L.

Hagiography. Writings devoted to the Lives of Saints (*zhitiya*) occupy a preeminent place in Old Russian literature. Frequently transcending the limits of the *vita* genre, Old Russian hagiographic compositions may conform to the schemes of other literary modes of expression such as sermons and chronicle accounts.

The earliest examples of Kievan hagiography were patterned after Byzantine models, especially the hagiographic collection of Simeon Metaphrastes (second half of the 10th century). Translations of Greek hagiography, produced in either the Russian lands or the Balkan Slavic area, were part of the oldest body of texts available to Kievan clergymen. Very soon, however, compositions connected with local cults appeared, expressing the needs of a church and ruling dynasty in search of spiritual legitimacy. Especially significant in this regard was the exaltation of the "passion sufferers" SS. BORIS AND GLEB by Monk NESTOR and an anonymous hagiographer whose aim was to affirm the dignity of the blessed dynasty embodied in Prince Yaroslav Vladimirovich (reigned ca. 1019–54). Also extremely important was Monk Nestor's *Life of Our Blessed Father Theodosius* (Zhitie prepodobnago ottsa nashego Feodosiya), which sought to confer special prestige upon the Kiev Monastery of the Caves.

From the earliest period of Old Russian literature, one can distinguish several types of hagiography. The life, deeds, and miracles of a Saint could be presented in a highly stylized, concise, and formulaic manner for the *sluzhba* (service) and the *chtenie* (liturgical reading), or could be offered in a more elaborate and detailed form as a *skazanie* (legend), *pokhvala* (eulogy) or *strast'* (passion). The size and makeup of a hagiographic text could also depend on the type of literary collections it might enter. Lives were included in collections such as the PROLOG (Synaxary), *Mineya* (Menology), and *Paterik* (Paterikon). Some of the best and most popular examples of Old Russian hagiography are to be found in the *Paterikon of the Kievan Monastery of the Caves* (Kievo-Pecher'skii Paterik).

Similar to Byzantine hagiographic writings, Russian Lives did not follow a single compositional and rhetorical scheme. A *zhitie* (Greek *bios*) could include or be accompanied by a section containing either the Saint's life experience (*politeia*) and—if referred to—spiritual accomplishments (*askēsis*) or a eulogy (*egkōmion*). In addition, the elements and features characteristic of the hagiographic genre could become part of texts with a quite different composition. The fact is that it is extremely difficult to distinguish clearly between hagiographic and non-hagiographic literature. Nor can one readily single out typical patterns which consistently occur in Old Russian Lives of Saints.

Hagiographic compositions written in close connection with the liturgical tradition would likely comply with general schemes—namely, introduction, family origins, childhood, adolescence, education, vocation, deeds, saintly death, and miracles. Yet any particular scene in the iconographic sequence which makes up the Life of a Saint could enter different types of narratives. This is the case, for example, with the portrayal found in the *Povest' vremennykh let* (Tale of Bygone Years, also called the Primary Chronicle [see LETOPISI]) of St. Andrew's apostleship and St. Theodosius's establishment of the cenobitic rule in the Kievan Monastery of the Caves. Typically hagiographic types of discourse such as the *pokhvala* (eulogy) or *molitva* (prayer) could easily make their way into oratorical compositions. This is what we find, for instance, in the portion of Metropolitan ILARION's *Sermon on Law and Grace* (Slovo o zakone i blagodati) which praises *Kagan* Vladimir Svyatoslavich for bringing the Christian faith to *Rus'*.

Because of the sacred nature of kingship among the Orthodox Slavs, the "Life of the Prince" (knyazheskoe zhitie) emerged as a particular type of hagiographic composition in Old *Rus'*. The true faith of the ruler was requisite in his role as the defender of his Orthodox subjects. In the *Life of* ALEXANDER NEVSKY (Zhitie Aleksandra Nevskago) the victor over the Swedes and the Teutonic Knights is depicted as a spiritual giant who is so well acquainted with the sacred texts that he can engage in and win a theological dispute with the representatives of the "Latin" faith. The image of the powerful yet pious and God-fearing ruler became a *topos* which was applied to many other Russian princes, from Dmitry Ivanovich Donskoi to Peter the Great.

Scholars have long debated the precise relationship between "secular" and "religious" elements in princely Lives. What seems important to emphasize, however, is that "secular" and "religious" motifs already coexisted in one of the main prototypes of Christian hagiography, namely, *Life of the Blessed Emperor Constantine* (*Eis ton bion tou makariou Konstantinou tou basileōs*) by Eusebius of Caesarea (early 4th century). The Constantinian model played a very significant role in Orthodox Slavic literature, most notably, in the Serbian princely *Lives*, some of which provided Old Russian writers with authoritative models in the period of the so-called Second SOUTH SLAVIC INFLUENCE.

Beginning in the late 14th century, the arrival of South Slavic churchmen and scholars radically affected all aspects of literary activity in the Russian lands. Hagiography in particular underwent important theoretical and technical changes, mostly (but not exclusively) under the impact of Hesychast doctrine. In Moscow Metropolitan Kiprian (Cyprian, 1390–1406), a Bulgarian Hesychast, rewrote Bishop Prokhor's *Life of Metropolitan Peter* (Zhitie Mitropolita Petra). In the second and third quarters of the 15th century the Serb PAKHOMY LOGOFET (Pachomius Logothetes) carried out similar rewriting and editorial activity in Novgorod, the Troitse-Sergiev Monastery, Moscow, and the Kirillo-Belozersky Monastery.

The purpose of these hagiographic revisions was to introduce to the Russian lands a new ideal of sainthood in accordance with the Hesychast notion of the path toward spiritual perfection. The changes undertaken influenced both the type of biographical in-

formation conveyed and the literary style. The use of synonyms, allusions, and interwoven syntactic units aimed to replace traditional icons of well-defined sainthood with partial visions of an indefinable perfection. The new image of sainthood was conveyed through similar techniques by contemporary icon painters.

One should note that the same devices were used in literary forms akin to the *zhitie*, especially in panegyrics. Another expatriate from the Bulgarian lands, the Kievan Metropolitan Grigory Tsamblak (died ca. 1420) provided a typical example of Hesychast hagiography in his highly sophisticated *Encomiastic Sermon* (Slovo pokhval'no), written to eulogize Evtimy (Euthymius) of Trnovo, the last patriarch of medieval Bulgaria (1375–93). The most important Russian hagiographer in this period was Epifany Premudry (EPIPHANIUS THE WISE, died ca. 1420). In his writings, above all in his *Life of Stefan of Perm* (Zhitie Stefana Permskago), Epiphanius presented what is considered the most typical example of a Hesychast-inspired way of writing, usually referred to as *pletenie sloves* (word weaving).

The diffusion of the "new style" reflected the pan-Orthodox attitude of a sophisticated elite. Yet this process of cultural unification often was at odds with, and eventually would be superseded by, the centralizing policies of Moscow. Indeed, until Muscovite supremacy was firmly established in the reign of Ivan III (1462–1505), different styles, both conservative and innovative, coexisted in the various principalities of the Russian lands. The lives and deeds of local saints and sacred rulers could be celebrated either in a traditional manner or in the more elaborate style of the Hesychast "word weavers" and politically-inspired rhetoricians. Smolensk, which was dynastically linked to Lithuania until the early 16th century, long remained attached to old-fashioned hagiographic celebrations of its local bishop Avraamy (*Life of the Blessed Avraamy of Smolensk*—Zhitie prepodobnago Avraamiya Smolenskago). Smolensk also produced the wonderful "hagiographic" legend on the young hero Merkury (*The Tale of Merkury of Smolensk*—Povest' o Merkurii Smolenskom). The twin principalities of Murom-Ryazan brought forth the highly popular hagiographic tale on Peter and Fevronia (*Povest' o Petre i Fevronii*), in which some fabulous elements are present. Novgorod gave birth to entire hagiographic cycles devoted to Varlaam Chutinsky, Archbishop Ioann, and Archbishop Moisei. Legendary elements are especially abundant in the hagiographic accounts on the deeds of Archbishop Ioann, who made a pact with the devil and sometimes acted as a magician.

When in the 16th century Moscow became the center not only of a nascent empire but also of a state-dominated church, the need for an established body of hagiographic writings became of paramount importance. The victory of IOSIF VOLOTSKY (1439–1515) and his followers over the Hesychast-inspired spiritual descendants of NIL SORSKY (1433–1508) led to the adoption of new, "official" patterns of sainthood. The revision of the hagiographic corpus was closely connected with attempts to produce complete and authoritative texts of the Holy Scriptures. In fact, one may speak of single philological enterprise which began with the activity of the Novgorodian circle of Archbishop Gennady (1484–1504) and which culminated in the preparation of the monumental *Monthly Readings* (MINEI CHET'I) of Metropolitan MAKARY (Macarius, 1542–63). In order to establish a new hagiographic code in Muscovy, the church headed by Makary recognized new local cults while deemphasizing certain existing traditions. Some modern scholars have seen in Makary's hagiographic policy the beginnings of a state-minded and censorship-dominated culture which would remain a pervasive feature of Russian spirituality well into the 20th century.

In the TIME OF TROUBLES the presence of Catholic activists in the Russian lands undoubtedly affected many aspects of Russian religious life, including the very ideal of sainthood and the writing of hagiographies. The *Lives of Saints* (Żywoty Świętych, 1579), by Piotr Skarga (1536–1612), the spiritual leader of Counter-Reformation Poland, may have provided both Ruthenian and Muscovite writers with important models. It remains a matter of dispute to what extent new types of hagiographic writings such as the *Life of* YULIANIYA LAZAREVSKAYA (Zhitie Yulianii Lazarevskoi), the first *zhitie* of a Russian saintly woman, could have been influenced by Western trends.

One should note, however, that the anti-Latino-Polish attitudes which developed after the Polish intervention brought about the restoration of traditional Orthodox Slavic spiritual and rhetorical schemes. As early as the Time of Troubles, the exaltation of the Muscovite Patriarch Germogen (Hermogenes) contributed notably to the reaffirmation of old hagiographic ideals. In the 17th century new collections of the *Minei chet'i* were compiled by German Tulupov (1627–32), Ioann Milyutin (1646–54), and Dimitry Tuptalo ROSTOVSKY (1689–1705). Towards the end of the century a new trend in hagiography was initiated by the OLD BELIEVERS. While the *Lives* of counter-heroes such as Ivan Neronov, Boyarynya Morozova, and Kirill Vygoretsky had much in common with their opponents from the established church, their particular audience and intent frequently required different modes of expression. The supreme hagiographic model for the Old Believers was provided by the so-called Autobiography of AVVAKUM (1620–1682), known under the title *Life of Archpriest Avvakum* (Zhitie protopopa Avvakuma).

Bibliography: D. I. Abramovich, ed., *Pam'jatky movy ta pys'menstva davn'oji Ukrajiny.* Vol. 4: *Kyevo-Pechers'kyj pateryk.* Kiev, 1930. (Reprint. in *Slavische Propyläen,* no. 2. Munich, 1964.) V. P. Adrianova-Peretts, "Zadachi izucheniya 'agiograficheskogo stilya' drevnei Rusi," *TODRL* 20 (1964); pp. 41–71. ———, "Syuzhetnoe povestvovanie v zhitiinykh pamyatnikakh XI–XIII vv." In *Istoki russkoi belletristiki.* Ed. Ya. S. Lur'e. 1970. Pp. 65–107. J. Allissandratos, *Medieval Slavic and Patristic Eulogies.* (Studia Historica et Philologica, no. 14.) Florence, 1982. N. P. Barsukov, *Istochniki russkoi agiografii.* 1882. D. Čiževskij, "On the Question of Genres in Old Russian Literature." *Harvard Slavic Studies* 2 (1954); pp. 105–15. L. A. Dmitriev, "Syuzhetnoe povestvovanie v zhitiinykh pamyatnikakh XIII–XV vv." In *Istoki russkoi belletristiki.* Ed. Ya. S. Lur'e. 1970. pp. 208–62. ———, *Zhitiinye povesti russkogo severa kak pamyatniki literatury XIII–XVII vv.* 1973. V. A. Yakovlev, *Drevne-Kievskie religioznye skazaniya.* Warsaw, 1875. N. Ingham, "The Limits of Secular Biography in Medieval Slavic Literature, particularly Old Russian." In *American Contributions to the Sixth International Congress of Slavists, Prague, August 7–13, 1968.* Vol. 2: *Literary Contributions.* 1968. pp. 181–99. A. P. Kadlubovskii, *Ocherki po istorii drevne-russkoi literatury zhitii svyatykh.* Warsaw, 1902. V. O. Klyuchevskii, *Drevnerusskie zhitiya svyatykh kak isticheskii istochnik.* 1871. D. S. Likhachev, "Sistema literaturnykh zhanrov drevnei Rusi." In *Slavyanskie literatury, V Mezhdunarodnyi s"ezd slavistov.* (1963), *Doklady sovetskoi delegatsii.* Pp. 47–70. ———, *Chelovek v literature drevnei Rusi.* 2d ed. 1970. R. Picchio, "Models and Patterns in the Literary Tradition of Medieval Orthodox Slavdom." In *American Contributions to the Seventh International Congress of Slavists, Warsaw.* Vol. 2: *Literature and Folklore.* 1973. Pp. 439–67. N. Serebryanskii, *Drevnerusskie knyazheskie zhitiya.* (*Obzor redaktsii i teksty*). 1915. Dj. Trifunović, *Azbučnik srpskih srednjovekovnih književnih pojmova.* Belgrade, 1974. Pp. 46–78. R. P.

Hérzen, Aleksándr Ivánovich (1812–70), a leading writer, journalist, editor, and founder of POLYARNAYA ZVEZDA and KOLOKOL. With some exceptions, Herzen's contributions to Russian literary history are divided by his departure from Russia in January of 1847. Up to this date, as one of the promising group of young authors which included DOSTOEVSKY, TURGENEV, and GONCHAROV, he wrote essays, philosophical studies, and fiction; after 1847 he turned to nonfictional modes of literature and devoted himself to émigré journalism. In the later period, his work expressed one of the more influential of social-political voices in Russian intellectual history of the 19th century.

Herzen was the son of a well-to-do Russian nobleman, I. A. Yakovlev, and his German common-law wife; the child was given his surname by his father. His broad education combined Western and Russian sources, including Voltaire, Rousseau, Schiller, and Schelling, on the one hand, and GRIBOEDOV, PUSHKIN, and church literature, on the other. Before entering Moscow University he received lessons in basic Russian Orthodox doctrine from a priest and was introduced to philology by Ivan Protopopov, a graduate of the Ryazan Seminary. Strong influences on his maturing values and ideas were provided by Nikolai OGARYOV, a distant relative who was to become a lifelong friend, by Natalie Zakharyina, a deeply religious young woman who became his wife, and by Alexander Witberg, an architect and mystic who was to live with Herzen during his exile and who inspired him with the visions and symbols of Boehme, Swedenborg, Eckartshausen, Paracelsus, and Masonic literature. Herzen entered the Department of Physics and Mathematics at Moscow University in 1829. Together with Ogaryov he took part in a circle of students who debated heatedly the progressive ideas—mainly of French utopian socialist origin—then active in Europe. Herzen completed his studies in June of 1833 and approximately a year later was arrested, along with members of his group. After serving his internal exile as a government clerk in the provincial cities of Perm and Vyatka he married and, in 1840, was allowed to establish residence in St. Petersburg. An unfortunate choice of words in a letter resulted in a second, albeit briefer period of exile, on this occasion in Novgorod. In 1842 Herzen obtained permission to return to the more cosmopolitan section of the country and to live in Moscow. The following five years marked the growth of his reputation as a leading young writer and essayist. In this period, together with Vissarion BELINSKY, he gave essential direction to the ideological syndrome that came to be known as WESTERNISM. Writing under the pseudonym of Iskander he published a series of essays on philosophy and the natural sciences, and brought out the major texts of his fiction.

Herzen's departure for Europe in 1847 was soon followed by events of both a historical and a personal nature that affected the future course of his work. The breakdown of the revolutionary movements of 1848 increased a pessimism he already felt about Western society. In 1851 a shipwreck took the life of his mother and son; Natalie died the following year after an unhappy liaison with Georg Herwegh, a minor German poet. In 1852 Herzen moved to London where he was soon joined by Ogaryov, newly arrived from Russia. The two men were to spend most of the remainder of their lives together. Herzen's affair with Ogaryov's wife did not hinder their friendship or their cooperation as editors of émigré publications which were to have a unique impact on Russian public opinion during the 1850s and 1860s. Thanks to judicious investments and the laxity of the Russian government in allowing him to get the bulk of his capital out of the country, Herzen was financially secure and able to sponsor not only his own works but to contribute to journals like Proudhon's *Voix du Peuple.* The Free Russian Press, founded by him, began its activities in 1853 with pamphlets and brochures on the pressing issues of the day. The journal *Polyarnaya zvezda* was begun in 1855 (and enthusiastically received by Lev TOLSTOI among other readers) and the newspaper *Kolokol* started a ten-year run with an initial issue brought out in 1857.

The influence of Herzen's press was most prevalent in the period of the mid-1850s up to the emancipation of the peasants in 1861. During this time he expressed the cherished hopes of liberal thought and was widely read throughout Russia. After the emancipation Herzen thought of reconciliation with Alexander II but the presence of his country's soldiers in Poland led him to continue his criticism of the Russian government. Disagreements with the crude political and cultural manners of radical intellectuals like Dmitry PISAREV and Nikolai CHERNYSHEVSKY also brought him into conflict with the Russian left (see "Very Dangerous!!!" [1859]). The popularity of *Kolokol* gradually suffered a decline, although expressions of jealousy over its influence and Herzen's finances were made known by no less a figure in the political arena than Karl Marx. Herzen stopped publishing the newspaper in 1867, briefly attempted revival of a French edition, and gave up *Kolokol* soon thereafter. His life, in any case, was in its final chapter. *My Past and Thoughts,* begun in 1852, was completed in 1868 and Herzen died two years later.

A full literary overview of Herzen's works must include, of course, the pre-1847 fiction, but because of important readers such as Tolstoi, Turgenev, LEONTIEV, and Dostoevsky who were influenced by his ideas, must also touch on his philosophical studies, social-political essays, and autobiography. In spite of differences in genre and changes in intellectual history the texts all gravitate to one core motif, already expressed in Herzen's first serious essay of 1832, "On the Place of Man in Nature." In reviewing Linnaeus, Bacon, Joseph Priestley, and Lorenz Oken, the young writer arrives at a strong defense of qualities of "freedom and will" supporting the "high origins of our soul." Most of his early work proposes a similar concern for the latest theories of science or society, and responds to them with an unwavering defense of the transcendent properties of the human personality. In Herzen's mature texts this defense developed into a passionate rejection of all moral, political, and historical checks to the spiritual dignity and value of the individual.

Herzen's first fictional work, "The Legend," united hints of utopian socialism and the transformation of religious values in the social and psychological theories of Fourier, Saint-Simon, and Pierre Leroux, with Russian kenotic ideas. The latter motifs are expressed in the exalted spiritual qualities of St. Theodora. The text is a modern reworking of a saint's life found in the Russian MINEI CHETYI, or church calendar reading.

A second work of short fiction, "Elena," was written during the years 1836 to 1838. The central character, a nobleman, is driven mad by a bad conscience over his shameful treatment of his mistress, the abandoned Elena. The sentimental plot is made lively by supernatural themes in the style of Hoffmann and ZHUKOVSKY and a mocking narrative technique reminiscent of GOGOL and Pushkin. Out of the then available literary traditions Herzen—not unlike Dostoevsky who was to write "The Double" and "The Landlady" some ten years later—places primary emphasis on those fictional strategies that incorporate psychology in approaching moral issues. Social criticism is hinted—in keeping with Rousseau—through the high rank of Elena's seducer, but the ultimate determinant of the protagonist's sad destiny is his own self-imposed feeling of guilt.

Two sketches, "From Roman Scenes" (1838) and "William Penn" (1839) further develop religious-social issues in the prisms of utopian socialism and kenoticism. "The Notes of a Certain Young Man" (1840–41) shows a refinement of imagery and caricature reminiscent again of Gogol's inspired humor; as in "The Portrait" and *The Inspector-General*, the narrative is directed at the disfiguring personal and social attributes which dim "the spark of the divine" in man. Such short pieces of fiction eventually gave way to preoccupation with the text of *Who Is to Blame?* (Kto vinovat?) The novel was serialized during 1845 and 1846 and published in book form in 1847. Herzen's intentions for the work were expressed in his review of a minor French play by Arnould and Fournier, entitled *Huit ans de plus*.

Who Is to Blame? is constructed around the love-triangle of Lyubonka Krutsiferskaya, her husband, and the nobleman Beltov. The protagonists are reminiscent of different literary traditions. Lyubonka is the product of sentimentalism, unable to break away from the role of victim in society. Lyubonka's major flaw is that she is unable to attain the ideal of feminine emancipation and self-expression advocated by George Sand. Krutsifersky is placed in the literary context of the NATURAL SCHOOL, a character devoid of free will and crushed by his environment. Beltov comes out of ROMANTICISM and assumes literary properties of the "superfluous men" made famous by DOBROLYUBOV's essay and Turgenev's short story of 1850. All three characters are unable to find a settled place for themselves in Russian society; their unhappiness is partially due to deficiencies in the environment but is much more a result of their own internal weaknesses. Beltov, in particular, as the most promising of the three, is made to bear the author's displeasure directed at failed expectations and the breakdown of his love for Lyubonka. The mutual inability of wife and lover to overcome the constricting social conventions of marriage joins with Krutsifersky's own deficiencies in courage, dignity, and self-assertion to illustrate Herzen's ideas of moral-psychological blame.

Before his departure from Russia, Herzen wrote two other pieces of fiction of some note, "The Thieving Magpie" (1848) and "Doctor Krupov" (1847). The first provides a passionate indictment of the dehumanizing conditions of serfdom; in it Herzen tells the story of a peasant-actress, the human property of a brutal nobleman. "Doctor Krupov" is narrated by a skeptical seminary-educated physician, and is the story of Lyovka, a YURODIVYI boy. Lyovka, a simple-minded, unspoiled, and innately moral peasant, is contrasted against the hypocrisies and debasements of society. His story acts as a point of culmination in the early fiction, and looks forward to later writings of the European and British periods. Krupov serves as Herzen's alter ego in depicting the transformation of religious impulses into secular hopes for social-political reform. As a peasant "holy fool," Lyovka points back to the native sources of kenoticism and forward to Herzen's delineation of the Russian peasant's spiritual capacities as the foundation for a new, communal society. Primary emphasis is placed on the dignity and unbending individuality of Lyovka's basic Russian ethos. After completing "Doctor Krupov" Herzen planned to write another major work of fiction entitled *Duty Before All*. It remained unfinished, however, due to his new interests in Europe.

Key evidence for the interpretation of Herzen's belles lettres is

provided by his essays. Important philosophical statements after the early "On the Place of Man in Nature" were made in *Dilettantism in Science* (1843–44) and *Letters on the Study of Nature* (1845–46). The last two works responded to intense study in Hegelian philosophy and the sciences, and, in both instances, used such sources for additional ammunition to be brought to bear in the defense of the individual. Herzen expresses fascination with Hegel's dialectic and historical grasp, but argues that the coming of the Absolute Idea involves "personalities" rather than "abstract norms;" he is wary, moreover, of the "indifferent fate" suggested by the Hegelian march of ideas. In a similar vein, science is understood to confirm human freedom, while nature is defined to be devoid of meaning, "mute" and "incomplete" without man.

Such concern for the dignity and centrality of the individual reached its apex in Herzen's essays written under the influence of Left Hegelianism and Ludwig Feuerbach. In "Whims and Reflections III. New Variations on Old Themes," published in *Sovremennik* in 1847, a radical individualism leads Herzen to develop psychological categories focusing on the notion of self-interest. Egoism is seen to be the proper medium for human beings to express their rightful centrality in all things, and self-interest is contrasted to self-induced expressions of inferiority and degradation in society. The core view of personality offered here looks back to the values of human dignity, free will, and the God-related nature of man provided by Herzen's early religious sources; but Feuerbach also pointed to a new form of the individual's self-aggrandizement in the actual world and suggested a haven of personal freedom and fulfillment for man in the midst of the vile jokes played on the human condition by history.

Herzen understood one such joke, made at the expense of Western hopes of progress, to be the evolution of the middle class into the leading force of civilized society. The bourgeoisie, he noted in the essays of *Letters from France and Italy* (1847–52) and *From the Other Shore* (1847–50) represented the epitome of the mediocre, banal, and non-individual in human affairs. The vulgar and petty materialistic concerns of the middle class represented a grotesque debasement of the high spiritual destiny of man, and worst of all, a vulgar caricature of the noble self-aggrandizement Herzen had envisioned. This view of the bourgeoisie would have a strong effect on Russian men of letters. Dostoevsky used such a perspective in *Winter Notes on Summer Impressions*, and Konstantin LEONTIEV turned to Herzen to develop his own cruel rejection of the "average man" and European history, anticipating the views proposed by Nietzsche.

Herzen's ideas on history, expressed in "Robert Owen" and *From the Other Shore*, influenced another major writer, Lev Tolstoi, and inspired the historical speculations that went into *War and Peace*. Herzen totally rejected the notion that history progressed to some predestined utopia. He defined historical processes, in terms reminiscent of Schelling and TYUTCHEV, as a vast, stormy ocean buffeting the small human craft. The shore was unseen in this view, but the haven for man was his own personal life. The most ludicrous of men were those who thought they could chart and control the future outside of the immediate realities of their own individual existence.

Flaws in progressive theories and Western society, as Herzen understood them, gave him added impetus to reaffirm the vision of the Russian peasantry's unique destiny in history. Essays such as "The Russian People and Socialism" (1851) developed an appreciation of the peasantry's ethos and gave hope to the Russian intelligentsia that their country had an indigenous contribution to offer humanity. Herzen deeply influenced both the left and the right wings of Russian political opinion in this regard and provided an important stimulant to the ideas of Russian populists such as Nikolai MIKHAILOVSKY.

The chef d'oeuvre of Herzen's mature years—begun in 1852 and worked on until 1868—were his memoirs, *My Past and Thoughts*. In combining history, personal reminiscences, philosophical observations, anecdotes, and sociopolitical analyses, he created a unique hybrid genre, epic in scope yet highly personal in style and content. The major motifs of the memoirs are grouped around a grand synthesis of Herzen's life and the key cultural phenomena of the 19th century. Since its writing, *My Past and Thoughts* has provided a primary source for studies of Western and Russian intellectual history. On its own stylistic account, it has contributed a rare merger of analytical clarity and metaphoric talent to Russian literature.

Works: Polnoe sobranie sochinenii i pisem. Ed. M. K. Lemke. 22 vols. 1915–25. (Useful for its commentary.) *Sobranie sochinenii.* 30 vols. 1954–64.

Translations: Selected Philosophical Works. Trans. Leo Navrozov. Moscow, 1956. *From the Other Shore and The Russian People and Socialism: An Open Letter to Jules Michelet.* Trans. Moura Budberg and Richard Wollheim. London, 1956. *My Past and Thoughts; The Memoirs of Alexander Herzen.* Trans. Constance Garnett; ed. Dwight McDonald; introd. Isaiah Berlin. New York, 1973. *Who Is to Blame?: A Novel in Two Parts.* Trans. Margaret Wettlin. Moscow, 1978.

Secondary literature: E. H. Carr, *The Romantic Exiles.* 1933. Georges Florovsky, *Puti russkogo bogosloviya.* Paris, 1937. (Reprint 1963.) ———. "Iskaniya molodosti Gertsena," *Sovremennye zapiski,* no. 39 (1929), pp. 274–305, no. 40 (1929), pp. 335–67. R. Labry, *Alexandre Ivanovič Herzen, 1812–1870.* Paris, 1928. Martin Malia, *Alexander Herzen and the Birth of Russian Socialism, 1812–1855.* 1961. Nicholas Rzhevsky, *Russian Literature and Ideology.* 1983.

N. Rz.

Hilarion, see ILARIÓN.

Hilferding (Gilferding), Aleksándr Fyódorovich (1831–72), historian and collector of BYLINY, spent his youth in Warsaw, where his father served under the viceregent of Poland. In 1852 he graduated from the historical-philological faculty of Moscow University. In 1856 he became consul in Bosnia and Hercegovina, later holding leading positions in the Asian Department and in the Committee for the Affairs of the Polish Kingdom. He combined his service with scholarly activity. In 1871 and 1872 he undertook collection trips for *byliny* in Olonets, where he fell ill and died.

Hilferding's first works were devoted to the study of the Russian language, Slavic literatures, and the history of the Balkan Slavs. This work led to his election as a corresponding member of the Academy of Sciences. His travelogue "Bosnia, Hercegovina and Old Serbia" (Bosniya, Hertsegovina i Staraya Serbiya, 1859) contains observations on Serbian and Croatian folk poetry, a few texts recorded by him, and some descriptions of singers of heroic poetry and their manner of presentation.

Hilferding's field trip to Olonets was undertaken for an on-the-spot study of the ancient epic tradition and its carriers, a tradition discovered by RYBNIKOV ten years earlier. As a SLAVOPHILE, Hilferding looked upon this tradition as the second link (after the South Slavic epic) of a common Slavic folklore. In Olonets he met a number of new singers and also rerecorded some *byliny* from Rybnikov's informants. This gave him an opportunity to make essential conclusions on the character of the epic tradition, which were outlined in his essay "The Olonetsian Province and Its Folk Rhapsodies." His model collection was published posthumously in 1873, containing 318 texts, which were arranged—for the first time—according to individual singers, with brief characterizations of the singers appended.

Works: Sobranie sochinenii. 4 vols. 1868–1874. *Onezhskie byliny.* 3 vols. 4th ed., 1949–1951. (1st ed. in one vol., 1873)

Secondary literature: M. K. Azadovskii, *Istoriya russkoi fol'kloristiki.* Vol. 2. 1963. Pp. 226–29. V. G. Bazanov, "A. F. Gil'ferding i ego 'Onezhskie byliny.'" In *Onezhskie byliny.* Vol. 1. 1949. Pp. 1–28. Yu. M. Sokolov, "Po sledam Rybnikova i Gil'ferdinga," *Khudozhestvennyi fol'klor* 2–3 (1927), pp. 3–33.

F. J. O.

Hippius (Gíppius), Zinaída Nikoláevna (1869–1945), born in Belev (District of Tula) into the family of the super-procurator of the St. Petersburg Senate, later chief justice in Nezhin (District of Chernigov). With the exception of a few months spent at the Kiev Institute for Girls (1877–78) and later in the Fisher private classical school in Moscow (1882), Hippius received her education at home. Her favorite author was DOSTOEVSKY. She went on to distinguish herself as a prolific poet, fiction writer, playwright, essayist, memoirist, and critic. Her activities in the religious and philosophical societies of St. Petersburg and the fashionable literary *soirées* which she organized added to her fame in Russian literary circles.

For Hippius, literature was a profound spiritual experience. It was, she felt, a means of embodying the unity of the transcendental and the phenomenal. Challenging the social and ideological approach to creative art, she insisted on paying more respect to universal culture, to the mystery of aesthetic beauty and harmony and to what for her were the eternal properties of art—love of God, Christian ethics, spiritual elation, and religious transports. Her own law of art was formulated in the aphorism: "Art should materialize only the spiritual." Hippius' poetry and prose present her spiritual experiences in strikingly, uncannily concrete imagery. Colors, sounds, images, and moods blend in the eerie spectre of her universe, a physical and emotional void instilling mystery and dread. These attitudes, however, are always counterbalanced by ideal strivings and a passionate faith in God and His mercy. In essence, these poems are spiritual psalms, reminiscent of devotional hymns or chants in praise of God, such as "Gloria in Excelsis."

At the turn of the century Hippius, intensely preoccupied with religious and socio-ethical matters, advocated an apocalyptic Christianity based on a belief in the Second Coming. Her narratives, resembling medieval novelettes in their mysticism, verbal refinement, sophistry, and wry humor, promote the humanity of the Third Testament and treat psychological problems by way of introspective analysis. Her novels and plays also reflect the poet's views on the religious and socio-ethical questions of the time; yet her main concern remained with God and freedom in the love of Christ.

As a critic, Hippius wrote many unconventional essays on literature, religion, and political issues. They were published in leading Moscow and St. Petersburg literary journals and newspapers under the pseudonyms Anton Krainy, Roman Arensky, Lev Pushchin, Comrade Herman, and Vitovt. Containing stimulating comments on the leading writers of the day, these essays also passed judgment on significant events in the literary circles of St. Petersburg, Moscow, and Paris. Moreover, Hippius often engaged in spirited exchanges of opinion on current ideas with Andrei BELY, Valery BRYUSOV, Maksim GORKY, Mark Vishnyak, Anton Kartashev, and Pavel Milyukov.

In her quest for "the Kingdom of Apocalyptical Christianity, this miraculous union of Heaven and earth," Hippius organized the central religious circle in St. Petersburg. She also initiated the Religious-Philosophical Meetings in St. Petersburg (1901–03) and the publication of a new literary journal, *Novyi put',* (1903–05), which printed the works of symbolist writers and published the reports of the Religious Philosophical Meetings. Among Hippius' closest associates at that time were Dmitry Filosofov, Vasily ROZANOV, Pyotr Pilsky, Nikolai BERDYAEV, Aleksandr Benois, Valentin Nouvel, Lev Bakst, Vladimir Hippius, Nikolai MINSKY, Aleksandr BLOK, Andrei Bely, Fyodor SOLOGUB, Serafima Remizova, Poliksena Solovyova (Allegro), Marietta SHAGINYAN, Dmitry MEREZHKOVSKY, Anton Kartashev, Tatyana and Natalya Hippius.

Hippius welcomed only the initial phase of the Russian Revolution, which abolished autocracy and promised freedom. After the October Revolution, however, she and her husband Merezhkovsky left St. Petersburg on 24 December 1919. Together with Boris Savinkov and General Glazenap, they tried to organize military opposition to Bolshevism in Poland, but President Pilsudski's peace with Bolshevik Russia put an end to their activities for the "Russian cause" there. They left Warsaw on 20 October 1920, for Paris via Wiesbaden.

In 1925 Hippius published her reminiscences, *Living Faces* (Zhivye litsa), and in 1928 at the First Congress of Writers in Exile she was honored by King Alexander of Yugoslavia with the Order of St. Sava for her contribution to Russian literature and culture. In 1926 the Merezhkovskys organized a new literary and philosophical society, *The Green Lamp,* an offshoot of their famous Sunday *soirées,* where the discussions centered on poetry, philosophy, religion, and metaphysical concepts. *Radiances* (Siyaniya), a volume of poetry published in exile in 1938, testifies that she had retained full control and lost none of her skills in versification.

Hippius' insistence on specific aesthetic, religious, and philosophical qualities of the literary work helped set the stage for a new 20th-century literary movement, Russian SYMBOLISM. She never relinquished the premise which she formulated at the turn of the century, namely, that art is real when it guides the reader toward the spiritual and stimulates his search for God. Her philosophy retains its validity even in the light of modern existentialism, for her central themes—the search for God, problems of good and evil, her intense interest in psychology, her idiosyncratic treatment of love, marriage, and sexual ambivalence, and her sense of responsibility toward oneself and one's fellow men—are indeed relevant even in today's cultural climate.

Works: Collected Poetical Works. Vol 1: 1899–1918. Vol. 2: 1918–1945. First comprehensive edition; compiled, annotated and with an introduction by Temira Pachmuss. Munich, 1972. *P'esy: Collected Dramatical Works.* Ed. and introd. Temira Pachmuss. Munich, 1972. (With Dmitri Mereschkowski and Dmitri Philosophoff,) *Der Zar et la Révolution.* Munich, 1908. (From the French, *Le Tsar et la Révolution*, Paris, 1907.) *Literaturnyi dnevnik: 1899–1907.* St. Petersburg, 1908. Reprint Munich, 1970. *Nebesnye slova i drugie rasskazy.* Paris, 1921. (With D. S. Merezhkovskii, D. V. Filosofov, and V. A. Zlobin,) *Tsarstvo Antikhrista.* Munich, 1921. *Sinyaya kniga. Peterburgskii dnevnik: 1914–1918.* Belgrade, 1929. Reprint Tel-Aviv, 1980. *Chto delat' russkoi emigratsii.* Paris, 1930. *Dmitrii Merezhkovskii.* Paris, 1951.

Reprint editions with introd. by Temira Pachmuss (all Munich: Fink Verlag): *Zhivye litsa.* Prague, 1925. Reprint 1971. *Chortova kukla/Roman Tsarevich.* Moscow, 1911 and 1913. Reprint 1972. *Novye lyudi/Pobediteli.* St. Petersburg, 1907, 1898. Reprint 1973. *Zerkala. Vtoraya kniga rasskazov.* St. Petersburg, 1898. Reprint 1977. *Tret'ya kniga rasskazov.* St. Petersburg, 1902. Reprint 1977. *Further reprint editions:* (With introd. by Temira Pachmuss:) *Alyi mech': Book IV of Short Stories.* Newtonville, Mass., 1977. *Chernoe po belomu: Book V of Short Stories.* Newtonville, Mass., 1977. *Lunnye murav'i: Book VI of Stories.* Newtonville, Mass., 1977. (Prideaux Press reprints:) *Poslednie stikhi.* Letchworth, Herts., 1974. *Ivan Ivanovich i chort.* Letchworth, Herts., 1979. *Vlyublennye.* Letchworth, Herts., 1979.

Translations: Selected Works of Zinaida Hippius. Trans. and ed. Temira Pachmuss. Univ. of Illinois Press, 1972. *Between Paris and St. Petersburg: Selected Diaries of Zinaida Hippius.* Trans. and ed. Temira Pachmuss. Univ. of Illinois Press, 1975. *Women Writers in Russian Modernism: An Anthology.* Trans. and ed. Temira Pachmuss. Univ. of Illinois Press, 1978. *A Russian Cultural Revival: A Critical Anthology of Emigré Literature before 1939.* Ed. and trans. Temira Pachmuss. Univ. of Tennessee Press, 1981. *Modern Russian Poetry: An Anthology.* Ed. Vladimir Markov and Merrill Sparks, 1967. Pp. 56–89. *See also: Lewanski*, p. 262.

Bibliography: A. Barda, *Bibliographie des oeuvres de Zenaïde Hippius.* Paris, 1975.

Secondary literature: Antonina Filonov Gove, "Gender as a Poetic Feature in the Verse of Zinaida Gippius." In *American Contributions to the Eighth International Congress of Slavists.* 1978. Pp. 379–407. S. Makovskii, *Na Parnase Serebryanogo veka.* Munich, 1962. O. Maslenikov, "Disruption of Canonical Verse Norms in the Poetry of Zinaida Hippius." In *Studies in Slavic Linguistics and Poetics in Honor of Boris O. Unbegaun.* New York, 1968. Pp. 89–96. ———, "The Spectre of Nothingness: The Privative Element in the Poetry of Zinaida Hippius," *SEEJ* 4 (1966), pp. 299–311. Olga Matich, *The Religious Poetry of Zinaida Gippius.* Munich, 1972. M. Nevedomskii, "80-e i 90-e gody v nashei literature." In *Istoriya Rossii v XIX veke.* Vol. 9. Moscow, 1911. Temira Pachmuss, *Zinaida Hippius: An Intellectual Profile.* Carbondale, Ill., 1971. ———, ed. *Intellect and Ideas in Action: Selected Correspondence of Zinaida Hippius.* Munich, 1972. Renato Poggioli, *The Poets of Russia: 1890–1930.* 1960. M. Shaginyan, *O blazhenstve imushchego: poeziya Z. N. Gippius.* Moscow, 1912. Yu. Terapiano, *Vstrechi.* New York, 1953. Pp. 36–81. A. Volynskii, *Bor'ba za idealizm.* St. Petersburg, 1900. Pp. 297–310. ———, *Kniga velikogo gneva.* St. Petersburg, 1904. Pp. 430–46.

T.A.P.

Historical Drama. Among the earliest Russian dramatic works—generally school dramas—were two historical plays: Yu. M. (Georg) Hübner's *A Play About Tamerlane* (Temir-Aksakovo deistvo, 1675) and Feofan PROKOPOVICH's *Vladimir* (1705). While retaining the eclecticism of school drama, these plays directed their focus away from common themes of universal history, hagiography, allegory, and ancient mythology to a specific historical setting. *Tamerlane* was a thinly disguised commentary on the political rivalry between Russia and Turkey; quite appropriately it ended with lavish praise for the beneficent rule of Tsar Alexis. Prokopovich's play recounted the story of Vladimir's conversion to Eastern Orthodoxy and the subsequent Christianization of ancient Rus; it too focused on political mat-

ters and emphasized the wisdom of cultural enlightenment. Although Christian doctrines continued to be prominent in these two works, they were considerably less important than questions of political behavior, nationalism, and secular ideology. The critical shift from a fundamentally religious framework to a political world—similar to the change that occurred in 16th-century English chronicle plays—laid the groundwork for the development of Russian historical drama.

In the 18th century historical drama initially took the form of ceremonial spectacles which were panegyric plays that used lavish stage decorations and costumes to celebrate Russian autocrats. These were simple literary works that relied on rituals and served primarily as court entertainment. In the second half of the 18th century several neoclassical tragedies were written that were based on episodes of Russian history. Prominent among these works were A. P. SUMAROKOV's *Dimitry the Impostor* (1771) and Ya. B. KNYAZHNIN's *Vadim of Novgorod* (1789). While relying on the basic tenets of neoclassicism—highly rhetorical style, the three unities, abstracted characters, a central conflict between passion and reason—Sumarokov focused on several important political issues: the tyranny of absolute autocracy, enlightened leadership, and nationalism. Like Sumarokov, Knyazhnin also introduced key features of historical drama—the spirit of political freedom, democratic rule, patriotism—and fashioned a tragedy that was rooted in a Russian historical context.

The true development of Russian historical drama occurred only in the early 1800s when dramatists such as V. A. OZEROV, S. N. Glinka, M. V. Kryukovskoi, A. A. SHAKHOVSKOI, and others wrote numerous plays that celebrated Russia's military victories, heroic rulers, and glorious national heritage. Their plays—approximately forty entered the repertoire—rarely addressed critical historical issues; questions of historical sources, political intrigues, and the behavior of medieval rulers, for instance, were generally ignored in favor of panegyric verse, passionate declarations of love, and the conventional elements of neoclassical drama. Of the many plays on the Russian stage, Ozerov's *Dimitry Donskoi*, the story of Russia's triumphant defeat of the Tatars in 1380, was by far the most popular.

After 1815 leading Russian critics—among others, O. M. SOMOV, A. A. BESTUZHEV, P. A. PLETNYOV—began to examine the accuracy of historical drama, the presentation of historical characters, and the general problems of dramatic structure and style. Critical of patriotic drama, which they saw as derivative of outmoded literary traditions, they urged Russians to develop more mature forms of drama. The most important response to their clarion call was made by Aleksandr PUSHKIN. Influenced primarily by Shakespeare and A. W. Schlegel, Pushkin wrote *Boris Godunov* (1825), a work that was intended to revolutionize Russian drama. Unlike earlier Russian dramatists, Pushkin depicted the events of the TIME OF TROUBLES (1598–1605) accurately and truthfully. Following Nikolai KARAMZIN's famous account of this period, he cast Boris as the murderer of the young tsarevich Dimitry (Tsar Ivan IV's son) and made the guilt of the tsar-usurper the main theme of his work. What was truly remarkable about *Boris Godunov* was the novelty of its dramatic form. Singlehandedly Pushkin destroyed the prevailing conception of Russian neoclassical tragedy by dividing his play into twenty-three short unnumbered scenes, introducing different levels of language and numerous characters, and avoiding an unambiguous political or moral message. Unfortunately these bold formal innovations were not understood or appreciated by Pushkin's contemporaries and *Boris Godunov* was generally dismissed as a shapeless dramatic fragment. Pushkin's influence on Russian drama was not felt until the mid-19th century when Modest Musorgsky used Pushkin's text to compose his opera *Boris Godunov* and A. N. OSTROVSKY and A. K. TOLSTOI tried their hand at writing historical plays.

What was most surprising in the evolution of Russian historical drama was the reappearance in the 1830s of the patriotic play. Of the many dramatists who wrote patriotic works—P. G. Obodovsky, R. M. Zotov, N. A. POLEVOI—the most popular was Nestor KUKOLNIK. His best known work, *The Hand of the Almighty Saved the Fatherland* (Ruka vsevyshnego otechestvo spasla, 1834), the title taken from Ozerov's *Dimitry Donskoi*, used a distant historical setting to glorify the Russian State, its customs, political order, and people. The main characters, Pozharsky and Minin, attain a saint-like stature as they mobilize the army against Russia's enemies.

But instead of creating dramatic conflicts, Kukolnik resorted to long rhetorical passages and lavish theatrical decorations which embellished the patriotic themes.

After the eventual demise of the patriotic play in the 1840s there were several types of historical drama. One popular form was the costume play that combined the glory of national heroes and the exotic setting of an historical period with the general features of melodrama: complicated plots, mysterious abductions, illicit (but vague) love affairs, unexpected meetings, and coincidences. The most important works were L. A. MEI's *Tsar's Bride* (Tsarskaya nevesta, 1849) and *The Maid of Pskov* (Pskovityanka, 1859); both were later transformed into successful operas by Rimsky-Korsakov. Running parallel to costume drama was the chronicle play. Drawing on Pushkin's *Boris Godunov* as a model, Ostrovsky, N. A. Chaev, and D. V. Averkiev wrote several plays that depicted in great detail historical characters and events. In the two best known chronicles—*Kozma Minin, Sukhoruk* (1862) and *Dimitry the Pretender and Vasily Shuisky* (1867)—Ostrovsky focused on critical political issues, introduced historical sources into the dramatic text, depicted the *narod* (people), and raised important religious and ideological questions. For all their ethnographic detail, though, chronicles were long, unwieldy works that played a small role in the development of Russian drama.

The most important historical dramatist of the latter half of the 19th century was A. K. Tolstoi who wrote a historical trilogy: *The Death of Ivan the Terrible* (Smert' Ioanna Groznogo, 1866), *Tsar Fyodor Ioannovich* (1868), and *Tsar Boris* (1870). In these works Tolstoi introduced many historical figures, speech patterns of Old Russian, and various Russian customs. Like Pushkin before him, he shunned conventional modes of dramatic structure—in particular the central love episode—and based his plays on the development of distinct historical personalities. With artistic skill Tolstoi revealed the psychological underpinnings of his characters. The interaction of Ivan, Fyodor, and Boris, as well as the finely etched minor characters, motivates the dramatic action and leads to the exploration of different modes of political rule.

In the early years of the 20th century, historical drama played an insignificant role on the Russian literary scene. Patriotic plays, costume drama, and chronicles continued to be written by dramatists such as N. A. Navrotsky and I. P. Shpazhinsky but they were rarely performed in major theaters and did not draw the attention of critics. After the Revolution, though, historical drama made a comeback. Numerous plays were written whose subject matter ranged from literary figures (e.g., Pushkin or Lermontov) and revolutionary leaders (primarily Stenka Razin and Pugachov) to Russian tsars and heroic military exploits. Like earlier Russian works, Soviet plays advocated public values of loyalty to the State, patriotism, and the struggle against foreign enemies. But Soviet dramatists—N. Lerner, N. Shapovalenko, D. Smolin, V. Solovyov, A. N. TOLSTOI (among others)—had to contend with Marxist conceptions of history and a shifting Party line toward the Russian past. Thus historical drama in the Soviet period became a clear handmaiden of political ideology. And this may explain why major 20th-century Russian writers have not been attracted to this genre.   M. G. P.

Historical novel, The.

The "father" of the Russian historical novel was N. M. KARAMZIN, whose tales *Natalya the Boyar's Daughter* (Natal'ya Boyarskaya Doch', 1792), and *Marfa the Magistrate* (Marfa Posadnitsa, 1802), set in the time of Novgorod, enjoyed enormous success with the Russian public.

The tales (povesti) of the early and mid-1820s and the novels of the late 1820s and 1830s were inspired by the new nationalistic spirit engendered by the War of 1812, and by the appearance of N. M. Karamzin's *History of the Russian State* (1818–25). Sir Walter Scott's novels, many of which had been translated into Russian in the 1820s, provided the most important literary stimulus.

Karamzin's *History* in many ways prepared the ground for the historical novel. It became a source and an aesthetic artistic inspiration for Russian writers. In dealing with historical figures like Ivan the Terrible and Boris Godunov, Karamzin relied on a psychological interpretation of character, so that the sections of the *History* devoted to these two approached the genre of a historical novel.

In the mid-twenties A. BESTUZHEV-MARLINSKY (1797–1837), F. GLINKA (1786–1880) and others wrote a variety of tales on historical topics, but these were still only the precursors of the true historical novel. A. Bestuzhev-Marlinsky's tale *Roman and Olga* (1823) set in the year 1396 is probably the best-known work written at that time, but it exemplifies the view of Bestuzhev-Marlinsky and many of his fellow writers that intuition alone was sufficient to secure correct historical insight.

M. N. ZAGOSKIN's novel *Yury Miloslavsky or the Russians in the year 1612* (1829) is generally considered to be the first full-fledged Russian novel in prose, and the first Russian historical novel. It adhered closely to Sir Walter Scott's literary methods, and was apparently derived almost entirely from Scott's *Legend of Montrose*. Even so, *Yury Miloslavsky* was greeted by PUSHKIN, ZHUKOVSKY, and KRYLOV as a great literary event, as a truly Russian novel. Zagoskin's contribution lies in his innovative use of language to create an illusion of antiquity. He also makes use of his skill as a dramatist in using dialogue rather than description or exposition, in the use of colloquial speech, and the oral speech of the common people. As in all of his works Zagoskin portrays the spiritual superiority of the Russians over the decadent West. That is why *Yury Miloslavsky* is the only one of Zagoskin's historical novels to have survived over the years, and to be published and republished in the Soviet Union.

In the 1830s the historical novel assumed a preeminent position on the Russian literary scene. Virtually every professional writer tried his hand at historical fiction. Major writers include F. N. BULGARIN (1789–1859), K. P. Masalsky (1820–61), I. I. LAZHECHNIKOV (1792–1869), N. A. POLEVOI (1796–1847), A. F. VELTMAN (1800–70), and R. M. Zotov (1795–1871). The most popular of these was Lazhechnikov, the author of three historical novels, *The Last Page* (1831–33), *The Ice Palace* (1835) and *The Infidel* (1838). *The Ice Palace* which deals with an attempt on the part of Russian patriots to undermine the political power of Biron, the German favorite of Empress Anna Ioannovna in the winter of 1740 was very popular before and after the Revolution. It has come out in Soviet editions every two or three years since 1924, irrespective of the political ideology or theory of history in force at any given time. For many it is Lazhechnikov, and not Zagoskin, who is viewed as the founder of the Russian historical novel and the "red Russian Walter Scott."

Although the writers listed above produced a large number of historical novels, the best works of the period are by Pushkin, the unfinished *The Blackamoor of Peter the Great* (1829), *The Captain's Daughter* (1836); and by GOGOL, *Taras Bulba* in its final form (1842).

By 1840 romanticism and the vogue for historical novels had disappeared. The collected works of such writers as Lazhechnikov and Zagoskin continued to be published, but no new historical novels of any significance appeared until 1861 when A. K. TOLSTOI's *Prince Serebryany* was published. *Prince Serebryany* stands out in contrast to the period in which it was published because it follows in the Sir Walter Scott tradition associated with both romanticism and nationalism. The subject is Ivan the Terrible. The author takes a stand against the senseless slaughter of innocent people but at the same time glorifies the deeds of those who repel the invader and protect Russia's borders. A. K. Tolstoi's novel is derived from Zagoskin's *Yury Miloslavsky* much in the same way as *Yury Miloslavsky* was derived from Scott's *Legend of Montrose*.

L. N. TOLSTOI's novel *War and Peace* (1861–64) stands quite alone, for it is unconnected with the tradition of the 1830s or with the tradition of A. K. Tolstoi. While no one will dispute the fact that *War and Peace* is a great novel, there is still some controversy as to whether it should be classified as a historical novel, since it gives a distorted presentation of the major historical characters, Napoleon, Kutuzov, and Alexander I. Furthermore, it is antihistorical in its approach, and strives to discredit the traditional view of history.

The true revival of the historical novel came in the 1870s and 1880s when a small number of writers interested in popularizing history and in furthering social and political aims wrote an extremely large number of works covering a major portion of Russian and in some instances world history. These include G. P. Danilevsky, Vsevolod Solovyov (1849–1903), Daniil Mordovtsev (1830–1905), and Count Eugène Salias de Tournemir.

At the turn of the century, the symbolists V. BRYUSOV (1873–1924), and D. MEREZHKOVSKY (1865–1941) attempted to raise this form of literature to a higher artistic level, and used it as a medium for the universal truths they wanted to communicate. V. Bryusov's *The Fiery Angel* (1908), *The Altar of Victory* (1913) and Merezhkovsky's trilogy, *Christ and Antichrist: Julian the Apostate* (1896); *Leonardo da Vinci* (1901); and *Peter and Alexis* (1905) are the major works of this third period.

But it is in the period since 1925 that the historical novel has seen its greatest quantitative growth in Russia. Unlike the end of the 19th century when a few writers were responsible for nearly all historical fiction published, the historical novel in the Soviet Union has been the product of many individuals, not all of them professional writers. Between 1925 and 1970, for example, more than 500 Soviet writers authored more than 1,000 historical novels and *povesti*. In 1925 there appeared three novels now considered classics, namely, Yury Tynyanov's *Kyukhlya*, Olga Forsh's *Clad in Stone* and Aleksei Chapygin's *Razin Stepan*. All three treated the revolutionary aspects of history. All tried to explain the Revolution of 1917 by concentrating on "the genealogy of the Revolution" and reflected the individual author's views and feelings on the Revolution, rather than some official governmental policy.

The historical novel developed most rapidly during the RAPP period (1928–1932) when writers who could not or would not comply with demands that they write on contemporary themes "escaped" into the field of historical fiction. The exaggerated popularity of the genre may also be viewed as an antidote to the Pokrovsky school of historiography which left no room for the role of the personality in history. Even as late as 1934 when the Pokrovsky school was officially abolished, critics still used Pokrovsky's slogan "History is politics projected into the past" to condemn virtually all Soviet historical novelists. However, it was precisely during the period of 1928 to 1934 that A. N. TOLSTOI published what is still the best Soviet historical novel, *Peter the First* (Book 1 1929, Book 2 1934, Book 3 1945), a novel which was clearly contrary to official policy at that time.

However, by 1935 writers were being exhorted to refute the charges of the "fascist falsifiers of history" by stressing the heroic and invaluable moments in the histories of their respective countries. The campaign urging writers to turn to the historical novel gained momentum rapidly, and by 1937 writers were told that there were enough heroic figures in Russian history to suffice for many generations of artists. The very historical analogies that were criticized in the early thirties were welcomed by the government. Stalin's statement of 7 November 1941 in which he said "Let the many images of our great ancestors, Aleksandr Nevsky, Dmitry Donskoi, Minin and Pozharsky, Suvorov and Kutuzov inspire us in this war" merely repeated on a somewhat higher and more official level what critics, historians, and party leaders had been writing about for the previous four years.

During World War II historical themes became important especially as they stressed Russian victories over the Germans, or Russian resistance to the Tatars and other invaders of the country. During the war many of the older writers had turned to historical themes. In the immediate postwar period Soviet literature was devoid of works on contemporary themes at the very time when efforts were being made to rebuild and restore a devastated country. A. ZHDANOV's speech in 1946 in which he criticized writers for withdrawal from contemporary themes was an attempt to allocate "literary talents" in much the same way as RAPP did in the late twenties and early thirties. The publication of new titles dropped, and it was not until 1956, after the denunciation of the "cult of personality" that the number of new titles increased significantly and have continued at a steady growth to the present day. The fluctuations in the number of new titles reflect Soviet policy and internal politics.

Throughout the 1970s the historical novel continued to enjoy popularity and success. Whenever official policy discouraged the publication of new historical novels, publishers used their allocation of paper to reprint old, safe, historical novels, so that the Soviet public always had the same or even larger number of copies of historical novels available in the stores.

As has already been noted the first major theme of the Soviet historical novel was the "genealogy of the Revolution." To the three novels first published in 1925 one might add G. Shtorm's *Ivan Bolotnikov* (1930), V. I. Shishkov's *Emelian Pugachev* (1938–1947), Stepan Zlobin's *Stepan Razin* (1951), Vasily SHUKSHIN's *I Came to Give you Freedom* (1971), and even Bulat OKUDZHAVA's *A Taste of Freedom* (1971), a novel about the Decembrist Paul Pestel. What could be called the genealogy of the centralized state is represented by such works as A. N. Tolstoi's *Peter I*, V. Kostylev's three-volume

Ivan the Terrible (1944–1947), V. Yazvitsky's four-volume *Ivan III* (1946–1951), S. Borodin's *Dmitry Donskoi* (1942), and Aleksii Yugov's two-volume *The Warrior* (1946–1949) about Aleksandr Nevsky. In the seventies Dmitry Balashov emulates Karamzin with his novels *Marfa the Magistrate* (1972), *Great Novgorod* (1977) and *The Younger Son* (1977) set in the period 1263–1304 just after the death of Aleksandr Nevsky when Nevsky's sons do battle with the Tatar horde and take the first steps in founding Moscow.

Tied to this theme are the novels of exploration, conquest and settlement of new lands, particularly of the Far East. To this group belong such novels as Artyom Vesyoly's *Gulyai Volga* (1932) about Ermak, the novels by Ivan Kratt about the Russians in Alaska, *Baranov's Island* (1945) and the *Ross Colony* (1950) and N. Zadornov's novel *To the Pacific Ocean* (1950) which deals with the 1848 expedition of Captain Nevelskoi to the Amur region.

The biographical historical novel, and especially the fictionalized biographies of the classical 19th century writers, have a special place in Soviet literature as a whole. In the period 1925 to 1970, 455 or almost half of the 1,010 historical novels and tales (*povesti*) published were set in the 19th century, and 118 of these or twenty-six percent were concerned with a major Russian author. Twenty-two of these novels dealt with Pushkin, eleven with LERMONTOV, eight with Gogol, and eleven with SHEVCHENKO. Major works on Pushkin have been authored by L. P. GROSSMAN, S. N. SERGEEV-TSENSKY, Yu. N. TYNYANOV, A. N. Novikov, and V. P. Voevodin. More novels and tales keep appearing on these literary themes. To be noted are Andrei SINYAVSKY's *In the Shadow of Gogol* (1975) and *Strolling with Pushkin* (1976).

It can safely be said that both in quantity and overall quality in the realm of the historical novel, Soviet writers have outshone most of their 19th-century counterparts. Writers continue to give new interpretations to traditional subjects, and strive to write what might be viewed as "the definitive novel" on a given topic. Some writers do escape into the past, and the historical analogies they present are not entirely lost on the reader.

Bibliography: S. Petrov, *Russkii istoricheskii roman XIX veka.* 1964. S. M. Petrov, *Russkii sovetskii istoricheskii roman.* 1980. L. I. Twarog, "The Arithmetic of the Soviet Historical Novel." In *Studies of the Institute for the Study of the USSR.* Munich, 1971. Pp. 83–105.
L. T.

Historicism (*istorizm*). The term denotes an author's approach to history or the degree to which his work reflects specific historical characteristics of the time he describes. In Russia the concept of historicism developed in the first half of the 19th century under the influence of a growing national awareness and Sir Walter Scott's novels. Vissarion BELINSKY saw an organic bond between literature and history and believed that a writer could re-create the past and the present of his nation more vividly and accurately than a historian. In contrast to Belinsky's concern for contemporaneity and social progress, Apollon GRIGORIEV's concept of historicism included the depiction of an eternal all-human ideal as revealed in religious, moral, and linguistic traits of the Russian people. Russian aesthetic thought, except that of the SYMBOLISTS, has been more receptive to Belinsky's view of historicism than to Grigoriev's.

LENIN's insistence that any phenomenon be analyzed in its specific historical context is mirrored in the definition of SOCIALIST REALISM which calls for "the truthful, historically concrete depiction of reality in its revolutionary development" (*Literary Gazette,* 3 September 1934). The approach to history depends on the Communist Party's policy. In the mid-1930s, preparing for war, the Party urged writers of historical fiction to shift emphasis from revolutionary to patriotic themes. In the heyday of nationalism (1946–53) literature had to praise nearly everything Russian, while earlier works were purged of unflattering descriptions of tsarist times. Post-Stalin relaxation of controls notwithstanding, writers are still required to adhere to politically motivated historicism.

Readings: Yu. Andreev, *Russkii sovetskii istoricheskii roman: 20–30–e gody.* 1962. M. Friedberg, "Soviet Literature and Retroactive Truth," *Problems of Communism* 3, no. 1 (1954), pp. 31–39; V. Terras, *Belinsky and Russian Literary Criticism: The Heritage of Organic Aesthetics.* 1974.
H. E.

Hylaea (Giléya), literary avant-garde group based in Moscow (1910–13). Hylaea constitutes the first stage of cubo-FUTURISM. Hylaea was founded in the winter of 1910 by three brothers, David, Nikolai, and Vladimir BURLYUK, and by Benedikt LIVSHITS, while vacationing at the Burlyuks' estate, Chernyanka, not far from the city of Kherson. Hylaea was the ancient Greek name for that region, and it was adopted by the founders as a symbol of primitive simplicity for a new trend in art and literature. Other members of the group were Vasily KAMENSKY and Velimir KHLEBNIKOV. Both had already collaborated with the Burlyuk brothers in the publication of the almanac *Sadok sudei* (1910). In 1911, Hylaea acquired two new members, Vladimir MAYAKOVSKY and Aleksei KRUCHONYKH.

Although the Hylaeans' dominant activity was literature, many among them were artists as well as poets. The Hylaeans worked closely with leading art groups and participated in discussions of modern art at various exhibitions. In 1912, Hylaea entered into an alliance with Jack of Diamonds, a group of artists, and the next year it was allied with the Union of Youth. In the first stage, the Hylaeans displayed a tendency towards primitivism, characterized by three main elements: childhood, prehistory, and Russian folklore. The painters more closely associated with the Hylaeans were Mikhail Larionov and Natalya Goncharova, who illustrated their books and miscellanies. Larionov's art is believed to have had an impact on the poetry of Khlebnikov and Kruchonykh because of its primitive features.

The first collective publication of the Hylaeans was the almanac, *Poshchechina obshchestvennomu vkusu* (Slap in the Face of Public Taste, 1912). It carries the homonymous manifesto in which the principles of what would eventually become known under the name of cubo-futurism are boldly outlined: rejection of the past, urbanism, technology, and word-oriented poetry. Another important manifesto, more programmatic than the previous one, appeared in the second almanac, *Sadok sudei II* (A Trap for Judges II, 1912). In 1913, the magazine *Soyuz molodezhi* devoted a whole section to the poetry of the Hylaeans. In the same year, a major publication appeared, *Trebnik troikh* (Missal of the Three). Still another remarkable collection was published in 1913, *Troe* (The Three), dedicated to the memory of Elena GURO.

In the second half of 1913, the name, futurists, appears in connection with the Hylaeans. One of their almanacs was issued under the title, *Futuristy, Gileya, Dokhlaya luna* (Futurists, Hylaea, Croaked Moon), and the title page read: "The miscellany of the only futurists in the world, the poets of Hylaea." Later, the word "cubo" was added to the new name. The motives for a name change are a matter of speculation. The Hylaeans maintained that it was the press that started calling them futurists. However, it is not unreasonable to assume that some of the Hylaeans welcomed the publicity benefits of being associated with a movement that was already known all over Europe. (For further developments of the Hylaea group, see "futurism").

Bibliography: V. D. Barooshian, *Russian Cubo-Futurism 1910–1930: A Study in Avant-Gardism.* 1974. K. Khardzhiev, K. Malevich, M. Matyushin. *K istorii russkogo avangarda.* Stockholm, 1976. A. Lawton, "Russian and Italian Futurist Manifestoes," *SEEJ* 20 (1976), pp. 405–20. B. Livshits, *The One and A Half-Eyed Archer.* Trans. John E. Bowlt. 1977. V. Markov, *Russian Futurism: A History.* 1968. A. L.

Iamb, see SYLLABOTONIC VERSIFICATION.

Ideinost' (ideological content, commitment). In prerevolutionary Russia the word *ideinost'* was occasionally applied in assessing the ideological profundity and significance of literary works. Mikhail SALTYKOV-SHCHEDRIN wrote about passionate *ideinost'* in some novels by George Sand ("Abroad," 1881); while Georgy PLEKHANOV saw *ideinost'* in the moral pathos of Henrik Ibsen's plays ("Henrik Ibsen," 1906). In the Soviet Union where literature is viewed in Marxist terms as an ideological phenomenon, *ideinost'* has acquired a distinct political coloration, becoming virtually synonymous with *partiinost'* (Party-mindedness)—the propagation of the Communist Party's official philosophy and policy. Theorists of SOCIALIST REALISM, perpetuating the view of proletarian literary organizations of the 1920s, maintain that the chief task of literature lies in the ideological education of the masses in the spirit of Communism. The most intense implementation of *ideinost'* took place during the last years of Stalin's rule. It was prompted by the Party's Central Committee resolution of 14 August 1946, which condemned what it called ideologically empty, apolitical, and decadent tendencies in Soviet literature and stated that writers must have no concerns other than those of the state. As a result, literature embarked upon an unusually false idealization of Soviet life, an unprecedented glorification of Stalin, and a crude vilification of the West.

After Stalin's death the official emphasis on *ideinost'* continues to be strong. It is claimed that Communist *ideinost'* enables writers to reveal in depth the revolutionary practices of the Soviet people, to heighten the aesthetic quality of their works, and to create the world's most progressive literature.

Readings: The Central Committee Resolution and Zhdanov's Speech on the Journals "Zvezda" and "Leningrad". Bilingual ed. 1978. Yu. Lukin, "Partiya i khudozhestvennaya kul'tura razvitogo sotsializma," *Vlit* 1982, no. 3, pp. 3–39. [G. Nedoshivin], "O kommunisticheskoi ideinosti iskusstva sotsialisticheskogo realizma." In *Osnovy marksistsko-leninskoi estetiki.* 1960. H. E.

Ignátiev, Iván Vasílievich (pseud. of Kazansky, 1892–1914), poet, critic, publisher.

Ignatiev began by writing for various newspapers and magazines in St. Petersburg. *Okolo teatra*, a collection of his early pieces (stories, sketches, parodies, poems), appeared in 1911. He subsequently joined the ego-FUTURIST group of poets (then led by Igor SEVERYANIN). A good organizer, he did much to bring the group to public attention, and became a distinctive, if minor, presence on the St. Petersburg literary scene.

As an ego-futurist, Ignatiev first published several issues of a newspaper, *Peterburgskii Glashatai* (1912). This was followed by a series of "poeza-concerts"—public readings by the ego-futurists arranged so as to appeal to a mass audience through a mixture of overt social snobbery and *épatage*. The next venture, a publishing house (1912–1914) also named *Peterburgskii Glashatai*, proved more lasting. A number of brief miscellanies (*almanakhi*) with works by the ego-futurists were published. Some of them featured poems by symbolist notables BRYUSOV and SOLOGUB—testimony to the ego futurists' literary kinships. Ignatiev also published individual collections of poems (by Vadim SHERSHENEVICH, Vasilisk Gnedov, etc.).

Ignatiev's promotional activities were supplemented by original writings. He attempted to fill the role of ego-futurism's historian-theoretician. In a 1912 article he pointed to intuition as its basis, and defended ego-futurism against charges of a lack of originality. After Severyanin's break with the group (November 1912), Ignatiev became its leader. He continued to emphasize intuitivism and extreme individualism, but also began to stress verbal experimentation (like the rival cubo-futurist movement). In late 1913, in the pamphlet *Ego-Futurizm*, his most extensive theoretical-polemical attempt, Ignatiev credited the group with various innovations and enrichments of poetic technique, and acknowledged its connections to symbolism.

Ignatiev's original poems (publ. in the various miscellanies; also in the posthumous collection *Eshafot. Ego-futury.* (Moim lyubovnikam—posvyashchayu), St. Petersburg, 1914) show little talent. Some are obscurely metaphysical; others offer verbal experiments analogous to those of the cubo-futurists, including visual poems, and use of "transsense" (ZAUMNYI) elements.

Secondary literature: Dm. Kryuchkov, "Pamyati Ivana Vasíl'evicha Ignat'eva. [Nekrolog]." *Ocharovannyi strannik.* Fasc. 3. 1914. Vladimir Markov, *Russian Futurism: A History.* 1968. (Contains bibliography). H. B.

Igor Tale, see SLOVO O POLKU IGOREVE.

Ilarión (Hilarion), Metropolitan (11th century). Considered by modern scholarship a central figure in religious and cultural life during the reign of Grand Prince Yaroslav Vladimirovich (ca. 1019–54), Ilarion is regarded as one of the initiators of Kievan ecclesiastic literature. Though only scanty information is provided by historical sources, many conjectures have been advanced about Ilarion's life and literary activity. Our main source of information is the POVEST' VREMENNYKH LET (Tale of Bygone Years), which relates that in the year 1051 "Yaroslav appointed Larion a Russian as metropolitan in [the cathedral of] St. Sofia, having assembled the bishops." The *Tale of Bygone Years* also informs us that "Larion" had come from Berestovo, the residence of Prince Yaroslav south of Kiev, to the site of the future Monastery of the Caves. According to the account about St. Anthony found in the *Paterikon of the Monastery of the Caves* (Kievo-Pecherskii Paterik), which was written by Bishop Simon of Vladimir to the monk Polikarp in the early 13th century, Ilarion received the monastic tonsure and was prepared for the priesthood by Anthony, the first abbot of the Monastery of the Caves.

A 15th-century "Synodal manuscript" (now in the Historical Museum in Moscow) contains a short "Confession of Faith" which ends with a first-person statement by the "monk and priest Ilarion." He declares that he was "consecrated and installed in the great and God-protected city of Kiev to be in it metropolitan, pastor, and teacher. This was the year 6559 [1051], when the beneficent Kagan Yaroslav, son of Vladimir, reigned." Nothing is known about Ilarion after 1051.

A number of works have been attributed to Ilarion, often on the flimsiest of grounds. The only attribution which still is generally accepted relates to an extremely complex work known as the *Sermon on Law and Grace* (Slovo o zakone i blagodati). One of the main arguments in favor of this attribution is that the *Sermon* immediately precedes the "signed" Confession of Faith included in the above-mentioned Synodal manuscript.

One cannot say with any certainty what the original makeup of the *Sermon* was. The textual documentation which has come down to us is relatively late. All known codices but one (which, according to O. M. Bodyansky goes back to the 14th century) date from the 15th and the 16th century. It is important to emphasize that these codices betray clear traces of scriptorial intervention.

In 1906 N. K. Nikolsky divided the thirty-two known manuscripts into four redactions, namely, the "extensive," the "shortened," the "interpolated," and the "interpretative" redactions. It is noteworthy that the "extensive" redaction is preserved only in the above-mentioned Synodal manuscript. Only this codex contains all four sections of the work indicated by its title: namely, (1) On the Law given through Moses and on the Grace and Truth which came into being through Jesus Christ; (2) and when the Law departed Grace and Truth filled the whole earth and faith spread to all the nations, and also to our Russian nation; (3) and a eulogy to our Kagan Vladimir, from whom we were baptized; (4) and a prayer to God from the whole of our land. Scholars have long debated whether sections 3 and 4 belong to the *Slovo* or represent either textual additions or separate appendices.

A central motif developed in the *Sermon* is the superiority of the age of Christian Grace over that of the Jewish Law. This opposition is symbolized by the biblical story about Sarah the freewoman and Hagar the handmaid. Relying on the allegorical teaching of St. Paul (Galatians 4:21–31), Ilarion means to suggest that Christian *Rus'* has been born not "of a slave girl, but of a mother who is free." Of crucial importance for the general meaning of the *Sermon* is the theme of the continuity of God's redeeming intervention. The conversion of all the nations, including *Rus'*, is seen as the confirmation of God's promise. Newly-converted *Rus'* is thereby exalted as the product of providential design and Prince Vladimir is praised as the chosen instrument of divine Grace.

The contrast between Law and Grace has given rise to many interpretations, many relating to Ilarion's aim to proclaim the full dignity of the Russian lands converted by Vladimir. The *Sermon* appears to have been rather popular throughout the Orthodox Slavic community, as evidenced by the inclusion of part of its textual material in works such as the Serbian *Life of Simeon Nemanja* (Žitije Simeona Nemanje) written by Domentijan (ca. 1210–64).

Bibliography: J. Fennell and A. Stokes, *Early Russian Literature.* 1974. Pp. 41–60. L. Müller, *Des Metropoliten Ilarion Lobrede auf Vladimir den Heiligen und Glaubensbekenntnis.* (Slavistische Studienbücher, no. 2.) Wiesbaden, 1962. ———, *Die Werke des Metropoliten Ilarion.* (Forum Slavicum, no. 37.) Munich, 1971. N. Nikol'skii, *Materialy dlya povremennogo spiska russkikh pisatelei i ikh*

sochinenii (X–XI vv.) 1906. Pp. 75–122. R. Picchio, "The Function of Biblical Thematic Clues in the Literary Code of 'Slavia Orthodoxa.'" *Slavica Hierosolymitana*, 1 (1977), pp. 1–31. N. N. Rozov, "Sinodal'nyi spisok sochinenii Ilariona—russkogo pisatelya XI v.", *Slavia* 32 (1963), pp. 141–75.   H. G.

Ilf, Ilyá and **Petróv**, Evgény (pseud. of Ilyá Arnóldovich Faínzilberg, 1897–1937, and Evgény Petróvich Katáev, 1903–42), a team of satirical writers and journalists. Both writers were from Odessa, but they met in Moscow in 1925, while both were on the staff of *Gudok*, a magazine for railway workers. They had both had some success as journalists, writing mostly satirical feuilletons, but were quite unknown to the general public. In the fall of 1927, Valentin KATAEV, Evgeny's elder brother and already a successful writer, suggested facetiously that the two write an adventure novel together and gave them the theme of *Twelve Chairs* (Dvenadtsat' stul'ev). They took him up on it and by January 1928 had produced their novel, which was a huge success. Its plot (the chase for a treasure hidden in one of twelve chairs, each of which was sold to a different party) gave Ilf and Petrov a chance to draw up sharply satirical scenes of Soviet life under the NEP. They also created one of the most popular heroes of Soviet literature, the *picaro* Ostap Bender, a crafty, cynical, and witty rogue who meets a world of honest plodders, dull bureaucrats, and greedy philistines with sovereign nonchalance and supercilious irony. Ilf and Petrov continued their collaboration with a series of feuilletons, a short novel, *A Pure Soul* (Svetlaya lichnost', 1928), and a cycle of satirical novellas, "1001 Days, or a New Scheherazade," over the pseudonym "F. Tolstoevsky." In 1931 they produced their second hit, *The Golden Calf* (Zolotoi telenok), for which they resuscitated Ostap Bender (whom they had let be killed by a fellow treasure-hunter in *Twelve Chairs*). In *The Golden Calf*, Bender, wishing to become a millionaire, decides that the simplest way to achieve this will be to find a Soviet multi-millionaire and relieve him of one of his millions. The satire here is, if anything, even sharper than in *Twelve Chairs*; and it attacks the Soviet system under Stalin's first Five-Year Plan. Accordingly, it was received coldly by official Soviet criticism. In 1933–34 Ilf and Petrov travelled in Western Europe and in 1935–36 they made a six-month automobile trip across the United States which they described in *One-Storied America* (Odnoetazhnaya Amerika, 1936), a perceptive and entertaining travelogue, on the whole favorably disposed toward many aspects of American life (college football, for example). After Ilf's death, Petrov wrote nothing of significance (mostly film scenarios). He died in a plane crash as a war correspondent.

Works: Sobranie sochinenii. 4 vols. 1938. *Sobranie sochinenii.* 5 vols. 1961.

Translations: Lewanski, pp. 262–63.

Secondary literature: B. Galanov, *Il'ya Il'f i Evgenii Petrov.* 1961. A. A. Shcherbina, "Iskusstvo smeshnogo i nasmeshlivogo slova," *RLit* 17 (1974), no. 1, pp. 200–09. T. N. Sintsova, *I. Il'f i E. Petrov: Materialy dlya bibliografii.* 1958. John L. Wright, "Ostap Bender as a Picaroon," *Proceedings: Pacific Northwest Conference on Foreign Languages* 25 (1974), pp. 265–68.   V. T.

Ilyá Múromets, see *BYLINA*.

Ilyín, Iván Aleksándrovich (1883–1954), religious philosopher, jurist, and political scientist, also historian and art and literary critic; educator, public lecturer, publicist, and editor. After graduation from the Moscow University Faculty of Law (1906) and research work in Germany and France, Ilyin taught for ten years (1912–22) at Moscow University and several other institutions of higher learning in Moscow. After the Revolution, as an active foe of Bolshevism, he was arrested on six occasions and then expelled from Russia in September 1922. Ilyin spent the next 16 years in Berlin, where he taught at the Russian Scientific Institute, gave public lectures in Germany and other European countries, contributed to the Russian émigré and German press, and edited a journal, *Russkii kolokol* (1927–30). In 1934 he was removed from the Institute by the Nazis, but in 1938 succeeded in establishing himself in Switzerland. For the last 16 years of his life he lived in Zürich-Zollikon.

Ilyin's printed legacy amounts to several hundred articles in newspapers and reviews and to over thirty books (several of them in German) and booklets which could be grouped into four major categories: philosophy and religion, law and political science, literature and the arts, Russian and Soviet Studies.

Brought up on the philosophical systems of the great German idealist philosophers and author of a remarkable two-volume study of Hegel, *Filosofiya Gegelya kak uchenie o konkretnosti Boga i cheloveka* (Hegel's Philosophy as Teaching on the Concreteness of God and Man, 1918), Ilyin, nevertheless, maintained that the philosopher's true task consists not in constructing a philosophical system, but in object-oriented contemplation and thinking. First of all, a philosopher must be, then act, and only then philosophize. His own philosophy, developed in the spirit of Socrates, Ilyin perceived as a series of acts (resulting in books) about acts.

Ilyin expounded his aesthetic principles in his book *Osnovy khudozhestva; O sovershennom v iskusstve* (The Foundations of Art; On the Perfect in Art, Riga, 1937) and his literary-critical views in *O t'me i prosvetlenii; Kniga khudozhestvennoi kritiki; Bunin, Remizov, Shmelev* (On Darkness and Enlightenment; A Book of Artistic Criticism; BUNIN, REMIZOV, SHMELYOV; finished 1938, publ. Munich, 1959) and *Russkie pisateli, literatura i khudozhestvo* (Russian Writers, Literature, and Art; ed. by N. P. Poltoratskii, Washington, D.C., 1973). In addition to Bunin, Remizov, and Shmelyov, Ilyin applied his principles of spiritual-aesthetic analysis also to the creative work of MEREZHKOVSKY. Among the Russian classics of the 19th century, Ilyin dealt mostly with Pushkin, Tolstoi, Dostoevsky, and Gogol. (His valuable German lectures on them remain, however, still unpublished.) He wrote also on Russian poetry and Russian folklore.

For Ilyin's biography, bibliography, and posthumous evaluation see: I. A. Il'in. *Nashi zadachi; Stat'i 1948–1954 gg.* Paris, 1956. Vol. 2, pp. 611–67. *See also:* N. O. Lossky, *History of Russian Philosophy.* New York, 1951. Pp. 387–89. *Hegel bei den Slaven.* Ed. D. Tschiževskij. Darmstadt, 1961. Pp. 360–68, *Russkaya literatura v emigratsii.* Ed. N. P. Poltoratskii. Pittsburgh, 1972. Pp. 177–90, 271–87, 376, 381–82. *Russkaya religiozno-filosofskaya mysl' XX veka.* Ed. N. P. Poltoratskii. Pittsburgh, 1975. Pp. 240–50. N. P. Poltoratskii, *I. A. Il'in i polemika vokrug ego idei o soprotivlenii zlu siloi.* London, Canada, 1975.   N. P. P.

Ilyinsky, Oleg Pávlovich (1932–   ), poet, critic, literary historian, and scholar in the history of ideas. In exile from the Soviet Union since 1944, Ilyinsky (who transliterates his name as Iljinskij) studied in Munich and New York City, receiving a Ph.D. from New York University in 1970. He is the author of five collections of poetry published in 1960, 1962, 1966, 1976, and 1981, all of them entitled *Stikhi* (Poems).

The world of Ilyinsky's poetry is a concrete one abounding in figures, objective visual thinking being of central importance. The classically romantic tradition, refracted by ACMEIST and post-FUTURIST tendencies, serves as the basis of his aesthetics. R. Pletnyov has characterized Ilyinsky's thinking as phenomenological, with the poet's life and his artistic work as an instance of oneness within a subjectively biographical world-view. Among the observable foreign influences on Ilyinsky are Hölderlin, Goethe, and Ossian. The problem of time (time seen as non-existent, as in Bergson and Proust) is one of Ilyinsky's leading themes, for him, culture and remembrance are of one and the same nature. Ilyinsky presents life as a logical and organic complex, with unobtrusive religious feeling as the background. A craftsman of the poetic word and of rhythmically closed form, Ilyinsky unites idealist philosophy with a lucid modernist perception of the visual arts.

Secondary literature: I. Chinnov, Review of *Stikhi* (1966), *Novoe russkoe slovo*, 3 Feb. 1967. R. Pletnev, "O poezii i stikhakh O. Il'inskogo," *Novoe russkoe slovo*, 29 Jan. 1967. A. Rannit, Review of *Stikhi* (1966), *SEEJ* 14 (1970), pp. 364–65. Yu. Terapiano, Review of *Stikhi* (1960), *Russkaya mysl'* (Paris), 18 March 1961.   A. R.

Imaginism, see IMAGISM.

Imagism, literary avant-garde group (1919–27), headed by the poet and theoretician, Vadim SHERSHENEVICH. Russian imagism made its appearance on the literary scene with the publication of the manifesto, "Declaration" (Deklaratsiya), in the magazine, *Sirena* (30 January 1919), signed by the three founding members—Vadim Shershenevich, Sergei ESENIN, and Anatoly MARIENGOF as well as Ryurik IVNEV and the painters, Boris Erdman and G. Yakulov. Later, other poets joined the group. Among them were Aleksandr Kusikov, Ivan Gruzinov, Matvei Roizman, and Nikolai ERDMAN. This group resided in Moscow, but a few years later a second group of imagists appeared in Petrograd (see below).

"Declaration" is more revealing of the imagist preoccupation with securing a place for themselves in the competitive literary arena, than of their literary program. The manifesto is mostly a harsh attack against FUTURISM (the movement they intended to replace), the main charge being (contrary to all evidence) that futurist poetry was based merely on content and disregarded all problems of form. The imagists declared that, unlike the futurists, they believed in "the representation of life through the image and the rhythm of images," and that they will write their poems in the "*vers libre* of images." These fundamental principles of imagist poetics are not developed in "Declaration." However, they recur and are discussed in subsequent manifestoes and individual works, especially in the writings of Shershenevich. Although a precise and programmatic formulation of imagism was never issued, the imagists often dealt with problems of literary theory. The main theoretical contributions by individual poets are: Shershenevich's $2 \times 2 = 5$ (1920), Mariengof's *Buyan-Island* (Buyan-ostrov, 1920), Esenin's *Maria's Keys* (Klyuchi Marii, 1920), and Gruzinov's *The Basics of Imagism* (Imazhinizma osnovnoe, 1921). Another point which the imagists constantly stressed in their ongoing verbal war against the futurists was that the latter had turned into a conservative group, supportive of the government, while the imagists themselves valued their independence, their revolutionary ideals, and their "romanticism."

The Russian imagists regarded every word in its poetic function as a potential image (the "word-image"). They believed that by juxtaposing selected words in a "chain of images" the word's potential would be realized. Consequently, the concept of image did not carry any visual or ornamental connotation for the poets of this group. Rather, it was an extension of the perception of the poetic word as a phonetic entity, which can be traced back to the works of A. VESELOVSKY and A. POTEBNYA. It informed the SYMBOLIST aesthetics and inspired the radical experiments of the futurists. While the Russian imagists shared the common belief that the image contained in the word is the very essence of poetry, they differed considerably in their creative works. However, it is possible to indicate some general features of imagism: (1) bold experimentation with rhythm and rhyme; (2) use of unusual and striking imagery, primarily shock effect images with obscene or blasphemous associations; (3) an attempt to create a new syntax (through omission of adjectives and verbs); (4) a new prosodic system, the "*vers libre* of images," also called the "catalogue of images" or the "chain of images"; (5) the long "lyrical *poema*," as a favorite genre. Not all of these points were fully realized in the imagists' poetic practice, and not all of them would characterize every individual imagist. However, they do characterize imagism as a whole.

The Russian imagists, like the futurists before them, took into their hands the task of publishing and advertising their works. As a means of publicity, they relied on numerous acts of hooliganism and the consequent scandals. However, while these juvenile pranks helped them to gain notoriety in the literary world, they also distinguished themselves in several worthier endeavors. They founded a publishing house, Imagists (Imazhinisty), and promoted the sale of their publications in two fashionable bookshops. They established the Association of Free Thinkers, designed to serve as a facade for the Order of the Imagists, which could not obtain official recognition from the government; then, within the Association of Free Thinkers the imagists promoted their own activities. They opened a café, The Stable of Pegasus, where they offered intellectual soirées of poetry reading and discussion; later, when the Stable of Pegasus had to close down because of government pressure, the imagists opened another similar establishment, Café Galosh, and after that still another one, The Mouse's Hole. They also rented the movie theater, Liliput.

The imagists issued several collections of verses, among them: *The Foundry of Words* (Plavil'nya slov, 1920), *Us* (My, 1920), *The Peddlers of Happiness* (Korobeiniki schast'ya, 1920), *Golden Boiling Water* (Zolotoi kipyatok, 1921), *The Horse Garden* (Konskii sad, 1921), *The Imagists* (Imazhinisty, 1925). Another worthy undertaking was the publication of the journal, *Gostinitsa dlya puteshest-vuyushchikh v prekrasnom* (An Inn for Travellers in the Beautiful). Only four issues appeared, the first in 1922 and the last in 1924. However, during those years the journal provided a forum not only for poetry and theory, as was the case with previous imagist publications, but also for artists and theatrical figures to voice their views on art. The journal was divided into several sections: manifestoes, poetry, articles, letters, and reviews. Here, besides the imagist poets, one can find artists such as B. Erdman, G. Yakulov, and Fernand Léger, and representatives of the theater such as V. Sokolov and A. Tairov. It is impossible to determine an imagist aesthetics from the pages of *Gostinitsa*, since all the authors display a great degree of individuality. In the same issue there may be two or three contradictory articles, and the poetry may not correspond to the theory. The journal reflects alliances and conflicts within the group, and consequent general changes of direction (as the imagists themselves recognized on several occasions, the group was split into the right wing—Esenin, Kusikov, Gruzinov, and Roizman—and the left wing—Shershenevich, Mariengof, Nikolai and Boris Erdman, and Yakulov). In the first issue, the imagists show a tendency to regress into classicism and nationalism, but later they come back to their typical radical pronouncements in matters of poetics, and to their westernizing outlook. This fact may be explained by the fact that Shershenevich, the leader of the radical wing, did not participate in the first issue, and his presence had some influence on the journal only later.

The year 1924 marks the beginning of the end for the imagists. Sergei Esenin, the most popular and beloved among them, committed suicide in 1925. His death, in the eyes of many, meant the death of imagism, and the authorities took advantage of the situation to discredit the imagists. A distorted view of Esenin and his role in the imagist group was born in those days. Esenin was presented to the public opinion as the country boy with an innate gift for poetry, as a pure soul with a populist and Slavophile bent, and as a passionate lover of the motherland. The authorities explained his association with the imagists by stating that he was co-opted by the group and misled into believing that they shared the same views on poetry. Imagism, supposedly, needed a popular poet such as Esenin in its ranks in order to justify its existence. Finally, the imagists were more or less overtly accused of having driven Esenin to his death. The most recent Western studies on the subject have begun to dismantle the myth of Esenin (which is still alive and well in the USSR). Reputable Western scholars now believe that Esenin was not necessarily the best poet among the imagists, and that he actually benefited from his association with the group. However, his relationship with his fellow imagists was not an easy one. It was complicated by personal rivalry and jealousy (well known is his obsessive attachment to A. Mariengof and his sense of betrayal when the latter married the actress Anna Nikritina), and by a public statement in which Esenin (together with Gruzinov) declared that the imagist group was disbanded (*Pravda*, 8/31/24). This statement was totally arbitrary, since Esenin was not the leader of imagism (as the imagists argued in their rebuttal), and he had even been expelled from the Order by that time. However, the announcement was prophetic, and a few months later, after Esenin's death, imagism began its gradual decline. *The Inn* was terminated, and the number of imagist publications was considerably reduced. Only two collections of poetry, issued in 1926, are worthy of note, Mariengof's *Poems and Poemas, 1922–1926* (Stikhi i poemy, 1922–1926) and Shershenevich's *And Now for a Summary* (Itak itog). In the summer of 1927, the group was dissolved.

There was another group of imagists in Petrograd, less important than the Moscow group. The Petrograd imagists were active from 1922 to 1925. They were headed by Grigory Shmerelson, a protegé of Shershenevich, who before becoming involved with imagism published a collection of verses in a futurist vein. The other members of the group were: Vladimir Richiotti (pseud. of Leonid Turutovich), I. Afanasiev-Solovyov, Semyon Polotsky, and Volf Erlikh. This group published only one collective volume of poetry, *In a Carriage of Inspiration* (V kibitke vdokhnoveniya, 1923), but its individual members published several books. In general, their verses reveal the influence of the Moscow imagists, both in their urbanist, antiaesthetic imagery and in their use of free verse and irregular rhyme. Little is known of the relationship between the two groups. However, that

some collaboration took place is evidenced by a joint collection of poetry by Shmerelson and Shershenevich, *The Fig* (Shish, 1924), and the participation of the Petrograd imagists in the last issue of *Gostinitsa*. Furthermore, Esenin, after his break with the Moscow imagists, sought the support of the Petrograd group, which in turn considered itself honored by their association with such a celebrity.

Soviet critics have generally blasted imagism and considered it irrelevant to the development of Soviet poetry. However, a clear imagist influence may be noted in such movements or groups as the "nichevoki," expressionism, and Futurism in its early stage. Furthermore, some imagist elements infiltrated the works of some proletarian poets and the Smithy (KUZNITSA).

The name, imagism, has been a matter of speculation for many literary historians and critics since it suggests a possible connection with another avant-garde group, the Anglo-American imagists. Russian critics of the 1920s tended to see a greater connection between the Russians and the Anglo-Americans than contemporary critics. The prevalent opinion today is that notwithstanding some superficial similarities, the Russian group did not have any connections with the London imagists. Rather, the name is believed to have an Italian etymology. There is reason to think that the Russian term, "Imaginism" (*imazhinizm*) derives from the Italian word, *immagine* (image). The term was devised by Shershenevich, an admirer and translator of the Italian futurist poet, F. T. Marinetti, several years before the birth of imagism. Marinetti, whom Shershenevich called, "the first imaginist," consistently maintained that "a poem is an uninterrupted series of images (*immagini*)." The choice of the name suggests that Russian imagism is an offspring of Shershenevich's futurist background, rather than a local version of Anglo-American imagism. For this reason, some Western scholars use the term, imaginism, to refer to the Russian movement. However, others prefer the term, imagism (even if it may generate some confusion), in order to stress the movement's connection with the "image" and to avoid any association with the verb "to imagine."

Bibliography: (this bibliography includes only the most recent works on imagism, in English; for the works contemporary of imagism, and/or works by the imagists, see bibliographies in the volumes listed below): A. Lawton, "Shershenevich, Marinetti, and the 'Chain of Images'." *SEEJ* 23 (1979), pp. 203–15. ———, *Vadim Shershenevich: From Futurism to Imaginism*. 1981. V. Markov, *Russian Imagism, 1919–1924*. Giessen, 1980. G. McVay, *Esenin: A Life*. 1976. ———, "Yesenin's Posthumous Fame and the Fate of His Friends," *The Modern Language Review* 67, no. 3 (July 1972), pp. 592–602. N. Å. Nilsson, *The Russian Imaginists*. Stockholm, 1970. C. F. Ponomareff, "The Image Seekers: An Analysis of Imaginist Poetic Theory, 1919–1924," *SEEJ* 12 (1968), pp. 275–96.   A. L.

IMLI, see *INSTITUT MIROVOI LITERATURY.*

Inber, Véra Mikhailovna (1890–1972), poet and writer. The daughter of the owner of an Odessa publishing house, Inber was close to literary and artistic ideas from her earliest years, and, from 1910 onwards, made regular contributions to newspapers and journals. During the years 1910 to 1914 Inber studied in Paris and had her first collection of verse, *Melancholy Wine* (Pechal'noe vino), published there privately in 1914. Inber's early literary endeavors such as this collection and the next one, *Bitter Delight* (Gor'kaya uslada, 1917), reflect the influence of French and Russian SYMBOLISM, although she shortly moved to a more restrained, more narrative style. Inber was in Moscow when the Revolution occurred, spent the Civil War years in Odessa and then moved back to Moscow in 1922. During the early 1920s Inber moved closely with the literary CONSTRUCTIVISTS and, along with Ilya SELVINSKY and Kornely ZELINSKY, made a vital contribution to the activities of the Literary Center of the constructivists, e.g., to their publication *State Plan of Literature* (Gosplan literatury, 1925). From 1924 through 1926 Inber worked as a journalist in Paris, Brussels, and Berlin, but although she travelled widely in the West, she harbored a suspicion of European and American culture while never losing her love of Russia. Inber lacked the experimental impetus of Selvinsky and Zelinsky and, ultimately, preferred a conservative, narrative style for her poetry and stories. In the years 1941 to 1944 Inber lived in Leningrad and her diary of the blockade, *Almost Three Years* (Pochti tri goda, 1946–47) and her long poem *Pulkovo Meridian* (Pulkovskii meridian, 1942–46), for which she received a Stalin Prize, are among the most moving literary evocations of that tragic time. Inber investigated many themes and genres including poetry for children, dramaturgy and even opera libretti.

Works: Izbrannye proizvedeniia. 3 vols. 1958. *Kak ya byla malen'kaya.* 2d ed. 1961. *Vdokhnovenie i masterstvo.* 2d ed. 1961. *Za mnogo let.* 1964.

Translations: One poem in *Modern Russian Poetry*, ed. Vladimir Markov and Merrill Sparks. 1967. Pp. 730–31. *See also Lewanski,* p. 263.

Secondary literature: I. Grinberg, *Vera Inber: Kritiko-biograficheskii ocherk.* 1961. J. E. B.

Institút mirovoí literatúry im. Gór'kogo (IMLI, 1932–), Institute of World Literature, organized on 17 Oct. 1932, in commemoration of the 40th anniversary of M. GORKY's creative activity. The first director of IMLI, Ivan Luppol, author of *The Creative Path of M. Gorky* (Tvorcheskii put' M. Gor'kogo, 1932), designed far-reaching perspectives for his Institute and in 1937 organized Gorky's Archive and a Gorky Museum under the auspices of IMLI. At present the Gorky Archive holds approximately 80,000 documents, and the Museum more than 22,000 items. The main task of IMLI was defined as research in Russian literature, the literatures of the Soviet Republics, and foreign literatures (ancient and modern). IMLI is the center of Gorky studies, Soviet literature, and SOCIALIST REALISM. It holds annual Gorky Conferences (*Gor'kovskie chteniya*). Under the auspices of IMLI, voluminous surveys of English, American, German, and French literature have been published. IMLI has initiated translations of Gide, Thomas Mann, Proust, and other European authors.

While INSTITUT RUSSKOI LITERATURY (IRLI) works primarily on Russian literature of the eleventh to the early twentieth centuries, IMLI concentrates on the early Soviet period and modern times (the works of Gorky, MAYAKOVSKY, ESENIN, SHOLOKHOV). IMLI has published a number of works on literary theory: *Theory of Literature*, vols. 1–3, 1962–64; *Problems of Textual Criticism*, vols. 1–4; *History of Soviet Russian Literature*, vols. 1–3, 1958–61. Since 1957 IMLI, in conjunction with the UNION OF SOVIET WRITERS, has been publishing the journal *Questions of Literature* (Voprosy Literatury).

Bibliography. Sovetskoe literaturovedenie i kritika: Bibliograficheskii ukazatel'. 1969. P. 75. N. Yanevich, "Institut mirovoi literatury v 1930-e–1970-e gody," *Pamyat'* 5(1982), pp. 83–164. N. P.

Institút rússkoi literatúry (*Púshkinskii Dom, IRLI*, 1905–), Institute of Russian Literature (Pushkin House). An Academy institution for the study of Russian literature, organized in 1905 as an archive and museum of Russian literature, in honor of Pushkin. Its first director, Nestor Kotlyarevsky, succeeded in attracting numerous donations and gifts of historical items for it. In 1913 Kotlyarevsky began the publication of the Chronicle of Pushkin House (Vremennik Pushkinskogo Doma). In 1918 Pushkin House became part of the Russian Academy of Sciences. In the first postrevolutionary years it grew into a center for the preservation of Russian culture, and its manuscript department saved many invaluable private archives of Russian writers and artists. In 1922 publication of these materials began, thus building the foundations of modern textual criticism and preparing the future Academy editions of Russian classics (to date twenty-one Academy editions in print).

In 1929, along with other Academy institutions, Pushkin House underwent a purge organized by the Leningrad Regional Committee of the Communist Party. Its director, Academician S. F. Platonov, was discharged, arrested, and exiled; many of its affiliates were sentenced to hard labor. The organizational principles of Pushkin House were changed. During the directorship of A. LUNACHARSKY (1931) it merged with the Institute of Russian Literature. For changes in the Academy structure and purges in Pushkin House, see *Pamyat': Istoricheskii Sbornik* (N.Y. and Paris, 1978, 1980), 1, pp. 386–91; 4, pp. 469–95.

In the 1930s, Pushkin House, a branch of the Soviet Academy of Sciences, widened the scope of Academy publications. Along with the publication of archival materials (*Chronicles of the Pushkin Commission, Literary Heritage*, etc.) it began to study the history, theory and poetics of Russian literature and criticism. Since 1958 Pushkin House has been publishing a professional journal, *Russian Literature*. A complete account of Pushkin House publications and archival holdings can be found in *Pushkinskii Dom: Bibliografiya trudov* (1981).

Bibliography: V. Baskakov, "Iz istorii sozdaniya Pushkinskogo Doma i ego deyatel'nosti v 1905–1917 gg.", *RLit* 1979, no. 3, pp. 97–111. ———, "Pushkinskii Dom v 1918–1930 gg.", *RLit*, 1980, no. 1, pp. 89–100. ———, "IRLI (Pushkinskii Dom) v 1930–45 gg.", *RLit*, 1980, no. 2, pp. 109–21. Loren R. Graham, *The Soviet Academy of Sciences and the Communist Party, 1927–1932.* 1967. N. Izmailov, "Iz vospominanii o Pushkinskom Dome, 1918–1928," *RLit*, 1981, no. 1, pp. 89–106. A. Rostov, "Delo chetyrekh akademikov," *Vozrozhdenie*, 1958, nos. 81–84. N. P.

Instrumentation (instrumentóvka), a term used to describe the effects created by the arrangement of sounds in works of poetry or, less often, prose. Since the number of phonemes in any language is miniscule in comparison to the number of words, some sound repetition is inevitable in any kind of writing. Instrumentation, though, results from a selective and significant interplay of phonemes, which is meant to be perceptible and in some way to enhance the work. The most apparent form of instrumentation is often RHYME, which may furthermore be "enriched"; that is, the sound or sounds immediately preceding the rhyming vowels may be similar or identical. Instrumentation can be achieved through other means as well, such as alliteration, assonance, consonance, and—when entire words rather than just individual phonemes are repeated—anaphora and chiasmus. The rhythmic effect created by the regular alternation of such features as stressed and unstressed syllables (i.e., rhythm) is often considered part of the same phenomenon. Sound repetitions may be more complex and subtle than those created by, say, simple alliteration. In the second line of TYUTCHEV's "Silentium!" ("I chúvstva i mechtý svoí") the four pronounced consonants in the second word recur over the last two words, and the repetitions of the phoneme [i] are also noticeable. As is the case here, repetitions are not always in the same order; there may be inversion or a more complex form of rearrangement. Often groupings of similar sounds, either instead of or in addition to identical sounds, are involved: voiced and unvoiced consonants, different resonants, or related vowel sounds (such as [o] and [u]). Instrumentation may occur within a single line, but it may just as well be spread over several lines or throughout an entire work. The significance of instrumentation varies; at times it is merely one more feature that helps to organize a poem, at others it is closely related to efforts at creating euphony or musicality. Of particular interest are the possible links between sound and meaning. While efforts to specify narrow inherent meanings for particular sounds have been controversial, poets have clearly made efforts to assign semantic significance to given sounds in ways that go beyond the obvious example of onomatopoeia. The repetition of key sounds may suggest relationships between individual words and lines and may also serve to enhance a particular mood or meaning, at least within the context of a given poem. The role played by instrumentation varies greatly from poet to poet and from work to work; it was of special importance for Russian poetry from the 1890s through the 1920s, when such movements as SYMBOLISM, with its special interest in euphony, and futurism, with its advocacy of ZAUM', caused poets to pay renewed attention to the sound elements of their verse.

Bibliography: Dwight L. Bolinger, "Rime, Assonance, and Morpheme Analysis," *Word* 6 (1950), no. 2, pp. 117–36. Osip Brik, "Zvukovye povtory." In *Poetika*, 1–2. 1919. Pp. 58–98. Kiril Taranovsky, "The Sound Texture of Russian Verse in the Light of Phonemic Distinctive Features," *IJSLP* 9 (1965), pp. 114–24. Wladimir Weidlé, *Embriologiya poezii: Vvedenie v fonosemantiku poeticheskoi rechi.* Paris, 1980. B. S.

Intermedia (intermédiya), a comic-satirical interlude in 17th- and 18th-century school drama. While the main body of the spectacle had a serious religious content based on a biblical text and was presented in SLAVONIC, the intermedia featured burlesque humor in the vernacular, often a carnivalesque travesty of the serious part.

Bibliography: A. I. Beletskii, *Starinnyi teatr v Rossii.* 1923. V. Vsevolodskii-Gerngross, *Russkii teatr ot istokov do serediny XVIII v.* 1957.   V. T.

Iósif Vólotsky (Iosif of Volokolamsk, 1439–1515). A leading figure in the religious and political life of Muscovite Russia. He proclaimed the sacred mission of the Muscovite ruler and supported the right of the Church to temporal power and material possessions. Iosif's polemical writings had a decisive impact on the intellectual and literary trends of his time. He was born Iosif Sanin of a noble family in the village of Yazvitsa in the district of Volokolamsk, or Volok (hence "Volotsky") Lamsky. In 1460 he received the tonsure from Pafnuty, abbot of the Borovsk Monastery, whom he succeeded as abbot in 1477. In 1479 Iosif founded a new monastery some eight miles from Volokolamsk. With Iosif's acquisition of power and prestige, his monastery grew to be one of the most influential and wealthiest monasteries in Muscovy. A large part of Iosif's activity was made possible by the active support of Ivan III (1462–1505). In 1507 Vasily III (1505–33) removed the Monastery of Volokolamsk from the jurisdiction of the local prince and placed it under his direct protection. Iosif supported and defended this action, claiming that it protected the monastery from the demands of lay authorities and affirmed the inviolability of monastic possessions.

In his defense of the established order, Iosif did not hesitate to eliminate any form of opposition. He was especially relentless in his determination to crush the "heresy" of the so-called *Zhidovstvuyushchie* (Judaizers). Iosif played a role in all major ecclesiastical decisions of his time, most notably, those taken at the Council of 1503, where he emerged as the leading spokesman of the *Styazhateli* (Possessors) against the party of the *Nestyazhateli* (Non-Possessors). His supporters, referred to as *Osiflyane* (Josephites), came to dominate the religious life of Muscovite Russia.

Among Iosif's many tracts and epistles, two works emerge as true expressions of his ideological attitude, namely, *The Enlightener* (Prosvetitel') and the *Monastic Rule* (Monastyrskii ustav). *The Enlightener,* which consists of an introduction entitled "Tale of the Recent Heresy" (Skazanie o novoyavivsheisya eresi) and sixteen chapters, is a fundamental source of information on the *Zhidovstvuyushchie* up to 1505. In the later portions of *The Enlightener,* Iosif develops to the extreme his views on the absolute nature of the ruler's power, which is granted by God himself. Citing Agapetus, Iosif asserts that "a tsar in his nature is like unto all men, but in power is like unto God almighty."

The *Monastic Rule* has come down to us in two redactions—a short version consisting of eleven chapters and a long redaction made up of nine chapters, which was written just before Iosif's death and is called his *Spiritual Testament* (Dukhovnaya gramota). The *Monastic Rule,* especially in its later redaction, focuses on the formal aspects of monastic life, in particular on the themes of discipline and punishment.

Bibliography: I. U. Budovnits, *Russkaya publitsistika XVI veka.* 1947. Pp. 66–109. I. P. Eremin, "Iosif Volotskii kak pisatel'." In his *Literatura drevnei Rusi: Etyudy i kharakteristiki.* 1966. Pp. 85–199. J. Fennell, "The Attitude of the Josephians and the Trans-Volga Elders to the Heresy of the Judaisers," *SEER* 29 (1951), pp. 486–509. J. Fennell and A. Stokes, *Early Russian Literature.* 1974. Pp. 151–57. N. A. Kazakova and Ya. S. Lur'e, *Antifeodal'nye ereticheskie dvizheniya na Rusi XIV–nachala XVI veka.* 1960. Ya. S. Lur'e, *Ideologicheskaya bor'ba v russkoi publitsistike kontsa XV–nachala XVI veka.* 1960. Pp. 75–284. *Poslaniya Iosifa Volotskogo.* Eds. A. A. Zimin, Ya. S. Lur'e, and I. P. Eremin. 1959. *Prosvetitel', ili Oblichenie eresi zhidovstvuyushchikh. Tvorenie prepodobnogo ottsa nashego Iosifa, igumena Volotskogo.* 4th ed. Kazan, 1904.   R. P.

Ipát'evskaya létopis' (Hypatius Chronicle) see LETOPISI.

IRLI, see *INSTITUT RUSSKOI LITERATURY.*

Ishútin, Nikolaí Andréevich (1840–79), revolutionary, was born in Serdovsk near Saratov, the son of a merchant and a noblewoman. He attended Moscow University, where he took up revolutionary activities. At this time he was an ardent follower of the social philosophy outlined by CHERNYSHEVSKY in the novel, *What Is To Be Done?* Abandoning his studies because they led to a "bourgeois existence," he gave himself over entirely to revolutionary activities of a "populist" type. Becoming more radical as his revolutionary schemes were frustrated, Ishutin adopted the methods of NIHILISM and terror. Within a revolutionary group known simply as The Organization (*Organizatsiya*) and composed largely of declassed students, Ishutin formed a small conspiratorial group called "Hell" (Ad). This secret society exacted the most extreme loyalty and devotion by its members, any of whom might be shot if they committed the slightest breach of discipline. Soon the aim of "Hell" became individual acts of terrorism against state officials, and the Tsar himself. Ishutin hit upon the idea of exaggerating the importance of his tiny circle, to which he gave the pompous, mythical name of "European Revolutionary Committee." One of the group's heroes was the Italian revolutionary Mazzini; Marx's International was considered too moderate. It is possible that D. V. Karakozov, who attempted to assassinate Tsar Alexander II in 1866, collaborated with Ishutin and his group. Ishutin, in fact, was arrested in connection with the Karakozov case. It was later revealed that Ishutin regarded the killing of the head of the Russian state as "destabilizing," a shock which could set off social revolution. Ironically, Ishutin, orphaned as a small child, had been raised by the Karakozov family in Saratov Province.

Ishutin was condemned to death for revolutionary activities but as he was led to the scaffold (not unlike the case of the writer Dostoevsky), the sentence was abruptly commuted to forced labor for life. He died of tuberculosis in a prison hospital in 1879 and, like his collaborator, Karakozov, just before he died, showed signs of insanity.   A. L. W.

Iskandér, see HERZEN.

Iskandér, Fazíl Abdúlevich (1929–   ), poet, short-story writer, and novelist. A native of Georgian Abkhazia, he graduated from the Gorky Literary Institute in 1953 and published his first book of verse, *Mountain Paths* (Gornye puti) in 1957. Subsequent collections soon followed. However, since 1966, Iskander is best known for his prose. He has published numerous short stories, most of which appear in collected volumes, and two novels, *The Goatibex Constellation* (Sozvezdie kozlotura, 1970) and *Sandro from Chegem* (Sandro iz Chegema, 1973). In addition, he has published abroad and contributed to the illegal collection, *Metropol.*

Although Iskander writes in Russian, the bulk of his stories are set in Abkhazia and outlying regions of Georgia. His work, largely autobiographical and narrated in the first person, describes with great charm and humor the exploits of a principal figure, usually the author-narrator and other colorful characters. Characteristically, Iskander's humor is uncomplicated and good-natured. That is to say, with a unique ability for the comic, he is able to shift his focus from human frailties to social evils without arousing offense. This artless quality may be traced to Iskander's early stories which are presented from the illogical, and yet telling viewpoint of a child. In "My Uncle—A Man of High Principles" (Moi dyadya samykh chestnykh pravil, 1964), for example, a ridiculous little boy who is filled with exaggerated notions of patriotic duty derived from journalistic warnings, concludes that his crazy uncle is a foreign spy. Thus, Iskander makes light of a situation reminiscent of the great purges. In his later work, this innocent tone is best illustrated in his widely acclaimed novel, *The Goatibex Constellation,* in which he provides a highly amusing description of an overzealous bureaucrat's campaign to gain Party support for the proliferation of a new superbreed of animal, the goat-ibex. Although the novel is essentially a political satire of the Khrushchev era, directed at Trofim Lysenko and his Michurinist school of agrobiology, the trials and tribulations of our young author, and his bouts with nostalgia and his lyrical digressions are given equal consideration. A growing number of Iskander's works display modifications of his narrative style. For example, his second novel, *Sandro from Chegem* is a series of anecdotes and portrait sketches featuring the customs and folklore of the Caucasus. Further, while his love story, "The House on the Lane" (Dom v pereulke, 1966) takes place in Abkhazia, it is narrated in the third person, basically non-humorous, and involves characters unfamiliar to the author.

Works: Trinadtsatyi podvig Gerakla, Sovetskaya Rossiya, 1966. Zapretnyi plod, Molodaya gvardiya, 1966. Pervoe delo, Detskaya literatura, 1972. Sozvezdie kozlotura. In *Derevo detstva, 1970. Sandro iz Chegema, Novyi mir, 1973, nos. 8–11.*

Translations: The Goatibex Constellation. Trans. Helen Burlingame. Ann Arbor, 1975. "Kocheruky." Trans. Marcia Satin. In *Ardis Anthology: Recent Russian Literature. 1975.*

Secondary literature: Vickie Babenko, "Fazil Iskander: An Examination of His Satire," *RLJ* 106 (1976), pp. 131–42. Edward J. Brown, *Russian Literature since the Revolution. 1982.* Helen Burlingame, "The Prose of Fazil Iskander," *RLT* 14 (1976), pp. 123–65.

B. A.

Iskra (The Spark), illustrated satirical journal published in Petersburg from 1859 to 1873 (weekly 1859–73, twice weekly 1873). Founded by the caricaturist N. A. Stepanov and the poet V. S. KUROCHKIN. Its pointed social satire and witty caricatures rapidly made *Iskra* one of the most popular publications of the 1860s. Although not among the journal's regular contributors, DOBROLYUBOV, NEKRASOV, SALTYKOV-SHCHEDRIN, and HERZEN ("Ogurchikov") all published there. After 1861, *Iskra* adopted an increasingly radical stance, critical of the 1861 reforms, and allied itself with SOVREMENNIK in the journal polemics of the period. Hounded by difficulties with the censorship, from 1870 on *Iskra* appeared without illustrations and ceased publication in 1873.

C. T. N.

Isocolon. In Greek rhetoric the term isocolon referred to a formal device which consisted in the use of series of *equal cola*, that is, syntactic segments with an identical number of either syllables or words. The device was known to Latin rhetoricians, who called it *compar* or, more generally, *exaequatum membris* (*membrum = colon*). The same device was also used in medieval Latin prose. Riccardo Picchio has employed the term to describe similar rhythmo-syntactic structures which occur in a large number of Old Russian and Balkan Slavic texts. Old Russian "isocolism" is characterized by series of syntactic segments which contain an equal number of stresses. The place of accentuation is not relevant and each stressed unit may consist of either a single word or a word plus clitic(s). It is important to emphasize that this type of rhythmo-syntactic organization was based on isotonism rather than isosyllabism. Because the number and not the place of accents was important, an isocolic scheme could be preserved when texts were transferred from an area with a different accentual system (as in the case of the transfer of texts from the Balkan Slavic territory to the Russian land).

Isocolic series might be of different types: "plain" (2/2/2/2 or 5/5/5/5); "alternant" (2/3/2/3 or 3/5/3/5); and "framed" (3/4/4/3 or 5/5 3/4/3/4 5/5). The individuality of each colon depends on its logical autonomy and can be emphasized by formal markers such as rhyme, alliteration, and phono-semantic cross signals. A great number of these formal variations could easily fit any syntactic structure marked by an isocolic grid.

Isocolic structures were used in diverse ways by various writers in different periods. They were frequently an essential component of new stylistic trends such as *pletenie sloves* (word weaving). Although a basic and consistent type of segmentation in Old Russian prose texts, isocolic structures are also to be found in the works of modern Russian writers such as A. S. PUSHKIN, N. V. GOGOL, F. M. DOSTOEVSKY, and I. E. BABEL. In addition, they might have played a part in the formation of modern Russian verse. Isocolic regularity and embryonic verse structures coexist in a number of 17th-century texts. In the middle of the 18th century V. K. TREDIAKOVSKY presented the isocolon as an old prose feature in contradistinction to his new verse structures which recognized the foot as the basic unit of the line. He observed that even though "the clauses of the so-called rhetorical isocolon are also divided into almost equal segments, still these clauses are not verse."

Bibliography: M. Colucci, "Note su L'armata a cavallo." *Spicilegio Moderno* 3/4–5 (1974); pp. 3–44. ———, "E possibile una constitutio textus della 'Zadonščina'?" *Spicilegio Moderno* 7 (1977); pp. 36–62. M. Colucci and A. Danti, eds., *Daniil Zatočnik. Slovo e Molenie.* (Studia Historica et Philologica, no. 4.) Florence, 1977. Pp. 197–243. E. Hercigonja, *Srednjovjekovna književnost.* Povijest

hrvatske književnosti, no. 2. Zagreb, 1975. Pp. 140–86. R. Picchio, "On the Prosodic Structure of the Igor' Tale," *SEEJ* 16 (1972); pp. 147–62. ———, "The Isocolic Principle in Old Russian Literature." In *Slavic Poetics: Essays in Honor of Kiril Taranovsky.* Ed. R. Jakobson, C. H. van Schooneveld, and D. S. Worth. 1973. Pp. 299–331. ———, "Vărkhu izokolnite strukturi v srednovekovnatá slavjanska proza." *Literaturna misăl* 24, no. 3 (1980); pp. 75–107. ———, "Simmetrie prosodiche in Dostoevskij (Osservazioni sulla tradizione medievale nella prosa russa)." In *Dostoevskij nella coscienza d'oggi.* Ed. S. Graciotti. Florence, 1981. Pp. 27–46. M. Ziolkowski, "The Style and Authorship of the *Discourse on Dmitrij Ivanovič Donskoj.*" Ph.D. diss., Yale University, 1978.

H. G.

Istómin, Karión (ca. 1650–1717), poet and pedagogue. A monk, Istomin was a disciple of SIMEON POLOTSKY, whose work he continued after the latter's death in 1680. While serving with the Moscow state typography (Pechatnyi dvor) from 1679 to 1701 as a scribe, proofreader, and eventually as its head, he translated a variety of works from the Latin and authored a number of schoolbooks and didactic works, such as a "Large Primer" (Bol'shoi bukvar', 1696) and an encyclopedia of learning, covering grammar, poetics, arithmetic, astrology, etc., under the title *Polis*, both in rhymed syllabic verse. He also wrote rhymed prayers, epitaphs, and exhortations. Like his colleague Silvestr MEDVEDEV, Istomin was a supporter of Sofya Alekseevna, whom he addressed in panegyric verse during her regency. Unlike Medvedev, he managed to survive the transfer of power from her to Peter I (to whom he had at one time addressed a "Book of Instruction").

Bibliography: I. P. Eremin, "Karion Istomin." In *Istoriya russkoi literatury.* Vol. 2, pt. 2. 1948. Pp. 355–60.

V. T.

Iván IV Vasílievich (1530–84), one of the major and most controversial figures in Russian history. Ivan had a decisive impact on the development of Muscovite culture in general and Muscovite literature in particular. With the death of Vasily III in 1533, Ivan nominally became Grand Prince at the age of three. His childhood and adolescence were dominated by his fear of the boyars who sought to limit princely power in Muscovy. From 1547, when he proclaimed himself "Tsar," Ivan asserted his imperial majesty against the boyars. He began to act as the "terrible" (*groznyi*) monarch whom subsequent generations would either celebrate or condemn as a mythical symbol of absolute power. During his long reign, radical changes took place in the social order and the political, religious, economic, and cultural fabric of Russia. Ivan dominated the stage as the military leader who conquered Kazan and whose power extended to Siberia, the Muscovite sovereign who dreamt of ruling the Polish-Lithuanian Commonwealth, the Tsar who combined the contrasting majesties of Christian autocrat and Tatar khan, and the ruler who, by supporting the followers of IOSIF VOLOTSKY, made of the Russian Church an instrument of his *raison d'état.* At the same time, Ivan asserted himself as the political reformer of Muscovite society, the cruel and merciless opponent of the boyars, the inspirer of a new class of nobility (*dvoryanstvo*), and the codifier of church and state law through his STOGLAV (Book of One Hundred Chapters) and *Sudebnik* (Code of Law).

Different opinions have been advanced as to Ivan's literacy and sophistication. It appears that Ivan took an active part in polemical writing and was directly involved in the production of several official (or semi-official) works, including the *Kniga stepennaya tsarskogo rodosloviya* (Book of Degrees of the Tsar's Genealogy) (see STEPENNAYA KNIGA). Modern scholarship has devoted special attention to Ivan's *Perepiska* (Correspondence) with Prince Andrei Mikhailovich KURBSKY. In June 1564, Kurbsky accepted the protection of Sigismund, King of Poland and Grand Prince of Lithuania, and participated in a military campaign against Muscovy. The *Perepiska*, shortly initiated by Kurbsky, expresses the contrasting views of two leading public figures in Muscovy, namely, the Grand Prince and the most learned representative of the boyar aristocracy. Ivan's two letters to Kurbsky reveal stylistic features which reflect his personal character. As Kurbsky's interlocutor, he is adept at playing with irony, arrogance, pathos, a sense of majesty, and Christian piety.

The texts of the *Perepiska* have come down to us in 17th-century codices. Whether and to what extent these codices preserve the "original" phrasing allegedly penned by Ivan and Kurbsky remains an open question. It is extremely difficult to trace the history of textual changes within what might well be an "open tradition," that is, a tradition characterized by the method of free scriptorial intervention typical of Old Russian textual transmission. Whatever the precise contribution of Ivan and Kurbsky might have been to the formation of these letters, the texts that make up the *Perepiska* are the expression of an ideological debate which was not limited to their time but which would endure well into the 17th century and in which Ivan and Kurbsky would play highly symbolic roles.

Of no less importance for the study of Ivan's personality and literary style are his *poslaniya* (epistles) addressed to, among others, the abbot of the Kirillo-Belozersky Monastery, Jan Rokyta, a minister of the Czech Brethren, Vasily Gryaznoi, Elizabeth I, Queen of England, Johann III, King of Sweden, and Stefan Batory, King of Poland. From the late 16th century on, succeeding generations have been fascinated by Ivan's life and his time. Both in Russia and the West, posterity has made of him a very popular literary subject, the symbol of an age.

Bibliography: I. U. Budovnits, *Russkaya publitsistika XVI veka*. 1947. Pp. 280–96. J. Fennell, ed. and trans., *The Correspondence between Prince A. M. Kurbsky and Tsar Ivan of Russia 1564–1569*. 1955. J. Fennell and A. Stokes, *Early Russian Literature*. 1974. Pp. 173–90. E. Keenan, *The Kurbskii-Groznyi Apocrypha. The Seventeenth-Century Genesis of the "Correspondence" Attributed to Prince A. M. Kurbskii and Tsar Ivan IV*. 1971. D. S. Likhachev, ed., *Perepiska Ivana Groznogo s Andreem Kurbskim*. 1979. D. S. Likhachev and Ya. S. Lur'e, eds., *Poslaniya Ivana Groznogo*. 1951. B. Nørretranders, *The Shaping of Czardom under Ivan Groznyj*. Copenhagen, 1964. R. G. Skrynnikov, *Ivan Groznyi*. 1975. V. Tumins, ed., *Tsar Ivan IV's Reply to Jan Rokyta*. (Slavistic Printings and Reprintings, no. 84.) The Hague-Paris, 1971. N. N. Zarubin, *Biblioteka Ivana Groznogo. Rekonstruktsiya i bibliograficheskoe opisanie*. 1982.   R. P.

Ivánov, Geórgy Vladímirovich (1894–1958), poet, prose writer, essayist, memoirist and literary critic. Ivanov started his literary career under most auspicious circumstances. At the age of eighteen, being enlisted in the St. Petersburg Cadet Corps and after a short flirtation with Ego-FUTURISM, he published his first collection of poetry and was formally accepted into the the POETS' GUILD (Tsekh poetov), the predominantly ACMEIST association, then dominated by GUMILYOV. His further books received critical acclaim from such various quarters as BLOK, BRYUSOV, and Gumilyov himself. He became a familiar figure in the St. Petersburg bohemian artistic milieu. In 1921 he married the poetess I. ODOEVTSEVA and the next year they emigrated and settled in Paris. Soon he began to exercise a significant influence within the Russian émigré community there, having joined the literary circle *Zelyonaya lampa* (The Green Lamp), founded by D. MEREZHKOVSKY and Z. HIPPIUS, and became, together with G. ADAMOVICH, the principal figure of the so-called Parisian Note (PARIZHSKAYA NOTA). Never regularly employed and having made many illwishers through his *penchant pour épatage*, Ivanov led the last years of his life in semi-starvation, was forced to move to a nursing home and died there in misery and desperation. Only recently has he begun to be recognized as one of the leading Russian poets of the 20th century.

Ivanov's emigration conveniently divides his work into two periods. The Russian period (1912–23) manifests his attraction to a kind of ornamental poetry, however skillful and ingenious. Affinities with SEVERYANIN and KUZMIN can be traced, and a preoccupation with details and particulars, characteristic of the Acmeist poetics. The manner is capricious, here and there sparkling with charming though slightly perverse naiveté. Praising highly the formal mastery of Ivanov's second book, *The Chamber* (Gornitsa, 1914), Blok writes: "Listening to such verse . . ., one can start weeping . . . about the fact that there can exist such frightening lines about nothing." In his later period, having fully appreciated his tragic emigration experience, Ivanov grew immensely as a poet. Already in *The Roses* (Rozy, 1931) his artistic power goes far beyond the narrow limits of the "Parisian note." In *A Portrait Without Resemblance* (Portret bez skhodstva, 1950) and in his final chef d'oeuvre, *Posthumous Diary* (Posmertnyi dnevnik), his subject matter becomes human existence in its ultimate and irreconcilable despair verging on the apocalyptic. Ivanov's lyrical hero is a man of two worlds, of Russia and exile (the nostalgic vision of St. Petersburg constantly haunts his imagination), of an irrevocable past and a terrifying future, a self-mocked mocker, for even his own art—with the very sublime meaning it implies—is of doubtful value. He is totally conscious of his mortality: "It may be that as a poet I shall not die, / But I am dying as a human being." (Dopustim, kak poet ya ne umru / Zato kak chelovek ya umirayu.) Death makes nonsense of the universe and provides a sufficient reason to reject the world and its alleged creator. Ivanov's principal philosophical preoccupation is thus theodicy, a major theme in Russian classical literature, poignantly introduced by Lermontov, who was undoubtedly on many occasions one of the sources of his inspiration. Ivanov's torment is akin to the "rebellion" of a Dostoevskian hero.

This constitutes the psychological basis of the nihilistic relativism of which Ivanov was often accused. However, the authentic and passionate expression of his personal and universal torture overshadows all pragmatic or ethical implications and suggests an "elective affinity" with the French *poètes maudits*, especially Rimbaud and Verlaine. Ivanov's poetry, though replete with echoes and allusions, is never rhetorical or declarative. On the contrary, his voice is "whispering," as R. GUL aptly phrased it. It was the same critic who perceptively noticed Ivanov's affiliation with the literary legacies of ANNENSKY and ROZANOV, and with their relaxed, subdued, and intimate tone. Ivanov displays this tone with virtuosity in a great variety of technical means. In Ivanov's prose work *Disintegration of the Atom* (Raspad atoma, 1938), the intermingling of shocking and tender descriptions caused an outrage similar to the reaction to the early novels of Henry Miller. It prefigures, however, much of the later aesthetic search of such authors as, for example, Michel Leiris. The ambitious novel *The Third Rome* (Tretii Rim) was never finished. Ivanov's memoirs, *Petersburg Winters* (Peterburgskie zimy, 1928), are a creation not factual but mythopoeic and because of this caused a controversy and a series of misunderstandings.

Works: Otplytie na ostrov Tsiteru. 1912. *Pamyatnik slavy*. 1915. *Veresk*. 1916. *Sady*. 1921. *Lampada*. 1922. *Otplytie na ostrov Tsiteru*. 1937. *Peterburgskie zimy*. 2d ed. 1952. *Stikhi 1943–1958*. 1958. *Sobranie stikhotvorenii*. 1975. *Izbrannye stikhi*. 1980.

Translations: Modern Russian Poetry. Ed. Vladimir Markov and Merrill Sparks. 1967. Pp. 408–27. *Russian Poetry: The Modern Period*. Ed. John Glad and Daniel Weissbort. 1978. Pp. 279–83.

Secondary literature: I. Agushi, "The Poetry of G. Ivanov," *Harvard Slavic Studies* 5 (1970), pp. 109–58 (has bibliography of works by Ivanov). P. Bitsilli, "Georgii Ivanov, Otplytie na ostrov Tsiteru," *Sovremennye zapiski* 64 (1937), p. 458. V. Blinov, "Proklyatyi poet Peterburga," *Novyi zhurnal* 142 (1981), pp. 66–87. R. Gul', "Georgii Ivanov," *Novyi zhurnal* 42 (1955), pp. 110–21. N. Gumilev, *Pis'ma o russkoi poezii* (1923). In his *Sobranie sochinenii* (1962–1968). Vol. 4. Pp. 292–93, 341–43. Vladimir Markov, "Georgij Ivanov, Stixi 1943–1958," *SEEJ* 17 (1959), pp. 286–87. P. Potemkin, "Georgii Ivanov, Sady," *Novosti literatury* 1 (1922), p. 55.   V. B.

Ivánov, Vsévolod Vyacheslávovich (1895–1963), prose writer and dramatist. Born in Lebyazh'e, a village in the Semipalatinsk region, the son of a teacher, Ivanov left home as a teenager and wandered throughout Siberia, the Urals, and Kazakhstan. Like GORKY, he supported himself by working as a laborer, sailor, actor, dervish, and at other odd jobs. He began publishing in 1915. A fellow traveler, Ivanov was affiliated with the Cosmists, a subgroup of the Proletarian Writers, and the SERAPION BROTHERHOOD.

Ivanov's best known work, *Armored Train No. 14–69* (novella 1922, play 1927) is the central part of a trilogy. Together with *The Partisans* (1921) and *Colored Winds* (1922), it deals with the civil war. This, like a number of his works written during the 1920s, is set in Siberia and the Far East and describes the Red Partisans. Filled with violence and cruelty, the narrative of *The Armored Train* is fragmented; its imagery is visual, and its style laconic. By avoiding first person narrative, and by using the cinematographic device of presenting events through a series of rapidly shifting still images,

Ivanov achieves emotional distancing. This is reinforced by the inclusion of material such as statistics, lists, reports, songs, and sounds which provide the narrative structure with a rich and varied texture.

After 1930 Ivanov conformed to the demands of SOCIALIST REALISM by simplifying his style and in his selection of subject matter. His most interesting work in this period is the autobiographical novel *Adventures of a Fakir* (1934–35), rewritten and published in 1960 as *We are Going to India*, in which he portrays his experiences as a circus performer. In *Parkhomenko* (1939), an idealized biography of a civil war general, Ivanov returned to the civil war theme. *On the Battlefield of Borodino* (1943) and *During the Taking of Berlin* (1946) are his major contributions to World War II literature. His reminiscences, *Meetings with Maksim Gorky*, were published in 1947.

Ivanov's works are usually set in exotic regions of Central Asia and the Far East. The characters are passionate and violent, and represent a mixture of East and West. His early prose is ornamental, colorful, and inventive; the dialogues are realistic and colloquial, with careful attention to form and style. Often apolitical, the stories are dominated by primitive emotions which unleash animalistic passions and drives, resulting in violence, brutality and cruelty. By contrast, his later works (1930 and after) are relatively tame, and less interesting.

Works: Sobranie sochinenii. 7 vols. 1928–31. *Sobranie sochinenii.* 8 vols. 1958–60. *Sobranie sochinenii.* 1973. *Sed'moi bereg. Rasskazy.* 1922, 1981. *Sonety.* Kharbin, 1978 (reprint of 1930). *P'esy.* 1979. *Tsvetnye vetra, povest'.* Petersburg, 1980 (reprint of 1922 ed.). *Chudesnye pokhozhdeniya portnogo Ivana Fokina.* 1980. *Dikie lyudi, Rasskazy.* Ann Arbor, Mich. 1980.

Translations: The Saga of the Sergeant. New York, 1932, 1966. *Armored Train 14–69 (A Play in Eight Scenes).* Trans. Gibson-Cowan and A. Grant. New York, 1933. *The Trans-Siberian Express.* Moscow, 1933. *The Adventures of a Fakir.* New York, 1935; Connecticut, 1975. *I Live a Queer Life. An Extraordinary Autobiography.* London, 1936. *Parkhomenko.* Moscow, 1959. *The Islanders.* Ann Arbor, 1978.

Secondary literature: E. J. Brown, *Russian Literature Since the Revolution.* 1982. Pp. 74–75. A. Fadeev, "O tvorchestve V. V. Ivanova." In *Za tridtsat' let.* 1957. V. Polonskii, "O tvorchestve Vsevoloda Ivanova," *Novyi mir* 1 (1929). *Russkie Sovetskie pisateli-prozaiki.* Vol. 2. 1964. M. Shcheglov, "Vsevolod Ivanov." In his *Literaturno-kriticheskie stat'i.* 1958. N. Yanovskii, *Vsevolod Ivanov.* Novosibirsk, 1956. N. Zaitsev, *Dramaturgiya Vs. Ivanova.* 1962.

H. S.

Ivánov, Vyacheslav Ivánovich (1866–1949), poet, critic, and scholar, was born 28 February 1866 in Moscow. He lost his father, a minor government official, at the age of five and was brought up by his mother, a deeply religious woman. In 1886, having received a scholarship to study the Classics at Berlin University, Ivanov became a student of the great historian Theodor Mommsen. He wrote a thesis on the Roman fiscal system under his direction. Later his main interest in classical philology, in the cult of Dionysos, led to a doctoral dissertation, *Dionysos and Pre-Dionysianism* (1923). A divorce from his first wife and eventual marriage to the writer Lidiya Zinovyeva-Annibal led to years of peregrination, then to the establishment of a brilliant literary salon in Petersburg, the famous *bashnya* (tower), in 1905. After the publication of his first book of verse, *Lodestars* (Kormchie zvezdy, 1902), Ivanov became one of the leaders of the SYMBOLIST movement and soon its principal theorist. In 1907 Ivanov's wife died and he eventually married her daughter from her first marriage, Vera. After Vera's death in 1920, Ivanov accepted a professorship of the Classics at Baku University. In 1924 he finally received permission to leave Russia with his children. Ivanov spent the rest of his life in Italy. He held a professorship of Russian literature at the University of Pavia from 1926 to 1934. He converted to Catholicism in 1926. In 1934 Ivanov was elected professor of Slavic literatures by the University of Florence, but the government failed to approve his appointment. Ivanov then moved to Rome and lived there until his death on 16 July 1949, active as a poet and scholar until the last day of his life.

Ivanov's Neoplatonic philosophy and aesthetic theory are derived from Goethe, German idealist philosophy, and Vladimir SOLOVYOV. Nietzsche is a major influence in some areas of Ivanov's

oeuvre. Ivanov saw life as a process in which the Godhead manifests itself in an ascending hierarchy of forms, with the artist's inner vision (Ivanov uses the term *forma formans*) at the summit of this hierarchy. In the celebrated dialogue, "Correspondence from Two Corners" (1920), between M. O. GERSHENZON and Ivanov, the latter asserts his faith in the continuity of human culture and an ascending historical teleology, ruled by a divine principle, and rejects the evidence, presented by his opponent, of the current decline of civilization and the seemingly haphazard quality of its development. Ivanov's aesthetic, stated in essays gathered in the volumes *Following the Stars* (Po zvezdam, 1909) and *Furrows and Landmarks* (Borozdy i mezhi, 1916), perceives the creative imagination as a quintessential form of energy, engaged in a dialectic movement *a realibus ad realiora*. A work of art is the realization of human striving for the divine and for harmony with the cosmos. Ivanov sees every form of individuation (Titanism, solipsism, mangodhood) as something to be overcome by a principle of universal community (*vselenskaya obshchina*), one of whose expressions is the choral drama (*khorovoe deistvo*) of classical tragedy. Ivanov advocated a revival of the drama as a public religious function with active audience participation ("Wagner and Dionysian Drama," 1905, and "On Action and Drama" [O deistvii i deistve], 1919).

The poetry of Ivanov's earlier collections, *Lodestars* (1902), *Translucence* (Prozrachnost', 1904), *Eros* (1907), *Cor ardens* (1911), and *Tender Secret* (Nezhnaya taina, 1912), is manneristic, often esoteric, and sometimes hermetic. It features epigraphs and echoes from the classics of antiquity, Dante, Goethe, Byron, Pushkin, etc., as well as frequent allusions to classical mythology, archaisms, manneristic conceits (such as calling falling stars "the tears of eternity"), cosmic and elementary imagery (such as the "inner sky" and the "inner sea"), Mediterranean landscapes, and Neoplatonic or Neohellenic ideas. This poetry is closest perhaps to that of the later Goethe, who had a pervasive influence on Ivanov. Some of Ivanov's poems are written in classical meters, such as the alcaic and sapphic strophe. Some resemble Pindaric odes. Ivanov's favorite form, however, was the sonnet.

In the years of turmoil and suffering after the Revolution Ivanov developed a more personal lyric voice. His cycles of twelve *Winter Sonnets* (Zimnie sonety), written between Christmas 1919 and February 1920, and nine sonnets *De profundis amavi*, written in the summer of 1920, are acknowledged to be the summit of Ivanov's art. After his emigration, Ivanov wrote relatively little poetry, but his nine Roman sonnets, written upon his arrival in Rome in 1924, again display his virtuosic mastery of the sonnet form. Ivanov concluded his career as a lyric poet with another burst of creativity, the poems of his *Roman Diary* (Rimskii dnevnik, 1944). The poetry of Ivanov's advanced years is characterized by a limpid simplicity, sparing use of poetic devices, and restrained rhythms.

Ivanov also explored the dramatic genre. His tragedies *Tantalus* (1905) and *Prometheus* (written in 1916, published 1919) follow the form of Greek tragedy. Their plots are restatements of classical myths in terms of Ivanov's philosophy, while their structure serves as an illustration of Ivanov's ideas about the ascent and descent of the spirit, where descent to the reality of incarnation must complement the soaring of the spirit toward the ideal.

Ivanov's posthumously published *Tale of Tsarevich Svetomir, as Told by a Holy Monk* (Povest' o Svetomire tsareviche: Skazanie startsa-inoka), parts of which were completed, from Ivanov's drafts, by Olga Deschartes, editor of Ivanov's *Collected Works*, is a unique work. Stylized to read like a medieval romance (a *povest'* or *skazanie*), *The Tale of Tsarevich Svetomir* is also a religious allegory, a recapitulation of the imagery, the leitmotifs, the visions, and the concepts of Russian symbolism, as well as an account of Ivanov's own searchings, strivings, and ultimate arrival at a mature and secure faith.

Ivanov was a masterful translator of poetry, translating Pindar, Alcaeus, Sappho, Aeschylus, Dante, Petrarch, Goethe, Novalis, Byron, and Baudelaire, and others. He was also a remarkable literary critic and scholar, with major contributions to the interpretation of Pushkin, Gogol, and Dostoevsky. In his essays on Dostoevsky, collected in English under the title *Freedom and the Tragic Life* (1952), Ivanov sought to interpret Dostoevsky as a tragic artist and to demonstrate the mythmaking and theurgic power of his "novel-tragedies."

Works: Sobranie sochinenii. Ed. Olga Deschartes and D. V. Ivanov. 1971– . (Three volumes have appeared so far.) *Svet vechernii.* (Poems) Introd. Sir Maurice Bowra; commentary O. Deschartes. Ed. Dimitri Ivanov. 1962.

Translations: Freedom and the Tragic Life: A Study in Dostoevsky. 1971. For translations of Ivanov's poetry, *see Lewanski,* p. 265. Also, "The Winter Sonnets." Trans. Mary Jane White. In *Russian Poetry: The Modern Period.* Ed. John Glad and Daniel Weissbort. 1978. Pp. 169–72.

Secondary literature: S. Averintsev, "Poeziya Vyacheslava Ivanova," *VLit* 19 (1975), no. 8, pp. 145–92. Maria Banerjee, "The Narrator and His Masks in Vyacheslav Ivanov's Tale of Tsarevich Svetomir," *CASS* 12 (1978), pp. 274–82. Armin Hetzer, *Vjačeslav Ivanovs Tragödie Tantal: Eine literarhistorische Interpretation.* Munich, 1972. I. V. Koretskaya, "O 'solnechnom' tsikle Vyacheslava Ivanova," *IAN* 37 (1978), pp. 54–60. Albert Leong, "The *Zimnie sonety* of Vyacheslav Ivanov," *Pacific Coast Philology* 6 (1971), pp. 43–49. Aleksis Rannit, "Vyacheslav Ivanov and His *Vespertine Light:* Notes from My Critical Diary of 1966," *RLT* 4 (1972), pp. 265–88. Robert H. Stacy, "The Poetry of Vjačeslav Ivanov: Some Critical Comments." In *Symbolae in Honorem Georgii Y. Shevelov.* Ed. W. E. Harkins et al. Munich, 1971. Pp. 383–90. Carin Tschöpl, *Vjačeslav Ivanov: Dichtung und Dichtungstheorie.* Munich, 1968. James West, *Russian Symbolism: A Study of Vyacheslav Ivanov and the Russian Symbolist Aesthetic.* 1970.   V. T.

Ivanóv-Razúmnik, R. V. (pseudonym of Ivanóv, Razúmnik Vasilievich, 1878–1946), ideologue and literary critic. Born into a gentry family and educated at St. Petersburg University, Ivanov-Razumnik is best known as a sponsor of the Scythian movement, one of the "fellow-traveler" groups of the early 20th century. According to Ivanov-Razumnik, the Russians were (in pseudo-ethnological terms) a half-Asiatic, half-European people; following the Revolution, which they welcomed as a blood-bath that would wash away the harmful effects of years of European influence, the Scythians would be free to follow their own destiny. Of the writers associated with this movement, Aleksandr BLOK is the most important (see his poem, "Scythians"), while Evgeny ZAMYATIN subjected Scythianism to harsh criticism. Ivanov-Razumnik's interest in socio-ideological problems is also evident in his once popular *History of Russian Social Thought* (1907). As a literary critic, he noted essential differences between the DECADENTS and the SYMBOLISTS; appreciated BELY's novel, *Peterburg;* pointed out the shallowness of ARTSYBASHEV's novel, *Sanin,* and of the writings of KUPRIN; and distinguished (in the manner of BELINSKY) between the true artist, who "renders" (*pokazyvaet*) reality, and the belletrist, who merely "tells about" (*rasskazyvaet*) reality. In the field of politics, Ivanov-Razumnik was early associated with the Social Revolutionaries and was arrested and imprisoned on numerous occasions both before and after the Revolution. Arrested and exiled several times between 1921 and 1941, he was finally set free and was living in Pushkin when the area was occupied by German troops. Deported to Germany, both he and his wife eventually died there.

Bibliography: See The Memoirs of Ivanov-Razumnik. Tr. P. S. Squire. London, 1965. (With full bibliography.) Brief notice in R. Stacy, *Russian Literary Criticism: A Short History* (1974).

                                            R. H. S.

Ivásk, Yúry Pávlovich (1907– ; has also published under the names George Ivask, B. Afanasievsky, G. Issako, Aleksandr Korn, and over the initials B. A. and Yu. I.), poet, scholar, and essayist, born in Moscow. After the Revolution Ivask's family emigrated to Estonia, where he took a law degree at the University of Tartu. Ivask was displaced to Germany by the War and immigrated to the United States in 1949, where he embarked upon an academic career. He received his Ph.D. in Russian literature from Harvard in 1954 and taught at several American universities until his retirement from the University of Massachusetts (Amherst). Ivask now lives in Amherst. A prolific scholar, Ivask is the author of essays on BELY, DOSTOEVSKY, MANDELSHTAM, PUSHKIN, and TSVETAEVA, among others, a monograph on LEONTIEV, which appeared in VOZROZH-DENIE (1961–64), a two-volume edition of Leontiev's works in English (1969), selections from the works of FEDOTOV (1952) and ROZANOV (1956 and 1977), and an anthology of Russian émigré poetry (1953). Ivask has also contributed many articles, notes, and reviews to the émigré press.

Ivask's early poetry, gathered in the collections *Northern Shores* (Severnyi bereg, 1938) and *Imperial Autumn* (Tsarskaya osen', 1953), was influenced by ACMEISM and the Parisian note (PARIZH-SKAYA NOTA). Ivask's irrepressible metaphysical imagination first appears fully in "Glory" (Khvala, 1967) and "Cinderella" (Zolushka, 1970), where a striking fusion of motifs from pre-Petrine Muscovite and Russian folk culture with a refined Western sensibility is brilliantly accomplished. Ivask has found a distinctive style of his own in his *poema* (referred to by himself as a "cycle of lyric verse") *Homo ludens,* published in *Vozrozhdenie,* 1973, nos. 240–42. It is the autobiographic odyssey of a Russian poet, which takes the persona from childhood in prerevolutionary Moscow to Livonia and the heartland of archaic Eastern Slavdom in the Pskov region, and on to emigration to Western Europe and America, a journey accompanied all the while by a wealth of allusions to historical events, art, and literature. Ivask happily synchronizes an intimate personal note with a mature thinker's worldly wisdom and an erudite *ars poetica.* The whimsical, impressionistic, remarkably palpable imagery of *Homo ludens,* coupled with Ivask's uninhibited play with sound patterns and onomatopoeia, symbolizes the idea of art as sacred play which transforms a very real world into a paradise of gladness, plenitude, and marvels (*rai* [paradise] appears as a magic word and label even in Ivask's earlier poetry). Ivask has suggested that he owes his style in part to the metaphysical poets of the baroque (echoes of them appear in *Homo ludens*) and that his repeated visits to Mexico have been an important source of inspiration to him. *Homo ludens* is a creation of mature craftsmanship and originality. It has had an impact in the Soviet Union, where a SAMIZDAT edition has appeared. At the writing of this article Ivask was working on a new collection of his poetry, to be entitled "A Petit-Bourgeois" (Meshchanin, in the positive, Pushkinian meaning of that word).

Translations: R. H. Morrison, ed. and trans. *America's Russian Poets.* 1975. Pp. 45–51.

Secondary literature: Laszlo Dienes, "On the Poetry of Yuri Ivask," *World Literature Today* 53 (1979), pp. 234–37. Valentin Evdokimov, "Igra pera i podvig vdokhnoven'ya: Man'erizm i tragizm 'igrayushchego' cheloveka," *Vestnik RKhD* no. 127 (4/1978), pp. 131–41. Temira Pachmuss, *A Russian Cultural Revival: A Critical Anthology of Émigré Literature before 1939.* 1981. Pp. 433–37. (Biographic and critical note, translations of some poems.)   V. T.

Ívnev, Ryúrik (pseudonym of Kovalyóv, Mikhaíl Aleksándrovich, 1891–1981), poet and novelist, was born in Tiflis, into a military family. He graduated from Moscow university with a degree in law, in 1912. In 1909, Ivnev published a few poems in a student collection, but his first volume of verses, *Self-Immolation* (Samosozhzhenie, reprint. 1917), appeared in 1913. Until 1916, Ivnev was associated with FUTURISM. He collaborated with the Ego-futurists, the CENTRIFUGE, and the Mezzanine of Poetry. His publications of those years include, *The Flame is Blazing* (Plamya pyshet, 1913) and *The Gold of Death* (Zoloto smerti, 1916). In 1918, Ivnev became secretary to the Minister of Culture, A. LUNACHARSKY. In 1919, Ivnev joined the group of IMAGISTS, and signed their first manifesto. He contributed numerous poems to imagist collections, almanacs, and the journal, *Gostinitsa dlya puteshestvuyushchikh v prekrasnom.* He also published a volume of poetry, *Sun in the Grave* (Solntse vo grobe, 1921) and a book of criticism, *Four Shots at Esenin, Kusikov, Mariengof, Shershenevich* (Chetyre vystrela v Esenina, Kusikova, Mariengofa, Shershenevicha, 1921). Ivnev's poetry is more decadent than avant-garde, and therefore it is untypical of both futurism and imagism. His main theme is death as purification of the flesh, often colored by religious fanaticism. Ivnev shows an aesthetic indulgence in images of physical violence or decay, and a tendency to the macabre. Ivnev's poetry presents such motifs as, homosexuality, madness, guilt, crucifixion, Christ, and the apocalypse.

Ivnev was also a novelist. His novels include: *The Unhappy Angel* (Neschastnyi angel, 1917), reminiscent of BELY's prose; *Love Without Love* (Lyubov' bez lyubvi, 1925) and *Open House* (Otkrytyi dom, 1927), both dedicated to the bohemian life of the cultural circles of

Tiflis and Baku; and *The Novel's Hero* (Geroi romana, 1929), a negative portrait of the Russian emigration. In later years, Ivnev translated Georgian poets and continued to write both poetry and prose. His most recent publications are collections of memoirs, short stories, and poems: *At the Foot of Mtatsminda* (U podnozhiya Mtatsmindy, 1973), *Selected Poems, 1912–1972* (Izbrannye stikhotvoreniya, 1912–1972, 1974), *Hours and Voices. Poems. Memoirs* (Chasy i golosa. Stikhi. Vospominaniya, 1978).

Secondary literature: B. Gusman, *100 poetov. Literaturnye portrety.* Tver, 1923. V. Markov, *Russian Futurism: A History.* 1968. ———, *Russian Imagism. 1919–1924.* Giessen, 1980. G. McVay, "Black and Gold: The Poetry of Ryurik Ivnev," *OSP* n. s. 4 (1971), pp. 83–104. V. Shershenevich, *Komu ya zhmu ruku.* 1921.

A. L.

Izbórniki Svyatosláva of 1073 and 1076. A general title applied by Russian scholars to two large miscellanies (*izborniki*) containing primarily ecclesiastic and didactic writings. The Izborniki are preserved in two Old Russian codices compiled by a certain "Ioann the Scribe" in 1073 and 1076 in Kiev. The full text of 1073 is known to us in many later copies (about twenty), which date from the 13th to the 17th century. The Izbornik of 1076, on the other hand, is not known to us in any other complete copy, although a part of its textual material is to be found in some of the most popular Old Russian miscellanies, such as *The Emerald* (Izmaragd) and *The Bee* (Pchela). The scribe Ioann produced the two codices for the Kievan Grand Prince Svyatoslav Yaroslavich. It appears, however, that the two miscellanies originally were compiled in Bulgaria for Tsar Simeon at the beginning of the 10th century. For this reason, Bulgarian scholars usually refer to them as *Miscellanies of Simeon* (Simeonovi sbornitsi).

Clearly dependent on Byzantine models, the Izbornik of 1073 contains 383 excerpts, both large and small, from the works of approximately thirty authoritative Christian writers. In addition to patristic writings by, among others, Basil the Great, Cyril of Alexandria, and Maximus the Confessor, one finds texts dealing with general erudition and an index of canonic and prohibited books. Modern scholars have devoted particular attention to the section *On Figures* (O obrazekh), translated from the treatise by George Choeroboscus entitled *Peri tropon poietikon.* Twice in the Izbornik of 1073—namely, fol. 2ʳ and fols. 263ᵛ–264ʳ—there occurs a eulogy of Prince Svyatoslav, which apparently represents an adaptation of a text originally composed to praise Tsar Simeon. Indeed, the name *Simeon* is preserved in other codices.

The Izbornik of 1076, parts of which appear to be less dependent on Greek models, contains forty-eight excerpts (both large and small) from the writings of John Chrysostom, Basil the Great, and other Church fathers, the Scriptures (Wisdom of Jesus, the Son of Sirach), hagiographic literature (including the Paterikon), and collections of proverbs and sayings, as well as instructions from a father to his son. Scholars have shown special interest in the brief text entitled *Sermon by a Certain Monk on the Reading of Books* (Slovo nekoiego kalugera o ch'[tenii] knig), which opens the Izbornik of 1076. Given its emphasis on the spiritual benefits derived from the reading of a carefully established body of texts, one may regard the *Sermon* as a guide for reading the entire miscellany.

Bibliography: V. S. Golyshenko et al., eds., *Izbornik 1076 g.* 1965. [S. Kozhukharov], "Simeonovi Sbornitsi." In *Rechnik na bălgarskata literatura.* Vol. 3. Sofia, 1982. Pp. 268–70. T. S. Morozov, ed., *Izbornik velikogo knyazya Svyatoslava Yaroslavicha 1073 goda.* (Obshchestvo lyubitelei drevnei pis'mennosti, no. 55.) 1910. B. Peichio, *Filosofskijat traktat v Simeonovija sbornik.* Sofia, 1977. R. Picchio, "The Impact of Ecclesiastic Culture on Old Russian Literary Techniques." In *California Slavic Studies: Issues in Medieval Russian Culture.* Ed. H. Birnbaum and M. Flier. 1983. Pp. 247–79. N. P. Popov, "L'Izbornik de 1076, dit de Sviatoslav, comme monument littéraire," *Revue des études slaves* 14 (1934), pp. 5–25. ———, "Les auteurs de l'Izbornik de Sviatoslav de 1076," *Revue des études slaves* 15 (1935), pp. 210–23. B. A. Rybakov, ed., *Izbornik Svyatoslava 1073 g. Sbornik statei.* 1977. Ševčenko, I., "On Some Sources of Prince Svyatoslav's 'Izbornik' of the year 1076." In *Orbis Scriptus: Dmitrij Tschižewskij zum 70. Geburtstag.* Ed. D. Gerhardt et. al. Munich, 1966. Pp. 723–38.

H. G.

Izmaílov, Aleksándr Efímovich (1779–1831), journalist, writer, and fabulist, combined a career in the civil service with his literary activities. A member of the Free Society of Amateurs of Letters, Sciences, and Arts (VOL'NOE OBSHCHESTVO LYUBITELEI SLOVESNOSTI, NAUK I KHUDOZHESTV) since 1802, he was its president from 1816 to 1825. He was the publisher of several periodicals, the most long-lived of which was the journal *Blagonamerennyi* (1818–26). Izmailov's fables are sometimes fresh and to the point. However, he owes his place in Russian literature to a novel, *Eugene, or the Results of Bad Upbringing and Bad Company* (Evgenii, ili Pagubnye sledstviya durnogo vospitaniya i soobshchestva, 1799–1801). While belonging to the genre of the *conte moral,* whose "oriental" variety Izmailov also cultivated (the hero's last name is *Negodyaev,* lit. "Good-for-Nothing;" he is seduced by a fellow student named *Razvratin,* lit. "Débauché," and a French adventurer called *Pendard,* from *pendre,* "hang"), the novel contains some robustly realistic descriptions, including some of rather intriguing vice, and in general stands out among its sentimentalist contemporaries. "Too late as an adventure novel, too early as a social novel" (STENDER-PETERSEN), it failed to catch on, and Russian literature would have to wait thirty years until the appearance of more similar works.

Works: Polnoe sobranie sochinenii. 3 vols. 1890. *Poety-satiriki kontsa XVIII—nachala XIX v.* 1959.

Translations: [Fables.] In Leo Wiener, *Anthology of Russian Literature* 1902–03. Vol. 2 and in Charles Thomas Wilson, *Russian Lyrics in English Verse.* 1887.

Secondary literature: I. A. Kubasov, *A. E. Izmailov.* 1901. S. A. Vengerov, *Kritiko-biograficheskii slovar' russkikh pisatelei i uchenykh.* Vol. 6. 1904. Pp. 92–108.

V. T.

Jákobson, Román Ósipovich (1896–1982) was born in Moscow on 11 October 1896, the son of a chemical engineer and prominent industrialist. He was educated at the renowned Lazarev Institute of Oriental Languages, from which he graduated *cum laude* in 1914, and at Moscow University, in which he enrolled in the same year. He studied in the Slavic Section of the philological faculty, attending the seminars of famous linguists and Slavists such as D. N. Ushakov, M. M. Pokrovskij, V. K. Porzeziński, V. N. Shchepkin, N. N. Durnovo, and L. V. SHCHERBA. In 1917 he spent a semester at Petersburg University studying Sanskrit with A. A. SHAKHMATOV, under whose guidance he also started his first research on the reconstruction of the *Igor Tale* (see SLOVO O POLKU IGOREVE). In October of 1918 Jakobson received his master's degree from Moscow University and was appointed, as his teacher Shakhmatov had been, a special Research Associate, thus becoming a candidate for a chair in philology.

Jakobson's academic training predisposed him to treat language as a *functional system* rather than advocating the historical-comparative approach characteristic of the neogrammarian doctrine. Moreover, following the Russian scholarly tradition, he was prepared to link the study of language with that of literature and folklore as an object of joint investigation.

No less important than his formal training was the artistic milieu in which the young Jakobson grew up. As early as 1913–1916 he associated with the most important avant-garde painters and poets, including Kazimir Malevich, Pavel Filonov, Velimir KHLEBNIKOV, A. E. KRUCHONYKH, and V. V. MAYAKOVSKY; his close friendship with Mayakovsky lasted until the poet's suicide in 1930. Even earlier, he became acquainted with the European pictorial experiments of the French post-impressionists and cubists, whose paintings he saw in the galleries of the Russian millionaire art collectors Morozov and Shchukin.

In the spirit of Moscow University, and drawing on his experience in experimental poetry and painting, in 1915 Jakobson, together with six other students, founded the Moscow Linguistic Circle, and he served as its president until 1920. The group also included poets, Mayakovsky among them. Here Jakobson began his serious investigation of language as a *system,* taking as his object of study the language of poetry—the most marked, semioticised form of discourse (see *The Newest Russian Poetry: Approaches to Xlebnikov;*

Selected Writings 5, pp. 299–354). This work was presented and discussed, in 1919, at the Circle, and it had widespread repercussions for the study of poetry. Under the influence of the Moscow Circle a group of literary scholars founded a similar association in Petersburg known as the OPOYAZ (an acronym standing for "Society for the Study of Poetic Language"). The association worked in close contact with its Moscow colleagues, especially with Jakobson, who was its co-founder, as well as the co-author (with Yu. TYNYANOV) of its program, "Problems in the study of literature and language" (1928; *SW 3*, pp. 3–6 and *SW 5*, pp 564–66). The innovative approach of the two groups later became renowned under the name of the Russian FORMALIST School.

Two basic factors explain Jakobson's personality and his intellectual makeup: the first is his belonging to and strong identification with the generation and milieu unique for its creativity and power, and instrumental in forming the character of our century; second, his understanding of the role of language as central to all human endeavor. Thus linguistics encompasses all that is human, as Jakobson voiced it in his often-quoted paraphrase of Terence: "Linguista sum: nihil linguistici a me alienum esse puto." These fundamental factors endowed him with the energy and confidence that permitted him to achieve what he did, in spite of historical disasters that led to years of enforced peregrination and often threatened his life.

In 1920 Jakobson went to Czechoslovakia as a translator, and eventually a cultural attaché, of the first Soviet Red Cross Mission. After several years he left the Mission but remained in Czechoslovakia to resume his studies at Prague University, from which he received a doctorate in 1930. In 1931 Jakobson began teaching at T. G. Masaryk University in Brno, but because of difficulties caused by academic conservatives, he assumed a chair of Russian Philology and Old Czech Literature only in 1937. The Czechoslovak period has been characterized by Morris Halle (1979, p. 336) as one which "saw the full development of his scientific genius." In Czechoslovakia, as in Moscow, Jakobson established close ties with Czech and Slovak poets, writers and artists, including V. Nezval, J. Seifert and L. Novomeský, and became a member of the Czech avant-garde artistic group *Devětsil*. Among Jakobson's endeavors to organize international scholarly cooperation, his supreme achievement was the establishment, in 1926, of the Prague Linguistic Circle, which he founded together with Vilém Mathesius and several other Czech and Russian scholars (notably J. Mukařovský, P. G. BOGATYREV and N. S. TRUBETZKOY). He remained the vice-president of the Circle for thirteen years and contributed many works to its renowned series *Travaux du Cercle linguistique de Prague*.

In 1939, fleeing the Nazi occupation, Jakobson went to Scandinavia, first to Denmark, then to Norway; after the occupation of Norway he was again forced to escape, this time to Sweden. He was a visiting lecturer in three Scandinavian universities, Copenhagen, Oslo, and Uppsala. There Jakobson continued his work on phonology and also worked on the Paleosiberian languages (*SW 2*, pp. 98–102). But his main accomplishment of that period was the monograph *Kindersprache, Aphasie und allgemeine Lautgesetze* (*SW 1*, pp. 328–401), first published in Uppsala in 1941. In this study Jakobson presented for the first time evidence for linguistic structure from the areas of language acquisition and speech pathology, a project that he "cherished for many years ..." and that he managed to realize thanks to the "wealth of the medical libraries of Stockholm" (*Dialogues*, pp. 39) and the help of the head of the psychiatric clinic in Uppsala.

In 1941 Jakobson came to the United States. As in his years in Czechoslovakia, he met with a reserved and even hostile reception from conservative linguists, who managed to block his way to a permanent university position for nearly five years. From 1942 to 1946 Jakobson was professor of general linguistics and Czechoslovak studies at the Ecole Libre des Hautes Etudes, the university in exile founded by French and Belgian scholars. After several years as a visiting professor of general linguistics at Columbia University, only in 1946 was Jakobson appointed T. G. Masaryk Professor of Czechoslovak Studies. In 1949 Jakobson was invited by Harvard University to assume the Samuel Hazzard Cross Professorship of Slavic Languages and Literatures, and from 1960 he held a joint appointment as professor of linguistics. In 1957 Jakobson was named an Institute professor at the Massachusetts Institute of Technology.

The main areas that had always captivated Jakobson's mind were: the general theory of language (including poetics), neurolin-

guistics, and Slavic studies. Each of these areas he either totally reshaped, or enriched with fundamental contributions. Jakobson's principal contribution to the science of language, and a turning point in the development of both modern linguistics and the science of man, is his theory of phonology. Jakobson's new approach, developed in close collaboration with N. S. Trubetzkoy, forced a revision of the concept of the phoneme, which until then was assumed to be the smallest component of language. He showed that the phoneme could be further resolved into a set of specific properties or *distinctive features*. These properties, defined in articulatory/motor/acoustic terms, are *relative* in character, and form *binary oppositions* which make up the phonemic *system* of language. A phoneme as a global unit does not stand in any clear relation to another phoneme, but sets of distinctive features (such as strident vs. non-strident, voiced vs. voiceless, etc.) are the necessary and sufficient components for the specification of the phonemes of a given language. This reduction provides "the minimum number of the simplest operations that would suffice to encode and decode the whole message" ("Phonology and Phonetics" [with M. Halle], *SW 1*, p. 498). His phonological theory contains another important principle, that of *markedness*. The marked member of an opposition, according to Jakobson, is the member that carries more information than its partner. In this way he established the *hierarchical* nature of phonemic oppositions and of phonemic systems as a whole. Another concept elaborated in this framework concerned the relation of the *invariant* to *variation*, an idea Jakobson adapted from topology in mathematics. Thus the distinctive features retain their invariant properties amidst a continuous stream of contextual variations.

These principles, which were first developed and refined in the field of phonology, were subsequently applied by Jakobson to all other levels of language—in particular to morphology, resulting in studies of the Russian case system, of the structure of the Russian verb, and of the nominal and pronominal inflections (*Russian and Slavic Grammar: Studies 1931–1981*). Jakobson's morphological investigations not only revolutionized the theory of grammar, but found important applications in language teaching as well. Jakobson's general theory of language, whose basis was phonology, profoundly influenced other branches of the science of man (see *Roman Jakobson: Echoes of His Scholarship*). His thinking left a particularly strong impact on anthropology, as has been testified by C. Lévi-Strauss, with whom Jakobson worked at the Ecole Libre des Hautes Etudes (see *Six Lectures on Sound and Meaning*, Preface by C. Lévi-Strauss).

Fundamental to Jakobson's theory of language is his revision of the doctrine of F. de Saussure, whose *Cours de linguistique générale* he received in 1920. Most basic was Jakobson's reassessment of the Saussurean opposition between synchrony (language as a static system) and diachrony (its dynamic, developmental aspect). According to Jakobson, the very opposition is false because it excludes the role of the time factor in the present moment of the language state and thus creates an erroneous disruption between past and present in language processes (*Dialogues*, pp. 56–78). In contradistinction to Saussure, who considered the linguistic sign to reflect an arbitrary connection between sound and meaning, Jakobson insisted upon the close and intricate ties between the two parts of the sign (*signans* and *signatum*). He showed that these ties are intrinsic in a number of linguistic phenomena: derivational processes, folk etymology, sound symbolism, etc. Saussure's conception of the pure *linearity* of language was contradicted by the existence of distinctive features, the fundamental manifestation of *simultaneity* in the system of language. Jakobson also proved that simultaneity manifests itself on all other levels of language, most conspicuously in the connection between speech event and narrated event, which encompasses simultaneously two different realms of time ("Shifters, Verbal Categories, and the Russian Verb," *SW 2*, pp. 130–147).

These and other aspects of Jakobsonian theory were guided by semiotic considerations. Moreover, Jakobson not only emphasised the semiotic character of language as a system "among other systems of signs," but worked to develop semiotics as a discipline of its own. He contributed a pivotal study to the classification and typology of semiotic systems, with special attention to language ("Language in Relation to Other Communication Systems," *SW 2*, pp. 697–708). In semiotics, his main inspiration came from the works of Charles Sanders Peirce, whom Jakobson considered the greatest American philosopher, and "the most powerful source of information" that he found in the United States (*SW 2*, p. v).

Next to semiotics in Jakobson's science of language stands the study of poetry as the most semioticised and one of the most important subcodes of the linguistic system. After having worked on poetics all his life, he found new insights into its development in the mathematical theory of information and within this framework built a model of language in operation. In this model Jakobson showed, on the one hand, the integration of poetry and the poetic function into the speech event, and on the other the specific role of poetic usage, focusing on the linguistic material itself ("Linguistics and Poetics," *SW 3*, pp. 18–51). Next to the problem of parallelism, one of the chief issues of his theory of poetics, which continued to occupy Jakobson for the last twenty years of his life, was the "poetry of grammar and grammar of poetry" (*SW 3*). Using poetic examples from a vast number of languages and cultures, he pointed out the specific role that grammatical categories play in poetry. First, the regularity of their distribution is comparable to that of metrical patterning. Moreover, grammatical categories, with their obligatory meanings and their power of abstraction, are transformed in verbal art into truly poetic "grammatical tropes."

Jakobson's most significant contribution to neurolinguistics is reflected in the title of his study "Two Aspects of Language and Two Types of Aphasic Disturbances" (*SW 2*, pp. 239–59). Basing himself on the pioneering work of the Polish linguist Mikołaj Kruszewski, Jakobson showed that our entire linguistic activity gravitates around the axis of selection and the axis of combination. By relating these two axes to brain structure and to the two basic types of speech disturbances, Jakobson made, as is widely recognized, one of the major contributions to aphasiology (see Luria, in *Echoes*, pp. 237–53). In this way he also provided rigorous proof for his theory of poetic language. The two axes in question are connected respectively with the metaphoric and metonymic poles in our language activity, since a process of selection underlines the metaphoric operation, while combinatorial procedures are related to the metonymic operation. The structure and function of the brain are thus reflected in the two types of discourse, poetry and prose, the metaphoric tendency being typical of the former and the metonymic of the latter. A further contribution to neurolinguistics is Jakobson's pioneering work on the language of schizophrenia, exemplified in his analysis of a late poem by F. Hölderlin (with Grete Lübbe-Grothues) "Ein Blick auf *Die Aussicht* von Hölderlin," *SW 3*, pp. 388–446). Contrary to accepted views, Jakobson showed that a schizophrenic is capable of producing a work of art of high quality, although in a highly idiosyncratic form. In his monograph *Brain and Language: Cerebral Hemispheres and Linguistic Structure in Mutual Light* (1980), drawing on data provided by clinical research in various countries, Jakobson reached a number of linguistic and semiotic conclusions concerning the mechanism and capacity of human thought and communication.

Metrics, and particularly Slavic versification, occupied a special place in Jakobson's scientific discoveries. In the Prague period he wrote and published his fundamental work *On Czech Verse, Particularly as Compared to Russian* (1923; *SW 5*, pp. 3–130), in which he analyzed Czech and Russian versification in terms of the dominant difference in their linguistic material, fixed stress and free stress respectively, while vocalic quantity, hitherto considered as the decisive feature in the Czech system, was shown to be the "secondary feature." One of his main conclusions was that these two different prosodic features provide for each verse system the basic unit of opposition in its rhythmical pattern, and that this pattern, rather than the metrical scheme, determines the nature of verse. He devoted a number of studies to various metrical systems, from Slavic to Chinese (*SW 5*, pp. 3–215). His theory found its most complete shape in two of his late studies: "Linguistics and Poetics" (referred to above) and "My Metrical Sketches, a Retrospect" (*Linguistics* 17, 1979, pp. 267–99 and *SW 5*, pp. 569–603). Aiming at an integrated theory of versification, Jakobson showed that in Slavic tradition both accentual and syllabic types of verse reveal the same rhythmic principle, namely the alternation of these two elements: stressed versus unstressed syllable and syllable nucleus versus syllabic margin, respectively. For Russian versification, he established that in binary meters the fulfillment of downbeats (metrically stressed syllables) is not a rule but a strong tendency, while the unfulfilled downbeats yield a statistically predictable pattern. In Russian ternary meters, on the other hand, the fulfill-

ment of downbeats is a rule. His work on diachronic Slavic metrics, with special attention to oral epic verse forms, led to his comprehensive study "Slavic Epic Verse: Studies in Comparative Metrics" (*SW 4*, pp. 414–63). His findings allowed him not only to reconstruct common Slavic verse forms, but also to align these findings with the metrical evidence of Vedic Sanskrit and Greek, thereby making a fundamental contribution to the reconstruction of Indo-European metrical prototypes.

In his research in Slavic studies, Jakobson followed the same integrated approach he displayed in every area of his scientific endeavor. He held that the Slavic unity is defined most importantly by the common language patrimony. This patrimony, in turn, determines the stock of poetic (literary) devices common to all Slavic peoples. These factors permit the reconstruction and thus the explanation of changes in national literary developments by enabling one to distinguish between borrowings, convergences, and coincidences. Jakobson's main efforts were focused on reconstructing the archaic forms of Slavic oral and written tradition. His chief interests included the Russian oral epos, the BYLINY, whose poetics points to their remote past and "betray a genetic kinship with archaic folklore forms of Slavic and even Baltic peoples" (*SW 4*, pp. 647). He refuted both of the persistent fallacies that, on the one hand, the Russian oral epic texts represent unqualified historical documents, and, on the other, that "no historical events are reflected in the epos"; instead, Jakobson insisted that all factors—historical, social, and literary— must be taken into account in terms of their transformation into the intrinsic design of the folk epos itself. In his extended analysis of the so-called *Vseslav Epos*, a *bylina* about a prince-werewolf (*SW 4*, pp. 301–68), he also demonstrated how myth is transformed through historical and literary factors: "An ancient Slavic myth, an international literary model, and domestic historical facts are intimately fused in the Vseslav epos." These "threefold ingredients," are not "totally disparate layers mechanically brought together," but "components of a poetic whole which are mutually coordinated and adapted to an artistic design" (*SW 4*, p. 356). The written medieval monument that occupied Jakobson during his entire life was the Russian epic poem composed on the threshold of the 12th and 13th centuries, the *Slovo o polku Igoreve* (*Igor Tale*). Since, after the burning of Moscow in 1812, the poem survived only in two late 18th-century transcriptions, some skeptics have questioned the authenticity of the *Slovo*. Jakobson began working on this Russian masterpiece in his freshman year at Moscow University in a proseminar of the prominent Slavist S. K. Shambinago. His first study on the *Slovo* was written in 1916, under the guidance of A. A. Shakhmatov: "Language and Orthography in the 'Slovo o polku Igoreve'," published in 1929 by S. Eremin among Shakhmatov's papers (see *SW 4*, pp. 653ff.). Jakobson sought to reconstruct the original text beneath the later layers of Musin-Pushkin's copy. In 1932, Jakobson explicitly refuted the unfounded skepticism of the French Slavist André Mazon concerning the authenticity of the *Slovo* (see *SW 4*, pp. 49–50). During his professorship at the Ecole Libre des Hautes Etudes in New York, Jakobson engaged in a seminar (together with the Belgian medievalist and Byzantinist Henri Grégoire) devoted to a detailed examination of the questions raised by Mazon. The seminar unequivocally rejected the doubts about the authenticity of the monument. In the years 1945 to 1947 Jakobson prepared a critical edition of the *Slovo*, accompanied by historical and philological essays, and including a reconstruction of the original text along with a translation into modern Russian (*La Geste du Prince Igor'*, 1948; *SW 4*, pp. 106–300). He returned to the *Slovo* in the early 1960s in order to challenge a new wave of skepticism, raised this time by the Soviet historian A. A. Zimin. In refuting Zimin's repertoire of doubts, Jakobson showed that the *Slovo* is the link that connects the *Hypatian Chronicle*, with its entries of the 12th century, with the ZADONSHCHINA of the 14th century, and is not—as Zimin claimed—an imitation of the latter text (see *SW 4*, pp. 656ff.). Much of Jakobson's argumentation is based on an analysis of the sound pattern of these three texts. He was reassured as to the value of such an approach by the publication of F. de Saussure's work on anagrams (*Mercure de France*, pp. 243ff.) in 1964. With Saussure, Jakobson held that the archaic "*fureur du jeu phonique*" was a tenacious feature of the poetic traditions of diverse Indo-European peoples. Jakobson's analysis of paronomastic patterns in the *Slovo* revealed an eloquent anagram of Igor's brother Vsevolod, clearly linking the *Slovo* to the pre-Mongolian Kievan period, an epoch whose literature displays this tendency as its most characteristic trait.

Jakobson's medieval studies also included wide-ranging investigations of the historical background of these texts in terms of both their origins and their first interpretations. He showed that the romantic era, in its failure to understand the Middle Ages, had reached a faulty conception of medieval verbal art. Jakobson's reanalysis of this art gave a new perspective not only to its historical origin but also to the cultural and political position of the Russians and the Slavs in the European and Eurasian world.

Of the greatest interest and importance is Jakobson's original reinterpretation of the Byzantine mission to the Moravian Slavs in the second half of the 9th century. The activities of the mission, conducted by two monks from Macedonia, Cyril (or Constantine the Philosopher) and his brother Methodius, resulted in the creation of a language suitable for the liturgy of the Slavic peoples, known today as Old CHURCH SLAVONIC. Jakobson became particularly interested in this subject in the 1930s while working on the Czech Middle Ages and the Hussite epoch of the Reformation. During the 1950s and 1960s he devoted two fundamental studies to this topic (*SW 6*, forthcoming), and returned to the question twice in the 1980s (see *Dialogues*, chap. XV; *SW 6*). Jakobson saw the significance of the Cyrillo-Methodian mission in its anticipation of the linguistic battles for national self-determination during the Reformation, when the possession of a sacred language was a powerful symbolic act. In his last paper, delivered at Wellesley College shortly before his death ("More on the Enlightener"; *SW 6*.) Jakobson emphasized another aspect of Constantine's legacy, namely his "appeal for equality which at the same time stands as a principle of individuation." As he has shown, Constantine's "inspiring tenet" of equality and individuation has had enormous consequences for the history of the Slavic peoples. Jakobson's contribution has significant ramifications not only for history, but also for semiotics, sociolinguistics, and social anthropology.

The understanding of the role of Cyrillo-Methodian ideology led Jakobson to his reassessment of Old Church Slavonic poetry, in its Russian, Czech, and Bulgarian variants. He concentrated on "verse relics" in the hagiographical literature and especially on the Slavic hymnody, which he considered "the principal achievement of the two brothers' mission" (*SW 6*.) Particularly important are his studies "Saint Constantine's Prologue to the Gospels" (*SW 6*, pp. 191–206), "The Encomium of Constantine the Philosopher to Gregory the Theologian" (*SW 6*, pp. 207–39), and above all, "Sketches for the History of the Oldest Slavic Hymnody" (*SW 6*, pp. 286–346). Jakobson's innovative approach to these texts consists in revealing in them the metrical (i.e., poetic) principle in its Slavic, rather than Greek, version. The reconstruction of this system, which Jakobson compared to the cleaning of Russian icons at the turn of the century, hitherto unrecognized as art, occupied him as early as 1919, when he communicated his first discoveries in a letter to Shakhmatov, who initiated its publication; it appeared three years later in *Izvestiya Otdeleniya russkogo yazyka i slovesnosti Ross. Ak. Nauk* 24 (1922), no. 2.

A group of Jakobson's works which was still in progress involved the field of Slavic mythology. From his seminal article "Slavic Mythology" of 1950 (*Funk and Wagnalls Standard Dictionary of Folklore, Mythology and Legend* 2, pp. 1025–28), to a Harvard course in 1966 and a series of studies in the 1960s, to his last paper on mythology, presented posthumously at the International Congress of Armenian Linguistics in September, 1982 (*SW 7*, forthcoming), Jakobson worked on the reconstruction of comparative Slavic mythology and its broader application to Indo-European mythology. At the center of his attention was the Slavic pantheon and its relation to the Indo-European one.

In modern Russian literature, as well as in other Slavic literatures, Jakobson cast a fresh glance on a number of writers, uncovering hitherto unnoticed issues. One of his most fundamental ideas is the concept of the "poetic myth," i.e., a particular link between a writer's life and his work. In this link the borderline between the "hard facts" of biography and the symbolic expression of poetry is obliterated, and the traditional division between "Dichtung und Wahrheit" proves to be invalid (see "The Statue in Puškin's Poetic Mythology," *SW 5*, pp. 237–80; "On a Generation That Squandered Its Poets,"

SW 5, pp. 355–81; "What is Poetry ?", *SW 3*, pp. 740–50). Witness also his views on the "naive" TOLSTOI, on the "transrational" TURGENEV, on the philosophy of C. K. Norwid, on the LUBOK of Taras SHEVCHENKO, etc. One of the most original and important ideas, insufficiently noted by literary historians, is his concept of the role of the *generation*, a concept extending beyond simple and traditional temporal units of periodization in literature (*SW 5*, pp. 227–36).

A special chapter in Jakobson's scholarly work belongs to his organizational efforts in building international and interdisciplinary science. From the late 1920s through the 1930s he was an active organizer and participant in a number of programmatic congresses, including the first Congress of Slavists in Prague (1929) and the Congresses of Phonetic Sciences in Amsterdam and in Ghent (1932, 1938). Together with Trubetzkoy, Jakobson was also instrumental in arranging a series of phonological conferences convoked by the Prague Circle. In the United States, he co-founded the Linguistic Circle of New York (1943), and remained its vice-president until 1949. At MIT he co-organized and headed the Center of Communication Science, and from 1966 to 1969 engaged in interdisciplinary research at the Salk Institute for Biological Studies and at the Center for Cognitive Studies at Harvard University. He was also a member of the Center for Byzantine Studies (Dumbarton Oaks), where he conducted his Byzantino-Slavic research.

During the last twenty years of his life, his international influence and recognition grew rapidly: he received honorary degrees from twenty-six universities, the first from Cambridge (1960) and the last from Oxford (1981). He was an honorary member of nearly thirty learned societies.

Jakobson's 60th and 70th birthdays were marked by two massive Festschriften (*For Roman Jakobson. On the Occasion of His Sixtieth Birthday*, Mouton, 1956; *To Honor Roman Jakobson. Essays on the Occasion of His Seventieth Birthday*, Mouton, 1967); a third Festschrift, for his 70th birthday, was offered to him by his students (Slavica Publishers, 1968). A final book in his honor appeared in celebration of his 80th birthday (*Roman Jakobson: Echoes of His Scholarship*, Peter de Ridder Press, Lisse, 1977).

His energy for lecturing was legendary, and his tours took him throughout the United States and Europe, to South America and Japan. Beginning in 1956 he made a number of trips to the USSR to attend scholarly congresses and to give individual lectures, in Moscow, Leningrad, and Tbilisi. In his last Russian trip, in 1979, he lectured at his Alma Mater. He spoke to an audience of about a thousand people on "The Immediate Tasks of the Science of Language" (*SW 7*, forthcoming), and emphasized the great linguistic tradition of Moscow University.

Roman Jakobson died in Cambridge, Massachusetts, on 18 July 1982.

Works: Selected Writings. 7 vols. The Hague-Paris-Berlin-New York, 1962– . Vol. 1: *Phonological Studies* (1962; 2d expanded ed., 1971). Vol. 2: *Word and Language* (1972). Vol. 3: *Poetry of Grammar and Grammar of Poetry* (1981). Vol. 4. *Slavic Epic Studies* (1966). Vol. 5: *On Verse, Its Masters and Explorers* (1979). Vol. 6: *Early Slavic Paths and Crossroads* (1984). Vol. 7: *Contributions to Comparative Mythology. Recent Studies in Linguistics and Philology. Retrospections. Bibliography* (forthcoming). (Ed.) *N. S. Trubetzkoy's Letters and Notes.* The Hague, 1975. *Six Lectures on Sound and Meaning.* Cambridge, Mass. and London, 1978. (With Linda R. Waugh,) *The Sound Shape of Language.* Bloomington, Ind., 1979. *Brain and Language: Cerebral Hemispheres and Linguistic Structure in Mutual Light.* Columbus, Ohio, 1980. *The Framework of Language.* Ann Arbor, Mich., 1980. (With Krystyna Pomorska,) *Dialogues.* Cambridge, Mass. and London, 1982. *Russian and Slavic Grammar: Studies 1931–1981.* Berlin and New York, 1983.

Secondary literature: Daniel Armstrong and C. H. van Schooneveld, *Roman Jakobson: Echoes of His Scholarship.* Lisse, 1977. Morris Halle, "Roman Jakobson," in *International Encyclopedia of the Social Sciences—Biographical Supplement.* Vol. 18 (David L. Sills, ed.) New York, 1979. Elmar Holenstein, *Roman Jakobson's Approach to Language.* Bloomington, Ind., 1976. *A Tribute to Roman Jakobson.* Berlin and New York, 1983. Linda R. Waugh, *Roman Jakobson's Science of Language.* Lisse, 1976.

K. P.

Journalism in Russia first emerged in the early part of the 18th century in Petersburg, nurtured by the newly founded Academy of Sciences. The publication, which may properly be considered the first Russian journal, began to appear in 1728 as a supplement to the newspaper *Sankt-Peterburgskie vedomosti* (Saint Petersburg News), which in that year was taken over by the Academy of Sciences and began to come out under the editorship of the German historian Gerhardt Friedrich Mueller (1728–30). During the course of its existence, this supplement, *Mesyachnye istoricheskie, genealogicheskie i geograficheskie primechaniya v Vedomostyakh* (Monthly Historical, Genealogical and Geographical Notes in the News), published articles on a variety of subjects, including the history of literature and theater, as a well as original and translated works of literature. Its contributors included LOMONOSOV and TREDIAKOVSKY. *Primechaniya* ceased publication in 1742. In 1755, the Academy of Sciences began to publish the first autonomous Russian journal, *Ezhemesyachnye sochineniya k pol'ze i uveseleniyu sluzhashchie* (Monthly Compositions for Profit and Amusement). The journal came out under the editorship of Mueller and closed down in 1764 when he was transferred to Moscow. Leading literary figures of the day and emerging young talents, many of them students of the Gentry Cadet Corps, grouped around the journal, and its contributors included Trediakovsky, SUMAROKOV, and KHERASKOV.

Beginning in 1759, the younger writers set out on their own to produce the first private journals in Russia: *Prazdnoe vremya v pol'zu upotreblennoe* (Idle Time for Good Use, 1759–60), published by former students of the Cadet Corps, and Sumarokov's *Trudolyubivaya pchela* (Busy Bee, 1759). Kheraskov, a former member of the Petersburg cadet circle, became the leading figure in establishing journal publishing in Moscow, drawing on students of the newly opened Moscow University as contributors. Kheraskov's first and most important journal was *Poleznoe uveselenie* (Useful Diversion, 1760–62), followed by *Svobodnye chasy* (Free Hours, 1763). As in Petersburg, the first Moscow journals spawned new publications: BOGDANOVICH's *Nevinnoe uprazhnenie* (Innocent Exercise, 1763) and V. Sankovsky's *Dobroe namerenie* (Good Intention, 1764). This brief initial flowering of literary journalism, centered around the academic institutions of Petersburg and Moscow, gave way to a period of inactivity which ended in 1769 with the appearance of CATHERINE the Great's *Vsyakaya Vsyachina* (All Sorts and Sundries). Inspired by the spirit of the ENLIGHTENMENT, Catherine's journal sought to raise the moral tenor of society through cautious, "smiling" satire directed at abstract vices. Educated society promptly responded to Catherine's initiative, and in 1769 alone, seven other satirical journals appeared in Petersburg. On the pages of these new journals, their author-editors pushed for more pointed social satire, aimed at specific abuses, including serfdom, and at recognizable public figures. Catherine's chief opponent in the ensuing polemic on the nature and limits of satire was Nikolai NOVIKOV, who, despite Catherine's growing displeasure and repressive tactics, managed to publish four journals during the period: *Truten'* (Drone) (1769–70), *Pustomelya* (Twaddler, 1770), *Zhivopisets* (Painter, 1772–73), and *Koshelek* (Purse, 1774). In 1774, the government crackdown following the Pugachev Rebellion effectively quashed the last remnants of satirical journalism. During the years that followed, until his arrest in 1792, Novikov remained a leading figure in journalism and publishing, taking control in 1779 of Moscow University Press. Among the numerous publishing projects undertaken by Novikov were a series of journals whose Masonic coloration reflected the editor's conversion to the order: *Utrennii svet* (Morning Light, 1777–80), *Moskovskoe ezhemesyachnoe izdanie* (Moscow Monthly Edition, 1781), *Vechernyaya zarya* (Twilight, 1782), and *Pokoyashchiisya trudolyubets* (Reposing Worker, 1884–85). Catherine also attempted indirectly to re-enter the field of journalism by exerting influence on the journal *Sobesednik lyubitelei rossiiskogo slova* (Interlocutor of Lovers of the Russian Word, 1783–84), published by the Academy of Sciences under the directorship of the Empress' friend and rival, Countess Dashkova. During its brief existence, the journal published works by almost all of the major writers of the time, including DERZHAVIN, FONVIZIN, Bogdanovich, Kheraskov, I. DMITRIEV, and Ya. KNYAZHNIN. Also during this period, journals began to appear in the provinces, although throughout most of its history, Russian journalism was to remain confined virtually exclusively to Moscow and Petersburg. Toward the end of the century, satirical journalism experienced

a revival in Fonvizin's *Drug chestnykh lyudei ili Starodum* (Friend of Honest People or Oldthink, 1788, circulated only in manuscript) and KRYLOV's journals, *Pochta dukhov* (Spirits' Mail, 1789), *Zritel'* (Observer, 1792), and *Sankt-Peterburgskii Merkurii* (1793). In the last decade of the 18th century, N. M. KARAMZIN became an active force in Russian journalism as the editor of the journal *Moskovskii zhurnal* (1791–92) and the almanacs AGLAYA (1794–95) and *Aonidy* (1796–99). Karamzin's publications reflected the increasingly SENTIMENTALIST orientation of Russian literature in both the literary works and the articles published on their pages. Aside from his own compositions, Karamzin published works by such notable literary figures of the age as Derzhavin, Dmitriev, Kheraskov, and KAPNIST. As the first Russian journal to separate the material it published into clearly defined sections, *Moskovskii zhurnal* may be identified as a forerunner of the 19th-century "thick" journals. As a rule, 18th-century Russian journals were fragile, short-lived institutions with few subscribers. They appeared irregularly, depending on the energy and private financial resources of their editor-publishers. The editors published primarily their own works or those of a small circle of friends, who also served as the journal's readers.

It was not until the 19th century, with the growth of the reading public, that Russian journalism took on a more businesslike and commercial character. The pattern of unprofitability and ephemerality which plagued 18th-century journalism remained largely intact through the first two decades of the 19th century, with the notable exception of the journal *Vestnik Evropy* (Herald of Europe, 1802–30), one of the relatively few long-lived journals in the history of Russian journalism. The journal owed its initial success to Karamzin, who served as editor from 1802–04, setting high standards for the selection of material to be published and attracting to the pages of the journal such writers as Derzhavin, Kheraskov, Dmitriev, and ZHUKOVSKY, who himself served as editor of *Vestnik Evropy* from 1808–10. Under Zhukovsky's editorship BATYUSHKOV, GNEDICH, VYAZEMSKY, and DAVYDOV contributed to the journal. After 1811, when M. T. Kachenovsky took over as editor, *Vestnik Evropy* grew increasingly conservative and abandoned its earlier sentimentalist bias to join the Shishkovite camp in its defense of CLASSICISM. In the early years of the century, a number of "Karamzinist" journals sprang up, primarily in Moscow, modelling themselves on Karamzin's *Moskovskii zhurnal* and championing sentimentalism in literature and Karamzin's views on language reform. The most important of these publications was P. I. Makarov's *Moskovskii Merkurii* (1803). For his part, Admiral SHISHKOV continued to wage the losing battle for classicism and the Greco-Slavonic tradition in the literary language in his reactionary journal *Chtenie v besede lyubitelei russkogo slova* (Reading in the Collegium of Lovers of the Russian Word, 1811–16). Other notable journals of the period included S. N. Glinka's reactionary *Russkii vestnik* (Russian Herald, 1808–10, 1824); N. I. GRECH's originally more liberal *Syn otechestva* (Son of the Fatherland, 1812–44, 1847–52), which in its early years published PUSHKIN, GRIBOEDOV, Krylov, KÜCHELBECKER, Gnedich, RYLEEV, Zhukovsky, and DELVIG, among others; and P. P. Svinyin's OTECHESTVENNYE ZAPISKI (National Annals, 1818–31), a conservative journal devoted primarily to articles on history and geography.

From the standpoint of literary trends, journalism in the 1820s was dominated by the clash between classicism (see NEOCLASSICISM) and ROMANTICISM. The former found its major defender in Kachenovsky's *Vestnik Evropy*, while the new infatuation with romanticism was reflected in a number of publications, including the almanacs POLYARNAYA ZVEZDA (Pole Star, 1823–25), published by BESTUZHEV and Ryleev, and *Mnemozina* (MNEMOSYNE, 1824–25), published by V. F. ODOEVSKY and Küchelbecker. In the late 1820s and into the 1830s, the main proponent of French romanticism was Nikolai Polevoi's MOSKOVSKII TELEGRAF (1825–34), while M. P. Pogodin's MOSKOVSKII VESTNIK (Moscow Herald, 1827–30) and, later, Nadezhdin's TELESKOP (1831–36) favored German romanticism. On an even more basic level, the 1820s and 1830s may be seen as a transitional period in the history of Russian journalism. Up until this time, journalism had been dominated by an elite group of literary "amateurs" from aristocratic backgrounds. Their publications, primarily short-lived literary journals and almanacs, were aimed at an exclusive readership, and on their pages poetry clearly predominated over prose.

Beginning in the 1820s, a new force entered Russian journalism—the RAZNOCHINETS—and hand in hand with this development went the increasing commercialism of the Russian journal. Journals geared to a mass audience began to appear, tailoring themselves to the less well-educated and provincial reader by concentrating more heavily on prose and varying their content with nonliterary features. This gave rise to the "encyclopedic" journal, marked as a precursor of the "thick" journal by its publication of articles devoted to diverse scholarly subjects, social problems, and even fashions, side by side with literature. Polevoi, himself the son of a tradesman, may be credited with founding the first "encyclopedic" journal in his *Moskovskii telegraf*. After 1825, the center of gravity of "respectable" journalism shifted to Moscow, and, until the late 1830s, Petersburg journalism was dominated by the publications of the "Petersburg triumvirate," Grech, Faddei BULGARIN, and Osip SENKOVSKY. In 1822, Bulgarin began to publish his *Severnyi arkhiv* (Northern Archive), which in 1829 merged with Grech's *Syn otechestva*. In 1834, A. F. SMIRDIN founded the "encyclopedic" journal BIBLIOTEKA DLYA CHTENIYA (Library for Reading, 1834–1864) and invited Senkovsky to take it over as salaried editor. Thus, *Biblioteka* became the first Russian journal to run as a commercial enterprise, dividing the publishing and editorial functions between two distinct figures and paying regular salaries to the staff and fees to the contributors. Like the publications of Bulgarin and Grech, *Biblioteka* was aimed at the "average" reader—clerks, tradesmen, and junior officers—and became the standard reading fare of the provincial landowner. Despite the hostility of serious literary people to the fawning patriotism and "yellow" journalism of the Bulgarin clique, they could not help but recognize the positive aspects of the new commercialism which was reshaping Russian journalism. Pushkin himself candidly admitted that he wanted to be paid for what he wrote and in the last years of his life turned increasingly from poetry to prose. Another key development in the 1830s which helped to pave the way for the appearance of the "thick" journal at the end of the decade was the emergence of the role of the literary critic as social critic, shaped initially by the *raznochinets* Vissarion BELINSKY in his writings for Nadezhdin's *Teleskop* and MOLVA (Rumor). The uneasiness of the post-Decembrist government with the growing socio-political voice of Russian journalism was reflected in the closings of a number of journals, including *Moskovskii telegraf* in 1834 and *Teleskop* and *Molva* in 1836. It was primarily the existence of a clearly definable "line," or socio-philosophical bias, determining the selection of material published in all departments of the journal and generally elaborated in the literary critical section which distinguished the "thick" journal from the "encyclopedic" journal. In 1838, A. A. Kraevsky obtained the rights to Svinyin's defunct *Otechestvennye zapiski* and reopened the overhauled journal at the beginning of the next year. The new *Otechestvennye zapiski* may be considered the first of the great 19th-century "thick" journals. Appropriately, Belinsky took over the management of the critical and bibliographical section of the journal toward the end of its first year. Belinsky's move from Moscow to Petersburg parallelled the renewed preeminence of the capital in Russian journalism during this period.

Journalism in the 1840s was marked by the ongoing controversy between the Moscow-based SLAVOPHILES and the Petersburg-based WESTERNIZERS. Unable to obtain permission to publish their own journal, the Slavophiles contributed, albeit rarely, to Pogodin's MOSKVITYANIN (Muscovite, 1841–56), and in 1845, the first three issues of the journal came out under the editorship of I. V. KIREEVSKY. In general, however, the Slavophiles found the "official nationalism" of *Moskvityanin* distasteful and preferred to publish their works in separate anthologies. From the beginning of the 1840s, the Westernizers' primary outlet for publication was *Otechestvennye zapiski*. HERZEN (Iskander), NEKRASOV, BAKUNIN, OGARYOV, GRANOVSKY, and BOTKIN, among others, joined Belinsky on the journal, and *Otechestvennye zapiski* soon established itself as the leading literary journal of the period, with TURGENEV and DOSTOEVSKY publishing their early works almost exclusively on its pages. In 1846, Belinsky, followed by the more radical wing of the Westernizers—Herzen (who emigrated abroad in 1847), Nekrasov, and PANAEV—broke with Kraevsky and left the journal. Nekrasov and Panaev obtained control of the journal SOVREMENNIK (Contemporary, 1836–66), which had been founded by Pushkin and which, during the decade since the poet's death, had stagnated under the

editorship of P. A. PLETNYOV. In 1847, the journal reopened with Belinsky as its chief literary critic. Despite the split in the Westernizer camp, a number of more moderate writers, most notably Turgenev, continued to publish in both journals. The "black seven years" following the revolutionary upheavals in Europe in 1848 were a bleak period in Russian journalism. In 1848, Nicholas I appointed a special committee headed by A. S. Menshikov to study the current state of journalism. The findings of the committee prompted the Third Department to issue severe warnings to the editors of *Otechestvennye zapiski* and *Sovremennik* and led to the formation of a permanent body, the "Committee of April 2" headed by the notoriously reactionary D. P. Buturlin, to oversee the workings of the press and censorship. The repressive atmosphere had a negative effect on the content of most publications, virtually putting an end to all journal polemics during the period. In the early 1850s, only the flagging *Moskvityanin* enjoyed a brief revival under the influence of its "young editors" (molodaya redaktsiya), centered around A. N. OSTROVSKY.

In contrast, the years following Alexander II's accession to the throne in 1855 and preceding the 1861 reforms were a period of unprecedented growth and vigor for Russian journalism. In the atmosphere of relaxed censorship which ensued, the Slavophiles finally received permission to issue their own journal, RUSSKAYA BESEDA (Russian Conversation, 1856–60), and Mikhail KATKOV began to publish his initially liberal and anglophile RUSSKII VESTNIK (Russian Herald, 1856–1906), which was to become the most brilliant literary journal of the 19th century. *Sovremennik* received an infusion of new blood with the addition to its staff of CHERNYSHEVSKY (in 1854) and DOBROLYUBOV (in 1856), who carried on the Belinskian tradition of "civic" criticism. Leading contemporary writers continued to publish on its pages, including TOLSTOI, Turgenev, Ostrovsky, and GRIGOROVICH. Even *Otechestvennye zapiski* made a fleeting comeback with the publication of PISEMSKY's *One Thousand Souls* (1858) and GONCHAROV's *Oblomov* (1859). This period also witnessed the beginnings of the émigré press. In 1855, Herzen, in residence in London, began to publish the almanac POLYARNAYA ZVEZDA (Pole Star) and, in 1857, the weekly newspaper KOLOKOL (The Bell, 1857–67), which was, at least until 1863, one of the most widely read and influential publications within the borders of Russia. All in all, this was an exhilarating period for the educated segment of Russian society, a time when the common striving for needed reforms, above all the abolition of serfdom, overshadowed party differences and created a rapprochement between the liberal and radical factions. This was reflected in the relatively cordial relations which obtained between the leading journals of the period. The "honeymoon," however, was short-lived. Already by the end of the 1850s, moderate writers began leaving the increasingly radical *Sovremennik*, primarily for the pages of *Russkii vestnik*. Tolstoi began to publish in Katkov's journal in 1859 and Turgenev in 1860.

In the 1860s, the split between liberals and radicals turned into an open confrontation, reflected in the heated journal polemics of the time. As a general rule, the best literary works continued to appear in the increasingly conservative *Russkii vestnik* well into the 1870s, while the most interesting criticism was produced by the radicals, notably Dobrolyubov (died 1861) and Chernyshevsky (arrested 1862) in *Sovremennik* and PISAREV in the journal RUSSKOE SLOVO (Russian Word, 1859–66). In 1861, Dostoevsky and his brother Mikhail received permission to publish the POCHVA journal VREMYA (Time), which was closed down by the government in 1863. In 1864, the Dostoevsky brothers were again allowed to put out a journal under the name EPOKHA, but the new journal never succeeded in recovering *Vremya*'s subscribers and was forced to go out of business for financial reasons in 1865. The 1860s also saw a new flowering of satirical journals, of which the most important was ISKRA (The Spark, 1859–73). In 1866, in the wake of Karakozov's attempt on the life of the Tsar, *Sovremennik* and *Russkoe slovo* were closed by the government. In the same year, G. E. Blagosvetlov, former editor of *Russkoe slovo*, opened the journal *Delo* (Deed, 1866–84) in collaboration with N. I. Shulgin, who served as official editor. *Delo* was conceived as a continuation of *Russkoe slovo*, and several articles by Pisarev appeared there in 1867–68. After the closing of *Sovremennik*, Nekrasov gained control of Kraevsky's *Otechestvennye zapiski*, and, in 1868, the journal began to come out under the editorship of Nekrasov, SALTYKOV-SHCHEDRIN, and G. Z. Eliseev. After Nekrasov's death in 1878, N. K. MIKHAILOVSKY also joined the editorial board. Contributors to the literary section of the journal included Nekrasov, Saltykov-Shchedrin, Ostrovsky, GARSHIN, PLESHCHEEV, NADSON, MAMIN-SIBIRYAK, and Gleb USPENSKY. Dostoevsky's novel *Podrostok* (The Adolescent) appeared in the journal in 1875. In the 1870s, *Otechestvennye zapiski* adopted an increasingly POPULIST orientation. Both *Delo* and *Otechestvennye zapiski*, the last survivors of the tradition of radical journalism of the 1860s, were closed by the government in 1884. In the last decades of the 19th century, the "thick" journal, which had dominated the intellectual life of Russia for decades, began to decline in importance. Challenged by the growing importance of newspapers and book publishing, by the appearance of "thin" illustrated journals—such as, *Niva* (The Grainfield, 1870–1917), *Rodina* (The Motherland, 1879–1917), *Ogonek* (Flame, 1879–83), and *Vokrug sveta* (Around the World, 1885–1917)—and by increasing numbers of specialized publications, the "thick" journal had difficulty competing in the new mass market. Nonetheless, several relatively durable publications in the old mold did appear during this period. The first of these was *Vestnik Evropy* (Herald of Europe, 1866–1918), which began publication in Petersburg under the editorship of M. M. STASYULEVICH, a retired professor of history. The journal was from the beginning a moderate liberal publication. During the course of its existence, *Vestnik Evropy* published a wide variety of writers, including Ostrovsky, Goncharov, Turgenev, Saltykov-Shchedrin (after the closing of *Otechestvennye zapiski*), A. K. TOLSTOI, Gleb Uspensky, ERTEL, FET, Pleshcheev, POLONSKY, Mamin-Sibiryak, HIPPIUS, N. M. MINSKY, and Vladimir SOLOVYOV. In the 1870s, with Turgenev acting as intermediary, Emile Zola became an active contributor to the journal. Among the "Parisian Letters" which he published in *Vestnik Evropy* were articles outlining his theory of the experimental novel. The music and art critic V. V. Stasov also published in the journal for many years. The popularity of *Vestnik Evropy* waned in the 1880s, and the leading writers of the last two decades of the century published primarily in the three remaining major "thick" journals, RUSSKOE BOGATSTVO (Russian Wealth, 1876–1918), RUSSKAYA MYSL' (Russian Thought, 1880–1918), and *Severnyi vestnik* (Northern Herald, 1885–1899). In the 1880s, under the editorship of L. E. Obolensky, *Russkoe bogatstvo* was oriented toward Tolstoian philosophy, and its literary section was generally uninteresting. In the 1890s, however, with N. K. Mikhailovsky as its unofficial editor, the journal attracted many of *Otechestvennye zapiski*'s former contributors and became a leading organ of populism, publishing almost exclusively realist writers. In contrast, *Russkaya mysl'*, a moderate liberal publication, emphasized the diversity of the writers whose works appeared on its pages, striving to publish the best-known writers of the day without regard for factional differences. The last of the major "thick" journals, *Severnyi vestnik* began publication in Petersburg in 1885 under the editorship of A. M. Evreinova. In the earliest years of its existence, Mikhailovsky and a number of other former contributors to the recently closed *Otechestvennye zapiski* played an active role in the running of the journal. During this period, CHEKHOV, Uspensky, Garshin, Mamin-Sibiryak, and Pleshcheev, among others, published in *Severnyi vestnik*. However, in 1888, Mikhailovsky left the journal, citing as his reason the incompatibility of his views with those of Evreinova, and one by one his sympathizers followed him. The final break with the populists came in 1889 over the participation in the journal of A. L. VOLYNSKY, and by 1892, Volynsky had become the leading voice on the journal. In his articles, Volynsky adopted an idealist stance, polemicizing with Mikhailovsky's utilitarian vision of art. Although far from being a SYMBOLIST himself, Volynsky supported the modernists insofar as they served his opposition to NATURALISM, and *Severnyi vestnik* was one of the few journals of the period in which the early symbolists —notably MEREZHKOVSKY, SOLOGUB, Hippius, BALMONT, and Minsky—could publish their works. In the 1890s, Tolstoi and LESKOV also published in the journal. *Severnyi vestnik* was forced to close in 1899 because of financial difficulties and trouble with the censorship. Beginning in the 1890s, a number of "legal Marxist" publications appeared, including *Novoe slovo* (New Word, 1894–97), *Nachalo* (Beginning, 1899), *Zhizn'* (Life, 1897–1901), *Mir Bozhii* (God's World, 1892–1906), and *Nauchnoe obozrenie* (Scientific Review, 1894–1903). BERDYAEV, P. B. STRUVE, and S. N. Bulgakov contributed to these publications along with LENIN and PLEKHANOV. The "legal Marxist" journals published primarily

realist writers—notably GORKY, VERESAEV, BUNIN, KUPRIN, and Chekhov—although works by Merezhkovsky, Hippius, Balmont, and Minsky appeared in *Nachalo* and *Zhizn'*. The first decade of the 20th century saw the rise of modernist art and literary journals in Russia. The first of these was the lavish art journal MIR ISKUSSTVA (World of Art, 1899–1904), which came out in Petersburg under the editorship of Sergei DIAGHILEV. Many of the symbolists published in the journal, including Hippius, Merezhkovsky, Sologub, BRYUSOV, BELY, ROZANOV, and Filosofov. In 1903, Merezhkovsky and Hippius began to publish the journal *Novyi put'* (New Way), which represented the wing of the symbolists oriented toward religion and philosophy. The journal was not successful and closed the following year. VESY (Scales, 1904–1909) was, of all the modernist journals, the most representative of the symbolist movement as a whole. Bryusov shared the editorship of the journal with S. A. Polyakov, and all the Russian symbolists contributed to the journal. During the first year of its existence, ZOLOTOE RUNO (Golden Fleece, 1906–1909) also published the entire spectrum of symbolists, but a split soon developed between the "mystical anarchists" of *Zolotoe runo* and the "first generation" symbolists of *Vesy*. The *Zolotoe runo* group, including BLOK, Vyacheslav IVANOV, Bunin, and ANDREEV, opposed *Vesy*'s preoccupation with questions of aesthetics and form. The year 1909 witnessed the closings of both major symbolist journals, and also saw the opening of a new modernist journal, APOLLON (1909–1917). Although originally without a definite orientation, *Apollon* became a forum for the developing ACMEIST school, with GUMILYOV as its chief theorist. During the course of its existence, *Apollon* published works by ANNENSKY, Gumilyov, Vyacheslav Ivanov, Balmont, Bryusov, KUZMIN, Sologub, AKHMATOVA, MANDELSHTAM, GORODETSKY, and NARBUT, among others. The 1917 Revolution marked a sharp break in the history of Russian journalism. Those prerevolutionary journals which continued to publish— including *Vestnik Evropy*, *Russkoe bogatstvo*, and *Russkaya mysl'* —were shut down by the new Soviet government in 1918. In their place a number of short-lived Soviet journals sprang up during the civil war years. During this period, the massive PROLETKULT organization was the most active group in publishing, issuing fifteen periodicals before the end of the civil war. The most notable of these were *Proletarskaya kul'tura* (1918–21), *Gryadushchee* (Future, 1918–1921), *Gorn* (Forge, 1918–20), and *Gudki* (Sirens, 1919). The FUTURISTS also issued several publications in these years, the most important being the newspaper *Iskusstvo kommuny* (Art of the Commune, 1918–19). A number of early Soviet journals did not represent any particular literary group. The most interesting of these were *Plamya* (Flame, 1918–20), *Khudozhestvennoe slovo* (Artistic Word, 1920–21), and *Tvorchestvo* (Creation, 1918–1921). The journal *Vestnik zhizni* (Messenger of Life, 1918–19) represented the first attempt to found a Soviet "thick" journal. After the Civil War, the ephemeral periodicals of the early years were replaced by more solid publications, including a number of "thick" journals created on the 19th-century model. The first of these was KRASNAYA NOV' (Red Virgin Soil, 1921–42), followed by MOLODAYA GVARDIYA (Young Guard, 1922–   ), OKTYABR' (October, 1924–   ), ZVEZDA (Star, 1924–   ), and NOVYI MIR (New World, 1925–   ). Another notable publication of this period was the critical and bibliographical journal PECHAT' I REVOLYUTSIYA (Press and Revolution, 1921–30). A number of specifically literary journals appeared as organs of the major literary groupings of the day. The futurists published LEF (acronym for "Left Front of Art," 1923–25), whose contributors included MAYAKOVSKY, Osip BRIK, A. M. Rodchenko, N. N. ASEEV, and Boris Kushner, as well as the formalist critics EIKHENBAUM and TOMASHEVSKY. *LEF* was superseded by *Novyi LEF* (New LEF, 1927–28). The Octobrists, a group of proletarian writers descended from the Proletkult, were represented by the journal NA POSTU (On Guard, 1923–25) and later by *Na literaturnom postu* (1926–32). Aside from the publications issued by the State Publishing House, about thirty private journals appeared during the NEP period. The most interesting of these were *Novaya Rossiya* (New Russia, 1922) and *Russkii sovremennik* (1924). The new "thick" journals played an important role in the development of Soviet literature during this period. The most interesting of these publications was *Krasnaya nov'*, which came out under the editorship of A. VORONSKY from 1921 until his removal from the post in 1927. Voronsky opposed the proletarian writers' claim to exclusive rights over Soviet culture and welcomed the works of the so-called fellow travelers on the pages of his journal. The fellow travelers also published in *Krasnaya nov*"s paler competitor, *Novyi mir*, as well as in *Zvezda*, the first "thick" journal to be founded in Petrograd. In contrast, *Oktyabr'* and *Molodaya gvardiya* published almost exclusively proletarian writers. In 1932, the Soviet Government consolidated its control over literature by liquidating all remaining literary groups. In 1934, SOCIALIST REALISM was proclaimed the only acceptable literary method, and for the next two decades, Soviet journalism shared the general colorlessness of Soviet literature as a whole. The most notorious incident in journalism of this period was ZHDANOV's attack in 1946 on the journals *Zvezda* and *Leningrad* for their publication of works by Akhmatova and ZOSHCHENKO. In the wake of Zhdanov's speech, *Leningrad* was closed, the editor of *Zvezda* was removed, and Akhmatova and Zoshchenko were expelled from the Writers' Union. After years of stagnation, Soviet journalism experienced a spurt of new growth with the appearance after Stalin's death of a number of new journals, including *Yunost'* (1955–), *Moskva* (1957–), and *Voprosy literatury* (1957–). In the early 1960s, the journal *Yunost'*, which had been founded by Valentin KATAEV and remained under his editorship until 1962, became the major publication outlet for a group of iconoclastic young writers, including Evgeny EVTUSHENKO, Andrei VOZNESENSKY, Vasily AKSYONOV, Anatoly GLADILIN, and Vladimir VOINOVICH. However, by far the most interesting journal of the period was the revitalized old "thick" journal *Novyi mir*. Under the editorship of Aleksandr TVARDOVSKY, *Novyi mir* published most of the major writers and works to appear in the Soviet Union during the post-Stalin period, most notably SOLZHENITSYN's *One Day in the Life of Ivan Denisovich*. Since Tvardovsky was forced to resign as editor in 1970, *Novyi mir* has lost its former brilliance, reflecting the general decline in Soviet literature in the 1970s. However, it remains the most prestigious literary journal in the Soviet Union. Its closest competitor is the relatively new journal, *Nash sovremennik* (Our Contemporary, 1956–), which in the 1970s was taken over by the "COUNTRY PROSE" writers and which regularly publishes the works of such writers as Valentin RASPUTIN, Vasily BELOV, Viktor Astafiev, Evgeny Nosov, Viktor Likhonosov, and Fyodor Abramov.

In the years since the 1917 Revolution, a second Russian journalism has grown up outside the boundaries of the Soviet Union, nurtured by three waves of emigration to the West. Many of the émigré journals proved to be interesting, but short-lived. The most durable of the publications produced by the first wave of emigration were SOVREMENNYE ZAPISKI (Paris, 1920–40), *Volya Rossii* (Prague, 1922–32), and NOVYI ZHURNAL (New York, 1942–). The main contribution of the second wave of emigrants which arrived in the West after World War II was the journal GRANI (Munich, 1946–). In the 1970s and 1980s, the third wave has spawned a proliferation of publications in Europe, Israel, and the United States. The most prestigious of these is KONTINENT (1974–), published in West Germany under the editorship of Vladimir MAKSIMOV. Both Solzhenitsyn and SINYAVSKY, the two major writers of the current emigration, contributed to the early issues of the journal. However, Solzhenitsyn now publishes exclusively in the Paris-based religious-philosophical journal *Vestnik russkogo khristianskogo dvizheniya* (Herald of the Russian Christian Movement), and in 1978, Sinyavsky began to publish his own journal *Sintaksis* in Paris.

Bibliography: Istoriya russkoi zhurnalistiki XVIII–XIX vekov. Ed. A. V. Zapadov. 1973. Robert A. Maguire, *Red Virgin Soil.* 1968. *Ocherki istorii russkoi sovetskoi zhurnalistiki, 1917–1932.* 1966. *Ocherki istorii russkoi sovetskoi zhurnalistiki, 1933–1945.* 1968. *Ocherki po istorii russkoi zhurnalistiki i kritiki.* Vol. 1. 1950. *Ocherki po istorii russkoi zhurnalistiki i kritiki.* Vol. 2. 1965. *Russkaya literatura v emigratsii.* Ed. N. Poltoratskii. Pittsburgh, 1972. *Russkaya periodicheskaya pechat' (1702–1894).* 1959. Gleb Struve, *Russkaya literatura v izgnanii.* New York, 1956.   C. T. N.

Kaménsky, Vasíly Vasílievich (1884–1961), poet and writer, was born on a steamboat on the Kama river near Perm, where he spent most of his early childhood. His father was a goldfield inspector. In 1905, Kamensky was arrested for political activity. In 1908, he published poetry in the journal *Vesna*, and later became its editor. A year later, he met David BURLYUK, joined his HYLAEA group, and took part in publishing *Sadok sudei* (A Trap for Judges, 1910). Kamensky published a novel in 1910, *The Mud Hut*, in which urban life is abandoned for the joy and beauty of nature. Kamensky was one of Russia's first aviators. In 1911, after surviving an airplane crash, however, he gave up flying. In 1913, Kamensky toured Russia with Burlyuk and MAYAKOVSKY to promote FUTURISM. He was the principal organizer of the Café of Poets during the immediate postrevolutionary period. In the 1920s, Kamensky's role in Mayakovsky's LEF group was minor.

Kamensky's poetry expresses a genuine love of, and communion with, nature in all its forms; it reflects linguistic and poetic features of KHLEBNIKOV's, KRUCHONYKH's and Mayakovsky's poetry. Like Kruchonykh, Kamensky uses transrational language (ZAUMNYI YAZYK) to experiment with the texture of sounds which evoke their own transrational meaning. Like Khlebnikov, he assigns concepts and characteristics to sounds. Like Mayakovsky, Kamensky breaks down words for verbal play; he declaims and sings his poetry. His major and most popular work, "Stenka Razin" (1915), is about a Don Cossack who led a peasant revolt in 1670.

Works: Ego-Moya biografiya velikogo futurista. 1918. *Eto i est' biografiya.* Tiflis, 1927. *Put' entuziasta.* 1931. *Zhizn' s Mayakovskim.* 1940.

Secondary literature: Vahan D. Barooshian, *Russian Cubo-Futurism 1910–1930.* The Hague, 1974. L. Efreimin, "Tvorcheskii put' Vasiliya Kamenskogo." In V. Kamenskii, *Izbrannye stikhi.* 1934. S. Gints, *Vasilii Kamenskii.* Perm, 1974. Vladimir Markov, *Russian Futurism: A History.* 1968.   V. D. B.

Kantemír, Prince Antíokh Dmitrievich (1709–44), poet and satirist. The polyglot and superbly educated son of the Moldavian ruling family, which had found refuge in Russia, Kantemir became his adopted homeland's first major representative of its own Age of Enlightenment. Deeply sympathetic with the Petrine europeanization of Russia and a member of Feofan PROKOPOVICH's "Learned Guard," Kantemir vigorously advocated educational reform and intellectual development. However, his direct participation in Russian life ceased in the early 1730s when he was appointed Russian ambassador, first to England and then to France. He remained abroad the entire last twelve years of his life.

Kantemir's greatest contribution to Russian letters consists of his nine satires. Although modelled on Horace and, especially, Boileau, Kantemir's satires are thoroughly russified and directed against the superficiality and obscurantism of Russian society, Russia's backwardness compared with the European world whose most progressive ideas Kantemir upheld. Most praised for his "gallery of types," Kantemir also succeeded in creating a satirist-narrator of engaging and individual personality (mock-modest, witty, shrewd) and in converting the Slavo-Russian literary language and the syllabic prosody (see SYLLABIC VERSIFICATION) into remarkably supple mediums. Well-known in manuscript copies, Kantemir's satires were published first in French translation (1749) and only in 1762 in their Russian original.

Kantemir also translated Horace and Aesop (in verse) and Fontenelle (in prose). Both to those translations and to his original works he appended copious notes and commentaries—the first to perform such a philological function in Russia. Kantemir also produced the only Russian manual of syllabic versification, especially interesting for its inclusion of Kantemir's own innovations.

Works: Sochineniya, pis'ma i izbrannye perevody. Ed. V. Ya. Stoyunin and P. A. Efremov. 2 vols. 1867–68. *Sobranie stikhotvorenii.* Ed. F. Ya. Priima and Z. I. Gershkovich. (Biblioteka poeta, bol'shaya seriya). 1956.

Translation: "Satire I: To My Mind." In *The Literature of Eighteenth Century Russia.* Ed. by H. B. Segel. Vol. 1. 1967.

Secondary literature: "Materialy yubileinogo zasedaniya, posvyashchennogo 250-letiyu so dnya rozhdeniya A. D. Kantemira." In *Problemy russkogo prosveshcheniya v literature XVIII veka.* 1961. Pp. 190–270. F. Ya. Priima, "Antiokh Dmitrievich Kantemir." In *Sobranie stikhotvorenii.* Ed. F. Ya. Priima and E. I. Gershkovich. (Biblioteka poèta, bol'shaya seriya. 1956. Pp. 5–52. L. V. Pumpyanskii, "Kantemir." In *Istoriya russkoi literatury.* Vol. 3, part 1. 1941. Pp. 176–212.   I. R. T.

Kapnist, Vasily Vasilievich (1738–1823), playwright and poet. A Ukrainian of Greek ancestry, Kapnist was born and raised on his family estate in Poltava. The Ukraine was dear to him and he served its interests often and at length in various official capacities. Although also otherwise occupied (the military, farming, etc.), Kapnist was an active and productive poet throughout his life. He became an intimate of DERZHAVIN, KHEMNITSER, and Lvov and together they comprised a poetry circle devoted to the study and imitation of Horace and the Anacreontica. Therefrom emerged Kapnist's splendid translations from Horace and his set of parallel, russified and personalized, imitations—among the finest examples of Horatiana in the history of Russian verse. While also writing odes and satires, it was principally *poésie légère* that Kapnist cultivated and with full justification he may be regarded as BATYUSHKOV's direct predecessor.

Keenly theatrical and blessed with extraordinary comic gifts, Kapnist produced his masterpiece in the five-act verse comedy *Chicanery* (Yabeda, 1798). Justly praised as a powerful satire depicting judicial corruption in a provincial town, the play also owes its high stature in Russian dramaturgy to certain technical achievements: brilliantly witty dialogue perfectly integrated with the verse, including the tour de force of a stutterer in iambic hexameter; ingenious modulations of tone that vitally enhance the play's meaning (e.g., the interaction of the sinister and the slapstick); full dramatic exploitation of stage props; and so on. *Chicanery* may be said to rival GRIBOEDOV's later, more famous masterwork and to stand as a worthy precursor to the greatest of all Russian comedies, GOGOL's *Inspector-General.*

Works: Sobranie sochinenii. Ed. D. S. Babkin. 2 vols. 1960.
Translations: See Lewanski, p. 266.
Secondary literature: D. S. Babkin, "V. V. Kapnist—kritiko-biograficheskii ocherk." In *Sobranie sochinenii.* Ed. D. S. Babkin. 2 vols. 1960. Pp. 12–65. V. G. Bitner, "Kapnist." In *Istoriya russkoi literatury*, Vol. 4, pt. 2. 1947. Pp. 485–500.   I. R. T.

Karamzin, Nikolai Mikhailovich (1766–1826) was the single most influential 18th-century Russian prose writer. Between 1789 and 1803 he left his important legacies in poetry and especially small prose forms. After 1803, he devoted the rest of his life to the writing of his monumental *History of the Russian State* (Istoriya gosudarstva Rossiiskogo, 1818–26, 12 vols.)

Karamzin, the second son of a retired army captain and a native of Simbirsk, between 1777 and 1781, boarded in Moscow at the school of Matthias Schaden (1731–97), professor of moral philosophy at the University. After graduating at Schaden's, he frequented literary and worldly salons in St. Petersburg and later Simbirsk; he projected translations of Voltaire, read, in his words, indiscriminately and gambled at the card table. At the death of his father in 1784 (he was four years old when his mother died), Karamzin met in Simbirsk the Moscow FREEMASON I. P. Turgenev (1752–1807). From this encounter, Karamzin later wrote the Swiss physiognomist and Mason Ja.-K. Lavater (1741–1801), "Everything was renewed in me" (Vse vo mne obnovilos') and that he was inspired to live "not without being of some use to people" (ne bespolezno dlya lyudei). The same year Karamzin entered the Masonic Lodge *Zlatoi Venets* (Golden Crown) in Simbirsk. In 1785, he moved to Moscow and joined Novikov's Friendly Learned Society (Druzheskoe uchenoe obshchestvo, 1781–ca. 1790) with over fifty members. Karamzin translated for the Society A. von Haller's *Vom Ursprung des Übels* (1734) and other spiritual and moral works, and he participated in their translation of C. C. Sturm's *Unterhaltungen mit Gott* (2 vols., 1768) and *Betrachtungen über die Werke Gottes* (2 vols., 1772). At this time Karamzin was especially close to the Mason A. A. Petrov (?–1793) and emulated his friend's simple, graceful style, purged of Church-Slavonicisms (see "A Flower on the Grave of my Agathon"—Tsvetok na grob moego Agatona, 1793). Karamzin and Petrov co-edited NOVIKOV's journal for children *Detskoe chtenie dlya serdtsa i razuma* (Children's Readings for Heart and Mind, 1785–89) and contributed his translations from the writer for children C.-F. Weisse (1726–1804), from Mme de Genlis's (1746–1830) *Veillées du Château* (1784), a collection of *contes moraux* for children, and from Anglo-German pastoral poets, notably the entire *Seasons* (1726–30) by J. Thomson and

the idylls (1756–72) of S. Gessner (1730–88). Karamzin's first original works also appeared in this journal, among them his first accomplished short story "Evgenii i Yuliya" (1789), where Karamzin with a simple, graceful prose style tempered the story's Masonic-religious theme of submission to the will of God. In *Children's Readings*, Karamzin followed the pedagogical principles of Rousseau's *Emile* (1762), which were very congenial to Novikov and his circle.

In May 1789, Karamzin left Russia on his European tour which, judging from the Masons' correspondence, they played some role in organizing, if not in financing. He returned 15 July 1790, to an unfriendly faction of Masons who accused him of cosmopolitanism (unpatriotic), ambition ("puffed with pride"), and of betraying Masonry: Prince N. N. Trubetskoi (1744–1821), A. M. Kutuzov (1749–97), I. V. Lopukhin (1756–1816), M. I. Bagryansky (1762/3–1813), et al. Notwithstanding their malicious accusations, Karamzin all his life shared the Masons' platonic love of freedom, equality, and brotherhood, some of the existential aspects of their philosophy, and more particularly the Mason Novikov's endeavor to spread "enlightenment" (i.e., education and the sciences) among the masses, and Novikov's interest in the national past, its monuments and history. He also counted Masons among his closest and dearest friends, intimates whom he frequently addressed and personified in his verse and prose, Petrov as "Agathon" and Pleshcheeva as "Aglaya". A. I. Pleshcheeva (died 1817) was married to the Mason A. A. Pleshcheev (1778–1862), Karamzin's life-long friend; in 1801, Karamzin married her sister E. I. Protasova (1767–1802). The role of Masonry in Karamzin's work was complex, almost dialectical, for there was a strong streak of scepticism in Karamzin. He wrote A. I. Pleshcheeva in 1790, "If my soul be immortal . . ." (much to her concern for Karamzin), and he pointedly contrasted the immortality of the soul as a Masonic "assurance" (uverenie) without proof, and as a "hope" (chayanie) of the "sceptic, but only in the good meaning of that word" in *Letters of a Russian Traveller*. The rational mind of Karamzin underlying his scepticism shunned the Masons' mystical, theological, not to mention alchemical pursuits, and their Church-Slavonicized, at times "hieroglyphic" style. Karamzin excluded from his first literary journal MOSKOVSKII ZHURNAL (1791–92) contributions which may best be termed *excessively* Masonic; however, he did publish Masonic articles by M. M. KHERASKOV, Petrov, F. P. Klyucharyov (1754–1820), and others, his own Masonic-inspired "Poeziya, 1787," and translations from foreign works widely read among the Masons. More subtly, underlying much of Karamzin's poetry and prose was a subtle interplay of Masonic-inspired idealism and scepticism toward this same idealism. Karamzin rarely sustained the idyllic, pastoral tone without lapses into a matter-of-fact or humorously ironic tone, alien to the former. Nowhere is this interplay, or bivocality, more striking than in his treatment of the Golden Age. Like the Masons, Karamzin frequently suggested that his idylls were not only about man's lost state in the Garden of Eden before the Fall but also about primal harmony on earth; however, unlike the Masons who believed Masonry would restore love and innocence on earth, Karamzin's arcadia was sceptical. Also his ideals of republicanism and freedom tended to wither under his sceptic's eye, but in the early 1790s this did not prevent occasional outbursts of enthusiasm for the French Revolution. In 1797, Karamzin began doubting the wisdom of Peter I's reforms, and under the reign of Alexander, his political views became markedly conservative, even "Slavophile," e.g., "Notes of Old and New Russia in Her Political and Civic Relations" (Zapiski drevnei i novoi Rossii v ee politicheskom i grazhdanskom otnosheniyakh, written Dec. 1810–Jan. 1811 for the Grand Duchess Ekaterina Pavlovna, and first published 1861). Under Alexander's reign Karamzin's scepticism became more subdued but so did his utopianism and idealism. His most important contributions to Russian literature, however, were written during the 1790s and early 1800s.

In 1791, Karamzin began publishing *Letters of a Russian Traveller* (Pis'ma russkogo puteshestvennika) in installments in *Moskovskii zhurnal*: letters from Germany, Switzerland, ending with the Traveller's arrival in Paris (continued in AGLAYA; 1st incomplete edition of *Pis'ma* in 1797, but publication of the final two volumes, with the complete letters from England and France, had to wait until 1801). Karamzin wrote *Pis'ma* independently from the few real letters he sent from abroad, and contrary to his claim in the 1797 edition he wrote *Pis'ma* in his study and consulted numerous and varied sources. He achieved the illusion of spontaneity, however, for which the epistolary form was ideally suited. This form also allowed the Traveler to pour into *Pis'ma* a wealth of information and create a sort of encyclopedia of West-European culture, especially belles lettres; also he provided a generous sampling of his favorite literary models (e.g., "Spring would not have been so beautiful for me, if Thomson and Kleist had not described all its beauties for me"). In depicting his tender, sensitive heart, at times mockingly, the Traveler frequently alluded to L. Sterne's *A Sentimental Journey Through France and Italy* (1768) and to passages from *Tristram Shandy* (1759–67). In the early 1790s Karamzin was crowned the "Russian Sterne," after the "French Sterne" in the late 1780s (C. Dupaty, 1746–88) and the "German Sterne" in the late 70s (J. F. Jakobi 1712–91). The informative character of *Pis'ma* and the Traveler's Sternian sensibility led Sipovsky to discern a "hybrid" journey, although Sterne's journey (over *six* times *smaller* in size) was "hybrid" too, if less obtrusively. In Russia *Pis'ma* generated a vogue for epistolary and diary-like journeys, which lasted until the 1820s, and launched on a grand scale in Russian belles lettres Sterne and German literature.

Karamzin's conception of *Moskovskii zhurnal* was also "encyclopedic": besides installments of *Pis'ma* it contained works by Karamzin in verse and in prose, Karamzin's translations, his reviews of Russian and foreign books, etc. The overall sentimental tone and manner of this journal's poetry and prose fiction was in keeping with the prevailing current at the time in West-European literatures; in addition, Karamzin's articles were often playful and ironic. In the tiny article "Frol Silin, a Virtuous Man" (1791) Karamzin related the virtuous deeds of a Russian saint-like peasant who was actually alive, and living in Simbirsk. In "Liodor" (1792), which introduced into Russian literature the theme of friendship, the hero Liodor (dressed in the costume of Goethe's Werther) began the tale of his sorrowful love for a beautiful Turkish woman, but the story was cut off before an unhappy ending. In "Natalya, the Boyar's Daughter" (Natal'ya boyarskaya doch', 1792) Karamzin gave a sentimentalized treatment of the historical period of Muscovy's struggle against the Lithuanians but lapsed into Shandean banter and parodied the Russian semi-folk novels of love and adventure (e.g. Komarov's *Milord Georg*, 1782). And in his famous "Poor Liza" (Bednaya Liza,—1792) Karamzin relied upon the hackneyed theme of lovers separated by their different social classes (set in vogue by Rousseau in *La Nouvelle Heloïse*, 1761), but Karamzin's narrator tempered with irony this story of his aesthetic experience of virtue in distress, and he contrasted his portrait of Liza as a pastoral peasant to that of her lover Erast, a young man from the gentry class, who was not evil but weak (the first successful portrait of a "superfluous hero"). Karamzin's pieces in *Moskovskii zhurnal* were very popular as was also the separate publication of a selection from among them under the title *My Trifles* (Moi bezdelki, 1794). The tiny size of Karamzin's prose pieces was an inducement for aspiring writers to emulate the first Russian author of classics in prose. Although Karamzin always gave his generous encouragement to beginning writers, already in 1797 he was critical of the new lachrymose trend, and advised writers "not to speak of tears incessantly ... this method to move your reader is most unreliable" (*Aonidy*, Vol. 2).

Some of the finest examples of Karamzin's prose style appeared in his *Aglaya* (I, 1794; II, 1795), a literary almanac with only Russian works (mainly Karamzin's). In tone *Aglaya* was different from *Moskovskii zhurnal*, less playfully humorous than poignant. The line from the opening dedication of *Aglaya* to A. I. Pleshcheeva in 1795 was programmatic, as Lotman observed: "We live in a sad world." In "The Island of Bornholm" (Ostrov Borngol'm, 1794) the Gothic props (Karamzin began experimenting with Gothic scenery and mood under the influence of Ossian in 1792, before A. Radcliffe's romances) conveyed an atmosphere of horror poetically keyed to the central couple's love which "is condemned by the laws." The doomed love of Orpheus and Eurydice, an important lyrical motif in "Athenian Life" (1795), Karamzin unfolded within the story's broader philosophical framework which juxtaposed man's innocence in Plato's time to man's greater knowledge, but also acquired cruelty, in modern times. And in "Sierra Morena" (1795), a remarkable experiment in lyrical prose subtitled "Elegiac Fragment," Karamzin followed three characters' stormy passions culminating in their separate retreats into a "sacred silence." Karamzin maintained the overall poignant tone

also in his philosophical essays. There was genuine pathos in his defense of knowledge and the sciences ("enlightenment") as a pursuit consistent with Orthodoxy and directed toward moral virtue, first in "Something about the Sciences, Arts and Enlightenment" (Nechto o naukakh, iskusstvakh i prosveshchenii, 1794) and more poignantly in the exchange between Melodor and Filalet (1795). The poet Melodor recorded his fears that in the aftermath of the French Revolution hatred toward the sciences threatened to precipitate the human race into barbarity; like Sisyphus and his stone, it would slowly rise, only to fall again. Melodor closed with an existential cry on the purposelessness of life, to which Filalet responded with a tightly reasoned argument in support of religious faith and belief in the progress of the sciences.

From *Aonidy* (1796–99, 3 vols.) may be dated the beginning of Karamzin's gradual disengagement from Russian belles lettres. His role was more limited in this almanac, Russia's first *Almanach des Muses*, which Karamzin conceived as a forum for established as well as beginning poets. Karamzin—whose poetry, paradoxically, was less lyrical than his prose—was also less innovative as a poet. Not only was Russian poetry at a comparatively advanced stage of development in the 1790s, but Karamzin's poetry was often indistinguishable from the light verses of his friend I. I. Dmitriev (1760–1837) author of graceful fables and "tender songs." However, Karamzin did also experiment with meter and poetic genres; notably, in "Graf Gvarinos" (1789) which anticipated Zhukovsky's ballads, and "Ilya Muromets" (1795), which was written in a new, allegedly "folk" meter, and treated the Russian epic hero humorously on the background of the fairy tale. The political and philosophical emphasis in Karamzin's last journal *Vestnik Evropy* (1802–03) surfaced even in its literary section. Karamzin raised the issues of republicanism and freedom in "Marfa Posadnitsa" (1803), a short story on the historical period of Novgorod's subjugation under Ivan III. He wrote a *pièce à thèse* in "The Sentimental and the Cold" (Chuvstvitel'nyi i kholodnyi, 1803), arguing that man's temperament and fate were largely in the hands of Nature and could not be changed at will by circumstances or man-made institutions and laws, contrary to the claims made by radical thinkers of the Enlightenment. He advanced his own ideas on happiness in "Discourse on Happiness" (Razgovor o schastii, 1802) and in "My Confession" (Moya ispoved', 1802), which was also related to the self-caricatures in Novikov's satirical journals (1768–74) and to the 18th-century West-European and Russian types of the immoralist. One notable exception to this journal's political and philosophical emphasis was Karamzin's unfinished semi-autobiographical "A Knight of Our Times" (Rytsar' nashego vremeni, 1802), which was inspired for the first half, Chaps. I–VIII, by Sterne's *Tristram Shandy* and for the second half, Chaps. IX–XIII, by Rousseau's account of his relationship with Mme de Warens in *Les Confessions* (1782–89). One year separated the publication of the two sections, and Karamzin in his foreword to the second one suggested that it be read as a "fragment."

Belinsky, although he certainly was not prejudiced in Karamzin's favor, recognized that Karamzin "launched a new epoch in Russian literature." Belinsky was referring in broad terms to the style, principally the prose style popularized by Karamzin, which he transformed from a heavy, cumbersome tool to a fine-tuned instrument. The transformation was brought about by Karamzin purging his prose style of Church-Slavonicisms, colloquialisms, and awkward conjunctions, and by his coining new words and expressions (often calqued from the French). Most impressively, Karamzin shortened the sentence period and restructured it upon logical but also rhythmical principles. The result was a supple prose style which was equally adapted to discourse on politics and current events, metaphysics and morals, literary criticism, and prose fiction. Karamzin, it is true, in the quest for *purity* of style (incidentally, not unrelated to his interest in Plato's philosophy) and its "pleasantness" (*priyatnost'*) favored words denoting general rather than particular ideas; however, the periphrastic style for which Karamzin has been criticized was less typical of him than of his imitators. Karamzin's innovative style is sometimes described as a "middle style," a term borrowed, somewhat inappropriately, from Lomonosov's "theory of three styles" which was mainly concerned with *poetry*; or as a "new style," the designation given it by its main opponent, A. S. Shishkov (1754–1841). Shishkov criticized in his *Discourse on the Old and New*

Style (Rassuzhdenie o starom i novom sloge, 1803) the Karamzinians' purified, rarefied, and excessively "pleasant" style, and their cult of "chepukha" (trivia) as he referred to the small forms they favored. Shishkov's patriotic and religious zeal in promoting a Church-Slavonicized, pre-Lomonosovian style won him the title "Slavophile" (Slavenofil), a word coined for him in 1809 by the Karamzinian BATYUSHKOV ("A Vision on the Shores of Lethe" [Videnie na beregakh Lety]); also Shishkov won a number of converts who on the eve of the Patriotic War banded together in his BESEDA LYUBITELEI ROSSIISKOI SLOVESNOSTI (1811–16). But it was already too late to set the clock back, and the battle was won, in the final analysis, by the Karamzinians (who later founded the ARZAMAS, 1815–18), even though, as TYNYANOV has shown, the debates were resumed during the 1820s by a younger generation of archaists and Karamzinians (Arkhaisty i novatory, 1929). The main contribution of Shishkov and his allies was to bring critical attention to the stylistic excesses of the Karamzinians, and to infuse the literary subject matter with a civic spirit. It is noteworthy that Karamzin, who never participated in the debates, was one of the first Karamzinians to take heed of the archaists' strictures. He raised significantly the level of Church-Slavonicisms in the style of his History, a work Pushkin praised for its "Karamzinian style, pure with a diamond's hardness" (1830).

In addition to laying down the basic principles of Russian prose style as we know it today, Karamzin also introduced artistic methods and ideas which were later picked up by poets and writers of prose, sometimes after an interval of several decades. The Karamzinian sentimental notion of the writer moving his readers to tears was shared by DOSTOEVSKY in "Poor Folk" (1846; and later, in individual instances, in virtually all Dostoevsky's works); it was explicitly stated by TOLSTOI as his objective in the foreword to his "Childhood" (1852). Even Karamzin's mawkish ending for "Evgenii i Yuliya," where loving tears sprinkling on the flowers around the tomb of the deceased hero were endowed with fertilizing powers, was echoed by TURGENEV for the ending of Fathers and Sons (1862). Very differently, Karamzin's Shandeism (Tristram Shandy, trans. 1804–07) became a literary vogue in the 1830s, culminating in the 1840s in the transference of the title "Russian Sterne" from Karamzin to GOGOL. Karamzin's lyrical use of mood in his nature descriptions was congenial to Turgenev's poetic temperament, as was perhaps best appreciated by Dostoevsky when in 1872 he satirized Turgenev in the character Karmazinov in The Possessed. Karamzin's suggestively symbolic use of storm imagery in "Poor Liza" was poeticized by Turgenev in On The Eve (1860) and dramatized by A. N. OSTROVSKY in The Thunderstorm (1860). And the intensely lyrical musical features of Karamzin's prose inspired a poet like A. A. FET, when in 1844 he wrote on Karamzin's use of the melodic name of the river Gvadalkvivir in "Sierra Morena" the short lyrical impromptu "Na vodakh Gvadalkvivira." Finally, philosophical themes treated by Karamzin for the first time in a lucid prose style turned up, for example in the form of defense of women's rights, as when arguments advanced by N. G. CHERNYSHEVSKY in What Is to Be Done? (1863) were anticipated, not by Rousseau as Chernyshevsky claimed, but by Karamzin in "Yuliya" (1796). Random examples such as these of Karamzin's lasting influence are an indirect but eloquent testimony to the versatility of Karamzin's prose style. Karamzin himself took a look at the diversity of expressions of his artistic temperament in his poem "Protei" (1798). This diversity was characteristic of the second half of the Russian 18th century, an age of experimentation in Russian literature, where Karamzin pointed the way to 19th-century prose fiction.

The importance of Karamzin is widely recognized by literary historians and linguists alike, yet to this day there is no academic edition of his works. From among his most influential articles many, like "Liodor," were never included in his collected works.

Works: Sochineniya. 8 vols. Moscow, 1803–04. Sochineniya. Ed. A. Smirdin. 3 vols. St. Petersburg, 1848. Izbrannye sochineniya. 2 vols. 1964. Polnoe sobranie stikhotvorenii. Ed. Yu. M. Lotman. (Bibl. poeta. Bol'shaya seriya.) 1966. Istoriya gosudarstva Rossiiskogo. Ed. P. Einerling. 3 vols. St. Petersburg, 1842–43. For Karamzin's private correspondence, largely scattered in various 19th-century journals and periodicals, see: Perepiska Karamzina s Lafaterom. Ed. Ya. Grot and F. Val'dman. St. Petersburg, 1893; Pis'ma N. M. Karamzina k I. I. Dmitrievu. Ed. Ya. Grot and P.

Pekarskii. St. Petersburg, 1866. There is no definitive biography of Karamzin; the closest approximation is: M. Pogodin, Nikolai Mikhailovich Karamzin. 2 vols. Moscow, 1866. The most comprehensive study of Karamzin's works until 1803 is: A. G. Cross, N. M. Karamzin, a Study of His Literary Career: 1783–1803. Carbondale, 1971. Classic studies on Karamzin include: V. V. Sipovskii, N. M. Karamzin, avtor "Pisem russkogo puteshestvennika." St. Petersburg, 1899. B. M. Eikhenbaum, "Karamzin." In his Skvoz' literaturu. Leningrad, 1924. Pp. 37–49. V. V. Vinogradov, "Neizvestnye sochineniya N. M. Karamzina." In his Problema avtorstva i teoriya stilei. Moscow, 1961. Pp. 221–365. A fine study of Karamzin's narrative techniques is given by Gunvor Birgitta Hammarberg in "Karamzin's Prose Fiction: The Poetics of Co-Creation" (Ph.D. Diss., University of Michigan, 1982). For Karamzin's political views until 1810, see R. Pipes, Karamzin's Memoir on Ancient and Modern Russia: A Translation and Analysis. Cambridge, 1959. Pp. 3–92.
T. P.

Karaváeva, Ánna Aleksándrovna (1893–), novelist, correspondent, and editor. The daughter of a petty official, Karavaeva graduated from the local gymnasium in 1911 and taught for two years in a village school before studying for three years in the History Department of the Bestuzhev Women's College in Petersburg. After the Revolution she taught in a Communist Party school in Barnaul, where she began publishing in 1922 and joined the Party in 1926. Her earliest works such as the story "The Wing" (Fligel', 1923) and the tale The Yard (Dvor, 1926) depicted peasant life in the Urals and petty bourgeois disenchantment with the new environment. A historical novel about the life of Ural artisans during the age of Catherine the Great The Gold Beak (Zolotoi klyuv, 1925) was followed by The Sawmill (Lesozavod, 1928), a novel depicting the industrialization of a village under Soviet rule. As the editor of The Young Guard (Molodaya gvardiya) in 1931–38, Karavaeva encouraged OSTROVSKY in writing The Making of a Hero (Kak zakalyalas' stal', 1935, Eng. trans., 1937) and wrote a series of tales about young people and their struggle for the revolutionary cause including Lena from Crane Grove (Lena iz Zhuravlinoi roshchi, 1938). Serving as a Pravda correspondent during World War II, she published a collection of patriotic sketches Stalin's Masters: Tales of People and Days (Stalinskie mastera: povestvovanie o lyudyakh i dnyakh, 1943), and depicted the struggle of the Soviet war effort in the trilogy Motherland (Rodina: Ogni, 1943; Razbeg, 1948; Rodnoi dom, 1950), which was awarded the Stalin Prize in 1951. A member of the editorial board of the journal Sovetskaya zhenshchina and of various international delegations which inspired a collection of memoir sketches Along the Roads of Life (Po dorogam zhizni, 1957), Karavaeva received numerous Soviet decorations and honors.

Works: Sobranie sochinenii. 5 vols. 1957. Grani zhizni: roman. 1963. Vechnozelenye list'ya: dnevnik pisatelya. 1963. Zvezdnaya stolitsa; zapiski i vospominaniya sovremennika. 1968.
Secondary literature: Literaturnaya entsiklopediya, vol. 5 (1931), pp. 102–04. Sovetskie pisateli: avtobiografii, vol. 1 (1959), pp. 511–24. Russkie sovetskie pisateli prozaiki, vol. 2 (1964), pp. 286–317.
A. M. S.

Kassíl, Lev Abrámovich (1905–70), writer, was born in Sloboda Pokrovskaya (now Engels), the son of a doctor. While studying aerodynamics in the faculty of physics and mathematics at Moscow State University in 1925, he published his first short story. In 1927 he worked with MAYAKOVSKY for Novyi Lef, decided to become a children's writer, and began his lifelong association with the magazine Pioner. Throughout the 1930s he covered major stories in many areas of science and technology for Izvestiya. His autobiographical novellas "Konduit" (1930) and "Shvambraniya" (1933) mirror the events of 1917 through the eyes of a child from the middle intelligentsia experiencing the breakdown of tsarist secondary education and the establishment of the first Soviet vocational schools. His books, written for adolescents as well as children, focus on exemplary personalities in many fields of Soviet life: sports (Goalie for the Republic-Vratar' respubliki, 1938; White Queen's Move-Khod beloi korolevy, 1956); the arts (The Great Opposition-Velikoe protivostoyanie, 2 vols., 1941–47); heroic children who lived during the war against the Nazis (*My Dear Boys*-Dorogie moi mal'chishki, 1944; *Street of the Younger Son*-Ulitsa mladshego syna, 1949, co-author M. Polyansky awarded a Stalin Prize in 1950, made into a film in 1962; *Early Sunrise*-Rannii voskhod, 1953). *Cup of the Gladiator* (Chasha gladiatora, 1961) describes the vicissitudes of Russian émigrés after 1917. *Be Ready, Your Highness!* (Bud'te gotovy, Vashe Vysochestvo!, 1964) probes the ethical ambiguities in the activities of an international Soviet Pioneer camp. *Mayakovsky—Himself* (1940, second amplified edition 1960) contains literary reminiscences. The romantic juxtaposition of fantasy and reality in Kassil's works, their emphasis on creativity and heroism, the way they combine lyricism with humor and satire, have won him perennial popularity among young readers.

Works: Sobranie sochinenii. 5 vols. 1965–66. "Avtobiografiya." In *Sovetskie pisateli.* Vol. 1. 1959.

Translations: Early Dawn. Trans. S. Rosenberg. Moscow, 1956. *The Hero's Brother.* Moscow, 1957. *The Land of Shvambrania: A Novel.* Trans. S. Glass and N. Guterman. 1935. *The Story of Alesha-Ryazan and Uncle White-Sea.* London and New York, 1935.

Secondary literature: V. Nikolaev, *Lev Kassil'.* 1955. ———, *Dorogami mechty i poiska: Tvorcheskii put' L'va Kassilya.* 1965. I. Svirskaya, *Tvorchestvo L. A. Kassilya.* 1955. C. N. L.

Katáev, Iván Ivánovich (1902–39), prose writer. Born in Moscow, he joined the Red Army in 1919, later studied economics at Moscow University, became a member of the Communist Party and perished during Stalin's purges on 2 May 1939.

Kataev began publishing in 1921 and was a member of the "PEREVAL" group. His novels *The Poet* and *The Heart* came out in 1929 and brought him recognition as a writer. Between 1928 and 1937 he published a number of short stories and novels dealing with the themes of industrialization, collectivization, and life in the Russian village. In 1930 his novel *Milk* was severely criticized for depicting the poor peasants as ignorant and prejudiced, while giving an excessively positive picture of a "kulak," the wealthy and religious peasant. Kataev's last work, *Under the Clear Stars*, written in 1937, was finally published in 1957.

Kataev's works raise moral and ethical questions. He avoids the stereotypical mold of SOCIALIST REALISM. His characters are rounded and his Communists empathize with their fellow men, including wealthy peasants and non-proletarians.

Works: Poet. 1928. *Serdtse.* 1928, 1931, 1935. *Zhena.* 1930. "Moloko," *Rovesniki* 7 (1930). *Dvizhenie.* 1932. "Leningradskoe shosse," *Krasnaya nov'* 11 (1933). *Na krayu sveta.* 1933. *Ledyanaya Ellada.* 1933. *Chelovek na gore.* 1934. *Otechestvo.* 1934. *Vstrecha.* 1934. *Izbrannoe: povesti i rasskazy, ocherki.* 1957. *Pod chistymi zvezdami.* 1969.

Secondary literature: E. J. Brown, *Russian Literature since the Revolution.* 1982. V. Goffenshefer, Introd. to *Izbrannoe* (1957). A. Makarov, "Razgovor po povodu..." In his *Literaturno-kriticheskie stat'i.* 1959. E. Mindlin, *Neobyknovennye sobesedniki.* 1968. ———, *Vospominaniya ob I. Kataeve.* 1970. H. S.

Katáev, Valentín Petróvich (1897–), prose writer, was born in Odessa. During the civil war he worked there as a journalist. In 1922 Kataev moved to Moscow and became a contributor to *Gudok*, *Pravda*, and *Trud*. During World War II he was a correspondent for *Pravda* and *Krasnaya zvezda*. From 1946 to 1954 he was on the editorial board of *Novyi mir* and in 1955 founded and, until 1962, was the editor of *Yunost'*.

After initial attempts to write poetry, Kataev began publishing short stories, novellas, novels, and plays. Because there are sharp stylistic and artistic differences, Kataev's work can be divided into three distinct groups: works written before 1930, characterized by parody, the grotesque, whimsy, and humor; works written between 1932 and 1964, generally adhering to the principles of SOCIALIST REALISM; and works written after 1964 in which he created his own genre and form.

Kataev began publishing short stories in 1916. His first novel, *The Island of Erendorf*, appeared in 1924 and his first play, *Squaring the Circle*, in 1927. Thematically, his works are topical, and timely. His early works (1919–24) deal with the civil war and world revolution. *The Embezzlers* (1927), Kataev's best known novel of the

twenties, is an adventure story set in Russia during the NEP. It is a satire of corrupt Soviet officials who travel throughout Russia in search of "high society." *Squaring the Circle*, premiered by the Moscow Art Theatre in 1928, is a comedy based on Kataev's own experiences related to the housing shortage in Moscow of the 1920s.

Time Forward! (1932) is Kataev's contribution to Five-Year Plan literature and has become a classic example of socialist realism. Inspired by MAYAKOVSKY's poem, "March of the Shock-Brigades," it depicts the construction of a metallurgical plant in Magnitogorsk. It conveys the excitement of workers who succeed in breaking the world's time record for pouring concrete thereby advancing Soviet technology by several decades. *Son of the Regiment* (1945) is set during World War II and earned Kataev the 1946 Stalin Prize. His longest work, *Waves of the Black Sea* (1936–61) is a historical novel in four parts. *Lonely White Sail is Gleaming* (1936), is set in Odessa during the 1905 Revolution and is partially autobiographical. *The Small Farm in the Steppe* (1956) describes the events of 1910 to 1912. *Winter's Wind* (1960) covers the civil war period while *Catacombs* (1961) depicts the revolutionary movement.

During the 1960s and 1970s Kataev began to create his own genre based upon experimentation with the treatment of time, memory, and narrative voice. In his semi-autobiographical series *The Holy Well* (1966), *The Grass of Oblivion* (1967) and *My Diamond Crown* (1966), Kataev deliberately dislocates and destroys the chronological concept of time and blurs the lines between fact and fiction, reality and dream. Memory is ordered on the basis of free association rather than chronology. He is intentionally subjective. In *The Grass of Oblivion*, Kataev pays homage to his masters, Mayakovsky and BUNIN, the two extremes of 20th century Russian literary tradition. He also presents a powerful and haunting portrait of the semi-fictitious Maria Zaremba, the "girl from the Soviet Party School" who, faithful to ideology, agrees to the execution of the man she loves.

Kataev is a rare phenomenon in Russian literature. An original and important writer of the 1920s, he maintained his writing and publishing activities during the Stalinist period. An officially sanctioned author and an important member of the Union of Soviet Writers, he continues to produce innovative and interesting work.

Works: Sobranie sochinenii. 9 vols. 1971–72. *Pochti dnevnik.* 1962, 1978. *Trava zabveniya.* 1967. *Raznoe. Literaturnye zametki. Portrety, Fel'etony. Retsenzii. Ocherki. Fragmenty.* 1970. *Razbitaya zhizn', ili Volshebnyi rog Oberona.* 1973. *Fialka, Teatr* 12 (1974). *Kladbishche v Skulyanakh.* 1976. *Povelitel' zheleza: avantyurnyi roman s prologom i epilogom.* 1977. *Ekho voennykh let.* 1979. *Almaznyi moi venets.* 1979, 1981.

Translations: The Embezzlers. New York, 1920; Conn. 1973; Ann Arbor 1975; *Time Forward!* New York, 1933; London, 1934; Bloomington, Indiana, 1976. *The Last of the Equipages; or A Million Torments.* 1934. *Squaring the Circle.* 1934, 1935, 1936, 1938. *The Path of Flowers.* 1935, 1936. *Peace is Where the Tempests Blow.* 1937. *Lonely White Sail.* London, 1937, 1976; New York 1938; Ann Arbor, 1971; *A White Sail Gleams*, Moscow, 1954, 1973. *The Blue Handkerchief.* Berkeley, Calif., 1944. *The Wife.* 1946. *Novels and Tales.* Moscow, 1949. *The Cottage in the Steppe.* Moscow, 1957. *The Small Farm in the Steppe.* London, 1958; Westport, Ct., 1976. *The Holy Well.* 1967. *The Grass of Oblivion.* 1969. *A Mosaic of Life or the Magic Horn of Oberon: Memoirs of a Russian Childhood.* Chicago, 1976.

Secondary literature: B. Brainina, *Valentin Kataev.* 1960. E. J. Brown, *Russian Literature Since the Revolution.* 1982. Pp. 100–03. K. Clark, *The Soviet Novel: History as Ritual.* 1981. R. Russell, "The Problem of Self-Expression in the Later Works of Valentin Kataev." In *Studies in Twentieth Century Russian Literature.* Ed. Christopher J. Barnes. 1976. Pp. 78–91. ———, *Valentin Kataev.* (Twayne's World Authors Series, 581.) Boston, 1981. *Russkie sovetskie pisateli-prozaiki. Bio-bibliograficheskii ukazatel'.* Vol. 2. 1964. T. Sidel'nikova, *Valentin Kataev. Ocherk zhizni i tvorchestva.* 1957. L. I. Skorino, "V. P. Kataev." In *Istoriya russkoi sovetskoi literatury.* Vol. 3. 1961. H. S.

Katénin, Pável Aleksándrovich (1792–1853), poet, playwright, translator, critic, and literary theorist. An officer of the elite Preobrazhensky Guards, Katenin took part in the major battles against

Napoleon. He fell afoul of the authorities for belonging to proto-Decembrist organizations and was exiled to his estate (1822–25).

Katenin was active in literary life from 1809 to the late 1830s. His ballads of 1815 and 1816, especially his adaptation of Bürger's "Lenore" ("Olga"), sought to counter ZHUKOVSKY's very successful efforts with his own Russian thematics, subliterary language, non-iambic meters, non-decorous detail, and the psychological development of characters. Katenin's comedy *Student* (1817), written with GRIBOEDOV, parodied Zhukovsky and BATYUSHKOV. His tragedy, *Andromakha* (1827) failed. From his estate he directed a malicious satire, "An Old Story" (Staraya byl', 1829) against PUSHKIN, for the latter's alleged flattery of Nicholas I. Nevertheless, Pushkin published a number of Katenin's critical essays in LITERATURNAYA GAZETA (1830), essays in which Katenin expounded his interesting and serious ideas on ROMANTICISM and on the need for a national literature. Katenin's better works, such as the narrative poems "Princess Milusha" (Knyazhna Milusha, 1834) and "Mstislav Mstislavich" (1820), draw on his fascination with concrete details of Russian antiquity. His verse story "Invalid Gorev" (1836) contributed to growing interest in non-heroic protagonists. Katenin translated or adapted a variety of Greek, Latin, French, German, and English works.

Katenin had everything—learning, languages, wit, intellect, awareness of stylistic levels, love of literature—except the ability to realize one of his own critical maxims: form should be an expression of content. Too often his verse seems an exercise in the use of unusual meters and crude language. Pushkin admired him chiefly for his mastery of the "mechanism" of verse and for his proud independence. A number of younger poets (including Pushkin, Griboedov, YAZYKOV, and KYUKHELBEKER) learned from his objections to the manner of Zhukovsky and from his attempts to open the language of literature to elements of archaic and folk Russian.

Works: Izbrannye proizvedeniya. Introd. and ed. G. V. Ermakova-Bitner. 1965. *Pis'ma P. A. Katenina k N. I. Bakhtinu.* 1911.

Secondary literature: Yu. M. Tynyanov, "Arkhaisty i Pushkin." In his *Pushkin i ego sovremenniki.* 1968. Pp. 23–121. W. M. T.

Katkóv, Mikhail Nikiforovich (1818–87), journalist and critic. Katkov's career was intertwined with the life of 19th-century Moscow. Born there, he attended Moscow University along with the great generation of his contemporaries in the mid-1830s, sharing their enthusiasm for German romantic philosophy. For a time he was closely associated with BELINSKY, who at one point thought him the "great hope of scholarship and Russian literature," and early entered the field of journalism, where he would make his mark.

Katkov studied in Germany under Schelling, wrote a dissertation in the field of Slavic philology, and then taught at Moscow University in the late 1840s. In 1851 he began the transition from scholarship to Russian literature by assuming the editorship of the newspaper *Moskovskie vedomosti*, which later became probably the single most influential journalistic organ of its time. In 1856 he received permission to found *Russkii vestnik*, which eventually became the leading literary monthly in Moscow and one of the most important such journals in Russia generally.

After the Polish uprising of 1863 Katkov's was the most prominent conservative voice in Russian cultural life. *Russkii vestnik* sometimes gave refuge to great writers under interdiction by the radical St. Petersburg critics, a group which included TURGENEV, Lev TOLSTOI and DOSTOEVSKY. The journal had no noteworthy critics except Katkov himself, who not only published critical articles but also served as a pre-publication advisor for some of the finest works of 19th-century Russian literature. He had a certain talent along these lines, even though his authors disliked him personally and disagreed with many of his political views. He was one of the great editors of his day.

Katkov was known as an Anglophile, but he also upheld what he perceived as Russian national principles, and sometimes criticized the government from the right.

Secondary literature: Martin Katz, *Mikhail N. Katkov: A Political Biography 1818–1887.* The Hague: 1966. Catherine T. Nepomnyashchy, "Katkov and the Emergence of the *Russian Messenger*," *Ulbandus Review* 1, no. 1 (1977), pp. 59–89. S. Nevedenskii [S. Tatishchev], *Katkov i ego vremya.* 1888. C. A. M.

Kátyrev-Rostóvsky, Prince Iván Mikhaílovich (?–1640), historian and memoirist. A courtier, Katyrev-Rostovsky was exiled by Tsar Vasily Shuisky in 1608 and returned to the Court by Tsar Mikhail Romanov to whose closer circle of followers he belonged. Charged with editing a chronicle of the TIME OF TROUBLES, authored by several writers, he made many additions, often based on his own recollections and including some verses at the end of the work. *A Tale of Bygone Years on the Development of the Capital City of Moscow* (Povest' ot prezhnikh let o nachale tsarstvuyushchego goroda Moskvy) is one of the first Russian historical works to show a distinct secular tendency, along with some Western influence in its perception of the world (Guido de Columna's *De Proeliis*, which was available in Russian translation, may have been one source of such influence) and a style which at times approaches that of popular narrative. Some passages from the *Tale*, such as a touching description of the beauty and innocence of Kseniya Godunov, or of the coming of spring in 1607, are often quoted as examples of a new beginning in Russian literature.

Works: Russkaya istoricheskaya biblioteka. Vol. 13. 2d ed. 1909.

Secondary literature: N. K. Gudzii, "K voprosu o sostave 'Letopisnoi knigi', pripisyvaemoi kn. I. M. Katyrevu-Rostovskomu," *TODRL* 14 (1958). V. T.

Kavérin (pen-name of Zil'ber), Veniamín Aleksándrovich (1902–), writer. Studied Russian and foreign literature at the University of Petrograd in the early twenties and graduated in 1924. He has written short stories, novels, plays, fairy tales, critical studies, essays, and autobiographical works. His earliest literary experience was with the SERAPION BROTHERS. Kaverin's collection of stories *Masters and Journeymen* (Mastera i podmaster'ya, 1923) marks his initial literary manner influenced by the German romantics. These stories are experimental. In them the author playfully twists time, space, and perception to any level of whimsical distortion. They foreshadow what has become Kaverin's narrative asset: a sense of suspense and a dramatic plot, to which in his mature works he adds insight into people's psyche and human relationships. His short satirical novel *The Troublemaker* (Skandalist, 1928) polemically portrays the intellectual petrification of older professors and the disintegration of the Russian formalist movement. *Artist Unknown* (Khudozhnik neizvesten, 1931) deals with the problem of the cultural lag in the Soviet society of the late twenties. The plot of the novel involves a philosophical dialogue between Shpektorov, an engineer, and Arkhimedov, a painter. At another level in the novel there unfolds a conflict in the techniques of representation. It is as if the author is treating the *what* and the *how* of the representation simultaneously. Both *The Troublemaker* and *Artist Unknown* demonstrate the measure of Kaverin's mastery as a thoughtful craftsman of the plot. Throughout the thirties, forties, and the early fifties Kaverin worked on conventional novels. In *Wish Fulfillment* (Ispolnenie zhelanii, 1934–35) and *Two Captains* (Dva kapitana, 1934–44) Kaverin follows the pattern of parallel development of two central characters. The first novel traces the *début dans la vie* of two students at Leningrad State University: a student of literature and a student of physiology. It is a "comparative study" in the sense that the second is successful where the first fails. In the next novel, the first captain is a prerevolutionary explorer who disappeared under enigmatic circumstances in the Arctic Ocean shortly before World War I; the second is a young Soviet Air Force captain who came to his maturity shortly before World War II. The working out of the unusual circumstances that link the two captains forms the substance of the novel. The third novel, *Open Book* (Otkrytaya kniga, 1956), narrates the story of a biologist. At a terrible personal cost she promotes a new biological theory against the old obsolete one with its vested interests in the atmosphere of Stalinist obscurantism. The underlying patterns of these novels are those of the adventure novel. However, these patterns are internalized and elevated to the level of an intellectual adventure, i.e., of intellectual quest and scientific discovery. From another angle these novels can be described as works reflecting the traditions of the *Bildungsroman*. However, the young protagonists as well the heroine of *Open Book* live incomplete destinies; they fail to reach the ultimate stage of self-fulfillment. All in all, Kaverin mostly avoids the stereotype from which novels suffered when designed according to to the doctrine of SOCIALIST REALISM. Post-Stalin literature witnessed a vigorous growth of short fiction. In the sixties Kaverin may have responded to this trend of reducing narrative format: only a significant episode and its dramatic development form the body of the narrative. The unfolding of the plot in itself conveys far-reaching philosophical implications. Kaverin's short fiction directs an incisive spotlight on the vital issues of the time: culture as it bears on the young Russian intelligentsia in the post-Stalin age; the lawlessness of the Stalinist period and the rehabilitation of the victims of Stalinism. In *A Piece of Glass* (Kusok stekla, 1960) an episode in the research work of a young physiologist ends in a ridiculously surprising reversal and hints at a wider issue of human relations that intellectuals face in the post-Stalin Russia. *Seven Pairs of Dirty Ones* (Sem' par nechistykh, 1962) reproduces a tragic episode during the transportation of a group of convicts in the White Sea. The plot of the story reveals the frightful discrepancy between legality and morality in the time of Stalin. It takes the outbreak of the War for this discrepancy to lessen. *Before the Mirror* (Pered zerkalom, 1971) again takes up the issue of the cultural lag. In *Artist Unknown* Shpektorov's exclusive dedication to laying the material foundations of socialism ended in a heroic forfeiture of personal self-fulfillment. Forty years later, Karnovsky, Shpektorov's alter ego in *Before the Mirror*, avoids the impasse by discovering the civilizing mission of art. Kaverin's autobiographical works, specifically his *Lighted Windows* (Osveshchennye okna, 1978), give an interesting account, among other things, of the events and the literary atmosphere of the early twenties.

Works: Konets Khazy. Bol'shaya igra. Fantasticheskie rasskazy. 1930. *Khudozhnik neizvesten.* 1931. *Sobranie sochinenii.* 6 vols. 1963.

Translations: The Larger View. New York, 1938. (Russian title: *Ispolnenie zhelanii.*) *Open Book.* Moscow, 1955. *Two Captains.* New York, 1942; Moscow, 1972. *The Unknown Artist.* Westport, Conn., 1973. *Devant le Miroir.* Paris, 1973. For translations of short stories, *see Lewanski*, p. 268.

Secondary literature: Elizabeth K. Beaujour, "Kaverin's *Before the Mirror*," *SEEJ* 24 (1980), pp. 233–244. Hongor Oulanoff, *The Prose Fiction of Veniamin A. Kaverin.* 1976. D. G. B. Piper, *V. A. Kaverin: A Soviet Writer's Response to the Problem of Commitment.* 1970.

H. O.

Kazakévich, Emmanuíl Génrikhovich (1913–1962), prose writer. After graduation from a Kharkov engineering trade school in 1930, Kazakevich went to the Jewish autonomous region of Birobidzhan (on the Amur river in East Asia), where he worked as an engineer and administrator. He soon became active in the local theater and newspaper. Kazakevich's early writings are all in Yiddish. He also translated a great deal of Russian literature into that language. Kazakevich fought with distinction in World War II. His war time experiences became the central topic of his stories and novels when he returned to civilian life. His first Russian short story, "The Star" (Zvezda, 1947), was a significant success. Some of his subsequent works, such as the story "Two in the Steppe" (Dvoe v stepi, 1948), were criticized for excessive "naturalism" and psychological complexity. These traits were avoided in the novel *Spring on the Oder* (Vesna na Odere, 1949), which won Kazakevich a Stalin prize. Kazakevich's later works, such as "Heart of a Friend" (Serdtse druga, 1953) and "In the Light of Day" (Pri svete dnya, 1961), tend to deal with moral conflicts under the extreme stress of war events. Kazakevich was also active as a critic, publicist, and public figure.

Works: Sobranie sochinenii. 2 vols. 1963. *Izbrannye proizvedeniya.* 2 vols. 1974.

Translations: Heart of a Friend: A Story. Trans. R. Dixon. Moscow, 1955. *The House on the Square* (Dom na ploshchadi). Trans. R. Prokofieva. In *Soviet Literature*, 1956, nos. 11 and 12. *Spring on the Oder: A Novel in Three Parts.* Trans. R. Daglish. Moscow, 1953. *Star: A Story.* Trans. L. Stoklitsky. London, 1950.

Secondary literature: A. Bocharov, *Slovo o pobeditelyakh: Voennaya proza E. Kazakevicha.* 1970.

V. T.

Kazakóv, Yúry Pávlovich (1927–83), short prose writer. Born in Moscow, he studied music (1946–51), taught at the Moscow Con-

servatory, and graduated from the Gorky Literary Institute in 1957. Kazakov began publishing in 1952 and was quickly proclaimed one of the "New Voices" in Russian literature. Between 1958 and 1973 he published fifteen collections of short stories, and then became almost completely silent.

Kazakov's short stories and sketches are set in northern and central Russian forests, villages, and provincial towns. Their central themes deal with emotions and the private life of the individual. His characters (both people and animals) are usually in physical and spiritual isolation, often outside their normal environment and frequently social misfits (the orphan in *Man'ka*, the drunkard in *The Outsider*, the blind hunting dog in *Arcturus*).

Kazakov's heroes, like some contemporary Russian intellectuals, escape from the Soviet urban landscape into the Russian past represented by rural Russia and its wooden church architecture. There they seek truth, genuine feelings, and real values. In *The Outsider* (1959), the beautiful river sunset transforms the drunkard, buoy-tender Egor, into an artist of song. In *Adam and Eve* (1962), the unhappy abstract painter finds peace and inspiration in the majesty and beauty of the northern island with its ancient wooden church. In *Goblins* (1960), Zhukov, director of the village club, whose job is to educate the ignorant peasants in the spirit of Communism and to dispel their superstitions, faces the truth while walking through the woods in the night when he discovers that he is terrified of goblins and crosses himself. His later stories, *The Little Candle* (1973) and *You Wept Bitterly in Your Dream* (1977), are autobiographical.

Kazakov's prose is impressionistic and lyrical in the tradition of TURGENEV, CHEKHOV, and PAUSTOVSKY. Written in a minor key, his stories contain beautiful descriptive passages, vivid imagery, and are filled with sounds, silences, and smells. His characters are psychologically portrayed. He employs a minimal use of dialogue. Emotions are often expressed through silences, internal monologues, and gestures. Kazakov is a fine artist whose stories are carefully crafted and economically drawn.

Works: Man'ka. Arkhangel'sk, 1958. *Na polustanke.* 1959. *Po doroge.* 1961. "Tri rasskaza ..." In *Tarusskie stranitsy.* Kaluga, 1961. *Rasskazy.* 1962. *Goluboe i zelenoe. Rasskazy i ocherk.* 1963. *Legkaya zhizn'.* 1963. *Krasnaya ptitsa.* 1963. *Selected Short Stories* (in Russian). New York, 1963; Oxford, 1964. *Zapakh khleba, rasskazy.* 1965. *Dvoe v dekabre.* 1966. *Kak ya stroil dom.* 1967. *Arktur—gonchii pes.* 1966, 1980. *Rasskazy.* Letchworth, Eng., 1968. *Osen' v dubovykh lesakh.* 1969. *Severnyi dnevnik.* 1973. *Goluboe i zelenoe.* Paris, 1973, Copenhagen, 1972, 1974. *Pervoe svidanie.* Paris, 1975. *Zapakh khleba, Nekrasivaya, O muzhestve pisatelya.* Letchworth, Eng., 1975. *Vo sne ty gor'ko plakal.* 1977. *Olen'i roga: rasskazy.* 1980.

Translations: Going to Town and Other Stories. 1964. M. Ginsburg, ed. and trans., *The Fatal Eggs and other Soviet Stories.* 1964. T. P. Whitney, ed., *The New Writing in Russia.* 1964. *The Smell of Bread and Other Stories.* 1965. *Arcturus: the Hunting Hound and Other Stories.* 1968. *Autumn in the Oak Woods.* Moscow, 1970.

Secondary literature: E. J. Brown, *Russian Literature since the Revolution.* 1982. Pp. 329–30. George Gibian, "Yurii Kazakov." In *Major Soviet Writers: Essays in Criticism.* Ed. Edward J. Brown. 1973. Pp. 321–32. M. Hayward and E. L. Crowley, *Soviet Literature in the Sixties: An International Symposium.* 1964. Karl D. Kramer, "Jurij Kazakov: The Pleasures of Isolation," *SEEJ* 10 (1966), pp. 22–31. H. Muchnic, *Russian Writers: Notes and Essays.* 1963. Yu. Nagibin, "Svoe i chuzhoe," *Druzhba narodov*, 1959, no. 7. V. Pertsovskii, "Osmyslenie zhizni," *VLit*, 1964, no. 2. L. Solov'eva, "Nachalo puti," *Novyi mir*, 1959, no. 9. G. Svirski, *A History of Post-War Soviet Writing: The Literature of Moral Opposition.* 1981.

H. S.

Kazakóva, Rímma Fyódorovna (1932–), poet and translator. After graduating from Leningrad University in history in 1954, Kazakova spent seven years in the Far East as a lecturer and editor. She published her first poetry in 1955 and her first volume of verse, *Let Us Meet in the East* (Vstretimsya na Vostoke, 1958), in Khabarovsk. Having moved to Moscow, she continued to publish poetry and translations from several languages. Kazakova's poetry, free of ideology and officious pathos, deals with human problems in carefully chosen and often original images, and a muted voice. Kazakova's earlier poetry, in particular, places her with the best of the "quiet school" of the late 1950s and early 1960s which sought to recover a mood of integrity and thoughtfulness in verse.

Works: Tam, gde ty. 1960. *Stikhi.* 1962. *Izbrannaya lirika.* 1964. *Pyatnitsy.* 1965. *V taige ne plachut.* 1965. *Poverit' snegu.* 1967. *Elki zelenye.* 1969. *Snezhnaya baba.* 1972. *Pomnyu: Stikhi raznykh let.* 1974.

Translations: "A Painting." In *Modern Russian Poetry*, ed. Vladimir Markov and Merrill Sparks (1967), pp. 810–11.   V. T.

Kázin, Vasily Vasilievich (1898–). A minor Soviet poet born in Moscow, Kazin worked as an editor of *Komsomolskaya pravda, Krasnaya niva,* and *Krasnaya nov'.* A member of "The Smithy" (KUZNITSA), a sub-group of the "Proletarian Writers," he had begun publishing poetry in 1914. Kazin is an official writer. His poetry is conventional in form and content. He follows official guidelines of party policy. His *White Sea Poem* (1936–62) glorifies the building of the Baltic–White Sea canal and applauds the corrective function that it played in reforming criminals. According to SOLZHENITSYN, this canal was built under inhuman working conditions primarily by forced labor (intellectuals and "kulaks"), thousands of whom died from cold, hunger, and exhaustion. Kazin's other works are similar in tone and verisimilitude.

Works: Antologiya revolyutsionnoi poezii. 1924. *Sbornik stikhov.* 1943. *Poemy sovetskoi Estonii.* 1950. *Stikhotvoreniya.* 1956, 1967. *Stikhotvoreniya i poemy.* 1957, 1964. *Lirika.* 1960. *Izbrannoe. Stikhotvoreniya i poemy.* 1967. *Izbrannoe.* 1978.

Translations: See Lewanski. p. 269.

Secondary literature: B. Bobovich, "Sovremennik bol'shoi epokhi," *Moskva,* 1957, no. 4. Z. Papernyi, (Introduction.) *Proletarskie poety pervykh let sovetskoi epokhi.* 1959. L. Polyakova, *Poeziya rabochego maya: Ocherk tvorchestva V. Kazina.* 1977.   H. S.

Kharms, Daniil Ivánovich (pseud. of Yuvachev, 1905–42), poet, writer. A native of Petersburg, by 1925, after two uncompleted tries at higher education (technical studies, film), Yuvachev made his debut with public readings of contemporary poetry. He already used the name "Kharms" (the most frequent of more than ten pseudonyms), which apparently derives from a combination of the English "charm" and "harm." 1925 also brought friendship with the poet Aleksandr VVEDENSKY. The end of 1927 saw the formation of OBERIU ("Association for Real Art"), in which both men figured prominently. This avant-garde group of poets and artists was publicly active until April 1930. During this time, Kharms began to write for children's journals edited by Samuil MARSHAK, and to work actively in the children's publishing house "Detgiz."

Spectacle was an important facet of *Oberiu* activity, and it allowed full play to Kharms' own proclivity for eccentric behavior, noted in memoirs about him. Making one's own life a piece of art was a key element of FUTURIST (even SYMBOLIST) practice; during the 1920s, Kharms indulged widely in play behavior, on and off stage.

During the thirties, Kharms' situation changed for the worse. At the end of 1931, he was arrested and imprisoned on charges of distracting people from the tasks of industrial construction with "transsense" poetry. Released in 1932, he was exiled for a few months, but returned to Leningrad later that year. He continued to make a living writing for children; however, this possibility became ever more limited, and the poet experienced real deprivation. Arrested in the summer of 1941, he died of starvation in prison.

Kharms' writing falls into two chronological periods: the *Oberiu,* and the mid- and late thirties. Initially, poetry predominates; there are also a few experimental plays. The poems range from highly patterned linguistic experiments akin to early works by Velimir KHLEBNIKOV, to longer dramatic texts, in which alogisms and violations of conventions abound. Anything can happen in these works: the plot is unpredictable or nonexistent; characters change drastically and without motivation; an inanimate object or animal may be endowed with speech; and linguistic (esp. grammatical) and stylistic rules are broken repeatedly. The poet's experiments with structure and technique are exemplified in his most outstanding achievement of this period, the play *Elizaveta Bam.*

Later years see a marked change, as Kharms' writing moves from verbal exuberance to stylistic simplicity and economy of means, from diverse, exotic thematics (works set in a mythologized nature, philosophical and mock-philosophical texts, etc.) to a background realism reflecting the Leningrad of the 1930s. The principal genres are tiny stories (termed *sluchai,* 'happenings,' by Kharms) and the poetry and prose of the so-called Blue Notebook. In these works, the dominant is a tension between an intensely observed surrounding world and the grotesque, which at any moment may intrude (often with considerable violence) among the minutiae. The novella *The Old Woman* (1939), influenced by the philosophical ideas of Kharms' friend Ya. S. Druskin about the possibility of miracles, brings together recurrent elements of his late works, and is perhaps the best of them.

Humorous, alogical works for children are also an important part of Kharms' literary heritage. They have many points of contact with his adult writing, and are almost exclusively the only part of his corpus which has appeared in print in the Soviet Union. Kharms' works for adults, long held in private archives, began to surface in the 1960s, as part of the rediscovery of the *Oberiu* school. A complete edition of his writings is being published in the West.

Works: Sobranie proizvedenii. Vols. 1–3. Ed. Mikhail Meilakh and Vladimir Erl'. Bremen: K-Presse, 1978–80 [Ongoing publication]. *Izbrannoe.* Ed. and introd. George Gibian. Würzburg, 1974. *Russia's Lost Literature of the Absurd: Selected Works of Daniil Kharms and Alexander Vvedenskii.* Ed. and introd. George Gibian. Ithaca and London, 1971. A. A. Aleksandrov, "Materialy D. I. Kharmsa v Rukopisnom Otdele Pushkinskogo Doma." In: *Ezhegodnik Rukopisnogo Otdela Pushkinskogo Doma na 1978 god.* Leningrad, 1980. Pp. 64–79 [numerous bibliog. references]. *Iz domu vyshel chelovek. Stikhi dlya detei, i ne tol'ko.* Rego Park, N. Y., 1982.

Translations: "(a railroad happening)." In *Modern Russian Poetry.* Ed. Vladimir Markov and Merrill Sparks. 1967. Pp. 724–27. "Death of the Wild Warrior." In *Russian Poetry: The Modern Period.* Ed. John Glad and Daniel Weissbort. 1978. Pp. 123–24.

Secondary literature: A. Aleksandrov and M. Meilakh, "Tvorchestvo Daniila Kharmsa." In *Materialy XXII stud. nauchnoi konferentsii. Poetika,* etc. Tartu, 1967. R. R. Milner-Gulland, "'Left Art' in Leningrad: The OBERIU Declaration," *OSP* 3 (1970), pp. 65–75. Alice Stone Nakhimovsky, "The Ordinary, the Sacred, and the Grotesque in Daniil Kharms's *The Old Woman,*" *SlavR* 37 (1978), pp. 203–16. M. Petrovskii, "Vozvrashchenie Daniila Kharmsa," *Novyi mir,* 1968, no. 8. Elena Sokol, "Observations on the Prose of Daniil Kharms," *Proceedings of the Pacific Northwest Conference on Foreign Languages* 26 (1975), no. 1, pp. 179–83.   H. B.

Khemnítser, Iván Ivánovich (1745–84), fabulist. The whole of Khemnitser's modest literary reputation rests with his achievements as an author of satires, witty epigrams, and fables, the last of which earned him a popularity rivaling KRYLOV's during the 19th century. As a member of N. A. Lvov's circle in the 1770s, he was introduced to the new aesthetics of the SENTIMENTALISTS as well as to NEOCLASSICAL norms. His writing reflects the confluence of these sources, strongly asserting the enlightened poet's obligation to expose society's flaws on the one hand while counseling the individual to accept the implacable circumstances of life on the other. Several satires, including "On Bad Judges," assume the more strident tone, taking as their theme various corrupt practices evident throughout the bureaucratic structure in Russia. As another, fragmentary satire, "On Profit-Seeking Poets" states, however, the satirist's truths are unloved and it was apparently that which decided the author against their publication.

The first edition of twenty-seven fables and tales, published anonymously in 1779, includes several free translations from the German fabulist Christian Gellert. The abstract, allegorical nature of his models coincided with Khemnitser's own convictions. In the literary debates concerning appropriate targets of satire, he took issue with contemporaries such as N. I. NOVIKOV who advocated the exposure of individuals to ridicule. Although Khemnitser frequently employed traditional Aesopian themes with immediate political implications, such as that of the lion which abuses its position of power, most remained within the limits of acceptability. Others, published only after their author's death, by Lvov and KAPNIST in 1799, were altered to reduce their stridency. From the standpoint of the fable's evolution, Khemnitser marks an intermediate stage between Sumarokov's forceful and often vulgar castigation of vice and Krylov's felicitous and entertaining union of didactic message with colloquial style.

Works: Polnoe sobranie stikhotvorenii. 1956.
Translations: Harold B. Segel, The Literature of Eighteenth Century Russia. Vol. 2. 1967.
Secondary literature: William Edward Brown, A History of Eighteenth Century Russian Literature. 1980.   P. R. H.

Kheráskov, Mikhail Matvéevich (1733–1807) was the author of Russia's first major epic, the Rossiada (1778), and a prolific writer of poetry, prose, and drama. Educated at the Petersburg Cadet Corps, Kheraskov spent much of his professional career in various jobs at Moscow University, where he worked from its founding in 1755, ultimately became one of its four curators (rectors) in 1778, and exerted important influence on its cultural activities (especially the University Press, which he himself first directed and then invited N. I. NOVIKOV to head in 1779). As one of the most devoted Russian Freemasons and the founder of a Masonic lodge of the Rosicrucian Order, Kheraskov produced some of the best, clearest, and most sophisticated examples of Masonic allegory in 18th-century Russia—especially his long novel Cadmus and Harmonia (Kadm i Garmoniya, 1789) and his epic poem Vladimir Reborn (Vladimir vozrozhdennyi, 1785).

During the early 1760s Kheraskov edited two literary journals at Moscow University—Useful Entertainment (Poleznoe uveselenie, January 1760–June 1762) and Free Time (Svobodnye chasy, January–December 1763). The former was the leading literary journal of its time and the only journal to devote most of its space to poetry. Among the writers in this journal were several who later produced some of the best works written in the third quarter of the 18th century, including D. I. FONVIZIN, I. P. BOGDANOVICH, V. I. MAIKOV, A. A. Rzhevsky, and Kheraskov himself. In 1772, Kheraskov brought together many of the same writers who participated in his first two journals in his third and last journal, Vechera (1772–73), which published works read at the literary salon organized by Kheraskov and his wife, the poetess Elizaveta Kheraskova. In addition to these three literary journals, Kheraskov also edited a 1767 three-volume translation of articles from the French Encyclopedia.

During the 18th century, Kheraskov was best known for his epic poems. Between 1761 and 1805 he wrote ten long poems, ranging in subject from a defense of science in The Fruits of Learning (Plody nauk, 1761) to a defense of faith and a decrial of excessive rationality in his Masonic allegory Vladimir Reborn (Vladimir vozrozhdennyi, 1785). For the most famous of these epics, the Rossiada (1779), which portrayed the 1552 capture of Kazan by Ivan IV as the decisive event in Russia's liberation from the Tatar yoke, Kheraskov was dubbed "the Russian Homer" and hailed as an equal of "the Northern Racine" (A. P. SUMAROKOV) and "the Russian Pindar" (M. V. LOMONOSOV). Given the fact that Russia's best poets had attempted to complete a major national epic for almost fifty years (beginning with A. D. KANTEMIR's abandonment of his Petriada dedicated to Peter the Great in 1730 and continuing with Sumarokov's one-page beginning of an epic about Dmitry Donskoi called the Dmitriada and Lomonosov's two cantos of Peter the Great), Kheraskov's completion of the full twelve cantos was indeed considered a major accomplishment and finally fulfilled the Russian ambition for their own national epic.

Kheraskov's three novels, Numa, or Flourishing Rome (Numa, ili protsvetayushchii Rim, 1768), Cadmus and Harmonia, and Polydorus, the Son of Cadmus and Harmonia (Polidor, syn Kadma i Garmonii, 1794) all use classical themes (taken especially from Plutarch's Lives and Ovid's Metamorphoses) as an allegorical focus for discussing both Russia specifically and the human condition in general. Although written in an archaic high style with awkward syntax (including sentences of up to 200 words), Kheraskov's novels reflect a very broad knowledge of classical and European cultures and often have interesting plots. The many levels of allegory in Cadmus and Harmonia prove that under the influence of the Western European baroque novel, Russian prose of the late 18th century had become more sophisticated and complex than is often realized.

In addition to his epic poetry and prose, Kheraskov wrote nine tragedies, five "dramas" (following the examples of Diderot, Lessing, and others), two comedies, a comic opera, a theatrical prologue, and many lyric poems in genres ranging from panegyric, "Anacreontic," and "moral" odes to sonnets, fables, and epigrams. Like his epic poetry and prose, many of Kheraskov's works in other genres (especially those written after the early 1760s) explore Everyman's search for faith, often allegorically opposing "paganism" (lack of true faith) to "Orthodoxy" (any "true faith," including that of the believing Mason). Many of Kheraskov's best lyric poems are written in anacreontic meter, but like most Masonic poets Kheraskov substituted a more Christian, moral, or didactic content for the usual anacreontic praise of wine, women, and song.

Although in 1779 DERZHAVIN called Kheraskov "the creator of the immortal Rossiada," in 1789 KARAMZIN called him the best contemporary Russian poet, and in the 1790s S. T. AKSAKOV recited his works with admiration, by the 19th century Kheraskov's "immortality" had died and his literary reputation was often unfairly destroyed by better poets like Prince V. A. VYAZEMSKY, who stated that Derzhavin's panegyric line in The Spring (Klyuch, 1779, rev. 1783) that Kheraskov had been nourished by "the water of poetry" was unintentionally "the best epigram against Kheraskov ... a surprisingly true and amusing expression."

Works: Tvoreniya, vnov' ispravlennye i dopolnennye. 12 vols. 1796–1800; 2d ed. 1807–12. Izbrannye proizvedeniya. Ed. A. V. Zapadov. (Biblioteka poeta, bol'shaya seriya.) 2d ed. 1961.
Translations: Selection from the Rossiada in: Harold Segel, ed., The Literature of Eighteenth-Century Russia. Vol. 2. Pp. 106–22.
Secondary literature: Stephen Baehr, "The Masonic Component in Eighteenth Century Russian Literature." In A. G. Cross, ed., Russian Literature in the Age of Catherine the Great. 1976. Pp. 121–40. William Edward Brown, "Mikhail Kheraskov and the National Epic." In A History of 18th Century Russian Literature. 1980. Pp. 246–67. Michael Green, "Kheraskov and the Christian Tragedy," California Slavic Studies 9 (1976), pp. 1–26. L. I. Kulakova, "M. M. Kheraskov." AN SSSR, Institut russkoi literatury, Istoriya russkoi literatury. Vol. 4. 1947. Pp. 320–41. A. V. Zapadov, "Tvorchestvo Kheraskova." In M. M. Kheraskov, Izbrannye proizvedeniya. 1961. Pp. 5–56.   S. B.

Khlébnikov, Velimír (real given name: Víktor) Vladímirovich (1885–1922), poet and poetic theorist. The son of an ornithologist, Khlebnikov studied mathematics and the natural sciences at Kazan and St. Petersburg Universities, but never graduated. He began to publish his poetry in 1908, when Vasily KAMENSKY printed some of his verses (they would have been called "surrealist" in the 1920s) in the weekly Vesna. In 1910, two poems by Khlebnikov, "The Thickets were Filled with Sounds" (Byli napolneny zvukami trushchoby) and "Incantation by Laughter" (Zaklinanie smekhom) appeared in the miscellany Studio of Impressionists (Studiya impressionistov) edited by Nikolai Kulbin. The first of these falls in line with the primitivism then in vogue in the visual arts and propagated vigorously by Mikhail Larionov. The second, Khlebnikov's most famous poem, is a "poetic exploration of the possibilities of morphological derivations inherent in the Russian language" (Vladimir Markov), as its twelve lines consist entirely of words derived from the root sme- "laugh." The title of the poem is quite proper, as its composition follows the model of magic rhymes and incantations known from Russian folklore. Khlebnikov went on to use the same technique often.

Also in 1910, Khlebnikov became one of the leaders of the Russian cubo-FUTURISTS, for whom he coined the Russian name budetlyane (from budet, "will be"). He participated in their miscellanies A Trap for Judges (Sadok sudei), I (1910) and II (1912), A Slap in the Face of Public Taste (Poshchechina obshchestvennomu vkusu, 1912), etc. and with A. KRUCHONYKH published the programmatic pamphlet "The Word as Such" (Slovo kak takovoe, 1913). Khlebnikov's ideas of that period must be seen in context with avant-garde visual art, since intimate links existed between the cubo-futurists and painters of the "Donkey's Tail," "Jack of Diamonds," and other modernist groups (Malevich, Goncharova, Larionov, Kandinsky, Tatlin, etc.) Khlebnikov's primitivism assumes various forms, such as cosmic mythology ("The Lightning Sisters"—Sestry molnii, 1915–21), a return to a primeval world of mythic imagination ("Shaman and Venus"—Shaman I Venera, 1912), excursions into a primordial proto-Slavic world ("I and E: A Tale of the Stone Age"—I i E: Povest' kamennogo veka, 1912), and other archaic utopias, but also descent to the vulgarity of the chapbook, popular romance, and urban kitsch in general ("Marquise Dezes"—Markiza Dezes, 1909), and even occasional dada. The element of parody and épatage is not altogether absent from this poetry, for instance in the delightful idyll "Nymph and Wood-Demon" (Vila i leshii, 1913). Very similar tendencies were in vogue in modernist painting at the time. There were cooperative ventures: modernist painters illustrated and designed futurist miscellanies and collections of verse, and designed the sets for their dramatic spectacles, such as Kruchonykh's "opera" Victory over the Sun, with music by M. Matyushin, a prologue by Khlebnikov, and sets by Kazimir Malevich.

Khlebnikov's theory of language, on which he bases his poetics, is related to the principles of cubism. He believed that certain basic meanings, inherent in the roots of words and in simple sound combinations, could be retrieved by reducing speech to its constituent elements and using these for poetic expression. Khlebnikov thus arrived at the principle of trans-sense (or: transrational) poetry (ZAUM'). In its most radical form it leads to poetic composition from speech sounds alone, though more often it assumes the form of a surrealist stream of consciousness, propelled by metonymic and metaphoric associations, puns, sound patterns (alliteration generating parallelism and paronomasia, etc.), and rhythm. Khlebnikov created a very large number of neologisms. Moreover, he tends to use existing words in other than their dictionary meaning, often in terms of what he sees as their original meaning ("etymologism").

An eccentric, Khlebnikov took a magic view of language, believing that there exists a deep organic link between the truth of language, as revealed to the poet, and the cosmic truth of the universe. He also engaged in numerological speculations, looking for the "laws of history." However, in spite of these and many other eccentricities, Khlebnikov was a poet blessed with an immensely fertile imagination who could produce poetry of great power and beauty. Much of his poetry was written spontaneously, without the benefit of editing and rewriting, a part of the creative process of most poets. Khlebnikov also wrote poetry almost incessantly, to the point of graphomania.

War and the Revolution caused Khlebnikov to write a number of more conventional works, both short and long. Thus, the narrative poems "The Night before the Soviets" (Noch' pered sovetami, 1920) and "The Nocturnal Search" (Nochnoi obysk, 1921) have a regular plot and are told in a taut, dramatic manner. Their language, while imaginative, is entirely proper to the subject at hand. "The Nocturnal Search" will stand comparison with any longer poem about the Revolution, including Blok's "The Twelve." However, Khlebnikov had not relinquished his surrealist, mystic, and transrational manner. His last major work, the dramatic poem "Zangezi" (Zangezi is Khlebnikov's Zarathustra) returns to the theme of a universal cosmic language, whose prophet is Zangezi.

Khlebnikov also wrote short prose fiction, whose themes are the same as those of his poetry, but whose style and language are classically clear and economical. Khlebnikov's dramatic pieces are short grotesque skits, for the most part, so "Death's Mistake" (Oshibka smerti, 1917).

Most of Khlebnikov's works were never published in his lifetime, largely because he did not bother to publish them. A good many of his works were lost irretrievably. Nevertheless, the extant corpus of his works is impressive. Khlebnikov was and probably will always remain "a poet's poet." He was held in very high regard by his contemporaries, such as MANDELSHTAM and MAYAKOVSKY. He blazed a trail for every conceivable "modernist" trend in Russian poetry, anticipating the manner and devices of IMAGISTS, CONSTRUCTIVISTS, OBERIUTY, etc. Futurists such as Mayakovsky, PASTERNAK, and ASEEV learned a great deal from Khlebnikov. Khlebnikov, who died alone and destitute in a provincial hospital, was long neglected in the Soviet Union. His legacy still asks for more serious research. Some pioneering work on Khlebnikov has been done in the United States by Vladimir Markov.

Works: Sobranie sochinenii. 5 vols. Introd. essays by Yu. Tynyanov and N. Stepanov. 1928–33. Reprint Munich, 1968–71. *Neizdannye proizvedeniya.* Ed. and notes by N. Khardzhiev and T. Grits. 1940. Reprint Munich, 1971. *Stikhotvoreniya i poemy.* Introd. N. Stepanov. 1960.

Translations: Modern Russian Poetry. Eds. Vladimir Markov and Merrill Sparks. 1967. Pp. 324–41. *Russian Poetry: The Modern Period.* Eds. John Glad and Daniel Weissbort. 1978. Pp. 33–45. *See also Lewanski,* p. 269.

Secondary literature: Henryk Baran, "On the Poetics of a Xlebnikov Tale: Problems and Patterns in 'KA'." In *The Structural Analysis of Narrative Texts.* Ed. Andrej Kodjak et al. 1980. Pp. 112–31. ———, "O nekotorykh podkhodakh k interpretatsii tekstov Vladimira Khlebnikova." In *American Contributions to the Eighth International Congress of Slavists.* 1978. Pp. 104–22. (With a bibliography.) N. Khardzhiev, "Mayakovskii i Khlebnikov." In *Poeticheskaya kul'tura Mayakovskogo.* By N. Khardzhiev and V. Trenin. 1970. Pp. 96–126. ———, "Novoe o Velimire Khlebnikove," *RusL* 9 (1975), pp. 5–24. Osip Mandel'shtam, "Zametki o poezii" (1923), *Sobranie sochinenii.* 1971. Pp. 260–65. ———, "Burya i natisk" (1923), *Sobranie sochinenii.* 1972, pp. 348–50. Vladimir Markov, *The Longer Poems of Velimir Khlebnikov.* 1962. ———, *Russian Futurism: A History.* 1968. V. V. Mayakovskii, "V. V. Khlebnikov" (1922), *PSS* 12 (1959), pp. 23–28. N. Stepanov, *Velimir Khlebnikov: Zhizn' i tvorchestvo.* 1975. Peter Stobbe, *Utopisches Denken bei V. Chlebnikov.* Munich, 1982. B. A. Uspensky, "On the Poetics of Chlebnikov: Problems of Composition," *RusL* 9 (1975), pp. 81–85. Ronald Vroon, "Velimir Khlebnikov's 'Razin: Two Trinities': A Reconstruction," *SlavR* 39 (1980), pp. 70–84. Willem G. Weststeijn, "Bal'mont and Chlebnikov: A Study of Euphonic Devices," *RusL* 8 (1980), pp. 255–96. R. Yakobson, *Noveishaya russkaya poeziya.* Prague, 1921.   V. T.

Khodasévich, Vladisláv Felitsiánovich (1886–1939), poet and critic, was born into the family of an artist of Polish descent. He was educated at a classical gymnasium and then attended Moscow University. Starting in 1905 he published his poetry in SYMBOLIST almanacs and journals. His first collections, *Youth* (Molodost', 1908) and *The Happy Little House* (Schastlivyi domik, 1914) are marked by the influence of symbolist poetics. After the Revolution, Khodasevich worked in various cultural organizations in Moscow. In 1920 he moved to Petrograd. By this time he had reached maturity as a poet in his collections *By Way of a Grain of Corn* (Putem zerna, 1920) and *A Heavy Lyre* (Tyazhelaya lira, 1922). In 1922 Khodasevich emigrated and went on to live in Berlin, Prague, Rome, and Sorrento, where he associated with M. GORKY for a time. In 1925 he settled in Paris, where he lived, plagued by ill health and need, devoting himself exclusively to literary work. He published in the émigré press (*Volya Rossii,* SOVREMENNYE ZAPISKI, etc.), and was editor of the literary section and permanent critic of the newspaper VOZROZHDENIE. Between 1922 and 1939 he published over 300 critical articles, a part of which were collected in a book, *Literary Articles and Memoirs* (Literaturnye stat'i i vospominaniya, 1954, later republished under the title *Izbrannaya proza* in 1982). Khodasevich's poems of his émigré period are not numerous, but of very high quality, for example, his cycle "European Night" (Evropeiskaya noch'). In 1927 Khodasevich published a volume of *Collected Verse* (Sobranie stikhov, republished in 1961), which did not include his first two collections. Khodasevich was also active as a historian of literature and memoirist: *Stat'i o russkoi poezii* (1922); *Poeticheskoe khozyaistvo Pushkina* (Pushkin's Poetic Household, 1924); *Derzhavin* (1931); *O Pushkine* (1937); *Nekropol'* (1939). He translated Z. Krasiński, Kh. Byalik, S. Chernikhovsky, etc.

Khodasevich's work was highly valued even in his lifetime. Authors as opposed to each other in their views and biases as Gorky and NABOKOV considered him to be the greatest Russian poet of the 20th century. A disciple of the symbolists, a contemporary and friend of the ACMEISTS, an implacable enemy of the FUTURISTS, Khodasevich to the very end refused to fit the mold of any of the established literary schools. He is considered to have been one of the creators of "Petersburg poetics," whose impact on Russian literature can be felt to this day, specifically in the case of I. BRODSKY. Khodasevich's basic motifs are the incompatibility of the spirit and the universe, the poet's tragic clairvoyance in a world of distortions and displacements. His poetry is built upon the contrast and contradiction between tradition and reality. In many ways, Khodasevich issues from the poetic culture of the 19th century, PUSHKIN and his pleiad in particular, but gives it a new meaning in a new historical setting. Hence, on the one side, is his neoclassical stylization, a penchant for "minor," private forms and genres (poetic aphorism, epigram, album or diary entry), the brilliance and elegance of his disciplined verse; on the other, a certain angularity, a prosaic quality, even roughness of lexicon and imagery, a sober keenness of observation, and a biliously ironic analysis of recent antipoetic and antispiritual forms of being. Such dualism gives Khodasevich's verse great plenitude and depth of meaning. A faith in the unshakable values of culture, a vivid sense of the past in the present, and at the same time, a physical horror of reality, a realization of the contemporary world as an eschatological catastrophe, all this links Khodasevich to MANDELSHTAM, and to T.S. Eliot as well. The acuity of his perception, sometimes approaching the grotesque, places him close to modernist prose as well. However, Khodasevich is more tragic than most of his contemporaries. From a melancholy scepticism, still connected with the mood of *fin de siècle*, he proceeds to a cruel cynicism and a sense of hopelessness. Life becomes for him an "iron gritting of cacophonic worlds," a region of existential emptiness and disintegration (cf. the frequent motif of mirror, window, and fall in his poetry). Along with this, Khodasevich's style is characterized by a laconic, dry, and lucid poetic script, intimate colloquial intonations, and by mockery next to reflection.

In his book on DERZHAVIN, Khodasevich proved himself a brilliant master of Russian prose. His slightly stylized, elegant narrative is a manifestation of a recurring characteristic theme: Derzhavin is perceived by Khodasevich as a paradigm of the poet in a clash with reality. Imbued with a vivid sense of history, this book remains the best biography of Derzhavin and an exemplar of its genre. Khodasevich's essays on Pushkin are devoted to investigation of Pushkinian *topoi*, recurring patterns, autoreminiscences, etc. Khodasevich was inclined to criticize the FORMAL school, viewing the poetic device as an indicator of worldview and personality structure. His method, which led him from formal and structural observations to biographic and psychoanalytic discoveries, is similar to that of AKHMATOVA and also, to some extent, anticipates contemporary semiotics (see STRUCTURALISM AND SEMIOTICS). The same method is applied in articles on ROSTOPCHINA, DELVIG, GOGOL, BELY, ANNENSKY, and others, all examples of creative, learned, as well as deeply personal criticism. Khodasevich's ironic reminiscences provide us with some quite unique material on the history of symbolism and the first years of the Revolution. Khodasevich's articles on émigré literature have also retained their value. Here he appears as an enemy of the literary establishment, promotes novelty, experimentation, and invites his fellow writers to take advantage, in every possible way, of their unique émigré experience. Perceiving his exile as both tragedy and duty, Khodasevich, along with Nabokov, became the most significant and original writer of Russian émigré literature.

Works: Sobranie sochinenii. 5 vols. Ann Arbor, 1981– . *Sobranie stikhov.* 2 vols. Paris, 1982. *Izbrannaya proza.* 2 vols. Rego Park, N.Y., 1982–83.
Translations: (ca. 35 poems), trans. Alexander Landman, *RLT* 8 (1974), pp. 45–64. (7 poems) in *Russian Poetry: The Modern Period.* Ed. John Glad and Daniel Weissbort. 1978. Pp. 157–64. *See also: Lewanski,* pp. 269–70.
Secondary literature: A. Belyi, "Rembrandtova pravda v poezii nashikh dnei," *Zapiski mechtatelei,* no. 5 (1922), pp. 136–39. ———, "Tyazhelaya lira i russkaya lirika," *Sovremennye zapiski,* book 15 (1923), pp. 371–88. N. Berberova, "Pamyati Khodasevicha," *Sovremennye zapiski,* book 69 (1939), pp. 256–61. ———, "Vladislav Khodasevich: A Russian Poet," *RusR* 11 (1952), no. 2, pp. 78–85. ———, *Kursiv moi.* Munich, 1972. (In English: *The Italics Are Mine.* 1969.) David Bethea, "Khodasevich's Poems in Blank Verse: The Pushkin Connection," *Topic,* no. 33 (1979), pp. 3–13. ———, "*Sorrento Photographs:* Khodasevich's Memory Speaks," *SlavR* 39 (1980), pp. 56–69. ———, "Following in Orpheus' Footsteps: A Reading of Xodasevič's 'Ballada'," *SEEJ* 25 (1981), pp. 54–70. ———, *Khodasevich: His Life and Art.* 1983. A. Chulkova-Khodasevich, "Vospominaniya o Vladislave Khodaseviche." In *Russica.* New York, 1981. Pp. 275–96. N. Gumilev, *Sobranie sochinenii.*

Vol. 4. Washington, 1968. Pp. 343–44. Roger M. Hagglund, "The Adamovič—Xodasevič Polemics," *SEEJ* 20 (1976), pp. 239–52. R. P. Hughes, "Khodasevich: Irony and Dislocation: A Poet in Exile," *Triquarterly,* no. 27 (1973), pp. 5–66. S. Karlinskii, "Pis'ma M. Tsvetaevoi k V. Khodasevichu," *Novyi zhurnal,* no. 89 (1967), pp. 102–14. John E. Malmstad, "The Historical Sense and Xodasevič's *Deržavin.*" In V. Khodasevich, *Derzhavin.* Munich, 1975. Pp. V–XVIII. N. Mandel'shtam, *Vtoraya kniga.* Paris, 1972. Pp. 160–62. O. Mandel'shtam, *Sobranie sochinenii.* Vol. 2. New York, 1971. Pp. 345–46. V. Orlov, *Pereput'ya.* Moscow, 1976. Pp. 144–56. R. Poggioli, *The Poets of Russia, 1890–1930.* 1960. Pp. 303–08. F. Radle, "Khodasevich—poet groteska." In *Vozdushnye puti,* book 4 (1965), pp. 256–62. M. Shaginyan, *Literaturnyi dnevnik.* 1923. Pp. 124–27. Z. Shakhovskaya, *Otrazheniya.* Paris, 1975. Pp. 184–87. V. Sirin [Nabokov], "O Khodaseviche," *Sovremennye zapiski,* 69 (1939), pp. 262–64. G. S. Smith, "Stanza Rhythm and Stress Load in the Iambic Tetrameter of V. F. Xodasevič," *SEEJ* 24 (1980), pp. 25–36. G. Struve, *Russkaya literatura v izgnanii.* New York, 1956. Pp. 141–46, 206–13, 220–22. Yu. Tynyanov, *Poetika, istoriya literatury, kino.* 1977. Pp. 172–73. V. Veidle, *Poeziya Khodasevicha.* Paris, 1928. ———, "A Double-Edged *Ars Poetica* (Vladislav Khodasevich)," *RLT* 2 (1972), pp. 339–47. ———, *O poetakh i poezii.* Paris, 1973. Pp. 34–52.

T. V.

Khomyakóv, Aleksei Stepánovich (1804–1860), poet, playwright, philosopher of history, and theologian, from a family of landowners. He received a degree in mathematics from Moscow University in 1821 and was associated with the Society of WISDOM LOVERS in the early 1820s. He published his poetry in MOSKOVSKII VESTNIK, the organ of Russian Schellingianism. His early verses are characterized by rhetorical pathos, a lofty view of the poet's calling, and a preview of his later SLAVOPHILE ideas. Khomyakov also wrote the historical tragedies *Ermak* (staged 1827, published 1832) and *Dimitry the Pretender* (Dimitrii Samozvanets, 1833), the latter in antiphon to PUSHKIN's *Boris Godunov.* As the Slavophile movement took shape in the late 1830s, Khomyakov became its most remarkable thinker and publicist. His essays, such as "On the Old and the New" (O starom i novom, 1839), "On the Possibility of a Russian School of Art" (O vozmozhnosti russkoi khudozhestvennoi shkoly, 1847), "On Contemporary Trends in the Area of Philosophy" (O sovremennykh yavleniyakh v oblasti filosofii, 1859), etc. are written in a lucid and eloquent, albeit somewhat archaic Russian, "free both from the Gallicisms of the Karamzin-Pushkin school and from the untidiness and vulgarity of later 19th-century journalism" (SVYATOPOLK-MIRSKY).

Although Khomyakov's theological writings were not even allowed to be published until 1879, his influence as a thinker extended to Russian Orthodox theology and to all those Russian writers who dealt with religious questions. Khomyakov's focal idea was that of *sobornost'* ("organic collectivity"), by which he defined the Church as the free unity of the faithful, a unity brought about by their common understanding of truth and their common love of Christ. Khomyakov's influence is strong in DOSTOEVSKY's *The Brothers Karamazov,* where a faith based on freedom and love, rather than on the law of God, and the concept of a universal community of all animate beings (implying universal responsibility for "all and everyone" and shared guilt for "all and everyone" as well) are the key ideas of Father Zosima, who speaks for the author. Dostoevsky's negative attitude toward the Catholic Church in the "Grand Inquisitor" chapter also has some traits which point to Khomyakov. Somewhat later, Khomyakov's ideas appeared in the philosophy of Vladimir SOLOVYOV and in Russian SYMBOLIST thought, Vyacheslav IVANOV's in particular.

Works: Sochineniya. 4 vols. 1861–73. 2d ed. 1879–82. *Polnoe sobranie sochinenii.* 8 vols. 1900–07. *Sochineniya.* 6 vols. 1915. *Stikhotvoreniya i dramy.* Introd. and notes by B. F. Egorov. 1969.
Translations: 13 poems, trans. Larry Andrews, *RLT* 8 (1974), pp. 72–82. *See also: Lewanski,* p. 270.
Secondary Literature: V. G. Belinskii, "Moskovskii literaturnyi i uchenyi sbornik na 1847 god" (1847), *PSS* 10, pp. 199–203. (A response to Khomyakov's "On the Possibility of a Russian School of Art.") P. K. Christoff, *An Introduction to Nineteenth-Century Rus-*

sian Slavophilism. Vol. 1. *A. S. Khomyakov.* The Hague, 1961. A. A. Gratieux, *A. S. Khomiakov et le mouvement slavophile.* 2 vols. Paris, 1939. E. A. Maimin, "Khomyakov kak poet." In *Pushkinskii sbornik.* Pskov, 1968. Mat' Mariya (E. Yu. Skobtsova), *A. Khomyakov.* Paris, 1929. V. Z. Zavitievich, *A. S. Khomyakov.* 2 vols. 1902–13. (With bibliography.) V. T.

Khvoshchinskaya, Nadézhda Dmítrievna, see KRESTOVSKY, V.

Khvostóv, Dmítry Ivánovich (1757–1835), poet, a count, attended the boarding school of Moscow University and Moscow University (1765–72). He was at one time Chief Procurator of the Holy Synod (1799–1802). Together with a few others, he published the journal *The Friend of Enlightenment* (Drug prosveshcheniya, 1804–06). He also worked on a "Dictionary of Russian Writers," which he never completed.

Khvostov grew up in a literary ambiancè (SUMAROKOV, A. Karin, V. MAIKOV) and began to write verse at the age of 18 or 20. He remained a strict classicist all his life. His early odes were entirely on the level of the literary standards of the times, and his translations of Racine (*Andromaque*) and Boileau (*L'Art poétique*) were quite successful. In 1802 Khvostov published his "Selected Parables from the Best Authors, in Russian Verse" (Izbrannye pritchi iz luchshikh sochinitelei rossiiskimi stikhami), where he absurdly exaggerated the practice of Aesop and Lessing to endow the personages of these fables with human qualities (doves who have teeth, pikes that give out a wail, etc.). From here on Khvostov was the butt of jibes by several generations of Russian writers, such as KRYLOV, PUSHKIN, ZHUKOVSKY, VYAZEMSKY, GNEDICH, IZMAILOV, and many others. In love with literature, good-natured, and by no means a fool, Khvostov stoically bore all this mockery. He printed his verses at his own expense, and himself bought up and reissued his collected works. In 1791 Khvostov was elected a member of the Russian Academy. In the mid-1800s he joined the informal literary circle of SHISHKOV and DERZHAVIN, and was one of the most active members of the "Collegium of Lovers of the Russian Word" (BESEDA LYUBITELEI RUSSKOGO SLOVA, 1811–16).

Works: Polnoe sobranie stikhotvorenii grafa Khvostova. 3d ed. Pts. 1–8. St. Petersburg, 1818–34. *Zapiski o slovesnosti.* In *Literaturnyi arkhiv.* Vol. 1. Moscow and Leningrad, 1938. [Poems:] *Poety 1790–1810-kh godov.* (Biblioteka Poeta. Bol'shaya seriya.) 1971. Pp. 424–46.

Secondary literature: P. O. Morozov, "Graf D. I. Khvostov," *Russkaya starina,* 1892, nos. 6–8. M. G. Al'tshuller, "Krylov v literaturnykh ob"edineniyakh 1800–1810-kh godov." In *Ivan Andreevich Krylov: Problemy tvorchestva.* 1975. Pp. 154–95. ———, "Neizvestnyi epizod zhurnal'noi polemiki nachala 19 veka ("Drug prosveshcheniya" i "Moskovskii zritel'")." In *Russkaya literatura 18 veka i ee mezhdunarodnye svyazi.* "18 vek" Sbornik 10. Leningrad, 1975. Pp. 98–106. M. A.

Kiev Academy (traditionally: Kiev Mohyla Academy), the oldest institution of higher learning in the Ukraine and in the East Slavic lands and their most important intellectual center in the 17th and early 18th century; Russia's first "window to the West." The Academy (then called a Collegium) came into existence in 1632 when the Kievan Metropolitan Petro Mohyla united the school of the Confraternity of the Epiphany (Bohojavlens'ke Bratstvo) with the newly established gymnasium of the Monastery of the Caves (the Lavra) and gave it a new Western-, Latinate- and Jesuit-influenced outlook and curriculum. (Although 1632 initiates the academic history of the Academy, its political and civic role begins with the founding of the confraternity school in 1615; from that time the Academy was officially supported by the Ukrainian Hetmans, by the Zaporozhian Cossacks, and later also by the elite of the Hetman State.) In 1694, during the Hetmanate of its greatest patron, Hetman Ivan Mazepa, the Collegium obtained the charter of an Academy (reaffirmed in 1701). In 1819, after a period of decline in the later half of the 18th century, the Academy was transformed into the Kiev Ecclesiastical Seminary, which existed until the Revolution of 1917.

Somewhat paradoxically, Mohyla's Western focus, with Latin the language of instruction (and Greek becoming quite peripheral),

was intended to revitalize and intellectually rearm Ukrainian and generally East Slavic Orthodoxy in the face of militant Polish Catholicism; in this, as witnessed by the imposing number of clerics, scholars, writers, political and civic leaders who graduated from the Academy, he was highly successful. The curriculum followed a basic Jesuit model: the lower or grammatical classes, dealing with etymology, grammar and syntax, and the intermediate (*humaniora*) classes of poetics and rhetoric; the higher classes had a two or three year course of philosophy; after 1694 a four year course of theology was also offered. In addition there were courses in languages—Slaveno-Ruthenian (i.e., bookish Ukrainian), Church-Slavonic, Polish, the all-important Latin, Greek, and Hebrew—in music, art and geometry; at the very end, courses in medicine and natural sciences were also offered. The spirit of the Academy was thoroughly scholastic, with Thomism as its prime mover; so, too, was its pedagogic praxis, with its vehicles of lectures, disputations and declamations. Fixed on this model, the Academy remained largely immune to the legacy of humanism, to rationalism and the era of scientific discovery that in the 17th and 18th centuries were reshaping the mind of Western Europe. The main focus of intellectual activity in Kiev was religious polemics. Kievan scholarship provided no innovations either in rhetoric or poetics, or in philosophy or theology. Despite that, however, its focus on Western models, particularly those of neighboring Poland, with its lively and developed literary culture (indeed Polish authors e.g., Jan Kochanowski in lyric and Piotr Kochanowski in epic poetry are taken as primary models), gave a new breadth and sophistication to Ukrainian and then to Russian literary culture.

The strongly clerical and theocentric thought of the Academy in the 17th century, coupled with the trauma of the twenty-year Ukrainian civil war following the death of Hetman Khmel'nyc'kyj in 1657, led many of its leaders to seek stability and legitimacy under the protection of the Orthodox Muscovite Tsar. (For their part, the Muscovites were initially highly suspicious of the Western-influenced Kievans; thus, for example, the first version of Dimitry ROSTOVSKY's MINEI CHET'I was declared un-Orthodox and revisions were demanded.) The clearest reflection of this search for legitimacy and order, and abnegation of Ukrainian political aspirations, is the quasi-historical *Synopsis,* written under the aegis of Innokentij Gizel' (?–1683), professor and rector of the Academy; while glorifying the Romanovs and depicting the Ukraine as their hereditary patrimony, it quite ignores the Cossacks and their elite who were the immediate protectors and patrons of the Academy.

By far the greatest patron of the Academy was Hetman Ivan Mazepa. During his rule (1687–1709) the Academy flourished as never before, receiving new buildings and endowments, expanding faculty and enrollments. (This patronage—as well as the reciprocal panegyrics of the academics, including the dedication to Mazepa of PROKOPOVICH's *Vladimir* in 1705—and the very fact that the school was known as the Mohyla-Mazepa Academy, is now consistently ignored in Soviet sources.) After the battle of Poltava (1709), the fortunes of the Academy declined. One of the most severe blows was Peter's decision, in 1721, to forbid the printing of Ukrainian books, with only religious works, resubmitted for censorship, and in Russian, permitted. A brief revival of the Academy's fortunes, and an updating of its curriculum occurred during the tenure of Metropolitan Rafail Zaborovsky (1731–42).

The Academy's impact on literary norms and conventions (e.g., syllabic poetry), especially through the vehicle of handbooks of poetics and rhetoric and the writing and staging of school dramas, was far-reaching. Even more pronounced was its impact on Russian education, beginning with the Slavonic-Greek-Latin Academy of Moscow (1687) which was modelled on, and whose faculty was largely trained in, the Kiev Academy. The most striking evidence of its important role and influence is the list of its faculty and graduates who left Kiev for St. Petersburg or Moscow both to lay the foundations for the subsequent flowering of Russian culture and to administer the Empire; e.g., such figures as Prokopovich, Stefan Yavorsky, SIMEON POLOTSKY, Epifany Slavynetsky and Arseny Satanovsky; the composers M. Berezovsky and A. Vedel; such officials as Chancellor Prince Aleksandr Bezborodko, Minister of Justice Dmytro Troshchinsky, or Minister of Internal Affairs Viktor Kochubei. G. G.

Kievo-Pechérskii Paterik, see HAGIOGRAPHY, OLD RUSSIAN LITERATURE.

Kingdom of India, History of, see SKAZANIE OB INDIISKOM TSARSTVE.

Kireevsky, Ivan Vasilievich (1806–56) together with A. S. KHOMYAKOV the principal architect of SLAVOPHILISM, was born into a cultivated and conservative gentry family. The Kireevskys had been based in the Tula–Orel area since before 1600. After the death of Vasily Ivanovich Kireevsky in 1812, his young bride, Avdotya Petrovna, married A. A. Elagin (1817) and in 1822 moved to Moscow. Although V. I. Kireevsky died when his children were very young, he left them with a powerfully based family tradition of integrated culture, simultaneously Russian and European.

Ivan Kireevsky was educated by tutors, several of whom were Moscow professors, and with constant reference to the advice of his godfather, the poet ZHUKOVSKY. D. M. Vellansky and M. G. Pavlov introduced him to German idealism, and particularly to the metaphysics of Schelling. In 1824 Kireevsky went to work in the archives of the Foreign Ministry in Moscow, thus becoming one of the aristocratic young idealists whom PUSHKIN immortalized as the "archive youth." He participated enthusiastically in several idealist circles of the period (the RAICH circle, the WISDOM LOVERS), published some important Pushkin criticism (MOSKOVSKII VESTNIK, 1828–29); and in January 1830 he sought solace from an unhappy love affair in a trip to Germany.

Kireevsky spent ten months there, visiting the University of Berlin briefly (where he met Hegel), but spending most of his time in Munich with his brother Pyotr Vasilievich. In the case of both brothers it is difficult to specify what the influence of Schelling, Oken, and Görres actually was, at the time or subsequently. Upon returning from Germany in the fall of 1830, Kireevsky founded a journal, whose name, *The European* (Evropeets) suggests its program: to inform educated Russia of the exciting intellectual events that had come to a head in the European revolutions of 1830. The government suppressed the journal after only two issues, however, prompted by a denunciation of Kireevsky's important essay, "The Nineteenth Century."

Kireevsky spent the 1830s in a state of semi-retirement from literary politics and even from literature; during this period he drew close to his brother and particularly to A. S. Khomyakov; the emergence of a Slavophile point of view was triggered by their collective hostility to CHAADAEV's Westernism. The earliest extant expressions of a thoroughgoing Slavophile point of view are Khomyakov's "On the Old and the New" and Kireevsky's "An Answer to Khomyakov," both written in 1839. Kireevsky's Slavophile vision, which he elaborated in a series of journal articles during the 1840s, laid particular stress on the Orthodox patristic foundation of old Russian culture and the historical communalism of the peasant *mir*.

In 1845 Kireevsky became the editor of Pogodin's MOSKVITYANIN for three issues and produced his "Survey of the Current State of Literature" for that journal. Toward the end of the 1840s, Kireevsky took on Father Makary, an elder of the Optina Monastery, as his spiritual adviser, an important relationship which lasted the rest of his life and contributed to his growing interest in the Fathers of the Eastern Church. In 1852 he wrote a long article for the Slavophile *Moskovskii sbornik* entitled "On the Character of the Culture of Europe and its Relationship to the Culture of Russia," in which he developed his ideas on the integral Christian civilization of old Russia and dwelt at length on the historical development of the Eastern and Western Churches. "On the Necessity and Possibility of New Principles in Philosophy" appeared in RUSSKAYA BESEDA at the end of 1856. It reflected his lifelong interest in philosophy, but like his other major articles it was really an extended comparison of what he regarded as the principles underlying the different civilizations of East and West. Kireevsky died of cholera on 11 June 1856 and was buried with his brother Peter, who survived him by only a few months, at Optina.

Works: Polnoe sobranie sochinenii. Ed. M. O. Gershenzon. 2 vols. Moscow, 1911.
Translations: "On the Necessity and Possibility of New Principles in Philosophy." In *Russian Philosophy*. Ed. James M. Edie et al. 3 vols. 1965. Pp. 171–213.
Secondary literature: P. K. Christoff, *An Introduction to Nineteenth-Century Russian Slavophilism: A Study in Ideas.* Vol. 2: I. V. Kireevsky. The Hague, 1972. A. Gleason, *European and Muscovite: Ivan Kireevsky and the Origins of Slavophilism.* 1972. E. Müller, *Russischer Intellekt in europäischer Krise: Ivan V. Kireevskij.* Cologne, 1966. N. Riasanovsky, *Russia and the West in the Teaching of the Slavophiles.* 1952. A. Walicki, *The Slavophile Controversy: History of a Conservative Utopia in Nineteenth-Century Russian Thought.* 1975.

A. G.

Kireevsky, Pyotr Vasilievich (1808–56) Slavophile and ethnographer, was born at Dolbino, a Kireevsky estate in Kaluga Province. Like his brother Ivan, he was privately educated in a patriarchal and conservative milieu, but one in close touch with the defining currents of 18th-century Russian culture, while being unusually sensitive to nascent literary romanticism, partly through the family's connection with the poet ZHUKOVSKY. In 1812 Kireevsky's father died of cholera; in 1817 his mother married A. A. Elagin, and the family moved to Moscow five years later. Pyotr Vasilievich was an unobtrusive member of several idealist circles of the 1820s; he was already notable for his shyness.

In 1828, Kireevsky published his first writings: a review of some published lectures on modern Greek literature and some translations from Calderon. The following year he spent several months abroad, mostly in Munich, where he was thoroughly exposed to the work of Schelling, Oken, and Görres. It is difficult to be specific about influences, but it seems likely that Schelling's ideas about mythology and religion as the deepest sources of European art had their effect on him.

The beginning of Kireevsky's activity as a song collector dates from the very early 1830s; the encouragement of PUSHKIN was important. An unpublished essay on Saint-Simon suggests that 1830 was the high point of Kireevsky's attraction to "progressive ideas." As the 1830s wore on, his interest in the Russian past and the folklore that expressed it continued to grow; he became a passionate opponent of CHAADAEV's WESTERNISM. Pyotr Vasilievich counted himself a devotee of "Slavism" almost before there was a Slavophile school, but he made no theoretical contribution to Slavophile doctrine, beyond polemicizing with POGODIN about the "submissiveness" of the people in "Old Russia" (*Moskvityanin*, 1845). After years of periodic concern about how to begin publication of his songs, Kireevsky presented some few annotated texts in *Moskovskii sbornik* (1852); but the challenging task of publishing the collection really began after his death and continues to this day. Kireevsky had no family of his own and died a few months after his beloved brother Ivan.

Bibliography: Pesni, sobrannye P. V. Kireevskim. 10 vols. 1860–1874; and *Novaya seriya,* vols. 1–2. 1911–29. M. K. Azadovskii, ed. *Pis'ma P. V. Kireevskogo k N. M. Yazykovu.* 1935. ———. *Istoriya russkoi fol'kloristiki.* 1958. A. Gleason, *European and Muscovite: Ivan Kireevsky and the Origins of Slavophilism.* 1972. *Pesni, sobrannye pisatelyami: Novye materialy iz arkhiva P. V. Kireevskogo, Literaturnoe nasledstvo* 79 (1968). A. D. Samoilov, *P. V. Kireevskii i ego sobranie narodnykh pesen.* 1971.

A. G.

Kirillov, Vladimir Timofeevich (1890–1943). An activist and poet who joined the Revolution as a boy and worked as a sailor on the Black Sea, where he took part in uprisings in 1905 and 1906. As a soldier at the front in 1917, he took a leading part in the rebellion against tsarist officers. He began publishing poetry in 1913. He was one of the leaders of the PROLETKUL'T, an organization he left in 1918 to found KUZNITSA (The Smithy) together with other proletarian poets committed to the production of lyric poetry free of political tutelage. Kirillov is a poet of revolutionary upheaval and his lines call for a clean break with the art and literature of the past in the name of a new proletarian culture. One of his most famous and most characteristic poems, entitled *We* (My, 1917), announces that "In the name of our tomorrow we will consign Raphael to the flames / Destroy the museums, trample underfoot the flowers of art." Such lines should not be taken literally but read in their temporal context as a hyperbolic statement of the poet's revolutionary fervor. Lenin's New Economic Policy, adopted in 1921, seemed to Kirillov and other "Smiths" a betrayal of their ideals, and a note of defeat crept into their published verse. Kirillov was arrested in 1937 and died in prison in 1943. He was rehabilitated posthumously in 1958.

Works: Stikhotvoreniya. 1958. *Stikhotvoreniya i poemy.* 1970.

Secondary literature: Z. S. Papernyi and R. A. Shatseva, In *Proletarskie poety pervykh let sovetskoi epokhi.* 1959.

E. J. B.

Kirsánov, Semyón Isaákovich (1906–72), poet, took a degree in philology in his native Odessa in 1925 and moved to Moscow the same year. He began to publish early, having joined the LEF group and being close to MAYAKOVSKY, with whom he toured the Soviet Union. Kirsanov was greatly influenced by Mayakovsky's poetic style. Like Mayakovsky, he produced a great deal of versified journalism, such as the *poema* "Five-Year Plan" (1932). Also like Mayakovsky, Kirsanov wrote a great deal of poetry in the first person singular, or with the poet's persona in the focus of attention, e.g., "My Name-day Poem" (Moya imeninnaya: Poema, 1927). Kirsanov's poetic style was marked by whimsical imagery, farfetched metaphors, a fondness for puns and conceits, and ample instances of symbolic patterning of sound and syntax. His rhythms and rhyming technique followed Mayakovsky's.

Kirsanov's penchant for fantastic themes led to versified science fiction, such as "Atom under Siege" (1933) and "Poem about a Robot" (1934), which at times produced intriguing insights. Among Kirsanov's poems of the 1930s there are some in which emotional suffering is expressed in haunting images and with a ring of truth: "Your poem" (Tvoya poema, 1937) and the cycles "Groaning while Asleep" (Ston vo sne, 1937) and "The Last of May" (Poslednee maya, 1937). During the war, Kirsanov worked as a war correspondent and produced his share of patriotic verse, such as the *poema* "Aleksandr Matrosov" (1946). He played a significant role in the THAW after Stalin's death. His *poema* "Seven Days of the Week" (1956) combines science fiction with moral allegory, describing the implantation of new, good and honest hearts in the chests of the Soviet people. Toward the end of his life Kirsanov turned more and more toward a versified *Naturphilosophie*, often in free verse. While much of Kirsanov's poetry is decidedly modern and even cosmopolitan in its outlook, he also cultivated the style of Russian folk poetry, e.g., in "The Tale of King Maks-Emelyan" (Skazanie pro tsarya Maksa-Emel'yana, 1962–64).

Works: Sobranie sochinenii v 4-kh tomakh. 1974–76.

Translations: (Selected translations from the cycle "Poets' Poem" [Poema poetov]) Trans. Mark E. Suino, *RLT* 8 (1974), pp. 22–44. *See also: Lewanski,* pp. 270–71.

V. T.

Kírsha Danílov, see BYLINA.

Kirshón, Vladímir Mikháilovich (1902–38), dramatist. Once active in RAPP, Kirshon began his career as a dramatic writer in 1920. His first play to attract attention was *Konstantin Terekhin* (1926), which he wrote together with Andrei Uspensky. A melodrama about the problems of adjustment of Soviet youth in the first decade after the Revolution, the work enjoyed a certain international renown. It became a part of the repertoire of the New York Theatre Guild in the late 1920s under the title *Red Rust*. Kirshon next wrote *The Rails Are Humming* (Rel'sy gudyat, 1927), a well-regarded play on the theme of industrialization. This was followed by *Gorod vetrov* (The City of Winds, 1929), dealing with revolutionary events in Baku in 1918 and written in the then popular episodic style of early Soviet drama. In 1930, Kirshon wrote the play for which he is best known, *Bread* (Khleb), an occasionally exciting work on the impact of the first Five-Year Plan on rural Russia and the liquidation of the *kulaks*. Although *Bread* has some vivid characters and is generally convincing, it was faulted for ideological deficiencies. Kirshon also wrote *The Court* (Sud) in 1933, about Communists in contemporary Germany, and his most successful play with the public, *The Miraculous Alloy* (Chudesnyi splav, 1934), a social comedy set against the background of the search for a certain alloy for airplane construction. In several articles in the late 1920s and early 1930s, Kirshon, like AFINOGENOV, pleaded for a Soviet drama of greater psychological depth and verisimilitude. His views resulted in sometimes sharp polemics with such advocates of a "romantic-monumental" drama as Vsevolod VISHNEVSKY and Nikolai POGODIN. Kirshon was eventually caught up in the purges of the late 1930s. He was condemned on a charge of Trotskyism and was executed on 28 July 1938.

Bibliography: L. Tamashin, *Vladimir Kirshon: Ocherk tvorchestva.* 1965.

H. B. S.

Klenóvsky, Dmítry Iósifovich (pseudonym of D. I. Krachkovsky, 1893–1976), émigré poet and essayist. Klenovsky was born into the family of a well-known Russian painter. In 1911 he graduated from the famous classical gymnasium in Tsarskoe Selo associated with the names of ANNENSKY, GUMILYOV, and AKHMATOVA. He then traveled extensively in Europe. In 1913 he enrolled in the law school of St. Petersburg University. From 1917 until 1922 he was in the military service. He moved to Moscow in 1918 and in 1921 to Kharkov, where he worked as a journalist. He published his first collection of poetry before the Revolution (*The Palette*— Palitra, 1917) under his own name; it was later discarded by the poet himself as juvenile and unsatisfactory. As there was another poet of the same name and surname, he decided to take a pseudonym.

His next volume did not appear until after he had left Russia in 1943 for Germany (*The Trace of Life*—Sled zhizni, 1950). It was followed by nine verse collections (including the posthumous *Last Poems*—Poslednee, 1977) of classical limpidity. Klenovsky is the leading poet of the second emigration and an accomplished master of lyrical and philosophical meditation. His pre-revolutionary background in Tsarskoe Selo left a profound impact on his poetic sensibility and endowed his art with painful lucidity and nostalgic poignancy. He was very correctly termed "the last of the Tsarskoe Selo poets, educated by the Acmeists" (N. Berberova). He inherited and transformed in a very personal way several features of the ACMEIST poetics: the simplicity and lyricism of his means of expression, an attention to every individual object, a melodic sonority, and a plasticity in sculpting his own artistic ego. Klenovsky's poetic vision is, however, complex and somber, lacking almost entirely the life-asserting enthusiasm of Gumilyov or early MANDELSHTAM and only rarely achieving a level of self-detachment that could resemble the serenity of late Akhmatova. Being under the influence of anthroposophy, Klenovsky never doubted spiritual reality, but more so in its occult than in its epiphanic aspect. Hence his inner conflict is a constant attempt at religious integration, never ultimately fulfilled; his striving for joy in a union with God, never accomplished. He relies on belief and thus cannot help the eroding influence of skepsis and pessimism. With an escape into nature or even into art not entirely satisfying, death gradually becomes the crux of his poetic world. Klenovsky's preoccupation with death, especially in his later volumes, comes to the verge of obsessiveness; in a less gifted poet, this kind of verse would become increasingly depressing, but Klenovsky always avoids the trap by means of his verbal mastery and a naturalness in his emphasis on personal existential torment "when one just cannot overcome a single line of torture every morning."

Works: Navstrechu nebu. 1952. *Neulovimyi sputnik.* 1956. *Prikosnovenie.* 1959. *Ukhodyashchie parusa.* 1962. *Razroznennaya taina.* 1965. *Stikhi.* 1967. *Pevuchaya nosha.* 1969. *Pocherkom poeta.* 1971. *Teplyi vecher.* 1975. "Avtobiografiya," *Sovremennik* 37–38 (1978), pp. 188–95. *Sobranie stikhov.* Vol. 1. 1980.

Translations: "Footprint of Life." In *Modern Russian Poetry*, Vladimir Markov and Merrill Sparks, eds. (1967), pp. 488–89.

Secondary literature: N. Berberova, "Poet Dmitrii Klenovskii." In *Sled zhizni. Literaturnoe zarubezh'e*, 1958, p. 45. A. Rannit, Review of *Stikhi* and *Pevuchaya nosha*, *SEEJ* 14 (1970), pp. 359–65.

V. B.

Klyúev, Nikolaí Alekséevich (1887–1937). The most talented of the so-called peasant poets, Klyuev became a semi-official composer of religious songs for a local *khlyst* (flagellant) religious sect. He was also involved in the *skopets* sect, whose members practised self-castration in the belief that this custom helped to achieve self-perfection. There are numerous references to these two sects in his poems. Klyuev's poems evidently first appeared in print in 1904. In 1907 Klyuev wrote to BLOK, who was troubled by the gap between the peasants and the intelligentsia, and the two established a friendship which was useful to Klyuev in getting his poems published.

Klyuev's early verse contained idyllic nature scenes, some local color and striking imagery, and individual poems written in a rather elevated, formal style which gave little indication of his later manner. This was a period of learning for Klyuev, and his work is often closely patterned after SYMBOLIST models, even though the fundamental image of an idyllic, rural Russia was already present.

Partly to attract attention, Klyuev adopted the pose of a "peasant poet," dressing in a peasant shirt and speaking with the *okan'e* pronunciation of the northern dialects.

Soon Klyuev moved away from his earlier symbolist models and consciously attempted to stress his roots as a people's poet, making broad use of dialect and folk imagery, combining Russian nationalism, eroticism, and deep religiosity. Later he was to add to all this a fascination with Western and Eastern mysticism. The result was probably the most unusual poetry ever created in the Russian language.

Replete with densely interlocking imagery and presented in a dialect difficult even for Russians, Klyuev's verse is not easily accessible to the average reader, who has shown a clear preference for the simpler images of another peasant poet—Sergei ESENIN. Esenin recognized Klyuev as his "teacher," but Klyuev rejected Esenin's later "hooligan" manner, and the strained (and possibly homosexual) relations of the two men ultimately contributed strongly to Esenin's suicide. Klyuev's long poem "The Fourth Rome" is an attack on what Klyuev saw as Esenin's betrayal of the peasant ideal. Later, when Esenin committed suicide, Klyuev wrote his powerful "Lament for Esenin" and recited it at the memorial service.

Without doubt, Klyuev's major achievements are his *poémy* (long poems), the best known of which is "The Burned Ruins" (Pogorel'shchina), in which the Russia of his dream is raped by the new Tatars. In it Klyuev describes a mythical village, which serves as an allegory of Russia. The village, guarded by Egory—Saint George the Dragon Slayer—is attacked by Saracens. Evil triumphs, Egory flees, the villagers die, and two monks commit an act of self-immolation. The Tatars slash at the icon of the Virgin, but its powdery paint settles on the earth only to blossom in the form of white flowers, while the bodies of the enemy blacken the road. The authorities, who had been variously depicted as Saracens, Tatars, the dragon, and the devil, arrested Klyuev in 1933, and little is known about his life after this point. He was exiled to the Narym area of Siberia. GORKY tried to help him, and he was transferred to the city of Tomsk in 1935, but he was rearrested there. In 1935 he reportedly attempted to save himself by writing a long poem entitled "The Kremlin," glorifying Stalin, Molotov, Voroshilov, and others, and ending with the lines "Forgive (me) or order (me) to die!" The circumstances of Klyuev's death are unknown. The Soviet *Brief Literary Encyclopedia* lists his death as having occurred in 1937, somewhere along the Trans-Siberian railroad. He had supposedly finished this period of exile and was returning to Moscow with, as he wrote, "a suitcase full of manuscripts." According to one version he died of a heart attack during the trip. According to another, he was executed by the authorities. The suitcase with the manuscripts was lost. Among other items, it is known to have contained the second and third parts of a large poem "Song of the Great Mother."

Although Klyuev was "posthumously rehabilitated" in the Soviet Union, he was not republished there until 1977, and his major achievement, his long poems, are still forbidden. The only serious Russian-language edition of his poetry was done in this country by Boris Filippov and Gleb Struve.

Works: Sochineniya. 2 vols. Ed. Boris Filippov and Gleb Struve. Munich, 1969.

Translations: Poems. Trans. John Glad. 1977.

Secondary literature: See introductory articles in *Sochineniya*, by Boris Filippov (in Russian) and Gordon MacVay (in English), vol. 1, and by Heinrich Stammler (in German) and Emmanuil Rais and Boris Filippov (in Russian), vol. 2. V. G. Bazanov, "Poema o drevnem Vyge," *RLit* 22 (1979), no 1, pp. 77–96. Jesse Davies, "The Life and Works of Nikolay Klyuyev," *New Zealand Slavonic Journal* 2 (N. S.) (1974), pp. 65–75.   J. G.

Klyúshnikov, Víktor Petróvich (1841–92), writer and journalist, was born in the Ukraine into a family of the gentry. Having graduated from the Physico-Mathematical Division of Moscow University in 1861, he worked as a journalist. His first novel, *Mirage* (Marevo), appeared in RUSSKII VESTNIK in 1864 and immediately drew attention for its sharply expressed ANTINIHILIST tendency. It had great success. In depicting the revolutionary strivings of the youth of the 1860s and the Polish uprising of 1863, Klyushnikov drew some fran-

tic young people (Leon and Inna Gorobets, Kolya, etc.), prone to daydreaming, a passionate yearning for virtue and justice, yet without any common sense or understanding of real life to back up these feelings. Hence sinister demonic self-seekers (Bronsky) gain control over these romantic dreamers and draw them into a senseless revolutionary struggle. The positive hero (Rusanov) seeks to gain an understanding of this complex and charged situation, and to discover the origin of this tragic "mirage." He gathers that the seeds of discord were sown in the 1840s, by LERMONTOV's despair, projected upon his hero Pechorin, and HERZEN's overwrought freethinking. Herzen's KOLOKOL is directly named the main instigator of this "bloody and revolting game." At the end of the novel, the heroine (Inna), having lost her illusions about the Revolution, accuses the revolutionary "seekers of glory" of being power-hungry and intent upon asserting themselves personally, while "the freedom of nations" is for them a mere "resounding pretext" under a "mask of nationality." The novel met with instant vehement rebuttals by journalists of the radical camp (PISAREV, V. ZAITSEV, SALTYKOV-SHCHEDRIN), but within a mere two years interest in Klyushnikov's work receded sharply and all of his subsequent works passed almost unnoticed: *Another Life* (Drugaya zhizn', 1865), *Great Ships* (Bol'shie korabli, 1866–74), *Gypsies* (Tsygane, 1869). This also goes for his short novel *Non-Mirage* (Ne-marevo, 1871), in which Klyushnikov, as though continuing the theme of *Mirage*, projects disillusionment in revolutionary ideals and a departure on a search for spiritual values in patriarchal principles. In the 1870s Klyushnikov published novels and short stories for young readers: "In Peter's Time" (Pri Petre, with V. Kelsiev, 1872), "A Family of Freethinkers" (Sem'ya vol'nodumtsev, with P. Petrov, 1872), "The Boy-Tsar" (Gosudar'-otrok, 1880), and was editor of the celebrated weekly *The Cornfield* (Niva), whose circulation at one time reached 250,000.

Works: Marevo: Roman v 4-kh chastyakh. 1865. *Ne-Marevo: Povest', Zarya,* 1871, nos. 2 and 4. *Tsygane: Roman v 3-kh chastyakh.* 1871. *Bol'shie korabli: Roman v 3-kh chastyakh.* 1874.

Secondary literature: A. Batyuto, "Turgenev i nekotorye pisateli antinigilisticheskogo napravleniya." In *Turgenev i ego sovremenniki.* 1977. V. Bazanov, *Iz literaturnoi polemiki 60-kh godov.* 1941. G. Byalyi, "Proza shestidesyatykh godov." In *Istoriya russkoi literatury.* Vol. 8, pt. 1. 1956. A. Coquart, *Dmitri Pisarev et l'idéologie du nihilisme russe.* 1946. Charles Moser, *Antinihilism in the Russian Novel of the 1860s.* 1964. D. Pisarev, "Serditoe bessilie ('Marevo')" (1865). In his *Sochineniya.* Vol. 3, 1956. Pp. 218–50. M. Saltykov-Shchedrin, "Nasha obshchestvennaya zhizn'" ('Marevo') (1864) and "'Tsygane': Roman Klyushnikova" (1871). In his *Sobranie sochinenii.* Vol. 6, 1968. Pp. 315–19. Vol. 9, 1970. Pp. 426–29. A. Skabichevskii, "Russkoe nedomyslie: 'Marevo' Klyushnikova" (1868). N. Strakhov, *Iz istorii literaturnogo nigilizma.* 1890. A. Tseitlin, "Syuzhetika antinigilisticheskogo romana," *Literatura i marksizm,* 1929, no. 2. V. Zaitsev, "Perly i adamanty russkoi zhurnalistiki ('Marevo')" (1864).   E. D. A.

Knut, Dovíd (pseudonym of Davíd Mirónovich Fíksman, 1900–55), poet, was born in Orgeev, Bessarabia. In 1922, together with Boris Bozhnev, Aleksandr GINGER, Boris POPLAVSKY, and Serge Charchoune, he organized the literary group *Palata poetov* (The Chamber of Poets) in Paris. He was married to Ariadne, daughter of the composer Scriabin. She was killed by the Germans for her active participation in the Jewish resistance during the Nazi occupation of Paris.

The originality of Knut's poetic talent, his personal intonation, and his fresh, unusual conceptions are obvious. He was very successful with ternary meters which he employed in slow, sorrowful, or exultant poetic meditations on the fate of the Jewish people. His lyrics are energetic, emotional, passionate, loud, and often solemn. One of the leitmotifs of Knut's poetry is man's persistent alienation from God, the world, and from himself. Biblical themes, eroticism with biblical overtones, and vigorous diction are salient traits of his verse. Knut's rhythmic texture with its imperative abrupt starts and stops, as well as his powerful images and striking epithets aid in creating the impression of speech compressed to the very limit of human endurance. To recognize Knut's peculiar poetic signature and his views on man and man's place in the universe, one needs to read only a few of his poems. His later works are more tolerant, simple, sincere, and restrained. Knut emigrated to Israel in 1949, where he worked for the Habin Theater. He died there from cancer.

Collections of Poetry (all published in Paris): *Moikh tysyacheletii* [Of My Millennia]. 1925. *Vtoraya kniga stikhov*. 1928. *Parizhskie nochi: tretii sbornik stikhov* [Parisian Nights: A Third Collection of Verse]. 1932. *Nasushchnaya lyubov': chetvertaya kniga stikhov* [A Vital Love: A Fourth Book of Verse]. 1938. *Izbrannye stikhi* [Selected Verse]. 1949. Knut also contributed to various Russian periodicals, anthologies, and literary almanacs in exile such as *Novyi korabl'*, *Perezvony*, *Chisla*, *Muza diaspory*, *Blagonamerennyi*, *Grani*, *Russkie zapiski*, *Volya Rossii*, *Sovremennye zapiski*, and *Svoimi putyami*.

Secondary literature: Temira Pachmuss, *A Russian Cultural Revival: A Critical Anthology of Emigré Literature before 1939*. 1981. Pp. 369–73. Andrei Sedykh, *Dalekie, blizkie*. New York, 1962. Pp. 260–65.   T. A. P.

Knyázev, Vasíly Vasílievich (1887–1937), poet and folklorist. The son of a Siberian merchant, Knyazev attended a teachers college in St. Petersburg in 1904–1905, but was expelled for political activities. He then pursued a career as a writer of satirical verse, journalist, and collector of folklore (proverbs, CHASTUSHKI). He joined the PROLETKULT movement after the Revolution and actively participated in its agitational activities. A member of the Red Guard, Knyazev published his verse in the Bolshevik press and in several collections, such as *Red Gospel* (Krasnoe Evangelie, 1918), *Red Peal* (Krasnyi zvon, 1918), and *Songs of a Red Bellringer* (Pesni Krasnogo Zvonarya, 1919). Some of his verses were set to music and became revolutionary songs. After the civil war, Knyazev continued his work as a folklorist, publishing *chastushki* and a *Book of Proverbs* (Kniga poslovits, 1930). In 1934, Knyazev published a novel, *Grandfathers* (Dedy), under the pseudonym Ivan Sedykh. It tells the history of a family of Siberian merchants. Knyazev became a victim of Stalin's purges in 1937.

Works: Kniga izbrannykh stikhotvorenii. 1930. *Poslednyaya kniga stikhov, 1918–1930*. 1933. *Za chetvert' veka (1905–1930)*. 1935. *Izbrannoe*. 1959.

Secondary literature: R. A. Shatseva, Introd. article in *Proletarskie poety pervykh let sovetskoi epokhi*. 1959. V. Sayanov, Introd. article in *Izbrannoe* (1959). I. S. Eventov, "Posle boevogo trekhletiya," *RLit* 17 (1974), no. 2, pp. 83–97.   V. T.

Knyazhnin, Yákov Borísovich (1742–91), playwright, poet, and translator. After a checkered career which included a conviction for embezzlement of government funds, Knyazhnin eventually found his calling in literature when appointed secretary to the Main Curator of Institutions of Education and Enlightenment in 1778. Knyazhnin translated a number of works from the French and Italian (Voltaire's *Henriade*, for example) and adapted several plays by Metastasio and Voltaire for the Russian stage. As an original playwright, he continued in the manner of SUMAROKOV (who was his father-in-law), writing both tragedies and comedies. Among the latter, the comic opera "Misfortune from a Coach" (Neschast'e ot karety, 1779) is best known. Knyazhnin's fame as a tragic poet rests largely with *Rosslav* (1784) and *Vadim of Novgorod* (Vadim Novgorodskii, 1789). The former is keyed on the conflict between a Russian nobleman's loyalty to his country and his love for a beautiful Swedish princess. It is set in Stockholm, where Rosslav is a prisoner of war, and features martial pomp, prison vaults, riots, executions, and an intricate plot at the end of which evil is defeated and virtue rewarded. *Vadim of Novgorod* is set in Novgorod under Ryurik the Varangian. Vadim must choose between loyalty to the republican traditions of his city and an honorable surrender to the victorious Ryurik. He chooses the former and suicide, and the tragedy is complete when Vadim's daughter, although in love with Ryurik, follows her father's example. *Vadim of Novgorod* was published only in 1793, after Knyazhnin's death, much to the displeasure of CATHERINE II, who recognized the republican tendency of the play and ordered it burned.

Works: Sobranie sochinenii. 4 vols. 1787. *Sochineniya*. 2 vols. 1847. *Izbrannye proizvedeniya*. Text, introd. and comm. L. I. Kulakova. 1961.

Translations: "The Ill-Fated Coach," trans. J. Eyre, *Slavonic Review* 22, no. 58 (1944), pp. 125–37. "Misfortune from a Coach." In Harold B. Segel, *The Literature of Eighteenth-Century Russia*. 1967. Vol. 2. Pp. 374–93.

Secondary literature: L. I. Kulakova, "Ya. B. Knyazhnin." In *Russkie dramaturgi XVIII v.* Vol. 1. 1959.   V. T.

Kóchetov, Vsévolod Anísimovich (1912–73), novelist and chief editor of *Literaturnaya gazeta* (1955–59) and *Oktyabr'* (1961–73), Secretary of Leningrad Division of the Soviet Writers' Union (1953–55) and member of editorial boards of the journals *Zvezda* and *Leningrad*. Kochetov represented the extreme pro-Stalinist faction of Soviet society and was one of the most powerful bureaucrats in the various writers' organizations. A prolific writer, he wrote mostly long novels, which have been published in large editions. Most notorious is his *Just What Do You Want?* (Chego zhe ty khochesh'?), in which four people are sent to the Soviet Union—supposedly to gather material for an album of old Russian art. In fact, they turn out to be spies, and one is even an ex-SS officer and a ruthless murderer.

In a formal sense the novel does not possess the tightly knit structure expected in a spy novel. The four Westerners arrive, engage in a series of dialogues which are in reality ideological harangues, and then leave. As the novel progresses, these speeches occupy increasingly more space. Characterization is "flat" (heroes and villains), and the dominant theme is patriotism. Cultural exchanges are described as attempts to destroy Soviet society; emigrés are "trash, the enemy, *kulaks*"; the use of the dove of peace is a religious symbol illegitimately used to replace the hammer and sickle; and the West is a Hitlerian aggressor.

The Ershov Brothers (Brat'ya Ershovy, 1958) is a novel of steel workers (dedicated communists) and their struggle with a bureaucrat who attempts to steal an invention. This is basically a moralistic novel rather than a political one, except for a confused attempt to link the negative characters with the Hungarian revolution. Kochetov was criticized in an article in *Pravda* for having depicted the intelligentsia as being tainted with un-Soviet views.

Secretary of the District Committee (Sekretar' obkoma, 1961) is another lengthy novel about the "Soviet man." The hero, Denisov, directs an area twice the size of Belgium. He discovers that the director of the neighboring district has been juggling the books, turns him in, and gets his job. The novel was severely attacked by A. Maryamov, then a member of the editorial board of Tvardovsky's journal *Novyi mir*. Maryamov attacked Kochetov's descriptions of female clothing as "pathological"; pointed out numerous banalities, instances of bad style, and even grammatical errors; characterized the nature descriptions as "saccharine"; and declared the novel to be "raw" and "tawdry." The review was written immediately after Kochetov's assumption of the editorship of *Oktyabr'* and intensified an old feud between Kochetov and Tvardovsky (going back to when Kochetov had used *Literaturnaya gazeta* to direct the anti-Pasternak campaign).

Works: Sobranie sochinenii. 1973–76.

Translations: The Zhurbins. Trans. R. Daglish. Moscow, 1953.

Secondary literature: John Glad, "Vsevolod Kochetov: An Overview," *RLJ* 32, no. 113 (1978), pp. 95–102. Terence M. Rickwood, "The Need for Revolutionary Vigilance: Kochetov's Novel *What Then Do You Want?* In *Proceedings: Pacific Northwest Conference on Foreign Languages*, ed. Walter C. Kraft. 1971. Pp. 112–25.   J. G.

Kochév'e ("nomadic settlement"), Parisian literary circle formed in the spring of 1928 by Marc Slonim, then literary editor of *Volya Rossii*, to unite and support the young writers and poets of the first emigration and to create for them a new, independent forum to discuss literary problems as well as their own works (and often works-in-progress), uninfluenced by politics, personalities, or cliques. Although initially envisioned as a closed workshop studio, the group quickly went public: from June 1928 it offered, with remarkable regularity, a weekly public lecture or debate every Thursday night. The first two seasons (1928–29 and 1929–30) were very active and quite successful, provoking many comments and discussions. By 1931–32, however, the group was in decline, the frequency of its meetings drastically reduced. According to Slonim himself (in his article on "Volya Rossii" in *Russkaya literatura v emigratsii*, p. 300) *Kochev'e* closed only in 1938 after 104 meetings. However, the last meeting for which we have published evidence took place early in 1934; and we know of at least fourteen meetings after the one labelled "one-hundredth" on 18 December 1930. Among the permanent "young" members of the group were V. Andreev, I. Boldyrev, B. Bozhnev, V. Fokht, G. Gazdanov, N. Gorodetskaya, A. Ladinsky, B. Poplavsky, S. Sharshun, M. Struve, and V. Varshavsky. They often gave readings of their new poems or stories as well as talks on a wide variety of topics. Among the interesting features of the group's activities were the critical analyses to which they publicly subjected each other's work; the attention paid to literary criticism (a series of "oral journals" on literary novelties along with regular papers); and to new writing from the Soviet Union (besides their natural interest in the work of fellow émigré writers). Several acknowledged ("older") figures of the emigration such as M. Osorgin, G. Adamovich, M. Tsvetaeva, G. Ivanov, B. Zaitsev, N. Berdyaev, and D. Svyatopolk-Mirsky strengthened the group by their occasional participation. Heated debates often arose thanks to the provocative positions assumed by various speakers (e.g., Mirsky on "provincial" Bunin, Slonim on the end of émigré literature, Gazdanov on Pozner's book on contemporary Russian literature). Quite a few of the artistic works first read at *Kochev'e* as well as several of the talks and the "oral reviews" were later published in *Volya Rossii*, *Chisla*, and elsewhere.

Bibliography: The following volumes of *Volya Rossii* contain accounts of *Kochev'e* activities: nos. 1, 2, 4, 8/9 (1929), no. 1/3 (1932). M. Beyssac, *La vie culturelle de l'émigration russe en France. Chronique 1920–1930.* Paris, 1971. A. Ladinskii, "Kochev'e," *Poslednie novosti*, 8 October 1931. M. Slonim, "Volya Rossii." in *Russkaya literatura v emigratsii*, ed. N. P. Poltoratskii (Pittsburgh, 1972).
L. D.

Kókorev, Iván Timoféevich (1825–53), writer. An author who later depicted characters of origins and social status similar to his own, Kokorev was born into a family of freed peasants in Zaraisk. Unable to continue his education beyond the fifth-year level in a Moscow gymnasium, he began working for the *Zhivopisnoe obozrenie* in 1843 at the age of eighteen. From 1846 until his death he worked for the Moskvityanin, where in 1850 he became a member of the editorial staff in charge of the "inside review" section of the journal.

Drawing upon Gogol and the natural school for plot line and tone, Kokorev published in this section his own sketches of Moscow (rather than the more usual depiction of St. Petersburg). Not straightforwardly naturalistic, Kokorev's depiction of people of the lowest calling, such as coachmen, cooks, waiters, and wood cutters, reflects Gogol's grotesquery plus the humor and style of the feuilleton combined with the technique of the vaudeville. Kokorev had excellent powers of observation, and with his first-hand knowledge of Moscow street life he captured the mores and daily existence of the lower classes and the poverty-stricken dregs of the city.

Kokorev's best work is considered to be the tale *Little Savva* (Savvushka), which was highly regarded by both Turgenev and Grigoriev.

Works: Ocherki i rasskazy. 3 vols. 1858. *Moskva sorokovykh godov.* 1959. *Sochineniya.* 1959.
Secondary literature: N. A. Dobrolyubov, "Ocherki i rasskazy I. T. Kokoreva," *Sobranie sochinenii* (1961–64), Vol. 4, pp. 265–71.
———, "Opyt otucheniya lyudei ot pishchi," *Sobranie sochinenii* (1961–64), Vol. 7, pp. 438–60. Peter Hodgson, *From Gogol to Dostoevsky.* 1976.
J. S.

Kólokol (The Bell) was a newspaper which began as a supplement to Aleksandr Herzen's and Nikolai Ogaryov's Polyarnaya zvezda. It was irregularly published, from 1857 to 1867, in London and Geneva. The newspaper marked a period of intense social-political debate in Russia beginning with the death of Nicholas I in 1856 and culminating in the emancipation of the serfs in 1861. Nurtured by the talented sensibilities of Herzen and Ogaryov, *Kolokol* expressed the cherished hopes and ideas of Russian liberal thought and exerted a strong influence both on writers and on Russian society at large. Freely smuggled and sometimes mailed into the country, it was passed from hand to hand or sold clandestinely in bookstores. The tissue-thin pages provided an uncensored forum for the poems of Ogaryov, Lermontov, and Nekrasov, for the studies of literary critics such as Annenkov and Dobrolyubov, and for the essays of politically inclined intellectuals such as Bakunin, Proudhon, Garibaldi, Michelet, and Mazzini. Primary genres were feuilletons, news items, letters, and articles on contemporary issues. Himself a major contributor, Herzen used *Kolokol* to bring out excerpts from his autobiography, *My Past and Thoughts.* Readers of note included Saltykov-Shchedrin, Tolstoi, Dostoevsky, and Turgenev. Tolstoi's interest in Herzen's historical principles and his visit to the London editorial office stimulated the writing of *War and Peace*; in their novels Turgenev and Dostoevsky undertook passionate debates with views expressed in the newspaper. Due to changing historical conditions, *Kolokol's* influence waned in later years. Herzen decided to stop publication with the 245th number. A French version of the newspaper was published during 1868 but quickly abandoned. An attempt organized in 1870 by Nechaev to bring out a new edition ended after six issues.

Bibliography: See the reproduction of *Kolokol*, 11 vols. Moscow, 1960–64. E. H. Carr, *The Romantic Exiles.* Boston, 1961. N. Rz.

Koltsóv, Aleksei Vasilievich (1809–42), poet. Born in Voronezh as son of a wealthy cattle dealer, Koltsov used to accompany his father's herds to distant markets. During these trips he learned of the life of the Russian peasantry, its joys and sorrows. Reckoning that a cowboy had little use for education, his father forced him to leave school early. However, Koltsov read poetry and soon decided to become a poet himself. In 1829 he made the acquaintance of N. P. Serebryansky, a brilliant student at the theological seminary in Voronezh, who gave him his first lessons in poetic technique and aesthetics. His first poems, even if little more than weak imitations of Merzlyakov, Dmitriev, Delvig, and Pushkin, awoke the interest of N. V. Stankevich, whom Koltsov met in 1830. The following year Stankevich introduced him to the members of his Moscow circle. The result was a lasting friendship between Koltsov and Belinsky, who was delighted to find a real "poet of the people." Regarding him as an expression of the Russian spirit, Stankevich and Belinsky in 1835 brought out the first volume of his popular songs, *Stikhotvoreniya Alekseya Kol'tsova*, which were instantly greeted with enthusiasm. Visiting Petersburg in 1836 Koltsov was hailed by a number of famous writers including Pushkin, Krylov, Vyazemsky and Odoevsky. All of them soon came to admire not only his songs, but also his character, his tact, and dignity. Unfortunately, his visits to Moscow and Petersburg were short and rare. He had to return to his cattle business in Voronezh, where he felt more and more lonely and miserable, all the time quarrelling with his despotic father: "My circle is narrow, my world is dirty; it pains me to live in it." Unable to break with his environment, he died after a long illness, having almost ceased to write.

Koltsov's poetry is usually divided into three categories: his early attempts to write in the accepted style of the Golden Age, his philosophical meditations (the so-called *dumy*), and his Russian songs. The poems of the two first sections, while in majority, are not very important. This is especially true of his philosophical poems. Highly influenced by the idealist circle of Stankevich, most of them show a poet trying his hand in a genre for which he is not intellectually prepared, being a self-taught man with only a year and a half of systematic schooling. "I understand something of the subject and the object," he tells Belinsky in 1836, "but I don't understand a bit of the absolute." Nevertheless, inspired by the Stankevich circle to reflect on the "mysteries of life and death," this child of nature was tempted into writing a number of undigested poems far below his achievements in the genre of the folk song. On the other hand, these songs, although not numerous, have secured him a permanent place as a classic. Inspired by a deep love of the Russian people and a genuine feeling of nature, Koltsov, in a naive and touching way reminiscent of Burns, sings of the broad rye fields of his homeland, of the yearning for freedom and space among the people. His pictures of agricultural labor and peasant life are not devoid of idealization, but he also tells us of heartbreaking human tragedies: "Ah, why did they marry me against my will to an old, unloved husband?" (1838) Unlike other peasant poets of the time, who are more or less insignificant imitators of literary verse, Koltsov makes use of many popular words and devices, and the meter of his verse is closely related to that of the folk song, with short lines and a fixed distribution of stresses. In the history of Russian poetry he is the first in a series of great peasant poets (Nekrasov, Esenin, Tvardovsky), bearing, in his best poems, comparison with any of them.

Works: Polnoe sobranie stikhotvorenii. Ed. L. Plotkin. 1958. *Sochineniya.* 2 vols. Ed. V. Tonkov. 1961.

Translations: Lewanski, pp. 272–73.

Secondary literature: E. Caffrey, *Kol'tsov: A Study in Meter and Rhythm.* Ph. D. diss., Harvard Univ., 1968. A. A. Moiseeva, *A. V. Kol'tsov: Kritiko-biograficheskii ocherk.* 1956. N. Skatov, *Poeziya Alekseya Kol'tsova.* 1977. V. A. Tonkov, *A. V. Kol'tsov.* 1965.

G. K.

Komaróv, Matveí (ca. 1730–1812). One of the first literary professionals in 18th-century Russia, Komarov adapted, edited and rewrote materials for publication, supplying prefaces and notes as required. His version of the Vanka Kain tale proved to be one of the most popular narratives of the period. Its first title (1777) was "Life and Adventures of the Russian Cartouche named Kain, the notorious scoundrel ..." (*Zhizn' i pokhozhdeniya rossiiskogo Kartusha, imenuemogo Kaina, izvestnogo moshennika ...*). Komarov rewrote the original first-person account by Ivan Osipov, a criminal who was sentenced to exile in Siberia, but later became virtually the police chief of Moscow. Komarov's version of "Vanka Kain" was reprinted throughout the 19th century, and was circulated among the "folk." Komarov's other works of a similar popular nature included "Tale of the Adventures of Milord George and the Brandenburg Margravine Friderika" (*Povest' o priklyuchenii aglinskogo* [sic] *milorda Georga i o brandenburgskoi markgrafine Friderike*) first printed in St. Petersburg in 1782, with further printings in 1786, 1789, 1791, and 1799. Komarov also edited and published popular pseudo-historical materials.

Secondary literature: I. R. Titunik, "Komarov's *Van'ka Kain* and Eighteenth-century Russian Prose," *SEEJ* 18 (1974), pp. 351–66.

D. W.

Konevskóí (pseud. of Iván Ivánovich Oréus, 1877–1901), poet and critic. An only child, Konevskoi received a thorough humanistic education, and read broadly in French, German, and English. Sometime between the ages of ten and twelve he started writing, and first published in 1896.

In 1897, Konevskoi entered the philological division of St. Petersburg University, where he participated in a student circle devoted to philosophy and art. During that year, and again in 1898, he travelled abroad. In 1900, a year before he graduated, the first collection of his works appeared. In the summer of 1901, Konevskoi drowned accidentally during a brief trip in the Baltic region.

Konevskoi came into literature as a younger member of the DECADENT wave of poets and writers, and his world-view and aesthetics are characteristic of this small, iconoclastic group. Thoroughly at home in Western European literature, he also experienced strongly the impact of Russian lyric, and wrote with special sympathy about TYUTCHEV and FET, in both of whom he found a mystical perception of the world — an awareness which, Konevskoi believed, also distinguished the contemporary generation. In tandem with his rebellion against ontology and skepticism about the validity of our basic perceptual categories came Konevskoi's rapturous vision of a mythologized Nature, filled with non-rational forces.

Brief philosophical lyrics constitute the body of Konevskoi's poetry. They form a kind of diary, characterized by the poet's youth and extreme idealism. Nature and mankind are principal objects of his reflection and emotion: they provide the stimuli for a complex intermingling of abstraction and lyricism which resembles the poetry of Wordsworth (without matching it).

Konevskoi combines an erudite Europeanism characteristic of fin de siècle intelligentsia with a deeply felt and subtly understood Russianness. His country's topography, climate and architecture prompt him to analysis, criticism and celebration. At times, however, Konevskoi's concerns are universal: indeed, he contemplates calmly a future intermingling and fusion of mankind's diversity into a single whole.

For all his depth of feeling and ideas, Konevskoi was not a successful poet. In part, this stems from aesthetic assumptions. In one essay, he denies that language possesses characteristics which would require the use of specific types of expressions or syntactic constructions; the sole inextricable essence of any language, he claims, is its lexicon. In consequence, syntax in his poems is difficult and overtly convoluted, sound texture is poorly orchestrated, and frequent violations of metrical expectations lack motivation on other levels of the text. In addition, too many of Konevskoi's works constitute a mere presentation of internalized rhetorical argumentation: tellingly, there are no love lyrics among his works. Far better, by comparison, is Konevskoi's prose, which includes both analytic essays and, although not titled as such, poems in prose. His peculiar blend of description, emotion, and ideas is far better suited for both such genres.

In spite of his brief life and limited literary output, Konevskoi's personality and writings had a considerable impact within literary circles. He was close to Valery BRYUSOV, whose genuine admiration for his younger contemporary is reflected in the memorial essay he wrote following Konevskoi's death and in poems dedicated to Konevskoi. (Bryusov also edited the posthumous edition of his friend's works). Similarly, Aleksandr BLOK also wrote about Konevskoi with considerable empathy, seeing in him a characteristic figure of the transition from Decadence to SYMBOLISM.

Works: Mechty i dumy. 1896–1899. St. Petersburg, 1900. *Stikhi i proza. Posmertnoe sobranie sochinenii. (1894–1901 gg.).* Moscow, 1904. Reprint Munich, 1971.

Secondary literature: V. Bryusov, "Ivan Konevskoi. Mudroe ditya." In *Dalekie i blizkie. Stat'i i zametki o russkikh poetakh ot Tyutcheva do nashikh dnei.* Moscow, 1912. Reprint: Valerii Bryusov, *Sobranie sochinenii v semi tomakh 1975 Vol 6 Pp. 242–49.* M. Gofman, ed., *Kniga o russkikh poetakh poslednego desyatiletiya.* 1910. Pp. 99–134. Reprint Munich, 1970. I. G. Yampol'skii, publ., "Ivan Konevskoi. Pis'ma k Vl. V. Gippiusu." In *Ezhegodnik Rukopisnogo Otdela Pushkinskogo Doma na 1977 god.* 1979. Pp. 79–98.

H. B.

Kóni, Anatóly Fyódorovich (1844–1927). Jurist and memoirist. An able member of the liberal Russian bar of the last three reigns, he was moderate enough to be made presiding judge of the court before which Vera ZASULICH was tried in 1878 for wounding the vicious General Trepov. Koni presided fairly and therefore controversially. The jury, with famous Russian illogic, acquitted her and she escaped to Europe. This scandal determined Koni's career, the relative disfavor of the régime and the hearty favor of the intelligentsia until 1917, and LUNACHARSKY's gift of a professorship of law at Petrograd University after the Revolution. It was also the wellspring of his writing, for in old age Koni wrote perhaps the most notable memoirs of any Russian early in this century, *On the Path of Life* (*Na zhiznennom puti*), published in five volumes from 1913 to 1929. A successor to ANNENKOV's memoirs, Koni reminisced at great, valuable, and fascinating length about the many official, political, and literary people he knew and remembered.

Works: Sobranie sochinenii. 8 vols. 1966–69.

F. B. R.

Kontinént (1974–   ), literary quarterly of the "third wave" emigration. Published by the Ullstein Publishing House (West Berlin) since 1974, under the editorship of Vladimir Emelyanovich MAKSIMOV (editor-in-chief), Viktor NEKRASOV, Natalya GORBANEVSKAYA, and Evgeny Ternovsky. Its editorial board is composed of Soviet dissidents and Western writers and journalists. *Kontinent* publishes mainly fiction as well as nonfiction written in Russian, but also pieces in other European languages. The emphasis is on fiction and poetry, but literary and art criticism, essays, documents, religious statements, etc., are also published. Among the journal's contributors have been, Iosif BRODSKY, Aleksandr GALICH, Anatoly GLADILIN, Aleksandr SOLZHENITSYN, Andrei SINYAVSKY, Vladimir VOINOVICH, and many others.

V. T.

Kópelev, Lev Zinóvievich (1912–   ), memoirist and German-literature scholar. An early convert to Marxism, he actively supported the government, participating in the confiscation of grain from the peasantry in 1933. He was depicted by SOLZHENITSYN in

The First Circle as Rubin, the communist who remains faithful to his ideals even after his arrest. A prominent dissident in the 1960s, Kopelev used his Moscow apartment as a meeting place for Western visitors and Soviet intellectuals. In 1968 he was expelled from the Communist Party, and in 1977 he was thrown out of the Union of Soviet Writers. He now lives and teaches in West Germany and has received the Peace Prize from the German Book Trade.

Works: Khranit' vechno. 1975. *Utoli moi pechali.* Ann Arbor, 1981. *Derzhava i narod.* Ann Arbor, 1982. *Na krutykh povorotakh korotkoi dorogi.* Ann Arbor, 1982.

Translations: To be Preserved. Trans. Anthony Austin. 1977. *The Education of a True Believer.* Trans. Gary Kern. 1980.

J. G.

Korolénko, Vladímir Galaktiónovich (1853–1921), writer, critic, publicist, translator, social activist. Born in Zhitomir of Ukrainian and Polish parentage, Korolenko studied at the Moscow School of Agriculture where his POPULIST activities led in 1876 to his arrest and exile to Kronstadt. A second arrest followed in 1877, and in 1881 he was banished for three years to Yakutsk, Siberia for refusing to swear allegiance to Alexander III. In 1879 Korolenko published his first literary work, the story "Episodes from the Life of a 'Seeker'" (Epizody iz zhizni 'iskatelya') which established his fundamental trait, a genuine love for people and a striving to find in each individual the best qualities of the human spirit. Siberia, however, was the source of his finest inspiration. He molded the raw material of his exile into literary shape producing a cycle of Siberian stories which appeared between 1880 and 1915. An incurable optimist, Korolenko believed in man's inherent goodness and the inevitable renewal of life. His fiction is anthropocentric, focusing particularly on man in his more primitive conditions and elemental brutishness set against the background of nature. The moment of the hero's awakening is crucial in every Korolenko story. He excelled in depicting the simple folk. His Siberian stories, for example, "The Falconer" (Sokolinets, 1885), "Fyodor the Homeless" (Fedor Bespriyutnyi, 1885) and "Cherkes" (1888), portray freedom-loving vagrants, escaped convicts, coachmen, etc., imbued with courage and seeking justice. "Makar's Dream" (Son Makara, 1885), the best story of the cycle, brought Korolenko instant recognition. A fantasy on Yakut and pseudo-Christian mythology, it dramatizes man's (and Korolenko's) belief in the ultimate victory of justice and truth. The Siberian stories emphasize mood, conveyed in a polished but simple style, and generally employ a stylized Korolenko exile as narrator. Predilection for lyrical expression and poetic nature descriptions to establish mood and setting reflects Korolenko's "fanatical admiration" for TURGENEV. Some stories ("Yashka," 1880, "At-Davan," 1892) approximate the reportage and suggest the influence of DostoEVSKY's documentary exposition; most of them strike a harmonious balance between the social message and literary execution. For their structure, most stories employ the *rahmenerzählung* device in combination with the SKAZ technique and many are based on Dostoevskian "diaphonic characterization." Korolenko's speech mannerisms, including prison *argot* and local dialects, serve as basic means of characterization. The Turgenevian poem in prose, "Lights" (Ogon'ki, 1901) reflects Korolenko's belief that persistent work will determine the form of future society; that man is "perpetually reborn" like life itself. As for literature, Korolenko believed that a synthesis of realism and romanticism would produce a new direction. "Legend about Florus, Agrippa, and Menahem, Son of Jehuda" (Skazanie o Flore, Agrippe i Menakheme, syne Iegudy, 1886), a polemic against TOLSTOI's doctrine of non-resistance, is an example of Korolenko's legends on an historical theme. He also cultivated the novella, mostly in sentimental romances. *The Blind Musician* (Slepoi muzykant, 1886) shows the hero overcoming his physical handicap and learning to serve others while the Dickensian *Without a Language* (Bez yazyka, 1895), Korolenko's longest and best-known novella and his most humorous work, portrays a Russian peasant stranded in America unable to communicate. Humanism, the salient feature of Korolenko's literary work, also marks his extensive publicistic activity. He denounced racial discrimination in "The Multan Sacrifice" (Multanskoe zhertvoprinoshenie, 1895–96), religious persecution in "House No. 13" (Dom No. 13, 1905), capi-

tal punishment in "An Everyday Occurrence" (Bytovoe yavlenie, 1910), and field court-martial in "Aspects of Military Justice" (Cherty voennogo pravosudiya, 1910–11). His last work, the autobiography *The History of My Contemporary* (Istoriya moego sovremennika, 1904–18, publ., 1922) is remarkable for its vividly drawn portraits and a valuable source of information about events and people from 1853 to 1884. Korolenko's literary criticism is contained in his essay-memoirs of his literary contemporaries.

Works: Polnoe sobranie sochinenii. Vols. 1–5, 6–8, 13, 15–22, 24, 50–51. Kharkov-Poltava, 1922–29. *Sobranie sochinenii.* 10 vols. 1953–56.

Translations: Lewanski, pp. 273–74.

Secondary literature: Victoria Babenko, "Nature Descriptions and their Function in Korolenko's Stories," *CSP* 16 (1974), pp. 424–35. G. A. Byalyi, *V. G. Korolenko.* 1949. R. F. Christian, "V. G. Korolenko (1853–1921): A Centennial Appreciation," *SEER* 32, no. 79 (1954), pp. 449–63. Maurice Comtet, *Vladimir G. Korolenko: 1853–1921. L'homme et l'oeuvre.* Paris, 1975. A. V. Derman, *Zhizn' V. G. Korolenko.* 1946. Natalia M. Kolb-Seletski, "Elements of Light in the Fiction of Korolenko," *SEEJ* 16 (1972), pp. 173–83. Lauren G. Leighton, "Korolenko's Stories of Siberia," *SEER* 49 (1971), pp. 200–13. N. V. Rostov, *V. G. Korolenko.* 1965.

L. P.

Kórvin-Pyotróvsky, Vladímir Lvóvich (Pyotrovsky until 1945, 1891–1966), poet, dramatist, and prose writer. Korvin-Pyotrovsky left Russia in 1920, after having fought in the White Army in the civil war. In the early 1920s in Berlin he was a member, together with V. NABOKOV, G. STRUVE, and others, of a literary circle grouped around the periodical *Vereteno.* He moved to Paris after Hitler came to power. During World War II he took part in the Resistance, was imprisoned, and barely escaped execution. He spent his last years in California and died in Los Angeles.

Korvin-Pyotrovsky's first poetic collections, *Absinth and Stars* (Polyn' i zvezdy, 1923) and *Stony Love* (Kamennaya lyubov', 1925), later repudiated by the author and never republished, are interesting, however, for their elaboration of fashionable expressionistic imagery within firm and traditional formal structures. His later and mature work, starting with *An Air Kite* (Vozdushnyi zmei, 1950), is collected in two volumes published posthumously as *The Guest Who Was Late* (Pozdnii gost', 1968–69). The roots of Korvin-Pyotrovsky's remarkable artistic achievement should be seen in the mainstream of Russian classical poetry, both preserved and transfigured by the experience of 20th-century realities. A poet of stature and elegance, never monotone (though he uses almost exclusively iambic tetrameter), Korvin-Pyotrovsky succeeded in creating a verbal sonority that echoes PUSHKIN's and meditations almost TYUTCHEVian in their insights into the existential issues of modern man. He produces his very original vision under the deceptive disguise of conservative perseverance. His novelty, using ADAMOVICH's appreciative phrase, never offends the eye, since it never excludes continuity.

An accomplished master, a creator of verse both transparent and transcendental, of dramatic poems of rare and austere harmony, among them his masterpiece "Beatrice" (on the story of Beatrice Cenci), Korvin-Pyotrovsky indeed merits a distinguished place on the Russian Parnassus.

Works: Primery g-na abbata. 1922. *Svyatogor-skit.* 1923. [With G. Rosimov:] *Veselye bezdelki.* 1924. *Beatrice.* 1929. *Porazhenie.* 1960.

Translations: Modern Russian Poetry. Ed. Vladimir Markov and Merrill Sparks. 1967. Pp. 480–83.

Secondary literature: G. Adamovich, "Stikhi V. Korvina-Pyotrovskogo," *Novoe russkoe slovo,* 10 April 1960. N. Andreev, "Polet 'polomanoi krivoi'," *Grani* 12 (1951). V. Blinov, "Poeticheskaya real'nost' Korvina-Pyotrovskogo," *Novyi zhurnal,* no. 138 (1980). L. Foster, *Bibliography of Russian Emigré Literature, 1918–1968.* 1969. Pp. 640–42. A. Frossard, *La maison des otages.* 1945. R. Gul', "V. L. Korvin-Pyotrovskii," *Novyi zhurnal,* no. 83 (1966). Yu. Ofrosimov, "Pamyati poeta," *Novyi zhurnal,* no. 84 (1966). K. Vil'chkovskii, "Literaturnye zametki o poezii Korvina-Pyotrovskogo," *Vozrozhdenie,* no. 53 (1956).

V. B.

Kostomárov, Nikolai Ivánovich (Ukr. Mykola Ivanovyč; 1817–85), along with SHEVCHENKO and Panteleimon KULISH an architect of the Ukrainian cultural and national re-awakening of the early 19th century, and, in the all-Russian context an outstanding and, at mid-century, immensely popular historian and ethnographer. Born in the Voronezh region of a Russian nobleman father and a Ukrainian peasant mother, he studied at Kharkov University (graduating in 1837) when it was the center of nascent Ukrainian romanticism, with a primary emphasis on folklore, ethnography and history (with I. SREZNEVSKY as an important influence), and defended his Master's thesis, *On the Historical Importance of Russian Folk Poetry* (Ob istoricheskom znachenii russkoi narodnoi poezii) in 1844. His commitment to populism, SLAVOPHILISM and to the Ukrainian cause ("Ukrainophilism") was already firmly set in this period.

Kostomarov's literary efforts in Ukrainian are centered in this period; they include two collections of poetry in an early romantic vein (ballads, historical and folkloric motifs) published under the pen name of Ijeremija Halka, and several historical plays. Kostomarov's most significant romantic text is the *Books of Genesis of the Ukrainian People* (Knyhy bytija ukrains'koho narodu, 1847), the programmatic statement of the Brotherhood of Saints Cyril and Methodius in which he, along with Shevchenko and Kulish, was a member; this Slavophile-federalist and millennarian program is a paraphrase of Mickiewicz's messianic *Books of the Polish People* (Księgi narodu polskiego).

After his arrest and exile in connection with the suppression (in 1847) of the Brotherhood, Kostomarov turned primarily to historical writing, and, to a lesser degree, to ethnography. In his many monographs he focused on 17th-century Ukrainian and Russian history, on the Ukrainian war of liberation against Poland, on Bohdan Khmel'nyc'kyj and the union with Russia, on the rebellion of Stenka Razin, and so on. As professor of Russian history at the University of St. Petersburg (1859–62) he had a reputation as a spellbinding lecturer, but political problems and official distrust of his heterodoxy led to his forced early retirement. At this time he also wrote several historical novels in Russian and contributed poetry, articles, and essays to Kulish's *Osnova* (1861–62).

Kostomarov was also an important literary critic and historian. His *Survey of Works Written in the Ukrainian Language* (Obzor sochinenii, pisannykh na malorossiiskom yazyke, 1842) is the first scholarly treatment of the subject. In his later years, especially after the Ems *ukaz* of 1876 which officially proscribed the use of Ukrainian in the Russian Empire, Kostomarov strove to defend—from a conservative and loyal position—the cultural rights of Ukrainians. His thesis of "the two *Rus* nations" (Ukrainians and Russians) within one all-Russian state exemplified his belief in the cultural, not the political validity of the Ukrainian national cause. Ultimately, his populism (*narodnyctvo*), i.e., his identification of Ukrainian literature with writing for and about the peasant masses (a literature "for home use") brought him to a near total estrangement from the Ukrainian national movement he did so much to foster.　　G. G.

Kostróv, Ermíl Ivánovich (1755–96), poet, came from the family of a peasant who had been made a sexton by petition of his village community. He attended the seminary in his native Vyatka, then the Slavo-Graeco-Latin Academy in Moscow, and finally Moscow University (1777–79), from which he received a bachelor's degree. He was officially appointed poet in residence of the University, which meant that he had to present verses for all solemn occasions. Frustrated by this position, he took to drink, fell ill, and died. In the eyes of subsequent generations Kostrov acquired the image of the romantic poet incarnate: independent, talented, and hopelessly impoverished. (See N. V. KUKOLNIK's play *Ermil Ivanovich Kostrov*, 1853; certain traits of Kostrov are probably reflected in Lyubim Tortsov, hero of A. N. OSTROVSKY's play *Poverty is No Vice*, 1853.) PUSHKIN and KYUKHELBEKER wrote poems in which they reflected on the lonely death of the forgotten poet-pauper: "Kostrov is dying obscurely in his garret." (Pushkin).

Kostrov was a contributor to the journals *Sobesednik lyubitelei russkogo slova*, *Zerkalo sveta*, etc. As a poet he continued the odic traditions of classicism, following LOMONOSOV. In his later verse the influence of DERZHAVIN is felt. The most important part of Kostrov's work are his translations. He translated Baculard d'Arnaud's novel *Zénothémis* (1775) in 1779, Voltaire's anti-war satire *La Tactique* (1773), also in 1779, and Apuleius' *The Golden Ass* (1780–1781, republished in 1911). Kostrov also translated the first nine books of the *Iliad* in Alexandrines (two editions, 1787 and 1811), as a heroic poem in the "high" style. He produced a complete prose version of Ossian (1792) in the spirit of early romanticism. Kostrov's translation served as the basis of the many versified translations and imitations of Ossian in the late 18th and early 19th century (V. OZEROV, A. Pushkin, and many others).

Works: Polnoe sobranie vsekh sochinenii i perevodov v stikhakh. Pts. 1–2. St. Petersburg, 1802. *Sochineniya.* (Polnoe sobranie sochinenii russkikh avtorov. A. Smirdin, publ.) St. Petersburg, 1849. [Poetry and excerpt from the 6th book of the *Iliad*:] *Poety 18 veka.* (Biblioteka poeta. Bol'shaya seriya.) Text by G. S. Tatishcheva. 1972. Vol. 2, pp. 112–90.

Secondary literature: Mark Al'tshuller and Ivan Martynov, "Materialy dlya biografii Ermila Ivanovicha Kostrova." In *Study Group on Eighteenth-Century Russia.* Newsletter 10. Ed. A. G. Cross. 1983. A. N. Egunov, *Gomer v russkikh perevodakh 18–19 vekov.* 1964. Yu. D. Levin, *Ossian v russkoi literature: Konets 18–pervaya tret' 19 veka.* 1980. P. O. Morozov, *E. I. Kostrov: Ego zhizn' i literaturnaya deyatel'nost'.* Voronezh, 1876. A. V. [A. S. Vereshchagin], "E. I. Kostrov." In *Vyatskie stikhotvortsy 18 veka.* Fasc. 1. Vyatka, 1897.　　M. A.

Kotoshíkhin, Grigóry Kárpovich (ca. 1630–67), diplomat and writer. A clerk in the Embassy Service under Tsar Alexis, Kotoshikhin defected to the West in 1664, and in 1666 entered Swedish service under the name of Ivan Selitsky. He was commissioned to compose a detailed report on life in Russia and produced thirteen chapters describing the daily life of the Imperial family, court ceremony, Muscovite officialdom, Moscow's relations with other powers, chancery procedures, municipal government, the military, commerce, the peasantry, and the life style of the Boyars. Kotoshikhin paints a very negative picture of Russian life, pointing out the backwardness, ignorance, rudeness, and dishonesty found everywhere. Kotoshikhin was executed in Stockholm for the murder of his landlord in a drunken brawl. His manuscript gathered dust in a Swedish archive until discovered by the historian S. V. Solovyov in 1837. When published in 1840, it created a sensation and was often used by WESTERNIZERS to undercut SLAVOPHILE claims about the virtues of pre-Petrine Russian society.

Works: O Rossii v tsarstvovanie Alekseya Mikhailovicha. 4th ed. 1906. Reprint, The Hague, 1969. *O Rossii v tsarstvovanie Alekseya Mikhailovicha.* With commentary by A. E. Pennington. Oxford, 1980.

Translations: Excerpts in Leo Wiener, *Anthology of Russian Literature.* Vol. 1. 1902–03.

Secondary literature: V. G. Belinskii, [Rossiya do Petra Velikogo]. In his *PSS*, Vol. 5, pp. 91–152. A. I. Markevich, *G. K. Kotoshikhin i ego sochinenie o Moskovskom gosudarstve v polovine XVII v.* 1895.　　V. T.

Kozlóv, Iván Ivánovich (1779–1840), poet and translator, was born in Moscow. He made an unusually rapid and brilliant career, first in the military and then in civil service. In 1821 he was struck by paralysis and two years later became totally blind. The long and cruel period of suffering made him dwell in the realm of the imagination; his personal tragedy led him to seek solace in poetry, which also helped him to earn a living. His poetry and personal plight attracted the attention and patronage of the court. Kozlov became a literary celebrity, hosting a well-known salon attended by ZHUKOVSKY, PUSHKIN and other poets and writers of the 1820s and 1830s.

Kozlov found meaning and inspiration in the poetry of Zhukovsky, with its sadness and longing for a better world, its melancholy view of earthly life. His earliest poems are full of echoes of Zhukovsky, carefully selected to parallel his own feelings. He studied and appropriated Zhukovsky's style, melodic structure, and imagery, but not his complicated symbolism. Kozlov's poetry is more concrete, more simple, at times naive in its acceptance of romantic themes. His verse is very rhythmic, the language liquid, its measure even and smooth. The facility in some of his lyric measures he learned from Pushkin and it is one of the chief merits of his poetry. His lyrics are deeply sincere and spontaneous; though not original thematically, they have an expressive harmony and, frequently, brilliance and apt phrasing.

Kozlov did many translations from Byron, Moore, Mickiewicz. The persisting charm of such free translations as Thomas Moore's "The Evening Bells" (Vechernii zvon, 1828) make them Kozlov's very own.

Kozlov was one of the first Russians to come under the influence of Byron and to translate him into Russian. His main work "The Monk" (Chernets, 1825), is a Byronic confessional poem, a tale of love, death, and revenge shrouded in an atmosphere of mystery.

From the beginning Kozlov's poetry enjoyed great success. "The Monk" had three successive printings; his works came out in three editions during his lifetime.

Kozlov's narrative poems had an important influence on Lermontov and his poetic technique on the poets of the school of "pure art" such as A. A. FET.

Works: Polnoe sobranie stikhotvorenii. (Biblioteka poeta.) 1960.
Translations: Lewanski, pp. 275–76.
Secondary literature: G. R. V. Barratt, *Ivan Kozlov: A Study and a Setting.* 1972. ———, "Somov, Kozlov, and Byron's Russian Triumph," *Canadian Review of Comparative Literature* 1 (1974), pp. 104–22.   A. Gl.

Kozmá Prutkóv, see PRUTKOV.

Krásnaya Nov' (Red Virgin Soil), a literary journal founded in 1921 with LENIN's personal approval. At a time when Russian literature seemed moribund, *Krasnaya nov'* was intended to attract and encourage new writers without imposing any political tests except for a general sympathy for the Revolution. As a typical "thick" journal, it featured various departments, but was most important for its belles lettres and its literary theory and criticism. Under the editorship of Aleksandr VORONSKY, a cultivated Bolshevik with an eye for quality, the journal published much of the best fiction and poetry of the 1920s, especially from the so-called FELLOW TRAVELERS, like OLESHA, LEONOV, BABEL and Vsevolod IVANOV. It also created an important body of Marxist criticism and theory, with such contributors as A. LEZHNEV, Dmitry Gorbov, and especially the prolific Voronsky himself. Soon the journal became entangled in the lively, often bitter literary polemics of the decade, and was the special target of NA POSTU, which resented its favored position in Party eyes, and accused it, with some justification, of promoting fellow-traveler writers at the expense of ideologically sounder proletarians. A change in the Party's policy toward literature led to Voronsky's dismissal as editor in 1927. The journal continued until 1942, under a succession of editors, but lost much of its old luster, eminence, and importance.

Secondary literature: R. A. Maguire, *Red Virgin Soil: Soviet Literature in the 1920's.* 1968.   R. A. M.

Krasnóv, Pyotr Nikoláevich (1869–1945), émigré writer. A general in the Tsar's Army, Krasnov played a prominent role in the civil war against the Bolsheviks. In the 1920s he published several novels in which he presented a conservative's version of the events which led to the overthrow of the Tsar and to the eventual victory of Bolshevism. Among these novels, the first, *From Double-Headed Eagle to Red Banner* (Ot dvuglavogo orla k krasnomu znameni, 1921–22), published in Berlin, gained wide popularity and was translated into several European languages. Its hero is a Russian officer whose life story unfolds against a broad panoramic background of the reign of Nicholas II. The novel is rather simplistic in its understanding of social and political developments, and amateurish in its construction, but it projected views which were those of many émigrés and right-wing Western readers. Krasnov's subsequent novels, such as *Fallen Leaves* (Opavshie list'ya, 1923) and *To Understand is to Forgive* (Ponyat'—prostit', 1923), had a lesser, but still a considerable success. Krasnov resumed his military and political activities in World War II, on the German side. After the War he was extradited to Soviet authorities by the Western Allies and was executed in Moscow.

Works: See Foster, pp. 652–55.
Translations: Lewanski, p. 276 (9 titles).   V. T.

Kravchínsky, Sergeí Mikhaílovich (1851–95), pseudonym—S. Stepnyak, POPULIST revolutionary and writer. Son of a military doctor and a graduate of an artillery academy, he was an active revolutionary after 1871. Member of *narodnik* organizations during the 1870s, he proved a gifted propagandist, both orally and in writing. Loyal to the goals of agrarian socialism, his views evolved from acceptance of those of LAVROV, then of BAKUNIN, and finally to strong support of constitutionalism. Already an author and editor of underground publications, he became an émigré after assassinating the Chief of Gendarmes in August 1878. Based in London, his writing career flourished as he consciously and successfully sought to influence Western public opinion in favor of what he pictured to be the selfless, idealistic struggle of Russian radicals against the oppressive autocratic Tsarist regime. Publishing in many languages, most of his books, beginning with *Underground Russia* (1882), were factual accounts of the revolutionary struggle and the abuses of the regime. His novels and a play featured the same themes. His model of the ideal revolutionary was also influential among radicals within Russia. Through articles in many journals and lectures, he sought to broaden the knowledge of the Western public about Russian subjects, especially major writers. Kravchinsky played a key role in the organization of the English Society of the Friends of Russian Freedom and edited its paper, *Free Russia*. He was also a founder of the Russian Free Press Fund which published abroad works by Russian authors representing the various ideologies of the opposition movement. During his last two years, he led an effort to organize a coalition of liberal and socialist groups to campaign for a constitution.

Works: Sochineniya. 2 vols. 1958.
Translations: Lewanski, p. 362.
Secondary literature: James W. Hulse, *Revolutionaries in London: A Study of Five Unorthodox Socialists.* 1970. Charles A. Moser, "A Nihilist's Career: S. M. Stepniak-Kravchinskij," *SlavR* 20 (1961), pp. 55–71. Donald Senese, "S. M. Kravchinskii and the National Front Against Autocracy," *SlavR* 34 (1975), pp. 506–22. Evgeniya Taratuta, *S. M. Stepnyak-Kravchinskii, revolyutsioner i pisatel'.* 1973.   J. A. D.

Krestóvsky, V., (pseud. of Nadézhda Dmítrievna Zayonchkóvskaya, née Khvoshchinskaya, 1824–89), poet and writer, lived in Ryazan most of her life, moved to St. Petersburg only in 1884. She began her literary career as a poet in the 1840s and 1850s (under her maiden name). When she gradually switched to prose in the 1850s, she published it under the pseudonym V. Krestovsky. When a real V. KRESTOVSKY appeared on the literary scene in 1857, she began to sign her pieces "Krestovsky—pseudonym." Her poems, stories, and novels consistently reflect the ideas of the progressive wing of the Russian intelligentsia. In the 1850s, the theme of suffering and lonely women who are not given a chance to apply their talents and idealism to a proper cause appears in several variations, as in the trilogy *Provincial Life in the Old Days.* In the 1860s and 1870s, themes of social protest and selfless work for the good of the people predominate, with women in key roles, as in "The Boarder" (Pansionerka, 1861), "Ursa Major" (Bol'shaya medveditsa, 1870–71), and "The Schoolmistress" (Uchitel'nitsa, 1880). In Krestovsky's late works, a mood of disenchantment and resignation takes over, as the ideals of the 1860s have failed to materialize. Krestovsky was a highly successful and popular writer in her day, although the artistic value of her prose is not great.

Works: Romany i povesti. 8 vols. 1859–66. *Sobranie sochinenii.* 2d ed. 5 vols. 1898. *Povesti i rasskazy.* Introd. M. S. Goryachkina. 1963.
Secondary literature: N. K. Mikhailovskii, "Smert' Zayonchkovskoi." In his *Polnoe sobranie sochinenii*, vol. 6 (1910). A. P. Mogilyanskii, "N. D. i S. D. Khvoshchinskie." In *Istoriya russkoi literatury.* Vol. 9, pt. 2. 1953. M. Tsebrikova, "Ocherk zhizni N. D. Khvoshchinskoi-Zayonchkovskoi," *Mir Bozhii*, 1897, no. 12.

V. T.

Krestóvsky, Vsévolod Vladímirovich (1840–95) came from an ancient family of Ukrainian gentry. Having enrolled in the

Historico-Philological Division of Petersburg University in 1857, he was close to PISAREV, took a fancy to radical ideas, and wrote for RUSSKOE SLOVO. But soon enough he attached himself to a circle of moderate Slavophile *littérateurs*: A. MAIKOV, L. MEI, A. GRIGORIEV, etc., and began to publish his verses and stories in the OTECHESTVEN-NYE ZAPISKI, VREMYA and BIBLIOTEKA DLYA CHTENIYA. In 1860 Krestovsky left the university to become a professional writer. His novel *The Slums of Petersburg: A Book about the Well-Fed and the Hungry* (Peterburgskie trushchoby: Kniga o sytykh i golodnykh, 1864) gained him great popularity. An exposé in the manner of the NATURAL SCHOOL, it depicts the life of different social strata, from wealthy high society to thieves and prostitutes. The novel is a fusion of sharp observations of actual fact (the author spent many hours in taverns and "dives," sketching his types from nature), sententious comments with a social and democratic tendency and a dose of eroticism.

In 1863 Krestovsky travelled to Warsaw to write sketches toward a planned novel on the Polish uprising, which appeared in RUSSKII VESTNIK under the title *The Flock of Panurge* (Panurgovo stado, 1869). Characters drawn from nature and detail based on personal observation appear here also, but the author's general attitude toward social problems has changed. Krestovsky takes a sharply negative view of Russia's radical youth of the 1860s, as well as of the Polish freedom movement. In 1874 he wrote a second book on the same events, *Two Forces* (Dve sily), and combined both into a dilogy entitled *The Bloody Bluff* (Krovavyi puf). Many of the heroes of the dilogy were actual participants of the Polish uprising (under fictitious names). The author's own position is stated by the physician Khvalyntsev, who gradually comprehends the senselessness of the movement of the 1860s, as far as Russian youth (the "nihilists") is concerned, but also recognizes the very real strength of the Polish movement, which has a tangible goal: to stand up to Russia. Krestovsky was chauvinist enough to declare that if Russia had not vanquished Poland in 1863, Poland would have conquered Russia. The next step of Krestovsky's political evolution is his shift to frankly anti-Semitic positions in the 1880s. He wrote a trilogy, *The Jews are Coming* (Zhid idet): *Egyptian Darkness* (1888), *Tamara Ben-David* (1890), and *The Triumph of Baal* (1892). From 1892 on Krestovsky was editor of the Warsaw newspaper *Varshavskii listok*.

Works: Sobranie sochinenii. 8 vols. 1899–1905. *Peterburgskie trushchoby*. 3 vols. 1935–37.
Secondary literature: Irina S. Ashcroft, "*Peterburgskie trushchoby*: A Russian Version of *Les Mystères de Paris*," *Revue de Littérature Comparée* 53 (1979), pp. 163–75. A. Batyuto, "Turgenev i nekotorye pisateli antinigilisticheskogo napravleniya." In *Turgenev i ego sovremenniki*. 1977. V. Bazanov, *Iz literaturnoi polemiki 60-kh godov*. 1941. G. Byalyi, "Proza shestidesyatykh godov." In *Istoriya russkoi literatury*. Vol. 8, pt. 1. 1956. K. Golovin, *Russkii roman i russkoe obshchestvo*. 1897. O. Miller, *Russkie pisateli posle Gogolya*. 1886. Charles Moser, *Antinihilism in the Russian Novel of the 1860s*. 1964. J. A. Rogers, "Darwinism, Scientism, and Nihilism," *RusR* 19 (1960), no. 1. A. Tseitlin, "Syuzhetika antinigilisticheskogo romana," *Literatura i marksizm*, 1929, no. 2. V. Zaitsev, "Rasskazy V. Krestovskogo: Peterburgskie tipy" (1865).

E. D. A.

Krizanic, Juraj (1617–83), a Croatian Dominican who travelled to the Ukraine in 1659 to inquire into the reasons for the religious schism between the Orthodox Church of the Polish Ukraine, which had entered a Union with the Roman Catholic Church in 1594, and the Orthodox Church of Muscovy, then went on to Moscow to work for a new Union. He proposed to Tsar Alexis a program of far-reaching reforms which would allow Muscovy to enter the community of Western nations without abandoning her traditions. Krizanic was convinced that Russia was destined to become a great power which would liberate the other Slavs from Turkish and German domination. He had little success, though, for he was soon (1661) banished to Tobolsk in Siberia. In his Siberian exile he wrote several works in a Common Slavic language created by himself. Among them were *Political Thoughts* (Politichnye dumy), *Discourse on Sovereignty* (Razgovori o Vladetelstvu), and a grammar of Russian. They are an important source of information on 17th-century Russia. Krizanic was finally allowed to leave Russia in 1676. His works were discovered and published only in the 19th century.

Works: Sobranie sochinenii. 3 vols. 1891–92. *Politika*. 1965.
Secondary literature: B. D. Datsyuk, *Yu. Krizhanich*. 1946. Thomas Eekman and Ante Kadić, eds., *Juraj Križanić (1618–1683), Russophile and Ecumenic Visionary: A Symposium*. The Hague, 1976.

V. T.

Kropótkin, Pyotr Alekséevich (1842–1921), libertarian philosopher and exponent of the theories of anarchist communism, was born in Moscow into an old aristocratic family which traces its lineage to the Ryurik dynasty. He was educated in the Corps of Pages and served as personal attendant to Tsar Alexander II. He was commissioned to serve in the Mounted Cossack regiment in Siberia where he became acquainted with liberal ideas. During his extensive travels in the regions of Siberia as a geographer he developed a theory about the structure of the mountains of Asia. He was an active member of the Russian Geographical Society. He became interested in radical ideas, expecially those of the famous anarchist Mikhail BAKUNIN.

Kropotkin returned to Russia after a visit to Switzerland where he joined Nikolai Chaikovsky's underground group. In 1874 he was arrested and imprisoned in the dreaded St. Peter and St. Paul Fortress. Two years later he escaped to Western Europe where he became an active participant in the rising anarchist movement. He founded the journal *Le Révolté* in which he published many of his political articles. In 1879 Kropotkin participated in the London International Anarchist Congress. In 1882 he was arrested by the French authorities and sentenced to five years imprisonment. He was eventually released from prison and settled in England where he lived until his return to Russia in 1917. He died in 1921.

Unlike Bakunin's anarchism which stressed the idea of collectivism, Kropotkin advocated the need of the individual consumer as a standard for the distribution of wealth. He emphasized the principle of mutual aid, and advocated the commune principle as the unit of social organization. Kropotkin rejected the idea of the state and stressed the principle of federalism without any political form. He regarded revolution as a natural development of man as a social being who is not in need of government. Kropotkin failed to reconcile his principle of mutual aid with his anarchistic love of freedom because he did not take into account the fact that social customs restrict freedom in most societies. Kropotkin saw morality as an extension of human good will beyond equity and justice.

Works: The State: Its Part in History. London, 1898. *Fields, Factories and Workshops*. London, 1898. *La Conquête du pain*. Paris, 1892. *The Great French Revolution*. London, 1909. *In Russian and French Prisons*. London, 1887. *Memoirs of a Revolutionist*. Boston, 1899. *Mutual Aid*. London, 1902. *Russian Literature*. New York, 1905. Reissued as *Ideals and Realities in Russian Literature*, New York, 1915. *Science and Anarchism*. Philadelphia, 1903. *The Terror in Russia*. London, 1909. *Etika*. Petrograd and Moscow, 1922.
Secondary literature: André Reszler. "Peter Kropotkin and His Vision of Anarchist Aesthetics," *Diogenes* 78 (1972), pp. 52–63.

L. J. S.

Kruchónykh, Aleksei Eliséevich (1886–1969?), poet and literary theorist, was born to a peasant family in Kherson province. In his early years, he took up painting in the Odessa Art School. In 1905, he was arrested and imprisoned for distributing Bolshevik literature. In 1906, he saw his vocation in teaching graphic arts. In 1907, he worked with the BURLYUK brothers—David, Nikolai, Vladimir—in promoting cubism in art. In 1912, he joined the cubo-FUTURIST group and was one of the signatories of its manifesto, "A Slap in the Face of Public Taste." During the revolutionary years 1917–1920, he organized, with Ilya Zdanevich, a poetic group, "41°", in Tiflis, Georgia. In the post-revolutionary period, he was a member of MAYAKOVSKY's LEF group.

Kruchonykh was the most prolific and effective theoretician of cubo-futurism and its most loyal and consistent advocate of trans-rational language (ZAUMNYI *yazyk*), or the destruction of meaning in poetry. Kruchonykh believed that transrational language would spell an end to Russian poetry's captivity to meaning, psychology, and philosophical pursuits from Pushkin to the symbolists. Kruchonykh remarked that his transrational poem, "*Dyr bul shchyl*," expressed "more Russian than all of Pushkin's poetry." For Kruchonykh, transrational language also reflected the confusion and chaos of modern life. In his poetry, Kruchonykh used arbitrary and logically meaningless but suggestive sound sequences expressive of certain emotions, and often combined transrational language with intelligible language. He often avoided punctuation, made grammatical errors, used typographical methods to emphasize words and sounds, assigned texture (*faktura*) to various sounds, and created new words to replace those in existence.

Works: Slovo kak takovoe. (With V. Khlebnikov). 1913. *Chort i rechetvortsy.* 1913. *Zaum'.* 1921. *Faktura slova.* 1921. *15 let russkogo futurizma.* 1928. *Pobeda nad solncem*: Ein futuristisches Drama von A. Kručenych. Trans. and commentary by Gisela Erbslöh. Reprint of original ed. Munich, 1976.

Secondary literature: Vahan D. Barooshian, *Russian Cubo-Futurism 1910–1930.* The Hague, 1974. Elizabeth K. Beaujour, "Zaum," *Dada* 2 (1972), pp. 13–18. Gerald Janacek, "Kručenych and Chlebnikov Co-Authoring a Manifesto," *RusL* 8 (1980), pp. 483–98. Nikolai Khardzhiev, "Sud'ba Alekseya Kruchenykh," *Svantevit* 1, no. 1 (1975), pp. 34–42. Vladimir Markov, *Russian Futurism: A History.* 1968. Pp. 40–48, 334–50. G. McVay, "Alexei Kruchenykh: The Bogeyman of Russian Literature," *RLT* 13 (1975), pp. 571–90. Viktor Shklovskii, "O poezii i zaumnom yazyke." In *Poetika.* Petrograd, 1919. Pp. 13–26.   V. D. B.

Krylóv, Iván Andréevich (1769–1844), journalist, playwright, and fabulist. Nowhere is the Russian satiric impulse realized more successfully than in the mature Krylov's fables. Although he did not complete his first translations of La Fontaine until 1805 and his first collection of original works until 1809, he was, both by temperament and early training, a man of the Age of Reason. His first comedies, although not distinguished, introduce characters such as the ignorant and cruel members of the landed gentry and the slavish imitator of foreign culture, common objects of the enlightened author's ridicule. In 1789, Krylov published a short-lived satirical journal, *Pochta dukhov*, modelled after earlier publications edited by NOVIKOV and EMIN, which consisted of social commentary in the guise of letters written by figures from the underworld. The device of making human foibles strange by describing them from the perspective of a naive, uncorrupted visitor was an established convention of the Oriental tale which Krylov used to didactic effect. Two of his contributions to the equally short-lived successors to *Pochta dukhov* deserve mention for their artistic maturity. "Kaib, An Oriental Tale," vividly depicts the insufficiencies of autocracy, thinly veiled as the account of the Caliph Kaib and his corrupt courtiers. The "Eulogy to the Memory of My Grandfather" must be considered a minor gem of Enlightenment satire, with its author inverting the whole eulogistic tradition to celebrate the folly and profligacy of his fictional relative.

The political implications of Krylov's fictional statements, made during a period of increasingly repressive rule, were sufficient to force the author to cease publishing, and the period of 1794 to 1802 saw his virtual disappearance from the literary scene. Only two plays, the comedy *The Pie* and a mock tragedy *Trumpf* can be dated from this period, the latter's satiric force, directed against the regime of Paul I, being sufficiently virulent to prevent its publication in Russian before 1871. Of the young Krylov's interest in verse the evidence stems primarily from such examples of the familiar letter as "To My Friend" (1793), rather than from attempts at the fable itself. The particular factors which prompted him to turn belatedly to the latter genre are difficult to determine; upon his return to Petersburg in 1806, he became associated with the cultural circle of A. N. Olenin, a group which placed considerable emphasis on the creation of a national literature with the aid of forms inherited from antiquity. Although many earlier authors, including SUMAROKOV and KHEMNITSER, had produced fables, Krylov displayed a unique talent for the genre and devoted himself exclusively to such writing after 1809. He shared with other fabulists the conviction that, by exposing both societal and individual faults to ridicule, reform could be attained within the context of the existing system. The essentially conservative nature of Krylov's satire is revealed by those works in which he derides individuals who express impatience with the status quo. In effect, the exuberant, unfocused satire of his youth, tempered by reflection and experience, yielded to a more indulgent commentary on human insufficiencies, inspired, in some instances, by particular events in the Russia of his day.

What distinguishes Krylov's fables is more the manner of their telling than the novelty of their message. At a time when the nation's authors were still struggling to establish the nature of their medium, he appears to have intuitively grasped the fable's amenability to a simple, colloquial style that appealed to the increasingly diversified body of Russian readers. Comparison of his earliest translations and reworkings of La Fontaine's fables with the originals gives some indication of the reasons for his success. Rather than the subtle irony and controlled diction characteristic of the 17th-century French classicist, there is a sense of everyday immediacy about the Russian versions that derives from the inclusion of concrete detail, character portrayal, and the succinct, colloquial narrative style. While retaining the genre's convention of using animals to symbolize basic human types, Krylov succeeds in fusing the general with the particular, his bears, donkeys, and nightingales expressing their distinctive qualities against a background that is unmistakeably Russian. He is also inclined to instruct by negative example and his forceful, concluding morals, some of which have passed into the realm of folk expression, are models of their kind.

It is the intrinsic aesthetic quality of Krylov's fables which is largely responsible for his enduring reputation but his works had topical relevance as well. His success at providing social commentary in fictional form established Krylov as one of the first in a long series of satirists who would contribute prominently to the shaping of modern Russian literature.

Works: Sochineniya. 2 vols. 1969.

Translations: Guy Daniels, trans. *Fifteen Fables of Krylov.* 1965. "Eulogy to the Memory of My Grandfather," *Satire Newsletter* 9 (1971). *See also:* Lewanski, pp. 277–81.

Secondary literature: V. Arkhipov, *I. A. Krylov: Poeziya narodnoi mudrosti.* 1974. Nikolay Stepanov, *Ivan Krylov.* (Twayne's World Authors Series, 247.) New York, 1973. V. V. Vinogradov, "I. A. Krylov i ego znachenie v istorii russkoi literatury i russkogo literaturnogo yazyka," *Russkaya rech'* 4 (1970), pp. 3–15. Franz Wiltschek, "La Fontaine und Krylov: Ein literaturwissenschaftlicher Vergleich," *Wiener Slavistisches Jahrbuch* 1 (1950).   P. R. H.

Krýmov, Vladímir Pímenovich (1878–1968), émigré writer. Before the Revolution, Krymov was active mainly as an editor and journalist. He travelled to America and the Far East, and wrote interesting travel notes. After the Revolution, he lived in London, Berlin, and Paris. At one time he edited the newspaper *Russkii golos*, supporting the position of SMENA VEKH. He also published a series of novels, the most significant of these being the trilogy *After Millions* (Za millionami, 1933), consisting of the novels *Apprenticeship with Sidor* (Sidorovo uchen'e), *They Used to Live Well in Petersburg* (Khorosho zhili v Peterburge), and *The Little Imp under the Table* (D'yavolenok pod stolom). Close to the picaresque genre, these novels give a panoramic and often colorful picture of Russian middle-class life from the viewpoint of a man of affairs (shady, for the most part). Krymov's style is smooth and folksy, he has an ear for colloquial speech, and his satire is sometimes to the point. His novels, some of which went through several editions, make for entertaining reading but are hardly serious literature.

Works: See Foster, pp. 664–66.

Translations: See Lewanski, p. 281 (five titles).

Secondary literature: Gleb Struve, *Russkaya literatura v izgnanii.* Pp. 126–28.   V. T.

Krýmov, Yúry Solomónovich (pseud. of Yu. S. Beklemíshev, 1908–41), prose writer. Born in St. Petersburg, Krymov was an engineer by profession, joined the Communist party in 1941, and was killed in battle 20 September 1941. Although Krymov began writing in the early 1930s, he is known primarily for his novel *Tanker "Derbent"* (1938). A classic of SOCIALIST REALISM, this work shows how, under the leadership of an "ordinary" communist, an undisciplined crew is transformed into an efficient and cohesive collective. Its theme is the use of socialist competition to inspire workers to productivity. This novel has been hailed by the Soviets as "one of the best works of Soviet prose of the 1930s." It has been made into a film and is reprinted almost annually.

Works: Tanker "Derbent." 1938, 1940, 1947, 1957, 1972. *Tanker "Derbent". P'esa.* 1939. *Tanker "Derbent". Inzhener.* 1963. *Povesti.* 1944, 1948.

Translations: Tanker "Derbent." Moscow 1940, 1960, 1962, 1971; *Tanker Derbent.* Conn. 1975 (reprint of 1940 ed.)

Secondary literature: P. Gromov, *Yurii Krymov. Ocherk tvorchestva.* 1956. L. P. Kozlova, *Yurii Solomonovich Krymov. Ukazatel' literatury.* 1956. M. Kuznetsov, *Yurii Krymov. Kritiko-biograficheskii ocherk.* 1951.   H. S.

Kryúkov, Fyódor Dmítrievich (1870–1920), prose writer, was the son of an ataman of Glazunovskaya Cossack settlement (*stanitsa*) in the Don Military Region. He graduated from the Petersburg Institute of History and Philology (1892) and taught in secondary schools in Orel and Nizhny Novgorod until 1906 when he was elected to the First State Duma. In 1907 he was sentenced to three months in prison for signing an antigovernment appeal prompted by the dissolution of the Duma. A liberal populist, he took a patriotic stance during World War I and actively opposed the Bolsheviks during the civil war, serving as secretary of the Don Cossack Assembly and editing the official newspaper of the Don Government. He died of typhus or pleurisy while retreating with the Whites.

Kryukov began his literary career in 1892 with sketches published in *Peterburgskaya gazeta* and with two historical tales about the Cossacks which appeared in different journals. For twenty years he was a regular contributor to the liberal journal RUSSKOE BOGATSTVO. Altogether he wrote over 200 stories, sketches, and essays; some of his stories approach the size of a short novel. Kryukov depicts various social strata, but is concerned mainly with the Don Cossacks. He vividly represents their way of life in such stories as "A Cossack Woman" (Kazachka, 1896), "Ripples" (Zyb', 1909), and "The Officer's Wife" (Ofitsersha, 1912). While rich in local color, Kryukov's stories suffer from weakly developed plots and protracted dialogues. Kryukov's style is that of a realist with a streak of sentimentality.

Works: Kazatskie motivy. 1907. *Rasskazy.* Vol. 1. 1914.

Translations: "In the Russian Village," *RusR* 1, no. 1 (February 1916), pp. 9–12.

Secondary literature: H. Ermolaev, *Mikhail Sholokhov and His Art.* 1982. Geir Kjetsaa, "Problema avtorstva v romane *Tikhii Don*," *Scando-Slavica* 24 (1978), pp. 91–105. V. Proskurin, "K kharakteristike tvorchestva i lichnosti F. D. Kryukova," *RLit*, 1966, no. 4, pp. 179–86.   H. E.

Küchelbecker, Wilhelm, see KYUKHELBEKER, Vilgelm.

Kudryávtsev, Pyotr Nikoláevich (1816–58), historian, critic, writer. Studied at the Moscow Theological Seminary, then graduated from Moscow University as a student of T. N. GRANOVSKY. In 1845 he went abroad for further study. On his return he was appointed lecturer in history at Moscow University. In 1850 he published *The Fates of Italy from the Fall of the Western Roman Empire to its Restoration by Charlemagne* (Sud'by Italii ot padeniya zapadnoi Rimskoi Imperii do vostanovleniya ee Karlom Velikim) and *Roman Women* (Rimskie zhenshchiny), as well as other articles on Italy. Kudryavtsev replaced Granovsky as professor after the latter's death (1857), edited Granovsky's works, and began his biography. As literary and art critic, he published regularly in *Teleskop, Moskovskii nablyudatel', Sovremennik*, and *Otechestvennye zapiski*. He published fiction under the pseudonym of A. Nestroev or A. N. An adherent of the "NATURAL SCHOOL," he still carried the seeds of romanticism in his choice of subjects, characterization, the subjectivity of the narrator and, at times, a slight melancholy, or supernatural coloring. His first story "Katen'ka Pylaeva" appeared in *Teleskop* (1836). Other stories followed: "Two Passions" (Dve strasti), "Bewilderment" (Nedoumenie), "Flute" (Fleita), "Mistake" (Oshibka), "A Flower" (Tsvetok). In some of these he reflected the contemporary Sandian theme of women's emancipation, and was one of the first to attempt to understand the dynamics of marriage and family. He also depicted the "superfluous" hero, and in one of his best stories, "The Last Visit" (Poslednii vizit) combined all these themes.

Works: Sochineniya. 3 vols. 1887–89. *Povesti i rasskazy.* 2 vols. 1866.

Secondary literature: V. G. Belinskii, "Russkaya literatura v 1841 godu," *PSS* 5, p. 582. I. I. Glukhovskaya, "P. N. Kudryavtsev i romantizm: k postanovke voprosa." In *Voprosy romanticheskogo metoda i stilya.* 1978. I. V. Kartashova, "O roli romanticheskikh traditsii i formirovanii natural'noi shkoly (Konets 30-kh–nachalo 40-kh godov)." In *Voprosy romantizma.* (Uchenye zapiski Kazanskogo gosudarstvennogo universiteta, 129, book 7.) 1969.   E. K. K.

Kuechelbecker, see KYUKHELBEKER.

Kúkolnik, Néstor Vasílievich (1809–68), dramatist and novelist. Kukolnik is known primarily as the author of patriotic plays on historical themes. The most famous of all, a great success in its day, was the five-act *The Hand of the Almighty Has Saved the Fatherland* (Ruka Vsevyshnego otechestvo spasla, 1832), set in the time of the election of the first Romanov (1613) and written in iambic pentameter blank verse. Other historical plays with Russian and Russian-related settings include *Prince Mikhail Vasilievich Skopin-Shuisky* (Knyaz' Mikhail Vasil'evich Skopin-Shuiskii); *The Boyar Fyodor Vasilievich Basyonok* (Boyarin Fedor Vasil'evich Basenok); *Lieutenant-General Patkul* (General-poruchik Patkul'), about the Russian ambassador of Peter I to the Saxon-Polish court; *The Orderly* (Denshchik), a historical drama set in Moscow in 1722; *The Statue of St. Christopher in Riga, or There Will Be War!* (Statuya Kristofa v Rige, ili Budet voina!), set in Riga in 1472; *Prince Daniil Vasilievich Kholmsky* (Knyaz' Daniil Vasil'evich Kholmskii), a drama in mixed prose and verse set in Pskov in 1474; and *Ivan Ryabov, an Archangel Fisherman* (Ivan Ryabov, Rybak arkhangelogorodskii). Kukolnik was also interested in the lives of artists who he believed had suffered for their art and with whom he could identify. It was this interest that motivated the writing of such plays as *Torquato Tasso* (1830–31), a "dramatic fantasy" in five acts in verse with an intermedium; *Giulio Mosti* (1832–33), a four-part "dramatic fantasy" in verse with an intermedium about a 17th-century Roman artist; *Ermil Ivanovich Kostrov* (1853), a five-act verse play about a Russian poet in Moscow in the late 18th century; *Giacobo Sannazaro* (1833), a "dramatic fantasy" in four acts in verse about a 15th-century Neapolitan poet; and *Domenichino*, a "dramatic fantasy" in verse about the Italian artist Giovanni Domenico Zampieri.   H. B. S.

Kulísh, Panteleimon Aleksándrovich (1819–97), after SHEVCHENKO the most central figure in the development of early 19th-century Ukrainian literature, and in the all-Russian context a prominent historian, ethnographer, and literary critic. The very range of Kulish's activities and initiatives suggests his importance for Ukrainian literature: innovative poet (moving from the then conventional Romantic Cossacophilism and folklorism of *Ukrajina* [1843] to meditative lyric, epic poetry, satire and even caustic polemic); prosaist, and most notably author of the first Ukrainian historical (Scottian) novel, *Čorna rada* (1857); tireless translator (of much of Shakespeare, Byron, Goethe, Schiller, Heine, Mickiewicz, as well as the Bible); antiquarian and ethnographer (see especially his highly successful two-volume *Notes on the South of Rus'* (Zapiski o Yuzhnoi Rusi, 1856); energetic organizer of literary life (particularly as editor of the first Ukrainian literary and cultural journal, *Osnova*, 1861–62); and, above all, ever-provocative critic and gadfly of Ukrainian society, willing to attack the most ingrained traits and cherished cults, be it nativist thinking, the Cossack legacy, or even aspects of Shevchenko himself.

Kulish's writings in Russian, almost exclusively in prose, also begin with folkloric stories and sketches and with the historical novel *à la* Scott *Mikhailo Charnyshenko or the Ukraine Eighty Years Ago* (Mikhailo Charnyshenko ili Malorossiya vosem'desyat let nazad). In the 1850s, following his arrest and brief exile for membership in the Brotherhood of Saints Cyril and Methodius (see KOSTOMAROV), Kulish turned again to the historical novel (e.g., *Aleksei Odnorog*, 1852–53, dealing with the TIME OF TROUBLES) and also to prose in the tradition of the NATURAL SCHOOL (*Yakov Yakovlich*, 1852, modelled on the theme of GOGOL's "Shinel'"). At this time Kulish also tried his hand at poetry in Russian, writing an autobiographic "novel in verse" entitled "Evgenii Onegin nashego vremeni". While only a very poor imitation of Pushkin's poetry, it does testify to Kulish's lifelong enthusiasm for the Russian poet. Historical fiction—novels, *povesti*, and stories—continued to be his major mode.

Kulish's renown on the all-Russian scene rested on his historical and critical efforts, with the Ukraine the focus in each field. Apart from the *Notes on the South of Rus'*, his major historical works were the three-volume *History of the Reunification of Rus'* (Istoriya vozsoedineniya Rusi, 1874, 1877) and *The Secession of the Ukraine from Poland* (Otpadenie Malorossii ot Pol'shi, 1888, 1889). In the large gamut of his literary scholarship, his biography of Gogol (1852, 1854, 1856) and his publication of Gogol's works and letters (1857, 1858) are major achievements. (He also published Shevchenko, M. Vovchok and other Ukrainian writers.) Of particular significance, too, are his articles (mainly in *Osnova*) on the interrelation of literature and folklore, and, even more, his very important study of the interrelation of Ukrainian and all-Russian literature (the epilogue to *Čorna rada*, 1857).   G. G.

Kuprín, Aleksándr Ivánovich (1870–1938) was, along with GORKY, BUNIN, and ANDREEV, a prominent figure in the so-called ZNANIE (knowledge) group of writers, who published regularly in the anthologies of the same name. Born into the family of a minor official in Narovchat, Penza Province, Kuprin lost his father before he was one and later accompanied his mother to Moscow, where his education beyond the early elementary years was at military academies. During this time he wrote verse, some of it satirical or political, some youthfully romantic, and published his first story, "The Last Debut" (Poslednii debyut, 1889). He then spent four years on active military duty before resigning his commission in 1894 and going to Kiev, where he became a professional writer. Besides publishing his works in newspapers and magazines, he earned money through a wide variety of jobs and gained the experience that, along with his military service, was to serve as the material for much of his writing. In 1901 Kuprin moved to St. Petersburg; his six-year association with *Znanie* began in 1902.

Kuprin's best-known works depict various social ills of his day. In *Moloch* (Molokh, 1896), a novella that helped bring him to the attention of a wide reading public, he wrote about the costs of industrial development: the factory, seen through the eyes of the hero, an engineer named Bobrov, appears to be a monster devouring the workers. The short novel *The Duel* (Poedinok, 1905) represents Kuprin at the height of his powers. Here an attack on the tedium and wretchedness of army life, and in particular on the brutality and uncwhen culturedness of the officers, is skillfully combined with a penetrating psychological portrait of the doomed protagonist, Romashov, himself an officer. Less successful is the longest of Kuprin's works, *The Pit* (Yama, 1908–15). Intended as an exposé of the evils of prostitution, its lack of a strong central figure and the disjointedness of the plot reduce its impact. Still, these three longer works typify some basic traits of his career. He was at his best when he had a strong central figure to provide a focus for his work or when he could indulge his talent for description; plots are usually of less interest. Second, for all that he often writes about the downtrodden or social injustices, few of his works are overtly political in the manner of, say, Gorky. Finally, the three stories roughly outline the curve of his career: rise to recognition in the late 1890s, popularity and literary success for about a dozen years after his move to St. Petersburg, and then a decline that seems to have set in even before the First World War.

During Kuprin's career he wrote many other types of works as well, ranging from factual sketches in "Kiev Types" (Kievskie tipy, 1895–97) and "The Laestrygons" (Listrigony, 1907–11) to romantic tales such as "Olesya" (1898) and "The Garnet Bracelet" (Granatovyi braslet, 1911); from sharply drawn uplifting portrayals of individual figures in "Gambrinus" (1907) and "Anathema" (1913) to grim depictions of death in "At the Circus" (V tsirke, 1902) and "The Horse Thieves" (Konokrady, 1903). Kuprin emigrated to France after the Revolution, but the late stories, most of which deal with the life he knew back in Russia rather than with French settings, rarely approach the level of his best writing prior to 1914. Already in failing health, he returned to the Soviet Union in 1937; he died and was buried in Leningrad just a little more than a year later.

Works: Sobranie sochinenii. 9 vols. Ed. N. N. Akopova et al. 1970–73.

Translations: Lewanski, pp. 282–83.

Secondary literature: V. N. Afanas'ev, *Aleksandr Ivanovich Kuprin: Kritiko-biograficheskii ocherk.* 2d rev. ed. 1972. Aleksandr Dynnik, *A. I. Kuprin: ocherk zhizni i tvorchestva.* Lansing, Mich., 1969. L. V. Krutikova, *A. I. Kuprin.* 1971. F. I. Kuleshov, *Tvorcheskii put' A. I. Kuprina.* 1963. Nicholas J. L. Luker, *Alexander Kuprin.* (Twayne's World Authors Series, 481.) 1978.   B. S.

Kúrbsky, Prince Andréi Mikháilovich (1528–83). The leading representative of boyar opposition to the autocratic rule of IVAN IV (1533–84) and the controversial author of polemical and historical writings. Kurbsky's "aristocratic" vision has been identified by modern scholars with various aspects of Muscovite conservatism, not only political but literary and linguistic as well. Yet as a representative of the "aristocratic party," Kurbsky also shared many views of the opponents of established church power such as Vassian Patrikeev and the intellectual group around MAKSIM GREK.

A descendant of one of the oldest princely families, Kurbsky played an important role as a member of the so-called *Izbrannaya rada* (Chosen Council). After suffering a military defeat on 3 April 1564, he abandoned his post as commandant (*voevoda*) of the city of Tartu (Derpt/Yuriev) in Livonia and joined the forces of Sigismund, King of Poland and Grand Prince of Lithuania. Shortly thereafter, Kurbsky initiated the celebrated *Correspondence* (Perepiska) with Ivan IV.

Kurbsky's reputation as a prominent 16th-century polemist rests in large measure on his *History of the Grand Prince of Muscovy* (Istoriya o velikom knyaze Moskovskom). In this work he not only relates historical events but presents his main political theories, which favor limited princely power and the sharing of governmental responsibility between the prince and the boyars. Numerous other original works and translations have been attributed to Kurbsky, often on the flimsiest of grounds. As regards these writings, the problem of authorship is compounded by the nature of the textual documentation, which reveals a good deal of scriptorial intervention.

Bibliography: O. Backus, "A. M. Kurbsky in the Polish-Lithuanian State (1564–1583)," *Acta Baltico-Slavica* 6 (1969), pp. 29–50. I. U. Budovnits, *Russkaya publitsistika XVI veka.* 1947. Pp. 280–96. J. Fennell, ed. and trans., *The Correspondence between Prince A. M. Kurbsky and Tsar Ivan IV of Russia 1564–1579.* 1955. J. Fennell, ed. and trans., *Prince A. M. Kurbsky's History of Ivan IV.* 1965. J. Fennell and A. Stokes, *Early Russian Literature.* 1974. Pp. 173–90. E. Keenan, *The Kurbskii-Groznyi Apocrypha. The Seventeenth-Century Genesis of the "Correspondence" Attributed to Prince A. M. Kurbskii and Tsar Ivan IV.* 1971. G. Z. Kuntsevich, ed., *Sochineniya knyazya Kurbskogo.* Vol. I: *Sochineniya original'nye.* (Russkaya istoricheskaya biblioteka, vol. 31.) 1914. D. S. Likhachev, ed. *Perepiska Ivana Groznogo s Andreem Kurbskim.* 1979. R. G. Skrynnikov, "Kurbskii i ego pis'ma v Pskovo-Pecherskii monastyr'," *TODRL* 18 (1962); pp. 99–116. A. N. Yasinskii, *Sochineniya knyazya Kurbskogo kak istoricheskii material.* 1889.   R. P.

Kúrochkin, Vasíly Stepánovich (1831–75), poet and journalist, the son of a freed serf, was educated at a Petersburg military school. After serving in the army until 1853, he devoted the rest of his life to literature. From 1855 to 1858 Kurochkin worked at the journal *Syn otechestva*, where his satirical verses and literary criticism were published. Critical acclaim came to him when his translations of Béranger's poetry were printed. The popular poems had three editions (1859, 1864, and 1874). During the latter 1850s, Kurochkin's satirical verses on social and political themes also enhanced the writer's reputation. In 1859 he joined the noted caricaturist N. A. Stepanov in the editorship of the journal ISKRA. In a short time *Iskra* led the field in its genre. With great causticity, the editors made fun of outmoded traditions and reactionary perspectives. The journal's humor was directed at castigating society's ailments, and the seriousness of its satire made *Iskra* comparable to the best of Western satirical journals. When Kurochkin left his editorship, *Iskra* went into decline (1870). In the year before his death, Kurochkin wrote feuilletons for the newspaper *Birzhevye vedomosti*. A collection of his writings was published in 1869. The writer's death was hastened when he took chloral hydrate, prescribed by a doctor.

Works: Stikhotvoreniya. Stat'i. Fel'etony. 1957. *Stikhotvoreniya.* 1962.

Secondary literature: N. A. Dobrolyubov, "Pesni Beranzhe: Perevody V. Kurochkina." In *Sobranie sochinenii* (1961–64), vol. 3, pp.438–54. N. K. Mikhailovskii, *Literaturnye vospominaniya i sovremennaya smuta.* 2d ed. 1905. Vol. 1, pp. 15–20. I. G. Yampol'skii, "V. Kurochkin." In *Istoriya russkoi literatury.* 1956. Vol. 2, pt. 2. ———, *Satiricheskaya zhurnalistika 1860-kh godov: Zhurnal revolyutsionnoi satiry "Iskra" (1859–1873).* 1964.   T. E. B.

Kushchévsky, Iván Afanásievich (1847–76), writer. Born in Barnaul, Kushchevsky was educated in the Siberian provinces before making his way to St. Petersburg in the mid-1860s. Lack of money, however, compelled him to leave the university and take up the most varied occupations. After a time, almost by chance he thought of becoming a writer, and produced a book (published serially in 1871, separately in 1872) displaying all the freshness of a first novel: *Nikolai Negorev; or, The Successful Russian* (Nikolai Negorev, ili blagopoluchnyi rossiyanin). Thereafter he wrote mostly stories and sketches for lesser-known liberal publications of the 1870s, in which he described the poverty of the working classes. But before long he succumbed to alcoholism and died a tragically early death.

His novel, however, remains a minor 19th-century classic. The narrator and central hero, Nikolai Negorev, seeks only his own advantage in life, and in the end makes a loveless marriage merely for the purpose of advancing his career. Much of the novel is given over to a description of the education of an entire generation, both in secondary school (here Kushchevsky follows in the tradition of POMYALOVSKY'S *Seminary Sketches*) and the university: Kushchevsky takes a generational cohort through childhood and youth. Nikolai's brother displays radical inclinations, as does a young woman, Sofya Lokhova, who finds Nikolai attractive. But Nikolai does not share their dedication: he is entirely too unfanatic, too humorous, too tolerant of human frailty to adopt their doctrinaire point of view. The novel has a vigor and charm—one can find no more precise word—which have commended it to generations of Russian readers.

Works: Nikolai Negorev ili blagopoluchnyi rossiyanin. 1958.
Translations: Nikolai Negorev; or, The Successful Russian. Trans. D. and B. Costello. 1967.   C. A. M.

Kúshner, Aleksándr Semyónovich (1936–), contemporary poet, was born in Leningrad, graduated from a pedagogical institute in 1959, and for ten years taught literature in night school. He was first published in 1957. Even his first collections showed a marked tendency to write about the simple, the everyday, the dim, and the unobtrusive ("The Carafe"—Grafin, "Two Boys"—Dva mal'chika). In this, Kushner differed from the poets of the avant-garde of the period of Khrushchevian liberalism (VOZNESENSKY, EVTUSHENKO, etc.). Among his contemporaries, Kushner stood out for precision of poetic finish, variety of intonations, and at the same time, simplicity of metaphor. He clearly favored the use of epithet in the creation of visual-sensual imagery. However, the mundane and everyday quality of Kushner's verses is in fact multidimensional and philosophically profound. "It's all a matter of foreshortening," said the poet himself ("There's a rainbow in your eyelashes").

In the 1970s, the "Petersburg theme" visibly grows in Kushner's poetry ("Day"—Den', "Garden"—Sad, "Canal"—Kanal) and eventually becomes its dominant. Through visual images of the city (its Summer Garden, the Neva, Gumilyov's "Crazed Streetcar") and the city's heroes, as imagined by the poet (ZHUKOVSKY, CHAADAEV, and perhaps DOSTOEVSKY and MANDELSHTAM—"The Neva Delta is Sloping," "The City is Unprecedentedly Weary," etc.), Kushner seeks to master the "chaos" of the world which surrounds him, create order in it, and humanize it. The theme of the "inquisitive double," which appears in Kushner's entire oeuvre ("Lie down

in a Swing"—Lech' v kachalku) balances, as it were, evil and good in our life, and in the midst of Kushner's hopeless, dead pessimism one meets a peculiar kind of consolation: "in pain," "in a sigh," in the very value of life ("Farewell, Love!"—Proshchai, lyubuv'!). Occasionally, a yearning for an unseen and unknown world ("Geography Lesson"—Urok geografii, "In Venice"—V Venetsii ...) breaks through in Kushner's poetry. Kushner does not claim "maître" status, nor does he need to bare any poetic passions. Kushner's poetry will appear occasionally in *Samizdat* and *Tamizdat*. He also writes poetry for children, and has translated the contemporary British poet Philip Larkin, who is apparently close to him. Kushner's creative career is not finished, of course. In his most recent collection, *Canvas* (Kanva), he has gathered the best poems of his preceding six books of verse. The poets of the so-called Petersburg School of the Bronze Age to some extent consider him "their own," although Kushner's connection with the traditions of the "maîtres" of that school (GUMILYOV, AKHMATOVA, KHODASEVICH) is an elusive one.

Works: Pervaya vstrecha. 1957. *Pervoe vpechatlenie.* 1962. *Nochnoi dozor.* 1966. *Primety.* 1969. *Pis'mo.* 1974. *Pryamaya rech'. Gorod i podarok.* 1976. *Golos.* 1978. *Kanva.* 1981.
Translations: (6 poems,) *Russian Poetry: The Modern Period.* Ed. John Glad and Daniel Weissbort. 1978. Pp. 243–48.
Secondary literature: G. Krasukhin, "I razgovor u nas sovsem inoi poshel," *Novyi mir*, 1970, no. 3. A. Marchenko, "Chto takoe ser'eznaya poeziya?", *VLit*, 1966, no. 11.   E. D. A.

Kuzmín, Mikhaíl Alekséevich (1875–1936), poet, prose writer, playwright, and critic who was associated with SYMBOLIST circles, and then close to the ACMEIST school. He was born in Yaroslavl, spent his childhood in Saratov and resided in St. Petersburg until the end of his life. He had a musical education, studied with Nikolai Rimsky-Korsakov, and set many of his own lyrics to music. He attended St. Petersburg University, travelled first to Egypt and Italy, and then to northern Russia to visit Old Believer settlements. During much of his career he was associated with small, experimental theaters and cabarets. After the Revolution he remained in the Soviet Union as a literary critic and died in 1936 of a chronic illness.

He was a prolific writer, but more esteemed in literary and artistic circles than known to a wide public. His genres were often the light ones, and his subjects esoteric. His connections with literary groupings were tenuous, and much of his work remains to be collected in a definitive edition. His youthful travels were undertaken as spiritual quests. On his return he became acquainted with the MIR ISKUSSTVA group of artists and art connoisseurs whose leader was Sergei DIAGHILEV. Through them he came into contact with Valery BRYUSOV and other symbolists and began to contribute to the influential symbolist journal, VESY (1904–09). Kuzmin shared with the symbolists a devotion to aestheticism, but he lacked their mystical tendencies. His religiosity was pious and ritualistic, and it was combined with an epicureanism and a deliberate airiness which were alien to the symbolists, who tended to be solemn. For some time Kuzmin was a resident at the "Tower" apartment of Vyacheslav IVANOV, which between 1905 and 1907 was among the most influential literary centers of St. Petersburg. Kuzmin's association with the Acmeist school came about, also, through personal contacts. However, his article "On Beautiful Clarity" (O prekrasnoi yasnosti, 1910) was perceived by the literary world as one of the manifestos of Acmeism. He was more directly connected with APOLLON, the Acmeist journal, than he had been with *Vesy*. But his work was most closely associated with the world of little theaters, and particularly with the cabaret *Brodyachaya sobaka* (The Stray Dog).

Kuzmin's reputation has rested primarily on his poetry, whose typical subjects are intimate moods, cultural reflections, and erotic, sometimes homosexual, attachments. Influences on his early work were his study of Plotinus and the poetry of *Sturm und Drang*; he valued especially the mystic aestheticism of Johann Georg Hamann. His first collection, *Nets* (Seti, 1908) includes a well-known cycle called "Alexandrian Songs" (Aleksandriiskie pesni) which are stylized pieces set in antiquity and often invoking a homosexual love. They raised a controversy around Kuzmin and probably restricted the subsequent sphere of his influence. Their free verse is an example of his rhythmic versatility and inventiveness. Next, Kuzmin set to music some poems written earlier in the style of 18th-century pastorals and published them in *The Carillon of Love* (Kuranty lyubvi, 1910). Subsequent collections were *Lakes in Autumn* (Osennie ozera, 1912) which is a high point in his idealization of homosexual love, and *Clay Doves* (Glinyanye golubki, 1914). A series of small books followed whose themes were by now familiar: *The Guide* (Vozhatyi, 1918); *To the Pair* (Dvum, 1918); *Echo* (Ekho, 1921) and *Draped Pictures* (Zanaveshennye kartinki, 1920), a frivolous piece of erotica which he had intended to remain private. In *Unearthly Evenings* (Nezdeshnie vechera, 1923) metaphysical concerns, latent since youth, and his studies of Plotinus, again came to the fore, now in connection with perceptions of transience and aging. *Parabolas* (Paraboly, 1923), whose experimental technique has caused it to be compared with French surrealism, has art rather than love as its subject. After *A New Carousal* (Novyi gul', 1924), a narrative structure made up of separate lyrics, came the book he considered his masterpiece, *The Trout Breaks the Ice* (Forel' razbivaet led, 1929), an autobiographical work in which the separate poems can be related to form a reasonably coherent story of homosexual love, betrayal, and reconciliation.

Although Kuzmin's prose is generally less significant than his poetry, his initial reputation owed much to his first novella, *Wings* (Kryl'ya, 1907); it is set in St. Petersburg and Italy and concerned with the cultural role of homosexuality in the past and present. Next came an adventure story called *The Adventures of Aimé Leboeuf* (Priklyucheniya Eme Lebefa, 1907), which is set in 18th-century France and concerns libertinism. Three collections of stories appeared between 1910 and 1913. In 1915 came *War Stories* (Voennye rasskazy), and finally *Travellers by Sea and by Land* (Plavayushchie-puteshestvuyushchie, 1915) which is a veiled story of bohemian life centered around the café *Brodyachaya sobaka*.

His plays, which appeared between 1907 and 1921, are all comedies. Several have historical, pseudo-religious settings, including *On Alexis, Man of God* (O Aleksee cheloveke bozh'em, 1907). His *Venetian Madmen* (Venetsianskie bezumtsy, 1915) is set in the 18th century and evokes the atmosphere of carnival.

Kuzmin was a virtuoso craftsman who has suffered in reputation from a lack of any affiliations to a school, from a suspicion of hedonism, and for his brief for homosexuality.

Works: Sobranie sochinenii. 9 vols. 1914–18. *Sobranie stikhov.* Ed. John E. Malmstad and Vladimir Markov. 3 vols. Munich, 1977–78.

Translations: Modern Russian Poetry. Ed. Vladimir Markov and Merrill Sparks, 1967. Pp. 206–33. *Wings. Prose and Poetry.* Trans. Neil Granoien and Michael Green. Ann Arbor, 1972. *Selected Prose and Poetry.* Ed. and trans. Michael Green. Ann Arbor, 1979.

Secondary literature: Joachim T. Baer, "Mikhail Kuzmin's *Aleksandrijskie Pesni*," *South Atlantic Bulletin* 41 (1976), no. 1, pp. 22–31. M. Green, "Mikhail Kuzmin and the Theater," *RLT* 7 (1973), pp. 246–66. S. Karlinsky, "Death and Resurrection of Mikhail Kuzmin," *SlavR* 38 (1979), pp. 92–96. John E. Malmstad, "Mixail Kuzmin. A Chronicle of His Life and Times." In *Sobranie stikhov.* Vol. 3. Pp. 9–319. Vladimir Markov, "Poeziya Mikhaila Kuzmina," In *Sobranie stikhov.* Vol. 3. Pp. 321–426.   E. Br.

Kuznetsóv, Anatóly Vasílievich (1929–   ), prose writer, was born in Kiev, where he lived through the German occupation. He began publishing in 1946, when some of his stories appeared in *Pionerskaya pravda*, a newspaper for children. Subsequently, Kuznetsov combined his studies (He graduated from the Gorky Institute of Literature in 1960.) with work on several construction sites, specifically the Irkutsk Hydro-Electric Plant. Kuznetsov's first success, *Sequel to a Legend; from the Diary of a Young Man* (Prodolzhenie legendy; zapiski molodogo cheloveka, 1957), based on that experience, was among the works which launched the new genre of the "youth story" (*molodezhnaya povest'*). After several further successful, though undistinguished, stories, Kuznetsov published a controversial novel, *Babi Yar* (Babii Yar, 1966), dealing with the murder of Kiev Jews by the Germans. In 1969 Kuznetsov defected to the West during a visit to London and subsequently published a new

version of *Babi Yar*, inserting passages cut by Soviet censors as well as passages left out by himself in anticipation of difficulties with the censor. Kuznetsov's prose is artistically undistinguished. Its merit derives from interest in its subject matter, which is considerable.

Works: Babii Yar, Yunost', 1966, nos. 8–10. New version *Novyi zhurnal,* no. 97 (1969), and as a separate book, Frankfurt, 1970.

Translations: Babi Yar; a documentary novel. Trans. by Jacob Guralsky. New York, 1967. *Babi Yar; a document in the form of a novel.* Trans. by David Floyd. New York, 1970. *Sequel to a Legend; From the Diary of a Young Man.* Trans R. Bobrova. Moscow, 1959.

Secondary literature: A. A. Amalrik, "An Open Letter to Kuznetsov," *Survey* 74/75 (1970), pp. 95–102. A. Rothberg, *The Heirs of Stalin.* 1972. Pp. 251–67.   V. T.

Kuznetsóva, Galina Nikoláevna (1902–76), émigré poet, prose writer, and memoirist. Kuznetsova left Russia in 1920, and after studying in Prague, she went to France (Paris and Grasse, where she lived with the BUNIN family). Following World War II she moved to the United States, where she worked for the United Nations and contributed to American Russian literary publications. Kuznetsova began writing in the 1920s, in a poetic-lyrical variety of realism (neoclassicism), close to the tradition represented by Bunin. Her most important publications came out in the 1930s: *Morning* (Utro, Paris, 1930), a collection of short stories, *Prologue* (Prolog, Paris, 1933), a novel, and *The Olive Garden* (Olivkovyi sad, Paris, 1937), a collection of poetry. In 1967 she published her penetrating memoirs about Bunin, *A Grasse Diary* (Grasskii dnevnik, Washington, D.C.)

Bibliography: G. P. Struve, *Russkaya literatura v izgnanii.* New York, 1956. N. P. Poltoratskii, ed., *Russkaya literatura v emigratsii.* Pittsburgh, 1972. *See also:* Foster, pp. 669–70.   L. D.

Kúznitsa (The Smithy), an organization formed by a group of proletarian writers, for the most part lyric poets, who seceded from the PROLETKUL'T in 1920. Among the founders were M. GERASIMOV, V. KIRILLOV, V. ALEKSANDROVSKY, and S. RODOV. Their statements at that time suggest that they wished to escape from the theoretical and practical tutelage of the *Proletkul't* and to offer writers "complete freedom in the choice of literary method and style." The Smiths were in full agreement with the *Proletkul't* as to the nature and function of literature as an instrument in the hands of a particular class: "Art is just as necessary for the proletariat as are its army, its transportation system and its factories.... It is becoming an exceptionally keen instrument for the organization of the future communist society." The poets of *Kuznitsa* sang of the power of labor and "the metallic world of machines," and labored at fashioning metaphors drawn from the world of work: "the morn lifts up its brick, the sun." Some of them (GASTEV, KAZIN) engaged in a kind of cosmic hyperbole, including the planets and the cosmos itself in the great wave of revolution. With the introduction of NEP in 1921 and the new emphasis on mundane tasks the romantic rhetoric of the Smiths lost favor, and many of them left the Party in melancholy disillusionment. *Kuznitsa* survived until the liquidation of all independent organizations in 1932.

Works of Smithy Poets: In Z. Papernyi, ed., *Proletarskie poety pervykh let sovetskoi epokhi.* 1959.

Secondary literature: A. Voronskii, "Prozaiki i poety Kuznitsy." In his *Literaturno-kriticheskie stat'i.* 1963.   E. J. B.

Kvítka, Grigóry Fyódorovich (Ukr. Hryhorij Fedorovyč, pen name Hryc'ko Osnov''janenko, 1778–1843), the first major modern Ukrainian prose writer, and one who, like virtually all Ukrainian writers of the first half of the 19th century, also wrote in Russian. Given the bilingualism of Ukrainian literature and society of that time, these works, like the Russian language writings of Hrebinka (GREBENKA) or KOSTOMAROV, or, indeed, SHEVCHENKO, are an integral part of the Ukrainian literary process and, at the same time, of the all-Russian imperial one (cf. UKRAINIAN ELEMENTS IN RUSSIAN LITERATURE). Born in a gentry family in Osnova (hence the pen name Osnov''janenko) near Kharkov, Kvitka's broad literary, cultural, and official activities are tied to the life of that provincial capital: he organized and headed its professional theater, was co-founder and editor of the journal *Ukrainskii vestnik* (1816–17), founder of a beneficial society, a school for women and a public library, chairman of the local nobility council and Chief Justice of the District Court.

Kvitka's Ukrainian prose, the first volume of which was published in 1834 as *Tales of Little Russia, as told by Grytsko Osnovyanenko* (Malorossiiskie povesti, rasskazyvaemye Gryts'kom Osnov'yanenkom), continues on the one hand the burlesque and comic tradition of Kotljarevs'kyj and the 18th century, while expanding it with satiric intent, and, on the other hand, introduces a new sentimental poetics. In Kvitka's own words, his most famous work, the novella *Marusja* (1834), was written to prove that not only the broadly comic, but also touching and gentle sentiments could be conveyed in Ukrainian. Though largely identified with a belated classicism, Kvitka was highly attuned to Ukrainian folk culture, both as literary (oral) source and narrative model (e.g., "The Witch of Konotop"—Konotops'ka vid'ma) and as ethnographic material (*Marusja*). His Ukrainian drama uses largely burlesque and vaudeville elements.

Kvitka's first Russian works (1816–17) are humorous essays mildly satirizing the local gentry. His first play, *A Visitor from the Capital, or Uproar in a Provincial Town* (Priezzhii iz stolitsy, ili sumatokha v uezdnom gorode), written in 1827 but published only in 1840, was used by Gogol as the basis for his *Inspector-General*. In his plays, especially the two parts of *Gentry Elections* (Dvoryanskie vybory, 1827–36); *Shelmenko, Community Scribe* (Shel'menko—volostnoi pisar'), and *Shelmenko, Orderly* (Shel'menko—denshchik); the satiric thrust (a continuation of the tradition of Fonvizin) is much sharper than in his early essays. The Shelmenko plays, especially the second, are significant in that they serve as a transition to Kvitka's Ukrainian works: the part of the title hero-scoundrel is entirely in Ukrainian. Kvitka's first novel, *Life and Adventures of Pyotr Pustolobov* (Zhizn' i pokhozhdeniya Petra Pustolobova, 1834) was stopped by the censor for the harshness of its satire; it was fundamentally reworked and published as *Life and Adventures of Pyotr Stepan's Son Stolbikov* (Zhizn' i pokhozhdeniya Petra Stepanova syna Stolbikova) in 1841. A year later Nekrasov reworked it into a comedy, *Adventures of Pyotr Stepan's Son Stolbikov. Pan Khalyavsky* (1840), a chronicle satire on the old Ukrainian gentry, was particularly well received by contemporary critics, including Belinsky. A separate theme in Kvitka's Russian prose is the recollection of the Ukrainian past, especially of the Kharkov region.

Translations: Marusia. Trans F. Livesay. New York, 1940.
Secondary literature: S. D. Zubkov, *Russkaya proza G. F. Kvitki i E. P. Grebenki v kontekste russko-ukrainskikh literaturnykh svyazei.* Kiev, 1979.

G. G.

Kyúkhelbeker (Kuechelbecker), Vil'gélm Kárlovich (1797–1846) poet, critic, Decembrist, was born in St. Petersburg of German parents. In 1811 he was placed in the newly established Lycée at Tsarskoe Selo with A. S. Pushkin and A. A. Delvig, who became his life-long friends. The intellectual and literary milieu of the Lycée had a strong influence on Kyukhelbeker: he began to write poetry, publishing his first work in 1815. He also experienced the awakening of social and political sympathies and became a member of an early Decembrist circle.

After graduation in 1817 Kyukhelbeker entered the Central Archive of the Foreign College as a civil servant, together with Pushkin and A. S. Griboedov. At the same time he began to teach Russian literature at the St. Petersburg Gentry Pension, where among his pupils was the future composer M. Glinka. He was active in the major literary societies and circles in St. Petersburg and hosted his own circle composed of Pushkin, Baratynsky, Delvig, Pletnyov and others. He was Secretary to the Society for the Propagation of the Lancaster Method of Education; member of the Masonic Lodge of Michael the Chosen. In spring, 1820 he became one of the editors of the best journal of the time, *Nevskii zritel'*. All this activity attracted the attention of the authorities; his friends considered it wise for him to leave the capital, and Kyukhelbeker was despatched as secretary to A. L. Naryshkin on his journey through Europe. Kyukhelbeker's travels, during which he met Goethe, lasted a year

and were abruptly interrupted when he delivered lectures on Russian literature at the Paris "Athénée." The political overtones of these lectures came to the attention of the police and the Russian Embassy ordered him to return to Russia.

In fall of 1821 his friends obtained for him a position in the Caucasus. Here he came under the influence of his colleague, A. S. Griboedov, and the literary group which favored a different linguistic reform than the one led by Zhukovsky and Batyushkov, which Kyukhelbeker had embraced until then. The so-called Young Archaists argued against polished diction, excessive mellifluousness, advocating Church Slavicisms, archaic expressions, and "Russian sounds." Because of a duel, Kyukhelbeker was expelled from his post and went to live on his sister's estate in Smolensk province.

In 1823 he moved to Moscow to publish a quarterly literary almanac *Mnemosyne* (1824–25) with V. F. Odoevsky. The popular almanac did not bring financial success and Kyukhelbeker was again forced to look for employment. In spring of 1825 he moved back to Petersburg. Shortly before the Decembrist uprising he joined the Northern Society. He was unusually active on 14 December, making an unsuccessful attempt to kill the Tsar's brother. Kyukhelbeker's death sentence was replaced by prolonged solitary imprisonment, later changed to exile in Siberia. The diary he kept during these years is a faithful mirror of his existence and the literary world of his youth which he viewed in retrospect. Deaf and blind during the last years of his life, Kyukhelbeker continued to write until his death from tuberculosis, in Tobolsk, in 1846.

Kyukhelbeker was a prolific writer, experimenting in various genres in poetry and prose. He wrote tales, travel sketches, novels, critical articles, and several plays. His early poetry is imitative of Zhukovsky, particularly admired by the Lycée poets; the conventional sentiments and phrases of his elegies and epistles are occasionally sincere, but lack facility and polish. Pushkin portrayed certain traits of Kyukhelbeker and the peculiar accent of unrelieved melancholy of his poems in the character of the elegiac poet Lensky in *Evgeny Onegin*. In contemporary criticism Kyukhelbeker was identified with "The Alliance of Poets"—Pushkin, Delvig, Baratynsky—whose chief genres, the friendship epistle and epicurean song, were widely parodied.

In the history of Russian poetry Kyukhelbeker is included among the Decembrist poets. A mixture of romantic elements and classical imagery and devices and the particular intensity which characterizes his poetry, are representative of Decembrist civic poetry. Thematically they show a sympathy with popular movements of resistance to despotism, love of civic freedom, a cult of heroism; his hopes for mankind are transformed into a spirited idealism and call to revolution: "To Akhates" (K Akhatesu, 1821), "On the Death of Chernov" (Na smert' Chernova, 1825). An important theme of his early and mature poetry is that of the chosen artist, persecuted by society for his exclusiveness and superiority. Kyukhelbeker also perceived himself in this romantic aura of the *poète maudit* as a result of his repeated conflicts and failures, as in "Poets" (Poety, 1820), "The Curse" (Proklyatie, 1824), "The Fate of Russian Poets" (Uchast' russkikh poetov, 1845).

In 1824 Kyukhelbeker published his famous article "On the Direction of Our Poetry, Particularly Lyric, during the Last Decade," proclaiming the need for a change in Russian literature. Under the influence of The Young Archaists, he attacked fashionable poetic genres and their style, which he declared to be an easily learnable technique, a ready-made mold that left the poet no idiom of his own. He condemned the fatuous epithet "hazy," which characterized the elegiac school as a whole; conventional keywords which invited predictable emotions and imagination; regularity of rhymes, all responsible for the monotony and homogeneity of contemporary poetry. Instead he called for an exploration of the resources of the ode, to give elevation to the subject and style that would be based on principles of archaic revival and oratorical strength, stressing the free, rich energy of the Russian language. His criticism, considered basically sound by Pushkin, tried unsuccessfully to break the spell of Zhukovsky and Batyushkov, conveying the right ideas but not the power of example—such as the ode "To God" (K Bogu) and the poem "Svyatopolk the Damned" (Svyatopolk Okayannyi), also published in *Mnemosyne*. The concentrated and difficult quality of his language and labored and fanciful archaisms, produced a style that had vigor and color, but because of the want of regularity and consistency was harmoniously rude and flat. Kyukhelbeker, rather incongruously, brought together Church Slavicisms and colloquial words and expressions, passages of Biblical and oratorial grandeur, and harsh, prosaic, platitudinous verse. One is also deterred by his style in his later works, such as his psalms, also stamped with unmistakable individuality of thought, energy and imagination, but clogged and petrified, lacking vocalic melody, resulting in passages that are rhythmically dead, and clumsy to the point of being ridiculous.

Kyukhelbeker is important primarily as a critic and journalist. He made a not entirely unsuccessful attempt to contribute to Russian poetry some qualities in which he thought it was defective and which were to emerge in the poetry of LERMONTOV and NEKRASOV.

Works: Izbrannye proizvedeniya v dvukh tomakh. (Biblioteka poeta.) 2 vols. 1967. *Puteshestvie. Dnevnik. Stat'i.* (Literaturnye pamyatniki.) 1979.

Translations: "To Alexander Griboyedov." In *The Book of Friendship: An International Anthology.* Ed. Elizabeth Selden. Boston, 1947.

Secondary literature: S. Karlinsky, "Trilogiya Kyukhel'bekera *Izhorskii* kak primer romanticheskogo vozrozhdeniya srednevekovoi misterii." In *American Contributions to the Seventh International Congress of Slavists, Warsaw, 1973*, pp. 307–20. I. M. Semenko, *Poety pushkinskoi pory.* 1970.　　　　　　　　　　A. Gl.

Ladínsky, Antonín Petróvich (1896–1961), émigré poet and writer. Having emigrated in 1921, Ladinsky lived mostly in Paris, where he contributed to SOVREMENNYE ZAPISKI, *Volya Rossii,* and other journals. His collections of poetry "Black and Sky Blue" (Chernoe i goluboe, 1930), "Northern Heart" (Severnoe serdtse, 1931), "Verses on Europe" (Stikhi o Evrope, 1937), "Five senses" (Pyat' chuvstv, 1939), and "Rose and Plague" (Roza i chuma, 1950) show a strong sense of history, but his historicism was not bookish, but animated, lyrical. In some ways he was undoubtedly indebted to Osip MANDELSHTAM, though he lacked that poet's genius. But Ladinsky was very talented. There is a blissful lightness about his rapid *dol'niki* (see TONIC VERSIFICATION). Russia was a mother to him, although he was in love with beautiful, but already frail and doomed Europe. He devoted more verses to her than to Russia. His poetry is tragic, but the tragic note in his verses is often sublated by serene rococo motifs (which style places him near KUZMIN), while his archaism goes back to DERZHAVIN. Ladinsky was distant from the metaphysical and at the same time nihilist Parisian Note (PARIZHSKAYA NOTA), which negated art and culture. Ladinsky had a certain influence on some émigré poets, such as CHINNOV, PERELESHIN, and IVASK. After World War II Ladinsky turned "Soviet patriot." In 1948 he was expelled from France and lived in a repatriation camp in Germany. He returned to Russia in 1955. His poetry was not published in the Soviet Union, hence he is known there only as a prose writer. Ladinsky published two historical novels in emigration, *Legion XV* (1937) and *Dove over the Black Sea* (Golub' nad pontom, 1938), and in the Soviet Union: *When the Chersonese Fell* (Kogda pal Khersones, 1950), *In the Days of Karakalla* (V dni Karakally, 1961), and *Anna Yaroslavna, Queen of France* (Anna Yaroslavna—koroleva Frantsii, 1961). His fiction also shows talent, but has no great literary value. His splendid lyric poetry is still awaiting critical recognition.

Secondary literature: G. P. Struve, *Russkaya literatura v izgnanii.* 1956. Pp. 340–43. Yu. Ivask, "Poeziya staroi emigratsii." In *Russkaya literatura v emigratsii.* Ed. by N. P. Poltoratsky. 1972. Pp. 57–58. In the USSR, only reviews of Ladinsky's prose fiction have appeared (by. V. Inber, V. Pashuto, P. Vainshenker, etc.). *See also: KLE* (1966), Vol. 3.　　　　　　　　　　G. I.

Lakshin, Vladímir Yákovlevich (1933–), literary historian and critic. Graduated from Moscow State University in 1955, Lakshin came into prominence as a member of the editorial board of *Novyi mir* (1962–70). In his studies of prerevolutionary literature Lakshin uses a biographical method, not unlike EIKHENBAUM's. He lays emphasis on the intimate relation between the literary work and the author's life. Therefore he disputes Eikhenbaum's earlier contention

that Tolstoi's "self-flagellation" in his diaries was merely a stylistic exercise. Nor does Lakshin underestimate the complexity of this relation. He believes that the presence of *prototip, protofakt, protosyuzhet* will educe specific overtones of meaning in fiction. However, Lakshin acknowledges that literary scholarship studies life as transmuted in the literary text. Hence he rejects the theory of Onegin's becoming a Decembrist because the text of the novel does not indicate this.

In his articles about Soviet literature, especially while affiliated with *Novyi mir*, Lakshin evaluated both literary works and critics. In a controversy over SOLZHENITSYN's works, Lakshin defended them on their aesthetic merits and their timeliness. (Subsequently, Lakshin and Solzhenitsyn drifted seriously apart.) Lakshin urged that normal working relations between critic, reader, and writer be restored: the critic should shake off the fetters of dogmatism inherited from the time of "personality cult;" he should appeal to the concrete reader; the writer should create works that convey a sense of authenticity of life to a knowledgeable public. Lakshin is one of the better Soviet critics. His literary studies are perceptive and practically free from distorting preconceptions.

Works: Lev Tolstoi i A. Chekhov. 1963. "Ivan Denisovich, ego druz'ya i nedrugi," *Novyi mir,* 1964, no. 1, pp. 223–45. "Pisatel', chitatel', kritik: Stat'ya pervaya," *Novyi mir,* 1965, no. 4, pp. 222–40. "Pisatel', chitatel', kritik: Stat'ya vtoraya," *Novyi mir,* 1966, no. 8, pp. 216–56. *Biografiya knigi: Stat'i, issledovaniya, esse.* 1979.

Translations: "Solzhenitsyn, Tvardovsky, and *Novy Mir.*" In *Solzhenitsyn, Tvardovsky and* Novy Mir. Trans. and ed. Michael Glenny. 1980. Pp. 1–81.　　　　　　　　　　H. O.

Lament. The function of the lament is to express grief in a conventionalized poetic form. The laments are referred to as *prichitaniya, prichet',* or *plach.* While funeral, wedding, and recruiting laments are the most widespread, there are also laments for specific tragic events that may occur in the village, such as conflagrations, a bad harvest, famine, or illness. The texts are improvised, but there is a common stock of poetic images and phrases which are selected by each individual performer and applied to the particular situation. Laments are performed as a recitative; in the north laments are long and have a more developed tradition, while in the south, laments are much shorter.

Funeral lament

Funeral laments are performed by women, usually close relatives of the deceased, but because of the complexity of the performance, often a specialist, the *voplenitsa* (wailer), sings in their name. The funeral ritual is separated into a series of episodes, with special laments associated with each: (1) *Plach-voproshenie* (lament-question)—the wailer addresses the deceased and asks why he has abandoned his family, begs him to open his eyes, and forgive any insults; (2) *Plach-opoveshchenie* (lament-notification)—the moment when friends and relatives come into the hut after learning of the death; the lament describes the deceased's premonition of death, then a description of his death follows; (3) the lament inside the hut as the women hear the coffin being constructed outside; (4) the coffin is brought into the hut, the coffin maker is thanked, the coffin is compared to a hut with no windows or doors; (5) lament on the removal of the coffin—the lamenter asks where the deceased is going; (6) lament on the road to the cemetery—the deceased passes by familiar fields and rivers for the last time; (7) lowering the coffin into the grave—the lamenter promises to visit the grave on ritual memorial days—on various days soon after the death, on the fortieth day, on the anniversary of the death, on "ancestral days" when the elements such as the wind are invoked to revive the deceased and the deceased is invited to come visit his home. Each episode has its own traditional motifs.

Wedding laments

The bridal lament is sung during various prenuptial rituals and describes the feelings of the bride toward leaving her home forever to live with her husband's family. The laments are sung up until the church ceremony, after which the bride must reflect joy in her new marriage. They are performed either by the bride or by the *vopleni-*

tsa. In the earlier rituals, such as at the *rukobit'e* (handshake), the focus is on the bride's difficulty in leaving her family, and she begs them not to force her to marry. As the wedding day approaches, the laments are directed toward her difficult life ahead. There is a certain order of laments within each ritual; for example, when the bride is first betrothed, she first sings a lament to her father, then to her mother, to her relatives, and to her girl friends. Each lament is different. In general there is no development of plot in the laments. The text is composed of an address, questions, repetitions, elements of dialogue, and exclamations. In the north the wedding lament has a more developed tradition. Depending on the area, the wedding lament may be sung to the same melody as the funeral lament.

Recruiting lament

Recruiting laments were addressed to the recruit either by his female relatives or by a *voplenitsa* who would sing in their name. These laments are often sung to the melody of wedding or funeral laments. The texts resemble funeral laments, especially when the lamenter complains of the hard work and difficulty she faces (and in the case of the wife, raising their children by herself) after the recruit has left for his extended military service. The recruiting laments only go as far back as the 18th century when Peter I initiated conscription. A recruiting lament was included by RADISHCHEV in *Journey from St. Petersburg to Moscow*.

Bibliography: Alex E. Alexander, *Russian Folklore: An Anthology in English Translation*. 1975. B. B. Efimenkova, *Severnorusskaya prichet'*. 1980. *Prichitaniya*. 2d ed. (Biblioteka poeta, bol'shaya seriya.) 1960. V. Ya. Propp, *Narodnye liricheskie pesni*. 2d ed. 1961. Roberta Reeder, *Down Along the Mother Volga*. 1975.

R. R.

Lavrént'evskaya létopis', see LETOPISI.

Lavróv, Pyotr Lavróvich (1823–1900), fifty-six pseudonyms, a leading theoretician of POPULISM (*narodnichestvo*), intellectual historian, sociologist, and editor of revolutionary journals. Of a substantial noble family, he pursued a military career, graduating from the Mikhailovsky Artillery Academy and rising to the rank of colonel by serving as a mathematics instructor in military schools. With encyclopedic intellectual interests, he was caught up in the intellectual ferment of the reform period after the Crimean War and became associated with the radical intelligentsia and their organizations. Primarily a scholar, he served as a teacher and collaborator rather than a leader in the populist movement. Court-martialed in 1866 and exiled to Vologda Province, he there wrote, under the pseudonym P. L. Mirtov, his most influential work, "Historical Letters" (1870). Escaping abroad in 1870, he played his most important role in the revolutionary movement as editor of *Vpered!* from 1873 to 1876. With a strong distaste for factional disputes, he resigned to resume his pedagogical and scholarly work. Later, he became an adherent of *Narodnaya volya* (The People's Will) because he saw that group as the guiding force of the socialist movement. From 1883 to 1886, he was co-editor of *Vestnik narodnoi voli* and continued to be loyal to populism until his death. During his years of exile, he was also a prominent figure in the international socialist movement.

A prolific writer in many fields, Lavrov's "anthropologism" was an effort to synthesize scientific, ethical, and social thought into one system. Co-founder with N. K. MIKHAILOVSKY of the Russian school of "subjective sociology," their emphasis was characteristically on the need to study ethical-moral phenomena in the social sciences by use of the subjective method as well as objective phenomena by the scientific method. Lavrov's greatest ambition was to write a history of the evolution of human thought by "critically thinking individuals" who by criticism of the status quo created the new ideals which became basic to the progress of society.

The attractiveness of the "Historical Letters" for the Russian radical intelligentsia was that Lavrov identified them as the key force in bringing social and economic justice to the masses of the Russian people through the realization of agrarian socialism. However, he stressed the intelligentsia must prepare themselves through careful study and then execute their moral obligation "to go to the people" to educate a significant cadre in these ideals. Only when a broad base was established in the countryside could a revolution be successful. Hence his followers were referred to as propagandists. Lavrov opposed premature revolts advocated by the Bakuninists as merely resulting in needless bloodshed and also the Jacobin seizure of power by a small group of professional revolutionaries for he wanted the people to control their own fate. While accepting Marxism as valid for Western Europe, he did not believe capitalism was inevitable in Russia and hoped it could skip that stage, for he detested bourgeois-liberal society.

Works: Izbrannye sochineniya na sotsial'no-politicheskie temy. 8 vols. 1934–35.
Translations: Historical Letters. Trans. James P. Scanlan. 1967.
Secondary literature: Alan Kimball, "The Russian Past and the Socialist Future in the Thought of Peter Lavrov," *SlavR* 30 (1971), pp. 28–44. Philip Pomper, *Peter Lavrov and the Russian Revolutionary Movement*. 1976.

J. A. D.

Lazhéchnikov, Iván Ivánovich (1792–1869), acclaimed by his contemporaries in the 1830s as the "Russian Walter Scott", made a career in government service. He began as a clerk in Moscow at fourteen, then served in the army (1812–19), in school administration (1820–37), as a Vice-Governor (1841–54), and as a censor for the St. Petersburg Censorship Committee (1854–58). His first publication, entitled "My Thoughts" appeared in 1807.

He continued to write and publish to the time of his death in 1869. He tried his hand at a variety of genres ranging from didactic stories, songs, poetry, memoirs, dramas, and novels dealing with contemporary life, to historical fiction including both dramas and novels. Today he is known only for the three historical novels which he wrote in the 1830s, *The Last Page* (1831–33), *The Ice Palace* (1835) and *The Infidel* (1838).

The Last Page is set in Livonia at the beginning of the 18th century during the war between Peter I and Charles XII of Sweden. *Ice Palace* deals with the attempt on the part of Russian patriots to undermine the political power of Biron, the German favorite of Empress Anna Ioannovna, in St. Petersburg in the winter of 1740. *The Infidel* describes the efforts of Ivan III to consolidate the Muscovite state in the period from 1490 to 1505. Like M. N. ZAGOSKIN and most of his contemporaries who wrote historical fiction, Lazhechnikov was a Russian patriot whose writing was influenced by Sir Walter Scott's novels, many of which had been translated into Russian in the 1820s, and by the wave of nationalism that swept Russia after the Napoleonic invasion of 1812.

Unlike many of his contemporaries, Lazhechnikov refrained from direct involvement with politics, and wrote predominantly on humanistic, patriotic, and educational topics. He developed the technique of blending history and fiction into an organic whole by following the precept that the writer may invent or alter historical episodes provided that such changes are essential for the artistic and ideological design of the work, and do not contradict well-known historical facts. He utilized some of M. N. Zagoskin's techniques of "historical stylization of language" in some of his works, but his best-known novel *Ice Palace* has almost no historical stylization. Later it was used effectively by both L. N. TOLSTOI and A. N. TOLSTOI.

Both *The Infidel* and *The Last Page* appeared in only two Soviet editions in the early 1960s, but *Ice Palace* has been published more or less continuously for the past 150 years, and with the exception of GOGOL's *Taras Bulba* or PUSHKIN's *Captain's Daughter*, is the only historical novel from the 1830s accorded this distinction. *Ice Palace* is popular in the USSR because both artistically and ideologically it fits in with the Soviet theory of the historical novel with its emphasis on patriotism, nationalism, and didacticism. *Ice Palace* is a tendentious novel which presents a pitiful image of Anna, the ruler of Russia, but which shows the Russian national struggle against foreign domination, and reminds Soviet citizens of their external enemies.

Most histories of Russian literature rarely give more than a few lines to Lazhechnikov, but if placed in its proper historical and geographic perspective, Lazhechnikov's fiction was an outstanding phenomenon which delighted both the public and many of Russia's eminent authors and critics.

Works: Polnoe sobranie sochinenii. S. Vengerov, ed. 12 vols. 1899–1901.
Translations: The Heretic. Trans. T. Shaw. Edinburgh and New York, 1844.

Secondary literature: Vitaly Wowk, *The Historical Novels of Ivan Ivanovich Lazhechnikov*. Ph.D. diss., Ohio State University, 1972.
L. T.

Lef (*Lévyi front iskússtva*—Left Front of Art), and **Novyi Lef**. A literary group formed in 1922 and made up largely of former members of the pre-war FUTURIST movement, together with some critics of a FORMALIST tendency. Its leading members were MAYAKOVSKY, O. BRIK, N. ASEEV, Boris Kushner, Sergei TRETYAKOV, N. Chuzhak, A. Rodchenko. Among those contributing to its journals (*Lef* and *Novyi Lef*) were V. SHKLOVSKY, Boris EIKHENBAUM, V. KAMENSKY, A. KRUCHONYKH, and Boris PASTERNAK (briefly). The principal purpose of the organization was to institutionalize the alliance of the former futurist avant-garde with the Soviet state, and to rationalize the production of art forms that would serve the revolution while at the same time utilizing the formal discoveries contributed by the avant-garde. Mayakovsky defined *Lef* as the "encompassing of the social theme by all the instruments of futurism."

The encouragement of innovative form in the service of the revolution attracted to the pages of *Lef* the work of many important artists of the twenties: Rodchenko in photography, EISENSTEIN and Dziga Vertov in film, MEYERHOLD in theater, BABEL in prose fiction. The first number of the journal featured Mayakovsky's long poem *About That* (1923), a prolonged cry of protest against the resurgence of the customary and the obvious in Russian life and art and in the mentality and mores of the Party itself. The struggle against BYT, by which he meant fixed hierarchical forms in art and life, was the consistent program of Mayakovsky and of his associates in *Lef*. The linguist G. VINOKUR and the critic Boris ARVATOV demonstrated on the pages of *Lef* that the language of the Party and the revolution had degenerated into fixed cliché formulas, had become a dead language unable to move anyone. During the last year of its life the *Lef* theoreticians developed the idea of literature as a craft and the writer as a craftsman whose activity should be determined by the "social demand" of his client, the proletarian state. The highest form of literary activity was, according to this theory, factual reporting: the writing of topical sketches, biographies, travel notes, and the like. The fixation of objective facts was to be required of the writer by the theoreticians of "literature of fact," rather than the creation of artistic wholes, which tend to "destroy or disfigure the *fact*." Thus the documentary novel of FURMANOV was to be preferred to FADEEV's plot development. This "factographic" emphasis is perhaps best exemplified in Mayakovsky's newspaper and advertising verse, and it led to acrid literary polemics and the rejection of most contemporary writing, both "fellow-traveller" and "proletarian."

The journal *Lef* ceased publication in 1925, but was revived as *New Lef* in 1927 under the editorship first of Mayakovsky then of Tretyakov. It ceased publication with the last number of 1928. Mayakovsky abandoned *Lef* in 1928, and in 1929 he formed a new organization, *Ref* (Revolyutsionnyi front iskusstva). The new organization, as he put it, would enable writers to devote their activities to "mass organizations carrying on agitational work: newspapers, agitprops, etc." *Ref* had a short life, however, since all independent literary groups were under pressure during 1929 to liquidate themselves and join RAPP. Mayakovsky abandoned *Ref* and joined RAPP in 1930.

Bibliography: *Lef*, nos. 1–7, 1923–25; *Novyi Lef*, 1927–28. E. J. Brown, *Mayakovsky: a Poet in the Revolution*. 1973. Chapter 8. Halina Stephan. *Lef and the Left Front of Art*. Munich, 1981.
E. J. B.

Left art, avant-garde art and literature of the 1920s, created as a manifestation of an "artistic revolution," and aimed at the development of a total aesthetic system which could lay foundations for Soviet culture. The term was initially applied to all non-realistic art practiced in post-revolutionary Russia; later it defined modern art which claimed to have a political function. The theory of left art assumed that revolutionary politics must have its equivalent in revolutionary art, while traditional art should be rejected together with reactionary politics. With the Revolution of 1917, experimental art devoted to formal innovation—such as FUTURISM, cubism, and suprematism—began to aspire to a social function as an instrument for the creation of modern mentality. In rejecting cultural traditions and developing new forms, the left artists intended to prepare ground for the emergence of a Communist culture which was to be shaped by man's involvement in modern technology.

The term "left art," a popular but an unclear designation, may have originated in the Arts Union (Soyuz deyatelei iskusstv), formed after the 1917 February Revolution. Within that organization, Osip BRIK, Nikolai Punin, and Vladimir MAYAKOVSKY formed the so-called left block, a starting point for their later function as the core activists of the left arts.

While the idea of left art received various interpretations depending on the medium, nevertheless the concepts involved existed as a unified aesthetic system. The major theoreticians were Osip Brik, who saw art as a creation of utilitarian objects; Nikolai Chuzhak, who viewed art as a method of life-building; Boris ARVATOV, who developed the theory of sociological poetics; Sergei TRETYAKOV, who created the concept of literature of fact; and FORMALIST critics Viktor SHKLOVSKY and Yury TYNYANOV, who promulgated the concept of the writer as a professional.

The theory of left art developed as a merger between the experimentation with forms practiced by pre-revolutionary avant-garde movements and the theory of the "organizational nature of art," proposed by Aleksandr BOGDANOV, the chief philosopher of the PROLETKULT. The left artists maintained that, while the earlier objective of art had been a presentation of a stylized reflection of reality, the new art had as its purpose an organization of reality in the spirit of modernity, a spirit which was equated with socialism. The innovative, fragmentary form of the new art was meant to challenge and activate the audience, providing it with approaches and structures appropriate for the rational organization of daily life and political activity. This analytic, functional approach allowed the artist to equate his creative methods with the methods of technology and science, while seeing his role as that of a professional, specializing in creating modern forms appropriate for the new Communist content of life and art.

The program of left art was a major step in incorporating the experimental artist into the socio-political fabric of the new state by casting him as a specialist, who conducted "laboratory experiments" in the development of new forms, or a craftsman, who created models of utilitarian objects appropriate for industrial production.

Left fine arts were intially led by non-objective painters, Kazimir Malevich and Vasily Kandinsky, who adhered to the idea of an artistic experiment as a laboratory of colors and shapes. In 1921 the movement became dominated by the CONSTRUCTIVISTS, who abandoned easel painting and moved into utilitarian design. Vladimir Tatlin, Aleksei Gan, Aleksandr Rodchenko, Vladimir and Georgy Stenberg, Varvara Stepanova, Lyubov Popova, and Aleksandra Exter adopted Osip Brik's theory of "industrial arts," in which art was defined as a production of useful objects, "things" formed by applying industrial techniques to art. Unlike Kandinsky and Malevich, who regarded art as a purely spiritual activity, the "production" group, influenced by Tatlin's "culture of materials" and his concept of "artist-engineer," became involved in furniture design (Rodchenko, Tatlin), advertisement and agitational propaganda (Rodchenko, the Stenbergs, El Lissitzky), design of clothes known as "prozodezhda" (Gan, Miller, Stepanova, Popova), design of textiles (Stepanova, Popova), layout and the artistic formation of books (Rodchenko, Lissitzky), and the design of exhibits and propaganda displays (Rodchenko, Lissitzky). In general, however, the left artists failed to realize their models in mass industrial production. As a result, they have often turned to designing sets for theater and to photography which offered a functional connection to reality through journalism.

Related to the constructivists were the left architects, Leonid, Viktor, and Aleksandr Vesnin, who together with Moisei Ginzburg, founded the Association of Contemporary Architects (Ob"edinenie sovremennykh arkhitektorov: OSA).

In literature, the left current was represented by the futurist poets: Vladimir Maiakovsky, Nikolai ASEEV, Sergei Tretyakov, Vasily KAMENSKY, Aleksei KRUCHONYKH, and, in some of his work, Boris PASTERNAK. Also regarded as left were the constructivist poets—Ilya SELVINSKY, Kornely ZELINSKY, Vladimir LUGOVSKOI, Vera INBER, and Eduard BAGRITSKY—who in 1924 formed the Literary Center of Constructivists (Literaturnyi tsentr konstruktivistov:

LTsK) and later competed with the futurists for the leadership of the left art movement.

In literature, the ideal of the production of "useful things" could be partially realized by the poet's direct involvement in educational and political propaganda (agitprop). An example of such an application of poetic skills was Mayakovsky's work for the Russian Telegraph Agency (Russkoe telegrafnoe agentstvo: ROSTA) and his advertising slogans for a department store. Far more, however, the poets were inclined to adopt the "laboratory" approach and interpret their experiments in form as a laboratory for the creation of the contemporary language (Grigory Vinokur). They even found a utilitarian application for the transrational language (zaumnyi yazyk; ZAUM') which they wanted to utilize in creating brand names for Soviet industrial products.

In the middle 1920s, the left theory of "social commission" cast the poet and the writer in the role of a verbal craftsman who would respond to the current social needs and interests of his audience by verbalizing them in literature. The function of the writer was to assure that the new political content would be expressed in a modern form appropriate to the progressive consciousness of the modern society. Since the impulse for such literature would come from the Soviet audience, "commissions" would be of a political nature and the left poetry and prose would become a politically engaged art. The concept of "social commission" as applied to poetry is best expressed in Mayakovsky's essay "How Are Verses Made" (Kak delat' stikhi, 1926).

With the gradual decline of interest in poetry in the second half of the 1920s, the futurists sought other ways to form a connection to Soviet reality and thus develop a legitimate social function for their art. They designed the program of "literature of fact" (literatura fakta), a major effort to change the genre system of literature. The new writing, aimed at the eventual dissolution of literature as an independent institution, projected a merger of literature with journalism, which would offer a precise reflection of contemporary reality with a focus on the conflicts mirroring the birth of the new society. Such a reflection was to be conveyed with an absolute minimum of an aesthetic stylization which inevitably results in a distortion of the subject matter. The focus on "material" was to allow the author to play his social role of shaping the consciousness of reality for the new Soviet audience.

Since several futurists and formalist critics were also involved in film production, film techniques noticeably shaped the forms and perspectives of "literature of fact." The new theory of literature was particularly influenced by Dziga Vertov's concept of "camera eye" (kino-glaz) and his "film truth" (kino-pravda), which interpreted the objectivity and the physical limitations of the camera as the means of standardizing the image of reality and thus created a basis for a collectivist point of view.

The most influential and lasting impact of left aesthetics is to be found in film and theater. In the context of left art, Sergei EISENSTEIN, working together with Sergei Tretyakov in the Proletkult, elaborated a theory of building a theatrical performance from "attractions" (attraktsiony), minute scenes which concentrated the emotions of the audience in such a way as to activate the viewer into reaching appropriate, politically conscious conclusions. This theory, later incorporated into the idea of montage, served as a basis of Eisenstein's film art. A high point in the history of theater was Vsevolod MEYERHOLD's program of "Theater October" and his concept of "biomechanics," based on his belief that the actor's technique and the general technique of the theater are inseparably connected with ideology and must express this connection directly. Meyerhold's "biomechanics"—based in body training, reflex psychology, and technology of labor—was meant to make the theater into a laboratory for the creation of the efficient, physically developed, universal people of the future socialist epoch.

In order to legitimize the program of left art as a valid proposal for the shaping of Soviet culture, the left artists formed several organizations and conducted widespread activity in Soviet cultural institutions. The organizational history of left art begins with the Association of Socialist Art (Assotsiatsiya sotsialisticheskogo iskusstva; Asis), formed by Osip Brik in 1917, and its continuation, Art of the Young (Iskusstvo molodykh: IMO), which was active in 1918 and 1919. Both associations consisted mainly of the futurists, the first artistic group which made the commitment to the new state,

and both had as its purpose the publication and the popularization of left art. The principles of the new art were first proclaimed in 1918, in the sole issue of The Futurist Gazette (Gazeta futuristov), put out by Mayakovsky, Kamensky, and David BURLYUK, who advocated the "democratization of art"—in which modern art was to find its audience through a direct encounter in everyday life. The first organ devoted to the development of the theory of left art was the newspaper Iskusstvo kommuny (1918–19), published by the Fine Arts Division of the Commissariat of Education (Otdel izobrazitel'nykh iskusstv: IZO). In 1919 the same group also attempted to form an organization of "Communists-Futurists" (Kommunisty-futuristy; Komfut), planned as a body which would design the culture of the new state along with the Communist Party which was to shape Russia's sociopolitical system. Komfut was led by Boris Kushner and Osip Brik, the latter nominated as the leader of the Komfut institute devoted to the development of the new culture based on the avant-garde aesthetics. However, when this group attempted to incorporate itself into the Party as an independent but connected organization, the Party turned down the request.

Left art experienced its highest popularity in the immediate post-revolutionary years, when it was promoted, almost to the exclusion of all other artistic currents, by institutions such as IZO, Petrograd Free Studios (Svobodnye masterskie; Svomas), Higher Technical-Artistic Studios (Vysshie khudozhestvennye masterskie; Vkhutemas); Academy of Artistic Culture (Institut khudozhestvennoi kul'tury, Inkhuk), and by the theatrical workshops of the Proletkult. But in 1920 LENIN sharply criticized the left artists' involvement in Soviet cultural institutions and subsequently their activities were curtailed. Three years later, they formed a new organization—the Left Front of the Arts (Levyi front iskusstv; LEF), which attempted to refine the principles of left aesthetics and to unite left artists in order to give them voice in Soviet cultural politics.

Lef existed as a loose association of futurist poets, constructivist artists, and formalist critics, occasionally joined by the constructivist poets, film-maker Dziga Vertov, and Sergei Eisenstein, then a theater director. Their journal Lef (1923–25) saw itself as a futurist-formalist organ, expressing also the interest of Inkhuk and Meyerhold's State Theatrical Institute (Gosudarstvennyi teatral'nyi institut; Gitis).

The idea of a common front of leftist artistic forces was essentially abandoned in 1925 when a convention of leftist groups, frustrated by difficulties in legitimizing the avant-garde in the Soviet state, failed to agree on the organizational character of their association. In 1927, the futurist core of Lef reappeared as an organization and began publishing a journal New Lef (Novyi Lef, 1927–28), which attempted to reorient left art toward the immediate sociopolitical reality. Narrower than Lef in the spectrum of the media which it covered, New Lef was devoted mainly to prose, literary criticism, film, and photography.

In 1928, Mayakovsky, who had officially acted as the leader of Lef, stepped down as the editor of New Lef and subsequently left the organization. In 1929, together with some other members of Lef (Brik, Aseev, Rodchenko), he organized the Revolutionary Front of the Arts (Revolyutsionnyi front iskusstv; Ref). Political pressures at the time of the cultural revolution forced the group to disband almost immediately and in 1930 Mayakovsky entered the Russian Association of Proletarian Writers (Rossiiskaya assotsiatsiya proletarskikh pisatelei: RAPP), thus giving up the idea of a separate avant-garde organization.

Although the left artists failed to establish the avant-garde as an equal partner in Soviet cultural politics, they succeeded in propagandizing their conviction that the new Soviet society required a functional, formally innovative art which would find its natural application in the process of industrial production and in everyday life of the state. Still, the Soviet government consistently refused to acknowledge their proposals for the social function of art and to grant legitimacy to their program.

From the time of their initial attempt to shape the Soviet culture through Komfut to their ultimate withdrawal from the scene, they were rebuffed by Lenin and his Commissar of Education Anatoly LUNACHARSKY, attacked by the proletarian writers, and criticized by the leading official journal KRASNAYA NOV'. Although in 1923, after the introduction of the New Economic Policy (Novaya ekonomicheskaya politika; NEP), the cultural administration, in an attempt to counteract pro-bourgeois sentiments, had given some support to the left art movement, by 1925, *Lef*, which was then representing left artists, failed to obtain recognition as a Communist group and was officially classified as a FELLOW TRAVELER (*poputchiki*) association. In the second half of the 1920s, the left artists put themselves still further in the service of the state by attempting to incorporate left art into the daily press, but did not manage to obtain official recognition for the program of "literature of fact." Ultimately, the aesthetics of left art lost all cultural-political impact with the introduction of SOCIALIST REALISM in 1934, which offered an official system for the formation of Soviet culture.

Since the late 1960s, left art has found a new appreciative audience in the West and has obtained a wide recognition as the most perfect artistic embodiment of Soviet revolutionary ideals. In the Soviet Union, despite a minor revival of interest, the left art theories are considered deviationist in the context of Marxist aesthetics.

Bibliography: Stephen Bann, ed., *The Tradition of Constructivism.* 1974. Vahan D. Barooshian, *Brik and Mayakovsky.* (Slavic Printings and Reprintings, 301.) The Hague, 1978. Stephanie Barron and Maurice Tuchman, eds., *The Avant-Garde in Russia 1910–1930: New Perspectives.* 1980. John Bowlt, ed., *Russian Art of the Avant-Garde: Theory and Criticism, 1902–1934.* 1976. Miroslav Drozda and Milan Hrala, *Dvacátá léta sovětské literární kritiky* (LEF-RAPP-Pereval). (Acta Universitatis Carolinae, Philologica Monographia, 20.) Prague, 1968. Gernot Erler et al., eds., *Von der Revolution zum Schriftstellerkongress: Entwicklungsstrukturen und Funktionsbestimmungen der russischen Literatur und Kultur zwischen 1917 und 1934.* (Veröffentlichungen der Abteilung für slavische Sprachen und Literaturen des Osteuropa-Instituts an der Freien Universität Berlin, 47.) Wiesbaden, 1979. Camilla Grey, *The Russian Experiment in Art: 1863–1922.* 2d ed. 1970. Bengt Jangfeldt. *Majakovskij and Futurism 1917–1921.* (Stockholm Studies in Russian Literature, 5.) Stockholm, 1976. Christian Mailand-Hansen, *Mejerhol'ds Theaterästhetik in den 1920er Jahren—ihr theaterpolitischer und kulturideologischer Kontext.* (Das slavische Institut der Universität Kopenhagen, Studier 8.) Kopenhagen, 1980. Vladimir Markov, *Russian Futurism: A History.* 1968. Anatolii Mazaev, *Kontseptsiya "proizvodstvennogo iskusstva" 20-kh godov: Istoriko-kriticheskii ocherk.* 1975. Fritz Mierau, *Erfindung und Korrektur: Tretjakows Asthetik der Operativität.* Berlin (GDR), 1976. Halina Stephan, *"Lef" and the Left Front of the Arts.* (Slavistische Beiträge, 142.) Munich, 1981. Boris Thomson, *Lot's Wife and the Venus of Milo: Conflicting Attitudes to the Cultural Heritage in Modern Russia.* 1978. Robert C. Williams, *Artists in Revolution: Portraits of the Russian Avant-garde, 1905–1925.* 1977. Gerd Wilbert, *Entstehung und Entwicklung des Programms der "Linken" Kunst und der "Linken Front der Künste" (LEF): Zum Verhältnis von künstlerischer Intelligenz und sozialistischer Revolution in Sowjetrussland.* (Marburger Abhandlungen zur Geschichte und Kultur Osteuropas, 13.) Giessen, 1976. Kestutis P. Zygas, *Form Follows Form: Source Imagery of Constructivist Architecture, 1917–1925.* (Studies in Fine Arts; the Avant-Garde, 15). Ann Arbor, 1981.   H. St.

Legends, see APOCRYPHA, FOLK SONG, FOLKTALES.

Leikin, Nikolaí Aleksándrovich (1841–1906), journalist and writer, came from the merchant class of St. Petersburg, a milieu which appears in most of his numerous novels, stories, and plays. Leikin's satirical, but inoffensive humor, whose butt is usually the rank ignorance and smug boorishness of well-to-do Russian businessmen, is often amusing, for instance, when a semiliterate Russian merchant and his slightly more genteel spouse explore Western Europe on a trip to the Paris World's Fair in *Our Folk Abroad* (Nashi zagranitsei, which went through more than twenty-five editions). Leikin was the publisher and editor of the comic magazine *Oskolki* from 1882 to 1905. It was here that young Anton CHEKHOV started his literary career, contributing over 200 stories between 1882 and 1887, most of them rather in the manner of Leikin.

Works: See Istoriya russkoi literatury XIX v. Bibliograficheskii ukazatel'. Ed. K. D. Muratova. 1962.

Secondary literature: L. Myshkovskaya, *Chekhov i yumoristicheskie zhurnaly 80-kh gg.* 1929. V. Rodionova, *A. P. Chekhov i yumor-*

isticheskaya zhurnalistika 80-kh gg. (Uchenye zapiski Moskovskogo pedagogicheskogo instituta im. V. I. Lenina. Vol. 115.) 1957. M. E. Saltykov-Shchedrin, "Povesti, rasskazy i dramaticheskie sochineniya N. A. Leikina" (1871), *Sobranie sochinenii* (1965–77), Vol. 9, pp. 421–25.   V. T.

Lelévich, G. (Labori Gilelevich Kalmanson, 1901–45), a critic and a poet notable chiefly as a literary theorist and organizer active in the proletarian movement. As early as 1917 Lelevich began writing lyrics describing and celebrating the revolutionary struggle, seen from the uncomplicated viewpoint of a devoted teenager. As a critic and theorist Lelevich was a sectarian supporter of a cultural revolution, and argued for the production of a proletarian literature free of contamination by "bourgeois" influences and exercising "hegemony" in the literary world. He represented, along with S. RODOV and B. Volin, the radical extreme in VAPP and RAPP, and he bitterly opposed the official policy of publishing talented writers in spite of their "class" affiliation. In the political struggles of the twenties Lelevich was clearly in opposition to the Party leadership, and may have been a member of the TROTSKY-Zinoviev opposition group. In 1937 he was labelled an enemy of the people and disappeared at that time. He was rehabilitated posthumously.

Works: Na literaturnom postu. Stat'i i zametki, Tver', 1924. "Stikhi raznykh let (s avtobiografiei)." In *Antologiya proletarskoi literatury.* 1924.
Secondary literature: V. Polonskii. *Marksizm i kritika.* 1927.
    E. J. B.

Lénin, Vladímir Ilyích (1870–1924) and literature. Lenin, the founder of Communism and first Communist dictator of Russia, was not a literary man, but his immense authority and example have been determinants of Russian literature in the Communist period. Lenin was an intensely verbal person: works of theory, ideology, history and some of imaginative literature were central to him. The meaning, the doctrine of written work was all-important, however, not the form or beauty. He inherited a complex of German romantic left convictions: that literature evolves in stages which reflect the economic and class development of each nation, that writers first perceive philosophical and social reality and by expressing it crystallize emerging phases of consciousness and move classes and nations; that the revolutionary movement must wage ideological and literary struggle to enlist the educated and the creative as well as the masses. He admired and was sentimentally moved by Shakespeare, Goethe, and Beethoven, not by any Frenchman. Of Russians he most praised PUSHKIN, GOGOL, TOLSTOI (whom he wrote about) and GORKY. He did not admire DOSTOEVSKY, and stated that he had been converted to revolution by CHERNYSHEVSKY's *What is to be Done?* Lenin's consequent belief was that since intellect and literature could move nations, Communist political and literary censorship would be necessary to safeguard his rule. Inspired by romantic-realist poems and novels of the 19th century, Lenin was puzzled and repelled by the SYMBOLIST and MODERNIST cultural movements of his own lifetime, and judged them reactionary flights from reality. All these convictions became baselines of future Communist policy on culture everywhere.

Lenin's own writings are graceless but vigorous in invective. His most ambitious work is *Materialism and Empirio-Criticism* (1907), a polemic against non-materialist philosophers. His most moving work, perhaps, is the incomplete *State and Revolution,* written in the exhilarating summer of 1917. In the years 1917 to 1919 Lenin's many speeches to Party groups and to the people, though inferior to TROTSKY's, moved millions to action, because of his position, program, and intensity. During his stormy rule, 1917 to 1922, he appointed LUNACHARSKY People's Commissar of Education, laid the foundations of future socialist culture, and used MAYAKOVSKY in the cause though he couldn't understand his poems. Although opposition writers were severely repressed and some poets (e.g., GUMILYOV) were shot, in retrospect Lenin's régime was milder than Stalin's in culture as in politics.

Works: Polnoe sobranie sochinenii. 5th ed. 55 vols. 1958–65. *O literature i iskusstve.* 2d ed. 1960.
Translations: Collected Works. 4th ed. 46 vols. Moscow, 1960–78.

Secondary literature: B. Byalik, "Osoboe zerkalo iskusstva: Perechityvaya stat'i V. I. Lenina o L. N. Tolstom," *VLit* 20 (1976), no. 7, pp. 113–44. V. V. Gorbunov, *V. I. Lenin i Proletkul't.* 1974. *Lenin i voprosy literaturovedeniya.* 1961. Adam Ulam, *The Bolsheviks.* 1965.

F. B. R.

Leónov, Leoníd Maksímovich (1899–   ), novelist and playwright was born in Moscow. His father, of peasant stock, was a self-educated poet and radical journalist who was exiled permanently to Archangel in 1910 for publishing subversive literature. Leonov attended a Moscow gymnasium from 1910 to 1918 and then moved to Archangel to work on his father's newspaper. In 1918 Archangel fell under Allied occupation, and when it was recaptured by the Bolsheviks in 1920 Leonov volunteered for service in the Red Army. He worked on a divisional newspaper in the Ukraine and was demobilized in 1921. In 1922 he published his first short story "Buryga."

His early stories, experiments in language and form, showed unusual facility in assimilating current styles—ORNAMENTAL PROSE, the SKAZ, the influences of GOGOL, LESKOV, REMIZOV, BELY, SALTYKOV-SHCHEDRIN, and DOSTOEVSKY. His most important stories of 1922–23 dealt with the impact of the Revolution on various social classes. "The Breakup of Petushikha" has to do with the clergy and the peasantry; "The Memoirs of Kovyakin" with the provincial intelligentsia; and his most important early (and very Dostoevskian) story, "The End of a Petty Man," with the Moscow intelligentsia. These stories record a picturesque yet doomed way of life as well as the violence and pain inflicted by the Revolution on the uncomprehending "little man," who is treated with much sympathy.

Leonov's first and most popular novel *The Badgers* (1924) is concerned with the antagonism between village and city during the NEP period. It describes a peasant revolt against Red Army grain collectors. The novel is panoramic, loosely structured, rich in anecdotes, and especially successful in its portrayal of the old trading quarter of Zaryadie in Moscow. The most interesting of the anecdotes is the satirical peasant tale of the giant king Kalafat, a rationalist who builds a tower to heaven so he can label and classify the stars, but as he climbs the tower it sinks under his great weight, so that he does not progress at all.

In 1927 Leonov described classical Russian literature as having that sense of moral complexity which he sought in his own work—"the literature of Everyman without his attachment to the transient conditions of his age, (which) serve only as material for creating a lasting picture of man on earth." And it was Dostoevsky, Leonov declared, who best embodied this aim.

Leonov's second novel *The Thief* (1927) clearly shows Dostoevsky's influence in its theme and concern for the darker recesses of the soul. It is about a civil war hero, Mitka Vekshin, who suffers a traumatic spiritual experience in killing a White Guard officer in cold blood. He is also disillusioned by the Bolshevik retreat from idealism in the NEP period. He degenerates into a leader of thieves. In shame and suffering he expiates his decline and works his way up as a Bolshevik leader. This was an interesting if unsuccessful effort to impart moral complexity to the static, stereotyped picture of the iron-willed Bolshevik. Leonov was more successful in dealing with social types like the "eternal" bureaucrat Chikelyov and the fallen aristocrat Manyukin. He also included an alter ego, the writer Firsov, who defends the autonomy of the author against anticipated Soviet criticism of *The Thief.*

With the advent of the First Five-Year Plan in 1928, Leonov, like other FELLOW TRAVELERS, moved from sympathetic neutrality to active support of the Soviet regime. His visit to Maksim GORKY in Italy in 1927 may have played a role. In less than a year he dashed off the novel *Soviet River* (Sot', 1930) about the construction of a paper factory. In hastening to publish this first social-command novel Leonov was probably hoping to set up an artistic prototype before the doctrinaire Marxist critics whom he hated could limit his freedom. He also found the new material and the new large audience a challenge to his imagination. And the problem of the new Soviet man posed in *The Thief* could now be looked at differently. Uvadiev, the hero of *Soviet River,* was a new Adam, not hindered in his audacity by any memory of culture, i.e., the history of past failures. Uvadiev has no personal life and no free time for anything except dreaming of Russia's material prosperity a century hence.

Leonov's "Dostoevskian" reservations about Communism are now expressed indirectly by a saboteur, Vissarion, who rages against rationality and materialism; while Vissarion rages, the Sot' River has flooded the area and cannot be controlled by the most heroic efforts of the rational Bolsheviks. Is this a covert comment on Vissarion's speech?

Leonov's second social-command novel *Skutarevsky* (1932) dealt with a talented individual's attempt to adapt himself to a collectivist society. The novel has echoes of the Industrial Party trial at which scientists belonging to the old technical intelligentsia were accused of sabotaging industrialization. Skutarevsky, world-famous, a fierce individualist, pro-Soviet but contemptuous of Soviet scientists and the masses, races against old age to finish his greatest project—the wireless transmission of energy. When this project fails he is humbled, reassesses himself, and becomes a true Bolshevik. As compared to the young, mediocre Soviet scientists and the gang of saboteurs, Skutarevsky is marvelously drawn. The novel ends on a note of faith that the talented individual (scientist or artist) can still work freely on themes supplied by the collectivist state.

Road to the Ocean (1935) was the first novel based on socialist realism, a formula promulgated in 1934. The novel is intricate, with four separate stories, many characters, and journeys into past and future. The new Soviet man is embodied in Kurilov, a cultured, old-time Bolshevik "with the shoulders of a stevedore and the forehead of Socrates." He is fatally ill, unable to work, but unafraid of death. Stifling his pain and loneliness, he spends his remaining months changing the lives of people and systematically dreaming of the future utopia of socialism, named "Ocean," which will also have tragedy but of a different kind. His personal protest against fate is so muted that he becomes an unconvincing model of the new man. Secondary characters are described more realistically except for some improbable transformations near the end.

During the next fifteen years Leonov wrote seven plays (he has eleven to his credit) and a short work of war fiction, *The Taking of Velikoshumsk* (1944). The plays included the prizewinning war play *Invasion* (1942) and *The Orchards of Polovchansk* (1938). His plays tend to be psychologically complex and he has had repeated problems with Soviet censorship.

In the bleakest period in all Russian literature, from 1950 to 1953, Leonov wrote *The Russian Forest* (1953), a long oblique commentary on the Stalinist period. It won the Lenin Prize in 1957. Vikhrov, a professor of forestry, supports forest conservation measures against his demagogic foe Gratsiansky, who argues that conservation would slow down the tempo of industrialization and is therefore treasonous. In 1936 he brings Vikhrov to trial—a trial which is a savage caricature of Stalinist trial procedures. Vikhrov knows he is prejudged, but fortunately he is saved by the intervention of the Communist Party. (This fairy-tale ending was unavoidable in 1953.) Vikhrov's daughter Polya embodies the new Soviet trait of selflessness but she is poorly drawn. The central symbol of the novel is the Russian forest, representing the continuity of past, present, and future.

Leonov's art has become more symbolic, the style is ornate, at times verbose, the syntax complex, the metaphors dense and precise—indeed, the language alone intimates a new reality, as if Leonov could breathe in the Stalinist period only by the verbal feats of his style and the art of his intricate flashbacks.

While revising all his works for a new collected edition Leonov spent two years making a "new version" (his phrase) of *The Thief* (1959). Leonov's real interest seems to be the expansion of Firsov's role as alter ego; Firsov incessantly speaks of the autonomy of the artist—which is paradoxical since the other changes made in the novel simplify the characters, turning them into black and white types in conformity with Soviet prescriptions. Leonov seems to have made these changes voluntarily. There is no easy explanation of this paradox.

Works: Sobranie sochinenii. 9 vols. 1960–62. *Teatr.* 2 vols. 1960. (Leonov has revised all his works. Original Russian editions should be used.)
Translations: The Badgers (Barsuki, 1925). Trans. Hilda Kazanina. London, 1947. *The Thief* (Vor, 1928). Trans Hubert Butler. New York, 1931. *Sot* (Sot', 1930). Trans. Ivor Montagu and Sergei Nolbandov. London, 1931. Republ. as *Soviet River.* New York,

1932. *Skutarevsky*. Trans. Alec Brown. London and New York, 1936. *Road to the Ocean* (Doroga na Okean, 1935). Trans. Norbert Guterman. New York, 1944. *Chariot of Wrath* (Vzyatie Velikoshumska, lit. "The Taking of Velikoshumsk", 1944). Trans. Norbert Guterman. New York, 1946. *The Russian Forest* (Russkii les, 1953). Moscow, 1966.

Secondary literature: L. Fink, *Dramaturgiya Leonida Leonova*. 1962. Helen Muchnic, *From Gorky to Pasternak*. 1961. Nathan Rosen, *The Fiction of Leonid Leonov*. Ph.D. diss., Columbia. Univ. 1961. *Russkie sovetskie pisateli-prozaiki*. 1964. Vol. 2. Pp. 662–721. Harold B. Segel, *Twentieth-Century Russian Drama*. 1979. Ernest J. Simmons, *Russian Fiction and Soviet Ideology*. 1958. Marc Slonim, *Soviet Russian Literature*. 2d rev. ed. 1977.   N. R.

Leóntiev, Konstantín Nikoláevich (1831–1891), writer, playwright, critic, philosopher, and publicist, came from a family of landowners. He studied medicine at Moscow University and participated in the Crimean War as a military surgeon. He began to publish his fiction in 1854 and received favorable attention. He then embarked upon a diplomatic career, serving in the Russian consular service on the island of Crete and in the Balkans (1863–73). In 1871, following a severe bout with malaria, he made a religious vow and spent a year on Mt. Athos. Soon after he resigned his position in the consular service to concentrate on his literary work. Leontiev's ideological manifesto, "Byzantinism and Slavdom" (Vizantinizm i slavyanstvo) appeared in 1871–72, without gaining much attention. Throughout his career as a writer and journalist, Leontiev was a maverick, whose brilliantly stated paradoxes were so much out of line with the concerns and thought patterns of his age that they met with little reaction, positive or negative. Leontiev's fiction, in spite of its penchant for psychological extremes and autobiographic, even confessional quality, lacks the breath of life and seems oddly detached, quite unlike his non-fiction. His best cycle of fiction, *From the Life of Christians in Turkey* (Iz zhizni khristian v Turtsii, 3 vols., 1876), was based on his experiences in the consular service.

Leontiev's criticism of TOLSTOI and DOSTOEVSKY is brilliant and often apt. In "Our New Christians: F. M. Dostoevsky and Count Lev Tolstoi" (Nashi novye khristiane, 1882) he charges that Dostoevsky's "rosy" Christianity is really heretical, as it promises men paradise on earth—according to the doctrine of utopian socialism and not the Bible. In his lengthy essay, "On the Novels of L. N. Tolstoi: Analysis, Style, and Drift" (1890, publ. 1911), Leontiev makes many just observations which go wholly against the grain of contemporary critical opinion, especially when Leontiev applies aesthetic criteria such as *bienséance*, good form, and style to Tolstoi's works. Vronsky of *Anna Karenina* is to Leontiev a highly positive character. *War and Peace*, he says, is a work of great political importance in that it gave the Russian people a positive self-image, contrasted against that of the French invaders. Altogether, Leontiev approves of the life-affirming epic plenitude of Tolstoi's novels, while disapproving of Dostoevsky's morbid psychologism.

Leontiev published two volumes of his essays under the title *The East, Russia, and Slavdom* (Vostok, Rossiya i Slavyanstvo, 1885–86). They contain his philosophy and eventually made Leontiev a classic, but they met with little response in his lifetime. Toward the end of his life, Leontiev spent more and more time at Optina Pustyn monastery, and in 1891 took monastic vows and settled in the Trinity-St. Sergius Monastery near Moscow, where he died. A brilliantly gifted, handsome, and energetic man, Leontiev, nevertheless, had a very unhappy life and never had a taste of real success.

Leontiev's fiction, such as his *Podlipki* (1861) and *Back Home* (V svoem krayu, 1864), never quite fulfilled the promise of his early works of the 1850s. Based largely on Leontiev's personal experience, it features tense conflicts, somewhat outré and devious psychology, and on occasion a flare-up of immoralism. There is a homoerotic strain in it. The language, though often emotionally charged, is somewhat flat and impersonal. Altogether, Leontiev did not succeed in making his ideas incarnate in his fiction. And yet his ideas were as intriguing and original as those of any of his contemporaries. Leontiev's pivotal conception was a wholly new, biological version of the cyclic theory of history, with each cycle comprising three stages: a first stage of "primitive simplicity," a second stage of exuberant growth and complexity, and a final stage of "secondary simplification" which ends in decline and decay. Leontiev believed that Europe had entered the third stage since the 18th century and that Russia had been infected by Europe's putrefaction. Leontiev's conception of a flowering civilization, for which he uses the term "Byzantinism," implies an autocratic and harsh state, a society racked by intense contradictions of extremes, such as blatant aestheticism and utter contempt for all aesthetic values, fervent religious faith and utter worldliness, extreme cruelty and the most delicate tenderness. In a general way, Leontiev anticipated the ideas of Oswald Spengler.

Leontiev's criteria are primarily and pointedly aesthetic. In fact, he perceives the aesthetic mode of cognition as the most universal and the highest, absolutely and historically. And yet Leontiev's aestheticism clashes with his ethics, as he knows that salvation depends on a denial of the very values which are the object of men's most vigorous and healthiest strivings at their aesthetic best. Intensely aware of this conflict, Leontiev welcomes a synthesizing and fruitful struggle between man's spiritual and aesthetic strivings, in the course of which religion will be refined and elevated, while art will become more spiritual. In order for both religion and art to flourish, this struggle should be as fierce as possible. Leontiev is an enemy of liberalism, tolerance, and compromise, all of which he believes to be detrimental to both religion and art.

Works: Sobranie sochinenii. 9 vols. 1912–14. "Moya literaturnaya sud'ba. Avtobiografiya." In *Literaturnoe nasledstvo* 22–24 (1935). Reprint, New York, 1965. *Egipetskii golub'. Ditya dushi*. New York, 1954. *Analiz, stil' i veyanie; o romanakh gr. L. N. Tolstogo*. (Brown Slavic Reprints, 3.) 1965. *Pis'ma k Vasiliyu Rozanovu*. Introd., comm. and postface V. V. Rozanov. Introd. essay B. A. Filippov. London, 1981.

Translations: The Egyptian Dove: The Story of a Russian (1881). Trans. George Reavey. Introd. and notes George Ivask. New York, 1969. *Against the Current: Selection from the novels, essays, notes, and letters of Konstantin Leontiev*. Trans. George Reavey. Ed. with an introd. and notes by George Ivask. New York, 1969. "The Novels of Count L. N. Tolstoj: Analysis, Style, and Atmosphere." In *Essays in Russian Literature. The Conservative View: Leontiev, Rozanov, Shestov*. Selected, ed., trans. with an introd. by Spencer E. Roberts. Athens, Ohio, 1968.

Secondary literature: N. A. Berdyaev, *Konstantin Leont'ev; ocherk iz istorii russkoi religioznoi mysli*. Paris, 1926. S. G. Bocharov, "'Esteticheskoe okhranenie' v literaturnoi kritike (Konstantin Leont'ev o russkoi literature)," *Kontekst*, 1977, pp. 142–93. P. Gaidenko, "Naperekor istoricheskomu protsessu (Konstantin Leont'ev—literaturnyi kritik)," *VLit* 18 (1974), no. 5, pp. 159–205. Yurii Ivask, *Konstantin Leont'ev: Zhizn' i tvorchestvo*. Bern and Frankfurt/Main, 1974. Stephen Lukashevich, *Konstantin Leontev (1831–1891): A Study in Russian "Heroic Vitalism."* New York, 1967. N. K. Mikhailovskii, "Zapiski sovremennika," *PSS*, Vol. 5 (1908). D. S. Mirsky, *A History of Russian Literature*. 1958. Pp. 339–46. Alexander P. Obolensky, "Essai critique sur l'esthétique de K. N. Leont'ev," *CSP* 15 (1973), pp. 540–55. Nicholas Rzhevsky, "Leontiev's Prickly Rose," *SlavR* 35 (1976), pp. 258–68. M. E. Saltykov-Shchedrin, "V svoem krayu K. Leont'eva" (1864), *Sobranie sochinenii*, Vol. 5 (1966), pp. 454–60.   V. T.

Lérmontov, Mikhaíl Yúrievich (1814–41), poet and novelist, was born in Moscow. His father, Yu. P. Lermontov, was a poor, retired army captain, apparently the descendant of a Scottish mercenary, who claimed his lineage from the 12th-century Scottish bard, Thomas the Rhymer. Lermontov's mother, M. M. Arsenieva, came from a wealthy, aristocratic family. She died when Lermontov was three years old, and he went to live with his grandmother, E. A. Arsenieva (née Stolypina) on her estate in Central Russia. Father and son were forcefully separated by a possessive, doting woman, intent on giving her only grandchild a proper upbringing. This imposed early estrangement from his father, and continuous family conflicts darkened Lermontov's early life and may have contributed to the poet's brooding and moody disposition.

Precocious and spoiled, Lermontov received a thorough early education at home, studying several foreign languages, including English. He also studied drawing and seriously pursued this hobby during his entire lifetime, leaving an extensive graphic legacy. As a boy he made several visits to relatives in the Caucasus; the grandeur and wild beauty of the mountain scenery left a lasting impression on him and were to be the subject of many of his works.

In 1827 his grandmother moved to Moscow to place Lermontov in the Moscow University Gentry Pension. Here he began to write poetry. His juvenile poems are close imitations of PUSHKIN, whose poetry he admired; a strong influence of Schiller and, especially, Byron, reveal his early literary tastes. Lermontov spent the summer vacation of 1830 on an estate near Moscow in the company of a distant cousin and her friend, E. A. Sushkova, who became the object of a boyish infatuation. The memory of this unhappy adolescent love haunted Lermontov for years, producing the need for savage poetic outpouring of scorn and agonized passion. In the fall he entered Moscow University, first in the Department of Ethics and Politics; later, in the Literature Department. During his two-year stay he made few friends and refrained from participation in literary and philosophical circles that flourished at this time, attended by such classmates as V. G. BELINSKY, A. I. HERZEN, and N. P. OGARYOV. His poetic output during the Moscow years was unusually large. In 1831 he fell in love with N. F. Ivanova, who inspired a cycle of poems and a drama, but showed no romantic interest in him, causing the young poet great emotional suffering. His subsequent attachment in 1832 to V. A. Lopukhina, possibly the deepest and most serious in his life, was also ill-fated, but remained a vision of ideal love in his lyrics and prose.

After a conflict with members of the University examination committee, Lermontov left Moscow for St. Petersburg, intending to continue his studies in the capital. In 1832 he enrolled in the School of Ensigns of the Guards and of Cavalry Cadets. These years show little effort at poetry except for some bawdy songs and pornographic poems, but he did devote time to writing prose. His major work was the historical novel *Vadim* (1832–34), which remained unfinished. In 1834 Lermontov was graduated as a cornet and received his commission in the Life Guard Hussars. Like other officers, he cultivated the personality of a cynical debauchee and society dandy, but his unattractive physical appearance, and lack of money and social position were not conducive to opening the doors of fashionable salons. Some of his experiences in the Petersburg *beau monde* were recorded in his unfinished society novel *Princess Ligovskaya* (1836).

In 1837 Lermontov achieved instant fame and notoriety for his poem "The Death of a Poet" written shortly after Pushkin's death in January of that year. The poem, circulated in handwritten copies, indicted court society and the Petersburg elite for inciting the poet to a bloody confrontation. When the poem came to the attention of the authorities, Lermontov was arrested, tried, and transferred to the Caucasus. A year later he was pardoned and returned to St. Petersburg. Now eagerly sought out by aristocratic circles and publishers of literary periodicals as a famous poet, his poetry began to appear regularly in print. In 1840 he published two volumes of poems and his novel *The Hero of Our Time* in book form. At that time he joined a secret political debating society, composed mainly of fellow officers, called by the number of its members, "The Sixteen." In the spring of that year a quarrel with the son of the French ambassador led to a duel. Lermontov was arrested for the second time and sent to a line regiment in the Caucasus on orders of the tsar himself. He distinguished himself in military expeditions and was recommended for awards for bravery, but these were not approved. In the summer of 1841 Lermontov went for a cure to the Pyatigorsk spa, where he mixed in local social life. His arrogant, injudicious conduct and disdainful and mocking attitude created many enemies. A former schoolmate, N. S. Martynov, a frequent butt of the poet's raillery, challenged him to a duel, in which Lermontov was killed 15 July 1841.

Lermontov's poetry and prose, like that of other romanticists, is self-centered and self-revelatory. His early lyrics (1828–36) are intensely introspective, autobiographical, and confessional, a poeticized diary of his private feelings and states of mind. The general nature of these poems is somber and melancholy; usual motifs are isolation, disillusionment, and despair. Love lyrics predominate, colored by a mood of morbid brooding, lonely pessimism, and the painful realization of the impossibility of love and happiness. Love motifs alternate with prophesies of the author's "terrible fate" in "The Prophecy" (Predskazanie, 1830). The poem "When rumor tells you" (Kogda k tebe molvy rasskaz, 1830) marks the appearance of a

"lyrical hero," a strong, proud individual, capable of lofty deeds and bloody crimes. His social sympathies are passionately given to causes of liberty: "The day will come" (Nastanet den', 1831), "For the common cause" (Za delo obshchee ... 1831). He is an avenger against the existing social state, a loner attacking the injustices and corruption of society, but fate-directed to an inevitably tragic, early end: "1831, June 11," "Romance to I ..." (Romans k I ..., 1831), "The Sail" (Parus, 1832). This image of himself that Lermontov had created and which appealed not only to his adolescent imagination but even to his more mature outlook, shows many of the moods of Byron's poetry in vogue at this time which deeply impressed the young poet. These moods are in part cultivated and in part genuine: they reflect his unhappy home life, the desolation of adolescent love, and a feeling of spiritual isolation that was inherent in his personality.

These early poetic exercises show Lermontov's method of using thematic and stylistic "ready-made material" (EIKHENBAUM). He borrowed and adapted tropes, expressions, and entire passages from Pushkin, ZHUKOVSKY, and other contemporary Russian poets, as well as from Byron, Moore, de Vigny, etc., while perfecting his technical ability and seeking his own authentic poetic voice, which is unmistakably heard in such early poems as "The Angel" (Angel, 1830). He used his own material in the same way, collating imagery, lines and passages from old poems to create new ones: "He was born for happiness" (On byl rozhden dlya schast'ya, 1832), "Meditation" (Duma, 1838), "Pamyati A. I. O[doevsko]go" (In Memory of A. I. O[doevsk]y, 1839). A literary practice of this kind was useful for his extensive experimentation with genres: generic specificity, previously dependent on style, became less pronounced and gave way to hybrids and new forms. Thus he infused the traditional lyrical, elegiac meditation with a vigorous rhetorical style, civic spirit, and emotional tension: "The Death of a Poet" (Smert' poeta).

Lermontov's mature lyrics (1837–41) have a more subdued spirit; the emotional excesses and temptation to overstatement are more controlled, as he searched for new forms of beauty and sublimity. The mode of expression is consciously calmer: "I, too, loved in former years" (Lyubil i ya v bylye gody, 1841). But the themes of early poems gain resonance in the poet's later work: "Don't trust yourself" (Ne ver' sebe, 1839), "I write to you" (Ya k vam pishu ..., 1840). A persistent note of melancholy inspired his best and most sincere poems: "It is dull and dreary" (I skuchno i grustno, 1840), "I step out onto the road alone" (Vykhozhu odin ya na dorogu, 1840). The grandiose personality of the "lyrical hero" is less autobiographical, more generalized, as the poet reflects upon his generation ("Meditation"), or is reduced to a romantic symbol in brief philosophical meditations: "Clouds" (Tuchki, 1840), "The Leaf" (Listok, 1841). Remaining a unique and superior individual, the author views society and his place in it in subjective lyrics with a serious moral purpose and civic themes: "January First" (1840), "The Prophet" (Prorok, 1841). The romantic theme of the heroic figure and "the crowd" contains a mingling of personal emotion and realistic observation as he indicts the falsity of the world and voices a new political realism: "The Last Housewarming" (Poslednee novosel'e, 1841).

His later poetry shows greater variety. There is an increase in narrative lyrics; the ballad and romance appear in a new form in which the story is obscured, yielding to personal emotions: "The Sea Princess" (Morskaya tsarevna, 1841), "Tamara" (1841). There is rhythmical innovation in folkloristic poems with an infusion of the popular spirit from folk epic, introduction of colloquial usage, and realistic imagery: "Borodino," (1837), "The Neighbor" (Sosedka, 1840). Nature plays an important role in his descriptive meditations; tempestuous nature in his Caucasian scenes reflects his own turbulent spirit; Russian scenes soothe his mind and serve as lyric mood pictures: "When the yellowing fields billow" (Kogda volnuetsya zhelteyushchaya niva, 1837), "Motherland" (Rodina, 1841). Occasional and album verses lend a lighter touch and sparkle with wit, charm, and warmth.

The general effect of Lermontov's style is a mixture of delicacy and strength: vigorous, dynamic lines and passages with a very fine musical and rhythmic sense, lucidity and exactness of diction. His mature style shows two voices—a tense, emotional, declamatory rhetoric and a mellifluous melodiousness. The first serves his serious oratorical lyrics with civic themes and reflects a directness of phrasing, rhetorical brilliance, polished aphoristic terseness, with specific stress on poetic statement. An important role is played by tropes, particularly the simile; the expanded simile frequently forms the structure of a poem with strong closing lines dissolving into a *pointe*: "Poet" (1838). The melodic style, cultivated in certain genres— romance, air, madrigal—is distinguished by a musical and rhythmic flow of the line, and depends greatly on lyrical intonation and melodic versification; ballad devices lead to rhythmic variety.

Lermontov possessed great technical mastery and ease of versification. His meter is predominantly varifooted iamb, less often ternary meter, with a preference for the amphibrach. The rhythm is expanded beyond the limits of a set scheme to suit movement through a variety of strong phrasing and frequent enjambement. He shows great skill and facility of rhyming: all masculine, all feminine patterns, unusual for his time; frequent dactylic rhymes; free patterns reinforced with masculine rhymed couplets and treble rhymes.

Lermontov's longer poetic works consist of almost thirty narrative poems. These are for the most part tales of adventure with a colorful setting and a lyrical mood. They all revolve around dramatic events and the idea of rebellion against constituted authority. The central character is a melodramatic, violent, proud individual, with a darkly hinted cloud of the sinister, a rebel, renegade, criminal, or fallen angel. Thematically the poems can be divided into two groups—poems with an exotic setting, mainly in the Caucasus, such as "Kally" (1830), "Izmail-Bey" (1832), and those set in medieval Russia, such as "Oleg" (1829), and "The Boyar Orsha" (Boyarin Orsha, 1835). Detail of landscape, ethnographic and folklore elements lend authenticity to specific national character. Descriptions of nature serve chiefly as background for the Byronic hero, are highly dramaticized, and incline to the tempestuous. The lyrical motif of self-representation can easily be discerned in them all: self-portraiture veiled under heroes of adventurous romance.

"The Novice" (Mtsyri, 1833), the most carefully constructed and polished of the poems is a poetic monologue, the confession of a young novice who, haunted by the memory of a free life and nostalgia for his native village, escapes his prison-like existence in the monastery and spends three days alone in the mountains, but loses his way and is brought back to his cell to die. Written in iambic tetrameter, the swiftly moving narrative carries the reader along by its vigorous style, and dynamic rhythm, phrasing, and diction.

Lermontov's most popular poem, on which he worked most of his life, "The Demon" (Demon, 1829–39), tells the story of the love of a fallen angel for a mortal. The Demon is yet another Byronic hero—a solitary, cold, bored, and titanic figure, a romantic rebel refusing to submit to authority, and defiant in his timeless isolation. This is Lermontov's most objective narrative poem, colored with dazzling imagery of the Caucasus, contrasting cosmic panorama with realistic detail of life in Georgia, and voluptuous in its imagery of the seduction scenes.

Lermontov's best "Russian" narrative poem, "The Song of the Merchant Kalashnikov" (Pesnya pro kuptsa Kalashnikova, 1837), is a stylized historical folk song, remarkably authentic in its imitation of the rhythm, diction, and structural devices of oral folk tradition. Set in the time of Ivan the Terrible, it is the story of the unextinguishable love of the Tsar's favorite bodyguard for the beautiful wife of a merchant. Told in an epic tone and with detached simplicity, it is a tale alive with swift action, dramatic episode, and vivid color.

Lermontov wrote five plays. His chief dramatic work, "The Masquerade" (Maskarad, 1835), is the only one the poet attempted to have published and performed, but he encountered difficulties with censorship. The play, written in four- and five-footed iambs, is a scornful picture of Petersburg society with a complicated plot of intrigue and murder. At the center of the play is Arbenin, a demonically destructive villain, sated with the world, contemptuous of society, mysteriously moody. His soliloquies are powerful emotional outpourings of hatred and defiance, in which he hints darkly at secrets in his past and deeds stained with crime. The play reflects Lermontov's own morbid dissatisfaction and quarrel with society at this time and shows his revolt against social and moral postulates. *The Masquerade* enjoys repertory status in the Russian theater and has attracted such directors as V. E. MEYERHOLD.

Lermontov's great reputation rests as much on his poetry as on his prose. He is generally recognized as the creator of the Russian realistic psychological novel, later developed by DOSTOEVSKY and

TOLSTOI. The appearance of realistic elements, characteristic of the poetry of his last years, is first visible in his early prose. In his depiction of the urban setting in *Princess Ligovskaya*, Lermontov concentrated on vivid and sharply observed details of the grim squalor of city slums, "physiological" elements that became an important focus of the NATURAL SCHOOL. In his most important novel, *A Hero of Our Time* (Geroi nashego vremeni, 1837–40), Lermontov gives a detailed, realistic psychological portrait of a Russian contemporary type. The hero, Pechorin, is the "superfluous man" of the 1830s, a clever, strong individual, born with an independent intellect and eager ambitions, but doomed to inactivity in contemporary Russia. Dissatisfied with life, he searches for an ideal that does not exist in reality. Not finding an outlet for his talents, he gives in to a permanent state of aimlessness, ennui, suppression of energy. He is self-absorbed, intensely self-analytical, dwelling on his own feelings and emotions, and becomes increasingly more alienated and isolated from society. Pechorin is the Russian version of the callous, egotistical Byronic hero, with his theme of protest and defiance, his cult of evil and demonism, but Pechorin is also a product of his own national history, political, social and economic conditions, and is approached from a new point of view, as a subject for analysis and criticism, rather than emulation.

This character study is brought about through a complicated narrative structure. The novel consists of a framed psychological cycle of five stories, with a complicated motivating sequence, united around the central character. There are several narrators. Generically, the stories present a great variety: the frame is a travel account, "Taman," a romantic adventure story told in realistic detail, "Princess Mary," a society tale in diary form. Each story reveals certain traits of the hero: "external" sketches show Pechorin through the eyes of others; "internal" characterization—Pechorin's diary—allows the reader to judge the character for himself. In this confessional monologue Pechorin exposes himself with extreme candor, revealing secrets of his private life, describing his multiple changing moods and states of mind, his powerful but transitory passions, his intense self-consciousness, super-sensitivity, positive impulses, all of which are outwardly carefully masked. The tone of the diary is ironic, cynical, and subjective, with stringent wit, a vein that was strong in Lermontov himself. Thus, contemporaries saw in Pechorin Lermontov's self-portrait; a depiction of his own antisocial conduct, contempt for established opinion and decorum, and his own intense individualism.

Lermontov is considered a great master of the pure, graceful, balanced prose style. His novel is rich in stylistic experimentation. Each narrator's speech is individualized: the mocking, lyrical style of the diary; the plain, halting speech of the old army captain; the lucid, restrained, dry prose of Pechorin, the narrator. The glowing lyric descriptions of the Caucasian setting are among Lermontov's best.

Works: Sobranie sochinenii. 4 vols. 1979–81.
Translations: Lewanski, pp. 286–96.
Secondary literature: I. Andronikov, *Lermontov: Issledovaniya i nakhodki.* 4th ed. 1977. A. V. Chicherin, "Stil' liriki Lermontova," *IAN* 33 (1974), pp. 407–17. B. Eikhenbaum, *M. Lermontov: Opyt istoriko-literaturnoi otsenki.* 1924. U. R. Fokht, *Lermontov: Logika tvorchestva.* 1975. M. I. Gillel'son and V. A. Manuilov, eds., *M. Yu. Lermontov v vospominaniyakh sovremennikov.* 1972. K. N. Grigor'yan, *Lermontov i ego roman* Geroi nashego vremeni. 1975. Janko Lavrin, *Lermontov.* New York, 1959. *Lermontovskaya entsiklopediya.* 1981. John Mersereau, *Mikhail Lermontov.* 1962. O. V. Miller, *Bibliografiya literatury o M. Yu. Lermontove (1917–1977).* 1980. Walter L. Reed, *Meditations on the Hero: A study of the Romantic Hero in Nineteenth-Century Fiction.* 1974. C. J. G. Turner, *Pechorin: An Essay on Lermontov's* A Hero of Our Time. 1978. B. T. Udodov, *M. Yu. Lermontov: Khudozhestvennaya individual'nost' i tvorcheskie protsessy.* 1973.   A. Gl.

Leskóv, Nikolaí Semyónovich (1831–95), Russian short story writer, novelist, and journalist. He was born 4 February 1831, at Gorokhovo, near Orel. His father was a legal investigator, the son of a priest, who, on completing the seminary had refused to enter the priesthood. Leskov's mother was of mixed gentry and merchant-class origin. Leskov thus had genetic links to three of the principal "estates," and he later had extensive contacts with peasants as well. The wide range of his social experience became for Leskov an important literary resource.

Leskov's father resigned from government service in 1839 and bought a small estate, which proved too small to provide adequately for his family. (Leskov was the eldest of seven children.) The father died in 1848, having spent his last years in depression and poverty; his wife was left to manage the family's affairs as best she could. Leskov for a time received private tutoring along with his cousins (one of his aunts had married a well-to-do local landowner); in 1841 he entered the Orel *gymnasium*, where he remained until 1846, dropping out before completing the course. This was the extent of his formal education. He first obtained employment as a clerk in the Orel criminal court, but in 1849 got himself transferred to Kiev, serving there as an army recruiting agent. In Kiev he greatly expanded his intellectual horizons through social contacts (an uncle was a professor at the university) and through wide reading. In 1853 he married, most unwisely as it turned out; much later his wife was committed to an insane asylum. (A later, informal marriage also came to an unhappy end after ten years.) In 1857 Leskov resigned from the service and entered private business as an employee of an uncle by marriage, a russified Scot who managed the estates of some wealthy noblemen. Though this employment lasted only until 1860, it involved extensive travels within Russia, providing Leskov with much material for his later writings.

Leskov began to write for publication in 1860, though at first only as a journalist. The journalist's life proved so attractive, however, that he moved to Petersburg intending to become a professional newspaperman. An unfortunate editorial he wrote for SEVERNAYA PCHELA concerning the Apraksin Market fire of May 1862, provoked the first political explosion of his life. Although his intent had been to exonerate the mass of university students from the charge of collusion with revolutionary arsonists (the proclamation *Young Russia* had just appeared, and it was widely believed that the fires had been set by student revolutionaries), the editorial was interpreted as an act of treason against the Left. The radicals' attack on Leskov was so vehement that for a time he was driven into the conservative camp, though his convictions remained those of a "gradualist," a liberal and fervent supporter of the reforms of Alexander II.

In the meantime, Leskov had begun to write fiction. His first story, "A Case That Was Dropped" (Pogasshee delo, 1862) already displays a technique he was to exploit intensively later, the "memoir," half fiction, half fact, whose narrating "I" is apparently the author himself, evoking colorful personalities and events from the world of the Russian provinces. Two similar stories followed shortly thereafter, and a small volume of the three together was issued in 1863. In that same year Leskov published a series of travel sketches from a trip through the Polono-Jewish territories of western Russia and Austria-Hungary. The journey ended in Paris, where he remained for several months, writing there a lengthy survey of the Parisian Russian and other Slavic émigré communities. Yet another excursion of 1863 was a government-subsidized investigation of illegal schools in the OLD BELIEVER communities of Riga and Pskov.

The year 1863 also marked a notable advance in Leskov's production of fiction. Three 1863 novellas rank among his very best works. "The Musk-ox" (Ovtsebyk) is a searching character study of a "rootless" religious dissident, an intellectual. "The Mocker" (Yazvitel'nyi) is the first of several treatments of the theme of the foreigner in Russia, partly drawn from the experiences of his British uncle. "The Life of a Peasant Martyress" (Zhitie odnoi baby) is a grim account of the hopelessly trapped and tragic life of a peasant girl, forced by her *kulak* brother into a distasteful marriage. It was Leskov's first work to display his extraordinary command of non-standard Russian.

No Way Out (Nekuda, 1864) was Leskov's first full-length novel. It is a *roman à clef* in which contemporaries could recognize many leading liberal and radical intellectuals, among them Leskov's friend, the Anglo-Polish journalist Artur Benni, concerning whom he later wrote a separate memoir, "An Enigmatic Man" (Zagadochnyi chelovek, 1870). Other than Benni's, most of these portraits are satirical, and the early 1860s are represented as a "comic time" enlivened by the antics of knaves and fools. Leskov's rupture with the

radicals was now complete; in a scathing review of 1865 the critic PISAREV read him out of all "honorable" literature. Though admitting it had many artistic faults, Leskov defended in later years the historical authenticity of *No Way Out*. In general, however, the long novel proved an uncongenial genre for him.

In the later 1860s, while continuing to work as a journalist, Leskov produced several fine works of shorter fiction, including some of his most famous. "Lady Macbeth of the Mtsensk District" (Ledi Makbet Mtsenskogo uezda, 1865) is a powerful story of sexual passion and crime in the merchant milieu. (It was the source of the libretto for Shostakovich's opera.) In "The Battle-axe" (Voitel'nitsa, 1866) Leskov demonstrated with dazzling skill the art of SKAZ, having the story related in colorful language obviously not the author's own. There were also failures, however, such as "The Islanders" (Ostrovityane, 1866), a bathetic replay of a hackneyed romantic theme. In 1867 Leskov also wrote his only play, *The Spendthrift* (Rastochitel'), a melodramatic evocation of crime and madness.

Likewise in 1867 Leskov began publishing the cluster of works that eventually, in altered and somewhat truncated form, became *Cathedral Folk*, the final version of which appeared in 1872. Though not free of the flaws that beset all Leskov's longer works, it is perhaps his best known. With regard to genre, Leskov insisted that it was not a novel, but a "chronicle," organized only by the sequence of events in time and without "romance." It provides a sympathetic picture of the life of the provincial Orthodox clergy, seemingly under attack from all directions—radical atheists, Old Believers, and indifferent officials, and subject to a harsh and corrupt ecclesiastical bureaucracy. The hero, Father Savely Tuberozov, is one of the most attractive portraits in Russian literature of an Orthodox clergyman.

The author, however, was by no means firm in his own Orthodox allegiance even at the time he wrote *Cathedral Folk*, and only three years later, in 1875, after a second trip to Western Europe, he broke decisively with the Church. Though he never joined any particular sect, he was more and more drawn to radical Protestantism. Repudiating all sacramentalism and "magic," he judged religions by their efficacy in raising their votaries' moral standards in this world. The Orthodox Church, he felt, supinely subservient to the state and with a poor and ignorant clergy, scarcely attempted, let alone accomplished, the basic mission of propagating Christ's teachings. Eventually, after 1887, Leskov was to become a believing Tolstoian, but in fact he had arrived at many of TOLSTOI's positions before Tolstoi did. As Leskov put it, their positions "coincided."

Fiction continued to pour from Leskov's pen. The last outburst in his long war with the "nihilists" was the novel *At Daggers Drawn* (Na nozhakh, 1870–71), even more diffuse than *No Way Out*. It was followed, however, by two of Leskov's most successful stories. "The Sealed Angel" (Zapechatlennyi angel, 1873) is a touching evocation of a group of pious Old Believers, their devotion to a beautiful icon, and the persecution inflicted on them by an obtuse government. "The Enchanted Pilgrim" (Ocharovannyi strannik, 1873) is a vivid autobiographical narrative by a runaway serf who passes through an extraordinary series of adventures before at last finding refuge in a monastery.

In 1874 Leskov undertook another "chronicle," *A Decrepit Clan* (Zakhudalyi rod), this one to be an epitomization of the gentry, of whose prospects Leskov took a pessimistic view. When his editor, KATKOV, made changes in the text without consulting him, Leskov broke relations with RUSSKII VESTNIK and stopped publication. Now on bad terms with both radicals and conservatives, Leskov was hard put to find publishing outlets. Nevertheless, his literary output continued unabated, both voluminous and diverse. *Years of Childhood* (Detskie gody, 1875) is a "problem story" on the subject of education. "At the Edge of the World" (Na krayu sveta, 1875) demonstrates what Leskov considered the hopelessness of Orthodox missionary efforts among primitive tribes in Siberia; it includes one of the most powerful blizzard stories in Russian literature. "Iron Will" (Zheleznaya volya, 1876) again takes up the theme of the foreigner in Russia, this time a German engineer. In "Episcopal Justice" (Vladychnyi sud, 1877) Leskov resurrected from his own memories as a recruiting agent a story illustrating the cruelty of Nicholas I's policy of conscripting underaged Jewish boys. In "The Unbaptized Priest" (Nekreshchenyi pop, 1877) Leskov uses Ukrainian folk humor to camouflage another attack on Orthodox sacramentalism.

The most formidable of all Leskov's anti-Orthodox satires, however, is *The Little Things in a Bishop's Life* (*Melochi arkhiereiskoi zhizni*, 1878–79), a series of portraits of actual bishops. Though some are noble and even saintly, the overall impression is one of pomposity and callous indifference to the needs both of the lower clergy and of the faithful. Though published intact in the last years of Alexander II's reign, the book was withdrawn from libraries in 1884 and could not be reprinted in its full text even in 1903.

To supplement his income in the period of literary ostracism, Leskov held for some years a part-time official position in the Ministry of Education. After 1881, however, his attitude was too glaringly at odds with the spirit of the new reign, presided over by his arch-enemy, Konstantin Pobedonostsev; and in 1883, refusing to resign, he was abruptly dismissed from his post.

In his later years Leskov took very seriously his moral responsibility to teach virtue through his art. He produced a remarkable series of portraits of *pravedniki* or "righteous ones," people who demonstrate that moral beauty and even sainthood are still possible. Among these are "Singlethought" (*Odnodum*, 1879), "Cadet Monastery" (*Kadetskii monastyr'*, 1880) and "Deathless Golovan" (*Nesmertel'nyi Golovan*, 1880). In a more secular vein, in 1881, Leskov produced one of his most celebrated works, "The Lefthander" (*Levsha*), another virtuoso display of the art of *skaz*. Another popular story of this period is "Pechersk Eccentrics" (*Pecherskie antiki*, 1883), in which Leskov genially retells several humorous anecdotes dating from his youth in Kiev. A quite different, somber note is struck in "The Toupee Artist" (*Tupeinyi khudozhnik*, 1883), a poignant evocation of the oppressiveness of serfdom and the cruelties it made possible. "The Sentry" (*Chelovek na chasakh*, 1887) is another moving story illustrating the grim, authoritarian spirit of Nicholas I's reign. The unfinished but impressive "Devil's Puppets" (*Chertovy kukly*, 1890) is a parable demonstrating the corrupting effect on artists of subservience to political authority.

After his "conversion" to Tolstoianism, Leskov placed even more stress on the didactic function of literature. He plumbed the Byzantine *Prolog* (brief saints' lives arranged according to the calendar) for a whole cycle of moralistic stories, slyly doctoring their plots to fit Tolstoian specifications. At the same time many of these stories present with obvious relish lush pictures of antique luxury and sensuality. (CHEKHOV described the series as a mixture of "virtue, piety, and fornication.") Some Tolstoian fables were given contemporary settings, however, one in particular, "Offended before Christmas" (*Pod Rozhdestvo obideli*, 1890) eliciting the rapturous approval of Tolstoi himself. Earlier, in the Prolog-based "Tale of Theodore the Christian and His Friend Abraham the Hebrew" (*Povest' o Feodore-khristianine i o druge ego Abrame zhidovine*, 1886) Leskov had preached a much-needed lesson of tolerance and fraternity between Christians and Jews. Leskov thus demonstratively reversed the anti-Semitic tendency of such earlier stories as "Yid Sommersault" (*Zhidovskaya kuvyrkalegiya*, 1882). In the meantime he had been commissioned by Petersburg Jewish leaders to write the privately distributed brochure, *The Jew in Russia* (*Evrei v Rossii*, 1884), by which they hoped to persuade the government to reduce or eliminate the legal disabilities imposed on Jews.

Perhaps the most memorable and artistically most successful work of Leskov's late years were satires of contemporary Russian society, which Leskov viewed with deep pessimism, seeing little but corruption and folly among the elite and darkness and savagery in the masses. "Night Owls" (*Polunoshchniki*, 1891) ridicules as a fraud (though without naming him directly) the touted Orthodox thaumaturge, Father John of Kronstadt. The title of "The Cattle-pen" (*Zagon*, 1893) is a metaphor for Russia as a whole, sealed off from European enlightenment by her own fatuity. "A Winter's Day" (*Zimnii den'*, 1894) depicts a purehearted Tolstoian girl alone in a degenerate milieu of police informers, extortionists, and sexual perverts. Finally, "The Rabbit Warren" (*Zayachii remiz*, written 1891–95, published 1917) ridicules the pervasive "police paranoia," the mentality that suspects a revolutionary behind every bush. Its humorous camouflage proved insufficient, and no magazine editor could be found brave enough even to submit it to the censors.

Leskov, who had suffered from heart disease for several years, died suddenly on 21 February 1895. His reputation had been somewhat eclipsed during his lifetime, partly because of his political non-conformity, partly because his best works are short stories and novellas rather than long novels. Since his death, however, his fame has continued to grow, later generations being more appreciative of his verbal ingenuity and immense narrative talent. Many later writers, such as REMIZOV, ZAMYATIN, and ZOSHCHENKO, have drawn inspiration from Leskov.

Works: Polnoe sobranie sochinenii. 36 vols. 1902–03. *Sobranie sochinenii.* 11 vols. 1956–58.

Translations: Lewanski, p. 296. *Satirical Stories.* Trans. and ed. William B. Edgerton. 1969. (With a bibliography.)

Secondary literature: Leonid Grossman, *N. S. Leskov; zhizn', tvorchestvo, poetika.* 1945. K. A. Lantz, *Nikolay Leskov.* 1979. Andrei Leskov, *Zhizn' Nikolaya Leskova po ego lichnym, semeinym i nesemeinym zapisyam i pamyatyam.* Moscow, 1954. Rprint. Orel, 1981. H. McLean, *Nikolai Leskov: The Man and His Art.* 1977. James Y. Muckle, *Nikolai Leskov and the "Spirit of Protestantism."* 1978.

H. McL.

Létopisi (Annals). A term which in the Old Russian tradition applies to various types of written records arranged in chronological order (*letopis'*, "writing for the year"). Old Russian *letopisi* may differ in a number of ways from Western annals and their features are better subsumed under the more general and conventional designation "chronicles." The inclusion of heterogeneous materials into *letopisi* frequently means that other compositional patterns prevail over the annalistic format. Entire texts, originally not related to any annalistic account, could become part of *letopisi* without necessarily losing their stylistic and ideological individuality. It is precisely their function as "carriers of texts" that makes Old Russian *letopisi* so attractive to literary specialists. Such a "classic" of Old Russian literature as the *Instruction of* VLADIMIR MONOMAKH (*Pouchenie Vladimira Monomakha*) has been preserved in the body of a chronicle account and nowhere else. Chronicle versions of Afanasy NIKITIN's *Journey beyond the Three Seas* (*Khozhenie za tri morya*) played their own unique role in the textual history of the work. If to historians *letopisi* are important primarily as factual sources, to literary scholars they represent a special type of *sbornik*, that is, an anthology of narrative compositions.

For more than two hundred years scholars have sought to describe and clarify the huge corpus of Old Russian *letopisi* which is known to us. From V. N. Tatishchev and A. L. Schlözer in the 18th and the early 19th centuries to A. A. SHAKHMATOV, M. D. Prisyolkov, M. N. Tikhomirov, and D. S. LIKHACHEV in the 20th century, specialists have focused on a set of problems connected with the compilatory nature of *letopisi*. The same textual material could be used by different compilers in diverse areas and periods. What this means is that one cannot identify the history of the individual textual components with the history of their larger compilatory contexts. Old Russian compilers could not only deliberately reelaborate texts and thereby produce new *redaktsii* (redactions) but could also combine preexistent historical accounts in new compositional schemes so as to create new *svody* (compilations).

The formal classification of *letopisi* traditionally is based on two main criteria: (1) the geographic area in which a given document was produced, or to which it thematically refers; and (2) the local linguistic features of the document. The term *izvod* (extraction) is used in reference to the latter grouping and aims to determine the linguistic provenance of the document.

The research carried out by scholars in the past two centuries has outlined the basic stages in the formation and development of Old Russian *letopisi*. Special attention has been devoted to the origin of chronicle writing in Old *Rus'*. What appears to be the oldest preserved annalistic *svod* is the *Tale of Bygone Years* (*Povest' vremennykh let*, also called the *Primary Chronicle*), which was put together around 1113. The *Povest' vremennykh let* (hereafter referred to as *PVL*) is contained in a number of codices. The most ancient of them are the *Lavrentievsky* codex, compiled by Monk Lavrenty in 1377 for Prince Dmitry Konstantinovich of Suzdal-Nizhny Novgorod, and the *Ipatievsky* codex, written in the Hypatian Monastery near Kostroma in the 1420s.

In some other codices, after the opening words "This is the tale of bygone years" (*Se povesti vremen'nykh let*), one finds the words "by a monk from the Caves Monastery of Feodosy" (*ch'rnoriz'tsa*

Feodosieva manastyrya Pecher'skago). This monk has been identified with Nestor, author of the *Life of Our Blessed Father Feodosy, Abbot of the Caves Monastery* (Zhitie prepodobnago ottsa nashego Feodosiya igumena Pecher'skago) and the *Reading on the Life and Slaying of the Blessed Passion-Sufferers Boris and Gleb* (Chtenie o zhitii i o pogublenii blazhennuyu strastoterptsu Borisa i Gleba). This attribution was first proposed by Tatishchev, who relied on certain manuscripts which ascribe the *PVL* to Nestor in accordance with a later tradition. For this reason the *PVL* is still frequently referred to as the "Nestor Chronicle."

More recent studies have cast doubt on the thesis that Monk Nestor was the author of the *PVL* and have recognized him, instead, as the compiler-reviser of a comprehensive edition of the work. Current scholarly opinion is that in about 1113 Nestor compiled the first redaction of the *PVL*, which has not been preserved. Abbot Silvester of the Vydubitsky Monastery near Kiev is credited with producing a second redaction, which is extant (completed ca. 1117). In a number of codices (including the *Lavrentievsky* codex), after the entry for the year 1110, one reads that in 1116 "Abbot Silvester ... wrote these books of annals" (Igumen Silivestr ... napisakh knigy si Letopisets). A third redaction was put together in 1118 at the behest of Prince Mstislav Vladimirovich by an unknown compiler. The redaction of 1117 appears to be the one found in the *Lavrentievsky* codex, whereas the *Ipatievsky* codex is based on the 1118 version.

Not only the history of the *PVL* but also its prehistory has been widely investigated. It is generally believed that historical records partially based on older oral traditions were first arranged as annals during the reign of Yaroslav Vladimirovich (ca. 1019–54). This enterprise might have been connected with the official acceptance of Christian law in *Rus'* and the consolidation of local political and ecclesiastical hierarchies. According to Shakhmatov, the next phase in the development of Old Russian chronicle writing was linked with the activity of Monk Nikon who established the technique of opening an entry for a given year with the words "In the year ..." (V leto ...). In Shakhmatov's opinion, however, it was only about the year 1095 that a readily identifiable compilation was put together, which he called the *Primary Compilation* (Nachal'nyi svod).

In addition to the textual material elaborated by Monk Nikon, the *Primary Compilation* included information collected outside the annalistic tradition, such as: (1) the events probably contained in an earlier compilation conventionally called the *Chronograph according to the Great Exposition* (Khronograf po velikomu izlozheniyu); (2) the tales about the raid on Constantinople by Askold and Dir (s. a., 866); and (3) the story about Igor's raid on Constantinople (s. a., 941).

No matter how accurate and trustworthy they may be, these attempts at reconstructing the genesis of Old Russian chronicle writing do not provide an exhaustive description of an extremely complex and largely undocumented process. There are good reasons to believe that there were other compilations of local records in addition to those which merged in the *Primary Compilation*. This hypothesis is confirmed by the fact that another important early body of annals, the Novgorod First Chronicle, contains material which appears to rely on a *svod* older than those which gave birth to the *PVL*.

Though opinions may differ regarding the nature and significance of the *PVL* as a historical document, it enjoys exceptional respect among literary scholars. The heterogeneity of its textual components results in a fascinating blend of different styles. In addition, the spiritual prestige of the *PVL* is enhanced by the presence of motifs which stress the unity of Old *Rus'* and its unique place in the Christian oecumene. Relying on the Byzantine *Chronicle* of George Hamartolus (and its continuation by Simeon the Logothete), the introductory section of the *PVL* deals with universal history, from the creation of the world to the time when the "Russian land arose" (Russkaya zemlya stala est') within the family of Slavic peoples. The annalistic account begins with the year 852, when at the beginning of the reign of the Byzantine Emperor Michael it "began to be called the Russian land" (nacha sya prozyvati Ruska zemlya). The *PVL* (according to the *Lavrentievsky* codex) goes up to the year 1110.

The textual history of the *PVL* illustrates a process which applied for centuries to the compilation of similar literary monuments

in many local centers. To record contemporary events, incorporate them in preexistent collections, and adapt the newly produced compilations to current needs became the basic tasks of monastic and princely scribes. Old Russian historical compilations became the repository for all kinds of writings, which often were mechanically inserted with little or no contextual adaptation or alteration. Thus, on the one hand, chronicles became anthologies of narrative compositions. On the other hand, the writing techniques developed by the compilers of chronicles sharply affected other types of literary activity. Old Russian *povesti* (tales) such as the *Tale of the Battle with Mamai* (Skazanie o Mamaevom poboishche) or the so-called *Tales on the Time of Troubles* (Povesti o Smutnom vremeni) cannot be separated from the narrative tradition which developed within chronicle writing. Much the same can be said about hagiographic compositions like the *Legend and Passion and Encomium of the Holy Martyrs Boris and Gleb* (Skazanie i strast' i pokhvala sviatuyu mucheniku Borisa i Gleba), and historical legends such as the *Tale on the Capture of Constantinople* (Povest' o vzyatii Tsar'grada), the *Chronograph* (Khronograf), and the *Book of Degrees of the Tsar's Genealogy* (Kniga stepennaya tsarskogo rodosloviya) (see Stepennaya kniga).

The *PVL* became part of later annalistic compilations, for which it provided a common introductory section. This is the case, for example, with the above-mentioned *Ipatievsky* codex (the oldest of the five extant copies of the *Ipatievskaya Chronicle*). The second section of this codex presents the so-called *Kievskaya Chronicle*, which relates events from 1117 to the end of the 12th century. The third section of the codex contains the so-called *Galitsko-Volynskaya Chronicle*, which deals with events from the beginning of the 13th century to the year 1289 (in the codex erroneously given as 1292). The *Kievskaya* and *Galitsko-Volynskaya Chronicles* were but two of a number of annalistic accounts which were compiled in several centers of the south Russian lands.

In the 12th century the rise of many religious and political centers in the Russian lands fostered chronicle writing that reflected the ambitions of local rulers and monasteries. Annals compiled in this period are usually grouped together on the basis of the political domain to which they belong. Scholars have focused particular attention on the chronicle writing which occurred in Vladimir-Suzdal and Novgorod. In the 13th century increasing feudal fragmentation under the Tatar "yoke" further underscored the local tendencies of Old Russian *letopisi*.

With the growth of Moscow from the 15th to the 17th century, new compilations were produced which reflected the pan-Russian ambitions of the Muscovite rulers. Among the most important of these compilations are: the *svod* of 1408, also known as the *Troitskaya Chronicle* (destroyed in the Moscow fire of 1812); the *Sofiiskaya Chronicle* (15th–early 16th century); the *Voskresenskaya Chronicle* (16th century); the *Nikonovskaya Chronicle* (16th century); and the *Novyi Letopisets* (New Chronicler, early 17th century). The *Pskovian Chronicles*—in particular, the *svod* of 1567—are among the most typical historical compilations which betray anti-Moscow tendencies. In the 18th century the activity of chronicle writers was mainly devoted to the revision of preexistent compilations. On the other hand, the vitality of the Russian chronicle writing is confirmed by the development of a new annalistic tradition in Siberia.

Bibliography: V. P. Adrianova-Peretts, *Povest' vremennykh let.* 2 vols. 1950. V. I. Buganov, *Otechestvennaya istoriografiya russkogo letopisaniya.* 1975. S. A. Bugoslavskii, "*Povest' vremennykh let* (Spiski, redaktsii, pervonachal'nyi tekst)." In *Starinnaya russkaya povest': Stat'i i issledovaniya,* ed. N. K. Gudzii. 1941. Pp. 7–37. S. Cross and O. Sherbowitz-Wetzer, ed. and trans., *The Russian Primary Chronicle. Laurentian Text.* Cambridge, Mass., 1953. R. P. Dmitrieva, *Bibliografiya russkogo letopisaniya.* 1962. V. S. Ikonnikov, *Opyt russkoi istoriografii.* 2 vols. 1891–1908. I. P. Eremin, *Literatura Drevnei Rusi (Etyudy i kharakteristiki).* 1966. G. M. Kloss, *Nikonovskii svod i russkie letopisi XVI–XVII vekov.* 1980. A. G. Kuz'min, *Nachal'nye etapy drevnerusskogo letopisaniya.* 1977. D. S. Likhachev, *Russkie letopisi i ikh kul'turno-istoricheskoe znachenie.* 1947. Ya. S. Lur'e, "K izucheniyu letopisnogo zhanra." *TODRL* 27 (1972), pp. 76–93. ———, *Obshcherusskie letopisi XIV–XV vv.* 1976. L. Müller, ed., *Handbuch zur Nestorchronik.*

Vol. 1: *Die Nestorchronik*. Vol. 2: *Textkritischer Apparat zur Nestorchronik*. Vol. 3: *Wörterverzeichnis zur Nestorchronik*, parts 1 and 2. (Forum Slavicum, vols. 48, 49, 50.) Munich, 1977–79. A. N. Nasonov, *Istoriya russkogo letopisaniya, XI–nachalo XVIII veka*. 1969. *Novgorodskaya pervaya letopis' starshego i mladshego izvodov*. 1950. D. Ostrowski, "Textual Criticism and the *Povest' vremennykh let*: Some Theoretical Considerations," *Harvard Ukrainian Studies* 5 (1981), pp. 11–31. *Polnoe sobranie russkikh letopisei*. St. Petersburg, Petrograd, Moscow-Leningrad, 1841– . M. D. Prisëlkov, *Istoriya russkogo letopisaniya XI–XV vv.* 1940. ———, ed., *Troitskaya letopis'. Rekonstruktsiya teksta*. 1950. *Pskovskie letopisi*. 2 vols. 1941–55. B. A. Rybakov, *Drevnyaya Rus', skazaniya, byliny, letopisi*. 1963. A. A. Shakhmatov, *Razyskaniya o drevneishikh russkikh letopisnykh svodakh*. 1908. ———, ed., "*Povest' vremennykh let*." Vol 1: *Vvodnaya chast'. Tekst. Primechaniya*. 1916. ———, *Obozrenie russkikh letopisnykh svodov XIV–XVI vv.* 1940. ———, "'*Povest' vremennykh let*' i ee istochniki." *TODRL* 4 (1940), pp. 9–150. M. N. Tikhomirov, *Russkoe letopisanie*. 1979. O. V. Tvorogov, "'*Povest' vremennykh let*' i '*Nachal'nyi svod*.' (Tekstologicheskii kommentarii)," *TODRL* 30 (1976), pp. 3–26.　　　　　　　　　　　　　　　　　　　　　　　H. G.

Levítov, Aleksándr Ivánovich (1835–77), writer. Born in the village of Dobroe in the Tambov province, Levitov entered the Tambov ecclesiastic seminary as the son of a country deacon, but reportedly left after receiving harsh punishment for reading GOGOL. In 1855 he was admitted into the Petersburg academy of medical surgery, only to be arrested and exiled to Vologda, apparently for participating in a student circle. Levitov was subsequently transported to Shenkursk in the province of Arkhangelsk, and experienced such difficult conditions in exile that he was afflicted by extended bouts of drunkenness for the remainder of his life. In 1859, having served out his sentence, he returned on foot to Lebedyan, where he found work as a tutor.

A large part of Levitov's life was spent in wandering across Russia. In 1860 he made his way to Moscow, lived in the slums, and in a way reminiscent of fellow authors F. M. RESHETNIKOV and N. G. POMYALOVSKY, endured a miserable existence. Levitov's life ended in a university clinic in Moscow after a lengthy struggle with tuberculosis.

Levitov began to publish in 1861 when the journal VREMYA printed his *Scenes from the Fair (Scenes from the Life of the Common People)* (Yarmarochnye stseny [Ocherki iz prostonarodnogo byta]). One of the gloomier authors of the developing inclination toward realism, Levitov's first works revealed a bond with the NATURAL SCHOOL, and—particularly in the naturalistic accuracy of dialogue—an affinity with the works of G. I. USPENSKY and V. A. SLEPTSOV.

Regarded as a forerunner of CHEKHOV and GORKY in theme and character types, Levitov addressed the ills of the times, particularly as embodied in the plight of tramps, peasants, and homeless pilgrims. He examined the tragic impact of the Reform on peasant villages in poignant sketches such as *Mundane Justice* (Mirskoi sud, 1862), *Fairytale and Truth* (Skazka i pravda, 1877), and *Omnivores* (Vseyadnye, 1876), and also captured the suffering of impoverished city dwellers in sketches and tales like *Moscow Beggars at Funeral Dinners* (Moskovskie nishchie na pominkakh, 1861), *The Morals of Moscow's Virgin Streets* (Nravy Moskovskikh devstvennykh ulits, 1864), *Figures and Tropes about Moscow Life* (Figury i tropy o moskovskoi zhizni, 1865), and in the collection published with M. A. Voronov titled *Moscow Holes and Slums* (Moskovskie nory i trushchoby, 1866). Similarly, Levitov devoted a number of short works to the corruption of village girls by the city, as in *Maidenly Sin* (Devichii greshok, 1874). In addition to his short works, Levitov's literary legacy includes one unfinished novel with the tentative title, *The Talking Monkey* (Govoryashchaya obez'yana), which depicts a young artist perishing from insanity and alcoholism.

Works: Sobranie sochinenii. 2 vols. 1884. *Sobranie sochinenii*. 8 vols. 1911. *Sochineniya*. 2 vols. 1932–33. *Sochineniya*. 1956.
Translations: "Shoemaker Cock-of-the-Boots." In Leo Wiener, *Anthology of Russian Literature* (1902–03), vol. 2.
Secondary literature: Rose Glickman, "An Alternative View of the Peasantry: The *Raznochintsy* Writers of the 1860s," *SlavR* 32

(1973), pp. 693–704. L. M. Lotman, "Levitov." In *Istoriya russkoi literatury*. Vol. 8. 1956. Mateja Matejić, "Major Themes in the Prose of A. I. Levitov," *SEEJ* 15 (1971), pp. 184–89. M. V. Nekhai, *Russkii demokraticheskii ocherk 60-kh godov XIX stoletiya: N. Uspenskii, V. Sleptsov i A. Levitov*. 1971. A. Silaev, *Liry zvon kandal'nyi: Ocherki zhizni i tvorchestva A. I. Levitova*. 1963. A. Strukov, *A. I. Levitov*. 1960.　　　　　　　　　　　　　J. S.

Lézhnev, A. (pseud. of Abrám Zakhárovich Gorélik, 1893–1938), Marxist literary critic and theorist, a member of the PEREVAL group and a regular contributor to the journal KRASNAYA NOV'. He played a leading role in the great literary debates of the 1920s, where he struck a middle position much like VORONSKY's: literature was neither propaganda nor mere craftsmanship, but rather, a "realistic" exploration, high in quality, of the complexities and contradictions of contemporary life, particularly in novel form. These features he found most promisingly (though not exclusively) embodied in the work of the FELLOW-TRAVELERS, and he became one of their vigorous advocates, much to the disapproval of the "OKTYABR'" group in particular. Like Voronsky, too, he developed an interest in the unconscious, intuitive nature of the creative process, and by the late 1920s had virtually redefined the writer's task as "seeing the world" with a freshness, immediacy, sincerity, and "humanism," unclouded by routine or ideology. At this point, however, literature was being mobilized for social service, largely by the RAPP, one of Lezhnev's major adversaries. By the early 1930s, he found it virtually impossible to function publicly as a critic and theorist, and he switched to the seemingly less controversial area of literary history. Nonetheless, he perished in the purges.

Works: Voprosy literatury i kritiki. 1926. *Literaturnye budni*. 1929. *Ob iskusstve*. 1936.
Secondary literature: Herman Ermolaev, *Soviet Literary Theories, 1917–1934*. 1963. Esp. pp. 80–85. R. A. Maguire. *Red Virgin Soil: Soviet Literature in the 1920's*. 1968. Esp. Chaps. VI, VII.　　　　　　　　　　　　　　　　　　　　　　　R. A. M.

Libedinsky, Yúry Nikoláevich (1898–1959), novelist, critic, and literary administrator. He was the son of a provincial doctor, and his formal education ended with the completion in 1918 of a secondary school course in Chelyabinsk. He joined the Communist Party in 1920 and served as a political commissar in the Red Army during the civil war. He was active very early in the proletarian literary movement, and his novel *The Week* (Nedelya), published in 1922, was one of the early successes of that movement. It appeared in a collection of stories and poems edited by A. K. VORONSKY and entitled *Our Day* (Nashi dni). That novel is an account of what happened to a local Soviet organization isolated and defenseless in a rural area where the peasantry was murderously hostile to the regime. Nearly all the members of the group are killed in an uprising which occurs when the Red Army detachment defending them is withdrawn. Libedinsky focuses on the individuals who formed the group and he reveals heroism cohabiting with doubt and inner conflict. Though realistic in its basic method, *The Week* bears the stamp of BELY in its frequent lyrical excursions. Libedinsky's *Tomorrow* (Zavtra, 1923) describes the disillusionment and moral deterioration of Party members following the "bourgeois revival" of NEP; the novel is frankly Trotskyist in its viewpoint. *Commissars* (1925) concerns the fading of ideals among Communist leaders no longer engaged in battle. *Birth of a Hero* (Rozhdenie geroya, 1930), Libedinsky's best novel, is a fictional protest against the developing conservatism of the Party, and against conformity and stagnation in its intellectual life. The novel figured prominently in the acrimonious literary debates of the period and it was heavily and authoritatively attacked soon after its publication. Libedinsky was a close associate of AVERBAKH and FADEEV in the leadership of RAPP, and in that capacity contributed in important ways to the development of the ideas and slogans dominant in the organization: "immediate impressions," the "living man," "for the removal of masks." Those ideas were condemned after the liquidation of RAPP in 1932 and Libedinsky was heavily attacked for his long association with Averbakh. He was in great danger again during the purge of 1937, but he survived and continued to be active in literature. His later lengthy novels *Mountains and People* (Gory i lyudi, 1947),

Dawn (Zarevo, 1952), *The Morning of Soviet Power* (Utro sovetov, 1958) are undistinguished contributions to Soviet didactic prose. His book of reminiscences *Contemporaries* (Sovremenniki, 1958; 1961) has considerable documentary interest in that it deals with a number of important figures in or near the proletarian literary movement, though of course it does not mention TROTSKY, an important influence in Libedinsky's young life, nor Averbakh, a long-time and close associate.

Works: Izbrannye proizvedeniya. 2 vols. 1958. *Rozhdenie geroya.* 2d ed. 1930. *General'nye zadachi proletarskoi literatury.* 1931. *Sovremenniki: vospominaniya.* 1961.

Translations: A Week. Trans. and introd. Arthur Ransome. New York, 1923.

Secondary literature: E. J. Brown, *The Proletarian Episode in Russian Literature.* 1953; 1971. Chap. 7. Lidiya Libedinskaya, *Zelenaya lampa.* 1966. A. Voronskii, *Literaturno-kriticheskie stat'i.* 1963. J. W. Weeks, *Yurii Libedinskii.* Ph. D. diss. Brown University, 1971.

E. J. B.

Lidin (real name: Gomberg), Vladímir Gérmanovich, (1894–), prose writer. Born in Moscow, Lidin was educated at Lazarev Institute of Eastern Languages and obtained a law degree at the University of Moscow in 1915. A prolific short-story writer since 1912, Lidin has been strongly influenced by CHEKHOV and BUNIN. His style is ornate and rhetorical. His earliest collection of stories, *Nothing Matters* (Tryn-trava, 1916), dealt with the bourgeoisie and the intelligentsia. Lidin volunteered for service with the Red Army in Siberia; his civil war experiences are reflected in *Stories of Many Days* (1923) and *Drab Days* (Myshinye budni, 1923). Many stories deal with the NEP period. His novel *The Price of Life* (Otstupnik, 1927), is a picturesque account of Moscow student life during the NEP. Lidin's favorite characters are strong-willed individualists, seekers of happiness, who triumph over nature and over weak-willed characters (as in *North*, 1925, *Seekers*, 1926, *Ships are Sailing*, 1926). In the 1930s Lidin began writing social command literature. A trip through the Far East inspired the novel *Grand or Quiet* (Veliki ili tikhi, 1932), about the construction of a Far Eastern hunting and fishing collective. In World War II Lidin served as a reporter for *Izvestiya* on the Belorussian front. His novel *Exile* (Izgnanie, 1947), is devoted to the first years of the war. Moscow postwar life and the Soviet intelligentsia are depicted in the novel *Two Lives* (Dve zhizni, 1950). Lidin's reminiscences of writers and artists are collected in *People and Encounters* (Lyudi i vstrechi, 1957, 1961, 1965).

Works: Sobranie sochinenii. 6 vols. 1928–30. *Sobranie sochinenii.* 3 vols. 1973–74.

Translations: The Price of Life (Otstupnik). New York, 1932. Reprint, 1973. *See also,* Lewanski, p. 297.

Secondary literature: Russkie sovetskie pisateli: prozaiki. 1964. Vol. 2, pp. 744–79.

N. R.

Likhachëv, Dmitry Sergéevich (1906–), leading Soviet specialist in Old Russian literature, whose many books and articles are highly influential both in the Soviet Union and abroad. Likhachëv is one of the foremost promoters of medieval Russian studies, the editor of numerous Old Russian literary monuments, and a literary theoretician. He has investigated all crucial aspects of the Old Russian literary heritage from the 10th to the 17th century. His book *Poetics of Old Russian Literature* (Poetika drevnerusskoi literatury, 1967) gave a new impulse to the study of the formal peculiarities of Old Russian writings. No less important are his studies on the place of Old Russian literature in medieval and humanistic Europe. Likhachëv's vision of an East European Pre-Renaissance (Vostochnoevropeiskoe Predvozrozhdenie) deserves special mention for its emphasis on the close connections between the literature of Old Russia and that of the Southern Slavs and the Byzantine world. On the basis of numerous analytic studies, Likhachëv has arrived at a comprehensive interpretation of the historical development of Old Russian literature, perhaps most clearly expressed in his *Development of Russian Literature from the 10th to the 17th century. Epochs and Styles* (Razvitie russkoi literatury X–XVII vekov. Epokhi i stili, 1973), and the *History of Russian Literature from the 10th to the 17th century* (Istoriya russkoi literatury X–XVII vekov, 1980), which was written under his general editorship and for which he provided the introduction and conclusion.

Probably Likhachëv's most influential theoretical work is his *Textology. On the Material of Russian Literature from the 10th to the 17th century* (Tekstologiya. Na materiale russkoi literatury X–XVII vv., 1962). The main purpose of this book is to describe and evaluate the particular conditions which affected the process of textual transmission in Old Russia. The work of the Old Russian scribes is seen as that of participants in the creation of a tradition rather than of simple "carriers" of textual material. In opposition to some traditional principles of Western textual criticism, Likhachëv's *Textology* concentrates not on the individuality of texts but on the "history of the text," which Likhachëv equates with the "history of textual changes." Likhachëv's theoretical formulations have been the object of considerable discussion (and even of dispute) among Western scholars.

Works: Russkie letopisi i ikh kul'turno-istoricheskoe znachenie. 1947. *Vozniknovenie russkoi literatury.* 1952. "Nekotorye zadachi izucheniya vtorogo yuzhnoslavyanskogo vliyaniya v Rossii." In *Issledovaniya po slavyanskomu literaturovedeniyu i fol'kloristike. Doklady sovetskikh uchenykh na IV Mezhdunarodnom s"ezde slavistov.* 1960. Pp. 95–151. *Tekstologiya. Na materiale russkoi literatury X–XVII vv.* 1962. *Chelovek v literature drevnei Rusi.* 2d ed. 1970. *Razvitie russkoi literatury X–XVII vv. Epokhi i stili.* 1973. *Poetika drevnerusskoi literatury.* 3d ed. 1979. (Ed.,) *Istoriya russkoi literatury X–XVII vv.* 1980.

Bibliography of Likhachëv's works: Dmitrii Sergeevich Likhachev. Materialy k biobibliografii uchenykh SSSR. (Seriya literatury i yazyka, no. 11. 2d rev. ed.) 1977.

R. P.

Lipkin, Semyón Izraílevich (1911–), poet and translator, was born in Odessa and graduated from the Engineering and Economics Institute in 1937. He started to write poetry in the late 1920s, being for a while a protegé of E. BAGRITSKY. However, the latter's "frenzied revolutionary romanticism" had a reverse effect on Lipkin, who refused to write "hymns to the new life" and instead went to translating, while writing poetry only for himself. During World War II Lipkin served on several fronts as a supply officer and wrote verses, but published very few of them. Instead, he published a book of sketches, *The Ship of Stalingrad* (Stalingradskii korabl', 1943). Later, Lipkin described his wartime impressions of the panic retreat in 1942, of "roadblock detachments," "checkpoints," Smershmen, and informers in his verse epic "Technician-Supply Officer" (Tekhnik-intendant, 1963, published in his collection, *Volya*, 1981). After the War, it appeared as though Lipkin had gone entirely into translating. He translated the Kabardinian folk epos and the verse epics of the Uzbek poet Alisher Navoi, Tadjik poetry and Firdausi, as well as contemporary Uzbek, Kirghiz, and Caucasian poets. However, at the same time, Lipkin continued to write his own verse. At times these were only fleeting travel impressions, caught at a glimpse ("The Caucasus below Me," "The Lezghinian Dance") and hardly polished poetically, yet also without any officious pathos or ideological passion. In almost every issue of DEN' POEZII, two or three poems by Lipkin would appear. Also, three collections of his poetry appeared between 1967 and 1977: *Eyewitness* (Ochevidets), *Eternal Day* (Vechnyi den'), and *Notebook of Being* (Tetrad' bytiya). However, not nearly everything Lipkin wrote was meant for publication. He would read much of his best verse only to his friends, and on rare occasions. Such were his *Mother of God* (Bogoroditsa, 1956), a cycle of verse on the prisoners of Gulag (1960), and poems on Jewish themes (printed in *Volya*). Of particular interest are Lipkin's verse epics *Nestor and Sariya* and *Tbilisi in April 1956*, as well as other pieces from the cycle *Leader and Tribe* (Vozhd' i plemya, printed in *Volya*). Here we hear about arrests and atrocities by the NKVD, secret murders in the Kremlin, Ordzhonikidze and Beria and, of course, Stalin, whose relentlessly naturalistic and wrathfully unmasking portrait is given in the verse epic on Tbilisi. Lipkin's best verse epic may be *Literary Reminiscences* (Literaturnye vospominaniya, 1974, in *Volya*), where the poet tells of Bagritsky, and of their joint visits to Ezhov's salon in the late 1920s. Lipkin's life went quite happily until 1978, when he submitted several of his unpublished poems to the almanac *Metropolis*. Hereafter, Lipkin was no longer published in the USSR and he re-

255

linquished his membership in the Union of Soviet Writers. In 1981, the Ardis publishing house, through the efforts of Iosif Brodsky, published Lipkin's book of verse, *Freedom* (*Volya*), which includes Lipkin's published and previously unpublished verse from 1936 to 1978.

Works: Ochevidets. 1967. *Vechnyi den'.* 1975. *Tetrad' bytiya* (Poetry and Translations). 1977. *Volya.* 1981.

Translations by Lipkin: Dzhangar. Kalmytskii epos. 1940. *Manas.* Kirgizskii epos. 1941. *Leili i Medzhnun.* A verse epic by A. Navoi. 1943. *Sem' planet.* A verse epic by A. Navoi. 1948. *Narty.* A Kabardinian epic. 1951. *Skazanie ob Bakhrame Chubine.* A verse epic by Firdausi. 1952. *Shakhname.* A verse epic by Firdausi. 1955. *Zafar i Zakhra.* A verse epic by Aibek. 1954. *Stranitsy tatzhikskoi poezii.* 1961.

Secondary literature: A. Keshokov, "Vtoraya zhizn' poezii," *Novyi mir,* 1957, no. 5. M. Popovskii, "Prorok i ochevidets," *Novyi Amerikanets,* no. 86, 3–9 October 1981.   E. D. A.

Literary criticism, Russian. Although one might reasonably claim that Russia only produced any literary criticism worthy of serious consideration during the 19th century and the early decades of the 20th century, in this survey we shall assume that Russian literary criticism begins, for all essential purposes, with the 18th century. The pseudoclassical normative criticism of this century in Russia, a concomitant of the largely derivative literature of the age, has of course some interest in its own right (reflecting as it does, for instance, various aspects of Enlightenment thought); but more than one observer has noted interesting similarities between, on the one hand, 18th-century Russian literature and criticism and, on the other, the literature and critical theory of postrevolutionary Communist Russia. As for pre-18th-century Russia, if we take the phrase "literary criticism" in its broadest meaning (i.e., as roughly synonymous with "writing about or commenting on works of literature"), we can go back to as early as the 11th century when, for example, a Byzantine Greek handbook (by Choeroboscus) on figures of speech was translated into Slavonic. But this and similar versions, as well as the usually off-hand remarks one can find here and there in old Russian literature concerning language and style, and even most of the later normative treatises on homiletics and rhetoric are primarily of interest to specialists.

It is safe to assume, then, that it is only by the 18th century that we find the written word being discussed and evaluated in terms of models drawn from Greco-Roman antiquity and on the basis of certain theoretical principles borrowed from West European neoclassical theory. Moreover, the treatment of the written word becomes more and more secularized as the heavy hand of Orthodoxy is somewhat relaxed. Baroque poetic usage is well represented by Skouphos' Greek *Rhetoric* (published at Venice in 1681) in the revised and russified version done by Kozma Grek in about 1705, while the direct influence of Boileau's *Art poétique* is apparent in the "Second Epistle" of the poet and man of letters, Aleksandr Sumarokov. But by far the most important name in the 18th century, not only in literature and criticism but also in the history of Russian science, is that of Mikhail Lomonosov. Lomonosov's *Rhetoric*, published in 1748, is the major document of Russian pseudoclassical poetics; perhaps it would be better to say "baroque poetics," since there is everywhere a marked predilection on the part of the author for such qualities as magnificence (*velikolepie*) and richness (*izobilie*) of expression and for various kinds of involved phrases (*vitievatye rechi*). A highly derivative compilation and hardly a work of genius (as some of Lomonosov's other achievements are often considered to be, especially in Russia), the *Rhetoric* draws heavily on the standard French handbooks by Caussin and Pomay and the *Ausführliche Redekunst* (1736) of Johann Christoph Gottsched, a professor at Leipzig. Essentially a "codex" of some 326 sections (about 280 pages of Russian text), it sets forth in quite elementary fashion the prescriptive (normative, legislative) rules of composition and allusion, with the implication that literary works are to be judged by these criteria (the juridical aspect of 18th-century thought is well known). There is a predominant emphasis on form and on decorum. The tradition of Roman school rhetoric is clearly manifest in the divisions of the work (*izobretenie = inventio, ukrashenie = ornatio,* etc.) and the full apparatus of ancient (mainly protreptic) rhetoric is exhibited, most of the examples being drawn from ancient authors. There is some quaint etymologizing and suggestions as to its utilization by the writer; a "psychophonetic" theory of the relationship between sounds and the emotions is outlined; and, in advocating odd and unusual verbal devices for winning the attention of the listener or reader, Lomonosov anticipates some of the ideas of the later Russian Futurists and Formalists.

A noticeable feature of both authentically classical (i.e., ancient Greek) and later pseudoclassical theory is the concept of a hierarchy of styles; it is not at all unusual, then, to find Lomonosov expounding such a hierarchy in his 1757 essay, "On the Uses of Church Books in the Russian Language." By "Church Books" he means works written in Church Slavonic, while the differences between his three styles are primarily lexical, depending on the ratio of Church Slavonic to Russian words. The high style (e.g., in odes and tragedy) should contain a high percentage of Church Slavonic; the middle style (e.g., in serious drama) requires a lower percentage; and the low style (e.g., in comedy and songs) should contain mainly Russian words. It was inevitable that, with the coming of preromantic ideas towards the end of the 18th century, such divisions should have been rejected, as indeed they were.

Beginning just before the turn of the century and throughout most of the 19th century, there is a marked shift of emphasis, both in literature and criticism, from form to content—from an overriding concern with the forms of expression to a concern with the writer's feelings themselves. In the early stages of romanticism—or Sentimentalism—the major figure is that of Nikolai Karamzin. Famous in his day as a historian and prose writer, he is mentioned here because he represents a link in literary theory and practice between Lomonosov and Pushkin and because he urged writers to do (as he himself was doing) two things: to reduce the three styles of Lomonosov to one—a middle style—closer to the spoken language of the educated; and to further enrich the Russian language by introducing neologisms and calques (or loan translations) from the languages of Western Europe. The first Russian author to translate Laurence Sterne and a great lover of Shakespeare, Karamzin was also influenced by—and a *vulgarisateur* of—the works of Rousseau, James Thomson, Goldsmith, Macpherson, and Ewald von Kleist. In 1815 those Russian writers sympathetic with Karamzin's views (the young Pushkin, Zhukovsky, Batyushkov, Vyazemsky and others) formed the Arzamas Society; but the classical and conservative literary tradition was strongly argued by Admiral Aleksandr Shishkov and his followers (including Griboedov) in the Beseda Society who equated, quite erroneously, the Russian and Church Slavonic languages. Another transitional figure was Aleksei Merzlyakov; although a member of the Karamzin circle, he was an academic classicist, a translator of Greek and Latin poetry, and the author of prescriptive handbooks.

The poets in the Arzamas Society and those close to Pushkin in the "Pushkin Pleiad" were, however, aristocrats with a traditional disdain for anything smacking of literary professionalism; whatever critical opinions they expressed were, to say the least, informal. In the case of Pushkin himself it is possible, nevertheless, to compile from his letters, his poetry (especially his novel in verse, *Eugene Onegin*), and his prose a good-sized volume containing a fairly consistent literary doctrine characterized by common sense and good taste (see Tatiana Wolff, *Pushkin on Literature*). This is not at all surprising, since we can see in his formal education, his reading, his background in general, and in his very language the marked influence of French 18th-century tastes and practices. Although there are some romantic thematic elements in Pushkin, his approach, so far as form is concerned, is severely classical (in the following century Andrei Bely refers to Pushkin's "Doric phraseology"). There is in Pushkin hardly any of the German romantic/idealist influence—aside from occasional parody and satire—which was to play such an important role in 19th-century Russian thought and literary theory. But not all the gentry poets of the age kept this respectful distance from Romanticism. Prince Pyotr Vyazemsky, for example, became an enthusiastic exponent of the movement. Nevertheless, Vyazemsky was a good friend of Pushkin's and their correspondence is, according to Mirsky (Svyatopolk-Mirsky), "a treasure house of wit, fine criticism, and good Russian." Three other writers of the period are occasionally mentioned as minor figures in this age of gentry criticism: Kondraty Ryleev, Aleksandr Bestuzhev, and Vilgelm

Kyukhelbeker. But all three were involved in something more than the avocation of letters: Ryleev was hanged and Bestuzhev and Kyukhelbeker were exiled for their parts in the abortive Decembrist revolt of 1825.

Alongside the gentry-critics of the early 19th century, all of whom were poets as well, we find in Orest SOMOV the closest approach to a professional literary critic prior to BELINSKY. Somov was an employee of the Russian-American Company who wrote his essay "On Romantic Poetry" in 1823 and began regular contributions to SEVERNYE TSVETY (a journal edited by another poet of the Pushkin Pleiad, Baron Anton DELVIG) in 1828. An apologist for the new romanticism and perceptive enough to recognize the potential talent of the young GOGOL, Somov was especially interested in the state of Russian prose. He saw that the Russian poetic language was well on its way to being an effective vehicle but that Russian prose was still comparatively immature and crude, inadequate to the demands for greater precision of expression and a satisfactory narrative style. As for Pushkin (who very soon was brilliantly to eliminate this shortcoming in Russian prose), Somov enthusiastically reviewed some of his verse, including portions of *Eugene Onegin*. While critical of certain details, he was on the whole positive in his reactions and even went out of his way to defend Pushkin against attacks by other critics. Somov also urged his fellow critics to be more objective and moderate in their discussions of literary works and to avoid polemics and vituperation, but this advice was hardly observed by the majority of the critics who followed.

One of the most influential developments in the 1830s in Russia was the tremendous impact on intellectuals of German romantic/idealist thought. Especially attractive, since it had more the appeal of a religion or mystical system than a critical philosophy was the organic *Naturphilosophie* of Friedrich Schelling. Although there are many, in various fields, who might be mentioned as examples of this influence, an important name in criticism is that of Nikolai NADEZHDIN. A journalist, academic, and amateur ethnographer as well as a critic, Nadezhdin proposed a synthesis of classicism and romanticism and saw the forms of art as features determined by the spirit of the age. But by far the most significant name in literary criticism before the middle of the century is that of Vissarion Belinsky. The first Russian professional critic and, in Soviet terms, the founder of "revolutionary-democratic" criticism, Belinsky wrote almost nothing but critical reviews and articles. A Westernizer and radical intellectual, all of his literary theory is strongly colored by German—especially organic—thought; even his concept of realism—that it represents something more than reality itself—is of German origin. While advocating "universal" qualities in literature, however, and emphasizing the importance of content rather than form, he set the tone for a large mass of subsequent Russian—and Soviet—criticism by insisting on the relevance of literature to actual social conditions. Condemned by some Russian critics and by critics in the West for his a priori approach as well as for his diffuse and journalistic style, Belinsky has also been regularly praised for his acuity of judgment and intensity of devotion to the significance of art and literature. The fact that Belinsky holds the high and pre-eminent place he does in Soviet Russian Marxist aesthetic and literary theory is not at all surprising; the very same German patterns of thought one notes in Belinsky were the ones that, to a great extent, shaped the taste behind those *obiter dicta* on literature in the writings of Marx which provide the basis for the general Marxist theory of literature.

Some of Belinsky's intensity is also evident in the output of his three epigones, Nikolai CHERNYSHEVSKY, Nikolai DOBROLYUBOV, and Dmitry PISAREV, the so-called civic critics. All three were typical "men of the sixties," in comparison with whom Belinsky and other "men of the forties" seem almost genteel; much more radical and strongly utilitarian in outlook, their narrowed vision, their crude didacticism, and their provincialism anticipate later Soviet practice in dealing with literature and the arts. The development of civic criticism in Russia with its anomalous extremes is unique and Western Europe offers nothing comparable. For Chernyshevsky, the author of *Studies in the Age of Gogol* (1856), the function of literature, an inferior reflection of reality to begin with, is didactic and edifying (as in the case of his single novel, *What Is To Be Done?*, which has been called the worst novel ever written). The civic critics also tended to read and interpret works of literature as sociopolitical documents and to discuss fictional characters as if they were real

people in actual environments; this tendency is especially apparent in the articles by Dobrolyubov (e.g., his essay, "What Is Oblomovism?", 1859). The *reductio ad absurdum* of civic criticism is represented by Pisarev who condemned the literature of the past (including Shakespeare and Pushkin) and felt that the best employment for an artist was to illustrate an insect identification guide. Two less notorious but still radical anti-aesthetic critics were Varfolomei ZAITSEV and Nikolai SHELGUNOV. The former provided the model for the doctrinaire socialist ideologist, Shigalyov, in Dostoevsky's *The Possessed*, while the latter, who lauded the novels of RESHETNIKOV as "popular [*narodnyi*] realism" and emphasized the importance of types, was an early apologist of what was later called "socialist realism."

In the publications of another group of critics in the second half of the 19th century we see some reaction against the extremes so evident in the civic critics. Because they turned away from a radical socio-political and utilitarian interpretation of literature towards a greater concern for intrinsic literary values, these men have been called the aesthetic critics, although in no sense were they devoted to purely aesthetic ends. On the whole, they are a fairly sensitive and genteel group, not given to journalistic vituperation and free of radical political persuasions. A good name to begin with is that of Valerian MAIKOV who very early noted some distinctive features in DOSTOEVSKY's prose. Called a "humanistic cosmopolite" by Belinsky (because he felt, for example, that national traits hinder human progress), Maikov's promising career was cut short by an early death. Stepan SHEVYRYOV was a leading Slavophile and professor of literature at Moscow University who wrote a *Theory of Poetry* in 1836 (the precursor of many similarly titled works to appear in Russia in subsequent decades); he also became the target of Belinsky's anger because he stressed the "genteel" and "elevating" qualities of literature. Vasily BOTKIN, a man of expensive and elegant tastes and a moderate liberal in his youth, moved towards aesthetic and subjective criticism after 1855 (exemplified in his 1857 study of the poetry of Afanasy FET). More substantial contributions to the aesthetic tradition were made by Aleksandr DRUZHININ, Apollon GRIGORIEV, and Stepan DUDYSHKIN. Druzhinin, who was also a novelist, was one of the first Russian critics to assert that literature should not be subordinated to social or political ends and to speak out in favor of the Pushkinian rather than the Gogolian tradition. Grigoriev, because of his strong attachments to the philosophy of Schelling and his interest in the more subtle and "ineffable" aspects of literature, is frequently called an organic or romantic critic. Markedly romantic and impressionistic tendencies are also observable in the writings of the apolitical critic Dudyshkin who has left us a fine study of Turgenev. Another intimate friend and admirer of both TURGENEV and Belinsky was the exceptionally broad-minded critic Pavel ANNENKOV. A wealthy landowner with aristocratic tastes, he wrote a study of Pushkin in the age of Aleksandr I and some valuable literary memoirs (*An Extraordinary Decade*).

Any survey of 19th-century Russian criticism would be incomplete if it ignored the names of the three great novelists of the age—Fyodor Dostoevsky, Ivan Turgenev, and Lev TOLSTOI. Though Dostoevsky wrote no single work wholly devoted to literary criticism or even sustained theorizing about the novel in particular, his essays of the early 1860s, his letters, his notebooks, and his *Diary of a Writer* are replete with comments on various aspects of the art of the novel and the problems of literary realism. These, along with the ideology in Dostoevsky, have been given added significance due to his tremendous influence—first in Russia during the Silver Age just prior to the Revolution and, later, outside of Russia during the 20th century. Like Belinsky, Dostoevsky's aesthetic theory owes a great deal to German—especially organic—thought. A veritable devotee of the idealism of Schiller during his pre-exile years, he went through a period of doubt before returning to this preoccupation with Schillerian ideals in later life (as evidenced in his last and greatest novel, *The Brothers Karamazov*). But the picture is complicated by Dostoevsky's devotion to the Russian Orthodox Church, his intense interest (a morbid interest in the opinion of some) in crime, cruelty, and suffering, and his marked Slavophile sympathies. Believing, like Kant, that the essential nature of reality is inaccessible to man, Dostoevsky held that the novelist can only perceive and describe the world as it is reflected in his ideas. "My idealism," he wrote, "is more real than their [i.e., other novelists'] realism." And his view that what others called his fantasy was the very essence of reality links him with such 20th-century Russian writers and critics as ZAMYATIN and SINYAVSKY; it also explains why Max Ernst once painted Dostoevsky seated among the surrealists.

In the case of Tolstoi we find absolutely no dalliance with German romantic or mystic-metaphysical thought. Though he admired Schopenhauer (easy to read and a misogynist), Tolstoi was rather a devotee of Jean-Jacques Rousseau and he reveals in almost every aspect of his thinking 18th-century French rationalist/classical predilections and tastes. In addition to the categorical remarks on literature in his letters and non-fiction, Tolstoi wrote what can only be called a notorious critical essay, *What Is Art?* (1897). Here Tolstoi ruthlessly rejects almost everything that has always been and is still considered great in literature (including his own novels), music, and painting on the basis of his own boldly stated criteria. These include simplicity, sincerity, and clarity; but the chief criterion of great universal art, appealing not to sophisticated elites but to great masses of people, is the ability to "infect" the reader, listener or viewer. This is Tolstoi's "infection (*zarazhenie*) theory", an adaptation of some statements by Eugène Véron in his *L'Esthétique* (1878). Tolstoi is hard on all forms of romanticism (romanticism, he wrote, comes from not looking into the eyes of truth) and is especially hard on the symbolist art of the age. His special animus against Shakespeare, revealed in another notorious work, *On Shakespeare and the Drama* (1906), recalls Voltaire's harsh opinions of the Bard for his failure to observe *les bienséances*.

Although Ivan Turgenev attended university lectures in Germany and once said that he was a German and not a Russian, we find in his literary preferences and tastes much more of a sympathy with French and English than with German traditions. He is also much less concerned than Tolstoi and Dostoevsky with problems of belief and the meaning of life and more with the art of the novel. As a novelist, he has never had the influence of his two peers, but on the other hand he is less often criticized from a technical novelistic point of view and has more than once been called a "novelist's novelist" in the West. Very Western and cosmopolitan, he associated intimately with some of the leading French writers of the time and received an honorary degree from Oxford, something difficult to imagine in the case of Tolstoi or Dostoevsky. In addition to his *Literary Reminiscences* (containing a chapter devoted to Belinsky), Turgenev wrote an interesting typological study, "Hamlet and Don Quijote" (1860), in which literary characters—and men in general—are divided into two categories: those whose endless ruminations prevent resolute action and those naive idealists whose performances are sad and ridiculous.

Among professional and occasional critics active near the end of the 19th and in the early 20th century some were primarily scholars, such as Aleksandr POTEBNYA whose theories of language interested the later formalists. Aleksandr VESELOVSKY was also a literary scholar concerned mainly with the genesis and migration of themes and motifs and with comparative literature, while Aleksandr PYPIN was a literary historian who viewed literature as a mirror of the history of ideas. Other critics were involved in political movements and continued the debate on realism and the relation of literature to life. Thus Aleksandr SKABICHEVSKY, a leading populist critic and the author of a *History of Russian Literature*, while rejecting radical realism, still saw literature as a moral force. Skabichevsky also noted some affinities between the poetry of TYUTCHEV and the symbolists, saw Turgenev as a writer closer to the Decadents than to traditional realism, and grievously under-rated the talents and future fame of Anton CHEKHOV. Nikolai MIKHAILOVSKY continued the Civic tradition in criticism and is best known for his essay on Dostoevsky, "A Cruel Talent" (1882). Criticizing Dostoevsky's apparently morbid preoccupation with pain and suffering, he also objects to lack of proportion in his novels, the atypicality of his characters, and a general lack of convincing motivation (*besprichinnost'*). Mikhailovsky much preferred the fiction of Tolstoi and his essay, "The Left and Right Hands of Count L. N. Tolstoi" (1875) is another treatment of the Janus-faced art of the enigmatic count. Finally, Georgy PLEKHANOV, the first important Russian Marxist and the first Russian Marxist critic, introduced Marxist analysis in his *Letters Without an Address* (1899–1900). Plekhanov saw the task of the critic as that of searching out "social equivalents" in the language of art.

Beginning in Western Europe in the 1880s, a neoromantic movement variously known as the DECADENCE, the Silver Age, the Age of SYMBOLISM, and MODERNISM very soon reached Russia. This movement, including post-symbolist ACMEISM and futurism, *was* in fact Russian literature up to the time of the Revolution. Though ultimately proscribed by the Soviet Communist authorities, this movement—complex and with many branches—persisted in its effects even after the Revolution and these influences are still apparent in Russian dissident art and literature today. Like their counterparts abroad, the Russian modernist critics were more often than not creative artists as well. As poets and critics, the modernists were frequently very erudite, had little or no interest in politics, were mainly concerned with the subtleties of spiritual and mental states, with impressionistic techniques, and with pure beauty, and were often preoccupied with the problems of non-Orthodox religious and mystical revelation. In this connection, the name of Vladimir SOLOVYOV is important, not so much as a critic as a philosopher-mystic and inspirer of religious symbolist poetry, although his clever parodies of Russian decadent verse are themselves a form of criticism. Vasily ROZANOV, an anti-rationalist, anti-Christian philosopher-critic and essayist, wrote articles on Pushkin and Gogol, but his best-known study is "The Legend of the Grand Inquisitor" (1894) in which he claims, as Blake did in the case of Milton, that Dostoevsky was doing something quite different than what he professed to be doing, that he was really (i.e., presumably without being aware of it) on the side of the Grand Inquisitor. But this interpretation is hardly tenable in the opinion of unprejudiced readers of Dostoevsky. Two other anti-rationalist philosopher-critics with special interests in Dostoevsky, Lev SHESTOV and Nikolai BERDYAEV, both left Russia after the Revolution and lived abroad. Shestov (his name often appears in its French form, Léon Chestov) is primarily a very learned critic of ideas and many of his works are readily available in English (e.g., *Athens and Jerusalem*). A number of Berdyaev's books have also been translated, including his study, *The World View of Dostoevsky*, which carries eulogy of Dostoevsky as religious thinker to extremes (the book ends by claiming that to have produced Dostoevsky is sufficient justification for the existence of the Russian people).

Some of the criticism of the period shows clearly a reaction against the Russian civic tradition. A. VOLYNSKY (pseudonym of Akim Flekser) gave needed recognition to the early Russian decadent/symbolist poets and defined symbolism as an artistic synthesis of the world of appearances and a transcendental world. Maksim Belinsky (pseudonym of Ieronim Yasinsky), the author of now long-forgotten decadent novels, also protested against didacticism in literature and defended pure art in the 1880s and 1890s but joined the Bolsheviks in 1917. N. MINSKY, the author of some extremely derivative decadent verse, vaunted art as superior to science, was one of the founders of the "Religious and Philosophical Society," and has been called "one of the first swallows of the modernist movement." In a pretentious essay, "In the Light of Conscience" (1890), he gives a Nietzschean critique of conventional morality and outlines some of the components of the decadent manner. In 1902 he published an article on Zola in the prestigious journal, MIR ISKUSSTVA (edited by Sergei DIAGHILEV), but by 1905 he was writing a "Workers' Hymn" and he later left Russia.

Somewhat more significant are the views of a number of major symbolist poets who very often wrote on the theory and practice of symbolism. Their differing outlooks point up the pluralistic and cosmopolitan aspects of Russian modernist thought which were all but suppressed in the years following the Revolution. Although Aleksandr BLOK is generally regarded as the greatest of the Russian symbolist poets, his sensitive critical articles (such as his review of a novel by Bely) are apt to be highly lyrical and subjective responses to another poet's lyricism. Valery BRYUSOV, a *doctus poeta* in the Alexandrian manner, viewed symbolism purely as literary method and not as a substitute religion. Very French in his affiliations and tastes, he wrote numerous articles on the symbolist movement, all of which are variations on Baudelaire's statement that poetry has no other end but itself. Konstantin BALMONT, whose Russian version of Poe's "The Raven" has been called better than the original, outlined an irrational theory of poetry in his "Poetry as Magic," while Andrei Bely, a poet and novelist of renown, was particularly interested in the mechanics of versification and the problems of verse rhythm, especially in the poetry of Pushkin. He founded a "Rhythmics Society" and, after the Revolution, wrote his *Rhythm as Dialectic* in which he attempted to combine poetic theory with Marxism. Another novelist and poet, Dmitry MEREZHKOVSKY, wrote *Tolstoi and Dostoevsky* (1902), excerpts from which are frequently cited in studies of the two novelists. Merezhkovsky's wife, Zinaida HIPPIUS, the poet and "*grande dame* of Russian Symbolism" (Victor Erlich), maintained a literary salon in St. Petersburg prior to the Revolution and contributed articles to the Russian journal *Vesy* and to *Mercure de France*. More eloquently than anyone else, she emphasized the vitalizing spirit of symbolism and the services of modernism in bringing Russian literature into closer contact with the artistic cultures of Western Europe. The acme of religious symbolism is found in both the poetry and criticism of Vyacheslav IVANOV. Known as "Vyacheslav the Magnificent," Ivanov was a classical scholar who eventually became a Roman Catholic and died in Rome. His study of Dostoevsky, *Freedom and the Tragic Life*, is the ultimate in a metaphysical or anagogic interpretation of the novels, while his collection of essays on symbolism, *Furrows and Boundary Markers* (1916) is replete with sibylline utterances as well as diagrams showing how the artist ascends to and descends from the transcendental world. More conventional professional criticism is represented by the writings of R. V. IVANOV-RAZUMNIK, one of the leaders of the "SCYTHIANS," a group of fellow-travelers. As a critic, Ivanov-Razumnik appreciated the differences between the decadents and the symbolists (e.g., he recognized the shallowness of the novels of KUPRIN and ARTSYBASHEV and the significance of Bely's novel, *St. Petersburg*) and—as Belinsky did before him—he differentiated between the true artist who "renders" reality and the belletrist who merely "tells about" reality. Another important fellow-traveler group was the "SERAPION BROTHERHOOD" and the major figure here is Evgeny Zamyatin. The author of an influential dystopian novel, *We*, and many short stories, his impressive essay, "On Literature, Revolution, and Entropy" (1923) is justifiably famous and the only Russian item, for instance, reprinted in Irving Howe's *Literary Modernism*. Claiming that the only future Russian literature now had was its past, he was able to leave Soviet Russia in 1931. Zamyatin spoke out in defense of freedom of expression, of irony in literature, and of heresy and revolution; although always something of a Marxist, his views are, in the best sense, enlightened.

The post-symbolist movements of Acmeism and futurism also produced poets who were at the same time good critics. Both movements were reactions against the lack of clarity and the religiosity of the late stage of symbolism, Acmeism making a return to clarity its specific goal and the futurists attempting to incorporate in their poetry something of the technological dynamism of the 20th century. All three of the major Acmeist poets—Anna AKHMATOVA, Nikolai GUMILYOV, and Osip MANDELSHTAM—wrote manifesto-like articles on the aims of their movement as well as sensitive studies of poetry and poets. Here the critical articles of Mandelshtam are the most outstanding; in particular his study of Dante, in which the analysis proceeds almost wholly by metaphor, is remarkable. Although the *enfant terrible* of Russian futurism, Vladimir MAYAKOVSKY, tried to shock in his statements on literature (e.g., *How Are Verses Made?*, 1926) as he did in his poetry, it was Viktor KHLEBNIKOV who wrote more provocatively, yet seriously on the language of poetry. Together with another futurist poet, Aleksei KRUCHONYKH, Khlebnikov elaborated the technique of "transmental" language (ZAUMNYI *yazyk*) and theorized about the "internal declension" of words (i.e., the supposed relationship between words like "brick"/"broke", "dim"/"dumb", etc.). Although the Party authorities tolerated futurism and many other schools and fellow-traveler groups for some time after the Revolution and the establishment of Soviet power, by 1932, with the organization of the UNION OF SOVIET WRITERS, they were effectively disbanded and outlawed.

Akin to futurism in its radical rejection of the past, Russian formalism (the only "school" of Russian criticism to have had any appreciable influence in the West) was a reaction against both the old civic tradition, with its emphasis on content and moral responsibility, and the aestheticism and idealism of the symbolists. It reflects, too, an aspect of modernism best exemplified in post-impressionist painting: a canvas no longer represents a "window," *through* which one sees something more or less familiar; rather the *surface* of the canvas with its arrangement of forms and colors *is* now the painting.

Having its own formal origin prior to the Revolution in two groups of linguistic scholars and students of poetic language in Moscow and St. Petersburg, formalism very soon became associated with one name in particular, Viktor SHKLOVSKY. For Shklovsky, a work of literature was simply the sum of the "devices" (his "Art as Device [*priem*]" appeared in 1917) employed by a writer in manipulating his verbal material. This was an extreme position, modified, however, as time went on, by Shklovsky himself and other formalists. In one sense it is true that all we have in a sonnet by Shakespeare is an arrangement of words, either in printed form or vocalized; but in another, more profound sense, such a view is essentially superficial, to say the least, and many contemporaries—including TROTSKY—took delight in poking fun at the formalist approach. But it was a refreshing and provocative theory which, while denying traditional "meaning" in literature, stimulated a renewed interest in meaning on the part of both linguists and poets. Among the various "devices" noted and named by Shklovsky, several, such as the "device of defacilitation," the "device of retardation," "laying bare the device," and—most famous—the "device of defamiliarization" (*priem* OSTRANENIYA), are frequently mentioned by contemporary critics in the West. The less stringent formalism of Yury TYNYANOV, the author of novels and short stories (including one of the greatest, "Second Lieutenant Kizhe"), is well presented in his collection of critical essays, *Archaizers and Innovators* (1929). For Tynyanov, literature is still a dynamic verbal structure but it is also functional integration, a "system of systems." Indeed, the formalist background of STRUCTURALISM is clearly seen in a paper by Tynyanov and the late Roman JAKOBSON published in 1928. It was, by the way, Roman Jakobson, later to teach at Harvard and M.I.T., who introduced Claude Lévi-Strauss to structuralist concepts.

Formalism came under attack by Party ideologists in the twenties and thirties, since it is blatantly anti-Marxist, not to mention anti-Belinskian. It is outlawed today and even present-day Soviet Russian structuralists, such as Yury LOTMAN, must disavow any connection with the heresy. Therefore other critics and literary scholars of Shklovsky's generation who were influenced by formalist theory had to tread very carefully after 1930. Boris EIKHENBAUM did formalist studies of Tolstoi, Gogol, and O. Henry and wrote *The Theory of the Formal Method* (1927). The most scholarly of the formalists, Boris TOMASHEVSKY, the author of a *Theory of Literature* (1925), produced important studies of Pushkin's verse rhythms and was also interested in thematics. Viktor ZHIRMUNSKY resisted formalism's neglect of the relations between life and literature and advocated a more pluralistic approach; but this, too, was dangerous and in the forties he was attacked by more orthodox Marxist critics for his "cosmopolitan" comparative studies. A more peripheral figure was that of Viktor VINOGRADOV, a recognised Pushkin scholar and author of *A History of the Russian Literary Language*; he dealt in quite traditional and academic—but safe—fashion with his research and was rewarded with the Order of Lenin and a Stalin Prize.

Official MARXIST-LENINIST literary theory and criticism have for the most part been represented by a regular succession of run-of-the-mill critics adhering closely to the Party line. Russian Marxism has never produced a critic comparable, for example, to the Hungarian Georg Lukács or the German Walter Benjamin; and whenever we encounter, from the twenties on, a Russian critic or literary scholar who has something unusual to say, he is without exception a dissident voice. The first major dissident voice was that of Lev Trotsky (murdered in Mexico in 1940) who, in his highly ironic *Literature and Revolution* (1924), pointed out that the attempt by the Party to produce a "proletarian" literature was itself un-Marxist. Nikolai Bukharin (executed in 1938) criticized his fellow Marxists for ignoring formalist insights and spoke out in praise of PASTERNAK while condemning the idolization of Mayakovsky, Stalin's favorite poet. The Russian Socialist Republic's first commissar of education, Anatoly LUNACHARSKY, although he criticized Eikhenbaum's formal analysis of Gogol as "soulless," was remarkably sensitive in other ways; he helped edit *Essays on the History of Russian Criticism* (1929–1931) as well as the valuable *Literary Encyclopedia*, begun in Moscow in 1929 but later withdrawn from publication. Aleksandr VORONSKY advocated a more humanistic interpretation of Marx and opposed enforced proletarianism; he even suggested that Soviet writers point out the vices of Communists as well as their virtues. Vyacheslav POLONSKY was another moderate Marxist critic; and

Pavel Sakulin, the author of *The Sociological Method in Literary Studies* (1925), was primarily a literary historian whose work is vitiated, according to later Marxist ideologists, by "idealistic concepts."

Then there were the early "hard-liners", such as Aleksandr Bogdanov, the advocate of proletarian literature and founder of Proletkul't in 1917; Vladimir Friche and Vladimir Pereverzev, both exponents of "economic determinism" in literature and literary studies; and Leopold Averbakh, the virtual dictator of early Soviet literature, who urged participation by writers in the first Five-Year Plan. The Stalin years (1924–53), including the Zhdanov purge following World War II, were particularly grim: a critic or literary scholar could get into serious trouble by just mentioning the name of an "enemy of the people" in his bibliography. Comparative studies were condemned and absurdities were prevalent: N. Chuzhak (pseudonym of N. F. Nasimovich), for example, regarded fiction as "opium for the people"; he wanted to "concretize" and "technicize" literature and urged the production of "factography" or literature of fact. There were theoretical disputes as to whether, for instance, tragedy could any longer be permitted even on the threshold of a classless society and whether or not Soviet Russian literature was a continuation of a "single stream" or something qualitatively new and different. Silence was imposed on Viktor Shklovsky, and one of the finest of Russian literary critics, Prince Dmitry Svyatopolk-Mirsky (author of the prestigious *History of Russian Literature*), who chose to return to Soviet Russia after many years abroad, was eventually arrested and perished in prison. Critics and students of Dostoevsky, such as Leonid Grossman and Mikhail Bakhtin, were especially hard hit, their research interrupted and their studies suppressed. Although the hard-line critics (including Aleksandr Dymshits and Aleksandr Surkov) continued in the majority after the death of Stalin, occasionally the voices of "soft" (but by no means anti-Communist) critics and editors such as V. Lakshin and, especially, Aleksandr Tvardovsky were heard. The official Marxist-Leninist Party line continued thereafter to be followed by a great mass of critics, among whom we might mention Kornely Zelinsky and Boris Suchkov. The former, a theorist of constructivism in the 1920s, in his *Soviet Literature: Problems and People*, forlornly attempts to picture the dismal expanse of Soviet letters as something exciting; the latter, in his *History of Realism*, unctuously criticizes Western fiction and writes on the "ethical significance of socialist realism as the literature of the new civilization." Less offensive at least are the structuralist studies of a few present-day Soviet literary scholars such as Yury Lotman, several of whose works are readily available in English. In structuralist analysis one can avoid many political and ideological pitfalls, while structuralist tendencies can, without any violent distortions, be found in Marx himself.

In the late fifties Andrei Sinyavsky, already an established literary scholar and critic in Russia, began to have serious misgivings about the course and nature of socialist realism. The result of his musings—dangerous, to be sure—on this subject was his essay, "On Socialist Realism," which appeared in translation in the West in 1959 under the pseudonym of "Abram Tertz." In a severe indictment of socialist realism and the "teleocratic" system behind it, the author suggests that Soviet socialist realist literature, far from being a new and bold continuation of the great 19th-century realist tradition, is actually more akin to the formal neoclassical literature of the 18th century. Citing many parallels in support of this claim, Sinyavsky also reveals many other perceptive insights in this brilliant essay. Like Zamyatin, he notes in particular the absence of irony, that "faithful companion of unbelief and doubt," in present-day Soviet Russian literature. Another excellent example of Sinyavsky as critic is his devastating article on the poetry—especially "The Bratsk Hydroelectric Plant"—of Evgeny Evtushenko. But Sinyavsky was inevitably arrested, tried, convicted, and sentenced to seven years of forced labor in 1965. Following his release, he managed to emigrate and now lives in France.

While it is hardly possible to deal here with the subject of Russian émigré criticism, we might in conclusion mention at least the name of one critic important not only in this category but in a somewhat larger context as well. Whereas Sinyavsky is, like Zamyatin before him, a modernist in every way, Vladimir Weidlé represents an older generation of Russian émigrés as well as older, more traditional views. Born and educated in St. Petersburg, Weidlé left Russia shortly after the Revolution, settled in Paris, and became a French citizen. Appointed a professor of Christian art at the Russian Theological Academy, he shows in his many later writings an interest in both art and literature and frequently draws analogies between the two. For Weidlé, a Westerner in more than one sense and a man of wide learning and culture, pre-revolutionary Russia was an integral part of Europe: non-Russians were attracted to Tolstoi, Dostoevsky, Turgenev, and Chekhov because they recognized or rediscovered in the writings of these men their own image. Weidlé is quite hard, however, on a good deal of modern art and literature. This is especially clear in his *The Bees of Aristaeus* (1954) where the author hopes that a new art will eventually emerge, like the bees of Aristaeus in Greek myth, from what he considers the corruption of contemporary art. But Weidlé's reputation was not limited to émigré circles: in *Problems of Literary Evaluation* (Yearbook of Comparative Criticism, Vol. II, University Park, Pennsylvania, 1969) an article by him appears along with contributions by Roman Ingarden, Luc Benoist, and David Daiches.

Bibliography: Vernon Hall, *A Short History of Literary Criticism*. 1963. V. I. Kuleshov, *Istoriya russkoi kritiki*. 1972. (For the Soviet view.) R. H. Stacy, *Russian Literary Criticism: A Short History*. 1974. René Wellek, *A History of Modern Criticism: 1750–1950*. 4 vols. 1955–65. W. K. Wimsatt and C. Brooks, *Literary Criticism: A Short History*. 1962.   R. H. S.

Literary Fund, see *Literaturnyi fond*.

Literary Gazette, *The*, see *Literaturnaya gazeta*.

Literary language, *literatúrnyi yazýk*, is equivalent not to "language of literature" but to "standard language," to the German *Hochsprache*. It is marked by a high degree of normativeness of pronunciation, grammar and syntax, and by society's keen awareness of the differences between a multipurpose neutral core, on the one hand, and a variety of regional, racial, professional, situational, and other dialects or jargons, on the other. Ability to recognize and use the neutral literary language is essential for every fully-franchised member of the community; conversely, since the literary language must serve the entire community in all its variegated verbal behavior, it must itself be polyvalent, i.e., suited for many purposes, which in turn assumes a high degree of stylistic differentiation. The language of literature, on the contrary, has a primarily self-conscious or poetic function, opposed to the literary language as aesthetic to communicative, innovative to conservative, centrifugal to centripetal. A literary language can exist only in a developed national state, one with a sufficiently broad and influential educated population, conscious of the existence of the national literary language and of the problems of its evolution. In Russia, such a state of national consciousness was reached only in the mid- to latter 18th century, but the events of that period were the organic outgrowth of the preceding 800 years of sociolinguistic evolution. During this earlier period, sometimes called "the prehistory of literary Russian," the sociolinguistic situation developed from polycentric, with several genre-dependent language types but no polyvalent neutral core, toward monocentrism, i.e., toward the creation of a neutral language in relation to which all social, regional, and other varieties came to be regarded as deviating from the norm. Only from this time can one properly speak of the "history of the Russian literary language," i.e., of the evolution of the neutral core itself, an evolution rising from the continuing dialectic interplay between the normative literary language and the constantly evolving and innovative social and literary genres (themselves the result of the nation's social and aesthetic development), whose vocabulary, syntax, etc., confront the literary language with new denotative and expressive forms, the relation of which to the established norms must continually be reevaluated.

Overall, the creation and subsequent development of the Russian literary language can be viewed as a sociolinguistic response to the two great macroevents of Russian cultural history. The first of these was the Christianization and Byzantinization of East Slavic culture in the 10th century, the second, the secularization and Europeanization of Russian culture in the 18th (the polytechnicalization and internationalization of Soviet culture in our own time can be seen as an outgrowth of secularization). In both macro-events, *Rus'*/Russia was thrust into sudden contact with more sophisticated foreign societies, whose achievements could be assimilated only by absorbing a wide range of new genres, for many of which the preexisting forms of expression were inadequate. In both, the immediate linguistic effect was an enormous influx of barbarisms on many levels (borrowings, calques, semantic loans, syntactic patterns, etc.), followed by a long and complex period of assimilation or elimination of these barbarisms.

We can infer that in pre-Christian *Rus'* there were few linguistically codified genres, mostly inherited from the Common Slavic period: the legal code, the heroic epic, the fairy tale, and probably the incantations of the pagan cult. These were all oral genres; writing was restricted to a few treaties recorded for the princely court, a small number of religious books imported by earlier missionaries from Byzantium, and some insignificant ownership marks on pots and spindles. This state of sociolinguistic equilibrium was radically upset by the adoption of Christianity as the state religion in 988 and the subsequent massive influx of new genres, primarily written. These genres were both religious (the Bible, Psalter, lectionaries, canon law, hagiography and patristics, etc.) and secular (chronicles, travel accounts, fictional tales and legends), and were written in a slightly adapted form of Old CHURCH SLAVONIC, a language closely akin to Old Russian in its phonology, inflectional morphology, and basic vocabulary, but patterned on Greek and far more complex than Old Russian in its syntax (hypotaxis, complex participial and relative subordination) and derivational morphology (suffixal formations and compounds calqued on Greek), not to mention the entire Christian theological and esoteric secular vocabulary.

The advent of literacy, reinforced by the continued cultural influence of Byzantium, led to the rapid development of new translations and original works in Kievan *Rus'*. It was in this local response to the newly-imposed Byzantino-Slavonic religious and cultural framework that the mass of borrowed words, forms, and language types began to interact with preexistent, autochthonous genre patterns. Some local writing merely reproduced the language of previously codified genres (Church Slavonic in new liturgical texts, archaic East Slavic in the first collection of Russian laws, *Russkaya Pravda*). Other, more or less imitative genres were influenced by, but did not merely replicate, the language of similar preexistent genres (Church Slavonic in hagiography, religious passages in the chronicles; East Slavic in the political and testamentary charters [*gramoty*]). Still other, more original genres, for which there were no precodified models, were relatively free to pick and choose from both Church Slavonic and East Slavic elements, mixing them as best suited the subject matter and the tonality of a given passage (e.g., the *Pouchenie* of VLADIMIR MONOMAKH or the *Povest' o razorenii Ryazani*), or even deliberately contrasting them for the artistic shock effect (the SUPPLICATION OF DANIIL Zatochnik). Such mixing occurred not only in basic language forms (Church Slavonic *zlat-*, gen. sing. fem. *dobryya* vs. ESl *zolot-*, *dobroě*), but also on the level of stylistic convention, as in the complex combination of Byzantine rhetoric and East Slavic epic formulae in the *Igor Tale* (see SLOVO O POLKU IGOREVE).

The overall developmental tendency through the 14th century (i.e., continuing past the Tatar invasion and the geographical dispersal of cultural centers) was toward the creation of a neutral, Russo-Slavonic written language, within which the more salient Church Slavonic or East Slavic elements began to acquire the status of deliberate stylistic markers, e.g., Church Slavonic incipits like *Se az rab bozhii ...* in civil charters. However, this unificatory tendency never came to fruition. For one thing, the Russian morphological system had changed radically since the 12th century: the dual number, vocative case, dative absolute, and most of the past-tense verb system (aorist, imperfect, perfect, pluperfect) had disappeared from the spoken language, with the result that these now obsolete forms were just as strange to the 15th century scribe as the esoteric calques from Greek. For another, during the 15th and 16th centuries all religiously oriented writing was subjected to a forced archaization and rebyzantinization, the ultimate source of which lay in the nascent Muscovite empire's search for historical legitimacy. This archaization, the Bulgaro-Serbian component of which should not be exaggerated, was striking but ephemeral in paleography and orthography (reintroduction of the back nasal vowel letter, spellings like

sr''d'tse for *serdtse*, etc.), but had more lasting effects in the activization of new derivational models (adjectives in *-tel'nyi*) and the return to florid stylistic devices of the Kievan period (e.g., antithetic parallelism in the *Slovo* of ILARION, reflected in EPIPHANIUS' *Life* of Stephen of Perm). The combined effect of archaization of the high written genres and rapid evolution of spoken Russian made much of Church Slavonic an arcane and obsolescent language. These events did not stop the interpenetration of Church Slavonic and East Slavic elements (cf. MAKSIM GREK's Russification of the Psalter, the gradual absorption of Church Slavonicisms into the legal codices, etc.), but did retard this process of interaction sufficiently to prevent the formation of a standardized language in this Middle Russian period.

Two additional developments helped slow the evolution of a neutral standard language. On the one hand, the spreading hegemony of Moscow in the late 15th and 16th centuries led to the creation of a national chancery language, which, freeing itself of earlier dialectisms (tsokanye, confusion of *s* and *sh* and of *ě* and *i*, etc.) and absorbing many elements from *gramoty* and the legal code and some from Church Slavonic, evolved into a codified written bureaucratese which would henceforth compete with the now obsolescent Church Slavonic in the new genres that were soon to appear. On the other hand, in the late 16th and the 17th centuries, when the effects of neo-Byzantinization were fading, there appeared the first currents of Westernization and secularization, as the Latinized and Polonized sermons, rhetorical works, drama, and syllabic verse of the Ukraino-Belorussian *Yugozapadnaya Rus'* began to reach Moscow; a third, Western element was thus added to the Church Slavonic and chancery genres. At just this time (latter 16th century) the printing press finally appeared among the Eastern Slavs, an event of dual significance for the future: first, the portion of the population affected by, and hence able to influence sociolinguistic developments, began to grow, thus laying the foundation for the future national (universally obligatory) literary language; second, the first grammars and dictionaries soon began to appear (*Adelphotes*, L. Zizany, P. Berynda, M. SMOTRITSKY) and, together with the introduction of formal schooling, created pressure for grammatical and lexical normalization, another prerequisite for a literary language. One specific form of normalization was the compromise between Ukrainian and Russian evident in the later, Moscow editions of Smotritsky's grammar and the verses of PROKOPOVICH.

However, these first steps toward normalization were barely a beginning, and were no match for the overwhelming flood of new genres (military, civil engineering, geographical, botanical, journalistic, belles lettres) and of concomitant linguistic borrowings (Latin, Polish, Dutch, German, English, French) which poured into Petrinic Russia in the early 18th century. Translations from Western languages brought uncontrolled hordes of loans and calques into a still heterogeneous language trying to cope with Church Slavonic archaisms, bureaucratic jargon, and Polono-latinate syntax and word order; the resulting malapropian chaos would take most of a century to sort out.

The post-Petrinic amalgamation of Church Slavonic, chancery, and foreign elements was due in part to the very novelty of these many new genres, artistic as well as technical: because they had no codified linguistic tradition, they were receptive to new combinations of elements which would have been incompatible in stabilized genres. This freedom of combination occurred at a time when the centripetal effect of increasing literacy prevented linguistic experimentation from moving too far away from the evolving inter-genre core. In equal measure, however, linguistic amalgamation resulted from conscious intervention on the part of men of letters: during the 18th and early 19th centuries, as never before or since, sociolinguistic development depended not only on general cultural change (education based on Russian rather than Church Slavonic, increasing knowledge of German and French, the rise of publicistic genres, etc.), but on the imprint of the individual scientific and artistic personality.

Peter the Great had already imposed a measure of simplicity and clarity on the translators of his Foreign Office. The young TREDIAKOVSKY, in spite of his classical Church Slavonic education (he was the last Russian writer to have learned Church Slavonic properly) continued this effort to bring written Russian closer to the spoken language (*Ezda v ostrov lyubvi*), although he retreated to a more conservative Church Slavonic position in his later years (as would KARAMZIN, GOGOL, and to an extent PUSHKIN after him). The major event of the mid-18th century, however, was the appearance of LOMONOSOV's grammatical and rhetorical works: whereas all previous normalization had been based on a highly artificial, Greek- and Latin-oriented Church Slavonic, there now existed a prescriptive *Russian* grammar. Furthermore, Lomonosov's misnamed "theory of three styles" (which in fact deals mostly with the incompatibility of only two stylistic layers, high and low), in eliminating from written genres the most peripheral lexical items (obsolete Church-Slavonicisms and vulgarisms, respectively), took the first prescriptive step toward the restriction of stylistically incompatible extremes, i.e., toward the creation of a relatively unified common core. Lomonosov's own language, however, was a mixture of Church Slavonic and dialectal elements (as, to an extent, were those of DERZHAVIN and RADISHCHEV after him), and seemed too coarse to the increasingly gallophilic nobility, who were more pleased (because more closely imitated) by the Westernizing SUMAROKOV. By this time, too, the literate public had acquired enough feeling for sociolinguistic differentiation to permit the utilization of Church-Slavonicisms, chancery clichés, vulgarisms, etc. for purposes of character delineation (FONVIZIN's *Brigadir*); that is, public consciousness of the interplay between center and periphery was growing.

The growing numbers and social importance of those who had been raised to speak French as well as, or even better than Russian intensified the already-apparent gallification of Russian in the late 18th century, sometimes in more subtle ways: simple borrowings gave way to the hidden borrowing of calques (*voyazh* to *puteshestvie*, Fr. *impression* to *vpechatlenie*, *à vol d'oiseau* to *s ptichyego poleta*) and semantic loans (*ploskii* 'flat' acquires the additional meaning 'banal' from Fr. *plat* 'flat, banal'). French syntax, so-called natural word order (subject before verb, modifier before modified, etc.) and calqued phraseology so penetrated the Russian salon and the literature which imitated it (Karamzin) that a new "high style" came into being, a style adequate to the limited needs of the aristocracy but, ignoring as it did both the stylistic riches of Church Slavonic (as SHISHKOV was quick to point out) and the resources of the spoken language, was of little use to most of a technically and politically developing society. Because of his own popularity, however, Karamzin's "centrist" morphology (avoiding neuter plurals in *-i*, feminine genitive plurals in *-ov*, but accepting genitives and locatives in *-u* from spoken Russian and *eishii/aishii* superlatives from Church Slavonic), as fixed in the increasingly sophisticated grammars of his own and subsequent decades (Barsov, GRECH), became the basic morphological model of the Russian literary language until the present.

Pushkin is rightfully considered the founder of the Russian literary language. Building on an already-codified morphology, his contribution was mostly syntactic and lexical. Pushkin rejected the complex gallicized syntax of the salon in favor of the simple subject–verb–object sentence, uncluttered by Karamzinian modifiers. Pushkin's flawless taste allowed him to achieve the century-old goal of combining Church Slavonic, chancery, Western, and spoken Russian elements into a homogeneous but stylistically differentiated medium. In his work, Church-Slavonicisms no longer seem clumsy or arcane, but are utilized for well-defined purposes, whether metrical (*Na beregu pustynnykh voln* but *Rodilsya na bregakh Nevy*) or for archaising coloration (e.g., in *Boris Godunov*). The fact that modern literary Russian is first crystallized in Pushkin's work is due less to *what* he did (which was, basically, only to continue his predecessors' efforts to eliminate incompatible peripheral elements and strengthen the neutral core) than to the fact that it was *Pushkin* who did it; his genial artistry was the crucible from which modern Russian was cast.

Some frequently cited post-Pushkinian developments belong more to historical stylistics than to the history of the literary language; these include LERMONTOV's return to a more elaborate, rhetorically connotative syntax and GOGOL's deliberate confrontation of incongruous elements as a device for characterization (cf. LESKOV and SALTYKOV). The literary language itself continued its slow grammatical evolution (coagulation of the second genitive and second locative into true case forms, development of the new masculine nominative plur. in *-á*, of *-shche* adverbs from participles, and of secondary prepositions like *vrode, so storony*, etc.), while economic

and technical evolution caused a proliferation of professional jargons. The main event of the mid- and latter 19th century, however, was the shift in the "center of genre gravity" from poetry to prose, and then from artistic to the publicistic genres; this development, dependent on the broadening literacy of Russian society, pushed aesthetically oriented writing permanently to the sociolinguistic periphery.

The salient events of the early 20th century were a violent but ephemeral spasm of acronyms during the war and the revolution, and a short-lived attempt by some determinedly proletarian writers to grant every dialectal quirk the status of a Tolstoi. In our own times, the internationalization and polytechnicalization of the Russian vocabulary proceeds apace, sometimes provoking puristic outcries on the pages of *Voprosy yazykoznaniya*. Church Slavonic morphemes like **trat* forms are fully integrated into the derivational system (Ozhegov: "*oxladit'*—*sdelat' xolodnee*"; "*vratar'*—*igrok, zashchishchayushchii vorota*"). Changing sex roles cause insignificant but interesting shifts in gender patterns (*Novyi vrach voshel* to *Novyi vrach voshla* to *Novaya vrach voshla*). Word order begins to reflect topic-and-comment arrangements (*A apel'siny,—u vas est'?*), and this and other aspects of educated *spoken* Russian are now being seriously investigated, for the first time. At a time when radio, television, and other oral media have acquired unprecedented influence, and when the best normative grammars (AN SSSR 1952/1960, 1970, 1980) waver between traditional and innovative descriptive choices, this may indicate the beginning of a potentially momentous reorientation in the core of the Russian literary language away from the written and toward the spoken word.

Bibliography: A. V. Issatschenko, *Geschichte der russischen Sprache*, 1–2. Heidelberg, 1980–84. B. A. Larin, *Lektsii po istorii russkogo literaturnogo yazyka (X–seredina XVIII v.).* 1975. V. D. Levin, *Kratkii ocherk istorii russkogo literaturnogo yazyka.* 1957. A. I. Sobolevskii, *Istoriya russkogo literaturnogo yazyka.* Ed. A. A. Alekseev. 1980. V. V. Vinogradov, *The History of the Russian Literary Language from the Seventeenth Century to the Nineteenth. A condensed adaptation* by Lawrence L. Thomas. 1969. E. A. Zemskaya et al., *Russkaya razgovornaya rech'.* Moscow, 1973– .

D. S. W.

Literary prizes (literaturnye premii). As a permanent feature of Soviet literary life, literary prizes were first established in 1939, and on 15 March 1941 the first winners of the Stalin prize for achievement in the fields of prose, poetry, drama, and literary criticism were announced. Since 1943, authors of film scenarios are also found among recipients of this prize. Altogether, over 200 authors were honored, with prizes ranging from 25,000 to 100,000 rubles. Among them were many nonentities, but also some outstanding writers and poets, such as KAVERIN, NEKRASOV, and TVARDOVSKY. After Stalin's death these prizes were initially renamed "State Prizes of the USSR", then discontinued, but reinstated in 1966. Besides State Prizes of the USSR. (announced on the anniversary of the October Revolution), Lenin Prizes (announced on Lenin's birthday, April 22) have also been awarded since 1956. Among Lenin Prize recipients are LEONOV (1957), Tvardovsky (1961), AITMATOV (1963), MARSHAK (1963), SIMONOV (1974), etc. Lenin Prizes have also been awarded posthumously, to M. SVETLOV (1967), for example. Several other literary prizes were established in the 1960s and 1970s, by various agencies, such as the Komsomol, the Academy of Sciences of the USSR, the Ministry of Defense, etc. Various regional prizes also exist. The total number of literary prizes awarded every year varies, but is generally high. Awards tend to be politically motivated, and the lists of prize winners give a fairly good picture of the political climate of the year in question.   V. T.

Literary Scholarship, see SCHOLARSHIP, LITERARY.

Literatúrnaya Gazéta (periodicals) (1) 1830–31, (2) 1840–49, (3) 1929– . (1) Edited by A. A. DELVIG (until he encountered problems with the censorship) and O. M. SOMOV, but inspired by A. S. PUSHKIN and P. A. VYAZEMSKY, who contributed prose, criticism, and verse. A literary newspaper forbidden to publish political news, this first *Literaturnaya gazeta* appeared once every five days and featured literary news and polemics, criticism, bibliographical notices, verse, prose fiction, and translations. Doomed from the outset by F. V. Bulgarin's denunciations and public attacks, by government hostility, by the amateurishness of its editors, by its relatively high price, and by its inability to attract more than a hundred subscribers, the paper nevertheless published excellent verse by Pushkin, Krylov, Baratynsky, Davydov, Kozlov, and the exiled Decembrist A. I. Odoevsky; criticism by Pushkin, Vyazemsky, Katenin, and Leigh Hunt; and the first Russian translations of Stendhal, Hugo, Mérimée, and Janin. It waged its fiercest polemics against Bulgarin's novels and journalism and against N. A. Polevoi's *History of the Russian People.* (2) Another Petersburg newspaper, but under different management, this one appeared in different years once, twice, and three times a week. Edited by F. A. Koni, A. I. Ivanov, N. A. Polevoi, and A. A. Kraevsky it featured articles by Belinsky and literary works by Grigorovich, Dal, and Nekrasov. (3) The present version has been, since 1934, an organ of the Writers' Union of the Soviet Union. It has appeared at various times once, twice, and now three times a week. Since 1947 it has been a straightforwardly political paper as well as a literary one, publishing speeches and officially controlled news of leading Soviet bureaucrats together with feuilletons and literary items. As such it has less in common with the original *Literaturnaya gazeta* than with its rival, the Severnaya pchela.

Bibliography: E. M. Blinova, comp., *"Literaturnaya gazeta"* *A. A. Del'viga i A. S. Pushkina. Ukazatel' soderzhaniya.* 1966.
W. M. T.

Literatúrnyi fond, Litfond (Literary Fund; actually: *Obshchestvo dlya posobiya nuzhdayushchimsya literaturam i uchenym,* "Society for the Support of Needy Writers and Scholars"), an organization founded in St. Petersburg in 1859. Among its organizers were N. G. Chernyshevsky, A. V. Druzhinin, N. A. Nekrasov, A. N. Ostrovsky, I. S. Turgenev, and other prominent men of letters. The organization was run by an executive committee of volunteer members, which was responsible for fundraising activities, such as concerts, amateur theatrical performances in which writers of some fame, such as Dostoevsky, Pisemsky, and Ostrovsky, participated, and (since the 1880s) publication of works of Russian literature. Among the authors who at one time received support from the organization were Dostoevsky, Garshin, Nadson, Nikolai and Gleb Uspensky, Maksim Gorky, etc. The organization also established several university scholarships, supported needy families of deceased writers, and on occasion acted as an organ of the literary profession in general, for instance, standing up for writers who were in trouble with the authorities, as on the occasion of Gorky's arrest in 1905. The organization existed until 1918. In 1934, a new Literary Fund was established as an affiliated organization of the Union of Soviet Writers. Its functions have included aid to needy writers, organizing research assignments and field trips, housing, and other logistic support. The Literary Fund runs writers' clubs, rest homes, and book shops. It is financed by a share, prescribed by law, of the proceeds from the sale of works of literature as well as from theatrical performances, by membership dues, and income realized from the organization's activities. The Literary Fund is run by an executive committee appointed by the executive committee of the Union of Soviet Writers.

Literature: see *KLE* 4, p. 323.
V. T.

Lívshits, Benedíkt Konstantínovich (1881–1939), poet and memoirist. After being expelled from Odessa University for his participation in a student demonstration, Livshits entered the Department of Law at Kiev University in 1905, graduating in 1912. Livshits decided to follow a literary career, moved to St. Petersburg in 1913, and quickly became a leading light in the literary bohemia there. Livshits first published his verse in 1910 in the journal Apollon (No. 11) and, until 1920, contributed to a number of modernist publications and signed several futurist manifestoes, including "Go to Hell" (Idite k chertu) and *Futurists: Roaring Parnassus* (1914). However, in comparison with the voluminous output of David Burlyuk, Khlebnikov and Mayakovsky, Livshits's poetical production was limited and also of a more classical bent. Livshits's knowledge and appreciation of European literature, especially French symbolist poetry, are evident from his own collections of poetry such as *The Flute of Mar-*

syas (*Fleita Marsiya: Stikhi 1907–1910,* 1911) and *Wolves' Sun* (Volch'e solntse: Stikhi 1911–1914, 1914). Although Livshits continued to write and publish during the Soviet period, including his remarkable memoirs of the Cubo-futurist era, *The One and a Half-Eyed Archer* (Polutoraglazyi strelets, 1933), his last book of verse appeared in 1928: *High Noon at Croton* (Krotonskii polden') and he turned increasingly to translation work. Livshits's last literary publication was his anthology *French Lyrics of the 19th and 20th centuries* (Frantsuzskie liriki XIX–XX vv., 1937). In 1937 Livshits was arrested and imprisoned. He died in a prison camp. During the 1960s he was rehabilitated, a procedure marked by the publication of a miscellany of his translations of Georgian poetry—*Kartvelian Odes* (Kartvelskie ody, Tbilisi, 1964).

Translations: Five poems in *Modern Russian Poetry.* Ed. Vladimir Markov and Merrill Sparks (1967), pp. 348–55. *The One and a Half-Eyed Archer.* Trans. by John E. Bowlt. 1977.
J. E. B.

Lokhvítskaya, Mírra Aleksándrovna (1869–1905), poet. The daughter of a renowned lawyer in St. Petersburg, Lokhvitskaya was educated at home and later at the Moscow Aleksandrinsky Institute, from which she graduated in 1888. Her early poetry appeared in such prominent journals as *Severnyi vestnik* and *Vsemirnaya illyustratsiya.* The first volume of her verse came out in 1895, and a year later she was awarded the Pushkin prize for poetry. A second award was announced on 27 August 1904, after the publication of her fifth volume of verse, and was conferred posthumously in 1905.

Lokhvitskaya, the Russian Sappho, was much admired as a poet at the turn of the century and literary journals printed her poetry eagerly. Valery Bryusov praised the artistic perfection of her verse, her colors, and the melodiousness of her stanzas. She skillfully conveyed both her maidenly dreams and the charms of sorcery—themes reminiscent of the Middle Ages. Her poems are striking in their sensual evocation of fragrances and their imaginative ingenuity, revealing the elemental force of life, and the flame of passion. The idea and music of the Song of Songs underlie Lokhvitskaya's entire work. Her emphasis is on the divine nature of the human flesh, the force of Eros in the human blood, and its harmony with everything earthly—sun, air, grass, water, trees. Her verse displays that craving for the realization of earthly existence which may be found in Salomé, Sulamith, Balkis, and Sappho, in the women of Burne-Jones, Dante Gabriel Rossetti, and in Aubrey Beardsley. A Hellenic cult of beauty is perfectly unified with orgiastic outbursts of oriental passion. With regard to technique, Lokhvitskaya excelled in sound symbolism, the elaboration of melancholy musical chords in the final stanza, and synchronization of rhythm, theme, and imagery. In her poems, Lokhvitskaya insisted on the need for women to express their individuality freely, to lay bare the passionate, erotic aspect of their emotions, to explore and portray elements of their nature which outmoded and stereotyped definitions of "female" and "femininity" had excluded.

Lokhvitskaya's later works, reminiscent of Blok's desire to be beyond all considerations of good and evil, heaven or hell, echo her feeling of loss, loneliness, isolation, and sorrow. Like other symbolist poets, Lokhvitskaya believed in a higher reality. This idea found expression in her verse in the form of eternal, ethereal gardens permeated with spiritual significance. The same ambiguity is inherent in the poetry of Zinaida Hippius and Blok: the spirit and the flesh, the divine and the demonic, faith and disbelief, the bright sunrise and the gloomy sunset, lofty, ethereal gardens and the dark impulses of human passion on earth.

Works: Stikhotvoreniya. 1896. *Stikhotvoreniya.* Vol. 2. 1896–98. 1898. *Stikhotvoreniya.* Vols. 1–5. 1900–04. *Pered zakatom.* 1908.
Secondary literature: Articles in *Russkoe obozrenie,* 1896, no. 12; *Sever,* 1897, no. 44; *Novoe vremya,* 1898, no. 17896; 1904, no. 10003; *Nedeli,* 1899, no. 1; 1900, no. 10; *Russkoe bogatstvo,* 1900, no. 8; 1903, no. 3; *Novyi put',* no. 1; *Novyi mir,* 1903, no. 120; *Vesy,* 1904, no. 2; *Istoricheskii vestnik,* 1904, no. 2; *Birzhevye vedomosti,* 1905, no. 9003; *Moskovskie vedomosti,* 1905, no. 253; *Vestnik Evropy,* 1908, no. 7; *Obrazovanie,* 1908, no. 4. See also: N. Ya. Abramovich, *Literaturno-kriticheskie ocherki.* Book 1. 1909. S. A. Andreevskii, *Literaturnye ocherki.* 1902. Samuel D. Cioran, "The Russian Sappho: Mirra Lokhvitskaya," *RLT* 9 (1974), pp. 317–35.

Temira Pachmuss, *Women Writers in Russian Modernism: An Anthology.* 1978. Pp. 85–113. K. R. [K. K. Romanov], *M. A. Lokhvitskaya.* 1908. ———, *Kriticheskie otzyvy,* 1915. A. Volynskii, *Bor'ba za idealizm.* 1900.   T. A. P.

Lomonósov, Mikhaílo Vasílievich (1711–65), the most outstanding man of science and letters from the Russian peasant class in the 18th century. Born near the town of Kholmogory, in the vicinity of the White Sea, Lomonosov learned to read early, developed a great thirst for knowledge and set off in pursuit of it to Moscow, where, pretending to be the son of a priest, he enrolled in the Slavo-Greco-Latin Academy in 1731. Mocked by some as a country bumpkin, he nevertheless advanced rapidly in learning, was admitted to the Imperial Academy of Sciences in Petersburg in 1736 and the same year became one of a small group of talented young Russians to be sent to Marburg, Germany, to study mining and chemistry—to gain skills which were more important for the Academy at that particular time than advances in Russian letters.

Lomonosov's interests as a student in Germany were much more universal than only science and included classical Greek and Roman authors, contemporary German poetry and literary scholarship and, as will happen among students, wine, women, and song. The latter three caused Lomonosov some problems both with his German professors and with the Academy in Petersburg. In 1740, he went to Freiberg to study under Professor Henckel, but soon left for a year's wandering in Europe which included marriage and, reportedly, a brief stint in the Prussian army, from which he was glad to escape and come back to Russia in 1741.

In 1742, Lomonosov was appointed Adjunct to the Academy, working mostly as a translator. From there, he steadily grew in power and scholarly accomplishment, becoming Professor of Chemistry at the Academy in 1745, establishing a chemistry laboratory in 1748, contributing to the founding of Moscow University in 1755 (it now bears his name) and rising to membership in the Chancellery of the Academy in 1757. In many of these endeavors he was greatly helped by his friend and protector Ivan Shuvalov, a favorite of the Empress Elisabeth and a rich and powerful Maecenas in the arts and sciences. Strong-willed, temperamental, and ambitious, Lomonosov did acquire significant enemies, both in the Academy, where he frequently clashed with some Russian and, particularly, German academicians over issues of scholarship and internal politics, and among Russian men of letters, notably SUMAROKOV and TREDIAKOVSKY. After the death of Elisabeth and the brief interlude of Peter's reign, the Empress Catherine II seemed rather cool to Lomonosov as he declined in health and fortune, stepping down to meet his death in 1765.

Lomonosov was deeply interested in a broad range of topics which today would be placed in the fields of art, humanities, and the social sciences. As early as 1733, he wrote a draft for a textbook in oratory which he may have utilized later for his lengthy "Short Guide to Rhetoric" (Kratkoe rukovodstvo k krasnorechiyu, 1748). In effect, this latter treatise was also a commentary on stylistics, a topic of great interest to Lomonosov in terms of the structure and the uses of the Russian language. Lomonosov wrote a major study of Russian grammar (1757) and a brief but highly significant "Foreword on the Utility of Ecclesiastical Books" (Predislovie o pol'ze knig tserkovnykh v rossiiskom yazyke) as a preface to the 1757 collection of his works. This preface set forth the proposition that ecclesiastical books, written in CHURCH SLAVONIC, basically a South Slavic dialect into which elements of Russian had entered over the years, is a language which made the intellectual dimension of civilization accessible to the Russian people, because it had itself inherited and assimilated to the Slavonic tongue the rich achievements of ancient Greek. This being so, Russian letters can now operate in two related but separate idioms: the Church Slavonic and the Russian vernacular. In terms of stylistic norms for the Russian literary language, as well as in those of genre distinctions, these two levels should be related to each other in three different ways: a "high" style, containing a large proportion of Church Slavonic words understood but not normally used by educated Russian speakers, which would be appropriate for heroic poems, odes or solemn public address; a "middle" style, in which words from the vernacular may be combined with assimilated Church-Slavonicisms to develop a language suitable for the theater, for epistles, eclogues, satires and

such, and finally, a "low" style, using for the most part words that occur only in Russian, to be used for comedies, humorous epigrams, and the like. Lomonosov's propositions gained legitimacy as the norm, and the actual development of Russian literary styles did follow them to some extent.

Russian versification, a topic closely related to stylistics, drew Lomonosov's attention as early as 1739 when, as a student in Germany, he read Trediakovsky's 1735 treatise on "The New and Brief Method for Composing Russian Verse." Agreeing with the basic principle that Russian verses should be measured in feet and not by syllabic count, Lomonosov did not accept Trediakovsky's notion that lines most appropriate for Russian poetry should consist of eleven or thirteen syllables, be scanned in trochaics, have an obligatory caesura on the seventh syllable and permit no alternation of masculine and feminine rhymes. Instead, he proposed to bring the versification reform to its logical completion and accept both bisyllabic and trisyllabic meters, measure lines by the number of feet per line, allow various combinations of masculine, feminine and dactylic (trisyllabic) rhymes and indeed, the mixing of verse feet within a line. To Trediakovsky's trochaics, he opposed the iambics as the most suitable measure of Russian verse. Lomonosov's system is basically unchanged until today, and most Russian poetry is even now being written in this syllabotonic mode.

Lomonosov showed a philosophical concern for the future of Russia in his treatise "On the Preservation and Increase of the Russian Nation" (O sokhranenii i razmnozhenii rossiiskogo naroda, 1761) and a nationalistic one for its honor in his polemics on history, where he opposed the "Scandinavian" hypothesis on the formation of the Russian state, maintaining instead that Slavs themselves were its creators. Among his other writings, there even exists a set of ideas for suitable subjects of monumental paintings depicting glorious episodes from Russian history.

In the exact sciences, Lomonosov's achievements do not stand out today with sufficient clarity to ascertain his proper stature within the framework of 18th-century science. He has not documented any major discoveries, nor has he proposed any basic new theories. His concerns seem to have been for the most part either practical or generally descriptive on the essayistic level. One original contribution was the surmise, based upon his astronomical observations in 1761, that the planet Venus is enveloped in a dense atmosphere. Lomonosov also did research on the solid and liquid properties of matter, on electricity, on the nature and origins of light, on the relationships between the weight and mass of physical bodies and on a number of problems in chemistry. The discovery and exploitation of Russian natural resources, especially in Siberia, was also one of Lomonosov's concerns, to which purpose he made efforts to promote surveying and mapping expeditions. Some have compared Lomonosov as a scientist to Benjamin Franklin in America, but such similarity extends basically only to the practical, experimental interests of both men, to their philosophical attitudes supporting a rational, technically competent view of life, and to their concern with pedagogical activities promoting general enlightenment. Lomonosov, however, was able to integrate a large poetic dimension into his overall scientific world-view, indeed, to be in essence a poet on a grand scale in everything he did. The main impetus of all his creative activity seems to have been an overwhelming, unceasing sense of wonder at the enormity and complexity, at the power and mystery of the universe, manifesting itself in the mind-boggling infinitudes of stars as well as in the subtle and manifold beauties of the microscopic worlds.

This sense of awe and wonder, and of power, is certainly present in Lomonosov's literary works. It manifests itself nobly in his "Evening Meditation Upon the Greatness of God" (Vechernee razmyshlenie o bozh'em velichestve, 1743), written on the occasion of a great display of northern lights. In this poem Lomonosov operates with extreme rhetorical contrasts in order to convey his amazement at the mystery of Nature which has lit a light in heavens without the sun: as a grain of sand upon the sea, as a feather in a holocaust or a speck of dust in howling wind, so does the poet lose himself in the vastness of the mysterious universe. Unable to provide an explanation for just this one phenomenon of northern lights, what, asks the poet, should the wise men of this world think of the greatness of the Lord?

The "Epistle on the Usefulness of Glass" sent to Shuvalov in

1752, although belonging to the "middle" style in terms of Lomonosov's own definitions, does contain the same spirit of admiring awe for the works of Nature even as he praises the uses to which this crystal has been put by the progress of civilization. The "Epistle" is in principle a forensic exercise, aimed at convincing the reader that glass is no less a noble substance than precious minerals and gold. For this purpose, Lomonosov even supplies glass with a mythological pedigree: it was born from the cataclysmic union of fire and earth in a grand volcanic eruption. The argument then proceeds from a down-to-earth discussion on how glass serves many practical necessities to a social commentary on how it can flatter our vanity. At this point, a political commentary is made apropos of the shameless exploitation of the American Indians by the exchange of cheap glass beads for land and gold. While praising glass as the substance from which telescopic lenses are made to observe the wonders of the stars, Lomonosov takes the occasion to denounce bigoted obscurantists in the Church who would forbid the dissemination of Copernicus' discoveries. Here he is careful to attack only the Western ecclesiastical figures, including St. Augustine. In each description of the various uses of glass, Lomonosov manages to convey a sense of humor and of noble astonishment at the wondrous complexity of both nature and the human mind.

The grandiloquent rhetoric of exalted admiration served Lomonosov as an excellent artistic device in the solemn odes which he was expected to write on various state occasions, celebrating military victories, birthdays or namesdays of royal personages, their coronations, weddings, royal births, and the like. The objects of his praise did perhaps occasionally fall short of the wonders of distant heavens; in fact, they may not even have been great rulers on earth, but for Lomonosov they provided suitable opportunities to give full play to the baroque exuberance of his high poetic style. When reality fell short of rhetorical vision, Lomonosov transformed it into an image, an idealized world of verbal splendor in which the flattered rulers may choose to recognize their own grandeur, and that of their domain. The empire and the nation of Russia, however, quickly became the main topic and the true object of praise in Lomonosov's odes, because the nation itself, its greatness and promise, was for him the true source of inspiration. The one Russian tsar Lomonosov truly admired was Peter I, a ruler of similar grand vision in the practical affairs of state as Lomonosov was in the realm of the word, possessing a similar determined will and energy. The praises of lesser monarchs who came after were therefore more like exhortations to follow Peter's example. Lomonosov's one unfinished heroic poem, entitled "Peter the Great," is exuberant and hyperbolic in praise of the tsar's victories and noble deeds, particularly in his wars with Sweden. It is written on a monumental scale, following the pattern of classical heroic epics, except that Lomonosov substitutes six-foot iambics for the Greek and Latin hexameters which Trediakovsky had faithfully tried to imitate in his *Tilemakhida*.

Religious topics also were given a significant place in Lomonosov's poetry. In accordance with the expectations of the time, he wrote paraphrases of Biblical psalms, sometimes engaging in a rivalry with Sumarokov and Trediakovsky, as in the translation of Psalm 143, where part of the issue was whether or not the iambic lines have a nobler ring and are therefore more suitable to elevated poetry than the trochees preferred by Trediakovsky. The "Evening Meditation on the Greatness of God," as well as its companion piece, "Morning Meditation," on the same, are two excellent examples of Lomonosov's original poetry on religious themes.

Writers of Lomonosov's talent, and of his stature at the Academy, were also expected to provide original Russian plays for the country's developing theater. Accordingly, when in 1750 the Empress Elisabeth ordered that Lomonosov and Trediakovsky should each write one tragedy, Lomonosov rather quickly produced his five-act play *Tamira and Selim*, dealing with the difficulties caused by emotional conflicts between love and duty, standard in classical tragedy, in the context of the rout of the Tatar prince Mamai by the Russian forces at the battle of Kulikovo in 1380. Lomonosov's play was soon performed and well received, even if it does not quite meet the measure of his accomplishments in odes and in heroic poetry. His second play, *Demofont* (1752), met with less success.

Like most other authors of the classical period in Russia, Lomonosov was quite prepared to descend from the sublime to the ridiculous, or at least to the humorous, in various satires and parodies castigating the evils of society and, in the case of Lomonosov's enemies, their real or imaginary personal faults, or their lack of competence as scholars and artists. Most notable among Lomonosov's works in this "low" genre is his "Hymn to the Beard," written around 1756, when he was involved in a struggle with the Church authorities over his Copernican scientific views. It is a mock panegyric to the "hair that is respected by all," (especially by the venerable fathers of the Orthodox church) even if, quite unfairly, it was not granted the honor of being baptised at the baby's birth, like his other, less noble parts.

By any measure, Lomonosov is a giant figure in Russian science and Russian letters of the 18th century. Most inspiring about him for future generations of Russians may well be the humble circumstance of his birth; the son of a peasant, he walked proud and free in the company of grandees, scholars, and poets, and established his mark upon Russian history.

Works: Izbrannye proizvedeniya. (Biblioteka poeta.) 1965. *Sochineniya.* 1961. *Polnoe sobranie sochinenii.* 1952. *Izbrannye filosofskie proizvedeniya.* 1950. *Sochineniya M. V. Lomonosova.* Ed. with explanatory notes by M. Sukhomlinov. 4 vols. 1891–98.

Translations: Lewanski, p. 297.

Secondary literature: P. N. Berkov, "Problema literaturnogo napravleniya Lomonosova," *XVIII vek*, no. 5, 1962, pp. 5–33. ———, *Lomonosov i literaturnaya polemika ego vremeni, 1750–1765.* 1936. W. E. Brown, *A History of 18th Century Russian Literature.* 1980. Chap. 5, pp. 74–110. S. Chernov, "Literaturnoe nasledstvo M. V. Lomonosova," *Literaturnoe nasledstvo*, no. 9–10 (1933), pp. 327–39. A. I. Dudenkova, "O postroenii obraza v lirike Lomonosova," *XVIII vek*, no. 5, 1962, pp. 70–79. A. I. Efimov, *M. V. Lomonosov i russkii yazyk.* 1961. W. C. Huntington, "Michael Lomonosov and Benjamin Franklin: Two Self-Made Men of the Eighteenth Century," *RusR* 18 (1959), pp. 295–306. B. B. Kudryavtsev, *The Life and Work of Mikhail Vasilyevich Lomonosov.* Moscow, 1954. E. Kulyabko, *M. V. Lomonosov i uchebnaya deyatel'nost' Petersburgskoi Akademii Nauk.* 1962. A. Kunik, ed., *Sbornik materialov dlya istorii Imperatorskoi Akademii Nauk v XVIII veke.* Vol. 1. 1856. M. D. Kurmacheva, *Petersburgskaya akademiya nauk i M. V. Lomonosov.* 1975. B. G. Kuznetsov, *Tvorcheskii put' Lomonosova.* 1956. *Letopis' zhizni i tvorchestva M. V. Lomonosova.* A. V. Topchiev, ed. 1961. *Literaturnoe tvorchestvo M. V. Lomonosova: issledovaniya i materialy.* P. N. Berkov and I. Z. Serman, eds. 1962. A. Martel, *Michel Lomonosov et la langue littéraire russe.* Paris, 1933. B. N. Menshutkin, *Russia's Lomonosov: Chemist, Courtier, Physicist, Poet.* 1952. D. K. Motol'skaya, "Lomonosov." *In Istoriya russkoi literatury.* Vol. 3: *Literatura XVIII veka.* Pt. 1. 1941. Pp. 264–348. P. Pekarskii, *Istoriya Imperatorskoi Akademii Nauk v Peterburge.* Vol. 2. 1873. I. Serman, *Poeticheskii stil' Lomonosova.* 1966. ———, "Poeziya Lomonosova v 1740-e gody," *XVIII vek*, no. 5, 1962, pp. 33–70. G. Vasetsky, *Lomonosov's Philosophy.* Moscow, 1968. V. P. Vomperskii, *Stilisticheskoe uchenie M. V. Lomonosova i teoriya trekh stilei.* 1970. A. Zapadov, *Otets russkoi poezii: O tvorchestve Lomonosova.* 1961.

F. R. S.

Lóssky, Nikolai Onúfrievich (1870–1965), Russian philosopher, in emigration after 1922. Lossky was born in Vitebsk *guberniya* and educated at the classical Gymnasium in Vitebsk and at St. Petersburg University. He was a professor of philosophy at St. Petersburg University, and during the 1920s and 1930s at the Free Russian University in Prague. He moved to the United States in 1947 and lectured for several years at the Russian Theological Seminary in New York. After 1952 he lived mainly in Los Angeles and Paris.

Lossky played an important part in bringing German philosophy to a Russian audience. He translated Kant's *Critique of Pure Reason* (1st ed., St. Petersburg, 1907; 2d ed., 1915) as well as Kant's dissertation of 1770 (1902, 1910) and Paulsen's monograph on Kant (1899, 1905). He also edited two Fichte translations (1905, 1906) and was co-translator of Kuno Fischer (1901–05).

In addition to several significant treatises on epistemology (he called his own position "intuitivism"), metaphysics, and theory of value, Lossky published (in English translation) *History of Russian Philosophy* (New York, 1951), two articles on Lev Tolstoi (1911 [reprint 1978] and 1928), and the book *Dostoevsky and His Christian Understanding of the World* (Dostoevskii i ego khristianskoe miroponimanie, New York, 1953), a thoughtful and sensitive interpretation of DOSTOEVSKY's mature religious position. Lossky's memoirs (Vospominaniya) were published posthumously (Munich, 1968).

Works: B. and N. Lossky, *Bibliographie des oeuvres de Nicolas Lossky.* Paris, 1978.

Translations: See: "Selected Bibliography." In *Russian Philosophy.* Ed. James M. Edie et al. 1965. Vol. 3, p. 320. "Intuitivism," *Russian Philosophy.* Vol. 3. Pp. 321–42.

Secondary literature: A. S. Kohanski, *Lossky's Theory of Knowledge.* Nashville, 1936. N. O. Losskii, *Vospominaniya. Zhizn' i filosofskii put'.* Preface and commentary B. N. Losskii. Munich, 1968. V. V. Zenkovsky, *A History of Russian Philosophy.* Trans. George L. Kline. 2 vols. London and New York, 1953. Pp. 657–75.

G. L. K.

Lótman, Yúry Mikhailovich (1922–), scholar. A graduate of Leningrad University, Lotman has been a professor at Tartu University since 1963. A specialist in Russian literature of the late 18th and early 19th century, he has published studies on RADISHCHEV, KARAMZIN, VYAZEMSKY, PUSHKIN, etc., all of which are marked by impeccable philological and historical scholarship. In the early 1960s Lotman developed the theory of a structural approach to the study of literature, based on the concepts and techniques of information theory and semiotics. (See STRUCTURALISM AND SEMIOTICS) His books, *Lectures on Structural Poetics* (Lektsii po struktural'noi poetike, 1964), *The Artistic Structure of* Eugene Onegin (Khudozhestvennaya struktura 'Evgeniya Onegina', 1966), *The Structure of the Artistic Text* (Struktura khudozhestvennogo teksta, 1970), *Essays in the Typology of Culture* (Stat'i po tipologii kul'tury. Pt. 1. 1970), *Analysis of the Poetic Text* (Analiz poeticheskogo teksta, 1972) have been widely discussed, have created a whole discipline (the structural-semiotic approach to culture), and have been widely translated. An exceptionally productive scholar, Lotman has also done some important organizational work. In 1964 he launched the series *Trudy po znakovym sistemam* (Studies in Sign Systems, Tartu), which has produced important contributions, including some by Lotman himself, to the structural and semiotic approach to culture in general and to literature in particular. At the same time, he has been an editor of the series *Trudy po russkoi i slavyanskim literaturam* (1959–) and of *Sēmeiōtikē*, a series of papers produced by participants in summer seminars on secondary modeling systems at Tartu University. Lotman has expanded his structural-semiotic approach to some areas beyond literature, such as the theater, film, the visual arts, and general culture.

Works: Lektsii po struktural'noi poetike. Vvedenie, teoriya stikha. Tartu, 1964. (Brown University Slavic Reprints, 5. Providence, 1968.) *Struktura khudozhestvennogo teksta.* Tartu, 1970. (Brown University Slavic Reprints, 9. Providence, 1971.) *Vorlesungen zu einer strukturalen Poetik.* Munich, 1972. (With a bibliography of Lotman's writings, pp. 229–34.) *Kunst als Sprache.* Leipzig, 1981.

Bibliography: Karl Eimermacher, *Arbeiten sowjetischer Semiotiker der Moskauer und Tartuer Schule.* Kronberg (Taunus), 1974. Karl Eimermacher and Serge Shishkoff, *Subject Bibliography of Soviet Semiotics. The Moscow-Tartu School.* Ann Arbor, 1977.

Translations: (Several articles.) In *Semiotics and Structuralism: Readings from the Soviet Union.* Ed. and introd. Henryk Baran. White Plains, N. Y., 1974. *Analysis of the Poetic Text.* Ed. and trans. D. Barton Johnson. (With a bibliography of Lotman's works comp. by Lazar Fleishman.) Ann Arbor, 1976.

Secondary literature: D. Barton Johnson, "The Structural Poetics of Yury Lotman." In *Analysis of the Poetic Text.* 1976. Pp. ix–xxx. Ann Shukman, *Literature and Semiotics: A Study of the Writings of Yu. M. Lotman.* Amsterdam, 1977.

V. T.

Lozina-Lozínsky, Aleksei Konstantinovich (1886–1916), poet and author of travel books, wrote under the pseudonym Ya. Lyubar'. Little is known of his life. In his early youth a hunting accident crippled him, leaving upon him severe and lasting psychological effects.

He had entered the Menshevik faction of the Russian Social Democratic Labor Party at the beginning of this century and took part in the events of the 1905 Revolution. In 1913 he travelled in Italy. Unable to bear the weight of his morbid obsessions and mental disturbances, Lozina-Lozinsky committed suicide at the age of 30, after several unsuccessful attempts. Our main biographical source on Lozina-Lozinsky, G. IVANOV, gives a characteristically anecdotal account of his personality.

Lozina-Lozinsky's first collection of poetry, *Contradictions* (Protivorechiya, 3 vols., 1912), presents us with a bizarre mixture of populist and decadent themes treated in an eclectic and epigonic manner. His further work, however, *Pious Journey* (Blagochestivye puteshestviya, 1916) and especially *The Trottoir* (Trottuar, 1916), indicates substantial growth of his artistic powers. Still subject to many literary influences, Lozina-Lozinsky acquires a poetic intonation unmistakably his own, where a special tension is created by the juncture of a relaxed and often almost conversational style with his dedication to social, cultural, and philosophical issues explored with the utmost seriousness. In his best pieces he can approach the subtlety of Heine's vision, lacking, unfortunately, the latter's sense of humor. The grotesque contraposition of the refined and the vulgar, naturalism as if expressed by a rococo littérateur, is characteristic of his verse. But frequently it works to the poet's advantage, especially in moments of mystical expectation when he, "the martyred and self-mocking Harlequin," looks forward to an encounter with his Master and Creator. Premature death prevented his further creative development.

Secondary Literature: G. Ivanov, *Petersburgskie zimy.* 1952. Pp. 98–103. *Peterburg, Petrograd, Leningrad v russkoi poezii.* 1975. Pp. 208, 467. A. Tarasenkov, *Russkie poety XX veka, 1900–1955.* 1966. P. 216.

V. B.

Lozínsky, Mikhaíl Leonídovich (1886–1955), poet, translator, and scholar. Lozinsky studied first law and then philology at Petersburg University. He published some poetry, rather in the ACMEIST manner, until he discovered his real calling in translation. He is considered to have been one of the great translators of both poetry and prose in all of Russian literature. Lozinsky's translation of Dante's *Divine Comedy* (1939–1945) is considered to be his finest work. He also translated Shakespeare, Cervantes, Molière, Corneille, Goethe, Schiller, Heine, Lope de Vega, Sheridan, and many others. Lozinsky also wrote some scholarly articles, particularly on the theory of translation.

Secondary literature: E. Etkind, "Iskusstvo perevodchika," *Inostrannaya literatura,* 1956, no. 3. A. Fedorov, "O tvorchestve Lozinskogo," *Zvezda,* 1946, no. 10.

V. T.

Lubóchnaya literatúra, or "chap" literature, Russian popular illustrated sheets and booklets produced by woodcut or copperplate printing from the 17th century up to the 1917 Revolution. The illustrations were the so-called *lubki* (sing. LUBOK), popular prints of a crude character with hand coloring; the text was usually carved from the same block or plate and printed below the illustration. Songs and other texts were printed in single sheets. Longer texts, such as tales, were printed on a series of sheets, usually on one side of the paper only and with an illustration on most or all of the pages, which were then loosely bound together into a booklet.

The *lubochnaya literatura* constituted a main staple of peasant and lower middle class reading. It contained a great variety of texts. Some were older works of manuscript literature from the Old Russian period, such as the 14th-century *Tale of the Battle with Mamai,* a heroic work celebrating the first great Russian victory over the Tatars in 1380. The 17th century contributed a number of comic and satiric texts, sometimes making fun of vested institutions such as the Church and the law courts, e.g., the "Kalyazin Petition," mocking the monastic rule, or "The Judgment of Shemyaka," satirizing the corrupt practices of the courts.

Another large group of texts were tales of chivalry coming into Russia in the 17th century: of these the most popular was *The Tale of* BOVA KOROLEVICH, of French origin. Another tale of heroic adventure, though of Eastern origin, is *The Tale of* ERUSLAN LAZAREVICH. Both these tales took on many stylistic traits of Russian folklore as they were reprinted. These tales served Russian readers as an early fiction of chivalry and adventure and as part of a young and burgeoning secular literature such as had scarcely existed before the 17th century.

The *lubochnaya literatura* likewise included many Russian epic songs (see BYLINA) and FOLKTALES. In modern times popular works by a number of individual Russian writers have been reprinted in this literature, including SUMAROKOV, KARAMZIN, PUSHKIN, LERMONTOV and GOGOL.

Though certain tales of the *lubochnaya literatura* underwent the influence of Russian folklore, either at the time of their composition or as they were progressively reprinted, still the reader must take care to distinguish the *lubochnaya literatura* from folklore as such. For one thing, it did not circulate in oral tradition but in printed texts. Also, though its publishers were no doubt close to the Russian people, they were not in any sense members of the milieu which performed Russian folklore.

Bibliography: V. Bakhtin and D. Moldavskii, *Russkii lubok XVII–XIX vekov.* 1962. F. I. Buslaev, "O russkikh narodnykh knigakh i lubochnykh izdaniyakh," OTECHESTVENNYE ZAPISKI, 1861, no. 9. N. K. Gudziy, *History of Early Russian Literature.* New York, 1949. Pp. 408–28, 432–37. D. A. Rovinskii, *Russkie narodnye kartinki.* 5 vols. 1881.

W. E. H.

Lubók (pl. *lubkí*), a form of popular print illustration introduced into Russia from the West early in the 17th century. The original technique used was that of the woodblock print, often with hand coloring, but this was replaced by hand-colored copperplate etchings and other techniques from the middle of the 18th century.

The *lubok* was usually rather crude, with bold outlines and large solid areas of hand coloring. Although one must suppose that the first artists were at least in part Westerners, the subject matter was rapidly russianized, and almost from the beginning we find illustrations of Russian folk and popular lore, including the legendary Firebird or the Baba Yaga, the witch. *Lubki* have several diverse styles, depending on the subject: there are religious prints, some of which substituted for icons, as well as popular and folkloristic ones; there is also a large number of comic and satiric prints. Some of these have masked political significance, as the celebrated "Mice Bury the Cat," a reflection of the death of Peter the Great, whose moustache presumably resembled a cat's whiskers.

The *lubok* illustration was frequently accompanied by a text: this was carved out in script on the same woodblock or copperplate below the picture. Texts included folk songs as well as folktales and other popular tales. Collectively, this literature is known as the LUBOCHNAYA LITERATURA ("chap" literature). Longer stories required a number of pages with illustrations and text; these were printed on one side of the paper only and loosely bound.

Originally produced for the upper classes, *lubki* rapidly descended in the social scale, and in the 19th century were sold to peasants and to members of the lower middle class. Their production continued until the Revolution of 1917.

Though crude, the *lubki* had an undeniable influence on modern Russian art, particularly on the radically modern painting of such artists as Mikhail Larionov (1881–1964) and Vasily Kandinsky (1866–1944). Though distinct in style from Russian folk decorative designs, the *lubok* has served in recent times as one of a variety of styles now equated with Russian folklore and folk art.

Bibliography: V. Bakhtin and D. Moldavskii, *Russkii lubok XVII–XIX vekov.* 1962. Yury Ovsyanikov, *Lubok/ The Lubok.* Moscow, 1968 (bilingual Russian-English publication). D. Rovinskii, *Russkie narodnye kartinki.* 5 vols. 1881.

W. E. H.

Lugovskoi, Vladimir Aleksándrovich (1901–57), poet. The son of a teacher, Lugovskoi served in the Red Army in the civil war and graduated from the military Pedagogical Institute in 1921. After his discharge from the Army in 1924, he concentrated on his literary career. His first collection of verse, "Summer Lightning" (Spolochi) appeared in 1926. Also in 1926, Lugovskoi joined the CONSTRUCTIVISTS and was one of the most active members of that group until 1930, when he joined RAPP. His constructivist mode appears strongest in his collection "Muscle" (Muskul, 1929). Moods of revolutionary enthusiasm and self-effacing service to the masses prevail in Lugovskoi's early poetry. His poetry of the 1930s is for the most

part utilitarian, serving the "building of socialism." Nevertheless, some of Lugovskoi's poems were branded politically harmful by *Literaturnaya gazeta* in 1937 and his career came to a stop until the Thaw. In the 1950s, Lugovskoi produced three more books of verse, which he and his critics considered his best: *The Sun's Circle* (Solntsevorot, 1956), *Blue Springtime* (Sinyaya vesna, 1958), and *Mid-Century* (Seredina veka, 1958). Lugovskoi's lyric verse epics of these collections present his philosophy of life, dealing with problems such as the individual and society, the drift of history, and such.

Works: Sobranie sochinenii. 3 vols. 1971.
Translations: See Lewanski, p. 298.
Secondary literature: P. Antokol'skii, "Vladimir Lugovskoi." In his *Puti poetov: Ocherki.* 1965. E. Solovei, *Poeticheskii mir V. Lugovskogo: Ocherk tvorchestva.* 1977.

V. T.

Lukin, Vladimir Ignátievich (1737–94). Of obscure though respectable origins, Lukin became a clerk in the Senate in 1752, then secretary to I. P. ELAGIN, Cabinet Minister in the Imperial court and censor of plays for the Empress CATHERINE later. He translated and freely adapted French plays to Russian manners and customs, and published several, with prefaces expounding his theories of translation, as *Works and Translations* (Sochineniya i perevody, 1765). His "original" (i.e. not translated) five-act comedy *The Spendthrift Corrected by Love* (Mot, lyuboviyu ispravlennyi, 1765) was an early example in the Russian theater of the fashionable *comédie larmoyante*, and was produced successfully at Court in 1765. It is "filled with pathetic and noble thoughts," depicts "Russian reality" by the introduction of merchants, usurers, and card-players, thus reflecting the passion for gambling in fashionable society (a passion to which Lukin was himself addicted). After the production of FONVIZIN's *The Brigadier* (1769) Lukin's work for the stage became outdated. He was attacked in the satirical journals (1769–70) for deriding "famous Russian authors" (SUMAROKOV in particular), and withdrew from the literary scene. His work was forgotten (PUSHKIN never refers to him) until 1868, when PYPIN published a monograph which revived interest in his work and influence in the 18th-century theater.

Works: Sochineniya i perevody. Ed. P. A. Efremov. 1868. *Shchepetil'nik* [after the French *Le bijoutier*]. In *Russkaya komediya i komicheskaya opera XVIII v.* Ed. and introd. P. N. Berkov. 1950.
Secondary literature: P. N. Berkov, *V. I. Lukin.* 1950.

D. W.

Lunachársky, Anatóly Vasílievich (1875–1933), old Bolshevik and first Communist Director of Culture. Born in Poltava, Lunacharsky was a cultivated and humane man and a revolutionary *intelligent*, though some colleagues called him slow and naive. A revolutionary from 1892, a Bolshevik on and off from 1903, he wrote Marxist literary criticism, including studies of LENIN's views of literature, and fourteen plays. Lenin, often annoyed by Lunacharsky's pluralism, nonetheless appointed him in 1917 People's Commissar of *Prosveshchenie* (*education* or *enlightenment*). Here Lunacharsky worked valiantly to save Russian culture during the civil war. He saved old buildings, even churches. He found jobs and ration cards for non-Communist writers. He tried to lay multiple foundations for the future Communist culture of Russia. He encouraged both Russian-German modernism and revived radical realism, granting no trend a monopoly franchise. He discouraged dogmatism and censorship, patronized poets as diverse as ESENIN, MAYAKOVSKY and MANDELSHTAM, constructivist artists, and foreign cultural radicals such as Isadora Duncan. Stalin naturally removed Lunacharsky from his post in 1929. He was the prime mover and remains the symbol of the semi-freedom and semi-cultural pluralism of Communist Russia before Stalin.

Works: Sobranie sochinenii, literaturovedenie, kritika, estetika. 8 vols. 1966–69.
Translations: Three Plays of A. V. Lunacharski: Faust and the City, Vasilisa the Wise, The Magi. London, 1923. *On Literature and Art.* Moscow, 1973. *The Bear's Wedding.* Trans. L. Zamkovsky and N. Borudin. London, 1926.
Secondary literature: Sheila Fitzpatrick, *The Commissariat of Enlightenment: Soviet organization of education and the arts under Lunacharsky.* 1970. Howard R. Holter. "The Legacy of Lunachar-

sky and Artistic Freedom in the USSR," *SlavR* 29 (1970), pp. 262–82. I. P. Kokhno, *A. V. Lunacharskii i formirovanie marksistskoi literaturnoi kritiki*. 1979.   F. B. R.

Lunts, Lev Natánovich (1901–1924), playwright, writer and literary theorist. After graduating from the Department of Philology at Petrograd University in 1918, Lunts took up a graduate fellowship in the Department of Western European Literature there. As a founder-member of the SERAPION BROTHERS in Petrograd in 1921, Lunts authored their manifesto "Why We Are 'Serapion Brothers'" (Pochemu my 'Serapionovy brat'ya', 1922) and was involved in most of their early activities. With his colleagues, FEDIN, KAVERIN, and TIKHONOV, in particular, Lunts sympathized with the FORMALISTS' elucidation of the literary process, but still maintained that art must be thematic and narrative—as he demonstrated in his fantastic story "Reference No. 37" (Iskhodyashchaya No. 37). Lunts also believed in the need for Russia to imitate Western literary models as he maintained in his article "Go West!" (Na Zapad! 1923). In 1923 Lunts left Petrograd for Germany to where his parents had already emigrated and, it would seem, was preparing to stay there when he died suddenly of a brain embolism in Hamburg. Lunts's play *Outside the Law* (Vne zakona, 1921) was prepared for production in Petrograd in 1923, but eventually was prohibited because of its ambivalent portrayal of Communism, a gesture that presaged the long suppression of Lunts's literary masterpieces in the Soviet Union.

Works: Vne zakona. Reprint Würzburg, 1972. *Obez'yany idut!* (1921). In *Veselyi al'manakh*. 1923. "V pustyne." In *Serapionovy brat'ya* (1922). Reprint Munich, 1973. *Gorod pravdy*. In *Beseda*, no. 5 (1924). "Iskhodyashchaya no. 37," *Rossiya*, 1922, no. 1. *"Rodina" i drugie proizvedeniya*. Israel, 1982.

Translations: Lev Natanovich Lunz, *The City of Truth: A Play in Three Acts*. Trans. by J. Silver. 1929. (Russian title: *Gorod pravdy*, 1924.)

Secondary literature: Wolfgang Kasack, *Lexikon der russischen Literatur ab 1917* (1976), pp. 225–26.   J. E. B.

Lvov, Nikolai Aleksándrovich (1751–1803), poet and scholar. The diversity of Lvov's interests and accomplishments justifies his designation as a latter-day Renaissance man. In addition to his literary activities, he was one of the era's foremost architectural authorities, a botanist and imperial advisor on coal resources. Although he apparently took his poetic talent lightly, much of his verse revealing an ironic attitude toward both self and subject, he rendered several important services to Russian poetry at a time when the question of its direction and cultural function was of particular issue. Other members of Petersburg's literary society, most notably DERZHAVIN and KHEMNITSER, regularly sought his judgements of their work. Both by example and by his work as translator and editor, Lvov heightened his contemporaries' awareness of the indigenous folk contribution to the whole of Russian culture. Doubtlessly inspired by Herder's example, Lvov published his "Collection of Russian Songs" (1790), in the preface to which he emphasized their worth for an understanding of the national character. A 1793 translation of an Old Norse saga sought to demonstrate the appropriateness of Russian popular verse forms for capturing the spirit of the original. Indeed, it was his insistence upon accentual (see TONIC VERSIFICATION) verse as being more expressive of the national character than the SYLLABOTONIC forms established by mid-18th century practice that distinguished Lvov's original verse. The surviving fragment of an epic poem *Dobrynya* (1796), which he had planned as a proof of his contention, consists of unrhymed lines with varying length and beat. Although general interest in the *dol'nik* would not develop for more than a century, Lvov must be credited with an early, nationalistically colored appreciation of its legitimacy as a poetic form.

Works: G. Makogonenko and I. Serman, eds. *Poety XVIII veka v 2-kh tomakh*. Vol. 2. 1972.

Secondary literature: William Edward Brown, *A History of 18th Century Russian Literature*. 1980. Hans Rogger, *National Consciousness in Eighteenth Century Russia*. 1970.   P. R. H.

Lyubomúdry, see WISDOM LOVERS.

Maikov, Apollón Nikoláevich (1821–1897), poet. Son of the artist N. A. Maikov, older brother of the literary critic Valerian N. MAIKOV, and great grandson of the 18th-century poet V. I. MAIKOV, he grew up in a very cultured environment and received a superb education. He studied at Petersburg University from 1837 to 1842, then traveled in France and Italy. He served as librarian at the Rumyantsev Museum (at that time located in St. Petersburg) and from 1852, for nearly forty-five years, on the Committee of Foreign Censorship.

Maikov began to write verse from the age of fifteen and published his first collection in 1842. He continued the PUSHKIN tradition in Russian poetry and was recognized, particularly in the sixties, for his aesthetic tendency which spurned the call to devote one's art to the problems of social reality. His topics are taken either from antiquity ("The Bacchante," 1841), or are based on meticulous and sensitive observation of nature ("Paysage," 1853, "In the Rain," 1856, "Swallows" and "Haymaking," 1856). There is joyousness in his poems of antiquity where the bacchantes frolic on the green moss to the tune of the timpani and flutes, and there is delight in the observation of nature, caring for all of its creatures including man. Everything is arranged to perfection in nature, and creation's harmony is Maikov's theme. Maikov's poetry is distinguished by its lyricism and its perfection of form. He was a master in the use of versification. Throughout his life he served only the cause of art.

Works: Polnoe sobranie sochinenii. 9th ed. Ed. P. V. Bykov. 4 vols. 1914. *Izbrannye proizvedeniya*. 1977.

Secondary literature: N. L. Stepanov, "Apollon Maikov." In *Istoriya russkoi literatury*. Vol. 8, Pt. 2. 1956. Pp. 284–301.

J. B.

Maikov, Valerián Nikoláevich (1823–47), literary critic. Born in Moscow, son of the painter N. A. Maikov and brother of the poet, Apollon, he graduated from St. Petersburg University, obtaining his *kandidat* degree in 1842 at age nineteen. The young Maikov was a promising scholar and the author of numerous works in a variety of areas (including a dictionary of foreign words). In 1846, following the departure of BELINSKY, he became head of the criticism section of OTECHESTVENNYE ZAPISKI, but in 1847 his life and career were cut short in a drowning accident. Although Maikov, influenced by Feuerbach and the utopian socialists, recognized social and civic values in literature and defended the Russian realistic tradition, he attacked Belinsky for his view that literature should be subordinated to societal needs. But Maikov also held (following Hegel) that national and particular traits are in fact obstacles to human progress and the realization of ideals; that art and literature should further—and represent—the emergence of universal human qualities and virtues. Such opinions incurred the ire of Belinsky who called Maikov a "humanistic cosmopolite." Whereas PLEKHANOV later (in 1911) emphasized the gap between Maikov's heterodox line of thought and that of Belinsky, the civic critics, and the Russian Marxists, Dmitry SVYATOPOLK-MIRSKY in his *History of Russian Literature* calls Maikov "one of the small number of genuine critics in Russian literature." Especially noteworthy is Maikov's essay "Something on Russian Literature in 1846" (Nechto o russkoi literature v 1846 godu) in which he points out the originality of Dostoevsky's psychological analysis of character.

Works: Kriticheskie opyty. 1891. *Sochineniya*. 2 vols. 1901.

Secondary literature: V. I. Kuleshov, *Istoriya russkoi kritiki*. 1972. Carroll Cargill Power, "V. N. Maikov's Contribution to Russian Literary Criticism," *Language Quarterly* 13 (1975), no. 3–4, pp. 38–42. Brief notice in R. Stacy, *Russian Literary Criticism: A Short History* (1974).   R. H. S.

Maikov, Vasily Ivánovich (1728–78), poet and satirist. The son of a provincial gentry family, Maikov was never properly educated, either at home or during his long army service, begun at age fourteen. His lack of sophistication was, however, more than compensated for by his innate intelligence and rich poetic gifts. Moreover, Maikov profited from his intimate acquaintance with many of the best minds and talents of the age (SUMAROKOV, KHERASKOV, I. P. ELAGIN, Z. G. Chernyshev, etc.).

The protégé of the masters of Russian NEOCLASSICISM, Maikov rendered signal service by providing one of its greatest and most applauded masterpieces, the mock-epic *Elisei, or Bacchus Enraged* (*Elisei, ili razdrazhennyi Vakkh*, 1771). Written in the canonical heroic meter (alexandrine couplets) and uniquely combining the two types of mock-epic (lofty language plus low subject matter and vice versa), *Elisei* exploits the real fact of a steep rise in the price of vodka to generate a rollicking, often hilarious tale, full of carnivalized drunkenness, sex, and violence, with a cast of characters from the Olympian gods to the riffraff of St. Petersburg. The very nature of mock-epic allowed for *literary* mockery and Maikov took full advantage of the opportunity, particularly against V. PETROV. In many respects *Elisei* was heavily influenced by the pornographic burlesques of I. BARKOV who is addressed in its proem under the sobriquet "Scarron."

Maikov's other verses include an earlier, more modest mock epic, based on a game of cards, and numerous fables, epistles, epigrams, etc. Maikov also wrote for the theater. But, after his mock-epic, the most outstanding of his works are no doubt his odes. Particularly impressive are his spiritual odes, strikingly baroque in character, among them a magnificent "Ode on the Final Judgement."

Works: Izbrannye proizvedeniya. Ed. A. V. Zapadov. (Biblioteka poeta, bol'shaya seriya.) 1966.

Translation: "Elisei, or Bacchus Enraged." In *The Literature of Eighteenth Century Russia*. Ed. H. Segel. Vol. 2. 1967.

Secondary literature: G. A. Gukovskii, "Maikov." In *Istoriya russkoi literatury*. Vol. 4, pt. 2. 1947. Pp. 201–26. A. V. Zapadov, "Tvorchestvo V. I. Maikova." In *Izbrannye proizvedeniya*. Ed. A. V. Zapadov. (Biblioteka poeta, bol'shaya seriya.) 1966. Pp. 5–52.

I. R. T.

Makárenko, Antón Semyónovich (1888–1939), educator and writer. Makarenko graduated in 1914 from the Poltava Teachers Institute. After various teaching jobs in the Ukraine he agreed in 1920 to organize a school for juvenile delinquents (*besprizornye*). This school—the Gorky Colony—was located near Poltava and later near Kharkov. In *The Road to Life*, published serially from 1933 to 1935, Makarenko described in vivid and dramatic detail, with a true storyteller's art, the various human, physical, and educational obstacles he had to overcome to create the Gorky Colony. Gorky acclaimed *The Road to Life* as one of the best works in Soviet literature.

At the invitation of the NKVD Makarenko set up a larger reform school, the Dzherzinsky Commune (1927–35), near Kharkov. He made this commune nationally famous for its economic productivity and the transformation of delinquents into "the new Soviet man." His educational theory combined manual work, schooling, military discipline, and an optimistic faith in human potential which he ascribed to his youthful reading of Gorky. Makarenko wrote a fictionalized account of the Dzherzinsky Commune in *Learning to Live* (1938).

His second most important work after *The Road to Life* was *The Book of Parents* (1937) in which he contrasted the upbringing of children in bourgeois families and in the ideal Soviet family. In this book poignant vignettes and subtle psychological analysis alternated with abstract theory.

In his last years Makarenko turned more and more to creative writing. He wrote stories for children, screen scripts, and a novel, *Honor* (1937), about his parents and the working-class milieu of his childhood.

Works: Sochineniya. 2d ed. 7 vols. 1957–58.

Translations: Learning to Live [trans. of *Flagi na bashnyakh*]. Moscow, 1953. *A Book for Parents* [trans. of *Kniga dlya roditelei*]. Moscow, 1954. Reprinted as *The Collective Family: A Handbook for Russian Parents*. Introd. Urie Bronfenbrenner. Garden City, N.Y., 1967. *The Road to Life* [trans. of *Pedagogicheskaya poema*]. Trans. Ivy and Tatiana Litvinov. 3 vols. Moscow, 1955. Reprinted by Peter Smith, Gloucester, Mass., 1973.

Secondary literature: Makarenko, His Life and Work (Articles, Talks, Reminiscences). Moscow, 1964. *Russkie sovetskie pisateli-prozaiki: Bibliograficheskii ukazatel'*. Vol. 3. 1964. Pp. 7–35.

N. R.

Makáry (Macarius), Metropolitan (1482–1563). Ecclesiastic who played a decisive part in the subordination of religious, political, and intellectual life to the interests of the Muscovite crown and state. His significance for Old Russian literature rests primarily on his role as initiator and organizer of vast editorial enterprises which aimed to affirm a new vision of Orthodoxy. Ordained in the monastery of Pafnuty Borovsky, Makary became a strong supporter of the so-called *Osiflyane* (Josephites), that is, the followers of IOSIF VOLOTSKY. After serving as archbishop of Novgorod, he became Metropolitan of Moscow in 1542. Under Makary's influence, IVAN IV assumed the title of "Tsar." Makary was the initiator of several church councils which sought to regulate both ecclesiastic and civil law. Of particular importance was the Council of 1551 which gave rise to the STOGLAV (Book of Hundred Chapters) and the *Sudebnik* (Code of Laws).

It is noteworthy that Makary actually promoted the use of printing in Muscovy. It was he who had Ivan Fyodorov trained for the production of the first printed church books (1564–65). Makary's most important undertaking was the new MINEI CHET'I (Monthly Readings; completed in 1552), on which he had already begun work in Novgorod. This revised hagiographic collection was made necessary by Makary's ecclesiastic-political actions (especially at the Councils of 1547 and 1549), which sought to replace locally-revered cults with saints that reflected better the unity of Muscovy as a church-state. Makary and his circle produced other important collections, most notably, the *Kniga stepennaya tsarskogo rodosloviya* (Book of Degrees of the Tsar's Genealogy, 1560–63) (see STEPENNAYA KNIGA), which represents the most authoritative expression of the dynastic ambitions of the Muscovite autocrats.

Bibliography: E. E. Golubinskii, *Istoriya Russkoi tserkvi*. Vol. 2. 1900. Pp. 744–875. A. V. Kartashev, *Ocherki po istorii Russkoi tserkvi*. Vol. 1. 1959. Pp. 424–42. N. Lebedev, *Makarii, Mitropolit vserossiiskii*. 1877. Makarii [Bulgakov], Metropolitan. *Istoriya Russkoi tserkvi*. Vol. 6. Pp. 209–94. I. I. Smirnov, *Ocherki politicheskoi istorii Russkogo gosudarstva 30–50kh godov XVI veka*. 1958. Pp. 194–202.

R. P.

Makóvsky, Sergeí Konstantínovich (1877–1962), poet, critic, art theorist, and memoirist. Son of the renowned painter Konstantin Makovsky and a celebrated beauty of the day, Makovsky from early childhood moved in the center of St. Petersburg artistic life. From 1909 to 1913 he edited the journal APOLLON, where he printed the poems of his "discoveries," Anna AKHMATOVA and Cherubina de Gabriak (pseudonym of Elizaveta Ivanovna Dmitrieva), and published several books, among them his *Collected Poems* (1905) and *Russian Graphics* (1916).

Devoted to art, Makovsky was interested only in the spiritual. Materialism was as alien to him as was the 20th-century spirit of experimentation in versification. Instead he looked for inspiration to the old and well-tested Russian poetic tradition. Heavy archaisms from the 18th-century (and from TYUTCHEV), a solemn tone, and a craving for a Pushkinian "concentrated solitude" were three distinguishing features of his poetic world. He accepted life with wisdom and sober gratitude—especially in Italy, where he could meditate on the Old Testament while admiring the ruins of ancient Rome. Makovsky was a writer of great spiritual culture.

Works: Siluety russkikh khudozhnikov. Prague, 1921. *Poslednie itogi zhivopisi*. Berlin, 1922. *Somnium Breve*. Paris, 1948. *God v usad'be: sonety*. Paris, 1949. *Krug i teni: pyataya kniga stikhov*. Paris, 1951. *Na puti zemnom: shestaya kniga stikhov*. Paris, 1953. *V lesu: sed'maya kniga stikhov*. Munich, 1956. *Eshche stranitsa: vos'maya kniga stikhov*. Paris, 1957. *Na Parnase serebryanogo veka*. Munich, 1962. *Requiem*. Paris, 1963. Makovsky also contributed to many Russian periodicals in the West, and his poetry was included in several anthologies.

Secondary literature: Yury Annenkov. *Dnevnik moikh vstrech: tsikl tragedii*. New York, 1966. Vol. 2, pp. 229–36. Innokenty Annensky. *Knigi otrazhenii*. 1979. Temira Pachmuss, *A Russian Cultural Revival: A Critical Anthology of Emigré Literature before 1939*. 1981. Pp. 382–83.

T. A. P.

Maksim Grek (secular name: Mikhail Trivolis, ca. 1475–1556), cleric, theologian, philologist, grammarian, and writer, was sent to Moscow from Mt. Athos in 1518 at the request of Vasily III, to perform a revision of translated texts in his library. A learned philologist, who had known several leading Italian humanists before dispatched to Russia, Maksim did a competent job of collating Slavonic texts with their Greek originals and soon was able to contribute his own translations of saints' lives by Symeon Metaphrastes (10th cent.), making a significant contribution to the Minei chet'i of Metropolitan Makary. Maksim's scholarly integrity eventually became his downfall. Influential Russian clerics disapproved of corrections he made in sacred texts, Maksim was accused of heresy, lost his position as the Grand Duke's librarian and translator, and spent over twenty-five years as a prisoner in various monasteries. He was allowed to continue his literary activities, though, and produced a number of didactic and polemic tracts in which he challenged not only the positions of the Josephites (see Iosif Volotsky), but the whole social order under emerging Muscovite absolutism. The best known of these is his "Homily Expounding in Detail and with Sorrow the Disorders and Outrages of Rulers and Authorities of Recent Times" (Inoka Maksima Greka slovo, prostranno izlagayushchee, s zhalostiyu, nestroeniya i bezchiniya tsarei i vlastei poslednego zhitiya), an allegorical presentation of Vasiliya (Greek. "the state"), a noble woman, grieving at the abuses suffered by her domain at the hands of her rapacious, dishonest, and cruel servants.

Works: Sochineniya. 3 vols. Kazan, 1859–62. *Sochineniya.* 3 vols. Sv.-Troitskaya lavra, 1910–11. Addenda to these: *TODRL* 1934, vol. 1, pp. 111–20; *Byzantinoslavica* 6 (1935–36), pp. 85–109; *Vizantiiskii vremennik* 14 (1958), pp. 164–74.
Secondary literature: V. S. Ikonnikov, *Maksim Grek i ego vremya.* 2d. ed. 1915.   V. T.

Maksimov, Sergei Sergeevich (literary pseudonym: Sergei Shirokov, 1917–67), prose writer, dramatist and poet, was born on the Volga into the family of a village school teacher. In 1934 he entered the Literary Institute in Moscow and published in the journals *Murzilka* and *Smena*, but his study there was interrupted by his arrest and incarceration in 1936. After five years in a concentration camp he was sentenced to internal exile. In 1942 he published his first book of poetry and stories, *Sumerki* (Twilight). In 1944 he left the Soviet Union. His first and only novel, *Denis Bushuev* (vol. 1, 1949; vol. 2, *The Revolt of Denis Bushuev*, 1956) was written entirely in the West and, together with a collection of short stories, a few poems and a play—all of them of secondary significance—comprises his literary legacy. An early death prevented the further development of Maksimov's talent, though his novel demonstrates its impressive initial qualities and remarkable artistic potential. It may well be that Maksimov is the only important prose writer produced by the Second Emigration, distinguished not so much by his subject-matter (the tragical experience of Soviet man was then a common enough topic), but by the relaxed maturity of his style and an insightful panoramic view of Soviet society. The rise and fall of the hero, a talented author, whose character presumably contains autobiographical elements, is traced from his humble peasant origins through the period of his officious celebrity to a dramatic confrontation with Stalin himself on aesthetic as well as political grounds. Certain literary influences, most prominently those of Sholokhov and Leonov, are perceptible but never dominating; the author's own vision and personality are inherently present. Written in a traditional realistic vein, Maksimov's prose is rich in observations and revealing details. His artistry stands comparisons with and perhaps surpasses that of the best specimens of Soviet prose writing of the thirties and forties. The early work of his namesake Vladimir Maksimov may possibly serve as a relatively recent analogue, reminiscent of Maksimov's achievement both in temperament and subject-matter.

Works: Taiga. 1952. *Goluboe molchanie.* 1953.
Translations: Denis Bushuev. 1957. *The Restless Heart.* Trans. H. Reigart. 1951.
Secondary literature: Literaturnoe zarubezh'e 15 (1958). V. Samarin, "Odisseya russkogo pisatelya," *Vozrozhdenie,* no. 207 (March 1969), pp. 115–21.   V. B.

Maksimov, Vladimir Emelyanovich (pseud., real name: Lev Alekseevich Samsonov, 1932–   ), poet, prose writer, and editor. With his father in prison after 1933, Maksimov grew up in orphanages and schools for juvenile delinquents. He then worked as a bricklayer and farmhand, but began to publish poetry as early as 1952. His first prose work to attract attention was the long short-story, "We Make the Earth Feel Homey" (My obzhivaem zemlyu, 1961), which appeared in the celebrated collection *Pages from Tarusa.* Another story, "Man Keeps on Living" (Zhiv chelovek, 1962) appeared in the journal Oktyabr' and was a major hit when made into a play (1965). Maksimov's career as a contributor to *Oktyabr'* and a member of its editorial board came to a halt when his first novel, *The Seven Days of Creation* (Sem' dnei tvoreniya, 1971) appeared in the West, receiving wide recognition. After Maksimov's second novel, *Quarantene* (Karantin) began to circulate in *Samizdat*, Maksimov was expelled from the Union of Soviet Writers in 1973 and emigrated in 1974. He settled in Paris, where he completed his third novel, *Farewell from Nowhere,* and assumed editorship of the journal Kontinent. Maksimov's prose deals with the neglected and alienated "lower" classes of Soviet society, giving awkward yet powerful expression to their feelings and dreams. The basic mood of Maksimov's art is somberly tragic, with a ray of light suggested by the hope of regeneration through Christian faith. His treatment of point of view and of time and space is highly irregular, his composition jerky, and his descriptions often overly naturalistic. However, Maksimov's prose has power and immediacy.

Works: Sobranie sochinenii. 6 vols. Frankfurt/Main, 1975–79.
Translations: A Man Survives. Trans. Anselm Hollo. 1963. *The Seven Days of Creation.* 1975. *Farewell from Nowhere.* Trans. Michael Glenny. 1979.
Secondary literature: Anne C. Hughes, "The Significance of 'Stan' za chertu' in Vladimir Maksimov's Literary Development," *Journal of Russian Studies* 36 (1978), pp. 19–26. Leonid Rzhevskii, "Triptikh V. E. Maksimova: Algebra i garmoniya," *Grani* 10 (1978), pp. 229–66.   V. T.

Mamin-Sibiryak, Dmitry Narkisovich (pseud. of D. N. Mamin, 1852–1912), short-story writer, novelist, and dramatist. The son of a priest, Mamin attended the Perm Theological Seminary and St. Petersburg University without completing his studies. His first story, "Elders" (Startsy, 1875) and his first novel, *In the Whirlpool of Passions* (V vodovorote strastei, 1876) were largely imitative. Mamin is best known for his novels of folk life in the Urals and portrayals of Siberian mining settlements, experiencing the growth of capitalism with the attendant exploitation of workers. Despite their lyric portrayal of the toiling masses, these works suffer from verbosity, artificial plots, and weak structure. Mamin's best novels are: *Privalov's Millions* (Privalovy milliony, 1883), a satirical treatment of the greedy bourgeoisie; *Mountain Nest* (Gornoe gnezdo, 1884), revealing a deep gulf between Ural industrialists and workers; *Wild Happiness* (Dikoe schast'e, 1884), depicting the moral bankruptcy of a merchant family; *Three Ends* (Tri kontsa, 1890), a study in the character of the Russian masses; *Gold* (Zoloto, 1892), which discredits populist ideas of "people's industry;" and *Bread* (Khleb, 1895), about the plight of starving peasants. Mamin's other significant works include *Siberian Stories* (Sibirskie rasskazy, 1895) and *Ural Stories* (Ural'skie rasskazy, 4 vols., 1888–1901). Mamin cultivated other genres as well, notably: dramatic works (*Gold Miners*—Zolotopromyshlenniki, 1877), sketches ("Fighters"—Boitsy, 1883), novellas ("Gordeev Brothers"—Brat'ya Gordeevy, 1891), publicistic essays ("From the Urals to Moscow"—Ot Urala do Moskvy, 1881–82), and legends ("Khantygayan Swan"—Lebed' Khantygaya, 1891). He also wrote autobiographical works (*Traits from Pepko's Life*—Cherty iz zhizni Pepko, 1894) and excelled in stories for and about children ("Emelya the Hunter"—Emelya-okhotnik, 1884, and "Gray Neck"—Seraya sheika, 1893), as well as fairy tales ("Alyonushka's Fairy Tales"—Alenushkiny skazki, 1894–96).

Works: Polnoe sobranie sochinenii. 12 vols. 1915–17. *Sobranie sochinenii.* 12 vols. Sverdlovsk, 1948–51. *Sobranie sochinenii.* 10 vols. 1958.
Translations: See Lewanski, p. 355.
Secondary literature: I. Dergachev, *D. N. Mamin-Sibiryak: Lichnost', tvorchestvo.* 1977. *D. N. Mamin-Sibiryak v vospominaniyakh*

sovremennikov. 1962. V. A. Kovalev, "D. N. Mamin-Sibiryak v sovetskom literaturovedenii (60–70-e gody)," *RLit* 22 (1979), no. 2, pp. 191–98.

L. P.

Mandelshtám (née Khazin), Nadézhda Yákovlevna (1899–1980), author of *Hope Against Hope* and *Hope Abandoned*, and wife of the poet, Osip MANDELSHTAM, was raised and educated in the intellectual and artistic circles of pre-revolutionary Kiev. Well-read, well-travelled, and well-versed in several European languages, including English, she was also abreast of the art movements of the early 20th century, having studied in the studio of Aleksandra Ekster. On 1 May 1919, she met Osip Mandelshtam, then on a visit to Kiev, in the basement cabaret, frequented by artists, actors, writers, and musicians, known as The Junk Shop. She claims this date in her memoirs as the beginning of "our life together," although it was not until March 1921 that Mandelshtam brought Nadezhda to Moscow. Officially married in Kiev in 1922, they returned to Moscow to live in the Herzen House until they could find a place of their own. Nadezhda Mandelshtam's close friendship with Anna AKHMATOVA dates from 1925. From 1934 to 1964, she lived "in exile" with Mandelshtam or alone (after his second arrest, 1 May 1938), devoting herself to the primary task of her life: the preservation of Mandelshtam's oeuvre and his "rehabilitation" (1956). The story of her incredible survival, her devotion to her husband and to the preservation of his work is told with passion and immediacy, eloquence and integrity, in two brilliant volumes of memoirs: *Hope Against Hope* (Vospominaniya) and *Hope Abandoned* (Vtoraya kniga). Overwhelming by the sheer force of verbal exuberance, wisdom, and sagacity, there is no doubt that "the voice of the eye-witness predominates over the cry of the victim" (J. BRODSKY).

Hope Against Hope concentrates on depicting Mandelshtam's last four years, from the time of his first arrest in May 1934 to the second arrest and disappearance on 1 May 1938. It concludes with a careful attempt to synthesize the various rumors and accounts pertaining to his last days. In addition, it is surely one of the finest accounts of life under Stalinism ever written.

Hope Abandoned is no ordinary sequel; it is a Book of Judgement. Not only does the survivor-heroine ruthlessly attack the moral deafness and moral degradation which supported Stalinism, but she celebrates her victory over time and her "faith in the abiding value of poetry and its sacramental nature."

On 29 December 1980, Nadezhda Yakovlevna died in Moscow in her tiny one-room apartment which, in the 1970s, had become a central meeting place for Soviet and foreign visitors and devotees.

Works: Vospominaniya. New York, 1970. *Vtoraya kniga.* YMCA, 1972.

Translations: Hope against Hope. Athenaeum, 1970. *Hope Abandoned.* Athenaeum, 1974. *Mozart and Salieri.* Ardis, 1973.

J. G. H.

Mandelshtám, Ósip Emílievich (1891–1938), poet and essayist. Son of a leather merchant with a passion for German philosophy, Emil Veniaminovich Mandelshtam, and a gifted piano teacher, Flora Osipovna Verblovskaya, Osip Mandelshtam was born in Warsaw but raised with his two brothers in the cultural milieu of St. Petersburg's bourgeois intelligentsia. He attended the Tenishev Commercial School, whose director, Vladimir Vasilievich Gippius, poet, member of the POETS' GUILD, and author of ingenious critical essays, Mandelshtam revered as a unique influence on his formative years. After graduation in 1907, he travelled abroad, first to Paris (1907–08) and, following an interim year in St. Petersburg, to Germany (1909–10), to study Old French literature at the University of Heidelberg. In St. Petersburg, he attended both Vyacheslav IVANOV's Tower and meetings of the St. Petersburg Society of Philosophy. His first published poems appeared in August 1910 in APOLLON. In 1911, he was baptized in the Vyborg Methodist Church, enrolled in the Department of History and Philology at the University of St. Petersburg, and joined Gumilyov's Poets' Guild, becoming an active member of the future ACMEIST nucleus.

Although Mandelshtam's initial poetic efforts were sent to Ivanov for comment and approval, by 1910 his essay, "François Villon," already expressed his basic Acmeist orientation. *Stone* (Kamen'), his first book of poems, appeared in 1913, concurrently with the publication of "François Villon" and the Acmeist manifestoes and programmatic verse in *Apollon.*

Stone brought Mandelshtam instant recognition as one of Russia's finest young talents. Technically elegant, full of original perceptions and striking details, his earliest poetry concerned the precise depiction of human culture, from the human body ("Given my body, what use shall I make of it") to the choreography of a tennis match; from the music of Bach and Beethoven to the comparison of "silence" and "muteness" ("Silentium"); from Hagia Sophia to Notre Dame. His programmatic poem, "Notre Dame," elucidates his manifesto, "Morning of Acmeism."

Mandelshtam's poetry divides easily into two major periods, the published collections (poems of 1908–25) and the unpublished notebooks (poems of 1930–37), preserved by his wife, Nadezhda Mandelshtam, until they could be printed abroad. The published poetry includes: *Stone* (Kamen', 1913; second, enlarged edition, 1916; third edition as *Pervaya kniga stikhov,* 1923); *Tristia* (1922; republished as *Vtoraya kniga,* 1923); and *Poems* (Stikhotvoreniya, 1928). *Poems* contains the early poetry plus twenty new poems, "1921–1925."

The poems of the 1920s differ from the earlier lyrics in their semantic density, form, and theme. Their inspiration is far more personal, meditative, and even metaphysical, evoking the dominant themes of Time, the Age, and the Poet. Experimentation with length, structural complexity, and rhythm, rhetorical questions, the contrasting motifs of power and frailty, and the emphasis on themes and images of contemporaneity, history, conscience, illness, death, darkness, and winter, bring these poems closer to the literary prose which dominates Mandelshtam's oeuvre in the 1920s and early 1930s. Compare the following with the self-confident optimism, relative simplicity, and emphasis on craft of "Notre Dame."

My age, my monster, who shall dare
To look into your eyes?
Whose blood shall ever glue together again
The vertebrae of two centuries?
(from #135, "The Age," 1923)

Star-salt melts in the barrel,
Icy water grows black.
Death grows purer, misfortune saltier,
As the earth moves closer to truth and to dread.
(from #126, "I was washing outside," 1921)

He who has kissed the wizened crown of time
Shall recall with filial tenderness
The moment time settled down to sleep
On a sheaf of wheat beneath his window.
He who has faced the age with lifted eyelids
   (Those two enormous sleeping eyeballs)
Shall know the voice of the river of time—
The eternal roar beguiling and certain!

. . . .
O life, fragile as clay! O dying age!
How I fear you shall be apprehended
By a stranger flaunting the bloodless smile
Of a man forced to forfeit his soul.
What agony to search out a lost word.
What torture to lift my aching eyelids
And with quicklime congealing in my blood,
To gather herbs for an alien race.
   (from #140, "January 1, 1924," 1924)

The last five collections, which comprise over two-thirds of Mandelshtam's poetry, assure his reputation as the finest Russian poet of the 20th century. As the early poetry is illuminated by the manifestoes and prose essays of the 1910s and early 1920s, so the later poetry reflects the prose of the later 1920s and 1930s. A trip to Armenia in 1930, Nadezhda Mandelshtam claims, returned the gift of poetry to Osip Mandelshtam. Armenia, the image of promise and hope, figures in *Fourth Prose* and *Journey to Armenia.*

The last five collections include: *The First Moscow Notebook* (October 1930–October 1931); *The Second Moscow Notebook* (May 1932–February 1934); *The First Voronezh Notebook* (April–July, 1935); *The Second Voronezh Notebook* (December 1936–February 1937); and *The Third Voronezh Notebook* (March–May 1937). During the 1930s, the poet's life became his basic lyric material, as distinct from the monuments of human culture represented in the early volumes and the predominantly Man-centered meditations of the 1920s.

The poet's personal life unites the five *Notebooks*, combining Mandelshtam's tragic vision—prescience of his own death and the death of culture—with his inimitable spirit of love and defiance. The *Notebooks* record the signs in the universe signaling that all is not lost and the imperatives demanded by the human soul that cannot be denied. They contain direct, impetuous, poignant utterances, mutterings, and expressions of feeling which do not merely record, describe or evoke, but overwhelm the reader in their immediacy: delight in the unexpected, joy at being alive, intimate revelations of this world's warmth and beauty as well as intimations and declarations of fortitude and courage in the face of Soviet reality and Time itself. The distance of unambiguous self-confidence, the ambiguity of the meditative thinker, and the outrage of the polemicist are tempered by the seeming simplicity of direct involvement or the intimacy of genuine conversation. The voice of the friend, companion, lover, or eyewitness reflects, despairs, fears, rages, rejoices, and judges.

The poetry of the *Notebooks* is defined by a verbal texture richer and denser than the poetry of any previous Russian poet. A limpid precision, sharpness of focus, and vivid, dynamic inner mobility endow these lyrics with a kind of grandeur or elegance rarely encountered in the 20th century. While *The First Voronezh Notebook*, although composed in exile, radiates the energy and joy of life in such poems as: (#299) "The Black Earth" (Chernozem), (#303) "What Street is This / Mandelshtam Street," or (#305) "I must live, even though I died twice," the later poetry also expresses the poet's uncanny sensitivity to mood changes, his inimitable perspicacity of the mystery of movement, and his awesome need to affirm conscience, consciousness, and the process of becoming, in such poems as: (#380) "Maybe this is the beginning of madness," (#384) "How I wish I could fly," or the concluding poem, (#394) "Toward the empty earth ..." in *The Third Voronezh Notebook*. Unfortunately, the density of sound patterns in the latter is impossible to render into English, for permanence resounds in the echo of footsteps, in the repetition of nouns and verbs of movement and accompaniment, and in the emphasis on the continuity and discontinuity of time past, present, and future. Presence and absence, permanence and promise are related to the reality of the earth, spring, and life, as well as to the potential of promise, spring, and resurrection:

> There are women kin to the damp earth,
> In whose every step reverberates sobbing;
> To escort the dead and be first
> To greet the resurrected is their calling.
> To demand caresses from them is criminal.
> To part with them is beyond endurance.
> An angel—today; a worm in the grave—tomorrow.
> A mere outline—the day after that.
> What was her step—becomes unrecognizable.
> Flowers are immortal. Heaven is whole.
> And what will be—is yet a promise.
> ("Toward the empty earth ...") 4 May 1937)

"François Villon," which may be regarded as Mandelshtam's first printed Acmeist manifesto, contains in embryonic form many thematic and stylistic elements of his future poetry and prose, including the intellectual and aesthetic dilemmas confronting him between 1910 and the early 1920s: (1) the image and role of the poet, (2) the nature and source of poetry and the poetic impulse, (3) the relationship of art to society or, on a more cosmic scale, to history or Time, and (4) the relationship between the poet and the reader.

Mandelshtam's essay "Pushkin and Scriabin" (begun in 1915, but completed only in the early 1920s), asserts that the poet's "consciousness of being right" is a fundamental characteristic of the "Christian artist," defined as a free spirit, absolutely unburdened by questions of "necessity." In direct contrast, his essays on CHAADAEV and Chénier (also dating from 1914–15) indicate the young poet's profound concern with intellectual and moral issues, his abiding interest in the problem of freedom and morality, and his serious concern over the question of the relationship of the artist to society. These essays provide an extraordinary insight into his self-image, foreshadowing the metaphor of the RAZNOCHINETS-*pisatel'*

(intellectual-author or "philological nihilist") which he applies to himself in his autobiographical *The Noise of Time* (1922–23) and, again in 1933, to Dante, PUSHKIN, and himself. "Pyotr Chaadaev" is particularly significant in that it implicitly associates the image of the *raznochinets-pisatel'* with Russia itself, identifying "moral freedom" as the essence of Russian national identity, establishing it as a vital source of every subsequent Russian writer's world view.

"Remarks on Chénier" contains Mandelshtam's revelation that, "Chénier ingeniously found the middle road between the classical and romantic manner." His own rejection of absolutes and concomitant striving towards meaningful synthesis is achieved in the essay, "On the Nature of the Word" (1922). Here he not only broadens his definition of Acmeism, but points out how the poet's duty to the State is a lesser form of moral commitment than confronting Time itself, in the name of "the word." Consequently, the poet's obligation is to educate his fellow "Men," not merely to educate the "citizens" of the State. The reader must constantly remind himself that the impulse behind Mandelshtam's conception of moral obligation is aesthetic, that is, it must not be politically or even philosophically justified. The moral imperative and moral freedom are perceived as eternal verities which the poet must reveal, celebrate and, ultimately, preserve.

> Acmeism is a social as well as a literary phenomenon in Russian history. With Acmeism a moral force was reborn in Russian poetry.... Until now the social inspiration of Russian poetry has reached no further than the idea of "citizen," but there is a loftier principle than "citizen," there is the concept of "Man."

As Mandelshtam matured, the bonds between his poetry and prose gradually tightened. Not only did the themes of his essays influence his poems, but by 1923, the major turning point in his life and literary career, the verbal fabric of his poetry found expression in his literary prose.

His literary prose, begun in 1922 and 1923, may be read as a series of autobiographical syntheses in which the autobiographical impulse mediates between the intellectual and aesthetic impulses. In these works, the poet subtly reveals aesthetic solutions to artistic, intellectual, and moral problems, solutions which emerge from the poet's unique "philological" focus—from his literal, Mandelshtamian "love of the word," from his "insatiable hunger for thought," and from his quest to determine "what is perceptible to the mind seeking unities and connections."

His first masterpiece of literary prose, *The Noise of Time*, was simultaneously the culmination of the first phase of his life as a poet—his artistic *rite de passage*—and an aesthetic declaration of intellectual maturity. Stylistically, it initiated a new phase in the poet's creative consciousness in that for the first time he recognized his autobiography as basic poetic material and began to make it the lyrical persona of his poems.

Furthermore, after 1923, certain secondary or even tertiary motifs in his earlier writings emerge as dominant autobiographical themes: the theme of the creative consciousness in an alien environment ("The Egyptian Stamp," "Fourth Prose," and "Journey to Armenia"); the Jewish theme (the Kievan sketches, "The Egyptian Stamp," and "Fourth Prose"); the theme of the creative process (as an organic phenomenon in "Journey to Armenia," as "performance" in "Conversation about Dante"); the theme of the reader (polemical essays of the late 1920s, "Journey to Armenia," and "Conversation about Dante"); the theme of death and immortality (works of the 1930s).

Following *The Noise of Time*, Mandelshtam's four major works of literary prose are: "The Egyptian Stamp" (1927), "Fourth Prose" (1928–30), "Journey to Armenia" (1931–32), and "Conversation about Dante" (spring–summer, 1933).

"The Egyptian Stamp" may be perceived as a second autobiographical act, in which Mandelshtam concentrates on the terrifying prospects for the mature creative consciousness in an alien environment, rather than on the reminiscences of formative childhood experiences. In his essay "The End of the Novel" Mandelshtam predicted: "The future development of the novel will be no less than the history of the atomization of biography as the form of personal existence, even more, we shall witness the catastrophic ruin of biography." "The Egyptian Stamp" fictionalizes this idea. The would-be author makes an abortive attempt to write a 19th-century biographical novel, but in the end, the third-person narrator expresses relief at being able to switch from third person to first.

Two years later, Mandelshtam no longer even considered the objective approach of the novel. His protagonist in "Fourth Prose" emerges triumphant over all forms of death and destruction, as a poet, Jew, and social outcast, cognizant of his rights as a poet and as a human being in an environment demanding his destruction. The passive surrealist dream and abortive novel—"The Egyptian Stamp"—yields to perverse literary exorcism. "Fourth Prose" is organized around the juxtaposition of the polemical and the lyrical. Sixteen prose vignettes, arranged like stanzas according to the musical paradigm of a theme and variations, take as their major theme, Man's response to the Old Testament Commandment: "Thou shalt not kill." The Jew, the outcast, and the genuine poet are associated with the field of images connected with Life and "the life of the word": escape, freedom, the Promised Land, the South, Armenia, creature comforts, fantasy, imagination, dreams, genuine literature, happiness, free verbal expression (including nonsense language and children's ditties), human dignity, justice, truth, pride, and perversity. Mandelshtam's Jewish consciousness reaches its peak in "Fourth Prose," as the synonyms, "Jew" and poet, reinforce, broaden, and universalize the moral and aesthetic power of the earlier image of the *raznochinets-pisatel'*. The writer finally merges his ideals of art as moral wisdom and art as celebration.

"Journey to Armenia" expresses Mandelshtam's experience of reprieve, or second birth. Like each of the poet's preceding works of literary prose, it functions as a summation and conclusion of a particular phase in both his personal autobiography and his creative consciousness.

"Conversation about Dante" is a counterpart to "Journey to Armenia," thematically and structurally. While the earlier work focuses on organic recurrence—physiological, philological and historical continuity, the life cycle, the relationship between the phenomenon of growth and the organic nature of memory—as a phenomenon of natural order, subtly enhanced by the Christian vision and the "philological" imperative, the latter attempts to reveal the instinct for form creation which underlies the immortality of art: the impulse behind the creative process—to preserve the eternal verities through human creativity and the phenomenon of the perpetuation of art through generations of readers. "Conversation about Dante" is Mandelshtam's last extant attempt to identify the impulse behind the text both for himself as poet and reader, and for his ideal "reader in posterity."

The boldness and originality of "Conversation about Dante" derive from Mandelshtam's interest in defining the effect of a great poet on himself as both reader and poet. The essay is thus directed toward the active poetic genius, the external model being Dante, the internal experience being his own creative cognition. "Conversation about Dante" also differs from the typical critical essay of the 1920s and 1930s in containing numerous autobiographical digressions which focus on the poet's own emotional, often physiological "love of the word," his fascination with verbal texture, phonology, sound harmony, and the relationship of the poetic impulse to the text.

Mandelshtam's insights into Dante's poetics, as well as into the "psychological foundation" of Dante's creative process—the relationship between the poet and the man, the link between his psychological and creative impulses—reveal much that is fundamental to Mandelshtam's own aesthetic vision. "Conversation about Dante" thus presents the autobiographical experience of a poet-"philologist" reading the work of an immortal poet while discoursing on his own poetic experience, defining and clarifying it. Hence, Mandelshtam's reference to Dante as a fellow *raznochinets* harks back to the imagery of *The Noise of Time*, for Dante could be considered a *raznochinets* only in terms of Mandelshtam's bold autobiographical metaphor:

> Dante is a poor man. Dante is an internal *raznochinets*.... Courtesy is not at all characteristic of him, rather something distinctly the opposite ... Dante does not know how to behave, does not know how to act, what to say, how to bow. I am not imagining this; I infer it from the numerous admissions of Alighieri himself.

The inner anxiety and painful, troubled gaucheries which accompany each step of the diffident man, as if his upbringing were somehow remiss; the man untutored in the ways of applying his inner experience or of objectifying it in etiquette, tormented and outcast, such are the qualities which both provide the poem with all its charm, with all its drama, and serve as its background, its psychological foundation.

The official date given on Mandelshtam's death certificate is 27 December 1938. As of his second arrest, 1 May 1938, he became a non-person. Only with the death of Stalin was the official "rehabilitation" begun in August 1956 conceivable. The commission appointed in 1957 by the Writers Union to oversee the poet's remains included the poet's widow, Nadezhda MANDELSHTAM, her brother, Evgeny Yakovlevich Khazin, the poet, Anna AKHMATOVA, the writer Ilya ERENBURG, and the critics, Z. S. Paperny, A. A. SURKOV and N. I. Khardzhiev. Not until 1973, however, did a large selection of his poetry appear in the Soviet Union in the Poet's Library series.

The first post-Stalinist collection appeared in New York in 1955. His *Collected Works* (1967–1971) were continually updated; a supplemental volume was added in 1981. This four volume Russian collection is now reasonably complete. Most of Mandelshtam's prose is now available in English in *Mandelstam: The Complete Critical Prose and Letters* and *The Prose of Osip Mandelstam*. Translations of his poetry are also available.

Works: Sobranie sochinenii. 4 vols. Ed. G. P. Struve and B. A. Filippov. New York, 1967–1981. Vol. 1 (Poetry). Introd. C. Brown, G. Struve, E. Rais (1964; 2d ed., rev. and expanded, 1967). Vol. 2 (Prose). Introd. B. Filippov (1966; 2d ed., rev. and expanded, 1971). Vol. 3 (Essays and Letters). Introd. G. Ivask, N. Struve, B. Filippov (1969). Vol. 4 (Supplementary). Ed. G. Struve, N. Struve, B. Filippov (Paris, 1981). *Stikhotvoreniya.* Ed. N. I. Khardzhiev. Introd. A. Dymshits. 1973 (2d ed. 1974).

Translations: The Complete Critical Prose and Letters. Ed. J. G. Harris. Trans. J. G. Harris and C. Link. Introd. J. G. Harris. Ann Arbor, 1979. *The Prose of Osip Mandelstam.* Ed., trans., and introd. C. Brown. 1967. *Selected Poems.* Trans. C. Brown and W. S. Merwin. 1974. *Complete Poetry of Osip Emilievich Mandelstam.* Trans. by Burton Raffel and Alla Burago. Introd. Sidney Monas. Albany, 1973. *Selected Poems.* Trans. and introd. David McDuff. 1974. *Poems.* Chosen and trans. James Greene. Forewords by Nadezhda Mandelstam and Donald Davie. 1978. *Selected Essays.* Trans. Sidney Monas. 1977. *Journey to Armenia.* Trans. Sidney Monas. 1979.

Secondary literature: Jennifer Baines, *Mandelstam: The Later Poetry.* 1976. Clarence Brown, *Mandelstam.* 1973. Stephen Broyde, *Osip Mandelstam and His Age.* 1975. Nikita Struve, *Ossip Mandelstam.* Paris, 1982. Kiril Taranovsky, *Essays on Mandelstam.* 1976. Articles by E. Etkind, G. Freidin, L. Ginzburg, J. G. Harris, C. Isenberg, J. Levin, G. Levinton, N. Å. Nilsson, O. Ronen, D. M. Segal, P. Steiner, K. Taranovsky, V. Terras, E. Toddes, and others are listed in the bibliographies to the above-mentioned books.

Memoirs: Nadezhda Mandelstam, *Hope against Hope.* 1972. ———, *Hope Abandoned.* 1974.

J. G. H.

Mandelshtám, Yúry Vladímirovich (1908–43), émigré poet and critic. A graduate of the University of Paris, Mandelshtam was married to the eldest daughter of Igor Stravinsky. A very highly educated person, Mandelshtam, along with KHODASEVICH, worked as a literary critic for the journal VOZROZHDENIE. Deported by the Gestapo in 1942, he died in a Nazi concentration camp, probably in 1943. Mandelshtam the poet was a disciple of Khodasevich and a member of the neoclassical poetic circle *Perekrestok*. Mandelshtam's was an erudite, intellectual, philosophical poetry in polished form with elements of ACMEIST precision as well as, later, the more passionate and emotional "Parisian note" (PARIZHSKAYA NOTA). His essays, collected in *Seekers: Essays* (Iskateli: etyudy, Shanghai, 1938), range in topic from Dante to Beethoven to Rilke. His collections of poetry: *An Island* (Ostrov, Paris, 1920), *Fidelity* (Vernost', Paris, 1932), *The Third Hour* (Tretii chas, Berlin, 1935), and the posthumous *Years* (Gody, Paris, 1950).

Bibliography: L. Foster, *Bibliography of Russian Emigré Literature 1918–1968.* Boston, 1971. Yu. Ivask, "Poeziya staroi emigratsii." In *Russkaya literatura v emigratsii.* Ed. N. P. Poltoratskii. Pittsburgh, 1972. T. Pachmuss, ed., *A Russian Cultural Revival: A Critical Anthology of Emigré Literature Before 1939.* Knoxville, Tenn., 1981. G. P. Struve, *Russkaya literatura v izgnanii.* New York, 1956. Pp. 331, 344. E. Sztein, *Poeziya russkogo rasseyaniya 1920–1977.* Ashford, Conn., 1978.   L. D.

MAPP, see RAPP.

Maramzin, Vladímir Rafaílovich (1934–), writer and film maker, was born in Leningrad, where he studied electrical engineering (1952–57) and worked as an engineer (1958–1965). After 1965, Maramzin, who had been publishing some prose since 1962, became a full time writer, authoring more than ten film scenarios and TV-plays. In the 1970s, he became progressively more active in SAMIZDAT. He was instrumental in publishing a Samizdat edition of the works of Iosif BRODSKY (1971–74) and published some of his own stories in Samizdat as well. After his arrest in July 1974, his long short-story, "The Story of Ivan Petrovich's Marriage," appeared in KONTINENT. In February 1975 Maramzin was convicted of having disseminated anti-Soviet propaganda, but was allowed to leave the Soviet Union later that year. He lives in Paris and has actively continued his literary activities.

Works: Blondin obeego tsveta. Ann Arbor, 1975. *Smeshnee chem prezhde.* Paris, 1979. *Tyanitolkai: Povesti i rasskazy.* Ann Arbor, 1981.

Secondary literature: Gabriel Laub, "Wladimir Kornilow und Wladimir Maramzin." In *Sowjetliteratur heute.* Ed. Gisela Lindemann. Munich, 1979. Pp. 195–207. Deming Brown, *Soviet Literature since Stalin.* 1979. P. 372.   V. T.

Mariengóf, Anatóly Borísovich (1897–1962), poet, playwright, and prose writer, was born in Nizhny Novgorod (now Gorky). He supposedly was of noble origin, although the true status of his family so far remains a matter of debate. As a youngster he lived in Penza, where he wrote his first poems which anticipated his later imagist poetry. In 1918, Mariengof moved to Moscow, where he took a job in the Central Executive Committee publishing house. Here, he met the young poets who were to become the leading exponents of IMAGISM, S. ESENIN, V. SHERSHENEVICH, and R. IVNEV.

From 1919 to 1927, Mariengof was an active member of the Order of the Imagists. He participated in the group's literary ventures, led a bohemian life, and indulged in dandyism. His extremely close friendship with Esenin, which lasted almost three years, became legendary. Mariengof's production of these years includes poetry, drama, criticism, literary theory, and memoirs. His book, *Buyan-Island* (Buyan-ostrov, 1920) is one of the fundamental texts of imagist poetics. Mariengof excels in the genre of the "lyrical *poema*," which the imagists inherited from BALMONT. Mariengof's most typical features are heteroaccentual rhyme and unusually long and intricate stanzas, which he later abandoned. His *poema*'s appeared both as separate books, such as *Magdalina* (1919) and *Pastry Shop of the Suns* (Konditerskaya solnts, 1919), and as collections, such as *I Show Off My Poetry* (Stikhami chvanstvuyu, 1920) and *Cloud-Flight* (Tuchelet, 1921). The main themes and motifs of Mariengof's poetry are: the Revolution in its anarchical and bloody aspects, love and sex, the city and its hellish atmosphere, and the suffering poet wearing the mask of the mad clown. Religious imagery is often used in conjunction with sexual imagery in expressions of violence. Mariengof was a prolific contributor to journals and almanacs, and occupied an important position among the editors of *Gostinitsa dlya puteshestvuyushchikh v prekrasnom.* Two plays belonging to his imagist period are *The Conspiracy of Fools* (Zagovor durakov, 1922) and *The Bipeds* (Dvunogie, 1925). Mariengof was also an original and skillful prose writer. He wrote two novels, *Cynics* (Tsiniki, 1928) and *Shaven Man* (Brityi chelovek, 1929?), and a book of memoirs, *A Novel Without Lies* (Roman bez vran'ya, 1927). The latter is a fascinating, although not totally reliable, account of the bohemian life of the imagists (Esenin's in particular).

In 1928, Mariengof moved to Leningrad. He no longer wrote any poetry worthy of note, but concentrated on writing for the theater and the cinema. Mariengof wrote several further plays, among them: *Taras Bulba* (1940), *Little Comedies* (Malen'kie komedii, 1957), and *Birth of the Poet* (Rozhdenie poeta, 1959).

Works: Roman bez vran'ya. Reprint. New York, 1978. *Tsiniki.* Reprint. Israel, 1978.

Translations: "We Lift the Heavens, the Heavens by the Ears." In *Modern Russian Poetry.* Ed. V. Markov and M. Sparks. 1967. Pp. 718–19.

Secondary literature: B. Gusman, *100 poetov. Literaturnye portrety.* 1923. V. Markov, *Russian Imagism. 1919–1924.* Giessen, 1980. G. McVay, *Esenin: A Life.* 1976. N. Å. Nilsson, *The Russian Imaginists.* Stockholm, 1970. V. Shershenevich, *Komu ya zhmu ruku.* 1921. V. Zavalishin, *Early Soviet Writers.* 1958.   A. L.

Mariya, Mat' or Monákhinya (religious name of Elizavéta Yúrievna Kuzminá-Karaváeva, *née* Pilénko, *en secondes noces* Skobtsóva-Kondrátieva, 1891–1945?), poet and critic, published her first book of verse before the Revolution, but developed her idiosyncratic style only after her emigration in 1919. Having taken holy vows, Mother Mariya continued to be actively involved in social work among her fellow émigrés and also continued her literary activities. Her religious poetry, conventional in its form, conveys the experience of a Christian facing a world which is not so much sinful as drab and indifferent with warm pathos and great intensity of compassion for human suffering. Mother Mariya published two volumes of saints' lives and also wrote several studies and articles on KHOMYAKOV, Vladimir SOLOVYOV, DOSTOEVSKY, BLOK, and others. Arrested by the Germans for having helped some Jews to hide, Mother Mariya died at the Ravensbrück concentration camp. A posthumous collection of her works, with reminiscences about her, came out in 1947, containing poems, two verse epics, "In Praise of Labor" (Pokhvala trudu) and "All Souls Day" (Dukhov den'), both written in 1942, and two *mystères* in verse, "Anna" and "The Soldiers" (Soldaty).

Works: Ruf'. 1916. *Zhatva dukha: Zhitiya svyatykh.* 2 vols. Paris, 1927. *Mirosozertsanie Vl. Solov'eva.* Paris, 1929. *A. Khomyakov.* Paris, 1929. *Dostoevskii i sovremennost'.* Paris, 1929. *Stikhi.* Berlin, 1932. "Vstrechi s Blokom," *Sovremennye zapiski,* no. 62 (1936), pp. 211–28. *Stikhotvoreniya i poemy, misterii. Vospominaniya ob areste i lagere v Ravensbryuk.* Paris, 1947. *Stikhi.* Paris, 1949.

Bibliography: See Foster, pp. 747–48.

Secondary literature: G. Struve, *Russkaya literatura v izgnanii.* 1956. Pp. 328–29.   V. T.

Markóvich, see VOVCHOK, Marko.

Marlinsky, see BESTUZHEV.

Marshák, Samuíl Yákovlevich (1887–1964), was born in Voronezh, the son of a factory foreman. His gifts developed early and were noted by the Maecenas D. Ginzburg, the art critic V. Stasov, and Maksim GORKY, who all helped him along. Marshak began to publish in 1907. From 1912 to 1914 he attended the University of London. In 1923 he began to publish books for children. He organized the *Detgiz* publishing house ("State Publishing House for Children's Literature") and several children's journals, attracting many major writers to this field, and in particular A. VVEDENSKY and D. KHARMS. Marshak's works for children were collected in his book *Fairytales, Songs, Riddles* (Skazki, pesni, zagadki, 1st ed. 1935). The best poems in this book, precise in their rhythms, well-composed, and not devoid of quaintness and whimsy, often steeped in the traditions of Russian and English folklore, are deservedly popular. Marshak's many plays for children were also successful, e.g., "Mrs. Cat's House" (Koshkin dom, 1945). Marshak's poetry for adults is epigonic. During the years of the Second World War and the Cold War, he also wrote a great deal of propaganda verse, expressing the official Soviet point of view. Marshak is widely known as a translator of English poetry (Shakespeare, Blake, Burns, Edward Lear, etc.). His translations show great versifying skill; however, Marshak tends to simplify the style and semantics of his originals.

Works: Sobranie sochinenii. 8 vols. 1968–72.

Translations: Lewanski, p. 301.

Secondary literature: N. Avtonomova and M. Gasparov, "Sonety Shekspira—perevody Marshaka," *VLit* 13 (1969), no. 2, pp. 100–12. Anna Bogdanova, "Samuel Marshak and his 'Children's Town' Theater." In *Through the Magic Curtain: Theater for Children, Adolescents and Youth in the U.S.S.R.* Ed. and trans. Miriam Morton. 1979. Pp. 11–17. L. Chukovskaya, *V laboratorii redaktora.* 2d ed. 1963. Pp. 219–334. K. Chukovskii, *Vysokoe iskusstvo.* 1964. Pp. 202–12. E. Etkind, *Poeziya i perevod.* 1963. Pp. 77–86. L. Panteleev, *Zhivye pamyatniki.* 1966. Pp. 362–442. B. Sarnov, *Samuil Marshak.* 1968. M. Tsvetaeva, *Izbrannaya proza v dvukh tomakh.* Vol. 2. 1979. Pp. 310–13. *Ya dumal, chuvstvoval, ya zhil: Vospominaniya o S. Ya. Marshake.* 1971. *Zhizn' i tvorchestvo Samuila Yakovlevicha Marshaka. Marshak i detskaya literatura.* 1975.

T. V.

Martýnov, Leonid Nikoláevich (1905–   ), poet, essayist, and journalist, was born in Omsk, Siberia, where he published his first verse in the journal *Iskusstvo* in 1921. He continued to publish mostly in Siberian journals (*Sibirskie ogni, Sovetskaya Sibir'*, etc.) in the 1920s and 1930s. While he was quite successful as a journalist and essayist, his poetry, never political or otherwise topical, attracted relatively little attention until 1955. Thereafter, he has been one of the most respected poets of the Soviet Union. Martynov's early poetry is marked by a withdrawal into a mythical region created from elements of the historical past, the folklore, and the ethnography of Northern Russia and Siberia (*Lukomor'e*, the title of Martynov's collection of 1945, is taken from Russian folklore, where it is a mythical region by the sea). Martynov's historical ballads ("Ermak," "The Swedish Prisoner," etc.) are written in conventional meters, but a wealth of enjambement along with colloquial phrase contours give them the character of folk verse (rayoshnik). Martynov's verses after 1955, without abandoning his former themes, expand into a more universal mythology, embracing modern civilization ("Daedalus," "Europe," "The Radioactive Island") and cosmic themes ("Hymn to the Sun," "Northern Lights"). Martynov is also a prolific translator from several European languages.

Works: Stikhi i poemy. 1939. *Lukomor'e.* 1945. *Stikhi.* 1955. *Novaya kniga.* 1962. *Pervorodstvo.* 1965. *Stikhotvoreniya i poemy.* 2 vols. 1965. *Izbrannaya lirika.* 1973. *Giperboly.* 1973. *Sobranie sochinenii.* 3 vols. 1976–77.

Translations: A Book of Poems. (Bilingual edition.) Trans. Peter Tempest. Moscow, 1979. Five poems in *Soviet Literature* 9 (1957), pp. 131–34.

Secondary literature: Valerii Dement'ev, *Leonid Martynov: Poet i vremya.* 1971. A. V. Nikul'kov, *Leonid Martynov.* 1969.   V. T.

Marxism in Russian literary theory and criticism. Marx and Engels never developed an aesthetic theory and even their sporadic comments on art and literature were not systematically investigated until the 1930s. The principles of a Marxist aesthetic theory were developed by prerevolutionary Marxist authors as a corollary of Dialectic and Historical Materialism. Georgy PLEKHANOV (1856–1918), along with Paul Lafargue in France and Franz Mehring in Germany, was the principal exponent of a Marxist aesthetic theory. His main thesis was that art, an element of the superstructure (*nadstroika*) of socio-economic life, was nevertheless an autonomous human activity, so that while its historical development was intimately linked with that of social labor and class struggle, the creative process itself was non-utilitarian, "disinterested" in the Kantian sense. Plekhanov also believed that all genuine art was historically linked with progressive and humanitarian ideas and that reactionary ideas would inevitably produce inferior art. Plekhanov's ideas were the basis of much subsequent Marxist aesthetics and criticism, specifically the writings of Vatslav VOROVSKY and Anatoly LUNACHARSKY before the Revolution, and of the critics of the PEREVAL group in the 1920s.

LENIN's statements relating to literature and the arts are found in six brief essays on TOLSTOI, a brief article, "Party Organization and Party Literature" (1905), some passages in *Materialism and Empirio-Criticism* (1909) and in his *Philosophical Notebooks*, as well as in his correspondence with GORKY. The principles which Soviet theorists have extracted from these sources are: the so-called theory of reflection (*teoriya otrazheniya*), according to which art is a reflection of objective reality in its dialectic development; the concepts of the class nature (*klassovost'*) and party-mindedness (PARTIINOST') of literature; an assumption of cultural continuity in art and literature, which in effect vetoed the development of "proletarian art;" and, finally, a demand that art be intelligible and appeal to the masses (NARODNOST'). The few and generally unoriginal statements of the "classics of Marxism" were gradually invested with an oracular authority by Soviet aesthetic theorists. In particular, Lenin's demand that all party literature follow the party line was interpreted as applying to Soviet literature under the wholly different conditions of party control over every aspect of public life.

After the October Revolution, Marxist thought was initially split into two camps, one which wanted to abandon the old culture and build a new, proletarian culture, and another which advocated the appropriation of existing bourgeois culture by the victorious proletariat. The Proletarian Culture movement (PROLETKUL'T), whose ideologue was Aleksandr BOGDANOV (1873–1928), flourished for several years, but faded quickly after the Party turned against it, specifically in a letter of the Central Committee of the Russian Communist Party, published in *Pravda*, 1 December 1920. The version of Marxist aesthetics which had the approval of the Party belonged to Anatoly Lunacharsky, People's Commissar for Education, and Lev TROTSKY, Commissar for War and unofficial second-in-command to Lenin. The views of both were close to Plekhanov's, as they saw a difference between a long range "historical utilitarianism" in art and short term catering to slogans of the day. Hence they felt that "the actual development of art, and its struggle for new forms are not part of the Party's tasks, nor is it its concern" (Trotsky). But both also emphasized the need for party-mindedness (*partiinost'*) in art, with Trotsky more intent upon using art as a tool of class struggle, and Lunacharsky rather serenely confident that an honest realism was the only suitable form for the art of a young and victorious class, such as the Russian proletariat. Lunacharsky was more inclined to give proletarian art a chance, while Trotsky believed that the period between the establishment of the dictatorship of the proletariat and that of a classless society would be too short to warrant the creation of proletarian art and literature. Both Trotsky and Lunacharsky believed that the Russian avant-garde's call to break with the feudal and bourgeois past had a meaning to a narrow circle of intellectuals only, whereas the proletariat, on the contrary, still faced the task of appropriating the old culture. Both Trotsky and Lunacharsky, along with the Soviet leadership at large, were convinced that art would flourish and play a significant role in the socialist society of the future. Trotsky, in particular, suggested that, since the historical process showed a steady growth of man's conscious control of his environment, art, too would move in that direction and thus get closer to technology.

The critics of the *Pereval* group (VORONSKY, LEZHNEV, etc.) proclaimed themselves Marxists and in general followed the line of social organicism established by Plekhanov and continued by Vorovsky, Lunacharsky, and Trotsky. They were engaged in a running battle with the theorists of LEF (BRIK, MAYAKOVSKY, etc.) who insisted that the revolutionary content of the new art demanded a revolutionary form. Neither side could draw any support from the classics of Marxism, simply because their works gave no answer to such questions as, for example, whether the new art should deal with the problems of building a socialist society in concrete, psychological terms, as Voronsky and his associates felt, or by hypostasizing and dramatizing goals and ideas, as Brik theorized and Mayakovsky practiced.

The theorists of RAPP shared with those of *Pereval* a preference for realist art and psychologically motivated characters, but while the latter would view contemporary life as it was, though from a Marxist viewpoint, AVERBAKH, LELEVICH, RODOV, and other members of RAPP saw the task of Soviet literature in reshaping the world in terms of their class-oriented Marxist ideology. While Voronsky charged them with projecting their theoretical views on reality, they reciprocated by accusing *Pereval* of insufficient alertness to ideology and "neo-bourgeois" tendencies. Neither party could rightfully claim that its position was supported by the classics of Marxism.

An effort to base literary theory and literary history on a solid foundation of Marxist dogma was made in the 1920s by several scholars, such as Vladimir FRICHE, editor of the journal *Literature and Marxism* (1928–29), Pavel SAKULIN, and Valerian PEREVERZEV. They

275

formed the so-called SOCIOLOGICAL SCHOOL of literary studies. Their basic conception, which they owed to Plekhanov, was that every aspect of literature, including even its formal elements such as genre, composition, imagery, and rhetoric, were determined by the writer's social consciousness. Literature was thus a faithful mirror of the social process. The sociological school failed to distinguish between the writer as a person essentially determined by his social milieu, and as an artist, i.e., the practitioner of a highly specific craft. It also identified social consciousness with ideology, perceived as the expression of class interest. The theorists of the sociological school polemicized with the FORMALISTS, who pointed out that the sociological approach underestimated the role of the artist's creative effort (Sakulin called it the "immanent" aspect of literature), and with theorists of the RAPP school, who charged that they were practicing sociologism without having a sociology, that is, paying insufficient attention to the active role of art as a tool of class struggle. The theorists of the sociological school were closer to Marxism in spirit, if not in letter, than any of their rivals (who, of course, all claimed to be Marxists) or any Soviet literary theorists who followed them. It was Friche who suggested that the basic genre of Soviet literature should be the "sociological production novel" (*proizvodstvenno-sotsiologicheskii roman*) without an individual hero and without "psychologism." He said so some years before this prescription was in effect applied in the production novels of the early 1930s. In spite of this, the theorists of SOCIALIST REALISM disowned the work done by the sociological school as "vulgar sociologism," on the alleged grounds that it had failed to understand the relations between art and society in dialectic terms.

In the 1920s the influence of the Party on literature was limited to exhortations of a general nature, such as the Resolution of the Central Committee of the RCP "On Party Policies in the Area of Literature" (*O politike partii v oblasti khudozhestvennoi literatury*) of 18 June 1925, which stated the need for a new artistic culture addressed to wide circles of workers and peasants. But a decree of the same body, dated 23 April 1932, "On Restructuring Literary and Artistic Organizations" (*O perestroike literaturno-khudozhest-vennykh organizatsii*) made it clear that the Party would henceforth control literature and the arts. All writers were to belong to a single organization, the UNION OF SOVIET WRITERS, whose first Congress, held in 1934, established the principles which have remained in force to this day.

Until the early 1930s Plekhanov was, at least tacitly, considered to have been the founder of Marxist aesthetics. Now Soviet scholars and the Hungarian Georg Lukács (then living in Russia) began to gather statements on aesthetics and literature by the classics of Marxism. A collection, *Marx and Engels on Literature: New Materials*, with a commentary by F. Shiller and G. Lukács appeared in 1933. Lenin's few statements on literature were also meticulously collected and quoted ad nauseam. It was then that Soviet literary and aesthetic theorists began to credit the classics of Marxism with having created a consistent—and, what is more, a new—aesthetic doctrine. This, in turn, put Soviet theorists under an obligation to produce a "scientific" aesthetic theory to fit the framework of "scientific socialism." Since Marx, Engels, and Lenin had hardly addressed themselves to specific problems of aesthetic or literary theory, these remained for Soviet theorists to work out. As a result, aesthetic theory in the Soviet Union shows more genuine diversity of opinion than any other area of social thought.

Another, rather unexpected development was that, while Marxist thought of the 1920s (RAPP, *Lef*, and the sociological school) was generally opposed to aesthetics as a separate discipline, socialist realist doctrine, at least since the 1950s, has embraced the idea of the sui generis quality of the aesthetic fact. In this, as well as in many specific details, socialist realist aesthetics and theory of literature are in fact a regression from Marxism to Hegelianism (in its Belinskian version, more or less). This became more and more evident when the period of the THAW produced some genuine discussions of aesthetic questions, inaugurated by the collection *Questions of Marxist-Leninist Aesthetics*, edited by P. S. Trofimov (1956). These discussions have dealt primarily with the question of the specificity of the aesthetic fact, the proper balance between application of the "Leninist reflection theory of art" and the notion, also credited to Lenin, that art should not only reflect but also help to change the world, and the degree to which historical determinism is valid in the

development of literature and the arts. A recurring question is that regarding the reality of extra-societal aspects of the aesthetic fact, stressed by the "naturists" (*prirodniki*) and minimized by their opponents, the "societalists" (*obshchestvenniki*). There is a third group, calling themselves "dialecticians" (*dialektiki*), whose efforts are directed at presenting the aesthetic fact as a function of the give-and-take of objective, social, and subjective factors. It would seem that these discussions, purportedly conducted within a framework of Marxist-Leninist thought, do not reflect any insights into the nature of the creative process, the reception of art by the individual and by society, or the relations between different art forms, which cannot also be found in Hegelian (or Belinskian) aesthetic theory. What new ideas and methods have made their appearance in Soviet aesthetic theory since the 1960s (STRUCTURALISM, SEMIOTICS, a quantitative approach to art [*iskusstvometriya*]) have no connection with the Marxist tradition, even if their practitioners will occasionally pay lip service to Marxism.

Bibliography: Lee Baxandall, comp., *Marxism and Aesthetics: A Selective Annotated Bibliography.* 1968. V. F. Berestnev and G. A. Nedoshivin, eds., *Osnovy marksistsko-leninskoi estetiki.* 1960. Aleksandr A. Bogdanov, *O proletarskoi kul'ture, 1904–1924.* 1925. Yurii Borev, *Estetika.* 1975. Margaret M. Bullitt, "Toward a Marxist Theory of Aesthetics: The Development of Socialist Realism in the Soviet Union," *RusR* 35 (1976), pp. 53–76. G. Fridlender, *K. Marks i F. Engel's i voprosy literatury.* 1962. M. Kagan, *Lektsii po marksistsko-leninskoi estetike.* 3 vols. 1963–66. M. Lifshits, *Karl Marks: Iskusstvo i obshchestvennyi ideal.* 1972. Robert A. Maguire, *Red Virgin Soil: Soviet Literature in the 1920s.* 1968. P. A. Nikolaev, *Vozniknovenie marksistskogo literaturovedeniya v Rossii* (metodologiya, problemy realizma). 1970. M. F. Ovsyannikov and V. V. Vanslov, eds., *Marksistsko-leninskaya estetika.* 1966. Edward M. Swiderski, *The Philosophical Foundations of Soviet Aesthetics: Theories and Controversies in the Post-War Years.* 1979. P. S. Trofimov, *Estetika marksizma-leninizma.* 1964. V. I. Lenin o literature i iskusstve. 4th ed. 1969. Raymond Williams, *Marxism and Literature.* 1977. A. Zis', *Iskusstvo i estetika: Traditsionnye kategorii i sovremennye problemy* (Art and aesthetics: Traditional categories and contemporary problems). 2nd ed. 1975.   V. T.

Matinsky, Mikhail Alekséevich (1750–after 1818), playwright and composer, was born the son of a house serf, but was able to attend the gymnasium of Moscow University. After having received his freedom in 1785, he taught at the Corps of Pages and at the Smolny Institute, and was employed as a translator by the State Commission for Educational Institutions. He enjoyed a reputation as a fine mathematician. Matinsky began his literary activities in 1774 with a translation of J. F. Gellert's comedy *Die Betschwester* (The Devotee). His fame rests with his comic opera, *The Arcades of St. Petersburg* (Sankt-Peterburgskii gostinyi dvor, 1781–82), set in the milieu of the tradition-bound merchant class and featuring a colorful Russian wedding ceremony.

Works: Russkaya komediya i komicheskaya opera XVIII v. Ed. and introd. P. N. Berkov. 1950.

Secondary literature: P. N. Berkov, "K biografii M. A. Matinskogo." In *XVIII vek, sbornik 3.* 1958.   V. T.

Matvéeva, Novélla Nikoláevna (1934–   ), poet, published her first poems in 1958 and her first collection in 1961, with immediate success. Matveeva often sets her poems to music and her personal appearances in which she accompanies herself on the guitar have been popular for many years. Her poetry is, however, serious and avoids the cliché and the obvious. Its basic devices are estrangement and unexpected metaphor. Altogether, her style resembles that of Marina TSVETAEVA.

Works: Lirika. 1961. *Korablik.* 1963. *Izbrannaya lirika.* 1964. *Dusha veshchei.* 1966. *Lastochkina shkola.* 1973.

Translations: "Narcissus." In *Modern Russian Poetry.* Ed. Vladimir Markov and Merrill Sparks. 1967. Pp. 808–9.

Secondary literature: Deming Brown, "'Loud' and 'Quiet' Poets of the Nineteen Sixties." In Benjamin A. Stolz, ed. *Papers in Slavic Philology 1: In Honor of James Ferrell.* Ann Arbor, 1977. Pp. 18–26. ———, *Soviet Russian Literature since Stalin.* 1978. Pp. 127–30.   V. T.

Maximus the Greek, see MAKSIM GREK.

Mayakóvsky, Vladímir Vladímirovich (1893–1930) was probably one of the great poets of the century. He was born in Bagdadi, Kutais region, Georgia, and lived there until 1906, when the family moved to Moscow. Georgian was the only language other than Russian in which Mayakovsky claimed expertise. His family was Russian, and his father was a forest ranger, though of noble ancestry. Mayakovsky's involvement with the Revolution began when he was a young boy. Early in 1908 he joined the Bolshevik faction of the Russian Social Democratic party and was elected, at the age of fourteen, to its Moscow committee. He was arrested for agitational work three times, and his third arrest in July 1909 resulted in imprisonment for six months, much of it in solitary confinement in Butyrki prison. After his release from prison Mayakovsky abandoned politics for a time and entered the Moscow Institute for the Study of Painting, Sculpture, and Architecture, where he planned to undertake a career as a painter. His meeting there with David BUR-LYUK, as he indicates in his autobiography *I Myself* (Ya sam), was decisive for his career. Burlyuk was already an established painter of the avant-garde and he has a place of modest importance in the history of modern European art. He was an influential organizer of art exhibitions which included the works of Larionov, Goncharova, Ekster, and others. He had also organized a group of innovative painters and poets under the name *budetlyane*, a russification of the term "futurist." He was involved in the publication of the first futurist collection, provocatively entitled *A Trap for Judges* (Sadok sudei, 1910), in which KRUCHONYKH and KHLEBNIKOV participated. The strength of Burlyuk's influence is borne out by Mayakovsky himself who in his autobiography calls Burlyuk "my real teacher."

The collection of poetry and prose published in 1912 under the title *A Slap in the Face of Public Taste* contained Mayakovsky's first two published poems, entitled "Night" and "Morning" (Noch' and Utro). The title of the collection as a whole was also that of the famous futurist manifesto, signed by Mayakovsky, Burlyuk, Kruchonykh and Khlebnikov, which consigned all past art (with a few exceptions) and nearly all contemporaries (except the futurists) to be thrown overboard from "the steamship of modernity." In 1913 the futurist group, Mayakovsky, Burlyuk, KAMENSKY, Khlebnikov, LIVSHITS, and (for a time) SEVERYANIN, undertook, for publicity purposes, a tour of the provinces which was a triumph of épatage and had some success in calling attention to the new departures of the European avant-garde in painting and poetry.

Mayakovsky's work published between 1912 and 1914 belonged to the futurist movement. A series of original and sometimes strangely moving lyrics, most of them devoted to city themes, appeared in futurist collections of verse and graphics during those years. His first book of poems appeared in 1913 under the title *Me* (Ya). A thin, lithographed volume, it contained four lyrics devoted to aspects of the poet's life in a kind of urban inferno, and featured the poet himself as a modern parody of Christ the Savior. His verse drama entitled *Vladimir Mayakovsky*, a *Tragedy* (1913) was produced as part of a futurist enterprise, alternating on the stage with Kruchonykh's *Victory over the Sun* (Pobeda nad solntsem). In both productions futurist poets and avant-garde painters were in close collaboration. The *Tragedy* sums up Mayakovsky's early concerns as a lyric poet. The play deals with the mutilation and enslavement of city dwellers and presents the poet (Mayakovsky, played by Mayakovsky) as a Christ figure who suffers for them all.

Mayakovsky's four narrative poems of the prerevolutionary period are an astonishing accomplishment, and it is on them that his reputation as a poet largely rests. *A Cloud in Pants* (Oblako v shtanakh, 1915) touches upon revolution, religion, and art as apprehended by a desperate lover who has been cruelly rejected; *The Backbone Flute* (Fleita pozvonochnik, 1915) is, once again, a male lyric on the theme of love's madness and pain; *War and the World* (Voina i mir, 1916) deals in fantastic imagery and outré language with the First World War, and ends with a utopian hope for a peaceful world when "Jesus Christ will play at checkers with Cain"; *Man* (Chelovek, 1917), regarded as the high point of Mayakovsky's prerevolutionary poetry, has its setting on our present earth, then in heaven, and at last in the far distant future, where nothing has changed and the greedy philistine still rules the planet.

The Revolution of October 1917 found in Mayakovsky a willing celebrant. He was active in the journal published by the Commissariat of Education, *Iskusstvo Kommuny*, and later he and his futurist and formalist associates formed the Left Front of Art (LEF), the purpose of which was to make the formal achievements of the avant-garde available to the revolutionary state. Much of his energy during the twenties was given to the writing and recitation of agitational and advertising verse, an ephemeral product which nevertheless reveals the verbal resources of a genuine poet. His agitational verse was ostensibly addressed to "the broad masses," but its formal sophistication and verbal complexity made it difficult for the newly literate, and it is doubtful that Mayakovsky ever had a mass following. Some of his works as an acknowledged propagandist are powerful poetic statements. *150,000,000* (1919) tells in a style which parodies the BYLINA (folk epic), the tale of a bogatyr-like Ivan in combat with Wilson, the champion of world capitalism; *Mystery-Bouffe* (Misteriya-Buff, 1918) mixes mystery-play motifs with vulgar comedy in a dramatic spectacle showing the conquest of the "Clean"— the bourgeois—by the "Unclean"—the proletariat; *Vladimir Ilyich Lenin* (1924) develops the story of Lenin's life as an archetypal myth of the savior sent by "History" just when he was needed; *Very good!* (Khorosho! 1927), written to celebrate the tenth anniversary of the October Revolution, presents itself as a "factographic" account of those years, but actually develops a political myth of the struggle against oppression, interspersed with tender and moving passages of a private nature. As a propagandist Mayakovsky produced graphic art as well as poetry, for instance *Windows of the Russian Telegraph Agency* (Okna ROSTA), more than 600 cartoon-like drawings accompanied by brief versified captions of great skill and versatility. Later (1923–25) he produced illustrated advertising jingles for the state stores, which was certainly the most literate advertising copy ever written.

During the 1920s political verse in various forms and on a great variety of topics alternated with lyric poetry: the poems "I love" (Lyublyu, 1922), *About That* (Pro eto, 1923), "Letter to Tatiana Yakovleva" (Pis'mo Tat'yane Yakovlevoi, 1928), "Letter to Comrade Kostrov on the Essence of Love" (Pis'mo tovarishchu Kostrovu o sushchnosti lyubvi, 1928), and his final poem, *At the Top of My Voice* (Vo ves' golos, 1930), are on a level with his best work.

In addition to his poetry and his graphic art, Mayakovsky produced thirteen film scenarios and two plays. Only a few of the scenarios were actually produced and shown, and only fragments of those are preserved. His two plays, *The Bedbug* (Klop, 1928) and *The Bathhouse* (Banya, 1930), both directed by Vsevolod MEYERHOLD, are satirical treatments of Soviet philistinism and the Soviet bureaucratic state.

Mayakovsky's verse may strike a reader as free of the conventional restraints of meter and rhyme, yet close analysis of his lines reveals a carefully structured and complex poetic artifice concealed but not destroyed by the breakup of the line into conversational phrase patterns. His earliest verse is actually faithful in form to the classical syllabotonic system; its impression of novelty is produced by unconventional syntax and diction, and by striking rhymes. In the cycle of poems entitled *Me* (1912) he introduced his characteristic verse line in which the organizing factor is the heavily accented syllable usually occurring three or four times per line, while the number of unaccented syllables between the accents may vary from none to six, offering rich possibilities for poetic emphasis. Rhyme is also essential to the structure of Mayakovsky's verse. Line and stanza boundaries are marked by rhymes, and the sense of a poem is often carried by its pattern of original and offbeat rhymes. His rhymes may be slant, heterosyllabic, consonantal, or paronomastic (punning), and always involve a radical rejection of canonical rhyming practice. Extravagant metaphors are a hallmark of his verse, frequently "realized" in the sense that the vehicle is taken literally and treated at length, as when his heart "on fire" with love becomes a burning building with firemen crawling all over it. Normal syntactic structures are characteristically deformed for the sake of metrical or rhyming emphasis, and the tender diction of lyric poetry alternates with the coarse vocabulary of the street. His verse as a whole, including even the so-called agitational component, is a notably original poetic invention.

Two contradictory themes dominate Mayakovsky's work. The first of these, alienation from the comfortable bourgeois world of established forms and values, is the leitmotif of all his early work, and it appears also in certain lyrics of the thirties. The poet's unrequited love is the vehicle which carries and concretizes his estrangement from the world and from life itself. His abused and battered heart—"burning," beaten to a tatter, a bloody paw run over by a train—is a recurrent image in the long early poems, though it also appears there as a bloody banner for revolutionaries. The manners and mores of the bourgeois world shut out the poet, who appears in one scene in an attitude of huddled despair. Thoughts of suicide are recurrent in the early works, and occur also in some of the later ones. The female object of his manic passion, always part of the alien philistine world, is either getting married (*The Cloud*), married and with "music on her piano" (*The Backbone Flute*), or in bed with a legal husband (*Man*). The poet's despair reaches cosmic proportions in the poem *Man*, which presents both the mythical Christian heaven and the future of the planet as dominated by the "solid ones," known to Sartre as "les salauds," the *meshchane* (philistines). His second theme, an opposite and answering note of optimism about man and the human future, appears in *War and the World*, *About That*, the two plays *The Bathhouse* and *The Bedbug*, and his last poem *At the Top of My Voice*, though even in those works discordant notes darken the bright images. His propagandistic work of the twenties was, in one way of looking at it, a kind of "occupational therapy" designed as a cure for the loneliness and despair of the poet himself, or of his lyrical spokesman. Some lyric poems of the twenties give eloquent voice to this effort to overcome alienation and to interact with fellow creatures: "Being Good to Horses" (Khoroshee otnoshenie k loshadyam, 1918) and "The Sun" (Solntse, 1922) are perhaps the best examples. His two plays *The Bedbug* and *The Bathhouse* offer evidence that he found the revolutionary state increasingly dominated by his old enemy, the philistine. And in his love life, which is faithfully reflected in the poems, he formed hopeless attachments to unattainable women, his grief and frustration curiously mirroring the agonies of his earliest lyric hero. His suicide in 1930 could come as a shock only to those who had not studied his life and work.

Both before and after the Revolution Mayakovsky was the center of important literary and artistic groups. The early futurists were a manifestation in Russia of a new and vital movement in European art. After the Revolution a number of innovatory artists, critics, and poets attached themselves to Mayakovsky, working first on the staff of the journal *Iskusstvo Kommuny* and later in the *Left Front of Art* (*Lef*). The most important of these was Osip BRIK, who "discovered" and published Mayakovsky in 1915 and remained a close friend and collaborator until the poet's death. Mayakovsky's early poems are dedicated to Brik's wife, Lily. Osip Brik was a theoretician and critic of literature, and one of the organizers of *Lef*. He wrote little, but his articles on poetic form, particularly "Sound repetitions" (Zvukovye povtory) and "Rhythm and Syntax" (Ritm i sintaksis) are brilliant formalist analyses of poetic language. He served Mayakovsky, who read very little, as a source of information and ideas, and he was probably the most articulate exponent in *Lef* of the theories of "social demand" and "literature of fact." A man of surpassing intelligence, he was apparently not strong either in performance or in principle. His connections with the Cheka are well documented. Nikolai ASEEV was a poet and a prominent member of *Lef*. His verse on revolutionary and industrial themes during the twenties and thirties was a skillfully made answer to the "social demand" promulgated by *Lef*. His long poem, *Incipit Mayakovsky* (1940) which received the Stalin prize in 1941, celebrates Mayakovsky as a revolutionary poet, creating a number of striking verbal images of the poet at his life and at his work. Vasily Kamensky was a poet, an early member of the cubo-futurist group and a participant in the tours and recitals of 1913. Probably his most important work is an account of his adventures with Mayakovsky: *Life with Mayakovsky* (Zhizn' s Mayakovskim, 1940). Sergei TRETYAKOV was an able writer and a proponent of radical innovation in all the arts. He worked on film with EISENSTEIN and with Meyerhold in the latter's theater. Among Mayakovsky's collaborators in *Lef* and *New Lef* should also be mentioned: A. M. Rodchenko, a brilliant photographer, artist, and master of the montage technique, the formalist critic Viktor SHKLOVSKY, Boris ARVATOV, an acute literary theorist who tried to integrate the formalist and sociological critical methods, and finally V. A. Katanyan, one of many less important figures close to Mayakovsky, and the one who has contributed the most complete record of his life: *Mayakovskii: Literaturnaya khronika* (1961).

Works: Polnoe sobranie sochinenii. 13 vols. 1955–61.

Translations: Herbert Marshall, trans. and ed., *Mayakovsky.* 1965. Patricia Blake, ed., Max Hayward and George Reavey, trans., *The Bedbug and Selected Poetry.* 1975. See also: Lewanski, pp. 302–04.

Secondary literature: E. J. Brown, *Mayakovsky; a Poet in the Revolution.* 1973. Roman Jakobson, "O pokolenii rastrativshem svoikh poetov." In *Smert' Vladimira Mayakovskogo.* Berlin, 1930. Trans. in E. J. Brown, ed., *Major Soviet Authors.* 1973. Pp. 7–32. N. Khardzhiev and V. Trenin, *Poeticheskaya kul'tura Mayakovskogo.* 1970. Vladimir Markov, *Russian Futurism: A History,* 1968. "Novye stroki Mayakovskogo." In *Russkii literaturnyi arkhiv.* New York, 1956. Z. S. Papernyi, *Poeticheskii obraz u Mayakovskogo.* 1961. Viktor Shklovskii, *O Mayakovskom.* 1940. (Trans. by Lily Feiler as *Maiakovsky and His Circle.* New York, 1972.) L. L. Stahlberger, *The Symbolic System of Mayakovsky.* The Hague, 1964. Victor Terras, *Vladimir Mayakovsky.* (Twayne's World Authors Series, 706.) 1983. W. Woroszylski, *The Life of Mayakovsky.* Trans. from the Polish by Boleslaw Taborski. New York, 1971.

E. J. B.

Medvédev, Silvéstr (secular name: Simon Agafonikovich, 1641–91) continued the work of SIMEON POLOTSKY in propagating the culture of scholastic humanism in Russia. Among the first generation of clerks from the Tsar's Privy Chancery to study at Polotsky's school at the Zaikonospassky monastery, Medvedev took monastic vows in 1677. Thereafter Tsar Fyodor placed him on the payroll of the court and he served as Polotsky's secretary and editor. He took his mentor's place at court after the latter's death in 1680, and inherited Polotsky's school as well as his private printing press until it fell under patriarchal control. He was a mediocre syllabic poet, and the author with Karion ISTOMIN of a historical account about the 1682 uprising of the Tsar's musketeers. He also compiled the first Russian bibliographical work. Between 1678 and 1689 he served as corrector of books at the Printing House under the patriarchal jurisdiction. His importance lies in his advocacy of neo-Latin enlightenment and his attempts to free learning from control by the Church led by the grecophile Patriarch Ioakim. A victim of the political struggle between his patron Sofiya and the Naryshkins who favored Ioakim, he lost his battle for the directorship of the first Russian academy to the Likhudi brothers. He was finally implicated in a plot against Peter I, and tortured and beheaded in 1691. However, his and Polotsky's vision of the academy was realized in 1701 when Stefan Yavorsky reformed the curriculum to include Latin learning, and prepared the ground for the emergence of a secular neoclassical literature.

Works: Medvedev's syllabic verse in English. In W. E. Brown, *A History of 17th Century Russian Literature.* Ann Arbor, 1980. Pp. 120–22. In Russian: In A. M. Panchenko, *Russkaya sillabicheskaya poeziya XVII–XVIII v.* 1970. Pp. 184–202.

Secondary literature: A. M. Panchenko. *Russkaya stikhotvornaya kul'tura XVII veka.* 1973.

P. H.

Mei, Lev Aleksándrovich (1822–1862), poet. Son of an impoverished country squire of German stock, Mei was first educated at the private boarding school of the nobility in Moscow, and from 1836 to 1841 at the Tsarskoe Selo Lyceum near St. Petersburg. After completing his studies there, he served in the office of the Moscow governor general. Literary interests drew him to the "young editorial group" at the MOSKVITYANIN. After 1853, Mei lived in St. Petersburg, devoting himself entirely to literary activity.

Mei began to publish in the mid-forties. His early verse marked him as one of those poets known for their lyrics in anthologies and as an advocate of the ideal of beauty which the poet serves unreservedly. Many of his lyrical romances were put to music by Glinka, Tchaikovsky, Borodin, Rimsky-Korsakov, Cui, Musorgsky, and Rakhmaninov. Starting with the mid-fifties Mei's poetry reveals social motifs in line with the tendency of the time. He became an important translator into Russian of Goethe, Schiller, Heine, Shakespeare, Milton, Byron, Mickiewicz, Shevchenko, and others. He transcribed the medieval "Igor Tale" (SLOVO O POLKU IGOREVE) into contemporary Russian (1841–50).

Mei is important for his historical songs, such as "The Veche Bell of Novgorod" (Vechevoi kolokol, 1839–40), and for his songs and poems dealing with folklore motifs, such as "Master" (Khozyain, 1849), unfulfilled love, longing for deliverance, such as "Twilight" (Sumerki, 1858), and disillusionment over his spent youth, "Hello—Hello!" (Au—Au! 1861). He is also the author of three verse dramas.

Works: Polnoe sobranie sochinenii. 3d ed. Ed. P. V. Bykov. 3 vols. 1910–11.

Secondary literature: S. A. Reiser, "Mei." In *Istoriya russkoi literatury.* Vol. 8, Pt. 2. 1956. Pp. 302–14. J. B.

Meierkhóld, see MEYERHOLD.

Meléty Smotrítsky see SMOTRITSKY.

Mélnikov, Pável Ivánovich (pseud. Andréi Pechérsky, 1818–1883), writer. A native of Nizhny Novgorod province, Melnikov graduated from the Kazan University Faculty of Letters in 1837 and subsequently worked for the government as a teacher, editor, statistician, researcher, and since 1850 was on "special assignment" in charge of Schismatic (Old Believer) Affairs for the Nizhny Novgorod region until his retirement in 1866. Melnikov's work for the government provided him with a great wealth of material on popular life between Volga and Urals. His early publications were ethnographic and demographic studies, and travel notes. Melnikov's first work of fiction, the story "On Who Elpidifor Vasilievich Really Was and What Arrangements Were Made for the Celebration of His Name-day in Chernograd" (1840), is a rather awkward imitation of GOGOL. After a long hiatus, Melnikov's long short-story "The Krasilnikovs" (Krasil'nikovy) appeared in MOSKVITYANIN in 1852. Many more followed in several different journals. Melnikov's stories of the 1850s paint a somber picture of Russian provincial life, rather in the manner of SALTYKOV-SHCHEDRIN (some of them did appear in SOVREMENNIK). After another long interval, Melnikov came forward with his main work, the epic novel *In the Woods* (V lesakh, 1871–74) and its sequel, *In the Hills* (Na gorakh, 1875–81), in which he presented a rich panoramic view of popular life in the region which he knew so well. His interest is centered in the Old Believer communities, which he had studied and energetically combated as a government official, and whose beliefs and customs, folklore, songs, and legends he presents with obvious sympathy. The political drift of Melnikov's work is that a great potential for economic and cultural progress is latent in the uneducated merchant class, if only it could be properly enlightened. Melnikov's language is rich and idiomatic. He has a perfect command of the local vernacular and its various nuances. Melnikov's works also have value as a historical source.

Works: Polnoe sobranie sochinenii. 14 vols. 1897–98. *Polnoe sobranie sochinenii.* 7 vols. 1909. *Sobranie sochinenii.* With a critical-biographical introd. by M. P. Eremin. 6 vols. 1963. *V lesakh.* 2 vols. 1936–37. *Na gorakh.* 1956.

Secondary literature: Thomas H. Hoisington, "Melnikov-Pechersky: Romancer of Provincial and Old Believer Life," *SlavR* 33 (1974), pp. 679–94. ———. "Romance—a Congenial Form: Mel'nikov-Pecherskii's *Grandma's Yarns* and *Olden Times*," *RusR* 36 (1977), pp. 463–76. ———. "Dark Romance in a Provincial Setting: Mel'nikov-Pecherskij's *The Krasil'nikovs*," *SEEJ* 22 (1978), pp. 15–25. L. M. Lotman, "Mel'nikov-Pecherskii." In *Istoriya russkoi literatury.* Vol. 9, pt. 2. 1956. ———, "Roman iz narodnoi zhizni." In *Istoriya russkogo romana.* Vol. 2. 1964. Pp. 405–15. V. F. Sokolova, "K voprosu o tvorcheskoi istorii romanov P. I. Mel'nikova-Pecherskogo *V lesakh* i *Na gorakh*," *RLit* 13 (1970), no. 3, pp. 107–18. V. T.

Merezhkóvsky, Dmitry Sergéevich (1865–1941), writer and religious philosopher, was educated at the Third Classical Gymnasium in St. Petersburg and at the Historical-Philological Faculty of the University of St. Petersburg, 1884 to 1888. In 1889 he married Zinaida HIPPIUS and they settled in St. Petersburg.

Eclectic and erudite, Merezhkovsky's literary corpus includes poetry, novels, dramas, critical essays, and translations from several languages including Greek. His importance, however, is primarily cultural: he was a popularizer of French symbolism in the 1890s, formulator and chief proselytizer of the "new religious consciousness" after 1900, and prophet of a religious revolution after 1905.

Poetry was his first means of literary expression. Influenced by MIKHAILOVSKY's and KOROLENKO's populism and by the "civic poetry" of NADSON and MINSKY, Merezhkovsky's first collection, *Verse* (Stikhotvoreniya, 1883–87, 1888) extolled peasant virtues and deplored the meaninglessness of everyday life. New themes—French symbolism, Nietzsche's philosophy, a new-found love for the beauties of classical antiquity, and certain problems in his marriage—inspired the verse of *Symbols* (Simvoly, 1892). Desiring a "new Parthenon" to be created by "god-like men on earth," Merezhkovsky still esteemed the Christian ideals of love and personal immortality, and was aware of the difficulty of reconciling them. *New Verse* (Novye stikhotvoreniya, 1896) treats the same themes, but Nietzscheanism is dominant.

As poetry proved inadequate to express complex ideas, Merezhkovsky turned to literary criticism, using famous writers such as CHEKHOV, Flaubert, and PUSHKIN as vehicles for his own views. These essays, subsequently collected in *Eternal Companions* (Vechnye sputniki, 1897), revived Russians' interest in great figures of world literature, past and present. In 1893, Merezhkovsky published his essay "On the Reasons for the Decline and on the New Trends in Contemporary Russian Literature." Defining literature as a cultural force, the essay charged that Russia lacked a great national literature, and blamed populist didacticism for impoverishing the content of literature and corrupting the language. Insisting that a purely secular literature would never reach the deeply religious people, Merezhkovsky advocated metaphysical idealism and symbolism. Extremely influential, the essay is a milestone in the development of Russian SYMBOLISM. Other important works of literary criticism are *L. Tolstoi and Dostoevsky* (1901–02), which treated the writers as symbols of "two [religious] truths," the flesh and the spirit, respectively; and *Gogol and the Devil* (1906), an attack on Christian asceticism and otherworldliness.

Tolstoi and Dostoevsky shows the impact of Merezhkovsky's "turn to Christ" in 1899. In 1900, he began to proselytize a "new religious consciousness" and a new form of Christianity based on the imminent Second Coming of Christ and a forthcoming Third Testament. Preaching that paganism (really Hellenism or Nietzscheanism) and Christianity were two halves of a yet-to-be-revealed higher truth, he, Hippius, and Dmitry Filosofov founded the Religious-Philosophical Society of St. Petersburg in 1901. Featuring debates between clergymen and intellectuals on burning issues of the day, such as Christian attitudes toward sex, the Society became a focal point of the religious revival of the early 20th century. The Merezhkovskys also founded *Novyi put'*, a revue, to serve as a showcase for the new spiritual and idealistic trends in literature. The clash of paganism and Christianity is also treated in Merezhkovsky's trilogy of historical novels: *Death of the Gods, Julian the Apostate* (1896), *Resurrection of the Gods, Leonardo da Vinci* (1901), and *Anti-Christ, Peter and Alexis* (1905).

Apolitical until 1904, Merezhkovsky interpreted the Revolution of 1905 as a religious revolution, harbinger of the Apocalypse and the establishment of the Kingdom of God on Earth. Having concluded that "Autocracy is from Anti-Christ," he attacked the Orthodox Church for its support of reaction, proclaimed a neo-Slavophile messianism, and scorned the bourgeois societies of the West for their *meshchanstvo* (philistinism). Closest to the Socialist Revolutionaries (because of their shared hostility to the state), but also linked to the Constitutional Democrats, Merezhkovsky insisted that socialism entails universal slavery and despotism. He also maintained that the Russian intelligentsia, despite its atheism, is practicing "Christianity without Christ" because of its selfless devotion to the people. Major works on these themes include: *Dostoyevsky: Prophet of the Russian Revolution* (1906), *The Coming Ham* (1906), and *Not Peace But A Sword* (1908).

The Merezhkovskys fled Russia in December 1919, lived in Poland (and worked with Piłsudski) until October 1920, then moved to Paris, where he died in December, 1941, a bitter opponent of Bolshevism to the very end. Works written in emigration stress religious themes and include novels and essays about the pre-Christian Near East.

Works: Polnoe sobranie sochinenii. 24 vols. 1914. (Includes works Merezhkovsky considered significant.) K. D. Muratova, *Istoriya russkoi literatury XIX–nachala XX veka* (1953) and C. H. Bedford (see below) contain complete bibliographies.

Translations: Death of the Gods (Julian the Apostate). London, 1901. *The Romance of Leonardo da Vinci.* London, 1902. *Tolstoi as Man and Artist with an essay on Dostoevsky.* Westminster, 1902. *Peter and Alexis.* London, 1905. For complete list, see Bedford.

Secondary literature: C. H. Bedford, *The Seeker, D. S. Merezhkovsky.* 1975. B. G. Rosenthal, "Nietzsche in Russia: The Case of Merezhkovsky," *SlavR* 33 (1974), pp. 429–52. ———, *D. S. Merezhkovsky and the Silver Age.* The Hague, 1975. ———, "Eschatology and the Appeal of Revolution: Merezhkovsky, Bely, Blok," *California Slavic Studies* 11 (1980), pp. 105–39. Heinrich Stammler, "Julianus Apostata Redivivus: Dmitrij Merežkovskij," *Welt der Slaven* 11 (1966), pp. 180–204. ———, "D. S. Merežkovskij: 1865–1965," *Welt der Slaven* 12 (1967), pp. 142–52. ———, "Russian Metapolitics: Merezhkovsky's Religious Understanding of the Historical Process," *California Slavic Studies* 9 (1976), pp. 123–39.
B. G. R.

Merzlyakóv, Alekseí Fyódorovich (1778–1830), university professor, poet, critic, and translator. Born into a provincial merchant family, Merzlyakov devoted exactly half of his life to an academic career as professor of literature, rising through all the ranks at Moscow University (1804–1830). Among his students at various times were Prince Pyotr VYAZEMSKY, Fyodor TYUTCHEV, Aleksandr POLEZHAEV, and Mikhail LERMONTOV. As a poet, he produced not only some traditional pseudoclassical verse, such as an "Ode on the Destruction of Babylon" (Oda na razrushenie Vavilona, 1801) but also a small body of romances and songs (*pesni*) in a stylized folk manner. While his conventional verse frequently elicited disparaging remarks from contemporaries (including PUSHKIN), his songs (some of which actually became popular) were praised by BELINSKY. These two sides of Merzlyakov's creativity are paralleled in his literary theory and criticism: although he was, as SVYATOPOLK-MIRSKY puts it, "an eclectic follower of senescent classicism" and the author of prescriptive handbooks such as *A Short Rhetoric* (Kratkaya ritorika ili pravila, otnosyashchiesya ko vsem rodam sochinenii prozaicheskikh, 1809–28), he was also a member of the KARAMZINian circle. Thus he stands as a transitional figure between the pseudoclassicism of the 18th century and the beginnings of romanticism. These "divided loyalties" are also evident in the fact that he was critical of many aspects of pseudoclassicism and admired Schiller but at the same time condemned the romanticism of ZHUKOVSKY. Merzlyakov's Russian versions of ancient Greek (Homer, Sappho, Theocritus, Moschus, Bion, Tyrtaeus) and Roman poets (Horace, Ovid, Tibullus, Propertius), with their careful attention to metrics, are among his best endeavors.

Bibliography: Stikhotvoreniya 1958. (With an introduction by Yury Lotman.) Brief notice in V. I. Kuleshov, *Istoriya russkoi kritiki* (1972).
R. H. S.

Meshchérsky, Prince Vladimir Petróvich (1839–1914), writer and publicist, published in SEVERNAYA PCHELA, *Moskovskie vedomosti,* and RUSSKII VESTNIK from 1860 on. His first major works are the *poema* "Tauris" (Tavrida, 1863) and *Sketches of Contemporary Social Life in Russia* (Ocherki nyneshnei obshchestvennoi zhizni v Rossii, 1868–70). Meshchersky not only took a stand against revolutionary movements but against liberal reform as well. Being closely associated with court and ecclesiastical circles, which subsidized his publications, including *The Citizen* (Grazhdanin, 1872–1914), *The Good* (Dobro, 1881), and *Friendly Discussions* (Druzheskie rechi, 1905), Meshchersky defended the privileges of the nobility and the perpetuation of the autocracy. Along with his public affairs commentaries, such as "Discourses by a Conservative" (Rechi konservatora, 1876), Meshchersky produced several ANTINIHILIST novels: *The Mysteries of Contemporary Petersburg* (Tainy sovremennogo Peterburga, 1876–77) and *Notes of an Adolescent Suicide* (Zapiski zastrelivshegosya gimnazista, 1875), as well as a series of novels exposing the mores and atheistic tendencies of the aristocracy: *Petersburg Women of High Society* (Zhenshchiny iz peterburgskogo bol'shogo sveta, 1874), *Petersburg Men of High Society* (Muzhchiny..., 1897),

One of Our Bismarcks (Odin iz nashikh Bismarkov, 1874), *Lord-Apostle in Petersburg High Society* (Lord-apostol v bol'shom peterburgskom svete, 1876), and others. In other novels, stories, and comedies, all characterized by forthright didacticism and blatant schematicism, Meshchersky promoted the same reactionary viewpoints. He is also the author of articles on TYUTCHEV, Lev TOLSTOI, Aleksei TOLSTOI, and DOSTOEVSKY, and of a series of memoirs, *Moi vospominaniya* (1897–1912).

Secondary literature: V. G. Korolenko, "Knyaz' Meshcherskii i pokoinye ministry," *Russkoe bogatstvo*, 1904, no. 12, pp. 155–61. I. Vinogradoff, "Some Russian Imperial Letters to Prince V. P. Meshcherskii (1839–1914)," *OSP* 10 (1962), pp. 105–58. A. Zayonchkovskii, "Aleksandr III i ego blizhaishee okruzhenie," *Voprosy istorii*, 1966, no. 8. For F. M. Dostoevsky's correspondence with Meshchersky, see: F. M. Dostoevskii, *Pis'ma.* 4 vols. 1928–59.
D. K. D.

Metrics, see VERSIFICATION.

Meyerhold, (Meierkhól'd) Vsévolod Emílievich (1874–1940), theater, opera, and film director, was born into a theater- and music-loving family in Penza. After gymnasium and a year's perfunctory study of law he entered in 1896 the theater class of Vladimir NEMIROVICH-DANCHENKO at the Moscow Philharmonia. Olga Knipper and he, the two gold-medalists at graduation, were taken by their teacher into the Moscow Art Theater, which Nemirovich had just founded (1898) with STANISLAVSKY. There Meyerhold at first played leading roles, but when in 1902 the company became a cooperative, those not invited to become shareholders, including Meyerhold, left to form their own "Cooperative of New Drama" which began touring the provinces. In Kherson and Tiflis Meyerhold directed and acted in plays, reflecting the Art Theater repertory and contemporary taste, by CHEKHOV, GORKY, Aleksei and Lev TOLSTOI, Ibsen, Hauptmann, and Przybyszewski.

Though Stanislavsky invited Meyerhold to direct an experiment in staging nonrealistic plays, the Theater Studio of 1905, the resulting productions of Maeterlinck's *Death of Tintagiles* and Hauptmann's *Schluck and Jau* did not satisfy him, and so he did not permit them to open. Meyerhold then served (1906–07) as director for the actress-manager Vera Komissarzhevskaya. However, here too his experiments in putting SYMBOLISM on stage succeeded only with Maeterlinck's *Sister Beatrice*, Leonid ANDREEV's *The Life of Man* and Aleksandr BLOK's *The Showbooth* (Balaganchik), in the last two of which Komissarzhevskaya did not even appear. Small wonder that the actress dismissed her director, who, however, the year after was appointed director at the Imperial opera and drama theaters of St. Petersburg.

During Meyerhold's next decade in this post (1908–18), he staged luxurious official productions, most often together with the designer Aleksandr Golovin. Among these his greatest successes were Molière's *Don Juan* (1910), Gluck's *Orpheus* (1911) and LERMONTOV's *Masquerade* (1917). But his innovative experiments under various auspices he wisely signed with a pseudonym, Doctor Dapertutto. Of these the pantomime *Columbine's Scarf* after Arthur Schnitzler (1910) along with the earlier *Showbooth* by Blok proved revelatory to him of the nature of theater.

After 1917 Meyerhold espoused the Communist cause, taking it into the theater with the slogan "October in the Theater," thus expressing his hope of a revolution in art as well as society. His first significant post-October production, Fernand Crommelynck's *Magnanimous Cuckold* (1922) emerged from his Moscow workshop, for which he devised a training system, "biomechanics," intended to give his actors basic physical gestures and movements with which to project action and reaction on stage. Thereafter at his own Meyerhold Theater he achieved innovative successes in staging the classics—OSTROVSKY's *The Forest* (1924), GOGOL's *Inspector General* (1926) and GRIBOEDOV's *Woe to Wit*, as he called the play (1928). He also produced Soviet writers, even, especially later, needling them for plays, thus Nikolai ERDMAN, Yury OLESHA, and Vladimir MAYAKOVSKY. The canon of Mayakovsky's dramatic work was staged by Meyerhold.

Meyerhold believed in the theater as art, not the imitation of reality, and therefore tried to give the actor basic forms with which consciously to communicate his meaning to an audience; he drew these forms from older traditions—Kabuki and the commedia dell'arte—and the practices of actors of the past. His pupils became not only actors, but also directors; notable among the latter are Nikolai Okhlopkov, and the film director Sergei EISENSTEIN.

Unfortunately, under Stalin, Meyerhold's conception of theater art was condemned as "formalistic," and his theater was closed in 1938; he died soon after his arrest in 1939. He has been posthumously rehabilitated as a victim of Stalinism.

Works: Stat'i. Pis'ma. Rechi. Besedy. 2 vols. 1968. *Perepiska, 1896–1939.* 1976. *Tvorcheskoe nasledie Vs. E. Meierkhol'da.* 1978.

Translations: Meyerhold on Theatre. Trans. and ed. by Edward Braun. 1969.

Secondary literature: Yurii Elagin, *Temnyi genii.* New York, 1955. 2d ed. 1982. Marjorie L. Hoover, *Meyerhold: The Art of Conscious Theater.* 1974. Konstantin Rudnitsky, *Meyerhold the Director.* Trans. G. Petrov. Ed. S. Schultze. Introd. Ellendea Proffer. 1981. Paul Schmidt, ed., *Meyerhold at Work.* 1980.   M. H.

Mikhailov, Mikhail Lariónovich or Ilarionovich (1829–65), poet, writer, translator, and revolutionary, was the son of a mining clerk and a Kirghiz princess. Mikhailov's grandfather was beaten to death when he demanded the freedom promised him by his dying owner, a member of the Aksakov family. The incident was described in S. T. AKSAKOV's *Family Chronicle.* Mikhailov was educated by tutors before attending St. Petersburg University (1846–48). His first literary work appeared in *Illustration* (Illyustratsiya) in 1845. Since his father did not approve of a career in letters, Mikhailov was forced to work in Nizhny Novgorod, but continued to submit verses to MOSKVITYANIN. In 1852, he returned to St. Petersburg and worked for SOVREMENNIK and the OTECHESTVENNYE ZAPISKI while attaching himself to the group of writers around DOBROLYUBOV and CHERNYSHEVSKY. In 1861 he travelled abroad. On his return, he was arrested for radical political activity and sentenced to six years at hard labor in Siberia where he died in 1865. Mikhailov wrote many stories, the best known of which was "Adam Adamych" in which the miserable life of a teacher of German is depicted. In 1854 Mikhailov published his novel *Birds of Passage* (Pereletnye ptitsy) which described the sordid life of traveling actors. In his lyrics and political satire, Mikhailov's themes were often radical. In the poems "Five" (Pyatero) and "In Memory of Dobrolyubov" (Pamyati Dobrolyubova) he called for the use of force to bring about social changes. Several of his agitational verses later became revolutionary songs, so "A Firm and Comradely Embrace" (Krepko, druzhno vas v ob"yat'ya, 1861). Mikhailov's translations from French, English, and German received much acclaim. His "Songs of Heine" (1858) were highly praised by Aleksandr BLOK.

Works: Sochineniya. Ed. B. P. Koz'min. 3 vols. 1958. *Sobranie stikhotvorenii.* 1969.

Secondary literature: P. S. Fateev, *M. Mikhailov—revolyutsioner, pisatel', publitsist.* 1969. M. K. Lemke, "Delo M. I. Mikhailova." In *Politicheskie protsessy v Rossii 1860–kh gg.* 2d ed. 1923.   T. E. B.

Mikhailóvsky, Nikolai Konstantinovich (1842–1904), with ten pseudonyms, including Gron'yar and Profan, leading theoretician of POPULISM (narodnichestvo) for four decades, literary critic, sociologist, and editor. Of petty noble origin, he was expelled from the St. Petersburg Mining Institute in 1863 shortly before graduation for participation in political demonstrations. While his first article was published in 1860, his most important work was as a literary critic and editor of OTECHESTVENNYE ZAPISKI from 1868 to 1884 and as chief editor of RUSSKOE BOGATSTVO from 1892 until his death in 1904. He and his collaborators made these two "thick" journals the most outstanding organs for "legal populism" within Russia. A critic in the tradition of BELINSKY and DOBROLYUBOV, he introduced to a large Russian audience the works of such contemporary West European thinkers as Comte, Proudhon, Spencer, Mill, and Marx as well as commenting on the Russian literary world. Particularly controversial were his sharply critical articles on DOSTOEVSKY and Lev TOLSTOI.

Consciously choosing not to emigrate, Mikhailovsky became the premier theoretician within Russia of agrarian socialism. Through-

out his career he remained a friend and trusted advisor of the radical intelligentsia, including those underground, and even contributed to illegal publications. During the 1890s, he was regarded as the most prominent opponent of Marxism by such figures as PLEKHANOV and LENIN. Four times, the government exiled him to the provinces.

Over four decades, Mikhailovsky was basically consistent in his worldview developed in the 1860s and 1870s. While differing on some points, he and Pyotr LAVROV, working independently, were the theoretical architects of populism and founders of the Russian school of "subjective sociology." Their ideas based on a synthesis of selected elements of Western and Russian thought were attractive to the radical intelligentsia who were taught that through the exercise of their free will they could within limits guide society toward their ideal of what it should be. According to Mikhailovsky, the key to social progress was the "struggle for individuality," the all-around development ("wholeness") of every person. Equating socialism with progress and justice for all, the intelligentsia, who all had gained their status at the expense of the working masses, had the duty to work for a social and economic revolution stressing egalitarianism. A "critical narodnik," Mikhailovsky did not accept the idea that the *opinions* of the masses were to be the guide for action, but rather their *interests* as defined in the ideal of those seeking a just society for all. He warned that the danger was great that the masses would follow a demagogue who would appeal to their opinions, but not advance their interests. The just society to be built in Russia was to be based on the socialist principles inherent in the *mir* (peasant community), although Mikhailovsky did recognize the harsh realities of village life and the need for raising the level of technology.

While acknowledging the relevance of Marxism for industrialized states, he denounced "metaphysical revolutionaries" and also classical economics, both basic to Marxism. His "subjective sociology" was based on the idea that the social sciences could not be reduced only to the study of objective phenomena (pravda-"truth") by using the methodology of natural science. For social sciences, there was a second aspect, subjective or moral truth (pravda-"justice"), which was of equal significance and required a different methodology. Neither type of truth should obscure the other in the study of society. Typical of Russian populists since HERZEN, Mikhailovsky hoped that Russia could skip the stage of bourgeois-dominated capitalism. While recognizing the importance of legal guarantees particularly of civil rights and supporting efforts to gain them, he felt that a constitution would be of only limited value to the working classes if there were not a social and economic revolution at the same time. To him, the bourgeois-dominated democracies of Western Europe were only instruments designed to exploit the working classes. Mikhailovsky's ideas on socialism were deeply influenced by the moralism of the French utopian socialists, particularly Proudhon. Among his key political articles were: "What is Progress?" (1869–70), "Idealism, Idolatry and Realism" (1873), "The Hero and the Mob" (1882), and his column, "Literature and Life" in 1894–96.

Works: Polnoe sobranie sochinenii. Vols. 1–8, 10. 1906–14. *Literaturno-kriticheskie stat'i.* 1957.

Translations: Dostoevsky: A Cruel Talent. Trans. S. Cadmus. 1978.

Secondary literature: James H. Billington, *Mikhailovsky and Russian Populism.* 1958. B. I. Gorev, *N. K. Mikhailovskii.* 1931. Arthur P. Mendel, *Dilemmas of Progress in Tsarist Russia, Legal Marxism and Legal Populism.* 1961. Alexander Vucinich, *Social Thought in Tsarist Russia: The Quest for a Science of Society, 1861–1917.* 1976.   J. A. D.

Mikula Selyaninovich, see BYLINA.

Miller, Orest Fyódorovich (1833–89), folklorist, specialist in medieval Russian literature. A graduate of Moscow University (1855), Miller was a professor at St. Petersburg University from 1870 until his death. His Master's thesis was entitled "On the Moral Element in Poetry, based on Historical Facts" (O nravstvennoi stikhii v poezii na osnove istoricheskikh dannykh, 1858), and his doctoral dissertation, "Ilya Muromets and the Heroes of the Kiev Cycle" (Il'ya Muromets i bogatyrstvo kievskoe, 1870). A student of Russian epic poetry, Miller was one of the most talented scholars of

Miller, Vsévolod Fyódorovich

the mythological school, which considered epic poetry as a reflection of folk consciousness. His works, and especially "Ilya Muromets," are credited for comparative analysis of a large number of *sujets* and their variants in Russian and Slavic epic poetry.

Bibliography: D. Yazykov. *Obzor zhizni i trudov pokoinykh russkikh pisatelei.* Fasc. 9 (1905).

Secondary literature: M. K. Azadovskii, *Istoriya russkoi fol'kloristiki.* Vol. 2. 1963. V. Ya. Propp, *Osnovnye etapy razvitiya russkogo geroicheskogo eposa.* 1958. *Slavyanovedenie v dorevolyutsionnoi Rossii: Biobibliograficheskii slovar'.* 1979. Pp. 239–240.

E. B.

Miller, Vsévolod Fyódorovich (1848–1913), folklorist, linguist, and ethnographer. One of the most brilliant members of the "historical school" in Russian folkloristics, renowned authority on Russian epic poetry. A graduate (1870) and professor of Moscow University (1884), director of the Lazarev Institute of Eastern Languages. In his early works, Miller studied the literary sources of Russian fairy tales. Later, in his book *Excursus into the Area of the Russian Folk Epic* (Ekskursy v oblast' russkogo narodnogo eposa, 1892), he discovered a deep influence of Persian epics on Russian epic poetry. His monograph, *Essays in Russian Folk Literature* (Ocherki russkoi narodnoi slovesnosti, 3 vols., 1897–1924), focused on studies regarding the historical value of *byliny* and their localization. His theory of an aristocratic and relatively late origin of the Russian heroic epos has had a deep impact on all later studies.

Bibliography: "Bibliograficheskii perechen' pechatnykh trudov V. F. Millera." In *Yubileinyi sbornik v chest' Vsevoloda Fedorovicha Millera.* 1900. B. Bogdanov, "Spisok uchenykh trudov Vsevoloda Fedorovicha Millera." In *Etnograficheskoe obozrenie,* 1913, no. 3–4. (The whole issue is devoted to Miller) M. N. Speranskii, "Spisok uchenykh trudov V. F. Millera." In *Otchet Imperatorskogo Moskovskogo Universiteta za 1913 god.* Pt. 1. 1914. (Also in *Drevnosti: Trudy Moskovskogo arkheologicheskogo obshchestva,* Vol. 24 (1914), pp. 11–39). *Istoriya istoricheskoi nauki v SSSR; Dooktyabr'skii period: Bibliografiya.* 1965. Pp. 329–30.

Secondary literature: M. K. Azadovskii, *Istoriya russkoi fol'kloristiki.* Vol. 2. 1963. V. E. Gusev, "'Istoricheskaya shkola' v russkoi dorevolyutsionnoi fol'kloristike." In *Ocherki istorii russkoi etnografii, fol'kloristiki i antropologii.* Fasc. 3 (1965). *Slavyanovedenie v dorevolyutsionnoi Rossii: Biobibliograficheskii slovar'.* 1979. Pp. 236–38.

E. B.

Mináev, Dmitry Dmitrievich (1835–89), poet and journalist, was from a gentry family of modest means. Educated in a military academy, Minaev left a government career in 1857 to begin full-time literary endeavors. While he was still in school, his poetry appeared in popular journals, and he began translating French, English, and Italian works. His translations were numerous, but did not always adhere to the original. Minaev's fame came from his satirical wit, expressed in poems, feuilletons, and epigrams usually published under a pseudonym: the journal ISKRA presented his verses under the title "The Poet Exposer" (Oblichitel'nyi poet); his feuilletons in RUSSKOE SLOVO were signed "An obscure man" (Temnyi chelovek); and in the 1870s, his witticisms for the *Peterburgskaya gazeta* were under the names "Major Burbonov" and "A common friend" (Obshchii drug). In 1860, Minaev's book *V. G. Belinsky* appeared with D. Sviyazhsky as the author. Minaev considered himself a liberal, but used his humor to attack both right and left. Known for his amazing versification and rhyme, he used his talent in glib polemics about social and political problems. He had a reputation for irritability and excessive drinking. As a playwright, Minaev was moderately successful. His comedy *The Liberal* was published in OTECHESTVENNYE ZAPISKI (1870) and *Finished Songs, or the Broken Nest* (Spetye pesni ili razorennoe gnezdo) received the Demidov prize for drama in 1875. His other comedies included *The Cashier* (Kassir, 1882) and *A Warm Nest* (Teploe gnezdyshko, 1883). Minaev's other major works were: *Rehashes* (Perepevy, 1859), *Eugene Onegin* (1863), *Ballads and Songs* (Dumy i pesni, 2 vols., 1863–64), *I Wish You Good Health* (Zdraviya zhelayu, 1867), *In the Twilight* (V sumerkakh, 1867), *Songs and Poems* (Pesni i poemy, 1870), *At the Crossroads* (Na pereput'i, 1871), *Songs and Satires* (Pesni i satiry, 1878), and *The Demon and Fairy Tales* (Demon i skazki, 1880).

Works: Stikhotvoreniya i poemy. Ed. with introd. and commentary by I. Yampol'skii. 1960.

Secondary literature: L. A. Belyaeva, "Vystupleniya D. D. Minaeva v zashchitu vozhdei revolyutsionnoi demokratii." In *Narod—geroi russkoi literatury.* Kazan, 1966. N. A. Dobrolyubov, "Perepevy" (1860). In *Sobranie sochinenii* (1961–64), Vol. 6. Pp. 211–20. M. E. Saltykov-Shchedrin, "V sumerkakh: Satiry i pesni D. D. Minaeva" (1868). In *Sobranie sochinenii* (1965–77), Vol. 9. Pp. 242–49.

T. E. B.

Minéi Chét'i (Monthly Readings). A collection of religious texts to be read on the feast day of each saint and arranged chronologically for the twelve months of the year. The Old Russian feminine singular substantive *mineya* was patterned after the Greek neuter plural mēnaia [biblia] (i.e., "monthly [books]"). The form *mineya* coexisted with the masculine singular *minei,* which frequently lost its etymological connotation (as in the formula *minei mesyach'nyi*).

The Old Russian *Minei* were introduced into *Rus'* from the South Slavic area, which had received the collection from Greek ecclesiastical literature. The fact that part of its textual material is to be found in the so-called Uspensky sbornik (late 12th–early 13th century) attests to the early presence of the work in the East Slavic territory. Subsequent Old Russian versions were adapted to local ecclesiastic traditions. It was only in the 16th century, however, that the *Minei* acquired a preeminent importance in the spiritual and literary life of the Russian lands. This is due to the monumental collection which the Muscovite Metropolitan MAKARY (1482–1563) prepared under this title.

Makary's original design for the *Minei* was limited to the compilation of Lives of saints either originally written in Slavic or translated from Greek. Later, particular significance was attached to the preparation of hagiographies for newly canonized Russian saints in accordance with the ecclesiastical policies established by Makary and his circle at the Councils of 1547 and 1549. In addition, the scope of the work was considerably expanded. The collection was now to include not only hagiographic writings but "all types of readings" (*vse knigy chet'i*), that is, "all holy books, collected and written, which are to be found in the Russian land." Thus, for example, in addition to the Lives and Eulogies of saints, we find in Makary's *Minei* entire collections such as *The Emerald* (Izmaragd) and *The Golden Chain* (Zlataya tsep'), the *Christian Topography* (Khristianskaya topografiya) of Cosmas Indicopleustes, and the polemical writings of IOSIF VOLOTSKY. This huge work was to serve as the expression of a new ecclesiastic order for Muscovite imperial Orthodoxy.

Although a critical edition of what became known as Makary's *Great Monthly Readings* (Velikie Minei Chet'i) was undertaken in 1868 on the basis of the three known versions of the work which date from the 16th century, it was never completed. What was published was the material for September, October, November (1–25), December (1–24 and 31), January (1–11), and April.

After Makary, other hagiographic collections known as *Minei chet'i* and prepared for liturgical purposes were produced on the initiative of German Tulupov (1627–1705), Ioann Milyutin (1646–54), and, most notably, Dimitry Tuptalo ROSTOVSKY (1689–1705). Also important was the hagiographic collection compiled for the Old Believers by the brothers Andrei and Semyon Denisov (1715).

Bibliography: A. V. Gorskii and K. I. Nevostruev, "Opisanie Velikikh Chet'ikh-Minei," *Chteniya v Obshchestve istorii i drevnostei,* 1884, no. 1, and 1886, no. 2. Iosif, Archimandrite, *Podrobnoe oglavlenie Velikikh Chet'ikh-Minei.* 1892. V. O. Klyuchevskii, "Velikie Minei Chet'i, sobrannye mitropolitom Makariem." In his *Otzyvy i otvety,* Vol. 3. (1914). Pp. 1–20. *"Velikie Minei Chetii," sobrannye mitropolitom Makariem.* 1868–1917. I. A. Shlyapkin, *Sv. Dimitrii Rostovskii i ego vremya.* 1891.

R. P.

Minsky (real name: Vilenkin), Nikolaí Maksímovich (1855–1937), poet and philosopher, was born in a Jewish family. He graduated from Petersburg University with a law degree (1879) and became an attorney. He began to publish his verse in 1876. He wrote "civic" verse in the vein of NEKRASOV and NADSON at first, but starting in 1884 (in an article, "An Ancient Controversy"—Starinnyi spor) began to criticize positivism and utilitarianism, to preach a cult of personality and beauty, and to promote mystic searchings. Together with A. VOLYNSKY and D. S. MEREZHKOVSKY, whose inferior he was in both talent and erudition, he was one of the first exponents of Russian modernism. Minsky also developed an eclectic philosophic doctrine, meonism (from the Greek mē on, "unbeing"), in which the influence of Nietzsche and Hindu philosophy is perceptible, for example, in his treatises, "In the Light of Conscience" (Pri svete sovesti, 1890) and "Religion of the Future" (Religiya budushchego, 1905). Minsky was one of the organizers of the "Religious-Philosophic Gatherings" (Religiozno-filosofskie sobraniya) which were to play a significant role in the history of Russian culture. Minsky's poetry of that period is characteristic of early Russian DECADENCE and SYMBOLISM. In 1905 Minsky published some revolutionary verse (very weak) and acted as the official publisher and editor of the Bolshevik newspaper Novaya zhizn'. He was arrested in connection with these activities and was eventually forced to emigrate. He lived in the West until his death in Paris. He did work for the Soviet embassy in London, but disapproved of Bolshevik practices from the vantage point of humanitarian socialism. Minsky's poetry, successful at one time, and avidly read by the likes of BELY and SOLOGUB (especially his verse epic "White Nights"—Belye nochi), is banal, cerebral, and rhetorical. Minsky also wrote plays: The Siege of Tul'chin (Osada Tul'china, 1889), Alma (1900), a trilogy: The Iron Apparition (Zheleznyi prizrak, 1909), A Small Temptation (Malyi soblazn, 1910), and Chaos (Khaos, 1912). Minsky translated Homer, Shelley, Maeterlinck, Yehuda ben Halevi, and others.

Works: Polnoe sobranie stikhotvorenii. 4th ed. 4 vols. 1907. *Ot Dante k Bloku.* Berlin, 1922.

Translations: Lewanski, p. 306.

Secondary literature: Yu. Aikhenval'd, *Siluety russkikh pisatelei.* 4th ed. Vol. 3. Berlin, 1923. Pp. 96–103. A. Blok, *Sobranie sochinenii.* Vol. 5. 1962. Pp. 277–84, 593–98. V. Bryusov, *Sobranie sochinenii.* Vol. 6. 1975. Pp. 235–41. A. Krainii [Zinaida Hippius], *Literaturnyi dnevnik.* 1908. Pp. 19–25. D. Merezhkovskii, *Polnoe sobranie sochinenii.* Vol. 18. 1914. Pp. 263–66. E. Mil'ton, "Vospominaniya o poete N. M. Minskom," *Novyi zhurnal*, no. 91 (1968), pp. 149–61. *Russkaya literatura XX v.* Ed. S. A. Vengerov. Vol. 1. 1914. Pp. 357–409. V. Solov'ev, *Sobranie sochinenii.* Vol. 6. 1912. Pp. 263–68. A. Volynskii, *Bor'ba za idealizm.* 1900. Pp. 354–64.

T. V.

Mintslov, Sergeí Rudólfovich (1870–1933), poet, playwright, novelist, memoirist, and bibliographer. The son of a well-known barrister, Mintslov graduated from the Nizhny-Novgorod Archeological Institute. As an officer he travelled extensively and began publishing in 1888, contributing to publications in Odessa, the Caucasus, and to Petersburg humorous journals and the newspaper *Rus'*. Beginning as a poet and dramatist, Mintslov soon gained recognition as a children's writer with *The Treasure* (Klad, 1902). As a historical novelist he wrote: *At the Dawn of the 17th Century* (Na zare XVII veka, 1899), *In the Storm; a Historical Novel of the Time of Peter the Great* (V grozu; istoricheskii roman iz epokhi Petra Velikogo, 1903), *A Forest Tale* (Lesnaya byl', 1904), and *In Lithuanian Forests* (V lesakh Litvy, 1905). Furthermore, he wrote ethnographic depictions of Siberia and the Far East: *The Fiery Path* (Ognennyi put', 1905) and *The Secret Mission* (Sekretnoe poruchenie, 1915). Having emigrated from Russia in 1916, Mintslov continued the historical tradition of Sir Walter Scott in *To the Sound of Oaks* (Pod shum dubov, 1919), *The Hussar Monastery* (Gusarskii monastyr', 1925), *Students' Adventures* (Priklyucheniya studentov, 1928), and *The Eagle Soars* (Orlinyi vzlet, 1931). Serving as the director of a Russian gymnasium in Yugoslavia for five years, Mintslov penned a whole series of memoirs including the retrospective diaries *In the Custom-House World* (V tamozhennom mire, 1917), *Trapezond Epic* (Trapezondskaya epopeya, 1925), *Petersburg in 1903–1910* (Peterburg v 1903–1910 godakh, 1931), and *The Labyrinth of Life* (Debri zhizni: dnevnik 1910–1915 gg., n.d.); travel sketches, such as *In Search of Dead Souls* (Za mertvymi dushami, 1921); and recollections of his youth, *Distant Days: Recollections, 1870–90* (Dalekie dni: vospominaniya, 1870–90, 1925) and *By the Fireside: My Youth* (U kamel'ka: moya molodost', n.d.). Of considerable value still today are Mintslov's prerevolutionary bibliographies: *The Rarest Books Published in Russia in the Russian Language* (Redchaishie

knigi, napechatannye v Rossii na russkom yazyke, 1904), *An Inventory of My Personal Library* (Opis' sobstvennogo knigokhranilishcha, 1905), and *A Survey of Notes, Diaries, Memoirs, Letters and Travel Notes Pertaining to the History of Russia* (Obzor zapisok, dnevnikov, vospominanii, pisem i puteshestvii, otnosyashchikhsya k istorii Rossii, 5 volumes, 1911–12).

Works: Stikhotvoreniya, 1888–1897. 1897. *Zhenikhi.* 1897. *Zhenskoe delo.* 1897. *Istoricheskie dramy.* 1917. *Tsar' Berendei.* 1923. *Sny zemli: roman.* 1925. *Zakat: roman.* 1926. *To, chego my ne znaem: rasskazy.* 1926. *Svyatye ozera: nedavnee.* 1927. *Svistopup: yumoristicheskie rasskazy.* 192?. *Proshloe: ocherki iz zhizni tsarskoi sem'i.* 192?.

Secondary literature: A. Amov, "Sergei Rudol'fovich Mintslov," *Istoricheskii vestnik*, 134 (1913), pp. 203–08. *Entsiklopedicheskii slovar'.* Suppl. Vol. 2 (1906). P. 190. P. Pil'skii, "Biograficheskii ocherk." In Mintslov's *Misticheskie vechera: zapiski obshchestva lyubitelei osennei nepogody.* 1930. Pp. 5–43. Gleb Struve, *Russkaya literatura v izgnanii.* 1956. P. 128.

A. M. S.

Mir Iskússtva (The World of Art) was a St. Petersburg circle toward the end of the 19th century which arranged concerts and lectures on various artistic and literary themes, launched a series of art exhibits, and founded a journal of the same name which lasted from 1898 to 1904. The goal of the journal was to educate the public in the great art of the past and present so that a renaissance in Russian culture would occur. The pages of the journal contained a wide range of articles on art, literature, music, and theater. The editor of the journal was Sergei DIAGHILEV. In his initial article, "Complicated Questions," he explains the eclectic nature of the journal, saying that every period and every individual creator of merit deserves attention, and that no great works can be created in Russia without a thorough knowledge of the art of the past.

While critics have often emphasized a disparity between the artistic and literary aspects of the journal, there were certain basic underlying assumptions. Both sections reflect the strong influence of Nietzsche in a rejection of Kant, utilitarianism, and a positivism which limited human knowledge to observable phenomena and the norm in human nature. The notion that satisfying man's material needs would bring him happiness was then strong in Russian culture which had turned to social rather than to metaphysical themes. The artist became a mirror or critic of reality. Most of the writers and artists in *Mir iskusstva* rejected this view. In his articles Diaghilev emphasized that a work of art is an expression of the creator's personality, of his unique genius. Hence all epochs became equally important. TOLSTOI's recent "What is Art" and the socially conscious artistic movement *The Wanderers* (peredvizhniki) frequently came under attack in the journal. Most writers in the journal wanted art to express abnormal, heightened states of mind, and some hoped art would address metaphysical questions such as the cause of evil and suffering and the relation of the flesh to the spirit. Diaghilev as well as others continually stated that they did not advocate art-for-art's sake, that ideas were as important to art as form; however, they also insisted that ideas had to be organically integrated into the work, and that the ideas themselves should not be limited to social issues.

One of the concepts that the artistic and literary sections had in common was the Nietzschean acceptance of evil and suffering as a necessary part of life. Vrubel's work, reproduced and discussed in the journal, reflects this. This is also true of BALMONT's article on Goya, in which he says that there are two poles of beauty: the harmony of the spheres and the poetry of horror. Goya reveals the demonic part of our souls which we must accept as part of our total personality. Lev SHESTOV's work, *Nietzsche and Dostoevsky*, which appeared in the journal, shows that for Nietzsche and DOSTOEVSKY, both evil and good are inevitable parts of the human condition, and that no social reforms will eliminate tragedy or suffering from life. N. M. MINSKY contributed a series entitled *Philosophical Conversations*, which also sees evil and suffering as a necessary part of life which must be incorporated into his new religion, meonism, which tries to reconcile rational and mystical knowledge.

One of the strongest statements against positivism that appeared in the journal was Dmitry MEREZHKOVSKY's "Tolstoi or Dostoevsky." According to Merezhkovsky, rational thought will not answer many of the basic questions of life. The work is essentially an examination of the personality of the authors conducted in order to understand their art. That Tolstoi is the seer of the flesh and Dostoevsky the seer of the spirit explains many aspects of their work. While Tolstoi's greatest works express emotion and thought through the flesh, i.e., through body movement and physical characteristics, and also exhibit an affirmation of earthly joy, Dostoevsky, in contrast, writes mainly of problems of the spirit. What is needed, says Merezhkovsky, is an artist who is a synthesis of both, and a form of Christianity which reconciles the flesh and the spirit.

The Nietzschean rejection of Christian asceticism and acceptance of pagan earthly joy in the flesh was also a major theme of articles by Vasily Rozanov and Andrei Bely, who also sought a synthesis of the joy of the flesh and of the spirit, and who thought Nietzsche had only come part way in renouncing the negative aspects of contemporary Christianity without creating a new religion in its stead. Nietzsche's influence can also be seen in a cycle of poems on the elements by Balmont which appeared in *Mir iskusstva*. The sun becomes a symbol of the affirmation of the joy of earthly life. These poems marked an important turning point in Balmont's career from poems focusing on Schopenhauerian despair to ones which emphasize an enjoyment of earthly life and acceptance of evil and suffering as part of this life.

Another theme that runs throughout the journal is the reconciliation of Russia and the West. Both Merezhkovsky and Diaghilev quote Dostoevsky as saying that the Russian's second homeland is Europe, and that to be Russian means at the same time to be in the greatest degree European and universal. Numerous pages of the journal are devoted to both Western and Russian art, music, theater, and literature, and even the last issues contain articles on Russian folk art alongside reproductions of contemporary Western avant-garde art.

Book illustration was treated as a serious art form in the journal, and headpieces and decorations were done by some of the best *Mir iskusstva* artists. The question of the artist's relationship to the text was discussed in relation to Alexander Benois' illustrations to Pushkin's "Bronze Horseman" which appeared in *Mir iskusstva*. It was pointed out he was successful because he did not merely supplement the literary work but illuminated it by expressing his own individual interpretation of the poem through visual images.

In 1903 when Merezhkovsky left *Mir iskusstva* to form his own journal, Diaghilev asked Chekhov to take over the literary section. In an interesting exchange of letters, Chekhov made it clear that every journal must have only one editor; in this case it must be Diaghilev; and he therefore refused. The journal continued for one more year and then ceased publication for lack of funds. However, it had played an important role. It not only educated the Russian public in great art of the past and present but served as a reflection of some major themes of the period. No study of this period in Russian culture would be complete without understanding the influence of this journal and how it reflected its epoch.

Bibliography: John E. Bowlt, *The Silver Age.* 1982. Janet Kennedy, *The* Mir Iskusstva *Group and Russian Art.* 1977. Renato Poggioli, *The Poets of Russia 1890–1930.* 1960. Bernice Rosenthal, "Nietzsche in Russia: The Case of Merezhkovsky," *SlavR* 33 (1974), pp. 429–52.   R. R.

Mírsky, see Svyatopolk-Mirsky.

Mnemosyne (Mnemozina), literary almanac (1824–25), published in four issues, subtitled *A Collection of Works in Verse and Prose.* Titled after the Greek goddess of memory because she was the mother of the muses by Zeus, *Mnemosyne* was edited by V. K. Kyukhelbeker and V. F. Odoevsky as an outlet for metaphysically oriented, romantic idealist poetry, prose, and criticism. The editors were closely associated with the Wisdom Lovers (*lyubomudry*), and the almanac featured a section devoted to philosophy. The almanac was also markedly political and expressed the patriotic ideals of Decembrist civicism. *Mnemosyne* thus united the political and metaphysical trends of Russian Romanticism, largely on the basis of a general concern for the historical past and national originality. Among the best contributors were Pushkin, P. A. Vyazemsky, A. S. Gri-

boedov, and E. A. Baratynsky. *Readings:* N. V. Koroleva, "V. K. Kyukhel'beker." In V. K. Kyukhel'beker, *Izbrannye proizvedeniya.* (Biblioteka poeta.) 2 vols. 1967.   L. G. L.

Modernism, Russian. The term modernism as applied to the context of Russian art and literature is a complex one. Ultimately, it denotes a chronology of ideas and personalities rather than a particular style, even though the approximate period 1900 to 1925 is identifiable with certain formal and thematic characteristics. Russian modernism is associated with audacious experimentation, artistic synthesism, forceful expression of individuality, and works of literature and art that stood in sharp opposition to traditional values. In general, the concept encompasses the movements of SYMBOLISM, CUBO-FUTURISM, ACMEISM, and CONSTRUCTIVISM and is linked to the pioneering achievements of writers and artists such as A. A. AKHMATOVA, Andrei BELY, A. A. BLOK, D. D. BURLYUK, P. N. Filonov, N. S. Goncharova, V. V. Kandinsky, V. V. KHLEBNIKOV, A. E. KRUCHONYKH, M. F. Larionov, K. S. Malevich, V. V. MAYAKOVSKY, B. L. PASTERNAK, A. M. Rodchenko, V. E. Tatlin and M. A. Vrubel.

It is difficult to establish precisely when modernism "began" in Russia. In the early 1900s the symbolists even argued that their movement had its roots in the poetry of TYUTCHEV and FET, i.e., in the early and mid-19th century, and some of the cubo-futurists, e.g., Larionov, regarded traditional folk art as a vital, creative stimulus. However, public awareness of a "new art" that rejected existing conventions seems to have arisen in Russia around 1889 when the critic V. E. Grabar first used the word "decadent" in the Russian press—a word that soon came to describe any literary or artistic trend that questioned the traditions of 19th-century realism and academic art. Still, from a more specific, literary standpoint, the first "modernist" manifesto was D. S. MEREZHKOVSKY's *On the Reasons for the Decline and on the New Trends in Contemporary Russian Literature,* published in 1892—a document that ushered in the symbolist era in Russia. Merezhkovsky, his wife Z. N. HIPPIUS and, on a different level, the idealist philosopher and poet V. S. SOLOVYOV, rejected the materialist worldview, attempted to imbue art with a mystical, messianic purpose, and outlined the first stages of a debate that dominated much literary thinking of early modernism, i.e., "Tolstoi or Dostoevsky?". Questioning the validity of TOLSTOI's realist approach to the world, Merezhkovsky felt that DOSTOEVSKY's concern with the inner contradictions of human nature and with man's religious quest presented the real departure point for an artistic and spiritual renaissance in Russia.

Merezhkovsky was a member of the St. Petersburg group of artists, writers and aesthetes known as MIR ISKUSSTVA (The World of Art). Led by the impresario and critic, S. P. DIAGHILEV and the erudite artist and critic A. N. Benua (Benois), The World of Art cultivated a deep and sincere love of "beauty," believing that Russia was on the threshold of a Silver Age and that she had every right to be considered an equal partner in the European cultural mainstream. Although The World of Art did not sponsor one particular aesthetic program, it was, as the critic and philosopher, D. V. Filosofov wrote, "a cult of dilettantism in the good and true sense of the word." The World of Art pursued its eclectic policy through its luxurious magazine *Mir iskusstva* (1898–1904) and its cycle of art exhibitions (1899–1906). The World of Art was very sympathetic to the international symbolist movement and contributed much to the fashionable discussions of art nouveau, arts and crafts revival, and the decorative arts. It is not by chance that many artist members of The World of Art such as L. S. Bakst, Benois, and M. V. Dobuzhinsky acquired their reputations as stage designers for Diaghilev's *Ballets Russes* in Europe and the United States between 1909 and 1929—the ballet being the most sophisticated of the synthetic art forms.

Although The World of Art was primarily an association of painters and graphists, the great symbolist poets and philosophers were at least acquainted with its members, and many contributed to the journal. Through contact with the poets Bely, Blok, Bryusov and Vyacheslav IVANOV, who were not all Petersburgians, the journal *Mir iskusstva* was a vehicle for the propagation of Russian symbolist philosophy. For example, Bely's important articles "The Forms of Art" (1902) and "Symbolism as Comprehension" (1904) first appeared on the pages of *Mir iskusstva*, defining the beliefs of the second, and more powerful, generation of symbolist writers—that we must seek to escape from the world of appearances to the ulterior reality, that certain images or symbols could facilitate this process, that art as cognition could save us from the crude materialism of science, etc. Blok's verse and dramaturgy express these sentiments, although not without ambivalence and occasional irony.

An important component of symbolism was its peculiar visual perception of reality: if the world of objects was not the real world, then the writer and artist had no need to concentrate on the exact depiction of these objects. Consequently, much symbolist art can be identified with a tendency towards approximation, generalization, or abstraction. In 1907 Bely even maintained that a possible path of artistic development was towards "non-objectivity [where] the method of creation becomes an *end in itself*" ("Art of the Future"). Neglect of the physical, three-dimensional world and evocation of mood and "landscapes of the soul" can be identified with the output of the principal symbolist painters of the Russian fin de siècle such as V. E. Borisov-Musatov, Vrubel, and the members of the Moscow Blue Rose group led by P. V. Kuznetsov. Their mysterious pictures painted in restrained colors (e. g. Borisov-Musatov's retrospective visions of vestal maidens, Vrubel's motif of the Demon inspired by LERMONTOV's poem of that name, Kuznetsov's images of young girls and babies) actually foreshadowed certain trends of later, abstract painting—removal of direct social and political relevance, concentration on color and other intrinsic elements for emotional response, manifestation of purely spiritual or psychological sensations.

There is no doubt that symbolism anticipated many of the ideas later developed by artists such as Kandinsky and Malevich. In fact, primary members of the Russian avant-garde, including Kandinsky, I. V. Klyun, Malevich, Rodchenko, began their careers as symbolists. Kandinsky's series of *Improvisations* and *Compositions* of 1910 onwards, while giving the impression of non representational canvases actually represent spiritual, often theosophical concerns. As Kandinsky wrote in his tract "On the Spiritual in Art" (1910–12): "Art is a *language whereby we speak to the soul ... of things that are the soul's daily bread and that it can acquire only in this form.*" Indeed, although Kandinsky developed a more geometric, more calculated style in the 1920s, his painting remained always committed to this spiritual dimension.

Symbolism dominated Russian literature and art of the early and mid-1900s, and its foremost representatives continued to create long after its decline. However, by the years 1907 and 1908 other styles and ideas came to the fore, often dramatically opposed to the ethereal, diaphanous visions of the symbolists. Two such movements emerged in the late 1900s. One sought to view a rose "because it is beautiful, not because it is a symbol of mystical purity" and in 1912 adopted the title ACMEISM or Adamism; the other, more intricate and more influential, was cubo-futurism. The Acmeists, led by Akhmatova, M. A. KUZMIN and N. S. GUMILYOV, favored lucid, straightforward descriptions of "life," uncluttered by transcendental philosophy: Akhmatova's love lyrics of the 1910s, such as "He Loved" (On lyubil, 1911) exemplify the Acmeists' pristine vision of the world. To some extent, Pasternak shared this direct and defined approach to the real world in his poetry and prose, even though, unexpectedly, he started his career as a member of the Centrifuge futurist group in Moscow. Acmeism was primarily a poetical movement and found no strong parallels in the visual arts, although the "neoclassical" style of K. S. Petrov-Vodkin and B. D. Grigoriev and some of the cubist paraphrases of N. I. Altman (such as his famous portrait of Akhmatova of 1914) bring to mind the polished and highly structured verse of Akhmatova and Kuzmin.

In contrast to the often contrived elegance of the Acmeists, the cubo-futurists, mostly from Moscow and the provinces, behaved like country bumpkins, boisterous and iconoclastic. This young generation of artists and writers led by Burlyuk, Goncharova and Larionov, wished to "primitivize" art by transferring methods from native artifacts such as the LUBOK, the store signboard, the icon, and the painted tin tray to their own studio paintings. In the bright colors, crude outlines and often humorous subject matter of peasant art, the new painters found sources of inspiration that injected a brute strength and vigor into the visual arts. This coincided with the exposure of French post-impressionist works (especially Gauguin and Matisse) in the Moscow collections of S. I. Shchukin and I. A. Morozov. Consequently, the works by Goncharova, Larionov,

Malevich and others of around 1910 often contain simultaneous references to the traditional arts of Russia and to contemporary Parisian trends. The culmination of this orientation occurred in the years 1912 and 1913 when these neoprimitivists declared that "The West has shown me one thing: everything it has is from the East" (Goncharova). A clear example of this reliance on Russian or "Eastern" culture is Larionov's painting called *Officer at the Barber's* (1909) based thematically and formally on an 18th-century *lubok* of a barber cutting off the beard of an Old Believer. The subject received many interpretations in the painting of D. Burlyuk and A. V. Shevchenko—and also in Mayakovsky's poem "They Don't Understand Anything" (Nichego ne ponimayut).

The above-mentioned artists constituted the first wave of the Russian avant-garde. While starting their experimental careers as neoprimitivists, they quickly assimilated other ideas such as French cubism and Italian futurism and produced their own aesthetic conclusions such as Rayonism (Goncharova and Larionov, 1912–14) and "everythingism" (Shevchenko, 1912–13). In their sharp opposition to cultural tradition, and in their formulation of new artistic values, the Russian artists were joined by important literary colleagues such as Khlebnikov, Kruchonykh, and Mayakovsky. In fact, the approximate period of 1910 to 1916 was marked by very close collaborations between painters and poets: some of the artists concerned (Larionov, Malevich, O. V. Rozanova) wrote poetry, some of the poets (Khlebnikov, Kruchonykh, Mayakovsky) painted and drew; painters and poets worked together on numerous avant-garde booklets such as *A Game in Hell* (Igra v adu, 1912, 1914), *The Word as Such* (Slovo kak takovoe, 1912), and *Explodity* (Vzorval', 1913); and many of them supported the same manifestoes, including the historic *A Slap in the Face of Public Taste* (Poshchechina obshchestvennomu vkusu), signed by D. Burlyuk, Kruchonykh, Mayakovsky, and Khlebnikov, and published in Moscow in December 1912. Their resonant words, "Throw Pushkin, Dostoevsky, Tolstoi, et al., et al., overboard from the Ship of Modernity," illustrated the essential impetus of the cubo-futurist movement.

Russian cubo-futurism was a many-sided phenomenon and accommodated many more isms than its title might imply. Although indebted to Western artistic and literary models, the Russians evolved much further in their artistic and linguistic experiments than, say, Picasso or Marinetti. For example, both Khlebnikov and Kruchonykh felt that the poet could invent his own vocabulary by compounding new words from roots with new prefixes and suffixes, as Khlebnikov demonstrated in his poem "Incantation by Laughter" (Zaklyatie smekhom, 1910), or by reducing language to its bare essentials, as in Kruchonykh's poem "Heights" (Vysoty, 1913), dependent upon only vowel sounds. Such poets also maintained that a new sensibility could be achieved if objects were removed from their usual contexts and reassembled in new ones, a procedure that they called transrationalism (ZAUM'). One of the highpoints of this tendency was the production of the cubo-futurist opera *Victory over the Sun* in St. Petersburg in December 1913 with transrational libretto by Khlebnikov and Kruchonykh, discordant music by M. V. Matyushin, and unorthodox sets and costumes by Malevich.

Malevich often resorted to combinations of visual non sequiturs as in his transrational painting *Woman at an Advertisement Kiosk* (1914). But surely his most spectacular extension of this transvaluation of values was the formulation of the system of geometric abstraction known as suprematism in 1915. Illustrating his new concept with his famous *Black Square* (1915), Malevich argued that art must reject its traditional narrative function and become an end in itself: "Our world of art has become new, nonobjective, pure" ("From Cubism and Futurism to Suprematism: The New Painterly Realism," 1916). Malevich developed suprematism both as a style of painting and then as an entire worldview, maintaining that objects, life itself, must be suprematized. The apex of Malevich's pictorial development was his *White on White* series of 1917–18 where the pure surfaces carry only delicate textural contrasts—anticipating American minimalist art by forty years. Actually, it is of interest to note here that the poet V. I. Gnedov dealt with a similar idea as early as 1913 when he published his "Poem of the End" (Poema kontsa)—a blank page.

The Russian cubo-futurists wished to "épater le bourgeois." Burlyuk's top hat, Larionov's painted face, and Mayakovsky's yellow vest both shocked and amused the Russian public. Of course, it is tempting to regard the antisocial stance of these poets and painters as one of political dissidence, but, except perhaps for Mayakovsky, they were not politically conscious, did not read subversive literature, and did not play constructive roles in the revolutionary movement. True, during the post-revolutionary period, Malevich, his follower El Lissitzky (L. M. Lisitsky), and other avant-garde artists looked back to these banquet years and interpreted their innovative ideas as "revolutionary movements in art, anticipating the revolution in the economic and political life of 1917" (K. Malevich, *On New Systems in Art*, 1919). Even so, we should be cautious in ascribing particular political views to artists and writers who had little interest in, or understanding of, ideological systems.

The October Revolution of 1917 transformed the outward structure of literary and artistic life in Russia. Although many cultural ideas from before the Revolution continued to flourish well into the 1920s, and although the cubo-futurists tended to associate their radical art with radical politics, the central question—"What should proletarian art be?"—did not receive a definitive answer until the early 1930s, i.e., until the imposition of SOCIALIST REALISM. The first few years of Soviet power were marked by a creative freedom when literary and artistic experimentation was encouraged by the political hierarchy, partly as a result of the tolerant attitude of A. V. LUNACHARSKY who became Minister of Education in 1918 (until 1929) and to whom Lenin relegated much of the overall responsibility for cultural activities. Of course, a practical question that faced all writers and artists immediately after October 1917 was whether to stay or to emigrate. The diaspora of the Russian intelligentsia just after the Revolution (in 1922, 100,000 Russians were living in Berlin) meant that all aspects of cultural life (publishing houses, exhibitions, commissions, audiences, etc.) were profoundly affected. Writers and artists such as Bely, BUNIN, SHKLOVSKY, TSVETAEVA, Marc Chagall (M. Z. Shagal), Naum Gabo (N. N. Pevzner), A. A. Ekster, and Kandinsky took up temporary or permanent residence abroad, laying the foundation of an entire émigré culture that flourishes to this day in Western Europe and the United States. However, most of the avant-garde, including Filonov, Malevich, Rodchenko, and Tatlin, did not leave Russia and never entertained the idea of emigrating.

Although the post-revolutionary period of Russian culture is extremely complex and heterogeneous, two basic trends can be distinguished, one thematic and "narrative," the other formal and "mechanical." Writers such as ESENIN and BABEL, perhaps even Mayakovsky, for example, whatever their philosophical differences, believed in the need to return to a descriptive art form concerned with the episodes of everyday life and accessible to the public at large. Esenin's poems such as "A Song about Bread" (Pesn' o khlebe, 1921) and Babel's stories of the civil war achieved immediate popularity because of this. A similar orientation away from "naked form" towards richer content was also identifiable with the work of the SERAPION BROTHERHOOD founded by L. N. LUNTS, V. A. KAVERIN and others in Petrograd in 1921. "Readability" was also a major component of the paintings and sculptures produced by the group of artists known as AKhRR (Association of Artists of Revolutionary Russia). Established in Moscow in 1922 by E. A. Katsman and others, this group asserted that "Our civic duty before mankind is to set down, artistically and documentarily, the revolutionary impulse of this great moment of history." To a considerable extent, this credo constituted an important precedent to socialist realism in the visual arts, and it is not surprising that Stalin's "court painters" of the 1930s, I. I. Brodsky and A. M. Gerasimov, started their careers as *akhrovtsy*.

One of the final, brilliant extensions of Russian modernism was constructivism, an interdisciplinary and, ultimately, international movement that many regarded as the true proletarian style. Founded in Moscow in January 1921 by G. A. and V. A. Stenberg and K. K. Medunetsky, constructivism quickly became identified with utilitarian art, with design and with the total restructuring of everyday life—from buildings to furniture, from dresses to porcelain. Constructivists such as K. S. Melnikov, L. S. Popova, Rodchenko and Tatlin believed that function determined form and advocated economy of material and absence of ornament as essential ingredients of the new art. In this respect, the constructivist designers shared common ground with the champions of the formal (FORMALIST) method in literary analysis such as B. M. EIKHENBAUM and Shklov-

sky, a fact demonstrated by their common support of the constructivist journals LEF and *Novyi Lef* edited by Mayakovsky in Moscow in 1923 to 1925 and 1927 to 1928. Tatlin's famous model for his *Monument to the Third International* (1919–20), Popova's textile and clothes designs of 1922 to 1924, Rodchenko's design for a workers' club in 1925 were exciting implementations of constructivist theory. Although constructivism was primarily a visual movement, it also attracted writers, movie makers and even musicians. The Literary Center of the Constructivists, founded in Moscow in 1924, strove to adapt the above principles to creative and critical literature, and its key supporters, V. M. INBER, I. L. SELVINSKY and K. L. ZELINSKY, declared that "Constructivism transferred into the field of art, changes on a formal level into a *system of maximum exploitation of subject* or into a system whereby all composite artistic elements are mutually and functionally justified". The very title of their principal collection of literary experiments, *State Plan for Literature* (Gosplan literatury, 1924) expressed their rational, scientific approach to the artistic process.

Parallel to the realist and constructivist tendencies of the early and mid-1920s, many other literary and artistic groups appeared and disappeared. Mention might be made of the IMAGISTS (imaginists) led by V. SHERSHENEVICH, A. B. MARIENGOF, Esenin and the painter G. B. Yakulov, the expressionists led by I. I. Sokolov, the nothingists led by B. S. Zemenkov, and Filonov's Collective of Masters of Analytical Art. However, as Bolshevik power consolidated and as the Party gave increasing attention to cultural policy, so the plurality of the modernist era yielded to greater homogeneity. In 1932 the Party issued its decree *On the Reconstruction of Literary and Artistic Organizations*, thereby liquidating all such groupings and advocating single unions for writers, artists, architects, and musicians. Finally, in 1934, the First Congress of Soviet Writers in Moscow, chaired by Maksim GORKY, declared socialist realism to be the "basic method of Soviet artistic literature and literary criticism, requiring of the artist a true, historically concrete depiction of reality in its revolutionary development." With the forcible and almost total imposition of socialist realism in the 1930s, the creative spirit of Russian modernism was lost. Only over recent years has the Soviet Union begun to rediscover and reappraise its extraordinary literary and artistic legacy of Russian modernism.

Bibliography: Stephanie Barron and Maurice Tuchman, eds., *The Avant-Garde in Russia, 1910–1930: New Perspectives.* 1980. John E. Bowlt, *The Silver Age: Russian Art of the Early 20th Century and the "World of Art" Group.* 1979. 2d printing, 1982. Vladimir Markov, *Russian Futurism: A History.* 1968. Avril Pyman, *The Life of Aleksandr Blok.* Vol. 1. 1979; vol. 2. 1980. Angelica Zander Rudenstine, S. Frederick Starr and George Costakis, *Russian Avant-Garde Art: The George Costakis Collection.* 1981. Robert C. Williams, *Artists in Revolution: Portraits of the Russian Avant-Garde, 1905–1925.* 1977.

J. E. B.

Modzalévsky, Borís Lvóvich (1874–1928), philologist, bibliographer, publisher of historical and literary sources. A graduate of St. Petersburg University, Modzalevsky was a scrupulous editor of historical and literary documents, who left excellent examples of in-depth commentaries. He was elected a correspondent member of the Academy of Sciences in 1918. Several of his publications, such as the Pushkin diaries and correspondence, serve as important reference sources for Pushkin scholars as well as for all researchers of early 19th-century history and literature. Modzalevsky also edited a series of collections of important articles and documents on Pushkin and his age, *Pushkin and his Contemporaries* (Pushkin i ego sovremenniki). His famous catalogue (kartoteka Modzalevskogo) which contains biographical references taken from published and archival sources, many of which are impossible to find in available reference works, is kept in the reading room of the Institute of Russian Literature (Pushkinskii Dom) in Leningrad.

Works: Biblioteka A. S. Pushkina (bibliograficheskoe opisanie). 1910. *Arkhiv Raevskikh.* 5 vols. 1908–1915. *Pushkin pod tainym nadzorom.* 3d ed. 1925.

Secondary literature: B. L. Kaplan, *Kratkii ocherk nauchnoi deyatel'nosti B. L. Modzalevskogo.* 1929. *Pamyati B. L. Modzalevskogo, 1874–1928: Biograficheskie daty. Bibliografiya trudov.* 1928.

E. B.

Molodáya Gvárdiya (Young Guard), a literary group, a journal, and a publishing house, all founded in 1922 as organs of the Communist Youth (Komsomol). The group soon declared affiliation with the larger "OKTYABR'" group, and in 1923 joined the MAPP, while retaining its identity, mainly through the journal, as a place where writers of and for Communist youth could come together. These included the poets Aleksandr BEZYMENSKY and Mikhail SVETLOV, and the future novelist Mikhail SHOLOKHOV. Eventually some members withdrew and joined the PEREVAL group.

As a publishing house, Molodaya Gvardiya is still active. It has issued many famous works of Soviet literature, and currently is responsible for more than a dozen journals, several literary almanacs, a newspaper, and the popular series entitled "Lives of Famous People" ("Zhizn' zamechatel'nykh lyudei"). It aims at younger or less sophisticated readers. The same can be said of the journal, which has continued to appear except for a hiatus between 1941 and 1956. Though covering a variety of fields, it is most important for its belles lettres. In the cultural controversies of the 1960s and 1970s, it consistently took a more "conservative" line.

Secondary literature: A. A. Maksimov, *Sovetskaya zhurnalistika 20-kh godov.* 1964.   R. A. M.

Mohýla, Pyotr, see KIEV ACADEMY.

Molénie Daniíla zatóchnika, see SUPPLICATION.

Molvá (Rumor), newspaper of "fashions and news," published in Moscow, 1831 to 1836 (weekly 1831, 1834–36; twice weekly 1832; three times weekly 1833). Founded by N. I. NADEZHDIN as a supplement to his journal TELESKOP, *Molva* generally published lighter material than *Teleskop*. In 1834 and 1836, *Molva* and *Teleskop* were merged, and *Molva* served as the critical and bibliographical section of the journal. BELINSKY began to contribute to *Molva* in 1833, and his first major critical work, "Literary Musings" (Literaturnye mechtaniya), appeared there in 1834. Both *Molva* and *Teleskop* came out under Belinsky's editorship during Nadezhdin's trip abroad in 1835. During the earliest period of the newspaper's existence, its contributors included I. V. KIREEVSKY, M. P. POGODIN, A. S. KHOMYAKOV, and S. P. SHEVYRYOV; under Belinsky's editorship, N. V. STANKEVICH, K. S. AKSAKOV, I. A. GONCHAROV, N. P. OGARYOV, and A. V. KOLTSOV. BAKUNIN, HERZEN, and V. P. BOTKIN became contributors in 1836. The 23 February 1834 issue of *Molva* contained a request to the readers by N. V. GOGOL for material on the history of the Ukraine. In October 1836, *Molva* and *Teleskop* were closed as a result of the publication of CHAADAEV's first "Philosophical Letter" in No. 15 of *Teleskop* for 1836.   C. T. N.

Mórshen (pseudonym, real name: Márchenko), Nikolaí Nikoláevich, émigré poet, was born in Kiev on 8 November 1917—"a genuine contemporary of the October Revolution," as he calls himself in a letter. His father was the well-known prose writer Nikolai Vladimirovich Marchenko, who used the pseudonym Narokov (sometimes: Knigochii). Morshen graduated from Kiev University in 1941, majoring in physics and specializing in x-ray analysis of metals. Starting that year, he led the migratory life typical of his generation: in 1941 the Germans took Kiev, in 1944 he found himself in Germany, then in a camp for displaced persons, and finally in the United States. His first published verses appeared in GRANI in 1948, and were followed by many further publications in *Grani*, NOVYI ZHURNAL, several anthologies, collections of verse, and almanacs. Morshen has published three volumes of verse: *The Seal* (Tyulen', Frankfurt, 1959), *Colon* (Dvoetochie, Washington, 1967), and *Echo and Mirror* (Ekho i zerkalo, Berkeley, 1979). There is much lyricism in the first book, if this term may be applied to those tragic and tragic-farcical miniatures rendering the pointless and hopeless day-to-day existence of the lyric *persona* under hammer and sickle, with utmost concision and great artistry. The lyric hero's biography is by no means complete, presenting no continuous line—rather a dotted line, a series of illuminated points in his consciousness, fragmentary and often self-sufficient—and no duration, only moments, but moments by no means frozen in time, not even by the horrors of life all around him. What saves the poet from that is the romanticism of youth, the *élan vital* of one who with all his might would like to survive, who refuses to surrender, who will straighten

up again. But when the biography of an epoch is itself catastrophic, personal biography is not determined by inner, psychological factors, but brutally and imperiously dictated by external forces. Therefore, the central idea of Morshen's first book is a kind of underground struggle of the principle of individuation against the fatalist determinism of his age. These momentary tragedies reach an extremely high degree of saturation: "He didn't live long: just forty years. / There isn't a word of truth in what you say. / He lived through two wars, a revolution, / Three famines, four changes of power, / Six states, two real passions. / Translated into years that makes about five hundred." The power of the horrors of Soviet life in Morshen's first book is generally not created by either naturalistic description or "cataloguing." An exception is the peasant who, driven by chronic starvation and all kinds of tribulations on his collective farm, hangs himself, leaving a note for his son, written in clumsy verse, apologizing for not having stuck it out, "because there ain't no force left in me." Otherwise, however, the tragic farce of life in the country of victorious socialism is made more hopeless because the horrors are not played upon: one hasn't the strength to help others, nor even the strength to feel compassion, because all one's strength is needed for simple survival. Egoism? No, one can be a hero for an hour, for a day, perhaps for a year, but how could one be a hero all one's life? Therefore, even while not voluntarily or even directly, one still has a part, albeit a passive one, in the crimes of Soviet justice: "'Comrades!' / He lowered his eyes, / which he knew he couldn't make behave. / 'Who is in favor of the death penalty for enemies of the people, is asked to raise his hand!' / They all did. He also raised his: 'In favor.' / Trying to think of nothing, / but to overcome that feeling of dizziness, / And, keeping aloof, / forget about it as quickly as possible. / Applause. That means, it is all right to leave, / Get out of the hallways of the university / Into the fresh air ..." Forget, no matter how and by what means: in nature, in music, in verse.... Here the romanticism of youth helps, of course, and so does the heroic image of a poet. Who? Why, GUMILYOV, of course. Accidentally hearing some lines of his verse, "dissenters recognize each other in my country." And so one withdraws from one's environment and becomes alienated from Soviet life. Perhaps Morshen's strongest verses are found in those dancing and jumping lines which tell us how, after a voluntary-forced parade before a rostrum of local and Republic level leaders on May the first or November the seventh, celebrating the happiness of the people, "two orchestras on three balconies play a Polish dance": Dance, popular masses! Life is so much happier, life is so much merrier!— "And then they dance a polka, / What a polka, polechka! / And they dance, Kolka and Olka, / Tolechka and Polechka! / And also the charming sounds of a waltz / Are played over their very heads, / and there's waltzing all over, / On shaking pavements everywhere. / Why then, amidst a noisy ball, / you alone wander about without rhyme or reason?.. / ... Join in / And share in this apportioned merriment!" We have here a magnificent "apportioned merriment" (*dozirovannoe vesel'e*) for rank-and-file toilers, and also an ironic rephrasing, so characteristic of Morshen's subsequent books of verse, of quotes from ancient salon romances ("the charming sounds of a waltz"), from Aleksei TOLSTOI and Tchaikovsky ("amidst a noisy ball"), and from PUSHKIN's "Bronze Horseman" ("on shaking pavements").

The Pushkinian principle, with its imperious attitude, with Pushkin's (and BLOK's) "secret" freedom, is profoundly alien to Morshen: give us external freedom, all of it visible, readily perceived! And thus, Morshen's second and third books of verse, which some critics have said are overly intellectual, are really nothing but poetic thought fully developed and active in freedom, albeit in the somewhat rarified air of a foreign country and its linguistic atmosphere. There are some formal searchings—only occasionally formalistic—with doubles running to meet each other from both ends of a line, making witty and entertaining word play: "Na rodine—schast'e!" / —Narod ... i ... neschast'e! / "Na rodine volya!" / —Narod ... i ... nevolya! (where the point is that of an ironic homonymy: "Back home—there is happiness!"—The People .. and ... unhappiness! "Back home there is freedom!"—The people ... and ... unfreedom!). Yet intellectualism is unavoidable in our age: how can a modern poet or writer free himself from what has been acquired by the culture of a thousand years? Nor can we escape our age of atomic power and computers. And thus Morshen's doubles and counter-doubles even graphically emphasize the intelligibility, rather than the intellectuality, and the inescapable dualism of man in our age. In his second and third books, Morshen seeks for new principles and devices of verse structure, new devices of verbal dynamics, neither continuous nor intermittent, necessarily, but somehow new, perhaps resembling a dotted line. The poet's personality, and that of his lyric hero, appear to double in echoes and mirrors, as existence itself turns double. However, Morshen is by no means a pessimist. He wants "the campaign against death to defeat the second law of thermodynamics," and through the pursuit of new and—ironically developed—old rhythms he seeks to give his verse a musicality that will overcome the discontinuity and inherently dot-like quality of life, giving it an infinite fluidity, compactness, and continuity, and replace even the period (Russ. *tochka* means "period" as well as "dot") of death by a colon (*dvoetochie*). Of course, wise poet and learned physicist that he is, Morshen realizes that ultimate wholeness and integrity are unattainable in poetry no less than in science—as is the ultimate meaning of being, which is beyond the poet's reach: "Neither my own, nor someone else's: nobody's/I lay on the earth, like a corpse./Birds began to sing. God remained silent." Perhaps the meaning of this is that God reveals Himself not in knowledge, and not in poetry either, but in faith, in mystic revelation. Perhaps, too, there is here an unconscious echo of the Fathers of the Church, who called God the "Lord of Silence," of speechlessness. For where the Word-Logos reigns, there is no place for words. In any case, Morshen is not merely a clever poet, but a wise one, who gives a great deal to our mind as well as to our poetic sense.

Works: Besides the collections and journals given above, Morshen's verses may be found in these anthologies and collections: *Na zapade.* Ed. Yu. Ivask. New York, 1953. *Literaturnoe zarubezh'e.* Munich, 1958. *Muza Diaspory.* Ed. Yu. Terapiano. Frankfurt/Main, 1960. *Chtets-deklamator* (New York, 1964). *Sodruzhestvo.* Ed. T. Fesenko. Washington, 1966. *Perekrestki*, nos. 2–6 (1979–82). *Russkii Al'manakh* (Paris, 1981).

Translations: Modern Russian Poetry. Ed. Vladimir Markov and Merrill Sparks. 1967. Pp. 494–95. *America's Russian Poets.* Ed. and trans. R. N. Morrison. 1975.

Secondary literature: L. Alekseeva, "O glavnom—stikhami ..." (*Tyulen'*), *Grani*, no. 41 (1959). Yu. Bol'shukhin, "Obretshie slovo." In *Literaturnoe zarubezh'e.* Munich, 1958. I. Chinnov, "Smotrite stikhi," *Novyi zhurnal*, no. 92 (1968). "Ekho i zerkalo" (anonymous review), *Kontinent*, no. 24 (1980). Boris Filippov, "Dvuedinyi (N. Morshen)." In *Mysli naraspashku*, kn. 2. Washington, D. C., 1982. L. Fleishman, "Neskol'ko zamechanii k probleme literatury russkoi emigratsii." In *Odna ili dve russkikh literatury? Mezhdunarodnyi simpozium.* Lausanne, 1981. Ya. Gorbov, "Novye knigi. Dvoetochie," *Vozrozhdenie*, no. 193 (1968). Yu. Ivask, "Ekho i zerkalo" (review), *Russkaya mysl'*, 27 December 1979. S. Karlinskii, "Dvoetochie" (review), *Novyi zhurnal*, no. 88 (1967). ———, "Morshen or a Canoe to Eternity," *SlavR* 41 (1982), pp. 1–18. Wolfgang Kasack, "Nikolaj Morschen," *Osteuropa*, 1981. Vladimir Markov, "Poeziya Nikolaya Morshena" (introd. essay to *Tyulen'*, 1959). B. Nartsissov, "Dva techeniya v russkoi poezii zarubezh'ya," *Vozrozhdenie*, no. 195 (1968). ———, "Pod znakom differentsiala: Poeziya Nikolaya Morshena," *Novyi zhurnal*, no. 125 (1976). I. Odoevtseva, "O Nikolae Morshene," *Novyi zhurnal*, no. 58 (1958). G. Struve, "Dnevnik chitatelya," *Novoe russkoe slovo*, 19 April 1981. F. Zverev, "Poety 'novoi emigratsii'." In *Russkaya literatura v emigratsii: Sbornik statei.* Ed. N. Poltoratskii. Pittsburgh, 1972.　B. F.

Moskóvskii telegráf, first Russian "encyclopedic" journal, published by Nikolai Polevoi. Came out in Moscow twice monthly from 1825 to 1834. The journal aimed at providing truly "encyclopedic" coverage of contemporary life, thought, and culture both in Russia and abroad, publishing articles on a wide variety of topics, ranging from literature, the arts, philosophy, and history to archaeology, agriculture, economics, and the natural sciences. During the earliest period of its existence, 1825 to 1828, Vyazemsky was an active collaborator in the running of the journal, and *Moskovskii telegraf* published works by Pushkin, Baratynsky, Odoevsky, Yazykov, Zhukovsky,

and Kyukhelbeker. The final break between *Moskovskii telegraf* and the "literary aristocracy" came in 1829, over an article by Polevoi critical of Karamzin's *History of the Russian State.* Beginning in 1831, Bestuzhev-Marlinsky published his stories almost exclusively in *Moskovskii telegraf*, notably *Ammalat-Bek.* The journal actively propagandized for romanticism in literature, especially French romanticism. This was reflected in the translations from foreign literature which appeared on its pages, including works by Balzac, Hugo, Musset, Alfred de Vigny, Merimée, Benjamin Constant, Eugène Sue, Walter Scott, James Fenimore Cooper, Washington Irving, Maturin, and E. T. A. Hoffmann. *Moskovskii telegraf* was closed in 1834 after publishing a negative review of N. V. Kukolnik's patriotic play, *The Hand of the Almighty Saved the Fatherland* (Ruka Vsevyshnego otechestvo spasla).　C. T. N.

Moskóvskii véstnik (Moscow Herald), journal published in Moscow from 1827 to 1830, under the editorship of M. P. Pogodin. *Moskovskii vestnik* was founded by the circle of "Wisdom Lovers" centered around D. V. Venevitinov. Active participants in the publication included A. S. Khomyakov, Pyotr and Ivan Kireevsky, S. P. Shevyryov, and V. F. Odoevsky. During the first years of the journal's existence, Pushkin published extensively on its pages. *Moskovskii vestnik* also published poetry by Venevitinov, Shevyryov, Khomyakov, Baratynsky, Davydov, Yazykov, and others. The journal's marked bias toward German literary romanticism and philosophy was reflected in its publication of translations of works by Goethe, Schiller, Tieck, Hoffmann, Jean Paul, and the Schlegels. By 1829, the departure from *Moskovskii vestnik* of most of its former contributors left Pogodin in control. The editor indulged his professional interest in history by filling the pages of *Moskovskii vestnik* with archival documents and articles on historical research, material too narrowly technical to appeal to a wide circle of readers. Never having enjoyed the success hoped for, *Moskovskii vestnik* was forced to close for lack of subscribers in 1830.　C. T. N.

Moskóvskii zhurnál, a literary journal, published by N. M. Karamzin, which came out monthly in Moscow from 1791 to 1792. The journal was composed largely of works by Karamzin, notably *Letters of a Russian Traveller* (Pis'ma russkogo puteshestvennika, installments appeared in every issue), "Poor Liza" (Bednaya Liza), and "Natalya, the Boyar's Daughter" (Natalya, boyarskaya doch'). The journal also published poetry by Derzhavin, Dmitriev, and Kheraskov, among others, as well as translations from foreign literatures, including excerpts from Sterne's *Sentimental Journey* and *Tristram Shandy* and works attributed to Ossian. The journal was markedly sentimentalist in character, challenging from the point of view of the new movement headed by Karamzin the rigid literary canon of classicism. *Moskovskii zhurnal* was the first Russian journal to contain permanent sections devoted to literary and theatrical criticism.　C. T. N.

Moskvá (Moscow), a Soviet "thick" journal published in Moscow beginning in 1957. Organ of the Writers' Union of the RSFSR and its Moscow division, it was notable for its publication of Mikhail Bulgakov's novel *The Master and Margarita* (no. 11, 1966, and no. 1, 1967). Contributors to *Moskva* have included M. Sholokhov, K. Paustovsky, V. Tendryakov, A. Yashin, K. Simonov, V. Nekrasov, Yu. Kazakov, V. Shukshin, N. Aseev, N. Zabolotsky, and E. Evtushenko. The journal has also published translations of works by Hemingway, Saint-Exupery, Faulkner, Steinbeck, Baudelaire, and Apollinaire.　C. T. N.

Moskvityánin (The Muscovite), a monthly (in some years twicemonthly) literary and historical journal published in Moscow (1841–56). The editor and publisher was M. P. Pogodin, and S. P. Shevyryov headed the section devoted to literary criticism. I. V. Kireevsky was the editor for three issues in early 1845 and after 1850 Pogodin and Shevyryov were joined by the so-called young editors (Ostrovsky, Pisemsky, Grigoriev, Melnikov-Pechersky and others); *Moskvityanin's* publication of their work considerably enhanced the journal's importance to Russian literature and temporarily tripled the number of subscribers. The editorial point of view was that of "Official Nationality," a brand of conservative nationalism which differed crucially from emergent Slavophilism on the cult of autocracy and dynasty. The "Official Nationalists" still regarded the Russian state as the center of Russian history, as opposed to the implicitly anarchist romanticizing of "the people," which was the hallmark of Slavophilism. Nor were the Slavophiles such passionate or patriotic enemies of "the West" as Pogodin and Shevyryov. *Moskvityanin* was also an important harbinger of the Panslavism of the 1860s and 1870s.

For Pogodin and Shevyryov, the "Westernizer" enemy was embodied above all in OTECHESTVENNYE ZAPISKI (founded in 1839) and the journalism of BELINSKY. The Slavophiles, lacking a journal of their own, sometimes published in *Moskvityanin*, and so did GOGOL, but they had a low opinion of it. In the mid-1840s, KHOMYA-KOV called it "that sufficiently sad sign of our intellectual life," and Gogol described the editors as "antediluvian old men who stick out their noses, then turn and flee." Subscribers fell to between 300 and 400 in the mid-1840s; lack of support finally forced Pogodin to cease publication in 1856.

Bibliography: N. P. Barsukov, *Zhizn' i trudy M. P. Pogodina.* 22 vols. 1888–1910. A. G. Dement'ev, *Ocherki po istorii russkoi zhurnalistiki 1840–1850 gg.* 1951. A. Gleason, *European and Muscovite: Ivan Kireevsky and the Origins of Slavophilism.* 1972. N. Riasanovsky, *Nicholas I and Official Nationality.* 1961. S. A. Vengerov, "Molodaya redaktsiya Moskvityanina," *Vestnik Evropy,* 1886, no. 2.
A. G.

Motif (Russ. *motív*), a recurring element of a literary work which can belong to the thematic, phonic, or compositional level of the work. It can be a word, a phrase, a sentence, a scene, an idea or a compositional pattern. The use of such motifs in literature goes back to ancient poetry. In modern literary criticism, the usage of the word *motif* has been influenced by musical criticism. In music, *motif* denotes the shortest intelligible melodic or rhythmic figure and it is often used as a synonym of *theme*. Musical purists contend that *theme* is a longer unit, and it consists of several *motifs*. However, Richard Wagner's usage of *leitmotiv* to denote a leading theme made the two almost identical. This usage of *motif* passed on to 19th-century literary criticism and to folklore studies. Owing to their dialectical bent and dislike of static definitions, the FORMALISTS did little to clarify the usage of the term. In *O teorii prozy*, V. B. SHKLOVSKY defined *motif* as the shortest possible unit of plot, and he occasionally replaced *motif* by *theme*. This static approach was soon abandoned. In *Morfologiya skazki*, V. I. PROPP dismissed the traditional use of *motif* as an analytical tool in folklore studies, and proposed to focus attention on *function* instead.

An oblique development of the *motif* controversy was Shklovsky's and EIKHENBAUM's use of the term *motivirovka* (motivation) which refers to the way in which a state of affairs in the plot changes into another state of affairs. The change is usually *motivated*, that is to say, the reasons for change are either stated explicitly or are implied. The formalist study of plot motivation contributed to the shifting of attention of later critics from the plot itself to interaction between it and the reader's expectations.
E. Th.

Muratov, Pável Pávlovich (1881–1950), writer and scholar, was born in Bobrov, Voronezh Province, and died in Ireland. A former artillery officer, he was a gifted and erudite writer. Prior to the Revolution of 1917, he was chiefly known as an art historian, a contributor to VESY, and later as the editor of an excellent though short-lived literary journal *Sofya* (1914). In exile after 1922, he continued writing about the history of art and republished some of his earlier works.

Muratov's stories are characterized by swiftly unfolding action, unusual plot collisions, an intentional lack of psychological development, and skillful stylization. The influence of Henri de Régnier is evident. Muratov admired Gérard de Nerval, about whom he wrote some brilliant and informative essays. His travelogues reflect a love for Italy and a subtle artistic touch in portraying a multitude of intimate details of historical and cultural significance. Muratov is also known as an excellent translator of Italian Renaissance novellas, and as a war historian. He spent World War II in England. Together with his Irish friend W. E. D. Allen, a historian and collector of Russian icons in Dublin, he wrote *The Russian Campaigns of 1944–45* (1946).

Works: Egeriya: istoricheskii roman. Berlin, 1922. *Kofeinya* [a comedy.] Moscow, 1922. *Morali.* Berlin, 1922. *Tri rasskaza.* Moscow and Berlin, 1922. *Obrazy Italii: putevye zametki* [travel notes]. Berlin, 1924. *Priklyucheniya Dafnisa i Khloi* [a comedy]. Paris, 1926. *Mavritaniya.* Paris, 1927. *Magicheskie rasskazy.* Paris, 1928. *Geroi i geroini* [historical études.] Paris, 1929, Muratov also published essays on art and short stories in *Volya Rossii, Okno, Vozrozhdenie,* and *Sovremennye zapiski.*

Secondary literature: L. Lyubimov, *Na chuzhbine.* Moscow, 1964. Temira Pachmuss, *A Russian Cultural Revival: A Critical Anthology of Emigré Literature before 1939.* 1981. Pp. 261–67. "Pisateli sovremennoi epokhi." In *Bibliograficheskii slovar'.* Vol. 1. 1928.
T. A. P.

Muravyóv, Mikhail Nikítich (1757–1807), poet and literary theorist. Most deservedly remembered for his "Pièces fugitives," Muravyov exemplifies the transitional nature of the poetic impulse in Russia during the final decades of the 18th century. NEOCLASSICISM's strict hierarchy of genres had already begun to erode as he began his literary activities in the 1770s and, while attempting the solemn ode as well as translations from the classics, including Sappho and Vergil, he was quickly attracted to the lesser genres favored by the SENTIMENTALISTS. Influenced by the practice of M. M. KHERASKOV and N. I. NOVIKOV, the latter of whom invited his contributions to the Masonic *Utrennii svet*, Muravyov emphasized self-cognition and emotional experience as the foremost concerns of the poet. Fragments of his diary, which he called "A Sentimental Journal," appeared in Novikov's publication, attesting to the intimate association of artistic and personal concerns in his writings.

Although he indulged in melancholy reflection on the transitory nature of human life, Muravyov gave particular emphasis to the positive aspect of man's earthly experience. One of the first to describe the Russian landscape realistically in poems such as "The Grove" (1777), Muravyov compares favorably with DERZHAVIN in his ability to convey concrete visual images through his verse. The importance of personal friendships, as opposed to professional recognition, is expressed in his numerous epistles to friends. They anticipate the further development of the friendly letter by the romantics in the early 19th century. Among his verses dealing with the torments of love, "Unfaithfulness" (1781) deserves mention as the first example of an original ballad in Russian. Others attest to Muravyov's interest in the romantic celebration of Slavic antiquity and his "Caledonian Ballad" (1804) reveals the immediate influence of Ossian. In its totality, Muravyov's verse, by virtue of both themes and form, must be considered an early if imperfect expression of the new aesthetic sensibility in Russia.

Works: Stikhotvoreniya. 1967.
Secondary literature: William Edward Brown, *A History of 18th Century Russian Literature.* 1980. R. Neuhäuser, *Towards the Romantic Age: Essays on Sentimental and Preromantic Literature in Russia.* 1974. Marija Teteni, "Rannee proizvedenie russkogo sentimentalizma," *Studia Slavica Academiae Scientiarum Hungaricae* 25 (1979), pp. 419–26.
P. R. H.

Musaget Publishing House, organized in Moscow in the autumn of 1909 by the so-called transcendentalists, the Moscow symbolists, Andrei BELY, E. K. Volfing (E. K. Medtner) and L. L. Ellis (L. L. Kobylinsky). Musaget effectively replaced the older Symbolist strong-holds, VESY and ZOLOTOE RUNO, which had ceased publication.

Musaget was not only a publishing house, but served as a meeting place for philosophical discussions, lectures, literary workshops, and other public presentations. Indeed, in the early spring of 1910, Bely brought V. Ivanov to Moscow to celebrate his entrance into the Musaget group. Others associated with the Musaget group and its publishing enterprise included G. A. Rachinsky, A. S. Petrovsky, A. Sizov, N. K. Kiselev and V. O. Nilender.

The Musaget Publishing House existed from 1910 to 1917. From 1910 to 1914, Musaget also published the Russian division of the international philosophical journal, *Logos,* subtitled "An International Yearbook on the Philosophy of Culture," headed by the philosophers F. A. STEPUN and S. I. Hessen, and from 1912 to 1916, it published the bi-monthly magazine, *Works and Days* (Trudy i dni), originally conceived as a diary for the three writers, A. BLOK, A. Bely, and V. Ivanov. However, Musaget soon divided into three separate publishing enterprises: Musaget itself, with an emphasis on literary works; Logos, with an emphasis on defining a philosophical basis for problems of culture; and Orpheus, with its dominant interest in mysticism. These three tendencies—aesthetics, metaphysics and mysticism—are presented in an essay-dialogue entitled "What We are Speaking About," signed by Cunctator, which appeared in the May–June, 1912 issue of *Works and Days*.

Musaget publications included A. Bely's collections of essays, *Symbolism* (1910) and *Arabesques* (1911) as well as his study of Tolstoi and Dostoevsky, *The Tragedy of Creative Work* (Tragediya i tvorchestvo, 1911). L. L. Kobylinsky-Ellis' *Russian Symbolists* was published in 1910, E. K. Volfing-Medtner's critical essays, *Modernism and Music* appeared in 1912, A. Blok's three volume set of *Collected Poems* in 1914, and V. Ivanov's essays, *Furrows and Boundaries* in 1916. In addition, Musaget published a number of first translations of classical and medieval texts.

Bibliography: A. Bely, *Mezhdu dvukh revolyutsii.* 1934. A. Blok, *Dnevnik.* 1928. O. Maslenikov, *The Frenzied Poets.* Los Angeles, 1952. K. Mochul'skii, *Andrei Belyi.* Paris, 1955.

J. G. H.

Muscovite, The, see *MOSKVITYANIN*.

Mythological school, a trend in folkloristics and literary scholarship, which arose in Western Europe in the romantic period. Its philosophical basis lies in the aesthetics of F. Schelling and A. and F. Schlegel. Their ideas were applied to folklore by the Heidelberg romantics and by the Brothers Grimm. The Grimms held that folk poetry was of "godly origin"; from religious myth there developed, during its evolution, the fairy tale, epos, legend, etc.; folklore was the unconscious and impersonal creation of a collective folk spirit. Carrying the methodology of comparative linguistics over to the study of folklore, the Grimms traced similarities in the folklore of various peoples to their common ancient mythology, to some kind of "proto-myth" (on the analogy of "proto-language").

The champions of the mythological theory were A. Kuhn, W. Schwarz, and W. Mannhardt in Germany, M. Müller in England, and others. Müller's "solar mythology" traced myths to the deification of stars, and Kuhn's and Schwarz's "meteorological theory" traced them to the deification of storms, lightning, and winds. Characteristic of Müller was his explanation of the rise of myths through "the disease of language," i.e., semantic change.

The mythological school had a strong echo in Russia. P. V. KIREEVSKY, under the influence of nationalist romanticism in Germany, became an enthusiastic collector of folk songs in the 1830s and 1840s. F. I. BUSLAEV, the first genuine Russian folklore scholar, considered himself a follower of the Grimms. A. N. AFANASIEV, a jurist by education, was the most typical representative of the mythological school; his *Poetic Attitudes of the Slavs Toward Nature* (Poeticheskie vozzreniya slavyan na prirodu, 3 vols., 1865–69) gives the fullest expression of this trend. Afanasiev took over the meteorological concept of Schwarz and the teaching of Müller about the connection between language and myth. In every legend, proverb, and song that he discussed, he sought to find echoes of myths about thunderstorms, clouds, and the conflict of darkness with light. A. N. VESELOVSKY in his earlier works of the 1860s and 1870s also followed the line of the mythologists. Later, however, Veselovsky and Buslaev became critics of the mythological theory and allied themselves with the theory of borrowing.

Bibliography: A. N. Afanas'ev, *Poeticheskie vozzreniya slavyan na prirodu.* 1865–1869. M. K. Azadovskii, *Istoriya russkoi fol'kloristiki* 2 (1963), pp. 47–84. V. E. Gusev, "Mifologicheskaya shkola." In *KLE*. Vol. 4. 1967. Pp. 874–76. Isidor Levin. "Afanas'ev, Aleksandr Nikolaevich." In *Enzyklopädie des Märchens*, Vol. 1. 1975. Pp. 127–37. Yu. M. Sokolov, *Russian Folklore.* 1971. Pp. 50–77.

F. J. O.

Nabókov, Vladimir Vladimirovich (pseud. Sirin, 1899–1977), Russian and American novelist, short-story writer, poet, memoirist, man of letters, translator, lepidopterist, and chess problemist. Born into a wealthy St. Petersburg family, Nabokov was trilingual from childhood. The family emigrated in 1919 and Nabokov attended Cambridge where he took a degree in Slavic and Romance literatures. From 1922 to 1937 Nabokov resided in Berlin where he married Vera Slonim in 1925. His nine Russian novels were written during the Berlin period as were most of the stories and poems. During the early years Nabokov supported himself by giving lessons, chiefly language and tennis, making translations, devising chess problems and the first Russian crossword puzzles, and writing reviews, essays, poems, and stories for émigré publications. By 1930, three novels had appeared and his reputation as the best new writer of the emigration enabled him to supplement his meagre income by giving readings throughout the European émigré community. In response to the Nazi menace, Nabokov and his family emigrated to France in 1937. The plays, *The Event* (Sobytie, 1938) and *The Waltz Invention* (Izobretenie Val'sa, 1938), were written in France as was the first of the eight English novels, *The Real Life of Sebastian Knight* (1941). A last, never-to-be-completed Russian novel, *Solus Rex*, was still in progress when Nabokov left for the United States in 1940 and his active career as a Russian writer ended. All of Nabokov's subsequent original fiction was in English.

In his early American years Nabokov taught at Wellesley College while also pursuing his professional interest in lepidoptery at the Harvard Museum of Comparative Zoology. From 1948 through 1959 he was Professor of Slavic Literature at Cornell University. Summers were spent traveling, writing, and butterfly-collecting. Only three novels, *Bend Sinister* (1947), *Lolita* (1955), and *Pnin* (1957), were composed during Nabokov's American stay. The memoir, *Conclusive Evidence* (1951), later revised and retitled *Speak, Memory* (1966), was also a product of this period as was its Russian recension *Other Shores* (Drugie berega, 1954). Much time was devoted to translations of Russian classics: *Three Russian Poets* (1944), LERMONTOV's *A Hero of Our Time* (1958), the anonymous epic, *The Song of Igor's Campaign* (1960), and the monumental, idiosyncratic, annotated edition of PUSHKIN's *Eugene Onegin* (1964) as well as the critical study *Nikolai Gogol* (1944). These, along with the posthumously published *Lectures on Russian Literature* (1981) are Nabokov's chief contributions to Russian letters during his American sojourn.

The American success of *Lolita* in 1958 restored to Nabokov the fortune that the Russian Revolution had deprived him of some forty years earlier. Now sixty, Nabokov emigrated once again, settling permanently in Switzerland, while retaining his American citizenship. The years in Switzerland saw the creation of *Pale Fire* (1962), *Ada* (1969), *Transparent Things* (1972) and *Look at the Harlequins!* (1974). Although Nabokov's last term of European residency was of great importance in his career as an American writer, it was also the time of the resurrection of his reputation as a Russian writer. All of the Russian novels (and almost all of the stories) were translated under the author's close supervision, and now found a new, much larger international audience, belatedly making Vladimir Nabokov one of the most widely read contemporary Russian authors.

Mary (Mashen'ka, 1926) and *Glory* (Podvig, 1933) are the most personal of Nabokov's novels and depict émigré life through the eyes of their young Russian heroes. They excel in their verbal precision but display what Nabokov later termed "a damp emotionalism" that opposes them to a second brace of novels, *King, Queen, Knave* (Korol', dama, valet, 1928) and *Laughter in the Dark* (Kamera obskura, 1932), which feature unidimensional characters and sensational, albeit hackneyed plots that are related with cool, technical brilliance. Yet another pair, *The Eye* (Soglyadatai, 1930) and *Despair* (Otchayanie, 1936), with their deranged, "unreliable" narrators, mark the appearance in the Nabokov canon of the psychological novel. Their basic structural device is the gap between the deluded narrator's account and the "reality" that the reader perceives through (and in spite of) that account. Although in part DOSTOEVSKY parodies, these books sound a key theme in Nabokov's works: the interrelation of two (or more) "realities," one more real than the other. This theme is also present in *The Defense* (Zashchita Luzhina, 1930), in which a chess master vainly strives to decipher and counter the chess-like attack of an unknown opponent who is replaying a sequence of biographical moves that once before led him to insanity.

Nabokov's ultimate reputation as a Russian writer rests upon his last two Russian novels. *Invitation to a Beheading* (Priglashenie na kazn', 1938) is a stunning, artifice-saturated tour de force almost without human dimension, or even plot. Cincinnatus, a young teacher, has been convicted of "gnostical turpitude" for he is different from his banal fellow citizens in their mythical totalitarian world. As he sits in his prison cell he records in his diary intuitions of an ideal world that is his true home. In due course, Cincinnatus is brought to the executioner's block and as the axe falls and the novel's stage prop world disintegrates, he arises and "makes his way in that direction where, to judge by the voices, stood beings akin to him." The surrealistic novel is literally structured upon an opposition of "this world" and "that world" with death the transition point between them. The book is susceptible of many interpretations but on one level the thematic opposition is between the circumscribed consciousness of the world of the hero versus that of the omniscient author—a recurrent Nabokov theme. The novel shows a stylistic and conceptual brilliance reminiscent of Andrei BELY encompassed within its elegant Nabokovian formal structure.

The Gift (Dar, 1937–38, 1952) dwells on the artist and the creative process rather than on the artifice of art. The protagonist, Fyodor Godunov-Cherdyntsev, is a young émigré writer living in Berlin in the late twenties. The more obvious plot line is the intricately patterned convergence of Fyodor and his beloved, Zina Mertz. The more fundamental line of development is the maturation of Fyodor's artistic talent (one of the gifts of the book's title) which culminates in his composition of *The Gift*. The novel is also a discerning critique of Russian literature, a penetrating appraisal of Russian intellectual and social history, and a harsh satire of the émigré literary scene. The love story and warmth of characterization absorb the reader and distract from the cunning plot which is modelled after a chess problem. *The Gift* is the finest fusion of the formal and human dimensions of Nabokov's Russian literary career.

Only a few of Nabokov's nearly fifty Russian short stories are memorable: "The Potato Elf" (Kartofel'nyi el'f, 1924), "A Guide to Berlin" (Putevoditel' po Berlinu, 1925), "The Return of Chorb" (Vozvrashchenie Chorba, 1925), and "Spring in Fialta" (Vesna v Fialte, 1936). In general, the short stories are less innovative than the novels and more grounded in the realities of émigré life. Nabokov published four volumes of poetry before turning to prose as his major medium. Although his output diminished sharply after 1930, over 300 Russian poems were published throughout his life.

Nabokov's Russian novels have been reprinted and have found a wide readership in the new "third wave" emigration. His reputation as a Russian writer has also been enhanced by his rendering of *Lolita* into Russian (1967), and by translations of his other English works. Nabokov's influence, already great among American and English writers, is now noticeable in the work of a few Soviet (as well as émigré) authors and his hotel suite at the Montreux Palace had become a place of pilgrimage for Russian literati (among others) in the years before his death. Nabokov's Russian heritage which had already enriched much of Western European literature has begun to come full circle.

Works: (All Russian titles with Ardis, Ann Arbor, Mich.) *Mashen'ka.* 1974. *Dar.* 1975. *Podvig.* 1975. *Vozvrashchenie Chorba.* 1976. *Drugie berega.* 1978. *Kamera obskura.* 1978. *Otchayanie.* 1978. *Soglyadatai.* 1978. *Vesna v Fialte.* 1978. *Korol', dama, valet.* 1979. *Priglashenie na kazn'.* 1979. *Stikhi.* 1979. *Zashchita Luzhina.* 1979. *Lectures on Russian Literature.* Ed. with an introd. by F. Bowers. 1980.

Translations: Invitation to a Beheading. 1959. *Laughter in the Dark.* 1960. *The Gift.* 1963. *The Defense.* 1964. *The Eye.* 1965. *Despair.* 1966. *Speak, Memory.* 1966. *The Waltz Invention.* 1966. *King, Queen, Knave.* 1968. *Mary.* 1970. *Poems and Problems.* 1970. *Glory.* 1972. *A Russian Beauty.* 1973. *Tyrants Destroyed.* 1975. *Details of a Sunset.* 1976. *Five Novels by V. Nabokov.* Introd. by Peter Quennell. 1979.

Secondary literature: Georgii Adamovich, "Vladimir Nabokov." In *Twentieth-Century Russian Literary Criticism.* Ed. Victor Erlich. 1975. Pp. 219–31. A. Field, *Nabokov: His Life in Art.* 1967. ———, *Nabokov: His Life in Part.* 1977. ———, *Nabokov: A Bibliography.* 1973. Ludmila A. Foster, "Nabokov in Russian Emigré Criticism," *RLT* 3 (1972), pp. 330–41. Jane Grayson, *Nabokov Translated: A Comparison of Nabokov's Russian and English Prose.* 1977. G. M. Hyde, *Vladimir Nabokov: America's Russian Novelist.* 1978. J. E. Rivers and Charles Nicol, eds., *Nabokov's Fifth Arc: Nabokov and Others on His Work.* 1982. W. W. Rowe, *Nabokov & Others: Patterns in Russian Literature.* 1979. Samuel Schuman, *Vladimir Nabokov: A Reference Guide.* 1979. *The Vladimir Nabokov Research Newsletter,* no. 1 (Fall 1978).

D. B. J.

Nadézhdin, Nikolaí Ivánovich (1804–56), publicist, literary critic, and ethnographer. The son of a deacon, Nadezhdin attended a Moscow theological academy but was expelled in 1826. His first articles were published in 1828 in *Vestnik Evropy* under the pseudonym of "Nikodim Nadoumko," attacking the romantic poets and even some of PUSHKIN's works. Meanwhile he imbibed German philosophy and wrote a Latin doctoral dissertation for Moscow University. In this dissertation ("On the Origin, Nature, and Fate of Romantic Poetry," defended in 1830) Nadezhdin asserted that forms of art are determined by the spirit of the age and he proposed a kind of synthesis of classicism and romanticism. He also criticized Russian romanticism on the basis, mainly, of Schelling's *Naturphilosophie*, influencing and prefiguring many of the views of BELINSKY (CHERNYSHEVSKY in his *Sketches of the Gogolian Period*, 1856, credits Nadezhdin with introducing German aesthetic theory into Russian literary thought). From 1831 to 1835 he was a professor in the sub-department of fine arts and archaeology at Moscow University and in his lectures in the early thirties likened Russians (in familiar terms!) to a horde of life-invigorating barbarians sweeping over a degenerate Europe. Also in 1831 Nadezhdin founded the monthly TELESKOP but this was closed down in 1836 for publishing CHAADAEV's "Philosophical Letter." Exiled to Siberia, Nadezhdin acquired an interest in ethnography. He returned from exile in 1838 and later, now quite reactionary, edited a publication of the Interior Ministry. A pioneer in historical geography, Nadezhdin became chairman of the ethnographic division of the Russian Geographic Society in 1848.

Secondary literature: N. K. Kozmin, *N. I. Nadezhdin.* 1912. V. I. Kuleshov, *Istoriya russkoi kritiki.* Yu. Mann, "N. I. Nadezhdin: predshestvennik Belinskogo," *VLit* 1962, no. 6.

R. H. S.

Nádson, Semyón Yákovlevich (1862–87), poet, began to write verse while still a schoolboy and published his first verse in 1878. He served as an officer until forced to resign his commission in 1884 because of illness. He died of consumption. Nadson began as a poet of the civic tendency of NEKRASOV's OTECHESTVENNYE ZAPISKI, though in a less vigorous and even more pessimistic vein. The poetry of his last few years, which made him a celebrity, is characterized by a conflict between pain and despair ("Our generation knows no youth") and dreams of ideal beauty. It is also rather schematic and "devoid of all life and strength" (SVYATOPOLK-MIRSKY), though rhetorically appealing and smoothly versified. Many of Nadson's poems were set to music.

Works: Polnoe sobranie sochinenii. 2 vols. 1917. *Polnoe sobranie stikhotvorenii.* Introd. G. A. Byalyi. 1962.

Translations: Lewanski, pp. 307–08.

Secondary literature: L. N. Nazarova, "Nadson." In *Istoriya russkoi literatury.* Vol. 9, pt. 2. 1956.

V. T.

Nagíbin, Yúry Márkovich (1920–), one of the best post-war Soviet short-story writers. Nagibin studied foreign languages and cinematography. His early stories dealt with the war, extolling the heroism of Soviet soldiers. Some stories demonstrate a redeeming sense of universality, for example, "A Man from the Front" (Chelovek s fronta). His "conflictless" stories on the kolkhoz theme during the late Stalin period have little aesthetic merit. Nagibin's better literary production comes after 1953. His Meshchera cycle of stories renews the tradition of TURGENEV's *A Sportsman's Sketches*: they conjure up the poetry of the life of hunters and fishermen; they celebrate the unassuming beauty of the Russian landscape; they stir up a civic concern about social ills ("the problem story"); they even hint at a re-emergence of the Russian tradition of the alienation between the intellectual and the peasant. Nagibin presents a wide cross section of the Soviet population in stories on varied themes. His characters are ordinary people in ordinary situations. Nagibin tries to discover the innermost self of his character as he or she experiences an illumination, a catharsis, and finally a new understanding of yet unrealized recesses of personality. In order to create this transformation Nagibin combines the effect of plot with a lyric comment akin to CHEKHOV's. This holds true of Nagibin's stories about attitudes between the sexes with their unexpected outcomes, as in "Gray Human Hair Wanted Immediately" (Srochno trebuyutsya sedye chelovecheskie volosy), and "Berendeev Forest" (Berendeev les); and his stories about children, such as "Winter Oak" (Zimnii dub), "Fourth Daddy" (Chetvertyi papa). Nagibin has also written travelogues. His American travelogue, "Flying Saucers" (Letayushchie tarelochki) is commendably even-handed.

Works: Chelovek s fronta. Rasskazy. 1943. "Khazarskii ornament" and "Svet v okne," *Literaturnaya Moskva* 2 (1956). *Izbrannye proizvedeniya.* 2 vols. 1973. *Berendeev les. Rasskazy. Ocherki.* 1978. "Letayushchie tarelochki. Puteshestviya po Amerike," *Nash sovremennik,* 1980, no. 2. *Sobranie sochinenii.* 4 vols. 1980–81.

Translations: Each for All. London, 1945. (Contains "The Man from the Front" and other stories). *The Pipe: Stories.* Moscow, 1954. *Dreams: Stories.* Moscow, 1959. "Chetunov, Son of Chetunov," "A Man and a Road," "The Echo." In *The New Writing in Russia.* Ed. and trans. Thomas P. Whitney. 1964. *The Peak of Success and Other Stories.* Ed. Helena Goscilo. Ann Arbor, 1983.

Secondary literature: I. Bogatko, *Yurii Nagibin.* 1980. Ellen Joan Cochrum, *Jurij Nagibin's Short Stories: Themes and Literary Criticism.* Ph.D. diss., Michigan State University, 1977. *Russkii sovetskii rasskaz.* Ed. V. A. Kovalev. 1970. (Chap. 8.)   H. O.

Na literatúrnom postú (On Literary Guard), established in 1926, was the main theoretical and critical journal of the VAPP, and later of the RAPP. The most active and influential member of the editorial board was Leopold AVERBAKH; others included Vladimir Ermilov, Vladimir KIRSHON, Yury LIBEDINSKY and Aleksandr FADEEV. This journal replaced NA POSTU, and differed in calling for higher standards for proletarian writers, in looking more favorably on FELLOW-TRAVELER and PEASANT WRITERS, in advocating the selective use of the cultural heritage, and in taking great interest in the workings of unconscious and intuitive factors in the creative process. For these views it was constantly attacked by RODOV and LELEVICH, diehard "Onguardists" who formed a leftist opposition within the RAPP. However, the editors of *Na literaturnom postu* also believed in the primacy of proletarian literature, and were highly, often savagely, intolerant of critics and groups with differing views, notably VORONSKY, PEREVERZEV, and the PEREVAL. The journal ceased to exist in 1932, when the Party abolished the RAPP and, in effect, all other literary groups.

Secondary literature: Edward J. Brown, *The Proletarian Episode in Russian Literature.* 1953.   R. A. M.

Na postú (On Guard), a journal of literary criticism and theory, established by the OKTYABR' group in 1923, and closed down in 1925. The editors were Grigory LELEVICH, Semyon RODOV and Boris Volin, who were known as "Onguardists" (*napostovtsy*); their views, collectively, were labeled "Onguardism" (*napostovstvo*). In the great literary debates of the 1920s, they were the most militant and influential advocates of the "Octobrist" line on the nature and role of proletarian literature. Though opposed to all non-proletarian theories, such as those of FORMALISM and LEF, their main target was VORONSKY, whom they accused of indifference to proletarian literature and favoritism toward the ideologically dubious FELLOW-TRAVELER writers. The ensuing exchanges, often extremely acrimonious, helped draw the hitherto reluctant Party directly into literary matters. A resolution of the Press Section of the Central Committee (18 June 1925) chided the Onguardists for crude factionalism and produced a split in the ranks of the Octobrists, which led to the group's—and the journal's—demise later that year. *Na postu* was succeeded by NA LITERATURNOM POSTU, with a whole new editorial board.

Secondary literature: Herman Ermolaev, *Soviet Literary Theories, 1917–1934.* 1963. Chap. 2.   R. A. M.

Nárbut, Vladímir Ivánovich (1888–1944), poet and writer, was born on the family estate of Narbutovka in Chernigov province. He spent his childhood among provincial small landowners. His experiences as a child gave him material for his later satirical poems. In his high-school years, he published four poems in the almanac, *Student Collection* (Studencheskii sbornik, 1909). Later, Narbut attended Petersburg University, where he studied in the department of history and philology. Narbut's first collection of poetry appeared in 1910, *Poems. Book I* (Stikhi. Kniga I). In that year, he started his collaboration with several Petersburg journals—*Gaudeamus,* GIPERBOREI, APOLLON, *Sovremennyi mir,* and others. In 1912, Narbut published a collection of short stories, *The Hunt* (Na okhote) and his second volume of poetry, *Hallelujah* (Alliluiya). The latter was confiscated by the censor because of its satirical treatment of the provincial landed gentry (a second edition was issued in 1922, in Odessa). The grotesque and vivid imagery, and the texture of the language, enriched by Ukrainian features, were reminiscent of GOGOL's prose (in fact, Narbut included epigraphs from Gogol and SKOVORODA). Notwithstanding his tendency towards anticlassicism and anti-aestheticism, Narbut joined the ACMEIST group, the POET's GUILD, in 1912. His poetry of those years, besides *Hallelujah,* includes the collections, *Love and Love* (Lyubov' i lyubov', 1913) and *Vii* (1915).

After the Revolution, Narbut became an active participant in the new Bolshevik order. He moved to Voronezh, where in the years 1918 and 1919, he worked as the editor of the newspaper, *Voronezhskie izvestiya* and of the magazine, *Sirena* (in this magazine, the newly born Moscow group of the IMAGISTS published its first manifesto). From 1920 to 1922, Narbut worked first in Odessa, as the director of the news agency, YUGROSTA, and then in Kharkov, as the director of RATAU. In these years, his poetry took a patriotic bent and showed Narbut's attraction to the themes of the Revolution and civil war, as evidenced by the collections, *War Poems* (Stikhi o voine, 1920), *Red Army Poems* (Krasnoarmeiskie stikhi, 1920), *Soviet Land* (Sovetskaya zemlya, 1921). In 1922, Narbut moved to Moscow, where he was actively involved in the press section of the Central Committee. He also founded and directed the publishing house, *Land and Factory* (Zemlya i fabrika). For a decade, Narbut did not publish any poetry. However, in 1933 and 1934, his verses reappeared in journals such as, *Novyi mir* and *Krasnaya nov'.* At that time, Narbut was experimenting with "scientific poetry" (a poetic concept introduced in France by René Ghil, in the 1880s, and applied among the Russians only by Narbut's fellow Acmeist, M. Zenkevich). Narbut died on 15 November 1944. The place and circumstances of his death are unknown. Official Soviet sources state that he was "illegally repressed," and posthumously rehabilitated.

Translations: One poem, "Portrait." In *Modern Russian Poetry.* Ed. V. Markov and M. Sparks. 1967. Pp. 366–67.

Secondary literature: N. Gumilev, "Pis'ma o russkoi poezii" (1923). In *Sobranie sochinenii* (1964–68). Vol. 4. Pp. 263–65, 300–01. B. Gusman, *100 poetov. Literaturnye portrety.* 1923. R. D. B. Thomson, "The Vision of the Bog: The Poetry of Vladimir Narbut," *RusL* 10 (1981), pp. 319–38. K. L. Zelinskii, *Na rubezhe dvukh epokh: Literaturnye vstrechi 1917–1920 gg.* 1959. M. Zenkevich, "Vladimir Narbut." In *Den' Poezii.* 1967. P. 226.   A. L.

Narézhny, Vasíly Trofímovich (1780–1825), a writer whose works crown the achievements of 18th-century Russian prose, but exert only an indirect influence on that of the 19th century. Born in the Poltava region of the Ukraine to an impoverished gentry family, Narezhny studied at Moscow University (1799–1801); without gaining a degree he entered the civil service, first, briefly, in the Caucasus (Georgia) and then in St. Petersburg; he remained a minor official and died in penury.

As a student, Narezhny tried his hand at poetry and drama; his play *Dmitry the Pretender* (Dmitrii Samozvanets) was published in 1804. His first prose effort was *Slavic Nights* (Slavenskie vechera, 1809), a collection of heroic Ossianic tales of the Kievan Rus' past. The successful formula came in the combination of adventure and satire of the picaresque novel. Narezhny's most famous work, *A Russian Gil Blas* (Rossiiskii Zhil'blaz, 1814) which openly calls attention to the generic model (Le Sage's *Gil Blas,* 1715–35), draws on the native tradition of social satire, especially of NOVIKOV, FONVIZIN, and KRYLOV but now encompasses the various strata of society and shows vice and iniquity in its endless manifestations. The acuity of Narezhny's satire, a satire animated by an Enlightenment rationalism and moralism (and not an "anti-gentry" democratism), and continuing the tradition of the Russian 18th-century satirical journals, is attested by the fact that the latter three parts of the novel were prohibited by the censor, and the first three confiscated soon after they appeared; the whole was published only in 1938. Similarly, his *A Black Year, or Mountaineer Princes* (Chernyi god, ili Gorskie knyaz'ya), which deals with social injustice and official corruption in the Caucasus—but not at all with the issue of Russian imperialism—while finished in 1818, appeared only posthumously, in 1829. The didactic concomitant of Narezhny's satire is best seen in his novel *Aristion, or Re-Education* (Aristion, ili Perevospitanie, 1822) which attacks the flaws of Russian education and counterposes the model of Rousseau's *Emile*.

A central moment in Narezhny's fiction is the Ukraine and its Cossack past. However, in such novels as *Zaporozhets* and *Bursak*, both published in 1824, and an unfinished novel on a Ukrainian Robin Hood, *Garkusha* (1850), the past is treated ahistorically and filtered through the prism of 18th-century sentiment and moralizing. All continue the picaresque mode. *Bursak*, probaly his best work, and *Two Ivans, or a Passion for Litigation* (Dva Ivana, ili strast' k tyazhbam, 1825) are particularly successful in their depiction of old-time Ukrainian society, its mores and *byt*. By virtue of his ability to frame a complex narrative and his comic gifts Narezhny ranks with such 18th-century writers as Defoe, Le Sage, Smollett and Fielding. But his style and language were out of step with the age; in 1841 BELINSKY saw him as the "forgotten forefather" of Russian novelists. In fact, Narezhny's influence is most evident in the work of his famous fellow Ukrainian, GOGOL—in the latter's use of satire and the picaresque, his focus on the Ukraine and its past, on the "little people" and provincial *byt*, in the specific motif of the quarrel of the "Two Ivans," and so on.

G. G.

Naródniki, see POPULISM.

Naródnost' (from *narod*, "people, nation," hence "popular and/or national quality"), a literary term which has played a key role in Russian literary criticism and literary theory since the romantic period. The term was first used by P. A. VYAZEMSKY and O. M. SOMOV in the early 1820s, to signify an author's faithfulness to distinctive traits of his national culture—not too different from the "local color" of the French romantics. In the 1840s, both SLAVOPHILES and WESTERNIZERS demanded *narodnost'* of Russian literature, but defined it differently, the former seeing it in Russia's Orthodox heritage and communal spirit (*sobornost'*), the latter believing that the Russian national spirit, having embraced Western civilization, was now in the process of creating its own national version of that civilization. V. G. BELINSKY sometimes distinguished *narodnost'* from *natsional'nost'*, with the latter referring to the nation as a whole, while *narodnost'* became a near-synonym of *prostonarodnost'* (from *prostoi narod*, "the common people"). Thus, Belinsky saw PUSHKIN as Russia's national poet (*natsional'nyi poet*) who, however, being entirely unknown to the common people, in a sense lacked *narodnost'*.

In the criticism of the 1850s and 1860s, e.g., in N. A. DOBROLYUBOV's essay, "On the Degree of *narodnost'* in the Development of Russian Literature" (O stepeni uchastiya narodnosti v razvitii russkoi literatury, 1858), the extent to which a work was directly concerned with the needs and aspirations of the common people (and was therefore intelligible to them) became the criterion not only of *narodnost'*, but of artistic quality in general. This view was also stated, with great vigor, in Lev TOLSTOI's essay *What Is Art?* (1898). Marxist critics adopted this view, but also insisted that the people should take possession of the "true" art of the past, even if it was produced by (or for) the bourgeoisie or the gentry. On these terms, then, the art of a Pushkin, TURGENEV, or GONCHAROV retroactively acquired the quality of *narodnost'*.

The aesthetic theory and critical practice of SOCIALIST REALISM give *narodnost'* a more important place than ever before, as it is made to refer to a content which represents the viewpoint and the interests of the people, in a form that is intelligible and congenial to the people. Hence *narodnost'* is seen as intimately linked, or in fact identical, with *partiinost'* (Party-mindedness, Party spirit).

Bibliography: N. A. Dobrolyubov, "O stepeni uchastiya narodnosti v razvitii russkoi literatury." In *Sobranie sochinenii* (9 vols.,

1961–64). Vol. 2. Pp. 218–72. N. Gei, *Narodnost' i partiinost' literatury*. 1964. L. G. Leighton, "*Narodnost'* as a Concept in Russian Romanticism." In his *Russian Romanticism: Two Essays*. 1975. Pp. 41–108. Victor Terras, *Belinskij and Russian Literary Criticism*. 1974. Pp. 92–101.

V. T.

Nartsissov, Borís Anatólievich (1906–82), émigré poet, was born near Saratov, of a Russian father and Estonian mother. After the Revolution his parents fled to Estonia, where Nartsissov was educated bilingually and received an M.A. in chemistry from the University of Tartu (1936). He served as an officer in the Estonian Army. Displaced to Germany by the War, Nartsissov then spent some years in Australia and in 1953 immigrated to the United States, where he worked in industry and for the United States Government as a research chemist until his retirement. Nartsissov began to publish poetry relatively late. He did, however, produce six collections, the last, *Stellar Bird* (Zvezdnaya ptitsa, 1978) being a compendium of earlier and some new poems. Nartsissov also published essays and reviews in literary journals and newspapers. He was a masterful, though not prolific translator of poetry, Estonian in particular.

Nartsissov's poetry, like that of other émigré poets, is the poetry of a world traveler. In addition to European land- and cityscapes from the extreme north to the Mediterranean, Nartsissov has produced some excellent Americana (his "Edgariana" cycle, devoted to his visits to Poe's haunts, is among his best) and some equally impressive verses on the "timeless land" of Australia. Nartsissov's scientific background shows in many of his poems, providing him with some of his bolder and more fantastic conceits. Some of his poetry is an expression of a scientific worldview, mythologized and presented in poetic form. For example, there is a cycle of poems about the human brain, illuminated from various aspects including the physiological—yet without becoming in the least prosaic or trivial. Nartsissov is very good at fusing a modern scientific-technological mythology with classical and biblical myths, for instance the biblical Apocalypse with its nuclear equivalent. Nartsissov's background shows in some poems in which he pays tribute to Estonia and her people. "The Estonian and the Rock" describes an Estonian farmer's tenacious struggle with his rocky field. "He who Chose to Stay" is a monument to Estonian freedom fighters who refused to leave their country, choosing "the noble lot of the few: to die, rifle in hand, on the threshold of their own house." Nartsissov, an austere poet, ordinarily foregoes the pursuit of euphonic patterns and sound symbolism, preferring to follow his unfailing sense of rhythm.

Works: Stikhi. 1958. Golosa. 1961. Pamyat'. 1965. Pod"em. 1969. Shakhmaty. 1974. Zvezdnaya ptitsa. 1978.
Translations: America's Russian Poets. Ed. and trans. R. H. Morrison. 1975. Pp. 62–67.
Secondary literature: Boris Filippov, "Pamyati poeta," *Novoe russkoe slovo* 13 March 1983, p. 5.

V. T.

National Annals, see OTECHESTVENNYE ZAPISKI.

Natural school, The (naturál'naya shkóla), as it was identified by adherents and opponents alike, has been characterized as the most important trend in Russian narrative prose in the mid-19th-century (ca. 1842–55). Serving as a transition from the influence of German romantic literature and idealist philosophy to a realistic approach associated with French social romanticism, the natural school moved from a blending of the natural world with the supernatural to the depiction of an ugly and imperfect natural world. However, the very concept of a "school" implies a more consistent literary approach than was actually present. Writers identified with the natural school were so designated because of their propensity at that time for certain shared elements of plot, style, and architectonics. Since the school coexisted with other schools and literary movements, all evolving and exchanging features, a rigorous definition of the natural school is inappropriate, but certain typical features associated with the school can be established.

The initial shift of attention toward the natural world was greatly assisted in the 1830s by the journalist N. A. POLEVOI's advocacy in MOSKOVSKII TELEGRAF of the social orientation of contemporary French literature. In the years that followed, the natural school developed as an amalgam of a variety of early influences reworked and synthesized in original ways with well-known features of work by Nikolai GOGOL, whose approach was indefatigably championed and recommended to other writers by the critic Vissarion BELINSKY.

Among these early influences were the French feuilleton and *physiologie*, the devices of the *école frénétique*, and the strong social and "philanthropic" orientation of contemporary French literature. Originally a journal column of information about current literature and public spectacles associated with Parisian cultural life, the feuilleton eventually was developed by Frédéric Soulié into the *roman feuilleton* when elements of the weekly columns were retained for further treatment in successive issues. Nearly all the rising authors of the natural school participated in the literary trend of writing feuilletons.

The *physiologie* was similar to the feuilleton, but was given more to the description of urban life and society after the 1830 Revolution. It conveyed neither the intimacy nor the stylized personality of the author nor the casual freedom of narrative associated with the feuilleton. In Russia, this PHYSIOLOGICAL SKETCH soon became a dominant literary influence.

In the third and fourth decades of the century, Russian writers (including Gogol) could hardly avoid the influence of the *école frénétique*, in which authors such as the young Balzac and Hugo, Jules Janin, Eugène Sue, Alexandre Dumas and others captured the imagination of readers with Gothic tales featuring unique plots, the rejection of sentimentalism, the introduction of vulgarity, tragic horror, torture, "nature in the raw," and the terrifying side of everyday life. Great swings in verbal formulation and in mood, as from horror to comedy, also reached Gogol and his contemporaries through the *école frénétique* and were assimilated and transformed by Russian literature.

Finally, current French literature was widely read in translation and discussed in Russian circles. The strong social orientation of works by authors such as Balzac, Hugo, Sand, and Sue (his muck-raking *Les Mystères de Paris* was enthusiastically received by Belinsky in 1844) was tremendously influential upon a sympathetic readership in Russia.

The natural school movement received its name from the ultra-conservative writer and journalist, F. V. BULGARIN, in an 1846 issue of SEVERNAYA PCHELA. Although Bulgarin's intention was to disparage writers who imitated Gogol's description of lowly characters, the term was adopted in Belinsky's articles to designate that branch of Russian realism which was associated with Gogol. In Gogol's work Belinsky professed to find the completion of the long struggle of Russian literature to become national and original by coming closer to Russian life. The publication of Gogol's *Dead Souls* in 1842 was a catalyst for Belinsky's efforts to alter the direction of Russian culture through his energetic and socially responsible criticism in OTECHEST-VENNYE ZAPISKI. Because it was a work by a Russian author of great artistic stature, *Dead Souls* provided a text from which Belinsky could discuss socially didactic art. Calling *Dead Souls* an expression of life "as it was" set on a lower plane, Belinsky quickly characterized it as an artistic representation of the contemporary position of Russian society. Though Gogol's characters were more grotesque than realistic, Belinsky used them to make the point that Russian reality was indeed grim. Forced to be circumspect in his criticism, Belinsky tirelessly defended *Dead Souls* as a description of ordinary, lowly, everyday life and as a "purely Russian and national creation." Few readers missed the implication.

Complicating the situation, however, is Gogol's other literary landmark of 1842, *The Overcoat*. Though at the height of his early work Gogol had characterized his approach as the antithesis of sentimental poetics and a step beyond romanticism, *The Overcoat* reflected the growth of civic sentimentalism in his work. As a result, after *Dead Souls* and *The Overcoat*, the natural school movement became involved in an intensified search for a new synthesis of Gogolian style with renovated sentimental forms, though the influence of the anomalies in Gogol's earlier work remained. Since Gogol had absorbed elements of markedly differing literary traditions, such as the comedy, the vulgar anecdote, the vaudeville, the Gothic tale, and the work of the *école frénétique*, the evolution of a consistent natural school approach was beset by conflicting tendencies.

The origin of the natural school dates from about 1842–43, when writers including the poet and publisher, N. A. NEKRASOV, D. V. GRIGOROVICH, I. S. TURGENEV, the revolutionary thinker and philosopher A. I. HERZEN, I. I. PANAEV, Gogol's fellow Ukrainian E. P. GREBENKA, and the ethnographer and lexicographer V. I. DAL were first brought together through *Otechestvennye zapiski*. Shortly thereafter, Fyodor DOSTOEVSKY (who at the time had been sharing a flat with Grigorovich) and M. E. SALTYKOV-SHCHEDRIN were also published in the journal. One may regard the first half of the forties as the initial phase of the movement, corresponding with the tendency of most of these authors, despite the appearance of *Dead Souls* and *The Overcoat*, to be primarily engaged in a process of russifying the French *physiologie*.

Works by many of the above writers appeared in two significant collections which became identified with the natural school: the two volumes of *A Physiology of St. Petersburg* (Fiziologiya Peterburga), which appeared in the spring and summer of 1845, and *A Petersburg Collection* (Peterburgskii sbornik, 1846). Initiated by N. A. Nekrasov, who recognized the potential of a Russian version of the French *physiologie* then selling well in the city's foreign bookstores, the *Physiology* consisted of "physiological sketches" presented as immediate observations depicting the life of St. Petersburg (though at times the images evoked are more reminiscent of Paris) as one might draw sketches from nature. In the *Physiology* various city workers were characterized, particularly petty clerks, the movement's favorite character. Grigorovich's *Petersburg Organ Grinders* (Peterburgskie sharmanshchiki) was typical of the collection for its treatment of a selected representative of the city's dregs. The *Petersburg Collection* was notable for the originality of the young contributors and offered a variety of genres, including works by Nekrasov, Turgenev, and, most important of all, Dostoevsky's *Poor Folk*. Belinsky was also a contributor, and the introduction to the *Physiology* contained his manifesto for the natural school in which he described the necessity of creating a realistic literature for the masses that would acquaint them with Russia's many facets. Writers, Belinsky maintained in the manifesto, should not only know Russian actuality, but must truly understand it and assess it.

Belinsky called for Russian writers to emulate Gogol by seeking their material in contemporary society and tirelessly defended his description of "life as it is," maintaining that Gogol had indeed captured the spirit of Russian life, though many highly stylized elements accompanied this "lowering of plane." Because of Belinsky's interpretation, these extraneous features appeared in the works of writers who, in responding to the call for an artistic representation of Russian reality, did not draw a clear distinction between that which was "realistic" and that which was Gogol's very personal style. This was a pattern characteristic of the second stage of the natural school movement after the mid-1840s.

As a result, the elements used by writers in their gravitation toward nature included the philanthropic emphasis upon the low-class origin of the principal characters (described by VINOGRADOV as the result of "the epidemic thirst for types, the desire to choose marionettes as symbols"), pointedly low-class subject matter, the squalor of dirty, littered, and malodorous surroundings, domestic cruelty, prosaic and depressing landscapes (easily provided by the St. Petersburg climate), the contrast between appearance and reality, and detailed attention to inadequate and inferior clothing, food, and furnishings. Considerable space is also devoted to mundane functions such as eating, smoking, coughing, and sneezing. The characters depicted are often sick, and always degraded. Their language is likely to be awkward, hesitant, and possibly vulgar. Life in the sketches, plays, and stories of the natural school was particularly bleak and banal, and as a consequence of this one-sidedness such depictions elicited attacks from both the SLAVOPHILES and the far right. Stylistically, however, one finds an inappropriate prevalence of grotesquery, humor, paradoxical hyperbole, metaphors and comparisons connecting main characters with animals and material objects, nonsense speech, a propensity for insignificant gestures and facial expressions, composition deliberately made uneven by frequent digressions, a mixture of styles, and the accumulation and emphasis of unimportant details, all largely the result of Gogolian SKAZ.

Belinsky's ardent defense of the natural school occasioned a considerable body of what could be termed "populist utilitarian" literature which, in keeping with his view of Russian reality, dealt with the most vital problems of life, accentuating the negative and im-

294

plying the need for change. Always opposed to romantic escapism, Belinsky held that true works of art such as *Dead Souls* do not contradict history but embody an idea which reflects the spirit of the times; and although he maintained that true artists were creators, not copyists, he did in fact champion a number of mediocre writers simply for their straightforward treatment of unadorned Russian life. Thus, while recognizing that authors like Ya. P. BUTKOV (see below) and Grigorovich were not artists, he nevertheless praised them as having "talent for" the physiological sketch.

One of the most important artistic realizations of the natural-school approach was Dostoevsky's *Poor Folk*, a work praised enthusiastically by Belinsky even before it appeared in 1846. *Poor Folk* offered almost all the features of the new school in style and composition. Indeed, Dostoevsky appears to have carefully planned *Poor Folk* from the beginning for submission to *Otechestvennye zapiski*, and consciously fashioned it in accordance with Belinsky's requirements. It is particularly significant as a work which, while meeting the thematic exigencies of the natural school, transcended the description of externals typical of the physiological sketch, avoided the Gogolian "view from above," and gave the reader a sense of new inner identification with the humiliated sensibility. For Belinsky, the publication of *Poor Folk* was an event of considerable magnitude as a model of the new orientation he so enthusiastically championed. It should be noted, however, that Dostoevsky never became as devoted to natural school poetics as Belinsky imagined.

After the publication of the *Physiology* in 1845, a number of authors associated with the natural school outgrew the "natural" style and made the transition to REALISM without Gogol's distinctive banter and stylistic devices. Many writers turned to realism within three or four years after they had contributed to the physiological anthologies. This is particularly evident in Turgenev's development in the later installments of *Zapiski okhotnika* (1847–52). One should not confuse the natural school with the NATURALISM that later evolved as a part of realism. The naturalism of the natural school comes nearer being unnatural; that is, it is a caricature of reality, a quality which the writers themselves sensed and for which they strove.

The work of Ya. P. Butkov, especially *Petersburg Heights* (Petersburgskie vershiny, 1845) has been described as a significant link between the work of Gogol and Dostoevsky. Appearing in the reactionary camp's *Severnaya Pchela*, *Petersburg Heights* was accompanied by Bulgarin's claim that the work was untainted by Gogolian caricature. In fact, some features associated with the natural school were so much a part of contemporary literature that even the reactionary Bulgarin and O. I. SENKOVSKY, (who wrote under the name of Baron Brambeus) indulged in prosaic descriptions and a general lowering of genre superficially similar to that which they attacked in the work of Gogol and his followers. Their understanding of "nature" and social reality was, however, markedly different from that of Gogol.

Other writers whose works were associated with the school were I. A. GONCHAROV, I. T. KOKOREV, the Ukrainian P. A. KULISH, A. I. LEVITOV, N. F. PAVLOV, A. N. PLESHCHEEV, F. M. RESHETNIKOV, V. A. SOLLOGUB, and N. K. USPENSKY.

Secondary literature: A. Beletskii, "Dostoevskii i natural'naya shkola v 1846 g.", *Nauka na Ukraine*, 1922, no. 4. V. G. Belinskii, "Fiziologiya Peterburga. Chast' pervaya," "Fiziologiya Peterburga. Chast' vtoraya," "Peterburgskie vershiny," "Petersburgskii sbornik," *PSS*, vol. 9 (1955), pp. 47–55, 214–21, 354–61, 543–81; "Vzglyad na russkuyu literaturu 1846 goda" and "Vzglyad na russkuyu literaturu 1847 goda," *PSS*, vol. 10 (1956), pp. 7–50, 279–359. A. Belkin, "Nekrasov i natural'naya shkola." In *Tvorchestvo Nekrasova*. 1939. Joseph Frank, *Dostoevsky: The Seeds of Revolt*. 1976. K. Harper, "Criticism of the Natural School in the 1840s," *SlavR*, 1956. Peter Hodgson, "Reluctant Naturalism." In his *From Gogol to Dostoevsky*. 1976. Pp. 37–72. V. I. Kuleshov, *Natural'naya shkola v russkoi literature XIX v.* 1965. N. I. Mordovchenko, "Belinskii v bor'be za natural'nuyu shkolu," *Literaturnoe nasledstvo*, 1948. Victor Terras, *The Young Dostoevsky*. 1969. ———, *Belinsky and Russian Literary Criticism*. 1974. V. V. Vinogradov, *Etyudy o stile Gogolya*. 1926. ———, *Evolyutsiya russkogo naturalizma*. 1929.

J. S.

Naturalism has had a more concrete existence in Russian literary practice than in literary theory. To be sure, in the 1840s Vissarion BELINSKY employed the phrase "NATURAL SCHOOL," but by that he designated authors who described the life of the common people in a straightforward manner emphasizing the need for social reform, writers we would call realists.

When the scientific worldview rose to dominance over the Russian mind in the 1860s, writers sought to reproduce reality in totally objective, or "scientific," ways. Writers like Vasily SLEPTSOV created whole dialogues which almost seem to have been recorded from an actual conversation. Other radical writers—in addition to concentrating their attention on individuals at the bottom of the social scale—took an interest in physiology and medicine, which they transferred to literature: they wished to describe the most unpleasant aspects of reality, as though they would equate literature with descriptions of repulsive diseases in a medical textbook. For example, in Nikolai USPENSKY's story "Rural Pharmacy" (Sel'skaya apteka), a doctor of uncertain qualifications acutely embarrasses a lady of gentle birth by striking up a conversation about pus: "I tell you that this pus stuff is a very important thing: in medicine we even define its taste."

Until Emile Zola published his theories on naturalism and the experimental novel in the early 1880s, naturalism in Russian literature designated primarily a lapse of taste in the lower reaches of realism; it was not a term for a theoretical movement. Modern Soviet literary theoreticians of SOCIALIST REALISM see in naturalism an aberration of the bourgeois mentality, and condemn it wherever it appears.

C. A. M.

Nazhívin, Iván Fyódorovich (1874–1940), prose writer. Born in Moscow, the son of a peasant timber merchant, Nazhivin began publishing collections of stories and sketches at the turn of the century: *Native scenes* (Rodnye kartinki, 1900), *Impoverished Russia* (Ubogaya Rus', 1901), *Before Dawn* (Pered rassvetom, 1902), *Cheap People* (Deshevye lyudi, 1903), *Amid the Graves* (Sredi mogil, 1903), *At the Doors of Life* (U dverei zhizni, 1904), and *In an Insane Asylum* (V sumasshedshem dome, 1905). His first novel, *Menè … Tèkel … Fares* (1907), depicted Russia and Europe on the eve of the Russo-Japanese War. Deeply influenced by the ethical teachings of TOLSTOI, Nazhivin wrote *My Confession* (Moya ispoved', 1912) and the biographical works, *From the Life of L. N. Tolstoi* (Iz zhizni L. N. Tolstogo, 1911) and *The Burning Bush: Tolstoi's Soul* (Neopalimaya kupina: dusha Tolstogo, 1936).

Having emigrated in 1920, Nazhivin penned numerous historical novels frequently characterized by an original point of view, of which the most famous were *Rasputin* (1923), *The Dogs* (Sobach'ya respublika, 1935), in which the events of World War I and the Revolution, featuring Lenin and the rise of the obsequious flunkey Peter to a revolutionary idol, are perceived and depicted from a dog's point of view, and *The Gospel according to Thomas* (Evangelie ot Fomy, 1935), where Christ is depicted objectively as a Messiah without miracles. The Revolution and Nazhivin's life in emigration inspired a series of memoirs: *Notes on the Revolution* (Zapiski o revolyutsii, 1921), *Amid Darkened Lighthouses* (Sredi potukhshikh mayakov, 1922), *The Intimate* (Intimnoe, 1922), and *On the Eve* (Nakanune, 1923). Nazhivin's thirty novels and some twenty collections rank him among the most prolific Russian writers in emigration. Nazhivin died in Brussels.

Works: Sobranie sochinenii. Vols. 1, 4–8. 1911–17. *'Ekleziast' i drugie rasskazy.* 1918. *Stepan Razin.* 1924. *Kazaki.* 1928. *Bes, tvoryashchii mechtu: roman iz vremen Batyya.* 1929. *Vo dni Pushkina.* 1930. *Bol'shevichka.* 1931. *Kreml', khronika XV–XVI vv.* 1931. *Iudei.* 1933. *Lilii Antinoya.* 1933. *Sofisty.* 1935. *Rastsvetshii v nochi lotus.* 1935. *Ostrov blazhennykh.* 1936. *Muzhiki.* 1937. *Molodezh.* 1938. *Nad Volgoi.* 1938.

Translations: Rasputin. Trans. C. Hogarth. New York, 1929. *A Certain Jesus: The Gospel According to Thomas. An Historical Novel of the First Century.* Trans. E. Burns. London, 1930. *The Dogs.* London and Philadelphia, 1931.

Secondary Literature: I. Nazhivin, "O sebe," *Novaya russkaya kniga*, no. 5 (1922), pp. 42–43. V. Polonskii, *Ukhodyashchaya Rus'*. 1924. Pp. 56–84.

Bibliography: Foster, pp. 802–05.

A. M. S.

Nekrásov, Nikolaí Alekséevich (1821–78), poet, writer, and publisher, is regarded as the leading representative of the "realist school" in Russian poetry. He was born on a country estate northeast of Moscow. His father was Russian, but his mother (as most biographers now admit) was Polish. It was she who awakened in young Nikolai an avid interest in poetry, and it was from her that he acquired compassion for the Russian peasant, whose hard life he later depicted in his poems. After graduating from a local secondary school, young Nekrasov went to St. Petersburg, where, in open defiance of his father's wishes, he sought admission to the university. Owing to his father's refusal to help him financially, Nekrasov had to wage an incessant battle against poverty and starvation while trying to eke out a meager subsistence through hackwriting and part-time tutoring. The adverse circumstances of his initial stay in St. Petersburg delayed the full development of his poetic talent. His first collection of romantic poems, published in 1840, evoked a negative reaction from contemporary Russian literary critics, among whom the most important was BELINSKY.

In 1842 Nekrasov became a book reviewer for OTECHESTVENNYE ZAPISKI. His reviews made a favorable impression on Belinsky, who eventually came to like the young author. He encouraged Nekrasov to continue writing poetry but insisted that he choose his themes from contemporary Russian social and political reality. As a result, in 1844 Nekrasov wrote his first "civic" poems, in which he expressed his concern for the Russian peasant's lot ("On the Road") and his repugnance at being a Russian landowner ("Homeland"). Both poems were subsequently published in the *Otechestvennye zapiski*.

In 1846 Nekrasov, together with some friends, purchased the journal SOVREMENNIK, founded by PUSHKIN in 1836, and became its co-owner and chief editor. Under his editorship, SOVREMENNIK became Russia's leading literary journal, publishing works by DOSTOEVSKY, TOLSTOI, TURGENEV, Belinsky, CHERNYSHEVSKY, and DOBROLYUBOV, as well as by Nekrasov himself. His concern for the Russian peasant was reflected in a number of poems published in his journal during the years 1846–1866. The most representative of these are "The Unreaped Row" (1854), "Vlas" (1854), "A Forgotten Village" (1855), and "On the Volga" (1860). *The Peddlers* (1861) is regarded by many critics as most illustrative of his ability to compose poetry in the spirit and style of Russian folklore; it may also be regarded as a prime example of Nekrasov's skill in re-creating the rhythm and style of Russian folksong. This fairly long poem is really a series of shorter poems about traveling peasant vendors. Another long poem about the peasantry is *Red-Nose Frost* (1863), in which Nekrasov presents Russian peasant life in its diverse aspects, with poignant realism as well as lyricism. It is significant that many of these poems were written and published in the years following the abolition of serfdom in 1861. Evidently, Nekrasov did not believe in social change by decree. He continued to call attention to the peasant's plight, in poems like "Orina, a Soldier's Mother" (1863), "The Railroad" (1864), and others. The latter poem, telling of the misery of peasant laborers employed on railroad construction in Russia, angered the authorities. In 1866 *Sovremennik* was suspended indefinitely, after twenty years of publication under Nekrasov's editorship.

However, in 1867 Nekrasov succeeded in acquiring *Otechestvennye zapiski* and became its editor-in-chief. The burden of his editorial duties and wearisome dealings with government censors did not prevent him from writing and publishing a number of outstanding works. Foremost among them is his longest poem about the peasantry, *Who is Happy in Russia?*, begun in 1863 and nearly completed by the time of the poet's death in 1878. Conceived as a poetic encyclopedia of Russian peasant life in the period following the abolition of serfdom, it is actually a folktale narrating the odyssey of seven Russian peasants who wander the length and breadth of Russia in a fruitless search for a happy man. But *Who is Happy in Russia?* is more than just a peasant travelogue similar to *The Peddlers*; it is a dynamic and colorful picture of the Russian peasantry in the years 1863 to 1876. In addition to the narrative poetry of the kind just mentioned, Nekrasov's lyric poems increased notably in quantity during the 1874 to 1877 period. The lyrical note was particularly strong in his last collection of poems, entitled *Last Songs* (Poslednie pesni) and published in 1877. It sounded loud and clear in a poem addressed to his "Muse of vengeance and grief" (Muza mesti i pechali) but meant for the Russian people.

Nekrasov died in early 1878. At his funeral, he was compared in a eulogy by Dostoevsky to his great predecessors, Pushkin and LERMONTOV.

Nekrasov has been called by some Russian critics "a poet of grief and anger" (*poet pechali i gneva*), because of his preoccupation with his country's social ills bred by the age-old system of serfdom. His poetry not only provides the key to the understanding of his complex personality but also reflects all the important political and social changes which occurred in Russia between 1845 and 1875.

He wrote under conditions that were vastly different from those prevailing during the lifetime of Pushkin and Lermontov. In the early 1840s Belinsky admonished all Russian writers, including poets, to use their art for the betterment of Russian society; in the 1850s Chernyshevsky's negation of all spiritual values sounded a death knell for the poetry of eclectics like FET; in the 1860s Dobrolyubov and PISAREV refused to recognize poetry except as a medium for revolutionary propaganda. Nekrasov, although he did not subscribe to all the views of the Russian POPULISTS (*narodniki*), felt a moral obligation to speak for the Russian peasant, whose misery he knew and sympathized with. His lifelong interest in peasant life and problems continued until his very death.

The best of Nekrasov's poems are those in which he expresses either his love for his Polish-born mother or his compassion for the long-suffering Russian peasant. Judged solely on its artistic merits, there is little doubt that his best poems were written between 1860 and 1865. An example is his lyric poem "A Knight for an Hour" (1860), in which Nekrasov combined his idealization of his mother with an expression of his feeling of failure and his fear of death. As for the period between 1865 and 1877, *Who is Happy in Russia?* stands out among the otherwise rather mediocre production of his waning years as a monument to his poetic genius. In his *Last Songs* there are two remarkable lyric poems, "Excerpts from the Poem *Mother*" and "Lullaby." In the closing stanza of "Lullaby", the image of his mother seems to assume superhuman proportions, that of "Mother Russia," who brings a final message of comfort and hope to her loving son.

In our present-day assessment of Nekrasov it is well to keep in mind that he was, first and foremost, a lyrical poet singing his feelings. The best among his poems are the subjective ones, in which he suffers with others or accuses contemporary Russian society both directly and by implication. Here belong many of his poems written in the years 1845 to 1865: "On the Road," "Homeland," "On the Volga," *The Peddlers* and *Red-Nose Frost*. His poetic preoccupation with the Russian peasant is evident in all of them, reaching its apogee in his long narrative poem *Who is Happy in Russia?* But there is another group of poems, just as subjective and lyrical, addressed to his mother, to whom he devoted his personal lyrics, "A Knight for an Hour," "Excerpts from the Poem *Mother*," and "Lullaby." Genuineness of feeling transmuted into lyrical singing, sometimes rough-hewn in form but often exquisite, characterizes Nekrasov's best poems.

Nekrasov did not succeed in creating a school of his own: no "peasant" poets came in his wake. But he, more than any other Russian poet, made his contemporaries aware of the existence of the peasant and his problems. Truly, he did point out the evils of serfdom prior to 1861 and the shortcomings of the Emancipation after 1861; but he rendered his most valuable service to Russian literature by the artistry with which he did it. Few poets could sing of the beauty of the Russian countryside as Nekrasov did. Few knew as much as he about the Russian peasant. Still fewer could express the truth as artistically and as powerfully.

It would be idle to deny Nekrasov's greatness despite his occasional failures as a writer and publisher. His imaginative perception, his complete artistic individuality, his poetic inspiration, and the folksong-like melody of many of his poems, were the traits which made his poetry so refreshingly different from that of the eclectics like Fet and others.

A. F. KONI, a personal friend of the poet, commented in his reminiscences of him: "The poetic and moral values that Nekrasov gave to Russian society are so great that they should obliterate all his defects." This, of course, is not an objective statement. However, objectivity in judging Nekrasov's contribution to Russian poetry was precisely what his contemporaries lacked. His poems, with their stark realism of detail, new rhythms, and unvarnished earthy language, shocked many of his contemporaries who equated poetry with the classical elegance of Pushkin and Lermontov, and his theme of "vengeance and grief" seemed shocking to them. The controversy about the poet's greatness lasted through the first decade of the 20th century, when it was finally settled in his favor by the formalists, who pointed out that Nekrasov was an accomplished artist and a bold innovator in addition to being a continuator of the great traditions of Russian poetry.

Writing in an age of prose, Nekrasov faced a dilemma that neither Pushkin nor Lermontov had faced: how to prevent his "civic conscience" from affecting his poetic integrity. He found a way out of this dilemma by giving in his poems an artistic presentation of important social problems of contemporary Russia.

Works: Polnoe sobranie sochinenii i pisem. Ed. V. E. Evgen'ev-Maksimov, A. M. Egolin, and K. I. Chukovskii. 12 vols. 1948–52. *Sobranie sochinenii.* 8 vols. Ed. and comm. K. I. Chukovskii. 1965–67.

Translations: Lewanski, pp. 309–12.

Secondary literature: Sigmund S. Birkenmayer, *Nikolaj Nekrasov: His Life and Poetic Art.* The Hague, 1968. K. Chukovskii, *Masterstvo Nekrasova.* 4th ed. 1962. B. O. Korman, *Lirika N. A. Nekrasova.* 2d rev. ed. 1978. *O Nekrasove: Stat'i i materialy.* 4th ed. Yaroslavl', 1975. V. G. Prokshin, *N. A. Nekrasov: Put' k epopee.* 1979. G. Tamarchenko, "Vremya stavit' voprosy (Obzor literatury o Nekrasove)," *VLit* 18 (1974), no. 7, pp. 237–71.

S. S. B.

Nekrásov, Víktor Platónovich (1911–), prose writer, born in Kiev, he received a degree in architecture, worked as an actor, fought at Stalingrad, and after 1945 served as a journalist. His first novel, *In the Trenches of Stalingrad* (1946), won him immediate recognition, the 1947 Stalin Prize, and established him as a writer. Hailed in Russia as the best World War II novel, it is an honest and realistic account from the point of view of field officers and simple soldiers. Party leadership and political indoctrination officers are presented negatively. Nekrasov avoids the norms of SOCIALIST REALISM prescribed for a war novel and shows how "heroic deeds" are committed in an unheroic manner by unheroic individuals. His characters are individualized through their speech which is colorful and colloquial. Written in a realistic manner, his prose is simple, terse and journalistic.

During the 1950s, Nekrasov wrote a number of short stories about the War. In 1959 he successfully protested the plan to build a Park of Culture and Rest on the site of Kiev's infamous Babi Yar. During the 1960s, he traveled through Europe and the United States, published the novella *Kira Georgievna* (1961), books on travel, and reminiscences. He also wrote commentaries on art, architecture, film, and literature. His 1965 war story, *It Happened at Mamai Mound,* circulated in SAMIZDAT. He was severely attacked by officialdom and praised by readers for the honesty in his works. These include *In His Home Town* (1954), which deals realistically with the problem of a soldier returning home from the front; *Kira Georgievna* (1961), which also deals with the theme of "return," but this time from a Stalinist concentration camp (it also focuses on the subject of art and creativity), and *Both Sides of the Ocean* (1962), which portrays the United States in a positive and objective manner, an unusual perspective for a Soviet writer.

In 1972 Nekrasov was expelled from the Communist Party which he had joined in 1944. In 1974 all of his manuscripts (including one about Babi Yar) were confiscated, and he was permitted to leave the Soviet Union. He lives in Paris, where, until recently, he was editor of KONTINENT.

Nekrasov's prose is realistic and straightforward. He is a good prose writer whose works communicate basic honesty and human dignity.

Works: V okopakh Stalingrada. 1947. *V rodnom gorode.* 1955. *Pervoe znakomstvo: Iz zarubezhnykh vpechatlenii.* 1958. *Sudak.* 1960. *Vasya Konakov. Rasskazy.* 1961. *Kira Georgievna.* 1962. *Izbrannye proizvedeniya. Povesti, rasskazy, putevye zametki.* 1962. "Po obe storony okeana," *Novyi mir,* 1962, no. 11. "Novichok. Tsar'-ryba. Iz Kasablanki v Darnitsu," *Novyi mir,* 1963, no. 11. *Na kryl'yakh pobedy.* Khabarovsk, 1963. *Vtoraya noch'. Rasskazy.* 1965. *V zadannom raione.* Khabarovsk, 1965. "Sluchai na Mamae-

vom Kurgane," *Novyi mir,* 1965, no. 12. *Puteshestviya v raznykh izmereniyakh.* 1967. "Dedushka i vnuchek," *Novyi mir,* 1968, no. 9. "O vul'kanakh, otshel'nikakh i prochem," *Grani* 74 (1970). *V zhizni i v pis'makh.* 1971. *Zapiski zevaki.* Frankfurt, 1976.

Translations: Kira Georgievna. New York, 1962. *Front-line Stalingrad.* London, 1962, 1970. *The Third Flare; Three War Stories.* Moscow, 1963. *Both Sides of the Ocean.* London and New York, 1964. *The White Guard.* London, 1971.

Secondary literature: Yu. Bondarev, "Molodost' chuvstv," *Literaturnaya gazeta,* 17 June 1961. Deming Brown, *Soviet Literature since Stalin.* 1978. Pp. 173–75. E. J. Brown, *Russian Literature since the Revolution.* 1982. P. 387. V. Bykov, "Byt' dostoinym nashego chitatelya," *Novyi mir,* 1963, no. 11. L. Plotkin, *Literatura o voine.* 1967. A. P. Reilly, *America in Contemporary Soviet Literature.* New York, 1971. M. Shcheglov, *Literaturnaya kritika.* 1971. K. Simonov, "V nogu s vremenem," *Literaturnaya gazeta,* 26 April 1955. G. Svirski, *A History of Post-War Soviet Writing: The Literature of Moral Opposition.* Ann Arbor, 1981.

H. S.

Nelédinsky-Melétsky, Yúry Aleksándrovich (1752–1828), poet, served in the Army (1770–85) and subsequently held important posts in the civil service. He began to write poetry in the 1770s and published his verses in various journals of the KARAMZIN school, such as *Moskovskii zhurnal, Aonidy,* and *Vestnik Evropy.* Neledinsky-Meletsky was at his best in the more intimate lyric genres of the epistle (*poslanie*) and the song (*pesnya*). In his songs he successfully introduced elements of folk poetry. Neledinsky-Meletsky also translated French poetry. Though later forgotten, Neledinsky-Meletsky was well respected by his contemporaries and some of his songs, for example, "When I walk down to the river" (Vyidu ya na rechen'ku, 1796), were popular at one time.

Works: Stikhotvoreniya. 1876. *Polnoe sobranie stikhotvorenii.* In *Russkaya poeziya.* Ed. S. A. Vengerov. Vol. 7 (1901). Selection in *Poety XVIII v.* Vol. 2. 1958.

Translations: Lewanski, p. 312.

Secondary literature: L. I. Kulakova, "Neledinskii-Meletskii." In *Istoriya russkoi literatury.* Vol. 4, pt. 2. 1947. P. A. Vyazemskii, "Yu. A. Neledinskii-Meletskii." In his *Polnoe sobranie sochinenii,* Vol. 7 (1879).

V. T.

Nemiróvich-Dánchenko, Vasíly Ivánovich (1844 or 1845–1936), journalist and writer, brother of Vladímir NEMIROVICH-DANCHENKO. From a military family and educated in the Corps of Cadets, Nemirovich-Danchenko won early fame as a war correspondent in the Russian-Turkish War of 1877–78. He was equally successful reporting on the Russian-Japanese War of 1904–05 and World War I. Nemirovich-Danchenko emigrated after the Revolution and died in Prague. A phenomenally prolific writer, Nemirovich-Danchenko published some 250 books: novels (war as well as social), short stories, poetry, travel notes, ethnographic sketches, memoirs, etc. Nemirovich-Danchenko's fiction reflects his journalistic base. It features vivid descriptions and lively action, but tends toward the predictable, melodrama, and superficial psychological motivation.

Works: Sobranie sochinenii. 18 vols. 1910–15. *Novoe sobranie sochinenii.* 1916.

Translations: Lewanski, p. 312.

V. T.

Nemiróvich-Dánchenko, Vladímir Ivánovich (1858–1943), cofounder with Konstantin STANISLAVSKY of the Moscow Art Theater, theater director, teacher, and playwright, early recognized the merit of Anton CHEKHOV's play *The Sea Gull,* and as professor at the drama school of the Moscow Philharmonia, communicated enthusiasm for it to his students of the 1890s. He took the two gold medalists of his graduating class, Vsevolod MEYERHOLD and Olga Knipper, to play Treplyov and Arkadina in the first successful production of Chekhov's play, which launched the Moscow Art Theater in 1898. As the theater's dramaturg, he produced the early work of Maksim GORKY and the remaining major plays of Chekhov by the end of the first half-decade of this century. But he chose less well his own pale play, *In dreams* (V mechtakh, 1901), for performance and those of merely fashionable authors, Leonid ANDREEV and Semyon Yushkevich. He proved conservative in directing classics of the Russian repertory and in persisting in the theater's realistic tendency.

An important production of the music studio he organized in 1919, called after 1926 the Nemirovich-Danchenko Musical Theater, was Dmitry Shostakovich's *Lady Macbeth of Mtsensk District* (Katerina Izmailova, 1934).

Works: My Life in the Russian Theatre. Trans. John Cournos. 1936.   M. H.

Neoclassicism. The impulse to modernize and secularize Russian culture, so aggressively promoted by Peter the Great, found particular expression among that nation's writers during the neoclassical period. Working without benefit of the lengthy process through which aesthetic standards first articulated in the Renaissance had evolved in Europe, they were confronted with the necessity of devising modes for communicating a whole spectrum of sentiment alien to a medieval Church-dominated society. Not surprisingly, they responded by accepting the example of writers and critics with whom they had become familiar in the course of their exposure to European culture. In the case of those privileged to attend foreign universities, the influence of particular trends in artistic thought and practice was especially marked. Upon their return, such Russian writers added in idiosyncratic manner to a pattern dominated but not totally determined by neoclassical standards.

Given the particular status of French as the language of educated Russian society, the impact of prevailing aesthetic notions in that culture is understandable. Boileau's *Art poétique* (1674) offered a succinct statement of neoclassical doctrine and repeatedly served as the theoretical benchmark for Russia's poets. In addition to characterizing both major and minor poetic genres, Boileau dealt with the fundamental attributes of artistic creation. Throughout, his stress was upon the participation of judgement and discrimination in the writing process but he also insisted upon the requisites of poetic inspiration and genius. His recommendations concerning style had particular implications for the development of Russian verse: "Soyez simple avec art / Sublime san orgueil, agréable sans fard."

While Boileau's representation of neoclassical canon gained wide acceptance in Russia, that did not prevent even those schooled in his thought from imposing other, seemingly disparate practices upon that base. The *préciosité*, to which Boileau's insistence upon clarity and common sense was a reaction, held its own appeal for Francophiles. Mikhail LOMONOSOV's aesthetic preferences further indicate the degree to which individuals might deviate from the norm. Educated as a scientist and thus attuned to the Age of Reason, he published a grammar and contributed to the further definition of the literary language. Yet influenced by his exposure to the anachronistic practice of the German baroque, he made one of neoclassicism's established genres, the solemn ODE, the vehicle for rhetorically charged and deliberately complex expressions of patriotic zeal.

Augustan England's writers also contributed to the complexion of Russian neoclassicism, particularly after mid-century. The moral didacticism of Addison and Steele's satirical journals struck a responsive note, giving rise to analogous publications in the 1770s. Deistic philosophical concepts, especially as represented in Alexander Pope's *Essay on Man*, enjoyed considerable popularity and prompted several attempts, such as Vasily TREDIAKOVSKY's *Feoptiya*, to reconfirm the divine order of things, using scientific rather than religious truths.

Original aesthetic theorizing did not figure prominently in the work of the Russian neoclassicists. Accepting the ultimate authority of the ancients, they reiterated those tenets which had been elaborated by successive generations of critics and writers in post-Renaissance Europe. Feofan PROKOPOVICH's lectures at the KIEV ACADEMY, "De arte poetica" (1705) and "De arte rhetorica" (1706–07) represent an early attempt to familiarize students with the conventions governing verbal art. The poet's obligation to follow the example of the Greek and Roman writers (although Prokopovich frequently cited Tasso as a model), the inseparable linkage of the pleasing with the useful (*dulce et utile*), and the desirability of a clear but eloquent style all attest to Prokopovich's basically neoclassical conception of artistic form and function. His lectures on rhetoric deserve particular mention for their anticipation of Lomonosov's hierarchy of stylistic levels, each associated with particular poetic genres.

Although Prokopovich frequently invoked the authority of the

16th-century Italian writer Scaliger for his aesthetic judgements, Boileau became the most common referent and his treatise was repeatedly translated into Russian. Aleksandr SUMAROKOV relied upon the French writer to a considerable degree, his two *Epistles* of 1747 revealing a marked dependency. His advocacy of elegant simplicity, observance of the dramatic unities, and of genre distinctions were sufficiently like the French original to precipitate charges of slavish imitation by his contemporary, Trediakovsky. Given Sumarokov's opposition to the baroque intricacies of Lomonosov's aesthetic credo, it would appear that he sought validation of his own position by close association with established authority. And, although Sumarokov's pronouncements came but a decade before the neoclassical standard began to weaken, the combination of his ideas and practice would have notable impact upon the tone and style of later verse. Moreover, the comparatively strong emphasis which he gave to lesser genres in the neoclassical hierarchy, such as the fable and the song, gave impetus to their development and popularity among authors in the second half of the century.

By contrast to Sumarokov's doctrinaire endorsement of recent French thought, Lomonosov's *Rhetoric* (1744) depended upon the remote and rather obscure authority of a 17th-century Jesuit priest, Nicolas Caussin, for its advocacy of *eloquentia* in support of *doctrina*. As its title suggests, Lomonosov was as much concerned with the emotive oratorical act as he was with the subject matter per se. Although Sumarokov did not deny the participation of feeling and imagination in the composition of verse, the two men differed sharply in their estimates of the contribution made by deliberate stylistic ornamentation. In other respects, however, Lomonosov showed greater affinity for the reasoned temper of the age. His three styles, governing the relationship between genres and lexical levels, were of use in defining the literary language and found acceptance among his contemporaries. Similarly, his enthusiastic use of literature to promote civic virtue coincided with the views of others.

Both metrical and lexical reform occupied Russia's authors during the period and though practice outpaced theory on occasion, several original statements concerning verse reform did appear. As early as 1735, Trediakovsky produced "A New and Brief Method of Composing Russian Verse," in which he recognized word accentuation as the primary determinant of regular metrical patterns. He did not completely abandon the older syllabic conception of versification until 1752 when, with the poetic example of Lomonosov's solemn odes as proof, he was prompted to acknowledge the equal suitability of iambic and trochaic verse in Russian. An article completed in 1755, "On Ancient, Medieval and Modern Russian Verse", further enhanced Trediakovsky's critical stature, being unique among 18th-century literary documents in its assumption of a historical perspective.

Lomonosov's 1739 "Letter on the Rules of Russian Versification" strengthened the case for syllabotonic verse, taking issue with Trediakovsky's earlier restrictions against the iambus, masculine rhyme, and trisyllabic feet. Antiokh KANTEMIR, by contrast, in his "Letter of Khariton Makentin to His Friend on the Composition of Verse" (early 1740s) insisted upon the primacy of the line rather than the foot, although admitting to the usefulness of word stress for improving rhythmic organization of the line. Kantemir's defense of a modified syllabic system placed him in a nominally reactionary position, but his practical success in composing short verse lines with regular rhythm contributed still another dimension to the ultimate shape of Russian verse.

Rather than a unified and relatively static doctrine, Russian neoclassicism embraced a heterogeneous combination of elements which, if sometimes incompatible in the purely aesthetic sense, served individual purposes and escaped the general scrutiny that a more coherent artistic community might have given them. Eclectic in their practice, Russia's 18th-century authors generally showed greater interest in the applicability of particular principles and genres to the resolution of issues provoked by a nascent awareness of national identity. By the end of the century, the neoclassical sensibility had outlived its usefulness, being supplanted by others which more completely satisfied collective cultural expectations.

Despite differences in aesthetic stance, writers during the first half of the century accepted the neoclassical hierarchy of forms with little hesitation; only later did the increasing influence of other literary movements effect a shift in artistic preferences toward the lesser species of verse. Foremost among the genres were the solemn ode, the epic, and the tragedy, all of which, by definition, were concerned with elevated themes of general rather than particular significance. Imitation of both ancient and modern masters being considered highly appropriate, the Russians, beginning with Kantemir, attempted a series of epic poems devoted to Peter the Great and other figures of national importance. Voltaire's *Henriade*, one of the most popular of the contemporary models, celebrated Henry IV and lent legitimacy to the representation of analogous leaders of the Russian state. As late as 1779, Mikhail KHERASKOV, in his *Rossiada*, sought to provide the appropriate account of national accomplishment and character.

Despite its stature and stimulative effect upon European drama, the classical tragedy did not evoke a strong response in Russia. Sumarokov, "Russia's Racine," set an early example, closely following the prescribed dramatic structure although altering the traditional cast of characters. His protagonists, of appropriately noble birth and locked in conflict between reason and passion, were fewer in number than in his French models' plays, thereby reducing plot complexity. A similar reduction in the use of confidants prompted Sumarokov to increase the number of monologues, imparting a ponderous quality to the works that contributed to their relatively short-lived popularity. In his choice of themes, he alluded to events from Russia's past without making any attempt at historical accuracy. *Dmitry the Pretender* was perhaps the most significant of his nine tragedies, both because it anticipated Aleksandr Pushkin's *Boris Godunov* thematically and because it reflected the playwright's indebtedness to Shakespeare for specific dramatic effects.

Of Sumarokov's tragedian successors, the most important was Yakov KNYAZHNIN, who made his rather auspicious debut with *Dido* (1769). As was commonly the case with Russian borrowings of classical material, Vergil's epic was not a direct source but had been filtered through the dramas of two 18th-century French authors. Yet in his depiction of the principal's passions, Knyazhnin recaptured something of the original; in general, the author's attraction to SEN-TIMENTALISM prompted him to give greater emphasis to the characters' emotional experience than strict observance of neoclassicist rules would have dictated. Open violation of the tragedy's conventions made *The Clemency of Titus* (1778) the most significant of Knyazhnin's contributions to the structural evolution of Russian drama. With respect to theme, however, his *Vadim of Novgorod* (1789) must be so recognized despite the fact that it reverts almost totally to neoclassical conventions of form. Regarded by Catherine as dangerously anti-monarchical, the play in fact depicts the seemingly insoluble conflict between freedom and the necessary authority of the ruler. These were issues repeatedly addressed by a score of the age's more enlightened authors in various genres and Knyazhnin's particular interpretation places him among that liberal group.

Equally elevated and of greater consequence to the development of Russian verse was the solemn ode. Trediakovsky may be credited with the formal introduction of the genre for, in 1735, he composed his "Triumphal Ode on the Capture of the City of Gdansk" in syllabic verse, the immediate inspiration for which was Boileau's "Ode sur la prise de Namur," but which ultimately traced back to Pindar and Horace. Yet it was Lomonosov's 1739 "Ode on the Capture of Khotin" which demonstrated the suitability of iambic verse to Russian and established the genre's place in that literature. The ode was marked by the rhetorical embellishments peculiar to its author's aesthetic convictions but, in its grandly abstract treatment of the military triumph, it was typical of its kind. A total of seventeen works, addressed to five different rulers, provide the basis for Lomonosov's reputation and initiated a literary practice that would extend into the early 19th century.

Consonant with his view of the poet as civic spokesman, Lomonosov devoted the majority of his odes to themes of national consequence, including the coronation and anniversaries of rulers, Peter the Great's particular accomplishments, and the importance of science to the country's well-being. Although the extravagant images and language of these odes lends a bombastic quality to them, there are several in which the union of elevated style and subject is more felicitous. His two "Meditations," celebrations of divine omnipotence with the aid of spectacular evidence drawn from the realm of scientific observation and speculation, aptly capture the several elements of Lomonosov's artistic impulse in a harmonious whole. Depictions of the sun's fiery surface and the cold splendor of the aurora borealis help to evoke that sublime sentiment which was the response sought by odists of the period.

Among Lomonosov's contemporaries there was greater disagreement over the style than the subject matter appropriate to the solemn ode. Consonant with his own convictions, Sumarokov criticized what he regarded to be unnecessary complexities in his compatriot's work and his "Nonsense Odes" deliberately parodied Lomonosov's style. At least in theory, Sumarokov argued for simpler, more direct expression of the odist's inspiration. Epigones, including Vasily PETROV, continued the association of rhetorical excess with the solemn ode, trivializing the genre by extolling events as inconsequential as an equestrian tournament staged for the entertainment of Catherine the Great. Increasingly subject to parody because of such inept application, the ode still retained an appeal by virtue of its traditional rank.

It was rescued from being totally discredited by imaginative reformulation in Gavriil DERZHAVIN's practice and thus modified, formed the base for some of the century's best formal verse. After a decade's apprenticeship in the Lomonosovian tradition, Derzhavin declared his independence in 1779, doubtlessly influenced by the growing influence of sentimentalism and a more lyric trend in verse. The odes that he published over the next dozen years collectively reflect the diversity of sources available to the Russian writer at that point. Of his major works, the religious ode "God" (1784) clearly follows Lomonosov's example in structure and, to a degree, in style. Its primary distinction, forcefully stated in the poem's latter half, lies in its positive assessment of man's place in the "great chain of being." While the theme had been common enough for several centuries, Derzhavin's particular phrasing is compelling evidence of a rational, secular perspective on life.

Greater originality is evident in the series of odes which Derzhavin dedicated to Catherine. The panegyric purpose is realized in completely unconventional manner. Using a conversational middle style distinctly unlike that prescribed by Lomonosov, the author of "Felitsa" (1782) contrasts his and other courtiers' indulgent, pampered lives with the monarch's purposeful, efficient rule. A late example of Derzhavin's innovative use of odic tradition appears in "The Waterfall" (1791–94) in which realistic nature imagery combines with Ossianic atmosphere as background for a meditation on the transient nature of human fame. Despite Derzhavin's successes, the solemn ode did not provide further inspiration for his younger contemporaries who were given increasingly to the expression of intimate personal thought rather than to broad civic statement.

Neoclassical canon did provide a place for poetic genres other than the epic and the solemn ode. Less thoroughly imbued with literary tradition than their European counterparts, the Russians responded quickly to those alternatives, as a consequence of which several minor species of verse enjoyed considerable popularity. The anacreontic, devoted to celebrations of earthly pleasure, attracted early attention and was redirected to a number of unexpected purposes. From Kantemir's unpublished translation of the *Anacreontea* in the 1730s to Nikolai Lvov's 1794 rendition, there was continuing interest in conveying the sense and spirit of the original Greek works to a Russian audience. In addition to numerous imitations, however, authors sought to subvert the genre to more serious purposes. In his programmatic "Conversation with Anacreon" (1758–61), for example, Lomonosov captured the light, dancing mood of the traditional meter while condemning its frivolous themes, urging that they be replaced with more serious paeans to national heroes. In contrast to this overly zealous application of civic design, Kheraskov appropriated the anacreontic meter for the equally incongruous contemplation of abstract moral qualities and the vanity of human pursuits, all inspired by the author's Masonic convictions. Still another adaptation of the anacreontic occurred in Derzhavin's 1779 occasional verse "On the Birth of a Royal Son in the North," where the poet makes an early, flawed effort to revitalize the panegyric by combining its themes with the imagery and metrical qualities characteristic of the lesser genre.

One of the genres recommended by Sumarokov for the simplicity of its expression was the song. Although none of his own was published during his lifetime, he composed more than 100 original examples of that sort. While typical expressions of neoclassical concern for the general rather than the individual, their focus on emotional experience still places them on a different plane than the impersonal declarations of civic pride and public virtue contained in the ode. Full development of the literary song's potential would not come until a transitional generation, more accepting of private feeling as the proper material for verse, appeared toward the end of the century. In the case of Mikhail POPOV, a follower of Sumarokov, however, there were early indications of an interest in combining folk materials with the literary. He excelled in the simple expression of conventional sentiment and, in two of his songs, experimented with the imitation of popular verse structure.

Another of Sumarokov's followers, Aleksei RZHEVSKY, cultivated the elegy, a genre which, by definition, had to do with the emotional expression of anguish and loss. Consistent with the age's tendency, it also was characterized by a basically impersonal poetic stance and Rzhevsky describes ostensibly personal experience without reference to the specifics of the relationship which might confer a sense of immediately felt grief. As in the case of the song, those receptive to the aesthetics of sentimentalism gradually introduced truly subjective elements into their verse. Mikhail MURAVYOV's "New Lyrical Experiments" (1776), include several laments in which he mourns the passage of youth, lack of poetic inspiration and the general emptiness of life. There is no question but that these sentiments retain much of the traditional elegy's rhetorical posture, yet an occasional glimpse of the individual artist is evident. Fuller accommodation of the neoclassical tradition to lyric verse may be found in Derzhavin's 1794 "On the Death of Katerina Yakovlevna". Combining the meter of folk verse with imagery and sentiments drawn from more formal literature, the poet gives clear testament to the depths of his personal loss.

Of signal importance, both to the specific definition of Russian neoclassicism and to the more general outline of modern Russian literature, was satire's emergence as a major genre. Well founded in the Latin verse of Horace and Juvenal, it subsequently appeared in a variety of poetic and prose forms. Kantemir, whose residence in England and France gave him a sound knowledge of both cultures, was instrumental in establishing satire as a serious vehicle for social commentary. His early translations of several of Boileau's satires were quickly followed by original works in a similar vein. The first, "On the Detractors of Learning. To My Mind" (1729), was, as its title implies, an expression of confidence in the fruits of enlightenment and an attack upon ignorance as both a social and political evil. As in the other eight satires which he would write during the next decade, Kantemir was concerned with the immediate problems of Russian society which he depicted in a relatively simple and direct manner. While the didactic motivation was one shared with his European models, he departed from most of them in the pointedness of his commentary. The substance of his remarks was sufficient to prevent publication of the satires during Kantemir's lifetime but their widespread circulation in manuscripts insured their impact upon other writers of the period.

Several authors were to follow Kantemir's example quite faithfully, producing verse devoted to the condemnation of particular vices. Toward the end of his career, Sumarokov reaffirmed the commitment to biting satire of the Juvenalian sort, choosing as the object of his attack the Russian nobility. Frontal assault upon entrenched interests of the autocracy could be a hazardous enterprise, however, and the Russian satirist resorted frequently to a variety of Aesopian devices in his commentary on human foibles. Among the more subtle of these was paraphrase of the Scriptures; Derzhavin's "To Rulers and Judges" (1779) was a reworking of the 81st Psalm and, while more admonition than actual satire, it was prompted by the same enlightened urge to secure social change through artistic commentary. Denis FONVIZIN, who was to distinguish himself as a comic playwright with "The Brigadier" and "The Minor," composed two early verse satires, of which "The Fox as Panegyrist" relies upon the fable's conventions for its indictment of the court of Empress Elizabeth.

The fable proper enjoyed particular popularity and, although Ivan KRYLOV did not demonstrate his unique command of the genre until well after the demise of neoclassicism generally, the intellectual inspiration for his work must be traced to that period. Although

regarded as one of the minor poetic forms, the fable had had several distinguished masters, La Fontaine being the immediate source for virtually all of the Russians. Sumarokov's *pritchi*, a heterogeneous collection of verse tales and anecdotes, included a number modeled after the French fabulist. Uneven in both style and moral explicitness, the actual fables include several with the succinct, direct manner of statement that would figure as a prominent feature of Krylov's style. Ivan KHEMNITSER, whose reputation depends entirely upon his collection *Fables and Tales*, is perhaps the most conventional of the neoclassical fable writers, dealing largely with abstract notions of vice and virtue, eschewing the intrusions of "low style" that sometimes occur in Sumarokov's work and that Krylov used to great advantage, and contenting himself with the stock animal characters inherited from antiquity.

As the culminating expression of its kind, Krylov's fables reflect the interplay of social and aesthetic forces in post-Petrine Russia. Both in his choice of literary vehicles and in his implicit view of the poet as a spokesman for reason and common sense, he proved his identification with 18th-century values. Yet in his sensitive use of colloquial Russian, he satisfied the expectations of the early romantics who, in their discovery of the "folk," advocated a literary language devoid of the arbitrary equations between genre and style that had restrained many of the neoclassicists. Most worthy of note is the fact that Krylov's practice did much to secure the satiric tradition in the national literature, for, if the fable itself was to find only infrequent practitioners, the gently sly Aesopian spirit would infect many writers of subsequent generations.

Verse held undisputed position as the means for expressing serious artistic notions so that the growing popularity of prose after mid-century might be construed as further evidence for the erosion of neoclassical standards. The practice of the Russian satirists indicates the degree to which doctrinal purity was readily sacrificed to immediate artistic and social purposes. That Nikolai NOVIKOV's journals of the 1770s took their inspiration from the coffee houses of England rather than from Greece and Rome presented no philosophical problems. If one compares the themes in such conventional poetic forms as the fable and the satire with those in prose, including the Eastern tale, mock renditions of traditional genres, and epistolary fiction, it is abundantly apparent that all were united by a common commitment to enlightened criticism of existing personal and societal vices. CATHERINE THE GREAT herself placed the stamp of legitimacy on prose satire when, in 1769, she began publication of her own journal *Vsyakaya vsyachina* with a bow of acknowledgment to *The Spectator*. Novikov responded to the imperial invitation to promote social change through well modulated satire by founding the first in a series of journals, TRUTEN'. For a brief period of time, his efforts, together with those of another author and editor, Fyodor EMIN, were tolerated but the pointedness of their attacks was too much for Catherine to tolerate and, in 1774, the last of Novikov's journals were forced to suspend publication. As the name of one of the fictitious correspondents in *Truten'* implies, Novikov's stance was thoroughly in keeping with the enlightened spirit of the age. Pravdulyubov (Truth Lover) is the *raisonneur*, frequently encountered in neoclassical comedy and a constant advocate of the proposition that "a man shows more love of humanity who tries to correct vice than a man who shows indulgence for it." To the degree that prose satire was dominated by such positive moral spokesmen, it adhered to the prescription for general, abstract representation yet the force of satire, as Russia's writers were quick to demonstrate, was best realized through explicit portrayals of the transgressor. The best of 18th-century satirical writing is distinguished by this tendency to dwell on the negative characterization rather than its positive counterpart.

In their efforts to enhance the power of their wit, satirists like Krylov did not shrink from the parodistic use of established genres, celebrating in mock heroic style the dubious talents and accomplishments of their intended victims. If the ultimate purposes of their parodies was instructive, that of some of their contemporaries was increasingly less so. The balance which neoclassicism had originally struck between aesthetic and didactic intention shifted toward the former as writers came to perceive their function in more personal terms. Like those individuals who violated genre boundaries in an effort to restore vitality to civic statement, the parodists realized the insufficiency of rigidly defined forms but their response was to exploit those insufficiencies for the entertainment of an audience that had become more sophisticated in its literary tastes.

Of the genres susceptible to parody, the epic had been frequently exploited, with numerous European examples including Pope's *The Rape of the Lock*. Certain qualities of the two most successful mock epics in Russian, Vasily MAIKOV's *Elisei or Bacchus Enraged* (1771) and Ippolit BOGDANOVICH's *Dushenka* served to distinguish them from the *vers de societé* toward which Western authors tended. Consistent with the growing concern for an identifiably national literature, both authors included detail that marked their verse as distinctly Russian. Maikov, who retained the traditional form, achieved his effect by making a coachman his hero and describing his checkered adventures, interspersed with those of the gods. Russia's rural landscape and populace, rather than the vague outlines of the classical world or the salons of high society provide the setting. Bogdanovich created a sense of separation from established practice by more formal means, his retelling of the Amor and Psyche myth employing a free verse form reminiscent of folk poetry.

If there was a theoretical recognition of sorts for such parody (Sumarokov had included the mock epic among the recognized genres although Boileau had not) by virtue of its relationship to the elevated original, the novel received none. For some thirty years, from the time that Trediakovsky's translation of Tallement's *Voyage à l'isle d'amour* appeared, there were objections to this alien species on formal and substantive grounds. As late as 1759 Sumarokov would dismiss the novel's aimless mass of weavings as being inimical to the neoclassical vision of rational order. Yet it is the case that, beginning with the publication of Emin's *Inconstant Fortune* (1763), narrative prose entered into an uneasy coexistence with the established genres. The literary romance provided the basic material for Emin's early works but despite their concern with love and adventure, they partly conformed to the expectations of their critics, supplying readers with a good account of the political ideas of the Enlightenment. However attractive the texture and appearance of the sugar coating, Emin also offered instruction concerning enlightened rule that seemed intended for Catherine herself. Of all the novels he wrote, *The Letters of Ernest and Doravra* (1766) anticipates literary trends to the greatest degree in its focus on the sensibility of noble lovers. But the fact that Emin abandoned the novel form after its publication must also be noted. His turn to satire in 1769 as editor of the *Adskaya pochta*, one of the journals founded in response to Catherine's call for such writing, might be regarded as an expression of renewed confidence in the forms and themes sanctioned by neoclassicism.

Where Emin faltered, others, most notably Mikhail CHULKOV, persisted in the creation of original fiction. Following an early attempt at a medieval romance, *The Mocker* (1766–68), that indiscriminately combined fact and fantasy, he produced the first picaresque novel in Russia, *The Comely Cook or The Adventures of a Depraved Woman* (1770). As its subtitle suggests, the novel did not excoriate vice so much as it capitalized upon it to provide entertainment for its bourgeois reader. Further evidence of its design for a popular audience is provided by its fairly consistent use of the low narrative style which is only occasionally disrupted by the intrusion of rhetorical flourishes. Viewed in the cultural context of the era, these initial attempts at the novel, so clearly at odds with the persisting but weakening set of neoclassical standards, are a harbinger of a general change in aesthetic values.

Topical comedy had engaged playwrights since the time of Aristophanes and it was natural that the genre should be enlisted by Russian authors in their efforts to correct the vices of their compatriots. With the imprimatur of neoclassical aesthetics to legitimize their practice, they developed a comedy of manners, founded largely upon the example of Molière and his followers, which held considerable popular appeal. Its most accomplished practitioner, Denis Fonvizin, might be regarded from a dual perspective, both as representing the culmination of the 18th century's inclination to prescribe amusing cures for social ills and as preparing the way for the more realistic comedies of the following century.

The distinction was one of degree; from its inception, Russian comedy built upon the twin traditions of the French stage, which directed its barbs against both individual and universal foibles. Ivan

ELAGIN and the group around him were instrumental in shaping the development of comedy. All agreed that, while the works of French authors were appropriate for adaptation, it was essential to the didactic effect that the spectator comprehend objects of ridicule as having a direct relationship to his own society. Vladimir LUKIN, in part responding to what he perceived as the alien nature of Sumarokov's "Harlequins" and "Pasquins," sought to russianize his adaptations more fully although he did not advocate the creation of original comedies. Still adhering to the notion of imitation, as the preferred aesthetic exercise, he simply replaced names and settings to a sufficient extent to evoke a vaguely Russian mood.

Fonvizin also belonged to the Elagin group and it was he who provided the Russian stage with its first truly original comedies. As early as 1764, he was working on what was ultimately to appear as *The Minor* in 1781. The central issue in this draft, education or the lack thereof, was of foremost concern to the leaders of Russian society. Rather than treating his theme in abstract fashion, Fonvizin tied it to unambiguously Russian practice, including the deplorable attitudes of the ignorant landed gentry toward their serfs, and particularly in *The Brigadier* (1769), the Gallomania that prompted uncritical acceptance of equally ignorant foreign tutors. An additional inviting target for the satirist playwright was the widespread corruption in government, with bribery and the capricious administration of the law drawing particular attention. Vasily KAPNIST's scathing attack on judges and lawyers in *Chicanery* (1793) was of such virulence as to delay its performance and publication for some five years.

Even at its most original, however, Russian comedy continued to observe many of the conventions of its French neoclassical models. Positive characters retained their roles and attributes assigned by Molière's successors, with identifiably Russian names and mannerisms being given to the negative and secondary figures. If Fonvizin's Mitrofan was a typical expression of the gentry's indifference to education, his Starodum and Pravdin were direct transplants of the *raisonneur* whose explicit purpose was to impress the spectator with the play's message. (Interestingly, the finished version of *The Minor* featured two such characters although the early draft had but one.)

Entertainment contended more openly with edification in the comic opera. Popov's *Anyuta* (1772) had inspired a number of playwrights with its presentation of peasant dance and song while Knyazhnin's *Misfortune from a Carriage* (1793) depicted the peasant as a sentient being, a result of sentimentalism's influence. The latter's satire of the superstitious gentry confirms its relationship to comedy proper but any claim to serious purpose in the comic opera quickly faded as it was transformed into vaudeville.

While modern Russian literature is commonly dated from the beginning of the 19th century, the concepts and practices upon it of the neoclassical period exerted an appreciable influence upon it. In some instances, renewed interest in the genres and rhetorical style favored by the 18th-century poet confirm that legacy. Yet it is the underlying notion of the artist as enlightened public spokesman, charged with the mission of inspiring his listener to socially virtuous action, that most clearly suggests a conceptual continuity. More than a structured exercise in aesthetics, Russian neoclassicism reflected a convergence of artistic and philosophic convictions upon the cultural issues confronting a young nation and though the formal solutions it offered fell into disuse, something of its spirit remained.

Works: C. L. Drage and W. N. Vickery, eds., *An XVIIIth Century Russian Reader.* 1969. A. V. Kokorev, comp., *Khrestomatiya po russkoi literature XVIII veka.* 1965. G. P. Makogonenko, comp., *Russkaya literatura XVIII veka.* 1970.

Translations: Harold B. Segel, ed. and trans., *The Literature of Eighteenth-Century Russia.* 2 vols. 1967.

Secondary literature: William Edward Brown, *A History of 18th Century Russian Literature.* 1980. A. G. Cross, ed., *Russian Literature in the Age of Catherine the Great.* 1976. J. G. Garrard, ed., *The Eighteenth Century in Russia.* 1973. B. P. Gorodetskii, ed., *Istoriya russkoi poezii v dvukh tomakh.* Vol. 1. 1968. P. R. H.

N.E.P. (New Economic Policy), economic policy practiced by the Soviet government from 1921 to 1928. It made concessions to private enterprise in agriculture, trade, and light industry. It led to a revival of the country's economy, but was deplored by many loyal communists as a sell-out of the ideals of the Revolution. The New Economic Policy came to an end with the launching of Stalin's first Five-Year Plan.

V. T.

Nestor (ca. 1056–after 1113). One of the few known writers in early Kievan literature and the first prestigious authority in the history of two basic Old Russian "genres," namely, HAGIOGRAPHY and chronicle (LETOPISI) writing. For about a century, from the pathbreaking studies of A. L. Schlözer to the critical revision carried out by A. A. SHAKHMATOV, Nestor's name was at the center of the controversy surrounding the origins and textual history of the *Tale of Bygone Years* (Povest' vremennykh let), also called the *Primary Chronicle*. Long considered the author of the *Primary Chronicle*, Nestor is now recognized as the compiler-reviser of a comprehensive edition of the work (ca. 1113). There is no doubt about his authorship of two hagiographic compositions: the *Reading on the Life and Slaying of the Blessed Passion-Sufferers Boris and Gleb* (Chtenie o zhitii i o pogublenii blazhennuyu strastoterptsu Borisa i Gleba) and the *Life of Our Blessed Father Feodosy, Abbot of the Monastery of the Caves* (Zhitie prepodobnogo ottsa nashego Feodosiya igumena pecher'skogo). The style of these two works frequently has been studied in order to determine Nestor's precise contribution to the extant text of the *Primary Chronicle*.

The only direct biographical data we have about Nestor is contained in the *Life of Our Blessed Father Feodosy*. At the end of this work Nestor informs the reader that he gathered his information about Feodosy shortly after the latter's death during the abbacy of Stefan (1074–78). Further details about Nestor's life and literary activity have been indirectly reconstructed by M. D. Prisëlkov on the basis of internal evidence drawn from Nestor's two hagiographic compositions and the *Primary Chronicle*.

Secondary literature: S. A. Bugoslavskii, "K voprosu o kharaktere i ob"eme literaturnoi deyatel'nosti prepodobnogo Nestora," *Izvestiya Otdeleniya russkogo yazyka i slovesnosti imp. Akademii nauk* 19 (1904), nos. 1 & 3. N. Nikol'skii, *Materialy dlya povremennogo spiska russkikh pisatelei i ikh sochinenii (X–XI vv.).* 1906. Pp. 395–434. M. D. Prisëlkov, *Nestor-Letopisets. Opyt istoriko-literaturnoi kharakteristiki.* 1923. A. L. Schlözer, *Nestor. Russische Annalen in ihrer slavonischen Grundsprache.* 4 vols. Göttingen, 1802–09. Russian Trans., A. Shletser, *Nestor, perev. s nemetskogo D. Yazykova.* St. Petersburg, 1809. A. A. Shakhmatov, *Razyskaniya o drevneishikh russkikh letopisnykh svodakh.* 1908. (Reprint in *Russian Reprint Series*, no. LIX. The Hague, 1967.)

H. G.

Nestor Iskander (15th century). An early 16th-century manuscript (Collection of the Troitse-Sergiev Monastery No. 773) containing the *Tale on the Capture of Constantinople* (Povest' o vzyatii Tsar'grada) includes an epilogue to the tale which identifies a certain "much sinning and lawless Nestor Iskinder" as the author-narrator. ("Iskinder" seems here to be the Turkized form of "Alexander.") Yet nothing certain can be ascertained about either the origins of the *Tale* or its alleged author. On the basis of the information provided by this epilogue—found only in the Troitse-Sergiev codex (apparently, the oldest version of the *Tale*)—it has been suggested that Nestor was a Slav of Russian origin who was captured by Turks at an early age, embraced Islam, and participated in the siege and capture of the imperial city in 1453. Nestor subsequently combined his eye-witness account of the siege and final battle with the tales of Greeks who had observed these events from the other side (i.e., from inside the city).

The *Tale*, which widely circulated in the Russian lands between the 16th and the 18th century, has come down to us in many manuscripts which reveal numerous redactional variants. The prestige of the *Tale* is attested by its inclusion in the Russian *Khronograf of 1512* and in the most important chronicle collections of the 16th century. Scholars have long debated as to whether the *Tale* is an original work or a translation from the Greek. At the present time, it is generally believed that the *Tale* was written on the basis of heterogeneous Greek materials.

The *Tale*, as it has come down to us in its oldest version, consists of thematically distinct sections. It is difficult to determine whether they were put together by an "original" compiler or added to a narrative core at different stages. The account of the foundation, flowering and final ruin of Constantinople is presented in a prophetic tone as the expression of providential design. Constantinople is doomed from the moment the light of divine grace abandons the city. Only at the end of the *Tale* can the reader establish a connection between the fall of the imperial city and the providential role played by the Russian lands. Prophecies by Methodius of Patara and Leo the Sage and the *Vision of Daniel* are cited to herald the eventual Christian return to the sacred city. In the Greek text of the *Vision of Daniel* this liberation will come from a "blonde" or "fair-skinned people" (xanthon genos). In the *Tale* the Greek xanthon genos is rendered as *rusii rod*. Both readers and scribes could not fail to establish a link between the qualifiers *rusii* ("tawny, light brown") and *russkii* ("Russian"). Such historiosophic views could easily become popular in the period which followed the proclamation of an autocephalous Russian Church (1458) and which was marked by Russian ambitions to inherit the historical mission of Constantinople.

Bibliography: S. N. Azbelev, "K datirovke russkoi Povesti o vzyatii Tsar'grada turkami." *TODRL* 17 (1961), pp. 334–37. G. P. Bel'chenko, "K voprosu o sostave istoricheskoi povesti o vzyatii Tsar'grada." In *Sbornik statei k 40-letiyu uchenoi deyatel'nosti akad. A. S. Orlova.* Leningrad, 1934. Pp. 507–13. L. A. Dmitriev and D. S. Likhachëv, eds., *Pamyatniki literatury drevnei Rusi: Vtoraya polovina XV veka.* Moscow, 1982. I. Duichev, "La conquête turque et la prise de Constantinople dans la littérature slave contemporaine," *Byzantinoslavica* 17 (1956), pp. 276–340. Leonid, Archimandrite. *Povest' o Tsar'grade (ego osnovanii i vzyatii turkami v 1453 g.) Nestora-Iskandera XV v.* (Pamyatniki drevnei pis'mennosti i iskusstva, no. 62). 1886. Reprint in *Russkie povesti XV–XVI vv.*, ed. M. O. Skripil' (1958), pp. 55–78. M. O. Skripil', "'Istoriya' o vzyatii Tsar'grada turkami Nestora Iskandera." *TODRL* 10 (1954), pp. 166–84. N. A. Smirnov, "Istoricheskoe znachenie russkoi 'Povesti' Nestora-Iskandera o vzyatii turkami Konstantinopolya v 1453 g.", *Vizantiiskii vremennik* 7 (1953), pp. 50–71. M. N. Speranskii, "Povesti i skazaniya o vzyatii Tsar'grada turkami (1453) v russkoi pis'mennosti XVI–XVII vekov." *TODRL* 10 (1954), pp. 138–65. B. O. Unbegaun, "Les relations vieux-russes de la prise de Constantinople," *Revue des Etudes Slaves* 9, nos. 1–2 (1929), pp. 13–38.

H. G.

Nevskii al'manakh (The Neva Almanac), popular illustrated literary almanac, published annually (1825–33) in St. Petersburg by E. V. Aladyin (1796–1860); revived in 1847–48 as a philanthropic venture. A typical collection of poetry and prose—short lyrical pieces, ballads, album verse and occasional miscellany, romantic and sentimental tales—patterned after the successful almanac *Polyarnaya zvezda*. The almanac featured the works of almost every major and minor poet and writer of the time: A. S. PUSHKIN, V. A. ZHUKOVSKY, E. A. BARATYNSKY, N. M. YAZYKOV, P. A. VYAZEMSKY, F. V. BULGARIN, I. I. KOZLOV, A. S. KHOMYAKOV, O. M. SOMOV, V. I. Tumansky, A. E. Izmailov, D. I. KHVOSTOV.

Pushkin published several short works: eight excerpts from "The Fountain of Bakhchisarai" (1827) and a scene from the tragedy *Boris Godunov* (1828), all with illustrations by S. Galaktionov; excerpts from *Eugene Onegin* (1829), with illustrations by A. Notbek, later ridiculed by the poet in epigrams.

In 1827 the almanac encountered problems with censorship when Aladyin reprinted the tales of Somov and A. A. Bestuzhev from the unpublished almanac *Zvezdochka* which authorities suppressed after the Decembrist uprising.

The diminutive, carefully and elegantly produced volumes of *Nevskii Al'manakh*, usually prefaced with an engraved portrait of a member of the Russian Imperial family, appended with popular music, enjoyed a great commercial but not critical success.

Bibliography: Nikolai Smirnov-Sokol'skii, *Russkie literaturnye al'manakhi i sborniki XVIII–XIX vv.* 1965. (See index.) ———, *Rasskazy o prizhiznennykh izdaniyakh Pushkina.* 1962. Pp. 537–46.

A. Gl.

New Review, The, see *NOVYI ZHURNAL*.

Nihilism. A global and confusing term which, when employed in a Russian context, almost always has reference to the radicalism of the 1860s. The term had been occasionally employed by earlier Russian writers—with various meanings and imputations—but its real career in Russia began when it was memorably applied by Ivan TURGENEV to radicals of the younger generation in *Fathers and Children* (1862); for a considerable period of years thereafter it was fashionable in Russia to call all sorts of radicals—or even mere social non-conformists—"nihilists." Among the broadest strata of Russian public opinion, then, "nihilist" had roughly the same specificity in meaning that "bolshie" had in England after the First World War or "commie" had in the United States of the 1950s. Richard Stites put the matter well when he wrote recently that "nihilism was not so much a corpus of formal beliefs and programs (like populism, liberalism, Marxism) as it was a cluster of attitudes and social values and a set of behavioral effects. In short, it was an ethos." (Pp. 99–100).

Among the most important of these nihilist attitudes was a powerful emphasis on individual emancipation and development and the concomitant hatred of all those barriers that held individuals back from what they might make of themsleves: traditional social roles; restrictions of caste or sex; religious and other archaic attitudes—the celebration of self-sacrifice, for example. This stress on the personal development of the individual has often seemed narrow, selfish, or "bourgeois" to hostile critics of varying persuasions, and it has been correspondingly difficult to avoid linking this aspect of nihilism to the breakdown of the traditional social order in Russia and the emergence of a more modern and variegated society—particularly as the nihilists appeared just as the emancipation of the serfs inaugurated a period of national self-questioning and reform.

This powerful individualist impulse (of a sort which in Russia has always been regarded with suspicion) was accompanied by other attitudes which made it easier to swallow: in particular, the view that the ultimate purpose of the emancipation of the individual was the promotion of the collective good. Altruistic and civic attitudes were important in the gestalt of nihilism, but it was generally regarded as inappropriate for tough-minded and realistic people to make direct reference to their own idealistic humanism, except under special circumstances, often provided by an intimate circle of friends. One was obligated to challenge the archaic and barbarous Russian society in public, to insist on the destruction of all that prevented the flowering of the individual personality. That this heroic iconoclasm masked altruistic social goals could be respectably referred to only in the philosophical vocabulary of what was known as "rational egoism," a point of view derived from the English philosophical radicals which suggested that the fervent pursuit of individual advantage (properly understood) would lead ineluctably to social betterment for the larger society.

The rather different radical values of POPULISM, centering as they did around the Russian peasant, set forth the proposition that educated Russians (and ultimately Europeans) had a great deal to learn from the peasantry's communal institutions. Strongly nihilist critics like Dmitry PISAREV (1840–68) believed no such thing, nor did they have any faith in the creative capacities of Russia's peasant masses. That strand of Enlightenment thinking which exalted the Noble Savage, so strong elsewhere in Russian culture, was quite lacking among the nihilists.

Central to the notion of personal emancipation and development generally held by those who thought of themselves as nihilists was the ideal of a scientific education, resolutely secular and utilitarian in outlook and propagated with missionary zeal. A powerful image of the ideal was the doctor-scientist, which is no doubt why Bazarov, the nihilist hero of *Fathers and Children*, spends so much time in the novel dissecting frogs. Scientific rationalism provided the key to elevating the superstitious Russian masses out of their age-old poverty and backwardness; and it would also work as a healthy solvent to all the sentimental and outmoded notions that comprised the intellectual stock of older "educated" people. European popularizers of philosophical materialism—Jakob Moleschott (*The Life Cycle*), Ludwig Büchner (*Force and Matter*)—had a brief but powerful vogue in the Russia of the early 1860s, and the merest reference to their books in a journal article or conversation was tantamount to a philosophical declaration. Auguste Comte was venerated, if not

actually very widely read; and great respect was accorded to Henry Buckle's efforts to produce a scientific history stressing climate, geography, and topography.

Conservative social attitudes and religion were obvious targets for the nihilists; it is slightly surprising to find them so set against aesthetic values, but from their point of view they were surely right, as the reverence for artistic genius and achievement was ultimately to prove a major distraction to Russian intellectuals in their crusade for revolutionary transformation. "Boots are better than Shakespeare," proclaimed Pisarev, and he demoted Beethoven and Raphael to the level of chefs and billiard players. CHERNYSHEVSKY (whose populism was shot through with nihilist attitudes) maintained that art was an aesthetically inferior substitute for "concrete reality," and that its justification lay in the moral judgment that it was able to pass on that reality, thus leading ultimately to its improvement. In Chernyshevsky's Master's dissertation, "The Aesthetic Relations of Art to Reality" (1855) we find ourselves again in the extravagantly Benthamite milieu from which so much of the nihilist spirit derives.

Much of what is most striking and memorable about "nihilism," however, cannot be understood with reference to ideas or programs alone—Mill's utilitarianism or Feuerbach's anthropologism or whatever. What is most memorable about this phenomenon is now largely stylistic: the quality of the rage against the established order, the naive extravagance of the attack against it. This is partly to be explained by the youth of the participants; even more central was the idealist coloration of the culture against which Pisarev and Nikolai DOBROLYUBOV (1836–61) were so militantly arrayed. The violence of the attack against "art," for example, becomes at least slightly more intelligible, even at moments more sympathetic, when we force ourselves to realize how shot through with a pretentious German idealist worship of art and artists the intellectual atmosphere of the 1830s and 1840s had been. Most of us feel no need these days to devalue art any further, but it is conceivable that we might have felt differently had we been born in Russia in 1835. Many of us have felt an episodic urge to be useful, but we might have experienced it with greater passion, shame and longing had we been fortunate enough to have been brought up in one of the seductively privileged gentry "nests" that we now know only from the Russian literature of the period.

Like the European and American radicalism of the 1960s, nihilism advertised itself with clothing and hair styles, most of which expressed various forms of political and sexual emancipation. Among the men, long hair and moustaches suggested rebellion (as they generally have in Western culture); among women it was short hair. Male nihilists generally dressed casually, or in old or soiled clothing, or in something which suggested that the wearer was skeptical of the social occasion and ironic about or hostile to the level of dress prescribed by the traditional society. In the late 1850s rebels of a more populist turn of mind were beginning to affect peasant costume, and this was soon a recognized means for any radically minded individual to indicate that he stood for a more democratic and free society in Russia.

But if clothes (and their employment to defy social convention) were important to the male nihilist, they were much more so to his female counterpart; and in general it may be said that the *nigilistka*'s challenge to the established order was more serious, far-reaching, and daring than that of the male. His rebellion could be seen as a not untraditional kind of wild oats or bohemianism; hers suggested drastic changes in the position of women in society, which in turn strongly suggested a new order more generally. It is not irrelevant to point out that a man like Turgenev, who was politically a Westernized liberal but socially conservative, could produce the magnificent, ambiguous portrait of Bazarov, but when he turned (in the same novel) to the female nihilist (Evdoksiya Kukshina), his hostility overflowed into a portrait that was scarcely more than a cartoon. The short-haired, simply-dressed young woman, without crinolines or parasols, often wearing dark glasses and talking of serious subjects (and sometimes smoking if she could manage it) was greeted by traditional society with a much greater and less controlled hostility than her male counterpart—at least until the male became associated with active revolutionary activity. Of course both the male and female nihilist did a good deal of posing, which would under the best of circumstances have exposed them to ridicule, but the mockery which the *nigilistka* attracted was seldom good-natured. Her rejection of the romance of traditional society, of herself as a passive sexual object and her assertion of her own autonomy was more deeply shocking and repugnant to men in Russia (a society profoundly aristocratic in its values) than in France, England, or Germany.

Although it is more than merely a "nihilist novel," Chernyshevsky's *What Is To Be Done?* (1863) must be mentioned in any discussion of literature and the nihilist spirit. Thousands of gallons of ink have been spilt over this strange novel, rather lifeless for most Western readers now, except during periods of extreme revolutionary excitement. But in the Russian society of the day—and in Russia's revolutionary subculture down to LENIN's time and beyond—*What Is To Be Done?* provided memorable pictures, or role models, of radicals in action. The militant, extravagantly rational figures demonstrate how society was to be reorganized and how men and women should begin to live their lives on a basis of equality and comradeship. However the novel may bore, amuse, or bewilder us now, the evidence of its importance is unmistakable: it is a fundamental document of the Russian Revolution.

What Is To Be Done? is only the best known of a good many "nihilist novels" of the time, but the ethical-political quarrels of the period called forth at least an equal number of novels on the other side (in one way or another), and in the history of Russian literature the "ANTI-NIHILIST NOVELS" are the more significant. They may, of course, be studied virtually without reference to the role played in their genesis by the polemics of the period, but the question of nihilism is unmistakably posed by them nonetheless. Several of Turgenev's novels (in addition of course to *Fathers and Children*) may be understood in part as anti-nihilist polemics—*Smoke*, and particularly *Virgin Soil*, in which the chief protagonist was drawn both from Dobrolyubov and Pisarev. Ivan GONCHAROV's last major work, *The Precipice*, makes some shift at portraying the mentality of a nihilist, and Nikolai LESKOV's work abounds in nihilist portraits and polemics. The problem of radicalism was a vital one for Leskov, as Charles Moser has observed. Aleksei PISEMSKY's *Troubled Seas* is the most important of his several works with nihilist themes or characters.

The most important writer who could be described as an anti-nihilist is of course Fyodor DOSTOEVSKY, for whom the problems of atheism and socialism were inextricably linked with the religious ideas so central in his work. Both *Crime and Punishment* (1866) and *The Idiot* (1868) contain nihilist portraits, but in *The Possessed* (1872), the ultimate form of which was profoundly shaped by newspaper reports of Sergei Nechaev's revolutionary activities, Dostoevsky produced the greatest of the Russian novels directed against the Russian radicalism of the day.

Since "nihilism" describes not a group of doctrines but a shifting set of attitudes, it is particularly difficult to sketch out its career after the first decade or so in which the term was widely employed. The revolutionary elitism it described, for example, gradually ceased to be called "nihilism," but in a way it survived and prospered among those radicals who were disposed to be skeptical of the revolutionary capacities of the Russian people: the Russian "Jacobins" or "Blanquists." The aspiration for personal liberation that nihilism represented became one pole of all subsequent Russian radicalism, coexisting uneasily with the primitivism, moralism, and collectivism characteristic of Russian populism. Perhaps the most enduring and clearest traces of nihilism may be seen in the women's movement, where the themes and behavior patterns initially branded as "nihilist" were central to Russian radical feminism for several generations, although even here a more specifically political spirit and a more defined set of objectives gradually replaced the spontaneity and the violence of the nihilist revolt.

Bibliography: N. G. Chernyshevsky, *What Is To Be Done? Tales About New People*. 1961. Charles A. Moser, *Antinihilism in the Russian Novel of the 1860s*. 1964. Dmitry Pisarev, *Selected Philosophical, Social and Political Essays*. Moscow, 1958. Philip Pomper, *The Russian Revolutionary Intelligentsia*. 1970. Richard Stites, *The Women's Liberation Movement in Russia: Feminism, Nihilism and Bolshevism, 1860–1930*. 1978. Ivan Turgenev, *Fathers and Sons (Children)*. Available in numerous translations and editions. Franco Venturi, *Roots of Revolution*. 1960.   A. G.

Nikiténko, Aleksándr Vasílievich (1804–77), literary historian, censor, and memoirist. Son of a serf, Nikitenko had no right to a higher education. However, a star graduate, he was given his freedom in 1824 and finished the university four years later. Painfully aware of his lowly origins, Nikitenko worked hard to gain dignity and respect and soon made a brilliant career. In 1833 he was appointed official censor, in 1836 professor of Russian literature at the University of St. Petersburg, and in 1855 member of the Academy of Sciences. Contrary to the prevailing biographism, his doctoral dissertation *On Creative Force in Poetry, or, on the Nature of Poetic Genius* (1836) stressed the importance of an aesthetic-philosophical approach to literature, pointing out that "the historical study of literature irrespective of general philosophical elements is impossible." The idea of a joint aesthetic-philosophical and historical method was further developed in his *History of Russian Literature* (1845). As editor of the journal SOVREMENNIK (1847–1848) Nikitenko defended the "NATURAL SCHOOL," however, calling upon writers to supplement their criticism of the "vices of society" by describing positive phenomena. "Destroy the abuses, but be anxious not to touch the principles" was the careful advice given by the censor Nikitenko to the writers of Russian realism. Extremely valuable are his autobiographical notes (1804–24) and diary (1826–77) published after his death. Apart from being an interesting human document this almost daily record offers a wealth of material on the literary, historical, and social life of the Russian people during a period of more than fifty years.

Works: Dnevnik I–III. 1955–56.
Works in English: The Diary of a Russian Censor. Abridged, ed. and trans. Helen Saltz Jacobson. 1975.   G. K.

Nikítin, Afanásy (15th century), a merchant from Tver known as the author of the *Journey beyond the Three Seas* (Khozhenie za tri morya). The account of Nikitin's journey beyond the three seas—Caspian, Indian, and Black—to India from 1466 to 1472 has come down to us in several versions (some attested only as fragments) either as autonomous texts or as part of chronicles. Most modern editions of the work are based on the late 15th-century *Troitsky* manuscript with variants from the 17th-century *Undolsky* codex. The *Journey* was first published by N. M. KARAMZIN in the sixth volume of his *History of the Russian State* (Istoriya gosudarstva Rossiiskogo, 1818).

According to the *Journey*, Nikitin and his trading party set sail with two ships for the Caucasian principality of Shirvan. Near Astrakhan their boats were attacked by Tatars and plundered. The smaller ship was lost in a heavy storm and was "smashed against the coast." Rescued by the ambassador of Shamákha (Azerbaijan), Nikitin eventually made his way to Derbent, Baku, and across the Caspian Sea to Persia, where he stayed for ten months. He then decided to cross the Indian Sea to India. After spending four years there, he returned to his homeland by way of Ethiopia, Arabia, Persia, Armenia, and the Black Sea. Nikitin did not succeed in returning to his native Tver, but died before reaching Smolensk.

Nikitin's *Journey* occupies a unique place in Old Russian Literature. Although the *Journey* can be compared to works of pilgrimage literature (*palomnicheskaya literatura*) such as Abbot Daniil's *The Life and Pilgrimage of Daniil, Abbot of the Russian Land* (Zhit'e i khozhenie Daniila Rus'skyya zemli igumena), its style does not depend on the symbolic code of ecclesiastic writings; rather, the work represents an immediate response to concrete emotions and experiences. Nikitin's treatment of the exotic sharply distinguishes his account from those of Western travelers and merchants such as Oderico da Pordenone and Niccolò de' Conti.

What has especially attracted the attention of scholars is the response of Nikitin the Christian to his Islamic environment. It is difficult to say, however, whether he actually converted to Islam or whether he managed to survive by accommodating himself to a peculiar religious symbiosis. Nikitin often comments on his fate in quasi-lyrical terms, sometimes switching to a bizarre mixture of Oriental tongues, namely, Turkic, Arabic, and Persian dialects. It is noteworthy that at the end of the *Journey* one finds an enigmatic prayer written in Arabic.

In addition, Nikitin's "Russian" has also been the object of considerable discussion. The extent to which his "language" does not rely on Church Slavonic models but is based on a local dialect remains an open question. From the viewpoint of the literary scholar, however, what is especially appealing in the *Journey* is the abundance of "marvellous" scenes presented as concrete and perceptible experiences and therefore worthy of unconditional admiration.

Secondary literature: V. P. Adrianova-Peretts, ed., *Khozhenie za tri morya Afanasiya Nikitina v 1466–1472 gg.* 2d rev. ed. 1958. L. A. Dmitriev and D. S. Likhachëv, eds., *Pamyatniki literatury drevnei Rusi: Vtoraya polovina XV veka.* Moscow, 1982. G. Lenhoff, "Beyond Three Seas: Afanasij Nikitin's Journey from Orthodoxy to Apostasy," *East European Quarterly* 13 (1979), pp. 431–47. N. S. Trubetskoi, "'Khozhenie za tri morya' Afanasiya Nikitina, kak literaturnyi pamyatnik." In *Three Philological Studies.* (Michigan Slavic Materials, no. 3.) 1963. Pp. 23–51. (Rptd. from *Versty,* 1 [1926].) M. N. Vitashevskaya. *Stranstviya Afanasiya Nikitina.* 1972. A. A. Zimin, "Novye spiski 'Khozheniya' Afanasiya Nikitina," 13 (1957), pp. 437–39. H. G.

Nikitin, Iván Sávvich (1824–61), poet. Like his predecessor KOLTSOV, Nikitin came from a well-to-do but uneducated middle class family of Voronezh. He was educated at a seminary, but never graduated, and went on to become an innkeeper and bookdealer in Voronezh. Nikitin wrote a great deal of rather conventional nature poetry. As many as sixty of his poems were eventually set to music. His claim to fame rests, however, with his "realistic poems of the life of the poor" (Mirsky), both rural—"The Ploughman" (Pakhar', 1856), "The Beggar" (Nishchii, 1857), "Smouldering Ruins" (Na pepelishche, 1860)—and urban—"The Tailor" (Portnoi, 1860), "Mother and Daughter" (Mat' i doch', 1860), etc. Nikitin's main work is the verse epic "The Kulak" (1857). Nikitin's "realistic poems" are overshadowed by NEKRASOV's. While the life of the poor is described vividly enough, Nikitin rarely finds the right balance between literary and popular language, or a proper relation between the point of view of his subjects and his own. Much of his poetry is derivative, as even DOBROLYUBOV pointed out, and sometimes it is simply semi-literate. But at times it has a ring of genuine feeling. Nikitin also wrote some revolutionary poems which were widely read in manuscript, but could be published only in 1906.

Works: Sochineniya. 4 vols. 1960–61. *Polnoe sobranie stikhotvorenii.* Preface N. I. Rylenkov. Introd. and comm. L. A. Plotkin. 1965.
Translations: See Lewanski, p. 313.
Secondary literature: N. A. Dobrolyubov, "'Kulak,' Poema I. Nikitina." In *Sobranie sochinenii* (1961–64). Vol. 3. Pp. 152–59. ——, "Stikhotvoreniya Ivana Nikitina." *Sobranie sochinenii* (1961–64). Vol. 6. Pp. 155–78. V. A. Tonkov, *I. S. Nikitin: Ocherk zhizni i tvorchestva.* 1964. *"Ya Rusi syn!: K 150-letiyu so dnya rozhdeniya I. S. Nikitina.* Voronezh, 1974. V. T.

Nikolaeva (pseud. of Volyánskaya), Galina Evgénievna (1911–63), writer. Nikolaeva graduated from Gorky Medical School in 1935 and served as a doctor in World War II. She wrote poetry, short stories, and sketches since 1939, but is known primarily for two novels. Her fiction is characterized by a concern for contemporary moral and social problems, a precise analysis of feelings, and a realistic style.

Her first novel, *Harvest* (Zhatva, 1950) won the State Prize in 1951. It dealt with a returning World War II veteran, his wife who had matured during the war through a love affair and her responsible work at the kolkhoz, and the wife's lover. Critics found the ending in which the backward kolkhoz is transformed into a model one falsely optimistic.

Nikolaeva's most important novel was *The Running Battle* (Bitva v puti, 1957). This was the first novel to portray the reactions of Russians to Stalin's death (his burial is described at length). The novel has three motifs. The selfless Party engineer Bakhirev opposes the demagogic careerist Valgan, director of a tractor factory, who is isolated from the workers. The puritanism of the Stalin period is rejected in the account of a love affair between the married Bakhirev and a girl. A new theme appearing from 1955 on, "repression" under Stalin, is exemplified here in the character of the husband.

Nikolaeva left unfinished a novel about physicists. She was awarded the Red Banner of Labor.

Translations: Harvest. Moscow, 1952. New York, 1953. *The Newcomer; the Manager of an MTS and the Chief Agronomist.* Moscow, 1955 (?). *Two Collective Farms. The Tractor Kolkhoz.* Moscow, 1950, 1952.
Secondary literature: Russkie sovetskie pisateli-prozaiki. 1964. Vol. 3. Pp. 215–33. N. R.

Nikolev, Nikolai Petróvich (1758–1815), poet and dramatist, was brought up in the house of Princess E. R. Dashkova, where he received an excellent education from various tutors. He was made a member of the Russian Academy in 1792. Nikolev went blind when he was only twenty.

Nikolev was primarily a dramatist. His tragedy *Sorena i Zamir* enjoyed great popularity (1784, staged 1785, published 1787). It was at one time withdrawn from the stage for some thrusts at tyranny featured in it, but was allowed to return by Catherine II. Among Nikolev's comedies, the comic opera *Rozana and Lyubim* (1776) enjoyed the greatest success. In his comedy *The Vain Poet* (Samolyubivyi stikhotvorets, 1775) Nikolev, who considered himself to be the greatest playwright of his time, tried to put down SUMAROKOV. An adherent of CLASSICISM, Nikolev nevertheless joined DERZHAVIN in introducing elements of parody and folklore in his verses ("Two Odes on the Capture of the City of Ochakov by Victorious Russian Forces on the 6th day of December, 1788"). Nikolev stated his classicist ideas in a "Lyric-Didactic Missive to E. R. Dashkova" (1791, 2d ed. with "Supplementary Notes," 1796), fashioned after Boileau's treatise. In the second edition of his "Missive" Nikolev took a stand against SENTIMENTALISM. Nikolev's literary activities initiated a vehement polemic in which he was supported by F. Karin, D. Gorchakov, D. KHVOSTOV, N. Shatrov, I. KRYLOV, and others, and was opposed by N. KARAMZIN, I. DMITRIEV, V. KAPNIST, P. VYAZEMSKY, and others.

In 1806 Nikolev composed a solemn poem celebrating Prince Bagration (it is mentioned in Tolstoi's *War and Peace*). In 1812 he left Moscow for Tambov, where he wrote poems and epigrams attacking Napoleon. After Nikolev's death, his friends attempted to establish a cult of the deceased poet, gathering annually to commemorate the day of his death, devoting essays to him, and publishing a book to honor him (*A Memorial to N. P. Nikolev by his Friends,* 1819).

Works: Tvorenii N. P. Nikoleva. 1795–98. (Only 5 volumes appeared, instead of a planned 10.) *Rozana i Lyubim.* Ed. and comm. P. N. Berkov. In *Russkaya komediya i komicheskaya opera 18 veka.* 1950. Pp. 196–216. *Samolyubivyi stikhotvorets: Komediya v 5-ti deistviyakh.* Text, biographic note, and comm. M. O. Yankovskii. In *Stikhotvornaya komediya kontsa 18-nachala 19 v.* (Biblioteka poeta. Bol'shaya seriya.) 1964. Pp. 70–174. *Sorena i Zamir.* Text, comm. and biographic note V. A. Bochkarev. In *Stikhotvornaya tragediya kontsa 18-nachala 19 v.* (Biblioteka poeta. Bol'shaya seriya.) 1964. [Poems] In *Poety 18 veka.* (Biblioteka poeta. Bol'shaya seriya.) Vol. 2, pp. 18–111. (With a biographic note by I. Z. Serman.)
Secondary literature: M. G. Al'tshuller, "'Liro-didaticheskoe poslanie' N. P. Nikoleva." In *Russkaya literatura.* (Uchenye zapiski Leningradskogo universiteta, no. 339. Seriya filologicheskikh nauk, fasc. 72). 1968. Pp. 208–14. M. A. Arzumanova, "Iz istorii literaturno-obshchestvennoi bor'by 90-kh godov 18 v. (N. P. Nikolev i N. M. Karamzin)," *Vestnik Leningradskogo universiteta,* no. 20 (1965), seriya istorii yazyka i literatury, fasc. 4, pp. 73–83. Yu. V. Stennik, "Lomonosov i Nikolev (Nekotorye tendentsii v razvitii zhanra pokhval'noi ody poslednei chetverti 18 veka)." In *Poetika i stilistika russkoi literatury.* Pamyati akademika V. V. Vinogradova. 1971. Pp. 59–68. M. A.

Nikúlin, Lev Veniaminovich (1891–1967), prose writer. Born in Zhitomir, he studied at the Moscow Commercial Institute. Nikulin began writing in 1911, was a member of the Soviet diplomatic mission in Afghanistan in 1921–22, became a member of the Communist Party in 1940, and died in Moscow 9 August 1967. Nikulin is the author of novels, plays and reminiscences. His first work, *Fourteen Months in Afghanistan* (1923), is semi-autobiographical. In 1951 he was awarded the Stalin prize for *Russia's Faithful Sons* (1950), an historical novel about the 1813–14 campaign of the Russian armies against Napoleon. His reminiscences include *Moscow Dawns* (1954) and *People and Wanderings: Reminiscences and Meetings* (1962). Nikulin is a conventional and official Soviet writer.

Works: Sochineniya. 3 vols. 1956. *Moskovskie zori.* 1956. *Rossii vernye syny.* 1958. *Chekhov, Bunin, Kuprin: literaturnye portrety.* 1960. *Trus.* 1961. *Lyudi i stranstviya: vospominaniya i vstrechi.* 1962. *S novym schast'em.* 1963. *Tukhachevskii.* 1963. *Mertvaya zyb'.* 1965. *Gody nashei zhizni.* 1966.

Translations: The Swell of the Sea. Arlington, Virginia, 1972.

Secondary literature: I. Kramov, *Literaturnaya gazeta,* 6 Feb. 1962. F. Levin, *Literaturnyi kritik* 2 (1938). Grigorii Svirskii. *Na Lobnom meste.* London, 1979. H. S.

Nil (Neilus) Sórsky (1433–1508). A central figure in the history of Russian spirituality, the initiator of a new mystical trend in Russian monasticism, and the inspirer of subsequent generations of opponents to the temporally-oriented policies of the Muscovite Church. Although few details are known about Nil's biography, his spiritual experiences and ideological responses to contemporary events can be fairly accurately drawn from his writings. Given the enormous prestige which Nil enjoyed during his lifetime, it is surprising that no Life (*Zhitie*) of him has come down to us. Some scholars have advanced the hypothesis that manuscripts containing accounts of his life were destroyed in 1538 when the Kazan Tatars raided the Vologda district. It has also been suggested that these manuscripts were burned by representatives of the Muscovite Church. In any event, it is noteworthy that there is no evidence to suggest that Nil was formally canonized. Although one finds traces of a church service to him, it appears to have reflected only local veneration with no official sanction. Only in 1903 was the name of Nil Sorsky placed in the official ecclesiastical calendar of the Russian Church (for May 7).

The most direct source of information about the life of Nil Sorsky is provided by the scribe of a 17th-century manuscript containing his *Monastic Rule* (Monastyrskii ustav). The scribe relates that in his time it was said that Nil had been born and educated in Moscow. He also informs us that Nil died on 7 May 1508, at the age of 75; from this one can deduce that 1433 is the year of his birth. From a letter written shortly after Nil's death, one learns that his family name was Maikov. Nil received the tonsure at an early age in the Kirillo-Belozersky Monastery during the abbacy of Kassian (1448–69). His first spiritual guide was the *starets* Paisy Yaroslavov, a follower of Hesychast prayer and devotional practice in accordance with the Athonite model. It was probably under Paisy's influence that Nil undertook the emblematic journey to Constantinople and Mount Athos, the two traditional centers of Eastern Christianity. It is unclear where he stayed and for how long he remained away from the Russian land. If one considers Nil's familiarity with both the classical texts of the Hesychast movement and the main ecclesiastical issues discussed by his contemporaries in the Greek and Balkan Slavic lands, one may assume that the period of his training outside Russia was not of short duration.

Upon his return to the Russian land, Nil left the monastery of St. Kirill and moved about 15 versts away to swampland near a river called the Sora or Sorka (hence the name "Sorsky"). This occurred during the reign of Metropolitan Geronty (1473–89). There he built a cell where he planned to live in total isolation. Shortly thereafter, however, Nil attracted a small group of pupils and formed a "skete" (*skit*), that is, a small community of cell monks (*kelliotai*) in imitation of similar communities on Mount Athos. This brotherhood, though never large, marked the beginning of a prestigious and enduring community which later came to be known as the *Zavolzhskie startsy* (Trans-Volga Elders).

Despite a life spent in relative isolation, Nil's reputation as a learned and pious man appears to have been considerable. In 1490 he was present, along with Paisy Yaroslavov, at a council convened by Archbishop Gennady of Novgorod to deal with the so-called *Zhidovstvuyushchie* (Judaizers). His opposition to the use of violence in the enforcement of religious law displeased the ecclesiastical authorities. Only once more did Nil participate in official church matters. In 1503 he roundly condemned the party of the *Styazhateli* (Possessors), that is, the defenders of monastic holdings. However, Nil did not engage in a protracted dispute with his opponents, pre-

ferring instead to dedicate the remaining years of his life to quiet prayer and meditation.

The writings of Nil Sorsky include: (1) the *Recommendations to Disciples* (Predanie uchenikom); (2) the extremely popular—about 200 manuscripts are known from the 16th to the 19th century—*Monastic Rule* (Monastyrskii ustav), usually entitled in the manuscripts *Nil's Chapters on Mental Activity* (Glavy [Nila] o myslennem delanii); and (3) a short *Testament* (Zaveshchanie), a prayer and several letters. In his writings Nil presents both the theory and practice of spiritual purification. The main guide to perfection is represented by the divine Writings, whose message can be assimilated both with the aid of a spiritual teacher and through individual study. Nil's attitude towards the holy Scriptures is marked by a preeminent concern for the critical evaluation of the texts. In his opinion, a devout reader should be very careful to distinguish truly inspired writings from texts (such as certain hagiographies) which reflect recent legendary motifs. What is remarkable in Nil's "textual criticism" is his "scientific" technique of collating codices in order to discuss textual variants.

Relying on the precepts of a mystical tradition which goes back to the very origins of Christian thought, Nil conceives of spiritual purification as a psychological process of liberation both from false images which captivate the mind and from passions (*strasti*). In his *Monastic Rule* he instructs his pupils on how to combat the eight sources of passion, namely, gluttony, fornication, covetousness, anger, sadness, acedia, vainglory, and pride. When one is free of all passions, one can strive for complete purity of heart and spiritual tranquillity (*hēsychia*/*bezmolvie*), and thereby prepare oneself for divine contemplation. As an aid in the process of spiritual liberation, Nil recommends certain physiological methods (such as body-posture and holding of the breath) and a special type of "mental prayer" (*umnaya molitva*) known as the "Jesus Prayer" and consisting in the constant repetition of the formula, "Lord, Jesus Christ, Son of God, have mercy upon me (a sinner)."

The brotherhood of Nil Sorsky was committed to work, apostolic activity, and especially poverty. The extent of Nil's dependence on Hesychast doctrine remains an object of dispute among scholars. Because of its originality, his thought cannot always be identified with dogmatic Hesychasm. It is clear, however, that Nil Sorsky was the product of a general tendency which spread among the Orthodox Slavs as a consequence of the Hesychast spiritual and cultural revival. The basic tenets and intellectual methods of Nil Sorsky's movement in the Russian land had much in common with trends which developed among the Bulgarians and Serbs beginning in the second half of the 14th century. Like the "Trnovo School" of Patriarch Evtimy and its diaspora (represented by churchmen and scholars such as Konstantin Kostenetski, Kiprian and Grigory Tsamblak), Nil Sorsky's monastic community focused on typically Hesychast concerns, most notably, (1) the spiritual ascent of purified souls towards God through strict devotional practices, and (2) textual criticism based on the interdependence of correct writing and correct doctrine. Although Nil Sorsky resolutely refused to engage in any religious or political struggle, his teachings provided his followers with a theoretical approach which would play a central role in the clash between the *styazhateli* (possessors) and the *nestyazhateli* (non-possessors).

Bibliography: A. S. Arkhangel'skii, *Nil Sorskii i Vassian Patrikeev, ikh literaturnye trudy i idei v drevnei Rusi. Istoriko-literaturnyi ocherk, I: Prepodobnyi Nil Sorskii.* St. Petersburg, 1882. Reprint in *Russian Reprint Series,* 20, The Hague, 1966. J. Fennell and A. Stokes, *Early Russian Literature.* 1974. Pp. 157–64. F. von Lilienfeld, *Nil Sorskij und seine Schriften. Die Krise der Tradition im Russland Ivans III.* Berlin, 1963. Ya. S. Lur'e, *Ideologicheskaya bor'ba v russkoi publitsistike kontsa XV—nachala XVI veka.* 1960. Pp. 285–345. G. A. Maloney, *Russian Hesychasm. The Spirituality of Nil Sorskii.* (Slavistic Printings and Reprintings, No. 269.) The Hague-Paris, 1973. *Pamyatniki drevnei pis'mennosti i iskusstva.* Vol. 179. Ed. M. S. Borovkova-Maikova. 1912.

R. P.

Nílin, Pável Filíppovich (1908–   ), prose writer, was born in Irkutsk. After working at various other jobs, Nilin became a journalist, at first in Irkutsk, later in the Ukraine, and finally in Moscow. His first book, *Man Moves Up: Sketches of Ordinary Life* (Chelovek idet v goru; Ocherki obyknovennoi zhizni, 1936), dealing with the coal miners of the Donets basin quite in the spirit of Five-Year-Plan literature, is nevertheless remarkable for its factual accuracy and a genuine interest in people. It was made into a successful film and launched Nilin's career as a writer and film maker. After experiencing some difficulties during the ZHDANOV years, Nilin came fully into his own with his short novel *Cruelty* (Zhestokost', 1956, made into a film of the same title in 1959). In this and in several subsequent prose works and films, Nilin deals with the delicate issue of clashes in Soviet life between the humane ideals of communism and a callous disregard for them in actual practice, as in officially sanctioned violence.

Works: Zhestokost'. Ispytatel'nyi srok. 1957. *Cherez kladbishche.* 1962. *Chetyre povesti.* 1970. *Znakomoe litso. Povesti.* 1975.

Translations: Comrade Venka, 1959. *Cruelty.* Trans. J. Guralsky. Moscow, 1958. "On Probation" [Ispytatel'nyi srok]. *Soviet Literature* 3 (1957), pp. 3–98. "Unquenchable Flame." In *Road to Victory* London. 1945.

Secondary literature: Deming Brown, *Soviet Russian Literature since Stalin.* 1978. P. 260. V. Kardin, *Povesti Pavla Nilina.* 1964. L. Kolobaeva, *Pavel Nilin: Ocherk tvorchestva.* 1969.   V. T.

Northern Bee, The, see SEVERNAYA PCHELA.

Novel, the Russian. The Russian word *roman* covers both "novel" and "romance." A distinction is made in Russian between *roman* and *povest'*, where the latter may be a short novel (or romance) or a long short-story. Within the range of works referred to as *roman*, one has to deal with continuity and/or uniformity based on a variety of criteria, such as novelistic genre (the PICARESQUE NOVEL, for example), mood (serious or humorous, for example), narrative structure (the EPISTOLARY NOVEL, for example), and literary models followed (PUSHKIN's *Eugene Onegin*, for instance). As early as in the case of A. N. RADISHCHEV's *Journey from Petersburg to Moscow* (1790), elements extrinsic to the novel as such must be considered in determining a novel's place in Russian literature. The influence of nonfiction as well as of other forms of verbal art (the drama, for example) is also a factor. Hence the classification of the novel in Russian literary criticism tends to be based on both intrinsic and extrinsic criteria. We have then, the "social novel" (since BELINSKY), the "psychological novel," the "ideological novel" (a term coined by Boris Engelhardt), the "nihilist" and the "antinihilist novel," but also the "novel-epopoeia," the "novel-tragedy" (a term applied to DOSTOEVSKY's novels by Vyacheslav IVANOV), the "polyphonic novel" (M. M. BAKHTIN), and so on.

Pre-Petrine literature features translations of a few late Hellenistic and Byzantine romances, such as the ALEKSANDRIYA, *The Deeds of Devgeny* (Devgenievo deyanie, a Russian version of the Byzantine romance *Digenis Akritas*), and *The Story of Apollo, King of Tyre* (Istoriya o Apollone korole Tirskom), as well as a good many Western romances of chivalry. Some of the better known among the latter are *The Story of Prince Bova* (Istoriya o Bove koroleviche, from the Italian *Buovo d'Antona*, which in turn goes back to the Old French *Histoire de Beuves d'Hanstone et de sa amie Sosianne fille du roi d'Armenie*, by Pierre du Ries) (see BOVA KOROLEVICH); *The Story of the Brave Prince Peter of the Golden Keys and the Beautiful Princess Magilena of Naples* (Istoriya o khrabrom knyaze Petre Zlatykh-Klyuchakh i o prekrasnoi korolevne Magilene Neapolitanskoi, from the French *Histoyre du vaillant chevalier Pierre filz du conte de Prouence et de la belle Maguelonne fille du roy de Naples* [Lyons, 1490], via the Polish); *The Story of Melusina* (translated in 1677 from the Polish version of 1671 of a German translation of the Old French romance); *The Excellent, Useful, and Entertaining Tale of Otto, Roman Emperor, and his Spouse, Empress Olunda* (Povest' izryadnaya, poleznaya zhe i uteshnaya ob Ottone, tsesare Rimstem, i o supruge ego, tsesarevne Olunde, from a Polish version of the French romance *Florent et Lyon, enfants de l'empereur de Rome*, via the German *Geschichte vom Kaiser Octavianus*); and *The Tale of Prince Bruntsvig of the Czech Lands* (Povest' o Bruntsvige koroleviche Cheshskiya Zemli, from the Czech). Several of these romances found their way into the chapbook (LUBOK) and the Russian FOLKTALE, and thence back into literature. Thus, Pushkin's *Tale*

of Tsar Saltan (Skazka o tsare Saltane) is loosely based on the folk-tale of *Bova korolevich*.

A native tradition of the adventure novel began in the age of Peter the Great, with the picaresque *Story of Frol Skobeev, a Russian Nobleman* (Istoriya o rossiiskom dvoryanine Frole Skobeeve) and the exotic *Story of Vasily Kariotsky, a Russian sailor, and the Beautiful Princess Irakliya of Florence* (Istoriya o rossiiskom matrose Vasilii Kariotskom i prekrasnoi korolevne Iraklii Florenskoi). Another source of what would later be the novel was the edifying moral tale, an early example of which is *The most Wonderful and Amazing Story of a certain Merchant, Foma Grudtsyn, about his Son Savva* (Povest' zelo prechudna i udivleniya dostoina nekogo kuptsa Fomy Grudtsyna o syne ego Savve, ca. 1660), a Russian variant of the Faust legend. Both of these genres also entered the literature of *lubok*.

In the 18th century an increasing number of Western romances and novels belonging to the higher level of contemporary literature (earlier translations were from "folk literature") were translated into Russian, beginning with V. K. TREDIAKOVSKY's translations of Abbé Paul Tallement's *Voyage à l'Isle d'Amour* (1730), John Barclay's *Argenis* (1757), and Fénelon's *Aventures de Télémaque* (1766, in hexameters!). *Robinson Crusoe* was translated between 1762 and 1764, *Don Quixote* in 1769, *Manon Lescaut* in 1790. By the end of the century a reading public existed to make translations of popular novels commercially profitable. The novels of Richardson, Sterne, Fielding, Smollett, Rousseau, Ducray-Duminil, Léonard, Goethe, etc., were routinely translated and soon enough imitated. Thus, fourteen novels by Ducray-Duminil appeared in Russian between 1794 and 1809, and ten novels by Ann Radcliffe during the same time span.

Rather awkward imitations of the love and adventure novels of the baroque were produced by Fyodor EMIN (1735–70), Matvei KOMAROV (1730s–1812?), Vasily Lyovshin (1746–1826), Pyotr Zakharyin (1750–1800), and others. The sentimental epistolary novel was introduced by Emin's four-volume *Letters of Ernest and Doravra* (Pis'ma Ernesta i Doravry, 1766), patterned after Rousseau's *Julie*. The novels of Nikolai Emin (1760–1814), *Roza* (1786) and *Play of Fate* (Igra sud'by, 1789), were imitations of Goethe's *Werther*, while Pavel Lvov's *A Russian Pamela, or the Story of Mary, a Virtuous Peasant Girl* (Rossiiskaya Pamela ili Istoriya Marii, dobrodetel'noi poselyanki, 1789) followed Richardson. Lyovshin and Aleksandr Benitsky (1781–1809) wrote satirical "journeys" and philosophical "oriental tales" in Voltaire's manner. The genre of the *conte moral* is represented by Aleksandr Izmailov's novel of manners, *Eugene, or the Detrimental Effects of Bad Upbringing and Company* (Evgenii ili pagubnye sledstviya durnogo vospitaniya i soobshchestva, 1799–1801). Aleksandr Radishchev's *Journey from Petersburg to Moscow* (Puteshestvie iz Peterburga v Moskvu, 1790) uses the form of Sterne's *Sentimental Journey* to advance a critique of the Russian social order from the viewpoint of an enlightened *philosophe*.

All of these works were artistically inferior to the works which they tried to imitate. In fact, less ambitious forms of narrative fiction aimed at simple entertainment were often superior to them, as, for example, Mikhail CHULKOV's *The Comely Cook* (Prigozhaya povarikha, 1770), the Russian *Moll Flanders*, or Matvei Komarov's *Unfortunate Nikanor, or Adventures of a Russian Nobleman* (Neschastnyi Nikanor ili Priklyucheniya rossiiskogo dvoryanina, 1775). They continue the tradition of the picaresque adventure novel, which is then raised to a higher level of realism and some social critique in Vasily NAREZHNY's *A Russian Gil Blas, or the Adventures of Gavrila Simonovich Chistyakov* (Rossiiskii Zhil'blaz ili pokhozhdeniya Gavrily Simonovicha Chistyakova, 1814). The adventure novel was refined by the addition of local and/or historical color in the novels of Narezhny (1780–1825) and Grigory Kvitka-Osnovyanenko (1779–1843), while an element of social satire was added to the novel of picaresque adventure by Faddei BULGARIN, whose *Ivan Vyzhigin* (1829) meant a step forward toward the social novel of the mid-19th century. The immense success of Bulgarin's novel was due largely to the middle-class ethos of its broad panorama of Russian provincial life, which appealed to the rapidly growing middle-class readership.

The romantic age launched the Russian novel on the road to genuine achievement. Aleksandr Pushkin's novel in verse *Eugene*

Onegin (1823–31), whose form is derived from Byron's *Don Juan* and similar works, and whose structure owes much to Sterne, defies classification. It is the first great Russian novel and a major influence far beyond its age. A novel of manners (Belinsky called it an encyclopedia of Russian life) and a family novel, a literary autobiography and a philosophy of life and of art, *Eugene Onegin* is a masterpiece of ambiguity. Its tight versification (*see* ONEGIN STROPHE) stands opposite a casual narrative; an apparently aimless plot eventually leads to the perfect symmetry of an hourglass; a light and graceful narrative voice produces what is really the saddest of all Russian stories; and prosaic subject matter is converted into charming poetry. *Eugene Onegin* was the first Russian novel to create Russian types who would be seen as emblems of their generation and their social class. Its successor in the latter sense was Mikhail LERMONTOV's *A Hero of Our Time* (Geroi nashego vremeni, 1840), whose romantic setting (the Caucasus and the Crimea) and Byronic hero made it a more "romantic" work than *Eugene Onegin*. It is structurally intriguing: composed of what were initially several separate short-stories, it presents the hero from several different points of view, gradually revealing his personality. Lermontov's novel also belongs to the "confession" genre, very popular in his age. Nikolai GOGOL's epopoeia *Dead Souls* (1842) is formally a picaresque novel, even in the traditional sense that it was meant to end with the *picaro* reformed and starting a good Christian life, but like *Eugene Onegin* and *A Hero of Our Time* it defies classification. It is, among other things, a POEMA (as its subtitle states) about the dead souls of Russia and the hope for their resurrection.

Besides these great works, which cannot be assigned to a particular novelistic genre, Russian literature of the romantic age produced a multitude of works which are readily classified. The great demand for adventure novels was met largely by translations of popular foreign authors such as Alexandre Dumas *père* or Captain Marryat, but Russian writers such as Aleksandr VELTMAN, Osip SENKOVSKY, and Nikolai POLEVOI contributed their share. The Walter-Scottian historical novel found its most successful practitioners in Mikhail ZAGOSKIN (1789–1852) and Ivan LAZHECHNIKOV (1792–1869). Pushkin's *The Captain's Daughter* (1834–36), a work of depth and originality, is also a pure vintage Waverley novel. Gogol's *Taras Bulba* (1835) is a mixture of historical romance and Gothic tale. The historical novel has been a fixture in Russian literature ever since the romantic age. From its tradition, mostly undistinguished, there emerged occasional remarkable offshoots, such as TOLSTOI's *War and Peace*.

A. F. Veltman (1800–70), a prolific and talented romantic novelist, wrote quasi-historical, utopian, and picaresque novels which resemble those of Jean Paul in their free play of fantasy, whimsical humor, and wide range of subject matter. A distinguishing mark of his art is the ample use of folklore, with plots moving in and out of the land of the Russian fairy tale and folk epic. The utopian genre is also represented by Vladimir ODOEVSKY's unfinished utopian novel *The Year 4438* (4438-oi god, published as late as 1926). The romantic *Künstlerroman* is represented by N. A. Polevoi's *Abbadonna* (1834) and by F. M. Dostoevsky's first major novel, the unfinished *Netochka Nezvanova* (1848–49), among others. The Gothic tale of horrors, represented mostly by translations, had its Russian practitioners also: Aleksandr BESTUZHEV-MARLINSKY (1797–1837), Aleksei PEROVSKY-POGORELSKY (1787–1836), and even Gogol, whose unfinished early novel *The Hetman* (1830–1832) definitely belongs to this genre.

The NATURAL SCHOOL of the 1840s developed a style which was still romantic in the narrator's (or implied author's) ironic detachment from his subject matter, usually the low life of the big city. It was influenced by the French "frenetic school," popular in Russia, whose works were a mixture of romantic and naturalistic elements. Dostoevsky's short novel *The Double* (1846) is a case in point, as it combines a fantastic plot (the hero is a madman who develops a *Doppelgänger* complex) with a carefully drawn realistic setting. An interest in social problems and in the social underdog was a dominant trait in the works of the natural school, much as in their French antecedents. Dostoevsky's *Poor Folk* (Bednye lyudi, 1846), Aleksandr HERZEN's *Whose Fault?* (Kto vinovat? 1845–1847), and Dmitry GRIGOROVICH's *The Village* (Derevnya, 1846) and *Anton Goremyka* (1847) may serve as examples.

The growth of the Russian novel was inextricably linked with the growth of the Russian monthly journal (the so-called thick journal). Most novels, including the most famous ones, such as *Anna Karenina* or *The Brothers Karamazov*, initially appeared in installments in such journals. The Russian novel's link with journalism was by no means limited to the technical aspect (publishing in installments had some effect on novelistic structure). Publishers such as Andrei Kraevsky (1810–99) of the OTECHESTVENNYE ZAPISKI, Mikhail KATKOV (1818–87) of RUSSKII VESTNIK, and Nikolai NEKRASOV (1821–78) of SOVREMENNIK exerted considerable control over the content of their journals, including a certain amount of censorship of accepted works. A novel's message was generally in accord with the journal's tendency and was judged, by readers and critics alike, largely on the merits of ideas expressed in it.

The great age of the Russian novel was launched by Ivan TURGENEV, whose first novel *Rudin* appeared in *Sovremennik* in 1856. It was followed by five more novels, each addressing itself to a new stage in the development of Russian society. The most famous of these, *Fathers and Sons* (Ottsy i deti), which appeared in *Russkii vestnik* in 1862, created the "type" of the Russian NIHILIST. The last, *Virgin Soil* (Nov'), published in *Vestnik Evropy* in 1876, was an attempt to analyze the POPULIST movement of the early 1870s. Turgenev was joined by Ivan GONCHAROV, whose *Oblomov* appeared in 1859. Fyodor Dostoevsky, who resumed his career after ten years of exile, began his *Notes from the House of the Dead* (Zapiski is mertvogo doma) that same year. Aleksei PISEMSKY scored his greatest success with *One Thousand Souls* (Tysyacha dush) a year earlier. The 1860s then saw *War and Peace* (1865–69) by Tolstoi, *Crime and Punishment* (1866–67) by Dostoevsky, and the emergence of some younger talented novelists, such as Konstantin LEONTIEV (1831–91) and Nikolai LESKOV (1831–95).

The Russian realist novel of the 1860s and 1870s deals with contemporary Russian life in broad panoramic terms. It is conscious of the historical events of which its action is a part. It always carries a message, social, moral, or ideological. Almost invariably it allows one to place the author in the political spectrum of the decade. One can speak of "nihilist" and "ANTINIHILIST" novels. The aesthetic of the Russian realist novel is involved in a *contradictio in adiecto*, demanding that the novel present "real life" (with inevitable allowances to propriety, censorship, and such), yet also claiming for the novel a certain generalizing and even prophetic power, in that it expects the characters and plots of these novels to be "typical" of contemporary society and its basic trends. Such symbolic power was attributed to the novels of Goncharov, Turgenev, Pisemsky, and others, by leading critics, such as DOBROLYUBOV, GRIGORIEV, and ANNENKOV. Dostoevsky, more ambitious than his rivals, actually suggested that his novels not only recognized trends in contemporary Russian society, but also foreshadowed its future.

The plot and structure of the Russian realist novel show great variety. Turgenev had a preference for "staging" his novels, with the plot amounting, in essence, to the intrusion of a stranger into a seemingly stable setting, which would return to its initial state after the stranger's eventual departure. Goncharov and Pisemsky tended toward a biographic plot. Dostoevsky's taut, dramatic plots, whose action extends over a few days only, as a rule, are built around a capital crime. Leskov liked a broad panorama of action, with the plot organized in space rather than in time. Tolstoi begins with his "confession" type *Childhood, Adolescence*, and *Youth*; later shows a preference for a plot which features a crisis in the hero's (or heroine's) life, as in *The Cossacks, Anna Karenina*, and *Resurrection*. The broad panoramic canvas of *War and Peace* and *Anna Karenina* is organized in terms of space as much as time.

Narrative technique likewise shows great variety. Tolstoi is closest to the pattern, established by Fielding, of a strong omniscient narrator who not only firmly controls his characters, but also judges them. Tolstoi's strong narrative voice makes his novels "monologic" as against Dostoevsky's "polyphonic" novels. In Turgenev's novels, on the contrary, the presence of the narrator is minimal, as are his insights into his characters' inner life. Dostoevsky has been credited by M. M. Bakhtin for having created the polyphonic novel, where the narrator's voice joins those of the major characters to generate a multivoiced dialogic narrative.

The Russian realist novel tends to be rich in context and subtext. It usually relates, through reference and allusion, to the social and literary scene of the day, and to other works of literature. The text often carries a more or less concealed polemic subtext, in which characters and events have a direct relevance to specific political issues and public figures or act as a response to earlier works of literature. Thus, the antinihilist novels of Dostoevsky, Pisemsky, and Leskov seek to discredit radicals and liberals in general, as well as particular political opponents and their works. Thus, Turgenev is lampooned as Karmazinov, a conceited and effete "great writer," in Dostoevsky's novel *The Possessed* (1871). The extremely negative image of the Russian gentry painted in novels by radical authors, such as *The Golovlyovs* (Gospoda Golovlevy, 1872–76) by Mikhail SALTYKOV-SHCHEDRIN, would be understood as a political statement by many readers. The novels of Turgenev, in particular, produced heated discussions about the authenticity of the social types presented by him.

The Russian novel was also a vehicle of outright political propaganda, being almost the only public forum in which controversial issues could be discussed rather freely. Thus, Nikolai CHERNYSHEVSKY's *What is to be Done?* (1863) became by far the most effective piece of socialist propaganda in the 19th century. Russian naturalist novelists, independently of Zola, concentrated, like the French novelist, on a certain segment of society or some aspect of regional life, often with the implied intent to awaken the conscience of the public to suffering and injustice. For example, Dostoevsky's *Notes from the House of the Dead* (1860–62) described the horrors of prison life in Siberia. Fyodor RESHETNIKOV's *The People of Podlipnoe* (Podlipovtsy, 1864) shocked the public with a depiction of the grinding poverty among the Finnish *permyaki* of the Northeast. Nikolai POMYALOVSKY's *Seminary Sketches* (Ocherki bursy, 1862–63), a work which like Dostoevsky's *House of the Dead* has the form of a novel, paints a bleak picture of life in an Orthodox seminary. Pavel MELNIKOV's (pseud. Andrei Pechersky) masterful "ethnographic" novels *In the Woods* (V lesakh, 1871–74) and *In the Mountains* (Na gorakh, 1875–81) vividly described life between the Volga and the Urals, especially among OLD BELIEVERS. Their tendency was to put in focus the native virtues of simple Russian people.

Russian literary critics generally paid much less attention to novelistic technique, structure, style, and symbolic detail than to a novel's ideological tendency. Nevertheless, reviews and essays by critics such as Belinsky, SHEVYRYOV, Dobrolyubov, Grigoriev, DRUZHININ, Annenkov, Leontiev, and STRAKHOV, to name but a few, contain occasional remarks which show that they were well aware of the problems inherent in the art of the novel. The notebooks, correspondence, diaries, and critical comments of novelists such as Turgenev, Dostoevsky, and Tolstoi show that they were at all times alert to the intricacies of their craft, commenting on the choice of a proper narrative voice, point of view, consistency of plot, plausibility and concreteness of characters and setting, as well as questions of style and language, proper social or regional diction in the dialogue, for example. A wealth of intrinsic and extrinsic evidence suggests that the major novelists of the 19th century perceived their novels as works of art, and so as integral wholes. Thus, foreshadowing symbols methodically prepare the dénouement of the plot in *Fathers and Sons*, in *Crime and Punishment*, and in *Anna Karenina*. In each case the distribution of such symbols throughout the novel indicates the author's continuous awareness of his novel as a whole. In each case a pattern of ironies, ambiguities, and parallelisms also suggests that these novels must be treated as integral works of art. The authors' statements about their novels also show that they conceived of their works as organized structures reflecting a definite conception of the world.

Nevertheless, the 19th-century novel also retains its syncretic quality. Many novels are composed of heterogeneous elements, including nonfiction, which are not wholly integrated into the plot. Even Dostoevsky's dramatic novels contain such elements as inserted letters, essays, and stories (told by the narrator or one of the novel's characters), Platonic dialogues, anecdotes and character sketches, confessions, speeches, many quotations and allusions to various works of literature and to the Bible, literary and social criticism, and other elements which do not advance the plot and may not even contribute to the development of the *sujet* of the novel.

Between 1880 and 1905 (approximately) the Russian novel was in decline, although a large number of novels continued to be published. The impressionistic style of writers such as GARSHIN, CHEKHOV, and KOROLENKO, which dominated the period, favored

the short story. It took some time until the SYMBOLIST movement infused the Russian novel with new vigor. Valery BRYUSOV, with his *The Fiery Angel* (Ognennyi angel, 1907–08), and Dmitry MEREZHKOVSKY with his trilogy *Christ and Antichrist* (Khristos i antikhrist, 1896, 1901, 1905) discovered new possibilities in the historical novel, without introducing any innovations in novelistic style or structure. But Aleksei REMIZOV (1877–1957), Fyodor SOLOGUB (1863–1927), and Andrei BELY (1880–1934), the latter two of whom established themselves as major poets before becoming novelists, created an entirely new kind of novel.

Remizov's novels *The Pond* (Prud, 1907) and *The Clock* (Chasy, 1908), and Sologub's *The Petty Demon* (Melkii bes, 1907) were a more radical departure from the realist novel than their plots and characters might have suggested. What was fundamentally new about them was that their language and imagery were activated and manipulated to generate as many effects as plot and characters in the old novel. The symbolic effect of stylistic patterns and recurrent imagery in these novels was aimed at evoking irrational fears, existential anguish, and a sense of doom and chaos. To some extent, such prose had been anticipated by Gogol. In Bely's *Petersburg* (1913–16), the text of the novel (and even the plot) is generated by a wealth of literary echoes, verbal associations, intricate patterns of recurrent imagery, geometric forms, colors, and outright "language games"— all of it "cerebral play," and unlike the realists' efforts toward an objective view of their society. Bely's novels feature a variety of new devices, including a great deal of *erlebte Rede* (or *erlebtes Gefühl*), where the narrative voice appropriates the speech and/or the emotions and sensations of its subjects, most interestingly so in *Kotik Letaev* (1917), where the subject is the experience of a child, beginning from his mother's womb and up to the age of five.

While the structure of the Russian symbolist novel does not altogether abandon conventional plot and character delineation, it follows none of the conventional lines of composition. It is a collage of heterogeneous images, formulaic phrases, literary echoes, scraps of dialogue, allusions to events of the day, and so forth, fragmenting and reshaping objective reality to form patterns that are symbolic of certain moods or ideas, such as the "yellow peril" and the mood of impending catastrophe in *Petersburg*.

Contemporaneously with the symbolist novel, Russian literature developed some other new tendencies. Ivan BUNIN, a disciple of Chekhov, developed an impressionistic narrative style of lyric nuances, fragmentary suggestive images, and subtle rhythmic and sound patterns in *Sukhodol* (1911) and *The Village* (1909–10). Maksim GORKY's novel *Mother* (1907), a mixture of his usual naturalist manner and an allegoric representation of the Russian Revolution, was hardly an artistic success, but it was to be the prototype of a whole new genre of Russian—and world—literature, namely, that which was to become known as the SOCIALIST REALIST novel.

The Revolution influenced the development of the Russian novel in several ways. It provided a generation of writers with subject matter. While the World War failed to inspire a single major novel, revolution and civil war were treated in numerous novels, of which several were remarkable. There were treatments falling under the category of "revolutionary romanticism," such as *The Iron Flood* (Zheleznyi potok, 1924) by Aleksandr SERAFIMOVICH. There were panoramic novels, fashioned after Tolstoi's *War and Peace*, for instance, Mikhail SHOLOKHOV's *The Silent Don* (Tikhii Don, 1928–40) and Aleksei TOLSTOI's *The Road to Calvary* (Khozhdenie po mukam, 1919–41). There were expressionist approaches, featuring the emotional impact on the Russian intellectual of the horrors, but also of the heroism and lofty hopes of the Revolution, such as Konstantin FEDIN's *Cities and Years* (Goroda i gody, 1924). There were novels of the documentary type, such as Dmitry FURMANOV's *Chapaev* (1923), which is remarkable for its introduction of a wholly new point of view, that of a proletarian and Party activist of Soviet vintage. There were also some remarkable novels of the Revolution which are symbolist both in their "ornamentalist" narrative devices and in their tendency to give a dual meaning to events described: a direct physical meaning and a metaphysical or allegoric meaning. Such are, for example, Boris PILNYAK's *The Naked Year* (Golyi god, 1922) and Andrei PLATONOV's *Chevengur* (1930, published in 1973).

In most instances, the narrator's point of view was that of an intellectual who finds his way to an acceptance of the Revolution, as in Mikhail BULGAKOV's *White Guard* (Belaya gvardiya, 1924). Less often, the Revolution was perceived through the eyes of a genuine proletarian, and often, the result left much to desire, as in Artyom VESYOLY's *Russia Washed in Blood (Rossiya krov'yu umytaya,* 1926). But in Aleksandr FADEEV's short novel *The Rout* (Razgrom, 1927), a consistently proletarian point of view and a distinctly "Soviet" morality were successfully integrated with Tolstoian psychological realism and a carefully structured narrative.

Few of the novels which deal with the period of reconstruction, or of the "production novels" of the 1930s, are as successful. There are novels whose authors' point of view is still that of a fellow traveller and which are artistically on a high level. There are also novels in which a proletarian viewpoint prevails, but none of them are artistic successes. Yury OLESHA's short novel *Envy* (Zavist', 1927) belongs to the former. It is, even today, the most "modern" novel ever written in Russian, featuring stream of consciousness, Freudian symbols, intricate subtexts, cinematic techniques in its descriptive passages, multiple perspective, and other ultra-modern "ornamentalist" devices. However, *Envy* remained a dead end. Fyodor GLADKOV's novel *Cement* (1925), which takes a proletarian viewpoint, carried the day. It became the prototype of the socialist realist production novel, whose plot features a critical juncture in the history of a production site, transportation unit, research institute, etc., where proletarian characters provide the constructive element, and assorted class enemies provide the destructive.

The production novel became the norm once the first Five-Year Plan was launched. Even without its political function, it presented a significant departure from the general tendency taken by the novel in the 20th century. It meant a return to 19th-century naturalism, lengthy digressions into nonfiction based on more or less substantial research (often of a technical nature), and the reduction of character to social type. In a manner reminiscent of the 19th-century *roman-feuilleton,* the Soviet socialist realist novel would directly respond to the latest political and economic events. For example, Sholokhov's *Virgin Soil Upturned* (Podnyataya tselina, 1932) was a response to Stalin's article "Dizzy with Success" of 2 March 1930, dealing with problems encountered by the collectivization of agriculture, while Leonid LEONOV's most important novel, *The Russian Forest* (Russkii les, 1953) was an exercise on Stalin's program of soil conservation and reforestation.

The "liberal" novels of the THAW period after Stalin's death differed from the "orthodox" ones only in their tendency. Thus, Ilya ERENBURG's novel *The Thaw* (1954–56) and Vladimir DUDINTSEV's *Not by Bread Alone* (Ne khlebom edinym, 1956) follow the master plot of the production novel. The social type to which their characters belong still determines their moral stature and function in the plot, although there has been a shift in the definition of some types.

The socialist realist novel is uniform and predictable in the same sense other established conventional novelistic genres (say, the detective novel) are. The master plot is played out in a great variety of different settings, and since the characters are determined by their social position and occupation, rather than by any personal traits, their variety is effected not so much by psychological criteria as by circumstances of occupational nature. Of course, not all Soviet novels are of the socialist realist "production" type. The HISTORICAL NOVEL continues to occupy an important place. Science fiction is at least as important as in the West and has been used to express thoughts which could not be stated in a novel set in contemporary Russia. The adventure novel continues to exist as literature for adolescents. There is also the satirical picaresque novel, whose best known practitioners were Ilya ILF and Evgeny PETROV. Nevertheless, the spectrum of the Soviet novel is considerably narrower than that of the 20th-century novel in the West. This goes for the serious novel as well as for "entertainments." In the former, not only political, social, and ideological restrictions account for the relatively narrow scope of the Soviet novel, but also the exclusion of the subconscious, the abnormal, and the frankly erotic. As for the latter, the adventure thriller, the detective story, the love romance, and other forms purported to have no social, educational, or moral value are frowned upon, although a market for them certainly exists.

A recovery from the stagnation of the novel under the socialist realist aesthetic proceeded along several lines. The war brought relief from the production novel and produced several novels of some merit. The "thaw" after Stalin's death produced not only a move-

ment toward honesty in literature, but also a tendency away from the schematic plots and characters of the production novel. The "socialist" component of socialist realism is eliminated or toned down in works of the rural school (DEREVENSHCHIKI), which feature the point of view of characters untouched or unaffected by the ideology of the socialist state. Such are, for example, the novels of Fyodor Abramov, *Brothers and Sisters* (Brat'ya i sestry, 1958) and *Two Winters and Three Summers* (Dve zimy i tri leta, 1968), or Vasily BELOV's *That's How It Is* (Privychnoe delo, 1966). Such is essentially the point of view of Aleksandr SOLZHENITSYN's *One Day in the Life of Ivan Denisovich* (Odin den' Ivana Denisovicha, 1962), even though the hero's consciousness is consistently filtered through that of the narrator.

A return to the psychological novel and hence to the personal concerns of life (identity crises, generation gap, family relations) was another way to break the canon of socialist realism. It is significant, though, that virtually all psychologically oriented fiction since the Thaw belongs to the genre of the short story and in almost every other way also follows the tradition of Chekhov. Among the short novels written in this vein, Vera PANOVA's *Seryozha* (1955), in which the world is seen through the eyes of a little boy, Vasily AKSYONOV's *Ticket to the Stars* (Zvezdnyi bilet, 1961), featuring a group of rebellious teenagers, and Andrei BITOV's *Such a Long Childhood* (Takoe dolgoe detstvo, 1965), which deals with adolescent psychology, stand out.

The "realist" component of socialist realism has been more resistant to change. Much of what is in violation of the canon of the realist novel has appeared in SAMIZDAT editions, or abroad. Mikhail Bulgakov's *The Master and Margarita* (Master i Margarita), fantastic and unconventionally structured (it features a multi-levelled plot and a novel-within-the-novel), was allowed to appear in 1966, a quarter of a century after it had been written. Boris PASTERNAK's celebrated novel *Doctor Zhivago* (1957), essentially unpolitical, but heavy with religious symbolism and allegory, has never appeared in the Soviet Union. Its narrative superficially resembles that of a 19th-century novel of the biographic type, but has, in addition to a great deal of foreshadowing and symbolic imagery, the extra feature of a network of correspondences between the narrative and the "Poems of Yury Zhivago," attached to the novel.

The literature of *samizdat* and of the "third wave" of *émigrés* features novels which lustily flaunt the canons not only of socialist realism, but also of realism. We find here a distinct preference for "modernist" devices. Sasha SOKOLOV's *School for Fools* (Shkola dlya durakov, 1976) views the world through the consciousness of a retarded boy, while Venedikt EROFEEV's *Moscow-Petushki* (1977) does the same through an alcoholic's delirium. Andrei Bitov's *Pushkin House* (Pushkinskii dom, 1978) features subtle play with point of view and estrangement. Georgy VLADIMOV's *Ruslan the Faithful: The Story of a Guard Dog* (Vernyi Ruslan: Istoriya karaul'noi sobaki, 1975) is a moral allegory in the tradition of Tolstoi's *Yardstick.* Aleksandr ZINOVIEV's *Yawning Heights* (Ziyayushchie vysoty, 1976) is a satirical anti-utopia *à clef.* Vladimir VOINOVICH's *The Life and Extraordinary Adventures of the Soldier Ivan Chonkin: A Novel-Anecdote in five parts* (Zhizn' i neobychainye priklyucheniya soldata Ivana Chonkina: Roman-anekdot v pyati chastyakh, 1975) names its genre in the title. It stands to reason that a response to Soviet reality would seek its outlet in the fantastic, the surrealistic, and the absurd. It is also understandable that a great symbolist novel which answers this description has never been published in the USSR, although it was written half a century ago: Andrei Platonov's *The Foundation Pit* (Kotlovan, published in the West in 1973).

Bibliography. General: A. S. Bushmin et al., eds. *Istoriya russkogo romana.* 2 vols. 1962–64. D. S. Mirsky, *A History of Russian Literature from Its Beginnings to 1900.* 1958.
Pre-Petrine and Eighteenth Century: Wm. E. Brown, *A History of 17th-Century Russian Literature.* 1980. ———, *A History of 18th-Century Russian Literature.* 1980. V. D. Kuz'mina, *Rytsarskii roman na Rusi: Bova, Petr Zlatykh Klyuchei.* 1964. D. S. Likhachev, *Poetika drevnerusskoi literatury.* 2d ed. 1971. N. K. Piksanov, *Starorusskaya povest'.* 1923. A. Pypin, *Ocherk literaturnoi istorii stareishikh povestei i skazok russkikh.* 1857.
Nineteenth Century: B. I. Bursov, *Lev Tolstoi i russkii roman.* 1963. Richard Freeborn, *The Rise of the Russian Novel.* 1973. Hen-

ry Gifford, *The Novel in Russia: From Pushkin to Pasternak.* 1964. V. Kirpotin, "Tipologiya russkogo romana," *VLit* 1965, no. 7. Janko Lavrin, *An Introduction to the Russian Novel.* 1947. B. S. Meilakh, ed., *Russkaya povest' XIX veka.* 1973. Helen Muchnic, *Russian Writers: Notes and Essays.* 1971. V. G. Odinokov, *Problemy poetiki i tipologii russkogo romana XIX v.* 1971. F. D. Reeve, *The Russian Novel.* 1966. Viktor Shklovskii, *O teorii prozy.* 1929. ————, *Povesti o proze: Razmyshleniya i razbory.* Vol. 2. 1966. N. A. Verderevskaya, *Russkii roman 40–60-kh godov XIX veka.* 1980.

Twentieth Century: Deming Brown, *Soviet Russian Literature since Stalin.* 1978. Edward J. Brown, *Russian Literature since the Revolution.* 1982. Katerina Clark, *The Soviet Novel: History as Ritual.* 1981. L. F. Ershov, *Russkii sovetskii roman: Natsional'nye traditsii i novatorstvo.* 1967. Geoffrey Hosking, *Beyond Socialist Realism: Soviet Fiction since Ivan Denisovich.* 1980. D. Mirsky, *Contemporary Russian Literature, 1881–1925.* 1926. Gleb Struve, *Russian Literature under Lenin and Stalin, 1917–1953.* 1971. Gleb Struve, *Russkaya literatura v izgnanii.* 1956.　　　V. T.

Novella, see SHORT STORY.

Novikóv, Nikolaí Ivánovich (1744–1818), journalist, critic, and publisher. Initially in the military, Novikov then served as secretary with CATHERINE II's Commission for the drafting of a new code of laws (*Ulozhenie*). After the Commission's dismissal in 1769 he devoted himself to journalism, editing the satirical journals TRUTEN' (1769–70), *Pustomelya* (1770), *Zhivopisets* (1772–73), and *Koshelek,* (1774), all modelled after *The Tatler* and *The Spectator* of Addison and Steele. The tendency of these journals was that of the liberal Enlightenment. In 1772 Novikov published his *Essay of a Historical Dictionary of Russian Writers* (Opyt istoricheskogo slovarya o rossiiskikh pisatelyakh), the first work of its kind by a Russian author, and from 1773 to 1775 a serial, *Old Russian Library* (Drevnyaya rossiiskaya vivliofika), in which he brought out some important historical source material. He also started a scholarly journal, *Uchenye vedomosti* (Learned News). In 1779 Novikov moved to Moscow, where he played an important role as a Freemason, philanthropist, publisher, and journalist. As a publisher, he produced translations of a large number of works of Western literature (Shakespeare, Rousseau, Diderot, Beaumarchais, Lessing, etc.). He also published several journals and the newspaper *Moskovskie vedomosti,* (1779–1789), with a weekly supplement for children (1785–89). All of these activities were halted by the government in 1789. In 1792 Novikov was arrested and kept in prison until the death of Catherine II. In 1796 her son Paul I had him released, but he was never allowed to resume his publishing or journalistic activities and retired to his country estate.

Works: Izbrannye sochineniya. Introd. G. P. Makogonenko. 1951. *N. I. Novikov i ego sovremenniki: Izbrannye sochineniya.* Comm. L. B. Svetlov. *Satiricheskie zhurnaly N. I. Novikova.* Ed. and introd. P. N. Berkov. 1951.

Translations: Lewanski, p. 314.

Secondary literature: P. N. Berkov, *Istoriya russkoi zhurnalistiki XVIII v.* 1952. G. Gareth Jones, "Novikov's Naturalized *Spectator.*" In *The Eighteenth Century in Russia.* Ed. J. G. Garrard. 1973. Pp. 149–65. G. P. Makogonenko, *Nikolai Novikov i russkoe prosveshchenie XVIII v.* 1952. Gilbert H. McArthur, "Freemasonry and Enlightenment in Russia: The Views of N. I. Novikov," *CASS* 14 (1980), pp. 361–75. Max J. Okenfuss, "The Novikov Problem: An English Perspective." In *Great Britain and Russia in the Eighteenth Century: Contacts and Comparisons.* Ed. A. G. Cross. 1977. Pp. 97–108. L. B. Svetlov, *Izdatel'skaya deyatel'nost' N. I. Novikova.* 1946.　　　V. T.

Nóvikov-Pribói, Aleksei Sílych (real name: Novikov, 1877–1944), writer. A sailor in the Tsar's Navy since 1899, Novikov served on the cruiser *Orel* when it sailed from the Baltic to the Pacific with the Second Pacific Squadron during the Russian-Japanese War of 1904–05. His ship was sunk in the naval battle of Tsushima and Novikov was captured by the Japanese. After his return to Russia he published two brochures about the battle, taking a sharply critical view of the Tsar's Navy. The brochures were confiscated and Novikov

emigrated. After the Revolution, Novikov used his naval background in writing many sea tales and his main work, the novel *Tsushima* (1932–35), called by some a "fictionalized documentary" (Westwood). *Tsushima* was widely acclaimed and won a Stalin prize. Novikov's long-lasting popularity with Soviet readers is due to his subject matter more than to his craftsmanship as a writer.

Works: Sobranie sochinenii. 6 vols. 1929–31. *Sobranie sochinenii.* 5 vols. 1963.

Translations: The Sea Beckons: Short Novels and Stories. Trans. B. Isaacs. Moscow, 1956. *The Captain.* London, 1936, 1946. *Tsushima.* Trans. E. and C. Paul. New York, 1937.

Secondary literature: V. Krasil'nikov, *A. S. Novikov-Priboi: Zhizn' i tvorchestvo.* 1966. J. N. Westwood, "Novikov-Priboi as Naval Historian," *SlavR* 28 (1969), pp. 297–303.　　　V. T.

Nóvyi Lef, see LEF.

Nóvyi mir (New World), Soviet "thick" journal, which began to appear monthly in Moscow in 1925 as an organ of the Soviet Writers' Union. In the 1920s, although it published many of the best writers of the day, *Novyi mir* took second place to A. VORONSKY's *KRASNAYA NOV'.* Contributors to the journal during this period included BABEL, MAYAKOVSKY, PASTERNAK, LEONOV, A. TOLSTOI, PRISHVIN, GORKY, and GLADKOV. In the 1930s and 1940s, *Novyi mir* suffered from the general decline of Soviet literature under Stalin. The most notable works published during these years were SHOLOKHOV's *Virgin Soil Upturned* (Podnyataya tselina) and the fourth book of *Quiet Flows the Don* (Tikhii Don) and V. Vishnevsky's *Optimistic Tragedy* (Optimisticheskaya tragediya). The journal's most brilliant period came in the post-Stalin years when *Novyi mir* came out under the editorship of Aleksandr TVARDOVSKY (1950–54, 1958–70). During these years, the journal published most of the best and, at times, politically explosive works to appear in the Soviet Union since Stalin's death, notably V. POMERANTSEV's article "On Sincerity in Literature" (1953), V. DUDINTSEV's novel *Not by Bread Alone* (1956), and SOLZHENITSYN's *One Day in the Life of Ivan Denisovich.* The content of the journal has declined somewhat since Tvardovsky's forced retirement from the editorship in 1970, but *Novyi mir* remains the most prestigious literary journal in the Soviet Union.

Bibliography: Edith R. Frankel, *Novy Mir: A Case Study in the Politics of Literature, 1952–1958.* 1981. A. Solzhenitsyn, *Bodalsya telenok s dubom.* Paris, 1975.　　　C. T. N.

Nóvyi zhurnál (New Review), the oldest and culturally most important Russian émigré literary-political review in existence. The first issue of this quarterly appeared in New York in 1942; by June 1982 a total of 147 issues had been published. *Novyi zhurnal* was founded by M. A. ALDANOV and M. O. Tsetlin; from 1946 to 1959 it was edited by M. M. Karpovich, from 1959 to 1966 by R. B. GUL, Yu. P. Deinike, and N. S. Timashev; from 1966 to 1975 by R. Gul, from 1975 through 1976 by R. Gul (editor-in-chief), G. A. Andreev, and L. D. Rzhevsky; and since March 1981 by R. Gul and E. L. Magerovsky. Zoya Yurieva is the secretary.

In many respects, *Novyi zhurnal* was a successor to the main émigré "thick" review of the pre-war period, the Paris-based SOVREMENNYE ZAPISKI (1920–40). The founders of *Novyi zhurnal* saw its task in the defense of a free Russia and continuation of the spiritual contribution to world culture made by Russia in the past. Later (No. 100, 1970), the review's position was defined as defense of the civic, political, and creative freedom of man, and as an affirmation of Russia's cultural identification with Europe, and the review itself as an organ of struggle against the anti-culture of despotic Bolshevism-Communism.

R. B. Gul, who has directed *Novyi zhurnal* for nearly a quarter of a century, singles out four periods in the history of the review: (1) from its foundation until the end of World War II (1945), (2) from the end of the war to the "thaw" in the USSR which came after Stalin's death (1953), (3) from the mid-1950s to the mid-1960s, and (4) from the mid-1960s to the present. The first period was characterized by a certain isolation and an emphasis on political topics. During the second period, *Novyi zhurnal* published the works of many well-known Russian authors who remained in Europe, mostly in France, as well as the works of some of the new émigrés, former

Soviet citizens. The "thaw" allowed *Novyi zhurnal* to penetrate into the Soviet Union and to publish the works of several Soviet authors. From the mid-1960s on, *Novyi zhurnal* has been receiving manuscripts directly from Soviet authors, critical of or actively opposed to the regime, who in one way or another "chose freedom."

During the over forty years of its existence, *Novyi zhurnal* has published a great number of important contributions in all of its sections: poetry and fiction, the arts, memoirs and documents, politics and culture, bibliography, and necrology.

Bibliography: Roman Gul', "Novyi zhurnal." In *Russkaya literatura v emigratsii.* Ed. Nikolai P. Poltoratzky. Pittsburgh, 1972. Pp. 321–31 (in Russian) and 384–85 (in English). This article is based on two articles previously published in *Novyi zhurnal* (Nos. 87 and 100) and later reprinted in: Roman Gul', *Odvukon'.* New York, 1973. Pp. 159–81 and 182–83.   N. P. P.

Oberiúty—participants in the *Oberiu* (Ob"edinenie real'nogo iskusstva, "Association for Real Art"), a Leningrad avant-garde literary and artistic group active from 1927 to 1930. Daniil KHARMS, Aleksandr VVEDENSKY, Nikolai ZABOLOTSKY, Nikolai Oleinikov, Igor Bakhterev, Konstantin VAGINOV, Boris (Doifber) Levin, Yury Vladimirov, and others were members.

Oberiu arose as a result of Kharms' and Vvedensky's efforts during 1925 to 1927 to unify the Leningrad literary and artistic avant-garde, succeeding several earlier groups with partially overlapping membership. One was the circle of *zaumnik* (transsense) poets headed by Aleksandr Tufanov, in which Kharms and Vvedensky briefly participated. Another, and more important, was the group centered around the avant-garde "Radix" theater: it included various figures who became Kharms's and Vvedensky's associates in *Oberiu.*

The "left" orientation of Kharms's and Vvedensky's efforts at organizational unity is reflected in some of the names (utilized or hypothetical) of the group during its formative period: "Left Flank", "Academy of Left Classics", etc. "Oberiu" was adopted in the autumn of 1927, when the group affiliated with the Leningrad House of the Press, to avoid controversy which at that time was becoming associated with an explicit avowal of "leftism" in art in the Soviet Union.

The *oberiuty* debuted in January 1928 at the House of Press with an evening entitled "Three Left Hours." It included readings by members of the group in a highly theatrical setting, as well as the performance of Kharms's play *Elizaveta Bam.* Irreverent, iconoclastic spectacles continued during the next two years, and won the *oberiuty* a place in Leningrad's cultural life. However, few of their works were printed; *Archimedes' Bath*, a collection planned in 1929, which was to include contributions by FORMALIST critics and such writers as KAVERIN and OLESHA, came to naught. For several of the *oberiuty*, the only chance to publish lay in children's literature. Kharms, Vvedensky, Zabolotsky, Oleinikov and Vladimirov worked for the Detgiz publishing house under Samuil MARSHAK. Their writings for children show a strong imprint of *Oberiu.*

Created almost on the eve of collectivization and the industrialization effort, *Oberiu* was decidedly out of step with the times. Its brief existence ceased after the April 1930 publication of the pogrom-like article "Reactionary Juggling," in which, among other points, its members were labelled "class enemies." Friendships and creative contacts among several of the *oberiuty* continued during the 1930s, but at this point the group no longer existed.

The *Oberiu* program was stated in a declaration published prior to its first public evening. The declaration protested the increasing restrictions on experimentation by such figures as the painters Filonov and Malevich, and the theater producer Terentiev. Polemicizing with "transsense" (ZAUM') poetry (of the purely phonic variety, as advocated by Tufanov), it celebrated "concreteness", and discussed the *Oberiu*'s striving to clear away conventional contextual associations of words and objects, and to reveal what the *oberiuty* regarded as their "absolute," fundamental meanings.

As the manifesto admitted, the *oberiuty* took different paths to achieving their goal of attaining the concrete in art. A common element in their practice involved the dissolution or segmentation of the depicted object, and reliance on collisions between verbal units taken out of their traditional contexts so as to produce new semantic effects.

In experimenting with syntagmatics and in subverting customary textual hierarchies, the *oberiuty* continued certain futurist practices, especially those of Velimir Khlebnikov and Aleksei KRUCHONYKH. Their deliberate alogism and their desire to uncover the underlying reality of objects also brought them close to other contemporary movements (cf. the ideas of Malevich and Filonov, SURREALISM, and expressionism).

The *Oberiu* association was an important stage in the creative biographies of its various members, but it does not encompass the full scope of their art. Bakhterev continued to create within the *Oberiu* framework; others, however, such as Zabolotsky, Kharms, and Vvedensky, underwent an evolution in their world-view and poetics.

The writings, not to speak of the very existence, of the *oberiuty* were almost totally unknown until the 1960s, when a rediscovery of the group began in the Soviet Union, and when their writings, circulated in *samizdat* form, began to exert an influence on the contemporary avant-garde. Complete editions of both Kharms and Vvedensky, produced by the Leningrad scholar Mikhail Meilakh, are being published in the West.

Works: Daniil Kharms, *Polnoe sobranie sochinenii.* 3 vols. Bremen, 1978–80 [Ongoing publication]. N. M. Oleinikov, *Stikhotvoreniya.* Introd. L. S. Fleishman. Bremen, 1975. *Russia's Lost Literature of the Absurd: Selected Works of Daniil Kharms and Alexander Vvedenskii.* Ed. with an introd. by George Gibian. Ithaca, 1971. Aleksandr Vvedenskii, *Polnoe sobranie sochinenii.* Vol. 1. Ed. Mikhail Meilakh. Ann Arbor, 1980. [Introd. very important; ongoing publication.] Nikolai Zabolotskii, *Stikhotvoreniya.* Ed. Gleb Struve and Boris Filippov. Washington, 1965.

Secondary literature: Fiona Björling, "*Stolbcy*" by Nikolai Zabolockij. Analyses. (Stockholm Slavic Studies, 8.) Stockholm, 1973. Lidiya Chukovskaya, *V laboratorii redaktora.* 1960. Ilya Levin, "The Fifth Meaning of the Motor-Car: Malevich and the Oberiuty," *Soviet Union/Union Soviétique*, Vol. 5, pt. 2 (1978), pp. 287–300. R. R. Milner-Gulland, "'Left Art' in Leningrad: the OBERIU Declaration," *OSP* 3 (1970), pp. 65–75. Alice Stone Nakhimovsky, *Laughter in the Void: An Introduction to the Writings of Daniil Kharms and Alexander Vvedenskii.* (Wiener Slawistischer Almanach, Sonderband 5.) Vienna, 1982. [Selected bibliography.]   H. B.

Oblomovism (*oblomovshchina*) is the term GONCHAROV coined in *Oblomov* for the inertia of his indolent hero. It is a tribute to the mythic power of the novel that "Oblomovism" has become a living part of the Russian language, along with "Don Quixotism" and "Hamletism." An enormously influential essay by the radical critic Nikolai DOBROLYUBOV, "What is Oblomovism," diagnosed it as an ailment of the Russian gentry, made passive by their dependence on the labor of serfs. For Dobrolyubov, Oblomov is the crystallization of a distinctively Russian literary type initiated by PUSHKIN's Eugene Onegin. The typical Russian hero is a member of the educated gentry, often highminded but ineffectual, alienated or, in the epithet of Russian criticism, "superfluous." Dobrolyubov also suggests that "Oblomovism" is a weakness of the Russian temperament, and for others it has been an expression of the "Russian soul." What Dobrolyubov dismisses is the compelling attractiveness of Goncharov's hero. Another, less pronounced current in Russian criticism, originated by the conservative critic Apollon GRIGORIEV and the aesthetically inclined Aleksandr DRUZHININ, has been kinder to Oblomov, emphasizing his human warmth and poetic imagination. Like so much in Russian thought, "Oblomovism" has provided a focus for ideological argument, with traditionalists taking a more benign view and progressives striking harsh notes. The arguments of criticism tend to recapitulate the arguments of the novel—of Stolz and Oblomov—except that Goncharov, like any great artist, is less interested in winning debater's points than in tracing the implications of ideas and attitudes for human life.

Bibliography: N. A. Dobrolyubov, "What is Oblomovitis." In *Belinsky, Chernyshevsky, Dobrolyubov: Selected Criticism.* Ed. Ralph E. Matlaw. 1962. A. V. Druzhinin, "Oblomov, roman I. A.

Goncharova." In *I. A. Goncharov v russkoi kritike*. Ed. M. Ya. Polyakov. 1958. Apollon Grigoriev, "I. S. Turgenev i ego deyatel'-nost'." *Sochineniya*. Vol. 1. 1876.   M. E.

óbraz, a literary term important in Russian literary criticism and literary theory. Its dictionary meanings are: (1) shape, form, appearance, (2) mode, manner, (3) image, (4) icon, sacred image. In aesthetic and critical usage it is routinely used in conjunction with the adjective *khudozhestvennyi*, "artistic," and acquires the meanings of an "aesthetic object" and of a "symbol."

In BELINSKY, the usage of *obraz* coincides with that of German *Bild*, "image," in Hegelian aesthetics, where it means both "shape, form, appearance" as well as "symbol." In this usage, the Russian (and the German) term also stand for "aesthetic idea," as opposed to "intellectual idea," so in Belinsky's celebrated definition of art as "*immediate* contemplation of truth, or thinking in *images*" (*myshlenie obrazami*). More precisely: "Truth was revealed to mankind first of all in *Art*, which is *truth made sensible*, that is, truth expressed not in an abstract idea but in an image (*obraz*), and moreover, in an image which is not a conventional symbol (as was the case in the East), but an *idea-turned-flesh*, a full, organic, and immediate manifestation in the beauty of its form, with which it is fused as inseparably as the soul is with the body." ("Gore ot uma," *PSS* 3, p. 423).

While Belinsky and his more sophisticated followers never considered *obraz* to be a visual image, or even a form directly related to any of the senses, their conception nevertheless created a narrow view of the creative process and the work of art. It implied that the mental activity involved in artistic creation (imagination) was fundamentally different from thought in other areas. It also meant an endorsement of the notion that an "inner vision" precedes the execution of a creative intuition (often called "poetic idea" by Belinsky and his successors).

Belinsky's conception was hardly challenged by 19th- and early 20th-century Russian critics. Even the Marxist LUNACHARSKY repeated Belinsky's definition, calling the work of art "a philosophy in images" (*filosofiya v obrazakh*). Only in FORMALIST criticism was it debunked, along with other concepts of organicist aesthetics, both in a psychological sense (regarding the creative process), and in a structural sense (regarding the nature of the work of art). The formalists SHKLOVSKY and JAKOBSON argued that great poetry can very well be imageless (*bezóbraznaya pocziya*) and that poetic creation must neither proceed by way of conceiving images, nor be necessarily holistic.

But in SOCIALIST REALIST literary theory and criticism, *obraz* once again occupies a central position. A great deal of theoretical literature has been and is still being devoted to it, and the term is an essential ingredient of textbooks in literary theory and aesthetics. It is defined as follows in *KLE*: "The artistic image is a universal category of artistic creation, being the method and form of mastering life specific to art, the 'language' of art and at the same time its 'expression'." The artistic image is thus perceived as an aesthetic universal which creates a bridge between objective reality and subjective human strivings. It is perceived as having cognitive power. Furthermore, it is seen as fully involved in the dialectic of the historical process, as it not only depicts, but also helps to change reality. The "inner form" (*vnutrennyaya forma*) of the artistic image, i.e., its ideological specificity and complexity, interacts organically with its outward form (rhythm, sound patterns, visual imagery), as well as with its sociohistorical function.

Bibliography: V. G. Belinskii. "Ideya iskusstva." In *PSS* (1953–59), vol. 4, pp. 585–602. Victor Erlich, *Russian Formalism: History—Doctrine*. 2d ed. 1965. Pp. 174–76 and 230–32. L. I. Timofeev, "K ponimaniyu termina 'obraz'." In *Osnovy teorii literatury*. 4th ed. 1971. Pp. 65–76. V. V. Vinogradov. "K sporam o slove i obraze," *VLit*, 1960, no. 5.   V. T.

Óbshchestvo lyubítelei rossíiskoi slovésnosti (Society of Amateurs of Russian Letters, 1811–1930), a learned society affiliated with Moscow University, which produced important serials, such as *Trudy OLRS* (20 vols., 1812–21), sponsored the publication of major scholarly works, such as V. I. DAL's *Tolkovyi slovar' zhivogo velikorusskogo yazyka* (4 vols., 1863–66), and initiated the erection of monuments to PUSHKIN (1880) and GOGOL (1909). Virtually every major Russian writer and literary scholar at one time addressed a meeting of the Society, with DOSTOEVSKY's "Discourse on Pushkin" (1880) the most celebrated of these occasions. Among the Society's presidents were M. N. ZAGOSKIN, A. S. KHOMYAKOV, M. P. POGODIN, I. S. AKSAKOV, A. N. VESELOVSKY, and P. N. SAKULIN. The Society continued its work after the October Revolution, but was liquidated in 1930.

Bibliography: P. N. Sakulin, "Obshchestvo lyubitelei rossiiskoi slovesnosti," *Pechat' i revolyutsiya*, 1927, book 7.   V. T.

Óbshchestvo lyubomúdriya, see WISDOM LOVERS, SOCIETY OF.

Ócherk, see SKETCH.

Odes. With antecedents going back to the 1670s (e.g., SIMEON POLOTSKY), odes figure most prominently in Russian poetry and most integrally with the literary system approximately from the 1730s to the 1830s. During the period of most intense cultivation, the genre included several different types: the panegyric ode (*oda pokhval'naya/torzhestvennaya*), the spiritual ode (*oda dukhovnaya/bozhestvennaya*), the Anacreontic and Horatian odes.

Honorifically linked with the ancient Pindaric ode, the Russian panegyric ode developed under European baroque and neoclassicist models. Lofty in language, solemn in tone, elaborately metaphoric and sonorous, this type of ode served as vehicle for suprapersonal ideological and political expression, employed typically "on occasion"—victories, landmarks in the life and reign of monarchs, the New Year, etc. It was LOMONOSOV, crucially influenced by the German odists (e.g., Günther), whose version proved overwhelmingly decisive; even its very stanzaic form—a unit of one quatrain plus two tercets in rhymed iambic tetrameter—became emblematic. The ode shaped by Lomonosov afforded equally an opportunity for voicing the highest national ideals and aspirations and an outlet for obsequiousness and chauvinism. Mandatory for all practicing poets in the 18th century, it underwent very conspicuous automatization and banalization. It was the frequent object of parody. DERZHAVIN, in addition to his Lomonosov-like odes, created a unique serio-comic type in his "Felitsa odes." RADISHCHEV, RYLEEV, and some other poets of the late 18th and early 19th centuries converted its panegyric purpose to that of bold political agitation. Marginally represented in Russian poetry after the 1830s, the panegyric ode reappeared, in modern transformation, in the 20th century with MAYAKOVSKY and enjoyed a later vogue with Stalin's adulators.

The Russian spiritual ode arose in connection with the practice of versifying the psalms. Other parts of the Bible also played a role but it was the lyric hero of the psalms with his creature-to-Creator relationship that served as the key element for original spiritual odes. As with their Western counterparts, Russian versions featured the vanity and transitoriness of human existence, the mystery and majesty of God and His universe, immortality, and similar themes. Again, Lomonosov was the paragon with his famous "Morning" and "Evening Meditations". TREDIAKOVSKY, SUMAROKOV, and virtually all other 18th-century poets made significant contributions, but the masterpieces of the Russian spiritual ode are Derzhavin's, e.g. "God" (Bog). Produced in enormous quantities, this type of ode did not, however, develop a canonical form of its own, frequently experimented with but as frequently adopting the form of the panegyric ode. With their close relationship in other respects, hybrid formations of these two ode types were common, an outstanding example being Derzhavin's "Waterfall" (*Vodopad*). Later, the spiritual ode merged into the romantic lyric in general.

The Anacreontic ode would seem, by its origin as light poetry devoted to "wine, women and song," not to stand on a par with panegyric and spiritual odes, but such was not the case. Not only did it bear the title "ode" and the authority of antiquity, it was also interpreted as a vehicle for expressing an opposition of values: personal vs. public interests, moral perfection vs. worldly success, love and friendship vs. power and glory, simplicity and naturalness vs. magnificence and grandiloquence, etc. Challenged by Lomonosov's rejection of Anacreontic values in favor of their opposites, Russian neoclassicists energetically cultivated the Anacreontic ode. In Sumarokov's hands it often served for literary polemic;

KHERASKOV and his Masonic associates particularly exercised its moralistic possibilities. Later, with KAPNIST, it resumed its light, and with Derzhavin, its erotic-bibulous character. As such it enjoyed its last popularity with the poets of "The Golden Age."

For the Russian Anacreontic ode prosodic equivalents were sought, choice devolving signally, although not exclusively, upon stanzaless, unrhymed trochaic or iambic tetrameter. The Horatian ode, in contrast, did not, except experimentally, achieve special formal identity. Translations of Horace's odes were legion throughout the 18th century, from KANTEMIR, and into the 19th century, Kapnist's being particularly successful. These translations frequently included adaptation to Russian—and even the poet-translator's personal circumstances—so that the border between them and the numerous original poems inspired by Horace was extremely fluid. Like the spiritual ode, the Horatian ode was refracted through a special image of the poet, here confronting not God and the universe but, as in the Anacreontic ode, the human condition. Worldly-wise, stoic in principle but epicurean in practice, with pessimism tempered by irony and humor, this Horatian image held enormous appeal and was realized most fully and vividly in Derzhavin.

Bibliography: G. A. Gukovskii, "Is istorii russkoi ody XVIII veka." In *Poetika*, Vol. 3. 1927. ———, *Russkaya poeziya XVIII veka*. 1927. Pierre R. Hart, "Continuity and Change in the Russian Ode." In *Russian Literature in the Age of Catherine the Great* 1976. Pp. 17–43. Yu. Tynyanov, "Oda kak oratorskii zhanr." In *Arkhaisty i novatory*. 1929. Pp. 48–86.   I. R. T.

Odóevsky, Aleksándr Ivánovich, Prince (1802–39), romantic poet and Decembrist, a model of the idealist poet and impractical revolutionary. As a young officer of the Guards he formed close associations in the early 1820s with A. S. GRIBOEDOV, A. A. BESTUZHEV, and K. F. RYLEEV. He joined the Decembrist Northern Society in the winter of 1824–25, and died in an epidemic in the Caucasus. Only fifty-seven poems have survived. A few poems were published before 1825, several appeared anonymously in 1830–31 in LITERATURNAYA GAZETA and SEVERNYE TSVETY. The early verses show that Odoevsky was a free-thinker who rejected the sentimental-elegiac manner of the early Russian romantics and glorified the Russian past. He wrote fine nature poems, verses on historical themes, and songs. He celebrated the Romantic hero-rebel and victim of crass society, and is remembered best for his poetry of imprisonment and exile, especially his reply to Pushkin's "Message to Siberia."

Secondary literature: M. Briskman, "A. I. Odoevskii." In *Polnoe sobranie Stikhotvorenii*. (Biblioteka poeta.) 1958. S. M. Klyuev, "Aleksandr Ivanovich Odoevskii (1802–39)," *Russkaya Rech'*, 1977, no. 6, pp. 30–38.   L. G. L.

Odóevsky, Prince Vladímir Fyódorovich (1803 or 1804–1869), writer, music critic, educator, and public servant. Born and educated in Moscow, Odoevsky developed an early interest in literature, becoming a member of the FREE SOCIETY OF AMATEURS OF RUSSIAN LETTERS and of the circle around S. E. RAICH. He was president of the Society of WISDOM LOVERS (1823–25) and co-editor, with V. K. KYUKHELBEKER, of MNEMOZINA (1824–25). In 1826 Odoevsky moved to St. Petersburg where he continued to be active as a writer, critic, and editor. Starting in 1846, he was deputy director of the Petersburg Public Library and director of the Rumyantsev Museum. When the Museum was transferred to Moscow in 1862, Odoevsky returned there.

Odoevsky is important in several areas. He is the principal exponent of Russian "philosophical romanticism," a knowledgeable adherent of Schelling's philosophy (he also knew Schelling personally and corresponded with him), who followed the example of the German romantics in using the short-story form to effect a fusion of philosophic thought and the reality of human life. His *Russian Nights* (Russkie nochi, 1844) are patterned after E. T. A. Hoffmann's *Die Serapionsbrüder*: Personalized narrators trade stories and between stories discuss the stories and the questions raised in them. Like Hoffmann, a music critic of some merit (he was also an amateur composer), Odoevsky gave much thought to the artist's calling, the traits which distinguish the creative individual, and the relationship between artist and society. These thoughts find

reflection in stories such as "Sebastian Bach," "Beethoven's Last Quartet," "Opere del Cavalière Giambatista Piranesi," and "The Painter" (Zhivopisets).

Odoevsky was also one of the most competent exponents of the Russian "society tale." His stories "Princess Mimi" (Knyazhna Mimi, 1834), "Princess Zizi" (1839), etc. combine social critique and perceptive psychology with a gentle irony. Furthermore, Odoevsky wrote some interesting phantastic tales, in the manner of E. A. Poe rather than of Hoffmann, as he himself said. The phantastic element in his stories has two sources: an interest in mysticism (Jakob Böhme, Swedenborg, Saint Martin, Franz von Baader) and an equally strong interest in the potential of science for the future of mankind (Odoevsky was himself an amateur inventor). Stories of a mystic bent are "Cosmorama" (1840), "The Salamander" (1842), and "The Possessed" (Besnuyushchiesya, 1842). Odoevsky's utopian phantasy "The Year 4338" (published in full only in 1926) contains many specific details of technical, social, and political nature which have already come true.

Odoevsky, a busy public servant for most of his life, whose social life took him to the highest circles of society, had little time for literature after the mid-1840s. But he contributed greatly to the progress of public education and musical culture in Russia. Close to the SLAVOPHILES, he was nevertheless an enlightened and highly cultured European, one of the most attractive figures of 19th-century Russian literature.

Works: Sochineniya. 3 vols. 1844. *Russkie nochi*. Ed. S. A. Tsvetkov. 1913. Reprint Munich, 1967. *4338 god. Fantasticheskii roman*. 1926. *Povesti i rasskazy*. Introd. E. Yu. Khin. 1959.

Translations: Russian Nights. Trans. Olga Koshansky-Olienikov and Ralph E. Matlaw. Introd. Dr. Matlaw. New York, 1965.

Secondary literature: V. G. Belinskii, "Sochineniya knyazya V. F. Odoevskogo" (1844), *PSS*, Vol. 8 (1955), pp. 297–323. Simon Karlinsky, "A Hollow Shape: The Philosophical Tales of Prince Vladimir Odoevsky," *Studies in Romanticism* 5 (1966), pp. 169–82. P. N. Sakulin, *Iz istorii russkogo idealizma. Knyaz' V. F. Odoevskii*. Vol. 1, pts. 1–2. 1913. Heinrich Stammler, "Fürst Wladimir Fjodorowitsch Odojewskij, der philosophische Erzähler der russischen Romantik." In *Fürst Wladimir F. Odojewskij, Russische Nächte*. Trans. Johannes von Guenther and Heinrich Stammler. Munich, 1970. Pp. 367–410.   V. T.

Odóevtseva, Irína Vladímirovna (pseud. of Iraída Gustávovna Ivánova, née Heinicke, 1901–), poet and novelist. Born in Riga, Odoevtseva became a member of the Acmeist POETS' GUILD and published her first volume of verse, *Court of Wonders* (Dvor chudes, 1922) in Petersburg. She emigrated with her husband, the poet Georgy IVANOV, in 1923. During the following three decades Odoevtseva published several novels and a number of short stories. Her prose, fluent and entertaining, was successful with the public and was translated into several languages, including English. In the 1950s Odoevtseva returned to poetry, producing several collections: *Kontrapunkt* (1951), *Verses Written While Ill* (Stikhi napisannye vo vremya bolezni, 1952), *Stikhi* (1960), *Ten Years* (Desyat' let, 1961), *Solitude* (Odinochestvo, 1965). Odoevtseva's poetry, remarkable for its formal discipline, displays an acute aesthetic sensitivity which often leads her to capricious, sometimes surrealist, associations of images, and a nagging awareness of death.

Works: (Novels:) *Nasledie* (n.d.), *Angel smerti* (1927), *Izol'da* (1931), *Zerkalo* (1939), *Ostav' nadezhdu navsegda* (1954). (Memoirs:) *Na beregakh Nevy* (1967). *Na beregakh Seny* (1983).

Translations: All Hope Abandon. Trans. F. Reed. 1949. *Out of Childhood*. Trans. and illustr. D. Nachshen. 1930.

Bibliography: See Foster, pp. 835–38.   V. T.

Ogaryóv, Nikolái Platónovich (1813–1877), poet, essayist, and co-editor with Aleksandr HERZEN of POLYARNAYA ZVEZDA and KOLOKOL. Ogaryov's poetry incorporated romantic subjects, nature and love motifs, peasant themes, satire, and civic issues. He wrote some unfinished prose fiction but his reputation rests primarily on his verse and sociopolitical activity.

Ogaryov was born into a well-to-do gentry family. His education was fairly typical for the Russian upper class and combined Western ideas with native, largely religious, cultural influences. Early poems such as "Christ" (1836), "The Christian" (1838), and "My Prayer" (1838) reformulated Russian Orthodox values into the contemporary language of romanticism. Contact with utopian socialism in turn served the transformation of Christian ethical impulses into a vision of imminent change in morality and society; a discussion group, organized around Ogaryov and Herzen in Moscow University, acted as an influential forum in which such ideas were aired. Other poems written by Ogaryov in the 1830s and early 1840s reflected themes of romantic idealism and his readings in Schelling, Goethe, and Lermontov. Pantheism and melancholy on the German model, thus, are evident in "Night" (1838) and "Among the Graves, I, in the Evening Hour" (1838), while a free rendition of Goethe's "Der Fischer" is skillfully presented in "Nocturno" (1840?). Among the most successful of such early works is "The Old House" (1839), Ogaryov's first published piece of verse. It expresses a well-tuned nostalgia for the past and for the passing of youthful hopes. Ogaryov's romantic inclinations were further revealed in verse renditions of the Hamlet motif, in a cycle of poems to friends: "To A. Herzen" (1833?), "To Friends" (1837), "To Tuchkov" (1839), and in a lifelong attraction to music. Ogaryov was fond of musical imagery, included musical directions in his poetry, and gave musical titles to his works: "I Tempi" (1835), "Aurora-Walzer" (1843?), "Scherzo" (1863–64). He himself composed a number of musical scores; to many 19th-century Russians, indeed, he was primarily known through popular folk and revolutionary songs such as "The Village Watchman" (1840), "The Prisoner" (1850), and "Freedom" (1858).

A neglected part of Ogaryov's poetic endeavor was a secret cycle of love lyrics brought together under the title of *Buch der Liebe* (1841–44). The poems—only published in their entirety in the 1950s—were addressed to E. V. Sukhovo-Kobylina, sister of the famous playwright. Inspired equally by Heinrich Heine and personal experience, these verses combine a sad irony stimulated by unattainable love with a profound appreciation of nature reminiscent at its best of FET. Ogaryov never revealed his feelings for Sukhovo-Kobylina and was not particularly fortunate in his relationships with other women. His first marriage, to Marya Roslavleva, proved to be disastrous; his wife refused to give him a divorce and helped to ruin him financially. His second wife, Natalya Tuchkova became Herzen's mistress (although not to the detriment of the deep friendship of the two men), and only the last, a former London prostitute named Mary Setherland, provided Ogaryov with solace and companionship in his old age. TURGENEV later included traits he saw Ogaryov demonstrate in his relationship with Marya Ogaryova in the protagonist of *A Nest of Gentlefolk*, Lavretsky.

Ogaryov's sociopolitical poems included verse based on a historical pessimism reminiscent of Herzen's ideas: "The Year 1849" (1849), "Die Geschichte" (1856); social criticism: "To Korsh" (1856), "Contemporary" (1858); partially autobiographical verse delineations of the Russian landowner's empty existence and ineptitude: "The Village" (1847), "The Gentleman" (1840s); poems on the Decembrists: "In Memory of Ryleev" (1859); and sentimental pieces full of outrage over government injustice such as "To Mikhailov" (1861) and "The Student" (1868)—the last parodied by DOSTOEVSKY in *The Devils*. Ogaryov's political verse opened the first issue of *Kolokol* and marked its last number. Among the most interesting experiments he undertook in this genre was "A Panorama of the Eastern Question" (1869) in which the folk *raeshnik* form is used for purposes of political satire.

Ogaryov's poetic legacy would have been considerably enhanced if he had completed a number of his long poems. The major part of his creative energy after his departure from Russia in 1856, however, was spent on editorial duties and articles on a wide range of social and economic issues of the sort he wrote during the years 1856 to 1858 for *The Polar Star* and *Kolokol* under the heading of "Russian Questions." The long poem "Yumor" (from the French *l'humeur*), begun under the influence of PUSHKIN and incorporating the concluding rhyme of the *Onegin* stanza, showed special promise as a plotless, first-person rendition of a superfluous man's ideology. In it Ogaryov calls on moments of his own intellectual biography, emphasizes the erosion of early ideals, and marks his passage into skepticism and political squabbles. The first two parts were completed in 1841, the third towards the end of the 1860s, and the re-

mainder of the work only exists in drafts. Other poems such as "The Village" (1847) and "Matvei Radaev" (1856–58) also remained unfinished. Out of the longer works Ogaryov did complete, "The Winter Way" (1855) demonstrates his talent in the use of nature imagery and a skillful control of meter.

Works: Stikhotvoreniya i poemy. Ed. S. A. Reiser. (Biblioteka poeta.) 2d ed. 1956. *Izbrannye sotsial'no-politicheskie i filosofskie proizvedeniya.* 2 vols. Ed. M. T. Yobchuk and N. G. Tarakanov. 1952–1956.

Translations: See Lewanski, p. 315.

Secondary literature: M. Gershenzon, "Lirika Ogareva," *Vestnik Evropy,* no. 9 (1903), pp. 292–312. ———, *Obrazy proshlogo.* 1912. V. A. Putintsev, *N. P. Ogarev.* 1963.

N. Rz.

Óksman, Yulián Grigórievich (1894–1970), historian and philologist, a specialist in 19th-century Russian history and literature. A graduate of Petrograd University (1917), he became a professor of that university in 1923. He was executive director of the Leningrad Institute of Russian Literature (Pushkinskii Dom) from 1933 to 1936. He was in prison from 1936 to 1945, and after his release a professor at Saratov University (1946–1957) and a senior researcher at the Institute of World Literature. In the 1920s Oksman established himself as the best connoisseur and editor of sources on the history of the DECEMBRISTS. A major organizer of the edition of Pushkin's Collected Works, famous for its textological quality, he also left excellent studies on Ryleev, Pushkin, Garshin, Herzen, Turgenev, and Belinsky (*Chronicle of the Life and Works of Belinsky—Letopis' zhizni i tvorchestva Belinskogo,* 1958). Oksman was one of the most influential "practical" textologists in Soviet philology, a brilliant lecturer and organizer of philological studies.

Bibliography: N. M. Chentsov, *Vosstanie dekabristov: Bibliografiya.* 1929. (Index.) *Dekabristy: Otryvki iz istochnikov.* Ed. Yu. G. Oksman. 1926. R. G. Eimontova and A. A. Solennikova, *Dvizhenie dekabristov: Ukazatel' literatury, 1928–1959.* 1960. K. D. Muratova, ed., *Istoriya russkoi literatury 19 veka: Bibliograficheskii ukazatel'.* 1962. *Ot Kapitanskoi dochi k Zapiskam okhotnika; Pushkin-Ryleev-Kol'tsov-Belinskii-Turgenev: Issledovaniya i materialy.* Saratov, 1959.

E. B.

Oktyábr' (October), a literary group and journal. The group was formed in 1922 in Moscow by young writers, all members of the Communist Party or the Komsomol, who wished to revise the languishing proletarian culture movement (See PROLETKULT, KUZNITSA). They believed that the proletariat must create its own literature, which would be topical and propagandistic, would enjoy predominance, and would best develop through a mass organization modeled on the Party. To these ends they set up the MAPP, took over and reinvigorated the VAPP, and established two important journals: NA POSTU (1923), and *Oktyabr'* (1924). The group's leading critics and theorists were Leopold AVERBAKH, Semyon RODOV, Georgy LELEVICH, Illarion Vardin, and Boris Volin; the most famous poet was Aleksandr BEZYMENSKY; the best prose writers, Yury LIBEDINSKY and Dmitry FURMANOV. The Octobrists, chronically intransigent and contentious, opposed all non-proletarian literary groups, but especially the journal KRASNAYA NOV' and its editor VORONSKY. A Resolution of the Press Section of the Central Committee (18 June 1925) rebuked them for factionalism, and enjoined them to work toward a more broadly based organization that would attract PEASANT and FELLOW-TRAVELER writers to proletarian ideals. As a result, the group split and folded that same year. But a "left" wing, led by Vardin, Lelevich and Rodov, long continued to reiterate the old positions; a "right" wing, under Averbakh, undertook to devise a new literary program, which was embodied partly in the Federation of Organizations of Soviet Writers, (FOSP, 1926), and mainly in the RAPP.

Oktyabr' was established as a "thick" journal with several departments. But it was most important for its belles lettres, the work mainly of proletarian writers. While echoing the views of *Na postu* and NA LITERATURNOM POSTU, it survived them both, became an organ of the UNION OF SOVIET WRITERS, and continues to this day. In the cultural controversies of recent years, it has consistently supported the "conservative" line.

Secondary literature: Herman Ermolaev, *Soviet Literary Theories, 1917–1934.* 1963.   R. A. M.

Okudzháva, Bulát Shálvovich (1924–   ), poet and writer, was born in Moscow of Georgian and Armenian parents. He volunteered for the front in 1942. At the war's end he entered the Philology Department of Tbilisi University, graduating in 1950. For the next five years Okudzhava taught in a village school in the Kaluga area, where his first volume, *Lyrics* (Lirika, 1956), appeared. At this time, Okudzhava began to perform his verses, which he accompanied on the guitar. After his second volume, *Islands* (Ostrova, 1959), he widened the scope of his writing: in addition to two more volumes of verses, *The Merry Drummer* (Veselyi barabanshchik, 1964) and *March the Magnanimous* (Mart velikodushnyi, 1967), he also published short prose works, "So Long, Schoolboy" (1961), "Promoksis" (1966), and three historical novels, *Poor Avrosimov* (Bednyi Avrosimov, also known as *A Sip of Freedom*, Glotok svobody, 1969), *Merci, or the Adventures of Shipov* (Mersi, ili pokhozhdeniya Shipova, 1971), and *Journey of Dilettantes* (Puteshestvie diletantov, 1979). His collection of songs and poems, *Arbat, my Arbat* (Arbat, moi Arbat) appeared in 1976. From the early sixties on, Okudzhava's elegiac, gently ironic songs, his most successful genre, have been recorded and sung by his post-Stalinist audiences, especially the urban youth. His principal themes—the brutality of war, human frailty, the enduring presence of hope—are dominated by lyricism even in his most humorous, critical, or self-critical pieces. He manages to combine breadth of vision with artistic understatement and generosity of spirit. His songs, technically modest, lack strict rhyme, meter, or even a set text. They often describe contemporary urban life, imbued with a sense of mystery. They are nevertheless consciously shaped, the concluding stanza usually providing an unexpected twist, a commentary, or a circular reiteration of earlier stanzas.

Works: Izbrannaya proza. 1979. *Proza i poeziya.* 5th ed. Frankfurt, 1977. *Arbat, moi Arbat.* 1976.

Translations: Bulat Okudzhava: 65 Songs. Trans. Eve Shapiro. Ed. Vladimir Frumkin. Ann Arbor, 1980. (Bi-lingual text.)

Secondary literature: G. Krasukhin, "To grusten on, to vesel on …" *VLit,* 1968, no. 9, pp. 40–54.   N. C.

Old Believers. There were two generations of Old Believer writers. The first was a spontaneous movement within the Church which launched an ideological campaign against Nikon's reforms of the Church ritual and books after they were accepted by the Council of 1666–67 which condemned the Old Belief as heretical. The second represented an organized school in the Vyg commune at the beginning of the 18th century. The introduction of the spoken word into the literary language, the dramatic, concrete narration of contemporary events, and the focus on their authors' and protagonists' personal responses to these events were the major contribution of the first generation to Russian literature. These innovations transformed previous poetic tradition and represented a step forward in freeing the word from domination by myth, pointing to the literary discoveries of the 19th century. The writings of the second generation lacked the innovative dynamic nature of those of the first. Under the leadership of the Denisov brothers, the Vyg school drew on the mainstream genres and poetics of the late 17th century. It espoused the scholastic aesthetics of the KIEV ACADEMY, inimical to the first generation, and produced sacred biographies in syllabic verse while remaining faithful to the traditional Old Believer themes of the end of the world, the reign of the Antichrist, and the benefits of life in the wilderness.

The fugitives and exiles of the first generation upheld the messianic penitential tradition which had sanctified the Third Rome since the rise of Muscovy. Their writings helped form a self-conscious movement, and inspired masses of the Russian people to stand up against the Westernizing official Church and State. The most gifted of the Old Believer writers was the Archpriest AVVAKUM. His autobiographical saint's life, a confession to the reader and to the monk Epifany, is an outstanding monument of Old Russian literature. Its lively vernacular language even drew accolades from the Westernizer TURGENEV. Others deserving of mention are Avva-

kum's co-exile at Pustozersk, the monk Epifany, who presented Avvakum with his own confessional, autobiographical saint's life, the monk Tikhon, the author of the incantatory "Abyss" and other works, the monk Avraamy, one of several Old Believers who wrote *virshi* such as were popular in the first half of the century. Other contributors were the priest Efrosin who composed the "Denunciatory Writing on the New Path of Suicidal Death" in 1691 to oppose the growing practice of self-immolation among dissenting peasant communities, the monk Feoktist who attempted sacred biography in his notes on the life of Ivan Neronov, and the anonymous author of the traditional life of the Boyarina Morozova.

The best of these writers used the word as a transforming spiritual force, and a witness to each man's personal responsibility in the providential unravelling of contemporary events. Their works mirrored the impending fulfillment and end of sacred history. Language, form, personal feeling, and experience tended to achieve and transcend their limits. The Old Believers naturally espoused the high style Slavonic canonized in the publicistic writings of the age of IVAN IV, but also used the "low" native Russian vernacular in historical and biographical narrative. This allowed for popular folk forms of *raeshnyi* (see SKAZOVYI STIKH) and accentual verse and of parody, as well as for self-consciously Orthodox literary usages. Both the Archpriest Avvakum and the monk Tikhon felt the need to use drawings of the universal order to illuminate the outer moral and spatial limits immanent in their poetic statements. The "Abyss" of Tikhon portrayed extreme emotional pathos. It reproduced the cries of the damned at the Last Judgement in a repetitive chant without narrative structure. The words possessed the force of repentance and could save one from hellfire. Efrosin's "Denunciatory Writing" focused in gruesome and naturalistic detail on the body's passage from life to death during immolation, perhaps to expose the victim's delusions of spiritual transformation. In general, Old Believer genres transcended their limits as well, and combined various religious and publicistic functions.

Bibliography: Ya. L. Barskov, *Pamyatniki pervykh let russkogo staroobryadchestva.* 1912. N. Nikol'skii, *Pamyatniki drevnei pis'mennosti i iskusstva,* vyp. 108 (1895), pp. 1–154 has Efrosin's "Denunciatory Writing". N. I. Subbotin, *Materialy dlya istorii raskola za pervoe vremya ego sushchestvovaniya.* 1875. V. I. Malyshev, *Pustozerskii sbornik.* 1975. I. M. Kudryavtsev, "Sbornik XVII v....," *Zapiski otdela rukopisei GBL,* vyp. 33 (1972), pp. 148–213. A. I. Mazunin, *Povest' o boyaryne Morozovoi.* 1979. For a general discussion of Old Believer writing see: *Istoriya russkoi literatury Akademii Nauk.* Vol. 2. 1948. Pp. 302–42.   P. H.

Old Church Slavonic, see CHURCH SLAVONIC.

Old Russian literature. The term "Old Russian literature" (*drevnyaya russkaya literatura*) generally is used to refer to all forms of "literary" activity in "Old Russia" from the 11th to the 17th centuries. However, the very notion of Old Russian literature has long been and still remains the object of wide-ranging disputes. Scholars have debated the question of whether the written documents produced in the centuries loosely defined as the "pre-Petrine age" should be granted the same "literary" dignity which has been conferred upon "Russian literature" of the modern period. In addition, the legitimacy of the qualifier "Old Russian" has been challenged by those who are unwilling to define as "Russian" a spiritual heritage belonging not only to the Great Russians but to the Ukrainians and the Belorussians as well. Nor has this qualifier been well received by scholars who hesitate to apply the modern concept of "nation" to medieval and premodern cultures. The terminological problem is compounded by the ambiguity of the term *russkii*, which is used with reference to both medieval *Rus'* and modern *Rossiya*.

It is important to remember that any historiographic formula (including Old Russian literature) possesses a high degree of conventionality and reflects a chosen point of view. What is seen as Old Russian literature can also be examined with different criteria and viewed from other perspectives. Given that "Old Russian" authors shared a religious and cultural patrimony with their fellow writers in the Serbian and Bulgarian lands, one can readily evaluate their work as the expression of a larger, supranational community, which can be defined as SLAVIA ORTHODOXA (i.e., Orthodox Slavdom). The fact that the Eastern and Balkan Slavs were under the spiritual jurisdiction of Orthodox churches traditionally bound to Constantinople was of decisive importance. Throughout *Slavia orthodoxa*, the art of writing was reserved for ecclesiastics and literary activity was directed by church authorities. The unity of purpose underlying a large part of "Orthodox Slavic literature" is evidenced clearly by the fact that texts could circulate from one end of the community to the other, that is, from the Aegean Sea to Novgorod and even to the islands of the White Sea. This degree of interchange could not have been possible without the existence of a common linguistic medium, namely, CHURCH SLAVONIC. Yet one should not believe that this linguistic medium was homogeneous. While pan-Orthodox Slavic elements made of its higher levels a supranational language, local variants characterized texts with more limited circulation. It is therefore possible to speak of a supranational "Church Slavonic linguistic community" within which there could develop local traditions such as "Old Bulgarian," "Old Serbian," and "Old Russian," or even "Old Kievan," "Old Novgorodian," and "Old Pskovian."

As regards the "literary" dignity of Old Russian literature, the main critical debates have focused on the question of whether the texts to which this historiographic formula refers actually exhibit "literariness," that is, whether they can be considered works of verbal art. Those unwilling to recognize the "literary" prestige of Old Russian literature have insisted on the following points: (1) Old Russian writers disregarded any form of "fiction" and produced works of a purely practical and utilitarian character; (2) Old Russian authors were not guided by theoretical principles equivalent to Western "poetics" and "rhetoric"; and (3) Old Russian writers wrote only in prose and completely ignored "poetry," that is, any type of "verse." The defenders of Old Russian literature have argued in response that: (1) the use of different levels of meaning and semantic figures was technically equivalent to the use of "fiction"; (2) no autonomous theory of literature was needed in a society which relied on church doctrine for every aspect of human activity, including literature; and (3) Old Russian texts are not entirely written in plain prose and exhibit complex combinations of rhythmo-syntactic units which can play a role similar to that of "poetry."

Another major problem in the study of Old Russian literature is presented by the dating and attribution of the literary monuments which have come down to us. The manuscripts which contain these monuments frequently betray so many traces of scribal intervention that it becomes exceedingly difficult to date a given text in its entirety. Not bound by any sort of "copyright," Old Russian scribes were free to introduce extensive changes into many texts. The very idea of authorship was alien to a large portion of Old Russian literature. Even works for which the name of an author was preserved in the process of textual transmission might ultimately keep very little of the author's original wording.

Thus, on the same page one may well find textual materials produced centuries apart and arranged in a new context. What this means is that a work originally written in an older period can be read only in later texts. At times, literary scholars are beset with perplexities, for they are uncertain whether to ascribe a given work to one age because of its origins, or to another because of its textual characteristics. For this reason, it is no easy task to construct a history of Old Russian literature based on a succession of different writing techniques.

The fact is that not a single history of Old Russian literature written in the past century has offered a periodization which relies on formal criteria. Instead, scholars have had recourse to historiographic schemes which chiefly depend on political and social events. Hence, the history of Old Russian literature currently is expounded in accordance with established sociopolitical categories such as the "literature of Kievan *Rus'*," the "literature of Muscovite Russia," the "literature of the TIME OF TROUBLES," the "literature of the centralized Russian state," and so forth. And even if specialists increasingly have made use of formulae such as the "period of stylistic simplicity," the "age of ornamental style," the "style of monumental historicism," and the "age of imperial rhetoric," their descriptions frequently have served to illustrate the characteristics of a period defined according to extraliterary criteria.

The origins of Old Russian literature coincide with the Christianization of Kievan *Rus'* during the reign of Prince Vladimir Svyatoslavich (ca. 988). The organization of a missionary church required the training of a clergy which was capable of reading and expounding apostolic texts in a standardized language intelligible to the local populace. This language had already acquired full liturgical dignity in Bulgaria, where Prince Boris had granted protection to some surviving members of the Cyrillo-Methodian community following its dissolution in Great Moravia towards the end of the 9th century. Many of the books needed for the newly established church were brought to *Rus'* from the Balkan Slavic area. It appears, however, that very soon writing centers were established in *Rus'* and local scribes began producing new copies of religious books. These local scribes may be seen as the initiators of a literary tradition which was to develop and eventually embrace all aspects of spiritual life in the Russian lands. Scribes operating in isolated cells, or working either for the ecclesiastical administration or in the service of secular dignitaries, added to their copying activities other, more demanding tasks such as compiling and adapting various texts, translating from the Greek language, and writing pages of their own.

At the dawn of Russian Christianity translated literature represented the largest and most influential corpus of writings. This situation remained unchanged for centuries. The first translations (almost exclusively from Greek) were made with the aim of fulfilling liturgical needs and providing believers with a basic body of didactic and edifying writings. Other texts which dealt with both religious and secular matters gradually were translated, but not always with the formal approval of the ecclesiastical authorities. Collections of heterogeneous texts very quickly became a typical expression of Old Russian book writing. In this regard, one should note that it is difficult to distinguish readily between "official" and "non-official" literature, or between "ecclesiastic" and "secular" writings. Within the same miscellany one might find officially-sanctioned hagiographies interspersed with apocryphal literature or historical accounts.

Translations could either be produced in Old *Rus'* or be based on preexistent translated texts brought from the Balkan Slavic area. The oldest dated monument of Old Russian literature is a work known as the *Ostromir Gospel*. It is an *Evangelie-aprakos*, that is, a collection of Gospel readings for feast days, which was copied from a Balkan Slavic model for the Novgorod *posadnik* (alderman) Ostromir in 1056–57. The *Tetraevangelion* (Chetvero-evangelie), service books such as the *Ieratikon* (Sluzhebnik), the *Agiasmatarion* (Trebnik), and the *Horologion* (Chasoslov), selections from the Old Testament (Parimiinik) and the Psalms (Psaltyr') are only some of the writings which comprised the corpus of translated literature for liturgical purposes.

At the boundary between canonic and apocryphal literature lay the historical and interpretative versions of the PALEYA. Collections such as the *Monthly Readings* (MINEI CHET'I), *Synaxary* (PROLOG), and *Paterikon* (Paterik) contained various types of hagiographic writings. Encyclopaedic compilations, which were based largely on Byzantine prototypes, included patristic and didactic literature. The oldest compilations of this kind are the IZBORNIKI SVYATOSLAVA of 1073 and 1076. In later periods, collections such as the *Hexaemeron* (Shestodnev) of John the Exarch, the *Physiologus*, and the *Christian Topography* of Cosmas Indicopleustes, which enjoyed tremendous popularity throughout the entire Byzantino-Slavic community, made their way to the Russian lands.

With the growth of writing centers and the formation of a more demanding reading public, other types of literature were transferred from the Greek area to *Rus'*. As early as the 12th and the 13th centuries, the Eastern Slavs were acquainted with the Byzantine *Chronicles* of John Malalas and George Hamartolus (and its continuation by Simeon the Logothete), Flavius Josephus' *History of the Jewish War* (known in Russian copies as *Povest' o razorenii Ierusalima* [Tale on the Destruction of Jerusalem], the *Romance of Alexander* by Pseudo-Callisthenes, the epic poem *Digenis Akritas*, the *Tale of Barlaam and Josaphat*, and the *Tale of Akir the Most Wise*.

Original (i.e., non-translated) literary compositions in the Russian lands were largely patterned after the models provided by translated literature. Yet with a cultural environment more ecclesiastically oriented than in the Byzantine area, the range of themes and forms were notably more restricted in Old *Rus'*. The principal types of writings (or "genres," as they are often called) can be reduced to: (1) homiletics, (2) hagiography, and (3) chronicles. However, each of these three main types of literature reflected thematic and formal categories which were so broadly conceived that they could easily embrace different sub-types (or "subgenres"). One should remember that the most typical Old Russian book was a collection or miscellany. It is modern scholarship which has isolated individual textual units from their miscellaneous contexts in an attempt to reconstruct particular thematic and formal trends in the history of Old Russian literature. Scholars have conventionally selected a body of representative Old Russian literary works and arranged them in accordance with the schemes of sociopolitical history.

A homiletic work which has often been selected to symbolize the birth of an autonomous and locally inspired Kievan literature is the *Sermon on Law and Grace* (Slovo o zakone i blagodati) by Metropolitan ILARION (11th century). This rhetorically elaborate and sophisticated work has been interpreted as a patriotic exaltation of the local Christian tradition of Old *Rus'* and its initiator Prince Vladimir Svyatoslavich in opposition to, though not formally against, Byzantine spiritual hegemony. A contemporary of Ilarion, Luka Zhidyata (first Russian bishop of Novgorod, 1036–60), ushered in a different form of preaching which was less bombastic and directed to a wider audience.

The legitimacy of the "blessed" lineage of Prince Yaroslav Vladimirovich (reigned ca. 1019–54) was proclaimed in a number of hagiographic compositions which eulogized the holy martyrs BORIS AND GLEB (?–ca. 1015). For one of these works we have an authorial tradition—to a certain Monk NESTOR is attributed the *Reading on the Life and Slaying of the Blessed Passion-Sufferers Boris and Gleb* (Chtenie o zhitii i o pogublenii blazhennuyu strastoterptsu Borisa i Gleba). Monk Nestor (ca. 1056– after 1113), who is one of the very few known authors of the early period of Old Russian literature, also wrote the *Life of Our Blessed Father Feodosy, Abbot of the Monastery of the Caves* (Zhitie prepodobnago ottsa nashego Feodosiya igumena pecher'skago). Nestor also played a decisive role in putting together the first authoritative body of chronicle writings. His name has been linked with the compilation of the *Tale of Bygone Years*, also known as the Primary Chronicle or Nestor Chronicle (Povest' vremennykh let), a work which modern readers have come to look upon as a typical expression of medieval Russian spirituality. Among the works which literary historians have isolated from their miscellaneous contexts to illustrate the early flowering of Old Russian literature are the *Instruction of* VLADIMIR MONOMAKH (Pouchenie Vladimira Monomakha) and *The Life and Pilgrimage of Daniil, Abbot of the Russian Land* (Zhit'e i khozhen'e Daniila Rus'skyya zemli igumena) (See DANIIL, Abbot). While the *Pouchenie* provided models for later didactic literature as well as a prototype for "autobiography," the *Life and Pilgrimage* inaugurated the particular "genre" of pilgrimage literature (*palomnicheskaya literatura*).

From the 12th through the 14th centuries, the Grand Principality of Kiev gradually lost its hold on the Russian lands. What is frequently referred to as the "period of feudal fragmentation" was marked by constant internecine struggles. In 1240, the former "mother" of the Russian lands fell to the Tatar hordes. It would be 140 years before the ascending power of Moscow would challenge the supreme authority of the Great Khan. In these three centuries Old Russian writings no longer expressed the ambitions of a new and united Christian state. Instead, the literature of the period was dominated by the motifs of struggle with internal and external enemies, exaltation of local princes, prelates or saintly men, and laments over the ruin of the Russian land. The political and religious characteristics of this age are masterfully synthesized in the celebrated *Igor Tale* (SLOVO O POLKU IGOREVE). The formal peculiarities, textual documentation and thematic emphasis of the *Slovo* remain the object of widespread controversy. Nevertheless, this remarkable literary monument clearly reflects the conflict between individual (or local) passions and the ideal of a united Christian *Rus'* in the strife-ridden age embodied by its heroes.

In the 12th century homiletics apparently attained a high level of rhetorical sophistication. The *Epistle to the Priest Foma* (Poslanie k presviteru Fome) by Metropolitan Kliment Smolyatich of Smolensk is unique for its references to the "pagan" authorities Homer, Aristotle, and Plato. The best examples of ornate eloquence in the 12th century are the eight sermons of Kirill, Bishop of Turov. A century later, the fears and despair of an eyewitness to Tatar cruelty were expressed in the five sermons of SERAPION, Bishop of Vladimir. Very close to the technique of religious preaching, though governed by a more complex and enigmatic code, are the *Discourse* and SUPPLICATION of Daniil Zatochnik (late 12th–early 13th century). In these two main redactions of the work it is not clear whether the rhetorical speaker seeks to convey a precise message or prefers to play with variations on more than one theme.

Characteristically, the main hagiographic hero of this age is not an ecclesiastic but a prince. The *Life of* ALEKSANDR NEVSKY, originally written shortly after the prince's death in 1263, was continuously reelaborated well into the 16th century. Later compilers of hagiographic collections added to the *Life* the short *Tale on the Ruin of the Russian Land* (Slovo o pogibeli Ruskyya zemli), which portrays in lyrical terms a spiritual landscape sharply different from that of a victorious Russian land guided by an inspired prince. In this work the glorious times are no more and "in these days the Christians are suffering."

Yet the essence of Old Russian religiosity was not to be found in the Orthodox patriotism of the prince and his entourage. It was rather located in the monastic communities of Old *Rus'*, which were devoted not to the events of this world but to obedience, charity, and the contemplative calling. It was in the Kiev Monastery of the Caves that the most celebrated monument of Old Russian monastic hagiography was gradually compiled. The *Paterikon of the Monastery of the Caves* can be read as a *florilegium* of hagiographic sketches and scenes. In other parts of *Rus'* lives of saints were written in a more routine manner and helped to crystallize topoi and formulae in the Old Russian literary tradition. A good example of this conventional hagiographic style is the *Life of the Venerable Avraamy of Smolensk*, written about the middle of the 13th century by a disciple of Avraamy named Efrem.

Chronicle writing, too, reflected the political and cultural limitations in the period of feudal fragmentation and the Tatar onslaught. Instead of putting together annalistic bodies such as the *Tale of Bygone Years*, writers and compilers fashioned thematically connected annalistic cycles and accounts of particular events which soon acquired the functional individuality of *povesti* (tales). The so-called Tatar Cycle (i.e., stories dealing with the Tatar invasion) culminated in the highly dramatic *Tale on the Capture of Ryazan by Batu* (Povest' o razorenii Ryazani Batyem). The so-called *Galician-Volhynian Chronicle*, which relates local events in 13th-century southern *Rus'*, contains excellent examples of the developing "genre" of the *voinskaya povest'* (military tale).

Fifteenth–sixteenth centuries

Both literary scholars and political historians tend to view the period from the late 14th century to the late 16th century as the age in which the spiritual world of Old *Rus'* was gradually replaced by a different political and cultural system shaped by the ascending power of Moscow. The waning of Tatar supremacy was symbolically marked by the victory of the Muscovite Grand Prince Dmitry Ivanovich Donskoi over the Khan Mamai on the battlefield of Kulikovo on 8 September 1380. It would be another hundred years, however, before Russian subjugation to the Tatar yoke would come to an end. In the 15th century Moscow expanded its rule over the Russian lands. One by one, such old and illustrious principalities as Murom-Ryazan, Smolensk, Novgorod, Tver, and Pskov fell to the Muscovite Grand Prince. The only power capable of challenging Muscovite hegemony was the Lithuanian Grand Principality, which was dynastically united with Poland after 1385.

Two main currents can be placed against the historical background of the 15th century, namely, (1) the "Second SOUTH SLAVIC INFLUENCE" and (2) what might be described as the increasing presence of Western models in the cultural life of the Russian lands. Whereas relatively little attention has been placed on the latter trend, the Second South Slavic Influence has been the object of wide-ranging investigations. It was the Turkish occupation of a large part of Balkan Slavdom at the end of the 14th century which encouraged the migration of South Slavic scholars and churchmen to the Russian lands. These Bulgarian and Serbian expatriates contributed to the establishment of new standards in the literary language and affected the very conception of literary activity. Both the existence of a number of cultural centers competing with Moscow and the rising prestige of Russian Orthodoxy—especially after the fall of Constantinople (1453), when the Russian Church retained the autonomous status it had acquired de facto in 1448—seem to have played an important part in the spread of new trends.

The most striking characteristic of the literature connected with the Second South Slavic Influence was a formal technique known as *pletenie sloves* (word weaving). This technique consisted in combining words to form synonymic or paronomastic series marked by a dense network of phonic correspondences. The purpose of this device was to *suggest* a given idea by referring to it through the convergence of related terms rather than to *identify* this idea with one term only. The use of *pletenie sloves* reflected the Hesychast theory of knowledge. In the same way that the Hesychast method of prayer and devotional practice aimed to reach the divine through degrees of spiritual purification, so did the Hesychast screening of verbal interconnections seek to approximate the perfect correspondence between the signifier and the signified.

Hesychasm played a dominant role in the spread of new literary trends connected with the Second South Slavic Influence. Kiprian and Grigory Tsamblak, two Bulgarian prelates linked with the "Trnovo School" of Evtimy, the last patriarch of medieval Bulgaria (1375–93), contributed notably to the establishment of innovative literary standards after they were installed as the metropolitans of Moscow (1390–1406) and Kiev (1415–ca. 1420) respectively. In the middle of the 15th century the Serb PAKHOMY LOGOFET (Pachomius Logothetes) introduced to Novgorod and Moscow innovative hagiographic techniques of South Slavic origin. The influence which South Slavic writers exerted was paralleled by similar tendencies originating among the Eastern Slavs. For this reason, one can speak of an "Orthodox Slavic revival" which affected the entire Church Slavonic linguistic community. The outstanding local representative of the new style was Epifany Premudry (EPIPHANIUS THE WISE, ?–ca. 1420), who occupies a preeminent place in Old Russian hagiography as the author of the *Life of Stefan of Perm* and the *Life of Sergius of Radonezh*.

The new style was applied to both ecclesiastical and worldly themes. The central figure of political hagiography connected with the early exaltation of Moscow is the Grand Prince Dmitry Ivanovich (reigned 1359–89), called "Donskoi" for his victory over the Tatars beyond the Don River. Prince Dmitry is portrayed as the ideal Christian soldier in the well known ZADONSHCHINA. This controversial monument has attracted considerable attention primarily because of its textual correspondences with the *Igor Tale*. The culminating point in the hagiographic portrayal of the victor on the battlefield of Kulikovo is the anonymous *Discourse on the Life and Death of the Grand Prince Dmitry Ivanovich* (Slovo o zhitii i o prestavlenii velikago knyazya Dmitriya Ivanovicha). At times, this work is reminiscent of the style of writers such as Epifany Premudry and Pakhomy Logofet. This *Discourse* is connected thematically, though not formally, with the *Chronicle Account of the Battle with Mamai* (Letopisnaya povest' o Mamaevom poboishche) and the *Tale of the Battle with Mamai* (Skazanie o Mamaevom poboishche). Together with the *Zadonshchina*, the latter two works form what is conventionally called the "Kulikovo Cycle."

The Russian response to Western schemes can be viewed as the consequence of Muscovite ambitions to establish its hegemony over rival principalities and to play a leading role in the Christian world. In order to compete with Latino-Germanic Europe, Russian culture had to come to grips with universal models such as the Holy Roman Empire and Roman Christianity. These two Roman concepts could apply to the Imperial power of Constantinople as well. Russian apologetic and polemical literature could also rely on some critical-philological criteria elaborated by Western humanists to construct their historical,—or rather historiosophic—theses. Here, too, one can observe a convergence of Latin and Greek humanistic trends.

Some textual-critical and linguistic principles, which reached Russia from the Byzantine area as a result of the Second South Slavic Influence, could coexist with similar humanistic techniques known from contacts with the West.

In 1461–62, on the basis of the *Tale of the Council of Ferrara-Florence* (Povest' o Ferraro-Florentiiskom sobore) written by Simon of Suzdal, a highly rhetorical and bombastic work was compiled. The work, often attributed to Pakhomy Logofet, is entitled: *Discourse selected from the Sacred Scriptures, which is directed to the Latins, and an account of the convening of the eighth Latin council, and of the deposition of the perfidious Isidore, and of the installation of the metropolitans of the Russian land; and finally a eulogy for the pious Grand Prince Vasily Vasilievich of all Rus'* (Slovo izbrano ot Svyatykh pisanii, ezhe na latynyu, i skazanie o s"stavlenii osmago sbora latyn'skago, i o izverzhenii Sidora prelestnago, i o postavlenii Rustei zemli mitropolitov; po sikh zhe pokhvala blagovernomu velikomu knyazyu Vasiliyu Vasil'evichu vseya Rusi). Here one finds a compact collection of the most typical forms of religious and political rhetoric, which aimed to apotheosize the Muscovite church and state.

The central idea of a *translatio imperii* is enunciated clearly in the final section of the *Tale on the Capture of Constantinople*, attributed to a certain NESTOR ISKANDER. A variation on the *translatio* theme is contained in the *Tale of the Babylonian Kingdom* (Povest' o Vavilonskom tsarstve), where the symbol of imperial dignity is transferred from the East. The *Legend of the Princes of Vladimir* (SKAZANIE O KNYAZEKH VLADIMIRSKIKH) elaborates on the motif of the transfer of imperial dignity from both Rome and Byzantium. In this work Muscovite princes are descendants of the Roman Emperor Augustus Caesar and have received the headgear of the Byzantine Emperor Constantine Monomachus (*shapka Monomakha*). There are clear textual correspondences between the *Skazanie* and a *Poslanie* (Epistle) about the headgear of Monomakh written by Spiridon-Savva.

In 1480, when Ivan III was facing the army of the Tatar Khan Ahmad on the Ugra River, Archbishop Vassian Rylo of Rostov composed the *Epistle to the Ugra* (Poslanie na Ugru), which exalted the sacred power of the Muscovite ruler. According to Archbishop Vassian, Ivan III was the "pious, Christ-loving, well-born, God-crowned, God-confirmed ... most glorious and shining sovereign amongst tsars." Approximately thirty years later (1511), another apologist of Muscovite power, the Monk Filofei of the Eleazar Monastery in Pskov, proclaimed in a renowned letter to Vasily III: "In all the universe you are the only Tsar of Christians.... Hear me, pious Tsar, all Christian kingdoms have converged in yours alone. Two Romes have fallen, a third stands, a fourth there shall not be."

Novgorod preserved its independence until 1478, when it fell to Moscow, and its rich literary heritage became part of the Muscovite pan-Russian cultural system. The last decades of its independence were marked by a concerted effort to organize into textually revised bodies the local patrimony of chronicles, hagiographic legends, and various historical tales. A corpus of Novgorodian Chronicles had been established as early as the 12th century by the priest German Voyata. In 1432 Archbishop Evtimy updated and reshaped this corpus. The many stories about saintly Novgorodian churchmen such as Varlaam Khutinsky and Archbishops Ilya-Ioann and Moisei became extremely popular as cycles.

Novgorodian literature contains many remarkable historiosophic motifs which are especially evident in semi-miraculous stories such as the *Life of Savvaty and Zosima*, written by the Monk Dosifei in the early 14th century, and the *Narration on the End of Novgorod* (Skazanie o kontse Novgoroda). Yet the richest and most puzzling narrative composition regarding the old city, its sacred ambitions and its destiny, is the *Tale on the White Cowl* (Povest' o belom klobuke). The pseudo-philological reliability and anti-Catholic significance of the *Povest'* are illustrated in a sort of epistle-foreword written by Dmitry Gerasimov and addressed to Archbishop Gennady. Dmitry Gerasimov, known as *Tolmach* (i.e., a "translator-interpreter"), was active in the early 16th century and represented Vasily III at the court of Pope Clement VII (reigned 1523–34). The *povest'* which Gerasimov offers, however, was apparently put together before him. The work is a variation on the widespread theme of the transfer of insignia from Rome and Constantinople to the Russian lands. It contains references to the theme of Moscow the "Third Rome" similar to those enunciated by Monk Filofei. Interestingly enough, the fantastic story which could be used by Novgorodian and later by Muscovite propagandists appears to be connected with the *Donatio Constantini*, that is, with a medieval myth which had recently been unmasked in the West by the humanistic philology of Lorenzo Valla (ca. 1407–57).

The Muscovite conquest of principalities such as Pskov, Tver, Smolensk, and Murom-Ryazan in the 15th and the early 16th centuries marked the end of limited yet vital traditions which only partially survived as literary echoes of a bygone age. The end and past glories of Pskov are evoked in a work entitled *The Capture of Pskov, How Grand Prince Vasily Ivanovich Captured It* (Pskovskoe vzyatie, kako vzyat ego knyaz' velikii Vasilii Ivanovich). The futile ambitions of Tver were emphatically affirmed in Monk Foma's *Encomiastic Discourse on the Grand Prince Boris Aleksandrovich* (Slovo pokhval'noe velikomu knyazyu Borisu Aleksandrovichu). Smolensk's glorious past found its best literary interpretation in the miraculous and heroic deeds of Merkury of Smolensk (Povest' o Merkurii Smolenskom), who in the third decade of the 13th century defeated the Tatar Khan Batu and carried his own severed head back to the walls of the city. However, the only historical legend of the period which reveals authentic elements of "literariness" is connected with the twin principalities of Murom-Ryazan. The *Tale of Peter and Fevronia* (Povest' o Petre i Fevronii) combines themes of different types and origins into a stereotypical yet highly dramatic plot. No less interesting for its literary appeal is Afanasy NIKITIN's *Journey beyond the Three Seas*, which relates the astonishment experienced by an Orthodox Slavic merchant from Tver when transplanted to Islamic India.

The trend towards centralization of political power in the Russian lands was paralleled by the strengthening of a new ecclesiastical apparatus no less politicized than its secular counterpart. From the 15th century on, this state-church alliance proved to be extremely effective in eliminating any sort of opposition. In an age when Western humanism was not totally unknown, dissidents and even "free thinkers" made their presence felt in several Russian principalities. Most of these "opponents" and their writings were branded as "heretical" and as such were anathematized. Only a few documents from this "heretical" literature have survived. In some cases, we have nothing but titles which were included in an index of prohibited books. It appears, however, that at the end of the 15th century many such works enjoyed wide diffusion. Among them were: (1) treatises on popular astronomy and astrology such as the *Reader of the Stars* (Zvezdochtets), the *Book of the Six Wings* [of the seraphims], i.e., of the six chapters (Shestokryl), and the *Lunary* (Lunnik); (2) a book of logic influenced by al-Ghazāli's reelaboration of Maimonides' work; (3) the political tract *The Doors of Aristotle* (Aristotelevy vrata); and (4) *The Secret of Secrets* (Tainaya Tainykh).

The main center of "heretical" activity was Novgorod. The accounts provided by ecclesiastical authorities inform us of the heretical sect known as the *Strigol'niki* (Shearers), which was active towards the end of the 14th century. About a century later, another conspicuous movement called the *Zhidovstvuyushchie* (Judaizers) confronted the church with concrete dogmatic and philological problems. It was partly in response to the *Psalter of the Judaizers* (Psaltyr' zhidovstvuyushchikh), a huge collection of biblical texts, that the Novgorodian Archbishop Gennady headed a circle of specialists and prepared an edition of the complete Bible (completed in 1499).

Archbishop Gennady (1484–1504) initiated a systematic repression of the Judaizers and other heretics. His inquisitional activity was continued by IOSIF VOLOTSKY (1439–1515) and his followers, known as *Osiflyane* (Josephites) or *Styazhateli* (Possessors). The way in which the official church dealt with heresy and its policy of encouraging monasteries to acquire temporal possessions was resolutely opposed by NIL SORSKY (1433–1508) and his Hesychast-oriented followers, called *Zavolzhskie startsy* (Trans-Volga Elders) or *Nestyazhateli* (Non-Possessors).

Under Ivan III (1462–1505) and Vasily III (1505–33), the process of centralization was brought to completion. The Muscovite state now spanned a huge territory, extending even beyond the Ural Mountains. The next Muscovite ruler, IVAN IV (1533–84) embodied the "menacing" (groznyi) majesty of an autocratic tsar and the

strength of a class of nobles (dvoryanstvo) faithful to the crown and opposed to the old aristocracy (boyarstvo). The radical political, social, economic, and religious changes which took place in 16th-century Russia decisively affected all aspects of cultural activity, including literature. The very notion of writing activity was transformed. The traditional figure of the anonymous scribe and compiler was now replaced by individual authors engaged in ambitious projects and ideological polemics. In the works of 16th-century authors, the spirit of ascending imperial unity contrasted with the defense of partisan interests or the aspirations of sectarian groups.

The most intense and sophisticated opposition to the church and state came from writers culturally linked with the old aristocracy and spiritually allied with the followers of Nil Sorsky. A critical role in the anti-establishment party was played by a direct disciple of Nil Sorsky, the Prince Vasily Ivanovich Patrikeev, who assumed the monastic name of Vassian Kosoi. Vassian's two major polemical works are *A Discourse in Response to Those Who Slander the Truth of the Gospels* (Slovo otvetno protivu kleveshchushchikh istinu euangel'skuyu) and the *Dispute with Iosif Volotsky* (Prenie s Iosifom Volotskim). As a result of his activity, Vassian was arrested in 1531 and sent as a prisoner to Iosif Volotsky's monastery at Volokolamsk, where he died some time before 1545.

Vassian's friend and disciple, MAKSIM GREK (1480–1556) underwent even greater trials. In 1518 Maksim had brought to Moscow the richness of his experience received first at Mount Athos and later in Italy. Yet because of his ideas and acquaintance with the opponents of the church and state establishment, he spent thirty-one years in prison. Maksim was directly or indirectly involved in the writing of more than one hundred and fifty works.

The representatives of official literature and ideology all shared a fervent desire to assemble a single all-embracing corpus of writings under the guidance of a perfect doctrine and to construct models for a new imperial society. In his many orations and epistles Metropolitan DANIIL (1522–39) expressed the political and ecclesiastical vision of the Possessors and the supporters of a hard line against any form of opposition to the official teachings of the Muscovite Church. Metropolitan MAKARY (1542–63) was the initiator and organizer of vast editorial enterprises, most notably the new *Minei chet'i*, which was the greatest and most ambitious work produced in the Russian lands up to that time.

Ivan PERESVETOV, an adventurer who had come to Moscow in the late 1530s from the Polish-Lithuanian Commonwealth and who had studied Ottoman institutions in the Romanian lands, introduced to Russia the "Turkish myth." About 1550 he wrote his most important work, the *Tale of Sultan Mahmed*, which advanced the idea that it was necessary to combine the "Christian faith" with a "Turkish order." To reach this goal, the Christian tsar Ivan IV was to exert his "terrible power" (groza). The name of Ivan IV himself is linked with a number of writings, including his celebrated and controversial *Correspondence* with Prince Andrei Mikhailovich KURBSKY (1528–83). The "terrible" tsar was also the main hero of a number of writings which celebrated his deeds. The *History of the Kingdom of Kazan* (Istoriya o Kazanskom tsarstve), with its merging of epic and quasi-liturgical strains, occupies a central place in the literature of what may be termed the "Age of Ivan the Terrible." The same sacred solemnity and bombastic grandiosity characterizes the *Book of Degrees of the Tsar's Genealogy* (see STEPENNAYA KNIGA.)

Sixteenth-century Russia was dominated by the idea of reorganizing and reducing to a harmonious whole all aspects of social life. This concern inspired many different types of works, from the ecclesiastical STOGLAV (Book of a Hundred Chapters) and the juridical *Code Of Laws* (Sudebnik) to the didactic DOMOSTROI, which focuses on the "management of the household" and aims to provide practical norms of moral behavior.

Throughout the 15th and 16th centuries one can detect in many works the formation of a historical, or pseudo-historical, awareness of a tradition which linked the new Muscovite age with the glorious past of Kievan *Rus'*. Political writings of the time insist on the continuity of a dynastic mission inaugurated by Prince Vladimir Svyatoslavich and developed by Muscovite rulers from Dmitry Ivanovich Donskoi to Ivan IV Vasilievich. In the late 16th century a peculiar literary monument known as the *Legend on the Kievan Heroes* (Skazanie o Kievskikh bogatyryakh) was compiled. In this work themes and motifs reminiscent of the oral epos are inserted into conventional narrative structures. Vladimir's faithful knights of Kievan era, however, behave like Muscovite dignitaries and speak like Muscovite bureaucrats.

Seventeenth century

The Time of Troubles was a turning point in the spiritual history of Russia. Although the Polish aim of making Russia part of a Catholic-dominated Europe ultimately failed, Old Russia did not survive the ordeal. Despite the revival of Orthodox Slavic patriotism as a result of the conflict with Catholic Poland, writers who were active after the installation of the Romanov dynasty in 1613 could not ignore the ideas, literary principles, and techniques introduced by the invaders. To a large extent, 17th-century Russian literature can be viewed as a response to the newly discovered world of Western verbal art. This response was not always the same, but the rules which had governed the old literary system for centuries ultimately were so shaken that writers could no longer operate within the system. Yet though the embryo of a new literary system was created, it was not brought to maturation. The Petrine Age would initiate a new revolution. The 18th century in Russia would replace the late humanistic models introduced from Poland and the Ruthenian lands with models taken from Germany, France, and later England.

During the Time of Troubles old-fashioned Orthodox Slavic rhetoric was used primarily in defense of holy Russia against the onslaught of Catholic Poland. The Muscovite Patriarch Germogen was glorified as the embodiment of Russian spiritual dignity and resistance to the invaders. Patriarch Germogen is the central figure in the *New Tale of the Most Glorious Russian Tsardom* (Novaya povest' o preslavnom Rosiiskom tsarstve), written during the winter of 1610–11. Also important in this regard is the highly rhetorical *Lament on the Capture and Final Destruction of the Highest and Most Luminous Muscovite State* (Plach o plenenii i o konechnom razorenii prevysokago i presvetleishago Moskovskago gosudarstva), compiled in 1611–12.

Many other works are devoted to the description of the main events in the Time of Troubles. Prose is frequently interspersed with embryonic verse segments and adorned with a number of innovative formal devices. Works such as the *Tale on the Honored Life of Fyodor Ivanovich, Tsar and Grand Prince of All Rus'* (Povest' o chestnom zhitii tsarya i velikago knyazya Fedora Ivanovicha vsea Rusi), written no later than 1603, the *Tale of 1606* (Povest' 1606 goda), the *Tale of This Book of Former Years* (Povest' knigi seya ot prezhnikh let, 1626), also known as the *Chronicle Book* (Letopisnaya kniga) and often attributed to Prince Ivan Mikhailovich KATYREV-ROSTOVSKY (but probably written by Prince Semyon Ivanovich Shakhovskoi), and Ivan Timofeev's *Chronicle* (Vremennik), compiled between 1616 and 1619, enjoyed great popularity and are important both as literary documents and as historical sources. Perhaps the most typical expressions of the stylistic variety and narrative complexity characteristic of the period are the *Account* (Skazanie) by Avraamy Palitsyn, completed in 1620, and the *Tale on the Death and Funeral of Prince Mikhail Vasilievich Skopin-Shuisky* (Povest' o smerti i o pogrebenii knyazya Mikhaila Vasil'evicha Skopina-Shuiskago), put together no later than 1612.

The main carrier of Western influence from Poland to Russia was the Ruthenian land. The church Union declared at Brest in 1596 marked the beginning of a religious and military campaign which was accompanied by intense cultural propaganda. The *Compendium of the Rules of Slavonic Grammar* (Grammatiki Slavenskiya pravilnoe Syntagma), published at Vevis (near Vilnius) in 1618–19 by Melety SMOTRITSKY, contained a chapter on versification which introduced Russian readers to the art of writing verse. Though Smotritsky's own theories were not immediately influential, the fashion of composing in verse gradually spread to the Russian lands. The first Russian poets wrote in types of "pre-syllabic" rhymed verse called *virshi*. In the first half of the 17th century the best known exponents of *virshi* were the priest Ivan Nasedka (1570–1660), Prince Ivan Andreevich Khvorostinin (died 1625) and Prince Semyon Ivanovich Shakhovskoi (died 1654).

The formation of a system of versification in 17th-century Russia has not been totally explored. Scholars have usually focused on the transition from various types of loosely constructed verse to a codified system of SYLLABIC POETRY in the second half of the century.

SIMEON POLOTSKY (1629–1680) is generally credited with introducing syllabic poetry to Muscovy. Polotsky began writing poetry in Polish and Latin. Later, he switched to the vernacular standard of the Ruthenian land and then to the type of Church Slavonic codified by Smotritsky. The Church Slavonic syllabic poetry which Polotsky wrote after his arrival in Moscow in 1664 represented both an importation of Western patterns and a restoration of the local linguistic tradition. Among the most important disciples and successors of Polotsky were Silvestr MEDVEDEV (1641–91) and Karion ISTOMIN (ca. 1650–ca. 1717).

The introduction of poetry into a literary world which had been dominated by prose for about six centuries was the most tangible evidence of the waning of the Old Russian tradition. Yet no less dramatic were the innovations that affected such established "genres" as the *povest'*. For the first time in Russian literature, the linear sequence of events was replaced by intricate "plots" reminiscent of Western novels.

Equally significant is the presence of explicitly erotic motifs. In the narrative cycle known as *Tale on the Beginnings of the Reigning City of Moscow* (Povest' o nachale tsarstvuyushchego grada Moskvy) Andrei, the son of Yury Dolgoruky, suffers a martyr's death because he fails to satisfy his wife's carnal appetite. Prince Daniil Aleksandrovich of Suzdal abducts two young brothers and his wife sins with both of them. Temptresses are frequent characters in 17th-century *povesti*. Concupiscence and virtue are the leitmotifs in the very popular story about the merchant Karp Sutulov (*Povest' o nekotorom goste bogatom i o slavnom o Karpe Sutulove i o premudroi zhene evo, kako ne oskverni lozha muzha svoego*), and vice and seduction are the sure road to success for the rogue Frol Skobeev (*Istoriya o rossiiskom dvoryanine Frole Skobeeve*). Similar ingredients are to be found in *The Tale of Savva Grudtsyn* (*Povest' o Savve Grudtsyne*). The new literary taste, which assured the success of these *povesti*, also depended on the translation and adaptation of Western tales such as the legends on Beuve d'Antone and Mélusine and certain novellas by Boccaccio.

A peculiar mixture of biblical motifs and adventure story in poetic form close to that of the oral tradition is to be found in the *Tale on Sorrow and Misfortune* (Povest' o Gore i Zlochastii) (see GORE-ZLOCHASTIE). A break with the pious tradition of Old Russia is more than evident in a number of works which introduce the hitherto unknown categories of parody, satire, and humor. This is the case, for example, with the *Shemyaka's Judgment* (Sud Shemyakin), the *Tale of the Drunkard, How he entered Paradise* (Slovo o brazhnike, kako vnide v rai), and the *Service in Honor of the Tavern* (O sluzhbe kabaku).

Changes in the hagiographic "genre" were less dramatic. The *Life of YULIANIYA LAZAREVSKAYA*, written about 1625, has been viewed as innovative, inasmuch as its protagonist is a woman and lay person. Yet the biblical models and compositional patterns of traditional hagiography play an essential role in this *Life*. Important innovations in the hagiographic genre were introduced in the second half of the 17th century in the so-called autobiography of Avvakum (1620–82), known under the title *Life of Archpriest Avvakum* (Zhitie protopopa Avvakuma). Here the break with tradition was actualized by a defender of that very tradition. And it was precisely Avvakum's attempt to restore a traditional spirituality that entered into conflict with the mentality of the new age.

The birth of drama in Russia during the reign of Tsar Aleksei Mikhailovich (1645–76) was the clearest evidence that a new literary system was replacing the old one and that the very notion of verbal performance was being adapted to Western models. Yet it is perhaps symptomatic of the process of literary change in 17th-century Russia that Russian drama was born out of the merging of Western influence and Orthodox Slavic restoration. The German pastor Gregory's *Action of Artaxerxes* (Artakserksovo deistvo) derived from a Germano-Protestant tradition, while Simeon Polotsky's dramas, *On King Nebuchadnezzar* (O Navkhodonosore tsare) and *Comedy on the Parable of the Prodigal Son* (Komidiya pritchi o bludnom syne), were Church Slavonic adaptations of dramatic techniques elaborated mainly in Polish and Ruthenian Jesuit schools.

Bibliography: V. P. Adrianova-Peretts, *Ocherki poeticheskogo stilya Drevnei Rusi.* 1947. ———, *Drevnerusskaya literatura i fol'klor.* 1974. ———, *Russkaya demokraticheskaya satira XVII veka.*

2d ed. 1977. V. P. Adrianova-Peretts and V. P. Pokrovskaya, *Drevnerusskaya povest'*. 1940. A. V. Arsen'ev, *Slovar' pisatelei drevnego perioda russkoi literatury. IX–XVII veka (862–1700 gg.)*. 1882. R. Auty and D. Obolensky, eds., *An Introduction to Russian Language and Literature*. 1977. Pp. 56–110. N. P. Barsukov, *Istochniki russkoi agiografii*. 1882. W. E. Brown, *A History of Seventeenth-Century Russian Literature*. Ann Arbor, 1980. I. U. Budovnits, *Slovar' russkoi, ukrainskoi, belorusskoi pis'mennosti i literatury do XVIII veka*. 1962. D. Chizhevskii [Tschižewskij], *Geschichte der altrussischen Literatur im 11., 12. und 13. Jahrhundert—Kiever Epoche*. Frankfurt, 1948. ———, *History of Russian Literature from the Eleventh Century to the End of the Baroque*. The Hague, 1971. L. A. Dmitriev and D. S. Likhachev, eds., *Izborniki (Sbornik proizvedenii literatury Drevnei Rusi)*. 1969. R. P. Dmitrieva, *Bibliografiya russkogo letopisaniya*. 1962. N. F. Droblenkova, *Bibliografiya sovetskikh russkikh rabot po literature XI–XVII vekov za 1917–1957 gg*. 1961. ———, *Bibliografiya rabot po drevnerusskoi literature. Part 1: 1958–1962 gg., Part 2: 1963–1967 gg*. 1979. A. S. Eleonskaya et al., *Istoriya russkoi literatury XVII–XVIII vekov*. 1969. I. P. Eremin, *Literatura Drevnei Rusi (Etyudy i Kharakteristiki)*. 1966. ———, *Lektsii po drevnei russkoi literature*. 1968. J. Fennell and D. Obolensky, eds., *A Historical Russian Reader. A Selection of Texts from the Eleventh to the Sixteenth Centuries*. 1969. J. Fennell and A. Stokes, *Early Russian Literature*. 1974. S. F. Gekker, "Ukazatel' istochnikov." In *Slovar' russkogo yazyka XI–XVII vv*. 1975. C. Gribble, *Medieval Slavic Texts. Vol 1: Old and Middle Russian Texts*. 1973. N. K. Gudzii, *Istoriya drevnei russkoi literatury*. 7th rev. ed. 1966. Eng. trans. *History of Early Russian Literature*. New York, 1949. ———, ed. *Khrestomatiya po drevnei russkoi literature*. 8th ed. 1973. *Istoriya russkoi literatury*. Vol. 1: *Literatura XI–nachala XIII veka*. Vol. 2, pt. 1: *Literatura 1220–1580-kh gg*. Vol. 2, pt. 2: *Literatura 1590–1690 gg*. 1941–48. V. M. Istrin, *Vvedenie v istoriyu russkoi literatury vtoroi poloviny XVII v*. Odessa, 1903. ———, *Ocherk istorii drevnerusskoi literatury domoskovskogo perioda (11–13 vv.)*. 1922. V. A. Kolobanov, et al., *Bibliografiya sovetskikh rabot po drevnerusskoi literature za 1945–1955 gg*. 1956. V. V. Kuskov, *Istoriya drevnerusskoi literatury*. 3d rev. ed. 1977. D. S. Likhachev, *Tekstologiya. Na materiale russkoi literatury X–XVII vv*. 1962. ———, *Razvitie russkoi literatury X–XVII vv. Epokhi i stili*. 1973. ———, *Velikoe nasledie*. 1975. ———, *Poetika drevnerusskoi literatury*. 3d ed. 1979. ———, ed., *Istoriya russkoi literatury X–XVII vv*. 1980. D. S. Likhachev and G. P. Makogonenko, eds., *Istoriya russkoi literatury. Vol. 1: Drevnerusskaya literatura; Literatura XVIII veka*. 1980. D. S. Likhachev and A. M. Panchenko, "Smekhovoi mir" drevnei Rusi*. 1976. L. E. Makhnovets', *Ukrajins'ki pys'mennyky. Biobibliografichnyj slovnyk. Vol. 1: Davnja ukrajins'ka literatura (XI–XVIII st.)*. Kiev, 1960. S. Matkhauzerova, *Drevnerusskie teorii iskusstva slova*. Prague, 1976. A. A. Morozov, "Problema barokko XVII–nachala XVIII v. (Sostoyanie voprosa i zadachi izucheniya)," *RLit*, 1963, no. 3, pp. 3–38. A. A. Nazarevskii, *Bibliografiya drevnerusskoi povesti*. 1955. N. Nikol'skii, *Materialy dlya povremennogo spiska russkikh pisatelei i ikh sochinenii (X–XI vv.)*. 1906. A. S. Orlov, *Kurs lektsii po drevnei russkoi literature*. 2d ed. 1939. *Pamyatniki drevnei pis'mennosti i iskusstva*. 1877–1925. *Pamyatniki literatury drevnei Rusi*. 1978– . A. M. Panchenko, *Russkaya stikhotvornaya kul'tura XVII veka*. 1973. R. Picchio, *Storia della letteratura russa antica*. Milan, 1959. 2d rev. ed. Florence-Milan, 1968. ———, "The Impact of Ecclesiastic Culture on Old Russian Literary Techniques." In *Medieval Russian Culture* (California Slavic Studies, no. 12), ed. H. Birnbaum and M. Flier. 1983. Pp. 247–79. *Polnoe sobranie russkikh letopisei*. St. Petersburg, Petrograd, Moscow-Leningrad, 1841– . A. N. Pypin, *Istoriya russkoi literatury*. Vol. 1: *Drevnyaya pis'mennost'*. Vol. 2: *Drevnyaya pis'mennost'; Vremena Moskovskogo tsarstva; Kanun preobrazovanii*. 2d rev. ed. 1902. M. N. Robinson, *Bor'ba idei v russkoi literature XVII veka*. 1974. ———, *Literatura drevnei Rusi v literaturnom protsesse srednevekov'ya (XI–XIII vv.)*. 1980. A. I. Sobolevskii, *Perevodnaya literatura Moskovskoi Rusi XIV–XVII vekov. Bibliograficheskie materialy. Sbornik Otdeleniya russkogo yazyka i slovesnosti imp. AN 74* (1903), no. 1. M. N. Speranskii, *Istoriya drevnei russkoi literatury*. 3d ed. 2 vols. 1920–21. A. Stender-Petersen, *Geschichte der russischen Literatur*. Trans. from the Danish by W. Krämer. 2 vols. 3d ed. Munich, 1978. A. Stender-Petersen and S. Congrat-Butlar, eds., *Anthology of Old Russian Literature*. New York, 1954. F. Thomson, "The Nature of the Reception of Christian Byzantine Culture in Russia in the Tenth to Thirteenth Centuries and its Implications for Russian Culture," *Gandensia* 5 (1978); pp. 107–39. N. S. Trubetzkoy, *Vorlesungen über die altrussische Literatur*. (Studia Historica et Philologica, no. 1.) Florence, 1973. *Trudy Otdela drevnerusskoi literatury*. Moscow-Leningrad, 1934– . O. V. Tvorogov, *Literatura Drevnei Rusi*. 1981. N. V. Vodovozov, *Istoriya drevnei russkoi literatury*. 1966. S. A. Zenkovskii, *Medieval Russia's Epics, Chronicles, and Tales*. 2d rev. ed. New York, 1974.

R. P.
H. G.

Olésha, Yúry Kárlovich (1899–1960). A major Soviet novelist, short-story writer, and occasional playwright, poet, essayist, journalist, translator, and film scenarist. Born in the Ukrainian town of Elisavetgrad (now Kirovograd) on 3 March 1899, Olesha was the only son of a middle-class Polish Catholic family (his older sister Wanda died of typhus in 1919). His father, a former landowner, moved the family to Odessa in 1902, where he worked as an excise official in a vodka distillery. Olesha distinguished himself as a student. He began to write poetry while at the Rishelevsky Gymnasium in Odessa, and during his two years of legal studies at Novorossiisk University he participated in Odessan literary discussion groups, where he struck up friendships with the young writers Ilya ILF, Valentin KATAEV, and Eduard BAGRITSKY. In 1919 he rejected the monarchist sympathies of his parents, who later fled to Poland, by volunteering for the Red Army. Olesha soon began to work as a journalist-propagandist, a vocation that carried him first to Kharkov (1921), and then to Moscow (1922), where he joined the staff of the successful railway journal *Gudok*. His caustic, satirical verse, written under the pseudonym Zubilo [Chisel], was quite popular, while his literary aspirations were sharpened by constant contact with other staff members (Ilf and Petrov, Kataev, Isaak BABEL, and Mikhail BULGAKOV). Two collections of his verse were published in 1924 and 1927, the latter year also seeing the appearance of his finest work, *Envy* (Zavist'). He soon adapted this novel for the stage under the title *The Conspiracy of Feelings* (Zagovor chuvstv, 1929); he did the same in 1930 with *Three Fat Men* (Tri tolstyaka), a novella-fairytale about revolution in an imaginary country, apparently written around 1924 but published in 1928. These works catapulted Olesha into the first rank of Soviet writers: *Three Fat Men* was later adapted by others for opera, radio, and film (twice), while *Envy* was praised almost everywhere until its rich ambiguities began to trouble critics devoted to ideological purity and clarity. Before 1932 Olesha also wrote several excellent short stories, the most highly regarded being "The Cherry Pit" (Vishnevaya kostochka), "The Chain" (Tsep'), "Love" (Lyubov'), and "Liompa", and his only original play, *A List of Benefits* (Spisok blagodeyanii, 1931). During the Stalinist darkness, Olesha fell almost silent, apparently surviving on translations, a few second-rate stories, and film scenarios. Olesha's last, lengthy, quasi-autobiographical work, *No Day without a Line* (Ni dnya bez strochki, 1965), was compiled and edited from a large and varied collection of writings on which he was working at the time of his death in 1960.

The immediate impact of Olesha's best works, even on unsophisticated readers, is produced first of all by the palpable presence of the *creating* author. Olesha sees our world with extraordinary acuity, and he conveys it with imagery both apt and altogether original (e.g., torches which "flow in the wind like fiery beards"). His great liking for indirect description, especially through simile and metaphor, creates an effect which has been called "estrangement" (OSTRANENIE). Habitual, conditional responses to experience are shattered by such evocative imagery, and the world is suddenly, momentarily reborn for the reader.

Olesha spoke of this ever-changing and eternally new world as "invisible" to those lacking attentiveness and imagination. His solitary, intensely personal, even solipsistic vision shaped his art along familiar modern lines. In his novel *Envy*, Kavalerov possesses this special artistic vision, but like many artists in twentieth-century literature he cannot escape the frustration and loneliness of the eccentric outsider. His ability to "capture" and manipulate external reality in his verbal art gives him a sense of mastery and control; he enjoys viewing the world through the wrong end of binoculars or from great heights, thereby diminishing it and magnifying himself. His belief in the power of his art is undermined, however, by his repressed awareness that it depends in part on an illusion. So he also dislikes things, and sometimes fears them at close range ("Things don't like me"), recognizing their alien otherness. But "things like" Kavalerov's benefactor-foe, Andrei Babichev, who is in Kavalerov's eyes the embodiment of the new social order, of another conception of the individual, and of a philosophy which offers no spiritual escape from the iron laws of alien matter. When fear of his enemy overwhelms Kavalerov, Babichev seems to be transformed into an inanimate thing, into stone or a machine.

Such existential perceptions combined with a lack of religious belief (the "invisible world" is empirically real) and an awareness of human moral frailty created the conceptual uncertainties and ambiguities, and the thematic dichotomies so characteristic of Olesha's best work (e.g., the old world vs. the new, the individual vs. the collective, spiritual vs. material values, the irrational vs. the rational, and so on). The story "The Cherry Pit" depicts rather convincingly a reconciliation between the forces of social and historical "progress" and faith in the value, and in some sense the efficacy, of artistic creativity. Otherwise Olesha's work is a brilliant record of the unresolved hopes and doubts which preoccupied the Russian intelligentsia in the early postrevolutionary era.

Works: Ni dnya bez strochki: iz zapisnykh knizhek. 1965. *Povesti i rasskazy.* 1965. *Izbrannoe.* 1974.

Translations: Envy (available in several editions). *Complete Short Stories and Three Fat Men.* Trans. Aimee Anderson. Ann Arbor, Mich., 1979. *No Day without a Line.* Trans. Judson Rosengrant. Ann Arbor, Mich., 1979.

Secondary literature: Elizabeth K. Beaujour, *A Study of the Artistic Imagination of Jurij Olesha.* 1970. William E. Harkins, "The Theme of Sterility in Olesha's *Envy*." In Edward J. Brown, ed., *Major Soviet Writers: Essays in Criticism.* 1973. Pp. 280–94. Nils Åke Nilsson, "Through the Wrong End of Binoculars: An Introduction to Jurij Oleša," in Edward J. Brown, ed., *Major Soviet Writers; Essays in Criticism.* 1973. Pp. 254–79.

K. N. B.

Onégin strophe. The Onegin stanza, like the SONNET, has fourteen lines, but its rhyme scheme is unique: $AbAbCCddEffEgg$, where capital letters are used to indicate feminine rhymes and small letters the masculine. The first twelve lines contain the three possible arrangements for two rhyme sets in a quatrain: alternating, adjacent, and enclosed; they are followed by a concluding adjacent masculine rhyme pair, which provides a rhythmic closure to the entire stanza. *Eugene Onegin*, for which PUSHKIN invented this form, and nearly all subsequent works employing the stanza are written in iambic tetrameter. The Onegin strophe proved to be very well-suited to Pushkin's needs in his verse novel. The use of a fixed form helped impart a sense of unity and regularity to the work. At the same time the particular rhyme scheme he chose offers a change in the pattern after every quatrain and lacks the confinement of the Petrarchan sonnet, in which the repetition of the Ab rhyme throughout the first eight lines would be difficult to sustain over a long work. Also, the length of the rhyme pattern enabled Pushkin to treat topics, or at least self-contained parts of topics, within the stanzas, so that they come to function as miniature "chapters." Indeed, enjambement between stanzas is rare, occurring only about ten times in the entire eight chapters of the novel.

Scholars have been unable to find independent stanzas that employ this rhyme scheme in any earlier work by other poets, but it does begin to appear after *Eugene Onegin*. Pushkin himself employed it for "The Genealogy of My Hero," an eight-stanza fragment from the uncompleted narrative poem *Ezersky*. Among other poets, LERMONTOV perhaps used it more than anyone else, most notably in "The Tambov Treasurer's Wife." YAZYKOV's poem "The Linden Trees" is notable for adhering to the rhyme scheme of the Onegin stanza but being written in iambic pentameter. Other poets to use the stanza include several parodists, as well as Vyacheslav IVANOV and Maksimilian VOLOSHIN. The form is so well known that its borrowing is nearly always acknowledged, either directly at the beginning of the poem or indirectly through references to Pushkin.

Bibliography: L. P. Grossman, "Oneginskaya strofa." In *Pushkin.* Vol. 1. 1924. Pp. 117–61. A. A. Ilyushin, "K istorii Oneginskoi strofy." In *Zamysel, trud, voploshchenie . . .* 1977. Pp. 92–100. M. A. Peisakhovich, "Oneginskaya strofa v poemakh Lermontova," *Filologicheskie nauki* 49, no. 1 (1969), pp. 25–38. G. O. Vinokur, "Slovo i stikh v *Evgenii Onegine*." In *Pushkin.* 1941. Pp. 155–213. B. V. Tomashevskii, "Strofika Pushkina." In *Pushkin: Issledovaniya i materialy.* Vol. 2, 1958. Pp. 111–33.

B. S.

Opoyáz (*Óbshchestvo izuchéniya poetícheskogo yazyká*, "Society for the study of poetic language"). The *Opoyaz* was a loosely structured scholarly society whose members were students at Petersburg University. They were both stimulated by, and dissatisfied with, the ways of studying literature in the academy, and shortly before World War I they began to gather privately to discuss their own ideas and those of the established scholars. The first members of the *Opoyaz* were V. B. SHKLOVSKY, L. P. Yakubinsky, B. M. EIKHENBAUM, O. M. BRIK, B. Kushner and E. D. Polivanov. Among other adherents and sympathizers were Yu. N. TYNYANOV, V. V. VINOGRADOV, S. I. Bernshtein, V. Kazansky and B. V. TOMASHEVSKY. Out of their discussions emerged three slim volumes entitled, respectively, *Sborniki po teorii poeticheskogo yazyka* (vols. 1–2, Petrograd 1916–17) and *Poetika. Sborniki po teorii poeticheskogo yazyka* (vol. 3, Petrograd 1919). The acronym *Opoyaz* was coined by the members themselves following the revolutionary and military fashion prevalent in Russia at that time.

In 1919, the group received official recognition as a learned society. This meant both an assignment of office space and material remuneration. At that time, says the *Opoyaz* sympathizer B. V. Tomashevsky, the society assumed the form of a committee in which "Viktor Shklovsky was president, Boris Eikhenbaum his deputy, and Yury Tynyanov his secretary." Owing to personal contacts between the Petersburg *Opoyaz* and the Moscow Linguistic Circle, the two groups eventually merged and began to be referred to as the Petersburg and Moscow *Opoyaz*, or the adherents of the "formal" method, the label which some members tried to avoid for political reasons.

The *Opoyaz* was dissolved in 1923, but its membership was largely absorbed by a better-structured and more political organization LEF (*Levyi Front Iskusstva*, the Left Front of Art, 1923–25). Eventually, former members of the *Opoyaz* joined the faculties of Soviet universities and research institutes, and continued their work under new auspices. The five-volume *Poetika*, published by the Leningrad Institute of Art History from 1926 to 1929, was largely authored by one-time *Opoyaz* adherents, and it displayed a strong FORMALIST influence. In the 1930s, formalism became a proscribed doctrine and the former *Opoyaz* associates repudiated it explicitly or implicitly.

The three volumes of *Sborniki* contain the seeds of many formalist arguments. They also contain remnants of the idealistic theories of art which the young scholars absorbed in the course of their university studies. This inconsistency indicates that the authors did not at that point perceive the implications of the views which they so enthusiastically proclaimed. Judging by a large number of typesetting mistakes, the articles had not been proofread. They were typeset by the authors themselves on an old machine for printing business cards.

These shortcomings did not prevent the *Sborniki* from becoming a spectacular scholarly success. The *Opoyaz* members made a plea for a new nonrepresentational poetics whose reference point would be language rather than reality. They wanted to change the traditional way of studying and reading literature as an appendix to history or as a reflection of human problems and aspirations. They wanted literature to be viewed rather as a linguistic artifact possessed of its own laws and structure. Normative criticism which flourished in Russia before the 1917 Revolution, was to be replaced by descriptive criticism.

The first step in initiating this approach was to separate literature from nonliterary discourse. This separatist tendency is reflected in the full title of *Sborniki* which mentions *poetic* language rather than just language, as well as in the heavy concentration, in the articles themselves, on the phonic level of literary works. It is argued that both in poetry and in artistic prose, the degree of verbal organization is significantly higher than in nonliterary discourse. This shows itself in the abundance of phonic and semantic parallelisms and repetitions, and in the "internal evolution" of poetic language which can be observed within any language that has produced a literature.

It is this internal evolution rather than philosophical influences external to literature, that accounts for literary changes and innovations.

While the *Opoyaz* members did not entirely succeed in proving their hypotheses, they generated much interest in the problems of literary language, among Western scholars in particular. The easy acceptance of their theories by Western Slavicists has been one of the instances of modern Russia's influence on the West.

Bibliography: B. V. Tomashevskii, "La nouvelle école d'histoire littéraire en Russie," *Revue des études slaves* 8 (1928), pp. 226–40. Victor Erlich, *Russian Formalism: History-Doctrine.* New Haven, 1982.

E. Th.

Ornamentalism, prose style. This problematic term has no precise definition. It is used most often in reference to a pervasive stylistic tendency in Russian fiction during the early postrevolutionary era (1920–25), most notably in the early works of Nikolai Nikitin, Vsevolod IVANOV, Isaak BABEL, Konstantin FEDIN, Leonid LEONOV, Aleksandr Malyshkin, and Nikolai Ognev. These writers and others were influenced in varying degrees by Boris PILNYAK, whose works are widely viewed as a bridge between the postrevolutionary era and earlier experiments in prose by Aleksei REMIZOV and Andrei BELY. Such patterns of influence have led some critics to understand ornamentalism as the Russian expression of a general modernist literary tendency (1900–30). A few have abandoned the notion of a particular historical period and use this term to refer to a stylistic "type" recurrent in the Russian tradition since the 16th century. Those who would limit ornamentalism to the early 20th century still emphasize its direct connections with the "second line" of 19th-century Russian prose (e.g., GOGOL, LESKOV, DAL), whose intricate verbal tapestries contrast with the unobtrusive, transparent prose of PUSHKIN, TOLSTOI, and CHEKHOV.

Such fluctuations in temporal perspective are predictable because this term implies nothing about a writer's world view, inevitably conditioned by time and place. Rather, it suggests that the familiar literary products of idea and value (theme, character, story, message) are suppressed in a piece of ornamental prose by a shift in its compositional center of gravity toward expressive means. Linguistic textures, stylistic richness and variety—not meaning—are ostensibly the raison d'être of works which are in open rebellion against the traditional genres of the novel and short story. The devices of rhetoric and declamation, word play, striking imagery, musicality—a complex mixture of alliterations, assonances, consonances, repetitions (leitmotifs), and phrase rhythms—are typical, while narration is sometimes fragmentary, a montage of diverse, juxtaposed narrative styles drawn from the nonliterary and oral (SKAZ), the solemn and philosophical, from diaries, documents, newspapers, prayers, ancient chronicles, political slogans and speeches, and so on. Recent studies show convincingly, however, that meaning is often elusive, but not absent, in the difficult works of major representatives of this stylistic tendency. For all its excesses, the postrevolutionary tradition in particular deserves renewed, sympathetic study.

Bibliography: G. L. Browning, "Russian Ornamental Prose," *SEEJ* 23 (1979), pp. 346–52. P. Carden, "Ornamentalism and Modernism." In G. Gibian and H. W. Tjalsma, eds., *Russian Modernism: Culture and the Avant-Garde, 1900–1930.* 1976. Pp. 49–64. Hongor Oulanoff. "The Impact of the 'Ornamental' and 'Dynamic' Prose." In his *The Serapion Brothers: Theory and Practice.* The Hague, 1966. Pp. 53–71.

K. N. B.

Osorgin, Mikhaíl Andréevich (real name: Ilyín, 1878–1942), journalist and writer. A graduate of Moscow University Law School (1902) and successful journalist, Osorgin was briefly imprisoned as a participant in the Moscow uprising of 1905. He spent the next ten years (1906–16) abroad, working as a foreign correspondent of *Russkie vedomosti* and other Russian periodicals. His *Sketches of Contemporary Italy* (Ocherki sovremennoi Italii, 1913) helped to spread the ideas of the Italian futurists. (Osorgin also translated from the Italian, e.g., Carlo Gozzi's *Princess Turandot*, 1923.) In spite of his leftist past, Osorgin was expelled from the Soviet Union in 1922, along with a group of other "bourgeois" writers and scholars. He eventually settled in Paris, writing articles and reviews for

several émigré publications, but mainly for SOVREMENNYE ZAPISKI. In the mid-1920s he began to concentrate on his fiction. His first novel, *Sivtsev Vrazhek* (1928), dealing with the early years of the Soviet regime, was a significant success. Three more novels followed: *A Witness of History* (Svidetel' istorii, 1932), *A Book of Ends* (Kniga o kontsakh, 1935), and *The Freemason* (Vol'nyi kamenshchik, 1938). Osorgin also wrote his memoirs: *A Man's Things* (Veshchi cheloveka, 1929) and *Times* (Vremena, 1955). Osorgin's fiction is marked by his journalistic background. It features elements of the documentary, describing events which had made newspaper headlines at one time. Osorgin's style is fluent, though a bit facile, and has a touch of the light irony of a newspaper feuilleton.

Works: Iz malen'kogo domika. Riga, 1921. *Povest' o sestre.* Paris, 1931. *Chudo na ozere.* Paris, 1931. *Proisshestviya zelenogo mira.* Sofia, 1938. *Povest' o nekoei devitse.* Tallinn, 1938. *Po povodu beloi korobochki.* Paris, 1947. *V tikhom mestechke Frantsii.* Paris, 1946. *Pis'ma o neznachitel'nom, 1940–1942.* New York, 1952.

Translations: Quiet Street (Sivtsev Vrazhek). 1930. *My Sister's Story.* Trans. N. Helstein and G. Harris. 1932. Donald M. Fiene, trans. and introd., "Osorgin's 'Original Chess-Playing Robot,'" *RLT* 3 (1972), pp. 97–105. *Selected Stories, Reminiscences, and Essays.* Trans. D. Fiene. 1982.

Secondary literature: Donald M. Fiene, "M. A. Osorgin—The Last Mohican of the Russian Intelligentsia (On the One-Hundredth Anniversary of His Birth)," *RLT* 16 (1979), pp. 93–105. Gleb Struve, *Russkaya literatura v izgnanii.* 1956. Pp. 119–20, 272–74.

V. T.

Ostranénie (defamiliarization, making it strange). In his programmatic essay "Art as strategy", V. B. SHKLOVSKY speaks of *ostranenie* as a means of destroying the automatization of perception which sets in in daily life. He argues that the aim of art is to make us *see* things instead of merely *recognizing* them. Art isolates phenomena from their usual contexts and makes them appear "strange"; we stare at them instead of merely recognizing them. Shklovsky's examples of *ostranenie* come from the works of Lev TOLSTOI. For example, in the story "Kholstomer," man's world is seen and commented upon by a horse. This way of presentation, contends Shklovsky, "defamiliarizes" the familiar and makes us see it anew.

Shklovsky's concept of *ostranenie* has its roots in an idealistic theory of language which he absorbed in his youth from Andrei BELY and the other SYMBOLISTS. It was later reinterpreted by Marxist critics and made to appear what it originally was not. Fredric Jameson shifted the notion of *ostranenie* from the realm of perception to the realm of philosophy of history. For him, Shklovsky's intention in introducing *ostranenie* was not to say something about the ends of art but rather to underscore the falsity of the idealistic theory of history as a continuum rather than as a series of ruptures with the past. *Ostranenie* foregrounds the element of rupture and thus can be regarded as an element of a dialectical literary theory. Jameson's interpretation, however, shows a lack of familiarity with Shklovsky's idealistic beginnings.

Bibliography: F. Jameson, *The Prison-House of Language.* 1974. Pp. 50–54. V. B. Shklovskii, "Iskusstvo kak priem." In his *O teorii prozy.* 1929. Pp. 7–23. E. M. Thompson, *Russian Formalism and Anglo-American New Criticism.* The Hague, 1971. Pp. 54–70.

E. Th.

Ostróvsky, Aleksándr Nikoláevich (1823–86), a leading 19th-century playwright and pioneer of theater rights, has perhaps been taken too much for granted as a classic in Russia, but is virtually undiscovered abroad. Son of a well-to-do Moscow business lawyer, Ostrovsky owed his pro forma nobleman's status to his father's second marriage to a Swedish baroness. Educated in languages with private tutors, he did well in gymnasium despite nightly attendance at the theater, but failed in the study of law undertaken at his father's wish. The father then got his son a job as clerk of commercial court (1843–51), while the son began publishing in various journals his observations of the Moscow district beyond the river, and of the lawsuits and corruption of business life.

His first play, *Bankruptcy* (Bankrut, 1847), appeared anonymously in the *Moskovskii gorodskoi listok*, where it was favorably noted by the literary critic Apollon GRIGORIEV. Noteworthy for its depiction of business people, not previously the heroes of literature, it shows an older businessman, declaring bankruptcy for profit, whom his son-in-law and accomplice then leaves in the lurch, allowing him to go to debtor's prison.

Ostrovsky began reading a later version of the play, now entitled *A Family Affair* (Svoi lyudi—sochtemsya, 1849) at literary gatherings. Mikhail POGODIN, editor of *Moskvityanin*, was so impressed by one of his readings with the actor Prov Sadovsky that he published the play in his magazine (March 1850). However, censorship permission to produce the play proved unattainable, for Imperial officials, fearful of taking responsibility, passed the play on finally to Emperor Nicholas I himself, who thought the play's portrayal of business people harmful. He requested a report on Ostrovsky, and when nothing adverse was found, placed the author under police surveillance so as to find something. Because of the surveillance Ostrovsky lost his civil service job.

Pogodin now asked Ostrovsky to edit the *Moskvityanin* with a board of his own choice, hoping to revitalize the magazine with a younger staff. Though Pogodin had guaranteed the new editor a free hand, Ostrovsky found himself subject to interference from his employer; furthermore, the parsimonious Pogodin could hardly bring himself to pay, for example, for the two more plays Ostrovsky published in *Moskvityanin*, *The Poor Bride* (Bednaya nevesta, 1852) and *Stay In Your Own Lane* (Ne v svoi sani ne sadis', 1853). Yet from now until the end of his life Ostrovsky was dependent on his literary income, for his father had cut him off when he refused to abandon his common-law wife, Agafya Ivanovna (last name unknown). Fortunately, *Stay In Your Own Lane* provided Ostrovsky's breakthrough into the theater. Its success at the Maly Theater, Moscow, in 1853 swept two more of his plays onto the boards in this, his first year in the theater. One of the two, *The Poor Bride*, realistically shows the unfortunate position of women in Ostrovsky's time, whose only hope of economic security was in marrying for money, not love. Though at moments the author parodies the romantic archetype, he states no thesis, but merely implies one in the relentless realism characteristic of both his first plays. Commenting on *The Poor Bride*, Grigoriev pronounced: "The question from whom to expect a new word [in Russian literature] can already be answered directly: ... in this new work ... we find new hopes for art."

Pogodin in the *Moskvityanin*, Grigoriev and the other Ostrovsky-appointed editors, and eventually Ostrovsky himself espoused SLAVOPHILISM and a more positive view of the Russian people. Ostrovsky, who had been all too realistically critical in both of the first plays he had failed to get past the censor, now tried a new tack in *Stay In Your Own Lane* and the third play, to be staged in 1853, *Poverty's No Vice* (Bednost' ne porok). He wrote to Pogodin on 30 September 1853: "My bent is beginning to change; my view of life in my first play seems to me youthful and too harsh. Let my fellow-Russian be glad rather than sad at seeing himself on stage." Undoubtedly the "new bent" meant less Ostrovsky's espousal of Slavophilism than the realization that to improve people through the theater, one's plays had to be seen. For, like Friedrich Schiller, Ostrovsky believed in the theater as a moral institution and had so declared in a written statement submitted to the Imperial authorities during his vain attempt to get performance permission for *A Family Affair*. Declaring that we must each use our God-given talent and that his was for writing comedies, he called comedy "the best form for the attainment of moral goals." Finally in 1858 *A Family Affair* was staged when Ostrovsky yielded and added a wordless gesture in the end to suggest that vice might, after all, be punished.

In 1856 Ostrovsky began publishing in SOVREMENNIK, where most of his plays were to appear until the magazine's closure (1866). Ostrovsky's next play, *A Profitable Post* (Dokhodnoe mesto, 1857) shows the near surrender and moral collapse of a young civil servant committed to honesty when he and his wife must suffer poverty while all around them take bribes.

Ostrovsky's perhaps best play—certainly his best known—*The Storm* (Groza, 1860), grew out of a trip to the sources of the Volga, which he was commissioned to make by the Marine Ministry in 1856–57. City-born and bred, Ostrovsky experienced the country and the forest more intensely as an adult. He spent all the sum-

mers of his mature working life writing plays at Shchelykovo, an estate acquired by his father which he and his brother Mikhail bought from their stepmother in 1867 after their father's death. Several of his best plays are set in fictional river towns, *The Storm* in Kalinov, and *Fiancée Without Fortune* (Bespridannitsa, 1878) in Brakhimov. Ostrovsky planned a series, never completed, titled "Nights on the Volga." The 1860s closed with a high government honor, the award of the Uvarov Prize for *The Storm* on the written recommendation of Ivan GONCHAROV.

The critic DOBROLYUBOV, surveying Ostrovsky's plays of the 1850s, saw them as criticizing the benighted business world, "The Dark Kingdom," as he called it, and especially the *samodur* or domestic tyrant who oppresses all within his power—even a whole town. In a second article the critic viewed the tragic end of the heroine Katerina in *The Storm* as a protest against the play's two tyrants. Another critic, Dmitry PISAREV, three years later more correctly thought Katerina of too simple and lyric a nature for conscious protest. Married off for money, Katerina begs for her husband Tikhon's love, but he is too busy escaping his mother's domination. Katerina falls in love for the first time with Boris, who has just come to live with his uncle-guardian. Boris and Katerina meet just once in a forest ravine. The dramatic break of a thunderstorm from which everyone has taken shelter causes Katerina to confess her fault before the whole town. She is now the prey of one *samodur*, her mother-in-law, while Boris' uncle, the other tyrant, sends him away. Left thus alone, Katerina throws herself into the river. The Czech composer Leoš Janáček based his opera, *Katya Kabanova* (1921), on *The Storm*.

After the emancipation of the serfs in 1861, Ostrovsky's plays reflect the social change of the time. *The Diary of a Scoundrel* (Na vsyakogo mudretsa dovol'no prostoty, 1868) shows how an ambitious young man, determined to make it to the top by flattery and insinuation, is unmasked only in the nick of time. *Easy Money* (Beshennye den'gi, 1870) contrasts the hard-working self-made man with the charming impoverished aristocrat. In *The Forest* (Les, 1871), two Bohemians, a tragic and a comic actor, expose the former's aunt as the selfish, despoiling landowner that she is, while they also liberate from her dominance a young couple in love. The plot of *The Forest* is so artfully contrived that with the sums of money involved it finally comes full circle, allowing Ostrovsky to claim that he could write a "well-made play," as good as the French. Of course, money is a key factor in Ostrovsky's reflections of the new capitalist society.

Ostrovsky also wrote historical plays, notably *Dream on the Volga* (Voevoda, subtitled Son na Volge, 1865), and a charming folklore play on the change of seasons, *The Snow Maiden* (Snegurochka, 1873), both of which have been made into operas. Further, the late plays are among the best of Ostrovsky's work. Several show a profligate landed aristocracy, deprived of serf labor, trying to get its share of the new prosperity in railroads and industry, for example, *Wolves and Sheep* (Volki i ovtsy, 1875), *The Final Sacrifice* (Poslednyaya zhertva, 1878), *Fiancée Without Fortune*, *Career Woman* (Talanty i poklonniki, 1882), *Guilty Without Guilt* (Bez viny vinovatye, 1884).

The last two plays have actress heroines, the calling in which women have equal if not more than equal rights with men, and one with which Ostrovsky, who spent his life in the theater, was intimately familiar. Indeed, Ostrovsky achieved certain important reforms for actors and the theater. He initiated an upward revision of the 1827 scale of fees paid dramatic authors and opera composers. He got the dramatic author's copyright extended from five to fifty years. Further, he helped to found the Actors' Club, which gave performers a meeting place better than the tavern and served to train actors in tryout performances. Finally, he hoped to found a national theater outside the Imperial censorship and monopoly, and was attempting to do so when the emperor abrogated the monopoly.

Works: Polnoe sobranie sochinenii. 12 vols. 1973–80.

Translations: Five Plays of Alexander Ostrovsky. Trans. and ed. Eugene K. Bristow. 1969. *Easy Money and Two Other Plays.* Trans. David Magarshack. 1970. *Plays.* Trans. Margaret Wettlin. Moscow, 1974. See also: *Lewanski*, pp. 316–17.

Secondary literature: Marjorie L. Hoover, *Alexander Ostrovsky.* (Twayne's World Authors Series, 611.) 1981. E. Kholodov, "Vokrug Ostrovskogo," *VLit* 20 (1976), no. 4, pp. 226–60. K. D. Muratova, *Bibliografiya ob A. N. Ostrovskom, 1847–1917.* 1974. A. I. Revyakin, *Iskusstvo dramaturgii A. N. Ostrovskogo.* 2d rev. ed. 1974. M. H.

Ostróvsky, Nikolaí Alekséevich (1904–36), Soviet novelist, was born in Viliya, Volhynia province. His life exemplifies the ultimate display of will and political fanaticism. The son of a worker, he joined the Komsomol and the Red Army at the age of fifteen, fought against the Poles in 1920, and subsequently held leading positions in Ukrainian Komsomol organizations. Suffering from war wounds and grave illnesses, bedridden and blind since 1928, he decided to serve the Bolshevik cause with his pen. His book *How the Steel Was Tempered* (Kak zakalyalas' stal', 1932–34) was partly written by himself and partly dictated to others. He called it a book of reminiscences, but it was published as a novel. The book is largely autobiographical, focusing on its heroic protagonist, Pavel Korchagin. It is a plotless, fragmentary work with numerous episodic characters and clear-cut heroes and villains. Life is presented as worth living only if it is dedicated to the revolutionary liberation of mankind on Communist terms. The critics barely noticed the book until 1935 when the Party decided to use it as an important tool for political education of youth. The book is still being published in large printings and studied in secondary schools. Yet it is doubtful that Korchagin's political fervor has strong appeal for contemporary Soviet citizens in view of their ideological scepticism. Ostrovsky's second novel, *Born of the Storm* (Rozhdennye burei, vol. 1, 1936), dealing with the 1918–19 revolution in the Western Ukraine, remained unfinished.

Works: Sochineniya. 3 vols. 1967–68.
Translations: Born of the Storm. 1939. *Hail, Life! Articles, Speeches, Letters.* Trans. H. Altschuler. Moscow, 1955. *How the Steel Was Tempered. A Novel.* Trans. R. Prokofieva. Moscow, n.d. *The Making of a Hero* [= How the Steel Was Tempered]. Trans. A. Brown. 1937.
Secondary literature: A. Karavaeva, *Kniga, kotoraya oboshla ves' mir (Sud'ba knigi).* 1971. M. Slonim, *Soviet Russian Literature: Writers and Problems, 1917–1977.* 2d ed. 1977. Pp. 185–87. S. Tregub, *Zhizn' i tvorchestvo Nikolaya Ostrovskogo.* 2d ed. 1975. N. Vengrov, *Nikolai Ostrovskii.* 2d ed. 1956. H. E.

Otechestvennye zapiski (*National Annals*, 1839–84), founded by A. A. Kraevsky, a friend of LERMONTOV, was considered the leading journal of the WESTERNIZERS during the fourth and fifth decades of the 19th century. Poems by Lermontov, NEKRASOV, and TURGENEV, political writings by HERZEN, and critical articles by BELINSKY appeared in its pages. Belinsky urged Russian writers to depict Russian society and its problems in a realistic manner, thus sounding a death knell for Russian romanticism. He received strong support from Nekrasov, who had joined the staff of *Otechestvennye zapiski* in the early 1840s as a book reviewer and literary contributor.

However, in 1846 Nekrasov, together with his friend I. I. PANAEV, bought the journal SOVREMENNIK and became its co-owner, editor, and publisher. As a result, *Otechestvennye zapiski* lost its chief literary critic, Belinsky, as well as its most important contributors, Panaev and Nekrasov himself. The publisher of the journal, Kraevsky, expressed his resentment at this by stating in an editorial of 1847: "Not one article by Belinsky, Panaev, or Nekrasov will ever be printed in *Otechestvennye zapiski* as long as this journal is published by us."

In the years 1846 to 1866 *Otechestvennye zapiski*, deprived of its best staff writers, in sharp competition with *Sovremennik* for paid subscriptions, fared rather badly under Kraevsky's management. The situation became even worse in 1867, when DUDYSHKIN, the acting editor of the journal, passed away. *Otechestvennye zapiski*, whose readership was declining rapidly, became an unprofitable venture for Kraevsky.

The journal was rescued from oblivion by Nekrasov whose thriving *Sovremennik* had been closed down by the authorities in 1866. He approached Kraevsky with the proposition of leasing or buying *Otechestvennye zapiski* from him. By that time Kraevsky's hostility toward Nekrasov had abated, and he was willing to come to terms. An agreement was signed in 1867, whereby Nekrasov took over the journal on a lease and became its editor-in-chief.

Otechestvennye zapiski, under the combined editorship of Nekrasov and SALTYKOV-SHCHEDRIN, became the leading journal of the Russian populists (*narodniki*) in the 1870s, with contributions by G. I. USPENSKY, F. M. RESHETNIKOV, N. K. MIKHAILOVSKY, and other populist writers. The novelist V. M. GARSHIN and the poet S. I. NADSON also published in it. Nekrasov himself, though busy with his editorial duties, wrote, and published in his journal many shorter and longer poems, among which the most outstanding were "Grandfather" (1870), "Recent Times" (1871), "The Contemporaries" (1875), a major portion of his monumental work, *Who is Happy in Russia?* ("The Last One," "A Peasant Woman," and "A Feast for Everyone," 1872–76), and the last collection of poems published during his lifetime, *Last Songs* (1877).

After Nekrasov's death in 1878, the journal, deprived of its chief editor and literary contributor, had to rely increasingly on lesser writers. Many of these, especially political ones, were closely associated with the Russian revolutionary movement of the 1870s and 1880s. Despite increasing government censorship, *Otechestvennye zapiski* continued publication until 1884, when it was closed for political reasons. S. S. B.

Otsúp, Nikolaí Avdéevich (1894–1958), poet and critic, a younger friend and disciple of Nikolai GUMILYOV, was born and educated in Tsarskoe Selo. A talented poet and a member of the ACMEIST POETS' GUILD and later of the Petrograd "Union of Poets," Otsup emigrated from Russia to Berlin in 1922. He studied at the University of St. Petersburg and the University of Paris. Otsup translated Russian poetry into German and edited the literary journal *Chisla* (Paris, 1930–34), in which he aspired to unite Acmeism with the Parisian avant-garde. Arrested by the Germans during World War II and confined to a concentration camp, he escaped and participated in the Italian Resistance. After the defense of his doctoral dissertation on Gumilyov in Paris after the war, he became a professor of Russian there. Otsup published selected poems of Tyutchev in French and compiled an edition of Gumilyov's poetry, *N. Gumilëv. Izbrannoe. Predislovie i redaktsiya N. Otsupa.* 1959.

As a poet, Otsup gave much thought to the formal aspects of his poetry, writing without "mystical haze" or "mystical allusions." His poems—airy, precise, lyrical, expressive, and cold—are composed in strict adherence to the rules of prosody. They have a profound and pure sound. His constant manipulation of temporal and spatial planes is another characteristic of his aesthetics. The imagery is vivid and the rhythm restrained. Otsup was also an erudite and perceptive critic.

Works: (Collections of poetry:) *Grad.* Petrograd, 1921. *V dymu.* Berlin, 1926. *Zhizn' i smert': stikhi 1918–1958.* 2 vols. Paris, 1961. *Dnevnik v stikhakh: 1935–1950.* Paris, 1950. Otsup also published a long poem, *Vstrecha* (Paris, 1928), consisting of several separate poems. (Novel:) *Beatriche v adu.* 1939. (Drama in verse:) *Tri tsarya.* 1958. (Essays:) *Literaturnye ocherki.* 1961. (Reminiscences:) *Sovremenniki.* 1961. "O sebe," *Novaya russkaya kniga*, 1922, nos. 11–12, pp. 42–43.
Translations: Two poems, in *Modern Russian Poetry.* V. Markov and M. Sparks, eds. and trans. 1967. Pp. 456–59.
Secondary literature: Obituaries in *Grani*, 1958, no. 40, p. 51, and in *Vozrozhdenie*, 1959, no. 86, pp. 135–40. Temira Pachmuss, *A Russian Cultural Revival: A Critical Anthology of Emigré Literature before 1939.* 1981. Pp. 243–53. T. A. P.

Ovéchkin, Valentín Vladímirovich (1904–68), writer and playwright. One of not many figures of Soviet literature with real experience in rural life and agriculture, Ovechkin managed a collective farm from 1925 to 1931 and worked for the Komsomol and the Party at various rural sites before concentrating full-time on his work as a rural reporter (*sel'skii korrespondent*) in 1934, and subsequently on his fiction: *Tales from a Collective Farm* (Kolkhoznye rasskazy, 1935). A war correspondent in World War II, Ovechkin returned after the War to his concern for the Soviet collective farm. His sketches and stories gathered in *District Routine* (Rayonnye budni, 1952–56), while unquestioningly loyal to the Party and its ideology, often expose administrative inefficiency, inflexible and dogmatic management, Party functionaries interested only in advancing their careers, and other shortcomings in the administration of rural Russia. A series of plays, *Into the Wind* (Navstrechu vetru, 1958), *Summer Rains* (Letnie dozhdi, 1959), *Time to Reap the Fruits* (Vremya pozhinat' plody, 1960), and *Let It Happen* (Pust' eto sbudetsya, 1961), and a number of short stories are likewise devoted to the problems of rural Russia. Ovechkin's well-meant criticism was not heeded (reviewers shrugged it off as related to the past only) and his disappointment led to a nervous breakdown and a suicide attempt.

Works: Izbrannye proizvedeniya. 2 vols. 1963. *Stat'i, dnevniki, pis'ma.* 1972. *Zametki na polyakh.* 1973.

Translations: Short stories, in *Soviet Literature* 10 (1954), pp. 3–62. "Guests in Stukachi." In *Russian Literature since the Revolution.* 1948.

Secondary literature: N. Atarov, *Dal'nyaya doroga: Literaturnyi portret V. Ovechkina.* 1977. P. Carden, "Reassessing Ovechkin." In *Russian and Slavic Literature.* Ed. Richard R. Freeborn, R. R. Milner-Gulland, and Charles A. Ward. 1976. Pp. 407–24. Deming Brown, *Soviet Russian Literature since Stalin.* 1978. Pp. 223–25. L. Vil'chek, *Valentin Ovechkin: Zhizn' i tvorchestvo.* 1977.

V. T.

Ozerov, Vladisláv Aleksándrovich (1769–1816), dramatist. Of an old but impoverished noble family, Ozerov attended the Corps of Cadets where he developed a lively interest in theater. His career as a dramatist began with the five-act tragedy *Yaropolk and Oleg* (1798), a static play in rhymed alexandrines in the style of traditional 18th-century Russian tragedy. His subsequent works adhered less rigidly to the conventions of classicist drama. Both syntax and diction were now brought closer to the patterns of conversational speech. Elements of SENTIMENTALISM and pre-ROMANTICISM also began to manifest themselves, above all in the treatment of the love theme. After *Yaropolk and Oleg*, Ozerov scored considerable success with three plays written in rapid succession: *Oedipus in Athens* (Edip v Afinakh, 1804), a five-act drama in alexandrines, with choruses, which was dedicated to the poet DERZHAVIN and staged on 23 November 1804; *Fingal* (staged 8 December 1805), a three-act verse drama inspired by the Ossianic poems; and the dramatic work for which he is best known, *Dimitry Donskoi* (1806; staged 14 January 1807), a patriotic five-act verse tragedy ostensibly about the Russian victory over the Tatars in 1380 but containing allusions to the contemporary conflict with the French. Ozerov's last play, *Poliksena*, was, like *Oedipus in Athens*, classical in setting. It was staged on 14 May 1809 and dramatizes the story of Poliksena, who yearns to die in order to be reunited with Achilles. The play met with little success notwithstanding Ozerov's mastery of French classicist tragic form. Ozerov's popularity as a dramatist brought him considerable personal anguish. *Dimitry Donskoi* became the butt of parodies, the most notorious by GRIBOEDOV, while the circle of conservative archaists led by Admiral SHISHKOV, offended by Ozerov's sentimentalism and romanticism, sought to ruin his career and reputation.

Works: Tragedii. Stikhotvoreniya. Ed. I. N. Medvedeva. 1960.

H. B. S.

Pachomius Logothetes (Pakhómii Logofét, 15th century), called "the Serbian," author. Pachomius arrived in Russia some time between 1429 and 1438, coming from Mt. Athos. A monk, he was the first known "professional writer" active in Russia (STENDER-PETERSEN). He lived in Novgorod, the Trinity-St. Sergius Monastery, Moscow, and Beloe Ozero. Pachomius authored a series of saints' lives, including a vita of Metropolitan Alexius of Moscow and a new version of the vita of St. SERGIUS OF RADONEZH by EPIPHANIUS THE WISE, as well as liturgic texts devoted to various saints, including one to Sts. Pyotr and Fevroniya. Pachomius also authored the initial version of the *Russian Chronograph* (1442) and has been thought by some scholars to have had a hand in the composition of SKAZANIE O KNYAZ'YAKH VLADIMIRSKIKH. Pachomius is one of the strongest exponents of the "second SOUTH SLAVIC INFLUENCE" on Russian letters and of the ornate style (*pletenie sloves*) which came along with it. His writings are veritable mosaics of artful epithets, similes, and metaphors. His syntax is complex and virtuosic, featuring long, involute periods with a multitude of rhetorical figures. The general tone of Pachomius' writings is highly emotional, with a great deal of high pathos, panegyric hyperbole, and apostrophe.

Works: Zhitie mitropolita vseya Rusi svyatogo Aleksiya. 1877–78.

Secondary literature: V. Yablonskii, *Pakhomii Serb i ego agiograficheskie pisaniya.* 1908.

V. T.

Paleography is the study of older forms of handwriting, which enables one to read old handwritten books and documents, and to determine their dates and places of origin. It has long been regarded as one of the ancillary historical disciplines, together with epigraphy, papyrology, diplomatics, codicology, textual criticism, etc. Originally cultivated by historians and antiquaries, these disciplines soon proved their worth to archivists, librarians, curators, and cataloguers of manuscripts, as well as to historians of literature and historical linguists—in short, to everyone who deals professionally with old handwritten or inscribed texts.

For some time now, however, paleographers have been more and more inclined to insist that all of the above ancillary historical disciplines are in fact not ancillary disciplines at all, but the separate parts of a new independent field of scholarship comprehensively treating older written texts in all their complexity. This new science does not yet have a commonly accepted name; of the various names so far proposed for it, perhaps the most satisfactory is "archeology of the book." The one disadvantage of this name is that it appears to exclude the study of legal documents and inscriptions. One of its advantages is that it may readily be broadened to include the study of the earliest printed books (incunabulistics): it has long been recognized that a strict separation of incunabula from manuscript books has no scholarly warrant.

Both the position of paleography as a scholarly discipline, as well as its methods have been critically examined during the last several decades. In the 19th century, paleographers were content to determine the date and place of a manuscript's origin by impressionistically comparing it with those dated and placed manuscripts known to them. Such impressionistic comparisons, of course, are no better than the experience and judgement of the paleographers who make them; and, being subjective, they do not readily lend themselves to the accumulation of precise data from one generation of scholars to the next. Recently paleographers have tried to come to grips with the problem of making such comparisons as objective as possible, so that the results of any paleographer's investigations can be independently reproduced and verified by any other paleographer, and can be combined and accumulated for the benefit of posterity, just like results of research in any of the sciences. Steps have also been taken to devise new tools and new laboratory techniques for the objective study of manuscripts: microphotography, microscopy, radiography, digital image processing, Fourier-transform analysis of holograms, and various kinds of mathematics have all been tested and found useful; and they will probably soon be joined by methods for comparing inks through the quantitative analysis of trace elements contained in them, and by reliable carbon 14 dating of parchment. Unfortunately, Slavic paleographers have fallen somewhat behind their Western colleagues in these respects; the specialist in CYRILLIC or GLAGOLITIC paleography who wants to stay up-to-date must be prepared to spend a large fraction of his working time studying recent advances in Greek and Latin paleography.

Cyrillic paleography took shape as a scholarly discipline during the 19th century, and received its standard treatment in several manuals published during the first three decades of the 20th century. It customarily distinguishes three successive types of Cyrillic writing: uncial (*ustav*), semiuncial (*poluustav*) and cursive (*skoropis*), each of which can be further subdivided into several local and temporal varieties. Uncial is the oldest. It was created ca. 900 A.D. in Bulgaria, and spread rapidly to all the other Slavs whose higher cultures and written literatures were shaped by BYZANTINE INFLUENCE. It derives from one of the contemporary varieties of Greek uncial writing, supplemented by additional letters which have been borrowed from the Glagolitic alphabet and calligraphically reworked to conform to the style of the Greek uncial. Semiuncial (which has no equivalent in Greek writing) probably first appeared in the 14th century. It is customarily treated as the result of a gradual development from uncial, which was impelled by a need for greater scribal efficiency. Cursive, which probably first appeared in the 15th century, subsequently developed from semiuncial in the same way, for the same reason.

This rather simple evolutionary scheme has been subjected to profound criticism by the doyen of Cyrillic paleographers, Vladimir Mošin, who sketched the main lines of a much more sophisticated scheme in his "Methodological Notes about the types of Cyrillic Writing" (1965). Examining South Slavic as well as East Slavic Cyrillic scripts, he observed that one can find contrasts between calligraphic and practical, every-day Cyrillic writing even in the oldest period, that—contrary to the common view—cursive is as old as semiuncial, and that there are also minuscule varieties of Cyrillic alongside the more common majuscule varieties. The traditional three-fold classification of Cyrillic writing is therefore inadequate, as are the common explanations of the origin of semiuncial and cursive. Mošin's observations are very much to the point, and his criticisms fully warranted. It is unfortunate that his article, written in Serbo-Croatian and published in a Latin-alphabet journal at Zagreb, has not had the influence it merits on the development of Cyrillic paleography during the last twenty years.

Glagolitic paleography is younger and less well developed than Cyrillic, and it still has not received anything like a standard treatment in any manual; the existing manuals do not stand up very well under critical examination. In practice, one operates with two principal types of Glagolitic writing: an older type, found in a number of early manuscripts and inscriptions; and a younger type of Croatian origin, which seems to have taken shape in the 13th century. The older type clearly represents the first Slavic alphabet, invented by Constantine (Cyril) in 863 A.D.; it is not a development from any earlier type of writing, but rather the product of its inventor's creativity, lightly influenced by his knowledge of other alphabets. The younger type, which clearly developed under the influence of Latin-alphabet Gothic writing used in Croatia, represents a deliberate revision of the older type. In addition, there is a cursive Glagolitic script, first clearly attested in the 15th century.

The study of early Cyrillic and Glagolitic writing is more difficult than is commonly admitted, because very few manuscripts earlier than the 14th century can be dated with any precision by non-paleographical means. The oldest explicitly dated Cyrillic manuscript now extant is Ostromir's Evangeliarium, written according to its colophon in 1056–57 A.D. This is an East Slavic manuscript; the oldest explicitly dated South Slavic manuscript is Miroslav's Evangeliarium, written according to its colophon during that prince's reign (+1199). In all, no more than about forty dated Cyrillic manuscripts earlier than the 14th century are known to exist, as against more than four hundred undated ones. The oldest explicitly dated Glagolitic manuscript is probably a Psalter written at Senj in 1359. There are also a small number of early legal documents and inscriptions which can be dated by non-paleographic means.

Cyrillic and Glagolitic printing first appeared toward the end of the 15th century. Well into the 18th century, however, liturgical books constituted almost the entire output of most Cyrillic and Glagolitic presses, with the result that the craft of the scribe was not superseded by the art of the printer until relatively modern times, and is not entirely dead even today among conservative Slavic religious communities (especially some of the groups of Old Ritualists). Consequently, Cyrillic paleography must extend its domain to a much later age than Greek or Latin paleography.

Bibliography: M. Bošnjak, *A Study of Slavic Incunabula.* Zagreb, 1968. L. V. Cherepnin, *Russkaya paleografiya.* Moscow, 1956. Petar Djordjić. *Istorija srpske ćirilice.* Belgrade, 1971. I. V. Yagich (Jagić), "Glagolicheskoe pis'mo," In *Entsiklopediya slavyanskoi filologii,* III/3 1911. Pp. 51–262. E. F. Karskii, *Slavyanskaya kirillovskaya paleografiya.* Leningrad, 1928. *Metodicheskoe posobie (Metodicheskie rekomendatsii) po opisaniyu slavyano-russkikh rukopisei dlya Svodnogo kataloga rukopisei, khranyashchikhsya v SSSR,* I, II/1–2. Moscow, 1973, 1976. V. Mošin, "Metodološke bilješke o tipovima pisma u ćirilici," *Slovo* 15–16 (1965), pp. 150–82. *Paleografski album na južnoslovenskoto kirilsko pismo.* Skopje, 1966. ———, "Najstarata kirilska epigrafika." In *Slovenska pismenost: 1050–godišnina na Kliment Ohridski.* Ohrid, 1966. Pp. 35–44. V. V. Panashenko, *Paleohrafiya ukrayins'koho skoropysu druhoyi*

polovyny XVII st. Kiev, 1974. N. N. Rozov, *Kniga drevnei Rusi.* Moscow, 1977. ———, *Kniga v Rossii v XV veke.* Leningrad, 1981. V. N. Shchepkin, *Uchebnik russkoi paleografii.* Moscow, 1918–20. (= *Russkaya paleografiya.* Moscow, 1967.) A. I. Sobolevskii, *Slavyano-russkaya paleografiya.* 2d ed. St. Petersburg, 1908. V. Štefanić, "Prvobitno slovensko pismo i najstarata glagolska epigrafika." In *Slovenska pismenost: 1050 godišnina na Kliment Ohridski.* Ohrid, 1966. Pp. 13–33. J. Vajs. *Rukovět hlaholské paleografie.* Prague, 1932. L. P. Zhukovskaya. *Razvitie slavyano-russkoi paleografii.* Moscow, 1963. L. P. Zhukovskaya and N. B. Shelamanova, "Instruktsiya po opisaniyu slavyano-russkikh rukopisei XI–XIV vv. dlya Svodnogo kataloga rukopisei, khranyashchikhsya v SSSR." In *Arkheograficheskii ezhegodnik za 1975 god.* Moscow, 1976. Pp. 24–40.   R. M.

Paleyá. A collection of writings which either recount or expound events and figures from the Old Testament—hence the name *Paleya,* from the Greek *palaia* [diathēkē] "Old [Testament]." The original Greek *Paleya* was compiled in 9th-century Byzantium. Via the South Slavic area it made its way to Old *Rus',* where it enjoyed great popularity until the 17th century. The Old Russian *Paleya* which was translated from the Greek bears the title, *Book on the Genesis of Heaven and Earth* (Kniga bytiya nebesi i zemli). Known as the *Historical Paleya,* it presents an abbreviated exposition of Old Testament history up to the reign of King David which is supplemented by apocryphal stories such as *On Solomon and Kitovras* and *Judgments of King Solomon.*

In the 13th century another collection called the *Interpretative* (tolkovaya) *Paleya* was compiled in the Russian lands. In its interpretation of scriptural passages its polemical aim was to demonstrate the superiority of the Christian faith over Judaism. Relying on works such as the *Testaments of the Twelve Patriarchs* (Zavety dvenadtsati patriarkhov), the *Hexaemeron* (Shestodnev) of John the Exarch, and the *Christian Topography* (Khristianskaya topografiya) of Cosmas Indicopleustes, this version of the *Paleya* also incorporated numerous apocryphal and legendary motifs.

Bibliography: V. M. Istrin, "Zamechaniya o sostave Tolkovoi Palei," *Izvestiya Otdeleniya russkogo yazyka i slovesnosti imp. Akademii nauk* 2 (1897), nos. 1 and 4; and 3 (1898), no. 2. ———, "Redaktsiya Tolkovoi Palei," *Izvestiya Otdeleniya russkogo yazyka i slovesnosti imp. Akademii nauk* 10 (1905), no. 4, and 11 (1906), nos. 1–2. *Paleya tolkovaya po spisku, sdelannomu v g. Kolomne v 1406 g. Trud uchenikov N. S. Tikhonravova,* nos. 1–2, 1892–96. A. N. Popov, "Kniga bytiya nebesi i zemli (Paleya istoricheskaya) s prilozheniem sokrashchennoi Palei russkoi redaktsii." *Chteniya v Obshchestve istorii i drevnostei rossiiskikh pri Moskovskom universitete,* 1881, no. 1, pp. 1–172. M. N. Speranskii, "Yugoslavyanskie teksty 'Istoricheskoi Palei' i russkie ee teksty." In his *Iz istorii russko-slavyanskikh literaturnykh svyazei.* 1960. Pp. 104–47. A. A. Shakhmatov, "Tolkovaya paleya i russkaya letopis'." In *Stat'i po slavyanovedeniyu,* 1904, no. 1, pp. 199–272.   H. G.

Pámyat' (Memory, New York/Paris, vols. 1–5, 1978–82), collection of archival documents and articles on Russian literature, history, and culture, edited by *Tamizdat.* The Soviet authors of *Pamyat'* have had to conceal their identities under pseudonyms. The publications cover the time span from 1906 to 1977. The editors seek to save from oblivion materials which are inadmissible for consideration in the Soviet Union, on account of official standards of Soviet historiography, such as concern the fate of different informal circles of Russian intellectuals, Menshevik activities in the first post-revolutionary decade, or a bibliography of Soviet prisoners press from 1921 to 1935. The title of the collection suggests its methods of publication: presenting the text in its completeness, relating it to a wider context built by similar sources and by additional information obtained from letters of readers to the editors, thus restoring a true, undamaged *memory* of the epoch. I. Voznesensky's article "Names and Fates," 1:353–410, and its further discussion in vols. 2 and 4 may serve as an example. All publications are annotated. The annotations provide bio-bibliographical data and historical references, advance new problems for discussion, and suggest new areas of investigation (for example, the fate of Tolstoian communities in the USSR.). A work of a free uncensored press, *Pamyat'* continues the traditions of HERZEN's Russian Free Press editions, and is also related to SOLZHENITSYN's *Gulag Archipelago*. Publications on Gulag are central in every volume, and the theme of Gulag is emphasized in the editors' preface.

The entire sum of rescued documents is subdivided into sections titled: Memoirs; From the History of Culture and From the History of the Russian Church; Varia; and Reviews, Addenda, Letters to the Editors. This flexible structure contributes to a versatile discussion of materials and allows inclusion of documents ranging from the antisemitic Beilis trial (1906) to the most recent reports issued by the Soviet dissidents R. Pimenov, A. Marchenko, A. Sakharov, and others.

Bibliography: N. Perlina, "*Memory* and *Amnesia*: A New Russian Free Press," *Survey*, 1982, no. 2 (115), pp. 176–84.

N. P.

Panáev, Iván Ivánovich (1812–62), writer and journalist. Of noble birth, Panaev in 1844 abandoned a career in the civil service to become a professional writer. In 1847 he and Nikolai NEKRASOV took over a foundering SOVREMENNIK and made it into a leading literary journal which was also financially profitable. Panaev was himself a prolific contributor to the feuilleton section of *Sovremennik* and was also skilful at writing verse parodies. His fiction follows the trend of the moment and is second rate at best. He began with "SOCIETY TALES" in the 1830s. In the 1840s he produced a number of "PHYSIOLOGICAL SKETCHES" in the manner of the NATURAL SCHOOL. His short novel, *Relatives* (Rodstvenniki, 1847), presents his version of the "superfluous man." In the 1850s Panaev was one of the leading advocates of the emancipation of women, as is evident in his novel *Provincial Lions* (L'vy v provintsii, 1852). A recurrent theme of Panaev's fiction is the conflict arising from the encounter of a weak and spoiled young aristocrat and a strong-willed and idealistic woman of lower social standing.

Works: Polnoe sobranie sochinenii. 6 vols. 1888–89. *Izbrannye proizvedeniya.* Introd. F. M. Ioffe. 1962. *Literaturnye vospominaniya.* Ed. and introd. I. Yampol'skii. 1950.

V. T.

Panáeva (née Bryánskaya, Avdótya Yákovlevna, 1819– or 1820–93), writer and memoirist. Married to the writer I. I. PANAEV since 1837, Panaeva was de facto for many years the common law wife of Nikolai NEKRASOV. She was an active collaborator of both writers and published many stories and several novels of her own. Her fiction deals with the topical problems of the times, and particularly with the emancipation of women, as in her novel *A Woman's Lot* (Zhenskaya dolya, 1862). Panaeva's memoirs (Vospominaniya, 1889–90), while not always reliable as to the facts, contain interesting impressions of her contemporaries and are one of the main sources of our knowledge of the literary ambience of the 1840s and 1850s.

Works: Semeistvo Tal'nikovykh. Introd. K. I. Chukovskii. 1928. *Vospominaniya.* Introd. K. I. Chukovskii. 1956.

Secondary literature: K. I. Chukovskii, *Zhena poeta.* 1922. Richard Gregg, "A Brackish Hippocrene: Nekrasov, Panaeva, and the 'Prose in Love'," *SlavR* 34 (1975), pp. 731–51. Marina Ledkovsky, "Avdotya Panaeva: Her Salon and Her Life," *RLT* 9 (1974), pp. 423–32.

V. T.

Panfyórov, Fyódor Ivánovich (1896–1960), prose writer. Of peasant origin, Panfyorov began writing in 1918. His works are set in the Russian village and usually deal with the theme of collectivization. His best-known novel is *Bruski: A Story of Peasant Life in Soviet Russia* (1928–37) in which he paints a broad picture of peasant life. His characters are individualized: their coarse language is alive. *The Struggle for Peace* (1945–48) is the first volume of a trilogy about World War II. The first two parts earned him Stalin Prizes for 1948 and 1949. His last novel, *Mother Volga* (1960), paints a surprisingly bleak picture of life on a collective farm. Although a mediocre craftsman, Panfyorov was a capable and prolific "official" writer whose works generally adhered to the demands of the Party and the style of SOCIALIST REALISM.

Works: Sobranie sochinenii. 6 vols. 1958–60. *Volga matushka reka.* 1960. *Bruski, Roman.* 1979.

Translations: And Then the Harvest. 1939. *With Their Own Eyes.* Moscow, 1942. *Soviet War Stories.* 1944. *Bruski: A Story of Peasant Life in Soviet Russia.* Hyperion, Conn., 1977.

Secondary literature: E. J. Brown, *Russian Literature Since the Revolution.* 1982. Pp. 150–51. M. Shkerin, "Romany Fedora Panferova," *Zvezda*, 1951, no. 3. V. A. Surganov, *Fedor Panferov. Literaturnyi portret.* 1961.

H. S.

Panóva, Véra Fyódorovna (1905–73), prose writer and playwright. Born in Rostov-on-Don, she was self-educated, worked as a journalist, wrote her first play in 1933, and began publishing prose in 1946. A recipient of three Stalin Prizes (1947, 1948, and 1950), she lived in Leningrad from 1940 until her death.

Panova's reputation as a writer was established by her war novel *Fellow Travelers* (Sputniki, 1945, in English *The Train*) for which she received the 1947 Stalin Prize. Set on a hospital train during World War II, this work does not comply with the norms of SOCIALIST REALISM for a war novel. Its focus is on individuals and their private lives. Her second novel, *The Factory* (Rabochii poselok, 1947), brought her the 1948 Stalin Prize, followed shortly by a barrage of criticism. Set in a factory settlement in the Urals, it opens with the sound of a prolonged factory whistle. Although intended as a Soviet industrial novel, much of its action takes place in the private rooms, minds, and diaries of individuals. Her third work, *The Bright Shore* (Yasnyi bereg, 1949), brought her the 1950 Stalin Prize and represents her expiation for previous deviation. Set on a collective farm, it is conflict-free and complies with the demands of socialist realism.

Panova's *Span of the Year* (Vremena goda, 1953) was the first book of the post-Stalin period to focus on personal problems and the individual. It depicts corruption among bureaucrats, the new upper class of Soviet society. This work again brought severe criticism to Panova.

During the 1950s she wrote a cycle of works about children (*Seryozha, Valya,* and *Volodya*). Told from the point of view of youngsters, her sentence structure captures their innuendos, thought processes, and speech patterns. During the 1960s Panova turned to medieval religious Russia for inspiration and wrote a cycle of historical works, *Faces at Dawn* (Liki na zare, 1969).

Loyal to the Party and cautious, Panova was a prolific, officially approved writer. Her prose is conventional, straightforward and realistic. Her portrayal of individuals, particularly women and children, is sympathetic and psychologically astute. She conveys the feminine point of view and shows, among other things, that Soviet women are still treated as second-class citizens.

Works: Izbrannye sochineniya. 2 vols. 1956. *Sobranie sochinenii.* 1969–70. *Izbrannye proizvedeniya.* 2 vols. 1980. *Zametki literatora.* 1972. "Svad'ba kak svad'ba," *Teatr* 1 (1973). *O moei zhizni, knigakh i chitatelyakh.* 2 vols. 1980.

Translations: Time Walked. Leningrad, 1957, Cambridge, Mass., 1959. *The Factory.* Hyperion, Conn., 1977 (reprint of 1949 ed.). *Span of the Year.* Hyperion, Conn., 1977 (reprint of 1957 ed.). *A Summer to Remember.* 1962, 1965. *Serezha and Valya.* 1964. *Sputniki.* 1965. *On Faraway Streets.* 1968. *Seryozha: a few Histories from the Life of a very Small Boy.* Moscow. 1974. *Selected Works.* Moscow, 1976. *The Train.* 1978.

Secondary literature: Deming Brown, *Soviet Russian Literature since Stalin.* 1978. Pp. 177–78, 287–89. E. J. Brown, *Russian Literature Since the Revolution.* 1982. Pp. 194–96. S. Fradkina, *V mire geroev Very Panovoi.* Perm, 1961. Xenia Gasiorowska, *Women in Soviet Fiction, 1917–1964.* 1968. L. Kopelev, "Zhivye obrazy russkoi stariny," *Literaturnaya gazeta,* 15 March 1967. A. Ninov, *Vera Panova. Ocherk tvorchestva.* 1964. L. Plotkin, *Tvorchestvo Very Panovoi.* 1962. M. Shaginyan, "'Vremena goda'. Zametki o novom romane V. Panovoi." In her *Ob iskusstve i literature.* 1958.

H. S.

Parallelism, as defined by Aleksandr VESELOVSKY, is not the comparison or identity of elements but their juxtaposition. There can be a parallelism of objects or actions or both. "Pearls roll / tears roll" is a case where both the objects and actions are related; "an apple rolls where it will / a girl goes where she will" is based on a comparison of action alone. Veselovsky called the parallelism in folk poetry "psychological parallelism" since it reflected the people's inclination to see parallels and resemblances everywhere, and their tendency to express their mental state through images from the external world, particularly from nature. Parallelism is thus an indirect way of communicating emotion or the implications of a situation.

Often a song will begin with a picture from nature: "Dew fell on the dark forest," and then the human situation is described; grief has overtaken the speaker's dear one. Usually the parallelism begins the song and sets the mood or portrays the basic situation, and then the song focuses on the human character. The song may also be divided into two stanzas, where one stanza is entirely devoted to the figurative image and the second to the real image. In a robber song the first stanza describes the freedom of a bright falcon who attacked other birds and is now imprisoned in a golden cage; the second stanza tells of a young man who was free, who sailed the blue sea, attacked foreign ships, and now sits in a dungeon. Very frequently most of the stanza will be devoted to the figurative image, such as in a soldier song where a pine tree is described standing sadly on the steep shore, an ermine gnawing its roots and bees weaving around it. In the last few lines we learn the girl's sweetheart has been recruited. In some cases there is an alternation between the figurative images and the human situation. In one love song, for example, a cuckoo cuckoos in the damp forest; in the next verse Mashenka grieves for her beloved; then the image of a garden drying up is compared to Mashenka's sweetheart leaving her. Sometimes the parallelism takes the form of an address at the beginning of the song: "My grey dove, you are flying away from the nest, abandoning me / Dear one, brave young man, you are leaving, abandoning me." In some cases there is implicit parallelism, where only the figurative part is provided, and the human situation which it illuminates is understood through the traditional imagery employed. If a song is limited, for example, to a description of a swan being taken by a falcon from her flock, it is understood that this refers to a bride being taken by the groom from her girlfriends. Negative parallelism, another form of comparison, is also popular in Russian folk songs: "It is not the white dawn that has come to my window / but my sweetheart has come to visit." This device is also popular in the BYLINY. Another version of this type of parallelism is to provide an image and then negate it: "You are an evil golden snake! You crawl along the grass, it dries up, the flowers in the field fade! / No, brothers, it is not an evil snake, it is a beautiful woman who has led to my destruction." Then the hero tells how he has been betrayed by her. Usually the figurative images are not interpreted, but in some songs their meaning is revealed, as in a SOLDIER SONG where three types of trees in a garden are enumerated, then their symbolism is explained: "The cypress is my dear daddy; the sweet apple tree is my dear mother; the green pear tree is my young wife."

Parallelism can be found in different types of FOLK SONGS, and there is usually a stock set of images associated with each genre. In a love song, for example, a cuckoo cuckooing is compared to a girl grieving for her lost love. In robber and prisoner songs the captive hero is compared to a bird once free which is now sitting in a gilded cage. The plight of a soldier is compared to wormwood, or trees bending in grief.

Another form of parallelism is syntactic parallelism, which is popular in *khorovod* (folk dance) and game songs. The stanzaic structure remains the same, but the content differs. One song is based on the girl's response to her father's suggestion as to whom to marry. In the first stanza her father suggests an older man, in the next a younger man, and in the last a man her own age. She refuses the first two and accepts the last suggestion. In another case syntactic parallelism appears in couplets:

Through the forests she walks—
All the forests to her bow;
Through the meadows she walks—
All the meadows turn green beneath her feet;
Along the fields she walks—
All the fields appear in splendor before her.

In its rich and varied forms, parallelism is one of the major devices employed in Russian folk songs.

Bibliography: Alex E. Alexander, *Russian Folklore: An Anthology in English Translation.* 1975. V. Ya. Propp, *Narodnye liriche-skie pesni.* 2d ed. 1961. Yu. M.Sokolov, *Russian Folklore.* 1971. Pp. 520–21. Roberta Reeder, *Down Along the Mother Volga.* 1975. A. Veselovsky, "Psikhologicheskii parallelizm i ego formy v otrazheniyakh poeticheskogo stilya." In *Poetika.* Vol. 1. 1913. Pp. 130–226.

R. R.

Parízhskaya nóta (Parisian note), a literary term which became current in Russian émigré literature in the early 1930s and is linked with the literary criticism of Georgy ADAMOVICH. This "note" was only geographically connected with Paris, the center of Russian émigré life. It reflected the tastes, moods, and persuasions of many émigré poets and writers of the young generation. The Parisian note dissociated itself from such literary tendencies as the "civic" (Soviet propaganda poetry, in particular), the prophetic rhetoric of the SYMBOLISTS, the experimentation and *épatage* of the FUTURISTS, and even the apology of culture found in ACMEISM, even though Adamovich was himself a disciple of GUMILYOV. The Parisian note also avoided every kind of West-European aestheticism (*l'art pour l'art*). What it expected from poetry was a miracle that would completely transform life. It had its share of romantic utopianism, but also enough irony for any form of rhetoric and mannerism in poetry. The Parisian note demanded simplicity, even spareness of poetic statement, rejected metaphor, and asked the poet to speak only of the most important: evil in this world, suffering, death, reaching out to God, even against a background of doubt. Adamovich occasionally almost identified the Parisian note with the poetry of Innokenty ANNENSKY. He also sympathized with the moral didacticism of Lev TOLSTOI. The Parisian note was best expressed in the poetry of Anatoly SHTEIGER, Lidiya CHERVINSKAYA, and the early Igor CHINNOV, as well as in the prose of V. Varshavsky and Yury FELZEN. Virtually all members of the younger generation of émigré poets and writers responded to the Parisian note in one way or another. However, V. F. KHODASEVICH and V. V. NABOKOV were sharply critical of it.

Bibliography: Georgii Adamovich, "Poeziya v emigratsii" and "Nevozmozhnost' poezii" (The impossibility of poetry). In *Kommentarii* (1967). Yu. Ivask, "Poeziya staroi emigratsii." In *Russkaya literatura v emigratsii.* Ed. N. P. Poltoratsky. 1972. Pp. 45–69.

G. I.

Párnok, Sófiya Yákovlevna (1885–1933), poet, critic, and translator. Her poems first appeared in print in the almanacs, *Protalina* (1907) and *Ogni* (1910). Parnok published several collections of poetry, *Poems* (Stikhotvoreniya, 1916), *Vine* (Loza, 1922), *The Roses of Pieria* (Rozy Pierii, 1922), *Music* (Muzyka, 1926), and *In a Soft Voice* (Vpolgolosa, 1928).

Parnok was an ACMEIST at heart, as evidenced by her verses which tend towards simplicity of form and clarity of thought. Her main themes—love, death, art, solitude—are often embodied in mythological and biblical images. V. BRYUSOV, in his review of Parnok's collection, *The Roses of Pieria*, writes: "Parnok chose as models the poets of ancient Greece, in particular Sappho, and composed verses with ancient meters, reminiscent of the sapphic strophe. This resulted in fragmented lines, which must be read in a special, artificial way in order to perceive any rhythm." Parnok joined the "Lyric Circle," whose members included V. KHODASEVICH, K. Lipskerov, G. Shengeli, and L. GROSSMAN. The group showed a classical orientation and favored harmony and order as opposed to the antiaestheticism of other contemporary groups (first among them, the FUTURISTS and the IMAGISTS).

Parnok was also a prolific critic and translator. Under the pseudonym of A. Polyanin, she contributed critical articles to several journals, and translated Baudelaire, Paul Roux, Proust, Giraudoux, etc. Soviet and Western criticism have devoted very little attention to this poet.

Works: Sobranie stikhotvorenii. Ann Arbor, 1979.
Translations: Two poems in *Modern Russian Poetry.* Ed. V. Markov and M. Sparks. 1967. Pp. 368–71.
Secondary literature: A. Berkova, "Rozy Pierii. Stikhi," *Pechat' i revolyutsiya,* no. 3 (1923), pp. 263–64. V. Bryusov, "Sredi stikhov," *Pechat' i revolyutsiya,* no. 4 (1923), pp. 134–38. S. Polyakova, "Vstupitel'naya stat'ya." In *Sobranie stikhotvorenii* (1979).

A. L.

Parody (*paródiya*), in the broadest sense a literary genre in which a given work is imitated with the purpose of rendering it ridiculous or otherwise attacking it; in a narrower sense, a work in which a certain form, style, or idiom is applied to a subject or content for which it is unsuited. In the latter case, "parody" may be distinguished from "travesty," where a content which is valid per se is given a pointedly inappropriate or inferior form. Parody ranges from lighthearted humor to bitter sarcasm. It may have a satirical edge. It is a form of literary and social criticism. It may be a form of literary polemic, in which case it may turn into a *parodie sérieuse*. Sometimes the parodic effect intended by the author is ignored by the reader, or is lost when the readership ceases being familiar with the subject of parody. Some Russian FORMALISTS, and Yury TYNYANOV in particular, saw parody as an integral and necessary part of all original creation, inasmuch as any original work relates in some specific way to some other work(s), earlier or contemporary. Mikhail BAKHTIN developed a theory of parody in a broad context of his conception of "the other voice" (*chuzhoi golos*) and also drew attention to its role in the carnival tradition.

Although elements of parody may be found in Russian FOLK VERSE and in pre-Petrine literature (e.g., the "Petition of the Monks of Kalyazin Monastery"—Kalyazinskaya chelobitnaya), parody as a distinct genre first appears in the classicist period, when every major genre has its parodic equivalent: the mock-heroic epic (V. MAIKOV's "Elisei, or Bacchus Enraged," 1771), A. SUMAROKOV's parodies of LOMONOSOV's odes (Lomonosov himself was not averse to composing in a parodic style: "Hymn to the Beard," 1757), and I. KRYLOV's parody of the classicist tragedy, *Podshchipa* (1799). The SHISHKOV-KARAMZIN controversy and the advent of ROMANTICISM generated a wealth of parodic works by K. BATYUSHKOV, I. DMITRIEV, A. SHAKHOVSKOI, N. POLEVOI, A. PUSHKIN, and many others. Pushkin, in particular, was a master of parody, in verse ("Ruslan and Lyudmila") as well as in prose ("A History of the Village of Goryukhino"). Parody had a heyday in the 1860s and 1870s when the "civic" poets of the Left parodied the poetry of romantic epigoni and "aesthetes," while writers of the Right parodied the works of liberal and radical authors. Among the former, D. D. MINAEV, V. S. KUROCHKIN, N. L. Loman, and other poets of ISKRA, as well as N. A. NEKRASOV and M. E. SALTYKOV-SHCHEDRIN stand out, among the latter F. M. DOSTOEVSKY's and N. S. LESKOV's anti-nihilist novels, which contain a wealth of parodic elements, deserve mention. The apolitical parodies of Kozma PRUTKOV were aimed at vapid "pure art," epigonic romanticism, self-satisfied philistinism, and officious loyalty. With the advent of modernism and a rapid succession of new schools, parody was again in full flower in the 1890s and 1900s. The plays of CHEKHOV elicited a wealth of parodic response (by V. P. Burenin, etc.), as did the stories of the young GORKY (by A. I. KUPRIN, etc.). The poetry of the SYMBOLISTS was parodied by V. S. SOLOVYOV, A. A. Izmailov, etc. The parodic element was strong throughout in the poetry of V. MAYAKOVSKY, and he and the FUTURISTS were themselves aggressively parodied in the daily press. The element of self-parody is also considerable in some of the MODERNIST poets, as in A. BLOK ("The Fair Show Booth"), Igor SEVERYANIN, and Mayakovsky. With political satire at a premium in the early years of the Soviet period, parody also flourished. The satire of Aleksandr Arkhangelsky (1889–1938), Demyan BEDNY, ILF AND PETROV, I. ERENBURG, etc., contains significant elements of parody. A collection of parodies under the title "Parnassus on End" (Parnass dybom, 1925) enjoyed great popularity at the time. Literary parody, generally of an innocuous nature, has continued to be featured by Soviet satirical journals (*Krokodil*) and will occasionally appear in "thick" literary journals as well. A new flowering of the art of parody emerged in the literature of SAMIZDAT and Tamizdat, as in the works of SOLZHENITSYN (e.g., the chapter "The Traitor Prince" in *The First Circle*), ZINOVIEV, AKSYONOV, VOINOVICH, etc.

Bibliography: B. Begak, N. Kravtsov, and A. Morozov, *Russkaya literaturnaya parodiya.* 1930. *Mnimaya poeziya.* Introd. Yu. N. Tynyanov. 1931. *Russkaya Stikhotvornaya parodiya.* Introd. and notes A. A. Morozov. 1960. Dmitrij Tschiẑewskij and Johann Schröpfer, eds. *Russische literarische Parodien.* Wiesbaden, 1957. *Secondary literature:* M. M. Bakhtin, *Problems of Dostoevsky's Poetics.* Trans. R. W. Rotsel. 1973. P. N. Berkov, "Iz istorii russkoi parodii XVIII–XX vv." In *Voprosy sovetskoi literatury*, Vol. 5 (1957). A. A. Morozov, "Parodiya kak literaturnyi zhanr," *RLit*, 1960, no. 1. "Parnas dybom! (Iz istorii sovetskoi literaturnoi parodii)," *VLit*, 1967, no. 10. Yurii N. Tynyanov, "Dostoevskii i Gogol' (K teorii parodii)." In *Arkhaisty i novatory.* 1929 (reprint. Munich, 1967). Pp. 412–55.
V. T.

Paronymy, see TAUTOLOGY.

Partiinost' (Party-mindedness, Party spirit), the cardinal principle of SOCIALIST REALISM, presupposes creation of works reflecting the official ideology, policy, and views of the Soviet Communist Party. Its theoretical foundation rests on Lenin's statement that materialism includes *partiinost'*—an obligation to adopt "the standpoint of a definite social group in any assessment of events" ("The Economic Content of Populism and the Criticism of It in Mr. Struve's Book," 1894–95). The need for *partiinost'* has also been deduced from Lenin's article "Party Organization and Party Literature" (1905), though in it Lenin demands *partiinost'* only from members of the Social-Democratic Party and refers primarily, perhaps exclusively, to their political writings. Some Soviet theorists contend that *partiinost'* has always been present in literature, beginning with Homer or Aeschylus; others distinguish feudal, bourgeois, and proletarian stages in literary *partiinost'*; and still others insist that *partiinost'*, as exemplified by Maksim GORKY's *Mother* (1906), could have emerged only in a time of proletarian socialist revolution.

The propagation of *partiinost'* intensified markedly in 1931 when the Party instructed the Russian Association of Proletarian Writers (RAPP) to abandon its reliance on Georgy PLEKHANOV's literary views and to create an aesthetics based on Lenin's philosophy. *Partiinost'* tends to absorb other principles of Socialist Realism, such as ideological tendentiousness, adherence to the Marxist class theory, Communist humanism, and NARODNOST' (national spirit). Implementation of Leninist *partiinost'* is said to enhance the aesthetic quality of literature and insure the most objective portrayal of life in its revolutionary development toward Communism.

Bibliography: H. Ermolaev, *Soviet Literary Theories, 1917–1934: The Genesis of Socialist Realism.* 1963. G. Kunitsyn, *Eshche raz o partiinosti khudozhestvennoi literatury.* 1979. N. Shneidman, "The Russian Classical Literary Heritage and the Basic Concepts of Soviet Literary Education," *SlavR* 31, no. 3 (1972), pp. 626–38.
H. E.

Pasternák, Borís Leonídovich (1890–1960), poet and prose writer, one of the great modern masters of Russian literature. Pasternak was the elder son of artist Leonid Pasternak and pianist Rozaliya Kaufman. He was born, brought up, and lived most of his life in Moscow. His early years were spent in a richly cultural artistic atmosphere. He showed early promise in both art and music, and under the impact of Scriabin studied musical composition for six years (1903–09). Pursued by vocational doubts, however, he read philosophy at Moscow University (1908–13), and an enthusiasm for Neo-Kantianism took him to Marburg University to study under Hermann Cohen in the summer semester of 1912.

Contacts with Moscow literary circles and his reading of Russian SYMBOLIST literature (BLOK, BELY, and others) and of works by Hamsun, Ibsen, Przybyszewski, and Rilke probably first stimulated Pasternak's own literary endeavors, and around 1909 he wrote translations of Rilke and pieces of autobiographically based prose and verse. Pasternak's publishing debut was in 1913 with the *Lirika* poetic group, and in 1914 a first verse collection *Twin in the Stormclouds* (Bliznets v tuchakh) appeared. The same year he joined Sergei Bobrov's moderate FUTURIST group, TSENTRIFUGA, and until 1917 published polemical articles and verse in a variety of futurist miscellanies. Topical "urban", symbolist and ego-futurist elements did not obscure the original talent and personality in Pasternak's early poetry, which was characterized by alliterative orchestration, novelty of rhyme, rhythmic and lexical variety, and by virtuosic metaphor. Pasternak met MAYAKOVSKY in spring of 1914, and some of his wartime verse registered Mayakovsky's influence. Two prose stories "The Mark of Apelles" (Apellesova cherta 1915, published

1918) and "Letters from Tula" (Pi'sma iz Tuly 1918, published 1922) reflected Pasternak's attempt to purge himself of the alien "romantic manner," and an article called "Some Propositions" (Neskol'ko polozhenii 1918, published 1922) also dwelt on the aesthetic and ethical reasons for resisting the current vogue for poetic rhetoric and self-dramatization. Meanwhile some poems of Pasternak's second verse collection *Over the Barriers* (Poverkh bar'erov 1917) demonstrated how emotion and the poet's romantic self-image could be successfully absorbed and used to dynamize metaphoric landscapes.

Partially lamed by a childhood accident, Pasternak was rejected for military service and spent part of World War I engaged in clerical work in the Urals, only returning to Moscow after the February 1917 Revolution. An amorous affair of summer 1917, intensified by revolutionary exhilaration and experiences of a journey to the Saratov area, inspired the verses of *My Sister Life* (Sestra moya zhizn'). This important poetic cycle circulated widely before its publication in 1922 and earned Pasternak acclaim as a major modern poet. The cycle celebrates love and nature experience as the rapturous revelation of a creative life-force. In it luxurious and explosive imagery combines and sometimes contrasts with the disciplined quatrain form, occasional colloquial idiom and elliptical syntax. The same freshness of vision was also captured in the prose story "Zhenya Luvers' Childhood" (Detstvo Lyuvers, 1918, published 1922) in which a child's developing awareness of surrounding objects, human beings and moral concerns is evoked, transcending the arbitrariness of ordinary psychological description and subverting the orderly severity of the unpoetic adult world.

Pasternak's euphoria over the social liberation of February 1917 and his initial sympathy for the Bolshevik October coup rapidly cooled. He did not regard politics as a primary human or artistic concern, and as a member of the liberal intelligentsia he was disaffected by Bolshevik tyranny and doctrinaire excess. The prose story "Aerial Ways" (Vozdushnye puti, 1924) illustrated how the forces of history and revolution take no account of individual human concerns and wishes, and the incompatibility of the lyrical and the historical established already in a prerevolutionary article, "The Black Goblet" (Chernyi bokal, 1916), was reiterated in a revolutionary setting in the prose extract "Lovelessness" (Bezlyub'e, 1918).

But Pasternak's infection by the spectacular aspect of revolution, and his desire to believe, "belong," and respond to new realities brought changes in his writing. After a fourth volume of lyrics, *Themes and Variations* (Temy i variatsii, 1923), his poetry of the 1920s was mainly epic or narrative in design. "The Lofty Malady" (Vysokaya bolezn', 1923–28) contained reflections of the civil war and described idealistic intellectuals as "music in the ice," writing placards on the "joy of their own sunset" and contrasting with the figure of LENIN, fearful yet admirable in his relentless logic, willpower, and mastery of events. *The Year 1905* (Devyat'sot pyatyi god, 1926) reconstructed the events and personal recollections of the 1905 Revolution in several chapters of galloping anapaestic verse. *Lieutenant Schmidt* (Leitenant Shmidt, 1927), also set in the 1905 Revolution, described the naval mutiny led by Schmidt and imbued the hero with some Christ-like, sacrificial qualities that also emerged in Pasternak's later prose and lyrics. *Spektorsky* (written 1924–30, published complete 1931) was a novel in verse, showing episodes of a young poet's life before and after the Revolution, in which the hero shared the author's own historical passivity and fatalism. The same qualities emerged in the central character of a prose companion-piece, "The Story" (Povest', 1929).

Pasternak's futurist experience and friendship with Mayakovsky led him in 1923 to join the latter's LEF (Left Front of Art) group, but the association was brief, for he disliked the "applied art" mentality and corporate artistic activities of the LEFT ART movement. In the laissez-faire conditions of the arts in the 1920s, Pasternak ranked as a literary FELLOW TRAVELLER. Among cognoscenti he had enthusiastic followers, but he was hounded by orthodox proletarian critics for his persistently bourgeois, hermetic outlook, "subjective idealism," "individualism," and complexity. The autobiographical *Safe Conduct* (Okhrannaya gramota, 1931) attracted similar charges. The book was not a conventional autobiography, but a record of individuals (notably Scriabin, Rilke, and Mayakovsky), and of mainly pre-revolutionary incidents that helped shape the author's artistic personality. In the work Pasternak also represented creativity as a form of "energy" that displaced the whole of reality, releasing showers of random metaphor and imagery whose function was to speak symbolically, on the poet's behalf, and as though without his participation.

Pasternak's first marriage, to Evgeniya Lurie, broke up in 1931 after nine years, largely as a result of his new infatuation with Zinaida Neigauz, who eventually became his second wife. In summer 1931 Pasternak travelled with his new consort to the Caucasus, and new friendships blossomed with Georgian poets Iashvili, Tabidze, and Chikovani. Love lyrics and Georgian impressions loomed large in a further verse collection *Second Birth* (Vtoroe rozhdenie, 1932). The title evidently implied a form of renewal, and in the verses Pasternak spoke of and demonstrated his striving towards a new and "unprecedented simplicity." The poetry also hinted at a new-found optimism and reconciliation of lyrical and social elements, while still emphasising the seriousness and tragic potential of the poet's calling. But artistic rebirth was short-lived. When independent artistic groups were disbanded in 1932 and the new UNION OF SOVIET WRITERS assumed control of literary affairs, one of its primary functions was to impose conformity and adherence to the principles of socialist realism. Pasternak was officially recognized as a major poetic talent, and for a time he perhaps naively showed willingness to participate in official literary life. He was a leading, though oblique and idiosyncratic speaker at the First Congress of Writers in 1934, and he was in the Soviet delegation to the Paris Conference of 1935 in Defense of Culture. But he recognized the dangers of being cast as an approved "court poet" and was privately revolted by the tyranny of Stalinism. After 1935 his flow of original writings virtually ceased, and his few recorded public statements were sharply critical of official interference with artistic freedoms. Earlier cajoling and muffled criticism of Pasternak now became openly hostile, and as colleagues and friends disappeared in the purges of the later 1930s, Pasternak resorted to poetic translation as a safer livelihood. His renderings of Georgian poets pleased Stalin and may have helped to preserve his liberty; they were followed by Russian renderings of Byron, Keats, Petöfi, Verlaine, and Becher. In the years of World War II and the later 1940s he also translated the major tragedies of Shakespeare, and these remain the standard versions used for staging the dramas in Russia. Two further major translating achievements were Pasternak's versions of Goethe's *Faust* (1953) and Schiller's *Maria Stuart* (1958).

Within Russia, the war brought some ideological relaxation and concession, and a revival of morale. Some of Pasternak's earlier verse was reprinted and two new collections appeared. *On Early Trains* (Na rannikh poezdakh, 1943) and *Breadth of Earth* (Zemnoi prostor, 1945) handled patriotic themes while eschewing all hackneyed official rhetoric; in simple, unforced language Pasternak described everyday local scenes, evoking a sense of communion with common folk at work and at war. The postwar ideological clampdown of "ZHDANOVISM" in the arts again forced Pasternak into silence. Surrounded by terror and suspicion, he labored on with translations while working away in secret on the manuscript of a prose novel. He cherished long-standing ambitions to work in this genre, but its mastery had not come naturally. Several earlier prose writings, including "Lovelessness," "Zhenya Luvers' Childhood," and "The Story," appeared to be, and were conceived as preliminary fragments of larger works. Themes, characterizations, names, and situations from prose fragments published between 1918 and 1939 now re-emerged in the novel *Doctor Zhivago* which Pasternak completed in 1955. The central hero, Yury Zhivago, was the author's near-contemporary and partial alter ego, a Moscow doctor and poet who died in 1929, leaving a legacy of inspired poetry that formed the final chapter of the novel. For the account of Zhivago's early life, wartime and revolution experiences, and his eventual retreat to the Urals following the Bolshevik takeover, Pasternak drew generously on his own personal recollections. Zhivago was also used as a partial mouthpiece for the author's own philosophical and artistic beliefs. His apparent weakness and inability to shape and influence his own fate or that of his family caught up in the revolutionary storm had been adumbrated in Pasternak's earlier prose. But these qualities were presented not as faults, but as signs of Zhivago's awareness of his own inescapable, divinely ordained sacrificial mission as an artistic witness to the tragedy of his age. This was also reinforced in "Hamlet" and other items in the poetic appendix which closely identified the creative poet's predicament with that of the suffering Christ. Creativity and compassionate involvement in the fates of other men thus emerged as the foundations of immortality and of a new Christian existentialism that owed something to BERDYAEV and other 20th-century Russian religious philosophers. Lara Antipova, the central heroine, was a woman whose vital and natural, yet vulnerable femininity inspired Zhivago to poetic creation, while at the same time driving her husband Pasha to make political commitments that eventually reduced him to sterility and destroyed him. *Doctor Zhivago* owed much to the 19th-century social-historical novel, but countered the quasi-scientific determinism of that genre by the use of coincidence, subjective distortion of historical chronology and atmosphere, and by blurring the characterization of some central characters—features which some commentators have regarded as flaws in the novel.

Doctor Zhivago was rejected for publication in the USSR, but its publication (1957) and acclaim in the West, followed by the award of the Nobel Prize for Literature (1958) unleashed a bitter official campaign against Pasternak, forcing him to reject the award. In the late 1950s Pasternak composed a further book of transparent and reflective verse, *When the Weather Clears* (Kogda razgulyaetsya, 1957), and a second "autobiographical essay," *Avtobiograficheskii ocherk* (1957); both books came out first in the West, but were later printed in the USSR also. A historical drama, *The Blind Beauty* (Slepaya krasavitsa), was left incomplete at Pasternak's death; surviving extracts depict Russia's emergence from tyranny to emancipation and enlightment in the late 19th and early 20th century and suggest that the work was conceived as a form of aesopian comment on Stalinist and post-Stalinist Russia.

Despite official opprobrium, Pasternak's funeral at Peredelkino writers' settlement near Moscow was attended by thousands, and his villa and grave are still places of pilgrimage. A gradual posthumous rehabilitation of Pasternak by the Soviet literary establishment has occurred, though the novel *Doctor Zhivago* has still not been published in the USSR.

Works: Doktor Zhivago. Milan, 1959. *Sochineniya.* Ed. G. P. Struve and B. A. Filippov. 3 vols. Ann Arbor, 1961. *Stikhotvoreniya i poemy.* Ed. L. A. Ozerov. Moscow-Leningrad, 1965. *Slepaya krasavitsa.* London, 1969. Also in: *Prostor* (Alma Ata), no. 10 (1969). *Vozdushnye puti (Proza raznykh let).* Ed. E. B. and E. V. Pasternak. Moscow, 1982.

Correspondence: Renate Schweitzer, *Freundschaft mit Pasternak.* Vienna, 1963. Marina Cvetaeva, Boris Pasternak, Rainer Maria Rilke, *Il settimo sogno: Lettere 1926.* Rome, 1980. *Perepiska s Ol'goi Freidenberg.* Ed. E. Mossman. New York and London, 1981.

Translations: Doctor Zhivago. Trans. M. Hayward and M. Harari. 1958. *I Remember: Sketch for an Autobiography.* Ed. and trans. D. Magarshack. 1960. *Poems 1955–1959.* Trans. Michael Harari. 1960. *The Poetry of Boris Pasternak 1914–1960.* Trans. G. Reavey, 1960. *In the Interlude.* Trans. H. Kamen. 1962. *Fifty Poems.* Trans. L. Pasternak-Slater. 1963. *Letters to Georgian Friends.* Ed. and trans. D. Magarshack. 1968. *The Blind Beauty.* Trans. M. Hayward et al. 1969. *Collected Short Prose.* Ed. and trans. C. J. Barnes et al. 1977. *The Correspondence of Boris Pasternak and Olga Freidenberg 1910–1952.* Ed. and trans. E. Mossman. 1982. *My Sister Life* and *A Sublime Malady.* Trans. Mark Rudman with Bohdan Boychuk. Ann Arbor, Mich., 1983.

Secondary literature: D. Davie and A. Livingstone, eds., *Pasternak: Modern Judgements.* 1969. Guy de Mallac, *Boris Pasternak: His Life and Art.* Norman, Okla., 1981. V. Erlich, ed., *Pasternak: A Collection of Critical Essays.* 1978. L. Fleishman, *Boris Pasternak v dvadtsatye gody.* Munich, 1980. ———, *Stat'i o Pasternake.* Bremen, 1977. H. Gifford, *Boris Pasternak: A Critical Study.* 1977. A. Gladkov, *Meetings with Pasternak.* Ed. and trans. M. Hayward. 1977. (Original: *Vstrechi s Pasternakom.* Paris, 1973.) O. R. Hughes, *The Poetic World of Boris Pasternak.* 1974. O. Ivinskaya, *A Captive of Time.* 1978. (Original: *V plenu vremeni.* Paris, 1978.) N. A. Nilsson, *Boris Pasternak: Essays.* 1976. D. L. Plank, *Pasternak's Lyric: A Study of Sound and Imagery.* The Hague, 1966. G.

P. Struve, ed., *Sbornik statei, posvyashchennykh tvorchestvu Borisa Leonidovicha Pasternaka.* Munich, 1962.

C. B.

Paterik (Patericon), see HAGIOGRAPHY, OLD RUSSIAN LITERATURE.

Pathos (*páfos*), a literary term whose meaning in Russian criticism has been different, since BELINSKY, from that which it has in Aristotle and the Aristotelian tradition. Following Hegel, who defined pathos as "the rich, powerful individual quality in which substantial movements of the Spirit are brought to life, achieving reality and expression," Belinsky used *pafos* essentially in the meaning of "poetic form in which an idea becomes incarnate," or even as a synonym of "poetic idea." Belinsky speaks of "the pathos of reality," sees humor as the pathos of GOGOL's *Dead Souls*, and defines humor as "negative pathos." In contemporary Soviet criticism, *pafos* is widely used in this broad Belinskian meaning. Expressions such as "humanist pathos" or "the pathos of building a socialist society" are common usage.

V. T.

Paustóvsky, Konstantin Geórgievich (1892–1968), prose writer, was born in Moscow. A descendant of Zaporozhian Cossacks, he spent his early years in Kiev, studied at the University of Kiev (1911–13) and later at Moscow University (1913). Between 1913 and 1929 he wandered through various parts of Russia, supporting himself as a streetcar conductor, medical orderly at the front, teacher, and journalist. He published his first story in 1912 and his first collection of short stories, *Sea Sketches*, in 1925. During the post-Stalin era Paustovsky conducted a seminar on prose at the Gorky Literary Institute in Moscow. He was nominated for the Nobel Prize in 1965. He died in Moscow.

Author of short stories, novellas, novels, plays, and reminiscences, Paustovsky, like Diderot, believed that "art consists in finding the extraordinary in the ordinary." During the 1920s he wrote romantic stories and sketches filled with exotic descriptions, unusual situations, and populated by characters who escape reality and exist in a dream world. A good example is his story *Labels for Colonial Goods* (1924).

Most of Paustovsky's work does not fit the framework of SOCIALIST REALISM and shows that he never succumbed fully to official pressures. His *Kara-Bugaz* (1932) and *Kolkhida* (1934), which deal with the theme of industrialization and the building of Communism, are historic adventure novels. During World War II when most Soviet writers were extolling patriotism and heroic deeds, Paustovsky wrote the first part of his autobiography, *Distant Youth* (1946) and a novel, *Smoke of the Fatherland* (1944), which tells the story of the Russian intelligentsia on the eve of the war.

During the post-Stalin years, Paustovsky continued to focus on the individual, producing some of his most important works. *The Golden Rose* (1955), a book about "literature in the making," consists of a series of stories and fragments dealing with creativity, artistry, the role of a writer, and the function of literature. Between 1945 and 1963 Paustovsky wrote his reminiscences, *Story of a Life* (Povest' o zhizni), considered by many to be his best work. Published in six parts, it covers more than a fifty year period in the life of Russia. His reminiscences about the Revolution and civil war years are particularly exciting and interesting. Historic and cosmic events are presented from the narrator's point of view with focus on the personal and the particular.

An acknowledged master of Russian lyrical prose, Paustovsky is considered one of the finest Russian stylists of the 20th century. In the tradition of BUNIN and PRISHVIN, whom he acknowledged as his masters, his prose is lyrical and contemplative. It is balanced and economical. His works are verbal landscapes filled with sounds, smells and nuances. They are "impressionistic" mood pieces.

Although chronologically Paustovsky belongs to the first generation of Soviet writers, his works earned him popularity and a place among the "new voices" of the 1960s. As a teacher and writer, Paustovsky had a great impact on such writers as KAZAKOV and Balter. In addition, he distinguished himself as the editor of the two volume collection, *Literary Moscow* (1956) and *Pages from Tarusa* (1961). These were attempts to introduce new writers to the reading public as well as to publish writers who either perished or were suppressed during the Stalin era. Always outspoken in defense of honesty, moral values, and the freedom of individual writers, Paustovsky came out in 1966 in defense of SINYAVSKY and DANIEL, an act which earned him the respect, admiration and love of many contemporary Russian writers.

Works: Sobranie sochinenii. 8 vols. 1966–70. *Poteryannye romany.* Kaluga, 1962. *Povest' o zhizni.* 1962. *Kniga o khudozhnikakh.* 1966. *Blizkie i dalekie* ("Zhizn' zamechatel'nykh lyudei"). 1967. *Naedine s osen'yu.* 1967. *Selected Stories* (in Russian). Oxford, 1967.

Translations: Selected Stories. Moscow, 1949. *The Flight of Time.* Moscow, 1956. *Rabbit's Paws.* 1961. *Story of a Life.* 1964, 1967, 1968, 1969, 1982. *Childhood and Schooldays.* 1964. *Slow Approach of Thunder.* 1965. *The Golden Rose.* Moscow, 1965? *In that Dawn.* 1967. *Years of Hope.* 1968. *Southern Adventure.* 1969. *The Magic Ringlet.* 1971. *The Restless Years.* 1974. *Selected Stories.* Moscow, 1974. *The Black Gulf.* Hyperion, Conn., 1977 (Reprint of 1946 ed.). *A Book About Artists.* Moscow, 1978.

Secondary literature: E. A. Aleksanyan, *Konstantin Paustovskii—novellist.* 1969. B. Balter, "Strana Paustovskogo," *Literaturnaya Rossiya,* 26 February 1965. P. Henry, [Introduction] in *Selected Stories.* Oxford, 1967. V. Il'in, *Konstantin Paustovskii.* 1967. L. Levitskii, *Konstantin Paustovskii; Ocherk tvorchestva.* 1963. V. Shklovskii, "Schast'e otkryvat' mir," *Izvestiya,* 15 February 1975. M. Slonim, *Soviet Russian Literature, Writers and Problems. 1917–1977.* 1977. Pp. 118–22. G. Svirski, *A History of Post-War Soviet Writings: The Literature of Moral Opposition.* 1981.

H. S.

Pávlov, Nikolaí Filíppovich (1803–64), writer. The son of a Moscow house serf, he was freed in 1811, entered a Moscow theatrical school, and finished in 1821. Pavlov worked briefly as an actor, then enrolled in the philology department of Moscow University, completing his studies in 1825.

Though his poetry appeared early in Moscow journals, Pavlov's literary career began with translations. In 1831, writing for the journal TELESKOP, Pavlov became the first to translate Balzac, with whom he was later often compared. Four years later, Pavlov's socially critical *Three Tales* (Tri povesti, 1835) brought him considerable notoriety. Refreshingly contemporary, the tales combined insights into social power with an implicit protest against the regime of Nicholas I. "Name Day" (Imeniny), the most successful of the three, describes the tragic life of a talented serf musician. Although the *Three Tales* passed censorship, Nicholas I suppressed further editions. In 1837, Pavlov married the poetess and heiress Karolina Yanish (PAVLOVA) and adopted the life style of Moscow's beau monde.

In 1839, Pavlov published the collection *New Tales* (Novye povesti), which included two more works devoted to high society, plus *The Demon* (Demon), notable for featuring a petty clerk as the main protagonist. During the next decade, many outstanding writers gathered at the Pavlov home. Though Pavlov himself was less active, his letters in response to GOGOL's *Selected Passages from Correspondence with Friends* were praised by BELINSKY and reprinted in SOVREMENNIK.

In the fifties, Pavlov authored critical and essayistic articles, but became increasingly more conservative. Publisher of the newspapers *Nashe vremya* (1860–63) and *Russkie vedomosti* (1863–64), Pavlov adopted a pro-government stance which led to epigrams at his expense in liberal journals pointedly satirizing his transformation.

Works: Povesti i stikhi. 1957.

Secondary literature: V. G. Belinskii, "O russkoi povesti i povestyakh g. Gogolya" (1835), *PSS* 1 (1953), pp. 280–84. E. C. Shepard, "Pavlov's 'Demon' and Gogol's 'Overcoat'," *SlavR* 33 (1974), pp. 288–301. V. P. Vil'chinskii, *N. F. Pavlov.* 1970. J. S.

Pávlova, Karolína Kárlovna (née Jänisch, 1807–93), poet. The daughter of a professor of Moscow University, she moved in literary circles early, meeting PUSHKIN, BARATYNSKY, VENEVITINOV, etc. In 1828 and 1829 she had a liaison with the Polish poet Adam Mickiewicz, whose memory she cherished all her life. In 1837 she married the writer Nikolai Filippovich PAVLOV. Her family had come into a substantial inheritance and the Pavlovs ran a brilliant literary

salon in Moscow for a number of years. In 1853 their marriage broke up; Pavlova left Russia and spent the rest of her life abroad, mostly in Dresden, where she died. Pavlova wrote poetry in three languages. Her first collection was in German: *Das Nordlicht: Proben der neuen russischen Literatur* (1833). It contained translations from the Russian (Pushkin and others) and her own verses. Subsequently Pavlova translated a great deal of Russian poetry into German. In 1839 a collection in French, *Les préludes par m-me Caroline Pavlof née Jaenisch* appeared in Paris. In the 1830s and 1840s Pavlova regularly published her poetry in various Russian journals and met with considerable success. BELINSKY spoke of the "noble simplicity of these diamond-like verses, diamond-like in their hardness and in their poetic brilliance" ("Russkie zhurnaly" (1839), *PSS,* 3, p. 191). Pavlova's novel in verse and prose, *A Dual Life* (Dvoinaya zhizn', 1848), deals with the problem which is also focal to her poetry: the alienation of a sensitive and thoughtful soul and its striving to rise above a shallow and corrupt society. Pavlova continued to write Russian verse abroad and also translated German poetry into Russian. She died forgotten and in poverty. Her poetry was rediscovered by the symbolists. BRYUSOV, in particular, found the form of her poetry intriguing and stimulating.

Works: Sobranie sochinenii. Ed. and introd. V. Bryusov. 2 vols. 1915. *Polnoe sobranie stikhotvorenii.* Intro. P. P. Gromov. 1964.

Translations: Lewanski, p. 323.

Secondary literature: L. Grossman, *Vtornik u Karoliny Pavlovoi.* 2d. ed. 1922. B. Rapgof, *K. Pavlova. Materialy dlya izucheniya zhizni i tvorchestva.* 1916. Barbara H. Monter, "From an Introduction to Pavlova's *A Double Life,*" *RLT* 9 (1974), pp. 337–53. Munir Sendich, "Moscow Literary Salons: Thursdays at Karolina Pavlova's," *Welt der Slaven* 17 (1972), pp. 341–57. ———, "*Ot Moskvy do Drezdena:* Pavlova's Unpublished Memoirs," *RLJ* 102 (1975), pp. 57–78.

V. T.

Peasant writers and poets. A movement in the early 20th century aimed at creating a secular literary tradition based on folk culture. It became recognized after Nikolai KLYUEV (1887–1937) wrote a letter to Aleksandr BLOK in 1907 in which he made claim to be a "people's poet." The movement lasted until 1937.

Klyuev is generally recognized as the "father" of the peasant school, although the most popular member was undoubtedly Sergei ESENIN (1895–1925). Other peasant writers were Sergei Klychkov (pseudonym of Sergei Leshenkov, 1889–1940), Pyotr Oreshin (1887–1938), Pavel Radimov (1887–1967), Rodion Berezov (pseudonym of Rodion Akulshin, 1896–   ), Pavel Druzhinin (1890–   ), Pavel VASILIEV (1910–37), Pimen Karpov (1884– or 1887–1963), and Aleksandr Shiryaevets (pseudonym of Aleksandr Abramov, 1887–1924).

While the FUTURISTS waxed eloquent over the wonders of the new machine age, the peasant writers and poets were moved by a strong revulsion for industrialization. Oreshin wrote of "dead blind steel crawling across the world," and Klyuev described the tractor as an "iron vampire sucking blood from the earth." The peasant writers glorified the village and longed to return to the simple life of rural Russia. At the same time the futility of their dream was evident even to them, and their writings are often of a tragic bent.

The most unique member of the movement, and perhaps of all Russian poetry, was Nikolai Klyuev, who actually began his poetic career with relatively conventional verse. Within a short time, however, he had developed a style rich and even startling in its imagery. His language is replete with dialect, and he makes frequent allusions to exotic eastern motifs, Slavic pagan gods, sectarian legend. His major work (or, at least, that which has survived) consists of his long poems (*poemy*): "Fourth Rome," "Lament for Esenin," "Mother Sabbath," "The Burned Ruins."

Esenin started out with idyllic poetry about his native Ryazan and became a follower of Klyuev, whom he referred to as his "teacher." While Esenin's verse lacks the complex imagery of Klyuev's work, it struck a chord with Russians of all classes. Esenin moved to Moscow and later to Leningrad, where his involvement with the imagists and his alcoholism radically altered his verse. The term "Eseninism" came to be used pejoratively to refer to carousing and a generally bohemian way of life.

Sergei Klychkov wrote largely poetry until 1925, when he switched to prose, which he felt was a better vehicle for his rural ideology. He is the author of four novels: *The Sugar German* (1925), *The Prattler of Chertukhino* (1926), *The Last Lel* (1927), and *Prince of This World* (1928). Klychkov's work is written in a highly ornamental style and is rich with pantheistic and Manichean imagery, and he is generally viewed as a follower of Klyuev. Virtually all his prose work revolves around a contrast between reality and dream, fact and fantasy. Pyotr Oreshin is the author of more than fifty books—primarily poetry. His imagery lacks the rich uniqueness of Klyuev's or Klychkov's writings, and he devotes himself to descriptions of everyday life in the countryside. He was viewed by the government as being a representative of the middle class of the peasantry (*serednyaki*), and an attempt was made to win him over to the cause of the Revolution. Ultimately, however, he joined the other peasant writers and poets in a severe condemnation of the new order of things.

Aleksandr Shiryaevets, who took his name from his native village of Shiryaevo, avoided elaborate stylization and imitated such folk genres as the song, the tale, and the CHASTUSHKA.

Pavel Radimov was a poet who was best known for his painting, which was impressionistic in nature and usually depicted scenes of country life. Critics often noted interrelations between his poetry and his painting.

Pavel Druzhinin and Rodion Berezov were both members of the literary group PEREVAL. Druzhinin was an imitator of the early Esenin and also wrote a good deal on religious topics. Berezov writes both prose and poetry and has been one of the most prolific émigré writers. Pavel Vasiliev wrote poetry rich in imagery and reminiscent of the folk song. Pimen Karpov was a prose writer who was first noticed by Tolstoi. His two autobiographical novelettes, *Riding the Sun* (1933) and *From the Depths* (1956), attracted a certain amount of attention.

When the government encountered stiff opposition to its collectivization policies, it decided to "destroy the *kulaks* (well-to-do peasants) as a class," and in the process declared the peasant writers and poets to be representatives of "*kulak* literature" or—just as dangerous—"*kulak* sympathizers."

By 1937 Klyuev, Klychkov, Oreshin, and Vasiliev had all been arrested and never returned. Akulshin-Berezov emigrated, and the other peasant writers and poets gave up literature until the period of de-Stalinization. Klyuev, Klychkov, Oreshin, and Vasiliev have all been "posthumously rehabilitated"—that is, the government now admits they never committed any crimes.

There is a certain continuity between the writings of the peasant poets and prose writers and the works of recent "rural writers," but the latter are often city dwellers or former villagers visiting the village, not peasants writing about their own lives. The lack of real peasant authors is a tragedy for Russian literature, as it means that Russian folklore is not being integrated into modern secular literature.

Bibliography: Rodion Berezov, *Iosif Prekrasnyi: poemy.* San Francisco, 1959. Nikolai Klyuev, *Sochineniya.* Ed. Boris Filippov and Gleb Struve. 2 vols. Munich, 1969. ———, *Poems.* Trans. John Glad. Ann Arbor, 1977. Gordon McVay, *Esenin: A Life.* 1976. Petr Oreshin, *Izbrannoe: Stikhi.* 1968.
J. G.

Pechat' i revolyútsiya (Press and Revolution)—Soviet journal of bibliography and criticism which came out monthly in Moscow from 1921 to 1930. Its editor-in-chief was V. P. POLONSKY. LUNACHARSKY served on the editorial board, and BRYUSOV was among the early contributors, along with N. N. ASEEV and A. K. VORONSKY. The journal originally aimed at a wide readership and at providing an "encyclopedic" overview of current developments in printing, publishing reviews and surveys of books on a wide range of subjects as well as articles on the technical and graphic aspects of printing. *Pechat' i revolyutsiya* gradually exhibited a greater interest in questions of literary history and methodology and engaged in polemics with the FORMALISTS, criticizing the formal method in literature espoused by members of OPOYAZ from a Marxist point of view (see especially bk. 5, 1924). Toward the end of the 1920s, the journal increasingly specialized in articles on the theory and history of literature and art and became an outlet for the "vulgar sociologism" of PEREVERZEV and his students. In 1929, Polonsky was forced to resign and was replaced by V. FRICHE. In its last year the journal was controlled by Litfront. *Pechat' i revolyutsiya* was closed in June 1930.
C. T. N.

Pechérin, Vladímir Sergéevich (1807–1885), romantic poet and religious activist, was educated at Petersburg University and in Berlin where he earned his academic degree in 1833. In 1831 and 1832 he wrote poetry, translated Schiller and Greek lyrics (*Syn otechestva*, 1831; *Nevskii al'manakh*, 1832). In 1836, when sent on a business trip to Europe, Pecherin defected and converted to Catholicism (1840). He spent the rest of his life in Redemptorist monasteries in the West and died in Dublin, Ireland. Pecherin's contacts with the secular world were quite limited, yet he corresponded with Aleksandr NIKITENKO (his former schoolmate, who left several notes on Pecherin in his *Diary*) and with Aleksandr HERZEN. Herzen wrote about Pecherin in his memoirs (*Polyarnaya zvezda*, 1861, no. 6) and also published some of Pecherin's poems in his *Vol'naya russkaya pechat'* ("The Triumph of Death," "A Submarine City"). In his memoirs Herzen placed Pecherin among the generation whose flower was crushed by the tyrannical regime of Nicholas I. Through Herzen's influence, Pecherin's name came back into Russian culture of the 1860s and 1870s. (KATKOV's article in *Moskovskie vedomosti*, 2 August 1863; Ivan AKSAKOV in *Den'*, 2 September 1865; P. I. Bartenev in *Russkii arkhiv*, 1870, no. 11). The image of Pecherin as portrayed by Herzen found a polemic echo in the novels of DOSTOEVSKY: *The Possessed* (Karmazinov's fiction), *A Raw Youth* (Versilov), and *The Brothers Karamazov* (Ivan's "Grand Inquisitor").

Works: Poety 1820–1830 gg. Ed. L. Ginzburg. 1972. Vol. 2, Pp. 453–88. *Literaturnoe nasledstvo* 62, pp. 463–84 (Pecherin's correspondence with Herzen and Ogaryov).
Secondary literature: M. Gershenzon, *Zhizn' Pecherina.* 1905. *Istoriya Molodoi Rossii.* Moscow and Petrograd, 1923. A. Lipski, "Pecherin's Quest for Meaningfullness," *SlavR* 23 (1964), pp. 239–57.
N. P.

Pereléshin, Valéry (1913– , pseud. of Valéry Frántsevich Salátko-Petrýshche), poet, translator, and critic. Born in Irkutsk, Pereleshin took degrees in law and theology from Kharbin University, where he also studied Chinese. He has lived in Peking, Shanghai, Tientsin, and since 1953 in Rio de Janeiro. In Pereleshin's early verse the ACMEIST poetics of GUMILYOV prevails, but more recently he has leaned toward a neobaroque style, setting off poetic phrases by somewhat rough prosaisms and using conceits as well as complex metaphors which are sometimes difficult to unravel. Not a few of his poems are devoted to China and Brazil, with the latter quaintly fused with Russia in a utopian island called Rozilia-Brassiya. Pereleshin's most mature and original collection of verse, "Ariel" (1976), is dedicated to a young Soviet poet with whom Pereleshin had been in correspondence but whom he had never met. This addressee is a Russian version of Shakespeare's Mr. W. H. Pereleshin's erotic poetry is very dynamic, combining stormy passion, at times even naked lust, with a feeling of warm tenderness for his beloved Ariel. A striving for impassivity and Nirvana is Pereleshin's antithesis to his passions. These peripeties of juxtaposed realia, symbolized by him in the image of a swing, enrich and dramatize Pereleshin's lyrics. The sonnet is Pereleshin's favorite form. Moreover, he uses exact rhymes of a type which has long since disappeared from Russian poetry. But such conservatism does not prevent Pereleshin from being a very modern poet, as his slight formal pedantry is wed to the feverish sensibility of 20th-century man. Pereleshin is one of the best translators of Chinese classics. He has also successfully translated Coleridge's "Rime of the Ancient Mariner," St. John of the Cross, the ballads of Villon, Portuguese and English poems by Pessoa, among others. He has also translated KUZMIN's "Alexandrian Songs" into Portuguese. His autobiographic "Poem without a Subject" (Poema bez predmeta) and his "Poem about the Universe" (Poema o mirozdanii) are current in Russia.

Works: (Collections of verse:) *V puti.* 1937. *Dobryi ulei.* 1939. *Zvezda nad morem.* 1941. *Zhertva.* 1944. *Yuzhnyi dom.* 1968. *Kachel'.* 1971. *Zapovednik.* 1972. *S gory Nevo.* 1975. *Ariel'.* 1976.

Yuzhnyi krest. 1978. (Translations of Chinese poetry:) *Stikhi na veere.* 1970. Tsui Yuan's "Li Sao." 1975.

Secondary literature: Yurii Ivask, Introd. to *Ariel'* (1976). Simon Karlinsky, "A Hidden Masterpiece: Valery Pereleshin's *Ariel,*" *Christopher Street* 2, no. 6, December 1977. P. P. Lapiken, "Tsui Yuan'. *Li Sao, poema, v stikhotvornom perevode Valeriya Pereleshina,*" *Novyi zhurnal,* no. 121 (1975), pp. 285–88. Aleksis Rannit, "O poezii i poetike Valeriya Pereleshina: Shest' pervykh sbornikov poeta (1937–1971)," *RLJ,* no. 106 (1976), pp. 79–104. ———, "Valerii Pereleshin posle *Kacheli,*" *RLJ,* no. 113 (1978). Vivian Wyler, "Quando traduzir ser um ato de gratidão," *Jornal de Brasil,* 8 September 1979.   G. I.

Peresvétov, Iván Semyónovich (16th century), political writer. A West Russian nobleman from the Polish-Lithuanian Commonwealth, Peresvetov served the Kings of Poland and Hungary, before going to Moldavia and finally arriving in Moscow around 1538. Twice he presented his works to IVAN IV, whose policies actually resembled those recommended by Peresvetov. In his "Tale of Sultan Mohammed" (Skazanie o Magmet-saltane) and "Tale of Emperor Constantine" (Skazanie o tsare Konstantine), Peresvetov comes out with a strong endorsement of the "Turkish" form of government and justice, that is, absolute power for the monarch, an efficient centralized administration, and rigorous and swift law enforcement. Peresvetov was vehemently opposed to the oligarchic rule which he knew from his native Grand Duchy of Lithuania, and suggests that only a strong and severe ruler can put an end to the luxury, corruption, and depredations of the feudal lords who create only disorder and misery for the people. An absolute ruler should see to it that men in responsible positions be appointed by merit rather than by privilege. Peresvetov's pamphlets are written in the vernacular, with elements of the chancery style of his age and few Slavonicisms. They are vivid and interesting.

Works: Sochineniya. Text A. A. Zimin. Comm. Ya. S. Lur'e. 1956.

Secondary literature: E. Donnert, "Gesellschaftstheorien und Staatslehre in Russland an der Schwelle der Neuzeit," *ZS* 16 (1971), pp. 392–406. D. Svak, "K voprosu ob otsenke deyatel'nosti Ivana Peresvetova," *Studia Slavica Academiae Scientiarum Hungaricae* 24 (1978), pp. 55–80. A. A. Zimin, *I. S. Peresvetov i ego sovremenniki.* 1958.   V. T.

Perevál (Mountain Pass or Divide), a literary grouping which developed in the winter of 1923–24 around the journal KRASNAYA NOV'. The name itself was lifted from an essay by A. VORONSKY, editor of that journal, who had spoken of a breakthrough from the meager present of Soviet literature into a rich and vigorous future (*Krasnaya nov',* 1923, October/November). Among the group's early members were M. Golodny, M. SVETLOV, and A. VESYOLY. From 1924 to 1928 the group published six volumes of miscellanies, among whose authors were E. BAGRITSKY and A. PLATONOV. A manifesto of *Pereval,* published in *Krasnaya nov'* (1927, no. 2), was signed by fifty-six writers, among whom were, in addition to those mentioned, D. Gorbov, A. Karavaeva, I. KATAEV, A. LEZHNEV, and M. PRISHVIN. A majority of these writers were members of either the Communist Party or the Komsomol.

The aesthetic principles of *Pereval* were formulated by the critics A. Voronsky, especially in his book *Art as Cognition of Life and the Contemporary Scene* (Iskusstvo kak poznanie zhizni i sovremennost', 1924), A. Lezhnev, in essays collected in the volumes *Contemporaries* (Sovremenniki, 1927) and *Literary Working Days* (Literaturnye budni, 1929), and D. Gorbov, in his book *In Search of Galatea* (Poiski Galatei, 1929). The aesthetic of *Pereval* was identified as "organic realism" by these theorists, whose dependence on BELINSKY and PLEKHANOV is often acknowledged by them. They profess to be Marxists and believe that "consciously or unconsciously, a scholar or artist fills orders which he has received from his class" (Voronsky). A distinctive trait of *Pereval* aesthetics is a trust in the cognitive powers of art and the artist's intuition, in contrast to the constructivist ideas of LEF and the emphasis on Party guidance of RAPP. Specifically, the critics of *Pereval* believed that the new art of the Soviet period would intuitively grasp the principles of the "new truth of life." Also, they emphasized the objectivity of true art

and suggested that the theorists of the PROLETKULT and *On Guard* (NA POSTU) movements were equally guilty of subjectivism, the former by virtue of their futuristic "goal-directedness" (*tseleustremlennost'*), the latter by virtue of their fixation on social class which would not allow them to see the facts of life. Furthermore, the critics of *Pereval* believed, again with Plekhanov and with some support from Engels, that a great artist would see and tell the truth even if as a man he was on the wrong side of the movement of history. As for contemporary Soviet literature, the critics of *Pereval* held that much of it was either cold, abstract propaganda, or crass naturalism (*bytovizm*) without the spark of an ideal. They also found enough outright opportunism, writing to order, toadyism, rose-colored glasses, and playing-it-safe—all of which, they felt, were vestiges of a bourgeois presence in Soviet literature, but which in actual fact were the traits of emerging SOCIALIST REALISM. The "organic realism" of *Pereval* was based on historical optimism, and specifically on a belief that the Revolution did not need the shrill hyperbole of MAYAKOVSKY or the doctrinaire schematism of the Onguardists, that realism was the natural and only proper style of a young, vigorous, and victorious class.

These principles and the literary practices resulting from them led to almost incessant polemic exchanges between *Pereval* and rival groups, *Lef* and RAPP in particular. As a result of the pressures generated by these polemics, members of *Pereval* began to defect to RAPP in 1929. Nevertheless, the group published two further miscellanies under the title *Contemporaries* (Rovesniki, 1930 and 1932) and an anthology, *Pereval'tsy* (1930). *Pereval* ceased to exist after the Party decree of 23 April 1932 which put an end to all literary groupings. Many of its members, including I. Kataev, Lezhnev, Vesyoly, and Voronsky, perished in the purges of the 1930s.

Bibliography: Edward J. Brown, *Russian Literature Since the Revolution.* 1982. Pp. 156–65. Miroslav Drozda and Milan Hrala, *Dvacátá léta sovětské literárné kritiky (LEF-RAPP-PEREVAL).* Prague, 1968. G. Glinka, *Na perevale.* New York, 1954. *Literaturnye manifesty: Ot simvolizma k Oktyabryu.* Vol. 1. 1929. Reprint Munich, 1969. Pp. 272–83. Robert A. Maguire, *Red Virgin Soil: Soviet Literature in the 1920's.* 1968.   V. T.

Perevérzev, Valerián Fyódorovich (1882–1968), literary scholar and theoretician of the sociological method. Pereverzev studied natural sciences and mathematics at Kharkov University, but was dismissed and arrested for his revolutionary activities in 1905. He spent six years in exile, arriving in Moscow in 1911, where he published a book on DOSTOEVSKY (1912, but written while in exile) and another on GOGOL (1914). Their radical application of PLEKHANOV's ideas about the social basis of literature gained immediate attention. After the Revolution, Pereverzev became a leading figure in the attempt to found a Marxist science of literature through participation in prestigious institutions such as the Communist Academy, as a teacher at Moscow University, and through his many publications in such major journals as *Pechat' i revolyutsiya* and *Literatura i marksizm.* He was also an editor of the *Literary Encyclopedia* (1929–30). Pereverzev was the most intransigent of all the sociological critics. He argued for the absolute dominance of economic determinism: one should pay attention only to a writer's position in the history of production techniques. A writer's subconscious was formed of images deriving from his place in the class struggle. If a writer is a proletarian, the images that dominate his work will be proletarian. "Nobody has the power to change his style," he said in 1929. Pereverzev gathered a number of disciples around him: their joint publication, *The Study of Literature* (1929), occasioned fierce debate and led to charges of "vulgar sociologism" and deviationism. Pereverzev was arrested in 1938 and spent the next eighteen years in a labor camp. He was rehabilitated in 1956 and praised on his eighty-fifth birthday in *Literaturnaya gazeta.* His last book, on ancient Russian literature, was written while in prison and published posthumously in 1971.

Works: Gogol'–Dostoevskii: Issledovaniya. Ed. V. V. Pereverzev. Introd. M. Ya. Polyakov. 1982.

Secondary literature: Robert Louis Jackson, "The Sociological Method of V. F. Pereverzev: A Rage for Structure and Determinism." In *Literature and Society in Imperial Russia 1800–1914.* Ed. William Mills Todd III. 1978. Pp. 29–60.   J. M. H.

Peróvsky, Aleksei Alekséevich (1787–1836), romantic storyteller known by the pseudonym Antony Pogorelsky, was the illegitimate son of Count A. K. Razumovsky and the Countess Maria Sobolevsky. Because of the misalliance of his parents, Perovsky and his siblings were named after the Perov estate. Educated by tutors, Perovsky entered Moscow University in 1805 and received a Doctorate of Philosophy in literature in 1807 after presenting extensive lectures in Russian, German, and French, which were published. After several government positions and distinguished service in the War of 1812, Perovsky retired to his Pogorelsk estate, where he helped with the education of his nephew, the future writer Count Aleksei Konstantinovich Tolstoi. In 1825 Perovsky published in the journal *Novosti literatury* the fantastic tale "The Poppyseed-Cake Woman of Lafertovo," which Pushkin satirized in his story "The Coffinmaker" (Grobovshchik). In 1828 Perovsky published *The Double, or My Evenings in the Ukraine*, a series of conversations between the author and his double, which imitate Hoffmann's *Serapion Brothers*. In 1829 Perovsky was elected to the Russian Academy and also published his magical tale "The Black Hen" (Chernaya kuritsa), which became popular and brought the author into the literary circle of LITERATURNAYA GAZETA headed by PUSHKIN and DELVIG. When the beginning of Perovsky's novel *The Girl from the Convent* (Monastyrka) appeared in *Literaturnaya gazeta*, there was much favorable criticism, but critical acclaim diminished with the publication of the second part in 1833. The book, however, remained popular through the 1830s and 1840s. Perovsky was a major Russian romantic writer with a tendency toward realistic description. He is known for his imagination, humor, literary tact, and realistic observation.

Works: A. Pogorel'skii, *Sochineniya.* 2 vols. 1853. A. Pogorel'skii, *Dvoinik, ili moi vechera v Malorossii, Monastyrka.* Introd. N. L. Stepanov. 1960. A. Pogorel'skii, *Chernaya kuritsa, ili Podzemnye zhiteli.* 1945.
Secondary literature: A. I. Kirpichnikov, "Antonii Pogorel'skii." In *Ocherki po istorii russkoi literatury.* 1896.   T. E. B.

Pésenniki, see SONGBOOKS.

Peter and Fevroniya, SS., see HAGIOGRAPHY, OLD RUSSIAN LITERATURE.

Petrashévsky Circle. A loosely organized group of young intellectuals who met at the St. Petersburg apartment of M. V. Butashevich-Petrashevsky (1821–66) from the mid-1840s. The circle's Friday meetings featured reading and discussion of papers on social, philosophical, and literary topics given by members. Petrashevsky's private library contained a number of prohibited books, French utopian socialist literature in particular. The tenor of some discussions was accordingly subversive by the standards of the reactionary and inflexible administration of Nicholas I. Some members of the circle, to be sure, and in particular a small group headed by S. F. Durov went further and had obtained a printing press on which they planned to print anti-government proclamations. Among the members of the circle were several writers, F. M. DOSTOEVSKY, A. N. PLESHCHEEV, and A. I. Palm being the most prominent. With one or two members of the circle being police informants, it was only a question of time before it would be routed. In the early morning hours of 23 April 1849, thirty-three members of the Petrashevsky circle were arrested and taken to Sts. Peter and Paul Fortress. Some of them, including Andrei and Mikhail DOSTOEVSKY, were released for lack of incriminating evidence. But twenty-one were taken to Semyonovsky Square on 22 December 1849 where they were subjected to a mock execution before being sent to Siberia to serve prison terms of various lengths.

Texts: Filosofskie i obshchestvenno-politicheskie proizvedeniya petrashevtsev. 1953. *Poety-petrashevtsy.* 1957.
Secondary literature: N. F. Bel'chikov, *Dostoevskii v protsesse petrashevtsev.* 1971. T. I. Usakina, *Petrashevtsy i literaturno-obshchestvennoe dvizhenie sorokovykh godov XIX v.* Saratov, 1965.
V. T.

Petrúshka, a form of Russian PUPPET THEATER and the name of its principal character. Petrushka seems to derive from Western European puppet theater with a source in the Italian commedia dell'arte with its figure of Pulcinella (compare English Punch). A Dutch traveller, Adam Olearius, made a print illustration of the Petrushka theater as early as 1736.

The Petrushka theater was performed at carnivals, fairs, and on the streets. One performer played a barrel-organ; the other manipulated the puppet figures from behind a screen. Texts of the play have been recorded in the last two centuries which show that the episodes of the play are relatively stable. Petrushka is a fearless prankster; he defeats his opponents both with his wit and with blows from his club. He is a sworn foe of the established order.

In the play's action Petrushka marries, buys a horse from a gypsy, falls from the horse and must be cured by the physician-apothecary; further on he encounters a German, a Tatar, an army corporal, and the police. He always emerges victorious as he routs his enemy with his club.

Stravinsky's ballet *Petrushka* (1911) is a celebrated reworking of the puppet theater story.

Bibliography: Yu. M. Sokolov, *Russian Folklore.* 1950. Pp. 501–02. Russell Zguta, *Russian Minstrels.* 1978. Pp. 112–20. ———, "Origins of the Russian Puppet Theater: An Alternative Hypothesis," *SlavR* 33 (1974), pp. 708–20. P. N. Berkov, *Russkaya narodnaya drama XVII-XX vekov.* 1953. Pp. 18–19, 113–23.
W. E. H.

Petróv, Vasily Petróvich (1736–99), poet. Born of a clerical family, his early life beset with hardships, Petrov possessed powerful ambition and intelligence which enabled him to secure a classical education at the Moscow Academy and, subsequently, a position there as teacher. His first published verse, an ode celebrating Catherine II's lavish carousel of 1766, so delighted the Empress that Petrov was installed at court as her personal reader and translator. There Petrov enjoyed a life of privilege, wealth and close personal relations with Catherine and her favorites—the addressees of the gorgeous and fulsome odes that comprise the bulk of Petrov's poetry. The plaudits conferred by Catherine and her courtiers upon Petrov were little echoed by the Russian literary community of the time. As a rule Petrov was the butt of ridicule, lampoon and parody. While excoriating the "official," servile, and insolently self-serving nature of Petrov's odes, the vehement condemnation also inadvertently testified to the formidableness of Petrov's poetic talent—a fact not denied even by recent Soviet scholars. Part of the dilemma over Petrov resides in the discrepancy between his poetic practice and the mainline of literary development at the time: Petrov revived and transformed into his own style the older traditions of LOMONOSOV and, especially, TREDIAKOVSKY. G. A. Gukovsky aptly describes him as "perhaps the last great representative of the tradition of ingenious verse ... going back to the courtly Baroque ... and ultimately to the Latin erudite poetry of the Renaissance."

Among other works Petrov produced a masterly translation in verse of the *Aeneid* and, after a two-year stay in England, a prose translation of the first three cantos of *Paradise Lost*.

Works: Poety XVIII veka. Ed. G. P. Makogonenko and I. Z. Serman. (Biblioteka poeta, bol'shaya seriya.) 1972. *Russkaya poeziya.* Ed. S. A. Vengerov. Vol. 1: *XVIII vek.* 1897.
Translations: "On the Victory of the Russians over the Turkish Fleet." In Leo Wiener, *Anthology of Russian Literature* Vol. 1. 1902.
Secondary literature: G. A. Gukovskii, "Iz istorii russkoi ody XVIII veka," *Poetika* 3 (1927), pp. 129–47. ———, "Petrov." In *Istoriya russkoi literatury*, Vol. 4, pt. 2. Pp. 353–63. I. Z. Serman, "Biograficheskaya spravka." In *Poety XVIII veka.* Ed. G. P. Makogonenko and I. Z. Serman (Biblioteka poeta, bol'shaya seriya.) 1972. Pp. 319–25.   I. R. T.

Physiological sketch. An important influence upon the early growth of Russian realism, the Russian physiological sketch developed in the 1840s from the French *physiologie*. Similar to the *feuilleton*, also popular in Russian literature at that time, the French *physiologie* grew from weekly newspaper columns devoted to Parisian life and society after the 1830 Revolution. Less stylized than the more personal and casual *feuilleton*, which treated current literature and cultural events, the *physiologie* gradually developed into an exposé of the miserable conditions that existed in urban France. Bearing the connotation of truth, actuality, or nature as it is, the term "physiological" implied nearly photographic accuracy and a "scientific" method of observation and categorization then sweeping the natural sciences. Forerunner of this movement toward descriptive naturalism was the French collection, *The French Described by Themselves* (Les Français peints par eux-mêmes, 1840), which was quickly echoed by the Russian imitation, *Us, Described from Nature by Russians* (Nashi, spisannye s natury russkimi, 1841–42), published by A. P. Bashutsky. M. Yu. LERMONTOV's *The Caucasian* (Kavkazets) was to have appeared in a subsequent edition of *Us* had not the censorship suppressed further publication.

Though the physiological sketch at first enjoyed only limited success and was generally limited to individual contributions to periodicals, it became a significant genre in Russian literature by the mid-forties. This was achieved with the help of the aesthetics promulgated by the progressive critic V. G. BELINSKY, who sought a "realistic" reflection of contemporary Russia, and through the publishing acumen of N. A. NEKRASOV, who saw revived potential for a russified counterpart of the French *physiologie* after the commercial success in Russia of Eugène Sue's *roman-feuilleton*, *The Mysteries of Paris* (Les mystères de Paris) in 1843. Through the efforts of Belinsky and Nekrasov, two illustrated almanacs appeared, a two-volume set entitled *Fiziologiya Peterburga* (1845), and another, *Peterburgskii sbornik* (1846). Offering a variety of genres, including essays, poetry, and sketches, both almanacs found a receptive public. The collections featured work by V. I. DAL, E. P. GREBENKA, Nekrasov, I. I. PANAEV, D. V. GRIGOROVICH's *Petersburg Organ Grinders* (Peterburgskie sharmanshchiki), articles by Belinsky, and, most prominently, F. M. DOSTOEVSKY's *Poor Folk* (Bednye lyudi).

In its Russian form, the physiological sketch described the lower strata of St. Petersburg and Moscow in an informal and frequently humorous tone capturing the jargon of daily conversation in settings (often reminiscent of Paris) such as marketplaces, garrets, and streets. Realia such as street signs and refuse were visibly present in the background, while sounds and smells of the locale contributed an additional natural dimension to the descriptions. Among the subjects favored by the physiological sketches were petty clerks (the favorite choice), water carriers, artists, writers, prostitutes, and others who seldom appeared in earlier literature. Some responded to the call for verisimilitude with indecorous descriptions of questionable literary taste, but care was taken to avoid explicit moralizing or dwelling upon social implications.

Though the physiological sketch had socially progressive implications, the genre was well received even by conservative critics such as Faddei BULGARIN, who briefly authored such sketches himself until the unmitigated reality began to pall upon him. His reactionary SEVERNAYA PCHELA published two collections of physiological sketches by Ya. P. BUTKOV titled *Petersburg Heights* (Peterburgskie vershiny I and II, 1845), which were in fact used polemically as a response to GOGOL's caricature and grotesquery. The initial impetus for I. S. TURGENEV's *Zapiski okhotnika* (1847–52) may also be found in the physiological sketch.

Of the more established writers, Dal, SOLLOGUB, and Panaev contributed much to the development of the genre, particularly by treating rural settings and the lowest rung of the social ladder, the serf. Among the younger writers who actually shared the social origins of the characters depicted in their own physiological sketches were Butkov, Grebenka, and I. T. KOKOREV, all of whom died by or before their early thirties. Though Belinsky did not consider the physiological sketch an artistic literary form, he defended it as a necessary step toward objective mimesis. An exercise in descriptive naturalism, the sketches contributed to the development of the NATURAL SCHOOL, to the work of the "serious" naturalists, and ultimately to the rise of Russian realism.

Bibliography: J. T. Baer, "The 'Physiological Sketch' in Russian Literature." In *Studia Litteraria Russica in Honorem Vsevolod Setchkarev*. 1974. Pp. 1–12. V. G. Belinskii, "Fiziologiya Peterburga" (chast' pervaya), "Fiziologiya Peterburga" (chast' vtoraya), "Peterburgskie vershiny," "Peterburgskii sbornik," *PSS*, Vol. 9, pp. 543–81. P. Hodgson, *From Gogol to Dostoevsky*. 1976. V. I. Kuleshov, *Natural'naya shkola v russkoi literature XIX v.* 1965. A. G. Tseitlin, *Stanovlenie realizma v russkoi literature (Russkii fiziolo-*

gicheskii ocherk). 1965. V. V. Vinogradov, *Evolyutsiya russkogo naturalizma*. 1929. T. Yakimovich, *Frantsuzskii realisticheskii ocherk 1830–1848 gg.* 1963.   J. S.

Picaresque novel (*plutovskoi román*). The genre developed in Russia in the 18th century under the influence of Western models, such as *Histoire de Gil Blas de Santillane* (1715–35) by Lesage. A native example existed in the anonymous *Tale of Frol Skobeev* (Povest' o Frole Skobeeve) from the turn of the 17th century. *The Comely Cook, or Adventures of a Lewd Woman* (Prigozhaya povarikha, ili Pokhozhdeniya razvratnoi zhenshchiny, 1770), by Mikhail CHULKOV, and *Detailed and Veracious Stories of two Crooks: the First being that of the Celebrated Russian Thief, Robber, and Former Moscow Detective, Vanka Kain* (Obstoyatel'nye i vernye istorii dvukh moshennikov: pervogo rossiiskogo slavnogo vora, razboinika i byvshego moskovskogo syshchika Van'ki Kaina, 1779), by Matvei KOMAROV, are early Russian adaptations of the genre to a Russian setting. In the 19th century, the picaresque novel in its traditional form is represented by V. T. NAREZHNY's *A Russian Gil Blas, or the Adventures of Prince Gavrila Simonovich Chistyakov* (Rossiiskii Zhilblaz, ili Pokhozhdeniya knyazya Gavrily Simonovicha Chistyakova, 1814), F. V. BULGARIN's *Ivan Vyzhigin* (from *vyzhiga*, "crook", 1829), and A. F. VELTMAN's *Adventures, Extracted from the Ocean of Life* (Priklyucheniya, pocherpnutye iz morya zhiteiskogo, 1846–63), among others. Elements of the picaresque novel appear in some works by major authors, as in GOGOL's *Dead Souls*, DOSTOEVSKY's *The Gambler*, and LESKOV's *The Enchanted Pilgrim*. However, while the biographic novel is a prominent form of Russian realism, its hero rarely bears the traditional traits of the *picaro*. The one purely picaresque hero, not counting Chichikov of Gogol's *Dead Souls*, who has earned proverbial status in Russia is Ostap Bender, hero of the satirical novels *Twelve Chairs* (1928) and *The Golden Calf* (1931) by Ilya ILF AND Evgeny PETROV. Benya Krik, gangster hero of several of Isaak BABEL's Odessa tales, has been almost as popular, but he is further removed from the traditional *picaro*.

Bibliography: V. F. Pereverzev, *U istokov russkogo real'nogo romana*. 1963. Jurij Striedter, *Der Schelmenroman in Russland*. 1961.   V. T.

Piksánov, Nikolaí Kiryákovich (1878–1969), historian of Russian literature, bibliographer, and textologist. A graduate of Dorpat (Tartu) University (1902), Piksanov was a professor of Moscow and Leningrad Universities, and a corresponding member of the Academy of Sciences (1931). He published studies of GORKY, GRIBOEDOV, LERMONTOV, PUSHKIN, and Russian FREEMASONRY. He was one of the originators of specialized literary bibliography, combined with suggested topics for further study (*seminarii*). Piksanov was also one of the first to proclaim the history of the creation of literary works one of the main subjects of textology. Most important and best known were his studies of Griboedov, which he began at the beginning of his scholarly career and continued through all his life.

Bibliography: "Nikolai Kir'yakovich Piksanov." In *Materialy k bibliografii uchenykh SSSR*. 1968. A. I. Barsuk, *Pechatnye seminarii po russkoi literature, 1904–1963: Istoriko-bibliograficheskii ocherk*. 1964. N. I. Zheltova, *Tvorcheskaya istoriya proizvedenii russkikh i sovetskikh pisatelei: Bibliograficheskii ukazatel'*. 1968.

Secondary literature: P. N. Berkov, *Vvedenie v izuchenie istorii russkoi literatury XVIII veka*. 1964. Pp. 185–87. R. I. Kuz'menko, *Nikolai Kir'yakovich Piksanov*. 1968.   E. B.

Pilnyák, Boris (pseud. of Boris Andréevich Vogau, 1894–1937?), a major Soviet novelist, short-story writer, and occasional journalist during the early post-revolutionary era. Born in Mozhaisk, Pilnyak spent his youth in provincial towns in Moscow province and in the middle-Volga area settled by German colonists, from whom his father descended (the provincial town and rural Russia are persistent settings in his work). His father, a veterinarian, and mother, a teacher, were active in the POPULIST movement and seem to have fostered his bookish inclinations. Pilnyak spent the years of revolution and civil war in Kolomna and, often enough, in travel searching for food. Although he began publishing short stories regularly after 1915, he also graduated in 1920 from the Moscow Commercial Institute with a speciality in economics—perhaps as insurance against more years of poverty (Pilnyak later acquired a reputation as a bon vivant). However, after the publication of his novel *The Naked Year* (Golyi god, 1921) he swiftly became, and remained for several years, the dominant figure in Soviet literature. His numerous works from the period 1921 to 1923—obviously difficult and apparently fragmentary, plotless, and stylistically heterogeneous—were widely imitated (among them "Cowwheat" [Ivan-da-Mar'ya, 1921], "Ryazan-Apple" [Ryazan'-yabloko, 1921], "The Blizzard" [Metel', 1921], "The Third Capital" [Tret'ya stolitsa, 1922], "Black Bread" [Chernyi khleb, 1923]), and "Pilnyakism" became a critical catchword. His highly mannered, dynamic, "ornamental" prose together with a predilection for primitivism and for the ancient folkways of the Russian peasantry have led critics to view Pilnyak as the main bridge from BELY and REMIZOV to the postrevolutionary generation of writers. His great accomplishment in this regard, *Machines and Wolves* (Mashiny i volki, 1924), appeared just as interest was waning in him and in the literary tendency he had epitomized.

From 1924 on, Pilnyak's prose reflected to a degree the general shift in literary taste toward the canons of traditional realism. He worked almost exclusively within the genres of the short story and tale (*povest'*), the best of which are perhaps "Mother Earth" (Mat' syra-zemlya, 1924), "Beyond the Portage" (Zavoloch'e, 1925), *A Chinese Tale* (Kitaiskaya povest', 1927), and "Ivan Moscow" (Ivan-Moskva, 1927). Numerous works from the later twenties incorporate even more extensively than earlier Pilnyak's travel experiences (e.g., *Roots of the Japanese Sun* [Korni yaponskogo solntsa, 1926]). During the decade from 1922 to 1932, Pilnyak traveled widely within the Soviet Union and in Europe, visited the Middle East, made two lengthy trips to the Far East (1926, 1932), and spent five months in the United States (1931), where he was briefly and unproductively under contract to MGM. His often disagreeable impressions of American life, gathered during extensive travel by automobile, were published in *O.K.: An American Novel* (O'kei: amerikanskii roman, 1932).

The peculiar subtitle of this volume illustrates one of several techniques used by Pilnyak after 1929 to alert readers to the politically skewed contents of his writings. In the fall of 1929 he had fallen victim to an organized campaign of vilification, ostensibly in response to the publication of his "slanderous" story "Mahogany" (Krasnoe derevo) among White Guardists in Berlin; in fact, as Chairman of the Board of the All-Russian Union of Writers, he was the scapegoat used to organize obedience through fear in the literary community as the First Five-Year Plan was initiated. His novel *The Volga Falls to the Caspian Sea* (Volga vpadaet v Kaspiiskoe more, 1930) is widely—and mistakenly—understood as his literary and moral collapse under this terrible political pressure. Another scandal, far less vicious but never forgotten, surrounded the publication and immediate suppression in January 1926 of "The Tale of the Unextinguished Moon" (Povest' nepogashenoi luny); the story contained what was viewed as an attack on Stalin in its scarcely fictionalized rendition of rumors that the death during an operation of the popular military commissar M. V. Frunze (31 Oct. 1925) was in fact a political murder. Other rumors have suggested the publication of this story was part of an unsuccessful plot to discredit and oust Stalin. True or not, Pilnyak certainly included among his wideranging acquaintances and close friends a number of politicians from the Kremlin's almost inaccessible inner circles (Karl Radek was an intimate, he knew TROTSKY, and was on good terms with several Trotskyites); he also associated occasionally with members of the secret police. These political connections and involvements remain obscure, but they help to explain the wealth and privileges Pilnyak enjoyed for a time. They also made his arrest inevitable during the purges. Although Soviet sources now claim that he died in 1941, evidence exists that he was shot shortly after his arrest in October 1937. Pilnyak married three times and left three children.

Recent studies have indicated the inadequacy of the traditional understanding of Pilnyak's best-known (early) works, that they are montages heterogeneous in material and organized (if at all) through the "musical" techniques of refrain and variation. Like Pilnyak's imitators, critics have rarely passed beyond the coruscating verbal textures at the surface of his works, and have ignored or dismissed his riddles and hints at hidden meanings. If his tales became less opaque and capriciously complicated over time, he never abandoned the creation of the intricate puzzle. This suggests that Pilnyak was an allegorist—as he twice admitted himself. The thematic center of his allegories—at once intensely personal and yet derivative—is located in a set of philosophical problems commonly associated with the modern period. Pilnyak read modern philosophy and he knew Russia's philosophical-literary tradition; he recognized in his private experience and in Russia's contemporary historical experience the interrelated problems of faith and value: Is there immanent in life generally, or in history (as the Marxists claim), an affirmable meaning which can generate values, or do men live in a valueless void? From this perspective his early works are meditations on this question in relation to history; they move between the poles of narrational contemplation and narrative "fact," and the narrator's search for meaning in apparent historical chaos characteristically ends with an irresolute metaphorical restatement of the question. After 1925 Pilnyak moved toward metaphysical nihilism: The gods of Heaven and History are analogous illusions, and men satisfy their longing for order and meaning in ways shaped by their culture. BYT—the cultural cocoon of life style and mores—became even more central to the thematic structure of his works; it explains the conviction implicit in them that the present always repeats, in one way or another, the past. For Pilnyak, the sole, man-centered source of affirmable meaning became virtue and love, grounded in the conviction that human life has value regardless of logic. The fullest expression of this vision, and a good example of Pilnyak's puzzle-making, is *The Volga Falls to the Caspian Sea*. Ultimately, then, his work should be viewed, not as eccentrically Russian, but as fully representative, in matter and manner, of important tendencies in European modernism.

Works: Krasnoe derevo. Berlin, 1929. *Sobranie sochinenii.* 8 vols. 1929–30. *Volga vpadaet v Kaspiiskoe more.* 1930. *Izbrannye proizvedeniya.* 1976.

Translations: The Volga Falls to the Caspian Sea. Trans. Charles Malamuth. 1931. Reprint 1970. *The Tale of the Unextinguished Moon and Other Stories.* Trans. Beatrice Scott. 1967. *Mother Earth and Other Stories.* Trans. Vera T. Reck and Michael Green. 1968. *The Naked Year.* Trans. A. R. Tulloch. 1975. *See also:* Lewanski, p. 324.

Secondary literature: Kenneth N. Brostrom, "The Enigma of Pil'njak's *The Volga Falls to the Caspian Sea*," *SEEJ* 18 (1974), pp. 271–98. ———, "Pil'njak's *Naked Year*: The Problem of Faith," *RLT*, no. 16 (1979), pp. 114–53. Peter Alberg Jensen, *Nature as Code: The Achievement of Boris Pilnjak.* Copenhagen, 1979. Robert Maguire, "The Pioneers: Pil'njak and Ivanov." In his *Red Virgin Soil: Soviet Literature in the 1920s.* 1968. Vera T. Reck, *Boris Pil'njak: A Soviet Writer in Conflict with the State.* Montreal, 1975.

K. N. B.

Pisarev, Dmítry Ivánovich (1840–1868), journalist and critic, was born at Znamenskoe, the Pisarevs' family estate in Orel province. He attended school in Petersburg, studied philology at Petersburg University, and acquired the degree of Candidate of Philosophy in 1861. As a student, he contributed some articles and reviews to a journal "for adult young ladies," *Rassvet*. In 1861 Pisarev began to write for G. E. Blagosvetlov's journal RUSSKOE SLOVO, soon establishing himself as that journal's leading critic and essayist. In July 1862 Pisarev was arrested for his authorship of a revolutionary pamphlet, seized during a police raid on an underground printing press. He spent over four years at St. Peter and Paul's Fortress in Petersburg. A year after his arrest, but still before his trial which resulted in a two-year, eight-month prison term, he received permission to write and to continue publishing in *Russkoe Slovo*. Much of his best work was written in prison. After his release Pisarev went on writing for several journals (*Russkoe Slovo* was closed by the authorities in 1866), including OTECHESTVENNYE ZAPISKI and *Delo*. The last years of his life were clouded by fits of severe depression (he had spent some time in a mental institution in 1860). His death (by drowning, at Dubbeln beach near Riga, 16 July 1868) may have been a suicide.

Pisarev was the nihilist par excellence among the critics of the 1860s, and the only one to welcome TURGENEV's Bazarov (in *Fathers and Sons*) as essentially a correct statement of his position ("Bazarov," 1862). Pisarev's philosophy, an attempt to rethink morality in terms of a modern scientific world view, was a blend of materialist positivism and a puritanic work ethic ("Sketches on the History of Labor," 1863). Pisarev scoffed at the teleological and dialectic thinking of Hegelians like BELINSKY and was, in turn, put down as a "vulgar materialist" by Marxists like PLEKHANOV. A believer in the power of science (he wrote some popular science articles) and education (he wrote "Our University Education," 1863), he did not, however, share the POPULIST illusions or the revolutionary optimism of his contemporaries.

In his essay "The Abolition of Aesthetics" (1865), Pisarev drew what he felt was the correct conclusion from CHERNYSHEVSKY's *Aesthetic Relations of Art to Reality*, namely that if absolute Beauty does not exist, as he thought Chernyshevsky had demonstrated, aesthetics and aesthetic criticism have no more value than alchemy or astrology. He accordingly refused to review works in "aesthetic terms," i.e., to discuss their structure, composition, and style, but rather judged them according to their "truth content" and "social usefulness." Pisarev's review of DOSTOEVSKY's *Crime and Punishment* ("Struggle for Survival," 1867–68) purposely analyzes not the predicament of its hero as presented in the text of that novel, but the plight of the social type represented by him.

Pisarev's most significant contribution was a brilliantly executed demolition of the organic criticism of Belinsky and DOBROLYUBOV, and of the high opinion held by most Russian critics of the role played by literature in the progress of Russian society. Pisarev demonstrated that the social significance attributed to PUSHKIN's works by Belinsky was really an insertion of Belinsky's own ideas into Pushkin's text ("Pushkin and Belinsky," 1865). He also debunked Dobrolyubov's interpretation of OSTROVSKY's drama *The Thunderstorm* ("A Ray of Light in the Dark Kingdom," 1860) which, he said, made an adulterous love affair into a harbinger of a moral revolution ("Motives of Russian Drama," 1864), and the social satire of SALTYKOV-SHCHEDRIN, which he presented as mere "Flowers of Innocent Humor" (1864). Pisarev's basic device is a clever confusion of empirical and poetic truth, justified by his denial of the reality of the latter. Pisarev's utilitarianism is more straightforward than Dobrolyubov's. He is willing to leave pure art and aesthetic criticism to "aesthetes" or "idealists," much as an adult will allow a child to indulge in aimless play. Mature "realists," though, will demand more serious fare ("Realists," 1864).

Cultured, well-educated, and well-read, Pisarev was by far the most gifted of the literary NIHILISTS. His writings are well reasoned, entertaining, and often witty. They have little of the heavyhanded doctrinaire pedantry of the critics of SOVREMENNIK, nor any of their personal venom. Inasmuch as Pisarev was ultimately among the losers historically, he has been and still is neglected and underrated in the history of Russian criticism.

Works: Polnoe sobranie sochinenii. 6 vols. 5th ed. 1909–13. *Sochineniya.* Ed. Yu. S. Sorokin. 4 vols. 1955–56.

Translations: Selected Philosophical, Social, and Political Essays. Moscow, 1958.

Biography: L. A. Plotkin, *D. I. Pisarev: Zhizn' i tvorchestvo.* 1962.

Secondary literature: Edward J. Brown, "Pisarev and the Transformation of Two Russian Novels." In *Literature and Society in Imperial Russia, 1800–1914.* Ed. W. M. Todd III. 1978. Pp. 151–72. J. Forsyth, "Pisarev, Belinsky and *Yevgeniy Onegin*," *SEER* 48, pp. 163–80. V. Kirpotin, *Radikal'nyi raznochinets D. I. Pisarev.* 1934. S. S. Konkin, "Pushkin v kritike Pisareva," *RLit* 15, no. 4, pp. 50–74. F. Kuznetsov, "Pisarev: Teoriya 'realizma' i literaturaya kritika," *VLit* 12, no. 7, pp. 109–34. G. V. Plekhanov, "Literaturnye vzglyady N. G. Chernyshevskogo" (1909). In *Estetika i sotsiologiya iskusstva.* 2 vols. 1978. Vol. 2. Pp. 326–37. V. A. Tsybenko, *Mirovozzrenie D. I. Pisareva.* 1969. V. Tunimanov, "Printsip real'noi kritiki: Evolyutsiya Pisareva v 1860-e gody," *VLit* 19, no. 6, pp. 153–85. Constantin D. Ushinsky. "Une Question à résoudre: Le 'Réalisme' de Dmitri Pisarev," *CSP* 18, pp. 141–53. ———, *D. I. Pisarev: Social and Literary Criticism.* Nordland Publ. n.d.

V. T.

Pisemsky, Aleksei Feofiláktovich (1821–81). Born in Kostroma province, after a local secondary education Pisemsky matriculated at Moscow University, where he paid rather more attention to the theater than to his academic specialization, mathematics. A junior

member of the memorable generation of the 1840s, he made his debut in print in 1848 with an obscure story entitled "Nina." He attracted more attention two years later upon the publication of his novelette *The Simpleton* (Tyufyak, 1850), the story of a young idealist who perishes when his illusions about life are destroyed.

At this point Pisemsky was accepted—on the recommendation of his friend the dramatist Aleksandr OSTROVSKY—into the circle of MOSKVITYANIN, the leading Moscow literary journal of the early 1850s. There he published his first play, *The Hypochondriac* (Ipokhondrik), in 1852, as well as the first work of a three-story cycle *Sketches of Peasant Life* (Ocherki iz krest'yanskogo byta), which made his reputation as a chronicler of the life of the common people. Indeed, after he moved to St. Petersburg from Kostroma in late 1854, St. Petersburg literary society regarded him as the epitome of the coarse peasant, a person of few social graces who spoke with a distinct provincial accent.

That, however, did not prevent him from making his career, and the end of the decade saw him at the height of his literary reputation. In 1858 he joined the staff of the literary journal *Biblioteka dlya chteniya*, and later became its editor. And in the years between 1858 and 1861 he published his three finest works: the novel *One Thousand Souls* (Tysyacha dush, 1858)—the title refers to the number of serfs a landowner should possess to be considered wealthy; the play *A Bitter Fate* (Gor'kaya sud'bina, 1859); and the novelette *An Old Man's Sin* (Starcheskii grekh, 1861).

The hero of *A Thousand Souls*, Kalinovich, an enormously ambitious young man from the provinces, makes his way to the capital intending to rise through the bureaucracy. In order to achieve that objective he takes a wealthy wife in a loveless marriage, abandoning the girl he had loved in the provinces, as well as a number of his principles and scruples. He is rewarded by a rapid promotion to the posts of vice-governor, then governor, of his home province. Once he has grasped power, he seeks to use it to enforce social justice and to punish wrongdoers, but his political enemies are mighty as well and eventually succeed in having him removed from his position. The novel's last part transmits a strong social message, and caused many critics to view the entire book as a "novel of exposure," one which emphasized the defects of the existing order. Pisemsky, however, took a cynical view of human nature in general, believing that everyone was actuated by greedy self-interest. That view led him to deny the very possibility of meaningful social reform.

A Bitter Fate is a tragedy of peasant life revolving about a peasant's discovery that, during his prolonged absence, his wife has given birth to a child by their serf-owner, whom she loves. Enraged, he murders the child, then is captured when he seeks to escape. Ultimately he recognizes the evil he has done and asks forgiveness of all those whom he has offended as he accepts his punishment. The plot possesses a certain dread inevitability which derives both from a husband's righteous pride and the social structure of Russian serfdom under which some human beings "owned" other human beings. At the time it appeared contemporaries appreciated the stature of *A Bitter Fate*, and in 1859 it received an official Uvarov prize, along with Ostrovsky's *The Storm*.

An Old Man's Sin partly follows the Gogolian tradition which Pisemsky prided himself upon continuing. It chronicles the psychological suffering of a lonely middle-aged bureaucrat. He has always been the soul of rectitude, but when a beautiful woman deliberately turns his head, he consents to embezzle government money for her sake. He is detected in his crime, and at his trial discovers that the object of his love had been taking purely selfish advantage of him. Finally he commits suicide, for he cannot bear to exist in a world in which scoundrels triumph and beauty conceals only corruption.

In the early 1860s Pisemsky crossed swords with the radical intelligentsia—which was then attaining cultural hegemony—in a series of satirical feuilletons. The response to them led him, in 1863, to his move to Moscow, where he resided for the rest of his life. He made a fictional rebuttal to his enemies through a large novel designed as a vast canvas of contemporary life, *Troubled Seas* (Vzbalamuchennoe more, 1863). Although it contained typically corrupt representatives of the establishment, the book sought primarily to demonstrate that the young radicals of the 1860s were quite as self-centered and greedy as their elders whom they attacked so mercilessly: Pisemsky castigated the radicals as "witty windbags" and "good-for-nothings of all sorts, always ready to fill their emptiness with whatever you like."

In the late 1860s Pisemsky published a second novel designed as a grand picture of a historical epoch, though now he chose a period to which he looked back fondly in *Men of the 1840s* (Lyudi sorokovykh godov, 1869). But, because of his earlier rupture with the radicals, this novel and all his later writings were mostly ignored.

In the 1870s, Pisemsky wrote several plays directed against nascent capitalism with its inhuman thirst for gain. The best of them, *Baal* (Vaal, 1873), also dealt in an enlightened way with the question of woman's place in society. Two years earlier, in one of his best-constructed novels, *In the Whirlpool* (V vodovorote, 1871), Pisemsky had offered a young woman radical as his heroine; although she ultimately perishes, she remains staunch in her convictions. However, this ideological shift leftward did not restore Pisemsky to the good graces of the critics, who paid very little attention to his last two novels: *The Bourgeois* (Meshchane, 1877) and *The Masons* (Masony, 1880).

Pisemsky died in early 1881—a week before DOSTOEVSKY—and was buried in Moscow's Novo-devichy monastery.

Works: Sobranie sochinenii. Ed. A. P. Mogilianskii and M. P. Eremin. 9 vols. 1959.

Translations: One Thousand Souls. Trans. Ivy Litvinov. 1959. *A Bitter Fate.* Trans. Alice Kagan and George Noyes. In *Masterpieces of the Russian Drama*, vol. 1. 1933 (reprint 1961). *The Simpleton.* Moscow, 1959.

Secondary literature: Charles A. Moser, *Pisemsky: A Provincial Realist.* 1969. Petr Pustovoit, *A. F. Pisemskii v istoru russkogo romana.* 1969. ———, "Istoriografiya izucheniya tvorchestva A. F. Pisemskogo," *RLit*, 19 (1976), no. 4, pp. 224–32.

C. A. M.

Platónov (originally Kliméntov), Andrei Platónovich (1899–1951), writer and critic, was born in Voronezh into a working class family. He started working on the railroad at fifteen, served in the Red Army in the civil war, then graduated from a polytechnical institute in 1924 and worked as a land reclamation and electrical engineer in Voronezh oblast. He published articles, verse, and essays in local journals and newspapers starting in 1918. His first book, *Electrification*, appeared in Voronezh in 1921. In it Platonov fervently preaches the "revolutionary power" of electricity which will effect a fundamental change in "human nature." Platonov's dreams of a new "electric" age were also reflected in his science fiction trilogy, "Descendants of the Sun" (Potomki solntsa), "The Lunar Bomb" (Lunnaya bomba), and "Ethereal Trail" (Efirnyi trakt). Simultaneously, Platonov also launched his career as a poet. His book of verse, *Light-Blue Depth* (Golubaya glubina, 1922) was sympathetically reviewed by V. BRYUSOV.

The years 1922 to 1925 brought a break in Platonov's literary activities. He was so heavily engaged in his work in the electrification program that he considered literature a "distracting," merely "contemplative," activity. He even began to move up the ladder of Soviet trade union hierarchy, participated in an all-union congress of hydro-technicians in Moscow, and subsequently worked with great enthusiasm on land reclamation projects in the Tambov area, all for the sake of "mankind's bright future." His personal participation in the building of this future and his private experience gained here provided him with a wealth of material for his fiction. Starting in 1926, Platonov's stories began to appear again in journals such as *Vsemirnyi sledopyt, Molodaya gvardiya, Krasnaya panorama, Krasnaya nov'*, etc.

In 1927 Platonov published his first collection of stories, *The Sluices of Epiphany*, entitled after the lead story. It also contained the stories "Gradov City" (Gorod Gradov) and "The Sandy Schoolmistress" (Peschanaya uchitel'nitsa). In "The Sluices of Epiphany," Platonov comes up with an original interpretation of certain authentic historical facts, namely, those connected with the attempt of Peter I, early in the 18th century, to build a waterway connecting the Baltic, Black, and Caspian Seas. It was not by accident that Platonov focused his attention on this grandiose, yet unrealized project of the great emperor-revolutionary. Neither Peter himself, nor the excellent, talented British engineer Bertrand Perry took into account the multifaceted elements of human life, but acted as strong individuals of an "arithmetic turn of mind" always do, confident of their own rightness. Meanwhile, as Platonov saw it, these elements of popular life, no matter how pitiful, poor, primitive, and senseless, are still closer to the truth than "blind" and heartless dogmatism. Mankind, of course, will have to suffer from the actions of these "possessed supermen," though the latter, too, will be punished terribly. This story, programmatic for Platonov in the 1920s, shows an influence of the philosophy of Nikolai FYODOROV, who quite specifically considered the division of humanity into "clever" organizers and "dumb" laborers, to be perhaps the greatest of all human tragedies. By the mid-1920s Platonov had become a defender of those "worn out by oppression" yet maintaining their "practical good sense" for the true goal of humankind, the defeat of death. These ideas were to develop and become more concrete later. *The Sluices of Epiphany* appeared at a time of sharp confrontation between the Bolsheviks and the intelligentsia, and was received favorably by official reviewers. Platonov moved to Moscow and from 1927 on was a professional writer.

In his subsequent collections, *Secret Man* (Sokrovennyi chelovek, 1928) and *The Origins of a Master* (Proiskhozhdenie mastera, 1929), Platonov developed the special "Platonovian" type of the "secret" dreamer, a man "unburdened" by education or culture (which is "condensed intellect" in Platonov's interpretation), yet "animated" (odukhotvoren, one of Platonov's favorite words) by the idea of a common weal. Like Foma Pukhov ("Secret Man"), he dreams of fully renouncing his individuality and merging with the universal life of nature and of history. The result is an almost masochistic drive not to spare oneself, to perish for the sake of the common cause. Such feelings make the "secret man" unintelligible and alien to those around him; hence came his spiritual anxiety, loneliness, and feeling of doom. At this stage, Platonov had not conclusively defined his relationship to the "secret man," even though he felt an affinity for him.

The story, "The Origins of a Master", is the first part of the novel *Chevengur*, fully published as late as 1972 and in the West only. This is also a novel about a "secret man," one who set out to find happiness in the country of victorious socialism in 1921. On his peregrinations Aleksandr Dvanov meets some other men who are equally possessed by "secret ideas," and they all travel together to the fantastic city of Chevengur, where communism is being built at an "accelerated pace." One of Dvanov's companions is obviously patterned on the image of Don Quixote; his beautiful damsel's name is Rosa Luxemburg. In the mind of this possessed "knight" of the revolution, dreams of universal happiness are linked to pathological necrophilia: from the very beginning, he loves a dead woman, imagines the process of her decay in the ground, and the revolution is for him "the last vestige of her body", which he hopes to revive by the victory of the proletariat all over the world. Altogether, Platonov describes scenes of death and destruction quite purposely in a sober, businesslike manner, as though nothing out of the ordinary were happening. Imperfect human beings, insufficiently prepared for life under communism, must die as soon as possible, yielding their place to future generations who will ultimately resurrect them (according to Fyodorov's theory). However, Platonov's novel has a very pessimistic ending: together with "Chevengur communism," the smallest young boy—the "future generation,"—also dies. The author seems to be asking the question: who, then, will live and resurrect his ancestors in the future city of the Sun? Doesn't this look like the universal destruction and end of the human race? Only the first part of *Chevengur* (where these global ideas find as yet no reflection) was published. Subsequently, neither GORKY's sympathy (see *Literaturnoe nasledstvo*, vol. 70) nor the support of the leading Party line critic, A. VORONSKY, could help to publish the novel. The 1930s brought a new period in Soviet literature, with sincerity and serious analysis of contemporary events no longer in demand, and new views regarding the development of socialism even less welcome. Stalin's regime needed thoughtless and primitive support of the Party line. This is why those of Platonov's stories which were published, such as "Doubting Makar" (Usomnivshiisya Makar, 1929) and "Benefit" (Vprok, 1931), featuring "doubt" and an ironic presentation of "enthusiasts" of the cultural revolution in the countryside, provoked a campaign of sharply negative official criticism. Platonov no longer appeared in print for some years. However, these were precisely the years of his creative flowering. He wrote a whole series of satirical and and philosophic tales (published only posthumously, for example, "Dusty Wind"—Musornyi veter) and around 1930 or a little later finished his short novel *The Foundation Pit* (Kotlovan), published only in the West so far.

In *The Foundation Pit*, the theme and composition of *Chevengur* are repeated in many details, though the action takes place ten years later in the years of the collectivization of agriculture. Enthusiasts of a world commune plan to build a home for the world proletariat, a kind of socialist paradise. But in fact they are merely digging a pit, a huge common grave for mankind of the future, because from its very inception the idea of this mad utopia is based on violence and death to those who are *called* "bourgeois," "kulaks," "kulaks' helpers," etc., in the name of those who are *declared* "bearers of class truth." Platonov was one of the first to recognize the vast role of language in social processes. The turns and direction of history, as well as millions of human lives do in actual fact depend on *how* to call, or on what *word* to use in designating a given social phenomenon. The deformation of the Russian language, so consistently shown by Platonov even in the 1920s, mirrors the process by which a normal social consciousness is destroyed in the first socialist state in the world. People are losing the language of their fathers and are beginning to use the artificial jargon (lexically as well as syntactically) of the "building of socialism." It is not Platonov, of course, who creates this language for his characters. Rather, he *takes* it, in a condensed and integrated form from its real bearers and prototypes. It suffices to glance through some Soviet periodicals of the 1920s and early 1930s (later this process was stopped by official fiat from above) to see that writers as well as their heroes, officials of the government, and the "great leader of nations," Stalin himself, all tried to speak and write precisely that jargon of "building socialism." In the stories "Benefit" and "Doubting Makar," but especially in *The Foundation Pit*, Platonov's attitude toward "socialist enthusiasm" and its "animated" heroes had become clearly satirical. Simultaneously, though, the writer had a premonition of the approaching somber shadows of a national tragedy.

In 1937, after a break in Platonov's publications, his collection *Potudan River* (Reka Potudan') appeared. Here Platonov had switched to different, seemingly quite neutral themes: love, the complex nuances of the human psyche, and such. However, everything in life is now overshadowed by a sense of doom. And this was precisely the year when Soviet writers received orders to write "how life had become better, how life had become happier." It was no surprise that Platonov's book again received hostile reviews. From the mid-1930s to the beginning of the war, Platonov published mainly reviews and essays (under the pen-name "F. Chelovekov") in the journals *Literaturnyi kritik*, *Literaturnoe obozrenie* and *Detskaya literatura* (Children's Literature). But when Platonov attempted to gather these pieces in a separate volume and publish them in 1939, only a few advance copies appeared, and the book was never properly distributed. In 1970, a full thirty years later, *A Reader's Meditations* (Razmyshleniya chitatelya) finally appeared, published by the *Sovetskii pisatel'* (Soviet writer) publishing house.

From 1942 to the end of the war, Platonov worked as a war correspondent on several fronts. The war years brought a certain relaxation of the controls imposed upon literature by the regime. Platonov was once more printed in newspapers and journals. His collections of war stories appeared one after another, and reviewers quite benevolently praised Platonov's "high artistry." However as early as November 1946, immediately after ZHDANOV's famous report on the journals *Zvezda* and *Leningrad*, a new wave of persecution was initiated against Platonov. His story "Ivanov's Family," published in *Novyi mir*, became the main target of these attacks. It is hard to see how V. Ermilov, a critic whose special function was to launch such attacks, could see a "slander against Soviet reality" in that calm and well-meaning story of Lieutenant Ivanov, who returns home after the war to join his family and quite naturally experiences certain psychological stress situations. Furthermore, "Ivanov's Family" (a variant title is "The Return"—Vozvrashchenie) is one of Platonov's simplest stories in both plot and language, and even has an optimistic ending. Nevertheless (perhaps by personal order of Stalin himself, who disliked Platonov's works even in the 1930s), the story was declared to be "anti-Soviet" and Platonov's name was removed from the history of Soviet literature. He was allowed, however, to work for the *Detskaya literatura* publishing house, rewriting folktales.

By the end of the 1940s, Platonov was a very sick man. He had caught tuberculosis from his son, who had returned from a camp and was dying in his parents' care. After the catastrophe of 1946 and 1947, he could not think of publishing original stories. The most somber prophecies of the author of *Chevengur* and *The Foundation Pit* were now coming true: the cultural revolution launched by "secret" dreamers and enthusiasts left no place for any creativity, save that of officious optimism and the glorification of "constructive ideas." Platonov could not survive in the world of Stalin's ever deepening "pit," and he died at 52 years of age in 1951, one of the darkest years of Russian history. After his death, there remained a huge archive of his published and unpublished works and letters. A part of it went to *TsGALI* (Central State Archive for Literature), and another to the writer's heirs. After Stalin's death and the exposition of his crimes, publication of Platonov's works began slowly. A volume of *Selected Stories* was the first to appear in 1958. It was followed by a number of further collections in the USSR. However, the novels *Chevengur* and *The Foundation Pit*, as well as the stories "Juvenile Sea" (Yuvenil'noe more), "Benefit," and some others have to date only been published in the West.

Works: Elektrifikatsiya. 1921. *Golubaya glubina.* Krasnodar, 1922. *Epifanskie shlyuzy.* 1927. *Sokrovennyi chelovek.* 1928. *Proiskhozhdenie mastera.* 1929. "Usomnivshiisya Makar," *Oktyabr'*, 1929, no. 9. "Vprok," *Krasnaya nov'*, 1931, no. 3. (Also in *Opal'nye povesti.* New York, 1955) *Reka Potudan'.* 1937. *Odukhotvorennye lyudi.* 1942. *Rasskazy o rodine.* 1943. *V storonu zakata solntsa.* 1945. "Sem'ya Ivanova," *Novyi mir*, 1946, nos. 10–11. *Izbrannye rasskazy.* 1958. *V prekrasnom i yarostnom mire.* 1965. *Razmyshleniya chitatelya.* 1970. *Chevengur.* Paris, 1972. *Kotlovan.* Ann Arbor, 1973. *Sharmanka. P'esa v trekh deistviyakh.* Ann Arbor, 1975. *Izbrannye proizvedeniya v dvukh tomakh.* 1978. "Yuvenil'noe more," *Ekho* (Paris), 1979, no. 4.

Platonov's correspondence with Gorky. Literaturnoe nasledstvo, vol. 70 (1964). "Pis'ma k Gor'komu." In *Arkhiv A. M. Gor'kogo.* Vol. 10, book 2. 1965.

Translations: The Foundation Pit. (Bi-lingual edition.) Trans. Thomas Whitney. Ann Arbor, 1973. *Collected Works.* Trans. Thomas P. Whitney, et al. Ann Arbor, 1978. *Chevengur.* Trans. A. Olcott. Ann Arbor, 1978.

Secondary literature: L. Averbakh, "O tselostnykh masshtabakh i chastnykh Makarakh," *Na literaturnom postu*, 1929, no. 21–22. V. Bryusov, "Sredi stikhov," *Pechat' i revolyutsiya*, 1923, no. 6. V. Eidinova, "K tvorcheskoi biografii A. Platonova," *VLit*, 1978, no. 3, pp. 213–28. V. Ermilov, "Klevetnicheskii rasskaz A. Platonova," *Literaturnaya gazeta*, 4 January 1947. A. Fadeev, "Ob odnoi kulatskoi khronike," *Krasnaya nov'*, 1931, no. 5–6. M. Geller, "Soblazn utopii," *Ekho*, 1979, no. 4. ———, *Andrei Platonov v poiskakh schastya.* Paris, 1982. A. Gladkov, "V prekrasnom i yarostnom mire," *Novyi mir*, 1963, no. 11. A. Gurvich, "Andrei Platonov," *Krasnaya nov'*, 1937, no. 10. Marion Jordan, "Andrei Platonov," *RLT* 8 (1974), pp. 363–72. V. Levin, "Beseda s kritikom Ermilovym," *Literaturnaya gazeta*, 17 October 1964. L. Shubin, "Andrei Platonov," *VLit*, 1967, no. 6. E. Tolstaya Segal, "Stikhiinye sily. Platonov i Pil'nyak," *Slavica Hierosolymitana* 3 (1978). ———, "K voprosu o literaturnoi allyuzii v proze Andreya Platonova," *Slavica Hierosolymitana* 5–6 (1981). V. Turbin, "Misteriya A. Platonova," *Molodaya gvardiya*, 1965, no. 7. *Tvorchestvo A. Platonova: Stat'i i soobshcheniya.* Voronezh, 1970. V. Varshavskii, "Chevengur i Novyi grad," *Novyi zhurnal*, no. 122 (1976), pp. 193–213. Genrika and Aleksei Yakushev, "Struktura khudozhestvennogo obraza u Andreya Platonova." In *American Contributions to the Eighth International Congress of Slavists.* Ed. Victor Terras. 1978. Pp. 746–77. Henryka Yakushev, "Andrei Platonov's Artistic Model of the World," *RLT* 16 (1979), pp. 171–88.

Bibliography: A. Kiselev and V. Maramzin, "A. P. Platonov," *Ekho*, 1979, no. 4, 1980, nos. 1–4.

E. D. A.

Plavilshchikov, Pyotr Alekséevich (1760–1812), playwright and actor. On graduating from Moscow University in 1779, Plavilshchikov joined the company of the St. Petersburg theater, and later that of Moscow. He played Pravdin in FONVIZIN's comedy *The Minor* (1782), but was better known for his roles in tragedy and drama. His first comedy, *The Correction, or Good Kinsfolk* (Ispravlenie, ili dobrye rodstvenniki, 1785), borders on the "tearful," and depicts the hero Plamen leading a dissolute life in general, although he is also virtuous owing to the teachings of his late mother. The characters have speaking names, are drawn from the bourgeoisie or gentry, and moralize frequently. Plavilshchikov's one-act comedies in prose, *Miller and Sbiten-seller Rivals* (Mel'nik i sbitenshchik soperniki) and *Kuteikin's Plot* (Sgovor Kuteikina), are sequels to ABLESIMOV's successful comic opera *The Miller* and Fonvizin's *The Minor* respectively. *Kuteikin's Plot* introduces Eremeevna, Skotinin, and others. Peasants appear in Plavilshchikov's five-act comedy *The Landless Peasant* (Bobyl', 1790, published 1792): some are wealthy, coarse, and wicked, others hardworking, poor, and ingenious. *The Landless Peasant* remained in the repertoire of the Imperial theaters until 1822. Plavilshchikov's *The Shopman* (Sidelets, 1803) has a merchant-class setting exploited by Ostrovsky in the 1850s and later. Rejecting LUKIN's method of translating and adapting foreign plays to Russian manners, Plavilshchikov's comedies are original. However, he supported Lukin's pleas for a Russian national theater, and wrote the first theoretical essay on acting and theater to be published in Russia (1792).

Works: Sochineniya. 4 vols. 1816. *Russkaya komediya i komicheskaya opera XVIII v.* Ed. and introd. P. N. Berkov. 1950.
Secondary literature: L. I. Kulakova, *P. A. Plavil'shchikov.* 1952.
D. W.

Plekhánov, Geórgy Valentínovich (1856–1918), revolutionary, theorist of Marxism, and critic, came from the rural gentry. He initially pursued a military career, but soon switched to the Petersburg Mining Institute. On 6 October 1876 he led a student demonstration organized by the Land and Freedom (Zemlya i volya) group, escaped arrest, and went underground. After several years of energetic revolutionary activity, Plekhanov left Russia in January 1880 and spent the next thirty-seven years abroad. In 1881 he discovered Marxism, whose principal Russian ideologue and propagator he soon became. Plekhanov became one of the founders of the Marxist Freedom for Labor (Osvobozhdenie truda) group in 1883 and was one of the leaders of the Second Internationale. He eventually joined LENIN and contributed to his journals *Iskra* and *Pravda.* Following the Second Congress of the Russian Social Democrat Workers Party in 1903, Plekhanov sided with the Mensheviks. He returned to Russia after the February Revolution, but died soon after, on 30 May 1918.

A prolific lecturer, political journalist, essayist, and social critic, Plekhanov also wrote many scholarly essays in which he tackled problems of social and intellectual history, art, and literature from a Marxist point of view. Some of these essays are: "Gleb Uspensky" (1888), "T. G. Shevshenko" (1890), "Belinsky and Rational Reality" (1897), "The Literary Views of V. G. Belinsky" (1897), "N. G. Chernyshevsky's Aesthetic Theory" (1897), "The Proletarian Movement and Bourgeois Art" (1905), "A Critique of Decadence and Modernism: Henrik Ibsen" (1906), "The Literary Views of N. G. Chernyshevsky" (1909), "Dobrolyubov and Ostrovsky" (1911), and "Art and Society" (Iskusstvo i obshchestvennaya zhizn', 1912–13).

Plekhanov was the first Russian to develop a MARXIST aesthetic. Much of his thinking was done in discussions of the aesthetic theories of BELINSKY, CHERNYSHEVSKY, and PISAREV, whom he faulted for lacking a historical dimension and for failing to recognize the specificity of art, and hence its dialectic relationship with other social phenomena. In his *Letters without an Address* (1899–1900), Plekhanov stressed the social origin of art and its original connection with labor and communal activities. In his essay "French Dramatic Literature and French Painting of the Eighteenth Century from a Sociological Viewpoint" (1905) he tried to demonstrate how art, while a sui generis activity, is generated by, intimately interacts with, and enhances the social structure of its age, in the case in question, the aristocratic regime of 18th-century France. Plekhanov thus deals with art as a superstructure of the socio-economic base. Beauty in art is then not an absolute, but a function of sociohistorical truth. Tendentious art is not non-art, but much of it is bad art, because its tendency is reactionary. Plekhanov was convinced that a disinterested pursuit of truth in art would necessarily produce

a progressive tendency. Hence, true art had to be socially useful. Plekhanov followed Belinsky in assuming that a true artist's creative intuition would, if given enough time, overcome and neutralize his ideological prejudices, and that even a talented and sincere expression of reactionary, and therefore false, ideas would have to be bad art.

Plekhanov's sociological approach to art allowed him to explain various aspects of modernist art, such as formalism, mysticism, decadence, political indifference, and *l'art pour l'art*, as an expression of the bourgeois artist's despair in and escape from the depressing reality created by his social class. On the other hand, Plekhanov insisted that the creative process in art had to be disinterested and non-utilitarian, so that the relation between art and sociopolitical life, and class struggle in particular, would be dialectic, rather than one of direct ("mechanistic") dependence. On these grounds, Plekhanov candidly criticized Chernyshevsky's *What is to be Done?* and GORKY's *Mother,* although he did not deny that these works were politically useful. It was this Kantian strain in Plekhanov's aesthetic that has been rejected by most Soviet literary theorists, who charge him with insufficient attention to correct ideology. However, Plekhanov's aesthetic gained wide acceptance and is found almost in its entirety in LUNACHARSKY and the critics of PEREVAL. After having been in almost total eclipse during the Stalin years, Plekhanov has been cautiously resurrected.

Works: Sochineniya. 24 vols. 1923–27. *Estetika i sotsiologiya iskusstva.* 2 vols. 1978. *Filosofsko-literaturnoe nasledie G. V. Plekhanova.* 3 vols. 1973–74. *Literatura i estetika.* Introd. B. I. Bursov. 1958.
Translations: Art and Society (trans. of *Iskusstvo i obshchestvennaya zhizn'*). Introd. Granville Hicks. 1936. "Ibsen, Petty Bourgeois Revolutionist." In *Ibsen,* ed. by Angel Flores. 1966. *Unaddressed Letters. Art and Social Life.* Trans. A. Fineberg. Moscow, 1957.
Secondary literature: V. G. Astakhov, *G. V. Plekhanov i N. G. Chernyshevskii.* 1961. ———, *Literaturno-esteticheskie vzglyady G. V. Plekhanova v sovetskoi kritike (20-e i nachalo 30-kh godov).* 1973. Samuel Haskell Baron, *Plekhanov; the Father of Russian Marxism.* 1963. D. Cherkashin, *Esteticheskie vzglyady G. V. Plekhanova.* 1959. Peter Demetz, "Georgy Valentinovich Plekhanov (1857–1918)." In *Marx, Engels and the Poets: Origins of Marxist Literary Criticism.* 1967. Pp. 189–98. M. Rozental', *Voprosy estetiki G. V. Plekhanova.* 1939. E. N. Zaslonova, *Plekhanov ob esteticheskom ideale.* 1965.
V. T.

Pleshchéev, Aleksei Nikoláevich (1825–93), poet, prose writer, playwright, critic, and journalist, came from a noble family, was educated at a military school in St. Petersburg, then attended Petersburg University. In 1845 he began to attend the meetings of the PETRASHEVSKY CIRCLE and simultaneously started a career as a poet and writer, publishing in SOVREMENNIK and in OTECHESTVENNYE ZAPISKI. He was arrested and tried with the other members of the Petrashevsky Circle in 1849. His death sentence was commuted to service in the ranks in Orenburg province. Having returned from exile in 1859, Pleshcheev continued his literary activities in the progressive camp. He wrote poetry, fiction, and several plays (in the 1860s), but mostly criticism and journalistic pieces. He also did many verse and prose translations from various languages. Pleshcheev's poetry and prose are generally representative of their period: his verses of the Petrashevsky Circle period are marked by lofty romantic idealism, while his prose of the same period belongs to the NATURAL SCHOOL; in the 1860s he writes poetry very much in the vein of NEKRASOV and prose with a strong message of social and civic protest. A solid journeyman of his trade, Pleshcheev lacked an individual style.

Works: Izbrannoe. Introd. essays N. M. Gaidenkov and V. I. Korovin. 1960. *Polnoe sobranie stikhotvorenii.* Introd. M. Ya. Polyakov. 1964.
Translations: Lewanski, p. 325.
Secondary literature: N. A. Dobrolyubov, "Stikhotvoreniya A. N. Pleshcheeva" (1858). In his *Sobranie sochinenii.* Vol. 3. 1962. Pp. 360–69. N. S. Garanina, "Literaturno-kriticheskoe nasledie A. N. Pleshcheeva," *Vestnik MGU,* Seriya 7, 1961, no. 3. V. N. Maikov, "Stikhotvoreniya A. Pleshcheeva." In his *Sochineniya.* 1901. Vol. 2. M. E. Saltykov-Shchedrin, "Novye stikhotvoreniya A.

Pleshcheeva" (1863). In his *Sobranie sochinenii*. Vol. 5. 1966. Pp. 417–21. I. A. Shchurov, "Lirika A. N. Pleshcheeva." In *Pisatel' i zhizn'*. Vol. 3. 1966. ———, "Belinskii i Pleshcheev," *RLit* 12 (1969), no. 2, pp. 134–38.   V. T.

Pletnyóv, Pyotr Aleksándrovich (1792–1865) poet, critic, journalist, educator, was born in Tver, the son of a clergyman. He received his early education at the St. Petersburg Pedagogical Institute. In 1814 he began his life-long career as a teacher in various institutes in St. Petersburg. He was tutor of Russian language and literature to members of the Imperial family. In 1832 he was made Professor of Russian Literature at St. Petersburg University; in 1840, rector, a post he held until 1861. Pletnyov died in Paris and was buried in St. Petersburg.

He began his literary activity in 1818 when he joined the circle of V. K. KYUKHELBEKER, whose members included PUSHKIN, DELVIG, BARATYNSKY and others. Pletnyov was active in the leading literary societies of the capital and published widely in journals and almanacs. He was especially close to A. A. Delvig, taking an active part in the publication of the almanac SEVERNYE TSVETY and, later, LITERATURNAYA GAZETA. During the 1830s Pletnyov was very close to Pushkin, helping the poet with the publication of his works. Pushkin dedicated *Evgenii Onegin* to Pletnyov. After Pushkin's death Pletnyov took over the publication of his journal, SOVREMENNIK.

Pletnyov is a poet of the "Pushkin Pleiad." His poetic output is modest, but charming and polished. His earliest works are poetic exercises and imitations of ZHUKOVSKY. His later poems attain greater originality. He experimented successfully with anthological lyric genres: "Night" (Noch', 1827), "The Sea" (More, 1827). His style and versification are polished and lovely, individual lines attaining perfect elegance: "To Pushkin" (K A. S. Pushkinu, 1822), "To the Manuscript of Baratynsky's Poems" (K rukopisi B[aratynsko]go stikhov, 1821). While these poems are full of reminiscences, they do have a sincere quality and are marked by an atmosphere of tenderness and sad regret which is made personal by a concrete autobiographical subtext. Throughout his short poetic career he remained, above all, a lyric poet even though he advocated the civic function of poetry: "To Vyazemsky" (K Vyazemskomu, 1822), but he did not possess the temperament or the radiant force of lyricism to rise above the conventional.

Pletnyov stopped writing poetry in the late 1820s and turned to criticism. As a critic he analyzed literary works along the lines of traditional poetics; his mild and kindly criticism was intended to encourage literary production rather than spark controversy or provoke polemics. He is the author of several literary portrait studies of his contemporaries—Pushkin, Baratynsky, Krylov, Zhukovsky—that have importance for literary history and shed light on contemporary life.

Works: Sochineniya i perepiska. 3 vols. 1885. Selection in *Poety 1820–1830-kh godov*. (Biblioteka poeta.) Vol. 1. 1972. Pp. 318–47.

Secondary literature: A. Krukovskii, "Pletnev kak kritik," *Filologicheskie zapiski*, 1916, fasc. 1.   A. Gl.

Pnin, Iván Petróvich (1773–1805) poet, publicist. Pnin was the natural son of field marshal Prince N. V. Repnin. He received his education at the Moscow University Gentry Pension and the Artillery Engineers Cadet Corps. He served in the military and civil service.

He began to write poetry while at the Pension, where the literary tradition was strong and literary interests were encouraged. He began to devote himself seriously to literature in the 1790s. In 1798 he published the literary and political *Sankt-Peterburgskii zhurnal*, with A. F. Bestuzhev, the father of the four Decembrists, which was encouraged and subsidized by the young Grand Duke Alexander and his circle of friends. Pnin was active in the newly established "FREE SOCIETY OF AMATEURS OF LITERATURE, SCIENCES and ARTS," and became its president in 1805.

In his publicistic works he appears as a student of the French Enlightenment, a deist, and a follower of A. N. RADISHCHEV, whom he admired and knew personally, and whose tradition of social protest he continued. His chief publicistic works are the "Essay Concerning Enlightenment in Russia" (1804) in which he explained the idea of class enlightenment, while promoting the cause of abolishing serfdom, and his eloquent defense of the rights of illegitimate children,

"A Cry of Innocence Ignored by Laws" (1802). His publicistic works have a certain literary value: his prose is sober, forceful and extremely lucid.

As a poet Pnin is grouped with the "Poety-radishchevtsy" (followers of Radishchev) because their poetry is characterized by lofty civic lyrics. Pnin is a transitional poet. He blends classical 18th-century literary convention and current social and political ideas in complex ways. His poems show a clear influence of the poetics of the didactic and philosophical odes of LOMONOSOV and DERZHAVIN and the new SENTIMENTALISM of KARAMZIN. Thus themes of social protest appear within the context of the inner and emotional world of the new lyric hero. Pnin's meter and rhyme schemes recall Derzhavin, although thematically their points of view are clearly polemical. Pnin is thoroughly classical in his diction: his style follows the models of Russian classicism in the abundant use of tropes for achieving the nobility and elevation appropriate to theme and genre, abstractions and generalizations, as in "God" (Bog, 1805) and "Man" (Chelovek, 1805).

Works: Sochineniya. Introd. essay and ed. I. K. Luppol. 1934. (Poetry:) *Poety-radishchevtsy*. Introd. essay by V. N. Orlov. 1961. (Selection:) *Russkie prosvetiteli*. Vol. 1. 1966.

Secondary literature: I. K. Luppol, "I. P. Pnin i ego mesto v istorii russkoi obshchestvennoi mysli." In his *Istoriko-filosofskie etyudy*. 1935. V. N. Orlov, *Russkie prosvetiteli 1790–1800-kh godov*. 2d ed. 1953.   A. Gl.

Póchva ("The soil"), **póchvenniki** ("men of the soil"), **póchvennichestvo**, terms applied to a group of intellectuals of the 1860s and after, who were initially gathered around the journals of the DOSTOEVSKY brothers, VREMYA (1861–63) and EPOKHA (1864–65). The leading *pochvenniki*, besides the Dostoevskys, were N. N. STRAKHOV and A. A. GRIGORIEV. The *pochvenniki* were close to the SLAVOPHILES in claiming that the educated classes of Russia had lost contact with the soil, i.e., with the masses of the people, and should make every effort to recover their roots. However, unlike the Slavophiles, the *pochvenniki* did not advocate a return to the culture of pre-Petrine Russia, but instead expected that the Russian people would create a synthesis of Western and Russian-Orthodox culture. Grigoriev and Dostoevsky saw PUSHKIN as a Russian who had succeeded in creating such a synthesis and had pointed Russia in the right direction. The *pochvenniki* combated the radicals and liberals, charging that both were assuming artificial, theoretical positions, without any foundation in the "soil." They also polemicized with the Slavophiles, considering their positions too theoretical as well.

Bibliography: F. M. Dostoevskii, "Dva lagerya teoretikov" (1862). In his *PSS*. Vol. 20. Pp. 5–22. ———, "Pushkin (A Sketch)" (1880). In his *The Diary of a Writer*. Trans. and annot. Boris Brasol. 1949. Pp. 967–80. Linda Gerstein, *Nikolai Strakhov*. 1971. Apollon Grigor'ev, "Razvitie idei narodnosti v nashei literature so smerti Pushkina" (1861). In his *Sochineniya*. Ed. V. S. Krupich. 1970. Pp. 243–79. ———, "Zapadnichestvo v russkoi literature" (1861). In his *Sochineniya*. Ed. V. S. Krupich. 1970. Pp. 280–332. Nikolai Strakhov, *Bor'ba s zapadom v nashei literature*. 3 vols. 3d ed. 1897–98.   V. T.

Poéma (verse epic). The verse epic made its appearance in Russian literature in the early 18th century when the classicist verse epic, a well established and much cultivated genre, was transplanted into Russian poetry. Russian poets followed the acknowledged examples of European classicism (Voltaire, Milton, Camoens, etc.), as well as Boileau's theory of genre. In Russia, M. KHERASKOV thus defined the classical verse epic: "The epic *poema* contains some important, memorable, famous event, which has occurred in this world and has caused some important change affecting the entire human race … or it sings of an event which has occurred in a certain state and serves the whole nation's glory, peace, or finally, its transition to a different condition." (1779).

The first attempt to create a classical verse epic was A. KANTEMIR's "Petriad" (1730), which remained unfinished (only the first canto was completed) and in manuscript (it was published as late as 1859). Practically unknown to contemporaries, written in syllabic verse, Kantemir's verse epic had no influence on the further development of the genre.

M. Lomonosov's "Peter the Great" (Pyotr Velikii, 1756–61) was a more significant event. It was structured according to all the rules of the classical epopoeia, presenting an important historical event, featuring a majestic and noble hero, and exhibiting mythological elements, digressions into the past, a solemn "high style," etc. However, Lomonosov only completed the first two cantos. The task of creating the Russian classical epic was eventually fulfilled by M. Kheraskov in his *Rossiada* (1779). Kheraskov correctly stated in his preface that "this work is the first of its kind in our language." *Rossiada* tells of the capture of Kazan by Ivan the Terrible in 12 cantos. It has elements of the miraculous, and features conceits (*vymysly*).

The classical verse epic continued its existence until the 1830s. The most significant exercises in this genre belong to S. A. Shirinsky-Shikhmatov, who introduced strong lyric elements into his epic poems. Other epic poems of the late 18th and early 19th century (I. Zavalishin's *Suvoroida*, 1796, D. Kashkin's *Aleksandriada*, 1836, etc.) do not rise above the level of epigonism.

The epic poem in travesty was more popular in the 18th century than the solemn epic itself. This genre arose as parody of the classicist heroic epic and either relates great and celebrated events in low, coarse language (the burlesque, e.g., Scarron's *L'Enéide travestie*, 1648–52), or trivial, comical events in pointedly lofty, solemn language (the mock-heroic epic, e.g., Boileau's *Le lutrain*, 1674–83). In Russian literature these two forms were frequently combined. The Russian mock-heroic epic was created by V. Maikov, whose "The L'hombre Player" (Igrok lombera, 1763) describes a game of cards in solemn "high style." In Maikov's "Elisei, or Bacchus Enraged" (Elisei ili razdrazhennyi Vakkh, 1771), the devices of the burlesque are mixed with those of the mock-heroic epic. Other works which may be assigned to the latter genre are the literary-satirical poems of M. Chulkov, "Verses on a Swing" (Stikhi na kacheli, 1769) and "The Lamentable Fall of Certain Poets" (Plachevnoe padenie stikhotvortsev, 1769), as well as Ya. Knyazhnin's "The Battle of the Poets" (Boi stikhotvortsev, the 1760s), discovered only recently, in 1971. A peculiar variant of the epic in travesty is found in I. Bogdanovich's "Dushenka" (1783), an elegant version of Apuleius' "Amor and Psyche" and A. Lafontaine's novel *The Love of Psyche and Cupid*.

The burlesque in its pure form appeared in Russia toward the end of the 18th century. It is represented by rather weak reworkings of classical themes, such as E. Lyutsenko's "Rape of Proserpina" (1795) or "Vergil's *Aeneid*, Turned Inside Out," by N. Osipov (1791–96). The latter is probably also the author of the burlesque, twice removed, "Dushenka," an obscene, scabrous reworking of Bodganovich's poem. Its manuscript is preserved in the archive of G. Derzhavin (Manuscript Section of the M. E. Saltykov-Shchedrin State Public Library in Leningrad.)

The exacerbation of the Shishkov-Karamzin controversy produced two mock-heroic epics in the 1810s: the anti-Shishkov "A Dangerous Neighbor" (Opasnyi sosed, 1811) by V. Pushkin, and the anti-Karamzin "Rape of the Fur-Coats" (1811–15) by A. Shakhovskoi. The latter has reached us only in a toned down printed version. The mock-heroic epic had a substantial influence on Pushkin's "Ruslan and Lyudmila" (1820), which may be considered the crowning work of this particular genre.

The descriptive epic poem showed a considerably less pronounced development. The only example of this genre worth mentioning here is S. Bobrov's *Tavrida* (1798), or *Khersonida* (1804), in its second version, a work which has its example in Thomson's *The Seasons*. The didactic poem, likewise, showed a minimal development. Kheraskov's "The Fruits of Learning" (Plody nauk, 1761) may serve as an example.

The next stage in the development of the Russian verse epic belongs to the romantic period and is initiated by the influence of Byron's "Eastern poems." This type of verse epic is characterized by the following traits: (1) Its *sujet* is dominated by a single hero, a strong, somber, romantic personality; his inner world and his conflict with his environment are described. (2) The composition of such a verse epic is characterized by devices such as "things unsaid" (*nedoskazannost'*), inner monologues, fragmentariness, an aura of mystery. (3) The action is set in some exotic country (the East, the South, a gypsy camp, etc.); sometimes the exotic function is taken over by moving the action into the past. (4) While the classical verse epic was written in Alexandrines, the romantic *poéma* gravitates to-

ward the iambic tetrameter. Pushkin's so-called southern *poemy* are built according to these parameters: "The Prisoner of the Caucasus" (1821), "The Fountain of Bakhchisarai" (1823), "The Gypsies" (1824), in which, however, the hero's historical determinants, his imbeddedness in the cultural and social problems of Russian life in the 1820s, are more pronounced than in Byron. K. Ryleev's historical *poéma* "Voinarovsky" (1824) is written in the manner of Pushkin, who also approved of it.

Baratynsky's "Edda" (1825) is purposely juxtaposed to the colorful romanticism of Pushkin's *poéma*, being constructed basically along the same Byronic parameters, but visibly toned down. Here the hero has changed into a rather banal officer, and the heroine, from a charming southern beauty, into a Finnish girl (*chukhonka*), while the place of action has been transferred to Finland, a locale well known to every Petersburg reader. Baratynsky's other *poemy*, "The Ball" (Bal, 1828) and "The Gypsy" (Tsyganka, 1831), describe the realia of life in society. K. Pavlova continued in Baratynsky's manner in her *poemy*, "A Double Life" (Dvoinaya zhizn', 1844–47) and "The Quadrille" (Kadril', 1843–59).

I. Kozlov's *poéma* "The Monk" (Chernets, 1825) may be mentioned as an example of "national romanticism," while A. Podolinsky's "Div and Peri" (1827), though not without merit and possessed of luxuriant Eastern color, was an imitation of Thomas Moore, and already an epigonic work. The romantic *poéma* reached its conclusion in Lermontov, who created the perfect image of a spiritually strong romantic hero, both in the astral plane ("The Demon," 1829–39), and in the terrestrial ("Mtsyri," 1839). The romantic *poéma* became one of the most prolific genres in all of Russian literature. According to V. Zhirmunsky's count, over 200 such poems and "fragments" were produced in the 1820s and 1830s.

In the later Pushkin, the romantic *poéma* evolves into works of a historical or social-philosophic perspective: "Poltava" (1829), "The Bronze Horseman" (1833). In the 1840s and 1850s there appears in Russian literature a type of verse epic which may be called a "*poéma* of manners" or a "real life *poéma*." Pushkin's "The Little House in Kolomna" (1830) may be assigned to this sub-genre. *Poemy* of this type describe day-to-day living and everyday situations. Such are, for example: I. Turgenev's "Parasha" (1843); V. Kyukhelbeker's "The Orphan" (Sirota, 1833–34); "Two Destinies" (Dve sud'by, 1843–44) and "Mashenka" (1845) by A. Maikov; "Up the Volga" (Vverkh po Volge, 1862) by A. Grigoriev; N. Ogaryov's unsuccessful and imitative *poéma* "Humor" (Yumor, 1857, 1869) and "The Village" (Derevnya, 1847). N. Nekrasov's *poemy* about peasant life, such as "Red-Nose Frost" (Moroz krasnyi nos, 1863), "Peasant Children" (Krestyanskie deti, 1863), etc., his historical *poemy*, such as "Russian Women" (Russkie zhenshchiny, 1871, 1872) and "Grandfather" (Dedushka, 1870), as well as his contemporary-publicistic *poemy*, such as "Sasha," also belong to this group. In their content, they all gravitate toward prose, and their verse form may appear somewhat artificial. Nekrasov's huge unfinished verse epic, "Who Has a Good Life in Russia?" (Komu na Rusi zhit' khorosho, 1865–77), which breaks down into separate fragments, illustrates the general crisis of *poemy* of this type.

Nevertheless, later, in the 1930s and 1940s, attempts were made to resurrect the realistic *poéma* of manners. During that period it aspired to a more epic, and even monumental quality, pretending to depict the typical hero of the period and thus approaching, in a way, the novel in verse. Characteristically, the titles of such verse epics often bear the hero's name, as is the case with Pushkin's *Evgeny Onegin*: "Lieutenant Schmidt" (1927) and "Spektorsky" (1931) by B. Pasternak, or "Vasily Tyorkin" (1941–45) by A. Tvardovsky.

At about the same time the historical *poéma* of manners made its appearance (S. Esenin's "Anna Snegina," 1925; E. Bagritsky's "Duma of Opanas," 1926). However, it quickly degenerated into simple "political paraphrase": "Vladimir Ilyich Lenin" (1924) by Mayakovsky, "Ulyalyaevshchina" (1924) by I. Selvinsky, "Strana Muraviya" (1936) by Tvardovsky, and many others.

At the turn of the century, the epic element was displaced from the *poéma* and the "lyric *poéma*" (the title of a cycle of poems by V. Bryusov, 1904; as a poetic term it was first used by L. Dolgopolov) made its appearance and developed rapidly during the first decade of the century. Such a *poéma* virtually lacks a *sujet*. It is focused on the author himself and on his lyric experience. It may feature the meditations of an auctorial "I" (V. Bryusov, "The Shutins"

—Zamknutye, 1901), or a dream (A. Blok's "Night Violet" —Nochnaya fialka, 1906), or a lyric event, such as the author's unhappy love (V. Mayakovsky's "A Cloud in Trousers," 1915). Sometimes the hero remains unnamed and is not identical with the author, but is yet the latter's alter ego, so that the lyric experiences and thoughts of such a hero are indeed those of the author himself (A. Blok, "The Garden of Nightingales"—Solov'inyi sad, 1915). The development of the lyric *poema* continues after the Revolution: A. Bely, "The First Rendezvous" (Pervoe svidanie, 1921), S. Esenin, "The Black Man" (Chernyi chelovek, 1925), V. Mayakovsky, "About That" (Pro eto, 1923). Marina Tsvetaeva's "*Poema* of the End" (Poema kontsa, 1924) and "*Poema* of the Mountain" (Poema gory, 1924) are imbued with a tense lyric pathos.

However, the basic tendency in this development of the lyric *poema* after the Revolution points toward the disappearance not only of the last vestiges of a *sujet*, but of the lyric hero as well, who is now dissolved in the masses (Mayakovsky's "150,000,000", 1920). What is left of the *poema* is the epoch itself, while the poet's attitude toward it is anything but simple—as in Blok's "The Twelve" (1918), where the *sujet* is insignificant and is, so it seems, pushed into the background by the ominous steps of History. In A. Akhmatova's "Requiem" (1935–43), the auctorial lyric "I" does not play a noticeable role. The heroine's soul is dissolved in the nation's grief, in the nightmare of Stalin's terror. The steps of history, perceived at some distance (20–30 years) are also heard in Akhmatova's "*Poema* without a Hero" (1940–62), in which the author continues the tradition of Blok. The absence of a hero (and hence of a *sujet*) is declared even in the title of this work.

Having jettisoned both *sujet* and hero, the "lyric *poema*" exhausts itself and ceases to exist as a genre. A sense of the death of the genre is clearly present in A. Voznesensky's *poema* "The Masters" (Mastera, 1959), which disintegrates into separate fragments, so that its author is forced to exclaim in the end: "But where's the *poema*? There is no *poema*!" Later, Voznesensky wrote a book, "The Triangular Pear: Forty Lyric Digressions" (1962), where only the digressions are left of the *poema*. A collection, "Heart of Achilles" (1966), begins with a "Lament for Two Unwritten *Poemy*."

In contemporary Russian literature there exist two distinct tendencies in the development of the *poema*. On the one side, there are the unwieldy, heavily publicistic, often primitive *poemy* of E. Evtushenko, such as "Bratsk Hydroelectric Plant" (Bratskaya GES, 1965) or "Mama and the Atom Bomb" (Mama i atomnaya bomba, 1982). On the other, there are some attempts to revive the genre. Such are, for example, S. Lipkin's epic-memoiristic *poemy* about Stalin's terror ("Nestor and Sariya," 1963), the war ("The Technician-Intendant," 1963), and about his encounters with Bagritsky and Ezhov ("A Literary Reminiscence," 1974). A search for new forms can be discerned in the fantastic-absurd *poemy* of V. Sosnora, "The Living Mirror" (Zhivoe zerkalo, 1979) and "One Day of Loneliness" (Odin den' odinochestva, 1979), and in V. Krivulin's ironic *poema*, "Nine *Repliques*" (Devyat' replik, 1980).

Bibliography: L. Dolgopolov, *Poemy Bloka i russkaya poema kontsa 19–nachala 20 vekov.* 1964. *Iroi-komicheskaya poema.* (Biblioteka poeta. Bol'shaya seriya.) 1933. A. N. Lur'e, *Poeticheskii epos revolyutsii.* 1975. E. A. Maimin, *O russkom romantizme.* 1975. Yu. V. Mann, *Poetika russkogo romantizma.* 1976. I. G. Neupokoeva, *Revolyutsionno-romanticheskaya poema pervoi poloviny 19 veka.* 1971. A. N. Sokolov, *Ocherki po istorii russkoi poemy 18 i pervoi poloviny 19 veka.* 1955. V. M. Zhirmunskii, *Bairon i Pushkin.* 1978. M. A.

Poetics, a branch of philology which studies the structure of works of literature. In a narrower sense, poetics studies the system of aesthetic means applied in the text of a work of verbal art. There is, for one, *descriptive* poetics, whose purpose is the reconstruction of the path from inception to definitive text. Sometimes, *structural* poetics is singled out; here, an effort is made to understand the work of art within the general system of texts of a given type by studying artistic devices on different levels, from elements of poetic language to plot and *sujet*. More current is the concept of *historical* poetics, which studies the development of particular artistic devices (epithet, rhyme, etc.) or categories (space, time), as well as the movement of literary *sujets*, mythological motifs, types, and genres.

Russian poetics as a scholarly discipline developed through direct transfer of foreign literary theories (Aristotle, Horace, Boileau, Lessing, the Schlegel brothers, Schelling, Hegel, Lévi-Strauss, etc.) A. N. Veselovsky is considered to have been the founder of Russian historical poetics. A. A. Potebnya asserted the intimate connection between poetics and linguistics as well as the study of myth; he viewed poetic language as "imaginative thinking" (*obraznoe myshlenie*). An even closer tie between poetics and linguistics was postulated by the Russian formal school, members of the Opoyaz group (R. Jakobson, Yu. Tynyanov, B. Eikhenbaum, V. Shklovsky, M. Polivanov), and subsequently by the Prague Linguistic Circle (B. Trnka, R. Wellek, J. Mukařovský, N. Trubetskoi, R. Jakobson, etc.) Some basic principles developed by this school (viewing language as a system of signs having a functional character) played a major role in the development of structural linguistics. The studies of the Russian folklorist V. Propp are a peculiar synthesis of historical and structural poetics. The works of M. Bakhtin, in which certain principles were suggested for the description of the structure of prose texts ("polyphony" in the novels of Dostoevsky) and a systematic study of the poetics of the "alien" (traditional) motif and of the "alien word" (*chuzhoe slovo*) were first introduced, have had a considerable influence on the study of literature everywhere. There have been, in Russian poetics, periods of fascination with so-called exact, mathematical, and statistical methods (B. Tomashevsky, G. Shengeli, A. Kolmogorov, M. Gasparov, etc.). During the last decade, the semiotic school (Yu. Lotman, B. Uspensky, V. Toporov, A. Pyatigorsky, B. Gasparov, etc.) has gained international recognition.

Bibliography: M. M. Bakhtin, *Problemy poetiki Dostoevskogo.* 2d ed. 1963. (In English: *Problems of Dostoevsky's Poetics.* Trans. R. W. Rotsel. 1973.) ———, *Estetika slovesnogo tvorchestva.* 1979. A. Belyi, *Simvolizm.* 1910. M. L. Gasparov, *Sovremennyi russkii stikh.* 1974. V. V. Ivanov, *Ocherki po istorii semiotiki v SSSR.* 1976. R. Jakobson, *Selected Writings.* Vols. 3–4. 1966–68. Yu. M. Lotman, *Struktura khudozhestvennogo teksta.* (Brown University reprint.) 1971. ———, *Analysis of the Poetic Text.* Ed. and trans. D. Barton Johnson. 1976. *Poetics.* Vols. 1–2. Warsaw, 1961–66. A. A. Potebnya, *Iz zapisok po teorii slovesnosti.* 1905. *Problemy poetiki: Sbornik statei.* Ed. V. Bryusov. 1925. V. Ya. Propp, *Morfologiya skazki.* 1928. 2d ed. 1969. (In English: *Morphology of the Folktale.* 2d ed. Rev. and ed. Louis A. Wagner. 1968.) *Sbornik statei: Akademicheskie shkoly v russkom literaturovedenii.* 1975. *Sborniki po teorii poeticheskogo yazyka* (OPOYaZ). Fasc. 1–2 (1916–17), fasc. 3 (1919), fasc. 4–6 (1921–23). *Sēmeiōtikē: Trudy po znakovym sistemam.* Vols. 1–12. Tartu, 1964–81. B. V. Tomashevskii, *Poetika.* 1931. Yu. N. Tynyanov, *Problema stikhotvornogo yazyka.* 1965. (In English: *The Problem of Verse Language.* Ed. and trans. Michael Sosa and Brent Harvey. 1981.) A. N. Veselovskii, *Istoricheskaya poetika.* 1940. V. M. Zhirmunskii, *Teoriya stikha.* 1975. M. A.

Poets' Guild, The (Tsekh poétov), founded in November 1911 by Nikolai Gumilyov and Sergei Gorodetsky, was an active group of primarily third generation modernist poets who gathered twice a month to discuss the poetic practice of its members and help them perfect their craft. According to N. Ya. Mandelshtam, this group broke away from Vyacheslav Ivanov's celebrated Academy of Verse which had been formed for similar purposes because "Ivanov made such a devastating attack on Gumilyov's 'Prodigal Son,' and his tone was so scathing and rude ... that Gumilyov's friends left the Academy of Verse and set up the Poets' Guild in opposition to it. Blok was invited to preside over it, but he quit almost at once. Six members of the Guild formed themselves into the Acmeist group." (*Hope Abandoned*, p. 38).

Members of the Guild included: Gumilyov, Gorodetsky, Mandelshtam, V. I. Narbut, A. A. Akhmatova, M. A. Zenkevich, M. L. Lozinsky, E. Yu. Kuzmina-Karavaeva, G. V. Adamovich, G. I. Ivanov, V. V. Hippius. It also included for a while: M. Kuzmin, F. Sologub, A. Blok. This first Guild lasted until 1914. At the end of 1920, a number of the members of the first Guild joined forces again under the same name and established the second Poets' Guild. They included: Gumilyov, Adamovich, G. Ivanov, Lozinsky, N. Otsup as well as I. Odoevtseva, V. A. Rozhdestvensky, S. E. Neldikhen, K. K. Vaginov, Mandelshtam, and others.

While the first Guild's official organ was the short-lived (1912–13) magazine, GIPERBOREI, "a monthly of poetry and criticism," edited by M. Lozinsky, the majority of the polemics of the Guild members appeared in APOLLON. With the coming of the First World War and the Revolution, Guild meetings ceased. However, its publishing ventures continued until 1918, namely, the three publishing labels, Poets' Guild, Hyperboreus, and Akme.

The second Guild published several almanacs including: a hectograph edition of *Novyi giperborei* (1921), *Drakon* (1921), and *Tsekh poetov* (1921–23; the last four issues were published in Berlin). Books were also published under the label, Poets' Guild from 1912 to 1914 and from 1921 to 1923.

The nucleus of the first Poets' Guild gradually formulated new aesthetic canons with the emphasis on craft, which began as literary polemics against SYMBOLISM and FUTURISM but soon became the source of manifestoes promoting the new literary movement known as ACMEISM.

Bibliography: Tsekh poetov. Berlin, 1922 (Ardis reprint).

J. G. H.

Pogodin, Mikhail Petrovich (1800–75), historian and journalist, was the son of an enserfed steward of Count Saltykov; the entire Pogodin family was manumitted in 1806. Pogodin was educated at the First Moscow Gymnasium and Moscow University, his principal intellectual interests being philology, literature, archaeology, and especially early Russian history. He defended his Master's dissertation in 1825 ("On the Origins of Rus'") and published his doctoral dissertation on Nestor and his contribution to the Primary Chronicle in 1834. In 1826 Pogodin became a professor of history at Moscow University; for the next nine years he taught primarily "universal history." In 1835 he received a chair in Russian history, which he occupied for nine years.

Pogodin's most important historical work relates largely to the earliest period of Russian history and dates principally from the first twenty years of his academic career. His seven-volume *Studies, Lectures and Remarks* contains much of this work. His early *Historical Aphorisms* already suggests the extent of his romantic historicism and Russian exceptionalism. Pogodin was also important as a collector of historical documents, coins, and objets d'art and also for his work in establishing relations with academic specialists on the Slavic world elsewhere in Europe.

Pogodin, together with his friend S. P. SHEVYRYOV, was a leading figure of "Official Nationality," a less romantic and more dynastically oriented current of romantic conservatism than SLAVOPHILISM, and a founding father of Panslavism. He edited MOSKOVSKII VESTNIK (1827–30) and MOSKVITYANIN (1841–56), in the latter journal polemicizing vigorously with BELINSKY's literary WESTERNISM and the historical theories of S. M. Solovyov and K. D. Kavelin. Pogodin died in 1875, his best historical work well behind him, excoriated by his enemies for pedantry, tactlessness, and avarice, but respected by Russians of a conservative bent, and by scholars and politicians concerned with questions of Slavdom in Russia and Europe.

Works: Issledovaniya, zamechaniya i lektsii M. Pogodina o russkoi istorii. 7 vols. 1846–54.

Secondary literature: N. P. Barsukov, *Zhizn' i trudy M. P. Pogodina.* 22 vols. 1888–1910. N. Riasanovsky, *Nicholas I und Official Nationality in Russia, 1825–1855.* 1961. ———, "Pogodin and Shevyrev in Russian Intellectual History," *Harvard Slavic Studies* 4 (1957), pp. 149–67. Edward Thaden, *Conservative Nationalism in Nineteenth-Century Russia.* 1964. Irene Zohrab, "'The Slavophiles' by M. P. Pogodin. An Introduction and Translation," *New Zealand Slavonic Journal*, 1982, pp. 29–87.

A. G.

Pogorelsky, Antony, see PEROVSKY.

Pogovorka, "saying" (pl. *pogovorki*). The Russian *pogovorka* is related to the PROVERB (*poslovitsa*), but the *pogovorka* is less than a complete sentence and the thought is often left implied or otherwise incomplete. Like proverbs, *pogovorki* often contain an element of moral advice, but the focus is vaguer because of the incomplete syntax. Proverbs are usually syntactically bipartite, while *pogovorki* are invariably monopartite (and hence usually unrhymed), while proverbs are often rhymed). In practice, however, *pogovorki* may

acquire a bipartite form and thus become proverbs: "measuring the wind" is a *pogovorka*, while "measuring the wind will spoil the weather" is a proverb. Note that the single phrase of the *pogovorka* normally corresponds to the first, or figurative part of the proverb.

Like proverbs, *pogovorki* are often metaphorical in their range of application. In the example, "kill two hares" (cf. "kill two birds with one stone"), the *pogovorka* would scarcely if ever be applied to the activity of hunting hares. The imagery and concerns of *pogovorki* are generally the same as those of proverbs, and their frequent use in modern Russian speech tends to give it a stylized, folksy character.

Bibliography: A. M. Novikova and A. M. Kokoreva. *Russkoe narodnoe poeticheskoe tvorchestvo.* 1969. Pp. 119–39.

W. E. H.

Polar Star, see POLYARNAYA ZVEZDA.

Polevoi (journalistic pseud.; family name Kampov), Boris Nikolaevich (1908–81), writer, was born in Moscow, where his father was a lawyer. His family moved in 1913 to Tver (now Kalinin). Polevoi graduated from a technical institute. From 1928 to World War II he wrote for local newspapers. His first work of fiction, *The Hot Shop* (1939), dealt with the creativity of factory workers who adopted socialist labor practices. From 1941 to 1945 he served as a war correspondent for *Pravda*. Much of his fiction derives from his wartime experience. His best-known novel is *A Story about a Real Man* (1946), a true-to-life story about a Soviet aviator shot down by the Nazis. When the aviator's legs had to be amputated, he painfully retrained himself and became a famous combat pilot. The novel won a Stalin Prize and is regarded as a classic of SOCIALIST REALISM. Sergei Prokofiev composed an opera about it in 1948. Polevoi's other war novels and stories are *We Are Soviet People* (1948), *Gold* (1950), *Far Back on the Home Front* (1958), and *Doctor Vera* (1966). His short-story collection *Contemporaries* (1952) extolled the builders of the Volga-Don Canal; and in 1962 he published *On the Wild Shore*, about the construction of a hydroelectric plant. He wrote two shorter works, *Silhouettes* (1974) and *Anyuta* (1977).

Polevoi's fiction clearly shows its journalistic origin. He prided himself on drawing his characters and subject matter directly from Soviet life. His style is journalistic. His heroes are inspired by socialism to perform remarkable feats in peace and war. Although his characters act predictably and lack psychological depth, the action is always gripping and the setting—nature, a factory, air combat—is vividly realistic.

Polevoi was a Party member from 1940, the editor of the magazine *Yunost'* from 1962 until his death, and secretary of the Writers Union of the USSR from 1967. He received many awards.

Works: Samye blizkie. Izbrannye rasskazy. 1961. *Izbrannye proizvedeniya.* 2 vols. Introd. B. Galanov. 1969.

Translations: See Lewanski, pp. 325–26.

Secondary literature: Edward J. Brown, *Russian Literature since the Revolution.* 1982. Pp. 223–25. B. Galanov, *Boris Polevoi. Kritiko-biograficheskii ocherk.* 1957. N. Zheleznova, *Nastoyashchie lyudi Borisa Polevogo.* 1978.

H. S.

Polevoi, Nikolai Alekseevich (1796–1846), journalist, critic, dramatist, and historian. Born in Irkutsk the son of a merchant, Polevoi received no formal education. Although he began publishing as early as 1817, he only became prominent in literary circles after he moved to Moscow in 1820. From 1825 until 1834 he published (along with his brother, the minor critic Ksenofont) the MOSKOVSKII TELEGRAF; as one of the first Russian non-gentry ideologists, he criticized the nobility, lauded the virtues of the merchantry, and strongly defended the tenets of the new romanticism. Of special interest are the polemics between Polevoi's journal and VESTNIK EVROPY (founded by KARAMZIN), then edited by M. T. Kachenovsky, a spokesman for classicist and conservative positions. Polevoi's liberal views in general and, in particular, his critical review of a chauvinistic play by Nestor KUKOLNIK resulted in the closing of his journal in 1834. A year earlier Polevoi had completed his controversial *History of the Russian People* (begun in 1829) which was written as a refutation of Karamzin's *History of the Russian State* (1818). Called by SVYATOPOLK-MIRSKY a "sciolistic and pretentious" work, Polevoi's *History* (parodied by PUSHKIN in his posthumous *History of the Manor of*

Goryukhino) led to more polemics with such journals as SEVERNYE TSVETY. In 1834 Polevoi moved both to the right and to St. Petersburg where he wrote for *Syn otechestva* and SEVERNAYA PCHELA. He was also the author of some sentimental melodramas and did a prose translation of *Hamlet* which was produced in Moscow in 1837 with the famous actor Mochalov in the title role.

Works: Sochineniya. 1903.
Secondary literature: V. E. Evgen'ev-Maksimov and V. G. Berezina, *N. A. Polevoi: Ocherk zhizni i deyatel'nosti.* Irkutsk, 1947. V. I. Kuleshov, *Istoriya russkoi kritiki.* 1972.   R. H. S.

Polezháev, Aleksándr Ivánovich (1804– or 1805–38), poet; an illegitimate son of L. Struisky, a rich landowner, and Agrafena, his servant girl, who was married to a district clerk named Polezhaev after the child's birth. A deprived child in his parents' home, Polezhaev was educated at a boarding school and then at Moscow University. His first poem, "Infidelity," was published in VESTNIK EVROPY in 1825. In 1826, influenced by the first chapter of PUSHKIN's *Eugene Onegin*, Polezhaev wrote a parodic imitation of it, *Sashka.* A freethinking and frivolous burlesque, *Sashka* was not destined for publication and circulated as a piece of hand-written literature. Informed of Polezhaev's writings, Nicholas I subjected Polezhaev to forced conscription and prohibited his promotion from the ranks. Polezhaev was sent to the Caucasus. In 1837 he escaped his regiment, was arrested, and died in an army hospital from tuberculosis.

Polezhaev's poems carry an imprint of Byronic romanticism. Their romantic gloominess is complemented by civic satire, philosophical and political nonconformism ("Funeral," "Chains," "Doom"). As A. GRIGORIEV noted, a Byronic poet of civic romanticism, Polezhaev was a poetic forerunner of LERMONTOV, who knew Polezhaev's works well and created his own poem *Sashka* as a poetic reply to Polezhaev's. Polezhaev sprinkles his works with quotations from the romantic poems of ZHUKOVSKY, Pushkin, and BARATYNSKY. ("The Song of the Captured Iroquois," "The Condemned," "Providence"). He creates an ambivalent image of the Caucasus, a romantic abode of free people and an area of routine garrison life.

Some of Polezhaev's works were published during his lifetime by N. Ketcher in 1832 (introduction written by BELINSKY). The posthumous editions of 1842 and 1857 were distorted by censorship, but many of his works were published by HERZEN and OGARYOV in *Vol'naya russkaya pechat'* in 1861. The Soviet edition of Polezhaev's *Complete Works* was compiled from archival sources. An essential part of his poetic heritage was found in the files of the Secret Police having been submitted there by an informer, Shervud (who also spied on the DECEMBRISTS). Polezhaev's real life and the interpretation he gave to it in his lyrics transformed him into a reverential figure for 19th-century Russian readers. As such he exemplified the tragic existence of a gifted personality destroyed by the tyrannical regime and by the tormenting conflicts of his own character.

Works: Polnoe sobranie stikhotvorenii. 1939. *Stikhotvoreniya i poemy.* 1957 (earlier editions included in bibliography).
Translations: "Song of the Captive Iroquois." In *Russian Poems*, trans. Charles Fillingham Coxwell (1929).
Secondary literature: V. G. Belinskii, "Stikhotvoreniya Polezhaeva" (1842), *PSS*, Vol. 6, pp. 119–60. A. I. Gertsen, In *PSS*, Vol. 8, pp. 165–68. N. Ogarev, *Izbrannye sotsial'no-politicheskie i filosofskie proizvedeniya* (1952), Vol. 1, pp. 447–49. I. D. Voronin, *A. I. Polezhaev; Zhizn' i tvorchestvo.* 2d rev. ed. 1979.   N. P.

Polish influence in Russian literature has three major components: (1) the impact of Polish Renaissance and baroque literature on the development of Russian syllabic poetry and drama in the 17th century; (2) Poles who became writers in Russian; and (3) Polish themes in Russian literature. (1) When scholars of the KIEV ACADEMY were invited to Moscow they brought with them a knowledge of 16th- and 17th-century Polish literature acquired during their stay at the Academy. The most outstanding of the Kievans were SIMEON POLOTSKY (1629–80), Daniil Tuptalo (St. Dimitry Rostovsky, 1651–1709, Metropolitan of Rostov), Stefan YAVORSKY (1658–1722), and Feofan PROKOPOVICH (1681–1736), Archbishop of Novgorod. The syllabic verse written by Polotsky, Yavorsky, and Prokopovich introduced the Polish metric system into Russia, while

the verse plays of Polotsky and Tuptalo laid the foundation of a Russian tradition of school drama. The most thoroughgoing baroque writer of 17th-century Russia was the Pole Jan Białobocki who wrote a Russian syllabic verse *Pentateugum* under the name of Andrei Belobotsky. A typical baroque celebration of death and the hereafter, the work is much indebted to German influence.

(2) Poles who made literary careers in Russian became more common during the period when Poland was partitioned between Austria, Prussia, and Russia (1795–1919). In the first half of the 19th century the most prominent Poles writing in Russian were Tadeusz Bułharyn (BULGARIN, 1789–1859), a deserter from Napoleon's army who became a Russian police agent and an ultrareactionary journalist, and Józef-Julian Sękowski (Osip SENKOVSKY, 1800–58), a well-trained Orientalist who began editing the famous BIBLIOTEKA DLYA CHTENIYA (Library for Reading) in 1834 and wrote under the pen name of Baron Brambeus (whose literary achievement Khlestakov takes credit for in GOGOL's play *The Inspector-General*). In the second half of the 19th century the principal writers of Polish or mixed Polish-Russian origin were Bolesław Markiewicz (Markevich), a once popular but now little-remembered writer of conservative stamp, and Vladimir KOROLENKO (1853–1921), an important literary figure best known for his stories with Siberian settings.

(3) In the modern period, Polish themes in Russian literature begin with the romantic period and have two general, though not exclusive, foci: the Polish insurrections of November 1830 and January 1863. Although direct Polish literary influence on the Russian is not extensive and in any case difficult to determine, one clear-cut case is the collection of patriotic and historical *Dumy* (Meditations, 1821–23) by the Decembrist poet Kondraty RYLEEV (1795–1826), which recall the similar, and earlier, *Dumy* by the Polish writer Julian Ursyn Niemcewicz (1758–1841). During his five-year exile in Russia from 1824 to 1829, the outstanding Polish romantic poet and dramatist Adam Mickiewicz (1798–1855) was warmly received by the Russian literary community, including Ryleev, the poet Ivan KOZLOV (1779–1840), and Prince Pyotr VYAZEMSKY (1792–1878) who became his first translators into Russian. Mickiewicz also made friends with PUSHKIN, but the November Insurrection of 1830 found them on opposite sides of the political fence. Pushkin's patriotic defense of the suppression of the uprising in 1831, the poem "To the Detractors of Russia," was answered in Mickiewicz's concluding poem to his romantic drama *Forefathers' Eve, Part III* (1832), in which Pushkin, unnamed, is accused of political toadying. The January Insurrection of 1863 evoked a sympathetic response among members of the Russian liberal intelligentsia. Aleksandr HERZEN (1812–70) openly espoused the Polish cause in the years 1861 to 1863, especially in his famous letter to the French historian Michelet, "The Russian People and Socialism," and in his essay "The Poles Forgive Us," while Korolenko's autobiographical *The History of My Contemporary* (the first part of which appeared in 1910 and the rest posthumously in 1922) contains vivid impressions of the predominantly Polish Volhynian region from which he came as well as of the Insurrection of 1863. In the 20th century, both before and after the reconstitution of an independent Polish state, Poles continued to make contributions to Russian literature. The major poet Bolesław Leśmian (1878–1937) in his younger years wrote poems in Russian which were published in the well-known symbolist journals *Zolotoe runo* (1906), *Vesy* (1907), and *Pereval* (1907). Stanisław Przybyszewski (1868–1927), one of the most widely translated writers of the Young Poland period, was highly regarded in Russia as the author of such typical fin de siècle works as the novel *Satan's Children* (originally published in German in 1897; Polish version, 1899) and the play *Snow* (1903). In the Soviet period, the best known Russian writer of Polish origin is Bruno Jasieński (Yasensky, 1901–41). An ardent Communist, Jasieński in 1925 emigrated to France where he was politically active. In 1927, for example, he organized in Paris a workers' theater made up primarily of Polish emigrants. Difficulty with the French authorities over his activities resulted in his expulsion from France in 1929. The Germans were no more hospitable and he finally took refuge in the USSR. His principal works in Russian are two novels: *I Burn Paris* (Ya zhgu Parizh, 1928), which he wrote originally in Polish while in France in reply to Paul Moran's anti-Soviet *Je brûle Moscou*, and *A Man Changes His Skin* (Chelovek menyaet kozhu), about socialist construction in Tadzhikistan

and published in the journal *Novyi mir* in 1932–33. Jasieński was also the author of a satirical anti-capitalist fantasy play, *The Mannequins' Ball* (Bal manekenov, 1931), which was never staged (apart from a Polish television production in 1980) and is not well known.

H. B. S.

Polónskaya, Elizavéta Grigórievna (1890–1969), poet. Born in Warsaw, Polonskaya attended school in St. Petersburg and studied medicine at the Sorbonne in Paris. She practiced medicine until 1931 and again during World War II. Polonskaya began her career as a poet under the guidance of GUMILYOV and CHUKOVSKY, publishing her first collection, *Banners* (Znamen'ya) in 1921. Subsequently she joined the SERAPION BROTHERHOOD and like some other poets of the avant-garde wrote a great deal of verse and prose for children (eleven children's books between 1923 and 1933). Having decided to become a professional writer in 1931, Polonskaya did a great deal of travelling as a roving correspondent for *Leningradskaya Pravda*, conveying her impressions not only in publicistic prose but in several volumes of poetry as well. She generally wrote public-spirited "occasional poetry," responding to political developments as well as to events of day-to-day living which she had witnessed. Her poetic style is clear and simple, approaching prose. But it is thoughtful and dignified. Polonskaya also published some stories and important memoirs and was a prolific translator from many languages.

Works: Izbrannye stikhi. 1935. *Stikhotvoreniya i poema.* 1960. *Izbrannoe.* 1966.

V. T.

Polónsky, Vyacheslav Pávlovich (real name: Gúsin, 1886–1932). A critic, editor, and historian of literature whose published work is a rich factual resource for the period of the twenties in Soviet literature. Polonsky was also important as an editor of two major literary journals, PECHAT' I REVOLYUTSIYA, from 1921 to 1929, and NOVYI MIR from 1926 to 1931. As a theoretician and critic of literature Polonsky opposed the narrow sectarianism of certain proletarian leaders and he defended and supported the work of non-communist and non-proletarian writers. His *Sketches of the Literary Movement of the Revolutionary Period* (Ocherki literaturnogo dvizheniya revolyutsionnoi epokhi, 1928) is a reasonably objective guide to the literature of the twenties, though written from a purely Marxist viewpoint. His essays on contemporary writers offer useful critical analyses and portraits of OLESHA, BABEL, FADEEV and PILNYAK, among others. Like VORONSKY and many others he rejected the theory of the "social demand" originated and propagated by the LEF group, and he held MAYAKOVSKY's publicistic poetry in low esteem. He was a specialist on BAKUNIN and published important works on his life and thought.

Works: Na literaturnye temy. 1968. *Ocherki literaturnogo dvizheniya revolyutsionnoi epokhi.* 1928. *O sovremennoi literature.* 1928; 3d. ed. 1930. *Bakunin.* 1922. *Materialy dlya biografii Bakunina.* 3 vols. 1923–33.

E. J. B.

Polónsky, Yákov Petróvich (1819–98), poet. Born into the Russian nobility, Polonsky attended Ryazan high school, later studied law at Moscow University, and served for four years in the office of the Tsar's governor general in Tiflis. In 1851, he came to St. Petersburg. Originally forced to earn his living by occasional work (literary honoraria, private lessons), he later became the editor of RUSSKOE SLOVO from 1858 to 1859, junior censor on the Committee of Foreign Censorship, and finally a member of the Council for the Administration of the Press.

As a Russian poet during the interval between the death of PUSHKIN (1837) and the revival of an aesthetic receptiveness in Russia forty years later, Polonsky published his collections of verse, *Scales* (Gammy, 1844) and *The Singer* (Sazandar [the Georgian word for "singer"], 1849) to limited critical applause. BELINSKY, DOBROLYUBOV and SALTYKOV-SHCHEDRIN berated him severely for the aesthetic emphasis and lack of civic-mindedness in his poetry. Polonsky tried to preserve his independence and made his place in Russian literary history as a poet of very fine and sensitive love lyrics: "Meeting" (Vstrecha, 1844), "The Woman Recluse" (Zatvornitsa, 1846), "Little Bell" (Kolokol'chik, 1854), and of poems evoking man's unfulfilled longing for peace and search for transcendence:

"Winter Path" (Zimnii put', 1844), "Night" (Noch', 1850). He is also the author of verse tales and novels which are less significant.

Works: Polnoe sobranie stikhotvorenii. 5 vols. 1896. *Stikhotvoreniya* 1954.

Secondary literature: B. M. Eikhenbaum, "Ya. P. Polonskii." In *Stikhotvoreniya.* 1954. Pp. 5–39. A. Lagunov, *Lirika Yakova Polonskogo.* 1974.

J. B.

Pólotsky, see SIMEON POLOTSKY.

Polyárnaya zvezdá (Polar Star), literary almanacs of two periods. (1) 1823–25 in three annual issues. The manuscript of a final *Little Star for 1826 (Zvezdochka)* was confiscated after the revolt of 14 December 1825. *Polyarnaya zvezda* was the platform of the romantics of the civic-Decembrist trend, edited by A. A. BESTUZHEV and K. F. RYLEEV, leaning to political poetry and prose in the ideal of civic Rome. Each issue was prefaced by a "Glance" (*vzglyad*) at Russian literature, written by Bestuzhev, the first a survey of the history of Russian literature through 1823, the others surveys of the years 1824 and 1825. The "Glances" were sociopolitical manifestos which championed national originality and independence from the French language, liberation from "servile" neoclassical imitation. The editors were not *comme il faut* among the literary aristocrats of the Pushkin pleiad, but attracted some of the best works by PUSHKIN, VYAZEMSKY, ZHUKOVSKY, GRIBOEDOV, BARATYNSKY, and others before being faced with competition from the pleiad's literary almanac SEVERNYE TSVETY in 1825. Bestuzhev's early romantic prose tales and Ryleev's *dumy* or political meditations on historical figures were featured, as were works by the literary plebeians N. I. GRECH, F. V. BULGARIN, and O. I. SENKOVSKY.

(2) literary and sociopolitical almanac published annually abroad from 1855 to 1862 in London and 1869 in Geneva by A. I. HERZEN and N. P. OGARYOV. The almanac's cover featured profiles of the five hanged Decembrists to show its origins in revolutionary tradition. It published suppressed poems of Pushkin, Ryleev, and LERMONTOV, BELINSKY's "Letter to Gogol," and writings of P. Ya. CHAADAEV. The new *Polyarnaya zvezda* was especially valuable for its publication of the memoirs of the Decembrists M. A. and N. A. Bestuzhev, M. S. Lunin, I. I. Pushchin, and others.

Readings: V. G. Bazanov, *Ocherki dekabristskoi literatury: publitsistika, proza, kritika.* 1953.

L. G. L.

Pomerántsev, Vladimir Mikhailovich (1907–7?), writer and critic. Pomerantsev became famous for an essay published in *Novyi mir* just after Stalin's death. Entitled "On Sincerity in Literature," the article was an attack on post-war Soviet literature for "varnishing reality" and avoiding politically distasteful topics. The article attracted broad attention, and Aleksandr TVARDOVSKY was fired from his position as chief editor of the journal (although he was subsequently reinstated).

Pomerantsev's first novel *The Used-Book Seller's Daughter* (Doch' bukinista) was first published in 1951 and was devoted to the conflict of ideas in post-war Germany. Pomerantsev also authored a number of short stories and novelettes, many of which were severely critical of Soviet life. His collection *House of Topics* (Dom syuzhetov) was originally passed by the censor and then forbidden while the book was in press. The printing plates were destroyed, and the book never appeared. Pomerantsev reportedly suffered a fatal heart attack when he was informed by telephone of the decision.

Works: "Ob iskrennosti v literature," *Novyi mir*, 1953, no. 12. *Doch' bukinista.* 1951. *Dom syuzhetov, Moskva*, 1965, no. 9.

J. G.

Pomyalóvsky, Nikolaí Gerásimovich (1835–63), writer. Pomyalovsky's is among the most characteristic lives of the literary generation of the 1860s. Born on the outskirts of St. Petersburg, the son of a Deacon, he received his early education at an ecclesiastical school, a Russian version of Dickens's Dotheboys Hall, which he later described in his *Seminary Sketches* (Ocherki bursy). Before long he rejected religious doctrine for the apparent certainties of materialist philosophy. In addition, although he had never been a good student, and lived only on the fringes of St. Petersburg University, he was interested in guiding others in enlightened ways, and his finest literary hero, Molotov, is a teacher.

His brief literary career opened in early 1861, when his novelette *Bourgeois Happiness* (Meshchanskoe schast'e) appeared in So-VREMENNIK, the leading radical literary journal. Later that same year he published his best-known work, *Molotov*. Molotov is the typical frustrated young idealist of the 1860s, and the story has to do with the conflict engendered by a love freely bestowed on him by the heroine, Nádya Dorogova, whose family expects her to move in much more conventional channels. Another major theme of the work is that of the sturdy independence of the individual from the institutions of his society. Superficially the story ends on a happy note, for Nadya and Molotov win through to "bourgeois happiness."

Despite the literary reputation which 1861 brought him (TURGENEV thought quite highly of his abilities), Pomyalovsky became addicted to alcohol and low companions. Only occasionally did he take hold and write something new before the consequences of his dissolute life led to his death in 1863, at the age of 28. Others of his generation believed that his life was emblematic of their time.

Works: Polnoe sobranie sochinenii. 2 vols. 1935.

Translations: Seminary Sketches. Trans. Alfred Kuhn. 1973.

Secondary literature: Rose Glickman, "An Alternative View of the Peasantry: The 'Raznochintsy' Writers of the 1860s," *SlavR*, 32 (1973), pp. 693–704. Isaak Yampol'skii, *N. G. Pomyalovskii: Lichnost' i tvorchestvo.* 1968.

C. A. M.

Poplávsky, Borís Yuliánovich (1903–35), émigré poet and writer. Poplavsky's poetry and fiction caused a sensation in the literary circles of Paris. His apocalyptic, delirious visions of perishing Europe and his grotesque portrayals of a new, huge, and doomed Babylon—clamorous Paris—impressed many Russian readers. A mystic immersed in the works of St. Thérèse and Jacob Boehme, Poplavsky was also influenced by Baudelaire, Nerval, Rimbaud, Laforgue, Apollinaire, and Breton. Poplavsky was an innovative poet: he enriched the Russian poetic vocabulary, freed the language from its habitual associations, disrupted logical ties and sequences, and introduced new, bold, and unexpected metaphors. Freedom and eccentricity—the two most characteristic traits of Poplavsky's poetry—led him to use airy and shining imagery. He was fond of surrealistic, bizarre images reminiscent of hallucinations. There is much music in his verse, which captivated his audience with its inimitable air of magic and with its sheer melodiousness. His craftsmanship, however, was deficient in many respects—monotonous rhythms, slipshod style, vulgarisms, awkward rhymes, and occasionally poor word choice. In this, Poplavsky's poetry resembles Igor SEVERYANIN's and Konstantin FOFANOV's, with their *Effekthascherei.* There are also echoes of MAYAKOVSKY in his verse, but Poplavsky considered himself much rather an heir to BLOK's mystical poetry, to the verse of LERMONTOV and PUSHKIN, and to the prose of ROZANOV and DOSTOEVSKY. His prose, lyrical and musical, abounds in unique observations and appropriate poetic vocabulary. Conveying a mood of profound and hopeless loneliness, it has greater expressiveness and artistry than his verse.

Works: (Verse collections:) *Flagi: stikhotvoreniya.* 1931. *Snezhnyi chas: stikhi 1931–1935.* 1936. *V venke iz voska: Chetvertaya kniga stikhov.* 1938. *Dirizhabl' neizvestnogo napravleniya: Stikhi 1924–1935.* 1965. (Novel:) *Apollon Bezobrazov,* published in *Chisla,* nos. 2–3 (1930), no. 5 (1931); *Opyty,* no. 1 (1953), no. 5 (1955), no. 6 (1956). Poplavsky contributed to *Krug, Vstrechi, Volya Rossii, Zveno, Sovremennye zapiski, Vozrozhdenie, Mosty, Grani,* and to the anthologies of émigré poetry *Na zapade, Yakor',* and *Muza diaspory, 1929–1960.* (Collected works:) *Sobranie sochinenii.* Ed. S. Karlinsky and A. Olcott. 3 vols. Berkeley, 1980–81.

Translations: Seven poems, *TriQuarterly,* no. 28 (1973), pp. 320–26. Two poems. In *Modern Russian Poetry.* Ed. Vladimir Markov and Merrill Sparks. 1967. Pp. 460–65. "Another Planet." In *Russian Poetry: The Modern Period.* Ed. John Glad and Daniel Weissbort. 1978. Pp. 153–54.

Secondary literature: Georgii Adamovich, "Literaturnye besedy," *Zveno,* no. 4 (Paris, 1928). Simon Karlinsky, "In Search of Poplavsky: A Collage," *TriQuarterly* 28 (1973), pp. 342–64. Anthony Olcott, "Poplavsky: The Heir Presumptive of Montpar-

nasse," *TriQuarterly* 28 (1973), pp. 305–19. Temira Pachmuss, *A Russian Cultural Revival.* 1981. Pp. 296–311. E. Rais, "O Borise Poplavskom (1903–1935)," *Grani* 114 (1979), pp. 156–84.

T. A. P.

Popóv, Mikhaíl Ivánovich (1742–90), poet, writer, and playwright. An actor with the court theater under Empress Elizabeth, Popov later attended Moscow University, worked as a secretary for Catherine II's Legislative Commission, and contributed some pieces to the satirical journals of the 1760s. His literary activities are characterized by a tendency toward elements of popular culture. Popov's "Songs, Composed by Mikhailo Popov" (1765) became the first Russian songbook printed under an author's name. He then participated in the publication of Mikhail CHULKOV's "Collection of Russian Songs" (Sobranie russkikh pesen, 1770–74). Popov also wrote elegies, parables, epigraphs, and made translations from the French. He produced a three-volume adventure novel, *Slavonic Antiquities* (Slavenskie drevnosti, 1770–71, 4th ed. 1794), and wrote the text of the first Russian comic opera, *Anyuta* (1772). (The music was by Evstignei Fomin.)

Works: Dosugi, ili Sobranie sochinenii i perevodov. 2 vols. 1772. (Poetry:) *Poety XVIII v.* Vol. 1. 1958.

Secondary literature: P. N. Berkov, *Russkaya komediya i komicheskaya opera XVIII v.* 1950. V. E. Gusev, "Mikhailo Popov—poet-pesennik." In *Rol' i znachenie literatury XVIII v. v istorii russkoi kul'tury.* 1966.

V. T.

Populism. Use of the term, *narodnichestvo,* translated as "populism," seems to have entered the Russian political vocabulary only in 1878 and to have become the standard label for the agrarian socialist movement in general during the ideological debates with the Marxists in the 1890s. The core of ideas common to the populists, *narodniki,* dated back to Aleksandr HERZEN and were predominant among the radical intelligentsia of the 1860s, 1870s, and 1880s. Only during the 1890s did Marxism emerge as a powerful contender, but populist principles continued to be widely influential and were basic to the platform of the Socialist Revolutionary Party, organized in 1902.

While the ideologues of the movement were deeply influenced by the ideas of West European philosophers and socialists, they asserted that Russia, due to its backwardness, could pursue a unique path of socio economic development. The key initial thinker of the movement was Herzen. Reacting to the failure of West European liberals in 1848 and influenced by the early French socialists, he condemned bourgeois-capitalist society and sought to have Russia skip that stage of development by entering directly into the stage of socialism. Idealizing the communal principles he believed still survived in the village *mir* as a basis for the construction of a new, just socioeconomic order based on self-governing communes, he called upon the radical intelligentsia to go to the peasants with this program which he thought the countryside would welcome. Vissarion BE-LINSKY in his literary criticism promoted the idea that it was the moral duty of the intelligentsia to bring about social change in Russia and introduced the ideas of many Western thinkers to his readers. Typically, both Herzen and Belinsky stressed the significance of the individual as a moving force in history. Nikolai CHERNYSHEVSKY, putting a heavy emphasis on the scientific study of society, preached a crude economic determinism and in detailed, realistic articles explored the operation of the *mir.* In his didactic novel, *What is to be Done?* (1863), he provided for young radicals a model of how a dedicated revolutionary should conduct his life. Pyotr LAVROV and Nikolai MIKHAILOVSKY in their "subjective sociology" developed what they regarded as a scientific system for the analysis of society. Continuing their predecessors' equating of progress with socialism, they both saw a central role for "critically thinking individuals" in inducing change in desired directions. Lavrov in his *Historical Letters* (1868) and Mikhailovsky in "What is Progress?" (1869–70) stressed the profound moral responsibility of the intelligentsia to engage in action to improve the life of the peasantry who through the centuries had been exploited to support the intellectual development of a small percentage of the population. While recognizing Marxism as valid for the analysis of West European capitalist society, they did not believe it applied to backward, predominantly rural Russia. In contrast to Marx, both Lavrov and Mikhailovsky did not accept the idea that all phenomena could be analyzed by the objec-

Posrédnik

tive methods of natural science, but rather insisted that a "subjective" method also had to be used to study the more complex, higher social sciences. Both defined the term "worker" broadly enough to include all toilers, both in countryside and town. Mikhailovsky in particular condemned both German metaphysics and classical economics, the two bases of Marxism. He did not believe that the German philosopher had discovered immutable laws of history.

As in the case of any broad ideological movement, there developed sharp differences on the pragmatic problems of realizing these goals. At least initially, most proponents of populism were *apolitical*, i.e., subordinated political goals to socioeconomic change for they believed that once the base was changed, the political system would become "just" and "free." Those advocating ideas of a Jacobin takeover of the state by an elite, e.g. Nechaev and TKACHEV, were broadly repudiated by the overwhelming majority of populists who believed the masses should determine their fate. BAKUNIN, particularly from 1872 to 1874, inspired many young populists, who participated in the "Going to the People" movement with his fervent belief that a few agitators could set off a spark of revolt that would initiate a spontaneous, primitive, mass uprising which would overthrow the hated institutions of the ruling class. After this success, the people would build a new life on the basis of their communal institutions. By 1875, blind faith in the immediate revolutionary potential of the peasant masses and the fragility of government institutions was thoroughly destroyed. Other radical youth, followers of Lavrov, were known as propagandists and advocated a slower process of going to the country to educate a cadre of peasantry in the ideas of socialism and revolution. Only after indoctrination of adequate numbers could a revolution be successful. During the "Going to the People," both groups had very little success in penetrating peasant communities. Harsh reality taught the revolutionaries that the repressive powers of the police made it virtually impossible to conduct sustained ideological work anywhere in the Empire. Relying primarily on individual terror against high officials and the ruler to gain by blackmail at least minimal political concessions, they succeeded in assassinating Emperor Alexander II in March 1881. This act provoked a strong reaction against any such concessions by the new Emperor. With the broad support of society, the organized movement was suppressed by the mid-1880s with the tradition of opposition being carried on only by isolated circles and émigrés. Most populists retreated to "small deeds" during the remainder of the 1880s and 1890s, although "Legal Populists," led by Mikhailovsky, worked to keep the broader goals of the movement in view.

During this period, the revolutionary movement grew from isolated circles numbering a few dozen members to a movement with hundreds of associates in a number of cities. The continuous underground movement with its professional "illegals" dates back to the mid-1870s when the techniques of tight conspiratorial organization were developed as a necessity for survival. Out of the Chaikovsky Circle formed in St. Petersburg in 1869 emerged a number of individuals who would play a continuous role in the movement during this whole period. Their contacts with circles in other cities, initially for the purpose of distributing radical literature, was evidence of the extent to which populist ideas were shared by radical students. Carried away by idealism, nearly 2,000 young people participated in the "Going to the People" movement during the summers of 1873 and 1874. By 1875, the movement and the Chaikovsky Circle had been decimated by police action. The survivors regrouped in the second *Zemlya i volya* (Land and Liberty) formed in 1876 and within two years had again established centers in a number of provincial towns. Severely harassed by the police, the more activist element decided it was time to pursue political objectives, by force if necessary. In 1879, the organization split into two parties, the short-lived *Chernyi peredel* (Black Partition) led by PLEKHANOV and other propagandists and *Narodnaya volya* (The People's Will) which pursued gaining political concessions with its activity more and more centered on planning terrorist acts. After the assassination of the Emperor in 1881, only isolated circles remained sporadically active through the 1880s and 1890s.

The underground and émigré presses of the movement were regarded as particularly important by revolutionary leaders as a significant direct challenge to the omnipotence of the regime as well as an important means to develop ideological unity among opponents of the government. The success of Herzen's KOLOKOL in influencing events within the Empire on the eve of Emancipation provided a model for such journalistic activity. The second *Zemlya i volya* and *Narodnaya volya* succeeded in publishing a number of issues of newspapers bearing their organizations' names. The success of émigré organs varied greatly. For the populist cause, the most important was *Vpered!* edited by Lavrov and published from 1873 to 1876. *Vestnik narodnoi voli* (1883–86) edited by Lavrov and Lev Tikhomirov was designed to keep the organization's spirit alive during the period it was being decimated by the imperial police.

The most successful legal "thick" journals in Russia during the last forty years of the 19th century were those of populist orientation. These include SOVREMENNIK, OTECHESTVENNYE ZAPISKI, and RUSSKOE BOGATSTVO. The book review sections were the most important for they were the means of introducing the reading public to Western thought. Reviews by such individuals as Belinsky, Chernyshevsky, and Mikhailovsky were in effect essays presenting their political viewpoint in AESOPIAN LANGUAGE. In other sections of the journal were serious studies of the Russian economy and peasant life. Economic essays by V. V. Vorontsov and N. P. Danielson (Nikolai-on) and articles on the history of the Russian peasantry by V. I. Semevsky first appeared in journals edited by Mikhailovsky.

Many of the literary figures identified with populism first published their works serially in those "thick" journals. Beginning with Belinsky, the populist critics established a virtual "censorship by the left" which judged a work by whether it was "progressive" and socially useful from their viewpoint. Art for art's sake was rejected as being morally irresponsible in a country where there was so much need for the fundamental reform of institutions to benefit the people. Themes stressing the life of the masses, particularly the peasantry, were predominant. Among the most outstanding authors were N. A. NEKRASOV, M. E. SALTYKOV-SHCHEDRIN, G. I. USPENSKY and N. N. ZLATOVRATSKY.

In the fine arts, the group of painters known as the "wanderers", including I. Repin, were influenced to turn to popular Russian subjects in a remorselessly realistic manner. In music, works by "The Five" of the neo-Russian school, e.g., M. P. Mussorgsky's "Boris Godunov," are cited as representative of the extent of the populist influence on intellectual life.

Bibliography: Alexander Gerschenkron, "Franco Venturi on Populism, A Review Article," *The American Historical Review* 78, no. 4 (Oct. 1973), pp. 969–86. P. S. Itenberg, "Narodnichestvo." In *Sovetskaya istoricheskaya entsiklopediya.* Vol. 9. Columns 922–935. Arthur P. Mendel, *Dilemmas of Progress in Tsarist Russia, Legal Populism.* 1961. Richard Pipes, "Narodnichestvo: A Semantic Inquiry," *SlavR* 23 (1964), pp. 441–58. Franco Venturi, *Roots of Revolution, A History of the Populist and Socialist Movements in Nineteenth Century Russia.* Trans. Francis Haskell. 1960. Alexander Vucinich, *Social Thought in Tsarist Russia, The Quest for a General Science of Society, 1861–1917.* 1976. Richard Wortman, *The Crisis of Russian Populism.* 1967.   J. A. D.

Poslóvitsa, see PROVERB.

Pososhkóv, Iván Tíkhonovich (1652–1726), economist and writer. From humble beginnings, Pososhkov rose to a position of wealth and influence by taking advantage of Peter the Great's mercantile policies. Toward the end of his life he set down the experience which he had gathered in a career which encompassed trade, manufacturing, mining, and finance, in several works the best known of which are *A Fatherly Testament* (Zaveshchanie otecheskoe, 1718) and *On Poverty and Wealth* (O skudosti i bogatstve, 1724), in which he develops a mercantilistic theory of political economy and maps out the tremendous economic potential of Russia. Pososhkov writes a lucid and vigorous Russian. *On Poverty and Wealth* earned Pososhkov no laurels. After the death of Peter the Great (1725) he was arrested and died in prison.

Works: Kniga o skudosti i bogatstve i drugie sochineniya. Ed. and comm. B. B. Kafengauz. 1951.
Translations: Excerpts in Leo Wiener, *Anthology of Russian Literature.* Vol. 1. 1902–03.   V. T.

Posrédnik (The Intermediary) was a publishing house organized to print inexpensive books and distribute them among the masses. Dismayed by the paucity of educational and morally elevating books then available to the popular audience, L. N. Tolstoi and V. G. Chertkov founded *Posrednik* in 1884. The firm was initially managed by Chertkov, with the active assistance of Tolstoi, and later (until 1897) by P. I. Biryukov, another of Tolstoi's associates. *Posrednik* was not the first attempt to improve the quality of the popular prints, but it succeeded where its predecessors had failed by allying itself with I. D. Sytin, one of the most successful purveyors to the popular audience, and making use of his effective network of itinerant peddlers to distribute its wares. Tolstoi himself wrote a number of works (his *Stories for the People*) for *Posrednik* and managed to persuade such other writers as V. M. Garshin, V. G. Korolenko, and A. M. Gorky to contribute as well. Biryukov estimated that at its height (in the 1890s) *Posrednik* distributed some 3,500,000 copies of its publications each year. Besides its own success, *Posrednik* influenced the reading habits of the masses by stimulating efforts similar to its own (nearly fifty such organizations were in operation by the turn of the century) and by causing the established popular publishers to add titles of somewhat higher quality to their traditional stock of adventure stories, romances, books on the interpretation of dreams, and the like. After the revolution of 1917 *Posrednik* devoted itself largely to the publication of children's books. It ceased operations in 1935.

Bibliography: Sorok let sluzheniya lyudyam. 1925. T. Lindstrom, "From Chapbooks to Classics: The Story of the *Intermediary*," *ASEER* 16, no. 2 (1957), pp. 190–201. S. I. Pozoiskii, *Lev Tolstoi—zhurnalist i redaktor.* 1964. [Esp. pp. 131–40.] I. D. Sytin, *Zhizn' dlya knigi.* 1960.

G. J.

Potebnyá, Aleksándr Afanásievich (1835–91), philologist, philosopher of language, and poetic theorist. A professor of Russian philology at Kharkov University from 1875, Potebnya did important work in comparative Slavic grammar, the history of the Russian language, Russian grammar and dialectology, and Russian and Ukrainian folk poetry. Potebnya's theoretical thought received little attention in his lifetime, but led to the emergence of the Kharkov school of literary scholars in the 1890s and 1900s (*see* SCHOLARSHIP).

Works: Mysl' i yazyk (1862). 5th ed. 1926. *Iz lektsii po teorii slovesnosti.* 2d ed. 1930.

Bibliography: O. O. Potebnya, Yubileinyi zbirnyk do 125-richchya z dnya narozhdennya. Kiev, 1962.

Secondary Literature: A. Belyi, "Mysl' i yazyk: Filosofiya yazyka A. A. Potebni," *Logos,* book 2 (1910). V. Khartsiev, "Osnovy poetiki A. A. Potebni." In *Voprosy teorii i psikhologii tvorchestva.* Vol. 2, fasc. 2. 1910. D. N. Ovsyaniko-Kulikovskii, *A. A. Potebnya kak yazykoved-myslitel'.* 1893.

V. T.

Potékhin, Aleksei Antipovich (1829–1908), writer and playwright, was born in Kineshma to impoverished gentry. He studied at the Demidov Lyceum under K. Ushinsky, graduating with a gold medal in 1849. Potekhin displayed an early interest in theater and acting. He served as an official in Kostroma, later supervised an estate. He began writing reviews in the early 1850s, and ethnographic sketches after participating in the Literary Ethnographic Expedition of 1856. His SLAVOPHILE leanings brought him in touch with the "young editorial staff" of the journal MOSKVITYANIN. Soon Potekhin began producing stories, novels, and plays. His plays, which were initially banned for their topical contents, eventually brought him fame. Appointed "artistic director" of the Imperial theaters, he managed dramatic troupes in St. Petersburg and Moscow, and helped to implement some much-needed reforms in the theater (1882–85). In 1900 he was elected an Honorary Academician.

Potekhin's oeuvre draws solely on contemporary Russian life. In his early period (1851–67) peasant themes dominated in his ethnographic sketches, stories, novellas, and novels: "Two Hunters" (Dva okhotnika), *Tit Sofronov Kozonok* (with pre-Tolstoian ideas, such as nonresistance to Evil by force), *Krushinsky,* and *Poor Gentry* (Bednye dvoryane). His novel, *A Peasant Girl* (Krest'yanka), with a peasant heroine brought up like a lady, has a unique dramatic sequel: *Sheepskin Coat—Human Heart* (Shuba ovech'ya—dusha chelovech'ya, 1854), in which the heroine weds a landowner. Devoid of nature, Potekhin's prose fiction characterizes through dialog while poeticizing peasants. They are shown as equals to noblemen in emo-

tions and learning ability, and superiors morally. Potekhin's expertise on the peasantry was applauded by Tolstoi. His plays are tightly structured, never repetitive thematically, marked by Slavophile idealism, proverbial titles, and individualized language. Happy endings are rare: a cruel fate dominates, aided by the power of money, parental egoism, domestic tyranny (*samodurstvo*), and xenophobia. Of the three character dramas, *Tinsel* (Mishura, 1858) is famous for the character of a corrupt official who refines his dubious talents through education. Post-reform relations between landowners and peasants are depicted in the play, *The Cut-Off Piece* (Otrezannyi lomot', 1865). Potekhin's comedies introduce the genre of the picaresque play and feature such themes as superstition among the gentry: *The Most Recent Oracle* (Noveishii orakul). The first to portray incipient peasant proletarization, Potekhin feared it even more than alcoholism: *Around Money* (Okolo deneg, 1876), *In the Village Commune* (Na miru), *Young Shoots* (Molodye pobegi). Recurrent themes are the search for matrimony, unhappy marriage, the gentry's adverse influence on the peasants: *The Sickly Woman* (Khvoraya), whose protagonist cannot survive among her kind. Vestiges of the ethnographic sketch emerge in *Peasant Children* (Krest'yanskie deti) and *Village Usurers* (Derevenskie miroedy). Potekhin is important as a pioneer and anticipator of Ostrovsky, Pisemsky, Dostoevsky, Lev Tolstoi, and Bunin.

Works: Sochineniya. 12 vols. 1903–05.
Secondary literature: S. V. Kastorskii, "Pisatel'-dramaturg A. A. Potekhin." In *Iz istorii russkikh literaturnykh otnoshenii XVIII–XX vekov.* 1959. S. Ketchian, "The Plays of Aleksei Potekhin." Ph. D. diss, Harvard Univ. (1974), unpublished.

S. K.

Póvest', see SHORT STORY.

Póvest' vremennýkh let, see LETOPISI.

Pre-Petrine Literature, see OLD RUSSIAN LITERATURE.

Primary Chronicle, see LETOPISI.

Pribaútka (joke), see PROVERB.

Princes of Vladimir, History of, see SKAZANIE O KNYAZ'YAKH VLADIMIRSKIKH.

Prishvin, Mikhail Mikhailovich (1873–1954), prose writer whose literary career straddles the pre- and post-revolutionary periods. Son of a rich merchant, he was born on his family estate, Khrushchevo, in Russia's North. While a student in Riga, Prishvin was arrested for revolutionary activity. After his release, he studied in Leipzig and in 1902 received a degree in agronomy. Prishvin developed an interest in folklore, linguistics, ethnography, and ornithology and traveled throughout Russia, Central Asia, and the Far East.

During the 1920s he remained independent of all literary groups and preserved his individualistic voice throughout the Stalin era. Although he lived in Moscow in the latter part of his life, he was happiest when in the country—hunting, fishing or just observing.

Prishvin is known primarily as the author of short stories and sketches about the nature and animals of Northern Russia. His first collection was *In the Land of Unfrightened Birds and Animals* (1907). This was followed by *Small, Round Loaf,* about the people of the North, their customs and legends. *The Black Arab* (1910) is based on his observations and experiences while traveling in Kazakhstan. His most important works of the twenties are *Calendar of Nature* (1935) and *The Chain of Kashchei,* an autobiographical novel published serially between 1923 and 1954. It is a collection of fragments and vignettes depicting 19th-century life in rural Northern Russia.

Prishvin's works of the 1940s and 1950s include *The Sun's Storehouse* (1945), which describes the Russian swamp lands and peat, their "hidden treasure." Significantly, only one sentence mentions World War II. *The Tsar's Road* (1957) describes the changes brought about by Peter the Great in the Far North. It focuses on a significant event of Peter's reign, the dragging overland of Peter's newly built fleet from the White Sea to the Baltic Sea. Prishvin's remarks on the enormous human cost of this venture allude to the Baltic-White Sea Canal, which was built by forced labor and opened in 1933.

The central theme in Prishvin's work is nature. His works are verbal landscapes. Nature becomes the subject of his stories rather than the background. Prishvin believed that by observing and understanding nature, man can understand the great truths of life.

Prishvin's prose style and choice of subject matter is often close to Sergei AKSAKOV's. Lyrical and realistic, it is a combination of poetry and scientific fact. A keen and careful observer, he records and presents what he sees. There is very little action in his works. His descriptions capture and communicate the slow rhythm of the seasons and the imperceptible and recurring movement of time. Prishvin gained his reputation as a writer after the Revolution. Never overly popular, and virtually unknown abroad, he maintained his artistic integrity throughout the Stalin era, continuing to produce finely written and artistically styled works.

Works: Sobranie sochinenii. 7 vols. 1927–30. *Sobranie sochinenii.* 6 vols. 1956–57. *Avtobiografiya.* In *Sovetskie pisateli.* Vol. 2. 1959. *Izbrannye proizvedeniya.* 2 vols. 1972. *Rodniki Berendekiya.* 1977. *Kak ya vstayu v predrassvetnyi chas: Miniatyury.* 1979.

Translations: The Black Arab and Other Stories. 1947. *The Lake and the Woods: or, Nature's Calendar.* London, 1951. Reprint Greenwood, Conn., 1976. *The Treasure Trove of the Sun.* New York, 1952. 1967. Also as: *The Sun's Storehouse.* Moscow, 1956, 1975. *Shiptimber Grove.* 1957. *Nature's Diary.* Moscow, 1958. *Boy and Ducklings.* Moscow, 1964 (?). *Jensheng: the Root of Life.* Hyperion, Conn., 1973 (reprint of 1936 ed.) *The Root of Life.* London, 1980.

Secondary literature: L. Borovoi, *Yazyk pisatelya.* 1966. G. Ershov, *Mikhail Prishvin.* 1973. A. Khailov, *Mikhail Prishvin. Tvorcheskii put'.* 1960. T. Khmel'nitskaya, *Tvorchestvo Mikhaila Prishvina.* 1959. I. Motyashov, *Mikhail Prishvin. Kritiko-biograficheskii ocherk.* 1965. K. Paustovskii, "Prishvin." In his *Sobranie sochinenii v vos'mi tomakh.* Vol. 3. 1967. M. Slonim, *Soviet Russian Literature: Writers and Problems, 1917–1977.* 1977. Pp. 109–15. A. Timrot, *Prishvin v moskovskom krayu.* 1973.   H. S.

Prismánova, Ánna Semyónovna (1898–1960, was married to Aleksandr GINGER), émigré poet. Contemporary critics were in agreement that Prismanova, in the 1930s one of the Parisian poets of the "young" generation, wrote poetry of considerable originality. Her versification is formally simple and conventional, though by no means lacking in sound patterning and rhythmic variety, but it is strong on creating an intriguing world of absurdist yet plastic images, and illogical yet somehow familiar relationships.

Works: Ten' i telo. Paris, 1937. *Bliznetsy: 2-aya kniga stikhov.* Paris, 1946. *Sol': 3-ya kniga stikhov.* Paris, 1949. *Vera; liricheskaya povest'.* Paris, 1960.

Translations: "Blood and Bone" (1946). In *Modern Russian Poetry.* Ed. Vladimir Markov and Merrill Sparks. 1967. Pp. 476–77.

Secondary Literature: G. Struve, *Russkaya literatura v izgnanii.* 1956. Pp. 336–37. Yurii Ivask, "Poeziya staroi emigratsii." In *Russkaya literatura v emigratsii: Sbornik statei.* Ed. N. P. Poltoratskii. 1972. P. 65.   V. T.

Prizes, see LITERARY PRIZES.

Production Novel, see NOVEL, SOCIALIST REALISM, SOVIET LITERATURE.

Prokopóvich, Feofán (Prokopovyč, Teofan; 1681–1736), Ukrainian clergyman, the most outstanding graduate of the KIEV ACADEMY and the most important writer as well as central Church and civic figure of the Petrine period. Born Eleazar, in a merchant's family in Kiev, he finished a Jesuit school and then the Kievan Academy, and converting to Uniate Catholicism, studied philosophy, the classics, and also the natural sciences at the Jesuit College in Rome. On returning to the Ukraine in 1704, he reconverted to Orthodoxy, assumed monastic orders and the name Feofan, and became a professor at the Kiev Academy, teaching philosophy and theology, as well as poetics, rhetoric, physics, and mathematics. In 1710 he became rec-

tor of the Academy. Having attracted the attention of Peter I (he had already accompanied the Tsar on the Prut campaign of 1711), he was called to St. Petersburg in 1715, where despite considerable opposition from the clergy (who suspected him of Protestantism) he became the chief organizer and propagandist of Peter's reforms. (In 1718 he became bishop of Pskov; in 1720 archbishop of Novgorod and de facto head of the Synod.) After Peter's death he continued to propagate the spirit of his reforms (and of royal absolutism), notably by organizing a "learned company" to which belonged such important figures as the poet Antiokh KANTEMIR and the historian Vasily Tatishchev.

More than any of his fellow Kievan writers and scholars, Prokopovich was a humanist with a strong rationalist bent. While belles lettres was only a part of his output (he also wrote histories, especially on Peter I, and treatises—theological, legal and literary-theoretical, e.g., his *De arte poetica libri tres*), its significance is great. Prokopovich wrote in Latin, Polish and Church Slavonic in its Ukrainian version; the latter writings were strongly russified in later editions. His tragicomedy *Vladimir* (1705), dealing with the introduction of Christianity in early *Rus'*, is largely an allegory on the reforms, and the obscurantist reaction, of his day; it is an excellent example of a school drama in thirteen-syllable verse, written according to the rules presented in his own poetics. His thirteen-syllable panegyric, *Epinikion* (1709), celebrating Peter's victory at Poltava appeared in Latin, Polish and his Ukrainian-influenced Church Slavonic. In his rare later poetry Prokopovich turned again to themes touching on the Ukraine (cf. "Zaporožec kajuščyjsja" or "Za mohyloju rjaboju"). Prokopovich's greatest impact, both in his time and on later literature, was through his numerous orations and sermons (slova i rechi). With their eloquence, passion, and sense of history, his orations, for example, on the victory at Poltava, on royal absolutism ("Slovo o vlasti i chesti tsarskoi," 1718; later developed in his famous 1722 treatise, *Pravda voli monarshei*), on the establishment of the Russian navy, on Peter's death, and so on, served as influential models for later 18th century Russian publicistic prose. In general, Prokopovich's transition from Kiev to St. Petersburg, from a basically scholastic baroque poetics to the first phase of a rationalist and secular classicism, is highly emblematic of the differing fortunes of 18th-century Ukrainian and Russian literature: the one declining into provincialism, the other developing into a dynamic Imperial literature. (See UKRAINIAN ELEMENTS IN RUSSIAN LITERATURE.)   G. G.

Proletkult (Proletkúl't, Proletárskie kul'túrno-prosvetítel'skie organizátsii—proletarian cultural and educational organizations). Under the leadership of the Marxist philosopher A. A. BOGDANOV and with the active cooperation of the future commissar of education A. V. LUNACHARSKY the *Proletkult* came into being early in 1917. The organization took upon itself the project of developing a distinctly proletarian literature and art. Lunacharsky and Bogdanov had been associates in the Party school organized on Capri in 1909, and both believed in the need to foster a "culture" proper to the new and rising class, the industrial proletariat. Certain passages in the works of Marx had stressed that the religion, art, and literature of a given epoch are a superstructure built upon the basis of productive relations which, in a society divided into classes, reflect the ideas developed by the dominant class. G. V. PLEKHANOV, applying the Marxist analysis to literature, maintained that "social consciousness is determined by social existence ... so-called belles lettres expresses the strivings and the mood of a given society, in a class society of the dominant social class." The ideologists of the *Proletkult* concluded as orthodox Marxists that since the bourgeoisie were destined to disappear as the dominant class, their art and literature would also disappear, to be replaced by a proletarian art and literature, created in part through the labors of the *Proletkult* itself.

The attitude of the *Proletkult* to the art and literature of the past was ambivalent. Some members, the poet KIRILLOV for instance, rejected all past art as the product of hostile classes and counseled "trampling the flowers" of such art. Bogdanov, Lunacharsky, and other theoreticians maintained, on the contrary, that the art of past ages could and should become the property of the working masses "through critically reworking it from the collective labor point of view." And Bogdanov himself used the term "the beautiful" in referring to the eternal values of great masterpieces.

Bogdanov contributed ideas of his own on the function of art, which he regarded not merely as a reflection of life from the viewpoint of a particular class, nor merely as an expression of its ideas, but as a means of organizing its collective strength. "The proletariat must have its own class art to organize its forces in social labor, struggle, and construction." Bogdanov insisted on the organizing role of art, and on the special task of the *Proletkult* in developing proletarian artists. For this purpose the organization set up a wide network of "literary studios" intended to train new writers in the techniques of literary creation.

The Party leadership was at first divided on the subject of the *Proletkult*, but by 1920 it had taken a firm stand against it, largely because of Bogdanov's claim to independence from Party and government authority. LENIN insisted that its work be subordinated to the commissariat of education, and TROTSKY opposed its basic premise, arguing that a specifically proletarian class literature did not exist and would not have time to develop before the establishment of a classless society. Lunacharsky remained a supporter of the *Proletkult*, but Lenin's strong opposition assured its decline and has determined subsequent Soviet accounts of its role and importance. It should be emphasized that Lenin had been an implacable opponent of both Bogdanov and Lunacharsky in the intra-Party philosophical debates that preceded the Revolution of 1917. The organization in its best days included a number of genuine poets, among them Kirillov, GASTEV, KAZIN, and GERASIMOV; it published many critical journals, and organized educational programs in which established writers and critics—BELY and KHODASEVICH, for instance—participated. It disappeared in 1932 when all separate literary organizations were liquidated.

Bibliography: A. A. Bogdanov, *Iskusstvo i rabochii klass.* 1918. N. L. Brodskii, ed., *Literaturnye manifesty ot simvolizma k oktyabryu.* Vol. 1. 1929. E. J. Brown, *The Proletarian Episode in Russian Literature.* 1953, 1971. Herman Ermolaev, *Soviet Literary Theories 1917–1934.* 1963. V. Khodasevich, *Literaturnye stat'i i vospominaniya.* New York, 1954. George Z. Patrick, *Popular Poetry in Soviet Russia.* 1929. *Proletarskie poety pervykh let sovetskoi epokhi.* 1959.

E. J. B.

Prólog. A collection of short hagiographic compositions occasionally supplemented by other didactic writings. The Prolog is arranged according to the calendar of saints and is patterned after the Greek Synaxary or Menology. The Old Russian designation *Prólog* arose through the mistaken identification of the title of the preface (Prologos) with the title of the entire work.

The Prolog was originally compiled in the 12th century, possibly in Constantinople, through the collaborative efforts of East Slavic and South Slavic scribes. Even the work's earliest redaction contains hagiographic accounts of both Greek and South Slavic saints, as well as of Russian saints such as Boris and Gleb, Princess Olga, and Feodosy Pechersky. Later versions of the Prolog were supplemented by extensive textual materials and enjoyed great popularity in the Russian lands. First printed in Moscow in 1641 (only the first half of the collection), the Prolog was published eight times in the 17th century. Nine editions of the work appeared in print in the 18th century. In the 19th century the Prolog's subject matter was used by Russian writers such as A. I. HERZEN, N. S. LESKOV, and L. N. TOLSTOI.

Bibliography: A. S. Dëmin, ed., *Literaturnyi sbornik XVII veka. Prólog.* 1978. N. I. Petrov, *O proiskhozhdenii i sostave slavyanorusskogo pechatnogo Prologa.* Kiev, 1875. A. I. Ponamarev, ed., *Pamyatniki drevnerusskoi tserkovno-uchitel'noi literatury,* nos. 2 and 4. 1896–98. *Prolog po rukopisi imp. Publichnoi biblioteki Pogodinskogo drevlekhranilishcha No. 58,* nos. 1–2. 1916–17. R. P.

Propp, Vladímir Yákovlevich (1895–1970), a leading folklorist, was of German ancestry. After graduating from Petrograd University in 1918, he worked as a high-school teacher and beginning in 1926 taught in higher educational institutions in Leningrad. In 1932 he began his teaching career in folklore at Leningrad University. He was named professor in 1938 and defended his doctoral dissertation in 1939.

Propp's fame is based on his *Morphology of the Folktale* (Morfo-

logiya skazki, 1928). Its publication was received almost with silence, and the work fell into oblivion. One reviewer, R. Shor, wished that the author "would give up these structures or base them on sufficient groundwork." However, the 1958 English version, though inadequately translated (new translation in 1968) scored an unparalleled success throughout the world. The work has been translated into numerous languages. When it was republished in the Soviet Union in 1969, E. M. Meletinsky, in his extensive appended survey of "the structural-typological study of the fairy tale," emphasized "the absolute dimensions of V. Ya. Propp's scholarly discovery."

Whether or not the basic notion on which the *Morphology* operates—the function of the folktale's dramatis personae—was discovered by Propp himself is disputable. Appearing simultaneously with Propp's, or maybe even a little earlier, was a project of the structural-morphological study of the fairy tale outlined by A. I. Nikiforov. The term "function" had been defined by Nikiforov in exactly the same way as by Propp, but while Nikiforov's article formulated the general program for such a study, it was Propp who carried this program to its ultimate conclusion and developed it into a full-sized book.

In his *Morphology*, Propp studied the Russian fairy tale as a single, organic whole. He concluded that all tales, however different their *dramatis personae* and their plots, had an identical sequence of functions and the same basic structure. These findings have been hailed as a major theoretical breakthrough in folklore. They have had a strong impact on structural analysis in other fields as well, particularly in anthropology, linguistics, and literary criticism. As some studies (such as Denise Paulme's and Alan Dundes') have demonstrated, Propp's analysis may have cross-cultural validity.

The *Morphology* was Propp's preparation for his other major work on fairy tales, *Historical Roots of the Magic Tale* (Istoricheskie korni volshebnoi skazki, 1946), which purported to clarify the origin of the fairy tale plot and the historical reality mirrored in it. Propp, as P. Saint-Yves had already done in 1923, considered the motifs which constituted the fairy-tale plot as a reflection of initiation rites. But since initiation was connected with the notion of death (the novice was supposed to die temporarily), a fairy tale reflecting initiation also had to reflect inevitably the idea of death. According to Propp, the novice was told at his initiation, in the form of myths, what was going to happen to him. The purpose of these myths was to disclose the meaning of the impending rites. When, at a later stage, myths were divorced from rites, the fairy tale was born.

Propp's work covers, in addition to Russia and Western Europe, classical antiquity, the East, the peoples of North Siberia, American Indians, African Negroes, Australian aborigines, and others. However, his endeavor to derive the fairy tale in its entirety from initiation rites led, on numerous occasions, to artificial and forced solutions. Also very problematic is his assumption that all primitive cultures are similar and that folklore forms can be traced to finite originals.

Propp's *Historical Roots of the Magic Tale* was received with a flurry of hostile criticism in the Soviet Union. One of the main objections was to the author's cosmopolitanism. The book was said to look more like a foreign than a Soviet work and to reflect more the tendencies of bourgeois folkloristics than those of the Soviet and the "brotherly Slavic nations." Due to Propp's abundant use of quotations from scholars like Frazer, Boas, Kroeber, and others, his work was compared to a London or Berlin telephone directory. The Folklore Sector of the Institute of Ethnography was forced to arrange a public meeting for criticizing this and other heretical works. Propp was subjected to a fierce assault by almost all of his colleagues, folklorists and ethnographers, who accused him of holding idealist positions and completely disregarding Marxist-Leninist methodology.

Propp's study of the Russian BYLINY, *The Russian Heroic Epic* (Russkii geroicheskii epos, 1955), is a complete reversal of his former research trends. Evidently under the pressure of previous criticism, Propp discarded as worthless all the results of the study of *byliny* done formerly by professional folklorists in Russia and abroad. Instead, he based his work exclusively on the ideas of the so-called revolutionary democrats, especially those of V. G. BELINSKY, whose work had come to be recognized as having general validity for Soviet folklore research. For Belinsky, *byliny* were "the absolutely original creation of the genius of the Russian people, in which the people expressed itself, its historical aspirations, and its national character."

Propp, following Belinsky literally, considered a correct interpretation of the ideology of *byliny* his prime task, since the national ideas expressed in them expressed also the ideals of the corresponding epochs. On the basis of their ideological contents, he assigned the *byliny* to different (hypothetical) periods of Russian history, beginning with the so-called primitive-communal system and ending with the contemporary communist regime. He did not escape the pitfalls of arbitrariness in his interpretation of the ideology of *byliny*, especially since he had not done the necessary groundwork for it—the study of *bylina* variants, their interrelations and chronology. Therefore, impartial critics have been able to single out as the prime merits of the work its patriotic pathos and its excellent bibliographic appendix.

Propp's last major work, *Russian Agrarian Holidays* (Russkie agrarnye prazdniki, 1963), is devoted to the Russian popular calendar. Its underlying theme is the assertion of a materialistic principle: in the celebration of every holiday Propp sees economic motivation, a desire to increase the fertility of the soil. Although based on secondary sources, the work contains some interesting observations and reinterpretations of known facts.

Propp also wrote a score of smaller studies on tales, heroic epic, historical songs, the characteristics of folklore as art, and other subjects. He eagerly participated in discussions and disputes that arose time and again.

Works: Istoricheskie korni volshebnoi skazki. 1946. *Russkii geroicheskii epos.* 2d ed. 1958. (1st ed., 1955.) *Russkie agrarnye prazdniki.* 1963. *Morfologiya skazki.* 2d. ed. 1969. (1st ed., 1928.)
Translations: Morphology of the Folktale. 2d ed. Rev. and ed. Louis A. Wagner, new introd. Alan Dundes. 1968. (1st ed., trans. Laurence Scott, introd. Svatava Pirkova Jakobson. 1958.) "Generic Structures in Russian Folklore," trans. Maria Zagorska Brooks, *Genre* 4 (1971), pp. 213–48.
Secondary literature: Mary P. Coote, "Beyond Morphology: Vladimir Propp's *Istoricheskie korni volshebnoi skazki*," *RLJ* 31 (1977), pp. 133–39. A. J. Greimas, "Le conte populaire Russe (Analyse fonctionelle)," *IJSLP* 9 (1965), pp. 152–75. Isidor Levin, "Vladimir Propp: An Evaluation of His Seventieth Birthday," *Journal of the Folklore Institute* 4 (1967), pp. 32–49. Claude Lévi-Strauss, "L'analyse morphologique des contes russes," *IJSLP* 3 (1960), pp. 122–49. E. M. Meletinskii, "Structural-Typological Study of the Folktale," trans. Robin Dietrich, *Genre* 4 (1971), pp. 249–79. Felix J. Oinas, "V. Ia. Propp," *Journal of American Folklore* 84 (1971), pp. 338–40. Archer Taylor, "The Biographical Pattern in Traditional Narrative," *Journal of the Folklore Institute* 1 (1964), pp. 114–29, esp. 121–29.
F. J. O.

Prosody, see VERSIFICATION.

Proverb. The Russian folk proverb (*poslovitsa*; pl. *poslovitsy*) is a rich genre which to a considerable extent survives and is still used in daily life. LENIN and, more recently, Nikita Khrushchev, were celebrated for their use of proverbs in their public speeches. The use of proverbs in modern Russian helps to give speech a folksy, stylized quality.

While proverbs have come down in oral tradition, there is no question that very many of them have a written origin as, for instance, in the Biblical Book of Proverbs. Still, they are changed in oral tradition and generally take on a syntax and lexicon so idiomatically Russian that they have every right to be counted a folk genre, one that is a Russian specialty.

Proverbs are short, concise expressions of general moral advice. Russian proverbs are rhythmic and are often rhymed. A bipartite structure is typical, with syntactic and semantic parallelism of the two parts, e.g., "The slower you go the farther you'll get." Proverbs give normative advice; some of them address directly the matter at issue, e.g., "Live a lifetime—learn a lifetime," but many are figurative and have a metaphorical or allegorical interpretation, e.g., "Until you've smoked out the bees, you can't eat the honey," i.e., one must get rid of obstacles in order to obtain some gain or enjoy some satisfaction.

Like much of Russian folklore, proverbs were greatly used by the peasantry, and many of them reflect peasant concerns and a peasant point of view, e.g., "Cabbage soup and porridge is our fare." Sometimes these go back in time to the period before the emancipation of the serfs in 1861, e.g., "You can't fill a duck's crop or a master's pocket," or "If there is no one to wear bast shoes, there will be none to wear velvet." But many also reflect middle class concerns and, in particular, commerce and trade, e.g., "If you don't cheat, you won't sell," or "Goods that lie idle won't feed you." In general the moral subjects of Russian proverbs tend to be specific and highly concrete, and there are relatively few proverbs of a generalized or abstract quality such as the adage, "If God does not bring it, the earth will not yield it." Still, proverbs tend to be generalized insofar as they are applied broadly to cover a range of metaphorically linked subjects.

Certain proverbs reflect past historical or even pre-historical circumstances, e.g., "A hungry Frenchman is glad to get a crow," a reference to 1812, or "Not everything's a mermaid that dives into the water," which would seem to go back to a period of literal belief in mermaids. Such proverbs probably survive because of their ability to be applied to metaphorically parallel situations.

Related to the proverb is the POGOVORKA, or saying. The *poslovitsa* (proverb) generally forms a complete sentence, while the *pogovorka* is less than a complete sentence. Also, the moral application of the saying is often vaguer. Another folk form related to the proverb is the *pribautka* (pl. *pribautki*), a characteristically Russian form of joke. Like the proverb, the *pribautka* is rhythmic and frequently rhymed, and in these formal characteristics much of its expressiveness is found. *Pribautki* often play with names or other words in context, e.g., "*Masha—radost' nasha*" (Masha is our joy). Others point out humorous contradictions, e.g., "Ah, how delicious goose legs are!" "Have you ever eaten them?" "No, but my uncle used to watch our master eat them."

The classic collection of Russian proverbs is the one prepared by Vladimir Dal and first published in 1861, *Poslovitsy russkogo naroda.*

Bibliography: Yu. M. Sokolov, *Russian Folklore.* 1950. Pp. 258–81. P. G. Bogatyrev, ed., *Russkoe narodnoe poeticheskoe tvorchestvo.* 1956. Pp. 264–82. V. P. Adrianova-Peretts, ed., *K istorii russkoi poslovitsy.* 1932.
W. E. H.

Prutkóv, Koz'má, a fictitious writer whose sayings became part of the Russian spoken language and whose satirical verses and plays attacked the bureaucratic and mundane aspects of Russian life in the mid-19th century. Created by two talented poets, Count Aleksei TOLSTOI and Aleksei Zhemchuzhnikov (1821–1908), with some contributions from the latter's brothers, Vladimir and Aleksandr, Prutkov became the personification of a particular type of bureaucrat, a self-satisfied, overconfident and vain director of an assay office. Prutkov was similar to Monsieur Prudhomme, the famous French fictional bureaucrat created by Henri Monnier in his "Scènes populaires dessinées à la plume" (1830). Prutkov's major trait, like Prudhomme's, was Philistine banality with a tendency toward pretentious rhetoric and petty emphasis. Prutkov's plays, *Fantasia* (1851), *Silk Lace* (Blondy, 1852), and *The Reckless Turk* (Oprometchivyi Turka, 1854) bordered on the absurd and trivial. *Fantasia* was performed at the Aleksandrovsky Theater in 1851, but the Emperor Nicholas I walked out during the performance and the audience booed the production to a halt. Prutkov's fame rests on his verses and cleverly ridiculous sayings. Prutkov's famous admonition to a civil servant for perseverance was *Bdi!* (grammatically correct imperative of an archaic *bdet'*, 'to hold a vigil,' but phonetically close to *bzdi!* 'flatulate!'). His philosophical advice became part of the language: "If you want to be happy, be it!" or "Death has been placed at the end of life, so that it might be more convenient to prepare for it." Prutkov's "Thoughts and Aphorisms" endeared the fictitious author to the reading public and his advice, such as "You can't fathom the unfathomable" (Nel'zya ob"yat' neob"yatnogo), was followed in the journal SOVREMENNIK through the 1850s and in the journals *Eralash* and *Svistok* in the 1860s.

Works: K. Prutkov, *Sochineniya.* Comp. with a postface by D. A. Zhukova. Notes by A. K. Baboreko. 1981. Koz'ma Prutkov.

Polnoe sobranie sochinenii. Ed. with introd. and commentary B. Ya. Bukhshtab. 1949. *Sochineniya Koz'my Prutkova.* 1965. A. K. Tolstoi, *Polnoe sobranie sochinenii.* 1907.

Secondary literature: P. N. Berkov, *Koz'ma Prutkov—direktor Probirnoi palatki i poet.* 1933.   T. E. B.

Psalms. The practice of versifying the psalms in the vernacular languages, common throughout Europe from at least the 16th century, appears in Russia in the late 17th century inspired by Polish examples. In Moscow, SIMEON POLOTSKY produced a Psalter in rhymed syllabic verse (*Psaltyr' Rifmovannyi*) in 1680. Polotsky's psalms were set to music, as was the established tradition. Several were incorporated into Russian songbooks which provided a repository for versified psalms and other sacred songs within the sphere of Russian ecclesiastical and popular-religious culture well into the 19th century. Meanwhile, during the 18th century, verse adaptations and paraphrases of the psalms also continued to play a role on the mainline of Russian literary development, first in the old SYLLABIC VERSIFICATION (KANTEMIR et al.) and then, from the 1740s, in the new syllabotonic system. TREDIAKOVSKY completed a versified Psalter in 1753 a part of which, like Polotsky's, was set to music. However, by mid-18th century the versified psalm adaptation had assumed a new and special importance. It became a kind of testing ground for the development of Russian verse techniques (for instance, SUMAROKOV's Psalter has virtually no two psalms prosodically identical, even containing examples of free verse; also, 18th-century verse competitions often featured the psalm adaptation). Moreover, as the psalm adaptation allowed scope for the poet's creative initiative, it powerfully promoted and conditioned the genre of the spiritual ode with which it remained closely associated throughout the 18th and into the 19th century.   I. R. T.

Puppet theater. The principal form of puppet theater in Russia is that of PETRUSHKA, a kind of Russian Punch, known since the 17th century. Another form is the so-called *vertep* (crèche) theater, originating in the 17th century in southwestern European Russia (i.e., the Ukraine and Belorussia) and spreading subsequently to other parts of Russia. The chief participants were divinity students, who adapted school plays as texts. The *vertep* was a vertical double box: in the top half sacred scenes were performed; in the bottom half, comic scenes. Both halves had tracks cut through the floor for manipulating the puppets, which were attached to rods.

The plays performed included Christmas plays on Christ's birth, the visit of the Wise Men, and the Massacre of Infants by Herod. Comic scenes, providing contrast and relief, drew on materials of everyday life and featured stock characters such as a peasant, soldier, gypsy, Jew, Cossack, or divinity student. There was also a "living *vertep*" performed by live actors.

Troupes of puppeteers visited Russia from Western Europe from the early 18th century. Marionettes were introduced from Germany in the 1770s.

Bibliography: P. G. Bogatyrev, ed., *Russkoe narodnoe poeticheskoe tvorchestvo.* 1956. Pp. 474–78. A. M. Novikova and A. V. Kokoreva, eds., *Russkoe narodnoe poeticheskoe tvorchestvo.* 1969. Pp. 333–35. V. N. Peretts, "Kukol'nyi teatr v Rossii," *Ezhegodnik imperatorskikh teatrov*, 1895–96. Russell Zguta, *Russian Minstrels.* Philadelphia, 1978. Pp. 112–20.   W. E. H.

Purism, a more or less organized program aimed at keeping a language free of foreign words and foreign influences in syntax and style, and/or maintaining certain norms of usage in educated written as well as oral discourse. Purism has been a major factor in the development of some East European literary languages, Czech, for example, but is a relatively minor phenomenon in the history of the Russian literary idiom. When thousands of foreign words entered the Russian language during and after the age of Peter the Great, and even the syntactic structure of the literary idiom was significantly affected by French, German, and Latin patterns, there existed no agency that might have checked this development. M. V. LOMONOSOV's epoch-making efforts to stabilize the literary idiom (*A Russian Grammar*, 1757, and "On the Usefulness of Church Books in the Russian Language," 1757) were not purist in their spirit. It was only the followers of A. S. SHISHKOV in the early 1800s who first sought

to eliminate Western loanwords as well as phraseological and stylistic calques from the language, replacing them with Slavic forms, including some neologisms, with little success. The Shishkovians were more liberal regarding the admission of popular usage (vulgarisms) into the literary idiom. Their opponents, the KARAMZINIANS, on the contrary, favored GALLICISMS, but were less liberal regarding vulgarisms.

The great literature of the 19th century, beginning with PUSHKIN, was generally anti-purist in theory as well as practice. Occasionally it met with purist criticism by such critics as F. V. BULGARIN, N. I. GRECH, N. A. POLEVOI, M. P. POGODIN, etc. The SLAVOPHILE journal MOSKVITYANIN generally followed a purist line. The critical and journalistic writings of the liberals and radicals (HERZEN, BELINSKY) greatly promoted the proliferation of foreign elements, such as loan translations of German philosophic jargon, in educated Russian speech. Vladimir DAL's monumental dictionary, *Tolkovyi slovar' zhivogo velikorusskogo yazyka* (1863–66), while it purports to reflect the living language of its time, written as well as oral, has a decided purist orientation, but had little effect on the development of the literary idiom.

The Revolution of 1917, much as the Petrine revolution of the early 1700s, brought a flood of foreign words (Marxist political jargon, new administrative and technological terms) as well as of vulgarisms into the usage of public discourse. As early as in the 1930s, efforts were under way to normalize the new Soviet idiom. D. N. Ushakov's four-volume *Tolkovyi slovar' russkogo yazyka* (1935–40) was a visible sign of a purist tendency to maintain the linguistic status quo. This trend was resumed in the 1950s when a section of "speech culture" (*kul'tura rechi*) was formed within the Academy of Sciences (1952) and charged with the production of orthoepic reference books. It also produced a series of symposia, "Questions of Speech Culture" (*Voprosy kul'tury rechi*). The tendency of most contributions to these symposia was purist. Ushakov's dictionary was superseded by S. I. Ozhegov's *Slovar' russkogo yazyka* (1st ed. 1949, many subsequent editions) and a four-volume *Slovar' russkogo yazyka* (1957–61) produced by the Academy of Sciences. Official language policy remains conservative. A significant fact is the removal of dialectisms from such a classic as SHOLOKHOV's *And Quiet Flows the Don*. The editorial practices of State publishing houses are quite stern and intolerant of vulgarisms, neologisms, macaronisms, and other deviations from the standard language.

V. T.

Púshkin, Aleksándr Sergéevich (1799–1837).

"National poet"

For all of the controversy that has surrounded his texts, Pushkin has no plausible rival for the romantic title of "national poet," and it was already extended to him by admirers during his lifetime, such as Nikolai GOGOL ("Some Words on Pushkin," 1834). Leaving aside for the moment the luminosity of his achievements in a dazzling array of genres or the ability of his texts to capture and define the crucial conflicts in Russian culture (Russia/the West, folk/gentry, religious/secular, state/individual), Pushkin's title rests primarily on the seminal nature of his writing.

His novel in verse, *Eugene Onegin* (1833), to give but one example of this impact, has left a number of settings, characters, and relationships to the RUSSIAN NOVEL. It is a commonplace, of course, to say that the novel as a genre "reflects" social and historical actuality, but the ability to render this actuality depends on codes and conventions, and it was Pushkin who, drawing on a plethora of European and Russian literary and social precedents, taught subsequent novelists (especially LERMONTOV, TURGENEV, and TOLSTOI) *what* sort of actuality to capture and *how* to encode it.

Pushkin's impact has been no less considerable on other modes of art. His lyrics have been set to music by such composers as Glinka; his narrative and dramatic works have been a continuing source of inspiration to Russian choreographers and composers, beginning with Glushkovsky's ballet *Ruslan and Lyudmila* (1821) and continuing through such famous appropriations as Mussorgsky's *Boris Godunov* (1869), Tchaikovsky's *Eugene Onegin* (1878) and *Queen of Spades* (1890), and Stravinsky's *Mavra* (1922). Given the difficulties that translators have encountered in capturing Pushkin's swift iambic tetrameters, subtle "poetry of grammar," and myriad stylistic levels, it is perhaps inevitable that Pushkin is best known abroad through these musical "translations."

Pushkin has been credited, moreover, with having created the modern Russian literary language. Gogol's essay opened a campaign for his canonization: "In him, as if in a lexicon, have been included all of the wealth, strength, and flexibility of our language. More than all others, he has pushed back its boundaries and showed all of its spaciousness." The campaign has been joined by such modern linguists as VINOGRADOV (see bibliography), who note that Pushkin not only admitted words from many different sources into his works, but established syntactic patterns and lexical principles for their use, thereby breaking limits set by NEOCLASSICAL rules and SENTIMENTALIST decorum. Arguments easily arise against this contention: there are levels of the language that Pushkin did not explore (mercantile, urban, clerical jargons, and the developing language of Russia's German-influenced metaphysics); his syntax has a spare, Voltairian quality that has hardly become a norm for Russian expository writing, influenced as it has been by academic and philosophical styles alien to the enlightened Westernized gentry of Pushkin's time; and it can no longer be taken for granted that Russian school children will immediately apprehend the Pushkinian texts. Nevertheless, that serious Russian scholars credit him with having created their literary language does show the extent to which Pushkin has been mythologized.

In one additional sense, Pushkin remains the "national poet" and this concerns his place at the center of the "Golden Age" of Russian literature. The hope-filled first decades of the nineteenth century—especially the years between the defeat of Napoleon and the crushing of the Decembrist uprising (1814–25) remain in the popular consciousness as an unprecedented and subsequently unrepeated time of cultural plenitude, grace, harmony, humor, and elegance. To the extent that Pushkin's best work captured these elusive qualities, it has a status in Russian culture unshared by other—no less considerable but frequently more "serious" and tortured—achievements.

Pushkinian texts: biographical and historical considerations

The literary milieu in which Pushkin grew to maturity—one dominated by the salons and familiar associations of Russia's aristocratic elite—demanded that a writer practice a variety of genres in order to avoid an ungentlemanly narrowness of interest. And Pushkin did them all—in verse, drama, and prose. His 800 letters are among the liveliest in the language. His 700 lyrics range from devastating epigrams to sentimental madrigals, from spiritual meditations to erotic fantasies, from dejected elegies to boisterous familiar epistles, from rebellious odes to celebrations of Imperial Russia, from "Imitations of the Koran" to "Songs of the Western Slavs." Their meters, rhyme schemes, and lexical virtuosity are no less protean (an epithet that GNEDICH and others were already using in Pushkin's time) than their subjects. His narrative poems include a mock-epic fairy tale ("Ruslan and Lyudmila," 1820); three Byronic "Southern poems" (1820–24); a romantic historical epic ("Poltava," 1828), several folk tales, (1831–32); several comic poems, from the still unpublished "Shade of BARKOV" (1816?) to the sacrilegious "Gavriiliada" (1821) to the highly original "Count Nulin" (1825) and "Little House in Kolomna" (1830); and his narrative masterpiece, "The Bronze Horseman" (1833). Pushkin's dramatic works include an historical play in twenty-three scenes, *Boris Godunov* (1825), four dramatic sketches (*The Little Tragedies*, 1830), and many fragments. His prose fiction consists of a completed historical novel, *The Captain's Daughter* (1836); a collection of stories (*The Tales of Belkin*, 1830); the psychologically profound "Queen of Spades" (1833); and many fragments of historical, adventure, and "society" fiction. His critical fragments and published essays—concerned primarily with Russian literature as an institution—fill two volumes of his collected works. His historical projects include *The History of Pugachev* (1833) and unfinished or fragmentary essays on 18th-century Russian history. A travesty of contemporary prose writing and literary life, "A History of the Village of Goryukhino" (1830), and a parodistic travel account, *A Journey to Arzrum* (1836), must also be listed among his achievements in prose.

While still a pupil at the Imperial Lyceum near St. Petersburg (1812–17), Pushkin developed an extraordinary feeling for the individual poetic genres and for the variety of moods, images, styles, and authorial personae that they required. An indifferent pupil—except in fencing, French, and dancing—he nevertheless became well read, especially in French and Russian literature, less so in the classics and in English (his substantial library would eventually contain several thousand books, two-thirds of them in foreign languages). The nephew of a salon poet, V. L. PUSHKIN, he gained entrée into Petersburg literary circles while still at the Lyceum and joined the ARZAMAS literary society and, later, the GREEN LAMP. He sought out, in his youth, the company of older contemporaries who represented a variety of literary tendencies—ZHUKOVSKY, KATENIN, DAVYDOV, and BATYUSHKOV—for instruction in the craft of poetry, for which he showed considerable talent by early adolescence. Like his fellow Arzamasians he developed a sense of poetry as play and as competition—competition with contemporaries and with the poets of other cultures, competition within the recognizable bounds of genre and style. He was, as all of this suggests, superbly aware of the conventions of literature, and it is one of the invariant characteristics of the Pushkinian text that the reader is made no less aware of these conventions—through reference, quotation, paraphrase, titles, epigraphs, and a host of other metaliterary devices. Increasingly as his career unfolded, he would set literary conventions against one another, parodying them, broadening their boundaries by attempting to combine them (*Eugene Onegin: A Novel in Verse*). As Pushkin's contemporary NADEZHDIN noted, with less admiration than a modern reader might, Pushkin was no less parodistic in his historical verse narratives than in his straightforwardly comic ones. In more positive terms it might be argued that Pushkin's are the first Russian texts to come adequately to grips with the wealth of cultural patterns that had been set in conflict by the Westernization of Russia during the 18th century. Certainly there is always something subtly formalistic and metaliterary about Pushkinian texts, always a dialogue with generic and individual precedents. But these dialogues with convention frequently serve a number of functions beyond competition and virtuosity: (1) exploring the extent to which world views are determined by literary and cultural stereotypes; (2) questioning the extent to which literary stereotypes are adequate for perceiving experience; and (3) through these essays in literary exploration, moving the world of art closer to the world of cultural and physical experience. In different ways the intersecting literary currents of the early 19th century (classicism, sentimentalism, ROMANTICISM, incipient REALISM) proposed relationships between literature and life—literature as an ideal model for behavior, polite social interaction as an aesthetic and ethical norm, the poet's life as an aesthetic creation, literature as the imitation of life. The Pushkinian text had—and has—a significance beyond its formal brilliance, not because it offers behavioral models or imitations of "reality" in any straightforward sense, but because it questions with unusual thoroughness and clarity these possible relationships between "literature" and "life."

The biographical moments relevant to Pushkin's production of such texts, aside from the details of education and literary association already mentioned, are those which illustrate his status on the margin of two social and cultural positions—"gentleman" and "author"—to which he devoted many of his most penetrating meditations in his letters, verse, notebooks, and critical essays.

Pushkin's very birth illustrates such marginality. He was descended both from an ancient noble family of pre-Petrine origins and (on his mother's side) from a captive Abyssinian who became a general through the patronage of Peter the Great's daughter. The contradictions of this descent—hereditary noble and recent creature, Russian and foreign—found a parallel in his precarious economic situation: the poet, desperate to maintain the noble independence of a gentleman (*chestnyi chelovek, honnête homme*) found himself during the 1830s increasingly forced by his and his family's lordly irresponsibility to depend both upon the modest income from his writings and upon the humiliating patronage of Nicholas I, who paid the poet's huge debts after his death. Pushkin's behavior—a series of duels, love affairs dutifully recorded in his famous "Don Juan list," ill-advised marriage to a teen-aged beauty, gambling, and free-thinking—often reveals an obsessive struggle to maintain gentlemanly status. Not only the variety of his writings, but also the pose of effortless creation that they frequently convey, bear the marks of a similar compulsion to be the independent gentleman-poet. Zhukovsky, posthumously examining Pushkin's papers, came to acknowledge the efforts that this pose demanded: "with what labor he wrote his light, flying verses! There is no line that had not been several times scribbled over."

The literary institutions of early 19th-century Russia—the patronage of the autocrat; the salons and familiar groups of the enlightened Westernized gentry; and incipient professionalism (journals, almanacs, purchases by booksellers)—offered no easy solution to the problem of realizing authorial talent while preserving noble independence. KARAMZIN had approached this goal by combining the possibilities that these institutions offered: as official historiographer he was protected from the censorship by the Tsar; as a landowner and a writer whose works found favor with the public he was freed financially from the necessity of state service; as a leading practitioner of the salon style he was welcomed in polite society. And Pushkin took cognizance of Karamzin's place amid these institutions in an article, "Fragments of Letters, Thoughts, and Comments" (1827). Yet his own attempts to chart a similar course ended in disaster. The 3,000 rubles that he received for his narrative poem "The Fountain of Bakhchisarai" (1824) had been the largest honorarium ever paid to a Russian poet, and he looked forward to practicing literature as a profession, but as such financial successes of the 1820s gave way to nearly hopeless attempts to establish periodicals of high quality (*Literaturnaya gazeta*, SOVREMENNIK), to bitter literary quarrels with BULGARIN and N. POLEVOI, to humiliation at court instead of the Autocrat's respectful attention, and to the vicious social intrigues that led to his death in a duel, Pushkin's early optimism disappeared.

Beyond these precarious situations on the margins of nobility and professional authorship, Pushkin's mature years were spent on the margins of public life: close enough to imagine a quasi-political rôle for himself, close enough for the future DECEMBRISTS to concern themselves with the political implications of his writing, close enough to obtain access to official archives and to be regarded by the Autocrat as an influence upon public opinion; yet removed from the various advisory, parliamentary, or administrative roles that Karamzin and contemporary French and English writers played. Exiled from the capital cities (1820–26) for his rebellious youthful verse, Pushkin was not able to take an active part in the Decembrist uprising. In all of his dealings with the Autocracy—in submitting works to its censorship, in proposing an educational program (1826), in attempting to found a political journal, in conducting historical research, or in fulfilling the trivial functions of a *kameryunker*—Pushkin was made to understand that enlightenment and talent counted less to the state than orthodoxy and obedience.

Consequently, the Pushkinian text became not only a place for the intersection of various cultural and aesthetic discourses, but a focus for social, literary, and political controversies. To the extent that the poet's place in society and the individual's role in the state continue to vex Russian culture, and plural modern societies in general, the Pushkinian text has remained vital and provocative.

The reception of these texts—leaving aside the veneration of them in Russian culture and the status of many lines as proverbs—has changed with each new cultural movement. But at least three broad critical strategies have been employed in almost every period. The first has been to appropriate fragments of the texts as exempla for homilies. Because of its variety, Pushkin's oeuvre lends itself conveniently to such enterprises. A second has been desperately to seek a "figure in the carpet"—a single model (political, metaphysical, religious) that can somehow account for the plenitude of themes, characters, and situations that the texts provide. A variant of this strategy is to deny that such a pattern can be found, and to fault Pushkin for it. Both variants, positive and negative, have particularly attracted late romantic and religious thinkers, such as DOSTOEVSKY (who saw the essence of Pushkin in his all-embracing "panhumanity") and Vladimir SOLOVYOV (who found that Pushkin lacked a unified core). A third strategic response to the frequently fragmentary and illusively allusive text has been a contextualizing one: to surround it with an overwhelming wealth of commentary (biographical, political, social, linguistic, etc.), in hope that this material will somehow fill the spaces between the lines of the texts and elucidate their "meaning." This last, ostensibly "objective", project—through which the contextual investigations at times take on a life of their

own—has produced many valuable and detailed reference works (see bibliography). It has been the particular enterprise of academic Pushkin scholarship, both Soviet and non-Soviet, pre- and post-revolutionary, but especially of the Pushkin scholarship centered in the Institute of Literature of the Soviet Academy of Sciences, the Pushkin House (see INSTITUT RUSSKOI LITERATURY).

Toward the "novelization" of verse: 1810s–20s

The development of Pushkin's career defies easy summarization because Pushkin—keenly aware of conventions, fashions, and traditions, and conscious as well of his own past achievements—constantly returned to the lyric genres (epistles, elegies, epigrams) and precedents (Anacreon, Chénier, Zhukovsky, DERZHAVIN, Batyushkov) of his youth, even as he used these "returns" to consider changes in his own authorial biography against the background of historical, biological, and seasonal change, and to use these considerations as a source of creativity. The title (and the plot) of his late lyric, " ... Afresh I visited" (1835) capture this typical movement. For his contemporaries, it was even more difficult to characterize Pushkin's development, for much of it was concealed. During the last decade of his life he worked at a feverish pace, starting many new projects, occasionally finishing them, and writing many of these fragments in a style as stark as a skeletal outline. Some of the work that he did complete, such as "The Bronze Horseman," could not be presented to the public because of censorship concerns. Yet such was his self-restraint and self-irony that many of these problems remained hidden from all but his closest friends, certainly from the reviewers who wrote that the sources of his inspiration had run dry.

One way of grasping Pushkin's mature work, which begins with his first published narrative poem "Ruslan and Lyudmila" (1817–20), would be to see this work tending toward two major achievements of the 1820s, *Eugene Onegin* (1823–31, pub. in full in 1833) and *Boris Godunov* (1825, pub. 1831), and then creatively departing from their themes, characterizations, styles, and authorial manner. Both of these verse works—the first subtitled *A Novel in Verse*, the second labelled an "Historical Tale" in draft—exemplify a process that M. M. BAKHTIN has called "novelization," the bringing together within a single work of conflicting discourses and world views, the challenging of orthodoxies, the voicing of cultural conflicts. Each, in its variety of moods and styles, draws upon the work that Pushkin did during the early 1820s in narrative poetry, and each illustrates Pushkin's daring transgression of stylistic and generic boundaries.

"Ruslan and Lyudmila" adapts a variety of precedents: Russian folklore, Western fairy tales, Ariosto, Voltaire, BOGDANOVICH, Russian medieval motifs, and others. Most importantly, it inaugurates the subsequently characteristic Pushkinian play with literary conventions, as it disrupts stylistic decorum and parodies other texts, especially Zhukovsky's ballad, "The Twelve Sleeping Maidens." For a decade Pushkin's elders, among them Batyushkov and Zhukovsky, had been discussing the possibility of a long poem on a Russian theme, and Pushkin's Decembrist friends longed for such a poem to provide rhymed civics lessons, but Pushkin's playful eroticism—reminiscent of Voltaire and Batyushkov—proved a slap in the face of such expectations. Consequently, a number of critics condemned it as trivial and formless, evaluations that many would later apply to *Eugene Onegin*. Meanwhile, the narrator's ironic tone, contrasting with the frequently elegiac and sentimental moods of the characters, produced a version of the multiple-voicing that would characterize his later narrative poems. This narrative's metapoetic awareness would be further developed in the three comic poems that followed it during the 1820s (titles above).

The next narrative poems that Pushkin composed were his "Southern Poems," and they represent a new stage in his engagement with European writing: a fascination with English literature—Shakespeare and Scott elsewhere, here the Byron who had overwhelmed Europe with his tremendously popular Eastern poems. Pushkin's attraction to these poems ("The Corsair," "The Giaour," etc.) with their disillusioned, rebellious hero-victim may be understood in the context of Pushkin's own situation: exiled, estranged from his family, harassed by the government. At the same time the structure of the Byronic poems attracted him as well: elliptical narratives with a variety of exotic scenes, each of which represents an emotional climax, and with virtual stylistic and thematic identity between the poet and his hero, who is a product of contemporary civilization. Pushkin's three Southern poems represent three distinct stages in his use of Byron's Eastern poems. The first, "A Prisoner of the Caucasus" (1820–21), features the expected Byronic identification of poet with hero. That the disillusioned hero, a captured Russian nobleman freed by a Circassian girl, remains nameless lessens his distance from the equally disillusioned poet. An epilogue and footnotes, however, introduce a different, metapoetic voice beyond that of the hero. The second Southern poem, "The Fountain of Bakhchisarai" (1822) addresses the identity between protagonist and narrator by dispensing with the Byronic hero altogether, constructing the plot around a confrontation of two harem girls each unable to understand the other's language. Nevertheless, the wealth of scenes, richness of detail, and sense of social constriction that the poem lavishly provides keep this, one of Pushkin's greatest popular and commercial successes, well within the range of fashionable Byronism.

The third poem, "The Gypsies" (1824) provides a different solution to the problem of the Byronic hero. The initial situation—disillusioned hero abandoning civilization for the liberty of a wild people—is, of course, Byronic. But the Gypsy tribe and the heroine constitute in this poem not merely foils for the hero (Aleko) and an occasion for local color but rather a society with an equally important part in the story and equal claim to the reader's attention. Aleko comes to live in this society, performs its menial tasks, and proves incapable of living with the gypsies' freedoms (he murders the heroine). This was seen by contemporaries as a process of containing and debunking the Byronic hero. Meanwhile, the plot (which begins with the hero joining the new society and ends with that society abandoning him) achieves a formal symmetry that stresses (as such symmetries frequently do in Pushkin) the working of fate, a fate that here takes the forms of passion and social necessity, but elsewhere will appear as "history," "nature," or "convention." The writing of "The Gypsies" coincided with the writing of the first chapters of *Eugene Onegin*. In the novel Pushkin dispenses with the exotic setting, but the idea of fate, manifested in structural symmetry, and the containment of the Byronic hero in a cross-fire of cultural patterns are carried over into the novel in verse.

Eugene Onegin (eight chapters, "Onegin's Journey," and fragments of a tenth chapter) is the product of eight years' work, and, indeed, a project that Pushkin contemplated continuing until the end of his life. Its chapters were published individually; and complete editions appeared in 1833 and 1837. Nearly every aspect of the novel suggests both aesthetic polish and the openness of the creative process. The highly ornate stanza, for example (fourteen lines of iambic tetrameters, employing masculine and feminine rhymes in three quatrains with alternating, plain, and crossed rhymes and a concluding couplet), is frequently opened up and made relatively conversational with enjambment between quatrains and even between stanzas. The plot, which opens in St. Petersburg and concludes there after trips to the countryside and to Moscow, seems shaped by an elegantly symmetrical double refusal of love: hero (Eugene) rejects heroine (Tatiana) and vice versa. Yet this plot (which covers the years 1819 to 1825) is constantly overshadowed by the author-narrator's digressions, many of which deal with his own authorial biography and with the process of writing his novel, as his "years to sober prose incline." Thus the digressions may be said to constitute a second plot, ever unfolding as the author-narrator's biography unfolds.

From its generically provocative subtitle to its concluding metaphor ("life's novel"), *Eugene Onegin* raises a series of problems concerning the relationship between literature and life and concerning the limits imposed on social action and artistic expression by a culture's grammar of conventions. Life and literature intersect at every turn, as the novel's two plots intersect. The author-narrator disconcertingly steps into the created world of his fiction to befriend Eugene (a move reminiscent of Byron's in *Don Juan*, which Pushkin much admired). The narrator's muse shades into the novel's heroine. She, Eugene, and Lensky (a poet) try to act out the patterns of the literature they read: epistolary novels (Tatiana), romantic and sentimental verse (Lensky), Byron and Constant (Eugene). Both Eugene, a dandy, and Tatiana, ultimately the hostess of a salon, play roles that unite the social and the aesthetic. All of the characters, including the author-narrator, share the syncretic culture of the Westernized gentry, and the relative success or failure of each depends upon his or her ability to use the conventions of this culture. The author-narrator develops from a child writing sentimental verse to the author of the "free novel," *Eugene Onegin*; Tatiana grows from a sentimental girl who automatically sees people in terms of literary stereotypes, to a thoughtful young woman who understands that life's imitation of literature can be a parody, to the hostess of a salon, the highest form of aesthetic creativity open to a woman of the time, one that had both aesthetic and moral force. As she grows in her ability to use the conventions of her culture, Eugene loses this ability, becoming ever more locked within his obsessions. Lensky never has any control over conventions. Yet all the characters, even the author-narrator, must pursue their ends within a novelistic world of daily life, from which there is no lasting retreat into the refuges of the romantic imagination—nature, dream, and primitive society.

Pushkin's historical drama in blank verse (iambic pentameter), *Boris Godunov*, moves toward the novelistic as well, primarily by setting discourses and world views (Counter-Reformation Poland, Medieval Muscovy) against each other, but also through its treatment of plot and characters. Set in 1598 to 1605 (Russia's "TIME OF TROUBLES") and drawing heavily on Karamzin's *History of the Russian State* for its events and treatment of these events, *Boris Godunov* opens as a conventional conspiracy play, centering around the attempts of Tsar Boris to conceal his part in the murder of the rightful heir to the throne, Prince Dmitry. But from this opening, which offered a traditional dramatic plot ("great" men confronting each other to produce great events, here the usurpation of a throne), *Boris Godunov* swiftly moved toward a more novelistic interpretation of history, as Sir Walter Scott had come to develop it. "History" becomes the property of more "average" individuals, embroiled in complicated and confusing clashes of nations, cultures, and religions. By the end of *Boris Godunov* Boris's secret has become irrelevant to all save Boris himself. The pretender's light-headedness, Boris's wavering and lack of control, and the failure of the plot to bring the two together in some grand confrontation are (together with the multiplicity of settings, the masses of people, and the range of human concerns and styles) such stuff as historical novels are made of, as, indeed, was the "Time of Troubles" itself, with its cultural, religious, ethnic, and social conflicts. Nicholas I (borrowing Bulgarin's reaction to the play) thought that Pushkin should have made it a novel à la Walter Scott. This testifies to the play's ability to provoke another level of awareness (generic) to a reader's experience of it. Scholars have, since Pushkin's time, sought other levels as well—"hidden" references to the French Revolution, to Alexander I's part in the assassination of his father, to the poet's own place in society, despite Pushkin's desire, expressed tongue-in-cheek, that the play not be tapped for allegorical meanings.

Obsessions, history, and "prose": the 1830s

During the last years of his life, Pushkin increasingly turned his attention toward psychological and social obsession, history, and "prose." In this he built upon the foundations laid in *Eugene Onegin* and *Boris Godunov*. The term "realism" does not adequately cover these movements—although Pushkinian texts of this period do show realistic development of character in social, historical, and economic contexts—because the texts continue to exhibit metaliterary concerns, an ironic self-awareness that was beyond the bounds of high literary realism.

"Prose" becomes not just the absence of rhyme and meter, but a way of thinking, a mode of human existence, opposed to the world of creativity, humor, and fancy; it appears as the prosaic, the ordinary, and also as the intellectual, the analytical. "Prose demands thought," as Pushkin put it. Pushkin's world of prose is, ultimately, a world of obsession and limitation, and his prose fiction fully develops these themes, beginning with a cycle of stories, *The Belkin Tales* (1830), each told by a culturally limited narrator (lieutenant colonel, provincial girl, shop assistant) and ostensibly gathered by the hopelessly naive landowner Belkin. The central story of this cycle, "The Gravedigger," exemplifies this process of limitation, as its Teutonic protagonist can never see beyond the profits he hopes to make from his cheated clients. Here there are no fewer games with multiple perspectives and literary allusions than in Pushkin's earlier work, although no author-narrator appears directly to control them. But when the obsessed, the prosaic, and the calculating reappear in *The Queen of Spades* (1833) in a more tragic plot, such metaliterary games do not figure so much in the reader's interaction with the text.

Pushkin's masterly *Little Tragedies* of this period (completed 1830, pub. 1832–39)—"The Covetous Knight," "Mozart and Salieri," "The Stone Guest," and "A Feast During the Plague"—while written in verse, constitute studies of greed, envy, obsession, and human limitation characteristic of the world of "prose."

Pushkin's interest in history runs parallel to his interest in prose. Awareness of the changes that had taken place during his own lifetime, awareness of the marginality of his family and class, the failure of the Decembrist uprising (in which a number of his friends had taken part), the peasant uprisings of 1831, the Polish rebellion of that same year—all of these contributed to his growing interest in history, particularly the history of revolutions and cultural conflicts, and his library testifies to his engagement with serious contemporary historians (such as Guizot, Michelet, Thierry, and Thiers) as well as with earlier Russian historians. Pushkin's historical studies, fictional and non-fictional, addressed the major Russian conflicts from the Time of Troubles to his own period. Such conflicts offered rich opportunities for his talents at cultural stylization.

The History of Pugachev (1833) and its highly compressed fictional counterpart, *The Captain's Daughter* (1833–36), show Pushkin's historical work at full maturity. In the former he analyzes the Pugachev rebellion of the 1770s against a carefully established background of social, political, and economic oppression. The ostensible leader of the uprising, Pugachev, is shown to be a mere screen onto which the Cossacks and peasants could project their resentments. The speed of the narrative brilliantly conveys the speed and scope of the uprising, which had badly shaken the Russian Empire. Lest Nicholas I miss the point, Pushkin provided him with a set of comments on his history. The narration of *The Captain's Daughter* and its editorial presentation provide, in themselves, a historiographical commentary on this national crisis. The story is told from the perspective of a young officer, Grinyov, caught up in the uprising and forced by his attachment to the heroine to move back and forth between the government's forces and the rebels; each side threatens at times to destroy him and his fiancée. This mode of presentation, familiar to Pushkin from Scott's novels, gives a bird's-eye view of the uprising. A second perspective, Grinyov's in older age, offers an interpretation of the events in terms of Enlightenment historiography, i.e. as a struggle of law and reason vs. cruelty and superstition. The limitations of this second perspective are revealed by the editor's perspective of 1836, manifest in epigraphs and in the organization of the text; it illuminates the conflict as one between the culture and government of the Westernized gentry (Catherine II's state) and the culture and government of the un-Westernized, Cossack Old Believers (Pugachev's state). What appeared to the naive young man and to the enlightened older Grinyov as anarchy, the Cossack army, is seen from this perspective as a cultural phenomenon with its own laws, beliefs, and political organization, no more violent and arbitrary than those of the Empress's state.

"The Bronze Horseman" (1833, pub. posthumously in 1837) represents the culmination of these historical interests in rebellion and cultural clash, of the movement toward a "prose" style, and of his concern with obsession. This, the last of Pushkin's iambic tetrameter narratives, centers around a flood that devastated Petersburg in 1824. In the midst of this natural disaster, a young civil servant undergoes a personal disaster when his fiancée is swept away by the flood. Driven to insanity, he threatens the Falconet monument to the city's founder, Peter the Great, and in his insanity imagines that the equestrian statue pursues him through the streets. This simple plot is presented through a variety of styles that recapitulate the history of Russian writing about Petersburg—18th-century odes to Peter's great plan, exuberant celebrations of the city's attractions (such as Pushkin himself crafted for *Eugene Onegin*, Chap. 1), studies of the depersonalizing center of the imperial bureaucracy (such as Gogol, Dostoevsky, and BELY would subsequently provide). It could be argued that the poem not only summarized these past perspectives, but anticipated those that would follow, teaching subsequent writers

to find madness, oppression, seething rebelliousness, and puzzled defeat among the non-aristocratic inhabitants of the capital. The many different critical readings of the poem demonstrate its power to evoke discussions about the tendencies, values, and costs of post-Petrine Russia's historical development. By leaving considerable space for the reader's imagination, by outlining the characters and setting in terms general enough to demand a wide range of commentary, and by offering many elegant and interpretation-provoking patterns of imagery and sound, "The Bronze Horseman" embodies the most enduring and culturally significant qualities of Pushkin's work.

Bibliography: B. P. Gorodetskii et al., eds., *Pushkin: Itogi i problemy izucheniya.* 1966. K. D. Muratova, ed. *Istoriya russkoi literatury XIX veka: Bibliograficheskii ukazatel'.* 1962.

Works: Polnoe sobranie sochinenii. 17 vols. 1937–59.

Translations: The Poems, Prose and Plays of Pushkin. Ed. Avrahm Yarmolinsky. 1936. (Has *Boris Godunov.*) *The Letters of Alexander Pushkin.* Trans. J. Thomas Shaw. 3 vols. 1963. *Eugene Onegin: A Novel in Verse.* Trans. and commentary Vladimir Nabokov. 4 vols. Rev. ed. 1975. *Three Comic Poems.* Trans. and ed. William E. Harkins. 1977. *Eugene Onegin.* Trans. Walter Arndt. 2d rev. ed. 1981. *Collected Poetry.* Ed. and trans. Walter Arndt. 1983. *Complete Prose Fiction.* Trans. Paul Debreczeny. 1983. *The Bronze Horseman: Selected Poems of Alexander Pushkin.* Trans. D. M. Thomas. 1983. *Mozart and Salieri; The Little Tragedies.* Trans. Antony Wood. 1983. See also: Lewanski, pp. 329–45.

Reference works: L. A. Chireiskii, *Pushkin i ego okruzhenie.* 1975. B. L. Modzalevskii, *Biblioteka A. S. Pushkina: Bibliograficheskoe opisanie.* 1910. J. Thomas Shaw, comp., *Pushkin's Rhymes: A Dictionary.* 1974. M. A. Tsyavlovskii, *Letopis' zhizni i tvorchestva A. S. Pushkina.* 1951. V. V. Vinogradov, *Yazyk Pushkina: Pushkin i istoriya russkogo literaturnogo yazyka.* 1935. ———, ed., *Slovar' yazyka Pushkina.* 4 vols. 1956–61.

Criticism and Biography: John Bayley, *Pushkin: A Comparative Commentary.* 1971. (Includes a useful bibliography.) D. D. Blagoi, *Sotsiologiya tvorchestva Pushkina: Etyudy.* 2d ed. 1931. Paul Debreczeny, *The Other Pushkin: A Study of Alexander Pushkin's Prose Fiction.* 1983. J. Fennell, "Pushkin." In ———, ed., *Nineteenth-Century Russian Literature: Studies of Ten Russian Writers.* 1973. G. A. Gukovskii, *Pushkin i problemy realisticheskogo stilya.* 1957. ———, *Pushkin i russkie romantiki.* 1965. Roman Jakobson, *Pushkin and His Sculptural Myth.* Trans. John Burbank. The Hague, 1975. Yu. M. Lotman, *A. S. Pushkin: Biografiya pisatelya.* 1981. ———, *Roman A. S. Pushkina Evgenii Onegin: Kommentarii.* 1980. A. Meynieux, *Pouchkine homme de lettres et la littérature professionelle en Russie.* Paris, 1966. D. J. Richards and C. R. S. Cockrell, eds. and trans., *Russian Views of Pushkin.* 1976. A. L. Slonimskii, *Masterstvo Pushkina.* 2d ed. 1963. Wm. M. Todd, *The Familiar Letter as a Literary Genre in the Age of Pushkin.* 1976. B. V. Tomashevskii, *Pushkin.* 2 vols. 1956–1961. Yu. N. Tynyanov, *Pushkin i ego sovremenniki.* 1969.

W. M. T.

Púshkin, Vasíly Lvóvich (1770–1830). A Moscow poet and salon figure, V. L. Pushkin is remembered primarily as the uncle of A. S. PUSHKIN, as the good-natured butt of his fellow ARZAMASIANS' jokes, and as the author of a lively comic poem "The Dangerous Neighbor" (Opasnyi sosed, 1811, published 1815 in Munich).

Pushkin received a splendid education in his Moscow home. He knew French, Latin, English, German, and Italian; during a journey through Europe (1803–04) he visited the theaters and leading salons of Paris; he was a devoted bibliophile and reader of Latin and French poetry. A retired guardsman and full-time spendthrift, Pushkin expended his literary energies in defending neoclassical French literature and the stylistic innovations of KARAMZIN, DMITRIEV, and ZHUKOVSKY against the attacks of Admiral SHISHKOV and his followers. Two epistles in stately Alexandrines (to Zhukovsky in 1810 and to D. V. Dashkov in 1811) and his comic poem represent the high points in these polemics and in the development of his modest talents. During the 1820s he engaged in minor skirmishes with Russia's growing romantic movement. An unfinished long poem that parodies romantic topoi, *Kapitan Khrabrov* appeared in fragments in several almanacs (1829–30). Heavily influenced by A. S. Pushkin's *Evgeny Onegin*, it remains a literary-historical curiosity. His slim volume of collected works (1822) features verse epistles, fables, epigrams, and other pieces of light verse.

A dedicated littérateur to the very end, his dying words were "How boring KATENIN's articles are." His nephew commented: "That's what it means to die like an honorable warrior on your shield, le cri de guerre à la bouche!"

Works: Sochineniya. Ed. and Introd. V. I. Saitov. 1893. Yu. M. Lotman, comp. and introd., *Poety 1790–1810-x godov.* 1971. Pp. 651–702. G. V. Ermakova-Bitner, ed. and introd., *Poety-satiriki kontsa XVIII-nachala XIX v.* 1959. Pp. 261–92. W. M. T.

Pushkin House (Pushkinskii dom), see INSTITUT RUSSKOI LITERATURY (Institute of Russian Literature).

Pyotr and Fevróniya, The Tale of, see HAGIOGRAPHY.

Pýpin, Aleksándr Nikoláevich (1833–1904), philologist, ethnographer, and historian, was born in Saratov, a relative of N. G. CHERNYSHEVSKY and graduate of St. Petersburg University. His Master's dissertation, "An Essay in the history of Old Russian Tales and Fairy Tales" (Ocherk istorii starinnykh povestei i skazok russkikh, 1857) is a useful work to this day. A corresponding member of the Academy of Sciences since 1891 and academician since 1898, Pypin was the author of about 1,200 publications. He is the creator of "three great compilations": *Istoriya russkoi literatury.* 4 vols., 1898–99, *Istoriya russkoi etnografii.* 4 vols, 1890–92, and *Istoriya slavyanskikh literatur.* 2 vols., 1879–81. Extremely broad in his interests and erudition, Pypin concentrated his main studies on modern Russian history and literature since the beginning of the 18th century. His monographs on the history of Russian FREEMASONRY: *Russian Freemasonry: the 18th Century and the First Quarter of the 19th* (Russkoe masonstvo [XVIII i pervaya chetvert' XIX v.], 1916), and religious movements in the early 19th century: *Religious movements under Alexander I* (Religioznye dvizheniya pri Aleksandre I, 1916), are still among the few valuable on these subjects. His edition of the collected works of CATHERINE II (vols. 1–5, 7–12; 1901–07) is the only available.

Bibliography: Ya. L. Barskov, *Spisok trudov akademika A. N. Pypina, 1853–1903.* 1903. *Materialy dlya biograficheskogo slovarya deistvitel'nykh chlenov Imperatorskoi Akademii nauk.* Pt. 2. 1917, Pp. 72–121.
Secondary literature: A. S. Arkhangelskii, "Trudy akademika A. N. Pypina v oblasti istorii russkoi literatury," *Zhurnal Ministerstva Narodnogo Prosveshcheniya,* 1904, no. 2, sect. 4, pp. 73–125. *Istoriya istoricheskoi nauki v SSSR. Dooktyabr'skii period: Bibliografiya.* 1965. Pp. 366–67. A. S. Myl'nikov, "Pypin, A. N." In *Slavyanovedenie v dorevolyutsionnoi Rossii: Biobibliograficheskii ukazatel'.* 1979. Pp. 286–89. E. B.

Radíshchev, Aleksándr Nikoláevich (1749–1802), is best known today as the author of *A Journey from Petersburg to Moscow* (Puteshestvie iz Peterburga v Moskvu), which he published anonymously in 1790 on his printing press. The work's subversive political overtones, compounded by its untimely appearance at the end of the ENLIGHTENMENT, and after the French Revolution, nearly cost Radishchev his life. The book was officially censored until 1905. That Radishchev came to be known as a politically revolutionary writer does little justice to his philosophical and artistic interests.

Radishchev's ancestry can be traced to two Tatar *murzy* who converted to Christianity under Ivan IV. Radishchev was born in the gentry class (without hereditary nobility), at Oblyazovo, in the province of Saratov. He learned to read and write from the *Book of Hours* and *Psalter*, like most children of the gentry, but with additional instruction from his very devout father. In Moscow, staying with his relatives, the Argamakovs, he was tutored (1757–64) by teachers from the university. He served in the Imperial Corps of Pages from 1764 to 1766. In 1766, he and his friend A. M. Kutuzov (1749–97) and ten other youths were selected by CATHERINE II to study law and related subjects at Leipzig University. At Leipzig, where he stayed from January 1767 to October 1771, Radishchev

distinguished himself, notwithstanding the physical deprivations and corporal punishments inflicted upon the group by their supervisor, a certain Major Bokum whom the authorities finally apprehended in 1772, several months after Radishchev and Kutuzov had returned to Russia. In St. Petersburg for little more than one year, both were made 9th-grade clerks processing court cases in the Senate. Radishchev was soon transferred to Count Ya. Bryus's staff as a consultant on questions of law in military courts. He joined the Masonic Lodge Urania and the English Club in 1773. In 1777 Radishchev entered civil service in the Commerce Collegium, and in 1790 was assistant director in the St. Petersburg Customs Office, with promotion to director due in August. But in June his *Journey* (printed with the censor's permission—he never read the book) came to the attention of Catherine, who saw in it evidence of a Masonic plot for her overthrow. Radishchev was imprisoned, and Catherine in a mock trial condemned him to death before "mercifully" commuting the sentence to ten years' exile in Siberia. Radishchev returned to Russia in 1797, under Paul, but remained in exile at Nemtsovo until 1801. Alexander I appointed Radishchev to the Commission for the Drafting of Laws in 1801. One morning in 1802, Radishchev, in the presence of his sons, swallowed the glass of sulphuric acid prepared for cleaning his uniform, and died the same day in terrible pain.

Numerous tragic incidents in Radishchev's life, to which he refers explicitly in his writing, confer on his works their intensely poignant emotional texture. In "Epitaph" (Epitafiya, 1783), written at the death of his first wife, Radishchev records his yearning to join her, but then questions the immortality of the soul. In "The Life of Ushakov" (Zhitie Ushakova, 1789), an essay which unfolds on the background of the Leipzig years, and in *Journey*, where autobiographical passages are frequent, Radishchev confides to Kutuzov, his addressee, that his soul is heavy with suffering and anguish; and in the remarkable "Diary of a Week" (Dnevnik odnoi nedeli), written around the time of Radishchev's imprisonment, his separation from his children and the uncovering of his debts generate a stream of consciousness on the theme of suicide. His momentous decision to write *Journey* came when, after the death of his first wife and under the pressure of his debts, he conceived a potentially lucrative book on the general topic of the humanitarianism of "Helvétius, de mémoire maudite," in Radishchev's later words. Already in 1773 Radishchev advanced in a note in his translation of Mably's *History of Ancient Greece* the Helvetian idea of selfish personal interest as the binding force in the social contract. And in "The Life of Ushakov," Radishchev claims that he learned from Helvétius's *De l'Esprit* (1758) the lesson in *morality* (deyatel'noyu naukoyu nravstvennosti) which he recognized in the students' impulse to respond in kind to a slap Bokum gave one of them. Radishchev shows that human social behavior is not governed by ideals of compassion and Christian love but by the universal principle: If you hit me my first impulse is to hit back. This response cannot be condemned on moral grounds since it is human. In *Journey*, with "empirical" material drawn from a broad spectrum of contemporary Russian life and even more so from the fund of Radishchev's life experience, but also with the aid of religious allegory, imagery, and language, Radishchev implores, and in some places vehemently demands of his reader (and perhaps more so of himself) that he embrace the principle of *revenge* as the true and rightful view of human social behavior. Moreover, in *Journey*, which unlike "The Life of Ushakov," is also concerned with the humanitarianism of this principle, Radishchev develops powerful prophesies of the strength for the individual and for society that will result from a conversion to this principle. The paradox of *Journey*'s "empirical" humanitarianism is easily but mistakenly understood as a call for an uprising of the masses against their ruler.

Beginning with *Journey*, Radishchev's first original work (not counting the love lyrics he destroyed), his creative writing assumes an eclectic character, even as he absorbs artistic features from Masonic literature; as in his *Journey* and later in "The Eighteenth Century" (Osmnadtsatoe stoletie, ca. 1800), and even in his "Apology" (Apologiya) of TREDIAKOVSKY's *Tilemakhida* (1766), where for his argument in defense of the Russian hexameter and of rhymeless verse Radishchev borrows directly from the treatises on the hexameter by Klopstock, who was much revered by the Russian Masons, and whose *Messiah* was translated by Kutuzov between 1785 and 1787. Radishchev's cult of expressiveness at the expense of clarity, as in "The Angel of Darkness" (Angel T'my, 1790s), partly an imitation of Milton's *Paradise Lost*, another work popular with the Russian Masons, and his penchant for archaic language, religious imagery, and allegory may be traced in part to Masonic influences. But a curiously distinctive feature of Radishchev's creative process is his dependence upon these sources in voicing his opposition to any and all expressions of religious ideology. Time and again Radishchev borrows the form of a moralizing, religious, or mystic work or genre to develop within it his own "empirical" ideas. For example, "A Hymn: The Creation" (Pesnoslovie. Tvorenie mira), an oratorio on the Creation (cf. Haydn's *Creation*, 1798), which Radishchev upon second thought removed from *Journey*'s chapter "Tver" where it was initially inserted directly following "Freedom, an Ode" (Oda Vol'nost'), shows God on the eve of the Creation prophesying that man will want to usurp His power. But God in His benevolence nonetheless endows man with an eternal source of bliss in the form of physical love; and the fragment ends after the act of Creation is described by the chorus in the terms of a delivery in childbirth. "The Life of Ushakov" develops, within the form of the Old Russian saint's life, the universal principle of revenge. *Journey* is in part inspired by the form of Masonic journeys and of Fénelon's *Télémaque*, an important model for them, even though, deliberately, the figure of Radishchev's traveler undergoes no moral change in the course of his journey. In addition, Sterne-Yorick, the "traveler-philosopher" of *A Sentimental Journey* (1768), helps Radishchev to conceptualize his hero even as Sterne's Christian humanitarianism, like the Masons' mysticism, is directly challenged in several passages of Radishchev's *Journey*. And "The Monument" (Pamyatnik, ca. 1801), an amusing structural riddle, ends with the "Apology" or praise of the hexameter which Trediakovsky adopted in translating Fénelon's *Télémaque* (in prose); but the section preceding the "Apology" parodies passages from the original, that is, the content or moral ideology of Fénelon.

Russian writers before Radishchev introduced into Russian belles lettres ideas current during the Enlightenment, but Radishchev is the first writer who did so with a new, pre-romantic emphasis on the self.

Works: Polnoe sobranie sochinenii. Vol. 1 (1938), vol. 2 (1941), vol. 3 (1952). *Puteshestvie iz Peterburga v Moskvu.* 1935. (Photomechanical printing of the original 1790 ed.) *Stikhotvoreniya.* Ed. V. A. Zapadov. (Biblioteka poeta, Bol'shaya seriya.) 1975.

Translations: A Journey from St. Petersburg to Moscow. Trans. L. Wiener. Ed. with introd. and notes by R. P. Thaler. Cambridge, Mass., 1958.

Secondary Literature: (The body of secondary sources on Radishchev is enormous with some of the finest work today coming from the area of the history of the writing of *Journey*.) M. G. Al'tshuller, "Literaturnaya zhizn' Tobol'ska 90-kh gg. XVIII v." In *Osvoenie Sibiri v epokhu feodalizma (XVII–XIX vv.)* Novosibirsk, 1968. Pp. 178–94. ———, "Vnov' naidennyi spisok *Puteshestviya iz Peterburga v Moskvu,*" *RLit* 12 (1969), no. 2, pp. 125–28. G. Gukovskii, "Radishchev kak pisatel'." In *A. N. Radishchev: Materialy i issledovaniya.* 1936. Pp. 141–92. L. I. Kulakova, "O datirovke 'Dnevnika odnoi nedel'l.'" In *Radishchev: Stat'i i materialy.* 1950. Pp. 148–57. P. G. Lyubomirov, "Rod Radishcheva." In *A. N. Radishchev: Materialy i issledovaniya.* 1936. Pp. 291–354. G. P. Makogonenko, *Radishchev i ego vremya.* 1956. Tanya Page, "A Radishchev Monstrology: The *Journey from Petersburg to Moscow* and Later Writings in the Light of French Sources." In *American Contributions to the Eighth International Congress of Slavists.* 1978. Pp. 605–29. I. Z. Serman, "A. N. Radishchev-pisatel' v issledovaniyakh poslednego desyatiletiya, 1965–1975," *RLit* 18 (1975), no. 4, pp. 180–91. G. Shtorm, *Potaennyi Radishchev.* 1968. T. P.

Raëshnyi stikh, raëshnik, see SKAZOVYI STIKH.

Raévsky, G., see OTSUP, Nikolai Avdeevich.

Raich (Amfiteátrov), Semyón Egórovich (1792–1855), poet, translator, journalist, was born in the village Rai-Vysokoe, in Orel Province, the son of a clergyman. He received his education in the Orel seminary, where he studied Latin and read the classics and began to write verses. He did not take his orders and moved in 1810 to Moscow, serving as tutor to various aristocratic families. For a number of years he was tutor to F. I. TYUTCHEV. He attended lectures at Moscow University, studying Italian language and literature. He was a member of the early Decembrist society "The Union of Welfare." In 1821 Raich published a translation of Virgil's "Georgics" in rhymed iambic pentameter, prefaced by an extensive study entitled "A Discourse on Didactic Poetry," which a year later he defended as his dissertation for a Master's degree in literature. He taught at the Moscow University Gentry Pension where among his charges was M. Yu. LERMONTOV. For several years he hosted a popular literary circle which was interested in literary theory, aesthetics and translation, and was close to the philosophical society, the WISDOM LOVERS. Raich published the members' works in his almanac *Novye aonidy* (1823); he later published the almanac *Severnaya lira* (1827) with D. P. Oznobishin and the journal *Galatea* (1829–30, 1839–40). In his later years he was active in the journal MOSKVITYANIN.

Raich's original poetic output is slight. His main works are the translations of Ariosto's "Orlando Furioso" and Tasso's "Jerusalem Delivered." His lyrics show many of the moods of ZHUKOVSKY's elegiac poetry and alternate with short classic pieces with epicurean motifs. His best known poem "To Friends" (Druz'yam, 1826) was set to music and enjoyed considerable popularity. His interest in Italian language and literature lent an unusual note to his style in which he attempted to reproduce the mannerism of the Italian, its voluptuousness, warm coloring, its complicated melodiousness and elegance of rhythmic patterns. The Italian note sounded clearly in his theoretical study "Petrarch and Lomonosov," in which he proposed to blend Italian euphony with the grandeur of Lomonosov's imagery. His experiments, theoretically significant, influenced the early poetry of Tyutchev and Lermontov.

Works: Poety 1820–1830-kh godov. (Biblioteka poeta.) Vol. 2. 1972. Pp. 5–31.

Secondary literature: M. Aronson and F. Reiser, *Literaturnye kruzhki i salony.* 1929. Pp. 123–28. *Literaturnye salony i kruzhki. Pervaya polovina XIX veka.* 1930. Pp. 139–40. A. Gl.

RAPP (*Rossiiskaya assotsiátsiya proletárskikh pisátelei*—Russian Association of Proletarian Writers) was the dominant proletarian literary organization from 1928 until the liquidation of all separate literary groups in 1932. During that period RAPP promulgated its program as the official line in literature. The organization was founded as VAPP (All-Union Association) in 1920 by a group of writers belonging to KUZNITSA (The Smithy). With the adoption of NEP and the postponement of a communist society to the indefinite future, VAPP split into two factions. The one calling itself "October" consisted of writers from the Young Communist League who contended that the Smithy faction was "retarding the development of young writers" and giving insufficient support to the Party program. In literary terms the division meant that the October (OKTYABR') group wished to abandon the lyrical and romantic note favored by the older Smithy poets in order to reflect and inspire the mundane labors of the proletariat in the period of reconstruction. The split in VAPP clearly reflected the Party's own retreat from world revolution in favor of restoring the economic life of the Soviet Union. The leaders of the October faction were Leopold AVERBAKH, Yury LIBEDINSKY, Aleksandr BEZYMENSKY, Semyon RODOV, G. LELEVICH, I. Vardin, and some others. They became the dominant group in VAPP and remained so until 1926. As spokesmen of VAPP they condemned nonproletarian writers and excoriated publishers who printed them and critics who showed them favor, such as Vyacheslav POLONSKY and Aleksandr VORONSKY. Their demand for "proletarian hegemony" over all literature led to a formal debate under the auspices of the Press Section of the Central Committee, the upshot of which was a resolution rejecting the demand for hegemony and calling for a more tolerant treatment of non-proletarian FELLOW TRAVELLERS of the Revolution (1925). A new leadership and somewhat modified policies were subsequently provided for the proletarian organization, and its name was changed to RAPP in 1928.

The program for literature promulgated after 1926 by the leading group—Averbakh, Libedinsky, KIRSHON, and FADEEV—favored realism of the classical 19th-century pattern, particularly the method and style of Lev TOLSTOI, who was presented to proletarian writers as a model to learn from and was widely imitated. The theorists tended to equate literary realism with materialism in philosophy and thereby a "dialectical materialist method" was discovered, according to which the real world should be presented as the struggle of opposites in society and in individual characters. The "dialectic of the individual psyche," a formula borrowed from CHERNYSHEVSKY, was the subject presented for the proletarian writer, and the principal slogan was "For the living man in literature." Works written in conscious conformity to the RAPP program included Fadeev's *The Rout* (1927), Libedinsky's *Birth of a Hero* (1930), and, perhaps, certain early chapters of SHOLOKHOV's *The Quiet Don* (1928). Their narrowly conceived and stylistically conservative literary program set the RAPP leadership at odds with a large and important segment of contemporary Russian literature: MAYAKOVSKY and LEF, the CONSTRUCTIVISTS, PEREVAL, and those fellow travellers who, like PILNYAK and ZAMYATIN, experimented with narrative technique. The RAPP leadership engaged in constant and bitter polemics with all its "enemies" and in 1930 other groups were discredited and encouraged officially to disband and join RAPP. Many of their members, Mayakovsky, for instance, joined RAPP during that year. "A tone of command" appeared in the pronouncements of the leadership, though internal dissension continued and in the debates of 1931 the program of the leadership was attacked as not in harmony with the current cultural line of the Party. A Party resolution liquidating RAPP and decreeing the formation of a single Union for all writers was published in 1932. Averbakh and some other members of the leadership were arrested and condemned as enemies in 1937.

Bibliography: E. J. Brown, *The Proletarian Episode in Russian Literature.* 1953, 1971. K. Eimermacher, ed., *Dokumente zur sowjetischen Literaturpolitik.* Stuttgart, 1972. Herman Ermolaev, *Soviet Literary Theories, 1917–1934.* 1963. S. Sheshukov, *Neistovye revniteli.* 1970.   E. J. B.

Raskól'niki, see OLD BELIEVERS.

Raspútin, Valentin, Grigórievich (1937–). Graduated from the college of humanities (istoriko-filologicheskii fakul'tet) of Irkutsk State University in 1959, Rasputin started writing in 1961. He belongs to the generation of Soviet writers who experienced neither the war nor the worst of Stalinist lawlessness directly. Therefore Rasputin's works do not suffer from the kind of constraint that these two inhibiting factors have exercised on older Soviet writers. During the early period of his writing career he published semi-journalistic sketches about life and work in the Siberian countryside. Rasputin made himself known nationally with his short novel, *Money for Maria* (Den'gi dlya Marii, 1967). Its plot is simple: a large sum of money is discovered to be missing when the accounts of a village store are audited, and Mariya, an honest but simple-minded woman, is responsible for the shortage. Thereafter, he published several other short novels which put him in the forefront of the writers of "COUNTRY PROSE". The best known of them are *The Final Stage* (Poslednii srok, 1970), a family drama about the dying of an old peasant woman; *Mark You This* (Zhivi i pomni, 1974), the tragedy of a deserter who in the last months of the war tries to return to his wife in Siberia; *Farewell to Matyora* (Proshchanie s Materoi, 1976), in which the construction of a new Siberian hydroelectric power dam necessitates the flooding of an island and the destruction of its long-established way of life. All these works deal with the life and hardships of Siberian villagers. Rasputin presents the life of his characters under extreme circumstances so as to elicit their ultimate psychological and moral response: anticipation of disgrace and imprisonment; imminent death; inevitability of doom; destruction of a proven way of life for the sake of a problematic progress. These dramatic situations are the measure of the villagers' vitality and insight into what constitutes the source of life. A powerful patriotic—*rusit* (the Russian equivalent of "100% American")—ethos runs through all these stories, and, undoubtedly, is one of the reasons for their popularity. In *Farewell to Matyora*, the author, blending his voice and thoughts with those of his old wise peasant women, fears for the identity of the archetypal Russian disappearing under the onslaught of frantic industrialization. In Rasputin's poetic and philosophical perception a wholesale modernization cannot redeem the loss of some traditional humane values rooted in nature

and inherent in his Siberian village. This Neo-Slavophilism is interwoven with modern notions of ecology. The author conveys his message, both concrete and poetic, in a prose akin to dialectal peasant speech. He uses folkloric symbolism and dreams, mostly to emphasize man's helplessness against the forces of fate. Altogether, Rasputin's complex prose has a sense of both completeness and ambiguity. Hardships have no easy solutions, and their moral is not unambiguous. A deserter is seen as just that, but also as one trapped by forces well beyond his control. And the latter condition carries its own moral, not as obvious as the former but far-reaching in another way. Rasputin's prose is circumscribed as to its societal material and theme. In this respect it is not easy to renew.

Works: Povesti. Foreword S. Zalygin. 1976. (Content: Proshchanie s Materoi; Zhivi i pomni; Poslednii srok; Den'gi dlya Marii.) *Uroki frantsuzskogo.* 1982.

Translations: Live and Remember. Trans. Antonina W. Bouis. 1978. *Farewell to Matyora: A Novel.* Trans. A. W. Bouis. 1979.

Secondary literature: Lewis Bagby, "A Concurrence of Psychological and Narrative Structures: Anamnesis in Valentin Rasputin's *Upstream, Downstream,*" *CSP* 22 (1980), pp. 388–99. Geoffrey Hosking, *Beyond Socialist Realism: Soviet Fiction since* Ivan Denisovich. 1980. Pp. 70–81. E. Starikova, "Zhit' i pomnit' (Zametki o proze V. Rasputina)," *Literatura i sovremennost',* 1976–77, Sbornik 16, pp. 213–36. Vladimir Vasil'ev, "Zhit' i pomnit'." In *Soprichastnost' zhizni.* 1979. Pp. 189–226.   H. O.

Rasskáz, see SHORT STORY.

Raznochíntsy, a social term referring to "people of diverse rank" or "people of no particular estate." These were a new breed within Russian society of mixed background below the gentry, including sons of the clergy who did not follow the calling of their fathers, offspring of petty officials and of impoverished noblemen, and individuals from the masses, who made their way, through education and persistent effort. Having emerged from provincial, clerical, and petty-bourgeois squalor, they rose with difficulty from poverty and social obscurity, frequently by tutoring, doing translation work, or through journalism. Already by the 1840s the *raznochintsy* showed a significant influence on the development of social life and culture. Even before the peasant reforms they made their liberal and democratic tendencies felt. Some of the most prominent representatives of the *raznochintsy* included the critics V. G. BELINSKY, N. G. CHERNYSHEVSKY, and N. A. DOBROLYUBOV.

Although in the 1840s the intelligentsia included individuals of all classes, it was still dominated primarily by those who came from the gentry. By the 1860s, however, prominence within the intelligentsia had shifted to the *raznochintsy*. Eventually precipitated by this shift in the center of gravity, the intelligentsia acquired a full sense of its own identity, which led, in fact, by the 1860s, to the adoption and currency of the very name "intelligentsia." Moreover, this change preempted what came to be known as the dichotomy between "fathers" and "sons." By the late 19th and early 20th centuries, the intelligentsia became to be dominated increasingly by commoners of more and more indeterminate origin, including LENIN, TROTSKY, and Stalin.   D. K. D.

Reading Library, see BIBLIOTEKA DLYA CHTENIYA.

Realism, a confused, but inescapable category of literary and art criticism. The term is a borrowing from philosophy, where it has a long history, the philosophical *realist* being one who believes in the independent existence of ideas, while his opponent, the *nominalist*, does not. In the arts, however, far from signalling belief in the primary reality of non-material ideas, *realism* has come to mean almost the opposite, emphasizing the obtrusive presence of the "real" world. Yet that core word, *real*, inevitably drags behind it a whole philosophical baggage train, including the central questions of epistemology, whether the world we perceive with our senses is *real* (or simply *is*), and if so, whether our knowledge of it, derived from sense impressions or otherwise, is *true*. To these age-old questions must be added the problem, especially crucial for literature, of whether language, our principal means of communication, can adequately convey to others the *truth* of what we experience.

The philosophical penumbra surrounding *real* is perhaps also responsible for another basic ambiguity in the use of the term *realism*. On the one hand, the word is used historically, to refer to a specific movement or period, one extending from about 1830 to about 1890, but with descendants still identifiable today. On the other hand, it is also used as a universal, ahistorical category, an attribute or quality of which literature and art of all periods may partake to some degree. In such usage *realistic* may become little more than a synonym for *truthful*. But even in the more limited sense, one that defines *realism* as a conscious orientation toward truth, especially unpleasant truth, as opposed to idealization or myth, "realistic" elements can be discerned in a host of writers and artists long before the 19th century: in art, Roman portrait sculpture and Flemish genre painting; in literature, medieval fabliaux and the picaresque novel beginning with *Lazarillo de Tormes*.

The notion of *mimesis*, or imitation of nature, as the "realistic" basis of art, of course, goes back to Aristotle, and the concomitant notion of *verisimilitude*, or faithfulness to nature, as the firmest foundation for aesthetic judgments, has an equally venerable history. The words *realism* and *realistic* are often used for conveying aesthetic value judgments, both positive and negative. As the Oxford English Dictionary puts it, "In reference to art and literature [*realism* is] sometimes used as a term of commendation, when precision and vividness of detail are regarded as a merit, and sometimes unfavourably, contrasted with idealized description or representation. In recent use it has often been used with implication that the details are of an unpleasant or sordid character."

In Soviet parlance *realistic* is even more frequently used as a qualitative signifier, invariably positive, and applied to works quite outside the period of historical "realism." The history of literature and art, like history itself, is perceived as an ascending curve, with "progress" being made, through addition of more and more "realism," until finally it becomes the dominant mode in the 19th century. It then acquires the fixed epithet *critical* and continues its progress down into the Soviet period, when the glorious plateau of *socialist* realism is at last reached. It is not clear what further ascent from there is to be expected.

Claims to truthfulness in representing the world are not, of course, limited to realists. This fact, in addition to the perennial difficulty of Pilate's question, led the early Russian FORMALISTS, in their effort to make literary studies rigorous and self-contained, to devise an intrinsic definition of *realism*, one that would avoid the troublesome epistemological issue. The most fruitful and provocative of these efforts was R. JAKOBSON's "Realism in Art" (1921). Realism, Jakobson maintained, is nothing more than the prevalence of metonymy (relationships of contiguity) over metaphor (relationships of similarity) as the fundamental trope. He later established this polarity as basic to any symbolic process and related it to depth psychology. Much later the STRUCTURALISTS followed this lead, Tzvetan Todorov managing to offer three definitions of *vraisemblance* none of which requires any assumptions (other than those of a naive, easily fooled reader) about "correspondence" between a literary text and "reality." Limitations of space preclude pursuing this theoretical issue here, but it should be recognized that in the West there is strong sentiment in favor of defining *realism* intrinsically as a species of illusionism, a system for tricking readers into believing (or at least suspending disbelief) in the "reality" of the text's world.

The word *realism* was in use among the Germans as early as 1800, but as a movement, a body of doctrine, realism took shape mainly in France. There by the 1830s critics were using the word to refer to detailed physical descriptions. Only in the 1850s, however, did *réalisme* become a slogan and a rallying cry. In 1857 the novelist and art historian Champfleury, a friend of the painter Courbet, published a volume of essays entitled *Le réalisme*, which is often taken as the movement's manifesto. It was written mainly in defense of Courbet's subject matter and style, especially his depiction of ordinary people in their ordinary activities. Before long *realism* acquired general European currency to signify various strongly asserted positions in contemporary literature and art. Most of the distinguishing features of realism, however, antedate the appearance of the term itself. Its true origins must therefore be seen as a series of impulses or tendencies that become increasingly dominant after about 1830. Though borderlines are blurred and some of these features can be found among writers usually considered romantics (just as "roman-

tic" features can be found among the realists), realism essentially began as a reaction against romanticism. These basic anti-romantic impulses can be briefly catalogued.

Where *romanticism* stressed the exceptional, the larger-than-life, the heroic, realism concentrated on the everyday, the average, the "typical." Where romanticism treated the individual as unique and independently valuable, realism perceived human beings as integral parts both of the system of nature and of society. Romanticism portrayed its heroes' behavior as motivated by their own ideas, passions, aspirations, and will; realism viewed peoples' lives as largely determined by social or biological forces beyond their control. The romantic author had no compunctions about obtruding his own reactions and reflections into his narrative; the realist author felt constrained to remain objective, dispassionate, to "let the facts speak for themselves." Proud of his title of "artist," the romantic author saw no reason to deny that his works were his own creation, the products of his imagination and even of inspiration vouchsafed from on high; for the realist, however, "imagination" connoted invention and even falsehood, and he deployed every technical means at his disposal to create the illusion that his fiction was fact. The realist was deeply impressed by the rapid development of natural science, which was making so many discoveries through precise observation of the material world, and the writer hoped that the same method would work in literature. Zola even made the extravagant claim that the "experimental novel" was a tool for discovering truth equivalent in method and equal in value to the scientist's laboratory. By no means all the "realistic" features were exhibited in every realist's work, and as noted above, some of the same tendencies can be detected among writers of the 18th century and earlier. Nevertheless, a sufficient concentration and conscious exploitation of them is present in the 19th century to justify calling it the classic period of realism.

In France the transition from romanticism to realism is adumbrated in the work of such ROMANTIC REALISTS (to use Donald Fanger's term) as Stendhal and Balzac. Both have strong links to romanticism, but both powerfully demonstrate basic realistic tendencies. Stendhal is a romantic in his cult of the individual at odds with society, but a realist in his careful representation of the dynamics of the society itself. His concern with psychological truth, with unvarnished representation of the realities of human motivation (from which TOLSTOI learned so much) has led some critics to label him a "psychological realist." Though the ironic tone in which he conveys them is too obtrusive to meet the objective standards of pure realism, events in Stendhal's novels appear to happen naturally, from causal interaction between the protagonists' impulses and actions and the world in which they move.

Balzac, more than Stendhal, illustrates the particular realistic impulse that assigns to literature the function of sociological analysis. In a vast series of interlocking novels he undertook a complete, "scientific" description of French society, with every class, every milieu given its due. Social historians have accepted his representations as both penetrating and true; Marxists in particular give Balzac great credit for telling the whole truth about the *embourgeoisement* of French society under the July monarchy, this despite his own aristocratic and legitimist sympathies. Engels further praises Balzac (incidentally, at Zola's expense) for depicting typical characters and circumstances; this concept of the *typical* remains important in the theory of realism, despite its abuse in Soviet times. Though romantic in his creation of "monster" characters enslaved by their passions, Balzac is strongly realist in his immensely detailed representations of the physical world. Balzac, and even more his contemporary Eugène Sue, exhibits another of realism's special proclivities, fascination with the "lower depths" of society. In *Les mystères de Paris* (1842) Sue titillated his bourgeois readers with lurid accounts of the degradation and crime of the slums; it was one of the social physiologies that inspired many imitators in Russia.

Whatever his sociological realism, Balzac remains thoroughly romantic in his lack of detachment, the *impassibilité* insisted upon by Flaubert, who proclaimed, "The author in his work must be like God in the universe, everywhere present, but nowhere visible." Balzac was far too visible to qualify as a "high realist." Thus the exemplar of high or non-romantic realism is Flaubert, and especially his *Madame Bovary* (1857). Here deromanticization is total. The milieu depicted is shallow and provincial, its characters limited and vulgar, their experiences banal. "I execrate [this] ordinary life," Flaubert lamented," ... but aesthetically I wanted, this time, and only this time, to get hold of it to the very bottom." Hidden behind the carefully wrought *impassibilité*, therefore, Flaubert's realism becomes a poetry of negation and disgust.

In Russia, even before the solid establishment of realism in France, important steps in a realistic direction had already been taken. Thus realism is perhaps the first major literary development whose Russian version is not a more or less belated response to ideas generated in Western Europe. To be sure, the 19th-century Russians are always keenly aware of current developments in the West, especially in France, but they come to realism almost by themselves, in their own way, and partly in advance of their Western colleagues. Doubtless Soviet claims to primacy should be viewed with skepticism, but it seems that if followed with caution, their application of the term "realistic" to certain features in the work of such pre-realist writers as PUSHKIN, GOGOL, and even the quintessential romantic, LERMONTOV, can be appropriate and illuminating.

One of the author's objectives in *Evgeny Onegin*, for example, is to deromanticize the Byronic hero, partly by removing him from his customary exotic setting and exposing him to the ordinary circumstances of the ordinary life of the Russian gentry—a more limited version of the Balzacian sociological impulse. The contrast in that novel of three geographically identified styles of gentry life, Petersburg, Moscow, and the country estate, proved an almost hypnotic model for later literary sociologists, especially Tolstoi. Pushkin's subjection of his hero to the ignominy of being rejected in love might also be considered anti-romantic and thus realistic. Yet in at least two respects *Evgeny Onegin* is as distant from canonical realism as it is possible to be. It never pretends to be anything other than an artifact, the product of a poet's workshop; several hundred elegant, fourteen-line stanzas in rhymed iambic tetrameter could hardly claim to be a "human document" emanating directly from life. And *Evgeny Onegin's* attitude toward itself, so to speak, is ludic, even the placement of its parts being represented as subject to the author's whims. Such a playful attitude toward literary form, which breaks the illusion of its inevitability, would be quite out of order in a full-fledged realist. Finally, *Evgeny Onegin* ostentatiously violates the Flaubertian imperative that the author must dissolve in his work. As the god of the novel's universe, Pushkin —or a narrator who shares much of his curriculum vitae—is notably palpable and present, lyrically associating and commenting feelingly on the action, though maintaining considerable ironic detachment from the characters.

Of all the labels assigned to Russian writers by their contemporaries and by subsequent generations, perhaps the most disputed has been the categorization of Gogol as a realist. It is an assignment that owes its origin to BELINSKY (though he never used the word), and on the strength of his authority it became canonical in the latter 19th century. Gogol's alleged realism was disputed only later by such symbolist or formalist critics as ROZANOV, BRYUSOV, MEREZHKOVSKY, BELY, and Vasily Hippius; and under their influence it has long become conventional in the West to stress the non- (or even sur-) realistic side of Gogol: the illogical absurdity of his plots, his exaggerated, ludicrous, unidimensional caricatures, his dreamlike sequences and unmotivated transitions, the lyrical or prophetic intrusions of his narrative voice—all features far removed from the prescriptions of high realism.

All this is granted; yet Belinsky was not wholly wrong either. Gogol himself, in a famous passage in *Dead Souls*, articulates a distinction between two basic classes of writers which approximates that between the romantic and the realist. The "happy" (i.e., romantic) writer, Gogol proclaims, turns aside from "tedious, repellent characters, impressive in their sad actuality" in favor of "characters who manifest the lofty dignity of man"; the "unhappy" (realistic) writer, on the other hand, dares to expose "all the frightful, shocking muck of trivia that engulf our life, the depths of those cold, fragmented, everyday characters with which our earthly path, often bitter and tedious, swarms." Gogol, needless to say, saw himself as an "unhappy" writer. He even uses a "scientific" metaphor almost worthy of Zola to describe the two kinds of art: "equally marvelous are the lenses that contemplate suns and those that convey the movements of unnoticed insects." Brandishing his microscope, Gogol thus lays claim to the title of the entomologist of Rus-

sian literature. It is his observations of human insects that validate whatever claim Gogol has to the looser title of "realist." As SVYATOPOLK-MIRSKY puts it, Gogol "was a realist in the sense that he introduced (as details and as material) innumerable elements and aspects of reality that hitherto had not possessed the freedom of literature."

After Gogol, the "realistic" strains in his work, as perceived by Belinsky, were continued and amplified in the 1840s by that heterogeneous group of writers who became known as the NATURAL SCHOOL. Belinsky's foreword to NEKRASOV's celebrated miscellany, *The Physiology of Petersburg* (1845), is sometimes taken as the manifesto of the school, but a fuller exposition of its principles is to be found in Belinsky's "View of Russian Literature in 1846." There he singles out "reality" and "truth" as the hallmarks of the movement: "Talents have always existed, but formerly they prettified nature, idealized reality, that is to say, depicted what did not exist, dealt with the fantastic, whereas today they deal with life and reality in their true light." These programmatic qualities of the natural school were best exemplified in Nekrasov's own contribution to the volume, "Petersburg Corners." These "corners" are literal: sections of filthy basement rooms rented out to people too poor to afford anything better. The corners' physical squalor matched the degradation and despair of their occupants—both potentialities later developed to the full by DOSTOEVSKY. The classic hero of the natural school, however, is the poor copy-clerk, harking back to Pushkin's Evgeny (from "The Bronze Horseman"), Lermontov's Stanislav Krasinsky (from *Princess Ligovskaya*), and Gogol's Akaky Akakievich (from "The Overcoat"). Dostoevsky's Makar Devushkin, from "Poor Folk" (which appeared in the second of Nekrasov's physiologies), is a polemically humanized version of Gogol's archetype.

The range of physiology, however, extended beyond the city and its slums. Its scrutinizing lens was also directed at the Russian countryside, revealing a human world notably different from that conventionally portrayed in earlier Russian literature, where peasants had seldom been more than dimly sketched background figures in the lives of gentry characters. "Khor and Kalinich," the first of TURGENEV's *Notes of a Hunter* (1847–51), had startled Russian readers by treating with dignity and seriousness, as fully developed, complex human beings, two peasant characters. At the other end of the social scale the *Notes* displayed some far from noble representatives of the nobility, though Turgenev was too subtle an artist to make the equation of "good" with "low" and "bad" with "high" too absolute. A harsher view of the misery of peasant life was found in the early stories of Turgenev's fellow physiologist, GRIGOROVICH, such as "The Village" (1846) and "Anton Goremyka" (1847). No doubt Russian rural physiologies were a genuine literary response to real Russian conditions and a reflection of the social forces that eventually led to the Emancipation. Nevertheless, it is a fact that peasant themes were much in vogue at this time in other countries as well, witness Balzac's *Les paysans* (1844), George Sand's *Jeanne* (1844), or Auerbach's *Schwarzwälder Dorfgeschichten* (1843–54), in addition to *Uncle Tom's Cabin* (1851–52). Clearly, the relationship between life and art in literary history is as complex as in literature itself.

At about the same time as the physiologies, Nekrasov began his long series of poems evoking the atmosphere of hopelessness and gloom felt as characteristic of the Russia of Nicholas I. Though gloom and realism often seem inseparable, the more literary connection of Nekrasov's poetry to realism is its deflation of poetic language. It is primarily he who freed Russian poetry from the conventional poeticisms of the "Golden Age" and enriched it with the hard roughnesses of prosaic diction.

Another early triumph of the natural school is GONCHAROV's *A Common Story* (1847), in which the hero, the provincial dreamer Aleksandr Aduev, is not only deflated in the eyes of the reader, but actually transformed, into a sleek, cynical, self-serving realist (in the non-literary sense), a careerist in the style of his uncle and mentor, who in the meantime has himself begun to wonder whether a life without ideals or love is worth living. As Milton Ehre has noted (applying an idea of Harry Levin's), the "realistic" tendency in *A Common Story* originates in parody, a parody of romanticism. Aleksandr's pretentious romantic effusions sound absurd in the sordid, self-seeking Petersburg epitomized by his uncle.

After Belinsky's death the very term "natural school" was outlawed by the censorship, but a substitute was soon found, the "GOGOLIAN TREND" (gogolevskoe napravlenie), the principles of which were spelled out in 1855 in a series of articles by CHERNYSHEVSKY. Despite Gogol's wrongheaded, reactionary ideas, Chernyshevsky maintained, his art had opened Russians' eyes to the pervasive disorder of their society and to the very possibility of using literature to tell the truth about it. This latter capacity Chernyshevsky now proclaimed as an imperative: literature (for which he otherwise had little respect) could at least be useful as a medium of instruction, as a vehicle of truth. Even before the Gogol articles, Chernyshevsky had published his celebrated master's dissertation, The Aesthetic Relation of Art to Reality (1855), in which he summarily downgrades art as an inferior surrogate for life. His argument is structured throughout as if one must make a choice between art and life, with art invariably the loser. A real apple is tastier than a painted one; only those who cannot view the sea need a picture of it; real human bodies are more beautiful than statues; and real human relationships are more rewarding than reading about them in novels. Realism as a drive to bring more "reality" into art thus became at Chernyshevsky's hands a move to substitute reality for art.

Essentially the same principles were upheld by DOBROLYUBOV. He too insists that literature is only a mirror, offering inferior reflections of life; he even uses the word realism in reference to its mimetic capacity. (The word had appeared in Russian in an 1849 article by Pavel ANNENKOV, but did not gain currency until the 1860s). In general, however, Dobrolyubov had little interest in literature as such; literary texts were used mainly as pretexts for disquisitions on the social problems "reflected" in them.

It was PISAREV who carried the assault on literature to its ultimate. In the scientific age, Pisarev averred, all art is outmoded. Even the cognitive function is no longer needed; there are better ways of discovering and reporting on the world. But since people are weak and seem to need such pablum, art can be conditionally allowed; and the critic can use literary texts for discussions of society itself, with literary types taken as social types. Pisarev's most successful application of this method was his article "Bazarov," in which he seized on Turgenev's hero, with all his roughnesses, as the long awaited "new man" in Russian society, the "realist." Thus Pisarev once again carries the terms realist and realism out of literature. Realist becomes a new euphemism for revolutionary, and realism stands for the doctrines of scientific materialism and socialism society was destined to embrace.

In the meantime, while being ignored or abused by the country's leading critics, Russian literary realists were reaching their greatest heights, turning out one after the other those masterpieces of prose fiction that still rank among mankind's greatest artistic achievements. The major realists all perform a ritualistic repudiation of romanticism, whether it had informed their own earlier work or not. Tolstoi, for example, at the end of "Sevastopol in May" (1855)—itself a sort of physiology—makes the somewhat melodramatic declaration that the hero of his story is Truth, "which I love with all the forces of my soul and which was, is, and always will be beautiful." Even as late as "The Cossacks" (1863) Tolstoi felt obliged once again to deflate the much deflated romantic hero, seizing the occasion to animadvert on Marlinsky (see BESTUZHEV). Likewise Dostoevsky, though with much unregenerate romanticism still latent within him, moved sharply in a realistic direction after his years of penance in Siberia. He exorcized the ghost of Gogol through parody in The Village of Stepanchikovo and Its Inhabitants (1858), revived his earlier fascination with the dregs of society (The Insulted and Injured, 1861), and produced a thinly fictionalized physiology of his Siberian prison experiences (Notes from the House of the Dead, 1862). Goncharov too, though he insisted that the artist's imagination was needed to illuminate reality, not merely reflect it, also claimed that in The Precipice he had "invented nothing: life itself did the writing."

The transition from romanticism to high realism is perhaps easiest to identify in the case of Turgenev. A letter to him of October 1852, from the same Annenkov who first used the word realism provides specifications for the change. Though full of praise for Notes of a Hunter, Annenkov urged Turgenev to put its techniques behind him and launch out in a new direction. In Notes, he wrote, "the element of contrivance [sochinitel'stvo] is too obvious" (in other words, the authorial presence is too obtrusive). Further, there is a question of genre. Annenkov asks Turgenev to give up "notes" and move to what was to become the classic vehicle for high realism, the big novel. And he wants a novel with a properly invisible, omniscient author: "I am absolutely expecting from you a novel with full authority over the characters and events and without exhibiting yourself (i.e., your authorship)." Turgenev agreed with alacrity: "I must take another road," he replied, "I have to find it—and bid farewell forever to my old manner."

For the next three decades Turgenev on the whole faithfully carried out Annenkov's prescriptions. He dutifully produced, one after the other, that series of topical novels in which he tried to encapsulate in literary form the vital questions of the day, the sea changes in Russian society; and in his short stories and novellas—perhaps in the last analysis artistically more valuable than the novels—he continued to explore some of the universals of human life, especially the man-woman relationship. Only toward the end of this long road did the "other Turgenev," the recidivist romantic, make a rather feeble reappearance as a purveyor of ghost stories such as "Klara Milich" (1882).

Partly under Turgenev's tutelage (though he chafed at it) Tolstoi also worked his way toward high realism. After the initial success of his military physiologies and of the acute psychological insights displayed in Childhood, Boyhood, and Youth (concerning which Chernyshevsky, of all people, coined the perfect descriptive phrase, "dialectics of the soul"), Russian literature seemed to leave Tolstoi behind. Stories like "Albert" and "Lucerne" were seen as tired replays of romantic themes; and even Family Happiness (1859), with its daring presentation of courtship and marriage from the woman's point of view, met a cool reception. The left wing of literature was continuing the physiological tradition with more stark reportage, offering pictures of poverty and degradation in every corner of Russian society; plebeian "factographers" such as Nikolai USPENSKY, POMYALOVSKY, and RESHETNIKOV were the rage. Ostensibly turning his back on literature, Tolstoi sulkily withdrew to his estate, eventually to emerge, in one of the most colossal comebacks of all time, with, of all things, a historical novel, something Russian literature had not seen—or at least taken seriously—for many years. It turned out to be the best historical novel ever written. Though realistic all right in its precision of detail, its psychology, its sociology, and its use of causality, not to mention the illusion of reality it imposes on the reader, it included many elements at odds with the reigning fashions of "plebeian realism." Not only was the patriotic, high-society theme anathema to the radicals, but so was the very escape into history, the lack of relevance to the burning issues of the day. And at least in one respect the author certainly did not meet the Flaubertian insistence on self-obliteration: on the contrary, Tolstoi was constantly coming out from behind the scenes to argue his views about determinism in history. In Anna Karenina, however, Tolstoi was a more complete realist, at least to the extent of bringing the action down to modern times and grappling with a whole host of questions, both contemporary, social, and eternal, "accursed" ones, as well as exposing with unexampled penetration the dialectics of its characters' souls. However, the basic plot nucleus, the sexual misbehavior of a high-society lady, once again seemed insultingly trivial to the radicals; and even Dostoevsky, though ostensibly full of admiration for the novel, sought to relegate it securely to an outmoded tradition, as the swan song of the Russian gentry.

In the critical pronouncements of his late years Tolstoi placed moral criteria, almost to the exclusion of aesthetic ones, as the basis for judging works of art. Nevertheless, he continued to insist that "beauty of form" and "clarity of exposition" were the same thing. And he recognized the importance of "talent," though talent too had a moral base: if not corrupted by the artist's milieu (as Maupassant's partly was), talent forces the artist, independently of his will, to love good and hate evil. It also, however, forces him "to see things not as he wants to see them, but as they are," i.e., to be a realist.

Though generally counted among the great realists, Dostoevsky's membership in this class is the most ambiguous; if a realist, he is the most romantic of them. He has been called "Gothic," for instance, in his predilection for stories of violence and crime, many of them exhibiting the "romantic agony," morbid fascination with suffering and humiliation. He creates several variants of the "infernal woman"—and the "infernal man" too—neither of whom could be called a realistic type. His characters live at a high pitch of excitement, frenzy, and even madness, so much so that many of his contemporaries thought they belonged to the realm of psychiatry, not literature. Nevertheless, most of the core criteria of realism are present in post-exile Dostoevsky. The theme of the physiology of Petersburg, for instance, reaches its very apotheosis in *Crime and Punishment*, where the slum, though "realized" in all its physical oppressiveness, becomes at the same time both psychologically and metaphysically symbolic.

Dostoevsky himself insisted that his was a special kind of realism, "realism in a higher sense." The extremes of psychological stress to which he subjected his characters were needed to expose the "depths of the human soul," resulting in "primordial, true realism," not the superficial kind practiced by others. Dreams and hallucinations might be needed to reach these depths. A special kind of vision was needed to perceive what was truly "typical" within the infinity of the world's realities: not just the statistically average, but those that reveal deep, underlying forces in society or in human nature, especially those that are incipient, destined to be fully manifested only in the future. Such "prophetic" phenomena are often unusual, exceptional: "What the majority call almost fantastic and exceptional sometimes constitutes for me the very essence of reality," he wrote. As Donald Fanger has shown, the "exceptional" in Dostoevsky is often incongruous or bizarre, i.e., grotesque. This grotesque, however, is often no longer comic, as it had been in Gogol, but borders uncomfortably on the tragic, since the reader is forced to identify closely with the ridiculed character.

In any event, the realism of Dostoevsky's late novels was clearly deviant, whether sick, romantic, or prophetic. It was disavowed by such leading period critics as MIKHAILOVSKY as neither "typical" nor admirable. Thus the perception of Dostoevsky's full stature, as artist and thinker, if not as realist, was left to the non-realist future. The "discovery" of Dostoevsky became one of the SYMBOLISTS' and post-symbolists' means of discovering themselves.

With the deaths of Dostoevsky and Turgenev and Tolstoi's loudly proclaimed withdrawal from literature, the great age of Russian realism seems to come to an end. In fact, of course, it did nothing of the sort: in the writings of such masters as SALTYKOV-SHCHEDRIN, LESKOV, Gleb USPENSKY, KOROLENKO, and GARSHIN, not to mention Tolstoi himself (whose withdrawal fortunately proved somewhat illusory), realistic writings of the highest quality continued to appear in Russia for many years. Only the grandeur of the big novels was not to be achieved again.

Late 19th-century Russian literature does, however, boast one figure whose stature as an artist is surely on a par with that of the great masters, CHEKHOV. Except for his avoidance of the classic genre of high realism, the big novel, Chekhov carries most of its traditions into the 20th century. It is true that some critics in the West, notably CHIZHEVSKY, have attempted to reclassify Chekhov as an impressionist, and indeed Chekhov's frequent use of single details to "light up" a whole scene, rendering it concrete and palpable, does recall some techniques of the impressionist painters. However, the usefulness to literary criticism of the category impressionist is questionable, and in any case most of the basic ingredients of realism are present, at least in the mature Chekhov. The verisimilitude of his stories and plays is surely as great as in any work of Tolstoi, i.e., the reader's or viewer's illusion that he is witnessing life "as it is." Chekhov was as vehement as Tolstoi in proclaiming truth as his ideal (though to be sure he did so in a letter, not in the text of a story). "Artistic literature is so called just because it depicts life as it really is," he wrote in 1887. "Its aim is truth—unconditional and honest." The range of Russian society depicted in Chekhov's works might easily qualify him as the Balzac of Russian literature: no other writer, with the possible exception of Leskov, casts such a wide net. Chekhov is as "dissolved" in his work as the most insistent Flaubertian could wish. He himself professed that "the artist should be, not the judge of his characters and their conversations, but only an unbiased witness." And again: "When I offer you a professor's ideas, trust me, and do not search in them for Chekhov's ideas." Despite these declarations of objectivity, however, Chekhov's ideas can generally be discerned or deduced from his artistic works; the point is rather that they are made inherent in the mode of presentation, not directly proclaimed in the author's own voice.

By the 1890s, however, Chekhov's realism, perfect as it was, had begun to seem to many younger writers a dead end. When he read "The Lady with the Pet Dog" (1899), GORKY wrote Chekhov, "Do you know what you are doing? You are killing realism.... No one can go along this path further than you; no one can write so simply about simple things as you can." The times, Gorky felt, called for a rebirth of the heroic: "Everybody wants something stimulating, bright-colored, not like life, but higher than life, better, more beautiful." Gorky's (quite sincere) praise for Chekhov's art is thus at the same time a declaration that it was time for realism to give way before a revival of romanticism, even at the price of repudiating truth in favor of a "beautiful lie." Gorky's own early tramp stories, with their homegrown exoticism and larger-than-life characters, popularized this reborn romanticism, even though paradoxically, Gorky later led the realist opposition to the symbolist and post-symbolist schools which dominated Russian literature in the early 20th century; still later he served (according to official Soviet historiography) as the connecting link in the transition from critical to socialist realism.

In any case, a reaction against realism was in full swing by the turn of the century. The center of literary gravity had shifted from prose to poetry, especially lyric poetry, to which the category of realism seems largely irrelevant. And even in narrative prose anti-realist tendencies become legitimized if not dominant. It therefore seems justifiable to state that realism, as a specific literary period or school in Russian literature, had come to an end by 1900. *Mutatis mutandis*, the same was true of other literatures as well. Many of the greatest works of 20th-century prose, though deeply indebted to 19th-century realism, have sought to transcend its limits and question its assumptions. Joyce's *Ulysses*, for example, on the one hand raises realism to the ultimate power by recounting in the most "complete" detail the events of "the dailiest of days." On the other hand, this same quotidian reality is located in a mythic context and sets off the broadest cultural reverberations. Likewise, Proust's reminiscential masterpiece, for all its sensory vividness, forces recognition of the subjectivity of all experience and also its elusiveness; the novel is full of retroactive discoveries that what the narrator once perceived as reality was only illusion. But could not the same discovery be made again? Thus the seemingly solid epistemological foundation of 19th-century realism, the belief that there is a knowable world about which we can tell the "truth," had been shaken, and literature was thrust back into the solipsistic prison of subjectivity. And even from there it could communicate only through a medium of suspect reliability, language.

Nevertheless, realism—or at least a simulacrum of it—refuses to die. In prerevolutionary Russia it was programmatic in the work of writers belonging to the Gorky-sponsored "ZNANIE" school, of whom the most eminent were KUPRIN and especially BUNIN. Bunin continued the tradition among the émigrés, and in Soviet Russia it inspired many leading prosaists of the 1920s, such as FEDIN, LEONOV, FADEEV, and SHOLOKHOV—this before the political bosses attached to it the questionable epithet "socialist" and imposed the result as dogma. It has acquired new life and distinction in the work of SOLZHENITSYN. And in the West, despite all the epistemological doubts raised or revived by contemporary schools of criticism, the ghost of realism still beckons to all those, readers and writers alike, who look to literature for truth about life.

Bibliography: Erich Auerbach, *Mimesis: The Representation of Reality in Western Literature.* 1953. George J. Becker, *Documents of Modern Literary Realism.* 1963. ———, *Realism in Modern Literature.* New York [1980]. V. Dneprov, *Problemy realizma.* 1961. Donald Fanger, *Dostoevsky and Romantic Realism.* 1965. Harry Levin, *The Gates of Horn.* 1963. Georg Lukács, *Studies in European Realism.* 1964. John Mersereau, Jr., "Toward a Normative Definition of Russian Realism," *California Slavic Studies* 6 (1971), pp. 131–44. S. M. Petrov, *Realizm.* 1964. Renato Poggioli, "Realism in Russia," *Comparative Literature* 3 (1951), pp. 253–67. Ernest J. Simmons, *Introduction to Russian Realism.* 1965. A. G. Tseitlin, *Stanovlenie realizma v russkoi literature.* 1965. René Wellek, *Concepts of Criticism.* 1963. H. McL.

Recruits' songs (*rékrutskie pésni*), see FOLK SONG, SOLDIER SONGS.

Renaissance, La, see VOZROZHDENIE.

Rémizov, Aleksei Mikhailovich (1877–1957), novelist, short-story writer, dramatist, poet, and memoirist. The son of a haberdasher, Remizov was raised in strict Russian Orthodox tradition in Moscow's Taganka section among impoverished workers and holy wayfarers. His study of natural science at Moscow University was curtailed by his arrest and expulsion in 1896 for participating in a student demonstration. Remizov developed an avid interest in Russian and Finno-Ugric folklore during eight years of repeated imprisonment and exile. In 1905 he settled in St. Petersburg, where he frequented SYMBOLIST circles, yet maintained a highly personal literary orientation.

Although marred by *moderne* vagueness, lyric fragmentation, abstractness, and verbosity, Remizov's two novels, the autobiographical *The Pond* (Prud, 1908) and *The Clock* (Chasy, 1908), do provide a graphic description of a world of pain and brutality, where chance misfortune appears to be manipulated by a malignant demon. Much more successful were three short novels in which he uses popular language and an intermediary narrator to cloak the author's personality and point of view in the SKAZ narrative tradition of GOGOL and LESKOV: "Sisters of the Cross" (Krestovye sestry, 1910), where the inhabitants of a single St. Petersburg tenement house represent a microcosm of human suffering and humiliation; "The Indefatigable Cymbal" (Neuemnyi buben, 1910; republished as "Povest' o Ivane Stratilatove," 1922; Eng. trans., *The History of the Tinkling Cymbal and Sounding Brass: Ivan Semenovich Stratilatov*, 1927), where the 19th-century poor-clerk theme is skillfully interwoven with the sacred and profane oral tradition to create a grotesquely humorous modernist work; and "The Fifth Pestilence" (Pyataya yazva, 1912), where literary parody and political commentary are combined in a Tolstoian tale of retribution for inhuman integrity.

Remizov's best short stories explore the psychology of children, sometimes focusing on disillusionment, "Princess Mymra" (Tsarevna Mymra, 1908), or on hope culminating in chance death, "The Cockerel" (Petushok, 1911). In later collections, *Spring Trifles* (Vesennee porosh'e, 1915) and *Amid the Swarm* (Sredi mur'ya, 1917), Remizov develops mood pieces with a unity of perception between child-protagonist and author-narrator.

Much of Remizov's writing was derivative in nature, beginning with adaptations of children's games and fairy tales in *Sunward* (Posolon', 1907) and apocryphal narratives in *Limonarium: A Spiritual Meadow* (Limonar': Lug dukhovnyi, 1907); then developing legends and folktales about the highly revered St. Nicholas, *St. Nicholas Parables* (Nikoliny pritchi, 1918), stories about various types of Russian women, *Russian Women* (Russkie zhenshchiny, 1918), and various non-Slavic ethnic tales, *A Siberian Cookie* (Sibirskii pryanik, 1919) and *E: Tibetan Rabbit Tales* (E: Zayashnye skazki tibetskie, 1921). He painstakingly researched and adapted the folk-drama *Tsar Maksimilian* (1920), and his penchant for blasphemous humor was manifested in *Forbidden Tales* (Zavetnye skazy, 1920) and *Tsar Dodon* (1921).

Remizov's profound compassion for Russia in revolution was expressed in a poignantly lyric, rhythmical prose lament, "The Lay of the Ruin of the Russian Land" (Slovo o pogibeli zemli russkoi, 1917) and in the lyric poem "The Red Banner" (Krasnoe znamya, 1917), which anticipated Blok's *The Twelve* by six months. Emigrating from Russia in 1921, Remizov convincingly portrayed the atmosphere of war-torn Petrograd in *Sounds of the City* (Shumy goroda, 1921) and *Spectre* (Mara, 1922). His predilection for Russia's past was reflected in *Russia in Documents* (Rossiya v pis'menakh, 1922) and in new adaptations of apocryphal tales, *Stella Maria Maris* (Zvezda nadzvezdnaya, 1928), *The Image of Nicholas the Miracle Worker* (Obraz Nikolaya Chudotvortsa, 1931), *Three Sickles* (Tri serpa, 2 vols., 1929) and folk legends, *A Tale of Two Beasts* (Povest' o dvukh zveryakh, 1950), *Tristan i Isolda* (1957), *Circle of Happiness* (Krug schast'ya, 1957).

Shunning new endeavors in prose fiction after the Revolution, Remizov developed a highly subjective hybrid memoir genre which combined a chronicle of postrevolutionary Russia, reminiscences, autobiography, biographical sketches, essays on life and literature, and a fantasy dream world: *Russia in a Whirlwind* (Vzvikhrennaya Rus', 1927), *Along the Cornices* (Po karnizam, 1929), *A Flute for Mice* (Myshkina dudochka, 1953), and a three-part biography of his wife, *In a Rosy Light* (V rozovom bleske, 1952). His life-long fascination with the world of dreams culminated in an original collection of his own dreams, *Martyn Zadeka* (1954), and in a penetrating critical commentary on Russian writers, *The Fire of Things* (Ogon' veshchei, 1954).

The influence of Remizov's early fiction and ornamental narrative style is readily apparent in the works of ZAMYATIN, PILNYAK, PRISHVIN, SHISHKOV and other Russian authors of the 1910s and 1920s. One of the most erudite, versatile, and innovative writers of the 20th century, Remizov was virtually unknown and ignored in the Soviet Union until the appearance of a selection, *Izbrannoe* (1973).

Works: Chortov log i polunoshchnoe solntse. 1908. *Sochineniya.* 8 vols. 1910–12. Reprint Munich, 1971. *Podorozhie.* 1913. *Dokuka i balagur'e.* 1914. Reprint (Slavische Propyläen, 122.) Munich, 1976. *Za svyatuyu Rus'.* 1915. *Ukrepa.* 1916. *Strannitsa.* 1918. *Besovskoe deistvo.* 1919. *Tragediya o Iude.* 1919. *V pole blakitnom.* 1922. *Krashenye ryla.* 1922. *Kukkha.* 1922. Reprint New York, 1978; Rego Park, N.Y. 1983. *Zga.* 1925. *Plyashushchii demon.* 1949. *Krestovye sestry.* Letchworth, Herts., 1969. *V rozovom bleske.* Letchworth, 1969. *Pyataya yazva.* Letchworth, 1970. *Vzvikhrennaya Rus'.* London, 1979. *Vstrechi. Peterburgskii buerak.* Paris, 1981. *Rossiya v pis'menakh.* New York, 1982. *Bibliography:* Hélène Sinany, *Bibliographie des oeuvres de Alexis Remizov.* Paris, 1978. Horst Lampl, "Bemerkungen und Ergänzungen zur Bibliographie A. M. Remizovs." *Wiener slawistischer Almanach* 2 (1978), pp. 301–26.

Translations: The Clock. Trans. J. Cournos. London, 1924. *The Fifth Pestilence*, together with *The History of the Tinkling Cymbal and Sounding Brass, Ivan Semyonovich Stratilatov.* Trans. with a preface by A. Brown. London, 1927. *See also Lewanski*, pp. 345–46.

Secondary Literature: Yurii Andreev, "Puti i pereput'ya Alekseya Remizova," *VLit* 21 (1977), no. 5, pp. 216–43. Renate S. Bialy, "Parody in Remizov's *Pjataja jazva*," *SEEJ* 19 (1975), pp. 403–10. Milena Karlova, "Osud i son pisatelya: O zhizni i tvorchestve A. M. Remizova." In *Russkaya literatura v emigratsii: Sbornik statei.* Ed. N. P. Poltoratskii. 1972. Pp. 191–97. Nataliya Kondryanskaya, *Aleksei Remizov.* Paris, 1959. ———, *Remizov v svoikh pis'makh.* 1977. H. Lampl, "Alexej Remizovs Beitrag zum russischen Theater," *Wiener slawistisches Jahrbuch* 17 (1972), pp. 136–83. D. Mirsky, *Contemporary Russian Literature, 1881–1925.* 1926. Pp. 281–91. N. Reznikova, *Ognennaya pamyat'.* 1980. Alex M. Shane, "Remizov's *Prud*: From Symbolism to Neo-Realism," *California Slavic Studies* 6 (1971), pp. 71–82. ———, "A Prisoner of Fate: Remizov's Short Fiction," *RLT* 4 (1972), pp. 303–18. ———, "An Introduction to Alexei Remizov," *TriQuarterly* 28 (1973), pp. 10–16. G. Slobin, "Writing as Possession: The Case of Remizov's 'Poor Clerk'." In *Studies in 20th Century Prose.* Ed. Nils Åke Nilsson. 1983. Pp. 59–79. G. Struve, *Russkaya literatura v izgnanii.* 1956. Pp. 104–07, 259–62.

A. M. S.

"Repression" and "Rehabilitation." Many of the biographies of Soviet writers in the *Kratkaya literaturnaya entsiklopediya* (*KLE*) are concluded by the stereotype formula: "Unlawfully repressed in [year follows], posthumously rehabilitated." Both terms cover a wide range of meanings. "Repression" may have been anything from expulsion from the Union of Soviet Writers (and hence disappearance from print) to prison, exile and execution. "Rehabilitation" may mean anything from full readmission to the ranks of Soviet writers and republication of all or most works to mere admission that the fate suffered by the writer was undeserved, without any action to restore his works to their former place in literature. Among the authors who appear in the present work, Babel, Gastev, Gerasimov, I. Kataev, Kharms, Kirillov, Kirshon, Klyuev, Knyazev, Mandelshtam, Narbut, Pilnyak, Tarasov-Rodionov, Tretyakov, Vasiliev, Vesyoly, Vvedensky, and others were "repressed" and eventually "rehabilitated."

Bibliography: John Glad, "The Soviet Concise Literary Encyclopedia: A Review Article," *SEEJ* 25, no. 2 (1981), pp. 80–90.

V. T.

Reshétnikov, Fyódor Mikhailovich (1841–71), writer. Born in Ekaterinburg (Sverdlovsk), into the family of a postman and former church deacon, Reshetnikov was raised by an uncle in Perm after his mother's death, and educated in a district school. He began work in 1859 as a petty official, but revealed his literary inclination through two sketches in the *Permskie gubernskie vedomosti* in 1861. Two years later, he found work in St. Petersburg as a clerk. Reshetnikov's first long work, *The People of Podlipnoe* (Podlipovtsy, 1864), aroused considerable attention when it appeared in NEKRASOV's progressive SOVREMENNIK. Dedicated to Nekrasov (who had been instrumental in the success of the PHYSIOLOGICAL SKETCH and a prominent member of the NATURAL SCHOOL), *The People of Podlipnoe* unsentimentally and with extensive detail provides an ethnographic sketch of poverty-stricken and downtrodden Finnish peasants of Perm who, like most of Reshetnikov's later characters, leave the land to take work in industrial or other non-agrarian situations (in this case, as barge haulers). It is said to have instilled a sense of guilt among the nobility and middle class, who came to understand better the peasants' human worth.

In *The Miners* (Gornorabochie, 1866), Reshetnikov faithfully captured the plight of Ural mineworkers, while his posthumously published *The Glumovs* (Glumovy, 1866–67, pub. 1880), described the onset of a strike among Ural workers after the reforms of 1861. Reshetnikov was the first to depict strikes in Russian literature. Paralleling 19th-century English industrial novels, *Where is it Better?* (Gde luchshe?, 1868) prefigured the spirit of Nekrasov's poem, "Who lives well in Russia?" (Komu na Rusi zhit' khorosho?), by portraying mine and railroad workers whose attempt to find a better life in St. Petersburg ends in a factory strike. Significantly, while N. V. USPENSKY's equally grim stories lost favor with the reading public, Reshetnikov's works remained viable because he directed attention to environmental causes and depicted peasants who attempt to escape hopeless immobility.

Reshetnikov also wrote an autobiographically inspired novella, *Among People* (Mezhdu lyud'mi, 1865), several short stories, sketches, and a novel, *One's Own Bread* (Svoi khleb, 1870), which addresses women's emancipation. Russia lost a promising writer when he died at the age of twenty-nine.

Works: Polnoe sobranie sochinenii. 6 vols. 1936–48. *Izbrannye proizvedeniya.* 2 vols. 1956.

Secondary literature: R. L. Glickman, "Industrialization and the Factory Worker in Russian Literature," CSS 4 (1970), pp. 629–52. ———, "An Alternative View of the Peasantry: The *Raznochintsy* Writers of the 1860s," SlavR 32 (1973), pp. 693–704. G. I. Lebedev, "Romany o rabochikh pisatelya-demokrata F. M. Reshetnikova," *Uchenye zapiski Shcherbakovskogo pedagogicheskogo instituta*, 1956. L. S. Sheptaev, "Tvorchestvo F. M. Reshetnikova." In *Proza pisatelei-demokratov shestidesyatykh godov XIX v.* 1962. Thomas J. Stacy, "F. M. Reshetnikov's *The Podlipnayans*." Ph.D. diss., U. S. C. (1974). (Trans. from the Russian, with an introd.) G. Uspenskii, "F. M. Reshetnikov." In his *Sobranie sochinenii.* Vol. 9. 1957.

J. S.

Retardation, see ZAMEDLENIE.

Revolution and literature. The October Revolution of 1917 had an immediate, powerful, and lasting effect on the world of Russian letters. It affected the lives of most writers already active, causing the death of some (such as Nikolai GUMILYOV, shot as a counter-revolutionary in 1921), the emigration of many (see EMIGRÉ LITERATURE), and a radical change in the personal circumstances of many more (e.g., Anatoly LUNACHARSKY, a minor littérateur, became Peoples Commissar of Education, while Pyotr KRASNOV, an important general and amateur writer, became a prolific professional writer in exile). Since the victorious Bolsheviks immediately installed their own brand of CENSORSHIP and greater pressure for conformity than had existed before the Revolution, Soviet literature soon assumed a character very different from Russian literature as it existed before the Revolution. (There was of course émigré literature to counterbalance this tendency.) The PROLETKULT movement sought to establish a new, proletarian culture and literature. The LEFT ART movement sought to create a MODERNIST art and literature in the service of the new social order. There was also a strong move toward utilitarian (didactic and propaganda) literature, even though direct government and Communist Party interference in the literary process came later. The new genre of "agit-poetry" was entirely a product of the Revolution. Its leading practitioner was Demyan BEDNY.

A cataclysmic event, which changed the life of a nation as few events have in recent history, the Revolution became a focus of attention for almost every writer or poet and became the subject of many important works, some of them written under the immediate impact of the Revolution. Such were Aleksandr BLOK's "The Twelve" (1918), some of Osip MANDELSHTAM's poems, such as "Twilight of Freedom" (Sumerki svobody, 1918), MAYAKOVSKY's *Mystery-Bouffe* (1918), Maksimilian VOLOSHIN's "Civil War: A Cycle on the Terror of 1920–1921" (Usobitsa: Tsikl o terrore 1920–1921 godov, 1920–1921), Boris PILNYAK's *Naked Year* (1922), Konstantin FEDIN's *Cities and Years* (1924), and Isaak BABEL's *Red Cavalry* stories (1923–24). In later years the Revolution was the focus of further major works such as Mayakovsky's "Good! A Poem of October" (1927), SHOLOKHOV's *The Quiet Don* (1928–40), Aleksei TOLSTOI's *The Way through Hell* (Khozhdenie po mukam, 1927–41), and PASTERNAK's *Doctor Zhivago* (1957).

Bibliography: M. Hayward and L. Labedz, *Literature and Revolution in Soviet Russia, 1917–1962: A Symposium.* 1963. D. S. Mirsky, *Contemporary Russian Literature, 1881–1925.* 1926. Leon Trotsky, *The History of the Russian Revolution.* 3 vols. Trans. M. Eastman. 1932. ———, *Literature and Revolution.* 1957. Avrahm Yarmolinsky, *Literature under Communism.* 1960. V. T.

Rhyme. Unlike English poetry and certain other literary traditions, where rhyme is used much less frequently in the 20th century than it was earlier, Russian continues to place great importance on rhyme. Both blank verse and free verse exist in Russian poetry, but they remain relatively minor forms when compared to the abundance of rhymed works.

Rhyme is based on identical or similar sounds in two or more words and takes place at or around the stressed vowels. Furthermore, in a rhymed poem the rhyme must occur at regular intervals, most often at the end of each line. As this definition implies, it is not sufficient to think of rhyme simply as an identity that occurs between two or more words at the end of lines, beginning with the stressed vowel and continuing to the end. In the first place, while rhyme words do occur regularly, they are not necessarily present in every line. It is possible, to take what is perhaps the most common instance, for a poem to be written in quatrains, with the even lines rhyming and the odd ones not. Second, while the great majority of rhyme does occur at the end of lines, a regular pattern of internal rhyming may occur as well or instead; consider the following excerpt from a poem by BALMONT:

Uskol'záyushchaya péna … Pominútnaya izména …	A–A
Zházhda výrvat'sya iz pléna, vnóv' izvédat' gnet okóv.	A–b
I v tumánnosti dalékoi, oskorblénnoi, odinókii,	C–C
Íshchet génii svetloókii neizvéstnykh beregóv.	C–b

Here the end of the first line rhymes with the caesura in the first and second lines; the third rhymes with the caesura in the third and the fourth. Other possibilities besides rhyming at the caesura exist; for instance, the ends of lines may rhyme with the beginnings of the same lines or of the following lines. However, the rhyme must occur regularly in the poem; random or occasional internal "rhymes" are a factor in the sound instrumentation of the poem, but they fall outside the regular rhyme scheme. Third, exact rhyme (*tochnaya rifma*) is only a special case; similarity of sounds can lead to rhyme just as well as identity, and for much of 20th-century Russian poetry approximate (*priblizitel'naya*) rhyme is extremely important. Fourth, and also of special significance for the modern period although employed earlier as well, is "enrichment"—the similarity or identity of sounds before the stressed vowel. Some would further distinguish between rich rhyme, which involves a consonant or two before the stressed vowel (*síla/sprosíla*, ka*príz/syurpríz*) and "deep" or "super-rich" rhyme, which extends back through at least the preceding vowel (*rokovói/vekovói*). Enrichment sometimes occurs with exact rhyme, but it is more common and of greater importance for approximate rhyme, where the focus of the rhyme sometimes shifts away from the very end of the line to a segment that includes the syllable or two preceding the rhymed vowel.

The signs used to indicate rhyme patterns in Russian also provide information about the clausula, which may be masculine, in which case the stress falls on the last syllable of the line and the first rhyme in a stanza would be marked *a*; feminine, with final stress on the next-to-last syllable and marked *A*; dactylic, with the stress two syllables from the end (*A'*); or hyperdactylic (*A''*). The second rhyme in a stanza is indicated by the proper form of the letter *b*, the third by *c*, and so forth. Unrhymed lines are indicated by *x*, *X*, *X'*, or *X''*, depending again on the type of clausula. The most common rhyme combinations include adjacent (*a a b b*), alternating (*a b a b*), and enclosed (*a b b a*). By far the most common stanza in Russian is the quatrain with alternating masculine and feminine rhymes (*a B a B* or *A b A b*, with the latter predominating). Rhyme in SYLLABIC POETRY was exclusively feminine, but already from the time of LOMONOSOV on the principle of alternating masculine and feminine rhyme was firmly established in Russian poetry. Dactylic rhyme was little used until well into the 19th century, while longer rhymes largely arose as the result of experiments by poets at the beginning of this century.

The description of Russian rhyme has, with certain modifications, traditionally followed the classification set forth by Viktor ZHIRMUNSKY in the 1920s and distinguishes among exact, approximate, and inexact rhyme. In this system the term approximate is essentially applied only to feminine or longer rhymes. It is used primarily when the only difference between two rhymed words occurs in the vowels following the stressed vowels, though it may also describe rhyme pairs in which one of the rhyme words ends in a [j] and the other does not. Some even employ the term when unstressed vowels are pronounced the same but spelled differently (*málo/snachála*). Inexact rhymes would then involve any difference, no matter how minor, in the consonants after the stressed vowel. While Zhirmunsky's descriptions of individual phenomena remain valuable, the terms approximate and inexact create a distinction that at times seems artificial. It seems more useful to speak of exact rhymes, liberties within the system of exact rhyming, and approximate rhymes (the term "inexact" is avoided since it implies that such rhymes are somehow imperfect rather than simply formed according to an alternate set of criteria). Certain liberties have always been taken even by those poets who normally adhered strictly to exact rhyme, though the nature and extent of those liberties does evolve with time. As TOMASHEVSKY has noted even the very concept of what is and is not rhyme, and in particular the parameters of exact rhyme, may well change from one era to the next; no absolute definition is possible.

The system of exact rhyme in Russian has always included the rhyming of voiced and unvoiced consonants in final position (*obéd/let*) and of the vowel pairs that reflect the hardness or softness of a preceding consonant (*telyáta/utráta*). Even *y* and *i*, which are not quite identical acoustically, are rhymed as a matter of course by all poets. Since the soft sign that appears after a sibilant has no effect on the pronunciation, pairs such as *kradësh'/nozh* also rhyme exactly. Similarly, silent consonants, such as a *t* between an *s* and an *n*, do not affect the quality of a rhyme: *strástnyi/prekrásnyi*.

Among the permissible liberties, the most common are the following: (1) Deletion of final [j] in feminine rhymes. Originally this was limited to cases in which one of the rhymed words was an adjective (*pólnyi/vólny*), but it was eventually extended to other parts of speech and to other vowels before the [j] (*síloi/unýlo*). In the 20th century this kind of deletion sometimes occurs in masculine rhyme pairs (*pryamói/tryumó*), where its effect is much more perceptible and it is better considered a form of approximate rhyme. (2) Rhyming of *-yi* and *-ii* with *-oi*. In the late 18th and early 19th centuries, adjectives such as *krásnyi* and *tíkhii* could be written with the ending *-oi* as well (the *-yi* is of CHURCH SLAVONIC origin). Under the influence of the orthography, poets came to treat these endings equally; thus LERMONTOV rhymed *nézhnyi* not only with *myatézhnyi*, but also with *myatézhnoi*. Such rhymes continued even after the spelling *-oi* was no longer found in the nominative masculine singular form of stem-stressed adjectives. (3) Rhyming of *k*, *g*, *kh*. Final *g* was pronounced like a fricative and therefore could be rhymed with *kh* (*drug/dukh*). At the same time poets continued to rhyme *g* and *k* in final position (*drug/zvuk*). Most likely by analogy rhymes of the sort *dukh/zvuk* also came into being. (4) Rhyming of final hard and soft consonants. Rhymes like *ottsóv/lyubóv'*, which some scholars would classify as inexact rhyme, occur in the poetry of DERZHAVIN, BATYUSHKOV, and other early poets. This one rhyme appears to have originated from a particular dialectal pronunciation,

but other rhymes involving hard and soft consonants (*sledít/zhit'*, *chudés/zdes'*) can also be found in the 19th century. (5) Open masculine rhymes. Normally, masculine rhymes ending in a vowel must have the same supporting consonant (*opornaya soglasnaya*): *straná/spiná*. However, there have always been a few exceptions to this rule. The preceding consonants may differ if they form a voiced/unvoiced pair (*nogá/stroká*); more commonly, the two consonants are "related" soft consonants (especially two different sonorants: *zaré/ogné*). Finally, a soft consonant and a plain [j] may serve as the two supporting consonants (*tvoyá/dityá [tvojá/dit'á]*). In the 20th century poets have sometimes ignored this principle and have used unrelated consonants in the supporting position (*nebesá/ushlá*).

Approximate rhyme occurs in proverbs, riddles, and other types of "minor" folk verse; in the literary tradition it was by no means rare even in the 18th century (Derzhavin in particular used it extensively), and while most 19th-century poets from PUSHKIN's time on came to rely almost exclusively on exact rhyme, approximate rhyme became widespread around the beginning of the 20th century and has been an important feature of Russian poetry ever since. Such rhyming is also common in other poetic traditions. Thus much of what is often called "near rhyme" in American poetry can be traced back at least to Emily Dickinson, who often based her rhymes on such minimal similarities as just non-final vowels (these/weep) or final consonants (clock/tick).

The main types of approximate rhyme in Russian are the following (unless otherwise stated, examples are from PASTERNAK): (1) *Unstressed vowels*. Rhymes based on a difference in the vowels that appear after the stress can be found well back into the 19th century; A. K. TOLSTOI used them extensively and justified his practice in an oft-quoted 1859 letter. By definition, the rhyme must be feminine or longer. Poets have generally perceived differences in unstressed vowels as less significant than those in consonants; for this reason some would prefer to classify these rhymes among the liberties allowed within exact rhyme rather than as approximate. (2) *Consonants*. Modern approximate rhyme arises largely out of differences in the consonants that follow the stressed vowel in rhymed words. These differences may be of three types: The most common of these is *deletion*, in which one of the words lacks one or more of the consonants that are present after the stressed vowel in the other. The deletion most often occurs at the very end of a word, but it may take place within it as well (*obrýv/dobrý*, *závtra/landsháfta*). Also used quite often is the *substitution* of one consonant for another: *obéikh/robéet*, *magazín/zim*. As the second example illustrates, closely related consonants are frequently involved in the substitution. Furthermore, as in both the rhymes here, enrichment may help compensate for the differences introduced by the substitution. More rare, though particularly effective when done successfully, is the *transposition* of two or more consonants. Sometimes transposition is used by itself (*móshkoi/namókshii*); in many instances it is combined with another type of consonant change (*chiriknuv/chernikoi*). (3) *Other types of approximate rhyme*. The most common of these is heterosyllabic (*neravnoslozhnaya*) rhyme, in which the rhymed words have a different number of syllables after the stress (*pténchik/zasténchivoi*). Usually, as here, one word has a feminine ending and the other word dactylic, though other combinations occur regularly as well. MAYAKOVSKY used this type of rhyme especially often. In heteroaccentual (*raznoudarnaya*) rhyme, often called wrenched rhyme in the English tradition, the rhyme vowel is stressed in one word but not in the other. KHLEBNIKOV and, in particular, MARIENGOF (note his *bóli/lik*) are among the poets who have employed it on occasion. *Consonances* are rhymes in which the stressed vowels differ (*ináche/inóchestv*); again, enrichment is quite common with this type of rhyme.

Some special phenomena that may arise in rhyming also deserve mention. Two of these by definition involve exact rhyme, the third can be used with either exact or approximate rhyme, and the fourth arose as a direct result of modern approximate rhyme. (1) Both *homonym* and *repetend* rhymes involve two words that sound alike. Repetend rhyme is the pairing of the same word, while homonym rhyme employs two words that sound alike but have different meanings. (2) *Echo rhyme* occurs when the final portion of one rhyme word includes all the sounds of the other (*ty/tshchetý*); such combinations occur most regularly among exact masculine rhymes. (3)

Compound (*sostavnaya*) rhyme, often called broken rhyme, means that the rhyme is extended over two or more words in either one or more members of a rhyme set. Traditionally, the last word would be a particle or a pronoun (*vék ei/véki*), but even in the 19th century, and much more frequently in the 20th, verbs, nouns, and other parts of speech are involved as well (*Gámleta li/nogám letali*—where the rhyme is hyperdactylic). (4) Since the increase in both the prevalence and kinds of approximate rhyme, the borders between rhyme sets (that is, the groups of two or more words that form individual rhymes) have sometimes become difficult to determine:

> Mne né v chem káyat'sya, Rossíya, pred tobói:
> Ne predavál tebyá ni mýsl'yu, ni dushói,
> A ésli v chúzhdyi krái fizícheski ushël,
> Davnó uzh pónyal ya, kak tó nekhoroshó ...

Here, does SEVERYANIN rhyme the third line with the first two (substitution) or with the fourth (deletion)? A comparison with the other stanzas in the poem reveals that he is using a scheme of aabb, but in light of modern rhyme practice this one stanza on its own could well have had a rhyme pattern of *a a a a*. When the distinction between rhyme sets becomes blurred in this way, the *b* rhyme is said to form a shadow (*tenevaya*) rhyme with the *a* rhyme.

The use of rhyme in Russian poetry has passed through several stages during the past 250 years. Essentially, Russian rhyme could be described as "mostly" exact since the establishment of SYLLABOTONIC VERSIFICATION in the 18th century. However, numerous exceptions were allowed, and a poet like Derzhavin could employ approximate rhyme more often than many a 20th-century writer. Still, by the 1820s a system of exact rhyme—along with the handful of liberties described above—had firmly taken hold. But even by then two types of change had begun to set in. First is the process that Zhirmunsky labeled the "decanonization" of exact rhyme. That is, the variety and use of approximate rhyme grew, albeit not always in a steady progression. Second, the nature of exact rhyme changes. As Roman JAKOBSON noted, rhyme becomes more and more "antigrammatical"; poets come to rely less on the relatively easy rhymes (particularly verbal rhymes) that were based on the pairing of words with the same grammatical ending. Also, the practice of combining masculine and feminine rhymes in each poem becomes less of a norm; poems written entirely in, for instance, masculine rhymes appear, and dactylic rhymes also become more than a mere curiosity. The major change, though, is the rise of an entire tradition of approximate rhyme during the first decades of the 20th century. The new method of rhyming does not appear all at once, but evolves gradually through innovations introduced by poets such as BLOK, KUZMIN, Khlebnikov, and Mayakovsky; further refinements have been made by certain contemporary poets. Exact rhyme has not disappeared; just as syllabotonic versification continues to be a viable (and indeed thriving) tradition despite the popularity of *dol'niki* and other forms of tonic versification, so too does exact rhyme retain its importance alongside modern approximate rhyme.

Bibliography: Thomas Eekman, *The Realm of Rime: A Study of Rime in the Poetry of the Slavs.* Amsterdam, 1974. Roman Jakobson, "K lingvisticheskomu analizu russkoi rifmy." In *Studies in Russian Philology.* (Michigan Slavic Materials, no. 1.) 1962. Pp. 1–13. D. S. Samoilov, *Kniga o russkoi rifme.* 1973. Michael Shapiro, *Asymmetry: An Inquiry into the Linguistic Study of Poetry.* Amsterdam, 1976. Chap. 4. J. Thomas Shaw, *Pushkin's Rhymes: A Dictionary.* 1974. B. V. Tomashevskii, "K istorii russkoi rifmy," *Trudy Otdela novoi russkoi literatury,* 1 (1948), pp. 233–80. B. O. Unbegaun, *Russian Versification.* 1956. Dean S. Worth, "On Eighteenth-Century Rhyme," *RusL* 3 (1972), pp. 47–74. V. M. Zhirmunskii, *Rifma: Ee istoriya i teoriya* (1923), reprint. in *Teoriya stikha.* 1975. A. L. Zhovtis, "Russkaya rifma 1960–1970-kh godov (zametki i razmyshleniya)," *RLit* 24 (1981), no. 3, pp. 76–85. B. S.

Rhythm, see VERSIFICATION.

Ritual Poetry (*obryádovaya poéziya*) performs different functions within the various rituals. In some cases the songs reflect the peasant belief that one can subject nature to one's will through special actions and words. Typical of this attitude are songs which are prophylactic (protection from evil forces), invocatory, divinatory, or homeopathic—by representing something in song it should come true. In some cases the songs pay homage to an anthropomorphized spirit such as Kupala (St. John's Eve), Maslenitsa (Shrovetide), and others. In many cases the words describe the ritual action itself, such as bringing eggs to the birch during *Semik* (Whitsuntide) and dancing a *khorovod* (round dance) around it, the removal of the *krásota* (maiden headdress) during the wedding ritual, or putting the body into the coffin during the funeral ritual. In the case of laments, they express the grief of one of the principal characters participating in the ritual.

Russian peasants celebrated two basic ritual cycles: the agricultural and the family. Agricultural rituals were timed to various holidays in the Christian calendar, although the rituals themselves were of pagan origin. Family rituals include wedding and funeral rituals (*see* CALENDAR POETRY; FOLK VERSIFICATION; LAMENT). R. R.

Ródov, Semyón Abrámovich (1893–1968), poet, literary theorist and critic, translator, Communist Party member since 1918. He began as a poet in 1912; though prolific, he was never recognized as a significant talent. In 1923, he abandoned poetry and embarked on the career as critic and theorist which determined his importance for Soviet literature. He broke with the KUZNITSA group, which he had joined in 1920, helped form the OKTYABR' group, and became an editor, along with Georgy LELEVICH and Boris Volin, of NA POSTU and of *Oktyabr',* where he was a militant advocate of the primacy of proletarian literature, and a virulent foe of non-proletarian writers, such as the FELLOW TRAVELERS and their supporters, especially VORONSKY. These views contradicted Party policy from the mid-1920s on, led to Rodov's expulsion from the executive board of the VAPP in 1926, and set him at odds with the RAPP, where he retained membership, but vigorously opposed its policies. In 1930 he helped form the Litfront group in a final attempt to assert the old Onguardist line. It was disbanded after four months; soon Rodov disappeared from public view for many years. He survived the purges, however, and after World War II began a third career as a translator.

Works: Moi sev (early poems). 1918. *Organizatsiya proletarskoi literatury.* 1925. *V literaturnykh boyakh.* 1926. *Na postu.* 1931.

Secondary literature: Herman Ermolaev, *Soviet Literary Theories, 1917–34.* Berkeley and Los Angeles, 1963. Chaps. 2–4. R. A. M.

Romance (*románs*), a short lyric poem, usually amatory, often of a sad, pensive nature, set to music. Sometimes the poet will himself anticipate the latter, and then the poem will bear the title (or subtitle) "Romance." In Russia, the romance makes its appearance in the 18th century. M. LOMONOSOV's popular poem, "The dark of night has veiled the sky" (Nochnoyu temnotoyu pokrylis' nebesa—sung by the hero of OSTROVSKY's drama *The Thunderstorm,* 1859) belongs to this genre. Some love poems by A. SUMAROKOV, such as "In vain I hide my heart's cruel pain" (Tshchetno ya skryvayu serdtsa skorbi lyuty), "Those hours have vanished" (Sokrylis' te chasy), etc., were also sung. The love songs of Yu. NELEDINSKY-MELETSKY were well known. G. DERZHAVIN called a type of poem close to the ballad a "romance," but also wrote several poems of the romance type, intended for vocal performance: "The Chiff-Chaff" (Penochka), "Nightingale in Dream" (Solovei vo sne), "A Whimsical Wish" (Shutochnoe zhelanie, a poem which became widely known as Tomsky's song in Tchaikovsky's opera *The Queen of Spades*), etc. Late in the century, I. DMITRIEV's romance "The Grey Dove Sighs" was widely popular.

The romance flowered in the early 19th century. Many of PUSHKIN's poems were set to music, e. g., "Did you hear?" (Slykhali l' vy), "The Black Shawl" (Chernaya shal'), etc. Among them is one of the most popular songs of the 19th century, "On a rainy evening in fall" (Pod vecher osen'yu nenastnoi), which the poet himself called "a romance." Some poems by ZHUKOVSKY are also so subtitled. A. DELVIG and N. YAZYKOV wrote romances. Verses by K. BATYUSHKOV ("Parting"—Razluka), and E. BARATYNSKY ("Dissuasion"—Razuverenie) were set to music. I. KOZLOV's "Evening Bells" (Vechernii zvon) and "Venetian Night" (Venetsianskaya noch') were phenomenally successful. M. LERMONTOV also wrote several romances. During that period there emerge two new themes of the romance: prison and the road. Such are "The Prisoner" (Uznik) by A. Pushkin, "A Prisoner's Song" (Pesn' uznika) by F. GLINKA, "A Wish" (Zhelanie) by M. Lermontov, "Winter Road" (Zimnyaya doroga) by A. Pushkin, "Troika" by F. Glinka, "Troika" by P. VYAZEMSKY, and many others.

As the romance became more and more popular, it entered urban folklore. About the middle of the 19th century, the gypsy romance made its appearance in Russian poetry. Aside of outright gypsy motifs, it is distinguished by a heightened emotionality, passion, and the theme of love and death. Gypsy romances by A. GRIGORIEV, such as "You, at least, speak to me" (O govori khot' ty so mnoi) and "Two Guitars" (Dve gitary zazvenev), and Ya. POLONSKY, such as "My campfire shines through the fog" (Moi koster v tumane svetit) were often sung. Similar poems by A. APUKHTIN were prodigiously successful: "Flies" (Mukhi), "Mad Nights, Sleepless Nights" (Nochi bezumnye, nochi bessonnye), "A Pair of Bay Horses" (Para gnedykh), etc.

The poetics of the gypsy romance and of the urban "folk" romance surfaced most distinctly in the later poetry of A. BLOK. In the early 20th century, the romances of A. Vertinsky, who composed his own lyrics and music and also performed his own work, enjoyed a wide popularity. Later, in the 1960s, the tradition of the romance was resumed by the "bards": B. OKUDZHAVA, A. GALICH, etc.

Texts: Pesni russkikh poetov (18–pervaya polovina 19 veka). Ed., introd. and comm. I. N. Rozanov. (Biblioteka poeta. Bol'shaya seriya.) 1936. *Pesni russkikh poetov.* Introd., ed., and comm. I. N. Rozanov. (Biblioteka poeta. Malaya seriya.) 1957.

Secondary literature: B. Eikhenbaum, *Melodika russkogo stikha.* In his *O poezii.* 1969. Yu. Lotman and Z. Mints, *"Chelovek prirody" v russkoi literature 19 veka i "tsyganskaya tema" u Bloka.* In *Blokovskii sbornik.* Tartu, 1964.   M. A.

Románov, Panteleímon Sergéevich (1885–1938), writer. Of the landowning gentry and without much success before the Revolution (he published his first story in 1911), Romanov succeeded in becoming one of the most successful Soviet writers of the 1920s and 1930s. He won his fame mostly with his satirical stories of the NEP period, in which he exposed some of the seamy sides of the new society, such as the ignorance, inefficiency, and boorishness of the new proletarian bureaucrats and the cowardice and cynicism of their "fellow traveller" aides—as in the short novel *Comrade Kislyakov* (Tovarishch Kislyakov, 1930; in English: *Three Pairs of Silk Stockings*, 1931). Romanov devoted a good deal of attention to the sexual revolution of the 1920s, sometimes describing its excesses too graphically by the standards of the next generation—as in the short novel *Without Cherry Blossoms* (Bez cheremukhi, 1926). In most of Romanov's stories there is a touch of vulgarity and unhealthy sensationalism (Struve), but they were a reflection if not of the actual experience of his generation, then at least of the image many of its members had created of themselves. Romanov also wrote in a conventional epic manner, as in his autobiographic novel, *Childhood* (Detstvo, 1926) and a lengthy epopeia, *Russia* (Rus', 5 vols., 1922–36), describing rural life in prerevolutionary Russia.

Works: Polnoe sobranie sochinenii. 12 vols. 1929–30.
Translations: See Lewanski, p. 347.
Secondary literature: Edward J. Brown, *Russian Literature since the Revolution.* 1982. Gleb Struve, *Russian Literature under Lenin and Stalin.* 1971. I. Vladislavlev, *Literatura velikogo desyatiletiya.* 1928.   V. T.

Romanticism. The concept and period of romanticism have not been treated well in Russia. In its time and subsequently Russian romanticism was imperfectly understood, eccentrically interpreted, and even denied to have existed. Anglo-American views have here been most strongly influenced by D. SVYATOPOLK-MIRSKY's often-quoted statement in *A History of Russian Literature* that the Russian poetry "contemporary with the great age of Romantic poetry in western Europe ... is not romantic; it is far more *formal*, active, selective—in short *classical*." This view reflects a persistent suspicion that Russia did not experience a fully legitimate romantic movement in the European sense, a suspicion first raised by the Russian romantics themselves. PUSHKIN once expressed doubt that Russia was experiencing a "true" romanticism; GOGOL tried to avoid the term romanticism; the critic BELINSKY habitually pointed to romanticism when denying that Russia possessed a truly national literature. Understandably, this view was readily endorsed by the Russian realists. TOLSTOI began his career by declaring he would write deliberately *not* like such romantic predecessors as LERMONTOV and BESTUZHEV-Marlinsky; Bazarov of TURGENEV's novel *Fathers and Children* uses the term romanticism to express his contempt for superfluous tradition; in his novel *What is to be Done?* CHERNYSHEVSKY dismissed romanticism as frail, insubstantial, irrelevant. This amalgamation of romantic doubt and realist hostility prevailed through the 19th century, so that it was only in the early 20th century that romanticism finally became the subject of major book-length studies. Unhappily, while the first serious scholars of romanticism proved that Russia did experience a romantic movement, they also obscured its history by cramming it into eccentric categories—individualism-nationalism-universalism, social-political-historical-philosophical romanticism, French-German-English Russian romanticism—these and other artificial schemes ruptured both the history and the concept of romanticism.

In the early 20th century, during the modernist period, it seemed that romanticism might finally come into its own in Russia. The Russian DECADENTS and SYMBOLISTS were drawn to romanticism to the same degree they distanced themselves from REALISM, and they even labeled themselves neoromantics. But modernism was suppressed in the Soviet period, study of modernism is still inhibited in Soviet scholarship, and even though modernist studies have flourished in Western Slavic scholarship we still do not have a serious comparative study of the relationships between romanticism and modernism in Russia. As for postrevolutionary literary history, it was especially in the Soviet period that romanticism was most seriously misinterpreted—so badly misinterpreted as to make the concept unrecognizable to specialists. Even though romanticism—or rather "revolutionary romanticism"—was given a prominent role in SOCIALIST REALISM and this role was officially endorsed by Stalin's cultural strongman A. A. ZHDANOV, the concept quickly came to be considered antithetical to the realism in the very term socialist realism and romantic idealism was rejected as hostile to dialectical materialism. Romanticism became a taboo subject in Soviet letters, and scholars of romanticism were disciplined or suppressed. The romantic movement was pushed forward in time by the encroachment of the "realistic" features of neoclassicism (which was even redefined as prerealism!) and back in time by the insistence on the supremacy of the realist period. The romantic period was literally squeezed out of literary history—assigned a short life from 1816 to 1825 and treated as a mere interlude on the inexorable historical path to realism. By 1953 Soviet scholars were so ignorant about romanticism that they actually defined it as a "recreation of surrounding milieu in all its reality" or studied it in stereotyped terms as "unrealistic" or "nonrealist."

Happily, this situation has changed. Beginning in 1957, in context with an all-union "Debate over Realism," scholars began to realize that by redefining romanticism in realist terms they had deprived realism of anything to be distinct from. For the first time in over three decades scholars began to suggest that romanticism was an important movement in literary history, that it was not necessarily realistic and not at all bad for being unrealistic, and that it had its own aesthetic premises worthy of study in their own right. It was found that the great critic Belinsky placed a high value on romanticism, that GORKY admired it, and that it had a prominent and by no means always negative place in the teachings of Marx and Lenin. By 1964 scholars were able to mount an all-union "Discussion of Romanticism" in which were raised most of the crucial questions that had already been raised and at least partly resolved by Western scholars, especially that controversial question, "Just What is Romanticism?" By the late 1960s collections and major studies of romanticism, considered on its own merits, were commonplace in Soviet scholarship. In the years since, scholarship on romanticism has grown to massive proportions and Soviet definitions are readily respected by Western specialists even despite their heavily ideological orientation. Indeed, where in the mid-1960s it seemed that romanticism would be left to a small band of Western Slavists, Soviet romantic studies have now completely overcome the heritage of almost a full century of neglect. On the basis of this new Soviet scholarship and Western studies it is now possible to define the Russian romantic movement along generally accepted historical lines.

The Russian romantic movement is roughly contemporary with the all-European movement: it covers at least the first half of the 19th century. As in Europe its roots can be traced back to the preromantic trends of 18th-century neoclassicism, both Russian and European, particularly to an increasing interest in the song and other folk forms, to experiments with variations on the ode, and to a growing preference for the elegy. The romantics themselves spoke of such neoclassicists as KHERASKOV, KHEMNITSER, KAPNIST, and MAIKOV as their predecessors, and they approved the "barbaric" violations of neoclassical principles in the poetry of the great poet DERZHAVIN. The SENTIMENTALIST interlude of the 1790s gave strong impetus to romantic creativity in Russia. In accordance with what is known as the "two-line" theory, a split between an active and a passive sentimentalism was carried over into the romantic movement. The radical attitudes of the sentimentalist writer A. N. RADISHCHEV were manifested in the romantic movement by the civic or Decembrist revolutionary romantics, and the acquiescent, conservative attitudes of the national historian and sentimentalist writer N. M. KARAMZIN were reflected in the passive, escapist poetry of the early romantic poets V. A. ZHUKOVSKY and K. N. BATYUSHKOV. The early romantic movement is even termed "Karamzinism" and is sometimes confused with sentimentalism because of Karamzin's strong influence. The romantic movement began at the turn of the century with Zhukovsky, Batyushkov, V. L. PUSHKIN, and others who were attracted to the aesthetic teachings of the German and English romantics; translated the ballads and other verse works of Bürger, Goethe, Schiller, Uhland, Southey, Scott, Wordsworth, and Coleridge; experimented with mixtures of styles and genres; and made the romantic elegy so markedly their own that they are termed "sentimental-elegiac poets." Romanticism reached its maturity in the 1820s with the appearance of Byron and BYRONISM, Pushkin's romantic, Byronic verse tales, the outbreak of a full-scale war on neoclassicism by vociferous champions of "the new, the modern, the so-called romantic school," and the literary and political activism of the writers who became known as the DECEMBRISTS after the failure of their revolt against the tsar in December 1825. The romantic movement suffered a severe setback during the reactionary aftermath of the Decembrist revolt, but romanticism remained controversial in a growing antagonism between the so-called Literary Aristocrats led by Pushkin and the newly rising Literary Plebeians who gained a monopoly over journals and publishing in the late 1820s. Poetry was dominant in the romantic movement throughout the 1820s, but in 1829 literature made a sudden turn to prose, and prose works dominated over the romantic verse tales of Pushkin and Lermontov in the 1830s. Pushkin began writing his prose tales and short stories at this time. Bestuzhev-Marlinsky rose to unprecedented heights of popularity with the appearance of his ultra-romantic Byronic prose tales. Tens of thousands of pages of historical novels were written by a pleiad of "Russian Walter Scotts." Gogol made his appearance with his Ukrainian folk tales and his Petersburg tales. Scores of prose tales appeared for the enjoyment of the newly literate and respectably large audience whom Belinsky indignantly labeled "lackeys" and the Literary Plebeians cultivated for great commercial profit. Lermontov's novel *A Hero of Our Time* appeared in 1841. In the late 1840s and 1850s the concept of a Russian literature growing organically from the soil (*pochva*) of national life (*pochvennichestvo*) was developed by the critic Apollon GRIGORIEV and found a reflection in some novels and short prose works. Grigoriev himself saw the plays of Aleksandr OSTROVSKY as a living proof of this conception. The school of sentimental philanthropism (so defined by Grigoriev) made the social underdog the hero of its stories, relieving his plight with a mixture of compassion, condescension, and irony. The rural version of this school had its most successful exponent in Dmitry GRIGOROVICH, whose stories (*povesti*) "The Village" (1846) and "Hapless Anton" (Anton Goremyka, 1847) were huge successes. The urban version, launched by Gogol's great short story "The Overcoat" (1842) and continued by the DOSTOEVSKY brothers and their Petersburg colleague Yakov BUTKOV, among others, created the genre of the "Tale of a Poor Clerk," which proliferated in the mid and late 1840s. Sentimental philanthropism was one manifestation of a general concern for the truth of "real life" and a tendency toward the "lower" genres which the

critic Belinsky promoted under the label of the "natural school." Belinsky championed Gogol and his *Dead Souls* (1842) as his model for it.

Russia's great metaphysical poet Fyodor TYUTCHEV made his appearance in the 1830s, and in the 1840s he and other late romantic poets wrote some of Russia's finest metaphysical poetry. These poets—called by some critics Eclectic or Parnassian—bravely continued the Poetic tradition against the hostility of the prose realists in the 1850s and 1860s. The rise of Russian realism in the late 1840s and 1850s marks the decline of romanticism in Russia, but even some Soviet scholars have ventured to apply the term romantic to the poet Nikolai NEKRASOV, and Western Slavists have discovered a true vein of romanticism in the works of HERZEN, Turgenev, Dostoevsky, PANAEV, DRUZHININ, and GONCHAROV.

Where the European romantics were unaware of their Russian contemporaries, the Russian romantics were intensely conscious of the European romantic movement and immediately responsive to its every new literary development. There is an irony here, for while the Russians fully appreciated the importance of originality in romantic aesthetics, and their contempt for the neoclassical principle of imitation was heightened by their need to liberate themselves from foreign as well as native 18th-century influences, they continued to place a high value on European romantic ideas and perceived in the very adaptation of foreign models a way to national literary independence. They were not unaware of the contradiction, and it was painful for them. Even worse, their attempts to break away from foreign influence and create an original national literature worked against them too: their cultivation of indigenous themes and values seemed to lead them away from the standard of European romanticism.

The problem was that, unlike the Germans, French, Italians, Spanish, and English, the Russians did not yet have a national literature in the Western sense, and it was precisely in the romantic period that they set out to do what their neoclassical predecessors had been prevented from doing by the principle of imitation: they were determined to liberate Russian culture from "slavish imitation" of European models and create a truly independent, nationally original literature. Russian romantic assertions of national feelings were thus far more pronounced than in Europe, and the Russian romantic movement was burdened by a concern for national originality (NARODNOST') far in excess of the comparable European preoccupation with *nationalité*, *Volkstümlichkeit*, or national distinctiveness (autochthony) that accompanied the rise of modern nationalism in the early 19th century. By the early 1820s national originality had become a virtual synonym for romanticism, and the Russian romantics were strongly attracted to romantic idealist teachings about national originality in the works of the Schlegels, Madame de Staël, Simonde de Sismondi, and J. P. F. Ancillon. In these teachings they found sensible formulae for adapting, rather than imitating, foreign values, and for developing them in independent ways suitable to their own national needs. But the traumatic question of Russia and the West—the search for guidance by and independence from European influences—led from the 1820s to the Slavophile-Westernizer controversy that rent Russian society in the 1840s and after. More than any other concern, national originality is the sine qua non of Russian romanticism.

This ambiguity of national identity made the Russian romantic movement even more confusing, variegated, and contradictory than other romantic movements. Soviet scholars explain this confusion by associating romanticism with the period of transition from feudalism to capitalism, periods of transition being by definition contradictory. Russian romanticism is in fact very dynamic, and literary polemics were more heated than in any other country except perhaps France. Partisan feelings ran high, journals managed to be controversial despite the vigilant censor, and literary groupings began to take form early in the century. The romantic period was a jumble of alliances, societies, circles, camps, discussion groups, schools, salons, "evenings," editorial programs, campaigns, cliques, coteries, and intrigues. Individuals tended to divide and join on specific aesthetic or philosophical questions, to move from one group to another, to belong to several opposing groupings simultaneously. Journals changed positions, or were closed by the government, or were coopted by rival commercial and literary powers. The romantics accused each other of being neoclassicists, thus adding confusion to the search for a definition of romanticism. Debates went on for years at a time in articles, essays, letters to the editor; criticism that quickly became anti-criticism, just as quickly became anti-anti-criticism.

The most important question of the early 19th century was the development of a Russian literary language: the modernization of a still awkward syntax, the relationship of the literary language to the models of European languages, the relationship to the Russian colloquial or "folk" language. *Literati* divided into two camps: the Karamzinian "modernizers" who sought to create a clearer language for the expression of "ideas and feelings" on the models of French and other more developed languages, and the ultra-conservative Shishkovites, led by Admiral A. S. SHISHKOV, who fought to protect the purity of the Russian language from the invasions of "frenchification." In actual fact, the Karamzinians strove to adapt, not crudely imitate, foreign-language models, and Shishkov was an admirer of French neoclassicism who denounced foreign linguistic influences in a Russian language filled with French and German syntactical and lexical calques. In 1815 this confrontation, clearly between neoclassicists and early romantics, was expanded into a free-for-all over the equally controversial question of the role of colloquialisms in literary works. This polemic, called the "battle of the ballad," dealt with the ballads of Zhukovsky, who was accused of using the elitist "language of the salon" in his translations of German and English ballads, and those of P. A. KATENIN, who cultivated folk words and Old Slavic archaisms. In actual fact, Zhukovsky's ballads are not markedly "French" and not devoid of colloquialisms, and Katenin's ballads have foreign calques and not overly many colloquialisms. And curiously, the polemic itself was between two supernumeraries who were markedly neoclassical in their taste—A. S. GRIBOEDOV, author of the great neoclassical comedy *Woe from Wit*, and N. I. GNEDICH, translator of *The Iliad*. If this tended to make the polemic confusing, it at least had a happy ending: Zhukovsky's superior ballads prevailed in literature and the Katenin-Griboedov championship of colloquial Russian resulted in the marvelously colloquial fairy tales and other folk genres of Pushkin and other men of the 1820s. And despite the confusion, the polemicists expressed clearly romantic opinions about language and style.

To read through the few existing journals of the early century is to witness the steady deterioration of neoclassical tastes in perfect ratio with the rise of romantic attitudes. By 1820 such names as Boileau, La Harpe, La Fontaine, Batteux, Marmontel, Montaigne, Voltaire, Racine, Corneille, and Du Marsais are gone from journals, while the names of Richardson, Sterne, Milton, Addison, Thomson, Young, Gray, Scott, Ann Radcliffe, Madame de Staël, Sismondi, Chateaubriand, Lamartine, Herder, Schelling, the Schlegel brothers, Schiller, Goethe, and other Romantics are standard fare. Ossian, night and the grave, Sturm und Drang, the Gothic and the supernatural, the folk song and the folk ballad—these are the increasing concerns of the 1810s. Shishkov's *Colloquy of Lovers of the Russian Word* (BESEDA LYUBITELEI RUSSKOGO SLOVA) remained powerful into the 1820s, but it was the reforms of the Karamzinians—first in the *Literary Friendship Society* and then in the high-spirited, parodistic society of ARZAMAS—that proved victorious. The early romantics include, in addition to Zhukovsky and Batyushkov, the sentimental-elegiac poets V. L. Pushkin, M. V. Milonov, and A. Kh. KHVOSTOV, the writer of songs Ya. A. NELEDINSKY-MELETSKY, the fabulists A. E. Izmailov and I. A. KRYLOV, the cultural activists A. I. Turgenev, D. V. Dashkov, and D. N. Bludov, the poet-hussar Denis DAVYDOV, and Prince P. A. VYAZEMSKY. Their journal during the first two decades was VESTNIK EVROPY.

Not until the early 1820s did the term romanticism actually appear in public print. This occurred in a major and long-lasting campaign from 1821 through 1825 in which romanticism was championed and neoclassicism attacked from all sides. Ironically, midway through the debate Pushkin suggested in a letter that the neoclassicists who were being so severely criticized no longer existed. He could find only two neoclassicists on the scene—the critic M. A. Dmitriev and the author of neoclassical comedies Prince A. A. SHAKHOVSKOI—and in this he was perfectly correct. The reputed antiromantic members of the Katenin circle, particularly V. K. KYUKHELBEKER, were more properly anti-Karamzinian romantics.

Katenin himself, who once proclaimed neoclassical allegiance, was the harshest critic of Griboedov's *Woe from Wit* for its neoclassical orientation. M. A. Dmitriev was really a literary conservative who never defended neoclassical principles; and while M. T. Kachenovsky turned *Vestnik Evropy* into an antiromantic bastion, he was also more of a conservative than a defender of neoclassicism. N. I. Gnedich and the neoclassical aesthetician A. F. MERZLYAKOV were respected by the romantics. Thus, by the 1820s neoclassicism was actually a straw man, and the debate over romanticism was fought by men who were devoted to romanticism: Vyazemsky, Bestuzhev-Marlinsky, V. F. ODOEVSKY, N. I. GRECH, F. V. BULGARIN, K. F. RYLEEV, Orest SOMOV, A. A. DELVIG, Katenin, and Kyukhelbeker. The most important result of the debate was the open espousal of romantic aesthetics and the introduction into Russia of the romantic questions that concerned Europe: ancient versus modern, North versus South, ideal versus corporeal, infinite versus finite, imitation versus originality, pre-Christian versus Christian creativity, plastic versus picturesque, Gothic versus Renaissance and the Age of Enlightenment, conditional principles of form and content, free expression and imagination, the development of a language of prose, the role of literary criticism, Byronism and the romantic verse tale, the romantic drama, the demand for *narodnost'*, local color, folklore, and historicism, the relationships between literature and history, politics, philosophy, religion, and science, revolution and protest, and, still going strongly, the question of the development of the Russian literary language.

By 1825 the debate evolved into rough but definable literary groupings of a new sort, each with its own weltanschauung and definition of romanticism. Among the most important of these new groupings was the so-called civic or Decembrist trend, those poets and writers who equated literature with the expression of socio-political ideals. Decembrist romanticism includes Bestuzhev-Marlinsky and Ryleev, Kyukhelbeker and Prince A. I. ODOEVSKY, Vyazemsky and Griboedov, Pushkin, Grech and Bulgarin, and any other writer of the time who cultivated civic themes in poetry and criticism. The civic trend formed around the literary almanac POLYARNAYA ZVEZDA in 1823 to 1825. In 1823 there also appeared the grouping of metaphysical poets, critics, and philosophers that grew out of the Moscow salon of Professor S. E. RAICH and propagated the teachings of romantic idealism, especially Schelling. The society known as the WISDOM LOVERS (*lyubomudry*) was founded that year, and in 1827 to 1829 the Russian Schellingists published the *Moskovskii vestnik*. The society was inspired primarily by the young poet and critic D. V. VENEVITINOV, who died in 1827, and its members were M. P. POGODIN, S. P. SHEVYRYOV, the brothers I. V. and P. V. KIREEVSKY, A. S. KHOMYAKOV, A. I. Koshelyov, and N. M. Rozhalin. The grouping also includes Kyukhelbeker, V. F. Odoevsky, and E. A. BARATYNSKY, whose poetry and writings were metaphysically oriented.

After 1825 Russian literature split into two large groupings, the Literary Aristocrats and the Literary Plebeians. This was the result of a major new development in Russian culture—the growth of a significantly large and, consequently, middle- and even lower-class audience. The former, known as the Pushkin Pleiad because of the poet's leadership, formed around A. A. Delvig's literary almanac SEVERNYE TSVETY and his newspaper LITERATURNAYA GAZETA, and later Pushkin's journal SOVREMENNIK. This group includes Pushkin, Delvig, Vyazemsky, Orest Somov, Zhukovsky, Denis Davydov, I. I. KOZLOV, N. M. YAZYKOV, P. A. PLETNYOV, Baratynsky, and a host of minor poets and writers. The Literary Plebeians gathered around N. I. Grech and F. V. Bulgarin's journal *Syn otechestva i severnyi arkhiv* and the latter's newspaper SEVERNAYA PCHELA. O. I. SENKOVSKY, publisher of BIBLIOTEKA DLYA CHTENIYA and author of low-taste prose works under the pen name Baron Brambeus, belonged to this grouping. The brothers N. A. and K. A. POLEVOI were at first competitors of the Grech-Bulgarin publishing monopoly, but they were co-opted in 1834 when their journal MOSKOVSKII TELEGRAF was shut down by the government. In the 1830s the Literary Plebeians attracted Bestuzhev-Marlinsky to their publications. Despised for their low taste in literature, their lack of artistry, and their commercial interest in a mass readership, they published most of the Russian Walter Scotts who aimed their historical novels at the new unsophisticated audience: M. N. ZAGOSKIN, I. I. LAZHECHNIKOV,

Anton POGORELSKY (A. A. Perovsky), R. M. Zotov, I. I. Kalashnikov, and K. P. Masalsky (Mosalsky). Bulgarin and N. A. Polevoi were also authors of historical novels, and the latter wrote his *History of the Russian People* as a democratic counterbalance to Karamzin's aristocratic *History of the Russian State*. Pushkin was the avowed enemy of the Literary Plebeians, and he decried their flood of *mauvais ton* works, but the new audience and the new taste were facts of life of the 1830s. Among the other new authors of the "lower taste" literature of the decade were A. F. VELTMAN, V. T. NAREZHNY, A. I. POLEZHAEV, V. G. BENEDIKTOV, and N. F. PAVLOV.

The 1830s saw the rise of Belinsky's NATURAL SCHOOL, his lifelong championship of social values in literature and the task of the critic to "extract social ideas" from the content of literary works. The natural school may be generally defined as a realization of Belinsky's romantic idealist concepts of naturalness, reality, sociality, contemporariness, and *narodnost'* in literature. The school cannot be defined without reference to Gogol whom the critic Belinsky considered (too hastily, as it turned out) to be the living proof of his theories of literature. Although Belinsky was a plebeian, his good taste in literature is beyond reproach and he did much to raise literary standards from the Grech-Bulgarin abyss. The SLAVOPHILES, whose ideas were largely derived from German romantic thought, began to form a group at this time. Among them were the KIREEVSKY brothers, the brothers K. S. and I. S. AKSAKOV and their father S. T. AKSAKOV, A. S. KHOMYAKOV, N. Ya. Danilevsky, and Yu. F. SAMARIN, as well as N. M. Yazykov, M. P. Pogodin, and S. P. SHEVYRYOV. Belinsky, a Westernizer himself, misjudged Gogol by not realizing how strong his Slavophilism was. Gogol was close to the Aksakov family and came under the reactionary influence of N. M. Yazykov. All alone in the 1830s is Russia's great romantic M. Yu. Lermontov.

The question of romanticism burned itself out in the 1830s, and the realist movement matured in the late 1840s and 1850s. It is very difficult to sort out the differences between romantic and realist phenomena because every literary development after the mid-1830s is usually labeled realist. There is a need to reconsider the entire question of late Russian romanticism. Indisputably Schellingian, for example, is A. A. Grigoriev's organic criticism, based on the belief that a national literature is a living entity that passes from infancy to youth to maturity to decline and death. The sentimental philanthropists, urban as well as rural, have also been too hastily labeled realists, for there are definite romantic qualities to the early novels of D. V. Grigorovich, A. V. Druzhinin, F. M. Dostoevsky, and other writers of the natural school of the 1840s. And even though literary groupings begin at this time to form around the lines of the Slavophile-Westernizer split, rather than clear-cut romantic-realist tastes, at least one grouping is clearly romantic: the eclectic or parnassian poets who expressed their faith in art for art's sake despite the hostility of the dominant social radical critics. Among these late romantic poets are L. A. MEI, A. N. MAIKOV, A. A. FET, A. K. TOLSTOI, and F. I. Tyutchev. A sadly neglected and very good late romantic poet is Karolina PAVLOVA.

Russian romanticism does not differ essentially from European romanticism in themes. The Russians were also preoccupied with death and the grave, madness and murder, magic and the supernatural, this world and the other world, escapism and rebellion, social protest and individual isolation, the spoiled *enfant du siècle*, rural and urban mores, exotic milieux and noble savages, the terror and pageantry of history, heroes of derring-do and tender heroines, love and passion. But romantic themes were given a Russian character and played out in Russian settings. Pushkin's Onegin and Lermontov's Pechorin, however Byronic they are, experience an unmistakable Russian ennui; and Bestuzhev-Marlinsky's Byronic heroes have markedly Russian failings. The same is true of the literary genres cultivated in Russia during the romantic period. The Russian romantics revolted against the same strictures of neoclassical prescriptions and found freedom of creativity by mixing forms and styles, favoring new or previously scorned forms, and associating old forms with new themes. But even though the genres cultivated by the Russians were with few exceptions the same preferred by their European romantic contemporaries, they were given a distinctly Russian character. Thus, while many of Zhukovsky's translations of

German and English ballads are faithful to their originals, many others are adapted to a Russian milieu. And while Pushkin's first romantic verse tales are very much influenced by Byron's model, he quickly found his own form and means of expression.

The three most popular verse genres of the early romantic period are the BALLAD, the ELEGY, and the song. Zhukovsky was Russia's great balladeer, and his strongest competitor in the genre was P. A. Katenin. The battle of the ballad revolved around the translations of Bürger's *Lenore* in three versions by Zhukovsky titled *Lyudmila*, *Svetlana*, and *Lenora*, and Katenin's version under the title *Olga*. Zhukovsky also made the elegy a highly admired form with his 1802 translation of Gray's "Elegy Written in a Country Churchyard," but the best of the sentimental-elegiac poets are K. N. Batyushkov, V. L. Pushkin, and Denis Davydov. The early Russian romantics performed marvelous experiments with the elegy and made it an intensely personal form of expression. Indeed, the elegy proved so popular that it eventually wearied Russians with its melancholy tone and ubiquitous nightscapes. The most popular author of Russian songs was Ya. A. Neledinsky-Meletsky, who paved the way for both Russian folk songs in literary form and the exotic songs of Greek, Italian, Spanish, Persian, and other national flavors that so attracted the men of the 1820s. The hussar poet Denis Davydov enjoyed great popularity for his rollicking poetry of wine, woman, song, and battle, and for his erotic verses. Russia's master of light verse in the early century was the epicurean poet Batyushkov. Less often cultivated, but very much appreciated, were the sonnet, the rondeau, and the *ottava rima*.

As in Europe, the epic was replaced by the ballad, and the ballad by the romantic verse tale (POEMA). In 1821 two events made the romantic verse tale and Byronism the rage in Russia: the appearance of Zhukovsky's translation of *The Prisoner of Chillon* and Pushkin's first Byronic verse tale *The Captive of the Caucasus*. Pushkin's verse tales, each less indebted to Byron, appeared throughout the 1820s: *The Fountain at Bakhchisarai, The Gypsies, Graf Nulin, Poltava*. His verse tales were followed by E. A. Baratynsky's *The Ball, The Concubine*, and *Eda*, and K. F. Ryleev's historical verse tales *Nalivaiko* and *Voinarovsky*. Pushkin wrote two of his best verse tales in the 1830s—*Angelo* and *The Bronze Horseman*—and Lermontov kept the genre popular through the 1830s with *The Novice* and *The Demon*. Bestuzhev-Marlinsky did not complete a fine historical verse tale published in fragments under the title *Andrei, Prince of Pereyaslavl*.

A uniquely Russian, or rather Slavic, genre cultivated in the mid-1820s was the DUMA or "meditation," a short historical poem featuring a hero of the people. The *duma*, written on the model of a 17th-century Ukrainian folk song and introduced to Russia from the Polish romantics, was the specialty of Ryleev. Together with Bestuzhev-Marlinsky, Ryleev also wrote a series of revolutionary "agitation songs" which were highly popular at Decembrist gatherings. These revolutionary works go with Pushkin's early songs and poems calling for the death of tyrants. Virtually every man of letters in the 1820s was a poet, and the romantic period is rich in lyric poetry. The most unusual and best known genre of the 1820s was Pushkin's novel in verse *Eugene Onegin*.

During the first decade of the century Russians were treated to a flurry of sentimental prose tales in the vein of Karamzin's "Poor Liza." All sorts of sad tear-jerkers appeared under the titles "Poor Masha," "Poor Dasha," "Poor Lizaveta," "Poor Louisa." The first three decades also saw the regular appearance in Russian journals of translations of European prose tales by Florian, Madame de Genlis, Ann Radcliffe, Goethe, Rousseau, Chateaubriand, Constant, George Sand, Jean Paul, and especially Hugo. The "instigator" of the Russian prose tale, as Belinsky called him, was Bestuzhev-Marlinsky, who began his career in 1821 before prose became acceptable. His early tales of history (a Russian and a Livonian "Gothic" cycle) and his society tales were very popular before 1825, and in 1830 he enthralled the new Russian reader with other Byronic society tales, naval adventure stories, tales of the supernatural, and especially his exotic tales of the Caucasus. Scott's Waverley Novels began to be published in Russian in the 1820s, and they paved the way for the flood of historical novels in the 1830s. Russia's first best-seller was a combination historical and picaresque novel by F. V. BULGARIN called *Ivan Vyzhigin*. Among the better historical works are M. N. ZAGOSKIN's *Yury Miloslavsky, or The Russians in 1612*, about the Time of Troubles, I. I. Lazhechnikov's *Ice Palace*, about the eccentric reign of Anna Ioannovna in the early 18th century, Pushkin's "The Captain's Daughter," and Gogol's "Taras Bulba." In the early 1830s Bestuzhev-Marlinsky hailed the historical novel as the culmination of the romantic development of all history, equating the word romanticism with the European word for the novel, *roman*. Only a few years later Belinsky began his successful campaign to reduce the historical novel to a sub-literary level.

The first Russian dramas to violate the neoclassical unities are V. A. OZEROV's historical dramas of the early 19th century. Pushkin's attempt at a romantic drama, *Boris Godunov*, was not successful in its time, and his *Little Tragedies* have been more greatly valued as literary texts than in performance. Gogol's great comedy *The Inspector General* enjoyed great success from the moment of its first appearance in 1836. Among the leaders of the Russian theater in the romantic period, as original dramatists, translators, or director-managers, were P. A. Katenin, M. N. Zagoskin, N. I. Khmelnitsky, A. I. Pisarev, Nestor KUKOLNIK, N. A. Polevoi, and, in opera, M. I. Glinka. To the drama in the romantic period may be added Lermontov's *Masquerade*.

Only two romantic prose novels have survived as great literature: Lermontov's *A Hero of Our Time* and Gogol's *Dead Souls*, both from the 1840s. V. F. Odoevsky's *Russian Nights*, a meandering metaphysical work in the style and spirit of Hoffmann's *Die Serapionsbrüder*, appeared in 1844. Among the more notable prose writers of the 1830s and 1840s are N. F. Pavlov, author of "society tales"; Orest Somov, whose Ukrainian folk stories were succeeded by Gogol's two volumes, *Evenings on a Farm near Dikanka*; A. F. Veltman, the main exponent of "romantic folklorism," author of humorous, ironic stories in the manner of Jean Paul; V. I. Dal, known for his Cossack stories and his "physiological sketches" of social mores; and Elena Hahn (GAN), who wrote in the manner of George Sand. Among the best prose tales of the 1830s are Pushkin's "Queen of Spades," a Hoffmannesque story of seemingly inexhaustible ambiguities, and his five *Tales of Belkin*. Among Gogol's Petersburg tales, "The Portrait" is a typical romantic *Künstler-novelle*, and "Nevsky Prospect" is at least partly so.

Russian romanticism is known to the West almost exclusively for the works of its three giants Pushkin, Gogol, and Lermontov. Belinsky's great stature as a critic has brought him to Western awareness, Griboedov is known on the world stage for his *Woe from Wit*, and three poets—Baratynsky, Tyutchev, and Fet—are so excellent as to have become at least generally known outside Russia. Less well known, but far more representative of the romantic literary standard and still highly valued in their own country's letters are Zhukovsky, Bestuzhev-Marlinsky, and V. F. Odoevsky. Many leading figures of the romantic period are known abroad in political rather than literary history, including Chaadaev, Herzen, and Bakunin. Many very good romantic writers—romantics at least in their early years—have been presented to the West as realists: Grigorovich, Dostoevsky, and S. T. Aksakov, for example. Western readers have remained ignorant of Russian romantics whose lives and works are fascinating: Denis Davydov, Vyazemsky, Katenin, Ryleev, Venevitinov, Karolina Pavlova.... Admittedly, it was not until the realist period that Russia produced the great writers who have had such a great impact on the West. But Russia's first modern national literature was created in the romantic period, and Russian romanticism still remains largely a blank in Western knowledge of the world romantic movement. The introduction of the Russian element into scholarship on romanticism would significantly change our view of what the world movement was, what it accomplished, how it affected the subsequent development of literary history.

Secondary literature: Dmitrij Čiževskij, *On Romanticism in Slavic Literature.* The Hague, 1957. Donald Fanger, *Dostoevsky and Romantic Realism: A Study of Dostoevsky in Relation to Balzac, Dickens, and Gogol.* 1965. *Istoriya romantizma v russkoi literature: 1790–1825.* 1979. *Istoriya romantizma v russkoi literature: 1825–1840.* 1979. L. G. Leighton, *Russian Romanticism: Two Essays.* The Hague and Paris, 1975. *Problemy romantizma.* 1967. *Russkii romantizm.* Ed. by K. N. Grigor'yan. 1978. V. V. Vanslov, *Estetika romantizma.* 1966.
L. G. L.

Romantic realism. A term applied by some scholars to fiction which combines certain romantic attitudes and devices with a realistic poetics. A pursuit of the metaphysical and the fantastic, the frequent use of symbols, a tendency to seek out the extremes of the human condition, vestiges of stylization along the lines of traditional genres (tragic vs. comic, sublime vs. grotesque) even though these opposites are demonstratively fused, and romantic irony may appear in a work whose setting, characters, plot, and language are those of the ordinary life of ordinary people in contemporary society, often urban. Major figures who may be viewed as "romantic realists" are GOGOL and DOSTOEVSKY.

Bibliography: Donald Fanger, *Dostoevsky and Romantic Realism: A Study of Dostoevsky in Relation to Balzac, Dickens, and Gogol.* 1965.
V. T.

Rosen (Rózen), Egór (Geórgy) Fyódorovich, Baron (1800–60), poet, translator, dramatist, critic, was born in Reval and received an excellent classical education at home. In 1819 he entered the military service. In 1835, through V. A. ZHUKOVSKY, he received the position of secretary to the Grand Duke Alexander and in 1838–39 accompanied him on his trip to Europe. Rosen retired in 1840, devoting the rest of his life to literature.

Rosen was a prolific writer with a genuine need for self-expression and enthusiasm for literature in a language that was not his native tongue. He learned Russian while in the military service by translating Russian poetry into his native German. In the 1820s he published original Russian verses in the leading almanacs and journals and thus received an introduction into the literary life of both Moscow and Petersburg. In 1830 he published, with N. M. Konshin, the almanac *Tsarskoe Selo* and in 1831 to 1833 *Altsiona*. Rosen was on friendly terms with PUSHKIN, translating one act of *Boris Godunov* into German, and contributing to SOVREMENNIK.

Rosen wrote lyrics, tragedies, poems, critical articles and prose tales. He is capable of inspired stanzas and there is true verbal vigor in some of his lines, but his poetry is afflicted with an insensitivity to stylistic levels of diction, creating disparities and lapses from the lofty to the colloquial and trivial. His fancy, although never exquisite is yet graceful, the rhythm frequently excellent. Rosen is remembered today as a minor poet of the Pushkin period and the author of the libretto for M. Glinka's opera *A Life for the Tsar* (1836).

Bibliography: Poety 1820–1830kh godov. (Biblioteka poeta.) Vol. 1. 1972. Pp. 551–79.
A. Gl.

Rostopchiná, Evdokíya Petróvna (née Sushkova, 1811–58), poet, playwright, and writer, published her first verses in 1831 and her first book of verse in 1841. A Moscow socialite, Countess Rostopchina was acquainted with ZHUKOVSKY, PUSHKIN, LERMONTOV, TYUTCHEV, and other major figures of Russian literature. Her love lyric won the praise of contemporaries and some forty of her poems were set to music. Her society tales, such as "Rank and Money" (Chiny i den'gi, 1838), "The Duel" (Poedinok, 1838), and "A Happy Woman" (Schastlivaya zhenshchina, 1852) received attention for their exposure of the emptiness of the life of the upper class. Rostopchina's later works, some satirical comedies, in particular, tended to carry a conservative message.

Works: Sochineniya. With a biographic sketch by S. Sushkov. 2 vols. 1890. Poems: in *Poety 1840–1850-kh gg.* Introd. B. Ya. Bukhshtab. 1962.
Secondary literature: V. G. Belinskii, "Stikhotvoreniya grafini E. Rostopchinoi" (1841). In his *PSS*, Vol. 5, pp. 456–61. N. A. Dobrolyubov, "U pristani: Roman v pis'makh grafini Evdokii Rostopchinoi" (1857). In his *Sobranie sochinenii*, Vol. 2 (1962), pp. 70–87. V. Khodasevich, *Stat'i o russkoi poezii.* 1922. Pp. 7–42.
V. T.

Rostóvsky, St. Dimítry (in Ukrainian: Danylo Savyč Tuptalo; 1651–1709) represents (with Stefan YAVORSKY and Feofan PROKOPO-VICH) the height of Ukrainian and KIEV ACADEMY influence in late 17th and early 18th century Russia. Born near Kiev in a Cossack family, Tuptalo attended the then Mohyla College from 1662 to 1665, was cowled and assumed the name Dimitry in 1668, traveled and preached in the Ukraine, Byelorussia and Lithuania and in the

1680s and 1690s was hegumen of various monasteries. In 1684, in the Kiev Caves monastery where he was official preacher, Tuptalo began his twenty year work on the MINEI CHET'I. In 1702 Peter I made Tuptalo metropolitan of Rostov, where along with his other duties he devoted special attention to the establishment of schools and curricula on the Kievan model. Though not supporting Peter's reforms, he did not join the opposition. He was canonized in 1757.

Tuptalo's poetry, largely religious and epigrammatic, is typical of the Ukrainian Baroque in its emphasis on formal devices, cabalistic word play, etc. His *Runo oroshennoe* (1680) exemplifies the fusion of moral teaching with arcane allegorical interpretations. In his Ukrainian period his sermons have a highly ornate rhetorical style; those of his Rostov period are simpler and more direct, and often aimed against the Old Believers (cf. "Rozysk o raskol'nicheskoi brynskoi vere," 1709). Of his several known school dramas two have survived—on the Assumption of the Virgin and a Christmas play; the latter (staged in Rostov in 1702) fuses Ukrainian and Great Russian linguistic elements and BYT. In the "historical" mode Tuptalo wrote several *letopisi* (e.g., on "world history") and his *Minei chet'i* in four parts, each for three months of the Church calendar (1689, 1695, 1700 and 1705). Tuptalo's *Lives of the Saints*, the first after the 16th-century *Menaea* of Metropolitan MAKARY, drew on several new sources—Skarga's Lives, the *Acta Sanctorum* of the Bollandists, the *Vitae sanctorum* of Surius—and unlike Makary's, was highly popular, with some ten editions in the 18th century alone.

G. G.

Rózanov, Vasíly Vasílievich (1856–1919), writer, critic, philosopher, and journalist. A graduate of the Historical-Philosophical Faculty of Moscow University (1880), Rozanov taught secondary school in the provinces until 1893 when he became a professional writer. He wrote mostly for A. S. SUVORIN's *Novoe vremya*, but also for various journals, such as MIR ISKUSSTVA and *Novyi put'*. As a political journalist, Rozanov was highly successful but also unprincipled. He generally supported the government and its policies and on occasion expressed odiously reactionary and bigoted opinions. Rozanov was singularly unglamorous personally, in spite of his brilliance. He made few friends and many enemies. His personal life was marred by an unhappy marriage in 1880 to Apollinariya Suslova, fourteen years his senior, and later by her refusal to accede to a divorce even after they had been separated for many years and Rozanov had several children by his second, common-law wife.

As a literary critic, Rozanov made some seminal observations which were soon taken up by his contemporaries, the SYMBOLISTS. His celebrated essay, *The Legend of the Grand Inquisitor by F. M. Dostoevsky* (Legenda o Velikom Inkvizitore F. M. Dostoevskogo, 1894), falsely assumes that the ideas of Ivan Karamazov are Dos-TOEVSKY's own (while in fact the whole plan of the novel is aimed at deflating and discrediting them), but it is the first piece of criticism to recognize fully the philosophic depth of the "Grand Inquisitor" chapter in particular, and of Dostoevsky's novels in general. In two shorter essays appended to the "Grand Inquisitor" piece, Rozanov boldly reversed the established view according to which GOGOL was the founder of Russian REALISM, suggesting that Gogol's fictional world was one of soulless caricatures, of characters who have pronounced appetites but lack the movements of the soul which alone make a character human. Rozanov followed Apollon GRIGORIEV in asserting that PUSHKIN was the true founder of Russian realism. Rozanov wanted art to present wholesome, ordinary people leading their useful lives, and found this ideal realized in the works of Lev TOLSTOI.

Rozanov's philosophy went against the grain of both main trends of 19th-century Russian thought. On the one side, Rozanov challenged the singleminded preoccupation of the Russian "progressive" intelligentsia with society and advocated a concern with personal and family happiness. On the other, he pointed out that Orthodoxy as embraced by right wing ideologues such as Dostoevsky or LEON-TIEV hinged on a firm belief in life in the hereafter. If there was none, monasticism, chastity, fasting, etc., were simply pointless and dangerous violations of the laws of nature. In both of these contexts, Rozanov brought in the topic of sex, equally ignored by both camps of his opponents. He preached a positive attitude toward sexuality, family life, the little joys of daily life (BYT), suggesting that these things, too, could be perceived as valuable and even sacred.

Furthermore, Rozanov, unlike almost every other Russian of his age, was willing to speak freely about problems related to gender and sexuality, including even homosexuality, which he did not consider an abomination.

Rozanov, not a systematic thinker, was at his best in wholly free, aphoristic prose, not unlike Nietzsche's (who had some influence on him). His books *Solitaria* (Uedinennoe, 1912) and *Fallen Leaves* (Opavshie list'ya, 1913–15) belong to the confession genre, presenting a free stream of thought and emotion, and touching a great variety of topics, always interestingly, often paradoxically, and at times profoundly. Rozanov's last book, *The Apocalypse of Our Times* (Apokalipsis nashego vremeni, 1917–18) is written in the same manner. In this truly tragic work, Rozanov's impressions and thoughts about the Revolution are of a rare, almost visionary perceptiveness.

Rozanov is considered to have been one of the great masters of the Russian language. Certainly he has few peers among writers of non-fiction. As a thinker, he has been ignored in the Soviet Union (for obvious reasons), but he may very well make a comeback some day.

Works: Literaturnye ocherki. 2d ed. 1902. *Kriticheskie etyudy.* 1904. *Bibleiskaya poeziya.* 1912. *Literaturnye izgnanniki.* 1913. *Sredi khudozhnikov.* 1914. *Izbrannoe.* Introd. and ed. Yu. P. Ivask. New York, 1956. *Neuznannyi fenomen.* (Brown Slavic Reprints.) Providence, 1965. *O Gogole.* Letchworth, Herts., 1970. *Legenda o velikom inkvizitore. Dve stat'i o Gogole.* (Reprint of 1906 ed.) Munich, 1970. *Temnyi lik: metafizika khristianstva.* Introd. George Ivask. Würzburg, 1975. *Lyudi lunnogo sveta: metafizika khristianstva.* Introd. George Ivask. Würzburg, 1977. *Religiya i kul'tura: Sbornik statei.* Paris, 1979.

Translations: Solitaria. Trans. S. S. Koteliansky. London, 1927. *Fallen Leaves.* Trans. S. S. Koteliansky. London, 1929. *Essays in Russian Literature; the conservative view: Leontiev, Rozanov, Shestov.* Sel., ed., trans. and introd. Spencer E. Roberts. Athens, Ohio, 1968. *Dostoevsky and the Legend of the Grand Inquisitor.* Trans. with an afterword by Spencer E. Roberts. Ithaca, 1972.

Secondary literature: Anna Lisa Crone, *Rozanov and the End of Literature.* Würzburg, 1978. (With a bibliography.) E. F. Goller-bakh, *V. V. Rozanov: Zhizn' i tvorchestvo.* Paris, 1976. Renato Poggioli, *Rozanov.* London, 1962. George F. Putnam, "Vasili V. Rozanov: Sex, Marriage and Christianity," CSS 5 (1971), pp. 301–26. V. Shklovskii, *Rozanov; iz knigi "Syuzhet, kak yavlenie stilya."* Petrograd, 1921. A. Sinyavskii, *'Opavshie list'ya' Rozanova, Sintaksis.* Ann Arbor, Mich., 1982. Mikhail M. Spasovskii, *V. V. Rozanov v poslednie gody svoei zhizni.* 2d ed. New York, 1968. Heinrich A. Stammler, "Apocalypse: V. V. Rozanov and D. H. Lawrence," CSP 16 (1974), pp. 221–44.

V. T.

Rozhdéstvensky, Robért Ivánovich (1932–), poet, was born in Kosikha in the Altai. His parents, both in the military, left for the front when the war began, leaving him in a children's home. In 1950 and 1951 he studied philology at Petrozavodsk University, then entered the Gorky Literary Institute, graduating in 1956. He began to publish his poems in 1950, and his first volume, *Flags of Spring* (Flagi vesny) appeared in Petrozavodsk in 1955, followed by *The Trial* (Ispytanie, 1956) and *Drifting Prospect* (Dreifuyushchii prospekt, 1959). Like EVTUSHENKO, Rozhdestvensky belongs to the post-Stalinist generation of poets whose works met with a tremendous response on the part of young readers, who looked to poetry in the sixties to give voice to their ideals, rebellion, and bravado. *Desert Islands* (Neobytaemye ostrova, 1962), *To a Contemporary* (Rovesniku, 1962), *Radius of Action* (Radius deistviya, 1965), and *Son of Vera* (Syn Very, 1966) belong to this period. His volumes *Seriously* (Vser'ez) and *Dedication* (Posvyashchenie), both 1970, demonstrated his versatility in handling a wide variety of subjects in his poetry. Later volumes include *Line* (Liniya, 1973), *Before the Holiday* (Pered prazdnikom, 1974), *All Begins with Love* (Vse nachinaetsya s lyubvi, 1977), and *The Seventies* (Semidesyatye, 1980). In 1972 he was awarded the Komsomol Prize for literature. Rozhdestvensky's writings continue the tradition of declamatory, at times rhetorical poetry which finds its 20th-century antecedents in MAYAKOVSKY's verse. A wide variety of thematic material contained in his verse—foreign travel, love, civic consciousness, space flight—provides a kind of poetic chronicle of his interests. Although somewhat more varied formally in his later work, Rozhdestvensky's primary artistic "restlessness" is expressed in the content, not the structure of his verse. The poems themselves often take the form of an apostrophe, a letter, or a dialogue of questions and answers on a given theme.

Works: Izbrannye proizvedeniya. 2 vols. 1979.

Translations: A Poem on Various Points of View and Other Poems. Trans. Geoffrey Dutton et al. Melbourne, 1968.

Secondary literature: Lev Anninskii, "Zametki o molodoi poezii," *Znamya,* 1961, No. 9, pp. 197–212.   N. C.

Rubtsóv, Nikolai Mikhailovich (1936–71), a poet of the "new wave" of the 1960s, was born in the North (Archangel oblast). He was orphaned at five, brought up in children's homes, received a grade school education, worked as a stoker on fishing vessels, then as a factory worker at a Leningrad plant. He began to write verse in 1953. In 1962, after having given a successful recital at the Leningrad House of Writers, Rubtsov was admitted to the Gorky Literary Institute. His verses now began to appear in the journals *Yunost'* and *Oktyabr'.* Rubtsov's first verses, "I've got oil all over me, I've got grease all over me" (Ya ves' v mazute, ya ves' v tavote) caught the public's attention by their pointed épatage of poetic aesthetics, their unusual metaphors, and skillful selection of colloquial rhythms. However, none of these qualities was later characteristic of Rubtsov's poetry.

In the collection "Star of the Fields" (Zvezda polei, 1967) entirely different themes, intonations, and a wholly different lyric hero make their appearance. Rubtsov becomes a poet of the remote Russian North, its sparse nature, gloomy forests, dismal swamps, and taciturn, secretive people: "My Country is Silent" (Tikha moya rodina), "A Small Russian Light" (Russkii ogonek), "Kind Filya" (Dobryi Filya). Obviously following ESENIN in this, Rubtsov describes the life of nature as he sees and feels it, without trying rationally to extrapolate particular truths from its harmonious wisdom. This is why Rubtsov avoids metaphors, preferring similes and epithets which give precision and concreteness to his images. The main thing about his poetry is its mood. A polemic immediately erupted around "Star of the Fields." Some critics were enraptured by the "tranquility," "ancientry," and "homeyness" of Rubtsov's poetry and proclaimed him the *maître* of a new wave of Russian poetry of the 1960s, which demonstratively moved away from "the posing and the manifestos" of the poetic avant-garde (EVTUSHENKO, VOZNESENSKY). Other critics took an ironic view of Rubtsov's "romantic dejection" and declared him the poet of "Russia of the pine forests," a Slavophile, and even a nationalist (*rusotyap*). In Rubtsov's subsequent collections, "Rustling Pines" (Sosen shum) and "Green Flowers" (Zelenye tsvety), a further evolution toward elegiac and philosophic meditations in the manner of Tyutchev and Baratynsky may be observed. An anxiety-ridden and tragic perception of the world emerges from them. The theme of death appears more and more often: "Winter Night" (Zimnyaya noch'), "The Procession Advances" (Idet protsessiya), "Nightfall" (Nastuplenie nochi), "The End" (Konets). It was as though the poet had a premonition of his tragic death at the hands of the woman whom he considered to be his wife. Real fame came to Rubtsov only after his death. Since 1971 as many as five collections of his poetry have been published, a biography of the poet has appeared, and many articles have been devoted to him, the best of these being by A. Pikach in *Questions of Literature* (Voprosy literatury), 1977, no. 9.

Works: Collections: *Lirika* (1965), *Zvezda polei* (1967), *Dusha khranit* (1969), *Sosen shum* (1970), *Zelenye tsvety* (1971), *Poslednii parokhod* (1973), *Izbrannaya lirika* (1974), *Podorozhniki* (1976), *Stikhotvoreniya* (1977).

Secondary literature: V. Kozhinov, *Nikolai Rubtsov.* 1976. Critical articles, surveys, and reminiscences have appeared in *Literaturnaya Rossiya,* 22 September 1967, *Literaturnaya gazeta,* 22 November 1967, *VLit,* 1969, no. 1, *Druzhba narodov,* 1969, no. 2, *Sever,* 1971, nos. 2, 3, 1972, nos. 1, 7, *Moskva,* 1973, no. 3, *VLit,* 1974, no. 3, 1977, no. 9, *Vologodskii komsomolets,* 29 August 1976 (reminiscences of R. B. Taigin). *See also Den' poezii,* 1967, 1968, 1972, 1976, and 1981.   E. D. A.

Russian Colloquy, see RUSSKAYA BESEDA.

Russian Herald, see RUSSKII VESTNIK.

Russian language, the. Russian is the official language of the USSR spoken by 183 million people of whom 141 million declare it to be their mother tongue (according to the 1970 census). Together with Ukrainian and Byelorussian it belongs to the group of East Slavic languages which evolved from a Common Slavic ancestor, the hypothetical language of the Slavs which traces its origin to Indo-European, or more specifically to the Balto-Slavic branch of Indo-European.

Common or Proto-Slavic was formed between the first and second millennia B.C. and persisted until about the 7th century A.D. when it broke down into three different Slavic groups: East, West and South Slavic. While the original habitat of the Indo-Europeans remains hidden in the mist of prehistory, it is generally assumed that the oldest habitat of the Slavs was located between the Vistula and Dnieper and between the Pripet in the North and the Ukrainian steppes and Carpathian Mountains in the South.

Between the 5th and 7th centuries A.D. the Slavs expanded as far as Hamburg and the Adriatic Sea to the West and as far as the Balkans and Greece to the South. The Magyar invasion of the Pannonian plain in the 10th century brought about the separation of the Northern and Southern Slavs and coincided with the formation of separate Slavic states and linguistic entities. A separate East Slavic group emerged between the 7th and 12th centuries as a result of a number of phonemic, morphological, and lexical developments that set it apart from the other Slavic languages and brought about the division of East Slavic itself into three different linguistic areas. Among the earliest phonemic developments were some that East Slavic shared with South or West Slavic, while later changes proceeded parallelly in all or most Slavic languages (though they did not yield everywhere the same results). A third set of changes was unique to East Slavic.

East Slavic shared with South Slavic the changes kvě-, gvě- > cvě-, zvě- (Russ. cvet, zvezda; SCr. cvijet, zvijezda vs. Pol. kwiat, gwiazda); tl, dl > l (Russ. plël, mylo vs. Pol. plótl, mydlo); x > ś (in such forms as Russ. vse, séryj vs. Pol. wsze, szary); Pj > Pl' (Russ. zemljá, ljubljú vs. Pol. ziemia, lubię). East and West Slavic shared the changes ort-/olt- > rot-/lot- (Russ. róvnyj, lókot'; Czech rovný, loket vs. SCr. ravni, lakat) and the overlap of the groups tj, kti; dj with the results of the I or II palatalization (e.g., Russ. sveča, doč', meža; Czech svíce, dcera, meze). The change of the diphthongs tort/tolt, tert/telt into a disyllabic group (*polnoglasie*) was originally common to East Slavic and Lekhitic, but it was simplified in the latter to a single syllable (Russ. górod, bolóto; seredá, molót'; Pol. gród, błoto; środa, mlec).

The final dissolution of Common Slavic was marked by a number of losses in the East Slavic system of vowels and some acquisitions in its system of consonants. Thus the nasal vowels ę, ǫ yielded the vowels æ, u (Church Slavonic męso, rǫka > Russ. mjáso, ruká) with the subsequent change of original ě [æ] to ę; the strong jers ь, ъ coalesced with e and o, while the weak jers were dropped, giving rise to a new opposition between hard and soft consonants that entailed the change of ļ, ń, ŕ into palatalized l', n', r'. The syllabic sonants ŗ/ŗ', ļ acquired a preceding vocalic segment (e.g., červ', tvërdyj, pólnyj); the system of three prosodic features was reduced to a single feature of stress, though original length left a trace in the sequence vo- (vóstryj, vótčim, vótčina) and in the new vowel ǫ, the counterpart of the phoneme ę. Among the strictly East Slavic phonetic changes was the shift of je-, ju- to o-, u- (Russ. olén, ósen', odín; útro, užé, uxá) and the change of Če to Čo before hard consonants (Ukr. pšonó, žoná, vs. pšenýcja, ženýty). The last change was superseded in the Great Russian area by the shift of e to o after any soft consonant (Russ. berëza, vesëlyj, idëš', padëž). Less profound were the changes in East Slavic morphology that involved the establishment of the gen. sing. and nom.-acc. pl. ending -ě in "soft" -ja/-jo stems (zeml'ě; kon'ě), the pres. participle ending -a (bera, nesa), the instr. sing. ending -ьmь/-ьmь in -ol-jo stems (nosъmь, kon'ьmь), and the ending -tь in the third person sing. and pl. of the present tense. In addition to some words that East Slavic shared with West or South Slavic, it has some lexical items that are characteristically its own including loanwords from non-Slavic neighbors (e.g., Russ. *gruzd', ráduga, sapóg, kóška, sem'já, sórok, devjanósto; step', žémčug, grid', solomjá, skam'já*).

The Christianization of *Rus'* by way of Byzantium (in 988) gave rise to the creation of an East Slavic literature which was deeply influenced by Old CHURCH SLAVONIC (OCS), the literary language that had flourished for over a century among the Southern Slavs. In addition to the works imported from the South, the Eastern Slavs soon developed a literature of their own which included translated and original texts of a religious, legal, historiographical and poetic character (e.g., *The Lives of* BORIS AND GLEB, the works of Kirill Turovsky and Metropolitan ILARION, the *Russkaya Pravda*, the *Primary Chronicle*, the Igor Tale—SLOVO O POLKU IGOREVE). The language of these texts was not, as has sometimes been claimed, a slavish imitation of the South Slavic model, but a true symbiosis of Southern and native elements which were skillfully utilized for various stylistic and semantic purposes. It is noteworthy that even the oldest translations of liturgical texts (e.g., the *Ostromir Gospel* of 1056–57) were permeated with native Russian forms to such an extent that they are excluded from the canonical corpus of OCS.

The fall of Kievan *Rus'* and the fragmentation of Russia into feudal states which came in the wake of the Mongol-Tatar invasions accelerated the linguistic differentiation of East Slavic and led to the formation of three major linguistic entities, the antecedents of modern Great Russian, Ukrainian, and Byelorussian. The lack of a unifying political and cultural center prompted the development of a South-Western variant of Russian-Church Slavonic (attested in the Galician-Volynian Chronicles) and facilitated the penetration of South Slavic linguistic norms and a return to the more conservative language of Kievan *Rus'*. The latter developments gained particular impetus by the end of the 14th century when Russian Church Slavonic acquired a whole set of phonological, morphological, syntactic, orthographic, and stylistic traits that emanated from or were imported by refugees from the Balkans (the so-called Second SOUTH SLAVIC INFLUENCE). These included the greater use of non-*polnoglasie* forms, of *ju-* for *u-*, of *é* for *ó* before hard consonants, the writing of *jusy* and of Greek-inspired accentual marks, the use of South Slavic derivative forms, an intricate syntax and ornamental style (*pletenie sloves*). These developments had the effect of widening the gap between the written and the spoken language which had in the meantime evolved according to its own intrinsic principles. By the middle of the 16th century, when Muscovite Russia emerged as a new political and cultural force, the Russian language underwent a series of morphological and phonological changes that gave it its distinctive Great Russian stamp and deepened the difference between its dialects. The morphological changes included the hardening of the verbal endings -m', -t' (*dam', idët' > dam, idët*), the substitution of the pronominal endings -*ogo*/-*ego* by -*ovo*/-*evo*, the leveling of the plural nominal endings -*am*, -*ami*, -*ax*, the loss of consonantal alternations in the nominal inflection, the fixation of the reflexive particles -*s'a*/-*s'*, and the use of the pronominal forms *menjá, tebjá, sebjá*. Even more far-reaching were the changes in the system of grammatical categories which led to the loss of the dual and the vocative, the disappearance of the aorist, imperfect, and pluperfect, the increase of cases in the singular, the substitution of the old gender distinctions in the nom and acc. plural by an animate/inanimate opposition in the acc. pl. and the loss of inflection in the short adjectives. Phonetic changes have at the same time widened the distinction between the Russian dialects which differed originally by such isolated and localized features as *cokan'e* in the North and the use of *γ/h* for *g* in the South. The Northern and Southern dialects acquired such additional differentiating traits as *okan'e* and the loss of intervocalic *j* in the North and various types of *akan'e* and *ikan'e* and the change *šč, žš* to *šš, žž* in the South, whereas the dominance and integrating pull of Moscow contributed to the formation of a Central, transitional area which combines the typical consonantal feature of the former (the phoneme *g*) with the vowel reduction characteristic of the latter (*akan'e*). The 17th century marked the expansion and Westernization of Russia which brought with it a wave of POLISH INFLUENCES (via the Ukraine) and a rapid growth of secular (administrative, technical and scientific) literature matched by a disarray in its literary language. This state of affairs prompted attempts to establish a new norm of Church Slavonic (undertaken by scholars of Ruthenian origin, in particular by Melety SMOTRITSKY), or to create a new literary vehicle that would bridge the widening gap between the written and spoken language. The latter need was most clearly perceived by Western scholars who produced the first grammars of spoken Russian (W. Ludolf, M. Groening, E. Kopijewitz, J. L. Frisch). However, it is only the reforms of Peter the Great (the introduction of *graždanskij šrift* in 1708, the establishment of an official press and the journal *Vedomosti*) that laid the base for a modern literary standard whose edifice was completed only a century later. The first part of the 18th century produced a clash of conflicting styles and a quest for a neutral, unmarked norm which would be capacious enough to accommodate the new and older literary genres (the novel, comedy, the epic, the ode), the language of science and administration (*delovoj stil'*) and the everyday language of educated speakers. The path for the integration of the various styles into a unified literary language was prepared by a number of writers and grammarians (V. N. TREDIAKOVSKY, A. P. SUMAROKOV, N. M. KARAMZIN, M. V. LOMONOSOV) who rejected the return to Church Slavonic (advocated by such conservative Pan-Slavists, as Admiral A. S. SHISHKOV) in favor of a modern idiom which would expand the stylistic possibilities of Russian and give sanction to the Western loanwords and calques (of English, Dutch, German, and French origin) which streamed freely into scholarly and colloquial usage. A powerful impulse for this broadening of the linguistic potential of Russian and for the leveling of its diverse styles was provided by the translation of Western scientific works and belles lettres (especially from French). A compromise solution to the question of the clashing styles was advanced by Lomonosov (in his *Russian Grammar* of 1755 and *On the Usefulness of Church Slavonic Books for Russian* of 1757–58) who argued for the admission of three different "styles" (high, middle and low) that would vary according to literary genre, a proposal which lost its force with the advent of romanticism and its systematic fusion of literary genres. The creation of a modern literary standard was the work of PUSHKIN and his followers, who succeeded in blending the three basic strands of Russian, i.e., the spoken language, Church Slavonic, and Western borrowings, into a cohesive though flexible norm in which the preponderance of one or another component is determined by the thematic, stylistic and literary character of the given text. The spread of education and the communicative media have further contributed to the elimination of regional variants and of jarring colloquialisms and to the advance of a standard *spoken* language which has made deep encroachments into the speech of the urban centers, so that dialectal Russian is now essentially confined to the countryside. The phonetic norm of the spoken language is based on the Old Moscow pronunciation (fostered by the Moscow Art Theater and the Maly Theater of that city), though other phonetic norms (especially the pronunciation of Leningrad) are not proscribed. Institutes for the study of the Russian language, normative grammars and dictionaries, orthoepic tools are forever on guard for the purity of the standard language, while stylistic variants in morphology, syntax and accentuation are widely tolerated. The Russian Revolution, which granted official recognition to the various languages of the Soviet Union (including the languages of the two Slavic minorities, Ukrainian and Byelorussian) and which raised the level of general education, has considerably promoted the spread of Russian as a language of administration and of obligatory instruction. Among the after-effects of this spread has been a deeper penetration of Russian into the languages of the non-Slavic minorities and a pronounced russification of Ukrainian and Byelorussian.

Bibliography: R. I. Avanesov and S. I. Ozhegov, *Russkoe literaturnoe proiznoshenie i udarenie.* 1960. F. P. Filin, *Proiskhozhdenie russkogo, ukrainskogo i belorusskogo yazykov.* 1972. A. I. Gorshkov, *Istoriya russkogo literaturnogo yazyka.* 1969. N. Yu. Shvedova, ed., *Russkaya grammatika*, 1/2. 1980. B. Unbegaun, *La langue russe au XVI-e siècle.* Paris, 1935. G. O. Vinokur, *Russkii yazyk.* 1945. V. V. Vinogradov, *Ocherki po istorii russkogo literaturnogo yazyka 17–19 vekov.* 1938.

E. S.

Russian Wealth, see RUSSKOE BOGATSTVO.

Russian Word, The, see RUSSKOE SLOVO.

Rússkaya beséda (Russian Colloquy), SLAVOPHILE journal, published in Moscow, 1856 to 1860. First periodical publication put out by

Slavophiles. Contributors included I. S., K. S. and S. T. AKSAKOV, I. V. KIREEVSKY, M. P. POGODIN, S. P. SHEVYRYOV, Yu. F. SAMARIN, Apollon GRIGORIEV, and A. S. KHOMYAKOV. The journal published poetry by the Aksakovs, A. K. TOLSTOI, TYUTCHEV, and Khomyakov (as well as PUSHKIN, ZHUKOVSKY, BARATYNSKY, YAZYKOV, and SHEVCHENKO.) Prose contributions included excerpts from S. T. Aksakov's *Family Chronicle* (Semeinaya khronika), *The Childhood Years of Bagrov Grandson* (Detskie gody Bagrova-vnuka), and *Literary and Theatrical Reminiscences* (Literaturnye i teatral'nye vospominaniya); "physiological" sketches by V. I. DAL; and works by OSTROVSKY, SALTYKOV-SHCHEDRIN, and Marko VOVCHOK.

C. T. N.

Rússkaya literatúra, see INSTITUT RUSSKOI LITERATURY.

Rússkaya mysl' (Russian Thought), a "thick" journal, came out monthly in Moscow, 1880 to 1918. During its early years under the editorship of S. A. Yuriev (1880–85), the journal had a SLAVOPHILE orientation, but soon discarded this position for a moderate liberal line sympathetic to POPULISM. After the closing of OTECHESTVENNYE ZAPISKI in 1884, many of its contributors moved to *Russkaya mysl'*. The journal prided itself on the diversity of its contributors, among them TOLSTOI, GORKY, CHEKHOV, KOROLENKO, Gleb USPENSKY, MAMIN-SIBIRYAK, LESKOV, GARSHIN, MEREZHKOVSKY, NADSON, CHERNYSHEVSKY, and ERTEL as well as the scholars S. A. VENGEROV and V. O. Klyuchevsky. After the 1905 Revolution, *Russkaya mysl'* shifted its orientation toward the right wing of the Kadet party under the editorship of A. A. Kizevetter and P. B. STRUVE, with Struve serving as sole editor from 1910 to 1918. During this period, a number of "vekhovtsy" (see VEKHI) contributed, including BERDYAEV and GERSHENZON, and the literary and critical sections of the journal were headed by BRYUSOV and HIPPIUS respectively. The journal adopted a hostile stance toward the October Revolution and was closed down by the Soviet government in 1918. After his emigration, Struve renewed publication of *Russkaya mysl'* in Sofia in 1921 and then in Prague in 1922–23. During the latter period, the journal published works by REMIZOV, BUNIN, and TSVETAEVA. Struve succeeded in putting out one more issue of *Russkaya mysl'* in Paris in 1927 before the journal's final demise.

C. T. N.

Rússkaya stariná (Russian Past), historical journal, published monthly in Petersburg, 1870 to 1918. Primarily interested in post-Petrine Russian history, the journal published historical articles and documentary materials, such as letters, diaries, reminiscences, notes, and autobiographies, notably KYUKHELBEKER's diary and notes by the Decembrists M. A. Bestuzhev and M. I. Muravyov-Apostol. *Russkaya starina* also printed previously unpublished works by Russian writers, including KRYLOV, BATYUSHKOV, RYLEEV, BARATYNSKY, DELVIG, ZHUKOVSKY, and A. K. TOLSTOI, as well as newly discovered stanzas from *Evgeny Onegin* and fragments from *Dead Souls*.

C. T. N.

Rússkii véstnik (Russian Herald), a "thick" journal published by Mikhail KATKOV, came out monthly in Moscow, 1856 to 1906. Originally a liberal, anglophile publication, after the 1861 reforms *Russkii vestnik* became increasingly more conservative. The earliest and most important period in the journal's history corresponded roughly with the "golden age" of the Russian novel, and during these years, most major works of Russian literature were published in *Russkii vestnik*, including TURGENEV's *Fathers and Sons*, TOLSTOI's *Anna Karenina*, and all four of DOSTOEVSKY's major novels. GONCHAROV, LESKOV, PISEMSKY, SALTYKOV-SHCHEDRIN, S. T. AKSAKOV, OSTROVSKY, FET, TYUTCHEV, A. K. TOLSTOI, and ANNENKOV, among others, published in the journal. After Katkov's death in 1887, *Russkii vestnik* lost what remained of its former importance, but survived under various editors as an organ of extreme reaction until it finally ceased publication in 1906.

Bibliography: Catharine Theimer Nepomnyashchy, "Katkov and the Emergence of the *Russian Messenger*," *Ulbandus Review* 1, no. 1 (Fall 1977), pp. 59–89.

C. T. N.

Rússkoe bogátstvo (Russian Wealth), a "thick" journal, was published monthly in Petersburg, 1876 to 1918 (from Nov. 1914–March 1917 issued under the name *Russkie zapiski* [Russian Notes]). In the early 1880s, a group of liberal POPULISTS began to form around the journal, but under the editorship of L. E. Obolensky (1882–92) the journal became increasingly oriented toward Tolstoian philosophy, occasionally publishing articles by TOLSTOI. In the 1890s, led by N. K. MIKHAILOVSKY and V. G. KOROLENKO, the journal shifted to a markedly populist stance. During this period, *Russkoe bogatstvo* published primarily realist writers, including GORKY, KUPRIN, ANDREEV, VERESAEV, BUNIN, and Gleb USPENSKY. In his critical articles Mikhailovsky attacked the early symbolists, among them MEREZHKOVSKY, HIPPIUS, and SOLOGUB, arguing for the social responsibility of art. After the 1905 Revolution *Russkoe bogatstvo* became an organ of the popular socialists. The journal was closed by the government in 1918.

C. T. N.

Rússkoe slóvo (Russian Word), monthly journal, was published in Petersburg 1859 to 1866. During the earliest period of the journal's existence, Ya. P. POLONSKY and Apollon GRIGORIEV served as editors. The critical section consisted primarily of articles by Grigoriev, and *Russkoe slovo* published works by a diverse selection of writers, including DOSTOEVSKY, FET, MAIKOV, MEI, and Marko VOVCHOK. Polonsky and Grigoriev left the journal in the summer of 1859. In 1860, G. E. Blagosvetlov became editor of the journal and began gathering around *Russkoe slovo* a group of radical writers and critics. PISAREV made his debut in *Russkoe slovo* in December 1860 and soon became the journal's leading critic and ideologist. The years during which Pisarev contributed to *Russkoe slovo* (1860–65) were the most productive of his career, and most of his major articles appeared in the journal. *Russkoe slovo* was closed by the government in 1866 after Karakozov's attempt on the life of Alexander II.

C. T. N.

Rýbnikov, Pável Nikoláevich (1831–85), ethnographer and folklorist. A graduate of the Historico-Philological Faculty of Moscow University in 1858, Rybnikov was exiled to Petrozavodsk in Olonetsk province in 1859 for belonging to a revolutionary circle. He served there in the Governor's office and went on to make a moderately successful career in the civil service. During his stay in Olonetsk province Rybnikov discovered a living epic tradition among the peasants of the region and collected many BYLINY and other forms of FOLK POETRY, as well as ethnographic material. His *Songs, Collected by P. N. Rybnikov* (Pesni, sobrannye P. N. Rybnikovym, 4 vols., 1861–67) included 224 *byliny*. In an article, "A Collector's Notes" (in vol. 3 of *Songs*), Rybnikov recorded his observations regarding the performance of *byliny* by particular singers and raised the question of the relation between tradition and individual performance.

Works: Pesni, sobrannye P. N. Rybnikovym. 2d ed. Ed. A. E. Gruzinskii. 3 vols. 1909–10.

V. T.

Rýleev, Kondráty Fyódorovich (1795–1826), romantic poet and Decembrist. Ryleev was a fanatic idealist in his life and poetry who proclaimed his political attitude in the line, "I am a citizen, not a poet." He was a leader of the Northern Society of the DECEMBRIST conspiracy who formed a conspiracy within a conspiracy in support of plans for a republic, recruited assassins and planned the extermination of the imperial family, instigated the revolt of 14 December 1825, and died on the scaffold. He was a perfect altruist who dreamed of liberating the Russian people and sought martyrdom. He was a proclaimed plebeian, hostile to the literary aristocrats.

As a poet Ryleev is remembered for lyric poems, satires, a series of "Agitational Songs" co-authored with A. A. BESTUZHEV, romantic verse tales, and the verse genre known as the *duma* or "meditation" which was his specialty. The DUMA is a short historical poem of varying lengths which in Ryleev's practice glorified a hero of the national past. Ryleev's heroes are democratic champions of a popular cause, symbols of a historical event or "spirit of the time." He developed the genre on a late 17th-century Ukrainian song form and was aware of the popularity of the form in Poland. Lamartine's political "Meditations" were a model. Among his best verses in the genre are "Oleg the Wise," "Svyatoslav," "Svyatopolk," "Dmitry Donskoi," "Bogdan Khmelnitsky," and "Nataliya Dolgorukaya." Like Ryleev himself, Ryleev's heroes died martyrs to a noble cause and freedom.

Ryleev's verse tale *Voinarovsky* (1823–25) dramatizes the martyrdom of the nephew of the Ukrainian hero Mazepa, with guarded expressions of sympathy for Ukrainian national aspirations. The tale is a pre-enactment of his own fate in the figure of Mazepa and Bestuzhev's in the hero of the title. Pushkin's verse tale *Poltava* is in part a polemic with Ryleev's democratic interpretation of the revolt against Peter the Great. The verse tale *Nalivaiko* (1823–25) treats the leader of the 16th-century Cossack uprising and again celebrates the struggle of the people against autocracy.

Especially remarkable in Ryleev's oeuvre are the "Agitational Songs"—rollicking satires on the autocracy, Petersburg society, landowners who "skin" and "fleece" their serfs, and the Romanov family. They are among the best Russian revolutionary songs.

From 1823 to 1825 Ryleev edited the literary almanac POLYARNAYA ZVEZDA with Bestuzhev, using it as a vehicle for the expression of the civic, sociopolitical ideals of Decembrist literature. His literary and political positions are well expressed in this activity, and he stated his ideology in an 1825 essay titled "Some Thoughts on Poetry." In this essay, which grew out of a correspondence with Pushkin, Ryleev defined the essence of poetry as "spirit of the time"—the content of poetry as opposed to Pushkin's preference for form. Ryleev viewed literature as primarily a political phenomenon, and in his essay he opposed not only Pushkin's formal values, but the Schellingian definition of poetry as philosophy, espoused by the WISDOM LOVERS (*lyubomudry*).

The most striking aspect of Ryleev's poetry is its emotional expression of his desire to die a martyr. Both in his meditations and his verse tales he praised heroes who died for a noble cause, leaving no doubt that his execution as a Decembrist revolutionary was truly the consummation of a love of death.

Bibliography: A. G. Tseitlin, "K. F. Ryleev." In K. F. Ryleev. *Stikhotvoreniya.* (Biblioteka poeta.) 1956. Franklin Walker, "K. F. Ryleev: A Self-Sacrifice for Revolution," *SEER* 47 (1969), pp. 436–46.
L. G. L.

Rzhévsky, Aleksei Andréevich (1737–1804), poet. Of ancient Russian noble lineage, Rzhevsky devoted most of his adult life to public service, occupying a variety of posts such as deputy to the Legislative Commission, official of the State Bank, vice-director of the Academy of Sciences. His active participation in Russian literary life was short but prolific: during the early 1760s he published some 225 items, mostly verse, in literary journals; in the late 1760s he added two verse tragedies. Utterly forgotten by later generations, Rzhevsky was rediscovered only in the 1920s thanks to the scholarship of G. A. Gukovsky.

Rzhevsky was an ardent admirer of SUMAROKOV whose active partisan he became in the controversies between Sumarokov and LOMONOSOV that raged around mid-century. In his own poetry Rzhevsky, in part, diligently imitated the classicist master, achieving particular success with fables and satires. At the same time, Rzhevsky wrote a large number of lyrics which, while *generically* classicist—elegies, idylls, songs, etc.—were startlingly out of kilter with the Sumarokov style in displaying blatant features of the highly mannered tradition of *poësis curiosa*, such as shaped poems, poems consisting of exclusively one-syllable words, poems that could be read three different ways, and conceit and riddle poems. Thus Rzhevsky stands out as a particularly extreme example of that peculiar co-existence of BAROQUE and CLASSICIST poetics which characterizes Russian verse throughout the 18th century.

Works: Poety XVIII veka. Ed. G. P. Makogonenko and I. Z. Serman. Vol. 1. 1972.
Secondary literature: G. A. Gukovskii, *Russkaya poeziya XVIII veka.* 1927. Pp. 151–82. I. Z. Serman, "Biograficheskaya spravka." In *Poety XVIII veka.* Ed. G. P. Makogonenko and I. Z. Serman. 1972. Pp. 189–94.
I. R. T.

Saints' Lives, see HAGIOGRAPHY.

Sakúlin, Pável Nikítich (1868–1930), literary historian and theorist of sociological method. Sakulin taught at Moscow University where he had a reputation as a social activist and a solid scholar before the Revolution. His dissertation, *From the History of Russian Idealism: Prince V. F. Odoevsky* (1913) is remarkable for its comprehensive treatment of the 1820s and 1830s and is still one of the best works on romanticism in Russia. After the Revolution, Sakulin became head of the FREE SOCIETY OF AMATEURS OF RUSSIAN LITERATURE and was active in a number of Soviet publishing and academic institutions. In a series of books and articles throughout the 1920s Sakulin sought to found a Marxist literary scholarship that would avoid the excesses of FORMALISM on the one hand and of VULGAR SOCIOLOGISM on the other. As a result, of course, he was attacked by both sides: by EIKHENBAUM (1924) as well as Medvedev (1926), who said Sakulin's method was a "sociologism without sociology." BAKHTIN (under the name of Voloshinov) also attacked Sakulin in his 1926 article "Discourse in Life and Discourse in Art." In such works as *Russian Literature and Socialism* (1922, 1924) and, particularly, *The Sociological Method in Literary Study* (1925), Sakulin argues that a literary work is shaped by the interaction of the author's individual artistic activity as it engages the immediate social conditions in which he is working as these, in their turn, are shaped by long term historical forces. These three conditions result in three different levels or aspects in the work: the immanent, deriving from the author; the causal, determined by social factors; and the constructive, resulting from the action of historical forces (never very well defined by Sakulin). Sakulin insisted all three should be treated as a unity, but had difficulty himself in applying this principle in such works as *The Aesthetics of Tolstoi* (1929, the same year he was made an Academician).

Secondary literature: Pamyati P. N. Sakulina. Moscow, 1931. P. S. Nikolaev, "Pavel Nikitich Sakulin," *VLit*, 1969, no. 4.
J. M. H.

Saltykóv-Shchedrín, Mikhaíl Evgráfovich (Pseudonym: N. Shchedrin) (1826–89). The man now considered the greatest satirist of 19th-century Russia was born in the province of Tver to a father of older but impoverished gentry stock, and to a mother from a wealthy Moscow merchant family. His mother set him a very negative example by her concern solely with material acquisitions, and later became the prototype for several rather unpleasant fictional characters in his works.

After growing up on the family estate—with sojourns in Moscow in season—Saltykov entered the lyceum at Tsarskoe selo. Upon completing his education there in 1844, he took up the bifurcated career which he would pursue for nearly the next quarter-century: he entered government service, where in time he rose to the rank of provincial vice-governor despite his radical political views; and he began to publish in the journals OTECHESTVENNYE ZAPISKI and SOVREMENNIK, with which he would long be associated. It is worth noting that as a literary man Saltykov consistently negated that which he was supposed to defend in his capacity as a government official.

The ideological split within him manifested itself when—after the publication of his first two important works and the onset of governmental reaction following the European revolutions of 1848—Saltykov was exiled to Vyatka in April of 1848 for almost seven years (although, astonishingly, he was still employed as a government official during that time). After Nicholas I's death in 1855, Saltykov returned to the capital, where he once more plunged into literary life, and continued his bureaucratic career, in addition to marrying. It was at this time that Saltykov's first important larger work appeared. It was, characteristically, a cycle of sketches gathered into a book. In *Provincial Sketches* (Gubernskie ocherki, 1856–57), he satirized the psychology of the bureaucrats among whom he worked, the very notion of bureaucratic rule in society. Bureaucracy, after all, functions on the basis of rules which seek to reduce the richness of human behavior to codified generalizations. Thus Filoveritov, one of Saltykov's satirical heroes, deals with people in terms of logical syllogisms, attempting to determine whether the regulations are satisfied; he cannot respond to an applicant in purely human terms. Whether a crime has actually been committed, he says, does not concern him: he must merely decide whether a matter has been "proven or not proven" by the rules of evidence.

In 1858 Saltykov arrived in Ryazan with the objective of reforming the local administration, but soon found himself at odds with his colleagues and superiors and moved on to Tver in 1860, just when the emancipation of the serfs was being prepared. The nobility of that area were relatively liberal in their support of the impending reform, but Saltykov was yet further to the left, and he continued to express his views forcefully in print. Thus by 1862 he had abandoned government service—for good, he evidently believed—to devote himself to journalism.

Saltykov considered founding his own journal, to be called *Russian Truth* (Russkaya pravda), after the name of the medieval Russian legal code, which would work for reform through law (though law implies bureaucracy, one might note in passing). When he did not receive official permission to begin his own journal, he joined forces with CHERNYSHEVSKY's *Sovremennik*, then the leading organ of radical thought in Russia. After Chernyshevsky's arrest in 1862, Saltykov was for a while the journal's most prominent figure, both because of his relative seniority and because of his literary talent, and he continued to write sketches, literary criticism, and social commentary. Temperamentally, indeed, he was a genuine "nihilist," both politically and philosophically: he could discover little or nothing worth preserving in existing Russian society, which he criticized mercilessly, but he deliberately refrained from setting forth his notions of how a just society might be organized, and even criticized Chernyshevsky's communal blueprint for a future society as set forth in the novel *What Is To Be Done?* (1863), arguing that the future would create social forms quite different from those which the radicals then envisioned, and that their dreams of today were a form of despotism over the world of tomorrow.

A fine polemicist, Saltykov fought on two major fronts during 1863 and 1864. On the one hand he carried on a running battle with Dmitry PISAREV and the *Russkoe slovo* group, rivals of the *Sovremennik* group for the leadership of the radical movement, in what DOSTOEVSKY dubbed the "schism among the nihilists"; and, on the other hand, he polemicized with Dostoevsky and his group. Though Saltykov did not care for *What Is To Be Done?*, he also disliked Dostoevsky's rebuttal to it, *Notes from Underground* (1864), and wrote a satire on Dostoevsky's journalistic endeavors entitled "Swallows" (Strizhi). Dostoevsky responded with counter-blasts, in which, for example, he defined the guiding principle of radical journalism as "malice for malice's sake." The Saltykov-Dostoevsky encounter pitted Russia's two greatest satirical polemicists against each other in a display of intellectual fireworks.

However, internal differences of opinion with his *Sovremennik* colleagues caused Saltykov in 1864 to rejoin the government bureaucracy. He served first in Penza, then in Tula, and finally again in Ryazan, full of old friends and enemies, where he began publishing *Letters on the Provinces* (Pis'ma o provintsii) in *Otechestvennye zapiski*, which by then had taken up the radical banner after the closing of *Sovremennik* and *Russkoe slovo* in 1866. But now the combination of bureaucratic service and satirical publications critical of the established order was more than his superiors could tolerate, and he was asked to resign. He then became a senior editor of *Otechestvennye zapiski*, along with NEKRASOV, and thenceforth dedicated himself entirely to journalism and writing.

In 1869 Saltykov began publishing his finest satirical work, *History of a Town* (Istoriya odnogo goroda), a bitterly satirical parody of Russian history cast as a historical chronicle of the town of Glupov (Stupidville). The book includes a superb list of the town's rulers from 1731 to 1826: one, for example, was "so short he could not ingest lengthy pieces of legislation." But the book's chief thrust is directed against Ugryum-Burcheev (a parody of the powerful statesman Count A. A. Arakcheev under Alexander I), a man for whom all questions have been resolved, who seeks to impose unquestioning, military obedience upon the townspeople. Holidays in the military colony he establishes differ from ordinary days in that even stricter discipline is imposed upon the population. For no particular reason he decides to move the site of the town to a place which requires the damming of a river, and when the dam bursts he attributes the catastrophe to treason. His power over the miserable Glupovites evaporates upon his sudden death. In *History of a Town* Saltykov not only mocked the errors of Tsarist social planners of the past, but issued a veiled warning to some of his ideological allies against draconic social regimentation in the future as well.

In the first half of the 1870s Saltykov published several further books, including *Pompadours and Pompadouresses* (Pompadury i pompadurshi); *The Diary of a Provincial in St. Petersburg* (Dnevnik provintsiala v Peterburge); and *Gentlemen of Tashkent* (Gospoda Tashkenttsy). A new target of his satire at this time following the abolition of serfdom and the decay of the landowning class was the rising capitalist entrepreneur, a man of no aristocratic background who thought only of profits.

In the latter half of the 1870s, a melancholy epoch in Russian history, Saltykov published serially his best-known "novel"—or cycle of stories—*The Golovlyovs* (Gospoda Golovlevy). In an atmosphere of unrelieved gloom the author describes the inexorable decline of a family through deaths—caused by alcoholism and despair—of each of its individual members. The domineering but energetic matriarch of the family, Arina Petrovna, devoted great effort to building the family's fortunes, but her descendants fritter away what she has accumulated as they go down to ruin, or else—in the case of Porfiry Petrovich, the book's central character—destroy themselves spiritually by their greed for material things. Porfiry Petrovich is, moreover, the epitome of the religious hypocrite: remarkably self-centered, he has a paralyzingly pious adage for any situation. But he too succumbs to the curse of his family—alcoholism—stimulated by his unbridled imagination, which leads him to busy himself solely with fantastically intricate calculations on trivial matters. He is in the midst of "empty space," both physically (the desolate Russian landscape) and spiritually (the absence of any genuine values in his life). In the end he commits a form of suicide, the only logical end for a person and for an entire family deprived of all spiritual roots.

The Golovlyovs is perhaps the greatest radical 19th-century Russian indictment of the institution of the contemporary family. This novel and others of Saltykov's works also included assaults against the institution of private property and the institution of the state; in short, it condemned the principal elements of contemporary society. But his critique was essentially negative, and the most one can do is make a few positive extrapolations from them. In one of his enjoyable *Fables* (Skazki), for example, a governor argues that the entire apparatus of local government simply hinders the normal flow of human existence: apparently Saltykov would have liked a peaceful anarchism, where each individual was permitted to live his own life.

After Nekrasov died in early 1878, Saltykov's life was linked almost wholly with *Otechestvennye zapiski*: he and it were considered the grand old institutions of radical intellectual life until the journal's suppression by the government in 1884. It was a severe personal blow to him. In the ten years before its suppression, Saltykov published, in addition to *The Golovlyovs*, several other volumes of satire on contemporary conditions, such as *The Sanctuary of Mon Repos* (Ubezhishche Monrepo, 1878–79), *Contemporary Idyll* (Sovremennaya idilliya, 1877–83), and *Letters to My Aunt* (Pis'ma k teten'ke, 1881–82). Because much of his satire in these and other volumes was embedded in contemporary historical conditions (his language, in particular, contains numerous echoes which have faded away for those of us reading him a century later), it is difficult to follow Saltykov without a specialized knowledge of his period. His more abstract *Fables*, however, are of more universal application and can be enjoyed even by those with little knowledge of Russian history. One of the best-known of them, "Tale of How One Peasant Fed Two Generals" (Povest' o tom, kak odin muzhik dvukh generalov prokormil) describes two retired, highly placed civil servants who find themselves on an island in danger of starving because they have no notion of how to catch or gather the fish, animals and fruits with which the island abounds until they find a "lazy peasant" and put him to work for them. He even builds them a boat and takes them back to St. Petersburg, whereupon they reward him with "a glass of vodka and a silver penny."

In the latter half of the 1880s, with his journal gone and his health deteriorating, Saltykov reverted to the past with a fictionalized autobiography, *Old Days in Poshekhonie* (Poshekhonskaya starina, 1887–89). Here he depicts the life of the landed gentry during his youth, but by no means in an idealized light: for example, he condemns most strongly the institution of serfdom on which his family's livelihood depended (that at least was one negative social institution which had been abolished in his lifetime), and depicts his mother as a landowner whose main function is to be "furious" at her servants over trifles and to appear to her children only on those occasions when they required punishment. The apostle of negation remained true to his nature to the end. Saltykov died in 1889 in St. Petersburg and is buried among many colleagues in the Volkovo cemetery.

Works: Sobranie sochinenii. Ed. S. A. Makashin et al. 20 vols. 1965–77.

Translations: Fables. Trans. Vera Volkhovsky. 1977 (reprint of 1931 ed.). *The Golovlyov Family.* Trans. Samuel Cioran. 1977. *The History of a Town.* Trans. S. Brownsberger. 1982. *See also: Lewanski,* pp. 351–52.

Secondary literature: A. S. Bushmin, *M. E. Saltykov-Shchedrin.* 1970. Milton Ehre, "A Classic of Russian Realism: Form and Meaning in *The Golovlevs," Studies in the Novel* (North Texas State) 9 (1977), pp. 3–16. I. P. Foote, "Quintessential Saltykov: *Ubezhishche Monrepo," OSP* 12 (1979), pp. 84–103. I. T. Ishchenko, *Parodii Saltykova-Shchedrina.* Minsk, 1973. Valerii Kirpotin, *M. E. Saltykov-Shchedrin: zhizn' i tvorchestvo.* 2d rev. ed. 1948. S. Makashin, *Saltykov-Shchedrin na rubezhe 1850–1860 godov: Biografiya.* 1972. *M. E. Saltykov-Shchedrin v vospominaniyakh sovremennikov.* 2 vols. 2d rev. ed. 1975. E. Pokusaev, *Gospoda Golovlevy M. E. Saltykova-Shchedrina.* 1975. Kyra Sanine, *Saltykov-Chtchédrine: Sa vie et ses oeuvres.* Paris, 1955. William Mills Todd III, "The Anti-Hero with a Thousand Faces: Saltykov-Shchedrin's Porfiry Golovlev," *Studies in the Literary Imagination* 9 (1976), no. 1, pp. 87–105.

C. A. M.

Samárin, Yúry Fyódorovich (1819–76). The son of a socially prominent family with good connections at court, Samarin was at first tutored by a French teacher in St. Petersburg who imbued him with a highly cosmopolitan attitude toward Western European languages and cultures. Later his family moved to Moscow, and he was placed under the supervision of Nikolai NADEZHDIN, who would soon become a prominent academic and journalist. Through Nadezhdin, Samarin became more conscious of his native roots. That consciousness was strengthened by his study with Mikhail POGODIN at Moscow University, who aroused in him a deeper interest in things Russian, so that he eventually undertook a dissertation on Feofan PROKOPOVICH and Stefan YAVORSKY.

In the 1840s Samarin joined the SLAVOPHILE circles of KHOMYAKOV and Konstantin AKSAKOV, and became known as one of their principal figures. In addition, he published a few literary articles advancing Slavophile viewpoints. At this point, however, most of his time was taken up with bureaucratic service, in which his progress was not always smooth. After the death of Nicholas I and the subsequent liberalization of Russian intellectual life, Samarin collaborated with such Slavophile publications as *Russkaya beseda,* and also assisted in the detailed preparation for the emancipation of the serfs in 1861, which—like everything else—he interpreted in Russian national terms. Indeed, in an early version of the proclamation accompanying the emancipation, which he drafted, he placed the event in a Slavophile context.

After a few more years devoted to implementing the Great Reform, Samarin dedicated the last twelve years of his life to writing on various topics. He published a discussion of the Jesuits and their attitude toward Russia, composed a multi-volume work on the nationalities inhabiting the Russian borderlands, and edited Khomyakov's theological writings. But the great propagandist of the Russian spirit also visited Western Europe regularly, and it was in Berlin that he died in 1876.

Works: Yurii Samarin, *Sochineniya.* 12 vols. 1877–1911.

Secondary literature: Gerda Hucke, *Jurij Fedorovič Samarin: Seine geistesgeschichtliche Position und politische Bedeutung.* Munich, 1970.

C. A. M.

Samizdát, literally, "self-printed," a play on official *gosizdat* (State Publishing House). A phenomenon in which manuscripts of books, copies of typescripts or mimeographed letters, petitions, appeals, poetry, etc., are circulated, at first among presumably close friends, then to a wider public. Given the lack of a free press, *samizdat* (along with *tamizdat* and *magnitizdat*—see below) is probably the primary outlet for free Russian literature.

Samizdat first became important as a vehicle for disseminating belletristic works in the early 1960s, when several "underground magazines," such as *Phoenix,* and *Sintaksis,* were circulated, as well as the poems of Esenin-Volpin. With the SINYAVSKY-DANIEL trial in 1965 *samizdat* became an important outlet for dissent when the trial transcript was compiled by Aleksandr Ginzburg and circulated widely after the defendants were sentenced; copies also came out to the West. In addition to the transcript, many of the statements and protests defending the writers were circulated, including one letter signed by sixty-three Moscow writers and a famous letter in which Lidiya CHUKOVSKAYA, daughter of the eminent Soviet children's writer and critic Kornei CHUKOVSKY, violently criticized novelist Mikhail SHOLOKHOV for his condemnation of Sinyavsky and Daniel and his collaboration with the regime.

Samizdat served not only as a medium for belles lettres; in 1968, which was designated by the United Nations as International Human Rights Year, the growing democratic movement began to issue a *samizdat* bulletin, *Chronicle of Current Events,* in which violations of civic and human rights by the Soviet authorities were scrupulously documented. In addition to information about individual instances of repression—for religious beliefs, expressions of nationalism, attempts to emigrate, etc.—the *Chronicle* has devoted particular issues to specific problems: one issue, for instance, commemorates the 40th anniversary of the Stalinist repression of the Crimean Tatars, a small ethnic minority which was forcibly removed and brutally relocated during World War II at the cost of a large number of lives. The *Chronicle* was matched by a number of other, similar journals produced by, among others, Ukrainians, Lithuanians, Baptists, Pentacostalists, and Jews.

Samizdat serves as a literary outlet for bypassing the official censorship of certain topics, themes, and experimental styles. Much of the early, often amateurish poetry which appeared in *samizdat* was characterized by a personal, lyric or "negative" tone, which was officially proscribed. Also, *samizdat* fiction has often portrayed contemporary or historic Soviet reality in a manner inconsistent with the doctrine of SOCIALIST REALISM, either by overly negative (by official standards) depictions or by subject matter (such as the forced-labor camps) virtually taboo in the Soviet Union, except for a very brief period under Khrushchev when a few works like SOLZHENITSYN's *One Day in the Life of Ivan Denisovich* were published. Among the most significant fiction dealing with the Stalinist era which circulated in *samizdat* were Solzhenitsyn's *First Circle* and *Cancer Ward,* Lidiya Chukovskaya's *Going Under* and *Deserted House,* VOINOVICH's *The Life and Extraordinary Adventures of Private Ivan Chonkin,* and SHALAMOV's *Kolyma Tales.* A parallel *samizdat* memoir literature also dealt with the Stalinist era, notably in Evgeniya GINZBURG's *Journey into the Whirlwind* and *Within the Whirlwind* and Nadezhda MANDELSHTAM's *Hope Against Hope* and *Hope Abandoned.* A number of important nonfiction studies of Stalinism also circulated, such as Roi Medvedev's *Let History Judge* and his brother Zhores Medvedev's *The Rise and Fall of T. D. Lysenko.*

One of *samizdat*'s most important contributions has been to provide Russian readers access to their own literary and philosophical past. Many of the works by such eminent 20th-century poets as MANDELSHTAM, AKHMATOVA, and TSVETAEVA, as well as prosaists like PLATONOV and PASTERNAK have become available to Soviet readers only through *samizdat* channels, for even when such works are officially published, they usually appear in such small editions as to be virtually unavailable to most Soviet citizens. It was through *samizdat,* first, that the entire text of BULGAKOV's classic *The Master & Margarita* reached Soviet readers; it is still only through *samizdat* that *Doctor Zhivago* is available.

In recent years *samizdat* has continued as a viable medium for the publication of free Russian literature—especially since it is frequently smuggled out to the West for publication. *Samizdat* works published abroad are then circulated among the émigré community, smuggled back into the Soviet Union, and broadcast and discussed in Russian-language radio programs directed at the Soviet Union. Through this connection with *tamizdat* (contraction of *tam,* "there" and *izdat,* "publication"), a *samizdat* work can easily become known to millions of Soviet citizens. Also significant is the interconnection with *magnitizdat* (contraction of *magnitofon,* "tape recorder," and *izdat*). With the appearance of the tape recorder many clandestine recordings of political matters, foreign radio programs and, especially, the songs of such Soviet "bards" as Aleksandr GALICH, Vladimir Vysotsky, and Bulat OKUDZHAVA are made available. Soviet-generated *magnitizdat* recordings are often circulated in *samizdat* form and are published in the West.

Bibliography: Abraham Brumberg, ed., *In Quest of Justice: Protest and Dissent in the Soviet Union.* 1970. *The Chronicle of Current Events.* Issues 1–11. Michael Meerson-Aksenov and Boris Shragin, *The Political, Social and Religious Thought of Russian Samizdat.* Belmont, Mass., 1977. Peter Reddaway, ed., *Uncensored Russia: Protest and Dissent in the Soviet Union.* 1972. Josephine Woll, *Samizdat: A Bibliography of Dissident Soviet Literature.* 1983.

J. W.
J. G.

Satire, an indispensable literary term with a confused history. Authorities invariably disagree about its precise meaning, some regarding it as a genre or "kind" of literature (Dr. Johnson defines it as "a poem in which wickedness or vice is censured"), others as a tendency or "spirit" that can inform almost any genre (comedy, tragedy, epic, novel).

The word itself is derived from Latin *satira*, earlier *satura* (sc. *lanx*), literally "full plate," idiomatically "bowl of mixed fruits." *Satura* was first used metaphorically to indicate a poetic medley set to music and sung on the stage; only later did it come to mean a particular type of didactic poem aiming to improve society or individuals by ridiculing their vice or folly. The Romans, via Quintilian, claimed satire as their exclusive invention, for once a genre not adapted from the Greeks, a claim that can be accepted if the term is defined narrowly enough. The satirical *spirit*, however, would seem to be as old and as widespread as mankind itself, dissatisfaction with forms of social organization, or with individual behavior within those forms, being clearly endemic in our troubled species, and the use of ridicule as a means of correction or social control being almost as popular as the rod of chastisement. Recent seekers of the ultimate roots of literature, such as Robert C. Elliott, have found "satirical" elements in the pre-literate cultures of many peoples, where they often perform a religious or magic function, such as a "curse" laid upon an enemy or malefactor. Among the archaic Greeks the earliest "satirists," such as Archilochus (680–640 B.C.), were believed to possess magic powers—to sting, cut, wound, or even kill with words.

The Romans, however, were responsible for the creation of satire in the restrictive sense, i.e., a particular genre of poetry. Such "satires" were written in hexameters and usually constructed as a dialogue between the Satirist, representing common sense and morality, and his deviant Adversary, who is put to shame. The Romans considered Gaius Lucilius (c. 180–102 B.C.) the progenitor of this form, but its greatest practitioners were Horace, Persius, and Juvenal, whose satires remained the classic exemplars of the form for all who essayed it later. Yet even in Roman times the strict genre limits of satire were fading, and Roman literature has left us two exemplary satirical novels, *The Golden Ass* of Apuleius and the *Satyricon* of Petronius. The title of the latter, incidentally, is one manifestation—or perhaps source—of a bit of etymological cross-fertilization that has proved fecund through the ages. The rude, ribald satyrs had long before given their name and spirit to the Greek "satyric" drama, and the "satyric" spirit pervaded "satire" long after the satyrs themselves had been forgotten. (Not the least example of the satyr-satire confusion are the titles of two celebrated Russian satirical magazines, SATIRIKON [1908–14] and *Novyi Satirikon* [1913–18]).

The history of post-classical satire in the narrow sense can be succinctly summarized. Verse satire was revived in the early 16th century by such Italian poets as Ariosto, Alamanni, and Berni. The form they revitalized was then transplanted to Paris by Mathurin Régnier (1573–1613) and after him polished to a high lustre by Boileau (1636–1711), who both elegantly translated Juvenal's satires and wrote a dozen of his own. Ever afterwards the models of Horace, Juvenal, and Boileau loomed large before anyone presuming to write verse satire. Certainly they did before that remarkable literary pioneer, Prince Antiokh KANTEMIR, who was the first to write verse satire in Russian. First "tuning up," as it were, with

direct translations from Boileau and Horace, Kantemir moved on to the method later known as *sklonenie na nashi nravy* (transposition to our customs)—which is in fact exactly what Boileau had done to Juvenal. Kantemir produced nine original poems in the prescribed "satire" form. His caustic portrayal of "our customs," however, with its all too vivid representation of prevalent abuses and foolishness, apparently touched too many raw Russian nerves, and his satires could not be published in the original until 1762. By that time their impact was considerably lessened, partly by the fact that their syllabic versification now seemed hopelessly old-fashioned. In the meantime, SUMAROKOV, the legislator of Russian classicism, in his "Second Epistle" (1748) had set forth the rules for writing "satires" ("In satires we must revile vices / And make pompous folly laughable"), first seizing the occasion to animadvert on poor Kantemir ("beneath him Pegasus was lazy"). Sumarokov himself turned out eight creditable specimens of verse satire. Of these the best known are "On Nobility" (O blagorodstve), which recycles a theme that goes back to antiquity, disparity between nobility of birth and nobility of character, and had already been vigorously worked in Kantemir's Second Satire; and "Instruction to a Son" (Nastavlenie synu), in which a dying father gives his son lurid lessons in wickedness.

Later in the 18th century effective verse satires were written by KAPNIST, whose "First and Last Satire" (1780) summarily indicts a whole array of fools, rogues—and poetasters; and by KHEMNITSER, whose six pungent satires, however, were not published until a century later. At the very end of the century Ivan DMITRIEV published translations of Juvenal's *Satire VIII* (again the "nobility" theme) and of Pope's "Epistle to Dr. Arbuthnot," and he wrote several verse satires of his own, among them "What Other People Say" (Chuzhoi tolk, 1795), which ridicules the pompous "Pindaric" odes still being ground out by the *epigonoi* of LOMONOSOV. Long before the end of the 18th century, however, the borders of the genre were eroding, and such a work as DERZHAVIN's "Felitsa" (1783), though in form an ode, is largely a satire in spirit. In the early 19th century the traditions of verse satire, though with considerably greater formal freedom, were continued by such poets as Dmitry Gorchakov, whose "biting verse, knowledge of the world, and purity of style" were praised by PUSHKIN, and Aleksandr VOEIKOV (see the volume *Poety-satiriki kontsa XVIII–nachala XIX v.*, ed. G. V. Ermakova-Bitner). As late as 1816 Prince VYAZEMSKY, in his "To My Pen" (K peru moemu) was following the model of Boileau's *Satire VII* in reviewing the literary controversies of the day.

Satire in the larger sense, i.e., all literature, of whatever genre, whose aim is to ridicule folly and vice, is of course a subject of vast dimensions; the number of "satirists" of this kind is indeed legion. In European literature, after the Romans most authorities trace the satirical spirit through the medieval *fabliaux*, Rutebeuf, and the *Roman de Renart* down to the Renaissance, when it bursts forth with vigor in Boccaccio, Rabelais, Erasmus's *In Praise of Folly*, and the *Epistolae obscurorum virorum*. In the French 17th century the satirical impulse is strong in the comedies of Molière, the fables of La Fontaine, the maxims of La Rochefoucauld, and the *Caractères* of La Bruyère. In Spain it is also a powerful force, manifesting itself, inter alia, in Cervantes's great masterpiece and in the picaresque novels of Alemán and Quevedo. In Germany it displays itself in Brant's *Narrenschiff*, Fischart's *Geschichtsklitterung* (an adaptation from Rabelais), and Grimmelshausen's *Simplicissimus*. It flourished gloriously in 18th-century France, inspiring Voltaire's *Zadig, Candide,* and *Micromégas*, Montesquieu's *Lettres persanes*, Diderot's *Neveu de Rameau*, and finally Chénier's *Iambes*. In England the satiric spirit speaks bitterly and caustically in Swift, wittily and cuttingly in Pope, with elegant informality in Addison and Steele, exuberantly in Fielding and Smollett, playfully in Sterne. In Germany it shows itself in Wieland's *Geschichte der Abderiten*; in Italy, in Parini's *Il giorno* and Alfieri's *Satire*; in Poland, in the witty poems of Krasicki. In the 19th century satire becomes even more diffuse, less focused as a genre, but the force of its spirit is still powerfully felt—for instance, in Byron's *Don Juan*, Hoffmann's *Kater Murr*, Heine's *Atta Troll*, in many novels of Balzac, Dickens, and Thackeray, and in Hugo's *Châtiments*. In the 20th century it is still readily discernible in many plays of Shaw, in the early poems of Eliot, in novels by Aldous Huxley, Orwell, and Waugh, in works by the great Czechs Hašek and Čapek, in Brecht and Beckett, and it is obviously still very much alive.

In Russia the satirical spirit can be descried in oral folklore of indeterminate antiquity, notably in anti-clerical *skazki*, of which Pushkin's "Tale of the Priest and Balda, his Hired Hand" (Skazka o pope i o rabotnike ego Balde) is a creative adaptation. In written literature some critics discern satire in the medieval SUPPLICATION OF DANIEL THE EXILE. It appears less ambiguously in several 17th-century tales, such as the *Kalyazin Petition (Kalyazinskaya chelobitnaya)*, which mocks laziness and debauchery among monks, the *Tale of Ersh Ershovich* (a parody of contemporary court procedures), and *Shemyaka's Judgment* (Shemyakin sud), another satire of courtroom venality, based on a migratory folktale.

In the 18th century, besides the verse satires already discussed, satire in the larger sense is to be found in the journals of CATHERINE II, NOVIKOV, EMIN, and others, modelled on those of Addison and Steele. It also appears powerfully in comedy, both in prose and in verse, the outstanding examples of the former being FONVIZIN's two masterpieces, *The Brigadier* and *The Young Hopeful*. The Empress herself, flourishing the Horatian motto *ridendo castigat mores*, produced a number of satirical comedies, such as *Oh, the Times* (O, vremya, 1769, an adaptation of Gellert's *Die Betschwester*), *Mrs. Grumbly's Name-day* (Imeniny g-zhi Vorchalkinoi, 1772) and *Mrs. Gossip and Her Family* (G-zha Vestnikova s sem'ei, 1772). Sensitive to criticisms of her regime, Catherine favored a "kindly" satire, one directed generally at social foibles, not at specific abuses or malfunctioning institutions. In the 1780s, however, she herself wrote three comedies satirizing the Masons.

Satirical bite can be felt in many other comedies and comic operas of the 18th century, including many written with more talent than Catherine's. Examples are LUKIN's *Curio Shop* (Shchepetil'-nik, 1765), NIKOLEV's *Conceited Versifier* (Samolyubivyi stikhotvorets, 1775), a lampoon on Sumarokov; Matinsky's *St. Petersburg Bazaar* (Sankt-Peterburgskii gostinyi dvor, 1781); KNYAZHNIN's *The Braggart* (Khvastun, 1784–85) and *The Eccentrics* (Chudaki, 1790); and Kapnist's famous *Chicane* (Yabeda, 1793). The tradition of satirical verse comedy carries into the early 19th century, inspiring such works as SHAKHOVSKOI's *Lipetsk Spa; or, A Lesson to Flirts* (Lipetskie vody; ili, urok koketkam, 1815); it reaches its apogee in GRIBOEDOV's masterpiece, *Woe from Wit* (Gore ot uma, 1824). The parallel tradition of satirical prose comedy reaches its apogee a decade later, in GOGOL's *Inspector General* (Revizor, 1836), which reworks, but with a verve and imaginative power all its own, the familiar 18th-century themes of official corruption and greed along with provincial backwardness and boorishness.

Outside the theater, some brilliant satirical verse was produced in the 19th century, much of it by poets whose major poetic achievements lay elsewhere. An exception was KRYLOV, whose salty, pungent fables are not only his masterpiece, but rank in world literature among the greatest specimens of the fable genre. The protean PUSHKIN worked a satirical vein in *Graf Nulin* (1825) and *The Little House in Kolomna* (Domik v Kolomne, 1830), and there is a potent satirical dimension in *Evgeny Onegin* itself. BARATYNSKY's *The Ball* (Bal, 1828) also has a strong satirical side, as do LERMONTOV's *Sashka* (1835–36) and *The Treasurer's Wife from Tambov* (Tambovskaya kaznacheisha, 1837–38).

In the later 19th century the greatest poet-satirist is undoubtedly NEKRASOV. The targets of his early satirical poems are mostly such traditional ones as the bribetaker and the miser ("A Contemporary Ode" [Sovremennaya oda] and "Lullabye" [Kolybel'naya pesnya], both 1845) and the hypocrite ("A Moral Person"—Nravstvennyi chelovek, 1847); but some take more specific aim, e.g., "The Philanthropist" (Filantrop, 1853), which bitterly mocks the false charity of the "Society for the Visitation of the Poor," whose chairman was Prince V. F. ODOEVSKY, himself a poet. Much later, "Contemporaries" (Sovremenniki, 1875), under the guise of parodies of anniversary speeches, takes aim—heavily camouflaged because of censorship—at such conservative stalwarts as Count Dmitry Tolstoi, the Minister of Education. Nekrasov's most formidable achievement in satire is undoubtedly his long poem *Who Can Be Happy in Russia?* (Komu na Rusi zhit' khorosho?, 1864–76), in which seven peasant pilgrims conduct, as it were, a sociological survey of the country. It is less bitter and pessimistic in tone than much of Nekrasov's work.

In the middle years of the 19th century a number of minor poets contributed verse, some of it effective, to the left-wing satirical

magazine *Iskra* (1859–73), among them Vasily KUROCHKIN, MINAEV, and Veinberg. Not all satirical poetry came from the radicals, however; one of its best specimens is the liberal Aleksei TOLSTOI's *Popov's Dream* (Son Popova, 1882).

After Gogol the most formidable prose satirist of the 19th century is undoubtedly SALTYKOV-SHCHEDRIN. His early works, such as *Provincial Sketches* (Gubernskie ocherki, 1856–57) are still quite moderate and even optimistic in tone. The colors become darker, however, in *The History of a Town* (Istoriya odnogo goroda, 1869–70), in which the "town," Glupov (Stupidville) synecdochically represents the whole history of Russia, seen as an unremitting series of coarse and cruel absurdities. The "Aesopian language" required to squeeze such works through the censorship, however, as well as the camouflaged references to specific persons and events, render these texts inaccessible to modern readers without extensive commentaries. Toward the end of the century effective prose satire was produced by the young CHEKHOV in, for example "Death of an Official" (Smert' chinovnika, 1883) and "Sergeant Prishibeev" (Unter Prishibeev, 1885) and by the old Leskov in "Night Owls" (Polunoshchniki, 1891), "The Cattle Pen" (Zagon, 1893), "A Winter's Day" (Zimnii den', 1894), and "The Rabbit Warren" (Zayachii remiz, written 1894–95).

Satire is not a signal feature in Russian literature of the great Silver Age, but its indomitable spirit nevertheless inspired such masterpieces as Blok's *Balaganchik* (1906) and Bely's *First Meeting* (Pervoe svidanie, 1921). The prerevolutionary satirical traditions were continued in the emigration by such experienced professionals as TEFFI, AVERCHENKO, and Sasha CHORNY. A group of them even brought off a short-lived Parisian revival of *Novyi Satirikon*. And there is a pervasive satirical strain running through all the work of Vladimir NABOKOV.

One of the surprises of the 20th century, however, has been the vitality of satire in Soviet Russian literature; indeed, a good deal of the most interesting writing produced in the Soviet Union, especially in the early years, could be called satirical. The NEP period was particularly fruitful satirically, partly because the bars of censorship were lowered further than they were to be again for many years, partly because the regime encouraged ridicule of "bourgeois" and "petty bourgeois" attitudes and styles, whose rebirth the NEP had made possible. And at a deeper level, according to Marxist theory there were inevitably "bourgeois" survivals in the consciousness of many unregenerate Soviet citizens, and satire was an appropriate tool for extirpating them. Thus would "mankind, laughing, take leave of its past." This comfortable doctrine, however, became less viable as time passed and "bourgeois survivals" somehow appeared even in persons born long after 1917.

The following are a few outstanding examples of NEP satire: ERENBURG's novel *The Extraordinary Adventures of Julio Jurenito and His Disciples* (Neobychainye pokhozhdeniya Khulio Khurenito i ego uchenikov, 1922); BULGAKOV's stories, collected as *The Diaboliad* (D'yavoliada) and *The Fatal Eggs* (Rokovye yaitsa, both 1925), followed by his suppressed plays *Zoika's Apartment* (Zoikina kvartira, written 1926) and *The Crimson Island* (Bagrovyi ostrov, written 1928); ERDMAN's plays *The Mandate* (Mandat, 1925) and *The Suicide* (Samoubiitsa, written 1928, suppressed); several works by Andrei PLATONOV, not all of them published, especially *The City of Gradov* (Gorod Gradov, 1926) and "Doubting Makar" (Usomnivshiisya Makar, 1929); many short stories and novellas by ZOSHCHENKO; MAYAKOVSKY's two plays *The Bedbug* (Klop, 1928) and *The Bathhouse* (Banya, 1929); and ILF and PETROV's picaresque novel *Twelve Chairs* (Dvenadtsat' stul'ev, 1928).

Conditions for satirists became much more difficult after the advent of Stalinism, but some remarkable specimens nevertheless appeared, such as Zoshchenko's *Youth Restored* (Vozvrashchennaya molodost', 1933) and Ilf and Petrov's *Golden Calf* (Zolotoi telenok, 1932). Other works were written "for the drawer" and came to light only much later, such as Bulgakov's *Master and Margarita* and *Heart of a Dog* (Sobach'e serdtse) and SHVARTS's play *The Naked King* (Golyi korol', written 1934, published 1960). By the end of the thirties satire had virtually disappeared from Soviet literature, although in his play *The Dragon* (Drakon, 1944) Shvarts, under the guise of satirizing fascism, managed to bring the theme of the corrupting effects of dictatorship perilously close to home. To this day Soviet satirists confront almost insuperable obstacles of taboo and censorship, but some, such as OKUDZHAVA, manage to sing their way around them; others, like the STRUGATSKY brothers, project their satire into science fiction. Some of the most talented, however, such as Tertz-SINYAVSKY, VOINOVICH, AKSYONOV, ZINOVIEV, and the late Aleksandr GALICH, have been forced into emigration.

Bibliography: Robert C. Elliott, *The Power of Satire: Magic, Ritual, Art.* 1960. L. F. Ershov, *Satira i sovremennost'.* 1978. I. S. Eventov, *Lirika i satira.* 1968. A. M. Makarian, *O satire.* 1967. Ronald Paulson, ed., *Satire: Modern Essays in Criticism.* Englewood Cliffs, N. J. [1971]. A. Z. Vulis, *Sovetskii satiricheskii roman.* Tashkent, 1965. David Worcester, *The Art of Satire.* 1940.   H. McL.

Satirikón, a satirical journal. Came out weekly in Petersburg, 1908 to 1914, under the editorship of A. T. AVERCHENKO. In 1913, a number of the journal's contributors began to publish a new journal, *Novyi satirikon* (New Satiricon), also edited by Averchenko. Sasha CHORNY, TEFFI, Leonid ANDREEV, KUPRIN, A. TOLSTOI, A. GRIN, S. MARSHAK, ERENBURG, BABEL, MANDELSHTAM, and MAYAKOVSKY published in *Novyi satirikon.* The journal's illustrators included Kustodiev, Korovin, Benois, and Bakst. *Novyi satirikon* was closed by the Soviet government in 1918. In 1931, an attempt was made to renew publication of *Satirikon* in Paris, but the journal lasted less than a year. During this period, contributors to the journal included BUNIN, Kuprin, REMIZOV, and Sasha Chorny.   C. T. N.

Sávva Grúdtsyn, The Story of, see NOVEL.

Schism, see OLD BELIEVERS, AVVAKUM.

Scholarship, literary. *Nineteenth century.*

Literary scholarship (*literaturovedenie*) as an independent discipline developed only toward the middle of the 19th century, when it became distinct from the history of letters (*istoriya slovesnosti*), understood as history of Russian letters as a whole, and from the history of language as a branch of linguistics. Its development was prepared by over a century of collecting and systematizing the facts of old as well as modern Russian literature, and by normative aesthetics which played an exceptionally important role in the development of modern Russian literature: Contrary to the usual order of things, the theory of Russian SYLLABOTONIC VERSIFICATION of V. D. TREDIAKOVSKY ("A New and Concise Method for the Composition of Russian Verse," 1735) and M. V. LOMONOSOV ("A Letter on the Rules of Russian Versification," 1739) were not generalizations of accumulated experience, but on the contrary, a theoretical discovery of forms so adequate to the spirit and structure of the Russian language that they have been fruitfully realized in various poetic genres for nearly 250 years now.

The first successful systematization of the facts of the history of Russian literature is Nikolai NOVIKOV's "Essay of a Historical Dictionary of Russian Writers" (Opyt istoricheskogo slovarya o rossiiskikh pisatelyakh, 1772), in which for the first time not only the newer, printed, but also the older, manuscript literature is treated. The first attempts at a fusion of the categories of POETICS (no longer purely normative, but understood as a part of AESTHETICS) with the conception of a historical development of literature were made in V. G. BELINSKY's literary criticism, another preparatory stage of literary scholarship. S. S. SHEVYRYOV's two-volume *History of Russian Letters, Primarily of the Older Period* (Istoriya russkoi slovesnosti, preimushchestvenno drevnei, 1846), "a serious impulse for later researchers" (N. K. Gudzy), must be assigned to the proximate prehistory of Russian literary scholarship.

F. I. BUSLAEV, the founder of the Russian MYTHOLOGICAL SCHOOL, was a student of Shevyryov's. He started out as a linguist and historian of language in the 1840s, but expanded his research to folklore and literature proper in the 1850s and 1860s. Buslaev was also first to transfer the methods of a historical-comparative study of language to oral poetry and to literature. Moreover, he was first to posit the problem of the connection between literature and folk poetry, as well as the problem of the transition from mythological thinking to the traditions of folk poetry, and hence to motifs and *sujets* of literature proper.

The methodology of the comparative study of literature was worked out in a variety of different dimensions even by the mythological school. It was based on a confrontation of folkloric and ancient literary texts (Buslaev's university lecture, "On Folk Poetry and Old Russian Literature," 1859), collation of all recorded variants of a given work of oral poetry to the end of establishing its "stratification" (*sloevoi sostav*, O. F. MILLER, *Comparative-Critical Observations on the Stratification of the Russian Folk Epic* [1869]), and comparison of *sujets* of Russian folk tales and folk songs with analogous *sujets* found in the oral poetry and literature of other Slavic nations (A. A. AFANASIEV, *Poetic Attitudes of the Slavs toward Nature*, 1865–69). Seeking to reduce a given literary or folkloric *sujet* to its mythological source, the Russian mythological school carefully registered, checked, and elaborated all possible explanations for an observed similarity of representations and poetic *sujets* among different peoples, from a theory of a common "primary myth" (*pramif*) from which these *sujets* had originated, to a theory of borrowing and a conception of "independent genesis" (*samozarozhdenie*) of motifs under similar historical conditions.

The Russian mythological school had the attractive trait of being free of any dogmatism in pursuing its hypotheses or theoretical ideas, a readiness to accept or check out any new thought or discovery, and a capacity for self-criticism. Thus, Buslaev, in 1874, spoke ironically of his own illusions of the 1850s, concerning an alleged national character imprinted upon folk poetry: "How many such idols of national adoration have been smashed by the theory of literary borrowing alone!" (F. I. Buslaev, "Migrating Stories and Tales," *Russkii vestnik*, 1874, no. 5, p. 31). Or, for another example, speaking of A. Afanasiev's one-sided explication of myths as exclusively "natural," A. A. Kotlyarevsky notes, also not without irony, that one can of course see in the "arrows" of Ilya Muromets "vestiges of mythical metaphors" standing for bolts of lightning, but that one can equally well perceive them as "an ordinary weapon of the age before firearms," which will be no less plausible (A. A. Kotlyarevskii, *Sochineniya*, vol. 2, 1889, pp. 295–96).

The merits of the mythological school in the history of Russian literary scholarship are great. First of all, it gave some meaning to the grandiose body of oral poetry, which it gathered and subjected to critical and comparative analysis, thus creating the foundation of Russian FOLKLORISTICS. It was also the mythological school that established the continuity of connections between literature and the development of a national language as well as of oral poetry; this connection becomes more complex, but it never disappears throughout the entire history of the Russian nation. Furthermore, the mythological school, and in particular F. Buslaev in his critique of S. Shevyryov's course, made a first selection of those works of Old Russian literature, from among the whole mass of literary monuments (primarily religious-ecclesiastic, which Shevyryov included in his course, in order to corroborate his notion of the fundamentally Christian and ecclesiastic character of Russian literature), which could be considered properly poetic. Finally, the meticulousness and variety of approaches to comparative study practiced by the mythological school served as an example to succeeding directions, and the material of literary parallels gathered by it could also be used by its successors.

The mythological school created a deep foundation upon which all the following academic schools could build. Among the members of that school, only Buslaev started his activities a decade earlier than the other major literary scholars in Russia. Almost all his students and followers belonged to the generation of scholars born in the 1830s or even the 1840s, much as the more prominent representatives of other schools, which emerged after the mythological school, but were active simultaneously with it. The traditional order in which these schools are treated is a matter of presentation rather than historical succession—which could not have developed within a single generation of scholars. It was precisely this circumstance that determined the intensity of interaction between these schools and the ease with which a literary scholar would move from one school to the other, taking along his entire accumulated arsenal of research devices and intellectual habits.

Within the framework of post-reform Russia, the cultural-historical school (*kul'turno-istoricheskaya shkola*), more directly linked to the drift of the times than others, was the most influential and numerous. To it belonged A. N. PYPIN, N. S. TIKHONRAVOV, A. I. Storozhenko, I. N. Zhdanov, A. A. Shakhov, A. I. Kirpichnikov, among others. Within the school itself, though, there existed certain essential differences, exemplified by two names: A. N. Pypin and N. S. Tikhonravov. Issuing from the principles of the West-European cultural-historical school of Hippolyte Taine, its Russian followers made some important changes in the very concept of "milieu" (*sreda*) to which the development of literature was placed into a causal dependance. To Pypin, "milieu" is primarily the socio-political and ideological life of a country. Here the influence of the ambience of Sovremennik, in which Pypin's literary activities began and his personality was formed, is evident. Although he was not a follower of Chernyshevsky's philosophy, or of his sociopolitical views, he still retained a certain charge of civic-mindedness and broad social interests. This was reflected in his prevailing interest in general cultural and sociohistorical progress, to a certain extent at the expense of perceiving literature as verbal art. Like most of the members of the cultural-historical school, Pypin was tremendously productive. In his scholarly works an interest in the history of social thought noticeably prevailed over problems connected with aesthetic values, though in theory he did not reject an aesthetic approach to literature. Even the themes of many of his works indicate this: "Social Trends in Russia under Alexander I" (Obshchestvennoe dvizhenie v Rossii pri Aleksandre I, 1871), "A Characteristic of Literary Opinions from the 1820s to the 1850s" (Kharakteristika literaturnykh mnenii ot 20-kh to 50-kh godov, 1873), "Belinsky, His Life and Correspondence" (1876), etc. Also, Pypin authored many multi-volume research works which added whole layers of cultural movements and historical-cultural material to Russian literary scholarship: *A History of Slavic Literatures* (with V. D. Spasovich, 1879), *A History of Russian Ethnography* (4 vols., 1890–92), *A History of Russian Literature* (4 vols., 1898–99), etc.

With the years, Pypin's interest in general culture extended further into the past. His works encompass the whole extent of Russian letters, from the most ancient times to current events of literary life. Also, more and more new facts of the nation's cultural history were introduced into his research: ancient Russian fairy tales and stories, the apocryphal literature of old Russia, the "secret" (*potaennaya*), i.e. uncensored literature after the introduction of the printing press, Russo-Slavic literary relations, etc. A flagging interest in versified forms and a tendency to view literary facts as a source or illustration of the general historical or general cultural development of the nation are the direct results of the neglect of the aesthetic approach, which are visible not only in Pypin's own works, but also in those of his students and followers.

N. S. Tikhonravov represents another variant of the cultural-historical school. His work is characterized by the same wide range of interests, as it spans the whole thousand years of Russian letters. But the concept of "milieu" as treated by him is closer to a history of national customs and habits, the way of life, and cultural attitudes, the "national spirit," so to say, though not to be understood in a narrowly nationalist sense. On the contrary, Tikhonravov had inherited the devices of the comparative-historical method from F. I. Buslaev and made full use of them, as he sought to understand the development of Russian national artistic culture as the result of a wide range of mutual relations and crossfertilization, yet also dependent on a national factor which receives, incorporates, and transforms these influences. In Tikhonravov, the living connection between the cultural-historical school and the traditions of the mythological school becomes quite obvious. Unlike Pypin, Tikhonravov openly declared himself opposed to using aesthetic criteria in the selection and evaluation of works of literature for a course in literature, rejecting such an approach as extra-historical without even drawing a line between the normative poetics of classicism and poetics as a part of aesthetics in Belinsky's interpretation (see Tikhonravov's review of *A History of Russian Letters, Old and New*, by A. D. Galakhov, which later appeared under the title, "The Tasks of the History of Literature and Methods of its Study," 1876). Nevertheless, Tikhonravov knew very well what works belonged to the "column of literature" (*literaturnyi ryad*) and established certain regularities that were specific to that "column." He was the first to observe the inner consistency of the development of literature in Russia, proving, for example, that the birth of a new post-Petrine literature was not at all a full break with tradition, since an orientation toward Western examples had been prepared by the three preceding centuries of literary life in Muscovy, so in the spreading of

the secular tale, original as well as translated, and in the infiltration of secular and fairy-tale motifs into the saints' life (see Hagiography). A significant portion of these "secular tales" were first published by Tikhonravov in his *Annals of Russian Literature and Antiquities* (Letopisi russkoi literatury i drevnostei, 1859–63), and some of them he discovered himself, such as the famous "Tale of Savva Grudtsyn."

The high esteem in which Tikhonravov held the artistic highlights of Russian literature is evidenced by his scholarly edition of Slovo o polku Igoreve (1866, new ed. 1868), in which he introduced many emendations of the text of 1800 using the methods of historical criticism. His wide range of interests is reflected also in his studies of the early Russian theater and his edition of thirty plays dating from the late 17th and early 18th century, which had been previously unknown (*Russian Dramatic Works, 1672–1725*, 1874). The third volume of this edition was to contain a study of and a commentary to these plays, but remained in manuscript due to the publisher's bankruptcy.

In the area of modern Russian literature, Tikhonravov's choice of authors and works to which he devoted his attention testifies to his good taste. It suffices here to mention his scholarly edition of the works of Gogol, unsurpassed to this day. Tikhonravov's generalizations do, however, show on occasion the influence of Russian literary criticism of the age preceding his, for instance, when he follows Belinsky in identifying the literature of exposé and satire (*oblichitel'no-satiricheskoe napravlenie*), from Kantemir, Novikov and Derzhavin to Gogol, as the truly national and original branch of Russian literature, free of imitation. To be sure, Tikhonravov as a rule refrained from aesthetic analysis of literary texts. But the manysided textological and cultural-historical commentary of each text to which he devoted his scholarly attention created an exhaustive supply of material for any kind of analysis, not excluding the aesthetic. Hence the charge of "underestimation" of the aesthetic meaning of works of fine literature, raised even by N. K. Gudzy, does not seem quite just.

It seems necessary to distinguish the comparative-historical *school* as a particular direction of Russian literary scholarship from comparative-historical *methods* of research, which were used by scholars of all schools, beginning with A. N. Pypin's early study, *An Essay in the Literary History of Ancient Russian Stories and Fairy Tales* (Ocherk literaturnoi istorii starinnykh povestei i skazok russkikh, 1857), which appeared two years earlier than the *Panchatantra* with Theodor Benfey's introduction, which is commonly taken as the start of European literary comparativism. The main difference lies here in the fact that comparison and establishing parallels are now no mere device of research, but to a considerable extent its aim as well, as they serve the task of reducing national literatures to a single and coherent process, the development of world literature.

The first steps of comparativism on Russian soil were made, as is commonly assumed, by V. V. Stasov's book *The Origin of Russian Byliny* (Proiskhozhdenie russkikh bylin, 1868), which generated a major polemic and thus promoted the spreading of the comparative method. V. V. Stasov created no school, as he himself shifted his interest from literature to research in the non-verbal forms of contemporary Russian art, painting and music. The most typical figure of "pure comparativism" in Russia was Aleksei N. Veselovsky. It was precisely in his works that the connection between the comparative-historical direction in Russian literary scholarship and later Westernism as a form of Russian liberalism appeared very clearly. This may explain his exceptionally wide fame, not quite commensurate with his achievements as a scholar. His book, *Western Influence in Modern Russian Literature* (Zapadnoe vliyanie v novoi russkoi literature), published as a series of articles in the journal *Vestnik Evropy* (1879–1881), went through five editions as a separate volume. Though considering himself a student of Pypin, Aleksei Veselovsky did not strive, as Pypin had, to link the literary process to the entire body of the cultural and general historical conditions of a given period. With rare boldness and occasional brilliance, he connected literary phenomena of different ages and countries, suggesting influence or direct borrowing. In so doing he not only had to lift a given work of literature from the context of its national history and culture, but also tended to view the work itself not as an artistic whole, but rather as an aggregate of motifs and structural elements (images, elements of plot, sometimes entire episodes or scenes), more or less fortuitously combined by the author as a result of various criss-crossing "influences" of foreign literature. The general picture of post-Petrine Russian literature appeared, in the light of his theories, as a "period of discipleship" (*uchenicheskii period*) in relation to Western Europe which extended through the entire 18th century and up to the middle of the 19th, not excluding even PUSHKIN and LERMONTOV.

However, the comparative-historical school is not limited to this liberal-Westernizing tendency, which left no visible trace in the further development of Russian literary scholarship. An original and most important contribution by this school belongs to Aleksei Veselovsky's older brother, Aleksandr N. VESELOVSKY. The method of confrontation, of establishing similarities and differences, is for him a path toward the establishment of general regularities in the development of world literature. As he chaired the department of general literature at St. Petersburg University (in Moscow it was held by A. I. Storozhenko, in Kiev by N. P. Dashkevich), Veselovsky saw the object of his course in clarifying how international cultural connections developed and evolved, where literary borrowing and influence had taken place, and where "independent genesis" of analogous phenomena, or a fundamental transformation or reworking of "foreign" forms had happened. Veselovsky proposed to build the integrated process of a universal historical evolution of world literature only on the basis of facts. Veselovsky overcame the earlier notion, widely held by scholars, which made general literature the sum total of West-European literatures, showing not only that Russia and the Slavic nations had actively participated in this process, but also demonstrating the importance of the role played by Byzantium as a mediator of literary interchange and mutual influence between East and West (see his dissertation, "Slavic Legends about Solomon and Kitovras and Western Legends about Morolf and Merlin," 1872).

The school of Aleksandr Veselovsky synthesized the rational peculiarities and achievements of all the other schools existing in Russia. But most of all, Veselovsky leaned upon the ideas and discoveries of the mythological school, and particularly of his teacher, F. I. Buslaev, who had said: "The nationhood of every people destined to have a great future (and the Russian people are such) possesses a special faculty to transform into its own property whatever will enter it from the outside. Consequently, when a researcher points out foreign influences on old Russia, he does no harm to our national identity, but on the contrary, supports it, because it has emerged as an independent entity from all foreign accretions, accepting only those foreign elements which agree with its own essence" (F. I. Buslaev, *Istoricheskie ocherki russkoi narodnoi slovesnosti i iskusstva*, 1861, vol. 2, p. 80). Veselovsky extended this idea to all peoples, large and small, developing a theory of "converging currents" (*vstrechnye techeniya*): "A borrowing presupposes in the recipient not a vacant space, but a converging current, a similar direction of thought, analogous forms of fantasy." Veselovsky had conceived this idea much earlier, during the first few years after his graduation from the university. The inception of his "historical poetics" belongs to the same period. It became the principal task of his life as a scholar. It developed, it would seem, under the influence of the lectures of G. Steinthal, a student of Hegel and W. von Humboldt, which he had attended in Berlin in 1862. Under the influence of these lectures, Veselovsky came to the conclusion that the subject of literary scholarship must be defined separately from its neighboring disciplines: the history of science, philosophy, religion, morality, etc.: "Within the domain of the history of literature there will thus remain only the so-called belles lettres (*izyashchnye proizvedeniya*), and it will become a branch of aesthetics, history of belles lettres, historical aesthetics" (A. N. Veselovskii, *Istoricheskaya poetika*, 1940, p. 396). However, only in 1871, as he was launching his course of general literature, did Veselovsky return to this idea in terms of a direct and principal task of literary scholarship: "To investigate how the new content of life, that element of freedom which comes streaming in with each new generation, permeates old forms, those unavoidable forms into which every previous development had to be cast" (*Istoricheskaya poetika*, p. 52).

Veselovsky repeatedly returned to the task of developing poetics from the history of literature, with the latter conceived as a history of literary forms, as in his "Iz lektsii po istorii liriki i dramy" (1882), "Iz lektsii po istorii eposa" (1884), "Iz istorii epiteta" (1895), and "Poetika syuzhetov" (1897–1906).

In the 1890s Veselovsky made an attempt to develop historical poetics as a separate and coherent discipline ("Iz vvedeniya v istoricheskuyu poetiku," 1893; "Tri glavy iz istoricheskoi poetiki," 1899). This he accomplished by selecting, from among a great number of literary forms which have withstood the test of time, the history of kinds and genres (*istoriya rodov i zhanrov*) for a pivot and framework of historical poetics. "The history of poetic kinds is the best verification of their theory," he wrote in his article, "History or Theory of the Novel?" In his "Three Chapters from Historical Poetics," Veselovsky pursues the process in the course of which the poetic forms of epic, lyric, and drama developed from an original syncretic state all the way to "the separation of the epos into folk epic and literary epic" (*prostonarodnyi i khudozhestvennyi*), that is, to the development of the novel.

Veselovsky could only finish the first part of his historical poetics which dealt with primitive society and the beginnings of literature. He was unable to demonstrate the regularities of the literary process in all of its stages. His immediate disciples and followers failed to continue the work started by Veselovsky, and the problems formulated by him continue to be worked on by literary scholars of different directions and views to this day.

The last school to emerge during the 19th century was the psychological school, linked to the eminent linguist A. A. POTEBNYA. Potebnya himself can be considered the bearer of the conceptions and methods of the psychological school only in a conditional sense, though without his strong influence it would have lacked any originality with regard to Western "aestho-psychology" in the manner of Emile Hennequin. More precisely, the psychological school developed at Kharkov University in the 1890s as a result of an encounter between Potebnya's theories and Western "aestho-psychology." It is therefore necessary to keep separate the contribution which Potebnya himself made to literary scholarship, on the one side, and the role of the psychological school, which emerged only after Potebnya's death.

A follower of W. von Humboldt in considering language as an energy, as an organ of cognition and a tool of creating (rather than merely expressing) thought, Potebnya had investigated the mechanism involved in the development and growth of Slavic languages on the basis of the laws of associative thinking. This led him to the postulation of a three-tiered structure of the word. Its external (acoustic) form, he thought, goes back to primary interjections, that is to primitive reactions to external stimuli. The "inner form" contains a visual representation which connects a new object of verbal signification with an old word already existing in the language. The actual meaning of a word is only the third link in this chain. The requirement of the mediatorship of an "inner form," always associative-figurative, in the forming of new words is connected to Potebnya's assumption that language is in itself a form of poetry, a poetic-cognitive energy of popular consciousness ("Thought and Language," 1862). This faced Potebnya with a new set of problems, no longer so much linguistic, as literary.

Potebnya's linguistic poetics, developed primarily only in his lectures ("Iz lektsii po teorii slovesnosti," 1894; "Iz zapisok po teorii slovesnosti," 1905), is based on a direct analogy between his understanding of language as poetry, on the one hand, and of poetry as a product of language, on the other. He asserted that every work of verbal art, from proverbs and fables to novels and other complex verbal structures, is composed of the same three basic elements as the word: external form, i.e., the verbal composition of the work; the inner form, that is, its imagery, including representations of its characters and of the events in their lives; and the actual content or idea of the work, to be grasped through the symbolic force of the "inner form."

Assigning cardinal importance to the cognitive power of poetry, Potebnya insisted on its autonomous and specific content, irreducible to abstract ideas obtained by science or other forms of cognition. One of the merits of Potebnya's theory with regard to literary scholarship may be seen in the fact that after a lengthy hegemony of the cultural-historical school, he, like Veselovsky, drew the attention of scholars toward the specificity of literature. But unlike Veselovsky's, his attention was focused not so much in the aesthetic specificity of literature as distinct from other "letters" (*slovesnost'*), as in its specificity as verbal creation and in its connection with the life and the history of language. Here he also drew directly on the traditions of the mythological school, as represented by Buslaev, and perhaps Afanasiev.

Potebnya's influence was strongest in the area of linguistic poetics and linguistic stylistics. His assertion of an identity of the laws of language and those of poetic thought led to a fusion of poetics and linguistics and to the discarding of the aesthetic approach to poetry. As a result, the artistic whole of a work of poetry was lost from sight, as it disintegrated into a multitude of purely verbal forms of imagery.

The psychological school leaned only on one aspect of Potebnya's teaching: his idea that poetic cognition is an individual creative act, generated by inner stimuli. It was Potebnya who asserted what was later taken up by Maksim GORKY, namely that a theme arises in the author's consciousness as a question, while the work of literature is a means by which consciousness seeks to work out an answer to its own question, that answer being the idea of that work. Here, the communicative function of the word and of verbal art amounts not so much to transmitting ideas to other people, as to a capacity to elicit in the reader's consciousness certain analogous, albeit not identical representations and ideas, based on his own arsenal of representations. From this position, there arose an increased interest in the psychology of the creative process and of the creative personality, as well as of the reception of a work of art. However, these problems, linked to the active role of art in the course of history, were treated by the next generation of literary scholars who were inspired by Potebnya's ideas.

Potebnya's first followers and founders of the psychological school, such as D. N. Ovsyaniko-Kulikovsky and A. G. Gornfeld, combined the problem of the psychology of the creative act with the heritage of the cultural-historical school and thus converted the history of literature into material for the study of "social psychology" and its history, as in Ovsyaniko-Kulikovsky's *History of the Russian Intelligentsia* (1906–11). Even the poetic images of the main heroes of the classics of literature were viewed, in this context, as material toward a classification of "psychological types" of Russian society during a given epoch.

Russian literary scholarship, born with great delay as late as the middle of the 19th century, nevertheless produced several scholars of high caliber, who not only gave a powerful impetus to the development of theory, but also provided ample material for succeeding generations of scholars. Scholars belonging to a variety of schools and directions keep returning to this day to their ideas and to the tasks set by them.

Twentieth century

The term *literaturovedenie* (literary scholarship), which combines the theory and the history of literature, became current in Russia only at the turn of the century, after Aleksandr Veselovsky had proposed to develop the theory of literature from its history. Literary scholarship, as it had developed by the end of the 19th century, also included several auxiliary disciplines, such as bibliography, the study of source materials (*istochnikovedenie*), textual criticism (*tekstologiya*), etc.

In the beginning of the 20th century, the cultural-historical school (N. A. Kotlyarevsky, S. A. VENGEROV, V. V. Sipovsky, V. N. Peretts, E. A. Lyatsky, etc.) and the comparative-historical school, dominant among specialists in the literatures of Western Europe (F. D. Batyushkov, Aleksei N. Veselovsky, E. V. Anichkov, K. F. Tiander, etc.) had retained their influence in academia. No new conceptions or methods were advanced in those years, as the traditional schools seemed to continue to exist by inertia, gathering, systematizing, and interpreting additional literary material. The relaxation of CENSORSHIP after the Revolution of 1905 helped this work. Mention must be made of the archival research and commentatorial work of M. K. Lemke on the history of Russian censorship, as well as his collections and editions of A. I. HERZEN, N. A. DOBROLYUBOV, and other writers, whose very names were previously prohibited in print. In these years, a whole series of periodicals and collections appeared, devoted especially to the publication of new archival materials and research ("Golos minuvshego"—Voice of the Past, "Russkie propilei"—Russian Propylaea, "Pushkinist," etc.)

The tendency of Russian literary scholars to switch from one school to another, in evidence even earlier, now turned into a conscious effort to synthesize methods and conceptions developed up to that point and to build from these elements a unified structure of the "literary process" (*literaturnyi protsess*). Such striving for a synthesis is characteristic primarily for a number of scholars of the cultural-historical school. As early as 1906 there appeared a brochure by V. V. Sipovsky, "History of Literature as a Science" (Istoriya literatury kak nauka), critical of earlier and contemporary Russian and West-European schools (from Taine to Wilhelm Scherer and Ferdinand Brunetière). Taking Aleksandr Veselovsky for his point of departure, Sipovsky does not, however, suggest to resume Veselovsky's grandiose project to create a historical poetics. Rather, Sipovsky reduces Veselovsky's idea to an "ideal structure" which will help to perfect an "evolutionary theory" of literary scholarship, applicable to all countries and nations. In this interpretation, historical poetics is merely an "elegant ready scheme, independent of all historical and geographic fact," though "in some instances" convenient as a means to explain the ways of literary progress.

Subsequently this idea was detailed and developed by P. N. SAKULIN, now in terms of a "sociological school," in his programmatic serialized edition, "The Science of Literature, Its Results and Perspectives" (Nauka o literature, ee itogi i perspektivy). The final (15th) fascicle of the series bears the significant title, "A Synthetic Construction of the History of Literature" (Sinteticheskoe postroenie istorii literatury, 1925). All these attempts at a "synthesis" for the sake of "economy of thought," at substituting a "convenient" scheme for an integral worldview, a scheme which only requires the mechanical insertion of the actual facts of literary development, remained fruitless in a scholarly and theoretical sense, as could be expected of eclecticism made into a principle.

New problems and aspects of the study of literature were advanced by an academic school, which had developed under the influence of A. A. Potebnya's philosophy of language and theory of verbal creation, still in the 19th century. The first two decades of the 20th century saw the activities of a group of philologists at Kharkov University, where Potebnya himself had taught for many years (1857–91) and where his follower, D. N. Ovsyaniko-Kulikovsky, even then a distinguished scholar, also held a chair (1888–1905). This group, only later designated as the psychological school, produced a number of talented literary scholars, who were interested in questions of the psychology of the creative process and of the reception of the work of art, philosophy of language, and linguistic poetics (A. G. Gornfeld, V. I. Khartsiev, T. Rainer, B. A. Lezin, etc.) This group published collections of articles under the title *Problems of the Theory and Psychology of Art* (Voprosy teorii i psikhologii iskusstva), of which 8 volumes appeared between 1907 and 1923. It gradually gained considerable influence in Russian literary scholarship and criticism. However, this school was not quite free of eclecticism either. In their effort to overcome the enlightener's rationalism which affected Potebnya, who viewed poetry merely as another form of cognition, his followers sought to wed his theory now to the aesthetic ideas of Vladimir SOLOVYOV, then again to the neo-Kantian aesthetic of G. Rickert or G. Simmel, or even to the intuitivism of Henri Bergson.

In literary scholarship as in other branches of knowledge, the general crisis of positivism led to a reactivation of philosophic idealism. After Veselovsky and Potebnya, a new and serious step forward was made by some literary theories which developed outside academia. Such were the contributions of Vyacheslav IVANOV and Andrei BELY, poets and theoreticians of the so-called younger generation of Russian SYMBOLISM. The younger Symbolists were distinguished from the many other schools and tendencies of poetry in the early 20th century by a heightened sense of the historical responsibility of art. Being conscious, though not very consistent followers of the religious-philosophical doctrine and the aesthetic conceptions of Vladimir Solovyov, they were convinced that poetry is not only a form of cognition, but also a powerful creative and life-building force of history, capable of awakening the creative potential and the spiritual needs of the masses. The conception of art as a force that could transform life, in spite of its utopian nature, placed serious problems of literary scholarship before its theorists, requiring acquisition and reworking of all the valuable work done by previous Russian literary scholarship, and especially by A. N. Veselovsky and A. A. Potebnya. In this respect the studies of Vyacheslav Ivanov are of particular importance, since it was he who was the first after Veselovsky to take a step toward the creation of a historical poetics. Responding to Nietzsche, he dealt with various aspects of the development of tragedy, and of the theater at large, from the Dionysian mysteries of ancient Greece, of the essence of tragedy and its historical evolution throughout the history of European culture, as well as of the contemporary condition and possible renaissance of tragedy as the most "communal" (sobornyi) of arts, demanding a "common emotion" (edinochuvstvie) on the part of artist and audience, so in his essays "On the Crisis of the Theater" (O krizise teatra, 1909), "On the Essence of Tragedy" (O sushchestve tragedii, 1912), "The Aesthetic Norm of the Theater" (Esteticheskaya norma teatra, 1916), "On Action and Act" (O deistvii i deistve, 1919), and "Multitude and Individuality in the Theatrical Act" (Mnozhestvo i lichnost' v deistve, 1920). Two chapters of his doctoral dissertation, Dionysus and Predionysianism (Dionis i Pradionisiistvo, 1923) are also devoted to these problems ("Pathos, Catharsis, Tragedy" and "The Origins of Tragedy"). Ivanov's three essays on DOSTOEVSKY, as well as his book on Dostoevsky, written in German (1932), are a must for every student of Dostoevsky.

A cycle of studies by Vyacheslav Ivanov devoted to problems of the psychology of the creative process and the reception of art advances beyond the framework of positivism and individual psychology. In his "Symbolics of Aesthetic Principles" (Simvolika esteticheskikh nachal, 1905), "Boundaries of Art" (O granitsakh iskusstva, 1913), and a course in poetics taught at Baku University (1921–23), the problems worked out by him, while inherited from preceding schools, emerge as aspects of an integrated philosophical and aesthetic worldview, establishing "symbolism as a worldview," rather than a separate direction in literature.

If a global and synthetic approach is characteristic of Vyacheslav Ivanov, the second most important theoretician of Russian symbolism, Andrei Bely, uses primarily an analytic approach to problems of literature. Sharing Vyacheslav Ivanov's general aesthetic views, which go back to Vladimir Solovyov (temporary disagreements, connected with the "mystic anarchism" of Ivanov, and later with the anthroposophy of Bely, are immaterial here), Bely separates poetry from the history of art, and lyric poetry from among a variety of poetic kinds and genres, and studies it from the side of the versified form specific to this genre. Continuing the analytic separation of his subject, Bely then selects the iambic tetrameter and proceeds to anatomize it by way of a meticulous count of all deviations from the "regular" meter, establishing the existing variety of rhythmic variations within its boundaries. Only following Bely's studies, which entered into his book, Symbolism (1910), did the study of VERSIFICATION become a separate discipline of Russian literary scholarship. Even today scores of university professors and hundreds of graduate students are working out the details of the statistics of rhythmic variations, using the methods, terminology and nomenclature of versification theory first developed by Bely.

Meanwhile Bely himself, leaving his discovery to academic scholarship, went on to problems of the melodics of verse (in his studies of 1922–23) and to an intonational theory of verse rhythm, which he developed in a monograph, "Rhythm as Dialectics" (Ritm kak dialektika, 1929). Bely made his principal discovery at the extreme end of his analytic separation, showing convincingly, first, that verse genres are distinguished from artistic prose by a specific expressiveness of intonational movement, fixed by verse rhythm; second, that in lyric poetry an indissoluble unity of intonational gesture and verse rhythm is precisely that element of "content-and-form" (formosoderzhanie) which creates the artistic wholeness of a lyric poem; and third, that an inimitable intonation, artistically fixed by equally inimitable rhythms, transmits to succeeding generations the unique and idiosyncratic "voice" of every genuine poet. In a genuine work of lyric poetry, rhythm "is given forever: the poet dies, but the intonation is written into it." Thus, Bely's specialized and inherently analytic studies in versification led him back to problems of general aesthetics. As far as lyric poetry is concerned, he gives entirely new

answers to questions regarding this genre of verbal art, such as the problem of artistic wholeness, unity of form and content, the connection between the artist's individual originality and the general artistic meaning of his works.

After the Revolution of 1917 the traditional schools of Russian literary scholarship gradually became inactive, retaining their importance only in academic teaching. On the surface at least, scholarly life was dominated during the first decade of the Soviet regime by two vociferous schools: the formal school (see FORMALISM) and that particular variety of sociological literary scholarship which called itself MARXIST and hence raised a claim to "hegemony."

The first shoots of a formal approach to literature appeared even before the Revolution as theoretical backup of certain slogans of the Russian FUTURISTS (budetlyane), as in V. SHKLOVSKY's "Resurrection of the Word" (Voskreshenie slova, 1914) and his articles in the first two Collections in the Area of the Theory of Poetic Language (Sborniki po teorii poeticheskogo yazyka, 1916, 1917), as well as the articles in the same collections by Osip BRIK (on sound repetition) and L. P. Yakubinsky (on "glossemolinkage"—glossemosochetanie). This was a polemic against the symbolists and against the "linguistic poetics" of the followers of Potebnya, and for the futurists' "word as such" (samovitoe slovo) and their break with classical traditions. However, the origin of the formal school must be dated by the publication of the miscellany Poetika in 1919, in which, in addition to reprints from the two preceding collections of the OPOYAZ, there also appeared B. M. EIKHENBAUM's article, "How Gogol's Overcoat Is Made" (Kak sdelana "Shinel'" Gogolya), as well as his bibliographic note on German studies in the areas of "acoustic philology" and metrics. In the same miscellany, Shklovsky goes beyond polemics about language, as he formulates the main principles of the formal school (see his articles, "Art as Device" and "The Connection between Devices of Plot Construction and General Stylistic Devices"—Iskusstvo kak priem, Svyaz' priemov syuzhetoslozheniya s obshchimi priemami stilya). Soon enough several other talented scholars from the Russian Institute of the History of the Arts in Petrograd (Yu. N. TYNYANOV, B. V. TOMASHEVSKY, V. M. ZHIRMUNSKY) and the Moscow Linguistic Circle (R. O. JAKOBSON, P. G. Bogatyrev, G. O. VINOKUR, etc.) joined this movement. There appeared a series of monographs which applied the formal principle to the history of literature, such as Yu. N. Tynyanov's Dostoevsky and Gogol: On the Theory of Parody (1921) and B. M. Eikhenbaum's The Melodics of Russian Lyric Verse (1922).

The history of the Russian formal school may be divided into two periods. Between 1919 and 1923 the circle of its participants grew. At the same time it worked out its methods of research and introduced new material. Its difference from the formal method in Western art history and literary scholarship is clearly defined. It amounts to a certain extremism of the Russian formalists in the realization of their principle of a "material aesthetics," as the essence of artistic literature is reduced to a combination of "material" (verbal and factual) and "devices," specifically the formalization (oformlenie) and "defamiliarization" of this "material," while the category of content is banned beyond the boundaries of literary scholarship as "extra-aesthetic."

The second period in the development of the formal school (1924–30) is marked by certain losses in membership, as some scholars returned to more traditional conceptions and methods. Even in 1922 there arose a polemic featuring V. Zhirmunsky, at first against B. Eikhenbaum and later against all that distinguished the Russian formal school from a similar direction in the West (along the lines of Oskar Walzel) and from the "acoustic philology" of E. Sievers. At the time even Zhirmunsky himself stayed within the limits of a "material aesthetics," as did the followers of the formal method in the West. G. Vinokur and later V. V. Vinogradov left to pursue problems and methods of linguistic stylistics, while O. Brik and V. Shklovsky returned to journal criticism and belles lettres.

Meanwhile the Leningrad group of literary scholars (B. Eikhenbaum, Yu. Tynyanov, and B. Tomashevsky) went through an inner evolution within the formal school and increased its membership, drawing on their students at the Institute of the History of the Arts (G. A. GUKOVSKY, L. Ya. GINZBURG, T. Yu. Khmelnitskaya, etc.) This evolution led the group to a study of problems of general aesthetics in the area of poetics, and to a move toward a deeper historicism in the history of literature. In his Problems of Poetic Language

(Problemy stikhotvornogo yazyka, 1924), Tynyanov raises the question of the artistic wholeness of the work of poetry and of the "constructive factor" (konstruktivnyi faktor) which makes for this wholeness, that is, of one of the main criteria of artistic quality (khudozhestvennost'). He asserted that "the unity of a work is not a closed symmetric whole, but an expanding dynamic wholeness (tselostnost'); its elements are not connected by a static sign of equality or addition, but always by a dynamic sign of correspondence and integration." This meant that not only for Tynyanov himself, but also for the entire formal school, the stage of description, survey, systematization, and nomenclature of literary forms and their elements had come to an end, and that it was now facing more complicated theoretical tasks of aesthetic analysis and evaluation. This was recognized by B. Tomashevsky in a letter to V. Shklovsky, dated 12 April 1925 (see *Slavica Hierosolymitana*, 3 [1978], pp. 384–88).

Literary-historical studies produced by the formal school during this period go beyond the study of an isolated "thing" (veshch') or correlation of "things," as "literary life" (literaturnyi byt) and "literary relations" of a given age, and hence prevailing tastes, friendly relations, the personality and biography of writers, in a word, that which M. BAKHTIN at the time called "the ideological horizon of an epoch," were introduced more and more intensively. There was an increased interest in archival, epistolary, and journal material of a given period, as well as in writers of the "second and third rank" (see, e.g., Tynyanov's *Arkhaisty i novatory*, L. Ginzburg's studies of Vyazemsky, etc.) Even in B. Eikhenbaum's studies of that period (on Lermontov and L. TOLSTOI), the "historical destiny" of these writers moves to the forefront, which is quite in agreement with the author's observation that "creation is the act of becoming conscious of oneself in the stream of history." The principal merit of the formal school lies with its predominant concern with the specific traits of verbal art, both in poetics, and in particular, in the history of "literature proper" (literaturnyi ryad). These problems could no longer be avoided by subsequent directions of Russian literary scholarship, while the onesidedness of their solution was overcome, very largely with the aid of "former formalists."

During the first period of the existence of the formal school the polemic initiative had been largely on its side. Starting with the mid-1920s, it worked under conditions of constant critical attacks on its principles. Objections which touched upon the essence of the problems involved were raised mainly by independent critics who were not associated with any particular school. The most significant example of this criticism is the book *The Formal Method in Literary Scholarship* (Formal'nyi metod v literaturovedenii, 1928), written in the main by M. M. Bakhtin, but published under the name of P. N. Medvedev, who gave it a semblance of a Marxist approach to the subject. But the heaviest polemic attacks came from the side of official criticism, such as a discussion in the journal PECHAT' I REVOLYUTSIYA, concluded by an article by A. V. LUNACHARSKY in 1924; repeated discussions in 1925 and 1927; systematically negative reviews in literary journals, etc. After the "year of the great change" (1929), a broad and systematic persecution of non-Marxist ("anti-Marxist") directions in all areas of the humanities began, serving the purpose of their total unification. Even though formalism was officially condemned only in 1936, the formal school actually dissolved in 1930. Shklovsky published an article, "A Monument to a Scholarly Error" (Pamyatnik nauchnoi oshibke, *Literaturnaya gazeta*, 27 January 1930). Other formalists switched to "applied" literary scholarship: textual preparation, commentaries, and introductions or postfaces of new editions of old authors. This circumstance determined for many years to come the high quality of book editing in Russia. The very term tekstologiya (TEXTUAL CRITICISM) belongs to B. Tomashevsky, as does the scientific elaboration of the methods of this discipline.

Marxist literary scholarship of that period had by no means a unified direction. Rather, it was distinguished by a medley of theoretical "positions" (ustanovka) and levels of sophistication, from worship of a "psychology of collectivism" in the PROLETKULT movement and implacable opposition to the principle of individuality found in RAPP, to more elaborate historical-literary conceptions and theoretical structures. By 1929 there existed two variants of Marxist literary scholarship, one of them headed by V. M. FRICHE and the other by V. F. PEREVERZEV. Both had made their debut as Marxist literary scholars even before the Revolution. Both considered PLEKHANOV to have been the founder of Marxist literary scholarship in Russia, yet each dealt with the Plekhanovian tradition in an entirely different manner.

V. Friche produced a truly immense number of concrete examples for Plekhanov's basic formula suggesting a firm causal dependance of literary evolution on the evolution of economic structure and successive changes in the interaction of social classes. He applied Plekhanov's version of Marxism more consistently than Plekhanov himself, who possessed a well-developed literary taste and therefore easily departed from his own understanding of "class analysis" when making literary judgments. Friche refused to go a step beyond Plekhanov's conceptions, rigidly subjecting the entire history of European literatures to the principle of economic determinacy. Having advanced the category of style as central in the history of literature, he would then establish the automatic dependance of a change in style on a change in the methods of production and the ascendancy of a new ruling class. The rather flat determinism of Plekhanov's "scientific aesthetics" became quite sterile in Friche's "concretizations," essentially exercises in a dead scholasticism. In Friche's followers, primarily critics of the RAPP camp, these traits were enhanced by their personal ignorance and aggressiveness in the struggle for "hegemony" in the literary life of the country (something quite alien to Friche himself). But his deadening dogmatism made him a convenient official figure. He occupied key administrative posts in the area of literary scholarship until his death in 1929.

"The School of Pereverzev" presented a substantially different version of Marxist literary scholarship. While he also held on to "Plekhanovian orthodoxy," Pereverzev was a man capable of conceptual thought and interpreted Plekhanov quite liberally in order to advance "class analysis" to the level of systems of imagery and the artistic texture of a work of art. This goal was realized by him with the greatest consistency in his books on Dostoevsky and on Gogol. Pereverzev paid serious attention to only one type of literary image, namely that of the hero, considering all other forms of literary imagery to be mere means toward the characterization of a work's personages. The old definition of poetry (taken by Belinsky from Hegel, and by Plekhanov from Belinsky) which said that poetry is "thinking in images," was changed by Pereverzev to say that poetry is "the thinking of images," that is, the opinions and thoughts of the heroes of works of literature, invariably expressing those of the author himself. According to Pereverzev, even a writer of genius has no access to the psychology or thought patterns of individuals belonging to a class environment other than his own. Here he uses, after his own fashion, a treatment of art as play, which Plekhanov had taken from Schiller: a writer, says Pereverzev "plays" the roles of his personages, not becoming "reincarnate" in them, but merely "dressing up" in the costumes of people of various ages and social classes. All this was of course a most naive vulgarization of the sociological method in general and of Marxist conceptions of class ideology in particular.

However, it was precisely this liberty of Pereverzev's interpretation of Plekhanov's "scientific aesthetics" that allowed him to introduce into his "class analysis" some apt observations on certain literary texts and even to maintain a certain independence of verbal art from political dictate. Thus, he develops a theory of "parallel ranks" (parallel'nye ryady) of ideology which depend similarly on the "base," but not on one another. Hence came his denial of an essential role played by preliminary "ideal intent" (ideinyi zamysel) in a work of literature and his demand that the researcher should remain "eye to eye" with the work. All this contradicted not only Plekhanov, but also LENIN's principle of the PARTIINOST' of literature, as well as the right and the duty of party politics to invade the sphere of literary creation. Pereverzev's concrete literary valuations also went against the official view. Thus, he identified Dostoevsky as a "petit-bourgeois" but nevertheless a "great artist and psychologist," and his novel *The Possessed*, not as a libel of the Revolution, as Lenin and Gorky had said, but a prophetic revelation of the petit-bourgeois quality of the Russian revolutionary attitude. If one adds to this that Pereverzev gave the 1922 and 1928 editions of his book on Dostoevsky a "Preface" in which he speaks of an inevitable "dissolution" (rastvorenie) of the Russian revolutionary attitude in the element of the Russian petite bourgeoisie, one cannot deny him the virtues of courage and sincere conviction. It came as no surprise that Pereverzev drew a following among young literary scholars (he taught at Moscow State University and held no "leading" positions), the so-called Pereverzevian School (I. Bespalov, G. Pospelov, U. Fokht, etc.), which even came out with a collective volume of articles, *Literaturovedenie* (1928).

The above makes it clear why measures directed at a unification of literary scholarship did not start with a persecution of the formal school (which never claimed to speak in the name of Marxism), but rather with a discussion, "On Pereverzev's Conception," which became the first of a series of "discussions," sanctioned by the Party leadership with the intent of provocation: views existing in a given area were to be brought out into the open, whereupon the Party would choose who should be victorious and who should be routed. The initiators of these discussions, conducted in print at first, were some critics of the RAPP group (G. Gorbachev, V. Ermilov, Yu. LIBEDINSKY, etc.). Oral discussions began at the Communist Academy in November 1929 and were joined by L. AVERBAKH, V. Sutyrin, V. KIRSHON, and others. These discussions went on for nearly two months in a tone of genuine debate. But in January *Pravda* published an article against "Pereverzevianism" (*pereverzevshchina*) and the methods of discussion underwent a sharp change. Political accusations were voiced, and not only against Pereverzev himself, concerning his former Menshevism, but also against his students, for their insufficiently resolute renunciation of their teacher. At this point, renunciations took on a massive character (it seems that only U. Fokht did not join them), so that the Pereverzevian School was routed certainly not by the force of argument, a development which now became typical of the fate of Russian literary scholarship.

The victors' triumph was short-lived. Two years later they were in turn liquidated without any discussion, by a simple decree of the Central Committee of the Communist Party, "On the Restructuring of Literary and Artistic Organizations" (O perestroike literaturno-khudozhestvennykh organizatsii, 23 April 1932). A few years later, members of both directions were for the most part "repressed": Pereverzev, but also Bespalov, who had renounced him, and Gorbachev, Averbakh, Kirshon, and others. Pereverzev was the only one of them to return after his rehabilitation.

In the 1930s and 1940s still another prolonged literary discussion took place, connected with the emergence of a new version of Marxist literary scholarship not anticipated earlier. In the process of preparing, but especially after the appearance of the first volumes of the *Collected Works* of Marx and Engels, there began the study and systematization of their utterances on art and literature. Taken as a whole, these utterances presented a system of aesthetic views which was quite incompatible with what heretofore had gone for Marxist literary scholarship. In 1932, M. A. Lifshits's article on the aesthetic views of Marx appeared in the 6th volume of *Literaturnaya entsiklopediya*, and in 1933 an enlarged version of it ("Karl Marks i voprosy iskusstva") came out as a separate brochure. Lifshits also prepared a chrestomathy, *K. Marks i F. Engel's ob iskusstve* (1st ed. 1933, 2d much enlarged ed. with commentary by G. FRIDLENDER and A. Vygodskii, 1938).

Much more so than his brochure, Lifshits's chrestomathy was "an attempt to present the views of Marx on the general course of the historical process from a side never illuminated before." In fact, this was not only an attempt to reconstruct, from a multitude of isolated statements, an integrated aesthetic of Marx, but also a new version of Marxism, a new interpretation of historical materialism which included all the elements of a traditional philosophy of culture: an integrated model of the history of mankind, its past, present, and future; "the meaning of history," given by the historical evolution of the "human essence" or the "essential powers of man," which in the communist future were to form the "universal individual" (corresponding to the "universal" development of productive forces and social relations); the role of the ever deepening contradictions in this process during the epoch of civilization. In this version of Marxism, art and poetry could claim an incomparably more important and independent role than had appeared earlier, so that the followers of a "Plekhanovian orthodoxy" in literary scholarship now found themselves cast into the role of exponents of "VULGAR SOCIOLOGISM." Their demand for a "class analysis" of literature had lost its overriding importance and acquired a totally different meaning: in "ideological forms" which mirror the views

and interests of a given social class, artistic and literary values may be developed which retain their importance for succeeding generations as achievements of mental culture. "Class analysis" is actually needed in order to make accessible and meaningful in contemporary terms precisely those permanent achievements of culture which had come about in a framework of class limitations and class prejudices.

As for the alleged fact that literature is "determined" by economic facts, "class existence" (*klassovoe byt'e*), and such, the real content of this problem was now linked primarily to the development of literature as a particular form of "mental production" (*dukhovnoe proizvodstvo*) along with other kinds of artistic activity. According to Marx, this had happened only as a result of the "great division of labor" (*velikoe razdelenie truda*), physical and mental, and the emergence of private property and antagonistic social classes. The matter was thus reduced to the perfectly traditional problem of the emergence of various forms of art and poetry from primeval syncretism. Altogether, this new version of Marxist literary scholarship "rehabilitated" almost the entire set of problems which the traditional schools of Russian literary scholarship had dealt with, and in particular that of the specific nature of art in general and of verbal art in particular.

In contradistinction to the formal school and "vulgar sociologism" this new direction recognized the independent cognitive potential of belles lettres, assuming that the creative writer can penetrate those aspects of human relations, emotions, and movements of the soul which are hardly accessible to conceptual, theoretical cognition. Thus, the specific quality of belles lettres starts even with its object of cognition, that is, the specific quality of its content, inseparably linked to the specific nature and variety of its forms and to the regularities inherent in the "column of literature" (*literaturnyi ryad*). But the role of art and poetry is not exhausted by their cognitive powers. They also are a creative force in the history of mankind and society. In artistic creations we find fixed and secured that particular level of inner capabilities and creative potential which human nature has attained at a given point in the course of history. This view returned literary scholarship to those problems which had been advanced by the Russian symbolists in connection with their conception of "life-building art" (*iskusstvo-zhiznestroenie*), though here the power of art to change man and life was asserted in the name of historical materialism and was linked to the task of educating the roundly developed "universal" individual of the future.

The list of such "returns" to old problems, though requiring further rethinking and elaboration, could be extended. The main thing was, however, that in every case the matter at hand did not amount to the "application" of ready Marxist truths to literary material, but rather required factual investigation of each problem and new theoretical interest in the subject. Not surprisingly, then, the new version of Marxist literary scholarship attracted a significant number of young literary scholars, both of the "writing" and the merely reading variety. As early as in 1933 a journal of literary studies, *Literaturnyi kritik*, was founded, becoming the organ of this new version of Marxist literary scholarship, and in 1936 a critical-bibliographic periodical, *Literaturnoe obozrenie*, was attached to it. The number of contributors to this journal grew rapidly, contributing to the consolidation of "the trend" (*techenie*), as this direction of Marxist literary scholarship got to be called. Among the most active collaborators of the journal were V. Aleksandrov, I. Vertsman, V. Grib, F. Levin, M. Lifshits, G. Lukács (who was residing in Moscow at the time), A. Makedonov, I. Sats, E. Usievich, Yu. Yuzovsky, a. o. The "trend" was also supported by some philosophers, such as M. Rozental, who was responsible editor of *Literaturnyi kritik*, V. Kemenov, and others.

The journal printed articles on the history of Russian and foreign literature, on the theory of literature, and on general aesthetics. As far as questions of contemporary literature were concerned, the journal took a rather independent position. It spoke out against "bureaucratic optimism," and "illustrative" literature (as in a discussion of *Slava* by Viktor Gusev), and against everything that was later called "glossing over of reality" (*lakirovka deistvitel'nosti*). *Literaturnyi kritik* was first to come up with a serious review and evaluation of A. MAKARENKO's *A Pedagogic Epic*, Yu. KRYMOV's *The Tanker* Derbent, and A. TVARDOVSKY's *The Land of Muraviya*. It was the only journal which ardently supported Andrei PLATONOV (in spite of Stalin's terrible "resolution" on one of his stories) and gave him an opportunity to engage in literary work as an essayist (under the pseudonym F. Chelovekov).

The struggle of the journal against "vulgar sociologism" was perhaps the only instance of successful ideological struggle which did not involve the use of "organizational" pressure from above. All this caused the "trend" and its journal to become unpopular in wide circles of literary mediocrity, both in the recently formed UNION OF SOVIET WRITERS as well as among critics whose vanity *Literaturnyi kritik* had offended. The situation led to a new literary polemic which began in November 1939. It was launched by articles by E. Knipovich in *Internatsional'naya literatura* (no. 11) and *Literaturnaya gazeta* (15 November 1939), directed against G. Lukács's book *From the History of Realism* (Iz istorii realizma). M. Lifshits responded in an article, "One is Tired of It" (Nadoelo, *Literaturnaya gazeta*, 10 January 1940), to which Knipovich replied with her own article, "Nothing You Can Do" (Nichego ne podelat', *Literaturnaya gazeta*, 15 January 1940). The discussion lasted for several months and involved many authors and several periodicals. On the "attacking side" (besides Knipovich), V. Ermilov, I. Altman, and V. Kirpotin, then better known as a major government official in literary affairs, figured most prominently. Nevertheless, the "trend" defended itself quite actively and for a while it seemed that it might win. By that time, people were already accustomed to seeing Party leadership act as arbiter in all kinds of arguments, including those in the humanities, and the Party was indirectly supporting the struggle against "vulgar sociologism," condemning an analogous "vulgarization" found in the conceptions of the late historian M. N. Pokrovsky, and was also favoring the idea of NARODNOST' in literature, which gave a "Marxist" foundation to the pre-war restructuring of Stalin's propaganda along nationalist-patriotic lines.

However, the debate was stopped while still in full swing, and again by a purely "organizational" decision. A decree of the Central Committee of the Communist Party, "On Literary Criticism and Bibliography," in the journal *Partiinoe stroitel'stvo* (1940, No. 22) stated, among other things, that "publication of the journal *Literaturnyi kritik*, isolated from writers and from literature, needed to be stopped," and that the journal *Literaturnoe obozrenie* would be handed over to the Gorky Institute of World Literature (see INSTITUT MIROVOI LITERATURY, "to be reorganized into a bibliographic manual of recommended titles in the area of belles lettres." The literary scholars of *Literaturnyi kritik*, too convinced of the superiority of their version of Marxism, were not considered fit to conduct Stalin's policies in the area of culture and were shown their place.

After the victory over Hitler's Germany, when an organized offensive was launched against all forms of artistic culture (by the decree of the Central Committee on the journals *Zvezda* and *Leningrad* of 14 August 1946 and other analogous directives), literary scholarship was among the first to feel the brunt of the attack. A. FADEEV, head of the Union of Soviet Writers, declared in a report to that body that Aleksandr Veselovsky and his school were "the main progenitor of kowtowing before the West as practiced by a certain branch of Russian literary scholarship in the past as well as in the present." This served as a signal for a general "working over" of prominent literary scholars in print as well as at well-attended public meetings. Thus, at the Philological Faculty of Leningrad University, V. Zhirmunsky, B. Eikhenbaum, V. PROPP, M. Azadovsky, and many others were subjected to public insults. They were asked to make a public renunciation of the ideas of Veselovsky, as well as of their own works. "The persecution of scholarship assumed the form of harassment of scholars. A police action which had begun in such organs of defamation as *Kul'tura i zhizn'* and *Literaturnaya gazeta* expanded directly to institutions of higher learning and scholarly institutes.... All scholarly analogies were labelled "cosmopolitanism," a term which had a terrible ("political") meaning," writes O. M. Freidenberg in her *Memoirs*, referring to the year 1948.

After the article "On a Certain Antipatriotic Group of Theatre Critics" (*Pravda*, 28 January 1949), the campaign against "cosmopolitanism" reached its height. To quote Olga Freidenberg: "Moral and intellectual pogroms spread over the whole body of Russia like a deadly plague.... Those active in cultural life who had Jewish names were subjected to moral lynching. You should have seen the atmosphere of pogroms which went on in our Faculty.... The whole university was routed. All the main professors were dismissed. Killing off the remainders of the intelligentsia goes on without interruption." Heart attacks and strokes were not the worst of the effects of being "worked over." Some of the scholars were arrested, as were G. A. Gukovsky in Leningrad ("posthumously rehabilitated"), L. E. Pinsky and other literary scholars in Moscow, E. G. Spivak in Kiev ("posthumously rehabilitated"). Unfortunately, it is impossible either to present, or to understand the history of Russian literary scholarship during a whole quarter of a century (1929–53) without investigating circumstances which are quite outside the sphere of scholarly thought.

Khrushchev's "Thaw" and the entire post-Stalin period of Russian literary scholarship produced works of lasting value precisely because the results of the labors of "independent" literary scholars who during those years had hardly gone beyond their teaching duties and had written "for their desk drawers" (*v stol*) only, entered scholarly circulation during this period. Olga Freidenberg, who is quoted earlier in this article, may serve as an example. The organizer of the first department of classical philology during the Soviet period (Leningrad University, 1932), she managed to publish her doctoral dissertation, "The Poetics of Sujet and Genre" (1936), but from that time until her death in 1955 could publish nothing except brief résumés of her numerous works, in which she connects the evolution of language with the transition from "mythological" thinking to the forms of artistic literature. These works were beginning to get published only in the 1970s. L. Vygodsky's book on problems of the psychology of the creative process and the reception of art, *The Psychology of Art* (Psikhologiya iskusstva), written in 1925, was only published in 1965. The best-known and perhaps the most flagrant example of such belated—though in this case happily not posthumous—recognition is the fate of the works of M. M. Bakhtin. It may be added that during the post-Stalin period the works of many "repressed" literary scholars, such as G. A. Gukovsky, P. N. Medvedev, D. P. SVYATOPOLK-MIRSKY, and others, were either published or republished, as were the works of earlier scholars, some of them classics already: Yu. Tynyanov, B. Eikhenbaum, B. Tomashevsky, V. Zhirmunsky, V. V. Gippius, A. P. Skaftymov, and others. Thus, it becomes clear that a reconstruction of the continuity of Russian literary thought, even in general outline, is becoming possible only today—in spite of everything that has stood in the way of such task.

Bibliography, 19th century: B. M. Engel'gardt, *Aleksandr Nikolaevich Veselovskii*. 1924. N. K. Gudzii, *N. S. Tikhonravov*. 1956. ———, "O russkom literaturovedcheskom nasledstve," *Vestnik MGU* (Istoriko-filologicheskaya seriya), 1957, no. 1. ———, *Izuchenie russkoi literatury v Moskovskom universitete (Dooktyabr'skii period)*. 1958. ———, *Vozniknovenie russkoi nauki o literature*. 1975. ———, *Akademicheskie shkoly v russkom literaturovedenii*. 1975. I. Ivan'o and A. Kolodnaya, "Esteticheskaya kontseptsiya A. Potebni." In A. A. Potebnya, *Estetika i poetika* (1976). N. V. Os'makov, *Psikhologicheskoe napravlenie v russkom literaturovedenii: D. N. Ovsyaniko-Kulikovskii*. 1981. A. N. Pypin, "Voprosy literaturnoi istorii," *Vestnik Evropy*, 1893, no. 10. V. F. Shishmarev, *Aleksandr Veselovskii i russkoe literaturovedenie*. 1946. S. V. Smirnov, *Fedor Ivanovich Buslaev*. 1978. D. E. Tamarchenko, "Istoricheskaya poetika A. N. Veselovskogo," *Zvezda*, 1939, no. 5. N. S. Tikhonravov, *Zadachi istorii literatury i metody ee izucheniya* (1876). In his *Sochineniya*. Vol. 1. 1898. A. N. Veselovskii, "O metode i zadachakh istorii literatury kak nauki" (1870). In his *Istoricheskaya poetika*. 1940. V. M. Zhirmunskii. "Istoricheskaya poetika A. N. Veselovskogo." In A. N. Veselovskii, *Istoricheskaya poetika*. 1940.

20th century: E. L. Belkind, "Teoriya i psikhologiya tvorchestva v neopublikovannom kurse lektsii Vyach. Ivanova v Bakinskom gos. universitete (1921–1922)." In *Psikhologiya protsessov khudozhestvennogo tvorchestva*. 1980. G. M. Fridlender, "K. Marks i F. Engel's o literature." In *KLE*, Vol. 4 (1967). Mikhail Lifshits, *Karl Marks. Iskusstvo i obshchestvennyi ideal*. 1979. P. N. Medvedev, *Formal'nyi metod v literaturovedenii*. 1928. (The greater part of this text belongs to M. M. Bakhtin.) V. F. Pereverzev, ed., *Literaturovedenie. Sbornik statei*. 1928. *Russkaya nauka o literature v kontse*

XIX–nachale XX v. 1982. P. N. Sakulin, *Sinteticheskoe postroenie istorii literatury.* 1925. *Sovetskoe literaturovedenie za 50 let.* Moscow, 1967. *Sovetskoe literaturovedenie za 50 let.* Leningrad, 1968.

A. T.
G. T.

School drama began as a pedagogical exercise during the Renaissance. In order to familiarize students with classical Roman drama and at the same time to further their knowledge of Latin, plays of Plautus, Terence, and Seneca were staged. The repertoire of classical plays was also augmented by works written in Latin by contemporary authors in imitation of the classics. For the sake of relief from the seriousness of the play proper, short skits or "interludes" of a comic character and in the vernacular language were performed between the acts. During the Counter-Reformation, school drama was cultivated by the Jesuits as another weapon in the campaign against Protestantism. In their adaptation of the traditional school drama of the Renaissance, however, the Jesuits developed their own repertoire. This consisted mainly of material taken from the Bible or from the lives of saints and often made use of abstract allegorical figures. Productions were frequently elaborate, involving music and complex stage machinery capable of a wide range of special effects. This type of school drama was integrated into the program of the academies operated by the Jesuits in the late 16th and 17th centuries in Poland. When the KIEV ACADEMY was founded in 1632, the Polish Jesuit schools provided the model. School drama patterned after that of the Jesuit institutions but adapted to Orthodox needs also became a regular feature of the Academy's curriculum. It was from this tradition that SIMEON POLOTSKY drew when he was invited to write dramatic works for the new court theater of the Tsar Aleksei Mikhailovich. Both the *Tragedy of King Nebuchadnezzar, or The Golden Calf,* based on the Book of Daniel, and the *Comedy of the Prodigal Son,* a dramatization of the New Testament parable, conform generally to the pattern of the Jesuit school drama but lack allegorical figures. More traditional in this respect were the plays, mostly on biblical subjects, by Daniil Tuptalo, the Metropolitan of Rostov (Dimitry ROSTOVSKY), for the students of the monastery school which he founded in Rostov. The best known of these are *The Birth of Christ* (Rozhdestvo Khristovo), *The Resurrection of Christ* (Voskresenie Khristovo), and *The Ascension Play* (Uspenskaya drama). A superior dramatist to Polotsky, Tuptalo achieved a greater degree of realism by interweaving the comic characters and episodes normally found in the interludes with the main action of the play. But like Polotsky he wrote exclusively in syllabic verse. School drama continued to be cultivated in Russia after the establishment of public theaters in the early 18th century, most notably in the Slavonic-Greek-Latin Academy in Moscow which was opened in 1687, and in the Moscow Hospital, the first Russian medical school (founded in 1706).

Bibliography: I. M. Badalich and V. D. Kuz'mina, *Pamyatniki russkoi shkol'noi dramy XVIII veka (po Zagrebskim spiskam).* 1968. *P'esy shkol'nykh teatrov Moskvy.* Ed. A. S. Demin. 1974.

H. B. S.

Science fiction, see UTOPIAN LITERATURE.

Scythianism, Scythians (*skifstvo, skify*), a conception of Russia's historical identity widespread in the early 20th century. It was based on the notion of an inherent duality in the national character of the Russian people: half-European and half-Asian. Aleksandr BLOK's poem "Scythians" (Skify, 1918) is a celebrated expression of this idea. Other symbolists, such as Andrei BELY and Vyacheslav IVANOV likewise used both the term and the idea, following the lead of Vladimir SOLOVYOV. More specifically, "Scythianism" meant an affirmation of Russia's Asian identity, understood as spontaneous and dynamic, though also savage and chaotic. The "Scythian" element was prominent in the HYLAEAN stage of Russian FUTURISM (1912–13). In an essay, "Scythians" (1918), Evgeny ZAMYATIN sees the "Scythian" as the eternal nomad, always in revolt against the constraints of civilization and hence a born revolutionary. A truly creative individual must therefore be a "Scythian." In 1917 and 1918 a group of writers and poets identified themselves as "Scythians" (*Skify*). The group's ideologue was the critic R. V. IVANOV-

RAZUMNIK, and Andrei Bely, Sergei ESENIN, and Nikolai KLYUEV belonged to it, among others. Two volumes of an almanac, *Skify,* appeared in 1917 and 1918. It was taken as continuing the political line of the earlier *Zavety* (Testaments, 1912–14), an organ of the Social Revolutionaries. A "Skify" publishing house of the same political direction existed in Berlin in the early 1920s, organized by E. G. Lundberg (1887–1965).

Bibliography: E. Zamyatin, "Scythians." In *A Soviet Heretic: Essays* by Yevgeny Zamyatin, ed. and trans. Mirra Ginsburg. 1970. Pp. 21–33.

V. T.

Seifúllina, Lídiya Nikoláevna (1889–1954), writer and playwright. Although she was the daughter of an Orthodox priest and a member of the Social Revolutionary Party (1917–19), Seifullina, a schoolteacher by profession, succeeded in making a spectacular career as a Soviet writer. Her stories of the early 1920s, dealing with the effect of the Revolution on simple men and women in Western Siberia, her home region, were generally well received. Unlike other Soviet writers of that period, Seifullina gave unpretentious, realistic accounts of what had happened, or could have happened in the Russian countryside. Her short novel, *Virineya* (1924), which tells the tragic story of a peasant woman's struggle for true emancipation, was made into a successful play and staged even abroad. Other stories, such as "Mulch" (Peregnoi, 1922) and "Lawbreakers" (Pravonarushiteli, 1922), were more optimistic, showing how the Revolution gave former misfits a fresh start. After the 1920s Seifullina was not very productive as a writer of fiction, but was very active as a journalist and educator.

Works: Sobranie sochinenii. 6 vols. 1929–31. *Sobranie sochinenii.* 4 vols. 1968–69.

Translations: "The Old Woman." In *Azure Cities. Stories of New Russia.* Ed. Joshua Kunitz. 1929. "The Lawbreakers." In *Soviet Literature,* ed. George Reavey and Marc L. Slonim. 1934.

Secondary literature: V. Kardin, *Dve sud'by: Lidiya Seifullina i ee povest'* Virineya. 1975. A. Voronskii, *Literaturno-kriticheskie stat'i.* 1963. N. Yanovskii, *Lidiya Seifullina: Kritiko-biograficheskii ocherk.* 2d ed. 1972.

V. T.

Selvinsky, Ilyá (real given name: Karl) Lvóvich (1899–1968), poet, playwright, and writer. Born in Simferopol (Crimea), the son of a furrier, Selvinsky led an eventful life. He worked at odd jobs, including stevedore and circus wrestler, then graduated from the Moscow University Faculty of Social Sciences (1923). A leader of the Literary Center of CONSTRUCTIVISTS since its inception in 1924, Selvinsky brought out his first volume of verse, *Records* (Rekordy), in 1926. Successful in his literary endeavors, Selvinsky nevertheless continued to live an adventurous life. In 1929 he worked as an instructor of fur farming in Kirghizia. In 1933 he participated in a polar expedition and thereafter travelled widely in Europe and Asia. All these experiences are amply reflected in his works. He served as an officer in World War II and continued to be restlessly active until the end of his life.

Selvinsky was the only major figure among the constructivists who actually followed their theoretical program. He consciously and consistently integrated every aspect of his work with its poetic intent. This involved not only vocabulary and dialect (such as thieves' cant, Odessa Jewish, Gypsy, technical jargon, etc.), but also syntax, rhythm, imagery, and general style. Selvinsky was also one of the first Soviet writers to do serious technical research toward his literary work and to view writing poetry as a goal-directed rational activity.

Selvinsky's specialty was the long (sometimes very long) verse epic. The first of these, "The Ulyalaev Uprising" (Ulyalaevshchina, written in 1924, published in 1927), deals with the rout of a counter-revolutionary peasant uprising by communist forces. The next, "A Poet's Notebooks" (Zapiski poeta, 1928) consists of two parts: the "autobiography" of a poet with many philosophical and aesthetic digressions, and a collection of the poet's verses, "The Silken Moon" (Shelkovaya luna). There followed "Fur Business" (Pushtorg, 1929), almost a novel in verse, whose plot is that of a standard socialist realist production novel: an honest communist administrator battles careerists and bureaucrats; the forces of reaction are routed in the end.

Selvinsky's plays, also in verse, followed the trends of the times. The satirical grotesque *Pao-Pao* (1932), his contribution to Five-Year-Plan literature, features the humanization of an ape (with bourgeois traits) through socialist labor. The most successful of Selvinsky's plays, *A Polar Bear named Umka* (1933), deals with the "leap" of a primitive arctic people across several historical stages into socialism. Selvinsky was not the only Soviet writer to use these particular themes. The humanization of an ape named socialism appears, in travesty to be sure, in E. ZAMYATIN's skit "The Visitor from Africa" (1929–30). A. FADEEV's novel *The Last of the Udege* (1930–33) deals with the integration of a primitive tribe into socialist society. Starting in the late 1930s, Selvinsky followed the prevailing trend toward historical works and produced a series of historical plays, still in verse, culminating in a trilogy, *Russia* (Rossiya), in each of whose parts a simple but heroic man named Chokhov appears at a crucial juncture of Russian history alongside Ivan the Terrible, Peter the Great, and Lenin, respectively (1944–57).

In his later years, Selvinsky reworked several of his earlier works, so "The Ulyalaev Uprising" (1956). It had been criticized for making the *kulak* Ulyalaev more interesting than its communist heroes. Selvinsky changed it all by making Lenin his central character. Shortly before his death, Selvinsky published an autobiographic novel, *Oh, My Youth!* (1966). All along, Selvinsky continued to write lyric poetry, however, generally tamer and more conventional than the poems of his constructivist days. Their earthy concreteness yields to a more philosophic bent. Selvinsky summarized his ideas about poetics and versification in the volume *Studio of Verse* (Studiya stikha, 1962).

Works: Izbrannye sochineniya. 2 vols. 1960. *Sobranie sochinenii.* 6 vols. 1971– . *Izbrannye proizvedeniya.* 1972.

Translations: Modern Russian Poetry. Eds. Vladimir Markov and Merrill Sparks. 1967. Pp. 652–53. *See also: Lewanski,* p. 350.

Secondary literature: Rainer Georg Grübel, "Das frühe Werk Il'ja Sel'vinskijs: Der Entwurf einer konstruktivistischen Poetik," *Wiener slawistischer Almanach* 6 (1980), pp. 83–107. O. Reznik, *Zhizn' v poezii: Tvorchestvo I. Sel'vinskogo.* 1972. Gleb Struve, *Russian Literature under Lenin and Stalin, 1917–1953.* 1971. Pp. 190–91.

V. T.

Semiotics, see STRUCTURALISM AND SEMIOTICS.

Senkóvsky, Ósip Ivánovich (Sękowski, Józef Julian, 1800–1858), writer, critic, scholar, and publisher, came from the Polish gentry and graduated from the University of Wilno in 1819. A brilliant student of oriental languages, he travelled widely in the Near East and worked as an interpreter for the Russian consular service. He was made a professor of Arabic, Persian, and Turkic languages at St. Petersburg University in 1822. He held this chair until 1847 and published many scholarly papers in the field. Senkovsky began to write for Russian periodicals soon after he moved to Petersburg, though he also continued to publish in Polish. From 1834 to 1847 he was the publisher and editor of BIBLIOTEKA DLYA CHTENIYA, a journal which he made into a substantial commercial success. He was himself one of its main contributors, publishing his highly entertaining fiction under the pen name "Baron Brambeus." Senkovsky put his immense learning and the experiences gathered during his travels to excellent use, as he presented a wealth of interesting scientific, historical, and anthropological information in a casual and amusing manner, also lacing his stories with a wry irony. As a critic, Senkovsky had erudition, common sense, and wit, along with his general facility of style. But he lacked empathy, generosity, and seriousness. Senkovsky had no real love or respect for Russian letters and failed to see the greatness of his contemporaries, PUSHKIN and GOGOL. His reviews of the latter's works, in particular, were written to show off the reviewer's ironic wit, rather than to convey an understanding of the work under review.

Works: Sobranie sochinenii. 9 vols. 1858–59.

Secondary literature: V. A. Kaverin, *Baron Brambeus.* 1966. Louis Pedrotti, *J. J. Sękowski: The Genesis of a Literary Alien.* 1965. V. Zil'ber [Kaverin], "Senkovskii (Baron Brambeus)." In *Russkaya proza.* Ed. B. Eikhenbaum and Yu. Tynyanov. 1926. Pp. 159–91.

V. T.

Sentimentalism (*sentimentalízm*) enters the historiography of Russian literature as a term designating a literary movement of 18th-century Russian literature comparatively late, at the end of the 19th century. In BELINSKY, and other 19th-century Russian critics, *sentimental'nost'* is used with reference to a particular aspect of style adopted by KARAMZIN and his school. Paradoxically, Karamzin is not generally viewed sympathetically by the experts on sentimentalism; after the censorship on RADISHCHEV's *Journey* was lifted, and increasingly during his embalmment as a prophet of the Russian Revolution, scholars working in the period show an overwhelming preoccupation with the presumed social and political usefulness of literary works written in the 1770s to the 1800s. Beginning in the 1930s and 1940s sentimentalism is defined in terms of two mutually antagonistic camps: one, headed by Karamzin and his followers, retreated from social struggle, while the other, led by Radishchev wrote with a politically revolutionary purposefulness and commitment. The definition is not a very useful one, as G. Smith shrewdly observes, for the distinction between the two sentimentalisms is developed "to a point at which they can no longer be understood as aspects of one and the same movement." Seeing sentimentalism as a literary movement overlooks the fact that the literature of sentiment, both in Russia and in the West, is not free from, but depends upon, the ideals and ideologies of the ENLIGHTENMENT and also of FREEMASONRY, and upon the literary trends and ideas of preromanticism for its ideas, genres and forms. A more balanced and productive approach is to explore sentimentalism as a *manner* or a mode of expression in vogue in Russia from the 1770s until the 1800s, which adapted itself to and absorbed a remarkable variety of ideas and ideologies, literary trends, and genres. In the historiography of the Western European literatures, increasingly since Van Tieghem's classic comparative study *Le Préromantisme* (1924–27), sentimentalism is subsumed under preromanticism; even though, ironically, sentimentalism in its Western European variants, particularly in France during the Revolution and Terror, is far more extreme and given to excesses (Monglond, *Le Préromantisme français*, 1966, Vol. 2) than in its Russian variant.

The word "sentimental" in England, Erik Eramätsa observes, was used in the 1740s in the sense of opinion, thought, judgment, and only acquires a distinctly emotional coloring in the 1760s, increasingly so after Sterne's *Sentimental Journey* (1768). In 18th-century Russia the corresponding word is not *sentimental'nyi* but *chuvstvitel'nyi*, from *chuvstvo*, "feeling," "emotion" ("sentiment" is ambiguous), and in philosophical prose, the human "sense." *Chuvstvitel'nost'*, close to French "sensibilité" and English "sensibility" (after the 1760s), is defined in the *Academy Dictionary* of 1794 as "the quality of a person who is moved by the unhappiness of another" (*Kachestvo trogayushchegosya cheloveka neschastiem drugogo*). (For *chuvstvitel'nyi* vs. *sentimental'nyi* cf. German *empfindsam* vs. *sentimental*.) No comparable semantic shift occurs with *chuvstvitel'nyi*, although the word's emotional value augments from the 1770s until the 1800s, and in the 1790s is compounded with another quality, "tender." The intrusion of the emotions, or emotional texture of a work, is not new in Russian literature, and has been traced back to the tales and songs of the Petrine period; it might as well be traced back to the "Skazanie knyazei BORISA I GLEBA" of the 11th century with the magnificent pathos and lyricism of Prince Gleb's laments (*plachi*). In any case, the emotional texture in works written before and after the 1760s is separated by the 18th-century "discovery" of the human senses and has its origins in Locke (*Essay on Human Understanding*, 1690): What we know derives ultimately from what our *senses* tell us, that is, from our *sensibility*. Upon this formulation are erected the 18th-century philosophical systems, from materialism and radical moral ideologies (which reached Russia beginning in the 1750s to 1770s) to the systems of Rousseau, the German pietists, and the Russian Masons. Literature of sentiment in Russia, as in the West, absorbed any one of these widely differing systems (including its social and political implications), and, with similar equanimity, any one of a variety of trends in preromanticism, from pastoral and idyll to the meditative and introspective poetry of night and graves, etc.

One of the earliest responses to Western European literature of sentiment in Russia dates from M. M. KHERASKOV's *Nun of Venice* (Venetsianskaya monakhinya, 1758), which inaugurates the Russian sentimental drama. The sentimental genre of the "tearful" drama (*slezlivaya* or *sleznaya drama/komediya*) originates in the "comédie larmoyante" of Nivelle de la Chaussée in 1730, and is furthered by Destouches (first Russian trans. 1758): it sought to moralize in comedy not with laughter but with tears. In Russia it was promoted in the 1760s by V. I. LUKIN's "Forewords" and his single original comedy *The Spendthrift, by Love Corrected* (Mot lyubov'yu ispravlennyi, 1765). SUMAROKOV looked askance and grumbled at "this new and vile kind of tearful comedies" (*sei novyi i pakostnyi rod slezlivykh komedii*) and in 1770 complained about it in a letter to Voltaire. But the new dramas continued to be listed on contemporary billboards next to neoclassical titles, and to make inroads into the Russian theater. After the "comédie larmoyante" came the "drame bourgeois" of Diderot, very popular in Germany, where Lessing in 1760–61 translated Diderot's discussion of the genre in *Entretiens sur Le fils naturel ou Les épreuves de la vertu*. *Le fils naturel* was first translated in Russia in 1764 (before the first stage performance in France), and four translated editions of the work appeared in two years. In this new genre the playwright sought to moralize less with tears than with "tender" emotions, to "attendrir," and he addressed the masses creating on stage the ambiance of their class. "Drame bourgeois" is translated "zhalostnaya tragediya/komediya" (pitiful tragedy/comedy) or simply "drama," and rarely by the more faithful "meshchanskaya drama" (from *meshchanin*, "bourgeois"). After the 1770s, translations continued to appear, notably of Beaumarchais's *Eugénie* (1767; first Russian trans. 1770), and later Kotzebue (first Russian trans. 1790). But original Russian sentimental drama was well represented also, with P. Potyomkin's *Triumph of Friendship* (Torzhestvo druzhby. Drama, 1773), M. I. Veryovkin's *In Point* (Toch' v toch'. Zhalostnaya komediya, 1774), Kheraskov's *Friend of the Unfortunate* (Drug neschastnykh. Sleznaya drama, 1774), *The Persecuted* (Gonimye. Sleznaya drama, 1775), and *Thralldom* (Nevol'nichestvo. Drama, 1780), I. A. Teil's *Virtue Rewarded* (Nagrazhdenie dobrodeteli. Drama, 1780) and *Feeling Beneficence* (Chuvstvovanie blagotvorenii. Drama, 1787), to name a few; and later after Kotzebue: N. Ilyin's *Liza, or a Triumph of Gratitude* (Liza ili torzhestvo blagodarnosti. Drama), V. Fyodorov's *Liza and the Consequences of Pride and Seduction* (Liza i sledstviya gordosti i obol'shcheniya), etc. Very successful at the time were endeavors to bring together drama and music in the comic opera (first "comic opera": Pergolese, *La padrona serva*, 1733) and in the 18th-century melodrama (originating from Rousseau's *Le Devin du village*, 1752). Popov's *Anyuta* (1772), the first Russian comic opera, is sentimental; many more followed, including V. I. MAIKOV's *A Rural Festival, or Virtue Rewarded. A Pastoral Drama with Music* (Derevenskii prazdnik ili Uvenchannaya Dobrodetel'. Pastusheskaya drama s muzykoi, 1777), and the surge of Russian sentimental comic opera in the 1780s, e.g., *A Sailor's Day and Night* (Matrosskie sutki), *Farmers' Diligence Rewarded* (Nagrazhdennoe userdie zemledel'tsev), *A New Family* (Novoe semeistvo), and of the Russian sentimental melodrama, including NIKOLEV's *Rozana i Lyubim* (1781) and A. Ya. KNYAZHNIN's sentimental melodramas on mythological themes. Sentimental drama in Russia and in the West is largely forgettable; nevertheless, some Russian experiments were innovative. For example, in *Rozana i Lyubim* Nikolev includes an interlude showing on stage a storm with thunder followed by clearing, with the specification: "Muzyka otvechaet nepogode" (music responds to storm), and provides directions for coordinating the states of mind of the characters with the music. This seems to anticipate the dramas of OSTROVSKY and CHEKHOV.

Russian sentimental poetry makes its debut a little later, in the 1770s and 1780s, when it was ushered in by the Masonic journals edited by NOVIKOV. In 1778, *Utrennii svet* (1777–80) opened the way to the vogue of Young's *Night Thoughts* (1742–43) with the Mason A. M. Kutuzov's translation (from a German translation) of the first eight songs. The next year DERZHAVIN wrote the first Russian "night" ode, "Na smert' kn. Meshcherskogo." Early translations of Gray's poetry of graveyards in *Pokoyashchiisya trudolyubets* (1784–85) and Macpherson's Ossianic poems (1762–63), in the 18th century assumed to be genuine translations from the Gaelic, appearing in A. Dmitriev's translation of 1788, provided a third eminently preromantic catalyst for sentimentalism. In the 1770s M. N. MURAVYOV wrote the first Russian sentimental elegies inspired by the poetry of night and graves. Also in 1778 Muravyov published in *Utrennii svet*

the first Russian manifesto of sentimentalism, "Dshchitsy dlya zapisyvaniya" (*dshchitsy* from Fr. "tablettes" here meaning diary). Beginning in the late 1770s in the Masonic journals the older generation of poets such as Kheraskov, V. I. Maikov and Muravyov, and a pleiad of younger poets rallied in the common aspiration, in their words, to "pour feeling (*chuvstvitel'nost'*) into the heart." But in Russian sentimentalism, in poetry much as in drama, the new manner was not one of *opposition* to neoclassicism. The ode of LOMONOSOV is not alien to Muravyov when he writes lyrical *Odes* (1775) any more than to Derzhavin when he composes "night" and "Ossianic" odes ("Na vzyatie Izmaila," 1790, "Vodopad," 1791). Rather, both renew the ode by pouring into it emotions incompatible with Lomonosov's lofty patriotism. Similarly, sentimentalism renewed the neoclassical forms, now frequently infused with Masonic themes and ideas: the ELEGY, idyll (written under the influence of Thomson's *Seasons*, 1727–30, and the German pastoral poets) and the epistle (*poslanie, pis'mo*). The FABLE (*basnya*), which was practiced as much if not more than in neoclassicism, in its sentimental variant is "simplehearted" (*prostoserdechnaya*) in the fables of KHEMNITSER (*Basni*, 1st ed. 1779), and even more so in N. A. Lvov, NELEDINSKY-MELETSKY, and especially I. I. DMITRIEV (*Basni*, 1st ed. 1795). Even when the sentimental manner in Russian poetry was at its height, after the 1790s, the older generation of poets, particularly Derzhavin and Kheraskov, continued to appear in print in sentimental journals, such as *Chtenie dlya vkusa, razuma i chuvstvovanii* (1791–93) and *Priyatnoe i poleznoe preprovozhdenie vremeni* (1794–98), edited by V. S. Podshivalov, and *Muza* (1796), edited by I. I. Martynov, in Karamzin's poetic almanac *Aonidy* (3 vols., 1796–99), and later in P. A. Sokhatsky's *Ippokrena ili Utekhi lyubosloviya* (1799–1801, with about 100 contributors, including Radishchev and ZHUKOVSKY). It should also be remembered that Russian sentimental poetry was an occupation of the aristocracy. In the salons of the upper classes light poetry inspired by the *vers fugitifs* of Voltaire, Bernis, Dorat, Delille or Parny (Muravyov's "ubegayushchie stikhi") was recorded in the album or sung to musical accompaniment and later published in collections like I. I. Dmitriev's *Karmannyi pesennik* (1795). Beginning in the late 1770s and increasingly after the 1790s Russian sentimental poets in anticipation of the romantic poets followed the preromantic trend of turning to the past for the national spirit not only of their country but also of other nations and ages. The quest to intuit the spirit of classical antiquity, particularly Greece, led to innovative experiments with metrics in N. A. Lvov's translations from the original Greek of Sappho in 1778 and of Anacreon in 1794 and to Radishchev's similar interests and experiments with Greek meters since the 1780s. As regards the national spirit in Christian times, this preromantic trend reached Russia from Germany where it was most pronounced. Bürger idealized the ballad and romance as a pure poetic form for the German national spirit, and in 1774 wrote his ballad *Lenore* (which Sir Walter Scott and Zhukovsky translated at about the same time). Herder added momentum to the trend with his work on folklore. In Russia numerous collections of native folklore appeared in the 1760s to 1790s (mostly alloyed with the sentimental manner). After the 1790s Russian folklore was intensively assimilated into poetry: Karamzin humorously sentimentalizes the Russian BYLINA in the fragment "Il'ya Muromets" (1794); Radishchev in "Bova" spun the Russian folktale together with autobiographical and humorously erotic elements; and Kheraskov in *Bakhariana* wove a Russian fairy tale into a Masonic allegory. N. A. Lvov (who headed an influential circle) saw in Russian folklore the repository of the Russian national spirit; in *Dobrynya. Bogatyrskaya pesn'* (1796) he urged the writing of poetry that was national in form and content, and that developed the themes of the Russian *byliny*, folktales, and of Russian history.

The blossoming of sentimental prose began in the 1790s; however, not under the direct influence of Rousseau's *Nouvelle Héloïse* (1761), read in Russia beginning in the early 1760s, Goethe's *Werther* (1774) or Richardson's novels (1740s–50s; read in Russia at the *end* of the century) but of Karamzin's *Moskovskii zhurnal* (1791–92), in particular of the first installments of Karamzin's *Letters of a Russian Traveller* (Pis'ma russkogo puteshestvennika, 1791–1801) and short tales, like his "Poor Liza" (Bednaya Liza, 1792). In 1794 Karamzin was crowned the "Russian Sterne," a title he retained at least until 1807, when Shakhovskoi parodied Karamzin and Zhukovsky in the hero Fialkin ("Mr. Violet") of his comedy *A*

New Sterne (Novyi Stern). *Moskovskii zhurnal* also launched Sterne in Russia on a grand scale (first excerpted trans., 1779). Sterne continued to be popular with Pushkin, Gogol, and Tolstoi, and as late as in the 20th century Shklovsky discovered in Sterne the device of *obnazhenie priema* ("baring the device"). Eighteenth-century readers in the West and in Russia valued the tender feelings, which Sterne evokes with ironic humor and with considerably greater talent than Diderot in his first *drame bourgeois*. In Russian sentimental prose the Western European epidemic of tenderness began to make its appearance in a significant way in the 1790s. The heart and soul are "tender," "tenderness" (*nezhnost'*) surfaces in a languid gaze, on the cheeks, or an elbow; even as a "tender man" (*nezhnyi muzhchina*); meanwhile, tears "poured onto the soft turf" (Karamzin, *Letters*), "poured and bathed the wilted grass" (Kamenev, 1804), and "dropped onto the misty green where they united with the evening dew" (V. V. Izmailov, 1795), not unlike in the famous scene of Yorick-Sterne at the grave of Father Lorenzo. But in Russia, unlike in the West, a *poetic* of the tear was developed in sentimental prose: the tear turns into a "drop of silvery water," or a "pearl" that rests poised "trembling on my eyelid" (Klushin, 1793), and it "glisten[s] on black eyelashes under the languid light of the moon like a transparent diamond" (N. P. Milonov, 1805), or it turns into a mirroring sphere ("the ray from the moon played on his tear drop") in a manner evocative of Derzhavin's poetry of reflection. Russian prose became "poeticized," as Lotman notes regarding the prose of Karamzin, and this factor above all saved the sentimental manner in Russia from the excesses of its Western European variants; also it allowed for the healthy expression of irony and humor, e.g., "[one tear] rolled from her *right* eye ... she answered and wiped the *other* tear glistening on the *lower eyelash of her left eye*" (*Letters*, italics Karamzin's), or self irony, "We each let roll one more little tear" (*po slezinke*, Kamenev, 1796). The humanitarianism of Sterne was his second most important attribute for 18th-century sentimentalists both in Russia and in the West. Kamenev refers to Sterne as a "chuvstvitel'nyi filosof," and the arch-sentimental Raynal in his *Histoire des Deux Indes* (1784) effusively eulogizes Sterne as "le defenseur de l'HUMANITE de la LIBERTE et de la VERITE." Similarly, Karamzin in *Letters* cites a passage on "Sweet Liberty" from *Tristram Shandy*; elsewhere he also alludes to the little Starling of Liberty on Yorick-Sterne's symbolic coat of arms; and in the writing of his *Journey* the image of the Traveler-Philosopher appeals to Radishchev as an artistic principle of organization. In Sterne, and generally in sentimentalism, the humanitarianism of the Enlightenment is treated in a tender manner in scenes dramatizing the powers of human sympathy. And in Russia, increasingly after the 1790s, writers pour forth feelings of compassion, e.g., for the mother of a dead child in "My Feelings over the Grave of Good Mary" (Chuvstva moi nad grobom dobroi Marii, 1794), for a merchant's daughter doomed to the sequestered life of women in her class in "Lake Pereslavskoe" (Pereslavskoe ozero, 1795), for a serf sold as a recruit in "Dark Forest, or Feeling Human Misery and Beneficence" (Temnyi les ili Chuvstvo bedstvii chelovecheskikh i blagotvoreniya, 1796), etc. Comparable treatments of the humanitarian theme extended into the 19th century and, in Russia, culminated in the literature of the Natural school on the "little man." Equally important are the first probings by sentimental writers in Russia into the psychological expressiveness of their characters' posture, gestures, glance, etc. They prepared the way for the Russian novel.

After the 1790s some sophistication in the Russian prose style was appreciable for the first time on a large scale. A mere sixty years after the *first* secular book on love was printed in Russia in 1730 (Trediakovsky's translation *Ezda v ostrov lyubvi*), Karamzin and his school tamed a prose style which even in the 1770s and 1780s bristled with Slavonicisms (see Church Slavonic), colloquialisms, bureaucratic jargon and syntax, and unassimilated foreign words, into a "tender style" (*nezhnyi slog*—the expression is Karamzin's). At the same time, however, the form of the novel was all but abandoned, and was not practiced at all by Karamzin and his followers. (For a long time no distinction was made between *povest'* and *roman*, prose fiction; there is none even for Sipovsky in 1911). After the 1790s, the Western European sentimental novel, which earlier Emin and P. Yu. Lvov had made some feeble attempts to implant, sank under the deluge of tiny prose forms, the size of an

essay; eighteen pages in Muravyov's "A Suburban Dweller" (Obitatel' predmestiya) and Izmailov's "Momentary Bliss" (Minutnoe blazhenstvo), twelve small pages in "The Lake, or Nature Feeling Overcome by Despair" (Ozero ili chuvstvo prirody pobezhdennoe otchayaniem), eleven small pages in "Dark Forest, or Feeling Human Misery and Beneficence," ten pages in Izmailov's "My Feelings over the Grave of Good Mary," six pages in "The Fugitive" (Beglets), three pages in "To the Village" (K selu), etc. The epistolary novel which Emin attempted to introduce in the 1760s shrank to small sentimental epistolary essays, such as "Fragment" (Otryvok) by A. Stolypin, or "Some Letters from My Friend" (Neskol'ko pisem moego druga) and a few "Friendly Letters" (Druzheskie pis'ma). Confessional literature (Rousseau's *Confessions*, I, 1782; II, 1789) was also short in Russia, e.g., M. V. Sushkov's "Russian Werther" (Rossiiskii Verter), and shorter still, Radishchev's "A Week's Diary" (Dnevnik odnoi nedeli). And imitations of the form of Sterne's *Sentimental Journey* flood the Russian literary scene only after the 1800s. It appears that the "tender style" is achieved in some measure at the expense of the *size* of the prose form. In this process the direct influence of foreign small prose forms (e.g., the "contes moraux" of Florian and Genlis) probably played a less important role than experimentation with language, most interestingly as a *melodic* means of "pouring feelings into the heart." The sentimental manner of Radishchev in his *Journey* is very different. His style is not "tender" but barbaric; also he omits nature descriptions and his humanitarianism does not rest on the power of human sympathy; these are tangible indications that he integrated the sentimental manner with an ideology of the Enlightenment which was profoundly alien not only to Karamzin and Sterne but also to Diderot and Raynal.

The "epidemic" of sensibility in the last third of the 18th century in Russia witnessed no "explosion" (Monglond) in the literary any more than in the political or social implications of the image. Indeed, over this period, and with full consciousness of the sentimental manner precisely as a *manner*, its "triviality" was stressed. Not only the opponents of sentimentalism, but also, implicitly, its exponents exposed the "triviality" of this manner, as when Karamzin and I. I. Dmitriev published their works under the title of "trifles" (*Moi bezdelki*, 1794, *I moi bezdelki*, 1795). The sentimentalists' self-abasement is ironically deceptive in the light of their lasting contributions, of which perhaps the most important one was the process of absorption in literature of the ideas and trends of the Enlightenment and of preromanticism.

Works: (With the notable exception of Radishchev, 20th-century collections and anthologies of Russian sentimental works are scarce, especially of sentimental prose.) S. L. Ginsburg, ed., *Russkii muzykal'nyi teatr 1700–1833 gg. Khrestomatiya*. 1941. Yu. Lotman, ed., *Poety 1790–1810-kh godov*. (Biblioteka poeta, Bol'shaya seriya.) 1971. G. P. Makogonenko and I. Z. Serman, eds., *Poety XVIII veka*. (Biblioteka poeta, Bol'shaya seriya.) Vol. 2. 1972. P. A. Orlov, ed., *Russkaya sentimental'naya povest'*. 1979.

Secondary literature: M. P. Alekseev, ed., *Shekspir i russkaya kul'tura*. 1965. K. A. Nazaretskaya, "Literaturno-khudozhestvennye vzglyady i tvorchestvo masonov v ikh znachenii dlya formirovaniya sentimentalizma i predromantizma," *Uchenye zapiski Kazanskogo gosudarstvennogo universiteta*, CXXVIII, 4 (1969), pp. 79–95. P. A. Orlov, *Russkii sentimentalizm*. 1977. L. V. Pumpyanskii, "Sentimentalizm." In *Istoriya russkoi literatury*, Vol. 4 (1947), pp. 430–45. I. Z. Serman, *Derzhavin*. 1967. K. Skipina, "Chuvstvitel'naya povest'." In *Russkaya proza*. Ed. B. Eikhenbaum and Yu. Tynyanov. 1926. Reprint 1963. G. S. Smith, "Sentimentalism and Preromanticism as Terms and Concepts." In *Russian Literature in the Age of Catherine the Great*. Ed. A. G. Cross. 1976.   T. P.

Serafimóvich (real name: Popóv), Aleksándr Serafímovich (1863–1949), writer and journalist. The son of a Don Cossack officer, Serafimovich attended St. Petersburg University from 1883 to 1887, but was arrested on suspicion of revolutionary activity and exiled to Archangel province in 1887. After his return from exile in 1890, Serafimovich pursued a career as a writer and journalist in the progressive camp, at first in the Don region and then in Moscow. A member of the Znanie group, he had considerable success with his stories and sketches, rather in the manner of Maksim Gorky, dealing with social problems, class conflict, and the evils of capitalism. An immediate and ardent supporter of the Revolution, Serafimovich produced one of its classics, the short novel *The Iron Flood* (Zheleznyi potok, 1924). An example of revolutionary romanticism, it makes an effort to show how an elemental movement of disorganized masses of oppressed humanity is turned into a disciplined fighting force by a heroic Bolshevik leader. Toward the end of his life, Serafimovich played the role of a grand old man of Soviet literature, writing little of any consequence, but holding important positions in the literary establishment. Serafimovich is greatly overrated in official Soviet criticism.

Works: Sobranie sochinenii. 10 vols. Ed. and comm. G. Neradov. 1940–48. *Sobranie sochinenii.* 7 vols. 1959–60.

Translations: The Iron Flood. New York, 1935. *Sand and Other Stories.* Trans. G. H. Hanna. Moscow, 1955.

Secondary literature: R. Khigerovich, *Put' pisatelya. Zhizn' i tvorchestvo A. Serafimovicha.* 3d ed. 1963. ———, *'Zheleznyi potok' A. Serafimovicha.* 1968. Vera Lafferty, "A. S. Serafimovich's Forgotten Novel, *City in the Steppe* (1912)," *CSP* 16 (1974), pp. 202–20.
V. T.

Serapion Brothers, The (Serapiónovy brát'ya). In his autobiography, KAVERIN speaks of ten Serapion Brothers. He must refer to Konstantin FEDIN (1892–1977), Il'ya Gruzdev (1892–1960), Vsevolod IVANOV (1895–1963), Veniamin Kaverin (1902–), Lev LUNTS (1901–24), Nikolai Nikitin (1897–1963), Vladimir Pozner (1905–?), Mikhail SLONIMSKY (1897–1972), Nikolai TIKHONOV (1896–1979), and Mikhail ZOSHCHENKO (1895–1958). There were also four "Serapion Maidens," among them the poetess Elizaveta POLONSKAYA (1890–1969). The Serapion Brothers emerged as a literary group on 1 February 1921. The poetic name that they assumed after E. T. A. Hoffmann's hermit Serapion indicated their liking for free fantasy and humaneness. They did not aspire to start a new literary school. What united these budding writers and poets in 1921 was their dedication to the individual freedom of the creative act, to belles lettres, and to one another as brothers. This is the substance of Lunts's polemical article "Why We are Serapion Brothers" (Pochemu my Serapionovy Brat'ya). It was an assertion of creative pluralism. This stance could not have survived long. It ran counter to the cultural values imposed subsequently. The Serapions used to meet at the Petrograd House of Arts where they had the benefit of ZAMYATIN's lectures about literary craftsmanship. At their meetings they discussed from a technical point of view the merits and flaws of the works they recited, heard outside speakers such as SHKLOVSKY, and debated problems of literature. These debates revolved around the status of literature with regard to craftsmanship, the deeper purpose of literature, and ideology. In *Gorky among Us* (Gor'kii sredi nas) Fedin tells about his debate with Lunts on the subject of the *how* versus the *what* in a work of literature. Lunts defended the notion of the *how*, i.e., the craftsmanship of writing which can be mastered by disciplined study, whereas Fedin insisted on the primacy of the *what*, i.e., the significance of the subject matter. All these debates reflected the Serapions' concern for the integrity of literature: trivializing literature by an unworthy but "well made" subject matter is as bad as debasing the aesthetic value of a literary work for the sake of political ideology (see "The Serapion Brothers' Reply to Sergei Gorodetsky," *Novaya Rossiya* 1, p. 160). The Serapions took up a wide part of the literary spectrum. Tikhonov and Polonskaya established themselves as poets. Tikhonov continued the ACMEIST line of poetry. Polonskaya in her lyric poetry responded to the events of the Revolution. Lunts wrote prose, drama, and polemical articles. Gruzdev wrote critical articles. Pozner emigrated. The largest group (Fedin, Ivanov, Kaverin, Nikitin, Slonimsky, and Zoshchenko) became prose writers. Just as the other "brothers," the Serapion prosaists shared a sense of renewal and experiment. For Kaverin, renewal would come from a new *syuzhetnaya proza*, i.e., a prose moved by an ingenious suspenseful plot, a literature of action and thought. E.g., his bizarre experimental story "The Purple Palimpsest" represents a structure of double reversal and interchange: people's daily work is superimposed over their true vocation. Inasmuch as literature of action and suspense was felt to be characteristically Western, Lunts advocated in his programmatic

article "Go West" (Na Zapad) that the "brothers" learn from Western writers such as R. L. Stevenson. However, the fiction of the majority (Ivanov, Nikitin, Slonimsky) dealt with the events of ordinary life. They drew their inspiration from their experience of the war and the Revolution, toward which they shared a dual literary attitude: to show the extraordinariness of the Revolution as if ordinary (especially Ivanov); to perceive the gory side of war (Slonimsky, Ivanov). Stylistically, they (especially Nikitin) used "ornamental prose" after BELY's "poetic prose." Fedin and Zoshchenko reached maturity earlier than the other "brothers." Fedin wrote *Cities and Years* (Goroda i gody, 1924), one of the first major novels of Soviet literature, in which he combined an experimental plot with a psychological mode of narrative reminiscent of Dostoevsky and about the fate of the Russian intelligentsia during the war and Revolution. Zoshchenko, the master of the *skaz* technique, parodied the speech of his contemporary uneducated philistine, contrasting seriousness with humor. Under their poetic name the Serapion Brothers published only one work: *Serapionovy Brat'ya. Al'manakh pervyi* (1922). The almanac showed how different the Serapion Brothers were as littérateurs. It was natural that subsequently they should evolve their individual art, not to speak of the pressure of the time. Kaverin's "Speech Not Held at the Eighth Anniversary of the Order of the Serapion Brotherhood" (Rech', neproiznesennaya na vos'moi godovshchine ordena Serapionovykh Brat'ev), of February 1929, represents a symbolic landmark of the disintegration of the Serapion Brotherhood. The Serapion Brothers will be remembered as a particularly creative group of Russian writers at the early stage of post-revolutionary literature.

Works: Serapionovy Brat'ya: Al'manakh pervyi. Peterburg, 1922. *Serapionovy Brat'ya: Zagranichnyi al'manakh.* Berlin, 1922. Lev Lunts, "Pochemu my Serapionovy Brat'ya," *Literaturnye zapiski*, no. 3 (1922). ———, "Na Zapad," *Beseda*, no. 3 (1923). (Trans. in Kern's *Critical Anthology.*) Konstantin Fedin, *Gor'kii sredi nas: Dvadtsatye gody.* 1943. V. Kaverin, *Osveshchennye okna.* 1978.

Translations: The Serapion Brothers: A Critical Anthology. Ed. Gary Kern and Christopher Collins. Ardis, 1975.

Secondary literature: Gary Kern, "Introduction." [Critical essay on the Serapion Brothers.] In *The Serapion Brothers: A Critical Anthology.* Hongor Oulanoff. *The Serapion Brothers.* 1966.
H. O.

Serapion of Vladimir (?–1275), preacher and writer, was for many years Archimandrite of the Kiev Cave monastery and was made Bishop of Vladimir in 1274. His five extant sermons are among the finest examples of homiletic eloquence in the Kiev period. They display a sophisticated use of all the figures and tropes of Byzantine rhetoric (parallelism, antithesis, climax, rhetorical question, apostrophe, rhythmic phrasing, etc.), combined with a pathos which seems genuine. Serapion's sermons deal with the Tatar invasion, perceived as God's punishment for the many sins of the Russian princes and their people. Serapion vigorously reproaches his audience for not having taken this chastisement to heart, but continuing in their selfish and godless ways.

Text: E. V. Petukhov, *Serapion Vladimirskii, russkii propovednik XIII v.* 1888. (Excerpts:) A. D. Stokes, *Khrestomatiya po drevnei russkoi literature.* 1963. Pp. 110–11.

Secondary literature: N. K. Gudzii, "Gde i kogda protekala literaturnaya deyatel'nost' Serapiona Vladimirskogo?" *IAN* 11 (1952), no. 5.
V. T.

Sergéev-Tsénsky, Sergéi Nikoláevich (pseudonym of S. N. Sergeev, 1875–1958), novelist and short-story writer. The son of a schoolteacher, Sergeev graduated from the Glukhovsky Pedagogical Institute in 1895, taught for ten years, and began publishing in 1898. After initial attempts at poetry—*Thoughts and Dreams* (Dumy i grezy, 1901), he turned to prose, documenting negative aspects of provincial Russia in "Forest Swamp" (Lesnaya top', 1907). His predilection for historical themes and individual psychology was apparent in his first novel, *Babaev* (1908), which described the events of 1905 in a provincial town. Subsequent works depicted various social strata—bourgeois industrialists in "Movement" (Dvizhenie,

1910), police and army officers in "Police Officer Deryabin" (Pristav Deryabin, 1911), and diverse intellectuals in "Inclined Elena" (Naklonnaya Elena, 1914) and "Transfiguration" (Preobrazhenie, 1914). The latter inspired the title for the massive four-part, twelve-volume epic cycle *The Transfiguration of Russia* (Preobrazhenie Rossii, 1914–58), unified by the same major characters and basic theme—the necessity of transforming both the individual and bourgeois society. Unmatched in scope and structure in Soviet literature, *The Transfiguration of Russia* describes prerevolutionary Russian society, World War I, and the February Revolution. *Brusilov's Break-Through* (Brusilovskii proryv, 1943), the most significant of three volumes devoted to World War I, represented the first attempt to vindicate the Russian Imperial Army in Soviet letters.

Sergeev-Tsensky's most popular work, however, is the extensive three-volume historical épopée *The Ordeal of Sevastopol* (Sevastopol'skaya strada, 1937–39), which describes the Crimean war and the defense of Sevastopol in 1854 and 1855.

Works: Sobranie sochinenii. 10 vols. 1955–56. *Sobranie sochinenii.* 12 vols. 1967. *Radost' tvorchestva: Stat'i, vospominaniya, pis'ma.* 1969.

Translations: Lewanski, pp. 350–51.

Secondary literature: G. Makarenko, *S. N. Sergeev-Tsensky.* 1957. P. Pluksh, *S. N. Sergeev-Tsenskii.* 1968. I. Shevtsov. *Orel smotrit na solntse.* 1963.
A. M. S.

Sergius, St. The *Vita of St. Sergius of Radonezh* (Zhitie sv. Sergiya Radonezhskogo) is one of the most significant works of Russian HAGIOGRAPHY. It is traditionally ascribed to EPIPHANIUS THE WISE. Sergius (Varfolomei before taking holy vows), Muscovy's most important saint, was born between 1314 and 1322 and died in 1392. He had a key role in the development of Russian monasticism and in the colonization of the Northeast by Muscovy. Both benefited greatly from the practice, established by Sergius, of creating hermitages in the wilderness (which eventually would become monasteries, then towns). Sergius was also one of the first churchmen to cast his lot firmly with the policies of the Grand Prince of Moscow. The Vita of Sergius exists in several different redactions. It has not come down to us in its original form, but in the form it was given by PAKHOMY LOGOFET, who eliminated important biographic facts and concentrated on the hagiographic-rhetorical aspect of the text.

Bibliography: The Vita of St. Sergii of Radonezh. Trans., introd., and notes Michael Klimenko. Houston, 1980. (With bibliography.)
V. T.

Sévernaya pchelá (The Northern Bee), newspaper (1825–64), a four-page sheet whose notoriety in Russian literary history greatly exceeds its size and quality. Founded by BULGARIN, it was edited by him alone until 1831, when it became a daily and was jointly edited by GRECH, and finally (from 1860) by P. S. Usov. As a reward to Bulgarin for his activities as an informer and unquestioning supporter of the autocracy, the newspaper became the only private one in Russia allowed to print political news, which was fed to it in small portions by the Gendarmes, the only daily in Petersburg, and the only paper read at court. It enjoyed considerable influence between the late 1820s and the mid-1840s.

In addition the paper published works by PUSHKIN, KRYLOV, and GRIBOEDOV and a number of sections generally written by Bulgarin himself: "New Books," "Literature," "Odds and Ends," "Humor," "Manners." Grech provided letters from abroad and notes on grammar. Bulgarin aimed for a readership of what he called the "middle class"—the gentry, bureaucrats, merchants, and townspeople. The paper's criticism defended "morality" and "nationalism", but these were rather loosely interpreted to fit commercial considerations. Thus Bulgarin reviewed Pushkin's works warmly enough until Pushkin began to take part in the rival LITERATURNAYA GAZETA (1830–31), at which point Bulgarin launched a smear campaign against him. Subsequent reviews blasted GOGOL, NEKRASOV, and DOSTOEVSKY, but praised LERMONTOV's *Hero of Our Time* in exchange for a bribe.

In 1860 the paper acquired a more liberal tendency, publishing works by SLEPTSOV, LEVITOV, RESHETNIKOV, and Marko VOVCHOK as well as articles about Nekrasov, SALTYKOV-SHCHEDRIN, HERZEN, and DOBROLYUBOV.

Bibliography: M. K. Lemke, "Faddei Bulgarin i 'Severnaya pchela.'" In his *Nikolaevskie zhandarmy i literatura: 1826–1855 gg.* 2d ed. 1909. N. L. Stepanov, "'Severnaya pchela' F. V. Bulgarina." In *Ocherki po istorii russkoi zhurnalistiki i kritiki.* Vol. 1. 1950.
W. M. T.

Sévernye tsvetý (Northern Flowers), almanac, (1) 1825 to 1832, (2) 1901 to 1911.

A. A. DELVIG compiled and edited the first three issues of this famous and profitable almanac, a collection of verse, essays, and fiction that appeared at the beginning of each year in an elegant, pocket-sized volume with several illustrations. Orest SOMOV served as co-editor for the fourth through eighth volumes; PUSHKIN and PLETNYOV replaced Delvig, who had died, for the final issue. Publishing short works (or fragments of longer ones) by over eighty Russian authors, *Severnye tsvety* provides an accurate index of the state of Russian letters during this period. Its verse included fragments of Pushkin's *Eugene Onegin*, many of his lyrics, "Graf Nulin," and "Mozart and Salieri." Excellent verse by VYAZEMSKY, ZHUKOVSKY, KRYLOV, and BARATYNSKY graced the almanac, as did translations of Byron by KOZLOV, and early lyrics by YAZYKOV. The fictional offerings represent a variety of genres but tend to illustrate Somov's points about the poverty of Russian prose. However, Pushkin and GOGOL did publish promising fragments of prose fiction here. Long critical surveys by Pletnyov and Somov helped readers to orient themselves in the swiftly changing literary landscape. These, like the literary selections, favored young Russian writers sympathetic to European romanticism and to the Karamzinian tradition in Russian letters.

Revived by V. Ya. BRYUSOV, *Severnye tsvety* remained elegant, supportive of young poets, and partial to lyrics and short fiction. The first two issues published most of the prominent modernist poets, fiction by CHEKHOV and BUNIN, and works by earlier poets (Pushkin, TYUTCHEV, FET) to whom the SYMBOLISTS were sympathetic. The remaining issues were more narrowly symbolist in orientation. The final issue included works by GUMILYOV and KUZMIN.

Bibliography: Severnye tsvety, I–V [1901–1911]. Munich, 1972. (Texts and cumulative index.) John Mersereau, Jr., *Baron Delvig's Northern Flowers, 1825–1832; Literary Almanac of the Pushkin Pleiad.* Carbondale, 1967. V. E. Vatsuro, *"Severnye tsvety": istoriya al'manakha Del'viga-Pushkina.* 1978.
W. M. T.

Severyánin, Ígor (pseudonym of Ígor Vasílievich Lotaryóv, 1887–1941; after taking Estonian citizenship in 1918, Severyanin changed his family name to Severyanin-Lotaryov), poet and translator. Born in St. Petersburg, Severyanin attended a science-oriented secondary school (*real'noe uchilishche*) in Cherepovets and planned to become an engineer, but his love of poetry soon prevailed. From early childhood he was a passionate devotee of opera and concerts, took singing lessons, and later learned to play the piano professionally. Contrary to the opinion of several critics that Severyanin was a primitive or that, as SVYATOPOLK-MIRSKY wrote: "His originality was that he had the boldness to present everything in its naked naiveté and to give the philosophy of a hairdresser's assistant the gait of an almost Nietzschean individualism," he was actually a cultured man who spoke several languages and was well read in literature, poetics, and music theory.

Severyanin started as a belated but legitimate child of 19th-century romanticism. Although at the beginning he used traditional verse schemes, he soon directed his consummate skill and intuitive methods of creation against the mechanical usage of well-established poetic rhythms. His early booklets, starting with 1904, contained sentimentalities and triteness but were also notable for rare melodic power in their love and nature poems. By 1909 Severyanin's sense of verse design sharpened, and he started to write with the intention of irritating the bourgeois public and intellectual snobs. The critics did not recognize the true, ironic message of his biting social commentary, but instead thought that he was tastelessly praising the decadence of pre-revolutionary society. However, Severyanin successfully introduced vulgarity as a poetic and aesthetic subject and device, and was followed in this by MAYAKOVSKY with *expressionistic* power.

Severyanin's first substantial volume was *Thunder-seething Goblet* (Gromokipyashchii kubok, 1913), which in two years ran through seven editions and brought him the recognition of SOLOGUB, BRYUSOV, GUMILYOV, BLOK, and KHODASEVICH, among others. In this book, Severyanin caught both the sensuous flavor of lush wording and its concentrated sculpturality, reworking classic forms into a style of new energy, movement, musicality, and rhythmic richness, especially of iambic and anapestic forms. His metric variations are among the richest of Russian poets. He was also always innovative in rhyme technique and was the first to use dissonant rhymes convincingly. Later, in his book *Old and New Poets* (1921), H. Visnapuu called Severyanin "a new Pushkin," and Mayakovsky viewed him as "Pushkin's neighbor." These are overstatements, but if applied to the purely rhythmical springiness and spark-flinging (*iskrometnost'*) of Severyanin's verse, a quality recognized by Gleb STRUVE, the compliments are probably valid. Severyanin also demonstrated this Pushkinian rhythmic facility in his translations of Pushkin's French verse, and after Pushkin, Severyanin and KUZMIN are the only significant masters of light verse in Russian. This quality of energy and lightness is also demonstrated in his brilliant and lively, sometimes ironical SONNETS. For him, poetic rhythm was the prime physical and emotional constituent of poetic meaning both in serious and in frivolous verse. Severyanin repeatedly told this critic that his rhythm—heightening, regulating, and manipulating prosodic movement—was a purely physiological and distinctly sexual phenomenon. Early in his career, Severyanin recited his poems by half-singing with his masculine-lyrical baritone voice of beautiful timbre and perfect vocal technique, and later, after the Revolution, in a simple, slightly incantational manner. His tumultuous successes before large, hysterical crowds were similar to those of Elvis Presley. In 1918, he was elected Russia's "King of Poets," Mayakovsky receiving second place and BALMONT third.

With his ingenious technical versatility and gift for discovering complex verbal rhythmics, trochaic and dactylic caesuras, and mannerist but readily understandable neologisms, Severyanin produced many books of verse, very uneven in their intellectual quality but rhythmically always inducing in the reader a state resembling a collective melismatic hypnosis. His poems rely less on thematic structure than on patterns of mood, and often must be read, without much thought about their contents, as abstract orchestral verse-creations of intense traditional as well as futurist rhythmic momentum. Although Severyanin was against the metrical break, many of his poems are distinctly futuristic, having the characteristic futurist qualities of rhythmical dynamism, dramatic vowel and consonant power, speed of wording, and modernist, in part technological, imagery.

Severyanin's influence has been little studied, yet is discernible in, among others, Bryusov, Mayakovsky, PASTERNAK, Georgy IVANOV, the Polish poets J. Tuwim, J. Lechoń, and K. Wierzyński, the Swedish poet K. Södergran, the Estonians H. Visnapuu and V. Adams, and many minor poets. By the 1930s a critical reaction had set in, and Severyanin was roundly condemned for alleged "superficiality." M. TSVETAEVA, however, after hearing him recite his poems in Paris in 1932, called him the only nightingale among living Russian poets. Though translated into almost all the European languages, Severyanin was almost forgotten for some fifty years, but his poetry has once again been recognized in recent years, in the West by V. MARKOV, N. Andreev, K. Taranovsky, and O. Ronen, and by the Soviet critics B. Smirensky and N. Khardzhiev. His work has been analyzed in two dissertations by Helen Lauwers (Leuven) and Christina d'Audino (Rome), Lauwers' study being the first extended investigation of Severyanin's metrical system. In the Soviet Union, a large collection of his *Stikhotvoreniya* (Poems) was published in 1975, though the selection was biased in accordance with the rules of Soviet censorship.

As a translator, Severyanin rendered many European poets, his principal interest being Estonian poetry. In book form, he compiled and translated the anthology *Poety Estonii* (1928) and separate collections of H. Visnapuu (1922), A. Rannit (1938, 1940), and M. Under (1939). While faithful to the strict metrical patterns of the originals, his verse translations are occasionally distant from them in content, but they are always living, vibrant poetry.

Works: Vervena. 1920. *Rosa oranzhevogo chasa.* 1925. *Adriati-*

ka. 1932. *Klassicheskie rozy.* 1934. *Medal'ony.* 1935. *Ocharovatel'nye razocharovaniya.* 1939 (unpublished manuscript kept in TsGALI, Moscow).

Translations: Modern Russian Poetry. Ed. Vladimir Markov and Merrill Sparks. 1967. Pp. 342–47. *See also: Lewanski,* p. 351.

Secondary literature: K. Chukovskii, "Ego-futuristy." In his *Futuristy.* 1922. Pp. 37–61. N. Khardzhiev, "Mayakovskii i Igor' Severyanin," *RusL* 6, no. 4 (1978), pp. 307–46. L. Khrapovitskii [L. Reisner], "Cherez Bloka k Severyaninu i Mayakovskomu," *Rudin* 7 (1916). *Kritika o tvorchestve I. Severyanina* [collective book of reviews and articles on Severyanin's poetry, no editor]. 1915. A. Lunacharskii, "Futuristy," *Kievskaya mysl',* 17 May 1913. V. Markov, "Ego-Futurism." In his *Russian Futurism: A History.* 1968. Pp. 61–116.

A. R.

Shaginyán, Mariétta Sergéevna (1888–1982), born in Moscow, the daughter of a brilliant doctor and aristocratic mother. She earned an M.A. degree in philosophy in 1912 and eventually a doctorate in philology in 1945. At fifteen Shaginyan began writing for newspapers on topical issues, art, and literature. In her first collection of verse *First Encounters* (Pervye vstrechi, 1909) simple children's pleasures coexist with symbolist ambiguity evoking HIPPIUS. Shaginyan moved to St. Petersburg to be near the MEREZHKOVSKYS, acting as liaison with the masses in the religious quest of their "trinity." The collection *Orientalia* (1912) brought her fame. These are stylized poems on exotic Moslem Caucasian themes with earthy passions. Some are mellifluous songs; poignant Armenian poems and the philosophical "Ode to Time" flesh out the collection. A pilgrimage to her idol Goethe's Weimar (1914) found expression in *Journey to Weimar.* Her cycle of nine metaphysical and philosophical verse plays with intriguing ideas includes *Separation for Love* (Razluka po lyubvi), on a kingdom where married couples are given the "sacrament of separation" should they fall in love.

After the Revolution, while continuing work for major newspapers, Shaginyan pioneered in prose fiction, such as in her anti-Freudian novel *One's Own Fate* (Svoya sud'ba, 1923) and her eclectic novel *Kik* (1929) which combines a medley of genres from poem to report. The civil war on the Don and new people are romanticized in a tragic vein in a trilogy of diverse genres: *Change* (Peremena, a novel), *Adventures of a Society Lady* (Priklyucheniya damy iz obshchestva, a novella), and "Agitvagon," a story. Shaginyan displays a sense of fun in creating the pen name "Jim Dollar" for the alleged American worker in Russia, "author" of the successful series *Mess Mend* (1923–25), which combines an adventure plot with revolutionary ideology in the manner of the SERAPION BROTHERS. A public figure often engaged in investigative reporting, such as on Caucasian mines, Shaginyan spent four years in mountain villages to write her famous *Journey through Soviet Armenia* (1950). Her *Hydrocentral* (Gidrotsentral', 1931) was among the first novels on industrialization promoting the leitmotif of creative socialist labor. A second version appeared in 1949. All her major pieces were reworked in the 1940s. Trips abroad resulted in essays interlacing history with contemporary scenes and portraits of the people. An ardent researcher, Shaginyan discovered two lost operas in preparing a historical novel on the Czech composer Josef Mysliveček, *Resurrection from the Dead* (Voskreshenie iz mertvykh, 1964). Her historical documentary novels on Lenin, for which she spent two winters in Simbirsk collecting material and making discoveries in other cities, were awarded a Lenin Prize (1972): *The Ulyanov Family* (Sem'ya Ul'yanovykh, 1938–57), *The First All-Russian* (Pervaya Vserossiiskaya, 1965), and the essays *Four Lessons with Lenin* (Chetyre uroka u Lenina, 1970). Shaginyan's pictures of early impressions, often brutally frank, intermeshing philosophical ideas in refined style with insightful reminiscences on Hippius and the times—*Man and Time* (Chelovek i vremya)—appeared in 1980. Prolific and versatile, Shaginyan authored seventy-nine books.

Works: Sobranie sochinenii. 9 vols. 1971–73.

Translations: "Three Looms." In *Azure Cities: Stories of New Russia.* Ed. Joshua Kunitz. 1929. *Mess-Mend.* Tr. S. Cioran. 1984.

Secondary literature: A. A. Margaryan, *Marietta Shaginyan.* Erevan, 1956. Konstantin Serebryakov, "*The Truth of Time:* A New Book by Marietta Shaginyan, Hero of Socialist Labor, Lenin and State Prize Winner," *Soviet Literature,* 1980, no. 9, pp. 107–13 (preceded by Shaginyan's "Man and Time," trans. Helen Tate, pp. 33–107). L. Skorino, *Marietta Shaginyan—khudozhnik*. 1975.　　　S. K.

Shakhmatov, Aleksei Aleksándrovich (1860–1920); leading linguistic authority of prerevolutionary Russia, Professor of Russian philology at St. Petersburg University, academician, student of Russian dialects and of Old Russian monuments.

Shakhmatov devoted most of his scholarly career to the study of Russian, in particular to the history of the Russian language. His works in comparative Slavic grammar, in history, paleography and philology were all ancillary to his central concern with the development of Russian from its earliest origin to the modern period. Like his teacher Fortunatov, he also studied the structure of Russian, especially its syntax and the parts of speech. His major (posthumously published) works in this field include *Russian Syntax* (Sintaksis russkogo yazyka, 1–2, 1925–27) and *An Outline of Contemporary Literary Russian* (Ocherk sovremennogo russkogo literaturnogo yazyka, 1941[4]). Together with Fortunatov he worked on the reform of the Russian alphabet which was implemented in 1917.

Shakhmatov's reconstruction of the history of the Russian language was elaborated on the basis of CHURCH SLAVONIC and Old Russian monuments. With the rise of modern dialectology he switched his attention to the study of Russian dialects in which he sought an answer to historical questions. He was an indefatigable organizer and participant in dialect expeditions and prepared a *Program* for the collection of dialect material which he helped to publish in the *Materialy* of ORYaS (Society of the Russian Language and Literature). Several of his dialect descriptions have hitherto retained their scholarly value. Shakhmatov devoted special attention to the formation of the East Slavic tribes and languages and the migration, mixture, and original habitat of the Slavs on which he advanced bold, and sometimes speculative, hypotheses. His outstanding work as a linguist was matched by his activity as a philologist and editor of Old Russian texts. His chief contribution in this field was the edition of the *Primary Chronicle* which he attempted to reconstruct in its various stages and ramifications by applying to it the comparative method practiced in linguistics. Though hardly acceptable in its details, this work has served as a model of textual analysis and has laid the foundation of contemporary Slavic textology.

Secondary literature: M. G. Bulakhov, *Vostochnoslavyanskie yazykovedy.* Vol. 1. Minsk, 1976. Pp. 280–96. V. V. Kolesov, "Znachenie lingvisticheskikh trudov A. A. Shakhmatova dlya sovremennogo slavyanskogo yazykoznaniya," *Voprosy yazykoznaniya,* 1971, no. 2, pp. 53–61. S. P. Obnorskii, Introduction to *A. A. Shakhmatov: 1864–1920. Sbornik statei i materialov.* 1947.　　　E. S.

Shakhovskoi, Aleksándr Aleksándrovich (1777–1846), a prolific dramatist whose major contribution was in the area of high comedy in verse. Shakhovskoi's talents lay especially in diction and verse. Creating characters more individualized than Russian comedy had known previously, he crafted a more natural dialogue appealing for its sparkle and wit. By ending the hegemony over Russian verse drama of the iambic alexandrine line of the 18th century, he paved the way for the greatest comedy in verse in the Russian language, GRIBOEDOV's *Woe from Wit.* Descended of an old aristocratic family, Shakhovskoi developed an early interest in the stage and left military service in 1802 to assume the directorship of the imperial theaters. Shortly afterward he was sent to France to recruit actors for the Petersburg French troupe and to familiarize himself with the French stage. Shakhovskoi wrote comedies, tragedies, vaudevilles, satires, and so-called magical operas. His best works for the stage are *Semi-Lordly Fancies, or Home Theater* (Polubarskie zatei, ili domashnii teatr), a prose comedy written and produced in 1808 and reflecting the popularity at the time of serf theaters; *The Cossack Poet* (Kazak-stikhotvorets, 1812), a VAUDEVILLE with a Ukrainian setting generally recognized as the first Russian vaudeville; *A Lesson for Coquettes, or The Lipetsk Spa* (Urok koketkam, ili Lipetskie vody, 1815), an immensely popular comedy set in the last year of the war with Napoleon and poking fun at unpatriotic Russian aristocrats who disdain their own country as well as at SENTIMENTALISM and early ROMANTICISM (the play aroused controversy for what was

commonly believed to be a satirical portrait of the poet ZHUKOVSKY); *All in the Family, or the Married Fiancée* (Svoya sem'ya, ili zamuzhnaya nevesta, 1817), which he wrote together with Griboedov and Khmelnitsky; and *Don't Listen If You Don't Want To, But Don't Interfere With Lying* (Ne lyubo—ne slushai, a lgat' ne meshai, 1818), a one-act comedy in which he first used iambic lines of varying length for rendering conversational speech. Shakhovskoi eventually was reconciled with Zhukovsky and took a more tolerant attitude toward romanticism. In this spirit he wrote several "romantic comedies" and "magical comedy-ballets," a few of which were based on works by PUSHKIN. After the appearance of Griboedov's *Woe from Wit,* Shakhovskoi virtually abandoned the genre of high comedy in verse about contemporary life. His verse play *Aristofan, ili Predstavlenie "Vsadnikov"* (Aristophanes, or The Presentation of "The Horsemen") which premiered in Petersburg in 1825, was an attempt to duplicate Griboedov's success, but in a play with a historical setting. The work, however, never achieved the same distinction as *Woe from Wit.* Although a lifelong political conservative, Shakhovskoi lost his position in the imperial theaters in the wake of the Decembrist uprising and never thereafter returned to theatrical administration. He remained active as a dramatist, however, until his death.

Works: Komedii. Stikhotvoreniya. Ed. A. A. Gozenpud. 1961.
Translations: The New Sterne. A Comedy in One Act. Trans. J. Eyre. In *American Slavic and East European Review* 4, no. 8–9 (Aug 1945), pp. 80–92.　　　H. B. S.

Shalámov, Varlám Tikhonovich (1907–82). A prose writer and poet, Shalamov has become known chiefly for his *Kolyma Tales,* in which he describes life in the Soviet forced-labor camps in northeastern Siberia.

The artistic manner of the stories is similar to that of CHEKHOV, although the overall effect is strikingly different: a brief plot devoted to one incident (occasionally more diffuse than that of Chekhov), an objective dispassionate narration intended to provide a contrast to the horror of the moment, and a very abrupt ending, often intended to be subtly ironic. There is a pantheistic surrealism in Shalamov's work. In the story "Fire and Water," magical mushrooms with caps cold as snakeskins grow taller than the bushes, while people live in tents lower than the rocks. Water and fire become primordial forces, on the periphery of whose competition man barely survives. Fire scampers through the dry grass like a snake, runs up tree trunks, roars and topples them. A growling river is as muscular as a wrestler, ripping up trees and flinging them into the current. The shore of the river is the shore of life, and a tiny boat becomes a metaphor for man's tremulous journey through that life.

Kolyma Tales presents a mosaic of individual moments intended to impart an understanding and achieve an emotional impact in their totality. Powerful as the individual stories are, they achieve their greatest effect when taken together. Shalamov was a writer who respected the rights of the reader in the creative process, and he consciously avoided making conclusions for him. His tone is strikingly dispassionate, and his narrator's calm acceptance of incredible brutality is inevitably startling.

Kolyma Tales are intended both as fiction and historical testimony, and it is truly difficult to separate aesthetic evaluation from historical appraisal in them. The British historian Robert Conquest, for example, used the stories as one of his major sources in studying Kolyma.

Shalamov was evidently arrested for some unknown "crime" in 1929 while he was only twenty-two and a student at the law school of Moscow University. He was sentenced to five years in Solovki, a former monastery that had been confiscated from the Church and converted into a concentration camp. In 1937 he was arrested again and sentenced to five years in Kolyma. In 1942 his sentence was extended "till the end of the war"; in 1943 he received an additional ten-year sentence for having praised the effectiveness of the German army and having described Ivan BUNIN, the Nobel laureate, as a "classic author of Russian literature." He appears to have spent a total of seventeen years in Kolyma.

By his own admission, SOLZHENITSYN barely touches on Kolyma in *The Gulag Archipelago.* He asked Shalamov to co-author *The Gulag Archipelago* with him, but Shalamov—already an old, sick man—declined. Nevertheless, Solzhenitsyn writes: "Shalamov's experience in the camps was longer and more bitter than my own, and I respectfully confess that to him and not me was it given to touch those depths of bestiality and despair toward which life in the camps dragged us all."

Shalamov did manage to smuggle *Kolyma Tales* out to the West, and they were published in German and French (and only much later in English). The Soviet authorities then forced him to sign a statement, published in *Literaturnaya gazeta* in 1972, in which he stated that the topic of *Kolyma Tales* was no longer relevant after the 20th Party Congress, that he had never sent out any manuscripts, and that he was a loyal Soviet citizen.

Once Shalamov had renounced *Kolyma Tales*, he was permitted to publish his poetry in the Soviet Union, although it is so deeply intertwined with his prose work that one wonders what meaning these poems might have for Soviet readers who know nothing of his life and work.

The poems—rhymed, metered, and very traditional—began to appear in literary journals in 1956. Four small collections were published between 1961 and 1972. The poems are touched with a strong pantheism and are dedicated to nature.

Works: Kolymskie rasskazy. London, 1980.

Translations: Kolyma Tales. Trans. John Glad. 1980. *Graphite.* Trans. John Glad. 1981.

Secondary literature: John Glad, "Art out of Hell: Shalamov of Kolyma," *Survey* 107 (1979), pp. 45–50.　　　　J. G.

Shálikov, Pyotr Ivánovich (1767 or 1768–1852), writer and journalist, the son of a Georgian prince of moderate means, was educated by tutors, served in the army, and in 1799 resigned his commission in the rank of Premier-Major to devote himself to his literary pursuits. He published the journals *Moskovskii zritel'* (1806), *Aglaya* (1808–12), and *Damskii zhurnal* (1823–33), and was editor of the *Moskovskie vedomosti* (1813–36).

As a poet and prose writer, Shalikov was a lifelong follower of sentimentalism and a disciple of KARAMZIN and DMITRIEV. He gained literary fame by his volumes of verse, *Fruits of Free Emotions* (Plod svobodnykh chuvstvovanii, 3 pts., 1798–1801), and their sequel, *Flowers of the Graces* (Tsvety gratsii, 1802). In his prose works, such as *A Journey to the Ukraine* (Puteshestvie v Malorossiyu, 1803), *A Second Journey to the Ukraine* (Drugoe puteshestvie v Malorossiyu, 1804), and *A Journey to Kronstadt in 1805* (Puteshestvie v Kronshtadt 1805 goda, 1817), Shalikov followed the tradition of sentimental journeys established in Russia by Karamzin (*Letters of a Russian Traveller*) and continued by V. IZMAILOV (*A Journey to Southern Russia*).

As a journalist, Shalikov came forward with sharply worded essays and epigrams against the Shishkovians. Karamzin and Dmitriev, while speaking ironically of Shalikov's excessive sentimentality, patronized him. In the 1820s and 1830s Shalikov, now an epigone of sentimentalism, was the butt of some ridicule, as in some epigrams by PUSHKIN and, most probably, by LERMONTOV as well. Pushkin was, however, rather good-humored toward Shalikov as a person and even called him "that amiable minion of Nature" ("Conversation between a Bookseller and a Poet," 1st ed., 1825). Shalikov venerated Pushkin and addressed enthusiastic verses to him. He died at a ripe old age, having survived his literary fame by many years, probably the last Russian sentimentalist.

Works: Sochineniya knyazya Shalikova. Pts. 1–2. Moscow, 1819. *Istoricheskoe izvestie o prebyvanii v Moskve frantsuzov 1812 goda.* Moscow, 1813. [Poetry:] In *Poety 1790–1810-kh godov.* (Biblioteka poeta. Bol'shaya seriya.) Leningrad, 1971. Pp. 629–50. (With a biographic note by E. N. Dryzhakova.)

Secondary literature: M. G. Al'tshuller, "Neizvestnyi epizod zhurnal'noi polemiki nachala 19 veka (D. Khvostov i P. Shalikov)." In *Russkaya literatura 18 veka i ee mezhdunarodnye svyazi.* "18 vek" Sbornik 10. Leningrad, 1975. Pp. 98–106. L. A. Chereiskii, *Pushkin i ego okruzhenie.* Leningrad, 1976. Pp. 466–67.

　　　　M. A.

Sharshún, Sergei Ivánovich (Charchoune, Serge, 1888–1975), painter and writer. Born in Buguruslan, Russia, Sharshun moved to Paris in 1912. Although as a painter he was associated with many major artists of the century from as early as 1913, as a writer of Russian prose he first attracted attention only in the early 1930s when he published excerpts from his original novels in *Chisla* (1930–32). Most of them, however, were published before the Second World War only in mimeographed form. After a long hiatus Sharshun returned to considerable literary activity in the 1960s, publishing several new volumes and republishing several old ones, many as parts of his "solipsist epic" called *The Hero is More Interesting than the Novel* (Geroi interesnee romana). Sharshun described himself as a "magic realist." V. Markov has called him "the other Russian dadaist" (along with Ilya Zdanevich). Sharshun's own memoirs about his role in the French dadaist movement were published in *Vozdushnye puti*, no. 5 (1967).

Works: Dolgolikov. Paris, 1934, reprint 1961. *Put' pravyi.* Paris, 1934. *Iano Grustneishii ili khozhdenie k istokam ottsovskoi krovi.* Paris, 1951.

Secondary literature: M. Andreenko, "Zhurnal Sharshuna." In *Russkii al'manakh.* Ed. Z. Shakhovskaya. Paris, 1981. A. Bosquet and R. Guerra, *Charchoune.* Paris, 1973. W. Copley, *Charchoune.* London, 1961. G. P. Struve, *Russkaya literatura v izgnanii.* New York, 1956. Pp. 300–01. Yu. Terapiano, "S. I. Sharshun kak pisatel'," *Russkaya mysl'*, 22 January 1976.　　　　L. D.

Shcheglóv, Mark Aleksándrovich (1925–56), Soviet Russian literary critic. Despite a life-long struggle against an ultimately fatal disease (tuberculosis of the bone), Shcheglov completed his undergraduate studies in 1953 and began graduate studies in Russian literature at Moscow University. Here, in seminars conducted by such eminent scholars as N. K. Gudzy and S. M. Bondi, Shcheglov demonstrated an exceptional range of knowledge and interest in literary analysis. His limited reputation as a critic, however, is based upon a small corpus of writings produced in a mere three years, between the publication of his first critical article, "Peculiarities of Lev Tolstoi's Satire" (Osobennosti satiry L'va Tolstogo, 1953) and his early death at the age of thirty. Although his name is occasionally mentioned by Western scholars (e.g., his "sharp commentary on Soviet drama and literary criticism" in Edward J. Brown's *Russian Literature Since the Revolution*), the bulk of his criticism is quite conventional, replete with such concepts and terms as "types," "thinking in images," and "revolutionary significance." Shcheglov's main interests were in the writings of Lev Tolstoi but here, too, there is hardly anything distinctively new or perceptive, although his essay on *The Death of Ivan Ilyich* might well be included in a critical anthology. Two of his more interesting articles are his essay "Correctness of Details" (Vernost' detalei, 1953) which deals with the importance and function of details in the technique of realism; and his 1956 essay on Aleksandr GRIN in which he claims that this unusual writer's fantasies are not a withdrawal (ukhod) from reality but rather an entry (prikhod) into life.

Works: Literaturno-kriticheskie stat'i. Ed. V. Lakshin. 1965.

　　　　R. H. S.

Shchérba, Lev Vladímirovich (1880–1944), theoretical linguist, founder of the Leningrad School of phonology, student of Russian grammar and lexicology. As a student and follower of Baudouin de Courtenay, Shcherba advanced the theory of phonology in two of his major works: in his master's thesis which dealt with the Russian vowels (*Russkie glasnye v kachestvennom otnoshenii*, 1912) and in his doctoral dissertation which described the Lusatian dialect of Mužakov (Vostochnoluzhitskoe narechie, 1915). Problems of phonology were also taken up in his *Fonetika frantsuzskogo yazyka* (1969, 9th ed.) which confronted the phonemic system of French with that of Russian. In the footsteps of Baudouin, Shcherba also formulated a three-fold system of phonetic, phonemic, and morphophonemic notation, whereas the relations of speech and language are discussed in his *Yazykovaya sistema i rechevaya deyatel'nost'* (1974) and in *O troyakom aspekte yazykovykh yavlenii i ob eksperimente v yazykoznanii* (1931) which attempt to overcome the Saussurian antinomy between *langue* and *parole*. Thus Shcherba distinguished a passive command of language based on the knowledge of the ready-made linguistic elements from an active command which involves a dynamic and creative usage of the former and which affects modifications of their values. Shcherba saw the foremost task of linguistics in the synchronic comparison of languages and in the formulation of general linguistic laws. In addition to the study of natural languages and the live process of social communication, he emphasized the importance of gestures and of linguistic pathology (aphasia and the language of deaf-mutes). He participated in the adaptation of the Russian alphabet to the minority languages of the Soviet Union and wrote several major studies on the classification of dictionaries and on lexical problems. As a practical lexicographer, he contributed articles to the *Defining Dictionary of the Russian Language* (edited by Ushakov) and co-authored a Russian-French dictionary (1939; 1969⁹). Shcherba's involvement in Western scholarship, his theoretical concerns and his consistent structural approach to questions of phonology, grammar, and lexicology made him one of the most enlightened linguists of pre-war Russia.

Bibliography: M. G. Bulakhov, *Vostochnoslavyanskie yazykovedy.* Vol. 3. Minsk, 1978. Pp. 285–302. M. I. Matusevich, L. R. Zinder, and B. A. Larin, Introduction to *L. V. Shcherba: Izbrannye raboty po yazykoznaniyu i fonetike.* Vol. 1. 1958. V. V. Vinogradov, *Istoriya russkikh lingvisticheskikh uchenii.* 1978. Pp. 154–81.

E. S.

Shcherbína, Nikolaí Fyódorovich (1821–69), poet. Son of an impoverished country squire of the Don region and of a Greek mother, he received early training from his mother, and later studied at the Taganrog high school. He knew ancient Greek well. Shcherbina began studying law at Kharkov University in 1841, but lack of funds forced him to seek occasional employment as a private teacher with the country squirearchy of the Ukraine. In the 1850s he worked as assistant editor of the *Moskovskie gubernskie vedomosti* and later in St. Petersburg as secretary without portfolio to the Associate Minister of Education, Prince P. A. VYAZEMSKY.

Shcherbina began to publish at the age of seventeen: his sonnet "To the Sea" (K moryu) appeared in 1838 in *Syn otechestva* (Vol. 3, Pt. 2). An essay on modern Greek songs appeared in the periodical *Mayak* in 1844. The first collection of Shcherbina's verse, *Greek Poems* (Grecheskie stikhotvoreniya, Odessa, 1850), indicates his love for Greek antiquity and the ideals of ancient Greek civilization. In the 1860s Shcherbina wrote primarily satirical verse and two cycles of satirical prose.

Shcherbina is important for his verse celebrating themes of ancient Greece ("Bathing"—Kupan'e) and for daring to proclaim the lofty mission of the poet ("The Poet"—Poet) as a servant of "elevated thought" and "truth" at a time when radical critics emphasized the need for a socially relevant poetry. In his satirical works (poetry and prose) Shcherbina is evenhanded in directing his barbs towards both the left and the right of the political spectrum.

Works: Polnoe sobranie sochinenii. 1873.
Translations: Lewanski, p. 352.
Secondary literature: I. Aizenshtok, "N. F. Shcherbina." In N. F. Shcherbina, *Stikhotvoreniya.* 1937. Pp. 5–33.

J. B.

Shchipachóv, Stepán Petróvich (1898–), poet and Party functionary. Of peasant background, Shchipachov served in the Red Army from 1919 to 1931, publishing his verse mostly in local newspapers, pamphlets, and such. In 1934 he graduated from the literature department of the Institute of Red Professorship (*Institut Krasnoi professury*) and, having developed great facility as a versifier, soon found his lyric style: "singable" classical meters, mostly iambic, dealing with old themes (love, nature) as well as with new ones (the building of a socialist society, or even of the "Palace of the Soviets"), in moderately literate language and readily accessible imagery. World War II found Shchipachov doing his duty writing "Frontline Verses" (Frontovye stikhi, 1942). He earned several Stalin prizes for his efforts. Shchipachov's success continued almost unabated after the THAW, as his verse epics, such as "Song of Moscow" (Pesn' o Moskve, 1968) and "Twelve Months around the Sun" (12 mesyatsev vokrug Solntsa, 1969) properly merged tales of the past with paeans to a dynamic present and a glorious future. Shchipachov's works have appeared in large editions and have been translated into many languages of the Soviet Union and the Soviet bloc.

Works: Izbrannye proizvedeniya. 2 vols. 1972. *Proza.* 1972. *Rusyi veter.* 1972.
Translations: See *Lewanski,* pp. 352–53.
Secondary literature: Valerii Dement'ev, *Stepan Shchipachev: Ocherk zhizni i tvorchestva.* 1956. ———, *Sad pod livnem: Lirika Stepana Shchipacheva.* 1970. Vladimir Ognev and Berta Brainina, "Stepan Shchipachev," *Soviet Literature,* 1979, no. 1, pp. 133–37.

V. T.

Shelgunóv, Nikolai Vasilievich (1824–91), radical (in Soviet terms, "revolutionary-democratic") literary critic of the late 1860s and 1870s. A civil servant of gentry origin, he visited the exiled Aleksandr HERZEN in London (1858–59), collaborated with CHERNYSHEVSKY on SOVREMENNIK, and, shortly afterwards, because of his radical political involvements and writings, was arrested and imprisoned for almost two years. This was followed by several years of internal exile. As a critic, Shelgunov was influenced by the views of BELINSKY and the latter's "civic" epigones, Dobrolyubov, Chernyshevsky, and Pisarev, although he frequently expressed divergent opinions. His critical articles began in 1868 with "Russian Ideals, Heroes, and Types" in which he lauds literature as an arena of political struggle (for him PUSHKIN, LERMONTOV, and TURGENEV are belletrists and belong to an "aesthetic school") and emphasizes the importance of representative types in fiction (as opposed to eccentric, individualized characters). In "Popular [*narodnyi*] Realism in Literature" (1871) he finds this "radical" or "critical" realism, in contrast to the "manor" realism of GONCHAROV, exemplified in the novels of Fyodor RESHETNIKOV (Shelgunov's "popular realism" is sometimes noted as a precursor of "socialist realism"). In his "Sketches of Russian Life" (posthumous, 1895) Shelgunov sees in Pushkin the beginnings of a Russian national consciousness and evaluates him more sympathetically. Towards the end of the 1870s Shelgunov shows a certain disillusionment with literature as a political force and his later journalistic activities are concerned mainly with current events.

Works: Sochineniya (various editions, 1871–1904). *Literaturnaya kritika.* 1974.
Secondary literature: See brief notice in R. Stacy, *Russian Literary Criticism: A Short History* (1974).

R. H. S.

Shershenévich, Vadím Gabriélevich (1893–1942), poet, theoretician, translator, playwright, and screenwriter, graduated in physics and mathematics from Moscow University, but devoted his life to literature. His name was at first associated with FUTURISM, and later with IMAGISM. His first collections of verses, *Patches of Earth Free of Snow* (Vesennie protalinki, 1911) and *Carmina* (1913) reveal the influence of SYMBOLIST and ACMEIST poetry. Shershenevich's futurist period starts with the collections, *Romantic Face Powder* (Romanticheskaya pudra, 1913) and *Extravagant Scent Bottles* (Ekstravagantnye flakony, 1913). In these collections, Shershenvich moves from the salon poetry of SEVERYANIN to the tragic urbanism of MAYAKOVSKY. Shershenevich's last collection of futurist verses, *Automobile Gait* (Avtomobil'ya postup') was issued in 1916.

In 1913, Shershenevich founded the futurist group, Mezzanine of Poetry, which included K. Bolshakov, R. IVNEV, and L. Zak. The group issued three almanacs, *Vernissage* (Vernissazh, 1913), *Feast During the Plague* (Pir vo vremya chumy, 1913), and *Crematorium of Common Sense* (Krematorii zdravomysliya, 1913), to which Shershenevich contributed articles, essays, and poetry. In the same year, Shershenevich published his first theoretical treatise, *Futurism Without a Mask* (Futurizm bez maski). This was followed by a second treatise, *Green Street* (Zelenaya ulitsa, 1916), which reiterated the main points of Shershenevich's poetic theory. Namely, that the essence of poetry lies in the "word-image" (a fresh metaphor not automatized by use) and that a poem must be an uninterrupted "chain of images." Shershenevich credits the Italian futurist, F. T. Marinetti with this idea. Shershenevich's translations of *Manifestoes of Italian Futurism* (1914), *The Battle of Tripoli* (1916), and *Mafarka, The Futurist* (1916) witness to his interest in the Italian poet. Other translations include works by Laforgue, and a treatise by C. Vildrac and G. Duhamel. The latter served as the basis for Shershenevich's theory of the "*vers libre* of images," in his imagist book, $2 \times 2 = 5$ (1920).

In 1919, Shershenevich together with S. ESENIN and A. MARIEN-GOF founded imagism. Later, I. Gruzinov, A. Kusikov, R. Ivnev and others joined the imagists. Shershenevich's contribution to imagist poetry includes three volumes of verses: *Just an Ordinary Horse* (Loshad' kak loshad', 1920), *Cooperatives of Happiness* (Kooperativy vesel'ya, 1921), *And Now for a Summary* (Itak itog, 1926), a tragedy: *The Eternal Jew* (Vechnyi zhid, 1919), a long *poema*: *Crematorium* (Krematorii, 1919), and a drama in verse and prose: *Absurdity from Beginning to End* (Odna sploshnaya nelepost', 1922). He also contributed articles and poetry to the imagist journal, *Gostinitsa dlya puteshestvuyushchikh v prekrasnom*. Within the spectrum of the avant-garde, Shershenevich was a left-winger. His radicalism is evidenced by his bold experimentation with new poetic forms, his daring, if impractical, theoretical statements, his use of anti-aesthetic imagery, his favorite theme of the poet as a rebel and an outcast.

During the civil war, Shershenevich worked with Mayakovsky for the news agency ROSTA. After imagism was disbanded, he wrote for the theater and the cinema. He translated Shakespeare, Corneille, and Brecht. His memoirs, *The Magnificent Eye-Witness* (Velikolepnyi ochevidets) remain unpublished. Shershenevich died in Barnaul, Siberia on 18 May 1942.

Translations: One poem, "When like a nut," in *Modern Russian Poetry*. V. Markov and M. Sparks, eds. 1967. Pp. 714–17.

Secondary literature: A. Lawton, *Vadim Shershenevich: From Futurism to Imaginism*. 1981. ———, "Shershenevich, Marinetti, and the 'Chain of Images'," *SEEJ* 23 (1979), pp. 203–15. ———, "Vadim Shershenevich: A Futurist Westernizer," *RLT* 12 (1975), pp. 327–44; reprint in *The Ardis Anthology of Russian Futurism*. 1980. V. Markov, *Russian Futurism: A History*. 1968. ———, *Russian Imagism. 1919–1924*. Giessen, 1980. N. Å. Nilsson, *The Russian Imaginists*. Stockholm, 1970. C. F. Ponomareff, "The Image Seekers: An Analysis of Imaginist Poetic Theory, 1919–1924," *SEEJ* 12 (1968), pp. 275–96.   A. L.

Shestidesyátniki, literally "men of the 1860s." The term usually designates the group of "civic poets" headed by NEKRASOV, who were noted for their caustic and humorous satire during the socially disruptive period before and after the emancipation of the peasants in 1861. Under the influence of CHERNYSHEVSKY and French socialism, the *shestidesyatniki* stressed the didactic in their poignant writings, which judged politics, society, and art by utilitarian populist ideals. They wrote in all genres, but excelled in allegory, caricature, feuilleton, and punning epigram. They often disguised the subversive and the erotic in AESOPIAN LANGUAGE and avoided censorship by deliberate indefiniteness or exaggeration. The sarcasm of the *shestidesyatniki* was directed against the government, which was presented as running a police state; the gentry, which was depicted as a class of oppressors; Philistinism in society and politics; and "pure art," which was considered pointless, if not immoral. Many of their poems were used by major Russian composers in songs, and in 1905 and 1917, *shestidesyatniki* lyrics were used in revolutionary chants and marches. Because of censorship and police surveillance, many of the *shestidesyatniki* wrote under pseudonyms. Major *shestidesyatniki*, such as DOBROLYUBOV, MIKHAILOV, MINAEV, NIKITIN, and others are listed individually in this volume.

Many writers of lesser importance were significant in the literary history of the period. Vasily Ivanovich Bogdanov (1837–86), a naval surgeon, published in several satirical journals: *Iskra, Oskolki, Budil'nik*. He taught the young Sofya Bers (Lev Tolstoi's wife) and was warmly remembered in her memoirs. He wrote the lyrics of one of the most popular revolutionary songs, "Dubinushka." Viktor Petrovich Burenin (1841–1926) was a major contributor to *Iskra* from 1863 to 1865. He later published in SOVREMENNIK and *Vestnik Evropy*. Because of Burenin's article against KATKOV, in 1872 issue 15 of *Iskra* was confiscated by the authorities. In the mid-1870s Burenin deserted the ranks of the "progressives" and turned reactionary. Grigory Zakharovich Eliseev (1821–91) began his literary career as a professor of theology in Kazan where he wrote theological treatises, but in 1858 moved to Petersburg and soon became one of the leaders of the revolutionary intelligentsia, co-editor of *Iskra, Sovremennik* and OTECHESTVENNYE ZAPISKI. His many articles almost always appeared anonymously. His claim to fame is that he is the pro-

totype of Rakitin in DOSTOEVSKY's *The Brothers Karamazov*. Ivan Ivanovich Golts-Miller (Gol'ts-Miller) (1842–71), an active revolutionary, wrote the poem "Listen" (Slushai) which became a famous revolutionary song. Golts-Miller published in *Sovremennik* and in *Otechestvennye zapiski*. Nikolai Loginovich Loman (1830–92) wrote humorous parodies of major poets in the "pure art" school. Loman's poems were printed in *Iskra* under the pseudonym N. G. Gnut. Iliodor Ivanovich Palmin (Pal'min) (1841–91) also worked for liberal and conservative journals because of his poverty, but wrote mainly on social themes for *Iskra*. CHEKHOV valued him as a poet and friend. Palmin wrote the lyrics of the popular revolutionary song, "Requiem" ("Ne plach'te nad trupami pavshikh bortsov," 1865). Pyotr Vasilievich Shumakher (1817–91), a contributor to *Iskra*, was noted for "To My Countrymen" (Moim zemlyakam, 2 vols., 1873–80), a collection of witty, but politically inflammatory poems, which I. S. TURGENEV helped him publish in Berlin. Aleksei Pavlovich Snitkin (1829–60) was a promising young humorist and poet-satirist who wrote under the pseudonym "Ammos Shishkin" for *Iskra*, before dying of a cold after appearing in a production of *The Inspector-General* for a theater fund, together with Dostoevsky, Turgenev, and PISEMSKY. Dostoevsky praised Snitkin in a letter to A. I. Shubert (3 May 1860). Pyotr Isaevich Veinberg (1831–1908) had a large following for his funny poems published under the pseudonym "Heine from Tambov" in *Iskra* and other journals. Veinberg was a noted translator from English, French, and German. Gavriil Nikolaevich Zhulyov (1836–78) was one of the most popular poet-humorists on the staff of *Iskra*. Zhulyov, a successful actor in the Aleksandrinsky Theater, published under the pseudonym "A Melancholy Poet" (Skorbnyi poet).

Bibliography. Editions: *Poety "Iskry."* With an introd. by I. G. Yampol'skii. 2 vols. 1955. *Poety 1860-kh godov*. 1968.

Secondary literature: G. M. Lebedeva, *Satiricheskii zhurnal "Iskra"*. 1959. I. G. Yampol'skii, *Satiricheskaya zhurnalistika 1860-kh godov*. 1964.   T. E. B.

Shestóv (pseud. of Lev Isaákovich Shvártsman, 1866–1938), philosopher and critic. Born in Kiev into the family of a wealthy businessman, Shestov had a choice of several careers. He held a law degree, successfully managed the family's textile business, was musically gifted and had a fine voice. But his real interest was in philosophy and literature. In 1895 he went abroad and lived in Italy and Switzerland until 1914. During this period he wrote prolifically and quickly earned the reputation of an original thinker and fine stylist. His first book, *Shakespeare and His Critic Brandes* (1898) received little attention, but his second book, the provocative *Tolstoi and Nietzsche: Philosophy and Preaching* (1900) created a lively controversy, as Shestov had boldly taken Nietzsche's side against TOLSTOI, calling the former's stand against traditional values more honest than Tolstoi's unctuous moralism. Several more books followed: *Dostoevsky and Nietzsche: The Philosophy of Tragedy* (1903); *The Apotheosis of Groundlessness* (Apofeoz bespochvennosti, 1905; translated into English as *All Things Are Possible*, 1920); *Beginnings and Endings* (Nachala i kontsy, 1908, translated into English as *Penultimate Words and Other Essays*, 1916). Even in these early works one can recognize the positions of what was later to be called "existentialism," specifically a dogged insistence on assuming the viewpoint of the concrete human individual. Shestov takes up the thoughts of DOSTOEVSKY's anti-hero in "Notes from Underground" (1864), challenging modern scientism and moral rationalism, and defending the reality of human free will.

Shestov and his family spent the years 1914 to 1919 in Russia, then emigrated to France, where Shestov gradually gained an eminent position as a philosopher. He lectured widely, taught at the Sorbonne, and saw his works translated into the major Western languages. Shestov was a thinker who was not afraid to restate and reformulate his thoughts, and his last books, *In Job's Balances* (Na vesakh Iova, 1929), *Kierkegaard and Existential Philosophy* (1936), and *Athens and Jerusalem* (Afiny i Ierusalim, 1938), while they do not add much to the philosophic substance of his earlier writings, are dialectic and stylistic masterpieces whose power and charm are equal to Kierkegaard's and Nietzsche's. The central idea developed here is a vigorous rejection of rationalism in all of its aspects, whether it be a scientific worldview which subjects man to inexorable laws of nature, the laws of logic with their theorems of no contradiction and sufficient reason, or universally obligatory moral rules. To Shestov, the real critique of pure reason says that if man is to trust reason, he must accept for a fact that his life, short and full of suffering, will end in total extinction. Unwilling to accept this, Shestov chooses the road to faith in God, which alone can give man freedom and joy.

Shestov's importance is threefold. His limpid prose is unsurpassed in 20th-century literature: his only peer as an essayist is Osip MANDELSHTAM. As a philosopher, Shestov is one of the most important exponents of existentialism. As a literary critic, he made important contributions to our understanding of Dostoevsky, Tolstoi, CHEKHOV, TURGENEV, and others.

Works: See "The Works of Lev Shestov" in *A Shestov Anthology.* Ed. with an introd. Bernard Martin. Athens, Ohio, 1970. Pp. 322–28. "Turgenev: Glava iz neopublikovannoi knigi," *Glagol* 2 (1978), pp. 131–39. *Turgenev.* Ann Arbor, 1982.

Secondary literature: V. F. Asmus, "Lev Shestov i K'erkegor," *Filosofskie nauki,* 1972, no. 4. Nathalie Baranoff, *Bibliographie des études sur Léon Chestov.* Paris, 1978. N. Baranova-Shestova, *Zhizn' L'va Shestova.* 2 vols. Paris, 1983. James M. Curtis, "Shestov's Use of Nietzsche in His Interpretation of Tolstoi and Dostoevsky," *Texas Studies in Literature and Language* 17 (1975), pp. 289–302. V. Erofeev, "Ostaetsya odno—proizvol: Filosofiya odinochestva i literaturnoe kredo L. Shestova," *VLit* 19 (1975), no. 10, pp. 153–88. R. V. Ivanov-Razumnik, *O smysle zhizni: F. Sologub, L. Andreev, Lev Shestov.* 1908. David Patterson, "Šestov's Second Dimension": In Job's Balances," *SEEJ* 22 (1978), pp. 141–52. Louis J. Shein, "Lev Shestov: A Russian Existentialist," *RusR* 26 (1967), pp. 278–85.

V. T.

Shevchénko, Tarás (1814–61), Ukrainian romantic poet. Shevchenko provided in his poems the raison d'être of the modern Ukrainian nation. The mythic poet became a national prophet. The Ukrainian identity, as evoked by Shevchenko, was necessarily separate from Russia, its history, and culture. Yet the relationship of the poet, who was born a serf and spent ten years in internal exile, to Russian literature is lasting though complex and ambivalent. It is all the more difficult to perceive because of the official Soviet interpretation which is based on the alleged overwhelming and beneficent influence of Russian literature on all the non-Russian literatures of the USSR. In actual fact, the Russian literary ambience was to Shevchenko as much of a repellent as a stimulus.

If one regards language as the main determinant of literature, Shevchenko also belongs to Russian literature since he wrote two long poems, two plays, and nine long short stories (not counting his diary in exile) in Russian. Significantly, all of them are of much poorer quality than his Ukrainian poems and, as G. Grabowicz has convincingly argued recently, belong to a different, more controlled mode of expression. Most of Shevchenko's contemporaries among the writers in the Ukraine wrote some of their works in Russian, but their contribution to Russian literature was very limited. Of those Ukrainians who wrote exclusively in Russian, only GOGOL stands at the very pinnacle. Shevchenko was an admirer of Gogol and in a poem dedicated to him stressed their different roles of "laughing" and "crying." One could detect some impact from Gogol's *Taras Bulba* on Shevchenko's historical poems. In terms of influence Shevchenko was also susceptible to ZHUKOVSKY, BARATYNSKY, and RYLEEV. Shevchenko admired the latter as one of the Decembrists. He was equally sympathetic to the émigré writings of HERZEN. But while admiring Russian revolutionaries and dissidents, Shevchenko retained his own ideal of a Christian revolution in which a reawakened Ukraine would play a prime part. His uncompromising rejection of tsarist social and national policies did not lead him, contrary to Soviet scholars' interpretations, to the camp of CHERNYSHEVSKY and DOBROLYUBOV. In 1860, at the time of his supposedly close relationship with Chernyshevsky, Shevchenko wrote that "the day passes and so does the night ... but the apostle of truth and knowledge does not come."

Not all Russian writers regarded Shevchenko as favorably as did Herzen and Chernyshevsky. His main critic was BELINSKY who on several occasions, especially in a review of the poem "Haidamaky," severely censured Shevchenko for trying to develop a viable literature in Ukrainian. Belinsky tolerated some Ukrainian writers (KVITKA), but thought that Ukrainians should write in Russian, like Gogol, if they wanted to be read and appreciated by a wide public. When, in 1847, Shevchenko, along with other Ukrainian intellectuals, was arrested for belonging to the secret society of Sts. Cyril and Methodius, Belinsky applauded this harsh act against what he believed to be a misguided liberalism. For his part, Shevchenko defended his works and was pursuing a concept of NARODNOST similar to that which Belinsky advocated for Russian literature. Although Belinsky was unfamiliar with the political poems of Shevchenko he sensed, quite rightly, that they pointed in a separatist direction. Ukrainian cultural separatism with all its political implications, was unacceptable to most Russian intellectuals, with the exception of Herzen. Rather, most of them regarded the Ukraine as a part of Russia and were patronizing towards Ukrainian romantic literature. OGARYOV, writing in 1861, considered Shevchenko to be a poet native to Russia. There were also those like Apollon GRIGORIEV, who recognized the uniqueness of Shevchenko's works and regarded him as the first great Slavic poet. Like many others, he thought of Shevchenko primarily as a *narodnyi poet,* and the image of the "peasant poet," with its inevitable comparison to the Russian self-taught poet KOLTSOV, stuck to Shevchenko for a long time.

Shevchenko's first collection of poems, *The Minstrel* (Kobzar, 1840) received mixed reviews in the Russian periodical press. Most recognized his poetic talent, but some regretted that he wrote in Ukrainian, not in Russian. The viability of Ukrainian literature was severely undercut by the arrest of Shevchenko and KULISH in 1847. There followed a prolonged period of official repression of Ukrainian publications, which culminated in the so-called Valuev circular in 1863 and the Ems *ukaz* in 1876, prohibiting Ukrainian literature. Many Ukrainian books came to be printed in Galicia (Austro-Hungary), assuring the survival of that literature. As an author persecuted in the Russian Empire, Shevchenko received, both in his lifetime and after his death much support from many Russian critics and intellectuals (Dobrolyubov, PYPIN, Ovsyaniko-Kulikovsky). Most of his political poems, however, were unknown and remained unpublished until after 1905. Several Russian writers who knew Shevchenko (TURGENEV, LESKOV, POLONSKY) left sympathetic memoirs of him.

Shevchenko's impact on Russian literature was manifold and lasting. During his life minor Russian poets (A. PLESHCHEEV, V. KUROCHKIN) translated Shevchenko's poems and admired his work. Others (FET, PISEMSKY) viewed him with hostility. Some Russian revolutionaries (Stepnyak-KRAVCHINSKY) were ardent admirers of Shevchenko's poetry, while its masterful translations into Russian were accomplished by the modernists BRYUSOV and SOLOGUB. Other well-known Russian writers who translated Shevchenko were MEI, KRESTOVSKY, BUNIN, PASTERNAK, and TVARDOVSKY. The only case of any genuine influence of Shevchenko's poetry on Russian literature can be attested in E. BAGRITSKY's "Duma pro Opanasa." K. CHUKOVSKY and M. ZOSHCHENKO wrote fine appreciations of Shevchenko. In general, the poet was perceived by Russian writers as a martyr for the Ukrainian cause and an original peasant poet. This image of Shevchenko is closer to the truth than the official Soviet one of the revolutionary democrat and a friend of Russia.

Works: Povne zibrannja tvoriv v shesty tomakh. Kiev, 1963–64. F. Ya. Priima, *Shevchenko i russkaya literatura XIX veka.* 1961. G. Luckyj, ed. *Shevchenko and the Critics.* Toronto, 1980.

G. L.

Shevyryóv, Stepán Petróvich (1806–64), literary historian, critic, and minor poet. Shevyryov, born into a Saratov gentry family and educated in Moscow, contributed some early verse to SEVERNYE TSVETY in 1826. He met PUSHKIN and began his publicistic work by joining the staff of the MOSKOVSKII VESTNIK in 1827, although by profession he was an academic (from 1834 a professor of Russian literature at Moscow University). His youthful enthusiasm for German romanticism soon developed into an extreme form of Russian nationalism, which led him directly into the SLAVOPHILE camp. In 1835 he joined the staff of the *Moskovskii nablyudatel'* and it was an article of his in this journal the same year on GOGOL's *Mirgorod* that aroused the ire of Belinsky who excoriated Shevyryov the following year in *Teleskop.* Shevyryov, who viewed Gogol as a distorter of reality and a poet of the "absurdity of life" (Belinsky considered

Gogol a realist), also spoke of such things as the "genteel" and "elevating" qualities in literature. But Pushkin admired Shevyryov (not least because the latter wrote some devastating criticism of Pushkin's *bête noire*, Faddeí BULGARIN). In 1841 Shevyryov joined MOSK-VITYANIN and his essays on Pushkin (*Sochineniya Pushkina*, 1841) are considered among his best efforts. In 1841 he also began a series of articles condemning the corrupting influence of the West on Russian thought and literature and later wrote his *History of Russian Literature, Primarily Ancient* (Istoriya russkoi slovesnosti, preimushchestvenno drevnei, 1846–60). For reasons of health he went abroad in 1863 and died in Paris in 1864.

Works: Istoriya russkoi slovesnosti, preimushchestvenno drevnei. 4 vols. 1846–60. *Lektsii o russkoi literature, chitannye v Parizhe v 1862 g.* 1884. *Stikhotvoreniya.* 1939.

Secondary literature: Brief notices in V. I. Kuleshov, *Istoriya russkoi kritiki* (1972), and R. Stacy, *Russian Literary Criticism: A Short History* (1974).

R. H. S.

Shirínsky-Shikhmátov, Prince Sergeí Aleksándrovich (1783–1837), Russian poet, was educated in the Corps of Naval Cadets (1795–1800) and in 1800 was assigned, in the rank of a midshipman, to the Naval Committee of Learning (*Morskoi uchenyi komitet*), affiliated with the Admiralty and headed by A. S. SHISHKOV, whose faithful and consistent disciple he became. From 1804 to 1827 he was a tutor at the Corps of Naval Cadets. On 25 March 1830 he took holy vows, assuming the name of Anikita. In the years 1834 to 1836 he made a pilgrimage to Jerusalem. In 1836 he was made an archimandrite with the church of the Russian embassy in Athens, where he died the following year. Shirinsky-Shikhmatov was elected to the Russian Academy in 1809 and was a member of the Colloquy of Lovers of the Russian Word (BESEDA LYUBITELEI RUSSKOGO SLOVA) from 1811 to 1816.

Shirinsky-Shikhmatov's literary career began with a translation of Pope's *Essay on Criticism* in 1806. His best-known works are the lyric *poema* "Pozharsky, Minin, Hermogenus, or Russia Saved" (1807) and "Peter the Great: A Lyric Epopoeia in eight cantos" (1810). Shirinsky-Shikhmatov consistently followed the literary principles of *Beseda*, as his verses are characterized by a solemn "high" style, avoidance of foreign words, and a wealth of Slavonicisms. A significant feature of his poetics is an absence of verb rhymes, which gives them a certain inner tension. Shirinsky-Shikhmatov tried to extend his solemn high style to all forms of literature, as for instance in "On my Dear Brother's Return to our Native Land" (1810). His activities elicited sharp criticism on the part of Arzamas. He was ridiculed by BATYUSHKOV, Vasily and Aleksandr PUSHKIN, VYAZEM-SKY, etc. But among the so-called young archaists (KATENIN, GLINKA, etc.) his works met with some favorable attention. KYUKHELBEKER, in particular, valued him highly for his revival of the high odic genre.

Works: [Poetry, excerpts from verse epics:] *Poety 1790–1810 godov.* (Biblioteka poeta. Bol'shaya seriya.) Biografic note and comm. by M. G. Al'tshuller. Leningrad, 1971. Pp. 365–423.

Secondary literature: Mark Al'tshuller, "Shikhmatov bezglagol'nyi..." *Novoe russkoe slovo*, 2 August 1979. V. Kyukhel'beker, "Razbor poemy knyazya Shikhmatova 'Pyotr Velikii'" (1825). *In* V. K. Kyukhel'beker, *Puteshestvie. Dnevnik. Stat'i.* Ed. N. V. Korolëva, V. D. Rak [M. G. Al'tshuller]. Leningrad, 1979. Pp. 469–92. *See also the index under* Shirinsky-Shikhmatov. P. A. Shirinskii-Shikhmatov, *O zhizni i trudakh ieromonakha Anikity, v mire knyazya S. A. Shikhmatova.* 2d ed. St. Petersburg, 1858.

M. A.

Shishkóv, Aleksándr Semyónovich (1754–1841), writer and statesman. Thoroughly conservative in both political and literary attitude, Shishkov sought to defend the Russian literary language against what he regarded as its unjustified Europeanization by KARAMZIN and his followers. His "Discourse on the Old and New Style in the Russian Language" (1803) asserted that Old CHURCH SLAVONIC was "the root and source" of Russian, and following LOMONOSOV's prescription, Shishkov urged the preservation of three stylistic levels, accommodating the ecclesiastical and colloquial languages in varying degree. Rather than permitting calques largely patterned after the French, he recommended that Slavic roots be used for any new ex-

pressions. A second, more productive aspect of the "Discourse" was its advocacy of the simple language of the folk as an additional source for literary Russian. Shishkov was reacting against the mannerisms characteristic of the Karamzinians' literary practice but his promotion of folk genres had positive implications for the subsequent development of Russian literature. Among his several "Conversations about Literature" (1811) is a study in which he correctly describes the fixed epithets and other lexical and structural features of Russian folk poetry.

Publication of the "Discourse" and later statements in a similar vein provoked considerable debate, with opposing positions being assumed by Shishkov's own Society of Lovers of the Russian Word (BESEDA LYUBITELEI RUSSKOGO SLOVA) and the more liberal ARZAMAS group. A variety of the era's more conservative thinkers and writers, including DERZHAVIN, KRYLOV and GRIBOEDOV, were attracted to the former. In addition to its literary significance, their debate marked the beginning of the protracted conflict between SLAV-OPHILES and WESTERNIZERS.

Works: Zapiski, mneniya i perepiska. Vols. 1 and 2. Berlin-Prague, 1870.

Secondary literature: N. I. Mordovchenko, *Russkaya kritika pervoi chetverti XIX veka.* 1959.

P. R. H.

Shishkóv, Vyacheslív Yákovlevich (1873–1945), novelist, essayist, and short-story writer. The son of a merchant's employee, Shishkov graduated from the Vyshnevolotskoe Technical School in 1891 and worked as a civil engineer based in Tomsk from 1894 to 1914. His yearly expeditions along the rivers of Siberia were a source of rich ethnographic material which inspired numerous travel sketches in local newspapers. In 1912 he drew close to the neorealists REMIZOV and ZAMYATIN, and Petersburg journals began publishing his stories about wanderers, "Vanka Khlyust" (1914); Siberian peasants, "The Beauty" (Kralya, 1913); and ethnic minorities, "They Prayed" (Pomolilis', 1912) and "The Quick Verdict" (Sud skoryi, 1914). The appearance of his first collection *Siberian Tales* (Sibirskii skaz, 1916), and a short novel depicting peasant life, *Taiga* (1916), established his literary reputation. After the Revolution Shishkov gave up engineering for full-time writing; he published colorful novels about revolutionary partisans, *The Gang* (Vataga, 1924) and *Lake Peipus* (Peipus ozero, 1925), and several volumes of humorous stories about the new Soviet environment, "A Performance in the Hamlet of Ogryzovo" (Spektakl' v sele Ogryzove, 1924) and *The Celebration* (Torzhestvo, 1925). His penchant for a large canvas led to *Wanderers* (Stranniki; English trans., *Children of Darkness*, 1931), a novel about homeless delinquents spawned by war's destruction; *Grim River* (Ugryum reka, 1933), a two-volume epic about mercantile exploitation in Siberia; and ultimately the three-volume Stalin prize winning historical narrative *Emelyan Pugachev* (1941–47), which combined a balanced description of the famous 18th-century rebel with a broad panorama of the epoch of Catherine the Great. An original and interesting writer with a sense of humor and a predilection for colloquial narrative, Shishkov is much underrated and relatively unknown outside of Russia.

Works: Polnoe sobranie sochinenii. 12 vols. 1926–29. *Neopublikovannye proizvedeniya—Vospominaniya o V. Ya. Shishkove—Pis'ma.* 1956. *Sobranie sochinenii.* 8 vols. 1960–62.

Translations: Lewanski, p. 353.

Secondary literature: V. Bakhmetov, *Vyacheslav Shishkov.* 1947. A. Bogdanova, *Vyacheslav Shishkov.* 1953. I. Izotov, *Vyacheslav Shishkov.* 1956. M. Maizel, *Vyacheslav Shishkov.* 1935.

A. M. S.

Shkápskaya (neé Andreévskaya), Maríya Mikhaílovna (1891–1952), poet, was born in St. Petersburg into a highly cultured family. Her mother, a Russian German, suffered from a nervous disorder, a fact which is partly reflected in some verses of Shkapskaya's collection "The Blood Ore" (Krov'-ruda). While still in secondary school, Shkapskaya participated in the activities of student groups of the Social Revolutionaries, distributing illegal literature and taking part in revolutionary demonstrations. She was expelled from school and stripped of the right to enter any educational institution of the Russian Empire. She eventually graduated from the émigré gymnasium in Paris, where she also attended the lectures of Henri Bergson. She then graduated from the faculty of letters of Toulouse University in 1914. Her first verses were published in 1910. Marriage and the birth of her children played a decisive role in her development as a poet. Her verses (her first volume came out in 1920) were hailed by writers of such diametrically opposed views as Maksim GORKY and Father Pavel FLORENSKY. The former wrote to Shkapskaya in January 1923: "You ... have taken to a new and very wide road. No woman before you has spoken so truthfully and in so firm a voice of her significance as a woman." Father Florensky placed Shkapskaya's verses, compressed to the utmost limit in their form and emotional tension, above TSVETAEVA's and perhaps even AKHMATOVA's (at the time not yet the author of "Poem without a Hero"). The thematics of Shkapskaya's poetry is essentially limited to the experiences of a wife-lover-mother. Love, conception, pregnancy, birth or abortion, the death of a child, jealousy, "a woman's Golgotha": "Having experienced love's captivating Eden, give birth to a child she knows not why ..." ("Blood Ore"); "My body was without an outlet, and burnt by black smoke. The black foe of the human race stood there, bent over it rapaciously. And to him, forgetting my pride, I gave my blood to the end, for the single hope of a son with dear features." These themes had not often been treated in this fashion. Many had written about a woman's lot, but all too often these were "lady writers." Shkapskaya's verses praised even pregnancy as "temptation of a blessed burden": "To walk down the street as a queen, proud of her dual fate. To know that your blind womb has been called upon, and that it is to be both sovereign and slave ..." Or: "To be like a beast, like a wild she-wolf, unquenchable in her forest anguish, when the time has come to be again embodied and be once more alone and separate." A woman cannot—and should not—acquiesce to where "there could be loveless conceptions, without being marked by a terrible sign of God":

> Couple upon couple— man and wife,
> In a dance of love, one after another.
> . . . .
> Let us drop the seed and gather the fruit,
> We sow wind and reap the whirlwind.
>
> ("A Stern Master's Drum")

And God, that "stern master," observes a stern law—of heredity, of immutable, unconscious traditions and impulses. He ("The Shrewd Sower") watches the "hours of conception," "meager, sickly, feeble human seeds." And how terrible is the death of an infant, but the birth of a dead child is more terrible yet: "Only a silent trace in the heart, flesh of my flesh, vein of my veins." But the most tragic of all is an abortion: "... and my blood flowed, without drying, not joyfully like last time, and later our disconcerted eyes were not gladdened by an empty cradle. Once again, pagan fashion, we make human sacrifices for our children's life. And Thou, oh Lord, dost not rise from the dead in answer to this crunching of infant bones" ("Mater Dolorosa"). A mother, even if she is a believer, when her children are still small, does not care much about Christ, and the mother asks Him to pass by her "peaceful house"—let the Lord come to see her "later some time, but only not today":

> Not like modest Martha—more warmly and closer,
> Like ardent Mary will I meet Thee.
> But now, Lord, the masters of my days are
> Thine rivals—my dear little babes.
>
> ("Mater Dolorosa")

Blood ore, love-pain-jealousy-despair, that whole "woman's Golgotha," overshadow, and push back God. And there is another thing: Man in general cannot accept death, but a mother certainly will not accept the death of her son. And if a mother cannot forgive God her son's death, she certainly will never forgive it to the Revolution. Shkapskaya had the courage to write, in 1921, a poem entitled "To Louis XVII" (in "A Stern Master's Drum"), which sharply and adamantly condemns the murder of Tsarevich Aleksei who, like Louis XVII before him, "delivered his ancient ransom" for all the sins and injustices of old Russia:

> But I remember, with grief and clearly, that
> I am a mother, and our law is simple:
> We are innocent of this blood,
> As we were innocent of that other.

Father Pavel Florensky called Shkapskaya a true Christian at heart. Perhaps it would be more apt to call her the Vasilisa Rozanova of Russian poetry, for, like Vasily Rozanov, she restored in her lyrics the sacred rights of the *flesh*. Also, the high tragedy of a woman's lot. "Shkapskaya's verses weep over what was not to be" (E. Zhiglevich, introd. essay to M. Shkapskaya, *Stikhi*, 1979). Shkapskaya's fate was a tragic one. As a poet, she was suppressed in the very zenith of her creative life: her verses were no longer printed after 1925, and starting that year she began to work on a history of Leningrad factories. She became a travelling correspondent-feuilletonist of the Leningrad *Vechernyaya Krasnaya Gazeta*, and the various achievements of the workers of the *Krasnyi vyborzhets* plant, of the weavers of Samarkand, of the cotton growers of Tadzhikistan became the subject of her essays and of whole books. So did, when the war came, Nazi atrocities. All of these things are written in a literate, even lively style, but her poetic creativity was stopped in the very flower of her creative powers.

Works: (Poetry:) "Mater Dolorosa." Petersburg, 1920. (2d ed. Berlin, Revel, 1921). "Chas vechernii." Petersburg, 1921. "Baraban strogogo gospodina." Berlin, 1922. "Krov'-ruda." Berlin, 1923. "Yav': poema." Moscow, 1923. "Kniga o Lukavom Seyatele." Moscow, 1923. "Zemnye remesla." Moscow, 1925. (Poems in Prose:) "Tsa-Tsa-Tsa" (kitaiskaya poema). Berlin, 1923. (Selected Poems:) *Stikhi*. With introd. essays by B. Filippov and E. Zhiglevich. London, 1979. (Contains poetry and "Tsa-Tsa-Tsa"). (Sketches:) *Sama po sebe*. 1930. *Voda i veter*. 1931. *Pyatnadtsat' i odin*. 1931. *Chelovek rabotaet khorosho*. 1932. *Eto bylo na samom dele*. 1942. *Puti i poiski*. 1968.

Translations: Marie Trommèr, *Poems by Women Poets of Russia*. Brooklyn, 1941.

Secondary literature: A. Bakhrakh, "Vspominaya Shkapskuyu," *Novoe russkoe slovo*, 9 December 1979. N. Berberova, "Baraban Strogogo Gospodina" (review), *Novaya russkaya kniga*, 1922, no. 8. V. Bryusov, "Sredi stikhov," *Pechat' i revolyutsiya*, 1923, no. 1. B. Filippov, "Zadushennyi talant," *Novoe russkoe slovo*, 1 May 1973. ———, "O zamolchennoi." In M. Shkapskaya, *Stikhi*. 1979. M. Gor'kii, "Dva pis'ma." Publik. Arkhiva Gor'kogo, *Rabotnitsa*, 1968, no. 3. G. Lelevich, "Krov'-ruda"—"Zemnye remesla" (review), *Krasnaya nov'*, 1925, no. 1. "Mariya Shkapskaya, *Stikhi*. London, 1979" (review), *Kontinent*, no. 23 (1980). Innokentii Oksenov, "Krov'-ruda" (review), *Zvezda*, 1925, no. 4. Z. Shakhovskaya, "Stikhi Marii Shkapskoi," *Russkaya mysl'*, 13 December 1979. V. Sinkevich, "Dvoinaya sud'ba: O stikhakh M. Shkapskoi," *Novoe russkoe slovo*, 27 January 1980. E. Zhiglevich, "Dve bespredel'nosti byli vo mne ..." In M. Shkapskaya, *Stikhi*. 1979.   B. F.

Shklóvsky, Víktor Borísovich (1893–   ), literary scholar, essayist, and novelist. Born into the family of a mathematics teacher, Shklovsky studied philology at the University of Petrograd. In 1916, he co-founded the OPOYAZ, which later developed into the FORMALIST movement. In 1920 and 1921, he taught creative writing at the Institute of Art History in Petrograd. In his capacity as a specialist in literary craft, he was informally associated with the SERAPION BROTHERS and with the FUTURIST poets of the LEF group. The years 1922 and 1923 Shklovsky spent in Berlin where he published his two most successful novels: *Zoo: or, Letters not about Love* (Zoo. Pis'ma ne o lyubvi, ili Tret'ya Eloiza, 1923) and *A Sentimental Journey; Memoirs 1917–1922* (Sentimental'noe puteshestvie: vospominaniya 1917–1922, 1923).

In the later 1920s Shklovsky dissociated himself from the formalist movement to the point of recanting his former views in LITERATURNAYA GAZETA in 1930. In post-Stalinist Russia, however, he returned to these views in a series of articles and books. In that respect, Shklovsky's writings are typical of the evolution which many Soviet scholars have undergone: they followed the approved paths of scholarship in the harshest years of Stalin's rule, but they sought to work creatively in periods of political relaxation.

On the Theory of Prose (O teorii prozy, 1925) is Shklovsky's most important work. It contains essays on literary craftsmanship and analyses of individual works. Shklovsky's literary ideas are grounded in the belief that presentation of "real life" in literature is not accomplished through the so-called content but through form. The formal aspect of a literary work consists of such "devices" (*priemy*) as defamiliarization (OSTRANENIE), defacilitation (*zatrudnenie*), retardation (ZAMEDLENIE), parallelism, contrast, and many others. In the opening essay of the collection, Shklovsky declared that all works of art are merely sum totals of the devices used in them. Depending on the definition of the word "device," this statement can be understood as shocking or as self-evident; however, many readers of Shklovsky were unaware of the Kantian background of his theory, and they perceived it as shocking. Subsequent essays examined the "stringing together" of literary devices in novels and stories. The title hero of *Don Quixote* was thus viewed as an accident of plot construction rather than as a consciously conceived character. His personality came about because the author wanted to include in the novel various witty sayings and monologues. On the other hand, Sterne's *Tristram Shandy* "laid bare" the constructional principles of the novel as genre by means of digressions and authorial asides and disclaimers.

Shklovsky's second major area of interest was the cinema. Here too his early work is of the greatest value. In *Literatura i kinematograf* (1923), he analysed those cinematographic techniques which make the cinema different from the theater. Predictably, Sergei EISENSTEIN's plotless movies containing rapid shifts of scenery and subject matter, won Shklovsky's praise.

Shklovsky's biographies and novels are attempts to put into practice the principles to which he adhered as a critic. *Zoo, or Letters not about Love* is a collection of thirty letters exchanged between an autobiographical character residing in Berlin and one Alya (modelled on Elsa Triolet) in Petrograd. The letters provide fragmentary insights into moods and thoughts of the major character but offer virtually no plot. Similarly, *Lev Tolstoi* (1963) provides a fragmentary but insightful biography together with an analysis of Tolstoi's major works.

Of Shklovsky's post-Stalin writings, the most characteristic is *The Bow-String: On Incompatibility of the Compatible* (Tetiva: o neskhodstve skhodnogo, 1970). Here he discusses literary genres and strategies in a way similar to that of his early formalist years, except that his vocabulary is updated and his presentations are better structured than in *On the Theory of Prose*. The title image of the bowstring is taken from Plato's *Symposium* and is meant to illustrate the principles of dialectical thinking and their application in literature.

Shklovsky is the least academic of all formalists. His critical and novelistic styles share a predilection for short paragraphs consisting of only one sentence. His way of arguing is sometimes chaotic and poorly organized; on balance, it can be described as evocative rather than logical. Shklovsky amply uses asides and shifts of subject matter. His frequently voiced admiration for *Tristram Shandy* suggests that he incorporated Sterne's novelistic technique into his essays. His evocative style, however, was also influenced by the tradition of Russian literary criticism which has favored "notes" (*zapiski*) and "musings" (*razmyshleniya*) over more structured forms of writing. On the other hand, the brevity of Shklovsky's paragraphs is reminiscent of Biblical style.

Viewed from a perspective of several decades, Shklovsky appears to have been a catalyst rather than an original thinker. He popularized a number of concepts which can be traced back to the idealist philosophies of Kant and Hegel but which received a new emphasis in formalism. He has been an agent of modernization in Russian literary criticism. He shares with Yury TYNYANOV the honor of being the most indispensable member of the Russian formalist movement.

Works: Khod konya. 1923. *Tret'ya fabrika.* 1926. *Material i stil' v romane L. N. Tolstogo Voina i mir.* 1928. *Matvei Komarov zhitel' goroda Moskvy.* 1929. *Kratkaya, no dostovernaya povest' o dvoryanine Bolotove.* 1930. *Zhitie arkhiereiskogo sluzhki.* 1931. *Chulkov i Levshin.* 1933. *Marko Polo.* 1936. *Zametki o proze Pushkina.* 1937. *Minin i Pozharskii.* 1940. *O Mayakovskom.* 1940. *Vstrechi.* 1944. *Za i protiv: Zametki o Dostoevskom.* 1957. *Khudozhestvennaya proza: Razmyshleniya i razbory.* 1959. *Zhili-byli.* 1962. *Sobranie sochinenii.* 3 vols. 1973–74.

Translations: Zoo; or Letters not about love. 1971. *A Sentimental Journey; Memoirs 1917–1922.* 1970. *Mayakovsky and His Circle.* 1972. *Third Factory.* 1977. *Lev Tolstoi.* Moscow, 1978.

Secondary literature: Richard Sheldon, *Viktor Shklovsky: an in-*

ternational bibliography of works by and about him. 1977. ———, "The Formalist Poetics of Viktor Shklovsky," *RLT*, Vol. 2, pp. 351–71.   E. Th.

Shmelyóv, Iván Sergéevich (1873–1950), novelist and short story writer, was raised in Moscow. His first works were published by GORKY's publishing house *Znanie*. After the October Revolution Shmelyov lived in the Crimea where he witnessed the bloody executions of the Russian intelligentsia by the Bolsheviks. In 1922 he left Russia and became a leading émigré writer in Paris.

The Russian Orthodox religious tradition forms the most important source of inspiration for Shmelyov's work. He will also be remembered for his manipulation of Russian folk speech. Shmelyov's narratives are marked by a rhythmical and declamatory melodiousness, and his style reaches a high level of lyrical and epic contemplation in *The Summer of the Lord* (Leto Gospodne, 1933). Delicate colors, refined designs, and a spiritual fragrance are inherent in this work. As a writer of long novels, Shmelyov frequently lacks a sense of moderation and is occasionally guilty of an uneven, flamboyant style. But in his shorter stories he demonstrates perfect control of his material. He greatly admired the works of LESKOV and DOSTOEVSKY, and the artistic devices he favored and used most effectively (SKAZ and "dream-logic") may be related to the narrative modes of these writers. Shmelyov's fiction is, however, more impassioned and boisterous, except for his pious descriptions of religious life in Muscovite Russia amidst the radiance of Russian Easter and the tolling of church bells. In exile, Shmelyov was also interested in the theme of a simple Russian's encounter with Western Europe. Shmelyov's most famous works include "The Man from the Restaurant" (Chelovek iz restorana, 1912), a humanitarian story about a waiter; "The Inexhaustible Cup" (Neupivaemaya chasha, 1921), a poetic tale about a miraculous icon; and "The Sun of the Dead" (Solntse mertvykh, 1926) and "About an Old Woman: New Stories about Russia" (Pro odnu starukhu: novye rasskazy o Rossii, 1927), which describe the Bolshevik terror of the civil war.

Works: Na skalakh Valaama: putevye zapiski 1897. *K svetloi tseli: pervaya kniga rasskazov.* 1910. *Oni i my: vtoraya kniga rasskazov.* 1910. *Rasskazy.* Vol. 1. 1910. *Rasskazy.* Vols. 1–8. 1912–18. *Vinograd: rasskazy.* 1923. *Grazhdanin Ukleikin: rasskazy.* 1923. *Zabavnoe priklyuchenie: rasskazy.* 1927. *Stena: rasskazy.* 1928. *Istoriya lyubovnaya.* 1929. *V"ezd v Parizh: rasskazy o Rossii zarubezhnoi.* 1929. *Puti nebesnye.* 1931–38. *Bogomol'e.* 1935. *Nyanya iz Moskvy.* 1937. *Izbrannye rasskazy.* 1955. *Povesti i rasskazy.* 1960. *Inostranets.* Introd. I. A. Il'in. 1962. *Svet vechnyi.* 1966.

Secondary literature: Pamyati Ivana Sergeevicha Shmeleva: sbornik. Ed. V. A. Maevskii. 1956. Articles in: *Sovremennoe slovo*, 1911, no. 10; 1912, nos. 5, 11; 1914, no. 1; *Russkie vedomosti*, 1911, no. 7; 1916, no. 229; *Put'*, 1911, no. 1; 1912, no. 7; *Novoe vremya*, 1912, nos. 12914 and 12938; *Russkoe bogatstvo*, 1912, no. 3 and no. 4; *Utro Rossii*, 1912, no. 248; *Vestnik Evropy*, 1912, no. 5; 1914, no. 3; 1915, no. 3; *Rech'*, 1912, no. 332; *Utro*, 1914, no. 2499; *Russkie zapiski*, 1915, no. 10; 1916, no. 6; *Zhurnal zhurnalov*, 1915, nos. 6, 31; *Birzhevye vedomosti*, 1915, nos. 14635, 15157; *Ezhemesyachnyi zhurnal*, 1915, no. 6; *Russkaya volya*, 1917, no. 8; *Russkaya mysl'*, 1916, no. 9. A. P. Chernikov, "I. S. Shmelev i I. A. Bunin: Po materialam perepiski," *RLit* 1980, no. 1, pp. 169–75. M. M. Dunaev, "Rabota I. S. Shmeleva nad povest'yu 'Chelovek iz restorana'," *Filologicheskie nauki*, 1978, no. 1, pp. 74–81. ———, "Svoeobrazie tvorchestva I. S. Shmeleva: K probleme 'bytovizma' v proizvedeniyakh pisatelya," *RLit* 21 (1978), no. 1: pp. 163–75. Temira Pachmuss, *A Russian Cultural Revival.* 1981. Pp. 132–55.

                                                                            T. A. P.

Shólokhov, Mikhaíl Aleksándrovich (1905–84), Soviet novelist, born in Kruzhilin, near Vyoshenskaya stanitsa, in the Don Military Region. Not a Cossack by origin, he was the son of a Russian who had no steady occupation and an illiterate maid of Ukrainian ancestry. His formal education ended in 1918 when the civil war came to the Upper Don region. For the greater part of the war Sholokhov lived within or near the combat zone, witnessing the anti-Bolshevik uprising of the Upper Don Cossacks in the spring of 1919. In the early 1920s, after the Reds' victory in the Don region, he worked for the new regime as a teacher, clerk, and tax inspector and served in food-requisitioning detachments, taking part in the fighting against anti-Soviet guerrillas. Much of what he saw in the period from 1918 to 1922 found its way into his works. He began his literary career in the early 1920s with plays and short stories, none of which have been preserved. In October 1922 he went to Moscow where he joined the group of Komsomol writers called "The Young Guard," though he did not formally belong to the Komsomol. With this group he attended seminars in creative writing. His first published work, the short story "The Test" (Ispytanie, 1923), appeared in a Komsomol newspaper. Altogether about thirty of his stories came out between 1923 and 1927 in various periodicals and in collections entitled *Tales of the Don* (Donskie rasskazy, 1926) and *The Tulip Steppe* (Lazorevaya step', 1926). A nature lover, fisherman, and hunter, Sholokhov returned to the Don countryside in 1924 and settled down in Vyoshenskaya in 1926. In the fall of 1925 he started working on a book about the Cossacks' role in the Revolution and later expanded this project into the four-volume epic *The Quiet Don* (Tikhii Don, 1928–40). He observed closely the collectivization of agriculture, and made it the subject of his second novel, *Virgin Soil Upturned* (Podnyataya tselina, 1932–60). Both novels had serious difficulties with editors and censors. Volume one of *Virgin Soil Upturned* was printed only after Stalin interceded on Sholokhov's behalf. During the 1933 famine Sholokhov saved thousands of lives by persuading Stalin to send grain to the Upper Don region. In 1938 the security police concocted a counterrevolutionary case against Sholokhov, but Stalin, apparently changing his mind, spared the author in order to promote him as a symbol of Soviet cultural achievements.

During World War II Sholokhov served as a reporter for Soviet newspapers, visiting various sections of the front. His war output was limited to one short story, several sketches, and excerpts from his new novel *They Fought for Their Country* (Oni srazhalis' za rodinu, 1943, 1944). After the war he intensified his activity in political journalism but accomplished relatively little in fiction. He wrote one short story, completed volume two of *Virgin Soil Upturned* (1960), and added new chapters to *They Fought for Their Country* (1949, 1954, 1969).

A Communist Party member since 1932, Sholokhov was the foremost figure of the Soviet literary establishment. He was a member of the Party Central Committee, a deputy of the Supreme Soviet, twice a Hero of Socialist Labor, and the recipient of Stalin and Lenin Prizes for literature. By 1980 almost 79 million copies of his works had been published in the Soviet Union in 974 editions and eighty-four languages.

The dominant theme of Sholokhov's short stories published between 1923 and 1927 is the bitter political strife within a village or a family during the civil war and the early 1920s. The motif of man's cruelty to man runs through the majority of the stories. Their usual ending is a violent death. Horror and suffering are presented with epic calmness. Sholokhov sympathizes with the Soviets, but a number of his stories are impartial, nonpolitical, and concerned with purely human problems. Taken as a whole, the stories demonstrate Sholokhov's rapid development from an imitative apprentice into an original author with a keen eye for detail, intimate knowledge of the racy Cossack dialect, an earthy sense of humor, and a penchant for tense situations. In their dramatic, comic, and stylistic features the stories foreshadow *The Quiet Don* and volume one of *Virgin Soil Upturned*. Sholokhov's war sketches are predominantly agitational, as is his story "The Science of Hatred" (Nauka nenavisti, 1942), which portrays German atrocities in order to arouse hatred for the enemy and to discourage Soviet soldiers from surrendering. In the story "The Fate of a Man" (Sud'ba cheloveka, 1957) Soviet patriotism is wedded to the theme of personal grief caused by the war. The ill-fated protagonist's account of violence and hardships sharply contrasts with the scene of natural serenity in the opening pages.

Sholokhov's principal work is *The Quiet Don*. Set in the period from 1912 to 1922, it presents a broad picture of the Don Cossacks' life in peacetime and during the fateful years of war and revolution. The author views man primarily as a part of nature, with love, procreation, and perpetual renewal being the very essence of existence. Human feelings and actions are often related to processes occurring in nature, depicted with striking vividness and keen attention to details of shape, color, sound and smell. There is no complete identification of man with nature, however. The complexities

of man's spiritual and emotional life are unknown to nature; on the other hand, man surpasses nature in cruelty and destructiveness. *The Quiet Don* is the only major Russian novel that offers a broad portrayal of the simple people's life and has a common man as its protagonist. The novel is an unusual work for Soviet literature in that it treats historical events with considerable impartiality as it describes the Whites' struggle against the Reds. Its likable protagonist, Grigory Melekhov, is ideologically uncommitted. In his search for justice he vacillates between the Reds and the Whites, his preferences determined both by his innate traits and by social, economic, and historical peculiarities of the Cossack milieu. However important, his political and war experiences are overshadowed by the story of his passionate and tragic love, which illustrates the author's idea that almost every true love ends in forced separation or loss.

The Quiet Don abounds in sharp, true-to-life situations arising from personal or sociopolitical conflicts. This realism of intense confrontation imparts a dramatic quality to the novel. The Cossack characters are full-blooded individuals, and their dialogue is superb. In his own narrative Sholokhov liberally employs dialecticisms and the imagery of the Cossack folk poetry. The plot unfolds smoothly, except in volume two, which is fragmented and overpopulated with episodic characters.

Like *War and Peace*, *The Quiet Don* combines the characteristics of family and historical novels. But if Tolstoi immortalizes the triumph of both the Russian people and the nobility, Sholokhov portrays the destruction of the centuries-old existence of the Cossacks as a unique segment of Russia's population. This outcome gives Sholokhov's epic an air of somberness absent from Tolstoi's. Sholokhov conveys a less optimistic view of the goodness of human nature. His characters, as a rule, kill their fellow men without feeling repugnance or pangs of conscience, whereas Tolstoi's characters experience instinctive aversion to their genocidal acts. There are many more instances of killing in *The Quiet Don* than in *War and Peace*, and in some of his Bolshevik characters Sholokhov introduces a new type of killer, the ideological one. He perceptively captures the beginning of what was to become the hallmark of the 20th century: massive genocide sanctified by totalitarian ideologies.

Some artistic features in *The Quiet Don*, such as chronological arrangement of the narrative, attention to detail, and certain methods of characterization and psychological analysis, may be attributed to Tolstoi's influence. Still, these similarities are outweighed by the difference in style. In its vocabulary and extensive use of tropes, color, and daring syntactical constructions, *The Quiet Don* manifests a closer kinship with the Soviet ornamental prose of the 1920s than with Tolstoi and Russian 19th-century realism.

The Quiet Don has over 2000 similes. One-fourth of them are provided by the characters, a sign of the picturesqueness of their speech. The novel's metaphors and epithets are imaginative and diverse. A great variety of these tropes are applied to the word "silence," an abstract noun that is not easy to describe. Sholokhov's palette in *The Quiet Don* contains over one hundred hues, and more than 3000 color words appear in the novel. Color words are usually employed in their literal sense. The same is true of "black" and "light blue" (goluboi), with the difference that these words are used symbolically more often than other color adjectives. Sholokhov's figurative use of "black" attests to the influence of the popular tradition which links this color with painful or condemnable aspects of life. The author is more subtle in his symbolic application of "light blue." He associates it with a sunlit day, suggestive of beauty, hope, and joy which nature offers to man. But man fails to take advantage of the offer, turning instead to a life of self-inflicted misery and frustration. In scenes of violent death, the joyfulness and tenderness implicit in "light blue" are contrasted with the ultimate display of human cruelty.

In 1965 Sholokhov received the Nobel Prize for *The Quiet Don*. The award rekindled allegations that he could not have written all or part of the novel because of his young age or pro-Soviet orientation. In the Soviet Union various versions of such allegations have circulated by word of mouth since 1928. In the West Sholokhov's authorship was questioned in print by an anonymous Soviet critic, by Aleksandr SOLZHENITSYN, and by Roi Medvedev. None presented any convincing evidence for plagiarism, and all three have named the Don writer Fyodor KRYUKOV as the most likely author of *The Quiet Don*. That this hypothesis is untenable can be demonstrated by an examination of the novel's historical sources and by a comparative study of Sholokhov and Kryukov with respect to their lives, literary styles, and world outlooks. A computer-assisted investigation of selected passages from the works of the two writers carried out by a group of Scandinavian scholars produced additional evidence against Kryukov's authorship.

Throughout the years Soviet censors made numerous deletions in *The Quiet Don*, chiefly in politically undesirable descriptions of the Reds. That the novel has survived as a remarkable work of art is due largely to the fact that relatively little space is devoted to the Bolshevik camp. Some 250 deletions, ranging from one word to several pages, remain unrestored in present-day Soviet editions, including the English-language edition entitled *And Quiet Flows the Don*. The British translation, which has been published in England and America under the titles of *And Quiet Flows the Don* (vols. 1–2), *The Don Flows Home to the Sea* (vols. 3–4), and *The Silent Don* (4 vols.), contains even more severe cuts than its Soviet counterpart.

Virgin Soil Upturned describes the collectivization of agriculture in a Don Cossack village. The novel's heroes are dedicated Communists who must overcome the Cossacks' hostility to collective farming and the organized resistance of former White Army officers. The agricultural upheaval is portrayed from the official viewpoint. The novel's political apex is the appearance of Stalin's article "Dizzy with Success," which condemns the excesses committed during collectivization and seems to give the peasant a choice between private and collective farming. The true, compulsory nature of collectivization is indicated in the remarks of two characters, but this sensitive subject is not developed. Opponents of the Soviet regime are shown predominantly in dark colors. The novel has no such independent characters as Grigory Melekhov. Its protagonist, an industrial worker from Leningrad, is rather flat, though its Cossack characters are more convincing and colorful. The only politically unadulterated love story is that of a local Communist for his dead wife. Unfolded in moving reminiscences, it strikes a tragic note of irrevocability. The reminiscences are set against a natural background, emphasizing Sholokhov's conception of the unity of man and nature. *Virgin Soil Upturned* contains proportionately fewer landscapes than *The Quiet Don*, and some of them are introduced to demonstrate the triumph of socialized agriculture.

Written almost thirty years apart, volume one and volume two of *Virgin Soil Upturned* are quite different. Volume one conveys the immediacy of an eyewitness report. The dramatic events of collectivization rapidly follow one another, generating tension and suspense. Relief is provided by the funny tales and mishaps of an old man, a type of popular storyteller. In volume two Sholokhov abandoned any effort to become a chronicler of collectivization. The volume covers only two summer months of 1930. The reader learns nothing about the repression and famine of 1932–33. Volume two is filled with static material, notably with various stories narrated by the characters and with comic episodes presented by the author in the form of anecdotes. Some situations and characters are chronologically out of place, reflecting the author's adjustments to the Party line under Khrushchev. The representation of life as inexorably moving toward socialism and the identification of the Party's interests with those of the people make volume two a typical work of socialist realism. Because of Sholokhov's politicization of his fiction and a certain exhaustion of his creativity, volume two is artistically inferior to its predecessor and especially to *The Quiet Don*. The English translation of volume one is entitled *Virgin Soil Upturned* in Great Britain and *Seeds of Tomorrow* in the United States. The translation of volume two is called *Harvest on the Don* in both countries. The Western translation of the novel is preferable to the Soviet one, which is based on the bowdlerized 1952 edition and retains later revisions concerning Stalin.

The unfinished novel *They Fought for Their Country* was conceived as a trilogy about World War II. Its published portions describe fighting in the Don region and provide flashbacks into the characters' prewar lives. One of the characters is a Red Army general recently released from a Soviet concentration camp and totally dedicated to the Soviet regime. The published portions are strongly propagandistic and ultraorthodox. Sholokhov avoids any serious queries about the war and focuses on the positive, the trivial, and the comic. Much of the imagery is familiar, and descrip-

tions of nature contain nothing new in terms of philosophical symbolism, lyrical intensity, or aesthetic power.

In most of his speeches and journalistic writings Sholokhov follows the official policy of the day. He extols the Party's guidance over literature and launches singularly vicious attacks on Western leaders and dissident Soviet writers. Yet he sharply criticizes the low quality of Soviet literature and the industrial contamination of rivers and lakes.

Sholokhov's claim to an enduring place in world literature rests on *The Quiet Don*. This monument to the Don Cossacks is of universal significance, offering an original and sensitive treatment of the eternal themes of love, death, and humanity.

Works: Donskie rasskazy. 1926. *Lazorevaya step': Rasskazy.* 1926. *Tikhii Don.* Vols. 1–2 (1928–31), vol. 3 (1933), vol. 4 (1940). *Podnyataya tselina.* Vol. 1 (1932), vol. 2 (1960). *Slovo o rodine.* 1951. *Sobranie sochinenii.* 8 vols. 1980.

Translations: And Quiet Flows the Don. A Novel in Four Books. Trans. S. Garry. Rev. and completed by R. Daglish. Moscow, 1959. Various editions under the title *And Quiet Flows the Don* contain Vols. 1 and 2 of the novel only. A translation of Vols. 3 and 4 has appeared under the title: *The Don Flows Home to the Sea.* Trans. S. Garry. New York, 1941. (And several other editions). *Seeds of Tomorrow.* Trans. S. Garry. New York, 1935. (= *Podnyataya tselina,* vol. 1). Also under the title: *Virgin Soil Upturned. 1. Seeds of Tomorrow.* Trans. S. Garry. New York, 1959. A translation of Vol. 2 has appeared under the title: *Harvest on the Don.* Trans. H. C. Stevens. 1st ed. London, 1960. *The Science of Hatred.* 1943. *Tales of the Don.* 1962. *One Man's Destiny and Other Stories, Articles, and Sketches, 1923–1963.* 1967. *At the Bidding of the Heart: Essays, Sketches, Speeches, Papers.* 1973. See also: *Lewanski,* pp. 354–55.

Secondary literature: C. G. Bearne, *Sholokhov,* 1969. D*, *Stremya Tikhogo Dona: Zagadki romana.* 1974. H. Ermolaev, *Mikhail Sholokhov and His Art.* 1982. V. Gura, *Kak sozdavalsya Tikhii Don.* 1980. V. Gura and F. Abramov, *M. A. Sholokhov: Seminarii.* 2d. ed. 1962. G. Kjetsaa, "Problema avtorstva v romane *Tikhii Don," Scando-Slavica* 24 (1978), pp. 91–105. G. Kjetsaa et al., *The Authorship of The Quiet Don.* Oslo, 1984. M. Klimenko, *The World of Young Sholokhov: Vision of Violence.* 1972. I. Lezhnev, *Put' Sholokhova: Tvorcheskaya biografiya.* 1958. R. Medvedev, *Problems in the Literary Biography of Mikhail Sholokhov.* 1977. H. Muchnic, *From Gorky to Pasternak: Six Writers in Soviet Russia.* 1961. pp. 304–40. K. Priima, *S vekom naravne: Stat'i o tvorchestve M. A. Sholokhova.* 1981. E. Simmons, *Russian Fiction and Soviet Ideology: Introduction to Fedin, Leonov, and Sholokhov.* 1958. Pp. 163–252. D. Stewart, *Mikhail Sholokhov: A Critical Introduction.* 1967. L. Yakimenko, *Sholokhov: A Critical Appreciation.* Moscow, 1973. ———, *Tvorchestvo M. A. Sholokhova.* 1964.

H. E.

Short story, the Russian. In the theory of literature the short story is basically a short form of epic narrative. While this may seem to be a simple enough statement, the multitude of definitions is evidence of the lack of consensus among critics as to what constitutes this prose genre. Is the primary qualification a simple issue of quantitative criteria, such as the number of words or pages, or are there qualitative and formal differences that mark it as a distinctive genre in its own right? The existence in Russian of such different terms as *povest', rasskaz,* even *novella,* which are all subsumed by the general definition of "short form," complicates the problem. To muddy the situation still more, throughout the 19th century, the terms *povest', poema, rasskaz,* and even *roman* were used interchangeably, and were practically synonymous. For general purposes in this article though, the use of "short story" will be more than valid. At best we can define the short story as a hybrid and flexible form which differs, because of its laconic form and concise narration, from the telescoping novel form with a wide epic frame. Indeed, the evidence is strong that the short story is a fairly distinct art form and while there are no such rigid rules as govern the German "novella" with its prescriptive structure for all times and places, there are certain definite features that inform this genre.

Given the reduced scope of the short form, the cast of characters is similarly diminished; instead of the full illumination required to unravel complex problems, varied points of view, conflicts, and numerous protagonists in a novel, the short story uses rigid economy. As CHEKHOV so aptly put it, in a short story it is better to say too little than too much. The ideal, of course, is to give the reader precisely enough information needed to grasp the central idea. Classic economy of form, lean clarity, and taut explosiveness blend well with the oral tradition from which the short story descends. As an important early theoretician of the genre, E. A. Poe, pointed out, the success of the short story form depends upon the reader being able to take it in at one sitting. The Russian words *povest'* and *rasskaz* indicate clearly the sense of "telling." In the structure of a successful short story, the story-teller plays an important role in that it is his voice that unifies the narrative, and creates a "wholeness" and coherence of effect, while contributing at the same time to the immediacy of its impact.

In no wise should the short story be taken only as a transitional genre, a laboratory for a future novel. Because of its flexibility, the short form can contract or expand at will, giving it the opportunity to acquire new methods and means of expression. We witness an incredible wealth and variety of themes, approaches, and views. In the system of genres in Russian prose the short form is one of the most productive modes.

We may define the appearance of N. KARAMZIN's short story, "Poor Liza" in 1792, as the beginning of modern Russian literature, as well as the trailblazer for the short form. Although SENTIMENTALISM as a literary school was evident in Russia as early as the 1770s, both translations and original Russian novels with their unwieldy, immensely long format did not presage a successful career for prose fiction. It took Karamzin to distill and develop the new vehicle of expression in which sentimentalism was best exemplified in Russia. In his seminal tale he steers clear of philosophic and moralistic commentaries and concentrates entirely on the psychological development of the love relationship between the protagonists. The sentimental cult of feeling was reinforced by graceful, soft, and melodious prose. A simple syntax structure, the rhythmic cadence and the lyric style helped to evoke the sweet melancholy that constituted the ultimate essence of sentimentalism. Since everything was seen through the eyes of the narrator, his speech, consisting of elegiac memories, heartfelt apostrophes, touching outpourings of emotions, and dramatized monologues, became paramount to the genre. Event and the figure of the narrator created a new system, as the paradigm for the sentimental tale was established. It is fair to state that variations on the theme of seduced innocence or disappointed ideals ruled the short form for the next several decades. Karamzin's epigones continued to publish countless stories with such moving titles as "Poor Masha" by A. E. Izmailov (1795), "Unfortunate M-v" by A. I. Klushin (1793), "The Dark Grove, or the Monument of Tenderness" by P. T. Shalikov (1798), "Desperate Love" by A. Stolypin (1795), etc.

Two of Karamzin's stories, "Sierra Morena" and "The Island of Bornholm," begin the first phase of Russian ROMANTICISM, bearing the obvious stamp of Ossianic poetry with its gloomy landscapes, characteristic fragmentary narration, and an undercurrent of mystery and terror. Karamzin's historical tales, "Natalie, the Boyar's Daughter" (1792) and "Marfa, Mayor of Novgorod" (1803), also helped to create a solid tradition for this subgenre in the 19th century.

The importance of the decade of 1825 to 1835 cannot be overestimated. In those years the short story was not only the most popular genre; it also acquired a new significance as writers viewed it as particularly suitable for the expression of a multitude of ideas, philosophical, ethical, aesthetical, or even satirically social. PUSHKIN stated that the short story had to be an indispensable part of a journal. BELINSKY, in his important article "On the Russian Short Story and the Stories of Mr. Gogol" (1835) wrote: "The short story is our daily bread, or bed-side book." To show how far the importance of this genre was taken, the publisher of MOSKOVSKII TELEGRAF, N. POLEVOI, advocated in 1828 that the aim of the romantic short story was to convey to the reader a new look at existing conditions and thereby become "an act of cognition."

The name of Aleksandr BESTUZHEV-Marlinsky literally towers in the literature of the 1820s and 1830s and extends to almost all the subgenres of prose. The influence of Walter Scott's historical novels, the exoticism of Byron's narrative poems, ZHUKOVSKY's legends and ballads, and Karamzin's heritage contributed to the establishment of romanticism in Russia. An outgrowth of this was a new interest in history. In his historical tales, e.g., "Wenden Castle" (1821), "Neuhausen Castle" (1824), "The Tournament at Reval" (1825), Marlinsky turned to the Baltic and Slavic Middle Ages. Other writers followed Marlinsky's lead in their historical tales, but switched the locale to the Ukraine, where the lure of the free life of Ukrainian peasants pictured as a harmonious society drew O. SOMOV to legends and folkloric stories with a fantastic element, such as "The Suicide" (1830), "The Mermaid" (1829), "The Werewolf" (1829), "The Kiev Witches" (1833). Marlinsky too explored the possibilities of the fantastic. In "An Evening at a Caucasian Spa" (1824) and in "The Cuirassier" (1832), and other stories Marlinsky delved into the extraordinary and the mysterious.

The influence of the German romantics led to the discovery of another world, a supra-rational, supra-sensual world with its own laws that coexists with the world we call real. The fantastic stories of the era deal with both levels. In the first truly fantastic tale, A. POGORELSKY's "The Old Vendor of Poppy Seed Cakes" (1825), reality and romantic fantasy are inextricably linked. Another well-known fantastic story with a romantic-mystical story line is Tit Kosmokratov's (V. Titov) "The Isolated House on Vasilievsky Island" (1829), allegedly inspired by Pushkin. Prince Vladimir ODOEVSKY, however, is the only authentic Russian romantic story teller in the true German mold, with alchemy, spiritualism, dreams and chiromancy peopling his stories. In addition to such stories as "The Ghost" (1838), "The Sylph" (1837), "Kosmorama" (1840), "The Salamander" (1842), where the real world is contrasted with ideal beauty, he produced a cycle of stories entitled *Russian Nights* which can be called *contes philosophiques*. In them contemporary life is shown as senseless, intellectually insignificant, and without any spiritual values. Like E. T. A. Hoffmann, his example, Odoevsky sees a tragic incongruity between the ideal for which man thirsts and his environment.

Romanticism in all its various facets came to dominate the literary scene in the 1830s. However, the most important strain of the short story was still that which tackled the problem of man's relationship to his society. Again, it was Marlinsky who was the founder and prolific practitioner of the "society tale" as it came to be known. These "society tales" were of major import for the future of Russian fiction, since they ultimately led to the discovery of new classes, problems, and heroes. The center of gravity now moved from idyllic country life into the urban salons. The tales are set in the elegant residences of the nobility, and the conflict is centered on the extraordinary individual's refusal or inability to conform to the rigid, dehumanizing, deadening rules of society. The new subject matter, as well as new narrative techniques, contributed to the popularity of the genre. Marlinsky's story "The Test" (1830) with its decor of the inevitable elegant lady's boudoir and the equally inevitable ballroom, and a duel functioning as its central motif, became the prototype for a multitude of stories that followed. With time, this theme grew into something more meaningful than an observation on the vanity of the leisure class. In "The Frigate 'Hope'" (1832) the hero is not only in conflict with Petersburg society, he is also in conflict with himself. An interesting development of the society tale occurs in Odoevsky's "Princess Mimi" (1834) and "Princess Zizi" (1839), where he focuses on the tragic fate of old maids in a milieu in which the primary aim of women is the acquisition of a husband. N. F. Pavlov's "Auction" (1835) goes further; only the supremacy of convention and the destruction of romantic ideals remain—the title truly reflects the ballroom as a market place.

An important variant of the romantic tale was the *Künstlernovelle*, a story dealing with the artist, the genius for whom there is obviously no room in a sterile society. Some of Odoevsky's best stories ("The Last Quartet of Beethoven," 1830, "Opere del cavaliere Giambattista Piranesi," 1832, and "Bach," 1835, later incorporated into *Russian Nights*) deal with the problem. Piranesi escapes from reality into the world of fantasy, namely, insanity, a theme that is heard more and more frequently. Madness, of course, is the central metaphor for the irreconcilable discord between the poetic ideal and social reality.

N. Polevoi's "The Painter" (1834) and "Abbadonna" (1834), A.

Timofeev's "The Artist" (1834) gradually bring in realistic elements of lower class life into the subject matter of the romantic artist. A. F. Veltman's "Furious Rolland" (1835) transforms the romantic motif of the artist into a grotesque story of mistaken identity. Finally, V. A. Sollogub's "Story of Two Galoshes" (1839) can be seen as the epitome of the genre: the sad tale of an artist is placed within a paradoxical narrative about the adventures of two galoshes.

Belinsky perceptively saw in the stories of the 1830s the beginning of a new direction; what had started as a romantic convention gradually turned into serious ethical and social critique. Romantic tales began to speak of forbidden topics; for instance, Pavlov's "Dagger" (Yatagan, 1835) exposes the spirit of cruelty and oppression among the military under Nicholas I. His "Nameday" (Imeniny, 1835) illustrates the destruction of artistic talent in a serf.

Russian prose fiction then began to move from the heroic to the non-heroic, from the picturesque to the commonplace. I. Panaev, Polevoi, M. Pogodin and V. Dal (among others, of course) are responsible for the transition. Stories such as Pogodin's "Beggar" (1826), or Polevoi's "Tales of a Russian Soldier" (1834) portend the evolution into the realistic tale. The new heroes, a beggar or soldier, integrate conventional sentimental themes into an observation of life (bytopisanie) among the lower classes. Dal's "Bedovik" (The Loser, 1839) is particularly note-worthy in that it almost eliminates plot. Insofar as the romantic stories leaned heavily on plot, on the unusual event, on love-passion and the duel unto death, the elimination of these factors left much of the burden of the narrative on the depiction of daily life with its details.

Even though Pushkin's "Tales of Belkin" (1831) came earlier than the decline of the Karamzin-Marlinsky tradition, they predicted, to a remarkable degree, the evolution the short story was to undergo. In terms of structure, Pushkin was able to expand and lend sophistication to the first person narrator and the traditional frame. By having the "implied author" speak through the voice of Ivan Petrovich Belkin, who himself was presumably giving the story as told by various narrators, Pushkin made it impossible to discern the role Belkin himself has in the telling of the stories. Thus, the author hides behind the mask of Belkin, and Belkin hides behind the masks of the different narrators. While Pushkin quite deliberately uses conventional plots, his protagonists are ordinary people who live in a sunny world where there is no real malice or intrigue, and where no one actually gets hurt. These tales play upon the reader's expectation of tragic endings, revenge, and ghosts; instead the reader is delightfully disappointed. We must also remember that Pushkin's predilection for "naked simplicity" rendered a great service to the cause of literary prose. If future writers did not follow the concision and tautness of his elegant and bare verbal flow, nonetheless, the verbiage and somewhat "purple prose" of Marlinsky were left behind.

Pushkin's "Queen of Spades" (1834) presents a further step in the evolution of the society and fantastic tales. In the new mercantile society, it is gold and not rank that motivates ambition. Ghosts and demons are now shown to be part of the inner psyche and not as supernatural beings sent from above. The internalization of man's passions spells the beginning of the future psychological novel.

To stress the significance of the short-story genre of that time, it would be well to consider Lermontov's Hero of Our Times (1841) referred to as Russia's first psychological novel. The work is structurally a cycle of five stories, including the quintessential society tale ("Princess Mary"), the Caucasian adventure story ("Bela"), a semi-fantastic story set in the traditional officer's milieu ("The Fatalist"), and a miniature gem, the story about exotic bandits, "Taman".

Of no less significance for the future of the short story were Gogol's first volumes, Evenings on a Farm near Dikanka (1831), featuring a curious combination of all the paraphernalia of the supernatural (witches, devils, mermaids), Ukrainian folk legends and motifs, as well as realistic detail. All these elements are given a novel treatment, for the "implied author" distances himself and gives full play to Rudy Panko (the "editor") and his friends. In the second part of the Dikanka stories a different group of narrators appears; some have gone, others come in. We learn that the manuscript of "Shponka" by Kurochka was used for baking pies. This playful tone is a far cry from the emotionally saturated romantic narrators; the emphasis is now on "orality" as contrasted with the previous "literariness." The last story, "Shponka," is no longer a

folk or fairy tale: Gogol moves into the real world in which Shponka is a most unromantic hero. It is also a very static novella, and now the enchanting and comical qualities of the preceding tales disintegrate into the grey fog of pedestrian existence.

On the surface, the Mirgorod stories (1835) seem very dissimilar. The romantic element is strongly present only in "Vii" and "Taras Bulba" in which demonic possession and the ancient heroism of the Cossacks for the glory of Orthodox Russia are vividly related. On the other hand, "Ivan Ivanovich and Ivan Nikiforovich" is a frankly absurd story of the quarrel between two neighbors, while the charm of "Old World Landowners" is a nostalgia for a time when culinary delights seem to have been the sole base of marital accord and only purpose in the life of a provincial couple. The common denominator of these works is the realism and homely humor that permeate them.

After the exoticism of the Ukraine and the dreariness of the provinces, Gogol moves to a depiction of Petersburg. Gogol's capital figures as a magic phantasmagoria. Alongside the glittering panorama there exists another level, peopled by lowly clerks, poor artists, tailors, prostitutes, opium dens and asylums for the insane. In this seething metropolis Gogol's romantic dreamers founder, as in "The Portrait" (1834) and in "Nevsky Prospect" (1835). In "Nevsky Prospect", the city of Petersburg is fragmented, dehumanized and rendered grotesque. Even those that appear whole on the exterior are rotten and withered inside. The beautiful woman whom the poor artist Piskarev sees on Nevsky Prospect and falls in love with is a prostitute whose divine mouth emits a stream of foul language. The only escape for Piskarev from this horrible reality is in the dreams granted by drugs, from which he eventually dies. The little clerk-hero of "Notes of a Madman" (1835) whose grandiose and totally unrealistic dream of engaging the love of his superior's daughter only underscores his insignificance, also sinks into madness.

Gogol, too, was drawn into the literary mainstream by his choice of subjects. The overtly supernatural story "The Portrait" (a Künstlernovelle) with its traditional devil as tempter, describes the betrayal of true art for material success, and the insanity and demise that follow are the inevitable result of the artist's spiritual death.

The theme of "The Overcoat" (1842), the life of a poor clerk, was certainly not new by that time, yet probably few stories have had as varied and controversial a history of critical analysis. Interpretations of it range from an indictment of the existing social and political reality to an assessment of the hero as a new saint, to a cruel depiction of a dehumanized puppet. The whole structure overturns the usual definition of a short story, for this is not one event in the life of Akaky Akakievich, but his whole life or parody of life from birth and christening to his death and resurrection. Akaky Akakievich, who in his lifetime could not articulate a whole sentence, after his death becomes a ghost and literally acquires the "manhood" he lacked during his life.

Gogol's realism is of a peculiar nature, permeated as it is with symbolic patterns of evil that distort and corrupt life. And yet the Gogolian narrator will not allow our sympathies to settle fully on his characters; he never allows the reader's compassion to develop. At the crucial moment, the tone which a second ago was full of pathos, makes an unexpected, radical twist toward bathos, or turns coldly ironical, or frivolously chatty. It is probably these features that make Gogol one of the most exciting, fully contemporary, yet not quite graspable writers of world literature.

Gogol was widely assumed to be the "father" of what came to be called "the NATURAL SCHOOL." Writers of the calibre of Panaev, Grigorovich, Dal, Butkov (as Yury Lotman suggests, guided by Belinsky and by Gogol's example), begin to identify literature with the study of society. This study found its best reflection in the compact, plotless little stories called PHYSIOLOGICAL SKETCHES, ruthless in their description of the prose of life. Inspired by the spirit of analysis, there was now an attempt by writers to understand the mainsprings of society, the laws of life, the anatomy of reality. The physiological sketch was so powerful and flexible an instrument that it spilled over easily into other genres, namely, the short story and the novel, since there were no really hard and fast borders between them. It is hard to find a rigid category for Panaev's "Onagr" and "Akteon" (1841–42), Grebenka's "Senya" (1842), Sollogub's "High Society" (1840) or "The Pharmacist's Wife" (1841).

F. M. Dostoevsky began his career with "Poor Folk" (1844–45), more strictly a short novel than a story, but quickly followed by "The Double" (1846), "The Landlady" (1847), "Mr. Prokharchin" (1846), "White Nights" (1848) and other short stories. Dostoevsky continued with the Petersburg setting and the lives of the lower classes and the dreamers. He also added to the mythology of Petersburg, a phantom-like city, colossal, cold, behind whose facade looms another reality, teeming with specter-like creatures.

The successors of Gogol's poor clerks are humanized by Dostoevsky. No longer helpless puppets, they display the first semblance of rebellion in which we hear the self-assertion inherent even in the poorest and most insignificant of men. For the first time in literature the psychology of poverty is investigated, rather than its conditions. Dostoevsky's "double" is an emanation of the protagonist's troubled fantasies and not a supernatural being sent by malevolent fate. His poor clerks succumb under the weight of their one obsessive idea which hides in the "underground" from the real world. These tales hold the essence of Dostoevsky's future novels, exploring as they do the rebels, the dreamers, the obsessive single idea, the confessional narrative, and exploiting the structural center of Dostoevsky's works, the device of antithesis.

At the same time the followers of the "natural school" (Butkov, Grebenka, Panaev, Galakhov) came out with a plethora of stories about the "insulted and injured"; but their heroes are frankly victims abused by society and described with a lack of psychological depth, thereby making them simply a sociological or even political statement.

In the 1840s attention also turned to the peasant as a new topic. No longer the non-existent idyllic figure of Karamzin, he now emerges as the serf of Russian reality. Nonetheless, Grigorovich's two tales, "The Village" (1846) and "Anton Goremyka" (1847), still to some extent idealize their characters while revealing the cruelty of the owners and the desperate misery of the serfs. Yet it was not until Turgenev's *Sportsman Sketches* (1852) that the peasant theme attained its full significance. Turgenev's stories bear none of the didacticism of Grigorovich. More importantly, those of the *Sketches* that feature peasants reflect Turgenev's interest in unusual characters, as exemplified by the poetic and meek (Kasyan, Kalinych, Lukeriya), or by proud and independent natures (Biryuk, Diky Barin). Turgenev is obviously attracted by the exceptional rather than by the typical.

The narrator's wanderings through the villages and forests allow for a wide range of portraits, and the narrator is always either a witness, a participant, or the interlocutor. Opportunity and coincidence, not a predetermined choice, become the guiding artistic principle. The inspired singing in "The Singers," the charm, simplicity, imagination, and daring exhibited by the village boys of "Bezhin Meadow" convey the inherent possibilities of the *moujiks*, who are a far cry from the debased creatures of Grigorovich. The overall effect is not to provide a realistic description of the typical peasant; the reader is much more impressed by the lyrical and impressionistic means with which the writer sets the emotional tonality of each story. While known primarily as the author of novels, Turgenev devoted himself as well to the writing of short stories, which encapsulate the ideas and world view that dominate most of his oeuvre: "Diary of a Superfluous Man" (1850), "A Quiet Spot" (1854), "Faust" (1856), "Asya" (1858), "First Love" (1860), a.o. Turgenev's great external mark was the concision that he applied with a rare felicity. Although most of his stories are framed by the traditional first person narration (which by then had been thoroughly exhausted), Turgenev was able to inject it with a new vitality. He deepened and intensified psychological analysis, focusing solely on the sharply etched outlines of the plot, yet veiling everything with a lyricism seldom heard in Russian prose. Turgenev gave birth to a new form of story blending a poetic mood with a sharp perception of the psychological realities inherent in human nature, all couched in rhythmic prose.

The era of the 1850s, especially the second half, with the Crimean War, rumors of the emancipation of the serfs, a new monarch, a fresh historic ambience, saw a startling literary flowering. New journals, authors, ideas, and themes proliferated, as well as new aesthetic attitudes to reality, changes in genre, and an expansion of forms. TOLSTOI radically changed the treatment of the peasant theme in "The Cossacks" (1862). In his Caucasian and "Sevastopol" stories (1856) he set out to destroy the existing romantic convention of martial heroism, and gave an objective, almost naturalistic painting of modern war.

In the second half of the 1850s and the beginning of the 1860s, Tolstoi shifted his interest from psychological analysis to ethics. "Two Hussars" (1856), "Albert" (1858), "Lucerne" (1857), "Three Deaths" (1858), "Polikushka" (1862) and "Yardstick" (1860–85), are much more dogmatic and moralistic than the earlier stories. Throughout this fiction, the opposition between the superiority of natural man with his proximity to nature and authentic nobility, and the inferiority of the sophisticated, civilized world is revealed.

By the end of the 1850s the short story attained supremacy among literary genres, as the form that best reflected contemporary demands, containing various discursive possibilities—lyricism (effusions of feeling), publicistic statements, drama, and satire. The political, social and intellectual ferment of the time led to a reevaluation of the traditional literary hero. There was hardly a story of the time that did not tackle this problem in its own way, for example, S. Kaloshin's "Your Old Friend" (1850), V. Likhachov's "The Dreamer" (1854), M. Avdeev's "Tamarin's Notes" (1852). At the same time, the familiar "little man", or the "poor artist," feature in stories by A. PLESHCHEEV, N. Khvoshchinskaya, A. PISEMSKY, I. KOKOREV, M. MIKHAILOV, and others. A. Pisemsky and A. Pleshcheev added protagonists from a new class, the small bourgeoisie, and in particular the rising heartless and greedy capitalist.

The 1860s set the stage for another subgenre of the short story by a new group of democratic writers, anti-romantic, anti-aesthetic, anti-sentimental: A. LEVITOV, V. SLEPTSOV, F. RESHETNIKOV, N. USPENSKY, N. POMYALOVSKY and M. E. SALTYKOV-SHCHEDRIN. These new writers of radical conviction based their works on material from real life, a sober and matter-of-fact accumulation of realistic details. N. Uspensky's *Provincial Customs*, and his other stories, depict the terrible greyness of provincial life and the spiritual and economic poverty of villages. Reshetnikov's *The People of Osinov* (Osinovtsy) and *The People of Podlipnaya* (Podlipovtsy), 1864, produced a ruthless representation of downtrodden peasants. The sketch tradition definitely helped to expand the genre of the short story; instead of focusing on the descriptive, it grew into little dramatic scenes presenting different opinions and arguments. V. Sleptsov's "The Foster Child" is an excellent example of such realistic dialogue: an unfortunate mother meets with different travellers during her hopeless search for her child. G. USPENSKY is the most significant representative of the new sketch-type story in which artistic and publicistic elements are combined organically. His semi-journalistic, semi-imaginative sketches of peasant life show the disillusionment in POPULIST ideas. The cycle *Ruin* (Razorenie), in which there is no real plot, nature description, or psychological analysis, possesses a special density and laconicism.

As a genre the short story continued to develop and evolve and its flexibility contributed to its protean quality. The short story gradually acquired an "open structure," absorbing the structural qualities of other genres. This can serve as an explanation of why some writers (e.g., I. Turgenev, L. Tolstoi), alternated between the short story and the novel.

The 1870s, though, were not the most propitious era for the short form except for Turgenev and N. LESKOV. Tolstoi, for instance, avoided the short story in the 1870s. As Mirsky has pointed out, Leskov's two key virtues are as narrator of vivid anecdotes and as a virtuoso with language. His superlative narrative gift and the vigor of his verbal expression are quite outstanding. Stories like "The Left-handed Smith and the Steel Flea" (1882) and "The Amazon" (1866) strike the reader with the spirit of folk story-telling that works in a way different from the literate efforts of other writers. Leskov removes himself from the narrative, and keeps at the center of the quasi-oral presentation the teller of the story with his own idiosyncratic style, his own amusing way of "fracturing" the Russian language with malapropisms. Leskov's characters are imbued with an excess of emotions and drive, the best-known example being "Lady Macbeth of Mtsensk" (1865), whose heroine murders her father-in-law, then her husband, and finally draws her lover's mistress with her into the swirling waters of the river in which they both drown. In other tales, for example, "The Mountain" (1890), Leskov focuses on the Byzantine legends of the PROLOG, and the general idea of the tale—that faith moves mountains—is clothed in the archaic style of the Prolog.

The master of a new synthetic form in the 1870s was M. E. Saltykov-Shchedrin. Possessing the temperament of a satirist, publicist, and polemicist, he wrote stories, such as "The Funeral," "A Sore Spot," "Gentry Boredom," and "Old Age Sorrow" (1881), which seem to sum up ordinary life and ordinary people; although the total is inevitably sad, even tragic, in these tales, Saltykov-Shchedrin is less of a cruel satirist, and more of an adherent of a sad Chekhovian humor. Behind each individual, there is a "domestic" drama, behind every outcome, sensitively and psychologically depicted, he shows the reasons in an abnormal social climate.

The Golden Age of the Russian novel traditionally ends with the deaths of Dostoevsky, Turgenev, and Goncharov. While the last decades of the 19th century are considered a "time of crisis," thus accounting for the increase of the small epic form and the waning of large novels, this was an exciting time for the short story with such writers as A. CHEKHOV, I. BUNIN, V. KOROLENKO, L. ANDREEV, A. KUPRIN, and V. GARSHIN. The particular style of these writers became possible as a result of some profound changes in the art of prose. The methods of exploring the human heart and consciousness reached such refinement and depth that they gave birth to new aesthetic dimensions. We have to consider the impact of contemporary poetry (especially FET's "Evening Lights" and Turgenev's "Senilia"), which undoubtedly intensified the lyrical and philosophical strains in the epic genre. A fusion of lyricism with prose is to be found in the works of almost all the writers of the period. Moreover, there was a renewed interest in folklore, legends, fairy tales, Biblical stories, parables and allegories (e.g., Leskov, "The Buffoon Pamfalon"; Garshin, "Legend of the Proud Agei"; Korolenko, "Makar's Dream"; Chekhov, "The Student"; Gorky, "The Old Woman Izergil"; Kuprin, "Sulamith"; Bunin, "The Death of the Procurator"; Andreev, "Judas Iscariot". These forms were preeminently flexible and accessible to outpourings of lyrical feeling merged with epic breadth and philosophic depth.

V. Korolenko's first works were immediately greeted with enthusiasm and recognized as innovative. While "Prokhor and the Students" and "In the Factory" reflected his populist leanings, "The Blind Musician" (1886) and "Makar's Dream" (1885) were stories of mood, full of emotional poetry and undying faith in the human soul.

V. Garshin too, can be called an innovator in the genre of the short story of the 1880s. His "Four Days" (1877) written during the Turkish War created a sensation. "The Red Flower" (1883) is a remarkable example of the spirit of compassion in the ubiquitous lunatic asylum tales of the period. In general, Garshin's stories are a hybrid of philosophical-psychological study and allegory.

Meanwhile Tolstoi's stories are significant for the new direction in which he was moving. "The Prisoner of the Caucasus" is a first attempt in which he eschews psychology, digressions, and descriptions. His tales for the common people written in the 1880s were based on popular or medieval genres: parables, legends, apocrypha, lives of saints and clothed in a very concise form. He also employed an almost lapidary, wholly unadorned narrative form in "The Death of Ivan Ilyich" (1886), "Kreutzer Sonata" (1889), "Father Sergius" (1898), "The Devil" (1901), "Master and Man" (1895), and "Hadji Murat" (1904), all dealing with the "eternal" questions, placing the heroes in tragically inescapable situations, emphasizing the fundamental contradictions of life and the ceaseless and tragic struggle between the rational and animal principles in man.

There is no doubt that the profound aesthetic reform of the short form was first realized by Guy de Maupassant in the West, and was felt acutely by A. Chekhov in Russia. L. Tolstoi thus qualified Chekhov's contribution to literature: "I think Chekhov created for the world new, absolutely novel forms of fiction, the like of which I have never met anywhere." The Chekhovian short story gave a new and more perfect depiction of reality. In comparison with Turgenev, Leskov, or Garshin, Chekhov increased the element of objectivity and authorial distancing to an unprecedented degree. The Turgenevian manner of lyric confessionalism seemed to Chekhov obsolete and exhausted. Another feature of Chekhov's art was the nontraditional conception of plot. The charge that Chekhov's stories are plotless is simply a failure to understand Chekhov. Plotlessness here means the absence of the conventional "intrigue." In such stories as "The Bishop" or "The Student," even the rudiments of plot in the usual sense of the word, are absent. The basis of the plot is a certain spiritual state of the hero.

Chekhov's stories can be described as little more than scenes whose almost every detail represents a crucial point and evokes associative responses which, when combined with action, serve to develop the forward movement of the plot; no detail is ever superfluous.

Chekhov believed that it was not necessary to portray something especially extraordinary or sensational or even entertaining; in his stories what seemed unimportant becomes important, what seemed petty, becomes momentous, and what seemed simple becomes complex. "Lady with a Pet Dog" is a wonderful example of how what was a banal, pedestrian episode—a casual love affair at a vacation resort—becomes a beautiful, pure, and great love. Very often what is important is not what happened, but what did not happen. Many stories are structured thus: something is supposed to happen, but *nothing* happens and that is more terrible than anything else.

Chekhov's first stories afforded amusement. His serious period began at the end of the 1880s with "The Steppe" (1888), "Lights" (1889), and "A Boring Story" (1889). In the younger Chekhov there was more external motivation, along with the introduction of a vivid and unusual situation. In the mature Chekhov, the plot canvas is extraordinarily simple, the narrative is always close to the hero, catching the moment in his life which allows the author to bare most fully the psychology of the character and his conflicts. "Ward No. 6" and "Ionych" contain a whole life, but the depth is so compacted, the denseness of the material so striking, that they fit into a few pages. Because the stories are about a life that never took shape, a dénouement is impossible. The absence of a finale is due to the absence of a beginning. Most of the mature Chekhov's stories convey the tragedy of the prose of life and man's essential loneliness. Never in the history of literature has human loneliness been described with such passion as in "The Bishop" or "A Boring Story." Often, the revelation that one's life has been lived uselessly, fruitlessly, badly, incorrectly, occurs only before the face of death, as for the coffinmaker Yakov Bronza ("Rothschild's Fiddle"), Professor Nikolai Stepanovich ("A Boring Story"), and Dr. Ragin ("Ward No. 6").

In other stories there is capitulation before the reality of life: "At Home," "Ionych," "Anna on the Neck." At other times the moment of revelation is the spiritual culmination of the story—the hero's eyes are opened now not only to himself, but to the whole world. He sees the falsehood of a life that had seemed normal. The impression of suddenness is created by the fact that the occasion for the revelation was an insignificant event. These "reflecting" Chekhovian heroes move from darkness to "illumination." Chekhov's total range of ideas is enormous, because he felt that no matter how sad life might be, it was still beautiful. But to appreciate it man had to be free; free not only of external tyrannies, brutal fathers, and heartless officials, but of internal tyrannies of anger, selfishness, and cupidity.

In addition to several novels, A. I. Kuprin wrote some interesting stories, quite new in Russian literature at that time—stories of action, even with elements of sensationalism, for example, "Lieutenant-Captain Rybnikov" (1906), a tense spy story.

A curious phenomenon at the turn of the century was Leonid ANDREEV in whose works symbolism and impressionism are combined with realism. Andreev tried to explore the farthest boundaries of realism in "neorealism," which he saw as a synthetic art capable of depicting the "unreal in the real," the symbol in the concrete. Andreev represents well the anticipation of the new coming, an apocalypse, a prophetic feeling of impending total change, the existential crisis experienced by so many at that time. In "The Life of Father Vasily" (1903), Andreev issues a challenge to God; the modern Job can bear all the personal sorrows with which he has been afflicted—it is the injustice toward men and society that finally breaks his faith. "The Wall" is a modern allegory in which nameless heroes ("the lepers") face the eternal enemies of man—the "wall" and "night." "The Governor" (1906) and "Story of the Seven Hanged Men" (1908), written in the aftermath of the 1905 Revolution, are prophetic in tackling the modern question about the right to break the fundamental law of life, as they deal with the horror of an execution or the justice of political terrorism.

The Nobel laureate Ivan Bunin reaches back to Turgenev and

Chekhov. Bunin freely acknowledged his kinship to the former, and yet his stories are sui generis. Bunin developed and took the short story to new heights of perfection. He gave it that unsurpassed, free, and extraordinarily flexible structure which avoids the strict contours of plot and seems to emanate spontaneously from the course of life. Bunin relinquishes a total resolution and adamantly refuses to offer any moral conclusions. At the forefront is a lyric mood always linked with an idealized elegiac past, never to be regained. Bunin's stories have no dynamic plot or intrigue. The main emphasis is a heightened attention to the "change of mood." The stories are literally poems in prose in their musicality, rhythmical language, rich employment of metaphors and poetic similes. The density of artistic details many of which may, at first glance, seem fortuitous, is striking. One gets the impression Bunin is simply enumerating everything that he hears and sees without exception. It is really not so, for so many of his concrete words and meanings contain an allegorical significance, a symbolic sub-text. At the center of his field of vision is a mood, a state of mind and thoughts associated with that mood and born of it. In his studies, "Silence," "In the Alps," "A Night's Lodging", one can almost see colors, detect smells, hear sounds. Yet the presence of death is the only reality in Bunin's stories. His heroes constantly think of death because they love life so acutely, because they are so much a part of it. One of the most poignant stories in world literature is "Light Breathing;" nor do "Grammar of Love," "Mitya's Love," and "Sunstroke" lag far behind. Other striking stories of love and death are "Chang's Dreams" (1916) and "The Gentleman from San Francisco" (1915).

Maksim GORKY brought in a new vigorous strain into the literature of the 1890s with his stories of tramps, bandits, exoticism, ultra-romantic individuals, and the lower depths. He is dominated by two main tendencies: an optimistic, romantic, elevated view of man, a hymn to man's inherent nobility, pride, and beauty; and a soberly realistic view of the ugly conditions of reality. One cannot really draw a hard and fast line between the two, as his stories are a fusion of the two systems. If "Makar Chudra" (1892) and "Old Woman Izergil" (1895) reflect his romanticism, "Grandfather Arkhip and Lenka" (1894), "On the Rafts" (1895), "Konovalov," "Out of Boredom," and "The Orlov Couple" (all 1897) represent the ultra-realistic side of Gorky. The moving story, "26 and One" is a good example of the fusion of both systems.

The relatively brief period of Russian modernism was cut short by non-literary causes: World War I, the Revolution, civil war. The symbolists who reigned at the beginning of the 20th century were not especially interested in the short genre. However, F. SOLOGUB and V. BRYUSOV contributed to it. The same refined aesthetic and somewhat mystical mood that marked their poetry and novels were reflected in the short form. Sologub's special predilection for exploring morbid sensuality, and his basic identification of peace and beauty with death, and of the sun as the source of evil is given free rein in stories like "Dear Page" and "Lady in Fetters." His limpid, balanced, poetic prose, governed by a keen sense of measure, creates a paradoxical impression when used to depict his morbid world view, and makes for the special secret charm of Sologub (Mirsky). There is a coldness and cruelty in Bryusov's prose. The lack of compassion is all the more underlined by the icy flame of sensual exaltation, and a desire to penetrate into the farthest recesses of human perversity. His visions of sensuality and abnormality are, however, only pageants of loud color. It is impossible to move on from modernism without mentioning A. REMIZOV. His ornamental prose proved to have a profound influence on the younger generation of writers. The dominating purpose of Remizov's prose was to cleanse the spoken language of the debris of various European languages that had accumulated in thick layers during the modern period of Russian literature, and to invigorate the literary language with the force and raciness inherent in colloquial speech ("The Fifth Plague," "The Incessant Tambourine," "Sisters of the Cross").

The 1920s heralded a new flowering of the genre. Actually, the short story reached new heights during this period. It is not difficult to observe how the romanticism of the epoch combined with the more somber aspects of its atmosphere, and to understand why it was precisely the short story that captured its almost apocalyptic chaos. One must warn the reader of a very curious fact—namely, that in all the voluminous prose of the 1920s one cannot see Man;

rather, what one catches sight of are glimpses of life: trains, elemental storms, people loving, dying, quarreling, wandering along the Russian plains, fighting. Here one glimpses an arm, there an eye, here a quick glance at some fragments of clothing. Nowhere though is a whole man to be seen. The writers seem to be able only to observe, not to create.

The big question facing the writers of the period was what aesthetic devices could immortalize the Revolution and the civil war. Most writers found it impossible to depict this new life within traditional forms. That is why a highly metaphoric and tense artistic manner marks the first stories of the period and helps to create its mythology. The feeling of the extraordinary exclusiveness of their experiences, their spontaneous apprehension of the elemental storm of history, their organic bond with the times allowed some young, often inexperienced writers, to create a new and exciting prose. A literary group, "The SERAPION BROTHERS," encouraged spontaneity, a hectic phraseology, a dense verbal flow, a profusion, even over-profusion of images, the use of regional dialects and local color.

Elemental force as an integral, organic manifestation of the Russian Revolution is vividly portrayed in Vsevolod IVANOV's "Armored Train 14–69" (1921). Although Ivanov took a discrete episode from the time of the civil war, he was able to render a generalized picture of a national struggle. His Siberian peasants have a very foggy understanding of the Revolution; they rise to shake off social shackles rather than to make a political, proletarian revolution. To convey the stormy, uncontrollable, elemental force of the national revolt, Ivanov uses a verbal style in which one can hear the disparate, angry shouts of the partisans, exclamations of indignation, short energetic phrases which all merge into a single, musical strain of triumph.

A. Malyshkin's long short-story "The Fall of Dair" (1921) about the legendary siege and taking of the Perekop isthmus by the Red Army, presents this military exploit as the final confrontation of two worlds, one of which is doomed. Bereft of all concrete details and incidents that would contradict the elevated romantic tone, the story is saturated with allegory and symbols. The main character is the nameless mass, actually compared to a horde. Individuals are simply physical signs, such as "a dishevelled sailor." Malyshkin rejects literary canons, and strives to find new forms appropriate to the events described, which he attempts to clothe in "monumental prose." A. Neverov's "Tashkent, the Bread City" (1921) presents another aspect of the civil war. The famine, the cold, the epidemics, the country devastated by the Volga famine in which there were twenty million victims, are incorporated in a ghastly picture of hungry, suffering people turned into savages for a piece of bread, of dirty hordes full of fleas, wet from the rain, cold from the winds, sick with typhus, crammed into trains already filled to capacity.

As the ascetic ideals of military communism gave way to the prosaic life under the New Economic Policy and the romantic dreams of "the blue cities" of the future were replaced by the greyness of bourgeois life, in itself a relic of the past, the satiric mode began to replace the heroic. On the opposite sides of the spectrum are satirical, yet humorous descriptions of the new Soviet society which the short story accommodated beautifully, as we see in M. ZOSHCHENKO, V. KATAEV, ILF and PETROV. The common denominator between the two seemingly contradictory tendencies (heroic and satirical) were heightened expressivity and a sharpened play of shadow and light.

B. PILNYAK is an especially interesting literary phenomenon of the time. An unashamed eclectic, he borrowed mainly from BELY and REMIZOV. Using fragments from newspapers and documents, plagiarizing himself, creating an incredibly ornamental style and complicated structure, he creates a style which is symbolic of a new cosmology. The Russia he sees is in the death struggle being waged, belongs to the Asian Mongol hordes. The qualities of European civilization, order and symmetry, are doomed to be swept away by the *moujiks* who have arisen as a spontaneous, elemental force: "Sankt-Piter-Burkh" (1921), "The Third Metropolis" (1923), "Snowstorm" (1921), "Ivan-Moskva" (1927).

Compared to others, I. BABEL's *Red Cavalry* (1926) has survived not only as a historical testament, but as an ever-living aesthetic experience. Babel's observing and participating narrator selects vivid, unusual, extraordinary characters: a holy fool who finds himself by chance in the army ("Sandy the Christ"), a sadist who kills pitilessly ("The Life and Times of Pavlichenko"). If his contemporaries showed the revolutionary masses rather than individual faces, Babel's interest was not so much in the events of the war, as in the human beings involved in the bloody campaigns. The bespectacled intellectual narrator is often at odds with the rough Cossacks ("My First Goose"). In "Dolgushev's Death," Babel shows how an intellectual's false compassion has no legitimate place in this world of death. This antithesis between the primitive Cossack cavalry men and the humane intellectual or the idealistic Jew, is organic for Babel. But then, time and again, he depicts the romance of war in poetic tones and glowing colors, while admitting the failure of "civilized" protagonists in slightly sad, melancholy tones. The lofty lyricism of the authorial tone, the musical rhythm of his prose, the pathos of his inflection, render an indelible picture of a world torn apart by contradiction, a paradoxical closeness of beauty and extreme ugliness, of the heroic and the comic. V. SHKLOVSKY's words exemplify beautifully the principle of Babel's style: "Babel ... speaks in the same tone of voice of the stars above and gonorrhea." A more restrained, but highly sophisticated ornamentalist prose style appears in the stories of Yu. OLESHA and Yu. TYNYANOV. Olesha's tales, "Liompa" (1927), "I Look into the Past" (1929), "Chain" (1929), "Love" (1928), and "The Cherry Stone" (1929), combine lyrical memories of the past, ironically sober meditations about the present, and a bold romantic prognosis concerning the future. Tynyanov's experiments with prose, for example, "Lieutenant Kizhe" (1928), a veritable tour de force, reveal him to be a part of the modernist movement; it is not for nothing that the modernist composer, Prokofiev, set the story to music.

The period of the Five-Year Plans and Collectivization in the 1930s was a time of huge novels. These grandiose projects required a larger epic stage, although writers such as M. PRISHVIN ("Naked Spring," 1940) and K. PAUSTOVSKY ("Kara-Bugaz," 1932, "Colchis," 1934) continued in the tradition of the short story, with poeticization of nature tinged with an almost sacred awe of its beauty. Here one must single out Andrei PLATONOV as representing one of the peaks in the realm of the short form. Platonov's tales are colored by a troubled sensitivity straining toward spirituality, toward the inner light in man, and by the seductive magic of a language which acts as a prism through which the consciousness of his characters is broken to reveal their innermost essence. His stories, "The Foundation Pit," "Third Son," "Fro," "Potudan River," "At Dawn," and others, showed a truthfulness that was a counterpoise to the simplistic optimism of the period. Even under most adverse conditions Platonov dared to experiment and take risks. In "The Return," published directly after the war, Platonov showed the possibility of bridging war literature with the new prose that would see light only later.

The monumental Stalinist prose of the end of the 1940s was certainly not conducive to the short form. But then World War II was still alive (it still is) among the Russians, and stories based on war experiences, semi-documentary or fictional, continued to be churned out. From simply describing war-time episodes with the paradigmatic ingredient—patriotic fervor that always triumphs over personal needs—the post war story eventually had to move into another plane. Now that the war was over it was necessary to draw up accounts and to look squarely at Soviet man and his future. M. SHOLOKHOV's "The Fate of Man" (1956) is a good example of this tendency. The war stories of Yu. NAGIBIN, E. KAZAKEVICH, K. SIMONOV, Yu. BONDAREV, and V. BYKOV all deal with an individual and his attitudes and conduct at a time of intense struggle between life and death. The main trend that had been "War and Man," now changed to "Man and War." New problems, themes, and images permitted a new focus; what in the by-now distant and legendary terrible days seemed relatively unimportant, acquired a new meaning. The past was experienced anew—V. Astafiev's "In Broad Daylight", S. Voronin's "The Sunlit Valley", Yu. Goncharov's "War", Yu. Nagibin's "The Pilot's Death", all tackle the problem of how to adjust that heroic and noble past to the dreary prose of today.

The Thaw Period (post-1956) began with a renewal of the short form. There was the sketch that would imperceptibly veer into the story proper. V. OVECHKIN, E. DOROSH, G. Troepolsky, V. TENDRYAKOV, and V. NEKRASOV are contributors to this genre. In general, the stories of the 1950s changed focus in order to concentrate on

daily life, on events almost unnoticeable at first glance, rather than on vivid characters and fates. Also, there now developed an orientation toward the exploration of ethical conduct. The lyric element again came into its own in the 1950s. K. PAUSTOVSKY continued his stories based on "free narration," not tied together by any plot or integrated structure ("In the Depth of Russia," 1951, "Brief Encounters," 1954). This form allowed a self-conscious attempt to tie together disparate personal experiences in order to create a modicum of harmony in a fragmented world. Some stories, like Nagibin's "The Mysterious House", or F. Abramov's "Once Upon a Time There Lived an Old Woman" have an allegorical flavor. Here "free narration" with a mosaic-like composition and an intricate plot, unmotivated by events, flows like a continuous lyrical monologue, with the basic purpose of evoking a spontaneous emotional reaction from the reader. The plot develops like a "stream of emotions." For instance, Yu. KAZAKOV's portrait of 90-year-old Martha in "Pomorka," emerges like the visage on a darkened icon, whose traits are rendered indistinct by the ages; but with a few strokes the author who intuits rather than knows, sketches in her past when she was young and beautiful and passionate, and her hard life and multiple losses evoke a lyric empathy. Kazakov began his career by maintaining an open polemic against the simplification of the human psyche, against avoiding the contradictions of the times: "At the Train Stop" (1959), "On the Road" (1961), "An Easy Life" (1963), "Smell of Bread" (1965). Kazakov's lyric feelings spill over into the meditations of his protagonists, into their emotions, moods, into the landscape. Kazakov's roots go back to Turgenev and Bunin.

V. AKSYONOV is undoubtedly one of the most interesting writers since the 1960s. His success stemmed particularly from the fact that he identified himself with the younger urban generation, and that that generation recognized itself in his fiction. His stories are laconic to the utmost, and he never tries to find simplistic or one-sided answers to any of the problems he pictures. By following Aksyonov's stories we can trace his path from initial attempts to find direct answers to the question of the ethical sense of human existence, to his intense efforts to break out of a magic circle of the entanglements of ordinary life. While he started as the "defense lawyer" for his generation, through the years he has gradually become its judge. More and more, a sad note of questioning creeps in. To be courageous in the face of an evil "class enemy" turns out to be much simpler than coping with evil in everyday life ("Catapult"). The loss of "wholeness," "integrity" in the hero may not come from a lack of personal strength, but be due to a social problem. Aksyonov's evolution is interesting not only for itself, but because it reflects the common quest of the younger prose writers of the 1960s. This is by no means a claim that there is or was a homogeneous group; the prose of young writers is varied in style, problematics, and ideology. Nonetheless, they seem to share a certain moral determination, an incessant wish to understand and reflect the frequently contradictory images of contemporary life.

The most popular literature today is the so-called COUNTRY PROSE, limited almost entirely to the short genre, and the names most frequently associated with it are those of A. SOLZHENITSYN and his heroine Matryona ("Matryona's House"). Even earlier, Yu. Nagibin's "The Poacher" (1965) had touched upon a new theme, an awareness of nature and man's destructive attitude to it. One can even include the prose of such writers of the 1950s as Ovechkin ("Provincial Prose"), S. Voronin ("Unwanted Glory"), S. ANTONOV ("Empty Run"), E. Dorosh ("The Little One"), S. ZALYGIN ("Red Clover"), P. Nilin ("Acquaintance with Shishkov"), and V. Tendryakov ("Potholes") as the emergence of the theme of man and nature.

Country prose, at present, represents a yearning to resurrect a country arcadia, an idyllic village world which has become, especially in our troubled times, a last preserve for spiritual values. In stories by Kazakov, V. BELOV, V. SHUKSHIN we observe the inhabitants of Russian villages and sketches of monochromatic Russian nature not simply as objects of artistic analysis and aesthetic contemplation, but as a very strong statement of the true norms of mankind, of an active meaningful life with attendent notes of nostalgia. One detects in these stories a palpable sense of the danger of loss, of forgetting the traditions of an ancient people that was always nourished by man's spiritual bonds with the earth, by close daily contact with the life of nature in all its many aspects. Even while describing the harshness of that kind of life, man's closeness to earth that gives birth and a final resting place to all, is paramount.

Among the pleiade of modern writers, V. Shukshin's name stands out conspicuously. Many of his heroes lose their sense of life when normal human contacts are broken. They seem to break out of the normal course of life not because of external pressures, but because of some mysterious impulses that acquire such domination that the hero cannot withstand their force and acts in a way that complicates his life seriously, even irrevocably ("Snowball Tree"). An actor, movie director and script writer, Shukshin uses cinematic devices in his prose, and specifically a dynamic development, rather unlike other country prose writers. From the very first lines he leads the reader to focus on the significant, as in "Ticket to the Second Show", "Nonresistor Makar Zherebtsov", "The Offense", and "Repartee". Shukshin is not interested in open subjective lyricism; his tendency to use the third person is due to the fact that an objective form of narrative allows him more latitude in employing various devices and means of revealing reality. Behind random external events or even the daily routine of life, Shukshin tries to find the genuine significance of a situation.

Country prose is the most active genre in short form prose today. F. Abramov, S. Nikitin, V. Belov, V. Astafiev, V. Fyodorov and many others are actively practising it. Since the death of Shukshin, the name of V. RASPUTIN is foremost ("Money for Mariya").

The 1970s have been interesting from another point of view: there have been more stories dealing with the problems of individual concerns in connection with the shortfalls of modern life. I. GREKOVA's first story "Beyond the Checkpoint" (1962) throws a fresh glance at the world of modern science. Her volume *Under the Streetlight* (1960) takes in many areas—work, daily life, people's relationships, different ages and social situations. Best of all are the stories dealing with the life of intellectuals in an urban environment: from the office to the hairdresser's, to the library, to the communal apartment. Zoshchenko's influence is perceptible in Grekova's refined sensitivity to jargon, colloquialisms, and the ability to employ them in an ironic way, as well as to use them as expressive verbal characteristics. While "A Week Like Any Other" by N. Baranskaya was severely criticized, the true life picture it presents, of the extreme energy it takes a young woman to survive in today's world as mother, wife and professional, offers a relatively objective and critical view of contemporary Soviet life.

It seems evident, then, that the short form is today, in the Soviet Union as elsewhere, the most dynamic genre by far. Isaac Bashevis Singer writes, "I prefer the short story because only in a short story can a writer reach perfection more than in a novel. When you write a novel, especially a long novel, you are never the ruler of your writing, because you cannot really make a plan of, say 500 pages and keep to the rules or keep to the plan. While in a short story there is always the possibility of being really perfect."

Bibliography: Deming Brown, *Soviet Russian Literature since Stalin.* 1978. Geoffrey Hosking, *Beyond Socialist Realism: Soviet Fiction since Ivan Denisovich.* 1980. D. S. Mirsky, *A History of Russian Literature from Its Beginnings to 1900.* 1958. G. Struve, *Russian Literature under Lenin and Stalin.* 1971. *Russkaya povest' XIX veka.* Ed. B. S. Meilakh. 1973.   E. K. K.

Shpet, Gustáv Gustávovich (1879–1937), philosopher and exponent of Husserl's phenomenology in Russian philosophical circles. Shpet studied under the neo-Kantian G. I. Chelpanov at Kiev University. In 1910 Shpet was appointed instructor in philosophy at Moscow University. He published many works on epistemology, history of philosophy, aesthetics, and psychology. He also translated into Russian some of the works of Byron, Dickens, and Thackeray. He died in a Siberian labor camp in 1937.

While still a student Shpet published his anti-metaphysical work, *The Problem of Causality in Hume and Kant* (Problema prichinnosti u Yuma i Kanta). His other works were developed along anti-metaphysical and anti-religious lines. He regarded the history of philosophy as a progression from folklore (*mudrost*) through metaphysics to strict science. Philosophy, according to Shpet, is a "basic science" underlying all special sciences.

In his *Appearance and Meaning* (Yavlenie i smysl), Shpet developed the view that philosophy is concerned primarily with the study of pure data of social consciousness. Hence, the philosopher's starting point must be of a sociological nature. Shpet was the first of the phenomenological philosophers to turn his attention to the problem of the meaning of history. He was closer to Hegel in his understanding of the essence of history, when he stated that "we proceed from sensuous reality as a riddle, towards its ideal basis, in order to solve this riddle by interpreting reality, through an examination of reason in reality itself, which is realized and embodied."

Shpet's interest in social phenomena led him to elaborate his views in works dealing with social psychology and the role of language in social intercourse. He became interested in the works of William James and he translated James's *A Pluralistic Universe* into Russian in 1911. His *Outline of the Development of Russian Philosophy* (Ocherk razvitiya russkoi filosofii) is an important contribution. Shpet also published works on P. D. Yurkevich, Aleksandr HERZEN and Pyotr LAVROV.

Works: Istoriya kak problema logiki. 1916. *Esteticheskie fragmenty.* 3 vols. 1922–23. *Vvedenie v etnicheskuyu psikhologiyu.* 1927. *Vnutrennyaya forma slova.* 1927.

Secondary literature: V. V. Zenkovsky, *A History of Russian Philosophy.* Trans. G. L. Kline. Vol. 2. 1953.   L. J. S.

Shteiger, Anatóly see STEIGER.

Shukshín, Vasíly Makárovich (1929–74), writer, actor, and filmmaker, was born of peasant parents in Srostki in the Altai, completed seventh-grade schooling, then worked in a variety of jobs before entering the All-Union Institute of Cinematography in Moscow in 1954, where he studied in the Department of Directing with M. I. Romm. He began to write stories as part of his Institute education. His first published story, "Two on a Cart" (Dvoe na telege), appeared in 1958. Shukshin graduated from the Institute in 1961. By 1963 the first collection of his stories, *Rural People* (Sel'skie zhiteli), appeared, followed a year later by his first full-length film, "There Lives a Lad" (Zhivet takoi paren'), which won the Golden Lion of Saint Mark Award at the 16th Venice Film Festival.

Shukshin excelled as a writer, director, and actor. He published four more collections of stories—*There, Far Away* (Tam, vdali, 1968), *Countrymen* (Zemlyaki, 1970), *Characters* (Kharaktery, 1973), and *Conversations under a Clear Moon* (Besedy pri yasnoi lune, 1974)—as well as the play *Energetic People* (Energichnye lyudi, 1974), and two historical novels, *The Lyubavins* (Lyubaviny, 1965) and *I've Come to Give You Freedom* (Ya prishel dat' vam volyu, screenplay 1968, novel 1971) before his death from a heart attack at age forty-five. Posthumous collections of his stories include *My Brother* (Brat moi, 1975), *In Fall* (Osen'yu, 1976), *Before Dawn* (Do tret'ikh petukhov, 1976), *I Want to Live* (Okhota zhit', 1977), *Point of View* (Tochka zreniya, 1979), and *Stories* (Rasskazy, 1979). Major films written and directed by Shukshin include "Your Son and Brother" (1965), for which he was awarded the Vasiliev Brothers State Prize, "Strange People" (Strannye lyudi, 1969), "A Bench by the Stove" (Pechki-lavochki, 1972), and his most famous film "Snowball Berry Red" (Kalina krasnaya, 1974), for which he was posthumously awarded the Lenin Prize in 1976.

One of the most gifted of the COUNTRY PROSE writers (derevenshchiki), Shukshin most typically depicts the deracinated country hero in an anarchic, at times self-destructive search for freedom (*volya*). He excels in incorporating spoken Russian into his work as a tool for characterization. His short stories, his most successful genre, often involve an unexpected twist in the hero's pursuit of an unrealizable goal. His hero's tragicomic suffering at the hands of unsympathetic authorities or exasperated women often culminates in a classic Russian *skandal*. Shukshin's writing has been enthusiastically received by readers of enormous social, educational, and political diversity within the Soviet Union, in part as a result of his success in depicting the fundamental transition from country to city in Soviet society.

Works: Izbrannye proizvedeniya. 2 vols. 1975. *Kinopovesti.* 1975.

Translations: Vasily Shukshin: Snowball Berry Red and Other Stories. Trans. Donald M. Fiene et al. Ann Arbor, 1979. *I Want to Live: Short Stories.* Trans. Robert Daglish. Moscow, 1973.

Secondary literature: D. M. Fiene and B. N. Peskin. "The Remarkable Art of Vasily Shukshin," *RLT*, no. 11 (1975), pp. 174–78. Geoffrey A. Hosking, "The Fiction of Vasily Shukshin." In *Vasily Shukshin: Snowball Berry Red and Other Stories*. Pp. 3–18.

N. C.

Shvarts, Evgény Lvóvich (1896–1958), dramatist and writer of children's fiction. Shvarts had two closely related literary careers, that of a gifted writer of children's literature and that of a dramatist. Apart from his many works for young readers and his association with Samuil MARSHAK at the State Children's Publishing House (DETGIZ), Shvarts was also on the staff of the children's literary magazines *Ezh* and *Chizh*. His early experience as an actor and later collaboration with the Leningrad Children's Theater and Nikolai Akimov's Theater of Comedy enabled him to bring a first-hand knowledge of the stage to his dramatic writing. His first play, *Underwood* (Undervud, 1929), about how a young girl foils the attempted theft of a student's typewriter, exhibited the interplay of realism and fairy-tale elements characteristic of his best plays. The author of over a dozen dramatic works, Shvarts is best known for *The Naked King* (Golyi korol', 1934), *The Shadow* (Ten', 1940), and *The Dragon* (Drakon, 1943–44), all of which have been translated into English. The first two are based on tales by Hans Christian Andersen, while *The Dragon* derives from Charles Perrault's legend of Sir Lancelot and the dragon. Despite their fairy-tale character, lively dialogue, and abundant humor, the plays address such adult issues as authoritarianism, militarism, racism, anti-intellectualism, social and political corruption, and man's capacity for evil as well as good. Their implications for Soviet reality are barely masked by their fairy-tale exterior, which may explain the difficulties in bringing them to the stage. *The Naked King* was produced for the first time only in 1960, while *The Shadow* and *The Dragon* were pulled off the boards in 1940 and 1944, respectively, after only a few performances. They were revived in the early 1960s when a relatively more liberal climate after Stalin's death made possible new productions and the first printed collections of Shvarts' plays (1956, 1962).

Works: Evgenii Shvarts. *Klad*, etc. Ed. S. Tsimbal. 1962. *Three Plays*. Introd. and notes by Avril Pyman. Pergamon Press, 1972.

Secondary literature: J. Douglas Clayton, "The Theatre of E. L. Shvarts: An Introduction," *Etudes Slaves et Est-Européennes* 19 (1974), pp. 24–43. Irina H. Corten, "Evgenii Shvarts as an Adapter of Hans Christian Andersen and Charles Perrault," *RusR* 37 (1978), pp. 51–67. ———, "Evgeny L'vovich Shvarts: A Biographical Sketch," *RLT* 16 (1979), pp. 222–43. ———, "Evgenii L'vovich Shvarts: A Selected Bibliography," *RLT* 16 (1979), pp. 333–39. Amanda Metcalf, *Evgenii Shvarts and His Fairy-Tales for Adults*. (Birmingham Slavonic Monographs. 8.) 1979.

H. B. S.

Simeón Pólotsky (Samuíl Emel'yánovich Petróvskii-Sitniyanóvich, 1629–80), poet. Simeon Polotsky separated poetics from theology and became Russia's first professional court poet, placing the word at the service of the State and setting the trends for 18th-century literature. He dedicated his life and work to Russia's transition from a sacred state with a penitential messianic ideology to enlightened absolutism and empire. Together with Paisios Ligarides, he helped prepare the Church Council of 1666–67 which officially deposed the Patriarch Nikon and condemned the Old Belief. His polemical tract of 1667 against the OLD BELIEVERS, the Rod of Governance, involved a defense of the new aesthetics realized in the icon painting of Simeon Ushakov and his school. He used his own extensive literary corpus as a didactic tool for introducing the culture of scholastic humanism into Russia. He communicated his new worldview and aesthetics in SYLLABIC VERSE, adapting to Slavonic the method of versification practiced in Poland.

A native of Polotsk in White Russia, Simeon was educated in the KIEV ACADEMY and the Jesuit College at Wilno where he mastered Latin and Polish. In 1656 he became a monk and taught in the Orthodox Brotherhood School in Polotsk. He settled in Moscow in 1664. The following year he opened a school for the clerks of the Tsar's Privy Chancery at the Zaikonospassky monastery, teaching grammar, Latin, poetics, and rhetoric. In 1667 he was made tutor to the Tsarevich Aleksis and later to Fyodor, Sofiya and the young Peter I. In 1678 he set up the first printing press independent of patriarchal control in the Kremlin. In 1680, he drafted a plan for what

was to become the first institution of higher learning, the Slavonic-Greco-Latin Academy realized later under Peter I.

In the 1670s he wrote the first plays for the court based on the Jesuit school drama, "The Comedy about the Parable of the Prodigal Son," published posthumously in 1685, and the "Tragedy on Nebuchadnezzar the King." He wrote and prepared the first Russian collection of poems in 1677–78, the *Many-Flowered Garden*, the first sermons in verse collected in *Spiritual Dinner*, and *Spiritual Vespers* published posthumously in 1681 and 1683 respectively, the first *Rhymed Psalter* to be sung at home, published in 1680 and adapted to music by Titov, and the first panegyric odes to the sovereign collected the same year in *Rifmologion*.

Simeon Polotsky espoused the moderation, reason, and civic virtue of classical tradition as interpreted by the neo-Latin authors. This tradition represented for him world learning and culture. His "baroque," artificial, "cultured" manner of communicating it was his antidote to the "ignorant" mythic, organic worldview of the masses and of traditional Eastern Orthodoxy. His abstruse syllabic verse deformed the native accentual system and required a declamatory style of reading; his lexicon combined Russian, Slavonic, Greek, and White Russian words; his syntax was elaborate and complicated. His principles of verbal organization were external, often elaborate and usually visually oriented. Equating scholastic reasoning with truth, he relied heavily on allegory and projected analytic linear thinking onto phenomena. He estranged them from their native contexts and combined unlike things, natural and mythological, to transform them into an abstract model of the universe which served to illustrate a given truth.

His emphasis on civic themes and his classicizing didacticism set a precedent for 18th-century literature. His *Rhymed Psalter* stood at the beginning of the tradition of poetic adaptations of the Psalter to comment on contemporary issues and values. Likewise, his play, the *Prodigal Son* addressed the contemporary problem of Russian youths leaving for the West without adequate learning, and heralded Russian literature's preoccupation with the consequences of westernization. His poems introduced the abstract satire of manners and provided models for the language and style of the panegyric ode in praise of the monarch, the empire and its military activities.

Works: Izbrannye sochineniya. Ed. I. P. Eremin. 1953.

Translations: S. Zenkovsky, *Medieval Russia's Epics, Chronicles and Tales*. 1974. Pp. 517–18. W. E. Brown, *A History of Seventeenth Century Russian Literature*. Ann Arbor, 1980. Pp. 117–20.

Secondary literature: I. P. Eremin, commentary in Simeon Polotskii, *Izbrannye sochineniya*. 1953. Pp. 223–61. A. M. Panchenko, *Russkaya stikhotvornaya kul'tura XVII veka*. 1973. Dm. Zhukov and L. Pushkarev, *Russkie pisateli XVII veka*. 1972. Pp. 199–335.

P. H.

Simonov, Konstantín (Kiríll) Mikhaílovich (1915–79), prose writer, poet, and dramatist. Born in Petrograd, he published his first work in 1934, graduated from the Gorky Literary Institute in Moscow in 1938, and in 1939 began working as a journalist. During World War II he was a correspondent for *Krasnaya zvezda*, editor in chief of NOVYI MIR (1946–50, 1954–58), and editor of LITERATURNAYA GAZETA (1938, 1950–53). The recipient of six Stalin Prizes, a Lenin Prize, and Hero of Socialist Labor, he was a member of the Communist Party and Deputy of the Supreme Soviet. As secretary of the UNION OF SOVIET WRITERS, he was active in establishing its conservative policies. A prolific writer, Simonov authored poems, novels, novellas, short stories, and plays. During the 1940s and 1950s Simonov was quite popular with the reading public. Between 1937 and 1939 he published *The Victor*, a poem about Nikolai OSTROVSKY, a number of other poems and several collections of lyrical poems. Some of his love poems, such as "Wait For Me and I'll Return," and "With You and Without You," became part of Russian popular culture of the war period. Simonov is the author of ten plays, of which *A Fellow from Our Home Town* (1941) and *Russian People* (1942) received Stalin Prizes.

While a war correspondent Simonov began his major novels dealing with the war. *Comrade in Arms* (1952) is set in Mongolia during the Japanese skirmish of 1939. In 1943 and 1944 Simonov published *Days and Nights*, about the battle of Stalingrad, the first part of his trilogy about World War II. The second part, *The Living* and the Dead (1959–71, 1974 Lenin Prize), describes the Soviet defeat in the early part of the war. The final part of the trilogy, *Soldiers are not Born* (1963–64), returns to the slaughter at Stalingrad. During the 1970s, he published the *Notebooks* which served as the basis for his war novels.

Simonov was a skillful, officially approved writer in tune with the spirit of his times. His poetry is melodious, though often sentimental and trite. His plays are dramatically weak and blatantly propagandistic. His prose represents his best work. Although Simonov's novels enjoyed great popularity when first published, they are no longer very popular.

Works: Sobranie sochinenii. 6 vols. 1966–70. *Sobranie sochinenii.* 1979, 1980. *Na Literaturnye temy. Stat'i 1937–1955.* 1956. "Sluchai s Polynnym. Povest'," *Znamya*, 1969, no. 8. *Poslednee leto.* 1970–71. *Tridtsat' shestoi i sem'desyat pervyi.* 1972. *Ot Khalkhingola do Berlina.* 1973. *Dvadtsat' dnei bez voiny. (Iz zapisok Lopatina). Povest'.* 1973. *Segodnya i davno.* 1974. *Esli dorog tebe tvoi dom...; poemy, stikhotvoreniya, povest'.* 1982.

Translations: On the Petsamo Road. Moscow, 1942. *Stalingrad Fights On.* Moscow, 1942. *The Russian People.* 1942. *No Quarter.* 1943. *The Russians.* 1944. *Four Soviet War Plays.* 1944. *The Death Factory Near Lublin.* 1944. *The Lublin Extermination Camp.* Moscow, 1944. *Days and Nights.* 1945. *Friendship is the Most Important Thing in the World.* 1946. *The Russian Question.* Sydney, 1947. *The Whole World Over.* 1947. *Friends and Foes.* Moscow, 1951. *Victims and Heroes.* 1963. *The Living and the Dead.* Hyperion, Conn., 1968 (Reprint of 1962 ed.); Moscow, 1975. *Liberation.* Moscow, 1974.

Secondary literature: E. J. Brown, *Russian Literature Since the Revolution.* 1982. S. Fradkina, *Tvorchestvo Konstantina Simonova.* 1968. M. Slonim, *Soviet Russian Literature: Writers and Problems, 1917–1977.* 1977. I. L. Vishnevskaya, *Konstantin Simonov. Ocherk tvorchestva.* 1966.
H. S.

Sinyávsky, Andrei Donátovich (1925–   ), literary critic and prose writer. As the author of a number of critical studies on Russian poetry (including a widely appreciated introduction to Pasternak's verse in the series "Library of a Poet"), Sinyavsky had acquired a certain status as a literary scholar even before his arrest. Secretly, however, under the pseudonym "Abram Terts," he wrote an article on Soviet socialist realism, two short novels (*Lyubimov* and *The Trial Begins*), a number of short stories, and a collection of aphorisms (*Unguarded Thoughts*). These works were smuggled abroad for publication and engendered in the KGB an intensive search for the author. In 1965 Sinyavsky was imprisoned together with Yuly DANIEL. He was finally released in 1971 and in 1973 was permitted to emigrate to France, where he is a professor of Russian at the Sorbonne.

Sinyavsky's essay "On Socialist Realism" is an attack on officially accepted doctrine and a call for a literature of the grotesque and phantasmagoric fantasy. Sinyavsky converted theory into practice in such works of fantasy as *Lyubimov* and "Pkhents." In *Lyubimov* the protagonist uses mass hypnosis to convince the residents of a small town that he can turn a river into champagne and create a utopian state. In "Pkhents" the hero is a being from outer space.

Unguarded Thoughts is a collection of aphorisms, dominated (as is so much of his work) by a sense of irony and unusual frankness—within the Russian literary tradition—in its free treatment of sex. A similarly structured work is *A Voice from the Choir*, which appeared after Sinyavsky's emigration to the West and consists of excerpts from letters he wrote to his wife from camp.

Sinyavsky, who claims to prefer to be Terts rather than Sinyavsky, usually tries to maintain very separate personalities as Terts and Sinyavsky. The critic writing under the name Sinyavsky is scholarly and serious, while the Terts half of his personality attempts to shock, to be irreverent, to maintain a constant ironic joking. This attitude was particularly evident in *A Stroll with Pushkin*, in which Terts describes Pushkin as "our Charlie Chaplin, a contemporary fake Petrushka, all duded up, who's figured out how to strut around in rhyme." The book was the subject of heated criticism on the part of émigré critics, who viewed it as an insult to the memory of the poet. Supposedly written in camp by memory, *A Stroll with Pushkin* contains a number of references to obscure 19th-century Russian journals—a circumstance which led Roman Gul, for example, to

claim that Sinyavsky was not telling the whole truth in the matter. Sinyavsky responded that the book had actually been written in camp and defended it as an attempt to prove to himself at the time that he had not been totally destroyed by the experience.

Kroshka Tsores, a fantasy with autobiographical elements, is the story of a bookworm who brings misfortune upon his family, inadvertently being the cause of death of his five brothers. The book is attributed to Terts, but as an ironic narrative device the protagonist bears the name "Sinyavsky." Sinyavsky the literary character is short, suffers from feelings of inadequacy and inferiority, and, finding himself rejected by women, ultimately comes to prefer books to the fair sex.

Sinyavsky-Terts openly admits that his art is intended only for the intelligent, educated reader, and this exclusivity must be viewed as still another rejection of the doctrine of socialist realism with its insistence that literature appeal to the man on the street.

Sinyavsky also confesses to being "painfully troubled by the gap between [his] generation and the generation of writers working in the first part of the twentieth century.... It is essential that we build a bridge back to that culture." He has been compared with BELY, PILNYAK, ZAMYATIN, REMIZOV, and OLESHA, among others.

Since his arrival in the West, Sinyavsky has published a major critical study of GOGOL, *In the Shade of Gogol*, and a book on Vasily ROZANOV, *Rozanov's* Fallen Leaves ("Opavshie list'ya" Rozanova, 1982).

Translations: On Socialist Realism. Trans. George Dennis, introd. Czeslaw Milosz. 1960. *Fantastic Stories.* 1963. *The Makepeace Experiment.* Trans. Manya Harrari. 1965. *On Trial: The Soviet State versus "Abram Tertz" and "Nikolai Arzhak."* Trans. Max Hayward. 1966. *For Freedom of Imagination.* Trans. and introd. Laszlo Tikos and Murray Peppard. 1971. *Unguarded Thoughts.* Trans. Manya Harrari. 1972. *A Voice from the Chorus.* Trans. Kyril FitzLyon and Max Hayward. 1976.

Secondary literature: Margaret Dalton, *Andrei Siniavsky and Julii Daniel': Two Soviet "Heretical" Writers.* Würzburg, 1973. Andrew R. Durkin, "Narrator, Metaphor, and Theme in Sinjavskij's *Fantastic Tales*," *SEEJ* 24 (1980), pp. 133–44. Richard Lourie, *Letters to the Future: An Approach to Sinyavsky-Tertz.* 1975.
J. G.

Sirin, see NABOKOV.

Sixties, Men of the, see *SHESTIDESYATNIKI*.

Skabichévsky, Aleksándr Mikhailovich (1838–1910), publicist and literary critic. Born into the family of a civil servant in St. Petersburg, Skabichevsky completed university studies there and began writing for the periodical press. From 1868 to 1884 he was a collaborator on the criticism staff of OTECHESTVENNYE ZAPISKI and he considered this period his most productive. At first influenced by the radical critics (CHERNYSHEVSKY, DOBROLYUBOV, and PISAREV), he later became involved with the POPULIST (*narodnik*) movement and, while continuing to regard literature as a potent moral force, he broke in part with the radical tradition, holding BELINSKY responsible for what he considered the poor showing of Russian letters in the seventies. For a while, however, Skabichevsky felt that the Russian writer must not try to reproduce objectively the real world but rather supplement and otherwise distort this reality in conformity with an ideal. Then, in connection with his historico-philosophical concept of two phases in European thought (abstract and practical), he modified his view and held that art should *not* distort reality (see his *Life in Literature and Literature in Life*, 1882). In the early nineties he wrote his once popular *History of Recent Russian Literature, 1848–1890* (Istoriya noveishei russkoi literatury 1848–1890, 1891) as well as his *Sketches on the History of Russian Censorship* (Ocherki istorii russkoi tsenzury 1700–1863, 1892) and he came into conflict with the decadents. Shocked at first by decadent theory and practice (he polemicized with MEREZHKOVSKY and made disparaging remarks about CHEKHOV), he later recognized decadence as a legitimate development, replacing as it did the pedestrian "prose" of everyday life with the "poetry of spiritual exaltation."

Works: Sochineniya. 2 vols. 1903.

Secondary literature: R. Stacy, *Russian Literary Criticism: A Short History.* 1974. James West, *Russian Symbolism.* 1970.

R. H. S.

Skaz, from the Russian *skazat'*, "to tell," may soon enter the international literary lexicon; no other culture seems to have produced an unambiguous name for the second of its referents.

In Russian the word is used in two senses. The first, which has not crossed the Russian frontier, is a vague genre designation of oral folk narrative, almost always in prose. It is approximately equivalent to "tale" in English. Semantically, *skaz* lies on neutral ground somewhere between *skazka*, which specifies that the contents are unreal, magic, fantastic, and *byl'*, whose contents are claimed as "true." *Skaz*, however, carries the additional information that the narrated events are represented as having taken place in the present or recent past. If, as is frequently the case, the narrator experienced the events personally, the *skaz* is a form of reminiscence. Often it is found on the border between an ordinary speech event (e.g., an anecdote from personal experience, on the order of "Listen to what happened to me today!") and a work of oral narrative art destined to survive and be transmitted by others. In written literature the equivalent of *skaz* is *rasskaz* or *povest'*, but some writers have occasionally labelled literary works *skaz* in order to place them in a "folk" cultural context. The word is used, for example, in the original title of LESKOV's famous "tale" of the squint-eyed left-hander from Tula and the steel flea (*Skaz o tul'skom kosom Levshe i o stal'-noi blokhe*). It happens that this work is also a *skaz* in the second sense, but Leskov's intent in the title was only to give his text the genre designation it would have been assigned by its putative folk narrator.

It is the second meaning of *skaz* that has been internationalized. Here too, however, there has been a lack of complete agreement concerning the term's precise meaning, such eminent literary theoreticians as EIKHENBAUM, VINOGRADOV, and BAKHTIN having differed over its definition. The early FORMALISTS singled out "orientation toward oral speech" as the distinguishing feature of *skaz*. (It was understood, of course, that the "oral speech" in question was an illusion: a literary text remains an aggregate of visual symbols reproduced on a page, and these can render no more than a highly selective sampling of the contours of an actual oral utterance.) This striving for (illusionistic) "orality" was said to stem from a wish to liberate the literary lexicon from the canons of "genteel" literary discourse, invigorating it with infusions from living speech, especially that of lower-class, uneducated, or provincial narrators. In his famous article on GOGOL's "Overcoat" Eikhenbaum stressed, however, that it was not only a question of enriched vocabulary, but of making written literature simulate a real oral performance, "in which a special role is played by articulation, mimicry, phonic gestures, etc." TYNYANOV went even further, claiming that the narrator's oral performance becomes (at least in imagination) an oral performance by the *reader*: "The *skaz* makes the word physically palpable.... The reader enters into the story, begins to articulate, gesticulate, and smile; he no longer reads the story, but plays it."

These "oral" definitions of *skaz* ultimately proved unsatisfactory, however. There was no evidence that all or even most *skazy* produce the "Tynyanov effect" on all readers. And there were literary works, such as many short stories by ZOSHCHENKO, which seemed to embody the most essential feature of *skaz* (that the narrative is presented in "marked" language deviating from the literary norm), but where no oral performance was specified or even implied. A more rigorous definition of *skaz* was subsequently worked out, using ideas derived from Bakhtin's celebrated work on the poetics of DOSTOEVSKY, his notion of a variable "narrative voice," the "author's voice" (*avtorskaya rech'*) contrasting with "someone else's voice" (*chuzhaya rech'*). As A. P. and M. O. Chudakov put it in the *Kratkaya literaturnaya entsiklopediya*, *skaz* is "a special type of narrative structured as emanating from a person distanced from the author (whether concretely named or presumed), and one who possesses a distinct manner of discourse." Applying a concept developed earlier in Germany, it could be said that the *skaz* is a narrative related in *erlebte Rede* or "quoted speech," i.e., language marked as not the author's own.

Though frequently used, "oral" markings are only one variety of the signals that can indicate distance between "author's" and "someone else's" voice; they are no longer a requirement of *skaz*. In Gogol's "Tale of How Ivan Ivanovich Quarrelled with Ivan Niki-forovich," for example, there is no indication of oral performance, but in the very first paragraph the absurdly excessive outpourings of rapture over Ivan Ivanovich's accoutrements notify the reader that these judgments and emotional responses are "someone else's," not to be taken seriously as those of a literate author. Though likewise not a requirement of *skaz*, this phenomenon of emotional and judgmental distance between narrator and author (and therefore reader) frequently accompanies the required stylistic distance. A tension is thus created, forcing the reader to distrust the narrative and discount the narrator's values and attitudes. Leskov's "Battle-axe" (Voitel'nitsa) and "Night Owls" (Polunoshchniki) are characteristic examples of this procedure. And as the ultimate twist, in many of Zoshchenko's stories a character called "the author" uses debased language and expresses philistine attitudes that cannot be those of the real author. "Framing" of the story with an explicit narrative *mise en scène*, though likewise frequent, is also not an obligatory feature of *skaz*. And correspondingly, most authorities deny the appellation *skaz* to such works as the many "framed" stories by TURGENEV which are said to have been related orally (after dinner, over cigars and liqueurs), but whose narrators speak in exactly the same literary Russian that Turgenev writes.

Though examples of *skaz* can be found in most literatures, Russian literature has been especially rich in this art. Among its greatest practitioners have been Gogol and Leskov in the 19th century and REMIZOV, ZAMYATIN, BABEL, and Zoshchenko in the 20th.

Bibliography: M. Bakhtin, *Problemy poetiki Dostoevskogo.* 2d ed. 1963. B. Eikhenbaum, "Illyuziya skaza." In *Skvoz' literaturu.* 1924. Pp. 152–56. H. McLean, "On the Style of a Leskovian *Skaz*," *Harvard Slavic Studies* 2 (1954), pp. 297–322. Irwin R. Titunik, "The Problem of *Skaz* in Russian Literature." Ph.D. diss., Berkeley, 1963. ———, "Mixail Zoščenko and the Problem of *Skaz*," *California Slavic Studies* 6 (1971), pp. 83–96. V. Vinogradov, "Problema skaza v stilistike," *Poetika* 1 (1926), pp. 24–40.

H. McL.

Skazánie (from *skazat'*, "to tell"), a genre of Old Russian and of folk literature which may be defined as a prose narrative relating an event or events of the past, or of mythical nature. In modern literature, *skazanie* is best translated by "legend." V. T.

Skazánie o knyaz'yákh Vladímirskikh (History of the Princes of Vladimir, late 15th or early 16th century), a fabricated history which establishes the descent of the Princes of Vladimir, and hence of Moscow, from the rulers of ancient Babylon, Caesar Augustus, and the Emperors of Byzantium. The part dealing with Russian history proper concentrates on the Christian virtues of the rulers and on the happy union between Church and sovereign. As history, this part, too, is largely fictitious. The *Skazanie* is composed in the ornate and prolix style which came to Russia in the course of the "second SOUTH SLAVIC INFLUENCE." Along with the later STEPENNAYA KNIGA (Book of Generations), it was used by Ivan IV to legitimize his claim to being the rightful head of all Orthodox Christendom.

Text: Appendix to I. Zhdanov, *Russkii bylevoi epos. Issledovaniya i materialy* (1895). (Excerpts:) A. D. Stokes, *Khrestomatiya po drevnei russkoi literature.* 1963. Pp. 155–57.

Secondary literature: R. P. Dmitrieva, *Skazanie o knyaz'yakh Vladimirskikh.* 1955. ———, *K istorii sozdaniya 'Skazaniya o knyaz'yakh Vladimirskikh',* TODRL, Vol. 17 (1961). V. T.

Skazánie o Mamáevom Poboíshche. An early 15th-century version, preserved in manuscripts of the 15th to 19th centuries, of the 1380 battle on the Kulikovo Field. The *Skazanie* contains more factual detail about this important campaign than the chronicle account or the ZADONSHCHINA, but is stylistically less cohesive than the other two versions. In genre, it is a mixture of dispassionate chronicle record and boisterous military tale, as this genre had developed through such works as the *Jewish Wars* of Josephus Flavius and the *Tale of the Destruction of Ryazan* (Povest' o razorenii Ryazani: "the snapping of lances' breaking and the clanging of swords' clashing" etc.). The *Skazanie* is deliberately modeled on an earlier tale of a successful warrior-prince, the *Life of* ALEXANDER NEVSKY, as the far more poetic *Zadonshchina* was modelled on the *Igor Tale* (SLOVO O POLKU IGOREVE); its source is clear not only in the overall narrative plan, but also in many detailed episodes (such as the beneficent role of SS. BORIS AND GLEB, who appear in visions to Russian warriors in both works) and even in phraseological minutiae. The *Skazanie* was also strongly influenced by folk imagery (howling wolves, soaring falcons, plangent swans, etc.) borrowed directly from both the *Zadonshchina* and the *Igor Tale*, and, above all, by the ponderous commonplaces of medieval Christian piety. The attempt to combine these stylistically disparate frameworks into a coherent work of literary art is only intermittently successful; except for a few effective battle scenes, the *Skazanie* is better suited for philological analysis than for aesthetic enjoyment.

Bibliography: S. K. Shambinago, *Skazanie o Mamaevom Poboishche.* 1907. M. N. Tikhomirov, V. F. Rzhiga, L. A. Dmitriev, *Povesti o Kulikovskoi bitve.* 1959. D. S. Likhachev and L. A. Dmitriev, *Slovo o polku Igoreve i pamyatniki Kulikovskogo tsikla.* 1966.   D. S. W.

Skazánie ob Indïiskom tsárstve (History of the Kingdom of India), the Slavic version of the *Legend of Presbyter John*, widely current in medieval Russia. It describes the marvels of India, a blessed land ruled by a wise Christian ruler. The Slavic version (from the Latin) has been determined to have originated in Serbia in the 13th century. The Russian version eventually entered Russian folklore, where it appears in the *bylina* about Dyuk Stepanovich.

Bibliography: A. S. Orlov, *Perevodnye povesti feodal'noi Rusi i Moskovskogo gosudarstva XII–XVII vv.* 1934. M. N. Speranskii, "Skazanie ob Indiiskom tsarstve," *IAN* 3 (1930), bk. 2.   V. T.

Skázka, see FOLKTALE.

Skázovyi stikh. The general term *skazovyi stikh* covers several types of spoken verse in Russian folklore, including *balagánnyi, govornói, lubóchnyi, rayóshnyi,* and *skomoróshii stikh. Skazovyi stikh* represents the main verse form in the small poetic genres, that is, proverbs, sayings, riddles, wisecracks (*pribaútki*), speeches of the master-of-ceremonies at a folk wedding (*prígovory svádebnogo drúzhki*), cries of hucksters and traders (*výkriki raznóshchikov i torgóvtsev*), and some incantations. However, spoken verse may also be utilized in folk plays, the PUPPET THEATER (PETRÚSHKA), peep show (*rayók*), folk tales, and inscriptions on broadsides (LUBÓK). Spoken verse constitutes one aspect of the common Slavic patrimony in Russian folklore (JAKOBSON, Taranovsky).

Skazovyi stikh is based on syntactic prosody in which the phrase represents the chief organizing feature, although rhyme may also be employed. The most common type of spoken verse possesses a bipartite intonational structure consisting of two phrases; each phrase (colon or syntagma) contains two words, the first of which bears a word stress and the second a phrase stress. While the number of syllables in a phrase is ordinarily free, the number of stresses may be the same; rhyme may mark the phrase boundaries or internal rhyme may occur within phrases. Grammatical and syntactical parallelism, etymological figures, and various kinds of sound repetition may further contribute to the integration of a work in *skazovyi stikh* (Jakobson).

The proverb "Khoroshá brázhka, da malá cháshka" (The beer is good, but the mug is too small) contains two rhymed phrases, has two stresses per phrase, displays complete grammatical and syntactic parallelism, and evinces vowel harmony, that is, all stressed vowels are identical. The proverb "Bogát shól v pír, a ubóg brél v mír" (He went rich to the feast and walked poor into the world) consists of two rhymed phrases, displays grammatical and syntactic parallelism, and has three stresses in each phrase. Sound play may become highly prominent in such miniature poems. For instance, the names are chosen so as to produce internal rhymes in the tripartite proverb "Artamón za limón, a Simán za timán, a Vlás za kvás" (Artamon for lemon, Simon for caraway, Vlas for kvass). The riddle "Édu, édu—slédu nétu, rézhu, rézhu—króvi nétu"—"voda" (I go and go—no trace, I cut and cut—no blood—water) contains two rhymed lines in trochaic tetrameter, evinces grammatical and syntactic parallelism, and except for the contrasting word "krovi" exhibits vowel harmony.

Rayoshnyi stikh (or *rayóshnik*) and *skomoroshii stikh* have the same organizational features as other kinds of *skazovyi stikh*; however, they are predominantly humorous or satirical, possess energetic speech rhythm, and frequently emphasize grotesque, absurd, or crude naturalistic elements. While the lines are usually rhymed in pairs, the number of syllables and stresses per line may vary widely. One example from Sheptaev will suffice: "Nemnógo u menyá rzhí,/nét vo mné lzhí./I oní togó ne znáyut/ból'she togó pytáyut./I uchiníli nado mnóyu putém:/mázali dvázhdy kózhu knutóm." (I haven't got much rye,/there's no falsehood in me./But they don't know this and torture me so much more./And they gave me the proper treatment:/twice they tanned my hide with the knout.)

Literary writers have from time to time utilized *skazovyi stikh*, the earliest instances of which occur in the *Primary Chronicle*. Spoken verse was employed in *Molenie Daniila zatochnika* (Taranovsky) (see SUPPLICATION OF DANIEL THE EXILE), in petrified formulas in legal documents from the 15th through the 17th centuries (Timofeev), and in satirical tales and intermedia of the 17th and early 18th century. PUSHKIN used *skazovyi stikh* in his "Skazka o pope i o rabotnike ego Balde" and MAYAKOVSKY utilized it in his poems modeled on the *lubok*.

Bibliography: P. G. Bogatyrev, "Khudozhestvennye sredstva v yumoristicheskom yarmarochnom fol'klore." In *Voprosy teorii narodnogo iskusstva.* 1971. Pp. 450–96. R. Jakobson, "Studies in Comparative Slavic Metrics," *OSP* 3 (1952), pp. 58–62, and "Vliyanie narodnoi slovesnosti na Trediakovskogo." In *Selected Writings.* Vol. 4. 1966. Pp. 613–33. V. V. Mitrofanova, "Ritmicheskoe stroenie russkikh narodnykh zagadok," *RFolk,* 1971, no. 12, pp. 147–61. D. Samoilov, *Kniga o russkoi rifme.* 1973. Pp. 29–68. L. S. Sheptaev, "Russkii rayoshnik XVII veka," *Uchenye zapiski Leningradskogo gos. ped. inst. imeni A. I. Gertsena,* 87 (1948), pp. 17–43. M. Shtokmar, "Stikhotvornaya forma russkikh poslovits, pogovorok, zagadok, pribautok," *Zvezda Vostoka,* 1965, no. 11, pp. 149–63. K. Taranovsky, "Formy obshcheslavyanskogo i tserkovnoslavyanskogo stikha v drevnerusskoi literature XI–XIII vv." In *American Contributions to the Sixth International Congress of Slavists* 1. 1968. Pp. 377–94. L. I. Timofeev, *Ocherki teorii i istorii russkogo stikha.* 1958. Pp. 203–36. I. I. Voznesenskii, *O sklade ili ritme i metre kratkikh rechenii russkogo naroda.* Kostroma, 1908.   J. O. B.

Sketch (*ócherk*). The literary sketch is a minor but influential and popular prose genre combining in varying proportions journalistic and literary elements. The sketch is solidly based on external reality, on what is factual and typical. This material can be extremely varied, ranging from a description of a landscape, a milieu, or a character to statistics and scientific facts. This assorted material is unified and commented on by a first-person narrator who is the central figure in the sketch, and who generally represents the views of the author. The narrator presents himself as an eyewitness or vouches in some other way for the authenticity of what he describes. He is free (within reason) to invent and imagine other details—even other characters and episodes—that will make his point clearer and more vivid. What is most important is that a character and his milieu be *typical*. Hence a character is drawn in broad strokes, with no attempt at individualization or psychological depth. He is a static figure who is never shown in conflict with any other character (although there may be accidental meetings, arrivals, or departures); the result is that he never changes or develops as would be the case in a short story. Since there is no need of conflict, plot is either weak or non-existent, and the space usually given to plot in a story is taken up instead by extended descriptions of character and milieu. Whatever movement there is in a sketch occurs through the logical progression of the narrator's argument or of his investigation of a problem, in the course of which he brings to bear his army of facts, observations, portraits, and episodes.

The history of the literary sketch goes back to the satirical writings of La Bruyère in France, Addison and Steele in England, and Novikov and Krylov in Russia. However, it was Balzac who established the distinctive form of the sketch and made it popular. From 1825 to 1844 he worked out his "physiologies" of the Parisian grocer, rentier, official, journalist, etc. The prestige of the natural sciences, especially zoology, persuaded Balzac that the scientific method could be applied to the study of man. Like a zoologist Balzac examined how man is shaped by his milieu, by his past history, and how he can be classified according to profession and character type. The physiology might be an exhaustive, scientific study of a profession, or of the history of a boulevard.

BELINSKY urged Russian writers to create similar sketches anatomizing various professions and social layers in Petersburg and Moscow. Between 1839 and 1848, 700 sketches were produced. These depicted not only the middle class but also the way of life of poor people, drunkards, and outcasts.

The two most important anthologies of physiological sketches were compiled by N. A. NEKRASOV: *The Physiology of Petersburg* (1845) and *The Petersburg Sbornik* (1846). These included sketches by Belinsky, Nekrasov, GRIGOROVICH, PANAEV, DOSTOEVSKY, SOLLOGUB, TURGENEV, and HERZEN. The most famous physiologists, including DAL, Grigorovich, Panaev, and Nekrasov, published collections under their own names.

The popularity of the physiological sketch led to the rise of the NATURAL SCHOOL. The sketch became part of the short story (*rasskaz*), the most popular literary genre of the 1840s. Thus PUSHKIN described the hard life of the station-master; Dostoevsky, the life of the poor bureaucrat; GOGOL, the life (somewhat romanticized) of Nevsky Avenue. Of greater importance, the physiological sketch influenced the methods of description of the major Russian realistic writers who grew up in the 1840s. "Oblomov's Dream" by GONCHAROV is a physiology of the gentry class; Turgenev's "Khor and Kalinych" in *A Sportsman's Sketches* is a physiology of the peasant; TOLSTOI's *Sevastopol in December* is a physiology of the soldier; and Dostoevsky's *House of the Dead* is (except for the psychologizing) a physiology of the criminal.

The physiological sketch proved too objective and confining in its structure and faded out in the 1850s. From 1860 to the 1880s SALTYKOV-SHCHEDRIN used the sketch to satirize government officials. The sketch was used forcefully from the 1860s to 1917 by Gleb USPENSKY (*The Power of the Land*), SLEPTSOV, and others to describe the hard life of the peasantry.

In the Soviet period the sketch became extremely popular for documenting historic events and for travel books. In the 1920s it was the medium of SERAFIMOVICH, FURMANOV, SHAGINYAN, and GORKY to describe the war years and the NEP period; in the 1930s sketches were written by TIKHONOV, PAUSTOVSKY, PRISHVIN and ILF AND PETROV (*Little Golden America*). The World War II years were chronicled by SIMONOV, V. GROSSMAN, ERENBURG, and LEONOV; and in the postwar period the sketch was used by TENDRYAKOV, KAZAKOV, Abramov, and V. NEKRASOV. OVECHKIN and DOROSH have written sketches describing village life.

With so many Soviet writers turning out sketches, the boundaries between the journalistic sketch, the literary sketch, the short story, and other genres have become unclear and subject to vigorous and continuing dispute.

Bibliography: Deming Brown, "The Očerk: Suggestions Toward a Redefinition." In *American Contributions to the Sixth International Congress of Slavists.* Vol. 2: Literary Contributions. 1968. Pp. 29–41. P. K. F. "Ocherk." In *Literaturnaya entsiklopediya.* Vol. 8 (1934). Pp. 381–88. G. N. Pospelov, "Sketch, Literary (*ocherk*)." In the *Great Soviet Encyclopedia*, trans. of 3d ed. 1978. Vol. 19. P. 682. A. G. Tseitlin, *Stanovlenie realizma v russkoi literature.* 1965.   N. R.

Skobtsóva, Elizavéta Yúrievna, see MARIYA, MAT'.

Skomorókhi (sing. *skomorókh*), "minstrel," though the translation fails to convey the very broad and diversified functions as entertainers the *skomorokhi* very likely held. In their long history these popular, often itinerant entertainers seem to have been musicians (instrumentalists as well as singers), dancers, actors, jugglers, puppeteers, and bear-wrestlers. Though there is considerable dispute as to which forms of folk and popular art the *skomorokhi* actually performed and which they may have influenced, there is little doubt that they played an enormous role in helping to shape modern Russian folk art and popular art as we know them.

The term *skomorokh* is of uncertain origin. The word first appears in a Russian chronicle as early as the year 1068. The *skomorokhi* seem to have had a pagan, ritual function in the early Russian period, and they may have practised sorcery. All this would apparently imply that they were indigenous and Russian, but they very probably were influenced by foreign itinerant entertainers, including the German *Spielmänner*, who visited Russia in the medieval period, and perhaps by Byzantine mime entertainers, who are depicted in early frescoes on the walls of the Cathedral of St. Sophia in Kiev.

The pagan link and general condemnation of secular entertainments brought the *skomorokhi* into conflict with the Russian Church, and itinerant *skomorokhi* were especially persecuted. Settled ones seem to have enjoyed a lower middle-class status and some prosperity. The northwest Russian city of Novgorod, a member of the Hanseatic trading league, was a center for the *skomorokhi* in the late Middle Ages, but the fall of Novgorod to Moscow in 1570 brought the beginning of their decline, and in 1648 Tsar Aleksei Mikhailovich outlawed the *skomorokhi* entirely.

Genres of folklore cultivated or influenced by the *skomorokhi* include the epic song or BYLINA, especially the so-called *skomoroshina*, a term which denotes humorous narrative songs sometimes depicting the activities of the *skomorokhi* themselves. FOLKTALES, PROVERBS, incantations and other forms of folklore also seem to have been cultivated by them. The Russian puppet theater of PETRUSHKA was a particular specialty, and an old print illustration made by the Dutch traveller Adam Olearius as early as 1736 shows them performing in various ways and, in particular, putting on a scene from the Petrushka puppet play.

Bibliography: A. A. Belkin, *Russkie skomorokhi.* 1975. A. S. Famintsyn, *Skomorokhi na Rusi.* 1889. N. Findeizen, *Ocherki po istorii muzyki v Rossii.* Vol. 1. 1928. Pp. 45–170. Russell Zguta, *Russian Minstrels.* 1978.   W. E. H.

Skorpión. A publishing house (1900–16) founded in Moscow by the art patron S. A. Polyakov for the furtherance of the SYMBOLIST literary movement. Its policies were guided by Valery BRYUSOV, who assumed thereby a role of leadership in the symbolist movement. *Skorpion* introduced Western symbolists such as Paul Verlaine, Emile Verhaeren, and Stanislaw Przybyszewski, and published contemporary Western art criticism. It published many of the best works of the major Russian symbolists, beginning with Konstantin BALMONT (*Burning Buildings*—Goryashchie zdaniya, 1900), and including Bryusov, Andrei BELY, Fyodor SOLOGUB, Zinaida HIPPIUS, and Vyacheslav IVANOV. *Skorpion* published five issues of a symbolist miscellany (*al'manakh*) called SEVERNYE TSVETY (1901–1904 and 1911) after the 19th century miscellany edited by Anton DELVIG; it included some works by the realists Anton CHEKHOV and Ivan BUNIN, as well as some archival material relating to authors of the 19th century. Between 1904 and 1909 *Skorpion* published the symbolists' leading literary journal VESY which contained works by all the outstanding symbolists, reports from correspondents on literature and art in Western European countries, essays on literary theory, and literary and art criticism. The books published by Skorpion were noted for distinguished art work by the artists of the MIR ISKUSSTVA group associated with Sergei DIAGHILEV.

Bibliography: Evgenii Anichkov, "Poety Skorpiona." In *Literaturnye obrazy i mneniya 1903 g.* 1904. Pp. 143–84. Andrei Belyi, *Nachalo veka.* 1933. Valery Ya. Bryusov, *The Diary of Valery Bryusov (1893–1905).* Ed., trans., and introd. Joan Delaney Grossman. 1980.   E. Br.

Skovorodá, Grigóry Sávvich (Ukrainian: Hryhorij, 1722–94), Ukrainian philosopher and poet, was born in the village of Chernukhy in Poltava province and spent most of his adult life in the so-called Slobidska Ukraine (Kharkov region). Skovoroda wrote in the heavily russified Ukrainian language spoken by the gentry of that region and in Latin. He was a student at the Kiev Mohyla Academy and as a young man visited Western Europe. From 1769 until his death he was an itinerant philosopher and preacher. He wrote several philosophical treatises, often in the form of dialogues, as well as *Kharkov Fables* (Kharkovskie basni) and a collection of poems *Sad bozhestvennykh pesen* (Orchard of Divine Songs, 1757–85). His view of life is ahistorical (no mention of current events) and his philosophy is based on Christian morality. He preached and practised non-attachment, simple living, and meditation. Popular with the peasants during his life, he was later the hero of a cult among some POPULISTS. Today a different image is foisted upon him—that of a friend of the working people.

Skovoroda's influence on Ukrainian literature was limited because of his universality and because of his language, which became unacceptable in the 19th century. Many Ukrainian writers (P. KULISH, T. SHEVCHENKO, P. Tychyna) either tried to emulate him or wrote about him. Russian scholars and writers (V. KAPNIST, N. LESKOV, S. Balukhaty, V. Bonch-Bruevich) were also attracted to Skovoroda. Great interest in Skovoroda was shown by L. TOLSTOI who wrote a popular article about him in 1907. There are some parallels between some tenets of both men's philosophies.

Works: Povne zibrannja tvoriv. 2 vols. Kiev, 1973.
Secondary literature: L. Makhnovets, *Hryhorij Skovoroda.* Kiev, 1972. D. Tschiževskyj, *Skovoroda: Dichter, Denker, Mystiker.* Munich, 1974.
G. L.

Slavia orthodoxa. A historiographic formula first introduced by Riccardo Picchio in 1958 to define a cultural community made up of Orthodox Slavs who shared common spiritual models and linguistic standards from the beginning of our millennium until the birth of individual national cultures in the 18th and 19th centuries. This vast community of peoples stretched from the Balkans (modern Bulgaria, Macedonia, Serbia, and for several centuries the Romanian lands) to the East Slavic territory (corresponding to the modern nations of Russia, the Ukraine, and Belorussia). The peoples of Slavia orthodoxa belonged to the spiritual jurisdiction of the Eastern Orthodox Church. Other Slavic peoples, namely, the Croats, Slovenes, Czechs, Slovaks, and Poles, owed their allegiance to the Roman Church until the Age of the Reformation and Counter-Reformation and formed the community of *Slavia romana*.

Picchio's conception of Slavia orthodoxa refers not to a particular ecclesiastical jurisdiction, administrative unit, or territorial entity, but rather to a cultural tradition. In his opinion, the boundary lines between the Orthodox Slavic community and *Slavia romana* were never fixed in a definitive way. Among the Slavs there were zones of mixed or overlapping influence up to the dawn of the Modern Age. The literary community of Slavia orthodoxa relied on the use of a common linguistic medium, that is, CHURCH SLAVONIC in all its variations. The formula "Church Slavonic community" is used to define the linguistic characteristics of Slavia orthodoxa.

Bibliography: C. Backvis, "Quelques études sur l'histoire de la littérature en Russie," *Revue belge de philologie et d'histoire* 40 (1961), pp. 864–87. H. Birnbaum, "Towards a Comparative Study of Church Slavic Literature." In his *On Medieval and Renaissance Slavic Writing.* The Hague-Paris, 1974. Pp. 13–40. E. Hercigonja, *Srednjovjekovna književnost,* Povijest hrvatske književnosti, no. 2 (Zagreb, 1975), pp. 46–47. D. S. Likhachev, "Neskol'ko zamechanii po povodu stat'i Rikkardo Pikkio," *TODRL* 17 (1961), pp. 675–78. R. Picchio, "La 'Istorija slavěnobolgarskaja' sullo sfondo linguistico-culturale della Slavia ortodossa," *Ricerche Slavistiche* 6 (1958), pp. 103–18. ——, "Die historisch-philologische Bedeutung der kirchenslavischen Tradition," *Die Welt der Slaven* 7 (1962), pp. 1–27. ——, "A proposito della Slavia ortodossa e della comunità linguistica slava ecclesiastica," *Ricerche Slavistiche* 11 (1963), pp. 105–27. ——, "Questione della lingua e Slavia cirillometodiana." In *Studi sulla Questione della lingua presso gli Slavi.* Ed. R. Picchio. Rome, 1972. Pp. 7–120.
H. G.

Slavonicisms, see CHURCH SLAVONIC.

Slavophilism. An important intellectual movement which arose among Russian intellectuals in the 1830s and has undergone periods of development, atrophy, and revival up to the present time. Slavophilism has essentially been a prolonged effort at national self-definition by Russian thinkers in opposition to the tendency (both in Russia and in the European world) to substitute more general and less national forms of social identity for traditional and pre-industrial ones. It was also a reaction to the assertion that the only difference between Russia and other European nations was that Russians were less far advanced along the universal highway toward civilization or, as Russians themselves early learned to say, "more backward." The historical origins of Slavophilism are thus to be found primarily in the reaction of privileged social strata in Russia to the experience of Westernization. This response was crucially shaped by European romantic and counter-revolutionary thought, in particular by the romantic revolt against the universalist claims of the European Enlightenment and industrial civilization.

Also central to the development of Slavophilism has been an opposition to the extreme claims of the Russian state as the sponsor of these alien ("Western", "European") forms of modernity and the construction of alternative typologies of what is truly Russian. Slavophilism's latent hostility to the state has emerged with particular clarity and force when the Russian (or Soviet) state has been unambiguously perceived as forcing alien values on the Russian people, or depriving them of a national identity necessary to their spiritual well-being. As national leaders have tried to stress order, regularity, discipline and uniformity in social life, they have helped foster a cult of the opposite values: spontaneity, generosity—all those qualities invoked by the phrase "broad Russian nature." Perhaps above all, Slavophiles have set themselves against the secularization process in Russia, and an exaltation of the particular spiritual depth and historical destiny of the Orthodox Church has always been a central aspect of the Slavophile weltanschauung. The Slavophile hostility to the state as the agent of Westernization has on occasion reached almost anarchist extremes, as in the journalism of Konstantin AKSAKOV (1817–60), and in the abundant and influential writings of Aleksandr HERZEN (1812–70), whose mature views contain a strong dose of Slavophilism, albeit in radical form.

But Slavophilism has always been ambiguous about the state in Russia, torn between criticizing it as a negative and "alien" force in modern history (at times almost making it into a negative "principle") and hoping that somehow an authoritarian and traditionalist state might come into existence, which would both reflect and defend the "traditional" values of Holy Russia. Of the two most influential founders of Slavophile ideology, Ivan KIREEVSKY (1806–56) was a strong anti-statist, while Aleksei KHOMYAKOV (1804–60) wrote and spoke much more positively of the historical achievements of the Russian state, which had after all carved out (and now guaranteed) a large-scale territorial and national arena within which Russian spiritual values could flourish. Neo-Slavophiles of the present, like Aleksandr SOLZHENITSYN, are scathingly critical of the Soviet state as the agent through which an extreme brand of alien "Western" values (Communism) has been forced on Russia, but they show little sign of philosophical hostility to a Russian state per se. Whatever their expressed political philosophies, however, almost all those sympathetic to the deepest impulses of Slavophilism have been powerfully conscious of the continued existence in Russia of a powerful and activist state which is shaping its citizens into social identities chosen by what the Slavophiles regard as a deracinated elite, for the good of an artificial and imposed system. Just as Peter the Great tried to make his unruly and unschooled subjects into European agriculturalists and entrepreneurs, so LENIN tried to make them into secular and disciplined industrial workers. Eventually the policies adopted to this end reactivated the impulse to preserve and venerate old values.

The pre-history of Slavophilism lies in Russia's experience of Westernization in the 18th century: in the celebration of the freedom and simplicity of village life reflected in SUMAROKOV's poetry; in the spiritual and philanthropic impulses of Russian FREEMASONRY and its hostility to the gallomania of the court in St. Petersburg; in the quite different critiques of Westernization offered by M. M. SHCHERBATOV (1733–90) and the historian N. M. KARAMZIN (1766–1826). But it was not until the hegemony of the Enlightenment had been shattered and the triumph of romantic and counterrevolutionary European social thought engendered by the French Revolution prevailed that the intellectual weapons were at hand for Russian intellectuals to conceive a systematic ideology of opposition to the more than a century of state-sponsored Westernization they had undergone. The organic thinking of Herder, and the idealism of Fichte and Schelling were most important in this process.

The first formulations of a distinctively Slavophile point of view took place at the end of the 1830s; these initial efforts stemmed from conversations among the Kireevsky brothers and Aleksei Khomyakov, stimulated by Pyotr CHAADAEV's withering critique of

Russia's historical isolation from the Roman and Mediterranean heart of European history and development. By the beginning of the 1840s a Slavophile party was forming in the salons of Moscow, and as the political rigors of Nicholas' regime began to soften, the first Slavophile journalism began to appear in Russian periodicals. Four figures dominated this period of "classical Slavophilism." Although Ivan Kireevsky's younger brother PYOTR (1808–56) contributed very little by way of theoretical formulation, he was an important source of stimulus and even inspiration. Konstantin Aksakov was the most single-minded and narrow; but what might seem to be intellectual defects actually helped him produce the most daring idealization of the moral and spiritual qualities of the Russian people. Ivan Kireevsky and Khomyakov were the central thinkers of Slavophilism and it was in their arguments and conversations that the basic tenets of the ideology were laid down. In the writings of these men, all of whom came from self-consciously traditional Russian families, there is a good deal of aristocratic elitism, which suggests the earlier opposition of boyar clans and great families to the pretensions of the autocracy. The subsequent history of Slavophilism, however, was to demonstrate that it need have little or no connection with the aspirations of traditional elites.

Taken together, Kireevsky, Khomyakov and their younger colleagues (which might include Ivan AKSAKOV (1823–86) and Yury SAMARIN (1819–76) put forward a view of pre-Petrine Russia which could also be understood as a political program for their own time. They described medieval Russia as a patrimonial monarchy, centered upon a communalism (*sobornost'*) which was ultimately grounded in ecclesiastical doctrine, but which found its most dramatic expression in the *mir* and other institutions of peasant collectivism, on the one hand, and in the old *Zemskii sobor* and other assemblies which allegedly represented the values and opinions of Russian society to the Tsar, on the other.

With the growth in the unchecked power of the autocracy (the Slavophile argument ran) and its reliance on Western values, much of the integral Christian civilization of pre-Petrine Russia had been lost, but the classical Slavophiles insisted that important fragments had been preserved in a largely unselfconscious way by the Russian peasant. They regarded him as a communal being to whom Roman law and private property were alien, whose spiritual faculties had not been fatally damaged by Western rationalism. He still lived in a religious universe that included his social world; he was not yet touched by alienation. But intermingled with the Slavophile veneration for the Russian peasant was a clear strain of gentry elitism: although the peasants had managed to *preserve* the values of Old Russia in their ethos and institutions, the renewal of Russia's religious civilization in the present could only be work of Russia's educated elite— of people, that is, like themselves.

Between 1840 and 1870, Slavophilism became a serious element in Russian literary culture through its complex impact on writers like GOGOL and DOSTOEVSKY, and more indirectly, as broader strata of public opinion became aware of the debate between the Slavophiles and WESTERNIZERS over the meaning and direction of Russian culture. Slavophilism had a substantial effect on other literary and philosophical points of view after 1860 (while its own internal coherence became less clear)—on Pan-Slavism, which took some of its varied notions of Russia's superiority to German or, broadly speaking, Western nations from Slavophilism, and on the anti-Western literary nationalism of the Dostoevsky brothers, Apollon GRIGORIEV and Nikolai STRAKHOV, whose battle cry was "return to the soil," in the 1860s.

The reign of Alexander II and the "Era of the Great Reforms" made possible something closer to political careers in Russia, which had the effect of chastening some of the more extravagant manifestations of the Slavophile spirit. The surviving Slavophiles and their younger adherents became more eclectic and practical. One sees this with semi-liberals like Aleksandr Koshelev (1808–83), as well as with men like Yury Samarin and Ivan Aksakov, who in different ways came to terms with the Russian state and moderated Slavophile religious messianism in the direction of ordinary nationalism and Pan-Slavism. With the unfolding of this Slavophile "reconciliation with reality," the opposition between the romantic nationalism of the older Slavophiles—which had placed the Russian people at the center of a historical utopia—and the Official Nationalism of

POGODIN and SHEVYRYOV—which had exalted the role of state and dynasty in Russian history—tended to disappear.

As the conservative heirs of classical Slavophilism developed its nationalism and messianism, the Slavophile tendency toward idealization of the peasantry and an anarchistic hostility to the state was picked up by the new Russian radicalism which was developing in the late 1850s and 1860s and may be called by the generic term POPULISM (*narodnichestvo*). Starting with Aleksandr Herzen and Afanasy Shchapov (1830–76), a good many radicals of the period from 1855 to 1881 took from Slavophilism the proposition that the state had played a cruel and anti-national role in Russian history (as well as an anti-popular one), and that Russia's future lay in developing the moral qualities and social institutions of the Russian peasantry. Unlike the classical Slavophiles, however, the populist followers of Herzen saw the Russian peasant not as inherently religious and apolitical, but as an instinctive fighter for freedom and an unselfconscious anarchist. His communal values were not religious and patriarchal, but a form of primitive socialism. The populists also appropriated other aspects of Slavophile doctrine: the notion that Russia need not follow what appeared to be the general path of West European development, but might also evolve along indigenous lines; and the messianic view that the growth of Russian communal institutions might show the West European nations a way out of the social impasse to which the development of industrial capitalism had brought them.

Although the vitality of Slavophilism within Russian culture seemed to have been waning toward the end of the 19th century, the so-called Russian Religious Renaissance of the early 20th century was strongly marked by Slavophile themes and preoccupations. The founding father of this revival of idealism and theism was Vladimir SOLOVYOV (1853–1900), whose philosophical aims had much in common with those of Ivan Kireevsky—the restoration of modern man to a condition of spiritual integration. At the same time, as Walicki points out, Solovyov had no interest in the historical utopia of Slavophilism, or in its critique of Western historical development. Solovyov's disciples—Nikolai BERDYAEV, Sergei Bulgakov, Semyon FRANK—eventually accepted a heavily Slavophile version of Orthodoxy, even as the official church was finally recognizing the theology of Khomyakov, which it had spurned for almost half a century.

For decades it seemed that the Russian revolution and the evolution of Soviet culture had brought the existence of Slavophilism as a vital force in Russia to an end. It seemed bookish, archaic, without social support. But in the last fifteen years, Slavophile doctrines have undergone a significant revival both within the Soviet Union and among dissident circles abroad, as Russian intellectuals have discovered whole chapters of their cultural history which have been systematically neglected or suppressed since the Revolution. An interesting aspect of this Slavophile revival is that Lenin has been cast in the role traditionally assigned to Peter the Great: the evil titan who subverted Russia's spiritual inheritance and national identity and forced the Russian people to venerate the golden calf of Western values.

It is not yet clear what the cultural fruits of the powerful but eclectic Slavophile revival will be, despite the adherence of such great writers as Aleksandr Solzhenitsyn. And the nativist impulses which have helped revive Slavophile doctrines have also inspired more atavistic and chauvinistic points of view from the Russian past. But the desire of Russians to reappropriate such central aspects of their cultural past cannot but stir the sympathies of a foreign observer, even if the full meaning of what he is witnessing is not yet clear.

Texts: A. S. Khomyakov, *Polnoe sobranie sochinenii.* 8 vols. 1900–14. I. V. Kireevskii, *Polnoe sobranie sochinenii.* 2 vols. 1911.

Translations: James M. Edie, James P. Scanlan, and Mary-Barbara Zeldin, eds., *Russian Philosophy* 3 vols. 1965. Vol. 1, pp. 155–269. (Essays by Ivan Kireevsky and Aleksei Khomyakov).

Secondary literature: Peter K. Christoff, *An Introduction to Nineteenth-Century Russian Slavophilism.* Vol. 1: A. S. Khomiakov. The Hague, 1961. Vol. 2: I. V. Kireevsky. The Hague, 1972. Vol. 3: K. S. Aksakov (Princeton, 1982). Abbott Gleason, *European and Muscovite: Ivan Kireevsky and the Origins of Slavophilism.* 1972. Nicholas Riasanovsky, *Russia and the West in the Teaching of the Slavophiles.* 1952. Andrzej Walicki, *The Slavophile Controversy:*

History of a Conservative Utopia in Nineteenth-Century Russian Thought. 1975. A. G.

Sleptsóv, Vasíly Alekséevich (1836–78), writer. Sleptsov attended Medical School at Moscow University in 1854 and 1855, then left for Yaroslavl, where he tried his hand at acting. Returning soon to Moscow he was in government service from 1857 to 1862. As a result of a walking tour in the provinces, he published in 1861 a cycle of sketches, *Around Vladimir and Klyazma* (Vladimirka i Klyaz'-ma), in *Russkaya rech'*, describing the terrible poverty and desolation of both the peasant masses and the gentry. In 1861 Sleptsov moved to Petersburg where he collaborated in SOVREMENNIK. In 1862 and 1863 a new cycle, *Letters about Ostashkov* (Pis'ma ob Ostashkove), appeared in that journal. Ostashkov, though a small town, was touted for its cultural life. Sleptsov showed the superficiality of this model town and depicted the exploitation of its people. A fervent adherent of women's emancipation, he was co-founder with N. V. Stasova, M. V. Trubnikova and R. N. Engelgardt of popular courses for women. He also founded a women's commune, "Znamenskaya kommuna," in 1863 and 1864, but had to disband it because of police harassment. In connection with Karakozov's attempt to assassinate Alexander II (1866), Sleptsov was arrested. After his release he helped to found the journal *Zhenskii vestnik* (Herald of Women), but after a few months broke off with it. From 1868 to 1872 he worked in OTECHESTVENNYE ZAPISKI. New sketches of city life followed: "Petersburg Notes" (Peterburgskie zametki), "News of Petersburg Life" (Novosti peterburgskoi zhizni), "In the Slums" (V trushchebakh), and "Scenes at the Police Station" (Stseny v politsii). The years 1861 to 1865 were particularly important for his fiction: "Foster Child" (Pitomka), "Night Lodging" (Nochleg), "Pigs" (Svin'i), and "Evening" (Vecher) were published, among others. In 1865 his novella "Hard Times" (Trudnoe vremya) appeared in *Sovremennik*. Basically a work directed against the "liberal" intelligentsia, the novella contrasts a typical nihilist of the 1860s, Ryazanov, with a landowner who talks well, but whose good deeds (a school, medical clinic) are shown to be only philanthropic crumbs. A novel, *A Fine Man* (Khoroshii chelovek), was left unfinished. Terseness and laconicism were Sleptsov's hallmarks, and while his plots are ordinary, he combines serious thought with a refined artistic realization. In the last few decades some unpublished manuscripts of his have been discovered.

Works: Polnoe sobranie sochinenii. 1888. *Sochineniya.* Introd. K. Chukovskii. 2 vols. 1957. *Izbrannye proizvedeniya.* Ed. M. Semanova. 1970.

Translations: "Choir Practice." In *The Humor of Russia.* Ed. Ethel Lillian Voynich. 1895. Reprint 1911.

Secondary literature: William C. Brumfield, "Sleptsov Redivivus," *California Slavic Studies* 9 (1976), pp. 27–71. K. Chukovskii, "Zhizn' i tvorchestvo Vasiliya Sleptsova." In his *Lyudi i knigi.* 1960. M. L. Semanova, "Tvorchestvo V. A. Sleptsova." In *Proza pisatelei-demokratov 60-kh godov.* 1962. E. K. K.

Slóvo o polkú Ígoreve (The Tale of Igor's Campaign). The greatest, but also the most puzzling work of medieval Russian literature, the Igor Tale (*IT*) is a complex artistic response to an insignificant historical event.

Historical background

According to the Hypatian Chronicle, on 23 April 1185, without the knowledge of Grand Prince Svyatoslav of Kiev, Igor Svyatoslavich of Novgorod-Seversk and three of his princely relatives set out to attack the Polovtsian army in the steppe, some 400 kilometers to the south. Disregarding the bad omen of a total solar eclipse on their way (1 May 1185), the Russians pressed on, crossing the height of land (*shelomyan'*) between the Don and Dnepr basins and making contact with the Polovtsian troops, near the Syuurli, the afternoon of May 10. After a single volley of arrows, the Polovtsians fled or pretended to flee, allowing the pursuing Russians to capture their tent encampment, with its women, children, and rich booty. Rather than retreat with their spoils, under cover of darkness, the tired Russian forces spent that night in the Polovtsian camp, where, the next morning, they were surrounded by the full Polovtsian army.

Cut off from water, the Russians fought all that day (May 11) and through the night, but by noon on May 12 all but fifteen of their army had been killed or captured; Igor himself was wounded in the arm and taken prisoner. The victorious Polovtsians immediately went north to sack the now defenseless Pereyaslav and Seim countrysides, while Igor began some five weeks of comfortable captivity, from which he escaped in mid-June of 1185.

Textology and authenticity

The *IT* was composed no later than 1 October 1187, the death date of Prince Igor's father-in-law Yaroslav Osmomysl of Galich, mentioned in the *IT* as still living. Almost nothing is known of its subsequent history, although it is cited briefly in the margin of a 1307 Pskov *Acts of the Apostles* and served as stimulus for the late-14th-century ZADONSHCHINA (mss. 15th-17th centuries). It was preserved in a single 16th-century copy, bound together with several other Old Russian works in a manuscript volume purchased by Count A. Musin-Pushkin in 1795 and announced publicly by KARAMZIN in the *Spectateur du Nord* (Hamburg) in 1797. The manuscript itself is thought to have perished in the Moscow fire of 1812, but not before it had been copied for Catherine's private library, in 1795–96, and published, by Musin-Pushkin and collaborators, in 1800. Some, but not all of the problems of interpretation of the *IT* are due to the fact that it can be approached only through these two late versions of a lost 16th-century manuscript, itself a graphically archaizing and occasionally faulty copy of the 12th-century original (or of some intermediate copy).

The authenticity of the *IT* has sometimes been called into question, and it is true that, at first reading, the work is strikingly different from almost everything else we know in old Russian literature. However, this is entirely a matter of imagery and genre (see below). The philological evidence of the *IT*'s authenticity is incontrovertible: the text abounds in accurate Old Russian forms that simply could not have been reconstructed in the 18th century, and probably not even in the 16th (e.g., the genitive dual *vayu* in *ne vayu li zlachenymi shelomy po krovi plavasha?* 'were not your (two) golden helmeted ones carried off by the blood?' 127). Attacks on the authenticity of the *IT* have always come from amateurs, while its defenders have been philologists with professional competence in 12th-century Russian language and culture.

Content and style

If the grammar and vocabulary of the *IT* no longer pose a serious problem, the same cannot be said of its content and style. Despite certain similarities with such works as the *Slovo o pogibeli russkoi zemli*, the *Povest' o razorenii Ryazani*, and even the *Molenie Daniila Zatochnika*, the *IT* remains unique among all known works of Old Russian literature. In genre and style, it is a hard work to define, too heterogeneous and too subtle for the supposed "monumental simplicity" of its epoch.

The *IT* is frequently and wrongly referred to as an epic; it is not. Only one-tenth of its brief 218 verses (in R. Jakobson's critical edition) actually describe the attested events of 1185, and even these are presented in such a kaleidoscope of metaphor and metonymy that one must know the real story by heart in order to appreciate the poem. Reality is presented in brief, almost cinematographic flashes, interspersed with lengthy authorial digressions into other times and places. Real time and space are almost ignored in the *IT*. In verses 6 and 7, for example, we learn that Igor, filled with martial spirit, has set out with his brave host against the Polovtsians; "Then," begins verse 8, skipping over eight days and some 260 kilometers of marching, "Igor looked up at the bright sun and saw all his troops covered by its [the eclipse's] shadow." There follow five verses in which Igor urges his men to battle, and another five in which the author compares his own and old Boyan's poetic techniques, during which another five days of marching pass unnoticed, for in verse 18 we suddenly return to the reality of Igor's meeting with Vsevolod, who had come from Kursk by a different route. Verses 53 to 56 show Vsevolod in battle, his golden helm gleaming as he cuts off pagan Polovtsian heads, but the next eleven verses digress to events of the beginning of that century, and only in verse 69 do we return to the battle of 1185. The entire disastrous end of the battle is disposed of in just four, mostly metaphoric verses (70–73): "They fought one day, they fought another, on the third day at noon Igor's standards fell. There the brothers parted on the bank of the swift Kayaly. There the bloody wine ran dry. There the brave Russians finished the feast: they gave their guests to drink, and themselves lay down for the Russian land."

The next 111 verses—very nearly half of the poem—hardly deal with real events at all, and then only tangentially: in verse 84, "For Kiev, brethren, groaned in grief, and Chernigov in attacks", refers to the Polovtsian incursions into the Pereyaslav and Seim territories; verse 121 reads, "Lo, in Rimov they cry out beneath the Polovtsian sabres, as does Volodimir beneath his wounds"; in verse 91, "Here Prince Igor dismounted from his golden saddle into the saddle of a slave", refers to his capture. The other 108 verses of this long section contain laments of the Russian women in verses 82 and 83, and of Igor's wife Yaroslavna in verses 167 to 183; the two *prichitanie*-like passages frame the intervening material. The "Dream of Svyatoslav" in verses 93 to 99 and its interpretation by his boyars in verses 100 to 110 are followed by his "golden word" apostrophe to Igor and Vsevolod in verses 111 to 119, a set of authorial appeals to other princes (Vsevolod Great Nest, verses 123–126; Ryurik and David Rostislavich, verses 127–129; Yaroslav Eight-Thought of Galich, verses 130–132; Roman of Volhynia and Mstislav The Mute, verses 133–139; the latter's brothers Ingvar and Vsevolod, verses 140–142; and, after a digression in verses 143–148, Yaroslav of Chernigov, verses 149–152), and an extensive folkloric digression on the werewolf Vseslav of Polotsk in verses 153 to 163. These thematically identifiable passages are interspersed with (and themselves contain) exclamations of authorial woe ("Too far has flown the falcon!" [79], "The times have turned a-turvy!" [120], "O, the Russian land must groan!" [164]); and a wealth of nature metaphors of defeat and dejection ("The grass bows down in complaint, the tree bends to earth in grief" [74], "Two suns [Igor and Vsevolod] grew dark, two purple columns died out and sank into the sea" [103], "the tree has shed its foliage for no good cause" [136]).

Only in the last thirty-odd verses does the *IT* return to historical reality: Igor escapes from the Polovtsian camp. His nineteen-day homeward journey is presented with no attention to real time and space ("Prince Igor leapt like a stoat to the canes ... flew off like a falcon" 188, 191), and is interrupted by a conversation between Igor and the River Donets ("Oh Donets! no little grandeur is yours, having cradled a prince on your waves," [195]), a dialogue between Gza and Konchak on how best to capture Igor, and a final Boyanic aphorism ("It's hard for a head without its shoulders, but it's mean for a body without a head—The Russian land without Igor," [210]). But all's well that ends well: "The sun shines in the sky: Prince Igor in the Russian land." [211].

Imagery

The *IT* compensates for its paucity of real information by an extraordinary panoply of imagery. If real time and space are almost entirely ignored, poetic time and space are central to the poem. Poetic time in the *IT* is of two sorts. On the one hand, events (real or imagined) are temporally localized in day or night, dawn or dusk, i.e., within the contrast of alternating light and dark that played an important role elsewhere in Old Russian literature (e.g., ILARION's *Sermon on Law and Grace*): "Groaning night awoke the birds with thunder" [28]; "the carts scream at midnight" [30]; "bloody dawns precurse the day" [43]; "Vsevlav ... ranged like a wolf in the night" [159]; "The rays of evening died out: Igor sleeps" [185]; etc. The vocabulary of this temporal location is repetitious: "morning" occurs ten times in the *IT*, "night" and "midnight" nine, "light" eleven. On the other hand, poetic time appears in the contrast of "then" and "now", of "old" and "new", as the author juxtaposes the events and the poetry of his own day with those of the more glorious past ("We must begin our song according to the real events of our time, and not according to the fancy of Boyan" [2]; "from old Vladimir to the Igor of today" [6]; "interweaving the glories of both borders of this time" [14]; "Is it any wonder, brethren, for an old man to grow young?" [117]; "Having sung our song to the princes of old, we must now sing to the young" [215]; etc. The contrast of old and new/young is also reflected in the *IT*'s insistence on family rela-

tions, especially cross-generational: parent and child, grandparent and grandchild, uncle and nephews, mothers and sons: the author is "Boyan's grandchild" [15]; and Boyan himself is "the grandchild of Veles" the cattle-god [17]; the Polovtsians are "children of the devil" [52]; the Chernigov troops "echo their forefathers' glory" [115], just as Izyaslav "touched the glory of his grandfather Vseslav" [144]; whereas the author reproaches the "grandsons of Vseslav" with having "jumped out of your grandfather's glory" [149–50]. Older men, as older times, are seen as better and wiser than what followed them in an elaborately iterated set of images reflecting the bare historical reality that Igor and his host had been insubordinate to their elder and superior, Grand Prince Svyatoslav of Kiev.

Space, too, is more poetic than real. The *IT* is particularly rich in vertical imagery: upward motion is positive, provided the subject is (actually or associatively, e.g., grass, trees, falcons) Russian, while downward motion by such subjects is negative; the evaluations are reversed if the subjects are (actually or associatively, e.g. Div, swans, grey ravens) Polovtsian. Positive vertical imagery is concentrated at the beginning and end of the *IT*: "Boyan raised his fingers to the living strings" [5]; "Igor looked up to the bright sun" [8]; "Let us mount our swift steeds, brethren" [11]; "Igor flew off like a falcon" [191]; "the sun shines in the sky" [211]; "Igor rides up the Borichev slope" [213]. Throughout the entire central section of the poem, however, negative images predominate: "Igor's standards fell" [70]; "The grass bowed in complaint, and the tree bent to earth in sorrow" [74]; "two purple columns sank into the sea" [103]; "the tree cast down its foliage for no good cause" [136]; etc. The briefer positive imagery of the poem's beginning and end form a perhaps ironic framework for the sad central content of the poem.

Nature and natural phenomena are the reference point for most of the *IT*'s metaphorics. Over two dozen different species of bird and animal figure in the action: the Russians are falcons, the Polovtsians swans (their totemic bird); Boyan runs in thought "like a grey wolf over the land, like a dove-grey eagle beneath the clouds" [3]; "horses neigh" [18], "eagles with their scream call the beasts to the bones" [31], "foxes bark at the scarlet shields" [31], "Prince Igor ran off like a stoat to the reeds, like a white duck to the water, Mounted his swift steed, dismounted from it as a white-pawed wolf" [188–89]. Even more luxuriant is the vocabulary of the landscape and the weather; over 60 percent of the *IT*'s phrases contain the name of some natural phenomenon. Igor's troops, their Polovtsian foes, and the author's imagination range across earth, steppe, hill and ravine, in shadows, darkness, and light. Water is everywhere, in rivers, streams, currents, lakes, oceans, swamps, and even in the dew, not to mention the frequent mists and rain, stormclouds and storms, winds and waterspouts, thunder, lightning, and eclipse that sweep across the landscape.

Rich as the *IT* is in natural phenomena, it is richer yet in names; over 70 percent of the poem's verses contain toponyms or anthroponyms, which together total over 330. Boyan sang praise "to old Yaroslav, brave Mstislav, who slew Rededya before the Kasog host, to handsome Roman Svyatoslavlich" [5]; "Horses neigh beyond the Sula, fame resounds in Kiev, trumpets blare in Novgorod, standards stand in Putivl, Igor awaits his dear brother Vsevolod" [18]; "Here Germans and Venetians, here Greeks and Moravians sing praise to Svyatoslav, reproach Prince Igor" [90]; "You have iron breastplates beneath Latin helmets ..., many lands,—Huns, Lithuanians, Jatvagians, Deremelians and Polovtsians—have cast down their lances" [135]. The cumulative effect of these many topo- and anthroponyms, combined with the extraordinary variety and specificity of flora, fauna, and weather phenomena, is one of both concretization and universalization of the author's view of his land and its people; he seems to have been everywhere and know everybody, and the artistic portrait he draws is less that of a minor prince in an unsuccessful battle than that of all Kievan *Rus'* itself.

With its many dozens of specified people and peoples, animals, places, and natural phenomena, its broad and rapidly shifting backgrounds in time and space, and its near-total absence of story line, the *IT* manages to avoid fragmentation and to achieve artistic unity only through what we may call its "communicative intensity." People, animals, plants, and things are in constant and usually verbal communication with each other throughout the poem. The eclipse is a "sign" ignored by Igor [8–13], although its shadow blocks his path [27]. Birds, animals, and things speak out: swans sing [4], night groans and beasts whistle [28], jackdaws talk [35] and even talk in their own tongue [65], the earth rumbles [49], standards declare [50], the host bellows like an aurochs [128], grass grows noisy [187], etc. This unifying communicative intensity, binding together into a single pan-Russian speech scene all the specifics described above, is implemented on several levels. In addition to the *verba dicendi* just adduced, there is extensive direct (quoted) speech: Igor addresses his troops [8–13]; Vsevolod gives Igor a pep-talk [19–25]; Svyatoslav retells his dream [93–99], is answered by his boyars [100–10], and responds with his "golden word" [111–19]; the Russian women lament [82–83], as does Princess Yaroslavna [168–83]; the River Donets exchanges compliments with Igor [192–96]; Gza and Konchak discuss strategy [203–08]; and there are several brief citations from Boyan's poetry [4, 145–46, 162–63, 209–10]. The author addresses his reader (or listener: the *IT* has characteristics of both written and oral poetry) [1–7]; and apostrophizes Boyan [14–18], the Russian land [32, 47], and several absent princes [53–56, 123–42, 149–52]. Overall, very nearly half the poem consists of direct address. The level of communicative intensity is raised by the large number of vocatives, imperatives, and first- and second-person verb forms, as well as by the many verbs and nouns denoting communicative acts of one sort or another: words, tales, songs, groans, whistles, orders, shouts, calls, caws, barks, neighs, trills, and simple announcements; the *IT* is full of crackling, ringing, resounding, trumpeting, and bewailing, and with more than fifty lexical items of this sort, many of which occur repeatedly (*rechi* 24 times, *peti* and *pesnya* 14 times, etc.), it is a very noisy poem. At the center of this complex and disparate communicative network, which links old and new, friend and foe, man and nature, stands the unknown author himself. If not actually speaking, he is listening and interpreting, and the sum total of the messages he sends and receives is his own, personal vision of his land and time. The ubiquity and strength of the authorial persona determines the work's genre: the *IT* is an extended social lyric.

Bibliography. V. P. Adrianova-Peretts, ed., *Slovo o polku Igoreve*. 1950. *La geste du Prince Igor'. Epopée russe du douxième siècle.* Ed. Henri Grégoire, Roman Jakobson and Marc Szeftel. New York, 1948. B. A. Rybakov, *Russkie letopistsy i avtor "Slova o polku Igoreve".* 1972.———, *"Slovo o polku Igoreve" i ego sovremenniki.* 1971. V. L. Vinogradova, ed., *Slovar'-spravochnik "Slova o polku Igoreve".* 1965ff.　　　　　　D. S. W.

Sluchévsky, Konstantín Konstantínovich (1837–1904), poet and prose writer, was born in the family of a senator. He quit a military career to study philosophy and natural sciences in Western Europe and received a Ph.D. from Heidelberg University. After his return to Russia in 1866, Sluchevsky held major positions in the civil service, and toward the end of his life was director of the *Pravitel'stvennyi vestnik* and held a high position (*gofmeister*) at court. Sluchevsky began to publish his poetry in 1857. His early verses, greeted enthusiastically by Apollon GRIGORIEV and TURGENEV, were however attacked by critics of the NIHILIST camp. After a long period of silence Sluchevsky returned to poetry in 1871. During the last years of his life his salon was frequented by BALMONT, BRYUSOV, and SOLOGUB, upon whom he exerted a certain influence.

Sluchevsky's poetry is a connecting link between late romanticism and modernism. Tragic motifs, a penchant for sharp psychological collisions, and an aesthetic of the Ugly and Abnormal are peculiar to it. Sluchevsky is close to DOSTOEVSKY in many ways (this includes even common themes and motifs), as well as to the French *poètes maudits*. Sluchevsky's style is peculiar: he uses grating prosaisms, alogical metaphors, and does not shrink from scholarly or officialese jargon. His verse is heavy and amusical. Sluchevsky's stylistic disharmony and his attention to the Tragic inherent in day-to-day living are a preview of many later phenomena of Russian lyric poetry. Certain similarities to Sluchevsky have been observed in BLOK, ANNENSKY, and even PASTERNAK. Sluchevsky's verse epics, *Snowbound* (V snegakh, 1879) and *Eloa* (1883), follow the romantic tradition, that of LERMONTOV in particular. Sluchevsky's prose is less significant: a novel, *From Kiss to Kiss* (Ot potseluya k potseluyu, 1872), and *Thirty-Three Stories* (1887).

Works: Stikhotvoreniya i poemy. 1962. *Zabytye stikhotvoreniya.* Munich, 1968.

Translations: Lewanski, p. 357.
Secondary literature: James Bailey, "The Metrical and Rhythmical Typology of K. K. Slučevskij's Poetry," *IJSLP* 18 (1975), pp. 93–117. V. Bryusov, *Dnevniki 1891–1910.* 1927. ———, *Sobranie sochinenii.* Vol. 6. 1975. Pp. 231–34. Yu. Ivask, "Sluchevskii," *Novyi zhurnal,* no. 79 (1965), pp. 270–84. V. Kozhinov, *Kniga o russkoi liricheskoi poezii XIX veka.* 1978. Pp. 242–57. S. Makovskii, *Na Parnase "Serebryanogo veka".* Munich, 1962. Pp. 65–86. S. Zen'kovskii, "Traditsiya romantizma v tvorchestve Konstantina Sluchevskogo." In *American Contributions to the Seventh International Congress of Slavists.* 1973. Pp. 567–97.　　　T. V.

Slútsky, Boris Abrámovich (1919–), contemporary poet, was born in the Ukraine, graduated from the Gorky Literary Institute in 1941 and published his first verse that same year. He served in World War II, was a political instructor in the Army, and joined the Communist Party. After the War, Slutsky slowly returned to poetry, working on war themes for the most part. As early as in 1954 and 1955, he wrote his poems on Stalin's suspiciousness and megalomania ("The Boss"—Khozyain, "God"—Bog), which became immensely popular, but only when they were published in *Literaturnaya gazeta* on 24 November 1962 (they were never republished). Other poems by Slutsky dealing with wartime atrocities and various negative sides of Soviet life were published by *Samizdat* in the late 1950s. However, during the period of Khrushchevian liberalism, Slutsky took a cautious wait-and-see position and actually voiced some criticism of Boris PASTERNAK in connection with the latter's having published his novel *Doctor Zhivago* in the West. In the many collections in which his poetry appeared after 1957, Slutsky avoided commenting directly on topical political issues, this despite the fundamentally publicistic nature of his poetry. His verses, even those included in the volume *Pages from Tarusa,* are marked by a dramatic quality, and straightforward moral characterization, but also a certain spiritual poverty, wary vagueness, and the shiftiness of the political worker. As far as their artistic quality is concerned, Slutsky's verses are distinguished by the prosaism of their imagery and intonations, and often go without metaphor or rhyme. In 1965 some leading Soviet journals featured a discussion as to whether or not Slutsky's verses should be considered poetry. Perhaps, "The Year Hand" (Godovaya strelka), where the poet published some of his early post-war poetry, is the best of his collections. It is, however, difficult to see a difference between these and his later poems. It would seem that Slutsky has not experienced any kind of poetic evolution: it is always the same declarative rationality with him, and the same poetic minimum ("How Tenacious of Life Women Are"—Do chego zhe zhenshchiny zhivuchi, "Poetry"—Poeziya). Since 1960, Slutsky regularly publishes in the central organ, *Den' poezii.* In the issue of 1981 he came forth once more with heavily structured "factual" verses, through the text of which the outlines of some hidden complexes vaguely appear ("Hand and Soul"—Ruka i dusha, "Humiliation in a Dream"—Unizhenie vo sne). It is possible that there are some unpublished poems in the poet's archives. His disciple, who is also the author of the introductory essay in *Den' poezii,* drops a hint to this effect. But for the time being, it may be said that Slutsky has far outlived his poetic apogee which he reached during the days of the poetic renaissance of the Thaw years.

Works: Pamyat'. 1957. *Vremya.* 1959. *Segodnya i vchera.* 1961. *Rabota.* 1964. *Izbrannaya lirika.* 1965. *Pamyat'. Stikhi 1944–1968. Sovremennye istorii.* 1969. *Godovaya strelka.* 1971. *Dobrota dnya.* 1973. *Prodlennyi polden'.* 1975. *Neokonchennye spory.* 1978.
Secondary literature: V. Leonovich, "Odin urok v shkole Borisa Slutskogo," *Den' poezii,* 1981. V. Ognev, "Zhizn' i masterstvo," *Den' poezii,* 1960. A. Urban, "Stikhi i rabota," *Zvezda,* 1965, no. 1. L. Lazarev. "Kogda proza stanovitsya poeziei," *VLit,* 1967, no. 1.　　　　　　E. D. A.

Sména vekh (Change of Landmarks), a collection of essays by six émigré publicists: Yu. V. Klyuchnikov, N. V. Ustryalov, S. S. Lukyanov, A. V. Bobrishchev-Pushkin, S. S. Chakhotin, and Yu. N. Potekhin, published in Prague in July 1921 (2d ed., 1922). Differing in individual views, the authors were united in a common appeal to the émigrés to revise their earlier attitudes toward the Revolution of 1917, Bolshevism, and Soviet authorities, cease all armed struggle against them, and start collaborating with them.

Yu. V. Klyuchnikov ("Change of Landmarks") wrote that the latest developments inside Russia indicated that the recent revolutionary extremism of the Bolsheviks was over and that Russia was entering a period of rapid and powerful evolutionary process, which must be helped in every possible way.

N. V. Ustryalov ("Patriotica") concluded that the new economic policies (NEP) and the unification of Russian territories under the Bolsheviks testified to their evolution, even if only tactical at first, from communism toward a bourgeois order, nationalism, and great power status; the Bolsheviks had started on their own Thermidorian path, and the Revolution was no longer the same.

S. S. Lukyanov ("Revolution and Authority"—Revolyutsiya i vlast') refuted the view that there was a revolution in February 1917: for him, that was just a coup; the true Revolution took place in October, since it was the Bolsheviks who recognized that only the popular masses, the peasantry, and the proletariat, could supply the proper social base for the Revolution; the intelligentsia's task now was "honestly to give a helping hand to the Motherland."

A. V. Bobrishchev-Pushkin, who wrote the longest essay, "The New Faith" (Novaya vera), and went even farther than the other authors in his acceptance of the Bolshevik Revolution, believed that the Revolution had already reached its Thermidor and that the main thing now was to avoid any additional bloodshed.

S. S. Chakhotin, whose article by its very title, "To Canossa!" (V Kanossu!), expressed the essence of the entire collection, urged the émigrés to do penance and, through collaboration with Soviet authorities, contribute to the education of the masses and to the economic rehabilitation of the country.

Yu. N. Potekhin, in "Physics and Metaphysics of the Russian Revolution" (Fizika i metafizika russkoi revolyutsii), insisted that only the October Revolution was a genuine people's revolution, and that now under the people's pressure the Bolsheviks' internationalism was gradually receding; it was no longer Russia that served the purposes of the Third International, but the Third International that was beginning to serve the national goals of Russia; the intelligentsia must abandon its former negative attitude toward the October Revolution and respond to the call: "To work! Home! To our motherland!"

Smena vekh aroused significant interest due to its timing and its relation to the recent, and heated, Vekhi dispute, as well as to the fact that the authors of the collection came from the liberal or liberal-conservative camp of the intelligentsia and had been actively associated with the White movement in the civil war. In this respect, and generally speaking, the most important of the six authors were Ustryalov and Klyuchnikov. Ustryalov, a jurist who had taught at Moscow University, was chairman of the Eastern section of the central committee of the Kadet (Constitutional Democrat) Party and a director of the press bureau of Admiral Kolchak's White government. He "changed landmarks" even before the Whites left the Crimea, and living in the Far East, in Harbin, published there a collection of revisionist articles, *In a Struggle for Russia* (V bor'be za Rossiyu, 1920). Klyuchnikov, also a former Kadet and professor of international law at Moscow University, took an active part in the anti-Bolshevik uprising in Yaroslavl in 1918, later became minister of foreign affairs in the Kolchak government, and in 1921 was living in Paris. Ustryalov and Klyuchnikov openly expressed their past ideological indebtedness to *Vekhi* and *Vekhi*'s main spokesman, P. B. STRUVE. It was therefore natural that the reaction to *Smena vekh* was concerned with the earlier dispute around *Vekhi* as well as with the new ideological and political platform of Ustryalov, which he himself defined as National Bolshevism, i.e., an attempt to use Bolshevism for national purposes.

Among the émigrés, the position of the leftist anti-Bolshevik sector was most spiritedly expressed by the Socialist-Revolutionary M. V. Vishnyak, an editor of the Paris-based review *Sovremennye zapiski*. Vishnyak's criticism of *Smena vekh* was uncompromisingly negative. He associated *ustryalovshchina* (Ustryalovism) with the psychology of personages so devastatingly depicted by SALTYKOV-SHCHEDRIN, and people of the Klyuchnikov type with Faddei BULGARIN.

The point of view of the moderately rightist camp of the emigration was best put into words by P. B. Struve, who also condemned Ustryalov's National Bolshevism and the collection *Smena vekh*. Bolshevism, wrote Struve, is objectively antinational, and the incon-gruity of National Bolshevism consists in its idealization of Bolshevism in the light of those very principles which Bolshevism negates. For him, *Smena vekh*, by its ideological content and its psychological character, was "the exact opposite of *Vekhi*."

The reaction to *Smena vekh* was not confined to the emigration alone. As a consequence of the military defeat of the White Army and the introduction of the new economic policy (NEP), a "change of landmarks" mood became evident also among intellectuals inside Russia. In order to further demoralize the intelligentsia and increase its acceptance of the new regime, the Bolsheviks, in the beginning, actually promoted *Smena vekh* in Soviet Russia itself.

The relatively freer conditions of the early 1920s allowed a small group of intellectuals to express their views of *Smena vekh* in a collection of essays, *On the Change of Landmarks*, published in Petrograd in 1922. Of the four authors of this collection—A. S. Izgoev, J. Clemens, P. K. Guber, and A. B. Petrishchev—the most prominent was Izgoev, a co-author of the initial *Vekhi*. Comparing *Vekhi* and *Smena vekh*, Izgoev concluded that in spite of some external similarities with *Vekhi* ideas found in the essays by Klyuchnikov and Ustryalov, the two collections were fundamentally irreconcilable and their authors belonged to two morally and spiritually different types of the intelligentsia.

Still, inspired by the interest which *Smena vekh* aroused among émigrés as well as inside Russia, the *smenovekhovtsy* started a weekly magazine under the same title in the fall of 1921. Published in Paris and edited by Yu. V. Klyuchnikov, the weekly lasted some five months, after which it was superseded by a daily newspaper, *Nakanune*, appearing in Berlin under the editorship of Klyuchnikov and G. L. Kirdetsov, with S. S. Lukyanov, B. V. Dyushen, and Yu. N. Potekhin as the other main contributors. The newspaper lasted until mid-1924. In contrast to the weekly magazine, which paid little attention to literature, the newspaper had a weekly literary supplement, edited first by Aleksei TOLSTOI and later by Roman GUL, in which both émigré and Soviet authors participated.

Smena vekh, and *smenovekhovstvo* (changing landmarks) in general, had practically no influence on wider political circles of the emigration. However, in literary circles the call for a change of landmarks, leading to a return to Soviet Russia and to collaboration with Soviet authorities, had a certain effect. But once the role of *smenovekhovtsy* had been played out, they were discarded by their new masters. The personal fates of most of the authors of *Smena vekh* were sad ones. Ustryalov was choked to death with a lace on the Siberian express taking him from the Far East to Moscow. Klyuchnikov and Potekhin died in the USSR under unclear circumstances. Lukyanov was beaten to death during interrogation in the Ukht-Pechersky "corrective labor" camp.

Bibliography: Smena vekh, weekly magazine, nos. 1–20, Paris, 29 October 1921 to 25 March 1922. (No. 6, of 3 December 1921, includes reviews of the collection *Smena vekh* published in the Soviet and pro-Soviet press; no. 10, of 31 December 1921, reprinted an account of a dispute devoted to the collection, which took place at the *Dom literatorov* in Petrograd.)

Secondary literature: Roman Gul', *Ya unes Rossiyu; Apologiya emigratsii.* Vol. 1: "Rossiya v Germanii." New York, 1981. Pp. 173–78, 193–203, 68–97. *O smene vekh.* [Petrograd:] Izdatel'stvo "Logos" pri Dome literatorov, 1922. Gleb Struve, *Russkaya literatura v izgnanii.* New York, 1956. Pp. 30–40. Petr Struve, "Istoriko-politicheskie zametki o sovremennosti," *Russkaya mysl'*, 1921, no. 5–7, pp. 208–24. ———, "Proshloe, nastoyashchee, budushchee; Mysli o natsional'nom vozrozhdenii Rossii," *Russkaya mysl'*, 1922, no. 1–2, pp. 222–31. I. Ya. Trifonov, "Iz istorii bor'by Kommunisticheskoi partii protiv smenovekhovstva," *Istoriya SSSR*, 1959, no. 3, pp. 64–82. ———, *V. I. Lenin i bor'ba s burzhuaznoi ideologiei v nachale nepa.* 1969. Mark Vishnyak, "Prof. N. Ustryalov, 'V bor'be za Rossiyu'," *Sovremennye zapiski*, 1921, no. 3, pp. 217–75. ———, "'Smena vekh'," *Sovremennye zapiski*, 1921, no. 8, pp. 380–85. Robert C. Williams, "'Changing Landmarks' in Russian Berlin, 1922–1924," *SlavR* 27 (1968), pp. 580–93. ———, *Culture in Exile; Russian Emigrés in Germany, 1881–1941.* 1972. Pp. 264–79.   N. P. P.

Smirdín, Aleksándr Filíppovich (1795–1857), pioneering bookseller, publisher, and owner of a famous subscription library on

Nevsky Prospect in St. Petersburg. Born to a merchant family and schooled by a local deacon, Smirdin was apprenticed to a Moscow bookseller. In 1817 he left for St. Petersburg to work for another bookseller, Plavilshchikov, whose business he inherited. In 1832 the establishment moved to a fashionable address on Nevsky Prospect, an event celebrated by a housewarming (*novosel'e*) to which many of the prominent writers of the time were invited. Soon Smirdin's publishing enterprises—books, journals (among them the BIBLIOTEKA DLYA CHTENIYA), miscellanies, library, and press—acquired such a hold over Russian letters that BELINSKY called the 1830s the "Smirdin period in Russian literature." The consequences of this monopoly, and of Smirdin's generous honoraria to such writers as PUSHKIN, KRYLOV, SENKOVSKY, and BULGARIN were hotly debated. However, few Russian writers refused his offers, which held out the possibility of a new, professional, institutionalization of Russian literature, previously the province of gentlemen-amateurs.

Smirdin lacked the education and taste to interact creatively with his authors. Yet his bookstore-library provided a popular meeting place for them, and its catalogue (1828) was an important bibliographical resource. Moreover, Smirdin helped to canonize a Russian literary tradition by publishing the works of over seventy contemporary and 18th-century Russian authors in moderately priced editions. The annual subscription to his library was too high to attract a mass public, but it did extend the availability of Russian literature to a broader readership. Only in the late 1840s did Smirdin attempt truly cheap editions. But cheated by some of his authors (such as Bulgarin), overextended by his honoraria, undercapitalized, and forced to compete with other booksellers for a small reading public, he fell into bankruptcy.

Bibliography: T. Grits, V. Trenin, and M. Nikitin. *Slovesnost' i kommertsiya. (Knizhnaya lavka A. F. Smirdina)*. 1929. N. P. Smirnov-Sokol'skii. *Knizhnaya lavka A. F. Smirdina*. 1957.
W. M. T.

Smithy, The, see KUZNITSA.

Smotritsky (Ukrainian: Smotryc'kyj), Melety (Christian name: Maksym; 1577 or 1579–1633), a Ukrainian bishop, writer, and scholar prominent in the religious conflicts and polemics of the early 17th century, whose importance for Russian literature stems above all from his authorship of one of the earliest and most influential East Slavic grammars. Smotritsky's father was Herasym (?–1594), scholar, writer, and polemicist, and first rector of the Ostroh school. Here the younger Smotritsky began his studies before going on to the Jesuit College in Vilno and then studying at the universities of Leipzig, Wittenberg and Nuremberg. In 1617 he became a monk, assuming the name Melety, and in 1620 bishop of Vitebsk and Mstislav and archbishop of Polotsk. Although long an ardent and officially persecuted defender of the Orthodox faith and opponent of the Union of 1596, Smotritsky switched to the Uniate position in 1627 and in his last writings defended his new allegiance.

Smotritsky is the author of several important works of polemical literature, most of them written in Polish (a reflection of the bilingualism of 17th-century Ukrainian literature). The most important and eloquent of these is his *Threnos* (1610), a lament, signed Teofil Ortolog, and styled as the "weeping of the holy, universal, apostolic Eastern Church" at her present decline, specifically the defection of her best sons, the Ukrainian nobility, to the Polish-Catholic camp. His sermon on the death of archimandrite Leonty Karpovich (1620) is in Ukrainian.

By far the most influential work, frequently reprinted and used as a model, is his *Hrammatiky slavenskija pravylnoe sintagma* (1619) a commodious handbook of Church Slavonic grammar, with many examples, with a clear concern for style and norm, and with a short concluding section on prosody and metrics. While conscious of the differences between the spoken and the written language, and while concerned for the purity of the latter, Smotritsky's grammar reflects Ruthenian (Ukrainian and Byelorussian) influences and the author's own western Ukrainian origins. Intended for teachers, the grammar is a compilation (drawing on Byzantine, Greek and Latin grammars, especially those of Melanchthon), but also a scholarly and innovative work. It remained an authoritative work throughout the 17th and well into the 18th century: it was reprinted (anonymously and with various changes) in Moscow in 1648, in a more faithful edition in

1721, and yet again in 1755; it exerted a great influence on LOMONOSOV (who knew it by heart, calling it his "gate of learning," and used it as a model for his *Rossiiskaya grammatika*) and a number of other Russian grammarians.
G. G.

Socialist realism is the official artistic method of Soviet literature. The emergence of the term "socialist realism" was predetermined by the decision of the 17th Conference of the Soviet Communist Party (30 January–4 February 1932) to establish a socialist economic basis and a classless society during the Second Five-Year Plan (1933–37). This involved shifting emphasis from the proletarian facets of the Soviet state to socialist ones. On 23 April 1932, the Party Central Committee passed a resolution abolishing all proletarian organizations in literature and the other arts and decreeing the formation of a single Union of Soviet Writers. The Party's next step in unifying literature was to introduce a single artistic method. The Party discarded as impractical the "dialectical-materialist creative method" hitherto propagated by the Russian Association of Proletarian Writers (RAPP), and decided to replace it with a method whose name—socialist realism—would suggest a closer relation both to the Party's political activity and to literature. It is impossible to ascertain who coined the term "socialist realism"; what is known is that it emerged during meetings of a special five-man commission created by the Politburo of the Central Committee to deal with questions arising from the 23 April resolution. Stalin was among the members of the commission.

The Party took complete control over the implantation of socialist realism. Its trusted functionaries—Ivan Gronsky, editor of *Izvestiya*, and Valery Kirpotin, chief of the Literary Division of the Party Central Committee—were appointed, respectively, chairman and secretary of the Organizing Committee of the Writers' Union. The earliest known public reference to socialist realism was made by Gronsky at a literary meeting in Moscow on 20 May 1932: "The basic demand that we make on writers is: write the truth, portray truthfully our reality that is in itself dialectic. Therefore the basic method of Soviet literature is the method of socialist realism" (*Literaturnaya gazeta*, 23 May 1932). The next statement on socialist realism was essentially identical with Gronsky's definition; it appeared on 29 May 1932, in a *Literaturnaya gazeta* editorial written by Kirpotin. On 26 October 1932, Stalin described socialist realism as the truthful depiction of that which leads life toward socialism and called writers engineers who build human souls. The crucial event in the history of socialist realism was the first plenary session of the Organizing Committee of the Writers' Union (29 October–3 November 1932) at which Gronsky and Kirpotin gave an extensive formulation of its precepts and imposed it on the literary profession represented by more than 500 writers. Three basic sources of socialist realism—literature, Marxism, and Soviet reality—were brought out at this session and during a large-scale discussion in periodicals which lasted until the opening of the First All-USSR Writers' Congress in August 1934.

The official Soviet viewpoint has always been that socialist realism originated in literature, primarily in its proletarian segment. In 1932 Maksim GORKY was proclaimed the founder of socialist realism. His major works, especially *Mother* (1906), were extolled as genuinely socialist and revolutionary because Gorky presented the revolutionary struggle for socialism, showed the Party's leadership in it, aroused hatred for exploitation, and promoted the spirit of collectivism. Aleksandr FADEEV's *The Rout* (1927) served as an example of socialist realism in that it revealed the Bolsheviks' role in organizing the Red guerrillas, displayed confidence in the final triumph of the Revolution, and gave a lucid and logically motivated description of psychological experiences. Other proletarian novels, such as Dmitry FURMANOV's *Chapaev* (1923), Aleksandr SERAFIMOVICH's *The Iron Flood* (1924), and Fyodor GLADKOV's *Cement* (1925), were regarded as characteristic of socialist realism thanks to the correct sociopolitical approach of their authors. Representation of revolutionary movements and the belief in historical progress were viewed as manifestations of socialist realism in historical fiction.

No doubt certain tendencies classified in the years 1932–34 as socialist realism had existed in literature before the proclamation of this method. What mattered was the fact that only the Party was entitled to determine which features were to be sanctioned and promoted as socialist realism. Moreover, the principles of socialist realism were drawn not only from literary works but also from Marxist teaching and from various statements made by Marx, Engels, and Lenin.

The existence of Marxism was considered to have been precisely the reason why Gorky wrote socialist realist works before the establishment of socialism. Since Marxism created no literary theory, dogmatic theorists of socialist realism treated as sacrosanct any truism that Marx or Engels said about literature. Thus Engels' view that "realism ... implies, besides truth of detail, the truth in reproduction of typical characters under typical circumstances" (Letter to Margaret Harkness, April 1888) became part of the canon of socialist realism. "Typical circumstances" were understood as the essential features of an epoch seen from the Marxist viewpoint, while "typical characters" were to embody distinctive traits of their respective classes. The concept of the typical was to be applied so as to designate not the most common phenomena but rather trends presumably leading toward communism, a demand which resulted in a greatly distorted representation of Soviet conditions.

LENIN's insistence in *What Is To Be Done?* (1904) that Social Democrats should be able to imagine the future results of their political activities was used to substantiate the concept of revolutionary romanticism as an ingredient of socialist realism. The function of revolutionary romanticism was to depict both the heroism of the builders of socialism and their dreams of a communist millennium.

The cardinal principle of socialist realism, PARTIINOST' (Party-mindedness), was deduced from Lenin's statement that *partiinost'* meant an obligation to adopt openly "the standpoint of a definite social group in any assessment of events" ("The Economic Content of Populism and the Criticism of It in Mr. Struve's Book," 1894–95). Lenin's article "Party Organization and Party Literature" (1905) was also quoted in support of *partiinost'*, though in it Lenin demands *partiinost'* primarily, perhaps exclusively, in the political writings of the Social-Democratic Party. The theorists of socialist realism later interpreted *partiinost'* in literature as propagation of Party policy and ideology.

Lenin's theory of reflection was made the philosophical foundation of artistic representation of reality. Since this theory considers sensory perceptions to be reflections of the objects of a material world existing independently of the perceiving subject, the essence of art was said to lie in the artist's ideas and images insofar as they reflect reality. The degree of correspondence between artistic images and objective reality was judged to be closer in the works of writers professing Marxist ideology. The aesthetic value of a work was virtually equated with its ideological and political effectiveness.

The Marxist idea that the proletariat is the sole legitimate heir to world culture determined the attitude of socialist realism toward literature of the past. The study of literary heritage was deemed vital, but with the understanding that even the greatest writers of the past could not have presented a complete and true picture of life due to the inherent defects of their non-Marxist world outlook. "Nobiliary" and "bourgeois" realism of the 19th century were generally thought to be more congenial to socialist realism than any other nonproletarian literary movement of the past. The sociologically minded Balzac and Stendhal were seen to be closer to socialist realism than TOLSTOI or DOSTOEVSKY, who were held to have been excessively preoccupied with moral, philosophical, and religious problems. Nineteenth-century realism was termed "critical" because of its negative view of contemporary society. Socialist realism, on the contrary, was to affirm the Soviet way of life. A greater right to be considered predecessors of socialist realism was accorded to the 19th-century satirist Mikhail SALTYKOV-SHCHEDRIN and the critics BELINSKY, CHERNYSHEVSKY, and DOBROLYUBOV. They were usually called the ideologists of a peasant-bourgeois-democratic revolution and held in high esteem for having advocated a civic-minded art. The impressive poetic legacy of Russian SYMBOLISM was rejected because its exponents were believed to represent philosophical and aesthetic reaction. Foreign revolutionary literature was regarded to be in the initial stage of socialist realism.

From the very introduction of socialist realism, Soviet reality emerged as its most important source. The predominant view was that actual experience in building socialism should take precedence over the theoretical study of Marxism-Leninism. To enhance the subordination of literature to the Party's political aims, Gronsky declared in February 1933 that the concept of socialist realism was formulated by Stalin. The writers were urged to study Stalin's speeches in order to create works of unprecedented artistry and ideological profundity. Literature had to depict the Bolshevik as the most typical man of his age, a strong-willed member of the Party that rebuilds the world. Works dealing with topical themes of socialist construction from a correct ideological position were propagandized as the foremost achievements of socialist realism, especially if they illustrated Stalin's views. This was the case with Mikhail SHOLOKHOV's *Virgin Soil Upturned* (1932–60), Fyodor PANFYOROV's *Bruski* (1928–37), and Gladkov's *Power* (1932–38), though the last two novels are less than mediocre artistically.

Essentially socialist realism is the reflection of the Party's political and ideological priorities at any given time. The utilitarian, didactic function of socialist realism is manifest in its definition as formulated in the bylaws of the Writers' Union and endorsed by the First All-USSR Writers' Congress: "Socialist realism, being the basic method of Soviet literature and literary criticism, demands from the artist the truthful, historically concrete depiction of reality in its revolutionary development. At the same time, truthfulness and historical concreteness of the artistic depiction of reality must be combined with the task of ideologically remolding and educating the working people in the spirit of socialism" (*Literaturnaya gazeta*, 3 September 1934). This peculiar concept of truth in socialist realism promotes false idealization of Soviet reality and precludes the description of its numerous negative aspects.

Until Stalin's death socialist realism was primarily a product of his policy and personal tastes. In 1935 Stalin stressed the significance of propaganda poetry by calling Vladimir MAYAKOVSKY the best Soviet poet, thus automatically elevating him to the status of principal initiator of socialist realism in poetry. During the preparation for war in the mid-1930s, writers of historical fiction were instructed to shift focus from revolutionary to patriotic themes, and the principle of *narodnost'* (popular spirit) became closely associated with traditional Russian patriotism. On 14 August 1946, the Party Central Committee passed a resolution virtually forbidding writers to have any concerns other than those of the state. As never before, socialist realism glorified heroes of socialist labor, worshipped the Party and Stalin, vehemently attacked the West, and admired everything Soviet and many things Russian. Literary theorists, particularly the head of the Writers' Union, Fadeev, vigorously championed revolutionary romanticism as the most appropriate vehicle for portraying the lofty ideals, dreams, and heroism of Soviet man. Many earlier Soviet works were reprinted with heavy censorial revisions mirroring the stricter political and puritanical requirements of socialist realism.

The post-Stalin period brought no radical changes into the theory of socialist realism. Its principles of Communist *partiinost'*, NARODNOST', and IDEINOST' (ideological commitment) remain inviolable. The Party leader retains supreme authority in literary matters. Khrushchev's emphasis on the kinship between *partiinost'* and *narodnost'*, because the Party supposedly expresses the people's aspirations, was reflected in the 1959 bylaws of the Writers' Union, which stated that *partiinost'* is the highest form of *narodnost'*. On the other hand, a certain relaxation of political controls, the growing ideological indifference of the Soviet people, and sharp attacks on socialist realism in Poland, Hungary, and Yugoslavia prompted its theorists to tone down their dogmatism in questions of secondary importance. Today socialist realism allows writers to use a greater variety of artistic devices than it did under Stalin, but practices deemed characteristic of the literature of the absurd or of works with Freudian or decadent tendencies are still banned as the offsprings of alien ideologies. Some theorists maintain that revolutionary romanticism is in fact the second distinct method of Soviet literature, while the majority considers it a facet or component of socialist realism. Theorists differ as to whether socialist realism and socialist literature are synonymous or whether socialist realism is the basic, ideologically most mature method within a large body of socialist literature. The universality of socialist realism is strongly underscored, with works by Henri Barbusse, Louis Aragon, Theodore Dreiser, and Anna Seghers being cited as examples.

In the course of de-Stalinization under Khrushchev the framework of socialist realism was widened to include, on a limited scale, the previously forbidden themes of Stalin's purges and Soviet concentration camps. A certain degree of objectivity was allowed in the portrayal of World War II, collective farming, and everyday Soviet life. Critical realism was revived in such works as Vladimir DUDINTSEV's *Not by Bread Alone* (1956), Aleksandr YASHIN's *Levers* (1956), and Vitaly Syomin's *Seven in One House* (1965). Yet their authors were taken to task by orthodox critics, and the limits of official toleration were demonstrated by the savage persecution of Boris PASTERNAK for daring to express his non-Marxist philosophy in *Doctor Zhivago* (1958).

The post-Khrushchev period has been marked by a partial rehabilitation of Stalin, a stricter regimentation of literature, and increased demands to depict Soviet achievements. The contemporary brand of socialist realism is evinced in Aleksandr Chakovsky's novels *Blockade* (1968–75) and *Victory* (1978–81), which describe World War II, international relations, and Stalin from the Party's viewpoint. By contrast, a considerable number of writers avoid heroic and epic subjects, concentrating instead on the complexities of human relationships in daily life, particularly in love and marriage. Works of this kind are represented by Irina Velembovskaya's *The Sweet Woman* (1973) and Yury TRIFONOV's *Preliminary Results* (1970) and *Another Life* (1975). A prominent place in contemporary literature is taken by the so-called COUNTRY PROSE whose chief exponents—Viktor Astafiev, Vasily BELOV, Valentin RASPUTIN—blend their unembellished depiction of the countryside with a sympathetic attitude toward traditional peasant values. Although village prose and works about daily life can hardly be called socialist realism, they are tolerated because they are not inimical to the Soviet regime and satisfy the readers' craving for better literature.

From the day of its introduction socialist realism has stifled creative potential by placing severe philosophical and artistic restrictions on writers. The best works written in the Soviet Union—those by Pasternak, Osip MANDELSHTAM, Mikhail BULGAKOV, and Aleksandr SOLZHENITSYN—do not belong to socialist realism. Even Sholokhov's *The Quiet Don* (1928–40), acclaimed by Soviet critics as a model of socialist realism, was written with a degree of impartiality incompatible with this method, and was therefore subjected to extensive censorship. There would have been many fewer works of socialist realism had the Party not exerted pressure on the writers. In Poland, Yugoslavia, Hungary, Czechoslovakia, and Rumania, where the political supervision of literature is less stringent, socialist realism has not won the dominant position it has in the USSR.

Bibliography: K. Clark, *The Soviet Novel: History as Ritual*. 1981. A. Dremov and V. Popkov, *Narodnost' iskusstva sotsialisticheskogo realizma*. 1981. H. Ermolaev, *Soviet Literary Theories, 1917–1934: The Genesis of Socialist Realism*. 1963. M. Hayward, "The Decline of Socialist Realism," *Survey* 18, no. 1 (1972), pp. 73–97. G. Hosking, *Beyond Socialist Realism: Soviet Fiction since Ivan Denisovich*. 1980. C. V. James, *Soviet Socialist Realism: Origins and Theory*. 1973. N. Khrushchov, *The Great Mission of Literature and Art*. 1964. K. Marx and F. Engels, *Über Kunst und Literatur*. 2 vols. 1967–68. E. Możejko, *Der sozialistische Realismus: Theorie, Entwicklung und Versagen einer Literaturmethode*. 1977. A. Ovcharenko, *Sotsialisticheskii realizm i sovremennyi literaturnyi protsess*. 1968. N. Piksanov, ed., *Sotsialisticheskii realizm: Bibliograficheskii ukazatel'*. 1934. H. G. Scott, ed., *Problems of Soviet Literature: Reports and Speeches at the First Writers' Congress*. 1935. N. N. Shneidman, *Soviet Literature in the 1970s: Artistic Diversity and Ideological Conformity*. 1979. *Sotsialisticheskii realizm segodnya: Problemy i suzhdeniya*. 1977. *Sovetskaya literatura na novom etape: Stenogramma pervogo plenuma Orgkomiteta Soyuza sovetskikh pisatelei (29 oktyabrya–3 noyabrya 1932)*. 1933. A. Tertz [A. Sinyavsky], *On Socialist Realism*. 1960. H. E.

Society of Amateurs of Russian Letters, see OBSHCHESTVO LYUBITELEI ROSSIISKOI SLOVESNOSTI.

Society tale, The, a genre popular in Russia during the 1830s, took its content from the manners and mores of the upper class. In a plot centered upon a romantic encounter involving two members of the beau monde, these works revealed many details of aristocratic life. Furniture, clothing, daily routines, and evening entertainments surrounded the love intrigue and defined its parameters, which the arranged marriages, adulterous affairs, and flirtations which consumed most of the energies of the idle privileged.

While society life appeared in the Russian literature that preceded and followed the society tale, the genre presented a unique perspective on the theme, for it occurred at a time during which the aristocracy grew aware of its disintegrating social and political influence. Dandyism and the cult of *ton* are displayed in the genre as an attempt by the upper class to fend off the encroaching bourgeois ethic that would eventually dominate the latter 19th century.

The more successful examples of the genre were produced by writers who possessed first-hand experience in these elite social circles. Count V. A. SOLLOGUB, Prince V. F. ODOEVSKY, the Countess E. P. ROSTOPCHINA, A. A. BESTUZHEV, and N. F. PAVLOV wrote tales which reflected their intimate positions in the drawing rooms of Petersburg and Moscow. While the attempts at the genre by PUSHKIN remained unfinished, his novel in verse, *Eugene Onegin*, had a marked influence on the works that were to follow. O. I. SENKOVSKY, M. A. Markov, and N. N. Veryovkin, who were not of this class, wrote satiric imitations which distorted the social complexities that formed the genre's foundation. The society tale was often a path by which women entered the literary arena. The works of E. A. GAN and M. S. ZHUKOVA were immensely popular and displayed the social limitations and difficulties encountered by women of fashion.

Society literature was also a popular tradition in Western Europe. Balzac's *Scenes from Private Life* and Bulwer-Lytton's *Pelham* were among the fashionable novels from France and England which appear to have had influence on the development of the society tale in Russia. A. U.

Sociological method, the, a general term for several attempts made during the period from roughly 1900 to 1930 to erect a specifically Marxist science of literature by such men as PLEKHANOV, SAKULIN, FRICHE, and PEREVERZEV. Earlier attempts had been made, of course, to relate insights of the new science of sociology to the study of literature by Taine, Guyau, Herbert Spencer, and others. But it was the Russians who sought most insistently to tie the study of literature to specifically Marxist ideas about class struggle and the determining role of economic base on the ideological superstructure. The first principle of this group is contained in Plekhanov's review of VOLYNSKY's survey of Russian critics: "social *consciousness* is determined by social *being* ... For a person adhering to this view, it is clear also that literary critics who undertake to evaluate a given work of art must first of all elucidate precisely what aspect of *social* (or *class*) consciousness is expressed in this work." There were, of course, several ways one might go about doing this. Debates very early developed on the question of just *how* determining social factors were in shaping a given work. Plekhanov represented the side that felt individual authors had relatively little to contribute as individuals to the work: what they did was more or less fated by their class and the historical situation in which they worked. They were moved by a kind of afflatus, by economic and historical forces larger than any individual will. A counter to this view was represented by the work of Aleksandr BOGDANOV. Bogdanov was rather more of a philosophical activist who believed individual men could shape texts and history according to their intentions. The rest of the critics who tried to establish a sociological method can be organized between these two extremes: Sakulin belongs more to the Bogdanov line, Friche and (especially) Pereverzev went even farther than Plekhanov in the opposite direction.

Each of these men had established careers as leftist intellectuals and literary scholars before the Revolution: Sakulin published his great study of ODOEVSKY in 1913. It was an encyclopedic attempt to create a balance between an individual talent and the distinctive features of the 1820s and 1830s in Russia. He was closer to the Bogdanov pole and was less doctrinaire about the determining role of impersonal social forces. In such works as his 1928 *Theory of Literary Styles* he argued that a literary work was composed of three elements: the artistic activity of the writer, the effects of immediate social phenomena, and the force of more slow-working historical trends. He sought to join social context with immanent features of the text.

On the other side, Friche was the great proponent of Plekhanov. In his various studies of West European literature he sought to show that the history of literature was the story of a constant struggle among different styles, each of which represented a different class.

Friche grounded this theory in a crude psychologism, arguing that individual heroes should be avoided in future literature, their places to be taken by whole classes as they battled each other.

The most extreme representative of the Plekhanov line was V. F. Pereverzev, a man who sought to relate the smallest formal details of Dostoevsky and Gogol to their social infrastructure. Dostoevsky was an uprooted petty bourgeois intellectual, thus the emphasis in his novels on urban alienation and split personality; Gogol came from the petty landowning class, thus "images and moods imbued with the environment of landowners take up the most prominent place in his work." In 1930 the Communist Academy condemned Pereverzev's approach as "vulgar sociologism," a move that virtually ended the independent search for a sociological method in the Soviet Union, as all criticism—not only the formal method but the sociological method as well—was enjoined "to be closely connected with the guiding criticism of the literary politics of the Party."

Bibliography: Robert Louis Jackson. "The Sociological Method of V. F. Pereverzev: A Rage for Structure and Determinism." In *Literature and Society in Imperial Russia, 1800–1914.* Ed. William Mills Todd III. Stanford, 1978. Pp. 29–60. Daniel Lucid, *Preface to Revolution: Russian Marxist Literary Criticism, 1883–1917.* Ph.D. diss., Yale University, 1972.   J. M. H.

Sokolóv, Borís Matvéevich (1889–1930), ethnographer and folklorist, and **Sokolóv, Yúry Matvéevich** (1889–1941), folklorist and literary scholar. Born as twins in Nezhin, Ukraine, they grew up in Moscow, where their father was a professor at the university. They studied language, literature, and folklore at Moscow University. As students, they undertook, thanks to V. F. Miller's encouragement, study and collecting trips to Novgorod province during two summers, resulting in the publication of *Tales and Songs of the Belozero Region* (Skazki i pesni Belozerskogo kraya, 1915). After graduating from the university in 1911, they continued their work at the university and taught in high schools and in a Teachers Institute.

In 1919, Boris was appointed Professor at Saratov University. There he investigated the ethnography of the Volga region and established the ethnographic museum of Saratov district. After he returned to Moscow in 1925, the brothers jointly began intensive research and published a guide for collectors of folklore, "Poetry of the Village" (Poeziya derevni, 1926). In the summer months of 1926 through 1928 they organized and directed an expedition, designated "In the footsteps of Rybnikov and Hilferding," to the Olonets region, under the auspices of the State Academy of Fine Arts. The purpose of this expedition was to investigate the fate of byliny and historical songs in this area since the collecting activities of Rybnikov and Hilferding in the 1860s and 1870s. The byliny obtained on this expedition were not published until 1948.

Beginning in 1929, the Sokolovs jointly brought out a series of booklets on Russian folklore for a correspondence course in teacher training. The sections on the historiography of folklore, byliny, folk tales, and religious verses were written by Boris, and those on the remaining genres and on Soviet folklore by Yury.

Boris devoted much energy to organizing the Central Museum of Ethnology, which became one of the great museums of Europe. He was director of this museum almost until his death in 1930. Yury held the position, in the 1930s, of professor of folklore in the Institute of History, Philosophy, and Literature and in the Moscow State Pedagogical Institute. In 1939 he was elected a member of the Ukrainian Academy of Sciences and worked as director of the Folklore Institute of the Academy in Kiev until his death in 1941.

The brothers gave their fervent support to government policies, however repressive they were. Boris participated in the carrying out of collectivization in Kaluga district. Yury ended up endorsing the changes in folkoristics that were pressed by the government in the mid-1930s, and greeted warmly the new folklore created to extoll Stalin and his cohorts.

The brothers were enthusiastic propagandists of folk art, popularizers of folklore and folkloristics. The most important works of Boris were his studies of byliny and historical songs, sections of a lecture course on Russian folklore, and a lengthy article "Excursus in the Poetics of Russian Folklore" (1926).

Yury was the author of theoretical studies on the mutual relations between literature and folklore, on the specifics of folklore, and on the problems of its study. Though the textbook *Russian Folklore* (Russkii fol'klor, 1938) carries only his name as the author, it must be considered a common work of both brothers. It grew out of a survey of Russian folklore prepared for their correspondence course. Certain chapters that were written by Boris for this course were revised by Yury for inclusion in *Russian Folklore.* Many chapters were completely rewritten and others were substantially revised. Thus *Russian Folklore* is essentially the product of a revision and enlargement of the textbook for the correspondence course. The work, now partly antiquated, is a curious document of folkloristics at the height of the Stalin regime.

Works: B. M. Sokolov, "Ekskursy v oblast' poetiki russkogo fol'klora," *Khudozhestvennyi fol'klor* 1 (1926), pp. 30–53. ——, *Skaziteli.* Moscow (no date). "The Gradual Contraction of Images." In *The Study of Russian Folklore.* Ed. F. J. Oinas and S. Soudakoff. 1975. Pp. 169–84. Yu. M. Sokolov, *Pop i muzhik.* 1931. ——, *Barin i muzhik.* 1932. ——, *Russkii fol'klor.* 1941. (1st ed., 1938). ——, *Onezhskie byliny.* Ed. V. Chicherov. 1948. ——, *Russian Folklore.* Trans. Catherine Ruth Smith. Introd. Felix J. Oinas. 1971. (1st ed., 1950.) B. M. and Yu. M. Sokolov, *Skazki i pesni Belozerskogo kraya.* 1915. ——, *Poeziya derevni.* 1926.

Secondary literature: E. Gofman and S. Mints, "Brat'ya B. M. i Yu. M. Sokolovy." In Yu. M. Sokolov, *Onezhskie byliny.* 1948. Pp. 9–31. E. V. Pomerantseva, "O teoreticheskikh vzglyadakh Yu. M. Sokolova," *Ocherki istorii russkoi etnografii, fol'kloristiki i antropologii* 5 (1971), pp. 201–12. E. Pomerantseva and V. Chicherov, "Boris Matveevich Sokolov," *Sovetskaya etnografiya,* 1955, no. 4, pp. 97–105.   F. J. O.

Sokolóv, Sásha (Aleksándr Vsevolódovich, 1943–), émigré novelist and poet, was born in Canada where his father was Soviet military attaché. Growing up in Moscow, Sokolov studied journalism at Moscow University, working briefly for a provincial newspaper, and then from 1969 through 1971 for *Literaturnaya Rossiya* where he wrote reviews and articles. Sokolov's first novel, *A School for Fools* (Shkola dlya durakov, 1976), was written while he was a gamekeeper on the upper Volga. Considering the experimental novel unpublishable in the Soviet Union, Sokolov sent the manuscript abroad before emigrating in late 1975. Since coming to North America, Sokolov, a Canadian citizen, has published two other avant-garde novels.

School for Fools is the first person account of the mental landscape of a nameless, schizophrenic adolescent. The boy's disordered perceptions literally shape the language, the manner, and the content of the narrative which deals with his attempts to come to terms with the elemental experiences of love, sex, and death in the small worlds of his special school, his family, and the dacha community where he summers. The novella progresses largely through a complex pattern of phonetic associations and many of its characters seem to emerge out of stream-of-consciousness word play. The language is of great beauty and wit with poetically organized lists as the dominant stylistic device. Upon its appearance the novella was hailed by Vladimir Nabokov as "an enchanting, tragic, and touching book." It has been widely translated.

The Russian title/idiom of Sokolov's *Between Dog and Wolf* (Mezhdu sobakoi i volkom, 1980), refers to twilight when normally discrete phenomena are blurred, if not indistinguishable. The major device of this language-centered novel, the realized metaphor, is exemplified by its title which retains its idiomatic sense "twilight" while simultaneously projecting a literal meaning. The plot emerges from the narrator's inability to distinguish between a real dog and a real wolf—a failure that leads to his murder in a bizarre reenactment of the Oedipus myth amid the headwaters of the upper Volga. The skaz narrative draws heavily upon backwoods argot, intermixed with sections of literary parody, and yet others of sparkling, whimsical poetry. The events of the narrative are both enriched and obscured by their co-occurrence in multiple time dimensions. The novel, one of startling originality, difficulty, and daring, received the 1981 Andrei Bely Prize from the samizdat Leningrad literary journal *Chasy.*

Sokolov's third novel, *Palisandriya,* appeared in 1984.

Works: Mezhdu sobakoi i volkom. Ann Arbor, 1980. *Shkola dlya durakov.* Ann Arbor, 1976.

Translations: A School for Fools. Trans. Carl Proffer. 1977.

Secondary literature: D. Barton Johnson, "A Structural Analysis of Sasha Sokolov's *School for Fools*: A Paradigmatic Novel." In *Fiction and Drama in Eastern and Southeastern Europe.* Ed. H. Birnbaum and T. Eekman. 1980. Pp. 207–37. ———, "Sasha Sokolov's *Mezhdu sobakoi i volkom* and the Modernist Tradition." In *Russian Literature in Emigration: The Third Wave.* Ed. Olga Matich with Michael Heim. 1984. Pp. 208–17.   D. B. J.

Soldier songs date back to the period when conscription began under Peter I. The entire cycle of a soldier's life is described in song. Recruiting songs describe the grief expressed by the soldier upon hearing he has been selected, his signing up with the clerks, and the shaving off of his curls. In many songs the loss of his curls is similar to the removal of the bride's maiden headdress in the wedding songs—it marks a passage in life from one role to another. In a soldier-love song a recruit's sweetheart grieves over the loss of her beloved. One popular song tells of the conflict in a family over which of three sons should be selected.

The actual life of a soldier is described in vivid colors. Many songs tell of the difficulty of campaigns, nights without sleep, hours standing in formation. Often the soldier sadly remembers his parents, his wife and children: he thinks of a garden in which each tree represents one of his family; he imagines he is a bird and flies back home. A soldier's life frequently is described metaphorically in terms of the family life he was forced to abandon: his home is the steep mountain, his bed the damp mother earth, his wife his rifle. In some cases the soldier exhibits no fear of the coming battle, but in most songs he complains of his life which is "more bitter than wormwood." Battles often last for three days, with no food or drink, always on horseback and fighting until one's sword becomes dull. Agricultural imagery is used to describe battles, where fields are ploughed by horses' hooves, the earth sown with soldiers' heads and watered with blood.

A soldier may return home after twenty or more years, only to confuse his daughter with his wife, who has aged and turned gray since he saw her last. A grieving mother may greet her wounded son, or the soldier not returning may send instead his bloodied shirt to be washed by his wife's tears. The death of a soldier usually does not occur in battle, but alone under a tree. He may address the tree as "mother," asking it to lower its branches and cover his white body; or he may address his horse, asking him to return home and tell his wife he has married another—a swift bullet, and was betrothed by a sharp sword. As in folk lyrics in general, the focus is not on the events themselves in the soldier's life, but on the thoughts and emotions they evoke within him and others affected by these events.   R. R.

Sollogúb, Count Vladímir Aleksándrovich (1813–82), writer. Born into an aristocratic family of Polish descent in St. Petersburg, Sollogub was educated at home, then completed studies at the University of Dorpat (Tartu) in 1834. Early in his career he served in the ministry of foreign affairs, then as an official in the Tver region. On close terms with the most prominent authors of the times, he published in 1837 the short stories "Three Bachelors" (Tri zhenikha) and "Two Students" (Dva studenta) in SOVREMENNIK. After 1839, much of his work appeared in OTECHESTVENNYE ZAPISKI, where his "Story of Two Galoshes" (Istoriya dvukh kalosh) attracted the attention of V. G. BELINSKY.

Sollogub married the daughter of a prominent courtier, M. Yu. Vielgorsky, and established a salon of literature and music in his home. In the forties, he produced a number of "society novellas" such as *The Lion* (Lev), and *High Society* (Bol'shoi svet), which depicted the emptiness and vanity of St. Petersburg social life.

Two of Sollogub's works generally included among those of the NATURAL SCHOOL are *The Little Dog* (Sobachka, 1845), which describes theatrical life and provincial officialdom, and *The Traveling Cart* (Tarantas, 1845), his most successful work. *The Traveling Cart* satirically reveals Russia's depressing provincial life through the traveling notes of a SLAVOPHILE and a landowner journeying from Moscow to Kazan. Though he discounted Sollogub's more optimis-

tic prophesies for the future, Belinsky took advantage of the realistic elements to direct a polemic at Slavophiles and conservatives in Moscow. Sollogub subsequently abandoned such literature for vaudevilles and articles about music and theatrical life.

In 1856, Sollogub was named court historiographer. He produced a light comedy, *The Official* (Chinovnik), was sent abroad in 1858 to study the European theatre, and wrote the comedy *Proof of Friendship* (Preuve d'amitié [Dokazatel'stvo druzhby]), performed in Paris in 1859. In 1865, Sollogub published an antinihilist poem "Nihilist" (Nigilist) and a comedy in which the hero is a nihilist thief. At the end of his life he became involved in the study of prison affairs.

Works: Sochineniya. 5 vols. 1855–56. *Vospominaniya.* 1887. *Vospominaniya.* 1931. *Vodevili.* 1937. *Tarantas.* 1955. *Povesti i rasskazy.* 1962.

Translations: The Tarantas. Travelling Impressions of Young Russia. 1850. *His Hat and Cane. A Comedy in One Act.* Trans. members of the Bellevue dramatic club of Newport. Boston, 1902.

Secondary literature: V. G. Belinskii, "Tarantas" (review, 1845), *PSS,* Vol. 9 (1955), pp. 75–117. N. A. Dobrolyubov, "Sochineniya grafa V. A. Solloguba" (review, 1857), *Sobranie sochinenii,* Vol. 1 (1961), pp. 520–43.   J. S.

Sologúb, Fyódor Kuzmích (1863–1927), symbolist poet, short story writer, novelist, and dramatist. Born Fyodor Teternikov in St. Petersburg, the son of a household maid, he was educated at a Teachers' Institute and taught school, primarily mathematics, in various provincial towns and in St. Petersburg until 1907. He has always been best known for the novel *The Petty Demon* (Melkii bes, 1907), a satire of provincial society. His poetry, short stories, and novels began to appear in the 1890s. Before the Revolution he published eight books of verse, six novels, a number of volumes of short stories, and several plays. He was a major figure in the SYMBOLIST movement, but did not participate in their organizational enterprises, such as journals and societies, or in their doctrinal disputes. His work was considered by all to be especially representative of the DECADENT current within the movement, but his philosophy was idealist. Moreover, his decadent tendencies were somewhat abated during the second half of his career. In 1908 he married the playwright Anastasiya Chebotarevskaya, who committed suicide after the Revolution, in 1921. He remained in the Soviet Union, but was unable to publish original works after 1923. He was chairman of the Leningrad Union of Writers when he died in 1927.

His poetry is essentially metaphysical, but it consists in moods and responses to nature, sometimes to cityscapes. It is abstract in motivation; there are few signs of autobiographical occasions in it. It is, however, highly imaginative in imagery, sometimes set in ancient or medieval times, and it became increasingly exotic and fantastic throughout his first period. His first book, published in 1896, is called *Poems, Book I,* and his next three volumes were to bear similarly modest titles. The first features a vague and causeless melancholia together with pastoral scenes; the second, also published in 1896, shows escapist reveries and an inclination to spleen. The following two "books," published in 1904, elucidate the philosophical problems that underlie the novels and short stories. The reader is confronted with two pessimistic philosophies, one, a Gnostic dichotomy with an evil earth and distant ideal, or a Schopenhauerian monism of an endless, aimless, and therefore cruel, round of existences in death and resurrection. A constant symbol of evil is the dragon or serpent which is the life-giving sun. *To the Homeland* (Rodine) is a response to the national defeat in the Russo-Japanese War; and *The Serpent* (Zmii) to the failure of the Revolution of 1905. Like other symbolists, he was sympathetic to the revolutionary cause before 1917. *The Fiery Circle* (Plamennyi krug, 1908) is a large volume summarizing all his poetic tendencies; death, however, is one of its most prominent themes.

The most significant of Sologub's numerous collections of short stories were the first, *Shadows* (Teni, 1896), *The Sting of Death* (Zhalo smerti, 1907), and *Decaying Masks* (Istlevayushchie lichiny, 1909). Central to the short stories as a whole is a romantic, dichotomous view of the universe and a nostalgia for an ideal that is both aesthetic and spiritual. Almost all of the stories of the first two volumes feature schoolchildren as protagonists; they are variously caught in the toils of the earthly, or drawn to, or representative of, a love, a perfection, or an innocence, that escapes adults; nearly all die. Some stories in *Decaying Masks* (no longer devoted so exclusively to children) show the social problems and violence of the Revolution of 1905. Some stories are realistic in method, others deal in the supernatural.

Sologub's most notable novels appear to evolve one out of the other. The first, *Bad Dreams* (Tyazhelye sny, 1896), is the partly autobiographical story of a schoolteacher repelled by the stagnation of his provincial surroundings. It was also influenced, however, by French decadence, particularly Joris Karl Huysmans' depiction of Des Esseintes in *A Rebours*. The novel also combines Gogolian satire, Dostoevskian moral problems, and Turgenev's social meliorism. Sologub's second novel, *The Petty Demon*, is simpler in construction and more successful. The hero, Peredonov, is again a provincial schoolteacher, but he is sunk in his stagnant environs and both are satirized. Instead of decadence, he suffers from a homicidal paranoia. The young people in the book display an aesthetic relationship to life that is typical of the symbolist movement.

A second period of Sologub's work is discernible when philosophical pessimism was to some extent alleviated. Harbingers of this change were his first two lyric dramas, *The Gift of the Wise Bees* (Dar mudrykh pchel), and *Conquest of Death* (Pobeda smerti), both of which suggest that love survives death or becomes eternal through the medium of death. The first play was staged in 1907 by Vsevolod Meierkhold at the innovative Komissarzhevskaya Theater. Sologub wrote many more plays; *Nocturnal Dances* (Nochnye plyaski, 1908) is a rendering of the fairy tale in which princesses wear out their apparel at night; its message is the triumph of the aesthetic over the commonplace. Among the short stories of *A Book of Charms* (Kniga ocharovanii, 1909) are several in which miracles, comparable to certain Biblical events, emanate from the human vision and yet alter reality. A twenty-volume *Collected Works* appeared in 1913 and 1914; it contained a volume of new verse (almost all triolets) called *The Charms of the Earth* (Ocharovaniya zemli). The *Collected Works* concludes with a trilogy of novels called *The Created Legend* (Tvorimaya legenda), which was Sologub's most ambitious statement of his new worldview: the creative imagination dictates to reality. The protagonist, still a provincial Russian schoolteacher, is endowed with magic powers and becomes king of the fabulous United Isles in the Mediterranean, whose Queen Ortruda is an alter ego of the Russian heroine Elizaveta.

After the October Revolution Sologub's new prose works, which included a novel, short stories, and a play, were weaker. But his poetry became even firmer, simpler, and more optimistic. He lived by translations because his original works were considered too "untimely" for publication. His works have seldom been republished in the Soviet Union because their idealistic philosophy and fantasies run counter to SOCIALIST REALISM.

Works: Sobranie sochinenii. 20 vols. 1913–14. *Stikhotvoreniya.* 2d ed. Ed. with an introductory article by M. I. Dikman. (Biblioteka poeta. Bol'shaya seriya.) 1975. *Rasskazy.* Introd. Evelyn Bristol. Berkeley, 1979.
Translations: The Petty Demon. Trans. Andrew Field. New York, 1962. *The Kiss of the Unborn and Other Stories.* Trans. Murl Barker. Knoxville, 1977. *Bad Dreams.* Trans. Vassar W. Smith. Ann Arbor, 1978. *The Created Legend.* Trans. Samuel D. Cioran. 3 vols. Ann Arbor, 1979. See also Lewanski, pp. 359–61. *Modern Russian Poetry.* Ed. Vladimir Markov and Merrill Sparks. 1967. Pp. 90–111.
Secondary literature: Anastasiya Chebotarevskaya, ed., *O F. Sologube: Kritika, stat'i i zametki.* 1911. Stanley J. Rabinowitz, *Sologub's Literary Children: Keys to a Symbolist Prose.* Columbus, Ohio, 1980. Galina Selegen', *Prekhitraya vyaz'.* Washington, D. C., 1968.

E. Br.

Soloúkhin, Vladímir Alekséevich (1924–), poet and prose writer, was born in the village of Alepino, Vladimir region. He graduated from the Vladimir Engineering Technicum in 1942 and served in the army until 1945. His first poems were published in *Komsomol'skaya pravda* (1946). He finished The Gorky Literary Institute in 1951 and became a magazine writer. A member of the Communist Party, he is active in the UNION OF SOVIET WRITERS.

Although Soloukhin began his literary career as a poet and continues to write poetry, he is known primarily as a writer of prose sketches, stories, novels, and essays. He is a "village writer" (*derevenshchik*, see COUNTRY PROSE) with rural Russia the usual setting for his works. Using first person narration, the themes which dominate are: love for Russia and its countryside, nature, antiquities, and architectural monuments. *Vladimir Country Roads* (Vladimirskie proselki, 1953), a lyrical journal of a walking trip with his wife in his native central Russia, contains lively descriptions of the pleasures of discovering flowers, birds, and peasant life. In *A Drop of Dew* (Kaplya rosy, 1960) he meditates on the fate of the Russian village and peasant.

In 1966 Soloukhin published *Letters from the Russian Museum* deploring the destruction of churches and icons in the Soviet Union. He asks what other country in the world would level a church in order to replace it with a swimming pool (The Church of Christ the Saviour in Moscow). Soloukhin accuses the Soviets of destroying the Russian spiritual heritage and roots. He continues this theme in *Slavic Notebook* (1965) and *Black Boards* (1969, the "black boards" are old icons). His *Third Hunt* and *Grigorovy Islands* (1967) are excursions and lectures on mushroom picking and ice fishing.

There is ambiguity in Soloukhin's position where his love for the Russian village does not seem to extend to love and concern for the hungry (Svirsky). His attitude towards Russian Orthodoxy is also ambivalent. On one hand he is willing to eliminate services in order to preserve church buildings but on the other hand he identifies icons with prayer. These ambiguities reach down to Soloukhin, the man. A sophisticated, educated, well-traveled Party member, all told, a modern man, he still behaves and plays the role of his characters. Svirsky notes that Soloukhin dresses in a sheep-skin coat, a peasant hat, big felt boots, ("valenki"), speaks Russian with Northern intonations, and at home is surrounded by his ancient manuscript and icon collection. Soloukhin's intense nationalism and Slavophilism places him firmly in the ranks of the village writers.

Works: Izbrannye proizvedeniya. 2 vols. 1974. *Izbrannaya lirika.* 1970. *Rasskazy.* 1971. *Argument.* 1972. *Oleninskie prudy.* 1973. *Po griby.* 1974. *Venok sonetov.* 1975, 1977, 1978. *Skazaniya.* 1975. *Rybii bog.* 1975. *Slovo zhivoe i mertvoe; Stat'i, ocherki, vystupleniya.* 1976; *Prekrasnaya Adygenbe; Povesti i rasskazy.* 1976; *Sedina; Novaya kniga stikhov.* 1977. *Kameshki na ladoni.* 1977. *Stikhotvoreniya.* 1977. *Med na Khlebe, povesti i rasskazy.* 1978. *Nozhichek s kostyanoi ruchkoi; Rasskazy.* 1978. *Vremya sobirat' kamni; ocherki.* 1980. *Pisatel' i khudozhnik; Proizvedeniya Russkoi klassicheskoi literatury v illyustratsiyakh Il'i Glazunova.* 1979. *Stikhotvoreniya.* 1982.
Translations: A Walk in Rural Russia. 1967. *Searching for Icons in Russia.* 1971, 1972. *White Grass.* Moscow, 1971. *Triptych for four-part chorus of mixed voices,* a cappella. 1980.
Secondary literature: Deming Brown, *Soviet Russian Literature since Stalin.* 1978. Pp. 237–43. E. J. Brown, *Russian Literature since the Revolution.* 1982. P. 298. G. Hosking, *Beyond Socialist Realism; Soviet Fiction since Ivan Denisovich.* 1980. Yu. Kazakov, "A Word of Introduction." In V. A. Soloukhin, *White Grass.* 1971. G. Kucherenko, "Posmotrim ob'ektivnei...," *Oktyabr',* 1967, no. 3. I. Kudrova, "Rasskazy Vladimira Soloukhina," *Novyi mir,* 1964, no. 11. L. Lyubimov, *Vladimir Soloukhin.* 1970. Grigori Svirski, *A History of Post-War Soviet Writing: The Literature of Moral Opposition.* 1981.

H. S.

Solovyóv, Sergeí Mikhaílovich (1885–1942), poet and theologian, a nephew of Vladimir SOLOVYOV and a second cousin of A. BLOK. Solovyov graduated, in classics, from Moscow University in 1911. In his youth, he was an intimate friend of Blok and BELY, and privy to their mystic searchings. He published in symbolist journals and over the years several books of his verse appeared: *Flowers and Incense* (Tsvety i ladan, 1907), *Crurifragium* (1908), *April* (1910), *A Princess's Flower Garden* (Tsvetnik tsarevny, 1913), *Return to my Native Home* (Vozvrashchenie v dom otchii, 1916), also, a verse epic, *Italy* (1914). Solovyov also wrote prose fiction, as well as critical and philosophical essays. His poetry is bookish and stylized; it was criticized by Blok, not always justly. Around 1916, Solovyov was ordained a priest and in 1923 he joined the Catholic Church (*orientali ritu*). He published a biography of Vladimir Solovyov (1916), his reminiscences of Blok (1925), and wrote a monograph, *The Life and Creative Evolution of Vladimir Solovyov* (published 1977). After the Revolution Solovyov taught Greek, Latin, and versification. He also translated Vergil, Seneca, and others. Arrested in 1931, he became mentally ill and died in a psychiatric hospital.

Secondary literature: A. Belyi, *Na rubezhe dvukh stoletii.* 1930. ———, *Nachalo veka.* 1933. ———, *Mezhdu dvukh revolyutsii.* 1934. ———, *Vospominaniya o A. A. Bloke.* Munich, 1969. A. Blok, *Sobranie sochinenii.* Vol. 5. 1962. Pp. 151–56, 298–300, 632–33. *Aleksandr Blok v vospominaniyakh sovremennikov.* Vol. 1. 1980. Pp. 503–04. V. Bryusov, *Sobranie sochinenii.* Vol. 6. 1975. Pp. 312–17. G. Struve, "Ob odnom stikhotvorenii S. Solov'eva," *Mosty,* no. 10 (1963), pp. 179–84. Ieromonakh Antonii Venger, "Materialy k biografii Sergeya Mikhailovicha Solov'eva." In S. Solov'ev, *Zhizn' i tvorcheskaya evolyutsiya Vladimira Solov'eva.* Pp. 1–12. "Iz vospominanii sestry Marii." In S. Solov'ev, *Zhizn' i tvorcheskaya evolyutsiya Vladimira Solov'eva.* Pp. 13–15.   T. V.

Solovyóv, Vladímir Sergéevich (1853–1900), a philosopher, writer, poet, and teacher who influenced both the modern course of Russian literature and key philosophical and religious texts of his culture. Solovyov's works figure prominently in the evolution of Russian SYMBOLISM, and provide the basis for a full understanding of Dmitry MEREZHKOVSKY's ideas, for a reading of Aleksandr BLOK's poetry, and for a grasp of Vyacheslav IVANOV's theoretical essays. Solovyov's intellectual concerns responded to the internal tensions of Russian history on the brink of the contemporary era, and his literary heritage, on its own account, is most profitably viewed in the light of the vital cultural paradoxes and dilemmas of the late 19th century.

Environmental factors are of little help in explaining the full range of aesthetic and philosophical vision, but much of what Solovyov wrote can at least be anticipated in his family milieu. He was the son of Sergei M. Solovyov, an eminent historian and rector of Moscow University. Solovyov the father was the author of a multi-volume Russian history which gave primary impetus to the professional methodology of the historical sciences developed by V. Klyuchevsky and others. His son was undoubtedly inspired by the analytical manner of academic discourse and the encyclopedic impulse demonstrated in his father's attempt to synthesize the Russian past. Of equal importance in early years was Solovyov's paternal grandfather, a priest, who took him to church and gave him a direct introduction to Russian Orthodoxy, as well as his mother Poliksena Vladimirovna, and his nanny, Anna Kolerova, who were deeply religious women. As a result of such family influences, Solovyov knew intimately religious literature in early childhood and grew up in an everyday routine structured by observation of the church calendar and Orthodox ritual. By the age of fourteen, however, he stopped attending services and in the following years of his late youth, until another, later reversal of ideas turned to total atheism. Such fluctuations between an extreme religiosity and the attempt to deal with it by breaking away to secular modes of thought marked the entire course of his intellectual development and reflected, in turn, the larger processes of Russian culture, as it entered the 20th century.

As a student of Moscow University, Solovyov attended both the Department of History and Philology and the Department of Physics and Mathematics. During 1873 and 1874 he abandoned the university and spent the entire academic year in the Moscow Theological Academy. In 1874 he returned to the Department of History and Philosophy to defend his master's thesis, "The Crisis of Western Philosophy: Against the Positivists." He followed that essay in 1880 with a doctoral dissertation entitled "A Criticism of Abstract Principles." Both studies were favorably received and helped him obtain teaching positions in the academic institutions of Moscow and Petersburg. At the beginning of 1878 he gave a series of public talks which drew a large audience; they were subsequently published under the title *Lectures on Godmanhood.* During one such lecture, given shortly after his doctoral defense, Solovyov introduced a plea for mercy concerning the revolutionaries who had just assassinated Alexander II. As a result of a reprimand by the Minister of Public Education, he resigned his teaching position and from that point on devoted himself exclusively to literary and philosophical work. The later stages of his life were marked by two unhappy infatuations

with women and by ill health; he managed, nevertheless, to produce a large body of poetry, literary criticism, translations, and encyclopedia articles. He added to his earlier academic essays by writing influential studies in history and philosophy entitled *The Spiritual Foundations of Life* (1884), *The History and Future of Theocracy* (1887), *L'Idée russe* (1888; Russian translation 1909), *La Russie et l'église universelle* (1889; Russian translation 1911), *The Meaning of Love* (1892–94), *The Justification of the Good* (1897), *Three Conversations (On War, Progress, and the End of History)* (1900), and *A Short Tale of Antichrist* (1900). On his deathbed in 1900 he reaffirmed his work's pathos of universal love by praying in Hebrew for the Jewish people.

As can be expected from his biography, Solovyov's writings were inspired by an attempt to make religion (and not an empty "religiosity" as he labeled the unthinking adherence to religious customs) a practical and valid part of modern society. The grand synthetic designs often noted in studies of his works were, in large part, created out of the attempt to reconcile current and fashionable ideas of Russian progessive thought with basic religious values. With the exception of a predilection for Spinoza acquired in his youth, the telling feature of his intellectual development was that it followed a reverse historical course: from Feuerbach, Büchner, PISAREV, John Stuart Mill, Darwin, and Schopenhauer, he turned back to study German idealism (Kant, Hegel, Schelling) and the history of Christianity. After his encounter with the Catholic Bishop Juraj Strossmayer, a Croat, he expressed the impulse to make religion socially actual through the formulation of a theocratic plan in which the major churches (with an initial emphasis on Catholicism) would merge with the Czar's political sphere in a synthesis leading to universal harmony. Two of his better known poems, "Ex Oriente Lux" (1890) and "Panmongolism" (1894) incorporate respectively the SLAVOPHILE hope of a positive role for Christian Russia in such a historical process and a mockery of Russian nationalism before the apocalyptic possibilities of the East. The fluctuation between the optimistic and skeptical views of history present in the two pieces of verse was not incidental or merely the result of biographical vicissitudes but reflected an intrinsic part of Solovyov's intellectual method. He always assumed a type of dialectic in which the expected criticism and skeptical appraisals of his cherished beliefs and hopes were anticipated, as it were, in the ironies and debunkings of his own writings. The negative polarity, nevertheless, was not his final resting place; the process of affirmation and rejection was a way of attempting to arrive at a grand synthesis of universal truths applicable to all spheres of human existence.

In addition to Hegel's dialectical method Solovyov's mature metaphysics responded to Schelling's notion of a world soul and to the passionate reception of reality in the mystical writings of Jacob Boehme, Paracelsus, Swedenborg, gnosticism, and the cabala. Poems such as "We Did Not Come Together Without Reason" (1892) showed existence moving to a total organic merger of the spiritual and the material in which love, the prime force of being, would triumph over chaos. Much of this philosophical vision suggests a not unusual sublimation of religious sensibility into Neoplatonism and idealism; the world, as Solovyov defined it in his essays and poetry, evolved to reconciliation and harmony but its contemporary nature was dual with a transcendent, eternal reality underlying the symbols and shadows of earthly life ("In the Dream of Life We Are Shadows, Shadows" [1875], "Dear Friend, or Do You Not See" [1892]). Among the most successful of the texts describing the spiritual and nearly pantheistic meaning Solovyov attributed to nature was a verse cycle written during the years 1893 to 1895. Images of Lake Saima and the Nordic landscape led him to the vision of an "entrance to a kingdom of spirits" in the "reflection of northern lights" ("On the Road to Upsala" [1893]). Such poems continued the traditions of three Russian writers—ZHUKOVSKY, TYUTCHEV, and FET—who provided the strongest literary influence on his verse. In other works, including "To A. A. Fet" (1897) and "In Memory of A. A. Fet" (1897), the debt was directly acknowledged.

Solovyov's key philosophical concepts were the notions of Godmanhood and Sophia. The vision of Godmanhood—a perfect, eternal reality to which humanity inevitably progressed—profoundly affected audiences at Solovyov's lectures and stimulated the historicocultural constructs of Merezhkovsky, BERDYAEV, and Vyacheslav Ivanov. Sophia—in a core meaning the universal feminine principle of love and reconciliation between human beings which led to world harmony—was the most influential contribution of Solovyov's metaphysics to Russian literature. The "Eternal Friend," as Solovyov characterized her, was celebrated in a verse cycle including "My Tsarina Has a Tall Palace ..." (1875–76), "The Eye of Eternity" (1897), "Das Ewig-Weibliche" (1898), and "Three Meetings" (1898). The last of these poems is the best known and describes Solovyov's three encounters with Sophia: in church as a young boy, in the British Museum during his trip abroad in 1875, and in the Egyptian desert. Characteristically, the visions are set in a light and humorous poetic context reminiscent of PUSHKIN and LERMONTOV; the last meeting, thus, is preceded by an encounter with Arab natives who are prone to robbery of tourists rather than mystical experience. Nevertheless, Sophia appears even in this imperfect and skeptical world, and it was such a triumphant assertion of transcendent reality in the worst conditions of existence which profoundly inspired Russian symbolism and the works of Blok, BELY, and Ivanov devoted to various forms of the Beautiful Lady.

Complementing his seminal influence on the weltanschauung of the symbolists and on the religious and philosophical revival undertaken by Sergei BULGAKOV, Pavel FLORENSKY, Evgeny Trubetskoi, Nikolai Berdyaev, and others, Solovyov's stylistic accomplishments contributed to the technical history of Russian literature. Thus, *Three Conversations* and *A Short Tale of Antichrist*, in addition to their effect on Russian apocalyptic ideas also provided a skillful refinement of the literary genre of philosophical dialogue, as undertaken in Herzen's *From the Other Shore* and Dostoevsky's "Bobok." It has been suggested not without reason that Solovyov was the prototype for Dostoevsky's Alyosha, although his intellectual modalities, it can be argued, are equally reminiscent of Ivan's trenchant debates with the Grand Inquisitor. Throughout his poetry Solovyov formulated his Neoplatonic views in arresting metaphors synthesizing with equal passion and clarity the material and the spiritual aspect of reality. Students of his verse have noted that his literary talent was particularly manifest in the creation of a unified vision of experience out of maximally polarized images like earth and sky, night and day. Oxymora, thus, were particularly developed elements of his poetic style.

Although Solovyov wrote a few essays on art such as "The General Meaning of Art" (1890) and "Beauty in Nature" (1899), his aesthetic principles were most forcefully expressed in literary criticism and poetry. Motivated, again, by the urge to trace absolutes of unity and harmony in concrete sociohistorical forms, he defended Nikolai CHERNYSHEVSKY and defined art as having an objective existence. He parodied as decadent the ideas of pure and independent art that he saw in early Russian Symbolism ("The Russian Symbolists," 1895), and valued Dostoevsky not for his work's "beauty of form" but for turning literature into "a real force, that enlightens and transforms all of the human world." ("Three Talks in Memory of Dostoevsky," 1881–83). The role of the artist for him was largely theurgic; that is, he wanted writers and poets to serve the task of changing reality into a perfect realm reminiscent of Dostoevsky's Golden Age. Such world-beauty, in his view, was formed out of specific ethical action. The true artist, as Perseus, undertakes a moral battle with the monster-evil of the world and as Orpheus saves beauty from death and non-being ("Three Deeds," 1882). In a series of essays on Fet, Tyutchev, A. K. TOLSTOI, and Ya. POLONSKY, he analyzed the lyric poet's intimate understanding of nature's hidden meanings, and in articles such as "On the Meaning of Poetry in Pushkin's Verse" (1899), "Pushkin's Fate" (1897), and "Lermontov" (1899) outlined the ethical example he expected of such writers.

The peculiar dialectic of Solovyov's work led him to write a number of parodies and satires which were directed at, among other subjects, the very notions of high artistic purpose and prophecy which he also postulated. The literary forms he used in this endeavor included nonsense verse, moral tales, and plays. *The White Lily* (1878–80), an example of the last genre, combined mystical vision with mockery of the poet-prophet. In reading such works it is appropriate to note that Solovyov was in love with the niece of A. K. Tolstoi, and that KOZMA PRUTKOV influenced his literary sense of humor. Solovyov's heavily ironic juxtapositions (for example, a romantic hero who devours seven legs of lamb in "The Mysterious Guest"), wicked puns, and vulgar images, however, surpassed all

earlier models and achieved a new degree of self-parody in Russian literature.

Solovyov's influence on Russian culture made itself felt in a number of other ways. In addition to his friendship with Dostoevsky, he debated or was on intimate footing with Ivan AKSAKOV, Vasily ROZANOV, N. F. FYODOROV, Konstantin LEONTIEV, Nikolai STRAKHOV and a host of other leading Russian intellectuals. His epistolary talents were remarkable; D. S. SVYATOPOLK-MIRSKY does not hesitate to rank his correspondence as second only to Pushkin's. In 1891 he was appointed editor of the philosophical sections in the Brockhaus-Efron Encyclopedia, and he contributed a number of entries including substantive studies of Kant, Hegel, and Leontiev. His literary and philosophical preoccupations were reflected in translations of Schiller, Heine, Vergil, Petrarch, Dante, Mickiewicz, Longfellow, and Tennyson. Finally, his comic plays, *Alsin* (1876–78), *The White Lily* (1878–80), and *The Gentry's Revolt* (1891), are of special interest in the light they shed on the origins of Russian symbolist theater.

Works: Sobranie sochinenii. 2d ed. 10 vols. 1911–14. This publication has to be supplemented by texts published abroad such as *La Russie et l'Eglise Universelle* (Paris, 1886), and *L'idée russe* (1886). Solovyov's letters: *Pis'ma.* 4 vols. 1908–23. A convenient and reliable collection of his verse, plays, and translations is: *Stikhotvoreniya i shutochnye p'esy*, introd. and comm. Z. G. Mints. 1974.
Translations: War, Progress, and the End of History. Trans. A. Bakshy. 1915. *The Justification of the Good.* Trans. N. Duddington. 1918. *Russia and the Universal Church.* Trans. H. Rees. 1948. *A Solovyov Anthology.* Trans. N. Duddington. Ed. S. L. Frank. 1950.
Secondary literature: A. Belyi, "Vladimir Solov'ev (Iz Vospominanii)." In *Arabeski.* 1911. Nicholas Berdiaev, *Dream and Reality.* 1950. A. Blok, "Rytsar'-monakh," "O sovremennom sostoyanii russkogo simvolizma," and "Vladimir Solov'ev i nashi dni." In vols. 5 and 6 of Blok's *Sobranie sochinenii.* 1962. V. Bryusov, "Vladimir Solov'ev: Smysl ego poezii." In Bryusov's *Dalekie i blizkie.* 1912. Georges Florovsky, *Puti russkogo bogosloviya.* Paris, 1937. Pp. 308–21, 382–88, and 554–57. P. A. Gromov, *Blok, Ego predshestvenniki i sovremenniki.* 1966. V. Ivanov, "Religioznoe delo Vl. Solov'eva." In Ivanov's *Borozdy i mezhi.* 1916. Nicholas Lossky, "The Successors of Vladimir Solovyev," *SEER*, 1924, June, pp. 92–105. Oleg Maslenikov, *The Frenzied Poets: Andrey Biely and the Russian Symbolists.* 1952. K. V. Mochul'skii, *V. S. Solov'ev.* Paris, 1936. Renato Poggioli, *The Poets of Russia 1890–1930.* 1960. Pp. 116–41. V. Savodnik, *Poeziya Vl. S. Solov'eva.* 1901. E. N. Trubetskoi, *Mirosozertsanie Vl. S. Solov'eva.* 2 vols. 1913. V. V. Zenkovsky, *A History of Russian Philosophy.* Trans. George L. Kline. Vol. 2. 1953. Pp. 469–531.   N. Rz.

Solzhenitsyn, Aleksándr Isáevich (1918–), writer, was born in Kislovodsk, the only child of a mother from a gentry family and a father from peasant stock who interrupted university studies in Moscow to volunteer in 1914, became an artillery officer on the German front, served throughout the war, and died from a hunting accident six months before his son's birth. Solzhenitsyn grew up in Rostov on the Don, where his mother was a typist and stenographer. He enrolled in the physics department at the University of Rostov in 1936, began correspondence courses at the prestigious Moscow Institute of Philosophy, Literature, and History (MIFLI) in 1939, married Natalia Reshetovskaya 7 April 1940, finished university study in June 1941, taught mathematics and astronomy for a month at a secondary school in nearby Morozovsk, enlisted in the army in October, served as a driver of horse-drawn vehicles, requested and received a transfer to officer's candidate school, completed an abridged course in artillery, and went to the front in November 1942 as commander of a reconnaissance battery. Promoted to captain and twice decorated for bravery, he served uninterruptedly until his arrest 9 February 1945, after counter-intelligence agents intercepted letters to a friend containing oblique disparagement of Stalin. He was sentenced 7 July to eight years in prison.

During 1946 Solzhenitsyn worked at a camp near Moscow on a construction project. From then until 1950 he served as a mathematician in radio and telephone communications research at the Marfino "special prison," the Mavrino "sharashka" of *The First Circle* (V kruge pervom, 1968). In 1950 he and Reshetovskaya divorced. From 1950 to 1953 he worked at the Ekibastuz "special camp" in Kazakhstan for political prisoners, the setting of *One Day in the Life of Ivan Denisovich* (Odin den' Ivana Denisovicha, 1962), as unskilled laborer, bricklayer, and smelter. There he underwent surgery for cancer 12 February 1952. He was released from prison 5 March 1953 and sent into "eternal exile" to the Kazakh village of Kok-Terek, where he taught mathematics and physics at the secondary school and began writing in secret. At the Tashkent Oncological Health Center, recreated in *Cancer Ward* (Rakovyi korpus, 1968), he was given radiation therapy in 1954 for a seminoma, pronounced cured, and sent back to continue teaching. In June 1956 he was freed from exile and appointed to teach in the Vladimir *oblast'* village of Torfoprodukt, where "Matryona's House" (Matrenin dvor, 1963) takes place. In January 1957 he remarried Reshetovskaya, and a month later he was officially rehabilitated. They settled down in Ryazan, where they taught mathematics at a secondary school and continued to write in secret.

The speech denouncing Stalin at the 22nd Communist Party Congress in 1961 emboldened Solzhenitsyn to submit *One Day* for publication to Aleksandr TVARDOVSKY, editor of the Moscow literary journal NOVYI MIR. Premier Nikita Khrushchev piloted a special resolution through the Central Committee authorizing its publication; it appeared in November 1962, and Solzhenitsyn found himself catapulted to literary fame by his first published work, not only for its intrinsic merits but for the very fact that the government was allowing fictional treatment of a formerly forbidden topic, life in Stalin's forced-labor camps. *Novyi mir* printed several of Solzhenitsyn's short stories: "Matryona's House" and "Incident at Krechetovka Station" (Sluchai na stantsii Krechetovka) in January 1963, "For the Good of the Cause" (Dlya pol'zy dela) in July 1963, "Zakhar-Kalita" in January 1966. Apart from a short article on style in LITE-RATURNAYA GAZETA, 4 November 1965, "You Don't Use Tar for a Whitener" (Ne obychai degtem shchi belit', na to smetana), nothing else by Solzhenitsyn has appeared in the official Soviet press. *Novyi mir* accepted *The First Circle*, but never published it, and the Secretariat of the Writers' Union prohibited the publication of *Cancer Ward* when it was already partially set in type. After Khrushchev's fall from power, Solzhenitsyn gradually became a literary pariah. In 1964 *Novyi mir* nominated him for a Lenin Prize, but he was rejected, denied permission to publish any long fiction, to teach, or to live in Moscow. The state security organs began a campaign of harassment against him, graphically described in *The Calf and the Oak Tree* (Bodalsya telenok s dubom, 1975), "literary sketches" chronicling his experiences from the time he first sought publication for his works until he was arrested 12 February 1974 on charges of treason, expelled the following day to West Germany, and stripped of his Soviet citizenship. He protested against his literary ostracism in an open letter of 16 May 1967 to the 4th Congress of Soviet Writers, where he also proposed sweeping changes in the policies of the Writers' Union. The letter was widely circulated at home and published abroad, but despite a petition on his behalf, his situation did not improve. An editorial in *Literaturnaya gazeta*, 26 June 1968, denounced him, and in 1969 he was expelled from the Union of Soviet Writers.

Meanwhile, the two novels that had circulated only through unofficial SAMIZDAT channels in the Soviet Union had won wide acclaim after their unauthorized publication in the West. On 8 October 1970 the Swedish Royal Academy awarded Solzhenitsyn the Nobel Prize for literature, in recognition of "the ethical force with which he has pursued the indispensable traditions of Russian literature," but he did not go to Stockholm to receive it. In 1972 he divorced Reshetovskaya, and in April 1973 married Natalia Svetlova, a mathematics teacher. The only works for which he authorized publication abroad were his novel *August 1914* (Avgust chetyrnadtsatogo, 1971) and his monumental survey of the Soviet forced labor system, *Arkhipelag GULag, 1918–1956* (3 vols., 1973–75), after state security organs confiscated his manuscripts. The appearance of the first *GULag* volume December 1973 in Paris evoked a virulent campaign of vilification in the Soviet press that culminated in his arrest and deportation. His wife and children joined him in March 1974, and nine months later he took possession of the Nobel Prize. The family lived in Zurich, Switzerland, until 1976, when they moved to the United States. Solzhenitsyn now resides in Cavendish, Vermont, with his wife, and three sons, Ermolai, Ignat, and Stepan.

In the autobiography written for the Nobel Prize Committee Solzhenitsyn declares: "From childhood I experienced a desire to write that was not inspired by anybody else, and I wrote a great deal of the usual adolescent rubbish." From age fourteen he belonged to a small group of students encouraged by a dedicated teacher to write verses and collaborate on a satirical newspaper and novels. In secondary school he also participated in theatricals, and only physical limitations kept him from pursuing drama instruction further. Allusions to MIFLI in his works indicate that his study there was a source of great pride, and his inability to finish a major disappointment in his life. He regarded mathematics as a means of finding steady employment while he was pursuing his primary literary interests. A Komsomol activist, he edited the wall newspaper for his university academic unit. As student and soldier he unsuccessfully submitted several pieces for publication. Though all his papers were destroyed after his arrest, available information suggests that his early stories and sketches were written in the spirit of the Soviet patriotism characteristic of the war years, and according to the canons of SOCIALIST REALISM, since he sent manuscripts to established writers like FEDIN and Lavrenyov.

His vicissitudes in prisons, concentration camps, and exile, recreated in the *GULag* volumes, changed his scale of values gradually, but totally and unalterably. From the time he went to Ekibastuz, in his words, "the most important years of my life began: years that put the finishing touches on my character.... I am true to the views and habits I worked out there." At Ekibastuz he had his first cancer operation and a personal encounter that led him back to the religious faith instilled in him as a child and abandoned in the years of his ambitions to excel according to Soviet ethical criteria. His psychological and spiritual crisis did not make him forget his literary aspirations, however. From 1948 he began developing a system of writing in rhyme, ten to twenty verses at a time, destroying his draft, and committing his poetry to memory. By the end of his imprisonment he had memorized 20,000 lines of poetry: two long narrative poems—*The Road* (Doroga), now lost, and *Prussian Nights* (Prusskie nochi, 1950, recorded by the author in 1969 and published in 1974)—a verse play, *Victory Celebration* (Pir pobeditelei, which he repudiated after security organs confiscated it in the 1960s), and a novella in verse, "Highway of Enthusiasts" (Shosse entuziastov, 1951), fragments of which have appeared in the periodical press. In exile he wrote the play *The Greenhorn and the Slut* (Olen' i shalashovka, 1954) and began *The First Circle* (1955–58).

Solzhenitsyn's immediate experience provides the point of departure for most of his fiction. *One Day* uses the perspective and the colorful language of an uneducated inmate in a special camp to formulate an oblique indictment of the Stalinist prison system and a powerful affirmation of individual integrity against formidable odds. The two novels on which Solzhenitsyn's fame primarily rests he has called "polyphonic," in the sense that they isolate a disparate group of characters in an enclosed space for a restricted period of time and delineate them in terms of the contrasting ways they meet some critical test of their ethical values. In *The First Circle* the space is the Mavrino special prison, the time two days, the characters incarcerated intellectuals, camp personnel, and figures from every echelon of the prison hierarchy, including Stalin himself. *Cancer Ward* assembles a heterogeneous collection of patients, people close to them, and hospital staff in a Central Asian cancer clinic. Each "polyphonic" novel has its psychological center in a character like the author, a prisoner (Nerzhin in *The First Circle*) or an exile (Kostoglotov in *Cancer Ward*) with a deep, probing moral sense. These and shorter works bear witness to what Solzhenitsyn has called a writer's prime concerns: "the mysteries of the human heart, the clash of life and death, and the overcoming of spiritual sorrow." In "For the Good of the Cause" the victory of cynicism over idealism arouses the narrator's open anger. In "Sketches and Mini-Stories" (Etyudy i krokhotnye rasskazy) he hymns the glories of sentience and decries everything that diminishes them. Short stories set in Central Asia, "Right Hand" (Pravaya kist'), and Central Great Russia feature an observer whose ethical vision expands when he belatedly appreciates the full significance of his own behavior ("Incident at Krechetovka Station") or another person's goodness ("Matryona's House," "Zakhar-Kalita").

Solzhenitsyn combines the personal and the historical in two generic contexts. In *Arkhipelag GULag*, his massive "experiment in literary investigation," begun in 1958 and finished in 1973, history dominates, in a systematic chronological account of the Soviet prison camp system unfolded with sustained moral outrage and interspersed with anecdotes from the experience of other inmates and Solzhenitsyn's own recollections. All royalties from these volumes go to the Russian Social Fund for Persecuted Persons and Their Families. The Afterword to *August 1914* implies that this whole enormous body of work has been written "only due to the peculiar circumstances of my biography and the multitude of my present impressions." In this work he articulates, for those who cannot speak for themselves, "the main truth, made up of more than just prisons, firing squads, concentration camps, and exiles, though they can't be totally avoided in writing the main truth." Nonetheless, "the primary project of my life," first conceived in 1936, is the cycle of historical novels entitled *Red Wheel* (Krasnoe koleso), of which the only "knot" yet published in its entirety is *August 1914*. Starting with the debacle of the Russian army in East Prussia at the beginning of World War I and interweaving the destinies of numerous fictional and historical characters, it aims at an interpretation of the October Revolution comparable in breadth and depth to *War and Peace* for the War of 1812, though Solzhenitsyn explicitly challenges and refutes TOLSTOI's philosophy of history. Despite chapters verbally reproducing cinema screen images, in the manner of Dos Passos, *August 1914* belongs, like the rest of Solzhenitsyn's writing, in the mainstream of 19th-century Russian realism, committed to the principle that the writer is "a kind of second government," to quote a character from *The First Circle*. In this role Solzhenitsyn has caused controversy wherever he has expressed his political views, using the same ethical and religious criteria to criticise materialism and falsehood wherever he finds it, and offering unsolicited advice to totalitarian and democratic governments alike.

Solzhenitsyn's best works are grounded in an authorial omniscience more subtle but no less authoritative than Tolstoi's. Despite the keen theatrical sense that informs his narrative prose, his plays—*The Greenhorn and the Slut* and *Candle in the Wind* (Svecha na vetru), 1960, published 1968—are the weakest part of his oeuvre. This can be attributed partly to his stylistic predilections. A traditionalist in narrative construction and characterization, he is an innovator in matters of language. With the notable exception of Ivan Denisovich, he is less interested in capturing the intonations of others than in creating a unique literary idiom of his own. Faithful to established principles of word formation and grammar, he constantly recombines roots and affixes, giving new semantic vitality to familiar syntactic structures. He shows the same skill as an ironist, hiding his emotions, and as a polemicist, giving them free rein. His rapid, nervous, dense, saturated, elliptical style compresses many complexities into a few words, like the Russian proverbs he often quotes. As both sympathetic observer of human suffering and stern adversary of violence and falsehood, Solzhenitsyn shows the same passionate commitment and literary virtuosity.

Works: Sochineniya. 6 vols. Frankfurt, 1969–70. *Avgust chetyrnadtsatogo.* Paris, 1971. *Prusskie nochi.* Paris, 1974. *Bodalsya telenok s dubom.* Paris, 1975. *Lenin v Tsyurikhe.* Paris, 1975. *Sobranie sochinenii.* 7 vols. Vermont and Paris, 1978– . *Skvoz' chad.* Paris, 1979. *P'esy. Kinostsenarii.* Paris, 1981. *Publitsistika.* Paris, 1981. *Krasnoe koleso. Uzel 1. Avgust 14-go.* 2 vols. Paris, 1983.

Translations: One Day in the Life of Ivan Denisovich. Trans. M. Hayward and R. Hingley. 1963. "We Never Make Mistakes." Trans. P. W. Blackstock. 1963. *For the Good of the Cause.* Trans. D. Floyd and M. Hayward. 1964. *Cancer Ward.* Trans. R. Frank. 1968. *The First Circle.* Trans. T. P. Whitney. 1968. *The Lovegirl and the Innocent.* Trans. N. Bethell and D. Burg. 1969. *Stories and Prose Poems.* Trans. M. Glenny. 1971. *August 1914.* Trans. M. Glenny. 1972. *Nobel Lecture.* Trans. F. D. Reeve. 1972. *Candle in the Wind.* Trans. K. Armes and A. Hudgins. 1973. *Letter to the Soviet Leaders.* Trans. H. Sternberg. 1974. *The Gulag Archipelago.* Trans. T. P. Whitney. 3 vols. 1974–78. *From under the Rubble.* Trans. M. Scammell. 1975. *Lenin in Zurich.* Trans. H. T. Willetts. 1976. *Warning to the West.* 1976. *Prussian Nights.* Trans. R. Conquest. 1977. *A World Split Apart.* Trans. I. I. Alberti. 1979. *Détente: Prospects for Democracy and Dictatorship.* 1980. *East and West.* 1980. *The Mortal Danger.* Trans. M. Nicholson and A. Klimoff. 1980.

Secondary literature: Hans Björkegren, *Aleksandr Solzhenitsyn.* Trans. K. Eneberg. 1973. J. B. Dunlop, et al., *Aleksandr Solzhenitsyn: Critical Essays and Documentary Materials.* 1973. K. Feuer, ed., *Solzhenitsyn.* 1976. D. Fiene, comp., *Alexander Solzhenitsyn: An International Bibliography of Writings By and About Him.* 1973. Andrej Kodjak, *Solzhenitsyn.* 1978. L. Labedz, comp., *Solzhenitsyn: A Documentary Record* (enlarged ed.) 1973. C. Moody, *Solzhenitsyn.* 1973. M. Nicholson, *Solzhenitsyn Studies: A Quarterly Survey* (Spring 1980–).

C. N. L.

Sómov, Orést Mikhaílovich (1793–1833), writer, literary critic, and journalist. Born into the Ukrainian gentry, Somov attended Kharkov University. He came to Petersburg in 1817 and soon became active in literary circles. He joined the FREE SOCIETY OF LOVERS OF RUSSIAN LITERATURE in 1818 and contributed to SEVERNYE TSVETY (1825–32), LITERATURNAYA GAZETA (1831–32), and other periodicals. Somov's essay, "On Romantic Poetry" (O romanticheskoi poezii, 1823), helped to introduce ROMANTICISM to the Russian public, although it was critical of some aspects of romanticism (as Somov saw it). Somov was in favor of cultivating the national spirit, Russia's historical heritage, and the traditions of folk poetry, but he was opposed to the mystic and elegiac tendencies of romanticism. Somov's Ukrainian tales make him a precursor of GOGOL.

Works: "Roman v dvukh pis'makh." In *Russkie povesti XIX v. 20-kh–30-kh gg.* Vol. 1. 1950. Several poems in *Dekabristy: Poeziya, dramaturgiya, proza, publitsistika, literaturnaya kritika.* 1951.

Translations: "Mommy and Sonny." In *Russian Romantic Prose: An Anthology*, ed. Carl R. Proffer. 1979.

Secondary literature: L. G. Leighton, *Russian Romanticism: Two Essays.* 1975. Pp. 52–54. John Mersereau, Jr., "Orest Mikhailovich Somov: Life and Literary Activities." In *Papers in Slavic Philology 1: In Honor of James Farrell*, ed. Benjamin A. Stolz. 1977. Pp. 198–224.

V. T.

Songbooks (*pésenniki*), collections of folk songs, popular songs, and literary texts set to music, which functioned as an intermediary between village and city culture. The first songbook compiled by Grigory Teplov, *Leisure Between Tasks* (St. Petersburg, 1759), consisted mainly of verses of SUMAROKOV and other court poets set to foreign melodic styles such as the French minuet and the Polish polonaise and mazurka. F. V. Trutovsky's *Collection of Simple Russian Songs with Tunes*, which appeared in the latter part of the 18th century, included both peasant songs adapted by him and songs of literary origin. A collection that had more authentic versions of the folk songs, *A Collection of Russian Popular Songs* (1790), was based on the selection and transcription of songs by N. A. Lvov and their harmonization by Ivan Prach. Another famous collection of this period is by Mikhail CHULKOV, *A Collection of Various Songs* (1770–74). While the audience for the previous collections was primarily the nobility, Chulkov intended his for a more popular audience. The work includes both traditional peasant songs and literary texts. He did not do his own transcription, but turned to songbooks in manuscript form. He apparently was also one of the first to use transcriptions sent to him from different areas in Russia. Numerous other songbooks appeared at this time, whose contents are revealed by their titles, such as: *A Selected Songbook, or a Collection of the Best of the Old and the Very Latest: Songs of the Tender Passion, Pastorals, Christmas Songs, Wedding Songs, Choral Songs, Theatrical, Merry, Simple, Popular, Drinking, Martial, Little-Russian, Satirical, and Other Russian Songs* (1792).

In the 19th century the songbooks were increasingly compiled with a popular audience in mind. This is reflected not only in the contents, but in the quality of the publications. By the end of the 19th century songbooks appeared as little notebooks in cheap editions. The books contained vaudeville, "gypsy" songs, and other popular songs which were often sung on stage in the taverns. Yu. M. SOKOLOV points out that the vast influence the songbooks must have had on oral folklore among all strata living in the city as well as on the peasants in the villages. The songbooks also illustrate the process by which a literary text is transformed when it becomes part of the oral repertory of the masses. Even in print the texts were often altered in different songbooks. In the majority of songbooks the authors were not even indicated. Thus the songbooks provide an example of the relationship between oral and literary poetry.

Readings: I. N. Rozanov, "Literaturnyi istochnik populyarnoi pesni," *Khudozhestvennyi Fol'klor*, no. 1 (1926). Yu. M. Sokolov, *Russian Folklore*. 1971.   R. R.

Sonnet. V. TREDIAKOVSKY wrote the first sonnet in the Russian language in 1735, two centuries after this form was established in Poland and other East European countries. This sonnet, actually a translation of a classical French sonnet by De Barrault, was composed, however clumsily, in accordance with the Petrarchan rules as laid down by Boileau and adapted to syllabotonic versification. A. SUMAROKOV's four sonnets, written some twenty years later, are much better technically and richer in emotional expression. However, it took some 150 years after Trediakovsky and Sumarokov for the sonnet form to establish itself firmly in Russia.

The real flowering of the Russian sonnet was during the SYMBOLIST movement, but there were notable earlier attempts. PUSHKIN left us three sonnets in all, not one of which can be termed correct and complete from the point of view of classical "laws;" they were: "Poet! Do Not Value the People's Love" (Poet! Ne dorozhi lyuboviyu narodnoi), "Not a Great Number of Paintings by Old Masters" (Ne mnozhestvom kartin starinnykh masterov), and "Stern Dante" (Surovyi Dant), this last a variant of Wordsworth's "Scorn Not the Sonnet." Nevertheless, it was then, at the beginning of the 19th century, that the preliminary rule for the Russian sonnet was fixed: a sonnet is written only in iambs, usually in pentameter or hexameter, rarely in three- or four-foot iambic lines. Trediakovsky had written his sonnet in trochees, however, and among the works of the first significant Russian sonnetist A. DELVIG, we have the one trochaic sonnet "What Flashed and Smokes in the Distance" (Chto vdali blesnulo i dymitsya). The Italian-born P. Buturlin was the next notable, devoted sonnetist, producing eighty lyrical and meditative sonnets, fifteen of them in impeccable Italian style. In the works of 19th-century poets, M. LERMONTOV, Ya. POLONSKY, K. PAVLOVA, and others, only the masterful sonnets of A. GRIGORIEV occupy a significant place. A. FET's nine sonnets are quite weak intellectually and technically as well, in the irregular usage of pentameters.

It was the Parnassian BUNIN and the symbolists BALMONT (who wrote over 350 original sonnets and numerous sonnet translations), VOLOSHIN, and especially Vyacheslav IVANOV who resurrected and recreated the sonnet in Russian, generally following the French rhyming scheme. Ivanov's early, perhaps very best sonnet "We Are Two Tree-Trunks Set Afire by a Thunderstorm" (My—dva grozoi zazhzhennye stvolà) must be singled out. This sonnet of truly epic power was first published in the collection *Pilot Stars* (Kormchie zvezdy, 1903) and then used as the magisterial sonnet of a *wreath of sonnets* published in the collection *Cor ardens* (1909–11). Ivanov victoriously ignored the "interdiction" against repetition; in fact, that very repetition is an organic element of his intention. In addition, he showed his great respect for the rules of sonnet versification by strict observance of caesura and exactness of rhyme. Not one of BRYUSOV's sonnets achieves such vitality, although some of them testify to a perfection of form, and sonnets are not always the best of the poetic legacies of Bunin, MEREZHKOVSKY, ANNENSKY, BLOK, SOLOGUB, KUZMIN, AKHMATOVA, and GUMILYOV. However, Bunin's famous sonnet "On the Height, on the Snowy Summit" (Na vysote, na snegovoi vershine) is one of the best examples of Russian classicist poetry in general.

Especial attention may be paid to I. SEVERYANIN's sonnets, some of them collected into his book *Medallions* (Medal'ony, 1934), in which, with the help of enjambments and lively wording (continuously using seven- and eight-syllable words within the sonnet line), he replaced the slow movement of the symbolists' and Acmeists' Russian sonnet form with an emphasis of freedom, speed, and spontancity within a classical structure. The best of these in part humoristic and ironic sonnets have the compressed force of Greek epigrams, particularly his "Sonnet XXX," the subject of which is a brilliantly ironic reflection on the tragic repetitiousness and decline of the sonnet itself.

Artistically, Ivanov's sonnet sequences "Winter Sonnets," "De Profundis Amavi," and his spectacular "Roman Sonnets," all in the collection *Vespertine light* (Svet vechernii, 1962), are the greatest

such in the Russian language (Bryusov, Balmont, Voloshin, and others also produced sonnet sequences). In these sequences, Ivanov, probably the best translator of Petrarch into *any* language, follows the Italian form of sonnet. In the "Roman Sonnets" the rhythm builds to a climax at the end of the octave but does not die away to silence in the closing lines of the sestet, to which Ivanov gives a new dynamic power of reflective tone and a great concentration of image, feeling, and language.

The decline of closed form in the 20th century adversely affected the Russian sonnet, too. Poets no longer wanted to observe caesura (in only one of his later, magnificent "Roman Sonnets" did Ivanov sustain caesura), also contenting themselves either with inexact rhymes or even unceremoniously breaking the rule of alternating rhyme structure; such are the experimental sonnets of S. KIRSANOV, I. SELVINSKY, and N. MATVEEVA. Distinctly not in accordance with the compositional theory of the sonnet, G. GOLOKHVASTOV wrote an entire book, *Half-Sonnets* (Polusonety, 1931), using only one quatrain and tercet for each. Finally, I. BRODSKY, too, has experimented with open-form sonnets.

The full canonization of the sonnet in Russian came late, namely with V. PERELESHIN, who has created over 600 and who, more than anyone else, has established the sonnet theoretically and creatively as one of the major Russian poetic forms. In his early sonnets of the 1930s and 1940s, he measured himself against his older contemporaries. The turning point for him occurred before his collection *Southern Home* (Yuzhnyi dom, 1968), for which he reworked earlier sonnets, replacing unsteady rhymes with exact ones and introducing severe caesura. The poet did similar work, perhaps his best, on the wreath of sonnets "Way of the Cross" (Krestnyi put'), published in the collection *Swing* (Kachel', 1971). The sonnet of the Italian type sometimes coexists in Pereleshin's work with a less rigid sonnet of the English type introduced by Surrey and used by Shakespeare. In Russian poetry, this English type of sonnet is rarely employed, but Pereleshin is its master-practitioner. He obviously prefers the Petrarchan sonnet to the Shakespearean, but he does not scorn the latter, to whose formal fluency he adds the exactness of faultless syllabic construction and caesura, bringing the accumulated energy of the three quatrains to an impressive sculptural close in the couplet. His are heavier, russianized English sonnets, full of somber intensity, and yet similar to Shakespeare's in their erotic Platonism.

                                                      A. R.

Sophia, Saint. The embodiment of divine wisdom (*Hagia Sophia*), a concept now known only to Eastern Christian Churches; in Russian Orthodoxy a personification represented on many icons. The concept played a major role in the works of some SYMBOLIST writers.

The doctrine of a feminine principle, perceived variously as the Divine Wisdom, or the World Soul, or the incarnation of the creative capacity of the Deity, ascends at least to Hellenistic times and was a feature of the Gnostic religion and some related Christian heresies. Constantine I established it in the Church and Saint Sophia became, like the Virgin Mary, the object of worship. Gnostic ideas were revived during the period of German romanticism, when *das Ewig-Weibliche* became a familiar concept. The influential Russian philosopher Vladimir SOLOVYOV assigned to Sophia an essential role in any ideal love between persons, as well as in a Christian millennium. She appears in his poem "Three Meetings" (Tri svidaniya) and others.

Symbolists whose works reflect the doctrine were Aleksandr BLOK, Andrei BELY, and Vyacheslav IVANOV. Blok's cycle *Verses about the Beautiful Lady* (1905) records a lyrical search for revelations of, or encounters with, the Lady. Bely anticipated the earthly sway of Sophia as Solovyov's "Woman Clothed in the Sun," an expectation he relinquished with the failure of the 1905 Revolution. For Ivanov, Sophia was an eternal metaphysical force, and like Christ, an intermediary between heaven and earth.

Bibliography: Hans Jonas, *The Gnostic Religion.* 1958. "Sofiya-Premudrost' Bozhiya," *Entsiklopedicheskii Slovar'*, eds. F. A. Brokgaus and I. A. Efron. 1900. Vol. 31, pp. 1–2. Vladimir Solovyov, *Russia and the Universal Church.* 1948. Ewa M. Thompson, "The Development of Aleksandr Blok as a Dramatist," *SEEJ* 14 (1970), pp. 341–51. Peter Zouboff, *Vladimir Solovyov's Lectures on Godmanhood.* Poughkeepsie, 1944.   E. Br.

Sosnóra, Víktor Aleksándrovich (1936–), contemporary poet, was born in the Crimea, suffered many misfortunes as a child (a winter in Leningrad under siege, orphanhood, the German occupation, the shooting of people close to him, etc.) He never received a systematic education, and worked as a mechanic at a Leningrad plant from 1958 to 1963. He began to read and publish his verse in 1960, enjoying the support of N. ASEEV, to whom Sosnora later dedicated one of his books (*Triptych*). Sosnora's first book of verse, *Rainstorm in January* (Yanvarskii liven') was noted by critics for its bold metaphors, free "spoken" intonations, a certain deliberate rhythmicality, and emphatic euphonic contours (e.g., "Snowdrifts"—Sugroby). Even at this early stage, Sosnora showed an interest in Old Russian themes and created poetic versions of the "Igor Tale," Russian BYLINY, and Russian chronicles ("The Year 1111"). These cycles entered Sosnora's second collection of verse, *Triptych*, which official critics called "insipid and sour." However, a well-known scholar, academician D. S. LIKHACHEV, declared himself in deep sympathy with Sosnora's poetic interpretation of Kievan Rus, even though there were many inaccuracies, linguistic absurdities, and outright fantasy in Sosnora's poems. Likhachev wrote a preface to Sosnora's third collection, *The Horsemen* (Vsadniki), crediting him with "living embodiment" of Russian antiquity and "authentic historical spirit." In spite of the academician's warm praise, Sosnora was received coolly in Moscow poetic circles, was invited only once to participate in the central *Den' poezii*, and remained essentially a "Leningrad poet." Also, he allowed himself to be published in *Tamizdat* from time to time. Sosnora's last collection which has appeared in the Soviet Union and is known in the West, *Crystal* (Kristall), bears evidence of a significant evolution undergone by the poet: his tense Aseevian rhythms have disappeared, and so have his Khlebnikovian phonetic experiments as well as historical themes and bright folk-style colors in the manner of Malyavin. Sosnora has turned externally calmer, more delicate. Pushkinian intonations may now be heard in his verse ("Crystal of love, crystal of hope"). Yet at the same time a certain hidden sadness permeates the poems of this collection, whether they be love poems ("Letters to You," "Crown of Sonnets") or philosophical poems "May the Earth Preserve You...."). Motifs of "living out one's days" and "remembrance of the deceased" ("Afterwards"—Posle) keep coming up, and the image of the "slave son" (nevol'nik-syn), who has become a symbol of humanity is reiterated ("No Dreams"—Net grez...). In 1979, the Posev publishing house in Frankfurt am Main issued Sosnora's collection, *The Flying Dutchman* (Letuchii gollandets), containing both prose and verse. Two verse epics, "Living Mirror" (Zhivoe zerkalo) and "One Day of Loneliness" (Odin den' odinochestva), in free verse, from this collection attempt to express in symbolic-fantastic imagery the same complex relations between poet and objective reality. The transition from these to rhythmic prose ("The Flying Dutchman"), also dealing with some kind of mystic-absurd existence, seems only natural. The other pieces of this collection also take the reader into an unreal world, where either time seems to have come to a stop, or everything is drowned in numbing banality. Sosnora's creative career has not run its full course yet. Most likely, not everything he has written has been published, and there have been some hints of new and interesting turns.

Works: Yanvarskii liven'. 1962. *Triptikh.* 1965. *Vsadniki.* 1969. *Aist.* 1972. *Kristall.* 1977. *Letuchii gollandets.* 1979.

Translations: Four poems, in *Russian Poetry: The Modern Period.* Ed. John Glad and Daniel Weissbort. 1978. Pp. 258–64.

Secondary literature: V. Betaki, "B mire molnii," *Kontinent*, no. 26 (1980). V. Portnov, "Po bylinam sego vremeni," *Novyi mir*, 1963, no. 2. V. Sobolevskii, "Poeziya i bubny," *Don*, 1967, no. 2.

E. D. A.

South Slavic influence made itself strongly felt on the higher culture and the written literature of the Russians and the other East Slavs (Ukrainians and Belorussians) at two times during the Middle Ages.

The first time was when Kievan *Rus'* officially converted to Christianity, traditionally in the year 988 A.D. (according to the Russian Primary Chronicle). The conversion took place under Byzantine auspices, and resulted in the virtual transplanting of one sector of Byzantine written literature and higher culture onto East Slavic territory (see "BYZANTINE INFLUENCE"). However, the immediate source of this transplanted culture was not Byzantium itself, but

Bulgaria and Macedonia, where the same sort of transplanting had taken place a century earlier. Many of the main features of Kievan literate culture derive directly from Bulgarian and Macedonian literate culture, and only secondarily from Byzantium: the use of CHURCH SLAVONIC rather than Greek, the large number of Church Slavonic texts translated from Greek, the CYRILLIC alphabet itself, etc. So strong was this current of influence that other, less powerful currents of literary influence from other Slavic lands can now be traced only by painstaking efforts of scholarship, and are hardly perceptible to the untrained eye (e.g., West Slavic influence in Novgorod, and probably Galicia, which was incorporated into the Kievan state only in 981 A.D.)

The second time when South Slavic influence made itself strongly felt on East Slavic written literature and higher culture was during the 14th and 15th centuries. At this time the East Slavs were divided between two states, the Grand Principality of Moscow and the Grand Principality of Lithuania, each of which rightly viewed itself as the legitimate successor of the Kievan state. This wave of influence, like the former one, made itself widely felt throughout East Slavic written literature and higher culture. It was not, as is commonly thought, the result of a large number of South Slavic refugees fleeing to other Slavic lands in the aftermath of the Turkish conquest of the Balkans. Rather, it was the result of the spread of a complex of religious ideas, which originated in Byzantium, passed to the Orthodox South Slavs and thence to the East Slavs, and eventually penetrated into every corner of Orthodox Christendom: this complex of ideas, known as hesychasm, was spread by the zeal of its adherents more than by any impersonal forces of political change. Unlike the first South Slavic influence, which was more a cultural transplant than an influence, the second South Slavic influence had a relatively slight impact on the East Slavs, and the character of the impact was different in each of the two East Slavic states. In the Muscovite state, the impact seems to have been strongest in the area of iconography and monastic practice; in the Lithuanian state, on the other hand, scribal practice seems to have been more strongly affected than iconography.

Bibliography: D. S. Likhachev, "Nekotorye voprosy izucheniya vtorogo yuzhnoslavyanskogo vliyaniya v Rossii," In *Issledovaniya po slavyanskomu literaturovedeniyu i fol'kloristike.* Moscow, 1960. Pp. 95–151. V. Moshin, "O periodizatsii russko-yuzhnoslavyanskikh literaturnykh svyazei X–XV vv," *TODRL* 19 (1963), pp. 28–106. I. Talev, *Some Problems of the Second South Slavic Influence in Russia.* Munich, 1973. D. S. Worth, "The 'Second South Slavic Influence' in the History of the Russian Literary Language," *American Contributions to the Ninth International Congress of Slavists*, I. Columbus, 1983. Pp. 349–72.

R. M.

Soviet literature. The Soviet *Concise Literary Encyclopedia* defines Soviet Literature as "artistic literature of the peoples of the Soviet Union, which originated after the Great October Socialist Revolution ... created in 72 languages of the peoples of the USSR." Since Soviet literature serves a political as well as artistic role in the Soviet Union, it is appropriate to consider also the definition espoused by the Central Committee of the Communist Party in greeting the 4th Congress of Soviet Writers in 1968:

> Born at a precipitous turn of history in the fire of Revolution, Soviet literature opened a new stage in the development of the artistic culture of humanity. Its international significance and authority are determined by the fact that it reflects the world-wide historical attempt at the revolutionary transformation of society, the struggle for socialism, and always carries to the people the lofty ideas of Communism, freedom, peace and progress.

In its absolute sense, Soviet literature includes all works of literature written and published in the Soviet Union since 1917 in all seventy-two languages of the fifteen Soviet Republics and thus includes the works of Kirghiz, Uzbek, Georgian, Ukrainian, Belorussian, Latvian, Estonian, Lithuanian and other nationalities. However, by definition, it also excludes the works of Russian writers in emigration, such as NABOKOV, BUNIN, TSVETAEVA, AKSYONOV, VOINOVICH, NEKRASOV, and SOLZHENITSYN. The situation is, however, not quite as simple as this definition implies since it is complicated by the fact that a number of émigré writers, such as Tsvetaeva, returned to Russia while others, like the poets AKHMATOVA and PASTERNAK, lived for many years in "internal emigration," and published in "SAMIZDAT" and "TAMIZDAT" some of their most important works dealing with the Soviet experience, *Requiem* and *Dr. Zhivago* respectively. Furthermore, recently a large number of established and officially recognized Soviet writers have published abroad important works dealing with the uniquely Soviet experience. Among these are writers who have been forced to follow their works into emigration. They include Viktor Nekrasov, Stalin Prize winner for *In the Trenches of Stalingrad*, Vladimir Voinovich, author of the *Soviet Anthem to the Cosmonauts* and of several short prose works, published in the Soviet Union, and of *Life and Extraordinary Adventures of Private Ivan Chonkin*, *The Ivankiad*, and *Pretender to the Throne*, published abroad, V. Aksyonov, who published *Colleagues*, *Ticket to the Stars*, *Oranges from Morocco*, *Half Way to the Moon*, and a number of short stories and novels in the Soviet Union while his *The Steel Bird*, *The Burn*, *Our Golden Bit of Rail*, and *The Crimea Island* were published abroad. Solzhenitsyn has had most of his major works published abroad only. The designation "Soviet literature" does not absolutely carry the meaning attached to it by the Soviet establishment. The problem of definition is further complicated by the fact that, for the Soviets, literature carries political connotations and implies a political and ideological commitment. Minorities are poorly represented and when national literature is discussed, only authors writing in the Russian language seem to be known and recognized by Soviet readers. The Soviets have indeed attempted to promote the idea of a single, multinational, multiethnic Soviet literature, but with few exceptions have been unsuccessful. Unless written in Russian, most of the works of Soviet national minorities are virtually unknown to the general public. There are exceptions. Writers like Chinghiz AITMATOV (Kirghiz), Fazil ISKANDER (Abkhazian), and Vasily BYKOV (Belorussian) are exceptions because, in addition to being outstanding artists, they write in Russian as well as in their native language. The Soviets are currently far from reaching the ideals expressed in their official definition of Soviet literature, and Soviet literature is hardly representative of all its peoples. Many minorities and nationalities such as the Ukrainians, Armenians, Latvians, Georgians, and Estonians do have rich traditions and cultures in which their literatures are rooted, and therefore cannot be considered and discussed as part of a homogeneous entity and should be discussed individually. Critics who write on Soviet literature in the West have struggled to define the term and explain the difficulties posed by these problems. To be inclusive it is apparent that, to a Westerner, a discussion of Soviet literature is basically a discussion of literature written in Russian after the Revolution, irrespective of place of writing or place of publication. Thus, in presenting and examining the development of Soviet literature, this discussion will concern itself with those authors who spent most of their professional life in the Soviet Union, or whose works were written in the Soviet Union or deal predominantly with the Soviet experience, regardless of the place of publication. The subject of this discussion then is Russian literature of the Soviet Period.

To understand Russian literature of the Soviet period the reader must understand the role and position of the writer in Russian society vis-à-vis the state on one side and his audience and/or readers on the other. There exists the 19th-century romantic tradition of the poet and writer, who like in PUSHKIN's "The Prophet," under the spell of the muse is transformed into a prophet, and who thereby, has been singled out by the gods to carry the *word* (understood as as *logos*)—the *truth* to the people. This commitment to truth, combined with a sincere belief in the didactic function of literature, is deeply ingrained in the consciousness of most Russian writers and in the way literature is perceived by his reader. What that truth is and what the best means of communicating the message are, varies depending upon the individual and the historical period during which he writes. What complicates the role of the Soviet writer is the fact that, since 1932, he has had but one official "patron," the state, and it has had a need to mobilize the writer's prophetic voice for its own purposes—for propagating its own goals. As his employer, publisher, editor, and censor, the Party has become "in loco parentis," the supreme authority, judge, teacher, and dictator. The writer in the Soviet Union is caught between two poles: his desire on one

hand to depict the truth, and to instill moral and ethical values, which his reader expects from him, and on the other hand, Soviet officialdom which expects the writer to be the faithful, unquestioning handmaiden of the state. It is this tension which places the Soviet writer in a unique and hazardous position, and which forces him to make extreme choices, perhaps even to go so far as to choose martyrdom in Siberia or emigration from his native land.

This situation creates two distinct groups of writers: those who, despite everything, have retained their independence and have protected their individual talent, creativity and "moral values," and the Party hacks or "official writers," who either sacrificed their talent, principles and individual values by placing them at the service of the Party, or never had any talent, but write according to pre-set formulae.

The early years of the 20th century were the "Silver Age of Russian Poetry" and witnessed the development of the Russian avantgarde in art and literature. The 1920s, following the Revolutions of 1917, were, despite the violence, fratricidal wars, physical deprivations, and economic shortages, years of dynamism and vitality in the arts. They were a continuation of the ferment and revolution in the arts which had begun in the decade preceding World War I, when Russian artists and poets, in addition to continuing the 19th century tradition of individuality and truth seeking, became closely interconnected with artistic developments in the West. Gradually, by the eve of World War I they had assumed a position of leadership in the arena of European art.

During the early post-revolutionary period and the civil war, poetry dominated the literary scene. Poets such as the symbolist BLOK, the ACMEISTS Akhmatova and MANDELSHTAM, the IMAGIST peasant-poet ESENIN, and the FUTURIST MAYAKOVSKY, appeared at mass readings and literary debates. They continued writing with the revolutionary fervor developed during the pre-revolutionary struggles. The revolution in the arts had preceded political revolution by almost a decade, therefore it was no surprise that Russian artists and writers assumed that they possessed the right to be the new leaders. Poets like Mayakovsky believed that they would bring about the final revolution, the "Revolution of the Spirit."

The first half of the 1920s was a period of unparalleled artistic excitement, innovation, creativity, and experimentation. There was a proliferation of literary groups, most of which lasted for a while, while others were short-lived, some with serious aesthetic beliefs which reflected the differences between the poetic schools and factions, others with little apparent philosophical foundation, but all engaged in lively, often vicious, debate with each other, each publishing its own manifesto, each broadcasting its own platform and position. These were the years which saw the birth of Soviet cinema under such brilliant directors as EISENSTEIN, Pudovkin, and Dovzhenko. It was a time of endless public literary debates concerning the function of art, the purpose of literature, and Russian literature in particular, the role of the artist in Soviet society, and, of course, the role of the individual. These were all part of the struggle between the various literary groups for hegemony in the arts. In the guise of various "isms" these groups and subgroups focused upon their respective uniqueness and on the differences which separated them from each other rather than on the points they had in common.

The older generation of symbolist poets, such as A. BELY in his *Christ Has Risen* and A. Blok in *The Twelve*, had an ambiguous relationship to the Revolution and perceived it in mystical and religious terms. The younger poets, especially Mayakovsky, and other CUBO-FUTURISTS who had been involved in revolutionary activity, greeted the Revolution with joy and great expectations. They hailed it as the flood which was sweeping away and destroying the old way of life which they firmly believed would be replaced by a new utopian ideal. Esenin, the peasant-poet, accepted it in his own way as a peasant revolution. Pasternak, who was loosely associated with the futurists, Tsvetaeva, who did not fit into any group, and the Acmeists Akhmatova and Mandelshtam continued to write and recite highly personal or philosophical, mostly apolitical poems. Mayakovsky was the dominant, most colorful, and most influential poet of the early 1920s. Through 1925 he and Esenin dominated the public literary scene. These two poets epitomized the dichotomy and major conflict in Russian literature of that period: the opposition between the city and the country; the modern urban, technological landscape and rural peasant Russia. Mayakovsky sang of city streets, squares, lanterns, and technological achievements, while Esenin wore a peasant shirt, spoke with a peasant lilt, and sang of races between the colt and the iron horse and bemoaned the destruction of the Russian village. These two poets often appeared at poetry readings on the same program which usually ended in arguments and fights.

Of all the poets and writers of the 1920s, Mayakovsky was the poet and the personality who best expressed and most closely embodied the spirit of his age and of his time. He was a member or organizer of the most radical and avant-garde literary groups and journals: the cubo-futurists, LEF and *New Lef*. A painter, poet, playwright, editor, and actor, he was a man of extremes who gave himself totally to his two passions: revolutionary art to revolutionize the spirit, and political revolution. He became "the trumpeter of the revolution" and when his dreams failed him, and his personal life failed as well, in the spirit of his age, he destroyed himself.

The cubo-futurists were the group which had the greatest impact on further formal developments in Soviet Russian literature of the 1920s. In their theoretical manifestoes and in their work, their primary concern was with formal aspects of the literary craft, with poetic language and poetic devices, form rather than content. They were attempting to renew poetic language by focusing on the word as such, its sounds and shapes. Representing both poets and painters, they attempted a total integration of the arts, particularly the visual and the written. They entered the artistic arena with a challenge to "public taste" and announced that a revolution in the arts had begun. Indeed, the futurists were the advance guard of the arts. Their poetic experimentation and searchings left a mark on the verbal texture, structure, and form of poetry and prose of the 1920s, and particularly on the development of the short story which replaced poetry as the dominant genre during the mid-1920s, while the Soviet novel had its roots in 19th-century realism.

The early post-revolutionary years, during the NEP era (1921–28), were a liberal period in politics with very limited government interference in the arts. The period was characterized by private enterprise and open political debates and struggles. As long as he was not opposed to or critical of the Revolution, the writer was free to choose his own form, style, and subject matter. He could publish and travel abroad without repercussion and with relative ease.

Competition and ideological differentiation among literary groups was officially supported by Bukharin, TROTSKY, and other Party leaders and was confirmed by a resolution of the Central Committee of the Communist Party of 18 June 1925, which stated that the Party policy on literature rejected any "legalized monopoly ... of any group or literary organization." The numerous and varied literary groups of the NEP period fall roughly into three general categories: (1) the Proletarian Writers, (2) writers affiliated with the futurists, *Lef* and *New Lef* under Mayakovsky's leadership, and (3) FELLOW TRAVELERS, members of the intelligentsia, unaffiliated with the Party or the government who had one way or another accepted the Revolution.

PROLETKULT (1918–24) was the parent organization of the various proletarian groups. Its purpose and ultimate goal was to educate and train writers of proletarian origin who would create a "genuine" proletarian literature. Thus art and literature would be created by and for the new victorious class. To achieve this goal *Proletkult* organized literary studios and workshops. While this effort was an abysmal failure, a number of writers who left *Proletkult* organized several separate groups, each advocating the creation of proletarian culture. The most important ones were the "Smithy" (see KUZNITSA), based in Moscow and "The Cosmist," based in Petrograd. Members of these groups were primarily poets of working class origin who favored the creation of "grand, monumental art," sang of the glories and wonders of steel furnaces, and glorified factories and industry. Members of the *Smithy* included Kazin, GERASIMOV, KIRILLOV, GASTEV, and GLADKOV, whose novel *Cement* has become a "classic of socialist realism."

An important literary group which stands by itself is PEREVAL (Mountain Pass) which branched off from the "Smithy." Led by the literary critic VORONSKY, it stressed humanism and its members focused on the changing nature of reality. *Oktyabr'* (October) was another Moscow-based group which in 1922 broke away from *Pro-*

letkult. It founded the literary journals NA POSTU and OKTYABR'. Although members of this group came from various class origins, most of them were young and militant in their points of view. They supported Party and government policies and advocated Party control in literature. They opposed experimentation and MODERNISM in literature. Their taste tended to be conservative and favored 19th-century realism. Among them were Zharov, UTKIN, SVETLOV, Doronin, Golodny, BEZYMENSKY, FADEEV, and others. Members of this group engaged in violent polemics with Mayakovsky and members of *Lef* and led vicious attacks on individual "fellow travelers."

The largest number of the most varied, creative, original, and talented writers were dubbed "fellow travellers" by Trotsky. Neither of proletarian origin nor members of the Party, they were primarily members of the intelligentsia and represented the best and the finest pre-revolutionary traditions and culture. Among them were such outstanding writers as BABEL, OLESHA, PILNYAK, BULGAKOV, V. KATAEV, ZOSHCHENKO, ILF AND PETROV, Erenburg, LEONOV, PRISHVIN, Aleksei TOLSTOI, and others. The "fellow travelers" also included the "SERAPION BROTHERS." This group published an "antimanifesto" which insisted on the preservation of differences and unique individual voices. E. J. Brown comments that "only in a very limited sense were they brothers, for they had nothing in common with one another except an organic revulsion against the use of literature for nonliterary purposes." This group originally included such varied and brilliant writers and critics as SHKLOVSKY, ZAMYATIN, LUNTS, Nikitin, Vsevolod IVANOV, Slonimsky, KAVERIN, and Boris Pilnyak. However, their ideals were not to be. By organizing VAPP in 1925, which in 1928 became RAPP, the proletarian writers eventually gained virtual control over literature. In 1932 the government officially dissolved all independent literary and artistic groups and organized the UNION OF SOVIET WRITERS, which all writers had to join if they wished to be considered writers, and in 1934, during the First Congress of Soviet Writers, membership in this union as well as adherence to the dogma of socialist realism became compulsory. This officially ended the period of creativity and experimentation in Russian literature and in the arts of Russia.

Another important, however small and short-lived, literary group of the 1920s was OBERIU (the Association for Real Art, 1926–30). In its concern with verbal experimentation, it had much in common with futurism. The works of the *oberiuty* are "absurd" and represent SURREALISM in Russia. Among them were the highly original poet ZABOLOTSKY, the young eccentric poet KHARMS and the poet-playwright, VVEDENSKY.

Thus the NEP era was represented in literature by a tremendous variety of points of view and styles, all of which were allowed to coexist. An overwhelming number of works written during the 1920s deal with the traumatic events of the Revolution and civil war. Short story writers such as Pilnyak, Babel, Zamyatin, Shklovsky and others, in an effort to depict the violence and horror of a world and morality turned upside down, created a style called "ORNAMENTALISM" characterized by the use of highly unusual, unexpected, and elaborate imagery and particularly by the device of estrangement. Other writers, like FURMANOV in his novel *Chapaev*, incorporated diaries, chronicles, and other factual material into their fiction, in an effort to produce the greatest degree of verisimilitude. During the mid-twenties, writers like V. Kataev in *The Embezzlers* began to produce adventure novels, while others like Leonov in *The Thief* wrote psychological novels. Zamyatin and Mayakovsky are the authors of the two major anti-utopias of the 1920s, *We* (1920) and *The Bedbug* (1928) respectively. The major recurring conflict and theme in the works of this period is the clash between the old and the new created by the transition to the new way of life. The best and most representative work dealing with this theme and one of the most interesting works from the structural and thematic point of view is Olesha's *Envy* (1928). The clash between the old and the new in the Russian village and the problems of collectivization are best depicted by Platonov, Vsevolod Ivanov, and Babel. Finally, the 1920s saw the development of satire, the subject of which was often "the new Soviet man"—the former ignorant laborer and proletarian, and now Soviet bureaucrat (Zoshchenko, Ilf and Petrov, and Mayakovsky's plays).

After Bukharin's loss of power, the reversal of the government policy of non-intervention in the arts, and the consolidation of literary groups, most of the works written during the first Five-Year Plan (1928–32) dealt with the themes of industrialization and collectivization. For the purpose of enlisting writers to aid in the government's industrialization program, the Party used RAPP. One of the best examples of the industrial novel is V. Kataev's *Time Forward* (1932). RAPP thus served as a tool in the government effort to control literature by helping with the process of consolidation, which was completed in 1932 when the Union of Soviet Writers was organized and the government ordered the elimination of all other groups. By imposing the dogma of socialist realism as the compulsory artistic method, and forcing all writers into membership in the Union of Soviet Writers, the Soviet government, with the assistance of the political police, took upon itself the control of style, language, and subject matter in literature and the arts and attempted to direct and censor the creative imagination of individuals. Not surprisingly, this effort has largely failed, and the majority of the writers who saluted and toed the line, have been mediocre, talentless bureaucrats, literary hacks rather than artists. During all the years of Stalin's reign, especially after the first writers' Congress in 1934 until Stalin's death in 1953, literature in the Soviet Union was under strict party control and writers had to adhere to the principles of socialist realism in style, selection of thematic material, and point of view.

One of the recurring thematic assignments given writers during the early 1930s was the promotion of industrialization and collectivization. Many of these works lack imagination and style. There are too many love affairs between the country maiden and her tractor. Among the "classics" of socialist realism written during this period are OSTROVSKY's *How the Steel was Tempered* (1934), Gladkov's rewritten version of *Cement*, and KRYMOV's *Tanker Derbent* (1938). During Stalin's purges of 1936 to 1938, when it became dangerous to write about almost anything that did not meet official demand, the printed pages were filled with innocuous poems about Russian nature, for example SHCHIPACHOV's poem "The Sunflower" (1937) describing a sunflower growing happily in its plot of dirt, or works glorifying "socialist labor and industrialization," such as KAZIN's *Belomorsk Poem* (1936–62), celebrating the building of the Baltic-White Sea Canal, or panegyrics to Stalin such as M. Isakovsky's "Song About Stalin" (1936). However, there were exceptions and some good books were written during this period. SHOLOKHOV finished his *Quiet Flows the Don* (1928–40). Several gems of Russian literature were written "for the desk drawer" and published much later. They include Bulgakov's masterpiece *The Master and Margarita*, Platonov's *Chevengur* and *Kotlovan*, Babel's stories about collectivization, "Gapa Guzhva" and "Kolyvushka," Akhmatova's *Requiem*, and parts of Pasternak's *Dr. Zhivago*.

In general, the 1930s were a period of centrally planned economy and of centrally planned literature. These were years of forced industrialization of national resources, forced collectivization of private peasant farms, and terrifying purges. These were tragic years for the Russian land, for the Russian people, and for Russian literature. This period began with Mayakovsky's suicide (April 1930) and ended with Marina Tsvetaeva's suicide in 1941 (after returning to Russia in 1939). It was a period which saw the destruction of an entire generation of the best Russian writers, critics, and artists. Arrested during the Stalinist purges of 1936, 1937, and 1938, they were either shot, or exiled to Siberia where many died of hunger, cold, and disease, or if they returned, did so as broken men. The list makes a very long obituary column and includes: Mandelshtam, Babel, Pilnyak, I. Kataev, Vvedensky, Kharms, Voronsky, Meyerhold, Zabolotsky, and many others.

During the World War II years (1941–1945) and immediately following, the situation improved slightly for the writer. The government needed the writer's help in spreading war propaganda. There was a general upsurge of patriotism and the feelings and interests of the writer coincided with the interest of the government. Artists like Akhmatova, who had not been published for years, had their poems published. TVARDOVSKY's poem *Vasily Tyorkin*, with a down-to-earth view of the war, was published serially, and so were a number of honest war novels. Among the best were PANOVA's *The Train* and Viktor Nekrasov's *In the Trenches of Stalingrad*. For a while, optimism prevailed. However, this was short-lived. On 21 September 1946, ZHDANOV inaugurated a new period of terror and purges in the literary community with an attack on the literary journals *Zvezda* and *Leningrad* for publishing the works of Akhmatova and Zoshchenko. He attacked Akhmatova for her lack of civic spirit, calling her "half-nun" and "half-whore." Zoshchenko was excoriated for writing "shallow and insipid" works. Both Akhmatova and Zoshchenko were expelled from the Union of Soviet Writers and the editors of the journals were removed from their positions. Zhdanov's speech was designed to tighten the levers of party control by enforcing socialist realism in the narrowest sense in order to require writers to devote their efforts to propagandize enthusiasm for post-war reconstruction and rehabilitation. As had happened in the 1930s, a number of so-called "classics of socialist realism" had to be rewritten to suit the current Party policy and ideology. Thus Gladkov's *Cement*, originally written in 1925, and rewritten in 1950. The same fate was accorded Fadeev's *The Young Guard*; originally published in 1945, it was rewritten in 1951. As during the 1930s, panegyrics to Stalin began to dominate the printed page. There was a plethora of officially approved highly propagandistic and ideological reconstruction novels such as Babaevsky's *Hero of the Golden Star* and *Light Over the Earth* (1948–49), both of which were awarded Stalin prizes and later, during "The Thaw," discredited as pure propaganda.

The decade following Stalin's death (1953–63), known as "The THAW," was characterized by reaction and rebellion against the limitations and restrictions of twenty-five years of Stalinism. It was a period of excitement and of moral, intellectual, and artistic ferment. There was an attempt to reintroduce freedom of expression and to restore honesty and sincerity in literature. There was a liberalization in the selection of subject matter, a renewed concern with moral and ethical questions and values, and a renewed interest in experimentation with form, style, perspective, points of view, and particularly with language. Writers attempted to rejuvenate and revise the stilted and ossified literary language by purifying it of clichés, bureaucratic jargon, ideological slogans and worn-out phrases. Writers like Aksyonov introduced slang, vulgarisms, and colloquialisms into the speech of their characters, thus rendering the substandard language of young "city slickers" and students. GREKOVA's characters speak their own mixture of technological and urban jargon, the intensity of which is determined by their level of education. Solzhenitsyn's characters speak a mixture of prison slang, regional peasant dialects, and bookish, Slavonic expressions.

"The Thaw" period witnessed the formation and maturing of new writers and artists. It was also a period of rehabilitation of a large number of writers and representatives of all the arts, who had perished or suffered during the years of Stalinist terror. Their works were republished or exhibited and the young generation of Russians were getting to know their own culture and literature of the 1920s. Such rehabilitated 19th-century classics as DOSTOEVSKY, whose works had hardly been reprinted since the Revolution, were again available. Although "The Thaw" produced a great number of new writers and artists and a great variety of works, it never quite became full summer and never quite matched the level of culture, experimentation, and variety of the 1920s. The arrest of the Leningrad poet I. Brodsky in 1963 and his subsequent trial, conviction, and sentencing to exile and hard labor on charges of "parasitism" signaled the end of "The Thaw" and coincided with the end of the Khrushchev era.

The Brezhnev era began with certain signs of renewed repressions and increased censorship and was symbolized by the 1966 trial and conviction of SINYAVSKY and DANIEL and their sentencing to the maximum term of hard labor for publishing abroad under the pseudonyms Tertz and Arzhak. This was of major significance to Soviet writers and intellectuals and had a number of repercussions. In the first place, it was the first political trial of the post-Stalin era, and the verdict, together with its severe penalty, carried an echo of the Stalinist purges, reminding people that not all of Stalin's camps had been liquidated. It was apparent that other arrests and prosecutions would follow. Secondly, petitions and letters of protest signed by large numbers of young and established writers marked what can be considered the beginning of these writers' dissident activity. Finally it evoked great furor and negative publicity for the Soviet State in the Western press. Because daring, or experimental, or critical works could not be published openly in the Soviet

Union, there was a great increase in the number of works which began to circulate in samizdat. By the end of the 1960s, the number of works published abroad (in tamizdat) with the permission and under the real name of the author also increased. Shortly following this trial, the brutal Soviet invasion and violent suppression of the "Prague Spring" in Czechoslovakia (1968), the destruction of the hopes of Czechoslovak and East European intellectuals, and the trials of GINZBURG, GALANSKOV, and Bukovsky, plus other repressive actions, stimulated the movement of writers into the ranks of dissidents.

Despite increasing censorship and repressions Aksyonov, Grekova, Okudzhava, Bitov, TRIFONOV, Voinovich, Iskander, Aitmatov, Kazakov and others continued to publish significant work. In addition, a number of writers concerned with the countryside and national Russian traditions, the so called "village writers" (derevenshchiki, see COUNTRY PROSE) were publishing and gaining recognition. They include Abramov, RASPUTIN, BELOV, SOLOUKHIN, SHUKSHIN, TENDRYAKOV, and others. Works written during the Stalin years but kept unpublished in the archives continued to appear. Bulgakov's brilliant novel The Master and Margarita came out in the journal Moskva (1966–67), a collection of Platonov's short stories was published, and there was a tamizdat publication of his Kotlovan and Chevengur. Babel's works and those of some others were also published.

Memoirs became an important and rich literary form during the 1960s and 1970s. After the publication of PAUSTOVSKY's The Story of a Life (1945–63) and Erenburg's People, Years, Life (1960–65), they began to appear with increased frequency, gradually spilling out into samizdat and tamizdat. They include Evtushenko's A Precocious Autobiography (1963), Olesha's Not a Day Without a Line, N. MANDELSHTAM's Hope Against Hope (1970) and Hope Abandoned (1974), Solzhenitsyn's The Calf and the Oak (1974), Ivinskaya's The Captive of Time, V. Kataev's cycle of memoirs, CHUKOVSKAYA's reminiscences about Anna Akhmatova, and many others. The 1960s and 1970s also witnessed an unprecedented output of "prison-camp" reminiscences. The most massive and detailed work is Solzhenitsyn's series, Gulag Archipelago (1973–75). Others include SHALAMOV's moving Tales of Kolyma (1966–75), KOPELEV's To Be Kept Forever, Ginzburg's Within the Whirlwind and Chukovskaya's haunting Olga Petrovna (1965, incorrectly published as The Deserted House) and Going Under (1972).

The last "grand event" of the 1970s was the "Metropol affair." A group of writers and painters issued four or five hand-prepared copies of an "almanac," the purpose of which was "to publish their works free of censorship." Edited by Aksyonov, Bitov, EROFEEV, Iskander and Popov, it purposely excluded contributions from dissident writers. It included works of established poets and prose writers alongside young and unknown writers. It contained satirical stories, poems, some material with sexual and homosexual references, and criticism. Popov and Erofeev who had just been accepted into the Union of Soviet Writers, were expelled. Aksyonov, Lisnyanskaya, and LIPKIN, resigned from the Union, and Aksyonov subsequently emigrated to the United States. A smuggled copy of Metropol was published in the United States. Thus ended the bold attempt of a small band of Soviet writers to free themselves from the embrace of their Soviet censor.

From the early 1970s and on into the 1980s repressions increased while greater numbers of writers published their works abroad and signed letters of protest. The usual consequence was expulsion from the Union of Soviet Writers, followed by harassment and eventual forced emigration from Russia. This was the case with Solzhenitsyn, Voinovich, Korzhavin, MAKSIMOV, Aksyonov, VLADIMOV, and others. Thus, the 1970s and early 1980s will probably be remembered in the annals of Soviet Russian literature as the decade of "the Diaspora." Chukovskaya has stated that the greatest tragedy befalling contemporary Russian literature and the Russian writer is the Diaspora. By being dispersed into all corners of the world, they are losing contact with their language, country, people, and especially with each other.

Literature in emigration or in tamizdat offers a tantalizing hint of what Soviet literature would be like and how it might develop if writers were left free to create as they wished. There would be a great diversity of themes and points of view. These tendencies are all represented by Russian writers currently in emigration: Solzhenitsyn represents the 19th-century realistic tradition; Maksimov pursues a search for religious faith; Sinyavsky follows the tradition of the grotesque; Voinovich continues the tradition of Gogol, Zoshchenko and Ilf and Petrov, showing that the great tradition of Russian satire is alive and well. Writers like Sasha SOKOLOV, a truly modern writer, experiment with the concepts of time, dream and reality. Erofeev, in his Moscow—End of the Line, explores the world of a drunken delirium while Oleshkovsky plunges us into the world of sex, violence, and vulgarity.

The Diaspora is a fact. Whether Russian writers in exile will be able to continue to write and be creative, without their mutual support, without their native soil, without the sharp prod of state censorship, and without the creative tension of repression, only time will tell.

Selected bibliography: P. Blake and M. Hayward, eds., "Dissonant Voices in Soviet Literature," Partisan Review, nos. 3–4 (1961). ———, Halfway to the Moon: New Writing from Russia. 1965. D. Brown, Soviet Russian Literature Since Stalin. 1978. E. J. Brown, Russian Literature Since the Revolution. 1982. K. Clark, The Soviet Novel: History as Ritual. 1981. V. Dunham, In Stalin's Time: Middle-Class Values in Soviet Fiction. 1976. M. Friedberg, Russian Classics in Soviet Jackets. 1962. X. Gasiorowska, Women in Soviet Fiction, 1917–1964. 1968. G. Gibian, Interval of Freedom; Soviet Literature During the Thaw, 1954–1957. 1960. G. Gibian and H. W. Tjalsma, eds., Russian Modernism; Culture and the Avant-Garde, 1900–1930. 1976. A. Gladilin, The Making and Unmaking of a Soviet Writer. Ann Arbor, Mich., 1979. M. Hayward and E. L. Crowley, Soviet Literature in the Sixties; An International Symposium. 1964. R. Hingley, Russian Writers and Soviet Society. 1979. J. Holthusen, Russische Literatur im 20. Jahrhundert. Munich, 1978. G. Hosking, Beyond Socialist Realism: Soviet Fiction Since Ivan Denisovich. 1980. P. Johnson, Khrushchev and the Arts; The Politics of Soviet Culture, 1962–1964. 1965. S. Karlinsky and A. Appel, eds., The Bitter Air of Exile: Russian Writers in the West, 1922–1972. 1977. W. Kasack, Lexikon der russischen Literatur ab 1917. Stuttgart, 1976. Kratkaya literaturnaya entsiklopediya. 9 vols. Moscow, 1962–78. R. A. Maguire, Red Virgin Soil: Soviet Literature in the 1920's. 1968. R. W. Mathewson, The Positive Hero in Russian Literature. 2d ed. 1975. H. Muchnic, From Gorky to Pasternak. 1961. K. Pomorska, ed., Fifty Years of Russian Prose: From Pasternak to Solzhenitsyn. 2 vols. 1971. Helen Segall, Majakovskii: A Tri-Dimensional View. Ph.D. diss., Bryn Mawr College, 1973. A. Siniavskii, On Socialist Realism. 1960. M. Slonim, Modern Russian Literature. 1953. ———, Soviet Russian Literature; Writers and Problems, 1917–1977. 1977. G. Svirski, A History of Post-War Soviet Writing: The Literature of Moral Opposition. 1979. H. Swayze, Political Control of Literature in the USSR, 1946–1959. 1962. L. Trotsky, Literature and Revolution. 1957. T. P. Whitney, The New Writing in Russia. 1964.   H. S.

Sovreménnye zapiski (Contemporary Notes), émigré "thick" journal published in Paris, 1920 to 1940. The editorial board of the journal was made up of the former Socialist Revolutionaries M. V. Vishnyak, A. I. Gukovsky (died 1925), V. V. Rudnev, N. D. Avksentev and I. I. Fondaminsky. However, from the very beginning the journal stated its intention to remain outside of Party politics, to speak for the entire emigration, and to attract a broad and diverse group of contributors. From its very first years, virtually every major prerevolutionary writer living in emigration published on its pages, including BALMONT, HIPPIUS (Anton Krainy), KHODASEVICH, TSVETAEVA, BUNIN, MEREZHKOVSKY, REMIZOV, Aleksei TOLSTOI, Leonid ANDREEV (posthumously), and Vyacheslav IVANOV (from 1936). While living in Berlin in the early 1920s, BELY also published in Sovremennye zapiski. In the 1930s, members of the new generation of writers who had begun their careers in the emigration began to contribute to the journal, most notably NABOKOV (V. Sirin). Although originally announced as a monthly publication, Sovremennye zapiski never managed to put out more than six issues per year, and only one issue appeared in 1940 before the fall of France.

Bibliography: Sovremennye zapiski, no. 70 (1940). Ardis reprint. Ann Arbor, 1983.   C. T. N.

Sovremennik, (The Contemporary), founded by PUSHKIN in 1836, was destined to become the most famous and widely read literary journal in 19th-century Russia. After Pushkin's death (1837), it was edited by his friend P. A. PLETNYOV until 1846, when it was purchased by I. I. PANAEV and N. A. NEKRASOV, the latter becoming its new editor. For the next twenty years (until 1866), it was Russia's leading literary journal.

In the first ten years of its existence, *Sovremennik* met with little success, chiefly because of its avowed romantic aestheticism which was out of date and could no longer attract substantial paying readership. Its chief contributors were I. S. TURGENEV and F. I. TYUTCHEV, whose poems appeared in it during the years 1836 to 1838. However, when the first issue of the journal under Nekrasov's editorship appeared in January 1847, it contained poems by Nekrasov and Turgenev, two short stories by the latter, a short novel by DOSTOEVSKY, political writings by HERZEN, and critical articles by BELINSKY. The subsequent popularity of *Sovremennik* as a literary journal was due as much to Nekrasov's literary genius as to his shrewd business sense. He certainly did not lack the latter, and he demonstrated it by securing the collaboration of the best literary critics of the time: Belinsky, CHERNYSHEVSKY, DOBROLYUBOV, and PISAREV.

Under the influence of Belinsky's ideas, Nekrasov turned *Sovremennik* into a periodical of the revolutionary democracy in Russia and, by the same token, the chief organ of the WESTERNIZERS. In the years 1846 to 1858, he published in his journal many outstanding prose works by distinguished writers like L. N. TOLSTOI, I. S. Turgenev, A. N. OSTROVSKY, I. A. GONCHAROV, A. K. TOLSTOI, as well as poems by himself. The controversial articles of the radical critic N. G. Chernyshevsky, published in *The Contemporary*, attracted the attention of the reading public.

However, the addition of Chernyshevsky in 1856 to the editorial staff of *Sovremennik* had far-reaching consequences for the journal. His radical views aroused the hostility of liberals like Turgenev, Tolstoi, ANNENKOV, BOTKIN, and GRIGOROVICH. The friction increased when N. A. Dobrolyubov, another radical critic, joined the staff in 1857. In the ideological battle that ensued, Nekrasov sided with his radical colleagues. The final break between the liberal and the radical writers of *Sovremennik* occurred in early 1858. As a consequence, the journal lost such first-rate contributors as Turgenev, both Tolstois, Goncharov, Grigorovich, Ostrovsky, and others; in their place came relatively unknown writers, among whom were A. N. PYPIN, N. G. POMYALOVSKY, and M. E. SALTYKOV-SHCHEDRIN. They were the ones who, together with Chernyshevsky, Dobrolyubov, Pisarev, and Nekrasov himself, set the political and literary tone of *Sovremennik* in the years 1858 to 1866.

Nekrasov's break with Turgenev and his group forced him to rely for the journal's success on the contributions of the radical writers and on his own poetic production. Fortunately, it was at that time that some of his best poems appeared, including "Reflections at the Grand Entrance" (1858), "On the Volga" (1860), "A Knight for an Hour" (1860), and several others. They were the kind of poems that would be widely read in Russia on the eve of the Emancipation, for they were vivid and moving descriptions of the Russian peasant's misery. In general, the "literature of accusation" (*oblichitel'naya literatura*) was the mainstay of *Sovremennik* during this period of the journal's existence. Nekrasov, a talented poet and a shrewd businessman, believed that this kind of literary fare was what most readers wanted. His belief proved correct. In due course, *Sovremennik* became the journal with the biggest circulation in 19th-century Russia.

However, the journal was also becoming the favorite target of Russian government CENSORSHIP because of its negative attitude toward the Emancipation Act of 1861. Nekrasov, in particular, sensed that little was going to change in the miserable existence of the Russian peasant, who was still at the mercy of the landowners. He continued to call the public's attention to the peasant's plight in a series of poems published in *Sovremennik* in the years 1861 to 1863. Among these were shorter poems like "The Crying of Children" (1861), "Orina, a Soldier's Mother" (1863), and the long narrative poems *The Peddlers* (1861) and *Red-Nose Frost* (1863). All these poems were enthusiastically hailed first by Chernyshevsky and then by Pisarev (who had been added to the journal's staff after Dobrolyubov's death in 1861).

In 1863, Chernyshevsky's political novel, *What is to Be Done?*

(*Chto delat'?*) was published in the journal. This angered the authorities, all the more so since the author was in prison waiting to be sentenced for his attempt to organize a Socialist Revolutionary Party. In 1864, the poem "The Railroad," telling of the misery of peasant laborers employed on railroad construction in Russia, was published in *Sovremennik*; this also drew the ire of the authorities. Consequently, Nekrasov was given a warning by the censor's office. The poems which followed, and were published in his journal (particularly, "Songs about the Free World" and "Ballet"), are proof that the warning went unheeded.

All these poems brought Nekrasov fame, but they made him very unpopular with Alexander II and his ministers, who regarded them as undermining the people's confidence in the ultimate success of the government-inspired program of limited social and political reforms. *Sovremennik* was feeling the brunt of increasingly harsher censorship. Finally, an attempt on Alexander's life by a terrorist in early 1866 provided the Tsar with the pretext to liquidate the radical press. Nekrasov, who had been forewarned of the danger threatening his journal, reportedly made a craven attempt to placate the authorities by composing and reciting a poem in honor of Count Muravyov, the Tsar's most powerful minister at the time. This did not save *Sovremennik*, however. The journal was ultimately suspended in the summer of 1866, after twenty years of publication under Nekrasov's editorship.

Sovremennik was not permitted to resume publication even after Nekrasov's death in 1878. It began to appear again only in 1911, but it was never able to regain its 19th-century status as Russia's most outstanding literary journal. In 1915, *Sovremennik* ceased publication, becoming a part of the history of Russian journalism.

S. S. B.

Sreznévsky, Izmaíl Ivánovich (1812–80); Professor at St. Petersburg University, foremost student of Slavic comparative grammar, historian of the RUSSIAN LANGUAGE, editor of Old Russian texts, paleographer and lexicographer. After a brief stint at political economy and statistics, Sreznevsky undertook a trip to Western Europe and to several Slavic countries where he collected ethnographic material and acquired a taste for the study of Slavic culture and folklore and the comparative study of the Slavic languages. In 1847 he assumed the Chair of Slavic philology at St. Petersburg University and became the leading authority in Slavic historical linguistics. His comparative linguistic approach and ethnographic research found expression in a number of works which deal with the sound systems and classification of the Slavic language (1843; 1845) and with the survivals of Slavic paganism (1846). He greatly advanced the study of Slavic PALEOGRAPHY by editing a number of Russian and Old CHURCH SLAVONIC texts and authored several books on the use of GLAGOLITIC and CYRILLIC among the Eastern Slavs. He was one of the first to recognize the chronological priority of the former over the latter. His editions of Old Church Slavonic and Old Russian manuscripts included such texts as the *Texte du Sacre*, the *Prague Leaflets*, the *Vatican Glagolitic Gospel*, the *Novgorod Chronicles* and the *Zadonshchina*.

At the center of Sreznevsky's interests was the history of the Russian language which he interpreted in the romantic spirit as a reflection of the Russian national character. The crowning of his life-long effort was, however, his *Materials toward a Lexicon of the Old Russian Language* (Materialy dlya slovarya drevnerusskogo yazyka po pis'mennym pamyatnikam, 3 vols. plus Supplement) which appeared between 1893 and 1911 (photocopy edition 1958). The materials for the *Dictionary* were culled from 2700 Old Russian and Church Slavonic sources and present the largest collection of Slavic medieval lexical elements (with quotations of contexts and etymological and grammatical explanations). Sreznevsky's *Dictionary* is only now being superseded by the *Dictionary of the Russian Language: XI–XVII Centuries* which is being published by the Institute of the Russian Language at the Soviet Academy of Sciences (A to M, 1875–1982).

Bibliography: M. G. Bulakhov, *Vostochnoslavyanskie yazykovedy.* Vol. 1. Minsk, 1976. Pp. 219–32. L. A. Bulakhovskii, "I. I. Sreznevskii: 1812–1880," *Russkii yazyk v shkole*, 1940, no. 6, pp. 75–81. I. V. Yagich (Jagić), *Istoriya slavyanskoi filologii*. 1910. Pp. 466–73.

E. S.

Stanislávsky, Konstantin Sergéevich (1863–1938), founder with NEMIROVICH-DANCHENKO of the Moscow Art Theater, actor, director, originator and teacher of the "Method" for actors. Stanislavsky showed an early love of the theater, in which he was supported by his wealthy parents. He performed leading roles, first as an amateur, then in his own professional company, for which he insisted on a genuineness beyond that of the Meiningen players. Thus, in preparation for *Othello* (1896) he went to Venice both to observe people and the scene there, and to acquire objects and fabrics to be used on stage. He sought realistic authenticity also in the first production (Aleksei TOLSTOI's *Tsar Fyodor Ioannovich*) of the theater he founded in 1898 with Nemirovich-Danchenko to be a people's theater after principles of OSTROVSKY.

The theater had its first success with CHEKHOV's *Sea Gull*, bringing at the same time the playwright his first success by their scrupulous presentation of a then new type of play. The Moscow Art Theater then staged the canon of Chekhov's work, as well as GORKY's early plays, with Stanislavsky both directing and acting. Stanislavsky worked out the "psychological realism" responsible for the theater's greatness. It was a system by which the actor, instead of declaiming lines, sought the inner reality of the experience he must convey—often without words. Stanislavsky did not, however, complete the formulation of his "Method," only one volume of which, *An Actor Prepares* (Rabota aktera nad soboi) had been published when he died.

Stanislavsky founded several studios with gifted disciples, two of whom, MEYERHOLD and Vakhtangov, continued as actors and directors in their own right. In the years 1922 to 1924 the Art Theater toured Europe and the United States. Only after the mid-1920s did it add Soviet plays to its repertory, thus Mikhail BULGAKOV's *The Days of the Turbins* (1926) and Vsevolod IVANOV's *Armored Train 14–69* (1927). Stanislavsky also taught acting to opera singers after 1922, and in 1935 founded his Opera and Dramatic Studio, to which he appointed Meyerhold as director after the closure of the Meyerhold Theater (1938). Actors and directors from abroad studied with Stanislavsky; thus Lee Strasberg's influential Actors' Studio in New York is "Method"-based.

Works: Sobranie sochinenii. 8 vols. 1954–61.
Translations: My Life in Art. 1924. *An Actor Prepares*. Trans. Elizabeth Reynolds Hapgood. 1936. *Building a Character*. Trans. Elizabeth Reynolds Hapgood. 1949.   M. H.

Stankévich, Nikolai Vladimirovich (1813–40). A poet and a philosopher, Stankevich was the leading figure in the circle which bore his name, one which played a major role in the development of ideas in Russia in the mid-19th century. Stankevich was the son of a well-to-do landowner of the Voronezh region, and spent his childhood on his father's country estate. In 1830 he enrolled in the literature faculty of Moscow University, where he became the center of a distinguished group of young men, most of them also students, who were later active in philosophy, literature, publishing, or politics. Stankevich suffered from tuberculosis, and on the advice of his doctors he travelled to Berlin in 1837, where he studied with the Hegelian philosopher, Karl Werder. He died in Italy in 1840.

It has been said that the Moscow Stankevich circle represented a kind of infancy of the Russian intelligentsia. In its discussions nearly all the problems that were to concern the Russian intellectual world during the 19th century were raised, but those problems were still in embryonic form, and lines of thought, each of which later developed a distinct character, were as yet undifferentiated. Among those associated with the circle early in their careers were the Westernizers BELINSKY and TURGENEV, the future Slavophile K. S. AKSAKOV, Ivan KLYUSHNIKOV and Vasily Krasov, both distinguished minor poets, the philosopher of anarchism, Mikhail BAKUNIN, M. N. KATKOV, later famous as a conservative literary theorist and publisher, and the liberal professor of history, Timofei GRANOVSKY.

Stankevich's own literary production was slight and has not been highly regarded. His lyrics, which appeared in a number of contemporary journals—*Babochka*, LITERATURNAYA GAZETA, TELESKOP, and *Molva*—express a kind of perplexity of spirit between the alternatives of chaste isolation within the self and involvement in "the world" and the concerns of other men. Their dominant theme is the duality of human nature and experience: there are "two paths" for man, the path of joy and the path of sorrow, but only the latter leads to heaven; "Two Ways of Life" is the title of a love poem that expresses the perplexing alternatives offered by the creature he kisses and the one to whom he addresses a fervent prayer. There are also poems reflecting on the renunciation of the material world and "overstepping the earthly bounds, becoming part of the universal life, which, filling you, is filled with you through love." The poems have their share of romantic clichés, but they are in the main philosophical poems, and they express concepts rather than feelings. Stankevich's verse tragedy *Vasily Shuisky*, published in 1830 when he was seventeen, is a romantic treatment of a real historical event of the TIME OF TROUBLES. A short story, *"Some moments from the life of Count Z."* (Neskol'ko mgnovenii iz zhizni Grafa Z.) tells of a young man moved by a holy urge to seek truth who travels to Moscow in order to find comrades who will help him in his search. Weak though it is both in plot and style the story does provide a vivid statement as to the meaning of the "circle" in the intellectual and spiritual life of its members.

Stankevich's correspondence is an important source on the operation and the function of "circles" in 19th-century Russia, and it is one of the prime documents in the study of Russian intellectual history. Stankevich's letters to his close friend Neverov, to Belinsky, Bakunin, Granovsky and others contain a continuing, spontaneous and lucid discussion of the philosophical issues that concerned the leading minds of the period. It is possible to trace in them the early absorption of the group with Schelling's romantic *Naturphilosophie*, their reading and discussion of Kant and Fichte as well as Schiller and Goethe, and their movement during the forties in the direction of Hegel. The correspondence also contains direct and uninhibited commentary on literary figures of the day, including PUSHKIN and GOGOL. Belinsky and other members of the circle spoke in the highest terms of Stankevich's intellectual and moral transcendence in their discussions, and of the debt they owed him.

Works: "Neskol'ko mgnovenii iz zhizni Grafa Z.", *Teleskop*, no. 21 (1834). *Stikhotvoreniya, Tragediya, Proza*. Ed. A. Stankevich. 1890. *Perepiska Nikolaya Vladimirovicha Stankevicha, 1830–1840*. Ed. A. Stankevich. 1914. *Poety kruzhka Stankevicha*. Ed. S. I. Mashinskii. 1964. *Izbrannoe*. 1982.
Secondary literature: E. J. Brown, *Stankevich and His Moscow Circle*. 1966. S. I. Mashinskii, "Stankevich i ego kruzhok," *VLit*, 1964, no. 5. For background, see: N. G. Chernyshevskii, *Ocherki gogolevskogo perioda russkoi literatury*. 1855. 1856.   E. J. B.

Stasyulévich, Mikhail Matvéevich (1826–1911), historian, journalist, civic activist. Graduated from Petersburg University in philosophy; in 1851 received the doctorate. From 1852 to 1861 he taught at the university. In the 1850s and 1860s he authored various historical studies: *History of the Middle Ages* (Istoriya srednikh vekov), among others. His public lectures were as popular as his courses. In 1861, because of government reaction to student unrest, he resigned together with his well-known liberal colleagues, K. D. Kavelin, B. D. Spasovich, B. I. Utkin, and A. N. PYPIN. The activity that earned him the greatest renown was his leadership of *Vestnik Evropy* (1866–1908), Russia's only liberal journal for many years. Stasyulevich chose a centrist position against the right (KATKOV's RUSSKII VESTNIK), as well as against the left, SOVREMENNIK and RUSSKOE SLOVO. From 1881–82 he was the editor of a political-literary newspaper *Poryadok* of similar moderate orientation. Throughout the 1870s he wrote many articles against government policies (for example, the Tolstoian reactionary reforms in education). The goals he advocated were a constitutional monarchy, enlightenment of the masses, representation, and freedom of the press. After 17 October 1905, Stasyulevich and his staff formed the Party of Democratic Reforms. Their views entailed the rejection of all violence and sudden social upheaval, and advocated a gradual evolution of reforms and economic, social and political guarantees. In 1909 he handed over the editorship to K. K. Arseniev. As a civic activist he participated in the social governance of Petersburg, especially in matters concerning elementary and secondary education. To commemorate his dedication to the improvement of Petersburg, he was named honorary citizen of the city. From 1874 to 1879 Stasyulevich edited

Russkaya biblioteka (Russian Library) that included works of Pushkin, Lermontov, Turgenev, Nekrasov and L. Tolstoi. He was also the author of literary reminiscences.

Works: Istoriya srednikh vekov v ee pisatelyakh i issledovaniyakh noveishikh uchenykh. 3 vols. 1863–65. *Opyt istoricheskogo obzora glavnykh sistem filosofii i istorii.* In *Vestnik Evropy,* 1866–1906. *M. M. Stasyulevich i ego sovremenniki v ikh perepiske.* 5 vols. 1911–13.

Secondary literature: K. K. Arsen'ev, "M. M. Stasyulevich" (obituary), *Vestnik Evropy,* no. 2 (February 1911). M. N. Gekker, "M. M. Stasyulevich i staryi russkii liberalizm" (obituary), *Sovremennik,* no. 4 (1911). A. F. Koni, "Vestnik Evropy." In his *Sobranie sochinenii,* Vol. 7 (1966).　　　　　E. K. K.

Stefan of Perm, St., see EPIPHANIUS THE WISE.

Steiger (Shteiger), Anatóly Sergéevich (1907–44), émigré poet. Baron Steiger, a Swiss citizen, was born on his father's estate near Kiev. After the Bolshevik coup d'état of 1917 he went to Constantinople, where he lived in the Mennonite orphanage for Russian children. Via Prague the Steiger family arrived in Paris, where Anatoly became close friends with Georgy ADAMOVICH, Boris POPLAVSKY and Georgy IVANOV. During World War II, while gravely ill, he worked as a journalist and conducted an open campaign against German propaganda for which he was denounced in the Nazi press. Steiger died of tuberculosis in a Swiss sanatorium on 24 October 1944.

Steiger's poetry represents the essence of the "PARIZHSKAYA NOTA." His verse is quiet, restrained, precise, and sincere, but he has his own intonation, style, and manner of lyrical expression. In his "diary-like" verse he treats "the most important," uses aphoristic sentences, and conveys his feelings in concise, compressed, often unfinished lines. Digressions, the interplay of light and shadow, a lack of melodiousness and color are also among the formal characteristics of his poetry, which is devoid of artificial poses, abstract thought, and undue familiarity. The basic leitmotif of Steiger's poetry is the *persona*'s sense of isolation and alienation from human society, nature, and God. Yet the intrusion of irony saves his verse from tones of pathos, shrillness, and affectation. Elements suggesting the passing of time and a prevalent mood of elegiac sadness combine in Steiger's poetry with a search for love and ultimate truth beyond the apparently incomprehensible and insipid surface of reality.

Bibliography. Collections of verse: *Etot den'.* 1928. *Eta zhizn'.* 1931. *Neblagodarnost'.* 1936. *Dvazhdy dva chetyre: stikhi 1926–1939.* 1950. Reprint 1982. His correspondence with Marina Tsvetaeva was published in *Opyty,* no. 8 (1957). He also contributed to *Sovremennye zapiski, Chisla, Russkie zapiski, Novyi korabl', Muza diaspory, Krug,* and *Vstrechi.*

Translations: Two poems, in *Modern Russian Poetry.* Ed. Vladimir Markov and Merrill Sparks. 1967. Pp. 466–67. Ten poems, in *TriQuarterly,* no. 28 (1973), pp. 428–30.

Secondary literature: Temira Pachmuss, *A Russian Cultural Revival: A Critical Anthology of Emigré Literature before 1939.* 1981. Pp. 360–63.　　　　　T. A. P.

Stender-Petersen, Adolf (1893–1963), Danish Slavist. Born in St. Petersburg, Stender-Petersen was first educated at the University of St. Petersburg (1912–15). He left Russia in 1916 and got his degree in Slavic philology at the University of Copenhagen. After some years as lecturer at the University of Gothenburg Stender-Petersen in 1927 got a chair in Slavic philology at the University of Tartu. From 1931 he was attached to the University of Arhus, where he became professor in 1941 and eventually Rector of the university. An excellent organizer, Stender-Petersen in 1952 assembled the Scandinavian Slavists to their first meeting in Arhus, where he was instrumental in forming the Association of Scandinavian Slavists and Baltologists and became the first editor of its periodical publication *Scando-Slavica.* As for breadth of knowledge, Stender-Petersen is generally recognized as the foremost Scandinavian Slavist. The author of some 150 works, he left important studies not only in literary history, but also in the fields of linguistics (loanwords) and history (Russo-Scandinavian relations). However, he was first and foremost a brilliant teacher of the Slavic literatures, especially those of Russia and Poland. A major contribution is his *History of Russian Litera-*

ture. Published in Danish in 1952, this three-volume work later appeared as *Geschichte der russischen Literatur I–II* (Munich, 1957) and is still regarded as one of the best surveys of Russian literature from its beginnings to the Revolution. Cutting down biography to a minimum and using the methods of the Russian FORMALISTS Stender-Petersen offers profound analyses of language and style, not forgetting the historical background. For a bibliography of his published writings, see *Scando-Slavica,* 10 (1964).　　　　　G. K.

Stepennáya kniga (The Book of Generations or The Book of Degrees). Actually, *Kniga stepennaya tsarskogo rodosloviya,* "Generational Book of Imperial Lineage," is only the beginning of a flowery title of nearly half a page in length. Composed between 1561 and 1563 at the initiative of Metropolitan Macarius (MAKARY) by his eventual successor as Metropolitan Athanasius (Afanasy), Archpriest Andrei, confessor to IVAN IV, it may have been patterned after a similar work by the Serbian Archbishop Danilo, the 14th-century *Carostavnik* or *Rodoslov.* It certainly made use of the earlier SKAZANIE O KNYAZ'YAKH VLADIMIRSKIKH. *The Book of Generations* is a fabricated history of Russia serving the purpose of demonstrating the legitimacy of the Moscow Tsar's claim to leadership of all Orthodox Christendom. This claim is substantiated by the assertion of the descent of Ryurik, founder of the Russian dynasty, from a legendary brother of Caesar Augustus, named Prus. The emphasis throughout is on the Christian virtues of the Russian rulers and on the inseparable union of Church and sovereign. *The Book of Generations* is composed in the ornate, precious, and prolix style characteristic of Muscovite rhetoric in the age of Metropolitan Macarius.

Text: Polnoe sobranie russkikh letopisei. Vol. 21, pts. 1 and 2. 1908–13. (Excerpts:) A. D. Stokes, *Khrestomatiya po drevnei russkoi literature.* 1963. Pp. 194–96.

Secondary literature: P. G. Vasenko, '*Kniga stepennaya tsarskogo rodosloviya' i ee znachenie v drevnerusskoi istoricheskoi pis'mennosti.* Pt. 1. 1904.　　　　　V. T.

Stoglav ("Book of a Hundred Chapters"), a code of regulations and opinions, formulated by the Church Council of 1551, gathered in Moscow at the initiative of IVAN IV and Metropolitan MAKARY. The Tsar figures prominently in this important document: it contains the text of his introductory address to the Council, as well as a series of questions which he addressed to the gathered churchmen, with their replies. The *Stoglav* contains many valuable details of religious as well as secular life in 16th-century Russia. Its fulminations against heresies, abuses, and superstitions are an interesting source of information about all of these.

Text: "Makarievskii stoglavnik." In *Trudy Novgorodskoi gubernskoi uchenoi arkhivnoi komissii,* fasc. 1. Novgorod, 1912.

Secondary literature: D. Stefanovich, *O Stoglave: Ego proiskhozhdenie, redaktsii i sostav.* 1909. Wayne Ford Barnette, "Stepennaja kniga: Sources, Their Adaption and Development," *Dissertation Abstracts International* 40 (1979): 2095A.　　　　　V. T.

Strákhov, Nikolaí Nikoláevich (1828–96), critic, essayist, and philosopher. The son of a priest, Strakhov attended a seminary and then St. Petersburg University, graduating with a degree in the natural sciences in 1851. He acquired a Master's degree with a thesis in zoology in 1857. After some years as a schoolteacher, Strakhov joined the staff of the DOSTOEVSKY brothers' journal VREMYA in 1861. It was his ill-conceived article, "A Fateful Question," concerning the Polish insurrection, which caused the suspension of *Vremya* by the government. After the demise of EPOKHA, which had succeeded *Vremya* in 1864, Strakhov worked for several other journals and in 1873 joined the staff of the St. Petersburg Public Library. Later he was also a member of the committee of Foreign Censorship. Strakhov's role in Russian literature is linked to his association with two of its giants. A Hegelian, who held an "organic" view of history, he played a major role in the formulation of the POCHVA ("the soil") ideology advocated by *Vremya* and *Epokha.* It seems likely that Dostoevsky, who lacked an academic background, acquired some of his philosophical ideas from Strakhov. Later, Strakhov edited a collection of articles by his fellow-*pochvennik*

Apollon GRIGORIEV (1876) and brought out the first posthumous miscellany of biographic materials on Dostoevsky (1883). He also wrote a major and very sympathetic review of *Crime and Punishment* (in OTECHESTVENNYE ZAPISKI, 1867) and generally advertised Dostoevsky's talent when few others did. After Strakhov had produced a cycle of thoughtful and perceptive essays on *War and Peace*, gathered in a book, *A Critical Analysis of 'War and Peace'* (Kriticheskii razbor 'Voiny i mira', 1871), he and TOLSTOI became friends. Their correspondence is of considerable importance for the study of Tolstoi. Also, Tolstoi entrusted Strakhov with proofreading his works, notably *Anna Karenina*. While Strakhov was a great admirer of Tolstoi's art, the two had their disagreements, especially when Tolstoi turned "nihilist" in the late 1870s.

Works: Bor'ba s zapadom v nashei literature. 3d ed. 3 vols. 1897–98. *Kriticheskie stat'i ob I. Turgeneve i L. Tolstom (1862–1885).* 1885. *Vospominaniya i otryvki.* 1892. *Zametki o Pushkine i drugikh poetakh.* 2d ed. 1892. *Filosofskie ocherki.* 1895. *Iz istorii literaturnogo nigilizma (1861–65).* 1890. *Kriticheskie stat'i (1861–1894).* 1902.

Bibliography: B. F. Egorov, "Bibliografiya pechatnykh trudov N. N. Strakhova." In *Uchenye zapiski Tartuskogo universiteta,* 1966, fasc. 184.

Secondary literature: A. S. Dolinin, "Dostoevskii i Strakhov." In his *Poslednie romany Dostoevskogo.* 1963. Pp. 307–43. Linda Gerstein, *Nikolai Strakhov.* Cambridge, Mass., 1971. U. A. Gural'nik, "N. N. Strakhov—literaturnyi kritik," *VLit* 16 (1972), no. 7, pp. 137–64.   V. T.

Structuralism and semiotics. In the Soviet Union, and within the Russian scholarly tradition more broadly, there is an intimate, inextricable relationship between *structuralism*, a holistic approach within the humanities and social sciences which emphasizes the systemic interconnectedness of the object studied, and *semiotics*, the study of signs and sign systems, and of their functioning in society.

Although their roots go back to the Stoics and to medieval speculation on language and logic, the two principal traditions of semiotics stem in modern times from the work on logic of the American philosopher Charles Sanders Peirce and the linguistic theories of Ferdinand de Saussure. In Russia, Saussure's ideas have proved dominant. The Geneva linguist's fundamental theoretical notions: of *langue* (system of rules of a language) vs. *parole* (actual realization in verbal practice); of synchronic (cross-section in time) vs. diachronic (evolutionary) description; of the verbal sign, made up of a signifier and a signified; of language as a system of signs, one of a number of such semiotic systems found in human society, provided the core concepts which allowed for an extension of these notions to neighboring fields of study.

Saussurean linguistics, which pointed the way to a more general science of signs at the beginning of this century, still plays a role in contemporary discussions. However, the role of linguistics for structuralism and semiotics does not stop here. Over the years, developments in linguistic science, whether binary oppositions in phonology or deep structure in syntax, have decisively shaped other areas of structuralist endeavor. Today, in applying semiotic methods in a number of disciplines, Russian researchers use methodologies advanced by different linguistic schools.

In Russia, Saussure's theory fell on fertile ground during the First World War, among the association of literary critics, linguists and poets who gathered within the OPOYAZ ("Society for the Study of Poetic Language," Petersburg) and the MLK ("Moscow Linguistic Circle"). Native scholarly tradition helped pave the way: the Kazan school of linguistics (J. Baudouin de Courtenay, M. Kruszewski); the Moscow school (F. FORTUNATOV and his students); and studies in stylistics (A. POTEBNYA). And they fit in with a wider intellectual climate in Europe which furthered the search for a new methodology for the humanities (Dilthey, Husserl, etc.)—one which recognized both the independent existence of phenomena in the humanities and the need for studying them through an autonomous methodology which did not rely on extraliterary factors for explanation. The scholars who embraced and developed Saussure's ideas (V. SHKLOVSKY, B. EIKHENBAUM, L. Yakubinsky, etc.) did not create a rigidly defined analytic approach. But despite the diversity of their interests, they were united, especially initially, in viewing the literary work as a verbal product and the material of verbal art as shaped by devices, expressive signs used to de-familiarize perception.

The mid-1920s moved the Russian scholars, now dubbed the FORMAL SCHOOL, to a new phase, associated particularly with the figure of Yu. TYNYANOV. In his work a new object of study appears: structure, understood as a dynamic assemblage of mutually interrelated elements. In Tynyanov's and Roman JAKOBSON's writings the notion of structure is joined by the related idea of function, understood and applied in several different ways. Another path out of early formalism was taken by V. PROPP in his pioneering 1928 monograph *Morphology of the Folk-Tale*, which described the magical folk-tale genre in terms of a higher-level invariant from which individual narratives may be generated in accordance with specific combinatorial rules.

The transition to structuralism in the Soviet Union overlapped with—and mutually reinforced—ideas being developed within the Prague Linguistic Circle, the principal center of semiotic and structuralist thought before World War II. Between 1926 and 1948, a constellation of scholars, mostly Czech and Russian (V. Mathesius, R. Jakobson, N. S. TRUBETZKOI, B. Havránek, J. Mukařovský, etc.) but also including participants from other countries, moved from a functionalist theory of language, the linchpin of which was the notion of the goal-directedness of a system, to a formulation of a semiotic conception of the literary work, with the concomitant consideration of the relationship of literary history to other aspects of human culture, and, ultimately, to questions of aesthetics within a broadly envisioned semiotics of art. The conflation of Czech traditions in aesthetics with the achievements of Russian formalism and Saussurean linguistics created a major, distinctive scholarly episode whose rich heritage continues to fuel current semiotic speculation and research.

The work of the Prague school was partially interrupted by World War II and was subsequently brought to a close by the general silencing of non-Marxist humanistic scholarship in post-1948 Czechoslovakia. The next phase of structuralism came in the United States. Expounded by Jakobson, the ideas of the Prague school found a sympathetic ear among some linguists, and among scholars from other fields, most notably C. Lévi-Strauss, whose development of structural anthropology, and, more specifically, of structural study of mythology, dates to this period. During the 1960s, through the medium of Lévi-Strauss' writings, as well as those of Jakobson and others, structuralism spread on the Continent.

Structuralist ideas reappeared in the Soviet Union at the beginning of the 1950s, initially in linguistics (in the phonological studies of S. Shaumyan). In the late 1950s, largely under the impetus of work in adjacent disciplines (cybernetics, information theory, automatic language processing), structural methods made further inroads in Soviet linguistics, where a group of scholars (Vyacheslav Ivanov, V. TOPOROV, A. Reformatsky, V. Zvegintsev, I. Revzin, I. Melchuk, etc.) led the way in the effort to relearn the old lessons of Saussure and assimilate newer developments in phonology, descriptive linguistics, logic, and transformational-generative syntax. A 1957 conference on synchrony and diachrony in linguistics proved a watershed in this regard.

Outside of linguistics in the narrow sense, the structuralist revival came about first in the ideologically neutral area of versification, where the linguistic-statistical method originally developed by B. TOMASHEVSKY, and extended by Trubetzkoi, Jakobson, and K. Taranovsky, was now pursued with great enthusiasm by mathematicians (A. Kolmogorov, A. Kondratov, A. Prokhorov, etc.) and literary scholars (M. Gasparov). From there, structuralist theory and analyses spread into other areas of research (literature, folklore, mythology, etc.), most notably in the writings of scholars associated with the Moscow-Tartu school of semiotics (Yu. LOTMAN, Ivanov, Toporov, D. Segal, T. Tsivyan, Yu. Levin, B. Gasparov, etc.). The tentative steps which heralded the rise of structural-semiotic research culminated in December 1962, with a Moscow symposium devoted to the structural study of sign systems, which was sponsored, in part, by the Sector of Structural Typology of Slavic Languages of the Soviet Academy of Science's Institute of Slavic and Balkan Studies, and the Linguistic Section of the Scientific Council on Cybernetics.

That the Sector of Structural Typology helped co-sponsor the 1962 symposium is indicative of its role in Soviet structural-semiotic investigations. Since 1964, the Department of History of Russian Literature at the University of Tartu in Estonia has been another major locus of structuralism and semiotics. Under the leadership of Yu. Lotman, Tartu has gained an international prominence, for a time overshadowing the contributions of the Moscow contingent.

Of major importance in the development of Soviet semiotics have been the several series of research papers published as part of the Tartu University's *Transactions*, especially the *Works on Semiotics* (Trudy po znakovym sistemam) and *Works on Russian and Slavic Philology* (Trudy po russkoi i slavyanskoi filologii).

Many of the articles in the semiotics volumes were first delivered as papers at a notable Tartu-sponsored institution, the so-called summer schools on semiotics in Kääriku. During the 1960s, these sessions, which attracted broad participation from Moscow, Leningrad and Tartu, became the matrix which helped give Soviet structuralism its cohesiveness and specificity. During the seventies, All-Union semiotic symposia in Moscow continued the Kääriku tradition.

Tartu, an institution of higher learning, took on a special role in Soviet semiotics. Lotman and his colleagues (Z. Mints, B. Egorov, etc.) trained a number of young researchers, some of whom have made their mark in scholarship, and created a climate in which semiotic-structural concepts shaped the intellectual perspective of many young people.

The "heroic period" of Soviet semiotics lasted until the mid-seventies, when two external developments affected the Moscow-Tartu group. One was the increasing pressure on the Soviet intelligentsia as a whole. Semiotics, born in the more liberal, relatively optimistic era of Khrushchevian reforms, found itself increasingly hampered, although the terms of discussion in semiotic-structural research had become firmly established. A second, related factor was emigration, which became substantial in the mid-1970s. Well-known scholars (A. Pyatigorsky, B. Ogibenin, D. Segal, E. Semeka, A. Zholkovsky, Yu. Shcheglov, B. Gasparov, and A. Syrkin), as well as more than a few younger researchers (e.g., L. Fleishman, I. Paperno), found themselves teaching and writing in the West.

Contemporary structural-semiotic research in the Soviet Union relies on some of the concepts and approaches developed at earlier stages in the growth of the structuralist methodology. Thus, in the work of Tynyanov and the Prague school, there was the crystallization of the notion of a *dynamic, historically-conditioned structure or system*—a concept which can be applied in the study of a single work of art or literature, of a literary movement, or of literature as a whole. The emphasis on the *function* of various elements within a given structure, and on the semiotic nature of art, anticipated modern emphasis on the study of the semantic aspect of semiotic objects. Similarly, the early morphological approach of Propp, prefigured the modern concern with the problem of *invariant and transformation*, while his subsequent study of semantic origins of elements of the folk-tale genre, prepared the ground for the strong Russian response to Lévi-Strauss' study of mythological semantics.

The richly multidisciplinary orientation of Russian formalism and the Prague school finds its continuation and broadening within the Moscow-Tartu school. Soviet structural-semiotic inquiries encompass a wide spectrum of concerns, and have made four major areas particularly their own: poetics and theory of literature; myth, folklore, and religion; non-verbal arts (painting, music, film, etc.); and culture.

Since 1964, a key term in Soviet discussions has been *secondary modelling system*, that is, a sign system superimposed upon and dependent on natural language. In the case of literature, myth, folklore, ideology, film and theater, natural language clearly plays a major role, making particularly viable the application of linguistic methodology and data in their study. In the case of essentially non-verbal sign systems, the "linguistic" approach has been somewhat looser, but the essential metaphor has held: Soviet semioticians have been concerned with establishing their specific *language* (languages), that is, determining the set of devices used systematically to generate and transmit meaning.

Basic concepts employed in structural linguistics have been used in the study of sign systems: *text* (seen as an elementary entity bearing a social function—the term "text" can be applied to different classes of objects); the *paradigmatic vs. syntagmatic plane; level* (linguistic and above, in accordance with the functioning of a given secondary system); *hierarchy* (of levels within a text, of semiotic systems within a culture); *opposition* (typically binary, as in phonology); and *distinctive feature*. One linguistic concept which has proved particularly important in Soviet structural-semiotic research is that of *structural typology*, which has been applied in a variety of comparative studies.

Information theory, cybernetics, and neurolinguistics also have provided needed hypotheses and terminology. From a semiotic perspective, man may be viewed as a mechanism that interacts with its surroundings, processing information internally and exchanging it with other members of his society. This transmission and receipt of information may be treated in terms of *codes* (sign systems) and *messages* (texts), and such information-theory terms as *channel, noise*, etc. yield significant insights into semiotic processes in society, especially as they are shaped by the twin axes of time and space.

Another operative concept is that of *culture*, which is regarded as a plurality of mutually interacting and mutually supported sign systems (codes). Within any given culture, as in natural language, a hierarchy of codes exists. At the deepest level, conscious and unconscious, of a member of a culture, an internalized "model of the world" is posited: built up from the interaction of the various semiotic systems, it depicts the universe (from macro to microlevels) and helps guide man's behaviour within it.

The systems of myth, folklore, literature and culture have attracted the most attention from the Moscow-Tartu semioticians, who have emphasized their empirical interrelationship, drawing far-reaching analogies and bringing results from one discipline to another. This pluralism results in part from the broad scholarly and intellectual interests of the researchers. More important, however, is the increasing realization, already found in the work of the Prague school, that the opposition between synchrony and diachrony, however fruitful at an early stage of analysis, is not adequate for dealing with dynamically developing sign systems. Whether it is natural language or culture as a whole, a sign system usually will not be homogeneous: it will contain strata from earlier periods of history, which must be analyzed in terms adequate to their archaic character.

Interest in myth and folklore on the one hand, and problems of etymology on the other, prompt an emphasis in Soviet semiotics on *reconstruction*, that is, reconstitution of texts and sign systems through special operations. Combining the typological method with the historical, this approach has been the hallmark of work in mythology, folklore, and religion. By using a vast array of linguistic and ethnographic data, its two leading practitioners, Ivanov and Toporov, have re-created, to name a few, the ancient East Slavic mythological system, a key Indo-European mythologem involving the thunder-god fighting a dragon, an apparently universal archaic symbol (the Cosmic Tree), and certain semantic universals (expressed in terms of binary opposition such as left-right, up-down, etc.) that ultimately underlie mythological-religious models of the world. The theory relied on by Ivanov and Toporov in their mythological studies has broader application. The procedure of reconstruction may be regarded as an algorithm into whose terms, at least in the abstract, most of the problems faced by students of various domains of semiotics may be translated. This applies, in particular, to the tasks facing the reader or the critic of a work of literature.

Major work on mythology has been carried out by E. Meletinsky, who has devoted numerous studies to the narratives of the North-Eastern Paleo-Asian peoples (the Chukchee, the Koryaks, and the Itelmen), as well as to classical myths. He has also published a separate monograph on the poetics of myth.

Soviet scholars have done a great deal of innovative work in the area of folklore. Three contributions have been particularly noteworthy. One is the work done by Meletinsky and his colleagues on the structure of the fairy tale. Combining the results of Propp's classic syntagmatic analysis with Lévi-Strauss' paradigmatic approach to myth, they have achieved a more abstract, semantically oriented version of the Proppian model. Another is that of G. Permyakov in the area of paremies (folklore cliches such as proverbs, sayings, etc.), at the interface of folkloristics and linguistics. Working on a large corpus of texts from different cultures, he has constructed an exhaustive three-level classificatory system (involving the linguistic, logico-semiotic, and artistic planes) and has clarified the place of paremies within the vocabulary system of language. The third is G. Levinton's semiotic analysis of the Russian wedding ritual.

The Moscow-Tartu structuralists have been particularly productive in the area of literature, both in the area of theory and its application to specific problems. Lotman gave a broad account of structuralism in literary studies in three early monographs; a structuralist-semiotic perspective also deeply informs his work on space in GOGOL's prose, on the prose of PUSHKIN, and on "Evgeny Onegin." B. Uspensky, blending methodology from linguistics, literary studies and the visual arts, discussed the problem of "point of view" in the artistic text. A. Chudakov devoted a book to the poetics of CHEKHOV's prose, analyzing rigorously various levels of this complex artistic phenomenon. An innovative theoretical model of literary evolution has been proposed by I. Smirnov. Toporov has analyzed the archaic, mythological element in DOSTOEVSKY's *Crime and Punishment*, in a monograph which initiates a series of studies on the complex of works he regards as a single "Petersburg text" in Russian literature. B. Gasparov has published a major study of Mikhail BULGAKOV's *Master and Margarita*.

Separate mention must be made of the theoretical work by Zholkovsky and Shcheglov, creators of a theory of "generative poetics," more recently termed "poetics of expressiveness." This analytical model, elaborated over the course of two decades and illustrated on a large number of diverse literary texts, originates in certain ideas expressed by Shklovsky, Propp, and the film director Sergei EISENSTEIN, and is based more immediately on the "meaning—text" linguistic theory of Melchuk. It attempts to construct a theory of how the various levels of the literary text are derived from its meaning. Rigorous, highly formalized, Zholkovsky's and Shcheglov's ideas fly in the face of basic tendencies of Soviet semiotics, which relies on a small number of heuristically applied concepts, and, unlike research conducted in Western Europe eschews theory-building and formalization. A subject of controversy in Soviet semiotic circles, the "poetics of expressiveness" found few followers in the Soviet Union, but has been received rather favorably by Western scholars, and continues to be developed by its authors.

Study of poetry, both of general problems of verse structure, and of the work of individual poets and movements, has occupied a special place in Soviet structuralism. Here, the connection between linguistics, versification and general poetics, traditional in Slavic scholarship, has proved the dominant shaping force. Mention has already been made of the revival of the linguistic-statistical study of verse at the start of the new structuralist phase; since then, an enormous amount of empirical research into rhythmical patterns in poetry (particularly the complex structures in 20th-century works) has been carried out.

Inter-level relationships within a poetic text, and problems of poetic semantics in general, have also preoccupied Soviet semioticians. Jakobson's ideas on the "grammar of poetry" and on the role of sound-meaning nexuses in poetic works, Tynyanov's discussion of the semantics of verse (in particular, the postulate that lexical units undergo semantic modification within the framework of a text or a unit of text), and Saussure's extensive research and theories about anagrams in ancient poetry have helped fuel much of the current research. In the sixties, statistical analysis of poetic lexicon (over the whole of a poet's creative life, within a given period, or within a collection) proved an important tool. Another, longer-lived approach has involved microsemantic analysis of individual works.

While no period of literature has been exempted from semiotic scrutiny (e.g., Lotman's work on medieval literature, V. Toporov's studies on BATYUSHKOV and ZHUKOVSKY, etc.), the poetic heritage of the period from the 1890s to the 1930s has been a special focus. ACMEIST writings, especially those of Osip MANDELSHTAM and Anna AKHMATOVA, came in for early and lasting attention, notably in studies by Segal, Levin, Ivanov, Toporov, M. Meilakh, Levinton, Tsivyan, R. Timenchik, and Zholkovsky. By and large, these have been based on the ideas of Tynyanov, on M. BAKHTIN's concept of the "alien word," and on the related notions of SUBTEXT and context advanced by K. Taranovsky in the United States. With their sophisticated semiotic mechanisms, Acmeist poetry and poetics have served to stimulate the semantic concerns of the structuralists; in

turn, the latter have been instrumental in restoring Acmeism to its rightful place in the Russian and world literary consciousness. SYMBOLIST poetry, especially that of BLOK, has also proved a favorite area of study over the years, especially during the recent period of the Blok centennial.

It should be noted that the study of these poets has combined the application of structural-semiotic concepts with a very high standard of philological and literary scholarship. Such a melding of old and new is a distinctive characteristic of the Moscow-Tartu school's approach to semiotics. Many of the Soviet scholars are trained in philology (Slavic, Oriental) and/or history of literature, and have a profound mastery of archival materials, dialectological and ethnographic data, etc. The kind of problems which have attracted the Soviet scholars, whether deep in the past, prior to the differentiation of the Indo-European linguistic unity, or involving the very difficult body of symbolist and post-symbolist works, involve both discovery and interpretation of new data, rather than, as is often the case in Continental semiotics, a reexamination of frequently analyzed texts and a questioning of the basic assumptions of semiotics itself. Finally, an openness to its intellectual antecedents in the more recent past, and, indeed, an active effort to rediscover them and bring them into scholarly circulation have been an important part of the Moscow-Tartu school's activity as a cultural force.

At an early stage in its development, the Moscow-Tartu school emphasized the need to publish and interpret archival materials so as to bring to general awareness major achievements of 20th-century Russian scholarship. The formalists were the initial object of this culture-preserving and culture-restoring program, which has also focused, among others, on the polymath Pavel FLORENSKY's work on symbolism; Olga Freidenberg's work on myth and literature; E. Polivanov's on linguistics and poetics; L. Vygotsky's on psychology of art and psycholinguistics; Eisenstein's on film, myth, and aesthetics; and Bakhtin's work on dialogism, theory of the novel, culture, and semiotics in general. Acquaintance with this scholarly heritage has done much to enrich the work of Soviet semioticians, though their attempts to reinterpret the past through a semiotic perspective must be treated with some caution.

Among nonverbal sign systems, painting received much attention initially. The publication of an old article by Florensky and of L. Zhegin's monograph on medieval icons (1970) were important events: B. Uspensky's own semiotic analyses of painting owe much to these prior writings. Ivanov and Toporov have also written about art, frequently in connection with their mythological studies. Research into the semiotics of music has thus far been rather limited: B. Gasparov has been the principal figure in this area.

The language of film has attracted increasing attention, in concert with a similar trend in the West (Metz, Chabrol). Interest in the semiotics of cinema has been stimulated by recognition of Eisenstein's role as a major, original theoretician of art, and by close study of both his cinematic heritage and his prolific writings (many of which still remain unpublished, even though a six volume edition of his works appeared in the 1960s). Eisenstein figures prominently in Ivanov's book on the development of Soviet semiotics. Lotman has considered problems of film composition in a brief but stimulating monograph.

The final major area of Soviet semiotics, and one in which Soviet researchers have made a major contribution, is the study of culture, understood as a mechanism for storage and transmission of collective, "noninherited" information. Approaches vary, and many of the studies already mentioned could be categorized under the broad rubric of typology of culture. Thus, much of the Moscow-Tartu work on myth is not viewed as self-contained, but as describing a universal stage in the development of human consciousness, traces of which reappear forcefully in the neo-mythological literature of MODERNISM.

Toporov's numerous writings on the Cosmic Tree, its sources and later reflexes recreate a period (some time following the Paleolithic epoch) in human culture in which a vast number of aspects and relationships of reality could be modelled through a single complex symbol. Enlarging on the ideas of the British philosopher R. G. Collingwood and other thinkers, Toporov has differentiated between various stages in human culture on the basis of a society's attitude towards history. Lotman and B. Uspensky, working principally with Russian materials, especially those of the 18th century and the early decades of the 19th, have proposed a variety of taxonomic schemes, based on different criteria (e.g., attitudes toward the past, attitudes toward what is considered as non-culture, attitudes toward mythological or nonmythological thought, etc.). Aside from the inherent theoretical interest of their studies, which combine psycholinguistics, Freudian theory, and literary and social history, the cycle of writings by these two scholars has richly illuminated important aspects of Russia's past.

One topic in semiotics of culture which has received much attention since the early 1970s is that of an archaic carnevalesque, unofficial layer in culture. Bakhtin's work on Rabelais provided the immediate stimulus and model for this, reinforced strongly, among a whole series of studies from several disciplines, by the results of two classic studies, Propp's (of ritual laughter in folklore) and Jakobson's (of an Old Czech mock mystery play). Ivanov has theorized that the "carnival" element, manifested in a range of texts from various spheres (literature, film, ritual, etc.) originates in an archaic method of a ritual neutralization of underlying binary oppositions. Lotman and B. Gasparov have discussed the carnival element in Blok's poem "The Twelve"; Lotman also has written about it in connection with Gogol. B. Gasparov also relies on this concept in his study of *Master and Margarita*.

Interest in the "carnival" element, and the corresponding need to account for historically-based differentiation in any theory of semiotic objects, are part of a broader tendency within the Moscow-Tartu school to move away from the application of logico-linguistic methodology to semiotic studies. Work on such topics as bilingualism (a situation with broad applicability to analysis of culture), semiotics of film (where the analogy with natural language is significantly weakened), and social aspects of language, reflect a search for a model which is more adequate to the complexity and diversity of semiotic phenomena. Reinforced by increasing evidence of parallels between molecular biology and linguistics, attempts continue at a synthesis which could embrace both the biological foundations of man's behaviour as a generator of signs and the full range of their cultural manifestations.

Bibliography: Karl Eimermacher and Serge Shishkoff, *Subject Bibliography of Soviet Semiotics: The Moscow-Tartu School*. (Michigan Slavic Publications, Bibliographic Series, 3.) Ann Arbor, 1977. *Translations of Primary Texts:* Vladimir Propp, *Morphology of the Folktale*. Trans. Laurence Scott. Bloomington, Ind., 1958. Roman Jakobson, *Selected Writings*. Vol. 2: Word and Language. The Hague, 1971. Boris A. Uspensky, *A Poetics of Composition: The Structure of the Artistic Text and Typology of a Compositional Form*. Trans. V. Zavarin and S. Wittag. Berkeley and Los Angeles, 1973. Pierre Maranda, ed., *Soviet Structural Folkloristics*. Vol. 1. The Hague and Paris, 1974. *Russian Poetics in Translation*. Vols. 1–9. Ed. L. M. O'Toole and A. Shukman. 1975–82 (ongoing series of translations). Henryk Baran, ed., *Semiotics and Structuralism: Readings from the Soviet Union*. White Plains, N. Y., 1976. L. Matejka et al., eds., "Soviet Semiotics of Culture. Special Issue," *Dispositio* 1, no. 3 (1976). Ladislav Matejka and Krystyna Pomorska, eds., *Readings in Russian Poetics: Formalist and Structuralist Views*. Cambridge, Mass., 1976. Ladislav Matejka and I. R. Titunik, eds., *Semiotics of Art: Prague School Contributions*. Cambridge, Mass., 1976. Daniel P. Lucid, ed., *Soviet Semiotics*. Baltimore, 1977. *PTL: A Journal for Descriptive Poetics and Theory of Literature*. Vol. 3, no. 3, October 1978 (Special Issue: Soviet Semiotics). Roman Jakobson, *Selected Writings*. Vol. 3: Poetry of Grammar and Grammar of Poetry. The Hague, 1981. Yuri Tynyanov, *The Problem of Verse Language*. Ed. and trans. Michael Sosa and Brent Harvey. Ann Arbor, 1981. Peter Steiner, ed., *The Prague School: Selected Writings, 1929–1946*. Austin, Texas, 1982. Alexander Zholkovsky, *Themes and Texts: Towards a Poetics of Expressiveness*. Ithaca, N. Y., 1984. *Secondary literature:* Victor Erlich, *Russian Formalism: History—Doctrine*. 3d ed. New Haven, Conn., 1981. V. V. Ivanov, *Ocherki po istorii semiotiki v SSSR*. Moscow, 1976. Roman Jakobson, *Coup d'Oeil sur le développement de la sémiotique*. (Studies in Semiotics, 3.) Bloomington, Ind., 1975. Roman Jakobson, ed., *N. S. Trubetzkoy's Letters and Notes*. The Hague and Paris, 1975. Giulio C. Lepschy, *A Survey of Structural Linguistics*. London, 1970. Ladislav Matejka, ed., *Sound, Sign and Meaning: Quin-*

quagenary of the Prague Linguistic Circle. (Michigan Slavic Contributions, No. 6.) Ann Arbor, 1976. E. M. Meletinskii and D. M. Segal, "Structuralism and Semiotics in the USSR," *Diogenes*, no. 73 (January–March, 1971), pp. 88–125. Krystyna Pomorska, *Russian Formalist Theory and its Poetic Ambiance*. The Hague and Paris, 1968. Thomas A. Sebeok, ed., *Current Trends in Linguistics*. Vol. 12: Linguistics and Adjacent Arts and Sciences. The Hague and Paris, 1974. (Especially important articles: E. Stankiewicz, "Structural Poetics and Linguistics"; F. Svejkovsky, "Theoretical Poetics in the Twentieth Century"; V. Ivanov, "Growth of the Theoretical Framework of Modern Poetics"; V. Toporov, "Folk Poetry: General Problems.") D. M. Segal, *Aspects of Structuralism in Soviet Philology*. (Papers on Poetics and Semiotics, 2.) Tel-Aviv, 1974. Irene Portis Winner, *Semiotics of Culture: The State of the Art. Rev. ed. 1981*. (Toronto Semiotic Circle, Monographs, Working Papers and Prepublications, No. 1.) Toronto, 1982.   H. B.

Strugátsky, Arkády Natánovich (1925–   ) and Borís Natánovich (1933–   ), writers of science fiction. Two brothers who began their careers as authors by writing for a juvenile audience, but soon switched to using science fiction thematics to satirize contemporary reality. In the 1960s they resurrected the anti-utopia and became the most popular and widely discussed science fiction writers in the Soviet Union. *It's Difficult to be a God* (Trudno byt' bogom, 1964) deals with life in a fascist state. *Predatory Things of the Age* (Khishchnye veshchi veka, 1965) has to do with the problem of a life's goal in a future materialistic society. In a world which has eliminated the need for work, people are in danger of turning into contented morons. *The Second Coming of the Martians* (Vtoroe nashestvie marsian, 1967) is Gogolian in manner and is intended as a satire on the bureaucracy and the super-patriot. In *The Snail on the Slope* (Ulitka na sklone, first part in *Ellinskii sekret*, 1966, pp. 384–462; second part in *Baikal*, 1968, no. 1, pp. 35–72, and no. 2, pp. 40–71) the unknown is symbolized by a giant forest being studied by an organization very similar to the KGB. The atmosphere is so oppressive that even machines are obsessed with the idea of escape. *The Fairytale of a Troika* (Skazka o troike, *Angara*, 1968, no. 4, pp. 3–17, no. 5, pp. 47–66) is a humorous political fable in which the universe is described as a skyscraper in which the sewer cleaners have seized power. In *The Inhabited Island* (Obitaemyi ostrov, *Neva*, 1969, no. 3, pp. 86–130, no. 4, pp. 85–127, no. 5, pp. 90–140) the government is using a network of transmitter stations to control men's minds. At the present time the political climate is such that the Strugatskys are no longer able to publish.

Works: Les. New York, 1981. *Obitaemyi ostrov*. New York, 1982. *Otel' u pogibshego al'pinista*. Moscow, 1982. *Zhuk v muraveinike*. New York, 1983. *Translations: The Final Circle of Paradise*. Trans. Leonid Renen. 1976. *The Ugly Swans*. Trans. Alice Stone Nakhimovsky and Alexander Nakhimovsky. 1979. *Beetle in the Anthill*. Trans. A. W. Bouis. Introd. T. Sturgeon. 1980. *The Second Invasion from Mars*. Trans. Antonina W. Bouis. 1980. *Space Apprentice*. Trans. Antonina W. Bouis. Introd. Theodore Sturgeon. 1981.   J. G.

Strúve, Gleb Petróvich (1898–   )—Russian émigré historian of literature and literary critic, poet, journalist, editor, translator, and educator. Born in St. Petersburg, the son of Pyotr Berngardovich STRUVE, he took part in the Great War and in the Russian civil war, in the Volunteer Army of General Kornilov. In December 1918 he fled from the Bolsheviks to Finland. In 1921 Struve graduated from Oxford University and for the next ten years worked as a Russian journalist and literary critic in Germany and France. Since 1932 he taught Russian literature at the School of Slavonic and East European Studies in the University of London. In 1946 he came to the United States, where he taught in the Department of Slavic Languages and Literatures of the University of California, Berkeley, until his retirement as Professor Emeritus in 1967. Later he was a visiting professor at several other universities.

Struve's incomplete bibliography of books, booklets, articles, essays, book-reviews, letters to the editor, etc. represents nearly fifty pages of small print. His two main works, however, are a history of Soviet literature and a history of Russian émigré literature. The first was published initially as *Soviet Russian Literature* (London, 1935) and then revised and republished in English and translated into French, German, Italian, and Russian (for limited use in the Soviet Union). His second standard work, *Russkaya literatura v izgnanii* (Russian Literature in Exile; New York, 1956) is being revised and translated into English.

A very important additional contribution by Struve to Russian literature and its history is a series of scholarly editions (jointly with Boris FILIPPOV) of the poetic works of PASTERNAK, GUMILYOV, MANDELSHTAM, AKHMATOVA, KLYUEV, and ZABOLOTSKY. Struve coedited, with N. A. Struve, M. TSVETAEVA's unpublished letters. For many years, he was coeditor of *California Slavic Studies* and the Boston *Studies in Romanticism*, and served on the editorial board of the *Yearbook of Comparative and General Literature*.

Struve was honored on several occasions. The 1973 AAASS "Award for Distinguished Contributions to Slavic Studies" emphasized, among other qualities and contributions, Struve's pioneering studies of Soviet Russian and émigré literature, his attention to new or unjustly forgotten writers, inspirational work with several generations of literary scholars, prodigious scholarship spanning the full history of Russian literature, "unique capacity for work, a rare degree of dedication, and a grand combination of scholarly and human integrity."

Works: Russkii evropeets; Materialy dlya biografii kn. P. B. Kozlovskogo. San Francisco, 1950. A book of poetry: *Utloe zhil'e; Izbrannye stikhi, 1915–1949.* Munich-Washington, D. C., 1965. 2d. suppl. ed., Berkeley, Calif., 1978.

Bibliography: Gleb Struve: A Bibliography. Comp. by Robert P. Hughes. Reprinted from *California Slavic Studies*, vol. 11 (1980), pp. 269–317.   N. P. P.

Strúve, Pyotr Berngárdovich (1870–1944), economist, sociologist, historian, philologist, and philosopher; publicist, editor, politician, and educator. A prominent Marxist in his youth, Struve, at the beginning of the century, turned to idealism and later to a religious *weltanschauung*. One of the leaders of the Russian Social Democrats and author of their first program, he later became a leader of the Liberals and Constitutional Democrats. During the civil war he was minister of foreign affairs in the government of General Wrangel and later one of the intellectual leaders of the moderately conservative elements of the Russian emigration.

Struve's academic career was associated mostly with the St. Petersburg Polytechnic Institute (since 1906), the Russian Faculty of Law in Prague (1922–25), and the Russian Scientific Institute in Belgrade (1928–41). In 1917 Struve was elected to the Russian Academy of Sciences. He was also awarded two doctoral degrees *honoris causa*, by Cambridge University (1916) and the University of Sofia (1939).

Much of Struve's energy and time was devoted to publicistic and editorial activities. Among his nearly a dozen editorial and publishing undertakings the most important was the "thick" monthly review RUSSKAYA MYSL' (Moscow-St.-Petersburg, 1907–18; Sofia, 1921; Prague-Berlin, 1922–24; Paris, 1927). Struve's name is closely associated also with three famous Moscow collections of essays: *Problems of Idealism* (Problemy idealizma, 1902), *Landmarks* (VEKHI, 1909), and *From the Depths* (Iz Glubiny, 1918; Paris, 1967), the latter conceived and edited by Struve himself.

By his intellectual interests, resulting in numerous and varied writings, Struve was an encyclopedist; by the general disposition of his mind an Aristotelian and pluralist; by his mature political world-outlook a liberal conservative. A great master of the Russian language and a stylist, he saw the word as an expression of the spirit. And, as has been rightly pointed out in the posthumous collection of his essays on Russian and West European literature which he wrote in exile, *Spirit and Word* (Dukh i slovo, Paris, 1981), Struve's method consisted in proceeding from the word to the spirit, and from the spirit to the word.

With regard to the Russian classics of the 19th century, Struve paid the greatest attention before the Revolution to LEV TOLSTOI, and in his later years to PUSHKIN. His essays on Tolstoi were republished as *Articles on Lev Tolstoi* (Stat'i o L've Tolstom) in Sofia, Bulgaria, in 1921. But he wrote also about Griboedov, Turgenev, Dostoevsky, Fet, Leskov, Chekhov, K. Aksakov, V. Solovyov, F. Sologub, Blok, Gumilyov, Voloshin, Bunin, Merezhkovsky,

Goethe, Walter Scott, Mérimée, Charles Nodier, Stendhal, A. Dumas père, Emile Zola, and many others.

Works: Collected Works in Fifteen Volumes. Ed. Richard Pipes. University Microfilms, Ann Arbor, Mich., 1970. *Bibliography of the Published Writings of Peter Berngardovich Struve.* Ed. Richard Pipes. University Microfilms International, Ann Arbor, Mich., 1980. *Dukh i slovo. Sbornik statei o russkoi i zapadnoevropeiskoi literature.* Paris, 1981.

Secondary literature: S. L. Frank, *Biografiya P. B. Struve.* New York, 1956. Richard Pipes, *Struve: Liberal on the Left, 1870–1905.* 1970. ———, *Struve: Liberal on the Right, 1905–1944.* 1980. N. P. Poltoratskii, *P. B. Struve kak politicheskii myslitel'.* London, Canada, 1981.   N. P. P.

Studio franco-russe, a relatively short-lived literary society in Paris, apparently the only major effort by Russian writers and intellectuals of the first emigration to establish formal contact with the French intellectual and artistic world and to launch cooperative programs to foster better mutual understanding and to study the cultural and literary interaction between France and Russia. After preliminary meetings in the spring of 1929 organized by Vsevolod Fokht, a young Russian writer and the principal driving force behind the *Studio*, the group began its regular series of monthly debates in October 1929, with one French and one Russian lecturer each presenting his respective point of view on a common topic, followed by general discussion. The manuscripts of the first four meetings (on topics such as anxiety in literature; the influence of French literature on the Russian; Dostoevsky; and Tolstoi) were published in *Rencontres. Soirées franco-russes ...* (ed. Robert Sebastien and Wsevolod de Vogt, Paris, 1930). The following ten pairs of lectures, with the debates ensuing each, from February 1930 to the *Studio*'s fourteenth and last meeting in April 1931, were all published in ten subsequent separate issues of the *Cahiers de la Quinzaine*, a Parisian literary journal close to Probus Corréard and Jean Maxence, Fokht's main French partners along with Sebastien. Among the highlights of the *Studio*'s work were talks by WEIDLÉ on Valéry (with the poet's personal participation), BERDYAEV on "East and West," Maritain on Descartes, ADAMOVICH on Gide, and FEDOTOV on "Spiritual Renewal in France and in Russia." Others, associated with *Studio* in one way or another, include André Malraux, François Mauriac, Georges Bernanos, Charles Péguy, André Maurois on the French side, and BUNIN, TSVETAEVA, ZAITSEV, BERBEROVA, Vysheslavtsev, TEFFI, Tsetlin, and Slonim on the Russian. Although Gleb STRUVE in his history of émigré literature regards the *Studio franco-russe* as a failure on the whole, its intrinsic interest and importance in the history of Russian-French literary relations is beyond doubt; after all, the only comparably "high-level" personal rapprochement between the two cultures occurred only once before, in the 19th century, thanks to TURGENEV. Moreover, the society's work, its publications and discussions were of such high caliber and quality that they certainly deserve more recognition even if the group has indeed failed to achieve any major breakthrough in bringing the two literatures closer to each other.

Bibliography: G. Struve, *Russkaya literatura v izgnanii.* New York, 1956. V. Veidle, "Frankorusskie vstrechi." In *Russkii al'manakh.* ed. Z. Shakhovskaya. Paris, 1981.   L. D.

Subtext, a literary term; as used by students of Russian SYMBOLIST and post-symbolist poetics, a work which serves as the source of an element repeated in another (usually subsequent) text. The concept was developed in the 1960s by Kiril Taranovsky and his school in analyzing the semantics of Osip MANDELSHTAM's poetry and prose; a similar approach to Mandelshtam, using the more traditional term "quotation," was proposed at about the same time by several Soviet scholars (members of the Moscow-Tartu school of semiotics) (see STRUCTURALISM AND SEMIOTICS).

Several different types of subtext may be distinguished. These range from a simple case in which a work serves as an impulse for the creation of an image or motif to situations in which the subtext measurably influences the message of the later work or is itself treated polemically in the subsequent work (the latter cases are more important in questions of interpretation).

Underlying the notion of subtext is the thesis that the works of certain poets and writers contain no haphazard components despite their reputation for being difficult, obscure, or even incomprehensible; such texts are in fact integrated structures, various elements of which are highly "motivated." Different types of semantic complexities may be encountered in these works: in many situations, identification of a subtext, or a group of mutually reinforcing (or even "competing") subtexts, and establishing its relationship to the work to which it is diachronically related, will provide the "missing piece" in a semantic puzzle.

Within this methodological framework, the concept of subtext is closely related to that of poetic *context*, by which is meant a body of works, however delimited, which contains the same or similar image as that found in the text under study; such a corpus, properly analyzed, can help uncover potential shifts in the meaning of an element of a text which are caused by its inclusion in a poetic structure. In certain situations, such as those of selfquotation (autoreminiscence), context and subtext overlap.

Study of subtexts has played a major role in elucidating the meaning of Mandelshtam's writings. It has also done much to illuminate AKHMATOVA's works, especially "Poem without a Hero", and continues to be applied with considerable success to such poets as BLOK, BELY, KUZMIN, MAYAKOVSKY, KHLEBNIKOV and PASTERNAK. Theoretical questions also have come to the fore, especially the task of establishing a typology of techniques and uses of quoting (within Silver Age literature and beyond).

Bibliography: Yu. I. Levin et al., "Russkaya semanticheskaya poetika kak potentsial'naya kul'turnaya paradigma," *RusL* 7/8 (1974), pp. 47–82. G. A. Levinton and R. D. Timenchik, "Kniga K. F. Taranovskogo o poezii O. E. Mandel'shtama," *RusL* 6, no. 2 (April 1978), pp. 197–211. Z. G. Mints, "Funktsiya reministsentsii v poetike A. Bloka." In: *Trudy po znakovym sistemam*, 6. Tartu, 1973. Pp. 387–417. O. Ronen, "Leksicheskii povtor, podtekst i smysl v poezii O. E. Mandel'shtama." In: *Slavic Poetics: Essays in Honor of Kiril Taranovsky.* R. Jakobson et al. eds. The Hague, 1973. Pp. 367–87. ———, "K istorii akmeisticheskikh tekstov. Opushchennye strofy i podtekst," *Slavica Hierosolymitana* 3 (1978), pp. 68–74. E. Rusinko, "Intertextuality: The Soviet Approach to Subtext," *Dispositio* 4 (1979), pp. 11–12, 213–35. Kiril F. Taranovsky, *Essays on Mandel'shtam.* Cambridge, 1976. *Tekst v tekste.* Trudy po znakovym sistemam, 14. Tartu, 1981. T. V. Tsiv'yan, "Zametki k deshifrovke 'Poemy bez geroya'." In: *Trudy po znakovym sistemam*, 5. Tartu, 1971. Pp. 255–77. A. K. Zholkovskii, "Zametki o tekste, podtekste i tsitatsii u Pasternaka." In: *Boris Pasternak: Essays.* Ed. N. Å. Nilsson. Stockholm, 1976. Pp. 67–84.

H. B.

Sukhovó-Kobýlin, Aleksándr Vasílievich (1817–1903), dramatist. Long overshadowed by the scandal in his personal life, Sukhovo-Kobylin's major dramatic work, the *Trilogy* (Trilogiya), consisting of *Krechinsky's Wedding* (Svad'ba Krechinskogo), *The Case* (Delo), and *Tarelkin's Death* (Smert' Tarelkina), has finally come to be regarded as a masterpiece of 19th-century Russian drama. A cultivated and learned aristocrat with a serious interest in philosophy, Sukhovo-Kobylin became embroiled in a sensational murder case following the mysterious death of his French mistress in 1850. The case dragged on for nearly seven years until Sukhovo-Kobylin was at last exonerated. Within a year after the court decision, Sukhovo-Kobylin left Russia for France, where he spent considerable time until his death at Beaulieu on the Riviera in 1903. The *Trilogy* grew out of the murder case. During his six-month incarceration in 1854, Sukhovo-Kobylin came to know at first hand the corruption endemic to the Russian state bureaucracy and the brutality of police methods. A long-time devotee of the stage, he decided to vent his feelings in a dramatic trilogy in which the imperial bureaucracy and police appear as incarnations of evil in a vision that grows progressively darker from play to play. *Krechinsky's Wedding*, which Sukhovo-Kobylin began and completed during his imprisonment in 1854, sets the stage for an indictment of unmitigated power and conviction. Modelled on the French "well-made play" (*pièce bien faite*) which Sukhovo-Kobylin knew well from his familiarity with the contemporary Parisian theatrical scene, *Krechinsky's Wedding* traces the attempted deception of Lidochka, the naive daughter of a wealthy provincial landowner named Muromsky, by a well-born scoun-

drel, Krechinsky, who views marriage to her as a remedy for his financial woes. A scheme to fleece a pawnbroker by means of a diamond pin borrowed from Lidochka backfires, but Krechinsky flees before the police can take him into custody. Circumstances implicate Lidochka in the attempted swindle, and Muromsky's frenzied efforts to clear her plunge him deeper into the labyrinth of tsarist bureaucracy. In its depiction of the corruption of the imperial administrative system, *The Case* (completed 1861) owes much to GOGOL's St. Petersburg stories. Following Muromsky's fatal heart attack, the officials who made a nightmare of his campaign to extricate his daughter from the web of bureaucratic entanglement fight among themselves for possession of money Muromsky was cajoled into offering as a bribe. This struggle between Varravin and Tarelkin, whom Sukhovo-Kobylin conceives of as degrees of evil in a world without justice, forms the subject of *Tarelkin's Death*, a phantasmagoric comedy remarkable for the modernity of its use of techniques of the absurd and grotesque. The play was begun in 1857 and finished only in 1869, the year in which the *Trilogy* was first published as a whole. Censors' objections necessitated a number of changes and *Tarelkin's Death* (under the title *Rasplyuev's Merry Days*, Rasplyuevskie veselye dni) was finally accepted for the stage in 1900. Its premiere took place in A. S. SUVORIN's Literary-Artistic Theater in St. Petersburg on 15 September 1900. Although the plays comprising the *Trilogy* have been staged a number of times in the 20th century, the most famous productions remain those of MEYERHOLD on 23 October 1917, at the Aleksandrinsky Theater, and especially in 1922 at Moscow's experimental GITIS theater. Meyerhold's first production in 1917 emphasized the play's tragic elements, but the more brilliant version of 1922 was presented in the spirit of a circus buffonade featuring clown routines and acrobatics and reflecting the great director's concepts of biomechanics and constructivism as well as his interest in the grotesque.

Bibliography: The Trilogy of Alexander Sukhovo-Kobylin. Trans. and introd. Harold B. Segel. 1969.

H. B. S.

Sumarókov, Aleksándr Petróvich (1718–77), poet, dramatist, journalist, and critic. Immensely productive and influential, Sumarokov was the first truly modern writer in the history of Russian literature. Descended of an old Muscovite family, his literary career was shaped by the modern European curriculum of the Corps of Cadets, which was established for the sons of the nobility in 1732. Here Sumarokov studied modern foreign languages and literatures, above all French, and saw dramatic productions on the school stage. Sumarokov's literary career began with two odes which he published in 1740, the year he completed his stay at the Corps of Cadets. Viewing himself as the first Russian secular writer liberated from the CHURCH SLAVONIC tradition and imbued with the then dominant French high classicism, Sumarokov believed that his mission was to lay the foundation of a new, modern, European-oriented Russian literary culture. To achieve this aim, he set about introducing virtually every current genre of European poetry and drama and drew up a literary program for the Russian language and Russian poetry, modeled on Boileau's *Art poétique*, which he presented in the form of two verse epistles written in 1747. Sumarokov wrote state, or formal, odes, spiritual odes (e.g., "On the Vanity of Man"—Na suetu cheloveka; and "Ode on the Vanity of the World"—Oda na suetu mira), Anacreontic, Horatian, and Sapphic odes, eclogues, idylls, elegies, sonnets, ballads, rondeaux, stances, madrigals, epigrams, songs (mostly on the theme of love), satires (among the best-known of which is "On Nobility"—O blagorodstve, wherein Sumarokov measures true nobility in terms of service to the state), a large number of fables (*pritchi*), folk tales (*skazki*), and choruses, including the well-known satirical "Chorus to a Perverse World" (Khor ko prevratnomu svetu) and "Second Chorus to a Perverse World" (Drugii khor ko prevratnomu svetu). Apart from the number of poetic genres with which he experimented, Sumarokov also contributed importantly to the development of the Russian literary language and Russian versification. Because of his modern European education, Sumarokov regarded the Church Slavonic language and literary tradition with contempt, cultivating instead the spoken language of the cultured people of the capital. In this respect, Sumarokov's impact on the formation of the modern Russian literary language was greater than that of any of his contemporaries. In the area of metrics, Sumarokov favored the iamb over the trochee, unlike TRE-DIAKOVSKY, and employed a more natural syntax and diction. How modern Sumarokov regarded himself as a poet and literary innovator in comparison to his contemporaries can be seen in several verse parodies mocking, on one hand, Trediakovsky's unwieldy syntax and fondness for the trochee, and, on the other, LOMONOSOV's baroque imagery which struck Sumarokov as outlandish and grotesque. While an important and influential poet embodying the outlook and aesthetics of classicism (see NEOCLASSICISM) and yet responsive also to the new sensibility of SENTIMENTALISM, Sumarokov is best remembered as a dramatist. He was the first modern writer of both comedy and tragedy in the history of the Russian stage. Stilted imitations of Molière and Molière's successors in the 18th century, Sumarokov's twelve comedies are of interest only to the historian. They include such plays as *Tresotinius* (1750), a satire of Trediakovsky, *An Empty Quarrel* (Pustaya ssora, 1750), *The Usurer* (Likhoimets, 1768), a satire on his father-in-law A. I. Buturlin, *The Guardian* (Opekun, 1765), and *Nartsiss* (1750), a satire of I. I. Shuvalov. Sumarokov's tragedies are by far more interesting. He wrote nine in all: *Khorev* (1747), *Hamlet* (1747), *Sinav and Truvor* (1750), *Artistona* (1751), *Semira* (1752), *Dimiza* (1756; later reworked under the title Yaroslav and Dimiza), *Vysheslav* (1770), *Dimitry the Pretender* (Dimitrii Samozvanets, 1771), and *Mstislav* (1774). Although generally conservative in his politics, Sumarokov opposed the privileges of the hereditary nobility and in his most provocative drama, *Dimitry the Pretender*, went so far as to suggest that even the illegitimate acquisition of a throne could be legitimized by good rule. More so than any other of his tragedies, *Dimitry the Pretender* provided the impetus to a politically engaged Russian tragic drama in the last two decades of the 18th century of which the best examples are N. P. NIKOLEV's *Sorena and Zamir* and Ya. KNYAZHNIN's *Vadim of Novgorod*. Sumarokov also held several important state positions. Shortly after leaving the Corps of Cadets he was appointed adjutant to Vice-Chancellor Count M. G. Golovkin. Later, he became adjutant to the Empress Elizaveta Petrovna's favorite, Count A. G. Razumovsky. In recognition of his contributions to the development of a Russian drama in 1756 he was named director of the newly organized Russian Imperial Theater. But because of his notorious inability to get along with people, his administration became embroiled in politics and petty squabbles and he was forced into retirement in 1761.

Bibliography: William Edward Brown, *A History of 18th Century Russian Literature.* 1980. Harold B. Segel, *The Literature of Eighteenth-Century Russia.* 2 vols. 1967. *Selected Tragedies of A. P. Sumarokov.* Trans. Richard and Raymond Fortune, introd. John Fizer. 1970.   H. B. S.

Superfluous man (*lishnii chelovék*), a traditional designation for a series of characters in Russian literature who are perceived—or regard themselves—as being in a state of disharmony with the world around them, rejecting it or being rejected by it. Since such disharmony is by no means limited to Russians, the category, a commodious one to begin with, can be stretched to include all sorts of "alienated," "outsider" figures from other literatures, such as Don Quixote, Alceste, Werther, Childe Harold, René, Adolphe, and even the hero of Rousseau's *Confessions.* "Superfluous men" can also, of course, be found outside of literature, in real life, and the category used as a typology manifested in history. As the definition implies, "superfluity" can be viewed from within, as a psychological syndrome, a state of mind; it can also be seen from outside, as a sociological phenomenon, a condition of society such that a significant class of people can find no useful place in it. In both cases a character's "superfluity" may be treated with approval or sympathy, e.g., as a manifestation of greater intelligence, sensitivity, or moral concern; or it may be condemned, e.g., as evidence of laziness, arrogance, or refusal to face realities. In answer to the question posed in HERZEN's title, the character can be "blamed" for his superfluity, or society "blamed" for making him so. Evocations of the superfluous man in Russian literature run the gamut of all these possible combinations of emphasis and attitude.

The term became current only after the publication in 1850 of TURGENEV's "Diary of a Superfluous Man" (Dnevnik lishnego cheloveka). The word "superfluous" had earlier been used in a similar sense, however, for instance, in a cancelled draft for *Evgeny Onegin*; and in any case the literary type as usually identified goes back at least to GRIBOEDOV's Chatsky and PUSHKIN's Onegin.

With regard to its "superfluous men," Russian literature shows evidence of complex interaction between "art" and "life," domestic social fact and international literary fashion. The crucial social fact was that the Russian gentry of the early 19th century found itself in a situation that almost guaranteed "superfluity." Assured of an unearned income, however modest, from their lands and the labor of their human chattels, gentlemen had been liberated since 1762 from the once concomitant obligation of service to the state. To be sure, many of them continued to "serve," but usually not very long or assiduously. Likewise, though they occasionally toyed with the task, day-to-day management of agricultural operations on their estates was a tedious job they generally preferred to leave to bailiffs. Russia lacked the alternative outlets often seized upon by energetic gentlemen in the West, such as the Church, business, or colonial administration. Thus non-serving Russian gentlemen were quite literally "superfluous": living off the labor of others, they were social parasites, consumers but not producers; and this fact lay heavy on their consciences, producing another recurrent cliché character of Russian literature (and history), the "repentant nobleman" (*kayushchiisya dvoryanin*).

On the other hand, gentleman writers, who were themselves "superfluous men" (in the sociological sense), were constantly affected by literary impressions and models imported from abroad. One of the most attractive of these importations was the romantic hero, proud but alienated, whose *schöne Seele* was afflicted with weltschmerz. Here was a magic formula for metamorphosing disapproval and guilt into self-satisfaction and pride. Alienation became admirable, and not only alienation from society but from nature. Nature eventually inflicts gray hair and flabby flesh on us all, at last rendering us superfluous in the most literal sense; and many literary heroes have revolted against the discomfort and injustice of this process, some even preferring to part with life suddenly, as Pushkin recommended, rather than waiting out an inglorious decay. But most frequently the revolt has been directed against the more remediable injustices of the social order. These were even more egregious in Russia than elsewhere, yet Russia's authoritarian government not only refused to consider independent initiatives for social remediation, but even prohibited most public discussion of social problems. The regime's rigidity turned potential reformers into revolutionaries and martyrs, as was demonstrated in December 1825; and the subsequent repressions of Nicholas I seemed to freeze Russia into a permanent state of backwardness and barbarism. Thrashing vainly about on this frozen ground, Russia's gentlemen of talent, education, and good will seemed doomed by history to frustration and despair, i.e., "superfluity."

The superfluous men succeed one another in Russian literature like the Biblical "begats." Chatsky, Onegin, Pechorin, Beltov, and hero after Turgenev hero, but especially Rudin and Lavretsky, who are considered more typically "superfluous" than the eponymous Chulkaturin of the *Diary*. (Chulkaturin rather anticipates DOSTOEVSKY's "underground man," a somewhat mutant species of the "superfluous" genus.) In *Fathers and Sons*, Pavel and Nikolai Kirsanov are conventionally "superfluous men," and Arkady is transformed into one; but Turgenev perhaps takes malicious pleasure in showing that the strong-spirited, self-willed plebeian Bazarov is also rendered "superfluous" in the course of the novel's action, first by unrequited love and then by the vagaries of the typhus microbe. GONCHAROV's Oblomov seems the very essence of "superfluity"; he was forced to do duty as DOBROLYUBOV's demonstration piece of the historical uselessness of the whole Russian gentry. Earlier, CHERNYSHEVSKY had made Turgenev's Gagin serve the same purpose, thus provoking a polemic with Herzen, himself a "superfluous man," who thought the "bilious ones" went too far in their wholesale repudiation of all progressive gentlemen. The Emancipation of 1861 marks the end of the "superfluous" line as usually interpreted, but specimens of disaffection and alienation are common in later literature as well, from CHEKHOV's Ivanov to OLESHA's Kavalerov and even PASTERNAK's Yury Zhivago.

Bibliography: P. V. Annenkov, "Literaturnyi tip slabogo cheloveka." In *Vospominaniya i kriticheskie ocherki* 2. 1879. N. F. Budanova, "Podpol'nyi chelovek v ryadu 'lishnikh lyudei'," *RLit* 19 (1976), no. 3, pp. 110–22. Ellen B. Chances, *Conformity's Children: An Approach to the Superfluous Man in Russian Literature.* 1978. Jesse V. Clardy and Betty S. Clardy, *The Superfluous Man in Russian Letters.* 1980. Robert Louis Jackson, *Dostoevsky's Underground Man in Russian Literature.* The Hague, 1958. Rufus W. Mathewson, Jr., *The Positive Hero in Russian Literature.* 2d ed. 1975.

H. McL.

Supplication of Daniel the Exile. Preserved only in manuscripts of the 16th to 18th centuries, the *Supplication* cannot be reconstructed in its original 12th-century (?) form referred to as the *Slovo*, nor can its author be identified. As a coherent literary work, it seems to date from early 13th-century Pereyaslavl. The contentual skeleton of the *Supplication* is an extended plea for princely support from the unknown Daniel, who for some reason had fallen upon hard times, been abandoned by friends and family, and exiled, perhaps to Lake Lacha near the headwaters of the Onega River. His appeal is full of abject flattery ("Thy voice is sweet, and honey flows from thy lips, and thy visage is beauteous" [15]; "Gold adorns women, and thou, Prince, thy people" [57]), and is based on the hope that the Prince will recognize his wit and intelligence, of which he himself holds a high opinion ("I am poor in dress, but rich in wit" [14]; "A brave man is quickly found, but a wise man is dear" [20]), qualities which are intended to outweigh his avowed cowardice ("Although not so brave in battle, I am mighty in words" [19]) and even his dishonesty ("You might say, Prince, that I have lied like a dog, but a good dog is favored by princes and boyars" [82]). Migrant motifs of mean wives and errant clergy also appear ("I should rather have an ox in my house than a mean wife" [67]; "Wherever there are weddings and feasts, there are the monks and the nuns and debauchery" [74]). The heavily aphoristic style draws on a variety of biblical and secular quotations and misquotations ("The foolish do not sow, neither do they plow, nor spin, nor weave, but only reproduce themselves" [62]), as well as folk or pseudo-folk sayings ("A poor wise man is like gold in a dirty dish, and a rich fool like a silken pillow stuffed with straw" [18]; "Even if a kettle had golden handles, its bottom would still be burnt and black" [37]; "If your clothes are clean, your speech is honored" [13]), and is couched in rhythmic cadences alternating between liturgical and folk genres, including the repeated onset, "O my Prince, my Lord!" (knyazhe moi, gospodine!).

Perhaps the most original feature of the *Supplication* is its exuberant SKOMOROKH humor, which takes the form of sudden, unmotivated shifts in viewpoint (Daniel usually extolls his own wisdom, but at one point suddenly parodies his own ego: "If I am not really wise myself, at least I have donned the robes of those who are, and have worn the boots of the reasonable" [51]), mockingly exaggerated rhetoric ("Place your heart's vessel beneath my tongue's torrent, that verbal sweetness may pour forth unto you more than the aromatic waters" [52]), and absurdly inappropriate metaphorics (for example, parodying epic onsets: "Let us then trumpet forth, o brethren, as in a gold-forged horn, in the wisdom of our wit, and let us begin to strike the silver organ in proclamation of sagacity", etc., [1]). At times, Daniel even seems to be teasing the Prince with dubious compliments, such as only a court jester could permit himself ("Water is mother to fish, as art thou, Prince, to thy people" [33]; "As the serpent is fearsome in its hissing, so art thou, Prince, in the multitude of thine armies" [57]). Overall, the *Supplication of Daniel the Exile* can be characterized as the only light-hearted and witty work of Old Russian literature.

Bibliography: Das Gesuch Daniils. Nachdruck von Zarubins Ausgabe Leningrad 1932 ..., Munich, 1972. *Daniil Zatochnik. Slovo e Molenie.* Edizione critica a cura di Michele Colucci e Angelo Danti. Firenze, 1977.

Secondary literature: D. S. Likhachev, "Sotsial'nye osnovy stilya 'Moleniya' Daniila Zatochnika," *TODRL* 10 (1954), pp. 106–19. K. Taranovsky, "Formy obshcheslavyanskogo i tserkovnoslavyanskogo stikha v drevnerusskoi literature XI–XIII vv." In *American Contributions to the Sixth International Congress of Slavists,* Vol. 1. The Hague, 1968. Pp. 377–94.

D. S. W.

Súrikov, Iván Zakhárovich (1841–80), poet. Though Surikov, a shopkeeper, lived in Moscow most of his life, his poetry follows the footsteps of KOLTSOV, NIKITIN, and NEKRASOV, treating mostly of the hard lot of the Russian peasant, of Russian nature, and of Russian children. Like theirs, many of Surikov's poems became popular songs: "Dubinushka," "The Mountain Ash" (Ryabina), "In the Steppe" (V stepi), and others. N. A. Rimsky-Korsakov's opera *Sadko* is based on Surikov's *poema* of that title. In 1872 Surikov prepared an almanac of poetry by beginning poets from his own class, *Dawn* (Rassvet), which led to the creation of a circle, eventually named the Surikov Literary and Musical Circle (Surikovskii literaturno-muzykal'nyi kruzhok). Later, similar circles of self-taught poets of the people were formed in other cities, and their members were often identified as *surikovtsy.* Sergei ESENIN is the most prominent one-time *surikovets.*

Bibliography: I. Z. Surikov i poety-surikovtsy. Introd. E. S. Kalmanovskii. 1966. N. I. Nezhenets, "Sud'ba 'Ryabiny'," *Russkaya rech',* 1978, no. 3, pp. 52–57.

Translations: two poems in C. M. Bowra, ed., *A Book of Russian Verse.* 1943.

V. T.

Surkóv, Aleksei Aleksándrovich (1899–), poet, writer, editor, and functionary, was born in the village of Serednevo, Yaroslavl Oblast. A Hero of Soviet Labor (1969), Surkov has been a member of the Communist Party since 1925 with an impressive service record. He was chosen head of RAPP in 1928, and has served on the editorial board of several Party periodicals, including *Literaturnaya ucheba* (1934–39). His first collection of poems, *Starting a Song* (Zapev) appeared in 1930. This was followed by further cycles of poetry during the next decade: *Verses* (Stikhi) and *At the Approaches to Song* (Na podstupakh k pesne) in 1931; *Offensive* (Nastuplenie) in 1932; *The Last War* (Poslednyaya voina) in 1934; *Home of the Brave* (Rodina muzhestvennykh) in 1935; *By Way of Song* (Putem pesni) in 1937, etc. In large part, the measure of success attained by these works has been attributed to Surkov's depictions of Soviet heroes of the civil war, in which he himself had participated.

During the years 1939 to 1945, Surkov was a war correspondent. He also completed a number of volumes of poetry devoted to war themes: *December on the Moscow Front* (Dekabr' pod Moskvoi, 1942); *The Roads Go West* (Dorogi vedut na zapad, 1942); *Offensive* (Nastuplenie, 1943); *Russia the Avenger* (Rossiya karayushchaya, 1944); *I Sing of Victory* (Ya poyu pobedu, 1946), and others. In these cycles, Surkov is concerned with such universal considerations as anger, grief, the striving for victory, and the soldier's longing for home. His work at this time and later is characterized by a severity of tone and limited coloration intermeshed with a high degree of lyricism. Surkov also completed a volume of essays, *Fires of the Great Urals. Letters of the Soviet Home Front* (Ogni Bol'shogo Urala. Pis'ma o sovetskom tyle, 1944). His collection of poems devoted to wartime experiences and meetings, *Peace to the World!* (Miru—mir! 1950), received the State Prize of the USSR in 1951. This was followed by later cycles of poetry: *East and West* (Vostok i Zapad,* 1957); *Songs of Mankind* (Pesni o chelovechestve, 1961); *What is Happiness?* (Chto takoe schast'e? 1969), and by a volume of literary criticism: *Voices of Time: Notes on the Margins of the History of Literature, 1934–1965* (Golosa vremeni. Zametki na polyakh istorii literatury, 1934–1965), which appeared in 1965.

Surkov served as editor of LITERATURNAYA GAZETA (1944–46) and of the journal, *Ogonek* (1945–53). From 1962, he has been chief editor of *Kratkaya literaturnaya entsiklopediya.* In 1953 he took over as First Secretary of the Union of Soviet Writers replacing A. A. FADEEV. He was made a member of the Supreme Soviet of the USSR in 1954 and was at one time a Candidate (alternate member) of the Central Committee of the Communist Party. He held other high positions in the course of his long Party career. Surkov has also translated poetry from Ukrainian, Belorussian, Bulgarian, Polish, Czech, Slovenian, Serbian, Hungarian, and Urdu.

Works: Sobranie sochinenii. 4 vols. 1965–66. *Posle voiny: Stikhi 1945–70 godov.* 1972. *Izbrannoe.* 2 vols. 1974.

Translations: Lewanski, pp. 363–64.

Secondary literature: O. Reznik, *Aleksei Surkov: Put' poeta.* 2d rev. ed. 1969. Konstantin Simonov, "Alexei Surkov," *Soviet Litera-

ture, 1979, no. 9, pp. 134–37 (followed by 7 of Surkov's poems). E. A. Vasilevskaya, "Poeziya grazhdanstvennosti: O voennykh stikhakh Alekseya Surkova," *Russkaya rech'*, 1976, no. 1, pp. 44–50.

D. K. D.

Surrealism. The impact of surrealism on Russian literature can be discussed only in very tentative terms. There has been little study of this question, and no definitive statement is possible.

Surrealism arose at a time unfavorable to its dissemination in the Soviet Union. The 1920s, however liberal by comparison with the Stalin period, were not a time for Russians to join Western writers and artists in decrying the presence of a barrier between man and the disintegrating world around him, in questioning the authority of reason, and in rejecting conventional categories of perception. Nor were they propitious times for implementing the surrealists' program to attain a higher reality: e.g., exploring the subconscious (in dreams, in delirial states, among the insane) and minimizing logical thought in poetry in favor of the hallucinogenic and the accidental (*écriture automatique*). That is not to say that the ideas of the surrealists may not have exerted an influence. Our knowledge of the inner life of Russian intelligentsia in the Soviet period is very incomplete. Many works originally written "for the drawer" continue to reach the light of day, and we must allow for the possibility that surrealism did play some role, however subterranean, in Russia's artistic life.

Scholars have pointed to the possible presence of a surrealist "mode of expression" in the works of several Russian writers, ranging from GOGOL ("The Nose") to NABOKOV (*Invitation to a Beheading*). There are two principal problems with this approach. First, to focus on poetics, largely to the exclusion of philosophical concerns, risks reducing surrealism to yet another variety of the grotesque. Whatever its links with earlier traditions in which the grotesque plays a major part (and they were acknowledged freely), surrealism's uniqueness as a complex phenomenon with serious philosophical underpinnings must be preserved when discussing its influence. Second, our changing, increasingly deeper understanding of 20th-century Russian literary movements renders dangerous attempts to find elements of surrealism in works which their creators did not acknowledge as such. Thus, MANDELSHTAM's novella *The Egyptian Stamp* has been identified as an example of surrealist prose. Yet, as has been shown, it is, like other Mandelshtam texts, a carefully crafted semantic montage, the product of a rational structuring of meaning which is very distant from a poetics which finds beauty in the happenstance.

We can identify a few writers whose art and life (often treated as phenomena of the same order) included some elements of surrealism. Thus, KHLEBNIKOV rejected 19th-century rationalism and often celebrated the primitive and the emotional in man. FUTURISM as a whole made iconoclastic behavior its trademark; it also relished the role of the accidental in art. IMAGISM relied on juxtaposition of unexpected images for aesthetic effect, while often reducing the narrative to a barely recognizable outline. Finally, there were the OBERIU writers, especially Aleksandr VVEDENSKY. Their public pose was similar to that of dada (surrealism's immediate source). And their early works, radical in their linguistic experimentation, and often featuring a nearly random assemblage of words and phrases, came perhaps the closest in Russia to the creations of surrealism.

Bibliography: Lyudmila A. Foster, "K voprosu o syurrealizme v russkoi literature." In *American Contributions to the Seventh International Congress of Slavists*. 1973. Pp. 199–220. Daniel Peter Gallagher, *The Surrealist Mode in Twentieth-Century Russian Literature*. Ph.D. diss., University of Kansas, 1975. Kleofas Hubert Rundzjo, *Surrealizm rosyjski*. Ph.D. diss., Brown University, 1976. Alice Stone Nakhimovsky, *Laughter in the Void: An Introduction to the Writings of Daniil Kharms and Alexander Vvedenskii*. (Wiener Slawistischer Almanach, Sonderband 5.) Vienna, 1982.

H. B.

Suvórin, Aleksei Sergéevich (1834–1912), Russian journalist and publishing magnate. Of humble provincial origin, he became prominent as a liberal journalist in the 1860s, first in Moscow, then in Petersburg, especially as a columnist for *Sankt-Peterburgskie Vedomosti* (pseudonym "Neznakomets"). For an article on CHER-NYSHEVSKY he was arrested in 1866. Suvorin also wrote articles on literary and other subjects for VESTNIK EVROPY. In 1876 he acquired control of the Petersburg newspaper *Novoe Vremya*, which he built into an organ of huge circulation and great influence, the center of a publishing empire. Beginning with its vociferous support for the 1877–78 war against Turkey, *Novoe Vremya*'s editorial stance was far to the right of Suvorin's earlier liberalism; the paper became a loud advocate of an aggressive foreign policy and a repressive domestic one, the latter particularly with respect to national minorities. Besides his newspaper, Suvorin was a publisher of books, including the mass-market "Cheap Library" of the classics, and also of the magazine *Istoricheskii Vestnik*. His firm enjoyed a profitable monopoly on the sale of books in railway stations.

Suvorin was a Maecenas of the theater. He was one of the organizers and subsequently the owner of the *Peterburgskii Malyi Teatr* (also known as the *Suvorinskii Teatr*). Moreover, he was himself a dramatist. His best-known plays are *Medea* (1883, written in collaboration with V. P. Burenin) and *Tatyana Repina* (1889), for which Chekhov wrote a sequel. Suvorin also wrote a novel, *V kontse veka; Lyubov'* (1893). His private diary was discovered and an edited version published in 1923; it shows that his personal opinions often differed from those articulated in his paper.

Suvorin was acquainted with most of the leading Russian writers of his time, among them both TOLSTOI and DOSTOEVSKY. He had a very ambivalent relationship with LESKOV, dating back to the time when both were obscure young journalists fresh from the provinces. And with CHEKHOV, twenty-six years his junior, Suvorin had a close friendship; many of Chekhov's most forthright and thoughtful letters were written to Suvorin. Their friendship cooled toward the end of Chekhov's life, especially over disagreement concerning the Dreyfus case, but was never fully extinguished. Because of Suvorin's politics and a contumelious characterization of him by LENIN, Soviet literary scholars are obliged to play down this relationship and in general to minimize Suvorin's services to Russian literature. Suvorin also carried on a voluminous correspondence with ROZANOV, who for years wrote a regular column for *Novoe Vremya*.

Works: Pis'ma A. S. Suvorina k V. V. Rozanovu. 1913.

Secondary literature: Simon Karlinsky, ed., *Anton Chekhov's Life and Thought: Selected Letters and Commentary*. 1973. D. S. Merezhkovskii, "Suvorin i Chekhov." In *Bylo i budet; dnevnik 1910–1914*. 1915. *Pis'ma russkikh pisatelei k A. S. Suvorinu*. 1927. I. Solov'eva and V. Shitova, "A. S. Suvorin: Portret na fone gazety," *VLit*, 1977, no. 2, pp. 162–99.

H. McL.

Svetlóv, Mikhail Arkádievich (1903–1964), poet and playwright. Svetlov joined the Komsomol in 1919 and fought with the Red Army in the civil war. His first book of poetry, *Tracks* (Rel'sy) came out in 1923, showing the traits that would always stay with him. His poems are topical, down-to-earth, sincere, and sentimental. Formally, they are simple, and their ballad style invites setting them to music. Svetlov's romantic-revolutionary ballad "Grenada" (1926) made the "poet of the Komsomol" a celebrity. His "Song of Kakhovka" (Pesnya o Kakhovke, 1935) was for years one of the most popular songs in the Soviet Union. Like so many devoted Young Communists, Svetlov took the retreat of Soviet society into the NEP very hard and expressed his bitterness in verse ("The Nepman," 1925). His poetry of the late 1920s and 1930s received mostly unfavorable reviews. A play, *Boondocks* (Glubokaya provintsiya, 1935), which depicted life on the collective farm as less than rosy, was attacked by *Pravda* and its run discontinued. Other plays were not published, or not staged. A war correspondent during World War II, Svetlov was never able to regain a solid position in Soviet literary life. He published two collections of verse after the War, but they were hardly noticed, and neither were his plays. A revival of Svetlov's fame occurred only after his death. In 1967 he was posthumously awarded a Lenin prize. Svetlov is an attractive, though hardly a major, figure.

Works: Sorok let moei liriki. 1959. *Stikhotvoreniya i poemy*. 1966. *Izbrannye proizvedeniya*. 2 vols. 1965. *Stikhi poslednikh let*. 1970. *P'esy*. 1970. *Sobranie sochinenii*. 3 vols. 1974.

Translations: "Granada," "Soviet Co-Ed," "From Poems about a Rabbi." In *New Directions. Anthology in Prose and Poetry*. 1949.

Secondary literature: N. Aseev, "Mikhail Svetlov." In his *Zachem i komu nuzhna poeziya.* 1961. E. Lyubareva, *Mikhail Svetlov: Kritiko-biograficheskii ocherk.* 1960. F. Svetlov, *Mikhail Svetlov: Ocherk tvorchestva.* 1967. Adol'f Urban, "Razmyshleniya ob itogakh," *Zvezda,* 1979, no. 4, pp. 198–213.   V. T.

Svinyin, Pável Petróvich (1787–1839), artist, collector of Russian art and manuscripts, historical novelist, ethnographer, historian, student of technology, editor of OTECHESTVENNYE ZAPISKI (1818–1830, 1839). Svinyin attended the Nobles' Pension at Moscow University and the Academy of Fine Arts, then joined the College of Foreign Affairs. He served in England, Philadelphia, and the Mediterranean, and was a member of the Academy of Fine Arts (1811) and the Russian Academy (1833).

Despite his education, travel experience, command of several languages (including English), enthusiasm, energy, and genuine artistic talent, Svinyin is remembered (if at all) largely as a figure of fun: as the object of epigrams (A. S. PUSHKIN, VYAZEMSKY), fables (A. E. Izmailov), and prose satire, such as Pushkin's "A Little Liar" (Malen'kii lzhets); and for his exaggerated patriotism, his well-meaning but often misplaced help of self-taught artists, and (above all) his persistent disregard for the conventional boundaries between fact and fiction. It has been argued that he served GOGOL (one of whose early stories he published) as a prototype for Khlestakov in the *Inspector General.* His accounts of his travels to North America (1815) touch upon statistics, religious practices, natural and artistic monuments, steamboats, Indians, and education.

Works: Opyt zhivopisnogo puteshestviya po severnoi Amerike. 1815.
Works in English: Sketches of Moscow and St. Petersburg. Philadelphia, 1813 and London, 1814.
Secondary literature: Avrahm Yarmolinsky, *Picturesque United States of America 1811, 1812, 1813, Being a Memoir on Paul Svinin.* 1930. (Reproduces fifty-two of Svinyin's watercolors.)   W. M. T.

Svyatopólk-Mirsky, Prince Dmítry Petróvich (1890–1939), literary historian and critic. Born into the titled aristocracy and educated at the University of St. Petersburg, Mirsky served in the White army during the civil war. Following the defeat of the Whites, he emigrated to Greece and then to England where he lectured at the London School of Slavonic Studies. In the twenties he contributed numerous articles to British and French periodicals and in 1926 his *History of Russian Literature* (written in English) was published. This now standard and familiar work, perhaps the most readable of all literary histories, is characterized by a refined taste and replete with perceptive and provocative insights. To be sure, Mirsky's judgments are occasionally erratic, revealing, for example, marked and often aristocratic prejudices (e.g., his sympathetic views of Count TOLSTOI and his final dismissal of the "real" DOSTOEVSKY as "food that is easily assimilated only by a profoundly diseased organism"). Another highly respected literary study by Mirsky is his *Pushkin,* also published in 1926, which is still one of the best introductions to and surveys of the works of Pushkin in English. In 1931 Mirsky surprised many by joining the British Communist Party; but the reason became clear when, in the following year, he returned to (Soviet) Russia. In 1934, however, an article he wrote criticizing a novel by Aleksandr FADEEV raised a storm of protest and he was arrested in 1935. On this occasion he was released, but he was arrested again in 1937 and disappeared in the Gulag.

Works: A History of Russian Literature. 1926 and subsequent editions, including a Vintage paperback. *Pushkin.* 1926 and subsequent editions, including a Dutton paperback.
Secondary literature: Nina Lavroukhine and Leonid Tchertkov, *D. S. Mirsky. Profil critique et bibliographique.* Paris, Inst. des études slaves, n. d. R. Stacy, *Russian Literary Criticism: A Short History.* 1974. Edmund Wilson, "Comrade Prince," *Encounter,* July 1955.   R. H. S.

Syllabic versification. A system of versification prevalent in Russia from mid-17th to the middle of the 18th century. In its customary definition, it is understood to be a method of composing poetry in lines of thirteen or eleven syllables, dividing them by a pause, or caesura, at the seventh and fifth syllable, respectively. The distribution of word stresses along these lines is not prescribed, except for two constants: the sixth and the twelfth syllable in the longer line, and the fourth and tenth in the shorter. The shorter lines, often octosyllabic, where the length of line and of an intonational-semantic unit tends to coincide, do not have a caesura. Syllabic lines are normally arranged in "feminine" rhymed couplets, requiring identity or close similarity of orthography and sound in the last two syllables of each pair of lines.

Syllabic poems are sometimes called *virshy,* (from the Latin "versus"), although this term describes a larger variety of Russian verse, beginning with pre-syllabic compositions, in which lines could be distinguished by their irregular rhymed endings, irrespective of the number of syllables in each. The earliest such verses, called *raeshniki* (see SKAZOVYI STIKH) in Russia, appeared at the beginning of the 17th century, in imitation of similar verses in Polish.

The principal model of Russian syllabic verse was the Polish system of versification, developed to its canonical form in the poetry of Jan Kochanowski (1530–1584) in the second half of the 16th century. In the Polish language, the word stress had stabilized on the penultimate syllable, thus permitting a natural distribution of feminine caesurae and clausulas, although these did not become "strong constants" until the 19th century, that is, long after the initial contacts between the Russian and Polish versification systems were made and after both systems had developed in their own separate ways. During the time of extensive Polish influence on Russian versification, the Russian poets, like the Poles, tended to vary the pre-caesura stress from feminine to masculine, and even to dactylic. The variable word-stress in Russian was especially conducive to such deviations from the standard pattern. In general, the stress in Russian carries semantic value and is therefore an important linguistic feature, highly perceptible to the speaker. In Russian syllabic versification, the presence of strongly felt but irregularly distributed stresses tended to disrupt the rhythmic flow of the line. In the Polish syllabic line, on the other hand, the function of word stress is minimal, and the perception of rhythm is determined by other factors. The discrepancy between the requirements of the syllabic line and the natural properties of the Russian language led to a gradual increase in the regularity of stress distribution and eventually to the replacement of the syllabic system by the syllabotonic, in the first half of the 18th century.

Among the most important practitioners of syllabic verse in Russian one may count SIMEON POLOTSKY (1629–80), a Kievan monk and graduate of the Mohyla Academy in Kiev—a school modelled on Polish Jesuit academies, in which the composition of verse was studied and practiced according to the Polish example. Another important author was Feofan PROKOPOVICH (1681–1736), a playwright and poet, a high dignitary of the Russian Orthodox Church and an active participant in the reforms of Peter the Great. He was a friend of Antiokh KANTEMIR (1708–44), author of well-known satirical poems castigating the social mores of the day, and perhaps the most talented poet to use the syllabic system. Kantemir felt it necessary to elaborate a theoretical description of Russian versification in his *Letter of Khariton Makentin to a Friend on the Composition of Russian Verse* (1743) in which he called for a much greater regularity of stress distribution than was common in the syllabic lines. He did not, however, propose the radical step of defining a Russian verse line in terms of a given number of verse feet as well as syllables, rather than syllables alone. This was accomplished by Vasily TREDIAKOVSKY (1703–69), a poet and scholar, who set in motion a reform of Russian versification with his treatise *A New and Brief Method for Composing Russian Verses* (1735). Trediakovsky concentrated on the classical thirteen- and eleven-syllable lines, reorganizing them in such a manner that they could be measured by trochaic feet, with a masculine caesura on the seventh and fifth syllable, respectively. Mikhailo LOMONOSOV (1711–65), an outstanding Russian poet and scientist of the 18th century, completed Trediakovsky's reform by developing full theoretical premises for the syllabotonic system of versification which is prevalent to this day.

Bibliography: Maria Dłuska, *Studia z historii i teorii wersyfikacji polskiej.* 2 vols. Cracow, 1948–50. I. P. Eremin, "Simeon Polotskii—poet i dramaturg." In Simeon Polotskii, *Izbrannye sochineniya.* 1953. P. 240. V. E. Kholshevnikov, "Russkaya i pol'-skaya sillabika i sillabo-tonika." In *Teoriya stikha.* 1968. V. N. Peretts, *Iz istorii razvitiya russkoi poezii XVIII v.* (= *Istoriko-literaturnye issledovaniya i materialy*, vol. 3.) 1905. ———, *Ocherki po istorii poeticheskogo stilya v Rossii.* (= *Istoriko-literaturnye issle-dovaniya i materialy*, vol. 4.) 1905. A. V. Pozdneev, "Die tonischen Elemente im russischen syllabischen Vers," *Zeitschrift für slavische Philologie*, 28 (no. 2, 1960), pp. 405–412. L. V. Pumpyanskii, "Ocherki po literature pervoi poloviny XVIII veka," *XVIII vek*, 1 (1935), pp. 83–132. L. I. Timofeev, *Ocherki teorii i istorii russkogo stikha.* 1939. ———, "Sillabicheskii stikh," *Ars poetica* 2, pp. 73–115. Jan Trzykadlowski, "Rytmotwórcza funkcja akcentu w wierszu staropolskim." Introduction to Karol Wiktor Zawodziński, *Studia z wersyfikacji Polskiej.* Wroclaw, 1954. Pp. xxvi–xlvii. *Virshi: Silla-bicheskaya poeziya XVII–XVIII vekov.* Ed. P. N. Berkov, with an introd. by I. N. Rozanov. 1935. K. W. Zawodziński, *Studia z wersy-fikacji Polskiej.* Ed. Janina Budkowska. Wroclaw, 1954.

F. R. S.

Syllabotonic versification. Although their position of absolute domi-nance has come to be challenged by the tonic meters and to a lesser extent by free verse, the so-called classical meters of the syllabo-tonic system—iambs and trochees (binary meters), as well as dactyls, amphibrachs and anapests (ternary meters)—have, taken as a group, been the most important for Russian poetry since the intro-duction of the syllabotonic system in the 18th century. Classical Russian syllabotonic poetry requires a fixed number of syllables between the ictuses (the positions that, according to the metrical scheme, may take stress). In iambic verse the ictuses are the even syllables (x x́ x x́ x x́ ...), in trochaic the odd (x́ x x́ x x́ x ...), and in the ternary meters they fall on every third foot, beginning with the first syllable in the line for dactylic meters (x́ x x x́ x x ...), the second for amphibrachs (x x́ x x x́ x ...), and the third for anapests (x x x́ x x x́ ...) The name of a given meter (sometimes called measure, or *raz-mer*) is determined by both the number and the position of the ictuses in a given line. Thus iambic trimeter lines have three ictuses located on the second, fourth, and sixth syllables; dactylic tetram-eter lines have four ictuses, located on the first, fourth, seventh, and tenth syllables. Usually all the lines in a poem have the same number of ictuses, and thus a single label, such as trochaic pentam-eter, is adequate for describing the entire poem. However, the lines may vary in length. When the different lengths form a regular pattern, the poem is said to be written in a mixed (*smeshannyi*) meter. A poem may contain iambic tetrameter lines alternating with others in iambic dimeter, or amphibrachic tetrameter lines alternat-ing with amphibrachic trimeter. As long as the same pattern is re-peated, the alternation may be quite complex. For instance, in BLOK's "Ispugom skhvachena, vlekoma ..." the first and third lines of each stanza are written in iambic tetrameter, the second in iambic dim-eter, and the fourth in iambic trimeter. When lines vary regularly, the meter is called variable (*vol'nyi*, often translated as "free," which causes confusion with free verse or *svobodnyi stikh*). By far the most common type of variable verse has been the variable iamb, which was widely used in fables during the 18th and 19th centuries.

For purposes of analysis the line is usually divided into three parts: the anacrusis, which contains the syllables preceding the first ictus; the stem, which consists of the syllables from the first through the last ictus; and the clausula, or the syllables that follow the final ictus. Compare, for instance, the iambic pentameter line, x x̀ x x̀ x x̀ x x̀ x́ (x) (x), with the anapestic trimeter, x x x̀ x x x̀ x x x́ (x) (x), where x́ indicates an obligatory and x̀ an optional stress. The former has a one-syllable anacrusis, a stem of nine syllables, and a clausula that may contain zero (in which case it is called masculine), one (feminine), two (dactylic) or, rarely, even more syllables. In the latter the anacrusis is two syllables, the stem has seven syllables, and the clausula may likewise contain zero, one, or more syllables. The clausula, which in rhymed poems reflects the pattern of mascu-line, feminine or other rhymes, has little effect on the lines' rhythm. The stem is of different lengths in poems containing mixed or vari-able meters, but otherwise it stays the same. The anacrusis is almost always constant throughout the poem in Russian syllabotonic meters, though there are rare examples of poems that mix the various types of ternary lines (for instance, anapests and amphi-

brachs). The anacrusis, unlike the clausula, does have a noticeable effect on the rhythm.

A few basic principles of Russian verse should be kept in mind: (1) The main prosodic element in Russian poetry is the distinction between stressed and unstressed syllables; all other considerations are of secondary importance. (2) The one absolute requirement that applies to nearly every line of Russian verse that has been written is the presence of a constant stress on the last ictus of the line. (3) While the precise way in which strong (potentially stressed) positions—that is, the ictuses—and weak positions occur in the line is important and there are noticeable rhythmic differences between, for instance, iambic and trochaic lines, "feet" as such exist only within the context of an entire line; it is not correct to speak of "mixing" various feet, such as iambs and anapests, in the same line. When the intervals between ictuses vary, the meter represents TONIC VERSIFICATION rather than syllabotonic. (4) Since the meters in mod-ern Russian are based on stress, the dominant feature for each meter can be expressed in terms of stressed or unstressed syllables: (a) In binary meters the metrical dominants are the weak positions, or unstressed syllables. The ictuses, other than the final ictus, only tend to be stressed, for omitted stresses are quite common. On the other hand, hypermetrical stressing on the weak positions is rel-atively infrequent; therefore, the lack of stress on these syllables is the most consistent feature of these lines. (b) Since ternary meters have two weak positions between the ictuses, the ictuses are normal-ly stressed and they become the metrical dominants. Hypermetrical stressing is somewhat more frequent than in the binary meters.

So far the discussion has been concerned primarily with meter, which specifies a set of norms to which lines in a poem must adhere. However, very few of the norms involve absolutes; for example, the schema for the trochaic tetrameter specifies only the zero anacrusis and the constant stress on the final ictus: x̀ x x̀ x x̀ x x́ (x). It further indicates that the even-numbered syllables are normally not stressed (the metrical dominants), while the first through third ictuses *may* carry stress (the metrical tendencies). *Rhythm*, on the other hand, is the actual pattern of stressing that occurs within the poem. The met-rical norms indicate the possible patterns of stressing on the line that constitute the *rhythmic variations* for a particular meter. Meter and rhythm interact. After just a few lines, a poem in trochaic tetram-eter creates the expectation of stresses on the odd syllables; when stress is omitted at an ictus (or, less commonly, when hypermetrical stressing occurs on one of the even syllables) the expectation is frus-trated. If stresses were to appear on every ictus in a trochaic or iam-bic poem, the rhythm would be monotonous. While other factors, such as word boundaries, have an effect, the rhythm of a poem is based primarily on the way in which it combines stressed and un-stressed ictuses.

The rhythmic tendencies that can be observed in the binary meters arise largely as a result of the obligatory stress on the final ictus and of the fact that stress in Russian words occurs at an aver-age rate of only once every 2.7 or 2.8 syllables. While ternary meters only rarely omitted a stress at an ictus in the 19th century, they do so more often in the 20th and have come to reveal patterns of stressing that follow the same tendencies as those for the binary meters. The *dol'nik*, the most common of the tonic meters, also omits stresses at ictuses in a manner that is reminiscent of iambic and trochaic verse. Kiril Taranovsky has expressed these tendencies in terms of two laws: (1) The law of the stabilization of the first ictus after the first weak position; and (2) the law of regressive accentual dissimilation.

The first law simply means that the first ictus in a particular type of line will be stressed relatively often if that ictus occurs after a weak position. If, on the other hand, the first ictus coincides with the first position in a line, then that ictus tends to be stressed rel-atively less often. Therefore the first ictus in iambic, anapestic, and amphibrachic lines has a propensity to bear stress, since in each case it follows a weak position. On the other hand, the first ictus in trochaic and dactylic lines coincides with the first syllable and is often left unstressed; in such poems the second ictus will be stressed more frequently.

The second law follows from the obligatory stress on the final ictus. If the next-to-last ictus is also stressed, then two stresses must occur within the space of three syllables. Since Russian words carry stress only a little more often than once every three syllables, binary meters will be most strongly inclined to avoid stress on the penultimate ictus. As M. L. Gasparov's figures for the frequency of stressing in the iambic pentameter without caesura in Soviet lyric poetry show, the same pattern continues throughout the line:

Syllable:	2	4	6	8	10
% of ictuses with stress:	82.5	72.3	84.1	38.9	100

Owing to the frequent omission of stress on the next-to-last ictus, the second ictus from the end will tend to bear a stress. However, stress here is not obligatory and therefore is not as strong as on the line's final ictus. The third ictus from the end will again be weak (that is, likely to omit a stress), but the tendency will be less pronounced than for the penultimate ictus. In other words, strong and weak ictuses alternate backwards from the end of the line in a wave-like fashion. The distinction between strong and weak ictuses is strongest at the end of the line, because of the obligatory stress on the last ictus, and becomes progressively weaker as one moves towards the beginning (hence the dissimilation is regressive).

Roman JAKOBSON has pointed out the special role of monosyllabic words in Russian poetry. Many one-syllable words, such as prepositions and conjunctions, are unstressed; others, such as pronouns, occupy a gray area; while verbs, nouns, and adjectives carry stress. But stress in all monosyllabic words differs from stress in words of two or more syllables, because it does not serve the important function of distinguishing between two words (e.g., *práva*, genitive singular of "law"; and *pravá*, short-form adjective of "right"). Since the stress in monosyllabic nouns and verbs is not functional, these are able to appear in the weak positions of lines written in binary meters and thereby create hypermetrical stressing. At the same time the stressed syllable of a polysyllabic word can not coincide with a weak position, for this would tend to have a disruptive effect. For example, it is not rare for a stressed monosyllabic word to appear at the very start of an iambic line and be followed by two unstressed syllables before the first stressed ictus, e.g., BARATYNSKY's "Snóv zolotýkh sud'bá blagáya ..." (of golden dreams the blessèd fate: x́ x x x́ x x́ x x́). But a polysyllabic word, stressed on the first syllable, will not be placed at the beginning of an iambic line by Russian poets. Also, one-syllable words, lacking word-distinguishing stresses, tend to appear more often on the weaker ictuses. In the trochaic tetrameter, for instance, the fourth, or last ictus, is a constant, the second will also be strong, and the first and third will be weak (as predicted by Taranovsky's two laws). Theoretically, then, the monosyllables should favor the first and third ictuses, and analyses of works written in this meter have shown the hypothesis to be correct. In general, words involved in hypermetrical stressing cannot be longer than the interval between ictuses in the particular meter. In practice, this means that in iambic and trochaic lines hypermetrical stressing is limited to monosyllabic words. In ternary lines, hypermetrical stressing may involve words of one or two syllables, though monosyllables are more common since they do not have as great an effect on the rhythm.

Since stress is omitted much more often at ictuses in binary lines than in ternary, the rhythm of binary lines provides much richer material for study. There is no theoretical limit for line lengths; they may range from a single ictus up to eight or more, though by far the most common lines range from trimeters through hexameters (i.e., from three ictuses through six). To illustrate the ways in which the rhythm of Russian verse may be analyzed, it is instructive to look closely at a single meter, the iambic tetrameter, which over the years has been the most common of the Russian meters.

The schema for the Russian iambic tetrameter is as follows: x x́ x x́ x x́ x x́ (x) (x). There are two ways to describe the usage of this or any other meter in a poem. One is "horizontally," that is, to consider all the possible rhythmic variations of lines written in the meter and then to see how often each of these variations is employed. The other is "vertically," or counting how often each ictus is stressed in all the lines of a poem.

The first method becomes awkward with some of the longer meters, since so many rhythmic variations can occur. However, it is quite practical for the iambic tetrameter, which has just eight possible variations:

Number of omitted stresses	Number of variation	Form	Example
0	I	x x́ x x́ x x́ x x́ (x)	Zheníkh blednél i bróvi sdvínul
1	II	x x x x́ x x́ x x́ (x)	Vospominán'ya prézhnikh lét
	III	x x́ x x x x́ x x́ (x)	Nerádostnym veshcháyut zvónom
	IV	x x́ x x́ x x x x́ (x)	Eë svyatáya krasotá
2	V	x x́ x x x x x x́ (x)	Nad rúkhnuvsheyu barrikádoi
	VI	x x x x́ x x x x́ (x)	Blagoukhánnuyu sigáru
	VII	x x x x x́ x x́ (x)	I velosipedíst letít
3	VIII	x x x x x x x x́ (x)	Khot' i ne bez predubezhdén'ya

The numbering of the variations follows that of Taranovsky; variations V through VII of the iambic tetrameter are ordered differently by some scholars. All the examples of iambic tetrameter lines, except for the seventh, are taken from the poems in Andrei BELY's collection *Ashes* (Pepel, 1909). Only I–IV and VI are common; the fifth variation is rare since most poets tend to avoid two unstressed syllables in a row, while both VII and VIII exist more in theory than in practice (the example for the seventh variation was invented by Bely).

The second method requires finding the percentage of times that a given ictus is stressed and comparing that percentage against the figure for other poems—perhaps with a part or all of the poet's other works in that meter or with a particular period in Russian poetry. In the iambic tetrameter stressing on the first three ictuses may vary considerably, and the relative frequency of stressing among the ictuses indicates the rhythmic structure of the poem as a whole. In theory the figures showing the usage of each rhythmic variation (the horizontal analysis) can also provide the information about the percentage of stressing on each ictus. For instance, only variations IV, V, and VI (and the virtually never used VIII) omit stress on the third ictus. By adding together the percentage of times that each of these forms appears and then subtracting the figure from 100, it is possible to obtain the percentage of stressing on the third ictus. However, it is difficult to carry out this operation mentally for three or four ictuses at once; therefore, even when percentages for rhythmic variations are given, a separate set of figures for the vertical picture, or stressing on each ictus, is usually provided as well. Following are Taranovsky's figures for *Evgeny Onegin*: first is the use of rhythmic variations and then the stressing at each ictus:

Variation	I	II	III	IV	V	VI
% of use	26.8	6.6	9.7	47.5	0.4	9.0

Ictus	I	II	III	IV
% of times stressed	84.4	89.9	43.1	100

Such information can be useful in a number of ways: it can illustrate the "background" for the works of a particular poet or era against which the rhythm of a given poem may be compared, help answer questions involving dating or scholarship, and show the predominant types of rhythm that are associated with a given meter. For instance, in the case of the iambic tetrameter, poets tended to stress the first ictus more heavily during the 18th century, which meant that they used the third rhythmic variation more and the fourth noticeably less than did PUSHKIN. In the 20th century many poets have come to use a rhythm that is closer to the 18th-century model.

In the case of longer lines the rhythmic analysis may be complicated by the presence of a caesura, or word boundary occurring at the same position throughout an entire poem. For example, until the 1820s the iambic pentameter was nearly always written with a caesura after the fourth syllable; as a result, stressing on the third ictus was very high, around 95 percent. When the caesura went out of use, stressing on the third ictus, as predicted by Taranovsky's second law, remained high, but not as high as before; therefore stressing throughout the line became somewhat more even. In still longer lines, such as the iambic hexameter, the caesura remains common. Poets have often employed a "strong caesura," in which the ictus preceding the caesura is constantly stressed. Sometimes the strong caesura is accompanied by certain other features, such as the non-metrical addition (or deletion) of a syllable or two at the caesura.

Still another factor affecting the rhythm is the interaction of the two laws formulated by Taranovsky. In iambic lines with an odd number of ictuses and trochaic lines with an even number, the two laws operate in harmony; as a result, there is generally a clear, wave-like rhythm throughout the line. But in the other binary lines the laws conflict. Since the combination of the two laws has a different effect on iambic and trochaic lines with the same number of ictuses, the most common rhythms for iambic and trochaic lines of the same lengths differ sharply. Thus in iambic tetrameter, percentage of lines stressing on the first ictus is usually fairly high (as a result of the first law) and that on the second just a bit higher (as a result of the second). Since the two laws conflict, the difference in stressing between the first and second ictuses is not great. But in the trochaic tetrameter, where the two laws operate in harmony, stressing on the first ictus is quite low (usually around 50–60 percent) and that on the second becomes a near constant—about 99 percent in Pushkin's use of this meter. As for ternary meters, until the 20th century omitted stresses occurred very rarely and then almost exclusively at the first ictus in dactylic lines. In the 20th century a few poets have taken to omitting stress more often, and in such works the rhythmic structure is generally in keeping with that found in the comparable binary meters. On the other hand, hypermetrical stressing has always been somewhat more common in ternary meters, with their two-syllable intervals between ictuses, than in the binary, and the location as well as the frequency of hypermetrical stressing may have some effect on the rhythm.

Bibliography: James Bailey, "The Basic Structural Characteristics of Russian Literary Meters." In *Studies Presented to Professor Roman Jakobson by his Students.* 1968. Pp. 17–38. ———, "Russian Binary Meters with Strong Caesura from 1890 to 1920," *IJSLP* 14 (1971), pp. 111–33. M. L. Gasparov, *Sovremennyi russkii stikh: Metrika i ritmika.* 1974. Roman Jakobson, "Ob odnoslozhnykh slovakh v russkom stikhe." In *Slavic Poetics: Essays in honor of Kiril Taranovsky.* 1973. Pp. 239–52. V. E. Kholshevnikov, *Osnovy stikhovedeniya: Russkoe stikhoslozhenie.* 1972. Kiril Taranovsky, *Ruski dvodelni ritmovi. I–II.* Belgrade, 1953. ———, "O ritmicheskoi strukture russkikh dvuslozhnykh razmerov." In *Poetika i stilistika russkoi literatury: Pamyati akademika Viktora Vladimirovicha Vinogradova.* 1971. Pp. 420–29; B. V. Tomashevskii, *O stikhe: Stat'i.* 1929. B. O. Unbegaun, *Russian Versification.* 1956. Viktor Žirmunskij, *Introduction to Metrics: The Theory of Verse.* 1966. (Trans. of *Vvedenie v metriku: Teoriya stikha,* 1925).

B. S.

Symbolism (*Simvolizm*), a literary movement which originated in France and which had ramifications in several national literatures and a florescence in Russia between 1900 and 1910. The Russian movement was, like the French, a resurgence of idealism and aestheticism. REALISM and positivism had enjoyed a long period of dominance in Russia before symbolism arose as a neo-romantic reaction. The French movement was perceived by the Russians as beginning with Charles Baudelaire and including Paul Verlaine, Stéphane Mallarmé, and Arthur Rimbaud. Russian symbolism was similarly accompanied by those morbid and sensational currents that were called DECADENCE, but it was more patently metaphysical than the French movement had been, partly under the influence of the Russian philosopher Vladimir SOLOVYOV. The principal Russian symbolists are usually separated into two waves; the first included Konstantin BALMONT, Fyodor SOLOGUB, Valery BRYUSOV, and Zinaida HIPPIUS, the second Aleksandr BLOK, Andrei BELY, and

Vyacheslav IVANOV. All were poets, but nearly every one also made significant contributions to the development of other genres. Blok introduced the lyric drama; Bely and Sologub owed their reputations more to their novels than to their poetry. The symbolist school in literature was associated with the graphic artists of the MIR ISKUSSTVA (World of Art) group, whose leader was Sergei DIAGHILEV. They were similarly close to the idealist philosophers Lev SHESTOV and Vasily ROZANOV. The symbolist movement had a broad success in Russia; many authors outside the school were influenced by its philosophical directions and technical innovations and contributed to its journals.

Among the first manifestations of symbolism in the early 1890s were translations from Baudelaire and other poets and periodical articles describing the major figures of the French school. In 1892 a transitional poet, Dmitry MEREZHKOVSKY, entitled a collection of his poetry *Simvoly* (Symbols); the poems resembled late romanticism. In 1893 he published a long essay that has since come to be regarded as the manifesto of the school; it was called "On the Causes for the Decline and on New Currents in Contemporary Russian Literature" (O prichinakh upadka i o novykh techeniyakh sovremennoi russkoi literatury). Citing the French poets as predecessors, he predicted the appearance in Russia of an idealist school, which he anticipated would draw on the "mysticism" of such Russian authors as DOSTOEVSKY and TOLSTOI. The first periodical to bring the symbolists together was the St. Petersburg newspaper *Severnyi vestnik*, which the publisher, Lyubov Gurevich, had bought in 1888 with the intention of making it into the first bulwark of idealism, a task which she attempted with the aid of a militant literary critic, A. VOLYNSKY. Informally associated with the editorship was another transitional poet, N. MINSKY, who propounded in his essay "By the Light of Conscience" (Pri svete sovesti, 1891) the first Russian philosophy influenced by Nietzsche. The first book of symbolist verse to win the approval of the critics and public was a collection by Balmont called *Under Northern Skies* (Pod severnym nebom, 1894), which featured melancholias, aspirations to spiritual attainment, and pastoral scenes. A *succès de scandale* was perpetrated by Bryusov, who, while still a Moscow university student, published, together with a collaborator, three miscellanies called *Russian Symbolists* (Russkie simvolisty, 1894 and 1895). They contain immature verse which was imitative of Baudelaire, Verlaine, and others, and which was ridiculed and parodied in the press.

A number of works representing the new currents appeared in the mid-1890s and established the movement on Russian soil. The school was almost always called decadence; in fact, the new works were characterized by an interest in psychopathology and a pessimistic view of the world that seemed to sort ill with the idealist philosophies which were propounded. Most authors accepted the appellation decadent without demurrer. Personal ties were formed in this period between the groups in St. Petersburg and Moscow which had arisen independently. Balmont, a Moscow poet, continued to be the most successful with the public. His themes developed rapidly into a coherent, and representative, philosophy. In *V bezbrezhnosti* (In Boundlessness, 1895) and in *Tishina* (Silence, 1898) his meditations intimate that nature and mankind both strive unceasingly and unavailingly towards a higher reality dimly intuited by them. Despondencies, revolts, and, in general, decadence, appeared to result from philosophical disillusionment. The leader of the St. Petersburg group was Merezhkovsky; he and Hippius, who was his wife, were at the center of a movement to renovate Russian Orthodoxy through the infusion of ideas from pre-Christian Greek philosophy. Merezhkovsky embarked on a trilogy of philosophical novels with historical settings whose general title was *Christ and Antichrist* (Khristos i Antikhrist), and whose thesis was that the "pagan" worship of the flesh will be joined with the Christian worship of the spirit in a future millennium. The first, *The Outcast* (Julian the Apostate) (1895), depicted not only the protagonist's struggle against Christ, but barbaric scenes comparable to those in Gustave Flaubert's *Salammbô.*

The second "decadent" to be accepted by the critics was Fyodor Sologub, whose initial reputation was owing to short stories published in the collection *Shadows* (Teni, 1896). A teacher until 1907 Sologub depicted schoolchildren suffering from the obsessions and delusions characteristic of the decadent mentality. In the novel *Bad Dreams* (Tyazhelye sny, 1896) he portrayed a schoolteacher concerned for social reforms, as in realistic novels, and yet afflicted by decadent hallucinations. The novel was influenced by Joris Karl Huysmans, as well as by GOGOL and Dostoevsky. A volume of poems, also published in 1896, featured melancholias and spleen, escapist dreaming, and pastoral imagery. Although he resided in St. Petersburg, Sologub did not participate in Merezhkovsky's religious movement.

Bryusov's first collection of verse *Chefs d'oeuvre* (1896) was still imitative of the French *poètes maudits* and was not taken seriously. His second volume, *Me eum esse* (1897), showed him more specifically as imitator of *Les Fleurs du mal* in that he expressed a disdain for humanity and a yearning for perfection, drew contrasts between evil and innocence, and was curious about the option for death. Bryusov, who came from a mercantile family, was eventually to conduct the most continuous and effective entrepreneurial activity for the school. Hippius earned a reputation for her striking poetry before it appeared in any collection; her initial publications were of short stories which have now been forgotten. The stories in *New People* (Novye lyudi, 1896) and *Mirrors* (Zerkala, 1898) portray people caught up in conflicts between conventional and ideal notions of human relationships, particularly as they relate to love, marriage, and class difference.

Decadence was even more characteristic of some lesser poets who were not successful with the press and public, but who were close to the major figures. Aleksandr DOBROLYUBOV published a collection called *Natura naturans. Natura naturata* (1895) containing innovative lyrics on death, religion, love, and nature. Other decadents were Vladimir Hippius and Ivan KONEVSKOI, whose untimely death was considered a loss to Russian poetry. The *Severnyi vestnik* rejected these poets, as well as Bryusov, for ideological reasons, and eventually even became intolerant of the decadent current in its chosen authors. Led by Minsky, the latter began to publish in other periodicals, and in 1898 *Severnyi vestnik* was closed. The authors defended their decadent elements from outside interference, and, in fact, decadence often functioned in their work as a symptom of an ideological disillusionment. Later, decadence was sometimes equated with an aesthetic view of literature and controversies then arose between partisans of theurgical and of aesthetic art. But during the fin-de-siècle years this inherent split was minimized while the school was still seeking recognition.

In the first years of the new century symbolism was established as a viable literary movement. Its aesthetic and religious elements were welcomed by some for whom the material ameliorism to which realism had dedicated itself began to seem inadequate. The successes of the writers were paralleled, and furthered, by the activities of the *Mir iskusstva* group of artists and art connoisseurs. Their journal, *Mir iskusstva*, which was published in St. Petersburg between 1899 and 1904, served as a new center for the movement. It introduced impressionist painting from Europe and revived an interest in 18th-century (pre-realist) Russian art, as did their series of exhibitions. The journal was open, in addition, to the creative works and essays of symbolist writers (it had a literary editor, D. Filosofov), and it accepted authors from both Moscow and St. Petersburg. Contacts were established with such eminent artists as Alexandre Benois and Leon Bakst, who served as editors of *Mir iskusstva* and who were later associated with Diaghilev in Paris. Ties were similarly formed with the idealist essayists, Rozanov and Shestov, who sometimes advanced their ideas in the form of interpretative essays on the works of such authors as Dostoevsky and Tolstoi. Philosophy as such was restricted in its development by the religious censorship; a body of philosophical literature grew up, therefore, around Russian fiction. In Moscow Bryusov was enabled by the patronage of S. A. Polyakov to found the *Skorpion* publishing house, which between 1900 and 1916 brought out a number of symbolism's best books and periodicals. Bryusov's devotion to the movement and his preference for aesthetic values over religious goals in art made him a fairly impartial manager. *Skorpion* editions were designed and illustrated by *Mir iskusstva* artists. Balmont and some other symbolists owe much of their reputation to the existence of this publishing enterprise.

Symbolism began to be welcomed by some of the intelligentsia as a resurrection of spiritual goals in cultural life. Some symbolists believed that the movement had overcome its stage of revolt, disbelief, and decadence. Merezhkovsky and Hippius viewed the movement as a "reevaluation of all values," not only in the spirit of Nietzsche, but of Neoplatonism. Together with Minsky and some interested clerics they founded a Religious-Philosophical Society in 1901 as a forum for their ideas. Their journal, *Novyi put'* was begun in 1903 as an organ for the society, but new creative works by the symbolists also appeared in it; in 1904 it was replaced, after censorship difficulties, by *Voprosy zhizni*.

A turn toward philosophical optimism is apparent in Merezhkovsky's *The Resurrection of the Gods (Leonardo da Vinci)*—Voskresshie bogi (Leonardo da Vinchi), 1899—the most successful and enduring novel of his career. Leonardo is, in his portrayal, the discoverer of ancient ideals of beauty and their power in human life; the book contributed to the "dawn" atmosphere present in symbolism at the beginning of the century. As a novel it is least spoiled by the networks of dichotomies that characterize not only Merezhkovsky's novels, but his essays, for example, his influential antithetic presentation of Tolstoi and Dostoevsky in 1901. The final part of Merezhkovsky's historical trilogy, *Antichrist (Peter and Alexis)*—Antikhrist (Petr i Aleksei), 1905, showed in its unexpected ambiguities a return of skepticism, or even pessimism, which reflected the worsening political situation. Orthodoxy, represented by Peter's son Alexis, now seemed the sole hope of the future.

Decadence did not vanish, but impotence and despondency tended, for a while at least, to be replaced as themes by manifestations of vigor and self-assertiveness. Symbolist works became, moreover, more candidly metaphysical. A sign of symbolism's success was the return of poetry to a wider public favor. In Balmont's new collections, *Burning Buildings* (Goryashchie zdaniya, 1900) and *Let Us Be Like the Sun* (Budem kak solntse, 1903) the nostalgia and the melancholies of his earlier books are rejected in favor of avowals of attainment and ecstasy. The latter moods rest on a new pantheistic view of the universe and a rather facile notion of being identified thereby with all phenomena. These moods are not incompatible with self-glorification and a willingness to go "beyond good and evil" which bespeak the influence of Nietzsche. An abundance of alliterations and vowel harmonies seemed to attest to an exuberance or intensity of feeling. Balmont's pastoral imagery now served his pantheism; exotic landscapes from Europe and various more tropical geographical areas began to appear. In life he cultivated the role of dandy and world traveller. New collections of his verse came out about twice yearly between 1903 and 1905. Bryusov achieved a reputation as a serious, even erudite, poet. In *Tertia vigilia* (1900) and *Urbi et orbi* (1903) he appeared as the inheritor both of French symbolism and of the Parnassians. He often posed as being splenetic, or ineffectual. Yet he drew portraits of mythical and historical figures and lauded physical might, courage, will power, and creativity. These exotic depictions frequently seemed to contain lessons in psychology for modern man. Bryusov's basic theme was the ubiquitousness of evil. He professed, however, to be dedicated only to aesthetic values in whose service he advised the artist to exercise both passion and cool observation. In these books Bryusov also popularized in Russian poetry the urban theme which he found in Emile Verhaeren and other Western writers.

Those who were least affected by the optimism of the "dawn" years were Sologub and Hippius. After the turn of the century Sologub's prose and poetry became even more trenchant in their denunciation of a material world without perfection, love, or beauty. A new collection of verse in 1904 contains arresting contrasts between a Gnostic, dichotomous world of good and evil, light and dark, and a Schopenhauerian universe of endless, aimless, amoral process. Death is viewed ambivalently as both a consolatrix and a source of horror. Sologub's imaginative imagery juxtaposes romantic and folkloristic pictures, such as of angels, stars, and witches, with simple scenes of the Russian countryside. His stories in *The Sting of Death* (Zhalo smerti, 1904) still depict children and young people who suffer from fantasies connected with unattainable ideals or with sordid reality; almost every protagonist ends in death. A fruit of his early years was his famous novel *The Petty Demon* (Melkii bes, which was not published until 1907), a Gogolian satire of provincial society. Hippius' poetry, which appeared in *Sobranie stikhov* (A Collection of Verse, 1904), depicts a personal dilemma. She aspires to a state of Christ-like ideal love and falls instead into arrogance and alienation. Hippius combined a restricted vocabulary and range of images with a subtle and complex feeling for rhythms, alliterations, and vowel patterns. In her stories she continued to portray characters who seek, or who fail to seek, an ideal love; she also took a liberal political stance in her sympathy for lower class characters.

Symbolism, as opposed to decadence, was thought to be exemplified in its purest form in the works of three new writers who joined the movement at the turn of the century. All wrote works which display a belief in the eventual spiritual ascension of mankind or in the possibility of mystical epiphanies. They epitomized the new "dawn" atmosphere. All three were influenced by the 19th-century Russian philosopher and poet Vladimir Solovyov. The latter assigned to SAINT SOPHIA, in Eastern Church doctrine the Holy Wisdom (*Hagia Sophia*), a role in earthly loves and in a future millennium. For some symbolists she was the animating spirit of the physical world. The first of the three to appear was Vyacheslav Ivanov, a classical scholar. His poems in *Guiding Stars* (Kormchie zvezdy, 1903) and *Transparencies* (Prozrachnost', 1904) are meditations blending Christian thought with Greek myth in tones of nostalgia, awe, and gratitude. Through the notion of a racial memory he equated the classical gods, as records of mankind's religious experience, with Christian entities. He was attracted to the cult of Dionysus and the idea of salvation through death and resurrection; he was much indebted to Nietzsche, especially in *The Birth of Tragedy*, as well as to Solovyov.

The youngest of the "second generation" symbolists were Blok and Bely, whose work contains many echoes of their friendship. Both were university students, Blok at St. Petersburg and Bely at Moscow. Bely's verse in *Gold in Azure* (Zoloto v lazure, 1904) was characterized by a mystical nostalgia, many skyscapes and a child-like whimsicality and preoccupation with creatures of folklore. His was the most innovative symbolist prose. Under the influence of Wagnerian ideas he published between 1902 and 1908 four "symphonies" in prose. All suggest the existence of an ultimate beauty and perfection that earthly creatures, sometimes kings and queens, may seek. The best-known of the "symphonies," *The Return* (Vozvrat, 1905) alternates realistic scenes of university life with fantasy scenes about a child, the alter ego of the protagonist. Blok's *Verses about the Beautiful Lady* (Stikhi o prekrasnoi dame, 1904) is a verse diary of a search for communion with Saint Sophia; the book marks the spiritual apogee of the Russian symbolist movement. The doctrine of Saint Sophia ascends to Gnosticism, which enjoyed a revival among early German romantics. It functioned in Russian literature as a specific instance of Goethe's Eternal Feminine.

The Russian movement was much altered in its course by the failure of the Revolution of 1905 and subsequent political repression. The symbolists were liberals and supported the revolutionary movement to end the autocracy. Sologub, who was of lower class origin, wrote verse lampoons for the underground satirical periodicals and published in the legal press a small book of patriotic and radical verse called *To the Homeland* (Rodine, 1906). Balmont joined the Social Democratic Party; he, Merezhkovsky and Hippius emigrated temporarily to Paris where Balmont published seditious verse in *Songs of an Avenger* (Pesni mstitelya, 1907) and Hippius and Merezhkovsky brought out a tract, *Le Tsar et la Révolution* (1907). Ivanov, on the other hand, returned from abroad out of patriotic feeling; he gave his energetic support to a newly devised tenet called mystical anarchism. Through the efficacy of a mystically shared racial culture, an obedience to the communal will was to be reconciled with the need for freedom. Both Blok and Bely began to romanticize the destiny of the nation, which they perceived as a mystical entity. The political disappointments of the times touched off metaphysical disillusionments in them. Henceforth Russian symbolism ceased to be a completely cosmopolitan movement; however wide its cultural perspectives, Russian symbolism was more or less preoccupied with the national character and fate.

Russian high culture was particularly brilliant during the period of political repression following the Revolution of 1905. Symbolist enterprises and circles were numerous; public sentiment was apparently attracted by the latent pessimism of this neo-romantic movement. The literary (and art) magazine *Vesy* (1904–1909) under the de facto editorship of Bryusov was one of the most opulent and informative in the history of Russian literature. It was published by *Skorpion* and featured the art work of the *Mir iskusstva* group, reports by foreign correspondents on literature and art in Western Europe, new creative work by the whole spectrum of Russian symbolists, and essays on doctrinal views by all parties. Its premises served as a center of the movement in Moscow. In St. Petersburg the Wednesday salon of Ivanov, known as "The Tower" in reference to his sixth-floor apartment, was between 1905 and 1907 a

meeting place for symbolists, as well as for kindred authors and artists, such as Mikhail KUZMIN and Maksimilian VOLOSHIN; some younger poets, for example Anna AKHMATOVA, were first recognized there. Ivanov was closely associated with the art and literary magazine ZOLOTOE RUNO (1906–1909) which was, from 1907 on, in the hands of the mystical anarchists. A debate arose between *Zolotoe runo* and *Vesy*, whose staff was itself divided between millennarists and those who, like Bryusov, saw in symbolism only a literary movement.

The period of creative work that followed the failed Revolution of 1905 was rich, but marked by a general return to pessimism. Cultural, popular, or national topics appeared in alliance with metaphysical subjects, and prose and drama assumed an equal weight with poetry. Blok was now a celebrity; his despair seemed to speak for, or meet with the sympathies of, educated Russians well beyond symbolist circles. His new lyrics appeared in a rapid series of small books; the first was *Nocturnal Violet* (Nochnaya fialka, 1906). He abandoned his earlier mystical aspirations for self-irony and showed himself tempted by earthly passions, perceived as a blasphemous denigration of his former quest. His new settings were urban, often in taverns. His first lyric drama, *The Fair Show Booth* (Balaganchik, 1906), epitomized the self-irony of the new period. Here Blok drew on the example of Maurice Maeterlinck and on the traditions of the commedia dell'arte. The play was staged at the innovative Komissarzhevskaya Theater by Vsevolod MEIERKHOLD. (The lyric theater in Russia was supported by an avant-garde current of staging that had arisen independently of symbolism, and in opposition to the realism of STANISLAVSKY.) Blok's *The Stranger* (Neznakomka, 1906) was even more symptomatic of the crisis of mysticism; in setting it matches his tavern verse. Blok was to surmount his self-irony only in a new mystical devotion to Russia, as in his cycle of lyrics, "On the Field of Kulikovo" (Na pole Kulikovom, 1908), whose title is a reference to a decisive medieval victory over the Tatars.

A symbolist novel which caught the public imagination was Sologub's *The Petty Demon* (Melkii bes, 1907); its accusatory depiction of provincial stagnation was considered timely, although the author had intended to portray evil as universal. His protagonist suffers not from decadence, as in the earlier novel, *Bad Dreams* (Tyazhelye sny, 1896), but from homicidal paranoia. Sologub's new short stories in *Decaying Masks* (Istlevayushchie lichiny, 1907) included some which were, in fact, meant to have a thinly veiled political significance. The culmination of his metaphysical pessimism was a volume of poetry published in 1908, *The Fiery Circle* (Plamennyi krug). It summarizes his previous themes, including his eternal devotion to a distant ideal, his vision of the universe as an evil process generated by a tyrannical Sun, and his spleen; but the most striking theme of the volume is an ambivalent fear of and desire for death. Yet Sologub was, in fact, undergoing a transition towards optimism. In his first lyric dramas, *The Gift of the Wise Bees* (Dar mudrykh pchel, 1907) and *Death's Conquering* (Pobeda smerti, 1907), he intimated that love transcends death's power. The plays have exotic, classical, and medieval settings and elevate beauty as the embodiment of a spiritual value. They were staged by Meierkhold and by Nikolai EVREINOV, also an innovative new director.

Other symbolists contributed to the impression of a general return to pessimism and decadence. Bryusov's new poetry in *Stephanos* (1906) exhibited his former tendencies, but the urban theme with its potential for the disturbing was more prominent. His short stories in *The Earth's Axis* (Zemnaya os', 1907) include a sensational novella, "The Republic of the Southern Cross" (Respublika yuzhnogo kresta), in which he depicts, as he does elsewhere, the catastrophic demise of a culture together with pathological behavior and atrocities; his message appears to be that human nature is evil, so society and the world must be. His ambitious historical novel, *The Fiery Angel* (Ognennyi angel, 1909), which probes the impact of occultism on medieval (and contemporary) culture, did not win the attention that was given to other novels whose cultural problems were more obviously contemporary. Bely's pessimism was as deep as was Blok's, but he was initially silent. In *Ashes* (Pepel, 1909) and *The Urn* (Urna, 1909) he satirized his own pathetic state, sometimes depicted as lunacy, and lamented the poverty and moral emptiness of Russian peasant culture; Russia is seen as a barren wilderness. In a major novel called *The Silver Dove* (Serebryanyi golub', 1910) he suggests that the relationship between the Westernized intellectuals and the superstitious, perhaps Asiatic, peasantry is a destructive one. Gogol's influence is obvious, as it had been in Sologub's *The Petty Demon*. Hippius published her fourth, fifth, and sixth volumes of short stories between 1906 and 1912; her best stories show public disasters and their attendant private psychological disorders. In 1910 she published a substantial collection of new, but no longer novel verse, about her decadent and Christian struggles.

There were outstanding writers who were merely close to the symbolist movement because of their themes or innovative techniques, and who may even have been welcome contributors to symbolist journals, but who were not counted among the inner circle because they had no mystical plane or otherworldly vision. One was the remarkable fiction writer Aleksei REMIZOV who experimented with innovative and folkloristic genres. Foremost among poets who were allied with symbolism was Innokenty ANNENSKY, whose poetic forebears were the French symbolists. His poems, collected in *Quiet Songs* (Tikhie pesni, 1904) and *The Cypress Chest* (Kiparisovyi larets, 1910) are characterized by melancholias and an appreciation of nature and the arts; his elliptical style focuses attention on the elusive and mysterious elements in the human psyche. Maksimilian Voloshin was also influenced by the French symbolists, but even more by the Parnassians. His poems feature elaborate imagery, but they are fundamentally philosophical meditations about the place of man in the universe. He often pictured exotic, mostly Mediterranean landscapes and cultures with their histories. His later poems protesting against the violence of the First World War, the Revolution, and civil war have been his best known. Mikhail Kuzmin, a prolific writer of verse, short stories, dramas, cabaret skits, and novels, won the reputation of a decadent aesthete with his first novel, *Kryl'ya* (Wings, 1907). His poetic subjects were often subtle aesthetic experience and delicate erotic relationships. His varied styles were sometimes clever pastiches. In his best known cycle of verses, "Alexandrian Songs" (Aleksandriiskie pesni, 1906), homosexual love appeared as a theme.

The success of the symbolist movement was marked by a flare-up of doctrinal controversies which reached a crisis in 1910. The split between beauty and truth, or aestheticism and mysticism was the deepest, but related issues were also debated. There were also rivalries among those who supported religious or cultural goals. Merezhkovsky had been the first leader of the latter tendency. When Ivanov became established in St. Petersburg he challenged Merezhkovsky's leadership of the "theurgically" oriented. Meanwhile, the mystical anarchists were hostile to every other faction. In Moscow Bely who was once the proponent of symbolism as a religious force, continued to insist on its efficacy as a cultural, or in fact as an epistemological system. Bryusov's *Vesy* was considered a bulwark of aestheticism. Yet Bely contended with him for the ideological direction of that journal. The heightened interest in national destiny engendered by the Revolution of 1905 resurrected the 19th-century conflict between SLAVOPHILES and WESTERNIZERS: should Russia as the embodiment of a religious force influence the West, or should Russia, as a poor and Asiatic culture, learn values from the West? The symbolist movement produced a number of volumes on aesthetic and cultural issues, among them *Symbolism* (Simvolizm, 1910), *The Green Meadow* (Lug zelenyi, 1910), and *Arabesques* (1911) by Bely and *By the Stars* (Po zvezdam, 1909) and *Furrows and Boundaries* (Borozdy i mezhi, 1916) by Ivanov.

The symbolist movement ceased to dominate Russian high culture after 1910. As eminent authors the symbolists continued to publish influential books, but they were joined, certainly in poetry, by vigorous new groups, in part an avant garde. At mid-career, the following symbolists were bringing out sets of their collected works: Balmont (1909-14), Sologub (1909-12; 1913-14), Blok (1911-12), Remizov (1910-12), and Merezhkovsky (1911-13). *Vesy* and the other symbolist journals ceased publication. A new periodical, *Apollon* (1909-17), launched by Ivanov and some of the younger poets, began to publish the best of the new creative works and to bring the news from abroad. The new groups included neorealists called ACMEISTS, whose leader was Nikolai GUMILYOV, as well as several factions of FUTURISTS—the cubo-futurists, ego-futurists, and Centrifugists, and others. All these groups rejected the mystical orientation of the symbolists while adopting their technical innovations. After 1917 members of this generation, which included Boris

PASTERNAK, Osip MANDELSHTAM, and Anna Akhmatova, were to displace the symbolists as Russia's leading poets.

In the period prior to the First World War the most successful Symbolists were those whose works show a serious interest in the national future and even in the subject of class conflicts, in however metaphysical a light these might be viewed. Purely philosophical meditations were now less successful. Ivanov's brilliant collection of verse, *Cor ardens*, published in 1911, was largely overlooked for this reason. Blok, however, was deeply engaged in his reflections on Russia's destiny, a pursuit reflected in a series of lyrics and essays in which he deplored the rift between the intelligentsia and the people. In other lyrics he became more generally responsive to the world at large, to Italy during a sojourn, for example, as well as to the arts and events of the times.

The national destiny and other worldly subjects inspired works by several other symbolists. Sologub rearranged his oeuvre in his collected works to reflect his new philosophical optimism and reconciliation with the material world. His *Collected Works* conclude with a trilogy of novels, *The Created Legend* (Tvorimaya legenda, 1914) whose lesson is that the imagination attuned to beauty dictates to reality, which copies art. The hero, a provincial schoolteacher as in *The Petty Demon*, is the embodiment of creative energy; disillusioned with the Revolution of 1905, he quits Russia to become king of the imaginary United Isles in the Mediterranean. Sologub was plainly a Westernizer. In Remizov's novel, *The Fifth Pestilence* (Pyataya yazva) published in 1912, Russia was perceived in a Slavophile light, as having in the untutored depths of the people a stream of mercy and spirituality that is spoiled by the introduction of Western notions of justice. Remizov did not portray a revolutionary movement here, but in his sympathy for the lower orders he was close to Blok. Bely in his extraordinary novel, *Petersburg* (1916), ridiculed both the radical movement of 1905 and the symbolists' metaphysical aspirations. Thus the novel is a bitter picture of the Russian culture that he knew best. Like the earlier novel *The Silver Dove*, it juxtaposes a Westernized elite with an Asiatic people, this time in an urban setting. This novel was the greatest single step in the direction of avantgardist Russian prose; it was remarkable for its absence of narrative transitions between scenes, and for its musical structure—repetitions in the form of leitmotifs, etc.

The symbolist movement disintegrated after the Revolution of 1917. In the first place, it was overshadowed by the poetry of the avant-garde generation. Second, the symbolists were dispersed physically because they were split by this revolution in their fealties; several remained in the Soviet Union while others became émigrés. The personal vicissitudes of both groups hampered the continuance of symbolist currents; moreover, mysticism and aestheticism were impeded from the beginning in the Soviet Union, and under SOCIALIST REALISM they were suppressed. Bryusov, Sologub, Bely, and Blok remained in the Soviet Union; the latter two poets again perceived the revolutionary movement as a spiritual upheaval on the part of the people. Blok produced one major piece, a long poem, "The Twelve" (Dvenadtsat', 1918) depicting the destruction of the old world at the hands of Red soldiers; the poem retains echoes of his mysticism in that it ends with the mysterious appearance of Christ. After a silence Blok died at the end of a famine winter in 1921. Bryusov served in the Ministry of Education; he published some original verse, but received more attention for his translations from Armenian poetry; he died in 1924. Sologub remained after an unsuccessful attempt to emigrate in 1921. He published a novel, short stories, and a play which suffer from a decline in his powers, but six small volumes of verse published between 1918 and 1922 show a continued growth and new simplicity. After 1923 he was able to publish only translations. He was Chairman of the Leningrad Union of Writers when he died in 1927. Bely continued to write experimental novels, the first and best of which was *Kotik Letaev* (the name of the protagonist, 1918) a first person narration of infancy heavily influenced by anthroposophy. In the twenties and early thirties he published several large novels, some autobiographical, some innovative, which have been neglected. In the thirties he published several volumes of memoirs of the symbolist period. He died in 1934.

Those who went into emigration—Balmont, Merezhkovsky, Hippius, and Ivanov—settled in France or Italy, where they lived and continued writing into the 1940s. They made few significant new contributions to Russian literature, and their audience dwindled. Balmont published much, but his verse was past its prime. Merezhkovsky and Hippius became the center, in Paris, of an anti-Soviet movement with religious coloration. Hippius published new verse in 1918, and a useful collection of reminiscences, *Living Faces* (Zhivye litsa, 1925). Otherwise, their works were usually essays and tracts. Ivanov, who defected to Italy in 1924, wrote excellent poems, including a cycle called "Roman Sonnets" (Rimskie sonety) and established multiple contacts with Western writers.

Symbolism, as a mystical and aesthetic movement, has been the object of disfavor in the Soviet Union, and little of its rich literature has been republished. Blok, who greeted the Revolution and died young, has fared the best, and Bryusov has been rewarded. In the sixties and seventies some works by Balmont, Bely, and Sologub have appeared; but Ivanov, Merezhkovsky and Hippius, the most religiously inclined of the émigrés, have not been republished in Soviet editions.

Bibliography: Andrei Belyi, *Na rubezhe dvukh stoletii. Vospominaniya.* 1930. —— *Nachalo veka. Memuary.* 1933. —— *Mezhdu dvukh revolyutsii. Vospominaniya. 1905–1911.* 1934. Evelyn Bristol, "Idealism and Decadence in Russian Symbolist Poetry," *SlavR* 39 (1980), pp. 269–80. Valery Y. Bryusov, *The Diary of Valery Bryusov (1893–1905).* Ed, trans., introd. Joan Delaney Grossman. Berkeley, 1980. Georgette Donchin, *The Influence of French Symbolism on Russian Poetry.* The Hague, 1958. Zinaida Gippius, *Zhivye litsa.* 2 vols. Prague, 1925. *Literaturnoe nasledstvo,* 27–28 (1937). Renato Poggioli, *The Poets of Russia. 1890–1930.* 1960. Avril Pyman, *The Life of Aleksandr Blok.* 2 vols. 1979–80. *RLT* 4 (1972): Symbolism.   E. Br.

Syuzhét (Fr. *sujet*, subject, topic). In his essay on Sterne's *Tristram Shandy,* V. B. SHKLOVSKY pointed out a difference between the simplest version of a story (*fabula*) and the unique presentation of that story in a literary work (*syuzhet*). *Fabula* is what is commonly called the summary of a story, and *syuzhet* is what actually happens with the story in a concrete narrative which uses such literary devices as RETARDATION (*zamedlenie*), OSTRANENIE and impeded form (*zatrudnenie*). In raising the issue of *syuzhet* versus *fabula,* Shklovsky tried to substantiate the FORMALIST thesis that narrative fiction does not amount to storytelling; that without literary devices, or without the *literariness* of literature, the stories would lose their zest and meaning.

It is significant that these two concepts were introduced in connection with *Tristram Shandy.* This novel can serve as an exaggerated example of what writers can do with the *fabula*: they can digress from it and actually talk about literary techniques, thus "laying bare the devices," and they can "string the motifs together" in a way which seems illogical from the standpoint of the *fabula.* For Shklovsky, *Tristram Shandy* was a welcome example of the difference between *syuzhet* and *fabula.*

However, the formalist definition of *syuzhet* raises more questions than it answers. Since everything in a narrative work can be regarded as a device used in the process of retelling the basic *fabula, syuzhet* merges with the notion of the literary work in its entirety. The novel *Anna Karenina* equals the *syuzhet* of *Anna Karenina.* Thus the concept loses its usefulness.

Bibliography: V. B. Shklovskii, "Parodiinyi roman." In his *O teorii prozy.* 1929. Pp. 177–204.   E. Th.

Tamizdát, see SAMIZDAT.

Tarásov-Rodiónov, Aleksándr Ignátievich (1885–1938), revolutionary and writer. A member of the Communist Party since 1905, Tarasov-Rodionov held a command position with the Red Army in the civil war and later was an examining magistrate of the Supreme Tribunal of the USSR (1921–24). As a writer, he belonged to the "Smithy" (KUZNITSA) group and was one of the organizers of the "October" (OKTYABR') group in 1922. His short novel, *Chocolate* (Shokolad, 1922), created a heated debate. It has a provincial Party functionary shot for allowing his flighty wife to accept a few bars of chocolate from class enemies. Like other old Bolsheviks, Tarasov-

Rodionov was disillusioned with the course taken by the Party during the NEP period and expressed his feelings in his fiction: "Grass and Blood" (Trava i krov', 1924). Subsequently he published a series of autobiographic novels and was immediately accused of having misrepresented the role of the Party in the Revolution. Tarasov-Rodionov was arrested and executed in Stalin's purges. He was "posthumously rehabilitated."

Works: Shokolad. Povest'. Reprint in *Opal'nye povesti.* New York, 1955. Reprint. Rego Park, N. Y., 1982.
Translations: February 1917. Trans. W. Drake. 1931. *Chocolate: A Novel.* Trans. C. Malamuth. 1932.
Secondary literature: V. Aleksandrova, *Literatura i zhizn'.* New York, 1969. Pp. 324–25.   V. T.

Tarkóvsky, Arsény Aleksándrovich (1907–) was born in Elizavetgrad, now Kirovograd, where he studied in the Higher State Literature Courses from 1925 to 1929. Until the early sixties, Tarkovsky was principally known as a translator of classical oriental poetry. Some critics see the philosophic strain in his own work as influenced by these Eastern poets, yet a more evident literary ancestor is TYUTCHEV.

His first volume of verse, *Before Snowfall* (Pered snegom, 1962), was followed by *The Earthly to the Earth* (Zemle—zemnoe, 1966), and *The Messenger* (Vestnik, 1969). That they are the work of a mature poet is clear not only from the poet's treatment of his subject matter ("not lyrical searches, but lyrical findings," as one critic has written), but also from the even control of artistic expression. His recent work includes *Poems* (Stikhotvoreniya, 1974), *Magic Mountains* (Volshebnye gory, 1978), and *A Winter Day* (Zimnii den', 1980).

Tarkovsky's writing combines a devotion to classical form, a designation of which he himself is suspicious, with a thematic concern for the concrete details of the modern world. His work, although dominated by the traditional iamb, uses a variety of meters, among them trochee, anapest, and amphibrach. His language, elevated, at times archaic, is reminiscent of DERZHAVIN's solemnity. Conscious of the word as artifact, he values its evocative quality without becoming absorbed in precious word-play. His treatment of the themes of art, love, nature, and the coming of old age, reflects his perception of the organic unity of historical past, often spanning centuries, with present and future, and brings into focus not only chronologically but also culturally diverse experiences.

Works: Stikhotvoreniya. 1974.
Secondary literature: Wolfgang Kasack, "Arsenii Tarkowskij," *Osteuropa,* no. 4 (1975), pp. 271–72. Adol'f Urban, "Ne podvodya itogi ... " *Zvezda,* 1975, no. 9, pp. 197–208.   N. C.

Tarsis, Valéry Yákovlevich (1906–). Editor, novelist, poet, dissident. Tarsis began publishing in 1929 and worked as an editor in the publishing house Khudozhestvennaya literatura from 1929 to 1937. He also translated thirty-four books from a variety of languages, including Ukrainian and Greek. He is the author of a four-volume epic novel entitled *The Beautiful and Its Shade* (Prekrasnoe i ego ten') and a trilogy *Free City* (Gorod razdol'nyi). He has also written three books of verse, various philosophical and political pamphlets, and some prose poetry. *The Bluebottle Fly* (Skazanie o sinei mukhe) is a political allegory of a philosopher who kills a fly and then asks himself why he cannot likewise kill people who get in his way. In 1961 Tarsis applied for permission to leave with his family for Italy. On 23 August 1962 he was incarcerated in the Kashchenko Psychiatric Hospital and kept there until February 1963 with a diagnosis of "expansive paranoia." He described his experience in *Ward 7,* whose title he modeled after Chekhov's *Ward 6.* On 21 February 1966 he was stripped of Soviet citizenship for "actions discrediting a Soviet citizen" and permitted to leave the USSR a few weeks later. This was the first such permission granted since the case of ZAMYATIN in 1932. He has persistently declared the USSR to be a fascist state, and the official Soviet reaction has been to accuse him of a "delirium of anti-Sovietism" and of having "sold his homeland for dollars." Tarsis currently resides in Berne.

Works: Sobranie sochinenii v 12-i tomakh. Frankfurt, 1966–70. *Nedaleko ot Moskvy. Roman.* Frankfurt, 1981.

Translations: The Bluebottle. Trans. Thomas Jones and David Alger. 1963. *Ward 7.* Trans. Katya Brown. 1965. *The Pleasure Factory.* Trans. Michael Glenny. 1967.   J. G.

Tautology can be defined as a device in which a combination of words that are similar in some way serves to emphasize and strengthen the meaning. A. P. Evgenieva limits the term to words having a common root: *grom gremit*, "thunder thunders," *krikom krichat'*, "shout with a shout," while BUSLAEV and POTEBNYA include synonym pairs. In a synonym pair the elements have a lexical relationship and belong to the same category of speech, while those words with a common root belong to different parts of speech. Evgenieva includes the following in her categorization of pairs with a common root (paronymy): (1) subject and verb (animate subject): *kuznets kuet*, "blacksmith forges," *pakhar' pashet*, "plougher ploughs," *vor voruet*, "thief steals," *bortsy borotsya*, "fighters fight"; (inanimate subject): *trubon'ka trubit*, "trumpet trumpets," *kosa kosit*, "scythe mows"; (subject—natural phenomena): *dozhd' dozhdit*, "the rain rains," *tuman tumanitsya*, "the fog fogs up." Sometimes the adjective rather than noun in the subject is coupled with the verb: *yasno svetel mesyats svetit*, "brightly shone the bright moon," *zasedelas' u starogo li sedaya boroda*, "the old man's gray beard was turning gray"; (2) verb and object (concrete object): *strelyat' strelochku*, "shoot arrow," *pisal pis'mo*, "wrote letter," *igrat' igru*, "play game"; (nonconcrete object): *razgovory razgovarivati*, "converse in conversation," *dumu dumat'*, "think a thought"; (3) instrumental case: *kosit' kosoi*, "mow with scythe," *vzglyanul vzglyadom neveselym*, "he gazed with an unhappy gaze"; (4) genitive case (rare): *ne budu est' tvoikh estvushek sakharshikh*, "I won't eat your sweet eatables"; (5) prepositional case: *na piru piroval*, "feasted at a feast," *vo gulyan'yakh ne gulyalosya*, "I did not (care to) stroll on a stroll." Almost all paired words with common roots appear in a combination of a verb with a noun in the nominative, accusative, or instrumental case. The combination of verbs with other cases is rare.

Another form of tautology is the tautological epithet: *medyanyi med*, "sweet honey," *rodnye roditeli*, "native parents." Sometimes several forms are combined: *diva divnogo oni tut divovalisya*, "here they marveled at the marvelous marvel."

Synonym pairs form another type of tautology frequently found in Russian folklore. All parts of speech may be used but synonym pairs are usually verbs or nouns. The components may have complete identity of meaning or an approximate similarity. Evgenieva includes the following types: (1) words common all over Russia: *glyazhu-smotryu*, "peer-look," *znayu-vedayu*, "know-have knowledge"; (2) a local dialect word combined with a word from the literary language: *krasa-basa*, "pretty girl," *rech'-pogovor'e*, "speech"; (3) one element is an archaism: *bit'sya-ratit'sya*, "fight"; (4) one word is foreign, although in general use: *mesyats-luna*, "moon" (*luna* is a loan-word); (5) words come into folklore from literary texts: *pora-vremya*, "time," *popy-ottsy dukhovnye*, "priests-spiritual fathers." Sometimes the synonyms are in the same syntactic position in parallel lines:

> Kak vse li-to v Tsari-gradi *po-staromu*
> Kak vse li-to v Tsari-gradi *po-prezhnemu*.
> (Is all in Tsargrad as of old,
> Is all in Tsargrad as before.)

Bibliography: Nina Borowska, "Redoublement des mots dans la poésie populaire russe," *Lingua posnaniensis* 3 (1951), pp. 260–91. F. I. Buslaev, *O prepodavanii otechestvennogo yazyka.* 1941. P. 180. A. P. Evgen'eva, *Ocherki po yazyku russkoi ustnoi poezii.* 1963. Pp. 98–298. A. A. Potebnya, *Iz zapisok po russkoi grammatike* 3. Kharkov, 1899. P. 522.   R. R.

Téffi, Nadézhda (pseud. of Nadézhda Aleksándrovna Buchinskaya, née Lokhvitskaya, 1872–1952), writer and poet. A younger sister of the poet Mirra LOKHVITSKAYA, Teffi was born in St. Petersburg. Though she distinguished herself as a writer of belles lettres as well as in journalism, poetry, and prose, the comic as well as the serious, her most significant early work was done for the St. Petersburg comic-satirical journal SATIRIKON and for the popular Moscow newspaper RUSSKOE SLOVO. Teffi also published her poems and short stories in several other periodicals, such as *Sever, Birzhevye vedo-*

mosti, Teatr i iskusstvo, and the first legal Bolshevik journal, *Novaya zhizn'*. When LENIN took control of that journal in November 1905, she withdrew (together with Zinaida HIPPIUS) from the editorial staff. Teffi left St. Petersburg in 1919 and in 1920 settled in Paris, where she went on to contribute short stories to various Russian periodicals. Some of her collections published in emigration contain pieces published earlier in Russia. Teffi also wrote a novel, *An Adventure Novel* (Avanturnyi roman, 1932), a volume of memoirs, *Reminiscences* (Vospominaniya, 1932), one-act plays collected in *Plays* (P'esy, 1934), and various other works. All her works reveal a keen sense of observation, wit, and humor. Her target is the humdrum of everyday life—the gray, dull, and uneventful. Human beings appear against this background as pitiful, intimidated, weak, often ridiculous, and always unhappy. The plots of Teffi's stories deal with psychology, political situations, and the social milieu. There are no fantastic elements; the language is lucid and the dialogue witty, though often tragic and gloomy at the same time. Fusing irony with bitterness and criticism with pity, Teffi depicts the vulgar, mundane existence of Russians in Paris and their little tragedies. They conceal their shallow natures both from themselves and from others by pretending to be something more than they are. As for her link with the Russian SYMBOLISTS, Teffi's "real reality" exists only as a dim reflection, a mirage for men on earth, while life here is dead and empty. In exposing the oddities of life and the bewildered state of Russian exiles, Teffi reveals an affinity with Mikhail ZOSHCHENKO, whose Soviet citizen is likewise unable to adjust to his new Soviet, and therefore alien, surroundings.

Works: (Collections of Poetry:) *Sem' ognei* (Seven Fires, 1910). *Sol' zemli* (The Salt of the Earth, 1910). *Passiflora.* Berlin, 1922. (Volumes of Short Stories:) *Yumoristicheskie rasskazy.* 1910–12. *I stalo tak ...* 1912. *Vosem' miniatyur.* 1913. *Karusel'.* 1913. *Miniatyury i monologi.* 1915. *Nichego podobnogo.* 1915. *Zhit'-byt'e.* 1916. *Nezhivoi zver'.* 1916. (Reprinted in exile under the title *Tikhaya zavod'*, Paris, 1921.) *Vchera.* 1918. *Chornyi iris.* Stockholm, 1921. *Vechernii den'.* Prague, 1924. *Gorodok.* Paris, 1927. (Reprint 1982.) *Parizhskie rasskazy.* Moscow, 1927. *Tango smerti.* Moscow and Leningrad, 1927. *Vsë o lyubvi.* Paris, 1930. *Kniga Iyun'.* Belgrade, 1933. *Ved'ma.* Berlin, 1936. *O nezhnosti.* Paris, 1938. *Zigzag.* Paris, 1939. *Zemnaya raduga.* New York, 1952. *Predskazatel' proshlogo.* Moscow, 1967. *Rasskazy.* Introd. O. Mikhailov. Moscow, 1971. See also: *Poety satirikona.* 1966.

Translations: All about Love. Trans. Darra Jane Goldstein. Ann Arbor, 1983.

Secondary literature: V. Bryusov, "Zhenshchiny poety." In his *Dalekie i blizkie.* 1912. Edythe Haber, "Nadezhda Teffi," *RLT* 9 (1974), pp. 454–72. Elizabeth B. Neatrour, "Miniatures of Russian Life at Home and in Emigration: The Life and Works of N. A. Teffi." Ph. D. diss., Indiana University, 1973. Irina Odoevtseva, "O Teffi." In *Russkaya literatura v emigratsii. Sbornik statei.* Ed. N. P. Poltoratskii. 1972. Pp. 199–207. P. Sh-v. *Teffi.* 1926. Temira Pachmuss, *Women Writers in Russian Modernism: An Anthology.* Urbana, 1978. Pp. 261–323. ———, *A Russian Cultural Revival: A Critical Anthology of Emigré Literature before 1939.* Knoxville, 1981. Pp. 106–31.

    T. A. P.

Teleskóp (The Telescope, 1831–36), with a supplement, *Molva*, was founded as a biweekly journal in Moscow, and became a weekly in 1834. Its founder and editor was N. I. NADEZHDIN, a professor at Moscow University. The journal, whose title page identified it as a "journal of contemporary enlightenment," published articles and reviews dealing with contemporary thought in philosophy, education, science, the arts, and literature. Its tendency was moderately progressive. *Teleskop* sought to advance a realistic national course in literature and the arts. Among its contributors were both future SLAVOPHILES, such as Konstantin AKSAKOV and Aleksei KHOMYAKOV, as well as future WESTERNIZERS, such as HERZEN, OGARYOV, and BAKUNIN. Vissarion BELINSKY also made his debut in *Teleskop*. His "Literary Reveries" appeared in *Molva* in 1834. The journal was closed in 1836, when the authorities belatedly recognized the "subversive" nature of P. Ya. CHAADAEV's first "Philosophical Letter," which had appeared in *Teleskop*. Nadezhdin was sent into exile and the censor who had passed the article lost his job.

Bibliography: Yu. N. Mann, "N. I. Nadezhdin, predshestvennik Belinskogo." In his *Russkaya filosofskaya estetika.* 1969.   V. T.

Temiryázev, Borís (literary pseudonym of Ánnenkov, Yúry Pávlovich, painter, theater designer, graphic artist, art critic, and memoirist, 1889–1974).

Temiryazev had already begun his career before the Revolution, but he acquired his celebrity, especially as a portrait painter, initially in the Soviet Union in the early twenties and later in emigration. An intimate member of the artistic milieu, he belonged to its upper echelons both in Russia and abroad, and a vivid description of it with many penetrating characteristics can be found in his monumental memoirs *Diary of My Acquaintances: A Cycle of Tragedies* (Dnevnik moikh vstrech: Tsikl tragedii, 2 vols., 1965–66). Under the pen name Temiryazev, apart from several fragments and tales which he contributed to SOVREMENNYE ZAPISKI and VOZROZHDENIE, Annenkov published a volume of semi-autobiographical prose, *A Tale of Trifles* (Povest' o pustyakakh, 1934), which is in fact a sort of novel, with a loosely connected plot. The action is set in Petrograd under the spell of revolutionary turmoil and is contained within the bohemian circles so familiar to the author. The main hero, a young painter of picaresque character, is constantly attempting to accommodate himself to the new reality through whatever means are available, though he experiences nothing but frustration and is forced ultimately to escape abroad. While literary activity was for Annenkov presumably the field of a secondary occupation, if not a simple hobby, his prose is by no means undistinguished. He displays considerable verbal skills, and Temiryazev's prose is in fact marked by many features which resemble Annenkov's graphics: its capricious firmness and extravagant persuasiveness of design, its elaborate craftsmanship which produces the effect of casualness and spontaneity, and its well-balanced penchant for the grotesque. As in the visual arts, his literary work conceals behind a façade of easygoing witty chat bitter meditations and merciless insights into human nature. It is next to impossible to trace any influences upon Temiryazev's prose: as with his pictures and graphics, it reveals a highly original, virtually unique vision and expresses it richly in a great variety of disguises.

Works: "Lyubov' Sen'ki Pupsika," *Zveno,* no. 222 (1927). "Tyazhesti," *Sovremennye zapiski,* no. 59 (1935), pp. 167–96, no. 64 (1937), pp. 79–97, *Russkie zapiski* 3 (1938), pp. 104–45. "Rvanaya epopeya," *Vozrozhdenie,* no. 71 (1957), pp. 42–61, no. 73 (1958), pp. 121–29. "Pobeg ot istorii," *Vozrozhdenie,* nos. 100–05 (1960).

Secondary literature: P. Courthion, *Iu. Annenkov.* 1930. B. Filippov, A. Rannit, and W. George. Introductory articles to *Dnevnik moikh vstrech.* E. Zamyatin and M. Kuzmin, Introduction to Yu. Annenkov, *Portrety* (1922).   V. B.

Tendéntsiya ("tendency") in literature. Although the root is Latin, this word in Russian is based on the German noun *Tendenz* (cf. the origin of the word *intelligentsiya*); this German origin is clearly seen in the Russian adjective *tendentsioznyi,* "tendentious," and the abstract collective *tendentsioznost',* "tendentiousness" (cf. the German *tendenziös*). As in English, the Russian *tendentsiya* may occasionally refer simply to the unpremeditated trend or "drift" observed in a particular age or author. But more often the Russian word, especially in present-day Marxist-Leninist usage, has very specific connotations and has become a technical term. Here it refers to the writer's very marked prejudices, preconceptions, or biases (ideological, social, political) which are overtly expressed in his works; formally, they are expressed in various ways: through calculated structure, idealized portraits, a *dénouement* that is not justified by the logic of the situation, etc. Some of this sense of "bias" was inherent in the German word (cf. our use of the term *Tendenzroman*) and is certainly present in the employment of *tendentsiya* by the 19th-century Russian critics (e.g., CHERNYSHEVSKY); but it is in Soviet Russian usage that the word *tendentsioznost'* represents a virtue and is even equated with PARTIINOST' or "party spirit." Difficulty arises when we are told that tendentiousness in literature makes for greater realism: thus the Soviet critic B. Bursov writes: "Tendentious works, rising above the facts of everyday life, do not cease to be realistic; on the contrary, their reality is thereby heightened."

The clue, of course, lies in an understanding of the concept of "socialist realism."

Bibliography: B. I. Bursov, *Voprosy realizma v estetike revolyutsionnykh demokratov.* 1953. *See also* the discussion of "tendentiousness" in T. Proctor, *Dostoevskij and the Belinskij School of Literary Criticism* (1969) and Andrei Zhdanov's pronouncement on tendentiousness quoted in R. Stacy, *Russian Literary Criticism: A Short History* (1974), p. 189.   R. H. S.

Tendryakóv, Vladimir Fyódorovich (1923–84), prose writer, was born in Makarovskaya village, Vologda province in the North of Russia. He moved to Moscow in 1945, where he initially studied film making but eventually graduated from the Gorky Literary Institute (1951). He was an editor of *Literaturnaya Moskva* (1958), a member of the Communist Party (1948), and a functionary in the Union of Soviet Writers.

Author of novellas, novels and sketches, Tendryakov was one of the new voices of the THAW. His first story was *Affairs of My Platoon* (1947), however his best works began to appear in the mid-1950s—*Potholes* (1956), *The Miracle Worker* (1958), *Three, Seven, Ace* (1960), *The Trial* (1961), *Tight Knot* (1956), *Beyond Today* (1959). Their usual setting is the remote northern regions of rural Russia, its small towns, villages, forests, and collective farms. His characters are "ordinary Russians," peasants, chairmen of kolkhozes, and other functionaries. He often indicts Soviet bureaucracy as a new elite whose inhuman callousness alienates them from the people.

Tendryakov's works also touch on education and upbringing. In *Beyond the Current Day* (1959) a school teacher is concerned with weaknesses in the Soviet educational system. In *A Topsy-Turvy Spring* (1973) a thirteen-year-old boy grows aware of the world around him and his place in it. *The Night after Graduation* (1974) focuses on the quality of education and the obligation to instill values. *Meeting with Nefertiti* (1964) attempts to define Stalinism and raises questions about art and creative freedom.

The conflict between good and evil is central to Tendryakov's works. The action in his stories often centers on a crisis situation, frequently death, in which the moral and spiritual world of each character unfolds in situations where they must make a decision. In *Potholes* (1956) Knyazhev sacrifices a life for a tractor. In *Death* (1968), the sixty-three-year-old Lykov, chairman of a wealthy collective, is dying. He has achieved success at the expense of women and children. He exploits the labor and energy of the workers as if they were his subjects. This imperial analogy is so well developed that after he dies we hear: Lykov is dead, long live Lykov.

Tendryakov was one of the most prolific and talented contemporary Russian writers. His works are a window into life in rural Russia. His stories touch the burning issues. He is an excellent storyteller, a fine craftsman, and his tales are carefully and systematically constructed. His prose is severe, robust, and strong, the language rich and varied. The vocabulary is permeated with the speech patterns and intonations of rural Russia. Tendryakov is a remarkable and interesting "village" writer.

Works: Sobranie sochinenii. 4 vols. 1978–80.

Translations: Chudotvornaya. Moscow, 1959. *Son-in-law.* Moscow, 195?. *Three Novellas.* New York, 1967. *Three, Seven, Ace and Other Stories.* London and New York, 1973. *A Topsy-Turvy Spring; Stories.* Moscow, 1978.

Secondary literature: Deming Brown, *Soviet Russian Literature Since Stalin.* 1978. Pp. 169–73, 280–82. E. J. Brown, *Russian Literature Since the Revolution.* 1982. Pp. 323–25. V. Klyuev, *Na perednei linii. Ocherk tvorchestva V. Tendryakova.* Minsk, 1963. V. Litvinov, "Tendryakov 'staryi' i Tendryakov 'novyi'," *Oktyabr',* 1961, no. 6. E. Sidorov, "Muzhestvo pravdy: O proze Vladimira Tendryakova." In Vladimir Tendryakov, *Sobranie sochinenii v chetyrekh tomakh.* Vol. 1. 1978. G. Svirski, *A History of Post-War Soviet Writing: The Literature of Moral Opposition.* 1981. I. A. Vilinkis, "Izobrazhenie zhizni. Zametki o proze Vladimira Tendryakova," *Sever,* 1965, no. 5. I. Vinogradov, "Za begushchim dnem," *VLit,* 1961, no. 1.   H. S.

Terapiáno, Yúry (Geórgy) Konstantínovich (1896–1980), poet and essayist, took a law degree at Kiev University, fought on the Southwestern front in 1917, and in 1919 joined the White Army as a volunteer. Having settled in Paris as an émigré, Terapiano organized the Union of Young Writers, among whose members were D. KNUT, and A. LADINSKY. Terapiano's poetics was based on the ACMEIST canon. To some extent, he expressed the "Parisian note" (PARIZHSKAYA NOTA). Terapiano abhorred rhetoric, but valued culture, the classical tradition, Homer, and French poetry. Some of his verses were devoted to Verlaine, Rimbaud, and Mallarmé. In Terapiano, a soldierly loyalty to Russia was wed to a love for Western culture, French in particular. He possessed a sense of moderation, avoiding extremes. In his poetry, he never experimented, and of all the Parisian émigré poets he was closest to the *maître* of the Acmeists, Nikolai GUMILYOV. Terapiano was a permanent collaborator of the newspaper RUSSKAYA MYSL' to which he contributed many reviews of new collections of verse (from the 1950s to the end of the 1970s). His memoirs of émigré literary life in Paris, *Encounters* (Vstrechi, 1953), are of considerable interest. Terapiano took an interest in Zoroastrianism and published a book on it. His collections of poetry are: *The Best Sound* (Luchshii zvuk, 1926), *Insomnia* (Bessonnitsa, 1935), *In the Wind* (Na vetru, 1938), *Earthly Pilgrimage* (Stranstvie zemnoe, 1950), *Selected Poetry* (Izbrannye stikhi, 1963), and *Sails* (Parusa, 1963). Terapiano edited an anthology of émigré poetry, *Muse of the Diaspora* (Muza diaspory, 1960). His prose work includes *Journey to an Unknown Land* (Puteshestvie v neizvestnyi krai, 1946).

Secondary literature: Yu. Ivask, "Poeziya staroi emigratsii." In *Russkaya literatura v emigratsii.* Ed. N. P. Poltoratsky. 1972. Pp. 60–61. Necrology by Yu. P. Ivask and poem by I. V. Chinnov, *Novyi zhurnal*, no. 144 (1981). Irina Odoevtseva, "Svetloi pamyati Yuriya Terapiano," *Russkaya mysl'*, 29 January and 6 February 1981. G. P. Struve, *Russkaya literatura v izgnanii.* 1956. Pp. 348–50.

G. I.

Terpigórev, Sergeí Nikoláevich (pseudonym Atava, 1841–95), writer, studied law at Petersburg University. Expelled in 1862 in connection with student disorders, he moved to Tambov where he lived until 1867. His first literary attempt was "A Hard Fate. A Story from a Troubled Past" (Cherstvaya dolya. Rasskaz is tyazhelogo proshlogo), published in *Russkii mir* in 1861. From then on he contributed to *Gudok, Golos*, RUSSKOE SLOVO, and *Sankt-Peterburgskie vedomosti*. His feuilletons, stories, and articles were mostly indictments of existing evils in Tambov. After his return to Petersburg he collaborated closely with NEKRASOV and SALTYKOV-SHCHEDRIN in OTECHESTVENNYE ZAPISKI and in *Telegraf.* In his works he exposed the alcoholism and ignorance rampant in the countryside, described the growth of capitalism, bureaucratic corruption, and advocated women's emancipation. His best-known work, a cycle of sketches, *Impoverishment: Sketches, Notes and Reflections of a Tambov Landowner* (Oskudenie. Ocherki, zametki i razmyshleniya tambovskogo pomeshchika), was published in *Otechestvennye zapiski* in 1880, with the second part, *Mothers* (Materi), appearing in *Novoe vremya* (1882). In the sketches Terpigorev described the failure of the postreform period, with the gentry bled white by the greed of the merchants and persisting in inertia, while the peasants lived in poverty and moral degradation. Nonetheless, Terpigorev was openly against violence and believed in the power of enlightenment. In the 1880s he published sketches and stories in RUSSKOE BOGATSTVO. From 1887 he collaborated constantly in *Novoe vremya* and *Istoricheskii vestnik* to which he contributed more than 600 Sunday feuilletons. His new cycle, *Shadows Disturbed* (Potrevozhennye teni, 1883–94) in *Istoricheskii vestnik* were sketches of the life of landowners under serfdom, in which he portrayed the "good old days," when the luxurious life and monstrous excesses of the gentry led to the tragic destiny of their peasants. However, Terpigorev was always able to blend tragic events with humorous scenes.

Works: "Vospominaniya" (posthumous), *Istoricheskii vestnik*, 1896, nos. 1–5. *Sobranie sochinenii.* 6 vols. 1899. *Oskudenie.* Introd. N. I. Sokolov. 2 vols. 1950. "Novyi barin." In *Russkie ocherki.* Vol. 2. 1956. "Marfen'kino schast'e." In *Russkie povesti XIX v. 80–90-kh godov.* Vol. 1. 1957. *Potrevozhennye teni.* Ed. N. I. Sokolov and N. I. Totubalin. 1959.

Secondary literature: G. T. Andreeva, "Fel'etony S. N. Terpigoreva (Atavy) v gazete *Telegraf*," *Voprosy filologii* 4 (1974), pp.

140–45. I. Gyul'mamedova, *Tvorchestvo Terpigoreva.* Baku, 1972. A. P. Mogilyanskii, "Terpigorev." In *Istoriya russkoi literatury* Vol. 9. 1956.

E. K. K.

Terts, Abrám, see SINYAVSKY, Andrei.

Textual criticism (Russ. *tekstológiya*), a literary discipline that provides retrospective examination of a text, attempts a chronological attribution, and establishes authorship and authenticity of a work. It establishes the definitive ("canonic") text of a work, thereby contributing to the field of book editing.

As a theoretical subject, textual criticism provides historical and textual commentary to a text and defines the various intra- and extratextual stimuli that eventually produced alterations in the initial authorial version (the cycling of smaller pieces into a larger unit; alterations in plot and composition; consecutive progression from one version to another; the influence of cultural-historical factors and censorship). The main task of textual criticism runs counter to the author's creative intent: while the author is interested in introducing his work as a self-gravitating, indivisible whole, textual criticism aims to single out small components for retrospective analysis. It is based on a diachronic interpretation of rough drafts, intermediary and definite version, as well as on historical analysis of the manuscripts proper. Textual criticism employs a variety of techniques: (1) hypothetical divination (the method of intellectually divining omitted or damaged parts of the whole, a method vital to the study of ancient and medieval texts); (2) conjectural reading (interpretation based on the likely omission of a passage or passages); (3) paleographic and polygraphic analysis; (4) lexicographic and stylistic analysis of preparatory drafts or disputed texts; (5) computer analysis of disputed passages and their further decoding; and (6) contextual analysis.

As an auxiliary discipline, textual criticism seeks to elaborate the basic rules for editorial practice. The Russian tradition of textual criticism distinguishes between facsimile editions, Academy editions (publication of the complete text with all its drafts and varia, with a commentary and indexes) and popular (or mass) editions, which are based on the definitive text of the Academy edition minus drafts and commentary. Common practice generally distinguishes between textual criticism of medieval manuscripts and that of modern sources. For Russia, the introduction of a secular alphabet (1704) and the spread of secular printing mark the onset of the modern period.

The origins of Russian textual criticism are to be traced back to the editorial practices of the 18th century: *The Project of Editing Russian Manuscripts* advanced by the Academy of Science in 1734, and the 1762 edition of the works of A. KANTEMIR. In 1778, Archimandrite Damascene (Dmitry Semyonov-Rudnev) adapted the basic methods of ecclesiastic textual criticism for the posthumous publication of *The Complete Works of Lomonosov.* Damascene grouped LOMONOSOV's works according to the latter's hierarchy of styles and genres and made a comparative analysis of Lomonosov's manuscripts and printed texts. Taken altogether, this made his 1778 edition a model for the Academy editions of the 18th and 19th centuries. The discovery of the *Igor Tale* (SLOVO O POLKU IGOREVE) and its publication in 1800 inspired archeographic, paleographic, linguistic, and editorial approaches (N. Gudzy, *The Destiny of the Printed Text of "The Lay of Igor's Campaign"*, 1951). A ten volume collection of Russian folk songs by P. KIREEVSKY (collected 1830–52, published posthumously, 1860–74) laid the foundations for an academic approach to the textology of folklore, distinguishing between variants and the dominant text, introducing generic nomenclature and methods of identification (M. Azadovsky, *A History of Russian Folklore Studies*, vols. 1–2, 1958–63). P. ANNENKOV's seven-volume edition of *Pushkin's Complete Works* (1855–57), as well as his *Sources for a Biography of A. S. Pushkin* (Materialy dlya biografii A. S. Pushkina, 1855) and *A. S. Pushkin in the Epoch of Alexander I* (1874) signalled the beginning of textual criticism as it applied to the classics of 19th-century Russian literature. As an editor Annenkov followed a generic and chronological order of publication and supplemented his edition with bio-bibliographical and textological notes. In many instances he deleted those lines which were placed into PUSHKIN's texts not by the poet, but by censors or editors and restored those originally found in Pushkin's manuscripts. Annenkov's edition broke the bans put on Pushkin's verses by the censorship of the poet's day (see *P. Annenkov and His Friends*, 1892, pp. 393–424). Annenkov's work inspired Ya. Grot's Academy Edition of *The Complete Works of Derzhavin* and L. Maikov's annotated edition of BATYUSHKOV.

Russian textual criticism developed further under L. Polivanov, N. TIKHONRAVOV and A. VESELOVSKY. Polivanov expanded the idea of a textual commentary, Tikhonravov revamped methods originally applied to medieval texts, and Veselovsky applied taxonomy to literary studies and employed a psychological approach to the text. In the beginning of the 20th century, S. VENGEROV undertook a set of bio-bibliographical editions on the history of Russian literature (*Sources for a Dictionary of Russian Writers*, vols. 1–4, 1900–17; *Russian Books. With Biographical Data on Authors and Translators: 1708–1893*, vols. 1–3, 1897–99). Vengerov organized a Pushkin seminar at Petersburg University and the students who participated in the preparation of a new annotated edition of Pushkin were later to play a leading role in raising textual criticism to an independent discipline in the humanities (M. Hofman, A. DOLININ, M. Azadovsky, V. Komarovich, S. Bondi). The works of P. Morozov and the successful decoding of the tenth chapter of Pushkin's *Eugene Onegin* (1910) made textual criticism into a combination of heuristic and analytical approaches.

As a discipline based on a diachronic interpretation, textual criticism depends on the availablity of authentic materials. The need for authentic sources was met by several Russian periodicals of an academic bent: *Russkii arkhiv* (1863–1917), *Russkaya Starina* (1870–1918), *Istoricheskii vestnik* (1880–1917) and *Byloe* (1906–25). These periodicals published a large number of historical and biographical materials from private Russian archives. In the early 1900s and during the first postrevolutionary decade the historical and literary archives newly available to scholars yielded fresh material for textual criticism: manuscripts and correspondence of Pushkin, DOSTOEVSKY, LERMONTOV, HERZEN, and the "revolutionary democrats." Prominent among the studies of this time are the works of the historians M. Lemke, P. Shchegolev and B. MODZALEVSKY. In 1905 Lemke began work on his collection *The Complete Works and Letters of Alexander Herzen* (1915–25, vols. 1–22). To prepare this edition Lemke contacted Herzen's son and daughters and included in his commentary excerpts from family archives, as well as memoirs written by members of Herzen's circle. He contacted the British Museum and Bibliothèque Nationale and organized a Herzen circle in Russia. Due to these efforts Lemke was able to find, attribute and publish a large number of Herzen's anonymous works. In many respects Lemke's edition of Herzen remains unequaled. Not only did he collect and preserve material unavailable from other sources, he also summarized and conceptualized the idea of Herzen's literary heritage. Lemke's work on the history of Russian CENSORSHIP and the Russian radical movement of the 1860s are immediate offshoots of his voluminous study of Herzen (M. Vandalkovskaya, *M. K. Lemke, Historian of the Russian Revolutionary Movement*, 1972). P. Shchegolev, editor of *Byloe*, and Boris Modzalevsky, one of the organizers of Pushkin House (INSTITUT RUSSKOI LITERATURY), undertook a systematic search for and publication of literary and historical documents. They advanced a complex approach for manuscripts under examination, thus bringing to life the question of the writer's contacts with his immediate and more distant cultural environment (B. Meilakh and N. Gornitskaya, *Seminars on Pushkin*, 1959).

In 1922 Modest Hofman published *Basics of the Study of Pushkin* (Pervaya glava nauki o Pushkine) where he formalized the methods and tasks of textual criticism and advanced the idea of a canonic text. His book provoked a lively discussion which eventually led to publication of G. VINOKUR's *A Critique of the Poetic Text* (1927) and B. TOMASHEVSKY's *The Writer and The Book: A Survey of Textology* (1928, 1959). While Vinokur discussed the theoretical aspects of textual criticism, the need to combine aesthetic, psychological, and heuristic approaches to the text, as well as the need for conjectural reading, Tomashevsky discussed the practical. He defined textual criticism as "applied philology" and provided descriptive definitions of the text and its history. He also specified different types of editions and provided a selective bibliography on textual criticism. In the early thirties the Soviet Academy of Sciences established two new series: *Zven'ya* (vols. 1–9, 1932–51) and *Literaturnoe nasledstvo* (1932–   ). These collections contain documents, ico-

nography, and bibliography, they examine the artistic ambience, the socio-historical and psychological atmosphere of different epochs in Russian culture, and provide primary sources for textual criticism of Russian poetry, prose, and journalism. *Literaturnoe nasledstvo* and *Zven'ya* set the groundwork for complete annotated editions of writers' works. In 1933 GORKY founded the still current Library of a Poet (Biblioteka poeta), a series of annotated editions which has published the works of approximately 400 authors to date.

The publication of the complete works of Pushkin, Dostoevsky, SALTYKOV-SHCHEDRIN, and USPENSKY, all of whom also contributed to the journalism of their day, further developed the field of textual heuristics. Textual heuristics discusses the problem of authorship on the basis of a theory of styles and helps to attribute anonymous works, polemic articles, feuilletons, and pieces of parodic poetry in Russian journals of the 19th and 20th centuries. *The Problem of Authorship and the Theory of Styles* (1961) by Viktor VINOGRADOV proved that several anonymous articles in Russian journals of the 1790s belonged to the pen of KARAMZIN and attributed various anonymous publications in *Literaturnaya gazeta* of 1830 and 1831 to Pushkin. He also worked out methods to differentiate between individual styles in anonymous Russian publications of the 1870s.

The four-volume collection *Problems of Textology* (1957–67) seeks to solve both practical and theoretical questions of textual criticism. The first volume suggests methods for establishing canonic texts and singling out the definitive version of 19th- and 20th-century works (GOGOL, NEKRASOV, MAYAKOVSKY, Gorky). Volume Two discusses problems of language and style in the framework of textual heuristics and brings forth the method of *negative attribution*, that is, a stylistic definition of plagiarism, forgery, and imitation. The third volume discusses principles of editing, annotating, and attributing epistolary texts, and the fourth discusses textual criticism of Soviet authors (FURMANOV, SERAFIMOVICH, GLADKOV, FADEEV, N. OSTROVSKY, SEIFULLINA). In many respects this fourth volume remains to this day a pioneering effort. While textual criticism of the 18th and 19th centuries operates with an exhaustive sum of documentary materials, historical knowledge, and scientific methods, the textology of Soviet literature does not. With exceptions made for the Soviet classics Gorky and Mayakovsky, the need for textual criticism of contemporary authors has been hotly debated up to the present. (Of ninety-two volumes of *Literaturnoe nasledstvo* only six are devoted to Soviet authors.)

The greatest obstacle to the development of textual criticism of modern authors is the system of prescribed aesthetic values and ideological definitions which reduces the number of manuscripts available for textological analysis. Even in the most exhaustive edition of Gorky (*Complete Works in 30 volumes*, 1949–54) certain items were deemed inadmissible for publication. The edition lacks Gorky's cycle "Untimely Thoughts," since they were polemically addressed to LENIN. For the same reason, the edition issued only selected correspondence from Gorky's archive. All publications of bio-bibliographical materials on Gorky or other figures of the Soviet era are equally selective and incomplete. (Complete editions of LUNACHARSKY or PLEKHANOV do not as yet exist.) Even as an auxiliary discipline, textual criticism of Soviet literature has rigid limitations in its development and application. Despite the massive bibliography of works by and about Lenin, there exists only one Soviet study dealing with the textological problems of Lenin's writings: S. Valk, *A Proposal of Rules for Editing the Works of V. I. Lenin* (Proekt pravil izdaniya trudov V. I. Lenina, 1926). No textological comparison of the different editions of Lenin's works has ever been undertaken. In the textual criticism of Soviet literature annotations based on comparative analysis rarely appear and the disappearance of realia and historical names from edition to edition (Trotsky, Bukharin, etc.) is routinely overlooked. The unofficial hand-written literature that has emerged as a reaction to censorship presents new problems for textual criticism. The regeneration of this type of literature necessitates the reinstitution of methods used in medieval textology. For example, hypothetical divination and conjectural reading seem to be the most effective approaches for such authors as PLATONOV and BULGAKOV (M. Chudakova, "The Creative History of the Novel *Master and Margarita*," *VLit* 20 (1976), no. 1, pp. 218–53). Even the issue of authorship remains problematic, although chronologically the Soviet period belongs to the recent past. M. SHO-

LOKHOV's *And Quiet Flows the Don* is but one example. Several poems of AKHMATOVA, MANDELSHTAM and other nonconformist writers which circulate in handwritten copies or are preserved orally provide a diversity of variants which cannot be reduced to one definitive text. In order to compile an academically reliable edition of these authors, methods from folklore textology must be applied. (While the Western four-volume edition of Mandelshtam by Inter-Language Literary Associates is the most exhaustive, the Soviet commentaries in the Library of a Poet Series are more useful for textological work.)

The emergence of SAMIZDAT and tamizdat literature distance the appearance of the printed text from the original manuscripts, which naturally impedes any textological approach to these materials. The inaccessibility of PASTERNAK's archives for an analysis of *Doctor Zhivago* is but one such case. Thus textual criticism, still a heuristic and analytic discipline, must readjust its methodology in order to be effective in this new cultural situation.

Bibliography: Istoriya russkoi literatury XVIII veka: Bibliograficheskii ukazatel'. 1968. Pp. 227–28.

Literature: M. Bulgakov, *Master i Margarita: Neizdannye otryvki i epizody.* Bern, 1967. K. V. Chistov, *Sovremennye problemy tekstologii russkogo fol'klora.* 1963. M. Chudakova, *Arkhiv M. Bulgakova: Materialy dlya tvorcheskoi biografii pisatelya.* In *Zapiski otdela rukopisei GBL.* 1976, vol. 37. G. Kjetsaa. "Problema avtorstva v romane *Tikhii Don*," *Scando-Slavica* 24 (1978), pp. 91–105. D. S. Likhachev. *Tekstologiya. Kratkii ocherk.* 1964. *Neizdannyi Bulgakov.* Ed. E. Proffer. Ann Arbor, 1977. *Osnovy tekstologii.* Ed. V. Nechaeva. 1962. (With a bibliography, pp. 482–98.) S. Reiser. *Paleografiya i tekstologiya novogo vremeni.* 1970. *Tekstologiya slavyanskikh literatur.* Ed. D. Likhachev. 1977.

In English: A. Cross, "Karamzin's First Story?" In *Essays in History and Literature.* Ed. L. Legters. Leiden, 1972. Pp. 38–55. G. Kjetsaa, "Written by Dostoevsky?", *Dostoevsky Studies* 1 (1980), pp. 73–88. E. Proffer, *An International Bibliography of Works by and on M. Bulgakov.* Ann Arbor, 1976. L. Sullivan and C. L. Drage, "Poems in an Unpublished Manuscript of the *Vinograd Rossiiskii*," *OSP* 1 (1968), pp. 27–48. N. P.

Thaw, the (1953–63), the period of relative artistic freedom which followed the oppressive years of Stalin's reign of terror, paralleled Khrushchev's tenure in power, and ended in 1963. Marked by a liberal and optimistic climate in the arts, it was characterized by three stages of development, paralleling domestic and international policies and crises during Khrushchev's reign (Hungary 1956, Poland 1956, Sputnik 1957, Cuba 1962).

Because the liberalization process was not continuous and because progress and achievements were followed by reaction, repression and setbacks, Western critics and scholars customarily refer to the Three Thaws. Each was built on the achievements of one stage and pushed liberalization several steps further in the succeeding stage. The label was taken from ERENBURG's novella *The Thaw* (Ottepel', *Novyi mir*, spring 1954), dealing with the concerns and hopes of the liberal intelligentsia during the first year following Stalin's death. Erenburg revealed the new Soviet man to be a corrupt and self-motivated bureaucrat, and the officially approved artist to be a mediocrity and a toady. Above all, it proved that certain topics such as Soviet concentration camps, individual emotions, personal problems, and even criticism of official art and public officials could be discussed without major consequence. Furthermore, it was a clear departure from SOCIALIST REALISM in that it depicted reality as it was. As one thaw followed another, even though there were regressions, writers realized that people were no longer shot or exiled for daring to say certain things, and were, therefore, encouraged to be more and more audacious.

The period was characterized by literary polemics and an open split between the liberals and the conservatives (or the dogmatists as some called them) who aligned themselves with the journals in which they published. More significantly, it was characterized by a growing optimism, enthusiasm, and excitement, especially in the early 1960s when every issue of the liberal journals *Novyi mir* and *Yunost'* published new and exciting works, including some by previously unknown writers. The desire to speak the truth and to be honest was a constant refrain. POMERANTSEV's *On Sincerity in Literature*, and VOINOVICH's *I Want to Be Honest*, epitomized the spirit of the period. Among Russian and Western intellectuals there was hope that a new era had arrived.

The initial domination by poets and poetry readings to enormous crowds, in such huge halls as the polytechnical institute or the Luzhinki Stadium, can perhaps be best envisioned by analogy to the effect of rock and roll music on Western youth. Crowds of people listened continuously for four to six hours to recitations by such poets as EVTUSHENKO, VOZNESENSKY, AKHMADULINA, OKUDZHAVA and others.

In addition to the publication of works on previously forbidden themes and the appearance of new young writers, there was a reappearance in print of the older prerevolutionary generation of writers. Some of the best writers of the 1920s who had either been silenced or executed began to be posthumously rehabilitated. They include the poets AKHMATOVA, TSVETAEVA, and ZABOLOTSKY, and the prose writers BABEL, BELY, BULGAKOV, OLESHA, PILNYAK, PLATONOV, ZOSHCHENKO and a number of others.

The first thaw, which lasted for a year, began during the first year after Stalin's death with the publication of four articles, all by writers of the older generation. The first, by O. BERGGOLTS, complained about the lack of lyric poetry in Russia. The second, by V. INBER, attacked the "steam shovel" school of poetry and its official encouragement. The third, "On the Writer's Works," by I. Erenburg, demanded that writers act as intellectual teachers. The fourth, by V. Pomerantsev, demanded honesty and sincerity in literature. These theoretical articles were quickly followed by works of fiction, among which the most important ones were PANOVA's novel, *The Seasons*, Zorin's play *The Guests*, and Erenburg's novella, *The Thaw*. The reaction to all this was fear in the party leadership which resulted in attacks on writers, and TVARDOVSKY's dismissal as editor-in-chief of *Novyi mir*.

The second thaw was a result of Khrushchev's "Secret Speech," 25 February 1956 at the 20th Party Congress. It was a guarded denunciation of Stalin. Liberals and writers, as a result, became exceedingly optimistic and began to work frankly on themes which had long been taboo. Outstanding literary events of this period included DUDINTSEV's *Not by Bread Alone* and the two volumes of *Literary Moscow* edited by PAUSTOVSKY, of which Volume 2 was particularly remarkable. It published young unknown writers, and introduced some of the best poets and writers of the 1920s whose names had been virtually unknown and unmentioned since the 1930s.

Frightened by the Hungarian uprising and the rebellion in Poland, officialdom gave in to the conservatives (dogmatists) and renewed its attacks. One of the casualties of this renewed repression was B. PASTERNAK whose *Dr. Zhivago* had been published in Italy (1957) and who was forced to refuse the 1958 Nobel Prize for Literature.

The beginnings of the third thaw coincided with the opening of the 22d Party Congress (October 1961), where Khrushchev launched his de-Stalinization policy. Openly denouncing Stalin, he performed the symbolic act of removing Stalin's body from the mausoleum in Red Square. These events were followed by a period of excitement in the intellectual community. There were poetry readings in huge halls and stadiums and a flood of daring publications, innovative in form, style, and subject, were offered by such "new voices" as KAZAKOV, AKSYONOV, Okudzhava, ISKANDER, Voinovich, BITOV, Balter, GREKOVA, Nilin, TENDRYAKOV, BYKOV, AITMATOV, NAGIBIN, Voznesensky, Evtushenko, Akhmadulina, Korzhavin, and others. Paustovsky published *Pages from Tarusa*. Memoirs began to be published, with reminiscences by Paustovsky and Erenburg. The high point of this period was the publication of SOLZHENITSYN's *One Day in the Life of Ivan Denisovich*, and Evtushenko's the *Heirs of Stalin* and his *Baby Yar*. This was disturbing to the political and conservative literary establishment. It triggered a reaction which began with the famous Debate at the *Manezh* exhibition where, in December 1962, Khrushchev attacked the artists and abstract art. Despite these attacks, 1963 saw the publication of some of the greatest works of the post-Stalin period: Solzhenitsyn's *Matryona's House, It Happened at Krechetovka Station*, and *For the Good of the Cause*, V. Voinovich's *I Want to be Honest*, and Tendryakov's *Potholes*, to name only a few.

It became clear that the thaw period had ended for good when, following the Cuban Missile Crisis, Khrushchev was forced to step down and power was taken over by members of the new bureaucratic elite. Tvardovsky was forced to resign as editor-in-chief of *Novyi mir*. The young Leningrad poet Iosif BRODSKY was arrested, tried, and convicted for parasitism.

The precedent had been set, the era of the thaw ended, and the beginning of a new era of repression signaled.

Bibliography: P. Blake and M. Hayward, *Half-Way to the Moon; New Writing From Russia.* 1964. D. Brown, *Soviet Russian Literature Since Stalin.* 1978. E. J. Brown, *Russian Literature Since the Revolution.* 1982. O. Carlisle, *Poets on Street Corners; Portraits of Fifteen Russian Poets.* 1968; G. Gibian, *Interval of Freedom; Soviet Literature During the Thaw, 1954–57.* 1960. M. Hayward and E. L. Crowley, *Soviet Literature in the Sixties; An International Symposium.* 1964. R. Hingley, *Russian Writers and Soviet Society.* 1979. P. Johnson, *Khrushchev and the Arts; The Politics of Soviet Culture, 1962–1964.* 1965. *Literaturnaya Moskva: Sbornik vtoroi.* Moscow, 1956. G. Svirski, *A History of Post-War Soviet Writing: The Literature of Moral Opposition.* Ann Arbor, Mich., 1979. H. Swayze, *Political Control of Literature in the USSR, 1946–1959.* 1962. *Tarusskie Stranitsy.* Tula, 1961. T. P. Whitney, *The New Writing in Russia.* 1964. H. S.

Theater, the Russian, produced its dramatist of international stature later than other European nations. Anton CHEKHOV (1860–1904) was first successfully performed by the Moscow Art Theater before he too stood with the "greats," just as Shakespeare was staged at the Mermaid and Globe Theaters in London, Molière at the Hôtel de Bourgogne in Paris, and Schiller in Weimar. Unmistakably performance has been essential to the development of great dramatic literature, as plays are, in turn, the lifeblood of the theater.

True, theater existed in Russia in primitive forms even before written literature. Theater is thought to have come to pre-Tatar Kievan Russia from Constantinople after Grand Duchess Olga and her suite had seen Byzantine theater there in 957 A.D. Vladimir Svyatoslavich (978–1015) may have seen performances of Biblical subjects in Kherson. Frescoes in St. Sophia Cathedral, Kiev, probably from the late 11th century, depict dancing figures, *gusli* (a kind of guitar) players and acrobats. Such entertainers, called SKOMOROKHI, who ranked as artisans of their craft like woodcutters or jewelers, are first mentioned in medieval chronicles in 1068. They were employed to sing, dance, do circus tumbling, or recite poetry and drama, or they performed in the streets. The Christian church, which suspected them of practicing magic and sorcery, and was indignant over their often outrageous participation in wedding festivities—to the point of their performing mock marriages—managed to have at least such excesses prohibited in 1648.

The medieval Church was itself the scene and sponsor of theater. Since the 4th century the Byzantine Church had dramatized Biblical texts and liturgical ritual, thus the washing of Christ's feet. With the Christianization of Kiev, Biblical subjects, for example "Susanna," and annual Christmas and Easter presentations, such as "The Passion of Christ," came to be performed. Other set pieces were devised, of which perhaps the most popular, "The Fiery Furnace" (*Peshchnoe deistvo*, 16th–17th centuries) showed three devout youths put in a furnace for their faith, but saved from the flames by an angel (after *Daniel*, 3). In Moscow Palm Sunday was celebrated by Christ's entry into the Kremlin on a white donkey. Such dramatizations had their heyday in the 15th and 16th centuries, continuing into the 17th. Religious street processions at Corpus Christi took place until the 1917 Revolution.

The oral tradition of popular plays descends from pagan celebrations of the seasons. Aleksandr OSTROVSKY's *Snow Maiden* (Snegurochka, 1873) is taken from popular pageants celebrating the advent of spring. In medieval Christian observance, *Mardi gras* or pre-Lenten festivities used *skomorokhi* among the animal masks. Some subjects of folk plays recur in Aleksandr AFANASIEV's collection, *Russian Folk Tales* (1855–64), for example "Judge Shemyaka's Verdict" (Shemyakin sud, nos. 319–20), the title of which is proverbial; it cynically means that it is the victim of a crime who must pay damages to his despoiler—and court costs as well. This bit of ironic folk wisdom entered the repertory of Fyodor VOLKOV's theater in Yaroslavl (1751).

The clown PETRUSHKA was central in some twenty-four episodes performed in PUPPET THEATERS at fairs and carnivals portraying Petrushka's marriage, his purchase of a horse, and his final descent to hell in the devil's clutches. Petrushka's end points to the two levels of the puppet stage, an upper for earth and a lower for hell. The lower level was needed also for the presentation at Christmas of *King Herod*.

A folk subject which occurs in some thirty-five variants is *The Boat* (Lodka); it has up to sixty scenes and other more specific titles: *The Robber Band* or *Captain, Stepan Razin, Ermak*, or in the 17th century, *Vladimir of the Iron Hand. Ermak* recounts the hero's battles with the Tatars. Ostrovsky's play *The War Lord* (Voevoda, subtitled *Dream on the Volga*, 1865) draws on the last variant about a Cossack band's opposition to authority.

In the 17th century a new use of drama in schools led to the first written texts. When Tsar Aleksei Mikhailovich twice visited troops in Polotsk in 1656, a monk, Simeon—called henceforth SIMEON POLOTSKY—at the Theological Seminary staged "declamations" by twelve pupils to honor these occasions. Later in Moscow the same Simeon Polotsky, now tutor to the tsar's children, wrote panegyrics praising the tsar, for example "The Russian Eagle" (Orel Rossiiskii), which were declaimed by pupils of the Slavic-Greek-Latin Academy. Most significant for the theater, Polotsky departed from his earlier monologues to write plays, so-called school dramas, two of which, *The Gospel Parable of the Prodigal Son* (Komediyapritcha o bludnom syne, 1685) and *The Comedy of Nebuchadnezzar* (O Navkhodonosore tsare, o tele zlate i o trekh otrotsekh v peshchi ne sozhzhennykh, 1673), are the oldest written Russian plays. To the frightening example of Nebuchadnezzar in the latter-named, earlier play Polotsky added the subject of "The Fiery Furnace," expanded into an entertainment with music and dance. *The Prodigal Son* was doubtless performed in 1663, also with interludes of music and dance, to judge by Protopop AVVAKUM's indignation expressed that year at the infiltration of the Orthodox Church by the "Romans," by which Avvakum meant that Polotsky had brought back school drama from the West and now taught "the craft of playing comedy."

Diplomats too brought theater news from foreign capitals. So Tsar Aleksei Mikhailovich commissioned a play about the Biblical Esther, *Artaxerxes*, from the pastor of the Moscow Lutheran church, Johann Gottfried Gregori, for his wedding in 1672. Though delays with workmen responsible for the theater and set prevented this play's performance on the wedding day, other historical and Biblical heroes were undoubtedly the subject of plays performed at various residences of the Tsar. In 1706, however, Peter I ended the government subsidy for such entertainments because they lacked general interest.

In the 18th century in addition to the court theaters of the tsar, other private theaters with serf actors trained in dance, music, and foreign languages were maintained by great nobles at their estates. For example, Prince Nikolai Sheremetiev's (1751–1809) troupe at Ostankino—finally with some ninety-five serfs—performed vaudevilles and opera in French with ballet and musical interludes.

Foreign theater companies also visited St. Petersburg for court and noble audiences, thus a commedia dell'arte troupe (1733), the German companies of Caroline Neuber (1740) and Ernst Ackermann (1747–52) and Sérigny's French troupe (1747–48). A military school, the *Sukhoputnyi shlyakhetnyi korpus*, also gave closed performances. All these theaters not only performed in other languages, but also were not open to the Russian-speaking public, though the private theaters of both the court and the nobility employed Russian actors.

The middle of the 18th century, however, marked important changes: original plays began to be written in Russian, and a theater open to the public was founded. Aleksandr SUMAROKOV (1717–77), himself an alumnus of the *Shlyakhetnyi korpus*, wrote a tragedy with a love plot and contemporary allusions, *Khorev* (1747). He also adapted *Hamlet* in a "tamed and orderly Russian version." Both were performed by the *Shlyakhetnyi korpus*. In 1751 the "public" (i.e., open to the general public) theater founded by the merchant's son Fyodor Volkov in Yaroslavl was transported at the Empress Elizaveta's expense with sets and actors to St. Petersburg to perform in her closed court theater at Tsarskoe selo. After a term of further education, to which Elizaveta assigned them at the *Shlyakhetnyi korpus*, Volkov and several of his actors in 1756 founded the first permanent professional theater open to the general public with Sumarokov as their director. The latter now wrote especially for this theater, tailoring his verse to Volkov's passionate style of declamation.

CATHERINE II showed great interest in theater, writing several bad plays herself. In 1777 she granted the privilege of running a "public" theater in St. Petersburg to the German manager Karl Kniper, who joined with the Volkov actor, Ivan Dmitrievsky (1734–1821), also director and coach for several companies. In Moscow the English circus artist, Mikhail Medoks (Michael Maddox), received the right to open a "public" theater on the Petrovka (1780–1805). Catherine also founded the *Direktsiya Imperatorskikh teatrov* to administer her court and public theaters—and to exercise censorship over the plays produced. In 1773 she ordered a theater, the Bolshoi, built in St. Petersburg, and in 1779 she founded the Imperial Theater School for the training of actors, singers, and dancers. She decreed subsidies, but for the foreign theater companies. Both "public" theater managers went bankrupt; Kniper's theater was taken over by the government in 1783, and Medoks' by the commander of the city of Moscow. So under Catherine the government became increasingly involved in theater administration.

The satiric comedies of Denis FONVIZIN and Vasily KAPNIST were staged at Kniper's and Medoks', as were the comic operas of Yakov KNYAZHNIN. Knyazhnin's heroic tragedy, *Vadim of Novgorod* (published 1793), was confiscated in print and prohibited for the stage, however. Kapnist's *Chicanery* (1798), first approved for publication, performance, and even dedication to the Emperor Paul, so shocked the court that it was forbidden after four performances, but then after 1805 performed without objection. The leading actor in *Chicanery*, Anton Krutitsky, was supplied by a government school, the *Vospitatel'nyi dom*, whose best acting pupils were assigned to Kniper's troupe. So the theater was subject to a constant flux of furtherance and hindrance from the government.

Both the classical dramatic theaters, the Maly in Moscow and the Aleksandrinsky in St. Petersburg, the equivalent of the Comédie Française in Paris and the Burgtheater in Vienna—both still functioning today—are foundations of the 19th century. The Maly goes back in part to the University Theater, founded (1757) at the new Moscow University; it soon became professional, appearing alternately with an Italian troupe at Locatelli's opera house, and after further divagations formed the nucleus of the company officially launched as the *Malyi teatr*, Moscow (1824).

A great actor, Mikhail Shchepkin (1788–1863), whose best roles reflect the Maly's early history, came to Moscow from performances in private theaters in the provinces, and with the help of a fund drive on his behalf bought his freedom from serfdom. His perhaps greatest role was as Famusov in GRIBOEDOV's *Woe from Wit* (1830). He also succeeded in quite different roles: Harpagon in Molière's *Miser* (1827), Shylock in Shakespeare's *Merchant of Venice* (1835) and SUKHOVO-KOBYLIN's disadvantaged "little man," Muromsky, in *The Marriage of Krechinsky* (1855). He even attempted several roles in Ostrovsky's plays, though with less successful projection of that author's more concrete realism.

Russian authors trying to write for the theater were mostly discouraged by censorship during the first half of the 19th century, so that actors found their best roles largely in foreign classics. The romantic actor Pavel Mochalov (1800–48) was a great Hamlet (1838), as well as Chatsky in Griboedov's play. He played other Shakespearean roles, Othello, King Lear, and Richard III, and in Schiller's *Robbers*, Karl Moor. Glikeriya Fedotova (1846–1925) played Shakespeare, and when Ostrovsky's plays entered the repertory, twenty-nine roles in his plays—the Snow Maiden by his request. Perhaps the greatest Katherine in Ostrovsky's *The Storm* was the creator of the role, Lyubov Kositskaya (1827–68), who entered the Maly playing Schiller's Luise Miller and Shakespeare's Ophelia (1847). Ostrovsky's friend, Prov Sadovsky, was also a great performer of his roles.

In the third quarter of the 19th century the Maly offered Russian classics—PUSHKIN's *Boris Godunov*, TURGENEV's *Month in the Country* and Sukhovo-Kobylin's *The Affair*, for example—and from the international repertory Goethe's *Egmont*, Victor Hugo's *Herna-*

ni, Lope de Vega's *Star of Seville*, Schiller's *Maid of Orleans* and Shakespeare's *Macbeth*. The termination of the Imperial theater monopoly and the consequent competition from private theaters may have impelled the Maly finally to play Ibsen (1892) and the new native realism with Leo TOLSTOI's *Power of Darkness* (1891). The leading actors at the Maly in the later 19th century were Mariya Ermolova (1853–1928), who splendidly projected both Schiller's romantic Joan of Arc and Ostrovsky's opportunist-feminist, the actress Negina in *Career Woman* (Talanty i poklonniki), and Aleksandr Lensky (1847–1908).

Though in England members of the nobility do not go on the stage, Lensky, the illegitimate son of Prince P. Gagarin, presents by no means an anomaly in Russia, where schools of the nobility nurtured actors. At the Maly, Lensky brilliantly played leading roles from 1876 till 1908, especially Hamlet (1871, 1877), Molière's Don Juan (1876), Karl Gutzkow's Uriel Acosta (1879), King Philip II in Schiller's *Don Carlos* (1894). The Russian repertory too was prominent in his achievement, including some thirty Ostrovsky roles. Great as an actor, he was also a great acting coach, insisting on training rather than inspiration as the basis of the actor's professionalism. Many of his ideas make redundant the later principles of STANISLAVSKY and NEMIROVICH-DANCHENKO. However, as director at the Maly in 1907, Lensky found that the stagnation of officialdom prevented his realizing sets and costumes, such as he envisaged in an age of theatrical renewal, and he, therefore, resigned shortly before his death.

The most important event of the outgoing 19th century was the founding in 1898 of the Moscow Art Theater by Konstantin Stanislavsky (1863–1938) and Vladimir Nemirovich-Danchenko (1858–1943); together they realized Ostrovsky's aspiration of a people's or public theater. The first production of the new theater, Aleksei TOLSTOI's *Tsar Fyodor Ioannovich* with Ivan Moskvin (1874–1956) in the title role, recreated the Russian past in luxurious detail; further, the humanity of the characters was conveyed without false declamation.

Still, the theater became truly itself only with the opening of Chekhov's *The Sea Gull* (1898), in which the truth of character and situation lay more in silence, gesture, and atmosphere than in spoken words. Olga Knipper (1868–1959) as Arkadina, Vsevolod Meyerhold as Treplyov, Stanislavsky as Trigorin realized in this production an ideal of ensemble, not "star" acting, which has given the theater its emblem of a sea gull.

By 1905 the Moscow Art Theater had perfected its unique style in classics of the realist renewal, major plays by Chekhov, Ibsen, Gerhart Hauptmann, and GORKY. Plays of a different ilk, such as Ostrovsky's *Snow Maiden*, succeeded less well, and those by symbolists like Maurice Maeterlinck, not at all. Stanislavsky called back Meyerhold, who had in the meantime left the theater, to experiment with projecting the new non-realist plays. But, however good in theory were the ideas of Meyerhold and his young stage designers, Nikolai Sapunov (1880–1912) and Sergei Sudeikin (1882–1946), in practice their productions of Maeterlinck and Hauptmann in the so-called Theater Studio of 1905 proved too ineffectual to open.

Meyerhold persisted, though, when the next year he was appointed to direct in the theater of the actress Vera Komissarzhevskaya. Though the set and costumes Sapunov created for Ibsen's *Hedda Gabler* were compellingly beautiful, Meyerhold's stubborn insistence on expressionless, monotone delivery of the lines again amounted to failure, as in 1905. However, he achieved success for Komissarzhevskaya in Maeterlinck's *Sister Beatrice*, in which he grouped his actors in set poses after medieval bas-reliefs. Meyerhold's remaining successes, Aleksandr BLOK's satiric one-act play, *The Showbooth* (Balaganchik), also designed by Sapunov, Leonid ANDREEV's *Life of Man* (Zhizn' cheloveka) and Frank Wedekind's *Spring's Awakening*, were achieved without Komissarzhevskaya herself playing any part, so that the actress-manager dismissed Meyerhold almost without notice in 1907.

The Pushkin Theater in Leningrad (The Leningrad State Academic Dramatic Theater dedicated to A. S. Pushkin), as the former Aleksandrinsky Theater is now called, traces its origin back to Volkov's troupe (1756), though, as such, it was founded in 1832 and named for the Emperor's wife Aleksandra. The wide orchestra pit of its red and gold auditorium—still with Imperial box—places stage action far away from the audience. Is this a reason for the heroic declamation by the tragic actor, Vasily Karatygin (1802–53)? In contrast, the Ostrovsky actor, Aleksandr Martynov (1816–60), excelled in portraying that author's often unheroic heroes. Another great actress of the Aleksandrinsky, Vera Komissarzhevskaya (1864–1910), was sufficiently dissatisfied with its conservatism to try founding her own theater. The innovator Vsevolod MEYERHOLD was director of the Aleksandrinsky from 1908 to 1918. Though at first confounded by the senior actors Konstantin Varlamov (1848–1915) and Yury Yuriev (1872–1948), he won them over with his perhaps greatest production, Molière's *Don Juan* (1910). In this and his other memorable production, LERMONTOV's *Masquerade* (1917), Meyerhold bridged the gap between actors and audience by building a platform over the orchestra pit and staging much of the action on the stage apron so achieved.

Meyerhold's productions at the Imperial theaters were most frequently designed by the great theater painter, Aleksandr Golovin (1863–1930), who also created the first *Fire Bird* by Igor Stravinsky for DIAGHILEV's Paris seasons. Golovin's colorfully painted backdrops on a shallow stage required placing the actors in his luxurious costumes far forward so that they might blend with the painted background. In experimental productions, which Meyerhold divorced from his official position by signing them with the pseudonym Dr. Dapertutto, he freed himself from the shallow-stage painted-curtain system of his Aleksandrinsky productions.

Two of Meyerhold's associates in the Theater of Komissarzhevskaya, Nikolai EVREINOV (1879–1953) and Aleksandr Tairov, became important directors in their own right. Evreinov directed Komissarzhevskaya in Gabriele D'Annunzio's *Francesca da Rimini* the season after Meyerhold's departure.

Tairov (1885–1950), whom Meyerhold had directed as an actor in the Theater of Komissarzhevskaya, founded in 1914 with the actress Alicia Koonen the perhaps most important non-realist theater besides Meyerhold's own, the Kamerny (Chamber) Theater (1914). His initial production, *Sakuntala* by the legendary Hindu Kalidasa, reflected his aim of showing eternal truths of life and death romantically and poetically. One of his productions, *The Veil of Pierrette* (1916), after Schnitzler, was reminiscent of Meyerhold's significant workshop production, *Columbine's Scarf* (1910), though lacking the latter's satiric bite. Unfortunately Meyerhold and Tairov, after intending to collaborate, quarreled over a review Meyerhold wrote of Tairov's *A Director's Notes* (Zapiski rezhissera, 1921). Meyerhold excoriated the "ballerina" movements which Tairov taught and swore to avoid such himself. For Tairov, like Meyerhold, used music and effective costumes and abstract or constructivist sets, the last designed by artists such as Aleksandra Ekster, the Veshnins, and Vadim Ryndin. With Koonen in the title role, Tairov's *Phaedra* (1922) was undeniably great. Tairov then turned to a foreign repertory not quite within reach of his theater: the plays of Eugene O'Neill and *The Threepenny Opera* by Bertolt Brecht. When Brecht's Russian friends deplored Tairov's production, Brecht, who saw it on his first Russian trip of 1932, deprecated its faults, preferring an inadequate production to none at all. Tairov worthily staged the Soviet classic, Vsevolod VISHNEVSKY's *An Optimistic Tragedy* (1933) with Koonen as the commissar. Tairov's theater was closed in the second half of the 1930s as "formalist," like Meyerhold's, though the director himself escaped the latter's cruel fate. Tairov had enjoyed a further advantage: His theater was allowed a foreign tour in 1923 and so first showed non-realist theater abroad, such as Meyerhold had pioneered. During the year of the tour Tairov's book, *A Director's Notes*, was also published in German under the title *Das entfesselte Theater* (The Theater Unchained), becoming the first statement of formalist theater principles to reach the West.

Stanislavsky's efforts to include plays besides realistic ones in the repertory of the Art Theater had not ceased with the failed Theater Studio of 1905. Maeterlinck's *Bluebird* was staged with fairy-tale effects in 1908, and in 1911 Gordon Craig staged *Hamlet* against a background of abstract cubes, a failure less for the design than for the inability of Stanislavskian actors to speak rhythmic verse. Two further studios were launched, of which the last, headed by Stanislavsky's pupil, Evgeny Vakhtangov (1883–1922), later the Vakhtangov Studio, was the most interesting.

Maeterlinck's *The Miracle of St. Anthony* officially opened the Vakhtangov Studio in 1921. Vakhtangov also directed August Strindberg's *Eric IV* (1921) for the First Moscow Art Theater Studio, in which Mikhail Chekhov appeared, and for the Habimah Theater, *The Dybbuk* (1922). Vakhtangov's own studio's most characteristic production was Carlo Gozzi's *Princess Turandot* (1922), in which he combined the comic playfulness of an earlier century with a satiric edge directed against our own. This last production was completed in part after Vakhtangov had become fatally ill with cancer. Had he lived, his talent promised to combine Stanislavsky's psychological depth with Meyerhold's inventive use of theatrical forms. One of Vakhtangov's pupils, Yury Zavadsky, became the director of the Mossovet Theater, Moscow, and another, Ruben Simonov, for many years headed the Vakhtangov Theater, Moscow.

After 1917 Soviet theaters came under the jurisdiction of Anatoly LUNACHARSKY's People's Commissariat of Education. In Petrograd a street pageant, "The Storming of the Winter Palace," celebrated the Revolution. Meyerhold staged MAYAKOVSKY's *Mystery-Bouffe* with volunteer actors, including the author, on the first anniversary (1918) of the Revolution, "the first Soviet play," as Lunacharsky called it. An updated version of *Mystery-Bouffe* was produced—again by Meyerhold—at the Theater RSFSR I in 1921. The previous year, for lack of new Soviet plays, Meyerhold adapted Emile Verhaeren's *Dawns* into the semblance of one (1920). For Meyerhold had created the slogan "October in the Theater!" (Teatral'nyi oktyabr'!), thus vowing a much needed revolution in the theater, as in the state and society.

While *Mystery-Bouffe* and *Dawns* alluded to revolutionary events in an innovative form, only in 1922 with Fernand Crommelynck's *The Magnanimous Cuckold* did Meyerhold try to wholly revolutionize acting and set design in the theater. He systematized the movements for actors, which as Dr. Dapertutto he had been teaching since 1914, now with the scientific designation "biomechanics." In *Cuckold* he demonstrated the use of these exercises, which were intended as a basic vocabulary of gesture and movement for the actor to combine on stage to convey his meaning. Further, he had the set designer, Lyubov Popova, construct "a machine for acting" with ramps, high platforms, and even a revolving mill wheel, an allusion to the miller hero of *Cuckold*. He called the "biomechanics" classes a "workshop," and opened them democratically to pupils from all backgrounds, as if anyone with proper training could become an actor. He dressed his trainees, the actors Mariya Babanova (1900–83) and Igor Ilyinsky (1901–), in factory coveralls, as if *Cuckold* with its acting machine on which they did their gymnastics were, like any other factory, part of the revolutionary effort to raise production. Finally, he and his colleagues in the workshop published a pamphlet, *The Set Roles of the Actor's Art* (Amplua aktera, 1922), to inform the actor-apprentices on the specialties of masters in their craft, that is, the roles of "young hero" or "heroine," "villain," "clown," etc., with comments on the aptitudes and physique required and examples from classical literature.

After the baldly abstract demonstration of movement and the movable set in *Cuckold* Meyerhold integrated his innovations in a series of great classics, such as Lunacharsky had encouraged the Soviet theater to return to with his 1923 slogan, "Back to Ostrovsky." Meyerhold made his production of *The Forest* (1924) a revolutionary challenge of youth against age and freedom against the tyranny of money, as well as an effective demonstration of expressive movement and CONSTRUCTIVIST set design. The production of Gogol's classic, *The Inspector General* (1926), integrated many innovative devices to heighten the play's satire of the bourgeoisie and become perhaps Meyerhold's Soviet masterpiece. The 1928 production of Griboedov's *Woe from Wit* had a set in height, though it was less effectively used to the same ideological end.

Among new Soviet authors Meyerhold produced Nikolai ERDMAN (1902–70), whose *Mandate* (1925) resorted to the absurd and slapstick in its satire of NEP racketeers and aristocratic revisionists. Erdman's second play, *The Suicide*, was never approved to open, though it was shown in dress rehearsal in 1932. Meyerhold produced Mayakovsky's last two plays, *The Bedbug* (1929) and *The Bathhouse* (1930), thus completing his staging of the canon of that author's dramatic work. Sergei TRETYAKOV (1892–1939), long associated with Meyerhold as play adaptor and instructor in the Meyerhold workshop, saw his anti-imperialistic play, *Roar China* (1927) on stage in an effective production directed by Vasily Fyodorov and revised by Meyerhold. But Tretyakov's next script for the Meyerhold Theater, *I Want a Child* (1927), remained before the play approval committee from 1927 until 1930 and despite revision, never received permission to open.

Clearly by the end of the 1920s it became increasingly difficult to find suitable new plays. Yury Olesha's *A List of Assets* (1931) and Vishnevsky's *The Last Decisive Battle* (1931) both made their ideological point in evaluating the two worlds, bourgeois and Communist. However, the play on a performance of which the Meyerhold Theater was closed by the government in 1938 was not new, nor Soviet, nor a great classic; still, with Alexandre Dumas fils' *Camille* (1934) Meyerhold is said to have achieved a beautiful production with a striking set furnished with genuine objects and with fine performances from his wife, Zinaida Raikh, in the leading role and Mikhail Tsarev (1903–) as Armand.

Stanislavsky, who at first after 1917 turned to the classics, then toured Europe and the United States with the Moscow Art Theater (1922–24), staged Soviet plays only in the latter half of the 1920s, that is, Mikhail BULGAKOV's play about conflicting loyalties during the civil war, *The Days of the Turbins* (1926) and the heroic epic of the same period, *Armored Train 14–69* (1927), after Vsevolod IVANOV's novel. Renouncing with greater age the leadership of the Art Theater, Stanislavsky went on working with its young actors on his Method, about which he published the first of two projected volumes, *An Actor Prepares* (Rabota aktera nad soboi, 1937).

Despite the 1930s' increasing hostility to artistic experimentation, Nikolai Okhlopkov (1900–67), Meyerhold's former workshop pupil and actor of his theater, directed his own highly innovative Realistic Theater from 1930 until 1937. In one typical production, Nikolai POGODIN's *Aristocrats* (1935), "realistic" snow was thrown by stage assistants on audience and actors alike, or again branches were pushed by the assistants past a stationary skier to give an illusion of his moving through the forest. Stage assistants, a device borrowed from the Oriental theater, had been used by Meyerhold-Dapertutto in his prerevolutionary production of Blok's *The Unknown Lady* (Neznakomka).

In Leningrad in the 1930s another non-realist director came to maturity. Nikolai Akimov (1901–68), who had studied theater painting under Mstislav Dobuzhinsky, designed for theaters in Moscow and Leningrad, and as design director of the Leningrad Theater of Comedy (1935–49), was remarkable especially for his witty, satiric set for Evgeny SHVARTS' ironic fairy tale of tyranny, *The Shadow* (1940). Named chief director of the Leningrad Lensoviet Theater in 1951, Akimov produced Sukhovo-Kobylin's *The Affair* (1955) in his own set, representing an oppressive, bottle-green-and-mahogany Imperial ministry office. From 1955 until his death Akimov directed the Leningrad Theater of Comedy, where he kept, above all, Shvarts and Sukhovo-Kobylin's entire trilogy in the repertory, designing the posters, as well as the sets, for his productions.

Again in Leningrad, the *Bol'shoi Dramaticheskii Teatr imeni Gor'kogo* or Gorky Theater is preeminent not only there but in the Soviet Union as a whole. The productions of classics by its director, Georgy Tovstonogov (1915–), equal those of the Moscow Art Theater in depth of feeling and panoramic view of a bygone society, but with an added mastery of climax and dramatic clash peculiar to Tovstonogov's Georgian temperament; to name a few: Griboedov's *Woe from Wit* (1962), *The Idiot* after DOSTOEVSKY (1966) and Gorky's plays, *The Petty Bourgeois* (Meshchane, 1966) and *Summer People* (Dachniki, 1981). Several of the Gorky Theater fine actors, Innokenty Smoktunovsky (1925–), Sergei Yursky (1935–) and Tatyana Doronina (1933–) are known abroad, thanks to their appearances in films shown in the West.

While the great names in 20th-century Russian theater confirm the designation "the director's century," one theater in the resurgence of the THAW after Stalin's death was an actors' group, the Moscow *Sovremennik* (Contemporary) Theater. Launched with the plays of Viktor Rozov in the late 1950s and specializing in recent plays, the *Sovremennik* has lately produced some classics, for example, a satire adapted after a prose work by Saltykov-Shchedrin, *Mr. Balalaikin* (1974). Could the young studio group led by the *Sovremennik* actor, Oleg Tabakov (1935–), be considered inner secession from the theater's increasingly "establishment" fame, or merely a training school, maintained by many Russian theaters? One "showcase" production of the youth group reflected intensive work

in body movement, though it was hardly significant as a play, but rather a near dance-drama of primitive tribal encounter entitled *Two Arrows* (Dve strely, 1980) by Aleksandr Volodin.

The youth studios or "branches" (*filialy*) of old theaters have since the end of the 1970s staged productions of often greater interest than the mother house. The Mayakovsky Theater "branch" was involved, like the *Sovremennik* studio, in tribal clash and body movement with Volodin's play, *The Lizard* (Yashcheritsa, 1981), while the Mossoviet studio, directed by Gennady Chernyakovsky, offered under conditions of discomfort to vie with New York Off-Broadway, Vyacheslav Kondratiev's *Sashka* (1981), not just another World War II play, but a sympathetic view of the common soldier's hard lot, and the tragedy of boys in soldier suits—on both sides.

Another highly regarded company, the Moscow Drama Theater, or Theater on the Malaya Bronnaya, as it is called, in addition to its superbly acted *Marriage* by Gogol, also stages late-night shows in its arena-type theater upstairs. A youth group as such, the *Molodezhnyi* (Youth) Theater of Leningrad, has also done a war play by Kondratiev in its hall improvised in the pavilion of a park. But its play by Volodin, though less "well-made" than Kondratiev's is the more novel: nominally a single play, it is actually three monologues and a one-act play connected by the theme of sympathy for women, *Four Songs in Inclement Weather* (Chetyre pesni v nepogodu, 1981).

Only the Moscow Theater of Drama and Comedy popularly known as the Taganka Theater, directed until 1983 by Yury Lyubimov (1917–), has remained exciting a quarter-century after it first drew attention in the "thaw." The variety and daring of its repertory, as well as the inventive, reliably unexpected manner of staging, have kept it in the forefront as possibly still the leading avant-grade theater of Russia. Launched in the late 1950s with productions of Brecht, poetry readings as revolutionary statements (Andrei VOZNESENSKY, Mayakovsky, Pushkin) and John Reed's *Ten Days That Shook the World*, it enters the 1980s with much sought-after unorthodox renderings of Bulgakov's *Master and Margarita*, Yury TRIFONOV's *House on the Embankment* and *The Exchange*, and Chekhov's *Three Sisters* recited in monologue and choral grouping in direct address to the audience. Its new larger building, connected with the other small house, allows programs by less established writers to be shown on the small stage simultaneously with major shows on the large one. Such a youth program, entitled *The Little Orchestra of Hope* (Nadezhdy malen'kii orkestrik, 1981), combined three one-acts, the first by Volodin, *A Woman and Children* (Zhenshchina i deti), the second, *Two Poodles* (Dva pudelya) by S. Zlotnikov, and the last, *Love* (Lyubov') by L. Petrushevskaya. Unlike the strong thrust of the major productions, the three plays with young actors left a whimsical impression.

The studio and youth-group theaters with their semblance of Off-Broadway only make clearer than ever the European mold in which Russian theater as a whole is cast. On the whole, the Russian theater is subsidized, government-approved theater and has been so since rulers in the 17th century first sponsored theaters. With the advantages of considerable financial security, and training and advancement for theater professionals, go the disadvantages of excessive seniority, lack of spontaneity, and censorship. With and despite all, the natural talent of Russians for performance has flourished.

Bibliography: Teatral'naya entsiklopediya. 5 vols. and 1 brochure. 1961–67. V. N. Vsevolodskii-Gerngross, *Istoriya russkogo dramaticheskogo teatra.* Vol. 1. 1977. *In English:* Marc Slonim, *Russian Theater from the Empire to the Soviets.* 1961. B. V. Varneke, *History of the Russian Theatre, Seventeenth through Nineteenth Century.* Trans. Boris Brasol. Rev. and ed. B. Martin. 1951.   M. H.

Theodosius, St. (Feodósii Pechérskii, ca. 1008–74). One of the central figures in early Russian religious history. Theodosius was the third abbot of the Kievan monastery of the Caves (*Kievo-Pecherskii monastyr'*) from around 1062 until his death. He established the first coenobitic rules in the Russian lands, patterning them after the rules of the Studios monastery in Constantinople. Theodosius figures prominently in the *Primary Chronicle*, and his spiritual prestige was enhanced by the remarkable popularity of monk Nestor's *Life of St. Theodosius*.

From the middle of the 19th century, there was a widespread tendency among Russian scholars (SHEVYRYOV, SREZNEVSKY, Petrov, SHAKHMATOV, Nikolsky) to attribute to Theodosius a large corpus of writings. Most of these attributions have proved unfounded. Current scholarly opinion links Theodosius with eleven rather short works: two epistles to Prince Izyaslav Yaroslavich; eight sermons; and a prayer "for all Christians." The oldest manuscript goes back to the 13th century, but most of our textual documentation is relatively late. (Two of Theodosius's works are preserved in South Slavic codices as well.) Given the changing function of texts such as sermons and prayers in ecclesiastic practice, it is difficult to determine whether Theodosius's works underwent adaptation in later periods and to what extent their attribution to an authoritative figure such as Theodosius might reflect the search for spiritual legitimacy.

Theodosius's writings are devoted to pastoral concerns and couched in a simple, priestly language. Occasionally, however, polemical fervor enlivens his style: thus, for example, in the highly sectarian *Slovo ... o věre krest'yanskoi i o latyn'skoi* (Sermon ... on the Christian and Latin Faiths) Theodosius offers a vivid and extremely emotional portrayal of members of the Latin Church as impious and impure people, to be avoided at all costs.

Bibliography: V. A. Chagovets, *Zhizn' i sochineniya prepodobnogo Feodosiya, Universitetskie izvestiya* (Kiev), 1901, nos. 6, 8, 10, 12. I. P. Erëmin, *Lektsii po drevnei russkoi literature.* 1968. Pp. 64–68. ———, "Literaturnoe nasledie Feodosiya Pecherskogo," *TODRL* 5 (1947), pp. 159–84. R. P.

Tikhonov, Nikolaĭ Semyónovich (1896–1979), poet, writer, and functionary. Born into a petit-bourgeois family, Tikhonov graduated from the Petersburg School of Commerce in 1911. He became a prolific poet and prosaist. His multifarious experiences occasioned his writings. A hussar during World War I, he was inspired by this experience to write his first collection, *The Horde* (Orda, 1922). Its verse has a distinct ACMEIST ring, somewhat harsh and compact, with GUMILYOV's commitment to the "Earth," glorifying a manly life of the Earth, both joyful and cruel. In prose, Tikhonov created a cycle of stories, *Military Horses* (Voennye koni, 1927), about horses at war. These stories are perceptive and well constructed. A Red Army man during the Revolution, Tikhonov poeticized his experience in his collection, *Mead* (Braga, 1922). The strains of its ballads are still Acmeist. Their heroic emphasis is poetically integrated into their structure, e.g., in "Ballad about Nails" (Ballada o gvozdyakh). Tikhonov owed his poetic detachment to his association with the SERAPION BROTHERS. In the twenties and thirties Tikhonov travelled extensively in Central Asia, the Caucasus, and Europe. Asia and mountains remained his preferred poetic topic: *Yurga* (1932), *Verses about Kakhetiya* (Stikhi o Kakhetii, 1935), the book of prose, *Nomads* (Kochevniki, 1931), and others. In them, the poetic and the topical coexist. In Tikhonov's better poems, the estranging exoticism of the setting along with the figures of the new Soviet managers achieve a valid poetic effect, as in "The People of Shiram" (Lyudi Shirama). Socialist construction attracted its share of Tikhonov's writings. Of particular interest are "The Blue Colonel" (Biryuzovyi polkovnik," 1927), "Chaikhana at Lyabi-Khouz" (Chaikhana u Lyabi-Khouza, 1927), "Oath in the Fog" (Klyatva v tumane, 1932), "Jokers" (Shutniki, 1932), and "Perennial Transit" (Vechnyi tranzit, 1933). Most of these stories deal with socialist construction in Soviet Central Asia. In them Tikhonov demonstrates his narrative skill. For instance, "Perennial Transit" depicts how the turmoil of socialist construction affects people's minds, telling about their inspired work and frustrations. During World War II, Tikhonov took part, as a poetic observer, in the defense of besieged Leningrad. His most significant contribution of the period was his long lyric poem "Kirov is with us" (Kirov s nami, 1941). In austere amphibrachic trimeter Tikhonov evokes this tragic hour. The symbolic figure of Kirov inspires the heroic population of Leningrad to save their city. After World War II, Tikhonov represented the Soviet Union at Soviet-inspired international meetings and was handsomely rewarded for his propagandistic verse. It has little intrinsically poetic interest. Tikhonov was a poet of talent. At his best he wrote competent verse. The reader can detect in it the influence of Gumilyov, KHLEBNIKOV, and PASTERNAK. At an earlier stage,

Tikhonov engaged in some experimentation, e.g., his narrative poem "Chess" (Shakhmaty, 1923) in which he poeticizes the Revolution in terms of a chess game. His better verse is his earlier work, e.g., poems in *The Horde, Mead*, "In Search of a Hero" (Poiski geroya, 1927), and poems of his pre-World War II lyrical cycles *Marvellous Excitement* (Chudesnaya trevoga) and *Autumn Walks* (Osennie progulki). The best of his prose are his shorter narratives with unusual plots spiked with a characterizing humor, such as *Military Horses* and the cycle *Roads of the East*. His literary reminiscences share orthodox historical values.

Works: Sobranie sochinenii. 7 vols. 1975.
Translations: See Lewanski, pp. 365–66.
Secondary literature: V. A. Shoshin, *Poet romanticheskogo podviga: Ocherk tvorchestva N. S. Tikhonova.* 2d rev. ed. 1978.

H. O.

Tikhonrávov, Nikolaĭ Sávvich (1832–93), scholar. A graduate of Moscow University (1853), Tikhonravov became a professor of Russian literature there in 1859 and was its Rector from 1877 to 1883. He was made an Academician in 1890. Tikhonravov was one of the main exponents of a *kulturhistorisch* approach to literature in Russia, seeking to understand authors and works in the context of their age and culture. Tikhonravov's main interests lay in the 17th and 18th centuries, but he worked on 19th-century authors (PUSHKIN, GOGOL) as well. He prepared editions of the "Life of Archpriest AVVAKUM," "The Tale of Savva Grudtsyn," two volumes of early Russian drama (*Russkie dramaticheskie proizvedeniya 1672–1725 gg.*, 1874), two volumes of Russian APOCRYPHA (*Pamyatniki otrechennoi literatury*, 1863), and other texts. Tikhonravov wrote important studies on Stefan YAVORSKY, Feofan PROKOPOVICH, N. I. NOVIKOV, and others. His annotated edition of Gogol's *Collected Works* (5 vols., 1889–1893), which death prevented him from completing, is considered one of the finest achievements of 19th-century philology in Russia.

Works: Sobranie sochinenii. 3 vols. 1898.
Secondary literature: N. K. Gudzii, *N. S. Tikhonravov.* 1956.

V. T.

Time, see VREMYA.

Time of Troubles, see TROUBLES, TIME OF.

Tkachóv, Pyotr Nikitich, (1844–86), critic and revolutionary, came from a family of landowners. As a student at the University of St. Petersburg, Tkachov took part in revolutionary propaganda activities and wrote articles for the opposition press. He collaborated with Sergei (The Eagle) Nechaev, perhaps in the writing of the famous Nechaev (BAKUNIN?) "Catechism" of revolutionary morality. In 1873, he left Russia and took up émigré activities—mostly writing—in Paris and elsewhere. For a time, Tkachov collaborated on Pyotr LAVROV's journal *Vpered* in Geneva. Having broken with Lavrov, whom he called a "gradualist" (*postepennovets*), Tkachov, together with likeminded radical revolutionaries, began in 1875 to publish *Nabat*. This was the publication in which Tkachov developed the idea, sometimes attributed to Louis Blanqui and later to V. I. LENIN, of carrying out a revolution by means of a small, professional group of revolutionary intellectuals.

In the many articles penned by Tkachov, later read enthusiastically by Lenin when he was in exile in Geneva around 1900, the somewhat shy, brilliant "P. N." decried the use of individual terrorism as advocated by the *Narodnaya Volya*. Yet he favored a post-revolutionary socialist application of terror to wipe out "class enemies," and the establishment of the "KOB," *Komitet obshchestvennoi bezopasnosti* (Committee of Public Security), an extraordinary anticipation both of Lenin's Cheka and Stalin's GPU, later KGB.

Tkachov left *Nabat* in 1879, after various editorial squabbles, settled in Paris, where he was to spend the rest of his life occupied mostly as a writer on the French Blanquist organ, *Ni Dieu, ni maître*. In 1881 the first signs of brain disease began to afflict Tkachov. In 1883, he was arrested by the Paris police when he was behaving strangely in a street. Sent to a mental hospital, Tkachov was placed under a doctor's care for the next three years. As his condition worsened (paralysis spreading throughout his nervous system), he slowly withered away and died on 5 January 1886. A few Russian émigrés paid tribute to him over a humble grave plot in the Paris Cimetière Parisien d'Ivry while Lavrov delivered a eulogy. Because the plot was not maintained, Tkachov's remains were exhumed in 1892 and placed in an ossuary. Thus, there is no trace left of the revolutionary, beyond the volumes of his writings.

Tkachov's "Proto-Bolshevism"

Numerous Russian and other European revolutionaries were familiar with the writings of Tkachov, the "Russian Blanquist." Some knew him through Russian contacts within Marx's International. Engels, for example, read Tkachov and also wrote an article in which he attacked Tkachov's views (in *Volksstaat*, 1874). Tkachov's letter replying to Engels was published in *Volksstaat* in the same year and became quite famous among such revolutionaries as Vera ZASULICH, Lavrov, PLEKHANOV, Lenin, who frequently referred to it in their own pamphlets and articles.

Tkachov's feud with Engels was monumental. It reflected Tkachov's deepest convictions, which were largely Russian-Jacobin in origin, in opposition to Marx and Engels, whom Tkachov found to be largely "metaphysical," in the Hegelian sense. Tkachov regarded Hegelian philosophy as "unmitigated nonsense," since it seemed to him to diminish the importance of human will; Tkachov's own philosophical bent leaned more toward voluntarism. Moreover, Tkachov had complained to Engels that the Western Marxists erred in their attempt to apply their philosophy to Russia. For example, Tkachov disputed the Marxist claim that Russia, like all other countries, would have to pass through a protracted historical period (during which socio-economic developments had to reach the "bourgeois" stage before "socialism" could be attained). In Tkachov's mind, somewhat like that of Lenin's Bolsheviks, Russia possessed special characteristics allowing her to "skip" ("jump," said Tkachov) intermediary stages and go on to the construction of socialism. One of the institutions that Tkachov thought would permit the *skachok* (leap) was the peasant commune, or *mir*, a unique collectivistic institution existing in the Russian village. "The idea of collective property," he wrote, "is so deeply entrenched ... that our people, despite their naiveté, stand immeasurably closer to socialism than the peoples of Western Europe."

Among the Bolshevist-like ideas developed by Tkachov (and to certain Soviet writers of the 1920s, making Tkachov a "forerunner" of Lenin) were: revolutionary elite, in power both before and after the revolution; dictatorship of the proletariat and the "permanently-revolutionary" worker's state; impatience with democratic procedures, rule of majority, the "snail-like passivity" of the populace, etc.; reliance on force to achieve revolutionary ends; Russia as an exceptional revolutionary breeding ground, and so on.

Works: Izbrannye literaturno-kriticheskie stat'i. 1928. *Izbrannye sochineniya.* Ed. Boris P. Kozmin. 6 vols. 1932–37.
Secondary literature: Albert L. Weeks, *The First Bolshevik: A Political Biography of Peter Tkachev.* 1968. (With a bibliography.)
A. L. W.

Tolstoi, Aleksei Konstantinovich (1817–75), is one of those writers whose reputation was overshadowed by the presence of the Big Three of Russian literature in the 19th century. A poet, playwright, novelist, and satirist, today he is remembered primarily for his only novel *Prince Serebryany* (1862), a novel dealing with the times of Ivan the Terrible, and his dramatic trilogy *The Death of Ivan the Terrible* (1866), *Tsar Fyodor* (1868), and *Tsar Boris* (1870). He is also known as a parodist for his part in co-authoring poems by Kozma PRUTKOV, a joint production of the author and Aleksandr and Vladimir Zhemchuzhnikov. These were parodies either on anthological poetry written by contemporary authors or on romantic poetry in general.

A. K. Tolstoi began his novel *Prince Serebryany* in 1840 when the heyday of the historical novel was drawing to a close, but when it was published in 1862 it was completely out of tune with the "realism" of the times, because it was still a romantic novel of the 1830s. Furthermore, it has many similarities with M. N. ZAGOSKIN's *Yury Miloslavsky*, in terms of plot development, the presentation of some secondary characters, and even of some individual scenes. The supernatural plays a part in both novels, again under similar circumstances, and patriotism is the unifying force in the novel. Despite all of the cruelties practiced by Ivan the Terrible, no one really deserts him, and all combine in the struggle against the Tatars who are the common enemy. *Prince Serebryany* continues to be published in the USSR, often in the Baltic Republics.

Tolstoi's major historical source was KARAMZIN's *History*. Not only did he rely on Karamzin for basic data about Ivan, but he also took virtually intact a number of incidents and descriptions which appear in Karamzin's *History*.

Much more important than his novel is the historical dramatic trilogy. Each drama is a self-contained unit, but all three are connected by historical chronology, and by characters and themes. The trilogy represents Tolstoi's preoccupation with that same historical period we find in his novel. His psychological characterization of the meek Tsar Fyodor in the second drama is extremely complex and modern. The character of Tsar Fyodor has often been compared with Prince Myshkin in DOSTOEVSKY's *The Idiot*. The trilogy and *Tsar Fyodor* in particular is performed with some regularity on the Soviet stage, and is published from time to time. A. K. Tolstoi is the most significant Russian historical dramatist of the 19th century.

Works: Polnoe sobranie sochinenii grafa A. K. Tolstogo. 4 vols. 1907.
Translations: A Prince of Outlaws. Trans. Clarence Manning. New York, 1927. *Czar Feodor Ivanovich.* Trans. A. Hayes. London, 1924. *The Death of Ivan the Terrible. A Drama in Verse.* Rendered into English verse by A. Hayes. London, 1926. *See also:* Lewanski, pp. 367–69.
Secondary literature: M. Dalton, *A. K. Tolstoy.* (Twayne World Author Series.) 1972. G. I. Stafeev, *Serdtse polno vdokhnoven'ya: Zhizn' i tvorchestvo A. K. Tolstogo.*
L. T.

Tolstoi, Aleksei Nikolaevich (1883–1945), a nobleman by birth, has been described as a man "who towards the end of his life became the most authoritative apologist for the Stalin regime." His death in 1945 was considered a great loss to Soviet letters and culture, second only to that sustained in the death of Gorky in 1936. Tolstoi's literary path went from SYMBOLISM to REALISM, from stories and novels about gentry life to fantastic tales, and then to historical novels. As a student at the Petersburg Technological Institute in the early 1900s, he came under the influence of the symbolists, and for a number of years he considered himself and was considered by others to be a poet and a symbolist. He was a war correspondent during World War I. After the Revolution he went into voluntary exile in Berlin and Paris, but returned to the Soviet Union in 1923. He brought back with him the novel *The Sisters* (1921), which was to be the first book of the trilogy on the Revolution, *Road to Calvary* (1921–40), *Nikita's Childhood* (1920), and the utopian novel *Aelita* (1922). Two other novels which today would be called science fiction followed: *The Revolt of the Machines* (1924), and *Engineer Garin's Hyperboloid* (1925).

In his novel *Peter the First*, the first part of which appeared in 1929, Tolstoi finally found the medium which best suited his needs. From this point his popularity increased, and he took a much more active part in the cultural life of the country. He promoted the compilation and publication of histories of literature of the nationalities of the USSR, and did much to ensure the publication of Russian folklore.

In 1939 he was elected to the Academy of Sciences. In 1941 he was awarded a Stalin prize for his novel *Peter the First*, and the following year for *Road to Calvary*. During the war he wrote articles denouncing the invader and boosting the morale of the Russian people. His drama, *Ivan IV* was finished in 1943, but death interrupted his work on the third book of *Peter the First*.

No other Soviet historical novel has been the subject of as much controversy as A. N. Tolstoi's *Peter the First*. Whereas most other authors altered their novels to meet the demands of Soviet criticism, Tolstoi's novel remained virtually intact to 1944. The few changes made by the author at that time did not radically alter the concept of the novel. With the official dissolution of the Pokrovsky School in 1936, Tolstoi's portrayal of Peter as a great historical figure received the approbation of critics, who saw what a great service Tolstoi had performed in overthrowing the personality-submerging concept of Pokrovsky.

Tolstoi made no attempt to uncover some new "truth" about Peter the Great. He utilized the trite and traditional material of his predecessors, the novelists D. S. MEREZHKOVSKY and D. L. Mordovtsev, and the historians S. M. Solovyov and V. O. Klyuchevsky, but he took this material without any of the historical and philosophical connotations previously ascribed to it. A. N. Tolstoi utilized effectively the techniques of Walter Scott in creating the fictional Brovkin family, which is in touch with both upper and lower levels of society and which permits Tolstoi to portray an unusually large segment of Russian life. Tolstoi knew just how much detail was necessary to render the atmosphere of the period, and he utilized genuine historical documents and the language of the period only to the degree that it was essential for his artistic purposes.

With the exception of PUSHKIN, who failed to complete the *Blackamoor of Peter the Great*, A. N. Tolstoi is the most talented writer to undertake a full-scale novel on the theme of Peter the Great. Not only is his *Peter the First* a successful novel, and the best of the Soviet historical novels, but it has won itself a place in Russian literature as a whole, as the best Russian historical novel to date on the theme of Peter the Great.

A. N. Tolstoi's popularity has remained unabated. In the USSR at least one edition of *Peter I* has appeared every year since 1945. The novel has been translated into all of the major languages of the USSR, and into most major world languages including English. *Peter I* is a "Soviet classic." Other works which appear with the same regularity, and which must also be considered as "Soviet Classics" include *Aelita*, *The Hyperboloid of Engineer Garin*, the trilogy *Road to Calvary*, and the folktales and fairy tales that A. N. Tolstoi rewrote for children.

Works: Polnoe sobranie sochinenii. 15 vols. 1946–53.
Translations: Peter the First. Trans. T. Shebunina. 1959. *Road to Calvary.* Trans. E. Bone. 1946. *See also: Lewanski*, pp. 369–70.
Secondary literature: A. B. Alpatov, *Tvorchestvo A. N. Tolstogo.* 1956. Xenia Gasiorowska, *The Image of Peter the Great in Russian Fiction.* 1979.

L. T.

Tolstoí, Lev Nikoláevich (1828–1910), writer, was born 9 September 1828 at Yasnaya Polyana, his family's estate, 200 km south of Moscow. He was the fourth of five children born to Count Nikolai Ilyich Tolstoi (died 1837) and Mariya Nikolaevna, née Princess Volkonskaya (died 1830). In 1847 Tolstoi received Yasnaya Polyana in the distribution of his parents' property. Thereafter, although occasionally absent (especially in the 1850s) for extended periods, he maintained the estate as his home. In 1862 he married Sofiya Andreevna Bers (born 1844), the daughter of a Moscow physician. Thirteen children were born of the marriage, ten of whom survived infancy. Tolstoi left Yasnaya Polyana for the last time in November 1910. He contracted pneumonia on his journey and died of heart failure on 20 November, aged 82, in the stationmaster's house at Astapovo (today called "Lev Tolstoi").

Educated and cared for by tutors, Tolstoi's early childhood was typical for his social class. He showed a gift for languages and a fondness for literature, including fairy tales, the poems of PUSHKIN, and the Bible, especially the Old Testament story of Joseph. After their father's death the children passed through the hands of a number of female relatives, finally (1841) being sent to live with an aunt in the provincial city of Kazan. In 1844 Tolstoi enrolled in the local university and began a notably unsuccessful career as a student. He did, however, develop a keen interest in moral philosophy. He steeped himself in the writings of Rousseau. He later listed Dickens, Schiller, Pushkin, LERMONTOV, D. V. GRIGOROVICH, TURGENEV's *A Sportsman's Sketches*, and Laurence Sterne, especially *A Sentimental Journey through France and Italy*, as also having made a "great impression" on him as a young man.

He left the university in 1847 without a degree and settled at Yasnaya Polyana. In 1851 he went to the Caucasus to join his brother Nikolai who was serving there in the army. He became a commissioned officer himself in 1854, serving first on the Danube and later in the Crimea. While in the army he began his literary career. His first published work, *Childhood*, appeared pseudonymously in SOVREMENNIK in 1852 and was greeted by general acclaim. It was followed by a sequel, *Boyhood*, and a number of tales of military life. When, in 1856, Tolstoi retired from the army and went to live in St. Petersburg, his reputation as a writer was already very considerable. He took an active part in literary circles and made the acquaintance of the leading writers and critics of the day. He was much in demand in the fashionable salons of the city. Stories of various types flowed from his pen.

He soon discovered, however, that he got on badly with his fellow writers and disliked his life as a literary celebrity. In 1857 he made his first trip abroad, and by 1859 he had decided to abandon literature in favor of more "useful" pursuits. He returned to Yasnaya Polyana to devote himself to the management of his estate and to the education of the children of his serfs. Thus began Tolstoi's first pedagogical interlude. He established a school at Yasnaya Polyana, and, in 1860 and 1861, he travelled extensively in order to acquaint himself with European, especially German, educational theory and practice. He resumed teaching on his return, but in 1862 he handed the bulk of the classroom duties over to others. He took upon himself the writing and publication of a periodical describing his theory of education and the pedagogical practice of his school. Twelve issues of *Yasnaya Polyana* appeared in 1862 and 1863. Tolstoi formulated his ideas most strikingly in "Who Should Learn to Write from Whom, the Peasant Children from Us or We from the Peasant Children?" ("Komu u kogo uchit'sya pisat', krest'yanskim rebyatam u nas, ili nam u krest'yanskikh rebyat?").

After his marriage Tolstoi became increasingly preoccupied with estate management, bent on achieving the ideal of the well-regulated life of a prosperous country squire. He published *The Cossacks*, a novel on which he had been working at intervals for ten years, in order to pay his outstanding gambling debts and enable him to enter into married life with balanced account books. Shortly thereafter he began his first long novel, *War and Peace*, a work of colossal proportions which occupied him until 1869.

In 1870 Tolstoi once again turned his back on literature and began a second period of preoccupation with pedagogical work. Over the next five years he wrote and compiled materials for a complete course of elementary education. He tested them in his school and revised them. The final versions were published in 1875 as *The New Primer* (Novaya azbuka) and *The Russian Readers* (Russkie knigi dlya chteniya). Tolstoi's materials eventually met with fairly general acceptance and were widely used in the nation's schools.

In 1873 Tolstoi's thoughts turned once again to literature, and in the course of the next four years he wrote his second long novel, *Anna Karenina*. His work on the later parts of the novel was disturbed by ever more frequent fits of emotional distress. This condition was brought on by his inability to find an acceptable answer to the question: "What meaning can a person's life have which would not be annihilated by the awful inevitability of death?" Tolstoi became more and more convinced that the bitter truth was that life is meaningless, that there is no escape from the power of death. By the mid-1870s Tolstoi was occasionally so depressed that he entertained thoughts of suicide. By 1878, however, his "crisis" had culminated in what is customarily referred to as a "conversion" to the ideals of human life and conduct which he found in the teaching of Jesus.

Tolstoi described the period of crisis and conversion in his *Confession* (Ispoved', 1882). The censor forbade its publication, a fate shared by many of Tolstoi's subsequent writings. Tolstoi regarded *Confession* as his first step along a new road in life, one which he hoped was secure from the lurking menace of the power of death. To Tolstoi the crisis and conversion meant a break with his past, especially his literary past. The convention of dividing his career into two parts (using 1878 as the year of demarcation) has a definite basis in the facts of his life, at least as these were understood by Tolstoi himself. It should not be forgotten, however, that most of the preoccupations, themes, purposes, and style of the "old" Tolstoi are present with greater or lesser clarity already in the work of the "young" Tolstoi.

Confession was, more specifically, the introduction to a group of three books on religion, written in the years 1880 to 1883 and thereafter considered by Tolstoi to be his most important work. The first volume, *A Study of Dogmatic Theology* (Issledovanie dogmaticheskogo bogosloviya), is a sustained polemic against the teachings of the established church. The second, *A Harmony and Translation of the Four Gospels* (Soedinenie i perevod chetyrekh evangelii), was Tolstoi's greatest religious labor. This heavily annotated work of exegesis demonstrates both his thorough acquaintance with the French, German, English, and Russian biblical scholarship of the 19th century and his fluent command of New Testament Greek. The last part of the religious trilogy is *What I Believe* (V chem moya vera), a reasoned statement of Tolstói's version of the Christian teaching.

Tolstói devoted the remainder of his life to the propagation of his religious views in publicistic essays, works of fiction, and in personal contacts with visitors and through correspondence. He dealt with a variety of subjects in his essays. *On Life* (O zhizni, 1886–87) offers the most extended discussion of that dualism of body (the "animal life of man") and spirit (the "true life") which is the philosophical heart of his teaching. *What Then Should We Do?* (Tak chto zhe nam delat'?, 1886) begins with a gruesomely realistic portrait of the poverty of the Moscow slums, which Tolstói had observed firsthand while helping conduct the Moscow census of 1882. He advocates the abolition of the use of money in favor of the direct exchange of services and the disestablishment of private property rights. He condemns philanthropy as a symptom of "the willingness of the rich to do everything for the poor except to get off their backs." *The Kingdom of God Is Within You* (Tsarstvo Bozhie vnutri vas, 1893) takes up two favorite themes: non-resistance to evil and anarchism. This work was among the several written by Tolstói which had a profound influence on Mohandas Gandhi. In *What Is Art?* (Chto takoe iskusstvo?, 1898) Tolstói gives a detailed account of his aesthetic thought. He also wrote many briefer essays on such subjects as the nature of religion, vegetarianism, famine relief (in which he took an active part in the early 1890s), and on the evils of alcohol and tobacco, patriotism, military conscription, war, terrorism (as practiced both by terrorists and by governments), and capital punishment.

Tolstói resumed literary activity in the mid-1880s with a series of stories written for the popular audience (i.e., for the common people, especially the peasants). To facilitate the publication and distribution of the "Stories for the People" he and his friend and disciple V. G. CHERTKOV founded (1884) a non-profit publishing house which they called The Intermediary (POSREDNIK). Tolstói also developed an interest in the drama and wrote his only major play, *The Power of Darkness*. The leading examples of Tolstói's fiction written for the educated audience also reflect his religious teachings. These include the short novels *The Death of Ivan Ilyich, The Kreutzer Sonata*, and *Master and Man*. He also wrote two more novels, *Resurrection* and *Hadji-Murad*, and more than a dozen short stories.

The last ten years of Tolstói's life were marred by intermittent ill health. He devoted such strength as remained to him chiefly to the compilation of vast compendia of morally and spiritually elevating extracts from the writings of sages of various epochs and cultures. These miscellanies reflect both Tolstói's wide reading in the world's wisdom literature and his lack of temerity in bending or adjusting the words of others to suit his own purposes. The largest of these compilations are *The Cycle of Reading* (Krug chteniya, 1904–08), *For Every Day* (Na kazhdyi den', 1907–10), and *The Way of Life* (Put' zhizni, 1910). Although not expressly so described by Tolstói, the miscellanies represent his version of the "perennial philosophy," the concept of which had been central to his view of religion from the early 1880s and even before.

Tolstói was the best-known Russian in the world during the last decade of his life. Tolstoian communities sprang up throughout Europe and in the United States. He was described in the newspapers as "the sage of Yasnaya Polyana" and "the conscience of humanity." His vast correspondence touched hundreds of people at a distance and many more came to visit him each year. He was a constant irritant to the authorities. His associates suffered exile and other manifestations of the government's displeasure, and he was himself excommunicated from the Orthodox Church in 1901. Most of the works written after 1880 were either banned outright or mutilated by the censor. His public stature in Russia and abroad, however, was such that his person, even in times of vigorous repression, remained inviolable. At home he was the center of a distasteful competition between his disciples, led by Chertkov, and his family, mainly his wife. Sofiya Andreevna made frequent and covert nocturnal searches of his private papers. It was the experience of lying sleepless in his darkened bedroom listening to his wife rustling through his papers in his study next door that finally prompted him

to leave Yasnaya Polyana for good and embark on the journey which ended in his death.

Tolstói was a multi-dimensional man. In his long career he had been a teacher and educational theorist, a philosopher and social critic, a successful farmer and paterfamilias, a soldier, and a prophet. Above all, however, he was a great artist, and it is on his fiction that his fame at present rests. The literary career of this "great writer of the Russian land" (as his contemporary Turgenev called him) may be divided into three parts: the early period of literary apprenticeship (1851–63), the period of the great novels (1863–77), and the later period of preoccupation with the message of his religious teaching (1878–1910).

The works of the early period may be regarded as the "school" in which Tolstói taught himself to write. He isolated the themes and developed the literary techniques which characterize his more mature writings. The spirit of trial and error is reflected in the journal which he began in 1847 and continued to keep, with greater or lesser regularity, throughout the remainder of his life. The journals, especially those of the 1850s, are one of the richest sources for the study of the development of Tolstói's literary style, so much so that their reliability as sources of biographical detail has always to be assessed in the light of the fact that they are also (according to some views, primarily) the record of his literary experiments.

Tolstói's first substantial literary endeavour, "The History of Yesterday" (Istoriya vcherashnego dnya) reflects the psychological self-analysis characteristic of the journals. Written in 1851, it was not submitted for publication, perhaps because its young author feared that its originality would occasion public rejection. The story is an account of the sequence of thoughts and feelings which pass through the mind of the protagonist in the course of a single day. Tolstói's fascination with the operation of the psyche found a more conventional outlet in *Childhood* (Detstvo, 1852), where it is cloaked in the format, familiar to contemporary readers, of childhood reminiscences. *Childhood* and its sequels, *Boyhood* (Otrochestvo, 1854) and *Youth* (Yunost', 1857), were conceived as parts of a tetralogy to be called *The Four Ages of Development* (the fourth volume was never written). The spontaneous impressions of the child as child alternate with the analysis of those impressions by the child grown up. The result is a combination of the lyrical representation of the memories of childhood (typical of the genre) and a detached, quasi-scientific investigation of the operations and growth of the conscious mind at various stages of its development.

The *Trilogy* (as the three novels are collectively called) abounds with autobiographical material, a feature characteristic also of Tolstói's later works. Another noteworthy element is the unconcealed presence of the author's voice (the author as narrator), a strategy which Tolstói seems to have adopted on the basis of his fascination with the work of Sterne. *Boyhood* and *Youth* continue the account of the child-hero's development through his late teens. In the former he discovers philosophy, and considerable attention is given to the phenomenon of the paralysis of the will when it seeks to be guided by reason alone. The distinction drawn here between the enervation arising from abstract mentation and the more practical philosophy in which the head and the heart cooperate remained thereafter a prominent motif in many of Tolstói's works, e.g., the tension between "reason" and "consciousness" in *War and Peace*. *Youth* concerns the hero's education in manners and concentrates on the theme of social comme il faut, a favorite target also in *War and Peace* (the characters of Berg and Vera) and *The Death of Ivan Ilyich*.

Tolstói's tales of military life reflect his experiences in the Caucasus and the Crimea. "The Raid" (Nabeg, 1853) and "The Woodfelling" (Rubka lesa, 1855) belong superficially to the familiar Russian genre of the Caucasian military tale. They contain an indirect polemic with the romantic clichés of fearless heroism, the glory of battle, and exaggerated patriotism characteristic of such earlier practitioners of the genre as Aleksandr BESTUZHEV (Marlinsky). Tolstói reduced the conventional exciting plots of such stories to the level of mere incidents which he used as a framework to display his true interest, a neatly categorized series of psychological portraits of the Russian soldiers and officers and their opponents, the mountain tribesmen. The stories blend the traditional Caucasian military tale of the 1820s with the strategies and devices characteristic of the NATURAL SCHOOL of the 1840s. Tolstói's interest in the latter, bespoken by his high opinion of Grigorovich (a leading practitioner of the "PHYSIOLOGICAL SKETCH"), is also reflected in "Notes of a Billiard Marker" (Zapiski markera, 1855) with its use of *skaz* (i.e., the interposition of a narrative persona, usually one with a "local color" value and characterized by dialectal or subliterary speech, between author and reader), and "The Snowstorm" (Metel', 1856), a physiological sketch of the Russian coachman.

The three *Sevastopol Stories* ("Sevastopol' v dekabre mesyatse," 1855; "Sevastopol' v mae," 1855; "Sevastopol' v avguste 1855 goda," 1856) are difficult to classify. They represent a blend of fiction and reportage with a startling admixture (in "Sevastopol in December") of the stylistic conventions of a tourist guidebook. They also (especially "Sevastopol in May") make extended use of the narrative device of stream of consciousness ("the dialectic of the soul" as it was called by the critic N. G. CHERNYSHEVSKY) with which Tolstoi had first experimented in "The History of Yesterday." The stories, especially the first of them, display the characteristically Tolstoian device of estrangement whereby familiar sights and events are made to seem new and striking by distorting or ignoring the conventions which usually govern our perception of them. This descriptive technique was to become a hallmark of Tolstoi's style. The *loci classici* are the account of Natasha at the opera in *War and Peace*, the description of the service in the prison church in *Resurrection*, and the ridiculing of the rehearsal of a Wagnerian opera in *What Is Art?* Finally, it was in "Sevastopol in May" that Tolstoi proclaimed that the "hero" of his fiction was not any of the characters who appeared in it but rather that which "I love with all the power of my soul" and which "has been, is, and will be beautiful," namely, The Truth.

The stories of the later 1850s illustrate several more of the themes and devices which became characteristic of Tolstoi's work. He had already touched upon death and various attitudes toward it in the *Trilogy* and the military tales. He devoted "Three Deaths" (Tri smerti, 1859) exclusively to this subject. The story describes the pain and anxiety attendant on the death of a wealthy noblewoman, the patient and uncomplaining acceptance of his death by a poor coachman, and the death of a tree. Despite his physical suffering, the coachman dies with less anguish than the noblewoman. The death of the tree is the least painful, because the tree is unaware that it is dying.

"Three Deaths" makes its point through comparison and contrast of the experiences of its three protagonists. This device, ubiquitous in Tolstoi's work, also forms the structural basis of "Two Hussars" (Dva gusara, 1856). He describes incidents from the lives of two Hussar officers, father and son. The comparison is distinctly unflattering to the younger generation, as the "progressive" critics of the time were quick to note and regret. They saw the story as proof of Tolstoi's disaffection from the liberal cause and of his recalcitrance in the face of their demand for literary works which would reflect modern ideas and ideals. Tolstoi added offense to innuendo with two stories based upon the experiences of his first trip to Europe. "Lucerne" (Iz zapisok knyazya D. Nekhlyudova. Lyutsern, 1857) contains a diatribe against the moral shortcomings of the values of "civilized" Europeans (especially the English) as compared with their rural brethren, and reminds us of Tolstoi's continuing interest in the ideas of Rousseau. "Albert" (1858) expresses the idea that art is valuable in itself and not merely as a medium for the communication of ideological or social concerns.

Tolstoi worked on *The Cossacks* (Kazaki, 1863) throughout the entire period of his literary apprenticeship, and it reflects the whole range of themes and stylistic techniques which then preoccupied him. The novel breaks new ground as well. More comprehensively and directly than in any other of his early works, Tolstoi here delves into the theme of the relationship between the individual and the group. The hero's (Olenin) inability to find a satisfying place for himself, the unattached individual, either in the Moscow society which he leaves at the beginning of the novel or the Cossack village which he leaves at the end is a foretaste of the investigation of the role of the individual in the context of the historical and social collective which Tolstoi will conduct in *War and Peace* and *Anna Karenina*.

The foundation of Tolstoi's reputation is the work of his middle period (1863–77). It was then that he wrote *War and Peace* and *Anna Karenina*, both of which are, by common consent, well up on the list of the greatest novels ever written. *War and Peace* defies facile categorization. It is a sui generis combination of the psychological novel, the *Bildungsroman*, the family novel, and the historical novel, with a liberal admixture of the scope and tone of the epic. Set amidst the historical conflict between the France of Napoleon and the Russia of Alexander I, it deals primarily with the events of the years 1805 to 1812 and ends with an epilogue set in about 1820. Against a backdrop of alternating periods of peace and war Tolstoi unfolds the stories of the Bolkonsky and Rostov families, and of Pierre Bezukhov.

The novel's epic qualities are most prominent in the account of Napoleon's invasion of Russia in 1812. All the classes of Russian society (with the exception of some portions of the St. Petersburg elite) unite in the defense of the homeland and in a spirit of national solidarity. On the family level it is the Rostovs who are the primary bearers of the epic spirit: the naturalness and spontaneity of Natasha; the courage and devotion of Nikolai; the scenes, most of which are associated with the Rostovs, of feasting and hunting, singing and dancing.

The novel as *Bildungsroman* is preoccupied with the moral and psychological growth of Andrei Bolkonsky and Pierre Bezukhov. Andrei passes from dreams of military glory to disillusionment, from dreams of honor in the career of statesman to disillusionment, from dreams of love to a final disillusionment which ends in a death which is, at least in part, a voluntary withdrawal from "vital life." Pierre's road is similarly bumpy. He passes, with intermediate periods of despair, from sensuality to Freemasonry and philanthropy to mysticism. At last he seems to find the truth which he has sought in the example of the peasant soldier Platon Karataev. In the "First Epilogue," however, it is suggested that Pierre has begun to slip away from that truth, too, as from its predecessors. Unlike Andrei, but like the novel itself, he continues along the undulating curve of life, from indeterminate beginnings to an indefinite and unspecifiable end.

The various aspects of *War and Peace* are united in a variety of ways. Tolstoi interweaves the fates of the fictional characters and connects them to those of the historical personages. The novel as a whole is marked by the vividness, fullness, and plasticity of description which is recognized as the hallmark of the Tolstoian manner. Life itself is, in a way, the unifying hero of this multi-dimensional book and Tolstoi is everywhere fascinated with its various aspects (youth and age, peace and war, mind and spirit, reason and intuition, the individual and the swarm) and its key moments: birth, love, and death. He raises many questions and explores many answers.

In one of its dimensions *War and Peace* is a historical novel. As a whole, however, it would be better described as a novel about history. Especially in the later parts of the novel proper and in the "Second Epilogue" Tolstoi is preoccupied with the investigation of the forces that move history. His primary target is the "great-man" theory of historical causation, both in direct argument and in his portrayal of Napoleon (the epitome of the great man) as limited, ineffectual, and essentially powerless to control the movement of history. The Russian commander Kutuzov, the salutary contrast to the pretentious Napoleon, succeeds precisely because he seeks to accommodate himself to the flow and flux of history rather than trying to manipulate it.

The "Second Epilogue" of *War and Peace* extends the discussion of historical causation into the realm of the more general philosophic question of freedom and necessity, a topic which was to retain a vital interest for Tolstoi throughout the remainder of his career. In reading Tolstoi, "freedom" and "necessity" can be understood as rubrics which summarize nearly all of his central thematic concerns. Under "freedom" come consciousness, life, the individual; under "necessity" fall reason (i.e., logic without intuition), death, the group. *War and Peace* explores the role of the individual within the group conceived of as the historical mass. Here is another unifying factor in the novel, for Tolstoi presents not only the involvement of the historical characters in the great events of history but that of the fictional characters as well. They all face situations which exemplify the tension between the immediacy of the individual's sense of freedom as individual and the feelings of powerlessness and constraint within the group. The intuitive freedom perceived by consciousness does battle with the indubitable necessity proven by reason, and from this war not one of the leading characters is allowed, in life, an unbroken peace. The same questions, cloaked in a different setting and explored in the context of another dimension of the "group," emerge again in Tolstói's second great novel.

Anna Karenina is an account of two marriages. The story of the ruin of Anna's in her adulterous affair with Count Aleksei Vronsky alternates with the story of the courtship and family life of Konstantin Levin and Kitty Shcherbatskaya. The two main characters, Anna and Levin, are brought together on only one occasion, however, so that while it is easy to see the contrast between these two characters and their respective fates, it is more difficult to understand the sense in which they are also comparable to one another.

At the beginning of the novel Anna is a highly respected member of society. She enters into a love affair and finds herself unable to conduct it discreetly. She abhors hypocrisy and deceit. She cannot be content with the stolen moments of passion in which so many of the women and men of her acquaintance indulge. Anna is caught between the power of the passionate "aliveness" within her and the equally pressing demands of the society to which she belongs. She finds herself in the position of serving two masters: her individuality, with its striving for freedom and self-expression through love, and her social self, with its need to belong to an authentic group context. As she herself says, she is, in her affair, "guilty, and yet not to blame." Anna commits suicide when she becomes convinced that Vronsky, the only remnant of social context remaining to her, wishes to leave her.

Levin's course is the reverse of Anna's. He begins as an acknowledged "outsider," an independent individualist, and gradually becomes ever more enmeshed in the web of social and familial constraints. Like Anna, he senses the tension between the force of his individual ideals and the obstructions of recalcitrant social reality. Unlike her, he finds a middle course which allows him to function with the social group while yet retaining a part of himself, what he calls on the last page of the novel his soul's "holy of holies," under his absolute control. In this hidden part of himself he is neither constrained nor obstructed by his continuing attachment to the group. His life, in this respect at least, is "full of the meaning with which I have the power to invest it."

In this respect the stories of Anna and Levin are truly comparable. Both experience the frustration of having their expression of themselves as individuals thwarted by an unmanageable social reality. As in *War and Peace* Tolstói had shown the powerlessness of individuals to force historical reality to conform to their own ambitions and plans, so here he explores their inability to realize the ideals of the free imagination in the context of society and the family. Although the group is of a different order of magnitude, the question is the same: wherein is a person free, wherein subject to the constraints of necessity. The hopeful implication of *War and Peace* that people are at least relatively free in the context of their personal and familial affairs is replaced in *Anna Karenina* by the suggestion that they are really free only within themselves, in that "holy of holies" which they alone may enter.

Tolstói devoted most of the first seven years of his later period (1878–1910) to non-fictional writing. When, in 1885, he returned once again to literature, he was determined to forswear the "nonsense" of his former style and to make all his fictional works conveyances for the message of the Christian teaching as he understood it. He distinguished between the educated and the popular audiences, and his first literary efforts were intended for the latter.

Tolstói's primary problem in writing "for the people" was to devise a style that was both accessible to them and commensurate with his artistic standards. He employed narrative models and subjects familiar from fairy tales, religious legends, and proverbs. He trimmed his customarily complex literary style to the bare bones, much as he had in the stories, especially "God Sees the Truth, But Waits" (Bog pravdu vidit, da ne skoro skazhet, 1872), written for *The Russian Readers*. To this simplified base he added, through appropriate lexical and syntactic selection, either a folkish or Biblical flavor. He consulted a well-known teller of folktales and was in the habit of eavesdropping on the conversations of simple folk in search of choice words and phrases. The stylistic innovation produced by these efforts is the chief glory of the collection of moral *exempla* which Tolstói called his *Stories for the People*. They represent a

genre unto themselves within Tolstói's work and include such gems as "What Men Live By" (Chem lyudi zhivy, 1882), "Where Love Is, God Is" (Gde lyubov', tam i Bog, 1885), "Two Old Men" (Dva starika, 1885), "How Much Land Does a Man Need?" (Mnogo li cheloveku zemli nuzhno?, 1885), and "The Three Hermits" (Tri startsa, 1886).

Tolstói's concern to bring the message of his teaching to the popular audience also led him into dramatic work. There were efforts afoot in the mid-1880s to develop a repertory of plays suitable for production in "popular" theaters. Tolstói, who had experimented briefly with and then abandoned the drama in the 1860s, was invited to contribute. In response he wrote *The Power of Darkness* (Vlast' t'my, 1886). This peasant tragedy, its five acts neatly apportioned to rising action, climax, and denouement, is constructed very much in the classical manner. As it happened, it was not produced for the popular audience, but it had a notable theatrical success in the 1890s under the direction of K. S. STANISLAVSKY. It has since remained a fixture of the Russian repertory. Tolstói's several later plays do not reach the level of *The Power of Darkness*. The best known is *The Fruits of Enlightenment* (Plody prosveshcheniya, 1889–90), a comedy in which Tolstói ridicules the spiritualism which was fashionable in the 1880s.

The major literary achievements of Tolstói's later period are to be found among the works which he wrote for the educated audience. Like the *Stories for the People*, these works are nearly all invested with the teaching; unlike them, they are written in a style which is much more typically Tolstoian. Tolstói seems to have felt that his peers were in need of instruction mainly with respect to the themes of death and sex, subjects which appear rarely and never, respectively, in the *Stories for the People*. The theme of death evoked the short novels *The Death of Ivan Ilyich* (Smert' Ivana Il'icha, 1886) and *Master and Man* (Khozyain i rabotnik, 1895). Both portray the encounter between a solid, respectable citizen and his death, an encounter which reveals that the very solidity and respectability of the lives of the protagonists was what was most wrong with them. Both works are painstakingly structured, densely allusive, and profoundly symbolic. It is here that Tolstói best succeeded in converting the raw material of his religious teaching into genuine works of art. The stories on the theme of sex are less well realized from the artistic point of view. *The Kreutzer Sonata* (Kreitserova sonata, 1889) aroused a storm of controversy. Tolstói was accused of advocating a celibacy so complete that it would, if practiced, result in the extinction of the human race. The pernicious results of sexual attraction are also the focus of *The Devil* (D'yavol, 1890—unfinished) and *Father Sergius* (Otets Sergii, 1898).

Tolstói's last long novel, *Resurrection* (Voskresenie, 1899) occupied him intermittently for eleven years. He published it to raise money for the transportation of the Dukhobors, a Christian sect with whose style of life he sympathized, to Canada. It is generally conceded that *Resurrection* does not compare well with its predecessors, and Tolstói himself felt that the novel was published before it had reached a fully satisfactory state of readiness. In *Resurrection* Tolstói attempts to provide a comprehensive account of the ills of contemporary society as seen from the vantage point of his religious teaching. The church, the government, the institution of private property, the judicial and penal system, the conventions of upper-class social life: all are mercilessly attacked and ridiculed. Tolstói uses his considerable gifts as a satirist with telling effect. *Resurrection* is also Tolstói's final fictional word on the perplexing question of freedom and necessity. He had left Levin (in *Anna Karenina*) in a state marked by the coexistence of an external, physiological obeisance to the laws of determinism and a spiritual, but wholly internalized, sense of freedom and individual worth. The hero of *Resurrection*, Prince Dmitry Nekhlyudov, strives to resolve this contradiction by externalizing the dictates of his spiritual consciousness. He abandons his position in society, turns his property over to his peasants, and follows the heroine (for whose ruin he feels responsible) into her Siberian exile. For the later Tolstói the mere recognition of the spiritual essence of man is no longer enough, even when (as in *The Death of Ivan Ilyich*) the recognition is total and entails the complete rejection of a life lived with the spirit submerged. Levin's compromise is replaced by Nekhlyudov's decision to act so as to remove from his life every vestige of dissonance with the commands of the spirit. Freedom seems at last to win its long struggle with necessity in the work of Tolstoi. The freedom exemplified in *Resurrection* is the freedom to act in accord with the requirements of the spirit, to control the fears and desires which were, for the later Tolstoi, the necessary adjuncts of the "animal life" of man, and to reject as irrelevant the physical death which was its determined end.

With his last remarkable work of fiction, *Hadji-Murad* (Khadzhi-Murat, 1904), Tolstoi's literary career seems to come full circle. This novel's Caucasian setting and descriptions of armed conflict and the warrior's life mark a recurrence of themes which had engaged Tolstoi's interest at the beginning of his career. He himself referred to *Hadji-Murad* as a return to his former manner of writing. Indeed, its stylistic artifice and the relative absence of the later Tolstoi's customary moral certitude are hardly in full accord with the principles expressed in *What Is Art?*. It was perhaps for this reason that *Hadji-Murad* was held back by Tolstoi and published only after his death.

Works: The definitive edition in Russian: *Polnoe sobranie sochinenii.* 90 vols. Ed. V. Chertkov *et al.* 1928–58.

Translations: Most of Tolstoi's published works have been translated into English, many of them more than once. A good collection is: *Oxford Centenary Edition of Tolstoy.* 21 vols. Ed. and trans. L. and A. Maude. 1929–37. (The Maudes were friends of Tolstoi and had the benefit of frequent consultation with him. As a general rule, their translations are the most satisfactory of those available.)

Correspondence: R. F. Christian, ed. and trans., *Tolstoy's Letters.* 2 vols. 1978.

Biography: N. N. Gusev, *Letopis' zhizni i tvorchestva L'va Nikolaevicha Tolstogo.* 2 vols. 1958, 1960. [A chronology of the documented facts. For more extensive details see the same author's series:] *Lev Nikolaevich Tolstoi: Materialy k biografii.* 5 vols. to date [the latest by L. D. Opul'skaya]. 1954, 1957, 1963, 1970, 1979. The standard biographies in English are: A. Maude, *The Life of Tolstoy.* 2 vols. 1930. E. J. Simmons, *Leo Tolstoy.* 1946. Also of interest: A. Tolstoy, *Tolstoy: A Life of My Father.* 1953.

Bibliography of critical studies: Russian sources (Soviet period only): N. G. Shelyapina *et al., Bibliografiya literatury o L. N. Tolstom.* 3 vols. [Coverage through 1967.] 1960, 1965, 1972. For criticism in English: D. R. and M. A. Egan, *An Annotated Bibliography of English-language Sources to 1978.* 1979.

Secondary literature: J. Bayley, *Tolstoy and the Novel.* 1966. I. Berlin, *The Hedgehog and the Fox* [concerns *War and Peace*]. 1953. S. P. Bychkov, ed., *L. N. Tolstoi v russkoi kritike.* 1960. R. F. Christian, *Tolstoy: A Critical Introduction.* 1969. ———, *Tolstoy's War and Peace: A Study.* 1962. B. M. Eikhenbaum, *Molodoi Tolstoi.* 1922. [English translation—*The Young Tolstoi* (Ann Arbor, 1972)] ———, *Lev Tolstoi.* 3 vols. 1928, 1931, 1960 [English translation of the second and third volumes—*Tolstoi in the Sixties* and *Tolstoi in the Seventies* (Ann Arbor, 1982)]. G. Gibian, *Tolstoj and Shakespeare.* 1957. H. Gifford, ed., *Leo Tolstoy* [anthology of criticism]. 1971. N. K. Gudzii, *Lev Tolstoi.* 1960. E. N. Kupreyanova, *Estetika L. N. Tolstogo.* 1966. K. Leont'ev, *Analiz, stil' i veyanie: O romanakh gr. L. N. Tolstogo.* 1911. K. N. Lomunov, *Dramaturgiya L. N. Tolstogo.* 1956. R. Matlaw, ed., *Tolstoy: A Collection of Critical Essays.* 1967. D. Matual, *Tolstoy's Translation of the Gospels: A Study.* 1985. L. M. Myshkovskaya, *Masterstvo L. N. Tolstogo.* 1958. V. Shklovskii, *Material i stil' v romane L. N. Tolstogo Voina i mir.* 1928. G. W. Spence, *Tolstoy the Ascetic.* 1967. E. Stenbock-Fermor, *The Architecture of Anna Karenina.* 1975. E. Wasiolek, *Tolstoy's Major Fiction.* 1978. G. J.

Tomashévsky, Borís Víktorovich (1890–1957), literary scholar, began to study philology after he had received a degree in electrical engineering in 1912. In the years 1921 to 1924, he taught literary theory at the Institute of Art History in Petrograd. From 1924 until his death he taught at Leningrad State University. His penchant for systematization of literary theory brought him close to the FORMALISTS. His two major works are *Teoriya literatury. Poetika* (1925; partial translation in *Russian Formalist Criticism: Four Essays*, 1965), and *The Writer and the Book: An Outline of Textual Study* (Pisatel' i kniga: Ocherk tekstologii, 1928). In the first work, Tomashevsky discussed "bound" and "free" motifs, differences between story and plot, and point of view. In the second work, he spoke of the usefulness of studying early variants of literary texts. Such study recovers the dynamism of texts and allows the reader to participate in the

creative process. Tomashevsky's studies of poetry are contained in his study, *On Verse* (O stikhe, 1929) where he followed Andrei BELY and Osip BRIK in arguing that Russian verse should not be looked upon from the perspective of metrical feet but from the perspective of line; the line of verse was, for him, the principal metrical unit.

Beginning with the 1930s, Tomashevsky devoted himself primarily to editorial work. He edited the works of Pushkin, Chekhov, Dostoevsky, Ostrovsky and Batyushkov, and he coedited *Tolkovyi slovar' russkogo yazyka* and several volumes of the series of literary documents LITERATURNOE NASLEDSTVO.

Works: Russkoe stikhoslozhenie. Metrika. 1923. *A. S. Pushkin.* 2 vols. 1956–61. *Pushkin i Frantsiya.* 1960.

Translations: "Thematics" (from his *Teoriya literatury*). In *Russian Formalist Criticism: Four Essays.* Trans. Lee T. Lemon and Marion J. Reis. 1965.

Secondary literature: C. J. G. Turner, "Tomashevsky's Literary Theory," *Symposium* 26 (1972), pp. 67–77.   E. Th.

Tonic versification. For a century and a half following the reforms of TREDIAKOVSKY and LOMONOSOV SYLLABOTONIC VERSIFICATION was employed for the great majority of Russian poetry. The handful of exceptions were mostly imitations of Greek and Latin meters: hexameters (including the elegiac distich) and logaoedic meters. Then, as part of the renewed interest in poetic technique around the beginning of the 20th century, poets began to experiment regularly with forms that were previously rare in Russian poetry. Thus *dol'niki*, various other tonic meters, and free verse all entered the repertoire of Russian poets at about the same time. Of these forms only *dol'niki* quickly achieved full acceptance; today they are as much a part of Russian poetry as iambs or anapests. The other tonic meters and free verse remained somewhat less widespread; even though MAYAKOVSKY helped popularize the other tonic meters during the 1910s and 1920s, they largely fell into disuse for the next couple of decades, to be revived only during the 1950s and 1960s.

Tonic versification (which, together with free verse, is often labeled "nonclassical" Russian poetry) is distinguished from the classical syllabotonic versification by its lack of a constant interval between the ictuses, or the positions in the line that may normally be stressed. Iambs and trochees maintain a one-syllable interval; for the ternary meters (dactyls, amphibrachs, and anapests) the interval is fixed at two syllables. *Dol'niki*, though, have both one- and two-syllable intervals between the ictuses. For the other tonic meters the intervals between ictuses vary over a greater range than for *dol'niki*, while the number of stresses per line remains constant, or nearly so.

Like binary or ternary meters, *dol'niki* lines may contain any number of ictuses, at least in theory. Usually the number of ictuses per line is fixed throughout the poem, but works may also consist of mixed *dol'niki* (in which lines of different lengths alternate according to some regular pattern) or variable *dol'niki* (where lines of different lengths appear in no regular sequence). Most poems have employed the three-stress or four-stress *dol'niki*, and during the early stages of the meter's development the three-stress form was by far the most common. Since this form has been studied most intensively, the following discussion focuses on it, but most of what is said applies equally well to lines of other lengths.

The scheme for the three-stress *dol'niki* is as follows: $0/2–1/2–1/2–0/2$, where the numbers separated by slashes represent the range for the number of syllables, the dashes represent ictuses, and the third ictus is shown to have an obligatory stress. In certain ways *dol'niki* resemble regular syllabotonic poetry. They are nearly always rhymed, and the clausula (the syllables appearing after the final stress) normally contains zero (masculine), one (feminine), or two (dactylic) syllables; longer endings, as in syllabotonic poetry, occur but are relatively rare. Hypermetrical stressing—that is, stressing which does not fall on an ictus—is limited to monosyllabic words or, when the interval between ictuses happens to be two syllables, to no more than disyllabic. If hypermetrical stressing does occur on a word with two syllables, then the unstressed syllable of the word may not fall at an ictus. As in both binary and ternary meters, hypermetrical stressing occurs most often on the anacrusis, or the syllables that precede the first ictus. Also, the only constant stress in *dol'niki* lines occurs on the final ictus; any other ictus may be left unstressed. As a result *dol'niki* have come to develop various rhythmical structures, and these have largely been in keeping with the laws elucidated by Kiril Taranovsky to explain the rhythmic characteristics of Russian iambs and trochees.

At the same time *dol'niki* differ from classical Russian syllabotonic verse in two ways. First, the anacrusis may vary within a given poem; the number of syllables may be both zero and one, or both zero and two, or one and two, or it may range from zero to two throughout a work. Within syllabotonic verse, the anacrusis does not vary in binary poems and does so only rarely in ternary poetry (which may then mix anapestic, amphibrachic, and dactylic lines within the same work). In recent years, though, the majority of *dol'niki* poems have come to exhibit a constant anacrusis, which most often consists of two syllables. Second, the interval between ictuses fluctuates between one and two syllables, and occasionally irregular intervals of zero or three syllables also turn up.

Even when fluctuations in the anacrusis are not considered, there are fourteen possible rhythmic variations for the three-stress line, depending on which of the ictuses are stressed (recall that only the third is a constant) and how the intervals between ictuses are distributed. Six of the variants have a one-syllable and a two-syllable interval; these might be called the "true" *dol'niki* lines. Four have two one-syllable intervals and, depending on the anacrusis, resemble regular iambic or trochaic meters; four have two syllables in both intervals and thus are like regular ternary lines, such as dactyls or anapests. (Note that in all tonic meters lines of the more regulated forms may appear in a poem. Thus a poem in *dol'niki* may include many lines that are, for instance, iambic or anapestic. A poem written in strict accentual verse many contain *dol'niki*, trochaic, dactylic, and other line types along with the accentual lines. A threshold figure of around 25 percent has been arbitrarily chosen for classifying poems. Thus in a sixteen-line poem written in what might appear to be amphibrachs, at least four of the lines would have to contain both a one-syllable and a two-syllable interval for the work to be classified as *dol'niki*. If only two of the lines were true *dol'niki*, the poem would be called a "transitional metrical form," essentially written in amphibrachs but containing a couple of irregular lines that make the work transitional between amphibrachs and *dol'niki*.) At the beginning of the 20th century, when *dol'niki* first appeared in the work of BLOK and other poets, they still strongly resembled ternary verse, out of which they apparently developed. Nearly all the ictuses bore a stress, and two syllable intervals predominated; many individual lines fit the norms for regular ternary verse. As *dol'niki* grew in popularity, the rhythmic variations with both a one-syllable and a two-syllable interval came to predominate and stress was omitted more frequently on either the first or second ictus. As a result regular patterns of rhythm began to emerge, as they long since had for the binary meters. *Dol'niki* soon lost their close connection with the ternary meters and are now best regarded as a fully independent form.

While *dol'niki* are a 20th-century innovation, they closely resemble the hexameter and logaoedic meters, both of which were employed in the 18th and 19th centuries. The hexameter contains six ictuses, with a zero anacrusis, either one or two syllables between each of the ictuses (but always two syllables between the fifth and the sixth), and required stresses on both the fifth and sixth ictuses. The ending was feminine and unrhymed. In practice Russian poets by the 19th century were almost always using two syllables between each ictus; therefore the line came to resemble a regular unrhymed dactylic hexameter. The meter was used by Trediakovsky (who *did* employ quite a few one-syllable intervals) for his *Tilemakhida*, and, after a period of disfavor, by GNEDICH for his translation of the *Iliad* and by ZHUKOVSKY for his rendition of the *Odyssey*. While the hexameter became an important meter for long verse translations, the elegiac distich appeared in many shorter works during the first half of the 19th century; it consisted of unrhymed couplets, in which the first line was a hexameter and the second a pentameter. The latter also has a zero anacrusis, but the ending is always masculine. The line is divided in two by a caesura, with either one or two syllables between the ictuses in the first half of the line and two in the second; the third ictus in both parts of the line is stressed: $-1/2-1/2 \angle //-2-2\angle$. The name pentameter derives from Greek and Latin, where the one-syllable intervals were always long (thereby creating spondees) and both the syllables in other in-

tervals were short. Since the system of metrics was based on a count of lengths, there were two and a half feet on either side of the caesura. In Russian, where length is not a factor, the six ictuses actually make this line a kind of "hexameter."

Logaoedic verse may be of two kinds; both differ from the usual *dol'niki* in that the ictuses appear at the same positions in each line of the poem, as in this work by TSVETAEVA:

> Ésli dushá rodilás' krylátoi—
> Chtó ei khorómy i chto ei kháty!
> Chtó Chingiskhán ei—i chtó—Ordá!
> Dvá na mirú u menyá vragá,
> Dvá bliznetsá—nerazrývno slítykh:
> Gólod golódnykh—i sýtost' sýtykh!

> x́ x x x́ x x x́ x x́ x
> x́ x x x́ x x x́ x x́ x
> x́ x x x́ x x x́ x x́
> x́ x x x́ x x x́ x x́
> x́ x x x́ x x x́ x x́ x
> x́ x x x́ x x x́ x x́ x

The intervals are again one or two syllables, and the anacrusis, which may contain anywhere from zero to two syllables, must by definition now remain fixed throughout the work. Some would prefer to limit the term logaoedic to the first kind: poems that adhere to traditional Greek and Latin forms, such as the sapphic and alcaic stanzas. However, even in the 18th century poets were writing what might be termed original logaoedic poetry, with the ictuses in fixed positions and both one- and two-syllable intervals on each line. With the tendency of much 20th-century *dol'niki* verse to be highly regular in form, many poems have appeared that could be labeled logaoedic or "regularized *dol'niki*," such as the above poem by Tsvetaeva.

Other tonic meters can be divided into two types: *strict accentual verse* (which most Soviet scholars currently refer to as the *taktovik*) consists of poems with a fixed number of ictuses per line and a limited range in the number of syllables between ictuses: generally from one to three syllables, more rarely from zero to two (as opposed to the one or two found in the *dol'niki*). The four-stress form is the most common in modern poetry, though poems with a three-stress line occur as well. *Loose accentual verse* (which Soviet scholars most often call accentual verse or pure accentual verse) need show only a certain regularity in the number of stresses per line and allows for complete freedom in the number of syllables between stresses. Since the intervals between ictuses are still somewhat regulated in strict accentual verse, it is possible to distinguish hypermetrical stressing and the occasional instances of unstressed ictuses. In other words, strict accentual verse maintains some interplay between meter and rhythm; loose accentual verse passes over into the realm of pure rhythm. A form of strict accentual verse has appeared in much folklore, especially in the BYLINA, and during the 19th century it was employed for literary imitations of folk verse, such as PUSHKIN's "Songs of the Western Slavs." The modern literary tradition of strict accentual verse arose around the beginning of the 20th century in the poetry of SOLOGUB, Blok, BALMONT, KUZMIN, and others. It became prominent only a decade or two later, thanks largely to the interest of such poets as Mayakovsky, ASEEV, and KLYUEV. By the mid-1930s, though, it fell into disuse and was not revived until the 1960s; Robert ROZHDESTVENSKY has used it especially often. Loose accentual verse is somewhat rarer than strict accentual, though otherwise its history is similar. It first appears in the literary tradition at the beginning of the 20th century, later was used regularly by a few poets, such as Mayakovsky, ESENIN, and SELVINSKY, and after a period of eclipse has been revived to a moderate degree in recent decades.

Bibliography: James Bailey, "Blok and Heine: An Episode from the History of Russian *dol'niki*," *SEEJ* 13 (1969), pp. 1–22. ———, "The three-stress *dol'niki* of George Ivask as an example of rhythmic change," *IJSLP* 13 (1970), pp. 155–67. ———, "The Development of Strict Accentual Verse in Russian Literary Poetry," *RusL*, no. 9 (1975), pp. 87–109. Richard Burgi, *A History of the Russian Hexameter*. 1954. M. L. Gasparov, *Sovremennyi russkii stikh: Metrika i ritmika*. 1974. V. E. Kholshevnikov *et al.*, eds., *Teoriya stikha*. 1968. A. N. Kolmogorov and A. V. Prokhorov, "O dol'nike sovremennoi russkoi poezii," *Voprosy yazykoznaniya* 12 (1963), no. 6, pp. 84–95 and 13 (1964), no. 1, pp. 75–94. G. S. Smith, "Logaoedic Metres in the Lyric Poetry of Marina Tsvetayeva," *SEER* 53 (1975), pp. 330–54.   B. S.

Toporóv, Vladímir Nikoláevich (1928–   ), philologist: specialist in Indo-European, Baltic, Slavic and Oriental studies. Has also written extensively on problems of general linguistics; theory of literature; poetics; anthropology; mythology; philosophy of history; semiotics. Since 1960, has worked as senior research fellow at the Institute of Slavic and Balkan Studies of the Soviet Academy of Sciences.

Toporov has played a major role in helping develop the Soviet semiotic-structural approach. He was the first head of the Sector of Structural Typology at the Institute (a group of scholars who have constituted most of the Moscow contingent of the Soviet semiotic school) (see STRUCTURALISM AND SEMIOTICS), and his vision of semiotics as encompassing not only linguistics and related disciplines, but also certain of the social sciences has been followed in the investigations pursued by that research team. The emphasis on research in typology of culture, where the principal object of research is the sign (or semiotic system) which functions as a hierarchically organized "model of the world," and which may be studied in its anthropological, cosmological and other aspects, is grounded in Toporov's early formulations.

Toporov's research on literature has had two principal loci. One involves close analysis of poetic texts, paying special attention to semantics: in particular, together with other scholars, he has established the fundamental role of intertextuality in ACMEIST poetics, and continues to lay bare the complexity of this phenomenon and its many sources. Another concern has been the "Petersburg theme" in Russian literature, which he has reexamined from a broad semiotic perspective, showing both its pervasiveness and its typological similarity to archaic mythological patterns.

Establishing the links between the ancient and the modern, reconstructing elements of archaic man's model of the world from later reflexes (in place-names and proper names, in the lower genres of folklore, in the works of modern writers) is a common denominator for a great many of Toporov's scholarly pursuits. Another recurrent element in his studies is his multiplex approach to semiotic objects: data from a variety of fields are used to solve a given problem, and the solution characteristically exhibits both a high degree of rigor in the handling of the data, and much daring in formulation of hypotheses to account for them.

An extraordinarily prolific scholar (no complete bibliography has appeared in print, but upwards of 300 published works would be a conservative estimate), Toporov has made important contributions in various disciplines. He has written on the locative case in Slavic languages; on problems of Slavic and Baltic dialectology (especially toponomastics); and on etymology in Slavic, Indo-Iranian, and other language families. He is the co-author of monographic descriptions of Sanskrit and Pali (with T. Elizarenkova); of monographs and articles on Slavic, other Indo-European and Ket mythologies (with Vyacheslav Vsevolodovich Ivanov). He has translated Buddhist works into Russian, and has written on Buddhism and other Indian religious-philosophical systems.

Bibliography (partial): Karl Eimermacher and Serge Shishkoff, *Subject Bibliography of Soviet Semiotics: The Moscow-Tartu School.* Michigan Slavic Publications, Bibliographic Series 3. Ann Arbor, 1977. S. D. Miliband, *Biobibliograficheskii slovar' sovetskikh vostokovedov.* Moscow, 1977. Pp. 552–53.
Works: Akhmatova i Blok. Ann Arbor, 1982.   H. B.

Trediakóvsky, Vasíly Kiríllovich (1703–69), poet, playwright, translator, theoretician of Russian versification and scholarly essayist on matters pertaining to philosophy, history, and the Russian language. Born in Astrakhan, in the Volga delta, to an Orthodox clergyman's family, he received his initial education from Catholic monks. Between 1723 and 1725, Trediakovsky studied at the Slavo-Greco-Latin Academy in Moscow, then left for Western Europe, where between 1727 and 1730 he studied mathematics, philosophy, and linguistics at the University of Paris and theology at the Sorbonne. In 1732 Trediakovsky became translator at the St. Petersburg Imperial Academy of Sciences, and a year later Secretary of the

Academy. In 1745 Trediakovsky and LOMONOSOV became the first native Russians to receive the rank of Professor at this initially German-dominated institution. Soon Trediakovsky became involved in sharp literary and personal disputes with Lomonosov, a powerful figure at the Academy, and SUMAROKOV, an aristocrat and celebrated playwright. The Academy ceased printing Trediakovsky's works, forcing him to express his views in prefaces to the various translations he continued to publish. Personal acrimonies, verging on persecution, drove Trediakovsky into solitude, where he continued to work doggedly, appreciated by none. In 1759 he was allowed to retire from the Academy and spent his last years with books, poverty and sorrow.

Trediakovsky's translations were creative in the sense that most of them broke new ground either in the composition of Russian verse, or in the development of written language, or both. Thus, the 1730 translation of Paul Tallemant's *Voyage à l'isle d'amour* for the first time introduced the Russian vernacular as the dominant idiom in secular literature, replacing CHURCH SLAVONIC. In 1751 Trediakovsky interspersed his translations of John Barclay's novel *Argenis* with original and translated verse passages, and in 1766 he published *Tilemakhida*, a skillful transformation of François Fénelon's *Les Aventures de Télémaque* into complex, unprecedented Russian hexameters based on the ancient Greek model.

Trediakovsky's philosophical treatise *Theoptia* (Feoptiya, 1754) tries to fit scientific knowledge into the shape of a poem for the greater glory of God. As an original poet, Trediakovsky is mostly remembered for his convoluted latinate syntax and clumsy vocabulary, increasingly loaded with Church Slavonicisms as time went on. He was, however, the first formally to introduce the genre of solemn ode into Russian poetry (1735), and the dry thicket of his poetic language does harbor an occasional blossom: a felicitous image, a melodious line, or a passage of noble intensity suggesting deep faith in the civilizing function of human letters as illuminated by the golden glow of classical antiquity.

History remembers Trediakovsky for his theoretical treatise *New and Brief Method for Composing Russian Verse* (Novyi i kratkii sposob k slozheniyu rossiiskikh stikhov, 1735), amended and supplemented in 1752. It is the first systematic attempt to replace the syllabic Russian versification with a syllabotonic one by modifying the previous eleven and thirteen-syllable lines to scan in regular trochaic pentameters and hexameters with a caesura marked by a stressed syllable. Trediakovsky's claim to have initiated the entire new Russian syllabotonic versification was successfully annulled by Lomonosov's accomplishments in verse theory and practice, but it does remain true that Trediakovsky was the first to insist that a regular alternation of stressed and unstressed syllables specifies the essence of a Russian verse line.

Works: Sochineniya Trediakovskogo. 2 vols. 1849. *Stikhotvoreniya.* 1935. *Izbrannye proizvedeniya.* 1963.
Translations: "A New and Brief Method for Composing Russian Verse," 1735, and "A Method for the Composition of Russian Verse," 1752, in Rimvydas Silbajoris, *Russian Versification: The Theories of Trediakovsky, Lomonosov and Kantemir.* New York, 1968. Pp. 36–68 and 100–28.
Secondary literature: G. I. Bomstein, "Trediakovskii-filolog i fol'klor," *XVIII vek* 5, pp. 249–72. Richard Burgi, *A History of the Russian Hexameter.* Hamden, Conn., 1954. C. L. Drage, "Trochaic Metres in Early Russian Syllabo-Tonic Poetry," *SEER* 37, no. 19 (1960), pp. 361–79. M. H. Heim, "Two Approaches to Translation: Sumarokov vs. Trediakovskij." In J. T. Baer and N. W. Ingham, eds., *Mnemozina. Studia literaria russica in honorem Vsevolod Setchkarev.* Munich, 1974. Pp. 185–92. S. Karlinsky, "Tallement and the Beginning of Novel in Russia," *Comparative Literature* 3 (1963), pp. 226–33. L. B. Modzalevskii, "Literaturnaya polemika Lomonosova i Trediakovskogo v 'Ezhemesyachnykh sochineniyakh'," *XVIII vek* 4, pp. 45–65. L. V. Pumpyanskii, "Trediakovskii." In *Istoriya russkoi literatury.* Vol. 3: *Literatura XVIII veka.* Part 1. 1941. Pp. 215–63.   F. R. S.

Tretyakóv, Sergei Mikhaílovich (1892–1939), playwright, writer, and literary theorist. After attending high school in Riga, Tretyakov enrolled in the Department of Law, Moscow University, graduating in 1916. He began to publish in 1913 and just before the Revolution moved closely with the ego-FUTURISTS. His first book of poetry appeared in 1919 in Vladivostok under the title *Iron Pause* (Zheleznaya pauza) and from that time until 1922 he played a crucial role in the organization of the Siberian futurist movement known as *Creation* (Tvorchestvo), collaborating with Nikolai ASEEV, Nikolai Chuzhak and David BURLYUK. In 1924 Tretyakov paid an extended visit to China where he taught Russian literature and collected the materials for several of his subsequent publications concerned with contemporary China. In the 1920s Tretyakov gained his reputation as an avant-garde dramatist with plays such as *Immaculate Conception* (Neporochnoe zachatie, 1923), *Roar, China* (Rychi, Kitai, 1926), and *I Want a Child* (Khochu rebenka, 1927), and he collaborated closely with EISENSTEIN at the PROLETKULT Theater, Moscow, and with MEYERHOLD. In the 1930s Tretyakov even wrote some movie scenarios. Tretyakov was one of the key members of the constructivist group and journals LEF (1923–25) and *Novyi Lef* (1927–28) and was a keen supporter of utilitarian art, design, and the "literature of fact." At this time he was close to MAYAKOVSKY, who exerted an appreciable influence on Tretyakov's own poetical endeavors, and to the artists Rodchenko and Stepanova. With them he believed that it was essential to adjust aesthetic criteria to the world of the factory and the machine. In 1930 and 1931 Tretyakov travelled in Germany, Denmark, and Austria. During the 1930s he translated a number of European authors, including Brecht. In 1937 he was arrested and imprisoned. He died in a prison camp but was rehabilitated during the 1960s.

Works: Den Shi-khua. Lyudi odnogo kostra. Strana perekrestok. Introd. V. Pertsov. 1962. *Slyshish', Moskva?!. Protivogazy. Rychi, Kitai.* 1966.
Translations: Roar China. Trans. F. Polianovskaya and B. Nixon. 1931.
Secondary literature: Lars Kleberg, "Ejzenštejn's *Potemkin* and Tret'jakov's *Ryči, Kitaj.*" *Scando-Slavica* 23 (1977), pp. 29–37. Fritz Mierau, "Sergej Tret'jakov und Bertolt Brecht: Das Produktionsstück *Xoču rebenka* (2. Fassung)." *ZS* 20 (1975), pp. 226–41. ——, *Erfindung und Korrektur: Tretjakovs Ästhetik der Operativität.* 1976. J. E. B.

Trifonov, Yúry Valentínovich (1925–81), novelist and short-story writer. Trifonov graduated from the Gorky Literary Institute in 1949. In the fifties and sixties he wrote about his experiences in Turkmenia, the major result of which is his novel *Thirst Aquenched* (Utolenie zhazhdy, 1963). His stories of that time describe his impressions of foreign travels. These earlier works convey a certain sense of the exotic and the heroic. In the late sixties Trifonov turned away from this, and embarked on what became his main literary contribution: his short novels about the Russian post-Stalin Moscow intelligentsia, *The Exchange* (Obmen); *Preliminary Stocktaking* (Predvaritel'nye itogi); *The Long Goodbye* (Dolgoe proshchanie); *Another Life* (Drugaya zhizn'); *The House on the Embankment* (Dom na naberezhnoi); *The Old Man* (Starik). In them Trifonov wrote about the first generation of Russian intelligentsia formed during the Soviet period and their children, treating of the middle echelon of the scientific and creative intelligentsia of both sexes. The time perspective is twofold, short-range and long-range. The main action is set in the short-range perspective, at a time between the last years of Stalin's rule and the early seventies. The duration of the main action tends to be short, as in *The Exchange*, whose story takes place in a year's time. It is in this short-range perspective that the mundane dramas occur: exchange of apartments, litigation about suburban property, money worries apropos of new fads, casual adulteries, generation gap, tangled career competition, professional failure, and intellectual snobbery. In Trifonov's modern city environment wide-spread interests complicate human relations. The Russian readers love these stories because they immediately recognize and identify with his picture of urban life. The long-range perspective adds another dimension to Trifonov's short novels. Flashbacks and reminiscences expand the scope of the stories and contribute to motivating them philosophically and historically. They tend to embrace the whole Soviet period, and in this long-range perspective it becomes clear that Stalinist rule has crippled a whole generation of Soviet intelligentsia. Trifonov, son of an "enemy of the people" (posthumously rehabilitated), is asking questions about

cowardly moral compromises. These works are free from the modes of SOCIALIST REALISM. The author does not perceive life in terms of an ideal. Reality has him view life in terms of an ideal lost. A low-keyed moral judgment is built into the conflicts. Trifonov's style combines matter-of-factness with understatement. The combination generates an ironic, morally intended, ambiguity. This aesthetic feature of Trifonov's prose transpires in the titles. "*The Exchange*" intimates that in the process of an apartment exchange better moral values surrender to less worthy ones. That a person can change stupendously for the worse is Trifonov's pervasive idea. *Preliminary Stocktaking* signifies that the protagonist's moral crisis is no more than a self-deception void of moral regeneration. "*The Long Goodbye*" is a formula of ironic condemnation: bidding farewell to Stalinist obscurantism has lasted too long. And still, for some it was a time of nostalgia. "*Another Life*" conveys an aspiration for a life of personal self-fulfillment free from Stalinist control. It is to Trifonov's credit that in his short novels he strives not to compromise with the complexity of human behavior.

Works: Izbrannye proizvedeniya. 2 vols. 1978. (Vol. 1: Rasskazy. Neterpenie: Roman. Preface by A. Turkov. Vol. 2: Obmen. Predvaritel'nye itogi. Dolgoe proshchanie. Drugaya zhizn'. Ocherki. Stat'i.) *Povesti.* 1978. (Obmen. Predvaritel'nye itogi. Dolgoe proshchanie. Drugaya zhizn'. Dom na naberezhnoi. Postface by A. Bocharov, "Energiya trifonovskoi prozy.") *Starik: roman.* 1979. *Utolenie zhazhdy: roman i rasskazy.* 1979.
Translations: Students: A novel. Moscow, 1953. "Thirst Aquenched," *Soviet Literature*, 1964, no. 1. "The Exchange," *RLT*, no. 5 (1973). *The Long Goodbye: Three Novellas.* Trans. H. P. Burlingame and E. Proffer. 1978. (The Exchange. Taking Stock. The Long Goodbye.) *The Impatient Ones.* Moscow, 1978.
Secondary literature: A. Bocharov, "V kratkom—beskonechnoe," *VLit*, 1974, no. 8, pp. 171–94. ——, "Vremya v chetyrekh izmereniyakh," *VLit*, 1974, no. 11, pp. 33–68. Deming Brown, *Soviet Russian Literature Since Stalin.* 1978. Pp. 167–69. Geoffrey Hosking, *Beyond Socialist Realism: Soviet Fiction since Ivan Denisovich.* 1980. Pp. 180–95. V. V. Kozhinov, "Problema avtora i put' pisatelya (Na materiale dvukh povestei Yuriya Trifonova)," *Kontekst*, 1977, pp. 23–47. B. Pankin, "Po krugu ili po spirali?" In *Literatura i sovremennost'.* Sbornik 16. Stat'i o literature 1976–1977 godov. 1978. Pp. 237–68. V. Sakharov, "Flamandskoi shkoly pestryi sor," *Nash sovremennik*, 1974, no. 5, pp. 188–91. N. N. Shneidman, "Iurii Trifonov and the Ethics of Contemporary Soviet City Life," *CSS* 19 (1977), pp. 335–51. H. O.

Trochee, see SYLLABOTONIC VERSIFICATION.

Trótsky, Lev Davidovich (1879–1940) and literature. Trotsky, revolutionary and actual organizer of Bolshevik victory in 1917 and the civil war, was also the greatest Russian orator and a notable writer, historian and critic. Largely self-educated, Trotsky absorbed German-romantic leftist culture, its emphasis on historical evolution, struggle, the new consciousness born in and spread by great thinkers and writers, the immense influence of literature and the necessity of enlisting it in the Revolution. From a non-religious Jewish family, Trotsky's outlook was not in any major way Jewish. As effective head of the St. Petersburg Soviet in the 1905 Revolution and as the "Danton of the Russian Revolution" in 1917, Trotsky became the greatest orator in Russian history in formal skill and political effect, far surpassing LENIN. His orations, long unknown in Russia, remain the greatest repository of the ideals, sentiments and language of the Bolshevik revolutionaries and masses.

In later life he wrote important discursive works. In *Terror and Communism*, 1920, he formulated the best case that can be made for police terror. In *The Revolution Betrayed*, 1934, he set forth powerfully the thesis underlying all Marxist criticism of Stalin, that a bureaucratic degeneration had corrupted the proletarian revolution. His masterpieces are his autobiography, *My Life*, 1930, and his three volume *History of the Russian Revolution*, 1931–33, in which his conflicting roles as eyewitness and political leader, idolizer of Lenin and impersonal Marxist theorist produce the greatest revolutionary account of the Russian Revolution.

In 1924 Trotsky published the most remarkable Communist consideration of literature itself, *Literature and Revolution*. Loathing

SYMBOLIST and MODERNIST departures from realism, he wickedly mocked "The small, lyric circle of AKHMATOVA, TSVETAEVA ... and God ... a doctor of female complaints," and Russia's other great Silver Age writers. He praised BLOK's *The Twelve* and MAYAKOVSKY's works but denied that they were truly revolutionary. He rejected pseudo-leftist attempts to abolish past culture and confine writing to genuine proletarians, insisted on censorship of counterrevolution but also on the autonomy of emerging socialist literature from clumsy Party dictation, and ended with a noble prose poem on the greatness liberated mankind could reach when given time to complete the effects of the Revolution: "The average human type will rise to the heights of an Aristotle, a Goethe or a Marx." Long suppressed in Russia, Trotsky's cultural outlook provides Communists with a broader alternative to Stalinism. The magnificent tragedy of Trotsky's life itself inspires works of historical and imaginative literature.

Works: Sochineniya. 21 vols. 1925–27. *Moya zhizn'.* Berlin, 1930. *Istoriya russkoi revolyutsii.* 3 vols. Berlin, 1931–33.

Translations: Writings of Leon Trotsky. George Breitman and Evelyn Reeds, eds. New York, 1969–73. *Literature and Revolution.* Ann Arbor Paperback, 1960.

Secondary literature: Isaac Deutscher, *The Prophet Armed.* 1954. ——, *The Prophet Unarmed.* 1959. ——, *The Prophet Outcast.* 1963.   F. B. R.

Troubles, Time of (*smútnoe vrémya*), the period (1598–1613) between the death of Tsar Feodor and the establishment of the Romanov dynasty. A period of unrest, civil strife, famine, and foreign intervention (by Sweden and Poland), it saw five tsars, including an impostor who reigned briefly as Tsar Dimitry (1605–06).
                                                              V. T.

Trubetzkóy, Nikolai Sergéevich (1890–1938) was born in Moscow. He came from one of those Russian families whose genealogy goes back to the Ryurik dynasty and which was renowned for its cultural and scholarly achievements. His father was professor of philosophy and Rector of Moscow University; both his grandfather and great-grandfather were scholars. Trubetzkoy received his primary and secondary education at home. In 1908 he enrolled in the Philological Faculty of Moscow University, where for two years he studied in the section of philosophy and later in the section of comparative Western literatures. In 1910 he shifted to comparative (Indo-European) linguistics. Among Trubetzkoy's teachers were famous followers of the FORTUNATOV school of Moscow linguistics, including the comparatist V. K. Porzeziński, the Slavicist V. N. Shchepkin and the classical philologist M. M. Pokrovsky. In 1913 Trubetzkoy graduated and was appointed a special research associate (*Ostavlennyi pri universitete*), thus becoming a candidate for a professorship. In the same year the university sent him to Leipzig, where he attended courses of K. Brugmann, A. Leskien, E. Windisch and B. Lindner, some of the leading representatives of the neogrammarian school of linguistics. There he also studied Sanskrit and Avestan. At this time he familiarized himself with the newly published and much discussed study by E. Sievers, *Rhytmisch-melodische Studien* (1912), which he assessed critically. In 1915 he received his master's degree at Moscow University and as a newly appointed *Privatdozent* of Comparative Linguistics he taught a course on Sanskrit.

The Revolution commenced years of wanderings for Trubetzkoy. From the Caucasus he went to Rostov, where he became Professor of Slavic Languages in 1918, but in 1919 he had to flee to Constantinople. In Bulgaria, his next stop, he was appointed *Dozent* of Comparative Linguistics at the University of Sofia. In 1922, supported by V. Jagić, Trubetzkoy was offered a professorship of Slavic Philology at the University of Vienna, and after the death of Jagić in 1923 he assumed the latter's chair in the same discipline.

Trubetzkoy's interests were extremely rich and diversified. In 1905, while still a gymnasium student, he made his first contribution to scholarship, publishing a number of works in *Etnograficheskoe Obozrenie*, an organ of the Moscow Ethnographic Society, whose president was the famous folklorist and ethnologist V. F. MILLER. By 1908 his interests gradually shifted to the study of Caucasian as well as to Finno-Ugric and Paleosiberian languages. A. A. SHAKH-

MATOV's monumental *Outline of the Earliest Period in the History of the Russian Language*, published in 1915, at once inspired Trubetzkoy's research on his own reconstruction of the sound system of Russian, questioning Shakhmatov's naturalistic methodology. This work, which was to occupy the rest of Trubetzkoy's life, entitled *Outline of a Prehistory of Slavic Languages*, was never finished, but some results and techniques of this life-long study were used by Trubetzkoy in other related areas.

One of the main and best known contributions of Trubetzkoy is his epoch-making book *Grundzüge der Phonologie* (1939; in English: *Principles of Phonology*, 1969); left unfinished, it was published posthumously and translated into his native Russian only twenty years later (*Osnovy fonologii*, Moscow, 1960). This concise yet thorough study of the world's sound systems is a landmark work in the history of linguistics: on the basis of data from some two hundred languages, Trubetzkoy articulated general principles of phonological organization that laid much of the groundwork for modern phonology. Trubetzkoy developed his phonological investigations in close collaboration with Roman JAKOBSON. The intellectual atmosphere and the international scope of the Prague Linguistic Circle, founded in 1926, whose member and co-organizer Trubetzkoy was, provided a congenial background for the development of his ideas. This period of his creative life is revealed in the 506-page volume of his letters to Roman Jakobson, a document of enormous importance. Saved from war and destruction, the letters were published by their addressee (Roman Jakobson, *N. S. Trubetzkoy's Letters and Notes*, Mouton, 1975). They constitute an invaluable supplement to many of Trubetzkoy's ideas.

Among Trubetzkoy's works on ethnology and national psychology the most important are *Europe and Mankind* (Evropa i chelovechestvo, 1920), translated into German, Japanese and recently into Italian; *The Legacy of Genghis Khan* (Nasledie Chingiskhana, 1925); and a collection of shorter works under the title *Towards the Problem of Russian Self-Awareness* (K probleme russkogo samopoznaniya, 1927). Trubetzkoy's ethnological works show that he conceived of all phenomena of human culture as one integrated whole. In *Europe and Mankind* he himself calls this principle "the rejection of egocentricity." This involved the rejection of any kind of fragmentation, embracing a holistic reconstruction of culture, built on most diversified empirical material. Trubetzkoy's linguistic studies are thus a part of this integrated whole, constituting at the same time the methodological nucleus of his investigations.

Trubetzkoy's other important contribution is his work on metrics, especially his studies of the Russian folk couplets, the CHASTUSHKA, as well as on Pushkin's folk stylizations. (See "O metrike chastushki" and "K voprosu o stikhe 'Pesen Zapadnykh Slavyan' Pushkina", in: *Three Philological Studies*, 1963.) Trubetzkoy's philological work on Old CHURCH SLAVONIC (witness his extraordinary descriptive treatment, *Altkirchenslavische Grammatik*, published posthumously) embraced literary and metrical questions as well as purely linguistic ones, as shown by his discovery of the poetic form of the "Pokhvala Konstantina Filosofa Grigoriyu Bogoslovu" ("Encomium of Constantine the Philosopher to Gregory the Theologian"). With this discovery, Trubetzkoy significantly enhanced the repertoire of Church Slavonic poetry (see "Ein altkirchenslavisches Gedicht," *Zeitschrift fur slavische Philologie* 11, 1934, pp. 52–54, and further *N. S. Trubetzkoy's Letters and Notes*, 289ff.).

In his studies on Russian literature Trubetzkoy applied, in his own words, "quite a dose of the [Russian] FORMALIST method", although his attitude to this innovative trend in literary studies, especially in the early period, was critical. The "dose" of formalism can be traced in his *Dostoewskij als Künstler* (Dostoevsky as Artist, 1964), a book based on a course he taught at the University of Vienna in the 1930s. The same is true about the *Vorlesungen über die altrussische Literatur* (Lectures on Old Russian Literature, Florence, 1973), and especially about his interesting short essay on Tolstoi, "The Literary Development of Lev Tolstoi" (Literaturnoe razvitie L'va Tolstogo), in the Appendix to *N. S. Trubetzkoy's Letters and Notes*, originally presented as a special lecture in 1935. Among Trubetzkoy's literary studies a particular place is occupied by his innovative analysis of a text of Russian literature of the 15th century, the travelogue written by the merchant Afonasy NIKITIN from Tver of his trip to India (see "'Khozhenie za tri morya' Afonasiya Nikitina kak literaturnyi pamyatnik," *Three Philological Studies*).

Trubetzkoy's ethnological and historical theories, with an emphasis on the importance of the Mongolian period in Russia as well as a concern for her ethno-geographical position, made him an important member of the EURASIAN movement (*Evraziistvo*). This movement was established and developed by eminent scholars in exile, including the economist and geographer P. N. Savitsky and the historians G. Vernadsky and Prince D. S. SVYATOPOLK-MIRSKY. The scientific, ideological, and political position of the movement was that Russia and Asia constitute an integral ethno-geographical and cultural unity. (See N. S. Trubetzkoy's "On the Turanian Element in Russian Culture" [O turanskom elemente v russkoi kulture] in *K probleme russkogo samopoznaniya*.)

In 1938, after the Anschluss of Austria, Trubetzkoy's apartment was brutally invaded and searched by the Nazis, who knew of the scholar's anti-fascist stand. This event considerably worsened the heart ailment from which he had suffered for some years. Trubetzkoy died on 25 June 1938.

Works: Evropa i chelovechestvo. Sofia, 1920. *Nasledie Chingiskhana*. 1925. *K probleme russkogo samopoznaniya*. 1927. *Grundzüge der Phonologie*. (Travaux du Cercle Linguistique de Prague, 7.) 1939. (In English: *Principles of Phonology*. Berkeley and Los Angeles, 1969.) *Three Philological Studies*. (Michigan Slavic Materials.) Ann Arbor, 1963. *Dostoewskij als Künstler*. The Hague, 1964. *Altkirchenslavische Grammatik*. 2d ed. Graz, 1968. *Vorlesungen über die altrussische Literatur*. Firenze, 1973.

Secondary literature: B. Havránek, "Bibliographie des travaux de N. S. Trubetzkoj," *Travaux du Cercle linguistique de Prague* 8 (1939). R. Jakobson, "Necrologie. Nikolaj Sergeevič Trubetzkoj," *Acta Linguistica* 1 (1939). Reprinted in Jakobson's *Selected Writings*, Vol. 2. The Hague-Paris, 1971. Pp. 501–16. ——, ed., *N. S. Trubetzkoy's Letters and Notes*. The Hague-Paris, 1975. A. Liberman, "N. S. Trubetzkoy's Letters and Notes," *Linguistics* 18 (1980).
K. P.

Trudolyubívaya pchelá (The Industrious Bee, 1759) was the first Russian journal devoted entirely to literature and one of the first two private journals in Russia, the other being *Prazdnoe vremya v pol'zu upotreblennoe* (Idle Time Well Used), founded several days earlier by a group of former students of the Petersburg Corps of Cadets. Edited by the noted writer A. P. SUMAROKOV, *Trudolyubivaya pchela* helped to break the "monopoly" of the government and its Academy of Sciences on Russian journalism and began the movement towards journalistic independence and opposition to the Russian status quo that was to culminate in the satirical journals of N. I. NOVIKOV of 1769–74. As is implied by the title of the journal (which used a favorite metaphor of classical and neoclassical moralism) the journal was largely moral and didactic and aimed to produce the kind of pleasant and useful pollen that would encourage its readers to "learn and exercise [their minds] ... like industrious bees." Most of the original works in the journal were written by Sumarokov himself and continued frequent themes from his previous writings, such as the distinction between a "nobleman" (dvoryanin) and a "noble man" (blagorodnyi chelovek) and even his literary polemic against M. V. LOMONOSOV. The journal contained a large number of satiric works, including a number directed against the courtiers of Empress Elizabeth, and published one of the first original Russian utopias—Sumarokov's short "The Happy Society: A Dream" (Son—schastlivoe obshchestvo). In addition to works by writers like A. A. Rzhevsky, V. K. TREDIAKOVSKY, and A. O. ABLESIMOV, the journal included translations of Longinus' *On the Sublime*, Voltaire's "Micromegas," and selections from Addison and Steele's *Spectator*, Ovid's *Metamorphoses*, Horace's *Satires*, and Livy's *History*.

Bibliography: P. N. Berkov, *Istoriya russkoi zhurnalistiki XVIII veka*. 1952. Pp. 117–24.
S. B.

Trúten' (The Drone, 1769–70), was the first and most important of the four "satirical journals" edited by N. I. NOVIKOV between 1769 and 1774, when CATHERINE II liberalized the censorship on certain kinds of satire and herself began the first satirical journal in Russia, *Vsyakaya vsyachina* (All Sorts and Sundries, 1769–70, under the nominal editorship of her secretary G. V. Kozitsky). Through "letters to the editor" signed with such tag names as "Pravdulyubov"

(Lovetruth), *Truten'* frequently attacked Catherine's journal, which it referred to as *nasha prababka* ("our great-grandmother") and parodied by beginning articles with the exact same words and, by implication, Catherine's policies themselves, which were not eliminating the problems in Russian society. The sharpest conflict between the two journals was on the nature of satire: while *Vsyakaya vsyachina* advocated a friendly, humorous, abstract satire "on vice" (*na porok*), *Truten'* supported a more biting satire on concrete instances of corruption and "on the people" responsible for it (*na litsa*). Unlike Catherine, who urged "indulgence" towards problems in society and government, Novikov wanted "cures" and, aided by collaborators like D. I. FONVIZIN, M. I. POPOV, F. A. EMIN, and A. O. ABLESIMOV, presented the journal as a "doctor" that would help cure the "diseases" of society.

In a series of letters from "Zabotin" (Concerned) called "Descriptions of Illnesses," *Truten'* attacked "diseases" like the harsh treatment of serfs by landlords who feel that "serfs are not people" or the laziness and corruption of many bureaucrats, and presented "prescriptions" for their cures under the signature of "Lechitel'" (The Curer). Despite a censor-baiting disclaimer that the title of the journal referred to the editor's own "vice" of laziness in writing very little and printing the works of others, Novikov selected a title which implicitly criticized harsh, lazy landowners by comparing them to the parasitic "drone" from which the journal derived its name. As its epigraph (from SUMAROKOV's 1752 satire "Beetles and Bees") stated: "They work but you eat their labor." Although *Truten'* criticized abuses of the landowning and governmental systems rather than the systems themselves, it may be seen as the initiator of the harsh criticism of the status quo that was to culminate in works like RADISHCHEV's *Journey from Petersburg to Moscow* in the late 18th century and the journalism of BELINSKY, CHERNYSHEVSKY, and DOBROLYUBOV in the 19th century.

Translations: Harold B. Segel, ed., *The Literature of Eighteenth-Century Russia*. 2 vols. 1967. Vol 1, pp. 255–300.
Secondary literature: P. N. Berkov. *Istoriya russkoi zhurnalistiki XVIII veka*. 1952. Pp. 156–212 and 252–58.
S. B.

Tsekh poétov, see POETS' GUILD, THE.

Tsentrifúga, see CENTRIFUGE, THE.

Tsvetáeva, Marína Ivánovna (1892–1941), poet, essayist, and critic. In 1931 a Paris-based Russian literary journal polled the numerous authors who had left Russia for emigration, asking them a single question: "What is your attitude toward your works?" Marina Tsvetaeva answered by quoting a poem she had written in 1913: "Scattered in bookstores, greyed by dust and time, / Unseen, unsought, unopened, and unsold, / My poems will be savored as are rarest wines— / When they are old." To emphasize the permanence of her opinion, she added a second date and signed her answer "1913–1931." Later, she called the lines "a formula for my auctorial fate."

The next ten years, Tsvetaeva's final decade, justified her pessimism. Initially welcomed by Russian writers and readers living in emigration, she now faced exasperated editors of the ever-fewer émigré journals who judged her new poetry incomprehensible and therefore unpublishable. Her perennial lack of money lapsed into outright poverty, yet she was the sole support of her husband, daughter, and son, who lived on her public readings and private begging.

As divisions within the emigration sharpened, the émigré community in Paris ascribed political overtones to Tsvetaeva's artistic solitude. Ominous changes occurred within her family. Misinformed about Stalin's Russia, her daughter returned to the Soviet Union. Her husband became an undercover Soviet agent and participated in a political assassination. Left with her son to face the opprobrium of the émigré community when her husband was exposed, Tsvetaeva followed her daughter; she and her son returned to the Soviet Union in 1939. There she wrote no new poetry, found no defenders, lost everyone but her son to arrests and execution, and finally surrendered her few remaining hopes to the cowardice and indifference of poets and writers who could have helped her. She committed suicide in 1941 in the wake of the German invasion and her evacuation from Moscow to Elabuga.

Seen in a broader perspective, however, Tsvetaeva's art and life belie the prophesied neglect. Her earliest publications were recognized and appreciated—and first of all by other poets, that most demanding audience. Early tributes came from Valery BRYUSOV, Maksimilian VOLOSHIN, and Osip MANDELSHTAM. Later, Boris PASTERNAK, Rainer Maria Rilke, and Anna AKHMATOVA joined the ranks of her admirers. Today, that peer recognition is sustained by the poet Joseph BRODSKY, foremost among Tsvetaeva's many champions. It can even be said that Tsvetaeva has regained popular appeal: among the new waves of émigrés from the Soviet Union, her life has won her as much esteem as has her work, for, in an era when so many languished in exile, and so many others capitulated to oppressors, Tsvetaeva wrote and lived as if isolation and torment were the very nectar and ambrosia of her godless, ungodly age.

Tsvetaeva is first of all a poet-lyricist, not only because the sheer volume and quality of her lyric poetry is remarkable, but also because her lyrical voice remains markedly audible in her narrative poetry, her prose, and her letters. Her lyric poems fill ten collections; the uncollected lyrics would add another, substantial volume. Her first two collections indicate their subject matter in their titles: *Evening Album* (Vechernii al'bom, 1910) and *The Magic Lantern* (Volshebnyi fonar', 1912). The poems present cameo scenes of a childhood and youth passed quietly in the nursery, study, and ballroom of a professorial, middle-class home in Moscow. The viewpoint is intimate but never trivial or banal; the poems reveal the young poet's mastery of the five standard SYLLABOTONIC VERSE meters and her inventiveness in devising uncommon stanza forms, traits of versification that persist in her later poetry alongside her characteristic innovations: the logaoedic lines and the inter-stanzaic enjambements.

The full range of Tsvetaeva's talent developed quickly and made itself evident in two new collections which share the same title: *Mileposts* (Versty, 1921) and *Mileposts: Book One* (Versty, Vypusk I, 1922). Three hallmarks of Tsvetaeva's mature style emerge in the *Mileposts* collections. First, Tsvetaeva dates each of her poems and publishes them, with a few exceptions, in strictly chronological order. All the poems in *Mileposts: Book One*, for example, were written in 1916 and form a kind of diary in verse. Secondly, there are cycles of poems which fall into fairly regular chronological sequence among the single poems, evidence that certain themes sought sustained expression and variation. One such cycle, in fact, announces the theme of *Mileposts: Book I* as a whole—the "Poems on Moscow." Two other cycles are dedicated to poets, the "Poems to Akhmatova" and the "Poems to Blok," which reappear, further amplified, in a separate volume, *Poems to Blok* (Stikhi k Bloku, 1922). Thirdly, the *Mileposts* collections reveal the essential dramatist in Tsvetaeva, her ability to don verbal masques, to speak as another character, to merge the dramatic and the lyric in monologues, dialogues, choruses, and one-sided perorations.

The small collection entitled *Separation* (Razluka, 1922) indicates yet another dimension of the poet's art, for it contains Tsvetaeva's first longer verse narrative, "On a Red Steed" (Na krasnom kone). The poem can be seen as a kind of prologue to three more verse-narratives written between 1920 and 1922. All four narrative poems draw on folkloric plots, language, and iconography, and Tsvetaeva acknowledges her sources in the titles of the two very long works, *The Maiden-Tsar: A Fairy-tale Poem* (Tsar'-devitsa: Poema-skazka, 1922) and the poem known in English as *The Swain* which has the subtitle *A Fairytale* (Molodets: skazka, 1924). The fourth folklore-style poem is called "Byways" (Pereulochki, published in 1923 in the collection *Remeslo*—see below), and it is the first poem which might not unreasonably be deemed incomprehensible in its otherwise marvelous play on sheer sound.

Tsvetaeva set her collection *Psyche* (Psikheya, 1923) somewhat apart when she gave it the secondary title *Romantika*, indicating that the groupings of poems by theme, unlike their counterparts in *Mileposts: Book One* (and, eventually, later collections) do not have a relevant chronological sequence. The volume contains one of Tsvetaeva's best-known cycles "Insomnia" (Bessonnitsa).

The years of Revolution and civil war brought special hardships to Tsvetaeva; her husband Sergei Efron was a White Army officer and Tsvetaeva was cut off and alone in Moscow while he fought on the Crimean front. These years produced the poems of *The Swans' Demesne* (Lebedinyi stan, Stikhi 1917–1921, published in 1957)

celebrating the White Army. In 1922 Tsvetaeva learned that Efron had survived and had left Russia. She took her young daughter Ariadna (born in 1912—another daughter had died in infancy from the wartime famines) and joined her husband in Berlin, from which city the family migrated first to Prague and later to Paris in 1925, the same year in which Tsvetaeva's son Georgy was born. Thus, Tsvetaeva's last two collections of lyrics were published by émigré presses, *Craft* (Remeslo, 1923) in Berlin and *After Russia* (Posle Rossii, 1928) in Paris. These two collections display the heights of Tsvetaeva's lyric power. The outpouring of cycles continues and accelerates. Their expanded thematic and vocal range encompasses the nocturnal secrecy of the twenty-three "Berlin" poems, the pantheistic exaltation of "Trees" (Derev'ya), the stoic renunciation of "Cables" (Provoda) and "Pairs" (Dvoe), and the tragic, proud credo of "Poets" (Poety). Again, the poems betoken future developments. Foremost among these is the voice of "the Greek Tsvetaeva" heard in the cycles "The Sibyl," "Phaedra," and "Ariadne." Tsvetaeva's beloved, ill-fated heroines reappear in two important verse plays, *Theseus-Ariadne* (Tezei-Ariadna, 1927) and *Phaedra* (Fedra, 1928), which form the first two parts of an uncompleted trilogy entitled *Aphrodite's Rage*. The satirist in Tsvetaeva is second only to the poet-lyricist. Several satirical poems, moreover, are among Tsvetaeva's best-known works: "The Train of Life" (Poezd zhizni) and "The Floorcleaners' Song" (Poloterskaya), both included in *After Russia*, and *The Ratcatcher* (Krysolov, published in 1925 and 1926 in journal installments), a long, folkloric narrative sometimes considered Tsvetaeva's greatest work. The target of Tsvetaeva's satire is everything petty and *kleinbürgerlich*. Unleashed against such middling, creature comforts is the vengeful, unearthly energy of workers both manual and creative. Thus, in her notebook, Tsvetaeva writes of "The Floorcleaners' Song": "*Overall movement:* the floorcleaners ferret out a house's hidden things, they scrub a fire into the floor ... What do they flush out? Coziness, warmth, tidiness, order ... Smells: incense, piety. Bygones. Yesterday ... The growing force of their threat must be stronger than the climax."

Similar themes permeate *The Ratcatcher*. Subtitled "a lyrical satire," the poem is based on a well-known, 13th century German legend. Its hero is the Pied Piper of Hameln who saves a town from hordes of rats and then leads the town's children away too, in retribution for the citizens' ingratitude. As in the other folkloric narratives, *The Ratcatcher*'s story line emerges indirectly through several speaking voices that shift from invective, to lyrical flights, to ironic understatement. Tsvetaeva's polyphony reaches its acme, both in the number of speakers—including the Piper's pipe—and the variety of tones. Varied too is the line length, ranging from three to twelve syllables, and the verbal texture with its neologisms (elsewhere relatively rare), its onomatopoeia, and its dazzling paronomasia, the central device of all Tsvetaeva's mature work.

Tsvetaeva's last ten years in emigration, from 1928 when *After Russia* appeared to her departure for the Soviet Union in 1939, have rightly been called the "prose decade." It was preceded, however, by two series of prose pieces: a set of short sketches related to the revolutionary and civil-war period from 1917 to 1920, and a set of literary essays dating from 1922 to 1931. The literary work comprises criticism, short tributes to the poets BALMONT, KUZMIN, Bryusov, Mandelshtam, and Rilke, and a portrait of the painter Natalya Goncharova.

The great prose decade opens with two essays that examine literature in the perspective of history and ethics: "The Poet and Time" (Poet i vremya) and "Art in the Light of Conscience" (Iskusstvo pri svete sovesti), both published in 1932. In 1933 Tsvetaeva's prose began to draw heavily on her past, although few of the some twenty prose pieces of this period can be called "autobiographical" in the usual sense of that word. Rather, the prose begins from Tsvetaeva's strongly-sensed duty to preserve a vanished past and then plunges beyond autobiography into a mythic recreation of her childhood that serves, in turn, as a metaphor for the genesis and destiny of the poet. This mytho-biography emerges in four long prose pieces. Written separately and published in rather misleading alternation with more conventionally autobiographical short works, "The House at Old Pimen" (Dom u Starogo Pimena, 1934), "Mother and Music" (Mat' i muzyka, 1935), "The Devil" (Chert, 1935), and "My Pushkin" (Moi Pushkin, 1937), present the ancestry and birth of the poet in quasi-autobiographical settings which, although charmingly authentic, function primarily as clues to the literary and mythical constants in which the poet's real life is lived.

The depth and originality of "Art in the Light of Conscience" finds a match in Tsvetaeva's two literary portraits of the period, "A Living Word about a Living Man" on the poet Voloshin (Zhivoe o zhivom, 1933) and "A Captive Spirit" on Andrei BELY (Plennyi dukh, 1934). Literary criticism too explores wholly new areas in the short essay on Goethe's and ZHUKOVSKY's "Erlkönig" (Dva lesnykh tsarya, 1934) and in the marvellous long study "Pushkin and Pugachev" (Pushkin i Pugachev, 1937).

Tsvetaeva rightly belongs in the quartet of Russia's greatest 20th-century poets along with Akhmatova, Mandelshtam, and Pasternak. And Tsvetaeva became conscious of her place very early on. Her correspondence, which comprises about three solid volumes, includes a remarkable exchange of letters with Pasternak and many other letters devoted to literature. Poetry and poets dominate all other themes in Tsvetaeva's work, a trait she shares with her great contemporaries. And other poets have most eloquently characterized Tsvetaeva's particular genius. Thus, Pasternak's praise of *Mileposts* can be extended to all Tsvetaeva's poetry: "I was immediately tamed by the lyrical power of Tsvetaeva's form, which had become her very flesh and blood, which had strong lungs, had a tight, concentrated hold, which did not gasp for breath between lines but encompassed without a break in rhythm whole sequences of stanzas, developing their innate elements." And Joseph Brodsky writes of Tsvetaeva's place in her epoch and in Russian literature: "Represented on a graph, Tsvetaeva's work would exhibit a curve—or rather, a straight line—rising at almost a right angle because of her constant effort to raise the pitch a note higher, an idea higher (or, more precisely, an octave and a faith higher.) She always carried everything she has to say to its conceivable and expressible end. In both her poetry and her prose, nothing remains hanging or leaves a feeling of ambivalence. Tsvetaeva is the unique case in which the paramount spiritual experience of an epoch (for us, the sense of ambivalence, of contradictoriness in the nature of human existence) served not as the object of expression but as its means, by which it was transformed into the material of art."

Works: Izbrannye proizvedeniya. Ed. V. Orlov. Moscow and Leningrad, 1965. *Pis'ma k A. Teskovoi.* Ed. V. Morkovin. Prague, 1969. *Neizdannye pis'ma.* Ed. G. Struve and N. Struve. Paris, 1972. *Izbrannaya proza v dvukh tomakh.* Ed. A. Sumerkin. New York, 1979. *Stikhotvoreniya i poemy v pyati tomakh.* New York, 1980. (Four vols. have appeared, with excellent essays and notes by Viktoriya Shveitser.)

Translations: Modern Russian Poetry. Ed. Vladimir Markov and Merrill Sparks. 1967. Pp. 429–49. *Russian Poetry: The Modern Period.* 1978. Pp. 140–48. *Selected Poems.* Trans. E. Feinstein. 1981. *A Captive Spirit: Selected Prose.* Trans. J. M. King. 1980.

Secondary literature: Joseph Brodskij, "A Poet and Prose." In *Izbrannaya proza v dvukh tomakh.* 1979. Vol. 1, pp. 7–17. ———, "On a Poem." In *Stikhotvoreniya i poemy.* 1980. Vol. 1, pp. 39–80. T. L. Gladkova and L. A. Mnukhin, comps., *Marina Cvetaeva: Bibliography.* Paris, 1982. Simon Karlinsky, *Marina Cvetaeva: Her Life and Art.* Berkeley, 1966. *Marina Cvetaeva: Studien und Materialen.* (Wiener Slawistischer Almanach, Sonderband 3.) Ed. Horst Lampl and Aage A. Hansen-Löve. Vienna, 1981.   J. M. K.

Tsvetkov, Aleksei (1947–), poet. Born in Stanisław (formerly Poland; presently Ivano-Frankivsk, Ukraine, USSR), Tsvetkov grew up in Zaporozhie. He studied chemistry at Odessa University, history and journalism at Moscow University, interspersing study with periods of extensive travel and newspaper work in Siberia and Kazakhstan. In Moscow, he supported himself with odd jobs (night-watchman, stage hand, proofreader). Some of Tsvetkov's early poems appeared in the Moscow weekly *Nedelya,* in the literary monthly *Yunost'* (hapax), and in provincial newspapers. He read his poetry at recitals in the VTO (the All-Union Theatrical Society), the Pedagogical Academy and *Dom Kompozitorov* (the Composers' Club). At one time, he participated in the work of I. Volgin's literary association *Luch* at Moscow University. After leaving the country into self(?)-imposed exile in 1975, Tsvetkov worked as a porter in a New York hospital, coedited the Russian daily *Russkaya Zhizn'* in San Francisco (1976–77) and earned a Ph.D. in

Russian literature at the University of Michigan. Presently, he teaches Russian language and literature at Dickinson College in Carlisle, Pennsylvania.

Tsvetkov's poems, some of which have appeared in Russian literary magazines and florilegia such as *Kontinent, Ekho, Vremya i my, Apollon, Glagol,* and some others (see *Bibliography*), have been collected in two books: *Sbornik p'es dlya zhizni solo* (A Collection of Pieces for Life Solo, 1978), and *Sostoyanie sna* (The State of Sleep, 1981). Among his credits is a Russian translation of Nabokov's "Pale Fire."

Sharing Tsvetkov's belief that poetry does not lend itself to translation, I do not regret that his poems have not appeared in English. I do regret, however, that his mastery of the Russian word cannot, at this time, be enjoyed by a wider audience in his homeland. For he is unquestionably among the finest, if not *the* finest, Russian poet of our time. His poetry is characterized by an unequaled sophistication and facility of technique, both formal and semantic (due in part to his vast and—rare in latter day Russian intelligentsia—profound erudition), juxtaposing the lofty and the common in self-reflexive irony; a provocative, insightful, often painful view of things—but let's not take ourselves too seriously. The presence in his poems of that unnameable, ungraspable, which is the difference between the live and the lifeless, makes it worthwhile to learn Russian to read Tsvetkov in the original.

Bibliography: Kontinent, no. 13, pp. 209–13, no. 20, pp. 89–93, no. 24, pp. 99–102. *Apollon* (Paris), 1977, pp. 141–42. *Ekho,* 2, 3 (1979), pp. 79–84. *Vremya i my,* no. 30, pp. 72–77. *Glagol* 1 (Ann Arbor, 1977), pp. 97–115. *Troe: Kuz'minskii, Tsvetkov, Limonov.* Los Angeles, 1981. *Sbornik p'es dlya zhizni solo.* Ann Arbor, 1978. *Sostoyanie sna.* Ann Arbor, 1981.   A. Le.

Tsyavlóvsky, Mstisláv Aleksándrovich (1883–1947), scholar. A graduate of Moscow University's Historical-Philological Division, Tsyavlovsky taught at universities in Nizhny Novgorod, Smolensk, and Moscow. He edited a broad range of material, from documents on the history of the Bolsheviks to GERSHENZON's letters, wrote many articles on PUSHKIN, and played a large part in planning and editing the ninety-volume Jubilee Edition of L. N. TOLSTOI's works. But his scholarly reputation rests first and foremost on his prodigious labors in ordering Pushkin's manuscripts (bound and gathered by the gendarmes immediately after Pushkin's death), in editing Pushkin's lyrics for the seventeen-volume Academy Edition (1937–59), and in chronicling Pushkin's life and works. Three of his projects, realized with the help of other scholars (especially his wife, T. G. Tsyavlovskaya), remain invaluable tools for the student of Pushkin's life and works: a collection of Pushkin's autographs (1935), a chronology of the publication of Pushkin's works during his lifetime (1914, 1938), and a monumental chronicle of the poet's life up to 1826. Several of Tsyavlovsky's major projects remain unpublished: a study of Pushkin's Lycee lyrics, an edition of Pushkin's youthful poem "Barkov's Shade" (Ten' Barkova), an history of Pushkin's manuscripts, a compendium of contemporary criticism of Pushkin's work, a bibliography of memoirs about Pushkin, and the final volumes of the chronicle of Pushkin's life and works.

Tsyavlovsky's work is largely factographical, and he aimed for objectivity and non-speculativeness in it. At the same time, his political background (he was a Bolshevik in his youth) to a certain extent governed the selection of contextual materials (political, conspiratorial, polemical) that he used to explicate Pushkin's texts.

Works: Stat'i o Pushkine. Introd. S. Bondi. 1962. (Contains a bibliography of Tsyavlovsky's work.) [With N. Sinyavskii], *Pushkin v pechati: 1814–1837.* 2d ed. 1938. ——— et al., *Rukoyu Pushkina.* 1935. *Letopis' zhizni i tvorchestva A. S. Pushkina.* 1951.
                    W. M. T.

Tur, Evgéniya (pseudonym of Elizavéta Vasilievna Salhias de Tournemir, 1815–92), prose writer, literary critic, and journalist. She received her education at home from the tutelage of such prominent intellectual figures as N. I. NADEZHDIN, M. P. POGODIN, and S. E. RAICH. Her first published works, the story, "A Mistake" (Oshibka, 1849) and the novel, *The Niece* (Plemyannitsa, 1850) appeared in *Sovremennik* and received positive acclaim from A. N. OSTROVSKY, I. S. TURGENEV, A. A. GRIGORIEV, and others. Her subsequent publications, the novel, *Three Periods of Life* (Tri pory zhizni, 1853) and the stories, "The Old Woman" (Starushka, 1856) and "On the Verge" (Na rubezhe, 1857) met with less success. At about this time, Tur began to develop new literary outlets both in criticism and, ultimately her most successful contribution, in children's literature. Her criticism, distinctly colored by overtones of Christian moralism and Rousseauism, appeared in the pages of *Russkii vestnik*, *Otechestvennye zapiski*, *Severnaya pchela*, and *Russkaya rech'*, the last of which she also edited in 1861 and 1862. Like her criticism, her children's books are imbued with Christian moralism, but its presence here is not inappropriate or inconsistent with the constructs of the genre.

Tur also adapted historical themes to represent her religious thought. Thus, appearing among her works are such titles as "Catacombs; a story from the early times of Christianity" (Katakomby; povest' iz pervykh vremen khristianstva, 1886), "A Sketch of the Life and Acts of Innokentii, Metropolitan of Moscow" (Ocherk zhizni i deyanii Innokentiya mitropolita Moskovskogo, 1884), and many more historical and religious themes. The most effective of these works is the novel *Pugachevians* (Pugachevtsy, 1874) which inspired the French, *Pougatcheff, d'après le roman russe de Salhias de Tournemire*," by Candiani, published in Paris in 1892.

Works: Povesti i rasskazy. 4 vols. 1859. *Semeistvo Shalonskikh.* 1879. *Poslednie dni Pompei.* 1882. *Knyazhna Dubrovina.* 1886. *Sergei Bor-Ramenskii.* 1888. *Vospominaniya.* (Incomplete, publ. in *Polyarnaya Zvezda*, 1881.)

Secondary literature: N. G. Chernyshevskii, "*Tri pory zhizni*, roman E. Tur," *PSS*, vol. 2 (1949). N. N. Golitsyn, *Bibliograficheskii slovar' russkikh pisatel'nits.* 1889.   C. T.

Turgénev, Iván Sergéevich (1818–1883), was raised on a vast manorial estate in the province of Orel. The wealth was his mother's, Varvara Petrovna née Lutovinova; his father contributed aristocratic lineage and the charm and looks to go with it. It was a marriage of convenience on his part, of frustrated passion on hers. She ran the estate; he spent his time in the idle pursuits and amorous escapades of a gentleman. The Lutovinovs were an unruly bunch, and Varvara Petrovna, as a child the victim of familial tyranny, exercised her power over her children and serfs (there were over 5000) with similar arbitrary brutality. Punitive to her subjects, this loveless woman could also be tantalizingly seductive in her relations with her favorite son, Ivan. His father was distant.

The witness and object of his mother's sadism, Ivan acquired in childhood a lifelong aversion to violence. Heir to his father's aristocratic charm, sensitive and urbane, he bore the scars of a painful childhood in the shape of melancholy and self-pitying hypochondria. Compromising by nature, he yet could be quite firm about his love of art and his hatred of serfdom whose indignities he knew only too well. His distaste for violence kept him at a remove from the revolutionary movements of his age. Even as a child he evinced a remarkable gift of observation—the barbarities of his upbringing had pushed him into a passive role. The cloud of Varvara Petrovna hung heavily upon him. He never married. Women in his fiction, when they are not idealized, can be frightful devouring monsters. The victim in childhood of arbitrary power, he came to see the world as capricious and hostile, "this indifferent, imperious, voracious, egotistical, invasive thing that is life, nature."

After passing through a conventional aristocratic education of governesses, tutors, and boarding school, Ivan entered Moscow University in 1833. A year later he switched to the University of St. Petersburg from which he received his degree in 1837. Nicknamed by his classmates "the American" for his democratic Westernist sympathies, he set out in 1838 for the Europe of his dreams, where, as he later put it, "the source of true knowledge was to be found." In Berlin Turgenev first displayed a knack for making friendships that were to place him close to the intellectual pulse of his age. Among others he met the future notorious anarchist but then Hegelian Mikhail BAKUNIN and the romantic philosopher Nikolai STANKEVICH. Stankevich made a great impression upon him, as did the brash and brilliant radical critic Vissarion BELINSKY, whom he met in 1843. Turgenev was "a man of the forties," sharing the exaltation of art and personal freedom of Russia's romantic generation. He soon outgrew Stankevich's airy soulfulness and was too much the moderate to be tempted by Belinsky's furious radicalism. Both men

provided the young, somewhat dilettantish aristocrat with models of serious commitment. Like many thinking Russians, alienated from the world of their fathers, stifled by the oppressiveness of their society, Turgenev was in search of a hero.

In 1843 he entered into a curious liaison with the celebrated operatic star Pauline Garcia-Viardot. Pauline was married; Turgenev adored her; it is not clear whether their love was ever consummated. He did have a daughter by one of his serfs, but with women of his own class he generally preferred intimate friendship. His relations with M. Viardot were good, and the Viardots furnished him, as he confessed, with the only true family he had ever known.

In 1852 Turgenev was arrested and, after a month in the guardhouse, confined to his estate for over a year. His "crime" was to have written a commemorative article upon the death of GOGOL, though he preferred to attribute his arrest to the publication of *Notes of a Hunter* (Zapiski okhotnika, 1852), a book that has been called Russia's *Uncle Tom's Cabin* for its exposure of the injustice and stupidity of serfdom. *Notes of a Hunter* was greeted with enormous enthusiasm, by progressives for its implicit attack upon serfdom, by SLAVOPHILES for its sympathetic treatment of the Russian peasant. The appearance in rapid succession of his first three novels—*Rudin* (1856), *A Nest of the Gentry* (Dvoryanskoe gnezdo, 1859), *On the Eve* (Nakanune, 1860)—placed Turgenev at the pinnacle of fame. There had been no continuous tradition of the novel in Russia, and in Turgenev the public at last discovered a first-rank novelist of contemporary life able to articulate the experiences and aspirations of the times.

Ironically, it was his best novel, *Fathers and Children* (Ottsy i deti, 1862), that caused his authority to plummet. The Left regarded the portrait of the radical Bazarov as a lampoon; the Right thought it too conciliatory. Times had changed. The precarious unity of progressive Russia of the age of Belinsky was destroyed by a new breed of men, many from the middling social stratum between gentry and peasant, who were avid for revolutionary upheaval. The moderate Turgenev broke with the organ of the WESTERNIZERS, SOVREMENNIK, when the radicals gained control, and quarreled with former allies, among them the great revolutionary Aleksandr HERZEN. Herzen was moving to a POPULIST position; Turgenev, as always, defended civilized values. Pained by the reception of *Fathers and Children*, depressed by heated Russian polemics, he abandoned his homeland to take up residence in Europe, first in Baden-Baden, then in Paris, where he could enjoy the comforts and sophistication of the Viardot home. He moved freely in European intellectual circles and became the first Russian writer to win a wide Western audience.

Turgenev tried his hand at poetry and drama before settling upon prose fiction. His poetry is undistinguished and derivative (of PUSHKIN and LERMONTOV, among others). It is noteworthy in that Turgenev is the only major Russian novelist of the realistic period tied to a poetic tradition. His fiction stands apart from the Russian pattern of expansive, openended form. It is meticulously crafted in the manner of poetry. In his employment of narrative structure he is more than any other Russian novelist an heir to the classical elegance of Pushkin, though the easy intimacy and emotionalism of his prose more closely resembles the sentimentalism of KARAMZIN than Pushkin's firm precision. Above all, the touch of a poet shows itself in a pervasive lyrical atmosphere, learned perhaps from Lermontov. Turgenev is always pressing against the limits of realism, sliding into idyllic or elegiac reverie.

His plays derive from the light VAUDEVILLES popular in his youth, but he produced one drama of distinction. *A Month in the Country* (Mesyats v derevne, 1850), by substituting realistic investigation of character for complication of plot, exerted innovative force in the Russian theater. Somewhat melodramatic, it nevertheless anticipates the plays of CHEKHOV in its reliance on tone. The play's format is repeated in the novels: an outsider enters the settled society of a gentry estate, and disturbs its routines, thereby illuminating its nature. As his novels are poetic, they are also dramatic. Action (usually single) is concentrated, characters play out miniature closed scenes, the whole is rounded off in classical symmetry.

Turgenev was also a master of short fiction. His stories tend to two types: a tale of romantic overtones that turns on the expression of a mood, and the more objective portrait of character and mores favored by the realists. *Andrei Kolosov* (1844), his first story, inaugurates a pattern, not only of the love stories but of the novels as well. A strong and weak man, the one "natural," the other given to debilitating self-analysis, are set in opposition, their characters tested by the challenge of a woman's love. Despite its too obvious schematism, the work has some of that charming blend of lyricism and irony that is Turgenev's hallmark. The lyrical *Three Meetings* (Tri vstrechi, 1851) is another archetypal love story, more concerned with evoking the ache of yearning than the pleasures of consummation. The narrative of *The Diary of a Superfluous Man* (Dnevnik lishnego cheloveka, 1850) veers between self-pity and self-mockery (reaching self-flagellation) typical of Turgenev's sensitive protagonists. The work gave the term "superfluous man" currency in Russia, not only for Turgenev's heroes, but for the many disillusioned and ineffectual men of the gentry who crowd the pages of 19th-century Russian literature. The touching *Mumu* (1852), a pathetic tale of a deaf-mute serf forced to drown his last connection to the world, a pet dog, belongs to the philanthropic manner of the 1840s.

Notes of a Hunter (1852), a collection of sketches of rural life under serfdom, is a masterpiece. The loose form of the sketch freed his narrative from calculated symmetry; the relegation of the narrator to the role of passive observer purged it of sentimentality—the two vices of his fiction. Turgenev is at his best when he treats the other. He tends to be self-indulgent with characters too much like himself. His realism, very much in the Russian tradition, never sinks into bare naturalism. It is moral and spiritual: "Every being studied with sincere sympathy," he wrote, "can free for us the truth which is the foundation of life." The bestowal of that "sincere sympathy" upon enserfed men and women had political impact, but *Notes of a Hunter* transcends its immediate situation to show us the truth of the human face.

The stories and novellas of the following decade are saturated with elegiac nostalgia. They are stories of regret over the fading of youth, the loss of the exalted hopes of Russia's romantic generation, and (Turgenev's favorite theme) the failure of love. *Faust* (1856) is indicative of Turgenev's ambiguous attitude toward romanticism, at once nostalgic and disillusioned. Its note of stoic resignation is increasingly sounded in his work. *Asya* (1858) and *First Love* (Pervaya lyubov', 1860) are among the finest of his love stories. The latter is a masterpiece of poetic evocation. Again Turgenev distances himself from his material (the narrator is a boy). The mix of youthful wonderment and perplexity is sensitive, the lyrical atmosphere still leaves space for the woman and the boy's father, who is his unwitting rival, to achieve dramatic fullness. The delicate ironies hinge on a contrast between the idealizations of innocence and the mysteries of adult passion. The poetically rich *A Tour in the Forest* (Poezdka v Poles'e, 1857) evokes Turgenev's image of nature—beautiful in its harmoniousness yet terrifying in its indifference to human fortunes.

Turgenev's novels are distinguished from his novellas not so much by length as by their broader social canvas. It was in the novels that he gave vent to his ambition to show "the body and pressure of the time." *Rudin* (1856) is a penetrating examination of a "man of the forties." Scathing in its exposure of the hollowness of romantic abstraction, it is also appreciative of Rudin's capacity for passionate (if aimless) conviction. The Slavophile leanings of *A Nest of the Gentry* (1859) have been viewed as a temporary retreat from his Westernism. However, a streak of conservatism runs through his work. Pessimistic and anxious, he, like many writers of the gentry, looked to the permanence of nature for solace. Liza is pious and traditional but she is also, like all of Turgenev's heroines, a natural flower in a sterile society. Along with nature, Turgenev's other sustaining value is art—embodied in the intensely romantic and eccentric composer Lemm. Lavretsky, whose story is handled with extraordinary delicacy, is the Turgenevian man of the middle—melancholy, lost, seeking to rediscover his Russian roots. Less successful is *On the Eve* (1860), where he attempted a heroic solution. The idealistic Elena, who flees vacuous Russian society with a Bulgarian revolutionary, is melodramatically overblown; Insarov, the man of action, is wooden. In *Fathers and Children* (1862) Turgenev recoiled from the abstract heroics of his previous novel. His conservative impulse reasserted itself. The fathers, mediocre as they may be, outlast the rebellion of their sons. Bazarov, caricaturing the positivism and utilitarianism of the radicals of the 1860s, denigrates aesthetic feeling, romantic love, the healing beauty of nature, and the sanctity of individual personality—in a word, all the cherished values of Turgenev's generation. He is brought to a point where he recognizes his terrible isolation and emptiness. Bazarov is an imposing creation, dramatic and vibrant. His accidental death—he is another Turgenevian casualty of arbitrary fate—vitiates tragic necessity, as his somewhat adolescent posturing denies him tragic magnitude. Turgenev never approached the tragic depth of Dostoevsky or the epic range and psychological acuteness of Tolstoi. He is a great writer of surfaces—of the observed scene. In *Fathers and Children* all his virtues—tact, intelligence, human sympathy, formal elegance—are at their peak.

His last two novels are a falling off. *Smoke* (Dym, 1867) is a bilious book, reflecting his bitterness at the manhandling he took from the Russian intelligentsia over *Fathers and Children*. Turgenev, however, did have a gift for the kind of sardonic satire Russians favor, and some pages ridiculing fuzzy radicals and diehard reactionaries (as usual, he seeks the center) are first rate. There is little to recommend *Virgin Soil* (Nov', 1877), a novel about the POPULISTS of the 1870s. Perhaps motivated by a desire to regain the favor of the young generation, or to recapture the idealism of his youth, it is a book without conviction, presenting a Russia concocted out of the head of a lonely exile.

Much of Turgenev's late prose, anticipating modernism, veers away from psychological and social interests to a purer narrative, sometimes fantastical, or to prose poetry. *Spring Torrents* (Veshnie vody, 1872) still has as its narrator one of Turgenev's introspective "superfluous" men, the "soft" Sanin, but the narrative of its final section—Sanin's seduction by the man-eating Mme. Polozova—is all from the outside. It is an extraordinary piece of writing, briskly paced, and alive. The slyly demonic though faintly comic Polozova is splendid. *King Lear of the Steppes* (Stepnoi Korol' Lir, 1870) again shows that Turgenev is at his best when at a psychological remove from his characters. Kharlov, the "Lear" of the story, is an awesome figure, larger than life, a creature more of the tall tale or yarn than of tragedy. The fantastic tales are less successful, smacking, in SVYATOPOLK-MIRSKY's biting phrase, of "the second-rate atmosphere of the medium's consulting room." The *Poems in Prose* (1879–83), originally titled *Senilia*, are for the most part miniature allegories of despair. Their language is flat. The reader in search of genuine lyricism would do better to turn back to the fiction. There he will discover that artful blend of realistic narration and lyrical coloring that is distinctively "Turgenevian."

Works: Polnoe sobranie sochinenii i pisem. 28 vols. 1960–68. M. P. Alekseev, ed., *Turgenevskii sbornik: Materialy k polnomu sobraniyu sochinenii i pisem.* 5 vols. 1964. *Nouvelle correspondence inédite.* Comp., annot. and introd. Alexandre Zviguilsky. 2 vols. Paris, 1971–72. Henri Granjard, ed., *Quelques lettres d'Ivan Tourguénev à Pauline Viardot.* Paris, 1974.

Translations: The Novels and Stories of Ivan Turgenieff. Trans. Isabel F. Hapgood. 16 vols. 1903–04. *Three Famous Plays.* Trans. Constance Garnett. 1959. *The Vintage Turgenev.* Trans. Harry Stevens. 2 vols. 1960. *See also: Turgenev in English: a checklist of works by and about him.* Comp. by Rissa Yachnin and David H. Stamm. With an introd. essay by Marc Slonim. New York, 1962.

Secondary literature: Isaiah Berlin, "Fathers and Children." In *Russian Thinkers.* Ed. Henry Hardy and Aileen Kelly. 1978. Richard Freeborn, *Turgenev: The Novelist's Novelist.* 1960. Henri Granjard, *Ivan Tourguénev et les courants politiques et sociaux de son temps.* Paris, 1954. Henry James, "Ivan Turgenieff." In *The Art of Fiction and Other Essays.* 1948. Eva Kagan-Kans, *Hamlet and Don Quixote: Turgenev's Ambivalent Vision.* Paris, 1975. M. K. Kleman, ed., *Letopis' zhizni i tvorchestva I. S. Turgeneva.* 1934. L. N. Nazarov and A. D. Alekseev, eds., *Bibliografiya literatury ob I. S. Turgeneve: 1918–67.* 1970. V. S. Pritchett, *The Gentle Barbarian: The Life and Work of Turgenev.* 1977. Leonard Schapiro, *Turgenev: His Life and Times.* 1978. A. G. Tseitlin, *Masterstvo Turgeneva-romanista.* 1958. Avrahm Yarmolinsky, *Turgenev: The Man, His Art, and His Age.* 1961. M. E.

Turovérov, Nikolaí Nikoláevich (1899–1972), émigré poet. Fought in World War I and with the White Army in the civil war. He was a sublieutenant (*podesaul*) of the Cossack Guard regiment. After the civil war he lived in Yugoslavia and France. He joined the French Foreign Legion as a volunteer during World War II. Turoverov published five collections of verse (1928, 1937, 1939, 1942, 1960). He owed his poetics entirely to GUMILYOV. Turoverov's distinction was to have introduced into Russian poetry themes of Cossack life on the banks of the "silent Don."

Bibliography: G. P. Struve, *Russkaya literatura v izgnanii.* 1956. Pp. 351–52. Yu. Terapiano, Necrology in *Russkaya mysl'*, 26 October 1972.   G. I.

Tvardóvsky, Aleksándr Trífonovich (1910–71), poet and editor-in-chief of NOVYI MIR (1950–54). A member of the Communist Party, the recipient of four Stalin Prizes and winner of the 1961 Lenin Prize, he was born of peasant origin in Zagorie village, Smolensk region. His father perished as a kulak during the collectivization. Tvardovsky studied at the Pedagogical Institute and the Moscow Institute of Philosophy, Literature and History, from which he graduated in 1939. During the 1930s he worked as a poet and correspondent for the Smolensk newspapers. During the Finnish war (1940) and World War II (1941–45) he was a war correspondent. He died at his country house near Moscow.

Tvardovsky's contributions were of major significance both as a poet and an editor. Although he wrote short stories, sketches and essays, he is known primarily for his long narrative poems and nature lyrics. His first narrative poem, *The Road to Socialism* (1931), describes life on a collective farm. *The Land of Muravia* (1934–36) established him as a poet, and won him his first Stalin Prize (1941). It is set in a Russian village during the period of collectivization. Its hero Nikita Morgunok is a peasant who refuses to join the collective and leaves in search of a land where he can own his own farm. When he learns that such a place does not exist, he good-naturedly decides to return to the kolkhoz. While the poem contains some of the clichés of socialist realism and is frankly propagandistic, collectivization is treated in a fairy-tale-like manner. The problems and tragedy of collectivization are glossed over and ignored.

During World War II, Tvardovsky published serially his widely popular epic poem *Vasily Tyorkin* (1942–45). It gave the Russians a folk hero whom they could love, with whom they could readily identify, and earned Tvardovsky his second Stalin Prize (1946). SOLZHE-NITSYN remembers "how soldiers at the front knew to a man the difference between *Tyorkin*, which rang so miraculously true, and all other wartime books" (*The Oak and the Calf*, p. 499). His *House at the Road* (1942–46), a poem about life in Russia under Nazi occupation, won Tvardovsky the 1947 Stalin Prize. His next epic poem, *Distance Beyond Distance* (1950–60), won him the 1961 Lenin Prize. Tvardovsky uses the image of a Siberian journey as a device for framing the work. Its tone is contemplative. As the author-narrator travels through the breadth of Russia, he also travels back and forth in time and space. Along the way he meets a friend returning home after seventeen years in a labor camp. At this point Tvardovsky reflects on the Stalinist period and its injustices. As a loyal Communist he concludes that Stalinism was evil, because it did not follow Leninism. In 1963 Tvardovsky published his satirical poem, *Tyorkin in the Other World*, where Tyorkin literally visits hell and discovers that life there is a distorted image of Soviet life.

One of Tvardovsky's last poems, *By Right of Memory* (1968), is autobiographical and contains his admission that his own father had been exiled as an "enemy of the people." It represents Tvardovsky's confession and admission of guilt before his father and a warning to future generations. Refused by the censors of *Yunost'* and *Novyi mir* (his own journal) this poem was published in Tamizdat by *Posev* in 1969. A loyal and devoted Communist, Tvardovsky began his career as a writer by strictly following the party line. It was only during the late 1950s that his transformation began to take place.

Tvardovsky is closely identified with *Novyi mir* and a distinct period (The THAW) in Russian culture. As editor-in-chief of *Novyi mir* for sixteen years, Tvardovsky will be remembered as the man who transformed this literary monthly into the most liberal Russian journal of the post-Stalin era. A powerful personality, prone to strong emotional attachments, he believed in his mission as a loyal Communist, yet was dedicated to truth, and felt the obligation to publish great literature on the pages of his journal. He introduced to the reading public some of the best contemporary writers: Solzhenitsyn, VOINOVICH, SINYAVSKY, NEKRASOV, GREKOVA, etc. He gave a

voice to such established writers as PASTERNAK, AKHMATOVA, MAN-DELSHTAM, TSVETAEVA, BABEL and many others who had either perished or become non-persons during the Stalinist era. The variety of styles, genre, and authors represented in *Novyi mir* under Tvardovsky's leadership was refreshing and exciting. During those years, Tvardovsky was constantly harassed by the bureaucracy. He temporarily lost his editorship in 1954, after publication of POME-RANTSEV's article on "Sincerity in Literature" (see The Thaw), but returned as editor in 1958, until, in 1970, he was forced to resign. He died a year later.

Works: Kak byl napisan "Vasilii Terkin"; otvet chitatelyam. 1952. *Sobranie sochinenii.* 5 vols. 1966–71. "Po pravu pamyati," *Posev*, October 1969, p. 54. *Stat'i i zametki o literature.* 1972. *Proza, stat'i, pis'ma.* 1974. *Sobranie sochinenii.* 1976. *Poeziya Mikhaila Isakovskogo.* 1980. *Izbrannye sochineniya.* 1981.

Translations: Tyorkin and the Stovemakers. Cheadle, England, 1974. *Vassily Tyorkin.* Moscow, 1975. *Selected Poetry.* Moscow, 1981. *See also: Lewanski*, p. 388.

Secondary literature: E. J. Brown, *Russian Literature Since the Revolution.* 1982. E. R. Frankel, *Novyi mir; A Case Study in the Politics of Literature.* 1981. V. Lakshin, "Novaya lirika Tvardov-skogo," *Den' poezii*, 1971. Zh. Medvedev, *Desyat' let posle "Odnogo dnya Ivana Denisovicha".* London, 1973. P. F. Roshchin, *Aleksandr Tvardovskii.* 1966. A. Solzhenitsyn, *The Oak and the Calf; Sketches of Literary Life in the Soviet Union.* New York, 1975. G. Svirski, *A History of Post-War Soviet Writing: The Literature of Moral Opposition.* 1981. A. Turkov, *Aleksandr Tvardovskii.* 2d ed. 1970. P. Vykhodtsev, *Aleksandr Tvardovskii.* 1958.   H. S.

Tynyánov, Yúry Nikoláevich (1894–1943), literary scholar and novelist. Born into a doctor's family, Tynyanov studied philology at Petersburg (Petrograd) University between 1912 and 1918. After graduation he worked as a French translator for the Comintern; between 1921 and 1930, he held a chair of literary history at the Institute of Art History in Petrograd (Leningrad). From 1931 until his death he worked as editor of the series *Biblioteka poeta* in the *Sovetskii pisatel'* publishing house.

The 1920s were Tynyanov's most creative period. At that time, he proved himself to be the most precursory (in regard to STRUCTUR-ALISM) of all FORMALIST scholars. In *Problems of Poetic Language* (Problemy stikhotvornogo yazyka, 1924), he eloquently argued for the "dynamism" of poetic language. In contrast to the other uses of language, in verse certain elements of language are suppressed, whereas others are foregrounded. Among the latter, rhythm is the most conspicuous. The relationship between the elements which are suppressed and those which are foregrounded, however, changes from line to line. At the same time, Tynyanov asserted that poetry acts on emotions rather than providing cognitive meaning.

In *Archaists and Innovators* (Arkhaisty i novatory, 1929) these postulates are applied to all literature. Literary works are dynamic verbal structures in which relationships between constructional factors, principles, and functions change from epoch to epoch and from work to work.

Tynyanov also wrote two novels dealing with the political and social oppression under Tsar Nicholas I: *Kyukhlya* (1925), commemorating the poet V. K. KYUKHELBEKER who was imprisoned and exiled to Siberia for his participation in the DECEMBRIST uprising, and *Smert' Vazir-Mukhtara* (1927–28; in English: *Death and Diplomacy in Persia*, 1938), about the playwright A. S. GRIBOEDOV who was killed in Teheran by an angry crowd while on a diplomatic mission. A similar novel about the destruction of PUSHKIN was attempted but never concluded: fragments of it were published in *Literaturnyi sovremennik* in 1935–37. Tynyanov's short story, "Second Lieutenant Kizhe" (Podporuchik Kizhe, 1927) was made into a popular movie in 1934.

Tynyanov's notion of literary dynamism anticipated the views of such Marxist theorists of literature and culture as György Lukács, and of some French and American structuralists and post-structuralists. His insistence on the ever-changing perception of the literary work, coincided with Lukács's notion of Marxist dialectics, Todorov's concept of literary genres and J. H. Miller's ideas about reader participation in the creation of works of literature.

Tynyanov's refusal to regard a literary work as pre-existing reality, fixed and immobile in its ontological status, was radically different from SHKLOVSKY's naively idealistic concept of the literary work as a sum total of devices. Tynyanov's theory of literary dynamism is profoundly dialectical in nature, and thus the most consistently Marxist of all formalist theorizing.

Works: Gogol' i Dostoevskii: k teorii parodii. 1921. *Sobranie sochinenii.* 2 vols. 1931. "Voskovaya persona," *Zvezda*, 1932, nos. 1–2. "Maloletnii Vitushinnikov," *Literaturnyi sovremennik*, 1933, no. 7. *Sochineniya.* 3 vols. 1959. *Pushkin i ego sovremenniki.* 1969.

Translations: Death and Diplomacy in Persia. Trans. A. Brown. 1938. "Second Lieutenant Likewise." In *New Russian Stories.* Ed. Bernard Guilbert Guerney. 1953. *The Problem of Verse Language.* Trans. and ed. Michael Sosa and Brent Harvey. Afterword by Roman Jakobson. 1981.

Secondary literature: J. Douglas Clayton, "Soviet Views of Parody: Tynianov and Morozov," *CASS* 7 (1973), pp. 485–93. V. Kaverin, ed., *Yurii Tynyanov: Pisatel' i uchenyi. Vospominaniya, razmyshleniya.* 1966. Reinhard Lauer, "Tynjanov (1894–1943)." In *Klassiker der Literaturtheorie: Von Boileau bis Barthes.* Ed. Horst Turk. Munich, 1979. Pp. 267–85. Anna Tamarchenko, "U istokov sovetskogo istoricheskogo romana," *Neva*, 1974, no. 10, pp. 179–87.

E. Th.

Typical, the (*tipichnost', tipicheskoe*). In literary criticism the word "typical" is usually applied to characters embodying essential personal, social, or national traits peculiar to a large number of individuals, a class, or a people. It can also be applied to conditions, events and ideas. The concept of the typical has gained a wide circulation in Russia since the 19th century. BELINSKY, DOSTOEVSKY, and GORKY believed that originality and profundity in literature depend on a writer's ability to create typical characters. Apollon GRIGORIEV contended that the typical must represent the eternal moral ideals of a nation, while DOBROLYUBOV perceived typical characters as products of sociohistorical conditions.

The concept of the typical has become an integral part of socialist realism, especially in view of Engels' statement that realism implies the portrayal of typical characters under typical circumstances. In conformity with the Communist Party's instructions, the typical is interpreted as corresponding not to the most common features of Soviet life but to the main tendencies in its development toward Communism. This interpretation leads to a highly embellished depiction of Soviet conditions and to the exclusion of such typical phenomena as the terror under Stalin or present-day alcoholism. The official attitude toward the typical can be seen in the case of Aleksandr FADEEV who was compelled to thoroughly revise his novel *The Young Guard* (1945) after the Party attacked him for describing supposedly nontypical aspects of the Soviet retreat and underground activities during World War II.

Bibliography: B. Küppers, *Die Theorie vom Typischen in der Literatur: Ihre Ausprägung in der russischen Literaturkritik und in der sowjetischen Literaturwissenschaft.* 1966. A. Revyakin, *Problemy tipicheskogo v khudozhestvennoi literature.* 1959. V. Terras, *Belinsky and Russian Literary Criticism: The Heritage of Organic Aesthetics.* 1974.

H. E.

Tyútchev, Fyódor Ivánovich (1803–73) was born on 5 December 1803 on the family estate of Ovstug (200 miles southwest of Moscow). Educated at home until his seventeenth year the precocious child was nurtured in that "patriarchal" atmosphere of piety, patriotism, and reverence for the throne which often characterized the Muscovite landed gentry of the period and doubtless helped shape the views of the future Slavophile. In apparent contradiction to these values was the hegemony, within the confines of the family at least, of French; and it was in that language that Tyutchev preferred to converse and correspond throughout his life. For the future poet, however, the most important formative factor was the unusually serious schooling provided by the learned young S. E. RAICH, an enthusiastic (if minor) poet and translator (from the Latin and the Italian), who was for years the boy's pedagogue, companion, and friend. It was to Raich that Tyutchev owed his excellent knowledge of the classical writers (he is said to have known much of Horace by

heart) and of Russian literature as well. It was under Raich's tutelage that the boy began to write verse. In 1816 (or 1817) Tyutchev was encouraged to join the "little academy" of fledgling poets organized by A. F. MERZLYAKOV, poet, literary theorist, and professor of literature at the University of Moscow. And in 1818 Tyutchev's "public" career was launched when his Derzhavinesque poem "The Nobleman (An Imitation of Horace)" was read by Merzlyakov himself before the Society of Lovers of Russian Literature.

In 1819 Tyutchev entered the Philological Faculty of the University of Moscow where after two years of study he received his degree as *kandidat*. In January 1822 he left for St. Petersburg to enroll in the Collegium of Foreign Affairs and in May was appointed to the Russian legation in Munich. A month later he left for the West, where he was to spend most of the next twenty-two years of his life.

For Tyutchev the German years were pivotal. For the man they were a "golden time," the "holiday of a wonderful youth" where he would grow into manhood, establish himself socially (Heine, Schelling, and Varnhagen von Ense were among his German acquaintances), marry twice, and become the father of three. For the poet they offered the cultural ambiance of German romanticism, which was to leave a lasting imprint on his verse. Appearing sporadically in Russian literary journals and almanacs of the second water, these poems could make no serious claim to the public's attention until 1836 when there appeared in PUSHKIN's *Sovremennik* a group of sixteen poems under the title "Poems Sent From Germany." It was characteristic of Tyutchev's aloof attitude towards his self-styled poetic "scribblings" (*virshi*) that the intercession of a former Munich friend Prince I. S. Gagarin was necessary for their publication under the quasi-anonymous initials "F. T."

Owning exceptional conversational skills and a passionate interest in international politics, Tyutchev nonetheless lacked a quality essential to any successful diplomat: a serious attitude towards his job. After seventeen years of slow progress along the diplomatic ladder his career came to an abrupt if temporary end in 1839, when having abandoned his post (Russian *chargé d'affaires* in Turin) without official permission in order to marry his second wife, he was fired from government service. It is an index of his attachment to the West that the jobless husband and father of three should have remained in Germany five more years before returning to Russia to settle and seek reinstatement.

With his reintegration into St. Petersburg society Tyutchev gained a measure of that recognition which he had been denied as a voluntary exile. An ardent and articulate patriot, he wrote sharply worded articles defending Nicholas' foreign policy ("Lettre à M. le Docteur Gustave Kolb" [1844], "La Russie et la Révolution" [1848], "La Question Romaine" [1850]), which aroused controversy both at home and abroad. An inveterate habitué of high society circles, he became, with his brilliant *mots* and oddly disheveled appearance, a striking figure in the salons of the capital city. Moreover through the efforts of NEKRASOV, who accompanied the republication of the *Sovremennik* poems with a glowing preface (1850) and TURGENEV, who edited the first collection of his verse (1854) Tyutchev the poet, heretofore all but unknown to the general public, won the acclaim of those authentic connoisseurs of superior poetry whose opinion matters most.

Although events on the international scene could stir Tyutchev inordinately (Russia's Crimean reverses were a source of particular distress) the most important single event of the Russian years was his liaison with Elena Aleksandrovna Denisieva. Since his Munich days Tyutchev had felt a need for a woman's love which neither of his marriages could satisfy. Extra-marital affairs were the consequence. But this liaison with an impoverished young noblewoman was of an unprecedented intensity and duration. For fourteen years (1850–64) Denisieva was in effect the poet's second wife, bearing him three children, nursing him when he was sick, seeking to amuse him during his frequent periods of irritability and melancholia. To these burdens was added the social stigma which attended their overt affair. Even more painful for the couple than the censure of society, however, was the nature of the love itself. For having sacrificed so much for her love, Denisieva would be content with nothing less than total possession of its object. Such a role Tyutchev, who could not completely forsake his duties as husband and father, was unable to fulfill. Quarrels, sometimes violent, ensued. The "last love" thus devolved into that "fatal duel" described in the remarkable "Denisieva cycle" of poems. Her health undermined by tuberculosis and, one may surmise, the emotional tension inherent in the liaison, Denisieva died in 1864.

Deeply shaken by his mistress's death the sexagenarian Tyutchev nonetheless continued to lead the life of a *mondain*, government official (he had been named chairman of the Committee on Foreign Censorship) and occasional poet (the lyrical output during these final years was meagre). In December 1872, however, a stroke left him partially paralyzed. Other strokes followed. On June 27, 1873 he was dead.

The relatively small corpus of Tyutchev's original poetry, if we exclude the circumstantial verse, may be divided into the poems about nature, the philosophical poems, the love poems, and the political or ideological verse. They will be considered here in that order.

The greatest nature poet that Russia has produced (such is the critical consensus), Tyutchev found his highly individual voice in Germany. Having shed the neoclassical manner of his early Russian juvenilia, he began in the 1820s to compress his perceptions of the Bavarian landscapes surrounding him into short lyrics which cultivate an intensive rather than extensive method of expression. Eschewing specific, closely perceived details (the telescope not the microscope is Tyutchev's preferred instrument), and content to describe those fiery sunsets, snowy peaks, and mountain rills which had inspired a generation of romantic poets (a Soviet critic has justly observed that Tyutchev's nature is that of a tourist) Tyutchev imparts to these familiar subjects extraordinary freshness, even strangeness. By finding an unexpected angle of vision he was able to perceive the surprising in the familiar, the unconventional in the conventional, and thereby achieve what all great poetry achieves, an alteration of our apprehension of reality. A sunset for example is transformed thus: "Already the earth has rolled the incandescent sphere of the sun from its head"; and the ensuing evening coolness: "A spring tremor like a stream, has run through the veins of nature, as if welling waters had touched her burning feet" ("Summer Evening"—Letnii vecher). A crepuscular landscape is described: "Like a spring sea at full tide the day brightening [!] is motionless" ("How Softly Wafts over the Valley"—Kak tikho veet nad dolinoi). A sudden spring storm is pictured: "One could say that Hebe had poured her thunder-bubbling goblet from the sky" ("Springtime Thunderstorm"—Vesennyaya groza). Such bold conceits may be compared instructively with the more normative perceptions of nature, at once more classical and more realistic, of Pushkin.

During the second German decade philosophical and subjective strains began to complicate and enrich Tyutchev's view of nature. Influenced by Schelling's *Naturphilosophie* the poet repeatedly describes the natural and human spheres as if they were parallel and analogous systems ("The stream, congealed, is growing dim"—Potok sgustilsya i tuskneet, "The Earth still looks sad"—Eshche zemli pechalen vid). Elsewhere ("Blue-grey shadows merging"—Teni sizye smesilis', "Spring"—Vesna) the world of nature is conceived as a place of refreshment or refuge for the poet's wearied or angst-ridden soul. And in others ("A hawk flew up from the glade"—S polyany korshun podnyalsya, "Look to the West ablaze"—Smotri, kak zapad razgorelsya) a landscape gives rise to philosophical or ideological speculations.

A somewhat different tone and style mark the nature poems of the Russian years. Subjective ruminations and *paysages moralisés* are met with less often, and animistic motifs—the famous "deaf and dumb demons" of "The Night Sky so Gloomy" (Nochnoe nebo tak ugryumo) notwithstanding—relatively rare. In the ascendant is a more impersonal apprehension of nature which may conceivably reflect the influence of Russian realism, now near its apogee. Memorable examples of this are the remarkable "There is in Early Fall" (Est' v oseni pervonachal'noi) and "Late in Fall" (Osennei pozdneyu poroyu). The relative frequency of autumnal motifs in these poems can plausibly be linked to the poet's approaching old age.

While it is impossible in all cases to distinguish between the nature poetry, charged as it often is with philosophical overtones, and those philosophical poems which are set in natural surroundings, the existence of the latter category is nonetheless clear. Here again the influence of German romanticism and Schelling in particular are evident. Thus, the phantasmagorical imagery of "Dream at Sea" (Son na more) describes the self-apotheosis of the poet and (a touch of Pascal here) its dangerous consequences. A trio of thematically linked poems ("What Art Thou Wailing about, Wind at Night"—O chem ty voesh', vetr nochnoi, "Day and Night"—Den' i noch', "Holy Night Has Risen"—Svyataya noch' na nebosklon vzoshla) proposes a radically dichotomous, almost Manichean universe, in which the lovely, warm, ephemeral day is opposed to the vast, chaotic, frightening, and yet mysteriously kindred abyss of night. "Silentium" with its celebrated apothegm, "the spoken word is but a lie" (later to become a rallying cry of the symbolists), proclaims the ultimate inexpressibility of human thoughts and feelings. In "Malaria" the poet mixes Pauline theology with a decadent sensibility when he declares that evil inheres in the loveliest phenomena of the external world and speculates that they may simultaneously be the heralds, the sweeteners, and the concealers of death's "terrible arrival."

The striking imagery and didactic, even dogmatic, tone of these poetic statements have led some critics (e.g., SOLOVYOV) to assume that they represent Tyutchev's own philosophical credo. The available evidence does not support this view. Not only is Tyutchev known to have rejected Schellingian metaphysics to the philosopher's face and disparaged German philosophy in general as "destructive," his own poetry contains far too many self-contradictions to be understood as a coherent philosophical system. Rather the poet seems to have appropriated Schellingesque images and ideas in order to express fears, conflicts, and predilections which he found in himself. Thus, to take a single instance, it seems less reasonable to see the recurring images of the abyss, night or chaos as an affirmation of the objective existence of Schelling's *Abgrund* or *Urgrund* than as projections of the poet's fascination with (and fear of) the "dark," i.e., the anarchic, destructive, or passionate, aspects of human experience.

Like Tyutchev's nature poetry his love poems undergo certain changes in tone and texture. Those of the German years tend to be lyrical epiphanies commemorating an especially poignant or passionate moment in a particular affair. Exhibiting at times an explicitly sensual strain ("With such sweet bliss"—S takoyu negoyu, s takoi toskoi vlyublennoi, "I love thine eyes"—Lyublyu glaza tvoi, moi drug) while emphasizing at others the illicit nature of the attachment ("Italian Villa"—Italianskaya villa), these poems are infused with a spirit of hedonism mixed with guilt which Solovyov's observation that for Tyutchev "the life of the soul concentrated in love [is] in essence an evil life" does much to illuminate.

The love poetry of the Russian period is contained almost entirely in the "Denisieva cycle" of poems. Central here is the theme of love as suffering. Stemming partly from society's "base" condemnation of his young mistress ("What you prayed for with love"—Chemu molilas' ty s lyubov'yu, "How lethally we love"—O kak ubiistvenno my lyubim) the theme is, more typically, rooted in the poet's gradual realization that their love is unequally shared, that he cannot give himself to her as wholly as she has to him ("Don't say, he loves me as before"—Ne govori: menya on, kak i prezhde, lyubit, "Don't trouble me with just reproach"—O ne trevozh' menya ukoroi spravedlivoi). By turns compassionate and angry, elegiac and self-flagellating, Tyutchev, now speaking in his own voice, now answering in hers, imparts to the sequence a dialectical movement capable of conveying psychological insights of unusual variety and depth. In more than a dozen lyrics written over a period of six years the poet transcribed the painful course of this self-styled "fatal duel" of lovers. By 1856, as if confirming the valedictory notes sounded in the poems themselves, he had lapsed into silence. Eight years later however the death of his mistress provoked a final creative outburst in such powerful evocations of grief as "O God, give burning suffering" (O Gospodi, dai zhguchego stradan'ya) and "How soothing art thou, nocturnal sea" (Kak khorosho ty, o more nochnoe).

The political verse occupies an inferior place in Tyutchev's oeuvre. Not devoid at times of satirical mordancy and wit (e.g., "There is a limit to long-suffering patience"—Net—mera est' dolgoterpen'yu) these poems very often amount to little more than rhymed rhetoric exalting Russia's messianic role in world history, prophesying her future greatness, and excoriating the Western enemy. Notable exceptions are "Those poor villages" (Eti bednye selen'ya), "Above this benighted crowd" (Nad etoi temnoyu tol-poi), and "Sea and Cliffs" (More i utes). The first two translate into moving images the Slavophile belief that the poverty, suffering, and Christ-like meekness of the Russian peasant mark him as God's chosen. In the last the chaotic and stormy seas (almost always a seminal image for Tyutchev) powerfully symbolize the forces of revolution furiously assaulting the lofty and impregnable cliff of Russian autocracy.

Tyutchev's poetic weltanschauung, like that of any great poet, cannot be neatly encapsulated. Nevertheless certain facts about his personality shed light on themes that are of central importance to his verse. Psychologically speaking, Tyutchev seems to have had no clearly felt sense of selfhood. An ardent Russian patriot, he preferred, whenever possible, to live in the West; deeply convinced that religion was essential to any healthy political or social order ("le lien ... qui retient, qui lie les faisceaux pour toute société historique") he himself was without faith; an enthusiastic Slavophile, his neglect of family, church, and that patriarchal mode of life which he so revered, was notorious. In view of this chasm separating theory from practice, the ideal from the actual, the comment of a contemporary that, nearing death, Tyutchev was trying to "ascertain his own identity" acquires special significance and invites comparison with his own admission that "only in [Denisieva's] love did I *realize my own identity*." In different ways both statements point to that inner emptiness which an *obiter dictum* (to his wife) that the sole aim of his existence was to "*avoid at all costs any serious encounter with myself*" and his neurotic aversion—repeatedly expressed in letters and poems—to such "annihilating" concepts as *orphanhood, separation, absence,* and *rootlessness* variously illustrate.

This *horror vacui* provides a suggestive context for some of the most basic motifs of Tyutchev's poetry. Thus, such diverse themes as a woman's passionate, self-surrendering love; the poet's fear of—and fascination with—the anarchic or chaotic aspects of existence; his wish to immerse himself in elemental, natural life; and his vision of nature as a harmonious, animate, and soulful being may be perceived as defenses against or expressions of an anguished sense of inner void.

On superficial inspection the "typical" Tyutchev poem might seem to exhibit, formally speaking, a conventional profile: a short (average length, 16–20 lines) poem consisting of *a b a b* or *a b b a* quatrains (sometimes disguised as octaves) in iambic tetrameter or, less frequently, pentameter. The language, free of colloquialisms, is consistently "poetic"; the tone, except for the political verse, predominantly lyrical. Closer examination, however, reveals interesting deviations from these norms. After 1830 non-iambic meters (the trochee in particular) make up nearly twenty percent of the total. Anticipating the more systematic metrical innovations of the symbolist poets are the *dol'niki*, anacrusis, and mixed meters which mark such celebrated poems as "Dream at Sea," "Silentium," "Sea and Cliffs," and "Last Love". Combined with occasional archaisms (e.g., *onyi, musikiiskii, ognevitsa, vodomet*), the generous use of compound adjectives (e.g., *boleznenno-yarkii, pyshno-zolotoi, tainstvenno-volshebnyi*), and a frequently oratorical mode of speech, these features make for a highly distinctive poetic texture.

Tyutchev's literary fortunes have fluctuated considerably according to cultural trends and political developments. Almost unknown until he was forty-five, he had won by the end of his life—the antipoetic bias of the age notwithstanding—the enthusiastic acclaim of such diverse literary judges as Nekrasov, Fet, Dobrolyubov, Dostoevsky, Turgenev, and Tolstoi. But it was not until the advent of the symbolist movement (Solovyov, Merezhkovsky, and Bryusov were among his most perceptive and admiring critics) that he gained recognition—among the *cognoscenti* at least—as the greatest lyric poet of the century after Pushkin. Although since 1917 his conservative political and religious views have discouraged frequent publication and wide dissemination of his works, Tyutchev's eclipse in the post-revolutionary years have been only partial. Such eminent Soviet scholars as G. I. Chulkov, Yu. N. Tynyanov, D. D. Blagoi, and V. V. Gippius have produced important studies of his poetry. And while the correspondence has received short shrift from Soviet editors and the political articles have been overlooked entirely, valuable scholarly editions of the verse have been brought out by Chulkov and K. V. Pigarev. The latter's *Zhizn' i tvorchestvo F. I. Tyutcheva* remains the most useful single work on the subject.

Works: Polnoe sobranie sochinenii. Ed. P. V. Bykov. 1913. (The only edition of Tyutchev's works which includes the political articles.) *Polnoe sobranie stikhotvorenii.* Ed. G. I. Chulkov. 2 vols. 1933. *Polnoe sobranie stikhotvorenii.* Ed. K. V. Pigarev. 1957. *Lirika.* Ed. K. V. Pigarev. 2 vols. 1966.

Translations: Eugene Kayden, *Poems of Night and Day.* 1944. Vladimir Nabokov, *Three Russian Poets.* 1944. Charles Tomlinson, *Versions from Fyodor Tyutchev.* 1960. Jesse Zeldin, trans. and introd., *Poems and Political Letters of F. I. Tyutchev.* 1974. *See also: Lewanski,* pp. 388–90.

Secondary literature: I. S. Aksakov, *Biografiya Fedora Ivanovicha Tyutcheva.* 1886. Borys Bilokur, *A Concordance to the Russian Poems of Fedor I. Tiutchev.* 1975. R. A. Gregg, *Fedor Tiutchev: The Evolution of a Poet.* 1965. I. A. Koroleva and A. A. Nikolaev, *F. I. Tyutchev: Bibliograficheskii ukazatel' proizvedenii i literatury o zhizni i deyatel'nosti, 1818–1973.* 1978. K. V. Pigarev, *Zhizn' i tvorchestvo F. I. Tyutcheva.* 1962. ——, *F. I. Tyutchev i ego vremya.* 1978. D. Strémooukhoff, *La Poésie et l'idéologie de Tiouttchev.* Paris, 1937.

R. G.

Ukrainian elements in Russian literature. Despite the long and close cultural and political proximity of the two nations, and despite the large number of studies dealing with selected aspects, moments, or periods in the history of Russian-Ukrainian literary relations, there is no comprehensive and synthesizing treatment of this problem. Indeed, the matter is seldom formulated as a historical scholarly problem: in the Soviet Union this relationship continues to be viewed through the dogmatic and teleological thesis of the Ukrainians' historical drive to "unify" with the Russians and with an implicit (and explicit) younger brother/older brother definition of the respective sides; in the West, it is a problem that is largely ignored.

The question of Ukrainian elements in Russian literature can be approached from several, frequently interconnected perspectives: the actual intellectual or formal influences or borrowings from the Ukrainian side; the broad range of Ukrainian themes, ranging from simple local color to more profound considerations of Ukrainian culture and history; the Ukrainian ethnic origins of various Russian writers and the effect this has on their creativity; the territorial connection, i.e., of Russian literature written in the Ukraine. The focus here is primarily on the first two categories, although the latter two are not insignificant. In general, this is a question fraught with complexity and ambiguity (the latter resulting not so much from tendentious interpretations as from fallacious historiography). Thus it must be noted that (1) as formulated here, this is only one half of a dynamic relationship (Russian elements in Ukrainian literature being its other half); (2) the nature of the relationship in a given period (e.g., ROMANTICISM) determines the range of elements that come into play (the relationship itself—from the 17th to the 18th, from the 18th to the 19th century, for example—is continually changing); and (3) what is most complicating is the fact that the very content of the customary terms, i.e., "Ukrainian" and above all "Russian," is shifting or in a state of becoming, and we are thus obliged to reconsider established historiographic formulas.

One such generally accepted formula, which we need not reconsider here, is that the literature of Kievan *Rus'* (it is essential to use this term rather than the—for this period—misleading "Russia"), i.e., of the 11th to the 13th century, is the common patrimony of the Eastern Slavs (later differentiated into the Russians, Ukrainians, and Byelorussians). Although there are various moments here that directly tie this literary creativity to the sphere of Ukrainian (south and west *Rus'*ian) history and culture—above all the territorial provenance, various linguistic features, the political-cultural specificity of various works (e.g., of the Galician-Volhynian Chronicle), and so on—they are not of the same order of phenomena as those subsumed by our topic.

The first period in which we can speak, with the usual meaning of the terms and indeed with much emphasis, of Ukrainian elements in Russian literature, is that of the late 16th to the early 18th century, corresponding to the periods of qualified Renaissance (i.e., sans humanism) and developed baroque in Ukrainian literature. Here, the relationship is mostly one of ever growing Ukrainian influences on Russian-Muscovite literature. To a large extent, Ukrainian literature and culture is here a conduit and mediator for Polish, and generally Western, influences and models. The first contacts and influences were in scholarship and book publishing. The 1581 Church Slavonic Bible printed at Ostroh (by the Russian Ivan Fyodorov) was soon known in Muscovy. The western Ukrainian (L'viv) lexicographer, Pamva Berynda, visited Moscow in 1624 and 1625; his Church Slavonic-Ukrainian dictionary, *Leksikon Slaveno-rosskii* (Kiev, 1627) became a model for later Russian dictionaries. In 1626 and 1627 Lavrentij Zyzanij, another Galician and also a lexicographer and a grammarian came to Moscow to print his catechism (*Katexizys*, 1627), but failed since it was deemed heretical; that same year, Kyrylo Trankvilion Stavrovec'kyj's collection of sermons, *Didactic Evangel* (Uchitel'noe Evangelie, 1619) was in fact burned. Still, in 1648 the famous Church Slavonic grammar of Meletij Smotryc'kyj (Russ. SMOTRITSKY) was reprinted in Moscow for the first of several times, and before that, in 1644, various Ukrainian works were translated in the *Book of Cyril* (Kirillova Kniga). In 1652 there appeared the translation of *Lithos*, a religious-polemical treatise written in 1644 under the aegis of Petro Mohyla. In 1649 the Ukrainian monks Arsenij Satanovs'kyj and Epifanij Slavynec'kyj are called from Kiev to Moscow by Tsar Alexis and begin their work in translations and lexicography; Slavynec'kyj, who had earlier been a professor at the KIEV ACADEMY and who founded in 1653 the first Greco-Latin school in Moscow, left after his twenty-six-year activity in Moscow a huge corpus of over 150 original and translated works. Visiting Moscow in the 60s and 70s were such major Ukrainian churchmen and writers as Innokentij Gizel', Lazar Baranovyč, and Ioanikij Galjatovs'kyj, the latter being the first of many Ukrainian preachers to gain popularity in Muscovy.

At the end of the 17th and the beginning of the 18th century, in the reign of Peter I, the Ukrainian influence, especially in Church matters and in education, was all-pervasive. (Cf. Kharlampovich's study *Ukrainian Influences on Russian Church Life—Malorossiiskoe vliyanie na velikorusskuyu tserkovnuyu zhizn'.*) This is apparent in terms of both quantity and quality: not only were the eminent churchmen and writers—Stefan YAVORSKY, Dimitry ROSTOVSKY and Feofan PROKOPOVICH—Ukrainians and graduates of the Kiev Academy, but also the broad ranks of the Church and educational establishments (e.g., sixteen of nineteen rectors of Moscow's Slavic-Greco-Latin Academy in the period 1700–64). The Ukrainian influence in literature as such was more circumscribed, but highly significant nonetheless. Already at the beginning of the 17th century Ukrainian anonymous *virši* (verses) were becoming popular. As argued by Čyževs'kyj (CHIZHEVSKY), their threefold effect is to establish the dominance of SYLLABIC VERSE, to introduce the genre of "spiritual verses" (dukhovnye stikhi), and to stimulate a baroque school poetry of an erotic and formalist cast. Syllabic poetry is particularly associated with the name of SIMEON POLOTSKY, a Byelorussian and graduate of the Kiev Academy. Subsequent innovations in syllabic verse are the work of the most accomplished graduate of this Academy—Prokopovich. In general, the genres in which Ukrainian influences in this period are most strongly felt all have an academic base: school drama, the favorite vehicle of Jesuit pedagogy and propaganda (the Jesuit curriculum was *the* model for the Kiev Academy), the religious sermon with its rules of rhetoric (cf. Rostovsky, Yavorsky, Prokopovich), and above all, the various treatises on poetics. Similarly, Kievan scholarship (despite, or perhaps because of its scholastic and pre-secular tenor) was highly popular in Russian—cf. Gizel's *Synopsis* (1694) or Rostovsky's MINEI CHET'I.

The first decades of the 18th century mark a profound though at first gradual shift as the Ukraine was transformed from a source of learning and enlightenment, a "window to the West," to an ever more somnolent province. The causes are various: the political decision to limit Ukrainian "separatism" and hence also cultural development (as exemplified by Peter's 1721 decree prohibiting the Kiev Academy to print new Ukrainian books); the brain drain to the center of Imperial power and opportunity (prominent Ukrainians continue to make civil and church careers in Russia); and not least the wages of the conservative, clerical and legitimist orientations of the Ukrainian intellectual elite. By mid-18th century there are few if any Ukrainian elements—even themes, let alone influences—in the Imperial Russian literary culture, a culture consciously modelled on the secular, rationalist West and on classicist poetics. When Ukrain-

ian themes do appear, as in the case of Vasily KAPNIST, above all in his "Ode on Slavery" (1783, published 1806), a passionate denunciation of the introduction of serfdom in the Ukraine, or in his occasional poems on the countryside or the historical past, they are occasioned by the writer's ethnic ties (which for Kapnist also take on the form of a fervent Ukrainian patriotism).

The 19th century presents a radically different picture, beginning with late classicism's discovery of an exotic Ukraine, with colorful customs and people. This discovery is introduced by a series of travelogues, starting with V. Izmailov's *Journey to Southern Russia* (Puteshestvie v poludennuyu Rossiyu, 1800–02), I. SHALIKOV's *Journey to the Ukraine* (Puteshestvie v Molorossiyu, 1803), and P. SUMAROKOV's *Leisure Hours of a Crimean Judge, or a Second Journey to Tauris* (Dosugi krymskogo sud'i—ili vtoroe puteshestvie v Tavridu, 1803). Such travel descriptions of the Ukraine and its countryside, its customs and its people continue well into the mid-19th century. In his bibliographically thorough study "The Ukraine in Russian Literature" (Ukrajina v rosijs'komu pysmenstvi, 1801–50), V. Sypovs'kyj lists twenty-three separate works, noting that, as one could expect, up to the 1820s these travelogues were written in the sentimental mode, often with echoes of Laurence Sterne; from the 1830s a realist poetics begins to predominate. The more important of these authors are V. Passek and I. Kulzhinsky (one of GOGOL's teachers).

These descriptions are, of course, only the tip of the iceberg. As shown in Sypovs'kyj's voluminous study, in the first half of the 19th century the actual number of individual works turning to a Ukrainian subject matter, works ranging from novels in several volumes to short sketches or poems, is just under 500. The categories into which he subdivides this vast material are: (1) narrative works dealing with the old Kievan Ukraine-*Rus'*, (2) narratives dealing with the 17th-century Ukraine, (3) the fantastic story, and (4) narratives dealing with Ukrainian life (BYT) of the 18th and 19th centuries. And here, even if we bracket out the first category (for although Kievan *Rus'* is as much a Ukrainian as a Russian theme, there is little doubt that for ZHUKOVSKY, or ZAGOSKIN or Zagorsky—just as at the end of the 18th century for CHULKOV, KHERASKOV or KARAMZIN—the turning to the subject of Vladimir, or Olga, or Ilya Muromets was a turning to the Russian past), and even if we realize that a great number of works listed here, by such Ukrainian writers as KULISH, KOSTOMAROV, KVITKA and others, despite being written in Russian, actually belong to Ukrainian literature, the dimension of this interest in things Ukrainian still remains impressively large; it is, in short, not merely a thematic interest but a programmatic and a theoretical one as well. At its core are the newly discovered romantic values: the authenticity and naturalness of the folk and its lore and local color, the power of oral poetry and of a "primitive" imagination, the purity of unspoiled nature, and, above all, a fascination with history.

Although an interest in the Ukrainian, specifically Cossack past is evident already in earlier, i.e., late classicist writings, e.g., in V. NAREZHNY's *Bursak and Zaporozhets*, the rationalist weltanschauung and sentimental convention submerge the actual historical reality—and indeed any empathy for or genuine curiosity about the past. Similarly, when the figure of the Cossack appears in A. SHAKHOVSKOI's *The Cossack Poet* (Kozak-Stikhotvorets, 1812) he comes from the world of vaudeville, not the past. A dramatic reversal of this occurs in the phase of pre-romanticism, which is largely coterminous with the writings of the DECEMBRISTS. Their historical interest, in turn, is quite frequently, and in the case of the prime representative here—RYLEEV—virtually exclusively focused on the Ukrainian past. In the course of the entire 19th century it is the Decembrists who provide the most intense and conscious utilization of Ukrainian elements. Their treatment of the subject is guided by an overarching sense of literature as civic statement and duty (cf. Ryleev's oft-cited dictum from the dedication to *Voinarovskii* (1825), "I am not a poet, I am a citizen"). In the several Decembrist works on the Ukrainian historical theme, N. GNEDICH's planned history of the Ukraine, F. N. GLINKA's *Zinobii Bogdan Khmel'nitskii ili osvobozhdennaya Malorossiya* (1819) and, of course, Ryleev's poem *Voinarovskii*, as well as his "Nalivaiko" and several other fragments, the Cossacks and the Ukrainian past in general are seen as the quintessential expression of the struggle for freedom. (Ryleev's willingness to so cast in *Voinarovskii* the officially anathematized Hetman Mazepa brought on recriminations even from close colleagues, and also PUSHKIN's rebuttal in his *Poltava*.) However, with their recourse to patriotism, didacticism and sentiment, the Decembrists—in the spirit of 18th century rationalism—saw little distinction between the past and present; it was precisely because of this that the past could give such clear lessons for the present.

In the period of romanticism proper the number of works focusing on the Cossack theme is smaller than in the preceding Decembrist phase, and some of them, e.g., Maksymovyč's *Bogdan Khmel'nitskii* (1833) echo a Decembrist poetics. Moreover, many such works written after the 1820s are by Ukrainians (Maksymovyč, Kvitka, Hrebinka [GREBENKA], and especially Kulish), and indeed (and not only because of the ethnic origins of their authors) part of Ukrainian literature. Both in the important works, Pushkin's *Poltava* (1828), Gogol's *Taras Bul'ba*, as well as "Vii" and "Strashnaya mest'," and in the weaker ones, e.g., BULGARIN's *Mazepa* (1833–34), the historical theme resonates with the symbolism of collective experience, the sense of a mysterious fate, even a "curse" hanging over a now-peaceful, but once so turbulent land. In Russian, as in Polish and in Ukrainian romanticism, we can speak of a myth of the Ukrainian past, of deeply symbolically coded statements of the "death" of the old Ukraine in the archetypal pattern of a rite of passage.

The other major vehicle in which the romantic interest in things Ukrainian is expressed is folklore and the fantastic. The preeminent figure here, of course, is Nikolai Gogol. His Ukrainian stories, *Vechera na khutore bliz Dikan'ki* (1831) and *Mirgorod* (1835) with their rich depiction of folk beliefs and customs, demonology and *byt*, had tremendous resonance and popularity in both Russian and Ukrainian society. As Kulish, his first biographer and fellow Ukrainian, observed, Gogol, more than any writer, made the Ukraine an object of great interest and appeal. But while such feelings could be (and were) rather short-lived for the cosmopolitan reader in Moscow and St. Petersburg, they had a profound effect on the Ukrainians, being for many the catalyst to their rediscovery of Ukrainian patriotism. Gogol's long-term effect on Russian literary culture, and specifically the literary language, was also profound: as was first observed by Kulish, Gogol's massive use of Ukrainianisms narrowed the distance between the two literary languages and also the two peoples; for EIKHENBAUM Gogol's effect was to redefine diction, in effect, "to lower Russian literary style without at the same time making it coarse."

In the broad gamut of works—prose and poetry, sketches, collections and studies—animated by or dealing with Ukrainian folklore and ethnography, the vast majority of the authors are Ukrainians: except for V. DAL and then the Ukrainians Gogol and O. SOMOV (Porfirii Baiskii) who are now traditionally studied in the framework of Russian literature, the rest are the very mainstream of Ukrainian literature, i.e., Kulish, Kvitka, Borovykovs'kyj, Bodjans'kyj, Hrebinka, Čužbyns'kij and others. In the range of works dealing with Ukrainian life and manners in the present, there are a few more Russian writers, i.e., again, Dal, POGODIN, Kulzhinsky, and Bulgarin, but the majority are Ukrainians (some, again, traditionally taken as Russian writers—Narezhny, Somov, Gogol).

This then puts directly the crucial issue noted at the outset: the demarcation between Ukrainian and Russian literature can hardly be drawn simply with the linguistic criterion. In fact, up to the 1860s all the Ukrainian writers, including the three founders of the national renascence—SHEVCHENKO, Kostomarov and Kulish—also wrote in Russian, often more than in Ukrainian. These works (e.g., Shevchenko's novellas and *Diary*) are traditionally taken as part of Ukrainian literature. Russian was an imperial lingua franca, and, at the outset, as argued by Kostomarov and Kulish, the common literary language of the two constituent *Rus'* nationalities, the Great Russians and the Ukrainians. Recourse to it—as in the first programmatic statement of Ukrainian national consciousness, i.e., the *Istoriya Rusov* (ca. 1812)—was in no sense a hedging on one's national consciousness. In short, the romantic (originally Herderian) identification of a people (Volk) with a language, and the belief that language is the sole and sufficient determinant of a literary tradition is certainly fallacious (cf. the various different national literatures in English or Spanish, or the problem of continuity as a given literature shifts from Latin to the vernacular, etc.). In the 18th century

and in the first half of the 19th century Ukrainian literature was bilingual, reflecting a bilingual society. Thus, too, much (though certainly not all) of what is subsumed by the designation of "Ukrainian element in Russian literature" is also part of Ukrainian literature. This applies, of course, to Gogol, particularly his early, Ukrainian stories; it does so not by virtue of his ethnic origins, or his thematics, but because his poetics and literary culture (the gamut of devices, subtexts, associations, humor, etc. etc.) coincide with that of Ukrainian literature—and indeed were so seen throughout the 19th century. At the same time, he is, of course, part of the all-Russian literary process and culture. This, in fact, is where the consideration of Ukrainian bilingualism has profound importance for the history of Russian literature, illustrating, as it does, how an imperial, *all-Russian* literature, in which Ukrainian literature was at first a provincial and "informal" subset, shifts and by the end of the 19th century is crystallized as a national, *Russian* literature.

In the second half of the 19th century there is no overarching or systematic, let alone theoretical, concern with things Ukrainian. For one, the poetics of realism dictates a focus on the immediate, not the exotic or distant; in large part, this is a consequence of a natural division of interests, with Ukrainian subjects becoming the domain of Ukrainian literature. There are individual writers who use Ukrainian themes or settings. Thus LESKOV's stories "The Unbaptized Priest" (Nekreshchenyi pop), "Ancient Psychopaths" (Starinnye psikhopaty), and "Cave Monastery Antiques" (Pecherskie antiki) and his novel *The Hare Park* (Zayachii remiz) draw on Ukrainian subject matter; beyond that Leskov wrote with empathy on Ukrainian culture, on Kiev, on Taras Shevchenko. Lev TOLSTOI also occasionally depicted Ukrainian characters, e.g., in "A Wood-cutting Expedition" (Rubka lesa) or "Sevastopol in August of 1855," or Ukrainian settings ("Two Old Men"—Dva starika); he wrote the conclusion to the legend "Forty Years" (Sorok let) which was first published by Kostomarov, and was particularly interested in the 18th-century Ukrainian philosopher SKOVORODA. At the turn of the century such writers as KUPRIN and ARTSYBASHEV and CHEKHOV depict a Ukrainian locale. V. KOROLENKO (himself a Ukrainian) often turned to the subject of Ukrainian *byt* and nature, e.g., in such stories as "Forest Murmurs" (Les shumit), "In Bad Company" (V durnom obshchestve), "The Story of My Contemporary" (Istoriya moego sovremennika), etc. While sympathetic to Ukrainians (cf. his defense of Ukrainian peasants in "The Tragedy of Sorochintsy"—Sorochinskaya tragediya) he was unmoved by the Ukrainian national-political cause. The life of I. BUNIN was closely tied to the Ukraine and sympathetic depictions of the land and people appear in such works as "Lika," "Rodion the Lyreman" (Lirnik Rodion) and *Arseniev's Life* (Zhizn' Arsen'eva). In Soviet criticism particular emphasis is placed on Maksim GORKY as a friend and supporter of Ukrainian literature. He indeed was close to the Ukrainian writer M. Kocjubyns'kyj and helped publish Ukrainian writers; Ukrainian characters and settings appear in his novel *Mother* (Mat'), in the stories "Removal" (Vyvod), "The Fair in Goltva" (Yarmarka v Goltve), and others. His attitude to Ukrainian political aspirations and later in the early Soviet period toward a truly autonomous Ukrainian literature was guarded and even hostile (as reflected, e.g., in his opinion, in 1926, that Ukrainian was a "dialect" and later the correction to this—that a single language in the Soviet Union was inevitable).

The Soviet period introduced further changes: while Russian writers continued to turn to Ukrainian themes, the onset of an official and obligatory SOCIALIST REALISM closely circumscribed their range and directed their tone. The most lively interest was focused on the Revolution and civil war in the Ukraine; a prominent subset here is formed by writers from Odessa: above all, E. BAGRITSKY with his *Lay of Opanas* (Duma pro Opanasa), I. BABEL, with the Ukrainian background of *Red Cavalry* (Konarmiya) and *Benya Krik*, and L. Slavin (*Intervention*—Interventsiya). M. BULGAKOV's *White Guard* (Belaya gvardiya, later as a play, *The Days of the Turbins*—Dni Turbinykh) is particularly negative in its depiction of the Ukrainian national forces in the civil war (a direct reply to this was the play *Sonata pathétique*—Patetyčna sonata—by the Ukrainian playwright M. Kuliš, which enjoyed a very popular but short run in Moscow). The civil war in the Ukraine is also treated in N. OSTROVSKY's novel *How the Steel Was Tempered*, A. SERAFIMOVICH's novel *The Iron Flood* (Zheleznyi potok, in which much of the dialogue is in Ukrainian), and the Revolution of 1905 in V. KATAEV's *The White Sail Gleams* (Beleet parus odinokii). Ukrainian motifs are found in the poetry of V. MAYAKOVSKY (e.g., "Kiev," "Debt to the Ukraine"—Dolg Ukraine, "Cast Iron Pants"—Chugunnye shtany), Demyan BEDNY (e.g., "The Rapids"—Porogi), S. GORODETSKY, N. ASEEV, V. INBER, N. TIKHONOV, N. Ushakov, and various others. But already in the afterglow of the Revolution, i.e., the 1920s, and certainly by the 1930s the Ukrainian theme has been narrowed to the expression of officially sanctioned sentiments. And here, just as in the case of the quintessential socialist realist hack F. GLADKOV who devoted a novel, *Energy* (Energiya, 1933–38), to the construction of the Dnieper Electric station, while also claiming, in 1934, that the Ukrainian language is being artificially revived—to the detriment of socialist construction, the distance between the platitude and true emotional and intellectual content is readily apparent. The paeans to Shevchenko, to Russian-Ukrainian brotherhood, to the beauty of the Ukrainian countryside, and so on, allow for easy anthologizing and quick oblivion. The rare exception to the mass of stereotypes and cliches, for example, I. Stadnyuk's novel *People Aren't Angels* (Lyudi ne angely, 1963–65), which deals with the horrors of collectivization and the artificial famine of 1933 is—despite its obligatory upbeat ending—all the more powerful in contrast.

A final rubric in the general problem are the writers, some Russians some Ukrainians, now writing and publishing in Russian in the Soviet Ukraine; for the most part they merit attention only collectively, as a sociological phenomenon, and not on their literary merit. Occasionally, as in the case of the young poet V. Kysel'ov, who began writing poetry in Russian and then turned to Ukrainian, they do signal an important literary phenomenon.   G. G.

Union of Writers of the USSR (Soyúz pisátelei SSSR), the only officially approved organization of professional writers and literary critics in the Soviet Union, was created by the 23 April 1932 resolution of the Central Committee of the Communist Party. The resolution liquidated all proletarian and, implicitly, all nonproletarian literary organizations and ordered the establishment of a single Union of Soviet Writers, to strengthen political control over literature. Union members were expected to uphold Soviet policy and accept SOCIALIST REALISM as their basic artistic method.

The Union has its branches in Soviet republics, provinces, Moscow, and Leningrad. Its membership grew from 1,500 in August 1934 to 8,773 in June 1981; it controls the Gorky Literary Institute and all major literary periodicals. No writer can hope for a systematic publication of his works without belonging to the Union. Expulsion from the Union removes or severely limits the possibility of being published, as was the case with Anna AKHMATOVA, Boris PÁSTERNAK, and Aleksandr SOLZHENITSYN.

Nominally, the Union's highest authority is vested in the All-USSR Writers' Congresses; actually, the Union is governed by the First Secretary of its Board and by the Board's Secretariat. Under Stalin there was only one Congress. Since 1971 Writers' Congresses have met every five years following Party Congresses. Their duration dwindled from sixteen days in 1934 to four to six days in 1959 to 1981 due to the growing bureaucratization of the Union; the proportion of delegates over forty years of age reached ninety-seven percent in 1981 (569 out of 588), reflecting the power of older, conservative writers.

Bibliography: Pervyi Vsesoyuznyi s"ezd sovetskikh pisatelei, 1934: Stenograficheskii otchet. 1934. "Schriftstellerkongresse," "Schriftstellerverband der UdSSR." In W. Kasack, *Lexikon der russischen Literatur ab 1917* (1976), pp. 335–40. R. Hingley, *Russian Writers and Soviet Society, 1917–1978.* 1979. *Vmeste s partiei, vmeste s narodom: Letopis' literaturno-tvorcheskoi deyatel'nosti Soyuza pisatelei SSSR mezhdu VI i VII s"ezdami.* 1981.   H. E.

Uspénsky, Gleb Ivánovich (1843–1902), writer and journalist. Uspensky's work is a bridge between the literature of the 1860s and the POPULIST writing of the 1880s. Born in Tula and educated in the provinces, he entered St. Petersburg University in 1861, just before it closed temporarily after radical student disturbances. He then transferred to Moscow University but could not continue because of his poverty, especially when his father's death in 1864 left him with the burden of supporting his family.

Uspensky published his first sketches—the favorite genre of the radical intelligentsia of that day—very early, in 1862, but began to make a reputation in 1866, with the appearance of *Manners of Rasteryaev Street* (Nravy Rasteryaevoi ulitsy), a cycle of sketches picturing the bleak hopelessness of ordinary Russian life, in the best nihilist tradition. The very title of his next important cycle, *Ruin* (Razorenie, 1869), points to the same approach to reality.

In the 1870s, with his financial situation strengthened, Uspensky travelled extensively and published his observations on life abroad. In the 1880s Uspensky worked closely with the journal OTECHEST-VENNYE ZAPISKI, where he brought out the sketches and stories dealing with peasant life incorporated into such cycles as *Peasantry and Peasant Labor* (Krest'yanin i krest'yanskii trud) and *Power of the Earth* (Vlast' zemli), in which he idealized the peasantry from a radical perspective, in a major contribution to the populist movement in Russia and elsewhere.

During the 1890s, Uspensky's life was darkened by mental illness, which did not leave him until his death in 1902 in St. Petersburg.

Works: Sobranie sochinenii. 9 vols. 1955–57.
Translations: Lewanski, p. 391.
Secondary literature: Nikita Prutskov, *Gleb Uspensky.* (Twayne's World Authors Series, 190.) 1972.   C. A. M.

Uspénsky, Nikolaí Vasílievich (1837–89), writer, cousin of prominent realist author, Gleb Ivanovich USPENSKY. The son of a village priest from the Tula district, Uspensky studied in the local seminary. In 1856 he enrolled in the St. Petersburg Medical-Surgical Academy, then transferred to the Historical Philology Department of the university, which he left to pursue a career as a writer.

Uspensky's first two sketches, titled *From The Life of the Common People* (Iz prostonarodnogo byta) were published in *Syn otechestva* in 1857; a third, *A Good Existence* (Khoroshee zhit'e) was printed by SOVREMENNIK. With this work Uspensky quickly gained the attention of liberal circles. N. G. CHERNYSHEVSKY was attracted by Uspensky's unflattering portrayal of peasants as brutish, greedy, ignorant, and inebriated, a characterization unfamiliar to the nobility. He regarded Uspensky's approach as showing greater understanding and compassion for the peasant than the typical romanticized and perhaps condescending view, and responded to the sketches with his famous article, "Isn't this the beginning of a change?" (Ne nachalo li peremeny?, 1861). Chernyshevsky was won over by what he saw as "the unadorned truth" about peasant life and the authoritarian peasant commune. Most often providing these insights through character dialogue, Uspensky, unlike F. M. RESHETNIKOV, gave little attention to environmental causes and details. Tinged with humor, his stories depict the misery of poverty-stricken peasants (*The Old Woman*—Starukha, and "Supper"—Uzhin), or their lack of rights and defenselessness as in *The Piglet* (Porosenok). Uspensky emphatically transmits the moral and spiritual results of these circumstances, including remarkable underdevelopment (*The Snake*—Zmei), general drunkenness (*A Good Existence*), thoughtless cruelty (*Thus It was Ordained*—Tak na rodu napisano) and, chiefly, the striking certainty that nothing can change, as in *The Old Woman, A String of Carts* (Oboz), and *The Sorceress* (Koldun'ya).

In his reform era sketches, Uspensky also described the difficult lot of the intelligentsia from various social levels, the life and mores of the clergy, and the speculative dealings of publishers. A regular contributor to *Sovremennik* by 1861, Uspensky undertook a journey through Europe with the publisher's support; however, a rift with Nekrasov and *Sovremennik* and waning public approval of his approach brought Uspensky into a lengthy creative crisis. Though he continued to write and even improve, his audience steadily diminished. In 1862, he accepted a teaching position at the Yasnaya Polyana School, followed by others at district schools and gymnasia. From 1884 onward, Uspensky led a nomadic life as a street buffoon, storyteller, and alcoholic, and finally ended his life in suicide.

Works: Rasskazy. Pts. 1–2. 1861. *Sochineniya.* 4 vols. 1883. *Rasskazy.* 1886. *Sobranie sochinenii.* 1931. *Povesti, rasskazy i ocherki.* 1957.
Translations: "The Village Schoolmaster" and "Porridge" in *The*

Humour of Russia. Ed. and trans. Ethel Lillian Voynich. London, 1895.

Secondary literature: I. V. Dedusenko, *Nikolai Uspenskii.* 1975. F. M. Dostoevskii, "Rasskazy N. V. Uspenskogo" (1861), *PSS*, Vol. 19 (1979), pp. 178–86. K. Chukovskii, "Zhizn' i tvorchestvo Nikolaya Uspenskogo." In his *Lyudi i knigi.* 1960. R. L. Glickman, "An Alternative View of the Peasantry: The *Raznochintsy* Writers of the 1860s," *SlavR* 32 (1973), pp. 693–704. M. V. Nekhai, *Russkii demokraticheskii ocherk 60-kh godov XIX stoletiya: N. Uspenskii, V. Sleptsov i A. Levitov.* 1971.   J. S.

Utkin, Iósif Pávlovich (1903–44), poet, was born in Khingan, Khabarovsk Region. He served in the Red Army (1920–22), began publishing verse in 1922, and graduated from the Moscow Institute of Journalism in 1927. He was killed in an army airplane crash 13 November 1944.

A minor poet, author of lyrical and narrative poems, his first major work was *The Tale about the Redheaded Motele, Mister Inspector, Rabbi Isaiah and Commissar Blokh* (1925) which dealt with the life of provincial Jewry after the Revolution. His *First Book of Poems* (1926) was followed by several others, among them *Publicistic Lyrics* (1931) and the autobiographical poem *Pleasant Childhood* (1933). During the early 1940s he began to write prose and was placed in charge of the poetry section of "Goslitizdat" (the Government Publishing House for Literature).

While his propaganda poems were weak, Utkin wrote some rather melodious lyrical poems, many of which were in accentual meter and have the flavor of folk songs. Natural phenomena, the environment, the Revolution and its aftermath, are presented from the human and personal point of view of an intellectual and a Jew. His lyrics enjoyed great popularity among the Soviet youth of the 1930s.

Works: Stikhotvoreniya i poemy. Introd. Z. Papernyi. 1961. *Stikhotvoreniya i poemy.* (Biblioteka poeta, Bol'shaya seriya.) Introd. A. A. Saakyants. 1966.

Translations: Lewanski, p. 391.

Secondary literature: A. Saakyants, *Iosif Utkin. Ocherk zhizni i tvorchestva.* 1969. I. Sel'vinskii, "Poeziya Iosifa Utkina," *Literaturnaya gazeta,* 2 December 1944. A. Tarasenkov, *Russkie poety XX veka, 1900–1955. Bibliografiya.* 1966.   H. S.

Utopian literature (Sumarokov through Odoevsky, c. 1750–c. 1850). With the opening of journals that were independent of the government in the late 1750s and the appearance of the first Russian novels in the 1760s, there began a strong interest in utopian literature in Russia. To some extent, this utopian literature reflected the marked tendency towards utopianism that had existed in Russian culture since Kievan times, and to some extent it represented a transfer to prose of some of the basic patterns and themes of contemporary Russian poetry, which often depicted an ideal time or place. Among the first works of utopian literature in Russia was A. P. SUMA-ROKOV's short *The Happy Society: A Dream,* (Son: Schastlivoe obshchestvo, 1759) that appeared in his TRUDOLYUBIVAYA PCHELA. The dream depicted a society run by the golden rule where laws are few and simple, justice is fair and fast, positions are obtained by merit, and there are no bribes, hereditary ranks, or favoritism. In his original version of *Chorus to the Debauched World* (Khor k prevratnomu svetu, 1763), Sumarokov expressed similar ideas in poetic form but censors forced him to dilute most of the satire and in its place he depicted a dog that simply barked the word "lout" (kham) as a would-be nonsense word for five lines because he does not "dare to sing satire."

When the first Russian novels appeared in the 1760s a number had utopian scenes. Most of these utopias were conservative or reactionary, and when they advocated change often looked backwards to old Slavic traditions like the peasant commune (the *mir* or *obshchina*) or the "patriarchal system" (rule based on tradition by a person venerated as a father who exercises absolute authority over his citizens) and criticized the Western-oriented policies begun by Peter the Great. Although there certainly were "radicals" among 18th-century Russian writers (e.g., A. N. RADISHCHEV), their ideas were seldom expressed in utopian form, and even the two "projects

for the future" in Radishchev's *Journey from Petersburg to Moscow* (in the "Khotilov" and "Vydropusk" chapters) did not use utopian conventions but presented arguments and blueprints for the gradual elimination of serfdom, the table of ranks, and court luxuries. Only in the 19th century, were liberal and radical ideas expressed in utopian form, as in the Decembrist Aleksandr Ulybyshev's *A Dream* (Son, c. 1819), which depicted a Russia of the future with no priests, monks, standing army, or despotism, but a thriving economy and a good system of justice and welfare.

Several 18th-century Russian utopias praised, rather than criticized, the status quo and depicted ideal societies that bore very close relationships to the institutions and policies of Catherine the Great's Russia, using imagery recalling that of contemporary panegyric odes to Catherine. For example, F. A. EMIN's *Fickle Fate* (Nepostoyannaya fortuna, 1763) describes a utopian "Kingdom of Pleasures and True Faith" where the Golden Age has been restored—a kingdom whose history and religion (Orthodoxy = "true faith") bear many similarities to those of Russia. Several similar "panegyric utopias," where Russia is praised through a utopian surrogate, occur in scenes in M. M. KHERASKOV's three novels—*Numa, or Flourishing Rome* (Numa, ili protsvetayushchii Rim, 1768), *Cadmus and Harmonia* (Kadm i Garmoniya, 1789) and *Polydorus, the Son of Cadmus and Harmonia* (Polidor, Syn Kadma i Garmonii, 1794). The best of these three, *Cadmus and Harmonia,* is a Masonic utopia which depicts the search of its hero, Cadmus (whose story is very loosely based on that told in Ovid's *Metamorphoses*), for his sister Europa (Russian: *Evropa,* which means also "Europe")—a search that is finally ended when he reaches the "promised land" of a people called the "Slavs" which is so pleasant and perfect that he abandons his search for Evropa (Europa/Europe). In short, several of these 18th-century Russian utopias encouraged the Russian reader to search for utopia at home.

Several 18th-century Russian utopias take place on the moon, including V. A. Levshin's *The Latest Journey* (Noveishee puteshestvie, 1784) and M. D. CHULKOV's *The Dream of Kidal* (Son Kidalov, 1789). Using plot, character, and setting culled from works ranging from Lucian's *Icaromennipus* and *True History* to the *Arabian Nights,* both works satirize the Russian interest in western science, which they condemn as antithetical to Russian faith, and both implicitly advocate a return to the principles of the old patriarchal system of the Slavs and the community of property represented by the Slavic peasant communes. A similar pacan to the prototype of the Slavic "patriarchal system" is contained in a description of the Kingdom of Prosperity to which the shipwrecked sailors are brought in P. Yu. Lvov's *The Russian Pamela* (Rossiiskaya Pamela, 1789)—a utopian land located on a distant island.

The strongest satire in 18th-century Russian utopian literature was written by Prince M. M. SHCHERBATOV in his *Journey to the Land of Ophir* (Puteshestvie v zemlyu Ofirskuyu, 1783–84) which was not published until 1891 because of its severe criticism of Peter the Great and his Westernization of Russia. Much of the utopia describes the city of Peregab (Petersburg) built by King Perega (Peter) "against the nature of things" which almost destroyed "the ancient example of virtue demonstrated by the greatest men in our history." Much of Shcherbatov's utopia describes the positive results of the purposeful destruction of this dystopian city and the resulting return to native principles and traditions.

Because of the animus towards Western-oriented science, there was little or no science fiction in 18th-century Russia—even in the utopias which took place on the moon. The first work of science fiction in Russia was probably Faddei BULGARIN's *Probable Fantasies, or Wanderings around the World in the Twenty-Ninth Century,* (Pravdopodobnye nebylitsy, ili stranstvovaniya po svetu v 29-om veke, 1824). The narrator, shipwrecked in the 19th century is revived after a 1000-year sleep in the city of Nadezhin ("Hope"), where people travel in prototypes of airplanes, automobiles, and submarines, and communicate over long distances through "hearing pipes" (telephones). Bulgarin's allegory *Improbable Fables, or A Journey to the Center of the Earth* (Neveroyatnye nebylitsy, ili Puteshestvie k sredotochiyu zemli) describes three cities in an underground world into which the narrator (like Holberg's Nils Klim) has fallen: Ignorantsia, Skotinia (Beastland), and Svetonia (Lightland)—which represent, the author informs us, ignorance, half-knowledge, and enlightenment. The capital of Svetonia is Utopia where the people have learned to subject their passions to reason and to love their neighbor and therefore are "as happy as it is possible for creatures endowed with passions and infirmity to be." Everyone works in Utopia, except the judges, who sleep for lack of cases. A third utopia by Bulgarin, *A Scene from Private Life in the Year 2028* (Stsena iz chastnoi zhizni v 2028-om godu, 1828) describes a future Russia where the legal system has become the most perfect in Europe.

The most interesting utopia of the first half of the 19th century is V. F. ODOEVSKY's *The Year 4338* (4338-y god, 1838) which takes place in a Mesmeric trance and describes a universe of the future divided between Russia and China, which each occupy a hemisphere. The work describes life one year before a predicted collision between the earth and Halley's comet that is supposed to destroy the world. Because of their remarkable scientific achievements (airplanes, telegraphs, outdoor central heating, etc.) men are convinced that a solution will be found and that life will go on as usual. But because this belief in science has replaced a belief in God, Odoevsky implies that the world will actually be destroyed. Odoevsky's utopia thus recapitulates the main theme which had dominated the Russian utopia since the last third of the 18th century: a belief that the "correct faith" (Orthodoxy) of Russia rather than correct science of the West will solve the problems of the world. This belief in the potential of Russia also characterizes the utopian dream in the last chapter of Vladimir Sollogub's *The Springless Carriage* (Tarantas, 1845) which is imagined by a young man of SLAVOPHILE views who has just returned from abroad hoping to find in his native land a "new, ideal world." In the dream, the carriage becomes like the flying troika of Russia which passes other nations at the end of Part 1 of GOGOL's *Dead Souls* and brings the ardent Slavophile to a utopian Russia of the future based strongly on native values where all the contemporary problems of rural Russia (drunkenness, filth, laziness, separation between the classes, poverty, ignorance) have been eliminated. Although this utopian dream is abruptly interrupted when the real carriage in which the dreamer is riding falls into a ditch (just at the point that the dreamer declares that "there is happiness on earth") and it has thus been interpreted as a parody on Slavophile utopian dreams (e.g., by V. G. BELINSKY), the context is quite ambiguous and the dream may well continue the basic emphasis of the early Russian utopia on the preservation of native values.

Texts: V. Guminskii, ed., *Vzglyad skvoz' stoletiya: Russkaya fantastika XVIII i pervoi poloviny XIX veka.* 1977. Contains excerpts or full texts of Levshin, Shcherbatov, Ulybyshev, Odoevsky, etc.

Translations: A. D. Ulybyshev, "A Dream." In *The Decembrist Movement.* Ed. Marc Raeff. 1966. Pp. 60–66. Leland Fetzer, ed. and trans., *Pre-Revolutionary Russian Science Fiction: An Anthology.* Ann Arbor, 1982. (Contains translations of Bulgarin, "A Plausible Fantasy" and Odoevsky, "The Year 4338.") "Pavel L'vov's *The Russian Pamela*: A Utopian Excerpt," *RLT*, special issue on the 18th century, forthcoming.

Secondary literature: Stephen Baehr, "The Masonic Component in Eighteenth Century Russian Literature." In *Russian Literature in the Age of Catherine the Great.* Ed. A. G. Cross. 1976. Pp. 121–39. (On Masonic utopias and especially Kheraskov's *Cadmus and Harmonia.*) ———, *The Paradise Myth in Eighteenth-Century Russia.* (Forthcoming.) Marina Rossi Varese, ed., *Utopisti russi del primo ottocento.* Naples, 1982. Pp. 7–41. (With a bibliography.) Nicholas P. Vaslef, "Bulgarin and the Development of the Russian Utopian Genre," *SEEJ* 12 (1968), pp. 35–43. S. B.

Utopian Literature (c. 1850–present). The term "utopian literature" is subject to so many definitions and can incorporate so many separate literary genres that it becomes not very useful, unless one speaks only of literature closely resembling the content and the rhetorical departure of Sir Thomas More's *Utopia*, or at least his understanding of the word itself (which he derived from the Greek *ou* and *topos*, denoting literally "no place"). If understood in More's usage (he sometimes employed the term *Nusquama* derived from the Latin *nusquam* or "nowhere" when he referred to his book), and if, in addition, one keeps in mind that the story of *Utopia* is told

by Raphael Hytloday (his family name derived from the Greek *hutlos* meaning "nonsense" and loosely translated as Raphael the Nonsense-speaker), then at least one half of More's design implies any other but a "real" place, that is a truly fictional place for the setting of his Book Two. Book One, on the other hand, consists of an unveiled satire on 16th-century England and as such constitutes a narrative, with a "real" place as its implied setting. It is important to note that More's respective settings *coexist* in the same time frame; prospective "future," if any, is only implied for England in the sense that it might imitate some of the customs of Utopians, including their communal living, moneyless economy, etc., which, if adopted, could turn England (also an island society) into Utopia almost overnight. More's narrator does not expect this to happen as he ends the book. In other words, utopia represents for More primarily a mental projection of a moral "ideal" attainable at *any* time, should the inhabitants of *any* commonwealth choose to embrace the ways of *Utopia*.

One of the few Russian writers in the 19th century to have kept More's basic elements intact, namely the *satire*, both temporal *and* fantastic setting and the nonsensical narrator (not so much in his name, but in the manner of his narration) was N. V. GOGOL. Of course, at first glance, Gogol's fiction is not anything like More's, and if More intended by his choice of the word *utopia* a possible pun on another Greek compound, *eutopos* (or "good place"), then the crux of Gogol's fiction is rather the portrayal of the obverse, or dystopia (a term introduced in the 1950s). Moreover, as opposed to More, Gogol in his mature fiction (*The Nose, The Overcoat* or *Dead Souls*) often fused the two worlds, the "real" and the "fantastic," in such a manner that the two became indivisible in his readers' mind, with the resultant effect of a colossal farce hardly suggesting the possibility of attainment of any utopia. Yet, neither the content nor the quality of Gogol's fiction is at issue for the purposes of the discussion here; rather it is the interpretation it received from the then-rising "civic school" of literary criticism, headed by V. BELINSKY. Gogol's literary practice was understood by Belinsky as a perfect "cleansing medicine" for Russia to embark on a path toward a society rather resembling the utopia of More (although More was not mentioned in the critical essays of the forties).

It should not come then as a surprise that it was a pupil of Belinsky, N. CHERNYSHEVSKY, who succeeded in molding an extremely important work of utopian character for the second half of the 19th century, the novel *What Can Be Done* (1862). Chernyshevsky's novel, however, represents a new brand of utopian literature and with a definite *future* in mind, a future predicated by the newly discovered presumed "laws" of historical process as posited by Marx (deriving his theory from Hegel's philosophical system). Ironically enough, most 20th-century definitions of *utopia* are far more indebted to Marx than to More and are understood as dealing with the possibilities of a social order set in the future, particularly the order coming about as a result of "predictable" advances in science and technology. Chernyshevsky's novel fulfills this definition. With the major theme centered on the emancipation of women and the *rational* division of labor, it is ultimately the woman protagonist's "dream" that provides a vision of future discoveries in science and technology. Among the images employed is that of the Crystal Palace which the new, classless society inhabits. Chernyshevsky obviously modelled this image on the real Crystal Palace erected of glass and steel as an architectural wonder at Sydenham for the Great London Exposition of 1852 (the year of Gogol's death).

Chernyshevsky's novel is hardly a work with primarily literary concerns, but rather a work of agitational and sociophilosophical character. At best, it is a second-rate work of fiction. Chernyshevsky did not set out to create a work in which sociopolitical concerns replaced literary ones; on the contrary, Chernyshevsky's novel was written to advance a priori political ideas camouflaged within a literary form. In this sense, the fact that one of the most important political pamphlets of V. I. LENIN bears the title of Chernyshevsky's work is not an accident of history, but a historical indication that the study of Chernyshevsky's "novel" belongs more to the area of history of political ideas than to literary inquiry. On the other hand, despite Marx's protestations to the contrary, and his reliance on the so-called scientific method of social history, much of Marxist idealism belongs to the realm of "fictional" future "reality," where the word *fictional* denotes precisely the primitive mechanism of literary fantasy as opposed to scientific method. Since the popular mind is not particularly bothered by the conceptual opposition of "good" science and "good" literature, this bridging of disciplines was highly successful in its time, and the work proved one of the most important political documents of 19th-century Russia.

In any case, achievements in technology seem to have been of far less importance to most major 19th-century Russian writers than achievements of the human spirit. On this point such disparate giants of Russian 19th-century literature as Dostoevsky, Turgenev, Tolstoi, or Chekhov would probably all unreservedly agree since they so often pitted man against technology in their works. Each of them, in turn, commanded respect unparalleled by any materialist philosopher in Russia, and it is probably not at all surprising that strictly "scientific utopian literature" fared quite poorly in their lifetimes. Furthermore, some major exponents of Russian realism were far more prone to exploit the romantic fascination with a metaphysical reality than their Western counterparts. This shifted Russian fiction in the heyday of realism from the realm of the "probable" to one dealing often with events of only "possible" or even improbable nature. Intrusion of the metaphysical world in the form of devils, apparitions or dream creatures into the physical existence of Dostoevsky's characters, for example, constitutes a fact of what he would call the state of human reality. In some of his works, such as in his famous triad from the *Diary of the Writer* in the mid-seventies, *Bobok, The Meek One* (Krotkaya) and *Dream of A Ridiculous Man* (Son Smeshnogo Cheloveka), Dostoevsky posits a prescription for achieving a moral "utopia" directly in contrast to any utopia founded on materialistic concerns such as advocated by Chernyshevsky's work. One of Dostoevsky's rejections of the latter came also in the Inquisitor's "utopia" (Ivan's monologue in the *Brothers Karamazov*). This, in turn, proved significant for the philosophical core (regarding the nature of human freedom) in one of the most famous Russian 20th-century *dystopias*, ZAMYATIN's *We*.

With the advent of the symbolist epoch, literature dealing with apparitions, time-travel, and excursions into altered states of reality became a commonplace in Russian literary culture and often formed a conscious return to some of the preoccupations of Russian and Western romanticism. Nonetheless, the fascination of the fin de siècle period with the romantic past harbored in some cases the seeds for the "romanticization" of the possible future as in S. Belsky's *Under the Comet* (Pod kometoi, 1910), a book which could be said to be a thematic return to V. F. ODOEVSKY's *The Year 4338*. Similarly, A. KUPRIN's *Liquid Sunshine* (1913) is based on the premise of the technological feasibility of capturing the energy of the sun in order to secure the future for the inhabitants of a cooling Earth. The project fails due to an insignificant but fatal mistake of its creator—a perfectly romantic touch of irony at the ending of the story. Kuprin's work is also significant in the sense that it is one of the first Russian literary creations bearing the unmistakable influence of *The Time Machine* by H. G. Wells, whose works were to be imitated in the Soviet Union particularly during the twenties. A curious blend of fantasy, science fiction and fairy tale was provided for Russian readers in the 1910s in F. SOLOGUB's *Created Legend* (Tvorimaya legenda) where the protagonist Trirodov succeeds in raising dead children from the grave to a zombie-like state, reducing his enemies to prisms, and using his gothic-like estate for a transformation into a spaceship capable of defying gravity.

Ultimately, it could be said that the arrival of the 20th century brought about two conceptually opposed forms of relating to the depiction of the future. For some of the adherents of a materialistic doctrine the future offered nearly limitless possibilities as an outcome of advances in science and often implied the conquest of space. The planet Mars seems to have been a particularly fascinating subject at the time. A. BOGDANOV's utopia *Red Star* is perhaps the most accomplished work among them, incorporating the aforementioned view of the future. First published in 1908, it was followed by a less successful sequel, *Inzhener Menni* (Menni, the Engineer), five years later. Bogdanov utilized his novel to foreshadow the future of Earth's history by presenting his readers with an account of the past and future history of Martian society (a non-ambiguous rehashing of Earth's history from the Marxist viewpoint) and using the context of the novel as an illustrative guide to social institutions of

the future. At the same time, the book raised the possibility of a space flight to Mars, interestingly enough, reinforced several years later by K. E. Tsiolkovsky's famous first theoretical designs for rocket propulsion which made interplanetary flight plausible.

On the other hand, it could be safely argued that the most prevalent form of envisioning the future in Russia at this time was one heralding doom. Suggested already in the midst of the second half of the 19th century by a score of important Russian writers and philosophers, the apocalyptic notion of the future was particularly evident in the work of Russia's famous philosopher of the time, Vladimir SOLOVYOV, to whom most Russian symbolist writers were indebted for their teleology. Perhaps the principal work of Solovyov in this regard is the one least quoted by cultural historians of Russia: entitled *Three Conversations*, it appeared at the turn of the century and prophesied, in one of the "conversations," the coming of the Antichrist in the near future. In some of his prophecies Solovyov was amazingly on the mark. Solovyov envisioned a United Nations Organization (the name in Russian for the United Nations is nearly identical to the one used by Solovyov), the creation of the state of Israel (one of the necessary ingredients, in Solovyov's view, for the Antichrist's arrival), and an Ecumenical World Council of Churches (Solovyov in fact envisions the erection of a monumental church in which churches of various rites will pray in different rooms to one Deity). The last days would be characterized by a world conflict on such a grandiose scale and with such advanced weapons as only likely in an all-out nuclear war. It is from Solovyov's cup that many of the famous Russian symbolists such as V. BRYUSOV or A. BELY have drunk in their own assessments of plausible futures.

Bely's famous novel *Petersburg* exploits the ambiguities and uncertainties of Russian life in the first decade of the 20th century. Although the author does not make it clear what *actual* future he foresees as the outcome of the cataclysm about to engulf the Petersburg society of 1905, it is patently clear that the physical acts within his fictional world will have metaphysical consequences along the lines envisioned by Solovyov. Bryusov also views the future with the profoundest misgivings in works such as *The Republic of the Southern Cross* or in *The Last Martyrs*, both published in a volume entitled the *Earth's Axis* (1907). As opposed to Bely's veiled portrayal of the future, Bryusov provides us with an outright anti-utopia in *The Republic of the Southern Cross*, the setting of which is located on the South Pole as the result of scientific advances enabling the population to be protected from the rigors of the Antarctic climate. The society is living in a controlled climate with an arching dome above it—that same "Crystal Palace" which Dostoevsky had rejected some forty years earlier. Just as Dostoevsky's *Notes from Underground*, so does Bryusov's entire work express his belief that material conditions alone are insufficient in providing human happiness. The inhabitants of the republic become possessed by a disease which forces them to exhibit anti-social tendencies and the entire population abandons its controlled scientific environment.

The allusion to the crystal palace forcefully re-emerges after the Bolshevik Revolution in Zamyatin's anti-utopia *We*, perhaps the most famous Russian work on the subject in this century. For Zamyatin, imagination is one of the prime ingredients of the human personality, with or without metaphysical connotations. The protagonist is a representative of another Crystal Palace society which to a large measure has succeeded in reducing its members to the level of robots. They work, sleep, and make love according to a prescribed schedule, punching their time cards; they do not have names, only numbers. They live in transparent quarters. The protagonist, a representative of the society and an engineer on a futuristic space-ship that is meant to conquer other worlds undergoes a personality split under the influence of love. His object of desire is in turn a female representative of a "free" society settled beyond the wall confines of the so-called Integral society within, and is one of the subversive elements intent on destroying the Integral. The plot proves abortive, and at the end of his diary, the protagonist undergoes an operation by the means of which his faculty for imagination is surgically removed. As in More's *Utopia*, the reader is introduced to two coexisting forms of social order, but neither is portrayed as desirable.

Needless to say, Zamyatin's dystopia *We* did not sit well within the framework of the future promised to the masses by the Bolshevik government which took control of Russian society in 1917. While it can be said that literary history rarely coincides in its ups and downs with the official history of any state, in the genre of literary utopia the year 1917 marks a clear diaeresis. Although the new regime itself overwhelmed the populace with the promises of political utopia in the near future, it could not tolerate any expression of a view challenging its own promises. In other words, the political reality of Soviet Russia made it soon impossible for Russian writers to publish works of fiction with a gloomy view of the future because any admonitory utopia would simply undercut the very foundation of Soviet rhetorical persuasion. While it is true that some writers, too much respected to be touched by the regime, such as BULGAKOV, were successful in producing science fiction of dystopic character in the twenties (in Bulgakov's case particularly *The Heart of a Dog* and *Fatal Eggs*), their voices were stifled by the early 1930s. A number of minor science-fiction writers too numerous to list here, appeared on the literary scene in the mid-twenties and science fiction began to be published in such special science-fiction journals as *Bor'ba Mirov*, *Mir priklyuchenii*, *Vokrug sveta*, *Vsemirnyi sledopyt*, and *Znanie—Sila*. It is interesting, however, that the period did not produce a great number of utopias *par excellence*. In fact only a handful, such as Ya. Okuniev's *Future World* or Nikolsky's *In a Thousand Years*, can be mentioned. A great majority of futuristic fiction at the time featured the fantastic adventure story in the form of a scientific or pseudo-scientific romance. This trend was particularly heralded by Aleksei TOLSTOI's *Aelita*, a humorous return to the Martian theme begun in Russia by Bogdanov. Perhaps for its description of love affairs with blue Martian women, the novel was an instant success and served as a model for the adventure-type science fiction prevalent in those years, particularly the so-called Red Detective (*Krasnyi detektiv*) popular in the second half of the twenties. V. SHKLOVSKY's and V. IVANOV's *Iprit*, M. SHAGINYAN's *Mess-Mend or Yankees in Petrograd* may serve as illustrations of the latter. In such fiction, the socialist state is invariably threatened by the futuristic imagination of representatives of capitalist societies. Perhaps ironically, the period also allowed for numerous translations of Western science fiction titles (over a hundred of them as counted by V. Lyapunov, appeared in translation between 1923 and 1930) with Verne and Wells by far the most popular.

While many pro-Soviet writers produced some samples of futuristic fiction at the time (*Ruler of Iron* by V. KATAEV, *Trust D.E.*, by I. ERENBURG; etc.), the second half of the twenties was dominated particularly by Aleksandr Belyaev who introduced as his common literary material the phenomenon of biological change in human beings. In his novels, the protagonists are usually scientists, surgeons capable of adapting men to unusual biological environs such as water (*The Amphibian Man*) or air (*Ariel*); they also succeed in adjusting the human brain to various forms of ESP and in making head transplants.

With the beginning of the thirties and the rise of the "cult of personality," it became increasingly more dangerous to "err" in any predictions of the future, and until the mid-fifties the former élan for science-fiction writing subsided, with periods of total disappearance of science-fiction books from circulation. Yet, there were almost heroic attempts in the thirties by major Russian writers to question Soviet present-day reality and its future. Among these, M. Zoshchenko's *Youth Restored* (*Vozvrashchennaya molodost'*, 1933), is an interesting attempt to combine fantastic fiction with the format of a scientific treatise with "scholarly" footnotes. The work provides a tongue-in-cheek treatment of the "elixir of life" theme revolving around the elderly protagonist's attempt to return his youth. M. Bulgakov's *Master and Margarita*, first published in an excerpted form almost thirty years after its completion (1966–67), is perhaps the most provocative and pioneering work of this period. Certainly destined to become one of the masterpieces of 20th-century Russian fiction, it is related to both More's and Gogol's fiction in being a merciless satire of Soviet reality, as well as in using duplex settings for its plot development. As opposed to former attempts, however, Bulgakov complicates his plot by shifting the plane of narration from present-day Moscow to the time of Christ's crucifixion in Jerusalem and finally to the eternal, metaphysical plane, the reworked "no-place", where his major protagonists finally find peace from their earthly troubles. Bulgakov sees no possible utopia in physical reality, filled with greed and pettiness which he so deftly portrays. In this sense, Bulgakov's novel is also a return to the philosophical precepts of Dostoevsky.

The first post-war Soviet writer of almost legendary fame among younger science fiction buffs was Ivan Efremov. His *Andromeda Nebula* (*Tumannost' Andromedy*, 1956), a large scale utopian novel set in the far future of interstellar travel, not only provided the impetus for the cosmic theme to become the prevalent subject of postwar science fiction, but in itself started the period of the "THAW" for science fiction. At the same time Efremov is one of those writers who express an unwavering view that societies of the distant future cannot have any other than the Communist form of social organization. At times, as in his novelette *The Heart of a Serpent*, Efremov takes up a situation formerly explored by a Western writer and transforms the plot to fit his preconceived idea of a more advisable resolution of the problem stated. Efremov also begins in a serious way to explore another facet of futuristic fiction of the post-Stalin era, namely that of contact with an alien civilization. Invariably, as opposed to frequent fears posited by various Western writers in their stories, such contact will have a happy resolution for Efremov.

The Soviet sixties witnessed a rapid rise both in the quantity and the quality of science-fiction stories produced in the USSR. Among the most able writers one should mention the brothers Arkady and Boris STRUGATSKY, Ilya Varshavsky, Valentina Zhuravlyova, E. Parnov, M. Emtsev, and a host of others. These years also witnessed the appearance of a most impressive, twenty-five-volume anthology of contemporary science fiction (*Biblioteka sovremennoi fantastiki*) which included selections from both Western and Soviet science-fiction writers, a publishing feat perhaps unrivaled in any language in its size and inclusiveness. For some strange reasons the Soviet government decreased the volume of science fiction publications in the late seventies by about ten-fold in comparison with the sixties and early seventies. One of the reasons may perhaps reside in the fact that science fiction became utilized by some Soviet writers for shrewd and often ingenious allusions to the present form of Soviet society and for implicit criticism of Marxist doctrine. Such is the case with many of the writings of the Strugatsky brothers whose contribution to science fiction is by far the most productive when compared with any other Soviet writer as well as the most satisfying from a literary point of view. On the other hand, even those writers who were seemingly innocent vis-à-vis the Soviet regime found in the sphere of science fiction productive avenues for interesting literary experimentation, often far removed from the precepts of socialist realism.

Bibliography: A. F. Britikov, *Russkii sovetskii nauchno-fantasticheskii roman*. 1970. Hans Foldeak, *Neuere Tendenzen der sowjetischen Science Fiction*. (Slavistische Beiträge. 88.) Munich, 1975. John Glad, *Extrapolations from Dystopia*. 1982. Glenn Negley, *Utopian Literature: A Bibliography*. 1977. Robert Scholes and Eric Rabkin, *Science Fiction: History, Science, Visions*. 1977. Darko Suvin, *Russian Science Fiction 1956–1974: A Bibliography*. 1976. ——, *Metamorphoses of Science Fiction: On the Poetics and History of a Literary Genre*. 1979. A. Lev.

Vaginov (pseud., real name: Vagingeim), Konstantin Konstantinovich (1899–1934), poet and prose writer. Vaginov started out as a member of the POETS' GUILD and published two collections of verse in the ACMEIST style: *Journey into Chaos* (Puteshestvie v khaos, 1921) and *Poems* (Stikhotvoreniya, 1926). In 1927, Vaginov joined the OBERIU group and his works became more aggressively modernist. His early prose, such as "The Monastery of Our Lord Apollo" (Monastyr' Gospoda nashego Apollona) and "The Star of Bethlehem" (Zvezda Vifleema), both 1922, is still fairly conventional. His later novels, *The Goat Song* (Kozlinaya pesn', 1928), *The Works and Days of Svistonov* (Trudy i dni Svistonova, 1929), and *Bambachada* (1931), follow the Oberiu aesthetic, featuring the grotesque, travesty, language games, verbal collage, an everpresent literary subtext, and pervasive romantic irony. They come as close to surrealism as anything in Russian prose of the 1920s. *The Goat Song* (the title is a pun on Gk. *tragoidia*, from *tragos*, "goat," and *oidē*, "song") draws a phantasmagoric picture of Leningrad as a cultural necropolis, populated by ex-intellectuals, now turned into faceless members of a Soviet petite bourgeoisie. The great cultural heritage of the City of Peter is relegated to the novel's subtext. Vaginov's last printed collection of verse, *Essays in Connecting Words by Way of Rhythm* (Opyty soedineniya slov posredstvom ritma, 1931), is among the last books of that period which openly professed an experimental, form-oriented attitude toward poetry. Vaginov's last cycle, "A Likeness of Sound" (Zvukopodobie), remained unpublished.

Works: Puteshestvie v khaos. 1921. (Reprint Ann Arbor, 1972). *Kozlinaya pesn'.* 1928. (Reprint New York, 1978).
Secondary literature: R. R. Milner-Gulland, "Left Art in Leningrad: The OBERIU Declaration," *OSP* 3 (1970), pp. 65–75. T. Nikol'skaya, "O tvorchestve K. Vaginova." In *Materialy XXII nauchnoi studencheskoi konferentsii.* Tartu, 1967.   V. T.

VAPP, see RAPP.

Vasiliev, Pável Nikoláevich (1910–37), Soviet poet. Of Siberian Cossack stock, Vasiliev attended school in Omsk, then enrolled in the Department of Far Eastern Languages at Vladivostok University to study Japanese (1926). Having scored some early successes with his poetry, he soon decided to become a poet and writer. He spent the next three years drifting from one place and one job to another (instructor of physical education, sailor on the Pacific, gold miner), but also published his poetry in various journals, as well as two books of travel sketches. In 1929 Vasiliev enrolled in a workshop for writers (*Vysshie gosudarstvennye literaturnye kursy*) in Moscow, but continued to travel a lot. He was arrested in 1932 and though soon released, had difficulty getting published thereafter. He now used the pseudonym "Mukhan Bashmetov," posing as a Kazakh poet in Russian translation. He also tried, futilely, to adapt his poetry to the political climate. In 1936 he was again arrested, "unlawfully repressed" in 1937, and "posthumously rehabilitated." Of the many poets who suffered this fate, Vasiliev was one of the most talented.

Though he never quite found his own style, Vasiliev did well in several manners which he adopted, as in that of the Russian folk ballad (of both the modern "urban," as well as of the traditional epic variety) and that of Kazakh gnomic folk poetry. Vasiliev's talent gravitated toward the epic genre. He was one of the few Russian poets good at writing in free and quickly changing rhythms, and used this skill effectively in his epic poems, most of which deal with the life of Siberian Cossacks, before the Revolution: "The Salt Rebellion" (Solyanoi bunt, 1933–34), "Sinitsyn and Co." (1934), and after: "Song of the Fall of the Cossack Commonwealth" (Pesnya o gibeli kazach'ego voiska, 1929–30), "The Kulaks" (Kulaki, 1933–34). Critics charged that Vasiliev was seeing the civil war and collectivization from the Cossack kulak's, rather than from the landless peasant's point of view, with the former developed with empathy and power, and the latter remaining pale and unconvincing. Vasiliev's *poemy* are characterized by their energetic rhythm, colorful imagery (often taken from, or stylized to resemble that of FOLK VERSE), and vigorous language. Vasiliev is at his best when he paints the plenitude and beauty of life in the Russian East with gladness and good humor, as in several poems devoted to a buxom beauty named Natalya.

Vasiliev is difficult to place. While he is often classed with the "PEASANT POETS," much of his poetry does not fit that category. He has little in common with ESENIN, although they share some themes. Vasiliev is the more interesting and more original poet, though he lacks Esenin's easy charm. At his best, Vasiliev may resemble KHLEBNIKOV.

Works: Stikhotvoreniya i poemy. Ed. S. A. Podelkov. (Biblioteka poeta.) 1968.
Translations: One poem ("Sister") in *Modern Russian Poetry*, ed. Vladimir Markov and Merrill Sparks (1967), pp. 704–07.
Secondary literature: Vladimir Markov, *Priglushennye golosa.* New York, 1952. Pp. 27–28. S. P. Zalygin, "Prostory i granitsy: O poezii Pavla Vasil'eva." In *Stikhotvoreniya i poemy.* 1968. Pp. 5–20.   V. T.

Vaudeville (*vodevil'*), a dramatic genre which dominated the Russian stage in the first half of the 19th century. A successor of the 18th-century comic opera, it developed under the direct influence of the French vaudeville (many Russian vaudevilles were adaptations of French texts to the Russian stage). The music, likewise, was largely unoriginal, though leading Russian composers of the period, such as A. N. Verstovsky (1799–1862), wrote vaudeville music. The vaudeville was superseded by the Viennese operetta around the middle of the century. The plot of a vaudeville generally presented scenes from contemporary life (often popular) with a satirical or topical twist. The critic BELINSKY, who rather liked and often reviewed vaudevilles, stressed that "being *à propos*" was essential to the genre. A typical vaudeville title would be "The Bakery, or a Petersburg German" (1843) or "A House on the Petersburg Side, or the Art of How Not to Pay Rent" (1838), both by P. A. Karatygin (1805–79), who also acted in the vaudevilles which he wrote. Literary feuds, such as that between SHISHKOVIANS and KARAMZINIANS, were also fought out on the vaudeville stage, and familiar literary figures would appear in caricature. The dialogue was often racy and actors were allowed to improvise their lines. The great Mikhail Shchepkin (1788–1863) scored some of his greatest successes in vaudeville. The plot was fast-moving, often paradoxic, and there had to be a surprise denouement. The musical part of the Russian vaudeville was less important than in its predecessor, the comic opera, or its successor, the operetta. Its satiric songs (*kuplety*) were not musically ambitious.

There are some prominent names among the authors of Russian vaudevilles: A. A. SHAKHOVSKOI, A. S. GRIBOEDOV, V. A. SOLLOGUB, and N. A. NEKRASOV. The most successful authors, besides Karatygin, who specialized in the vaudeville were Nikolai Khmelnitsky (1789–1845), Dmitry Lensky (pseud. of D. T. Vorobyov, 1805–60), Aleksandr Pisarev (1803–28), and Fyodor Koni (1809–79). Elements of the vaudeville penetrated into Russian comedy. GOGOL complained that the actor Nikolai Dyur, who played Khlestakov in *The Inspector-General*, spoiled the role by doing it "vaudeville fashion," but of course Gogol's comedies owed a great deal to the vaudeville. Some of OSTROVSKY's early comedies, with their profusion of song and dance, are not so far removed from vaudeville. Elements of the vaudeville may also be detected in the prose of the period, as in some early pieces by DOSTOEVSKY ("Another Man's Wife and the Husband under the Bed," "A Novel in Nine Letters") and even in his later stories "Uncle's Dream" and "The Village of Stepanchikovo."

Texts: Staryi russkii vodevil', 1819–1849. 1937. *Russkii vodevil'.* 1959.
Secondary literature: Vera Gottlieb, *Chekhov and the Vaudeville.* 1982. M. Paushkin, "Sotsiologiya, tematika i kompozitsiya vodevilya." In *Staryi russkii vodevil', 1819–1849.* 1937. V. V. Uspenskii, "Russkii klassicheskii vodevil'." In *Russkii vodevil'.* 1959.   V. T.

Vekhi (Landmarks), a collection of essays on the Russian intelligentsia by seven authors, published in Moscow in March 1909 in the wake of the first Russian Revolution of 1905. The seven, N. A. BERDYAEV, S. N. BULGAKOV, M. O. GERSHENZON, A. S. Izgoev, B. A. Kistyakovsky, P. B. STRUVE, and S. L. FRANK, severely criticized, each from his own perspective, the basic psychological and ideological tenets of the Russian intelligentsia—essentially the radical, or "circle," intelligentsia. The collection was initiated by M. O. Gershenzon, but expressed, on the whole, the ideas and sentiments propagated by P. B. Struve and like-minded authors.

The essays were preceded by a brief introduction, written by Gershenzon, which indicated that the Revolution of 1905 clearly demonstrated the bankruptcy of the ideals held dear by the intelligentsia for several decades. It confirmed the primacy of spiritual foundations of the individual and the society over superficial forms of sociopolitical institutions.

N. A. Berdyaev ("Philosophical Truth and the Truth-Justice of the Intelligentsia") criticized the circle intelligentsia for its tendency to approach philosophical teachings, and cultural phenomena in general, with purely political and utilitarian criteria rather than from the point of view of their absolute value—a subjective truth-justice being dearer to the intelligentsia than objective philosophical truth.

S. N. Bulgakov ("Heroism and Asceticism: From Reflections on the Religious Nature of the Russian Intelligentsia") observed that the intelligentsia took a heroic stand against Russia's past and present. This involved a maximalism of ends and means and led to the appearance of a new hero, the revolutionary student, who replaced, in the eyes of "society" (*obshchestvennost'*), the former ideal figure, the ascetic. Yet, despite superficial similarities, these two types of heroism, revolutionary and Christian, have in their essence absolutely nothing in common. And in as much as the simple Russian people remain Christian, they are more enlightened, though often illiterate, than the intelligentsia, which has become predominantly atheist.

M. O. Gershenzon ("Creative Self-Consciousness") discussed the deep schism between the suppressed creative will and the gluttonous consciousness in typical representatives of the intelligentsia. Characterized by this psychic duality leading to impotence, the intelligentsia is isolated from the Russian people, whose soul is qualitatively different. Instead of rebelling against the authorities, the intelligentsia must be grateful to them: their bayonets and prisons alone protect it from the people's rage.

A. S. Izgoev ("About the Intelligentsia's Youth: Notes on Its Mode of Life and Moods") writes that the driving ideal of the intelligentsia's youth is that of death; its main criterion, that of leftism. This ideal casts a spell over the minds of young people and paralyzes their conscience; instead of creating life, it destroys it. Because youth studies little and poorly, has no real love for a chosen profession, and prefers revolutionary superficiality, Russia is in dire need of qualified cadres of administrators and reformers.

B. A. Kistyakovsky ("In Defense of Law: The Intelligentsia and Legal Consciousness") concentrated on the intelligentsia's attitude toward law, especially on its lack of devotion to the ideas of the rights of the individual and of a *Rechtsstaat*, the latter being unavoidably based on the principle of compromise.

P. B. Struve ("Intelligentsia and Revolution"), in distinguishing between "intelligentsia" and "educated class" in general, noted that since the reception of West European atheist socialism in the 1860s the ideological form of the Russian intelligentsia consisted of a nonreligious rejection of the state and hostility to it. The constitutional Manifesto of 17 October 1905 signified a fundamental change in the political order of Russia formed in the course of many centuries. The intelligentsia, however, continued to inculcate the radicalism of its ideas upon the radicalism of the people's instincts, appetites, and hatreds.

S. L. Frank ("The Ethics of Nihilism: Toward a Definition of the Ethical Worldview of the Russian Intelligentsia") saw the fundamental antinomy of the ethical and cultural worldview of the intelligentsia in a contradictory combination of elements of nihilism and utilitarianism on the one hand, and of moralism and asceticism on the other. An accomplished representative of the intelligentsia must thus become a "militant monk of a nihilistic religion of earthly prosperity," i.e., a non-productive and morally deficient cultural type. The intelligentsia, therefore, is facing the difficult but necessary task of a reevaluation of old values and a creative mastering of new ones.

In view of the severe and unaccustomed criticism to which the authors of *Vekhi*, themselves prominent members of the intelligentsia, subjected their peers, it was in retrospect only natural that *Vekhi* aroused a deep and immediate reaction. The polemics around them took several forms: public meetings, lectures, papers, and discussions, book reviews and essays in newspapers and periodicals, and special collections of essays. The interest in *Vekhi* was such that in less than a year it ran through five editions. As a supplement to the fifth edition, which appeared early in 1910, Gershenzon published a bibliography of *Vekhi*. It contained by then already more than 160 titles.

Most of those who spoke or wrote about *Vekhi* treated them critically or inimically. (It is interesting to note that among the relatively few positive responses to *Vekhi* was an article by Andrei BELY in the symbolist review *Vesy*.) One of the most outspoken critics of *Vekhi* was V. I. LENIN, who branded them "an encyclopedia of liberal reneging." Attacks on *Vekhi* never stopped in the Soviet Union and since 1955 took a rather systematic character—thus only adding to *Vekhi*'s continued topicality.

Vekhi were, indeed, a very important (second) stage on the spiritual, ideological, and cultural path of a gifted segment of the Russian intelligentsia from positivism, materialism, linked with atheism and radicalism or revolutionism to metaphysical or religious and liberal or liberal-conservative foundations of a new world outlook. The first stage was represented by the collection of essays *Problems of Idealism* (1902), the third by the collection *From the Depths* (Iz glubiny, 1918). Published over seventy years ago, *Vekhi* are thus not simply a historical episode; they continue to be both an object of vehement political negation and a source of historical and ideological inspiration.

Texts: Landmarks: A Collection of Essays on the Russian Intelligentsia, 1909; Berdyaev, Bulgakov, Gershenzon, Izgoev, Kistyakovsky, Struve, Frank. Ed. Boris Shragin and Albert Todd. Trans. Marian Schwartz. 1977. *Vekhi (Signposts): A Collection of Articles on the Russian Intelligentsia*. Marshall Shatz and Judith Zimmerman, trans. and eds., *CSS* 2 (Summer 1968, pp. 151–74; Fall 1968, pp. 291–310; Winter 1968, pp. 447–63), 3 (Spring 1969, pp. 1–21; Fall 1969, pp. 494–515), 4 (Spring 1970, pp. 36–59; Summer 1970, pp. 183–98), and 5 (Fall 1971, pp. 327–61).

Secondary literature: Intelligentsiya v Rossii. 1910. Gisela Oberländer, "Die Vechi-Discussion (1902–1912)." Inaugural-Dissertation, University of Cologne, 1965. Nikolai P. Poltoratzky, "The *Vekhi* Dispute and the Significance of *Vekhi*," *CSP* 9 (1967), pp. 86–106. Christopher Read, *Religion, Revolution and the Russian Intelligentsia, 1900–1912: The* Vekhi *Debate and Its Intellectual Background.* 1980. Leonard Shapiro, "The *Vekhi* Group and the Mystique of Revolution," *SEER* 34, no. 22 (December, 1955), pp. 56–76. *V zashchitu intelligentsii.* 1909. *Vekhi kak znamenie vremeni.* 1910. Nicholas Zernov, *The Russian Religious Renaissance of the Twentieth Century.* 1963.   N. P. P.

Véltman (Vel'tman, Vel'dman), Aleksándr Fomích (1800–70), poet, writer, and scholar, was born in St. Petersburg, the son of a minor government official of Swedish descent. He attended boarding school and then a school which trained military quartermasters, in Moscow. Dispatched to Bessarabia as a military topographer in 1817, he served there until he resigned his commission in 1831, having attained the rank of a lieutenant colonel. He then held several civil service positions in Moscow, the last with a historical museum, the *Oruzheinaya palata*, whose director he was from 1852 to his death. Veltman published prolifically in Russian and Slavic history, archeology, ethnography, and philology ever since he had developed an interest in local antiquities during his stay in Bessarabia. His scholarship was more imaginative than sound. He was, however, elected a corresponding member of the Academy of Sciences in 1854.

Veltman began his literary career as a poet in 1828 and in 1831–32 published his first novel, *The Wanderer* (Strannik), a fanciful journey through Bessarabia with many literary, philosophic, antiquarian, and poetic digressions in the manner of Sterne and Jean Paul. There followed a steady flow of romantic novels and short stories which made Veltman one of the most popular writers of the 1830s and 1840s. Veltman's novels feature excursions into the distant past, as in *Raina, Queen of Bulgaria* (1843), set in 10th-century Bulgaria, and into the recent past, as in *The Lunatic: An Occurrence* (1834), set during the campaign of 1812. He explores the world of Russian folklore in *Koshchei the Deathless, a Tale of Old Times* (1833) and creates a utopian fantasy in *The Manuscripts of Martyn Zadeka: The Year MMMCDXLVIII* (1833). Among Veltman's devices were travel through time (*Aleksandr Filippovich Makedonsky* [1836], where the narrator rides into classical antiquity on a hippogryph), whimsical metamorphosis of historical personages (*General Kalimeros* [1840], where Napoleon has a romance with a Russian girl), and literary parody (*A New Emelya, or Metamorphoses* [1845], an antieducational *Emile*). Veltman's wealth of interesting detail, provided by his immense erudition, his delightfully unrestrained imagination which moves easily across the boundaries of time, space, and logic, and his cheerfully irresponsible humor are enhanced by an easy colloquial style.

The last twenty-five years of Veltman's life were devoted to a five-volume epopoeia, *Adventures Extracted from the Ocean of Life*, whose first volume, *Salomeya*, appeared in the years 1846–1848 and whose last volume, *Last in Line and Disinherited*, completed not long before Veltman's death, remained unpublished. The novels of this cycle are set in contemporary Russia and are a mixture of the picaresque adventure story and the realistic novel of manners. Their plots interlock, as the leading characters of one novel will appear on the fringes of another, and vice versa. Veltman, well respected by his contemporaries (BELINSKY and even DOSTOEVSKY and TOLSTOI praised him highly), was soon forgotten and is still awaiting a deserved revival.

Works: Priklyucheniya, pocherpnutye iz morya zhiteiskogo: Salomeya. Introductory essay and notes V. F. Pereverzev. 1957. *Strannik.* Ed. with an essay, "Aleksandr Vel'tman i ego roman *Strannik*," and notes by Yurii Akutin. 1977. *Povesti i rasskazy.* 1979.

Translations: "Travel Impressions." In *Russian Romantic Prose: An Anthology.* Ed. Carl R. Proffer. 1979.

Secondary literature: V. F. Pereverzev, "Predtecha Dostoevskogo." In *U istokov russkogo real'nogo romana.* 1937. S. A. Vengerov, *Kritiko-biograficheskii slovar' russkikh pisatelei i uchenykh.* Pp. 222–27.   V. T.

Venevitinov, Dmitry Vladimirovich (1805–27), romantic poet, critic, philosopher, artist, musician, was educated at Moscow University where he was immersed in German romantic idealist philosophy, particularly Schelling's *Naturphilosophie.* He was one of a group of young Muscovites known as the Archive Youths Circle, from their sinecures in the Foreign Ministry. He was a founder and leader of the WISDOM LOVERS (lyubomudry) who in the early 1820s propagated romantic idealist aesthetics and began the metaphysical trend in romantic poetry. Venevitinov first displayed his erudition in an 1825 article in which he decimated the neoclassical aesthetics of his teacher A. F. MERZLYAKOV. In the same year he showed himself a sensible critic of good taste in a polemic with N. A. POLEVOI over the first chapter of PUSHKIN's *Eugene Onegin.* His chief philosophical-critical work is "On the State of Enlightenment in Russia," written in 1826 as a plan for the journal *Moskovskii vestnik,* but not published until 1833 in his posthumous collected works. As a poet Venevitinov was influenced by Goethe and Byron. His poetry is conventionally romantic in themes, devices, and lexicon. An escapist rather than a rebel, he expressed longing for faraway places and the despair of the lonely poet in a cultural wasteland. Truly Schellingian, he believed in the lofty mission of the poet-philosopher: poetry is love of wisdom. He expressed strong national feelings in both his poetry and his criticism, and called for national originality in reaction to the neoclassical principle of imitation. His essay on enlightenment, in which he advocated removal from European influence except for a national immersion in German philosophy, leaves no doubt that he was an early Slavophile. Venevitinov was writing a novel titled *Vladimir Parensky* at the time of his death.

Works: Polnoe sobranie stikhotvorenii. (Biblioteka poeta.) 1960.

Translations: one poem ("Fatherland") in Avrahm Yarmolinsky, *A Treasury of Russian Verse.* 1949.

Secondary literature: Larry R. Andrews, "D. V. Venevitinov: A Sketch of His Life and Work," *RLT* 8 (1974), pp. 373–84. L. Tartakovskaya, *Dmitrii Venevitinov: Lichnost', mirovozzrenie, tvorchestvo.* Tashkent, 1974. Günther Wytrzens, *Dmitrii Vladimirovich Venevitinov als Dichter der russischen Romantik.* 1962.   L. G. L.

Vengerov, Semyon Afanasievich (1855–1920), scholar. A graduate of St. Petersburg University, on whose staff he remained all his life, Vengerov began his career as a scholar with a study of Turgenev (1875). *A History of Recent Russian Literature: From the Death of Belinsky to the Present* (1885) was confiscated by the government for allegedly subversive opinions expressed in it. Vengerov produced a series of monographic studies (on K. S. AKSAKOV, V.G. BELINSKY, N. V. GOGOL, I. A. GONCHAROV, A. F. PISEMSKY, etc.) as well as several theoretical and survey articles on 19th-century Russian literature, in all of which he treats literature as an integral part of socio-historical developments. Thus, in his study *Writer and Citizen: Gogol* (Pisatel'-grazhdanin: Gogol', 1913), Vengerov carefully investigates the factual and biographic basis of Gogol's fictional world. A scholar of inexhaustible energy, Vengerov was involved in several encyclopedic works: *A Critical and Biographic Dictionary of Russian Writers and Scholars, from the Beginnings of Russian Civilization to the Present* (Kritiko-biograficheskii slovar' russkikh pisatelei i uchenykh. Ot nachala russkoi obrazovannosti do nashikh dnei. 6

vols. 1886–1904, incomplete); *Sources for a Dictionary of Russian Writers* (Istochniki slovarya russkikh pisatelei. 4 vols. 1900–17, incomplete); *Russian Books* (Russkie knigi. 3 vols. 1897–99, incomplete). Vengerov edited and published a number of authors and works which had been previously prohibited, such as his *Russkaya Poeziya* (2 vols., 1893–1901).

Works: Sobranie sochinenii. 5 vols. 1911–19.

Bibliography: A. S. Polyakov, Trudy prof. S. A. Vengerova; *Bibliograficheskii perechen'.* 1916.   V. T.

Verbitskaya, Anastasiya Alekseevna (1861–1928), prose writer and playwright, came from a family of the gentry. Starting in 1887, she published her works in journals of a liberal orientation. Her best known works are the novels *Keys to Happiness* (Klyuchi schast'ya, in 6 books, 1909–13) and *The Yoke of Love* (Igo lyubvi, 1914–16), the short novel *The Story of a Life* (Istoriya odnoi zhizni, 1903), and the collection of short stories, *Mar'ya Ivanovna's Crime* (Prestuplenie Mar'i Ivanovny, 1899). Verbitskaya's work is largely devoted to questions of sex and the emancipation of women. She may be considered a precursor of today's feminist literature. Verbitskaya's involved plots, exalted style, as well as her candid treatment of love scenes, extraordinary for her time, combined to make her immensely popular. In the early 1900s she was considered a rival of Lev TOLSTOI, even though most critics did notice the vulgarity and pseudo-intellectualism of her works. Verbitskaya was a typical second-rate writer who translated the themes and motifs of her epoch into the idiom of mass literature. Verbitskaya's plays are somewhat more interesting, such as the comedy *Mirage* (Mirazh, staged 1895–1896, published 1909).

Secondary literature: K. Chukovskii, *Kniga o sovremennykh pisatelyakh.* 1914. Pp. 7–21. (An abbreviated version in his *Sobranie sochinenii,* vol. 6, 1969, pp. 10–21.) V. Kranikhfel'd, *V mire idei i obrazov.* Vol. 2. 1912. Pp. 155–81. Temira Pachmuss, ed., *Women Writers in Russian Modernism.* 1978. Pp. 114–19.   T. V.

Veresaev (pseud. of Vikenty Vikentievich Smidovich, 1867–1945), writer and scholar. Born in Tula, the son of a doctor, Veresaev acquired degrees in classical philology and medicine, and practiced medicine in Tula and later in St. Petersburg. He began to publish his fiction in 1887. His early stories, typical of socially oriented "critical realism," dealt with diverse strata of Russian society, but mostly with the searchings of young intellectuals for an ideal that would not be dashed to pieces by the facts of life, as in "No Way" (Bez dorogi, 1895) and "Pestilent Air" (Povetrie, 1898). Veresaev's autobiographic *Memoirs of a Physician* (Zapiski vracha, 1901) was a major success. His service as a physician in the Russo-Japanese War (1904–05) resulted in some fiction as well as non-fiction: *Tales about the War* (1906) and *At War* (Na voine, 1907–08). Starting in 1910, Veresaev also began to publish literary criticism: *Living Life* (Zhivaya zhizn', 1910–15), dealing with DOSTOEVSKY, TOLSTOI, and Nietzsche. After the Revolution, Veresaev continued to write in his former vein of scrupulous and observant socially concerned realism. In the novel *In a Blind Alley* (V tupike, 1922; English trans. *The Deadlock,* 1927) he registers the reactions of different types of progressively minded young people to the Revolution, without concealing that a morally pure person may have reason to reject as well as to accept it. His last novel, *The Sisters* (Sestry, 1933), repeats this pattern with regard to the collectivization of agriculture. Since the 1920s Veresaev devoted most of his energy to scholarly works and excellent translations of classical Greek poetry. His *Pushkin in Life* (Pushkin v zhizni, 1926–27), *Gogol in Life* (1933) and several other, similar works are based on carefully collected source material. Veresaev also wrote his memoirs: *My Youth* (V yunye gody, 1927) and *My Student Years* (V studencheskie gody, 1929).

Works: Polnoe sobranie sochinenii. 16 vols. 1928–29. *Sobranie sochinenii.* 5 vols. 1961.

Translations: The Memoirs of a Physician. Trans. S. Linden. Introd. and notes H. Pleasants, Jr. 1916. *The Deadlock.* Trans. N. Vissotsky and C. Coventry. 1927. *The Sisters.* Trans. J. Soskice. 1936.

Secondary literature: S. P. Borodin, *V. V. Veresaev: Zhizn' i tvorchestvo.* 1959. N. V. Galichenko, "Doctors as Writers: Veresaev and Bulgakov," *Proceedings: Pacific Northwest Conference on Foreign Languages* 24 (1973), pp. 273–80.   V. T.

Versification, historical survey of Russian. Prior to the 17th century the main source of Russian poetry was the folk tradition. While it is difficult to ascertain the precise extent to which FOLK VERSIFICATION influenced literary practice, at the very least direct imitations of folk poetry have occurred ever since the establishment of the SYLLABO-TONIC literary tradition in the 18th century. Of all the folk verse forms, the most widely studied has been the BYLINA. Several kinds of meters have been found in the *bylina*, but in most cases the lines typically exhibit an unrhymed dactylic ending (that is, two syllables follow the final metrical stress). Of the two most common meters, one is essentially trochaic, employing primarily but not exclusively pentameter and hexameter lines. As opposed to literary verse written in trochaic meters, the *bylina* shows fewer restraints on non-metrical stressing and occasionally even contains iambic lines along with the trochaic. The other common meter is similar to the strict accentual verse (or *taktovik*) (see TONIC VERSIFICATION) of modern literary poetry. It features a three-stress accentual line, in which the intervals between stresses usually consist of either two or three syllables. In many songs a large percentage of the lines contain stresses distributed in such a way that they too tend to develop a trochaic cadence. Literary imitations of folk verse, while quite varied in form, have frequently employed unrhymed dactylic endings and have also inclined to be trochaic or to employ a type of strict accentual verse.

Laments and songs likewise often have trochaic lines; of particular note is the trochaic 5 + 5 song meter, a ten-syllable form with a caesura after the fifth syllable and constant stress on the third and eighth syllables; this meter was popularized by A. V. KOLTSOV in his 19th-century songs. Spoken verse, as opposed to sung verse, is found in proverbs, riddles, magic spells, and the like. Unlike the epics and early lyric songs, which generally lack rhyme, all these shorter forms depend heavily on sound repetitions. For one early type of verse, the *rayoshnik* (see SKAZOVYI STIKH), rhyme is the sole organizing feature; it contains neither an equal number of syllables nor necessarily an equal number of stresses per line. Often humorous or satiric, the *rayoshnik*, with its usually paired rhymes, was used in traditional entertainments and in the inscriptions on the LUBOK, a type of popular print.

As for the earliest period of Russian literature, the clearest examples of poetry occur in the Orthodox liturgy, which included Russian recensions of Church Slavonic poetry. These in turn had usually been translated from the Greek. Since the translations not only maintained but at times even strengthened the syllabic symmetry of the originals, the Russian composers must have been aware of a poetic tradition. However, it is much more difficult to decide whether some of the works in Old Russian Literature—the *Igor Tale* (see SLOVO O POLKU IGOREVE), Ilarion's *Sermon on Law and Grace*, the SUPPLICATION OF DANIIL THE EXILE—may have employed verse as well. They all contain evidence of rhythmic organization, but it is clear that if there was a verse tradition at the time it must have involved a looser and less readily defined set of principles than that found in modern poetry. Other problems in discovering such a system of verse include the necessity to determine the original forms of the texts and the difficulty of knowing just how words were stressed in Old Russian. Of the several systems that have been suggested all could apply about as well to rhythmic prose as to verse. The most convincing effort to date is that of Kiril Taranovsky, who has suggested that there existed a tradition of religious verse (*molitvoslovnyi stikh*), the distinguishing feature of which was a tendency to mark the start of each line by using particular grammatical forms, syntactic structures, or literary devices like anaphora.

A definite literary tradition in Russia begins only with the rise of pre-syllabic verse (*dosillabicheskii stikh*) during the first three decades of the 17th century, a time when only a handful of poems were actually written in Russian. Works in both pre-syllabic and the later syllabic verse are sometimes referred to as *virshi*. During the pre-syllabic period, rhyme is the one constant feature of the poetry (much as was the case with the *rayoshnik*); both the number of syllables and the number of stresses on each line may vary. The rhyme is paired, but unlike the subsequent syllabic verse, pre-syllabic poetry allowed not only feminine, but also masculine, dactylic, and even hyperdactylic rhyme. Nor is the rhyme always exact; at times assonance or consonance were used instead. Perhaps as a result of the relatively loose rules for creating this type of poetry, the authors frequently resorted to acrostics as a way of further distinguishing their work from ordinary prose.

Pre-syllabic verse soon gave way to SYLLABIC poetry, and this shift resulted largely from the influence of SIMEON POLOTSKY. Although there was a fairly extensive body of work in pre-syllabic poetry by the mid-17th century, the number of poets was still small. A new method could quickly win favor throughout this limited group, and within a few years the pre-syllabic system had virtually disappeared. Simeon Polotsky's verse was based on Polish syllabic poetry, which he himself had written before coming to Moscow. The Polish versification principles then in vogue had been popularized by Jan Kochanowski, a 16th-century poet. All the lines within a given poem were of equal length (this of course is the basic feature of all syllabic verse); the most common line lengths for Polish poetry were thirteen or eleven syllables. Furthermore, the line was divided into two parts (7-6 or 5-6) by a caesura. While stress in Russian and English may appear on any syllable within a word, stress in Polish is always on the next to last syllable. Therefore both the ending and the caesura were normally feminine. However, the tendency to use feminine endings was less of a restriction on Polish writers than was isosyllabism. Given the nature of Polish stress, feminine endings were simply to be expected in the majority of cases; for that matter, masculine and dactylic endings were not absolutely forbidden and did occasionally occur when monosyllabic words or enclitics appeared at the caesura or the end of the line.

Russian took three of the four main features in Polish syllabic verse. It too (1) used lines of the same length throughout the poem (and, as in Polish, preferred poems with lines of thirteen or eleven syllables), (2) contained a caesura that divided the line into two halves or hemistichs (again, 7-6 or 5-6), and (3) used feminine endings, which normally formed rhymed couplets. However, the caesura in Russian was not necessarily feminine but could be masculine or dactylic as well. In practice, not all the poems were completely regular; sometimes rhymes were not adjoining but alternating, and lines within a single poem could even vary slightly in length. Still more rarely, poets would use an occasional non-feminine rhyme. One peculiarity of syllabic verse is the relative frequency with which strong stresses appear on contiguous syllables; the same phenomenon is found in syllabotonic poetry, but there its usage is much more circumscribed. During the period when syllabic poetry was predominant, from about 1670 through the 1730s, the first part of the line exhibited strong stressing on adjoining syllables about one time in five; the second part of the line contained such stressing approximately once every ten lines.

The seeming casualness with which poets employed adjoining strong stresses calls into question the extent to which syllabic verse served as a direct percursor of the SYLLABOTONIC system. For some seventy years syllabic poetry reigned supreme; its major practitioners, besides Polotsky, included Feofan PROKOPOVICH, Silvestr MEDVEDEV, Karion ISTOMIN, Antiokh KANTEMIR, and the young Vasily TREDIAKOVSKY. Yet within two decades after Trediakovsky had written his "New and Brief Method for Composing Russian Verse" of 1735, the syllabotonic system had almost entirely replaced syllabic poetry. Presumably, had syllabic poetry led directly into the syllabotonic system, poets writing syllabic verse would have gradually come to (1) decrease the amount of contiguous stressing and (2) favor trochaic rhythms, since Trediakovsky, who was the first to formulate a theory of syllabotonic poetry and who had originally written syllabic poetry himself, felt that trochaic meters were the most suitable for Russian. However, contiguous stressing, if anything, becomes slightly more frequent up until the time of Trediakovsky's reform. After the reform it drops dramatically in the late poetry of Kantemir and in Trediakovsky's subsequent syllabic poetry. As for trochaic rhythms, a tendency for lines to sound more trochaic should be accompanied first of all by a decrease in the frequency of a feminine caesura. Since the first hemistich usually had either five or seven syllables, a feminine caesura places a stress on an even syllable (either the fourth or the sixth), while in trochaic meters the ictuses are on the odd syllables. In fact, right up until the time of Kantemir and Trediakovsky about half of all the lines contain a feminine caesura and therefore necessarily lack a strongly trochaic rhythm.

Only after 1735 do both Kantemir and (especially) Trediakovsky consistently use masculine or, to a lesser extent, dactylic caesuras instead. Second, if purely syllabic poetry had been gradually developing into syllabotonic, the second hemistich of syllabic lines should also have begun to use trochaic rhythms more and more consistently. Since the second hemistich of both the eleven- and thirteen-syllable lines contains six syllables and has a required stress on the penultimate syllable, its schema is as follows: xxxxxx́x. Therefore, in lines without contiguous stressing, only five types of second hemistich are possible: (1) x́xx́xx́x (2) xxx́xx́x (3) x́xxx́x́x (4) xx́xxx́x (5) xxxxx́x. The first three of these resemble trochees and the fourth amphibrachs. The "theoretical expectation," which has been calculated using examples of prose, is that about 55 percent of the second hemistichs should be trochaic, assuming that poets were not striving to favor any one type of rhythm over the others. Indeed, poets stayed quite close to this theoretical figure until the 1730s, after which Trediakovsky abruptly began to use trochaic rhythms almost exclusively. Since the presence of feminine rhyme means that 55 percent of the lines would show a trochaic rhythm in the second hemistich even if poets were not attempting to use such a rhythm consciously, it is easy to see why some have felt that syllabic verse exhibited a trochaic cadence. But the failure of poets to exceed the 55 percent "norm" before Trediakovsky's time shows that they were not aware of, or at least not trying to emphasize, a trochaic rhythm. Furthermore, in the first hemistich, where the placing of stress was much more varied, there was no tendency to favor trochaic rhythms at all until after Trediakovsky wrote his essay. Every change that did take place occurred suddenly; just after Trediakovsky wrote his "Method," the feminine caesura virtually disappeared, the second hemistich became much more trochaic, and contiguous stressing dropped dramatically. Many scholars now therefore believe that the change to a new system was a "revolutionary" rather than evolutionary process.

Metrists are divided as to why the syllabic system gave way so abruptly and so completely. Some hold that the reasons are largely linguistic; languages like Polish, with fixed stress, tend to favor syllabic systems, in which stress plays little or no role as a distinguishing feature; on the other hand, languages like English, German, and Russian—in which stress appears at various positions in words and has therefore come to be quite prominent—prefer tonic systems, in which stress is the main prosodic feature of the language. Therefore the switch to a syllabotonic system in Russian is seen as a natural development, and the only question might be why the syllabic system reigned as long as it did. Others have cast doubt on some of these premises. For instance, Ukrainian, which phonologically is very close to Russian, retains a syllabic tradition; conversely, Polish, with its fixed stress, later came to use some syllabotonic poetry. Also, syllabic poetry is not necessarily unnatural to Russian; if anything, it puts fewer restraints on the language than the strict laws of syllabotonic poetry. If linguistic features are not the answer, then changes in the cultural background and outside influence must be considered paramount.

The answer seems to lie somewhere between the two positions. The cultural environment probably did play some role, since early in the 18th century there was a strong German influence in the Court and at the Academy of Sciences. German poetry was syllabotonic, and Mikhail LOMONOSOV based his important revisions of Trediakovsky's "Method" on German models. Lomonosov had picked up most of his ideas in Germany itself, but German poetry was also well known in Russia and some Germans in St. Petersburg even wrote early examples of Russian syllabotonic poetry. However, linguistic influences cannot be ignored. Russian folk verse, in which stress has always played a major role, shows that from the earliest times stress has been recognized as an important prosodic element in Russian. Also, according to some critics, syllabic verse, by putting few restraints on the language, was still perceived as close to prose. Therefore, syllabic poetry could be used to create successful satires and the like, but it appeared to be less suitable for the more formal genres, such as the ode and the narrative poem.

All this may help account for the rapid ascension of syllabotonic poetry once it first appeared, but the failure of syllabic verse to continue as at least a minor tradition is more difficult to explain. Perhaps the answer is that the circle of poets active during the first half of the 18th century was still relatively small and self-contained.

The influence of the new system could be quickly felt by every poet of any significance then active, and since the prevailing feeling seemed to be that syllabotonic verse was more suitable for serious poetry, the desire of every young poet to master the new method is not surprising. Furthermore, once syllabotonic poetry had been around for even a short while, changes took place in Russian poetic practice that made it difficult to reestablish a syllabic system. Almost from the start (or at least from the time of Lomonosov) Russian syllabotonic poetry mixed different kinds of rhyme in the same poem; thus a poem written in iambic tetrameter could have eight syllables (masculine rhyme), nine syllables (feminine rhyme) or even ten (dactylic rhyme). Hence isosyllabism, the basic feature of syllabic poetry, was no longer a governing principle for poems written in Russian. Second, a regular interval between stresses became the norm, and this feature soon assumed a greater importance than the caesura for determining the structure of the line. Third, long lines, common in Russian syllabic meters, gradually gave way to shorter lines of eight or nine syllables; this too lessened the need for the pause created by a caesura. Thus, of the three main features of Russian syllabic poetry, two—isosyllabism and exclusively feminine endings—became rarities, while the third, the caesura, became less prominent as Russian poetry moved into the 19th century. Certainly by the mid-19th century, syllabic verse had become quite foreign to the Russian ear.

Trediakovsky and Lomonosov were together largely responsible for the establishment of the syllabotonic system. The word "together," though, is not entirely appropriate, since the two men disagreed sharply over the new methods for composing poetry. Their arguments, which began over literary issues, soon grew into a bitter personal quarrel that eventually ruined Trediakovsky's career. In a sometimes more seemly fashion, disputes regarding the significance of each poet's contribution have continued ever since. For some time Lomonosov was considered to be the more important figure in the history of Russian verse theory, though more recent studies have tended to put Trediakovsky's theoretical work at least on a par with Lomonosov's and have generally attributed the latter's greater reputation to his superior skill as a poet. Today their work on verse theory is viewed, in spite of themselves, as a kind of joint effort; Trediakovsky made the original and perhaps more difficult breakthrough to the new system, while Lomonosov provided some needed modifications to Trediakovsky's ideas and thus created the kernel of the system that prevails in Russian versification to the present day.

Trediakovsky's "New and Brief Method for Composing Russian Verse" was published in April of 1735 by the Russian Academy of Sciences, where Trediakovsky had been working as a translator since 1732. In some ways Trediakovsky's "Method" was hardly a radical departure from accepted practice. As in regular syllabic verse, Trediakovsky advocated lines of thirteen or eleven syllables, with a caesura after the seventh or fifth syllable respectively. Also, he still wanted to use feminine rhymes exclusively. However, he introduced one crucial difference: instead of just specifying a constant stress on the line's penultimate syllable (for the sake of the feminine rhyme), he talked in terms of *feet*, which in turn implied a regular alternation of stressed and unstressed syllables. In other words, Trediakovsky was the first to draw attention to the importance of stress for Russian literary poetry. Indeed, he was careful to specify the difference between classical poetry, in which the main prosodic feature is length (the opposition between long and short syllables), and Russian, where stress fulfills the role played by length in Greek and Latin works. Furthermore, by talking of regular intervals between stresses, Trediakovsky also became the first to introduce the concept of rhythm into Russian verse practice.

At the same time Trediakovsky did not adapt all the features of what is now known as "classical" Russian verse. He did not include ternary feet in his schema and therefore referred to only four kinds of feet: the iamb (x x́), trochee (x́ x), pyrrhic (x x) and spondee (x́x́). In addition, he placed what now seem to be strange value judgments on the various feet. He believed that the best lines contained either all or mostly trochees, the worst were those consisting primarily or exclusively of iambs, and lines in which spondees and pyrrhics predominated were of middling value. In practice Trediakovsky wrote lines almost exclusively in his favored trochees. Another peculiarity of his theory is that it allowed not only "pyrrhic feet" and "spondees" (in modern terms, omitted stresses and hypermetrical stressing), but also the substitution in trochaic lines of an iamb for a trochee, as well as of a trochee for an iamb in iambic verse. However, these substitutions remained more a part of his theory than of his practice.

Many suggestions have been offered regarding the sources of Trediakovsky's theories. Least convincing are the assertions that a syllabotonic system already existed in Russia at the time of Trediakovsky's treatise. True, songbooks from the 17th century do contain a few syllabotonic lines, but these are scattered and appear to be incidental occurrences rather than evidence of an established verse tradition. Also, two German churchmen, Ernst Glück and Johann Paus, who came to Russia around the turn of the 18th century, translated many German poems into Russian, attempting to use the syllabotonic system of the originals. However, their verse practice differs noticeably from later Russian versification, and in particular from the ideas presented by Trediakovsky in 1735. For example, their use of stanzaic forms, their preference for iambic meters, and their approach to rhyme are all contrary to Trediakovsky's proposals.

Among the more likely sources, no single influence can be identified with any certainty as necessarily more important than the others. Very possibly Trediakovsky at least took his terminology, if not the very idea of syllabotonic poetry, from the Russian grammars of his time. Despite the predominance of the syllabic system within Russia during the late 17th and early 18th centuries, the grammars continued to describe classical prosody along with its feet and meters. Another possible influence stems from his trip to France in the late 1720s. His essay provides French translations for many terms, and he seems to have borrowed a few ideas, such as his rejection of enjambement, from Boileau's *Art poétique*. Third, Trediakovsky himself later referred to a "Dalmatian" text that he once owned, which contained a work in trochaic tetrameter (he was probably referring to a work by Ivan Gundulić, *The Tears of the Prodigal Son*—Suze sina razmetnoga, 1622). This book could well have helped incline Trediakovsky both toward syllabotonic poetry and toward the trochee, though he himself of course began with the longer line he knew from syllabic verse. German poetry, though not necessarily that of Paus and Glück, was probably yet another influence. Not only were many Germans connected with the Russian Academy of Sciences, but Trediakovsky himself translated German verse into Russian. Thus he was familiar with German syllabotonic poetry, though the types of lines he advocated for Russian syllabotonic poetry differed from the more common meters in German poetry. Possible Russian influences include folk poetry and syllabic versification itself. Folk poetry often exhibits a trochaic cadence, and at one point in his writings Trediakovsky refers to his interest in folk verse. Folk poetry may well have reinforced his conviction regarding the suitability of trochaic meters for Russian and the importance of stress as an organizing principle. Still, his continued use of the caesura and of feminine rhymes indicate that folk verse could not have been the sole source for his new system. Finally, while syllabic verse did not "evolve" into the syllabotonic system, its occasional use of trochaic cadences, especially in the second half of the line, may well have inclined Trediakovsky towards favoring the trochee for his new "Method." In short, his treatise appears to have grown out of his wide reading and his own experience as a poet; it does not derive from any one source but represents a distillation of many ideas and influences.

Only four years after the appearance of Trediakovsky's work, Lomonosov, then studying in Germany, sent back to the Russian Academy of Sciences his "Letter on the Rules of Russian Versification." Included with the letter, as an example of his new approach to writing poetry, was Lomonosov's "Ode on the Taking of Khotin." When he had left for Germany in 1736, he had taken along a copy of Trediakovsky's recently published "Method." Then during his stay abroad Lomonosov became acquainted with the principles of German verse practice. Thus the influence of German verse theorists can be seen throughout Lomonosov's letter, while his "Ode on the Taking of Khotin" in some ways imitates a poem by a contemporary German poet, Johann Günther. Even Lomonosov's opening point—that poetry should be faithful to the inherent qualities of the Russian language—may well derive largely from what German theoreticians were then saying to their own poets. Still,

by applying this idea to Russian, Lomonosov was breaking new ground. He was able to modify Trediakovsky's tentative introduction of syllabotonic principles in a way that made them less restrictive and less artificial for poets writing in Russian.

Like Trediakovsky, Lomonosov based his verse theory on the opposition between stressed and unstressed syllables. However, he went beyond Trediakovsky's proposals and drew closer to modern verse practice in at least seven ways. First, while Trediakovsky considered all monosyllables stressed, Lomonosov distinguished between words like *khram* and *svyat*, which carry stress, and others like *zhe* and *da*, which do not. Second, Lomonosov moved completely away from reliance on the old syllabic lines and admitted lines varying in length from trimeters to hexameters. Third, his system included ternary meters, anapests ($x x \acute{x}$) and dactyls ($\acute{x} x x$)—he says nothing about the amphibrach ($x \acute{x} x$)—in addition to the binary meters allowed by Trediakovsky. Fourth, he does not favor trochees; on the contrary, he notes that iambs are especially effective in solemn odes. Fifth, and also contrary to Trediakovsky, Lomonosov uses masculine and dactylic, as well as feminine rhyme; furthermore, he advocates using alternating as well as adjacent rhyme. Sixth, Lomonosov makes the caesura an optional feature even in long lines. Finally, he remarks that iambs and trochees are opposed to each other and does not recommend using both in the same line.

While Lomonosov's letter was to mark the end of the syllabic system in Russian poetry, it still differs from modern verse theory in two important details. First, according to Lomonosov, an unfulfilled ictus (what he called a pyrrhic foot) was a defect, and he suggested avoiding it except in songs, which he regarded as a less serious type of poetry. Lomonosov apparently borrowed this idea from German verse theorists, but in practice German poets actually omitted at least one stress in about 20 percent of all lines in their binary poetry. German averages about one stress per every two syllables, while in Russian stress occurs somewhat less frequently—about once in every 2.7 or 2.8 syllables. Therefore, it would be natural for Russian poets to omit stress on an ictus quite often in binary meters (which have an ictus once every two syllables). At first Lomonosov attempted to emulate his theory and strove to omit as few stresses as possible; as a result his first poems closely follow the pattern of German poetry in the percentage of unfulfilled ictuses. By the mid-1740s, however, he is already omitting stresses more often, thereby writing poems that are closer to the rhythms of subsequent Russian poetry and quite distinct from those of German. Sumarokov's poems from the same period omit still more stresses and may have had some influence on Lomonosov's practice. In any case, by the late 1740s Lomonosov was freely ignoring his own stricture against so-called pyrrhic feet. Second, in his letter Lomonosov talks about not just four types of meters (iambs, trochees, anapests, and dactyls), but six: he felt that iambs and anapests could be mixed on the same line to create another meter, as could trochees and dactyls. While the concept of different "feet" occurring on the same line is foreign to modern Russian verse theory, the classical hexameter (which imitated the Greek and Latin line of the same name by allowing trochees and dactyls to appear on the same line) was used a few times in the 18th century and continued to be written into the 19th.

While subsequent essays by 18th-century poets added relatively little to these two pioneering works, four other items deserve brief mention. The first work, Kantemir's "Letter of Khariton Makentin to a Friend on Composing Russian Verse" was written in 1743 and represents a last attempt to defend syllabic poetry. Khariton Makentin is an anagram of Antiokh Kantemir; thus the "Letter" was clearly Kantemir's own reply to Trediakovsky's "Method" of 1735. In some ways Kantemir was a reformer as well; he accepted enjambement, unrhymed syllabic verse, and rhymes other than feminine—none of which, in fact, were allowed by Trediakovsky. However, Kantemir still clung to the basic tenet of the syllabic system, for he felt that it was "superfluous" to consider feet in composing poetry. Two other works were both by Trediakovsky. In 1752 he published a new version of his "Method," called "A Method for Composing Russian Verse." Here Trediakovsky himself adopted most, but not all, the changes suggested by Lomonosov. For instance, he continued to believe that all monosyllabic words are stressed but admitted that some may be considered unstressed in a given poem owing to the exigencies of meter. His other essay dealing with poetic theory, "On the Ancient, Middle, and New Russian Versification"

(1755) provides a history of Russian verse practice. It is especially interesting for indicating some of the sources that led Trediakovsky to formulate his "Method" of 1735. Finally, during the 1770s, Sumarokov composed "On Versification." Writing somewhat later than his one-time colleague, Sumarokov was able to look back over his own verse practice and that of his contemporaries. He is the first to mention the amphibrach and thus is also the first to list the five types of meter that make up classical Russian verse; iambs, trochees, anapests, dactyls, and amphibrachs. He also recognizes that the "spondee" and the "pyrrhic" are not independent feet but result from permissible rhythmic variations in trochaic and iambic lines. This is the first theoretical statement to correspond almost exactly to our contemporary understanding of binary and ternary meters. Thus it reveals just how far syllabotonic prosody had advanced within forty years of Trediakovsky's first treatise.

Changes in Russian poetry did not cease with the reforms of Trediakovsky and Lomonosov. Even though the meters favored by Lomonosov and then Sumarokov dominated Russian poetry for over a hundred years, various poets—not least of all Sumarokov himself—experimented with a number of less common forms. Then during the 19th and especially the 20th centuries poets began using meters that were either rare or completely absent from 18th-century verse practice. A brief outline of these developments is given below; for the sake of clarity it focuses only on the usage of various meters, without going into the finer points of individual rhythmic forms.

Throughout the 18th century iambs were by far the favorite meters of all the leading poets, and the most widespread of the iambic meters was the "variable iamb" (vol'nyi yamb; often referred to in English as the "free iamb"). Poems composed in variable verse contain lines of different lengths that alternate in no regular pattern. (A regular alternation of, say, four- and three-foot iambs would be considered a "mixed iambic" meter.) Lines written in variable iambs during the 18th century usually were from two to six feet in length. The meter has traditionally been associated with fables, beginning with Sumarokov and achieving their greatest popularity in the works of KRYLOV. However, during the 18th century such iambs were employed in a wide variety of other genres as well, including odes, epistles, narrative poems, and dramatic works. The iambic hexameter rivaled the variable iamb in popularity. Though more works were written in variable iambs, the iambic hexameter accounts for a far greater number of lines; poets tended to use the iambic hexameter in the longer genres, such as dramas and narrative poems, while the variable iamb was most often employed in much shorter works. The third most common meter was the iambic tetrameter, which occurred in almost all genres. Well over 70 percent of all 18th-century poetry was written in just these three meters.

Still, the leading poets of the day experimented widely; by the end of the century there were few varieties of classical syllabotonic poetry that had not been tried in at least isolated instances. The iambic trimeter and mixed iambs were quite common; a few poems were written in iambic dimeter, and there were also some examples of the iambic pentameter, which did not achieve popularity until the 19th century. Trochaic lines ranged in length from the dimeter to the octameter, though only the trochaic tetrameter appeared with any great frequency and even that was largely limited to songs. Among the ternary meters, a handful of dactyls and amphibrachs were used, along with a very few lines in anapests. Trediakovsky combined dactyls and trochees in unrhymed lines in his imitation of the Greek and Latin hexameter. The resulting mixture of one- and two-syllable intervals between stresses resembled the modern dol'nik, though the latter is normally rhymed and has three or four instead of six stresses. Trediakovsky's most famous, or perhaps infamous, use of this meter was in his Tilemakhida, a verse translation of Fénelon's novel, Les Aventures de Télémaque. The work itself was ridiculed when it first appeared, though later commentators have treated it more kindly and the hexameter itself enjoyed a revival during the first half of the 19th century.

From 1800 into the 1830s a number of changes took place in Russian verse practice. The ternary meters became more common, thanks largely to ZHUKOVSKY's use of them in his ballads. Iambs on the whole lost a little ground, but they remained by far the most popular meters. The iambic pentameter emerged from the background to become a familiar meter in the works of Zhukovsky, and PUSHKIN. From the 1820s on, thanks largely to Zhukovsky and

Pushkin, the unrhymed iambic pentameter began to be used widely in dramatic works. By the 1820s the iambic tetrameter had replaced the variable iamb as the meter used in the greatest number of poems. Trochaic meters were employed with about the same frequency as before, the trochaic tetrameter continuing to account for the overwhelming majority of trochaic poems. The imitation of the Greek and Latin hexameter achieved new popularity when GNEDICH published the first part of his translation of the Iliad in 1813; the complete work came out in 1829 and was eventually followed by Zhukovsky's translation of the Odyssey in the same meter.

Pushkin's choice of meters closely followed the general verse practice of his day. The iambic tetrameter was his favorite meter, accounting for over 40 percent of his works and over half of his lines. He also resorted frequently to the iambic hexameter and pentameter as well as to variable iambs; in all, over three-quarters of his poetry was iambic. Nearly all of his trochaic poems were written in trochaic tetrameter. Pushkin did not show much interest in the ternary meters; although some of his contemporaries wrote fairly frequently in these meters, the ternaries were still significantly less common than trochaic meters. Pushkin's nonclassical verse included several examples of hexameters as well as imitations of folk poetry.

The picture begins to change among certain poets active already in the 1830s, and by the middle of the century the frequency with which individual meters are used changes markedly. Iambic meters remained the most common, but their share declined abruptly from over three-quarters of all poetry to about half. The iambic tetrameter held onto its position as the single most popular meter overall, but the variable iamb receded far into the background as the leading writers turned less and less often to the fable, the genre with which this form was most closely connected. The nonclassical meters just about held their own: the hexameters peaked about mid-century and then began a sharp decline, while imitations of folk verse and translations accounted for most of the remaining examples.

Two major developments marked this period. First, the trochaic and ternary meters both became far more common than before. The precise figures vary from decade to decade and from poet to poet, but for the period as a whole trochaic and ternary meters each accounted for about one-fifth of the poetry being written. Particularly startling was the increase in ternary meters, which appeared in such a small percentage of, for instance, Pushkin's or TYUTCHEV's poetry but which, during the 1870s and 1880s, were used in nearly one-third of the lyric poetry. Second, individual poets came to write extensively in a wider range of meters. Through the time of Pushkin each poet tended to favor no more than three of four meters and to use the others in his repertoire quite sparingly. Now, in addition to the variety of popular iambic meters, trochaic meters other than the tetrameter were employed fairly regularly. All the ternary meters began to be used with at least some frequency: throughout the first half of the 19th century amphibrachs were the most common, but by the 1870s anapests and dactyls were being used just as often.

At the end of the 19th and the beginning of the 20th century a more fundamental modification in Russian verse practice took place. Many of the symbolists and their successors in Russian poetry experimented freely with the new verse forms. As a result, various types of "nonclassical" Russian poetry came into regular use for the first time: dol'niki, strict accentual verse (also called the taktovik), loose accentual verse, and free verse. In all, about one-fifth of the poetry written during the first three decades of the 20th century was in some kind of nonclassical verse. Individual poets came to show a great variety in their verse practice: some continued to write primarily the classical verse of the 19th century, while those who were interested in the new verse forms differed widely in the extent and kinds of nonclassical poetry that they wrote. Among the first to compose large numbers of nonclassical poems were BRYUSOV, HIPPIUS, and BLOK. Soon dol'niki became a common meter in the poetry of GUMILYOV, AKHMATOVA, KUZMIN, TSVETAEVA, ASEEV, ESENIN, and others. MAYAKOVSKY and KHLEBNIKOV, along with other futurist and some imaginist poets, developed a tradition of accentual verse. Free verse never became widespread, but Blok, Kuzmin, and Khlebnikov all turned to it upon occasion.

From the 1930s through the 1950s nonclassical poetry, with the exception of dol'niki, virtually disappeared. Only toward the end of the 1950s were some of the forms used during the first third of the century resurrected. Today nonclassical verse has recovered much of its popularity and will probably remain a strong factor in Russian poetry. The *dol'nik* continues to be the most widely used nonclassical meter and has long since become a fully established meter in its own right. Some changes have also taken place in the distribution of the classical meters. Among both iambs and trochees, the pentameter line has gained popularity at the expense of the tetrameter. During the past thirty years or so the iambic pentameter has been used about as often as the iambic tetrameter. The trochaic pentameter, which was virtually unknown before the 1830s, is now seen far more frequently than the trochaic tetrameter, which was once the mainstay for all trochaic verse. Meanwhile, among the ternary meters, poets have come to show a clear preference for anapests and amphibrachs; dactyls now account for only about 10 percent or less of all ternary verse.

By no means has every poet shown an equal interest in the nonclassical meters. Even during the 1960s some individuals—such as Tvardovsky, Kazakova, and Mezhirov—used the classical binary and ternary meters as often as the typical poet from the beginning of the 19th century. Conversely, others—including Voznesensky, Rozhdestvensky, Slutsky, Soloukhin, and Okudzhava—have shown a strong propensity for the newer verse forms. For example, Voznesensky's favorite verse form has been the three-stress *dol'nik*, followed by the iambic tetrameter. He often likes to mix various meters in different sections of his poems, thereby creating polymetrical compositions. In all, various types of nonclassical verse, primarily *dol'niki*, account for about 30 percent of his poetry.

Thus the history of Russian versification is a record of constant change. The earlier developments, when the Russian poetic tradition was not yet well established, tended to be revolutionary: the rapid establishment of syllabic poetry, the annihilation of the syllabic system by syllabotonic versification. Since then innovations have been less drastic: the increased use of trochaic and ternary meters alongside iambic, the introduction of new forms at the beginning of the 20th century and their eventual acceptance alongside the continued use of syllabotonic meters. Indeed, the main trait since the 18th century has been the broadening of the metrical repertoire as new forms join rather than replace the old.

Bibliography: Folk poetry: James Bailey, "The Metrical Typology of Russian Narrative Folk Meters." In *American Contributions to the 8th Intl. Congress of Slavists*, 1. (1978). Pp. 82–103. M. L. Gasparov, "Russkii narodnyi stikh v literaturnykh imitatsiyakh," *IJSLP* 19 (1975), pp. 77–107. Roman Jakobson, "Studies in Comparative Slavic Metrics," *OSP* 3 (1952), pp. 21–66. M. P. Shtokmar, *Issledovaniya v oblasti russkogo narodnogo stikhoslozheniya.* 1952.

Old Russian Literature: Roman Jakobson, "The Slavic Response to Byzantine Poetry." In *Actes du XIIe Congrès international d'Etudes byzantines.* 1963. Pp. 249–67. A. M. Panchenko, *Russkaya stikhotvornaya kul'tura XVII veka.* 1973. Kiril Taranovsky, "Formy obshcheslavyanskogo i tserkovnoslavyanskogo stikha v drevnerusskoi literature XI–XIII vv." In *American Contributions to the 6th International Congress of Slavists.* Vol. 1. 1968. Pp. 377–94.

18th Century: C. L. Drage, "The Introduction of Russian Syllabo-Tonic Prosody," *SEER* 54 (1976), pp. 481–503. M. L. Gasparov, "Russkii sillabicheskii trinadtsatislozhnik." In *Metryka słowiańska.* Wrocław, 1971. Pp. 39–63. Rimvydas Silbajoris, *Russian Versification: The Theories of Trediakovskij, Lomonosov, and Kantemir.* 1968. G. S. Smith, "The Reform of Russian Versification: What More is There to Say?" *Study Group on Eighteenth-Century Russia: Newsletter* 5 (1977), pp. 39–44.

Modern Poetry and general studies: James Bailey, "The Verse of Andrej Voznesenskij as an Example of Present-Day Russian Versification," *SEEJ* 17 (1973), pp. 155–73. M. L. Gasparov, *Sovremennyi russkii stikh: Metrika i ritmika.* 1974. V. E. Kholshevnikov, *Osnovy stikhovedeniya: Russkoe stikhoslozhenie.* 1972. P. A. Rudnev, "Iz istorii metricheskogo repertuara russkikh poetov XIX–nachala XX v." In *Teoriya stikha.* 1968. Pp. 107–44. Kiril Taranovsky, *Ruski dvodelni ritmovi.* I–II. Belgrade, 1953. B. V. Tomashevskii, *Stilistika i stikhoslozhenie: Kurs lektsii.* 1959. K. D. Vishnevskii, "Russkaya metrika XVIII veka," *Uchenye zapiski Penzenskogo gosudarstvennogo pedagogicheskogo instituta,* no. 123 (1972), pp. 129–258.
                                                                B. S.

Vertép, see Puppet theater.

Vertinsky, Aleksándr Nikoláevich (1889–1957), poet, singer, variety actor, composer and memoirist, became an almost instant celebrity in 1915 when he started his performances on the stage of small theaters and variety theaters. Writing both the text and the music of his songs, he displayed extraordinary ingenuity in his performance, combining the most intimate vocal intonation with an eccentric plasticity of gesture. Very soon Vertinsky was recognized as master of the genre which was in fact his own creation—a kind of psychological novelette in verse and music to be performed through echoing the dying traditions of minstrels and jesters, carnival and commedia dell'arte. Despite the pretended decadence of the style and contents, Vertinsky's art stands very far from the vulgarized world of the trivial cabaret and has much more in common with the artistic search of expressionists like Meierkhold, or with the refined experiments produced in the same direction in the Weimar Republic. Vertinsky's tragicomic persona, in a bizarre way resembling that of Charlie Chaplin, was poignantly moving and cast an enormous spell over his audience. During his emigration period (1919–43) he was constantly on tour giving concerts in different European countries and his profoundly nostalgic art enjoyed invariable success. His poetry, set to music, frequently deals with ironic trivia, reminiscent of the amusing artificialities of the beau monde or the demi-monde; in a certain sense, I. Severyanin can be seen as his predecessor. But Vertinsky has a very different key—much more intimate and totally devoid of rhetoric. A certain correspondence with the work of Agnivtsev may be noticed here. But, in his best achievements, Vertinsky markedly surpasses this playful level; the game becomes serious and the status of an émigré, replete with miseries, acquires the dimension of tragedy: "Here only the alien cities have noise, and only the alien water is splashing and the alien star is shining in the sky." It was perhaps his inextricable Russianness that became the driving force behind Vertinsky's decision for repatriation in 1943. He was honored in the Soviet Union and even played parts in several films.

Works: "Chetvert' veka bez rodiny," *Moskva*, 1962, nos. 3–6. *Pesni i stikhi (1916–1937).* 1976. *12 pesen Vertinskogo.* 1980. *Zapiski russkogo p'ero.* 1982.
                                                                V. B.

Veselóvsky, Aleksándr Nikoláevich (1838–1906), scholar. A graduate of Moscow University (1858), Veselovsky became a professor of St. Petersburg University in 1872 and an Academician in 1880. He initially specialized in Romance philology, the Italian Renaissance in particular, but soon branched out into comparative study of literature, folklore, and Russian literature. His doctoral dissertation, "From the History of Literary Relations between East and West: Slavic Legends about Solomon and Kitovras and Western Legends about Morolf and Merlin" (1872), was indicative of the direction his research would take during the following decades. Veselovsky soon became the leading representative of the historical-comparative school of folkloristics in Russia, producing several studies about the historical background of Russian byliny. Veselovsky's historical-comparative studies eventually led him to the pre-Christian and pre-historical core of folklore and even literature, and he became an early exponent of an anthropological approach to these subjects, as in his "Investigations in the Area of Russian Spiritual Verses" (Razyskaniya v oblasti russkikh dukhovnykh stikhov, 1880–91). Veselovsky also published a number of theoretical essays on methodology, poetics, and aesthetics, such as "History or Theory of the Novel?" (Istoriya ili teoriya romana, 1886), "From an Introduction to Historical Poetics" (Iz vvedeniya v istoricheskuyu poetiku, 1894), and "Psychological Parallelism and its Forms in Reflexions of Poetic Style" (Psikhologicheskii parallelizm i ego formy v otrazheniyakh poeticheskogo stilya, 1898). Veselovsky created a new, essentially positivist approach to the study of literature and folklore, doing away with the Schellingian or Hegelian schemes of his predecessors. He was a great scholar whose works have lost none of their importance even today.

Works: Sobranie sochinenii. Vols. 1–6, 8, 16. 1908–38 (incomplete). *Izbrannye stat'i.* Introd. essay V. M. Zhirmunskii, comm. M. P. Alekseev. 1939. *Istoricheskaya poetika.* Introd. and notes V. Zhirmunskii. 1940.

Secondary literature: V. E. Gusev, "A. N. Veselovskii i problemy fol'kloristiki," *IAN* 16 (1957), no. 2. *Materialy dlya biograficheskogo slovarya deistvitel'nykh chlenov imp. Akademii Nauk.* Pt. 1. 1915. (With a bibliography of Veselovsky's works.)

V. T.

Véstnik Evrópy. Two distinct journals appeared under this title, the first between 1802 and 1830 and the later one from 1866 to 1918. The earlier *Vestnik Evropy* (Herald of Europe) was a biweekly literary journal, the most distinguished journal of the early 19th century, a champion of early romantic trends until 1820 and thereafter a bastion of anti-romantic criticism. Founded by N. M. KARAMZIN, edited by P. P. Sumarokov (1804), M. T. Kachenovsky (1805–07, 1811–13, 1815–30), V. A. ZHUKOVSKY (1808–11), and V. V. Izmailov (1814), but usually in fact by Kachenovsky, *Vestnik Evropy* oversaw the transition from SENTIMENTALISM to ROMANTICISM by publishing the poetry of "the new, the modern" and, later, "the so-called romantic school." Zhukovsky's translations of German and English ballads, the romantic elegies of the "sentimental-elegiac" poets Zhukovsky, K. N. BATYUSHKOV, and V. L. PUSHKIN, and criticism on behalf of new forms, styles, and language made the journal a showcase for innovation in the early years. A. S. PUSHKIN first appeared in *Vestnik Evropy* in 1814. In 1820 *Vestnik Evropy* took a sudden conservative turn with attacks on Pushkin's "Ruslan and Lyudmila." In the early 1820s it systematically criticized each of Pushkin's romantic verse tales, resisted the rise of BYRONISM, and challenged virtually every romantic innovation without ever taking a marked neoclassical position. It ceased to be a credible influence by 1825.

The new *Vestnik Evropy,* a liberal monthly journal, was founded by Professor M. M. STASYULEVICH and was devoted to history, politics, and literature in evenly divided departments. It published leading works by A. N. OSTROVSKY, I. A. GONCHAROV, and I. S. TURGENEV, as well as important works by the liberal scholars A. N. VESELOVSKY, P. N. Ovsyaniko-Kulikovsky, and A. N. PYPIN.

Bibliography: Ukazatel' k "Vestniku Evropy." Moscow, 1861.

L. G. L.

Vesý (The Scales). The leading literary journal of the SYMBOLIST movement, published in Moscow between 1904 and 1909 by the art patron S. A. Polyakov, who was also its nominal editor, *Vesy* was in fact edited by Valery BRYUSOV, whose major statement of doctrine, "The Keys of Mysteries" (Klyuchi tain), opened the first issue. *Vesy* reported on contemporary developments in art and literature in Western Europe and had regular foreign correspondents, such as René Ghil in Paris. *Vesy* was founded as a journal for criticism and information, but from 1906 on it featured creative prose and poetry as well. It included the work of all the major Russian symbolists, BLOK, BELY, SOLOGUB, Zinaida HIPPIUS, BALMONT, and Vyacheslav IVANOV, as well as writers close to symbolism such as Maksimilian VOLOSHIN and Mikhail KUZMIN also appeared. It also printed reproductions of art works by contemporary foreign and Russian artists. It was luxuriously designed and illustrated, often by artists of the MIR ISKUSSTVA (World of Art) group. Eventually it served as a vehicle of doctrinal disputes among those symbolists who wished to make of symbolism a religious or cultural movement, such as Bely and Ivanov, and those who saw in symbolism only an artistic movement. Bryusov, although a champion of the latter view, opened the door to controversies among all the more radical factions of symbolism. *Vesy* served the symbolist movement during its most productive years.

Bibliography: Andrei Belyi, *Nachalo veka.* 1933. Georgii Chulkov, "Vesy." In *Gody stranstvii.* 1930. Pp. 192–97. Nikolai Gumilev, "Poeziya v 'Vesakh'," *Apollon,* 1910, no. 9, pp. 35–41. K. Mochul'skii, *Valerii Bryusov.* Paris, 1962. Martin P. Rice, *Valery Briusov and the Rise of Russian Symbolism.* 1975.

E. Br.

Vesyóly, Artyóm (pseud., real name: Nikolai Ivánovich Kochkuróv, 1899–1939), playwright and writer. Of working class background and with only an elementary school education, Vesyoly joined the Communist Party even before the October Revolution and served in the Red Army all through the civil war. A political activist and member of the Cheka (political police), he contributed to the Bol-

shevik press since 1917. After the civil war, Vesyoly continued his education and turned professional writer, joining the PEREVAL group, and later RAPP. The style of his plays, *Jewelweed* (Razryv-trava, 1919) and *We* (My, 1921), and his stories, such as "Rivers of Fire" (Reki ognennye, 1924) and "My Native Land" (Strana rodnaya, 1926), resembles that of Boris PILNYAK in its ample use of verbal ornamentation, *skaz,* slang, and dialect expressions. Their plots express the chaotic, elemental aspect of the Revolution, sometimes in a manner resembling MAYAKOVSKY and KHLEBNIKOV. The revolutionized masses are their heroes. Vesyoly's main works are *Russia Drenched in Blood* (Rossiya, krov'yu umytaya, 1929–32), a novel about the Revolution and civil war, and *Have a Spree, Volga!* (Gulyai, Volga! 1932), a historical novel about the conquest of Siberia by the Cossack Ermak. Vesyoly was arrested in 1937 and disappeared from Russian literature until his posthumous rehabilitation in 1956.

Works: Izbrannye proizvedeniya. Introd. M. Charnyi. 1958.

Translations: (Excerpts from *Russia Drenched in Blood:*) *Bonfire, Stories out of Soviet Russia.* Ed. Sergei Konovalov. London, 1932.

Secondary literature: M. Charnyi, *Artem Veselyi.* 1960. V. Skobelev, *Artem Veselyi: Ocherk zhizni i tvorchestva.* 1974. O. V. Stekol'shchikov, "K istorii sozdaniya romana Artema Veselogo *Rossiya, krov'yu umytaya,*" *Filologicheskie nauki* 10 (1967), no. 2, pp. 25–36.

V. T.

Vígdorova, Frída Abrámovna (1915–65), short-story writer, novelist, and educator. Born into a family of teachers, Vigdorova completed the course at Moscow Pedagogical Institute herself and went on to teach secondary school. Her first novel, *The Daring Twelve* (Dvenadtsat' otvazhnykh, 1948), is the story of young "pioneers" (members of the Soviet youth organization) struggling against the oppression of Hitler's occupation. Vigdorova's works are all dominated by a single theme: the importance of pedagogy and the power of well-trained young minds. Vigdorova boldly spoke up for allowing children to see things their way and encouraging them to develop into thinking individuals, as in her essay "Empty Eyes and Magic Eyes" (Glaza pustye i glaza volshebnye) in the celebrated miscellany *Pages from Tarusa* (Tarusskie stranitsy, 1961). Much translated in the Eastern bloc languages, her works enjoy little popularity in the West.

Works: Doroga v zhizn', Povesti. 1957. *Semeinoe schast'e,* Povesti. 1965.

Translations: Diary of a Russian Schoolteacher. Trans. Rose Prokofieva. New York, 1960. "Empty Eyes and Magic Eyes." In *Pages from Tarusa.* Ed. Andrew Field. 1963. Pp. 301–09. "A Question of Ethics." Trans. Friederike F. Snyder, *RLT* 5 (1973), pp. 406–13.

Secondary literature: N. Pleshcheev, "Novaya povest' F. Vigdorovoi," *Narodnoe obrazovanie,* 1960, no. 2. N. Podorol'skii, "Povesti F. Vigdorovoi," *Narodnoe obrazovanie,* 1958, no. 3. N. Vengrov, "Uvlekatel'naya professiya," *Novyi mir,* 1950, no. 5.

C. T.

Vinográdov, Víktor Vladímirovich (1895–1969); Professor of Russian at Moscow University, academician, leading student of Contemporary Standard Russian, of the history of the Russian literary language, of Russian stylistics and poetics.

As a disciple of Shakhmatov and Shcherba, Vinogradov began his scholarly career with a study on the phonology of a Northern Russian dialect, but devoted most of his scholarly output to the semantic and stylistic aspects of the literary language, to its historical formation and to the language of writers. His basic ideas on the structure of Russian are contained in his *The Russian Language* (Russkii yazyk: Grammaticheskoe uchenie o slove, 1947) which analyzes all parts of speech and the function of Russian grammatical categories. Of particular interest in the book are Vinogradov's remarks on the history of the Russian linguistic tradition. The history of this tradition received special treatment in a number of Vinogradov's later studies, especially in his *From the History of the Study of Russian Syntax* (Iz istorii izucheniya russkogo sintaksisa, 1958). Vinogradov contributed a series of articles to the *Defining Dictionary of the Russian Language* (edited by Ushakov), and he considerably advanced the study of Russian vocabulary and phraseology by distinguishing the various stylistic layers of the lexicon and types of phraseological units. His *Outline of a History of the Modern Russian Literary Language* (*Ocherki po istorii russkogo literaturnogo yazyka XVII–XIX vv.*; 1938²) is the most thorough study of this subject and a turning point in the study of the Slavic literary languages. In the late twenties Vinogradov participated in formulating the "formal" method in the study of literature, but he soon departed from this approach by emphasizing the role of social and cultural contexts of literary works and the individuality of their authors. His method is best exemplified in the studies of such outstanding authors as PUSHKIN (1935; 1941), GOGOL (1925; 1926), DOSTOEVSKY (1929), AVVAKUM, and AKHMATOVA. In his late works he developed a theory of stylistics as a system of interacting linguistic conventions and literary genres. Through his work and scholarly standing Vinogradov contributed in the fifties to the suppression of Marrism and the acceptance of structuralism in Soviet linguistics.

Works in English: The History of the Russian Literary Language from the Seventeenth Century to the Nineteenth: A Condensed Adaptation into English. Introd. Lawrence L. Thomas. 1969.

Secondary literature: "Akademik Viktor Vladimirovich Vinogradov" (obituary), *Voprosy yazykoznaniya,* 1970, no. 1, pp. 3–18. M. G. Bulakhov, *Vostochnoslavyanskie yazykovedy.* Vol. 2. 1977. Pp. 89–122. N. I. Konrad, "O rabotakh V. V. Vinogradova po voprosam stilistiki, poetiki i teorii poeticheskoi rechi." In *Problemy sovremennoi filologii,* pp. 400–12.

E. S.

Vinokúr, Grigóry Ósipovich (1896–1947), linguist, textologist, historian of Russian literature and of the Russian literary language. Born in Warsaw, Vinokur graduated from Moscow University, was a member of the Moscow Linguistic Circle together with R. O. JAKOBSON and N. S. TRUBETZKOI, and became a professor of Moscow University in 1942. He was one of the best Soviet textologists and one of the main authorities on the history of the Russian literary language and historical stylistics. His contributions to textology were both theoretical and practical. In his book *Critique of the Poetic Text* (*Kritika poeticheskogo teksta,* 1927), Vinokur gave a highly original discussion of the problems and rules of textological reconstruction. In the 1930s, he became one of the main participants in the preparation of the Academy edition of PUSHKIN's *Collected Works* and prepared several volumes himself. *A Dictionary of Pushkin's Language* (*Slovar' yazyka Pushkina,* 1956–1961), an important landmark in Pushkin studies, was prepared under Vinokur's guidance, beginning in 1938. An accumulation of Vinokur's ideas on the history of the Russian language may be found in his book, *The Russian Language: A Historical Sketch* (*Russkii yazyk: Istoricheskii ocherk,* 1945, translated into French and German). Vinokur can be credited with pioneering studies of Russian FUTURISM (MAYAKOVSKY, KHLEBNIKOV).

Bibliography: R. M. Tseitlin, *Grigorii Osipovich Vinokur (1896–1947).* 1965. (Bibliography of Vinokur's works, pp. 85–92) G. O. Vinokur, *Izbrannye raboty po russkomu yazyku.* 1959.

E. B.

Vinokúrov, Evgény Mikhaílovich (1925–), poet, was born in Bryansk, a soldier's son. After completing the ninth grade, he entered artillery officers' school; at seventeen he was in command of an artillery unit. His first volume, *Verses on Duty* (*Stikhi o dolge*), appeared in 1951, the same year he graduated from the Gorky Literary Institute, where he has taught since the mid-sixties. In 1956, two more volumes appeared: *War Lyrics* (*Voennaya lirika*) and *Sky Blue* (*Sineva*), the latter praised by PASTERNAK for its originality. The late fifties and the sixties were a most prolific period for Vinokurov. Of the twelve books which appeared in as many years, among the most significant were *Admissions* (*Priznaniya,* 1958), *A Human Face* (*Litso chelovecheskoe,* 1960), *Word* (*Slovo,* 1962), *Music* (*Muzyka,* 1964), *Characters* (*Kharaktery,* 1964), *The Bounds of the Earth* (*Zemnye predely,* 1965), and *Gesture* (*Zhest,* 1969). His collected essays, *Poetry and Thought* (*Poeziya i mysl'*), appeared in 1966. His works of the seventies—*Metaphors* (*Metafory,* 1972), *Per Force of Things* (*V silu veshchei,* 1973), *Contrasts* (*Kontrasty,* 1975), *Space* (*Prostranstvo,* 1976), *Home and World* (*Dom i mir,* 1977), *She* (*Ona,* 1977), *The Lot* (*Zhrebii,* 1978)—and his most recent work, *Reverence* (*Blagogovenie,* 1981) reflect more careful re-working, are more contemplative, less aphoristic. A mas-

ter of the poetic sketch, Vinokurov has broadened his range of subject matter, but preserved his love of concrete details and interest in apparently simple truths, which, upon reflection, gain in significance and complexity. His collected essays, *Remains in Force* (*Ostaetsya v sile*), appeared in 1979. Vinokurov shows little interest in formal experimentation. With his keen ear for spoken Russian, he often relates autobiographical episodes in a subdued, reflective tone: "pencil sketches," as one critic has described them.

Works: Izbrannye proizvedeniya. 2 vols. 1976.

Translations: Selected Poems. Trans. Alex Miller. Moscow, 1979. (Bilingual text.) *The War Is Over.* Trans. and ed. Anthony Rudolf and Daniel Weissbort. Cheadle Hume, Cheshire, 1976.

Secondary literature: Pierre Forgues, "The Young Poets," *Survey,* no. 46 (1963), pp. 31–52.

N. C.

Vishnévsky, Vsévolod Vitálievich (1900–51), prose writer and dramatist, born in St. Petersburg. He volunteered for the front in 1914, participated in the October Uprising in Petrograd, fought in the Red Cavalry and became a political worker in the Baltic and Black Sea fleets. Vishnevsky began publishing in 1920, was editor of *Krasnoflotets,* a war correspondent during the Finnish war, participated in the defense of Leningrad in 1941 and 1942, and in 1944 became editor of *Znamya.* A member of the Communist Party, he received the 1950 Stalin Prize for his hagiography of Stalin, *The Unforgettable Year, 1919.*

Though he also wrote short stories and novels, Vishnevsky is known primarily for his plays, most of which deal with the Revolution and civil war. His initial play, *First Cavalry* (1929), still part of the repertoire in Soviet Theaters, depicts the Cossacks as active and enthusiastic supporters of the Bolshevik cause. Vishnevsky's classic of Soviet theater, *Optimistic Tragedy* (1933), portrays a group of Communists, led by a female commissar, struggling to transform an anarchistic group of seamen into a disciplined division of the Red Army. He utilized a number of innovative theatrical devices, among them a chorus and a narrator who comment on the action. Generally, his plays are mass spectaculars with impressive crowds on stage.

Vishnevsky was an innovative writer who sacrificed his talent serving Party and State. He will be remembered in the history of Russian literature as a falsifier of historical fact and as an official writer whose works are blatantly tendentious, propagandistic, and represent archetypal models of socialist realism.

Works: Sobranie sochinenii. 5 vols. 1954–60. *Izbrannoe.* 1966. "Avtobiografiya," *Sovetskie pisateli,* vol. 1 (1959). *Dnevniki voennykh let: 1943, 1945.* 1974, 1979.

Translations: Dialogue on "We are from Kronstadt." n.p., n.d. *An Optimistic Tragedy.* New York, 1937.

Secondary literature: O. K. Borodina, *Vsevolod Vishnevskii (Ocherk zhizni i tvorchestva).* 1958. K. Rudnitskii, *Portrety dramaturgov.* 1961. M. Slonim, *Soviet Russian Literature: Writers and Problems 1917–1977.* 1977. Pp. 284–85.

H. S.

Vladímir Vsevolódovich Monomákh (1053–1125), Grand Prince of Kiev (1113–25), author of an *Instruction* (*Pouchenie*), addressed to his children. The *Instruction,* written around 1117, has been preserved as a section of the Lavrentievsky codex of the Primary Chronicle (see LETOPISI). The *Instruction,* an established genre of Byzantine literature (it is represented in the IZBORNIK SVYATOSLAVA of 1076), bears here an autobiographic and personal nature, as it creates a vivid picture of the concerns and labors of an active and capable ruler, tireless warrior, and mighty hunter.

Works: Khudozhestvennaya proza Kievskoi Rusi XI–XIII vv. Comp. and comm. by I. P. Eremin and D. S. Likhachev. 1957. (Excerpts:) A. D. Stokes, *Khrestomatiya po drevnei russkoi literature.* 1963. Pp. 39–44.

Secondary literature: A. S. Orlov, *Vladimir Monomakh.* 1946.

V. T.

Vladímov (real name: Volosévich), Geórgy Nikoláevich (1931–), writer and critic, took a law degree in Leningrad, but then turned to literary criticism, and published his first short novel, *The Great Ore* (*Bol'shaya ruda*) in 1961. A "production novel," it nevertheless has some ironies and possibly an allegoric message which are unflattering to the Soviet effort: the hero, a shock worker, ruins much of what he does by his own rashness and is killed in an accident as he raises the first load of ore from a new mine. In 1967 Vladimov addressed an open letter to the Fourth Congress of the Union of Soviet Writers, demanding that the Congress take up SOLZHENITSYN's letter on censorship and stressing the need for free discussion. Vladimov's manuscript, *Faithful Ruslan* (Vernyi Ruslan, written 1963–65), appeared first in SAMIZDAT, then in GRANI, no. 9 (1975). *Faithful Ruslan* is an allegory of Soviet society. Its hero is a good, honest, hard-working dog, intelligent enough to become an efficient Gulag guard dog, but incapable of understanding who or what he is working for. When the Gulag he works at is closed, his world collapses. *Faithful Ruslan* contains a wealth of sharp observations on various types of Soviet man. Ruslan's canine traits, though not as skillfully developed as the equine traits of Tolstoi's "Yardstick," or the feline of Hoffmann's "Murr the Cat," are also in evidence throughout. Vladimov's short novel *Three Minutes of Silence* (Tri minuty molchaniya, 1969), set on a Soviet fishing trawler, is a tightly structured study of man under extreme stress.

Works: Bol'shaya ruda. 1962, 1971. *Tri minuty molchaniya, Novyi mir,* 1969, nos. 7–9. *Vernyi Ruslan.* Frankfurt, 1975.

Secondary literature: Vladimir Chernyavskii, "Gibel' geroev," *Grani,* no. 106 (1977), pp. 204–28. Geoffrey Hosking, *Beyond Socialist Realism: Soviet Fiction since Ivan Denisovich.* 1980. Pp. 154–61. A. A. Kots, "Khudozhestvennoe svoeobrazie prozy G. Vladimova," *Uchenye zapiski Permskogo universiteta,* no. 241 (1970). A. Terts, "Lyudi i zveri," *Kontinent,* no. 5 (1975). V. T.

Voeikov, Aleksándr Fyódorovich (1779–1839), poet, critic, and journalist, was a professor of Dorpat (now Tartu) University (1814–20), co-editor (with N. I. GRECH) of *Syn otechestva* (1821–22), *Russkii invalid* (1822–38), *Novosti literatury* (1822–26), *Slavyanin* (1827–30), and *Literaturnye pribavleniya k Russkomu invalidu* (1831–39), and a member of the Russian Academy, the Amicable Literary Society, and Arzamas.

Voeikov was educated at the Moscow University boarding school (1791–96), where he made friends with the Turgenev brothers and with ZHUKOVSKY. In 1814 he married Zhukovsky's niece, Aleksandra Protasova (celebrated by the latter under the name of Svetlana). As a result of this marriage Voeikov could enter the circle of the best writers of his age: Zhukovsky, BATYUSHKOV, KRYLOV, BARATYNSKY, etc. Voeikov's literary friends often overestimated his poetic gifts.

Voeikov wrote many epistles in verse, translated Delille's descriptive poem *Les Jardins* (1782) under the title "Gardens, or the Art to Decorate Rural Views" (Sady, ili iskusstvo ukrashat' sel'skie vidy, 1816), translated Vergil, and wrote a didactic poem in four cantos, entitled "The Arts and Sciences" (Iskusstva i nauki). Voeikov's best work is his satire in verse "The Madhouse" (Dom sumasshedshikh), in which Russian littérateurs from SHISHKOV, Batyushkov, KHVOSTOV, SHALIKOV, etc., to BELINSKY and POLEVOI are made fun of in witty rimes. Voeikov was writing this satire during the course of almost his entire literary career, from 1814 till 1839 (at least four redactions are extant), eliminating antiquated pieces and replacing them with new ones. The satire was never published in Voeikov's lifetime, but circulated in numerous copies.

Works: [Poems:] *Poety satiriki kontsa 18–nachala 19 veka.* (Biblioteka poeta. Bol'shaya seriya.) Leningrad, 1959. Pp. 295–320. (With a biographic note by G. V. Ermakova-Bitner.) *Poety 1790–1810-kh godov.* (Biblioteka poeta. Bol'shaya seriya.) Leningrad, 1971. Pp. 259–302. (With a biographic note by E. N. Dryzhakova and Yu. M. Lotman.)

Secondary literature: N. I. Grech, *Zapiski o moei zhizni.* Moscow and Leningrad, 1930. Yu. M. Lotman, "Satira Voeikova 'Dom sumasshedshikh'." In *Trudy po russkoi i slavyanskoi filologii,* vol. 21. *Uchenye zapiski Tartuskogo gosudarstvennogo universiteta,* fasc. 306. Tartu, 1973. Pp. 3–45. N. V. Solov'ev. *Istoriya odnoi zhizni: A. A. Voeikova—"Svetlana."* 2 vols. Petrograd, 1915–16.

M. A.

Voinóvich, Vladímir Nikoláevich (1932–), writer, was born in Stalinabad (now Dushanbe) in Tadzhikistan, Soviet Central Asia. His father, of Serbian origin, was a journalist and translator of Serbian

literature. His mother, a school teacher, was Jewish. Voinovich had five years of schooling. He worked on a collective farm, on construction projects, and in a factory. From 1951 to 1955 he served as a private in the Red Army. Having published some verse he applied for admission to the Gorky Institute of World Literature and was rejected. Voinovich then worked as a carpenter and taught evening classes in Kazakhstan. In 1960 he obtained a job with Moscow Radio, and became famous as the author of the unofficial anthem of the Soviet cosmonauts. His first short story "We Live Here," published in 1961 in NOVYI MIR, won critical acclaim. It was a realistic account of young people on a collective farm. By 1973 Voinovich had published five other stories and a historical novel about the revolutionary Vera Figner. The story "I Want to Be Honest" aroused much controversy for its depiction of cynical builders of an apartment house. However, Voinovich got into serious trouble with the authorities only when he protested against the trials of SINYAVSKY and DANIEL in 1966 to 1968, and against the expulsion of SOLZHENITSYN from the Writers' Union. (He described Solzhenitsyn as "the greatest of our citizens.") On 21 February 1974 Voinovich was himself expelled from the Writers' Union and could no longer publish in the Soviet Union. In "An Incident at the Metropole" (Proisshestvie v "Metropole", 1975), he charged that the KGB had tried to poison him in 1975. Voinovich's major work, the satirical novel *The Life and Extraordinary Adventures of Private Ivan Chonkin,* written between 1963 and 1970 and enjoying a lively circulation in SAMIZDAT, had to be published abroad. In *The Ivankiad,* published in the United States in Russian in 1976, he recounted his difficulties in getting an apartment in Moscow, and painted an unflattering picture of top bureaucrats. On 21 December 1980 Voinovich and his family were forced to emigrate to West Germany. In 1981 he gave a series of lectures at the Bavarian Academy of Fine Arts in Munich; in 1982–83 he was a visiting fellow and teacher at Princeton University.

Voinovich's main theme is the difficulty of having a personal identity in a state-controlled system whose values are closer to fantasy than to reality. In his big comic epic, through a peasant antihero named Ivan Chonkin, Voinovich deflates the whole Soviet way of life, including the NKVD. The further adventures of Chonkin are related in *Pretender to the Throne.* Voinovich's extraordinary satirical talent and imagination have led some Western critics to acclaim him as a new GOGOL.

Works: "My zdes' zhivem," *Novyi mir,* 1961, no. 1 (January). *Stepen' doveriya (povest' o Vere Figner).* 1973. *Zhizn' i neobychainye priklyucheniya soldata Ivana Chonkina.* Pts. 1 and 2. Paris, 1975. (Pt. 1 was published in *Grani,* no. 72 [1969]). *Ivan'kiada.* Ann Arbor, 1976. *Pretendent na prestol (novye priklyucheniya soldata Ivana Chonkina).* Paris, 1979. "Proisshestvie v 'Metropole'." *Kontinent,* 5 (1975). *Putem vzaimnoi perepiski.* Paris, 1979. (Several short stories and some biting letters to the government.)

Translations: The Ivankiad. Ann Arbor, 1976. *The Life and Extraordinary Adventures of Private Ivan Chonkin.* 1977, 1978. "Incident at the Metropole." 1977, 1978. *In Plain Russian.* 1979. *Pretender to the Throne: The Further Adventures of Private Ivan Chonkin.* 1981.

Secondary literature: Geoffrey Hosking, *Beyond Socialist Realism: Soviet Fiction since Ivan Denisovich.* 1980. Pp. 136–54, 243–46. Edward J. Brown, *Russian Literature Since the Revolution.* 1982. Pp. 365–70.

N. R.

Vólkov, Fyódor Grigórievich (1729–63), actor and creator of leading roles in Aleksandr SUMAROKOV's tragedies, was called by Vissarion BELINSKY "the father of the Russian theater." Volkov used the fortune he inherited from his factory-owner stepfather to found a "public" theater in Yaroslavl, that is, not the private court theater of an aristocrat (1750). In 1756 the troupe was invited to St. Petersburg to perform before the Empress Elizabeth, and then given an auditorium in which to open its Russian Public Theater with Sumarokov as director. The dramatist directed Volkov as hero in his plays, tailoring the verse to suit the actor's passionate temperament and "natural" declamation. Upon Sumarokov's retirement in 1761 Volkov succeeded him as director. Volkov participated in the plot against Peter III. He was given the task of organizing the festivities for the coronation of CATHERINE THE GREAT, during which he caught cold and died.

M. H.

Vol'noe obshchestvo lyubitelei slovesnosti, nauk i khudozhestv, see FREE SOCIETY OF AMATEURS OF LETTERS, SCIENCES, AND ARTS.

Vol'noe obshchestvo lyubitelei rossiiskoi slovesnosti, see FREE SOCIETY OF AMATEURS OF RUSSIAN LETTERS.

Voloshin, Maksimilián Aleksándrovich (1877–1932), a poet, translator, and artist associated with the SYMBOLIST movement but never a member of its inner circles and unlike the symbolists in some aspects of his work. He was born Maksimilian Kirienko-Voloshin in Kiev; after the early death of his father he was reared by his mother in the southern Crimea. He attended the law faculty at Moscow University, was expelled for political activity, spent a half year in central Siberia, and moved to Paris to complete his education. He travelled widely in Mediterranean areas and returned often to Russia. He was a contributor to the symbolist journals VESY and ZOLOTOE RUNO and later to the ACMEIST periodical APOLLON. In 1917 he moved permanently to Koktebel in the Crimea where his house became a refuge for writers and artists of any political persuasion. His pacifist poems deploring the cruelties of World War I and the Revolution have always been his most popular. His most representative books are *Poems* (Stikhotvoreniya, 1910), *Iverni* (1918), and *Poems* (Stikhi, 1922). He was unable to publish in the Soviet Union after 1923, but an exhibit of his aquarelles was shown in 1927. He died at Koktebel.

Voloshin shared some traits, such as his interest in exotic lands, with the Russian symbolists, but the influence of French poetry on his work was probably stronger. He acknowledged the Parnassians, especially José Maria de Hérédia, as his predecessors. Voloshin's poems typically consist in intimate meditations. They are often set in specific Mediterranean areas or in Paris, and concern culture or art. Although personal in tone, they display broad historical and philosophical perspectives, and have been criticized as overly detached. He called himself a "neo-realist," which may be the best label for him; it shows not only his distance from the symbolists, who disdained mere realism, but also his closeness to the Parnassians, including Leconte de Lisle and Sully-Prudhomme, and their Russian heirs, the Acmeists.

Voloshin's early poems are often set in Paris, where he pictures the Tuileries, for example, and elsewhere abroad. A cycle describing the stained glass windows in the cathedral at Rouen ("Ruanskii sobor") was considered the epitome not only of his dispassionateness, but also of his ornate style. Many of the later poems are set in Russia, and of those, most in the Koktebel environs, which he habitually describes as a craggy wilderness. In the cycle "Cimmerian Dusks" (Kimmeriiskie sumerki) he first pictured its cliffs, meager soil, small flowers, and nearby sea. Other poems are set in St. Petersburg, Moscow, and elsewhere. Throughout his work he frequently alluded to mythological, and sometimes Biblical, events, a device that made his subjects seem larger than life in spite of their modest details. An example is "Odysseus in Cimmeria" (Odissei v Kimmerii).

Voloshin's fundamental subject was, in fact, philosophy, as became increasingly clear with time. He once said of his formative period that the six months he spent in Siberia "with camel caravans" had altered his views of mankind and the universe henceforth. He was pessimistic in that he regarded evil and suffering as inextricable elements both of nature and of the human character. Melancholia pervades his poetry, and his alleged detachment is perhaps more nearly an un-Russian cynicism. These philosophical views place him close to the humanistic pessimism of the Parnassians, who were basically atheistic. For many years it appeared that Voloshin differed from the Russian symbolists in his total lack of mysticism, while he concurred with some despairing attitudes typical of DECADENCE, for example, in his opening line "I am tired of being with people" (Ya byt' ustal sredi lyudei).

But the World War, Revolution and civil war brought to his work a new phase in which he displayed a faith and a cause. He deplored atrocities and brutalities (newly depicted in his poetry) on the part of any political faction whatsoever. He depicted the sufferings of Russia as a nation, invoked its dismal history, and expressed his belief in its Christian essence and mission. *Anno mundi ardentis* (1916) is about the First World War. *Deaf-mute Demons* (Demony glukhonemye, 1919) opens with a cycle, "The Angel of Revenge"

(Angel mshcheniya) in which Russians learn to live in violence; a second section shows the ruthlessness of the French Revolution; it contains a well-known poem, "The Head of Madame de Lamballe" (Golova Madam de Lambal'); the last cycles concern the history and meaning of the nation. Voloshin's pacifism continues in *Poems about Terror* (Stikhi o terrore, 1923).

Masks of Creation (Liki tvorchestva, 1914) contains Voloshin's literary criticism. He was a translator of Emile Verhaeren, Paul Claudel, and other French poets.

Works: Demony glukhonemye. Kharkov, 1919. *Stikhi o terrore*. Berlin, 1923. *Stikhotvoreniya*. Ed. L. A. Evstigneeva. Introd. S. S. Narovchatov. 1977. *Stikhotvoreniya*. 2 vols. Ed. B. A. Filippov, G. P. Struve, and N. A. Struve. Vol. 1. Paris, 1982.

Translations: Lewanski, p. 393. *Modern Russian Poetry*. Ed. Vladimir Markov and Merrill Sparks. 1967. Pp. 498–523. *Russian Poetry: The Modern Period*. Ed. John Glad and Daniel Weissbort. 1978. Pp. 99–100.

Secondary literature: Valerii Bryusov, "M. Voloshin." In *Dalekie i blizkie*. 1912. Pp. 172–73. Ilya Ehrenburg, *People and Life, 1891–1921*. New York, 1962. L. T. Kupriyanov, *Sud'ba poeta (Lichnost' i poeziya Maksimiliana Voloshina)*. Kiev, 1978. Evgenii Lann, *Pisatel'skaya sud'ba Maksimiliana Voloshina*. Moscow, 1927. Marina Tsvetaeva, "Zhivoe o zhivom (Voloshin)." In her *Proza*. New York, 1953. Pp. 135–202. Duffield White, "Vološin's Poems on the Revolution and Civil War," *SEEJ* 19 (1975), pp. 297–309.

E. Br.

Volýnsky, A. (pseud. of Akím Lvóvich Flékser, 1863–1926), literary critic and art historian. In 1889 Volynsky began working for *Severnyi vestnik* where he published his literary criticism and eventually took over the editorship. When the journal was closed in 1898, he turned to scholarship in the area of art and theater, writing articles such as "Leonardo da Vinci" (1900) and editing the memoirs of Richard Wagner (1911). His work on DOSTOEVSKY continued past the closing of *Severnyi vestnik* and culminated in his major study, *The Reign of the Karamazovs* (Tsarstvo Karamazovykh, 1901). Volynsky's study perceives not only the characters but the plot itself as a function of realistic psychology. It contains many perceptive observations, not a few of which anticipate "discoveries" by later critics. Volynsky's was one of the earliest voices in Russian literary criticism to deplore the integration of Russian literature into political life started by BELINSKY, calling it a pernicious sellout of the integrity, freedom, and autonomy of art (see his *Russian Critics*, 1896). After 1917, Volynsky concentrated on the study of dance.

Works: Bor'ba za idealizm: kriticheskie stat'i. 1900. *Tsarstvo Karamazovykh*. 1901. *Russkie kritiki*. 2d ed. 1907. *Dostoevskii*. 2d ed. 1909.

Secondary literature: N. K. Mikhailovskii, "O g. Volynskom i russkom chitatele." *PSS*, 2d ed. Vol. 10. 1913. G. V. Plekhanov, "Sud'by russkoi kritiki: A. L. Volynskii." *Sobranie sochinenii*. Vol. 10. 1925.

C. T.

Voprósy literatúry, see INSTITUT MIROVOI LITERATURY IM. GOR'KOGO.

Vorónsky, Aleksándr Konstantínovich (1884–1943), Marxist editor, literary critic and theorist, came from a family of Tambov priests but joined the Social Democrats (later Bolsheviks) at an early age. His first critical efforts appeared in a Party newspaper in 1911, under the pseudonym of "Nurmin." After the Revolution he was named editor of the newspaper *Rabochii krai* (Workers' Region) in Ivanovo-Voznesensk. In 1921 he was transferred to Moscow and appointed editor of a major new literary journal, KRASNAYA NOV', which was enormously successful and made him one of the most respected and influential men of letters in Russia. Additional activities included founding the *Krug* (Circle) Publishing House, co-editing *Prozhektor* (The Searchlight), a popular journal, and serving as mentor to the PEREVAL literary group. Shifts in the Party's policy toward literature proved his undoing. In 1927 he was dismissed from *Krasnaya nov'* and thereafter lived a precarious existence under suspicion of "Trotskyism" until his final arrest in 1937. Presumably he died in prison. Recently he has been undergoing a "rehabilitation."

As a critic, Voronsky was prolific, covering the entire range of contemporary Soviet literature. He called for large-scale works of high quality, especially novels, which would address the complexities of modern society while responsive to the great 19th-century traditions. He expected writers to be sympathetic to the Revolution but not ideologues, and he doubted that a separate "proletarian" literature could develop. These views made him an advocate of the FELLOW-TRAVELER writers and the target of abuse by other Marxist literary groups, especially OKTYABR'. As a theorist, he drew heavily on PLEKHANOV, but was also interested in the psychology of creativity and perception, and eventually redefined art's purpose, in terms soon deemed un-Marxist, as restoring, through "immediate impressions," a lost harmony with a pristine state of "objective beauty."

Works: Iskusstvo i zhizn'. 1924. *Literaturnye tipy.* 1926. *Iskusstvo videt' mir.* 1928.

Secondary literature: R. A. Maguire, *Red Virgin Soil: Soviet Literature in the 1920's.* 1968.   R. A. M.

Voróvsky, Vatsláv Vatslávovich (1871–1923), revolutionary, Soviet diplomat, publicist, and literary critic, joined the "Workers Union" (*Rabochii soyuz*) in 1894, while a student at Moscow Technical University and went on to live the life of a professional revolutionary. He was imprisoned, exiled, and forced to live abroad for long periods of time. A capable publicist, he wrote for LENIN's ISKRA and for a variety of other periodicals, legal and illegal. About one quarter of his articles were devoted to literature. After the Revolution he served as a diplomat in Scandinavia and Italy. Vorovsky was assassinated by an anti-communist émigré while representing the USSR at an international conference in Lausanne.

Vorovsky, who called himself a *kritik-publitsist*, saw literature as "artistic reflection of life," produced by dialectic interaction of objective economic and political reality, social factors (such as belonging to a class on its way "in" or "out"), subjective traits of the artist's personality, and his creative talent. An orthodox Marxist, Vorovsky criticized BELINSKY and DOBROLYUBOV for their disregard of the historical dimension and of the role of class struggle in literature. But his practical criticism was similar to theirs, being largely a sociological analysis of plots and characters, and a search for social types as catalysts of social change ("Bazarov and Sanin," 1909). He judged contemporary authors, such as Leonid ANDREEV, BUNIN, GORKY, and KUPRIN, essentially by the extent to which he considered them to be in step with the times, i.e., attuned to the revolutionary situation in Russia. He blamed Andreev's failure on that writer's lack of a progressive ideological basis ("Leonid Andreev," 1910), but also faulted Gorky for his iconographic and allegoric development of the heroine of *Mother* ("More about Gorky," 1911), though approving of the novel's political message. While in favor of realist art, Vorovsky was inclined to tolerate "revolutionary romanticism," so long as it was a genuine echo of "an as yet faint voice of new life about to be born" ("Maksim Gorky," 1910). Here as elsewhere Vorovsky uncritically accepted the traditional tenets of organic aesthetics, crediting the artist with an intuitive grasp of the drift of history. Vorovsky believed that modernist art and literature were expressions of the decadence, stagnation, and despair of the bourgeoisie ("On the Bourgeois Nature of Modernism"—O burzhuaznosti modernistov, 1908). Vorovsky, however, insisted that a writer could very well see beyond the scope of his social class—simply because objective reality was there ("Turgenev as a Public Figure"—Turgenev kak obshchestvennyi deyatel', 1908).

Bibliography: Sochineniya. 3 vols. Moscow, 1931–33. *Literaturnaya kritika.* Moscow, 1971. I. S. Chernoutsan, "V. V. Vorovskii," In *Istoriya russkoi kritiki.* Ed. B. P. Gorodetskii et al. Moscow, 1958, vol. 2, pp. 565–93. N. F. Piyashev, *Vorovskii.* Moscow, 1959.   V. T.

Voskresenie (Resurrection, 1917–28), a religious-philosophical circle organized in Petrograd by Aleksandr Meier and Kseniya Polovtseva. Supporters of mystical anarchism in 1905 to 1907, Meier (1875–1939) and Polovtseva (1887–1949) were seeking opportunities to imbue the turbulent revolutionary element of Russian life with spiritual ideas. During the ten years of their activities (ca. 1917–27), Meier and Polovtseva attracted to their circle no fewer than 200 intellectuals who considered the circle to be an expression of individual and social consciousness. As Polovtseva formulated it, they

viewed *Voskresenie* as a "crucible to test the ideology elaborated by the intelligentsia for its capability to accept and fuse religion and communism." The same social sentiments were expressed by the circle's journal *Svobodnye golosa* (Free Voices, Petrograd, 1918, no. 1–2), edited by G. FEDOTOV, and similar emotions are to be found in the memoirs of N. P. Antsyferov, historian and author, who was a member of *Voskresenie* from 1918 to 1922: "We dreamed that ... our restrained conversations would give birth to new ideas, that we were the nucleus of the new Saint-Simonists, successors to Pierre Leroux, Lamennais, and George Sand." The minutes of the meetings held in 1921 and 1922 reveal the circle's strong interest in the societal and communal aspects of Christian and socialist teachings. Although the religious orientation of the circle grew stronger from 1922 to 1927, its participants were in close touch with members of other informal groups of secular nature: the literary scholar Pumpyansky and the artist Maria Yudina participated in a seminar on Kant; the philosopher S. ASKOLDOV lectured before an informal group called the Academy of Cosmic Sciences; and the artist K. Petrov-Vodkin belonged to the Free Philosophical Society. These close contacts with other circles contributed to a free convergence of ideas, and inspired the creativity of members. Among the works written by the participants of *Voskresenie* are N. Antsyferov's *Dostoevsky's Petersburg* (1921) and *Lamennais* (1922), A. Meier's philosophical writings, 1917–24 (repr. in Paris, 1982), some articles by G. Fedotov, later included in his *Profile of Russia* (Paris, 1967), and a book by L. Pumpyansky, *Dostoevsky and Antiquity* (1922).

In 1928 and 1929 most of the participants of *Voskresenie* were arrested. Accused of conspiratorial activities toward restoration ("resurrection", in the GPU's interpretation) of the Tsarist regime, they were sentenced to hard labor in prison camps.

Literature: N. Antsyferov, "Memoirs," *Pamyat'*, 1981, no. 4, pp. 55–152. O. I. Yatsevich, "From Recollections," *Pamyat'*, 1978, no. 1, pp. 93–154. N. P. Antsyferov, "An Episode from Solovki History," *Pamyat'*, 1978, no. 1, pp. 331–36.   N. P.

Vostókov, Aleksándr Khristofórovich (1781–1864), linguist, palaeographer, historian of Slavic literatures. Born in Arensburg (Livonia), the illegitimate son of Baron Ch. von Osten-Saken, he graduated from the Corps of Cadets (Sukhoputnyi Shlyakhetnyi Kadetskii Korpus) and the Academy of Fine Arts in St. Petersburg. Vostokov began as a poet and translator of Slavic songs, and was prized by PUSHKIN, ZHUKOVSKY, and VYAZEMSKY. In 1815 he started to work as an archivist at the Manuscript Division of the Imperial Public Library in St. Petersburg and was also invited by Count N. P. Rumyantsev to catalogue his collection of Russian and Slavic manuscripts (1824–44). As a linguist, palaeographer, and historian, Vostokov made several outstanding contributions to Slavic studies. In 1820 he discovered the Bulgarian origin of Old Slavonic. In 1842 he published his *Description of Russian and Slavonic Manuscripts of the Rumyantsev Museum*, a landmark in Russian and Slavic palaeography. His *Dictionary of Church-Slavonic* (2 vols., 1858–61) and *Grammar of Church-Slavonic* (1863) laid a ground for later studies in Slavic lexicography and linguistics.

Works: Opisanie russkikh i slovenskikh rukopisei Rumyantsevskogo muzeuma. 1842. *Slovar' tserkovno-slavyanskogo yazyka.* 2 vols. 1858–61. *Grammatika tserkovno-slovenskogo yazyka, izlozhennaya po drevneishim onogo pamyatnikam.* 1863. *Perepiska A. Kh. Vostokova v povremennom poryadke.* 1873. *Stikhotvoreniya.* 1935.

Secondary literature: N. Grech, *Pamyati Aleksandra Khristoforovicha Vostokova.* 1864. B. L. Kandel', et al., *Russkaya khudozhestvennaya literatura i literaturovedenie: Ukazatel' spravochno-bibliograficheskikh posobii s kontsa XVIII veka po 1974 god.* 1976. P. 157. *Slavyanovedenie v dorevolyutsionnoi Rossii: Biobibliograficheskii slovar'.* 1979. I. I. Sreznevskii, "Obozrenie nauchnykh trudov A. Kh. Vostokova." In A. Kh. Vostokov, *Filologicheskie nablyudeniya.* 1865. V. I. Sreznevskii, "Zametki A. Kh. Vostokova o ego zhizni." In *Sbornik ORIAS*, 1902, no. 6, pp. 1–114.   E. B.

Vovchók, Markó (1834–1907), pseudonym of Maria Vilinska who later married O. Markovych, a Ukrainian ethnographer, exiled for his participation in the Brotherhood of Sts. Cyril and Methodius. She was born into a russified Polish gentry family in Orel province.

After her marriage she lived in the Ukraine and shared her husband's interest in Ukrainian folklore. Her collection of short stories *Folk Tales* (Narodni opovidannja) was published in 1857 by P. KULISH. They were warmly received by Ukrainians, above all by SHEVCHENKO, and in 1859 were translated into Russian by I. TURGENEV as *Ukrainian Folk Tales* (Ukrainskie narodnye rasskazy). These stories depart from romantic models and are regarded as the first realistic prose pieces in the Ukraine. Later some doubts were cast on their authorship (some people refused to believe that she could write so well in Ukrainian) but were eventually dispelled. Marko Vovchok continued to write in Ukrainian but at the same time began to write in Russian. The liberal and radical Russian intellectuals (HERZEN, DOBROLYUBOV, CHERNYSHEVSKY, PISAREV) welcomed her stories as a protest against serfdom. From 1859 to 1867 Marko Vovchok lived mostly abroad and continued writing in Ukrainian and Russian, as well as translating into Russian Jules Verne, Bolesław Prus and co-translating Charles Darwin. Her "Marusia" was very popular in France.

Marko Vovchok's high reputation in Ukrainian literature rests on her short stories from peasant life as well as on the short novel *Boarding-School Girl* (Instytutka, 1860), regarded as a masterpiece by Ivan Franko. The decision to devote herself more fully to Russian literature and journalism was influenced by the official bans (1863–1876) on Ukrainian publications in Russia. Her Russian works comprise the novels *A Living Soul* (Zhivaya dusha, 1868), *A Journey inside the Country* (Puteshestvie vo vnutr' strany, 1871), and *A Warm Nest* (Teploe gnezdyshko, 1873). In spite of the fact that she was very prolific in Russian (in 1896–99 a seven-volume edition of her works appeared), she never rated very highly as a novelist.

Works: Tvory. 6 vols. Kiev, 1955–56.
Secondary literature: A. E. Zasenko, *Marko Vovchok.* Moscow, 1958.
G. L.

Voznesénsky, Andréi Andréevich (1933–), poet, was born in Moscow, a scientist's son. He graduated in 1957 from the Moscow Architectural Institute and, encouraged by PASTERNAK to pursue writing, began publishing his poetry in newspapers and "thick" journals. With EVTUSHENKO, an outstanding representative of the post-Stalinist "young poetry," Voznesensky first received critical attention with the appearance of "Masters" (Mastera) and "Goya" in 1959. His first two volumes, *Parabola* and *Mosaic* (1960), were followed by *40 Lyric Digressions from the Poem "Triangular Pear"* (40 liricheskikh otstuplenii iz poemy "Treugol'naya grusha," 1962), *Antiworlds* (Antimiry, 1964), *Heart of Achilles* (Akhillesovo serdtse, 1966), *Shadow of Sound* (Ten' zvuka, 1970), *A Look* (Vzglyad, 1972), *Let the Bird Out!* (Vypusti ptitsu! 1974), *Violoncello Oak Leaf* (Dubovyi list violonchel'nyi, 1975), *Master of Stained Glass Windows* (Vitrazhnykh del master, 1976), and *Temptation* (Soblazn, 1978). Voznesensky's official status has risen and fallen repeatedly since 1963 when Khrushchev denounced him as a "bourgeois formalist": in 1967 he became a member of the Praesidium of the USSR Writers' Union and in 1979 he was awarded the State Prize for poetry. His participation in the publication of the unofficial literary almanac *Metropolis* (Metropol', 1979) once again involved him in controversy.

Voznesensky's verse explores a wide range of technical devices: polymetric lines, graphic verse (*Shadow of Sound*), and prose poetry (*A Look*). He delights in shocking the reader with stylistically inappropriate rhymes or deliberately far-fetched metaphors. The associative quality of his verse is often dependent on visual, concrete imagery. The precarious coexistence of civilization and technology, the interplay of history and contemporary life, the vulnerable position of the poet in society are themes which predominate in his work. Although at times publicistic, Voznesensky is more concerned with challenging artistic rather than political norms.

Works: Dubovyi list violonchel'nyi. 1975.
Translations: Nostalgia for the Present: Poems by Andrei Voznesensky. Trans. Robert Bly et al. Ed. Vera Dunham and Max Hayward. 1978. *Antiworlds and the Fifth Ace: Poetry by Andrei Voznesensky.* Trans. W. H. Auden et al. Ed. Patricia Blake and Max Hayward. 1973.
Secondary literature: "Andrei Voznesensky: The Art of Poetry

XXVI," *The Paris Review*, no. 78 (1980), pp. 95–109. James Bailey, "The Verse of Andrej Voznesenskij as an Example of Present-Day Russian Versification," *SEEJ* 17 (1973), pp. 155–73. W. Gareth Jones, "A Look Round: Poems by Andrei Voznesensky," *The Slavonic Review*, 1968, no. 1, pp. 75–90.
N. C.

Vozrozhdénie (La Renaissance, renascence), Russian émigré literary and political review published in Paris from January 1949 through March 1974. It appeared as a continuation of *Vozrozhdenie* which was founded as a daily on 3 June 1925, transformed into a weekly newspaper in 1936, and temporarily discontinued on 7 June 1940, on the eve of the fall of Paris. From January 1949 through December 1954 the review appeared once every two months; from January 1955 it was changed into a monthly. Like the newspaper, the review was subsidized by the prominent Russian-Armenian businessman and public figure, A. O. Gukasov (1872–1969). After his death, the review continued as a monthly under very difficult conditions. Later, its publication became irregular and, after No. 243, it ceased to exist.

Vozrozhdenie, officially called *tetradi* (the French *cahiers*), was first edited by I. I. Tkhorzhevsky (1949), then by S. P. Melgunov (1949–54), after whom, for several years, there was no formal editor. Editorially, the review was directed mainly by E. M. Yakonovsky (1954), G. A. Meier (1955), I. K. Martynovsky-Opishnya (1956–60), and Prince S. S. Obolensky and Ya. N. Gorbov (1960–74; the latter two became official editors in January 1970).

From the very beginning, the review's credo was formulated by I. I. Tkhorzhevsky as "greatness and freedom of Russia; dignity and rights of man; continuity and growth of culture." This credo, reprinted in each issue of *Vozrozhdenie*, was a further concretization of the general political and cultural world outlook which the first editor of the newspaper *Vozrozhdenie*, P. B. STRUVE, defined as "liberal conservatism." On the whole, the review remained faithful to Tkhorzhevsky's and Struve's principles, in spite of certain fluctuations to the "left" or to the "right" (in its last years, more to the "right").

During the quarter of a century of its existence, *Vozrozhdenie* published many valuable contributions. Some of its issues were in part, or mostly, thematic: No. 3 was devoted to PUSHKIN, No. 70 to Russian literature in exile, No. 76 to Russian painting, No. 77 to TURGENEV, Nos. 80 and 107 to L. TOLSTOI, No. 82 to Rimsky-Korsakov, No. 87 to GOGOL, No. 96 to CHEKHOV, etc.

For "Contents" of *Vozrozhdenie* see: No. 6 (nos. 1–6, 1949), No. 23 (nos. 7–23, 1950–1952), No. 36 (nos. 24–36, 1952–1954); from No. 48 (nos. 37–48, 1955) through No. 227 (nos. 217–227), "Contents" were published yearly; from No. 228 (1971) through No. 243 (1974), only monthly.

Bibliography: G. Meier, "*Vozrozhdenie* i belaya ideya," *Vozrozhdenie*, nos. 42, 43, and 44 (June, July, August 1955); reprinted in his book *U istokov revolyutsii*. Frankfurt, 1971. Pp. 121–242.
N. P. P.

Vrémya (Time, 1861–63), a "literary and political journal" published in St. Petersburg by the DOSTOEVSKY brothers, Mikhail Mikhailovich and Fyodor Mikhailovich, with the latter its de facto editor. Among its regular contributors were A. A. GRIGORIEV, V. V. KRESTOVSKY, A. N. MAIKOV, L. A. MEI, Ya. P. POLONSKY, and N. N. STRAKHOV. Much of its fiction as well as nonfiction was provided by Fyodor Dostoevsky himself, among whose contributions were *Notes from the House of the Dead*, *The Insulted and Injured*, "A Series of Articles on Russian Literature," and "Winter Notes on Summer Impressions." *Vremya* was the organ of the POCHVA ("the soil") movement, advocating a return of the educated classes to "the soil" of Russia's simple people and their Christian faith. As such, *Vremya* engaged in polemics with the radical Left, whom it charged with having abandoned the historical values of the Russian nation for artificially transplanted foreign ideologies, as well as with the extreme Right, whose reactionary ideas it also challenged. *Vremya*, while generally in sympathy with the SLAVOPHILES, was opposed to their notion of a return to pre-Petrine culture and very much considered Russia a part of Europe. *Vremya* was shut down by the government in 1863 after an acrimonious polemic with M. N. KATKOV's RUSSKII VESTNIK. The formal reason for such action was

Strakhov's article on the Polish insurrection, "A Fateful Question," which the censors misunderstood as taking a pro-Polish position. *Vremya* was succeeded by EPOKHA in 1864.

Literature: V. S. Nechaeva, *Zhurnal M. M. i F. M. Dostoevskikh 'Vremya' 1861–1863*. 1972.   V. T.

Vulgar sociologism, a term used to describe the more extreme ideas of critics such as V. M. FRICHE and, in particular, V. F. PEREVERZEV. During the 1920s several men who had been leftists and who had established scholarly reputations before the Revolution sought to establish a Marxist science of literature. Pereverzev was the most radical of these scholars. In his 1912 study of DOSTOEVSKY Pereverzev had already sought to show that the characteristic features of that novelist's art were mere subfunctions of the class struggle. The reason why Dostoevsky is such a great "poet of the city" is because he was born into the RAZNOCHINTSY, the uprooted petty bourgeois. The class he represents expresses its anxieties in his work: threatened at one end of their existence by capitalist exploiters and by the stirrings of the oppressed masses at the other, it was no wonder his world is pervaded by a sense of foreboding and peopled by split personalities. Pereverzev taught that the literary image openly manifested forces that were otherwise socially and psychologically unconscious. He reduces the base/superstructure model to its most radical extremes, as even P. N. SAKULIN, another sociological critic had already pointed out in his introduction to the Dostoevsky book. Throughout the twenties serious questions about Pereverzev's method were raised by Marxist theoreticians, culminating in a resolution in the spring of 1930 of the Communist Academy directed specifically against him. The resolution, published in No. 4 of *Press and Revolution* in that year, accused his method of treating literature only as a passive thing, shaped but not shaping, therefore unable to be a tool for social change. The artist was seen as utterly determined by his class outlook and unable to remake himself. Finally, both the work and creator were cut off from party influence in so ideologically fated a world as Pereverzev presupposed. Friche, who held somewhat similar views to Pereverzev, died before the campaign against vulgar sociologism reached its peak, but Pereverzev was arrested in 1938 and rehabilitated only in 1956.

Literature: Literaturnye diskussii. Bibliograficheskii vypusk. Moscow, 1931. Pp. 1–10.   J. M. H.

Vvedénsky, Aleksándr Ivánovich, (1904–41), poet and writer, was born in St. Petersburg, in an upper middle class family. His father was an economist, and his mother (of noble descent), a gynecologist. Vvedensky attended the L. D. Lentovskaya gymnasium, and after graduation, in 1921, enrolled in the department of Oriental Languages at Petrograd University. However, very soon he abandoned academic studies. From 1923 to 1926, Vvedensky worked in the linguistics department of the Institute of Artistic Culture (GINKH-UK), where he collaborated with the futurist, Igor Terentiev, on a research project on the nature of the poetic text. There, he became acquainted with a number of artists, such as Malevich, Tatlin, Matyushin, Mansurov, and Ender. In the mid-twenties, Vvedensky was active in several Left-wing literary associations, among them the *zaumniki* group founded by Aleksandr Tufanov. Following in the steps of the FUTURISTS (especially KHLEBNIKOV's), the *zaumniki* sought the roots of a universal language as the basis of their poetic compositions. In 1928, Vvedensky became a member of a newly constituted group, OBERIU (an approximate acronym for "Association of Real Art"). Some other members of the group were: D. I. KHARMS, N. A. ZABOLOTSKY, K. VAGINOV, and N. M. Oleinikov. The Oberiu manifesto appeared in the *Afishi doma pechati* (*Posters of the House of the Press*, No. 2, 1928, 11–13), and in part reflected the principles of Vvedensky's poetics. In the two years of its existence, the *Oberiu* dedicated itself mostly to stage activities. The group organized shows which included music, dramatic action, film screenings, poetry reading, and discussions. Vvedensky used to recite his scandal-provoking verses on stage, and afterwards to defend them in heated debates. The *Oberiu* was forced to disband in 1930. In the following years, Vvedensky worked closely with S. MARSHAK in the field of CHILDREN'S LITERATURE, and produced numerous books (poetry, prose, translations, and a play for the Obraztsov Puppet Theatre). He also contributed to the journals, *Ezh* and *Chizh*. However, he never ceased to write adult poetry, and some of his best works belong to his later years (for example, "Christmas-Tree at the Ivanovs,"—Elka u Ivanovykh, 1938). In 1936, Vvedensky moved to Kharkov, where he lived until his arrest, in 1941. He died that same year during the evacuation, under unclear circumstances. In the late 50s he was rehabilitated, and some of his children's books were reprinted.

Vvedensky writes in a grotesque and absurd vein. He treats universal themes such as life, death, time, and eternity in a Dada-like manner devoid of emotions. Vvedensky learned the lesson of futurism and IMAGISM in matters of poetic form and built his poems on analogical juxtapositions of images. His rhythms and rhymes tend towards primitivism. A good number of his works consists of mini-plays in verse, or simply poems in dramatic form. During his lifetime, only two poems appeared in print, in the collections of the Leningrad Poets Union, *Collection of Poems* (Sobranie stikhotvorenii, 1926) and *Bonfire* (Koster, 1927). Only one fourth of Vvedensky's works have been preserved in manuscripts by his friends and are now being printed outside of the Soviet Union.

Works: Izbrannoe. Ed. W. Kasack. Munich, 1974. *Polnoe sobranie sochinenii.* Vol. 1. Ed. Mikhail Meilakh. Ann Arbor, 1980.

Translations: One poem, "Where," in *Russian Poetry: The Modern Period.* John Glad and Daniel Weissbort, eds. 1978. Pp. 125–28.

Secondary literature: M. Meilakh, "Tvorchestvo A. Vvedenskogo." In *Materialy XXII nauchnoi studencheskoi konferentsii.* Tartu, 1967. ——, "Aleksandr Vvedenskii," *RLT* 11 (1975), pp. 479–80. In the same issue, the poem "Potets," pp. 481–87. R. R. Milner-Gulland, "'Left Art' in Leningrad: The OBERIU Declaration," *OSP* 3 (1970), pp. 65–75. Alice Stone Nakhimovsky, "About Vvedensky's *Conversations*," *Ulbandus Review* 1, no. 1 (1977), pp. 107–11. (Followed by trans. of text.)   A. L.

Vyázemsky, Prince Pyotr Andréevich (1792–1878), critic, polemicist, poet, archivist, translator (Constant's *Adolphe*), prose stylist, epistolarian. The son of an aristocratic "Voltairian", Vyazemsky received a fine literary education at home and in the Jesuit Pension in St. Petersburg. He would eventually learn German, English, and Italian, but his strongest cultural affinities were always for French thought and literature of the 18th century. His quick wit, precocious talents, and connections (his brother-in-law was KARAMZIN), soon brought him into public literary life, and his polemical personality propelled him into nearly every literary and intellectual controversy from the early 1810s to the 1840s. His personal life was no less tempestuous. He fought the French at Borodino (1812), squandered a huge fortune, and was fired from his post in Warsaw because of his liberal sympathies (1821). Never trusted by Nicholas I and unrepentant concerning his anti-government writings, Vyazemsky served, against his inclinations, twenty years in the Ministry of Finance. Meanwhile, his liberalism became increasingly incompatible with the radical beliefs of younger generations. As head of the Censorship from 1856 to 1858, Vyazemsky was attacked by reactionary officials (and forced to quit the post) and also by such radicals as HERZEN, who sought to embarrass Vyazemsky by publishing the rebellious verses of his youth in the underground press. Vyazemsky spent most of his last years abroad, having survived his friends, his readers and all but one of his children.

Vyazemsky's friendships with Karamzin, DMITRIEV, BATYUSHKOV, ZHUKOVSKY, Denis Davydov, A. S. PUSHKIN, BARATYNSKY, and later with GOGOL, YAZYKOV, and TYUTCHEV, and his participation in ARZAMAS shaped his published criticism and journalism (MOSKOVSKII TELEGRAF, LITERATURNAYA GAZETA, SOVREMENNIK), although he often criticized his authorities in his familiar correspondence with them. Vyazemsky argued against Admiral SHISHKOV and his followers on behalf of Karamzin and Zhukovsky (1810s), against the critics of Karamzin's *History of the Russian State* (1820s and 1830s), against the "classical" opponents of Pushkin's romantic narrative poems (1820s), against BULGARIN and Nikolai POLEVOI on behalf of the "aristocratic" poets (1829–late 1830s), and against SLAVOPHILES, Hegelians, and radical critics of the 1840s and 1850s. Vyazemsky's attachments, ridiculed by the younger generation, made him an invaluable archivist of the Golden Age, and he released volumes of documents for publication. His sketches on Moscow life— "Antediluvian or Anteconflagration Moscow" (1865), "Griboedov's

Moscow" (1878), "An Old-Fashioned Moscow Family" (1877)—are especially illuminating. Vyazemsky's notebooks reveal his considerable ability to catch lively conversation on the fly and to fix it on the page with wit, paradoxes, and lexical peculiarities intact. Like Vyazemsky's letters—especially the correspondence with A. I. Turgenev (1812–44)—the notebooks offer a detailed account, shaped by the ideology and aesthetics of the enlightened Westernized gentry, of early 19th-century culture and society.

Vyazemsky's critical essays are marked by a conversational, polemical manner. BELINSKY called Vyazemsky the best critic of his time (1842), and Pushkin gave him credit for inventing the Russian "metaphysical" [i.e., conceptual, analytic] language (1822). Vyazemsky's criticism—unsystematic, and certainly unmetaphysical—remained grounded in such classical concepts as clarity, logic, and appropriateness. He is remembered as an early supporter of ROMANTICISM, but the romantics he greeted—Byron, Stendhal, Constant—were those closest to the political ideals and satirical, analytical traditions of the Enlightenment, and he was drawn to romantic literature for its local color, formal innovations, and political protest, not for its metaphysics or celebration of the irrational. Vyazemsky's concern for Russian literature as an institution led him to write about 18th-century authors (LOMONOSOV, DERZHAVIN, SUMAROKOV, Dmitriev). His pioneering monograph on FONVIZIN (1848) is remarkable for its attention to social and literary contexts.

Vyazemsky's verse is competent, often unpolished, sometimes excellent. He began with Batyushkov-like exercises in "light poetry," and he remained loyal to this tradition in his criticism. But his mature verse often features archaic diction, convoluted syntax, and metrical schemes (especially Alexandrines) that were uncommon in this school. He reached maturity with two elegies, "First Snow" and "Dejection" (1819) and with the brilliant "Indignation" (1820), which takes the form of an elegy, but draws on the lofty lexicon and thematics of the Russian odic tradition. Believing that "a poet should sometimes seek inspiration in the newspapers," Vyazemsky devoted much of his talent to topical epistles, fables, epigrams, and satires, such as "The Russian God" (1818, pub. 1854 in London).

Works: Polnoe sobranie sochinenii. 12 vols. 1878–96. *Ostaf'evskii arkhiv knyazei Vyazemskikh.* Ed. V. I. Saitov. 5 vols. 1899. *Stikhotvoreniya.* Ed. and introd. L. Ya. Ginzburg. 1958. *Zapisnye knizhki: 1813–1848.* Ed. V. S. Nechaeva. 1963.

Translations: See Lewanski, p. 394.

Secondary literature: M. I. Gillel'son, *P. A. Vyazemskii: Zhizn' i tvorchestvo.* 1969. I. A. Paperno and Yu. M. Lotman, "Vyazemskii—perevodchik 'Negodovaniya.'" In *Uchenye zapiski tartuskogo gosudarstvennogo universiteta.* Vol. 369. Tartu, 1975.

W. M. T.

Vysótsky, Vladímir Semyónovich (1938–80), poet, singer, actor and composer. During his short life, Vysotsky became a cult figure for millions of his contemporaries. A gifted actor, he worked with Yu. Lyubimov at the Taganka Theater and also became a popular movie-star. His fame is due, however, to his being, together with A. GALICH and B. OKUDZHAVA, a leading representative of the so-called bards and minstrels movement which was initiated in the sixties and reached its peak in the mid-seventies and which only in a very circumspect way can be juxtaposed with the corresponding cultural developments in Western pop and rock music.

Vysotsky, like the other "bards," composed both the verses and the tunes of his songs and performed them in person and, when his public performances were barred, began to tape his singing; those tapes were then eagerly duplicated by his admirers and, as a result of a chain reaction, began to circulate in hundreds of thousands of copies in every stratum of Soviet society, thus creating a totally new phenomenon within the unofficial culture: "magnitizdat." It is difficult to overestimate the impact that "magnitizdat" produced on the minds of the people, especially those of the young generation. But Vysotsky's work is by no means only a social phenomenon; it is an accomplished art on its own merits, and as a poet he deserves critical attention. Vysotsky's poetry has immediate appeal, independent of social and intellectual distinctions, which can itself be regarded as a manifestation of true art. His songs, psychologically poignant and reflecting the feeling of abandonment and debasement so widespread in Soviet society, are often politically pointed. He has

an ability for combining satire and lyricism almost in the same line. His world is a multidimensional one where, in the bizarre yet real mixture of guilt and innocence, the moral orientation is not lost: "I do not like it when they shoot you in the back and also I am against shooting into your face." In many ways Vysotsky's hero is the "underground man," but of the Soviet mold, always enmeshed, whatever his moral or intellectual profile, in existential problems and struggling in vain to get rid of the frightening predicament in which he finds himself. One of his most powerful images is that of a man as a submarine, dreaming to reach the very bottom of the ocean in order that "his bearings not be taken." This can be read as a very apt symbol of the human condition in totalitarian society. Vysotsky's verse or records were never published in the Soviet Union during his lifetime.

Works: Pesni russkikh bardov, teksty. Vols. 1–4 (1977–78). 1981.

Secondary literature: P. Leonidov, *Vladimir Vysotskii i drugie.* 1982. I. Rubanova, "Vladimir Vysotsky." *Aktery sovetskogo kino* 11 (1972), pp. 90–105. P. Zveteremich, *Canzoni russe di protesta.* 1972.

V. B.

Wedding ritual songs. The wedding ritual takes place in the autumn after harvest or in the winter, and depending on the region, extends over a few days or lasts several weeks. It is divided into two basic cycles: the prenuptial and postnuptial. The prenuptial rituals consist of matchmaking, the *smotriny* when the groom and his family come to look over the bride and her family, the *rukobit'e* and *sgovor* or final agreement between the parents, the *devichnik* at which the bride says farewell to her girl friends, the ritual bath, and the wedding day rituals before the *venchanie* (the church ceremony when the couple exchanges wreaths—*venets*). The mood of the songs before the wedding ceremony is sad; bridal laments are sung about the difficult life ahead for the bride (see LAMENTS). The postnuptial rituals take place at the wedding feast in the home of the groom. At the wedding feast *velichal'nye* (panegyric) songs are sung to the various participants of the wedding ceremony, praising them in idealized terms. At this time *koril'nye* (mocking) songs are also sung, making fun of the various participants. The order of the episodes may be different in different regions.

There are several types of lyric songs that accompany the various rituals. The ritual wedding songs are associated with particular rituals, such as the bath or the matchmaking ceremony, and describe the ritual. Other songs are not related to specific rituals, but must be sung only during the course of the wedding and focus on marriage themes. Other lyrics are often sung during the wedding rituals, such as at the *devichnik*, but are also sung on other occasions as well. While the prenuptial lyrics are elegiac in mood, depicting the future marriage as tragic, the postnuptial lyrics represent the bride as happily married and glad to be serving her husband well. The songs are sung by a chorus, usually by the bride's girl friends in her home at the prenuptial rituals, and by girls from the groom's village in his home where the postnuptial celebration takes place. The lyrics differ in many ways from the bridal laments. Unlike the laments, they are not improvised during the performance, but a fixed variant is agreed upon ahead of time which will be performed. The songs are much more idealized than the laments; the bride is depicted as a princess or swan in a fairy tale landscape, and the groom as a strong prince breaking down city walls with his boyars to capture the bride, or as a falcon swooping down and taking the swan from her flock. Decorative epithets add to the idealization. The groom has winding curls and a silken lash, the girl crimson cheeks and brows of sable. Parallelism is a favorite device, where a scene in nature such as a falcon capturing a swan is compared to the situation between the prospective bride and groom. Gradual narrowing of imagery is another typical device. While the bridal laments are sung as a recitative, the wedding songs are much more melodious.

Although not directly part of the wedding ritual, around Easter time, especially on Foma (St. Thomas) Sunday (the week after Easter), *v'yuniny* songs are sung to couples who have married the previous winter. The couple is depicted as weavers of a nest, and the song praises them, and portrays an idyllic picture of a family nest.

Bibliography: Alex E. Alexander, *Russian Folklore: An Anthology in English Translation.* 1975. D. Balashov and Yu. Krasovskaya, *Russkie svadebnye pesni.* 1969. N. P. Kolpakova, *Lirika russkoi svad'by.* 1973. Yu. G. Kruglov, *Russkie svadebnye pesni.* 1978. V. Ya. Propp, *Narodnye liricheskie pesni.* 2d ed. 1961. Roberta Reeder, *Down Along the Mother Volga.* 1975. Yu. M. Sokolov, *Russian Folklore.* 1971.

R. R.

Weidlé (also: Veidle, Vladímir Vasílievich, 1895–1979), art historian, critic, and poet. Weidlé published in several languages besides Russian, mostly in French. His prize winning book *Les Abeilles d'Aristée; Essai sur le destin actuel des lettres et des arts* (1954) is an energetic attempt to determine, from an analysis of its art and literature, the direction in which Western civilization is headed. Like Oswald Spengler, he sees Western civilization in decline since the romantic period. Weidlé's work on Byzantine and Russian iconography is among the best in the field. Weidlé also took a lively interest in Russian literature, writing many reviews of works by contemporary authors (BLOK, PASTERNAK, among others). As a theorist of literature (and art in general), Weidlé defended a traditional organic approach to art. He insisted, on the one hand, that the modern tendency to isolate and abstract an "aesthetic" component from the work of art leads to an irreversible separation of understanding from appreciation, and on the other, that artistic expression requires the medium of an existing form, however flexible. Therefore, Weidlé challenged the premises of both FORMALISM (of which he felt modern STRUCTURALISM was merely an extension) and SURREALISM as inconsistent with the nature of art. Early in his life and again toward the end of his career, Weidlé wrote Russian poetry, often drawing on his impressions as a traveler and a student of art. His verse is polished and elegant.

Works: Umiranie iskusstva; razmyshleniya o sud'be literaturnogo i khudozhestvennogo tvorchestva. Paris, 1937. *Le icone bizantine e russe.* Firenze, 1950. *Vechernii den'; otkliki i ocherki na zapadnye temy.* New York, 1952. *Russia: absent and present.* Trans. A. Gordon Smith. New York, 1952. (Originally in French.) *Zadacha Rossii.* New York, 1956. *Bezymyannaya strana.* Paris, 1968. *Posle "Dvenadtsati": Prinoshenie krestu na mogile Aleksandra Bloka.* Paris, 1973. *O poetakh i poezii.* Paris, 1973. *Zimnee solntse: iz rannikh vospominanii.* Washington, D. C., 1976. *Na pamyat' o sebe: Stikhotvoreniya, 1918–1925 i 1965–1975.* Paris, 1979. "Beneath the Surface of Foreign Words and/or Aleksis Rannit," *Journal of Baltic Studies* 11 (1980), pp. 187–98.

Bibliography: Foster, pp. 322–27.

Secondary literature: R. H. Stacy, *Russian Literary Criticism: A Short History.* 1974. Pp. 243–47.

V. T.

Westernism. In order to discuss Westernism in Russia, one must have a working definition of "the West"; there are many to choose from, though not all work. It seems generally accepted by now that "the West" is least of all a point on the compass, and that when we speak of it we are invoking a complex of cultural attitudes, forms, and institutions which took shape on the Western fringe of the Eurasian land mass after 1500, and which have been changing the rest of the world increasingly rapidly over the last several hundred years. Some definitions—perhaps one could describe them as ultimately Hegelian—describe Westernization as a process by which the remainder of the planet has been forced to accept the *universal* cultural, economic and political values which were worked out in the dynamic centers of Europe, values centering around rationalism—scientific thinking, the modern state and its bureaucratic *modus operandi*, even Western art, architecture, and music. Along with the values and forms of Western life has come its terrible energy and restlessness that we often call Faustian or Promethean. Why all these worldshaking things originally developed in the Western part of Europe is a historical problem with which we do not have to deal here.

In the course of the last half-century in particular, educated people in almost every society on the face of the earth have been forced to arrive at some definition of "the West"; it is part of Russia's particular historical destiny to have provided the arena where the opposition between the values of a local society and "the West" was first referred to in these "modern" terms. Initially (in the 17th and

18th centuries) the contrast was between Russia and "Europe," the latter term having a broader and more purely descriptive meaning than "the West." Russia seemed to be a part of Europe, but it had barely experienced (or had missed entirely) many of those major phases of development that defined the essence of Europe's common inheritance and contemporary cultural cohesion: classical antiquity; the Renaissance; the Reformation; the rise of scientific thinking. Because Russia had experienced these things very little or very differently from the heart of Europe, there was some disposition among European thinkers of the day (such as Leibniz) to regard Russia as a tabula rasa, upon which all sorts of benevolent and unheard of projects might be sketched. Such schemes were intriguing to Peter the Great (1689–1725) and many members of his entourage, who shared the implicit scorn of Leibniz (or the explicit scorn of Voltaire) for Russia's past.

In any event, Russia submitted with amazing wholeheartedness to the cultural values, myths, prejudices, and even objects emanating from France and elsewhere in Europe, undergoing almost a century of apprenticeship to French classical literature, German and Scandinavian governmental institutions, Italian architecture, and English mathematics and science. Peter felt that Russia's survival in the European world of the early 18th century meant "becoming European," by which he already meant something quite close to what many "third world" leaders have meant more recently by becoming "modern" or "Western." Like many of them, Peter began by trying to emulate the military might of Europe and ended by attempting to import an entire alien civilization, employing the considerable powers and resources of the Russian autocracy in the effort. If Peter was not technically the first advocate of "Westernism" in Russia, his was on such a heroic scale as to make it inevitable that he would be regarded as the founding father.

By the end of the 18th century and the beginning of the 19th, the Russian economy and Russian culture had become more like those of West European nations, but in a most complex fashion. Most of the tiny Russian elite had become strikingly Europeanized (at least on the surface), to the point that French had almost entirely replaced Russian as the language of educated society. The remainder of the nation, however, had not heeded Peter's call (or been forced to heed it); in particular, the vast peasant majority of the population still lived more or less as their parents, grandparents, and great-grandparents had done. Here too was a pattern which would become familiar to all those subsequently interested in what we have come to call "non-Western societies."

Despite the apparent success of Russians in appropriating European ideas of literary tragedy, verse forms, carriages, and perfumes, by the beginning of the 19th century there were abundant signs that Westernism and the Westernization process were going to be subjected to a more conscious and careful scrutiny than had earlier been the case. The most substantial and compelling (but by no means the only) reason for this was that the rise of romanticism in European culture was persuading intellectuals of the central importance of the nation and the nation's past; the cosmopolitanism of the 18th century was everywhere on the defensive. This cultural change presented Russians with a particularly severe dilemma. The values and myths of their intellectual world were still predominantly Petrine, but the Petrine message was that the Muscovite past was brutal, uncivilized, and best forgotten. Now the very European sages that Peter had instructed his subjects always to consult were telling them that in order to continue becoming European they had to exhume, venerate, and develop their Russianness.

Two points of view, essentially, coalesced out of this national-cultural identity crisis: nationalist groups (of which by far the most important was the SLAVOPHILES) representing a nativist reaction against Russia's cultural borrowing; and the less cohesive majority of Russia's educated elite who believed that Russia should continue its policy of cultural Westernism. Even in these quarters, however, there was now much mockery of the francophilia that had been the height of good form just a few years earlier.

It was the Slavophiles and the "Official Nationalists" who largely brought about the transition from the vague contrast between Russia and Europe, which had been common coin among the elite for so long, and the now increasingly ideological comparison of Russia and "the West." The first-generation Slavophiles were almost all from old, historically conscious families, and their attack on Westernization and on the denigration of Russia's past had a pronounced aristocratic dimension to it; classical Slavophilism had something of the "old boyar" tone of earlier aristocratic opposition to the autocracy, of a kind which had not been politically significant since the early 18th century. At about the same time, dynastically oriented conservatives such as S. P. SHEVYRYOV and M. P. POGODIN (the "Official Nationalists") were exalting the Russian state and dynasty and criticizing "the West," whose apparently glittering achievements in politics, economics and culture they regarded as having been founded on a violence and oppression which had inevitably produced the social rebellion and class conflicts of contemporary Europe. The Slavophile critique agreed with these points to some extent, but cut deeper in that the Slavophiles clearly saw that intellectual and social rationalism were the central values in the increasing power of the West European nations. In their zeal to combat the sinister secularism and radicalism of "the West," the Slavophiles created a historical utopia, idealizing pre-Petrine Russia into a commonwealth of Christian communities, united by the spirit of the Orthodox Church and ruled over by a benign and patrimonial monarch, who never transgressed the limited sphere of traditional rulership. "Old Russia" had not been very much like this, but the Slavophile tableau was arresting and attracted many of the most conservative and consequent opponents of Westernization.

Those out of sympathy with these new nationalist currents found themselves rather on the defensive. Because an unself-conscious Westernism had been the norm during the century since the death of Peter the Great, its new nationally oriented opponents had the more interesting position at first; they were also able to take advantage of the more prosaic currents of patriotism which had been stimulated not only by the romantic nationalism of the intellectuals, but by the major role which Russia had played in the defeat of Napoleon and in the politics of the Restoration.

Like the Mensheviks three-quarters of a century later, the Westernizers were given their sobriquet in the heat of battle; what was intended as a pejorative they elected to wear as a badge of honor. In the almost 150 years since the great debate began, "Westernizer" and "Westernism" have been used in diverse ways, with many a subtle (and not so subtle) shade of meaning. Still, it is generally accurate to say that all proponents of "Westernism" have either regarded Russian civilization as vitally related to larger entities (Christendom, Europe) or undergoing more universal processes ("modernization," revolution), than those provided by a purely national life and they have defined their sense of themselves accordingly. One does not want, of course, to exaggerate the consciousness or seriousness of either the nativists or the Westernizers. Once the debate had become part of the intellectual universe of educated Russians, it was quite possible to take the blandest, most pro forma stand for Westernism—really intending to say no more than that one advocated some vague notion of progress or recognized oneself as part of a cultural whole whose outer boundaries were European.

But in the 1840s, and on occasion since then, Westernism has had much more specific meanings. The leaders of the party of Westernism during the first phase of the debate were Aleksandr HERZEN (1812–70), the historian Timofei GRANOVSKY (1813–55), and the literary critic Vissarion BELINSKY (1811–48), and for them Westernism had a specific meaning which derived from the Hegelian frame of reference in which much of the debate about Russian nationhood was taking place. They saw European history moving dialectically through ever higher stages of development toward the achievement of a new civilization which would reconcile the individualism which was the finest flower of the liberal era with the communal and socialist values which they also prized. This march of civilization, in which they felt called to participate, also had as an essential task endowing the politically inert majority of the Russian population, which had hitherto remained altogether outside the historical process, with the consciousness and capacity to shape its own destiny. For these men, "Westernism" entailed both an understanding of themselves as Europeans and a belief that the most vital political processes of which they were destined to be a part were not Russian but European or worldwide, and profoundly progressive.

Pyotr CHAADAEV (1794–1856) represented another tendency within Russian Westernism—more sparsely represented in the culture than the Hegelian-radical brand, but nonetheless important for that. Chaadaev insisted that Russia's tragedy was having been cut off by her history from the Roman-Mediterranean world, the heart of the

high classical and Christian civilization of Europe; the hope of his Westernism was that Russia, thanks in large part to Peter the Great, might be able to return to that world. Rome was the capital of his "West"; the capital of young Herzen's "West" was where the *Weltgeist* had established itself. Chaadaev can not really be said to have had followers, but his writing and persona have never lost their appeal and one can pick up echoes of his point of view in some writings of Vladimir SOLOVYOV (1853–1900) and in the weltanschauung of Osip (1891–1937) and Nadezhda (1899–1981) MANDELSHTAM.

The Westernism of Belinsky in particular continued to be a shaping force in Russian literary culture for generations (continues to be so, in a sense, to this day), but the purely "Western" social radicalism of the 1840s really gave way after the Crimean War to populist currents of radicalism with a strong nativist component. In some respects the scientific elitism of Dmitry PISAREV (1840–68) and his adherents should be counted as Westernism, but it did not last long as a distinct point of view within Russian radicalism. N. G. CHERNYSHEVSKY (1828–89) was the heir of both Belinsky and Herzen, however selectively he developed their ideas. His conception of the historical process was thoroughly regular and universalist, and he drew on the main lines of Enlightenment theory for his journalism and criticism: the 18th-century materialists; the French Utopian socialists; the English philosophical radicals; the anthropologism of Ludwig Feuerbach (1804–72).

Russian Westernism may be considered to have reached its apogee with Marxism, particularly before LENIN made Bolshevism into Marxist orthodoxy, russifying it significantly in the process. Marxism is universalist, rather than national; it stresses the overcoming of the past, rather than its recovery or renewal; it glorifies the culture of rationalism, secularism, and industrialism. It is therefore a major historical irony that so much of Soviet cultural history can be read as the steady infiltration of a kind of textbook Westernism (Marxism-Leninism) by all sorts of nativist and anti-Western elements: patriotism, nationalism, and chauvinism in varying combinations; veneration of the Russian past; and in the last dozen years or so, the explicit re-emergence of Slavophilism, not only among anti-Soviet dissidents, but in veiled forms among members of the establishment as well.

Despite the official internationalism of Soviet politics and culture today, it is not so easy to discover proponents of Westernism or people who could really be described as Westernizers in the way SOLZHENITSYN can be designated a Slavophile. Russians are as eager to acquire Western technology as they were in Peter's time, but they are rather less childlike about "learning from the West"; they pay homage to an internationalist ideal (the world revolution), but its contents are increasingly mixed with Russian blood and soil. Perhaps Andrei Sakharov is the most prominent representative of some of the most attractive attitudes of Westernism, now on the defensive, and not only in Russia: the necessity of worshipping other than merely the household deities; the ability and willingness to criticize one's own nation in a reasonably objective fashion; the capacity to take seriously the old chestnut that we inhabit one world. That the Russian Westernizers seldom lived up to the more moderate and humane statements of their creed—and in fact reserved their greatest enthusiasm and loyalty for the most extreme and one-sided forms of Westernism—does not finally diminish the power of the ideal or the importance of the tradition of civilized cosmopolitanism as a vital aspect of Russian culture.

Bibliography: Cyril Black, *The Dynamics of Modernization.* 1966. Martin Malia, *Alexander Herzen and the Birth of Russian Socialism.* 1961. Nadezhda Mandelstam, *Hope Against Hope.* 1970. Raymond McNally, *The Major Works of Peter Chaadaev.* 1969. Lewis Mumford, *The Myth of the Machine:* Vol. 2. *The Pentagon of Power.* 1970. Andrei Sakharov, *Progress, Coexistence and Intellectual Freedom.* 1968. Benjamin Schwartz, *In Search of Wealth and Power: Yen Fu and the West.* 1964. Victor Terras, *Belinskij and Russian Literary Criticism: The Heritage of Organic Aesthetics.* 1973. William Woehrlin, *Chernyshevskii: The Man and the Journalist.* 1971. A. G.

Wisdom Lovers, Society of (Óbshchestvo lyubomúdriya, ca. 1823–25). The "Lyubomudry" were a circle of Moscow University graduates and young men employed in the Moscow Archives of the Ministry of Foreign Affairs (hence the nickname "arkhivnye yunoshi," archive youths) who met secretly to discuss and debate philosophical problems. "Obshchestvo lyubomudriya" (Society of Philosophers), as the circle called itself formally, was founded in 1823 with the intention of initiating a new philosophical tradition in Russia. The Greek word philosophy was translated into an archaic Russian equivalent—"lyubomudrie." The circle was composed of V. F. ODOEVSKY (President), D. V. VENEVITINOV (Secretary), I. V. KIREEVSKY, A. I. Koshelev and N. M. Rozhalin. Others, close to "the Philosophers" in spirit and certain views on literature, were M. P. POGODIN and S. P. SHEVYRYOV, members of the circle of S. E. RAICH, which was also frequented by "the Philosophers," thus resulting in a certain fluidity of membership.

The members studied German metaphysics and read Kant, Fichte, Spinoza and others. They were particularly devoted to the transcendental philosophy of Schelling and made pilgrimages to Germany to meet and study with the philosopher in person. The actual philosophical point of view and their individual interests varied. Odoevsky was interested in the pantheistic systems of Spinoza and the Russian philosopher G. SKOVORODA. Kireevsky and Koshelev were ardent supporters of Schelling's idealistic philosophy and searched for "religious truths." The atmosphere of feverish zeal and transcendental enthusiasm which animated the meetings of these disciples of Hegel and Schelling is fictionalized in Odoevsky's cycle of stories *Russian Nights* (Russkie nochi, 1844).

Most of the members of the circle were interested in literature. Their literary tastes and critical judgements were permeated by a transcendental trend of thought and show a strong influence of doctrinal preconceptions. Although they all published their works in various journals, they longed to have a journal of their own. In 1824 Odoevsky began to publish a quarterly literary and philosophical almanac *Mnemosyne* with V. K. KYUKHELBEKER, which in its format was very close to a journal. The almanac undertook to acquaint its readers with the new romantic aesthetics and philosophy and to establish a new national Russian literature. The works of "the Philosophers" published in the almanac reveal a general parallelism with the idealist and historicist movement of ideas which gives German romanticism its essential character. Thus in an article, "An Excerpt from the Dictionary of the History of Philosophy," Odoevsky popularized Schelling's thought about the constant development of the human spirit, making art, religion, and philosophy the highest manifestations of universal reason. Among other contributors to the philosophical section of the almanac was the Moscow University professor of philosophy, M. G. Pavlov, who was responsible for the philosophic enthusiasm of his former students.

The leading poet of "the Philosophers," was Venevitinov; Odoevsky, the leading prose writer. The members shared Kyukhelbeker's views expressed in his critical articles about changes that had to be made in contemporary literature. His views were later taken up by S. P. Shevyryov. These poets advocated poetry with serious philosophical themes, with a style that could express ideas rather than emotions.

After the Decembrist uprising in 1825 "the Philosophers" discontinued their formal meetings and destroyed the protocols of the society so as not to attract the attention of authorities. Most of "the Philosophers" united again in 1827 around the journal *Moskovskii vestnik*. Kireevsky, Koshelev, and KHOMYAKOV later formed the group of thinkers known as SLAVOPHILES, continuing many of the ideas of "the Philosophers."

Texts: V. F. Odoevsky, *Russian Nights*. Trans. Olga Koshansky-Olienikov and Ralph E. Matlaw. Introd. Ralph E. Matlaw. 1965.

Secondary literature: M. Aronson and S. Reiser, *Literaturnye kruzhki i salony*. 1929. Pp. 128–32. Abbot Gleason, *European and Muscovite: Ivan Kireevsky and the Origins of Slavophilism*. 1972. *Literaturnye salony i kruzhki. Pervaya polovina XIX veka*. 1930. Pp. 141–50. V. I. Sakharov, "Vstrechi s Shellingom. (Po novym materialam)." In *Pisatel' i zhizn'*. 1978. Pp. 167–80. P. N. Sakulin, *Iz istorii russkogo idealizma. Knyaz' V. F. Odoevskii*. Vol. 1, pt. 1. 1913. W. Setschkareff, *Schellings Einfluss in der russischen Literatur der 20er und 30er Jahre des XIX Jahrhunderts*. Leipzig, 1939.

A. Gl.

Woe-Misfortune, The Tale of, see GORE-ZLOCHASTIE.

Women and Russian literature. Due to peculiar historical, social, and political conditions in Russia, the woman question in Western terms did not arise until the late 18th century and did not appear in literature until the early 19th. In the middle of the 1550s, *A House Ordered* (DOMOSTROI) dealt only with the proper methods of keeping wives and daughters—locked in the women's part of the house (*terem*), obedient to the patriarch of the household, the father or husband. Peter the Great let the women out of the *terem* with, judging by the biting satire of CATHERINE THE GREAT and FONVIZIN, disastrous results for their morals and no advantage to their intellectual development.

Several conditions unique to Russia influenced the position of women in society and thus in literature, both as writers and fictional characters. First, Russia was the only European country with an autocratic government as late as 1917. Second, serfdom was not abolished until 1861. Third, government control had been exercised over public speech and the printed word since 1792. These political and social conditions could not but influence the position of women and their portrayal in literature. Heroines were of noble birth (as were the heroes and initially the authors themselves) and were joined by the intelligentsia and the middle class following the arrival of the RAZNOCHINTSY. The image of the long-suffering peasant woman (*mnogostradal'naya baba*) was introduced as part of the anti-serfdom movement and was largely neglected by fiction until the Revolution. In Soviet literature, the development of the woman question has followed a separate pattern.

The traditional first model of Russian womanhood is PUSHKIN's Tatiana (*Evgenii Onegin*, 1823–31), KARAMZIN's Poor Liza (1792) being just a distant cousin of Richardson's Clarissa, a garden variety of Western sentimentalism. Tatiana earned her distinction both by behaving honorably (virtuously is perhaps a better word) and by daringly usurping a man's privilege to declare love without being asked first. Pushkin, however, shared Lamartine's opinion that all a woman needed to be was lovely, sweet, and virtuous. He can hardly be considered a promoter of woman's rights.

The first writers to draw attention to the existence of woman's problems were, after all, women: Elena GAN (1814–42, pseud. Zinaida R-va), Karolina PAVLOVA (1807–93), and Maria ZHUKOVA (1804–55). They represented the trend known as George-Sandism, demanding a woman's sentimental emancipation: her right to love—virtuously, to be sure, within wedlock, but freely choosing a husband herself. Moreover, the three follow GRIBOEDOV in blaming, first, the girls' superficial education which hardly prepares them to make a wise choice, even if they were in a position to do so; next, the milieu—banal provinces in the case of Gan's heroine in *The Useless Gift* (Naprasnyi dar, 1842), and the shallow and hypocritical beau monde in Pavlova's *A Double Life* (Dvoinaya zhizn', 1848) and Zhukova's *Society's Judgement* (Sud obshchestva, 1840); and finally, the parents, whose only concern was to find their daughters a husband suitable by their own standards. In general, all these novels are meant to illustrate the sad lot of girls brought up exclusively to be dependent females with underdeveloped minds, capable only of deep feeling and unquestioning obedience. Men's novels of the forties, like HERZEN's *Who is to Blame?* (Kto vinovat? 1847) and DRUZHININ's *Polin'ka Saks* (1847), illustrate BELINSKY's opinion that women, which indeed created for love and motherhood, still need more spiritual outlets for their energies, and blame society for women's "harem" conditions. S. T. AKSAKOV in *Family Chronicle* (Semeinaya khronika, 1846–56) portrays women nurtured by the patriarchal family condition as silly, ignorant, stultified by domestic tyranny, or cunning and intriguing or, when intelligent, vainly trying, like Aksakov's mother, to build a tolerable life while tied to a mediocre, weak-willed husband. None of these authors offers a viable solution, except perhaps sensible education for girls and a change of attitude for parents and husbands who treat women like their inanimate property.

This proprietary attitude prevailed on all social levels, from the fate of the heroine of PISEMSKY's *A Thousand Souls* (Tysyacha dush, 1858), a duplicate of Gan's or Pavlova's "poor rich girl," to that of the peasant heroine in his *A Hard Lot* (Gor'kaya sud'bina, 1859). Moreover, if the latter's lot was hard, indeed, so was her husband's, since both were the personal property of the wife's lover, the squire. The image of the long-suffering peasant woman was first presented by D. V. GRIGOROVICH in his *The Village* (Derevnya, 1846), and by TURGENEV in *A Sportsman's Sketches* (Zapiski okhotnika, 1847–52). Her miserable condition became a part of the strivings of the liberal intellectuals for the abolition of serfdom, and was painted primarily as a detail of the whole dark picture. NEKRASOV, however, singled out in a poetic tribute, "Frost the Red-Nosed" (Moroz Krasnyi-nos, 1863), that slave of slaves, crushed by poverty and hard work, the peasant wife, widow, and heroic mother of orphaned children.

DOSTOEVSKY and OSTROVSKY each present a whole gallery of women. Yet, neither the former, bard of the humiliated and the injured, nor the latter, discoverer of the "dark kingdom" of Moscow merchants, deals basically with the "woman question." Dostoevsky's heroines, whether "infernally" proud, or gentle to the point of self-abnegation, are primarily foils to his heroes, whose tortured souls are being probed in their religious or ontological struggles. Ostrovsky's women, like his men, are indigenous to the larger panorama of Russian BYT and social conditions. Still, both authors vividly portray the enslavement of women by their domestic tyrants—parents, husbands, or guardians—and by abject and/or genteel poverty from which a girl cannot escape except by selling herself (with luck, honorably, into marriage). So it is with Dostoevsky in *Poor Folk* (Bednye lyudi, 1847), *Crime and Punishment* (Prestuplenie i nakazanie, 1866), or *The Gentle Soul* (Krotkaya, 1877); and Ostrovsky in *The Poor Bride* (Bednaya nevesta, 1852), or *The Dowerless Girl* (Bespridannitsa, 1879); while in his *The Storm* (Groza, 1860), suicide is the escape.

For Lev TOLSTOI the woman question simply did not exist except, as in his opinion expressed in 1905 in an afterword to CHEKHOV's "The Darling" (Dushechka, 1899), "a vulgar fashionable movement confusing both men and women." He considered a woman's calling (and her superiority to man) to be her sublime capacity for love and sacrifice, exemplified by the loving selfless half-wit, Darling. Even the two revolutionaries, Maria Pavlovna and Vera in *Resurrection* (Voskresenie, 1899) fit the pattern: they sacrifice their personal lives in the cause of their suffering brethren. Tolstoi's good women, as in *War and Peace*, are innocent as girls and become chaste wives and dedicated mothers, like Natasha and Princess Marie, or useful, selfless spinsters, like Sonya; adulteresses, like Hélène Bezukhov, wreak evil and perish by it—even the lovely heroine of *Anna Karenina* (1877). Hence, there is no need to develop a woman's mind, still less her imagination. A worldly, frivolous education makes even blameless girls into traps for masculine lust and leads to tragedies, such as in *The Kreutzer Sonata* (Kreitserova sonata, 1889); while carnal passion breeds crime, as in *The Power of Darkness* (Vlast' t'my, 1887).

"The vulgar movement" dates in real life from the reforms of Tsar Alexander II, and is variously reflected in literature in the works of such dissimilar writers as Turgenev, GONCHAROV, POMYALOVSKY, and CHERNYSHEVSKY. It was the latter's effort to formulate the image of a truly emancipated woman in *What Is to Be Done* (Chto delat'?, 1864) that created Vera, the novel's heroine. She escaped the tyranny of her home by contracting a fictitious marriage to a progressive young student who educated her mind and eventually, by faking suicide, set her free to marry another. She founded a cooperative workshop for seamstresses, studied, and earned a degree in medicine. Another Vera in Goncharov's *The Precipice* (Obryv, 1869), manifested her freedom from prejudice by allowing herself to be seduced by a confirmed nihilist, repented, and married a former suitor. Turgenev's Marianna in *Virgin Soil* (Nov', 1877) eloped with an enthusiastic populist to help him in spreading revolutionary propaganda among peasants. When he committed suicide having become disappointed in the cause, Marianna lost her own interest in it, and married a level-headed liberal. Interestingly, the only genuinely emancipated woman in the novel is Mashurina, a cruel caricature of a female revolutionary. Another Turgenev heroine who embraced a lofty political cause is Elena in *On the Eve* (Nakanune, 1860). The cause is the liberation of Bulgaria; Elena eloped with a consumptive freedom fighter, and after his death continued his work alone. It will be observed that all the heroines seeking emancipation achieved it only with the help of men, on men's initiative and, basically, for men's sake. Even Pomyalovsky's Nadya, whose emancipation consisted in rebelling against her bourgeois family, and who refused to marry an influential bureaucrat in favor of an impecunious enlightened suitor, has had her mind and will developed by that very suitor (in *Molotov*, 1858).

Chekhov's only heroine to choose revolutionary activity over the routine of comfortable marriage is Nadya, in *The Bride* (Nevesta,

1903), and she too was set on that path by a male cousin. Otherwise to Chekhov—humane and liberal though he was—woman's emancipation was not a matter of deep concern. Like Turgenev, he preferred sweet and charming, if socially useless, girls to cold efficient activists—witness his Misyus and Lidiya respectively in *House with an Attic* (Dom s mezoninom, 1895). He portrayed, of course, intelligent women languishing in the *poshlost'* of provincial life, as in *Three Sisters* (Tri sestry, 1901), and talented idealistic girls vainly striving to serve Art, like Katya in *A Dreary Story* (Skuchnaya istoriya, 1889) and Nina in *The Seagull* (Chaika, 1895). Yet, theirs were not specifically feminine problems, but frustrations and goals shared within common social conditions with men. His characters seek refuge from despair and heartache in work, Chekhov's panacea for all the ills of the present and the only hope for the future of humanity. But women can find an added solace in religion and sacrifice, as does gentle Sonya, while nothing but alcohol is left for Dr. Astrov (*Uncle Vanya*, 1900).

Women writers, though widely read in Russia, contributed but little to the greatness of Russian literature, which has no George Sand, Jane Austen, or George Eliot. Their works followed contemporary intellectual and social trends mainly insofar as these affected the position of women in family and marriage, and otherwise continued a slightly updated trend of George-Sandism. Their heroines, as themselves, did not actively fight for their civic and political rights, economic independence, and an education which would make it possible. Few were interested in the plight of women who worked for a living. There were no prototypes of Mrs. Gaskell's *Mary Barton* in Russia, though certainly there were models for governesses like Brontë's *Jane Eyre* and, not existing elsewhere but easily found at home, models of miserable, oppressed peasant women. They created no original individuals within typical situations, no Anna Karenina or Mme Bovary, but rather stereotyped characters and conditions in which they confront their typical problems. Suffragette heroines, such as H. G. Wells's *Ann Veronica*, were unthinkable in Russian conditions, whether coming from the pen of a male or a female writer.

Evgeniya TUR (pseud. of Elizaveta Salias-de-Tournemir, 1815–92) published between 1840 and 1890 a number of essays on lives of distinguished women, among them George Sand; several novels on romantic loves of elegant heroines who had the good taste of preferring low-born teachers to aristocratic wastrels; and finally specialized in juvenile fiction—similarly proper, while liberally oriented. Lidiya Veselitskaya (pseud. Mikulich, 1857–1936) denounced in her *Mimochka* stories (1883–93) the superficial, trivial education received by rich middle-class girls at home and in boarding schools. Nadezhda Sokhan'skaya's (pseud. Kokhanovskaya, 1823–84) contribution to women's emancipation must be considered of a negative kind. A follower of the SLAVOPHILE trend, she portrayed in her numerous literary and journalistic writings the provincial milieu and its patriarchal family, as rooted in old-Russian traditions, piety, and virtues. Her path to women's happiness led through modesty and unquestioning obedience; she generously dispensed "national Slavic" paraphernalia: folk customs and costumes, rustic singing and dancing in the open air, and traditional wedding ceremonies, as for instance in *An After-dinner Visit* (Posle obeda v gostyakh, 1858) and *Kirill Petrov i Nastas'ya Dmitrova* (1862).

In contrast, Nadezha Khvoshchinskaya (pseud. V. KRESTOVSKY, 1824–89) represents the spirit of the sixties. Her heroines, like those of Gan, Pavlova, or Zhukova, still yearn for emotional freedom and suffer from the insensitivity of a frivolous beau monde; but her novels are also an indictment of a bureaucratic, money-mad society which victimizes or corrupts idealistic young men and naive girls, and Katya in *The Big Dipper* (Bol'shaya medveditsa, 1871), like Turgenev's Marianna, is a populist. Also her *The Boarding-School Girl* (Pansionerka, 1861) is an entirely new type of heroine. Lyolenka, seventeen, naive, ignorant, and submissive to her petty despotic parents, is unique among her contemporaries in fiction in that, having rejected her parents' choice of husband and having left their home, she is genuinely free and happy without love or marriage, earning her living and living alone.

Avdotya Panaeva (pseud. N. Stanitsky, 1820–93) is remembered for her *A Woman's Lot* (Zhenskaya dolya, 1862), the *Memoirs* of her literary salon (1889), and her long and unhappy liaison within a marriage à trois with Nekrasov, who also collaborated with her on some of her novels. Her *The Talnikov Family* (Semeistvo Tal'nikovykh, 1848), rejected by the censor as "undermining parental authority," was discovered only posthumously. That saga of a swarm of unwanted children, neglected by parents, abused by alcoholic relatives and an ignorant governess, is comparable only to Saltykov-Shchedrin's *The Chronicle of Poshekhonie* (Poshekhonskaya starina, 1887–89) where children, brought up by a servile governess, were divided into those "dear" or "odious" to the heart of their despot mother. Panaeva's narrator, believed to be Panaeva herself, escapes from the inferno of her home by marrying at sixteen the first man to ask her. To quote one of the personages of Ostrovsky's plays: "The girl has no skills, no learning—what is she fit for except for marriage?"

With the turn of the century, and through the next two decades, the woman question in literature fell into disfavor. The modernists and even the "fellow travellers" of the 1920s, did not concern themselves with it. Womanhood for BLOK meant his quest for the ideal Beautiful Lady, who could also materialize in a suburban tavern as the Unknown Woman; for BRYUSOV it was the collective object of his famous one-line poem: "O, cover your pale legs!" or Renata the witch, in *The Fiery Angel* (Ognennyi angel, 1907); for BELY, the half-wit "Angel Peri" in *Petersburg* (1913), or evil sexuality incarnate, Matryona in *The Silver Dove* (Serebryanyi golub', 1909). Modernist women poets, Zinaida HIPPIUS, Anna AKHMATOVA, and Marina TSVETAEVA, did not deal with women's emancipation in their lyrics, and Hippius's prose reveals her fascination with the mysterious element of the *Ewig-Weibliche*, not voting rights.

Anastasya VERBITSKAYA (1861–1928), however, is a champion, a believer in Stanisław Przybyszewski's (1868–1927) concept of a free "naked soul": sexuality expressed through art and hysteria. Her Manya, the heroine of *The Keys to Happiness* (Klyuchi schast'ya, 1908–13), seeks freedom from the fetters of social prejudice by bearing a child out of wedlock, finds spiritual fulfillment in barefoot dancing, achieves equality with men by having two lovers simultaneously, and, failing nevertheless to find her identity, commits suicide. She does have certain socialist leanings, but these are marginal interests.

Thus, between GORKY's Malva and Verbitskaya's Manya, no heroine raised the banner of women's rights. *Malva* (1897) is a proletarian version of the mysterious Eternal Femininity. A fisher-woman with a beautiful restless soul, she is free in her material independence, her contempt for property, and frank sexuality. The first proletarian heroine, however, is not Malva but Pelageya Nilovna, the middle-aged, workman's widow in Gorky's *Mother* (1906). She achieved this status through her contact with socialist underground activists, developed class-consciousness, and followed in her son's steps by distributing revolutionary pamphlets. For Lidiya Seifullina's *Virineya* (1924) whose sexual behavior used to scandalize her neighbors, the road to class-consciousness led through love for a true Bolshevik: she died for him and for the Revolution.

Gorky, a pureblood Marxist, shared Marx's ideas on the woman question as part of the proletarian revolution. Therefore, when with its advent, women were officially liberated, acquiring complete legal equality with men, the woman question ceased to exist for him, as for all the proletarian writers of the 1920s. There remained, however, the necessity of making women aware of using their rights, and the first writers who undertook the task created in their zeal model heroines larger than life. Of these, Zhenya in *Love of Three Generations* (Lyubov' trekh pokolenii) and *Vasilisa Malygina* (both 1923), by Aleksandra Kollontai (1872–1952) and Dasha in *Cement* (1925) by GLADKOV (1883–1958), are the most representative. All three women are totally dedicated to the Communist Party, despise bourgeois prejudices and love of property, and exercise their right to equality with men, Dasha by being unfaithful to her husband, Vasilisa by divorcing hers, and young Zhenya by carrying on two affairs simultaneously and considering both "unimportant as drinking a glass of water." However lofty the New Heroine's principles were—and perhaps because of them—her image was considerably altered in the Party-approved model of the next period. Dasha, who in order to work full time at *Zhenotdel* (a women's section of the Communist Party, 1919–1929) neglected her home and placed her child in an orphanage where it eventually died, proved too ambitious an example to emulate. Zhenya's casual promiscuity resembled too much the "free love" of Verbitskaya to be compatible with

Marxist ideals. Vasilisa, class-conscious and a factory worker, who left her unfaithful husband, determined to raise their child all by herself, was more acceptable, and her type contributed one of the patterns for a proletarian woman under SOCIALIST REALISM.

Socialist realism is a watershed in the history of Russian literature. Established in 1934, it limited creative writing to one goal: ideological education of the reader, and one method: presenting Soviet reality—people and environment—in its revolutionary development, that is, not as they are today but as they are expected to become tomorrow. Henceforth, literary trends were determined by the degrees to which Soviet writers were compelled to follow these basic rules, or were able to deviate from them. The woman question, then, can be considered only within this context, as one assumed to have been solved. Parental authority no longer extended beyond the age of legal majority, that of a husband did not exist, divorce was available practically on demand, education was equal for both sexes, as was access to all professions, thus assuring economic independence. However, with equal rights came equal duties. At the peak of socialist realism (1946–54) a typical heroine was, indeed, the hero's equal: she was just as industrious, as good a Soviet citizen guided by the Party, successful and happy in the work of building socialism. On occasion, she even surpassed him. In war novels (an evergreen subject for decades after World War II) she vied with men in heroism on the battle line, in partisan activities, and usefulness on the home front. She also lived up to the high standards of the new Soviet family's morals and values which, under the watchful eye of the Party, excluded sexual licence, adultery, or ideological deviations. Kollontai's Zhenya was succeeded by her namesake, a student in V. Dobrovolsky's *Zhenya Maslova* (1950). Gladkov's Dasha was followed by *kolkhoznitsa* Dunya, innovator, citizen, and homemaker, in Galina NIKOLAEVA's *The Harvest* (Zhatva, 1950). Heroines of the post-war Soviet-educated intelligentsia were: the efficient director of a goldmine in Antonina Koptyaeva's *Tovarishch Anna* (1950), good mother and a wife, proud but capable of forgiving a repentant husband's momentary aberration; and the brilliant engineer Nonna, content to take the second place in her husband's life, his work taking the first, in *The Factory* (Kruzhilikha, 1947) by Vera PANOVA.

After Stalin's death, when it became gradually possible not, to be sure, to oppose socialist realism, but to write unostentatiously outside its pale, the woman question emerged in a new guise. First came the revival of the ancient problem of dissimilarity in emotional attitudes of men and women: the very words "love, marriage, infidelity" seemed, as of old, to have a different meaning for either sex, and to affect women's lives more significantly than men's. The first harbingers of the phenomenon were not so much ERENBURG's *The Thaw* (Ottepel', 1954) or DUDINTSEV's *Not by Bread Alone* (Ne khlebom edinym, 1956), though their respective heroines left their husbands, resenting their bureaucratic insensitivity to everything except work (a trait hitherto considered a communist virtue), but *Elena* (1955) by Kseniya Lvova (1897–). The success of this maudlin novel revealed the readers' longing for a true-to-life heroine, one "who has everything" in terms of civic rights, and yet can want something more out of life than marriage to a good Soviet citizen; Elena ruins her marriage by taking a lover, an engineer like herself and a married man.

This new form of George-Sandism invaded Soviet literature progressing through the 1960s and 1970s, and into the 1980s. Women's economic independence and legal equality proved to offer no emotional help in love affairs; in fact, it rather encouraged philanderers, who felt no responsibility towards a "good pal" of female gender, like Nikandrov in ZALYGIN's *The South-American Variant* (Yuzhno-amerikanskii variant) or Chuzhinov in GRANIN's *Rain in a Strange City* (Dozhd' v chuzhom gorode, both 1973). In classical marital triangles, the trauma of breaking up a home, severing familiar ties, hurting the children, often would prevent the now-obtainable divorce, leaving both romance and marriage in ruins, as for instance, in Nikolaeva's *Battle on the Way* (Bitva v puti, 1957), or GLADILIN's *Forecast for Tomorrow* (Prognoz na zavtra, 1972). Women—usually strong, sometimes just average, but always self-supporting—valiantly accepted the necessity of rebuilding their lives. Their tragedy was the sudden loneliness: a trust was shattered, a husband or a lover, in the words of a heroine, had overnight become a stranger, as in *In Summer, in Town* (Letom v gorode, 1965) by Irina GRE-

KOVA (pseud. of Elena Ventsel). Variations on that theme have been contributed chiefly by women writers. A few examples follow: Panova's *A Farewell to the White Nights* (Provody belykh nochei, 1960); *The Red Light* (Krasnyi svet, 1971) by Nora Adamyan (pseud. of Eleonora Adamova, 1910–); *Nobody, Ever* (Nikto, nikogda, 1971) by Natalya Davydova (1925–); *A Sweet Woman* (Sladkaya zhenshchina, 1973) by Irina Velembovskaya (pseud. of Irina Shukhgalter, 1922–); *Hearken to Your Hour* (Uslysh' svoi chas, 1976) by Maiya Ganina (1927–); *May It Perish* (Propadi ono propadom, 1972) by Viktoriya Tokareva (1937–). Another disconcerting aspect of the present-day woman question was presented by Natalya Baranskaya (1908–) in a novelette *A Week like Any Other* (Nedelya kak nedelya, 1969), which could have been entitled "the emancipated woman's dilemma": how to be a breadwinner, career woman, wife, mother, and homemaker all at once? After the Revolution, Kollontai had envisaged a utopian answer: communal houses where services—cleaning, mending, cooking, and child-care—would be provided by the State, leaving women free to work in their chosen professions and use the leisure time in cultural activities. Fifty years later, Baranskaya's Olga, a promising scientist, a happily married mother of two, is torn between her working hours at the Institute, the shopping, done during the lunch break, and, in the evening the cooking, the house chores, and attending to the children, home from their kindergarten. Not surprisingly, no time is left for any cultural or social activities. Olga's husband helps occasionally and acknowledges her equal rights, but this is no general solution, especially since not all husbands are so cooperative, and divorced and single mothers have nowhere to turn for help. Finally, a third aspect is gaining in popularity in the Soviet fiction. Judging by the heroines of Lipatov's (1927–79) novel, *A Tale without a Plot, Beginning, or End* (Povest' bez syuzheta, nachala i kontsa, 1978) and Grekova's *The Faculty* (Kafedra, 1978), emancipated women are still subject to the biological urge of building a nest, and a primordial feminine longing for a mate who is reliable, wise, and—stronger than themselves. Thus, apparently, the woman question has come full circle and, possibly, to the verge of starting anew.

Bibliography: A. Chudinov, *Istoriya russkoi zhenshchiny v posledovatel'nom razvitii eya literaturnykh tipov.* 2d. ed. St. Petersburg, 1873. Carolina de Maegd-Soëp, *The Emancipation of Women in Russian Literature and Society.* Ghent, 1978. Xenia Gasiorowska, *Women in Soviet Fiction: 1917–1964.* Madison, 1968. M. Portugalov, *Zhenshchina v russkoi khudozhestvennoi literature XIX veka.* St. Petersburg, 1914. Carl and Ellendea Proffer, eds., *Women in Russian Literature, Russian Literature Triquarterly* 9 (1974). N. Trubitsyn, *Obshchestvennaya rol' zhenshchiny v izobrazhenii noveishei russkoi literatury.* Moscow, 1907.   X. G.

Workers' songs fall into four basic categories: (1) oral works by the workers; (2) literary works which entered the oral system and were modified; (3) written songs by proletarian poets; and (4) songs by the revolutionary intelligentsia. Dating many of these works is difficult since the majority were recorded during the Soviet period, as much as two centuries after their origin.

It is assumed that the earlier songs, which often reflect no protest, date from the 18th century. One describes the building of the Ladoga Canal in St. Petersburg. In the first half of the 19th century, songs were optimistic. In them the owner promised the workers that everything would get better, or men found life in the village boring, preferring the factory and amusements of the city. Most songs were about specific professions. In the factories and metallurgical mines in the Urals and Siberia, peasants from many different areas resettled and their songs were a fusion of folklore traditions from their native regions. In these songs there were complaints of long working hours, extreme reprisal for disobedience, and child labor. By the mid-19th century there were motifs of running away from the factory or mine, and of staged protests against working conditions in particular establishments. The textile workers in central Russia complained of mutilation by machines, and the coal miners in the Don Basin feared cave-ins and other dangers they faced working in the mines. The songs often consisted of couplets connected by a general theme such as bad working conditions, but with no prescribed sequence, so that the order and number of couplets varied. A favorite motif was "For whom is it worse?" The miners address the peasants

saying their own life is much more difficult. There are also love songs about girls whose sweetheart has left the village for the factory. In the 1870s the POPULISTS wrote and disseminated songs among the proletariat as well as the peasants.

While the songs in the middle of the century were generally related to specific professions and establishments and were mainly an expression of the dissatisfaction of the workers, the songs of the 1890s were devoted to the proletariat in general and urged armed uprising. Many of the songs were written by proletarian poets such as Moiseenko and Shtripan under the strong influence of literary models. Marches and hymns were written as well as satirical songs. They were spread orally, and by leaflets, and underground newspapers. Often they reflect specific events such as Bloody Sunday of 1905. Works by earlier revolutionaries such as RYLEEV and BESTUZHEV became popular and were imitated. The texts of these later songs were much more stable than the earlier texts, which were more under the influence of folklore. Songs of the 1890s also reflected the influence of popular culture, such as gypsy songs and "cruel romances."

Songs would vary over time. For example, the famous "Oh, that Mining Work" (O, se gornye raboty) at first mainly described the mining process, and only incidentally mentioned the difficulties of the work; in later variants the description of the labor process is vastly reduced, and the difficulties and bad conditions are emphasized. Motifs and formulae would be borrowed from folk lyrics such as the soldier song and applied to life in the factory or mines. Songs composed in response to a specific event would be modified to fit other similar events. "The Whip" (Nagaika), for example, first composed by students in connection with the suppression by mounted police of a student demonstration in 1899, was later enlarged with material relating to Bloody Sunday. There were also translations of famous revolutionary songs such as the "Varshavyanka" and the "Internationale." Thus the workers' songs represent a wide range of types, from those closely associated with peasant folk lyrics with many variations to those which were under the influence of literature and remained as relatively fixed texts; the earlier texts were more concrete and localized and expressed grievances, whereas the ones at the turn of the century called for armed uprising and finally for political overthrow of the tsar.

Bibliography: O. B. Alekseeva, *Ustnaya poeziya russkikh rabochikh.* 1971. V. Chichirov, "Pesni i stikhi proletariata v periode massovogo rabochego revolyutsionnogo dvizheniya (1890–1907)." In *Voprosy teorii i istorii narodnogo tvorchestva.* 1959. Pp. 159–227. K. E. Korepova, "Nekotorye problemy izdaniya rabochikh pesen," *RFolk* 19, pp. 178–86. *Pesni russkikh rabochikh.* 2d ed. (Biblioteka poeta.) 1962. *Ustnaya poeziya rabochikh Rossii.* Ed. V. G. Bazanov. 1975.   R. R.

Yakubóvich, Pyotr Filippovich (1860–1911), poet, short-story writer, and literary critic. A professional revolutionary, Yakubovich was born of gentry parents in Isaevo, Novgorod province. After graduating from St. Petersburg University in 1882, he joined the revolutionary group, The People's Will, and was arrested in 1884. Eleven years of prison, hard labor, and exile in Siberia failed to break his revolutionary spirit. His faith in the inevitability of a revolution in Russia was reflected in "The Cloud" (Oblako, 1892) and "In the Year of Hunger" (V golodnyi god, 1892) and the atmosphere of the revolutionary period in "Red Snow" (Krasnyi sneg, 1905) and "Land" (Zemlya, 1907–08). He employed various pseudonyms, notably "P. Ya." and "Ramshev" for poetry, "L. Mel'shin" for prose, and "P. F. Grinevich" for literary criticism. He began publishing poetry, "My Path" (Moya doroga), in 1878 and his first collection, *Matvei Ramshev's Verses* (Stikhotvoreniya Matveya Ramsheva), appeared in 1887. An admirer of NEKRASOV, Yakubovich wrote "civic" poetry depicting the revolutionary as a fearless fighter. His poetry, with its dominant motifs of "just anger" and "revenge," is lucid and simple but artistically weak. It reflects his sympathy with people's suffering, his dream of the brotherhood of men, and his faith in the victory of justice. Yakubovich's principal work, the autobiographical *In the World of Outcasts* (V mire otverzhennykh, 1895–98), was the best penological study to appear after DOSTOEVSKY's *Notes from the House of the Dead*. He portrays criminals with remarkable objectivity, yet detects in them flashes of humanness and dignity. In 1901 he published the collection of stories *Life's Stepchildren* (Pasynki zhizni) and in 1904 the critical *Essays on Russian Poetry* (Ocherki russkoi poezii).

Works: Stikhotvoreniya. 2 vols. 1898–1901. *Pasynki zhizni. Rasskazy.* 1918. *Vol'naya russkaya poeziya vtoroi poloviny XIX veka.* 1959. *Stikhotvoreniya.* 1960. *V mire otverzhennykh.* 2 vols. 1964.

Translations: "The Ninth Wave" (rendered into English verse by A. Blackwell), *Russian Review* (New York) 1, no. 2 (March 1916), p. 84.

Secondary literature: A. N. Bakh, *Zapiski narodovol'tsa.* 2d ed. 1931. E. P. (Demyan Bednyi), "Pevets bor'by i gneva," *Zvezda,* no. 18 (1912). B. N. Dvinyaninov, *Mech i lira.* 1969. V. G. Korolenko, *Voina, otechestvo i chelovechestvo.* 1917. I. I. Popov, *P. F. Yakubovich.* 1930. I. D. Yakubovich, *P. F. Yakubovich.* 1967.　　　　L. P.

Yanóvsky, Vasíly Semyónovich (1906–　), émigré writer and physician. Yanovsky first belonged to the "Paris school" of Russian émigré writers, publishing three novels and numerous short stories and other pieces in Paris or Berlin in the 1930s. After coming to the United States in 1942, he entered the American literary scene in 1967 with the publication of *No Man's Time* (with a foreword by W. H. Auden). Since his novel *The Great Transfer* (1974) Yanovsky has switched to writing in English. His unusual novels are generally fictional speculations on religious and philosophical themes, strongly influenced by the ideas of BERDYAEV, Bergson, FYODOROV, and FEDOTOV: there is in them, as one critic put it, a "quest for humanism, social justice, and the transfiguration of a grossly material world through transcendent philosophy as well as action."

Works: Koleso. Paris-Berlin, 1930. *Mir.* Berlin, 1931. *Lyubov' vtoraya.* Paris, 1935. *Portativnoe bessmertie.* New York, 1953. *Amerikanskii opyt.* First in *Novyi zhurnal,* 1946–48. Reprinted in book form, New York, 1982. *No Man's Time.* New York, 1967. *Of Light and Sounding Brass.* New York, 1972. *The Great Transfer.* New York, 1974. *Medicine, Science and Life.* New York, 1978.

Bibliography: Foster, pp. 1229–31. "Yanovsky" in *Contemporary Authors.* Vol. 97–100, pp. 577–79.　　　　L. D.

Yáshin (pseud. of Aleksándr Yákovlevich Popóv, 1913–1968), poet and prose writer, was born into a peasant family of Vologda province. He graduated from a technical school and worked as a teacher. His first verses were printed in *Pionerskaya Pravda* when he was fifteen. His first collections, *Songs to the North* (Pesni Severu, 1934) and *The Northern Woman* (Severyanka, 1938), sing the praises of the "new" and "happy" life on the collective farm quite in the customary official style. Yashin graduated from the Literary Institute in 1941 and promptly joined the Communist Party. He then worked as a war correspondent, publishing verses and sketches in the usual spirit of socialist realism, glorifying the heroism of Soviet warriors. His *poema* "Alyona Fomina" (1949), in which post-war village life was described in idealized rose-colored hues, brought him a Stalin prize. There is some evidence (Svirsky, p. 82) that there were some truthful strophes in it, dealing with the plight of the Vologda peasantry, but that Yashin was ordered to excise them, and did, allegedly "with tears in his eyes."

The turning point in Yashin's career came in 1956, when he published his story "The Levers" (Rychagi) in the almanac *Literaturnaya Moskva.* This story was among the works which launched the literature of recantation (*literatura otrecheniya*), as a movement toward truth and sincerity arose in Russian literature after Stalin's death. Simple and meticulously precise in its details, the story deals with collective-farm leaders who have been made into "levers" of the Party. Their whole life is pervaded by lies and falsehoods. The story literally shocked the Soviet readership, which then still had had little experience with the truth, and scored an extraordinary success, although it was sharply condemned by leading Party ideologues. Akin to "The Levers" was the story "A Vologda Wedding" (*Novyi mir,* 1962), which mercilessly exposes the bitter truth about the daily grind of Soviet life. It was also denounced by the official critics.

Yashin's poetry after 1956 likewise reveals a complete spiritual

revival in that it wholly renounces the falsehood and dogmatism of his earlier works. It is no accident that the favorite image of these poems is renewal, springtime, nature's awakening: "As though I were Reborn" (Kak budto rodilsya ya zanovo), "They've washed the Windowpanes" (Promyli v oknakh stekla), "The Butterfly came back to Life" (Babochka ozhila), among others. In the poetry of these years lyric motifs prevail: meditations on the ways of the world, self-criticism, a yearning for goodness and sincerity. Yashin's poetic images are simple and unassuming, at times primitive. His best collection is *Barefoot through the Land* (Bosikom po zemle). Yashin continued to write prose also, deepening his reflections about the Russian countryside, the psychology of mental dependance ("The Orphan"), and in general on the truth about life in the countryside. In a posthumous story, "Shortness of Breath" (Korotkoe dykhanie), a personal drama of Yashin's last years, his infatuation with the poetess Veronika Tushnova, apparently has found its expression.

Collections of Verse: Pesni Severu. 1934. *Severyanka.* 1938. *Na Baltike bylo* ... 1942. *Gorod gneva.* 1943. *Zemlyaki.* 1946. *Alena Fomina.* 1949. *Sovetskii chelovek.* 1951. *Sovest'.* 1961. *Bosikom po zemle.* 1965. *Den' tvoreniya.* 1968. *Bessonnitsa.* 1968. *Prose:* "Rychagi," *Literaturnaya Moskva,* Vol. 2. 1956. "Sirota" and "Vologodskaya svad'ba," *Novyi mir,* 1962, no. 12. "Ugoshchayu ryabinoi," *Novyi mir,* 1965, no. 6. "Korotkoe dykhanie," *Zvezda,* 1971, no. 5. *Collected works: Izbrannye proizvedeniya.* 2 Vols. 1973.

Secondary literature: Yu. Burtin, *Novyi mir,* 1969, no. 10. F. Abramov, *Novyi mir,* 1973, no. 4. (Verses from Yashin's diaries and reminiscences of his daughter) *Sever,* 1973, nos. 4 and 9. G. Svirskii, "Na lobnom meste," *Overseas,* 1979. (Personal reminiscences.)
　　　　E. D. A.

Yásnaya Polyána, the name of L. N. TOLSTOI's ancestral estate, was also the title of a monthly journal on education which he edited and published in 1862 and 1863. In 1859 Tolstoi had founded a school in which he taught the peasant children of his estate. He devoted much study to educational theory and travelled extensively in Europe to observe the pedagogical practices of the time. *Yasnaya Polyana* was the forum in which he discussed his findings, described the practices of his school, and set forth his own ideas on education and teaching. In all, twelve issues of the journal appeared. Simultaneously, Tolstoi published a series of "Yasnaya Polyana Booklets." These contained reading material suitable for school children, including a few stories written by pupils of Tolstoi's school. The journal did not enjoy great success, although notice was taken of it (and of Tolstoi's ideas on education) by such influential critics as N. G. CHERNYSHEVSKY and N. A. DOBROLYUBOV, and by F. M. DOSTOEVSKY's journal VREMYA.

Of the numerous articles written by Tolstoi for the journal the most significant are: "On Popular Education" (O narodnom obrazovanii), in which he discusses his general theory of education for the people; "On the Methods of Teaching the Rudiments" (O metodakh obucheniya gramote), in which he describes his pedagogical strategies in teaching children to read and write; "Who Should Learn to Write from Whom, the Peasant Children from Us or We from the Peasant Children?" (Komu u kogo uchit'sya pisat', krest'yanskim rebyatam u nas ili nam u krest'yanskikh rebyat?), an essay on the proper cultivation of the innate aesthetic values of the pupils; and "Yasnaya Polyana School in November and December" (Yasnopolyanskaya shkola za noyabr' i dekabr' mesyatsy), an account of the school's day-to-day operations.

Bibliography. The articles written by Tolstoi for *Yasnaya Polyana* are collected in volume 8 of L. N. Tolstoi, *Polnoe sobranie sochinenii* (1928–58). Seven of them, including those mentioned above, are available in English translation in *Tolstoy on Education,* trans. L. Wiener (1967). For discussion of the substance of Tolstoi's articles on education see G. R. Noyes, *Tolstoy* (1918), chapter 4, and A. Maude, *The Life of Tolstoy* (1930), vol. 1, chaps. 7 and 8. On Tolstoi and *Yasnaya Polyana* see N. Smirnov, *Lev Tolstoi— redaktor zhurnala* Yasnaya Polyana (1972).　　　　G. J.

Yavórsky, Stefán (Simeón, 1658–1722), poet and preacher, was born in Galicia of Russian or Ukrainian parents. He attended the KIEV ACADEMY, then Polish and Lithuanian universities. Returning to

Kiev, he took holy orders and taught at the Academy where he became "poet laureate" and earned a reputation as a brilliant preacher. This latter distinction so impressed Peter I that, despite Yavorsky's extreme reluctance, the tsar had him consecrated Metropolitan of Ryazan and Murom and, subsequently, appointed to a series of offices requiring Yavorsky's residence in Moscow and St. Petersburg. Although occupying eminent positions (such as president of the Holy Synod), Yavorsky's life in Russia was a troubled one, as he did not sympathize with Peter's reforms and was also fiercely distrusted by the conservative Russian clergy. He was never allowed to return to Kiev.

Yavorsky enjoyed considerable literary repute during his lifetime. Author of magnificent baroque sermons and of theological tracts that figured prominently in the religious polemics of the time, he was also a tri-lingual poet. His masterpiece, an elegy-farewell to his library, is in Latin and belongs to the tradition of neo-Latin humanism. In Polish, as well as Latin, he produced typically baroque heraldic, panegyric, and occasional poems. Among his CHURCH SLAVONIC verses, his epitaph-cycle entitled "Emblemata et Symbola" proves him to have been an adept of the baroque lyric as well.

Yavorsky's literary fame all but vanished after his death. Ironically, many of his finest verses came to be attributed to his more prestigious arch-rival, Feofan PROKOPOVICH. The difficult task of reconstructing Yavorsky's full literary legacy is only now in progress.

Works: Selected letters in *Trudy Kievskoi Dukhovnoi Akademii,* 1866, no. 4. Selected sermons in *TKDA,* 1874, nos. 7, 10, 12; 1875, nos. 1, 3, 5, 9, 10; 1877, no. 4. Latin elegy in S. I. Maslov, *Biblioteka Stefana Yavorskogo.* Kiev, 1914. "Emblemata et Symbola." In I. P. Eremin, "K voprosu o stikhotvoreniyakh Feofana Prokopovicha," *TODRL* 16 (1960). Also in A. M. Panchenko, *Russkaya sillabicheskaya poeziya XVII–XVIII vv.* 1970.

Secondary literature: E. Bolkhovitinov, *Slovar' o russkikh pisatelyakh Greko-Rossiiskoi Tserkvi.* Vol. 2. 1827. Pp. 251–62. R. Lużny, "Stefan Jaworski—Poeta nieznany," *Slavia Orientalis* 16 (1967), no. 4, pp. 363–76. Ju. Šerech, "Stefan Javorsky and the Conflict of Ideologies in the Age of Peter I," *SEER* 30 (1951), pp. 40–62. F. A. Ternovskii, "Mitropolit Stefan Yavorskii (Biograficheskii ocherk)," *Trudy Kievskoi Dukhovnoi Akademii,* 1864, nos. 1, 3, 6.
I. R. T.

Yazýkov, Nikolaí Mikhaílovich (1803–47), poet. Yazykov, born to a landowning family whose wealth supported him throughout his life, was sent to St. Petersburg for schooling, which he did not complete. It was here that he wrote his first verse, largely under the influence of BATYUSHKOV and ZHUKOVSKY. In 1822 he entered the relatively free and European University of Dorpat (now Tartu), where he spent nearly seven years and produced the poetry that won him the admiration of his contemporaries, among them PUSHKIN, who proclaimed this verse "intoxication." During these years he made the acquaintance of Zhukovsky, DELVIG, Pushkin, and (probably) RYLEEV. In 1829 Yazykov left for Moscow without receiving his diploma and took up nominal government service. Here his circle of acquaintance consisted mainly of former members of the "WISDOM LOVERS" and of future SLAVOPHILES: Ivan and Pyotr KIREEVSKY, A. S. KHOMYAKOV (who married Yazykov's sister), Konstantin AKSAKOV, M. P. POGODIN, and S. P. SHEVYRYOV. Determined to devote himself to verse projects more serious than the celebrations of "wine, women, and song" that had made his reputation, Yazykov studied the Bible, religious literature, and Russian folklore. He prefaced the first collection of his works (1833) with a poem, "To a Poet" that announced this commitment to a poetics of prophesy, religious significance, and moral purity. Soon, however, serious illness (*tabes dorsalis*) forced him to return to his Simbirsk estate (1833–38), then to make the rounds of European spas (1838–43). During these travels he was befriended by Nikolai GOGOL, but their stay in Rome together did not prove satisfactory to either, and Yazykov returned to Moscow, where, having survived his talent, he died. He devoted his last years to attacks on various "Westernizers" (CHAADAEV, BELINSKY, GRANOVSKY, HERZEN). Two more collections of verse (1844, 1845) received generally hostile reviews.

Yazykov is remembered principally for his student songs, which, like Denis DAVYDOV's hussar songs, presented a strikingly original

persona and an image of "freedom" to a culture that longed for both. This image of Yazykov as the bold, impulsive, inspired, liberty-loving student-poet was confirmed in lyric epistles by Pushkin (1826) and BARATYNSKY (1831), in Gogol's essay on Russian poetry (1846), and in MANDELSHTAM's "Stikhi o russkoi poezii" (1832). Although at times sophomoric in their sexual, religious, and political libertinism, Yazykov's verses of the 1820s, such as "In cordial harmony with wine" (Ot serdtsa druzhnye s vinom, 1823), often achieved a brilliant synthesis of technique and theme. Yazykov's iambic tetrameters were remarkable for their rapidity of tempo, realized through his frequent use of pyrrhic feet and long intervals between syntactic breaks. Although not entirely without precedent—Davydov, Schiller, Byron, KATENIN, Ryleev, GNEDICH, and Pushkin attracted at various times his admiration—Yazykov's verse had an unmediated quality, a lack of literary references, that was unusual at the time. His "elegies" had little in common with the examples of that genre that Batyushkov, Zhukovsky, and Pushkin were offering the Russian public. Featuring explicit, sensual detail and political defiance, they constituted something of an attack on the genre. See, in particular, "Inspiration of proud freedom!" (Svobody gordoi vdokhnoven'e! 1824) and "Blest who could on the couch of night (Blazhen, kto mog na lozhe nochi, 1831).

Yazykov's post-1833 verse is generally considered a departure from his exuberant work of the 1820s. His tempos slowed down, his generally superficial "free-thinking" yielded to equally superficial Slavophilism, his elegies became more "dejected" (to use the terminology of the time), and he tried his hand at new genres—dramatic scenes, folk tales: "The Firebird" (Zhar-ptitsa, fragments 1836–45, separate edition 1857), verse narratives ("Serzhant Surmin," 1845; "Lipy," 1846), and polemical epistles: "To the Other Side" (K nenashim, 1844); "To Chaadaev" (1844). His gifts did not prove equal to these new tasks—the narratives proved less kinetic than even his descriptive poems of the earlier period, such as "Trigorskoe" (1826), or "Two Pictures" (Dve kartiny, 1825), and the epistles—spiteful and witless—discomfited his allies as much as his opponents. Yet even in these years of physical and poetic degeneration, Yazykov wrote several lyrics that recalled his early promise: a verse epistle to Davydov (1835) that moved Pushkin to tears (reports Gogol), and a metapoetic meditation, "Earthquake" (Zemletryasenie, 1844) that Zhukovsky called the finest Russian lyric (same source).

Works: Yazykovskii arkhiv. Vol. 1. *Pis'ma N. M. Yazykova k rodnym za derptskii period ego zhizni* (1822–1829). 1913. *Polnoe sobranie stikhotvorenii.* Ed. and introd. M. K. Azadovskii. 1934. *Polnoe sobranie stikhotvorenii.* Ed. and introd. K. K. Bukhmeier. 1964.

Translations: See Lewanski, pp. 394–95.

Secondary literature: V. N. Orlov, "Yazykov." In his *Puti i sud'by.* 1963. I. M. Semenko, "Yazykov." In her *Poety pushkinskoi pory.* 1970.
W. M. T.

Yuliániya Lazarévskaya, St. The Tale of Yulianiya Lazarevskaya uses hagiographical conventions to present a story of daily life and a family chronicle. It was written soon after 1614 by the protagonist's son Druzhina-Kalistrat Osoryin (1570–1640), a member of the gentry serving as Officer of the Peace in Murom the last fifteen years of his life. He drew on the domestic ideal of the 16th-century DOMOSTROI to portray his mother, Yulianiya Yustinovna Osoryina (died 1604), called Lazarevskaya after her husband's village of Lazarevo near Murom. She manifests exemplary good sense and piety while raising a family and looking after the extensive estate and household of her husband in the periods of severe famine and pestilence which lasted into the reign of Boris Godunov. However, during her childhood, and especially after the murder of her eldest son by a serf, she exceeded the ideal of the House Orderer and took on the attributes of a lay saint, mortifying her flesh, subjecting herself to poverty through extensive works of charity, living in chastity with her husband's permission and praying at home when unable to go to church. Her son makes her the focus of supernatural activity during and after her lifetime. Osoryin's creation of the image of a saint out of his own mother, neither nun nor princess, represents a step forward in the larger cultural process of granting the private individual within his daily life the power to serve and even to define the supernatural, a process which brought new aspects of human and social reality into the domain of literary representation during the 17th century.

Bibliography: For an English translation of the tale see: S. A. Zenkovsky, *Medieval Russia's Epics, Chronicles and Tales.* 1974. Pp. 391–99. For an early 17th century Russian version see: M. Skripil', *Russkaya povest' XVII veka.* 1954. Pp. 39–47. The most extensive critical treatment has been given by F. Buslaev, "Ideal'nye zhenskie kharaktery drevnei Rusi," in his *Istoricheskie ocherki* 2, pp. 238–68.   P. H.

Yuródivye (holy fools, God's folk), usually an abbreviation of *yurodivye Khrista radi* (fools for the sake of Christ). These were men and women, usually of peasant origin, both Orthodox and sectarian, who wandered around and behaved as if they were mad, and who allegedly did so not because they were mentally ill but for the sake of humility. The opinions of Russians on that subject have always been divided. While a majority of the society perceived *yurodivye* as deeply religious and spiritual, a minority (including some ranking members of the Russian Orthodox Church) saw them as a group of mentally disturbed people who either would not or could not join organized society. The behavior of *yurodivye* entailed such characteristics as nakedness, striking neglect of bodily needs, striking fondness for iron objects, vagrancy, soothsaying, clairvoyance, and a tendency to commit apparently immoral acts including sacrilege and even murder. While in Kievan Russia *yurodstvo* (*yurodivyi*-like behavior) was a rare phenomenon, in Muscovite Russia it became common. Some *yurodivye* were actually canonized as saints. The number of those canonized however is significantly lower than the customary figure of thirty-six which was quoted in G. P. FEDOTOV's *The Russian Religious Mind.* In 19th-century Russia, a vast body of hagiographical literature was created to explain and justify religious veneration of *yurodivye.* One way to legitimize their claim to religious orthodoxy was to emphasize a connection between them and the small group of Byzantine ascetics known as *saloi.*

In spite of the Church's uneasy tolerance of the veneration of *yurodivye,* historical evidence suggests that they derived more from a shamanic tradition than from the Christian one. Shamanic characteristics include paranormal behavior similar to that of the *yurodivyi,* as well as ornamental use of iron, nakedness, speech disorders, clairvoyance and the use of musical instruments to attract attention.

Nineteenth-century Russian literature made vast use of *yurodivye.* PUSHKIN, TOLSTOI, DOSTOEVSKY, GARIN-Mikhailovsky, MELNIKOV-PECHERSKY, ZAGOSKIN, MEREZHKOVSKY, BUNIN, and others presented in their works portraits of *yurodivye* of both sexes. Some of the popular characters of 19th-century Russian fiction: Pierre Bezukhov in Tolstoi's *War and Peace* and Prince Myshkin in Dostoevsky's *The Idiot,* seem to be modelled on *yurodivye.* *Yurodstvo* is one of the important concepts in the interpretation of Russian literature and culture.

Bibliography: E. M. Thompson, *The Holy Fool in Russian Culture.* Forthcoming.   E. Th.

Zabolótsky, Nikolaí Alekséevich (1903–58), poet. Zabolotsky's father was an agronomist, of peasant stock. The poet's childhood and youth were spent in a remote rural area and in small provincial towns, such as Urdzhum of Vyatka province, where he graduated from secondary school. He then attended the Leningrad Herzen Pedagogical Institute, graduating in 1925. Zabolotsky began to publish his verse as a student. At one time he belonged to the OBERIU group of poets, which advocated a palpable "thingness" (*veshchnost'*) in art, meaning that the artist should present "a concrete object cleansed of its literary and everyday shell." Zabolotsky also collaborated with the *Oberiuty* in two journals for children, *Ezh* and *Chizh,* headed by S. Ya. MARSHAK. His work for these journals and writing books for the State Publishing House for Children (*Detgiz*) was, more or less, Zabolotsky's only source of income. He produced tales for children, such as "The Bogyman" (Bukan) and "Rubberheads" (Rezinovye golovy), in 1928 and 1929,

as well as translations, reworked for children, of *Till Ulenspiegel* by Charles de Coster (1934) and *Gargantua and Pantagruel* by Rabelais (1935). Elements of absurdism, blatant grotesque, and a Khlebnikovian "word as such" (*samovitoe slovo*), all of which are characteristic of *Oberiu,* also appear significantly in Zabolotsky's first (and best) book of verse, *Columns* (Stolbtsy, 1929). It was greeted with enthusiasm by its cultured leadership as well as in literary circles, as by N. S. TIKHONOV, the literary scholar N. L. Stepanov, who spoke of its "Rabelaisian" quality and "the pathos of the mundane and of the embodiment of things" found in it (*Zvezda,* 1929, no. 3), and others, but was given a hostile reception by orthodox Soviet critics. The latter were particularly incensed by Zabolotsky's verse epic, "A Celebration of Agriculture" (1929–30, eventually published fully in *Zvezda,* 1933, nos. 2–3). Critical reviews of this work simply amounted to denunciations of Zabolotsky to the GPU-NKVD: "Spiteful buffoonery and mockery of socialism" (A. Selivanovsky, *Poets and Poetry* [Poety i poeziya, 1933], p. 215); "Zabolotsky's put-on tomfoolery is the mask of an enemy of collective farms, a hater of socialism, and a defender of the landowner peasant-kulak" (V. Ermilov, in *Pravda,* 21 July 1933); the poet's view of Soviet reality "turns into a rebellious petty bourgeois' reactionary protest against victorious socialism" (S. Malakhov, in a collection of articles, *Struggle for Style* [Bor'ba za stil', 1934], pp. 119–33). A whole pack of watchdogs of orthodoxy attacked Zabolotsky. Almost the entire issue of that particular number of *Zvezda* was withdrawn; a sub-chapter of Zabolotsky's poem, "The Exile," dealing with a peasant victim of collectivization, was cut out and pasted back into the journal in a shortened and distorted version, now under the title "The Enemy"; only then was the journal returned to distribution. Zabolotsky managed to publish a *Second Book of Verse* in 1937, greeted with more howls of "pantheism," "Klyuevism" (*klyuevshchina*), and "out of step with Soviet psychology." In 1938 he was arrested, convicted of alleged participation in a wholly fantastic terrorist organization "headed by N. S. Tikhonov and K. A. FEDIN, enemies of the people." The most striking thing about these charges was that they were made precisely at a time when the very "leaders" of that terrorist group were beginning their rapid rise to high echelon rank in the world of Soviet letters. In camp, Zabolotsky did heavy physical labor for a long time (*KLE* hollowly notes that he worked as a "builder"), later worked as a draftsman and laboratory worker. As a result of persecution, prison, and camp life Zabolotsky developed serious heart trouble. Moreover, after his release in 1946 he was not allowed to live in Leningrad or Moscow, but had to stay with different friends of his, mostly at their summer houses around Moscow. He eventually settled in Tarusa, a small town on the Oka river. Zabolotsky died of a heart attack, at fifty-five years of age.

Zabolotsky's poetry is divided into two sharply distinct periods: before camp, and after. Before camp, it is the strange and curiously fascinating world of *Columns,* a world of reified souls, and of not merely animate but even personified and anthropologized things. The "thingness" of Zabolotsky's images reaches hyperbolic proportions, while the manner in which they are constructed and the poetic form used throughout present a highly original fusion of 18th-century mock-heroic poetry before DERZHAVIN (sometimes even earlier syllabic rimes) and Khlebnikovian patterns in lexicon and imagery. The influence of painting is also apparent, specifically that of 17th-century genre painting, as well as that of Zabolotsky's contemporary, Pavel Filonov and his "school of analytic art." Here, for instance, is a Leningrad back yard, where the atoms not only of human day-to-day living, but of human consciousness as well, have been broken up: "Around it: a system of cats,/a system of pails, windows, firewood/suspended, dividing a dark world/into multiple narrow realms of back yards.../...where my youth is hung up to dry...." The world of DOSTOEVSKY's doubles, of GOGOL's "Nose," and of KHLEBNIKOV's "Planks of Fate"—a world of entropy, where man is a *mē on,* an imaginary value, with "a dense hell of existence" around him, a world where people "wheeze in tireless passion," where "straight bald husbands sit, like rifle shots," and stereotyped, identical Ivanovs trudge to their daily labors. Nor are they all that happy in their "chicken coop of joy," the thick broth of philistinism which is everywhere, be it at a "people's home" or at a beer garden named "Red Bavaria."

"A Celebration of Agriculture" is a multi-layered, highly original work in which Zabolotsky's tragic-farcical and heroic-satirical—yet entirely serious—verse images create, now a polyphonically harmonized *poema*, then again a dissonantly dramatized satire. The disintegration of the world, caused by man's rapacious husbandry, his oppression of animals and fellow humans, will have to be superseded by its free and loving transfiguration, enriching even Nature herself. Zabolotsky speaks of universities for horses, academies for cows, of wise animals and rational machines, much as he does of lucidly reasoning people. Meanwhile, obtuse materialist dogmatism, whose exponent in the poem is the Soldier, to whom the world is merely hostile to man, a mere dance of atoms, so that "nature understands nothing, and cannot be trusted," is incapable of a creative transfiguration of the world. Zabolotsky remains true also to what is immediately given through the senses and the subconscious, but he has abandoned the outright trans-rational and absurdist ways of the *Oberiuty*. He is sustained by a Pushkinian faith in reason, and the legions of phantoms, nocturnal flocks of "witches, fleas, and corpses," recede (together with the weird figures of Filonov's paintings) into "semi-being" (*polubytie*): "Candidate of past centuries, / commander of new years, / my Reason, these little monsters / are only fiction and ravings... / ... unconsolable grief / is something that does not exist in this world... / High is the abode of this Earth..." Yet we see in this sweep of death and decay not only "something that does not exist in this world." Zabolotsky's unfinished poem, *Lodeinikov*, features that very same sweep of live decay, the triumph in untransfigured nature, of death: "Over the garden, there went a rustle of a thousand deaths."

The tragic problem of our and the world's subjection to death always tormented Zabolotsky, who yearned to be confirmed in his faith in immortality, not generic, but individual. This yearning for human immortality did not leave the poet even in his second, post-camp, period. It was not only persecution, prison, and camp that had "pacified" the poet: a certain inclination toward classicism and harmony was surely triggered in him also by the advent of maturity, as TYUTCHEV naturally began to supplant Khlebnikov. Even in Zabolotsky's highly interesting correspondence with K. E. Tsiolkovsky (1932), other moods and thoughts appear, as they do also in some poems of the first period, such as "Yesterday, Meditating about Death" (Vchera, o smerti razmyshlyaya, 1936), where a classical, and in fact a classicist note may be discerned, while their form becomes mint-traditional: "And insufferable pain of separation pierced my heart." Thus, in a poem, "Metamorphoses" (Metamorfozy, 1937), the poet struggles with himself, seeking to assert both personal, human immortality as well as the eternal changeability and mortality of phenomena, yet right there he, as it were, dilutes such immortality in cosmic panpsychism, or pantheism. But then, individuality remains unchanged and unique even in this flow of transformations, though it be only in name: "How the world changes! / And how I change myself! / Only I'm still called by the same name. / But in fact that which is called 'me,' / is not me alone. There are many of us. I am alive... / ... Oh, how many dead bodies / have I separated from my own body!..."

During the second period, insofar as the poet was able to express this under the conditions of Soviet censorship, there is much more faith in this wholeness and harmony of human individuality, as well as faith in its actual immortality. Also, there is more simple and unaffected love, not only for nature, but also for individual people. Zabolotsky writes of aged prisoners on the Kolyma and their freezing death, of a woman who waits for her husband, or lover, to return from the wars, or from a Soviet camp. His form has now become entirely traditional. These are no longer literary frescoes, but poetic easel painting. Nevertheless, even during the second period, lines of striking poetic plenitude and dramatic quality will appear, for example, in the poem "Thistles" (1958): "I dreamed of a high prison cell / and bars, black as night, / behind the bars, a fairy tale bird, / the one whom nobody can help. / But I live, too, and badly, it seems, / for I haven't the strength to help her. / And a wall of thistles rises / between me and my joy." After his return from prison camp, Zabolotsky earned his living mostly by doing translations. But his translations, too, were often masterpieces, as was his versified translation of the *Igor Tale* (1938–46), of Shota Rustaveli's *Hero in a Tiger Skin* (final version, 1957), of poems by V. Pshavela, and others, which will remain unsurpassed for a long time.

Works: Stikhotvoreniya. Moscow, 1948. *Stikhotvoreniya.* Moscow, 1957. *Stikhotvoreniya.* Moscow, 1959. *Izbrannoe.* Moscow, 1960. *Stikhotvoreniya.* New York and Washington, 1965. *Stikhotvoreniya i poemy.* (Biblioteka poeta.) 1965. *Izbrannye proizvedeniya.* 2 vols. Moscow, 1972.

Translations: 5 poems in *Modern Russian Poetry.* Ed. Vladimir Markov and Merrill Sparks. 1967. Pp. 682–95. 11 poems in *Russian Poetry: The Modern Period.* Ed. John Glad and Daniel Weissbort. 1978. Pp. 110–22.

Secondary literature: B. Filippov, "Put' poeta." In his *Stat'i o literature.* London, 1981. (Also in *Stikhotvoreniya.* New York and Washington, 1965.) A. Makedonov, "Puti i pereput'ya N. Zabolotskogo." In his *Ocherki sovetskoi poezii.* Smolensk, 1960. Robin Milner-Gulland, "Zabolotsky and the Reader: Problems of Approach," *RLT* 8 (1974), pp. 385–92. ———, "Grandsons of Kozma Prutkov: Reflections on Zabolotsky, Oleynikov, and Their Circle." In Richard Freeborn, R. R. Milner-Gulland, and Charles A. Ward, eds., *Russian and Slavic Literature.* 1976. Pp. 313–27. E. Rais, "Poeziya N. Zabolotskogo." In *Stikhotvoreniya.* New York and Washington, 1965. A. Rannit, "Zabolotskii—a Visionary at Crossroads of Expressionism and Classicism." In *Stikhotvoreniya.* New York and Washington, 1965. I. Rodnyanskaya, "Poeziya N. Zabolotskogo," *VLit,* 1959, no. 1. *Vospominaniya o Zabolotskom.* Moscow, 1977. M. Zoshchenko, "O stikhakh Zabolotskogo." In *Rasskazy, povesti, fel'etony, teatr, kritika.* 1937.   B. F.

Zadónshchina, a highly poetic account of the 1380 battle on the Kulikovo field, in which Grand Prince Dmitry Ivanovich ("Donskoi") defeated the Tatar armies of Khan Mamai, signalling the beginning of the end of Tatar hegemony over the Russian lands. The Kulikovo Field battle, which began disastrously for the Russians but then turned into a resounding victory, was a mirror image of the 1185 Kayaly River battle in which the forces of Prince Igor were annihilated. Correspondingly, the *Zadonshchina* is a mirror literary image of the *Igor Tale* (SLOVO O POLKU IGOREVE). The original *Zadonshchina* was composed no later than 1393 (the extant mss. date from the late 15th to latter 17th centuries) by the otherwise unknown Sofoniya Ryazanets, who, according to R. JAKOBSON's brilliant conjecture, deliberately appended it to his own just-finished copy of the *Igor Tale*; Sofoniya himself says, "First I wrote the Lament of the Russian land, adducing it from books, and then I wrote the Lament and the Praise of Grand Prince Dmitry.... Let us append one Slovo to another (*s"stavim Slovo k Slovu*" 7–9; verses are cited according to Jakobson and Worth 1963). This diptych structure explains not only the massive borrowings from the *Igor Tale* into the *Zadonshchina* (since the latter was a deliberate replique to the former), but also the occasional and otherwise enigmatic borrowings from the *Zadonshchina* into later mss. of the *Igor Tale*, and from both texts into the SKAZANIE O MAMAEVOM POBOISHCHE.

Like the *Igor Tale*, the *Zadonshchina* is written not in verse, but in a rhythmic prose sometimes approaching the *taktovik* or the dolnik. Like its earlier model, the *Zadonshchina* refers back to the days of Boyan ("let us praise the prescient Boyan, wise bard of Kiev town. For that prescient Boyan would raise his wise fingers up upon the living strings and sing the praise of Russian princes" 13–14). No less than its predecessor, the *Zadonshchina* abounds in direct speech. The author addresses the reader, "Let us go up upon the Kiev hills and glance out at the Dnepr and at all the Russian land..." (4; note the enduring symbolic role of Kiev, centuries after it had lost its military and cultural importance.) The warrior brothers urge each other on: "Brother Andrew! Let us not spare our lives, for the Russian land and the Christian faith!" (37). Nature speaks as noisily as in the *Igor Tale*: "steeds neigh in Moscow, trumpets sound in Kolomna" (19); "carts squeal between Don and Dnepr" (44); "grey wolves howl on the river Mecha" (45); "Ravens often croak, jackdaws speak their own tongue, eagles scream, wolves howl fearsomely, and foxes bark at the bones" (50). The *Zadonshchina* shares with its prototype a fascination with topo- and ethnonyms: "We have swift steeds beneath us and gold armor on us, Cherkassian helmets, Muscovite shields, German lances, Frankish pikes, swords of Damascus steel" (63). It makes equal use of the folk lament: "Mikula Vasilievich's wife Marya lamented early on the Moscow ramparts, saying, 'Don, Don, swift river! You have torn through the stone mountains, you flow into the Polovtsian land. Rock my master back to me, [my] Mikula Vasilievich!" (94–95). The poetic effect is not lessened by the fact that the Don flows through no stony hills, nor were the Polovtsians relevant in 1380. The *Zadonshchina* makes even greater use of negative parallelism than the *Igor Tale*: "Grey wolves ran up to attack the Russian land. Those were no grey wolves, but the pagan Tatars who had come..." (45–46); "Then the fierce stormclouds came together, and in them blue lightning flashed, great thunderclaps thundered. [No,] that was the sons of *Rus'* who came together with the pagan Tatars..." (77–78; cf. 38, 48, 69, 80, 106, 122, 128).

The *Zadonshchina*, although deliberately imitative of the *Igor Tale*, also shows clearly that two hundred years had passed since its model came into existence. By 1393, some 12th-century realia and attitudes were no longer comprehensible. Thus, the *Igor Tale* refrain, "O Russian land, thou art already beyond the culmen [*za shelomyanom*; the height-of-land separating the Don from the Polovtsian-controlled Dnepr basin]" becomes the nonsensical "O Russian land! for the first time thou art as things were under King Solomon [*za Solomonom tsarem*]" (51); the foreboding anti-Virgin bird-figure Div of the *Igor Tale* is converted in the *Zadonshchina* into a harmless or even positive figure ("Divo cries beneath the Tatar sabres" (104); [at the Russians' victory] "Divo has been cast down upon the land" (149), retaining no trace of the violent sexual imagery inherited from Indo-European). Unlike the *Igor Tale*, the *Zadonshchina* sometimes shows a chronicler's concern for specific names and numbers: "from the Kalka battle to the rout of Mamai was 160 years (15) [only four years off]; "The posadniki rode out of Novgorod with 70,000 soldiers" (23); "And there are 70,000 brave Lithuanians with us, seasoned troops [all]" (41); "Brother Volodimer Ondreevich! We two are brothers to each other, and our generals [*voevody*] are appointed, seventy boyars, firm Belozersk princes,— Fedor Semenovich and Semen Mikhailovich, Mikula Vasilievich, the two Olgerdovich brothers, Dmitry Volynsky, Timofei Voluevich, Ondrei Serkizovich, Mikhailo Ivanovich" (61). Note how troops seem to come in seventies—even Mamai came against *Rus'* with "nine hordes and seventy princes" (*devyat'yu ordami i s'' sem'yu desyat knyaz'mi* 161).

The most noticeable difference between the *Igor Tale* and the *Zadonshchina*, however, is that the latter presents its events in a firmly Christian framework. Mamai and his troops are usually referred to as "pagan"; the epithet occurs twenty-six times in the work's 180 lines. The Russians always fight "for the Russian land and for the Christian faith" (eight occurrences), and the *Zadonshchina* is, in general, sprinkled with Christian phraseology typical of the chronicles: before setting out to do battle, the princes "pray to God and His Immaculate Mother" (16; *idem*, 53, 126); Baty's bloody conquest is taken as evidence that "God had punished the Russian land for its sins" (160); before the final victory, Dmitry prays, "O Lord my God, I have placed my faith in you, that I not shame myself forever, and that my foes not mock me" (125). This consistently Christian viewpoint reduces the importance of natural phenomena in the *Zadonshchina*, compared to the *Igor Tale*: in the 12th century, the pagan (or *dvoeverie*) interconnections among man, beast and plant were still very much alive, and the natural world was as much a protagonist as the princes and their cohorts; but by the late 14th century, man's dependence on the Christian God had reduced Nature to a mere decorative background. Nonetheless, the *Zadonshchina*, linguistically and stylistically less enigmatic than the *Igor Tale*, is hardly less consistent as a self-contained work of verbal art.

Bibliography: Roman Jakobson and Dean S. Worth, *Sofonija's Tale of the Russian-Tatar Battle on the Kulikovo Field.* The Hague, 1963. D. S. Likhachev and L. A. Dmitriev, *Slovo o polku Igoreve i pamyatniki Kulikovskogo tsikla*, Moscow-Leningrad, 1966. *Povesti o Kulikovskoi bitve.* Moscow, 1959.　　　　　D. S. W.

Zagóskin, Mikhaíl Nikoláevich (1789–1852), dramatist, novelist, and short-story writer, a civil servant who eventually became the director of Moscow Theaters, first made his reputation as a playwright. His first play, "A Comedy Versus Comedy" (1815), was well received by the public. Today he is remembered primarily as a his-

torical novelist, or more accurately, as the author of what is generally considered to be the first Russian prose novel, and the first Russian historical novel, *Yury Miloslavsky, or The Russians in 1812* (1829). Zagoskin became a literary hero overnight. PUSHKIN, ZHUKOVSKY, and KRYLOV, among others, responded with exaggerated praise to the novel which went through four editions in three years.

Zagoskin was also the first of a whole school of historical novelists who flourished in the 1830s, including F. V. BULGARIN, I. I. LAZHECHNIKOV, N. A. POLEVOI, A. V. VELTMAN, and R. M. Zotov. The war of 1812 and the emergence of romantic ideology in the 1820s in Russia intensified the feeling of national self-awareness which led to an interest in the national past, and this interest in turn led to the development of historical fiction, and of the historical novel in particular. Sir Walter Scott's novels, many of which had been translated into Russian in the 1820s, served as models for the developing Russian historical novel.

In writing *Yury Miloslavsky*, Zagoskin borrowed from Scott the techniques and devices of structure and development, motifs, the compositional function of characters and the methodology of reconstructing historical time. Like Scott, Zagoskin combines the elements of a love story with an adventure story. The protagonist is an imaginary character who comes from a stratum of society which gives him access to characters at all levels of society. A close comparison of *Yury Miloslavsky* and some of Scott's novels leads to the conclusion that in *Yury Miloslavsky* there is more of Scott than of Zagoskin, and that *Yury Miloslavsky* is a Russian adaptation of Scott's *Legend of Montrose*.

Yury Miloslavsky is Zagoskin's expression of his patriotism, and an affirmation of Russia's spiritual superiority over the West. In order to present the most glorious aspects of the Russian national spirit, he selected a historical period which was parallel in many ways to the recently experienced Napoleonic invasion, namely the TIME OF TROUBLES, a period of interregnum, civil strife, occupation by Polish armies, and the expulsion of the foe. It is this attention to the Russian national spirit that made it possible for his novel to be greeted so enthusiastically by his contemporaries and even by the Soviets today. The only work by Zagoskin to be published in the USSR, it was published first in 1956, and has continued to appear at three or four year intervals. Zagoskin's other historical novels are *Askold's Grave* (1833), set in the time of Prince Vladimir's Kiev, *Brynsky Forest* (1846), set in the first years of the reign of Peter the Great (1848).

Although Zagoskin is indebted to Sir Walter Scott, his own contribution lies in his innovative use of language to create an illusion of antiquity. The dramatist in him shows through in the preponderance of dialogue over description or exposition, and in the use of colloquial speech, and the oral speech of the common people.

Works: Polnoe sobranie sochinenii. Biographical essay by A. O. Kruglyi. 1898.
Translations: The Young Muscovite, or The Poles in Russia. Ed. F. Chamier. New York, 1834.
Secondary literature: Miriam G. Schwartz, *M. N. Zagoskin as a Historical Novelist.* Ph. D. diss., The Ohio State University, Columbus, 1978.　　　　　L. T.

Zaitsev, Borís Konstantínovich (1881–1972), writer, essayist, and critic. Born in Oryol, Zaitsev studied at the Moscow Technical Institute, the St. Petersburg Mining Institute, and at Moscow University Law School, but never graduated from any of these institutions. He began to publish in 1901. In 1921 and 1922 he was chairman of the Moscow Union of Writers. In 1922 he emigrated to Paris, became one of the leading émigré writers, and contributed to various Russian periodicals in France.

Zaitsev's early works are in the tradition of TURGENEV's novels about life on the manor, with their nostalgic lyrical mood and an extremely personal style. His later works display some mystical tendencies, but his style remained transparent, the arrangement of sentences rhythmical and melodious. In pursuit of higher spiritual goals, Zaitsev's hero is a confirmed individualist, at odds with material reality and with all utilitarian and social ideals. Inner freedom is his most precious treasure. Zaitsev is a writer of melancholy and quiet resignation. His works are marked by gentle humor. He poeticized the "prosaic" details in his texts by changing the position of an epithet, or by imparting a dactylic meter to a sentence in order to heighten its emotional effect. The prosaic movement of speech thus changes into poetic, verse-like arrangements. Zaitsev frequently transforms the authorial narration into an indirect monologue. The angle of vision shifts from one person to another, producing a picture of impressionistic fragmentation. Some of Zaitsev's works have a folkloristic flavor, created by stylized speech, supernatural events, and a journey in search of a mystical essence.

Besides his fiction, Zaitsev published in exile several volumes of his reminiscences: *Moscow* (1939), *Silence* (Tishina, 1948), *Youth* (Yunost', 1950), *En Route* (V puti, 1951), *The Tree of Life* (Drevo zhizni, 1953), *Tranquil Dawns* (Tikhie zori, 1961), and an autobiographical account of his boyhood in the country: *Gleb's Journey* (Puteshestvie Gleba, 1937). Furthermore, three literary biographies: *The Life of Turgenev* (Zhizn' Turgeneva, 1932), *Zhukovsky* (1951), and *Chekhov* (1954), and several other nonfiction works, such as *Italy* (Italiya, 1923) and a collection of sketches about Moscow, *St. Nicholas Street* (Ulitsa sv. Nikolaya, 1923). Zaitsev also wrote several religious works: "The Life of St. Sergius of Radonezh" (Prepodobnyi Sergii Radonezhskii: zhitie, 1925), "The Heart of Abraham" (Serdtse Avraamiya, 1925), "Alexis, Man of God" (Aleksei Bozhii chelovek, 1925), "Mount Athos: Travel Notes" (Afon: putevye zapiski, 1928), "Valaam: Travel Notes" (Valaam: putevye zapiski, 1936), and "The River of Time" (Reka vremen, 1968). All of these works often resemble "poetry in prose" and are imbued with music and mysticism. Zaitsev translated Dante's *Divine Comedy* into Russian in 1961, and wrote several lyrical and plotless short stories about Raphael and Emperor Charles V, as well as a short play about Don Juan.

Works: Strannoe puteshestvie. 1924. *Zolotoi uzor.* 1926. *Anna.* 1929. *Dom v Passy.* 1935.

Translations: Anna. London, 1937.

Secondary literature: N. Ya. Abramovich, *Literaturno-kriticheskie ocherki.* Book 1. 1909. K. I. Chukovskii, *Ot Chekhova do nashikh dnei.* 1908. Zinaida Gippius, *Literaturnyi dnevnik, 1899–1907.* 1908. A. G. Gornfel'd, *Knigi i lyudi.* Vol. 1. 1908. René Guerra, *Bibliographie des oeuvres de Boris Zaïtsev.* Paris, 1982. Temira Pachmuss, *A Russian Cultural Revival.* 1981. Pp. 156–76. N. Pervouchine, "La place de B. Zaitsev dans la littérature russe du XXᵉ siècle," *Etudes Slaves et Est-Européennes* 14 (1969), pp. 121–28. Also, articles and reviews in *Birzhevye vedomosti*, 1909, no. 11261; *Golos*, 1908, no. 3; *Krasnaya nov'*, 1926, no. 7; *Lebed'*, 1908, no. 4; *Moskovskie vedomosti*, 1907, no. 143; *Nasha zhizn'*, 1915, no. 4; *Nashi dni*, 1914, no. 3; *Novaya zhizn'*, 1911, no. 3; *Novoe vremya*, 1913, no. 13493; *Novyi mir*, 1926, no. 6; *Obrazovanie*, 1907, no. 2; *Put'*, 1913, no. 8; *Rech'*, 1907, no. 261; 1911, no. 348; 1912, no. 269; 1913, no. 232; 1916, no. 251; *Sovremennik*, 1913, no. 9; *Sovremennyi mir*, 1913, no. 11; 1916, no. 11; *Utro Rossii*, 1916, no. 351; *Vestnik Evropy*, 1913, no. 10; 1914, no. 9; *Vestnik znaniya*, 1915, no. 2; *Vesy*, 1907, no. 3; 1908, nos. 2 and 10; *Voprosy zhizni*, 1905, no. 1; *Zavety*, 1913, no. 6; *Zolotoe runo*, 1907, nos. 1 and 10.   T. A. P.

Zaïtsev, Varfolomeï Aleksándrovich (1842–82), literary critic and publicist. Born in Kostroma, he studied at the universities of St. Petersburg (law) and Moscow (medicine) but was expelled from the latter. A radically oriented "man of the sixties," he was especially close to PISAREV. Like Pisarev, Zaitsev was an anti-aesthetic critic, a mechanistic materialist (a "vulgar materialist" in present-day Soviet terms), and a "nihilist," markedly influenced by such German materialists as Büchner, Vogt, and Moleschott. He ridiculed German idealistic philosophy (e.g., Hegelianism) as "clownery," but admired Schopenhauer, interpreting him also as a materialist. He thought highly of NEKRASOV's verse (chiefly because its "hero" was always the Russian peasant) but disliked what he took to be LERMONTOV's abuse of poetic metaphor. From 1863 to 1865 Zaitsev was associated with the liberal journal, RUSSKOE SLOVO, and articles of his in this publication in 1864 responding to Saltykov-Shchedrin's criticism of Dostoevsky's *Notes from the House of the Dead* and CHERNYSHEVSKY's novel, *What Is To Be Done?*, were part of a protracted series of polemics known as the "nihilist schism" (*raskol v nigilistakh*—see Kozmin's monograph cited below). Zaitsev came

under police surveillance in 1865, was arrested in 1866, and spent several months in prison. In 1869 he fled abroad where, among other activities, he founded at Turin the first Italian section of the International. Towards the end of his life he completed his *Ancient History of the East* (Drevnyaya istoriya Vostoka, 1879) and *Ancient History of the West* (Drevnyaya istoriya Zapada, 1882). Shigalyov, the doctrinaire socialist theoretician in Dostoevsky's novel, *The Possessed*, is based on the figure of Zaitsev.

Works: Izbrannye sochineniya. 2 vols. 1934.

Secondary literature: B. P. Koz'min, "Raskol v nigilistakh," *Literatura i marksizm*, 1928, no. 2, pp. 51–107. F. Kuznetsov, *Publitsisty 1860-kh godov: Krug Russkogo slova: Grigorii Blagosvetlov, Varfolomei Zaitsev, Nikolai Sokolov.* 1969.   R. H. S.

Zalýgin, Sergeï Pávlovich (1913–), writer. Zalygin initially combined his career as a writer with the study of hydrology and land reclamation. In the 1940s he headed a hydrographic expedition to the Siberian Far North. He drew on his experiences as an engineer in the Hydrological and Meteorological Service in *Northern Tales* (Severnye rasskazy, 1947). Only in 1955 did he become a full-time writer. Since the mid-1960s he has built a reputation as an author of controversial fiction and a leading exponent of the new "COUNTRY PROSE." Zalygin's long short-story, *On the Irtysh* (Na Irtyshe, 1964) deals with the collectivization of a Siberian village in 1931, openly showing the cruelty and injustice involved in this action. The novel, *Salt Gorge* (Solenaya Pad', 1967) actually develops a communist leader as a negative type. Another novel, *The South-American Variant* (Yuzhno-amerikanskii variant, 1973), presents the extramarital affair of a successful woman scientist, who has an unsatisfying marriage, in a controversial manner. The novel, *The Commission* (Komissiya, 1975), raises the question of the relative value of Russia's traditional peasant culture and the new Soviet way of life.

Works: Izbrannye proizvedeniya. 2 vols. 1973.

Translations: "The Second Act." Trans. I. Litvinov. In *Soviet Literature* 12 (1952), pp. 77–81.

Secondary literature: Geoffrey H. Hosking, *Beyond Socialist Realism: Soviet Fiction since Ivan Denisovich.* 1980. Pp. 56–57.   V. T.

Zamedlénie, or *zaderzhánie* (retardation, lit. "slowing it down"), a literary strategy whose purpose is to prolong the "slow dance" (*tanets-khod'ba*) of art. It is also an element of a larger strategy of "staircase-like structure" (*stupenchatoe postroenie*), the step-by-step sequence in which a prose narrative unfolds. These concepts were formulated by V. B. SHKLOVSKY in *O teorii prozy* and were abundantly used by the early FORMALISTS. Shklovsky argued that in literature "form creates its own content," whereas in nonliterary discourse content creates form. Thus, in art, form is all. Since form comprises many kinds of repetition and parallelism, one can speak here of a tautological "slowing down" of an inevitable end. Rhyme and sound repetitions, synonyms and nonsense words in children's poetry and folk poetry, the framework structure in a series of tales, are all instances of *zamedlenie*, according to Shklovsky.

In fiction, the notion of *zamedlenie* merges with the notion of plot. In Shklovsky's analysis, the adventures and trials which the hero undergoes are merely a detour, a way of slowing down the arrival of the end of the story. Similarly, in his analysis of Friedrich Schiller's tragedy *Wallenstein*, B. M. EIKHENBAUM argued that Wallenstein's misfortunes and hesitations were of slight interest to the author and should not interest the critics either; what should matter in critical analysis is how these elements of plot satisfy "the compositional principles of tragedy" which require, among others, a slowing down of the stream of action. This rigid program for critics can be labelled vulgar formalism, and it was abandoned by later researchers who otherwise followed formalist tenets.

Bibliography: B. M. Eikhenbaum, "O tragedii Shillera v svete ego teorii tragicheskogo." In his *Skvoz' literaturu.* 1924. Pp. 84–151. V. B. Shklovskii, "Svyaz' priemov syuzhetoslozheniya s obshchimi priemami stilya." In his *O teorii prozy.* 1929. Pp. 24–67.   E. Th.

Zamyátin, Evgény Ivánovich (1884–1937), fiction writer, literary critic, dramatist, and editor. The son of an Orthodox priest, Zamyatin his first important work "A Country Churchyard" (Sel'skoe kladbishche), a free translation of Thomas Gray's elegy, in N. M. KARAMZIN's journal *Vestnik Evropy*. A close association with Karamzin and his circle had a great influence on the poet's literary tastes and point of view. In 1808 he took over the editorship of the journal and published many of his best early works in it. In 1812 the poet joined the Moscow militia. Zhukovsky witnessed the battle of Borodino from a nearby location and recorded his reaction in a patriotic hymn "A Bard in the Camp of Russian Warriors" (Pevets vo stane russkikh voinov), which established his poetic reputation and popularity. The year 1813 was a critical one for the poet: he proposed marriage to M. A. Protasova, the daughter of his half-sister. Even though his affection was returned, he was not permitted to marry her. This personal tragedy was to cast a sad and melancholy light on his life and poetry. That same year he moved to St. Petersburg and soon began his long career as a courtier, first as reader to the Empress Mother and teacher of Russian to members of the imperial family and in 1825 as tutor to the future Emperor Alexander II. A man of scrupulous honesty and honor, a person of great tact, unusual devotion and ability, a living example of "die schöne Seele," Zhukovsky spent his entire life interceding for friends and strangers alike before the tsar and members of the court. Among the poets and writers whose fates he helped to alter for the better were his close friend PUSHKIN, BARATYNSKY, SHEVCHENKO, GOGOL, and HERZEN.

All his life Zhukovsky was active in Russian literary life. In 1815 he helped found the semi-humorous circle ARZAMAS dedicated to the defense of the Karamzinian language reform which advocated an exceptionally precise, smooth, lucid, and melodious style with an easy well bred manner and flowing ease, and a natural spontaneous grace. For years he hosted his own literary evenings. He also belonged to the leading formal literary societies in Russia and was an active contributor to literary journals and almanacs.

In 1839 Zhukovsky retired from service and travelled abroad. In 1841 he married Elizabeth Reitern, the daughter of an artist, and settled permanently in Germany. He died in Baden-Baden April 12, 1852 and was buried in St. Petersburg.

Zhukovsky is the founder and leading representative of early ROMANTICISM in Russian literature. The bulk of his poetic production is either translation or adaptation; only a small number of works are original. "Almost everything of mine," he once noted, "is someone else's or about someone else, and yet it is all my very own." What made it original and significant for Russian literature was his new and fresh style.

The main genre associated with early Zhukovsky is the intimate, meditative elegy, later the short elegiac song. His elegy focused on the poetical expression of the inner world of the poet. Nature became a pretext for meditation and contemplation; a soothing sense was derived from the sight of innocent, idyllic simplicity, far removed from the artificiality of society, as in "Evening" (Vecher, 1806). Zhukovsky's choice of natural beauty has a suggestion of sadness, a mournful pathos, bathed in a haze of mystery and a haunting sense of loss—death of friends, passing of youth: "The Inexpressible" (Nevyrazimoe, 1819). Pensive and alone, the poet abandons himself to the harmony and grace of the setting (which is an actual place) and the reflections it suggests: "Evening," "Slavyanka" (1815). The poet draws his inspiration from the sadness of eventide, twilight, the paling light, and all that that hour of the day holds of the sense of foreboding and mystical atmosphere that is best suited for his temperament. His was not a temperament given to powerful feelings of rapture or exaltation but a sensitive soul, capable of delicate impressions, tempered passions, a taste for peaceful emotions and a restrained tone: "Pevets" (The Singer, 1811).

The quiet melancholy awakened by the contemplation of nature is expressed in words of moving simplicity and melodic sweetness. Delicate shades of emotions or dreams are each set off with carefully picked epithets, rich in suggestion of atmosphere. The subtlety of feeling and shadings require a very fine sense of word values and musical expression, so that the strong focus on style in Zhukovsky's elegies was of great theoretical importance for Russian poetry.

The central theme of many of his elegiac short songs is the pathetic sense of regret for what once has been, a longing for perfection, for an ideal, nostalgia for innocence, as in "Song" (Pes-

nya, 1818), and "The Inexpressible" (Nevyrazimoe). The theme of idealized innocence and beauty finds poignant expression in such lyrics as "Dreams" (Mechty, 1812), and "Lalla Rookh" (1821); the desire to escape from reality into an ideal, fantastic world echoes hauntingly in "Spring Feeling" (Vesennee chuvstvo, 1816). This peculiar accent of elegiac melancholy reflects his own unhappiness and frustration of his love for Protasova. All of Zhukovsky's poetry is steeped in this melancholy, subjective mood, and mystical haze ("Elisium," 1812)—his original works and his translations, his elegies and ballads.

The poetics of Zhukovsky's elegiac style show a melodic system based on intonational patterns and rhythmic mobility. A musical design is seen in the very composition of a poem (such as strophic punctuation). Typical devices of melodization consist of interrogative and exclamatory intonation with complicated inversions and repetitions (anaphore, refrain) and variations linked to syntactical patterns, as the melody swelled or subsided with the needs of the musical suggestion. Zhukovsky experimented with various meters and rhyme schemes; toward the end of his life he preferred hexameters and blank verse.

In 1808 Zhukovsky published the ballad "Lyudmila" whose subtle diffusion of the supernatural element marked a new trend in his poetry, eventually earning him his nickname, "the Balladier." Most of Zhukovsky's thirty-nine ballads are free translations from Goethe, Schiller, Bürger, Zedlitz, and others. They are, again, experimentations in style and, as such, led to numerous polemics. The genre of the ballad with its robust local color and naive simplicity of character, as well as its narrative style contradict the idea of the refinement of the poetic idiom. Zhukovsky's beguiling style transmits the subtle sensation of mystery and vague sense of dread by means of carefully selected correspondences of images and sounds, and shrinks from the appearance of true popular spirit, folk elements, coarseness, and dissonance.

The third genre associated with Zhukovsky's name which laid down new canons of taste and standards for poetical diction is the friendship epistle. Epistles show a side of Zhukovsky that is totally different from the overall impression of his poetry and person: the charm of a warm and spontaneous wit, an affectionate nature made for friendship. This is the "Arzamas" side of the poet, who was the initiator of the ludicrous and playful tone of that circle; the inoffensive mockery and familiar playfulness is also reflected in his letters. The familiar epistles, these conversations in verse, possess a special quality of language—a chatty conversational manner, an informal tone, which demand an exceptionally precise, clear style with an easy turn of thought and language, and civil elegance ("Epistles to Prince Vyazemsky and V. L. Pushkin," 1814). They show a strange mixture of classical and romantic elements, a style at once elegiac and anacreontic, haunted by classical memories: Greek and Roman names, mythological allusions, classical forms appear, as in "To Voeikov" (1814).

During the 1820s Zhukovsky turned to translating longer poetic works—Byron's "The Prisoner of Chillon," Moore's "Death of the Peri," Scott's "The Eve of St. John." During the 1830s and 40s he completed his major translations of epics and episodes, "Nal and Damayanti" from the *Mahabharata* and "Rustem and Zorab" from Firdausi's *Shah-Name*. His major effort as translator was his life's work, the translation of the *Odyssey*.

Zhukovsky's great achievement as a poet lies in the creation of a poetic language and in his translations and adaptations which introduced Russians to European poetry. His strength lies primarily in the magic beauty of style, the "captivating sweetness" (Pushkin) of his music; a style so striking and alluring that it lent itself readily to imitation and worked itself out into formulas. Zhukovsky was eclipsed only by Pushkin in public favor and overshadowed only by the daring efforts of the remarkable generation of poets whom he inspired and who constitute the Golden Age of Russian poetry. The mystical elements of his poetry were to have a strong attraction for symbolists and he was to be rediscovered in the Silver Age.

Works: Polnoe sobranie sochinenii. 12 vols. Ed., biogr. sketch, and comm. A. S. Arkhangel'skii. 1902. *Sobranie sochinenii*. 4 vols. Introd. I. M. Semenko. Text and comm. V. P. Petushkov, 1959–1960. *Sochineniya v trekh tomakh*. 1980.

Translations: Lewanski, pp. 398–99.

was born in Lebedyan and grew up in provincial central Russia. He joined the Bolshevik Party while studying at the St. Petersburg Polytechnic Institute, and was imprisoned and exiled in 1905. Upon graduation as a naval engineer in 1908, he joined the faculty and began publishing technical articles and fiction. The literary fruit of his exile in 1911, the short novel "Uezdnoe" (1913; Eng. trans., "A Provincial Tale," 1967), brought him national recognition as an ardent humanist inexorably opposed to brutality, ignorance, and inhumanity, and drew him into the neorealists grouped around the journal *Zavety*—writers Aleksei REMIZOV, Mikhail PRISHVIN, Vyacheslav SHISHKOV and critic IVANOV-RAZUMNIK. His second short novel, "Out in the Sticks" (Na kulichkakh, 1914), depicts the drunken debauchery of a Siberian military garrison and resulted in the confiscation of the journal and a court trial. In the long story "Alatyr" (1915), a gallery of ridiculous dreamers humorously enlivens provincial tedium, while an earthy primitivism is manifested in the stories "The Womb" (Chrevo, 1915) and "The Diehards" (Kryazhi, 1916). The most distinctive aspect of Zamyatin's early fiction, however, is his ornamental prose style characterized by grotesque synthesis, impressionistic animal imagery, and SKAZ narration.

During World War I Zamyatin continued his dual career of engineer and novelist, supervising the construction of Russian icebreakers in England, while writing satirical tales on urban bourgeois conformity—"The Islanders" (Ostrovityane, 1918) and "The Fisher of Men" (Lovets chelovekov, 1922). He occupied a central position in the cultural revival after the October Revolution, editing the journals *Dom iskusstv, Sovremennyi zapad* and *Russkii sovremennik* as well as Russian translations of H. G. Wells, O. Henry, Anatole France, Romain Rolland, and Jack London for the World Literature Publishing House; serving on the executive boards of numerous literary organizations; and lecturing on writing techniques in literary studios. Some of the lectures, published only posthumously, which influenced young writers such as the SERAPION BROTHERS provide excellent insights into the craft of writing. Among these are the programmatic "Contemporary Russian Literature" (Sovremennaya russkaya literatura, 1956) and the revealing "The Psychology of Creative Work" (Psikhologiya tvorchestva, 1956).

Zamyatin's post-revolutionary prose is characterized by a systematic modernist color symbolism, a highly elliptical style, the intensification of acoustical and rhythmic qualities, and the systematization of imagery systems, best exemplified in the frequently anthologized stories "Mamai" (1921) and "The Cave" (Peshchera, 1922) as well as in the fine, but less known "The Nursery" (Detskaya, 1922). As a former Bolshevik Zamyatin welcomed the Revolution, but criticized its excesses in polemical articles and political fables under the pseudonym M. Platonov in leftist socialist revolutionary newspapers such as GORKY's *Novaya zhizn'* and Viktor Chernov's *Delo naroda*. Later, his clever, meticulously crafted literary essays extolled integrity and freedom, while ridiculing repression and sycophancy—"I Am Afraid" (Ya boyus', 1921), "About This Day and Age" (O segodnyashnem i sovremennom, 1924; Eng. trans., "The Day and The Age," 1970), and "On Literature, Revolution, Entropy and Other Matters" (O literature, revolyutsii, entropii i prochem, 1924). Zamyatin's anti-utopian novel *We* (My, corrupt text 1927, complete text 1952; Eng. trans., *We*, 1924), which anticipated Huxley's *Brave New World* and inspired Orwell's *1984*, represents a unique synthesis of his professional mathematical training, the stylistic innovation of his fiction, and the polemical anti-philistinism of his critical essays. Derived from DOSTOEVSKY's critique of collectivist ideals, *We* prophesies the realization of a technological utopia in which the hypertrophy of the state and the machine threatens the very essence of man's creativity.

During the 1920s Zamyatin developed a deceptively simple, unobtrusive style based on the conversational literary language in a series of anecdotal novellas where literary parody joined gentle irony in depicting human frailty in accommodating to the new Soviet environment: "X" (Iks, 1926), "A Ten-Minute Drama" (Desyatiminutnaya drama, 1928), and "Martyrs of Science" (Mucheniki nauki, written 1931, published 1962; Eng. trans., "Another Turning of the Worm," 1931). He also penned two masterpieces of tragic passion: "The Yawl" (Ela, 1928), and "The Flood" (Navodnenie, 1929), inspired, respectively, by GOGOL's "Overcoat" and Dostoevsky's *Crime and Punishment*.

Zamyatin also wrote eight plays: three original works and five adaptations, of which the most famous is *The Flea* (Blokha, 1926), a lively folk play in the commedia dell'arte tradition based on Leskov's story "The Left-Handed Craftsman."

Frequent attacks on Zamyatin by Communist Party-line critics culminated in intense vilification in 1929; his books were removed from libraries, his plays were banned, and he was denied access to publication. He went abroad in 1931, spending his last years working on the unfinished novel *The Scourge of God* (Bich Bozhii, 1939), which stressed historic parallels between the conflict of 4th-century Rome with Attila and that of 20th-century Russia with the West.

From the contemporary perspective, Zamyatin's achievements as an astute critic-essayist equal his achievements as an original craftsman in fiction. Renowned in the West for his dystopian novel *We*, he remains virtually unknown in Russia.

Works: Bol'shim detyam skazki. 1922. Robert Maier. 1922. *Sochineniya*. 4 vols. 1929. *Litsa*. 1955. *Sochineniya*. 2 vols. Munich, 1970–82.

Translations: "The Cave." Trans. D. Mirsky. *Slavonic Review* 4 (1923). *We*. Trans. G. Zilboorg. 1924. "Mamai." In *Soviet Literature*. Ed. George Reavey and Marc L. Slonim. 1933. "God." In *New Russian Stories*. Ed. Bernard Guilbert Guerney. 1953. *The Dragon: Fifteen Stories*. 1967. (Contains "The Flood," "A Provincial Tale," "X," etc.) *A Soviet Heretic: Essays*. 1970. (Contains "Contemporary Russian Literature," "The Day and the Age," "I Am Afraid," "On Literature, Revolution, Entropy and Other Matters," "The Psychology of Creative Work," etc.) "The Islanders." 1972.

Secondary literature: E. J. Brown, "Brave New World, 1984, and We: An Essay on Anti Utopia: Zamyatin and English Literature." (Ardis essay series, 4.) 1976. C. Collins, *Evgenii Zamiatin: An Interpretive Study*. 1973. T. R. N. Edwards, *Three Russian Writers and the Irrational: Zamyatin, Pilnyak, and Bulgakov*. 1982. Pp. 36–86 and passim. V. D. Mihailovich, "Critics on Evgenii Zamiatin," *Papers on Language and Literature* 10 (1974), pp. 317–34. C. H. Rhodes, "Frederick Winslow Taylor's System of Scientific Management in Zamiatin's We," *Journal of General Education* 28 (1976), pp. 31–42. D. J. Richards, *Zamiatin: A Soviet Heretic*. 1962. A. M. Shane, *The Life and Works of Evgenij Zamjatin*. 1968. G. Struve, *Russian Literature under Lenin and Stalin, 1917–1953*. 1971. Pp. 43–50. A. Voronsky, "Evgenii Zamiatin," *RLT* 3 (1972), pp. 153–75. G. Woodcock, "Utopias in Negative," *SlavR* 64 (1956), pp. 81–97.
A. M. S.

Zasúlich, Véra Ivánovna (1849–1919), revolutionary, editor, translator, author of political articles. Of petty noble origin, she became a socialist by age seventeen and an "illegal" at twenty-six. Her attempted assassination of the Petersburg Military Governor in 1878 and subsequent acquittal by a jury provided a "model" of the selfless revolutionary totally dedicated to the people. While her act legitimized terror among some revolutionaries, she opposed it on principle as a POPULIST and subsequently as a MARXIST. A member of PLEKHANOV's propagandist wing of populism, *Chernyi Peredel*, she joined him and three other émigrés in founding the first significant Russian Marxist organization, the "Liberation of Labor" Group. From 1883 to 1905, she translated basic Marxist works, served as editor of *Iskra* and *Zarya*, and wrote occasional polemical articles advocating the Marxist viewpoint. While influenced by Plekhanov, her works reveal a certain independence of mind. She was profoundly concerned with maintaining Party unity and with developing an ethical base for the movement. She broke decisively with LENIN in 1904 over his elitist concepts which she felt would distort the Revolution. In ill health after her return to Russia in 1905, her writings were few, but consistently Menshevik. To her, the October Revolution was a perversion of Marxist theory.

Works: Sbornik statei. 2 vols. 1907. *Vospominaniya*. 1931. *Stat'i o russkoi literature*. 1960.

Secondary literature: Samuel H. Baron, *Plekhanov; the Father of Russian Marxism*. 1963. Jay Bergman, "The Political Thought of Vera Zasulich," *SlavR*, 38 (1979), pp. 243–58.
J. A. D.

Záum', literary term which originated among the Cubo-FUTURISTS, around 1913. *Zaum'* literally means "beyond the mind," and it is also referred to as *zaumnyi yazyk* (transrational language). *Zaum'* is the most radical expression of the new concept of poetry proclaimed by the futurists in their manifestoes. The poetic word, according to the futurists, had to be "self-sufficient," i.e., nonreferential. It had to be treated and perceived as the "word as such," a phonetic entity possessing its own ontology. *Zaum'*, therefore, is an experimental language which consists of neologisms rich in sound, but devoid of any conventional meaning. *Zaum'* is not organized by means of grammar and syntax, but by phonetic analogy and rhythm. This requires the capability on the reader's part to receive the message not through a rational process, but by intuition.

The concept of *zaum'* is associated primarily with the creative and theoretical works of A. Kruchonykh and V. Khlebnikov, although other poets practiced it (among them E. Guro, V. Kamensky, I. Zdanevich, I. Terentiev). The term *zaumnoe* (transrational) appeared for the first time in Kruchonykh's essay, "The New Ways of the Word" (Novye puti slova, *Troe*, 1913), but three poems written in the transrational language had already appeared several months earlier in the book, *Pomade* (Pomada). One of them has become the most famous example of *zaum'*:

Dyr bul shchyl
ubeshchur
skum
vy so bu
r l ez

Kruchonykh introduces these poems by saying that they are written "in my own language differing from all others: its words do not have a definite meaning." In the essay, "New Ways of the Word," Kruchonykh gives a more detailed definition of *zaum'*: "The word is broader than its meaning, the word (and its component sounds) ... is not simply logical, it is first of all transrational.... Therefore, we destroyed grammar and syntax, we realized that to convey [the essence] of contemporary frenzied life and the even more impetuous future we had to combine words in a new way, and that the more disorder we introduced in the structure of the sentences, the better." Kruchonykh reiterated these principles in a long series of declarations, manifestoes, and longer essays over the next fifteen years, and applied them in his creative works. Notable is the opera libretto, *Victory over the Sun* (Pobeda nad solntsem, 1913), with prologue by Khlebnikov.

The hallmark of Kruchonykh's production are the numerous mimeographed pamphlets, which often combine poetry, theory, and illustrations. Among the artists who illustrated them are: Rozanova, Kulbin, Malevich, Larionov, Goncharova, Tatlin, Rodchenko, and Kruchonykh himself. The following is a very partial list of Kruchonykh's pamphlets: *Declaration of the Word as Such* (Deklaratsiya slova kak takovogo, 1913), *Duck's Nest of Bad Words* (Utinoe gnezdyshko durnykh slov, 1914), *Explodity* (Vzorval', 1913 and 1914), *Game in Hell* (Igra v adu, 1912 and 1913, with Khlebnikov), *Worldbackwards* (Mirskontsa, 1912, with Khlebnikov), *Te li le* (1914, with Khlebnikov), *Pomade* (Pomada, 1913), *Lacquered Tights* (Lakirovannoe triko, 1919), *Zaum'* (1921), *Zaumniks* (Zaumniki, 1922, with Khlebnikov).

Although Khlebnikov participated in the creation of some of those pamphlets, his concept of *zaum'* differed considerably from Kruchonykh's. Khlebnikov's experiments were aimed at revealing the essential meaning of existing word roots as contained in consonantal sounds, in order to create a universal language by means of a rational process. Kruchonykh, on the contrary, considered *zaum'* as the manifestation of a spontaneous, non-codified language. He thought that a phenomenon close to *zaum'* occurred among the Russian religious sectarians, who in a moment of ecstasy would start speaking in foreign tongues. Khlebnikov's most ambitious attempt at creating *zaum'* poetry is represented by the long poem, *Zangezi* (1922). Another cubo-futurist, V. Kamensky, used *zaum'* in the first edition of his long poem, "Stenka Razin, the Heart of the People," (Serdtse narodnoe—Sten'ka Razin, 1918).

Of the many futurist groups, only "41°" was programmatically dedicated to the theoretical development and practice of *zaum'*. "41°" was born in Tiflis (Tbilisi), a refuge for many poets and artists fleeing the Revolution, and was active between 1917 and 1920. Kruchonykh emerged as the leader of the group. Other members were: Ilya Zdanevich, Igor Terentiev, and Nikolai Chernyavsky. The manifesto of the group which appeared in the newspaper, *41°* (1919), proclaims that *zaum'* is "the mandatory form for the manifestation of art." Another manifesto by Kruchonykh, "Declaration of Transrational Language" (Deklaratsiya zaumnogo yazyka, Baku, 1921), represents his definitive formulation of *zaum'*. Among the members of "41°", Zdanevich was the most consistent and refined practitioner of *zaum'*. His virtuoso handling of the transrational language is especially notable in his plays—a pentalogy of so-called *dra*. Four plays were published in Tiflis between 1918 and 1920, the last one was published in Paris in 1923, where Zdanevich spent the rest of his life as an émigré. Another member of "41°", I. Terentiev, is the author of a treatise on *zaum'*, *Treatise on Total Indecency* (Traktat o sploshnom neprilichii, 1920), which rivals Kruchonykh's pamphlets for its bold and original typographical features.

Only a few contemporary critics considered *zaum'* worthy of any serious attention. Kornei Chukovsky in the book, *Futurists* (Futuristy, 1922) and Baudouin de Courtenay in the two articles, "Word and Word" (Slovo i slovo, 1914) and "Towards a Theory of the 'Word as Such' and the 'Letter as Such'" (K teorii 'slova kak takovogo' i 'bukvy kak takovoi', 1914) expressed a rather unfavorable view of the transrational language. Viktor Shklovsky, on the other hand, defended *zaum'* as a legitimate form of art, in the articles, "Premises of Futurism" (Predposylki futurizma, 1915) and "Transrational Language and Poetry" (Zaumnyi yazyk i poeziya, 1916), and so did Roman Jakobson in his book, *New Russian Poetry* (Noveishaya russkaya poeziya, 1921).

Bibliography: V. Erlich, *Russian Formalism: History, Doctrine*. 1981. Z. Folejewski, *Futurism and Its Place in the Development of Modern Poetry*. 1980. G. Janecek, "Il'ia Zdanevič's 'aslaablič'e' and the Transcription of zaum' in Drama." In *L'avanguardia a Tiflis*. Venice, Italy, 1982. Pp. 33–44. ———, "Kruchenykh, Maker of Minimal Books," *Lightworks*, no. 14/15 (1982), pp. 48–49. V. Khlebnikov, *Snake Train: Poetry and Prose*. Trans. and ed. Gary Kern. 1976. V. Markov, *Russian Futurism: A History*. 1968. (See bibliography in Markov's book for the works of Kruchonykh, Khlebnikov, the 41° poets, and contemporary criticism.) T. Nikol'skaya, "Igor' Terent'ev v Tiflise." In *L'avanguardia a Tiflis*. Venice, Italy, 1982. Pp. 189–210. R. Tsigler, "Poetika A. E. Kruchenykh pory '41°'. Uroven' zvuka." In *L'avanguardia a Tiflis*. Venice, Italy, 1982. Pp. 231–58. A. L.

Zdanévich, Ilyá, see Zaum'.

Zelínsky, Kornély Lyutsiánovich (1896–1970), critic and literary theorist. Graduating from the Department of Philology at Moscow University in 1918, Zelinsky immediately turned his attention to critical and creative writing. In 1924 he became a founder-member, with Ilya Selvinsky, Vera Inber and others, of the literary constructivists, contributing much to the theory of the movement as elaborated by the Literary Center of the Constructivists in Moscow. Zelinsky participated in all the main constructivist publications in the mid-1920s, including *Changing Everything* (Mena vsekh, 1924), *State Plan of Literature* (Gosplan literatury, 1925) and *Business* (Biznes, 1929). In his theoretical essays Zelinsky identified economy of material, semantic condensation, and absence of ornament as key principles of constructivism, and he tried to apply them in his own critical analyses. At the end of the 1920s Zelinsky moved away from his predominantly formal considerations towards a renewed interest in narrative content as he argued in his book *Poetry as Meaning* (Poeziya kak smysl, 1929). After expressing his disenchantment with constructivism in an article entitled "The End of Constructivism" (Konets konstruktivizma, 1930), Zelinsky gave increasing attention to biographical work, writing appreciations of many Russian and Soviet writers, including Gorky, Inber, Fadeev, Shaginyan and A. Tolstoi. In the early 1960s Zelinsky published a number of essays on general questions of literary theory and practice such as "Literature and Man of the Future" (Literatura i chelovek budushchego, 1962) in which he demonstrated his broad knowledge of both Western and Eastern European literature. Of particular interest also are Zelinsky's memoirs of the revolutionary period, *At the Boundary of Two Epochs: Literary Encounters 1917–1920* (Na rubezhe dvukh epokh. Literaturnye vstrechi 1917–1920, 1960).

Secondary literature: Herman Ermolaev, *Soviet Literary Theories 1917–1934: The Genesis of Socialist Realism*. 1963. J. E. B.

Zhdánov, Andréi Aleksándrovich (1896–1948), Communist Party functionary, chief of the Leningrad Party organization, 1934 to 1944; secretary of the Central Committee, 1944 to 1948.

Zhdanov served several times as Party spokesman or "hatchet man" for cultural affairs. As such he was articulating official policy, obviously with Stalin's full approval; nevertheless, his name has provided a convenient label for the period of cultural oppression that marked the immediate post-war years. "Zhdanovism" (*zhdanovshchina*) thus signifies cultural Stalinism at its most repressive.

Zhdanov's first important literary pronouncement was made on 17 August 1934, when he "greeted" the first Congress of Soviet Writers on behalf of the Party and government. Citing Stalin's immortal formula, "writers are engineers of human souls," Zhdanov provided the assembled "engineers" with a mission and a method. The latter was to be called "socialist realism," a term now given official sanction. Zhdanov's definition of it, slippery as it is, has proved remarkably durable: "truthfulness and historical concreteness of artistic representation should be combined with the ideological remolding and education of the working people in the spirit of socialism."

In 1946 Zhdanov issued two ex cathedra literary pronouncements, of which a condensed and combined version was published. They were designed to amplify and interpret the Central Committee's decree of 14 August concerning the delinquent magazines *Zvezda* and *Leningrad*. Once again he voiced the Party's insistence on tight control over literature and reiterated its demand that writers devote themselves unstintingly to their assigned task, rallying the people around the Communist cause. The partial relaxations tolerated during the war were to be terminated forthwith. As examples of the individualist degeneration that had infected Soviet literature Zhdanov singled out Mikhail Zoshchenko and Anna Akhmatova, subjecting both to a scurrilous, bullying attack and raking over "sins" dating back to the early 1920s.

Zhdanov subsequently made similar pronouncements concerning philosophy (in June 1947, denouncing G. F. Aleksandrov's *History of Western European Philosophy*) and music (castigating the "elitist," discordant music of Shostakovich, Prokofiev, Khachaturian, and others).

Works: "Sovetskaya literatura—samaya ideinaya, samaya peredovaya literatura v mire." In *Pervyi s"ezd sovetskikh pisatelei; stenograficheskii otchet*. 1934. *Doklad o zhurnalakh "Zvezda" i "Leningrad."* 1946.

Translations: Essays on Literature, Philosophy, and Music. New York, [1950].

Secondary literature: Harold Swayze, *Political Control of Literature in the USSR, 1946–1959*. 1962. Avrahm Yarmolinsky, *Literature under Communism: The Literary Policy of the Communist Party of the Soviet Union from the End of World War II to the Death of Stalin*. 1960. H. McL.

Zhirmúnsky, Víktor Maksímovich (1881–1971), literary scholar. Born into a doctor's family, Zhirmunsky graduated in philology from Petersburg University in 1912. From 1919 until his retirement, he taught at that university. Together with B. V. Tomashevsky, he represents the academic wing in Russian formalism which did not reject the traditional philological methods of research. His best known work, *Vvedenie v metriku. Teoriya stikha* (1925; in English: *Introduction to Metrics: The Theory of Verse*, 1966) surveys the basic concepts of verse and applies them to Russian prosody. He points out the evolution of Russian poetry from its syllabotonic beginnings to the "tonic" structures of early 20th-century lyrics. His study takes into account the less systematic works by Brik and Bely on the same subject, as well as European developments in the theory of verse. Parallelling this study are Zhirmunsky's fine analyses of Pushkin, Akhmatova and Blok in *Problems of Literary Theory* (Voprosy teorii literatury, 1928), as well as some general theorizing on "classic" and "romantic" poetry in the same volume of essays. Of all the scholars who were associated with the Opoyaz, Zhirmunsky was probably least influenced by the Marxist approach to literature. The very concept of a classic-romantic duality to which he subscribed throughout his scholarly career, stands in direct opposition to the dialectical model of literature advanced by influential formalists such as Yu. N. Tynyanov.

Works: Kompozitsiya liricheskikh stikhotvorenii. 1921. *Valerii Bryusov i nasledie Pushkina*. 1922. *Bairon i Pushkin*. 1924. *Gete v russkoi literature*. 1937. [With Kh. Zarifov:] *Uzbekskii narodnyi geroicheskii epos*. 1947. *Epicheskoe tvorchestvo slavyanskikh narodov i problemy sravnitel'nogo izucheniya eposa*. 1958. *Skazanie ob Alpamyshe i bogatyrskaya skazka*. 1960. *Narodnyi geroicheskii epos*. 1962. *Drama Aleksandra Bloka "Roza i krest"*. 1964. *Sravnitel'noe literaturovedenie: Vostok i Zapad*. 1979. *Iz istorii zapadnoevropeiskikh literatur*. 1981. E. Th.

Zhúkova, Márya Semyónovna (1804–55), writer of short stories and sketches. Her first-published stories, "Evenings at Karpovka" (Vechera na Karpovke, 1837–38) brought her immediate and exceptional recognition and, in the phrase of V. G. Belinsky, "very, very deservedly." Her stories are not masterpieces of technique nor do they concern themselves with the social or political situation of the primarily foreign settings and citizens which form the frame of her narratives. When exhibited, her strong point is to capture a glimpse of human experience and transform it into something familiar, even if not traditionally represented or in its typical associative value context. Unfortunately, Zhukova is not consistent in her presentation of such insights and her stories often suffer with the burden of much that was already old at the time of its appearance in her work—sentimentalist representations of the passage of life and its woes, for example, including authorial sighs and laments, occur and even predominate in places to produce a maudlin, pathetic mood without realistic force. What undoubtedly endeared her to Belinsky was her ability to deform romantic clichés and produce fresh, more practical outlooks on love, human relations, etc. Belinsky's opinion which went unaltered from the beginning of her career through her final published work, "Sketches of Southern France and Nice" (Ocherki yuzhnoi Frantsii i Nitstsy, 1844), was essentially positive: her works suffer from compositional weakness and other flaws, are generally speaking "un-artistic" (*nekhudozhestvennye*), but "such stories can be pleasing and contain their own relative worth." That they were written by a woman he acknowledges with the exhortation that more men should write like her. Belinsky fully recognized that her works display no concern for social themes or change in the human condition, "but so much the better for us and for her." It seems he realized that the value of a new outlook was at least equal to social-political conviction in literature.

For today's reader, there are still passages in Zhukova's stories which are captivating. She is also interesting in the historical perspective both as a contemporary of Lermontov, to whose works there are certainly similarities, and additionally as a representative of the phenomenon of immense, but transitory, popularity.

Works: Vechera na Karpovke. 2 vols. 1837–38. *Povesti*. 2 vols. 1840. *Ocherki yuzhnoi Frantsii i Nitstsy*. 2 vols. 1844.

Secondary literature: V. G. Belinskii, "Vechera na Karpovke" (1838), *PSS*, vol. 2 (1953), pp. 566–75. ———, "Povesti Marii Zhukovoi" (1840), *PSS*, vol. 4 (1954), pp. 110–18. ———, "Ocherki yuzhnoi Frantsii i Nitstsy" (1844), *PSS* (1955), pp. 422–26. (All with lengthy excerpts from Zhukova's works.) N. A. Nekrasov, "Literaturnye novosti," *PSS i pisem*, vol. 12 (1953). C. T.

Zhukóvsky, Vasíly Andréevich (1783–1852), poet, translator. The illegitimate son of a wealthy landowner, A. I. Bunin and a captive Turkish woman, Zhukovsky was born in the village of Mishenskoe in Tula province. He received his early education in the Bunin family and provincial boarding schools. In 1797 he was placed in the Moscow University Gentry Pension. The Pension had a strong literary tradition, and Zhukovsky, who began to write poetry at the age of eight, was encouraged to pursue his writing. Here he formed those enthusiastic friendships which were recorded in his epistles and which endured during his entire lifetime. In 1801 he founded, with such close friends as the Turgenev brothers, A. F. Voeikov, and A. F. Merzlyakov, "The Literary Friendship Society" (Druzheskoe literaturnoe obshchestvo). This circle was especially interested in German and English preromantic literature and occupied itself with poetical translations. In 1802 Zhukovsky published

Secondary literature: V. G. Belinskii, "Stat'i o Pushkine," 2 (1843), *PSS*, Vol. 7, pp. 144–222. William E. Brown, "Vasily Andreevich Zhukovsky," *RLT* 8 (1974), pp. 295–328. Lidiya Ginzburg, *O lirike.* 1974. Pp. 19–50. Adrian Gizhitskii, "V. A. Zhukovskii i rannie nemetskie romantiki," *RLit* 22 (1979), no. 1, pp. 120–28. G. A. Gukovskii, *Ocherki po istorii russkogo realizma.* Pt. 1. *Pushkin i russkaya romantika.* Saratov, 1946. P. A. Pletnev, *O zhizni i sochineniyakh V. A. Zhukovskogo.* 1853. Irina Mikhailovna Semenko, *Vasily Zhukovski.* Boston, 1976. A. N. Veselovskii, *V. A. Zhukovskii. Poeziya chuvstva i "serdechnogo voobrazheniya".* 1904.

A. Gl.

Zlatovrátsky, Nikolaí Nikoláevich (1845–1911), writer. The son of a minor official, Zlatovratsky attended Petersburg Technological Institute, but never graduated and became a professional writer early, publishing from 1866 in the OTECHESTVENNYE ZAPISKI, ISKRA, *Budil'nik, Russkaya mysl'*, and other journals. He soon specialized in fiction and nonfiction dealing with peasant and working class life after the Emancipation, which he perceived from a right-wing POPULIST point of view. In his several series of sketches of village life, such as *Workaday Village Life* (Derevenskie budni, 1879), his many stories, all dealing with peasants or peasants turned factory workers, and his novels, *Peasant Jurors* (Krest'yane-prisyazhnye, 1874–75) and *Foundations* (Ustoi, 1878–83), Zlatovratsky combined realistic descriptions of post-Reform Russia with attempts to capture its characteristic types. He anticipated the Soviets' division of peasants into three classes: paupers (who are also "drunks"), middling (whom he calls "economic"), and rich (called *miroedy*, "devourers of the peasant commune, the *mir*"). Zlatovratsky also hoped to discover the secure foundations of Russian life in the peasant commune, but gradually grew disenchanted with his populist ideas. In the 1880s the focus of his fiction switched from the peasantry to the intelligentsia. His later stories also show an influence of Tolstoianism. Zlatovratsky concluded his career with some memoirs and autobiographic stories.

Works: Sobranie sochinenii. 8 vols. 1912–1913. *Izbrannye proizvedeniya.* Introd. A. Egolin. 1947. *Vospominaniya.* Introd. S. A. Rozanova. 1956.

Translations: "Old Shadows." In Leo Wiener, *Anthology of Russian Literature.* 1902–1903. Vol. 2.

Secondary literature: See *KLE*, Vol. 2, p. 1025.

V. T.

Známya (The Banner). (1) A short-lived art and literary journal published in Moscow between 1919 and 1922. In 1921 the journal was published simultaneously "in parallel" in Berlin in both Russian and German. The literary contributors constitute some of the best-known avant-garde or popular writers of the time: A. BELY, A. BLOK, S. ESENIN, N. KLYUEV, and V. SHERSHENEVICH, and others. Since one of the subjects frequently addressed in the theoretical articles was the constraint caused by the institutionalization of Marxism upon the production and the very nature of art and artistic literature, the journal did not survive the general political-literary consolidation of Soviet ideology.

(2) A monthly literary journal published in Moscow. First appearing in 1930 under the acronym *LOKAF* (Literary Union of Writers of the Red Army and Navy) it began its course as an outlet for chauvinistic literature devoted to military themes or about war or, in a broader understanding of the word, literature concerned with struggle (class struggle, the struggle of friends abroad against oppression and prejudices, etc.) Some important literary figures have published in *Znamya* (ILF AND PETROV, VOZNESENSKY) although the literary quality of contributions tends to be of secondary importance. Some well-known "progressive" foreign writers have been translated (Hemingway, etc.) and appeared in *Znamya* as well. *Znamya* continues to be published and is important in that the current official Soviet literary-political canon is overtly represented in both its original literature and its critical reviews.

Secondary literature: "Literaturnye zhurnaly 30-ykh godov." In *Istoriya russkoi sovremennoi literatury.* Vol. 2. 1960. "Literaturnye zhurnaly 40-ykh–50-ykh godov." In *Istoriya russkoi sovremennoi literatury.* Vol. 3. 1960.

C. T.

Znánie (Knowledge), a St. Petersburg publishing association (1898–1913) and its literary almanacs (1903–1913). The association was formed by members of the publishing commission of the former liberal Literacy Committee, headed by K. P. Pyatnitsky, to produce popular books in the fields of natural sciences, education, history, and the arts. In 1900 *Znanie* was joined by Maksim GORKY; in late 1902 he and Pyatnitsky became the only stockholders and began to publish collected and individual literary works by writers, mostly of the school of the so called critical realism. *Znanie* also published translations of books by foreign authors, both modern and ancient, as well as a series, *Deshevaya biblioteka* (Low-Priced Library), which included works by regular *Znanie* writers and by past and contemporary authors of socio-political literature. Especially popular, at the beginning, were the literary almanacs of the association, *Znanie*.

Preparatory work on the almanacs (their official name was *Sborniki tovarishchestva "Znanie"*—Collections of the Association *Znanie*) began in 1903. Initially, the contributors were mainly writers who had previously belonged to N. D. Teleshov's literary circle *Sreda* (Wednesday). The first issue of *Znanie*—for the year 1903—appeared on March 16, 1904, and contained works by L. ANDREEV, I. BUNIN, V. VERESAEV, N. GARIN, M. GORKY, S. GUSEV, A. SERAFIMOVICH, and N. Teleshov. They were later joined by E. CHIRIKOV, S. Yushkevich, Skitalets, S. Naidenov, A. Kipen, E. Tarasov, A. Sulerzhitsky, D. Aizman, and others. Among foreign authors whose works were published in *Znanie*, were E. Verhaeren, W. Whitman, G. Hauptmann, G. Flaubert, K. Hamsun, etc. However, as a consequence of the first Russian Revolution of 1905 and the intense literary-political conflicts of the time, a number of talented writers, such as L. Andreev, A. KUPRIN, V. Veresaev, Skitalets, S. Yushkevich, broke away from Gorky and stopped contributing to *Znanie*. Some new names appeared on the almanacs' pages—I. SHMELYOV, I. Surguchev, S. Kondurushkin, and others. But the decline was irreversible. Moreover, Pyatnitsky, who was practically in charge of all publishing matters, did not share Gorky's radical political views and related publishing plans. In 1911 Gorky, living abroad, passed his editorial functions to V. S. Mirolyubov. In 1912 he left *Znanie* altogether. The fortieth and last issue of *Znanie* came off press in February 1913; only 8,000 copies were printed (in 1906 the average was nearly 32,000; at the height of *Znanie* popularity, 65,000 copies were printed). In 1913, both the almanacs and the publishing house ceased to exist.

Texts: Arkhiv M. Gor'kogo. Vol. 4 (Gorky's letters to K. P. Pyatnitsky). Moscow, 1954. Vol. 7. Moscow, 1959. *M. Gor'kii i poety "Znaniya".* (Biblioteka poeta. Bol'shaya seriya.) Introd., text, and commentary S. V. Kastorskii. Leningrad, 1958.

Translations: An Anthology of Russian Neo-Realism: The "Znanie" School of Maxim Gorky. Ed. and trans. Nicholas Luker. Ann Arbor, 1982.

Secondary literature: B. S. Bugrov, "Dramaturgiya 'Znaniya'." In *Gor'kovskie chteniya.* Vol. 8. 1964. O. D. Golubeva, *Gor'kii-izdatel'.* 1968. *Istoriya russkoi literatury.* Vol. 10. 1954. Sect. "Proza," pt. 1: "Realisticheskaya proza. Gor'kii i 'Znanie'."

N. P. P.

Zolotóe runó (The Golden Fleece), a monthly art and literary journal which appeared in Moscow between 1906 and 1909. Its editor and publisher was the art patron N. P. Ryabushinsky. The first six issues of *Zolotoe runo* were dual language editions in French and Russian. Initially its de facto editor was Valery BRYUSOV and its contributors included all the major SYMBOLISTS, such as BLOK, BELY, SOLOGUB, and Zinaida HIPPIUS, as well as writers close to Symbolism such as KUZMIN, REMIZOV, and the essayist Vasily ROZANOV. After a controversy with Ryabushinsky in 1907 the journal remained in the hands of a faction of symbolists sympathetic to the doctrine of mystical anarchism, namely Vyacheslav IVANOV, Blok, and Georgy CHULKOV, the originator of the controversial thesis. The journal thereafter propagated the view that art by virtue of its metaphysical veracity must play a role in the cultural and religious life of the nation. For Ivanov art was ideally theurgy and mythmaking. Blok published "The People and the Intelligentsia" (Narod i intelligentsiya, 1909) and other articles in which he deplored a rift in the Russian national culture. The aesthetic view of art was attacked in the journal and identified with DECADENCE. A debate arose with another symbolist journal, VESY, which became known as the champion of individualism and aestheticism. This discord contributed to the decline of symbolism.

As a publishing house *Zolotoe runo* issued books by the symbolists Blok (*Zemlya v snegu*), Sologub (*Plamennyi krug*), and BALMONT, by Remizov, and by the artist Nikolai Rerikh.

Bibliography: Boris Mikhailovskii, "Zolotoe runo," *KLE*. Vol. 4, p. 351. William H. Richardson, "Chulkov," *MERSL*. Vol. 4, pp. 137–41. S. Yaremich, "Konets 'Zolotogo runa'," *Iskusstvo v yuzhnoi Rossii*, 1910, no. 8–9, pp. 378–81.   E. Br.

Zóshchenko, Mikhaíl Mikhaílovich, writer. He was born in 1895 in Poltava, the son of a Ukrainian painter of gentry origin, and an actress (née Surina). In 1904 the family moved to Petersburg, which became his permanent home. After finishing the gymnasium Zoshchenko matriculated in the law faculty of Petersburg University, but World War I had begun, and he soon volunteered for military service. In 1915 he was commissioned and sent to the front. During two years of fighting he was decorated and also wounded and gassed, with permanent damage to his health. In 1917 he served briefly as commandant of the Petrograd post office. The next year he volunteered for the Red Army "to fight against the nobility and landlords, a milieu I know quite well enough," as he later put it. Demobilized as physically unfit in 1919, he passed through a kaleidoscopic succession of diverse jobs.

Zoshchenko began writing stories in 1920, and his first book appeared in 1921. His stories were immensely successful with the reading public, and during the twenties and thirties he was the most popular living writer next to GORKY. He associated himself with the SERAPION BROTHERS, who were trying to assert the independence of art from politics, and he remained loyal to that principle as long as he could. In his stories, Zoshchenko's skeptical and ironic view of human life, and especially of any regime's ability to transform human nature, is camouflaged by his use of SKAZ. In the early "Tales of Nazar Ilyich, Mr. Sinebryukhov" his narrator is named and identified, an ex-soldier whose language is a bizarre hodgepodge of peasant Russian overlaid with misapplied journalese. In later works, however, no narrator is introduced, but the story is told in vulgar language and with expression of philistine attitudes that cannot be those of an educated author. Zoshchenko sometimes muddies the waters still further by calling such a narrator "the author." His trademark genre of the 1920s was the short-short story deriving situational humor from the many incongruities of everyday Soviet life; his focus on mundane realities proved a refreshing antidote to Communist bombast. He also wrote several more conventionally literary novellas, of which the most substantial is *Michel Sinyagin* (1930), an ambivalent account, both sympathetic and satirical, of the gradual descent to beggary, during the 1920s, of a pre-war aesthete and mama's boy.

During the 1930s, Zoshchenko came under increasing pressure to write in a more Soviet spirit. His subsequent work divides into two classes: serious, ideologically "correct" works; and works that preserve the ambiguities that had marked his earlier writings. Among the former is "The Story of One Reforging" (Istoriya odnoi perekovki, 1934), purportedly the truthful record of how a former criminal is transformed, while digging the White Sea-Baltic Canal as an NKVD prisoner, into a useful Soviet citizen. To the same "correct" category belong Zoshchenko's satirical biography of Aleksandr Kerensky and his saccharine *Stories About Lenin*, written for children. Much more interesting are the ambiguous works, especially *Youth Restored* (Vozvrashchennaya molodost', 1933) and *The Sky-blue Book* (Golubaya kniga, 1935). In these he sought to create a new literary form: a theoretical or philosophical argument to which fictional stories are attached as illustrations. *Youth Restored* purports to be a treatise on senescence; Zoshchenko's thesis about how the ill effects of aging can be delayed by the subject's willpower is then "illustrated" with a tale about an aging professor who runs off with his neighbor's young wife. *The Sky-blue Book* is a discussion of the influence on history of such "forces" as money, love, and perfidy; it is also "illustrated" with stories. There are clearly parodic elements in both these works, but the line between seriousness and mockery is intentionally unclear. In 1943, Zoshchenko

published the first installment of another work of literary "research," *Before Sunrise* (Pered voskhodom solntsa), in which he explored the causes for his own chronic unhappiness, among other things discussing the theories of both Pavlov and Freud. For such outrageous subjectivism in time of war Zoshchenko was censured and further publication halted (the remainder of *Before Sunrise* came out only in 1972).

In 1946, Zoshchenko was singled out, together with Anna AKHMATOVA, as sacrificial victims for demonstrating the new, toughened party line. Stalin's satrap Andrei ZHDANOV delivered a vituperative attack on him, and he was expelled from the UNION OF SOVIET WRITERS. Unable to publish original work, he lived mostly by translating. After Stalin's death he was gradually rehabilitated. New editions of his stories were published, but he did not succeed in producing much significant new work, and he does not seem to have written "for the drawer" during his period in disgrace. He died on 22 July 1958. Besides his fiction, Zoshchenko also wrote plays, such as *The Canvas Briefcase* (Parusinovyi portfel', 1944), an adaptation of a famous short story; and film scenarios, such as *Soldier's Luck* (Soldatskoe schast'e, 1943).

Works: Izbrannye proizvedeniya. 2 vols. 1968.
Translations: Lewanski, pp. 400–01.
Secondary literature: M. O. Chudakova, *Poetika Mikhaila Zoshchenko*. 1979. Rebecca Domar, "The Tragedy of a Soviet Satirist." In *Through the Glass of Soviet Literature*. Ed. Ernest J. Simmons. 1953. L. F. Ershov, *Iz istorii sovetskoi satiry: M Zoshchenko i satiricheskaya proza 20–40-kh godov*. 1973. H. McLean, "Belated Sunrise: A Review Article," *SEEJ* 18 (1974), pp. 406–10. *Mikhail Zoshchenko: stat'i i materialy*. 1928. Linda Hart Scatton, "The Neglected Zoščenko: An Integrated Approach to His Life and Works." Ph.D. diss., Harvard Univ., 1976. V. Shklovsky, "On Zoshchenko and Major Literature," *RLT* 14 (1976), pp. 407–14. Irwin R. Titunik, "Mixail Zoščenko and the Problem of *Skaz*," *California Slavic Studies* 6 (1971), pp. 83–96.   H. McL.

Zvezdá (The Star), a monthly literary journal reviving the "thick journal" tradition of pre-revolutionary Russia, was first published in 1924 in Leningrad. It was to a considerable extent an organ of literary FELLOW TRAVELERS. In particular, virtually all of the SERAPION BROTHERS published in it. In 1932 it became an organ of the UNION OF SOVIET WRITERS. Excoriated by ZHDANOV in 1946 for providing publication to such "derelicts and dregs" (*poshlyaki i podonki*) as Anna AKHMATOVA as well as Mikhail ZOSHCHENKO and other "Serapions" who, as Zhdanov quotes Serapion theorist Lev LUNTS, prefer "writing not for propaganda." *Zvezda* nonetheless remained in publication. The writings of such prominent writers as K. FEDIN, M. GORKY, N. TIKHONOV, A. TOLSTOI, and N. ZABOLOTSKY have appeared in *Zvezda*.

Bibliography: G. Brovman, "Zvezda," *VLit* 5 (1961), no. 2. N. I. Dikushina, "Literaturnye zhurnaly 1917–1929 godov." In *Istoriya russkoi sovetskoi literatury*. Vol. 1. 1958. I. M. Maiskii, "U istokov 'Zvezdy'," *Literaturnaya gazeta*, no. 15 (4 February 1964). A. A. Zhdanov, (Text of Speech in Russian and English.) In *The Central Committee Resolution on Zhdanov's Speech on the Journals "Zvezda" and "Leningrad."* Trans. Felicity Ashbee and Irina Tidmarsh. Royal Oak, Mich., 1978.   C. T.

I. GENERAL BIBLIOGRAPHIC WORKS AND SERIALS

(For more titles see Serge A. Zenkovsky and David L. Armbruster, *A Guide to the Bibliographies of Russian Literature*. Vanderbilt University Press, 1970.)

Academic Writer's Guide to Periodicals. Vol. 2: *East European and Slavic Studies*. Comp. and ed. Alexander S. Birkos and Lewis A. Tambs. The Kent State University Press, 1973.

American Bibliography of Slavic and East European Studies, 1956– . Bloomington, Ind., 1957– .

Ettlinger, Armei, and Joan Gladstone. *Russian Literature, Theatre, and Art: A Bibliography of Works in English, Published 1900–1945*. London and New York, 1947.

Fomin, Aleksandr Grigor'evich. *Putevoditel' po bibliografii, bio-bibliografii, istoriografii, khronologii i entsiklopedii litera-tury: Sistematicheskii ukazatel' russkikh knig i zhurnal'-nykh rabot, napechatannykh v 1736–1932 gg*. Leningrad, 1934.

Horak, Stephen M., comp. *Russia, the USSR, and Eastern Europe: A Bibliographic Guide to English Language Publica-tions*. Vol. 1: 1964–74. Vol. 2: 1975–80. Littleton, Colo., 1978–82.

Horecky, P. L. *Basic Russian Publications: An Annotated Bibliogra-phy on Russia and the Soviet Union*. Chicago, 1962.

——. *Russia and the Soviet Union: A Bibliographic Guide to Western-Language Publications*. Chicago, 1965.

International Committee for Soviet and East European Studies. *European Bibliography of Soviet, East European and Slavonic Studies*. Vols. 1 and 2. Birmingham, 1975–76. Vols. 3 and 4. Paris, 1981 83.

Knizhnaya letopis'. Organ gosudarstvennoi bibliografii SSSR. Mos-cow, 1907– .

Knizhnoe obozrenie. Moscow, 1966– .

Leningrad. Publichnaya biblioteka. Gazetnyi otdel. *Alfavitnyi sluzhebnyi katalog russkikh dorevolyutsionnykh gazet, 1702–1916*. Leningrad, 1958.

——. *Obshchie bibliografii russkikh knig grazhdanskoi pechati, 1708–1955: Annotirovannyi ukazatel'*. Ed. P. N. Berkov. Leningrad, 1956.

——. *Obshchie bibliografii russkikh periodicheskikh izdanii, 1703–1954*. Comp. M. V. Mashkova and M. V. Sokur-ova. Leningrad, 1956.

Letopis' gazetnykh statei. Moscow, 1936– .

Letopis' periodicheskikh izdanii SSSR. Moscow, 1933– .

Letopis' retsenzii. Moscow, 1934–57.

Letopis' zhurnal'nykh statei. Moscow, 1926– .

Maichel, K. *Guide to Russian Reference Books*. Vol. 1– . Stan-ford: Hoover Institution, 1962– .

Martianov, Nikolai Nikolaevich. *Books Available in English by Rus-sians and on Russia, Published in the United States*. 6th ed. New York, 1950.

Novye knigi SSSR: Ezhenedel'nyi bibliograficheskii byulleten'. Mos-cow, 1956– .

Schatoff, Michael, comp. *Half a Century of Russian Books, 1917–68: Bibliographic Index of Books Published Outside the U.S.S.R*. New York, 1969– .

——. *Half a Century of Russian Serials: Cumulative Index of Serials Published Outside the U.S.S.R*. 4 vols. New York, 1970–72.

Shibanov, P. *Katalog russkikh knig, starykh i novykh, zamechatel'nykh i redkikh*. Moscow, 1899. Reprint Col-ogne, 1981.

Simmons, J. S. G. *Russian Bibliography, Libraries and Archives: A Selective List of Bibliographical References for Students of Russian History, Literature, Political, Social and Philo-sophical Thought, Theology and Linguistics*. Twick-enham, England, 1973.

Smits, Rudolf, comp. *Half a Century of Soviet Serials, 1917–65: A Bibliography and Union List of Serials Published in the U.S.S.R*. Washington, D.C., 1968.

Sopikov, Vasilii Stepanovich. *Opyt rossiiskoi bibliografii*. 2d ed. Ed. V. N. Rogozhin, 5 vols. St. Petersburg, 1904–06. Reprint London, 1962.

Terry, Garth M. *East European Languages and Literatures: A Sub-ject and Name Index to Articles in English-Language Jour-nals, 1900–1977*. Oxford and Santa Barbara, Cal., 1978.

U. S. Library of Congress. *Guide to Soviet Bibliographies: A Selected List of References*. Comp. John T. Dorosh. Washington, D.C., 1950.

Whitby, Thomas J., and Tanja Lorković. *Introduction to Soviet National Bibliography*. Littleton, Colo., 1979.

Zalewski, Wojciech, comp. "Reference Materials in Russian-Soviet Area Studies," *RusR* 40 (1981), pp. 163–80.

Zdobnov, Nikolai Vasil'evich. *Sinkhronisticheskie tablitsy russkoi bibliografii 1700–1928, so spiskom vazhneishikh biblio-graficheskikh trudov: Materialy dlya istorii russkoi biblio-grafii*. Ed. B. S. Bodnarskii. Moscow, 1962.

Zernova, Antonina Sergeevna. *Knigi kirillovskoi pechati izdannye v Moskve v XVI–XVII vekakh: Svodnyi katalog*. Ed. N. P. Kiselev. Moscow, 1958.

II. COMPREHENSIVE BIBLIOGRAPHIC WORKS AND SERIALS COVERING RUSSIAN LITERATURE

Bukhshtab, B. Ya., ed. *Osnovnye izdaniya proizvedenii khudozhest-vennoi literatury na russkom yazyke*. Vol. 1. *Russkaya literatura dorevolyutsionnoi epokhi*. Leningrad, 1958.

Gul'binskii, Ignatii Vladislavovich. *Russkie pisateli: Opyt biblio-graficheskogo posobiya po russkoi literature XIX–XX st*. Rev. ed. With appendices: 1. *Literatura revolyutsionnogo perioda (1918–23 gg.)*; 2. *O proletarskom tvorchestve*; 3. *Voprosy poetiki*. Moscow, 1924.

Harvard University Library. *Twentieth Century Russian Literature: Classified Listing by Call Number, Alphabetical Listing by Author or Title, Chronological Listing*. Cambridge, Mass., 1965.

Katalog knig izdatel'stva "Khudozhestvennaya literatura" 1946–1966. Comp. K. S. Baskina et al. Vol. 1: *Russkaya klassicheskaya literatura. Russkaya sovetskaya literatura. Literatury narodov SSSR. Inostrannye literatury*. Vol. 2: *Literaturovedenie i kritika. Roman-gazeta. Alfavitnyi uka-zatel'. Spravochnye tablitsy*. Moscow, 1970.

Lewanski, Richard C., comp. *The Literatures of the World in English Translation*. Vol. 2: *The Slavic Literatures*. New York, 1967.

Line, Maurice B. *A Bibliography of Russian Literature in English Translation to 1900 (Excluding Periodicals)*. London, 1963.

Mez'er, Avgusta Vladimirovna. *Russkaya slovesnost' s XI po XIX stoletiya vklyuchitel'no: Bibliograficheskii ukazatel' proiz-vedenii russkoi slovesnosti v svyazi s istoriei literatury i kri-tikoi*. 2 vols. St. Petersburg, 1899–1902.

Modern Language Association of America. *MLA International Bib-liography of Books and Articles in the Modern Languages and Literatures*. New York, 1957– . (See East European Literatures.)

Moody, Fred, ed. *Ten Bibliographies of 20th Century Russian Liter-ature*. Ann Arbor, Mich.: Ardis, 1977.

Moscow. Gosudarstvennyi bibliotechnyi institut. *Bibliografiya khu-dozhestvennoi literatury i literaturovedeniya: Uchebnik dlya bibliotechnykh institutov*. Moscow, 1958–60.

Bibliography

Russian Plays: A Preliminary Catalogue. Comp. Leo Schmeltsman. New York, 193?

Sakharova, Evgeniya Mikhailovna. *Entsiklopediya russkoi zhizni; roman i povest' v Rossii vtoroi poloviny XVIII–nachala XX veka: rekomendatel'nyi bibliograficheskii ukazatel'.* Moscow, 1981.

Sipovskii, V. V. *Iz istorii russkogo romana i povesti: Materialy po bibliografii istorii i teorii russkogo romana.* St. Petersburg, 1903.

Smirnov-Sokol'skii, N. P. *Russkie literaturnye al'manakhi i sborniki XVIII–XIX vv.* Moscow, 1956.

Tsentral'nyi gosudarstvennyi arkhiv literatury i iskusstva. *Putevoditel': literatura.* Ed. N. F. Bel'chikov and A. A. Volkov. Moscow, 1963.

The Year's Work in Modern Language Studies. By a number of scholars. Ed. for the Modern Humanities Research Association. London, 1929/30– .

Zenkovsky, Serge A., and David L. Armbruster. *A Guide to the Bibliographies of Russian Literature.* Vanderbilt University Press, 1970.

Zheltova, Ninel' Ivanovna, and M. I. Kolesnikova, comps. *Tvorcheskaya istoriya proizvedenii russkikh i sovetskikh pisatelei: Bibliograficheskii ukazatel'.* Moscow, 1968.

III. ARCHIVES AND LIBRARIES

Access to Resources in the 1980's: Proceedings of the First International Conference of Slavic Librarians and Information Specialists. Ed. Marianna T. Choldin. New York, 1982.

Akademiya Nauk, S.S.S.R. Institut literatury. *Opisanie rukopisei i izobrazitel'nykh materialov Pushkinskogo doma.* 7 vols. Moscow, 1951–62.

Association of Research Libraries. Slavic Bibliographic and Documentation Center. *New Slavic Publications: A Guide to Selection and Acquisition in the Social Sciences and Humanities.* Washington, D.C., 1970– .

Bel'chikov, N. F., Begunov, Yu. K., and N. P. Rozhdestvenskii. *Spravochnik-ukazatel' pechatnykh opisanii slavyano-russkikh rukopisei.* Moscow and Leningrad, 1963.

Djaparidze, D. *Medieval Slavic Manuscripts: A Bibliography of Printed Catalogues.* Cambridge, 1957.

Grimsted, Patricia Kennedy. *Archives and Manuscript Repositories in the USSR; Moscow and Leningrad.* Princeton University Press, 1972.

———. *Archives and Manuscript Repositories in the USSR; Estonia, Latvia, and Belorussia.* Princeton University Press, 1981.

Resources for Soviet, East European and Slavonic Studies in British Libraries. Ed. Gregory Walker. Birmingham, 1981.

Wynar, Lubomyr R., and Pat Kleeberger. *Slavic Ethnic Libraries, Museums, and Archives in the United States: A Guide and Directory.* Chicago, 1980.

IV. BIBLIOGRAPHIC WORKS AND SERIALS ARRANGED BY PERIOD

1. Old Russian Literature

Bibliografiya rabot po drevnerusskoi literature, opublikovannykh v SSSR 1958–1967 gg. Comp. N. F. Droblenkova. Leningrad, 1978.

Bibliografiya sovetskikh rabot po drevnerusskoi literature za 1945–1955 gg. Comp. V. A. Kolobanov, O. F. Konovalova, and M. A. Salmina. Ed. D. S. Likhachev. Moscow, 1956.

Bibliografiya sovetskikh russkikh rabot po literature XI–XVII vv. za 1917–1957 gg. Comp. Nadezhda Feoktistova. Moscow, 1961.

Dmitrieva, R. P. *Bibliografiya russkogo letopisaniya.* Moscow and Leningrad, 1962.

Nazarevskii, A. A., ed. *Bibliografiya drevnerusskoi povesti.* Moscow and Leningrad, 1955.

2. 18th-Century Literature

Istoriya russkoi literatury XVIII veka: Bibliograficheskii ukazatel'. Ed. P. N. Berkov. Leningrad, 1968.

Moscow. Publichnaya biblioteka. *Russkie pisateli XVIII veka: rekomendatel'nyi ukazatel' literatury.* Comp. N. P. Zhdanovskii. Moscow, 1954.

Stepanov, V. P., and Yu. V. Stennik, comps. *Istoriya russkoi literatury XVIII veka: Bibliograficheskii ukazatel'.* Ed. P. N. Berkov. Leningrad, 1968.

U. S. Library of Congress. *Eighteenth Century Russian Publications in the Library of Congress: A Catalog.* comp. Tatiana Fessenko. Washington, D.C., 1961.

3. 19th-Century–Early 20th-Century Literature

Moscow. Publichnaya biblioteka. *Russkie pisateli pervoi poloviny XIX veka: Rekomendatel'nyi ukazatel' literatury.* comp. R. N. Krendel' et al. Moscow, 1951.

———. *Russkie pisateli vtoroi poloviny XIX–nachala XX vv. (do 1917 goda): Rekomendatel'nyi ukazatel'.* 3 vols. Moscow, 1958–63.

Muratova, K. D., ed. *Istoriya russkoi literatury XIX veka: Bibliograficheskii ukazatel'.* Moscow and Leningrad: AN SSSR, 1962.

———. *Istoriya russkoi literatury kontsa XIX–nachala XX veka: Bibliograficheskii ukazatel'.* Moscow and Leningrad: AN SSSR, 1963.

Petrovskaya, V. I., and E. M. Sakharova. *Klassiki russkoi khudozhestvennoi literatury: Dooktyabr'skii period.* Moscow, 1964.

Ryskin, E. I. *Bibliograficheskie ukazateli russkoi literatury XIX v.* Moscow, 1949.

———. *Osnovnye izdaniya sochinenii russkikh pisatelei XIX v.* 2d ed. Moscow, 1948.

Tarasenkov, A. K. *Russkie poety XX veka, 1900–55: Bibliografiya.* Moscow, 1966.

Vengerov, Semyon Afanas'evich. *Russkaya literatura XX veka, 1890–1910.* Moscow, 1914.

Vladislavlev, I. V. *Russkie pisateli: Opyt bibliograficheskogo posobiya po russkoi literature XIX–XX st.* Moscow, 1924.

4. Soviet Literature

Gibian, George. *Soviet Russian Literature in English: A Checklist Bibliography: a Selective Bibliography of Soviet Russian Literary Works in English and of Articles and Books in English about Soviet Russian Literature.* Ithaca, N.Y.; Cornell University Press, 1967.

Leningrad. Publichnaya biblioteka. *Russkie sovetskie pisateli-prozaiki: Biobibliograficheskii ukazatel'.* Ed. V. M. Akimov et. al. 7 vols. Leningrad, 1959–68.

Miller, T., comp. *Bibliographical Index to the Contributions to "Novyi mir" (1925–1934).* Ann Arbor: Ardis, 1983.

Moscow. Publichnaya biblioteka. *Sovetskaya literatura: Rekomendatel'nyi ukazatel'.* Moscow, 1957.

Sovetskaya khudozhestvennaya literatura i kritika: Bibliografiya. Comp. N. I. Matsuev. Moscow, 1952– .

Sovetskaya literatura. Dramaturgiya. Kinodramaturgiya: Rekomendatel'nyi ukazatel' literatury. Moscow, 1977.

Sovetskii roman, ego teoriya i istoriya: Bibliograficheskii ukazatel', 1917–1964. Comp. N. A. Groznova. Leningrad: AN SSSR, 1966.

Tarasenkov, A. K. *Russkie poety XX veka, 1900–55: Bibliografiya.* Moscow, 1966.

Vitman, A. M. *Vosem' let russkoi khudozhestvennoi literatury (1917–1925).* Moscow and Leningrad, 1926. Reprint Letchworth, Herts., 1972.

5. Emigré Literature

Foster, Ludmila. *Bibliografiya russkoi zarubezhnoi literatury, 1918–1968.* 2 vols. Boston, 1970.

Institut zur Erforschung der UdSSR. *Ukazatel' periodicheskikh izdanii emigratsii iz Rossii i SSSR, 1919–52.* Munich, 1953.

Khotin, Leonid, ed. *Abstracts of Soviet and East European Emigré Periodical Literature.* Pacific Grove, Cal., 1981– .

V. ANTHOLOGIES OF RUSSIAN LITERATURE

(For a complete list of anthologies of Russian literature, see *The Literatures of the World in English Translations: A Bibliography.* Vol. 2: *The Slavic Literatures.* Comp. Richard C. Lewanski. New York, 1967. Pp. 145–86.)

1. General Anthologies

Guerney, Bernard Guilbert. *The Portable Russian Reader: A Collection Newly Translated from Classical and Present-Day Authors.* New York: The Viking Portable Library, 1947.

———. *A Treasury of Russian Literature.* New York, 1943.

Yarmolinsky, Avrahm, ed. *Russians: Then and Now; A Selection of Russian Writing from the Seventeenth Century to Our Own Day.* New York, 1963.

2. Drama

Classic Soviet Plays. [In English translation.] Comp. Alla Mikhailova. Moscow, 1979.

Four Russian Plays. (Fonvizin, *The Infant*; Griboedov, *Chatsky*; Gogol, *The Inspector*; Ostrovsky, *Thunder*.) Trans. Joshua Cooper. Harmondsworth, England, 1972.

MacAndrew, A. R. *19th Century Russian Drama.* Introd. prefaces by Marc Slonim. New York, 1963.

———. *20th Century Russian Drama.* New York, 1963.

Magarshack, David, ed. and trans. *The Storm and Other Russian Plays.* New York, 1960.

Noyes, George Rapall, ed. and trans. *Masterpieces of the Russian Drama.* 2 vols. New York, 1960–61.

Pervye p'esy russkogo teatra. Comp. O. A. Derzhavina et al. Moscow, 1972.

Reeve, Franklin D., ed. and trans. *An Anthology of Russian Plays.* 2 vols. New York, 1961–63.

———. *Contemporary Russian Drama.* New York, 1968.

Tikhonravov, Nikolai Savvich. *Russkie dramaticheskie proizvedeniya 1672–1725 godov.* St. Petersburg, 1874.

3. Folklore

Afanas'ev, Aleksandr Nikolaevich. *Russian Secret Tales: Bawdy Folktales of Old Russia.* [In translation.] New York, 1966.

———. *Russkie narodnye skazki.* Ed. A. E. Gruzinskii. Moscow, 1913–14.

Alexander, Alex E. *Russian Folklore: An Anthology in English Translation.* Belmont, Mass., 1975.

Byliny; Russkie narodnye skazki; Drevnerusskie povesti. Comp. V. P. Anikin, D. S. Likhachev, and T. N. Mikhel'son. Moscow, 1979.

Chadwick, Norah, trans. *Russian Heroic Poetry.* Cambridge University Press, 1932.

Costello, D. P., and I. P. Foote, eds. *Russian Folk Literature: skazki, liricheskie pesni, byliny, istoricheskie pesni, dukhovnye stikhi.* [Texts in Russian, introduction and notes in English.] Oxford, 1967.

Dal', Vladimir Ivanovich. *Poslovitsy russkogo naroda: Sbornik poslovits, pogovorok, rechenii, prislovii, chistogovorok, pribautok, zagadok, poverii i pr.* 3d ed. 4 vols. St. Petersburg, 1904.

Poltoratskaya, M. A. *Russkii fol'klor: Khrestomatiya, stat'i i kommentarii.* New York, 1964.

Reeder, Roberta, ed. *Down Along the Mother Volga.* Philadelphia, Pa., 1975.

Russian Fairy Tales. Trans. by Norbert Guterman from the collections of Aleksandr Afanas'ev. Folkloristic commentary by Roman Jakobson. New York, 1973.

4. Poetry

Bowra, Cecil M., ed. *A Book of Russian Verse.* Trans. into English by various hands. London, 1943.

Dobson, Rosemary, and David Campbell, comps. *Seven Russian Poets.* St. Lucia, Queensland, 1979.

Glad, John, and Daniel Weissbort, eds. *Russian Poetry: The Modern Period.* [In translation.] University of Iowa Press, 1978.

Kuzminsky, Konstantin K., and Gregory L. Kovalev, eds. *The Blue Lagoon Anthology of Modern Russian Poetry.* Vol. 1. Newtonville, Mass., 1980.

Markov, Vladimir. *Priglushennye golosa: Poeziya za zheleznym zanavesom.* New York, 1952.

Modern Russian Poetry: An Anthology with Verse Translations. Ed. and introd. Vladimir Markov and Merrill Sparks. Indianapolis, 1967. [Bilingual edition.]

Obolensky, Dimitri, ed. *The Penguin Book of Russian Verse.* Baltimore, 1962.

———, ed. and introd. *The Heritage of Russian Verse.* Indiana University Press, 1976.

Orlov, Vladimir Nikolaevich. *Poety pushkinskoi pory: Izbrannye stikhotvoreniya.* Moscow, 1949.

The Oxford Book of Russian Verse. Chosen by the Hon. Maurice Baring. Oxford: The Clarendon Press, 1925. 2d ed. Ed. D. P. Costello. 1948.

Raffel, Burton, comp. *Russian Poetry under the Tsars: An Anthology.* S.U.N.Y. Press, 1971.

Russkaya poeziya XIX veka. Ed. A. Krakovskaya and S. Chulkov. Moscow, 1973.

Russkie poety: Antologiya. Ed. D. D. Blagoi et al. Moscow, 1965.

Sosnitskii, Arkadii, ed. *Russkaya poeziya: Izbrannye stikhotvoreniya russkikh poetov s biograficheskimi i poyasnitel'nymi primechaniyami.* Moscow, 1902.

Tebbutt, A. E., ed. *Russian Lyrical Poetry: An Anthology of the Best Nineteenth-Century Lyrics, Selected, Accented, and Arranged, with Notes.* [Text in Russian.] London, 1918.

5. Science Fiction

Fetzer, Leland, ed. and trans. *Pre-Revolutionary Russian Science Fiction: An Anthology (Seven Utopias and a Dream).* Ann Arbor, Mich.: Ardis, 1982.

Magidoff, Robert, comp. and ed. *Russian Science Fiction 1969: An Anthology.* N.Y.U. Press, 1969.

6. Short Stories

14 Great Short Stories by Soviet Authors. Ed. George Reavey. New York, 1959.

Modern Soviet Short Stories. Introd. and biogr. notes by George Reavey. New York, 1961.

The Penguin Book of Russian Short Stories. Ed. David Richards. Harmondsworth, Middlesex, England, 1981.

Yarmolinsky, Avrahm. *A Treasury of Great Russian Short Stories, Pushkin to Gor'ki.* New York, 1944.

7. Miscellaneous

Edie, James M., et al., eds. *Russian Philosophy.* 3 vols. The University of Tennessee Press, 1976.

Shein, Louis J., ed. *Readings in Russian Philosophical Thought: Philosophy of History.* W. Laurier University Press, 1977.

Skazki russkikh pisatelei. Comp. V. P. Anikin. Moscow, 1980.

Women Writers in Russian Modernism: An Anthology. Ed. and trans. Temira Pachmuss. University of Illinois Press, 1978.

8. Old Russian Literature

Gudzii, N. G., ed. *Khrestomatiya po drevnei russkoi literature XI–XVII vekov.* Moscow, 1965.

Khudozhestvennaya proza Kievskoi Rusi XI–XIII vekov. Ed. I. P. Eremin and D. S. Likhachev. Moscow, 1957.

Pamyatniki literatury drevnei Rusi; Nachalo russkoi literatury: XI–nachalo XII veka. Comp. and ed. L. A. Dmitriev and D. S. Likhachev. Moscow, 1978.

Skripil', Mikhail Osipovich, comp. *Russkie povesti XV–XVI vekov.* Moscow, 1958.

Stender-Petersen, Adolf, ed. *Anthology of Old Russian Literature.*

[Russian text with English commentary.] Columbia University Press, 1954.

Zenkovsky, Serge A., ed. and trans. *Medieval Russia's Epics, Chronicles, and Tales.* New York, 1974.

9. 17th and 18th Century

Derzhavina, Ol'ga Aleksandrovna, ed. *Panegiricheskaya literatura petrovskogo vremeni.* Moscow, 1979.

Manning, Clarence Augustus. *Anthology of Eighteenth Century Russian Literature.* New York, 1951.

Poety XVIII veka. Ed. G. P. Makogonenko. Leningrad, 1958.

Russkaya proza XVIII veka. Comp. G. Makogonenko. Moscow, 1971.

Russkaya sentimental'naya povest': Sbornik. Moscow, 1979.

Segel, Harold B., comp. *The Literature of Eighteenth Century Russia.* 2 vols. New York, 1967.

Sipovskii, Vasilii Vasil'evich, ed. *Russkie povesti XVII–XVIII vv.* St. Petersburg, 1905.

Skripil', Mikhail Osipovich, comp. *Russkaya povest' XVII veka.* Leningrad, 1954.

10. 19th Century–Early 20th Century

An Anthology of Russian Neo-Realism: The "Znanie School" of Maxim Gorky. Ed. and trans. Nicholas Luker. Ann Arbor, Mich.: Ardis, 1982.

The Ardis Anthology of Russian Romanticism. Ed. Christine Rydel. Ann Arbor, Mich.: Ardis, 1984.

Dekabristy: Antologiya. Comp. V. Orlov. Leningrad, 1975.

Folejewski, Zbigniew. *Futurism and Its Place in the Development of Modern Poetry: A Comparative Study and Anthology.* University of Ottawa Press, 1980.

Neuhäuser, Rudolf, comp. *The Romantic Age in Russian Literature: Poetic and Aesthetic Norms; An Anthology of Original Texts, 1800–1850.* Munich, 1975.

Peterburgskii sbornik. Comp. N. Nekrasov. St. Petersburg, 1846. Reprint Leipzig, 1976.

Proffer, Carl R., ed. *Russian Romantic Prose: An Anthology.* Ann Arbor, Mich.: Translation Press, 1979.

Proffer, Carl R., and Ellendea Proffer, eds. *The Ardis Anthology of Russian Futurism.* Ann Arbor, Mich.: Ardis, 1980.

———. *The Silver Age of Russian Culture: An Anthology.* Ann Arbor, Mich.: Ardis, 1975.

Russkie povesti XIX veka 20kh–30kh godov. Ed. B. S. Meilakh. 2 vols. Moscow, 1950.

Russkie povesti XIX veka 40kh–50kh godov. Ed. B. S. Meilakh. 2 vols. Moscow, 1952.

11. Soviet Literature

The Ardis Anthology of Recent Russian Literature. Ed. Carl R. Proffer and Ellendea Proffer. Ann Arbor, Mich.: Ardis, 1975.

Contemporary Russian Prose. Ed. Carl R. Proffer and Ellendea Proffer. Ann Arbor, Mich.: Ardis, 1982.

Dissonant Voices in Soviet Literature. Ed. Patricia Blake and Max Hayward. New York, 1962.

Glenny, Michael, comp. *Novy Mir: A Selection, 1925–1967.* London, 1972.

Glinka, Gleb, ed. *Na perevale: Sbornik proizvedenii pisatelei gruppy "Perevala": A. K. Voronskogo, Nik. Zarudina, Ivana Kataeva i dr.* New York, 1954.

Guerney, Bernard Guilbert, ed. and trans. *An Anthology of Russian Literature in the Soviet Period from Gorki to Pasternak.* New York, 1960.

Half-Way to the Moon: New Writing from Russia. Ed. Patricia Blake and Max Hayward. London, 1964.

"Metropol'": Literaturnyi al'manakh. Ann Arbor, Mich.: Ardis, 1979. In English: *Metropol: Literary Almanac.* Ed. V. Aksenov et al. New York, 1983.

Reeve, F. D., ed. and introd. *Great Soviet Short Stories.* New York, 1962.

Scammell, Michael, comp. *Russia's Other Writers: Selections from Samizdat Literature.* New York, 1971.

Vchera i segodnya: Ocherki russkikh sovetskikh pisatelei. 2 vols. ed. B. Agapov et al. Moscow, 1960.

Vo ves' golos. [An anthology of Soviet poetry with English commentary.] Comp. Vladimir Ognyev. Moscow, 1965.

Yumor i satira poslerevolyutsionnoi Rossii: Antologiya. 2 vols. Comp. Boris Filippov and Vadim Medish. London, 1983.

12. Emigré Literature

Karlinsky, Simon, and Alfred Appel, Jr., eds. *The Bitter Air of Exile: Russian Writers in the West, 1922–1972.* University of California Press, 1977.

Pachmuss, Temira, ed. and trans. *A Russian Cultural Revival: A Critical Anthology of Emigré Literature before 1939.* University of Tennessee Press, 1981.

Rovner, Arkady, et al., eds. *Gnosis Anthology of Contemporary American and Russian Literature and Art.* Vol. 2. New York: Gnosis Press, 1982.

Shakhovskaya, Zinaida, et al., eds. *Russkii al'manakh.* Paris, 1981.

Vne Rossii: Antologiya emigrantskoi poezii, 1917–1975. Ed. H. W. Tjalsma. Munich, 1978.

VI. HISTORY OF RUSSIAN LITERATURE

1. General Works

Auty, Robert, and Dimitrii Obolensky, eds. *An Introduction to Russian Language and Literature.* (Companion to Russian Studies, Vol. 2.) Cambridge University Press, 1977.

Baring, Maurice. *An Outline of Russian Literature.* New York, 1915.

Billington, James H. *The Icon and the Axe: An Interpretive History of Russian Culture.* New York, 1966.

Blagoi, Dmitrii D. *Ot Kantemira do nashikh dnei.* 2d ed. Moscow, 1979.

Davies, Ruth. *The Great Books of Russia.* University of Oklahoma Press, 1968.

Istoriya russkoi literatury. 11 vols. Moscow and Leningrad: AN SSSR, 1941–56.

Istoriya russkoi literatury v trekh tomakh. 3 vols. Moscow: AN SSSR, 1958–64.

Lavrin, Janko. *From Pushkin to Mayakovsky: A Study in the Evolution of a Literature.* London, 1948.

———. *A Panorama of Russian Literature.* University of London Press, 1973.

Mirsky, D. P. *A History of Russian Literature from its Beginnings to 1900.* Ed. Francis J. Whitfield. New York, 1958.

Muchnic, Helen. *An Introduction to Russian Literature.* Rev. ed. New York, 1964.

Osorgina, Antonina Mikhailovna. *Istoriya russkoi literatury (s drevneishikh vremen do Pushkina).* Paris, 1955.

Pypin, A. N. *Istoriya russkoi literatury.* 2d ed. 1902–03. 4 vols. Reprint The Hague and Paris, 1968.

Slonim, M. L. *An Outline of Russian Literature.* Oxford University Press, 1958.

Tschižewskij, Dmitrij. *Russian Intellectual History.* Trans. John C. Osborne and Martin P. Rice. Ann Arbor, Mich.: Ardis, 1978.

Walicki, Andrzej. *A History of Russian Thought: From Enlightenment to Marxism.* Trans. Hilda Andrews-Rusiecka. Stanford University Press, 1979.

2. Drama and Theater

O sovremennike i sovremennosti: Russkaya sovetskaya dramaturgiya nashikh dnei. Ed. A. O. Boguslavskii and M. M. Kuznetsov. Moscow, 1964.

Ocherki istorii russkoi sovetskoi dramaturgii. 3 vols. Leningrad, 1963–68.

Roberts, Spencer E. *Soviet Historical Drama: Its Role in the Development of a National Mythology.* The Hague, 1965.

Segel, Harold B. *Twentieth-Century Russian Drama: From Gorky to the Present.* Columbia University Press, 1979.

Varneke, B. *Istoriya russkogo teatra XVII–XIX vv.* 3d ed. Moscow and Leningrad, 1939.

———. *History of the Russian Theater, Seventeenth through Nineteenth Century.* Trans. Boris Brasol. Rev. and ed. Belle Martin. New York, 1951.

Vsevolodskii-Gerngross, V. *Istoriya russkogo teatra.* 2 vols. Leningrad, 1929.

Welsh, David J. *Russian Comedy 1765–1823.* The Hague and Paris, 1966.

3. Folklore

Propp, V. Ya. *Morphology of the Folktale.* Trans. Laurence Scott. Introd. Svatava Pirkova-Jakobson. 2d rev. ed. with a preface by Louis A. Wagner and a new introd. by Alan Dundes. University of Texas Press, 1968.

Sokolov, Yu. M. *Russian Folklore.* Trans. C. Ruth Smith. Detroit, 1971.

Wosien, Maria-Gabriele. *The Russian Folktale: Some Structural and Thematic Aspects.* Munich, 1969.

4. Novel

Clark, Katerina. *The Soviet Novel: History as Ritual.* University of Chicago Press, 1981.

Freeborn, Richard Harry. *The Rise of the Russian Novel: Studies in the Russian Novel from* Eugene Onegin *to* War and Peace. Cambridge University Press, 1973.

———. *The Russian Revolutionary Novel: Turgenev to Pasternak.* (Cambridge Studies in Russian Literature.) Cambridge University Press, 1982.

Garrard, John, ed. *The Russian Novel from Pushkin to Pasternak.* Yale University Press, 1983.

Gifford, Henry. *The Novel in Russia: From Pushkin to Pasternak.* London, 1964.

Istoriya russkogo romana. 2 vols. Ed. A. S. Bushmin et al. Moscow: AN SSSR, 1962–64.

Lavrin, Janko. *An Introduction to the Russian Novel.* New York, 1947.

Reeve, F. D. *The Russian Novel.* New York, 1966.

5. Poetry

France, Peter. *Poets of Modern Russia.* (Cambridge Studies in Russian Literature.) Cambridge University Press, 1983.

Hingley, Ronald. *Nightingale Fever: Russian Poets in Revolution.* New York, 1981.

Poggioli, Renato. *The Poets of Russia, 1890–1930.* Harvard University Press, 1960.

Struve, Gleb. *K istorii russkoi poezii 1910-kh godov.* Berkeley, Cal., 1979.

6. Short Story

O'Toole, L. Michael. *Structure, Style and Interpretation in the Russian Short Story.* Yale University Press, 1982.

Russkaya povest' XIX veka. Ed. B. S. Meilakh. Leningrad, 1973.

7. Old Russian Literature

Fennell, John. *Early Russian Literature.* University of California Press, 1974.

Gudzii, N. G. *Istoriya drevnei russkoi literatury.* Moscow, 1966. In English: *History of Early Russian Literature.* Trans. Susan W. Jones. New York, 1949.

Istoriya russkoi literatury X–XVII vekov. Ed. D. S. Likhachev. Moscow, 1980.

Orlov, Aleksandr Sergeevich. *Drevnyaya russkaya literatura XI–XVII vekov.* Moscow and Leningrad: AN SSSR, 1945. Reprint The Hague and Paris, 1970.

Robinson, A. N. *Literatura drevnei Rusi v literaturnom protsesse srednevekov'ya: Ocherki literaturno-istoricheskoi tipologii.* Moscow, 1980.

Sazonova, Yuliya Leonidovna. *Istoriya russkoi literatury: Drevnii period.* 2 vols. New York, 1955.

Tschižewskij, Dmitrij. *History of Russian Literature from the Eleventh Century to the End of the Baroque.* The Hague, 1960.

8. 17th and 18th Century

Berkov, Pavel Naumovich. *Istoriya russkoi komedii XVIII v.* Leningrad, 1977.

———. *Vvedenie v izuchenie istorii russkoi literatury XVIII veka.* 3 vols. Leningrad, 1964.

Blagoi, D. D. *Istoriya russkoi literatury XVIII veka.* 4th ed. Moscow, 1960.

———. *Ot Kantemira do nashikh dnei.* 2d ed. 2 vols. Moscow, 1979.

Brown, W. E. *A History of Seventeenth-Century Russian Literature.* Ann Arbor, Mich.: Ardis, 1980.

———. *A History of Eighteenth-Century Russian Literature.* Ann Arbor, Mich.: Ardis, 1980.

Demin, Anatolii Sergeevich. *Russkaya literatura vtoroi poloviny XVII–nachala XVIII veka: Novye khudozhestvennye predstavleniya o mire, prirode, cheloveke.* Moscow, 1977.

Drage, C. L. *Russian Literature in the Eighteenth Century: The Solemn Ode, The Epic, Other Poetic Genres, The Story, The Novel, Drama: An Introduction for University Courses.* London, 1978.

Gukovskii, G. A. *Ocherki po istorii russkoi literatury i obshchestvennoi mysli XVIII veka.* Leningrad, 1938.

Istoriya russkoi literatury XVII–XVIII vekov. Ed. A. S. Eleonskaya. Moscow, 1969.

Orlov, P. N. *Russkii sentimentalizm.* Moscow, 1977.

Serman, Il'ya Zakharovich. *Russkii klassitsizm. Poeziya. Drama. Satira.* Leningrad, 1973.

9. 19th and Early 20th Century

Andrew, Joe. *Writers and Society during the Rise of Russian Realism.* Atlantic Highlands, N. J., 1980.

Čiževskij, Dmitrij. *History of Nineteenth-Century Russian Literature.* Vol. 1. *The Romantic Period.* Vol. 2. *The Realistic Period.* Trans. Richard Noel Porter. Ed. Serge A. Zenkovsky. Vanderbilt University Press, 1974.

Hingley, Ronald. *Russian Writers and Society in the Nineteenth Century.* 2d ed. London, 1977.

Istoriya romantizma v russkoi literature. Vol. 1. *Vozniknovenie i utverzhdenie romantizma v russkoi literature 1790–1825.* Vol. 2. *Romantizm v russkoi literature 20–30kh godov XIX v., 1825–1840.* Moscow, 1979.

Istoriya russkoi literatury XIX veka. Ed. F. M. Golovenchenko and S. M. Petrov. 2 vols. Moscow, 1960–63.

Istoriya russkoi literatury vtoroi poloviny XIX veka. Ed. N. I. Kravtsov. Moscow, 1966.

Markov, Vladimir. *Russian Futurism: A History.* University of California Press, 1968.

———. *Russian Imagism, 1919–1924.* 2 vols. (Bausteine zur Geschichte der Literatur bei den Slaven, 15.) Giessen: Wilhelm Schmitz, 1980.

Mersereau, John Jr. *Russian Romantic Fiction.* Ann Arbor, Mich.: Ardis, 1983.

Mirsky, D. P. *Contemporary Russian Literature, 1881–1925.* New York, 1926.

Williams, Robert C. *Artists in Revolution: Portraits of the Russian Avant-Garde, 1905–1925.* Indiana University Press, 1977.

10. Soviet Literature

Brown, Deming B. *Soviet Literature since Stalin.* Cambridge University Press, 1978.

Brown, Edward J. *Russian Literature since the Revolution.* Harvard University Press, 1982.

Hingley, Ronald. *Russian Writers and Soviet Society, 1917–1978.* New York, 1979.

Hosking, Geoffrey A. *Beyond Socialist Realism.* New York, 1979.

Istoriya russkoi sovetskoi literatury. Ed. A. G. Dement'ev. 3 vols. Moscow: AN SSSR, 1958.

James, V. C. *Soviet Socialist Realism.* London, 1973.

Lomidze, G. I., and S. I. Khitarova. *Sovetskii roman: novatorstvo, poetika, tipologiya.* Moscow, 1978.

Maguire, Robert A. *Red Virgin Soil: Soviet Literature in the 1920s.* Princeton University Press, 1968.

Shneidman, N. N. *Soviet Literature in the 1970s: Artistic Diversity and Ideological Conformity.* University of Toronto Press, 1979.

Simmons, Ernest J. *Russian Fiction and Soviet Ideology*. New York, 1958.

Slonim, Marc. *Soviet Russian Literature: Writers and Problems, 1917–1977*. 2d rev. ed. Oxford University Press, 1977.

Struve, Gleb. *Russian Literature under Lenin and Stalin, 1917–1953*. University of Oklahoma Press, 1971.

Svirskii, Grigorii. *Na lobnom meste: Literatura nravstvennogo soprotivleniya (1946–1976 gg.)*. London, 1979. In English: Svirski, Grigori. *A History of Post-War Soviet Writing: The Literature of Moral Opposition*. Trans. and ed. Robert Dessaix and Michael Ulman. Ann Arbor, Mich.: Ardis, 1981.

11. Emigré Literature

Poltoratzky, Nikolai P. "Russian Literature, Literary Scholarship, and Publishing in the United States." In *Ethnic Literatures since 1776: The Many Voices of America*. Ed. Wolodymyr T. Zyla and Wendell M. Aycock. Lubbock, Texas: Texas Tech Press, 1978. Vol. 2, pp. 455–501.

Russkaya literatura v emigratsii: Sbornik statei. Ed. N. Poltoratzky. Pittsburgh, 1972.

Struve, Gleb. *Russkaya literatura v izgnanii*. New York, 1956.

VII. LITERARY THEORY AND CRITICISM

AN SSSR. Institut russkoi literatury. *Istoriya russkoi kritiki*. Ed. B. P. Gorodetskii. 2 vols. Leningrad, 1958.

Anikst, Aleksandr Abramovich. *Teoriya dramy v Rossii ot Pushkina do Chekhova*. Moscow, 1972.

Belinsky, Chernyshevsky and Dobrolyubov: Selected Criticism. Ed. and introd. Ralph E. Matlaw. New York, 1962.

Erlich, V. *Russian Formalism: History, Doctrine*. Yale University Press, 1981.

Freeborn, Richard Harry. *Russian Literary Attitudes from Pushkin to Solzhenitsyn*. London, 1976.

The Futurists, the Formalists, and the Marxist Critique. Ed. and introd. Christopher Pike. Trans. Christopher Pike and Joe Andrew. London, 1979.

Ginzburg, L. Ya. *O lirike*. 2d rev. ed. Leningrad, 1974.

Grigor'ev, Apollon Aleksandrovich. *Literaturnaya kritika*. Moscow, 1967.

Jackson, Robert Louis. *Dostoevsky's Underground Man in Russian Literature*. The Hague, 1958.

Kovalev, Valentin Arkhipovich. *Mnogoobrazie stilei v sovetskoi literature*. Moscow, 1965.

Kropotkin, Petr Alekseevich. *Ideals and Realities in Russian Literature*. New York, 1919.

Kuleshov, Vasilii Ivanovich. *Istoriya russkoi kritiki XVIII–XIX vv*. Moscow, 1972.

———. *Literaturnye svyazi Rossii i Zapadnoi Evropy v XIX veke (pervaya polovina)*. Moscow, 1965.

———. *Natural'naya shkola v russkoi literature XIX veka*. Moscow, 1965.

———. *Russkaya kritika XVIII–XIX vekov: Khrestomatiya*. Moscow, 1978.

———. *Slavyanofily i russkaya literatura*. Moscow, 1976.

Likhachev, Dmitrii Sergeevich. *Poetika drevnerusskoi literatury*. Leningrad, 1967.

———. *Tekstologiya: Kratkii ocherk*. Leningrad, 1964.

Literature and National Identity: Nineteenth Century Russian Critical Essays. Ed. and trans. Paul Debreczeny and Jesse Zeldin. University of Nebraska Press, 1970.

Lomunov, Konstantin Nikolaevich. *Razvitie realizma v russkoi literature*. 3 vols. Moscow, 1972–74.

Mann, Yurii. *Poetika russkogo romantizma*. Moscow, 1976.

Matejka, Ladislav, comp. *Readings in Russian Poetics*. (Michigan Slavic Materials, No. 2.) Ann Arbor, Mich.: Dept. of Slavic Languages and Literatures, 1962.

———. *Readings in Russian Poetics by M. M. Bakhtin et al*. Ann Arbor, Mich.: University of Michigan Press, 1971.

Mathewson, Rufus Wellington, Jr. *The Positive Hero in Russian Literature*. Stanford University Press, 1975.

Mordovchenko, Nikolai Ivanovich. *Russkaya kritika pervoi chetverti XIX veka*. Moscow: AN SSSR, 1959.

Nadezhdin, Nikolai Ivanovich. *Literaturnaya kritika. Estetika*. Moscow, 1972.

Nebel, Henry M., Jr., trans. and introd. *Selected Aesthetic Works of Sumarokov and Karamzin*. Washington, D. C., 1981.

Peretts, Varvara Pavlovna. *Ocherki poeticheskogo stilya drevnei Rusi*. Moscow: AN SSSR, 1947.

Plekhanov, G. V. *Literatura i estetika*. 2 vols. Moscow, 1958.

———. *Art and Society*. Trans. and introd. Granville Hicks. New York, 1936.

Readings in Soviet Semiotics. Ed. L. Matejka. Ann Arbor, 1977.

Roberts, Spencer, ed. and trans. *Essays in Russian Literature; the Conservative View: Leontiev, Rozanov, Shestov*. Ohio University Press, 1968.

Robinson, Andrei Nikolaevich. *Bor'ba idei v russkoi literature XVII veka*. Moscow, 1974.

Russkaya kritika. [Collected Essays by V. G. Belinsky et al.] Comp. M. I. Belousova. Leningrad, 1973.

Russkaya literatura i ee zarubezhnye kritiki: Sbornik statei. Moscow, 1974.

Rzhevsky, Nicholas. *Russian Literature and Ideology: Herzen, Dostoevsky, Leontiev, Tolstoy, Fadeyev*. University of Illinois Press, 1983.

Senelick, Laurence, ed. and trans. *Russian Dramatic Theory from Pushkin to the Symbolists: An Anthology*. (University of Texas Slavic Series, 5.) University of Texas Press, 1981.

Sobolevskii, Aleksei Ivanovich. *Zapadnoe vliyanie na literaturu Moskovskoi Rusi XV–XVII vekov*. St. Petersburg, 1899.

Stableford, Tom, ed. *The Literary Appreciation of Russian Writers*. Cambridge University Press, 1981.

Stacy, Robert H. *Russian Literary Criticism, a Short History*. Syracuse University Press, 1974.

Swiderski, Edward M. *The Philosophical Foundations of Soviet Aesthetics: Theories and Controversies in the Post-War Years*. Dordrecht, Holland, 1979.

Terras, Victor. *Belinskij and Russian Literary Criticism: The Heritage of Organic Aesthetics*. University of Wisconsin Press, 1974.

Twentieth Century Russian Literary Criticism. Ed. Victor Erlich. Yale University Press, 1975.

Tynyanov, Yury Nikolaevich. *Arkhaisty i novatory*. Leningrad, 1929.

Wellek, René. *A History of Modern Criticism*. 4 vols. Yale University Press, 1955–65.

Western Philosophical Systems in Russian Literature: A Collection of Critical Studies. Ed. Anthony M. Mlikotin. University of Southern California Press, 1979.

Wilson, Edmund. *A Window on Russia, for the Use of Foreign Readers*. New York, 1972.

VIII. ENCYCLOPEDIAS AND DICTIONARIES OF LITERATURE

Arsen'ev, Aleksandr Vasil'evich. *Slovar' pisatelei drevnego perioda russkoi literatury IX–XVII veka (862–1700 gg.)*. Ed. O. F. Miller. St. Petersburg, 1882.

Bédé, Jean-Albert, and William B. Edgerton, eds. *Columbia Dictionary of Modern European Literature*. 2d ed. Columbia University Press, 1980.

Berry, Thomas Edwin. *Plots and Characters in Major Russian Fiction*. 2 vols. Hamden, Ct., 1977.

Bol'shaya sovetskaya entsiklopediya. 3d ed. Ed. S. I. Vavilov. Moscow, 1970– .

Budovnits, I. *Slovar' russkoi, ukrainskoi, belorusskoi pis'mennosti i literatury do XVIII veka*. Moscow, 1962.

Dana, Henry Wadsworth Longfellow. *Handbook on Soviet Drama: Lists of Theatres, Plays, Operas, Ballets, Films and Books and Articles about Them*. New York, 1938.

Golitsyn, Nikolai Nikolaevich, knyaz'. *Bibliograficheskii slovar' russkikh pisatel'nits*. St. Petersburg, 1889–91. Reprint Leipzig, 1974.

Gusman, B. *Sto poetov*. Tver, 1923.

Harkins, William E. *Dictionary of Russian Literature*. London, 1957.

Kratkaya literaturnaya entsiklopediya. 9 vols. Moscow, 1962–75.

Kvyatkovskii, A. *Poeticheskii slovar'*. Moscow, 1966.

Literaturnaya entsiklopediya. Ed. V. M. Friche and A. V. Lunacharskii. 9 vols. Moscow, 1929–39.

Matsuev, N. *Russkie sovetskie pisateli: Materialy dlya biograficheskogo slovarya 1917–1967*. Moscow, 1981.

The Modern Encyclopedia of Russian and Soviet Literature. Ed. Harry B. Weber. Gulf Breeze, Fla.: Academic International Press, 1977–   .

Russkie pisateli. Biobibliograficheskii slovar'. (*Spravochnik dlya uchitelya*.) Ed. D. S. Likhachev et al. Moscow, 1971.

Snow, Valentine. *Russian Writers: A Bio-Bibliographical Dictionary*. [From the age of Catherine II to the October revolution of 1917.] New York, 1946.

Sovetskie pisateli: Avtobiografii. Comp. B. Ya. Brainina and E. F. Nikitina. 2 vols. Moscow, 1959.

Teatral'naya entsiklopediya. Ed. S. S. Mokul'skii. 5 vols. Moscow, 1961–67.

Utechin, S. V. *A Concise Encyclopedia of Russia*. New York, 1964.

Vengerov, S. A. *Istochniki slovarya russkikh pisatelei*. 4 vols. (A–Nekrasov). St. Petersburg, 1900–17. Reprint Leipzig, 1965.

———. *Kritiko-biograficheskii slovar' russkikh pisatelei i uchenykh ot nachala russkoi obrazovannosti do nashikh dnei*. 6 vols. 1st ed. St. Petersburg, 1889–1904 (incomplete). Vols. 1–2. 2d ed. St. Petersburg, 1915–18.

Zernov, Nikolai Mikhailovich. *Russkie pisateli emigratsii: Biograficheskie svedeniya i bibliografiya ikh knig po bogosloviyu, religioznoi filosofii, tserkovnoi istorii i pravoslavnoi kul'ture*. Boston, 1973.